THE CONCISE DICTIONARY OF ENGLISH CHRISTIAN NAMES

THE CONCISE DICTIONARY OF ENGLISH CHRISTIAN NAMES

by

E.G. WITHYCOMBE

OMEGA BOOKS

*This edition published 1988 by Omega Books Ltd.,
14 Greville Street, London, EC1N 8SB by arrangement with
Oxford University Press.*

First Published by Oxford University Press Paperback 1977

ISBN 1-85007-059-8

*Printed and bound in Great Britain by
Mackays of Chatham PLC, Chatham, Kent*

PREFACE TO THE THIRD EDITION

THE present edition contains about forty names not included in the previous editions, as well as a number of new cross-references. The main work of revision, as before, consists of many small corrections, emendations, and additions to existing articles, many of which reflect the changes in usage, frequency, and status of names that have occurred in the thirty years since the first edition was published. For many of these I am indebted to numerous friends and correspondents. One must be mentioned by name: Dr. R. B. Hetherington of Birmingham put at my disposition a mass of notes on christian names accumulated in the course of his genealogical researches.

E. G. W.

FEAST OF ST. NICHOLAS
1976

PREFACE TO THE SECOND EDITION

THE present edition contains some fifty names not included in the original issue, but the main work of revision has consisted in a multitude of small corrections, additions, and emendations, which affect almost every article, and for the greater number of which I am indebted to the kindness and learning of correspondents, unfortunately too numerous to name here. It would seem, judging by their letters, that my readers, hitherto, have all been amiable, witty, and well informed, and the pleasure which I have derived from their letters has more than compensated for the tediousness of revision. Though it is not possible to make acknowledgement of all such help, I must express my particular gratitude to Professor G. R. Driver, Professor Idris Foster, Professor Max Förster, the Very Rev. Dean Reidy of Tralee, Dr. C. Suffern, and Professor J. A. Twemlow, for the time and trouble they have spent on the book, though it would be impertinent in me to speak of the value of their help and advice.

It will be noted that pronunciation has been indicated whenever it is doubtful.

E. G. W.

ST. PHILIP'S AND ST. JAMES'S DAY
1949

PREFACE TO THE FIRST EDITION

Some apology, or at least explanation, may be expected for the addition of yet another to the list of books on this subject, which is already very long and is added to in almost every publishing season. It must, however, be stated frankly that they are for the most part almost valueless. There has been little change in this respect since the Rev. R. S. Charnock wrote in 1882, in the preface to his *Praenomina*: 'I cannot say I have been greatly edified by the perusal of many [books on the subject]. The unworthiness of works on this subject is caused by the fact that one author copies from another, and but few writers have more than a superficial acquaintance with two or three languages.' These strictures are still valid (*Praenomina* itself, incidentally, was no better than its predecessors). At the time when Charnock wrote, the primary source was still the lists of names with etymologies which form part of Camden's *Remaines* (1605), and these amusing but completely fanciful explanations were still solemnly put forward. Edward Lyford, a pious young man, of whom it is stated in the preface to his work that in six weeks he learned enough Hebrew for the purpose, in 1655 published a little book entitled *The True Interpretation of Christian Names*, the purpose of which he explains: 'I wish therefore, that all Christians were more seriously exhorted, not so much to use those Barbarous and Strange names, as Saxon, Sabin, and German names, which are now introduced amongst us, but rather, that as we are Christians, so we would use such names that become Christians (I mean) those Scripture names whose Interpretations and Etymologies might be suitable to our several estates and conditions.' Lyford copied the etymologies of non-Hebrew names almost word for word from Camden, and his own Hebrew etymologies are somewhat wild. His book was probably not much read, but Mrs. Thrale had a copy of it, and planned and partly executed a a work which she named *Lyford Redivivus*, which has never been printed.

The first attempt at seriously tackling the subject was made by Charlotte M. Yonge, the novelist, who in 1863 brought out a work in two volumes entitled *A History of Christian Names*; a revised edition in one volume was issued in 1884. This has ever since remained the standard work on the subject in English, and practically the whole substance of later books has been based on it, their authors, sometimes openly and sometimes tacitly, using it as a quarry. Before pointing out the deficiencies of this work it must be emphasized that it was a great deal better than anything which had gone before and, indeed, than most of its successors. Having regard to the author's equipment, to the sources then available, and to the fact that few at that time had any conception of applying historical methods to linguistic studies, it is indeed a remarkable achievement and assembles a great deal of miscellaneous information in a very readable form. Miss Yonge's modesty prevented her from philological flights of fancy, except when all her authorities failed her, but it also led her to adopt uncritically the pronouncements of those authorities, particularly the Germans. The etymological part of her book is to-day almost valueless, but it contains a mass of anecdotes and facts about the history of names, which are still of interest and value.

The next landmark in English studies of nomenclature was the posthumous publication in 1901 of *A Dictionary of English and Welsh Surnames* by Canon C. W. Bardsley, who had already published in 1873 a short work on the subject, and in 1880 *Curiosities of Puritan Nomenclature*. Bardsley's book was the fruit of thirty years' study and is a measure of the revolution which had taken place in linguistic studies in England during that period, which had witnessed the establishment, for example, of the Early English Text Society and the Rolls Series, and the launching of the *Oxford English Dictionary*. The necessity of an historical basis for philological speculations was now generally recognized by scholars, though the old army of happy guessers was still fighting a stiff rearguard action, and is indeed by no means extinct to-day, particularly in the field of place-name study. The foundation of Bardsley's work was an enormous mass of material collected by himself from both published and unpublished sources. Though his subject was surnames, he incidentally provides a most valuable corpus of material illustrative of medieval christian names, upon which the present work has drawn freely.

Of equal importance is Förstemann's monumental *Altdeutsches Namenbuch* which has likewise been of the greatest use for all names of Germanic origin.

The principal original sources of which use has been made will be found in the list of abbreviations, but a very much greater number of works have been consulted. The earliest recorded forms of each name are given. It will be noted that a majority of these are in Latin, and the rarity of early records in English is one of the chief difficulties in elucidating the history of difficult names. For the later history of uncommon names, Burke's *Peerage*, the *Baronettage*, and the *Landed Gentry* are invaluable.

There was an obvious difficulty at the outset in deciding which names to include in a book of this kind. The standard adopted is roughly that a name should have survived in use after the end of the fourteenth century (or been revived later). At the other end, it has not been felt possible, or even desirable, to deal with the flood of newly invented names in use at the present time in the United States of America, many of which have already crossed the Atlantic. Some of the commoner Irish and Welsh names have been included, since they are of obvious interest and are often used in England.

I wish here to express my gratitude to Dr. Onions and to both the late and present Secretary to the Delegates of the Press for their help and encouragement in the preparation of this book, and also to the late Sir Allen Mawer, but for whose teaching and example it would never have been written.

E. G. W.

ST. FRIDESWIDE'S DAY
1944

CONTENTS

LIST OF ABBREVIATIONS

ASC	Anglo-Saxon Chronicle
Ass	Assize Rolls
Bardsley	C. W. Bardsley, *Dictionary of English and Welsh Surnames* (pub. 1901)
Black	G. F. Black, *Surnames of Scotland*, 1946
Burke	Burke's *Peerage, Baronetage,* and *Landed Gentry*
C	Century
Cal Gen	*Calendarium Genealogicum*
Camden	Camden's *Remaines*, 1605 (pub. 1623)
Chester	Child-marriages, &c. in the diocese of Chester, 1661–6 (E.E.T.S. 108)
Chester Wills	Wills at Chester, 1545–1720
Cl	Close Rolls
Clerkenwell	Cartulary of St. Mary, Clerkenwell
CMY	Charlotte Mary Yonge, *History of Christian Names*, 2 vols., 1863. Revised ed. 1884
Cornhill Reg	Church Registers of St. Peter's, Cornhill
Cornish Reg	Cornish Church Registers
Cov	The Coventry Leet Book
Cur	Curia Regis Rolls
DB	Domesday Book
Exch R	Exchequer Rolls
f.	feminine
FA	Feudal Aids
FF	Feet of Fines
Förstemann	E. Förstemann, *Altdeutsches Namenbuch*
14th C Legendary	Early S. English Legendary, 14th C (E.E.T.S. 87)
GEC	G.E.C. *Complete Peerage*
Godstow	English Register of Godstow Nunnery, *c.* 1450 (E.E.T.S. 129–30)
HR	Hundred Rolls
Huntspill	Parish registers of Huntspill, Somerset
IPM	Calendar of Inquisitions Post Mortem
Keighley Reg	Church Registers of Keighley
Lancs Wills	Lancashire Wills (1531–1760)
Langland	William Langland, *Piers Plowman*
Linc	Lincoln Diocese Documents (E.E.T.S. 149)
Lond Marr Lic	Allegations for Marriage Licences issued by the Bishop of London, 1520–1828

Lyford	Edward Lyford, *The True Interpretation of Christian Names*, 1655.
m.	masculine
Magd.	Muniments of Magdalen College, Oxford.
N & Q	*Notes and Queries*
Notts P Reg	Nottinghamshire Parish Registers
OED	*Oxford English Dictionary*
Oseney	English Register of Oseney Abbey, *c.* 1460 (E.E.T.S. 133–4)
Ox Univ Reg	Register of Oxford University
Pat	Patent Rolls
Pipe	Pipe Rolls
Poll Tax	Poll Tax of West Riding of Yorkshire, 1379
Privy Purse Exp	Privy Purse Expenses of Henry VIII and Elizabeth
Prompt Parv	*Promptorium Parvulorum*
QW	Placita de Quo Warranto
Reg	Regesta Regum Anglo-Normannorum
St. Antholin	Church Registers of St. Antholin, Budge Row, 1538–1754
St. Columb Major	Church Registers of St. Columb Major
St. Dionis	Church Registers of St. Dionis, Backchurch, 1538–1754
St. Geo. Hanover Sq	Church Registers of St. George's, Hanover Sq., 1725–1809
St. Jas. Clerkenwell	Church Registers of St. James's, Clerkenwell, 1551–1754
St. Mary Aldermary	Church Registers of St. Mary Aldermary, 1558–1754
St. Mary at Hill	Records of St. Mary at Hill, 1420–1559 (E.E.T.S. 125–8)
Testa de Neville	Testa de Neville, or Book of Fees, temp. Hen. III–Edw. I
TRE	Tempore Regis Edwardi (In the Reign of Edward the Confessor)
Werburga	*Life of St. Werburga*, transl. 1573
Whitby Cart	Cartulary of Whitby Abbey
Yorks Recusants	A list of the Roman Catholics in the County of Yorks in 1604
Yorks Visit	Visitation of Yorkshire

INTRODUCTION

'Every person had in the beginning one only proper name', writes Camden, adding in his pleasant gossiping way, 'except the savages of Mount Atlas in Barbary, which were reported to be both nameless and dreamless.' Whatever be the truth about the savages of Mount Atlas, it is certainly true of the two main sources of English personal nomenclature, which are respectively Hebrew and Indo-European, that, with a few exceptions, they were originally based on the theory of one name for each individual.

Semitic Names

Semitic names, for the most part, consisted of two elements, so combined as to have an intelligible meaning, usually religious. The true meaning of the Hebrew names in the Old Testament is revealed by comparing them with those in the cognate Semitic languages, and these show that the explanations offered in the Old Testament are often only pieces of folk etymology; thus *Moses* has nothing to do with 'drawing up', nor 'Samuel', with 'hearing'.

The divine name was *Yaweh*, of which only the first element was used in making up personal names. The full name was too sacred to be uttered except in the high-priestly blessing on the Day of Atonement; either *'ădônāy* 'my lord' or *'ĕlôhim* 'God' was substituted for it. In course of time the vowels of these words were substituted for those of *Yahweh*, producing the absurd *Yehovah*, first in writing and then in speaking. This was written in European books with the Latin *j* for *y*, yielding *Jehovah*, which was pronounced with the sound of the English *j*. Further, *Yah-* was shortened to *Yô-* at the beginning of names, so that we get such pairs of names as *'Elîyāh* (English *Elijah*) = 'God (is) Jehovah' and *Yô'ēl* (English *Joel*) = 'Jehovah (is) God'.

The primitive Semitic doctrine seems to have been that a man's name was in some way an expression of his personality and that any one name could therefore apply to only one individual. In historic times, however, a limited number of these names had been adopted (chiefly those of patriarchs and their families) and were given to children instead of newly coined names. The ambiguity arising from the use of only a comparatively few names was obviated by the adoption of patronymics (e.g. Matt. xvi, *Simon Bar-Jonah*, i.e. 'Simon son of Jonah'). A boy received his name at his circumcision, and the giving of a christian name at baptism was probably derived from this Jewish custom.

Indo-European Names

Of the great Indo-European family of languages the general principle was also that of one name for each individual, the majority of names being compounded of two elements chosen from a stock of special name-words. Such elements were naturally for the most part words of good augury, but they seem, in most languages, to have been combined with no particular regard for meaning. As Professor Stenton writes:[1] 'Most compound names can be translated, but the translations often make nonsense. The men who coined the names *Frithuwulf* "peace-wolf", and *Wigfrith* "war-peace", were not concerned about their meaning. These are ancient names and they prove that at an early time the sense which a compound name bore was a matter of little importance . . . in most cases personal or family reasons determined the choice of a name, and speculation as to its meaning, if it came at all, came as an afterthought.' Sanskrit, Greek, Slavonic, Germanic, and Celtic names were all of

[1] *Introduction to the Survey of English Place-names*, p. 168.

this type, but there are also shorter names formed from the compound ones; examples of such pairs are Sanskrit *Indra-ketu*, *Indra*, Slavonic *Bogu-slav*, *Bogoj*, Greek *Νικο-κλῆς*, *Νίκων*, Celtic *Catu-rix*, *Catoc*, Scandinavian *Sig-urd*, *Siggi*, Old German *Hari-bald*, *Herilo*, Old English *Ceol-ric*, *Ceola*. These short names arose at an early date and established themselves in independent use, often superseding the longer compound names.

The special name-words of which personal names were composed were originally ordinary significant words, but with the passage of time some of them fell out of use in the spoken language, and others underwent phonetic and semantic changes to which personal names were not always subject. An example of this is the word *Os*, 'a god', which was often used as an initial element in Old English personal names, but is hardly ever found in independent use, having become obsolete at an earlier date than any written records of the language.[1] A modern French writer[2] says of such names: 'Fossiles de la langue, épaves de couches historiques submergées par les apports successifs des sédiments lexicaux, ils permettent de reconstituer des formes et des types disparus du parler courant.' The Frankish monk Smaragdus, who wrote at the beginning of the 9th century, shows that even as early as that there was no longer a clear understanding of the formation and meaning of Germanic names: thus he translated *Uuilmunt* ('will'+'protection') as 'volens bucca' (willing mouth), and *Ratmunt* ('counsel'+'protection') as 'consilium oris' (counsel of the mouth), confusing *mund* 'protection', with *mund* 'mouth'. The short uncompounded names were naturally even less comprehensible than the compounded ones; Redin[3] lists 736 such names in Old

[1] It occurs once, in the plural, in the Charms.
[2] Dauzat, *Les Noms de Personnes*.
[3] Redin, *Uncompounded Names in Old English*.

English, of which he classes 338 as intelligible and 398 as unintelligible.

Greek Names

In Greece a child was given its name on the seventh or tenth day after birth. The father chose the name and could change it later at his will. The eldest son was usually given the name of his paternal grandfather, later children those of other relatives. Thus Sositheus, a client of Demosthenes, named his eldest son after his own father, the second after his wife's father, the third after another relative of his wife, and the fourth after his own maternal grandfather. Sometimes, though rarely, a son bore the same name as his father, e.g. the orator *Demosthenes*; or a derivative of the father's name, e.g. *Phocion* son of *Phocos*; or a compound name with one of the same elements, e.g. *Philotheus* son of *Philocles*. If two persons bore the same name, and confusion was likely to be caused, ambiguity was avoided by adding the name of the father, either in the genitive case (e.g. *Δημοσθένης Δημοσθένους*) or with the suffix *-ίδης* or *-ιάδης*;[1] or by indicating their place of origin, the name of the tribe or deme being added for persons of the same town (e.g. *Δημοσθένης Δημοσθένους Παιανιεύς*, i.e. *Demosthenes* son of *Demosthenes* of the deme of *Paiania*), and the name of the country or town for foreigners (e.g. *Ἀγησίλαος Λακεδαιμόνιος*, *Agesilaus of Lacedaemon*). Women's names were formed in the same way as men's, but with feminine terminations; an unmarried woman was designated as her father's daughter, a married woman as her husband's wife, and a widow as her son's mother. Slaves were given short, often neuter, names. Nicknames, added to or substituted for the genuine name, were common, the most famous example being the philosopher Plato, who was named

[1] In Aeolic there was a patronymic in *-ιος* (e.g. *Αἴας Τελαμώνιος*, *Ajax* son of *Telamon*) which corresponds to the Latin names in *-ius*.

Aristocles after his grandfather, but received from his gymnastic master the nickname *Πλάτων* (from *πλάτυς*, broad), which practically superseded his real name. When such names were in general use they were written after the original name, preceded by the words *ὁ ἐπικαλούμενος* or *ὁ καί*.

Celtic and Slavonic Names

The Celtic system of nomenclature seems to have been much the same as the Greek, and it survived long after a system of regular surnames had been established in the rest of Europe.[1] It is noteworthy that a very large proportion of Greek personal names are composed of words denoting moral and intellectual qualities, while Celtic names have a preponderance of those concerned with physical attributes. Slavonic names were also very largely composed of two elements. The use of patronymics arose early in Russia, and they continue to be used down to the present day, though proper surnames came into use in the Middle Ages. Thus a Russian always has three names, the christian name, patronymic, and surname. The first two are generally used in addressing anyone who is known to the speaker; thus *Lef Nikolaivitch Tolstóy* would in general be addressed as *Lef Nikolaivitch*. The patronymic is regarded as honorific and is not used, e.g., in signing one's name, when the christian name and surname alone are used.

Roman Names

The Romans evolved a quite different system of nomenclature, which in its classical form consisted of three names, the praenomen (e.g. Marcus), nomen (e.g. Tullius), and cognomen (e.g. Cicero), and two other designations (the name

[1] Hereditary surnames were not generally used in Wales until the 17th century, and the names of the Highland clans were hardly used as surnames in the full sense of the word until the 18th century.

of the father and of the tribe): thus a full, formal appellation would be in the form *Marcus Tullius, Marci filius, Cornelia tribu, Cicero.* In very early times a man seems to have been known by a single name together with his father's name in the genitive case, e.g. *Marcus Marci*; but the name of the *gens*, or family, developed early. Finally, the cognomen, originally a personal nickname, then the name of a *familia* or branch of the *gens*, acquired importance and became the name by which a man was usually known in familiar speech, though until the time of Sulla only two names were recognized by the law, i.e. the praenomen and nomen (name of the *gens*) followed by the designation of the father, e.g. *Publius Cornelius Lucii filius.* The cognomen was first used in patrician families, which were distinguished from the plebeian by the use of three names. The general adoption of the system for all free men came towards the end of the Republic. The praenomen and nomen for the most part consisted of simple stems with the suffix *-us* or *-ius*, which correspond to some of the contracted forms in other languages (e.g. Celtic *Tontius* from *Tontio-rix*, Greek *Zeuxias* from *Zeuxippos*, &c.).

The praenomen was the name given to a male child nine days after his birth, and enrolled in the official list of citizens when he assumed the *toga virilis.* There are 36 known praenomina, though there may originally have been more. Varro (116–27 B.C.) gives a list of 32, of which 14 had by then fallen out of use. The 18 which remained were *Appius, Aulus, Decimus, Gaius, Gnaeus, Kaeso, Lucius, Mamercus, Marcus, Manius, Numerius, Publius, Quintus, Servius, Sextus, Spurius, Tiberius, Titus.* The number in general use was further reduced by the fact that some of these names were confined to certain patrician families (e.g. *Appius* to the *Claudii, Mamercus* to the *Æmilii*), that some families renounced the use of a certain praenomen which had been disgraced by one of their name, and that yet other families used only one or two (the

Domitii Aenobarbi, for instance, used only *Lucius* and *Gnaeus*).[1] It was, moreover, a common practice to give brothers the same praenomen. The Senate (A.D. 6) decreed that the eldest son alone should bear his father's praenomen. It was inevitable that such a system should lead to the wide use of nicknames to distinguish identically named members of a family, and in this way the cognomen arose. But though, e.g., *Publius Cornelius Scipio* might in later life be distinguished from his brothers or cousins as *Africanus*, we do not know how he was addressed in his youth and by his family. The imagination, indeed, retires baffled before the prospect of a Roman patrician nursery where all the boys might have the same name and the girls none at all.

The nomen belonged to all members of a *gens* and to all those attached to it (women, clients, and freedmen included). Almost all these names are adjectival in form, derived from some other personal or place-name, usually by the addition of the suffix *-ius*, *-aeus*, *-eius*, or *-eus*; Gauls used the suffix *-acus*, Etruscans *-nas* or *-na*, Umbrians *-enus*, *-ienus*.

The cognomen was originally a nickname or surname given to an individual by his friends or the public, which afterwards came to be used by a whole branch of a *gens*. The cognomen is usually more intelligible than the far older gentile name, being formed directly from names of places, events, physical characteristics, or else from praenomina or some other cognomen by the addition of the suffix *-inus* or *-ianus*. The *gens* could admit a new cognomen either for an individual or for a whole branch, and it was thus possible in the course of time for one person to bear several cognomina. Thus the Cornelian *gens* had a branch named *Scipio*, from which was later formed another named *Nasica*, and one consequently finds such names as *P. Cornelius Scipio Nasica Corculum* (the last being his personal cognomen). But in the best period people used only one

[1] A few of the plebeian families had praenomina of their own.

or at most two cognomina, and the occasion of a second was usually some feat of arms or an adoption; an adoptive son usually took all three of his adoptive father's names together with a derivative in *-anus* of the name of his own *gens.*

Women originally bore the name of the father's *gens* with another name placed before it; this, which often formally resembled the masculine praenomen, seems actually to have been more in the nature of a cognomen; thus besides *Gaia, Lucia, Publia,* &c., we find *Rutilia, Murrula, Rodacilla, Tertia, Secunda, Prima,* &c. These names went out of use about the middle of the Republican period, and women were known simply by the name of the *gens.* At the beginning of the Empire they took to personal names again, placing them after instead of before the name of the *gens* (e.g. *Iunia Tertulla*). Later there were fresh changes; two names were still used, but these were either the father's nomen and cognomen put into a feminine form (e.g. *Aemilia Lepida* daughter of *L. Aemilius Lepidus*), or the nomen of the father plus that of the mother (e.g. *Valeria Attia,* daughter of *L. Attius Atticus* and *Valeria Sextina*). These variations seem to have been chiefly a matter of fashion. Married women are often designated by their own names followed by that of the husband in the genitive case (e.g. *Agrippina Germanici Caesaris*).

Slaves originally had no official names of their own, but simply took their owner's praenomen in the genitive case followed by the suffix *-por* (= *puer* boy), e.g. *Marcipor, Publipor, Quintipor.* Later they were given Greek (often neuter) names followed by the owner's name in the genitive case. Freedmen used their own name as cognomen, the nomen of whoever freed them, and any praenomen they fancied.

During the later centuries of the Empire no strict rule was observed, and the number of names which a member of a great family could bear was very large. It was the fashion to use many cognomina in order to display the illustriousness of one's ancestry. Sometimes we find a man with two praenomina, two or more nomina, and a considerable number of cognomina. Moreover, the order in which the names were arranged became quite arbitrary, and it is often difficult to tell by which of them a person was usually known. Finally, there arose, particularly in the army and lower classes, a new kind of surname, called *signum* or *vocabulum*, which was at first a nickname but later became a genuine surname. The introduction and spread of Christianity seems not to have affected the existing usage in the matter of names.

It is difficult to judge how far the Roman system of nomenclature was adopted in the various parts of the Empire, but it is certain that at all events the upper classes in the more thoroughly romanized parts adopted it; examples are *L. Aurelius Augustinus*, a Numidian, better known as *St. Augustine*, and the 5th-century Gaul *C. Sollius Modestus Apollinaris Sidonius*. The hordes of barbarians who overran the Empire, however, obliterated the Roman system, and even in such countries as Gaul and Spain, where the Franks and Goths adopted the language of their victims, they for the most part kept their own names. For instance, Dauzat, speaking of France, says that in the 9th century, out of a hundred names chosen at random, one will find five or six of Latin origin such as *Honoré* or *Loup*, three or four Biblical ones, and all the rest Germanic. Conversion to Christianity made little difference in this respect, for though the Church has always favoured the use of the names of saints and deprecated purely heathen names, and was partly able to enforce its preference in the later Middle Ages, it seems not to have taken any strong line in earlier times. Heathens seem mostly to have retained their old names on baptism, though sometimes they were given a new one in its place (e.g. *Ceadwalla*, King of Wessex, after his abdication, went to Rome in 689 and was baptized by Pope Sergius in the name

Peter); but sometimes the new name was no more Christian than the old (e.g. the Dane *Guthrum*, who became Alfred's son by adoption at his baptism, was given the name Æthelstan, which was in the old tradition of the West-Saxon royal family).

Old English Names

The Germanic-speaking peoples had a simple system of nomenclature, with general features the same amongst them all, though with minor variations of detail. It may be said in general that cognate forms of most names exist (or may be presumed to have existed) in Old German (and its derivatives), Old English, Gothic, and Old Scandinavian. As with the Greeks and Celts, there is a single name for each individual, and the names are usually made up of two elements taken from a stock of special words used in name-making. Some of these words could be used only as a first element in a name (e.g. Old English *Æthel-*, *Ead*), others only as a second element (e.g. Old English *-weard*), while others could be used in either position (e.g. Old English *ric*, *beorht*). Men's names usually had a second element of masculine gender and women's names one of feminine gender, but there are some exceptions. In addition there were a number of short names which are of two kinds: (1) genuine independent names derived from a single root-word, (2) hypocoristic or pet-names formed from compound names, e.g. *Cutha* from *Cuthwulf*, &c., which sometimes acquired the rank of independent names. The available evidence seems to show that uncompounded names were relatively common both in England and on the Continent in the Migratory period, but became less so later. It should, however, always be remembered that the material for study of early names is almost entirely derived from lists of witnesses to charters, &c., and that such people were necessarily for the most part members of the ruling classes. There is some evidence that the uncompounded names continued to be used by the lower classes after they had been discarded by the upper. There is, e.g., a group of 11th-century English manumissions where a high proportion of the serfs bear uncompounded names; and surname material suggests that such names survived among this class long after the Norman Conquest: *Bugg* and *Wragg*, for instance, of which Matthew Arnold eloquently complains,[1] are almost certainly derived from the Old English personal names *Bugge* and *Ragge*, and there are a number of similar examples. But these names, with a very few exceptions (e.g. *Hilde*) did not survive as christian names after the 13th century, have not been revived since, and so do not concern us here.

Except in Scandinavia and Iceland, where patronymics and nicknames acquired a wide currency at an early date, the Germanic-speaking peoples used but a single name, family connexions being indicated chiefly by the devices of alliteration and variation. Alliteration (i.e. the use of names beginning with the same letter for members of a family) is of very early date, traces of it being found in Tacitus. It was particularly common in the Old English kingdoms, from the earliest recorded genealogies down to the Norman Conquest. Vocalic alliteration was commonest, but consonantal was also practised (e.g. SS. *Mildthryth*, *Mildburh*, and *Mildgyth*, daughters of *Merewald*). Alliteration was definitely of Germanic origin, but variation probably arose before the Germanic languages were differentiated from the main stock (traces of it are found, for instance, in Greek); it consists in giving to the child or children a name or names of which one element is the same as one in the name of the father (or occasionally mother) and the other is different. Variation could be either of the first element (e.g. *Eadmund* son of *Alkmund*) or of the second element (e.g. *Eadgar* son of *Eadmund*). In England end-

[1] *The Function of Criticism.*

variation was rather the commoner. Very rarely both elements represented parts of the parents' names, as in the classic example of St. *Wulfstan*: 'Pater Æthelstanus, mater Wulfgeua nominati . . . puero Wulfstanus vocabulum datum ex anteriore materni et ex posteriore paterni nominis compositum.'[1] But this never became a general fashion. In the East Saxon royal family *Sige-* was the commonest initial element, in Bernicia *Os-*, in Kent *Eormen-* or *Æthel-*, and in Wessex *Æthel-*, *Ead-*, and *Ælf-*.

A third method of showing family connexions was by the repetition of names, usually in alternate generations (e.g. naming a child after his grandfather). This was a late development and seems, indeed, to have been prohibited in early times, perhaps for religious reasons. It was practised in England to some extent in the 10th and 11th centuries, and there are a few examples of repetition between great-grandfather and great-grandson in the 7th century.

Women, in the Old English period, were named on precisely the same system as men with due regard to alliteration and variation on the names of the father's family.

The Danish invasions had no great effect on the general system of nomenclature in England, though the Danes and Norwegians, of course, used their native names. These were usually cognate with Old English names, but some specifically Norse ones, such as *Knud*, *Thorkill*, *Sweyn*, were introduced. They do not, however, seem to have become current outside the Danelaw, and were in any case reinforced later by the much greater influence of the Normans, many of whose names were of Norse origin.

EFFECTS OF THE NORMAN CONQUEST

With the Norman Conquest a great change came over the personal nomenclature of the English. So far as the upper

[1] *Vita Wulfstani* (11th C).

classes are concerned, it is almost true to say that the Old English names (with a few exceptions) had disappeared within two or three generations, and though, as we have seen, there is some reason to suppose that some of the uncompounded Old English names remained in use amongst the peasantry, they, too, had disappeared by the end of the 13th century. For example, in a list of 800 names of jurors and bailiffs in the Eyre of Kent 1313–14, the only Old English names found are two *Edmunds*, one *Edward*, one *Hereward*, and one *Aylwyn*. In a Poll Tax roll for the West Riding of Yorkshire in 1379 there is hardly a single Old English name. Those few names which did survive usually did so for one of two reasons: either they were names of saints (e.g. *Edward*, *Edmund*, *Hilda*, *Mildred*) or they were the names of former kings of the house of Wessex (e.g. *Alfred*, *Edgar*, *Ethelbert*); the first of these classes is the more numerous. The change was facilitated by the fact that the Norman names were largely drawn from the same ultimate sources as the English, being for the most part gallicized forms of Old German names, most of which had cognates in Old English, or else gallicized forms of Norse names, many of which were also familiar in England. Such Old English names as did remain in use were subject to a gallicizing process, the chief effects of which were: (1) *th* was either omitted (e.g. *Aylward*, *Aylwin* for *Æthelweard*, *Æthelwine*) or became *t* (as *Turbett* for *Thurbeorht*) or *d* (as *Adlin* and *Edlin* from *Æthelwine*); (2) final *-eald* became *-auld*, *-aud*, or *-old* (e.g. *Reynebaud*, later *Rainbow*, from *Regenbeald*); (3) *w* tended to become *v* before *a*, *e*, or *i*, and to disappear before *o* and *u* (as *Harvard* for *Hereweard*, *Ayloffe* for *Æthelwulf*, *Reynold* for *Regenweald*); (4) final *h* was replaced by *k*, and later by *-ge* (e.g. *Elphick*, *Alphege* from *Alfeah*). Some of these, however, were probably merely Norman *spellings*.

But these survivals are few and hardly noticeable among

the flood of *Williams*, *Richards*, *Roberts*, *Ralphs*, *Odos*, *Hughs*, *Walters*, which fill the records of the period. The Normans also brought with them a certain number of names of Latin and others of Breton origin (e.g. *Ives*, *Sampson*, *Alan*).

Growing Influence of the Church

Down to this time the Church in western Europe had had little influence on the names of its members. It is true that various Fathers and ecclesiastical writers and some synodal decrees had from time to time exhorted the faithful to give their children only the names of canonized saints or of angels, but their admonitions had not been much heeded, and in fact it was not until the Council of Trent (1545–63) that the Roman Catholic Church absolutely required the use of such names in baptism. By the end of the 12th century, however, the growing power of the Church to influence every aspect of life is reflected in the greatly increased use of the names of saints. To take only scriptural saints as an example, it may be observed that *Matthew*, *Peter*, *John*, and *Andrew* each occur once in Domesday Book, and are rare until the end of the following century; *Luke*, *Bartholomew*, *Philip*, *James*, *Paul*, *Simon*, *Michael*, are first recorded between 1185 and 1200, *Barnabas* in 1201, and *Mark* not until 1303. At the end of the 12th century the commonest man's name in the records is still *William* (15%) followed by *Robert* (11%), *Ralph* (10%), *Richard* (8%), *John* accounting for only 2 per cent. A hundred years later *William*, *Robert*, and *Richard* represent respectively 14, 11, and 10 per cent. of recorded names, but *John* has jumped to first place with no fewer than 25 per cent., and other scriptural names are well established. The change was even more noticeable in the case of women's names, the old Germanic names being almost entirely replaced by the names of scriptural and legendary saints. *Mary* is first found recorded as a christian name about 1203, *Anne* in 1218, *Joan* in 1189, *Elizabeth* in 1205, while of the names of the three great virgin saints, *Agnes*, *Catherine*, and *Margaret*, the first two are recorded in 1189 and 1196; *Margaret* came into use rather earlier owing to St. *Margaret*, sister of Edgar Atheling, who had Hungarian connexions, *Margaret* being used from an early date in eastern Europe.

Changes in the 12th and 13th Centuries

The first effect of this change in fashion was greatly to increase the number and variety of names; in the late 12th century and early 13th century there were probably more christian names in use than at any subsequent period until the 20th century. Some of the Old English names were still in use, there was the rich Norman stock with a sprinkling of Breton, in addition to the newly adopted saints' names which were drawn from Hebrew, Greek, Latin, and other tongues. But even this wealth of material seems not to have satisfied the eclectic taste of the period, and the oddest names are to be met with in late-12th-century records, e.g. *Aliena*, *Antigone*, *Camilla*, *Cassandra*, *Celestria*, *Extranea*, *Grecia*, *Hodierna*, *Idonea*, *Ismenia*, *Juvenal*, *Italia*, *Lavina*, *Leda*, *Melodia*, *Norma*, *Oriolda*, *Paris*, *Pavia*, *Pharamus*, *Splendor*. It will be noted that these are mostly feminine, and they no doubt represent the same love of novelty as led Mrs. Kenwigs to invent the name *Morleena* 'for the special distinction of her eldest child, in case it should prove a daughter', and still sways the minds of potential stars of stage and screen in their search for professional names. But as the 13th century advanced, the stock of names shrank rapidly, and of those still in use a comparatively small number were borne by an increasingly large proportion of the population. The five names *Henry*, *John*, *Richard*, *Robert*, *William* together accounted for 38 per cent. of recorded men's names in the

12th century, for 57 per cent. in the 13th century, and for 64 per cent. in the 14th century. The same tendency is to be observed in France; it has been calculated that in Paris at the end of the 13th century the names *Jehan* and *Jehane* were at least twice as frequent as the next commonest, *Guillaume* and *Marie.* This tendency continued until at least the end of the 18th century, though interrupted by temporary fashions, such as the use of Biblical names in the 17th century. It is easier to illustrate after the compulsory registration of baptisms begins, as is shown in the following tables which give percentages of total baptisms.

Commonest Men's Names

	1550–99	*1600–49*	*1650–99*	*1700–49*	*1750–99*
William .	22·5	15·5	18·5	20·0	20·0
John .	15·5	19·0	28·0	24·5	19·0
Thomas .	13·5	16·0	16·0	10·0	16·0
Total .	51·5	50·5	62·5	54·5	55·0

Commonest Women's Names

	1600–49	*1650–99*	*1700–49*	*1750–99*
Elizabeth .	25·0	14·5	22·0	19·0
Mary . .	17·0	20·5	20·0	24·0
Anne . .	10·0	11·5	14·0	14·0
Total . .	52·0	46·5	56·0	57·0

Rise of Surnames

To return to the 13th century, it is evident that such a limitation in the number of christian names must have led to a considerable amount of confusion, and this had no doubt some influence on the fairly general adoption of surnames in the 13th and 14th centuries. Surnames had been in use to some extent among the Norman nobility since the Conquest, though even by them they were not used consistently and were often not real hereditary surnames. A good example is the genealogy of the Fitzhugh family, which was founded by one Bardolph, the succession being Akaris Fitz-Bardolph, Hervey Fitz-Akaris, Henry Fitz-Hervey, Randolph Fitz-Henry, Hugh Fitz-Randolph, Henry Fitz-Hugh (fl. 1321). But the bearing of a surname of some sort became common in all classes of English society in the late 12th and early 13th centuries. A large number of these were patronymics; even more were place-names indicating the residence or place of origin of the bearer; others were names of trades or callings, and yet others were nicknames, sometimes descriptive, sometimes derisive. A man might very well be known at different times or in different places by different names (in the Battle Abbey Deeds, for example, the same man is referred to indifferently as John Hervy, John Fitz Hervie de Sudwerk, and John de London), and it was long before the custom of keeping to a single hereditary surname became general. The compulsory keeping of parish registers (from 1538) probably completed the process in England. In Wales even the gentry bore no hereditary surnames until the time of Henry VIII, who strongly advised the heads of Welsh families to conform to English usage; their use by other classes in Wales was by no means universal even in the 18th century. Borrow has a story of a Welsh 18th-century poet Twm o'r Nant (Tom of the valley) whose father's name was Evan Edwards, and who accordingly was in the habit of calling himself Thomas Evans, until it occurred to him that this might be taken as meaning that he was a bastard, after which he called himself Thomas Edwards. There are even parts of England (notably Yorkshire and Staffordshire) where, within living memory, the poorer classes seldom used their surnames except in legal documents, &c., men being known by such appellations as 'Tom o' Dick o' Mary's'.

Legal Aspect of Names

It is, indeed, by no means clear what a man's name legally is, or, indeed, whether there is such a thing as a legal name. The Church recognizes only the name given in baptism,[1] and there is some division of opinion whether a second name can be added to or substituted for the baptismal name at confirmation. Monks and nuns always take a new christian name in religion, and priests can change their christian name at ordination. Before the Reformation the unauthorized change of a christian name was a grave offence. It is recorded in the consistorial acts of the Bishop of Rochester that on 15th October 1515 one Agnes Sharpe appeared and confessed that she had 'of her own motion and consent, voluntarily changed at confirmation the name of her infant son to Edward, who was when baptized named Henry, for which she submitted to penance'. A beneficed clergyman of the Church of England is obliged to perform the ceremony of baptism when required to do so by a parishioner, and to give whatever names the godparents select; but, although the rubrics do not expressly say so, it is generally assumed that he may object to any name on religious or moral grounds. A Roman priest is authorized to add a saint's name to those chosen by the godparents, if these are unchristian or non-christian and circumstances are such that discussion and dissuasion are impracticable or impolitic. The Registration of Births Act (1874), though it makes provision for the insertion of a christian name, does not require such insertion, which remains permissive, not compulsory. Chief Justice

[1] e.g. in the rites of baptism, confirmation, and holy matrimony. Bishops sign only their christian names, followed by the name of their dioceses. Another vestige of this is to be found in the signatures of royal personages, e.g. *George R.*

Coke (1552–1634) says: 'It is requisite that a purchaser be named by the name of baptism and his surname, and that special heed be taken to the name of baptism, for that a man cannot have two names of baptism as he may have divers surnames'; and again: 'It is holden in our antient books that a man may have divers *names* at divers times, but not divers Christian names.' Sir Joseph Jekyll, Master of the Rolls, in 1730 in the case of *Barlow* v. *Bateman*, remarked: 'I am satisfied the usage of passing Acts of Parliament for the taking upon one a surname is but modern, and that anyone may take upon him what surname, and as many surnames, as he pleases, without an Act of Parliament.' This decision, however, was reversed by the House of Lords, and it is now usually assumed that a man's legal appellation is the christian name given him in baptism by his god-parents (or, alternatively, inserted in the registration of his birth) and the surname of his father or, in the case of an illegitimate child, of his mother.

Nicknames

The adoption of surnames was not in itself enough to prevent the ambiguity caused by the extensive use of a very few christian names, particularly as it was by no means uncommon in the 13th to 15th centuries to give more than one living child in the same family the same name; in particular it is quite usual to find brothers named John (e.g. the two sons of John Paston, Sir John Paston the elder (1442–79) and Sir John Paston the younger (died 1503)). Examples from 15th-century wills are bequests to 'Isabel and Isabel my daughters', and to 'Besse my daughter and Elizabeth my daughter'.[1] The difficulty was partly solved by the use (as in

[1] It has been suggested that one reason for giving the same name to more than one son was the custom of granting leases for three lives, i.e. to John Doe and his sons John and William; if one son died, there would still be one of the same name left to hold the lease.

the last-quoted example) of diminutives or pet-names; thus the common name *Bartholomew* appears variously as *Bat*, *Bate*, *Batty*, *Bartle*, *Bartelot*, *Bartelet*, *Batcock*, *Batkin*, *Tolly*. The French diminutive suffixes *-el*, *-on*, *-in*, *-ot*, *-et* are earlier than the English *-kin* and *-cock* and were used by all classes of the community, whereas the English ones are found only among the lower classes. The French diminutives were used either singly or in combination with each other and are found from the early 12th century; thus the Norman name *Hamo*(*n*) developed the diminutive forms *Ham-el*, *Ham-el-in*, *Ham-el-et*, *Ham-el-ot*, *Hamon-et*. They were used for both men's and women's names, but survived longer in the latter case; thus *Philpot*, *Wilmot*, *Marriot*, *Emmot* are found as women's names in the 16th and 17th centuries, and even later in Cornwall, long after such forms had ceased to be used by men. *-on*, which is always feminine in French and usually in English (e.g. *Alison*, *Marion*), was also sometimes used for men (e.g. *Gibbon* from *Gib*, a pet-form of *Gilbert*).

The vernacular suffixes *-cock* and *-kin* are first recorded about the end of the 13th century. *-kin* was possibly of Flemish origin, having been in use in the Low Countries from the 10th century. It is usually masculine, though occasionally feminine (e.g. *Malkin* or *Mawkin* from *Mary*), the earliest recorded examples being *Janekin*, *Malekin*, *Watekin*, and *Wilekin* which are found in 1250. It was most common in the second half of the 14th century. *Piers Plowman* (1362) has *Malkin*, *Perkin*, *Hawkin*, and *Watkin*; Chaucer uses *Jankin*, *Malkin*, *Perkin*, *Simkin*, and *Wilkin*; in 'The Tournament of Tottenham' (*c.* 1450) occur *Dawkyn*, *Hawkyn*, *Jeynkyn*, *Perkyn*, and *Tymkyn*. It will be noted that most of these are derived from the commoner christian names, and the same is true of compounds of *-cock*, examples of which are *Adcock* (from *Adam*), *Batcock*, *Hancock* (from *Jehan*), *Hitchcock*, *Simcock*, *Wilcock*. The origin of this suffix is obscure, but it seems probable that it is the Middle English *cok* (= French *coq*), used in the sense 'good fellow' (cf. modern slang 'old cock', &c.), though this sense is not recorded until much later than the first occurrence of the suffix in personal names (*c.* 1275). Christian names in *-kin* and especially *-cock* are rare after about 1450, though they survive in numerous common surnames.

There was another kind of pet-name, that formed by apocope or syncope from the original name, as *Will* from *William*, *Sim* from *Simon*, *Gib* from *Gilbert*, *Wat* from *Walter*; and these in turn gave rise to other, rhyming, forms, as *Dick* and *Hick* for *Ricard*, *Hitch* for *Richard*, *Hob* and *Bob* for *Robert*, *Hodge* for *Roger*. *Dick* is one of the earliest of these names to be recorded (*quidam Dicke Smith* Curia Regis Rolls 1220), and many of them are still in use, though it is curious to note that the once common forms with initial *H*, e.g. *Hob*, *Hodge*, *Hick*, *Hitch*, *Hudd* (for *Richard*, see Bardsley s.v. *Hudd*), *Hibb* (for *Ib* from *Isabel*), have all died out. There can be little doubt that the majority of peasants in the 13th to 15th centuries went by these rather uncouth names, which so nearly resembled the Old English uncompounded names which had been general among their forefathers before the Norman Conquest and had lingered on in occasional use until the 13th or 14th century. The *locus classicus* for these pet-names in literature is Gower's *Vox Clamantis*, where the poet describes the peasant's revolt of 1381:

> *Watte* vocat, cui *Thomme* venit, neque *Symme* retardat,
> *Betteque*, *Gibbe* simul, *Hykke* venire jubent;
> *Colle* furit, quem *Geffe* juvat, nocumenta parantes,
> Cum quibus ad dampnum *Wille* coire vovet.
> *Grigge* rapit, dum *Dawe* strepit comes est quibus *Hobbe*,
> *Lorkyn* et in medio non minor esse putat:
> *Hudde* ferit, quem *Judde* terit, dum *Tebbe* minatur,
> *Jakke* domosque viros vellit et ense necat.

These forms were mainly a plebeian usage, a sign of which is the later use of many of them as common nouns, e.g. *hodge* for a country labourer, *jack* and *dick* meaning 'man', 'fellow', and such phrases as *every Tom, Dick, and Harry.* In the 14th century there was scarcely a name in common use which had not one or more of such diminutives. After the Reformation, with the advent of Biblical names, the old French and English diminutive suffixes fell out of use, but the habit of using shortened forms of names for familiar use went on and still persists.[1]

It is instructive to note how age throws a cloak of respectability over names of plebeian origin. Thus the medieval *Jack, Tom, Dick, Bob, Will* are now used by all classes; the 17th-century *Sam, Ben, Joe* were freely used by the middle classes in the 19th century and would doubtless still be so used, but for the fact that their originals have gone out of fashion; but the modern *Les, Reg, Bert* have not yet had time to rise in the social scale.[2] This was true in 1944, but is no longer so. *Des, Ron, Vic, Doug, Cliff*, and many others are dotted, for instance, all over the pages of the *Radio Times* in 1976.

Use of Men's Names for Women

One other result of the increasing use of saints' names in the later Middle Ages was the adaptation of men's names to the use of women. In some cases a similar name was taken to be the equivalent; *Joan*, for instance, was given to girls whom it was wished to put under the patronage of St. *John.* In French the formation of feminines was perfectly easy, and these became, and have remained, common in France.

[1] Cf. Mr. Samuel Weller's comment on the name of Mr. Job Trotter: 'And a wery good name it is—only one I know, that ain't got a nickname to it.'

[2] *Reggie* and *Bertie*, for some obscure reason, have a much higher social standing than *Reg* and *Bert*.

Latin records of the 13th to 15th centuries show that the custom of giving masculine names to girls was also common in England; they appear in Latin with feminine endings, e.g. *Philippa*, *Nicholaa*, *Alexandra*, *Jacoba*, but it is clear that girls so named were in fact baptized and called *Philip*, *Nicholas*, *Alexander*, *James*, &c. For further details see under these names. Other names which were commonly used for girls were *Gilbert*, *Aubrey*, *Reynold*, *Basil*, *Eustace*, *Giles*, *Edmund*, *Simon*, *Florence*. *Nicholas* was particularly common as a girl's name in Scotland, where it was still current at the end of the 17th century. An interesting reference to this custom occurs in a 12th-century tract by Maurice of Kirkham to Gilbert of Sempringham, quoted by M. R. James ['The Salomites', *J. Theological Studies*, 35, 1934 (287–97)]. The writer was concerned to refute the heretical opinion that *Salome* was a man's name (i.e. that in *Mark* xv. 40 and xvi. 1, *Mary* and *Salome* represent not two, but one person 'Mary wife of Salome'). The Salomites, he says, make use of the vulgar argument that women often borrow men's names ('plerasque mulieres a viris sibi nomina solere mutuari'), giving as examples Alexander, Thomas, Eustace, and William. He then describes how he had crushed a scholar who was defending this opinion. ' "Were you never present in a baptistry when infants were being baptized?" "Yes, often." "Did you ever on such an occasion hear a boy named Beatrice or Gunnilda or Matilda or Godiva?" "Certainly not." "Then why should you suppose that the Jews should be in the habit of giving feminine names to males? Women's names or nicknames are given to lazy, slothful, effeminate persons, not in their baptism, but on account of their vicious life, as, for example, we formerly knew a Robert who for his infamous character was called Godiva." '

The Scots in the 18th century were very fond of making feminine forms of masculine names, quite regardless of euphony, possibly under French influence. Examples are

Abrahamina, *Adamina*, *Æneasina*, *Alexina*, *Angusina*, *Clementina*, *Davidina*, *Forbesia*, *Jacobina*, *Jamesina*, *Johnina*, *Philippina*, *Roberta*, *Robina*, *Stewartina*, *Vallentina*, *Williamina*. A few of these survive, but most of them have, happily, disappeared.

Names referring to Circumstances of Birth

Before we leave the pre-Reformation period there are one or two details which may be noted. Children were often christened with names referring to the day of their birth: *Christmas*, *Nowell*, *Easter*, *Pask*, *Whitsun*, *Pentecost*, *Epiphany*, *Theophania* or *Tiffany*, *Loveday*, and others were all used as christian names. It was the custom for a midwife to christen quick children before birth when it was feared that they might not be delivered alive. They were given neuter names such as *Vitalis*, *Creature*, *Chylde-of-God*.

The Reformation

The change in nomenclature which followed the Reformation was second in importance only to that caused by the Norman Conquest. Up to that time the number of Biblical names in use was comparatively small, consisting for the most part of those made familiar by the mystery plays, as *Adam*, *Eve*, *Noah*, *Sarah*, *Abraham*, *Isaac*, *Jacob*, *Joseph*, *Daniel*, *Sampson*, *David*, *Absalom*, *Susanna*, *Judith*, *Anna*, *Hester*, *Tobias*, *Jonah*. There were also a few names brought back by the Crusaders, such as *Baptist*, *Jordan*, *Elias*, and the names of the apostles, particularly *John*, *James*, *Simon*, *Peter*, *Bartholomew*, *Matthew*, *Philip*, *Thomas*, *Barnabas*; *Paul* and *Timothy* were also used, but were not common. With the Reformation all the names of non-scriptural saints fell into disgrace and were for the most part speedily disused. *Austin*, *Basil*, *Bennet*, *Blase*, *Brice*, *Christopher*, *Clement*, *Crispin*, *Denis*, *Fabian*, *Gervase*, *Hilary*, *Martin*, *Quentin*,

Theobald, *Valentine*, *Viel* were some of those which almost disappeared in the 16th century, and some of the apostles (e.g. *Simon Peter*) fared little better. The effect was even greater on the naming of women, for some of the favourite women's names were those of unscriptural saints, e.g. *Agnes*, *Cecily*, *Barbara*, *Katherine*, *Margaret*, *Ursula*. Since the disgrace of the calendar coincided in time with the dissemination of the English Bible, it was naturally to the Bible that people looked for new names, and since the names of the apostles had long been in use and were felt to savour somewhat of popery, it was the Old Testament names which now began to be used. Cartwright, writing in 1565, advised that 'They which present unto baptism ought to be persuaded not to give those that are baptized the names of God, or of Christ, or of Angels, or of holy offices, as of baptist, evangelist &c. nor such as savour of paganism or popery: but chiefly such whereof there are examples in the Holy Scriptures, in the names of those who are reported in them to have been godly and virtuous.'

Puritan Names

The next innovations were made by the Puritans, who, wishing to mark their children off from what they regarded as the godless masses, found that the more manageable of the Old Testament names were already in use. They accordingly took to such names as *Renovata*, *Donatus*, *Beata*, *Renatus*, *Rediviva*, *Desiderius*, *Desideratus*, *Deodatus*, all of which are recorded in the 16th century. Later they began to coin corresponding English names. Thus *Desiderius*, *Donatus*, and *Amor* are matched by *Desire*, *Given*, and *Love*, and as time went on many strange names were invented, of which the classic example is *Praise-God* Barebones. It is sometimes stated that these Puritan names are a mere myth, but that is because the mistake has been made of consulting parish registers of the second half of the 17th century, whereas the time when they were most rife was from about 1580 to 1640. Thus Thomas Heley, minister of Warbleton, called his children (born between 1583 and 1589) *Much-Merceye*, *Increased*, *Sin-denie*, and *Fear-not*; a contemporary Presbyterian minister called his *Persis*, *Renewed*, and *Safe-on-high*. Camden in his *Remaines* (1605) writes:

> 'If that any among us have named their children *Remedium amoris*, *Imago saeculi*, or with such like names, I know some will think it more than a vanity, as they do but little better of the new names, *Free-gift*, *Reformation*, *Earth*, *Dust*, *Ashes*, *Delivery*, *More-fruit*, *Tribulation*, *The Lord is near*, *More triall*, *Discipline*, *Joy again*, *From above*, *Acceptance*, *Thankfull*, *Praise-God* and *Live-well*, which have lately been given by some to their children with no evill meaning, but upon some singular and precise conceit.'

The more responsible religious leaders did not encourage this fashion: Cartwright, as we have seen, merely recommended the use of the names of virtuous persons mentioned in the scriptures, but his condition of *virtuous* was not always heeded, and during the 17th century there was hardly a name in the Bible which was not used, regardless of its associations, as a christian name, and the more thoughtful were scandalized by such names as *Antipas*, *Cain*, *Dinah*, *Tamar*, *Sapphira*, as well as pained by the cacophonies of *Bezaleel*, *Ezekiel*, or *Habakkuk*. Camden, who probably represented the normal point of view, wrote:

> 'In times of Christianity, the names of most holy and vertuous persons, and of their most worthy progenitors were given to stir up men to the imitation of them, whose name they bare. But succeeding ages (little regarding S. Chrysostom's admonition to the contrary) have recalled prophane names, so as now Diana, Cassandra, Hippolitus, Venus, Lais, names of unhappy disaster

are as rife somewhere, as ever they were in Paganism.[1] Albeit in our late reformation, some of good consideration have brought in *Zachary*, *Malachy*, *Jozias* &c. as better agreeing with our faith, but without contempt of countrie names (as I hope) which have both good and gracious significations.'

The judicious Calamy, writing his account of the ejected ministers at the end of the 17th century, says: 'This was a course that some in those times affected, baptizing their children *Reformation*, *Discipline* &c. as the affection of their parents stood engaged. For this they have sufficiently suffered from Profane Wits, and this worthy person [Sabbath Clark] did so in particular.' Anyone interested in these eccentricities may refer to Bardsley's *Curiosities of Puritan Nomenclature*, where he will find much information and entertainment. Here there is only room for a few detached remarks. There is no doubt that a fanatical minister had much influence in the matter of names: thus while Thomas Heley, mentioned above, was minister of Warbleton (1585–9) the parish registers show at least 100 eccentric names including *Sorry-for-Sin* and *No-merit*. One Edmund Snape, curate of St. Peter's, Northampton, in 1590 refused to christen a child Richard (after its grandfather) because it was not a scriptural name, but this seems to have been an exceptional case. Some typical Puritan families are those of Robert Pound of Canterbury, whose children (born between 1564 and 1592) were baptized *Abdias*, *Barnabas*, *Ezekiell*, *Philemon*, *Repentance*, and *Postumus*; and of Michael Nichollson of St. Peter's,

[1] Camden was probably thinking primarily of France, where the fashion of using classical names was very general among the nobility. It was also prevalent in Italy and Germany. Such names as *Lucrezia*, *Cesare*, *Alessandro*, *Olimpia*, *Diane*, *Hercule*, *Aurore*, *Achille* are examples. In England they were less common, but *Diana* was establishing itself, and there are occasional others such as *Apollo* Pepys (d. 1644), the great-uncle of Samuel Pepys. One of Camden's examples, *Cassandra* (q.v.), had been in general use in the Middle Ages.

Cornhill, who between 1589 and 1599 had *Bezaleel*, *Aholiab*, *Sara*, and *Rebecca*. Later examples are Zachary Crofton (d. 1672), whose sons were named *Zachary*, *Zareton*, *Zephaniah*, *Zelophehad*, and *John*; and *Jonathan* Grant (d. 1681), who had by his wife *Obedience* children named *Jedediah*, *Jonathan*, *Deodate*, *Elizabeth*, *Hadassa*, *Charity*, *Hannah*, and *Sarah*. Foundlings were obvious subjects for the ingenuity of Puritan ministers, and they were freely given such names as *Helpless*, *Repentance*, *Lament*, *Forsaken*, *Flie-fornication*; perhaps the climax of this kind of name was reached in the case of a poor little foundling girl baptized in 1644 at Baltonsborough, Somerset, in the name *Misericordia-adulterina*.

The more extravagant of these names died out gradually after the Restoration, and the permanent addition made to the stock of christian names in general use was (1) the large class of Biblical, especially Old Testament, names, (2) names such as *Faith*, *Hope*, *Charity*, *Prudence*. Of the Old Testament names, some became truly acclimatized and common, e.g. *Samuel*, *Benjamin*, *Joseph*, *Jacob*, *Sarah*, *Susan*, *Hannah*. Others, such as *Elijah*, *Amos*, *Zachary*, *Ebenezer*, *Caleb*, and many others, continued to be used by the sectaries and later by Wesleyans and Evangelicals in the Church of England, and died out only towards the end of the 19th century; examples still linger on, as for example three brothers recently still living in a Devon village, who were named *Shadrach*, *Meshach*, and *Abednego*. The permanent effects of Puritan nomenclature were greater in America. The settlers of the 17th century were very largely sectaries, and there was therefore an unusually high proportion of these names among them; *Preserved* Fish (1766–1846), for instance, could hardly have received such a name at that date in England. Besides the common Old Testament names there are others which have taken firm root in America, such as *Ira*, *Seth*, *Jedediah*, *Elihu*; and the commoner ones, *Benjamin*, *Samuel*, *Daniel*, &c., which are now rare in England, are still in general use in the U.S.A.

Surnames as Christian Names

An interesting post-Reformation development was the use of surnames as christian names. One of the earliest examples noted is Lord *Guildford* Dudley, son of the Duke of Northumberland and husband of Lady Jane Grey, whose mother's maiden name was *Guildford*. Another early example was Sir *Warham* St. Leger (1525–97), whose mother was d. and heiress of Hugh *Warham*, and whose nephew was also named *Warham* St. Leger. The fashion became fairly general among the landed gentry in Elizabeth's reign, and apparently gave rise to some criticism. Camden writes (1605):

'Whereas in late years Surnames have been given for Christian names among us, and no where else in Christendome; although many dislike it, for that great inconvenience will ensue: neverthe-less it seemeth to proceed from hearty good will, and affection of the godfathers to shew their love, or from a desire to continue & propagate their own name to succeeding ages. And is in no wise to be disliked, but rather approved in those, which matching with heirs generall of worshipfull antient families, have given these names to their heirs, with a mindful and thankful regard of them, as we have now, *Pickering Wotton*, *Grevill Varney*, *Bassingburne Gawdy*, *Calthorp Parker*, *Pecsall Brocas*, *Fitz-Raulf Chamberlaine*, who are the heirs of *Pickering*, *Bassingburne*, *Grevill*, *Calthorp* &c.'

He continues in virtuous indignation:

'Neither can I believe a wayward old man, which would say, that the giving of Surnames for Christian Names first began in the time of King *Edward* the sixt, by such as would be Godfathers, when they were more than half fathers, and thereupon would have persuaded some to change such names at the Confirmation. Which (that I may note by the way) is usuall in other Countries, as we remember two sons of King Henry the second of France, christened by the names of *Alexander* and *Hercules*, changed them at their Confirmation to *Henry* and *Francis*.'

Fuller in his *Worthies of England* (1662) has the following passage on the subject, s.v. *Besilius Fetiplace*:

> 'Reader, I am confident an instance can hardly be produced of a surname made Christian, in England, save since the Reformation; before which time the priests were scrupulous to admit any at the font, except they were baptized with the name of a scripture or legendary Saint. Since, it hath been common; and although the Lord Coke was pleased to say he had noted many of them to prove unfortunate, yet the good success in others confutes the general truth of the observation.'

These names were occasionally given to girls, e.g. *Essex*, daughter of Lord Paget (1609–78) and granddaughter to an Earl of Essex, and, in the 18th century, Johnson's friend Miss *Hill* Boothby; in such cases they were sometimes given a feminine termination, e.g. *Jermyna, Althama*. The fashion was confined to the nobility and landed gentry until the 19th century when it was imitated by the middle classes. Some of the more aristocratic surnames, e.g. *Percy*, *Sydney*, *Neville*, *Russell*, *Howard*, have now become genuine christian names, i.e. they are used without any family connexion. At the present time, though family names are still very generally given as a second or middle name, they are less frequent as first names. The use of surnames as christian names is now much more common in the U.S.A. than in England. It has been calculated that three out of four eldest sons of American families of any pretensions bear their mothers' maiden names either as first or as middle names. Compare the Spanish practice of combining the paternal and maternal surnames. Many surnames, for various historical reasons, have also become generally used in America as christian names, e.g. *Calvin*, *Chauncey*, *Dwight*, *Elmer*, *Jackson*, *Grant*, *Lee*, *Jefferson*, *Lincoln*, *Luther*, *Washington*, *Wesley*.

Use of Two or More Christian Names

Another fashion which became general in the 17th century was that of giving more than one christian name. Very rare, isolated examples have been noted earlier, e.g. John William Whytting, vicar of Egdean 1389–1432; John Philip Capel of Fineham 1363. But it is not until the beginning of the 17th century that the number of such names becomes noticeable. Camden, writing in 1605, says:

> 'But two Christian names are rare in England, and I only remember now His Majesty [James I], who was named Charles James, as the Prince his son Henry Frederick, & among private men Thomas Maria Wingfield [Rector of Warrington 1527–37] and Sir Thomas Posthumus Hoby.'

A few other early examples are Robert Browne Lilly, born 1593, son of John Lilly, his mother's maiden name being Browne; Arthur Rous Russhe, born 1564; Charles Maria Chute, born 1610; Gulielma Maria Postuma Springett, born 1640. It will be noted that the second name is usually either a surname or one chosen for religious or other obvious reasons, e.g. *Maria*, *Postumus*. The general spread of the fashion was probably due to the French influence first of Queen Henrietta Maria and later of the Court of Charles II. Charles II's natural daughter by Lady Shannon, who was born 1650 and later married the Earl of Yarmouth, was named Charlotte Jemima Henrietta Maria. In the 18th century this type of name was widely used, especially for girls, who were given three or more names, usually in latinized forms. Goldsmith was laughing at this kind of thing when he invented Miss Carolina Wilhelmina Amelia Skeggs, and at the use of romantic names in general in the Vicar's remarks on his daughters' names:

> 'Our second child, a girl, I intended to call after her aunt Grissel; but my wife, who during her pregnancy had been reading romances, insisted upon her being called Olivia. In less than

another year we had another daughter, and now I was determined that Grissel should be her name; but a rich relation taking a fancy to stand godmother, the girl was, by her directions, called Sophia: so that we had two romantic names in the family; but I solemnly protest I had no hand in it.'

The double names *Mary Anne* and *Anna Maria* are found only after the Revolution of 1688, and seem at first to have been given in honour of Queens Mary and Anne. These and similar combinations, such as *Mary Jane*, *Sarah Jane*, &c., were treated as a single name and commonly used in addressing a person so named well into the 19th century, gradually becoming confined to the poorer classes, and eventually dying out. In the Southern States of America this fashion is still common. Examples of the accumulation of many names are Maria Ann Isabella Margaretta Beatrix, wife of R. Venn, died 1762, and the son of Charles Stone a tailor of Burbage, Wilts, who in 1781 received the names Charles Caractacus Ostorius Maximilian Gustavus Adolphus. The worst offenders in this tasteless piling up of names have been the royal and noble houses both in this country and on the Continent, but in the mid-19th century the middle classes set themselves to imitate them in this as in so many other ways. The great Victorian novelists, Dickens, Thackeray, Trollope, constantly laugh at the fashion, which reminds one forcibly of that, already mentioned, which was current in the later years of the Roman Empire.[1]

[1] There is a difference of usage in Great Britain and the U.S.A. in the matter of initials when there is more than one christian name. The American generally gives the first name in full and the second only as an initial, e.g. Franklin D. Roosevelt, Elihu P. Root. The corresponding usage in England would as a rule be either Franklin Delano Roosevelt, or F. D. Roosevelt, or (with suppression of the middle name) simply Franklin Roosevelt. There was a correspondence on the subject in *N. & Q.* 1856; the American practice was then quite unfamiliar in England, and some correspondents suggested that the initial was merely inserted for

Revival of Obsolete Names

On the whole, however, the 18th century did not display any very great change in nomenclature beyond two limited fashions; one being that already noted of preferring the Latin forms of women's names (e.g. *Anna*, *Maria*, *Sophia*, *Olivia*, *Evelina*, *Cecilia*, *Juliana*, &c., instead of *Anne*, *Mary*, *Sophy*, *Olive*, *Aveline*, *Cecil*, *Julian* or *Gillian*); the other being a certain revival of Old English or medieval names, which was connected with the general interest in the 'gothic'; examples are *Edgar*, *Edwin*, *Alfred*, *Galfrid*, *Emma*, *Matilda*. This second tendency was much accelerated in the 19th century when a whole host of old-fashioned and long obsolete names came back into use as the result of several movements, both religious and literary. The first of these was the Romantic movement, and particularly the great influence of Scott's novels, which reintroduced such names as *Wilfrid*, *Guy*, *Roland*, *Nigel*, *Quentin*, *Amy*, &c.; the second was the Tractarian movement which revived the names of long-neglected saints such as *Aidan*, *Augustine*, *Alban*, *Theodore*, *Benedict*, *Bernard*, &c.; finally the medievalism of Tennyson and the Pre-Raphaelites brought back into use such names as *Lancelot*, *Hugh*, *Walter*, *Aylmer*, *Roger*, *Ralph*, *Ella*, *Alice*, *Mabel*, *Edith*. The fashion has continued ever since, every ten years or so producing new favourites—either names which had become altogether obsolete such as *Joyce*, or obsolete forms of names still in use such as *Gillian*.

distinction, and did not stand for a real name. A correspondent in Suffolk (a magistrate) informed me in 1963 that in the course of questioning American witnesses, he had twice met with cases where the middle initial of their names was said to represent no actual name. The most famous example of the middle initial of a name standing for nothing except itself is the S. in Harry S. Truman.

Modern Eclecticism

In the present century the taste in names has become more and more eclectic, and there are few European languages which have not been laid under contribution. This has been a natural development in the U.S.A. whose population is drawn from every European country, and to some extent that example may have influenced this country. There can be no doubt that at the present time one of the most powerful influences on the masses in this country, in this, as in so many other ways, is that of the American films. The names of American film actors and actresses (frequently fancy inventions of their own) are freely bestowed on the children of their 'fans'. Thus the registrar for Tottenham in 1938 stated that at least 20 per cent. of the parents of Tottenham chose 'cinema names' for their offspring, *Gary* and *Shirley* being the favourites. Other common names from the same source are *Carol*, *Maureen*, *Marlene*, *Myrna*, *Merle*. The great number and enormous circulations of cheap story magazines, the characters in which usually have somewhat fanciful names, has also, no doubt, had much the same effect. On the whole the names of boys remain simpler than those of girls, and in any case the old favourites, *John*, *Thomas*, *William*, *Henry*, *Richard*, *Mary*, *Elizabeth*, *Anne*, *Joan*, still retain first place.

Though in this country and the U.S.A. there is no legal restriction on the taste of parents in naming their children, many European countries have laws, more or less operative, with the object of regulating the matter. Thus in France the Revolutionary Law of 11 Germinal XI (1 April 1803), which is still in force, decrees that names shall be chosen only from those of persons known in ancient history, or in use in the various calendars. Good revolutionaries were averse to using names from christian calendars and availed themselves largely of the permission to use names from ancient history which was interpreted to include a good deal of mythology.

Such favourite French names as *Marcel*, *Jules*, *Aristide*, *Achille* came into use at this time. The rule is not now very strictly applied, but still has a restrictive effect. The law in Germany is that a name must not be used which cannot be proved to have been used before. Such regulations as these, even though they are not always rigidly applied, have, on the whole, had the effect of saving European continental countries from the flood of neologisms which has swept over U.S.A. and, to some extent, over Great Britain.

There is still, however, a strong conservative tendency, at least among readers of *The Times*, and a correspondent writing to that paper (11 Jan. 1950) states that the relative popularity of the ten commonest names for boys and girls respectively, as shown by announcements of births, in *The Times* during 1949 was as follows:—*John* (207), *Richard* (126), *Peter* (114), *David* (108), *Charles* (100), *Michael* (96), *William* (81), *Robert* (79), *Christopher* (77), and *James* (77) for boys; and *Ann(e)* (144), *Mary* (141), *Elizabeth* (132), *Jane* (101), *Susan* (83), *Margaret* (72), *Sarah* (57), *Caroline* (44), *Jennifer* (40), and *Frances* (38). In the previous year also, 18 of these names were in the first 20, but *William* has taken the place of *Anthony* and *Jennifer* of *Penelope*.

A

Aaron (m.): the name of the brother of Moses, first High Priest of Israel. It may be Egyptian, but the meaning is unknown. There was a Celtic saint named *Aaron*, but that was probably a different name. *Aaron* has been used occasionally as a christian name since the Reformation. Bardsley says he did not meet with a single English *Aaron* in medieval times, though it sometimes occurs as the name of a Jew; but there is mention of one apparently English *Aaron* in the Curia Regis Rolls for 1199.

Abel (m.): the 2nd son of Adam and Eve; the meaning of the name is obscure, but it is possibly the accusative of *ablu* 'son'. It was a favourite christian name in the 13th C and gave rise to various surnames, such as *Abel(l)*, *Abelson*, *Able*, and *Nabb(s)* (from the nickname *Nab*, cf. *Abel* in Jonson's *The Alchemist*, who is called *Nab*), *Ablet(t)* from the dim *Abel-ot*. It had some revival in the 17th C. It is still in use in France.

ABEL Cur 1205–6, 1207–9, HR 1273.
ABELOT HR 1273.

Abigail (f.): Hebrew signifying 'father rejoiced'; for *'ăbîgāl* with *ā* changed to hypocoristic *ai* for a girl; the name of the wife of Nabal and afterwards of David (1 Sam. xxv). It came into use in England in the 16th C and was common in the 17th C. From a character so named in Beaumont and Fletcher's play *The Scornful Lady* (1616) it became a slang term for a lady's maid and gradually went out of fashion, though it never became obsolete. CMY suggests that it may also have suffered through being the name of Queen Anne's unpopular favourite, Mrs Masham. In Ireland it was formerly used as an equivalent of the native Celtic name *Gobnait*. It is still in use in Co. Cork. *Abbey* was the usual abbreviation of it. The now quite common *Gail* (q.v.) may also be an abbreviation of *Abigail*.

Abner (m.): Hebrew 'the [divine] father (is) light'; the name of the cousin of Saul and commander of his army. One of the many

Old Testament names adopted after the Reformation, and still occasionally used in the USA.

Abraham (m.): Hebrew. The name of the patriarch was originally *Abram*, 'high father', but was changed to *Abraham*, 'father of a multitude'. *Abraham* occurs as the name of a priest in DB, and was in general though not frequent use in the 13th C. It was revived after the Reformation and was particularly popular in the Low Countries in the forms *Abram*, *Bram*. It is now commoner in the USA than in England (partly, no doubt, owing to its being Lincoln's name), and is there often abbreviated to *Abe*.

ABRAHAM DB 1086, Cur 1189–1207 *passim*, 1294 QW.
HABREHAM (a Jew) Magd. 1230–40.

Absalom (m.): Hebrew 'the [divine] father (is) peace'. The name of the unhappy son of David and Maacah was a favourite in the 12th and 13th C, usually in the French form *Absolon*, and was given by Chaucer to the lively young clerk in his *Miller's Tale*. It has not been much used since about the end of the 14th C.

ABSALOM Cur 1189–1207.
ABSOLON Cur 1197, 1200, 1210, 1213–15.

Acelin (m.): diminutive of Old French *Asce*, *Ace* from Old German *Azzo*. *Ezzelin* was the form in which it took root in Italy. There was another diminutive *Acelet*, and a f. form *Ascelina* also occurs in Latin records. Common in the 13th C, it gave rise to various surnames, e.g. *Aslin*, *Ashlin*, *Asling*, *Acelet*.

AZELINUS DB 1086.
ASCELINA Cur 1207.
ASCELYN HR 1273.
ACELIN HR 1273.
ASSELIN HR 1273.

Achilles (m.) [ăkĭ'lēz]: Greek Ἀχιλλεύς. The etymology of the name is obscure (it is possibly allied to the name of the river Ἀχέλωος.) This Homeric hero, unlike his rival Hector, was not a favourite in the Middle Ages and his name never came into general use. But there was a 3rd-C St. *Achilleus*, the apostle of Vienne, and consequently *Achille* has been not uncommon in France, where it is still used. The revival of classical names at the Renaissance led to an occasional use of *Achilles* by German princes, and it has been used, very rarely, in England.

Ada (f.): imported from Germany at the end of the 18th C. An early example is the name of Byron's daughter, *Augusta Ada*. It became very popular in the 19th C, but has now fallen out of favour. *Ada* is probably a pet form of some name in *Adal*, but there was an Old German m. and f. name *Eda*, *Æda*, *Etta*, *Ætte*, cognate with Old English *Eadda*, *Eadu* (see EDEN). The Hebrew *Adah* (an ornament) has been used occasionally since the 16th C, especially in America, and it may sometimes have been confused with *Ada*, cf. *Ada Nowell*, baptised at Feering, Essex, in 1573. *Ada* is also sometimes a pet-name for *Adelaide* (q.v.).

Adam (m.): Hebrew 'red', from the colour of skin. In medieval Latin the name was declined as though it were a noun of the first declension (e.g. nominative *Ada*). When it was used for a woman (as it frequently was) the Latin form was *Adama*. St. *Adamnan*, the 8th-C Irish saint, whose name means 'little Adam', is one of the earliest bearers of the name. It occurs once or twice in England before the Conquest, but always as the name of a monk. In DB it is the name of one tenant-in-chief and some sub-tenants, and its popularity increased rapidly in the 12th C. In 13th-C records it is one of the two or three commonest names (it is the name of Chaucer's Scrivener) and was a particular favourite in the North and in Scotland (e.g. *Adam* Bell, *Edom* o' Gordon). It gave rise to a multitude of surnames such as *Adam(s)*, *Adamson*, *Adcock*, *Addis(on)*, *Adkin*, *Atkin(son)*, and *MacAdam*. *Ade* and *Adekin* were pet-forms of the name. Like many of the favourites of the 13th C it lost ground in the 14th C, but came back into use after the Reformation and continued to be popular with the poorer classes down to the end of the 19th C. It is now (1976) very popular.

ADAM (genitive *Ade*) DB 1086, Cur 1187–1212 *passim*, Ass 1218–19 *passim*, HR 1273 *passim*, Exch R 1306.
ADECOCK IPM 1311.
ADEKIN Exch R 1306.
ADINET Exch R 1306.

Adela (f.): Old German *Athala*, *Adila*, *Edila*, &c., from *athal* 'noble'. The name was introduced into England by the Normans; it was borne by the 4th daughter of William I, who was named after her maternal grandmother, a daughter of Robert of France. The continued use of the name in France and Flanders was helped by veneration of St. *Adela*, daughter of Dagobert II, and Abbess of Pfalzel near Trèves, but it was never common in England. It was revived in the 19th C, probably in imitation of modern French *Adèle*.

Adelaide (f.): Old German *Adalhaid* or *Adalheidis*, compound of *athal* 'noble' and *haidu* 'kind', 'sort' (= English *-hood*). This became in Norman-French *Adelais*, *Adeliz*, *Aaliz*, *Aliz* (whence English *Alice* q.v.). *Adelaide* is the modern French version of German *Adelheid*, and is now the usual form of the name all over the Continent. The popularity of William IV's queen, 'Good Queen Adelaide', led to its general use in England in the 19th C, when it was often abbreviated to *Ada* or *Addy*.

ADELIZ SEU ADELIZA DB 1086.

Adeline (f.): another derivative of Old German *athal*, 'noble', introduced into England by the Norman Conquest. It was common in the Middle Ages in the forms *Adelin*, *Edelin* (cf. surnames *Adlin*, *Edlin*). A sub-tenant in DB is *Adelina joculatrix*. *Adelina*, Abbess of Poulangy (d. 1170), a niece of St. Bernard of Clairvaux, was venerated as a saint, and it was possibly to her that the (now disappeared) church of Little Sodbury, Glos., was dedicated. Lyford, 1655, gives *Adelin* as a f. christian name, but it must have been very uncommon at that date. *Adeline*, like *Adelaide* and *Adela*, came back into favour in the 19th C. See also ALINE.

ADELINA JOCULATRIX DB 1086.
ADELIN Cur 1201–3.
ADELINA, EDELINA Cur 1210–12.
EDELINA Cur 1213–15.
EDOLINA Magd. 1246–7, 1268–70.
ADELENA Magd. *c.* 1280–90.

Adolphus (m.): Old German *Athalwolf*, compound of *athal* 'noble' and *wolfa* 'a wolf'. The equivalent Old English *Æthelwulf* died out after the Conquest. *Adolphus* is a latinized version of the German form *Adelulf*, which was adopted in the 17th and 18th C by various German royal families and brought to England by the Hanoverians. It was sometimes abbreviated to *Dolly* in the 19th C. *Adolf* is the usual form in German to-day and *Adolphe* in French.

Adrian (m.): Latin *Hadrianus*, 'of the Adriatic'; the name of a Roman emperor and of several popes, one of whom, Adrian III, was beatified. It has never been a popular name in England, but occurs from time to time from the end of the 12th C. The earliest example noted occurs in the Curia Regis Rolls 1189. It is possible that the introduction of the name into England may have been due to its adoption by Nicholas Brakespear (died 1159), the only English pope, who took the name Adrian IV. There are several saints of this name, including *Adrian* Fortescue, executed in London, 1539.

ADRIANUS Cur 1189–1205.
ADRANUS, ADRIEN Clerkenwell 13th C.

Adriana (f.): (French *Adrienne*), f. form of *Adrian* (q.v.), used very rarely. The name occurs in Shakespeare's *Comedy of Errors*.

Aeneas (m.): the name of the Trojan hero was occasionally used in Italy and elsewhere after the Renaissance (e.g. Aeneas Sylvius Piccolomini (born 1405), Pope Pius II). But its chief use has been in Ireland and Scotland to translate the Gaelic *Aonghus* (Old Irish *Oeng(h)us*) or *Angus* (q.v.) (cf. the similar use of *Terence*, *Cornelius*, *Penelope*, &c.). The Clan Macdonell, for instance, have used *Aonghus* since at least the 15th C, and the Glengarry branch still use it and spell it *Aeneas*.

Agatha (f.): (French, German *Agathe*, Russian *Agafia*), from Greek ἀγαθός 'good', the name of a 3rd-C Sicilian martyr honoured in both Eastern and Western Churches. Her cult was very widespread and her name still appears in the Anglican Calendar; there are four English churches dedicated to her. *Agatha* was the name of the mother of Edgar Atheling, a daughter of the Emperor

Henry II, and also of one of the daughters of William the Conqueror. The medieval French form of the name was *Agace*, and *Agacia* is usual in Latin records of the 13th C. Prompt Parv (*c.* 1440) and Godstow (1450) give *Agase* and *Agas* respectively as the English for *Agatha*, and Bardsley gives several examples to illustrate the surnames *Agasson*, *Agace*, *Aggas*. It appears as *Agathie* in 1652. It is often abbreviated to *Aggie*.

AGATHA Cur 1186–1215 *passim*, FA 1303.
AGACIA HR 1273.
AGACE 14th C Legendary.
AGASE *Prompt Parv c.* 1440.
AGAS Godstow 1450.

Aglaia (f.): Greek Ἀγλαία, 'splendour', 'beauty', the name of one of the three Graces. It was also the name of a legendary saint, whence its use in France as *Aglaë*. It has been used very occasionally in England, probably directly from the Greek.

Agnes (f.): (French *Agnès*, Italian *Agnese*, *Agnete*, Spanish *Iñez*) from Greek ἁγνός, 'pure', 'chaste'. The original Latin form of the name was *Agnes* (*-etis*), but in the Middle Ages a form *Agneta* was commonly used. St. *Agnes*, a 3rd-C saint, was one of the most popular virgin martyrs and her cult was very widespread. Many legends gathered round her name, and unmarried girls celebrated the eve of her festival with semi-magical rites. There are five churches dedicated to her in England. From the 12th to 16th C *Agnes* was one of the commonest English f. names; in the 16th C it was one of the first three, the others being Joan and Elizabeth. The usual forms of the name were *Annis*, *Annys*, *Annais*; Prompt Parv (*c.* 1440) gives it as *Anneyce*. The common medieval *Annot* was almost certainly a diminutive of *Annis* and not of *Ann*, for it was very frequent at a date when *Ann* was still scarcely used in England. (It may, however, sometimes be for *Annora* (q.v.)) The names *Agnes* and *Ann* became confused at a later date, and in the case of King *v.* King (42 Eliz.) it was argued that they were 'all one name', though the court unanimously decided that they were 'several names'. Again in the case of Griffith *v.* Middleton (15 James I) it was held that

'Joan and Jane are both one name, but Agnes and Anne, Gillian and Julian are different'. Since Agnes was habitually pronounced, and usually spelt, *Annis*, the confusion was natural. A child was christened *Anese* as late as 1870 at Ducklington, Oxon., and *Anis* is still used as a gipsy name. In Welsh the name became *Nest* or *Nesta*, and it was used in Ireland as an equivalent of the Gaelic *Una* (q.v.) After the 16th C its popularity waned together with that of most of the non-scriptural saints, but it remained current among the poor, especially in the West country, until its revival in the 19th C. *Taggy* and *Taggett* were formerly nicknames for *Agnes*, but have now given place to *Aggy*. The Latin *Agneta* is also occasionally used. See also SENGA.

AGNES Cur 1187–1215 *passim*, HR 1273 *passim*.
ANNAIS Ass 1218.
ANNEYS(E) 14th-C Legendary.
ANNYS *Prompt Parv c.* 1440.
ANNES FA 1450.
ANNISE *Pills to Purge Melancholy* 1684.

Agneta, see AGNES.

Aidan (m.): Old Irish diminutive of *aid*, 'fire'; the name of a 7th-C Irish monk of Lindisfarne, the apostle of Northumberland, which appears in Old English as *Æthan*. Revived by the Tractarians in the 19th C.

Aileen (f.), see EILEEN.

Ailie, see ALISON.

Ailith, see ALDITH.

Aine, Aithne (f.) [aun'yē]. Old Irish *Aodhnait*, f. diminutive of *Aodh*, 'fire', modern Irish *Eithne*, was a favourite name in Ireland for centuries, sometimes semi-anglicized as *Ena* (q.v.) and often translated as *Anna* or *Hannah*. With the revival of Celtic names it is coming back into use in Scotland as well as Ireland.

Al(l)an, Allen (m.): A Celtic name of doubtful etymology. The name of a popular early Welsh and Breton saint, Bishop of

Quimper. It was introduced into England at the time of the Norman Conquest, notably by *Alain* Fergéant, Count of Brittany, and *Alain* le Roux, 1st Earl of Richmond, companions of the Conqueror, and soon became common. In French it was *Alain* and *Alein*, and the spellings *Allan* and *Allen* have both been used in England. *Alan* is the commonest form at the present time. From the 14th to 16th C it was usually *Aleyn*(*e*). It has always been most popular in the north and especially in Scotland (where it was perhaps confused with the old Gaelic name *Ailéne* or *Ailin*) and has given rise to a number of surnames. *Alain* is still a favourite in Brittany, but is not much used in the rest of France.

ALANUS Reg 1071–5, DB 1086, Cur 1189–1212, FA 1284.
ALEYNE 15th C *Brut*.
ALEYN *Prompt Parv c.* 1440.

Alard (m.): Old German *Adalhard*, compound of *athal* 'noble' and *hardu* 'hard'. *Adalhard* was the name of a 9th-C saint, cousin to Charlemagne. The equivalent Old English *Æthelheard* was also the name of a saint, an Archbishop of Canterbury (died 805), and *Alard* may represent a survival of this as well as of the German name, which was introduced into England by the Normans and continued in use until the 16th C. *Athelard* is found at Kirton, Lincs., in 1519.

ADELARDUS DB 1086.
ATHELARD Cl 1272, Kirton Parish Reg 1519.
ADELARD HR 1273.
ADERLARD HR 1273.
ADLARD Gedney Parish Reg 1598, 1610.
AYLARD HR 1273.
ALARD 13th-C documents *passim*.
ADELARD or ALARD Ox Univ Reg 1505.
ADLARD Gedney Parish Reg 1596, 1610.
ALART Privy Purse Exp 1530.

Alaric (m.): Old German *Alaricus*, compound of *ala* 'all' and *ric* 'ruler'; the name of several kings of the West Goths, notably Alaric I who sacked Rome in A.D. 410. Occasionally used as a christian name since the beginning of the 19th C.

Alastair, see ALEXANDER.

Alban (m.): Latin *Albanus* 'of Alba'. The name of the first British martyr has never been a favourite, but it occurs in the 13th C and survived the Reformation, e.g. *Alban* Hill died 1595. The name was used until the middle of the 17th C by the Thrale family of Sandridge Bury, Herts., no doubt from association with the neighbouring town of St. Albans. It was revived in the 19th C by the Tractarians, along with other names of pre-Augustinian saints, e.g. Aidan. Bardsley gives examples of a name *Albany* in the 17th C, which he regards as the same as *Alban*. It is still sometimes used. There was also a 4th-C French saint named *Albinus*, and the name *Albin*, still in use in Germany, was not uncommon in England in the 13th C and gave rise to several surnames. Yet another possibly connected name is *Albion*, e.g. Sir *Albion* Richardson KC, b. 1874.

ALBANUS Cur 1201.

Alberic (m.): Old German *Albirich*, compound of *alfi* 'elf' and *ric* 'ruler', the equivalent of Old English *Ælfric*, was introduced into England by the Normans in the form *Alberi*, *Auberi*, and in due course developed into *Aubrey* (q.v.). The Latin form of the name was *Albericus*, and in the 18th C the back-formation *Alberic* was made; it is still sometimes used.

Albert (m.): Old German *Adalbert*, compound of *athal* 'noble' and *berhta* 'bright', equivalent of Old English *Æthelbeorht*. The name, either in the Latin form *Albertus* or the French *Aubert*, is not uncommon in the 12th and 13th C, and it occurs in DB. It is impossible to be quite sure whether this points to a survival of the Old English name or to an importation of the continental form of it, but on the whole the latter is the more likely. The surnames *Albert*, *Albright*, &c., were formed from it. In the form *Halbert* the name survived in the North country until the 17th C and is still common on the Scottish borders. *Albert* was reintroduced from Germany in the 19th C on the marriage of Queen Victoria, and soon became very popular, especially among the poorer classes with whom it is still common. The Queen's own name never had anything like the same measure of popularity. *Albert* is commonly abbreviated to *Bert* in England and *Al* in America.

ALBERTUS DB 1086.
ALBERT Cur 1189–1205.
AUBERT Cur 1189–1205.
AYLBRICHT HR 1273.

Alberta, Albertine: f. of *Albert* (q.v.). Occasionally used in the 19th C during the period when *Albert* was in fashion. A writer to N & Q (4.10.1930) mentions the occurrence of the name *Albertine* in a diary kept in Lincs. 1865–93, and it was one of the christian names of the novelist Olive Schreiner (b. 1855 in Cape Province). *Alberta* may sometimes be the name of the Canadian province rather than a simple f. form of *Albert*.

Albery, see AUBREY.

Albin, Albion, see ALBAN.

Albin(i)a (f.): *Albinus* was a Latin cognomen, derived from *albus* 'white'. *Albina* was the name of a 3rd C saint. The name *Albina* or *Albinia* (common in Italy) was apparently first given in England to *Albinia* Cecil, born 1604. It has been retained in use to the present day in many families descended from her. See *The Albinia Book, being the History of Albinia Cecil, & others who have borne her name, with a new and particular account of the celebrated Albinia Bertie, Countess of Bucks and her immediate descendants*, by Albinia Lady Cust, 1929. The name now usually appears as *Albinia*, but *Albina* was frequent in the 17th and 18th C. The Italian name is often spelt *Albigna*, and *Albinia* is probably a phonetic rendering of that.

Albreda (f.): Old German *Alverat*, *Alvered*, *Alberad*, *Albrad*, compound of *alfi* 'elf', *radi* 'counsel', the equivalent of Old English *Ælfred*, was used both as a m. and as a f. name, and it is the f. use which seems to have survived in the name which appears in medieval records as *Albreda*. It was no doubt introduced into England by the Normans, and in the vernacular became *Aubrey*. Bardsley gives an example of *Albray*, and *Albreda* is common in 12th- and 13th-C Latin records. The use of the name (for women, but see AUBREY) seems to have come to an end before the 15th C.

ALBREDA Ass 1218, Cur 1187–1215 *passim.*
ALBRAY Yorks Poll Tax 1379.

Alda (f.): Old German *Alda*, 'old'. *Alda* or *Aldabella* was the name of the wife of Orlando and sister of Oliver in the Charlemagne romances, and the French form of the name, *Aude*, was not uncommon in England in the 12th C, and survived at least until the 14th C.

ALDA, Cur 1199, FA 1303.

Aldhelm (m.): Old English *Ealdhelm*, compound of *eald* 'old' and *helm* 'helmet'. *Eald* in compounds of this kind seems to have had the sense 'great'. It was the name of a Bishop of Sherborne (? 640–709), later venerated as a saint. It did not survive in use after the Norman Conquest, but was revived by the Tractarians in the 19th C.

Aldith (f.): Old English *Ealdgyth*, compound of *eald* 'old' and *gyth* 'battle', 'strife'. It survived the Conquest and was not uncommon until the beginning of the 14th C. In Latin records it usually appears as *Alditha*. Old English *Æthelgyth* also survived for some time in the form *Ailith*.

ÆLDIET, ÆLDIT, ÆLDID, ELDIT, ELDID, ALDGID, ALDIET, ALDID, ALDED DB 1086.
ADELID, AILIET, AILITH, AILID, ALITH, ALID DB 1086.
ALDITHA Cur 1189, 1200, 1210, Ass 1313.
ALDITH HR 1273.

Aldous (m.): *Aldus*, *Aldis*, or *Aldous* has been used as a christian name in England since at least the 13th C. It seems to have been almost confined to East Anglia, where it is still occasionally used, and where the surnames *Aldous*, *Aldis*(*s*), *Aldhouse*, &c., are common. Its earlier history is obscure, but there can be little doubt that it is the same as the Old German *Aldo* 'old', which corresponds to the Old English *Ealda*. *Aldo* took firm root in Italy and was often latinized as *Aldus* (cf. *Aldus Manutius* the famous printer of 'aldine' editions of the classics). There were two saints of the name, *Aldo* or *Aldus*, an 8th-C hermit of Bobbio whose relics are preserved at Pavia, and *Aldo* Count of Ostrevant, an 8th-C

Benedictine of the monastery of Hirson in Belgium. The writer *Aldous* Huxley (b. 1894) is the best-known recent example of the name.

ALDUS HR 1273.

Aldred (m.): Old English *Ealdred*, compound of *eald* 'old', 'great', and *ræd* 'counsel'. A fairly common pre-Conquest name which survived the Conquest, though not in wide use, and gave rise to the surnames *Aldred* and *Eldred*. *Eldred* occurs as a christian name as late as 1850 in Bucks. and is still used in the Lincolnshire half-blood gipsy family of Brown. It is still (1976) used in some other families.

EALDRED Reg 1066–9.
ÆLDRED(US), ÆLDRET, ELDRED, ALDRET, ALDRED DB 1086.
ALDRED(US) Cur 1189, HR 1273.

Aldwin (m.): Old English *Ealdwine*, compound of *eald* 'old', 'great', and *wine* 'friend'; it survived the Conquest and was not uncommon in the Middle Ages in the form *Aldwin*, *Aldin*; cf. the surnames *Aldin*, *Alden*, &c.

ELDUIN, ALDUIN DB 1086.
ALDEYN, ALDUN, ALDYNE HR 1273.
AUDOENUS Exch R 1306.

Alec, see ALEXANDER.

Alethea (f.) [ălethē′a or ălē′théa]: Greek ἀλήθεια, 'truth', came into fashion as a christian name in the 17th C. The Spanish Infanta wooed by Charles I as Prince of Wales was named *Maria Aletea*. Lyford 1655 gives the name as *Alethia*. The earliest example noted in England was *Alatheia* Talbot who married the Earl of Arundel in 1606. In 1670 Charles Savile married *Alethia* Mellingham, and the name has continued to be used in the Savile family. *Allathea* occurs in Lancs. in 1683. The spelling has always been liable to variation; thus Jane Austen writes the name of her friend sometimes as *Alethea* and sometimes as *Alithea* Bigge, and the name is also sometimes spelt *Aletheia*. *Alethea* is sometimes confused with *Althea* 'wholesome', the name of the mother of Meleager, which was used by Lovelace in his well-known poem 'To Althea from Prison'.

Alexander (m.): (French *Alexandre*, Italian *Alessandro, Sandro*, Gaelic *Alasdair*). Greek Ἀλέξανδρος, 'defending men', originally one of the epithets of Hera, and often applied as an alternative to Paris. It acquired general use at a later date as the name of the Macedonian conqueror. It was the name of an early convert to Christianity, one of the two sons of Simon of Cyrene who carried the cross for Jesus on the road to Calvary. The immense popularity of the Alexander Romance in the Middle Ages helped to make it a favourite christian name. An early example is *Alexander* of East Marcham, who distinguished himself in the wars during the reign of Stephen. In England it usually appears in the French form *Alysaundre*, and Prompt Parv (1440) gives *Alesaunder* as the English for *Alexander*. It was often shortened to *Saunder* or *Sander* and the surnames *Saunder(son)*, *Sa(u)nders*, *Sander(son)* as well as *Alexander* testify to its popularity. It has always been a particular favourite in Scotland, where it was probably introduced by Queen Margaret, sister of Edgar Atheling, her 3rd son being *Alexander* I of Scotland. The long reigns of *Alexander* II and III, which covered the period 1214–85, no doubt helped to consolidate its position, and ever since then it has been one of the commonest names in Scotland. In a list of inhabitants of Inverness in 1894 there were 584 Johns, and the next most frequent name was *Alexander* with 363. It is often shortened to *Alec*, *Alick*, *Alex*, or *Sandy*. It was early adopted into Gaelic as *Alasdair* (now often spelled phonetically *Alastair*, &c.). The Russian pet-form *Sacha* is occasionally used in England.

ALEXANDER Cur 1189, HR 1273, FA 1284, 1316.
ELEXANDER, ELYSANDRE FA 1284.
ALESAUNDER *Prompt Parv c.* 1440.
ALIZAUNDER Oseney 1460.
ALISAUNDER 15th-C Brut.
ALISANDRE AL. SANDRE HR 1273.
SANDER, SAUNDRE, SAUNDER HR 1273.
SAUNDER *Cocke Lorelle's Bote c.* 1515.

Alexandra (f.): this and *Alexandrina*, both f. forms of *Alexander*, are mainly Russian, and were popularized in England by the marriage of Edward VII when Prince of Wales to the Princess *Alexandra* of Denmark. But *Alexandra* is found in England in 1205 and *Alexandria* in 1218, and these may have been named after a 4th-C martyr, though they are more likely to be mere latinizations of *Alexander* used as a girl's name. The use of m. names for girls was far from uncommon up to the 15th C, especially when there were no sons in a family. Lyford 1655 gives *Alexander* as a f. name, and an early-14th-C English legendary gives *Alisaundre* as the name of the mother of St. Thomas of Canterbury. It is now commonly abbreviated to *Alex*. See also SANDRA.

Alexis (m.): Greek Ἀλέξιος, 'helper', 'defender', the name of a 5th-C Roman saint. It has always been used more in the Eastern than the Western Church, and is particularly common in Russia. The 20th-C fashion for Russian names has led to its being sometimes used in this country.

Alfred (m.): Old English *Ælfræd*, compound of *ælf* 'elf' and *ræd* 'counsel', was the name of *Alfred* the Great (849–901). The name *Ealdfrith* ('old' or 'great peace') borne by a 7th-C king of Northumberland, also sometimes appears as *Alfrid*. *Alfred* was latinized as *Aluredus* (= *Alvredus*), and from that came the French forms *Alveré*, *Auveré*, whence the Middle English *Alvery*, *Avery*, which seem to have superseded the native form of the name. *Alvery* survived until the 18th C; it was the name of one of the brothers of Robert Dodsley the bookseller and is still used in that family. *Alfred* was restored to favour with other Old English names in the 18th C. *Alured*, which has been used from time to time since the late 18th C, is a modern back-formation from the medieval Latin form of the name, of the same kind as Alberic, Galfrid, Hugo, Nigel, Reginald (qq.v.). *Alfred* is vulgarly abbreviated to *Alf*.

ALUEREDUS Reg 1086.
ALURED(US), ALURET, ALUERAD, ALUERD, ALUER, ELURET DB 1086.
ALVREDUS, ALUREDUS Cur 1189–1205.
ALUREDUS, ALFRIDUS FA 1285.

ALUREDUS, ALVREDUS FA 1303.
AUVERAY HR 1273.
AVEREY HR 1273.
AVERE Ox Univ Reg 1608.

Algar (m.): Old English *Ælfgar*, compound of *ælf* 'elf' and *gar* 'spear'. It survived the Conquest and gave rise to the surnames *Algar*, *Elgar*.

ALGAR, ÆLGAR, ÆLGER, ALGER DB 1086.
ALGAR FF *c.* 1160, HR 1273.
ALGOR HR 1273.
EYLGAR HR 1273.

Algernon (m.): Norman-French, meaning 'with whiskers' or 'moustaches'. William de Percy, companion of William the Conqueror and founder of the Percy family, bore this nickname (most Normans of that time were clean-shaven); cf. also Eustace II, Count of Boulogne, who was called *aux Gernons* or *als Gernons*, to distinguish him from his father, Eustace à l'œil. In the Whitby Cartulary William de Percy is called 'cognomento *Asgernuns*' and his son is 'filius Willielmi de Percy *Ohtlesgernuns*'. It was not until 400 years later that the sobriquet *as* or *al Gernons* was bestowed as a christian name upon his descendant, Henry *Algernon* Percy, 5th Earl of Northumberland (1478–1527). From that time it was commonly used in the Percy family, and transmitted by marriage to other families (e.g. *Algernon* Sidney's mother was a Percy). It has remained a mainly aristocratic name. It is sometimes abbreviated to *Algy*.

Alice (f.): from Old French *Aliz*<*Aaliz*<*Adaliz*<Old German *Adalheidis* (see ADELAIDE). By the 12th C it was being latinized as *Alesia*, *Alicia*, and was a very common name in England as well as France, its popularity being partly due to the influence of the literary type of '*Bele Aaliz*' in contemporary romances. It is still used in France in the form *Alix*. The Curia Regis Rolls of 1219–20 give a good example of the development of the name; one woman appears there in different places as *Athelesia*, *Aelesia*, *Aeleis le Neweman*. In England it was usually *Alys*, and was in time contracted to *Alse* (Lyford 1655 '*Alice* or *Alse*, abridged from

Ade-liz'). By the middle of the 17th C it was regarded as an old-fashioned, country name and fell into general disuse, until its revival in the middle of the 19th C by the romance writers, often in the latinized form *Alicia*. CMY says of it (1863) 'now with Constantia and Edith a favourite fancy name'. The publication of *Alice in Wonderland* in 1865 no doubt contributed to its further popularity. It is sometimes abbreviated to *Ally*, cf. Brome's *A Mad Couple Well Match'd* (1653). See also ALISON.

ALICIA Cur 1189–1215, FA 1303.
ALESIA Cur 1200.
AELEIS, AELESIA, ATHELESIA Cur 1219–20.
ALICE, ALISE HR 1273.
ALYS 15th-C Brut.

Alick, see ALEXANDER.

Aline (f.): very common from 12th to 15th C, usually appearing in the Latin form *Alina*, *Alyna*. It is almost certainly a development from *Adeline* similar to that of *Alice* from *Adalheidis*, but it was sometimes treated as a diminutive of *Alice*.

ALINA Cur 1187–1215 *passim*.
ALYNA, ATHELYNA FA 1346.
ALINE FA 1428.

Alison (f.): a pet-name for *Alice* (q.v.), formed by the addition of the suffix *-on* to the French *A(a)lis*. It was common in France from the 13th C and was often treated as an independent name. It was still common in England in the 17th C, especially in the North country, where it often appears as *Alicen*. It is particularly popular in Scotland, where it is sometimes abbreviated to *Ailie*. The *locus classicus* is the Middle English poem with the refrain 'From alle wymmen my love is lent, Ant lyht on Alisoun'.

ALISON Chaucer *Canterbury Tales c.* 1386.
ALISCEON, ALISON Yorks Wills 15th C.
ALISONE, ALYSON, ALSON Lincs Wills 1450–3.
ALICEN, ALLISON Yorks Recusants 1604.

Alma (f.): This name had a temporary vogue, following the battle of *Alma* 1854. The battle took its name from the river

Alma in the Crimea. No doubt the name was sometimes associated, in the minds of those giving it, with the Latin adjective meaning 'loving', 'kind', &c.

Almeric (m.): Old German *Amalricus*, compound of *amal* 'work' and *ric* 'ruler'; introduced into England at the Norman Conquest in the French form *Americ*, *Emeric*, and later common as *Aimeri*, *Amaury*, *Amery*, which gave rise to many surnames. *Almeric* is a modern back-formation from *Almericus*, a latinization of the German by-form *Almeric(h)*. The first example noted is in the will of Lord Kinsale, 1699, which is signed *Almarick* de Courcy.

AMALRICUS DB 1086.
AMAURI, AMAURY Cur 1189–1205, 1213–15.
AMERICUS HR 1273

Aloysius (m.) [ălōē′zēus]: see LOUIS. The name of a popular 16th-C Spanish saint, used in Britain only by Roman Catholics. A f. name, *Aloisia*, occurs in the 16th and 17th C in the parish registers of Hinton Charterhouse. This may be a f. form of *Aloysius*, or a latinized form of *Helewise* (q.v.).

Alphonso (m.): Old German *Adalfuns*, compound of *athal* 'noble' and *funsa* 'ready', 'apt'. It was carried to Spain by the Visigoths, and was borne by a series of kings of Asturias and Leon who in the 8th and 9th C fought successfully against the Moors. From that time *Alfonso* or *Alonso* has been a favourite name in Spain and has been borrowed occasionally in other countries.

Althea, see ALETHEA.

Alured, see ALFRED.

Alvery, see ALFRED.

Alwyn, see AYLWIN.

Amabel (f.) [ă′mabĕl]: this is apparently the Latin adjective *amabilis*, 'lovable'. It appears in Latin as *Amabilis*, *Amabilia*, *Amabilla*, and in the vernacular as *Amabel*, *Amable*, *Amiable* from the 12th C onwards. An early example was one of the three coheiresses of William Earl of Gloucester (died 1183). *Amabel* was later shortened to *Mabel* (q.v.), and was gradually superseded by it. It was uncommon between the 14th and the 19th C when it was revived, with other medieval names, e.g. by C. M. Yonge in *The Heir of Redclyffe* (1853); but in the 12th and 13th C it was a very common name. See also ANNABEL(LA), ARABEL(LA).

AMABILIS Cur 1189, 1219.
AMABILIA Cur 1218, FA 1284.
AMABILLA FA 1316.
AMABLE HR 1273, D'Urfey *Pills to Purge Melancholy* 1684.
AMABIL, AMABLE, AMIABLE Testa de Neville 13th C.

Amanda (f.): Latin 'fit to be loved', seems to be a 17th-C literary invention. It occurs in a Notts parish register of deaths for the year 1805, but was probably in use earlier than that. It is now (1976) very common, often abbreviated to *Mandy*. This popularity may well have been helped by the use of the name in Noel Coward's *Private Lives* (1930).

Amaryllis (f.): Latin, from Greek Ἀμαρυλλίς, used by Theocritus, Ovid, and Virgil as a name for a country girl, and borrowed by English poets (e.g. Milton). Sometimes used as a christian name in recent times.

Ambrose (m.): (Latin *Ambrosius*, French *Ambroise*, Italian *Ambrogio*); Greek ἀμβρόσιος, 'pertaining to the immortals'. It became popular in the West as the name of St. *Ambrose* the 4th-C Bishop of Milan. It occurs twice in DB and from time to time in the 12th and 13th C, and is given in Prompt Parv 1440 as an English name. In 1604 it occurs in a list of Yorkshire recusants, and it has been in regular though infrequent use during the last three centuries. The fairly common Welsh name *Emrys* is said to be a Welsh form of *Ambrosius*, and to go back to *Ambrosius Aurelianus*, the semi-historical 5th-C prototype of King Arthur.

AMBROSIUS DB 1087, Cur 1189–1213.
AMBROYS HR 1273.
AMBROSE *Prompt Parv c.* 1440.

Ambrosine (f.): a f. form of *Ambrose* (q.v.), borrowed from the French. *Ambrosina* occurs in Charles Dickens's Memoranda of unusual names in Privy Council Education lists (1855–65). *Ambrosia*, sister of Sir Philip Sidney was named after her uncle, *Ambrose*, Earl of Danwick. *Ambrosia* was d. of Sir Arthur Gorges (1588–1600).

Amelia (f.): (German *Amalie*, French *Amélie*), a hypocoristic form of an Old German name in *amal-*, such as *Amalburga* the name of an 8th-C Burgundian saint. Many Gothic royal names were compounded with this element, which may mean 'labour'. The name became confused quite early in Germany with *Aemilia*, from the name of the well-known Roman *gens*. It was not much used in England until the Hanoverian period, when it became very popular and was often anglicized as *Emily* (q.v.). Thus Princess *Amelia*, the youngest daughter of George III, was usually called Princess *Emily*. An early example is Fielding's novel *Amelia* (1751). In the Curia Regis Rolls for 1205 there occurs the name *Amilia*, *Amellia* which may be an early use of *Amelia*.

Amery, see ALMERIC.

Amfrid (m.): Old German *Anafrid*, compound of *ano* 'ancestor' and *frithu* 'peace'. It was introduced into England by the Normans and survived at least until the 14th C.

AMFRIDUS Cur 1189–1213.

Amice (f.) [ă'mis]: this name, very popular from the 12th to 15th C and surviving into the 16th C, appears in Latin as *Amisia*, *Amicia*. *Amisius* is also found, and *Amis* was certainly a m. name in French (e.g. the romance of *Amis and Amiloun*). There was a St. *Amicia* whose relics were highly venerated in the Cathedral of St. Pol-de-Léon. The origin of the name is obscure, and it is often confused with AMY (Latin *Amata* or *Amia*) (q.v.). Bardsley gives two entries from a Lincs. record of 1273 which come close together and almost certainly refer to the same person: *William fil. Amye* and *William fil. Amice*. The latest example he gives of the name is *Ameis* Austen died 1540. The surnames *Ames*, *Amies*, *Amis(s)*, *Aymes*, *Amison*, &c., probably derive from *Amice* rather than from *Amy*, which was much less common in the surname period.

AMICIA Cur 1187–1215, FA 1346, HR 1273.
AMIS Testa de Neville 13th C.

Aminta (f.): one of a number of literary coinages of the Restoration period. See also ARAMINTA.

Amos (m.): Hebrew 'carried'. The name of one of the minor Old Testament prophets, occasionally used since the Reformation and especially common in the USA.

Amphelisia (f.): the first occurrence of this name which has been noted is *c.* 1190, when Alan of Leigh gave land to Godstow together with his daughter *Amphelisia* to be a nun. The Abbess of Godstow from 1216 to 1230 was also of this name (and possibly the same person); she appears variously as *Felicia*, *Aunphelice*, *Amphelice*, *Felice*, *Amyfelyse*, *Anfelise*, *Amfelice* (the forms *Felice*, *Felicia* were no doubt attempts at replacing an unfamiliar by a familiar name). *Amflisa* Comyn is mentioned in 1303. Several examples have been noticed in the 16th C, spelt *Amphelicia*, *Amphelice*, *Amfelice*, *Amphillis*; *Amphillis* is found in 1770 at North Repps, and a writer to N & Q 1898 stated that *Amphelisia* and *Amphillis* were then still current in some families. No etymology can be offered; Charnock's suggestion of ἀμφίλαλος, 'speaking two languages', is not convincing.

AMFELISIA Magd. *c.* 1230.
AMFLISIA HR 1273.
AMFLIS Testa de Neville 13th C.
AUNFLIS HR 1273.

Amy (f.): this is Old French *amée*, Modern French *aimée*, past participle of the verb *aimer*, 'to love'. In England it was sometimes latinized as *Amata*, more often as *Amia*. Prompt Parv (*c.* 1440) gives *Amye* as the English, *Amia* as the Latin form. There was a 13th-C St. *Amata* of Bologna who may have helped to popularize the name, which does not seem to occur before about 1270. It was sometimes confused with *Amice* (q.v.). The best-known bearer of the name was *Amy* Robsart, the ill-fated wife of Robert Earl of Leicester, but it was not uncommon in the 17th C. Lyford, 1655, gives both *Amata* and *Aimie*. It seems to have fallen out of use in the 18th C, and its return to favour in the 19th C may have been due to the popularity of *Kenilworth* (1821), and later *The Heir of Redclyffe* (1853), where it is used as a pet form of *Amabel*.

AMYA HR 1273, Poll Tax 1379, FA 1346.
AMIA Testa de Neville 13th C.

Amyas (m.) [ā'mēas]: the etymology of this name is obscure. There was a m. name *Amis* (Latin *Amisius*) corresponding to the f. *Amice* (Latin *Amisia*) (q.v.), and there was also a French *Amé* (Latin *Amatus*), the name of a popular saint. The diminutive *Amiot* which occurs in England in the 12th and 13th C was probably formed from *Amé* or from the more common f. *Amée* (see AMY). *Amyas* or *Amias* may likewise be derived from *Amé*, though the formation is irregular. *Amias* is found as early as 1199 (Curia Regis Rolls) but was never common. Camden (1605) says 'We do now use *Amias* for this (i.e. *Aimé*) in difference from *Amie* the woman's name'. Kingsley's use of it for the hero of *Westward Ho!* (1855) was doubtless responsible for the modern revival of the name. *Amias* has sometimes been misread in old records and printed *Ananias*. See also ESMÉ.

AMIAS Cur 1189–1213, HR 1273.
AMIOT, AMISIUS Cur 1199.

Anastasia (f.): this and the m. *Anastasius* represent adjectives formed from the Greek ἀνάστασις, 'resurrection'. *Anastasius*, common in the Greek Church, was seldom used in the West, but *Anastasia*, the name of a 4th-C martyr mentioned in the Canon of the Mass, became a general favourite, and in medieval legend was attached to the Virgin's midwife. It is found in England from the 13th C, and Bardsley gives 16th- and 17th-C examples of *Anstey*, *Anstice*, *Anstes*, *Anstis*(*s*) all as christian names. Lyford 1655 gives the name as *Anastase*, and in the 18th C it regained its full stature and became *Anastatia*. It has been a particular favourite in Ireland, where it was used, amongst others, to translate the native *Aine* (q.v.).

ANESTASIA, ANASTASIA Cur 1219, 1220.
ANASTAS FA 1303.
ANNESTAS Magd. 1447.

Ancel (m.): Old German *Ansila*, a derivative of *ansi* 'a god'. A favourite Norman name, with diminutives *Ancelin* and *Ancelot*. It was sometimes confused with *Anselm* (q.v.). See also LANCELOT.

ANSELL' Testa de Neville 18th C.
ANSELLUS HR 1273.
AUNSELLUS HR 1273.
ANSELL St. Dionis 1545.

Anchoret (f.): is usually explained as being simply the word *anchoret*, 'an anchorite', but it does not occur on the Continent, and there is no parallel to a name formed in this way from a common noun in the Middle Ages. CMY was probably right in suggesting that *Ancret* (which is the earliest form) was an anglicization of the Welsh *Angharad*. This is strongly supported by the fact that the earliest occurrences of the name are in Welsh Marcher families such as the Le Stranges; or are Welsh, such as *Ancreta* daughter of Rhys ap Gruffudd, Prince of South Wales, who married a Lord of Kylsant in the 12th C. *Angharad* is found in Herefordshire in 1207. *Angharad* is the name given in the *Mabinogion* to Peredur's lady. The name may mean either 'much loved' or 'unloved' (the prefix *an* may have an intensitive or a negative force), but the former is the more likely. Later examples of it are *Ankerita* 1528, *Ancret* 1660, *Ancrett* 1791. Lyford 1655 gives it as *Anchoretta*. *Ingaretta* occurs in a 17th-C visitation of Cambridge and *Ingaret* is recorded in Shropshire in 1904.

Ancilla (f.): (Latin *ancilla*, handmaid), occasionally used as a christian name from the 17th C. It is found in Devon in the 17th and 18th C., and in Oxfordshire in the 19th. *Annzella*, which occurs at Eynsham (Oxon.) in 1824 may be a form of this name, or possibly a late survival of *Ancel* (q.v.).

Andrea (f.): the use of this name is comparatively modern and infrequent, though *Andrée* has long been a common name in France. It is simply a f. form of *Andrew* (Latin *Andreas*). *Andrea* occurs occasionally in medieval Latin records, but probably represents the ordinary m. name *Andrew* applied to a girl, i.e. the person in question was called *Andrew* in the vernacular and only acquired the distinctively f. ending when her name was turned into Latin. See ALEXANDRA for further discussion of this point. The earliest example noted of *Andrea* as a genuine christian name is *Andrea* Beeston, who appears in a list of Middlesex recusants in 1617.

Andrew (m.): (Latin *Andreas*, French *André*, Italian *Andrea*, Spanish *Andres*, German, Dutch *Andreas*, Russian *Andrei*); Greek *Ἀνδρέας*, from *ἀνδρεῖος* 'manly'. The name of the first disciple called by Jesus, the brother of Simon Peter, and patron saint of Scotland and of Russia. *Ἀνδρέας* is a genuine Greek name, found in papyri, but it is unlikely that St. *Andrew* had a Greek name, and in his case it was probably a translation of a Hebrew name. The great popularity of St. *Andrew* in the Middle Ages is shown by his having 637 churches dedicated to him in England alone (it is the fourth most frequent dedication), and is partly accounted for by an apocryphal history of St. Andrew and St. Matthew, which was declared heretical as early as the 5th C, but versions of which were widely read for many centuries; it was translated into Old English verse and prose. *Andrew* is not found in England applied to a native before the Conquest, but there is a sub-tenant called *Andreas* in DB. From the 12th C it became a general favourite and gave rise to many surnames such as *Andrew(es)*, *Anderson*, *Dandy*, *Tandy* (the last two from nicknames). It has naturally been particularly common in Scotland. The usual pet-form now is *Andy*.

ANDREAS DB 1086, Cur 1189–1213, HR 1273, FA 1302.
ANDREU HR 1273.
ANDEREWE Yorks Poll Tax 1379.
DANDI HR 1273.
DANDY QW 1292.

Aneurin (m.) [ănĕi′rin]: the name of a Welsh bard, supposed to have flourished about A.D. 600. Probably derived from Latin *Honorius*. It is still a common name in Wales. The older and better spelling is *Aneirin*. Often abbreviated to *Nye*.

Angel (m.): Greek *ἄγγελος* 'a messenger', used in the Septuagint to translate the Hebrew *mal'āk yĕhōwah* messenger of Jehovah, and adopted in most European languages as the name of these celestial visitors. *Angelos* was first used as a personal name in Byzantium, whence it spread to Sicily where there was a 13th-C saint of the name. *Angelo* has since been a fairly common name in Italy, *Ange* has been occasionally used in France, and *Angel* in England, where it occurs from 16th C onward, especially in Cornwall, as a man's name. Probably the best-known example of its use is in Hardy's *Tess of the D'Urbervilles* for Tess's husband *Angel* Clare. In the 17th C *Angel* was also sometimes used instead of *Angela* (q.v.).

Angela (f.): a f. form of *Angel* (q.v.). St. *Angela* Merici (d. 1540) founded the Ursuline Order of teaching nuns, and her name has been used occasionally in Italy and France (*Angèle*). CMY says 'occasionally used by lovers of ornamental names', and that *Angel* and *Angela* are sometimes found in the 17th C. It remained uncommon until the end of the 19th C. It was possibly Tractarian influence which led to its revival in the first place, for there is evidence of the name having been given to children born on the eve of St. Michael and All Angels. Lyford 1655 gives a name *Angeletta*, but there is no further evidence for its use.

Angelica (f.): f. of Latin adjective *angelicus*, 'angelic'. The name of the lady beloved by Orlando in the poems of Boiardo and Ariosto. Occasionally used in England, France, and Germany since the 18th C. The most celebrated bearer of the name was the painter Angelica Kauffman. *Angélique* is not uncommon in France.

Angelina (f.): a diminutive of *Angela* (q.v.), occasionally used in 19th C. Not uncommon in Italy, where there have been three saints of the name.

Angharad, see ANCHORET.

Angus (m.): this common Scottish name is identical with the Irish *Aonghus*, from Old Irish *Aengus*, 'one choice'. It was the name of a 9th-C saint, Bishop of Clonenagh, as well as of a legendary hero. See also AENEAS.

Anita, see ANN.

Anketil, Anketin, see ASKETIL.

Ann, Anna, Anne, Annette, Annie (f.): (French *Anne*, *Annette*, *Nanette*, German, Italian, &c., *Anna*, Spanish *Aña*, *Anita*). The usual Western form of the Hebrew *Hannah* (q.v.). The name is not given to the mother of the Blessed Virgin in the Bible, but appears in various apocryphal gospels. Her cult did not take hold until the 14th C, and it was not until after the Council of Trent (1545) that the observance of her festival was imposed upon the Roman Catholic Church. The name was a favourite in the Byzantine Empire, and was carried to Russia by the marriage in 988 of *Anna*, daughter of the Emperor Romanus, to Vladimir, Prince of Kiev. Her granddaughter *Anna* married Henri I of France (1031–60) and so introduced the name into the West. It occurs first in England about the beginning of the 13th C (1218 is the earliest record), but it was rare until the beginning of the 14th C, when it began to come into more general use, perhaps partly owing to the influence of *Anne* of Bohemia, queen of Richard II. Its popularity grew steadily after the beginning of the 16th C, and by the beginning of the 17th C it was one of the commonest English names, a position it retained for at least two centuries. There was an early tendency to confuse it with *Agnes* (q.v.). *Anna*, the Latin form of the name, came into fashion in the 18th C. The early diminutives were *Nan* and *Nanny*, but they came in time to be used as a term for a loose woman, and were replaced in the 18th C by *Nancy*. *Nan* has recently come into use again. In the 19th C the diminutive *Annie* was frequently used as an independent name. The French *Annette*, *Nanette* and Spanish *Anita* are occasionally used in England as independent names. The very common medieval *Annot*, which survives in Scotland and the North, was probably a diminutive not of *Ann* but of *Agnes* (q.v.). Bardsley remarks that one out of every ten Yorkshire girls was named *Annot* at a time when *Anne* or *Anna* is never found. The spellings *Ann* and *Anne* were used indifferently until recent times when spelling became more rigid. *Anne*, like *Marie*, was sometimes added to men's names in France. Lord *Anne* Hamilton (1709–48) was named after his godmother, Queen *Anne*. In the 18th and 19th C it was often joined with Mary, and both *Mary Anne* and *Anna Maria* were common.

Annabel(la) (f.): this puzzling name has always been primarily Scottish and was apparently not known on the Continent until modern times. One of its earliest occurrences is as the name of a daughter of Duncan, Earl of Moray, who in 1158 carried it into the Lucy family. Robert III of Scotland in 1367 married *Annabel* Drummond, who became mother of James I of Scotland. The name appears variously as *Annabel*, *Anabel*, *Anabill*, *Anabul*, *Annable*, *Annaple*, and is latinized as *Annabella*. It was in general use in Scotland at a time when *Anne* was practically unknown in Great Britain, and there is almost certainly no connexion between the two names. The most probable explanation is that *Annabel* was derived by a process of dissimilation from *Amabel* (q.v.). It is in favour of this explanation that *Amabel* seems not to occur in Scotland, in spite of its popularity with the Anglo-Normans in England. Poe's poem '*Annabel* Lee' has caused some revival in the use of this name in America and England and has even introduced it to France.

ANABEL Cl 1311.
ANABILLE Cl 1386.
ANABUL Cl 1379.

Anne, Annette, see ANN.

Annis, see AGNES.

Annora, see HONOR(I)(A).

Ansel, see ANCEL.

Anselm (m.): Old German *Ansehelm*, compound of *ansi* 'a god' and *helma* 'a helmet'. The name was chiefly used by the Lombards and was brought to England by St. *Anselm* (1033–1109), Archbishop of Canterbury, a Lombard by birth. It was never popular in this country, though it occurs from the 12th C onwards, sometimes spelt *Ancelm* through confusion with the common name *Ancel* (q.v.); conversely *Ansellus* of Laon is called *Anselmus* of Laon. *Anselm* was revived in the 19th C by the Tractarians.

ANSELMUS Reg 1078–85, Cur 1189–1213, FA 1284.
ANCELMUS FA 1284, 1303.

Anthea (f.): the f. of the Greek adjective ἄνθειος, 'flowery' (an epithet of Hera at Argos). It was used by pastoral poets in the 17th C (e.g. Herrick's poem 'To *Anthea*, who may command him anything') and passed into currency as a genuine, though never common, christian name. CMY does not mention it, but a writer to N & Q (23.12.1922) says: 'I know two families in which for several generations it has been usual to call a daughter *Anthea*.'

Anthony, see ANTONY.

Antigone (f.) [ănti′gŏnĕ]: Greek compound of ἀντι 'contrary', 'against', γόνος 'born', the name of the heroic daughter of Oedipus. The name occurs in a Curia Regis Roll of 1219 as *Antigonia* and Humphrey Duke of Gloucester (1391–1447) had an illegitimate daughter named *Antigone*. *Ismene*, the name of the sister of *Antigone*, is also found at about the same date (see ISMEN(I)A). The story of Oedipus and his children was probably familiar from the tragedies of Seneca.

Antoinette, Antonia (f.) [ăntwahnĕt′, ăntō′nĕ*a*]: these are respectively the French (diminutive) and the Italian f. forms of *Antony* (q.v.). Both were occasionally used in England in the 19th C and are still so used. There was a 3rd-C Byzantine saint *Antonia*, and a 3rd-C Portuguese saint *Antonina*, and some *Antonias* and *Antoninas* may be named after them rather than after *Antony*.

Antony, Anthony (m.) [ăn'tonĕ]: (Latin *Antonius*, French *Antoine*, Italian *Antonio*, German *Anton*(*ius*), Slav *Anton*); the name of a Roman *gens*, the most famous member of which was 'Mark *Antony*', the triumvir Marcus *Antonius*. The etymology is unknown. The later popularity of the name was due to St. *Antony* the Great, the Egyptian ascetic, whose cult was diffused in the West at the time of the Crusades. The Temptation of St. *Antony* was one of the favourite subjects of medieval art. He was regarded as the patron of swineherds, and a *St. Antony* or *Tantony* pig was one of the many names for the smallest of a litter; erysipelas was called St. *Antony's* Fire after an outbreak in 1089 when many were said to be cured after making intercession to him. The name *Antony* (*Antoine*) was particularly common in France after the relics of the saint were translated to Vienne. At a later date St. *Antony* of Padua (1195–1231), a favourite saint, no doubt contributed to the popularity of the name. (It is he, and not St. *Antony* the Great, who is invoked to find lost property.) *Antony* was fairly common in England from the 12th C, and has continued steadily in use. It was also common in Scotland and appears as *Anton* in Middle Scots. The intrusive *h* in the spelling *Anthony* was a late development, and seems not to appear before the late 16th C. It may have been the result of false etymologizing, for Camden (1605) derives the name from Greek ἄνθος. The *h* is, of course, silent, but there is some danger nowadays of a spelling pronunciation (already in use in USA), and the older spelling is to be preferred. The usual abbreviation of the name is *Tony*, which is found from the 17th C (e.g. in Brome's *Weeding of Covent Garden* 1658).

ANTONIUS Cur 1207–13. HR 1273.
ANTONY *Prompt Parv c.* 1440.

Aphra (f.): this was a not uncommon name in the 17th C, the best-known example of it being the woman dramatist *Aphra* Behn (1640–89), whose name is variously spelt *Afra*, *Aphra*, *Ayfara*. An earlier example is *Aphra* Hawkins, who died in 1605 aged 25. The name originated in a misunderstanding of a verse of the Book of Micah: 'In the house of *Aphrah* roll thyself in the dust', where *Aphrah* is in fact a word meaning dust.

Appoline (f.): Greek Ἀπολλωνία, 'pertaining to Apollo'. This was the usual English form of the name of St. *Apollonia*, a 3rd-C Alexandrian martyr who was said to have been tortured by having her teeth broken, and hence was invoked against the toothache. Bardsley says it was a favourite name before the Reformation and gave rise to the surname *Ap(p)lin*, but he gives no early examples of it, his first being 1593 (*Apeline*), 1609 (*Apoline*), and a later *Aplin*. *Appollonia Allathea*, daughter of William, Lord Widdington, was baptized in 1683 at Blackley, Lancs. It appears as *Appolonia* in Shropshire in 1787 and as *Abbelina* in New England in 1827. An old lady of 85 named *Appolina* died in 1938.

April (f.): the name of the month, used as a christian name in recent times (cf. *June*).

Aquila (m.): Latin *aquila* 'eagle', a cognomen in several Roman families. This was the name of the tent-maker with whom and his wife Priscilla St. Paul stayed at Corinth. It came into use in the 17th C, both as a man's and a woman's name, e.g. *Aquila* Moor (a man) 1695, and *Aquila* Burge (a woman) 1793, both in Huntspill parish register, and *Aquila* Cruso, Rector of Sutton, Sussex, 1633.

Arabel(la) (f.): this name, like *Annabel* (q.v.), was originally Scottish and is apparently unknown on the Continent. The earliest example noted is one *Orabilis*, daughter of Ness, Lord of Leuchars, and sometimes said to be a granddaughter of William the Lion, who married Robert de Quincy about the middle of the 12th C and became mother of Saer de Quincy, 1st Earl of Winchester. In 1255 Magdalen Laver was held by *Arabella* wife of John de Montpynçon. The name occurs in the 13th C in the forms *Arable*, *Orable*, *Orabell*. The Lady *Arabella* Stuart (1575–1615) was commonly called *Arbell* by her contemporaries, and Lyford 1655 gives both *Arbella* and *Orabilis* (which he derives from the Latin *orabilis*, 'easy to be intreated'). The probabilities seem to point to the derivation of this name from *Annabel* by a process of dissimilation (cf. the development of *Durham* from *Dunholm*). But there can be no certainty, and there is another factor to be considered. In the *chansons de geste*, *Orable*, *Oriabel*,

Oriabiaus occur as a m. name; *Orable* is also given as the name of a queen of Arabia; and the name of Arabia is variously rendered *Arabe, Arrabe, Arable, Arrable, Errabe, Esrabe, Erable, Araboi, Arabloi.* It is doubtful whether there can be any connexion between these and the 12th-C Scottish name, but the possibility cannot be altogether ruled out. *Arabel* and especially its latinized form *Arabella* came into fashion again in the late 18th and early 19th C, but it is not now much used.

Araminta (f.): one of the many literary coinages of the Restoration period, in this case possibly a conflation of *Arabell* and *Aminta* (qq.v.). Two early examples are *Araminta* Lundy, granddaughter of Rowland Davies, Dean of Cork (1650–1721), and *Araminta* Roberts, daughter of the 1st Earl of Radnor (1606–85).

Archelaus, see HERCULES.

Archibald (m.): Old German *Ercanbald*, compound of *ercan* 'genuine', 'simple', and *bald* 'bold'. Like other names in *ercan* (see Förstemann) it developed *A*-forms which were influenced by the supposed analogy with Greek names in *Archi-* (cf. *Theodoric*), and such forms as *Archembald*, *Archimbalt* appear at an early date. The name was brought to England at the Norman Conquest and appears in DB as *Arcebaldus*, *Arcenbaldus*, *Erchenbaldus*, while later versions are *Erkenbaud*, *Erchebald*, *Herchembaut*. There was a corresponding OE name *Eorconbeald* in use in the East Anglian royal family, many of whose members bore names compounded with *eorcan*, and some of the post-Conquest examples may represent a survival of it. St. *Eorkonweald* (died 693) is sometimes at a later date referred to as St. *Archibald*. *Archibald* survived in occasional use in England, especially in the North, and gave rise to the surnames *Archbell*, *Archbold*. But it was only in Scotland that it took permanent root and became really common. It has always been a particular favourite with the Campbells and Douglases. The usual abbreviation is now *Archie*, but *Baldie* still survives in Scotland. Like *Algernon* (q.v.) it is taken by comic writers as a typical aristocratic name. In the Highlands *Archibald* has commonly been used as a translation of Gaelic *Gillespie*. This has been explained as due to the mistaken notion that *-bald* in the former name = hairless, and was therefore the equivalent of Gaelic *gille* 'servant', 'shaven one', 'monk'.

ARCEBALDUS, ARCENBALDUS, ERCHENBALDUS DB 1086
ERKENBAUD Cur 1201–3.
ERCHEBALDUS FA 1303.
ARCHEBALD or ERCHENBALD Lyford 1655.

Aretas (m.): Greek Ἀρέτας for Ἀρέθας, Arabic *Hāritā*, the name of a series of kings of the Nabataeans. *Aretas* IV is mentioned in 2 Cor. xi. 32, being King at Damascus at the time of St. Paul's escape from there. The name was made use of in the 17th C, like many names occurring in the Bible, without much regard to its associations. The daughter of *Aretas* Seton, Governor of the Leeward Islands, married at the beginning of the 18th C Edmund Akers, ancestor of the present Lord Chilston, and from that time the name has been in regular use in the Akers (now Akers-Douglas) family.

Ariadne (f.): the Greek heroine Ἀριάδνη probably conceals an earlier Cretan goddess, and her name signifies 'the very holy one'. The name was borne by an obscure Phrygian martyr, and in the forms *Arianna*, *Ariane* has been used in Italy and France respectively. It has been used occasionally in England of late years, probably with no reference to the saint.

Armand, see HERMAN.

Armigil, see ERMYNTRUDE.

Armin, see HERMAN.

Arminel (f.): a rare name which seems to be confined to Devon, where it is still in use. There was an *Arminel* Cording in that county in 1797. It looks like a diminutive of *Armine*, the English f. form of French *Armand*, German and Dutch *Herman* (q.v.).

Arnold (m.): Old German *Arenvald*, compound of *arin* 'eagle' and *vald* 'power'. It early became *Arnoald*, *Arnald*, and finally

Arnold. The Normans brought it to England in the French form *Arnaud* or *Arnaut*, which accounts for the common Middle English *Arnott*. The occasional *Ernald*, *Ernold* which are found in the 11th and 12th C may represent a survival of the corresponding Old English name *Earnweald*. The modern form *Arnold* is probably a comparatively late back-formation from the Latin *Arnoldus* (cf. the supersession of *Harry* by *Henry*). It was a very popular name in the 12th and 13th C and gave rise to a number of surnames (e.g. *Arnold*, *Arnoll*, *Arnot*(*t*), *Arnould*, *Arnald*, *Arnall*, *Arnell*, *Arnet*(*t*). Later it fell out of use. Camden (1605) seems to regard it as a rare name, but mentions that 'it hath been common in the old family of the Boyses'. Bardsley, writing about 1870, says 'of course *Arnold* is now practically forgotten as a personal name in England'. That is far from being true to-day, when *Arnold* is once more a comparatively popular name.

ERNALDUS DB 1086.
ARNOLDUS Cur 1189–1213.
ARNALD or ARNAUD HR 1273.
ERNALD HR 1273.
ARNET HR 1273.

Artemisia (f.): Greek Ἀρτεμισία, 'belonging to Artemis'; the name of a queen of Caria in the 4th C B.C., who built the Mausoleum at Halicarnassus. The name has been in use since the middle of the 18th C in the family of Philipps of Picton, and has been carried by marriage into other families. A writer to N & Q (15.12.1934) states that there are a number of instances of its use in the neighbourhood of Lewisham, Greenwich, and Bermondsey.

Arthur (m.): the etymology of this name has been the subject of much speculation: it has been variously derived from Celtic *artos* 'a bear', Irish *art* 'a stone', and other Celtic words. It is more probably of Latin origin. There seems to have been a Roman *gens* named *Artorius*; Tacitus mentions an *Artoria Flacilla*, and Juvenal an *Artorius* (some MSS have *Arctorius* or *Arcturius*). There are other examples of Latin names naturalized and surviving in Wales (e.g. *Cai* or *Kai*, Arthur's seneschal = Caius; *Emrys* = Ambrosius), and it is significant that Gildas says that the leader of the Britons against the Saxons was a man of Roman race, Ambrosius Aurelianus.

The earliest recorded example of the name *Arthur* occurs (as *Arturius*) in Adamnan's life of St. Columba, where it is the name of an Irish prince killed in 596; the earliest mention of King *Arthur* is in Nennius (fl. 796). *Artor* and *Artur* are the names of tenants in DB. In the 13th C and thereafter it is usually *Artur*(*us*) until the 16th C when *Arthur*, *Arther*, *Artheur*, &c., are usual, though *Arter* is found as late as 1630, and the vulgar abbreviation *Arty*, which is still sometimes heard, may represent a survival of this. Never very common (until the 19th C), *Arthur* is most often found, in the Middle Ages, in counties bordering on Celtic districts, Cumberland, Yorkshire, Somerset, for example. It may be noted that the two early examples of its use for royal persons are also the result of Celtic connexions: *Arthur* Duke of Brittany, the unfortunate nephew of King John, was a Breton on his mother's side, and *Arthur* Tudor, elder son of Henry VII, was a Welshman. The name first appears in Scotland in the 13th C in the Galbraith family, whence it was carried by marriage to the Hamiltons. In the 19th C *Arthur* became very popular, chiefly, at first, on account of *Arthur* Wellesley, Duke of Wellington (he was named after his maternal grandfather, *Arthur* Hill, Viscount Duncannon, whose family had used the name since the 17th C). Apart from his general influence, Wellington had a number of godsons named after him, among them the Duke of Connaught, third son of Queen Victoria. Tennyson also, no doubt, had something to do with the revival of the name, both by his *In Memoriam* (commemorating his friend *Arthur* Hallam) and by his *Idylls of the King*. It is sometimes abbreviated to *Arty* (e.g. in *The Newcomes* 1854, *Kipps* 1905).

ARTUR(US) DB 1086.
ARTOR DB 1086.
AZER, AZOR(IUS), AZUR DB 1086.
ARTHURUS Cur 1189–1213, HR 1273.
ARTUR, ACUR, AZUR Cur 1189–1213.

Asenath (f.): '(woman) belonging to (Egyptian god) Neith.' The name of the Egyptian wife of the patriarch Joseph. It was occasionally used in the 17th C, and there was an *Asenath* Angel in

Shropshire in 1798. *Assenath* occurs in 1813 at Leasingham, Lincs. The gipsy name *As(h)ena* may be derived from it.

Asketil, Anketil (m.): Old Norse *Asketil*, compound of *âss* and *ketal*. The corresponding elements in Old English were *ôs* and *cytel*. Both are found chiefly in compound proper names; the first signifies 'god' or 'divinity', the meaning and derivation of the second are doubtful but probably have nothing to do with the common word kettle; it may be cognate with Old German *Kacili*, *Chacili*, *Chazili*, which Förstemann derives from a root *Caz-* cognate with *Cuth*. Old English *Oscytel* and Norse *Asketel* were both common in England before the Norman Conquest, and *Aschetil*, *Osketel*, *Askell*, *Astell*, *Oskell* are found as late as the thirteenth century. In the main, however, they were superseded by the Norman forms *Ansketil*, *Anketil*, and the still commoner *Anketin*. This once popular name fell into disuse in the course of the fourteenth century, but continued to be used in a few families. Camden (1605) says of *Anskettell* 'used much in the ancient house of Mallories', and *Anchitel* was used in the family of Grey (Earls of Stamford), e.g. *Anchitel* Grey, son of the 1st Earl born *c.* 1625, and the Rev. *Anchitel* Grey, son of the 5th Earl (1774–1833).

ARCHETEL, ARCHEL, ARCHIL DB 1086.
ANSCHITILLUS Reg 1087–94.
ANSCHETILLUS Lincs Survey 1109.
ANKETEL Cur 1189–1213, HR 1273.
ANKETIL HR 1273.
ASCHETIL, ASCHETIN, ASKETIN, ASCHETEL, ASTELL (one man) Whitby Cart 13th C.
ASTILL, ASTELL HR 1273.
ANKETIN QW 1273.

Aspasia (f.): Greek ἀσπασία 'welcome'; the name of the celebrated mistress of Pericles, and used by Beaumont and Fletcher for a principal character in their play *The Maid's Tragedy* 1619. It was occasionally used as a christian name in the 17th C. CMY has a story of finding the name in use for a village child, whose mother explained 'Her name 's *Aspasia*, but us calls her *Spash*'.

Astrid (f.): a Norse name, corresponding to the Old German

Ansitruda, compound of *ansi* 'god' and *drudi* 'strength'. It was the name of the mother of Olaf Trygvesøn, King of Norway, and of the wife of St. Olaf, and has been used ever since in the royal families of Scandinavia. Of recent years it has been used occasionally in England.

Athelstan (m.): Old English *Æthelstan*, compound of *æthel* 'noble' and *stan* 'stone', the name of a King of Wessex (925–40) son of Edward the Elder. It was a common Old English name, but seems not to have survived the Norman Conquest. Lord Herbert of Cherbury, in his autobiography, mentions a cousin named *Athelston* Owen, but this seems to be an isolated example. It was revived in the 19th C, perhaps as a result of Scott's use of it in *Ivanhoe*.

ÆTHELSTAN, ACHESTAN, ATHESTAN, ADESTAN, ADSTAN, AISTAN, ALESTAN DB 1086.

Athene (f.) [ăthē'nē]: the name of the Greek goddess Ἀθήνη is very ancient, and no explanation of its meaning is possible. In modern times it has occasionally been used as a christian name in this country, a notable example being the actress *Athene* Seyler.

Auberon (m.): a diminutive of French *Auberi* (see AUBREY). As *Auberon* or *Oberon* it is the name of the King of the fairies in the medieval romance *Huon of Bordeaux* and *A Midsummer Night's Dream*. Modern examples are *Auberon* Herbert and *Auberon* Waugh.

Aubrey (m.): from *Auberi*, the French form of *Alberich* (see ALBERIC). Introduced into England by the Normans, it was fairly common during the Middle Ages, sometimes in the form *Albery*. It has been used in the family of de Vere since the house was founded by Albericus de Vere, one of the Conqueror's companions, and they continued to bear it after it had fallen out of general use and before its restoration to favour in the 19th C. See also ALBREDA.

ALBERICUS DB 1086.
AUBRI HR 1273.

Aude, see ALDA.

Audrey (f.): a reduction of the Old English *Æthelthryth*, *Etheldreda* (q.v.), until the 17th C used as a pet-name for it, but now usually an independent name. St. *Etheldreda* appears as St. *Audry* in the early-16th-C life of St. Werburga, and *Audrey*, *Awdrie*, *Audrye*, &c., appear as christian names from about the same period. No doubt this pronunciation was current long before it was recorded in writing. It was in the 16th C that the word *tawdry* arose, at first to describe the necklaces sold at St. *Etheldreda*'s or St. *Audrey*'s (cf. the formation of Tooley St. from St. Olave) fair, and later for any cheap garish goods. *Audrey* was mainly used by the poorer classes, as is shown by Shakespeare's use of it for the country wench in *As You Like It*. It has had a revival of favour in the present C and is probably commoner now than at any time in the past.

Augusta (f.): f. form of *Augustus* (q.v.), first used by the German princes who had taken to using *Augustus* in the 16th C. It was introduced into England by *Augusta* of Saxe-Gotha, wife of Frederick Prince of Wales, and mother of George III, one of whose daughters was named *Augusta Sophia*. It became common in the 19th C, often shortened to *Gus* or *Gussie*. It is now quite out of fashion.

Augustine, Austin (m.): (French, German *Augustin*, Italian *Agostino*, Spanish *Agostin*): Latin diminutive of *augustus* 'venerable', 'consecrated'. The name was very common in England in the Middle Ages (it is not found before the Conquest) usually in the syncopated form *Austin*. It was probably the 6th-C St. *Augustine*, 1st Archbishop of Canterbury, as often as the 4th-C Bishop of Hippo, who was the sponsor of the English *Austins*. *Austin* has remained in use until the present day, though it lost much of its popularity after the Reformation and is now more familiar from the common surnames *Austin*, *Austen*. The full form *Augustine* has been used with some frequency in the last 100 years; it was one of the names revived by the Tractarians.

AUSTIN(US) Cur 1189–1213, HR 1273.

ASTIN HR 1273.
AUGUSTINUS Poll Tax 1379.
AUSTYN Poll Tax 1379.

Augustus (m.): Latin *augustus*, 'venerable', 'consecrated'. *Augustus* was adopted as a second name by some of the German princes after the Renaissance in imitation of the Roman emperors, and it soon became an ordinary christian name among them. It was introduced into England by the Hanoverians and was popular in the 19th C. It was often shortened to *Gus* or *Gussy* in familiar use. *August* is common in Germany and *Auguste* in France.

Aulay (m.), see OLAF.

Aurea (f.): Latin *aurea* 'golden'. *Aurea* Otway married a Lambarde of Sevenoaks in 1789, and the name has been used in the Lambarde and Battiscombe families ever since.

Aurelia (f.): the name of a Roman *gens*, a derivative of *aurum* 'gold'. There was an 11th-C French saint of the name, and *Aurélie* has been used in France for that reason. *Aurelia* has been used occasionally in England since the 17th C, probably directly from the Latin. Lyford 1655 gives *Aureola* as a f. christian name, giving its meaning as 'little pretty golden lady', but there seems to be no instance of its use. *Auriol* has recently come into use, presumably with some reference to *aurum*.

Aurelian (m.): Latin *Aurelianus*, a derivative of *Aurelius*, the name of a Roman *gens* (see AURELIA). The name of a 3rd-C Roman emperor of obscure origins, and also of a 6th-C saint, a Bishop of Arles. It was revived at the time of the Renaissance and has been used occasionally since, e.g. *Aurelian* Townshend the 17th-C poet.

Auriol, see AURELIA.

Aurora (f.): the Latin name for the goddess of the dawn. Since the Renaissance occasionally used in England, Germany, and

France (*Aurore*). It was the name of the Countess von Königsmark, sister of Count von Königsmark and mother of Marshal Saxe (b. 1696).

Austin, see AUGUSTINE.

Aveline, see EVELINA.

Avenel (m.): this name, not uncommon in the 12th and 13th C, first appears in England in DB. It appears to be a m. equivalent of *Aveline* (see EVELINA), from the same stem *Ava* and with double diminutive, in *-en* and *-el*.

AVENEL DB 1086, Cur 1189–1213.

Averil (f.) [ă'verĭl]: *Everild* (Latin *Everildis*), the name of a 7th-C Yorkshire saint, is probably a compound of Old English *eofor* 'boar', *hild* 'battle'. There is a well-attested cognate Old German *Eburhilt* (other forms are *Eburhild*, *Eberhild*, *Eurohildis*, *Eurildis*). *Everild* was not uncommon in the Middle Ages and was in use as late as the 17th C; it is still occasionally used in Yorkshire and *Everilda* survives as a gipsy name. But the usual form of the name is now *Averil*. *Averell* appears in 1604 in a Yorkshire list of recusants, side by side with the form *Everild*.

Avice, Avis (f.) [ā'vĭs]: this name seems to have been introduced into England by the Normans. It may be from Old German *Aveza*, a derivative of *Avi* (a common element in personal names) which is recorded by Förstemann. It was fairly common from the 12th to 14th C, and is found occasionally in the 16th to 18th C. Bardsley speaks of it as just coming into fashion again after two centuries of neglect, but a writer in N & Q at about the same time (1872) says: '*Avice*, if it is the same as *Avis*, is certainly not obsolete, for I have known more than one.' *Avis* is also a gipsy name. The surnames *Aves*, *Avis*, *Avison* are derived from it. In medieval records *Avice* is sometimes confused with *Amice* (q.v.).

AVICIA Cur 1196–1219.
AVICE HR 1273, St. Columb Major 1600.
AVIS Stepney Register 1590.
AVICE Lyford 1655.
AVEIS Binsey Church 1711.

Aylmer (m.): Old English *Æthelmær*, compound of *æthel* 'noble' and *mære* 'famous', was a common name before the Conquest, and the medieval *Aylmer* may sometimes represent a gallicization of it. But there was also a common Old German name *Agilmar*, which early appears as *Ailemar*, *Eilemar*, and this was brought to England by the Normans. *Aylmer* (e.g. Tennyson's Sir *Aylmer* Aylmer) was common in the Middle Ages and has never died out altogether. It gave rise to several surnames, including that of *Elmer* (q.v.), which has gained independent currency as a christian name in the USA, being the surname of two New Jersey brothers who played an active part in the American Revolution.

AYLMER(US) Reg 1066–70.
ÆGELMAER Reg 1066–70.
AELMAR, ÆILMAR, AILMAR, ALMER, AILMER, EILMER, ÆLMER, ELMAR, ELMER DB 1086.
AYLMER Cur 1207–9.
AYMAR HR 1273.

Aylwin, Alwyn (m.): both Old English *Æthelwine*, from *æthel* 'noble', *wine* 'friend', and Old English *Ælfwine* from *Ælf* 'elf', *wine* 'friend', could give a gallicized *Alwin* or *Aylwin*. The names survived the Norman Conquest and have never been altogether disused, though not common since the 12th C. They gave rise to the surnames *Alwin*, *Aylwin*, *Elwin*, and others. Theodore Watts-Dunton's novel *Aylwin* (1898) helped to revive the use of the name.

ADELUIN, AILUIN, ÆLUUIN, ÆLUIN, ALUUINE, ALUUIN DB 1086.
AILWIN(US), ALWIN(US) Cur 1189–1213.
ALEWYN, ALWYNE HR 1273.

Azariah (m.): Hebrew 'whom Jehovah aids', the name of a king of Judah. Occasionally used by Puritans in England and America.

B

Babette, see ELIZABETH.

Babs, see BARBARA.

Baldie, see ARCHIBALD.

Baldric (m.): Old German *Baldarich*, compound of *balda* 'bold' and *ricja* 'rule'; introduced into England at the time of the Norman Conquest. It remained popular in the 12th and 13th C, usually in the French form *Baldri*, *Baudri*; *Baudrey* occurs as late as the 15th C.

BALDRICUS DB 1086, Cur 1187–1219.
BAUDRE FA 1284.
BAUDRI FA 1346.
BAUDREY FA 1428.

Baldwin (m.): Old German *Baldavin*, compound of *balda* 'bold' and *vini* 'friend', and the cognate Old English *Bealdwine* are joint sources of this name. In DB there is mention of actual tenants of this name and also of tenants TRE. *Baldwin* was a particular favourite in Flanders, and it was probably Flemish influence which was responsible for the popularity of the name in England in the 12th and 13th C. The surnames *Baldwin*, *Bawden*, *Boden*, *Bowden* (the last three from French *Baudoin*), and *Bodkin* (from the diminutive *Baudkin*) are from it. Though less common in later centuries, it has never been altogether disused.

BALDEWYNE Reg 1066–70.
BALDUIN, BALDEWIN DB 1086, Cur 1187–1219.
BALDWYN, BALDEWYN, BALDEWYNE HR 1273.
BAUDUIN Testa de Neville 13th C.
BAWDEN Cornish Registers 1550.
BODWINE Clerkenwell 1694.

Balthasar (m.) [balthaz'ar]: *Belshazzar* ('Bel protect the king') appears in the Vulgate in the form *Baltassar* and in the Septuagint as βαλτασάρ. *Balthasar* is the name, in medieval legend, of one of the Magi. As early as the 2nd C it was believed that they were three in number and were kings, and by the 11th C the names *Balthasar*, *Caspar* (see JASPER), and *Melchior* had been attached to them. In 1164 Rainald of Dassel brought their supposed relics from Milan to Cologne, which thenceforward became a great place of pilgrimage and the centre of a widely diffused cult. *Baldassare* became a fairly common name in Italy, but *Balthasar* has rarely been used in England; Shakespeare gives it to a servant in *Much Ado about Nothing* and it is sometimes found in the 17 C.

Baptist (m.): Old French *baptiste*, Latin *baptista* from Greek βαπτιστής, 'one who baptizes'. This name, which is much used in Roman Catholic countries, usually with John (e.g. French *Jean-Baptiste*, Italian *Giambattista*) but also by itself and as a f. as well as a m. name (e.g. Italian *Baptista*), is uncommon in England, and seems not to have been used earlier than the Reformation; examples are Baptist Hicks, 1st Viscount Campden (1551–1629) and Baptist Wriothesley Noel (1798–1873). The f. form *Baptista* sometimes occurs in the 17 C, e.g. *Baptista Jones* who is recorded in 1619.

Barbara (f.): (French *Barbe*, Russian *Varvara*); f. of Greek βάρβαρος 'strange', 'foreign'. St. *Barbara*, a 3rd-C Syrian saint, was one of the four great virgin saints, and though her name never became as common as those of the others (Margaret, Agnes, Katharine), yet it was fairly popular from the end of the 12th C onwards. She was the patroness of architects and engineers, and invoked against thunder and lightning. The English form of the name was *Barbary*, and CMY says it was still so pronounced by poor people in her time. The French form *Barbe* and its diminutive *Barbot* also occur in medieval records, and both gave rise to surnames. It was still fairly common in the 16th C, but, like other names of non-scriptural saints, it tended to drop out of use after the Reformation. Bardsley writing *c.* 1870 says it is 'now of rarest use'. It was revived with other medieval names at the beginning of the 20th C. The usual modern abbreviation is *Babs*, which has been used at least since the 17th C.

BARBOT Cur 1203–5.
BARBATA, BARBOTA Cal Gen 13th C.

BARBERY St. Antholin 1581.
BARBERRY Cheshunt Church Reg 1692.

Bardolph (m.): Old German *Berhtolf*, compound of *berhta* 'bright', and *wulfa* 'wolf'. The cognate Old English *Beorhtwulf* was not very common, and the name was introduced into general use in England by the Normans, giving rise to several surnames, e.g. *Bardolph, Bardell.* Now obsolete, it is chiefly remembered for Falstaff's roistering companion in *Henry IV*, *Henry V*, and *The Merry Wives of Windsor.*

BARDOLPHUS Cur 1205.
BARDOLF alias BARDOL Cal Gen. 1261.
BARDULPHUS Testa de Neville 13th C.

Barnabas (m.): Hebrew 'son of exhortation or consolation'. The name of St. Paul's companion on many of his missionary journeys —'Joses, who by the apostles was surnamed *Barnabas* (which is, being interpreted, The son of consolation).' It is found in use as a christian name in England from about 1200. The English form of the name, *Barnabe* or *Barnaby*, survived in use until the early 19th C (e.g. Dickens's *Barnaby Rudge*), and has recently been revived. *Barn(e)y* is the usual diminutive.

BARNABAS Cur 1201.
BARNABE 14th C Legendary.

Barnard, Barnet, see BERNARD.

Barn(e)y, see BARNABAS.

Barret(t) (m.): Old German *Beroald*, compound of *bera* 'a bear', *wald* 'rule', later became *Berold*, *Berolt*, and in that form was introduced into England by the Normans; the Middle English form *Barrett* is a similar development to *Arnett* from *Arnold.* It was not uncommon in the surname period, but died out later.

BEROLDUS Pipe Roll 1159.
BARAT, BARET HR 1273.

Barry (m.): Irish *Bearrach*, a derivative of a word meaning 'spear'; until recent years confined to Ireland, but now not uncommon in England and the USA. The name of the poet Barry

Cornwall was an invention of his own—a partial anagram of his real name, Bryan Waller Procter.

Bartholomew (m.): Hebrew 'son of Talmai' ('abounding in furrows'); the patronymic of the Apostle *Nathanael* (q.v.), by which he is commonly known. It is not found in use in England before the Conquest, but it was very common from the 12th C onwards. The cult of St. Bartholomew was popular (there are 165 church dedications to him in England) and his relics were widely diffused. *Bartholomew*, with its diminutives *Bartle(t)* and *Bat*, gave rise to a number of surnames such as *Bartholomew*, *Bartle*, *Bartlet(t)*, *Bate(s)*, *Bateson*, *Bateman*, *Batcock*, *Batkin*, *Batt(s)*, *Batson*, *Batty*. In Ireland *Bartholomew* is used as an equivalent of Irish *Portholan*.

BARTHOLOMEUS Cur 1196, HR 1273, FA 1303.
BARTHOLOMEW HR 1273.
BARTELMEU HR 1273, 14th C Legendary.
BARTEL, BERTOL, BARTLY HR 1273.
BARTELOT HR 1273.
TOLY, THOLY HR 1273.
BERTYLMEW Coventry Mysteries 15th C.

Baruch (m.): Hebrew 'blessed', the name of the secretary and companion of the prophet Jeremiah. Used as a christian name from the 16th C, especially in the Midlands, e.g. *Baruch* Middlemore of Kings Norton (1548–86), *Baruch* Weston of Burton Dassett (fl. 1707).

Basil (m.): Greek *βασίλειος* 'kingly', the name of one of the great doctors of the Church, St. Basil the Great (329–79), brother of St. Gregory. The name has always been more common in the East than in the West, but it is found in England from the end of the 12th C. The Tractarians revived its use in the 19th C. See also BASILIA.

BASILIUS Cur 1196.
BASIL HR 1273.
BASILL St. Mary at Hill Reg 1486.

Basilia, Basilie (f.): now obsolete, but very common in England and France in the 12th and 13th C. It may be a f. form of the name *Basil* (q.v.), formed at a comparatively late date, or may have been taken from the name of an early Saint *Basilla*; but as *Basil* was at no time a common name in the West, and as St. *Basilla* was a very obscure saint whose cult was never of any great importance another possible source is the medieval 'Death of Pilate', in some texts of which St. Veronica is named *Basilia*. The usual English form of the name was probably *Basil*, though the French form *Basilie* sometimes occurs (cf. *Denis*, *Denise*). *Basilia* occurs only in Latin documents. The surnames *Bassil(l)*, *Bazell*, *Basley*, *Basely*, *Bazley*, are derived from it and testify to its former popularity.

BASILIA Cur 1187–1220 *passim*, HR 1273 *passim*.
BASSILLY Clerkenwell 1665.

Bastian, see SEBASTIAN.

Bat, see BARTHOLOMEW.

Bathsheba (f.): Hebrew 'daughter of satiety', 'voluptuous', the name of the wife of Uriah and afterwards of David. It occurs occasionally as a christian name in the Middle Ages in the form *Barsabe*, and more frequently after the Reformation, often as *Bathshua*, the form of the name in the Authorized Version of the Book of Chronicles.

Beata (f.) [bēā'ta]: f. of Latin *beatus* 'happy'. There was a St. *Beata* martyred in France under Aurelian, and it was possibly after her that the name was occasionally used in England from the 12th to the 18th C, when it seems to have died out.

Beatrix, Beatrice [bē'atriks, bē'atris] (f.): (French *Béatrix*, Italian *Beatrice*, *Bice*, Spanish *Beatriz*); Latin 'bringer of joy', the name of a 4th-C Roman saint, to whom the church of Bethersden, Kent, is dedicated. It occurs as the name of a sub-tenant in DB, and was fairly common from the 12th to 13th C. The two forms of the name are relics of the old French *cas-sujet Béatrix*, and *cas-régime Béatriz*; both occur in England, but the second was the commoner; in 1487 it appears as *Beautrice*, a little later as *Betteresse* and in 1604 as *Bettris*. *Bettrys* is still the Welsh form. The diminutives

Beatty, *Beton* were common in the Middle Ages and gave rise to various surnames. *Beaten* occurs in Cornwall as late as the 17th C. The name went quite out of fashion in the 17th and 18th C, and its revival in the later part of the 19th C was probably due to its many literary associations—Dante's *Beatrice* Portinari, Shakespeare's *Beatrice* in *Much Ado about Nothing*, and Thackeray's *Beatrix* Esmond. The name is not now generally abbreviated; when it is, it is usually to *Bee* or *Trix*(*ie*); occasionally, in the Italian mode, to *Bice*. It is interesting to note that the vulgar modern pronunciation of the name as a disyllable, and abbreviation of it to *Beat*, closely correspond to the medieval vernacular pronunciation.

BEATRIX Reg 1076–84, Cur 1187–1215, FA 1346.
BEATRICIA HR 1273.
BEAUTRICE St. Mary at Hill 1487.
BETRYS, BETTE Coventry Mysteries 15th C.
BETE or BETUNE *Prompt Parv c.* 1440.
BETON Yorks Poll Tax 1379.
BEATEN Cornish Reg 1637.
BETTRICE *Pills to Purge Melancholy* 1684.

Bedelia (f.): this obscure name is used in Ireland as a genteel substitute for Bridget [see also DELIA], and is also used in the USA.

Bee, see BEATRIX, BRIDGET.

Belinda (f.): Old German *Betlindis*; the second element is the Old German *lindi*, 'a snake', which formed the second element of a very great number of f. names; the meaning of the first element is uncertain. The name was perpetuated in the Charlemagne romances as that of Orlando's wife, but was not taken into ordinary use. Pope's use of it for the heroine of his *Rape of the Lock*, and Tate's in *Dido and Aeneas*, started a literary fashion, and it was occasionally used as a christian name in the 18th and 19th C (e.g. Maria Edgeworth's successful novel *Belinda* 1801). It is now (1976) not uncommon.

Bell (f.): used from the 13th C onwards as a pet-name for *Isabel* (q.v.).

Bella (f.): an abbreviation for *Isabella* (q.v.).

Ben, see BENEDICT, BENJAMIN.

Benedict, Bennet (m.): (French *Benoît*, Italian *Benedetto*, Spanish *Benito*). Latin *benedictus* 'blessed', the name of St. *Benedict*, the founder of the Benedictine Order (490–*c.* 542). It is not found as a christian name in England before the Conquest, but it soon afterwards became common, and a measure of its popularity is to be found in the number of common surnames derived from it, such as *Benn*, *Benson*, *Bennet*(*t*), as well as the rarer *Benedict*. The usual form of the name from the 12th to the 18th C (e.g. Dr. Johnson's friend *Bennet* Langton) was *Bennet* from the Old French *Beneoit*, *Benoi*(*s*)*t*, and Prompt Parv gives *Benet*, and Godstow *Bennet* as the English form of *Benedict*. There is also some evidence for an English form *Benedick*, derived directly from the Latin, e.g. the surnames *Benedick*, *Bendixson*, and Shakespeare's *Benedick* in *Much Ado about Nothing*. In modern times *Bennet* has fallen out of general use, but *Benedict* is occasionally met with, especially among Roman Catholics. It is sometimes abbreviated to *Ben*.

BENEDICTUS Cur 1167, HR 1273, Poll Tax 1379.
BENEDICT or BENETT HR 1273.
BENEYT HR 1273.
BENEDICUS HR 1273.

Benedicta (f.): (French *Benoîte*, Italian *Benedetta*, Spanish *Benita*); f. of Latin *benedictus* 'blessed'. Probably as a rule simply a f. form of *Benedictus*, the man's name, though there are one or two obscure saints *Benedicta*. It is found in England from the beginning of the 13th C. In Latin documents it appears as *Benedicta*, but in English ones it is the same as the m. name, i.e. *Bennet*. Lyford 1655 gives *Benet* or *Benedicta*, and *Bennitt* is found as a woman's name as late as 1690. The Latin form of the name was revived at the end of the 19th C, and lately the Spanish *Benita* has been introduced by way of America.

BENEDICTA Cur 1205, FA 1316.

Benjamin (m.): the youngest son of Jacob was originally named *Benoni* 'son of my sorrow', but later *Benjamin*, literally 'son of the south', interpreted as 'son of the right hand' (Gen. xxxv. 18). The name occurs very rarely in the Middle Ages, but came into general use in England after the Reformation. It was very common from the 17th to 19th C, but suffered a decline, like other Biblical names, at the beginning of the present century. It is a name which lends itself naturally to abbreviation, and *Ben* has at all times been the form of the name in ordinary use. *Benny* seems to be exclusively Jewish. In Ireland *Benjamin* frequently represents *Berihert*, the name of a Saxon saint whose cult flourished in Ireland. It is well established in certain families.

Bennet, see BENEDICT, BENEDICTA.

Berengaria (f.): f. of *Berenger* (q.v.). The queen of Richard I was named *Berengière*, which was latinized as *Berengaria*. The name did not take root in England, but there have been children named *Berengaria* in Southampton in the present century after the well-known transatlantic liner of that name.

Berenger (m.) [bĕr'enjĕr]: Old German *Beringaer*, *Beringer*, compound of *berin* 'a bear', *ger* 'a spear'; the name of one of the paladins in the Charlemagne romances. *Berengerius* occurs in DB, and it was in fairly common use throughout the 12th and 13th C, usually in the form *Bereng(i)er*, but the shortened form *Benger* occurs as early as 1201. The name died out in general use after the 14th C, but has been used down to the present day in a few families.

BERENGERIUS DB 1086.
BERENGARIUS Pipe Roll 1159.
BERENGER Cur 1201, HR 1273.
BERENGERUS FA 1285.
BENGER Cur 1201.

Berenice (f.) [bĕrenī'sĕ]: Macedonian form of Greek Φερενίκη, 'bringer of victory'. The name was borne by a 4th-C Syrian martyr, but was not used in England until after the Reformation, when it was occasionally employed on account of its occurrence in Acts xxv. 13. See also VERONICA.

Berinthia (f.): a name apparently coined by 18th-C dramatists. It occurs in Vanbrugh's *The Relapse*, Cibber's *Love's Last Shift* and Sheridan's *Trip to Scarborough*. It has been used as a christian name in some families, e.g. *Berinthia* Thornycroft b. 1875 in Notts.

Bernadette (f.) [bĕrnadet']: French f. diminutive of *Bernard* (q.v.), which has gained wider currency from St. *Bernadette* Soubirous (1844–79) of Lourdes. The name is sometimes used in England by Roman Catholics.

Bernard (m.): Old German *Berinhard*, compound of *berin* 'a bear', *hard* 'stern'. The cognate Old English name was *Beornheard* (Old English *beorn* having acquired the sense brave, noble). *Bernard* was introduced into England at the Norman Conquest, and occurs in DB as the name of one tenant-in-chief and several sub-tenants. It is also given as the name of two tenants holding TRE, and though these may have been English *Beornheards*, it is more probable that they were of continental origin. It was a common name from the 12th C onwards, often in the English forms *Barnard*, *Barnet*, which were usual until the 15th C. For the development of *Barnet* cf. *Arnet* from *Arnold*, *Barret* from *Berold*. The influence of St. *Bernard* of Clairvaux (1091–1153) may have had something to do with the popularity of the name, but it was well established on the Continent before his time. Its use declined after the Reformation though it survived in some families. Camden says: 'It hath been most common in the house of *Brus*, of *Connington* and *Exton*.' It was revived in the 19th C, probably by Tractarian influence. The diminutive *Bernie* is used in America.

BERNARDUS DB 1086, Cur 1186–1219.
BARNARD 15th C Brut.
BERNARD HR 1273.

Bernice, see BERENICE.

Bert, Bertie (m.): the somewhat plebeian *Bert* is the usual

diminutive of *Albert* (q.v.). *Bertie*, on the other hand, is more often from *Herbert* or *Bertram* (qq.v.), though it was the usual name by which *Albert Edward*, Prince of Wales (later King Edward VII) was known in his family circle. Both *Bert* and *Bertie* may be used for any name ending in *-bert*, e.g. *Cuthbert*.

Bertha (f.): (French *Berthe*, German *Bertha*, Italian *Berta*); primarily a Frankish name, a pet-form of some of the many names in *berhta* (Old English *beorht*) 'bright'. It was a favourite with the Carolings, having been the name of the mother of Charlemagne. The only occurrence in England before the Norman Conquest is *Bercta*, daughter of Charibert and queen of *Æthelbert*, King of Kent. After the Norman Conquest it was in regular though not frequent use, often appearing in the form *Berta*. It does not appear to have been much used after about the beginning of the 14th C, though Lyford 1655 gives it in his list of christian names. It came back into use with other old names in the 19th C, one of the earliest to use it being the poet Southey, one of whose daughters was named *Bertha*.

BERTHA, BERTA Cur 1205–15.
BERTA Werburga 1513.

Bertram (m.): (Latin *Bertramus*, German *Bertram*, French *Bertrand*, Spanish *Beltran*); Old German *Berahthraben*, compound of *berhta* 'bright' and *hraben* 'raven'; introduced into England at the Conquest (*Bertrannus* occurs in DB). The French form of the name, *Bertran(d)*, is much less common than *Bertram*, *Bartram*, which occur from the end of the 12th C. For the form *Bartram*, which survives as a surname, cf. *Barnard* from *Bernard*. *Bertie* is the usual diminutive.

BERTRANNUS DB 1086.
BERTRAM Cur 1198–1215.
BERTERAM HR 1273.
BARTREM Poll Tax 1379.
BERTRAN Lyford 1655.

Beryl (f.): Greek βήρυλλος (of doubtful etymology, see OED s.v.), the name of a precious stone. Its use as a christian name seems to be modern; CMY does not give it and no earlier example has come to light.

Bessie, Beth, Betsy, Betty, see ELIZABETH.

Bethia (f.) [bĕthī'ă]: Hebrew *bith-yah* 'daughter (i.e. worshipper) of Jehovah', the name of a daughter of Pharaoh and wife of Mered (1 Chron. iv). The name appears in the Septuagint as *βετθία*, in the Vulgate as *Bethia*, and in the Authorized Version as *Bithiah*. It is found in use as a christian name from the 17th C, being most popular in Scotland, possibly from its likeness to the Gaelic *Beathag*, a derivative of *beath* 'life'.

Beverley (m., f.): this is apparently a use of the surname, which is derived from *Beverley*, Yorks ('beaver stream'). It appeared in England at about the end of the 19th C as a m. name (e.g. *Beverley* Baxter MP (b. 1891) and *Beverley* Nichols the novelist (b. *c.* 1900)). A little later it became common as a f. name in the USA and this use has now spread to England. The American name may derive from Miss Courtney *Beverley* who m. William Randolph of Virginia early in the 18th C, and many of whose male descendants bore the name.

Bevis (m.) [bē'vis]: Frankish *Bobo, Bovo* (cognate with Old English *Bobba*) became French *Beuves* (cf. *Eudes* from *Eudo*, *Ives* from *Ivo*) by the addition of a final *s* to mark the nominative case, and in England, where the name was introduced at the Norman Conquest, it became *Beves* or *Bevis*, and was not uncommon in the 12th and 13th C. The popular romance of Sir *Bevis* of Hampton no doubt helped to keep it in use. Lyford 1655 gives a characteristically fanciful etymology '*Beavis*, Beautifull, Fr. as some will have it'. Richard Jefferies's novel *Bevis, the story of a boy* (1882) has been responsible for a slight revival of the name.

Bianca, see BLANCH(E).

Bice [bē'chĕ], see BEATRICE.

Biddy, see BRIDGET.

Bill(y), see WILLIAM.

Blanch(e) (f.): French f. of the adjective *blanc* 'white'. There were several saints *Candida*, and *Blanche*, which seems to have originated in Navarre and Castile, represents a translation of the Latin name. Candida was in some cases a translation of a Celtic name, e.g. *Guenolé*. There is, in the same way, some evidence that St. Candida was known in England as St. *Whyte*; thus Whitchurch Canonicorum was said to take its name from a chapel dedicated to St. *Whyte* (the fact that this is a false etymology is not relevant here). Similarly Chaucer says of his Duchess *Blaunche* 'And gode faire *Whyte* she hete'. One of the earliest examples of the name was *Blanca* of Navarre who married Sancho III of Castille (died 1156); her namesake and granddaughter (died 1252) married Louis VIII of France and became the mother of St. Louis. Her name, in the form *Blanch*, became fairly popular in France, and her granddaughter *Blanch* of Artois carried it to England, when she married Edmund, Earl of Lancaster (died 1296). Chaucer's *Duchess Blaunche*, the wife of John of Gaunt, was a great-granddaughter of *Blanch* of Artois. The name has never been common in England, but *Blaunch* occurs in the 15th C, and Lyford 1655 gives *Blanch* or *Blanchia*. Charles Lamb, writing about 1808, says '*Blanche* is out of fashion', and his sister bestowed it on the subject of a Cinquecento painting. They evidently regarded it as old-fashioned and romantic, and with other such names it had a revival of use during the 19th C. The Italian form *Bianca* is occasionally used in England.

Blase (m.): the etymology is obscure; there was a cognomen *Blasio* current in the Cornelian *gens*, and also one *Blaesus* in the Sempronian *gens*. *Blaesus* is Latin *blaesus*, 'splay-footed', 'deformed', 'stuttering', and *Blasio* may possibly be cognate with it. The cult of St. *Blasius*, Bishop of Sebaste, martyred in 316 and patron saint of wool-workers, was widely diffused in the Middle Ages, and was naturally popular in England where the wool trade was of so much importance. The only relic of the trade in Romsey, Hants (once a wool staple), is an inn called the *Bishop Blaise*. *Blase* or *Blaze* survived the Reformation and is found occasionally in the 17th C. The French form of the name was *Blaise* (e.g. *Blaise* Pascal) and the Spanish *Blas* (e.g. Gil *Blas*).

Blodwen (f.): a Welsh name from *blod-yn* 'flower' and *gwen* (m. *gwyn*) 'white'.

Bob(by), see ROBERT.

Bonamy (m.): French *bon ami* 'good friend', a not uncommon surname in France. Peter Dobrée of Guernsey in 1751 married Rachael *Bonamy*, daughter and heiress of Peter *Bonamy* of that island. Since that time *Bonamy* has been regularly used as a christian name in the Dobrée family and in others connected with them by marriage, e.g. *Bonamy* Price, the Victorian economist. [*Ex inf.* Prof. Bonamy Dobrée.]

Bonaventure (m.): Italian *bonaventura* 'good luck', the name of the great Franciscan scholar St. *Bonaventura* (Giovanni di Fidenza 1221–74). The name has occasionally been used by RC's in England, e.g. *Bonaventure* Gifford (1642–1734), Vicar Apostolic (*not* his name in religion).

Boniface (m.): Latin *bonifacius* 'well-doer', the name of a 3rd-C saint martyred at Tarsus, and adopted by a series of popes, beginning with Boniface I (418–22); it was given by Pope Gregory II, in 719, to St. Winfrid or Winfrith (680–755), the Apostle of the Germans. It occurs in England as a christian name from the 13th C, but did not long survive the Reformation, the latest example noted being *Bonyface* Tateham whose name occurs in a list of Roman recusants 1604. It became a surname and was given by Farquhar to the innkeeper in his play *The Beaux' Stratagem*, 1707, whence it was taken into use as a general term for an innkeeper. It may be noted that the name *Bonchurch* in the Isle of Wight, which is sometimes stated to be an abbreviated form of *Boniface church*, has nothing to do with this name; it was Old English *bana cerce*, the first element probably being Old English *bana* 'murderer'.

BONIFACIUS Cur 1207, HR 1273.
BONYFACE Cornhill Reg 1543.
BONEFACE Ox Univ Reg 1456.

Boris (m.) [bŏ'rĭs]: a favourite Russian name, said to signify 'fight'; occasionally used, like other Russian names, in England in the present century.

Botolf (m.): Old German *Bodoloff*, *Bodenolf*, *Bodolev*, an uncommon name of doubtful, possibly Slavonic, origin. St. *Botolf* or *Botulf* (died 680) is said to have first introduced the Benedictine rule into England, though it did not take root until three centuries later. *Boston* Lincs. is *Botulf's stone*, and *Botolphs* Sussex is also named after the saint. It is of rare occurrence as a christian name. *Botolfe* Thomas was baptized at Trull (Som.) in 1551.

Brenda (f.): this is a Shetland name, possibly a f. form of the common Norse *Brand* which is still current in Iceland and was in use in England until the 12th C. The present wide diffusion of the name *Brenda* is probably due to Scott's use of it for one of the two heroines of his novel *The Pirate* (1821). In Ireland it is nowadays regarded as a f. form of *Brendan*.

Brendan (m.): the name of a 6th-C Irish saint, frequently used in recent times in Ireland. The modern Irish spelling *Brenainn* indicates the pronunciation. Professor Max Forster derives it from Old Irish *brēn* 'stinking' and *find* 'hair'.

Brian (m.): a pet form of some name compounded with British or Irish **bre* 'hill' (cf. 9th-C Breton names *Brior*, *Brian*, *Briunal*). *Brian* or *Bryan* has from early times been a favourite in Ireland on account of the national hero *Brian Boroimhe*; but it was, during the Middle Ages, equally popular in England, where it was introduced from Brittany at the time of the Norman Conquest. *Brian* is the name of 2 sub-tenants in DB, and for several centuries it was a favourite, as the many common surnames derived from it testify (e.g. *Brian(t)*, *Bryan(t)*, *Briand*, *Bryanson*). It survived in Yorks., Westmorland, Cheshire, Lancs. until the 18th C, but gradually fell into disuse and came to be regarded as an exclusively Irish name. It is still used in Brittany and has come back into use in England during the present century.

BRIENUS DB 1086, Cur 1199.
BRIANUS Cur 1199–1219.
BRIAN HR 1273.

Brice (m.): St. *Britius* or *Brice*, Bishop of Tours 444, was responsible for the vogue of this name in England and France in the Middle Ages. It is probably of Celtic origin. *Brice* and the diminutive *Bricot* were fairly common in England in the 13th and 14th C and have left traces in the surnames *Brice, Bryce, Bryson, Brisson, Bricot.*

BRICE HR 1273.
BRICEUS FA 1316–46.

Bride, see BRIDGET.

Bridget (f.): the English form, derived through the Old French *Brigette*, from latinized *Brigitta*, adapted from Old Irish *Brigit*, later *Brigid* (modern Irish *Brighid* pronounced *brī'ĭd*). The etymology of the name is a primitive Celtic **briganti* 'the high one'. *Brighid* was the name of a Celtic fire goddess, and many of her attributes were incorporated in the legends which gathered round the name of the historical St. *Brighid* (453–523). The cult of St. *Brighid* was very popular in England as well as in Ireland. In English she was usually called *Bride* or *Bryde*, which represents the Irish *Brighde*, the genitive case of *Brighid*; thus a 14th-C Legendary has *seinte Bride*, Godstow 1450 gives *Bryde* as the English of *Brigida* (cf. also *Bridewell* in London). The earliest occurrence which has been noted in England as a christian name is the youngest d. of Edward IV, b. 1480, d. 1513, and it does not seem to have come into common use in Ireland until the 17th or 18th C. St. *Brighid* was known as 'the Mary of the Gael', and it is possible that her name, like that of the Blessed Virgin, was considered too sacred for ordinary use. It is significant that *Mary* came into general use in Ireland at about the same time as *Brighid*. They are now and have long been the two commonest names in that country. The common pet-form *Biddy* displays the same process of formation as *Fanny* from *Frances*, *Kit* and *Kester* from *Christopher*. The name of the Swedish St. *Brigitte* or *Birgitte* (1303–73), which is usually translated *Bridget* in English, was an independent Swedish name. French and German *Brigitte* may represent either the Irish or the Swedish name, as the cults of both saints had a considerable extension.

Brilliana (f.): Sir Edward Conway, 1st Lord Conway, and for some time governor of the *Brill* in Holland (held by the English 1585–1616), named one of his daughters (born *c.* 1600) *Brilliana* after the seat of his office. She later married, as his 3rd wife, Sir Robert Harley, and her name was used for several generations in the Harley family and spread by marriage into others. It occurs as late as 1844, and may still be in use. Lady Harley's sister was also given a name, *Helegenwach* (Dutch = Saints' lane), commemorative of her father's service in the Netherlands. She married Sir W. Smyth of Hill Hall, Essex, and had children, but it is not surprising that her very uneuphonious name should not have been perpetuated as her sister's more pleasing one was.

Britannia (f.): occasionally used as a woman's name in the 18th C.

Bronwen (f.): Welsh, 'white breast'; a common Welsh woman's name.

Bruce (m.): the use of this as a christian name in Scotland and to some extent in England appears to be of recent growth; CMY does not mention it. It is the surname of Robert de Bruce (1274–1329), liberator and King of Scotland. The family of *de Bruce* or *de Braose* took its name from *Braose* (now *Brieuse*) near Falaise in Normandy. It was spelt in various ways during the Middle Ages, when the family was a powerful one with branches all over England; some of the surviving forms are *Bruce, Browse, Brewis.*

Brunhild, Brynhild (f.) [brŏon'hild]: the name of one of the Valkyries in ancient German legend, probably a compound of Old German *brunnia* 'corslet' and *hild* 'battle'. It was introduced into England in the last century by the cult of Wagner.

Bruno (m.): Old German *brun* 'brown'; has survived in Germany, probably on account of St. *Bruno*, Archbp. of Cologne 953–65, and of *Bruno* of Cologne (1030–1101), founder of the Carthusian Order. *Bruno* occurs in England from time to time (e.g. *Bruno* Ryves, Dean of Chichester 1646), probably always as a borrowed name. But the cognate Old English ***brun*** was also used as a christian name both before and after the Norman Conquest until at least the end of the 13th C, and was probably the ancestor of some examples of the surname ***Brown*** (most of which, however, come from the common nickname ***le brun*** 'the brown') and certainly of the less common ***Brownson.***

Bryan, see BRIAN.

Brynhild, see BRUNHILD.

Bunty (f.): a pet-name, apparently dating from 1911, when the popular comedy *Bunty Pulls the Strings* had a great success on the London stage.

C

Cadwallad(e)r (m.): Welsh *cad* 'battle' and *gwaladr* 'leader', in use in Wales from at least the 7th C.

Caesar (m.) [sē'zar]: a cognomen in the Julian *gens*, of which the most famous member was Caius Iulius Caesar, after whom the name *Caesar* was borne as a title, first by all Roman emperors and later by the heirs apparent to the emperors. The German *Kaiser* and Russian *Czar* are both derived from it. Various etymologies have been suggested; Pliny derives the name 'a caeso matris utero', Julius Caesar having been delivered by the operation now known as *Caesarian* section, but this obviously is no explanation of a name which was already in use. Another early explanation was that it was from *caesaries*, a fleece or head of hair, whilst a third connects it with *caesius* 'bluish-grey'. It is not improbable that the name is in fact not Roman but Etruscan in origin. *Caesar* has been used occasionally as a christian name since the revival of classical nomenclature at the Renaissance. *Cesare* was fairly common in Italy in the 15th C (e.g. *Cesare* Borgia), and *César* has been used fairly often in France. There were two or three saints named *Caesarius* who may be partly responsible for its use in Latin countries. The earliest example noted in England is *Cesare* Adelmare (1558–1636), a Venetian who became physician to Queen Elizabeth and later dropped his patronymic, adopted the christian name of Julius, and in due course became *Sir Julius Caesar* and founder of a long line of physicians. A clergyman named *Cesar* Walpole died in 1613. *Caesar* Williamson was a Westminster scholar in 1627. Bardsley gives an example of a baby born in 1799, who was brought into the world by Caesarian section and bore, during his short life of 17 months, the names of *Julius Caesar* Thompson.

Caius, see GAIUS.

Caleb (m.) [kā'leb]: Hebrew 'bold', 'impetuous'. Used as a christian name after the Reformation (e.g. *Caleb* Willis, a Westminster scholar in 1585), and survived till the 19th C. It is still used in Scotland and the USA.

Camilla (f.): possibly of Etruscan origin; the name of the Queen of the Volsci, killed in battle by one of the followers of Aeneas (Virgil's *Aeneid* bk. vii). The name occurs in a Curia Regis Roll under the date 1205, but has not been noted between that date and the late 18th C. Mme D'Arblay's novel *Camilla* (1796) may have contributed to its later use.

Candace (f.): *Candace* appears to have been a dynastic title of the Queens of Ethiopia (cf. Pliny vi. 29, 'regnare feminam Candacen, quod nomen multis iam annis ad reginas transiit'). It occurs in Acts viii. 27 and has been used occasionally as a christian name since the 17th C. Mr. Collett of Woodbridge, in whose family the name has been used for at least 250 years, tells me that it was spelled *Candase* in 1675, and is pronounced *can'dis.*

Candia (f.): a name used in the Barrow family and other Quaker families. The first bearer of the name, *Candia* Palmer, was born while her father was on a voyage to *Candia* (now Heraklion), capital of Crete.

Candida (f.): Latin 'white'; the name of a 1st-C Neapolitan saint supposed to have been cured by St. Paul. See further under BLANCH(E). The name does not appear to have been used in England until recently, after its use by G. B. Shaw for the heroine of his play *Candida* (1898).

Canute, see KNUD.

Caradoc (m.): Welsh *Caradawg* 'amiable'. The British name was *Caratācos* of which '*Caractacus*' was a latinized form. A favourite christian name in Wales (cf. the surname *Craddock*). The equivalent Irish name *Carthac(h)* is often rendered in English by *Carthage*.

Carl (m.): = German *Karl*, see CHARLES. *Carl* is fairly common in USA where it is now used by people of all races.

Carmel (f.): Hebrew 'the garden', the name of a mountain in Palestine. The church and convent on the mountain, founded by St. Louis, are dedicated to the Blessed Virgin who, according to legend, frequented the neighbourhood with her infant Son. *Carmel* (*Carmen* in Spanish) is used as a christian name by Roman Catholics (cf. *Loretta*, *Lourdes*, &c.).

Carmen, see CARMEL.

Carol (m.): Anglo-Irish for Irish *Cathaoir* and *Cathal*, the latter of which is also often anglicized as *Charles*. Also an anglicization of Czech *Karel*, Dutch *Carolus* (see CHARLES); very common in USA and now becoming naturalized in England.

Carol (f.): this name, a favourite in the Southern States of the USA, has become, probably through the influence of the cinema, a very common name in England. It is presumably a shortened form of *Caroline* (q.v.), but see also CAROL (m.).

Carola (f.) [kă'rŏlă]: one of the f. forms of *Charles* (see also CAROLINE and CHARLOTTE). A *Carola* Harsnet is recorded in 1670.

It was probably coined by Royalists in the middle of the 17th C. It has never become common. A modern example is *Carola* Oman, d. of Sir Charles Oman the historian.

Caroline (f.): originally an Italian f. form (*Carolina*) of *Charles* (*Carlo*), which spread to south Germany and was introduced to England by George II's queen, Caroline of Brandenburg-Anspach. It became a favourite English christian name in the 18th C. The usual diminutive is *Carrie*, but *Caro* (e.g. Lady *Caroline* Lamb) and *Lina* are also used. There is an isolated example of its use as a man's name; the Rev. *Caroline* Robert Herbert was a godson of Queen Caroline. The spelling *Carolyn* has recently come into fashion.

Casimir (m.): Polish *Kazimier*, 'proclamation of peace'. The name spread from Poland, by intermarriage, to some of the German royal houses, and *Casimir* is not infrequent in France. It was sometimes, like *Ladislas*, used in England in the 19th C when there was much sympathy for the national aspirations of Poland. Its use in America may derive from *Casimir* Pulaski, a general in the War of Independence.

Caspar, see JASPER.

Cassandra (f.): Greek *Κασσάνδρα*, the name of the prophetic daughter of Priam and Hecuba. The Trojan war was a favourite theme of medieval poets and romancers, and medieval sympathies seem to have been entirely with the Trojans; we thus find *Cassandra*, like *Hector* (q.v.), a common christian name in the 13th and 14th C. It is first recorded about 1207, and though it became less common in the 15th and subsequent centuries, it never quite died out. In the 17th C it is found in Lincs, sometimes in the form *Cassandry*. The most notable later example is *Cassandra* Elizabeth *Austen*, the elder sister of Jane Austen, who was named after her mother, *Cassandra* Leigh of Stoneleigh, Warwick, in whose family it had been used from at least 1690. Dr. R. W. Chapman suggests that the popularity of La Calprenède's romance *Cassandre*, which was translated in the 17th C, may have helped to keep the name in use. The surnames *Cash, Cass, Case, Casson* are derived from the diminutive *Cass*.

CASSANDRA Cur 1207, 1210–13, FA 1302–3, HR 1273.
CASSE HR 1273.
CASSANDER Poll Tax 1379.

Catharine, Catherine, see KATHARINE.

Catriona, see KATHARINE.

Cecil (m.): Latin *Caecilius*, the name of a Roman plebeian *gens*, from the root of *caecus* 'blind'. There was a 3rd-C saint *Caecilius*, and *Cecil* was not uncommon in England in the Middle Ages, though much less common than the corresponding f. name. The present widespread revival dates back only to the end of the last century, and is a use of the family name of the Marquis of Salisbury. An early example was *Cecil* Rhodes (1853–1902) whose fame may have had something to do with the popularity of the name in the present century.

Cecil (f.), see CECILIA.

Cecilia, Cecily, Cicely (f.): (French *Cécile*, German *Căcilie*); Latin *Caecilia*, f. of *Caecilius* (see CECIL). St. *Cecilia*, martyred *c.* 177, was a Roman and presumably belonged to this family. She is mentioned in the Canon of the Mass and was regarded as the patroness of music; her name became a favourite one in the Western Church. It was introduced into England at the Norman Conquest (the Conqueror had a daughter of the name, Abbess of Caen), and soon became a favourite. The usual English form of the name was *Cicely* or *Sisley*. Lyford 1655 gives *Sisley* as an equivalent of *Cicely*. It was also sometimes abbreviated to *Cecil* (e.g. *Cecil* Matthews who in 1709 married the 1st Lord Talbot, and whose name has continued in use amongst her descendants). *Celia* is also sometimes an abbreviation of *Cecilia*, and *Sela*, *Sely* occur in 1221. The Latin form *Cecilia* was adopted in the late 18th C, probably in part on account of Mme D'Arblay's novel of that name (1782). *Sis*, *Ciss* were the diminutives of the name in the days of its general popularity (cf. Corbet's 'When Tom came home from labour, or Cis from milking rose'). See also CELIA, SHEILA.

CECILIA Cur 1197–1219, HR 1273, FA 1428.
CECILLE HR 1273.
CECELYA FA 1303.
CECILLIA FA 1346.
CECILIE Godstow 1450. CYCALYE, CYCLY, SYCILY Yorks Rec 1604.
SISLEY South Leigh Parish Register 1623.
SISCELLA 1656.

Cedric (m.) [sĕ'drik]: this now not uncommon name seems to have been invented by Sir Walter Scott for one of the characters in *Ivanhoe*, '*Cedric* the Saxon'. It was probably a mistake of Scott's for *Cerdic*, the name of the traditional founder of the West Saxon kingdom. *Cerdic* is itself a puzzling name, for it has the appearance of a Celtic rather than a Teutonic word and may be from *Caratacos* (see CARADOC). *Cedric* came into fashion as a christian name after the publication in 1886 of *Little Lord Fauntleroy* (it was the christian name of the hero of that book), and seems to have settled down to permanent use, unlike the hero's clothes, which were also once popular.

Celeste (f.): Latin *caelēstis* 'heavenly'. There was a St. *Celesta*, who no doubt sponsored the name, which is not uncommon in France. *Celestine*, which also occurs, is probably a diminutive of *Celeste*, and not taken from the papal name *Celestinus*. *Celeste* and *Celestine* are occasionally used in England. The m. name *Celestine* was formerly used to render the Gaelic *Gillespie*.

Celia (f.): the Italian name *Celia* is from the name of the *Caelian gens* and from it was derived the French *Célie*, used chiefly in romances. The English name *Celia*, however, is probably as a rule a form of *Cecilia* (q.v.). Shakespeare's use of it for the cousin of Rosalind in *As You Like It* is responsible for its modern vogue as an independent christian name. See also SHEILA.

Ceridwen (f.) [kerĭd'wen]: Welsh goddess of poetic inspiration, a not uncommon name for girls in Wales. Professor Max Förster derives it from *ceiridd a by-form of *cerdd* 'poetry', and *gwyn* (f. *gwen*) 'white', 'fair'.

Chad (m.): *Ceada* or *Chad* (d. 672), a monk of Lindisfarne who became Bishop of the Mercians and fixed his seat at Lichfield. The name is probably Celtic. There are a number of churches dedicated to St. *Chad*, and his name has been used since the Tractarian revival of such names, e.g. Rev. *Chad* Varah, founder of the Telephone Samaritans.

Charis (f.) [kă'ris]: Greek *χάρις* 'grace'; its use as a christian name is subsequent to the Reformation (cf. *Alethea*, *Sophia*). Spenser's *Charissa* in the *Faerie Queene*, a latinized form of *Charis*, is also occasionally used.

Charity (f.): Old French *charité*, from Latin *caritatem*. Like other names of abstract qualities this came into use as a christian name after the Reformation, and was fairly common in the 17th C. *Faith*, *Hope*, and *Charity* were sometimes given as names to triplets. *Cherry* is sometimes used as a pet name for *Charity* (e.g. in *The Beaux' Stratagem* 1707, and *Martin Chuzzlewit* 1843).

Charles (m.): (Latin *Carolus*, French *Charles*, Italian *Carlo*, Spanish *Carlos*, German, Scandinavian *Karl*, Dutch, Slav *Karel*): Old German *carl* (Old English *ceorl*) 'a man'. *Karl* or *Carl* was latinized as *Carolus*, whence the French *Charles*. The great popularity of the name in France and Germany was chiefly due to the renown of the Emperor *Charles* the Great, or *Charlemagne*. *Charles* was introduced to England by the Normans, but did not become common, though it is occasionally found from the 12th C, often in the form *Carle*, and gave rise to the surnames *Charles* and *Charlet* (from a diminutive). Prompt Parv gives it as *Charlys*. The use of the name in the house of Stuart did something to increase its popularity amongst Royalists in the 17th C and Jacobites in the 18th C, but it was not until the 19th C that it became really common, often in the pet-form *Charlie*. It was hardly used in Ireland until the 17th C, when it began to be used to translate various native names such as *Cathal* and *Cathaoir*. It is also used to translate Gaelic *Teàrlach*, the same name as the Irish *Turlough* (see TERENCE).

KAROLUS Cur 1205, 1207.
CARLE Cur 1205, 1210.
CHARLES HR 1273.

Charlotte (f.) [sharl'*ot*]: Italian *Carlotta*, f. form of *Carlo* (*Charles*); first given as a name to *Carlotta* (French *Charlotte*) of Savoy, wife of Louis XI of France. *Charlotte* was introduced into England in 1626 by the marriage of the 7th Earl of Derby to *Charlotte* de la Trémouille, whose name is usually spelt *Charlet* in contemporary records (*Caroletta* is also found in the 17th C). The name, however, remained rare until the marriage of George III in 1761 with *Charlotte Sophia* of Mecklenburg-Strelitz, who made the name popular as her predecessor had made that of *Caroline*. The popularity of the name, with the romantically inclined, may have been partly due to its use by Goethe for the heroine of his *Sorrows of Werther* (1774), and later to the Princess *Charlotte*, the daughter of George IV. The 17th-C spelling *Charlet* shows that the pronunciation of the name at that time was much the same as it is now; but there is some evidence that early in the 19th C it was sometimes made a trisyllable. In a correspondence in N & Q in 1908 Henry Bradley recalled that old people in Sheffield in his youth spoke of *Charlottē* Street; and another correspondent said he had quite recently heard a woman addressed as *Charlotty*. Great *Charlotte* Street, Liverpool, and *Charlotte* Street, Edgbaston, are still sometimes so pronounced. The usual abbreviation of the name is *Lottie* or *Lotty* (sometimes *Totty*), but *Charlie* is also occasionally used.

Charmian (f.): occasionally used as a christian name, being taken from Shakespeare's play of *Antony and Cleopatra*, where he gives it to one of Cleopatra's slaves. In Plutarch (Shakespeare's ultimate source) the name is *Χάρμιον*, 'a little joy', a neuter diminutive of *χάρμα* 'joy'; Greek slaves were often given neuter names. The usual pronunciation seems to be char'me*a*n, but shar'me*a*n is also common, and the name is sometimes confused with, and pronounced like, *Charmaine*, the name of a once popular song. The correct pronunciation would be kar'me*a*n.

Chaunc(e)y (m.): a surname of French origin, probably from a place-name, found in England from the 13th C; it was the name of the 2nd President of Harvard, Charles *Chauncey* (1592–1672), some of whose pupils gave it to their children as a christian name, whence it has gradually come into general use as a christian name in the USA.

Cherry, see CHARITY.

Chloe (f.) [klō'ĕ]: Greek χλόη 'a young green shoot', an epithet of Demeter. St. Paul (1 Cor. i. 11) mentions a woman of Corinth named *Chloe*, and the name was adopted, like most of those which occur in the Epistles, in the 17th C, but its main use has been by pastoral poets.

Chloris (f.): from Greek χλωρός, 'blooming', 'fresh'; given as a christian name by Lyford 1655, but there is little evidence for its use, except by poets in the 17th and 18th C.

Chris, see CHRISTABEL, CHRISTIAN(A), CHRISTOPHER.

Christabel (f.): the earliest occurrence of this name is in the Middle English romance of *Sir Eglamour d'Artois*, and it also comes in some versions (e.g. Percy's) of the *Ballad of Sir Cauline*. It was doubtless from Percy that Coleridge took it for his own poem. *Christable* occurs as a christian name in 1561, *Christabell* in 1604, *Christobelle* in 1687, *Christabel* in Cornwall in 1727; *Christobella* Lady Saye and Sele died in 1789 aet. 94. The etymology is puzzling, but it seems to be a compound of *Christus* and Latin *bella*, cf. *Dulcibel*, *Claribel*, *Rosabel*, &c. (qq.v.). Other examples of the use of *Christ* in compound names are the Old German (7th–9th C) *Cristemia*, *Cristehildis*, *Cristemberga*. The modern use of the name is probably, as a rule, consciously derived from Coleridge's poem. It is sometimes abbreviated to *Chris(sy)* or *Christy*.

Christian (m.): Latin *christianus* 'a christian'. The name is found from about 1200, but has never been common in this country. See further under CHRISTIAN(A) (f.).

Christian(a) (f.): (French, German *Christiane*): f. of Latin *christianus* 'christian'. The common noun and adjective *christian* are found in England only from the 16th C, the earlier word being the Old English *christen*. The name *Christian*, however, together with its Latin form *Christiana* (occasionally *Christiania*) are found from the end of the 12th C, and are rather commoner than *Christina* (q.v.) which is derived from the Old English *christen*. Prompt Parv 1450 gives *Kyrstyan* or *Kristyan* as the English for *Christiana*, and *Kirsty* is still used as a pet-name in Scotland. *Christian* was still common in the 17th C, but *Christiana* is now more usual, and *Christina* is commoner than either. *Christiania* is an occasional variant. The surnames *Christian*, *Christie*, *Christy*, *Christison* are among those derived from it. It is sometimes abbreviated to *Chrissy* or *Chris*. See also KIRSTEN.

CHRISTIANA Cur 1199, FA 1285, 1303, Cov 1424.
CRISTIANE Poll Tax 1379.
CHRISTIAN Cov 1424, Chester 1562.

Christina, Christine (f.): from Old English *christen*, 'christian'. The earliest example of the name noted is *Christina*, sister of Edgar Atheling, who was born in Hungary and fl. 1086. It has been in use in England ever since but, until recently, was not as common as *Christian* (q.v.). The diminutive *Tina* is sometimes used for *Christina*.

CRISTINA HR 1273, FA 1346.

Christmas (m., f.): this, like other names of Church festivals, was sometimes given to children born on that day (cf. *Pentecost*, *Easter*, &c.) and is found from the 13th C down to the present day. It gave rise to a not uncommon surname. It has now been largely replaced by *Noel* (q.v.).

Christopher (m.): (Latin *Christopherus*, French *Christophe*, Italian *Cristoforo*, Spanish *Cristoval*, *Cristobal*, German *Christoph*): Greek Χριστοφόρος, 'bearing Christ'. It was originally a word applied by Christians to themselves, meaning that they bore Christ in their hearts. St. *Christopher* was an early Christian martyr, to whose name was later attached the legend of a gigantic saint who carried the Christ-child across a river, and *Christopher* became an ordinary christian name. The sight of the image of St. *Christopher* was thought to be a protection from accidents and sudden death for the rest of the day ('Illa nempe die morte mala non morieris, Cristoferi sancti speciem quicumque tueris'), and it was therefore often depicted on the outside of houses and churches in Italy, Spain, and Germany. In England St. *Christopher* was, for the same reason, one of the commonest subjects for mural paintings inside churches. Always the patron of travellers, St. *Christopher* is now in Roman Catholic countries regarded as being the particular protector of motorists. Bardsley's earliest example of the name in England is of the 14th C, and he says he found none in the Hundred Rolls of 1273. There are, however, examples of the name in the Curia Regis Rolls for 1201 and 1220, though it is certainly uncommon until the 15th C when it becomes much more frequent (examples are *Christofre Crease* 1450, *Crysteffor Johnson* 1491, *Christouer Hobye* 1483). From the 16th C to the end of the 18th C the name was in fairly general use, often abbreviated to *Kester*, *Kit* (cf. the island of St. *Kitts*), or *Chris*. It suffered an eclipse in the 19th C, and CMY speaks as though it were little used in her time, but it has had a great revival in the present century. In Scotland the Lowland form of the name was apparently *C(h)rystal*, of which Black gives several examples. *Christopher* has often been used to render Gaelic *Gilcrist*.

CHRISTOPHERUS Cur 1201–3, 1220.
CRISTOFORUS Poll Tax 1379.
CRISTOFRE 14th-C Legendary, Linc 1450.
CHRISTOFUR St. Mary at Hill 1513.

Chrysogon (f.): Greek χρυσόγονος, 'goldborn'. St. *Chrysogonos*, a 4th-C saint, adviser of St. Anastasia, mentioned in the Canon of the Mass, was a man, and his name is found as a man's name (*Grisigion* Foule of Tenterden) in 1609. But it is more often found as a f. name, e.g. *Chrysogon* or *Grisigon* Stradling (*c.* 1550) of Co. Glamorgan, who married Anthony Porter of Aston Subedge, and whose christian name took root in the Cotswolds; later members of the Stradling family carried it to Essex and Somerset. The name is spelt variously *Chrysogon*, *Chrisoogone*, *Grisegond*, *Griso-*

gonia, Grisigion, Grissecon. It has not been noted in England earlier than the 16th C, and the reason for its use then is unknown.

Cicely, see CECILIA.

Cissy, see CECILIA.

Clara, Clare (f.): (French *Claire*, Italian *Chiara*): f. of Latin *clarus* 'bright', 'clear'; occurs in England from the beginning of the 13th C, in Latin as *Clara*, in English as *Clare*. It was apparently a f. form of *Clarus*, the name of at least two saints, a 3rd-C Bishop of Nantes and a 7th-C Norman saint; the latter gave his name to *St. Clair* in Normandy, from which came the well-known family of *St. Clair* or *Sinclair*. Later the popularity of the name was increased by St. *Clare* of Assisi (1193–1253), the friend of St. Francis and founder of the order of Poor Clares. *Clare*, though never common, is found in every century from the 13th onward. The latinized form *Clara* came into fashion in the 19th C, but both forms continued to be used.

CLARA Cur 1210, Poll Tax 1379.
CLARE Poll Tax 1379, Yorks Rec 1610, Lyford 1655.

Clarence (m.): the name of a dukedom created in 1362 for Lionel, 3rd son of Edward III, who had married the heiress of *Clare* in Suffolk. In Latin his title became *dux Clarensis* or *dux Clarentiae*. The title was later held by George, the brother of Edward IV and Richard III, and was revived for the 3rd son of George III, later William IV, and again for the elder son of Edward VII. It was probably after this last that *Clarence* came into use as a christian name at the end of the 19th C, but the hero of Maria Edgeworth's novel 'Helen' (1834) is named *Clarence* Harvey.

Claribel (f.): occurs in *The Tempest* as the name of the Queen of Tunis and appears to be formed on the analogy of *Christabel*, *Dowsabel*, *Mirabel*, &c.

Clarice (f.): apparently a French derivative of *Clara* (q.v.). It occurs in England as early as 1199 (*Claricia* in a Latin document), and was not uncommon in the 13th and 14th C in the forms *Clarice*, *Clarisse*, and gave rise to the surnames *Clarice*, *Claris*, *Clares*, and also, as Bardsley shows, *Clar(r)idge*, *Clardge*, *Clarges* (he gives an example of the same person referred to in a Hundred Roll of 1273 as *Claricia* and *Clarugge*). *Clarice* was popular on account of its occurrence in the romances, where it is the name of the wife of Rinaldo and sister of Huon of Bordeaux. The latinized form *Clarissa* was revived by Richardson in his novel *Clarissa Harlowe*.

CLARICIA Cur 1199, HR 1273, FA 1316, 1346, 1428.
CLARICE HR 1273.
CLARUGGE (or CLARICIA) HR 1273.
CLARISCIA Poll Tax 1379.

Clarimond (f.): Old French *Claremonde*, *Esclairmonde* occurs in various romances, notably in that of Huon of Bordeaux, and CMY states that *Clarimond* is found as a christian name in Devon in the 17th C. It is apparently a compound of Old German *munt* (Old English *mund*) 'protection', with Latin *clarus*, which was early borrowed by the Teutonic languages (cf. CLEREBOLD).

Clarinda (f.): this derivative of *Clare* is used by Spenser in his *Faerie Queene* and had a certain literary vogue in the 17th and 18th C. It was possibly confused with *Clorinda* which occurs in Tasso.

Clarissa, see CLARICE.

Claud(e) (m.): French, from Latin *Claudius*, the name of two famous Roman *gentes*, one patrician, the other plebeian, probably a derivative of *claudus* 'lame'. *Claude* has long been used in France, and it was adopted in the 16th C by the Hamilton family, who had French connexions, the first to bear the name being Lord *Claud* Hamilton (born 1543), Baron Paisley and ancestor of the Earls and Dukes of Abercorn, since whose time it has been used continuously in his family.

Claudia (f.): the f. form of the name of the Claudian *gens*, see CLAUD. *Claudia* is found in Lancashire in the late 16th C, probably taken from the 2nd epistle to Timothy where it occurs as the name of a Roman convert. The equivalent *Claude* has been used in France since Louis XII gave it to his daughter. The Welsh *Gladys* (q.v.) is said to be a form of the name.

Clemence, Clemency (f.): Latin *clementia* 'mildness', seems to have been used as a f. form of the man's name *Clement* (q.v.). From about 1200 *Clemence* (Latin *Clemencia*) is not uncommon in England; in the 16th C it appears as *Clemens*, later usually as *Clemency*, no doubt consciously equated with the abstract noun.

CLEMENCIA, CLEMENTIA Cur 1200, 1203, 1210, 1220.
CLEMENS Lincs 1534.
CLAMANCIA Owston Parish Reg 1676.

Clement (m.): Latin *clemens*, *-tis*, 'mild', 'merciful', the name of a saint, the first of the Apostolic Fathers and a disciple of St. Paul, and of many subsequent popes. St. *Clement* has over 40 church dedications in this country, and his name was a favourite one from the end of the 12th C until the Reformation; Bardsley gives some 15 surnames derived from it, including *Clement(s)*, *Clemens*, *Clemson*. The Tractarians revived the name in the 19th C, with reference rather to *Clement* of Alexandria than to the Pope. The diminutive *Clem* is found from the 13th C.

CLEMENS Cur 1199–1215.
CLEMENT HR 1273.
CLEM HR 1273.

Clementina, Clementine (f.): f. forms of *Clement* (q.v.), name of one of St. Ursula's 11,000 virgins. Sometimes used in the 19th C. *Clemence* and *Clemency* (q.v.) were used earlier. *Clementine* has probably been killed by the song of that name.

Clerebold, Clarenbald (m.): this name, which was common from the 11th C to the 14th C in England, is also found in Old German in the 10th C as *Clarebald*, *Clarembald*. It is a compound of *klâr* (borrowed from Latin *clarus*) and *bald* 'bold'. In England it gave rise to the surnames *Claringbold*, *Clarabut*, &c.

CLEREBALD HR 1273.
CLERENBALD Pipe Roll 1160.

Clifford (m.): a surname derived from a place-name (there are several villages of this name). Its general use as a christian name appears to date from the last quarter of the 19th C. Now (1976) commonly abbreviated to *Cliff*.

Clive (m.): the surname of Robert *Clive* (1725–74), the great servant of the East India Company. The name was originally chiefly given as a christian name by those who have connexions with India, and was perhaps first used in this way by Thackeray in *The Newcomes* (1853–5). It no longer has this connexion.

Clodagh (f.): Irish, the name of a river in Tipperary; seems to have been first given as a christian name to a daughter of the Marquis of Waterford, now Lady Clodagh Anson, and has been fairly often used since.

Clorinda, see CLARINDA.

Clotilda (f.): Old German *Chlotichilda*, compound of *hloda* 'loud' and *hildi* 'battle', the name of the wife of Clovis (465–511), King of France, whom she converted to Christianity. *Clotilde* has remained in occasional use in France, and *Clotilda* is sometimes used by English Roman Catholics.

Cnut, see KNUD.

Colette (f.): French diminutive of *Nicole*, now chiefly known in this country as the pen-name of a contemporary French novelist, but formerly not uncommon in England. It was latinized as *Coleta* or *Colecta*, and gave rise to the surnames *Colet*, *Collett*, *Collect*. Prompt Parv gives *Colette* as the English and *Colecta* as the Latin form, and *Colet* is found as late as 1635 in Lincolnshire. It was the name of the 15th-C reformer of the Poor Clares, who helped to end the Great Schism of the West, and is much favoured in modern Roman Catholic use.

COLETT HR 1273, Coventry Mysteries 15th C.
COLETTA FA 1316.
COLETA Poll Tax 1379.
COLLETTE Poll Tax 1379.
KALOTTE Langland *c.* 1360.

Colin (m.): French diminutive of *Col*, an abbreviation of *Nicholas* (q.v.). *Colin* is found in England from 1200 onwards, but not apparently as an independent name; it gave rise to the common surnames *Collin(s)*, *Collinson*. Spenser's *Colin Clout* seems to show that by the 16th C the name was regarded as a rustic nickname, and it gradually died out altogether. The Scottish *Colin*, still in use (sometimes by English as well as Scots), is a different name representing the Gaelic *Cailean*, which has been derived by some from *coileán* a young dog, a youth, and hence a cadet. The Irish form *Colán* has recently been revived.

COLINUS Cur 1200, HR 1273.
COLIN Poll Tax 1379.

Colum, Colm (m.): the Irish form of *Columba* (Latin 'dove'), the name of, amongst others, St. *Columba* (521–97), the apostle of the Picts, who was usually known as *Columcille*, 'Colum of the Church'. See also MALCOLM.

Comfort (m., f.): occasionally used as a christian name after the Reformation. A *Comfort* Dormer occurs in Bucks as recently as 1850.

Comyn (m.) [kŏm'ĭn]: formerly a christian name in Ireland and the Highlands of Scotland, but now usually a surname. It is Irish *Cuimin*, a diminutive of *cam* 'crooked'.

Conal(l) (m.) [kŏn'*a*l]: a common Irish name, derived from Old Celtic **Kuno-val-s* 'high-mighty'.

Conan (m.) [kō'n*a*n in England, konawn' in Ireland]: probably derived from the Old Celtic root **kuno-*, 'high'. Traditionally the name of one of the early British Bishops of London, and later of several Celtic saints. One of them, *Conan* or *Kynan Meriadech*, was said to have led a band of fugitive Britons to Armorica and to have been the ancestor of the Dukes of Brittany. The name still survives in Brittany, and it was brought to England by Bretons after the Norman Conquest, and became a fairly common christian name from the 12th to 16th C, giving rise to the surnames *Conan*, *Con(n)ant*, *Connand*, *Conning*, *Connon*.

CONANUS Cur 1199–1215.
CONAN FF 13th C, HR 1273.
CONAYN HR 1273.
CONANDUS FA 1428.
CONON Poll Tax 1379.

Conn, a common Irish name from Old Celtic **Kuno*.

Connie, see CONSTANCE.

Con(n)or (m.): Irish *Conc(h)ub(h)ar* 'high desire', a great name in Irish mythology, and for long a common christian name in Ireland, where it still survives.

Conrad (m.): Old German *Conrad*, *Chonrad*, compound of *conja* 'bold' and *rad* 'counsel'. The name of a 10th-C saint, Bishop of Constance. This is essentially a German name, but has been occasionally used in England, the earliest example noted being *Conrad* Nye, rector of Foxley, Wilts, from 1436.

Constance, Constantia (f.): Latin *constantia* 'constancy'. There was a saint of the name, a daughter of Constantine the Great. The name was introduced into England at the Norman Conquest (it was borne by one of the daughters of the Conqueror, who married Alain de Bretagne), and soon became common, being anglicized as *Custance*, which is found as late as 1561. In the 16th and 17th C *Constancy* came into use among the Puritans, but was not common. In the 19th C the Latin form *Constantia* was introduced, and CMY says of it that it 'at present reigns among the favourite fancy names, scarcely less inevitable than Alice or Edith'. *Constantia* has now given way to the simpler *Constance*. It is sometimes abbreviated to *Connie*.

CONSTANCIA Cur 1199, FA 1346.
CUSTANCIA Cur 1199.
CONSTANCE HR 1273.
CUSTANCE HR 1273, Poll Tax 1379.
CUSTANS Poll Tax 1379.
CUSTINS Broughton-by-Brigg Parish Reg 1604–5.

Constant (m.): occurs as a christian name in the 17th C, e.g. *Constant* Oates, brother of Titus Oates, and was probably the common adjective, not a form of *Constantine*.

Constantia, see CONSTANCE.

Constantine (m.): Latin derivative of *constans* 'constant', 'firm'. As the name of the first Christian Emperor, *Constantine* was early adopted as a christian name. *Constantine*, a Cornish saint, was said to have evangelized Scotland in the 6th C, and his name was borne by *Constantine* MacFergus (died 820), King of the Picts, and by three early (9th and 10th C) Scottish kings. There is one sub-tenant of the name in DB, and it was not uncommon in England as well as Scotland from the 12th to the 17th C, giving rise to the surnames *Costin*, *Costain*, *Considine*, *Constantine*, &c. *Costin* was the usual English form of the name in the Middle Ages and until the 17th C. It was particularly common in Devon and Cornwall. In Ireland it is used to render Irish *Connor* (*Conc*(*h*)*ub*(*h*)*ar*) and *Conn* (qq.v.).

CONSTANTINUS DB 1086, Cur 1200, 1205, 1210, Poll Tax 1379.
CONSTANS Cur 1200, 1213–15.
COSTIN Cur 1207.
COSTETINE Clerkenwell 1222.
COSTAINE or CONSTANTINE Keighley Reg 1586, 1597.
COSTANE, COSTAN Halifax Reg 1583, 1597.

Consuelo (f.) [konsooā'lo]: Spanish '(Our Lady of) Counsel'. Occasionally used by Roman Catholics, particularly in America (cf. MERCEDES, DOLORES). It is perhaps best known as the name of a novel by George Sand.

Cora (f.): apparently of American origin, and does not occur before the middle of the 19th C.

Coralie (f.): one of the numerous romantic names invented in France after the Revolution. It has been occasionally used in England.

Cordelia (f.): when used to-day, this name is probably always taken from *King Lear*. Shakespeare took (and slightly altered) the name from Holinshed where it appears as *Cordeilla*. It may be the same as *Cordula*, which appears in Welsh and Cornish calendars as the name of one of the companions of St. Ursula, and is found in German as *Kördula* or *Kordel*. *Cordell* or *Cordelia* Harvey was buried at St. Martin-in-the-Fields in 1636; *Cordelia* Parker died in 1689 in Cornwall, and several examples of the name have been noted in Lancashire in the second half of the 17th C, and one in Lincolnshire (Gedney Parish Reg) in 1763.

Corinna (f.): Greek, the name of a Boeotian woman poet, possibly a derivative of *κόρη* 'a maiden'. It was used in 17th- and 18th-C poetry, notably by Herrick, and has sometimes also been used as a christian name. The French use *Corinne* more often, probably on account of Mme de Staël's novel of the name.

Corisande (f.): a name from medieval romance; it is borne by one of the characters in *Amadis de Gaul*, and was used as a name for Diane de Poitiers. Disraeli named one of the heroines of his *Lothair* Lady *Corisande*.

Cormac (m.): of doubtful etymology. A common name in Irish myths and legends and still sometimes used, though commoner as a surname.

Cornelia (f.): the f. form of the name of the Cornelian *gens*, made famous by the mother of the Gracchi, a daughter of Publius Cornelius Scipio. It has been used occasionally as a christian name. An early example occurs in the baptismal register of South Leigh, Oxfordshire, in 1645. See also CORNELIUS.

Cornelius (m.): the name of a famous Roman *gens*, possibly derived from *cornu* 'a horn'. It was the name of the devout centurion (Acts x. 1) converted by St. Peter, and later of a 3rd-C martyred pope whose relics were taken to Compiègne and later to Rosnay in Flanders, whence the name became common in the Low Countries. *Cornelius* de Wyrley of Hanšworth, Staffs., lived at the beginning of the 15th C and the name was used for many generations in that family; *Cornelius* Clark, a carpenter of Oxford, fl. 1506–26; other examples are *Cornelys* Smythe 1504, *Cornelius*

Todd, son of a Presbyterian, born 1631, and *Cornelius*, son of Seth Wood, an ejected minister. *Cornelius* or *Corney* are often found in Ireland, where they came into use to translate the native *Conchubhar* (see CONNOR) or *Conn*.

Cosmo (m.): Greek κόσμος, 'order'; the name of one of the two martyrs *Kosmas* and *Damianos* whose supposed relics were revealed in a dream to St. Ambrose, and who became the patron saints of Milan. *Cosimo* or *Cosmo* became a favourite name in Italy, and was adopted by the Florentine family of Medici. It was the name of the 3rd Duke of Gordon (died 1752) whose father was a close friend of *Cosimo* III, Grand Duke of Tuscany, and since that time has been constantly used in the Gordon family, who have carried it by marriage into other Scottish families.

Costin, see CONSTANTINE.

Courtenay (m.): one of the considerable number of aristocratic surnames now often used as christian names. The family of *de Courtenay*, famous in the West country, took its name originally from *Courtenay* in the Île de France.

Cressida (f.): the rather complicated history of this name may be summarized as follows. In the Iliad, Hippodamia, daughter of Brises, is called *Briseis* (acc. *Brisëida*). Benoit de Ste Maure, the 12th-C poet who invented the story of Troilus in his *Roman de Troie*, took the name *Briseida* for his faithless mistress, apparently not realizing that it was simply a patronymic and could not apply to the daughter of Calchas. When Boccaccio took Benoit's story and refashioned it in his *Filostrato*, he presumably noted this mistake, and substituted the name of the other captive Greek maiden, *Chrysëis* (acc. *Chrysëida*) daughter of *Chryses* priest of Apollo, whom Agamemnon returned to her father at the command of the god. There is a passage in Ovid which might be misread to mean that she was in fact the daughter of Calchas. Boccaccio's *Criseida* was turned into *Criseyde* by Chaucer, and *Cressid* or *Cressida* by Shakespeare. That this name, a byword for faithlessness, should recently have been used as a christian name, is one of those aberrations of taste for which there is no accounting.

Crispin (m.): Latin *Crispinus*, a Roman cognomen, probably derived from *crispus* 'curled'. *Crispinus* and *Crispinianus*, shoemakers of Soissons, martyred *c.* 285, were considered the patron saints of shoemakers, and both *Crispin* and *Crispi(ni)an* were used as christian names in the Middle Ages. *Crispian* survived as late as 1587 at Gedney, Lincs., and *Crispin* still survives in occasional use.

CRISPINUS Cur 1201, 1207.
CRISPIANUS HR 1273.
CRISPIAN Gedney Parish Reg 1587.

Crystal (f.): sometimes used as a woman's name in modern times, presumably on the analogy of *Ruby*, *Emerald*, &c. *Crystal* or *Chrystal* is also a Lowland Scots pet form of *Christopher* (q.v.).

Cuddy, see CUTHBERT.

Curtis (m.): a common surname, originating in the nickname 'courteous' (*Curteis* is found as a personal name in 1199), and variously spelt; now sometimes used as a christian name.

Cuthbert (m.): compound of Old English *cuth* 'famous', *beorht* 'bright', a common Old English personal name, which survived the Norman Conquest, as being the name of St. *Cuthbert* (died 687), Bishop of Lindisfarne, whose body, preserved in Durham Cathedral, was said to work many miracles. There are 72 church dedications to him, mostly in the North of England where the name has chiefly flourished. It sometimes appears as *Cudbert*, and the pet-form *Cuddy* was formerly current and may have been the origin of the Scottish and Northern *cuddy*, an ass. *Cuthbert* lingered on in Yorkshire and Durham, chiefly among Roman recusants, after the Reformation, but went out of general use until it was revived by the Tractarians in the 19th C. During the War of 1914–18 *Cuthbert* was used as a slang term for an evader of military service, and it seems now to have gone out of fashion as a christian name.

CUDBRIHT HR 1273.
CUTHBRID Poll Tax 1379.

Cudbert 14th C Legendary.
Cuthbert Linc 1533, Cov 1530.
Cuddie, Cuddy Westmorland 1587.

Cynthia (f.): one of the titles of Artemis, meaning 'of (Mt) Cynthus', and the name of the mistress of Propertius. English writers in the later Middle Ages, struggling to spell *Sanchia* (q.v.), sometimes turned it into *Cynthia*, but the name was not really used until the Renaissance. It occurs from time to time in the 17th and 18th C and Mrs. Gaskell gave it to one of the characters in her novel *Wives and Daughters* (1866). CMY (1860) describes it as 'name of girls in America'. About the end of the 19th C it suddenly became fashionable in England for a time.

Cyprian (m.): Latin *Cyprianus*, 'of Cyprus', the name of a Bishop of Carthage, one of the first great Christian Latin writers, beheaded in 258 and mentioned in the Canon of the Mass. *Ciprianus* is found as a christian name in England at the beginning of the 13th C and at Cambridge University in the 16th and 17th C; it was revived by the Tractarians in the 19th C.

Ciprianus Cur 1199, 1200, 1219.

Cyriack (m.): Greek κυριακός, 'lordly'. St. *Cyriack* or *Cyr* of Iconium, the infant martyr son of St. Julitta, has 9 churches dedicated to him in the West of England, and *Cyriack* or *Syriack* has sometimes been used as a christian name, the best-known example being Milton's friend *Cyriack* Skinner.

Cyril (m.): Greek κυριλλός, probably a derivative of κύριος 'lord', 'master'. There were two saints of this name, both doctors of the Church, St. *Cyril* of Jerusalem died 387, and St. *Cyril* of Alexandria died 444. The name is first found in use in England in the 17th C (e.g. Sir *Cyril* Wyche *c.* 1620–90, named after Cyril Lukar the patriarch), but did not become generally used until the 19th C, when it was favoured, like other names of early Fathers of the Church, by the Tractarians. It is now a rather common name.

Cyrus (m.): Greek Κῦρος, from Persian *kuru*, 'throne'. The name of the great king of Persia occurs in the Old Testament and hence came into use among the Puritans. It has taken hold in the USA, where it is regularly used as a christian name.

D

Daisy (f.): a late-Victorian pet-name for *Margaret* (marguerite = daisy). It is sometimes used as an independent name.

Damaris (f.) [dă′m*a*ris]: the name of an Athenian woman converted by St. Paul (Acts xvii. 34), possibly a mistake for Greek *Damalis* 'a calf'. Like other New Testament names, it was adopted as a christian name by 17th-C Puritans and early examples occur at Gedney, Lincs., in 1597 and 1620.

Damian (m.): *Kosmos* and *Damianos* were brothers martyred in Syria in 303 under Diocletian. Their cult spread westward and was much increased by the supposed discovery of their relics at Milan by St. Ambrose. *Damianos* may be a derivative of Greek *δαμάζω*, 'to tame'. *Damian* is found in England as a christian name in 1205, and was in use for several centuries. See also COSMO.

DAMIAN Cur 1205.

Dandy, see ANDREW.

Daniel (m.): Hebrew 'God has judged'. *Daniel* is found in England before the Norman Conquest, but only as the name of monks or bishops. Its use as an ordinary christian name seems to have begun in the 12th C and it became common in the 13th and 14th C, giving rise to the surnames *Daniel(s)*, *Dann(son)*, *Dannet* (Lyford 1655 gives *Dannet* as a diminutive of *Daniel*). It was revived with other Biblical names in the 17th C and remained in general use down to the middle of the 19th C, when it became rare. This is no longer true; there was a sudden crescendo of popularity about 1968, and *Danny* is one of the commonest names in the present play-group generation. It has been particularly common in Ireland where it is used to translate the native *Domhnall* (*Donal*), and in Wales for Welsh *Deiniol.*

DANIEL Cur 1189–1215.
DANYELL Poll Tax 1379.
DANYLL Poll Tax 1379.

Dante (m.) [dăn'tĭ]: a diminutive of the Italian *Durante* (see DURAND), the christian name of the poet Alighieri and that by which he is usually known (cf. Michelangelo, Raphael, Leonardo). The name has been long obsolete in Italy, but is occasionally used in modern times after *Dante* Alighieri, e.g. *Dante* Gabriel Rossetti.

Daphne (f.): Greek *Δάφνη* 'bay' or 'laurel', the name of a nymph loved by Apollo and turned into a bush. CMY says of it, 'Daphne has not subsequently been used as a name except for dogs'; but about the beginning of the 20th C it began to be used as a christian name and is now quite common.

Darby (m.): CMY says this was the form of *Diarmaid* commonly used in Limerick and Tipperary. *Darby* occurs in the Liverpool Town Books from 1560, used in the family of Ulster (presumably of Irish origin). *Darby* Braye is recorded in London in 1609. The proverbial couple *Darby and Joan* are usually supposed to originate in a set of verses printed in the *Gentleman's Magazine* for 1735 (vol. v, p. 253), though *Darby* there may be a surname.

D'Arcy (m.): a name of territorial origin, derived from either Arcy-Ste-Restitue (Aisne) or Arcy-sur-Cure (Yonne). The English family of *Darcy* or *D'Arci* was founded by *Norman d'Areci*, one of the companions of the Conqueror, who was granted large estates in Lincs. In the 14th C a branch of the family settled in Ireland, and *Darcy* was there adopted as a christian name, at first perhaps as a translation of the native Irish *Dorchaidh.*

David (m.): Hebrew, originally a lullaby word meaning 'darling', then 'friend' generally. One of the first bearers of this name in Britain was *David* or *Dewi*, Archbishop of Menevia (died 601), the patron saint of Wales. From his time the name has been a favourite one in Wales. In Scotland it was the name of two kings, *David* I 1084–1153, and *David* II 1324–71, and has also always been common. In England it is not found before the Norman Conquest, but was common in the 12th C and has been used ever since, though never a favourite name. The surnames *David(son)*, *Davy*, *Davi(e)s*, *Davison*, *Davitt*, *Davidge*, *Daw(es)*, *Dawson*, and *Dawkins* are derived from *David* and its pet-forms *Davy*, *Davit*, and *Daw*, while *McTavish* is the Gaelic patronymic. In Ireland *David* has been used to represent Irish *Dathi*. At the present time it is enjoying a considerable degree of favour.

DAVID INTERPRES DB 1086.
DAVID Cur 1196–1220, FA 1285, Poll Tax 1379.
DAVY Cov 1471, 1494.
DAVIT HR 1273.
DAUE Poll Tax 1379.

Davina (f.): a Scottish f. form of *David*, found from the 17th C (e.g. *Davine* Dobenes 1639).

Dawn (f.): the use of this as a christian name is a 20th-C invention of novelette writers, which has sometimes been adopted in real life.

Deborah (f.) [dĕb′ŏră]: Hebrew 'a bee', the name of a prophetess, adopted by the Puritans in the 17th C, when it became a favourite christian name. It was borne by the youngest daughter of John Milton and, as readers of *Cranford* will remember, by the awe-inspiring Miss Jenkyns, who insisted on its being pronounced *Debōrah* in accordance with the usage of her late father. One can hardly imagine what her reaction would have been to the now frequent diminutive *Debbie*. In Ireland *Deborah* is sometimes used to represent Irish *Gobnait* (cf. *Abigail*).

Decima (f.): Latin 'tenth', see DECIMUS.

DECIMA Beckingham Parish Reg 1799.

Decimus (m.): Latin *decimus* 'tenth'. This, with *Septimus*, is the commonest of the numeral christian names. CMY says: 'Decimus and Decima are now and then to be found among us in unusually large families of one sex', but they were also used for tenth children in mixed Victorian families.

Deirdre (f.) [dĕr′drĕ]: the name of the heroine of 'The Sons of Uisneach', one of the Three Sorrowful Tales of Erinn, the subject of many plays and poems by modern Irish poets. The etymology of the name is doubtful. It was not known to CMY and its use as a christian name is quite recent, dating from the 'Celtic Revival' (Yeats's *Deirdre* 1907, Synge's *Deirdre of the Sorrows* 1910).

Delia (f.): an epithet of Artemis, derived from her birthplace *Delos*. It was a favourite name with pastoral poets in the 17th and 18th C. CMY mentions it as an occasional christian name, and it is still sometimes used. *Delia* or *Bedelia* is often used in Ireland by persons christened *Bridget* or *Brigid*—presumably as sounding more genteel.

Denis (m.): Latin *Dionysius*, Greek *Διονύσιος*, 'of Dionysos'; the name of the Areopagite converted by St. Paul at Athens (Acts xvii. 34), and of several saints, notably the apostle of the Gauls who was martyred near Paris in 272 and, as St. *Denys*, became the patron saint of France. There are 41 churches dedicated to him in England, where the name was introduced about the end of the 12th C and gave rise to the surnames *Den(n)is(s)*, *Den(n)ison*, *Denny*, *Dennett*, *Tennyson*. It occurs in the 15th C (*Deenys*, *Deenes* Scorchebefe) and still survived at the beginning of the 17th C, after which it went out of common use for a couple of centuries to be revived at the beginning of the 20th C. It is now in fairly frequent use. In Ireland, however, it has been used for some centuries as a substitute for the native *Donnchadh*.

DIONISIUS Cur 1200, 1221.
DYONISIUS Cur 1221.
DENES Poll Tax 1379.

Denise (f.) [dĕnēz′]: French *Denise*, Latin *Dionysia*, f. of *Dionysius* (see DENIS). *Denise* is probably now always a conscious borrowing from the French and is pronounced in the French manner; but *Denis(e)*, with its pet-forms *Dennet* and *Diot*, was a common English girl's name from the 12th C and survived till the end of the 18th C. Lyford 1655 gives *Denis* as a girl's name. A correspondent writes that she was christened *Denise* in the 1930's, and has always pronounced it dĕn′is. This may be a genuine survival of the older usage. In Latin records the name appears as *Dionysia*, and a list of Yorks Recusants 1604 mentions one *Dionis* Wilden which is presumably a shortened form of *Dionysia*. *Dionise* was borne by several members of the Markham family 1574–1631.

DIONISIA HR 1273, FA 1303.
DIONYCIA FA 1303.
DEONYSIA Cov 1449.
DIONIS Yorks Rec 1604.
DENOTE Langland *c.* 1362.

Denzil (m.): William Holles (16th C) married Anne, daughter and co-heiress of John *Denzell* Esq., of *Denzell*, Cornwall; their eldest son was named *Denzell*, and the name has been used ever since in that family and others connected with it. It is now usually spelt *Denzil*.

Deodatus, Deodonatus (m.): Latin 'given by, or to, God'. These, like *Adeodatus* and *Deusdedit*, were fairly common ecclesiastical names from the 7th C onwards, but unlike the similar Greek *Theodoros*, *Theodosios*, did not come into general use as christian names, though *Deodonatus* is found in England in 1205, and *Dieudonné* was sometimes used in the north of France and *Déodat* in the south.

Derek, Derrick (m.): *Diederick* or *Dirck* is the Dutch form of German *Diederich*, from Old German *Theodoric* (q.v.). *Dederick*, *Dyryke*, *Deryk* are found in England in the 15th C, borrowed, no doubt, from the Low Countries. Camden gives *Derric* as the English and *Terry* as the French forms of *Theodoric*. The name has been revived during the 20th C; it is now oftener spelt *Derek* than *Derrick*.

DEDERICUS Cl 1464.
DEDERIC Cl 1464.

Dermot, see DIARM(U)IT.

Desdemona (f.): sometimes used as a christian name in recent times after the heroine of Shakespeare's *Othello*. Shakespeare took her name, with the story, from Cinthio (*Hecatommithi* 1565) where it appears as *Disdemona*, possibly an adaptation from Greek δυσδαιμονία 'misery'.

Desideratus (m.): Latin 'desired'. Found as a christian name (probably ecclesiastical) in England in 1200. In France *Didier* from Latin *Desiderius* (the name of the last Lombard king of Italy and of a 7th-C French saint) was not uncommon in the Middle Ages. See also DÉSIRÉE.

Désirée (f.) [dāzērā']: French *désirée* from Latin *desiderata* 'desired'. *Désirée* is nowadays sometimes used as a christian name in England, but only as a loan from the French and pronounced and accented in the French manner. In the 13th and 14th C, however, *Desiderata* and *Desirata* occur from time to time in (Latin) records, and probably represent a latinization of some English form of the name which has not survived on record.

DESIRATA, DESIDERATA Cur 1210–12, FA 1302, 1316.

Desmond (m.): Irish *Deas-Mumhain* 'South Munster', came to be used first as a surname and then as a christian name in Ireland, and has recently come into use in England also. It is now (1976) fairly common, and is often abbreviated to *Des*.

De(r)vorguilla (f.): Gaelic 'true oath', the name of the foundress of Balliol College, Oxford, *Dervorguilla* of Galloway, widow of John de Balliol (d. 1269), who continued the foundation started by her husband. The name has been given occasionally to the daughters of patriotic Balliol men.

Diana (f.) [dīă'nă]: Latin name of the moon goddess (Greek *Artemis*), probably a derivative of *deus*. The use as a christian name was a Renaissance fashion (e.g. *Diane* de Poitiers) and it is first found in England in the 16th C, e.g. *Diana* Luttrell born 1580, *Diana* Cecil, daughter of 2nd Earl of Exeter born early in the 17th C, *Dyana* Sturdy 1618. It has never been a common name, but has been in regular use in e.g. the Manners family since the middle of the 18th C. Its comparative popularity in modern times may be due in part to Scott's *Diana* Vernon, heroine of *Rob Roy* (1817) and Meredith's *Diana of the Crossways* (1875). The abbreviation *Di* has been used since the 18th C (e.g. Lady *Di* Beauclerk (1734–1808)).

Since the above was written, the French form, *Diane*, has been widely used, usually pronounced dīan′, and is now (1976), probably commoner than *Diana*.

Diane, see DIANA.

Diarm(u)it, Dermot (m.): from Old Irish *di-fharmait* 'free from envy', pronounced *dī-ormwid*. The name of the lover of Grainne. The anglicized spelling *Dermot* has lately been reinforced in Ireland by *Diarm(u)id*. See also DARBY, JEREMIAH.

Dick, see RICHARD.

Digby (m.): the use of this surname as a christian name appears to have begun in the 19th C. An early example was Sir Matthew *Digby* Wyatt (1820–77), the architect, and the name has continued to be used in the Wyatt family, often as a first name. The surname was derived from *Digby* in Lincolnshire.

Diggory (m.): this apparently goes back to the medieval romance of *Sir Degore* or *Degarre*. An early example is *Digory* Wheare (b. 1574), Master of Gloucester College, Oxford. Goldsmith used *Diggory* as the name of a serving-man in *She Stoops to Conquer* (1773). It seems to be mainly Cornish. The explanation of the name given in the romance is that the hero as a child was found by a hermit and christened *Degarre* because

> Degarre nowt elles ne is
> But thing that not neuer what hit is
> Other thing that is neg3 forlorn also.

It is presumably derived from French *égaré*, 'strayed', 'lost', though it is not clear how; possibly the *s* of the reflexive form may have been mistaken for a *d*.

Dillian (f.): Dutch *Dilliana*, perhaps a derivative of Old German *Dilli*, *Dillo*. It is used in a few English families.

Dilys (f.): Modern Welsh *dilys* 'certain', 'perfect', 'genuine'. First used as name in Wales in the middle of the 19th C. Now often used in England.

Dinah (f.): Hebrew 'law suit', the name of a daughter of Jacob. It came into use in the 17th C (e.g. *Dinae* Shorthose 1629) and was a favourite name with the working classes until about the end of the 19th C. It seems sometimes to have been confused with *Diana*.

Dionys(ia), see DENISE.

Dionysius, see DENIS.

Dodo, see DOROTHEA.

Dolly, see DOROTHEA and ADOLPHUS.

Dolores (f.) [dolor'es]: Spanish, short for *Maria de Dolores*, 'Mary of the Sorrows'. The name of the Blessed Virgin was formerly seldom used in Spain, but attributive names such as this are common, e.g. (*Maria de*) *Mercedes*, (*Maria de*) *Consuelo*, (*Maria*) *Assunta*. *Dolores* is sometimes used by English, more often by American, Roman Catholics.

Dominica (f.), see DOMINIC(K). The f. form *Dominica* is used from time to time.

Dominic(k) (m.): (French *Dominique*, Italian *Domenico*, Spanish *Domingo*): Latin *dominicus*, 'of the Lord'. The name may have been given originally to children born on a Sunday (*dies dominica*). In England it is found as a monk's name in Anglo-Saxon times, but did not come into use as an ordinary christian name until the 13th C, in honour of St. *Dominic* (1170–1221), founder of the Order of Preachers. It was used at first as both a m. and a f. name, sometimes appearing as *Dominick*, sometimes as *Dominy*; *Domenyk* occurs in the 15th C. The name was never common in England, and after the Reformation was used almost exclusively by Roman Catholics until quite recently. It is now (1976) in more general use.

Donald (m.): Gaelic *Domhnall* (pronounced *Dawnal*), from Old Irish *Domnall*, from primitive Celtic **Dubno-walos* from **dubno-* 'world' and **walos* 'mighty'. It is one of the commonest Highland christian names and *Donal* is much used in Ireland, often as an equivalent of *Daniel*. Early examples of the name in England are *Doneuuald*, a Yorkshire sub-tenant mentioned in DB, and a *Donaldus* Sturmyn 1346.

Donatus (m.): Latin 'given'. The name of several martyrs as well as of the famous schismatic. *Donatus* may have been used in Britain before the Anglo-Saxon period—the Welsh *Dunawd* has been derived from it, and *Donat* is found in Ireland. In the Middle Ages it is found from time to time, both m. and f. usually in the form *Donnet*, and CMY records a female *Donnet* in Cornwall as late as 1755. For the development of *Donnet* or *Donat* from *Donatus*, cf. the word *donet* an elementary treatise, derived from the name (Aelius) *Donatus*, the author of a popular rudimentary Latin grammar widely used in the Middle Ages.

Donnet, see DONATUS.

Dora, see DOROTHEA.

Dorcas (f.): Greek δορκάς 'a roe or gazelle'. In Acts ix. 36 *Dorcas* is given as an interpretation of the Aramaic *Tabitha* (q.v.), the name of the charitable disciple raised from death by St. Peter. Both names became popular in the 17th C, and later *Dorcas* was the name given to a meeting of ladies to make clothes for the poor, in allusion to the story in Acts, where the poor are said to have wept over her, showing the coats and garments she had made for them.

Doreen (f.) [dor'ēn]: Modern Irish *Doirean*, probably an Irish adaptation of *Dorothy* (q.v.). It came into use in England about the beginning of the 20th C perhaps as a result of a novel of the name (1894) by Edna Lyall, an extremely popular writer in her day. It became one of the commonest names among the working classes, but has become less popular in recent years.

Dorinda (f.): an 18th-C coinage formed on the model of *Belinda* and *Clarinda* (qq.v.). It occurs in Farquhar's *The Beaux's Stratagem* (1707). It is still occasionally used.

Doris (f.) [formerly pronounced dōris]: this is a puzzling name. The first occurrence noted is *Doris* Dorcis Tabitha Mann, a New **Englander, in 1819. The name is not mentioned by CMY, and seems to have leapt into sudden popularity towards the end of** the 19th C. Forster, in his *Life of Dickens* (Book ix, ch. vii), quotes, from a memorandum book which Dickens kept between 1855 and 1865, a list of out-of-the-way christian names taken from Privy Council Education lists, amongst which occurs *Doris*.[1] It is the name of a character in Mrs. Oliphant's novel *Effie Ogilvie*, 1886. *Doris* is the name of a sea nymph in Greek mythology, Juvenal uses it for the mistress addressed in several of his poems, and it was the name of one of the four concubines of Agrippa the Prefect, whose conversion and martyrdom are related in the apocryphal *Acts of Peter*; but none of these seems to be a cogent reason for the sudden adoption of the name in late-Victorian England. It has been suggested that the later vogue of the name may have been helped by the actress *Doris* Keene (in *Romance*, 1914).

Dorothea, Dorothy (f.): (French *Dorothée*, German *Dorothea*, Italian, Spanish *Dorotea*); appears to be an arbitrary inversion of the name θεοδώρα, 'gift of God', which, like the m. θεοδώρος, was apparently a christian coinage. The legend of St. *Dorothea*, a 3rd-C Cappadocian martyr, is not found very early, and the name is not found in use in England until the end of the 15th C (e.g. *Dorothy* daughter of John Markham of Sedgebrook, Lincs., born *c.* 1494). It was very common in the later part of the 16th C when it was already abbreviated to *Doll*, and throughout the 17th C, often in the forms *Doll(y)* or *Dorat(e)*. It went out of fashion in the first half of the 18th C, came back *c.* 1750–1800, and then disappeared again until *c.* 1880. The pronunciation indicated by the 17th C spelling *Dorate* apparently survived in the 18th C. Miss

[1] I owe this reference to Professor John Butt.

D. K. Broster has called my attention to a grammar published by Newbery in 1769 in which the following occurs:

'*Q*. Does *h* never lose its sound after the *t*?
A. Yes, it is quite lost in these proper names, *Esther*, *Anthony*, *Thomas*, and *Dorothy*.'

The use of *doll* for a child's plaything is first recorded in 1700 (see OED s.v.), about the time when the christian name went out of fashion. Like Jill, Parnell, Nan, and other popular names, *Doll* came to be used as a generic name for a loose woman (cf. Shakespeare's *Doll* Tearsheet and Ben Jonson's *Doll* Common), which probably accounts for its temporary disappearance. *Dorothy* has been the usual form of the name in England, but *Dorothea* was sometimes used in the 19th C (e.g. *Dorothea* Brooke in *Middlemarch*). Besides *Doll(y)* the diminutives *Dot* and *Dodo* are used. *Dora*, now an independent name, came into use at the beginning of the 19th C. *Dora* Wordsworth (1804–47), the daughter of the poet, is an early example. Although named *Dorothy* after her aunt, she was always known as *Dora* after she grew up. *Dorothy* has been used to render Gaelic *Diorbhail*.

Dougal, Dugald (m.) [doo'gal]: Old Irish *dubhgall* 'black stranger', a name originally given by the Irish to the Norwegians, which later became a common christian name. It is now chiefly used in the Highlands of Scotland. The word *dubhgall* is still used in Irish and Gaelic to indicate an Englishman and in Modern Breton for a Frenchman.

Douglas (m., f.): Gaelic *dub(h)glas*, 'dark blue'. This very common Celtic river name (e.g. *Dawlish*, *Devil's Water*, *Dowles Brook*, *Dulas*, *Divelish* in England, *Douglas* in Ireland and Scotland, and *Dulas* in Wales) became the name of a great Scottish family, and, like other such names, also a common christian name. This use is not found, however, much before the late 16th C, when it was as commonly a girl's as a boy's name. Spenser's *Daphnaïda*, for instance, was written on *Douglas* Howard, wife of Sir Arthur Gorges, who also had an older cousin *Douglas* Howard who married, among others, Robert Dudley, Earl of Leicester. There was a connexion with Lady Margaret *Douglas*, d. of Margaret Tudor. Camden 1605 puts it among the women's christian names, and says of it, 'Of the Scottish surname, taken from the river *Douglas*, not long since made a Christian name in *England*'. It is now often used by people with no Scottish connexions.

Dowsabel, Dowse, see DULCIE.

Drogo (m.): Old German *Drogo*, Gothic *Draga*, a derivative of *dragen* 'to bear', 'carry'. The name was introduced into England at the time of the Norman Conquest (it was borne by several of the Conqueror's followers, notably *Drogo* de Monte Acuto, ancestor of the *Montagu(e)* and *Montacute* families), and became common, in the French form *Dru* or English *Drew*. *Drewsteignton* (Devon) was held by one *Drogo* in 1210 and is called Teyngton *Drue* in 1275; Littleton *Drew* (Wilts) was held by Walter *Drew* in 1242 and is called Littleton *Drewe* in 1316. It gave rise to the surnames *Drew(e)*, *Drews*, *Druce*, and survived as a christian name as late as the end of the 17th C; Lyford gives *Dru* in his list of names 1655, and a *Drugo* Cressener, a Hunts clergyman, died in 1679. *Drogo* was revived in the 19th C by the Montagu family (the 7th Earl of Manchester, born 1823, was christened William *Drogo*) and they have used it ever since.

DROGO DB 1086, Cur 1187–1219.
DRUET(TUS) or DROGO HR 1273.
DREW Lincs 1455.
DRUE Oseney 1460.

Dru, see DROGO.

Drusilla (f.): f. diminutive of Latin *Drusus*, a cognomen in use in the Livian *gens*, first assumed by the Livius who slew the Gaul *Drausus*. Livia *Drusilla* was the 2nd wife of Augustus, and another *Drusilla* was the daughter of Drusus Germanicus and sister and mistress of Caligula. Herod Agrippa I probably called his daughter *Drusilla* out of compliment to his patron Caligula; she is mentioned in Acts xxiv along with her husband Felix, Procurator of Judea. Like most other New Testament names, *Drusilla* was taken into use in the 17th C, and has been used from time to time since, more often in the USA than in England.

Dudley (m.): a surname derived from *Dudley* in Worcestershire, and made famous by the great family of *Dudley* which rose to power under the Tudors. It has been used as a christian name in the Ryder family, Earls of Harrowby, since the 17th C. Like many other aristocratic surnames, it came to be used as a christian name in the 19th C, with no reference to family connexion and it is now quite common.

Dugald, see DOUGAL.

Dukana (f.), see MARMADUKE.

Duke, see MARMADUKE.

Dulcie (f.): this seems to be a modern invention, not directly connected with the medieval *Dowsabel* (Latin *Dulcibella*), but formed immediately from the Latin *dulcis* 'sweet'. An early example is to be found in *Vice Versa* (1882). *Dowsabel* or *Dowse* (French *Douce*) were common in the Middle Ages, and gave rise to the surnames *Dous*, *Dowse*, *Dowson*, *Duce*, *Dewse*, and also *Dowsett* and *Dowsing* from the diminutives *Douset* and *Dousin*. The name was latinized as *Dulcia*. *Dowsabel* was still common in the 16th C, sometimes appearing as *Dowzable*, *Dussabel*, &c., and it was also used as a generic name for a sweetheart. Camden 1605 gives *Douze* and *Dousabel*. In the 18th C the Latin form *Dulcibella* was sometimes used, but CMY seems to regard it and *Dowse* as obsolete. *Dowsabel* was formed in the same way as *Christabel*, *Mirabel*, &c. (qq.v.).

DUSSABELE, DUSZABELL Writs of Parliament *c.* 1300.
DUCE, DOUCE HR 1273.

Duncan (m.): From Old Irish *Dunccan*, with a double suffix *-ec*+*-an*. It is a hypocoristic form from Old Irish *Dun-chadh* 'brown warrior'. The name of two early Scottish kings, Duncan I 1034–40, Duncan II 1094–5, it has always been a fairly common name in Scotland, but has not been adopted in England as other Scottish names have been. *Donecan* occurs, however, in DB as the name of a sub-tenant in Somerset. In Ireland *Donnchadh* is usually rendered by *Denis*.

Dunstan (m.): Old English, compound of *dun* 'hill', and *stan* 'stone', the name of the great Archbishop of Canterbury, *Dunstan* son of Heorstan 924–88. His memory was held in great reverence in the Middle Ages and his name is occasionally found in use; a *Donston* Chechelly occurs in London as late as 1529, probably named after the parish of his birth. The name went out of use after the Reformation until it was revived by the Tractarians in the 19th C.

DUNSTAN, DONESTAN, DUNESTAN DB 1086.
DUNSTAN HR 1273.
DONESTAN Poll Tax 1379.

Durand (m.): apparently from Latin *durantem* 'lasting'; the French *Durand*, Italian *Durante* were common in the Middle Ages. *Durand* was introduced into England by the Normans before the Conquest; in DB there is mention of several tenants of this name who held TRE. It gave rise to various surnames, e.g. *Durand*, *Durant*, *Durrant*, *Durrance*. *Durant* Hamelyn occurs in a volume of Inquisitions as late as 1428, and *Durant* is still used as a christian name by the gipsy family of Lovell. See also DANTE, the Italian diminutive form of the name.

DURAND(US) Reg 1079–83, DB 1086, Cur 1189–1212.
DURAND HR 1273.
DURANT HR 1273.

Dwight (m.): an English surname, perhaps derived from *Diot*, a diminutive of *Dionisia*. A John *Dwight* of Dedham emigrated to New England in 1635, and was founder of a numerous family, eminent among whom was Timothy *Dwight*, President of Yale, 1795–1817. It was probably in his honour that *Dwight* first came into use as a christian name in America, where it is now common. Cf. CHAUNC(E)Y.

Dymp(h)na (f.) [dĭmf'n*a* or dĭmp'n*a*]: Irish *Damhnait*, possibly a formation with the suffix *-aid* from *damhna* 'one fit to be'; the name of an Irish virgin martyr, sometimes used by Irish Roman Catholics.

E

Eamon, SEE EDMUND.

Easter (m., f.): like *Christmas, Pascal, Pentecost,* &c., *Easter* was formerly used as a christian name, and still survives in some families. When used as a woman's name it was sometimes confused with *Esther*. The pet form *Eacy* is occasionally used.

Ebenezer (m.): Hebrew 'stone of help' (the name of a stone raised by Samuel to commemorate the defeat of the Philistines, 1 Sam. vii. 12); adopted as a christian name by 17th-C Puritans, sometimes in the form *Benezer* (e.g. *Benazer* Wilson born 1668, son of an ejected minister). It continued in use among Dissenters and is still used in the USA, sometimes abbreviated to *Eben.*

Eda, Ede, see EDITH.

Edborough (f.): Old English *Eadburh*, compound of *ead* 'rich', 'happy', and *burh* 'fortress', was the name of an 8th-C saint, abbess of Minster, and survived until at least the 17th C. *Edborough* Butcher is mentioned in a Somerset will of 1582.

Eden (m., f.): Hebrew 'delight'; like some other Old Testament place-names, sometimes used as a christian name. A recent example was the novelist *Eden* Phillpotts. See also EDITH.

Edgar (m.): Old English *Eadgar*, compound of *ead* 'rich', 'happy', and *gar* 'a spear'. The first element was a distinguishing mark of the royal house of Wessex. *Eadgar* (944–75), the grandson of Alfred, was one of the most successful kings of that house; his name became a favourite among the English and survived the Norman Conquest. It was used, though infrequently, until about the end of the 13th C. It was revived in the 18th C, along with other Old English names, by romantic writers, but the reason for its greatly increased use in the 19th C was probably that it was the name of the hero of *The Bride of Lammermoor* (1819).

EDGAR, ETGAR DB 1086.
EDGAR Cur 1200.

Edith (f.): Old English *Eadgyth*, compound of *ead* 'rich', 'happy', and *gȳð* 'war'. A fairly common Old English name which survived the Norman Conquest, probably because of the popularity of St. *Eadgyth* (962–84), daughter of King Edgar. The marriage of Henry I to the English princess *Eadgyth* may also have helped to perpetuate the name, though she was usually known as Matilda or Mold. *Eadgyth* was sometimes confused with *Eadgifu*, compound of *ead* with *gifu* 'gift', which is also found after the Conquest, usually latinized as *Ediva*. *Edith* remained common all through the Middle Ages and never died out entirely, though it was infrequent from the 16th to 18th C. It came back into fashion in the 19th C.

The now obsolete but formerly common f. name *Ede* was from Old English *Eadu*, a f. name formed from the root *ead*. Camden 1605 says '*Ead* drawn from *Edith*', and Lyford 1655 says '*Eade* for *Edith*'; but it seems to have been an independent name earlier, was latinized as *Eda*, and often used in the diminutive form *Eden*. It gave rise to a number of surnames such as *Ede*, *Eade*, *Eadie*, *Eden*. An example of the christian name *Ede* occurs in a Notts Parish Register as late as 1765, but it seems now to be obsolete.

EADITA, EIDITA, EDGIDA, EDGED, EDIET, EDIED, EDIT, EDID DB 1086.
EDITHA Cur 1199, FA 1346.
EDITHE FA 1284.
EDA Cl 1255, HR 1273.
EDDE HR 1273.
EDDA Poll Tax 1379.
EDON HR 1273.
EDINE HR 1273.
EDDEN Poll Tax 1379.
EDAN, EDEN Poll Tax 1379.

Edmond, Edmund (m.): Old English *Eadmund*, compound of *ead* 'rich', 'happy', and *mund* 'protection'; the name of two kings of England, *Edmund* the Magnificent (922?–46), son of Edward the Elder, and *Edmund* Ironside (981?–1016), and of two saints, St. *Edmund*, King of the East Angles, martyred by the Danes in

870, and St. *Edmund* Rich (1170?–1240), Archbishop of Canterbury. It was common in the 11th C and occurs in DB. Henry III owed special devotion to SS. *Edward* and *Edmund*, and named two of his sons after them, which probably helped these names to survive at a time when many Old English names went finally out of use. *Edmund* was often written in the French form *Edmond* in the later Middle Ages. It was less common after the 15th C, but continued to be used in certain families, e.g. Courtenay, Montagu, Mortimer, Despenser, Murray, Douglas. In the 17th C *Edmund* and *Edward* were often confused. The Irish form of the name is *Eamon*, which is now often used, incorrectly, to render *Edward*.

EDMUND(US) DB 1086, Cur 1199–1219, HR 1273, FA 1316, Poll Tax 1379. EMOND Lincs 1450.

Edna (f.): this name occurs in various books of the Apocrypha, as the wife of Enoch, the wife of Raguel in *Tobit*, and twice in the book of *Jubilees*. Its etymology is unknown. It is not clear when it was first used as a christian name, but the first example noted is a character in C. M. Yonge's novel *Hopes and Fears* (1860). The modern vogue of the name is possibly due to the novelist '*Edna* Lyall', whose real name was Ada Ellen Bayly, of which her pen-name is a partial anagram. Her first novel *Won by Waiting* was published in 1879, and she soon became a best-seller.

Edred (m.): Old English *Eadred*, compound of *ead* 'rich' and *raed* 'counsel', the name of a King of England, *Eadred* (d. 955), son of Edward the Elder. One of the Old English names occasionally revived in the 19th C.

Edward (m.): (Latin *Edwardus*, French *Édouard*, German *Eduard*, Italian *Eduardo*, Portuguese *Duarte*); Old English *Eadweard*, compound of *ead* 'rich', 'happy', and *weard* 'ward', 'guardian'. It was the name of one of the greatest of the West Saxon kings of England, *Edward* the Elder, son of Alfred the Great, who reigned from 901 to 924; of a saint and martyr, the son of Edgar, who reigned from 975 to 978; and of *Edward* the Confessor, the last English king of the line of Alfred. These associations were sufficient to ensure the popularity of the name in the Old English period and its survival after the Norman Conquest. It occurs in DB and is found in 12th-C records. But the reason why *Edward*, unlike most Old English names, continued in general use after the end of the 12th C was undoubtedly the fact that Henry III's devotion to SS. *Edmund* and *Edward* led him to give their names to two of his sons. From the accession of *Edward* I in 1272 there was an *Edward* on the throne of England for over a century (until 1377). From that time it has been in regular use as a christian name and has shown very little fluctuation of fashion. It is one of the very few names of English origin which have been generally adopted on the Continent. The surnames *Edward(s)*, *Edwardes* were formed from it, but *Edwardson* is surprisingly rare. The nicknames *Ned* and *Ted* have been used since the 14th C; *Eddie* is modern.

EADUUARD, ÆDUUARD, EDUUARD, EDUARD DB 1086.
EDWARDUS Cur 1187–1219.

Edwin (m.): Old English *Eadwine*, compound of *ead* 'happy', 'rich', and *wine* 'friend', the name of the first Christian king of Northumberland (585?–633), and a fairly common name in the Old English period. It survived the Norman Conquest, and is sometimes found as a surname, but seems not to have been generally used as a christian name between the 13th and the early 19th C, though it is said to have been common in Lancashire in the 16th and 17th C.

EADUIN, ÆDUUIN, ÆDUIN, EDUUIN(E), EDUIN DB 1086.
EDUINUS Cur 1200–19.

Edwina (f.): a modern f. name formed from *Edwin*.

Effie (f.), see EUPHEMIA.

Egbert (m.): compound of Old English *ecg* 'sword', and *beorht* 'bright', the name of the traditional first King of all England (died 839) and of a Northumbrian saint (639–729). It seems not to have survived the Old English period, but was revived in the 19th C.

EGBERT DB 1086.

Egelina (f.): probably a Norman version of Old German *Agilina* from the root *Agil.* It is found in England in the 13th and 14th C and gave rise to the surnames *Eglon, Eglin, Eagling, Eggling.*

EGELINA FF 1257, FA 1346.
HEGELINA Testa de Neville 13th C.

Eglentyne (f.): Old French diminutive of *aiglente* from Latin *aculenta* 'prickly', a name for the sweetbrier (later erroneously applied to the honeysuckle). The earliest example of the word in OED is 1400, but *Aiglente, Aiglentine* are common as personal names in the *chansons de geste*, and *Eglentine* occurs in England as early as 1213 (Cur). *Eglentyne* was the name of Chaucer's Prioress. It was revived in the late 19th C, but has not come into general use.

Eileen (f.): Modern Irish *Eibhlin*, pronounced *ī'lēn* in Munster, but *ev'lēn* in Connaught. Also spelt *Aileen.* Often taken to be the Irish equivalent of *Helen*, but more probably an Irish development of *Evelyn* (q.v.). Often in pet-form *Eily.* Like many other Irish names it became common in England at the beginning of the 20th C.

Eithne, see AINE.

Elaine (f.): an Old French form of *Helen* (q.v.), which occurs in the *chansons de geste* and in Malory's *Morte d'Arthur.* It is not found in use as an ordinary christian name until after Tennyson's *Idylls of the King* (1859) had made familiar the story of Lancelot and *Elaine*, which he took from Malory.

Eldred (m.), see ALDRED.

Eleanor(a), Elinor (f.) [ĕ'lenor, ĕlĕänor'ă]: Provençal *Aliénor*, a form of *Helen* (q.v.), first introduced into England by *Eleanor* of Aquitaine (1122–1204), wife of Henry II, but its popularity was rather due to her descendant *Eleanor* of Castile (died 1290), queen of Edward I, in whose memory her husband erected the so-called '*Eleanor* crosses'. From the 12th to the 15th C the name usually appears as *Alienor, Eleanor, Elianor.* Its relation to *Helen* was apparently recognized as late as 1604 when a list of Yorkshire recusants calls the same person indifferently *Helen* and *Elinor*. The shorter *Elinor* came in in the 17th C, but the spelling *Elianor* also occurred, and no doubt the name was pronounced sometimes as a quadrisyllable, sometimes as a trisyllable. Its use was fairly steady in the 17th and 18th C (examples are *Elinor* (*Nell*) Gwyn 1650–87, *Elinor* Dashwood in *Sense and Sensibility* [1796] 1811). Dickens's 'Little *Nell*' (*Elinor* Trent) in *The Old Curiosity Shop* (1840) may have helped to increase the use of the name, which CMY, however, appears to have regarded as obsolete. The Italian form *Eleonora* is sometimes used. *Eleanor* is now usually so spelt and given in full, the pet-form *Nell* being used rather for *Helen*. See also LEONORA.

ALIENORA Cur 1199, 1213.
ELEANORA Cur 1205, 1207.
ELIANORA FA 1303, 1346.
ALIANORA FA 1428.
ELYENORA HR 1273.
ELINOR Yorks Rec 1604.
ELLENOR St. Michael, Cornhill 1687.
HELEANOR St. Michael, Cornhill 1690.

Eleazar (m.) [ĕlĕā'zar]: Hebrew 'God helped'; the name of the son of Aaron, the second chief-priest of Israel, and also of a son of Aminadab, one of David's captains. Not uncommon as a christian name in the 17th C.

Elfleda (f.): the later form of two Old English women's names, *Æthelflæd*, compound of *æthel* 'noble' and *flæd* 'beautiful', 'clean'; and *Ælflæd*, compound of *ælf* 'elf' and *flæd*. The first was the name of the most able of the daughters of Alfred, 'The Lady of the Mercians' (died 918), and the second of a famous abbess of Whitby (654–714?). Neither name long survived the Norman Conquest, but *Elfleda* was revived in the 19th C.

ÆLFLED(A), ALFLED(A), ALFLET, ELFLET DB 1086.

Elfreda, Elfrid (f.) [ĕlfrē'da, ĕlf'rid]: Old English *Ælfthryth*, compound of *ælf* 'elf' and *thryth* 'strength'; the name of the 2nd wife of King Edgar and mother of Ethelred the Unready. She was supposed to have killed her stepson Edward the Martyr.

The name did not survive the Norman Conquest but was revived in the 19th C.

Elgiva (f.): either Old English *Æthelgifu*, compound of *æthel* 'noble' and *gifu* 'a gift', or *Ælfgifu*, compound of *ælf* 'elf' and *gifu*, both common Old English names. The latter survived until the 13th C in the form *Elveva*. *Aileve*, which may represent either name, was also common in the same period. *Elgiva* is a 19th-C revival of a latinized form.

ÆILEUA, AILEUA, EILEUA DB 1086.
ÆLFGIUEE, ÆLUEUA, ALUIUA, ALUEUE, ALUEUA, ELUEUA DB 1086.

Eli (m.) [ē'lī]: Hebrew 'height'; the name of the high priest who brought up the prophet Samuel. It was taken into use as a christian name in the 17th C.

Elias [ĕlī'as], see ELIJAH.

Elihu (m.) [ĕlī'hū]: Hebrew 'God (is) he', 'he is God'; the name of one of the participants in the debate with Job, adopted as a christian name in the 17th C and still used in USA.

Elijah, Elias (m.): Hebrew 'Jehovah is God'. It was one of the most popular Old Testament names in the Middle Ages, the various vernacular forms of it being derived from the Greek form Ἠλίας. The English *Ellis*, French *Élie*, and the diminutive *Eliot* were all common in England, as is testified by the numerous surnames formed from them (e.g. *Ellis(on)*, *El(e)y*, *El(l)iot(t)*). *Ellis* gradually went out of fashion, though it is found in use as late as the end of the 15th C; in the 17th C the Puritans took to using *Elijah* (the form in which the name appears in the Authorized Version of the Old Testament). A well-known example of the name is Sir *Elijah* Impey (1732–1809), the friend and colleague of Warren Hastings. *Ellis* and *Eliot* are nowadays often found as christian names, but they are usually surnames being so used. *Élie* is still frequently used in France.

ELIS Cur 1199–1215, HR 1273.
ELYS HR 1273.
ELIAS FA 1316.

ELYAS FA 1303.
ELYE HR 1273.
ELIE QW 1292.
ELIOT Cur 1210.
ELYOT HR 1273.

Eliot, see ELIJAH.

Elisabeth, see ELIZABETH.

Elisha (m.): Hebrew 'God is generous', commonly latinized as *Eliseus*, the name of the disciple and successor of Elijah. Some of the medieval *Ellis's* may represent this name, though most of them are undoubtedly from *Elias* (i.e. *Elijah*). *Elisha* was occasionally used as a christian name in the 17th C and later, but was never common.

Elizabeth (f.): Hebrew *Elisheba*, 'My God (is) satisfaction', the name of the wife of Aaron and of the mother of St. John the Baptist. The Greek form of the name was Ἐλίσαβετ, the Latin *Elizabetha*; in England the spelling with a *z* has been usual, on the Continent that with an *s*. It was first used as a christian name in the Eastern Church, and made its way from Russia to Germany and the Low Countries and thence to France, where it was transformed into *Isabel* (q.v.), the usual English medieval form of the name. *Elizabeth* is found in England from time to time in the 13th and 14th C, but did not become common until the end of the 15th C. The medieval use of the name, such as it was, was probably a tribute to St. *Elizabeth* of Hungary (1207–31) rather than to the mother of the Baptist. There is only one English church dedication in this name, and it has given rise to no surnames. The cause of its later immense popularity was undoubtedly the long and successful reign of *Elizabeth* Tudor, who was presumably named after her grandmother *Elizabeth* of York and her great-grandmother *Elizabeth* Woodville, wife of Edward IV. At the end of the 15th C *Elizabeth* was still a comparatively rare name; by 1560 it accounted for 16 per cent. of female baptisms, and by 1600 for over 20 per cent., a position which it held for at least 200 years. No name has been more prolific of diminutives, many of which have from time to time established themselves as independent names, a circumstance which gave rise to the old riddling rhyme:

> Elizabeth, Betsy, Betty, and Bess
> Went out one day to find a bird's nest,
> They found a nest with five eggs in it,
> They each took one and left four in it.

The chief of these are the following: *Eliza* (used of the queen by 16th-C poets, and popular in the 18th and early 19th C; Charlotte Lucas in *Pride and Prejudice* calls *Elizabeth* Bennet *Eliza*, though her family call her *Lizzy*); *Betty* (fashionable in the 18th C until it became too common, was relegated to chambermaids and the like, and gradually died out, to be restored to fashion in the 20th C); *Bess*(*ie*) (common in the 16th C and revived in the 19th C to take the place of *Betty*); *Betsey*, *Lizzie* or *Lizzy*, *Tetty*, *Tetsy*, *Beth*; Scottish variants are *Elspeth*, *Elspie*, and *Elsie*, the last of which is now often used as an independent name, *Libby* and *Tibby*. The German *Elsa*, *Lise*, *Liesl*, Italian *Bettina* and French *Élise*, *Lisette*, and *Babette* are all occasionally used in England. *Elizabeth* and *Isabel* were early differentiated, but were sometimes treated as the same name as late as the end of the 15th C; e.g. in 1483 there is a record of one *Ysabell* or *Elisabeth* Cutler. *Elizabella* was a 16th-C coinage. See also LIL(L)IAN.

ELIZABETH Cur 1205.
ELIZABEZ Cur 1207.
ELIZABET FA 1303.

Elkanah (m.): Hebrew 'God has created', the name of the father of the prophet Samuel. Occasionally used as a christian name in the 17th C, and later in the USA. The best-known example of the name is *Elkanah* Settle (1648–1724), the city poet.

Ella (f.): the Norman-French christian name *Ela*, *Ella*, or *Ala*, which was fairly common in England from the Conquest till about the middle of the 14th C, was probably derived from Old German *Alia*, a f. name from the root *alja* 'all'. It was one of the medieval names revived in the 19th C by the Pre-Raphaelite writers, and has come into general use again. It is used in Ireland as = *Ellie*, a pet-form of *Ellen*.

ELLA Cur 1196, 1200.
ELA Cur 1210–12, FA 1284, 1303, 1346.
ALA Cur 1210–12.
HELE FA 1346.
ELIA FA 1346.

Ellen (f.): the earlier English form of *Helen* (q.v.), now treated as an independent name. In medieval records *Helen* usually appears as *Elen(a)*, *Elene*, *El(l)in*, &c., and these forms, together with the diminutive *El(l)ot*, are found as late as the 17th C. *Ellen* gradually fell out of upper-class use, and CMY seems to regard it as a Scotticism; but it survived among the poorer classes in England and had some revival of popularity in the later 19th C. It is very common in Ireland.

ELENA Cur 1213–15, FA 1346.
ELENE Lincs 1529.
ELLENE Lyford 1655.
ELLYN St. Mary at Hill 1507.
ELEN, ELLIN Chester 1561.
ELOTA, ELLOTA Poll Tax 1379.

Ellis (m.): see ELIJAH and ELISHA. *Ellis* is found in the 17th C as a woman's name, but this is a corruption of *Alice* (q.v.).

Elma (f.): not uncommon in the USA where it is usually an abbreviation of *Guglielma* (q.v.) The 8th Earl of Elgin's elder daughter (born 1842) was named *Elma*, a combination of parts of the mother's names *Elizabeth Mary*, and it has continued to be used in her family.

Elmer (m.): a surname derived from the christian name *Aylmer* (q.v.). It was the name of two New Jersey brothers who played an active part in the American Revolution, and is now a common christian name in the USA. But as late as 1655 Lyford gives *Elmer* as a christian name from *Ethelmer*, and it is possible that the American use may also represent a survival of this.

Eloisa, see HELEWISE.

Elsa (f.): German diminutive of *Elisabeth* (q.v.), now sometimes used as an independent name in England, probably after the heroine of Wagner's opera *Lohengrin.*

Elsie, Elspeth, see ELIZABETH.

Eluned, Luned (f.) [ĕli'n*e*d]: a Welsh name now occasionally used in England. See also LINNET.

Elvira (f.) [ĕlvē'r*a*]: this Spanish name is possibly from Old German *Alverat,* which became *Alvery* or *Aubrey* in English (see ALBREDA). It has occasionally been used in England since the beginning of the 19th C, perhaps from its associations with the Don Juan legend.

Emanuel (m.): Hebrew 'God with us', the name given to the Messiah in Isa. vii. 14, viii. 8. First used as a christian name by the Greeks (e.g. *Manuel* Comnenus), it spread westward and became particularly common in Spain and Portugal as *Manuel* or *Manoel,* with f. forms *Manuela, Manuelita. Manuel* and *Emanuel* are found as christian names in Cornwall in the 15th and 16th C, and *Immanuel* occurs sometimes in the 17th C, but in general the name has not been much used in England except by Jews, who sometimes abbreviate it to *Manny.*

Emblem, see EMMELINE.

Emerald (f.): the name of a precious stone, occasionally used in recent times as a christian name. See further under ESMERALDA and MERAUD.

Emery (m.): Old German *Emmerich,* compound of some element from the stem *Im-, Em-,* and *ric* 'ruler'; latinized as *Emericus. Emery* was introduced into England by the Normans and, though never common, survived both as a man's and as a woman's name until the end of the 18th C. The f. form occurs as *Emeria* in Lancashire in the 17th and 18th C. It is still used from time to time as a man's name, as also is *Emerick.*

EMERY Cur 1201.
EMERICUS FA 1284, 1316.
EMERIC HR 1273.

Emily, Emilia (f.): f. of Latin *Aemilius*, the name of a plebeian *gens*. Boccaccio's use of *Emilia* for the heroine of his *Teseide* helped to bring the name into use in the later Middle Ages, and Chaucer in his *Knight's Tale* anglicized it as *Emelye*. In FA (Heref) 1316 there occurs *Emulea* la Prys, which may be this name, and *Emerlee* is found in 1694. But it was not much used before the 18th C; George II's daughter, Princess *Amelia*, was usually called Princess *Emily*, and it was probably as a supposed equivalent of *Amelia* (q.v.) that *Emily* came into general use in the 19th C.

Emlyn (m.): a common Welsh name. It has been suggested that it is from Latin *Aemilianus*.

Emma (f.): Old German *Emma* or *Imma*, hypocoristic forms of names compounded with *ermin*, *irmin* 'whole', 'universal'. The name was introduced into England by *Emma*, daughter of Richard I, Duke of Normandy, who married (1) 1002 King Ethelred the Unready, and (2) 1017 King Cnut. It was a favourite Norman name, and was common from the 11th C onwards. The English form was *Em(m)*, which is found as late as the middle of the 18th C, and the diminutive *Emmot* was also common, giving rise to a number of surnames; Camden 1605 and Lyford 1655 give *Emmet* as a christian name. The form *Emma* was revived in the 18th C, probably under the influence of Prior's poem *Henry and Emma*, a paraphrase of the ballad of the 'Nut Brown Maid'.

EMMA Cur 1186–1219 *passim*, FA 1316, 1401.
EMME *Prompt Parv c.* 1440.
EMMOTE HR 1273.
EMMETE HR 1273.
EMMOT(A) Poll Tax 1379.

Emmeline (f.): Old French *Ameline*, *Emeline*, apparently formed from the common element *Amal-* (see AMELIA) with the diminutive suffix *-ine*. It was introduced into England by the Normans; one of the daughters of Aimeri, Vicomte de Thouars, who accompanied the Conqueror to England, was named *Ameline*. It was common throughout the Middle Ages in the forms *Emlin*, *Emblin*, and later *Emblem*. *Emblen* and *Imblen* occur in the 16th and

17th C, *Emlyn* in the 17th, and in Chichester Cathedral there is a memorial to *Emblem* Miller, died 1718 aet. 17. *Emblyn* Rogers, b. 1840 at Ashburton, Devon, is the latest example noted. The full form *Emmeline* was revived in the 18th C.

EMELINA Cur 1199–1219, Cl 1319.
EMELYNE QW 1292.
EMELYN Poll Tax 1379.
EMELINE Year Book 1422.
EMBLEMA Huntspill 1697, 1700.

Emrys (m.): see AMBROSE.

Ena (f.): used in Ireland as a semi-anglicization of the Irish *Eithne* (see AINE). It became popular in England on account of 'Princess *Ena*', Princess Victoria Eugénie Julia Ena, later Queen of Spain (born 1887).

Endymion (m.): Greek *'Ενδυμίων*, the name of the Latmian shepherd loved by Artemis. It was sometimes used as a christian name in the 16th and 17th C, e.g. *Endymion* Porter, the royalist (1587–1649).

Enid (f.) [ĕ'nid, ĕ'nid]: a Welsh name which came into use in England after the publication of Tennyson's 'Geraint and Enid' in the *Idylls of the King* (1859). It is commonly pronounced *ēnid* in England, but the Welsh pronunciation is *ĕnid.*

Enoch (m.): Hebrew 'trained', 'skilled', the name of a patriarch, father of Methuselah. It came into use as a christian name in the 17th C.

Eoín, see SEAN.

Ephraim (m.): Hebrew, possibly means 'meadows', the name of the 2nd son of Joseph. It came into use in the 17th C, and is still current in USA.

Erasmus (m.): from Greek *ἐράσμιος* 'beloved', 'desired', the name of a martyr of the Diocletian persecution and one of the 14 Holy Helpers. It is best known, however, as the name of the

Dutch scholar and reformer *Desiderius Erasmus* (1465–1536). *Erasmus* came into use in England in the later Middle Ages, particularly in the Eastern counties, probably through contact with the Low Countries. Examples are *Erasmus* Paston, died 1540, Sir *Erasmus* Dryden (1553–1632) in whose family the name has been used ever since, and *Erasmus* Darwin (1731–1802) grandfather of Charles Darwin, who was named after his great-grandfather Sir *Erasmus* Earle (1590–1667).

Eric (m.): Modern Norse *Eirik*, German *Erich*.

The second element is the common Teutonic root meaning 'ruler', 'government', the first is doubtful. The name was brought to England by the Danes (there is one tenant named *Iricus* in DB), but it seems to have soon died out. Its revival in the 19th C was helped by Dean Farrar's immensely popular school-story, *Eric: or Little by Little* (1858), and it is now a fairly common name.

Erica (f.): f. of *Eric* (q.v.). CMY does not mention this name, though she gives the Swedish form *Erika*. Its use in England seems to derive from the name of the heroine of Edna Lyall's very popular novel *We Two* (1884). A correspondent to N & Q mentions it as 'a curious name' in 1898. Some users of the name now identify it with Latin *Erica*, the botanical name for heather.

Ermengarde (f.): see ERMYNTRUDE.

Ermyntrude (f.): Old German *Ermentrudis*, *Ermandrud*, compound of *ermin* 'whole', 'universal', and *drudi* 'strength'. It was used in England in the 18th and 19th C by romantic writers and sometimes as an actual christian name. *Ermegarde*, with the same first element, is still common in Germany in the form *Irmgard* and was in use in England in the 12th to 13th C in the form *Ermengarde*, though this may have been a survival of the corresponding Old English *Eormengard*, which is on record. Old English *Eormengild* also survived and is found as late as the 19th C in the form *Armigil*.

Ernest (m.): Old German *Ernust*, Modern German *Ernst*, 'vigour', 'earnestness'. The name was apparently introduced into England in the late 18th C by the Hanoverians (e.g. *Ernest* Augustus, Duke of Cumberland 1771–1851), but did not come into general use until the middle of the 19th C. *Ernest* Jones (1819–69), a Chartist, was a godson of the Duke of Cumberland. The name *Ernis* or *Erneis* (Latin *Ernisius*, French *Hernays*, *Hernais*), which was common from the 11th to 13th C and gave rise to such surnames as *Harness*, was probably Old German *Arnegis* and not a form of *Ernest*. Lyford 1655 gives *Ernestus*, but specifies that it is German, and there is no evidence of its use in England at that time.

Ernestine (f.): f. form of *Ernest* (q.v.), occasionally used in the 19th C.

Esau (m.): Hebrew, etymology doubtful but possibly means 'blind'. The usual explanation 'hairy' is based on a philological error. The name of the elder son of Isaac. Occasionally used as a christian name since the 17th C.

Esmé (m., f.): the first occurrence of this name seems to be *Esmé* Stuart (1542–83), 6th Seigneur d'Aubigny and afterwards Duke of Lennox, cousin of James VI of Scotland, whose mother was French. His name, which is not found earlier in the family, and which was borne by his son and his grandson, was sometimes spelt *Aymie*, and it is possible that it is really the fairly common French name *Aimé* (see AMYAS). The name spread from the Stuarts to other Scottish families and eventually to England. It is not mentioned by CMY. It is now sometimes given to girls, probably from confusion with the old name *Ismay* (q.v.).

Esmeralda (f.): Spanish 'emerald'. It is used as a name in the romance of *Palmerin of England*, and Victor Hugo made use of it in his *Hunchback of Notre Dame*, since when it has sometimes been used as a christian name in England and France. See also EMERALD and MERAUD.

Esmond (m.): apparently Old English *Estmund*, compound of *est* 'grace', 'beauty', and *mund* 'protection' (Förstemann gives examples of names compounded with the cognate Old German *anst*). It was a rare name and died out in the 14th C. The modern

use of *Esmond* as a christian name is no doubt due to the influence of Thackeray's novel *The History of Henry Esmond* (1852).
ESTMŪND, ESTMOND HR 1273.
ESMOND Ass 1313–14.

Estelle (f.): a French dramatic name, possibly formed from *estoile* 'a star', used by Dickens for the heroine of *Great Expectations* (1860–1), and since then occasionally as a christian name in England.

Esther (f.) [ĕs'ter]: in the Old Testament book of this name, *Esther* is given as the Persian equivalent of the Hebrew *Hadassah* 'myrtle'; it is probably not, as usually supposed, from the Persian word for a star. In the Septuagint the name appears as Ἐσθήρ, whence Latin *Esthera, Hestera.* It is not found in use in England until the 17th C. Lyford 1655 gives both *Hester* and *Esther*, and the two forms were used indifferently. Racine's play gave the name some vogue in France, but it was at no time common in either country, and it is a strange coincidence that Swift's fate should have been involved with two women of this name, *Esther* Johnson and *Esther* Vanhomrigh. *Hetty* was formerly a pet-form of *Hester*. *Hadassah* was occasionally used in the 18th C.

Estrild (f.): Old English *Eastorhild*, compound of *Eastre*, the goddess of the rising sun, and *hild* 'battle'. *Estrild* survived in England until the 12th C. The Spanish *Estrella*, still sometimes used, came from the cognate Old German *Austrechildis*.

Etain (f.): Irish *Etaoin*; the name of the heroine of an Irish myth, popularized in the opera of *The Immortal Hour* (1922), since when the name has occasionally been used in England.

Ethan (m.): Hebrew 'perennial' properly applied to streams that run all the year round. The name occurs in 1 Kings iv. 31 and in the title of Psalm 89. *Ethan* Allen was a leading figure in the American Revolution, and the name has been fairly common in the USA.

Ethel (f.): *Ethel* seems not to have been an independent name in early times, though *Æthelu* occurs in Old English, corresponding to

Old German *Athala*. It seems to have arisen in the 19th C as a pet-form for such names as *Ethelburg*, *Etheldred*, *Ethelinda* (qq.v.). There was a correspondence in N & Q in 1872 about *Ethel*, which was then very fashionable. Several correspondents imputed its origin to Thackeray in *The Newcomes* (1853–5); others traced it to C. M. Yonge's *The Daisy Chain* (1856), in which the heroine is called *Ethel* as an abbreviation of her full name *Etheldred*. No doubt it was the popularity of these almost contemporaneous novels which caused the spread of the name.

Ethelbert (m.): compound of Old English *aethel* 'noble', *beorht* 'bright', the name of the King of Kent (560–616) who was converted to Christianity by St. Augustine, and also of a King of England (855–65), brother of Alfred the Great. It is doubtful if it survived the Norman Conquest (but see further under ALBERT), and if it did, it was only for a short time. A solitary example occurs at Cambridge in 1564. It was revived in the middle of the 19th C, an early example being *Ethelbert* (*Bertie*) Stanhope in *Barchester Towers* (1857).

AILBERT, AILBRIHT, AILBRIC, ALBERT, ALBRICT DB 1086.

Ethelburg (f.): Old English *Æthelburh*, or *Æthelburg*, compound of *æthel* 'noble' and *burh* 'a fortress'. The survival of the name down to the 19th C in London is no doubt due to the dedication of the Church of St. *Ethelburga* in Bishopsgate. There were two saints of the name, St. *Ethelburga* (d. 676) sister of Erkenwald, Bishop of London, and St. *Ethelburga*, Abbess of Farmoutiers, sister of SS. Etheldreda, Sexburga, and Withburga.

Etheldred (f.): Old English *Æthelthryth*, compound of *æthel* 'noble', and *thryth* 'strength'. St. *Etheldred* (630?–79) was Queen of Northumbria and founder and abbess of a convent at Ely. The present Cathedral at Ely is built over her remains and there are 12 other churches dedicated to her. From the 16th C the popular corruption *Audrey* (q.v.), now an independent name, was the usual form, but Lyford 1655 gives *Etheldred* or *Ethelred*, and there is a record of one *Etheltred* Daw (born 1728), whose name was corrupted to *Theldry*. The same person is named in Market Rasen

Parish Register as *Ethelia* in 1787 and *Theldred* in 1795. *Etheldred(a)* was sometimes used in the 18th and 19th C but is now supplanted by *Ethel* (q.v.).

Ethelfleda (f.): Old English *Æthelflæd*, compound of *æthel* 'noble' and *flæd* 'clean', 'beautiful'. See ELFLEDA.

Ethelinda (f.): Old German *Adallindis*, compound of *athal* 'noble' and *lindi* 'a serpent'. There appears to have been a corresponding Old English name *Æthelind*, and the name *Athelyna*, which occurs in 1346 FA may be a survival of it, though it more probably represents *Ethelwine*. *Ethelinda* is found in England from *c.* 1800 in the forms *Ethelinda*, *Athelinda*, and even *Earthelinda*. *Ethelenda* is still used by the gipsy family of Heron.

Ethelred (m.): compound of Old English *æthel* 'noble' and *ræd* 'counsel', a fairly common Old English name; one *Ethelred*, the brother of Alfred, was King of Wessex 866–71, and *Ethelred* son of Edgar was King of England 978–1016. It seems not to have survived the Norman Conquest, but was revived with other Old English names in the 19th C.
ÆTHELRÆD, ADELREDUS, EDRED, ADRED, AILRED, ALRET DB 1086.

Etta (f.): a pet-form of *Henrietta* (q.v.), occasionally used as an independent name.

Eubule (m.): Greek εὔβουλος 'he of good counsel', an epithet of Zeus. *Eubulus* occurs in 2 Tim. iv. 21 as the name of one of St. Paul's companions. It was sometimes used as a christian name in England after the Reformation (e.g. Sir *Eubule* Thelwall 1562–1630, one of the founders of Jesus College, Oxford). In the 17th C it was sometimes spelled *Ewball*; Lyford 1655 gives it as *Ybel*.

Eudo (m.): Old German *Eutha*, which Förstemann connects with Old Norse *jôdh* 'child'. It was introduced into England by the Normans and appears as *Eudes* and *Eudon* (representing Old French *cas-sujet* and *cas-régime*), and latinized as *Eudo*. *Udo* is found as late as 1507.

EUDO Reg 1070–7, DB 1086, Cur 1197–1219.
UDONA FA 1346.
EUDES Cur 1187–1219.

Eugene (m.) [ūjēn']: Greek εὐγένιος 'noble', 'well-born', Latin *Eugenius*. There were four popes of this name, the first (died 657) being venerated as a saint. *Eugenio* has been fairly common in Italy, but its wider diffusion was due to the fame of Prince *Eugène* of Savoy (1663–1736), the brilliant general after whom e.g. Richard Steele's 2nd son (born 1712) was named. *Eugene* is now sometimes used in England, oftener in USA where it is often abbreviated to *Gene*. *Eugenius* occurs in lists of early kings of Scotland, but it then represents a Gaelic name (see EWEN). In Ireland *Eugene* has come to be the English equivalent of *Eoin*, the Old Irish form of John, later replaced by *Sean* from French *Jean*. The relationship of *Eoin* to John was almost forgotten in the 19th C.

Eugenia, Eugénie (f.) [ūjēn'ēă, *ez*hānē']: Greek Εὐγενία 'nobility', 'excellence'; the name of a 3rd-C Roman martyr, a convert of SS. Protus and Hyacinthus. *Eugenia* is recorded in England in the 12th and 13th C. The French form of the name, *Eugénie*, was made fashionable in France by the Empress *Eugénie* (1826–1920), and is now sometimes used in England.

Eulalia (f.) [ūlā'lēă]: from Greek εὔλαλος 'sweetly-speaking', an epithet of Apollo; the name of a 4th-C martyr, the patron saint of Barcelona. It is fairly common in Spain and France (*Eulalie*), and is occasionally found in England, especially in Cornwall, e.g. *Eulalia* Sarat (died 1684), *Ulalia* Moyle (married 1657), both Cornish.

Eunice (f.) [ūnī'sē, ū'nis]: Greek Εὐνίκη, compound of εὖ 'well' and νίκη 'victory'; the name of the mother of Timothy, mentioned in Acts xvi. 1 and 2 Tim. i. 5. It came into use in England in the 17th C. The spelling *Unice* is found in Lincs. in 1617 and in New England in 1804. It is often pronounced as a disyllable; as CMY says: 'A favourite with English lovers of Bible names, though unfortunately usually pronounced among the lower classes after the most ordinary English rules of spelling: Younice.'

Euphemia (f.) [ūfē'mēă]: Greek *Εὐφημία* 'auspicious speech', hence 'worship of the gods', 'honour', or 'good repute'. The name occurs in the apocryphal Acts of Peter (*c.* 200) as that of one of the four concubines of Agrippa the prefect, who were converted and suffered death for their chastity. It was also the name of a 4th-C Bithynian martyr who has a place in the Roman Calendar. *Eufemia* or *Eupheme* is found in England from about 1200, and by the 16th C it was usually shortened to *Epham*, *Effum*, or *Effim*. Lyford 1655 gives *Eupheme*, but by his time the name was probably confined to Scotland, where it still flourishes, occasionally in the form *Eupham*, and often in the pet-forms *Effie* or *Phemie*. One of James Boswell's daughters bore this name. A m. form *Euphemius* occurs at Cambridge in 1629.

EUFEMIA Cur 1205, 1210, 1221, QW 1292, FA 1284, 1346.
EUFEMMIA HR 1270.
EUPHEMIA FA 1346, Poll Tax 1379.
EPHAM Yorks Rec 1604, Alvingham Parish Reg 1621.
FEMMOTA Magd. 1357.

Eusebius (m.) [ūsē'bēus]: from Greek *εὐσεβής* 'pious'; a common Greek name, the best known example being *Eusebius* of Caesarea (*c.* A.D. 264–*c.* 349), the ecclesiastical historian. It was probably after him that the name was used in the 17th C, e.g. *Eusebius* Hunt (Hunts Clergy List 1696), *Euseby* Pelsant 1642. Godstow 1450 gives *Euseby* as the English form of *Eusebius*, but there is no evidence of its use as a christian name at that date.

Eustace (m.) [ūs'tas]: there are two saints named *Eustachius* in the Roman Calendar, one of them having the same day as St. *Eustathius* in the Greek Calendar, and the two names are often supposed to be identical. But there is no trace of confusion between them at an early period, and though *Eustachius* is not easy to explain etymologically, that is no reason for confounding it with *Eustathius* (from Greek *εὐστάθης* 'tranquil', 'stable'). It may possibly be from *εὔσταχυς* 'fruitful'. The better known of the two saints *Eustachius* was a 2nd-C Roman soldier, whose legend included the story of his conversion, while hunting, by the vision of a crucifix between the horns of a stag. He was, like St. Hubert, a patron saint of huntsmen. His relics were transferred at an early date to St. Denis, and *Eustache* was a common French name. It was brought to England by the Normans and was fairly common in the 12th and 13th C. In Latin it appears as *Eustachius* or *Eustacius*, in English as *Eustace*, *Eustas* or *Ewstace*, and gave rise to the surnames *Eustace*, *Eustes*, *Eustis*. It has continued in infrequent use till the present day.

EUSTAC(H)IUS Reg 1076–84, DB 1086, Cur 1196–1215, FA 1303, 1316.
EUSTACE, EWSTACE HR 1273.

Eustacia (f.) [ūstā'sēă]: f. form of *Eustace* (q.v.). *Eustac(h)ia* is fairly common in Latin records of the 12th and 13th C. In the vernacular the m. and f. forms of the name were doubtless identical, and in 1521 there is mention of *Eustace* wife of William Malley. The Latin form *Eustacia* was occasionally used in the 18th and 19th C.

EUSTACHIA Cur 1200, 1205, 1207, 1213.

Eva, Eve (f.): Hebrew *Chawwa*, (?) 'lively', the name of the first woman. The Jews seem not to have used it, but it is found in use in England from about the end of the 12th C, and gave rise to the surnames *Eve*, *Eaves*, &c. *Eva* is the Latin, *Eve* the vernacular form of the name. In Ireland and Scotland it was used to represent the Gaelic *Aoiffe*, Modern Gaelic *Eubha*. Its revival in England in the 19th C was no doubt partly due to the popularity of 'little *Eva*' in *Uncle Tom's Cabin* (1852).

EVA Cur 1199–1219, HR 1273, FA 1303, 1346.
EVE FA 1284, 1486.
EVOTA Magd. 1426.

Evadne (f.): Greek *Εὐάδνη*, the name of the wife of Capaneus, who threw herself on her husband's funeral pyre. It was used by Fletcher for the heroine of *The Maid's Tragedy*. It is now sometimes used as a christian name, such use originating, perhaps, in the name of one of the characters in Sarah Grand's popular novel *The Heavenly Twins* (1893).

Evan (m.) [ĕ'van]: Welsh form of *John* (q.v.). It is usually considered to be derived from Latin *Iohannes* by way of vulgar Latin

Iŏvannes (cf. Italian *Giovanni*), but there are several phonological difficulties. The form *Evan* dates only from about 1500. Earlier forms were *Iefan* and *Ifan*, and in Middle English we find *Yevan*, *ȝevan*.

Evangeline (f.): this name appears to have been invented by Longfellow for the heroine of his narrative poem *Evangeline* (1847), as a f. form of the noun *evangel*. It is now fairly common in the USA and is also sometimes used in England.

Eveleen (f.) [ĕvelēn′]: Irish diminutive form of *Eva* (q.v.). It is often confused with *Evelina* (q.v.).

Evelina, Evelyn (f.) [ĕvelē′na, ē′velin]: Old German *Avelina*, a hypocoristic form of *Avi* (cf. the m. name *Avila*). The Normans introduced *Aveline* into England and it was common in the 12th and 13th C, giving rise to the surnames *Aveling*, *Eveling*, *Evelyn*, *Eveline*, &c. *Aveline* was still used as a christian name in the 17th C and *Avaline* is found as late as 1829 in New England. The Latin form of the name, *Evelina*, was revived by Fanny Burney for the heroine of her novel of that name (1778), and has been used from that time onwards. The shorter *Evelyn*, which is now commoner than *Evelina*, and is usually pronounced *ēvelyn*, has apparently come into being through association with the m. name *Evelyn* (q.v.). See also EILEEN.

AVELINA Cur 1189, 1200, HR 1273, FF 1430.
AVELYN Poll Tax 1379.

Evelyn (m.) [ē′velin]: as a man's name this seems to date only from the 17th C and to be derived from the surname *Evelyn*. The two earliest recorded examples are *Evelyn* Pierrepont, 1st Duke of Kingston (1665–1726), and Sir *Evelyn* Alston died 1750. Both their mothers were *Evelyns* by birth. The surname probably originated in the christian name *Aveline* (see EVELINA).

Everard (m.): Old German *Eburhard*, Modern German *Eberhard*, compound of *ebur* 'a boar' and *hardu* 'hard', cognate with Old English *Eoforheard*. It was introduced into England by the Normans in the French form *Everard* and was fairly common in the

12th and 13th C, giving rise to the surnames *Everard*, *Everit(t)*, *Everett*, &c. It has continued in occasional use ever since, notably in the Digby family.

EBRARDUS DB 1086.
EBERARDUS Cur 1213–15.
EVERARDUS FA 1284, Cur 1196–1215, HR 1273.
EVERITT St. Jas. Clerkenwell 1619.
EVERET Gedney Parish Reg 1783.

Everild, see AVERIL.

Ewen (m.) [ū′en]: this name, now mainly confined to Scotland, was once common in England, as may be seen by the surnames *Ewen*, *Ewing(s)*, *Ewan*, *Ewin*, &c. It is probably the same as Irish and Gaelic *Eoghan* 'a youth', which is frequent in Celtic legend and history. *Eoghan* is usually derived from Primitive Celtic **Esugenios* 'well-born', from which also is derived Old Welsh *Euguein* which later became Middle Welsh *Ewein*, *Ywein*, whence Modern Welsh *Owain*, *Owen* (q.v.). Mr. J. P. Blackledge of Ambleside informs me that the name *Ewan* has been in regular use in his family (until recently resident in the Ormskirk district of Lancashire) since the end of the 15th C.

Ezekiel (m.): Hebrew *Y'hezqēl* 'May God strengthen', the name of one of the major prophets. The English form comes from the Septuagint Greek Ἰεζεκιηλ through the Vulgate Latin *Ezechiel*. It was adopted as a christian name in the 17th C and has been common in the USA, where it is sometimes abbreviated to *Zeke*.

Ezra (m.): Hebrew 'help', the name of the author of one of the books of the Old Testament, taken into use in England in the 17th C (e.g. *Ezra* Grayle, a Presbyterian minister in 1648). It is still used in the USA and occasionally in England.

F

Fabian (m.): Latin *Fabianus* 'of *Fabius*' (the name of a Roman *gens*). *Fabius* may be derived from *faba* 'a bean', but this etymology is not certain. There was a 3rd-C Pope *Fabian* venerated as a saint and he is no doubt responsible for the survival of the name. Bardsley gives many examples of *Fabian* as a christian name in the 16th C, the earliest being in *Cocke Lorelle's Bote* 1515, but was unable to find anything earlier, though the existence of the surnames *Fabian*, *Fabyan* made it certain that the name was in use some centuries before. *Fabianus* does, however, occur as the name of a sub-prior of St. Albans *c.* 1200 and in a Curia Regis Roll of 1220, but he was of Italian origin.

Faith (f.): first used as a christian name after the Reformation. Lyford 1655 calls it 'a name commonly used'. In the 16th and 17th C it was given to boys as well as girls. Female triplets were often called *Faith*, *Hope*, and *Charity*. Not in CMY but now fairly common. See also FAY.

Fanny, see FRANCES.

Faramond (m.): Old German *Faramund*, compound of *fara* 'journey' and *mund* 'protection'. *Faramond* was the name of the legendary first King of France. It was introduced into England by the Normans and gave rise to a number of surnames, such as *Farrimond*, *Farman*, *Fairman*, *Fearman*. The *Ph* spelling occurs in Shakespeare's *Henry V*.

FARMAN(NUS) DB 1086.
FAREMANNE Pipe Rolls 1169.
FARMAN, FAIRMAN Writs of Parliament 1306.
FAREMAN Writs of Parliament 1316.
PHAREMAN Fines 12th C.

Farquhar (m.) [far'kar]: Gaelic *Fearchar*, from *fer* 'man' and *car* 'friendly'. The name of an early Scottish king. Still fairly common in the Highlands.

Faustus (m.): Latin *faustus* 'fortunate', 'lucky', the name of a 3rd-C Roman martyr. It was used as a christian name in the Middle Ages in Germany and Italy. In Germany it gave rise to the surname *Faust* or *Faustus*, which was borne by the 16th-C necromancer Johann *Faust*, who was the original from which the *Faust* legend arose.

Fay (f.): this name appears to be modern, first occurring in the 1890's. It may have been an abbreviation of *Faith* (q.v.) as in the case of the actress *Fay* Compton, or be the word *fay* 'fairy'.

Felicia (f.): the history of this name is much confused with that of *Phyllis* (q.v.). There was a St. *Felicia* of Nicomedia of unknown date, and the name, which is a f. form of *Felicius*, a 3rd-C derivative of *Felix* (q.v.), is found in use in England from the end of the 12th C. The vernacular form of the name was *Felice* or *Felis* (cf. French *Félise*): *Felice* occurs in *Piers Plowman*; Lyford 1655 says: '*Felice* see *Felix* in Men's names.' In 1577 the name is found spelt *Phelis*, and there seems little doubt that many of the 17th-C *Phyllis's* were really *Felice's*. The name was occasionally used in the 18th C, e.g. *Felicia* Hemans (1793–1835). A writer to N & Q in 1874 says: 'I have known 3 instances of the name *Felicia* being given in Cheshire. In one case it was always shortened to *Phyllis*.' G. M. Hopkins writing to Coventry Patmore in 1883 about one of his poems says: '*Felicia*—I do not understand the name. Is it a proper name, or the neuter plural of *felix*?' Patmore replied: 'I used the name *Felicia* because it *is* a name, and suggests itself as the female of *Felix*. *Felicitas* would not have done.' At the present time *Felicity* (q.v.) is much commoner.

FELICIA Cur 1199, 1218, FA 1303, 1316, 1401.
FELICE Oseney 1460.
FELISIA Poll Tax 1379.
FELIS Poll Tax 1379.
FILISIA Poll Tax 1379.
FILLYS St. Jas. Clerkenwell 1569.

Felicity (f.): Latin *Felicitas* 'happiness'. There were two saints *Felicitas*, one a 3rd-C Carthaginian martyr, and the other a widow said to have been martyred with her seven sons, and popularly identified with the mother of the Maccabees. But the name does not seem to have been used in England until the 17th C when many abstract nouns came into use as christian names. It is spelt *Phelisstie* in 1641.

Felix (m.): Latin *felix* 'happy'. The name of four popes and several saints, notably St. *Felix* the apostle of East Anglia, after whom *Felixstowe* was named. It was used in England in the Middle Ages, but not as often as the f. form (see FELICIA). It appears as *Felis* in the *chansons de geste*, and *Felyse* is given as the English form of *Felix* in Godstow 1450. *Felix* has been commonly used in Ireland to represent the Irish *Phelim*.

Fenella (f.) [fene'lă]: Gaelic *Fionnghuala*, from *fionn* 'white' and *guala* 'shoulder'. In Ireland it has often been rendered by *Penelope* (q.v.). The name was made generally known in England by Scott in *Peveril of the Peak*. *Finola* is the usual form in Ireland to-day.

Ferdinand (m.): compound of Old German *fardi* 'journey' and *nanthi* 'risk', 'venture'. The name was never very common in Teutonic countries, but was carried south by the Goths and became very popular in Spain (it was borne by many Kings of Castille) as *Fernando*, *Hernan(do)*, and also in Italy as *Ferdinando*, *Ferrante*. *Ferrand* was not uncommon in France and England in the Middle Ages, and gave rise to the surnames *Farrand*, *Farrant*, *Farren*, &c. By the 14th C, however, the name seems to have died out. In the 16th C the Italian form *Ferdinando* suddenly came into use in England. The earliest examples noted are Sir *Ferdinando* Heybourne (born 1558), and *Ferdinando* Stanley, later 5th Earl of Derby (born 1559). From then until the end of the 17th C *Ferdinando* was not uncommon, particularly in the landed families of the Midlands; it was also used regularly by some northern families such as the Stanleys and Hudlestons. In Ireland *Ferdinand* or *Fardy* is used to represent the Irish *Feordorcha*.

FERANT HR 1273.
FERRANT HR 1273.
FERENTUS Testa de Neville 13th C.

Fergus (m.): Old Irish *Fer-gus* from *fer* 'man' and Primitive Celtic **gustus* 'choice'. Mainly Scottish and Irish but occasionally used in the North of England, probably after *Feargus* O'Connor, the Chartist leader.

Fer(r)and, see FERDINAND.

Fer(r)y, see FREDERIC(K).

Finola, see FENELLA.

Fiona (f.): this name seems to have been invented by William Sharp (1855–1905) for his literary personality '*Fiona* Macleod'; he presumably intended it for a f. form of Gaelic *fionn*, 'fair', 'white'. Now (1976) fairly common as a christian name in England.

Firmin (m.): Latin *Firminus*, a derivative of the name *Firmius*. St. *Firminus* was a 5th-C Bishop of Metz. *Firmin* is found in England from the 12th to the 16th C and is still used in France.

FIRMIN HR 1273.
FIRMAN FF 1324.
FIRMINE FF 1552.
FYRMYN St. Dionis 1545.

Flavia (f.): f. of Latin *Flavius*, the name of a Roman *gens*, probably derived from *flavus*, 'yellow'.

Fleur (f.): French *fleur* 'flower'. Used as a christian name by Galsworthy in his *Forsyte Saga* (1926–30), and since then occasionally in real life.

Flora (f.): the name of the Roman goddess of flowers, which was adopted as a christian name in France (*Flore*) at the Renaissance, and carried thence to Scotland where it has been used ever since. *Flora* Macdonald, the Jacobite heroine, no doubt increased its popularity, and it is now often used in England, where it was formerly considered a suitable name for a spaniel but not for a woman. In the 13th and 14th C there are a few records of a name *Floria*, presumably the f. of Latin *Florius* 'of *Flora*'.

Florence (m.): Latin *Florentius*, from *florens* 'blooming'. There was a 3rd-C Roman martyr named *Florentius*, and also a Gaulish saint whose relics were preserved at Saumur. The name also occurs in the Old French romances, and was not uncommon in England in the Middle Ages. Lyford 1655 gives *Florence* as a man's name, but it does not seem to have survived the 17th C in England (Shelley's son, Percy *Florence*, was named after the city of his birth), though it has continued in use in Ireland (e.g. the inimitable '*Flurry*' Knox), where it was used to represent various native names.

FLORENCIUS Cur 1201–3, FA 1284, 1316.
FLORENCE HR 1273.

Florence (f.): Latin *Florentia* f. of *Florentius* (see man's name). *Florence* was used in the Middle Ages about equally as a man's and a woman's name, but whereas it died out as a man's it survived in use as a woman's name, e.g. *Florence* Vavzor 1621, and *Florence* Dombey in Dickens's *Dombey and Son* (1846–8). But it was rare until it was given a fresh impetus by the fame of *Florence* Nightingale (1820–1912), who herself received the name because she was born in Florence. Mrs. Gaskell, whose 3rd d. (b. 1842) was named *Florence*, wrote in 1852 to Miss Nightingale's sister: 'Babies *ad libitum* are being christened *Florence* here [i.e. at Manchester]; poor little factory babies whose grimed, stunted parents brighten up at the name'. In the 19th C it became common and was often shortened to *Florrie*, *Flo*, *Floy*, or *Flossie*.

FLORENTIA Cur 1196–1219.
FLORENCIA FA 1346.
FLORENCE Cl 1378, Lyford 1655.

Florian (m.): Latin *florianus* 'flowery', 'blooming'; the name of a 4th-C Roman saint invoked against fire and drought. It was occasionally used in the Middle Ages.

Flossie, see FLORENCE.

Flower (f.): this is found as a girl's name, occasionally, from the 17th C. Early examples are found in the parish registers of Hinton Charterhouse in 1625 and 1668.

Fortunatus (m.): Latin *fortunatus*, 'prosperous' 'lucky' a name adopted by or given to freedmen. Saints *Felix* and *Fortunatus* were martyred in 212 at Valence. Its use as a christian name has not been noted in England before the 17th C and it was probably a Puritan usage analogous to such names as *Donatus*, *Renatus*, *Desideratus*, &c. A number of examples of *Fortunatus* are cited in N & Q 192, No. 9 (3 May 1947).

Frances (f.): (French *Françoise*, Italian *Francesca*, Spanish *Francisca*, German *Franziska*): from Italian *Francesca*, f. of *Francesco* (see FRANCIS). The earliest record of the name *Francesca* seems to be *Francesca* da Rimini (died about 1288); the French *Françoise* appears about the same time. In England the name, like its m. equivalent, does not appear until the Tudor period, the earliest examples noted being *Frances*, daughter of Humfrey Cockayne, born about 1490, and Lady *Francis* Brandon (born 1517) daughter of Mary Tudor, god-daughter of Francis I of France, and mother of Lady Jane Grey. It was a favourite name with the aristocracy in the Elizabethan period, being spelt in the same way as the m. name and, like it, abbreviated to *Frank*. The distinctive spelling came in in the 17th C (e.g. *Francesse* Carpenter baptized at St. Giles Cripplegate 1644). Lyford 1655 says: '*Frances* see *Francis* in men's names'. The pet-form *Fanny*, from an earlier *Franny* (cf. *Biddy* from *Bridget*, *Kit* from *Christopher*), came in at the beginning of the 18th C, e.g. Pope's attack (1733) on John, Lord Harvey under the name of Lord *Fanny*. *Francie* and *Frankie* are also used as diminutives of *Frances*.

Francis (m.): (French *François*, Italian *Francesco*, Spanish *Francisco*, German *Franz*): Latin *Franciscus* 'a Frenchman'. The widespread use of this name on the Continent is undoubtedly due to St. *Francis* of Assisi (1182–1226), whose baptismal name was Giovanni, *Francesco* being a nickname said to have been bestowed by his father, who was on a business journey in France at the time of his birth. But the name may have been in use earlier, for in Curia Regis Rolls of 1200 and 1207 there is mention of a certain *Franceis*, though this, too, may have been a nickname rather than a proper christian name. The surname *Francis* seems to have originated thus, for early examples are all in the form *le Franceys*, &c. The earliest examples of the christian name noted in England are *Francis* Calthorpe of Norwich (1494), and *Francis* Southwick of Norfolk (1499). It is curious that the name did not become common until the 16th C, though the Franciscans established themselves early in this country and at the Reformation had some 80 convents here. An early example is *Francis* Russell, 2nd Earl of Bedford (1527?–85), and the growing power and influence of the Russell family in the 16th C may have had a good deal to do with its spread. *Francis* Drake, for example, was a godson of this *Francis* Russell, and one of *Francis* Bacon's aunts was married to his son, Lord Russell. The name was not much used in the 17th and 18th C except in families, such as those of Russell and Drake already mentioned, where it was firmly established. It gradually came back into favour in the 19th C and is now a common name. In the 16th C *Fraunce* was sometimes used as an abbreviation, as well as the more usual *Frank*.

Frank (m.): this name is now, and has been since the 16th C, the common abbreviation of *Francis* (q.v.). But it was not uncommon in England from the time of the Norman Conquest till about the middle of the 14th C, as an independent name representing the Old German *Franco* 'a Frank'. *Franco* occurs three times in DB and *Francus* once, and *Franco*, *Francus*, *Frank*, *Fraunk* occur with some frequency in the records of the next three centuries.

Freda, see WINIFRED.

Fredegonde (f.): Old German *Fridegundis*, compound of *frithu* 'peace' and *gundi* 'war'. This was the name of the queen of Chilperic I, an early Frankish king, and the French form of the name, *Frédégonde*, has been used from time to time in France and, very rarely, in England.

Frederic(k) (m.): (Latin *Fredericus*, German *Friedrich*, *Fritz*, French *Frédéric*, Italian *Federigo*): Old German *Frithuric*, compound of *frithu* 'peace' and *ric* 'ruler'. There was a corresponding, rather rare, Old English name *Freodhoric* which is probably behind the *Fredericus* who appears in DB as a tenant TRE. The medieval French form *Frery* or *Ferry* is occasionally found in the 12th C, but on the whole the name was uncommon until the 17th C. An early example was Henry *Frederick* Howard, 3rd Earl of Arundel (1608–52). Camden 1605 says: 'For *Frideric* the English have commonly used *Frery* and *Fery* which hath been now a long time a christian name in the ancient family of Tilney, and lucky to their house as they report'. (A '*Fred.* de Tilney' is recorded as early as 1360.) The real acclimatization dates from the 18th C, when the Hanoverians brought it in, e.g. *Frederick* Prince of Wales, son of George II. It very soon gained a firm footing and has for some 200 years been one of the commonest English men's names. It is usually shortened, in use, to *Fred* or *Freddy*.

Frederica (f.) [frĕdérē'kă]: the f. form of *Frederick* (q.v.), coined in Germany and first used in England in the 19th C.

Frideswide (f.) [frīds'wīd]: Old English *Frithuswith*, compound of *frith* 'peace' and *swith* 'strong'. St. *Frithswith* or *Frideswide* (died 735?) is said to have been the daughter of a king of Mercia and to have fled to Oxford to preserve her virginity from a royal suitor. She founded a convent at Oxford, and the Cathedral was raised over her remains, which were in 1289 translated to a splendid shrine. Her name is found in use up to the Reformation (Godstow 1450 says '*Fryswyde* English for *Frediswitha*') and even later. Lyford 1655 gives *Frideswid* as a woman's name, and it is found in use in 1593 (*Fridswed*), 1612 (*Fridiswid*), 1658 (*Friswead*), and 1706 (*Fridiswed*). It is now used mainly by Roman Catholics, except in and around Oxford, where it is in general, though not common, use, sometimes abbreviated to *Friday*. Corruptions of this name were common: for example, it occurs in Henley church registers as *Fridayweed* and *Freadeyweed* in the early 18th C.

Frusannah (f.): this name, occasionally used in the 18th and 19th C, seems to be an artificial combination of *Frances* and *Susannah*. Cf. *Rosanna*, *Saranna*.

Fulbert (m.): Old German *Filibert*, compound of *filu* 'much' and *berhta* 'bright'. St. *Filibert* or *Philibert* was the 7th-C founder of the Abbey of Jumièges, and the name was introduced into England by the Normans in the forms *Filbert*, *Fulbert*. It gave rise to the surnames *Filbert*, *Philbert*, *Philibert*, and also to the name of the *filbert* nut, so called because it ripened about the time of St. *Philibert*'s day (22 Aug. OS). *Fulbert* is given as a christian name by Lyford 1655, and is still used in a few families.

FULBERTUS Reg 1094–9.

Fulcher, see FULK(E).

Fulk(e) (m.) [fo͝olk]: Old German *Fulco*, a derivative of *Folc-* 'people'. The name was particularly common among the Burgundians and was hereditary with the Counts of Anjou. It was introduced into England at the time of the Norman Conquest, but attained its greatest popularity under the Angevins. It often appears as *Fawke* or *Fowke*, and gave rise to the surnames *Faux*, *Fawkes*, *Fowkes*, *Folk(es)*, &c. *Fulk(e)*, *Fawke*, *Fowke* are still found as christian names in the 17th C, but the name is now apparently obsolete, except in the Greville and Markham families, which have both used it since the 16th C, and in the gipsy families of Gray and Heron, who still use the form *Fowk*.

The allied compound name *Fulcher* (Old French *Fouchier*, Old German *Folkher*) was also common in the Middle Ages, and Lyford 1655 gives it in his list of christian names.

FULCO DB 1086, Cur 1196–1220, HR 1273.
FULKE HR 1273.
FOLKE Testa de Neville 13th C.
FOLKES HR 1273.
FOWKE HR 1273.
FOLC QW 1292.
FULK or FOWKE Ox Univ Reg 1567.

G

Gabel(l), see GABRIEL.

Gabriel (m.) [gā'brēel, gă'brēel]: (Italian *Gabriele*, Russian *Gavril*): Hebrew 'God is a strong man' or 'strong man of God', the name of the Archangel of the Annunciation. Never common, it occurs sometimes in the form *Gabel* or *Gabell*, from the 12th C and has never quite died out in England; it is not uncommon in Ireland. There are very few churches dedicated to the archangel, but it was a common dedication for bells, the angelus being rung on the *Gabriel* or *Angelus* bell.

GABRIEL Cur 1199, 1200, 1210, HR 1273, FA 1316.
GABELL HR 1273.
GABRYELL St. Mary at Hill 1480.

Gabriel(le) (f.) [gā'brēel, gă'brēel]: in the Middle Ages *Gabriel* (in Latin *Gabriela* or *Gabella*) was used as a woman's as well as a man's name. The Modern French *Gabrielle* is now sometimes used to distinguish the f.

Gaenor, see GUENEVERE.

Gail (f.): this name, imported from the USA since about the end of the War of 1939–45, is said to have originated as an abbreviation of *Abigail* (q.v.). It is now (1976) fairly common in England.

Gaius (m.) [gī'es]: Latin *Gaius* (less correctly *Caius*) for *Gavius* (from *gaudere* 'to rejoice'). A Roman praenomen. The Welsh *Kai* or *Kay* is said to be from *Caius*. The surname of John *Caius*, founder of Caius College, Cambridge, is usually supposed to be a latinized form of the English surname Kay. Several examples of *Gaius* as a christian name have been noted in Bucks. in the 19th C, and it is still occasionally used in Wales. This use is no doubt due to the occurrence of several persons named *Gaius* in the New Testament.

Galahad (m.): the name of the spotless knight, son of Lancelot, who alone achieved the quest of the Holy Grail. The name seems to have been invented by the author of *La Queste del' Saint Graal*; *Galahad's* ancestry as given there contains several Biblical names, and it has been plausibly suggested that *Galahad*, or *Galaad* as it is spelt in the earliest MSS, represents Hebrew *Gilead*. Rhys's attempted etymology from Welsh *gwalch* 'hawk' and *hâv* or *hâf* 'summer' is unconvincing. *Galahad* has occasionally been used as a christian name since Tennyson's *Idylls of the King* made the Arthurian legends generally known.

Galfrid(us) (m.): a modern antique (cf. ALURED) formed from the medieval Latin form (*Galfridus*) of *Geoffrey* (q.v.). An early example is *Galfridus* Mann, brother of Horace Walpole's friend and correspondent, Sir Horace Mann.

Galiena (f.): this name, which occurs not infrequently in 13th-C records, always, unfortunately, in Latin, may be Old German *Gailan(a)*, a derivative of *gail* 'lofty'. It may be the origin of the surnames *Gallon, Gallyon* which are found as early as 1273.

GALIENA Cur 1219, 1220.
GAUNLEYA, GANLEYA, GAUNLIENA Cur 1220.

Gamaliel (m.): Hebrew *Gamlī'ēl* 'my recompense (is) God' or 'the recompense of God'; Greek *Γαμαλιήλ* and Latin *Gamaliel* in the Vulgate. The 'recompense' is the male child so called. The name of the teacher at whose feet Saul of Tarsus had sat. It was used as a christian name in the 16th and 17th C, e.g. *Gamaliel* Cane, a Presbyterian minister in 1648 and *Gamaliel* Chase, Rector of Wambrook, Somerset, 1621. It has been used regularly in the Milner family.

Gamel (m.): apparently Old Norse *gamal* (= Old English *gamol*) 'old'. It first appears in the 10th C and was apparently of Danish origin. It was common, especially in the North of England, until the end of the 13th C, and gave rise to many surnames, such as *Gamble, Gammel(l)*, and *Gamlin, Gamlen, Gambling* from the diminutive *Gamelin*. It has long been obsolete in England but appears to survive in the Scottish *Gemmel*.

GAMEL DB 1086, HR 1273.
GAMELINUS DB 1086.
GAMELUS FA 1303.
GAMELLUS HR 1273.
GAMMELL Lincs. Will 1669.

Gareth (m.): the name which appears as *Gareth* in Malory's *Morte d'Arthur* is *Gahariet* in his French source, and probably results from a misreading or mis-hearing of some Welsh name. *Gareth* was given to a child baptized at Wigan in 1593 and has been used from time to time since Tennyson made it generally known in his *Gareth and Lynnet* (1872). It is now moderately common in Wales. The relatively modern name *Garth* is presumably a form of *Gareth*, and its use may derive from the hero of Florence Barclay's immensely popular novel, *The Rosary* (1909).

Garmon (m.): Welsh form of *Germanus*. See GERMAN.

Garnet (m., f.): the best-known example of this name is General Sir *Garnet* (later 1st Viscount) Wolseley (1833–1913), who had his name from his father, who had it from a great-uncle, Dr. John *Garnett*, Bishop of Clogher. The surname *Garnet(t)* came from the christian name *Garnet*, apparently a diminutive in *-et* of the common Anglo-Norman name *Guarin* (*Warren*). *Garnet* is now also sometimes a girl's name probably with reference to the precious stone (cf. *Ruby*, *Pearl*, &c.).

Garret, see GERARD.

Garth, see GARETH.

Gary (m.): this name, common in the USA, is apparently a pet-form of *Garret* (see GERARD). Its use in England dates from the 1930's, and was due to the great popularity of the film actor, *Gary* Cooper. It is now quite common.

Gaston (m.): this name appears first among the Counts of Foix and Béarn, and was introduced to France proper by *Gaston* Duke of Orleans, son of Henry IV. It is now a common French name and is also used in other countries. The etymology is doubtful, but, since the name sometimes appears in early records as *Gascon*, it may well be that it was originally a racial designation (cf. *Norman*, *German*, *Francis*). That this phonetic change could take place is shown by 13th-C records quoted by Bardsley which refer to the same man at one time as William de *Gasconia* and at another as William de *Gaston*.

Gatty, see GERTRUDE.

Gavin [gă′vĭn], see GAWAIN.

Gawain (m.): the character who appears as *Gauvain* in French, and *Gawayne* in English medieval versions of the Arthurian cycle, is in Welsh sources named *Gwalchmai*, a compound of *gwalch* 'hawk' and *Mei* the month of May. Geoffrey of Monmouth calls him *Walganus*, and it has been suggested that *Gwalchmai* had an alternative name *Gwalchgwyn* 'white hawk', which became *Walganus* and thence *Gauvain*. Prof. Max Förster considers that *Gawain* is a genuine Welsh name corresponding to Old Breton *Gauen* found in *Uuoi-gauan* (9th C). No one seems to have noticed in this connexion the existence of an Old German name *Gawin*, a derivative of *Gavja* 'a district of land', which is found from the 7th C. Förstemann gives several examples of it, the earliest a Bishop *Gavinus* 633, another Bishop *Gavienus* (of Tours), and persons called *Gavin* and *Goin*. The English *Gawayne*, *Gawn*, *Gawin* or *Gawen*, and the French *Gauvain*, *Gavin* were fairly common in the Middle Ages and were still used at the end of the 17th C. *Gavin* has survived in Scotland where it is still quite common.

GAWYNE HR 1273.
GAWYN Poll Tax 1379.
GAWIN Lond Marr Lic 1530.
GAWEN Lancs Wills 1669, 1680, 1687.
GAVIN Yorks Rec 1604.
GAWNE Ulverston Ch 1653.

Gaynor, see GUENEVERE.

Gemma (f.) [jĕ'ma]: Italian *gemma* 'a gem'. The name occurs once in an Assize Roll for 1218. In modern times it has been borrowed from Italy and seems to have established itself as an English name, possibly helped by a modern Italian saint, *Gemma* Galgani (d. 1903).

Gemmel, see GAMEL.

Gene, see EUGENE.

Genevieve (f.) [jĕn'evēv]: French *Geneviève* from Gaulish *Genovefa*; the first element is *genos* 'race', the second is doubtful. St. *Geneviève*, born *c.* 422 at Nanterre, is the patron saint of Paris, and the name is a favourite one in France. It was sometimes used in England in the 19th C (e.g. the actress *Genevieve* Ward). The form *Genovefa* is still used in Germany.

Geoffrey (m.): the modern name *Geoffrey*, from Middle English *Geffrey*, Old French *Geoffroi*, *Geuffroi*, seems to represent two, if not three, Old German names, (1) *Gaufrid*, (2) *Walahfrid*, and possibly (3) *Gisfrid*. The second element in all of these is *frithu* 'peace'. The first element of *Gaufrid* is *gavja* (Modern German *gau*) 'a district of land'; the first element of *Walahfrid* (gallicized to *Gualafrid*) is *valha* 'traveller', and of *Gisfrid*, *gis* from the same root as *gisel* 'pledge'. In early medieval Latin records, traces of these origins are to be found, the name appearing in many variants of three main forms *Gaufridus*, *Galfridus*, *Goisfridus*. Later come *Geofridus*, *Joffridus*, &c., a direct latinization of the current vernacular forms. In later times the name has been further confused with *Godfrey* (*Godefridus*) (q.v.), which during the Middle Ages was a quite separate name. *Geoffrey* was common in England from the 12th to 15th C, giving rise to many surnames, e.g. *Geoffrey(s)*, *Jefferies*, *Jefferson*, &c.; *Jeeves*, *Geve*, *Jephson*, *Jepson*, &c., from the abbreviations *Jeff*, *Geve*; and *Giffen*, &c., from the abbreviation *Giff*. *Geoffrey* was rather uncommon from the 15th to 19th C. It has now once more come into favour. It seems not to have taken root in Scotland.

GOSFRIDUS, GAUFRIDUS Reg 1071–5.
GOISFRIDUS, GAUFRIDUS DB 1086.
GOFFRIDUS Reg 1087–97.
GALFRIDUS HR 1273.
GEFFREI HR 1273.
GEFFREY, GEFFRAY HR 1273, Coventry Mysteries 15th C.
GEVE HR 1273.
GEFFRAI Exch R 1306.

George (m.): (Latin *Georgius*, French *Georges*, Italian *Giorgio*, Spanish *Jorge*, German, Danish *Georg*, Russian *Yuri*, Irish *Seiorse*): Greek *γεωργός* 'farmer' or 'tiller of the soil'. St. *George* was a Roman military tribune martyred at Nicomedia in 303. The dragon-killing legends were attached to his name later. His cult was brought to England from the East by returning Crusaders;

he was said to have come to their help under the walls of Antioch in 1089 and was then chosen as their patron by the Normans under Robert of Normandy, son of the Conqueror. There are 126 churches dedicated to him in England. But *George* as a christian name was slow in taking root. The earliest example noted is one *George* Grim at the end of the 12th C, and there are occasional occurrences in records of the 13th and early 14th C. Edward III had a particular devotion to St. *George* and in 1349, on St. George's Day, founded the order of the Garter, which he placed under his patronage, and dedicated to him the chapel of the order at Windsor. From this time he was regarded as the patron saint of England. But even after this the name was not much used, and Edward himself gave it to none of his seven sons, the only member of the royal family to bear the name before the 18th C being his great-great-grandson, George, Duke of Clarence (born 1449). The name was used in a few families (e.g. the Nevilles in the 15th C, and the Villiers's, who used it from the middle of the 16th C), but was rare until the advent of the house of Hanover in 1714, when an unbroken succession of King *George*'s for 116 years at last acclimatized the name, which has now acquired an extremely English flavour. The usual Scottish and North-country pet-form is *Geordie* which is often used as a nickname for a Northumbrian (cf. *Jock* for a Scot). *Dod* is still used in the northern counties of Scotland.

GEORGIUS Cur 1199, 1203, HR 1273, FA 1303, 1346, 1428, Poll Tax 1379.
JEORGIUS HR 1273.
GEORGE Magd. *c.* 1270–80.

Georgi(a)na (f.): these f. derivatives of *George* (q.v.) date from the 18th C, when *George* first became common in England. CMY says: 'The first English lady on record so called was a god-child of Anne of Denmark, who caused the child to be christened *Georgia Anna*.' But this must have been an exceptional case, and CMY may have made a slip here perhaps confusing the consort of James I with her great granddaughter Queen Anne, whose husband was Prince *George* of Denmark. *Georgiana* was pronounced jorjā'n*a* in the 18th C. *Georgina* was the commoner form in the 19th C, and was often abbreviated to *Georgie*. Another f. form of *George* is *Georgia*, which is chiefly used in the USA and is probably an adaptation of the name of the State.

Geraint (m.) [jĕrānt′]: Welsh form for Old British **Gerontius*, probably borrowed from Latin *Gerontius* from Greek *Γερόντιος* a derivative of *γέρων* 'old'. A letter from St. Aldhelm, dated 705, is addressed to a Cornish King *Geruntius*, which appears in the Anglo-Saxon Chronicle as *Gerente*. The modern pronunciation with soft instead of hard *g* is the result of French influence. The story of Geraint and Enid is in the *Mabinogion*, and was the subject of one of Tennyson's *Idylls of the King* (1859), since which it has occasionally been used as a christian name.

Gerald (m.): Old German *Gairovald*, compound of *ger* 'spear' and *vald* 'rule'. It was introduced into England by the Normans and was used regularly in the Middle Ages, but was by no means as common as *Gerard* (q.v.) with which, especially in Ireland and Wales, it was often confused. It seems to have died out in England about the end of the 13th C. About the end of the 19th C it became relatively popular, probably reintroduced from Ireland where it had been kept alive by the Fitzgeralds, and it is now much commoner than *Gerard*.

GEROLDUS, GERALDUS, GIROLDUS, GIRALDUS, GIRAUDUS DB 1086.
GEROLDIN Reg ? 1086.
GEROLT Reg 1094–9.
GEROLDUS Cur 1197, 1219.

Geraldine (f.): this name seems to have been invented by the poet Surrey who, *c.* 1540, celebrated the beauty of Lady Elizabeth Fitzgerald, daughter of the 9th Earl of Kildare, under the name of 'the fair *Geraldine*' (*Geraldine* = one of the Fitzgeralds). Drayton (1597) published in his *Heroicall Epistles* one entitled 'The Lady *Geraldine* to the Earl of Surrey'. It may have been from one or other of these that Coleridge took the name for use in *Christabel* (written *c.* 1800, first published 1816). But the use of *Geraldine* as a christian name seems to antedate the publication of *Christabel*, for *Geraldine* Jewsbury, the writer and friend of Mrs. Carlyle, was born in 1812, and in the cloister of Wells Cathedral there is an inscription in memory of *Geraldina* Eugenia Wallace (born 1811, died 1820).

Gerard (m.) [je'rard]: (French *Gérard*, German *Gerhard*): Old German *Gairhard*, compound of *ger* 'spear' and *hardu* 'hard'. Probably introduced into England by the Normans shortly before the Conquest (*Girardus* and *Gerardus* occur several times in DB), *Gerard* soon became a common name and remained so for several centuries. It gave rise to many surnames, e.g. *Garrard*, *Garrett*, *Garrod*, *Jerrard*, &c. *Garrard* and *Garret* represent the usual Middle English pronunciation of the name (cf. *Barnard* and *Barnet* for *Bernard*), and *Garret* is given as a christian name by Camden 1605 and Lyford 1655; the latter seems to regard it as an independent name and confuses *Gerald* and *Gerard*. *Gerard* is not now much used. *Garret* is still used in Ireland.

GIRARDUS, GERARDUS DB 1086, Cur 1199–1219.
GERRARDUS FA 1284.
GERARD Ass 1313, Exch R 1306.
GYRERD Poll Tax 1379.
GARRETT, GARRATT 16th C Royal Accounts.
GARRAT Newcastle Epitaph 1637.
GARIT Cheshire Burials 1678.

Gerbert (m.): Old German *Gairbert*, compound of *ger* 'spear' and *berhta* 'bright'.

Gerbold (m.): Old German *Gairebold*, compound of *ger* 'spear' and *balda* 'bold'.

These two names were not uncommon in England in the Middle Ages and gave rise to the surnames *Garbett*, *Garbutt*, *Garbott*.

GERBERTUS FA 1284.
GERBALD HR 1273.
GERBOD Pipe Roll 1164.

Gerda (f.) [ger'da]: in Norse mythology the name of the wife of the god Freyr. *Gerda* has been used as a christian name in England in the present century after the little girl in Hans Andersen's story of 'The Snow Queen'.

German (m.) [jer'man]: Latin *Germanus* 'a German'. There were two saints of this name, St. *Germain* of Auxerre (*c.* 378–*c* 448) and St. *Germain* of Paris (*c.* 496–*c.* 576). It was introduced into England by the Normans, and there is one *Germanus* in DB. It was not uncommon in the 13th C and gave rise to various surnames, e.g. *German(s)*, *Germain*, *Jarman*, *Jermyn*, &c. It has continued in infrequent use ever since.

GERMANUS DB 1086, Cur 1199, 1200, HR 1273, Poll Tax 1379.
GERMAYNE Yorks Rec 1604.
JERMAN Visitation of London 1634.

Gershom (m.) [ger'shŏm]: Hebrew 'bell', the name of sons of Moses and Levi. The Old Testament explanation 'stranger' is folk etymology. The name is now used mainly by Jews, but in the 17th C was found amongst English Puritans (e.g. *Gershom*, son of Seth Wood, an ejected minister) and survives in Scotland.

Gertrude (f.): Old German *Geredrudis*, *Geretrudis*, compound of *ger* 'spear' and *drudi* 'strength', the name of one of the Valkyrie. There were two saints of this name, St. *Gertrude*, Abbess of Nivelles (died 659), and St. *Gertrude*, surnamed the Great (1236–1311), a German mystic. The first of these was very popular in Brabant, and it was no doubt from the Low Countries that the name was introduced into England. It is found occasionally in the Middle Ages, and the surnames *Gatt(e)*, *Gattie* may be derived from *Gatty*, formerly the pet-form of the name. In the 16th and 17th C the name was fairly common and it is found spelt variously *Gartrude*, *Gartrite*, *Gethrude*, *Garthrite*. Lyford 1655 gives it as *Gertrud*. The will of Albinia, Lady Wray 1660, mentions 'my gentlewoman *Gartrett* South'. In the later 19th C *Gertrude* became a favourite name and was often abbreviated to *Gertie*.

Gervais, Gervase (m.) [jer'vāz]: Old German *Gervas*, compound of *ger* 'spear' and the Celt stem *vass-* 'servant' (cf. *vassal*). Sts. *Gervase* and *Protase* were said to be 1st-C martyrs, whose remains were opportunely discovered at Milan by St. Ambrose. The name was introduced into England by the Normans and was common in the 12th and 13th C, giving rise to the surnames

Gervas, *Gervis*, *Jarvis*, *Jarvie*, &c. It was rarer in later times, but *Jarvis* is found as a christian name as late as 1650 (*Jarvicius* in the Parish Register of South Leigh, Oxfordshire), and Lyford 1655 gives *Gervasius* or *Gerfast*. Some families have continued to use it, e.g. the families of Elwes, which has used the name since the time of Sir *Gervase* Elwes (died 1615), and Markham.

GERVASIUS Cur 1199–1219.
GERVASSIUS FA 1284.
GERVAS Lincs 1456.
JARVIS Yorks Rec. 1604.

Gideon (m.): Hebrew 'having only a stump (for a hand)', the name of one of the Judges over Israel. Adopted as a christian name by the English Puritans and French Huguenots, and still current in the USA.

Giffard (m.) [gĭf′*a*rd]: this, though long obsolete as a christian name, was common in the 11th and 12th C. It is apparently Old German *Gebahard*, *Gevehard*, compound of *gib* 'give' and *hardu* 'bold', 'fierce'.

GIFARDUS, GIFARTUS DB 1086.
GIFFARD HR 1273.
GYFFARD HR 1273.
GIFFORD HR 1273.

Gilbert (m.): Old German *Gisilbert*, compound of *gisil* 'pledge' and *berhta* 'bright'. The name was introduced into England by the Normans and is common in DB, though not found earlier. It was a favourite throughout the Middle Ages, as is shown by the numerous common surnames formed from it, e.g. *Gilbert*(*son*), *Gilbart*, *Gilson*; *Gibb*(*s*), *Gibson*, *Gibbon*(*s*), *Gibbin*(*s*) (from the common pet-form *Gib* and its diminutive *Gibbon*), *Gipps*, *Gilby*, *Gilpin*, &c. In the 15th C it is usually spelt *Gylbart* or *Gylbard* (cf. *Robart* for *Robert*, *Hubbard* for *Hubert*). It was common in Scotland from a fairly early date, being used as an equivalent of Gaelic *Gilbride*, 'servant of [St.] Bridget'. *Gib* was a common nickname for a cat (cf. Hamlet's 'from a paddock, from a bat, a gib, such dear concernings hide').

GISLEBERTUS DB 1086.
GILBERTUS Cur 1186–1220 *passim*, HR 1273.
GYLBARDE 15th C Brut.
GILEBERT HR 1273.
GILBERD Poll Tax 1379.

Gilchrist (m.): Gaelic 'servant of Christ'; now mostly a surname.

Giles (m.): Latin *Aegidius*, *Egidius*, derivative of Greek *αἰγίδιον* 'kid'. *Aegidius* became in French *Gidie*, *Gide* (which survives as a surname) and then *Gilles*, *Gile*, and *Gire*. St. *Giles* is said to have been a 6th-C Athenian who fled to France to escape the veneration aroused by the miracles he performed. He is the patron saint of cripples and beggars, and has 162 churches dedicated to him in this country. Medieval records of the name are usually of the Latin form *Egidius*, but there are a few examples of the vernacular. It was sometimes turned back into Latin as *Gilo* or *Gilius*. It was used as a woman's as well as a man's name.

EGIDIUS Cur 1199–1220, HR 1273.
GILO(NEM) Cur 1199.
GYLIS FA 1284.
EGIDIUS or GILIUS HR 1273.
EGIDIA or GILIA Cur 1201.

Gillian (f.) [jĭl'yan]: the popular English form of *Julian*(*a*) (q.v.); very common in the Middle Ages, especially in the diminutive forms *Gill*, *Jill*, *Gillot*, *Gillet* which gave rise to many surnames. *Gillot* or *Jillet* became a designation for a flighty girl, whence probably, by a process of syncopation, the word *jilt*. In the 17th C it was legally declared that *Julian* and *Gillian* were different names, like *Anne* and *Agnes* (qq.v.). *Gillian* went out of use in the 18th and 19th C, but has been revived in the 20th. *Jill* is now often given as an independent name. For forms, &c., see JULIAN(A).

Ginevra (f.) [jinĕv'ră]: the Italian form of *Guenevere* (q.v.). Occasionally used in England in the 19th and 20th C.

Gisela (f.) [jĭzĕl'ă]: Old German *Gisila*, derivative of *gisl* 'pledge'. It was the name of a daughter of Charles the Simple, who married Rollo 1st Duke of Normandy. *Gisèle* is not uncommon in France and it, or *Gisela*, is sometimes used by Roman Catholics in England.

Githa, Gytha (f.) [gīth'*a*]: a Norse name, probably derived from *guthr* 'war'. It is found in England in the 11th C, and has recently been revived. An early example is Countess *Gytha*, a Dane, wife of Godwin, Earl of Wessex (*c.* 1054).

Gladys (f.): Welsh *Gwladys. Gladusa* is found in Cumberland in 1207. It is commonly said that *Gwladys* is a Welsh form of the Latin *Claudia* (q.v.), and from an early date the *Claudia* mentioned in 2 Tim. iv. 21 was supposed to be a Welshwoman, and her name identified with *Gwladys*, though Welsh Bibles do not so translate it. Camden 1605 says: '*Gladuse* (Brit) for *Claudia*'. The adoption of the name in England seems to date from the 70's of the last century and in 1877 there was an interesting correspondence on the subject in N & Q. The first letter asked 'Is Gladys a male or female name, or a name at all—at least out of a novel?' All the replies treat the name as purely Welsh, except for one which says 'I have also seen a *Gladys*, and I have frequently met with the name in fiction'. Another says that in Caernarvonshire, where *Gwladys* is common, bearers of it commonly sign their name *Claudia*. One novel in which the name occurs is Ouida's *Puck* (1870), and this may well have been the origin of its use in England, where it is now common.

Glenda (f.): this name, which appears to have originated in the USA about the end of the 19th C, has recently become common in England, helped no doubt by the popularity of the actress, *Glenda* Jackson. It seems to have come to England via Australia rather than directly from N. America. It may have originated as a f. form of the common American *Glenn*, perhaps modelled on *Gwenda* (q.v.).

Gloria (f.): Latin *gloria* 'glory'. Came into use in the late 19th C, e.g. G. B. Shaw's *You Never Can Tell* (published 1898).

Glennis, Glynis (f.): a Welsh name, derived from Welsh *glyn*, 'a valley'. Now (1976) rather common in England.

Glyn (m.): Welsh *glyn*, 'a valley'. A very common Welsh christian name, now often used also in England.

Goddard (m.): Old German *Godehard* (Modern German *Gotthard*), compound of *Guda* 'god' and *hardu* 'hard'. Introduced into England at the Conquest in the Norman form *Godard*, it was common in the Middle Ages and survived in use until the 17th C. It is now used only as a surname.

GODARD Cur 1200, HR 1273.

Godfrey (m.): Old German *Godafrid*, compound of *Guda* 'god' and *frithu* 'peace'. There was a corresponding Old English *Godfrith*, but it was not common and the medieval *God(e)fry* seems to represent a Norman version of the Old German name rather than a survival of the Old English one. It was common in the 12th and 13th C and gave rise to the surnames *Godfrey*, *Godfree*, *Godfreed*, &c. In later times it has sometimes been confused with *Geoffrey* (q.v.), but was quite separate in the Middle Ages, appearing in Latin as *Godefridus* while *Geoffrey* was *Galfridus* or *Goisfridus*.

GODEFRIDUS DB 1086, Cur 1187–1220, Pipe Roll 1161.
GODFREY HR 1273.
GODEFRAY HR 1273.

Godiva (f.): Old English *Godgifu*, compound of *God* and *gifu* 'a gift'. *Godeva* is the name of a tenant in DB, and *Godefe* remained in common use until the 13th or 14th C, giving rise to the surname *Goodeve*. The most famous bearer of the name was *Godgifu* (*fl.* 1040–80), latinized as *Godiva*, wife of Leofric of Mercia, who founded several monasteries and is the heroine of the well-known Coventry legend.

GODEVA DB 1086.
GODIVA Cur 1200.
GODEFE HR 1273.
GOODIFE St. Jas. Clerkenwell 1606.

Godric (m.): Old English *Godric*, compound of *God* and *ric* 'ruler'. It seems to be a specifically Old English name, without any corresponding Old German form. It was very common in England before the Norman Conquest. The Normans used it as a nickname for an Englishman, and called Henry I and his queen *Godric and Godiva*, in allusion to her English blood and his supposedly English sympathies. It seems to have died out in the course of the 13th and 14th C, but not before giving rise to the surnames *Godrich*, *Goodrich*, *Goodrick*, *Goodridge*.

GODRIC(US) DB 1086.
GODRIGE HR 1273.
GODRICH(E) HR 1273.

Godwin (m.): Old English *Godwine*, compound of *God* and *wine* 'friend'; one of the commonest of Old English names. It survived the Conquest and its popularity is attested by the number of surnames formed from it, e.g. *Goodwin*, *Godwin*, *Godden*, *Goodden*, *Godding*, *Godin*, *Goding*, &c. (the last five being from the Anglo-French form *Godin*).

GODUIN(E), GODEUUIN DB 1086, Cur 1187–1220.
GODIN HR 1273.
GODUN HR 1273.
GAUDINUS Testa de Neville 13th C, QW 1347.

Goldwin (m.): Old English *Goldwine*, compound of *gold* and *wine* 'friend'. It was not uncommon in the Middle Ages, giving rise to the surnames *Goldwin*, *Golden*, *Goulden*, *Goulding*, &c., and was still in use as a christian name as late as 1730. (The well-known Victorian controversialist *Goldwin* Smith was named after an uncle, Thomas *Goldwin*.)

GOLDUIN DB 1086.
GOLDWYN HR 1273.
JOLDEWIN HR 1273.
GOLDING HR 1273.
GOLDIN(E) HR 1273.
GOLDWIN St. Geo. Hanover Sq. 1730.

Goodeth (f.): Old English *Godgyth*, compound of *God* and *gyth* 'war'. *Goditha* or *Godith* was common in the 13th and 14th C, and was sometimes confused with *Godefe* (see GODIVA). *Goodeth* is found as late as the 17th C.

GODITHA Cur 1200, FA 1303.
GUDYTHA Poll Tax 1379.
GOODETH Somerset Wills 1597, St. Jas. Clerkenwell 1661.

Gordon (m.): the name of a large and famous Scottish family, probably derived from *Gordon* in Berwickshire. The modern use of *Gordon* as a christian name is due to the enormous popularity of General Gordon (1833–85). It is now firmly established as a christian name.

Goronwy (m.) [gŏrŏn′wĕ]: a Welsh christian name still in use. A London parish register of 1641 has *Granaw* Evine son of *Granawa* Evine.

Grace (f.): Latin *gratia* 'grace'. *Gracia, Grecia, Gricia* occur as a woman's name in Latin records of the 13th and 14th C and possibly represent this name, though they may be a latinization of some name derived from Old German *grisja* 'grey'. *Grace*, like *Faith, Hope, Charity, Patience*, &c., came into use as a christian name after the Reformation, but it is also found fairly frequently in lists of Roman recusants in the early 17th C. It was sometimes also given to boys in the 17th C. It went out of fashion in the 18th C and its revival in the Victorian period may have been influenced by the fame of *Grace* Darling (1815–42). In Ireland it has been used to render the native *Grainne* (q.v.).

GRACIA Cur 1200, FA 1303, 1346.
GRECIA Cur 1213, FA 1346.
GRICIA FA 1346.
GRACE Chester 1562.

Gracilia (f.): from Latin *gracilis* 'slender'. Sometimes used as a f. christian name, probably from a mistaken derivation from *gratia*.

Graham (m.): the name of a large and famous Scottish family, originally a place-name. Its use as a christian name is comparatively recent, especially in England.

Grainne, Grania (f.) [grā′nyē]: Irish *Graidhne*, the name of Diarmuit's mistress; a popular Irish name, often rendered by *Grace* (q.v.). A notable example was *Grainne* or *Grace* O'Malley, the Amazonian princess who opposed the forces of Queen Elizabeth.

Grant (m.): a common surname, derived from the nickname 'le grand', applied to a tall man. This has become a very common N. American christian name, after General *Grant* (President of thc USA 1869–76), and is now coming into use in England.

Granville (m.): originally a surname derived from *Granville* in Normandy. *Grenville* is another form of it. *Granville* has been used as a christian name in the Leveson-Gower family since the early 18th C, and is now used more widely.

Gregory (m.): (Latin *Gregorius*, French *Grégoire*, Italian *Gregorio*, German *Gregor*): Greek *γρηγόριος* a derivative of *γρηγορέω* 'to be watchful'. It was the name of two fathers of the Eastern Church, St. *Gregory* Nazianzen (*c.* 325–*c.* 390) and St. *Gregory* of Nyssa (*c.* 331–*c.* 395), and of 16 Popes, beginning with St. *Gregory* 'the Great' (*c.* 540–604). The name is not found in England before the Norman Conquest, but was common in the 12th C and later. *Godstow* (1450) gives *Gregour* as the English for *Gregorius*. There are a great many surnames formed from it, e.g. *Gregory*, *Greg(g)*, *Grig(g)*, *Greggs*, *Griggs*, *Gregson*, *Grigson*, *Greig*. *Greg* and *Grig* were respectively North and South country forms of the diminutive. *McGregor* is a patronymic formed from *Gregor*, the usual Scottish form of the name.

GREGORIUS Cur 1187–1220, HR 1273, FA 1346, Cl 1386.
GREGORY HR 1273, Cl 1387.
GREG(E) HR 1273, Poll Tax 1379.
GRIGGE HR 1273.

Greta (f.): a Swedish abbreviation of *Margaret* (q.v.), sometimes also used in England in recent times. A solitary early example occurs in Assize Roll of 1218.

Griffin, Griffith (m.): Welsh *Gruffudd*. The second element is *udd* 'lord'. It was the name of several Welsh princes and has always been common in Wales, and also in the counties on the Welsh Marches, e.g. in Shropshire Feudal Aids 1428 there occur

Griffinus Hull and *Griffinus seu Griffith* Kynaston. Lyford 1655 gives both *Griffin* and *Griffith.*

Grimbald (m.): Old English *Grimbeald.* The second element is *beald* 'bold'; the first may be either *grim* 'savage', 'fierce', or *Grima* a name for Odin (from *grima* 'a mask'). St. *Grimbald* (*c.* 820–903) was a monk at St. Omer, who was invited over to England by King Alfred to help him with his educational work. He was the first Abbot of New Minster at Winchester, and after his death was venerated as a saint. Later his name was associated with the mythical early history of Oxford University. *Grimbald* was a fairly common name in the Middle Ages and gave rise to a number of surnames, e.g. *Grimbald, Grimbold, Grimble, Grimbly, Gribble,* &c. Camden in 1605 says: 'a name most usual in the old family of Pauncefoot'.

GRIMBALD(US), GRIMBOLD, GRIMBOL, GRIMOLD DB 1086, FA 1303.
GRIMBALD, GRIMBAUD HR 1273.
GRIMALDUS FA 1284.

Griselda, Grizel (f.) [grĭzĕl'da, grĭ'zel]: the second element of *Griselda* or *Griseldis* seems to be Old German *hild* 'battle', 'strife', the first may be Old German *grisja* 'grey', though an Old German name *Grishild* is not actually on record. It is also possible that it represents the recorded Old German *Cristehildis*, a compound of *Christ* and *hild.* It is not found in early use as a christian name in England, and its adoption was no doubt due to the literary influence of Chaucer, who took the story of Patient *Griselda* (the Clerk's Tale) from Boccaccio. Dekker wrote a play on the subject. The name is now used mainly in Scotland where it is still quite common, usually in the form *Grizel.* Lyford 1655 gives *Grishild,* but *Grissel, Grizzel* or *Grisel* were the usual forms by that time.

Guendolen, Gwendolyn (f.): a Welsh name of which the first element is the f. of *gwyn* 'white'. The earliest form is *Guenddoleu.* In the *Vita Merlini* it is the name of Merlin's wife and there was a saint of the name. It came into use in England in the 19th C.

Guenevere, Guinevere (f.) [gwen'evĕr]: Welsh *Gwenhwyvar,* the name of the wife of King Arthur. In Anglo-Norman the name became *Guenièvre*, and the English metrical romances give it as *Gwenore*, *Gonore*, *Ganor*, *Gaynore*, *Wannour*, *Wannore*. *Guener* and *Gueanor* occur in Lancashire at the beginning of the 17th C. In Scotland it became *Guanor*, *Vanora*, or *Wander*. *Gaenor* is still used in N. Wales, though no longer associated with *Guenevere*, and *Gaynor* is now sometimes used in England. *Gwenhevare* occurs as a christian name in Shropshire in 1431. In Cornwall the name has survived in the form *Jenifer* down to the present time. In the present century *Jen*(*n*)*ifer* has become fashionable in the rest of England. See also WINIFRED.

Gu(g)lielma (f.): Italian f. form of *Guglielmo* (William), sometimes used in England since the 17th C., particularly by members of the Society of Friends, since it was the name of the first wife of William Penn the elder, *Gulielma* Maria Springett (*c.* 1643–93). Sometimes shortened to *Elma*.

Guiscard (m.): one of the earliest recorded bearers of this name was Robert *Guiscard*, son of Tancred de Hauteville and conqueror of Sicily. It seems to be a purely Norman name. Förstemann suggests that it is a compound of the rare root *visc* and Old German *hardu* 'bold', 'hardy'. The Normans used the name a good deal in England and it appears as *Gwychardus* (cf. the modern name of Robert *Guiscard's* birthplace, Hauteville-la-*Guichard*), *Wiscard*, *Wyschardus*, &c., and gave rise to the surnames *Whiskard*, *Whisker*, *Wiscar*, &c.

WISCAR, WISGARUS DB 1086.
WISCARD HR 1273.
WYSCHARDUS Testa de Neville 13th C.
WICHARD HR 1273.
GWYCHARDUS FA 1303.
GUISCHARD or WISCHARD Lyford 1655.

Gunilda (f.): Old Norse *Gunnhildr*, compound of *gunn*(*r*) 'war' and *hild*(*r*) 'battle', 'strife'. There was a corresponding Old German *Gundichild*, but it was the Norse name which was introduced into England by the Danes; one of the daughters of King Knut was named *Gunhild*. The name survived the Norman Conquest, and was in use until the 14th C, often in the Norman form

Quenild. The English form seems to have been *Gunnell*. The surnames *Quennell* and *Gunnell* are derived from these forms. The word ***gun*** is probably from *Gunne*, a pet-form of *Gunhild* (see OED s.v. *gun*); an account of munitions at Windsor Castle in 1330 mentions 'una magna balista de cornu quae vocatur domina *Gunilda*', and doubtless the same nickname was later used for cannon.

GUNILDA Cur 1200, 1210, 1213.
GUNNILDA HR 1273, Cl. 1295.
GONNILDA HR 1273.
GUNNILDE HR 1273.
GUNNELL Testa de Neville 13th C.
QWINHILD Whitby.
QUENILDA Lancs Lay Subsidy 1332.

Gunnora (f.): Old Norse *Gunnvǫr* (late Old English *Gunware*); the first element is *gunnr* 'war'. The name was latinized by the Normans as *Gunnora*. It was a favourite Norman name and remained in use in England until the 14th C.

GUNORA Cur 1196–1220.
GONNORA FA 1285.
GUNNORA FA 1302.

Gunter (m.): Old German *Guntard*, compound of *gundi* 'war' and *hardu* 'bold', 'hardy', or Old German *Gunter* a compound of *gundi* and *harja* 'host'. Introduced into England by the Normans and fairly common in the 13th and 14th C. *Gunter* is found as a christian name as late as 1494. It gave rise to the surnames *Gunter*, *Gunther*.

GUNTERIUS Reg 1086–93.
GUNTER HR 1273, Cov 1494.
GUNTARD HR 1273.

Gussie, Gussy, see AUGUSTA, AUGUSTUS.

Gustavus (m.) [gustāvus]: Old German *Chustaffus*, the second element of which is *staf* 'staff'; the first element is doubtful, Förstemann suggests the root *Chud*, connected with Old German *chûton* 'to meditate'. *Gustaf* (or *Gosta*) is chiefly a Swedish name, but in the 17th C the fame of the Swedish king *Gustaf Adolf* (1594–1632) (*Gustavus Adolphus*, as he is usually called) spread it over Europe (e.g. German *Gustav*, French *Gustave*). In England the latinized form *Gustavus* has occasionally been used; an early example is *Gustavus* Barratt, christened at St. Giles Cripplegate in 1638.

Guy (m.): Old German *Wido*, from the root *vid* which is common in personal names; it is doubtful whether it is the same as Old German *witu* 'wood', or *wît* 'wide'. It was introduced into England by the Normans and appears in Latin records sometimes as *Wido*, sometimes as *Guido*. The French forms of the name were *Guy* and *Guyon* (representing the *cas-sujet* and the *cas-régime*, cf. *Hue* and *Huon*), and also *Wy* and *Wyon*; the diminutives *Wyat*, *Guyat* were also common. The surnames *Guy(s)*, *Guise*, *Guyon*, *Gye*, *Wyat(t)*, *Wiatt*, &c., are derived from it. It was in common use from the Norman Conquest until the 17th C, when *Guy* Fawkes drove it out of use for some 200 years. Its revival in the 19th C may have been helped by Scott's *Guy Mannering* (1815), and later by C. M. Yonge's *Heir of Redcliffe* (1853) whose hero was named *Guy*.

WIDO DB 1086, Cur 1189, FA 1316.
GWYDO HR 1273.
GUIDO FA 1285.
GY HR 1273.

Gwen(da) (f.): *Gwen* is the common pet-form of *Guendolen* (q.v.) and of other Welsh f. names compounded with *gwen* (f. of *gwyn* 'white' which is used as a man's name). It is now used as an independent name in England, as is occasionally *Gwenda*.

Gwladys, see GLADYS.

Gwendolyn, see GUENDOLEN.

Gwyn, see GWEN(DA).

Gwyneth (f.): Welsh *Gwynedd* the name of North Wales used as a f. name. Now often used in England.

Gytha, see GITHA.

H

Hacon (m.): Old Norse *Hakon*, modern *Haakon*, derivative of the stem *hag* 'useful', 'handy'. The name was introduced into England by the Danes and survived the Norman Conquest, *Hacun*, *Hacon* being not uncommon in the 12th C, after which it died out. It survived in Shetland, sometimes corrupted to *Hercules*.

HACUN, HACON, ACUN, DB 1086, Cur 1189, 1200.

Hadassah, see ESTHER.

Haidée (f.): from Byron's use of it in *Don Juan* (Canto ii) this is now occasionally used as a christian name in England. It is apparently a mistaken version of modern Greek *Haido*, found as a christian name in rural areas of Greece and derived from the verb *haideúo* 'to caress'. Less probable suggestions are that it was derived from αἰδώς (modesty) or due to mistaking the Turkish exclamation *haydi* meaning 'get along' or 'hurry up' for a personal name.

Hal, see HENRY.

Halbert, see ALBERT.

Ham (m.): the name of the eponymous ancestor of the 'Hamites', who lived in the 'hot' (Hebrew *hām*) south (Gen. x. 6 ff.) as distinct from the Semites, whose eponymous ancestor was called Sēm (Gen. x. 21 ff.), a name of unknown meaning. *Ham* has been used occasionally as a christian name since the 17th C (cf. *Ham* Peggotty in *David Copperfield*).

Hamish (m.): an attempt to render phonetically *Sheumais*, the vocative of *Seumas*, the Gaelic form of *James* (q.v.). Scott has a *Hamish* MacTavish, but the present vogue of the name seems to be due to the novels of William Black (1841–98), very popular in their day, in several of which he makes use of the name *Hamish*. The use of this pseudo-Gaelic form is to be discouraged.

Hamlet, Hamnet, see HAMO(N).

Hamo(n) (m.) [hā'mō]: Old German *Haimo* from *haimi* 'house', 'home'. The name was introduced into England by the Normans and soon became common. The two forms *Hamo*, *Hamon* represent the Old French *cas-sujet* and *cas-régime*. The diminutives *Hamelot*, *Hamelin*, *Ham(o)net* were all in general use and gave rise to the surnames *Hamlet(t)*, *Hamblet*, *Ham(b)lin*, *Hambley*, *Hamnet(t)*, &c. Shakespeare's only son was named *Hamnet* (after one of his godfathers). *Hamlet*, Prince of Denmark, bore a different name, the Icelandic *Amlóthi*, which appears as *Amleth* in Saxo, and was turned by English translators into the more familiar *Hamlet*. *Hamlet* and *Hamnet* survived into the 18th C (cf. *Hamlet* Winstanley, the painter, 1700–56). *Hamon* is still used in the Norfolk family of Lestrange and *Hamo* among Yorkshire gipsies belonging to one of the families of Smith. *Hamelen* is also a gipsy name. A modern example of *Hamo* is the sculptor Sir *Hamo* Thornycroft (1850–1925).

HAYMO Reg 1071–5.
HAMO DB 1086, Cur 1196–1220.
HAMMOND Cur 1200, 1210.
HAMUND HR 1273.
HAM(E)LIN DB 1086, Cur 1207, 1213.
HAMOND Exch Roll 1306.

Hannah (f.): Hebrew, a shortened form of *Hanani* and similar names, meaning 'He (= God) has favoured me'. The name of the mother of the prophet Samuel. The Greek form of the name, *Anna* (q.v.), was that in which it became acclimatized in Europe, but *Hannah* came into use at the Reformation, and was common in the 17th C. It has been in regular, though not frequent, use ever since. It is a favourite rural name in Ireland.

Hannibal (m.): Phoenician, the name of the great Carthaginian general. At a later date the name *Annibal* and its derivative *Annibalianus* were used in Rome. *Annibale* continued to be used in Italy (cf. the painter *Annibale* Caracci). *Hannibal* has been used as a christian name in Cornwall at least since the 16th C, e.g. *Hannibal* Gammon, Rector of Mawgan in Pyder 1619. It is doubtful whether this is the origin of the surnames *Hanniball*, *Honeyball*, &c.

Hardwin (m.): Old German *Hardwin*, compound of *hardu* 'hard', and *wine* 'friend'. It was introduced into England by the Normans, and became very popular, usually anglicized to *Harding*. It went out of use after the 13th C.

HARDUINUS DB 1086.
HARDWIN HR 1273.
HARDING HR 1273.

Harold (m.): Old English *Hereweald*, compound of *here* 'host', 'army', and *weald* 'power'. But the actual source of the modern name was probably the corresponding Old Norse *Harivald*, Modern Norse *Harald*, for it was amongst the Anglo-Danes that it particularly flourished, the most notable bearer of it being *Harald* Godwinson who contested the kingdom with William of Normandy. The name is found from time to time in the 12th and 13th C but was not common and seems to have died out altogether. It was revived in the 19th C.

HARALD(US), HAROLD, AROLD, HEROLD, HERALD, HERAL, ERAL, HEROULD, HEROLT, HAIRAUD DB 1086.
HAROLDUS Cur 1201–13.

Harriet (f.): the English form of French *Henriette*, a f. derivative of Henry (cf. *Harry* for *Henry*). *Henriette* was apparently invented in France in the 16th C and brought to England by Charles I's Queen, *Henriette Marie*, the daughter of Henri IV, who was usually called Queen Mary in England (e.g. in the liturgy). Her numerous god-daughters, however, were usually christened *Henrietta* (a latinization of *Henriette*, which became *Harriet* in speaking). *Harriet*, or *Harriot* as it was often spelt, was a very common name in the 18th and early 19th C. It was often abbreviated to *Harry* or *Hatty*, and sometimes to *Harty*.

Harry, see HENRY.

Hartley (m.): this surname, derived from the common place-name, is now fairly often used as a christian name, one of the earliest examples being *Hartley* Coleridge (1796–1849), the son of S. T. Coleridge, who was named after David *Hartley* the philosopher.

Harvey (m.): this is probably from *Hervé*, the French form of Breton *Haerveu*, the name of a favourite Breton saint and poet, a compound of Old Breton *aer* 'carnage' and *-uiu* 'worthy'. The name was introduced into England at the Norman Conquest and soon became common. In DB there are 11 tenants of this name, including two who had held TRE, and it continued in use throughout the 12th to 14th C, giving rise to the surnames *Harvey*, *Hervey*, *Harvie*, *Harveson*. There is no record of its use in the 15th to 18th C, but it occurs in the 19th C (e.g. *Harvey* Goodwin, Bishop of Carlisle, 1818–91) and is still sometimes used.

HERVEUS DB 1086, Cur 1187–1215.
HARVEY HR 1273.
HERVI HR 1273.

Hatty, see HARRIET.

Hawis(e) (f.): Old German *Hadewidis*, compound of *hathu* 'battle' and *vid* 'wide'. In French it became *Ha(u)eis*, *Haouys*, and was introduced in this form into England in the 12th C; it was in general use until the 14th C, giving rise to the surnames *Hawes*, *Haweis*, *Hawison*.

HAWIS Cur 1189, 1203, HR 1273, Testa de Neville 13th C, Freemen of York 1326.
HAWISIA FA 1346.
HAWISE HR 1273.

Hazel (f.): apparently a late-19th-C innovation. A correspondent in N & Q 1904 mentions it as one of several flower and plant names then growing in popularity.

Heather (f.): like *Hazel* (q.v.). It is mentioned in the same article in N & Q.

Hebe (f.) [hē'bĕ]: Greek *Ἥβη* 'youth', the goddess of youth and cupbearer to the gods. Sometimes used as a christian name.

Hector (m.): Greek *Ἕκτωρ*, the name of the heroic son of Priam; it is uncertain whether this is the same as the adjective ἕκτωρ 'holding fast'. In the Old French romances the name becomes *Ector*.

Hector is found as a christian name in the 13th C, but it was only in the Highlands of Scotland that it really took root and became common; this was probably due to its being used to translate Gaelic *Eachdonn*. *Ettore* is fairly common in Italy.

HECTOR Cur 1203–5.

Helen(a) (f.): Greek *Ἑλένη*, f. of *Ἕλενος* 'the bright one'. The wide diffusion of the name is not due to the fame of the fateful queen of Menelaus, but to St. *Helena* (died A.D. 338), mother of the Emperor Constantine. Many legends were early attached to her name, such as that of her discovery of the true cross. There are 135 churches dedicated to her in Great Britain. She was said to have been of British origin, the daughter of a British king, the Old King Cole of the nursery rhyme. Her name was popular in Celtic countries, especially Wales, from an early date. It was not used in England in the Old English period, but is found (*Elena*) soon after the Conquest. The common English form of the name has always been *Ellen* (q.v.), but *Helen* and *Helena* came in at the Renaissance. At the present time *Helen* is probably more common than *Ellen*. For another development see ELEANOR. The *Elaine* of Arthurian romance is a gallicizing of a Welsh form of *Helen*. Like *Ellen* it is often shortened to *Nell*. The German pet-form *Lena* is also sometimes used in England.

Helewise (f.) [ḥĕl'ewēz]: Old German *Helewidis*, compound of *haila* 'hale', 'sound', and *vid* 'wide'. The name was apparently introduced into England by the Normans, though in DB there is a *Helewis* mentioned as having held land TRE. It is fairly common in the 12th and 13th C. The surname *Elwes* is derived from it. After this it dropped out of general use, but in the 18th C there was some use of *Eloisa*, a latinization of *Héloïse*, the French form of the name, famous for its associations with the unhappy love of Abelard.

HELEWIS DB 1086.
HEILEWIS Cur 1189.
HELEVISA HR 1273.
ELWISIA HR 1273.
HELEWYS HR 1273.
ELEWYS HR 1273.

Helga (f.): a Norse name meaning holy. *Helga*, *Helge*, *Helghi* are found in DB as the names of tenants TRE, but the name does not seem to have survived in England. It has continued to be used in Scandinavia and has been carried thence to the USA where it is not uncommon. See also OLGA.

Heloise [hel'ōēz], see HELEWISE.

Henrietta (f.): this f. form of *Henry* was introduced into England by *Henriette Marie* (Latin *Henrietta Maria*) wife of Charles I. The English form *Harriet* (q.v.) quickly established itself, but *Henrietta* came back into use in the 19th C, often abbreviated to *Etta* and sometimes to *Hetty* (cf. *Hatty* from *Harriet*).

Henry (m.): (Latin *Henricus*, German *Heinrich*, *Heinz*, *Heine*, Dutch *Hendrik*, French *Henri*, Italian *Enrico*, Spanish *Enrique*); Old German *Haimirich*, compound of *haimi* 'house', 'home', and *ric* 'ruler'. This was latinized as *Henricus* and became *Henri* in French. There are five tenants of this name in DB, and the eight King *Henrys* in the 11th to 16th C are some measure of the popularity of the name in the Middle Ages, a popularity which has fluctuated very little since. *Henri* in English pronunciation became *Herry* or *Harry*, and this was the usual English form of the name until the 17th C. At the present time *Harry* is often regarded as a mere pet-form of *Henry* instead of the right English version of the name. The surnames derived from the various forms of this name are very numerous, including *Henry*, *Henryson*, *Harris*(*son*), *Harries*, *Herries*, *Henderson*, *Hendry*; *Hawke*, *Hawkins*, &c., are from *Halkin*, the diminutive of *Hal*, a favourite pet-form of *Henry*; *Her*(*r*)*iot* is from the diminutive *Henriot* (English *Herriot*). The form with intrusive *d* (e.g. the surnames *Hendry*, *Henderson*, &c.) was especially common in Scotland and Wales. Other common Welsh surnames are *Penny*, *Parry*, *Perry*, from *ap Henry*, &c.

HENRICUS DB 1086, Cur 1187–1220.
HANRY HR 1273, Testa de Neville 13th C.
HENRY or HANRY Testa de Neville 13th C.
HARRY or HERRY 15th C Brut.
HRERY Lincs 1459.
HARY *Cocke Lorelle's Bote c.* 1515.

HENDRY Newcastle 1562.
HENDEREYE St. Antholin 1601.

Hephzibah (f.): Hebrew 'my delight is in her', the name of the wife of Hezekiah. It came into use in the 17th C, but has been more common in America than in England. It is often spelt and pronounced *Hepzibah*, and in the early part of this century I knew a village girl of this name who was always called *Hepsie*.

Herbert (m.): Old German *Hariberct*, compound of *harja* 'host', 'army', and *berhta* 'bright'. There was a corresponding Old English *Herebeorht*, but it was not very much used, and the wide diffusion of the name after the Norman Conquest was no doubt due to its reintroduction from the Continent. *Herbertus* occurs many times in DB, and the surnames *Herbert*, *Herbertson*, *Herbison* are derived from it. After the 13th C, however, it went out of general use, though it lingered on in remote corners. It was revived at the beginning of the 19th C, an early example being *Herbert* Southey (born 1806), the eldest son of the poet, who was named after his uncle *Herbert* Hill, born in the 1740's. It became very popular in the later part of the century, possibly by association with the noble family of *Herbert* (cf. the history of *Sidney*).

HERBERTUS DB 1086, Cur 1187–1220, FA 1303, 1346.
HEREBERT HR 1273.
HARBERT Will of Henry Condell 1625.

Hercules (m.): Greek Ἡρακλῆς, Latin *Hercules*, of unknown etymology, the name of the son of Zeus and Alkmene. It was first used as a christian name in Italy (*Ercole*) at the time of the Renaissance, and spread to France, where *Hercule* is still sometimes used. *Hercules* is found as a christian name in England, though rarely, in the 16th and 17th C. It apparently continued to be used in Cornwall until the 19th C, but may have been confused with *Archelaus* (Matt. ii. 22). In Shetland it was used to render the Old Norse *Hakon* (see HACON).

Hereward (m.) [hĕr′*e*ward]: Old English *Hereweard*, compound of *here* 'army' and *weard* 'guard', 'protection'. The name was made famous by *Hereward* the Wake, the last leader of Saxon resistance against the Normans. It survived until the end of the 13th C and was revived at the beginning of the 19th C by the Wake family, which claims descent from the Saxon hero. Kingsley's novel *Hereward the Wake* (1866) helped to make the name generally known.

HEREUUARD, HERWART, HEREUUORD DB 1086.
HEREWARD Cur 1196, 1200, Testa de Neville 13th C.

Her(r)iot (m.): obsolete diminutive of *Henry* (q.v.).

Herman (m.): Old German *Hariman*, compound of *harja* 'host', 'army', and *mana* 'man'. The name was introduced into England by the Normans, and *Hermannus* occurs in DB. The French form of the name, *Armant*, *Armand*, became in English *Armin*, which survived until recently in Norfolk. The surnames *Harman*, *Harmon*, *Armand*, *Arment*, &c., are derived from it. The modern German *Hermann* is occasionally used in England, usually by families of German-Jewish origin. See also ARMINEL.

HERMANNUS DB 1086, Cur 1205, 1207.
HERMAN Pat 13th C.
ARMUNDUS Testa de Neville 13th C.
ARMAND FF 1348.
HARMAN Ox Univ Reg 1549.

Hermia (f.): this is apparently a f. name formed from *Hermes* (Greek *Ἑρμῆς*), the name of the messenger of the gods. The modern use is taken from one of the characters in *A Midsummer Night's Dream*. It is not known where Shakespeare found the name.

Hermione (f.) [hermī'ŏnĕ]: Greek *Ἑρμιόνη*, f. derivative of *Hermes*, the name of a daughter of Menelaus and Helen, the wife of Orestes. It was often used in 16th-C literature, notably by Shakespeare for the queen in *A Winter's Tale*, and it is from this that the modern use of *Hermione* as a christian name is derived. The German *Hermine* is a different name, probably a f. form of *Herman* (q.v.).

Hero (f.): Greek *Ἡρώ* the name of (1) a daughter of Danaus, (2) a daughter of Priam, (3) the beloved of Leander. The etymology of the word is doubtful; it is unconnected with the common noun *hero*, and may be from the name of the goddess *Hera*. The modern use of *Hero* as a christian name is the result of Shakespeare's use of it in *Much Ado about Nothing*.

Hester, see ESTHER.

Hetty, see ESTHER and HENRIETTA.

Hew, see HUGH.

Hezekiah (m.) [hĕzekī'ă]: Hebrew 'God is strength'. Brought into use by the Puritans in the 17th C.

Hilary (m., f.): late Latin *Hilarius* from *hilaris* 'cheerful'. St. *Hilarius* of Poitiers (died 368), a champion of the Church against Arianism and hence called the Athanasius of the West, was the cause of the popularity of the name (*Hilaire*) in France. It was not uncommon in England from the 13th to 16th C, and has continued in infrequent use ever since. Lyford 1655 gives it as *Hilarie*. It has become more common in recent years. In the 12th and 13th C it was also used as a woman's name (Latin *Hilaria*, *Illaria*, &c.), but that use seems to have died out altogether until it was revived at the beginning of the present century. CMY knows it only as a man's name.

YLLARIUS Cur 1203–5
HILLARIUS Cur 1207, FA 1346.
ILLARIUS FA 1284.
HILLARY St. Dionis Backchurch 1547, St. Peter Cornhill 1593.
ILLARIA Cur 1199.
YLLARIA Cur 1203, 1205, 1210.
HILLARIA HR 1273.

Hilda (f.): Old English *Hild*, probably a hypocoristic form of one of the names compounded with *hild* 'war', 'battle'. St. *Hild*, foundress and Abbess of Whitby (614–80), was much venerated in the Old English period and later. *Hilde*, *Hylde* (Latin *Hilda*) is found as a christian name until the end of the 13th C, and never died out in the neighbourhood of Whitby. The general use of the name was revived, like that of other names of Anglo-Saxon saints, by the Tractarians in the 19th C.

HILDE Cur 1201, 1203, 1210, HR 1273.
HILLDA HR 1273.
HYLDE Werburge 1513.

Hildebrand (m.): Old German *Hildibrand*, compound of *hildi* 'battle', 'strife', and *branda* 'sword'. The name was common in German medieval romances, but its general use as a christian name was probably due to St. *Hildebrand* (1000–85), Pope Gregory VII, one of the greatest of medieval popes. It was not uncommon in England in the 13th and 14th C and gave rise to the surnames *Hildebrand*, *Hildebrant*. It has occasionally been revived in modern times.

HILDEBRAND Cur 1200.
HEUDEBRAND, ODIBRAND Cur 1210.
HILDEBRANDUS HR 1273.
HILDEBRONDUS FA 1316.

Hildegard(e) (f.): Old German *Hildegard*, compound of *hildi* 'war', 'battle' and *gardi* probably a derivative of *gardan* 'to know'. St. *Hildegard*, Abbess of Bingen (died 1004) was much venerated, and her name has been used a good deal in Germany, and hence in modern times in USA. It is very rarely used in England.

Hippolyta (f.) [hĭpol′ĭtă]: Greek f. of *Hippolytus* (q.v.), the name of the queen of the Amazons, occasionally used in England in recent times, presumably on account of its occurrence in *A Midsummer Night's Dream*.

Hippolytus (m.) [hĭpol′ĭtus]: Greek Ἱππόλυτος 'letting horses loose', the name of the son of Theseus and Hippolyta, Queen of the Amazons. It was the name of a Roman saint martyred in 252. A church dedicated to him in Rome gave its name to a cardinal. *Ippolitus*, *Ypolitus* are found in the 13th C, and a 14th-C Legendary gives the name of the saint as *Ypolit*. The village of *Ippollitts* in Hertfordshire takes its name from the dedication of the church to St. *Hippolytus*, and exhibits many and strange perversions of the name, culminating in *Polledge*. Another church dedicated to this saint is that at Ryme Intrinseca in Dorset, and in 1607 a child in the neighbouring village of Holnest was christened *Epowlett*. *Hippolyte* is not uncommon in France.

YPOLITUS Cur 1200.
IPPOLITUS Cur 1207.
IPOLITUS Cur 1210, 1213.

Hiram (m.): Hebrew *Hîrām*, an abbreviated form of 'Ahiram' (Hebrew *'ăhîrām*) meaning 'my (or the) brother is high'; the reference is not to a human brother, but to the patron deity regarded as the divine 'brother' of the clan or tribe. The name of the King of Tyre who supplied cedar wood to David and his son Solomon. *Hiram* was a favourite name in the 17th C and has continued to be used in Yorkshire. It is also common in the USA.

Hob, see ROBERT.

Hodierna (f.): this name, which appears indifferently as *Hodiern(a)* and *Odiern(a)*, occurs from time to time in the 12th–14th C and was the name of the mother of Alexander Neckham and foster-mother of Richard I. Fr. Reidy has pointed out to me that on the Feast of the Epiphany the Collect in the Latin liturgy begins 'Deus qui *hodierna* die', &c., and suggests with much probability that the name may sometimes have been given to children born at that season, instead of the more usual *Theophania* (q.v.).

Hoel, see HOWELL.

Homer (m.): Greek *Ὅμηρος*, Latin *Homerus*. The name of the poet is sometimes used as a christian name in the USA. It was common in the Flesher family of Dumfries in the 17th C, and occurs in Charles Dickens's memoranda of unusual names from Privy Council Education lists (1855–65). A few modern examples have also been noted in England.

Honor(i)(a) (f.) [ŏn'or, hŏnōr'*a*, hŏnōr'ēă]: this was a common Anglo-Norman name, a derivative of Latin *honor* 'reputation', 'beauty', though the exact etymology is doubtful. There was a St. *Honoria*, one of the companions of St. Ursula, and a St. *Honorata* (French *Honorée*), either of whom may have been the sponsor of the name, which occurs in Latin records from the 12th–14th C as *Honora*, *Onora*, *Annora*. *Annora*, which is the commonest form, is a regular Anglo-Norman development, cf. Middle English *annour* for *honour* (see OED s.v. *honour*). It was carried to Ireland by the Normans and became a favourite name there, giving rise to the common *Nora* (q.v.). After the Reformation *Honor* or *Honour* was adopted as a christian name in England (cf. *Faith*, &c.), and in the 16th and 17th C was used as both a man's and a woman's name. It is now always f. *Honora*, *Honoria* came in again in the 18th C.

ANNORA Cur 1187–1215, FA 1302, 1316, HR 1273, Testa de Neville 13th C.
ANNOR HR 1273.

Hope (m., f.): used as a christian name from the 17th C. *Faith*, *Hope*, and *Charity* were often given as names to triplets. *Hope* is now used only as a girl's name.

Horace, Horatio (m.) [hŏr′*a*s, hŏrā′shĕō]: Latin *Horatius*, the name of a famous patrician *gens*, amongst whose members were the legendary three *Horatii* who fought the three Curiatii, and *Horatius* Cocles who defended a bridge across the Tiber single-handed. The chief glory of the name, however, and the reason for its survival, is the poet Horace, *Quintus Horatius Flaccus*, the son of a freedman who had adopted the name of *Horatius*. Its use as a christian name dates from the Renaissance, and seems to have started (as *Horatio*) in Italy (cf. Shakespeare's *Horatio* in *Hamlet*). The earliest example noted in England is Sir *Horatio* Vere (1563–1635), 1st Lord Vere of Tilbury. His grandson, 1st Viscount Townshend, was named *Horatio* after him, and in turn stood sponsor to one of the sons of his neighbour Sir Edward Walpole. The name was thenceforward much used by the Walpoles, sometimes written *Horatio*, sometimes *Horace*, but apparently usually called *Horace*. It was carried by marriage into the families of Suckling and Nelson. *Horatio*, 1st Viscount Nelson, received his name from his godfather and distant relative *Horatio* Walpole, 2nd Baron Walpole of Wolterton. It is a little surprising that the immense fame of the admiral did not bring his name into general use, but it remains for the most part still the peculiar property of a few families. *Horace* is rather more generally used.

Horatia (f.): f. form of Latin *Horatius* (see HORACE). Examples are Lady Anna *Horatia* Waldegrave, a grand-niece of *Horace* Walpole, and *Horatia*, daughter of Lord Nelson and Lady Hamilton. God-daughters of Nelson were also given this name.

Horatio, see HORACE.

Hortensia (f.): Latin f. from the name of the *Hortensian gens*. The Italian *Ortensia* was taken to France by *Ortensia* Mancini, niece of Mazarin, and was acclimatized there as *Hortense*. From France it has occasionally been borrowed in England.

Hosanna (m., f.): a Hebrew word which in Greek became ὡσάννα or ὠσάννα, in Latin *Hosanna* or *Osanna*. It was an exclamation in liturgical use amongst the Jews, meaning 'save now' or 'save pray', and was shouted before Jesus on his last entry into Jerusalem. The form *Osanna* was used in England from the Old English gospels until the 16th C when the versions of Tyndale and Coverdale have *Hosanna* or *Hosianna*. It is found as a christian name for both men and women from the beginning of the 13th C, usually in the French form *Osanne* or *Ozanne*; but it did not remain in use for very long. It seems to have been revived as a man's name in the 17th C, for Lyford 1655 gives *Hosanna* in his list of men's names. An *Hosannah* Johnson has been noted in 1880, but this was a woman.

Howard (m.): the use of this surname as a christian name is quite recent and there seems no particular reason for it except that it is the name of several noble families. The origin of the surname itself is doubtful; it seems sometimes to be from the name of the manorial officer, the *hayward*, and sometimes from a personal name *Howard*, *Heward*, *Hewerald* which occurs in the 11th and 12th C. There is no Old English name corresponding to it, but Förstemann gives one example of a name *Huguard*, apparently a compound of Old German *hugu* 'heart', 'soul', and *vardu* 'ward', 'protection', which may be the source of *Howard*.

Howell (m.): Welsh *hywel* 'eminent'. The corresponding Breton name *Hoel* was occasionally used in England in the Middle Ages.

Hubert (m.): Old German *Hugubert*, compound of *hugu* 'heart', 'mind', and *berhta* 'bright'. There was a corresponding Old English *Hygebeorht*, but it was not common, and the popularity of the name in the Middle Ages was undoubtedly derived from the cult of St. *Hubert*, Bishop of Liége, the patron saint of huntsmen. The surnames *Hubert*, *Hobart*, *Hubbard* (from the usual English form of the name), *Hubbert*, &c., are derived from it and testify to its former popularity, but it seems to have died out after the 14th C, and CMY treats it as obsolete. It was revived in the later 19th C and is now not uncommon.

HUBERTUS DB 1086, Cur 1187–1220.
HUBERT Cl 1270.
HUBARD Yorks Poll Tax 1379.
HOBARD Yorks Poll Tax 1379.

Hugh, Hugo (m.): there is an Old German name *Hugi* from *hugu* 'heart', 'mind'; but *Hugh* may equally represent a hypocoristic form of any of the numerous names compounded with *hugu*. It was introduced into England by the Normans and is frequent in DB. The French forms of the name were *Hugues* and *Hugon* in the north, *Hue* and *Huon* in the south (cf. *Ives* and *Ivon*, *Guy* and *Guyon*, the medieval *cas-sujet* and *cas-régime*). *Huchon* regularly appears in Scotland in the 14th–16th C. *Huon* is found as late as the 16th C in England. The Latin form was *Hugo*. All these gave rise to English versions of the name, which are illustrated by the many surnames derived from it, such as *Hugh*, *Hughes*, *Hugget* and *Huggin(s)* (from diminutives *Hug-et*, *Hug-in*), *Hew*, *Hewes*, *Heweson* (from the Scottish and North country *Hew*), *Hewet*, *Hewit(t)* (from the diminutive *Hew-et*), *Hewlett*, *Hewlitt* (from the diminutive *Hew-el-et*), *Hewling* (from the diminutive *Hew-el-in*), *How*, *Howes*, &c., from the southern form *How*, and many others. The name was already common in the 12th C, but became still more popular in the following century in honour of St. *Hugh*, Bishop of Lincoln (1135–1200), who was venerated in the North much as St. Thomas was in the South. Later, Little St. *Hugh* of Lincoln (1246?–55), a child supposed to have been martyred by the Jews, added to the popularity of the name. In Ireland and Scotland it has been used to render several Gaelic names, e.g. *Aodh, Eòghann, Ùisdeann.* The Latin form *Hugo* has sometimes been used in modern times.

HUGO Reg 1082, DB 1086, Cur 1199–1220.
HUGH HR 1273.
HOWE, HEWE *Prompt Parv* 1450.
HUGELIN Cur 1200, 1273.
HUGOLINUS DB 1086.
HUET HR 1273, Yorks Poll Tax 1379.
HUGLINE HR 1273.
HUELIN HR 1273.
HUGETHUN Exch R 1306.

Hulda (f.): Norse *Huldr*, 'muffled', 'covered'. Introduced into USA by Scandinavians.

Huldah (f.): Hebrew 'weasel', the name of a prophetess (2 Kings xxii.). Used occasionally in the 17th and 18th C.

Humbert (m.): Old German *Hunberct*, compound of *Huni* the folk-name, which probably originally meant 'giant', and *berhta* 'bright'. The name is most common, as *Umberto*, in Italy, but is also used in Germany, and occasionally in England by persons of German origin.

Humphr(e)y (m.): there was an Old English *Hunfrith*, a compound of the folk-name *Huni* (see HUMBERT) and *frith* 'peace'; but the widespread use of the name in the Middle Ages was due to the introduction by the Normans of the French *Onfroi* from the cognate Old German *Hunfrid. Humfridus* or *Hunfridus* occurs some score of times in DB. Later the French form of the name was latinized as *Onuphrius. Umfray, Humfrye, Humfrey* are some of the English forms; the spelling with *ph* instead of *f* is relatively modern. *Dumphry* and *Dump* were pet-forms, and the nursery hero Humpty-Dumpty probably contains an echo of this. *Humphrey* and *Humphries* variously spelt are common surnames. CMY says: 'From being a noble and knightly name, *Humphrey*, as we barbarously spell it, came to be a peasant's appellation, and is now almost disused.' Since then, however, it has come back into favour and fashion. See also OLAF.

HUMFRIDUS, HUNFRIDUS DB 1086.
UMFRIDUS Cur 1199–1220, FA 1346.
HUMFREDUS FA 1316.
UMFREY HR 1273.
HUNFRAY HR 1273.

Hyacinth (m.): Greek ὑακίνθος the name of a flower. St. *Hyacinthus* was a Roman martyr, brother of St. Protus. Used very occasionally. See also JACINTH.

Hypatia (f.): the name (presumably Greek) of a 5th-C Neo-platonist of Alexandria, killed by a Christian mob, the subject of Charles Kingsley's novel of this name. Examples of the use of the name in England are *Hypatia* Carlile (b. 1834) d. of Richard Carlile the deist, and *Hypatia* Bradlaugh (b. 1858) d. of Charles Bradlaugh the atheist.

I

Ia(i)n, see JOHN.

Ianthe (f.) [ĭăn'thĕ]: Greek Ἰάνθη (possibly a compound of ἴον 'violet' and ἄνθος 'flower'), the name of a sea-nymph, daughter of Oceanus and Tethys. In *The Siege of Rhodes* (1656) the name of the heroine is *Ianthe*, which is made to rhyme with 'dainty'. The first example noted of its use as a christian name is *Ianthe Eliza*, daughter of Shelley and Harriet Westbrook. Landor addressed some of his most pleasing poems to *Ianthe* (Sophia Jane Swift), and this may have helped to make the name known.

Ida (f.) [ī'da]: this name is found in Old German and is from the root *id-* (= Old Norse *idh* 'labour'). It was brought to England by the Normans, and *Ida* Countess of Boulogne is mentioned as a tenant-in-chief in DB. It continued to be used until at least the middle of the 14th C and was revived in the 19th C. The Old English *Ida*, a man's name, was from the same root. *Ida* has been used in Ireland as an equivalent of the native *Ita*.

IDA FB 1086, Cur 1199–1212, FA 1302, 1346.
YDA Cur 1201.

Idonea (f.) [idŏn'ēă]: this is a puzzling name, but it seems probable that it is related to the Old Norse *Idhuna*, the name of a goddess of spring, derived from the Old Norse *idh* 'work', 'labour'. It can scarcely be (what it looks like) the Latin adjective *idonea* from *idoneus* 'suitable', for there is no trace of it in the Romance languages. Förstemann records a f. name *Idina*, which is probably the same. It was common in England from the end of the 12th C; in Latin it appears as *Idonea*, *Idonia*, in the vernacular as *Ideny*, *Idony*, *Edony*. Examples of the name occur in later centuries. The surnames *Edney*, *Idney*, and possibly *Iddon*, *Idden*, are derived from it.

IDONEA Cur 1201–1218, FA 1284, 1303, 1346, *Times* 4 Feb. 1882.
YDONEA Cur 1203, 1207.
IDONIA Yorks Poll Tax 1379.
EDONIA Yorks Poll Tax 1379.
IDONY HR 1273.
IDENY Beetley, Norf Reg 1644.
EDNEY Notts P Reg 1754.

Ifor, see IVOR.

Ignatius, see INIGO.

Igor (m.) [ē'gor]: a Russian name of Scandinavian origin (=*Ingvarr*), sometimes used in England in recent times.

Ilbert (m.): Old German *Hildeberht*, compound of *hildi* 'strife' and *berhta* 'bright', introduced into England by the Normans in the French form *Ilbert*. It seems to have died out in the 13th C, but not before giving rise to the surnames *Ilbert*, *Ilberd*. There was a corresponding Old English *Hildebeorht*.

ILBERTUS DB 1086.
ILBERT Cur 1200, 1201, 1210, Pipe Roll 1159.

Imbert (m.): Old German *Isenbard*, compound of *isan* 'iron', and the folk-name *Bard*, found e.g. in *Langobardi*. Introduced into England by the Normans in the form *Isembert*, *Imbert*. It died out in the 14th C. *Imbart* still occurs in France.

ISENBARDUS Reg 1094–9.
IMBERT Cl 1267, 1313, Fines 1283.
ISEMBERD HR 1273.
IMBERTUS FA 1303.

Immanuel, see EMANUEL.

Imogen (f.) [im'ojen]: this name, from the heroine of Shakespeare's play of *Cymbeline*, has been used as a christian name during the last 50 years or so. *Imogen* appears to be a misprint in the Folio for *Innogen*, which is how the name appears in Shakespeare's source, Holinshed. *Innogen* is also the usual form in Geoffrey of Monmouth, who makes her the wife of Brutus. *Innogen* actually appears in the Quarto *Much Ado about Nothing* in the list of dramatis personae, as the name of the wife of Leonato, a character who does not appear in the play. Prof. Max. Förster suggests that *Innogen* is probably the same word as Old Irish *ingen* 'daughter', 'girl', from **eni-genā*, cf. Greek ἐγγόνη 'granddaughter'.

Inez (f.): Spanish form of *Agnes* (q.v.).

Ingaret, see ANCHORET.

Ingram (m.): either Old German *Angilramnus* or *Ingilramnus* (corresponding to Old English *Engelram* and *Ingilram*). The second element in either case is *hraban* 'raven'; the first is either *angil* 'angel', or *Ingil*, a derivative of *Ingvi*, an old hero-name. Both names were fairly common in Old German; but phonetically the Old French *Ingelram*, later *Enguerran*, is more likely to come from *Ingilramnus*. The name was brought to England by the Normans, a notable example being *Ingelram* Count of Ponthieu, brother-in-law of the Conqueror. *Enguerran* became in English *Ingran* and *Ingram*, and gave rise to the surnames *Ingram*, *Ingraham*, *Ingry*. It is found as a christian name as late as the 17th C.

It is sometimes found in use at the present day, but apparently always as an adaptation of the surname.

INGELRANNUS, INGELRAMNUS, INGRANNUS DB 1086.
INGELRANDUS Reg 1094–9.
INGELRAM Cur 1196, HR 1273.
INGERAM HR 1273.
ENGERAMUS FA 1303.
INGRAM Yorks Poll Tax 1379.
INGELRAMUS Yorks Poll Tax 1379.
INGRAMUS FA 1431.

Ingrid (f.): an Old Norse name of which the first element is from the hero-name *Ingvi* and the second *rida* 'ride'. *Ingerith* is found in England in the 13th C, but the name, like most Norse names, died out. It has sometimes been borrowed from Scandinavia in recent years.

INGREDE DB 1086.
INGERITH Cur 1205–13.

Inigo (m.): Greek *'Ιγνάτιος*, of unknown etymology. It was the name of a Bishop of Antioch, martyred between A.D. 104 and 117, identified by tradition with the child whom Christ set in the midst of the disciples. He was the reputed author of epistles to the Romans, the Ephesians, Polycarp, &c., which had a wide circulation. The name was used chiefly in Russia. In the West it was confined to Spain, where it is found from the 8th C as *Ignacio*, *Iñigo*, or *Eneco*. Its wider diffusion was due to St. *Ignatius* de Loyola (*Iñigo* Lopez de Recalde, 1548–98), founder of the Society of Jesus. The Jesuits carried his name with them, and as *Ignace* in France, *Ignaz* in Germany, it became fairly common. In England it has naturally not been much used except by a few Roman Catholic families. *Inigo* Jones, the architect, was named after his father, who always signed himself *Enego*, but named his son, in his will, *Inigue*. *Jenico* has been used in the family of Preston, Viscounts of Gormanstown, since about 1430 when Christopher Preston married the daughter of Sir *Jenico* d'Artois. This is apparently a Provençal form of Spanish *Eneco*.

Iolo (m.) [ī'olō]: Welsh, probably a hypocoristic form for *Iorwerth*, a compound of *iōr* 'lord', and *-gwerth* 'worth', 'value'. It is, however, commonly supposed to be derived from *Julius*. Cf. the alleged origin of *Gladys*, *Owen*, and *Emlyn*.

Ira (m.): Aramaic 'the stallion'; the name of a priest of David. It is used extensively in the USA, e.g. *Ira* D. Sankey (1840–1908) the evangelical hymn-writer.

Irene (f.) [īrē'nĕ, īrēn']: Greek *Εἰρήνη* 'peace'. A common Byzantine name also used in Sicily. It first appears in England *c.* 1880 (CMY does not regard it as an English name) and is now common. The American disyllabic pronunciation is now often used in England. *Renie* is a common abbreviation.

Iris (f.): Greek *Ἶρις* 'the rainbow'. The earliest example of this name which has been noted is in a list of christian names from Privy Council Education lists compiled by Charles Dickens between 1855 and 1865, apparently because of their oddity. A writer to N & Q 1904 gives it as one of the flower-names whose use was growing common.

Isa (f.): found chiefly in Scotland, and sometimes, at least, a pet-form of *Isabel* (cf. *Isa* Keith, cousin and correspondent of Marjorie Fleming). CMY says 'Isa is an old German feminine revived by a poetess of our own day'. She refers to *Isa* Knox (*née* Craig, 1831–1903) who contributed to the *Scotsman* over the name 'Isa'.

Isaac, Izaak (m.): Hebrew 'He (= God) may laugh', i.e. regard the bearer in a friendly light. Popular etymology connected the meaning with Sarah's laughter when she heard his conception foretold. The name of the son of Abraham and Sarah. It occurs twice in the Old English period as the name of a priest. *Isac* occurs twice in DB, and the name was used from time to time in the following centuries, sometimes, but by no means always, by Jews. The surnames *Isaac(s)*, *Isaacson*, *Isacke* are derived from it. After the Reformation it was much more commonly used. The spelling *Izaak* came in in the 17th C. The name has now almost completely dropped out of use.

ISAC DB 1086.
YSAAC (a Jew) Magd. 1207.
ISAAC HR 1273.
ISAKE Lincs 1534.

Isabel(la), Isobel (f.) [ĭz′*a*bel, (Scottish) ĭs′*o*bel]: this form of *Elizabeth* (q.v.) seems to have developed in Provence, and became almost universal in both Spain and France. Camden (1605) says of it: '*Isabel*—one with *Elizabeth*; if the Spaniards do not mistake, which always translate *Elizabeth* into *Isabel*, and the French into *Isabeau*.' *Isabella* Clara Eugenia, daughter of Philip II of Spain, signed her name *Isabel*, had coins struck 'Albert and *Elisabet*' and seals with *Isabella*. The names were still interchangeable in the 16th C; for instance a Berkshire yeoman in his will, 1542, names his wife *Isabel*, but in her own will, two years later, she is named *Elizabeth*. *Isabel* first appears in England in the 12th C, and its rapid spread may have been due to its being the name of three queens, *Isabel* of Angoulême, wife of King John; *Isabel* of France, wife of Edward II; and *Isabel* of France, 2nd wife of Richard II. In the 13th and 14th C it was one of the commonest female names in England. In the 15th and 16th C it is often spelt *Issabel*, sometimes *Esabel*. It gave rise to many surnames, such as *Isabell*, *Isbell*; *Ibb(s)*, *Ibson*, *Ibbison* (from the nickname *Ib*); *Nibbs*, *Tibbs*, *Libby* (from other nicknames); *Ibbetson* (from the diminutive *Ibbot*). The English form of the name is usually *Isabel*, or the latinized *Isabella*, which came in in the 18th C. *Belle* was a common pet-form in the 19th C. In Scotland *Isobel*, *Isbel*, or *Ishbel* and the nickname *Tibby* are used. Borrow's *Isopel* Berners was probably a phonetic reminiscence of the Scottish *Isobel*, in which the *s* is often pronounced hard. See also ISA.

ISABELE Cur 1196.
ISABELLA Cur 1199, Yorks Poll Tax 1379.
ISABEL(L) Ass 1284, HR 1273.
ISSABELL Lincs 1450, 1535.
EZABELL Cov 1471.
IBOT(A) Yorks Poll Tax 1379.
IBBET Cornish Parish Reg. 1579.

Isadora, see ISIDORE.

Isaiah (m.) [īzī'*a*]: Hebrew 'Jehovah is generous', the name of one of the greatest Hebrew prophets. It has been used, infrequently, as a christian name since the 17th C.

Isidore (m.) [ĭz'ĭdōr]: Greek 'Ἰσίδωρος; the meaning of the first element is doubtful, the second is from δῶρον 'gift'. The name was fairly common in ancient Greece, and it was early established in Spain, where it was the name of two notable saints, St. *Isidore* of Seville (560–636), a voluminous writer, and St. *Isidore* the Ploughman, the patron saint of Madrid, who lived in the 11th or 12th C. The name was adopted by the Spanish Jews, and outside Spain is mainly a Jewish name. It has been used in the Blake family of Menlough from the mid-17th C to the present day. The f. forms *Isidora*, *Isadora* are occasionally used.

Ismay (f.): this rather rare name is found from the 13th C, spelt variously *Ysemay*, *Isemay*, *Ysmay*, *Isamaya*, and it gave rise to the surname *Ismay*. *Ismey* is found in Ireland in the 18th C, and *Ismay* has been used in England in the present century. It does not seem to be found on the Continent. There is insufficient evidence on which to base an etymology, but it may perhaps be related to *Ismenia* (q.v.). See also ESMÉ.

YSEMAY HR 1273.
ISEMAY HR 1273.
YSMAY HR 1273.

Ismen(i)a (f.): this name is found from the 12th C in various forms. *Ismenia* occurs in Ireland as late as 1800. There are some signs that this and the possibly related *Ismay* (q.v.) may be of Irish provenance and possibly of Celtic origin. It is unlikely that they have anything to do with the Greek *Ismene*, the d. of Oedipus, although *Antigone* occurs as a christian name in the 13th C. In the 17th and 18th C *Emony*, *Emeny* are found as men's names, possibly a use of the surnames derived from this christian name. The gipsy family of Heron use *Emmannia* as a woman's name.

The name *Jesmond* which was common in North Lancashire in the 16th-18th C may be the same name. Other forms of it are *Jessimond*, *Jesmaine*, *Jismond*, *Gismon*.

ISMENA Cur 1199, 1200, 1201.
ISMENIA Cur 1218.
ISMEINA Cur 1213.
YMEISNA, YMENIA, YSMENA Cur 1200.
YSMEINA Cur 1207.
YSMENA Cur 1210.
ISMANIA, ISMANNA FA 1303, 1346.
IMANIA QW 1294.
EMONI HR 1273.
YMANYA HR 1273.
IMANIE HR 1273.
EMAYN Poll Tax 1379.
IMAYNE Poll Tax 1379.
IMYNE Chester Wills 1594.

Isobel, see ISABEL.

Isolda (f.) [ĭzŏl′d*a*]: whether a Celtic or a German origin should be assigned to the name of the heroine of the Tristan romances is doubtful, though phonetically the German seems more likely. *Essylt* occurs early in Welsh; *Isold*, *Isolt*, a compound of *is* 'ice' and *vald* 'rule', occurs in Old German as early as the 8th C. It was a common christian name in the Middle Ages, owing its popularity to that of the Tristan romances. It is usually recorded in the latinized form *Isolda*, but the spoken forms of the name were derived from the French *Iseut*, *Isaut*. *Ysolt* occurs in 1201, *Isowde*, *Isolde* in the 15th C, but the usual English form of the name was *Isot* or *Izot*, which in turn was often latinized as *Isota*. Bardsley gives no fewer than 12 surnames derived from it. He also gives an example of the christian name *Izett* in Ireland as late as 1891. A writer to N & Q in 1880 stated that *Isott* was then still current in Somerset. Another N & Q correspondent in 1877 wrote: 'the name *Isolda* may be rare at the present day, but it has not fallen into disuse. I am well acquainted with a lady of that name, and I learned from her that it was an old family name in both her father's and her mother's family.' CMY, however, seems to have regarded it as obsolete. Since then the name has had some revival, probably owing to the vogue of Wagner's opera *Tristan und Isolde*.

ISOLDA Cur 1199–1313, HR 1273, FA 1346, Yorks Poll Tax 1379.
YSOLT Cur 1201.

ISOTA Yorks Poll Tax 1379.
ISOTT Cornish Reg 1576.
ISYLTE St. Jas. Clerkenwell 1612.
ISSAT Yarborough Parish Reg 1734.

Isot(t) (f.), see ISOLDA.

Israel (m.): Hebrew; the sense is much disputed, but probably 'may God prevail'. Jacob was called *Israel* after his wrestling with the Lord, and thereafter the name was applied to the whole Jewish people. It has continued to be used as a personal name among the Jews, but seems not to have been used by Christians until the Reformation. It is found among 17th-C Puritans, and continued in use, mainly among the working classes, until the end of the 19th C.

Ivah (f.): apparently a use of an OT place name as a christian name (cf. *Sharon*). The AV has in 2 Kings xviii. 34 'Where are the gods of . . . *Ivah*?' (RV *Ivva*). *Ivah* is still used in at least one West Country family.

Ivo (m.): Old French *Ive*(*s*), *Ivon* (representing the *cas-sujet* and *cas-régime*). Förstemann derives it from Old German *Iv* 'yew'. The St. *Ives* who gave his name to the Hunts. town was a legendary person, said to have come to England from Persia in the 7th C. *Yvon*, *Yves* was the name of one of the 12 peers who fell at Roncesvalles, and it is common in Old French romances. It was brought to England at the time of the Norman Conquest, one of the best-known examples being *Ivo* Taillebois who married an Englishwoman, sister of Edwin and Morcar. It was a favourite name with the Anglo-Normans and it, and its diminutive, gave rise to many surnames, such as *Ive*(*s*), *Iveson*, *Ivatt*(*s*), *Ivett*(*s*), *Ivens*. In the Latin form *Ivo* it has been revived in modern times. *Yves* is still used in France. See also YVONNE.

Yvo Reg 1066–71.
Ivo DB 1086.
Yvo Cur 1196, Yorks Poll Tax 1379.
IVE HR 1273.

YVONUS Testa de Neville 13th C.
IVONE, YVONE HR 1273.
IVOTE HR 1273.

Ivor, Ifor (m.) [ī'vor, ē'vōr]: this name is mainly Irish, Scottish, and Welsh (there was a St. *Ivor* contemporary with St. Patrick), and is probably a borrowing of the Old Norse name *Ivarr* which was borne by several Danish Kings of Dublin in the 9th and 10th C. The Scottish surnames *MacIver*, *MacIvor* come from *Ivor*. *Ifor* is the Welsh spelling, and *Yfore* occurs in English records in the 13th C.

Ivy (f.): a late 19th-C invention. A writer in N & Q 1904 mentions it as one of the plant and flower names then gaining popularity.

J

Jabez (m.): Hebrew, meaning unknown. The etymology suggested in the OT 'because I bore him in sorrow' may well have been in the minds of some who gave the name in England, where it came into use in the 17th C and continued to be used, especially by Dissenters, until the 19th C.

Jacinth (f.): the name of a precious stone, from Old French *iacinte*, and ultimately from Greek ὑακίνθος (Hyacinth). *Jacinthe* and *Giacinta* are used respectively in France and Italy. *Jacinth* is found in use in England in the 17th C (e.g. in the Sitwell and Sacheverell families) as a man's name possibly with reference to Rev. xxi. 20 'the eleventh, a *jacinth*'.

Jack (m.): this, the commonest pet-name for *John* (q.v.), has caused a good deal of difficulty owing to the natural assumption that it must be derived from the French *Jacques* and should therefore logically represent *James* rather than *John*. The problem was cleared up by E. W. B. Nicholson in a little book entitled *The Pedigree of Jack and of Various Allied Names* (1892). He showed that there is no recorded instance of *Jack*, *Jak*, *Jacke*, or *Jakke* ever being used to represent *Jacques* or *James*, and that no statement in favour of the French connexion has been produced from any early writer. He then proceeded to elucidate and illustrate with examples the development from *Johannes* to *Jehan* and *Jan*, whence, by addition of the common suffix *-kin*, we get *Jankin*, which as a result of French nasalization becomes *Jackin*, and was finally shortened to *Jack*. There was a similar development from *Jon* to *Jock* (the Scottish form of the name). This process was complete by the beginning of the 14th C, by which time *Jack* was already established as a synonym for *man* or *boy*. The OED gives no fewer than 80 uses and compounds of *jack* as a common noun. The correctness of this derivation of *Jack* is confirmed by a passage in the *Historia Monasterii S. Augustini Cantuariensis c.* 1414: 'Mos enim est barbaricae locutionis et Saxonum, etsi non transponere, transformare tamen apocopando, et saepius syncopando: ut pro Thoma *Tomme* seu *Tomlin*; pro Johanne *Jankin* sive *Jacke*.'

Jackie (f.), see JACQUELINE.

Jacob (m.): Hebrew ăqōb; the meaning is much disputed. The name of the younger son of Isaac, who supplanted his elder brother Esau whence the popular explanation of the name as meaning 'he seized the heel' or 'he supplanted' (cf. Gen. xxv. 26). The name was a favourite one among the Jews, and was borne by two of the apostles. *ăqōb* became in Greek *'Ιάκωβος*, in Latin *Jacōbus*, but in late Latin it became *Ja·cŏbus* or *Ja·cŏmus*, from the former of which developed the Italian *Jacopo*, *Giacobbe*, Spanish *Jaco*, *Jago* or *Iago*, French *Jacques*, English *Jacob*, Welsh *Iago*; from the latter come Spanish *Jayme*, Italian *Iachimo*, *Giacomo*, Provençal *Jaume*, *Jacme*, Old French *James*, *Gemmes*, English *James*, *Jem*, *Jim*. See further under JAMES. *Jacob* is found four times in England before the Conquest, but always as the name of an ecclesiastic. After the Conquest there is little evidence of the use of *Jacob* except occasionally as the name of a Jew, though Godstow 1450 has 'St. Philip and St. *Jacob*'. *Jacobus* was, of course, the almost invariable form of *James*, &c., in Latin documents, and the surnames *Jacob*, *Jacobs*, *Jacoby*, if not of Jewish origin, are possibly from the Latin. The general use of *Jacob* as a christian name dates from the Reformation, and is due to the fact that the English translators of the Bible, while using the English form *James* for the two apostles, retained *Jacob* for the patriarch.

Jacoba, Jacobina (f.) [jakō'b*a*, jăkobē'n*a*]: *Jacoba* occurs from time to time in medieval Latin records as a woman's name. Probably the women in question were actually christened and called *James*. For example, one of the three daughters of Richard Emelden who died in 1333 is called *Jacoba*. In the proof of her age, 1339, one of the witnesses said he remembered the date of her baptism because 'it seemed to him wonderful that he called her by a boy's name when she was herself a girl'. She is usually called *Joan* in later records, but after her marriage to Sir Alan Clavering there is a reference to 'Sir Alan and *James* his wife'. In the 18th C Scottish Jacobites gave the names *Jacoba* and *Jacobina* to their daughters, and *Jacobina* still survives in Scotland.

Jacqueline, Jacquetta (f.) [jăk'*e*lēn, jakĕt'*a*]: French f. diminutive of *Jacques* (*James*), probably introduced to this country from Flanders and found from time to time from the 13th to 17th C. The English pronunciation of the names is preserved in the surnames *Jacklin* and *Jacket*. *Jacket* is found as a christian name as late as 1628. The full French form of the name has become common in the present century, often abbreviated to *Jackie*. *Jaquetta* is also sometimes used in recent times, probably taken from Shakespeare's *Love's Labour's Lost*.

JAKOLINA Cl H III.
JAKELINA Cl 1309.
JACLYN Yorks Poll Tax 1379.

Jael (f.): Hebrew *Jaalah* 'wild she-goat'. *Jael* the Kenite, who treacherously slew Sisera while he was her guest, would not seem to be an attractive person after whom to name a child, but *Jael* was a favourite Puritan name and continued in use during the 18th and early 19th C among Dissenters and in America.

James (m.): for the development of *James* from *Jacobus* and its etymology, see under JACOB and JACOBA. *Jame*(*s*) is found side by side with *Jacques* in Old French, the one being from *Jacomus*, the other from *Jacobus*, and it was *Jame* or *James* which took root in England where, however, it is not recorded until about a century after the Norman Conquest. The first recorded pilgrimage from England to the shrine of St. *James* in Compostella was in 1148, and the name *James* (*sic*, not *Jacobus*) occurs at the beginning of the 13th C, i.e. *James* de Houdernes and *James* de Bakepuz, so named in charters of King John. In the *Ancren Riwle c.* 1225 it is *Iame*, in the Testa de Neville *Jame*; in Chaucer's *Shipman's Tale* we find *Seynt Jame*; a 14th-C Legendary has *Seynt Iemes*, *Seynt Ieme* (cf. later vulgar *Jeames* and *Jem*), and 15th C Oseney *Jamys*. It will be noticed that most of these early examples are references to St. *James*. The saint meant is usually St. *James* the Great, the son of Zebedee, and not St. *James* the Less, the brother of our Lord; of 440 churches dedicated in this name in England, 414 are to the former and only 26 to the latter. It was the supposed tomb of St. *James* the Great which was the object of pilgrimage at Sant Jago de Compostella, the most famous shrine in Europe in the Middle Ages. The name was not very widely used in England in the Middle Ages, though it was more frequent in the North and in Scotland. The surnames *James*, *Jameson*, *FitzJames* (found in the 15th C) are, however, evidence that it was well established. The accession of *James* Stuart to the English throne in 1603 marks the beginning of the period in which it became a common English name. The usual diminutive is *Jim* or *Jimmy* (formerly *Jem* and *Jemmy*—cf. a burglar's *jemmy*), in Scotland spelt *Jamie*. The Gaelic *Seumas*, Irish *Seumus* are occasionally heard in England; more common is the monstrous pseudo-Gaelic *Hamish* (q.v.). There seems to have been a fashion for the French *Jacques* in the 16th C, and Camden says of it: 'which some Frenchified English, to their disgrace, have too much affected.'

JACOBUS Cur 1186–1220.
IAME Ancren Riwle *c.* 1225.
JAME Testa de Neville 13th C.
JAMES Magd. *c.* 1240.
JAMETTUS FA 1284.
JAKE, JAQUES Exch R 1306.
JACOMINUS FA 1305.

IAMES, IAME 14th-C Legendary.
JACOMYNUS FA 1428.
JAMYS Oseney 1460.
IAMES, IAMYS Lincs 1533.

Jamesina (f.) [jāmzē'na]: a Scottish f. form of *James*. See also JACOBA, JACOBINA.

Jan (m.): a dialectal form of *John* (q.v.). For a similar development, cf. *Jane* and *Joan*. It is occasionally used in Devon and Somerset nowadays, probably on account of 'girt Jan Ridd' the hero of *Lorna Doone*.

Jane (f.): the usual modern form of *Joan(na)* (see JOAN). It comes from Old French *Jehane*, and is not found much before the 16th C, *Joan* being the more usual medieval form of the name in England. *Jane* was very common in the late 18th and early 19th C, often in combination with other names, as *Mary Jane*, *Sarah Jane*, *Jane Anne*. It went out of fashionable use in the middle of the 19th C and came to be regarded as a typical maidservant's name. It has come back into fashion in the present century. *Janey* and *Jenny* are the usual diminutives. For *Janet* see separate article. The Gaelic form of the name is *Sìne* (phonetically rendered as *Sheena* or *Shena*); Irish is *Séadna*.

JANE Coventry Mysteries 15th C.

Janet (f.): a diminutive of *Jane* (q.v.). *Janeta* is not uncommon in medieval records. It is now chiefly used in Scotland and is generally given as an independent name sometimes in the diminutive form *Netta* or *Nettie*. *Jonet* and *Jennet* were other diminutives, from *Jone* and *Jeanne* respectively. *Jennet* is found as late as 1660, and Lyford (1665) gives '*Jennet* diminutive from *Jeane*'. *Jonet* has been occasionally revived in recent years. See also JESSIE.

Janice (f.): now (1976) a very common name, presumably invented in the USA as one of the various derivatives of Jane, which has for some reason taken the fancy of English parents.

Japhet(h) (m.): Hebrew 'may he expand', the name of one of the sons of Noah. Occasionally used as a christian name in the 17th C.

Jared (m.): Arabic *ward* = Hebrew *yered, yared* = Greek *ῥόδον* 'rose'. Occasionally used as a christian name, especially in the USA, since the 17th C.

Jaquetta, see JACQUELINE.

Jarvis, see GERVAIS.

Jason (m.): this name, occasionally used as a christian name since the 17th C, especially in USA, is not that of the Greek hero, but that of the author of the book of Ecclesiasticus and of a kinsman of St. Paul at Thessalonica who was persecuted on his account (Acts xvii. 5, Rom. xvi. 21). *Jason* was the English translators' rendering of the Greek *'Εάσων*, which was no doubt a hellenizing of some Hebrew name, possibly Joshua or Jesus. *Jason* has recently (1976) become fairly common.

Jasmin(e) (f.): one of the flower names that came into use at the end of the 19th C. The name is of Persian origin. It is still (1976) in use, unlike many of these names, and may owe something to the Persian *Yasmin*, the name of the heroine of Flecker's once popular play *Hassan* (1922).

Jasper, Caspar (m.): *Jasper* is the usual English form of *Gaspar* or *Caspar*, which was the traditional name of one of the Three Kings (*Gaspar*, *Melchior*, *Balthasar*) into whom medieval legend transformed the 'wise men' who came to Bethlehem to worship the infant Christ. The Gospels say nothing of their number or their names, but the legend evidently arose early. The three kings and their names appear in an 11th-C painting. Their supposed remains were translated from Constantinople in the 12th C and were ultimately enshrined at Cologne: *Kaspar*, in consequence, became a fairly common name in Germany; and *Gaspard* in France, *Gaspar* in Spain, *Gaspare* in Italy were not uncommon. *Jasper* or *Jesper* is first found in England in the 14th C, e.g. *Jasper* Woodlock (Magd. 1370) (cf. the surnames *Jasper*, *Jesper*), but the name has never been popular in this country. The etymology is unknown; it is probably of eastern origin. See also BALTHASAR.

Jean (f.): the usual modern Scottish form of *Jane* or *Joan* (qq.v.). It comes from the Old French *Jehane* (Modern French *Jeanne*) and was formerly common in England. Lyford 1655 says '*Jeane* see *Joane*'. The diminutive form of *Jean* was *Jennet* (see JANET).

Jedidiah (m.): Hebrew 'friend of Jehovah', one of the surnames or epithets of Solomon. Occasionally used by English Puritans. Still used in USA, where it is often shortened to *Jed*.

Jeffrey, see GEOFFREY.

Jehu (m.): Hebrew 'Jehovah is he'; cf. *Elihu*. Occasionally used by English Puritans.

Jemima (f.): Hebrew 'dove'; the name of one of the three daughters of Job, the others being *Keziah* and *Kerenhappuch*. All three were used, though not often, in the 17th C. A natural daughter of Charles II and Lady Shannon, born in 1650, was christened Charlotte *Jemima* Henrietta Maria. *Jemima*, in spite of its ugliness, became generally popular in the 19th C and was for a time a really common name. It is possible that it was regarded as a f. form of *James*.

Jenico, see INIGO.

Jennet, see JANET.

Jen(n)ifer, see GUENEVERE.

Jenny (f.): the usual pet-name for *Jane* (q.v.), properly pronounced *Jinny*, though a spelling pronunciation is now often heard. In Scotland, where it is the usual pet-form of *Janet*, the spelling pronunciation is general.

Jephthah (m.): Hebrew 'He (= God) opened (the womb for a first-born child)' or 'may He (= God) open, release (the bearer from harmful influences)'. Occasionally used by English Puritans.

Jeremiah, Jeremy (m.): Hebrew 'May Jehovah raise up, exalt'. The name of one of the great Hebrew prophets. The English form of the name, *Jeremy*, is found from the 13th C. *Jeremiah* and *Jeremias* (the Greek form) were adopted by the Puritans in the 17th C. There has been some revival of *Jeremy* in the present century and it is now (1976) very common. In Ireland it has been used to render the native *Diarmuit*. *Jeremiah* is particularly common in S.E. Ireland, perhaps because of the old tradition of a visit there by the prophet.

JEREMIAS Cur 1200, 1201, 1210.
JEREMY FF 1239.

Jerome (m.): Greek Ἱερώνυμος 'sacred name'. This was the name of a king of Syracuse (grandson of Hiero) and of a Rhodian peripatetic philosopher, and thirdly of St. Eusebius *Hieronymus* Sophronius (340–420) better known as St. *Jerome*, whose Latin translation of the Bible was the basis of the Vulgate. He was much reverenced in the Middle Ages and his name was used in Italy, where it became *Geronimo*, and France, where it was reduced to *Jérôme*. In England *Jeronimus*, *Geronim*(*us*) (variously mis-spelt) occur in Latin records from the end of the 12th C. The English pronunciation of the name is indicated by the surnames *Jerome*, *Jerram*, *Jerrems*, *Jarram*. *Ieram* occurs in 1556 and *Hierom* in 1675, but the initial *J* was usual. A f. form *Jeromia* occurs at Bury (Lancs.) in 1615.

JERONIMUS Cur 1199.
JERONIM Cur 1207.
GERONIM Cur 1200, 1201, 1210.
GEREMINUS, GERMINUS, JEREMINUM, JEREMIMUM (all the same man) Cur 1219–20.
GERONIMUS Cur 1219.

Jerry, diminutive of *Gerald*, *Gerard* or *Jeremy* (qq.v.).

Jervis, see GERVASE.

Jesmond, see ISMENE.

Jesse (m.) [jĕ′sĕ]: Hebrew 'Jehovah exists'. The name of the father of David; used as a christian name after the Reformation.

Jessica (f.): this name, the use of which is modern, is taken from Shakespeare's *Merchant of Venice.* It appears to be the Hebrew *Yiṣkāh* 'He beholds'. In the Authorized Version Gen. xi. 29 the name appears as *Iscah*, but in earlier translations it is *Jesca.*

Jessie (f.): a Scottish diminutive of *Janet* (q.v.), now often used as an independent name. Early examples of the name are *Jessy: or the Bridal*, a novel published in 1770, and Robert Tannahill's poem '*Jessie* the Flower o' Dunblane', which expressed his love for *Janet* Tennant (1770–1833) of Paisley. Burns in his last illness was nursed by *Jessie* Leuars. Early examples of the name in England are in Charlotte Brontë's *Shirley* (1849) and Mrs. Gaskell's *Cranford* (1853).

Jethro (m.): Hebrew 'abundance', 'excellence'. Used as a christian name after the Reformation. A notable example is *Jethro* Tull (1674–1741) the agriculturist.

Jevon (m.): Welsh *Yevan, Jevan,* forms of *Evan* (q.v.) or *John. Jevon* is still sometimes used instead of the usual *Evan.*

Jill (f.): a pet-form of *Gillian* (q.v.), now often used as an independent name.

Joab (m.) [jō'ăb]: Hebrew 'Jehovah (is a) father'. Used as a christian name after the Reformation.

Joachim (m.): Hebrew *Jehoiachim* 'May Jehovah raise up, exalt'. In apocryphal writings this was said to be the name of the father of the Blessed Virgin, and it was consequently used as a christian name, particularly in the Greek Church. *Joachim, Achim* or *Akim* is still fairly common in Germany and Russia. *Gioiachino* in Italy and *Joaquin* in Spain were also formerly in use. *Joachim* is recorded in England from the 13th C, but has never been in general use.
JOACHIM, JOACHIN HR 1273.
JOACHIM FA 1346.

Joan (f.): the most usual f. form of *John* (q.v.). *Jehane* or *Jehanne* became suddenly common in the 12th C in the south of France. The usual English form *Jhone, Johan* came into use soon after and was very common in the ensuing centuries together with its diminutive *Jonet*. By the 16th C it was the third commonest English female name and was apparently considered vulgar (e.g. Shakespeare's 'greasy *Joan* doth keel the pot') and was largely superseded by *Jane* (q.v.) which had developed from *Jehane*, whereas *Joan* came from *Johan* (cf. the parallel development of *John* and *Jan*, *Jock* and *Jack*). *Joan* was revived at the beginning of the present century (*Jane* having been overtaken by the fate which had earlier befallen *Joan*) and is once more a favourite name.

JOHANNA Cur 1189–1220, Yorks Poll Tax 1379.
JOHAN Yorks Poll Tax 1379.
JOHNE Lincs 1459.
JOHNA, JAHAN 15th-C Brut.
IONE Lincs 1535.
JONET Lincs 1450.

Jo(h)anna (f.): *Joanna* occurs in the Authorized Version of the New Testament in St. Luke's Gospel, once as the name of a man in the genealogy of Jesus, and again as the name of one of the women who ministered to Jesus. It is apparently a Greek spelling of Hebrew *Johanan* (see JOHN). It was first used as a women's christian name after the Reformation. *Johanna* was the usual medieval Latin form of *Joan* (q.v.), and was taken into use, like other medieval latinizations, in the 18th C.

Job (m.): Hebrew 'hated', 'persecuted'. The story of Job was a favourite subject of medieval plays, interludes, &c., and Bardsley would derive the surnames *Job*, *Jobson*, *Jobling*, *Jopling*, *Jupp*, *Jubs* from it. It is, however, more probable that the medieval name *Jupp* or *Job* represents an English equivalent of Old German *Joppo* (probably a hypocoristic form of *Judbert*, &c.). The Biblical name, however, came into use after the Reformation, though it was never common.

JOB, JOBBA, JOPPA, JOP HR 1273.

Jocelyn, Joscelin (m., f.): Old German *Gautelen*, *Gauzelen*, a combination of *Gauta* (from the same root as the folk-name *Goth*) and the suffix *lin* (= English *-ling*) which was not originally a diminutive. Förstemann gives many examples of the name from the 7th to the 11th C, including several in the form *Joscelin*. The name was introduced into England by the Normans (*Gozelinus* occurs 11 times and *Gos(c)elinus* 8 times in DB), and it was common throughout the Middle Ages, giving rise to the surnames *Joslin*, *Josselin*, *Joscelyne*, *Gosling*, and many other variants. It was rare after the 14th C, but has never altogether died out. The use of *Jocelyn* as a girl's name seems to be quite modern and is not mentioned by CMY.

GOZELINUS DB 1086.
GOSCELINUS DB 1086.
GOSELINUS DB 1086.
GOSCELINUS Reg 1087–97.
JOCELIN(US) Cur 1196, HR 1273, FA 1285.
JOSCELIN Cur 1199.
GAUSELIN Cl 1292.
GOSLINUS Yorks Poll Tax 1379.

Jock, see JACK, JOHN.

Joel (m.): Hebrew 'Jehovah is God'. This name of a minor prophet began to be used as a christian name after the Reformation. The common medieval *Joel*, *Juel*, *Jowell*, or *Jewell*, which gave rise to numerous surnames, is a different name, from the Breton *Judicael* or *Juhel*, the name of a saint who lived as a hermit in Ponthieu. It was introduced into England, with other Breton names, at the time of the Norman Conquest.

John (m.): Hebrew *Johanan* (Latin *Johannes*) 'Jehovah has favoured'. One of the commonest of Jewish names. As the name of both the Baptist and an Evangelist (each of whom had two festivals, the Nativity and the Decollation of St. John the Baptist, and the Nativity of St. John the Evangelist and St. John before the Latin Gate) *John* was marked out for popularity as a christian name. It was rare in England in the Old English period, though it occurs from time to time as the name of a priest or monk. In early times its chief use was in the Eastern Church, and it did not become common in western Europe until after the first Crusades.

The sponsor was probably more often the Baptist (who has 500 churches dedicated to him in England) than the Evangelist (181 dedications). Though *John* was a fairly common English name in the 12–15th C, its singular predominance over all other names came later. An analysis of names in the register of one church gives interesting results:

Period	*Percentage of all males baptized John*
1550–99	15½
1600–49	19
1650–99	28
1700–49	25
1750–99	19

It has been an equal favourite in other countries; French *Jean*, German *Hans* (from *Johannes*), Italian *Giovanni*, Spanish *Juan*, Russian *Ivan*, for example, are among the commonest names in their respective countries. The Welsh *Evan* and Irish *Sean*, *Shane* are noticed separately, as is also the nickname *Jack* (Scottish *Jock*). *Johnnie* is a less frequent diminutive. The Gaelic *Ian* (or better, *Iain*) is now increasingly used even in England. See also EUGENE. The number of surnames derived from *John* and its pet-forms is very great, e.g. *John(s)*, *Johnson*, *Jones*, *Jone*, *Jack(s)*, *Jackson*, *Jake*, *Jenkin(s)*, *Jenkinson* (from the diminutive *Jen-kin*); *Jennens*, *Jenyns*, *Jennings* (from the French diminutive *Jeanin*); *Jennett*, *Jenn(e)*, *Jennison*; *Hankin(s)*, *Hankinson*, *Hancock*, &c., from the diminutive *Hane-kin*, *Hane-cock*.

Jolyon, see JULIAN.

Jonah, Jonas (m.): Hebrew 'dove'. *Jonas* is the Greek form of the name. The story of the prophet *Jonah* was a favourite one in the Middle Ages, and *Jonas* is occasionally found in the 12th and 13th C. It became relatively popular after the Reformation, usually in the form *Jonah*, but is now seldom used.

JONAS Pipe Roll 1165, Cur 1213.

Jonathan (m.) [jŏn′*a*th*a*n]: Hebrew 'Jehovah has given (i.e. a son)'. The name of the son of Saul and friend of David. *Jonathas* (the Greek form) is found as a christian name in the 13th C, but its general use is subsequent to the Reformation.

JONATHUS CUR 1213.

Jonet, see JANET.

Jordan (m.): Hebrew 'flowing down', the name of the principal river of Palestine. There was an Old German personal name *Jordanes*, probably from the same root as Old Norse *jördh* 'land'. *Jordan* is found as a christian name in England from the end of the 12th C, and the probability is that its ultimate source was the Old German *Jordanes*, but that its continued use was due to confusion with the name of the river, which would be familiar to returning Crusaders, who were in the habit of bringing back Jordan water to be used in the baptism of their children. The surnames *Jordan(s)*, *Jordanson*, *Jordison*, &c., are derived from it. Bardsley also derives the surnames *Judd*, *Judson*, *Juggins*, *Juxon*, *Jewks*, &c., from Jordan by way of the nickname *Judd*. But there is no evidence connecting *Judd* with *Jordan*, and it is more probable that it was an Old English name cognate with Old German *Judo* which is recorded.

JURDANUS Cur 1196.
JORDANUS FA 1284, 1302.
JURDAN HR 1273.
JORDAN HR 1273.
JURDI HR 1273.

Joscelin, see JOCELYN.

Joseph (m.): Hebrew 'May Jehovah add' or 'Jehovah added' (i.e. children); the Greek form was *Joses*. The name was a favourite in post-exilic Israel; in the New Testament, for instance, there are *Joseph* of Nazareth the husband of the Blessed Virgin, *Joseph* of Arimathea, *Joses* brother of James, and *Joses* surnamed Barnabas. The early use of it as a christian name, however, was probably with reference to the patriarch (cf. *Abraham*, *Isaac*, *Jacob*). It occurs once or twice before the Norman Conquest as the name of a cleric, and during the Middle Ages it was in regular though infrequent use, cf. the surnames *Joseph*, *Josephs*, *Jessop(p)*, *Jessup(p)*. The pronunciation *Jessop* may have been influenced by the Italian *Giuseppe*, introduced by Italian Jews, for there is evidence that many of the medieval *Josephs* were Jews. The general and widespread use of the name dates only from the 17th C. In England it shared in the popularity of all Biblical names (the eponym in this case being the patriarch); and in Roman Catholic countries its use was enormously increased by the growing devotion to St. *Joseph*, husband of the Blessed Virgin. Until 1624 he had had no festival dedicated to him. The name occurs among RC recusants in England in the 17th C. In Italy and Spain, particularly, *Giuseppe* (pet-form *Beppo*) and *José* (pet-form *Pepe*, *Pepito*) became very common. The usual English nickname is *Joe*.

JOSEPHUS DB 1086, Cur 1203–1321, HR 1273.
JOSEP HR 1273.

Josephine (f.): French f. diminutive of *Joseph* (q.v.). The Empress *Josephine*, who is responsible for the modern vogue of the name, was actually named *Marie Josèphe Rose*, *Josephine* being a pet-name. *Josepha* was occasionally used in the last century, when the popularity of *Joseph* was at its height. *Josephine* is commonly abbreviated to *Josie* or *Jo*.

Joshua (m.): Hebrew *Jehoshea* 'Jehovah (is) generous' or 'Jehovah (is a) help'. *Jesus* and *Jeshua* are variant transliterations of the same Hebrew name, which was a favourite in post-exilic Israel. *Joshua* came into use as a christian name in England after the Reformation. In Spain and South America *Jesus* has been used as a christian name, probably given to children born on the feast of the Sacred Name of Jesus.

Josiah (m.): Hebrew 'May Jehovah heal' (i.e. the mother at the moment of birth). The hellenized form *Josias* is sometimes used. Camden mentions this as one of the names which came in after the Reformation. It was common in the 17th C, and has continued to be used to the present day in the Wedgwood family, by whom it is familiarly abbreviated to *Josh*.

Jotham (m.): Hebrew 'Jehovah is perfect'. Occasionally used in the USA.

Joy (f.): *Joia* is found as a christian name as early as 1199 and occurs from time to time in the 13th C. It looks like the ordinary word *joy* used as a christian name. It then died out, but was revived at the end of the 19th C and is now fairly common.

JOIA Cur 1199–1213.
JOHI, JOIHA Cur 1200.
JOYE FA 1285.

Joyce (m., f.): this common medieval name was used for both men and women in the forms *Josse*, *Goce*, &c. (Latin *Jodocus*, *Jodoca* or *Joceus*, *Jocea*). It is of Celtic origin, being the name of a 7th-C Breton saint, *Jodoc*, son of *Judicael*, a hermit of Ponthieu. His hermitage was at the place now called St. Josse-sur-Mer. His cult spread through North France, the Low Countries, and Southern Germany. The Dutch *Joos(t)* is a form of it. As a man's name it died out in England in the 14th C, but as a woman's name it survived, though in rare use. It has been noted in the 17th C, and in the 18th and 19th C survived in country districts. CMY says of it, 'once not uncommon amongst English ladies'. There was a correspondence on the subject in N & Q 1874 when one correspondent said: '24 years ago I used to lodge at the house of one *Joyce* Bell, at Cleator, Cumberland.' A further correspondence in 1896–7 produced evidence of the rare survival of the name in the Midlands. It was about this time that it was revived as a fashionable name, probably in part owing to Edna Lyall's use of it for the heroine of her popular historical novel 'In the Golden Days' (1885), and it is now once more in frequent use.

JOCEA Cur 1167, 1200.
JUICIA Cur 1210–12.
JOSSE HR 1273.
JOCEY HR 1273.
JOSSY HR 1273.

Jude (m.): Hebrew *Judah*, meaning doubtful, but possibly 'Jehovah leads' or 'He will be confessed', the name of the 4th son of Jacob and Leah. *Judas* is the hellenized form, and *Jude* an abbreviation of it. It was not used by the Jews until post-exilic times, when it became common. As the name of *Judas* Iscariot it never had a chance of being used as a christian name, in spite of the popularity in the Middle Ages of *Judas* Maccabaeus. The Authorized Version of the Bible in some places calls the apostle *Judas* ('not Iscariot'), *Jude*, and after the Reformation *Jude* was sometimes used as a christian name, as was also *Judah*, sometimes as a woman's name.

Judith (f.): Hebrew 'a Jewess', the name of the Hittite wife of Esau as well as of the slayer of Holofernes. It seems to have been introduced into England by the marriage of Æthelwulf (died 878) King of Wessex to *Judith* daughter of Charles the Bald. Another early example was *Judith* Countess of Huntingdon, niece of the Conqueror. It was not, however, until the 17th C that the name became common. The pet-form *Judy* is now sometimes used as an independent name, and in Ireland is also used for *Julia* (q.v.). JUDITA DB 1086.

Julia (f.): the f. form of *Julius* (q.v.). *Julie* has been common in France and *Giulia* in Italy since the 16th C. It is the name of a character in *Two Gentlemen of Verona*, and Herrick used it as the name of the mistress to whom many of his poems were addressed, but it seems not to have been used as a christian name until the 18th C. In the 19th C *Julia* was often used in Ireland to render *Sheila* (q.v.). The French form *Julie* is now often used as a pet-form of *Julia* and sometimes, especially in USA, as an independent name.

Julian (m.): Latin *Julianus*, a derivative of *Julius* (q.v.). There were some 10 saints of this name, but the best known of them is the legendary St. *Julian* the Hospitaller, the patron saint of travellers. The name is found in England from the 13th C, and the surnames *Julián*, *Julyan*, *Jolland*, *Jalland*, *Golland* are derived from it. The name *Jolyon*, which Galsworthy used for several characters in his *Forsyte Saga*, presumably derives from one of the medieval spellings of *Julian*. *Julian* was also the usual Middle English form of *Juliana* (q.v.).

JULIANUS FA 1285.
JOLANUS FA 1302.
JOLLANUS, JOLLAN Testa de Neville 13th C.
JOLIN HR 1273.

Julian(a) (f.): the f. form of *Julian* (q.v.). St. *Juliana* was said to have been martyred at Nicomedia under Gallienus and her relics were preserved at Brussels and Sablon. Her name was consequently a favourite in the Low Countries, and it was probably from there that it reached England towards the end of the 12th C. The usual English form was *Julian*, *Julyan*, or *Gillian* (q.v.), together with the diminutives *Gill*, *Jill*, *Gillot*, *Juliet*, *Juet*. It was one of the commonest girl's names from the 12th to 15th C, and there are many surnames derived from it, e.g. *Julian*, *Julien*, *Julyan*, *Jolyan*, *Juet*, *Jewett*, *Jowett*, *Gill*, *Gilson*, *Gillett*, *Gillott*, &c. By the 16th C *Jill* had become a synonym for a flirt or worse (cf. Shakespeare's 'flirt-gill'), and the word *jilt* comes from the diminutive *Gillot*. Another sign of the former frequency of the name is the common expression '*Jack* and *Jill*', which survives in the well-known nursery rhyme. This was no doubt the reason why the name went out of fashion in the 16th and 17th C. In the 18th C the Latin form *Juliana* came in and continued to be used in the 19th C. The older *Gillian* has been revived in the present century, and *Jill* (q.v.) is also now used as an independent name.

JULIANA Cur 1196–1220, HR 1273.
GILLIAN HR 1273.
GILLE HR 1273.
GYLLE Coventry Mysteries 15th C.
JUET HR 1273.
JELYAN *Cocke Lorelle's Bote c.* 1515.
GELIAN 1615 South Leigh Parish Reg.

Juliet (f.): the modern use of this name is undoubtedly taken from Shakespeare, who took it from the Italian *Giulietta* a diminutive of *Giulia* (see JULIA). But the medieval English *Julian* (q.v.) apparently had a similar diminutive, which appears as *Juet*, *Juetta*. There was also an occasional *Julitta* from St. *Julitta*, mother of St. Cyr.

Julius (m.): the name of a Roman *gens*, of which the most famous member was Caius *Iulius* Caesar. The Romans supposed the name to be derived from Greek ἴουλος 'downy', but there is no good evidence of this. It was first used as a christian name in Italy in the Renaissance period (*Giulio*), and the first instance recorded in England is Cesare Adelmare (1558–1636), a Venetian physician to Queen Elizabeth, who later dropped his patronymic, adopted the christian name of *Julius*, and in due course became Sir *Julius* Caesar. The family is still in existence and still uses the name *Julius*. The French *Jules* also dates from the 16th C. The Welsh name *Iolo* (q.v.) is sometimes said to be derived from *Julius*.

June (f.): the name of the month. Its use as a christian name dates from the present century (cf. *April*).

Justin (m.): a derivative of Latin *justus* 'just', the name of two Byzantine emperors, and of the writer *Justin* Martyr (died A.D. 163). The name has not been used much in England, oftener in Ireland where it is used to render some native name. The Welsh *Yestin*, *Iestin* is said to come from it. *Justin* Whitman was baptized in 1639 at South Leigh, Oxfordshire.

Justina (f.) [justē'n*a*]: f. of *Justin* (q.v.). St. *Justina* was a 4th-C martyr, the patron saint of Padua, and *Giustina* and *Justine* were current respectively in Italy and France. The first example noted is *Justina* d. of Lawrence Humphrey, President of Magdalen College, b. *c.* 1556. A solitary example of *Justiana* has been noted in 1640.

Justinian (m.): Latin *Justinianus*, a derivative of *Justinus* (see JUSTIN), the name of the 6th-C Emperor who caused the compilation of the *corpus juris*, and also of a 6th-C Welsh saint, the confessor of St. David. Occasionally used as a christian name. An early example is *Justinian* Baldwin, a Westminster scholar in 1567. Several examples occur in the baptismal registers of South Leigh, Oxfordshire, in the first half of the 17th C.

K

Karen (f.) [kah'ren]: Danish form of *Katharine* (q.v.), which has recently come into use in England as an independent name, probably borrowed *via* the USA where it was no doubt introduced by immigrants. *Karen* is now very common, and it has been suggested that this use was mainly due to the *Daily Mirror* strip cartoon 'Garth' in which a character named *Karen* was prominent in the 1940's.

Katharine, Katherine, Catharine, Catherine (f.): the name of a virgin martyr of Alexandria, died 307. The Greek form of the name was *Αἰκατερίνη* and the etymology is unknown. The Latin form was at first *Katerina*, later *Katharina*, with the spelling assimilated to that of *καθαρός* 'pure', the supposed origin of the name. Another fancied etymology was from Greek *αἰκία* 'torture'. The original form is preserved in the Russian *Ekaterina* (with pet-forms *Katya, Katinka*), and the earlier Latin form in the Italian *Caterina.* The legend of St. *Katharine*, who was said to have been broken on a wheel before decapitation, grew up in Syria, the chief centre of her cult being on Mount Sinai. It was brought to western Europe by early Crusaders, and the first reference to her in England is in a miracle play founded on her story and performed at Dunstable in 1100. In 1148 Queen Matilda founded a collegiate church and hospital of St. *Katharine* near the Tower. Her greatest popularity was in the 14th C. There are 62 English churches dedicated to her, and when bells came to be rung by wheel and rope they were often dedicated to St. Katharine, who had been broken on a wheel. The usual Old French forms of the name were *Caterine* and *Cateline* (the latter under the influence of the common diminutive suffix *-line*), and in Middle English it usually appears as *Katerine, Kateline*, or *Catlin* (cf. the surnames *Catlin, Catling*); the spelling with *th* came in about the 16th C, and in the 17th C the usual spelling is *Catherne, Katherne.* The name has been a steady favourite since its first introduction, changes in fashion only affecting the various pet-forms: *Kitty* seems to have been an early one, and by the end of the 16th C it had met the usual fate of common pet-names (e.g. *Jill*, *Nanny*, *Parnel*) and become a cant term for a loose woman. In the 16th and 17th C *Kate* was the common diminutive; *Kitty* came in again in the 18th and early 19th C, *Kate*, *Katie* in the late 19th C. All are now used, as well as *Cathy* and *Kay*. The Irish *Caitlin*, *Cathleen*, *Kathleen* from Middle English *Catlin*, is now often used in England. The pet-form *Kerry* is also used in Ireland. The Gaelic diminutive *Catriona* (pronounced kătrēē'onă), *Katrine*, and Danish *Karen* are also sometimes met with.

KATERINA Cur 1196–1215, HR 1273, FA 1428.
KATELINE HR 1273.
KATERINE, KATERYNE 15th-C Brut.
KATERYN Lincs 1456.
KYTTE Langland *c.* 1360, Coventry Mysteries 15th C.
KIT Yorks Poll Tax 1379.
KATE Coventry Mysteries 15th C.

Kathleen, see KATHARINE.

Katrine, see KATHARINE.

Kay (m.): this name, which has been occasionally used in recent years, is apparently taken from Hans Andersen's story of *The Snow Queen*. The name of Sir *Kay* the Seneschal in Arthurian romances is said to be from a Welsh form of Latin *Caius*. *Kay* is also used as a pet-form of *Katharine* (q.v.).

Keith (m.): a Scottish surname derived from place-name (there are several villages, &c., of this name). Its use as a christian name in England is fairly recent.

Kenelm (m.): Old English *Cenhelm* or *Cœnhelm*, compound of *cene* 'brave' and *helm* 'helmet'. *Cœnhelm* King of Mercia, who was murdered in 819, was venerated under the name of St. *Kenelm*. There are 8 churches dedicated to him. His cult was mainly confined to the Midlands, and it is there that the christian name *Kenelm* has flourished, e.g. in the Rutlandshire family of Digby, in which it is still current.

KENELM Cur 1201–3, Cov 1480.
KENHELM Lyford 1655.

Kenneth (m.): Gaelic *Cinaed*. The Welsh form of the name is found in *Cennydd* son of Gildas, a 6th-C Welsh saint and the Irish equivalent is *Canice*, after whom the town of Kilkenny was named and to whom the cathedral there is dedicated. It has been a favourite name in Scotland from the time of *Kenneth* (I) MacAlpine (died 860), 1st King of Scotland. In recent times it has been increasingly used in England by families with no Scottish connexions. Another Gaelic name, *Coinneach*, 'comely', from which is formed the patronymic Mackenzie, was also anglicized as *Kenneth*.

Kenrick (m.): Old English *Cynric*, compound of *cyne* 'royal' and *ric* 'ruler'. *Cynric* (died 560) was traditionally the grandson of Cerdic and 2nd King of Wessex. The name was fairly common in the Middle Ages, cf. the surnames *Ken(d)rick*, *Kenrack*, *Kenwright*, *Kenwrick* (for the epenthetic *d* in *Kendrick* cf. *Hendry* for *Henry*). The christian name survived into the 17th C.

CHENRIC, KENRIC(US) DB 1086.
KENWREC Pipe Roll 1161.
KENEWREC Pipe Roll 1161.
KENDRICK Chester Wills 1602.
KENRICK Chester Wills 1613.

Kentigern (m.): Gaelic *Ceanntighern*, Welsh *Cyndcyrn* 'chief lord', the name of the patron saint of Glasgow, where it was a favourite christian name in the 16th and 17th C and is found as late as the end of the 18th.

Kenward (m.): Old English *Kenweard*, compound of *cene* 'brave' and *weard* 'guard'. It became *Kenard* in Anglo-Norman and gave rise to the surnames *Kenward*, *Kennard*. Now long obsolete.

KENEWEARD DB 1086.
KENARD FF 1282, Lyford 1655.

Kerenhappuch (f.) [kĕr′en hăp′*u*k]: Hebrew 'horn of stibium' (eyelash paint), the name of one of the daughters of Job, the other two being *Jemima* and *Keziah* (qq.v.). It has been used from time to time since the 17th C, and in actual use is generally reduced to *Keren*.

Kester, see CHRISTOPHER.

Keturah (f.): Hebrew 'fragrance', occasionally used in USA.

Kevin (m.) [kĕ'vin]: Irish *Caomhghin*, Old Irish *Coemgen* 'comely birth'. The name of an Irish saint, common as a christian name in Ireland.

Keziah (f.) [kĕzī'*a*]: Hebrew 'cassia', the name of one of the daughters of Job (see also JEMIMA and KERENHAPPUCH). Used since the 17th C, especially in Evangelical circles; one of the Wesleys was named *Keziah*.

Kinborough (f.): Old English *Cyneburh*, compound of *cyne* 'royal' and *burh* 'fortress'. St. *Kyneburg* of Mercia (*c.* 657) was long venerated in the Midlands, where her name was in use as late as the 17th C. Lyford 1655 gives it as *Kinburga*. *Kimbery* Vowles occurs in a Somerset will of 1753. (Mr. Jeremy Morse tells me that the name has been used in his mother's family since the 17th C in the form *Kinbarra*, and that he knows of 4 persons at present bearing the name.)

Kirsten (f.): Scandinavian form of *Christian* or *Christine* (qq.v.), now often used in England, perhaps on account of the opera singer *Kirsten* Flagstad.

Kirsty, see CHRISTIAN(A).

Kit, see CHRISTOPHER, KATHARINE.

Kitty, see KATHARINE.

Knud (m.): a common Danish name perhaps related to Old German *kint*, Saxon *kind* 'kind', 'race'. It was introduced into England by the Danes and is familiar in the form *Canute* from the Latin version *Canutus*. It survived in use until the 13th C as *Note*, *Nute*, and the diminutive *Nutkin*, cf. the surnames *Nott*, *Nutt*, *Nute*, *Notson*.

NOTE HR 1273.

L

Lachlan (m.): a name much used by the McIntosh's and McLeans. It may be derived from Gaelic *laochail* 'warlike'.

Laetitia, see LETTICE.

Lalage (f.) [lăl'*a*jĕ]: Latin, a girl's name used by Horace, from Greek λαλαγέω 'babble'. Occasionally used as a christian name in modern times.

Lambert (m.): Old German *Landoberct*, *Landebert*, compound of *landa* 'land' and *berhta* 'bright'. There was a corresponding Old English name, but it was uncommon, and there is little doubt that the popularity of the name from the 12th to 15th C was due to Flemish influence. St. *Lambert*, a 7th-C Bishop of Maestricht, was much venerated in the Low Countries, and his name became a favourite there. In Middle English the form *Lambard* is found (cf. *Hubbard* for *Hubert*, *Robard* for *Robert*, &c.) and the diminutive *Lambin* and *Lambkin* were common. The name became rare after the 16th C but is still sometimes used.

LAMBERTUS DB 1086, Cur 1196–1215, HR 1273.
LAMBEKIN Cur 1213–15.
LAMBARD HR 1273.
LAMBIN HR 1273, Exch R 1306.
LAMBERT Cov 1574.

Lancelot (m.): this is undoubtedly a French double diminutive in *-el-ot* of the name *Lance* from the common Old German *Lanzo* from the root *landa* 'land'. Another diminutive of *Lance* was *Lancelin*. *Lance*, *Lancelot*, and *Lancelin* are found as christian names in England from the 13th C. The continued survival of *Lancelot* was due to the fame of the hero of Arthurian romance, a character who does not appear in Welsh or other early sources but was apparently invented by Chrestien de Troyes. The names were often confused with *Ancel* (q.v.) and its diminutive *Ancelot* and *Ancelin*. *Lancelot* seems to have been most popular in the North of England.

LANCE Ass 1218, HR 1273.
LANCELYN HR 1273.
LANCELOT Privy Seal Warrant 1380, Yorks Rec 1604.
LAUNCELETUS FA 1428.
LAUNSELOT Lincs 1526.
LANSLET St. Anne's Blackfriars 1641.

Laura, Lauretta (f.): the history and origin of this name are somewhat obscure. *Laurencia*, *Lauretta*, *Laura*, or *Lora* are all fairly common from the end of the 12th C; *Laurencia* is evidently a Latin f. form of the popular name *Laurence*, and it is possible that *Laura* was a pet-form of it, and *Lauretta* a diminutive of *Laura*. *Laura* occurs from time to time in the 16th and 17th C, and Lyford 1655 gives *Lora*, *Laurana*, *Laurentia*, and *Laureola* all as f. christian names. *Lora* was the usual Provençal spelling, e.g. of the name of Petrarch's mistress *Lora* de Sades. *Laura* is common in Wales and has latterly come more into favour in England after being neglected for some time. The pet-form *Lolly* is sometimes used.

LAURETTA Cur 1203–15.
LAURA Cur 1210–12.
LORA HR 1273, FA 1346, Yorks Poll Tax 1379.
LAURENCIA Testa de Neville 13th C.
LORETTA Testa de Neville 13th C.
LORE Godstow 1450.

Laurence, Lawrence (m.): Latin *Laurentius* 'of *Laurentum*', the name of a city, probably ultimately derived from *laurus* 'a bay tree'. St. *Laurence* the Deacon, martyred at Rome in 258, was a favourite saint in the Middle Ages, and there are 237 churches dedicated to him in England. *Laurence* occurs in England only as a monk's name before the Norman Conquest, and there is only one *Laurentius* in DB, but it soon became common and there are a great many surnames derived from it, e.g. *Lawrence*, *Laurence*, *Lawrenson*, *Lawrie*, *Laurie*, *Lowrie*, *Lawson* (from the nickname *Law*), *Larry*, *Larkin*. *Laurence* has been very popular in Ireland since the time of St. *Laurence* O'Toole (1130–80), Archbishop of Dublin, whose real name was the Irish *Lorcan*. *Larry* and *Lanty* are the usual Irish nicknames, *Laurie* is Scottish.

LAURENTIUS DB 1086.
LAURENCIUS Cur 1197, 1213–15, FA 1364.
LAURENCE HR 1273.
LARANCE Yorks Visit 1563, St. Mary Aldermary 1603.
LAW Yorks Poll Tax 1379.

Lavinia (f.): the name of the daughter of Latinus, the 2nd wife of Aeneas, of unknown etymology. It seems to have come into use, like other classical names, after the Renaissance, and is found at the end of the 17th C. In the 18th C it became something of a favourite, perhaps owing to the poet Thomson, who substituted it for Ruth in his version of the Book of Ruth. It is a favourite gipsy name. In the 13th and 14th C there is occasional record of a name *Lavina, Lavena* which may possibly be a version of *Lavinia* (which would be familiar from Virgil's *Aeneid*); on the other hand it may represent some such name as Old German *Leobuina* which is on record.

LAVINA Cur 1201, 1203.
LAVENA FA 1346.

Lazarus (m.): Greek form of Hebrew *Eleazar* 'God helped', used in the Authorized Version of the Bible for the brother of Martha and Mary and for the beggar in the parable of Dives and Lazarus. It is now an exclusively Jewish name, but was used as a christian name in the 17th C.

Leah (f.): Hebrew 'cow' (cf. *Rachel* and *Rebecca*), the name of the sister of Rachel and first wife of Jacob. It was first used as a christian name in England by 17th-C Puritans.

Lee (m., f.): a common surname, derived from Old English *leah* 'meadow', much used as a christian name in the southern USA, after the confederate general Robert E. *Lee* (1807–70). Now fairly common also in England.

Leila (f.) [lī′lə]: Persian, the name of the heroine of the popular tale of *Leila and Majnun*. Byron used it in *The Giaour*, and thus promoted its use as a christian name in the 19th C.

Lemuel (m.): Hebrew 'devoted to God', 'Godward', the name of a king mentioned in Prov. xxxi, sometimes used as a christian name in the 17th C, e.g. *Lemuel* Tuke, an ejected minister. The name is best known from Swift's hero *Lemuel* Gulliver.

Lena, see HELEN(A).

Lenore, see LEONORA.

Leo (m.): Greek *λέων*, Latin *leo* 'lion'; the name of thirteen popes. *Léon* is a fairly common name in France, and *Leon* or *Lyon* is found in England in the Middle Ages, usually as a Jewish name. *Leon* is now a common Jewish name in USA and *Leo* is occasionally used in England by Roman Catholics. See also LIONEL.

LEONIDEM (acc.) Cur 1199.
LEON Cur 1213–15, Exch R 1306.
LEO HR 1273.

Leofric (m.): compound of Old English *leof* 'dear' and *ric* 'ruler'; a common Old English name. It survived the Norman Conquest and gave rise to the surnames *Leverick*, *Leveridge*, *Loveridge*, &c.

LEOFRIC(US), LEURIC, LEOURIC, LEFRIC(US), &c., DB 1086.
LEFERICH, LEVERIGE, LEFRICH, LOVERICH, LOVERICK HR 1273.

Leofwin (m.): compound of Old English *leof* 'dear' and *wine* 'friend'; a common Old English name which survived into the 13th C and gave rise to many surnames, e.g. *Lewin*, *Levin*, *Levinson*, *Living(s)*, *Liven(s)*, &c. *Levin* is found as a christian name as late as the 17th C.

LEOFUUIN(US), LEOUUINUS, LEFUUIN(US), LEUUINE, LEUUIN, LEWIN DB 1086.
LEFWINUS Cur 1197.
LEFWYNE, LEFFEYNE, LEWINE HR 1273.
LEWIN QW 1292.
LEVIN St. Michael Cornhill 1626.

Leonard (m.): Old German *Leonhard*, compound of *levon* (Modern German *löwe*) 'lion' and *hardu* 'hardy', 'bold'. St. *Leonhard* was a 5th-C Frankish noble, converted with Clovis, who became a hermit near Limoges and the patron saint of captives. He was a favourite medieval saint in England and France and there are 177 English churches dedicated to him. *Leonard* is found as a christian name in England from about 1200. It has remained in steady though not common use from that time (cf. the surnames *Leonard*, *Lennard*, &c.) until the 19th C when it gradually increased in popularity. Lyford 1655 says of it: '*Leonard*, of a churlish disposition; a name fit for another Nabal.'

LEONARDUS Cur 1200, FA 1431.
LEONARD HR 1273, Yorks Rec 1604.

Leonie (f.) [lē'*onĕ*]: French f. of *Léon* (see LEO) occasionally used in England in modern times. *Leonia*, *Leonina* are found in the 13th C, evidently f. forms of the medieval *Lion*. In 1710 one *Lioness* Lee is recorded, but that seems to be a solitary freak.

Leonora, Le(o)nore (f.): *Leonora* is the Italian, *Léonore* the French, and *Lenore* the German form of this name. Its origin is not quite clear, but it may be a form of *Eleanor* (q.v.). The various forms of the name are not found in England until the 19th C; their introduction was no doubt due to literary and musical influences, e.g. Beethoven's opera of *Fidelio* (originally called *Leonora* after the heroine), Bürger's ballad of *Lenore*.

Leopold (m.): Old German *Leudbald*, *Luitpold*, compound of *leudi* 'people' and *balda* 'bold'. Names in *leud-* became *leo-* under the influence of Latin and Greek names. *Leopold* was occasionally used in England in the 19th C on account of the Queen's connexions (e.g. her favourite uncle *Leopold* King of the Belgians, after whom one of her sons was named).

Lesley (f.): this is the usual spelling of *Leslie* (q.v.) when used as a girl's name. It no doubt derives from Burns's 'Bonnie Lesley' who was *Lesley* Baillie who m. Cumming of Logie and d. 1843.

Leslie (m., f.): a well-known Scottish surname; the family took its name from *Leslie* in Aberdeenshire; early forms of the place-name are *Lesslyn*, *Lescelin*. The earliest example of its use as a christian name seems to be *Leslie* Stephen (b. 1832), but no reason for this seems to be recorded. The common use as a christian name seems to have begun in about the last decade of the 19th C, and no explanation of it can be offered. *Leslie* is now a common man's name but is sometimes also given to girls, when it is usually spelt *Lesley*.

Lettice, Laetitia (f.): Latin *laetitia* 'gladness'. It is not clear how or when the word came to be used as a christian name, but it was in general use in England in the 12th C and remained a favourite until the 17th C. The usual English form was *Let(t)ice*, but the French *Lece* (latinized as *Lecia*) was common in the 12th and 13th C. The surnames *Lettice*, *Lett(s)*, *Letson* (from the nickname *Lett*), and possibly some of the *Leesons* (from *Lece*) are derived from it. *Lecelin* a diminutive of *Lece* is also recorded. *Lettice* went out of fashion in the 18th C and was replaced by the Latin form *Laetitia*, but it has now come back into use. *Letty* is the usual pet-form.

LETICIA Cur 1199–1215.
LECIA Cur 1199–1215, HR 1273.
LETTICE HR 1273, Cl 1300.
LETYCE Coventry Mysteries 15th C.
LETE HR 1273.
LETIA HR 1273.
LECE HR 1273.
LECELINA Cur 1220.

Levi (m.): Hebrew 'pledged' or 'attached', the name of the third son of Jacob and Leah, and father of the priestly tribe. It was also the name of St. Matthew the apostle. Occasionally used as a christian name in the 17th C.

Lewis, Louis (m.) [lo͞o'is, lo͞o'ĕ]: (Latin *Ludovicus*, French *Louis*, Italian *Luigi*, Spanish *Luis*, German *Ludwig*): Old German *Chlodovech*, compound of *hloda* from the root *hlu* 'to hear' and *viga* 'fight'. The founder of the Merovingian line of Frankish kings, *Chlodowig* I (466–511), was called in Latin *Ludovicus* or *Clovis*, and later reduction produced the French Louis. It was, perhaps, the most popular of all names in France until the Revolution and was borne by no fewer than 18 kings. It was introduced into England soon after the Norman Conquest, the English form of the name being *Lewis* or *Lowis*, and gave rise to many surnames, e.g. *Lewis*, *Lewes*, *Lowis*, *Lowes*, *Lewison*, &c. It has been used a good deal in Wales, originally as an anglicization of *Llewelyn* (q.v.). The French pronunciation is often used in Lowland Scots, e.g. Robert *Louis* Stevenson. The Provençal form of the name was *Aloys*, and *Aloisio* was also sometimes used in Italy and Spain (see further ALOYSIUS). See also LODOWICK.

LEWIS Cur 1203.
LOWIS Cur 1210.
LODEWICUS FA 1428.

Liam (m.): Irish for *William* (q.v.)

Libby, see ELIZABETH.

Lil(l)ian, Lil(l)ias, Lily, Lilla(h) (f.): these names probably originated as pet-forms of *Elizabeth* (q.v.), cf. the German *Lili* for *Elisabeth*. *Lillian* is found as a christian name in England in the 16th C and *Lillias* at about the same time in Scotland; *Lilion* occurs as a surname as early as 1273 and looks like a diminutive in *-on* of *Lily*. Some of the many surnames *Lill(e)y*, *Lyly*, *Liley*, &c., may be from a christian name *Lily*, though it is not on record earlier than the 19th C, when it has no longer any connexion with *Lilian*, but is merely a flower-name adopted as a christian name. *Lil(l)ias* has remained principally a Scottish name. *Lillah* appears to be a 19th-C invention, perhaps a mixture of *Lily* and *Leila* (q.v.).

Lilith (f.): Assyro-Babylonian 'goddess of storms', misinterpreted as 'night-hag' from Hebrew *lail* 'night'. In Rabbinical literature the name of the first wife of Adam before the creation of Eve. *Lilith* has occasionally been used as a christian name in modern times.

Lina, see CAROLINE.

Linda (f.): this is a German name, not used in England until the end of the 19th C. It is from Old German *Lindi* or *Linda*, 'serpent', one of the commonest elements in Old German female names.

Lindsay (m., f.): the name of an ancient and famous Scottish family, and the surname of the Earls of Crawford. Early occurrences of the name are in the form 'de *Lindsay*', and the name may originally have been derived from *Lindsey*, a part of Lincolnshire, which incorporates the British name (*Lindon*) of Lincoln. *Lindsay* is widely used as both a m. and a f. name in Scotland and sometimes by English families with Scottish connexions.

Linnet, Lynnette (f.): the medieval French form of Welsh *Eluned* (q.v.). It has sometimes been used as a christian name since it became familiar from Tennyson's *Idylls of the King*. Often abbreviated to *Lyn* or *Lynne*.

Lionel (m.): apparently a French diminutive in *-el* of *Leon* or *Lion* (see LEO). In the reign of Edward III (who himself named one of his sons *Lionel*) there is mention of one *Leo*, *Lionel*, or *Lionet* de Bradenham. The surnames *Linnell* and possibly *Lyall*, *Lyell* are from it. Bardsley gives many examples of the christian name *Lyell* or *Lyonel* in the North in the 16th and 17th C.

LEONEL HR 1273.
LEONEL, LYONEL 15th-C Brut.
LIELLUS FA 1428.
LYONELL Yorks Rec 1604.

Lise(tte), see ELIZABETH.

Lizzy, see ELIZABETH.

Llewel(l)yn (m.) [hlĕwĕl'ĭn]: a common Welsh name also written *Llywelyn*. The first element is probably *llyw* 'leader'. From the 13th C it is found anglicized as *Leolin(e)* and this is found as late as the 17th C (e.g. Sir *Leoline* Jenkins born 1623, Principal of Jesus College, Oxford). Camden gives it as *Lewlin*, and Lyford 1655 says: '*Lewellin* like a lion; Latin.' *Lewis* (q.v.) has also often been used as an anglicization of *Llewelyn*. The correct spelling is *Llewelyn*, but *Llewellyn* is often written, especially by English writers, who are unaware of the pronunciation of Welsh *ll*. A f. form *Leolina* occurs in Cur 1213.

Lloyd (m.): Welsh *Llwyd* 'grey', a common Welsh christian name.

Lodowick, Ludovic(k) (m.): from *Ludovicus*, the Latin form of *Lewis* (q.v.) (cf. Italian *Ludovico*); used a good deal in the Highlands of Scotland since the 17th C.

Lois (f.) [lō'ĭs]: the name of the grandmother of Timothy, mentioned in 2 Tim. i. 5. The other members of the family who are named all have Greek names, and it seems probable that *Lois* is also Greek. It presumably came into use, like other out-of-the-way Biblical names, in the 16th or 17th C (Lyford 1655 gives it in his list of women's names), and the earliest occurrence noted is in 1583 in Springthorpe, Lincs., Parish Register. It became relatively common at the beginning of the present century.

Lola (f.): sometimes used in USA and less often in England. Originally a Spanish diminutive of *Dolores* (q.v.) and of *Carlota*.

Lora, see LAURA.

Loretta (f.): a name common in Roman Catholic use, derived from Our Lady of *Loreto* in Italy, a famous place of pilgrimage. *Lourdes* is used similarly as a christian name, but usually as a second name only.

Lorna (f.): this now frequent name was invented by R. D. Blackmore for the heroine of his extremely popular novel *Lorna Doone* (1869); he apparently formed it from the title of the Marquesses of Lorne.

Lottie, see CHARLOTTE.

Louis, see LEWIS.

Louisa, Louise (f.): *Louise* is the French f. of *Louis* (see LEWIS) and was not used in England before the 17th C. The earliest example noted is *Luese* Bencon 1646. *Louisa* was the usual form in the 18th C, when the name became a popular one. *Louisa* Countess of Berkeley (born 1694) granddaughter of *Louise* de Kéroual and Charles II, is sometimes referred to in contemporary records as *Lewes*. *Louie* is the usual pet-form. *Louise* has become a very popular name in recent years and is now (1976) one of the commonest f. baptismal names.

Loveday (f.): a common medieval christian name, which later became confined to Cornwall (where it still survives), sometimes in the form *Lowdy*. The name was originally given to either boys or girls born on a *loveday*, that is, a day appointed for a meeting between enemies, litigants, &c., with a view to an amicable settlement of disputes. It is a translation of Latin *dies amoris*. The christian name *Luveday* is recorded as early as 1205, though the earliest example of the noun given in OED is *c.* 1290. It is now given only to girls.

LUVEDAY Cur 1205.
LOVEDAY HR 1273.
LOVDIE Corn Par Reg 1578.
LOWDY Corn Par Reg 1601, 1622.

Lovell (m.): this appears to have been a diminutive in *-el* of the Anglo-Norman name *Love*. Another diminutive was *Lovet*. *Love* was apparently the English form of *louve* 'wolf'. *Lovel* and *Lovet* both occur in DB. The common surnames *Lovel(l)*, *Lowell*, *Lovet(t)*, *Lovat* are derived from them. *Lovel* was apparently also much used for dogs, e.g. the 15th-C rhyme on the favourites of Richard III, Ratcliffe, Catesby, and *Lovel*:

> The Rat, the Cat, and Lovel our dog
> Rule all England under the hog.

These names seem to have died out in the 14th or 15th C, but *Love* (the abstract noun) was used by the Puritans in the 17th C as a christian name.

LOVEL DB 1086, HR 1273.
LOVET DB 1086.
LOVE HR 1273.

Lucas, see LUKE.

Lucasta (f.): a name invented by the poet Lovelace, under which to address his mistress, who was possibly a member of the *Lucas* family. It has occasionally been used as a christian name since then.

Lucia, Lucy (f.): Latin f. of *Lucius* (q.v.). St. *Lucia* was a virgin martyred at Syracuse under Diocletian; she is said to have had her eyes put out, and was consequently regarded as the patroness of those suffering from diseases of the eyes. She was a popular saint in the Middle Ages and from the 12th C onwards *Lucy* or *Luce* was a favourite name in England. *Luce* continued to be used well into the 17th C. The Latin form *Lucia* came into use at the end of the 17th C. The diminutive *Lucette* (still used in France) is sometimes found in England in the Middle Ages. *Luciana*, which occurs in the 13th C, is probably a f. form of *Lucian* (q.v.), *Lucina*, also used in the 13th C, is probably another diminutive of *Lucy*. *Lucy* occurs as a man's name in some families, but in this case it is the surname used as a christian name.

LUCIA Cur 1196–1215, HR 1273, FA 1428.
LUCIE 14th-C Legendary.
LUCE HR 1273, 15th-C Brut, Yorks Rec 1604.
LUCY Godstow 1450.
LUCIANA Cur 1201–3.

Lucian (m.): Latin *Lucianus* from Greek *Λουκιανός*; the etymology of the name is uncertain but it was probably of Asiatic origin; both *Lucian* the 2nd-C satirist, and St. *Lucian* the 3rd-C martyr, were natives of Syria, and the 2nd-C heretic of the same name was from Asia Minor. *Lucianus* occurs as a christian name in 12th- and 13th-C records, but it was never common. Since the revival of learning it has been used occasionally, with reference to the satirist rather than the saint.

LUCIANUS Cur 1166, 1200, 1210.

Lucilla (f.): this is apparently a diminutive derivative of Latin *Lucius*, rather than of *Lucilius* which was the name of a Roman plebeian *gens*. St. *Lucilla* was a 3rd-C Roman martyr. *Lucille* is not uncommon in France and is occasionally imported into England.

Lucinda (f.): a 17th-C poetic variation of *Lucy* (q.v.) sometimes used as a genuine christian name.

Lucius (m.): a Latin praenomen, probably derived from *lux* 'light'. St. *Lucius* was Bishop of Rome from 253–4, and there were two later popes of the name. But it seems not to have been used as an ordinary christian name until the Renaissance, when *Lucio* became common in Italy. *Lucius* is found occasionally in England, e.g.

Lucius Cary, Viscount Falkland (1610?–43), and not infrequently in Ireland, where it has been used to render various native names.

Lucretia, Lucrece (f.): Latin, f. form of *Lucretius*, the name of a Roman *gens*. In the 15th C *Lucrezia* came into use in Italy and *Lucretia* or *Lucrece* has occasionally been used in England, probably with reference to *Lucretia*, wife of Collatinus, whose rape by Tarquin and her subsequent suicide were the immediate cause of the expulsion of the Tarquins from Rome. It was fairly common in Lancashire in the 16th–18th C. A *Lucresse* Briain occurs at Aston, Warwickshire, in 1603.

Ludovic(k), see LODOWICK.

Luke (m.): Latin *Lucas*, Greek *Λουκᾶς*, of or belonging to *Lucania*: the name of the third Evangelist. Both *Lucas* and the anglicized form *Luke* or *Luck* were commonly used in the Middle Ages. The name is not found in England before the Norman Conquest, and seems to have come into use in the 12th C. There are many surnames formed from *Luke*, *Lucas* and their diminutives, e.g. *Luke(s)*, *Lucas*, *Luck*, *Luckett*, *Lucock*, *Lukin*, *Luckin*, &c.

LUCAS Cur 1196–1215, HR 1273.
LUK(E) HR 1273.

Lydia (f.): Greek *Λυδία* 'woman of *Lydia*'. *Lydia* of Thyatira is mentioned in Acts xvi, and was, in apocryphal writings, identified with a daughter of Joseph of Nazareth. The name came into use in England in the 17th C.

Lynn(ette), see LINNET.

Lyulf, Lyulph (m.): Old English *Ligulf*, compound of *lig* 'flame, fire' and *wulf* 'wolf'. It appears in 11th-C charters as *Ligulf*, *Liulf*, *Lyolf*. It is still used in some Scottish families.

M

Mabel, Mabella (f.): the usual English form of *Amabel* (q.v.). *Mabella* is found as early as 1189; other latinized forms are *Mabilla*, *Mabilia*. The usual English forms were *Mabel*, *Mable*, or *Mably*. The surnames *Mabley*, *Mabb(s)*, *Mapp(s)* (from the nickname *Mab*), *Mabbit*, *Mabbot* (from the diminutive *Mab-et*, *Mab-ot*), *Mapson*, *Mappin* (from the diminutive *Mab-in*) are all derived from it. *Mabell* occurs in Yorkshire in 1604, and Lyford 1655 gives *Mabella*, but the name was rare from the 15th C. CMY says, 'it is still used among the northern peasantry', a remark which is left unaltered in the 2nd edition of her work (1884), though *Mabel* must by then have been returning into fashion. It was a favourite name in the last quarter of the 19th C.

MABELLA Cur 1189.
MABILLIA Cur 1196.
MABILIA HR 1273, FA 1284.
MABILLA FA 1303, 1346.
MABELL Yorks Rec 1604.
MABYLE, MABLY, MABILL, MABILE, MABLE, MABEL Godstow 1450.

Mace, see THOMAS

Madeline, Magdalen (f.): Hebrew 'woman of Magdala'. Devotion to St. *Mary Magdalene* was already growing in the 12th C, but was much increased by the supposed discovery of her relics in the 13th C when the distinctive epithet *Magdalen* was adopted as a christian name. In England the French form of the name, *Madeleine*, was further reduced to *Maudlin* and *Madlin*, which were still used in the 17th C. *Magdalen* seems to have come in after the Reformation (*Magdalen* and *Magdelne* occur in 1604), being no doubt taken directly from the Bible. Lyford 1655 gives it variously as '*Magdalene, Maudlin seu Magdalin*'.

MADELINA Ass 1221.
MAUDELEYN HR 1273.
MAWDELYN St. Jas. Clerkenwell 1562.
MAUDLIN St. Jas. Clerkenwell 1608.
MAGDALEN, MAGDELNE Yorks Rec 1604.

Madge, see MARGARET.

Madoc (m.): an old and favourite Welsh christian name, sometimes found also in the Welsh Marches. A derivative of *mad* 'fortunate'.

MADOCH DB 1086.
MADDOC Cur 1207.
MADOCUS FA 1346.

Magda (f.): German abbreviation of *Magdalena* (see MADELINE), occasionally used in England in modern times.

Magdalen, see MADELINE.

Maggie, see MARGARET.

Magnus (m.): Latin *magnus* 'great'. The first person to bear this name was *Magnus* I, King of Norway and Denmark, died 1047, son of St. Olaf. His father was a great admirer of Charlemagne, '*Carolus Magnus*', and the child is said to have been baptized by servants who thought *Magnus* was a proper name. It was subsequently borne by many kings of Norway and Denmark and became a popular name in those countries, whence it was introduced into Shetland, Scotland, and Ireland. Bardsley says that at the time of his writing *Magnus* was the tenth most frequent name in Shetland, where *Magnus*, *Magnusson*, *Manson* are common surnames. The Gaelic and Irish form of the name is *Manus* (cf. the surname *Macmanus*). The occasional occurrence of the name in the South may be connected with the church of St. *Magnus* the Martyr in London.

MAGNUS Cur 1200, 1207.

Mahalah (f.): Hebrew, possibly means 'barren', but more probably the name of a city used for a person. Occasionally used in England from the 17th C and taken to America where it was common until recently. *Mahala* occurs in Essex in 1792, and cf. Baring Gould's novel *Mehalah*. Kilvert's Diary for 26.2.1871 says, à propos a baptism: 'The name selected was, as far as I could make out, *Mahalah*, which Mrs. Jones declared to be the name of one of Cain's wives, on the authority of a book she had read, called the Life of Abel. She called her elder girl *Thirza*, which she says was the name of Cain's other wife'. See further under *Thirza*.

Maidie (f.): an occasional diminutive of *Mary* (cf. *Sadie* from *Sarah*).

Máire [mār'ĕ]: Irish form of *Mary* (q.v.).

Maisie (f.): *Maisie* or *Mysie* is a Scottish diminutive of *Margaret* (q.v.) now often used, especially in USA, as an independent name.

Malachi (m.) [măl'akī]: Hebrew 'my messenger'; an impossible name, probably borrowed by an editor from 'Behold! I send my messenger' (*Mal.* iii. 1) to provide an author's name for the book. Used as a christian name in England after the Reformation. *Malachy* is common in Ireland, representing *Maelaghlin*, the name of an Irish saint.

Malcolm (m.) [mal'kom or mah'kom]: Gaelic *maol-Columb*, 'servant' or 'disciple of Columb', a favourite Scottish name. It is occasionally found in England in the Middle Ages. Of late years it has come into use in England even with families who have no close Scottish connexions.

MALCOLUM DB 1086.
MAUKOLUM Cur 1207.
MALCULMUS FA 1303, 1316, 1346.
MALCULINUS FA 1346.
MALCOLINUS FA 1316.
MALCULMS FA 1428.
MAUCOLYN Werburge 1513.

Malise (m.) [mălēz']: Gaelic *Mael-Íosa*, 'servant of Jesus'. Traditional in, amongst others, the Gordon family. *Maolíosa* is still used in Ireland.

Malvina (f.): apparently invented by Macpherson in his Ossianic poems, perhaps to represent Gaelic *maol-mhin* 'smooth brow'.

Mamie (f.): an American diminutive of *Mary* (q.v.).

Manasseh, Manasses (m.) [m*a*năs'*e*, manăs'*ez*]: Hebrew 'one who causes to forget', the name of the first-born of Joseph. *Manasses* is, rather surprisingly, found as the name of a tenant-in-chief in DB, and again of one *Manasse* Saluernille in 1160. It has sometimes been used in Ireland to represent *Manus* (see MAGNUS). After the Reformation it was sometimes used by Puritans in England, and later in the USA.

Manfred (m.): Old German *Manifred*, compound of *mana* 'man' and *frithu* 'peace'. It was brought to England by the Normans, and there is a *Mainfridus* in DB, but it never took root here. Byron's poem of this name caused it to be used occasionally in the 19th C.

Manon, French diminutive of *Marie* (see MARY).

Manuel, see EMMANUEL.

Marah (f.) [mah'r*a*]: Hebrew 'bitter'. Sometimes used as a christian name in the 17th C.

Marcella (f.): f. of *Marcellus* (q.v.), the name of a Roman widow, a disciple of St. Jerome. *Marcelle* is not uncommon in France, and *Marcella* has occasionally been used in England. Lyford 1655 gives it as a diminutive of *Marcia*.

Marcellus (m.): Latin diminutive of *Marcus*; a cognomen of the Claudian *gens*. There were two saints of this name, one a 1st-C Roman martyr, the other a 4th-C Pope. *Marcello* has been used a good deal in Italy. The common French *Marcel* is one of the classical names adopted in the Revolutionary era. In England *Marcellus* has been used, very rarely, since the 16th C when a good many classical names first came into use as christian names.

Marcia (f.): f. of *Marcius*, the name of a Roman *gens*, probably derived from the name of the god *Mars*. It is sometimes used as a christian name, being regarded as a f. form of *Marcus* (q.v.).

Marcus, Mark (m.): Latin *Marcus*, a common Roman praenomen, and occasionally cognomen. It was probably derived from the name of the god *Mars* from some such form as *Marticos*. Though the name of one of the four evangelists, *Mark* (which is the English form, cf. *Luke* for *Lucas*) did not achieve widespread popularity until recent times, but it occurs from time to time in the Middle Ages and became a little commoner in the 19th C. The Latin form *Marcus* is found once in the 17th C, and has been used occasionally since the mid-19th C.

MARCUS HE 1273, FA 1303.
MARK(E) HR 1273.

Margaret (f.): (French *Marguérite*, *Margot*, German *Margaret(h)e*, *Gretel*, *Gretchen*, Italian *Margherita*): Latin *margarita* from Greek μαργαρίτης, 'a pearl'; the ultimate origin of the word is believed to be Persian. St. *Margaret* of Antioch, one of the Fourteen Holy Helpers, was supposed to have been martyred in the 3rd C, but nothing was known of her beyond that fact and her name, until apocryphal lives were written, which represented her as having overcome a dragon. She was one of the most popular medieval saints, largely, perhaps, because her last words were reported to be: 'Hearken to my prayer, O God, and grant to every man who shall write my life or relate my works, or shall hear or read them, that his name be written in the book of eternal life, and whosoever shall build a church in my name, do not bring him to thy remembrance to punish him for his wrong-doing.' She was also regarded as the patron of women in childbirth (e.g. a daughter of Henry III was christened *Margaret* because her mother had invoked the saint during her labour). Her name appeared in English litanies as late as the 17th C. The first recorded example of the name in England is St. *Margaret* (died 1093) sister of Edgar Atheling and wife of Malcolm III of Scotland, whose name may have been due to her Hungarian connexions (cf. *Christina*). The name soon became a favourite in both England and Scotland, and evolved a host of nicknames, abbreviations, and diminutives such as *Margot*, *Magge*, *Magot*, *Madge*, *Meg*, *Mog*. Bardsley gives more than 30 surnames derived from them. One form of the name, *Margery* or *Marjorie* (q.v.), was early regarded as an independent name. The nicknames *Mog* and *Meg* later gave rise to the rhymed forms *Pog*(*gy*) and *Peg*(*gy*). The Welsh form of the name is *Margiad* (see also MEGAN). In Scotland the pet-forms *Maggie*, *Maisie*, and *Mysie* have been chief favourites. *Maidie* is used in America. German *Greta*, Italian *Rita*, French *Margot* are now sometimes used in England. *Meta* was occasionally used in the 19th C. *Margaret* went somewhat out of fashion from the 16th to 18th C but regained its popularity in the later 19th C, and is now once more one of the most generally used of women's names.

MARGARETA Cur 1189, HR 1273.
MARGARETE, MARGARETT Lincs 1450.
MARGARETTE Lincs 1450.
MARKARET St. Mary at Hill 1494.
MARGAT Lincs 1534.
MARGYT Lincs 1540.
MERGET Oseney 1460.
MERGRET St. Mary at Hill 1498.
MAGOTE, MAGOTT HR 1273, Yorks Poll Tax 1379, Cov 1430.
MEGGOT Yorks Poll Tax 1379.
MAGGE HR 1273.
MEGGE HR 1273, Coventry Mysteries 15th C.

Margery, Marjorie (f.): *Margerie* was a French popular form of *Marguérite* (see MARGARET) and it is found in England as early as 1194; *Marjorie* was a less usual spelling but is of about the same age. *Margery* was regarded as a separate name as early as the 13th C, and all connexion with *Margaret* was soon lost. Lyford 1655 derives it from the name of the herb *marjoram*. In the 18th and 19th C *Margery* almost disappeared except among poor country people, but it is now general again. It is sometimes abbreviated to *Margy*. *Marjorie* is the usual spelling in Scotland.

MARGERIA Cur 1195, HR 1273, FA 1346.
MARGERY Prompt Parv *c.* 1440.
MARGERYE Lincs 1529.
MARJORIA Cur 1199, 1207, 1284, Yorks Poll Tax 1379.
MARJORY Yorks Poll Tax 1379.

Margiad, see MARGARET.

Maria (f.) [marī'a]: Latin form of *Mary* (q.v.); came into fashion in England in the 18th C and lasted well into the 19th C. This name has recently returned to popularity and is now quite common and usually pronounced marē'a. This may be a side effect of the age of the 'au-pair girl', who was frequently Italian or Spanish. A song in *Westside Story* may also have contributed to its revival.

Mariabella (f.): a compound, formed on the model of *Christabel*, *Claribel*, &c. (qq.v.), which came into use in the early 17th C and has continued to be used to the present day in some families.

Mariamne (f.) [mărĭăm'nĕ]: *Miriam* (q.v.) appears as *Mariamne* in Josephus; *Mariamne* is occasionally used as a christian name.

Marian(ne), see MARION.

Marie (f.) [mah'rĕ]: French form of *Mary* (q.v.) sometimes also used in England.

Mariel (f.): Bavarian diminutive of *Mary* (q.v.) sometimes used in England recently.

Marietta (f.): common in the USA, from the name of the town of *Marietta*, Ohio, founded 1788 and named after Queen *Marie Antoinette*.

Marigold, Marygold (f.) [măr'igōld]: this flower-name is mentioned as new in N & Q 1904. It has not become common.

Marilyn (f.): one of the many modern American variations on Mary, in this case popularized by the film actress *Marilyn* Monroe. It was no doubt her popularity that led to the widespread use of the name in England from about 1950.

Marina (f.) [marē'na]: St. *Marina* of Alexandria was a virgin martyr venerated in the Greek Church and sometimes identified with St. Margaret of Antioch. The etymology of the name is doubtful, though it is usually identified with the Latin adjective *marinus* 'of the sea'. A *Marina* de Beseville is mentioned in FA 1302. The name is found at Olney in the 18th C. A writer to N & Q in 1882 said: 'There is a family in this parish [South Stoke, Wallingford] who have used the name *Marina* (abbreviated to *Rena*) for some generations. I baptized the elder daughter by that name.' *Marina* or *Mairenni* is used by Northamptonshire gipsies. The marriage of Prince George to Princess *Marina* of Greece in 1934 gave a certain vogue to the name in this country.

Marion, Marian(ne) (f.) [măr'ĕon, mărēăn']: *Marion* was originally a diminutive in *-on* of *Mary* (q.v.). It was common in the Middle Ages and later. The spelling *Marian* led in the 18th C to the supposition that the name was really *Mary*+*Anne*, and *Mary Ann* was the first and chief of the double names which were so common then and in the early 19th C. The French *Marianne*, a later diminutive of *Marie*, is also sometimes used in England.

MARION Yorks Poll Tax 1379, FA 1402.

Marius (m.) [mă'rĕus]: the name of a Roman *gens*, probably derived from the name of the god *Mars*. *Marius* has been used occasionally in England since the revival of learning. *Mario* is very common in Italy, where it is apparently regarded as a masculine form of *Mary*.

Marjorie, see MARGERY.

Mark, see MARCUS.

Marlene (f.) [mărlā'na or marlēn']: a name devised for the German film actress *Marlene* Dietrich, by telescoping her original name of *Maria Magdalena*.

Marmaduke (m.): fairly common in Yorkshire from the 12th C onwards, particularly in the region round Thirsk, in the families of de Arell, de Thweng, and others. In DB Wellbury, about 13 miles from Thirsk, is said to have been held TRE by Fredegist and *Melmidoc*. This looks like Irish *Maelmaedoc*, 'servant of Maedoc', which would easily become *Marmaduc* (the usual medieval spelling) in Anglo-Norman. The name has remained very much localized in its use; Camden says of it, '*Marmaduc* a name common in the North', and it is still principally used in Yorkshire, often abbreviated to *Duke*. It was used, at least from the 17 C, by a Welsh family, the Lloyds of Middleton, with a f. derivative, *Dukana*.

MELMIDOC DB 1086.
MARMADUCUS Cur 1201, 1205, 1207, FA 1431.
MARMADUC Ass 1219.
MARMEDOKE Yorks Poll Tax 1379.

Martha (f.): apparently the f. of Aramaic *mar* 'a lord'; the name of the sister of Mary and Lazarus, whom medieval legend transported with her sister to Provence, where her name became a favourite one (*Marthe*). It was not, however, used in England until after the Reformation, when it became not uncommon and evolved the nicknames *Matty* and *Patty* (cf. *Meg* and *Peg*, *Molly* and *Polly*).

Martin (m.): Latin *Martinus*, apparently a diminutive of *Martius* 'of *Mars*'. St. *Martin* of Tours was a 4th-C soldier, later Bishop of Tours and apostle of Gaul; the story of his sharing his cloak with a beggar was a favourite subject of medieval art, and St. *Martin* was a favourite saint in England and in France; there are over 170 churches dedicated to him in England. *Martin* was a common christian name from the 12th C until the Reformation, and gave rise to many surnames, e.g. *Martin(s)*, *Marten(s)*, *Martinson*, *Martel* (from the diminutive *Mart-el*), *Martlet* (from the double diminutive *Mart-el-et*), and *Martinet* (from the diminutive *Martin-et*). After the 15th C the name was less common, but never fell into complete disuse. The names of the birds *martin* and *martlet* are derived from *Martin* (cf. French *martinet* 'swift', *martin-pêcheur* 'kingfisher').

MARTINUS Cur 1196–1220, FA 1428.
MARTIN Cl 1258, HR 1273.
MARTINET Exch R 1306.
MARTYN *Cocke Lorelle's Bote c.* 1515.

Martina (f.) [martĕn'*a*]: f. of *Martin* (q.v.). There was a St.

Martina, but the name when used in England and France (*Martine*) has probably usually been simply a f. form of *Martin*.

Mary (f.): (French *Marie*, Italian, German *Maria*, Russian *Marya*, *Masha*); Hebrew, probably 'wished-for child', less probably 'rebellion'. See further under MIRIAM, which is the same name. The consonants of the Hebrew word are M-R-Y-M, and when vowels were inserted in about the 7th C A.D. it became *Miryam*; the Septuagint, however, vocalized it as *Μαριάμ* (*Mariam*), and this is the usual form in the Greek New Testament both for the Blessed Virgin and for *Mary* sister of Lazarus, while *Μαρία* (*Maria*) is most often used for the other *Marys*. The Vulgate (probably owing to a mistaken idea that *Mariam* was an accusative in *-am*) adopted *Maria* for all of them. The name of the Blessed Virgin was long held to be too sacred for common use. The Sienese, for example, would allow no woman so named to practise the calling of a prostitute. In Spain, girls whom it was wished to put under the patronage of the Blessed Virgin were given names connected with her life or attributes, e.g. *Dolores*, *Mercedes*, *Asunción*, &c. The earliest example noted in Britain is *Mary*, 2nd d. of Malcolm III of Scotland and St. Margaret, b. *c.* 1082. From the 12th C, however, the name *Mary* gradually came into use in western Europe, and its growing popularity reflects the growing devotion to Our Lady. It is an indication of that growth that Bede in his list of churches gives only 3 dedicated to her; such dedications increased from the 12th C onwards, and there are now twice as many of them as of the next most common, those to St. Peter. *Mary* is first found as a christian name in England at the end of the 12th C; the diminutive *Mariot* is found about the same time; its use increased slowly during the next 3 centuries, *Mary*, *Mariot*, *Marion*, and the nicknames *Mall* and *Moll* (cf. *Hal* from *Harry*) becoming moderately common and giving rise to such surnames as *Maris*, *Marrison*, *Marrian*, *Marriot(t)*, *Marryat*, *Malleson*, *Mollison*, &c. *Mary* suffered an eclipse after the Reformation and was seldom used during Elizabeth's reign; it began to come back into use in the middle of the 17th C, and by the middle of the 18th C nearly 20 per cent. of female children in England were baptized in this name. In Ireland, where a quarter of the women are now called *Mary*, it was hardly used before the 17th C. In Irish, *Muire* is the form used for Our Lady, *Máire* or *Moire* being the common christian name. Several of the diminutive and pet-forms of the name are noticed separately, e.g. *Marion*, *Mariel*. *Mariot*, which was the most usual diminutive in the Middle Ages, was used in Cornwall as late as 1725. *Mally*, which was formerly much commoner than *Molly*, died out at the end of the 18th C. *Polly* is a rhyming nickname formed from *Molly* (cf. *Peg* from *Meg*). *Maidie* was formerly a Scottish pet-form. *Mamie* is a common diminutive in America. The French *Marie*, *Mariette*, *Marianne*, *Manon* are all occasionally used in England. For *Maria* see separate article. *May* is a late-19th-C coinage. The use of *Mary* as a second name (for men as well as women) arose on the Continent in Roman Catholic countries in the 16th C, and has occasionally been adopted by English Roman Catholics.

MARIA Cur 1203–10.
MARIOTA Cur 1205, 1210, HR 1273.
MARY Prompt Parv *c.* 1440.
MALKYN Coventry Mysteries 15th C.

Matilda, Maud(e) (f.): Old German *Mahthildis*, compound of *mahti* 'might', 'strength', and *hildi* 'battle', 'strife'. It was introduced into England by the Normans (William I married *Matilda* daughter of Baldwin V of Flanders), and was a favourite in the 12th and 13th C, gradually falling into desuetude in the 14th and 15th C. The Latin forms are *Matillis* or *Matilldis* as well as *Matilda*; the French were *Mahhild*, *Mahault*, *Molde*, or *Maud*, and these were all used in England, together with the nicknames *Till*, *Tillot*. Many surnames are derived from them, e.g. *Madison*, *Maud*(*e*), *Maudson*, *Mawson*, *Moulson*, *Mould*, *Mowl*(*e*), *Moult*, *Till*(*y*), *Tillison*, *Tilson*, *Tillotson*. It was very rare in the 16th and 17th C, but the Latin form *Matilda* was revived in the middle of the 18th C and became a great favourite. Tennyson's poem *Maud* (1855) was probably responsible for the revival of this medieval form of the name in the later 19th C. It occurs in *John Halifax*,

Gentleman (1856). The pet-forms *Matty*, *Tilly*, and *Tilda* were usual in the 19th C.

MATILDIS Reg 1082.
MATHILD, MATHILA, MATHELD, MATHILDIS DB 1086.
MATILDA Cur 1189–1215.
MATILLDIS FA 1284.
MATILLIS FA 1316.
MAULD Visit of Cheshire 1303.
MAUD Cl 1314.
MAUDE Godstow 1450, Lincs 1451, Cov 1486.
MOLDE, MOOLDE Godstow 1450.
MAWT Lincs 1455.
MAWDE Chester 1562.

Matthew, Matthias (m.): Hebrew *Mattathiah* 'gift of Jehovah', became *Ματθαῖος* or *Ματθίας* in Greek and *Matthaeus* or *Matthias* in Latin. The name was introduced into England by the Normans and *Mathiu seu Macy* is a tenant mentioned in DB. *Matheu* (latinized as *Matheus*) was the usual French form, together with the nickname *Mac(e)y*. From this are derived the surnames *Mayhew*, *Mayo(w)*, *Mayhow*, *Mace(y)*. *Mace* or *Macy* is sometimes found used as an independent name and latinized as *Maceus*, *Macius*. Another French diminutive was *Machin*, *Machon* which gave rise to the surnames *Machen*, *Machin*, *Machon*. *Mathew(s)*, *Mathewson*, *Matheson* (all spelt in many ways) are derived from the English *Mathew*; *Maton*, *Matkin*, *Matterson* are from the English nickname *Mat*; *Maycock* and *Maykin* from the nickname *May*, with the suffixes *-cock* and *-kin*. These surnames are only a selection of the derivatives of *Mathew* and they give some measure of its popularity in the 12th–14th C. It continued in general use, though less frequent, after the Reformation. The English versions of the Bible rendered the name variously, and in the Authorized Version *Mattathiah* is used in the Old Testament, *Matthew* for the Evangelist, and *Matthias* for the disciple who was chosen to take the place of Judas. *Matthias*, accordingly, was sometimes used in the 17th C as a christian name.

MATTHEUS DB 1086.
MATHEUS Cur 1166, HR 1273, FA 1316.
MATHIU SEU MACY DB 1086.

MATHIE, MATHEU 14th-C Legendary.
MATHEU Exch R 1306, Yorks Poll Tax 1379.
MATHEWE *Cocke Lorelle's Bote c.* 1515.
MATHY, MATHEY HR 1273.
MACIUS, MACE, MASSE HR 1273.
MAHEU HR 1273.
MAYE HR 1273.
MAYEU Writs of Parl 1300.

Matty, see MARTHA and MATILDA.

Maud(e), see MATILDA.

Mauger (m.): Old German *Malgar*, apparently a compound of *malv* from *malvjan* 'to grind' and *ger* 'spear'. The name was introduced into England by the Normans in the French form *Mauger*, which was used as a christian name until the 18th C in the Vavasour family which descended from one *Mauger* who held lands in vavasoury in the reign of Henry I. Lyford 1655 says of it: '*Maugre*, some make as it were *malgerius*, bearing evil.'

MALGERIUS DB 1086.
MALGER HR 1273.
MAUGER HR 1273, Writs of Parl 1300.
MARGRE Yorks Poll Tax 1379.

Maureen (f.) [mōr'ēn]: Irish *Máirín*, diminutive of *Máire* (*Mary* q.v.). *Maureen* has become general in England in the present century, the fashion probably coming via America.

Maurice (m.) [mŏr'ĭs]: Latin *Mauritius* 'a Moor'; the name of a martyr said to have belonged to the Theban legion and to have been martyred in Switzerland A.D. 286. The name is found in use in England from the 11th C, sometimes in the French form *Meurisse*, but more often in the English *Moris* or *Morris*. It gave rise to the surnames *Morris(s)*, *Maurice*, *Mor(r)ison*, *Morson*, *Morse*, *Morin*, and *Morcock*. *Maurice* has now replaced *Morris* as the usual spelling of the christian name. It has been used in Ireland to render the native *Moriertagh* (*Moriarty*) 'sea warrior'. The Welsh form is *Meuric*.

MAURICIUS Reg ? 1086, Cur 1196–1220.
MEURIK Testa de Neville 13th C.

MORIS FA 1346.
MORICIUS FA 1431.
MORYS Lincs 1459.
MORES Cov 1471.
MOURICE Cov 1539.
MAURIS 15th C Brut.
MERICK SEU MORRICE Lyford 1655.

Mavis (f.) [mā'vis]: an old name for the song-thrush. Marie Corelli seems to have been the first to use it as a christian name, in one of her novels, and it is now not uncommon.

Maximilian (m.): Camden gives the following account of the origin of this name: 'a new name, first devised by *Frederic* the third Emperor, who doubting what name to give his son and heire, composed this name of two worthy Romans, whom he most admired, *Q. Fabius Maximus*, and *Scipio Aemilianus*, with hope that his son would imitate their vertues (*Hieronymus Gebvilerius de familia Austriaca*).' It became a favourite name in Germany, particularly in the abbreviated form *Max*, and is occasionally used in England.

Maxine (f.): a favourite modern French girl's name, sometimes used in England and oftener in America. It is apparently a f. diminutive of *Max* (see MAXIMILIAN). *Maxencia* occurs in the 13th C, apparently a f. form of *Maxentius*, but there is no evidence of its survival.

May (f.): a 19th-C pet-form of *Margaret* or *Mary*, sometimes used as an independent name and associated with the name of the month (cf. *June*, *April*).

Maynard (m.): Old German *Maganhard*, compound of *magan* 'strength' and *hardu* 'hardy'. There was a similar Old English *Maegenheard*, but it was not common, and the fairly frequent use of *Maynard* after the Norman Conquest was probably due to its importation by the Normans. It appears as *Manard* in the 17th C.

MAINARD(US) DB 1086.
MAINARD Cur 1189–1203.
MAYNARD HR 1273.

Meave (f.) [māv]: Irish *Meadhbh*, the daughter of Eochaidh and heroine of many legends. In Ireland the name has often been rendered by *Mab* or *Mabel*, and it is usually stated that the English 'Queen *Mab*' is the same as the legendary Irish queen. This is, however, prima facie unlikely, and *Mab* in this case is no doubt the common abbreviation for *Mabel*.

Meg, see MARGARET.

Megan (f.) [meg'*a*n]: this Welsh name, now sometimes used in England, is apparently a fairly modern coinage, perhaps a diminutive of *Margaret*. The earliest example noted is *Megan* Lloyd George MP, d. of the Prime Minister.

Mehetabel (f.) [m*e*hĕt'*a*bĕl]: Aramaic 'God is active, treating well', a name which occurs in Gen. xxxvi. It came into use as a christian name after the Reformation and is recorded as early as 1578. It remained in use in villages until the 19th C and was transplanted to America where it is a favourite negro name.

Melanie, Melloney (f.) [mĕl'*a*nĕ]: Greek μέλαινα 'black'. St. *Melania* the elder and St. *Melania* the younger were a grandmother and granddaughter, Roman ladies devoted to St. Jerome. *Mélanie* is not uncommon in France, and was probably introduced into England by Hugenot refugees. It first appears in Devon and Cornwall in the middle of the 17th C (*Melloney* 1655, *Melanie* 1660, *Melony* 1748, *Melloney* 1770). It is still used in Cornwall.

Melchior (m.): Hebrew 'King of light' or 'the King (= God) is light', the name of one of the 'Three Kings' into whom medieval legend transformed the wise men from the East who visited Bethlehem. See BALTHASAR and CASPAR. *Melchior* has been used less often than the other two as a christian name. It occurs as *Melcher* at Manchester in 1592. In the 18th C it was used a good deal in Ireland, probably to represent some Irish name.

Melchisadek (m.) [melchiz'*a*dĕk]: Hebrew 'the King (i.e. God) is righteousness' or 'my King is righteous', the name of the priest-king of Salem who blessed Abraham, later taken as the type of Christ. The name was used occasionally from the 17th C.

Melesina, see MILLICENT.

Melicent, see MILLICENT.

Melior(a) (f.): this is apparently a purely Cornish name. The church of Linkinhorne, Cornwall, is dedicated to St. *Melior*. The name occurs in Assize Rolls as early as 1218 and FA in 1346 as *Meliora*, in the 17th C as *Melyear*, *Melyar*, *Mellier*, in the 18th and 19th C as *Meliora*. CMY says: '*Melior* is a Cornish name, probably an imitation of some old Keltic name. It is found as early as 1574, but is now probably ruined by Amelia.' (It has been pointed out to me that *Meliora* is the name of the sister of Melusine, the water-fairy in the medieval Lusignan romance.)

Melissa (f.): Greek *μέλισσα* 'a bee', also the name of a nymph, later used as a personal name in Greece. Italian 16th-C poets used *Melissa* as the name of a fairy, and in the 18th C it was occasionally used as a christian name in France and England.

Melloney, see MELANIE.

Melody (f.): this would seem to be the ordinary word *melody* but there is no clue to show how it came to be so used. It is recorded in Shropshire at the end of the 18th C and in Somerset *c.* 1880.

Meraud (f.): this Cornish name is usually taken to be a contraction of Middle English *emeraud* emerald, e.g. Lyford 1655: '*Meraud* perhaps by contraction from the pretious Emeraud stone.' *Esmeralda* was used as a christian name in Spain. But a *Merouda* Pygot is recorded in 1296, which is earlier than the earliest recorded occurrence of *emeraude*, and moreover there is no evidence that *emeraude* was ever shortened to *meraud*. On the whole it is probable that *Meraud* is a Cornish name, possibly a derivative of *mur* 'the sea' (cf. *Meriel* for *Muriel*).

Mercedes (f.) [mersā'dez]: Spanish elliptical for *Maria de Mercedes*, 'Mary of Mercies', an epithet of the Blessed Virgin. *Maria* was formerly seldom used as a christian name in Spain, being considered too sacred (see also DOLORES). *Mercedes* has been used a good deal in France and occasionally borrowed in England.

Mercy (f.): came into use as a christian name in the 17th C along with other similar names, e.g. *Faith*, *Hope*, *Charity*, &c.

Meredith (m.): a Welsh name (*Maredudd*), of which the second element is *iudd* 'lord'. It is still used as a christian name, though it is commoner as a surname. Lyford 1655 gives a characteristically fanciful etymology: '*Meredith*, but rather *Mere ductus* for *Mere-ducius*, brought together without mixing.'

Meriel, see MURIEL.

Mervyn (m.): a Welsh name now sometimes used in England, though usually by families of Welsh origin (e.g. two contemporary bishops, *Mervyn* Charles-Edwards and *Mervyn* Stockwood, and the writer and artist *Mervyn* Peake). The name was used in parts of England, notably Yorkshire, in the Middle Ages and gave rise to the surnames *Marvin*, *Mervin*, *Merfin*, *Mervyn*, *Murfin*, &c.

Meta, see MARGARET.

Methuselah (m.): Hebrew, first element 'man of', second element unknown. Occasionally used as a christian name in the 16th–18th C.

Micah (m.): a contraction of Hebrew *Micaiah* 'who is like Jehovah?' The name of one of the minor prophets, occasionally used as a christian name in England and USA since the 17th C.

Michael (m.): Hebrew 'Who is like the Lord?' The name of one of the archangels, the leader of the heavenly host, and hence the patron of the christian warrior. St. *Michael* and All Angels is one of the commonest church dedications (there are 687 in England and Wales) and the name was a favourite from the 12th C onwards, giving rise to a number of surnames, such as *Michell*, *Mitchell*, *Mitchelson*, *Mitchison*, which show that the common pronunciation was like that of the French *Michel*. *Mighel* was also a common medieval form of the name (cf. *Cursor Mundi* 'The sothfastenes and nothing hele, That thow hadest of seynt *Myghell*'), and this in turn was reduced to *Mihel, Miel,* or *Mial* (cf. the surnames *Mighill, Miall, Miell, Myhill*). Bardsley quotes Hudibras to show how this pronunciation persisted: 'At *Michael*'s term had many a trial, Worse than the Dragon and St. *Michael.*' The name was not used in Ireland much before the 17th C, but is now one of the commonest Irish names, often abbreviated to *Mick, Micky,* or *Mike.*

MICHAEL Cur 1196–1215, Ass 1218, FA 1303, 1346.
MICAHEL HR 1279.
MIKAEL HR 1279.
MICHELL Cov 1439, 13th C Brut.
MIHILL St. Michael Cornhill 1549.
MIGHELL St. Mary Aldermary 1598.
MYGHCHAELL St. Mary at Hill 1533.

Michelle (f.) [mēshĕl′]: French f. form of *Michel* (see MICHAEL), occasionally used in England, especially since the Beatles' song of that name.

Milborough, Milbury, see MILDRED.

Mildred (f.): Old English *Mildthryth*, compound of *milde* 'mild' and *thryth* 'power', 'strength'. Saints *Mildthryth* (died 700) and *Mildburh* (died 722?), daughters of a king of Mercia, and abbesses, were much venerated in the Middle Ages. The Middle English forms of the names were *Mildred* or *Meldred*, and *Milburh, Milbury,* or *Milborough. Milborough* survived in Shropshire till the 18th C and is still used (as *Milbrer*) by a gipsy family, the Locks. *Mildred* survived in infrequent use until the 19th C when it had a revival of popularity, and is now fairly common.

Miles (m.): Old German *Milo*, a name of doubtful etymology, possibly connected with Old Slavonic *milu* 'merciful'. The name was introduced into England by the Normans as *Miles* (*cas-sujet*) or *Milon* (*cas-régime*) and became fairly common, giving rise to the surnames *Miles, Mills, Milson.* It was less common from the 16th to 19th C but has been somewhat revived of late. In Ireland it has been used to render the native *Maolmuire* 'servant of Mary'.

MILO DB 1086, Cur 1196–1220.
MILON HR 1273.
MILES Coventry Mysteries 15th C.

Millicent, Melicent (f.): Old German *Amalasuintha*, compound of *amal* 'work' and *swintha* 'strong'; the name was current particularly among the Lombards and Burgundians, and appears early as *Malasintha*, whence *Melisenda*, the name of a daughter of Charlemagne. It was introduced into England in the French form *Melisent* at the end of the 12th C. The spelling *Milisent* occurs soon after, but *Melisent* was the more usual. *Millesant, Milicent* occur in the 15th C, and Lyford 1655 gives *Melicent*. *Millicent* is now the more usual form. In France there has been some confusion with *Mélusine*, the name of a water nymph (e.g. Maeterlinck's *Pelléas et Mélisande*). *Melesina*, a name which has been used since the 18th C in the Chenevix family and its connexions, probably derives from *Melusina* von der Schulenburg, Duchess of Kendal, whose daughter Petronella *Melusina* married Lord Chesterfield, the patron of Richard Chenevix, Bishop of Waterford. *Millicent* occurs as a man's name at Cambridge in 1584.

MELISENT Cur 1201.
MELISANT Cur 1213.
MILICENTA HR 1273.
MILLESENTA HR 1273.
MYLISANT Yorks Poll Tax 1379.

Mina (f.): pet-name for *Wilhelmina* (q.v.).

Minerva (f.): the name of the Roman goddess who was identified with the Greek Pallas Athene. It was probably of Etruscan origin and not, as is sometimes suggested, connected with *mens*. *Minerva* has occasionally been used as a christian name since the Renaissance, e.g. *Minerva* Dunn in Shropshire 1679.

Minna (f.): Old German *Minna* which may be from *minna* 'memory', 'love', or more probably from *min* 'small'. *Minna* was used in Shetland and parts of Scotland, and Scott's *Minna Troil* in *The Pirate* probably introduced it into England.

Minnie (f.): originally a Scottish pet-form of *Mary*. It became common in England in the 19th C and was often used as an independent name. Not in CMY.

Mirabel (f.) [mĭr'abel]: Latin *mirabilis* 'wonderful', 'glorious'. *Mirabella* or *Mirabilis* occurs in Latin records from the 12th C. The English form of the name was *Mirable*, *Mirabel*, and sometimes *Marabel* (cf. the surnames *Mirabel*, *Marrable*). It has not been noted between the middle of the 14th C and the beginning of the 19th C (*Maribella* Wise born 1810; *Mirabel* Saville born 1854). Congreve uses it as a man's name in *The Way of the World*.

MIRABILIS Cur 1210.
MIRABILLA FA 1346.
MIRABLE, MIRABEL HR 1273.

Miranda (f.): Latin *miranda* 'worthy to be admired'. Apparently invented by Shakespeare for the heroine of *The Tempest*, 'admired *Miranda*'. It is found at Rochdale in 1687 and in New England in 1827, and like other Shakespearian names (e.g. Cordelia, Hero, Imogen, Juliet) has been used a good deal in England in the present century.

Miriam (f.): Hebrew probably from *râma* 'high', 'longed for', 'desired', with prefixed *ma-*, hence 'wished-for child'. An alternative etymology is the accusative case of *merî*, 'rebellion', but this is less probable since this form of accusative died out very early and Semitic names are seldom if ever formed from the accusative case. For the phonology of the name see MARY. *Miriam* is the form of the name used in most versions of the Bible for the sister of Moses and Aaron. It came into use as a christian name in England after the Reformation, and is a favourite name among the Jews.

Moggy, see MARGARET.

Moira, Moyra (f.) [moy'ra]: apparently an attempt at rendering phonetically *Maire*, the Irish form of *Mary*. Not uncommon in England now.

Molly, see MARY.

Mona (f.): Irish *Muadhnait*, a diminutive of *muadh* 'noble', the name of an Irish saint. It has been used in England since the end of the 19th C, when many Irish names came into fashion.

Monday (f.): used as a christian name in the Middle Ages for children born on a *Monday*; Friday and Saturday were similarly used, cf. the surnames *Monday*, *Munday*, *Mundy*.

Monica (f.): the name of the mother of St. Augustine; the etymology is unknown; it is possibly of African origin. *Monique* is not uncommon in France. *Monica* occurs at Croston, Lancs., in *c.* 1640, and again at the end of the 18th C. It has become something of a favourite in the present century.

Montagu(e) (m.): the ancient and celebrated families of *Montacute*, *Montagu*, and *Montague* were founded by Drogo de *Montacute* or *Mont Aigu*, who came to England with the Conqueror and was granted lands in Somerset; he probably took his name from *Mont Aigu* near Caen. The use of *Montague* as a christian name is comparatively modern, and is paralleled by similar use of other names of noble families, e.g. *Cecil*, *Russell*, *Dudley*.

Morag (f.) [mōr′ag]: Gaelic, diminutive of *mor*(*a*) 'the sun'.

Mordecai (m.): Babylonian *Mardukâ* 'man of *Marduk*', i.e. a follower or worshipper of *Marduk*, the supreme god of Babylon. The name ought to be 'Mardecai', as the Septuagint's *Μαρδόχαιος* and the Vulgate's *Mardochaeus*, in agreement with the Babylonian form, show; but the Jewish scribes substituted *o* and *e* in the first two syllables as the characteristic vowels of *bōšeth* 'shame', thereby indicating their disapproval of a Jewish name containing the name of a heathen god. The name, from the Book of Esther, was used occasionally as a christian name during the 17th–19th C.

Morgan (m.): Welsh, cognate with Irish *Muirgen*. The first element is *mor* 'the sea'. It has been a favourite Welsh name from early times, and is used to render *Pelagius* in the Welsh Book of Common Prayer.

Morna (f.): Gaelic *muirne* 'beloved'.

Morris, see MAURICE.

Mortimer (m.): a surname from *Mortemer* in Normandy.

Morwenna (f.): St. *Morwenna* is the patron saint of *Morwenstow*. All that is known of her is a single mention in William of Worcester, 'Sancta *Morwinna*, virgo'; she is said to have been a daughter of St. Brychan. The name has continued to be used in Cornwall. The first element is probably *mor* 'the sea', and the name may be related to Welsh *morwaneg*, 'a wave of the sea'.

Moses (m.): the etymology of this name is obscure; it may be Egyptian rather than Hebrew. It became a favourite Jewish name after the dispersion. In Middle English it appears as *Moyse* or *Moyses* (cf. French *Moïse*), with the nickname *Moss*, and though some of the persons of this name recorded in medieval documents were Jews, it is possible that others were not. The surnames *Moyses*, *Moyse*, *Moyce*, *Moys*, *Moss* are apparently of this origin and point to the use of the name by non-Jews in the period during which surnames were coming into use. The 17th-C Puritans made use of *Moses* as a christian name, and it continued to be so used occasionally in the 18th C (e.g. the younger son of the Vicar of Wakefield).

MOYSES DB 1086.
MOSES Cur 1200, 1205, 1210.
MOSSE (a Jew) HR 1273.
MOSSEUS (a Jew) QW 1292.

Moyna (f.): an Irish name, perhaps *Muadhnait* (see MONA).

Moyra, see MOIRA.

Mungo (m.): Gaelic 'amiable', an epithet applied to St. Kentigern, and occasionally used as a christian name in Scotland, e.g. *Mungo* Park the explorer born 1771. It is most frequent in the saint's own city of Glasgow.

Murdoch (m.): Gaelic *Muireadhach* 'sea man'. Now usually a surname, but still sometimes used as a christian name. *Murdac* Miles occurs as the name of a sub-tenant in the Sussex DB. The Irish form of the name is *Murtagh*.

Muriel, Meriel (f.): this is a difficult name, probably of Celtic origin. There is an Irish name *Muirgheal*, compound of *muir* 'the sea' and *geal* 'bright'. *Mýrgjol* occurs in the Landnámabók as the name of a King of Dublin. *Muriel* is first found in Brittany and Normandy in the 11th C, when it seems to have been borne by several nuns, e.g. *Muriel* mother of Thomas of Bayeux, Archbishop of York (1070–1100), and a mysterious *Muriel*, apparently also a nun, to whom poems were addressed by Baudri de Bourgueil (1046–1130) and by Serlan de Bayeux (1050–1113). William I is said by Wace to have had a half-sister of the name. It does not appear to have been current elsewhere on the Continent, which supports the supposition that it was a Celtic name. The Normans brought it to England. *Muriel*, *Meriel*, and *Miriel* are common in the 12th and 13th C, giving rise to the surnames *Merrall*, *Merrell*, *Merrill*, *Muriel*, *Murrell(s)*: it was also a favourite name for English Jewesses, perhaps as a rendering of *Miriam*. Less common in later centuries, it survived in country districts; in a list of Yorkshire recusants in 1604, for instance, there are five women named *Meriall* or *Meryall*, and John Coke of Holkham in 1640 married *Meriel* Wheatley. CMY in 1863 wrote: 'an almost obsolete English name', but in her 2nd edition 1884 she altered this to 'both it and *Meriel* were once common and have lately been revived'. A correspondence in N & Q 1872–7 elicited the fact that it was then very rare. Lord Lyttelton wrote in 1874: 'The name Muriel is an eminent one in my family and my eldest daughter is so named. In our old letters it is spelt *Muriel*, *Meriel*, *Maryell*.' The revival of which CMY speaks may have been partly due to Mrs. Craik's immensely popular novel *John Halifax, Gentleman* (1856), one character in which is named *Muriel* 'after the rather peculiar name' of her father's mother. *Meriel* is still used in some families.

MURIEL Cur 1198, 1200, 1205, HR 1273.
MURIELLA Cur 1199, FA 1285.
MIRIELLA Cur 1199.
MIRIELD HR 1273.
MIRIEL, MIRIELDA Cur 1205, 1207.
MIRIALD Cur 1207.

Murtagh, see MURDOCH.

Myra (f.): this name appears to have been invented by Fulke Greville, Lord Brooke (1554–1628), who wrote love poems to a lady whom he so designated (e.g. in his poem 'I, with whose colours *Myra* dressed her hair').

Myrtle, Myrtilla (f.): the name of the shrub, first used as a christian name in the 19th C.

Mysie, see MAISIE.

N

Nadine (f.) [nah'dēn]: a French version of Russian *Nadezhda* 'hope'; occasionally used in England in the present century.

Nahum (m.): Hebrew 'consoling', the name of a Hebrew prophet, sometimes used as a christian name since the Reformation, e.g. *Nahum* Tate (1652–1715), the co-author of the metrical psalms.

Nan(ny), Nancy, see ANN.

Naomi (f.) [nā'omĕ]: Hebrew 'pleasaunce', the name of the mother-in-law of Ruth. It came into use as a christian name in the 17th C.

Napoleon (m.): Italian *Neapoleone* or *Napoleone*, apparently a derivative of *Neapolis* (Naples); the name of a 4th-C saint martyred at Alexandria. It was used by the Orsini and other Italian families in the Middle Ages and later, though never common. *Napoleone Buonaparte* gallicized his name as *Napoléon Bonaparte.* His name has not often been used in France, either in his lifetime or later; dictators in general seem to discourage the use of their own names, e.g. German parents were advised against calling their sons Adolf. There have been a few examples of its use in England.

Narcissus (m.): Greek νάρκισσος, the name of a flower and of the youth loved by Echo, who died for love of his own image. The name was a common one for Greek slaves. St. *Narcissus* was Bishop of Jerusalem in A.D. 195, and his name has occasionally been used in Italy. The English use of the name, which is post-Renaissance, is very rare and has reference to the Greek myth rather than to the saint.

Natalia, Natalie (f.): from Latin *natale* (*domini*), i.e. Christmas Day. St. *Natalia*, wife of St. Adrian, has a place in the Calendar of the Greek Church, and *Natalia*, with its diminutive *Natasha*, is a favourite name in Russia. *Natalie* is used in France and Germany and occasionally in England. More recently, *Natasha* is sometimes used as an independent name.

Natasha, see NATALIA.

Nathan (m.): Hebrew 'gift', the name of a prophet, occasionally used as a christian name since the 17th C, but mainly a Jewish name.

Nathanael, Nathaniel (m.): Hebrew 'God has given', the name of one of the apostles, generally known by his patronymic *Bartholomew* (q.v.). This name has only been noted once in the Middle Ages, but it became fairly common after the Reformation, often abbreviated to *Nat*.

Ned, see EDWARD.

Nehemiah (m.): Hebrew 'consolation of Jehovah', the name of one of the Hebrew prophets. A common name among the 17th-C Puritans.

Neil, see NIGEL.

Nell(y) (f.): a pet-form of *Ellen*, *Eleanor*, and *Helen* (qq.v.). *Nel* or *Nell* is not uncommon in medieval records, and though it is often a man's name (*Neil*), it is also sometimes a woman's. *Nell* Gwynn's name was *Eleanor*.

Nessie, Nest(a) (f.): Welsh diminutives for *Agnes* (q.v.). The most famous example of the name is the 11th-C Welsh princess,

Nest, mistress of Henry I. *Nesta* is recorded in Worcestershire and Gloucestershire as early as 1199.

Netta, Nettie (f.): Scottish diminutive of *Janet* (q.v.).

Neville (m.): this was originally a Norman surname, the family having been founded by Gilbert de *Nevil*, one of the companions of the Conqueror, who took his name from *Néville* or *Neuville* in Normandy. The family was widespread and powerful in the Middle Ages. The earliest example of its use as a christian name that has been noted is one *Nevil* or *Nevell* Kay in Lancashire at the beginning of the 17th C.

Niall, see NIGEL.

Nicholas (m.): Latin *Nicolaus* from Greek Νικόλαος, compound of *νίκη* 'victory' and *λαός* 'the people'. St. *Nicholas*, Bishop of Myra *c.* 300, is regarded as the patron saint of children, sailors, pawnbrokers, and wolves, and was much venerated in both Eastern and Western Churches. The name is found in use in England before the Norman Conquest, usually applied to a monk. DB mentions two men of the name, one of whom held TRE. In the 12th C it became a favourite, and some idea of its popularity in the Middle Ages can be gained from the number of common surnames derived from it. The usual English form of the name was *Nicol*, and Bardsley gives no fewer than 16 different spellings of the patronymic formed directly from it, in addition to the various spellings of *Nicolson*, and others formed from diminutives such as *Nicolin*, *Nicolet*, *Nick* (whence *Nixon*), *Cole* (whence *Cole(s)*, *Colley*, *Collis*), *Colin* (whence *Collin(s)*, &c.), *Colet* (whence *Collett*, &c.), *Colinet*. The intrusive *h* is found as early as the 12th C; *Nicholaus* occurs e.g. in *The Owl and the Nightingale*. The spelling of the name was probably influenced by medieval Latin spellings of Greek words containing χ, φ, θ, ῥ, which varied between *k/ch*, *p/ph*, *t/th*, *r/rh*. *Nicholas* became much less common after the Reformation. The usual abbreviations are now *Nichol* and *Nick*. *Colin* (q.v.) is now an independent name.

NICOLAUS DB 1086, Cur 1186–1220.
NICHOLAS HR 1273.

NICOLL HR 1273.
NICHOLE HR 1273.
NICHOL Yorks Poll Tax 1379, Cl 1348.
NYCOLAS Lincs 1535.

Nicodemus (m.): Greek *Νικόδημος*, a compound of *νίκη* 'victory' and *δῆμος* 'the people'; the name of 'the ruler of the Jews', who came to Jesus by night (John iii. 1–21). It was evidently a Greek name adopted by the Jews (cf. *Philip*). The apocryphal 'Gospel of *Nicodemus*' was very popular in the Middle Ages and was the basis of many passion plays. *Nicodemus* was a common name in the 17th C and survived into the 19th C.

Nicola, Nicolette (f.): Italian and French f. forms of *Nicholas* (q.v.). *Nicholaa* is not infrequent in medieval Latin records, but is no doubt merely a latinization of *Nicholas* when borne by a woman, who would in the vernacular have been simply *Nicol* or *Nicolas*. *Nicole*, *Nicolette*, *Colette* are fairly common in France and are occasionally borrowed in England.

Nigel, Niall, Neil (m.): the history of this name is complicated and rather obscure, but it is probably of Irish origin, *Niul*, a derivative of *niadh* 'champion'. From Ireland it must have been introduced fairly early into Iceland, where it appears as *Njal* (e.g. the *Njalssaga*) and thence to Scandinavia, and eventually to France by the Normans, in the form *Nel* or *Nele*. It was latinized as *Nigellus* and taken to be a diminutive of *niger* 'black'. In England it was well established amongst the Danes and Norsemen before the Norman Conquest, and in DB there are many tenants of the name holding both then and TRE. *Nel*, *Nele*, *Neel* appear to have been the usual forms of the name in England; it gave rise to the surnames *Neil*, *Neild*, *Neal*, *Nell*, *Nelson*, *Nielson*, &c., as well as *FitzNeel*. In the 15th C there arose a back-formation from the Latin *Nigellus*, e.g. Oseney 1460 has *Nygell*, *Nigelle*, but Lyford 1655 gives *Neale* as still in use. *Niall* is the correct form, *Neill* being the possessive case. Both *Neil* and *Nigel* are now mainly Scottish; *Niall* is the usual modern Irish form.

NIGELLUS DB 1086, Cur 1187–1220, HR 1273, FA 1346.
NEL HR 1273.

Nell HR 1273.
Neel Cl 1303, FA 1346.
Nele Yorks Poll Tax 1379.

Nina (f.) [nē′na]: Russian diminutive of *Anne* (q.v.) (cf. French *Ninon*, *Ninette*), occasionally used in England since the middle of the 19th C.

Ninian (m.): *Ninian* or *Ninias* was the name of a saint of British origin (died 432) who founded a church at Whithorn in Wigtownshire and evangelized the southern Picts. It is probably the same as *Nennius*, the name of the 8th-C British historian; the Irish *Ninidh* may be a cognate name. *Ninian* is now almost entirely Scottish, but it was formerly current in Yorkshire and Northumberland; it is, for example, frequent in early 17th-C lists of Yorkshire recusants.

Nita (f.) [nē′ta]: Spanish abbreviation of *Juanita*, itself a diminutive of *Juana* (= *Joan*). *Nita* is now occasionally used in USA and England.

Noah (m.): Hebrew 'long lived', literally 'long', being a shortened representation of the name of the Sumerian Noah, Zi-ud-sudda 'life of days long', in the Epic of Gilgamesh. It was not uncommon in the 17th C, and survived in use in the 18th and 19th C both in England and the USA as an independent name.

Noel (m., f.): Old French *nouel*, *noel* from Latin *natalis* (*dies*), used as a christian name for children of either sex born on Christmas Day. It was fairly common in the Middle Ages from about 1200, and gave rise to the surnames *Noel*, *Nowell*. *Christmas* was also sometimes used as a christian name. Cf. also *Tiffany*, *Pentecost*, *Easter*, *Midwinter*, *Loveday* which were all formerly used as christian names.

Noel HR 1273.

Nona (f.): Latin f. of *nonus* 'ninth'. Sometimes used for a ninth child (cf. *Decima*, *Octavia*), but also without reference to number.

Nonie (f.): pet-form of *Nora* (q.v.).

Nora(h) (f.): Irish abbreviated form of *Honora* (q.v.), now and for long past an independent name.

Noreen (f.) [nōr'ēn]: Irish *Nóirín*, diminutive of *Nora*, now often used as an independent name. *Norinna* is found in 1213.

Norma (f.): the modern use of this name seems to date from Bellini's opera *Norma* (1831), but one instance of it is recorded in 1203 (Cur). The etymology is obscure, though it may be Latin *norma* 'rule', 'precept', 'pattern'.

Norman (m.): Old English *Northman* and cognate Old German *Nordemann* were both used as christian names (cf. *German*, *Franco*). *Norman* was fairly common in England before the Norman Conquest, and in DB there is mention of several tenants of this name who had held land TRE. It continued in use for some centuries and gave rise to the surnames *Norman* and *Normand*, but died out in England about the 14th C, though it continued in Scotland where it is used as an equivalent of the MacLeod name *Tormond* (= Old Norse *Dormund*). CMY regards it as being in her time exclusively Scottish, and its modern revival in England may be due in part to her use of it in *The Daisy Chain* (1856).

NORMANN(US) DB 1086, HR 1273.
NORMAN HR 1273.

O

Obadiah (m.): Hebrew 'serving Jehovah', the name of one of the Hebrew prophets. It was a common christian name in the 17th C, and continued in use, particularly in America, until the 19th C.

Obedience (f.): rather common in the 17th C.

Octavia (f.): Latin f. of *Octavius* (q.v.).

Octavius (m.): Latin derivative of *octavus* 'eighth', the name of a Roman *gens*, the most famous member of which was the Emperor Augustus. It is sometimes used in England, but has naturally become somewhat rare in an age when eighth children are almost unknown.

Odette, see OTTILIA.

Odo (m.): Old German *Audo*, later *Odo* or *Otho*, derivative of *auda*, the equivalent of Old English *ead* 'rich'. It was introduced into England by the Normans, who used both *d* and *th* forms; thus in DB we find *Odo, Oddo, Otho, Otto*. The commonest form at a later date was *Otes* (the Old French *cas-sujet*). The surnames *Oddy, Oddie, Od(e)y, Odlin(g), Oat, Oat(e)s, Oatson*, and others are derived from it. Camden says '*Othes* an old name in England, drawn from *Otho*'. *Otes* is found in Cornwall as late as 1547, *Ottie* in 1597. *Odo* was used in Scotland to render the Gaelic *Aodh*. The diminutive *Odinel* was also used. *Otho* has been used in the Cooke family of Lancashire from the 17th C to the present time, and *Ot(h)i* is still used as a gipsy name. The name was revived in the form *Odo* in a few families in the 19th C. The modern German *Otto* is also now occasionally used.

ODO Reg 1067–71.
OTTO, OTHO, ODO, ODDO DB 1086.
ODO Cur 1189, FA 1346.
ODE, ODDE HR 1273.
OTES Cur 1189–1220, HR 1273, Yorks Poll Tax 1379.
HOTYS HR 1273.

Ogier (m.): Old German *Audagar, Autger*, compound of *auda* 'rich' and *ger* 'spear', so that it is the equivalent of Old English *Eadgar* (see EDGAR). It became *Oger* or *Ogier* in Old French, and was the name of one of the paladins of Charlemagne, *Ogier le Danois* or *Holger Danske*. It was introduced into England by the Normans and occurs some 7 or 8 times in DB. It was not uncommon in the 12th and 13th C and gave rise to the surnames *Odger(s)*.

OGER(I)US DB 1086.
OGER Cl 1270.
OGGERY Testa de Neville 13th C.

Olaf (m.): Old Norse *Anleifr*, of which the first element is cognate with Old German *ano* 'ancestor', and the second means 'relics', 'remains'. It was and still is a favourite name in all Scandinavian countries on account of *Olaf* Trygvasson (956–1000), King of Norway, and St. *Olaf*, King of Norway, died 1030, who introduced Christianity into that country. It was used by the Danes in England, but does not seem to have survived the Norman Conquest. In Gaelic the name became *Amhlaibh* (Aulay), whence the Hebrides surname *Macaulay*. It is often rendered by *Humphrey* in Ireland.

Olga (f.): a Russian name of Scandinavian origin, from Norse *helga* 'holy'. St. *Olga* (9th C) of Kiev was reputed to be the first Russian convert to Christianity. Used in England in recent times like other Russian names (cf. *Vera*, *Sonia*).

Olive, Olivia (f.): this is apparently Latin *oliva* 'olive', used as a personal name. In the Roman martyrology there is a St. *Oliva*, a virgin of Anagni of unknown date, and also a St. *Oliva*, venerated in the place so named and the patroness of olive-trees, which looks suspiciously as though she started life as a tutelary goddess. *Oliva* is found in Latin records in England as early as 1203 and was not uncommon in the 13th and 14th C, the usual English version being *Oliff* (cf. surnames *Olive*, *Oliffe*, *Olliffe*) and the diminutives *Olivet*, *Ollett*. *Olive* occurs in the 16th C and Lyford 1655 gives *Olive* as a christian name. In the 18th C the Italian *Olivia* came into fashion, and *Olive* survived only in rustic use, but it has now been revived. *Olivia* has maintained its place, probably on account of Shakespeare's *Twelfth Night*, when most of the 18th-C Italian and Latin versions of christian names have died out.

OLIVA Cur 1203–15, HR 1273, Yorks Poll Tax 1379.
OLIF Yorks Poll Tax 1379.
OLYFFE St. Columb 1579.
OLYFF St. Columb 1581.

Oliver (m.): the name of one of the most famous of the peers of Charlemagne and hence a favourite medieval name. The French form was *Olivier* and it has usually been taken to be the Old French *olivier*, *oliver* 'an olive-tree', from Latin *olivarius*. Alternatively it has been derived from Norse *Olaf* (q.v.). But there is no evidence for the existence of a name *Olivarius* and almost all the other names connected with the older versions of the Charlemagne cycle are of Teutonic origin, whilst derivation from *Olaf* is phonetically difficult. *Oliver* may therefore represent some such name as Old German *Alfihar* (which is on record and is the equivalent of Old English *Ælfhere* 'elf-host') adapted later to a fancied derivation from *olivarius*. For the phonetic development compare modern German *Olfert* from *Alfhard*, and *Olbrich* from *Alberich*. *Oliver* first occurs in England as the name of a subtenant in DB. It was moderately common in the Middle Ages (cf. the surnames *Ol(l)iver*, *Olver*, *Oliverson*; and *Ollier* from the Breton form of the name), and continued so in the 16th and 17th C. After the Restoration it went completely out of fashion owing to association with Cromwell, and it was not until the end of the 19th C that it came back into general favour. The old nickname *Noll* is now seldom heard.

OLIVERUS DB 1086, Cur 1199–1220.
OLIVER Cl 1249, HR 1273.
HOLIVER Yorks Poll Tax 1379.

Olivia, see OLIVE.

Olwen (f.): Welsh, literally 'white track'. In the Welsh tale of 'Culhwch and Olwen' it is said that 'fair white trefoils sprang up behind her wherever she went and for that reason was she called Olwen'.

Olympias (f.): Greek 'Ὀλυμπιάς 'of Olympus', the name of the mother of Alexander the Great, and also of a saint, a disciple of St. Chrysostom. It was on account of the saint, no doubt, that *Olimpe* became a christian name in France. *Olimpias* occurs in England in the 13th C. Lyford 1655 gives *Olympia*, and an *Olympia* Morshead was living in 1745, and other examples of the name are on record.

OLIMPIAS Cur 1207–15.

Oonagh, see UNA.

Ophelia (f.): probably Greek *ὠφελία* 'help', 'succour'. The name seems to have been coined by Sannazaro, in whose *Arcadia* (1504) it appears as *Ofelia*. John Rickman (born 1587) married *Ophelia* Marchant of Bath, but this appears to be an isolated example. Shakespeare's use of *Ophelia* in *Hamlet* has led to its occasional use as a christian name in England and USA.

Oriana (f.) [ōr'ĕahna]: *Oriande, Oriante* are frequent in Old French romances, e.g. as the name of the mistress of Amadis de Gaul. It is presumably a derivative of Latin *oriri* 'to rise'. Madrigal writers applied the name *Oriana* to Queen Elizabeth, and Ben Jonson used it for Anne of Denmark 'quasi *oriens Anna*'. *Oriana* Palfreyman of W. Toynton, Lincs., was excommunicated in 1602. Tennyson's 'Ballad of Oriana' owed the name to his friend *Oriana* Reinagle, daughter of R. R. Reinagle and *Oriana*, granddaughter of Sir Mitford Crowe.

Oriel (f.): Old German *Aurildis, Orieldis*, which Förstemann considers a compound of *aur-* (= *aus* 'fire'), and *hildi* 'strife'. The name was apparently introduced into England by the Normans, and is found in the 13th C as *Oriolt, Oriolda, Oriholt, Oriel*. It does not seem to have taken permanent root, and soon died out. The recent use of the name may be a revival, but is more probably a use of the name of *Oriel* College, Oxford, which is derived from the word *oriel* 'a window', for the history of which see OED s.v.

Original (m.): used as a christian name in the 16th–18th C, usually for a first-born son.

Orlando (m.): Italian form of *Roland* (q.v.). *Orlando* was not uncommon in England in the 16th C when there was a fashion for Italian names, e.g. *Ferdinando* (q.v.). The best-known example of the name is *Orlando* Gibbons the composer (1583–1625), one of whose brothers was named *Ferdinando*.

Osanna, see HOSANNA.

Osbert (m.): Old English *Osbeorht*, compound of *os* 'a god' (a word which is not recorded except in compounds) and *beorht* 'bright'. It was principally a Northumbrian name in the Old English period and survived the Norman Conquest, being reinforced by Norman French *Osbert* from cognate Old German *Ansobert*; it was not uncommon in the 12th–14th C, is found occasionally in subsequent centuries, was revived, with other Old English names, in the 19th C, and is now fairly common again.

OSBERT(US) Reg 1066, DB 1086, Cur 1196–1220, FA 1284, 1303, 1363.
HOSBERTUS FA 1285.

Osborn (m.): Old English *Osbeorn*, compound of *os* 'a god' and *beorn*, a poetical word meaning 'man' (the cognate Norse word *bjorn* means 'bear'). Both *Osbeorn* and the corresponding Norse name *Asbjorn* were in general use in England before the Norman Conquest, and were then reinforced by the Norman version. DB mentions several tenants named *Osbernus* and others who had held TRE. It remained in general use during the Middle Ages and gave rise to the common surnames *Osborn(e)*, *Osbourn(e)*, *Osbern*, *Osburn*. *Osberne* is recorded as a christian name as late as 1489, and Lyford (1655) gives it in his list.

OSBERN(US) DB 1086, Reg 1087–97.
OSEBERNE HR 1273.
OSBARN Yorks Poll Tax 1379.

Oscar (m.): Old English *Osgar*, compound of *os* 'a god' and *gar* 'spear'. Both this and the corresponding Norse *Asgeirr* were in use in England before the Norman Conquest, but do not seem to have long survived it. Macpherson in his Ossianic poems gave the name *Oscar* to the son of Ossian: the name also appears in some old Irish poems as *Osgar*, and had doubtless been carried to Ireland by the Danes. Napoleon's Ossianic enthusiasm caused him to bestow the name *Oscar* upon his godson, son of Bernadotte, who later succeeded his father as *Oscar* I, King of Sweden, and *Oscar* Wilde was a godson of *Oscar* II, King of Sweden, whom his father had treated and cured. The great vogue of *Ossian* on the Continent has led to the general use of the name *Oscar* there. CMY, in mentioning this, adds that with us, however, 'it has descended to dogs'. But in fact it has, since her time, been used a good deal in England and Ireland.

OSGARUS DB 1086.

Osmond (m.): Old English *Osmund*, compound of *os* 'a god' and *mund* 'protection'. Both it and the corresponding Norse *Asmundr* were in general use in England before the Norman Conquest, after which it was reinforced by the Norman version (*Osmond*). DB gives several tenants of this name and others who held TRE. St. *Osmond* Bishop of Salisbury (died 1099) was a Norman. The surnames *Osmond*, *Osmund*, *Osman*, *Osment*, *Osmint*, *Osmon*, *Osmand* are derived from it. It became less common after the 13th C, but examples have been noted at Cambridge in the 16th and 17th C, and Lyford (1655) gives it in his list of names.

OSMUND(US), HOSMUNDUS, HOSMUNT DB 1086.
OSMUND Cur 1199–1215, HR 1273.

Oswald (m.): Old English *Osweald*, compound of *os* 'a god' and *weald* 'power'. There was a corresponding Norse name *Asvald*. St. *Oswald* (605–42), King of Northumbria, and St. *Oswald* (died 992), Archbishop of York, no doubt helped to establish the popularity of the name, which has never (like most other Old English names in *Os*-) gone out of use. The surnames *Oswald*, *Oswell*, *Oswill* are derived from it. In the 16th, 17th, and 18th C the christian name *Oswald* is found in the forms *Oswell*, *Oswall*, or *Ozwell*. It has been in regular use in the Mosley family since the end of the 16th C.

OSUUALD(US), OSUUOLD(US), OSUUOL DB 1086.
OSEWOLD Chaucer *Cant. Tales c.* 1387.
OSWOLD 14th C Legendary.
OSWELL St. Antholin 1540.
OSWALL St. Mary Aldermary 1620.
OZWELL Cant Cath Reg 1744.

Oswin (m.): Old English *Oswin*, compound of *os* 'a god' and *wine* 'friend'. It remained in use until the 14th C. and was occasionally revived in the 19th C.

Ottilia (f.): *Odala*, *Odila*, *Otila*, *Odilia* are found in Old German as a woman's name, being a derivative of *othal* 'fatherland'. The corresponding man's name *Odila* occurs in Old English. St. *Ottilia* (French *Odille*) was a 7th-C virgin who became the patron saint of Alsace. *Ottilie* is not uncommon in Germany, and *Odille* and its diminutive *Odette* are fairly common in France. They are occasionally borrowed in England.

Otto, see ODO.

Owen (m.): a common Welsh name; in Middle English romances often spelled *Owain*, *Owayne*, *Ywain*. It has been supposed to be derived from Latin *Eugenius*; cf. *Emrys* from *Ambrose*, *Gladys* from *Claudia*, but see EWEN.

OUEN, OUUIN, OWINE DB 1086.
OUEIN Lib Lond 10th C.
UWEN ASC 10th C.
OENUS Pipe Roll 1164.
OWEN Cur 1200, Cov 1492, HR 1273.
OWEYN HR 1273.
OWYNE Cov 1524.

P

Paddy, see PATRICIA, PATRICK.

Padraig, see PATRICK.

Pagan (m.): Latin *paganus*, originally 'rustic', 'villager', later 'heathen'. Its use as a personal name appears to be late (cf. *Urbanus*). It was introduced into England by the Normans (*Edmundus fil. Pagani* occurs in DB), and it soon became common, the usual vernacular form of the name being *Payn* (cf. French *païen* 'pagan'); the surnames *Pagan*, *Pain(e)*, and *Payne*, and *Paynel*, *Paganel*, *Pannet* from diminutive forms, testify to its popularity. It did not, however, survive the Reformation as a christian name.

PAGANUS, PAGEN DB 1086.
PAGANUS Cur 1189–1220, FA 1303.
PAGAN Pipe Roll 1165, HR 1273.
PAYNE Cl 1249.
PAYN HR 1273.
PAGANE Godstow 1450.

PAGANEL or PAIN Writs of Parliament 1301.
PAYNEL HR 1273.

Pamela (f.) [pă'me*la*]: apparently invented by Sir Philip Sidney as the name of a character in his *Arcadia* (1590), and pronounced *Pamēla*. Richardson adopted it for the heroine of his first novel *Pamela* (1740), and the great vogue of that book led to its being sometimes used as a christian name. It is found in New England in 1812. CMY says: 'still not uncommon among the lower classes.' A writer in N & Q 1904 mentions it as an unusual name. Within the present century it has become rather fashionable. There seems to have been some doubt as to its pronunciation in the 18th C. Fielding, in *Joseph Andrews*, wrote: 'She told me that they had a daughter of a very strange name, *Pamĕla* or *Pamēla*; some pronounce it one way, and some the other.' It is now always pronounced *Pă'mela*.

Parnel, see PETRONELLA.

Pascoe (m.): Middle English *Pask* 'Easter'. Both *Pask* and the adjective *Pascal* were used as christian names in the Middle Ages. *Pascal* was still used as late as the middle of the 19th C and survives as *Pascoe* in Cornwall.

PASCHE HR 1273.
PASCOWE St. Columb 1571.
PASCOW St. Columb 1542.
PASKELL St. Columb 1608.

Pat, see PATRICIA, PATRICK.

Patience (f.): Like other abstract nouns, came into use as a christian name in the 17th C, e.g. Sir Thomas Carew, Speaker of the House of Commons in the reigns of James I and Charles I, had four daughters named *Patience*, *Temperance*, *Silence*, and *Prudence*. *Patience* was in the 17th C often also a man's name. It is sometimes abbreviated to *Patty*.

Patricia (f.): f. of *Patricius* (see PATRICK). *Patricia* occurs from time to time in medieval Latin records, but then merely denotes a woman bearing the name *Patrick.* Its use as a genuine christian name seems to have begun in Scotland in the 18th C, but it was uncommon until the present century, when it became popular owing to Princess Victoria *Patricia* Helena Elizabeth of Connaught (born 1886), usually known as Princess *Patricia.* It is frequently abbreviated to *Pat* or *Paddy.*

Patrick (m.): Latin *patricius* 'nobleman', the name adopted by the apostle of Ireland, whose original name was Sucat, when he was consecrated as a missionary. It has been chiefly used in Ireland and Scotland, but was common in the North of England from the 12th C (cf. the surnames *Patrick(son)*, *Pate(s)*, *Pat(e)y*, *Paton*, *Patten*, *Patti(n)son*, *Pat(t)erson*). In Scotland *Peter* was formerly used as a diminutive of *Patrick*, e.g. *Patrick*, Lord Robertson (1794–1855), 'Lord *Peter*, Who broke the laws of God and man and metre'. Black cites evidence that the two names were interchangeable in Scotland as late as 1867. In Ireland, where it is one of the commonest men's names, *Padraig* is the usual spelling and the pet-forms *Pat*, *Patsy*, *Pad*, *Paddy*, and *Packy* are in general use.

PATRICIUS Cur 1200–12, FA 1284, Yorks Poll Tax 1379.
PATERICK 14th C Legendary.
PATRYCKE *Cocke Lorelle's Bote c.* 1515.
PATTRIK St. Mary at Hill 1527.

Patty, see MARTHA, PATIENCE.

Paul (m.): Latin *paulus* 'small', the name of Saul of Tarsus after his conversion. *Paul* occurs in England before the Norman Conquest only as a monk's name. St. *Paul* was not an object of particular devotion in the Middle Ages; of 326 English churches dedicated to him, 283 are double dedications to SS. Peter and Paul, and of the 43 remaining ones, some at least were originally to the Celtic St. *Pol* or to St. *Paulinus.* I have found the christian name *Paul* recorded only 4 times in the 13th C (probably the same man in three cases), and there can be no doubt that it was a very rare name in the Middle Ages. Bardsley, it is true, says that it was one of the favourite names in the 13th C, but though he derived from it many surnames (e.g. *Paul*, *Pawl(e)*, *Paulin*, *Pawley*, *Paulet*, *Powell*, *Pollit*), it is significant that he does not give a single example of it as a christian name, and he was certainly wrong about the origin of some of these names. It was not until the 17th C that *Paul* had a certain degree of popularity, and even so it never equalled that of many other Biblical names. It has always been commoner in Spain (*Pablo*) and Italy (*Paolo*) and Russia (*Pavel*) than in England, France, or Germany.

PAUL Cur 1200, 1207, 1210.
POWEL Magd. *c.* 1260.
POWLE Coventry Mystery 15th C.

Paula (f.): a German f. form of *Paul*. Occasionally used in England in recent times. It is the name of the heroine of Pinero's popular play *The Second Mrs. Tanqueray*, which may have helped its use in this country.

Paulina, Pauline (f.): Latin *Paulina*, f. of *Paulinus* (q.v.). St. *Paulina* was a 4th-C martyr, and the name is occasionally met with in the 12th and 13th C. It has been most common in France, where *Pauline* is regarded as a f. form of *Paul*. *Paulina* and *Pauline* are both occasionally used in England.

Paulinus (m.) [pawlī'nus]: Latin derivative of *paulus* 'small'. St. *Paulinus* (died 644) was one of a second mission sent to Britain by St. Gregory to assist St. Augustine, and there are a number of churches dedicated to him. A *Paulinus* is mentioned in DB as having held land TRE and *Paulin* or *Pawlin* is not uncommon in the 12th and 13th C. The latest example noted is *Paulin* Phelips (died 1782) whose name occurs in a Hunts Clergy List.

PAULINUS DB 1086, Cur 1203, HR 1273, FA 1316.
PAULIN HR 1273.

Pearl (f.), used in recent times as a christian name (cf. *Ruby*, *Emerald*), and sometimes as a pet-name for Margaret (*margarita* = pearl).

Peg(gy), see MARGARET.

Penelope (f.) [penĕl'opĕ]: Greek *Πηνελόπη*, *Πηνελόπεια* (said to be connected with πήνη 'a bobbin'), the name of the faithful wife of Odysseus. It was first used as a christian name in the 16th C, e.g. *Penelope* (1562–1607) daughter of William Devereux, Earl of Essex, wife of Lord Rich and the *Stella* of Sir Philip Sidney. *Penelope* has never been common but has been used regularly since its introduction. It is rather more frequent in Ireland where it was used to render the native name *Fionnghuala* (see FENELLA). It is sometimes abbreviated to *Pen* or *Penny*. The gipsy name *Peneli* may be a form of *Penelope*.

Pentecost (m., f.): from Greek πεντηκοστή (ἡμέρα), 'fiftieth (day)', the Greek name for Whitsuntide. *Pentecost* is found as a christian name from the beginning of the 13th C and continued in general use until the 17th C. Occasional examples occur later, and it was in use in Cornwall until the end of the 19th C. It was used indifferently for men and women.

PENTECOST Pipe Roll 1165, Cur 1200–7, Cl 1331.

Perceval, Percival (m.): this name seems to have been invented by Crestien de Troyes in the 12th C for the hero of his poem *Percevale*; it is French *perce-val* 'pierce (the) valley'. There are not many early examples of its use as a christian name, the earliest noted being Sir *Percivale* Sowdon 1375. The surname *Perceval* is found rather earlier; it was a Norman name derived from the place-name *Percheval*.

PERCYVALLUS Yorks Poll Tax 1379.
PERCYVELL, PERSIVELL Yorks Rec 1604.
PERSEFALL St. Jas. Clerkenwell 1666.

Percy (m.): this is the name of the famous family which is descended from William de *Perci*, one of the companions of the Conqueror, who took his name from the village of *Perci* near St. Lô in Normandy. The use of *Percy* as a christian name seems at first to have been confined to persons connected with the family. The earliest example noted is Lord *Percy* Seymour (died 1721), son of the 6th Duke of Somerset and Lady Elizabeth *Percy*, heiress of the Percy family. His sister Lady Catherine Seymour married Sir William Wyndham, and her 2nd son, later Earl of

Thomond, was also called *Percy*. Another example was the poet *Percy* Bysshe Shelley (born 1792). The connexion between the Shelley and Percy families was very remote; the poet's grandfather married (as his second wife) the heiress of the Sidneys, Earls of Leicester, and the 2nd Earl had in 1615 married Dorothy *Percy*, daughter of the 9th Earl of Northumberland. She was mother of Algernon Sidney, 'the patron saint of the Whigs', and it may have been Sir Timothy's Whiggism rather than his snobbishness which made him call his son *Percy*. In the course of the 19th C the name became more and more generally used, and Shelley may himself have contributed to its popularity.

Perdita (f.) [per'dĭta]: from f. of Latin *perditus* 'lost'. Shakespeare invented the name for the heroine of *A Winter's Tale*: 'and for the babe Is counted lost for ever, *Perdita* I prithee call 't.' Like other Shakespearian names, it is now occasionally used as a christian name.

Peregrine (m.) [pĕr'egrĭn]: Latin *peregrinus* 'stranger' or 'traveller', later 'pilgrim'. St. *Peregrinus* (died 643) was a hermit near Modena who was regarded as the patron of Modena and Lucca. *Peregrine* is found, though always rare, as a christian name from the 13th C. The revival of the name may derive from *Peregrine* Bertie, born in 1555 in Brabant where his parents were exiles from the Marian persecution, the name having, no doubt, reference to the circumstances of his birth. The same reason may have led the poet Edmund Spenser to name one of his sons *Peregrine*.

PEREGRINUS Writs of Parliament 1291.

Perpetua (f.): f. of Latin *perpetuus* 'uninterrupted', 'perpetual'. St. *Perpetua* was a 3rd-C virgin martyred with St. Felicitas at Carthage and named in the Canon of the Mass. Her name is sometimes used by Roman Catholics.

Persis (f.): Greek *Περσίς*, 'Persian woman'; the name of a woman mentioned by St. Paul in Rom. xvi 'salute *Persis* the beloved'. It came into use as a christian name after the Reformation (the first example noted is 1579) and was fairly common in the 17th C.

Peter (m.): (Latin *Petrus*, French *Pierre*, Italian *Pie(t)ro*, Spanish *Pedro*, German *Peter*, Dutch *Pieter*, Norwegian *Peer*, Russian *Pyotr*): Greek *πέτρος* 'stone', a translation of Aramaic *Cephas*, the name given by Jesus to Simon son of Jonas. St. *Peter* appealed to the imagination of the medieval Church more than any other of the apostles (there are 1,140 churches dedicated to him in England, more than twice as many as to St. *Michael*, the next commonest); and his name was one of the commonest christian names in every country. It was introduced into England by the Normans and soon became a favourite. The usual form was the French *Piers*, which gave rise to numerous surnames such as *Piers*, *Pierce*, *Pearce*, *Pears(e)*, *Pearson*, *Pierson*; and *Perrin*, *Perkin(s)*, *Parkin(son)*, *Perrot(t)* from various diminutives. *Peters* and *Peterson* are much less common, and are usually Welsh (Welsh surnames are of later origin than English), and in fact the form *Peter* is not found before the 14th C, the earliest examples noted being *Petyr* in the alliterative *Morte Arthure* (*c.* 1355), *Petur of Westcote* mentioned in an Oseney MS of 1460, and *Petyr* which is given as the English equivalent of *Petrus* in *Promptorium Parvulorum*. From then onwards it gradually ousted the older form, though *Pearse* or *Peares* is still found in Elizabeth's reign. Lyford 1655 says '*Pierce* used for *Peter* formerly'. The Reformation struck a blow at the name which was so closely associated with the Papacy, and in the 17th and 18th C it was uncommon and regarded as rustic and old-fashioned. The sudden enormous popularity of the name in the present century is no doubt largely due to Barrie's *Peter Pan* (1904).

PETRUS DB 1086, Cur 1186–1220, HR 1273.
PETUR Oseney 1460.
PETYR *Prompt Parv c.* 1440.
PEROTE Exch R 1306.
PERES Yorks Poll Tax 1379.
PIERS 15th C *Brut*, Gedney Parish Reg 1734.
PERS *Cocke Lorelle's Bote c.* 1515.
PEARS, PEIRCE St. Columb 1641.

Petronella, Petronilla (f.): Latin f. diminutive of *Petronius*, the name of a Roman *gens*, possibly a derivative of *petra* 'stone'. The discovery of a tomb in Rome, inscribed *Filiae dulcissimae Aureliae Petronillae*, led to the belief that *Petronilla* was the name of a daughter of St. Peter, and, as St. *Petronilla*, she was invoked against fevers. The name was very common in the Middle Ages, when it was used as a convenient f. form of *Peter*. It is found in England from the 12th C and was early contracted to *Peronel*, *Pernel*, or *Parnel* (cf. the surnames *Parnall*, *Parnell*, *Parnwell*). *Pernel* or *Parnel*, for some reason, came to be used as a generic name for a priest's concubine, and is so used as early as 1362 in *Piers Plowman*. Later it meant any loose woman, and survived in dialectal use until the 18th C. The christian name *Parnel* or *Peternel* survived in Cornwall and Lancashire till the 18th C.

PETRONILLA Cur 1196, HR 1273, FA 1303, 1316.
PETRONELLA Cur 1207, FA 1303.
PETRONYL Godstow 1450.
PERNEL HR 1273.
PARNELL Lincs 1529, St. Mary Aldermary 1680.
PARONEL Yorks Poll Tax 1379.
PETERNELL St. Columb 1706.
PETRONEL St. Columb 1714.

Phelim (m.) [fē'lim]: Irish *Feiolim* 'the ever good'. A common Irish name, often translated by *Felix*.

Phemie, see EUPHEMIA.

Philadelphia (f.): Greek *Φιλαδελφία* 'brotherly love', the name of a city founded by *Attalus Philadelphus*, King of Pergamus. The church at *Philadelphia* was one of the seven mentioned in the Book of Revelation, and *Philadelphia* became a favourite Puritan name (Bardsley says he found no fewer than 100 examples of it in James I's reign) and Lyford gives it as a woman's name. It was occasionally used as late as the 19th C.

Phil(i)bert, see FULBERT.

Philemon (m.) [filē'mŏn]: Greek *Φιλήμων*, derivative of *φίλημα* 'kiss', and a common Greek name. St. Paul's epistle to *Philemon* led to its being used as a christian name in the 17th C, and it has been retained in a few families.

Philip (m.): Greek Φίλιππος 'lover of horses', the name of one of the apostles. It was common in England in the Middle Ages, as is shown by the number of surnames derived from it and its nicknames; there are 8 ways of spelling the simple patronymic *Philip*(*s*), besides *Philipson*, *Philp*(*s*), *Phelip*(*s*), *Phelps*, *Philpot*(*t*)(*s*) (from the French diminutive *Philip-ot*), *Philkin*, *Philcox*, *Phipps*, *Philson*, and others. *Phelyp* is found as a christian name as late as the end of the 15th C, and *Philip* was used as a nickname for the sparrow. The popularity of the name waned somewhat after the reign of Mary Tudor, when *Philip* of Spain became the enemy *par excellence*. Sir *Philip* Sidney was his godson, born while he was King Consort of England.

PHILIPPUS Cur 1186–1220, HR 1273.
PHELIPPE Exch R 1306.
PHELYP St. Mary at Hill 1491.
PHELYPP Coventry Mysteries 15th C.
PHILIPOT Yorks Poll Tax 1379.
PHYLYPP *Cocke Lorelle's Bote c.* 1515.

Philippa (f.): Latin f. form of *Philip* (q.v.). *Philippa* occurs in medieval Latin records, but women so named were actually called *Philip*, e.g. in the 15th-C Brut Queen *Philippa* is *Quene Phelip*, *Philippe*, or *Phillip*, and a daughter of Henry IV is *Dame Phelyp*. Lyford 1655 in his list of women's names says '*Phil* or *Philip* see in Men's names'. The modern use of *Philippa* is quite recent. It is sometimes abbreviated to *Pippa* (an Italian form) with reference to Browning's poem *Pippa passes*.

Phillida, Phillis, see PHYLLIS.

Philomena (f.) [fĭlōmē'na]: Greek Φιλοῦμενα, present participle of Φιλοῦμαι 'I am loved'. There was a St. *Philomena* of unknown date, and the name was occasionally used in the Middle Ages, e.g. *Philomena* Sturdi (HR 1273). The discovery of relics in a loculus marked '*Philomena*' in Rome in 1802 revived the name in Italy (*Filomena*).

Phine(h)as (m.) [fĭn'ēăs]: Egyptian 'the negro'. Used as a christian name in the 16th and 17th C (e.g. the two *Phineas* Fletcher's) and occasionally since.

Phoebe (f.): Greek Φοίβη, 'the shining one', an epithet of Artemis. St. Paul, in the Epistle to the Romans, recommends '*Phoebe* our sister', and the name came into use in England after the Reformation; the earliest example noted is in 1568. *Phebe* or *Phoebe* was fairly common in the 17th C, and has remained in use until the present day.

Phyllis, Phillis, Phillida (f.): Greek Φύλλις 'leafy', the name of a girl who hanged herself for love and was turned into a tree. *Phyllis* was used as a name in Greek and Roman pastoral poetry, and was adopted in England in the 16th C, when it became confused with *Felis*, the usual English form of *Felicia* (q.v.), so that it is often difficult to decide which name is meant. For instance, in a list of Yorkshire recusants of 1604 there are a number of cases of *Phillis*, *Philles*, *Phillice*, which almost certainly represent *Felice*, *Felis* rather than *Phyllis*. The 17th-C poets also used the form *Phillida*, and a *Fillida* was married at Leigh, Lancashire in 1620. *Phyllis* became almost obsolete in the 18th and 19th C, but suddenly came back into favour at the end of the 19th C, and is now common.

Phythian, see VIVIAN.

Piers, see PETER.

Pippa, see PHILIPPA.

Pleasance, Pleasant (f.): Old French *plaisance* and *plaisant* respectively (cf. *Clemency* and *Clement*); found as christian names from the 13th C onward. Dickens, who used the name for a character in *Our Mutual Friend*, noted it down in a memorandum of unusual names found in Privy Council Education List about 1855. *Pleasance* is still used in USA. *Pleasant* was a man's as well as a woman's name.

PLESENCIA Cl 1245.
PLACENCIA FA 1346.
PLESANCIA Year Book 1422.

Polly, see MARY.

Postumus (m.) [pŏst′ūmus]: Latin *postumus* 'last', 'later', applied to children born after their father's death. An erroneous idea that the word = post+humus led to the intrusive *h* in the English word *posthumous*, and it also often appears in the christian name. *Postumus* was usually given as a name to posthumous children. The first example noted is *Posthumus* Pownell born 1571, but it was more often given as a second name.

Primrose (f.): mentioned in N & Q 1904 as one of the flower-names then growing in popularity. Several examples (m. and f.) which occur in the 18th C. are no doubt cases of the use of the Scottish surname as a christian name; e.g. *Primrose* Fraser, 3rd wife of Simon Fraser, Lord Lovat, was probably named after her mother's sister-in-law, who was born *Primrose*.

Priscilla (f.): Latin diminutive of *Prisca*, the f. of the Roman cognomen *Priscus* (apparently the word *priscus* 'former'). *Priscilla* is the name of a woman mentioned in Acts xviii. 2, and was a favourite with 17th-C Puritans; the earliest example noted is *Precilla* Stevenson 1592. *Priscilla* is apparently also mentioned, in non-diminutive form, as *Prisca* in the Epistle to Timothy, and *Prisca* was also sometimes used as a christian name in the 17th C and later.

Protasia (f.): Latin f. of *Protasius*, a name of doubtful etymology. St. *Protasia* was martyred at Senlis *c.* 282 and her relics were enshrined in the cathedral *c.* 1191. It is difficult to account for the use of the name in England, which has not been noted before the late 16th C. Examples are found of various spellings, e.g. *Prothasey* at Lincoln in 1616, *Protezy* on a tombstone at Stoke-by-Nayland in the late 17th C; Sir Thomas Bodley (1545–1613) had a sister *Prothesia*, and a *Pertesia* Midwinter lived at Exeter in the reign of Elizabeth.

Prudence (f.): Latin *prudentia* 'prudence'. The name is found in use in the 13th C (cf. *Clemency*, *Pleasance*), and was revived, with other similar names, after the Reformation. It was rather common in the 17th and 18th C, often abbreviated to *Prue*.

PRUDENCIA Cur 1210.
PRUDENTIA Ass 1221.

Q

Queenie (f.): A pet-name, fairly common and sometimes used as an independent name in the 19th C. Dr. Johnson called Hester Maria Thrale 'Queen Hester', which was later shortened to '*Queeney*'.

Quenild, see GUNILDA.

Quentin, Quintin (f.): Latin *Quin*(*c*)*tinus*, a derivative of *quinctus* 'fifth'. The town of St. *Quentin* in the north of France was the burial place of St. *Quentin*, martyred *c.* 287, and the name became common in the district and was brought to England by the Normans. It is found in the 11th to 13th C and survived in Scotland until the 17th C. It has been revived in recent times, perhaps after Scott's *Quentin Durward.*

QUINTINUS DB 1086, Cur 1199, 1200, 1213, Pat 1492.

R

Rachel (f.): Hebrew 'ewe'; a common name among the Jews, but not used as a christian name in England until after the Reformation. In the 17th C, when it was used a good deal, it was often spelt *Rachael.*

Radegund (f.): Old German *Radagundis*, compound of *radi* 'counsel' and *gundi* 'war'. St. *Radegund* was a 6th-C Queen of the Franks, wife of Clothaire I, and there are several English church dedications to her. Jesus College, Cambridge, in 1490 took over the property and dedication of the nunnery of St. *Radegund*, and the full title of the college is 'The College of the Blessed Virgin Mary, St. John the Evangelist, and the glorious virgin St. *Radegund*, commonly called Jesus College, in the University of Cambridge'. The name is not recorded in the Middle Ages, but the parish registers of Bengeworth, Worcs., *c.* 1580, have examples of children of both sexes being christened *Radegund*, and Lyford gives it in his list of christian names.

Ralph (m.) [rāf, rălf]: Old Norse *Raðulfr* (= Old English *Rædwulf*, compound of *ræd* 'counsel' and *wulf* 'wolf'), became *Radulf* and then *Ralf*. It was in use in England before the Norman Conquest, after which it was reinforced by Norman influence; DB mentions tenants named *Radulfus* who had held TRE, and many at the time the survey was made. It developed into *Rauf* or *Raff*, and these were the usual forms of the name until the 17th C, when *Rafe* was more usual. *Ralf* occurs in the 16th and 17th C and *Ralph* in the 18th C, but the pronunciation of the name was still *Rāfe*. Recently, there have been signs that the spelling pronunciation *Rălf* (already general in Scotland and USA) is creeping into use. See also RAOUL.

RAUF, RAULF Reg 1066–70.
RADULF(US), RADOLF DB 1086, HR 1273.
RAFFE, RAUF HR 1273.
RAFE *Prompt Parv c.* 1440.
RAAF 15th C *Brut*.
RAUF Lincs 1455, Cov 1538.
RAFF Lincs 1533.
RAUFFE Lincs 1534.

Ranald, see RONALD.

Randal (m.): Old English *Randwulf*, compound of *rand* 'shield' and *wulf* 'wolf', was current in England before the Norman Conquest, after which it was reinforced by the corresponding Norman name derived from Norse *Ranðulfr*. The vernacular forms in the Middle Ages were *Ranulf* and *Randal*, which were latinized as *Rannulfus* and *Randulfus* respectively. The abbreviated form *Rand* and the diminutive *Rankin* were also common. The surnames *Randal(l)*, *Randell*, *Randle*, *Rand*, *Randson*, *Rance*, *Ranson*, *Ransom*, *Rankin(g)* are derived from *Randal* and *Rand*. *Rannulf* appears to be obsolete. *Randal* was less common after the 15th C, but has never altogether died out and is also used in the gipsy families of Smith, Boss, and Lee. 18th-C antiquarianism coined the form *Randolph* from Latin *Randulfus*.

RANNULFUS, RANDULFUS DB 1086.
RANULPHUS Reg 1093–1100.
RANNULFUS Cur 1186–1220.
RANDOLPH Cur 1201.

RANULF HR 1273.
RANULPH HR 1273.
RANDLE Cheshire 1290.
RANDULL Cov 1481, Chester 1565.
RAND Yorks Poll Tax 1379.

Randolph, see RANDAL.

Raoul (m.) [rah'ōōl]: French form of *Radulf* (see RALPH); not uncommon in England in the Middle Ages, especially in the diminutive forms *Raoulin*, *Raoulet*, whence the surnames *Rawle*, *Rawlin(gs)*, *Rawlinson*, *Rowlett*, &c. This form of the name died out with the use of French, but *Raoul* made its appearance again after the War of 1914–18, when it seems to have taken the fancy of British soldiers in France.
RAWLIN Exch R 1306.
RAULYN Writs of Parliament 1306.

Raphael (m.): Hebrew 'God has healed', the name of one of the archangels. It was used as a personal name among the Jews, and as a christian name in Italy in the Middle Ages. In England it was used not infrequently in the 16th and 17th C.

Ray (m., f.): usually a pet-form of *Rachel* or *Raymond* (qq.v.), but now sometimes used as an independent name. The scientist Sir *Ray* Lankester was named after John Ray, the 17th-C botanist, his father being secretary to the Ray Society formed to publish his works.

Raymond (m.): Old German *Raginmund*, compound of *ragan* 'counsel', 'might', and *mund* 'protection'. It was introduced into England by the Normans in the form *Raimund* or *Reimund*. The surnames *Raymond*, *Reymond*, *Rayment* are derived from it.
RAIMUNDUS DB 1086, Cur 1200, 1201, 1210.
RAYMUNDUS FA 1346.
REIMOND Cl 1245.
REIMUND HR 1273.

Rayner (m.): Old German *Raganher*, compound of *ragan* 'counsel', 'might', and *harja* 'army', 'folk'. There was a corresponding Old English *Regenhere*, but it was not much used, and the common medieval *Rayner*, *Rainer*, &c., was introduced by the Normans and derived from the Old German name. It was in general use from the 12th to 14th C and gave rise to the surnames *Rayner*, *Raynor*, *Reyner*, &c.

RAINERUS, RAINERIUS, RAYNERUS DB 1086, Cur 1186–1220.
REYNER HR 1273, Cl 1320.

Rebecca, Rebekah (f.): Hebrew possibly 'heifer', a common Jewish name, not used as a christian name until after the Reformation. It was much used in the 17th C. Sometimes abbreviated to *Becky*; *Beck* occurs in Brome's *The Sparagus Garden* (1640).

Regina (f.) [rĕjī′n*a*]: Latin *regina* 'queen'. Sometimes used as a christian name in the Middle Ages, probably with reference to the Blessed Virgin as Queen of Heaven. *Regina* and *Reina* occur in 13th-C Latin records. The spoken version of the name was probably the French *Reine*. *Regina* has continued to be used in Italy, Germany, and Scandinavia, and was occasionally revived in England in the 19th C.

Reginald, see REYNOLD.

René (m.) [rĕn'ā]: French, from Latin *renatus* 'born again'. St. *René* or *Renatus* was Bishop of Angers from 426, and his name became common in France. It has occasionally been borrowed in England, and *Renatus* was used in the 17th C (cf. Beatus, Desideratus, Fortunatus, &c.). The German f. name *Renate* is also sometimes used.

Renée (f.): French f. form of *René* (q.v.) sometimes used in England.

Renfred (m.): Old German *Raganfrid*, compound of *ragan* 'counsel', 'might', and *frithu* 'peace'. The name was introduced into England by the Normans and was not uncommon from the 12th to 16th C, appearing variously as *Reimfred*, *Reynfrey*, *Remfrey*, &c. *Renfry* was still used in Cornwall in the 19th C.

REIMFRED Cur 1186, 1220.
REYNFREY HR 1273.
REINFRIDUS Testa de Neville 13th C.

REMFREY St. Columb 1542, 1551.
REYNFRED Lyford 1655.

Reuben (m.): Hebrew possibly 'renewer', i.e. a child taking the place of one that has died; the name of one of the sons of Jacob and of a tribe of Israel. Its use in England dates from the 17th C.

Rex (m.): Latin *rex* 'king'. Its use as a christian name is modern and was not known to CMY. It is sometimes used as an abbreviation for *Reginald* (q.v.).

Reynard (m.): Old German *Raganhard* compound of *ragan* 'counsel', 'might', and *hardu* 'hard'. It was introduced into England by the Normans in the form *Rainard* or *Reynard*, but was never so common as *Rayner* and *Reynaud* (or *Reynold*) with which it is sometimes confused.

Reynold (m.) [rĕn′*o*ld]: Old English *Regenweald*, compound of *regen* and *weald*, both of which mean 'power', 'force', 'might', was not a very common name. After the Norman Conquest it was reinforced by French *Reinald* or *Reynaud* from the corresponding Old German *Raganald*, which became a favourite name. In Middle English it is usually *Rainald* or *Reynold* (latinized as *Rainaldus*, *Reynoldus*, and occasionally *Reginaldus*). The surnames *Reynold*(*s*), *Reynoldson*, *Rennell*, *Reynell*, *Rennison*, *Renaud*, *Renaut* are derived from it. In the 15th C such forms as *Raignald*, *Reignald*, *Reignolde*, *Reginalde* came into use. The reappearance of the *g* after several centuries of disuse may have been an early example of the effect of antiquarianism on names. Both *Reginald* and *Reynold* became much less common after the 15th C. Neither Camden nor Lyford gives them (though they have the German *Reinhold*), but *Reynold* has never quite died out in the West country, and *Reginald* was revived in the 19th C and is now common. See also RONALD. *Reginald* is often abbreviated to *Reg* [rĕj] or *Reggy* [rĕj′ĕ]; the earliest example of this which has been noted is in C. Reade's 'Love me Little, Love me Long' (1859).

RAINALD(US), RAGENALD, RAYNALDUS, RAYNOLDUS, REINOLD(US), RENOLDUS DB 1086.
REGINALDUS FA 1284.

REYNALD HR 1273.
REYNOLD HR 1273.
REYNAUD HR 1273.
RENAUT Testa de Neville 1379.
RAIGNALD Cov 1424.
REIGNALD Cov 1444.
REGINALDE Oseney 1460.
REGINALD or REYNOLD Oxf Univ Reg 1566.

Rhoda (f.): derivative of Greek *ῥόδον* 'rose'; the name of a girl mentioned in Acts xii. 13. It came into use as a christian name in the 17th C.

Rhona (f.): this rather uncommon name is not mentioned by CMY. It may possibly be a pet-form of a Welsh name, e.g. *Rhonwen* the Welsh version of the Saxon *Rowena* (q.v.). Watts-Dunton uses it as a gipsy name (*Rhona* Boswell in *The Coming of Love* (1897)).

Rhys (m.) [rēs]: a common Welsh christian name, the origin of the surnames *Reece*, *Rice*, *Price*, *Preece* (= *ap Rhys*).

Richard (m.): the existence of an Old English *Richeard*, compound of *ric* 'ruler' and *heard* 'hard', is not certain, though both elements were in use. The great popularity of the name *Richard* in the Middle Ages was due to importation from the Continent, the Normans bringing in French *Richard* (from the corresponding Old German *Ricohard*). The allied name *Richer* was also common until at least the middle of the 13th C. In Latin MSS. the abbreviations *Rich.* and *Ric.* are used for *Richer* and *Ric(h)ard*, respectively. *Richard* and *Ricard* were equally common in the Middle Ages, together with many nicknames and diminutives, such as *Rich(ie)*, *Hitch*, *Rick*, *Hick*, *Dick*, *Dickon*, *Ricket*, *Hicket*, which in turn gave rise to an immense number of surnames. *Richard* has maintained its position as one of the half-dozen favourite men's names with singularly little fluctuation of fashion, though it was rather less common in the 18th C. *Richie* is still used as a pet-form in USA, but *Dick* is universal in England. *Dick* and *Hick* (now obsolete) were among the earliest of this kind of rhyming nickname (cf. *Polly* from *Molly*, *Bob* from *Rob*, *Hodge* from *Roger*), the first example noted being a record in Cur 1220 '*quidam Dicke*

Smith'. *Dick*, like *Jack*, was formerly used as a colloquial term for 'man', 'fellow', &c., e.g. 'You are a gone *dick*'. The proverbial *Any Tom, Dick, or Harry* is indicative of the long-established popularity of the name. The peculiar pet-form *Hudde*, which was common in the 13th and 14th C, has long been obsolete, though its traces survive in the surnames *Hudd, Hudson*; Bardsley gives examples which prove that *Hudd* was a form of *Richard*, e.g. 'Ricardus dictus Hudde de Walkden', 'Ricardus de Knapton et Cristiana hud-wyf'.

RICARD(US) DB 1086, Cur 1186–1220, HR 1273.
RICARD Exch R 1306.
RYCHARDE *Prompt Parv c.* 1440.

Richenda, &c. (f.): *Richenda, Richarda, Richenza* are all from compounds of Old German *ric* (Modern German *reich*) 'ruler', and are recorded very early. They have occasionally been used in England as f. forms of *Richard* (q.v.). In the 16th C the diminutive *Richardyne* is found. Other compounds are *Richolda*, recorded in the 13th C, and *Richoard*, fairly common in Devon in the 17th C. *Richenda* was used by the Gurney's in the 18th C.

Rita [rē'ta], see MARGARET.

Robert (m.): Old English *Hreodbeorht* was reinforced at the time of the Norman Conquest by French *Robert* from the cognate Old German *Hrodebert*, a compound of *hrothi* 'fame' and *berhta* 'bright'. It occurs frequently in DB, and has been a favourite name ever since. The nicknames *Rob, Hob, Dob, Nob*, and (later) *Bob*, were all commonly used, and *Robin*, a diminutive form of *Rob*, was in the 13th C more usual than *Robert* itself. In Scotland the forms *Hab* and *Rab* are found in some districts (cf. *Tam* and *Tom*). *Rab* and *Roy* are used as diminutives of *Robert* in N. Ireland. Among the many surnames derived from *Robert* and its nicknames are *Roberts(on), Robins(on), Robson, Robeson, Nobbs, Hobb(e)s, Hobson, Hopkins, Dobb(s), Dobson*, &c. In Middle English the form *Robard* was not unusual (cf. *Hubbard* for *Hubert*), and is given in *Promptorium Parvulorum* as the English equivalent of *Robertus*. *Robin* is now sometimes used as an independent name.

RODBERTUS, ROTBERT(US), ROBERT(US) Reg 1071–5, DB 1086.
ROBERTUS Cur 1186–1220, HR 1273.
ROBIN Cur 1200, 1205, 1210, Cl 1276.
ROBYN Coventry Mysteries 15th C.
ROBARD St. Mary at Hill 1507.

Roberta, Robina (f.) [robert′*a*, robēn′*a*]: f. forms of *Robert* and *Robin* (q.v.). An early example is *Robina* Cromwell, sister of the Protector, but these forms have been used mainly in Scotland. Dickens, *c.* 1855, notes *Rubina* and *Rebinah*, which are presumably phonetic renderings of *Robina*, as occurring in Privy Council Education Lists.

Robin, see ROBERT.

Roderick (m.): Old German *Hrodric*, compound of *hrothi* 'fame' and *ricja* 'rule', was the source of Russian *Rurik* and of Spanish *Roderigo*, but has not taken deep root elsewhere. *Roderick*, however, is not infrequent in Scotland, where it is used to render the Gaelic *Ruaidhri* 'the red' (the Irish equivalent is *Rory*). It is used particularly by the Mackenzies and McLeods. The corresponding Welsh name *Rhydderch* was rendered as *Rotheric*; *Rothericus* son of Gryfin is mentioned in FA 1303 (cf. the surname *Protheroe* = *ap Rhydderch*).

Rodney (m.): a Somerset surname, derived from the village of *Rodney Stoke*. It is now well established as a christian name, after the famous admiral, Lord *Rodney* (1719–92).

Roger (m.): Old English *Hrothgar* was reinforced at the time of the Norman Conquest by French *Roger*, from the corresponding Old German *Hrodgar*, compound of *hrothi* 'fame' and *ger* 'spear'. *Rogerus* is frequent in DB, and *Roger* was a favourite throughout the Middle Ages. Together with its nicknames *Hodge* and *Dodge*, it gave rise to a multitude of surnames, e.g. *Roger(s)*, *Rodger(s)*, *Hodge(s)*, *Dodge*, *Hodgkins*, *Hodgkiss*, *Hotchkiss*, *Hodgkinson*, &c. The colloquial use of *Hodge* to denote an agricultural labourer is an indication of the former frequency of the name. After falling into desuetude in the 18th and 19th C (though it was always used in some families), *Roger* has now regained some measure of favour.

ROGER(I)US Reg 1071–5, DB 1086, Cur 1186–1220, HR 1273, Yorks Poll Tax 1379.
ROTGERIUS Reg 1088–91.

Roland, Rowland (m.): Old German *Hrodland*, compound of *hrothi* 'fame' and *landa* 'land'. As the name of the most famous of the peers of Charlemagne, *Roland* was a favourite in the Middle Ages and was introduced into England by the Normans (*Rolland* occurs in DB), the usual English form of the name being *Rouland* or *Rowland*. *Rowland* was, indeed, the usual spelling in the 17th and 18th C, and the modern *Roland* is a piece of archaizing.

ROLLAND DB 1086.
ROLANDUS Cur 1186–1220, FA 1316, 1428.
ROULAND Testa de Neville 13th C.
ROWLAND Lincs 1529, Lyford 1655.

Rolf (m.): Old German *Hrodulf*, compound of *hrothi* 'fame' and *vulf* 'wolf' (see RUDOLF), and the cognate Old Norse *Hrólfr*, developed into *Rolf* in Normandy (cf. *Ralph* from *Raðulfr*). It was introduced into England by the Normans and survived long enough to originate the surnames *Rolf(e)*, *Rolfes*, *Rolph*, but it disappeared fairly early, perhaps on account of its likeness to the more popular *Ralf*. It has been revived of late. *Rolf* was sometimes latinized as *Rollo*, which was occasionally used as a christian name in the 19th C.

ROULF, ROLF, ROLFT DB 1086.
ROLF HR 1273.

Rollo, see ROLF.

Roma (f.): the name of the city, recently used as a christian name (cf. *Florence*).

Romola (f.): [rŏ′mola]: a f. form of *Romolo*, the Italian version of *Romulus*. A saint *Romulus* occurs in the Roman Martyrology and *Romolo* was used, especially in and around Florence, e.g. the first Bishop of Fiesole bore this name. *Romola* is now sometimes given as a name in England after the heroine of George Eliot's novel of that name.

Rona (f.): this name, now sometimes given to girls, is apparently the name of two islands (derived from Gaelic *ronan*, a seal) used, perhaps, with an idea of its being a f. equivalent of *Ronald* (q.v.). It is also confused with the Welsh *Rhona* (q.v.).

Ronald (m.): *Ronald* and *Ranald* (Gaelic *Raonull*) are the Scottish equivalents of *Reynold* or *Reginald* (q.v.), but are derived from the Norse version of the name, *Rögnvaldr*. *Ronald* is now often used by persons of non-Scottish descent.

Rory (m.): Modern Irish form of Gaelic *Ruaidhri*, a derivative of *ruadh* 'red'. It is often rendered by *Roger*. See also RODERICK.

Rosa (f.): latinization of *Rose* (q.v.), which came into use in the 19th C.

Rosabel (f.): an 18th-C invention, formed on the model of *Christabel*, *Claribel*, &c.

Rosalie (f.) [rŏz'*a*lĕ, rōz'*a*lĕ]: this is apparently Latin *rosalia*, the annual ceremony of hanging garlands of roses on tombs. St. *Rosalia* was a 12th-C Sicilian recluse, patron saint of Palermo. Her name was used in Italy and spread to France, where *Rosalie* is not uncommon. It has sometimes been borrowed and used in England.

Rosalind (f.) [rŏz'*a*lĭnd]: Old German *Roslindis*, compound of (*h*)*ros* 'horse' and *lindi* 'serpent'. The name was carried to Spain by the Goths and took root there as *Rosalinda*. The modern use of it in England is probably owing to Shakespeare's *Rosalind* in *As You Like It*. Thackeray uses it in *The Newcomes* (1854) and Trollope in *The American Senator* (1877). *Rosaline* (e.g. in *Romeo and Juliet* and *Love's Labour's Lost*) is presumably the same name. This form has been used occasionally in recent times.

Rosamund, Rosamond (f.) [rŏz'amund]: Old German *Rosamunda*, compound of *(h)ros* 'horse' and *munda* 'protection'. In the Middle Ages, however, it was regarded as a Latin name *rosa*+ *munda* = 'pure or clean rose'. It was introduced into England by the Normans, a famous example being *Rosamund* Clifford (died 1176), the unfortunate mistress of Henry II. The surnames *Roseaman, Rosomon, Rosemond, Rosamund* are derived from it. *Rosamund*, unlike many names of Germanic origin, survived the Renaissance and was fairly common in the 17th C, usually spelt *Rosamond* (the French form, cf. *Edmond* for *Edmund*), held its own in the 18th and 19th C, and is now somewhat more common than it has been for several centuries.

ROSAMUNDA Cur 1205, 1207, HR 1273.
ROSEMUNDA FA 1303.
ROSAMOND FF 1282.
ROSSAMOND Yorks Rec 1604.
ROZEMAN St. Clerkenwell 1665.

Rose (f.): although this name has, from a fairly early date, been identified with the flower-name and latinized as *Rosa*, it seems actually to be a derivative of *(h)ros* 'horse' (cf. *Rosalind, Rosamund*). It was introduced into England by the Normans in the form *Roese, Rohese* (Latin *Roesia, Rohesia*), which became *Royse* (latinized as *Roysia*) and *Rose* in Middle English (cf. surnames *Royce, Royse, Rose*). *Promptorium Parvulorum* gives it as *Rose*, Latin *Rosa*.

ROESIA Cur 1199–1220.
ROHESIA, ROHEIS Cur 1164.
ROYSIA FA 1303.
ROSA FA 1316, HR 1273, Yorks Poll Tax 1379.
ROSEIA FA 1346.
ROSE FA 1316.
ROYSE Godstow 1450.
ROOS Lincs 1529.

Roseanna (f.) [rōz'ăna]: an 18th-C mixture of *Rose* and *Anna*.

Rosemary (f.) [rōz'marĕ]: the first occurrence of this name is *Rosemary* Dacre (afterwards Lady Clerk), b. 1745 at *Rose* Castle,

Cumb. The baptismal register gives her name as Mary, but her own account of her baptism gives it as *Rosemary*, and this name has been used since in the Dacre and Clerk families. It was unknown to CMY but has become common during the 20th C. For the circumstances of *Rosemary* Dacre's baptism see *Trans. of the Cumb. & West. Antiq. & Arch. Soc.* 8, 1886 (237).

Rosetta (f.): a diminutive of *Rose* (q.v.), sometimes used in the 18th and 19th C. The Spanish and Italian diminutives *Rosita* and *Rosina* are also sometimes used.

Rowena (f.) [rōē'n*a*]: this name seems to originate with Geoffrey of Monmouth, who gives it to the daughter of Hengist, with whom Vortigern fell in love. Some MSS give the name as *Renwein* or *Ronwen*. It may be Old English *Hrōðwyn*, a compound of *hreod* 'fame' and *wine* 'friend'. Scott used it for the Saxon heroine of *Ivanhoe*, and *Rowena* (like *Cedric* (q.v.)) came into use as a result of the popularity of that novel.

Rowland, see ROLAND.

Roy (m.): originally a Gaelic name, derivative of *ruadh* 'red'. It is now fairly common in England as well as Scotland and is used in N. Ireland as a diminutive of Robert.

Royston (m.): this use of the surname, derived from *Royston* in Yorks., as a christian name is difficult to explain. It became common, for no apparent reason, in the 1930's. Mr. J. M. Tradwell, however, has drawn my attention to Richard *Royston* (d. 1686) a prominent bookseller during the Commonwealth and Restoration period, who had a grandson (*Royston* Chiswell) and a great-grandson (*Royston* Meredith), named after him. The gap of 250 years between this and the modern use of the name is unbridged.

Ruby (f.): the name of a precious stone; its use as a christian name is modern (cf. *Diamond*, *Emerald*, *Pearl*, &c.).

Rudolf (m.): the Modern German form of Old German *Hrodulf* (see ROLF). Occasionally borrowed from Germany in recent times.

Rufus (m.): Latin *rufus* 'red-haired'; used by Jews instead of *Reuben*, and in USA sometimes by others.

Rupert (m.): Old German *Hrodebert* (see ROBERT) developed into Modern German *Rupprecht*. The name was first introduced into England by Prince *Rupprecht* of the Palatinate, the nephew of Charles I, whose name on English lips became *Rupert* (his contemporaries also often called him Prince *Robert*). It is the admiration felt for him that is responsible for the modern vogue of the name in England, which is not mentioned by CMY.

Ruperta (f.): f. form of *Rupert*, first used for a daughter of Prince *Rupert*.

Russell (m.): a surname derived from the nickname *russell* or *rousselle*, a diminutive of French *roux* 'red'. Its use as a christian name is paralleled by that of other names of famous families, e.g. *Cecil*, *Sidney*, *Mortimer*, *Montague*, and is comparatively recent.

Ruth (f.): a Hebrew or Moabitish name of doubtful etymology. First used as a christian name in England after the Reformation. *Ruthe* Evans 1589 is the earliest example noted.

S

Sabin(a) (m., f.) [săb'ĭn, sab'ĭn*a*, săbēn'*a*]: Latin *Sabinus*, *Sabina* 'Sabine man or woman', a common Roman cognomen. St. *Sabinus*, a 4th-C Bishop of Spoleto, and St. *Sabina*, a Roman matron martyred under Hadrian, ensured the survival of the name. Both became *Sabin* in English, and the name is found from the 12th C, giving rise to the surnames *Sabbe*, *Sab*(*e*)*y*, *Sabin*(*e*), *Saben*, &c. As a man's name it died out, but *Sabina* survived in rustic use until the 19th C and is not yet extinct.

SABINA Cur 1199–1215, FA 1303.
SABYN HR 1273, Coventry Mysteries 15th C.

Sacha (m.): Russian pet-form of Alexander, sometimes now used in England.

Sacheverell (m.) [s*a*shĕv'*e*r*e*l]: the surname of an ancient, but now extinct, family. The origin of the name is obscure; it is sometimes derived from the castle of *Saute de Chevreuil* in Normandy; but one example quoted by Bardsley from the year 1273, where it is given as *Saucheverel alias Sauzcheverel alias Saunz Cheverel*, looks like a Norman nickname '*Sans Cheverel*'; *cheverel* was Old French for a kid and for the leather made from kid-hide. In the early 18th C *Sacheverell* was often given as a christian name in honour of Dr. *Sacheverell* (1674–1724) the Tory preacher, and it is said to have survived in rural districts in the last century. The Sitwell family, who continue to use it to the present day take the name from William *Sacheverell* (1638–91) one of the founders of the Whig party.

Sadie, see SARA(H).

Saer, Sayer (m.): Old German *Sigiheri* (Old English *Sigehere*), compound of *sigu* 'victory' and *harja* 'the host' or 'people'. *Sagar*, *Saer*, or *Sayer* was a popular name in medieval England, and Bardsley lists some 20 or 25 surnames derived from it. It seems to have died out completely in the course of the 14th C.

SAGAR(US), SEGAR(US) DB 1086.
SAER Cur 1200.
SAERUS HR 1273.
SAYER HR 1273.
SAGARD Exch R 1306.

Salathiel (m.): Babylonian *Salti-ila* meaning 'the god is my . . .' (the meaning of the first element is unknown). This was taken over by the Hebrews as *Shaltiel* and sometimes Hebraized as *Šealtiel* 'request(ed) of God'. Both forms occur in the Book of Haggai. The Vulgate has Salathiel both there and in Matt. i. where it occurs in a genealogy as the father of Zerubbabel. It was used as a christian name from the 16th C (cf. Ben Jonson's epitaph on *Salathiel* Pavy, a child of Queen Elizabeth's chapel. *Salathiel*, son of *Salathiel* Symdsion was baptized in 1711 at Edgington, Wilts.

Sally, see SARA(H).

Salome (f.): originally Aramaic *Shalam-zion* 'peace of Zion', abbreviated to *Shalamzu*, and then hellenized as *Salome.* A favourite name in the Herod family. *Salome* was also the name of one of the women who ministered to Jesus, who was first at the sepulchre on Easter morning. It has been used as a christian name since the 17th C. It is now usually pronounced salō′mĕ, but the medieval pronunciation, according to Maurice of Kirkham (see p. xxxvii) was sal′*o*mĕ, with a tendency to suppress the final *e*.

Samantha (f.): this curious name has come into use since about 1970 as a name for female children and cats. The immediate source is undoubtedly the American television series *Bewitched*, where it is the name of the younger of two witches. This series has been shown on British TV and is very popular. Mrs. Rella Cohn of Chicago reports the occurrence of the name in a series 'best styled as American folk humor; a number of books by Marietta Holley appeared in the 1880's, in the titles of all but one of which the name Samantha was included'. Mrs. Cohn has now discovered examples of the name in New England families in the 18th C, but the ultimate derivation of the name is obscure.

Sam(p)son (m.): Hebrew 'child of Shamash (the sun-god)', 'sun child', rendered in Greek as *Σαμπσῶν*; the name of the great champion of the Israelites against the Philistines. *Samson* was the name of a Welsh bishop (fl. 550) who crossed over to Brittany and founded the abbey of Dôl, where he was buried and later venerated as a saint. It is impossible to say whether he was named after the Biblical *Samson*, or whether his name was of Celtic origin, but there is no doubt that the prevalence of the name in Brittany and Normandy, whence it was carried to England, was due to his fame. The name was common in England from the end of the 11th C, spelt sometimes *Samson* or *Sampson*, sometimes *Sanson* or *Sansum* (from French *Sanson*). An early example is *Samson*, Bishop of Worcester, brother of Thomas, first Norman Archbishop of York. The surnames *Sam(m)s*, *Sam(p)son*, *Sansom(e)*, *Sanson*, *Sansum* testify to its popularity. In the 17th C the name was reinforced by Biblical influence, but it died out after the Restoration.

SAMPSON *Reg* 1074–85.

SANSON DB 1086.
SAMSON Cur 1196–1215, HR 1273, FA 1431.
SAMPSON, SANSON, SAUNSUM Testa de Neville 13th C.
SAMPSON FA 1302, 1346.
SANSUM HR 1273.

Samuel (m.): Hebrew 'name of God' or 'Shum (is) God', for there is much evidence for a god called *Shum* or *Shem*. The name of one of the greatest of the Hebrew prophets, who anointed Saul as first king of Israel. *Samuel* was rare as a christian name in the Middle Ages, though examples occur in 12th-C records, and the surnames *Samuel*, *Samwell* occur as early as 1273. Not all of these were Jewish, though some may have been. After the Reformation *Samuel* became a favourite name, an early example being *Samuel* Daniel the poet (1562–1619). It continued in general use after the Restoration, when many Biblical names went out, and is still a common working-class name, usually abbreviated to *Sam*. In Scotland it has been used to render *Somerled* (Gaelic *Somhairle*), a borrowing from Old Norse *Sumarliði*, 'summer wanderer', 'viking', which came to be used as a christian name.

Sanchia (f.): Spanish and Provençal *Sancha* or *Sanchia*, f. of *Sancho*, from Latin *sanctus* 'holy'. Introduced into England by the marriage in 1243 of Richard, Earl of Cornwall, to *Sanchia*, daughter of the Count of Provence. Her name evidently puzzled English scribes, who write it in a variety of ways, including *Cynthia*, *Scientia*, and *Science*. The name occurs during the next four centuries, variously spelt *Sens*, *Sence*, *Sense*, *Saints*, *Science*, *Sanche*. An example is a record in 1620 of 'James Bynde and *Sanctia* or *Sence* his wife'. Lyford (1655) gives *Sanchia* in his list of women's names. *Sence*, *Senses*, *Saint*, and *Sayntes* occur in 18th-C and early-19th-C Lincs. records. *Sanchia* is still occasionally used.

Sandra (f.): Italian diminutive of *Alessandra*, now sometimes used as a diminutive of *Alexandra* (q.v.), and recently as an independent name.

Sandy, see ALEXANDER.

Sara(h) (f.): Hebrew 'princess'. The wife of Abraham, whose name was originally *Sarai* 'contentious', was later called *Sarah*. *Sara* is the hellenized form of the name. It is found in use in England as a christian name from the 12th C, usually in the form *Sarra*, but was not really common until after the Reformation, when *Sarah* becomes the usual spelling. In the 17th C the form *Sarey* is found (cf. the vulgar 19th-C pronunciation, e.g. '*Sairey Gamp*'). In the 18th and 19th C the compound *Saranna* (*Sara*+*Anna*) had a certain vogue. The usual pet-form of the name is *Sally* (cf. *Mally* for *Mary*, *Hal* for *Harry*); in USA sometimes *Sadie* (cf. *Maidie* for *Mary*). In Ireland *Sarah* has been used to render the native *Sorcha* and *Saraid*.

SARRA Cur 1189–1215, HR 1273, FA 1303, 1316.
SARA Yorks Poll Tax 1379.

Saul (m.): Hebrew 'asked for', the name of the first King of Israel, and later of *Saul* of Tarsus. Occasionally used as a christian name since the 17th C.

Scholastica (f.): f. of Latin *scholasticus*, Greek *σχολαστικος* 'scholar'. St. *Scholastica* was the sister of St. Benedict (*c.* 480–543) and the first nun of his order. Benedictine influence carried the name to England where it is found as a christian name from the beginning of the 13th C until the Reformation. A 14th-C Legendary gives *Scholace*, and Godstow (1450) gives *Scholast*, as the English form. Camden (1604) and Lyford (1655) both give *Scholastica* in their lists of women's names.

SCHOLASTICA Cur 1200, 1207, 1210, FA 1316, 1346, Salop Reg 1635.
SCHOLACE 14th C Legendary.
SCHOLAST Godstow 1450.

Sean (m.) [shawn]: Irish for *John* (q.v.), through Norman-French *Jean*. The original Irish form of the name was *Eoín*, which is becoming very common again in Ireland. Fr. Robert Davison OP has suggested that this may possibly be because the Gospels in Irish use *Eoín* for John, and the newly introduced vernacular liturgy has made this form familiar.

Sebastian (m.): Latin *Sebastianus* 'man of *Sebastia*' (a city of Pontus, from Greek *σεβαστός* 'venerable', modern *Sebaste*). St.

Sebastian was a Roman legionary martyred under Diocletian. His martyrdom, by being shot with arrows, was a favourite subject of medieval art. As a christian name, *Sebastian* was particularly common in Spain, and in France where it became *Bastien*. *Bastian* and *Sebastian* have been used in Cornwall at least since the 16th C and probably earlier, for the surnames *Bastian, Bastin, Bastion*, &c., would seem to be derived from them.

Secundus (m.): Latin 'second', sometimes used as a christian name.

Selina (f.) [selē'na]: the history of this name is obscure. The first example noted is 1619 *Zelina* Gardener. *Selinah* occurs in 1687, *Sillina* in 1697. *Celina* or *Selina* Finch, born about 1680, married the 1st Earl Ferrers, and her daughter *Selina* Shirley became the Methodist Countess of Huntingdon. The name has ever since been current in the Shirley and Finch families and in other families connected with them. There is no reason to identify the name, as is sometimes done, with Greek σελήνη 'the moon', and on the whole it seems as if CMY may be right in taking it to be from French *Céline* (Latin *Coelina*, derivative of *caelum* 'heaven') the name of a 5th-C saint, mother of St. Rémy. This is borne out by occasional spellings *Celina*.

Selwyn (m.): the surname *Selwyn*, which is first recorded in the 13th C, may be from the Old English *Selewine*, a compound of *sele* 'house' and *wine* 'friend', though that name was a rare one and has not been noted after the 11th C. The current use of *Selwyn* as a christian name (particularly common in Wales) may be after George Augustus *Selwyn* (1809–78), Bishop of New Zealand and later of Lichfield, after whom *Selwyn* College, Cambridge, was named. CMY, who was a great admirer of the bishop, does not mention this name.

Senga (f.): this name, common in parts of Scotland, is said to be simply a variant of *Agnes* (q.v.) obtained by spelling it backwards.

Septimus (m.): Latin 'seventh', often given to a seventh child in the 19th C, occasionally used without any numerical significance.

Seraphina (f.): Latin f. derivative of *seraph* (Hebrew 'noble', 'burning one'), the name of an early saint. Both it and the Spanish diminutive *Seraphita* were occasionally used in the 19th C.

Serena (f.): f. of Latin *serenus* 'calm', 'serene'. This name has been noted once in the 13th C, again in Notts in 1761, and in New England in 1830.

Serle (m.): Old English *Serlo*, Old German *Sarilo*, derivative of *sarva* 'armour'. The name was in use before the Norman Conquest, but was much commoner afterwards, being a favourite with the Normans; it died out after the 14th C. The surnames *Serle, Searl(e), Serrell, Serrill(s)* are derived from it.

SERLO DB 1086, Cur 1186–1215, FA 1346.
SERLE 15th-C Brut, HR 1273.
SERILL, SERELL Yorks Poll Tax 1379.

Seth (m.): Hebrew 'substitute', 'compensation', the name of one of the sons of Adam, born after the death of Abel. Only one pre-reformation example of its use as a christian name has been noted: *Seth* Denwall (fl. 1495–1525) master mason in the counties of Cheshire and Flint. Another early example noted is *Seth* Holywell (died 1557), whose name occurs in a Hunts. Clergy List. It was common in the 17th C but is now seldom used in England, though more common in the USA.

Seumus (m.): Irish form of *James* (q.v.).

Sewal (m.): Old English *Sigeweald*, compound of *sige* 'victory' and *weald* 'strength'. It survived as late as the 16th C.

SEWALLUS HR 1273.
SEWALE HR 1273.

Sextus (m.): Latin *sextus* 'sixth', occasionally used as a christian name for a sixth child, or a sixth son.

Shamus (m.): phonetic rendering of *Seumus*, Irish form of *James* (q.v.).

Shane (m.) [shawn]: phonetic rendering of *Sean*, Irish form of *John* (q.v.).

Sharon (m., f.): one of the Biblical place-names adopted as christian names by the English Puritans, and carried by them to N. America (cf. *Beulah*, *Gilead*). It was originally used as a m. name, a well-known example being the historian *Sharon* Turner (1768–1847). It is now (1976) predominantly f., and has become very common in England since about 1945. Its use in America was rather earlier.

Sheila (f.): phonetic rendering of *Síle*, the Irish form of *Celia* from *Cecilia* (q.v.). Now extensively used in England as an independent name. In the 19th C *Sheila* was often rendered by *Julia* in Ireland.

She(e)na (f.): phonetic rendering of Gaelic *Sìne* = *Jane* (q.v.).

Shirley (f.): this is apparently a surname (derived from a place-name) used as a christian name. The first example noted is the heroine of Charlotte Brontë's novel *Shirley* (1849), who, as an only child and an heiress, was given 'the masculine cognomen' *Shirley*, a family name. I have found no clue to the modern prevalence of *Shirley* as a christian name in the Southern States of USA. It has now become a common name in England, owing to the number of children named after the child film-star, *Shirley* Temple.

Sholto (m.): this name seems to be used exclusively by the Douglas family. It was first used by them at the beginning of the 18th C, when the genealogists had derived the family from one *Sioltaich Dhu Glas*, *Sioltaich* meaning 'sower'.

Sibyl (f.): Greek *Σίβυλλα*, Medieval Latin *Sibilla*, *Sibylla*, *Sibulla*, the name of the women who acted as mouthpieces of the ancient oracles. From about 200 B.C. collections of alleged sibylline oracles were written and propagated by the Jews, and later by Christians. St. Augustine admits the sibyl to the City of God, and in general it was believed that the sibylline oracles represented one form of divine revelation (cf. the *Dies Irae*, 'teste David cum Sibylla'). *Sibylla*, accordingly, came to be used as a christian name, and it was introduced into England after the Norman Conquest. Robert, Duke of Normandy, son of the Conqueror, married *Sibylla* of Conversane. From the 12th C onwards the name was common. Its spelling was erratic, and the misspelling *Sybil* is common to the present day. *Sibley* was the usual Middle English form of the name and is still occasionally used in Scotland. The surnames *Sibley*, *Sibbs*, *Sibson*, *Sibbet* are derived from it and its abbreviation *Sib*. *Sibyl* went out of fashion after the Reformation, but never became obsolete. Its revival in the 19th C may have been partly due to Disraeli's novel *Sybil* (1845). The Latin forms *Sibylla*, *Sibella* are sometimes used.

SIBILLA Cur 1196–1215, FA 1316, Yorks Poll Tax 1379.
SIBILIA HR 1273, Yorks Poll Tax 1379.
SIBILIE, SIBELY HR 1273.
SYBYLE, SYBBLY, SIBBE *Prompt Parv* 1440.
SIBELL Cov 1434.
SYBILL Lincs 1455.
SYBELL Lincs 1533.
SIBOTA Yorks Poll Tax 1379.
SYBBY *Cocke Lorelle's Bote c.* 1515.
SYBYLY Coventry Mysteries 15th C.

Sidney (m.): the *Sidney* family was founded in England by William *Sidney* or *Sydney*, the Chamberlain of Henry II, who came from Anjou. The name appears regularly in Latin as *de Sancto Dionisio*, &c., and there can be little doubt that it is a reduction of *St. Denis* (cf. Semple for St. Paul, Sellinger for St. Leger, Simbarb for St. Barbe). The use of *Sidney* as a christian name was no doubt partly due to the Whig idolization of the memory of Algernon *Sidney* (1622–83); one of the earliest recorded examples of the name is *Sidney* Beauclerk, 5th son of 1st Duke of St. Albans (born 1703). *Sidney* Herbert, Lord Herbert of Lea (born 1810), was no doubt named after his ancestress Mary *Sidney*, sister of Sir Philip *Sidney*. Another early example of the name is *Sydney* Dobell, the poet, born 1824. *Sydney*, New South Wales, was named after Thomas Townshend, 1st Viscount *Sydney* (1733–1800), who was Secretary of State at the time of its foundation.

Sidney (f.): this is not uncommon as a woman's name in Ireland, and is probably a survival of *Sidony* (q.v.) rather than the family name; see above.

Sidony (f.) [sĭd′onĕ]: this name was formerly used by Roman Catholics for girls born about the date of the Feast of the Winding Sheet (i.e. of Christ), more formally alluded to as 'the Sacred *Sendon*'. *Sendon* or *Sindon* (from Latin *sindon*, Greek σινδών 'fine cloth', 'linen') was used in Middle English for a fine cloth, especially one used as a shroud. The Sacred *Sendon* is supposed to be preserved at Turin. That *Sidony* or *Sidonia* = *Sindonia* is shown by an example from Shropshire, 1793, '*Sidonia* or *Sindonia* Wilden'. *Sidonie* is not uncommon in France, and the Irish *Sidney* (q.v.) is probably really *Sidony*. No early example of the name has been found, but it seems likely that the surname *Siddons* has this origin.

Siegfried (m.): Old German *Sigifrith*, compound of *sigu* 'victory' and *frithu* 'peace'. Occasionally used as a christian name in England since the end of the 19th C, no doubt under the influence of Wagner's *Ring* (cf. *Brunhild*).

Sigrid (f.): Old Norse *Sigridhr*, compound of *sig* 'victory', and the common suffix *-ridhr*, the meaning of which is not clear. In recent times the name has sometimes been borrowed from Scandinavia, but it was also used in the 13th C, when *Sirida*, *Sierida*, *Sigerith* are recorded.

Silas (m.): apparently a shortened form of Latin *Silvanus*, the name of the god of trees. The person called *Silvanus* by St. Paul in 2 Cor. i. 19 is usually identified with the *Silas* of Acts. Neither name is found in use in England before the Reformation. *Silas* became fairly common in the 17th C, and continued to be used in Dissenting circles in the 18th and 19th C. *Silvanus* or *Sylvanus* has also occasionally been used, e.g. *Silvanus* Spencer eldest son of the poet.

Silvanus, see SILAS.

Silvester, Sylvester (m.): Latin *silvester* 'woody', 'growing or found in a wood'. It was the name of three popes, the first of whom, St. *Silvester*, was said to have baptized the Emperor Constantine, to have cured him of his leprosy, and to have received in return the 'Donation of Constantine'. The name was not uncommon in the Middle Ages (it is first noted in 1200) and gave rise to the surnames *Silvester*, *Sylvester*. Though less common since the Reformation, examples have been noted in the 16th, 17th, 18th, and 19th C; one in 1580 and one in 1623 are of *Silvester* as a woman's name.

SILVESTER Cur 1200–1215, FA 1303.
SILVESTRE HR 1273.

Silvia, Sylvia (f.): Latin f. of *Silvius*, derivative of *silva* 'wood'. *Rhea Silvia* was the name of the mother of Romulus and Remus, and it was probably from this that *Silvia* came into use as a christian name in Italy at the Renaissance. Shakespeare's use of it for one of the two heroines of *Two Gentlemen of Verona* is probably responsible for its modern use as a christian name in England, though Mrs. Gaskell's novel, *Sylvia's Lovers* probably had some influence.

Simeon (m.) [sĭm'ēŏn]: Hebrew *Shimeon* 'hearkening' (or possibly 'little hyena'). It was a common name in Israel. English versions of the Old Testament usually render it as *Simeon*, occasionally as *Shimeon*. In the New Testament, however, it is rendered as *Simon* (q.v.), except in the case of the aged *Simeon* who blessed the infant Jesus in the Temple. *Simeon* was kept separate from *Simon* in the Middle Ages, and though not a common name it is recorded from time to time and gave rise to a surname. After the Reformation it was used rather more often.

SIMEON Cur 1200.
SYMEON HR 1273.

Simon (m.) [sīm*o*n]: the usual New Testament form of Hebrew *Shimeon* (see SIMEON). There was a Greek personal name *Σίμων*, derived from *σιμός* 'snub-nosed', and this probably influenced the later form of the name. No fewer than 8 persons of this name are mentioned in the New Testament as well as the aged *Simeon*. The great popularity of *Simon* as a christian name in the Middle Ages was due to *Simon Bar-Jonah* surnamed *Peter* (q.v.), the favourite apostle during that period. *Simon* almost rivalled *Peter* in frequency before the Reformation, and gave rise to a host of surnames, such as *Simon(s)*, *Sim*, *Sims*, *Simes*, *Syme*, *Sim(p)son*, *Simcock*, *Simcox*, *Sim(p)kin(s)*, *Simkinson*, *Sim(m)onds*, *Sinkins(on)*, *Sincox*, most of which are also found spelt with a *y*. The final *d* in *Simond* is a common development (cf. *Hammond* for *Hamon*), and *Promptorium Parvulorum* gives *Symounde* as the English form of Simon, while *Symond* is the usual spelling in the 15th and 16th C. The names *Simon*, *Simond'*, *Simund'* which occur in DB are probably not anything to do with *Simon*, but represent a Norman version of the name *Sigmund*, which existed in Old English as well as on the Continent. *Simon*, like *Peter*, went out of general use after the Reformation and has not since recovered its former popularity, though it is now more common than it has been for some centuries. The abbreviation *Sim* has been used since the 13th C. *Simon* has been used as a christian name by the Frasers of Lovat from the 12th C to the present day. In Ireland it has been used to represent the Irish *Sendn*.

SIMON Cur 1197–1215, FA 1284.
SIMOND HR 1273, Exch R 1306.
SYMOND Pat 1394, 15th-C Brut.
SYMOUNDE *Prompt Parv* 1440.
SYMKYN Cov 1480.
SYMME Coventry Mysteries 15th C.

Sis(sy), see CECILIA.

Siward (m.) [sē'ward]: Old English *Sigeweard*, compound of *sige* 'victory', and *weard* 'protection'. It was a common name before the Norman Conquest and continued in use until the 14th C, giving rise to the surnames *Seward*, *Seaward*, &c.

SEUUARD(US), SIUUARD(US) DB 1086.
SIWARDUS Cur 1197–1215, Pipe Roll 1159.
SYWARD(US) HR 1273.

Solomon (m.): Hebrew either 'little man of peace' or 'worshipper of (the god) Shalman', a well-known western semitic deity. *Salamon* was the usual medieval form of the name, which was not uncommon, and gave rise to the surnames *Salaman*, *Salmon*, *Salmond*, *Sammon*, *Sammond*, &c. The name died out about the beginning of the 14th C, but was revived by the Puritans in the 16th C. It is now used almost exclusively by Jews.

Somerled, see SAMUEL.

Sonia (f.) [sŏn′y*a*]: Russian diminutive of *Sophia* (q.v.). It came into use in England about 1920, perhaps as a result of Stephen McKenna's popular novel of that name (1917).

Sophia, Sophie (f.) [sofī′*a*, sōf′ĕ]: Greek *σοφία* 'wisdom', was first used as a christian name in England in the 17th C (cf. *Alethea*, *Charis*: the youngest daughter of James I, born in 1607, who only lived for a day, was christened *Sophia* after her maternal grandmother *Sophia*, wife of Frederick II of Denmark) and became common in the 18th C, being a favourite with German royal families. It was often anglicized to *Sophie* or *Sophy*. Admiral Croft, it will be remembered, wished that 'young ladies had not such a number of fine names. I should never be out, if they were all Sophys or something of that sort'. It went out of fashion during the later 19th C. *Sophia* has been used to render Gaelic *Beathag* (see BETHIA).

Stanislas (m.): Slavonic 'camp glory', the name of two Polish saints in the Roman calendar. Like another Polish name, *Casimir*, *Stanislas* has been used a good deal in France, and more rarely in England, chiefly by Roman Catholics.

Stanley (m.): a surname derived from a common place-name. It is not mentioned by CMY, and its use as a christian name is apparently a recent development, perhaps largely due to the popularity of the explorer Henry *Stanley* (1841–1904), whose real name was not *Stanley* but *Rowlands*. The earliest example noted is *Stanley* Baldwin (b. 1864). It is now a common christian name.

Stella (f.): Latin *stella* 'star'. The name was used by Sir Philip

Sidney to address Penelope Rich in the sonnet sequence *Astrophel to Stella* (*Astrophel* = lover of stars). Later Waller also used it, and Swift bestowed it as a pet-name on Esther Johnson. The modern use of the name is doubtless often due to these literary associations, particularly those with Swift. An early example is the use of *Stella* and *Vanessa* for two of the daughters of Leslie Stephen (1832–1904). By Roman Catholics it is associated with *Stella maris*, a title of invocation of the Blessed Virgin Mary. One medieval example of the name has been noted in a Yorks Poll Tax return of 1379.

Stephanie (f.) [stĕf′*a*nĕ]: French f. formed from Latin *Stephanus* (see STEPHEN), occasionally borrowed and used in England.

Stephen (m.): Greek *Στεφανᾶς* from *στέφανος* 'crown', a common Greek personal name, borne by the first christian martyr. *Stephanus*, *Stefanus* is found in England only as a monk's name before the Norman Conquest, but became a common christian name soon after. It occurs in DB. The surnames *Stephen(s)*, *Steven(s)*, *Stephenson*, *Stevenson*, *Steve(r)son*, *Stinson*, *Stim(p)son*, *Stenson*, *Steenson* are derived from it. *Stevyn* was the usual Middle English form.

STEFANUS DB 1086, Cur 1196–1220.
STEPHANUS HR 1273.
STEUEN Yorks Poll Tax 1379.
STEVEN Lincs 1450, *Cocke Lorelle's Bote c.* 1515.
STEVYN Lincs 1450, Cov 1491, *Prompt Parv* 1440.

Stewart, Stuart (m.): the name of the royal house of Scotland and of an extensive clan originated in the office of *steward*, the manager of a large household. Its use as a christian name, like that of a number of Scottish surnames (e.g. *Graham*, *Bruce*) seems to have begun in the latter part of the 19th C and has now spread to families with little or no Scottish connexion.

Susan(nah) (f.): Hebrew *Shushannah* 'lily', the name of the heroine of the apocryphal Book of *Susannah and the Elders*. The name is found occasionally in the 13th C, but did not become common until the 17th C, when it often appears as *Susanney* and

Shusan(na). This 17th-C use probably had reference to the *Susanna* mentioned in Luke viii. 3. In the 18th C it became very common, *Susan* being more usual, with *Sue* and *Sukey* as pet-forms. It was less popular in the later 19th C but is now again fashionable. The French *Suzanne* is also sometimes used.

SUSANNA Cur 1200, 1201, 1203, 1205, 1213.

Swithin, Swithun (m.): a derivative of Old English *swiþ* 'strong'. *Swithun*, Bishop of Winchester (died 852), received popular canonization and there are 35 churches dedicated to him. The name (usually in the incorrect spelling *Swithin*) is still occasionally used.

Sybil, see SIBYL.

Sylvanus, see SILAS.

Sylvester, see SILVESTER.

Sylvia, see SILVIA.

T

Tabitha (f.): the Aramaic equivalent of *Dorcas* (q.v.) 'roe' or 'gazelle'. Both names are given in Acts ix for the charitable woman who was raised up by St. Peter. *Tabitha*, like *Dorcas*, was common in the 17th C, and continued in use in the 18th and early 19th C.

Tace, Tacye (f.): this was a fairly common woman's name in the late 16th C and throughout the 17th C. Later it survived only among the Quakers. It is found (*Tacy*) as late as 1786. Lyford (1655) probably gives its origin correctly: '*Tace*, hold peace, hush! be silent, the imperative mood singular and indeed it is a fit name to admonish that sex of silence.' Camden (1605) gives much the same account of it.

Tadhgh, Teige (m.) [thīg]: Irish 'poet'. The name, a fairly common one, has been variously represented as *Teague*, *Thaddeus*, *Thady*.

Tagget, see AGNES.

Talbot (m.): this is now chiefly a surname, though occasionally used, like other surnames, as a christian name. Bardsley gives several instances of *Talebot* as a christian name in the 12th and 13th C. The famous and ancient family of *Talbot* took its name from its founder *Richard Talbot*, one of the companions of the Conqueror. The surname never appears in early records as *de Talbot*, and in the case of the original *Richard Talbot* was probably either a patronymic or (more likely) a nickname. Similar nicknames were *Taillefer* (found as a christian name as late as the end of the 13th C), and *Taillemache*, which gave rise respectively to the surnames *Telfer* and *Tollemache*. *Talbot* would be a compound of *tailler* 'to cut' and *botte* 'faggot'. At a later date *Talbot* was used (e.g. by Chaucer) as a nickname for a dog, and later still for a breed of dogs as well as (in heraldic language) for the dogs on the *Talbot* arms.

Tamara (f.) [tămār'ă]: a Russian name, probably of Caucasian origin, sometimes used in England in recent times, probably influenced by the popularity of the dancer *Tamara* Karsavina.

Tamasine, Tamsin, see THOMASIN.

Tancred (m.): Old German *Thancharat*, compound of *thanc* 'think' and *radi* 'counsel'. It later became *Thancred*, and in Norman French *Tancred*. In England, though not common, it gave rise to the surnames *Tancred*, *Tankard*.

Tanya, see TATIANA.

Tatiana (f.): the name of a martyr who suffered A.D. 225 and is venerated in the Orthodox Church. There are at least two others, as well as several saints *Tatianus*, all of whom seem to have been connected with Syria or Asia Minor and the name is possibly of Asiatic origin. *Tatiana* is a favourite Russian name, often abbreviated to *Tanya*, and is now occasionally used in England.

Ted(dy), see EDWARD, THEODORE.

Terence (m.): Latin *Terentius*, the name of a Roman *gens*, of unknown etymology. The poet, *P. Terentius*, was an African freedman, who took his name from his master. There was a 3rd-C Carthaginian St. *Terentius*, but it has not been used as a christian name, except in Ireland, where *Terence* or *Terry* is commonly used for the native *Toirdhealbhach* or *Turlough.*

Teresa, Theresa (f.) [terē'za]: (Latin *T(h)eresia*, Spanish, Italian *Teresa*, German *Theres(i)a*, French *Thérèse*). The origin of this name is obscure, and there is no real evidence for the usually accepted etymology from Greek θερίζω 'reap'. Θηρασία was the name of an island near Crete and of another near Sicily, and there may be some connexion between this and the personal name. It is first found as *Therasia*, the name of the wife of St. Paulinus, Bishop of Nola in the 5th C, who was converted by her. She was a Spaniard, and the name was for many centuries confined to the Iberian peninsula. There was a queen of Leon of this name in the 10th C, and it was firmly established in the royal house of Castile in the 11th C. It did not spread outside the Iberian peninsula until the 16th C, when the fame of St. *Teresa* of Avila (1515–82) carried it into all Roman Catholic countries. In recent times the popularity of the name in such countries has been increased by St. *Thérèse* of Lisieux (1873–97). It was not much used in England until the 18th C, when it was introduced by the admirers of the Empress Maria *Theresia* of Austria. It is now chiefly used in the abbreviated form *Tess* or *Tessa*. See also TRACY.

Tess(a), see TERESA.

Tetty, see ELIZABETH.

Thekla (f.) [tek'la]: Greek θέκλα, an abbreviated form of θεόκλεια a derivative of θεόκλης 'god-famed'. In early legends this was the name of a convert of St. Paul, the first woman martyr. Godstow (1450) gives *Tecle* as the English of *Tecla*, but there is no evidence of its use as a christian name until the 19th C when it was occasionally borrowed from eastern Europe.

Thelma (f.): apparently invented by Marie Corelli for the Norwegian heroine of her novel *Thelma: a society novel* (1887), and frequently used as a christian name since then. Pronunciation is not there indicated, but thĕl′ma seems to be more popular than tĕl′ma, though both are used.

Theobald (m.): Old German *Theudobald*, compound of *theuda* 'folk', 'people', and *bald* 'bold'. Names compounded with *theuda* were early changed to *theo-* under the influence of such Greek names as *Theodore*. There was a corresponding Old English name *Theodbeald*, and no doubt this survived after the Normans had introduced their version of the Germanic name. There are several subtenants mentioned in DB as *Tedbaldus*, *Teodbald*, *Tetbald*, which may well represent Old English *Theodbeald*. Later *Teobaldus* or *Theobaldus* is the usual Latin form, the vernacular being *Tebald* or *Tibald*, which survives in the surnames *Tibbald*, *Tibbles*, &c. Lyford 1655 gives *Tibald* as a form of *Theobald*, and Pope pilloried Lewis *Theobald*, the editor of Shakespeare, as *Tibbald*, explaining in a note that his name was so pronounced. Cf. also *Tybalt* in *Romeo and Juliet*.

TEDBALDUS, TEODBALD, TETBALD DB 1086.
TEBBALD Cur 1196.
THEOBALDUS Cur 1199–1220, FA 1303, 1316, 1428.
TEOBALDUS FA 1428.
THEOBALD HR 1273.
TEBBE HR 1273.
TEBAUD HR 1273.
TEBALD HR 1273.
TIBBOTT Chew 1699.

Theodora (f.): f. of *Theodore* (q.v.). First found in England in the 17th C. It has never been common. Sometimes abbreviated to *Theo*.

Theodore (m.): Greek θεόδωρος 'god's gift'. There were several saints of this name, which is common in the Eastern Church. In Russia, particularly, *Fe(o)dor* is a favourite. *Theodore*, Archbishop of Canterbury (602?–690), was a native of Tarsus in Cilicia. The name has not otherwise been noted in England before the 17th C. Horace Walpole used *Theodore* as the name of the hero of *The Castle of Otranto*, but it remained rare until the 19th C when it was favoured by the Tractarians. But the Welsh *Tudor* or *Tewdwr* is said to be of this origin. The American diminutive is *Teddy*.

Theodoric (m.) [thēŏd'orĭk]: Old German *Thiudoricus*, compound of *theuda* 'folk', 'people', and *ric* 'ruler'. There was a corresponding Old English name *Theodric*. It appears in DB as *Teodric*, *Theodric*, *Tedric*. The usual Middle English form was *Terry* from Old French *Thierry*, or *Terrick*; hence the surnames *Terr(e)y*, *Ter(r)ick*. Bardsley gives an example of *Terye* as a christian name as late as 1629. *Theodoric* was occasionally revived in the 18th C. *Terry* has been used as a christian name in recent times, but apparently always with reference to the surname. See further under DEREK.

TEODRIC, THEODRIC, TEDRIC DB 1086.
TERICUS, Cur 1199.
TERRY HR 1273.
TERRICUS HR 1273, Testa de Neville 13th C.

Theodosia (f.): f. of Greek *Theodosius* 'divinely given'. It is first found in use in England in the 17th C. It is less common than *Theodora*.

Theophania (f.): Late Latin *Theophania* from Greek *θεοφάνια* 'the manifestation of God', another name for the Epiphany. *Theophania* became *Tifaine* in Old French, and in French folk-lore *Tifaine* was thought to be the name of the mother of the Magi. It was given to girls born at the season of Epiphany, and is found in England from about 1200. It gave rise to the surnames *Tiffany*, *Tiffen*, *Tiffin*. *Tiffeny* survived in Cornwall until the 17th C. Bardsley also records an *Epiphany* there in 1695.

TEFFANY Cur 1200.
THEOPHANIA Cur 1205.
THEFFANIA Cur 1205.
THIFANIA HR 1273.
THIPHANIA Magd. 1305.
TIFFONIA Testa de Neville 13th C.
THEOFANIA Cl 1262, FA 1346.
TIFFANY Magd. 1315.
TIFFAN Yorks Poll Tax 1379.
TEFFAN Yorks Poll Tax 1379.
TYFFANY Coventry Mysteries 15th C.

Theophila (f.) [thēŏf'*ila*]: f. of *Theophilus* (q.v.). Occasionally used in the 17th C and later, e.g. *Theophila* Berkeley died 1653, and Sir Joshua Reynolds's mother *Theophila* Reynolds and his niece Mary *Theophila* Palmer (born 1757) who was usually called *Offy*.

Theophilus (m.) [thēŏf'*ilus*]: Greek θεόφιλος 'loved of God', the name of the man to whom St. Luke's Gospel and the Acts of the Apostles were addressed. It was first used as a christian name in England after the Reformation, and was common in the 17th C. It has continued to be used in the Hastings family since the time of *Theophilus* Hastings, 7th Earl of Huntingdon (born 1650).

Theresa, see TERESA.

Thermuthis (f.): occasionally used as a woman's christian name in the 18th and 19th C. Josephus gives Θέρμουθις as the name of Pharaoh's daughter who adopted the infant Moses. The grandmother, mother, and sister of Kilvert the diarist (1840–79) all bore this name. His sister was usually called *Thersie*.

Thirza (f.): Hebrew *Tirzah*, possibly 'acceptance', but more probably the name of a city used for a person (cf. *Mahalah*), a name which occurs in a genealogy in the Book of Numbers. CMY says this 'was probably the origin of *Thirza*, the name of Abel's wife in Gessner's idyll of *The Death of Abel*, a great favourite among the lower classes in England, whence *Thyrza* has become rather a favourite in English cottages'.

Thomas (m.): an Aramaic word signifying 'twin'; in the Gospels the name of one of the twelve apostles, also known as *Didymus*, the Greek for a twin. Eusebius says that his real name was *Judah*, and his nickname may well have been used by his companions to distinguish him from the two other Judahs, Judah the brother of James (St. Jude), and Judah of Kerioth (Judas Iscariot). *Thomas* is found in England before the Norman Conquest only as a priest's name, but with the advent of the Normans it soon came into general use. Two of the earliest Norman Archbishops of York were so named, *Thomas* of Bayeux (died 1100) and his nephew and successor (died 1112). In the later Middle Ages *Thomas* was one of the commonest men's names, and this was owing to the fame of St. *Thomas* of Canterbury (*Thomas* Becket, 1118–70), whose martyrdom made Canterbury the greatest object of pilgrimage in the country. From the 13th C onwards *Thomas* has been one of the half-dozen commonest men's names in England (cf. the expression *Every Tom, Dick, and Harry*). Most of the church dedications in this name were originally to St. *Thomas* of Canterbury, but Henry VIII, who had a special dislike to the memory of the recalcitrant archbishop, had them altered to St. *Thomas* the Apostle. The usual medieval abbreviation of *Thomas* was *Thome*, later (from the 14th C) *Tom*. The French diminutive *Mace* or *Macey* was also used. The surnames *Thomas*, *Thom(s)*, *T(h)om(p)son*, *T(h)omlin(son)*, *T(h)om(p)kin(s)* are some of those formed from it.

THOMAS DB 1086, Cur 1199–1220, HR 1273.
THOME HR 1273, Yorks Poll Tax 1379.
THOMASIN, THOMELIN Exch R 1306.
TOM Yorks Poll Tax 1379.
THOM Coventry Mysteries 15th C.
MACE Magd. *c.* 1200–10.

Thomasin(e) (f.): diminutive of *Thomas* (q.v.), found from the middle of the 14th C. *Thomasinus* and *Thomasina* both occur in FA 1346. *Thomas* was occasionally given to girls (*Thomasia* occurs in 14th- and 15th-C records), but the diminutive *Thomasin* soon became the usual f. form of the name. In the 16th and 17th C it appears as *Thomson*, *Tomson*, *Thomasing*, *Thomison* amongst other variants. Lyford (1655) gives it as *Thamasin* or *Thomasin*. As *Tamasine* or *Tamsin* it still survives in Cornwall.

THOMASINA FA 1346.
THOMESON St. Dionis 1538.
TOMSON St. Columb 1622.
THOMASIN Notts P Reg 1750.

Thork(et)ill (m.): a Norse name, compounded of *Thor* the name of the god, and a second element of doubtful meaning (see ASKETIL). It was adopted into Gaelic as *Torcail*, whence *Torquil*, a favourite name with the Macleods. It was introduced into England by the Danes and survived into the 13th C, giving rise to a number of surnames, e.g. *Thurkettle*, *Thurkle*, *Thirkell*, &c.

Thorold (m.): *Thorweald*, compound of *Thor*, the Norse name of the god known in Old English as *Thunor*, and Old English *weald* 'strength'; probably a semi-anglicization of Norse *Thorvald*. It is found after, as well as before, the Norman Conquest, though it was largely supplanted by the Norman-French version of the name, *Torold* or *Turold*, which survived until the 15th C. The surnames *Thorold*, *Thorald*, *Turrell*, *Turrill*, *Terrell*, *Tirrell*, *Tyrell* are derived from it.

TUROLD(US) DB 1086, Cur 1199.
THOROLD Cur 1200, 1201, 1203.
THORALD HR 1273.
TOROLD HR 1273.

Thurstan (m.): Danish *Thorstein*, compound of *stein* 'stone' with *Thor* the god's name. It was introduced into England by the Danes and survived the Norman Conquest, often in the gallicized form *Turstan* or *Turstin*. Lyford (1655) gives '*Turstan* alias *Trustan*'. *Thurstan* has continued to be used in Lancashire. The surnames *Thurstan*, *Thurston*, *Tustin*, *Tustian* are derived from it.

TURSTANUS, TURSTINUS, TURSTIN, TURSTEN DB 1086.
THURSTANUS HR 1273.
THURSTANUS, THRUSTANUS Cov 1449.
THURSTAN HR 1273.
TURSTAN HR 1273.
THRYSTAN St. Dionis 1544.

Tibby, see ELIZABETH.

Tiffany, see THEOPHANIA.

Tilly, see MATILDA.

Timothy (m.): Greek *τιμόθεος*, compound of *τιμή* 'honour', 'respect', and *θεός* 'god'. It was the name of the convert and companion of St. Paul, to whom two of his epistles are addressed. It did not come into use in England until after the Reformation. (The common surnames *Tims*, *Timms*, &c., are from an Old English name cognate with Old German *Thiemmo*, which developed into *Thim* or *Tim*.) *Timothy* has been used a good deal in Ireland (usually abbreviated to *Tim*) to represent the native *Tadhgh* (q.v.). A f. form *Timothia* occurs at Burtonwood, Lancashire, in 1702.

Tina (f.): a pet-form for names such as *Christina*, *Clementina*, but sometimes used as an independent name.

Tirzah, see THIRZA.

Titus (m.): a common Latin praenomen, of doubtful etymology. It was the name of a disciple of St. Paul, to whom one of his epistles is addressed, and has sometimes been used as a christian name since the Reformation (e.g. *Titus* Oates 1649–1705).

Tobias, Toby (m.) [tobī'*as*, tō'bĕ]: Hebrew *Tobiah*, 'Jehovah (is) good'. *Tobias* is the hellenized form of the name; *Toby* was the Middle English form (cf. *Piers Plowman* 'And can tell of *Tobye*, and of twelve Apostles'). The use of *Toby* as a christian name has not been noted before the Reformation, but the existence of the surnames *Toby*, *Tobey* (which are recorded in the 13th C) and the diminutive *Tobin*, *Tobyn*, makes it probable that it was in use then. This is the more probable since the Book of Tobit (*Tobit* probably = Greek *Tobides*, 'son of *Tobias*') was a great favourite in the Middle Ages. In the 17th C it was used a good deal.

Tony, see ANT(H)ONY.

Torquil, see THORK(ET)ILL.

Tottie, see CHARLOTTE.

Tracy (f.): this name, now common in England, is a fairly recent import from the USA, where it is, sometimes at least, a diminutive of *Teresa* (q.v.). Sometimes, however, it may have been taken from the surname of the film star Spencer *Tracy*. The surname *Tracy*, derived from Traci-Bocage in Normandy, was borne by a Norman family in Devon.

Tristram (m.): Celtic *Drystan* from *Drest* or *Drust* 'tumult', 'din'. The form *Tristan* was influenced by French *triste* 'sad', and the *Tristan* romances give this as the derivation of the name. *Tristan* is found as a surname in France as early as the end of the 12th C. The christian name occurs in England from 1189 in the form *Tristram*, which was the usual one in England, though it was exceptional in France. The intermediate form *Tristran* is found in one of the earliest French *Tristan* romances. The surnames *Tristram, Trustram, Triston* are derived from it.

TRISTRAM Cur 1189–1215, HR 1273.
TRYSTREM Yorks Poll Tax 1379.
TRISTIAN Lyford 1655.

Trix(ie), see BEATRIX.

Troth (f.): one of the many abstract nouns adopted as christian names in the 17th C. It was not uncommon during that century and continues to be used in some families. The following is an example of the way in which such names were handed down; Sir Thomas Tempest (died 1641) married *Troth* Tempest; their daughter married John Kennett, and her daughter *Troth* Kennett married William Bradshaw and had a daughter *Troth*.

Tryphena, Tryphosa (f.): derivatives of Greek τρυφή 'daintiness', 'delicacy'. *Tryphena* and *Tryphosa* are the names of women mentioned by St. Paul in Rom. xvi. 12, and were used a good deal as christian names in the late 16th and 17th C. *Tryphena* is no doubt the source of the gipsy name *Truffeni*.

Turlough (m.) [tur'lō]: Irish *Toirdhealbhach*. A common Irish name, often represented by *Terence, Terry*, or *Charles* (qq.v.).

U

Uchtred, Ughtred (m.) [ū'tred]: the second element is Old English *ræd* 'counsel', the first is obscure. It is found in the Old English period as *Uhtred* and *Wihtred*, survived the Norman Conquest, and has continued to be used in a few families.

UCTRED DB 1086.
UHTRED Pipe Roll 1161.
UHREDUS Cur 1189.
UGHTRED Cur 1200, 1210, 1213, Cl 1284.
UCHTRED Cur 1203, 1205.
UCHERED Lyford 1655.

Ulick, see ULYSSES.

Ulric (m.): Old English *Wulfric*, compound of *wulf* 'wolf' and *ric* 'ruler'. It survived the Norman Conquest and gave rise to the surnames *Woolrich*, *Woolridge*, &c. The modern form, *Ulric*, is apparently a revival of the Norman-French spelling, which occurs in DB.

ULRICUS, ULURIC DB 1086.
WLVRICUS Cur 1199.
WULURICH HR 1273.
WLFRIC HR 1273.
WLFRICHE HR 1273.

Ulrica (f.): f. of *Ulric* (q.v.), occasionally borrowed from German.

Ulysses (m.): *Ulixes* or *Ulysses* was the Latin name for the Greek hero *Odysseus*: it was probably from Etruscan *Uluxe*. The name has been used in Ireland to represent the native names *Ulick* and *Uileos*.

Una (f.) [English ūn*a*, Irish o͞on*a*]: *Una* (phonetically rendered as *Oonagh*) is an ancient Irish name, still in use, but often anglicized as *Winnie* or *Winifred* or translated as *Agnes*, from a fancied connexion between *Agnes* and the Latin *agnus* on the one hand, and *Una* and the Irish *uan*, a lamb, on the other. *Juno* is yet another rendering (cf. O'Casey's play 'Juno and the Paycock'). *Una* is also sometimes used in England after *Una* in Spenser's *Faerie Queene*, where it is the f. of Latin *unus* 'one' (in distinction to the false *Duessa*).

Unity (f.): an example of the use of abstract nouns denoting moral qualities which came into fashion in the 17th C. It occurs as the name of a widow at Wallingford in 1681. Another example is the Hon. *Unity* Mitford (d. of the 2nd Lord Redesdale).

Urania (f.): Greek *Οὐρανία*, the Muse of Astronomy (from *οὐρανός* 'the sky'). It was also an epithet of Aphrodite. Sir Philip Sidney addressed poems to *Urania*, which became a favourite poetic title in both France and England. It has been used as a christian name in some families and is still used in some gipsy families.

Urban (m.): Latin *urbanus*, 'of the town or city', like *paganus* 'a villager', came to be used as a personal name. *Urbanus* is one of those to whom St. Paul sends greetings in his Epistle to the Romans, and it was adopted by eight Popes, starting with St. Urban in the 3rd C. It was occasionally used as a christian name in the Middle Ages.

URBAN HR 1273.
URBANUS Testa de Neville 13th C.

Uriah (m.): Hebrew 'Jehovah is light' or 'Light of Jehovah'. In the case of '*Uriah* the Hittite', the Hittite *Ariya* or *Uriya* has been assimilated to the Hebrew name. Occasionally used as a christian name since the Reformation (e.g. *Uriah* Bankes 1648, a Presbyterian minister). It was never common, and if it needed a *coup de grâce*, it was given one by *Dickens* in the character of *Uriah* Heep in *David Copperfield*.

Urian, Urien (m.): this is a Welsh name, possibly derived from **Urbigenos* = town born, but it is found also in England in the Middle Ages, possibly as a result of its occurrence in the Arthurian romances.

URIAN HR 1273.
URYENE HR 1273.
URIANUS FA 1431.
URIAN or URANIUS Lyford 1655.

Urith (f.): The name of the patron saint of the church of Chittlehampton in Devon. William of Worcester identifies this saint with *Herygh*, an Irish saint, after whom he supposed the parish of St. Erth in Cornwall to be named. But *Herygh* was a man, and there appears to be no good reason for the identification. Camden says of Chittlehampton:—'a small village where *Hierytha*, Kalendar'd among the She-saints, was buried.' Nothing is known of this

Hierytha, and no suggestion can be made for the etymology of the name, which sometimes appears locally as St. *Wurth*. The form *Urith* occurs as a christian name about the beginning of the 17th C. Early examples are *Urith*, daughter of Thomas Shapcote of Shapcote married Sir Courtenay Pole of Shute (1618–95); *Urith*, daughter of Sir John Pole of Shute married (1693) Sir John Trevelyan, 2nd Bart. Another John Trevelyan, High Sheriff of Somerset in the reign of James I, married *Urith*, daughter of Sir John Chichester of Raleigh. The name is still used in the Trevelyan family.

Ursula (f.): Latin diminutive of *ursa* 'she-bear'. The legend of St. *Ursula* and the 11,000 virgins was popular in the Middle Ages, and the name was fairly common. It is also found from time to time in the 17th–19th C, and has lately become more frequent.

URSEL Cur 1200.
URSELL Cur 1207, HR 1273.
HURSEL HR 1273.
URCY HR 1273.
OURSE 14th C Legendary.
URSALAY, URSELEY Yorks Rec 1604.

V

Valentine (m., f.): Latin derivative of *Valens* 'strong', 'healthy' (cf. *Constantinus* from *Constans*, *Clementinus* from *Clemens*); the name of a 3rd-C Roman martyr. His feast day (14 Feb.) almost coincided with the festival of Juno Februata (15 Feb.), and the custom of drawing lots for lovers was transferred from the pagan to the christian festival. The name has never been common, but is found occasionally from the 12th C onwards. It is now used indifferently for men and women, and has been so since the 17th C.

VALENTINUS Cur 1196, 1200, 1203, 1205, FA 1284, Vis of Berks 1433.
VALANTINUS Cur 1210–12.
VALENTINE Cl 1553.

Valeria, Valerie (f.): Latin *Valeria*, f. of *Valerius*, the name of a Roman *gens*, probably derived from *valere*. St. *Valeria* was supposed to have been the wife of St. Vitalis, and mother of SS. Gervasius and Protasius, who were martyred at Ravenna in the 1st C. *Valeria* is common in Italy and *Valérie* is not uncommon in France and was imported into England as *Valerie* towards the end of the 19th C.

Valerian (m.) [*va*lēr'ĕ*a*n]: Latin *Valerianus*, derivative of *Valerius* the name of a Roman *gens* (see VALERIA). St. *Valerianus* was a Bishop of Auxerre, and *Valérian* has had some currency as a christian name in France. It is found in England in the 13th C and has been used by the Wellesley family from the Middle Ages to the present day.

VALERIANUS Cur 1213–15.

Vanessa (f.): invented by Swift as a partial anagram of the name of Esther Vanhomrigh (cf. his *Cadenus and Vanessa*), and occasionally used as a christian name since then.

Venetia (f.): said by CMY to be a latinizing of Welsh *Gwyneth* (q.v.). Sir Kenelm Digby's wife, *Venetia*, a famous beauty, is probably responsible for its occasional use.

Vera (f.): Russian *Vjera* 'faith'. CMY does not know this as an English name. Ouida in *Moths* (1860) and Marion Crawford in *A Cigarette-Maker's Romance* (1890) both used the name, but both thought it necessary to explain it. Its popularity at the beginning of the 20th C was probably due to the second of these novels. In modern Roman Catholic use it is apparently often used as an equivalent of *Veronica* (q.v.).

Vere (m.): the name of a famous family which derived its name from *Ver* in Normandy. The *de Vere* Earldom of Oxford became extinct in the 17th C, but Lady Diana de Vere, the heiress of the last earl, married the 1st Duke of St. Albans, and their 3rd son was named *Vere* Beauclerk (later Lord Vere of Hanworth). This is the earliest example noted of the use of *Vere* as a christian name. Like other similar names, it is now often used by persons with no connexion with the family.

Verena (f.) [verē'na]: the name of a virgin martyred under Diocletian. Her cult is one of the most ancient in Switzerland and Suabia, and there are many churches and chapels dedicated to her around the Lake of Lucerne. The name *Verena* has been used in England in recent times, possibly introduced from this favourite tourist region, but also probably with reference to its use in *The Heir of Redclyffe*.

Verity (f.): used as a christian name since the 17th C.

Vernon (m.): a surname of local origin (it is a very common place-name in France). Richard de *Vernon*, a companion of the Conqueror and founder of a famous family, came from *Vernon* (Eure). The use of *Vernon* as a christian name arose in the 19th C. An early example is *Vernon* Whitford in Meredith's novel *The Egoist* (1879).

Veronica (f.). from late Latin *veraiconica*, compound of f. of *verus* 'true' and *iconicus* 'of or belonging to an image'; the name given to a famous relic, a cloth supposed to retain the image of the face of Christ. Later *Veronica* was taken to be the name of the woman who had wiped His face with the cloth, and in some medieval apocryphal writings (e.g. the Acts of Pilate, the Book of Resurrection by Bartholomew) she was identified with the woman who was cured of an issue of blood. The name was also sometimes confused with *Berenice* (q.v.). *Véronique* has been used a good deal in France. Alexander Bruce, Earl of Kincardine (died 1681) married a Dutch lady, *Veronica* Sommalsdyck, and so introduced the name into Scotland; his great-grandson, James Boswell, gave the name to one of his daughters. In England it seems not to have been used until about the end of the 19th C.

Vesta (f.): the name of the Roman goddess of fire, sometimes used as a christian name in modern times.

Victor (m.): Latin *victor* 'conqueror', the name of an early Pope and of several martyrs. *Victor* is found in Curia Regis Rolls of

1200 and 1203 and a single example has been noted in 1585, but it was evidently rare in the Middle Ages, and its modern use in France seems to date from the Revolution. In England it came into general use in the later half of the 19th C, being regarded, probably, as a m. form of *Victoria.*

Victoria (f.): Latin *victoria* 'victory'. Said to occur in the Liverpool area 1617–1702, and a pauper named *Victoria* Chapman was buried at Moulton, Lincs., in 1681. Otherwise it has not been noted as a christian name in England before the 19th C. Queen *Victoria* (who was christened Alexandrina *Victoria*) was named after her German mother, Maria Louisa *Victoria.* The Queen's name was borne by her numerous godchildren and was sometimes given as a second name, but did not become generally popular and is now only rarely used. The Italian *Vittoria* and French *Victoire* are from the 3rd-C Roman martyr *Victoria.*

Viel, see VITALIS.

Vincent (m.): Latin *Vincentius,* derivative of *vincens* 'conquering'. There was a 3rd-C martyr of this name at Saragossa, whose cult was fairly extensive; and the name is found in England from the 13th C, giving rise to the surnames *Vincent, Vince, Vincey.* Later the fame of St. *Vincent* Ferrer, a 15th-C Spanish Dominican, and particularly of St. *Vincent* de Paul, the 17th-C French founder of the Vincentian Order of the Sisters of Charity, increased its use in Roman Catholic countries. It also became fairly common in England in the 19th C.

VINCENTIUS Cur 1200, 1203, 1205, 1210, Vis of Berks 1433.
VINCENT HR 1273.

Viola (f.) [vī'*ola*]: Latin *viola* 'violet'. The modern use of the name is due to Shakespeare's heroine in *Twelfth Night.* One of his possible sources has the name *Violetta,* which he may have shortened. *Viola,* however, also occurs as a name in Gower's *Confessio Amantis.*

Violet (f.): from Old French *violete,* diminutive of Latin *viola* 'violet'. *Violette* occurs as a christian name in the south of France in the Middle Ages, and there are a few instances in England, e.g. the wife of Sir John Chandos (died 1370). In the 16th C it is fairly common in Scotland, doubtless through French influence, and it has continued to be used there. It did not become general in England until the middle of the 19th C.

Virginia (f.): Latin f. of *Virginius*, earlier *Verginius*, the name of a Roman plebeian *gens*, probably cognate with *Vergilius* and of non-Latin origin. The story of *Paul et Virginie* (1786) made it popular in France. It came into use in England in the 19th C. The name arose independently in America where the first child born in America of English parentage (*Virginia* Dare, born at Roanoke, Aug. 1587) received the name of the plantation, which had been named in honour of Queen Elizabeth. It is much commoner there than in England.

Virtue (m.): used as a christian name in the 17th C and occasionally since.

Vitalis (m.): Latin *vitalis* 'of or belonging to life', 'vital'; the name of several early saints, SS. *Vitalis* of Bologna, Ravenna, and Rome. The name was introduced into England by the Normans and was not uncommon in the 12th–13th C, often in the French form, *Viel*. *Vyell* Vivian Esq. is found at Lancaster as late as 1799, but this may be a use of the surname. *Veitel* is still used in Germany.

VITALIS, FITELLUS, VITHELET, VITEL, FITEL, PHITELET DB 1086.
VITALIS Cur 1203, 1205, 1210.
VITAL Godstow 1450, Lyford 1655.
VIEL Cur 1210, 1213, HR 1273.
VITALIS or VIEL Testa de Neville 13th C.

Vivian (m.): Latin *Vivianus*, derivative of *vivus* 'alive'. St. *Vivianus* was a 5th-C martyr, who sometimes appears as *Bibianus*. The name is found in England from the 12th C, but has never been common. In the Middle Ages it was sometimes spelt *Phythian*, *Fithian*, &c.

VIVIANUS Cur 1199–1219, HR 1273.

VIVIAN St. Columb 1544.
FITHIAN HR 1273.
FITHIAN or VIVIAN Cheshire 1514.
PHYTHEON Chester Wills 1582.

Vivien (f.): Tennyson in his *Vivien and Merlin* used this form for French *Vivienne*, the name of the Lady of the Lake. The name probably originated in a misreading of MS *Ninian*, a Celtic name (see NINIAN). *Viviana*, which is found in medieval records, is a f. form of the man's name *Vivian* (q.v.).

W

Waldeve, see WALTHEOF.

Waldo, see WALTHEOF.

Wallace (m.): a Scottish surname (the equivalent of English *Welsh*, *Walsh*) used as a christian name after the famous patriot William *Wallace* (1272?–1305). This use is fairly recent and is not now confined to Scotland.

Walter (m.): Old German *Waldhar*, compound of *vald* 'rule' and *harja* 'folk'. It was a favourite with the Normans, and was introduced by them into England at the time of the Conquest. The corresponding Old English name *Wealdhere* was never common. *Walter* has been in use ever since its introduction, and gave rise to the surnames *Walter(s)*, *Watt(s)*, *Watkin*, *Watson*, *Waters*, *Gwatkin*, &c. *Wat* was the usual abbreviation until the 17th C, and apparently the full name was pronounced *Water* (cf. Shakespeare's 2 *Hen. VI*, IV. i. 31–5); *Water* occurs as late as 1670 in the parish registers of South Leigh, Oxfordshire.

WALTER(I)US DB 1086, Cur 1196–1220.
G(U)ALTER(I)US DB 1086.
WALTER HR 1273.
WAUTER Writs of Parliament 1313, Exch R 1306.
WATER Oseney 1460, St. Dionis 1579, St. Antholin 1563.
GWALTER St. Antholin 1640.
GUALTER St. Jas. Clerkenwell 1688.

Waltheof (m.): Old English *Wealdtheof*, compound of *weald* 'power', 'rule', and *theof* 'thief'. *Waltheof* Earl of Northumbria, executed by William I in 1076, and his grandson *Waltheof*, Abbot of Melrose (died 1159), were regarded by the English as saints, and miracles were said to be worked at their tombs. The name survived in use in the North as late as the middle of the 17th C in the form *Waldeve, Waldive*. Bardsley would derive the name *Waldo*, still used in some families, from *Waltheof* (cf. the 11th C forms *Waltheof, Waldeof*, and *Waldew* for the name of the Abbot of Crowland). There was, however, an Old German name *Waldo*, from Gothic *valdan* 'to reign'.

WALDEOF, WALTHEOF, WALDEW (Abbot of Crowland at end of 11th C).
WALDIEF Pipe Roll 1161.
WALDIVE Exch Dep 1661.

Wanda (f.): a German woman's name, derivative of Old German *vand* which probably meant 'stock' or 'stem'. *Wanda* has lately been used a good deal in England, possibly taken from a novel of that name by Ouida (1883).

Warner (m.): Old German *Warinhari*, compound of the folk-name *Varin* and *harja* 'folk'. It was introduced into England by the Normans in the form *Garnier*, and was fairly common in the 12th–14th C. The surname *Warner*, derived from it, is now often used as a christian name in the USA.

WARNER(I)US DB 1086, Pipe Roll 1159.
WARNER HR 1273.
WARINER HR 1273.
GERNER FF 1283.
GARNER Yorks Poll Tax 1379.

Warren (m.): Old German *Varin*, a folk-name. It was introduced into England by the Normans as *Warin* or *Guarin* and became common, giving rise to the surnames *Warren, Waring, Garnet* (from the diminutive *Guarin-et*), &c. It is rare after the 14th C, and when used as a christian name in more recent times is generally found to be a family name, e.g. *Warren* Hastings was named after his mother's maiden name. Lyford, it is true, gives

Warin in his list of names and it is said to occur in Manchester in the early 17th C.

WARINUS DB 1086, Cur 1199–1220, Testa de Neville 13th C.
GUARINUS DB 1086, Cl 13th C.
WARRENUS Testa de Neville 13th C.
WARIN HR 1273.
GUARIN Pat 13th C.

Wendy (f.): First used by J. M. Barrie in his play *Peter Pan* (1904), and frequently used since then as a christian name. The origin of the name was a pet-name for Barrie evolved by W. E. Henley's little daughter Margaret: 'Friendy' became 'Friendy-wendy', and eventually 'Wendy'.

Wilfred, Wilfrid (m.): Old English *Wilfrith*, compound of *will* 'will', and *frith* 'peace'. St. *Wilfrith* or *Wilfrid* (*c.* 634–709), Bishop of York and one of the foremost men of his day, has some 50 churches dedicated to him. His name seems not to have survived in use after the Norman Conquest, and has not been noted before the late 16th C. It was revived by the Tractarians in the 19th C and is now common.

Wilhelmina (f.): a f. form of *Wilhelm* (see WILLIAM), borrowed from the German or Dutch in the 18th C. An early example was *Wilhelmina* Newnham who m. the eldest son of Sir John Shelley Bt. in 1769. Cf. also Miss Carolina *Wilhelmina* Amelia Skeggs in *The Vicar of Wakefield* (1766). Sometimes abbreviated to *Mina*.

William (m.): Old German *Willahelm*, compound of *vilja* 'will' and *helma* 'helmet'. It became *Guilielm* and then *Guillaume* in French, and was introduced into England by the Normans in the 11th C, from which time it has held its place as one of the commonest men's names (from the 16th to 19th C, for instance, it averages 20 per cent. of baptismal entries in parish registers), tying with John for first place. At the present time it is (probably only temporarily) much less common. The usual abbreviation was *Will*. There is no direct evidence for the use of *Bill* as a nickname for *William* in the Middle Ages (the surnames *Bill*, *Bilson* may be from Old English *Bil*). There are many surnames derived from William and its diminutives, e.g. *William(s)*, *Williamson*, *Wilson*, *Willcock*, *Wilcox(son)*, *Wilmot* (from the common diminutive *William-ot*), *Wilkin(s)*, *Wilkinson*, *Wilk(e)s*, *Wilkie*, &c. (from the pet-form *Wil-kin*), *Willis*, *Willet*, *Willin(g)s*. *Gill*, *Gillot*, *Gillet*, &c., are sometimes from Old French *Guille*, an abbreviation for *Guillaume*, but may also be from the girl's name *Gill* (see JULIAN). *Wilmot* was often a girl's name, and occurs as late as 1702 in the parish register of Kemble.

WILLELM Reg *c.* 1067.
WILLELMUS DB 1086, Cur 1199–1220.
WILECOC HR 1273.
WYLYMOT Poll Tax 1379.
GILLET, GILLOT(IN), GILLIAME, GUILLOT Exch R 1306.
WYLL *Cocke Lorelle's Bote c.* 1515.
GILOW, GYLAW Poll Tax 1379.
GILMYN Poll Tax 1379.

Wilmot (f.) see WILLIAM.

Winifred (f.): Welsh *Gwenfrewi*. St. *Gwenfrewi* was said to be a Welsh princess martyred by Caradoc, and her well was, and still is, regarded as miraculous. The Latin life of the saint gives the name as *Wenefreda*, which was early anglicized as *Winifred*, and was sometimes confused with the Old English man's name *Winfrith*. It has not been noted in use in England until the 16th C, and then usually with a Welsh connexion; *Wynifreed* occurs in 1585, *Winefred* 1631, *Winfrith* 1646, *Winnifred* 1704, *Winefred* 1742. It is now often abbreviated to *Winnie* and sometimes to *Freda*.

Winston (m.): used as a christian name in the Churchill family since Sir *Winston* Churchill (born 1620), father of the first Duke of Marlborough, whose mother was Sarah *Winston*, daughter of Sir Henry *Winston* of Standish in Gloucestershire. The name is derived from a hamlet near Cirencester.

Wystan (m.): Old English *Wigstan*, compound of *wig* 'battle' and *stan* 'stone'. *Wigstan*, King of Mercia, murdered in 849 while still a boy, was later revered as a saint, and his memory long survived in the Midlands.

WYSTAN FF *c.* 1190.
WISTANUS FA 1431.

Y

Yolande (f.): apparently a medieval French form of *Violante*, a derivative of *Viola* (q.v.). It has been occasionally revived in modern times.

JOLENTA FA 1289, 1302.
JOLEICIA (*sic*, the same person as in the other references) FA 1346.

Yorick (m.): Shakespeare's source for this name in *Hamlet* has been much discussed, but it was probably a phonetic rendering of *Georg* (pronounced *Yorg*) the Danish form of *George*. Sterne made use of the name *Yorick* in his *Sentimental Journey* (1768), and since then it has occasionally been used as a christian name.

Yvonne, Yvette (f.) [ēvŏn', ēvĕt']: French f. diminutive of *Yvon*, *Yve* (see IVO). *Yvonne* has become fairly common in England in the present century. *Ivetta* occurs in Cur 1167.

Z

Zacchaeus (m.): Hebrew '*Zakkai*' an abbreviated form of *Zachariah* (q.v.), latinized as *Zacchaeus* (the Greek is *Ζακχιος*). It has also been explained, less probably, as identical with the Aramaic adjective *zakkai* 'pure'. *Zacchaeus* was the name of the publican of Jericho who climbed a tree in order to see Jesus pass by and later entertained him in his house (Luke 19). It was a common christian name in the 17th C.

Zacharias, Zachary (m.) [zăkarī'*as*, zăk'*ar*ĕ]: Hebrew 'Jehovah has remembered', the name of a king of Israel, and also of a prophet (whose name appears in the Authorized Version as *Zechariah*, a better spelling). *Zachary* seems to have been used occasionally in the Middle Ages, cf. the surname *Zachary*, which is recorded from the 16th C. It became popular with the 17th-C Puritans and lingered on in country use until recently.

Zedekiah (m.): Hebrew 'righteousness of Jehovah', the name of a king of Judah, sometimes used as a christian name in the 17th C.

Zenobia (f.): the name of a famous queen of Palmyra, probably a hellenization of some such name as *Zunab*. It was also the name of a 4th-C martyr. For some reason it came into use in Cornwall, where it occurs from about 1586. *Zenobe* Webb occurs in a Somerset will of 1694.

Zephaniah (m.): Hebrew 'Jehovah has concealed' (= 'protected') or 'stored up, treasured', the name of a Hebrew prophet, sometimes used as a christian name in the 17th C and later.

Zillah (f.): Hebrew 'shade', the name of the wife of Lamech. Occasionally used since the Reformation. It is a favourite gipsy name.

Zoë (f.): Greek *ζωή* 'life', used by Alexandrian Jews as a translation of the name *Eve*, and later as a christian name by the Byzantine Greeks. It was the name of a 3rd-C martyr who is in both the Greek and the Roman Calendars. Its use in England is recent. The earliest example noted is *Zoë* Skene, daughter of a British consul general at Aleppo, who in 1855 married the future Archbishop Thomson.

SOME COMMON WORDS DERIVED FROM CHRISTIAN NAMES

Aaron's beard: kinds of plant, especially Great St. John's wort. (Reference to Ps. cxxxiii. 2.)

Aaron's rod: kinds of plant, especially Great Mullein and Golden Rod. (Reference to Num. xvii. 8.)

abigail: lady's maid. (Character in Beaumont and Fletcher's *Scornful Lady*, perhaps with reference to 1 Sam. xxv. 24–31.)

Achilles tendon: tendon connecting heel (where alone Achilles was vulnerable) with calf.

Adam: *old Adam*, unregenerate condition; *Adam's ale* or *wine*, water; *Adam's apple*, projection of the thyroid cartilage of the larynx.

Adamite: child of Adam, human being, unclothed man; name of sects who imitated Adam in this respect.

Albert: kind of watch-chain, also a frock-coat. (From Prince Albert, consort of Queen Victoria.)

Alexandrine: pertaining to verses of 12 syllables, from the Old French romance *Alexandre* concerning *Alexander* the Great.

Alice blue: a colour. (Named after Alice Roosevelt, daughter of President Theodore Roosevelt.)

Andrew: *Merry-andrew*, mountebank's assistant, clown, buffoon.

Ant(h)ony: *Anthony* or *Tantony*, the smallest pig of a litter; (*St.*) *Anthony's fire*, erysipelas.

Bain-Marie: vessel containing hot water, for heating saucepans, from med. Latin *balneum Mariae*, from the name of a supposed Jewish alchemist, *Maria*.

Benedick: newly married man, especially confirmed bachelor who marries. (Shakespeare, *Much Ado about Nothing*.)

Benjamin: youngest child, darling. (Gen. xlii. 4.)

bertha, berthe: deep-frilling, (usually lace) collar to low-necked dress. (French *Berthe*, woman's name.)

Biddy: nickname for an Irish-woman, from the prevalence of the name Brigid in Ireland; hence *old biddy*, an old woman. Also used for calling chickens.

billy: (Australian) tin can used as kettle, &c., in camping out.

billycock: a hard felt hat (19th C) named from William (*Billy*) Coke, nephew of the Earl of Leicester (1752–1842), to whose order the first such hat was made. Still called a *coke* in the hat trade.

billy-goat: male goat. *Silly billy*, a foolish person, first used of William, Duke of Gloucester. When his cousin William IV gave the Royal Assent to the Reform Bill, Gloucester said 'Who 's silly Billy now?'

bob: (slang) a shilling. *Dry-*, *wet-bob*, *cricketing* or *boating* Etonian; *light-bob*, soldier of light infantry.

bobby: (slang) policeman. (From Sir Robert Peel, Home Secretary, 1828; cf. also *peeler*.)

Boniface: innkeeper. (Farquhar's *Beaux' Stratagem*.)

Caroline: of Charlemagne; of the time of Charles I and II of England. (From Latin *Carolus*.)

Catherine-wheel: circular spoked window or window-compartment; rotating firework; lateral somersault. (From the spiked wheel which was the instrument of St. Catherine's martyrdom.)

Charles's wain: the constellation Ursa Major. (Old English *Carles wægn*; wain of Arcturus, a neighbouring constellation, became wain of Arthur, who was confused with the other great hero of romance, Charlemagne.)

charley, charlie: a night watchman and, later, a fool (no explanation of these meanings). Also a pointed or 'vandyke' beard, from portraits of Charles I.

Charlotte: *apple charlotte, Charlotte Russe*, names of puddings (French).

cuddy: (Scottish) donkey; fool, ass; lever on tripod for lifting stones, &c. (Probably *Cuddy*, Scottish and North country diminutive of *Cuthbert.*)

Cyrillic: of the alphabet used by Slavonic people in the Eastern church, the invention of which was traditionally attributed to the Greek missionary *Cyril.*

dandy: (person) devoted to smartness, especially of costume; neat, smart, decorated. (Found from 1780 in Scotland, where *Dandy* is used as a pet-form of Andrew.)

Daniel: upright judge, person of infallible wisdom. (Dan. i–vi; *Merchant of Venice* IV. i. 223, 333.)

David and Jonathan: any pair of devoted friends. (1 Sam. xiii., &c.)

davit: crane at a ship's bow for hoisting anchor clear of side; one of a pair of cranes for suspending or lowering ship's boat. (Formerly also *david*, probably from the personal name.)

demijohn: bulging, narrow-necked bottle of 3–10 gal., usually cased in wicker. (Corruption of French *Dame Jeanne.*)

derrick: contrivance for moving or hoisting heavy weights; kind of crane with adjustable arm pivoted at foot to central post, deck, or floor. (Obsolete senses *hangman*, *gallows*, from the surname of a noted hangman at Tyburn, *c.* 1600.)

Diana: horsewoman, huntress. (*Diana*, goddess of the chase.)

dickens: devil, deuce. (From 1598; probably use of *Dickon* (= Richard), or the surname *Dickens*, as an alliterative substitute.)

dicky, dickey: donkey; (also *dicky-bird*) small bird; false shirt-front; pinafore or apron; driver's seat; servant's seat at back of carriage; seat at back of two-seater car. Some of these (e.g. first two) are certainly from the pet-name *Dicky* for *Richard.*

Dorcas: meeting of ladies to make clothes for the poor. (Acts ix. 36.)

doubting Thomas: incredulous person, from St. *Thomas* (John xx. 24–9).

Geordie: a nickname for a Northumbrian, from the north country form of *George.*

George: jewel forming part of Garter insignia.

gib: (obsolete) male cat. (From *Gib*, pet-form of *Gilbert.*)

Gregorian: of the plain-chant or plain-song ritual music named after Pope Gregory I; Gregorian calendar, correction by Pope Gregory XIII of the Julian calendar.

guy: effigy of Guy Fawkes burnt on 5 Nov.; grotesquely dressed person, fright.

Harry, Old: the devil.

hector: bluster(er), bully.

Herculean: pertaining to Hercules, especially 'a Herculean labour'.

hick: (US colloquial) countryman, farmer, provincial. (Possibly from *Hick* = *Dick*, cf. *Hodge*.)

hobby: favourite subject or occupation that is not one's main business; (archaic) small horse; (hist.) early type of velocipede; *hobby-horse*, wicker horse used in morris-dance, &c., child's stick with horse's head; rocking-horse; horse on merry-go-round. (From Old French *hobin*, *hobi*, probably variant of the name *Robin*.)

hobgoblin: mischievous imp, bogy, bugbear. (From *Hob* for *Rob*(*in*)+*goblin*.)

Hodge: typical English agricultural labourer. (*Hodge* for *Roger*.)

Isabel, Isabella: greyish yellow. From the female name; history unknown, though there are several apocryphal stories attached to the word.

jack: familiar form of the name John, especially as type of the common people, as *Jack and Jill*; *every man jack*, every individual; = *jack tar*, common sailor; labourer, man who does odd jobs, &c.; *Cheap Jack*, travelling hawker; *steeplejack*, man who climbs steeples, &c., to do repairs; (Cards) the Knave; machine for turning spit in roasting meat; figure of a man on a clock; machine for lifting heavy weights; machine for lifting axle off ground while cleaning or changing wheel; *boot-jack*, for pulling boots off; parts of various machines, &c.; pike, especially young or small one; *Jack Frost*, frost personified; *Jack-a-dandy*, dandy; *jackass*, male ass, dolt, blockhead; *laughing jackass*, Giant Kingfisher of Australia; *jack-boot*, large boot coming above the knee; *jackdaw*, thievish small crow haunting church towers; *Jack in office*, fussy official; *jack-in-the-box*, toy figure that springs out of box when opened, also kind of firework; *Jack-in-the-green*, man or boy (usually a sweep) enclosed in framework covered with leaves in Mayday sports; *jack-knife*, large clasp-knife for the pocket; *Jack of all trades*, one who can turn his hand to anything; *jack-o'-lantern*, will-o'-the-wisp; *jack-plane*, for coarse work; *jack* *pudding*, buffoon, clown; *jack-snipe* (small species); *jack tar*, common sailor; *jack-towel* (endless, hung from roller); *jack*, a small flag flown from a *jack-staff*, whence *Union Jack*, is probably the same word.

Jackanapes: formerly an ape, then a pert aping fellow, a coxcomb. First recorded *c.* 1450 as a nickname (*Jack Napes*) of William de la Pole, 1st Duke of Suffolk, whose badge was an ape's clog and chain. Later used as a quasi-proper name for an ape.

Jack Ketch: common hangman.

Jacobean: of the reign of James I; of St. James the Less.

Jacobin: (1) Dominican friar, originally Fr. member of the order, from the church of St. *Jacques* in Paris, near which their original convent was built; (2) member of a political club established in 1789 near the old convent of the Jacobin friars; (3) breed of pigeons with a cowl-like ruff.

Jacobite: (1) adherent of *James* II of England after his abdication, or of his descendants; (2) member of a monophysite heresy taking its name from *Jacobus* Baradaeus of Edessa (6th C).

Jacob's Ladder: plant (*Polemonium caeruleum*) with corymbs of blue or white flowers, and leaves suggesting a ladder; (Naut.) rope ladder with wooden rungs.

Jacob's staff: surveyor's iron-shod rod; instrument for measuring distances and heights.

jacobus: English gold coin struck in reign of James I.

jane: (American slang) woman.

jarvey: 19th-C slang for a coachman, perhaps in allusion to the emblem of St. Gervase, which was a whip.

Jehu: furious driver. (2 Kings ix. 20.)

jemimas: (colloquial) elastic-sided boots; galoshed cloth overboots.

jemmy: crowbar used by burglars; sheep's head as a dish.

jenneting: kind of early apple. (Probably from the name *Jeannet+ing*.)

jenny: locomotive crane; *spinning jenny*, mechanism for spinning more than one strand at a time; *jenny-wren*, popular and nursery name for the wren; *Jenny donkey*, female ass.

Jeremiah: doleful prophet or denouncer of the time.

Jeroboam: wine-bottle of 8–12 times ordinary size. ('A mighty man of valour' 'who made Israel to sin'—1 Kings xi. 28, xiv. 16.)

jerry: *jerry-builder*, *-building*, builder, building of unsubstantial houses with bad materials; *jerry-built*, so built; *jerry* or *jerry-shop*, low beer-shop; (slang) chamber-pot; *Jerry* (army slang) German soldier, the Germans. (Probably familiar form of the name *Jeremiah*.)

Jezebel: impudent or abandoned woman; woman who paints her face. (Jezebel, wife of Ahab.)

Jill or Gill: *Jack and Jill*, lad and lass.

jilt: woman who capriciously casts off lover after giving him encouragement; (rarely) man who treats woman thus. (Probably from obsolete *Gillot*, diminutive of *Gill* from *Gillian*.)

Jim Crow: (USA) negro.

Job: *Job's Comforter*, one who under guise of comforter aggravates distress; *Job's tears*, seeds of a grass used as beads.

Jock: Highland soldier. (*Jock* is scottish equivalent of *Jack*.)

jockey (n.): professional rider in horse races. (From Scottish *Jocky* = *Jacky*.)

jockey (v.): outwit, cheat. (From preceding in obsolete sense 'cheat'.)

Joe Miller: stale joke, chestnut. (From *Joseph Miller*, comedian, died 1735.)

joey: a fourpenny-piece (first issued in 1836, at the instance of Mr. Joseph Hume, whence it for some time bore the nickname 'joey'); a young Kangaroo; a clown.

John: *John Barleycorn*, malt liquor personified; *John Bull*, English nation, typical Englishman; *John Chinaman*, Chinaman; *John Doe*, fictitious character in law; *John Dory*, also simply *dory*, sea fish used as food; *John Company*, the Honourable East India Company.

johnny: fellow, especially fashionable idler; *Johnny Armstrong* (nautical slang), handpower; *Johnny Raw*, novice; *johnny-cake*, cake of (USA) maize-meal or (Australia) wheat-meal. (The last, however, possibly = journey cake.)

Jonah: person who brings, or is sacrificed lest he bring, ill luck. (Jonah i. 11–16.)

Jonathan: (*Brother*) *Jonathan*, personified people of, typical citizen of, United States.

joseph: chaste man; woman's long riding-cloak of 18th C.

judas: infamous traitor; peephole in door; (of beard, &c.) *Judas-coloured*, red; *Judas kiss* (see Matt. xxvi. 48); *Judas-tree*, tree with purple flowers appearing before the leaves (from tradition that this was the tree on which Judas Iscariot hanged himself).

Julian: of Julius Caesar; *Julian calendar* (introduced by him).

Kit-cat: *Kit-cat Club*, club of Whig-politicians founded under James II; member of this; *Kit-cat* (portrait), portrait of less than half-length, but including hands. (From *Kit Cat(ling)*, keeper of of pie-house where the club met.)

Lazarus: beggar, poor man; *lazar* (archaic), poor and diseased person, especially leper; *lazar-house, lazaretto*, hospital for diseased poor, especially lepers; building or ship for performing quarantine in; after-part of ship's hold used for stores. (From the name *Lazarus*, Luke xvi. 20.)

Lizzie, tin: model T Ford car.

louis: French gold coin of about 20 francs from Louis XIII to Louis XVI.

Lucretia: model of chastity, woman preferring honour to life.

Magdalen(e): reformed prostitute. (*Mary Magdalene* (Luke viii. 2), identified with the sinner of Luke vii. 37.)

magpie: European bird with long pointed tail, black and white plumage; variety of pigeon; (rifle shot that hits) outermost division but one of target. (*Mag*, abbreviation of *Margaret*, +*pie*.)

Marian: of the Virgin Mary, Mary Tudor, Queen of England, or Mary Queen of Scots.

marigold: kinds of plant with golden or yellow flowers. (*Mary* (the Blessed Virgin) +*gold*.)

marionette: puppet worked by strings. (From French *Marionette*, double diminutive of *Marie*.)

marry (interjection): (= the Virgin *Mary*).

martin: *St. Martin*, Bishop of Tours in 4th C; *Martinmas*, St. Martin's day, 11 Nov.; *St. Martin's summer*, fine season about this time; *martin, house-martin*, bird of swallow family (cf. French *martin-pêcheur*, the kingfisher).

martlet: the swift. (From French *martelet*, probably from *martinet*, diminutive of *Martin*.)

Mary: Australian slang for a native woman. 'Little Mary', nursery name for the belly.

maudlin: mawkishly sentimental, especially of tearful stage of drunkenness. (Middle English *Maudlin* = *Magdalen.*)

Michael: *Michaelmas*, feast of St. *Michael*, 29 Sept.

mick(e)y: temper, possibly, like Paddy, from the supposed short temper of the Irish, with whom this is a common name.

Moggy: cat, probably from an old pet-form of Margaret.

moll: prostitute, mistress of highwayman or gangster. *Moll* Cutpurse was the nickname of Mary Frith, a notorious criminal in the first half of the 17th C; cf. also *Moll* Flanders.

Moses: nickname for Jewish money-lender.

moses-basket: straw or rush cot for infant.

namby-pamby: insipidly pretty, mildly sentimental. (Formed on the name of *Ambrose Philips*, pastoral writer, died 1749.)

nanny: she-goat (cf. *billy-goat*); child's nurse and in some dialects child's word for grandmother = granny.

nap: a card game, also (betting) to put all one's money on a single horse. (Abbreviation of *Napoleon.*)

Napoleon: French gold twenty-franc piece of Napoleon I; kind of top-boot; the game of *nap*.

Neddy: donkey.

nelly: largest kind of petrel. (Perhaps from the name *Nelly.*)

Noah: *Noah's ark*, child's toy, large old-fashioned trunk or vehicle, small bivalve, detached fragment of flying cloud; *Noah's nightcap*, the plant eschscholtzia (from conical bud-sheaths).

Old Nick: the devil.

oliver: foot-operated drop hammer.

Paddy: nickname for Irishman (cf. *Biddy*).

paddy(whack): a rage, fit of temper. (From the supposed irascibility of the Irish.)

Paul: *Rob Peter to pay Paul* (see PETER); *Paul Pry*, inquisitive person (character in comedy, 1825).

Pauline: of St. Paul, as *the Pauline epistles*; member of St. Paul's School in London.

peeping Tom: type of prurient curiosity (in tale of Godiva).

Penelope: chaste wife. (From *Penelope*, wife of Odysseus.)

Peter: *Rob Peter to pay Paul*, take away from one to give to another, discharge one debt by incurring another; *Blue Peter*, blue flag with white square, hoisted before sailing; *Peter's fish*, haddock or other fish with marks supposed to have been made by St. Peter's thumb and finger; *Peter's-penny* or *-pence*, (Hist.) annual tax of a penny paid to the papal see.

philippic: plural, name of the orations of Demosthenes against *Philip* II of Macedon, hence applied to Cicero's orations against Mark Antony, and generally to any invective or denunciatory speech.

pierrot (f. pierrette): French pantomine character; itinerant minstrel with whitened face and loose white garment. (French diminutive of *Pierre*.)

Poll (parrot): a nick-name for a parrot, found from about 1630.

Reynard: (proper name for) the fox; a fox. (From Old French *Renart*, name of a fox in the *Roman de Renart*.)

Richard: *Richard Roe* typical name for defendant in ejectment suit (cf. John Doe).

Robert: *herb Robert*.

robin: also *robin redbreast*, a small red-breasted bird; (with or without epithet) kinds of American, Colonial, and Indian bird; *Robin-run-the-hedge*, ground ivy; *robin's eye*, herb Robert; *Robin Goodfellow*, a sportive goblin; *Robin Hood*, (type of) medieval outlaw.

Roger: *the jolly Roger*, pirates' black flag. *Roger* or *Sir Roger de Coverley*, a country-dançe and tune.

Roland: *a Roland for an Oliver*, effective retort.

Sally: *Sally Lunn*, sweet light tea-cake served hot; perhaps from name of girl hawking them at Bath *c.* 1800; *Aunt Sally*, game at fairs, in which players throw sticks at pipe in mouth of wooden woman's head.

Sam: *stand Sam*, bear the expense, especially of drink; *upon my Sam*, asseveration. (Possibly the personal name.)

Sam Browne: army officer's belt and straps. (From Gen. Sir. *S.* J. *Browne*.)

Sam(p)son: person of great strength, or resembling *Samson* (Judges xiii–xvi) in some respect; (Naut.) *Samson's post*, strong pillar passing through hold or between decks, post in whale-boat to which harpoon rope is attached. Hence *samsonite*, an explosive.

Sandy: nickname for a Scotsman. (The usual Scots abbreviation of *Alexander*.)

Sawney: nickname for Scotsman; simpleton. (Probably the same as *Sandy*.)

simony: buying or selling of ecclesiastical preferment. (From *Simon Magus* (Acts viii. 18.))

Sukey: (colloquial) *Sukey* or *black Sukey*, kettle. (*Sukey*, pet-form of *Susan*.)

tabby: watered fabric; brindled, mottled, or streaked cat; cat, especially female; gossiping woman, especially old maid; kinds of moth; kinds of concrete. (Some senses perhaps from *Tabitha.*)

Taffy: (colloquial) Welshman. (From Welsh *Dafydd* = *David.*)

tam o'shanter: round Scotch cap (bonnet) from name of the hero of Burns's poem so entitled (1790).

tantony pig: the smallest pig in a litter, from St. *Antony*, the patron saint of swineherds. Also a name for the woodlouse.

tawdry: see under AUDREY.

Teddy-bear: child's toy bear (named after *Theodore* Roosevelt).

Thomism: theological doctrine and philosophy of St. *Thomas* Aquinas.

timothy, timothy grass: a fodder grass. (From *Timothy* Hanson, who introduced it into North America.)

toby: jug or mug, usually in form of old man with three-cornered hat (also *Toby Fillpot*); *toby-frill*, broad turned-down goffered collar like Punch's dog *Toby's*.

tom: *Tom, Dick, and Harry*, persons taken at random, ordinary commonplace people; male animal, especially *tom-cat*; *long tom*, (naut.) long gun, especially one carried amidships on swivel-carriage; *Old Tom*, strong kind of gin; *Tom and Jerry* (USA), rum and water beaten up with eggs, &c.; *tomboy*, romping girl, hoyden; *tomfool*, fool, trifler, *tomfoolery*, foolish trifling, foolish knick-knacks, &c.; *Tom Fool*, type of witlessness; *tomnoddy*, blockhead, fool; *Tom Thumb*, a legendary dwarf, any diminutive person, dwarf variety of various plants; *Tom Tiddler's ground*, children's game, place where money can be had for the picking up; *tomtit*, kinds of small bird, especially titmouse.

tommy: *Tommy Atkins*, the British soldier, whence *Tommy* or *tommy* (slang), private in the army; (Mech.) kinds of wrench or turnscrew, (also *tommy-bar*) short bar for working box-spanners; bread, provisions, especially as given to workman in lieu of wages;

this system of payment, truck system (now illegal); *tommy shop* (formerly) in which *tommy* was enforced, (now) shop in works where provisions may be bought, any baker's shop; food carried by workmen; *tommy gun* (= Thompson, from inventor); *tommy-rot*, nonsense, absurd statement or argument, foolish course, undesirable state of things; *soft tommy* (naut.), soft or fresh bread.

Uncle Sam: government, or typical citizen, of USA.

valentine: *St. Valentine's Day*, day on which St. Valentine was beheaded and on which birds were supposed to pair, 14 Feb.; sweetheart chosen on this; amatory or satirical letter or picture sent to person of opposite sex on St. Valentine's day.

veronica: kinds of herb or shrub with blue, purple, pink, or white flowers; cloth with representation of Christ's face, especially one miraculously so impressed after being used by St. Veronica to wipe sweat from Christ's face.

Victorian: of person living in the reign of Queen Victoria; *early-Victorian*, of Victoria's reign, antiquated.

victorine: woman's fur tippet with long ends. (Perhaps named from Queen Victoria.)

will-o'-the-wisp: ignis fatuus, jack-o'-lantern. (Abbreviation of *William*; *wisp* = handful of (lighted) tow, &c.)

William, Sweet: name for a common garden flower, *Dianthus barbatus*, found from 1573.

TYPHOON STRIKE

Recent Titles by Julian Jay Savarin from Severn House

MACALLISTER´S RUN
PALE FLYER
TARGET DOWN

TYPHOON STRIKE

Julian Jay Savarin

SEVERN SH HOUSE

This first world edition published in Great Britain 1996 by
SEVERN HOUSE PUBLISHERS LTD of
9–15 High Street, Sutton, Surrey SM1 1DF,
by arrangement with Bloomsbury Publishing PLC.

CIP data for this book is held at the British Library.

ISBN 0-7278-4960-3

All the characters and events described in this story are entirely imaginary: any resemblance to real people, living or dead, or happenings present or past is coincidental.

Typeset by Hewer Text Composition Services, Edinburgh.
Printed and bound in Great Britain by
Hartnolls Ltd, Bodmin, Cornwall.

Prelude

March 1942. Oberleutnant Karl-Heinz Ketelheim was fed up. He was lost, and hated it. He was flying a lumbering, fully laden bomber and hated that too. What he really wanted, what he'd really hoped for when he'd gone into the Luftwaffe, was assignment to a fighter squadron. He was, after all, a Prussian, he fumed, and Prussians were warrior-knights. His modern steed should have been one of Willy Messerschmitt's wonders, the Me-109. Then he would have turned to give battle to the Tommies in their vengeful Spitfires when they had bounced his attack force of twenty-five aircraft, instead of going into the wild, evasive contortions about the sky that had subsequently separated him from the main group.

In a way, he was lucky, he supposed. He had watched all the section leaders and the raid commander himself go down in the first attack. His own manoeuvre had enabled him to escape the deadly British fighters – so far. He glanced anxiously about him through the faired cockpit of the Heinkel He-111H medium bomber, looking for the fighters. The sky was empty. He hoped their luck would hold.

'Look out for those damned Spitfires,' he ordered the other four members of his crew. 'And stay at gun positions.'

All non-commissioned personnel, each replied, 'Yes, Herr Oberleutnant.'

'What am I doing in this sitting duck?' he muttered to himself. If they made it back, he was going to request an immediate transfer to a fighter unit. He didn't care how many strings he had to pull.

He had never bought the ludicrous Nazi ethos, for whose practitioners – who included his entire crew – he harboured a well-concealed contempt; but he loved and believed in the glory of battle. In his mind, class was all and his connections were powerful enough, even these days, to get him the new assignment. He was emotionally more suited to fighters, he reasoned. He wanted the freedom to charge through the skies to take the battle to the enemy, the way the Me-109 escorts had. As was usual these days, however, the escorts had been too few.

'Müller!' he called to the bomb aimer, who doubled as nose gunner, in the lower nose section.

'Oberleutnant?'

'We're going to have to dump those bombs. We need more speed.'

'There's no target below. Just open fields. I think we're over Dorset.'

'He *thinks* we're over Dorset. Then we'll frighten some cows and deprive the Tommies of their breakfast milk.'

No one laughed.

'Get ready to dump when I tell you,' he snapped.

'Yes, Oberleutnant.'

Bunch of thick-headed peasants, Ketelheim thought disparagingly. What was he doing flying with such people?

The black Jaguar SS-100 was in beautiful condition. The day was unseasonably warm and the hood was down. The twenty-one-year-old at the wheel, in civilian clothes, drove it at a gentle pace along the country road, his left arm about the shoulders of the beautiful young woman at his side. She was just six months past her eighteenth birthday. There was a happiness about them that was frighteningly vulnerable.

The car was not his, but his father's pride and joy, and was on loan for this the last day of their two-day honeymoon.

Mindful of the shortage of petrol, they were not going far, only the five miles round the perimeter of the family's farm. It was the first time that the car had been out since the beginning of the war.

'Ah,' he said after a while. 'Here we are.'

He took his arm from her shoulders as he slowed down and turned into a narrow track that could easily be missed if one did not know what to look for, and was just wide enough to allow the car through. It rocked its way sedately along the bumpy ground, its exhaust rumbling powerfully. Soon they came to a small clearing, hidden from above by a canopy formed by the branches of tall trees. He brought the car to a halt, near the bank of a clear stream.

'This is it,' he told her, climbing out and waving an expansive arm. 'My secret place. I came here quite often as a boy. Walked across the fields.' He went round the side to open the door for her. 'Just right for our picnic. I wanted you to see it before I went back to the squadron. I've never brought anyone here before.' He looked at her anxiously. 'What do you think?'

'I love it.' She turned eyes, full of love, upon him. 'Thank you for bringing me to your secret place.' She put her arms about him, hugging him tightly. 'I feel I'm really part of you now, and that feels wonderful.'

'And I am so lucky,' he said, kissing her gently. 'Wife.'

It was then that they heard the faint sound.

He stiffened briefly, then relaxed. 'Must be one of ours. There's nothing of military value way out here. Let's get our picnic things.'

'Get ready to dump, Müller,' Ketelheim ordered. He knew the way home now. 'Then we turn for base.'

'Yes, Herr Oberleutnant.'

'All right. Now!'

* * *

He had listened to the growing sounds of the engines with mounting disbelief and anxiety. The uneven beat was too familiar; but because it did not make sense, he was slow to react. An instinct for survival, despite his own reluctance to accept that a bomber was overhead, made him yell, '*Megan! Move!*'

He had grabbed her and was dragging her unceremoniously, when the first bomb hit.

He came to, feeling cold and wet, and realized he was in the water. He got to his feet groggily and looked about him.

The Jaguar was in two pieces. Half, almost intact, was still on the bank. The other was a twisted mass of metal, wires and upholstery lying upside down in the stream. Bits of stuffing, looking like fluffy young chicks, floated aimlessly away. There was a big crater next to the remaining half of the Jaguar on the bank. Several trees were down, scorched and still smoking, the smell of their burning hanging in the air.

Of Megan, there was no sign.

'Oh my God!' he exclaimed softly, with mounting dread. A terrible fear began to envelop him, freezing his heart and chilling his blood, making him shiver with foreboding. He began to shout, a desperate wail in his voice. '*Megan! Megan!*'

He stumbled out of the water to begin frantically looking for her, a man demented, calling out her name over and over.

He found her eventually – pieces of her, scattered all over his secret place. There was not a mark upon him.

March 1944. The Typhoon, a great darting, predatory ghost, swept low over a landscape made deceptively tranquil by the drowsy twilight of the approaching dawn. The roar of its powerful engine ripped the tranquillity apart in a tearing bellow that was almost obscene. Yet the winged form that flitted between the trees, miraculously remaining unscathed as its silhouette appeared to shift insubstantially in the gloom, seemed remarkably graceful. This gracefulness belied its dreadful purpose, for there was murder in the heart of the man who piloted it.

The Hawker Typhoon 1B was a killing machine that was as dangerous to unwary pilots as it was to the enemy. Some of its pilots feared it so much that they tended to approach it with trepidation, knowing what it could do to them and already afraid of the possibility. They had good reason. Earlier versions had the disconcerting habit of shedding their entire tail sections, and despite the fact that these problems had eventually been ironed out, its pilots still viewed it with understandable caution. Many had not survived their first take-off. Others had nicknames for it, a good percentage of which were highly descriptive anatomically.

But the Typhoon was also a formidable weapon in the right hands, and Mike Pendrake loved it. He had flown both the sturdy Hurricane and the inimitable Spitfire in combat; but it was the Hawker monster that had stolen his soul. Much bigger and more brutal than the Spitfire, he called it the 'Beast' and felt he belonged to it. It had served him spectacularly.

It was noisy inside, the raw power of the 2100-plus horsepower Napier Sabre engine snarling its way into the cockpit he called the 'birdcage'. This had anachronistic side-opening doors rather like a car and he longed for the sliding bubble canopy of some versions, with its infinitely better all-round view; but he didn't care. What mattered was the thunderous power under his control, which, at his command, could unleash devastating havoc upon the enemy. Armed with four Hispano 20mm cannon and eight rockets, he deployed awesome fire-power. He could obliterate tanks, turn trains into starbursts of flame and steam, demolish buildings, tear roads apart, and convert railway lines into so much twisted metal and the sleepers into shrapnel. The more the devastation, the better he liked it.

He could drop bombs too, but the aircraft could only carry at most a pair of 1000-pounders at a time. He didn't like bombing missions. The drag and weight of the bombs slowed and restricted the manoeuvrability of even such a powerful aeroplane far too much for his liking. He preferred the current set-up. Once the rockets were gone he could take on even the Focke-Wulf Fw-190, which, with its top speed of 472mph in some variants, was still his meat. He hoped one or two would come out to play. This low down, they would be hopeless against him.

He banked the aircraft steeply on to a new heading, threading his way between a pair of tall trees whose very branches, barely visible arms, reached vainly for him. The dark shape of a building seemed to caress a wingtip as it flashed past.

'Hope I woke you up, you bastards,' he shouted into his mask. Darting fireflies of anti-aircraft shells, their tracers lighting up the gloom, followed him briefly. 'Too late, you dozy sods! You can't catch me!' He laughed. 'Better luck next time!'

Distorted by the mask, the strange noise did not sound like the laughter of a totally sane man.

He banked once more, then brought the wings level on to another heading. The parallel lines of a railway line gleamed dully before him in the pale light of the new day; but with the darkness at his back, he would not be spotted until it was much too late. He flew along the track so low it seemed as if he was about to land on it. Soon, just up ahead, he found what he was looking for.

The train was packed with ammunition and troops. Its importance was such that three flatbed anti-aircraft trucks were among its carriages. One of these was at the very end, to cover the vulnerable tail. The gunners were among the best, their weapons lethal. They were very alert. Even at this time of the day, only a very daring and perhaps foolish lone pilot would take them on and hope to achieve surprise.

But surprise was achieved.

It may have been a trick of the wind, but the deafening roar of the Typhoon did not come to them over the clatter of the train until far too late. A sharp-eyed gunner spotted the dark shape impossibly low and, disbelieving his own eyes, tried desperately to train his multi-barrelled gun, only to find he had run out of elevation. He could not bring the weapon to bear. *The target* was *too low!*

He yelled to his comrades in fear, rage and despair. He knew what was coming and, worse, knew he hadn't the slightest chance of being able to do anything about it.

Pendrake held the Typhoon steady as he swept down on them. He fired the rockets, watching as they whooshed off to explode along the length of the train. It had been beautifully done.

The rear anti-aircraft truck was lifted clean off the track, rolling in mid-air as its ammunition exploded as if in response to the rockets. Like a giant hand twisting a toy, it took the entire train with it. The ammunition wagons ripped apart, incinerating the carriages that housed the troops.

The Typhoon flew through a raging hell of fire, and Pendrake heard several thumps strike the aircraft. He knew no one had fired at him – they hadn't had the time – and assumed that bits of the exploding train had somehow reached him. But the aircraft felt OK. No serious damage, so far.

He banked away and wheeled round to survey his handiwork. Though he knew with the train off the track the anti-aircraft guns would be useless, he was still taking a chance. He was breaking his own rule of never going back to look. It was one of the best ways of getting pounced on by marauding fighters, out for revenge. There would also be survivors, and they'd be after his blood with anything to hand. Even a rifle bullet could down an unwary aircraft.

Yet he wanted to see.

His work had been terrible. The train was burning along its entire length. The engine lay on its side off the track, its steam shooting along the ground in a white jet before rising into the air, the last gasp of a dying behemoth. Then tracers began to reach for him. He swung away, out of range. No point wasting cannon shells. That train was going nowhere. The carnage on the ground and the haphazard nature of the firing had also shown that those lucky enough to survive had been very few indeed.

He felt good.

He kept the Typhoon low as he headed across the fields of Normandy for home. Behind him, the glow of the burning train was like a demonic sunrise. Despite the severe attrition of the years of war and their relative scarcity in the skies above France, there were still a fair number of enemy fighters around. It wouldn't take them long to come hunting. Pendrake kept a good look- out, while maintaining his ultra-low-level flight.

He did a thorough check of the aircraft. Everything was working as it should. Whatever had hit him, had done no damage.

Despite the increasing light of the day, it would still be difficult to spot him, and his rush for home did not mean he would run away from a fight. If anything, he'd be happy to oblige; but there was little point in making it easy for them. Yet though from time to time he glimpsed tiny specks high above him, none came down to look and it was with a slight feeling of disappointment that he made it safely back across the Channel, keeping low above the choppy grey waters.

1

Major Jack Halloran, in the uniform of the US Army Air Force, sat quietly in the office of the Royal Air Force station commander while the group captain, the Honourable William, Viscount Fox, read through the papers in the black folder he had brought with him.

Halloran had arrived at the station gates at about the time that Mike Pendrake had destroyed his train so spectacularly. The guards, surprised by the uniform, despite having seen many of the different kinds worn by Allied and Commonwealth forces during the course of their service, still took no chances and intially put the major through stringent security checks. The major was unperturbed, insisting only that he be taken directly to the station commander. This was done under heavy guard. No one had been allowed to look into his briefcase, or take it away from him.

Halloran now permitted himself the faintest of smiles as he waited patiently for Group Captain Fox to finish. The guards may have considered their checks rigorous. They had little idea of what a really tough security check was like. They should meet some of the people *he'd* had to deal with.

The group captain glanced up briefly. Halloran's smile disappeared.

'Something to amuse you, Major?' Bill Fox, as he preferred to be called, queried mildly.

'Er . . . no, sir!'

'Good.' Fox returned to his reading.

Halloran, Fox had noted, though in the uniform of an air force officer, was conspicuously bereft of pilot's or aircrew wings. The American did, however, sport a chestful of ribbons. Everyone knew the Americans were rather lax when it came to dishing out gongs. His own pilots tended to claim with graveyard humour that you had to die first, before the RAF would deign to give you one.

Still, Halloran appeared to have people of some influence in his corner. No less august a body than the War Office had underwritten his security status, and the contents of the papers he'd brought pointed squarely to the fact that the good major spent much of his time behind enemy lines. However, the part that interested Fox most was the blueprint for a very special squadron, to be trained for a particularly difficult task. Halloran's people were looking for someone to command it. Even at this early stage, they had already given the squadron a name.

Fox looked up once more. 'Why Cobra Squadron?'

Halloran cleared his throat. 'Its mission is . . . er . . . part of an overall . . . er . . . strategy, sir.' If the group captain did not already know about Cobra, the plan that was part of the tactics for the eventual invasion of continental Europe, it was not his place to give that information.

'Major,' Fox began, 'when people clear their throats before speaking to me I know they're either lying, or holding something back. However,' he continued before Halloran could protest, 'you are quite right. If it doesn't concern my responsibilities to this unit, I don't want to know. That satisfy you?'

Taken aback, Halloran said, 'Yessir!'

'Good,' Fox murmured as he slowly closed the folder. 'The people who sent you already knew what they were looking for. I think we may have your man. He's out on a rhubarb at the moment . . .'

'Rhubarb, sir?'

Fox smiled thinly. 'Something you don't know about,

Major? A rhubarb is a sort of prowling flight over enemy territory. We go out to make mischief. It's dangerous work . . . and the man I'm thinking of is on one at this very moment. He tends to get results. Bit mad, of course.'

Halloran was startled. 'Mad?'

'Ah. You're wondering whether a madman's the right sort of chap to command this . . . Cobra unit of yours.' Fox tapped at the folder. 'From what I've just read, that's exactly the type of chap you need. Mad, or suicidal. There are times when I think Flight Lieutenant Pendrake's both. There are also times when I think the people who dream these operations up are equally touched in the head . . .'

'It's my plan, sir,' Halloran said quietly as Fox paused.

Fox levelled upon the major the sort of gaze that one would expect of a scientist scrutinizing a laboratory specimen. 'Is it, by George? Astounding.'

'It *will* work, sir,' the major insisted. 'I've already got the backing. It's an operational necessity.'

'I've no doubt you do have, and I'm quite certain it is. You would not be here, and I would not just have read the contents of your folder.'

'You sound as if you might be changing your mind, sir.'

'Good Lord, no. I'm more convinced than ever he is your man.'

'Because he's mad?'

'No,' Fox replied calmly. 'Because he's damned good. Strangely enough, he is a good commander. Once took command of a full squadron during the worst times of the air war over this country, when both the CO *and* the deputy CO bought it on the same day. He whipped the demoralized squadron into shape and they eventually went on to take a grievous toll of the enemy. He was only twenty-one at the time and they called him the *old* man.' Fox gave a soft laugh. 'I'm the really old man around here. Thirty tomorrow. He's now twenty-three and covered in gongs, though it's the devil's own job to get him to wear them at all. Always improperly dressed, that man.'

'Then may I ask you something, sir?'

'Please do.'

'If he's so good, why is he still a captain . . . er . . . fight lieutenant? It can't be because of his dress sense, surely.'

'Sometimes,' Fox began seriously, 'being brave is not always the prerequisite for command. Or so I've been told. By rights, he deserves his own squadron, though there are those who will disagree.'

Pushing his luck, Halloran asked, 'So you think he was unfairly treated?'

Fox, a tall, elegant man whose own uniform was handmade in Savile Row, looked at Halloran steadily. His triangular face, adorned by the thinnest of dark lines upon his upper lip, was given greater effect by the fact that his neatly trimmed hair was almost blond. His dark eyes radiated a calm that Halloran found, despite himself, oddly relaxing. The ribbons of the DSO and the DFC nestled in splendour beneath the pilot's wings, above Fox's left breast pocket.

By contrast, Halloran, though almost as tall, was more solidly built. His crew-cut, less militarily brutal than Fox had expected, gave him an air of boyishness that was very misleading indeed. Among his friends and colleagues in the French Underground unit to which he'd been assigned, he was known as a very dangerous man; as dangerous as the snake they'd chosen as his code-name: the *fer de lance*, the spearhead.

'Pendrake's wife was killed in a bombing raid,' Fox said, 'when she'd been a bride for just two days. Damned awful luck. They were out in the country on a picnic, well away from the danger of bombs. The last day of their forty-eight-hour honeymoon. Then this lone aircraft went over, probably lost, dumping its load any old where. Blew her to bits. Nothing touched him. He's been fighting his own war ever since.'

Halloran, a man who'd seen many shocking things, suddenly felt sympathy for Pendrake. He knew something of what he must be going through. There'd been a young French girl who'd been part of his team in France; then the Gestapo had got her . . .

Fox was looking at him interestedly. 'I do believe I may have struck a chord somewhere.'

Halloran nodded.

'When he came to us about a year ago,' Fox continued, 'he'd been in so many battles it seemed as if he was hanging on to his sanity by a thread. But he hasn't let up, and is arguably the best and most aggressive pilot we've got.'

'If you recommend him, sir, I'll pass that on to my superiors. But I'd like to see him first, if that's OK.'

Fox nodded. 'Wait till he lands. Stay for breakfast. I can't promise an American bounty, but I'm sure you'll find ours sufficiently substantial.' Fox stood up. 'Let's see what they've got on offer in the mess, shall we?'

'I happen to like an English breakfast, sir,' Halloran confessed with a straight face as he too got to his feet, 'though some of the guys might think me crazy. When I ask for tea they think I've really flipped.'

'Gone native, have you?'

'Something like that, sir.'

'Good man.'

As they made their way out of the office, Halloran added, 'You're sure he'll make it back? If these rhubarbs are as dangerous as you've said . . .'

'He always makes it back. Don't be put off by his manner when you first meet him. Strange thing, isn't it, Major?' Fox continued mildly. 'When a man wants to die, the gods almost never grant his wish. Quite, quite remarkable.'

Halloran realized that Fox was looking directly at him.

The bellowing roar of a fast-approaching aircraft made virtually everyone on the station interrupt what they were doing and listen. Some, out in the open and newcomers to the airfield, at first believed it to be an attack and were already priming themselves for a headlong rush to the nearest shelter, when they noticed that other people had stopped wherever they were, to stare in the direction of the sound. As yet, nothing could be seen.

In the dispersal area, pilots due to fly halted their pre-flight preparations to do the same. One very young airman paused in the act of heaving himself on to the wing of the fifteen-foot-high aircraft, trying to identify the direction of the swelling thunder. In the various messes, diners left their tables to have a look. Most of them already knew who it was and waited for what would come next.

Leaving his own table, Fox said to Halloran, 'That's Pendrake. Let's go and meet him, shall we?'

'How do you know?' Halloran demanded as he hurriedly followed the group captain.

Fox put on his cap as they emerged into the crisp, brightening day. There was no wind to speak of and no early spring rain had fallen during the night, though there was a slight patina of frost on the grass.

'Everyone who's been on this station long enough knows . . . aircrew and groundcrew alike.' Fox came to a halt. 'We can see everything from here. Look at the runway.'

From where they stood, the far end of the runway appeared to dip out of sight. The crescendo of noise was closer but as yet, there was still nothing to be seen.

Then Halloran gave a gasp of astonishment as the bellowing Typhoon seemed to rise from the very ground itself, to hurtle at what he was certain was a height of bare inches, along the length of the runway.

'My God!' he exclaimed. 'His prop will hit!'

Fox said nothing.

Miraculously, the aircraft did not slam into the unforgiving earth. Instead, it pulled up into a steep climb, rolling swiftly as it did so. After the third roll it stopped, pulled on to its back, flicked into a ninety-degree bank, hauled round tightly, levelled out and was nicely placed to land along the runway's centreline.

It was only when he let out his breath the Halloran realized he'd been holding it.

'The guy can fly,' he remarked with soft admiration.

'Got some trade too,' Fox said. 'He always does. That's what those three rolls were about. Come on. I'll take you to Dispersal in my car. Get your first impression of him in person.'

At Dispersal, where aircraft were parked in small groups, the young pilot, with the barely visible thin blue ring of the rank of pilot officer on his shoulders, stood gaping as the Typhoon taxied towards them. Another pilot, barely older and with the slightly thicker rings of a flying officer, sauntered up.

'Catch a fly in that if you're not careful.'

The pilot officer snapped his mouth shut in embarrassment. 'Anyway,' he protested after a pause, 'too cold for flies.'

'Never too cold for those pests. Took one up once. Wretched thing had got into the cockpit. I went high, hoping it would die of oxygen starvation.'

'Did it?'

'Of course not. The thing kept buzzing around infuriatingly and tried to get inside my mask; and then I had to go into a furious evasion manoeuvre when I saw an enemy approaching from my starboard quarter.'

'What did you do?' the young pilot asked breathlessly.

'Not an enemy aircraft at all. The wretched insect had pasted itself to the canopy. At that angle, the speck looked like another aeroplane.'

The young pilot was not sure whether to believe the story or not, but said nothing. He looked towards the Typhoon, which had now stopped some distance away, and saw the station commander's car heading towards it.

'The station CO's going to congratulate him for those three victories.' There was a touch of wistfulness in the young pilot's voice. He had yet to successfully down an aircraft.

'Not three victories . . .'

'But he did three victory rolls.'

'Victory rolls . . . yes, but not for three aircraft. When you've been here a while, you'll recognize Old Scarface's codes. Like everyone else, each slow roll is a kill. But Mike Pendrake's fast rolls mean something else entirely. One means a tank or tanks . . . usually several when Mike gets truly going. Two rolls and it's some other ground target . . . artillery pieces, radars, ammo dumps, so forth. Three, and he's got a nice fat, juicy train. Must have been a good one. He was particularly exuberant just then.'

'So the old man's going to tell him off for the low approach?'

'No fear, old boy. Mike's the only person who gets lower than Foxy the Viscount, though strictly, the station CO shouldn't really go on ops any more. Now come on. Up you go. And stick to me. They still play very rough across the water.'

'Ye . . . yes. Yes, of course.'

The young pilot climbed into the cockpit of the Beast with trepidation.

The car drew up just as the huge propeller whirled to a stop. Fox and Halloran climbed out to walk slowly towards the Typhoon. Its ground crew were already beginning to busy themselves around it.

Halloran stared at the large aircraft with its aggressive, inclined stance, the brutish nose with its gaping intake beneath pointing upwards meanly. He moved closer to tentatively pat its flank as he would a wild, skittish horse that he half-expected to kick out at the slightest provocation.

'Ever flown one of these?' a strong voice, strangely cold, addressed him from above.

He turned to look. The helmet, with goggles raised, was still on and the oxygen mask, though now unhooked, still partially obscured the face. There was such a chill in the eyes that Halloran found he had to suppress a shiver.

'No . . . no,' he replied. 'I'm not a flyer.'

'I see.' It sounded like a condemnation. The eyes continued to survey him from their eyrie. 'American.' That sounded like a condemnation too.

'Yes. My name's Halloran.'

'Pendrake.'

'Yes. I know.'

If Pendrake thought that surprising, he gave no indication. 'I've flown with your compatriots when they were with the Eagle Squadrons. Good blokes.'

'I'm glad to hear it.'

'Of course, the Royal Air Force ironed out the rough edges.'

'Of course.'

Suddenly, helmet and mask came off. The face grinned. Halloran saw a long scar, like a sabre slash, running down the left side of the face from upper cheek to mouth, stopping just before reaching the corner. Yet the face, pleasant enough to look upon, was itself not distorted and almost handsome. Many women, Halloran decided, would find that scar dangerously attractive.

'Hullo, sir,' Pendrake called to Fox.

'Hullo, Mike. Got some more trade, did you?'

'A nice fat train. A pricey one, I think. Long job. Three flak cars, and lots of ammo. Went up like a gasworks. Must have been important.'

'It certainly sounds like it. Check with the Spy when you debrief. He may have had some news about it.'

'Will do.' Pendrake began to climb out of the Typhoon.

Halloran, his hand still on the aircraft, was apparently deep in thought as he watched Pendrake descend.

The pilot was of average height and slim, almost delicate. But there was an unnerving fire of such intensity burning within the eyes that it was enough to give an air of ferocious, relentless strength to his presence. His rich, dark hair bore faint streaks of premature greyness incongruous in one so young, low down on the temples near the ears. Like so many of his peers, Pendrake had grown up very quickly.

Halloran felt his hand move absently; then it came to a sudden halt. He'd felt something that was soft and sticky to the touch. He snatched his hand away, turning his head to see what it was.

'*Jesus!*' he heard himself shout.

Startled, both Pendrake and Fox turned to stare at him. Some of the ground crew rushed round.

Halloran had pulled a handkerchief out of a trouser pocket and was wiping his hand vigorously.

He pointed. 'Will you look at that?'

Everyone looked. A mangled hand was pulped to the fuselage.

'So that's what hit me,' Pendrake said calmly, as if it was something that happened every day. 'I flew through part of the explosion. The Tiffy rocked a bit and I felt some thumps. Thought it was bits of the train. Must have been flying bodies.'

'You flew *through* the explosion?'

Pendrake stared at Halloran. 'I was rather low.'

'I'll wipe it off right away, sir,' a horrified crewman offered.

'You most certainly will not!' Pendrake countered in a harsh voice.

The leading aircraftman stared worriedly at Pendrake, then glanced in appeal at the senior officers, before turning as a last resort to look at the non-commissioned officer in charge of the ground-crew team. Then it was back to Pendrake.

'Leave it,' Pendrake said.

'Sir, that's going to stink to high heaven . . .'

'Leave it,' Pendrake repeated, then turned to Fox. 'I'll be off to debriefing, sir, if that's all right.'

Fox nodded slowly. 'Give you a lift?'

'I'll walk, thank you, sir.'

Once more, Fox nodded.

Pendrake again turned to the aircraftman. 'Don't you dare wipe it off, LAC Thomas.'

He moved away without waiting for a reaction.

They all watched him go. Then Thomas turned to the group captain. 'What should I do, sir?'

'You heard the flight lieutenant, Thomas. Leave it for the moment. I shall be having a word with him.'

Leading Aircraftman Thomas looked relieved. 'Thank you, sir.' But he could not hide a look of revulsion as he glanced at the human remains on the aircraft.

'Are you going to let him leave that . . . that thing on there, sir?' They were on their way back to the car as Halloran spoke.

'Do you carry a rabbit's foot by any chance, Major?'

'No, sir.'

'Do you know anyone who does?'

'Well, yes, but . . .'

'And you have absolutely nothing which serves as one?'

Halloran took a few moments to reply. By then, they had reached the car.

He paused by the door. 'I have a small crucifix,' he eventually replied. 'It was given to me by a young girl . . . in France.'

Fox gave one of his thin smiles. 'I sense a few memories in those words.' He climbed in behind the wheel. 'Let

Pendrake have his rabbit's foot. Slipstream and the weather will eventually clean it off. Get in, Major.'

'Grisly stuff, sir,' Halloran said as he obeyed.

'War is grisly, Major, as you well know.'

As the car started off, the NCO, who had been following at a respectful distance, saluted. Fox raised a casual hand to his cap in response. The man returned to supervise the servicing of the Typhoon.

Halloran craned his neck round to glance at them. They were leaving the mangled hand scrupulously alone.

'How did he get that scar?' Halloran asked. 'You said he was not touched when his wife was . . . er killed. Combat?'

'Combat caused the situation, but not the injury. The scar is the result of an argument he lost with the gun-sight of a Hurricane during a wheels-up landing that went very badly wrong. Considering the aircraft was blazing at the time, he's lucky to be alive. Not a burn on him.'

'You were right, sir. He *is* mad, but lucky too.'

'I doubt very much he'd agree . . . that he's lucky.'

'Lucky or mad, he'll do,' Halloran said.

'I had a feeling you might say that,' Fox said. 'Now to persuade him.'

'Persuade him? You expect him to refuse?'

'He'll not refuse a direct order, Major. But I'm not going to make it an order. This has to be his free choice.'

There was a long pause before Halloran said, 'An observation, sir.'

'Observe away.'

'You worry about him.'

'I worry about all my pilots.'

'You know what I mean, sir.'

'Are there none of your people across the Channel about whom you worry especially?' Fox countered. 'The girl who gave you the crucifix, for example.'

There was another pause. 'The Gestapo got her,' Halloran said flatly.

'My dear chap. I am sorry.'

'Happened a while ago.'

'But you still remember.'

'Yes, sir.'

'I do think, Major,' Fox said after a while, glancing at him, 'that there is more in common between Pendrake and yourself than you'd care to admit.'

Halloran said nothing. In his mind's eye he could still see Jeanne-Anne's face. Although itself a vital part of the preparations for the eventual invasion, the mission was also for her. He would finally be getting the man who had betrayed her.

The 'Spy' was the unit Intelligence officer, a squadron leader called Stanley and whom everyone – including non-commissioned personnel – called 'Baldwin' out of earshot. It didn't help that his hair was rather thin on top.

Stanley had left the service and had already been too old for fighters when war had broken out. Undeterred by such minor problems, he had bluffed his way back in, lying about his age on rejoining, in order to get into combat. The acute shortage of skilled pilots during that fraught period worked in his favour. By the time the truth had been discovered, he already had five kills to his name. Unfortunately, reality had caught up and he'd been shot down, losing his right arm.

He considered himself lucky. His worst nightmare had been the thought of being trapped in a burning aircraft. He'd seen those who had got out too late.

Stanley looked up as Pendrake entered his small, standard-issue office, his eyes seeming bigger behind round, wire-framed spectacles.

'Hullo, Spy,' Pendrake greeted brightly. 'Use your phone?'

Stanley pointed to one of the two on his desk. 'Be my guest.' The other was the scrambler on which he received Intelligence reports.

'Thanks.' Pendrake picked up the instrument. 'This is Flight Lieutenant Pendrake,' he said into it as the operator answered. 'Get me Dispersal, please. Corporal Griffin.'

The was a brief wait as the call was put through and someone ran to find Griffin.

'Corp'l Griffin here, sir,' came the voice, slightly out of breath. Griffin had clearly been running.

'Ah, Corp. That little souvenir I brought back . . . cover it with clear dope, will you? That should hold it in place and kill the smell at the same time.'

'Dope . . . dope it over, sir?' Griffin sounded as if he wanted to vomit.

'We're not out of the stuff, are we?'

'No, sir. There's plenty around.'

Dope was the clear solvent used to stiffen the skins of those aircraft with fabric covering on their fuselages and wings. It was mainly for use on the station flight aircraft, some early-model Hurricanes allocated for the purpose of station air defence, should any raiders attempt to come over. Though the Hurricanes had their own pilots, the Typhoon boys always tried for a temporary swap, while the Hurricane men jealously guarded their mounts.

'Then do it, Corp,' Pendrake ordered.

'Yes, sir.' Griffin was obviously not happy about the idea, but he had little choice in the matter.

'Thank you.' Pendrake hung up.

Stanley was looking at him with interest. 'Souvenir? Smell? Caught a packet, did you?'

'You might say so.'

'Well, I'm not surprised. Got a report on your little jaunt, down the scrambler. I take it you were the one who hit that train?'

‘Waste of time trying to surprise you, Spy,’ Pendrake said. ‘Yes. That’s one of mine.’

Stanley passed him a form. ‘Here. Fill in the details. Usual stuff.’

Pendrake took a seat and began to write. When he’d finished, Stanley compared the report with some notes he had made.

‘It is the same one. The location and time match perfectly. You’ve raised merry hell over there. That train was full of reinforcements and ammunition for a vital rocket site. I’m not surprised you took some hits yourself. It would have been heavily defended. How many flak cars did it have?’

‘I counted three.’

‘You went after a train with *three* AA batteries? No wonder you took hits. You’ll be pleased to know you’ve also killed a general, and several of his staff officers. They’re going quite berserk and are seeking to take revenge on the French Resistance, whom they accuse of giving us the details of the train’s movements.’

Pendrake said nothing about the ‘hits’ he’d taken. Stanley would find out soon enough. It would be all over the station like wildfire.

‘The Groupie wants to see you when you’re finished here,’ Stanley added.

‘I’m hungry, Spy,’ Pendrake pleaded. ‘You know what it’s like when I come back from a successful foray. I could eat ten horses.’

‘He did say you could have breakfast first.’

‘A generous soul. Any idea what he wants to see me for?’ Pendrake was certain it was about the disembodied hand on his aircraft.

‘He didn’t say.’

Then Pendrake remembered Halloran. ‘There was an American with him at Dispersal. Some US Army Air Force major, but not a pilot. Anything to do with that?’

‘He didn’t say,’ Stanley repeated.

‘Trouble with you, Spy, is that you never say anything.’
‘Must be my high intelligence.’
‘Ha!’
‘Now there’s a good chap. Run along to breakfast then dash off to see the group captain.’ As Pendrake turned to go, Stanley went on, ‘Oh Mike . . .’ and when Pendrake had paused to look back at him, ‘Good work getting that train. You really hurt them.’
‘That’s what I’m here for . . . to hurt the bastards.’
‘How is it with Megan?’ Stanley, knowing a little about the tragedy, enquired gently. He studied Pendrake’s features with keen interest.
‘She’s still in my thoughts every day, Spy; every day for the last two years since it . . .’ Pendrake paused, face stony, remembering. ‘Exactly two years today, you know. It was warmer too. That’s why we went on that picnic. No time for a real honeymoon, of course . . . so the picnic was a sort of . . .’
Pendrake abruptly ended the sentence and went out.
Stanley watched him leave, and continued to study the retreating figure of the pilot through the crossed lengths of adhesive tape that starred his window. He knew and understood that Pendrake’s outward mask hid an almost unbearable inner turmoil.
‘God help you,’ he said in a low voice. ‘Poor devil . . .’

2

'Had a good breakfast?' Group Captain Fox asked.

'Yes, thank you, sir,' Pendrake answered.

'Sleepy?'

'Not at the moment. I can catch up later and be ready for my next flight.'

'No more ops for you today, Mike.'

Pendrake, still wearing the battledress he'd used for flying, looked surprised.

'But, sir . . .'

'No more flying today,' Fox told him firmly. 'There's an end to that.'

'Yes, sir.'

The group captain leaned back in his chair and studied Pendrake closely. 'How would you like your own squadron to command? Not temporary like the last time you took the job on, but fully confirmed. There's a half ring in it for you.'

Pendrake took this silently for some moments. 'Promotion, sir?' he said at last. 'And a squadron, to boot. Have I upset someone?'

'I can understand your cynicism, but this is genuine. Your talents are sought after.'

Pendrake gave a grim smile. 'Not grown tired of me, have you, sir?'

'You would know of it if I had. This is not an order. You are entirely free to choose.' Fox paused. 'I cannot tell you more at this stage – at least, until you've accepted. However, what I can tell you is that it will give you all the action you could possibly wish for.'

Pendrake looked interested. 'Dangerous?'

'Very.'

'In my place, would you take it on?'

'No. But then I don't have your talents.'

'I'm intrigued. This would not have anything to do with that American . . . Major Halloran, would it, sir?'

'I've gone as far as I can, unless you decide to accept.'

'I'll take it.'

Fox nodded. 'Thought you would.'

'You knew I would, sir.'

Again, Fox nodded. 'Yes. But I'll give you one last chance to refuse. There's no going back once you've accepted and once I have told you, there'll be a total security blackout. You will talk to no one about it, except those specified by your orders. Is that clear?'

'Sir.'

'Do you still wish to accept?'

'Yes, sir.'

'Very well.' Fox paused for several seconds, as if making his mind up about something. 'You are to be given command of a special Typhoon squadron, with the confirmed rank of squadron leader. They will be highly modified aircraft. Though the squadron comes under the aegis of No. 100 Special Duties Group in Norfolk, you will in fact be based nowhere in that vicinity. You will also have a certain degree of autonomy – something which will be much to your liking, I shouldn't wonder. The Special Duties attachment is really for the purposes of organizational channels, and security.

'You'll be equally pleased to know that the new sliding bubble canopy you've always wanted will be on these aeroplanes. Like the Tempest, they are Tiffies with the bugs removed. In fact, they're virtually Tempest Vs but more powerful, more agile, and of course faster. But I've been told they are classed as Typhoons, designated "S" for Special.

'You'll be going to a unit deep in the wilds of Gloucestershire tomorrow,' Fox went on, 'where you'll be met by Major Halloran, who will brief you. Your aircraft, and pilots, will be waiting. You will be responsible for their training, and conversion to type if that proves necessary. When you are operational, the squadron will be moved to a forward operating base. You'll be given full details of the mission by Halloran. My part in this has now ended. Questions?'

'A few.'

'Fire away.'

'Why can't I pick my own pilots?'

'That's not an option. You'll have to work with what you find out there.'

'I'll need at least one person who I know can fly the Tiffy, sir. If I've got to get these unknown bods properly trained, I must have this one person I do know and can depend on. If these are such special aircraft, it would be folly to risk a high attrition rate in training. I'll need help. There'll be casualties enough without loading the dice even more.'

Fox thought about this and seemed prepared to agree. 'Anybody in particular in mind?'

'Bingo Wilson, sir. He's up at the moment on a ranger with young Braddock. If you'll give him the gen when they return . . . or I shall, if you prefer.'

'I'll do it. All right, you can have Wilson. But that's it. I'll have to square it somehow with Squadron Leader Mitchell. No squadron commander is going to like losing his star pilot, plus another who's shaping up quite nicely.

'I did tell Halloran as he left,' Fox continued before Pendrake could reply, 'that if you did agree to take the job on, you might want to take someone with you and he hinted there was room to accommodate such a possibility.'

'Seems as if you had it all mapped out, sir,' Pendrake remarked drily, but managing to make it sound respectful.

'Can't watch over you for ever. I think you're just about ready for a move.'

'Is that what you've been doing? Watching over me?'

'Let's say some station commanders might not have understood you as I have.' Fox gave one of his thinner smiles.

'Am I that much of a problem?'

'Again, I'd prefer to say . . . a trifle unorthodox. Command will do you good.'

Pendrake gave one of his own rare smiles. 'I'll do my best.'

'Which is what I would expect of you.'

'I have a request, sir.'

Fox waited.

'I'd like to keep my current Tiffy,' Pendrake said.

'You mean you wish to hang on to that . . . that thing on the fuselage.' Fox did not look pleased. 'Besides, compared with your new aircraft, it will be underpowered, not as agile, and has the old canopy.'

'It can be modified, sir,' Pendrake insisted. 'They can bring it up to the same standard. It's practically new and has never been damaged in combat . . . and I'm certain work can be done to give it the new canopy.'

Fox was silent.

'I really would like to keep it, sir,' Pendrake added for good measure, pressing his case.

At last Fox said, 'I'll talk to Halloran, and he'll talk to his superiors. But I promise nothing.'

'Good enough for me, sir. Thank you.'

'Anything else?'

'If I can take the Tiffy, I'd like to fly it out. Bingo can travel by road with our gear.'

'Of course. And now, Squadron Leader designate, go and

get some rest. Make the most of it. You'll be needing all the rest you can get where you're going.'

'Yes, sir.'

Fox got to his feet and came round the desk. He held out a hand. 'Good luck, Mike. And don't let the Hun get on your tail.'

They shook hands.

'Thank you, sir. I won't.'

Karl-Heinz Ketelheim had succeeded in his desire to be transferred to fighters. Having managed to escape back across the Channel unscathed, he had immediately put in for his transfer and had pursued his goal with single-minded determination. He had shamelessly pulled every string he could, until he'd got his wish. However, his string-pulling had annoyed a senior staff officer so intensely that the officer took revenge by having him posted to the Eastern Front, hoping the Russians would do what the British had not and put an end to his career – permanently.

But Ketelheim had thrived in the eastern theatre. He had revelled in his mastery of his Me-109 and had found the shooting gallery of the Russian front much to his liking. To the chagrin of the staff officer, Ketelheim had returned a highly decorated major sporting a couple of top-grade Iron Crosses, with fifty air victories to his credit, and worse, without a scratch on him. Mere days after Ketelheim's return, the staff officer was killed in a bombing raid while on an inspection tour of Luftwaffe units near the Ardennes.

Ketelheim was further promoted and was returned to France, having been given command of a new unit flying Focke-Wulf Fw-190s. In addition to its normal defensive duties, the unit had a special task: the defence of the airspace above a particular area of Normandy. Within that airspace was a château. He had been told that at all costs the area was barred to all aircraft, including those with German markings making unauthorized entry. All Allied planes were pounced upon with alacrity, and two light transport aircraft with Luftwaffe markings that had failed to obey the ruling on unauthorized entry had also been shot down.

Ketelheim took his task very seriously indeed.

Pendrake could not have known that of the two aircraft he'd spotted high above him after he had destroyed the train, one had been piloted by Ketelheim, the man who had killed Megan.

Bingo Wilson returned from the ranger mission. Braddock did not. Visibly affected by the death of his wingman, Wilson reported to Stanley.

'I warned him over and over, Spy,' he began. 'I told him to stick to me. Then he spotted a 190 stooging around low down. Instead of checking for another as he should have, he broke formation and went after what he thought was a sitting duck. He ignored my orders to return. He was desperate to get a kill, you see. The young fool.'

Wilson paused while Stanley, doing what he was very good at, listened and watched him intently.

'Then before he could even get a good line,' Wilson continued, 'this . . . this second 190 came down like a shark. One slash and Braddock was a flamer. He never got out. I told him . . . I *told* him,' Wilson ended softly.

'Can't blame yourself, Bingo.'

'I was the leader, Spy. My responsibility.'

'You could hardly have got out of your aircraft and dragged him back by the scruff of his neck,' Stanley pointed out reasonably. 'Happens all too often, old son. Eager young sprogs wanting to make a mark. Easy meat for wily veterans.'

A miserable Wilson nodded in agreement. 'Someone like that must have done it. No wasted action. It was down and *bam*, goodbye Braddock. Whoever was flying that 190 knew his business. And another thing, the one Braddock was after broke away with perfect timing, as if it had all been set up. It was an assassination.'

'Aces of some sort?'

'Must be. There was something else very odd too. They just circled and then turned away, ignoring me completely. I can't believe they didn't spot me rushing down on them; but they weren't interested. They'd had a good start and I couldn't catch up. Besides, fuel was getting low. My Typhoon didn't frighten them. It was as if they knew there'd be another time.'

'Or were under instructions not to leave the area,' Stanley said mysteriously.

Wilson stared at him. 'What do you mean, Spy?'

'Random thoughts,' Stanley replied vaguely. 'All right, Bingo. Fill in the form then hop over to see the group captain.'

Wilson looked anxious. 'I'm being carpeted?'

'Good Lord, no. He wants to see you about something else entirely.'

'Any idea?'

'Why not wait until you see him? There's a good chap.'

Wilson gave up and began to write his report.

The WAAF officer opened the door to Group Captain Fox's office and announced, 'Flying Officer Wilson's here, sir.'

'Thank you, Miss Johnson. Send him in.'

'Sir.' Then the young woman stood back for Wilson to enter, closing the door after him.

Wilson, cap smartly on, marched in and brought himself to attention. He saluted briskly.

'At ease, Flying Officer Wilson,' Fox said. 'And don't look so worried, man. I'm not about to tear you off a strip. I heard about Braddock. Sorry it happened. Not your fault. I've lost a couple of eager beavers myself in my time, for exactly the same reason. You're not the first, and you won't be the last flight leader to lose a man that way. Doesn't help the way you feel, I know. But there you have it.'

'Yes, sir.'

'Well, Bingo. Think you're about ready to become a flight lieutenant?'

Wilson, though ordered to stand at ease, was still trying to maintain a smartly respectful stance. His eyes grew round in surprise.

'Well, sir . . . I mean, sir . . . I . . .'

'Yes?'

'Well, sir, there are others of greater seniority on the squadron . . .'

'Are you doubting my ability to choose whom I wish to promote?'

'No, sir! And . . . thank you, sir.'

'Thank you, Flying Officer Wilson,' Fox said drily. 'You won't have to worry about offending anyone on the squadron. You'll be leaving . . .'

His resolve weakened, Wilson broke his stance to look aghast at the group captain. 'Leaving, sir?' He sounded horrified. 'But . . .'

'Damn it, man! Let me finish.'

Wilson straightened sharply. 'Sir!'

'Yes. Well. Now where were we? Ah, yes, Mike Pendrake is moving to take command of a new squadron, with a new rank. He asked for you, though God knows why.'

Wilson gave an unrestrained grin. 'Ah well, that's different, sir.'

'I'm so glad you approve, Mr Wilson. I feel much better now.'

Wilson glanced at the group captain warily, but his superior's expression gave nothing away.

'The necessary arangements are already being made,' Fox went on. 'You will be briefed by Pendrake. You will discuss this posting with no one. There are no exceptions, save those with the need to know, until you arrive at your new unit. Am I perfectly clear?'

'Yes, sir!'

'That's it, Bingo. You leave tomorrow.'

'Yes, sir . . . and sir . . .'

Fox waited expectantly.

'I've enjoyed being here. I've enjoyed being in this command.'

'I'm sorry to see you go, young Wilson. Look after yourself and look after Mike. Give him all the support you can.'

'You can count on me, sir.'

Fox nodded. Wilson again drew himself to attention, gave another snappy salute and went out.

The first thing he did was to go in search of Pendrake, whom he found in the mess.

'Heard about Braddock,' Pendrake greeted him. 'Sorry.'

Wilson nodded soberly. 'Mitch Mitchell's got another letter to write to one more family. I think I ought to . . . you know . . . write one of my own to them. More personal. After all, I was the last friendly person to see him alive.'

'If you can handle it, it's a nice thought.' Then Pendrake went on, 'I take it you've just seen the old man?'

'Yes.'

'And how do you feel about coming along?'

'Sounds interesting.'

'It will be. We've got brand-new special Tiffies.'

Wilson looked suspicious. 'And what have we done to deserve such largesse?'

'All in good time.'

'Ah. Dangerous, is it?'

'Would I lead you into danger?'

'Frequently.'

They grinned.

'Come on,' Pendrake said. 'Let's go and drink to lost ones. Tomorrow will come soon enough.'

'Yes. Let's.' Wilson knew what Pendrake really meant.

The Château de St Sauveur was a magnificent mid-seventeenth-century edifice secluded by thick woods, in the wooded heart of Normandy. A two-storey, U-shaped building, it stood serenely within perfectly landscaped grounds, an oasis of unmatched calm in the insanity of a war that was tearing the rest of the world apart. It was as if the years of madness belonged to a totally different world, for not a blemish marred its structure. No shell, no bomb, no bullet had touched it. But this air of wholesome perfection hid a far from pleasant reality.

The manicured gardens were dotted with anti-aircraft weaponry. A solid platform had been built at the back like an outward extension of the eaves, upon which were mounted two four-barrelled cannons, again for air defence. At the ornate gates at the end of the long drive, a company of Panther tanks stood guard. Positioned on each side of the approach road, their formidable 75mm gun barrels pointed menacingly along it. Anything suspicious coming along that road would be blown to bits within seconds. They had also perfected a routine whereby they could move from a defensive to an offensive posture with alarming rapidity.

Within the woods themselves, more tanks lay in wait for any force stupid enough to attempt an assault. These were backed by several platoons of battle-hardened, well-armed Waffen-SS troops positioned throughout the area in a series of concentric defensive rings. It was defence in great depth. The Waffen-SS infantry wore the standard grey-green uniform, sometimes with a camouflaged smock. All the tank crews wore black.

Within the immediate environs of the château itself, and responsible for its protection, was a praetorian guard of more black-uniformed SS men. By themselves, they could stop a small army. They were well aware of that fact and were arrogantly proud of it. Like their comrades in the woods outside the château, they displayed a contempt for the Allied forces that was matched only by their equally naked contempt for their own countrymen who served in the Wehrmacht.

But the true horror existed out of sight, deep within the bowels of the château. Dungeons that had two hundred years before been converted for the infinitely more civilized purpose of housing an extensive wine cellar had in part been restored to their former use. It was here that the local Gestapo went to work on their victims. There was something obscene about the horrors they perpetrated upon their fellow human beings, while from time to time drinking the rare and lovingly collected wines from cut glasses, commandeered from the legitimate owners of the château. The family of the Baron de Malzey were virtual prisoners in their own home and were confined to one of the less attractive wings, under SS guard.

Two misguided attempts by some Resistance groups to rescue the family had ended disastrously, with heavy casualties and prisoners taken. There were other attempts, but for very different reasons. They, too, had failed spectacularly.

The new lord of the commandeered château was Emile Boucheron. Before the war, Boucheron had made a precarious living as a small-time garage owner and motor mechanic; but he had prospered enormously after the defeat of France. He was a man for whom the right time had come. Having decided he had found the winning side, he had readily offered to do business catering for some of the transport needs of the new overlords. This began in a small way, but soon burgeoned into a highly profitable operation. Before long, he was employing like-minded people. His influence with the invaders grew.

Then he discovered a source of even greater power. From the days when he had plied his one-man trade, he drew upon his knowledge of both the area and the people. He could tell with unerring accuracy those who would either support or be active in the Resistance, and those who would collaborate. He knew where they lived. He knew their families. He built up an impressive network of informers, people who owed him favours. His influence with his new-found friends became stratospheric. Soon, even general officers sought his company and advice on local matters. When the Château de St Sauveur was eventually acquired, Boucheron was installed as its new lord.

This arrangement served several purposes. The château provided the Gestapo with a handy operating base; it became an intelligence headquarters; it was a convenient and sumptuous location for the lavish entertaining of the Occupation elite; it gave visiting senior officers a place to stay; but most importantly of all, it afforded protection to Boucheron and his family, who could now never travel without a powerful escort. His enemies were many.

As the fortunes of the war began to turn against his protectors, so did he become more aware of his own vulnerability. A vaguely entertained hope that he would be taken to Germany soon died, and he was left with no illusions that his safety would be assured should a retreat become inevitable. It was therefore greatly in his interest that the Allies failed in their endeavours. To this end, he applied himself with great energy in ferreting out any items of intelligence that would be of use to his patrons, particularly anything to do with a possible invasion from across the Channel.

Boucheron's zeal surprised even the hardened thugs of the Gestapo. The more astute knew he was being driven by fear for his own skin but most merely made use of him and thought little more of it.

Boucheron had himself attended many torture sessions and had once actually outlasted his own SS bodyguards, who had been too sickened to continue watching and listening to the appalling screams. On that occasion, Boucheron had simply joined the torturers, between sessions, in depleting the stock of the baron's wine collection.

Jeanne-Anne Flahaut was just fifteen when she first met Halloran, two years before the outbreak of war, in Paris. One of the adventurous American students who had decided to 'do Europe' before settling into a pre-mapped career that had begun at an Ivy League university, Halloran had found himself warming to the quietly confident, green-eyed blonde he'd been introduced to by a group of new-found Parisian friends. She had seemed much older than her years.

A friendship had grown between them, but nothing more at that stage. Halloran travelled round France, doing odd jobs, living in different areas for a while and learning the language, which was eventually to stand him in good stead. He wrote to Jeanne-Anne frequently. He did not, like many of his peers, get involved in the civil war in Spain, and he was still in France when the first shots of the major war to come were fired on the Polish border.

In Paris he again met Jeanne-Anne, now seventeen. Everyone knew, she told him, that the war would eventually come to France and that if her country was invaded she would join the Resistance. People were already talking about doing so. It was also at that time that he found out that Jeanne-Anne was nearly eight years younger than him. Their friendship continued to remain platonic, much to Jeanne-Anne's annoyance. When the Wehrmacht inevitably stormed across the border, she was as good as her word and joined the Resistance. To celebrate doing so, she seduced him in an open field.

By now fluent in French, Halloran made his way to England and offered his services to the Crown, just as many of his compatriots were offering themselves as pilots for the RAF. His offer was taken up with alacrity. His knowledge of France and the language would be of great use, he was told. It was the beginning of a new kind of life he had never expected and one which turned him into Fer de Lance. It was also one that would eventually lead him to seek a terrible revenge upon the man into whose clutches Jeanne-Anne would subsequently fall.

Everyone at the Château de St Sauveur who had seen her would remember the day Jeanne-Anne was brought in. She had been arrested on a back road by two of the château's Gestapo men in a prowling car. They found material on her that indisputably linked her with the Resistance.

The SS guards in the grounds had stared in frank admiration at the proud and shapely young blonde, each with a sense of regret that she'd had nothing better to do with her time than join the Resistance. To them, it was a shameful waste.

Boucheron had been in residence that day and on seeing her brought in had intervened, saying he knew her. Perhaps he could help. He might get more information out of her, he suggested. The Gestapo allowed him some time.

He took her into a study. 'You don't remember me, do you?' he began.

He was a big man, and with his new status he had developed a passion for tight double-breasted suits that made him look like a Chicago gangster. His large face, topped by a head of lank, black hair, seemed permanently damp, as if the suit was trying to squeeze all the moisture out of him. His nose tended to shine when he got sexually excited and already it had begun to glisten. Once, twice, he drew his tongue slowly across his lower lip, as if priming it for action.

She stared at him. 'Should I?' she said. 'And why would I want to know someone who betrays his people to the Boche just so he can live in this place? What's it like? Stealing someone's home?'

Boucheron made a great show of being conspiratorial.

'Shhh! Keep your voice down! Many of them understand French, you know.'

'Why should I care?'

'You should. Because I can get you away from here.'

She laughed at him. 'From this fortress? With all your filthy SS infesting the countryside?'

'I have the authority of a general in this district,' he said pompously.

'The SS only listen to their generals,' she snapped back scathingly. 'They don't even obey the ordinary German generals. Why should they obey you?'

'They need me . . .'

'Yes. To betray your people! Collaborator!'

'Keep your voice down!' he hissed. 'And don't act high and mighty with me! I can help you. I am trying to save your life. But you must do something for me . . .'

'Of course,' she said contemptuously. 'And now it comes. Your eyes have been undressing me . . .'

'Don't be a fool! That was not what I meant. I can tell them you would be of better use to us if we let you go. You can become part of my network. I can tell them you will be our infiltrator. I will say I can force you to work for me because I have something I can use to pressure you.'

She stared at him. 'You have nothing. So how will they believe you? And what makes you think I would do anything once I am away from here?'

'I would not expect you to,' he said, genuinely surprising her. 'I want you to let the Resistance know I helped you escape . . .'

Understanding dawned. 'Your insurance policy. So you do not believe your Boche are so invincible? You are trying to save your miserable skin . . .'

'Listen! If I can get you away, I have much information that the Allies can use after the war . . .'

'So now you betray your friends.'

Boucheron had small, mean eyes. They became even

nastier. 'Don't play games with me, my girl. Have you any idea what these people will do to you, a beautiful young woman, to get you to talk? You will not die quickly, I assure you. Aren't you afraid?'

'Of course I'm afraid.'

'Then you will do as I say. You must. Anything I say.'

She said nothing.

His eyes studied her body. Again, his tongue stroked his lip. 'You should know me, you know. Your father stopped at my garage before the war, for fuel. Your family was going to the coast on holiday. To La Baule. You were a little girl then, just about to enter your teens, but already very pretty. You, your father, and your mother . . . a Jew.'

She paled. 'Wh . . . what?'

'You can't deny it. I know many things. People gossip all the time. I know that your mother is dead. She was pregnant that day. An unexpected baby. She and the baby died during childbirth. Your mother had married against her family's wishes and into another religion. They rejected her. You were brought up as a Catholic, your father's religion. But that won't save you if I tell my friends out there. To them, half a Jew, even a Catholic one, is still a Jew. After all, we all know with Jews the race is vested in the mother. They will treat you harshly enough as a member of the Resistance; but as a Jew . . .' There was no need for him to finish the sentence.

Jeanne-Anne had begun to tremble slightly.

Then Boucheron once more became reasonable. 'Listen to me. Do as I say. Let me help.'

There was a sharp knock on the door. 'Monsieur Boucheron! Are you all right?'

'I'm fine,' the Frenchman called. 'They're getting impatient,' he continued urgently to her. 'Well? Do you agree to my suggestions?' His eyes roved over her body yet again. Nose and face were glistening now. 'I think we should seal our . . . pact in a friendly manner. Don't you?'

There was no mistaking his intentions. Having exposed her secret, he now clearly thought she would do anything to avoid having it betrayed to the Gestapo.

She did what he never expected. She spat full into the large, moist face.

'Krötemann!' he yelled, reddening with anger as he wiped at the spittle with a large white handkerchief. The cruel eyes kept staring at her.

One of the Gestapo men came charging in, pistol drawn.

'Take the Jew slut down!' Boucheron ordered.

Krötemann stared from Jeanne-Anne to Boucheron disbelievingly. 'What? A Jew? Impossible.'

'You think she looks a picture of Aryan perfection?' he snarled. 'I know her family. Her mother was a Jew.'

Krötemann again looked from one to the other. Jeanne-Anne was glaring with unwavering contempt at Boucheron. With ludicrous correctness, he asked her, 'Is this true?'

'Yes,' she replied calmly.

Krötemann's correctness suddenly changed. '*Come on, bitch!*' he shouted. '*Move!*'

Boucheron followed them out. 'I'm coming to watch.'

In the dungeon, among all those bottles of rare wines, Boucheron watched as Jeanne-Anne was abused by her torturers. She was raped, her four interrogators taking turns, beaten, and raped again until her cries became piteous whimpers. It was this that even the SS bodyguards who had accompanied Boucheron could no longer stomach. In their minds, they still saw the beautiful young woman; not the mangled thing lying in her blood and urine, and who now whimpered like a badly injured puppy.

She never divulged any information.

Boucheron drank wine.

They did not finish the job of killing her. Instead, they took her out, flung her into a motorcycle sidecar and, under escort, drove her into the countryside. They dumped her by the side of a narrow road and left her there.

Several hours later a Resistance patrol found her crawling along, an inch at a time. She'd been willing herself to stay alive. They took the wreck of her body to her beloved Fer de Lance.

She remained alive just long enough to tell him, 'Boucheron.'

'They're ready for you now, Major. *Major?*'

Halloran jerked out of his reverie as the hand shook him by the shoulder. He looked up at the young Wren officer, his eyes slowing coming back into focus.

She stared at him anxiously. 'Are you all right, Major Halloran?'

'Yes, yes,' he said, getting slowly to his feet. 'Sorry. I guess I must have fallen asleep or something.'

'You certainly looked as if you were a long way away.'

Without thinking, Halloran placed a hand to his upper chest and felt the shape of the small crucifix beneath his clothes. Strange, he reflected, suddenly remembering her like that; the way they had found her. He felt a sudden heat behind his eyes.

The Wren continued to study him anxiously and misinterpreted the look in them. 'You seem in pain, Major. Is it an old wound?'

'You could say that.'

She began to reach forward solicitously. 'Need any help walking?'

'No thanks. I'm really OK. Guess I'd better hear what the brass has to say.'

He followed her down the corridor to the room where the senior staff officers awaited him.

3

Pendrake was about seven miles from the airfield, with the ancient city of Cirencester, at the junction of the Fosse and Ermine Ways, passing his right wingtip. He made his approach at full throttle – 'up the firewall' as an American Eagle Squadron pilot once described it to him – keeping the Typhoon low, almost skimming the ground. They wouldn't know he was there until the moment of his arrival.

Word had come from Halloran that modification to 'S' standard had been approved. He was thus very pleased that he had been able to take his own aircraft, truncated hand included, to the new posting.

Even this far inland, he still kept a constant lookout and it was during one of his repeated searches of the sky that he spotted two specks bearing down upon him, from the higher reaches. He was very aware that pilots of other Allied aircraft, and the gunners on the ground, sometimes tended to have difficulty in recognizing the Typhoon.

It was not as familiar a shape as the Spitfire or Hurricane, and he knew of at least one occasion when it was misidentified as a Focke-Wulf Fw-190 and the hapless pilot had found himself on the receiving end of the concentrated attention of four Spitfires. Only his flying skill had saved him, for by the time the eager Spitfire pilots had finally paused long enough to identify the RAF roundels, the Typhoon was no longer airworthy and the pilot had been forced to make an unscheduled descent by parachute.

Enraged, he had muttered bitterly when picked up that he should have given the Spits a dose of his cannon.

Pendrake kept a wary eye on the approaching aircraft, but did not alter his course. If they were Allied planes and they were incompetent enough to attack him, he would fight back. They *would* get a dose of *his* cannon.

They turned out to be Spitfires and, using the speed they had generated in the dive to catch up, peeled off beautifully left and right on either side of him, showing off the graceful, elliptical planform of their wings. They formatted on him, struggling slightly to keep up.

He waggled his wings at them as the greater top speed of the Typhoon began to leave them behind. They continued to maintain position, trailing him towards the airfield.

He took the Typhoon down to almost ground-scraping height as it bellowed its way along the runway. Then he broke smartly left, his wingtip making those watching gasp as they believed it was about to touch the grass beyond the runway, or that the aircraft itself would slam into one of the camouflaged buildings. But the Typhoon raced round the circuit to line up perfectly once more.

As he was turning, Pendrake saw that the trailing Spitfires had followed his approach pattern and had done the break in perfect formation, to follow him in for the landing. He lowered his wheels and landed smoothly. He was taxiing off the runway when the pair of Spitfires touched down.

On the break, he had seen a line of gleaming aircraft, positioned in a neat row in Dispersal. As he now taxied towards them, he saw they were the new S-type Typhoons. All were painted a uniform black, which gave them a powerful air of palpable menace, even as they stood waiting silently. Their bubble canopies glinted dully in the bright sun of a cold but clear day. Their RAF roundels and serial numbers were of such low visibility, the markings seemed to disappear into the paintwork. He realized that from the ground or in the air, it would be as if there were no markings at all. There were eighteen in all.

They were, he thought, absolutely beautiful and he felt

a thrill of anticipation surge through him. Now that he had landed and had actually seen the aircraft, the full meaning of what had occurred barely twenty-four hours before began to make an impression upon him. These were *his* to command.

A member of the ground crew directed him to a parking position at the head of the line of black Typhoons. He cut the engine, removed his helmet and paused for a moment to savour the sudden quiet, then climbed out. As he did so, he was aware that two more of the ground crew had joined the first. They were staring at a spot on the fuselage.

'It's what you think it is,' he said to them.

They jumped at the sound of his voice, drew to attention and saluted. One of them looked ill.

He waved a hand at them to relax.

The ill-looking one, a senior aircraftman, said, 'It's not really a hand, is it, sir? It's one of those things you get in a joke shop, isn't it, really?'

'What's your name?'

'Henderson, sir.'

'Well, SAC Henderson, it's not from a joke shop. It comes from a German on a train. Not sure of his rank, though. It must not be removed. Understand?'

'Yes . . . yes, sir!'

The other two stared at him dumbfounded. He left all three to it and began walking. Before long, everyone on the station would know of the incident. It was what he wanted.

He'd only gone a few yards when a staff car approached. A short distance away, the two Spitfires that had followed him in were being marshalled to a stop.

The staff car came to a halt and a wing commander, almost three inches shorter than Pendrake, climbed out. He was not wearing pilot's wings.

The officer walked up to him. 'Squadron Leader Pendrake?'

Pendrake stood to attention. 'Yes, sir.'

'That was quite an approach. Impressive. You had everybody gawping. And you can relax. I'm not really CO here. You are. My role is to see that the administration of this unit runs smoothly, while you get on with whatever it is they sent you here to do.' The wing commander held out a hand. 'My name's David Rhys.' There was a pleasant manner about Rhys that Pendrake found agreeable.

They shook hands. 'Mike Pendrake.'

'Yes. We were advised. Hop in, Mike. I'll take you to . . .'

'Just a moment.'

Rhys paused to follow Pendrake's gaze. The Spitfire pilots were hurrying towards them, helmets still on, leads flailing as they jogged. Pendrake removed his Mae West as they waited, took his forage cap from a pocket and put it on.

The Spitfire pilots stopped when they had reached the car, whipped off their helmets and snapped to attention. Both had the rank of flying officer.

'Sean Kelly,' one announced with an American accent, grinning. 'Boston Irish. And next to me is Jim Dodson, Yorkshire terrier. We're your welcoming committee, if you're Squadron Leader Pendrake.'

They were trying not to stare at his scar.

'I am,' Pendrake said. He glanced at Rhys. 'Know these two?'

Rhys nodded. 'Flew in yesterday. I authorized their . . . patrol.'

'I see. At ease, gentlemen,' Pendrake said to them. 'I thought I was about to have been the victim of poor recognition.'

'And had you been, sir,' Kelly asked boldly, 'would you have fought back?'

'Let's put it this way, Kelly. You would have found

yourself trying to dodge 20mm cannon shells. You might not have succeeded.'

Kelly stared at him. 'You mean that . . . er, sir?'

'I never joke about combat. If you are to be part of my squadron, you'll soon find that out. Have you two been assigned to me?'

'Yes, sir,' Dodson answered. 'We were told we had been selected for a new squadron and to leave immediately. At least they let us take our Spits.'

'From now on, you'll be flying something else, gentlemen.' Pendrake pointed to the line of Typhoons. 'Those are to be your new mounts.'

'We've had a good look at them, sir,' Kelly said. 'We all have. They look like mean beasts.'

'They are. Possibly more powerful than anything you've flown before, and very different to the Spitfire. Do you have any Typhoon time? Either of you?'

Kelly shook his head. 'Hurrybacks and Spits.'

'I was on a Typhoon conversion course,' Dodson ventured. 'I'd come from Hurrys. Then I was sent on to Spits.'

Pendrake looked at him. 'Why?'

'Had a problem with the take-off, sir. I was always swinging to the right – couldn't seem to compensate in time.'

'So they send you back to something even more powerful?' Pendrake shook his head slowly in disbelief.

'Perhaps they thought every little would help,' the Englishman explained awkwardly.

'Perhaps.' Pendrake looked at Kelly. 'Earlier, you said "we all have". Are the other pilots all here?'

'They must be, sir. There's twenty of us.'

'Very well, gentlemen. As you elected to be my welcoming committee, you can now go and round up all pilots. I'll see them in the briefing room in one hour. I now have things to discuss with Wing Commander Rhys. See you then.'

'Yes, sir,' they said together.

Pendrake and Rhys got into the car.

As it drew away, Kelly turned to look at Pendrake's Typhoon. 'What are those guys staring at?'

Dodson looked. There was a small crowd by the aircraft. 'Let's see.'

As they approached, the men parted to allow them through.

Kelly stared at the object of everyone's attention. 'Is this for real?'

Henderson answered him. 'The squadron CO said it was, sir. Said it came off a German on a train. He was joking, wasn't he, sir?'

'I dunno, guys,' Kelly said. 'One thing I reckon our new CO doesn't do, that's make jokes like this. Came off a German on a train, you said.'

'Yes, sir,' Henderson replied. 'He also ordered us to leave it just where it is. If you look closely, sir, it's been doped over to keep it in place.'

Kelly peered at the remains. 'But how in hell did that get there? Did he just put it on?'

'I've heard his name before,' Dodson was saying thoughtfully. 'I think it was on my old Hurricane squadron. I heard someone talking about . . .' he paused, looked at the ground crew and said, 'Sorry. We'd better leave you to your work.'

As they moved away, followed by uncomprehending stares, Kelly said, 'What's going on?'

'It may only have been someone shooting a line but if it's true, it's personal to the CO. I don't really want to gossip with the ground crew about him.'

'I get your drift. So? What's the story?'

'The way I heard it, he was married for two days when he and his wife got caught up in a freak bombing. Wasn't really a raid at all. Just one Heinkel, out in the country somewhere, I think. Story is it got lost and just dumped its bombs. She was killed.'

'The poor guy.'

'He went berserk in the air, killing anything with a black cross on it, moving or not.'

'Doesn't surprise me.'

'Mark you, I'm assuming it's the same Pendrake. Then on the Spit squadron, I heard he'd gone on to Typhoons and was a champion trainbuster. He's flown both the Spit and the Hurry, and now he's come here with a Typhoon to command his own squadron of Tiffies. It must be the same bloke.'

Kelly grabbed Dodson by the shoulders, turning him round. 'Now hold on. You're not telling me he attacked a train, it blew up, bodies flew through the air and one hit his plane?'

'Why not? He said it came off a train.'

'Aw, come on! He'd have to fly so low . . .' Kelly paused, remembering Pendrake's ultra-low approach.

Dodson watched comprehension slowly dawning on his companion's face. 'Exactly,' he said.

'Jeez!' Kelly said. 'What have we gotten ourselves into?'

'We're going to find out, Boston. We're going to find out.'

'Jeez!'

In the car, Rhys said, 'What would you like to do first?'

'I'll resist the temptation to inspect the aircraft immediately, sir,' Pendrake replied. 'I'll do that later. I want a quick check of the pilot records. What have they sent me?'

'A motley lot. Some very experienced, some fairly, and some not at all. You've got a mixed bag. In addition to the British contingent, you've got two Australians, a New Zealander, another American to add to Kelly, a Canadian, a Pole . . .'

'A Pole! Can he speak the kind of English that I can understand in the air? My Polish is . . . my Polish isn't.'

Rhys's features creased in a slow smile. 'He speaks it fairly well – when he wants to – and understands it exceedingly well – when he wants to.

'That's all I need.'

'Old Josef's a good type. Hates Nazis. Likes killing them.'

'Just the sort of man I want. Any more?'

'There's a Frenchman, and another Frenchman, only this one's from across the water. Quebecois. He's very fond of telling his fellow Canadian, Bill Mackenzie, that after the war Quebec will be free.'

'Does he actually mean that?'

'Oh, I believe as a French Canadian he enjoys ribbing Mackenzie. But you never know. This war will change many things. The world will change. Even in this country, things will never be the same again. The social strata will alter radically. It may not happen overnight, but it will do so quicker than many expect. But we've the job with the Hun to attend to first.'

There was a lull in the conversation as Rhys pulled over to allow a petrol bowser going in the opposite direction to pass.

'So practically half of my complement of pilots are Commonwealth,' Pendrake said as they began to move again, 'and Allied.'

'Will that cause you problems?'

'Absolutely not. All I want from them is the ability to fly the Typhoon without killing themselves, and to kill the enemy. To enable them to do that, I must turn them into hawks. Their souls will belong to me.'

Rhys glanced at Pendrake, noting how the scar seemed to have become a livid weal that faded again so quickly, Rhys thought his eyes had played tricks on him.

'Young Karen will help you with the paperwork,' Rhys went on. 'She . . .'

'Young Karen?'

'Yes. Karen Lewis. Section officer. She was sent to look

after the bumf. Bright. Very bright indeed. I believe she was seconded from the Air Ministry. Powerful people are moving things for you. They got me here. I was staff officer to an air vice-marshal before this little lot. Karen's already arranged all the relevant documents for you. She's got an office next to yours. We're going over now . . . unless you'd prefer to go to the mess first.'

'No, sir. I might as well start right away if I've got to meet my pilots within the hour.'

'Fine. And by the way, no need for the "sir". I'm David. In reality, you probably outrank me. I'm actually a university lecturer. I'm thirty-seven. When they pulled me in, they weren't sure what rank to give me. I think they felt wing commander was just high enough, so as not to make things awkward.' Rhys smiled deprecatingly.

'I'm sure your rank is deservedly earned,' Pendrake said. 'But I'll compromise. In private, it's David. Before the men and any junior ranks, it's "sir".'

'Fair enough,' Rhys said awkwardly after awhile. 'But you're making this rather difficult for me. When I was with the AVM it was easy. I was the subordinate. Here, you're the operational commander. I know nothing about combat.'

'You've got skills I haven't, or you wouldn't be here. Let's do this together, and we'll be fine.'

'Fair enough,' Rhys said again.

'I'm expecting two others,' Pendrake said. 'A US Army Air Force major . . .'

'Ah yes. Major Halloran. He's actually on his way. An Anson's bringing him over. He should be here by the time you're ready to meet the pilots.'

'Good. Then there's Bingo Wilson. He's my deputy. He'll be coming by road. I expect him to arrive sometime this afternoon.'

'We'll look out for him,' Rhys said. 'Ah. Here we are.'

They had pulled up before a long, low building, brick-built and camouflaged.

'Your fully self-contained headquarters,' Rhys went on as they climbed out of the car. 'It's been furnished to meet all your operational needs. Your offices are at this end, close to the entrance. The briefing room's at the far end.'

'Someone's certainly been preparing for this for some time.'

'Oh, I don't think it was built especially for your particular mission. But it was here, and available. It's been used before, I believe, for other . . . special missions.'

Pendrake looked at the building and nodded. 'By the way, talking of missions . . . I don't think it's a good idea to leave the aircraft where they are. They look nice and shiny and impressive lined up so neatly for inspection. But I'd feel more at ease if they were split into pairs and dispersed haphazardly about the place, when they're not in the hangars being repaired.

'They make juicy targets as they are. I know we're well away from the bombers and that the old raids are now virtually non-existent. But there are still intruders. I've been doing single intrusions myself. It takes only one . . . and you never know where a bomb might come from. Believe me, I do know what I'm talking about.'

Pendrake turned from his scrutiny of the building to look at Rhys, who thought he saw a strange intensity in the pilot's eyes.

'I'll have it done,' Rhys promised.

'Thanks. And my own aircraft is to be modified to "S" standard.'

'That's in hand. As a matter of fact, they're moving it into a hangar as we speak.'

'Thank you, David,' Pendrake repeated. 'Do you see? You've already proved my point. The team's working. Now, let's meet Section Officer Lewis.'

* * *

Karen Lewis was a rare creature. Though aware she was beautiful, she saw little reason to preen, or to make a song and dance about it. She had scant time for make-up and the only concession she made to beautifying herself was a touch of lipstick that was less red than contemporary fashion dictated. Her male admirers, who were legion, fell into two camps. Some were of the opinion that hers was the face of an angel. The others, that the reality surpassed even that description.

Fortunate to have been endowed with flawless skin, jet-black hair and vivid blue eyes, she never failed to impress at the very first meeting. Her body, while not slim enough to be described as willowy, had an unconscious sinuosity of movement that generated awe. Her service shoes, built for utility rather than beauty, could do nothing to detract from the perfection of her legs. In the person of Karen Lewis, nature had won hands down. She was just nineteen.

It was thus something of a shock to Rhys when he introduced her to Pendrake that, though pleasant and polite enough, the pilot failed to register the slightest flicker of interest in her, other than in the question of her duties. And though from what he knew of her Rhys was aware she never traded on her beauty, he thought he detected a slight disappointment in her.

'I'll leave you to it,' he now said, glancing from one to the other. 'And I'll have those aircraft dispersed,' he added to Pendrake. He held out a hand. 'Good luck.'

'Thank you, sir,' Pendrake said as they shook hands.

Pendrake waited until Rhys had gone before saying, 'Well, Miss Lewis, shall we get started?'

'Yes, sir.' She had a warm, comforting voice. 'This is your office,' she continued, pointing to a connecting door. 'I assumed you'd want to see all the pilot records. They're on your desk, with the experience of each individual itemized and graded.'

'My word,' he said as they entered the surprisingly

well-appointed room. 'This is better than the station commander's at my old unit.'

'I believe it was an American general's office, sir. There were some people here last year, working on an operation.'

'Were they?' Pendrake was astute enough not to ask whether she knew more about it. 'Well, it's our turn.' He looked at the large desk, on which documents were neatly arranged. 'My pilots?'

'Yes, sir.'

He went over to the polished-walnut swivel chair with its padded leather seat and sat down, testing it with a couple of swings to left and right. 'Nice being an American general. Very pleasing. And now, the paperwork.'

She came across to the desk and stood next to him, looking over his shoulder. He sensed her glancing at his epaulettes. They still bore the two blue rings of a flight lieutenant.

'I know,' he said. 'I'm improperly dressed. No time yet to sew the new ones on.'

'I thought that might be the case, sir. I've got the new ones, so if you'll give me your battledress blouse, I'll have them put on.'

'You must be a mind-reader, Lewis. But you don't have to . . .'

'I'd be happy to, sir.'

Pendrake gave in. 'All right.' He removed the blouse and handed it to her. 'I'll look through these records in the meantime.'

'Very good, sir.'

He did not look up as she went out, already engrossed in studying the flying experience of the pilots he'd been given to command.

Lewis had done a thorough job of collating the information. Rhys was certainly right about her. After a quick skim through the detailed breakdown by pilot, matters took a distinct turn for the worse; not because she had been inefficient, but because her remarkable efficiency had exposed to the light of day the motives of those who had set up the mission.

He waited for her to return, quietly fuming.

She entered with a smile that would normally have sent any man weak at the knees, carrying his newly be-ranked battledress blouse triumphantly. The smile vanished when she saw his expression. She paused uncertainly.

'Have I done something wrong, sir?'

'No, Lewis. You've done everything right.'

Still uncertain, she handed him the blouse. 'I don't understand, sir.'

'It's the information in here. I've got twenty pilots and if you add Wilson and myself, my complement's twenty-two. I've got eighteen brand-new aircraft, plus mine, making a grand total of nineteen. A well-equipped squadron . . . almost too well equipped.' Pendrake looked about him. 'We've been very well accommodated, and I've got you to hold my hand. I should be happy. And yet . . .'

'And yet, sir?'

Pendrake put his blouse back on and buttoned it as he considered his next words.

'And yet, Lewis.' He pointed to one of the neatly assembled files. 'Take Flight Lieutenant Keane. Australian, excellent combat record, shot down three times. Nothing wrong with that, except . . . Keane's barely out of hospital. The third time, he was badly wounded. Right shoulder's still stiff, and gives him pain. Not much use if he's going to be doing some hard turning at low level with Jerry on his tail.

'Then our Canadian, Mackenzie. Also a good record, also shot down . . . once. But over water, and he swallowed a lungful of oil-contaminated Channel. Though cleared for flying, I want to be certain those lungs are not going to be a liability. Captain Elmore, USAAF. Mustang pilot.

Pranged. Not in itself a problem. I've pranged. Once. I was on fire. Elmore's pranged *three* times, none because of enemy fire. Noted for particularly heavy landings.'

Pendrake hunted out another file while Lewis watched him silently. 'Our New Zealander, Knowles, was on Mosquitoes. No single-seat experience whatsoever. And as for the home-grown contingent, they've sent me *boys*, most of whom have flown nothing more powerful than an advanced trainer. Those Typhoons will have them for breakfast. It appears to me that with the exception of Wilson and myself, Kelly, Dodson, and our very own Pole, Josef Wojdat, who appears to have been trying to decimate the Jerry air force all by himself, I don't have a squadron. Now tell me something, Lewis . . . Wing Commander Rhys has informed me that you're very bright. What does this smell like to you?'

'They've given you a bit of a job, sir.'

'I would have used stronger language, but I'm thinking of a particular word, Section Officer Lewis.'

'What word is that, sir?'

'Expendable.'

The Avro Anson, a twin radial-engined light transport and training aircraft, banked sedately as it approached the airfield. Halloran peered down out of the oval window by his seat, to study the ground as it slowly moved across his field of view.

The place was much bigger than expected, until he realized it was rather like two separate units grafted together to make one. Yet both parts remained distinctly autonomous. The larger section, with its own runways, was a hive of flying activity over to the west. He'd been told that this was a major operational training unit, with a variety of aircraft in use. He wondered if that was where some of Pendrake's pilots had come from. As his window now passed over the Cobra Squadron section, he could make out the new Typhoons, haphazardly dispersed in pairs. He compared this with the neat lines of aircraft on the training unit.

His mouth twitched in a fleeting smile. Pendrake was already making his presence felt. Halloran approved of the precaution.

'You have seen something funny?'

Halloran turned to look at the speaker, dressed in civilian clothes, who was sitting across from him. The accent was French.

'Just observing a professional at work, Michel,' Halloran explained. 'The commander of Cobra Squadron has dispersed his airplanes, in order to minimize any damage that might be done by an unexpected strike against the airfield, even way out here.'

Michel Montcarneau nodded approvingly. 'I like the way he thinks. Perhaps we shall work well together.'

'I'd wait and see, Michel,' Halloran cautioned. 'I've met the guy briefly, just the once. But I've heard plenty. He's a tough customer.'

Montcarneau looked him straight in the eye. 'Someone once said to me when France fell, we are going to need some pretty tough customers.'

'Throwing my words back at me, Michel?'

'No. Just reminding you.'

The Anson throttled back as it lined itself up for the landing. Soon, it was settling itself gently on to the ground.

Rhys was waiting with his own staff car, with another nearby.

After introductions, Halloran said, 'Is the model ready, sir?'

'All taken care of,' Rhys answered. 'We've got a wide range of skills on site. Prior to our show with Jerry, some of the people who have worked on it had jobs requiring a very high degree of expertise, in toy factories. Others, like so many boys *and* girls, believe it or not, have built model aeroplanes since their childhood days. I've had both male and female personnel working on the construction. I think you'll be pleased with the result.'

'I'm sure we will, sir. Thank you. We'll check it out later. Better see our new squadron commander first. I see he's moved the airplanes.'

'Yes. Insisted we did so. Protection against surprise attack.'

'Understandable. It's what he's been doing to the Germans in Normandy. Be seeing you later, sir. We'll be on our way.'

Rhys pointed to the other vehicle. 'Car and driver at your disposal. Gentlemen.'

Halloran saluted. Montcarneau inclined his head slightly. Rhys gave them a brief wave at his cap and went back to his car.

In his office, Pendrake had heard the aircraft go over and had listened to and accurately identified the noise of its engines.

'Sounds like an Anson has just come in,' he remarked to Karen Lewis after a while as he continued to study the pilots' records. 'Could be Major Halloran,' he went on grimly. 'He's early. All the better. I can see him before I meet the aircrew. I want a few words with that man. He's got some explaining to do. If not him, then whoever's responsible for this selection of pilots.'

'Sir . . .' she began in what sounded like an attempt to calm him down. 'You may be confronting officers of senior rank. A squadron leader of one day's standing will have no chance . . .'

The ringing of the telephone on his desk cut into any retort he might have been inclined to deliver.

He picked it up. 'Flight Lieut . . .' Then he remembered. 'Squadron Leader Pendrake.'

It was Rhys. 'Major Halloran's arrived, Mike. He's got a French chap with him.'

'Pilot?' Pendrake enquired hopefully.

'No idea, old boy. He's a civilian. That is, he's in civilian clothes.'

'*Civilian?* Why has Halloran brought him? And what does a *French* civilian want with me?'

'You're about to find out. They're on their way.'

'I see. Thank you, sir. You heard that?' he added to Lewis as they hung up.

She nodded.

'You'd better get out there to greet them,' he said unenthusiastically. 'Whatever they're about, it's probably not going to improve my view of the day so far. I'm beginning to think, Lewis, that I was much better off as a flight lieutenant roving on my own across Normandy at night.'

'Yes, sir.'

He looked at her. 'No arguments?'

'For the time being, no, sir.'

'I see. Thank you, Lewis.'

'Sir.'

She went out, a thoughtful expression on her face.

Not long after, Pendrake heard voices and got to his feet, composing himself for the coming meeting.

The door opened and Karen Lewis stood there. 'Major Halloran and Monsieur Montcarneau, sir.'

'Thank you. Please send them in.'

She stood back, and the two men entered, Halloran carrying his brown leather briefcase.

'Good to see you again,' Halloran began with a grin, 'and congratulations on the promotion.'

'Thank you.' Pendrake remained civil.

'This is Michel Montcarneau.'

Pendrake held out his hand. 'Monsieur Montcarneau.' He noted that the Frenchman was studying him hard.

They shook hands as Halloran continued, 'Michel will be working closely with you. You'll find his information, and his help, invaluable.'

Pendrake glanced at Montcarneau before returning his gaze to the American. 'I shall be better able to judge that when I know precisely what I'm doing here.'

'And I'm here to put you in the picture,' Halloran said.

'Fully?'

Montcarneau glanced at Halloran, his eyes seeming to telegraph a message. 'I think, Major,' he interrupted quietly, 'I shall wait in the outer office. I believe you and Squadron Leader Pendrake should discuss certain matters first, without my presence.'

He did not wait for either to comment. He turned, and went out to Karen Lewis's office.

'That's Michel for you,' Halloran said drily. 'Circumspect as always.'

'Has he reason to be?'

Halloran seemed to pause to take stock. 'I get the feeling you're sore about something.'

'How long do I have before this unit goes on whatever mission has been planned for it?' Pendrake countered.

'A little under three weeks.'

Pendrake stared at Halloran as if the other had taken leave of his senses. '*Under* three weeks! Is this a joke?'

'It's wartime.'

Pendrake's eyes bored into Halloran's.

'Out there,' he began in a quiet but hard voice, pointing in the direction of Dispersal, 'in addition to my own, I've got eighteen spanking new aircraft. An almost lavish supply of equipment. Now why, I asked myself, not give me the pilots to match such wonderfully shiny aeroplanes?' He brought a hand firmly down on the papers on the desk. 'Do you know what I've got instead?

'On the face of it,' Pendrake went on, before the American could say anything, 'I've got a good complement of pilots.

Twenty. Then there's Wilson, who's on his way and, of course, the squadron commander. Me. More than enough from which, with time, to fashion a good fighting force. Unfortunately, most of my aircrew appear to be invalids, indifferent flyers or inexperienced boys! Now you tell me I've got just *three* weeks to turn this bunch into a fighting unit that's supposed to not only do the job, but survive long enough to get it done!'

Halloran said nothing.

'Major? I'm waiting for some explanation.'

'I know what's biting you,' Halloran said at last.

'You do?' Pendrake remarked coldly.

'You've got your own private war with the enemy . . .'

'What the devil do you . . .?'

'You've got to let her go some time,' Halloran ploughed on. 'I know about what happened to your wife. You're not the only person, and you won't be the last, to lose somebody close . . .' Halloran stopped, seeing the look that had come into Pendrake's eyes. *I'm looking into hell*, he thought.

For a moment, Pendrake did not trust himself to speak.

'Who . . . what . . . what gives you the idea that you know anything about it?' he eventually said in a voice so devoid of warmth that Halloran again felt the slight chill he'd experienced when they had first met, only a day before. 'You're now inside my head, are you? You've persuaded yourself that you understand *my* feelings? You *know*, do you? You know what it means to watch the woman you love almost beyond life itself, blown into tiny pieces of flesh and bone, so that it feels as if someone has cut your heart out and stuck it in a lump of ice?

'Shall I tell you what it's really like, Major? You see her blood, flash-dried on the ground. Too late, you discover you've stepped on it. You see bits of white sticking out of scorched trees and you look and realize you're staring at slivers of bone with the flesh hanging off them. You see strips of blackened cloth that only moments before were part of the dress she wore.

'You see something like a dark ribbon hanging off a branch. It takes you a while to understand that what you're looking at is a length of her intestine. You see a ripped shoe. You pick it up and out falls this . . . *thing* of pulped, burnt flesh. And at last you've got to accept that the horrible thing from the shoe, the slivers of bone, the ribbon of intestine . . . *is your wife*. She's all around you; on the ground, in the trees . . . *and she wouldn't have been there* if *you* hadn't taken her in the first place.

'So you know all that, do you? Would you like to hear more? Do I hate the bastards? Yes, yes, *yes*! And unless you can give me an exceedingly good reason, I'm going back to what I know I can do well. *Killing* them. I may be waging my private war, Major Halloran, as you've put it, but I'm not going to be responsible for getting those pilots killed while I'm doing so. And I shall have no difficulty whatsoever about reverting to my old rank, if that's what it takes.'

4

In the outer office, Section Officer Lewis had found it impossible not to hear what Pendrake had said. In his torment, he had spoken loudly. She bit at her lower lip.

Montcarneau had been watching interestedly. A truly beautiful young woman, he'd been thinking. In his early thirties, he had been a railway worker before the war. A far more sophisticated man than his exterior proclaimed, he thought he understood clearly the reasons for the anxiety she displayed.

'You like this man,' he said to her, zeroing in on the truth with perfect accuracy.

Unable to help herself, Lewis blushed. 'Of . . . of course not. I only met him today. He's . . . he's my superior officer.'

'So? That prevents you from liking him? You met him today, but you have known of him before. Yes?'

'Ye . . . yes.'

'Let me tell you something.' His eyes never left her. 'Five minutes after I met my wife, I knew she would be my wife. You have had some hours already.'

His directness was throwing her into confusion.

'Your-your-your wife. What has that . . .?'

'To do with your present anxieties for the brave but emotionally wounded squadron leader?' Montcarneau smiled. 'Who knows?'

'And where . . . where's your wife?'

'Serving France, as I am.'

* * *

In the squadron CO's office, an uneasy silence now reigned. Pendrake and Halloran were eyeing each other like a pair of stags marking out territory.

Then Halloran said, 'Let's sit down, for God's sake. I know nothing about the type of pilots they sent you. What do I know of pilots? I know what kind of man I wanted to command the squadron, that's all. The pilots were someone else's job. Like you, I've got to take what I get. If there's been a foul-up with them, there was nothing I could have done about it, and there is nothing I can do about it now.

'I can raise the matter with Personnel, if you want; but I don't hold out any hope. They'll say they gave us new airplanes and why do we think we deserve the best pilots too? Everyone wants top pilots right now. There's a lot of stuff going on. Things are hotting up. We're just a very small part of the whole picture.'

Halloran paused and absent mindedly felt for the small crucifix beneath his shirt to briefly pat it.

'Look,' he carried on in a reasoning voice. 'I'm sorry about what you had to go through. What more can I say? I'm not going to pretend I can begin to understand how you feel; but I've had my tough one too and, like you, I wanted to go out and shoot every goddam one of them by myself, all the way to Berlin. Believe me, I really felt like doing that. Stupid, of course.'

Halloran fell silent and became introspective. Pendrake kept his own silence and waited.

Then very quietly, almost as if talking to himself, Halloran told Pendrake about Jeanne-Anne. Frequently, he touched the crucifix beneath his shirt, as if searching for reassurance.

When Halloran had finished, Pendrake said nothing, but slowly took his seat. Halloran grabbed a chair, dragged it close to the desk back towards Pendrake, straddled it and sat down.

'Just as you blame yourself for your wife's death,' he said, 'I blame myself for what happened to Jeanne-Anne. I could have prevented her from carrying those documents that day. She would not have thanked me for it . . . but I could have stopped her.' He paused, seeing again in his mind's eye the wreck of the body that had been brought to him. 'We never had the chance to get married. I wanted it, but she didn't. Not in wartime, she said. I wanted what you had. I believed you should take everything that's handed to you today, in case you lost it tomorrow. Each of us, in our own way, still ended up losing what we valued most. So perhaps there's no difference. We each took our chances.'

Another silence fell.

'After that day,' Halloran continued, 'I wanted to attack the château with everything we had. Crazy, of course. We wouldn't have got near it. Other Resistance groups have tried before. They're probably still where they fell. But we have people working for us in there. That's how we've gotten to know what had really happened to Jeanne-Anne.' Halloran drew a ragged breath as he remembered. 'I saw her face every day. You know that? Every hellish day. I still do. Then at last, a chance came to strike back.' Halloran stood up. 'Come with me. I'll show you what your squadron is about to do. We're both going to pay those bastards back.'

'Your target,' Halloran said.

The accurately scaled model of the Château de St Sauveur and the surrounding landscape for miles around was on a large raised platform that seemed to fill the entire room. It was like a giant billiard table, with shaded overhead lighting hanging above it. There was just enough space to allow free passage around its perimeter. Outside in the corridor, armed guards stood on either side of the closed door. There were no windows.

Pendrake stared at the model. All the important trees,

their respective heights marked on small flags, and every hill, mound, valley and river or stream, was represented. Every gun emplacement, every flak tower, every group of soldiers, every tank and scout car was in place. Whoever had supplied the information had done on incredible job.

As if he knew what Pendrake was thinking, Halloran said, 'It took a year to get all the information. The local terrain is well known by our group. We gathered the rest from ordinary people going about their business and who happened to notice an emplacement here, a tank there; but most of all, we got valuable details from Michel, his wife – who's in the château . . .'

Pendrake was astonished. 'In the château?'

'Why yes. It's her castle. Well . . . her family's. Michel worked on the railways and kind of married above his station.' Halloran smiled at Montcarneau, who smiled fleetingly in return.

Pendrake looked at Montcarneau. 'Don't the Gestapo know you're her husband?'

'Was.'

'Was?'

'She's a widow.' Montcarneau gave another brief smile. 'Safer for her.'

'We've also got others in there,' Halloran rejoined. 'Boucheron's cousin, for one. To the Gestapo and Boucheron himself, and even the local people, he's a fervent collaborator. It was he who got word to us that on one of their regular sweeps, the Gestapo picked up a very senior district commander in the Resistance.

'Thing is, they have no idea they have him. He's simply someone among others they've arrested in a reprisal raid, and who looks like just another ordinary old man. He's been in one of the dungeons for months while they decide what to do with him. We've even thought they were going to release him. They sometimes do that with people they take so they can keep tabs on them, hoping they'll lead to bigger fish. At least, he'd be out.

'But his health is failing and if they go to town on him, he may not be strong enough to hold out. He knows too much. When I had the situation relayed to the Intelligence services, they came up with a suggestion to help both the plans for the eventual invasion, and ourselves. They asked me to come up with a plan of execution.'

'Execution,' Pendrake remarked drily. 'Sounds appropriate. And those imprisoned in the château?' he asked. He was walking round the model, studying it, searching out the best approach for a successful attack. He did not look up as he spoke.

'Casualties will be inevitable; but if you carry out the attack well, we might get lucky.'

Pendrake stopped to look at Montcarneau. 'What about your wife?' He thought it grimly ironic that his actions might do to the man's wife what the unknown enemy pilot had done to Megan.

'This is the family wing,' Montcarneau said, pointing to a section that had been painted red. 'You do not attack there. They have been given times of the day when they should all be in that part of the building. This will be the same period of time as your attack. From today, they will be doing this for the next four weeks. It will become a routine and their guards will not be suspicious. Also, one of the girls who works as a maid has got one of Boucheron's SS bodyguards interested in her. It was he who told her of what happened to Jeanne-Anne. Even they could not stomach what was being done; but Boucheron, the pig, stayed to watch and drank wine as he was doing so. The animal.'

'It will be a pre-dawn attack,' Halloran said evenly with some effort, clearly not wanting to think of Jeanne-Anne. 'That should ensure the Malzeys and those others working for us will be in the family wing. We'll never be absolutely sure, of course. Anything can happen. There are sometimes special evenings, when the local commanders are invited to dinner or a general comes visiting. The family are obliged to attend. As these things can go on all night, we've just got to hope the day you attack is not one of those; or that they'll find a way of getting back to their section of the château in time.'

'And the Gestapo prisoners?' Pendrake asked again, still not looking up.

'They take their chances. We can't risk warning them. They may talk under interrogation.'

Pendrake looked up. 'Bit tough on them.'

'It's tougher where they are. My Resistance group will think of a way of helping them on the day.' Halloran sounded as if he did not want to discuss it further.

'The Waffen-SS forces defending the area,' he went on, returning to the main subject, 'come from the 1st Waffen-SS Panzer Division. We'd like to keep them tied up there, permanently, so that they can't be used to reinforce their comrades in other areas. This is vital. In short, they must be pushing up daisies. The Resistance will mop up what you leave.'

Pendrake was again studying the model. 'This place is a fortress,' he said. 'We'll be running a gauntlet all the way in, and all the way back.' He moved along a side of the platform until he came to where an airfield had been positioned, with fighter aircraft upon its runway and in the dispersal bays. They were Fw-190s. 'And these fighters . . . I assume they're stationed so close in order to protect the airspace?'

Halloran nodded. 'I leave you to decide how best to sort them out.'

'I'm glad you're leaving something to me. Tell me . . . do the people who've sanctioned this expect any of us to come back alive?' Pendrake looked up once more, his eyes surveying the two men steadily. He'd made the question sound almost conversational.

Halloran and Montcarneau stared back at him silently.

'Just wondering,' he said, returning to his scrutiny of the model.

His brow furrowed as he began to visualize the tactics he would use to give the squadron the best possible chance of success, with the least number of casualties. In the ensuing silence, it was as if the others had ceased to exist as he immersed himself in the problem. They stared at him, watching as he moved round the table from time to time, sometimes stooping to peer along the edge of the platform, studying the various possible directions from which to mount the attack.

Lewis, her eyes fastened upon him, stared palely from a shadowed corner.

At last, he stopped prowling around the model and straightened, his attention on Halloran. 'Six more aircraft.'

'*What?*'

'I want six more aircraft.'

'You've already got *eighteen*. Brand new! Then there's yours, which is being modified. I had a hell of a job convincing the brass to let you take it. Now you want me to go back to them and say you want *six* more? They'll have my neck.'

'*We'll* be losing our necks if I don't get my aircraft. I need those extra Typhoons to make this thing work. No Typhoons, no mission. It will be a waste of time, and lives.'

Halloran stared at him in astonishment while Montcarneau looked on with clinical interest. In the gloom of her shadows, Lewis's eyes seemed hooded as she continued to fix them on Pendrake.

'Why six, for Pete's sake?' Halloran demanded.

'I want eighteen aircraft in the air on the mission. We're bound to suffer attrition during training, and on the practice runs. The extra six will give us sufficient margin. I must have eighteen fully operational Typhoons on the day. You want this job done, you get me my six aeroplanes.' Pendrake glanced at his watch. 'Time to meet my squadron.'

He went out, leaving them staring after him.

'How do you like that?' Halloran said, his eyes on the closing door. 'What does he expect me to do?'

'I would get him his six aeroplanes,' Montcarneau suggested.

They got to their feet in a rumble of chairs as Pendrake entered and climbed the low dais.

'Please take your seats, gentlemen.'

They complied, faces expectant, eyes questioning, most looking anxious and uncertain. The majority wore RAF uniforms, with those from the Commonwealth or Allied countries wearing the shoulder titles of their respective homelands. The Frenchman and the Pole wore their nations' uniforms while Elmore, the USAAF captain, had the exotic mix of an RAF pair of trousers topped by a USAAF tunic. Four of the British contingent were sergeant pilots. They looked very young and more anxious than most. They were the ones, Pendrake already knew, with the least experience.

There was another NCO pilot, a flight sergeant and slightly older, who had flown Hurricanes in combat and who had two kills to his credit. Pendrake had decided to put him in charge of the young sergeants.

'My name is Pendrake,' he began. As he started speaking, he was aware of Halloran, Montcarneau and Lewis entering the room. His eyes zeroed upon the USAAF officer. 'Captain Elmore, isn't it?'

Elmore got slowly to his feet. 'Yes, sir,' he drawled.

'Captain, you're improperly dressed.'

'Well, sir, it's like this,' Elmore began to explain in his Southern drawl. 'These here are my lucky pants. Had them since I was in the Eagle squadron. Never a scratch on me.'

'Did you wear them when you were transferred to the US Army Air Force?'

'No, sir.'

'Were you . . . scratched?'

'No, sir.'

'Captain, if you're going to remain with this unit, you will either find yourself a full Royal Air Force uniform with a relevant shoulder title attached, or find a proper pair of trousers to go with that tunic. This is not a carnival. Am I quite clear enough for you?'

Elmore, seeing a compatriot in the room and a major at that, looked to Halloran for guidance. Halloran gave him a cold stare in return.

'I'll be properly dressed, sir,' Elmore finally said.

'Good man. You may sit down.'

'Sir.'

'These two gentlemen,' Pendrake continued as Elmore resumed his seat, 'are Major Halloran and Monsieur Montcarneau. You'll be seeing them from time to time. Section Officer Lewis I'm sure you all know.'

The entire group beamed at her, including the fearful boy-pilots.

'Thank you, gentlemen,' he said drily. 'I see you do know her.'

They gave him nervous smiles, the tension easing.

'You may well be wondering what this unit is about,' he went on, 'and why you were chosen. You have come to Cobra Squadron. Its purpose is totally secret, and you will be given such information as is necessary at the appropriate times. You will discuss nothing about this unit to anyone. There are no exceptions. If any of you makes the slightest reference to the squadron outside these requirements, disciplinary action will be taken, and you will be replaced. This is the only warning you will receive.

'The job in hand is dangerous. I'm not going to pull

punches. I want pilots who know what to expect from the outset, and who can carry the job through. You will undergo rigorous training. You will fly better than you have ever flown before, and you will fight better than you have ever done before.

'You will all have seen the new aircraft. They are powerful beasts and they'll have you for breakfast if you do not first learn to master them, then merge with them. Make them extensions of yourselves until fighting with them becomes second nature. To survive at all, you will need to achieve that level of competence. Then, and only then, will you be ready to tackle the mission. Today is your day of rest. Make the most of it. From tomorrow, training begins in earnest. Any questions?'

Elmore was on his feet.

'Yes, Captain?' Pendrake kept his voice neutral.

'Well, sir . . . I've heard that these ships . . . these Typhoons have gotten a habit of losing their tails, or suffering a sudden disintegration. Imagine that happening with a Nazi on *your* tail. One kill to him without a shot. Friend of mine was flying in a squadron when the plane next to his simply came to pieces. They were not being fired upon by the enemy at the time.'

Pendrake noted that the boy-pilots looked decidedly queasy.

'In the first place,' he replied calmly, 'this no longer happens, and our aircraft are not ordinary Typhoons. They are solid, and I'd rather be in one of them under fire or in a hard fight, than in anything else flying today. However, if one does break up around you, come back and I'll give you another.'

There were slow smiles that turned into chuckles that turned into laughter at Elmore's expense. He sat down ruefully.

'Any more questions?' Pendrake asked when the laughter had subsided.

No one else raised a query.

'Very well,' he said. 'That is all for now, gentlemen. Thank you.'

They got to their feet as he left the dais and went out, followed by his three companions.

'You handled that well,' Halloran said as they walked back to the squadron offices. 'Nice and short. You slap Elmore down twice, but without rubbing his nose in it. Then you give them the old one-two, soft and hard. Everybody knows who's in charge. They know your bite is worse than your bark, but they also know you'll be fair. Not bad going for a new CO. They'll all be bracing themselves for what comes next, minds concentrated. It will be a matter of pride to succeed. That was pretty good going.'

'Early days,' Pendrake commented. 'I took the initiative. It doesn't mean it will hold. They're still in shock. Let's see what evolves.'

'I'll try for your planes,' Halloran announced suddenly.

Lewis, walking behind with Montcarneau, glanced surreptitiously at the Frenchman, who smiled vaguely.

'Excellent,' Pendrake said. 'I knew I could count on you.'

Halloran stopped, forcing the others to an abrupt halt. 'Well, I'll be . . . You play a mean game, Squadron Leader.'

'Not a game, Major,' Pendrake said. 'Never a game.'

The big green Mercedes 540K open-topped sports car roared along the approach road to the château. Its driver knew where each group of soldiers, tanks and armoured vehicles was positioned in the woods.

A patrol of twelve Waffen-SS, six to each side of the road and commanded by a lieutenant, paused when they heard the approaching car and turned alertly. The lieutenant recognized the car and ordered his men to attention. They snapped rigidly erect. The lieutenant gave a sharp salute as the car passed. The driver brought a hand to his elegant cap as he drove past.

'A fine body of men,' his passenger, Oberstleutnant Ketelheim commented. Ketelheim, resplendent in his Luftwaffe uniform, turned to glance back. 'Very smart, Franz.'

Franz Meckler, of equivalent rank in the Waffen-SS and an old friend, smiled proudly. 'My men are the best in the whole of the 1st Waffen-SS Panzer Division.'

'And of course, you're not biased.'

'The truth is not biased.'

They laughed.

Sitting with his left arm resting on the back of the driver's seat, Ketelheim looked at his friend.

'It's really good to see you, Franz. Who would have thought we'd meet up in Normandy? We spent all that time on the Eastern Front and never saw each other and now I find you're commanding a unit in the very area my planes have been sent to protect.'

'On the Eastern Front, there was the little problem of the Russians getting in the way.'

They laughed again.

'But we made them pay,' Ketelheim said with a chuckle.

'I can see by those Iron Crosses,' Meckler observed, 'that you extracted a high price.'

'You haven't done so badly yourself. A lieutenant-colonel at your tender age. And what that's I see? A Knight's Cross with Oak Leaves.'

Meckler grinned. 'I'm only a month younger than you are. So spare me the ancient sage act. So . . . from bomber pilot to fighter ace. How did you manage it?'

'Friends in high places,' they said together, laughing a third time.

Ketelheim gave the dashboard a pat. 'And your car! The times we had in it! How did you manage to get it out of Germany?'

They looked at each other. 'Friends in high places!' they chorused once more.

'And a few low ones,' Meckler added for good measure. 'I have a transport sergeant who can arrange anything. He has more brains than some generals I could mention.'

Ketelheim gave him a serious look. 'That's a change from the Franz of old.'

'Since the Eastern Front, Franz has changed a lot,' Meckler said, momentarily speaking of himself in the third person. 'I know you have never given much credence to the Party's ideals, Karl-Heinz. Yes, yes, I know. No use denying it to me, your oldest friend. When you have known someone from childhood to manhood, you understand a few things about him. I know also, you considered I was foolish to join the Waffen-SS . . . perhaps even disappointed in me. What would you have called it? Intellectually shallow. You used that term when we were students. You were talking about the SA Brown-shirts then.'

Ketelheim said nothing, waiting for his friend to continue.

'Well,' Meckler went on, 'I am going to shock you. You may have been right. The things I have seen on the Eastern Front. The things we have done . . . Oh, don't worry. I'm not suddenly going to throw away my uniform and shout I repent, I repent. It's much too late for me. But I will fight as ferociously as ever, with one important difference – it is no longer for an ideal. I will fight to save Germany. And we shall need to fight, Karl-Heinz. We . . . Germany, will be made to pay severely for the things that have been done in our name. Things we have done in our name.'

There was silence between them for a while as the car's exhaust note bounced off the trees.

Ketelheim was indeed shocked to hear such sentiments from his friend. He could well remember Meckler's first home leave in the smart new uniform of a junior officer in the Waffen-SS, and the piratical air with which it had been worn. Now, as a highly decorated senior officer and combat veteran, though the piratical air could still be discerned, there was a new attitude that seemed a contradiction to all that he thought he'd known about the man.

'Be very careful to whom you say these things, Franz,' Ketelheim now cautioned. 'That uniform, the rank and the Knight's Cross will be no protection if the boys in the black leather coats come sniffing.'

'I am a highly decorated senior officer in the 1st Waffen-SS Panzer Division,' Meckler said proudly. 'I command the forces in this area. I am the protection for their château. They need me. They would also have a rebellion on their hands. My men would take a terrible revenge on the corporal's thugs.'

'And don't let them hear you call the Führer the corporal,' Ketelheim said urgently, giving the impression of half-expecting to be heard, even in the car.

'The whole division might have something to say about it too,' Meckler said, as if Ketelheim had not spoken. 'With the rumours and counter-rumours flying about of an Allied invasion being imminent – though no one seems to know precisely *how* imminent – I don't think he would want to lose one of his best divisions. And we are one of the best . . . probably the best.'

'Just be careful, Franz.'

'There are other rumours,' Meckler said tentatively.

'What other rumours?'

'Rumours about saving the Fatherland from the current madness.'

Ketelheim stared at Meckler. 'I've been hearing rumours too, but I'm keeping well out of it. I'd advise you to do the same. I'm not interested in any coup, nor should you be . . . especially as a member of the Waffen-SS.'

'It's all right, Karl-Heinz. I'm not canvassing.'

'It still sounds to me as if you've been talking to some

very dangerous people . . . dangerous to your continuing survival. As I've said, that uniform will be no protection.'

Another silence descended. The 540K's exhaust boomed its arrogance. In the woods on either side of the road, the unseen eyes of the SS troops observed their passage, radioing on ahead, warning other troops of their approach. Every so often, they passed a foot patrol on the road, a motorcycle and sidecar, or troop carriers going in both directions, returning the salutes that were sometimes given.

'Change of subject,' Meckler said. 'When and where do you think the Allies will invade?'

'It's anyone's guess. Their aircraft are very active all along the coast, so they're gearing up for something big. That much is obvious enough. The *where* is as important as the when.'

'Yesterday,' Meckler said, 'the Wehrmacht took a pasting.' He spoke with thinly veiled contempt. 'In the early hours, *one* plane took out an ammunition train that was also full of troops, rocket fuel and staff officers. From what I've heard, they never even saw it coming until too late. They had *three* flak cars on that train. Not one fired. I can hardly believe it.'

'I had some action too, yesterday,' Ketelheim remarked. 'A pair of Typhoons. One of them made the classic mistake of going after a decoy. My wingman, Hauptmann Schiffer, played it beautifully. I came down and the Tommy was finished. He was not very good. I think he must have disobeyed his leader as I cannot believe any flight leader would have been so stupid.'

'What did the other one do?'

'Brave man. He came for us, but as we were just outside our area, we let him live. There'll be another time.'

They were now approaching the section where the tanks stood guard. Ketelheim looked at them with great interest as the snouts of the gun barrels appeared to be pointing directly at him.

'The way you've got this area locked up, it would be suicidal for anyone to try an assault. Those Panzers of yours send shivers down my spine.'

'Then think of what they will do to the enemy,' Meckler said, grinning. The pirate of old was back.

'Herr Oberstleutnant!' someone called from a tank, saluting. There was a great deal of warmth in the voice.

Meckler touched his cap in a casual salute.

'Your men clearly think highly of you,' Ketelheim observed.

'You'll notice that the man who shouted used the military rank. None of that political Obersturmbannführer stuff for me. Not any more. In my command, we use the military ranks.

'You'll also have noticed that all my Panzer and other armoured crews, like my motorized infantry, use the field-grey or camouflage, instead of the black favoured by some other commands. Very pretty, the black uniforms, but excellent targets in combat. Favourites for snipers. They'd stand out in these woods. My men are all completely loyal. Imagine what would happen if those fancy-dress merchants at the château moved against me.'

'No one minds about your use of the military rank?'

Meckler laughed sourly. 'I'm a hero! They humour me. The Gestapo specifically asked for my command for this duty. My men have a reputation for ferocity in battle. Now tell me, Karl-Heinz. Your pilots . . . what do they think of you?'

'I am fortunate in having an excellent bunch.'

'Then between us we can give the enemy a few nightmares.'

They laughed, their good humour returning. They continued laughing as, a short while later, they arrived at the château gates. The two black-uniformed Totenkopf

SS guards on either side clicked to rigid attention and gave arm-wrenching, outstretched salutes. A third raised the barrier, while simultaneously giving his own salute.

'*Heil Hitler!*' they barked in unison.

''Hitler,' Meckler responded in an indifferent mumble and waved a lazy hand at them. 'Concentration camp lackeys,' he muttered in a low voice to Ketelheim disparagingly.

Ketelheim gave a proper Luftwaffe salute.

The guards lowered their arms and the barrier, and gazed after the car poisonously as it rumbled its way up the long drive.

'They hate everybody,' Meckler added.

When he was summoned to the château and told he'd be picked up by the area commander of the Waffen-SS unit, Ketelheim had been astonished to discover it was Meckler. No one had seen fit to tell him before, nor had Meckler known Ketelheim was in command of the air element of the defensive screen.

Now, as a curve in the drive gave them a full view of the building, Ketelheim said, 'Someone's done well for himself. Whom are we going to see?'

'At least one general, possibly two.'

'Waffen-SS?'

'Wehrmacht,' Meckler replied. 'But the second general may be Waffen-SS. I don't know who it might be. Neither general lives here. This is more of a Gestapo headquarters. There are plenty of documents in this place that could hang a lot of people. Resistance if we remain in control, Germans and collaborators if we don't. Quite a den of iniquity.

'The actual resident of the château is a collaborator of some importance, and carries the honorary status of general.' Meckler sounded as if he wanted to spit.

Studying the building as they drew nearer, Ketelheim said, 'I'm not surprised he's a collaborator. This place is beautiful. He doesn't want it destroyed and has obviously managed to arrange a situation that would enable him to keep an eye on it.'

'Oh, *he's* not the owner. That's the Baron Malzey and his family. The good baron looks upon us with civilized contempt. The entire family is more or less under open restraint. It makes the Resistance behave. They tried a couple of rescues, but my troops wiped out both forces easily. They were then warned by the Gestapo that further attempts would result in the death of the family. They've behaved themselves after that; at least, for the time being.'

'You expect more attempts?' Ketelheim was surprised.

'Who knows with the French? In their place, I would try. So my men are always on the alert. As for the so-called 'general' in residence, Boucheron . . . before this, all he owned was a broken-down garage on a road that leads to the coast. In Germany, I would shoot such a man myself. It's no surprise the Resistance want his head. War elevates all sorts of people . . .' – Meckler paused – '. . . even corporals.' He grinned as they came to a halt.

Two more SS guards came up and gave the Nazi salute.

Ketelheim looked at Meckler warningly as they climbed out. Meckler waved a hand at his cap and strode past the guards in the manner expected of an officer of his rank in the Waffen-SS. Ketelheim followed suit.

They were met by a bare-headed Wehrmacht major as they entered. They removed their caps.

'Gentlemen,' the major greeted them. 'The generals are waiting for you. Please follow me.'

As they walked along a wide corridor hung with priceless paintings, two civilians in long black leather coats went past on their way out. Meckler gave Ketelheim a knowing glance.

They were shown into an ornately furnished room

where the generals were waiting. One was a Wehrmacht lieutenant-general, the other a Waffen-SS major-general of the 1st Panzer Division, whom Meckler recognized as his own corps commander.

5

Pendrake had checked every one of the new aircraft and had decided to take one up on a test flight. Halloran had taken off again in the Anson, on his way back to persuade his bosses to supply six more Typhoon Ss as Pendrake had requested. Montcarneau had been found a room in the officers' mess, but was currently in the model room inspecting the target to see if modifications would be needed. His job would be to talk Pendrake through every aspect of the area until he knew it almost as well as the Frenchman himself.

A sheet of paper in one hand and flying gear in the other, Pendrake went through the connecting door of his office and into Lewis's. She looked up from her desk as he entered and began to rise from her chair.

He waved the hand with the paper briefly to stop her. 'You don't have to do that every time I come in here. I'm going to take one of the aircraft up. Might as well show the motley bunch that these particular Typhoons do keep their tails intact.'

'You won't take any chances, will you, sir?' she said quickly, stopping suddenly as if the words had come out before she'd realized what she had said.

She found her eyes drawn almost without volition to the faint scar that made him look irresistibly dangerous. Yet she also sensed a strange vulnerability that was brought on, she knew, by the pain he kept deeply hidden within himself but which, as she had gleaned from his records, tended to find explosive release in the powerful rage of combat.

'What's the matter, Lewis? Not worried about me, are you? Major Halloran would be singularly annoyed if I went in. So would I, for that matter. Keep the faith, Lewis,' he added gently as he handed her the paper. 'I want the doc to see these men. Organize it, will you? And tell him, he must be ruthless. Anyone who flies must be absolutely fit to do so. He is also to annotate those he believes will be fit to fly at a later date.'

'Very good, sir.'

'And Bingo Wilson . . . if he arrives while I'm up, look after him, will you? He's got all my gear.'

'Yes, sir.'

He turned to go. 'Oh . . . have I got a car?'

'Parked in the CO's spot.'

'You're a treasure, Lewis,' Pendrake said as he went out.

'Yes, sir,' she said.

But the door had already closed. She stared at it for a while, then turned to the sheet of paper he had given her. She studied the names he had written, and picked up the phone to speak to the medical officer.

Captain Elmore was in the crew room trying to explain the intricacies of baseball to two of the sergeant pilots.

'It's rounders,' one said.

'Why is it whenever I try to explain the game to you guys,' Elmore complained, 'you always call it rounders? Like when I was with the Eagles. Our British ground crew used to say the same thing.'

'Because it is,' the other sergeant reasoned.

Elmore shook his head, as if in sorrow. 'I give up.' He glanced out of a window and saw Pendrake getting into the car that had been allocated as the squadron commander's vehicle. 'Hey . . . lookee here,' he went on softly. 'The old man's got his flying kit. This I want to see. Find the others. Let's get to Dispersal.' He hurried out of the room.

* * *

The smell of freshly made coffee greeted Meckler and Ketelheim as they entered. It was real coffee, not the ersatz stuff with which ordinary people had to make do back in Germany.

'Franz!' Waffen-SS Gruppenführer Friedrich Herrenbach came forward with a huge smile, hand outstretched. 'Good to see you.'

'Pleasure to be here, sir,' Meckler responded as they shook hands.

'And this,' Herrenbach continued looking at Ketelheim, 'must be the famous fighter ace, Oberstleutnant Ketelheim.' He shook hands with Ketelheim. 'Franz will hate me for saying this, but he brags about you a lot. I am very glad you're watching the skies for us.'

'Thank you, sir.'

Herrenbach turned towards his superior officer. 'May I present Generalleutnant Manfred von Stahlenbüren of the Abwehr.'

The Army Intelligence lieutenant general shook hands with each man as they brought themselves to attention, clicked their heels and gave him sharp little nods of respect.

Von Stahlenbüren indicated a gleaming seventeenth-century table with four chairs already in place. 'Please sit down, gentlemen.'

Next to the table was a smaller one with a coffee pot, milk and cream jugs, spoons and cups of pristine silverware. There were also spotlessly clean white napkins, and gilt-edged place mats bearing eighteenth-century maritime scenes.

As they all sat down a young civilian woman entered and laid the table, then poured coffee for each, waiting as they made their choice of milk or cream.

'Thank you, my dear,' von Stahlenbüren said to her in impeccable French. 'We'll take it from here.'

She gave him a pretty, dimpled smile and went out.

'Shame to think she'd heartily slit all our throats,' he remarked conversationally, 'given half the chance.'

'Surely not, sir,' Ketelheim began, finding that difficult to believe. 'She looks so . . .'

'Pretty? Don't let that fool you. Do you have a sister, or a girlfriend, or wife back home?'

'A wife and a sister, sir.'

'And if the French were in Germany, doing what we're doing here, what would you expect them to do?'

Ketelheim said nothing.

'Precisely,' the general said. 'Now drink your wonderful French coffee, gentlemen. I know many people back home who would give anything to taste this.' He took a swallow, then put the cup down. 'And now to business.'

'You will both be well aware,' he continued, breaking their expectant silence, 'that the Allies are planning a major invasion. For months, they have been carrying out probing attacks under the cover of normal bomb- ing raids, on all fronts, to keep us guessing. My Abwehr believe we should be alert all along the western coasts, from Denmark to the Spanish border; but we do have our favourite candidates . . . here in Normandy, or the Pas de Calais. The general consensus is the Pas. It makes more tactical sense. It's also a more direct route to the Reich, their ultimate objective.

'As a result of this, I am virtually certain you will get your fair share of interest down here. There will also be increased activity from the Resistance. You, Ketelheim, must ensure that your aeroplanes are secure on the ground and you, Meckler, keep your boys on their toes.'

'They always are, General.'

Von Stahlenbüren nodded. 'So Friedrich has been telling me. Keep up the good work. And as for you, Ketelheim, I am certain you will take care of any Tommy or Ami aircraft foolish enough to come into your pasture.'

'Count on it, General. Our Luftwaffe infantry are

permanently on the alert, guarding the airfield and the immediate area outside its perimeter.'

'Good,' the general said approvingly. 'The Abwehr has authorized its own probing flights, by night and by day, over Britain. We also use the cover of nuisance bombing raids. We're looking for units that are out of the ordinary, and use all kinds of aircraft for this work. Fighters on low-level search patterns; medium bombers to destroy identified special groups or airfields; parachute drops, E-boats and submarines making landfalls under cover of darkness to disembark specialist teams; even slow but quiet Storchs to drop agents to find out what's going on over there.

'Infiltrations are not easy. Although we have had our *Vertrauensmänner* in different countries – there are many here in France, for example, especially those used by our friends the Gestapo – it is not so easy with the British. Many are caught by the Tommies; but we still have a few at large. Your organization's own security units, Meckler, from the Security Service, like ourselves and the Gestapo, have made good use of these people who would earn the trust of their own kind, then betray them.'

The general gave a grim chuckle as he continued, 'The "trustful men" seems an ironic way to describe them. Good for us, bad for their own people. The hope is that these *V-männer* can send us information of the proposed invasion site and the date, in time to give us the opportunity to prepare the warmest reception.'

Everyone grinned at this. A meaningful silence then fell, causing both Ketelheim and Meckler to look questioningly at the two generals. It was Herrenbach who eventually spoke.

'You have also been probably aware,' he began, 'that certain rumours have been circulating.' He paused, watching their faces keenly for a reaction to his words.

Both subordinate officers stiffened slightly. They knew exactly what he meant.

'We've heard some loose talk,' Meckler finally offered cautiously.

'Loose talk.'

Both younger men were suddenly aware that the generals were looking at them very closely, definite messages in their eyes. They knew nothing more would be said in this Gestapo den; but they were also left in no doubt of the import of what had been disclosed, despite the apparently innocuous nature of the conversation.

'Be very careful, Franz,' Herrenbach advised, 'who you listen to. You too, Karl-Heinz.'

'Yes, sir,' they both said together.

'And now,' von Stahlenbüren said brightly, 'let us finish our coffee. Stay with us till evening, gentlemen. There is a dinner tonight. You will meet the owners of this beautiful *Schloss*, and other . . . interesting people. Meanwhile, enjoy the pleasures of the place. There are wonderful grounds, and very rare paintings. We shall see you both later.'

They all stood up, the junior officers springing to attention. All four shook hands, then Ketelheim and Meckler went out.

In the corridor, Meckler said in a low, urgent voice, 'Herrenbach's involved? And so cosy with the Wehrmacht, even though it is the Abwehr. I can't believe it!'

'We don't know that he is,' Ketelheim countered.

'I know my commander. It's what he doesn't say that matters in a situation like this.'

'In that case, let's take his advice. We know nothing, and we watch our step.'

Two black-uniformed SS came smartly towards them, boots gleaming.

'*Heil Hitler!*' they said, and stomped past.

''Hitler,' Meckler responded in his customary clipped way, pretending to be so fully absorbed in his conversation, he had barely registered their presence. 'I agree with you,' he added to Ketelheim when they were safely out of earshot.

Pendrake got out of the car, picked up his Mae West and slipped it on. He then got the helmet with its goggles attached and shut the car door. He began walking towards the nearest Typhoon, helmet in hand. A sergeant in charge of a servicing crew was standing nearby, supervising a couple of crewmen at work. One of the aircraftmen was in the cockpit.

The sergeant, having heard the car approach, had turned to await him. The sergeant saluted.

'At ease, Sarge,' Pendrake said. 'You are . . .'

'Sergeant Ransome, sir.'

'Right, Sergeant Ransome.' Pendrake placed his helmet on the wing and began to secure the life-jacket. 'This aircraft serviceable?'

'They all are, sir,' the NCO replied proudly. 'Just doing some extra checks. Nearly done.'

'Ready to fly, is she?'

'Yes, sir.'

'Armed?'

'Full load of ammo, sir. No rockets though, as you can see. But I can have them put on.'

'No need, Sarge. Won't be needing them. I'm taking her up for a test, but I hate flying an aircraft without teeth, irrespective of the flight. Never can be too careful.'

'Know what you mean, sir. I checked the cannons myself. She'll bite if you ask her to.'

'Good.' Pendrake looked up at the cockpit, where the aircraftman, head down, was still at work. 'Now if he'll get out of the office, I'll hop in.'

'Right you are, sir,' Ransome said. He looked up at the cockpit and bawled, 'Millar!'

'Yes, Sarge!' came the muffled acknowledgement.

'Get out of there! The CO needs the aeroplane!'

'Right away, Sarge! Just finishing.'

'Jump to it, lad!'

There was a brief pause, then, 'I'm done!'

Millar climbed out quickly, saw Pendrake waiting, and athletically slid down the wingroot to the ground.

'Sorry, sir,' he said to Pendrake, bringing himself to attention.

'Relax, Millar. It's all right. Do you recommend that I take her up?'

'Yes, sir! I've just been adjusting the throttle movement. Smooth as you could wish, sir. Like a hot knife through butter. I've done all the others. This was the last one.'

'He is good with the throttles, sir,' the sergeant confirmed. 'Got the touch. Makes them work like magic.'

'Then I shall have to find out.' Pendrake retrieved his helmet, put it on, then did a rapid but detailed pre-flight check.

The bigger wing of the "S" version enabled the four-cannon fit – two to each side – to be deeply recessed, instead of sticking out aggressively. They were still aggressive, but almost seemed to peep out of the leading edges by comparison. The rear fuselage was also bigger yet sleeker, and the tail more gracefully curved at the fin. The nose was longer too, with the cockpit set further back. She looked good.

Satisfied with his checks, Pendrake climbed aboard the black Typhoon. The parachute was already in the seat, which made life immensely easier, as scrabbling up to a cockpit which was nine feet off the ground while lugging the pack was hardly the stuff of elegance.

The crewmen moved back, two of them crouching some distance from either wing, holding on to lengths of rope to which the wheel chocks were attached.

Pendrake settled himself in, secured his harness, then looked right and left to make certain the aircraft was clear of obstructions. He immediately appreciated the unrestricted view the new bubble canopy afforded.

This is more like it, he thought.

He clipped on his oxygen mask and began his preparations for engine start. Throttle lever to starting position, propeller pitch control lever set, all fuel tanks full, centre fuselage selected, twin engine pumps low down on the right of the instrument panel set, starter cartridge inserted, starter button pressed . . .

The massive engine exploded into a powerful wall of sound and though Pendrake was familiar with the Typhoon bellow, the modified engine seemed to him to roar its challenge to the world.

'My God!' he whispered, enthralled. The ferocious power of the new engine was awesome. Yet it settled down to a remarkably smooth, but daunting rhythm. 'This will frighten the kids,' he added, thinking of the boy-pilots, 'but it's putting hairs on my chest!'

He checked his immediate environs once more, noting that the crewmen on the chocks were awaiting his signal. He also saw a group of people approaching, to stop a safe distance away. His pilots had come to watch him and almost certainly to pass judgement. All the better.

He moved the throttle forward, easing it gently. The engine roared gleefully in response, while he held the aircraft on the brakes. Millar had not exaggerated. The movement was smoother than anything he remembered on any Typhoon, or any other fighter, for that matter. He'd have to caution the new pilots about being over-eager with its use until they got to know the aircraft better; or it would run away with them.

He brought the throttle back. The engine responded without a hiccup. No tell-tale, oily smears on the windscreen. Forget the old Sabre. This was a beauty. He hoped the modifications to his own aircraft would be as good.

He gave a sharp outward wave with both hands and the chocks were hauled away. Aware that all eyes were on him, he taxied smoothly towards the runway, then lined up for take-off. He slid the canopy forward. It moved equally smoothly and clicked home, cutting out much of the engine noise, but still leaving enough to let him know it was there. A powerful vibration coursed through the entire airframe, making the Typhoon feel like a living being. Trifle with me, it seemed to say, and you're dead.

'Homebase, Homebase,' he called on the radio to the control tower. 'Cobra One calling. Scramble? Over.'

A green flare arced skywards. Time to go.

He opened the throttle wide. Now the beast was truly alive. The Typhoon hurled itself forward with an acceleration that almost took him by surprise. It did so much more rapidly than his old mount. He watched for the notorious rightward swing of all Typhoons. It was still there and as he applied left rudder to counter it, he realized he needed much less effort. The swing had not been totally eradicated, but it was much more subdued. There was none of the wild crabbing that had trapped so many novice pilots, some terminally, despite the fact that the Typhoon was a tough bird that could take amazing punishment. Even so, the less experienced pilots would have to be coached into using the correct trim inputs so as to make the best use of the aircraft's almost benign new trim set-up.

He eased gently back on the slimmed-down column with its familiar, laterally pivoting upper half and spade grip. The Typhoon surged into the air, eager to go. He brought the wheels up and held her at low level, letting the speed build. He glanced about him. The view out was quite a revelation.

At last. This was what he'd always wanted! Now he really could see the sky about him.

On the ground, the Cobra pilots were spread loosely in little groups. All followed the progress of the Typhoon keenly.

'He was wearing his Mae West,' one of the younger sergeant pilots remarked. 'He's not going over water. Why bother?'

'Why not ask him when he gets back?' someone else suggested.

The sergeant turned, and found himself looking into the steely blue eyes of the Australian, Dominic Keane.

'Oh. Hello, sir.'

'Benson, is it?'

'Yes, sir.'

'Well, Benson. How old are you?'

'Nineteen, sir.'

'How old?'

Benson looked embarrassed. 'Um . . . still three months to go, sir.' He had a rich Midlands accent.

'If you want to make it even to nineteen, Sergeant Benson, I'd advise you to wear yours at *all* times, even over land. I once got into a fight over land, but found myself over water. Like an idiot, I had not worn my Mae West. Scrambled without it. I was very glad not to have been shot down that day. It was a lesson I have never forgotten. Today you're getting it for free.'

'Yes, sir.'

The roar of the Typhoon was growing louder and they both turned to look.

'Where is he?' Benson asked.

'Search me.'

Then a black shape hurled itself from between two hangars and came at them.

'He's . . . he's going to hit!' Benson stammered and dropped to the ground.

Keane remained where he was and watched the great nose of the aircraft grow bigger. Then suddenly, it yanked upwards to fling itself into a steep climb. A series of fast rolls in the climb followed.

'You can get up now, Benson,' Keane said, staring upwards at the fast-diminishing shape. 'If that tail was going to come off, it would have done so just then. I think our CO's proving to us that this baby is going to stay in one piece whatever we do to her. Enjoy the fun.'

They all watched, many open-mouthed, as Pendrake put the Typhoon through its paces.

He was in his element. He pulled over the top of a loop and plunged earthwards. The powerful engine gave its howling bellow as the Typhoon hurtled down. The bigger wing gave it much-improved agility. He could see the airfield plan etched upon the ground beneath, as if on a model in an ops room. It continued to expand perceptibly as he lost altitude.

He began to ease back on the stick, progressively applying the pressure. He did not want to reach a speed where the controls became so stiff that he would be unable to pull out before hitting the ground. It had happened to many pilots.

But the control forces were well within the limits. The nose came up, the scything disc of the massive four-bladed propeller began to slide up the background of the sky as if greased on its surface, as the seven-ton aeroplane began to haul itself upwards. The forces of the pull-out pushed his head and neck towards his shoulders; a slight greying touched the edges of vision. He was experiencing forces of gravity under which, in later years, other pilots would wear special equipment to help increase the tolerance of the relatively frail human body.

Pendrake gave a heart-stopping display for about five minutes, throwing the aircraft about the sky with seemingly wild abandon. Then the Typhoon was shooting upwards once more. He pulled it on to its back, then rolled upright. At five thousand feet, he headed north-east from the airfield.

Elmore briefly removed his cap to scratch the back of his head.

'I'll say this for him,' he announced to Dodson, who was close by. 'He sure can fly.' The captain was now wearing a complete USAAF uniform.

'And if that kite was going to bend,' Dodson pointed out, eyes still on the Typhoon, 'it would have done so after what he's just put it through.'

'Yeah, yeah. I get the point. Hey. Where's he going?'

'As long as *he* knows, that's all right with me. A man who flies like that is going to want a lot out of us.'

'Yeah. Just what I was thinking. The blood from our veins. But that plane did sound real good. Reckon I'd hate to wash out of this outfit.'

'I'm certain he'll be pleased to hear that, Yank.'

'I'm no goddam Yankee. How'd you like it if I called you Scotch?'

'Scotch is a drink . . . the nectar of the gods. And I'm not a Scot.'

'See what I mean?'

The two Messerschmitt Bf-109Gs, coming from Cherbourg, had crossed the coast high above Lulworth Cove. They should have been spotted, but weren't. Flying at height to conserve fuel, they had each used an extra capacity ventral drop tank of 500 litres instead of the usual 300. With the tank in place, they had staggered to altitude over France, their performance improving as the fuel was used up and their all-up weight decreased. For the high transit over to southern England, they stayed on the ventral tank.

They were fortunate in not being caught by patrolling Spitfires, or Hurricanes. Their manoeuvrability would have been seriously compromised with the tanks still attached. Without them, the loss of the extra fuel would have made their return to base highly unlikely once they had become engaged in a fight.

Their mission objective effectively meant that getting into a dogfight would be a desperate, last resort. They were on a reconnaissance prowl and while they could attack ground targets with their cannon, dogfights were only to be entered into as defensive measures, if that proved to be the only means of escape.

This particular pair had survived many successful missions. They had caught out single Allied aircraft, shot up coastal airfields, sunk special forces assault craft training in British coastal waters, and even big Sunderland flying boats had been caught at their moorings. Intelligence supplied them with particular coordinates, and they would subsequently hunt down the target. They came from one of the type of units von Stahlenbüren had been talking about.

Today, however, they were tasked with searching out a special British unit. The information had been imprecise. There was no certainty that such an establishment even existed and their job was to either prove or disprove this, and get back to tell the tale. Definite confirmation would mean a night bombing raid by twin-engined Messerschmitt Bf-110 fighter-bombers.

They were passing high above Chippenham when they began their rapid and steep descent, engines throttled back, as if coasting down a precipitous hill. There was still some fuel left in their ventral tanks. Low down, they cruised towards their objective, their pilots marvelling that they had so far been undetected. No one had expected an intrusion from that direction, it seemed.

The pilots armed their specially mounted under-nose cameras, in preparation for a filming pass, if they did find the unit. They checked the sky about them. So far, so good.

Pendrake was making for an extensive beech wood in the Cotswolds. He intended to use it as a training area, deciding it would be a good place to introduce the squadron to the rigours of ultra-low flying.

'Assuming they can fly the aircraft in the first place,' he muttered to himself.

He went down to a thousand feet and covered the woods

in a wide circle, examining landmarks and the narrow valleys. He did that twice, discovering areas where he could fly below the treetops. There was even an old, ruined manor house among the trees which could serve as a stand-in for the château. He was on his third circuit, when a fast movement over to his right caught his eye.

At first he refused to believe it. *Two* 109s were passing within less than a mile of him, coming from the south-east. They had clearly not seen him, for they made no alteration of course and appeared to be heading in the direction of the airfield.

He did two things almost simultaneously. He slammed the throttle to the wall and radioed the airfield. The Typhoon seemed to leap forward as its engine smoothly gathered power. Millar's magic was working nicely.

'Homebase, Homebase,' he called urgently as he prepared himself for combat. 'Cobra One calling. Two bandits. Repeat, two bandits heading your way. Am giving chase. All Cobra Squadron pilots, do *not* take off. Repeat, all Cobra Squadron pilots do *not* take off. I want no dead heroes. Inform Keane. Over.'

'Roger, Cobra One. Receiving you loud and clear. Understand bandits approaching. No Cobra pilots to scramble. Inform Keane.'

'Cobra One, out.'

The Messerschmitts were still holding a tight formation. Pendrake saw the belly tanks as he curved in behind them, gaining rapidly.

Now to see how the Typhoon S really performed.

Keane watched the startled expression that appeared on every face as the sirens went.

'What the devil?' someone exclaimed. 'Must be a drill. Can't possibly be a raid.'

Then the Tannoy came on. '*Airfield defences man your*

guns! Man your guns! All other personnel to shelters! I repeat. All other personnel to shelters!'

'I'm scrambling!' someone shouted. 'Give me a helmet! Give me a helmet! I'll take one of the Spits!' It was Elmore.

Just then, one of the corporals ran up to Keane. 'Message from the control tower, sir!' he reported, wheezing from his run. 'It's from the squadron leader. No pilots are to take off. No dead heroes, he said. Message was for you specifically, sir!'

'Righto. Off you go, Corp.'

The corporal shot off to find a shelter.

'Hold it, Elmore!' Keane bawled at the American. 'To the shelter!'

'But . . .'

'Don't argue with me! *Move it!* CO's orders.'

Seeing the blaze in Keane's eyes, Elmore did not argue.

Pendrake had taken the Typhoon low, low down, a sleekly black hawk skimming the ground, closing in for the kill. He had positioned himself neatly in their blind spot, just beneath them. Had they been flying in a wider formation, the wingman might well have spotted him. But it was obvious they had wanted to bring as little attention to themselves as possible.

A wider formation or a wingman weaving to keep a good lookout would have quickly attracted attention, including among the non-vigilant. The poor rearward vision from even the 'Gustav' version of the 109 also counted against the enemy pilots. Pendrake found himself comparing it unfavourably, as he closed range, with the excellent vision afforded by the new canopy of the Typhoon he was now flying.

He selected the leading aircraft as the first target. The wingman, probably less experienced, would be shocked and slightly disorientated by the sudden demise of his leader. It would be a psychological advantage when the time came to attend to him.

Still unseen, Pendrake crept in nearer still. He couldn't afford to miss. He was not at all keen to take on a two-on-one engagement, in an aircraft he was still getting used to.

He was close enough. At that very moment the wingman spotted him. He could almost hear the shout as the pilot warned his leader. Both drop tanks went simultaneously, tumbling like silver pear drops. They were fast, but not fast enough.

Almost at the instant that the tanks went, Pendrake fired. The Hispano cannons were devastating. Tracer streamed ahead of him as they thumped out their killer song at the target 109. They ripped it apart, tearing it to pieces in a violent explosion that seared outwards in an expanding, boiling fireball. Then suddenly there was nothing. Something trailing a black plume tumbled to the ground. There was no parachute.

The second Messerschmitt leapt skywards like a startled minnow darting from a predatory pike. Pendrake hauled on the stick and the Typhoon bellowed after it, eating up the distance. But whoever the wingman was, he was no slouch and Pendrake soon realized he was not dealing with an inexperienced pilot after all. Perhaps he had taken the wrong one first.

They tore upwards in their aerial ballet of death, the black avenging Typhoon gaining in the climb on the smaller, camouflaged Messerschmitt. Just as it was about to come into range of the cannons, it twinkled to the left and plunged earthwards. Pendrake half-rolled in the climb and hauled on the stick. The Typhoon described a tight curving dive as it went after the 109. He again had the enemy aircraft before him. But it was banking tightly low down, heading south.

Pendrake understood instantly what was happening. The enemy pilot's primary concern was escape. Getting lower on fuel by the second, on his own, deep into enemy territory and very far from base, he had little choice. He would obviously only fight to survive long enough to get away. Pendrake also saw that his current course was taking them both towards the airfield.

'Homebase, Homebase!' he called urgently. 'Cobra One calling. Am chasing single bandit, heading towards you. Fighter, *not* bomber. Repeat. Fighter, *not* bomber. Call off the guns! Repeat. Call off the guns!'

The last thing he needed was some overexcited gunner, short on good recognition, blasting him out of the sky in error.

'Roger, Cobra. One bandit, fighter. Will call off the guns.'

'Cobra One, out.'

At the airfield, the Tannoy was again doing its stuff. '*Gunners stand down! Gunners stand down! Single bandit, fighter, heading towards the airfield. All other personnel remain in shelters. I repeat. All other personnel remain in shelters!*'

In one of the shelters, Sean Kelly said to Mackenzie, 'Strange. Why stand down the gunners?'

'It must mean the CO's on the tail of that bandit and doesn't want to get shot down by itchy trigger fingers. It happens. I've been hit by our own ack-ack. Blew a damn great hole in the wing of my Spit before those jokers woke up. I was not a happy boy, believe me.'

'Hang on,' someone else said. 'I hear something!'

Everyone listened. Very faintly but growing perceptibly louder, they could hear the high scream of an engine, counterpointed by a familiar bellow.

'I'll be damned,' Kelly exclaimed softly. 'The CO's bringing him home! I've got to watch this.'

'You can't go out there,' another voice cautioned. 'Fighters carry bombs too, you know.'

'I know. I've done it. But I'm not going to miss this for the world.' Kelly hurried out of the shelter.

'Hell,' Mackenzie said. 'If the CO's going to button up a bandit right over our heads, I'm not staying in this hole.' He followed Kelly out.

Soon, everyone was following suit.

The Tannoy blared again. '*Get back into those shelters! Get back into those shelters!*'

The other shelters were emptying too, as the noise of the two aircraft grew louder. People stood to gape upwards.

The person on the public address system gave up. 'Oh, what's the bloody use,' came the unguarded comment before the Tannoy was switched off.

Pendrake could see the airfield in the distance. The Me-109 was still low down, still fleeing, but with little real hope of escape in a straight race. The Typhoon was gaining inexorably.

Suddenly the enemy aircraft shot upwards, wrenching on to its back almost immediately, then pulling down as if about to complete a tight loop. But it rolled swiftly upright and was bearing down upon Pendrake in a head-on pass.

Pendrake was ready as soon as he'd seen the roll commence. Knowing what was coming, he broke hard left to displace, but continued the roll through 180 degrees, and pulled the stick hard. The 109 tried to correct and fired, but was going too fast. Tracers lanced the air and missed. The enemy pilot overshot and immediately began to turn hard as the Typhoon sliced in behind him. He jinked violently, trying to locate his black nemesis.

Pendrake had climbed and was now on his back looking through the top of the canopy at the Messerschmitt below him. It was again heading south. For the first time since Megan's death, he actually felt sorry for an enemy pilot and sensed a peculiar solidarity with the man, as one aviator to another. It was a terrible situation to be in. No matter how good the pilot might be, the strain would be overwhelming.

But the solidarity did not extend to wanting the enemy's survival. Pendrake was totally implacable. He remembered Megan's terrible death. He remembered also what had happened to the relatively inexperienced Braddock. He had done something exceedingly rash and the ace who had got him had not been merciful. As far as Pendrake was now concerned, the enemy pilot's only chance was to bale out. It was either that, or certain death. There were no other options.

In the Messerschmitt, Major Hans Brillermann was not thinking about baling out. He was thinking of getting back to pass on the information about the black aeroplane, and the others he could now see on the airfield. *This was the special unit!*

Even as he kept an eye out for the special Typhoon that had so efficiently shot down Leutnant Forschmeister, he triggered the camera. At least he'd have some photographs. Then he had to break off to go into another defensive manoeuvre, as he spotted the Typhoon curving down on his tail.

The epic battle came inexorably towards the airfield.

The screaming Messerschmitt tore upwards, followed by the snarling Typhoon, the clear bright sky of the late afternoon marking them out sharply as they danced high above the mellow Cotswold hills. They were two deadly predators engaged in a territorial battle in which the victory of the one would mean the demise of the other.

Elmore stood with both hands shading his eyes as he followed their choreography.

'Will you just look at that,' he said, mainly to himself. 'Nothing that 109 can do seems able to shake off the CO.'

'Wouldn't want that to happen, would you?' Dodson asked.

'Hell, no. But you got to feel sorry for the poor Nazi bastard.'

'You can feel sorry if you like. I want the CO to turn him into a flamer. If *you* were up there with *him* on your tail, he wouldn't be feeling sorry.'

The Messerschmitt was not giving up. It had now gone so low over the airfield that it seemed about to hit one of the hangars. But it screamed between them, with the Typhoon hot on its tail.

Pendrake flew between the hangars, reluctant to shoot for fear of stray shells causing havoc on the ground. The enemy pilot must have known it, and had deliberately employed the ruse.

They shot across the airfield, seemingly about to crash into something. The noise of their engines, from ground level, was at once terrifying and exhilarating. The entire station, it seemed, was now watching the contest.

Karen Lewis was outside the squadron building with Montcarneau. He glanced at her surreptitiously, noticing her anxiety; but there was something else too. She looked excited, and full of pride. Her lips were swollen and moist. Once, her tongue inched out like a shy pink animal, to lick slowly at the lower lip before quickly disappearing once more. It was, he thought, a most sensual act. He wondered whether Pendrake was even aware of the furnace he was stoking within her.

Montcarneau smiled to himself. 'He will be all right,' he said gently. 'It is easy to see who is the master in this trial by combat.'

His voice startled her, and she blushed.

'I know he'll be all right,' she said firmly, then added uncertainly, 'I do hope so.'

Her eyes anxiously followed the twists and turns of the jousting aircraft, now leaping once more for the heavens. It all looked so beautiful, she thought. A graceful prelude to death. Totally oblivious of the man standing next to her, she forced herself not to think of Mike Pendrake dying in an explosion of fire up there.

Watching as she craned her neck upwards, Montcarneau saw a tiny pulse flutter intermittently in the gentle curve of her throat, and smiled again to himself.

The end, when it came, was sudden and almost an anticlimax.

Major Hans Brillermann made a slight error of judgement, the pressure having at last got to him. He had left the airfield perimeter, once again low down, and had been herded into making too tight a turn by Pendrake. The 109 simply went into a high-speed stall and slammed into some trees beyond the airfield. It exploded in a great gout of flame on impact.

Pendrake came low across the runway, pulled into a steep climb and rolled slowly, twice.

'I'll be damned,' Kelly said. 'There must have been two of them, and he got both.'

People around them were cheering loudly. It seemed the whole station was doing so.

'He's going to be a tough act to live up to,' Mackenzie said.

'Or to please,' Kelly added.

Keane, standing to one side, heard the exchange. He rubbed his right shoulder absently. He'd been told he had an appointment with the medical officer.

He watched as the Typhoon came in for a most stylish landing.

6

The Messerschmitt had burned fiercely and by twilight was still smouldering. Several people went to have a look at it, some to take souvenirs, until they were forbidden to do so. However, the pilots had grabbed themselves a piece of wing with the black cross on it as a first trophy for Cobra Squadron.

Pendrake did not visit the crash site.

The aircraft recovery team had found pieces of wreckage scattered over a wide area. Among those was the under-nose camera, virtually intact, its exposed film in perfect condition. There was not much left of Hans Brillermann. Rhys ordered that the remains be properly buried.

'They can collect him after the war,' he said. 'After we've won.'

Pendrake was in a darkened room in the Photographic Intelligence Section with Rhys. The retrieved film had been developed and was now in a projector.

'All right, Sergeant Pascoe,' Pendrake said. 'Let's see what's on this.'

The WAAF sergeant in charge of the section started the projector. They watched as the silent film began to roll. It was remarkably sharp, and very clearly they saw how the doomed 109, still hoping for escape, had corrected its course to make deliberately for the airfield. The buildings and the aircraft were sharply detailed. There was also a zoom function that allowed detailed close-ups of the new Typhoons. It was very evident that some of the film had been shot during the dogfight, as the

Messerschmitt's flight between the hangars was clearly depicted.

'A very determined man,' Rhys commented as the film ended and the lights came back on.

'And brave,' Pendrake added, surprising himself.

The recovery team had so far found no documents by which to identify either Brillermann or his unit. Investigators were scraping away at such items of the wreckage that might yield identification numbers.

Then Pendrake voiced the thought that was in all their minds. 'Someone over there knows enough about us to have mounted this operation. The breach must have come from Halloran's people. There must be someone in his group in Normandy who's talking to the enemy. Perhaps even one of his much-vaunted infiltrators in the château.'

Rhys was looking steadily at him. 'Was that the reason you chose not to tell Montcarneau about this film?'

'I'm being careful until I see our good major again.'

'But Montcarneau has the local knowledge you need.'

'He can still do the job he was sent to do. If he, or someone close to him is responsible, it hardly matters now. He's not going anywhere. They never expected their recce aircraft to be shot down. Mounting the operation so soon after our deployment, they probably expected to catch us on the hop. And they would have, had I not gone up when I did.

'As for the 109s, they would have been keeping radio silence. When those at their base realize their aeroplanes are not returning, they'll assume they've simply been shot down; which could have occurred at any time during the flight.

'If it is Montcarneau,' Pendrake continued, 'we're actually quite secure. He can't risk further communication, now that we're alerted, even if he has no idea we've got the film. If the breach is in France, there may be more attempts, especially when we move to the forward airfield. From now on, those two Spitfires brought in by Kelly and Dodson will mount a standing patrol. I should have taken a leaf out of your book, sir,' he added ruefully. 'I'm thinking of my welcoming committee.'

'Oh, that,' Rhys said with an embarrassed smile. 'I assure you there was no tactical thinking behind it.'

'Even so, I've learned the lesson. The crews can rotate the duty. The younger pilots can get their hours in on the Spits, before I unleash the Tiffies upon them. The flight commanders can handle that when I've made my selections.'

'And meanwhile?' Rhys asked.

'Meanwhile, we treat Monsieur Montcarneau normally until we know one way or the other.' Pendrake turned to the sergeant. 'Sergeant Pascoe, as our most senior Photo Intelligence bod on the station, I leave it to you to ensure that this film remains secure until I ask for it, and that no one makes mention of it. This means *all* your personnel.'

'You may count on me, sir,' she vowed.

'I'm sure I can. One other thing – who knows about the camera having been found, apart from your people? Who actually found it?'

'Two members of my section saw one of the recovery team pick it up, sir. It was quite some distance from where the aircraft hit. They immediately took it from him and advised him to say nothing to the others unless otherwise instructed by you or the station CO, and brought it straight to me.'

'Good show. Well done. Then we'll leave it in your very capable hands.'

'Thank you, sir.'

Pendrake was on his way back to his office when he ran into Montcarneau.

'So, Squadron Leader,' the Frenchman began. 'I hear there were two of these Germans, and you got both of them.'

'Yes.'

'You are having quite a day. You are a formidable warrior.'

'Simply trying to stay alive, Monsieur Montcarneau.'

'Michel, please.'

'Michel.'

'And I shall call you Mike,' Montcarneau went on. 'We have the same name, so it is fitting. I think, Mike, you are too modest about your talents. I think what happened today is more than just trying to stay alive,' he observed shrewdly. 'We all saw what happened to the second aeroplane. He was outmatched.'

'I was lucky.'

'If that was only luck, then you know more than most of us. You know how to make it. Will you soon be going to dinner in the mess? We can go together.'

'I shall be going to dinner, but there are a few things to attend to first.'

Montcarneau nodded sympathetically. 'Ah, the joys of command. The young lady is still awaiting your return,' he continued, as if divulging a great secret. 'Very loyal, that one. She will stay until the morning if you do not dismiss her.'

Pendrake glanced at his watch in concern. 'Good heavens. She should have gone to the mess by now.'

Montcarneau gave his private smile. 'You are an excellent fighter pilot, Squadron Leader, and from what I have so far seen, you are already becoming an equally good commander. But there are other things which I believe you do not see.' He gave an expressive shrug. 'But maybe you do see, and do not want to. Hmm? I will see you in the mess.'

He went on his way, leaving Pendrake to ponder upon his words.

Lewis came to her feet as Pendrake entered.

'You're still doing it,' he admonished her.

She sat down quickly. 'Sorry, sir. Habit.'

'Then lose it. I'm not running a square-bashing camp.'

'Yes, sir. That was a very good show up there . . .' she went on, excitement bringing a slight breathlessness to her voice, '. . . getting those Jerries. Especially that last one.'

'I was lucky,' he told her, repeating his words to Montcarneau.

'I don't believe anyone on the station looks upon it as just luck, especially the pilots. A few of them came up to me to sing your praises.' She smiled. 'They made me promise not to tell you what they actually said. You're winning, sir.'

Despite her adherence to service discipline in maintaining just the right amount of familiarity, her startling blue eyes were betraying her. Pupils dilated, they seemed to want to swallow him.

Pendrake appeared totally unmoved by this. 'So far,' he remarked portentously.

Privately, he was very pleased that they currently held him in high regard. The spectacular downing of the Messerschmitts, especially the last one as she'd said, had put the fire into them. But that would not prolong the honeymoon period indefinitely. Things would soon change. When the rigours of the training to come started taking their toll, it would be interesting to hear what they thought about him then.

'Oh . . .,' she began, interrupting his train of thought, 'we've heard from Flight Lieutenant Wilson.'

'Bingo Wilson? Why isn't he here? I need him.'

'Seems as if a huge bomb had been lying unnoticed in a ditch for days, along the back road he was taking. The ditch was grassed over and full of water. Then the bomb exploded, leaving a big crater, cutting the road itself in two.'

'Is Bingo all right?'

'Oh yes. He wasn't there when it happened, but he's had to detour and got caught up in a convoy of Americans.'

'That would have pleased him. And when does he expect to be with us?'

'As soon as he can, sir.'

'Not much we can do in that case,' Pendrake admitted, adding lightly, 'After all, there is a war on, they tell me.' He studied her closely. 'And you, young lady, are quite tired. It's been a long day. By now, you should have been in the mess having dinner. I just saw Michel Montcarneau outside, on his way there. You ought to join him.'

'And you, sir?'

'What about me?'

'Are you off to the mess?'

'Not at this very moment, but I shall be along. I'm about to select the flight commanders . . .'

'Then you'll need all the information . . .'

'I can do that.'

'With my help, you'll get through it much more quickly, sir,' she said firmly. 'You've got to eat too.'

He looked at her steadily. 'Are you bullying me, Section Officer Lewis?'

'Just doing my job, sir.'

'I see. And you won't leave unless I make it a direct order.'

'No, sir. Although . . .'

'"Although"? You wouldn't be thinking of insubordination, would you?'

'Not quite, sir.'

'Not quite? One is either insubordinate, or one isn't. There are no half-measures.' A tiny smile came and went. 'I ought to know. And having no doubt heard of my . . . er, past exploits with the brass, so do you.'

'There you are, sir.'

'All right, Lewis. You win. Let's get cracking.'

'Yes, sir.' She beamed at him.

A string quartet was playing in the minstrels' gallery at the château. Its incongruity was heightened by the fact that the musicians were in the black dress uniform of the Totenkopf SS.

Glancing up at them from the dinner table, Ketelheim thought that the Gestapo who had organized it all were either totally oblivious of the irony or, as was perhaps most likely, playing another of their psychological games with the owners of the château. Meckler had informed him that this was a common occurrence, as though every so often the Gestapo needed to spice their days up a bit. It also sent an unmistakable message to the Resistance.

Before the dinner, Meckler had taken him on a guided tour of the defences within the grounds. All the patrolling guards were black-uniformed SS, but the anti-aircraft gunners were all Waffen-SS. Relations between the soldiers of the two branches of the organization were, at best, politely distant. The veterans looked upon the *die Toter*, as they offhandedly called them, as pampered brutes. While the 'brutes' looked upon the veterans as being too big for their boots and disrespectful, just because they had seen service on the Eastern Front and had a few Iron Crosses.

The fact was, the vets were secretly envied by guards of the Totenkopf, members of which sported their own Iron Crosses knowing they had been earned for activities that had required something rather less than valour. The veterans never let them forget it. Meckler made no attempt to rein in his men and on more than one occasion Ketelheim had urged him to be less blatant in his contempt.

As he now listened to the quartet's surprisingly excellent playing, the whole dinner seemed to him to be quite a bizarre event. In addition to the two generals, there were other high-ranking individuals. An Obergruppenführer from another SS Panzer division, and who outranked Herrenbach by one, was clearly of the type that Meckler had been talking about. This SS lieutenant general, whose name was Schlierhof and who wore a monocle, had arrived with a motorcycle escort of four outriders, and was resplendent in black. Meckler had whispered that he was certain Schlierhof's Panzer troops all wore black as well. Excellent target practice for the Allies, he'd added.

There were also two senior Gestapo men, in civilian evening wear. The most senior outranked every military person in the room. The Abwehr general was accompanied by another Abwehr officer, a Colonel Eigen. The only women at the lavish table were those of the Malzey family, and the woman who accompanied Boucheron, claiming to be his wife.

Ketelheim could see that though they disguised it tolerably well, the baron and his family felt humiliated by being forced to attend. He was certain that was the reason the Gestapo had demanded their presence in the first place. The whole thing, the well-stocked table, the two highly polished, eight-branched candelabra, the SS musicians, the high-ranking guests – especially of the SS – all together in the gilded banqueting room, was an exercise in deliberate humiliation. For the true owners of the château, nothing could be clearer.

They did not behave like conquered people and bore the invasion of their home with quiet dignity. Ketelheim found within himself a grudging admiration for them, and knew why. In the not too distant future, he believed, if the forces of the Reich did not hold the line in France and elsewhere, the people of Germany would soon be facing a similar situation, from an implacable foe bent upon revenge. He wondered how his own family would fare. The thought made him even more determined to do fierce battle with the enemy.

Ketelheim was seated next to the baron's oldest daughter, Mariette, a big-boned handsomely curved woman, not yet thirty, with rich, dark-brown hair and pale-brown eyes. On his left was her younger sister, Odile. She had the same strong build but was fairer, with long blonde hair that gleamed in the candlelight. Meckler was sitting on the other side of her and she was conversing politely with him, unexpectedly brown eyes attentive every time she glanced in his direction. Opposite Ketelheim was the forbidding presence of Schlierhof.

The SS lieutenant general suddenly looked up from his plate. The main course for the evening was a wild boar that had been hunted by SS troops, cooked by an SS chef, and served by young French women.

'Well, Ketelheim?' Schlierhof began. 'How do you find the boar? To your Prussian taste?' It sounded like a challenge.

Momentarily caught out by being so directly addressed, Ketelheim said, 'It is excellent, Herr Obergruppenführer.'

Schlierhof nodded in agreement, before turning to Meckler. 'Our SS cooks can show the Luftwaffe a thing or two, eh, Meckler?'

'To judge by this, Herr Obergruppenführer,' Meckler began diplomatically, 'you are right.'

'Of course I am right.' Schlierhof now looked along the table to where Waffen-SS Major-General Herrenbach was in conversation with the junior Gestapo man. 'Friedrich,' he went on expansively, generously mellowed by the Malzeys' excellent but ever-depleting wine stock, 'I like these two young officers. From what I've seen, they give me great confidence. I like the defensive set-up you've got here.'

Herrenbach gave a slight, courteous nod. 'Thank you. My confidence in them is equally strong.'

The monocle tracked round and fastened upon the baron himself. 'Now you tell me, Baron,' he said in tolerable French, 'despite your generosity with your home and your wines, you would like to see the back of us, eh? You must be hoping the Allies will come to your rescue.' There was the tiniest of smiles on his lips as if, having baited a trap, all he needed to do was wait.

'I do not want them to have this house either,' Malzey replied evenly.

The eye behind the monocle was unblinking, while the other seemed amused.

Schlierhof smiled. 'Well spoken.'

He continued eating, now and then glancing at the baron as if hoping to catch an expression that might betray Malzey's true feelings.

The higher-ranking Gestapo man, who had observed the exchange with some interest, now paused, fork in mid-air and turned to Schlierhof.

'Perhaps the Countess might be more forthcoming, Schlierhof,' he suggested, with just a hint of slyness as he glanced at Mariette. 'She lost her husband, you know.' He continued eating, as if losing all further desire to participate in the proceedings.

'Oh, I am sorry, madame,' Schlierhof said to her with a display of concern that Ketelheim thought was too heartfelt to be truly genuine. 'We were not responsible, I hope.'

'As a matter of fact,' she responded coldly, 'you were. Some of your SS.'

'Don't let her apparent disenchantment fool you, Schlierhof,' the Gestapo man said, concentrating on his plate. 'There is more.'

The SS lieutenant general looked at Mariette with a raised eyebrow, his monocle glinting in the candlelight. 'Madame?'

'The stupid Resistance,' she answered vehemently. 'They forced him to join. Now he's dead. I cannot forgive them.'

Schlierhof looked from her to the baron and back, as if trying to decide whether she really meant it. The baron was stony-faced. Schlierhof then glanced at Odile, who was now openly flirting with Meckler.

'It would seem, Herr Daggenau,' he said to the Gestapo chief, 'that there appears to be dissension between the generations.'

Daggenau shrugged.

Schlierhof smiled at Mariette in a way that Ketelheim thought bordered on the predatory.

She turned to Ketelheim. 'Tell me, Colonel,' she surprised him in English, 'do you believe the Allies will invade?'

Ketelheim glanced cautiously at the Abwehr general who nodded, just perceptibly, that he could answer.

'Well, madam,' he replied with ease in the same language, 'I believe they will. But we shall be ready for them.'

'But do you know where they intend to attack?'

'Wherever it may be, we shall be ready,' Ketelheim replied firmly. He noted that all the senior officers were pleased with his answer.

'Your English is very good, Colonel,' Mariette said, in an apparent change of subject. 'I am impressed.'

'I was an exchange student in England in the thirties.'

'And have you never thought that perhaps you might have killed some of your former friends? I do not mean to make a political point, you understand. I am, however, fascinated by the possibility.' Mariette, the Countess Malzey, gave a perfect impression of a woman who asked questions out of curiosity, but with no real interest in profound answers.

Aware of everyone's sudden, undivided attention, with the sole exception of the baron, who was locked away in a world of his own, Ketelheim said, 'Are there not Frenchmen currently killing former friends? And are they not of the same nationality?'

'Bravo!' Schlierhof exclaimed. 'I believe he has you there, Madame!' he finished in his passable French.

'I believe you are right, Herr Obergruppenführer,' she said to him in German.

The eyebrow raised itself once more. 'You are indeed someone of many linguistic talents,' he complimented her in his native tongue.

'One must have the skills of society, if one *is* society.' She made it sound as if this were quite distinct from being merely French, but encompassed all those who belonged to 'society' internationally. She gave the impression that Schlierhof was among this elite.

Schlierhof, clearly flattered, acknowledged the inclusion with a slight nod of the head. Daggenau looked on with an expression of smug disdain.

The dinner continued, the animated conversation among those at the table covering a wide range of subjects. Mariette played the slightly empty-headed aristo, while Odile flashed her eyes at Meckler. The baron, a slim, prematurely greying man, his countenance made pale by his repressed sense of outrage, ate in dignified silence, speaking only when spoken to and then only with the barest of civil replies. None of the baron's family exchanged a single word either with the collaborator Boucheron or with the woman who lived with him in the master's suite of the château as his 'wife'.

Strategically positioned about the table, the young French women who had served the dinner continued to do so on silent feet or waited patiently to be summoned. They listened in on the conversations while seemingly completely uninterested, their thoughts carefully hidden from all but themselves.

'That ought to do it.'

Pendrake straightened in his chair to survey his handiwork. Lewis, standing to one side, leaned forward slightly to have a better look. She was close enough for him to sense the warmth of her body. As she studied the four sheets of paper spread out on the desk, head to one side, a wing of her hair fell slightly forward, baring the neck and jawline. A hand moved absently to brush it back. It fell forward again almost immediately, so she left it alone.

Pendrake did not look at her, but kept his eyes firmly on sheets of paper on which he had written the names of the pilots, dividing them into three flights. The fourth sheet contained the names of those to be held in reserve.

She nodded slowly as she read.

'Approve, do you?' he asked.

She turned her head to look at him. The deep blue eyes were dark and startlingly near. 'It's not for me to approve, sir . . .'

'Come on, Lewis. Don't be so pedantic. What do you really think?'

'I think the allocation works very well. If you're happy with this final draft, I can have it typed up and put a copy on the squadron notice board in the orderly room, and one in the crew room as well.'

'Tomorrow morning. Not tonight. You can't have it typed up right away as everyone's long gone. And I won't have you remaining here to do it. The morning will be soon enough. Now let's get to the mess before they stop serving dinner.'

She straightened, automatically smoothing the skirt of her uniform, her movements unconsciously sensual. Again, he chose not to look at her.

As they were walking through her office on the way out, Wilson barged in, looking very tired.

'Bingo,' Pendrake exclaimed. 'At last! I'd given up hope of seeing you before morning. You look absolutely brassed off.'

'I am, I am,' Wilson said with feeling. 'I got caught up in an armoured convoy that had lost its way. That wretched bomb had blown a great hole in the road I'd intended using. I kept thinking if raiders came over, they'd have found a nice fat target with me in the middle.' He removed his cap and plopped it on Lewis's desk. 'But I see you had a much better time,' he continued to Pendrake, while looking at her. 'I ran into the stationmaster. He says you bagged a couple of 109s today. Lucky sod.'

'They came for a sniff, but found me upstairs. I was on a test flight.'

'You bagged them in one of the new jobs?'

'Yes.'

'Good are they, these new Tiffies?'

'Better. Very powerful, and the bigger wing makes for good agility. And as for the view . . . Find out all about it for yourself tomorrow.'

Wilson was still looking at Lewis. 'Will there be an introduction? Or are we waiting for hell to freeze?'

Pendrake shook his head in mock despair. 'Section Officer Karen Lewis, Flight Lieutenant Bingo Wilson, my deputy.'

She held out her hand. 'Sir.'

'Forget the sir,' he said as he shook it. 'And what he really means is that I'm his stooge.' He grinned. 'I'll carry the can when he makes a mess of things, which, granted, is not very often, thank God.'

'I'd watch him if I were you, Lewis,' Pendrake cautioned. 'He can be dangerous.'

Wilson grinned once more. 'Only a little.'

She looked at him with amusement. 'I'll watch him.'

'Yes, please,' Bingo Wilson said.

'If you're hungry,' Pendrake told him, 'join us for dinner.'

'Will they still be serving?'

'We'd better find out. I'm starving.'

They left the office and went out of the building. Outside in the gloom a patrolling sentry armed with a rifle, bayonet fixed, challenged them.

'*Halt! Who goes there!*' the man barked.

'Squadron Leader Pendrake, Flight Lieutenant Wilson, Section Officer Lewis,' Pendrake replied.

The man came forward and snapped to attention. 'Oh it's you, sir. Ma'am. No lights left on?'

'No.'

He peered at Wilson. 'Ah. You just came in, sir.'

'Yes,' Wilson replied drily. 'You nearly punctured me.'

'Sorry, sir. Never seen you before. Can't be too careful.'

'Quite.'

'Good job you did with those Jerries today, sir,' the sentry went on to Pendrake. 'Bloody good job. We came out of the shelters to watch. We enjoyed seeing you get that bastard . . . Oh, sorry, ma'am,' he said to Lewis.

'That's quite all right,' she assured him. 'I've heard worse. Goodnight.'

'Goodnight,' ma'am. Sirs.'

'Goodnight,' Pendrake said. 'Keep up the good work.'

'Sir!' The sentry cracked his boot down smartly, wheeled, and continued his patrol.

At the château, the dinner was over and the baron, as uncommunicative throughout as he'd been from the very start, had retired to his quarters as soon as he decently could. The musicians were still playing, but neither Ketelheim nor Meckler was at the table. Mariette and Odile had offered a personal tour of the parts of the château that had been allowed by the Gestapo. Forbidden areas included the Malzeys' separate quarters.

Schlierhof was not pleased. 'The woman has snubbed me for that Luftwaffe matinée idol,' he growled to Daggenau. 'A mere lieutenan colonel!' he added in outrage.

'He's hardly a matinée idol,' the Gestapo man told him smoothly. 'Such women are fickle, Herr Obergruppenführer. Anyway, let her have her fun while she still can,' Daggenau continued ominously, in rapid German. He glanced up to survey the French serving girls coldly. 'Leave us!' he ordered in French. He waited until they had all gone, before speaking again.

Outside, two blank-eyed Totenkopf SS guards stood at the door.

'The situation here at the château will not go on for ever,' Daggenau resumed. 'Eventually we shall have no further use for them and then . . .' He let the sentence die, having no need to explain further.

Schlierhof understood. 'Before you do anything to her, I must have her first.'

'Of course,' Daggenau said, considering that a foregone conclusion.

The carnal desires of the Waffen-SS lieutenant general amused him, but would be of future use. The time would come when the dossier he already had on the man would be of great value. If the Allies won, it would be a bargaining chip. If they didn't, it would be an instrument of power over Schlierhof.

Herrenbach had changed position to sit with the Abwehr general, and they discussed the possible options for countering the expected Allied invasion. If von Stahlenbüren already knew that his recce pilots Brillermann and Forschmeister had failed to return, he gave no indication.

Herrenbach noted Daggenau's conspiratorial expression as the Gestapo chief conversed with Schlierhof. Herrenbach did not trust Daggenau in the least. A man to watch constantly, he thought. A man who would be a very dangerous enemy indeed.

'So tell me, Mariette,' Ketelheim began in English as they strolled arm in arm along the wide corridor of the portrait gallery. Meckler and Odile trailed a short distance behind. 'Is your mother still alive?'

'Oh yes. It was not her night.'

'Not her night? What do you mean?'

'I must put this delicately. They would rather not attend these functions at all, but Herr Daggenau insisted. So they reached a compromise. My parents are adamant that if they must be forced to attend, only one should do so at any given time. Herr Daggenau agreed.'

'So your parents hate us strongly?'

'Do you want the truth? Or a diplomatic answer?'

'I always prefer the truth, no matter how harsh.'

She paused to look at him. 'You're an interesting German. My parents despise the Gestapo,' she added.

So do I, he told himself silently.

'She hates the SS – all kinds – almost as much,' Mariette went on, 'and the average German only less so. You allowed the Nazis to take power, you see. Her family originally came from Alsace, and she has a great love for the other Germany. This one is diseased, she says.'

He was silent for a long time.

'You did ask for the truth,' she reminded him as they walked on.

'I almost wish I hadn't. Any brothers?'

'Yes. Two.'

'And I take it they are in uniform?'

'Are you trying to find out whether my brothers are in the Resistance?'

'No. It was genuine curiosity.'

'They are both dead.'

This time it was Ketelheim who stopped. 'I am sorry. Believe me.'

She gave him a little tug, to move him on. 'But it is war. Is that what you were about to say?'

'It *is* war. What did they do?'

'My older brother died commanding his tank platoon in 1940. The other, younger than I am but older than Odile, was torpedoed in 1942. He was serving on a British warship.'

'I am not surprised your parents hate us. I am equally surprised you do not. After all, you have also lost your husband.'

'I am practical,' she said. She glanced back at Odile and Meckler. 'My sister seems to have taken to your friend. She has been attentive to him all evening.'

'And is she also . . . practical?'

'No. She's young, and I think follows a more basic urge.'

Mariette had paused once more, this time before a large portrait of a young woman.

'She's very beautiful,' Ketelheim said admiringly as he studied it.

'My mother.'

'Both you and Odile look like her, in different ways.'

'Are you saying we are beautiful?'

'Yes. Very.'

7

By 0700 hours the next morning, a new board in the station operations room carried the details of the new unit:

Cobra Squadron

Officer Commanding:	Sqn Ldr M. M. Pendrake, DSO, DFC, AFC.
2nd In Command:	Flt Lt D. G. Wilson, DFC.
Squadron Adjutant:	Section Officer K. Lewis.

There followed a list of all pilots by flight, and their current operational status, as well as that of all squadron aircraft.

On the squadron, some of the pilots were clustered round the orderly room notice board, while others studied the one in the crew room. The information on each was the same. The three flights were identified by number, instead of a phonetic or colour designation. Call-signs were also allocated identification numbers.

Pendrake, as CO, would always be Cobra One. Wilson was Cobra Two. The flight leaders were Cobra Double-One, Cobra Two-One, and Cobra Three-One respectively, the first number denoting the flight in question. Their seconds in command were Cobra One-Two, Cobra Two-Two and Cobra Three-Two. The remaining pilots were identified in chronological order, according to flight. As CO and deputy, Pendrake and Wilson could assume command of any flight. There were six pilots per flight, with a reserve of two, which was currently filled by the youngest pair of the sergeant pilots.

Keane was both surprised and pleased to find he had been given command of One Flight. He was due to visit the medical officer for his check-up, and had not expected it. He knew Pendrake was worried about the stiffness in his right arm.

He noted that the Pole, Josef Wojdat, was his second in command.

'Looks like you got me in your flight,' a familiar voice said at his shoulder.

'I have indeed, Captain Elmore. You won't give me any trouble, will you?'

'Who? *Moi?*'

Keane looked at him balefully. 'Give me any, and I'll have your guts for a kangaroo jockstrap.'

'You say such nice things.'

Lewis, walking past the crew room door, overheard the exchange and smiled to herself. They did not notice her as she went by.

At each board, voices competed with each other as their owners commented upon their allocations.

'Hey, Kelly!' someone shouted. 'You've got Three Flight. Are you sure you know how to fly?'

'I was flying my pa's crop-duster when I was twelve, boy!'

'God. You Yanks tell such tall tales.'

Laughter followed this.

'Well, well,' came Dodson's voice. 'He's given me command of Two.' He was standing next to Kelly.

'Is that good?' Kelly demanded. 'Or bad?'

'Time will tell, old son. Time will tell.' Dodson turned as he sensed someone approach to stand just behind him. 'Ah. Flight Sergeant Charlton. I see you're my number two. And in brackets, next to your name, what do you see?'

Charlton came closer to look, and made a sound of astonishment. 'P/O designate. He's recommended me for a commission! I'm going to be a pilot officer?'

'There you are. Who says there isn't a God? You're well overdue, old son. About time that Distinguished Flying Medal was properly recognized. Congratulations.' Dodson grabbed Charlton's hand and shook it vigorously.

'Well, sir,' the flight sergeant pilot said hesitantly. 'I haven't got it yet.'

'Who cares?' Kelly said expansively. 'It's as good as done. Put 'em here.' He, too, shook the bewildered Charlton's hand. 'And you can buy the first round in the mess.'

'I knew there was something wrong about being an officer,' Charlton said ruefully.

Soon, the others were grabbing his hand, patting him on the back, congratulating him.

Kelly, searching the faces about him, spotted Mackenzie entering the room. 'Hey, Mac. Seen the roster, buddy? You're my number two.'

'God help me,' the Canadian said.

Laughter again erupted as they relieved the tension that had built up within them. They were all very much aware of the dangers they were bound to face, and none allowed himself the luxury of thinking how many names would still be on the board when the mission was over.

A WAAF approached the group in the orderly room. 'Please go and sign for your books at the desk, gentlemen.'

'Books?' someone asked. 'What books?'

'Flying manuals, pilot's notes. For the Typhoon S.'

There was a loud, collective groan.

'We're pilots,' another complained. 'Not students.'

'You'll be dead pilots if you don't learn how to fly those Tiffies out there,' a firm voice said.

They all turned to see where it had come from.

Bingo Wilson was standing there, legs planted solidly, fists on hips, facing them. 'I'm Wilson, deputy squadron commander. I got in late last night after you lambs had dinner. And lambs to the slaughter you will be, if you don't get those books and *study* them. They'll save your lives. Might even make decent pilots of some of you. After you've all got and signed for His Majesty's property, I'll see you in the briefing room. Holiday's over, gentlemen.'

In his office, Pendrake called, 'Enter!' in answer to a discreet knock.

Lewis came in, looking bright and fresh. She carried a thin folder, held against her bosom.

'Ah, Lewis. Bright and early. Good. Slept well?'

'Yes, sir.'

'Excellent. Big day, today. It begins.'

'Yes, sir. When did you get in?'

Pendrake stalled for a moment. 'Well . . . er, had an early breakfast.'

'When, sir?' she insisted.

'What is this, Section Officer? Are you nannying me?'

'No, sir. But you'll be no use to the squadron if you're overtired.'

'I only got here at six. The whole station had been long awake.'

'How early, sir?' The blue eyes were insistent.

'Well . . . perhaps 0530 hours.'

She waited.

'Perhaps it was . . . earlier than that. I have plenty to do. This is not easy, you know. Two days ago I was carefree and happy on my lone missions over France. Today I've got twenty-one souls to keep alive in the air, counting Bingo Wilson.'

'Twenty-two.'

'I beg your pardon?'

'Twenty-two, sir. You. A tired pilot is no use to himself or the squadron. It's what you'd say to them.'

'And now you know what I would say to my pilots?'

'Yes, sir,' she said. 'I think . . .'

'All right! All right, Lewis. I've got the message. Now, have the manuals been distributed?'

'Being done as we speak.'

Pendrake nodded. 'Good. And . . .'

'Flight Lieutenant Wilson's got them filing into the briefing room.'

He stared at her. 'You're even finishing my sentences.'

'May I go on, sir?'

'Be my guest.'

'The MO will see Messrs Keane and Mackenzie soon after, plus any of the other pilots on your list. And' – she opened the folder and took out a single sheet of paper – 'this just came in. Thought you might like to see it straight away.' She handed it over.

It was a signal. He stared at it, then broke into a grin of satisfaction as he read:

'SIX FURTHER UNITS AGREED. DESPATCH SOONEST. H.'

'We're in business, Lewis. We've got our aircraft.'

'Yes, sir.'

'We could do with two extra Spits as well,' he remarked thoughtfully, 'for the standing patrol. Two waiting to scramble while two are in the air. It would also allow them to alternate the flying. Save the wear and tear on the aircraft. An hour up, an hour down.'

'We might be giving our luck a bit of a push, sir, asking for more. But it does seem that at the moment they'll give you anything you want. Rather accommodating of them.'

'It certainly looks like it, Section Officer Lewis,' Pendrake agreed, then added, 'The trouble is, the devil always wants his due. Makes me wonder about the price we may have to pay eventually.'

'That's something I have a feeling we'll find out soon enough, sir.'

'I'm not sure I do want to find out,' Pendrake said with a grim smile. He stared at the signal, as if hoping to see the answer already there. 'Oh, hang the consequences. Acknowledge receipt of the information to the originator of the signal and ask for two extra thoroughbreds.'

'Thoroughbreds, sir?'

'Halloran will know. If they do send them, we'll also know we really are the blue-eyed boys.'

'And then?'

'And then, Lewis, we worry. Because it will be uncomfortably apparent that the condemned are eating a hearty breakfast.'

'Yes, sir,' she said quietly. She glanced at the wall behind him. 'That's new. I noticed it when I came in.'

Pendrake twisted briefly round to glance up at the large framed copy of an aviation cartoon he'd hung there. It was of a Typhoon in an aggressive climb, the big chin scoop of the radiator filled with bared teeth, a fierce eye set a short distance on the upper nose behind the propeller spinner, and a single scar running from beneath the eye.

'I'm not sure who added the scar,' he explained, 'but it's not in the original artwork. Bingo gave this to me to celebrate my DFC. He brought it with him last night, so I thought I'd put it up. What do you think? Not overdoing it?' He sounded genuinely concerned.

'Not at all, sir. I would even say put it in the briefing room. It would amuse the pilots. Put them more at ease.'

'I'm not so sure . . .'

She looked at him.

'I'll think about it,' he said.

'I'll remind you,' she warned.

'I know you will,' he said, resigning himself to the fact.

'Why do you call him Bingo, sir?'

'Oh that.' He gave a brief chuckle. 'When everybody was yelling "Tally-ho" as they mixed it with Jerry, he shouted "Bingo". God knows why. Inevitably, the nickname stuck.'

* * *

The pilots were all seated when Wilson entered and mounted the low dais.

'All right, gentlemen,' he began. 'I trust you have all got your school books?'

A few comedians waved theirs at him.

'Very good. Now I do hope you can all read, because I shall be asking questions when the time comes.'

A loud groan greeted this.

'I know, I know. You're hard done by. You thought you had left school for good. Bad luck, gentlemen. The learning never stops. For my sins, I have been designated your chief instructor. It is my job to see that you are able to get those Typhoons into the air and back down again without bending them, or yourselves.

'Those of you who have flown Tiffies, however minimal your time, will be pleased to know that this is a very different beast altogether. It is very powerful, as you now all know . . . and for those of you bred on nightmare stories of the vanishing tail fin, you will have observed the squadron leader's somewhat exciting little demonstration yesterday.'

Loud chuckles, tinged with relief, followed these words.

'Yes, yes. It was impressive and we're very happy the Tiffy's no longer the tailless wonder. But that was the CO, and none of you comes close. But by the time I am finished, I would like to think that when any of you comes into contact with a 109, or, God help you, a 190, it will be Jerry who'll be hitting the silk as his aircraft disintegrates about him or, better yet, never lives to fly another day.'

He paused, eyes raking them.

'The thing is,' he went on softly, 'can you do it?'

'Yep,' someone said. 'We sure can.'

Wilson's eyes tracked and found Elmore. 'You are?'

'Elmore, sir. Captain, US Army Air Force, and south of the Mason–Dixon.' Elmore grinned.

'Well, Captain Elmore, you're the first.'

‘Me, sir?’

‘You, sir.’

‘First what?’

For reply, Wilson barked, ‘Flying Officer Kelly!’

‘Sir!’ Sean Kelly answered.

‘You, Mr Kelly, will be taking Captain Elmore under your wing for the first of a new series of patrols. From today,’ Wilson continued before Kelly could respond, ‘the CO has ordered a regular patrol of Spitfires up top to watch out for surprise visitors, like those we had yesterday, for the duration of our stay here. We shall all be taking turns, so those of you looking for Spit time will get a fair amount. And Mr Elmore . . .’

‘Yes, sir?’

‘When you bring that Spit back to earth, do so very gently indeed. I don’t know how you treat your girlfriends, but don’t treat that aeroplane like one of them. If you are gentle with the ladies, be even gentler with the Spit. Bend her, and I’ll bend you. Are you receiving me?’

‘Loud and clear, sir. Very loud and clear.’

‘Then I’m very glad your ears had a clean this morning. Mr Kelly, when we’re through here, both of you pick up your gear and get aloft. Time on patrol, one hour.’

‘Sir.’

‘One other thing . . . Messrs Keane, Mackenzie, Wojdat, Kelly and Dodson are to be my deputy instructors. With help from time to time from the CO, I shall convert each of you to the new Typhoon. Each in turn will teach those assigned to you. We’ve not got a lot of time, gentlemen, and there’s a big job ahead. Flight Sergeant Charlton . . .’

‘Sir?’

‘The CO wants a word with you afterwards.’

‘Very good, sir.’

‘All right, gentlemen. The Spitfire patrol roster will be on the notice board, as well as the training schedules for the day. Check that, and be ready for take-off at the appropriate times. In the meanwhile, I want you to study those manuals until you know the aircraft as well as you know yourselves and perhaps even better. All flight commanders not detailed for immediate take-off, make yourselves ready for a commanders' meeting with the CO. Mr Mackenzie, as deputy Three Flight, you'll stand in for Flying Officer Kelly while he's aloft and report to him afterwards. Thank you, gentlemen. That is all.'

Ketelheim and Meckler were on their way back to their respective units from the Château de St Sauveur. They had stayed the night at the invitation of the baron's daughters, but had not slept in the Malzey quarters. The baron would certainly not have allowed it in any case, even if the Gestapo would not have objected. The major part of the building, having been commandeered by the Gestapo, contained several bedrooms for use by military and political guests.

Both Waffen-SS generals, Schlierhof and Herrenbach, had left during the night, Schlierhof in a foul mood because Mariette had chosen to snub him for Ketelheim. At least, that was how he had preferred to see it.

Ketelheim and Meckler had an early breakfast by themselves, and had not seen the sisters again.

'So, Karl-Heinz?' Meckler now began as the Mercedes boomed its way along the narrow forest road. 'Will you see her again? We have been invited, after all.'

'If I have the time. But remember, I'm a married man. And you?'

'Most certainly, I shall see the delightful Odile. She has the most desirable body and I believe she would like to put it to good use.' Meckler laughed aloud in anticipation. 'And I, I am not married.

'You have made a very bad enemy in the Obergruppenführer, Karl-Heinz,' he went on soberly. 'Schlierhof's a very nasty customer. I've told you about the things we have done on the Eastern Front. Schlierhof revelled in it. His arms should be red up to the armpits. He belongs in a slaughterhouse. Forget the surface niceties of last night. He hates the Luftwaffe with a passion. As far as he is concerned, the Luftwaffe failed to defeat the Tommies in the Eagle Battle – what *they* call the Battle of Britain – failed on the Eastern Front, and is not doing enough to stop the Allied bombers . . .'

'*What?*'

'Don't snap at me, Karl-Heinz. I'm telling you what he thinks, and there are many like him who blame the Luftwaffe for their own failings.'

'If people interfered less in operational decisions,' Ketelheim said in a hard voice, 'perhaps we would have had more success. We have lost a lot of good men because of stupidity by . . .'

'Uh-oh. What's this? Am I hearing dangerous criticism from you? Yesterday, you were warning *me* against indiscretions.'

Ketelheim smiled grimly. 'In 1940, we did ask Fat Hermann for Spitfires.'

Meckler grinned at him. 'You've really got the bit between your teeth this morning. Calling the great Reichsmarschall Göring "Fat Hermann".' Meckler gave him a sly look. 'You're sure it's not because of the delightful widow?'

'I'm . . .'

'Yes, yes. You're married. Tell me then . . . how is it with you and Trudi? Remember, this is your best man you'll be answering.'

There was a very long silence. The car rumbled its way through the forest, watched by the unseen eyes of Meckler's soldiers.

'Before I took over this command,' Ketelheim began at long last in a flat voice, 'I went home on leave. Just back from the Eastern Front, I was eager to see her, of course. I could hardly wait. She wasn't there. No one knew where she was. I was beginning to think she'd been killed in a bombing raid while she was out. Two days later, she turned up. There was a man with her. Someone with high Party connections.' His lips tightened and a muscle in his jaw throbbed visibly as he remembered. 'While I was out in the East freezing in a miserable tent and longing for her, he was . . . she was . . .'

Ketelheim stopped, unable to put into words what his wife had got up to during his absence, and took a deep breath. He fell silent again as a shocked Meckler continued driving, glancing at him from time to time.

'I haven't seen her since,' Ketelheim said at last harshly, 'nor have I contacted her.'

They drove on in another long silence.

'I'm very sorry,' Meckler ventured at last, glancing out of the corner of his eye at his friend, as if unsure of Ketelheim's mood. 'I know how much you . . .' He stopped, then continued brightly, 'Let's take up that invitation. I'm not saying you should do anything with the merry widow; but a man needs a woman's company. And I don't mean going to a whorehouse. I mean a good, sophisticated woman like our hostess.'

'You're sure you're not being influenced by your loins?'

'I won't deny it. Odile does things to me. Yes, I want to satisfy myself in her. I want to spend a whole night exploring that marvellous body. A fighting man needs to be able to do that. But I also think it would do you some good to at least spend a little time with Mariette. What you do then is entirely your business. Read poetry to her, smell the flowers . . . anything. At times like these, who knows where we may be tomorrow? So, Karl-Heinz . . . what do you say? Shall we see them next week?'

'What about the Gestapo? Won't they have something to say about it? And your Obergruppenführer Schlierhof? You just warned me about him.'

'He's not *my* lousy Obergruppenführer. Herrenbach's

my commander. As for the Gestapo, I know we saw Daggenau and Schlierhof playing cosy-cosy; but let me tell you, Schlierhof would stab Daggenau in the back at the first opportunity, and Daggenau would return the favour.

'But Daggenau won't give us trouble; at least, not for the time being. He's too busy playing with his prisoners and hunting out the Resistance helpers in the district. His weasel of a deputy, Grüber, might sneak around a bit, but I don't think he'll do anything without Daggenau's say-so. And Daggenau would not want to lean on me and offend Herrenbach, who's a much tougher customer than Schlierhof, despite being the junior rank. Also, don't forget it's my troops guarding his little hell on earth. Well? Shall we accept the invitation?'

'I'll think about it.'

'Don't take too long.'

In the château, Odile and Mariette were having breakfast in Mariette's bedroom. Both women were still in their night clothes, with Odile wearing something under her dressing gown that would have driven Meckler insane with lust. When the gown came open, which was often, the short nightdress bared all of her long, strong legs and most of her thighs. There was no underwear beneath the exceptionally thin garment.

Despite the time of year, she possessed a light tan that was clearly a legacy of many years' worship of the summer sun. Of a generally bigger frame and taller than her older sister, she exuded an uninhibited and powerful sexuality as she sat cross-legged on the bed. Mariette's own sensual attractiveness was more subtle, but still evident.

Odile bounced slightly on the bed as she made herself more comfortable, her blonde hair a gleaming slow-motion curtain about her face.

'Well, they're gone,' she said. 'Did you mean it when you asked them back?'

Mariette nodded. 'Yes. As the commanders of the ground and air forces in the area, they're just what we need. We must cultivate them. But be careful, Odile. That Waffen-SS colonel is dangerous. He is nice and pleasant to you, but only because he wants you in bed. Do not forget what he really stands for.'

'I can handle him,' Odile said lightly.

'I am not so sure. What will you do when he thinks it's time he started undressing you?'

'I'll cross that bridge when I get to it.'

Mariette looked at her, brow furrowed. 'You're not really attracted to him, are you? Odile! That would be . . .'

'Don't worry. I know what I'm doing. I've done more dangerous things than this.'

'Perhaps. But this man is no fool. He's not like the others. If we are to continue being of use to the Resistance, we cannot be compromised . . .'

Odile hummed a little to herself then bit enjoyably into half a crusty roll, dipped in honey. 'And what about you?' She wiped a small, golden tendril that had slid off the edge of the roll and on to her full lower lip with a finger, then licked the finger clean.

'*Me?*' Mariette looked at her as if she'd taken leave of her senses.

'Yes. What about your airman? He thinks, like all those other idiots, you're a widow.'

'*My* airman? Don't be ridiculous. And besides, he's married.'

'How do you know?'

'Because, Odile, dear sister, I'm a married woman. I understand these things.' Mariette looked thoughtful. 'Although . . . I think he may have problems.'

'You know all that from just the one evening?'

'You can discover plenty, if you know what to look for. I caught him looking at you and Franz. There was a longing . . . no, no, not for you . . .'

Odile pouted. 'I am insulted,' she said theatrically.

'He was longing for someone else,' Mariette went on, ignoring her sister's interruption. 'There was a sadness in his eyes. His wife is either dead, or she is playing around and he knows it. I believe she is playing around. The sadness is not for someone who is dead, but for something that was once valuable and is now lost. The more I think about it, the more I'm certain I am right.'

'You're pretending that Michel is dead, and they all believe it. What kind of sadness do you show in your eyes?'

'Ah but you see, we're much better at it than men. We are experts at hiding what we really feel. It's not the expression on the face but what is hidden in the eyes. You're very good at it. You always were, even as a child.'

Odile gave her sister a sideways look, a tiny smile playing briefly about her lips. 'If you say so.'

'Look,' Mariette began in a change of subject, 'let's go for a little walk today. See if they've brought in any more guns or tanks, or changed positions.'

'We can always ask that horrible Grüber to accompany us,' Odile said with a giggle, 'to protect us from the soldiers. Grüber thinks I like him.'

'Be careful of him too. A rat like that is even more dangerous, especially when rejected. Meckler is someone who will react openly. Grüber will sneak behind your back. Remember what they did to Jeanne-Anne.'

Then something very strange happened to Odile. The sexual animal vanished. The laughing eyes grew chillingly cold.

'I'll never forget,' she said.

Helmut Grüber had been aptly described by Meckler. The man was indeed a weasel. He fitted perfectly the job description Hitler had laid down for the species he dubbed the *Gauleiter*. Grüber was the quintessential odious deputy, right-hand man, *éminence grise*. He could be relied upon to carry out any dirty work with great enthusiasm. A nonentity before the ascent of Hitler opened up a whole new world to him, he was the epitome of an inadequate who had suddenly found himself granted virtually unlimited power, within his own jurisdiction. He did what such people in his position invariably do: he abused it.

He had once been little more than a subsistence farmer in a small mountain village in Bavaria. Full of anger and frustration about his lot in life, he had been forced to endure from boyhood the taunts of his male peers and unending rejection by the village girls. They called him a weasel even then.

He had joined the Party in its very early days and quickly gained favour with its leadership for his ruthless espousal of the National Socialist ethos. Soon he was given a local command, then a district. When the Nazis eventually took over the reins of government, Grüber became a very powerful man indeed. Before long, the very girls who used to reject him began to seek favours from him. He made them pay, the only way that would please him; even the wives of those who had once taunted him.

High rank as Daggenau's number two had not blunted his desire to revenge himself upon all women. It simply meant he now had a wider selection to choose from; but even he would not dare go against Daggenau's orders as far as the Malzey sisters were concerned. However, it did not mean this prevented him from carrying out his normal duties. In matters regarding Gestapo activities in Occupied France, *all* French citizens were suspect.

Grüber was feeling particularly good that morning. He rolled out of bed, stood up and stretched his pale, thin body. His vulpine face, with its head of black strands of short, lank hair, turned to look at the bed as he brought his arms down. One of the French serving girls was lying beneath the rumpled bedclothes, back towards him. She was huddled in a foetal position, as if protecting herself. His lovemaking had been brutal, lacking finesse or any real emotion. It had been a service. Nothing more.

'You had better get back to your work,' he commanded harshly in bad, arrogant French. 'You will not forget our little arrangement, will you? *Will you?*'

'No . . . no, monsieur,' came an answering mumble.

'Good. As long as you remember that and you come to me when I require, your family will be safe. You will be replaced if you fail me, and you will all be transported. I know you miserable French are hoping for the invasion. Even if it does come, we will make them wish they never tried. They won't be able to save you, my lovely Agnès. Do you hear me?'

'Yes, monsieur.'

'Now get out. Put on your clothes. Hurry! I have work to do. You can wash somewhere else.'

Agnès Grappin got out of the bed, never once turning to face him and hurriedly dressed with trembling hands. She quickly left the room, her body hurting as a result of Grüber's sexual attentions and ashamed that for some time now she had been his spy in the château. On occasion, he had warned her that she was not the only one.

8

The soft knock made Pendrake look up from his desk. Lewis entered.

'Flight Sergeant Charlton, sir.'

'Ah yes. Send him in.'

She stood back and Charlton marched in, came to a halt and saluted.

'Flight Sergeant Charlton reporting as ordered, sir!'

'At ease, Flight.'

'Sir.' Charlton relaxed.

Pendrake nodded at Lewis and she backed into her office, closing the door softly. The two Spitfires, with Kelly and Elmore at the controls, roared overhead on their way to patrol altitude.

'How do you like the idea of being a pilot officer, Peter?' Pendrake began as the sounds of the Merlins faded.

'Very much indeed, sir. But it's taken me a bit by surprise. Very unexpected.'

'Fully deserved.'

'Did you put me up for it, sir?'

'Yes. No problem with confirmation. It will be made official very soon. You'll have to go away for a bit when our little show is over, but I hope you'll be coming back to us.'

'I'd like to, sir.'

Pendrake nodded. 'Pleased to hear it. I'd hate to lose you to some other unit. Until your scraper arrives, I've arranged for you to move to the officers' mess . . .'

'If I may interrupt, sir.'

'Go ahead.'

'Unless it's an order, sir, I wouldn't mind remaining with the other sergeant pilots until the rank does arrive . . .'

'Granted,' Pendrake said. 'In any case when we move from these salubrious surroundings to a forward airfield, we'll all be billeted together. There is something else I did want to mention. The other sergeant pilots are fairly green. I'd like you to take them under your wing, especially young Benson. Would you do that?'

'No trouble at all, sir. Leave it to me. I'll sort them out.'

'Thank you, Pilot Officer Charlton.'

Charlton grinned as Pendrake stood up to approach him. 'Sounds strange, hearing it.'

Pendrake held out a hand. 'Get used to it. Congratulations, Peter.'

'Thank you, sir.'

As Charlton went out, the phone rang. Pendrake reached over to the desk and picked it up.

'Squadron Leader Pendrake.'

'Ah . . . Mike.' It was Rhys.

'Yes, sir?'

'We've got a bit of a problem. Your aircraft.'

Pendrake waited.

'The Typhoon 1B you brought in,' Rhys explained. 'I'm afraid the mods are rather more complicated than at first thought. You see, the "S" versions you've got out there are actually all-new aircraft. Now that we've done a partial strip-down, it appears that bringing yours to an equivalent standard requires a major rebuild. That means a return to the factory.'

Pendrake, hiding his disappointment, said, 'That would take more time than we've got.'

'Precisely what I thought. Knowing one of the reasons you wish to keep the aircraft, we've come up with an idea – or rather Sergeant Ransome has – which we hope you'll approve of.'

'May I have a word with him?'

'He's on his way to you right now. I think you'll like the suggestion. Listen to what he has to say.'

'Very well, sir. I'll wait to hear.'

'You won't be disappointed. Are you settling in all right?'

'Yes, sir. Those two 109s are continuing to do me some good.'

Rhys gave a chuckle. 'Can't deny it was a rather spectacular way to begin your command. The mess for lunch?'

'If I can get away.'

'The joys of command.'

'Just what someone said to me yesterday.'

Rhys chuckled once more. 'Never a truer word, old boy.'

The ground-crew sergeant was ushered into the office five minutes later.

'I hear you've got a solution to our problem, Sergeant Ransome,' Pendrake began.

'It's just an idea, sir . . . but it's a way out, if you'll agree.'

'The wing commander's already explained about the difficulty of doing the job on site, so I'm open to any ideas you've got.'

'A little cannibalization, sir,' Ransome said, 'is what I'm thinking about. If we cut a panel about a foot square from your old aeroplane with the er . . .' He stopped, uncertain how to describe what he was thinking about.

'The hand,' Pendrake finished for him.

'Er . . . yes, sir. If we cut the panel, we can then cut a similar panel – an exact match – from the new aircraft. The panel with the . . . um . . . hand can then be flush-riveted to the new aeroplane, painted over and you'd never be able to tell the difference. The part that's been clear-doped will be exactly as before. There will be no structural penalty.

We've already checked where it would go. We also thought the Typhoon you used yesterday to get those 109s would be the perfect choice. It could be your new personal kite, sir. We'll transfer all your kills to it.' Ransome ended his words in a rush and waited for a reaction from Pendrake.

Pendrake turned, then stood perfectly still by his desk, to stare at the cartoon Wilson had given him. But he wasn't seeing the drawing. His eyes were looking into the past and seeing Megan's intestine on the scorched tree. His face paled and the scar on his cheek felt hot for a brief moment.

At last he turned towards Ransome once more. 'That old Tiffy and I have been through a lot together. All right, Sergeant. Do it. How long will it take?'

Clearly relieved, Ransome replied, 'It will be done in no time at all, sir. She'll be ready for flight this afternoon, if you need her.'

Pendrake nodded. 'That will be fine. Thank you.'

'Oh, and how would you like the aircraft kills put on, sir? Swastikas, like on the old Tiffy? Or black crosses on a faded white background?'

'Keep the swastikas, but not as bright as they currently are. In fact, make all the kills low-key. We don't want them to stand out in the air against our new black paintwork, do we?'

Ransome smiled. 'We certainly don't, sir. The blokes are quite excited by the number of kills you've got. They say it looks as if you've been wiping out the Jerries all by yourself, and it'll take hours to stencil them all on. They're exaggerating about the time, sir.'

'Exaggeration or not, just don't let Flying Officer Wojdat hear you say that. He might get upset if he thinks I'm leaving nothing for him. All right, Sergeant Ransome. Thank you for coming. I like your idea.'

'Sir.'

Ransome saluted smartly and went out.

Pendrake went through to Lewis's office. 'When are the flight commanders due?' he asked her.

'After the medical, sir. I thought it would be better to wait until then. Medicals began an hour and a half ago.'

'Which gives us . . .?'

'About forty minutes.'

Pendrake glanced at his watch. 'I've got just enough time to get to Dispersal, have a look around to see how things are progressing, then get back here. I'm going to see how Bingo Wilson's doing with the fledglings. Leave you to hold the fort?'

'Of course, sir.'

'Thank you, Karen.' It was the first time he had addressed her with anything approaching familiarity.

'Sir.'

At Dispersal, Wilson had four of the Typhoons occupied. None had been started and he was going from aircraft to aircraft, pointing out salient features to the pilots in the respective cockpits. By a fifth aircraft, Charlton was talking to Benson, the youngest of the sergeant pilots. Pendrake noted that one of the aircraft had been moved to a hangar and he could see two of Ransome's men working away at the left rear fuselage.

He caught up with Wilson as his deputy was stepping off one of the Typhoons. The day was mildly chilly, but with no wind to speak of and with a high but cool sun, was crisp and pleasant.

'How's it going, Bingo?'

Wilson glanced up at the cockpit where Wojdat was busy familiarizing himself with the layout. 'Old Josef's very quick. I'm thinking of authorizing his first flight.'

'And the others?'

'They're coming along . . . especially our New Zealander, Knowles. Amazing, really. For a man who's never flown single-seaters, he seems in his element.' Wilson smiled. 'Must have been a frustrated fighter pilot.'

'Aren't we all? Need me for anything?'

Wilson shook his head. 'No. But I'll yell if I do. Don't worry, Mike. I can handle it. You're the commander.' Wilson grinned. 'You've got serfs to do the dirty work now.'

Pendrake stuck his hands in his pockets and looked irresolute for some moments. 'What I want to do is get up there and fly.'

'Can't just do that any more, old son. You've got responsibilities now. Tell you what,' Wilson continued, relenting slightly, 'when I think they're good enough, you can take them flying. That should scare the pants off them.'

'I'd rather have them scared now than later. Flight commanders' meeting in . . . thirty minutes. If you've got any with you by then, send them on. You don't have to be there. No point interrupting the training. We'll talk later.'

'Right,' Wilson said as they walked towards another aircraft. 'Now push along, Mike, sir, and let me do my stuff.' He climbed on to the Typhoon and made his way up to the side of the cockpit. 'That, old son,' he said to the nervous pilot, 'is the supercharger lever. You don't want to mistake it for the throttle and grab at it in error. You might get a very nasty surprise. On the other hand, used judiciously, it will get you out of trouble . . . or should. Got it?'

The pilot nodded wordlessly, peering anxiously at the lever as if expecting it to jump up and bite him on the nose.

Pendrake gave a rueful smile and glanced upwards. There were high clouds in the otherwise clear sky. He could see a couple of specks describing a wide, slow circle. The Spitfire patrol.

'See you later, Bingo,' he called.

Wilson waved at him without turning round.

As he walked slowly back towards the staff car, the explosive start of one of the 2400-horsepower engines made him pause to look. Wojdat was getting ready for his flight. Pendrake decided to wait for the take-off.

The Typhoon began to taxi smoothly. Wojdat had clearly got a grip on things very quickly indeed. Pendrake watched keenly as the aircraft made its way towards the runway threshold, stopped, and Wojdat opened the throttle. The Typhoon bellow filled the air.

Then it was surging forward. Pendrake watched as the tail rose slightly as the Typhoon's great wing began to generate lift. Now the entire aircraft was off the ground, maintaining an infinitesimal raising of the nose. There was barely any swing to the right. The wheels came up. Wojdat continued to hold the aircraft low as the speed increased in a great rush.

Then the nose snapped up and the Typhoon hurled itself skywards.

'Not bad,' Pendrake said to himself approvingly. 'In fact, bloody good.'

'Not much I can teach him,' a distant voice said.

Pendrake turned to see that Wilson had paused in his tutorial to judge Wojdat's take-off. The pilot under instruction had a look of apprehensive envy as he turned his head to follow the Typhoon's flight.

Then Wojdat began to throw the Typhoon about.

'Show-off!' Wilson shouted at the cavorting aeroplane. He turned to his pupil. 'If you want to fly this thing like that nice man up there,' Pendrake heard him say loudly over the noise of Wojdat's exuberance, 'treat what I say to you like the Ten Commandments.'

Again, the pilot nodded wordlessly.

Pendrake smiled to himself as he entered the car. Bingo was doing all right. Wojdat too.

He checked the other aircraft, but forced himself not to

visit the hangar to see how the work on his own Typhoon was progressing. He returned to the squadron offices with ten minutes to spare, just as the Spitfire patrol came in to land.

'Was that a Typhoon I heard a short while ago, sir?' Lewis asked as he entered.

'Yes. Wojdat. Barely needed any instruction. If the others are half as quick I'll be a very happy man. Any news on the medicals?'

She handed him a folder. 'The flight commanders are in your office.'

'And any response to the Spitfire request?'

'Nothing as yet. No news . . .'

'Is not always good news.'

He opened the folder and quickly read through the sheets of paper. Everyone was cleared except for Keane, whose stiff right arm and shoulder needed more time.

He shut the folder and handed it back. 'Keane's not going to be too pleased.'

'He isn't,' she confirmed. 'You might have to calm him down.'

He nodded. 'I'll handle it. Kelly's just landed. I take it Mackenzie's deputizing?'

'Yes, sir.'

'No matter. I'll start immediately. They can liaise afterwards.'

'Very good, sir.'

'At ease, gentlemen,' Pendrake said as he entered his office. 'Let's make this informal. Grab seats wherever you can.' He went to his desk and sat down.

'Right,' he went on. 'This is as new to me as it is to you, so we're all going to have to help each other. You'll have realized by the almighty din a short while ago that we've got someone up already. That was our friendly Pole, Wojdat. Took to it like a veritable duck to water. I'm not expecting everyone else to be as quick, but I do expect fairly rapid progress. We do not have the luxury of time.'

'That puts me at a disadvantage, sir,' Keane said. 'The doc's *grounded* me,' he added, outraged by the medical officer's audacity.

'We'll dispense with the "sir" in here. I do appreciate your problem, Dominic. It's mine too. You're a bloody good pilot and as far as I'm concerned, a valuable flight commander. I do not intend to risk losing you, by forcing you into an aircraft while your arm and shoulder stand the slightest chance of inhibiting your flying ability. My reponsibility ensures that I take the doc's diagnosis seriously. I'd like to think that in my place, you'd do the same for me.' Pendrake's eyes held Keane's in their gaze.

Eventually, Keane took a deep breath and nodded slowly. 'You're right, I reckon. Only it's bloody frustrating. I've got to ask the boys to go up and do their best while I'm stuck on the ground. A flight commander who doesn't fly. Hell of a way to lead by example.'

'I do appreciate the difficulty. Your priority, therefore, is to get that wing working properly again. I'm going to need you for the show.' Pendrake grinned at him. 'Don't think you're going to sit it out.'

The Australian gave a reluctant, barely visible smile. 'As long as you mean that.'

'Oh, I do, even if it means I've got to get you up to scratch myself.'

'I'll hold you to that. So . . . what's the mission?'

Pendrake stood up. 'Come with me.'

They followed him through to Lewis's office.

'Any idea of the whereabouts of our French guest?' he asked her.

'With the wing commander, sir. He's being shown around. Shall I contact them?'

'No need. But if he makes contact, let me know immediately. We'll be in the model room.'

'Very good, sir.' There was a question in her eyes, but she did not voice it, and he ignored it.

'Gentlemen,' he said to the others, and walked out.

They trooped after him to the guarded room where the model of the château and its environs was installed. He switched the lights on as they followed him in. They stared at the display before them, each trying to work out what part it would eventually play in their lives.

'Find yourselves a good position from which to study this,' he told them and when they had, went on, 'This, gentlemen, is our target. Take a good, long look.'

There was a light wooden rod like an elongated swagger stick, leaning against the edge of the platform. Pendrake picked it up and began to indicate.

'Château. Primary target . . . but of virtually equal importance from a survival point of view – ours – are the defences . . . here, and here, and here, the château itself . . . Airfield with Focke-Wulf Fw-190s, and in and around the woods of the château, anti-aircraft emplacements, manned by the Waffen-SS. Within the grounds, more guns with these two multi-barrelled flak jobs just here, by the roof. There will be more of these nasties in the woods. Very, very dangerous and must be destroyed at the earliest opportunity. Take good note of their positions. Additionally, there are tanks and armoured vehicles, virtually all having some anti-aircraft capability.

'At the height at which we shall be operating, you can assume that light weapons will also be a threat to be considered. I intend to carry out a simultaneous, three-pronged attack.' The pointer was moving once more. 'The airfield, to neutralize the fighters; the woods, to engage the guns and tanks; and the château itself. We will be over the target area while it's still dark, but just before dawn. By the time dawn arrives, the attack should be long over and we'll be on the way home. One very important point: this red section of the château is not to be attacked . . . under *any* circumstances.

'I know we shall be attacking in poor light. However, any of you finding yourselves over the château must take note of your point of entry, which will then enable you to know exactly the position of the red zone. Memorize its relative position from any angle of entry. You'll have the opportunity to study this model as often as you like. On the day of the mission briefing, we'll have a detailed map on display.

'Timing will be vital. I shall cover that at a later date.' Pendrake straightened, holding the pointer in both hands across his lower body. 'You will all have seen from the model that I do not have to tell you how dangerous an undertaking this will be. Our best hope of success is to train rigorously, so as to carry out our attack with absolute precision and, hopefully, minimal or no casualties. If we do encounter fighters, we must also be able to take them on and *win*. We all know what happens to those who do not. They die.'

Pendrake stopped and studied their expressions. They were all staring at the model as if mesmerized, and were silent for a long while.

'Mother of God,' Mackenzie uttered at last, softly. 'The SS are growing like daisies in there.'

'Then we'll make sure they remain where they are. Permanently.'

'And those 190s,' Keane said. 'We've got to make sure they stay on the ground. Otherwise . . .'

Pendrake looked at him. 'That's your job, Dominic. I told you I needed you.'

Keane's eyes stared into his. 'Yes, sir.'

Keane had a reputation for very steady eyes, especially when first introducing himself. Don't call me 'Cobber' he would say, while those eyes zeroed in on the unfortunate victim. The eyes did not waver as they now looked at Pendrake.

'Can you do it?'

'Yes, sir,' Keane repeated.

Pendrake nodded, placed the pointer back against the platform, then leaned forward, resting his hands on the edge. He looked at each man, searching out their individual faces with probing eyes. The scar on his cheek glistened faintly in the hooded lighting.

'It's not going to be easy,' he told them, 'but it can be done. I cannot at this stage tell you the purpose of the mission. However, I can tell that our efforts will make a major contribution to the war effort in this theatre. There will also be ground forces in the area to mop up anything we leave standing.

'You'll be pleased to know that I have asked for, and we shall be receiving, six further Typhoons. This will give us a healthy margin with which to absorb any aircraft attrition. I intend to have three flights of at least six aircraft each, over the target area. If we keep the attrition rate down, we could have seven to each flight, plus myself. I shall be leading the attack on the château.

'Assume that we'll meet with ferocious resistance, so attack with your own ferocity to overwhelm the enemy. Don't give him time to think, and thus to react. If resistance is less than expected, then so much the better. Irrespective of enemy response, there will be no let-up in the aggressiveness of the attack. Remember, our business is killing Jerries, and there'll be plenty to go round. Originally, I was not going to inform you so soon. However, I've decided that since the available time is three weeks . . .'

'*Three weeks!*' It was Dodson.

'As I thought,' Pendrake said. 'Concentrates the mind wonderfully. Three weeks, gentlemen. That's all we've got.'

A short while after lunch, Pendrake got a call from Ransome.

'Can you come over to have a look, sir?' the ground-crew sergeant asked. 'We're nearly done.'

'On my way,' Pendrake said.

When he got to the hangar, the two aircraft were wing to wing. The difference between them was marked, the Typhoon S looking perceptibly bigger and meaner.

Ransome came up to him. 'Come and have a look, sir.'

Pendrake noted that the other members of the ground crew were eyeing him warily. It was obvious they weren't sure how to take the man who had downed the two Messerschmitts with such skill, but who also flew with the mangled hand of a dead enemy plastered to his aircraft.

Pendrake followed Ransome. The sergeant stopped by the left rear fuselage of the black Typhoon and pointed. It was a remarkable job. There was no indication whatsoever that the clear-doped remains had not been on the aircraft from the very beginning. It was only when Pendrake went over to look at his old 1B that the black panel on that aeroplane betrayed the change. They had done a straight swap.

'Fair exchange, sir,' Ransome explained.

'Indeed. A quite marvellous job, Sarge. My compliments.'

'Thank you, sir. We haven't done the change of kills as yet, but we've already put your two 109s on the blackbird.'

'I've decided to leave them where they are,' Pendrake said, looking at the markings beneath the cockpit rim. He gave the older Typhoon a gentle pat. 'She deserves her laurels. The blackbird can notch up her own tally,' he added, borrowing Ransome's nickname for the Typhoon S. 'And as you can see, she's already started.'

'Righto, sir. We'll leave the old kills on the 1B.' The sergeant peered up at the cockpit. The kills practically covered the side. 'Quite a score, sir.'

The first line of ten small swastikas denoted ten aircraft

downed. Beneath that were the silhouettes of twenty steam engines in double rows of ten. Next came tanks. There were twenty-five of those. The bottom line carried three rockets to show the sites destroyed, three patrol boats, and a radar antenna. Then on a line all by itself, was a silhouette that looked like part of a submarine.

'Did you really get a sub, sir?' Ransome enquired, staring at the marking.

'Just a third,' Pendrake replied. 'Three of us caught it just before dawn, limping along on the surface. It was heading towards the Cherbourg peninsula. It had either been hit in a battle somewhere and couldn't dive, or something had gone wrong and it was hoping to make it somewhere safe before daylight, from where it could later sneak down to the pens at St Nazaire. It would have managed it too except the dawn beat it, with the added bad luck that we happened to be there. We hit it with rockets before they could man their gun. Went down like a stone.'

'Well, sir, I agree with you. It would be a shame to rob the old girl of her glory.'

Pendrake gave the aircraft another pat before turning to Ransome. 'I'll leave you to it, Sarge. Thank you all,' he added to the ground crew. 'Excellent work.'

As he left, a Typhoon started up, while in the circuit another two were coming in to land.

Three days later all the squadron pilots, with two exceptions, had made at least two flights each in the new Typhoons. The exceptions were Keane, who waited in frustration for his arm and shoulder to get better, and Benson. Though he had flown a Spitfire patrol, Benson seemed to be having problems with the Typhoon. It was as if the aircraft intimidated him.

Even Elmore, who had no problems with the Spitfire and who on one occasion took off diagonally across the airfield, managed to land again with reasonable – by his standards –

gentleness. The landing-gear was still in one piece after two of his landings.

But the time had come for Benson to make his debut. It was a grey sort of day and a light rain had fallen earlier, leaving the grass sparkling as if with a mild frost. Charlton was standing outside the cockpit, giving last-minute words of encouragement.

'Now remember . . . move the throttle smoothly. Don't rush it, and you'll be all right. Watch out for the swing. It's gentle so *don't* over-correct. OK?'

Benson, helmet on, stared at him and nodded.

'Good man.' Charlton patted him once on the shoulder, then climbed down.

Wilson approached as Charlton moved a safe distance away from the aircraft. 'Is he all right?'

'As right as he'll ever be,' Charlton replied. 'Either he'll do it, or he won't.'

They watched as the Typhoon was started. No problem there. Benson used the throttle as he'd been instructed. The powerful engine settled down to a steady idle. Benson left the canopy open as he taxied towards the runway. The aircraft was handled perfectly.

'So far, so good,' Charlton murmured, following the Typhoon with his eyes as it made its way to the threshold. 'Now just remember what I said,' he went on, speaking to the distant Benson. 'Easy does it.'

The Typhoon stopped. The canopy was slid shut. The engine roared as Benson opened up the throttle. It began to roll forward. The tail came up. An incipient swing was corrected; but then it went too far the other way. Opposite correction was made as the speed built. Another swing, this time more pronounced, followed by another correction. The swing was reversed, quite violently.

Charlton watched in mounting horror. 'He's over-correcting! I told him to watch out. He's going to lose it!'

By now, the speeding Typhoon was swinging this way

and that. It left the ground briefly, to touch down again in mid-swing. It gave a sharp pivot and began to head off the runway. The engine rose to a screaming bellow before suddenly dying, then it roared again, fitfully. The aircraft was now off the runway and heading straight for a fuel bowser. The driver saw it coming and tried to move out of its way.

As if now with a mind of its own, the Typhoon seemed to correct itself and again headed for the speeding truck. The aircraft tried to take off, actually leaving the ground completely. Had it continued upwards, it would have vaulted the truck. Instead, in sank back to earth.

Charlton and Wilson watched in helpless despair as the inevitable occurred in what seemed to them like slow motion. The Typhoon collided explosively with the fuel truck. A great fireball expanded from the point of impact then began to fold in on itself before expanding rapidly once more. They felt the heat of the blast on their shocked faces.

Then they began to run towards the blaze, already knowing it was a pointless effort.

In the control tower, just before the impact, they'd heard Benson screaming in terror and frustration.

'*I don't want to die! I don't want to die!*' he'd repeated over and over.

Pendrake heard the explosion, rushed out of his office, through Lewis's, and outside. She was hot on his heels. They made it in time to see the blaze and the rising pall of smoke in the distance.

'Oh dear God!' she exclaimed softly.

'I'm going out there,' he told her sharply. 'Stay by the phone. If anyone rings, tell them where I've gone.'

She was staring at the fire.

'*Section Officer Lewis!* Did you hear me?'

She brought herself back with a start. 'Yes, sir!'

‘Better get back inside,’ he said in a gentler tone. ‘Not much you can do.’

‘No, sir. Who . . . who do you think it is?’

‘That’s what I’m about to find out. Now off you go.’

He ran to the car without waiting to see if she’d done as he’d ordered.

He brought the car to a skidding halt, got out and ran to where Wilson and Charlton were standing. The crash crews were already at the wreckage, but the fierceness of the flames was beating them back. Even if anyone had survived the initial impact, there would have been no chance of effecting a rescue.

‘Who was it?’ Pendrake demanded.

‘Young Benson,’ Wilson replied flatly, not looking round. ‘I hope he died when it happened. There was a driver in that bowser as well. Couldn’t have felt anything though.’

‘Damn it!’ Pendrake muttered tightly. ‘Damn it! What happened?’

‘Over-corrected, sir,’ Charlton answered. ‘I warned him about that. I warned him . . .’

‘Steady on, Peter. Not your fault.’

‘Perhaps if I hadn’t mentioned it, he wouldn’t have been so preoccupied with correcting the swing that he forgot everything else.’

‘You can’t take the blame for that. Everyone gets a warning about the swing first time out. Afterwards it becomes instinctive. Now push off, you two. Talk to the others. I’ll hang on here. Bingo, see that there isn’t too much gloom and despondency around.’

‘Yes, of course.’

They went off while Pendrake remained, staring at the fire as it continued to defeat the efforts of the crash crew to put it out, though it did not spread.

‘The first letter,’ he said to himself softly.

The scar on his cheek seemed to glow as it was reflected by the fire.

9

Pendrake went through to his office without saying a word to Lewis, only vaguely aware of her troubled eyes following him as he passed. He went up to his desk and stood there staring at the cartoon Wilson had given him, hands at his sides, fingers bunched tightly into fists. A soft knock sounded on the door behind him, but he did not respond.

Lewis slowly pushed it open and stood in the doorway, watching his rigid stance. She looked down and saw the tightly closed fists, which after a while came reluctantly open.

She entered, closing the door softly behind her, and went up to him. Tentatively, a hand reached out, intending to touch his shoulder, offering comfort. Then she hesitated, changed her mind and brought the hand back down.

'He was so young,' she said.

'We were all young, once,' he retorted with a harshness that surprised her. He whirled suddenly and the cold fire in his eyes startled and frightened her at the same time. 'And people die.' He turned from her once more. 'Now I must write my first letter as a commander. Was there something you wanted?'

The coldness of his tone struck at her and she blinked uncertainly.

'I . . . I just thought you might want someone to talk to . . .'

He walked round to his chair and sat down, the cold eyes looking up at her. 'About what, precisely? About death? This is wartime. People die singly, in their hundreds, their thousands, every day. Pilots are going down all over the place. What makes this so special?'

His words shocked her. 'You know you don't believe that, sir!'

'What I do or do not believe is not up for discussion. I've got a job to do. More of these men are going to die before it's over, and it's up to me to get as many of them over the target as possible. And that's what I'm going to do. I want all of them in the briefing room within twenty minutes. Pull them off whatever they're currently doing. If the Spitfire patrol is down, I want those pilots to attend. Thank you, Section Officer Lewis. Now please see that it's done.'

She was staring at him, the blue eyes suspiciously moist.

There was no warmth in his own eyes. 'I trust you have not lost the use of your limbs?'

'No. No, sir.' She tightened her lips, turned, and went out.

He waited until the door had closed behind her, then put his head in his hands.

Mackenzie was leading the Spitfires back to the airfield.

'Smoke!' he called to Wojdat in the second machine. 'How come we missed an attack?'

'We do not know it is an attack,' Wojdat said, eagerly checking that the two 20mm cannons and four .303 machine-guns of his Spitfire XIV were ready to fire, just in case. Wojdat didn't need an excuse for a scrap.

'Check us out,' Mackenzie ordered. Homebase would have warned of an impending attack, but you never know. It could have been a sneak approach that might have caught them by surprise and all communications could be down.

'Roger. Checking.' Wojdat pulled slightly behind and did a complete circle, scanning the sky about them for hostile aircraft. 'No bandits,' he eventually called regretfully.

It had been a source of constant disappointment to him

that since the downing of the 109s by Pendrake, no other enemy aircraft had seen fit to come calling. He would have been quite happy for such an event to occur every day . . . as long as he was part of the welcoming committee.

'Roger,' Mackenzie responded. 'Rejoin formation.'

'Roger. Rejoining formation.'

As Wojdat formatted on his wing, Mackenzie called the airfield. 'Homeguard to Homebase. Returning from patrol. Are you under attack? Over.'

'Not under attack, Homeguard. Repeat. *Not* under attack. You are cleared to land. Over and out.'

'What the . . . Did you hear that?'

'Yes,' Wojdat replied.

'Then what the hell happened?'

'We will find out soon, I think.'

Wilson was waiting for them when they landed, their faces registering profound shock when he told them what had taken place.

'Such a young boy,' Wojdat remarked softly, himself just twenty-two. He stared in the direction of the still-rising smoke, though the fire had by now been put out. 'He was not even nineteen.' He shook his head. 'This shit war. It takes all the innocents.'

'God damn it,' Mackenzie muttered.

'We'd better get along,' Wilson urged them. 'The CO wants to see everyone in the briefing room. He has a few strong words to say, I fancy.'

Pendrake stood before them grim-faced.

'I will not mince words,' he began. 'Benson is dead because he behaved foolishly.' He looked at the shocked expressions brought on by his comments and continued unrepentantly, 'Yes. You heard correctly. Benson was given clear instructions. He was particularly warned to remain calm. In short, he panicked and now he is *dead*. But I blame myself. Despite the fact that he handled the

Spitfire adequately and, given time, would have become a fine pilot, we do not have the time, and he was not yet ready for the Typhoon. I should have obeyed my instincts and rejected him as soon as I felt uneasy.

'I therefore give you fair warning – your first mistake, if you survive it, will be your last with this unit. I do not care what rank you are, how many hours you've got, how many kills, or how many aircraft you've flown. From now on, training will be intensified. If you're going to die, the enemy will be responsible. You will not be allowed the luxury of either ignorance or inattention. I will be absolutely ruthless with anyone who does not measure up. The manuals you were given were not doorstops. They're there for you to read, digest and understand. *Use them.* Flight Lieutenant Wilson!'

'Sir!'

'Carry on.'

'Sir.'

Pendrake stepped off the dais and went out.

'Jeez!' Elmore said to no one in particular. 'Some horsefly bit him in the butt? Why did he have to be so hard on Benson? The poor kid's dead, for Chrissakes. Fried to a . . .'

'Captain Elmore!' Wilson snapped.

'Yeah.'

'Shut it. Now everybody, back to work. I want each of you to make at least one Typhoon flight before nightfall.'

As they went out, Elmore found himself next to Kelly.

'What's with the CO, Sean? Doesn't he care about what happened to Benson?'

Kelly sighed. 'Sometimes I wonder if we come from the same country. Use your brains, Elmore. Of course he cares.'

'Got a helluva way of showing it.'

'If you live long enough to get a command, you might understand. Just.' Kelly walked on ahead.

'I only asked a simple question,' Elmore muttered to himself.

'Perhaps you are a simple man,' commented Wojdat, who was passing by.

'Great,' Elmore retorted. 'Now I've got a darned Polack on my back.'

But Wojdat was already out of earshot.

Back in his office, Pendrake laboured over the best way to compose the letter he needed to write to Benson's parents. Was there ever a best way? he wondered. How do you tell doting parents that their only son, barely nineteen, has burned to death in his aircraft?

'You don't,' he said aloud.

You tell them about a young boy, eager to do his bit, but frightened too. No. Don't tell them about being frightened, in case your own fears and your own hatred of the enemy permeate the letter. Don't spoil their picture of their son.

He paused, temporarily defeated, and suddenly began to appreciate the difficulties of Foxy the Viscount, his former CO, in similar circumstances.

'You knew what you were doing, you old schemer,' he said, 'when you recommended me for this command. I wish you could take it back.'

But Pendrake knew there would be no respite for him. The joys of command, as Montcarneau had so perceptively remarked.

He started on the letter for the third time.

Wilson and his fellow instructors took Pendrake's words to heart. For the next three days, the airfield echoed with the continuing bellow of Napier engines. It seemed there was never a moment when a Typhoon or two was not in the air.

Wilson pushed the pilots hard and from time to time Pendrake turned up at Dispersal to check progress. On each occasion, he went away feeling pleased, but giving nothing away. Keane was at last passed fit to fly, and the Australian put in as many hours as he possibly could until he caught up and then surpassed many of those who had started before him.

There were no other accidents. Elmore learned to take off in a straight line, and to land the aircraft smoothly. The time was fast approaching when they would all be taught to use the Typhoon in the role it was designed for: as a formidable fighting weapon, in all weathers, and at any time of the day or night.

Pendrake was so satisfied with progress that he gave them a day of rest, but they were still required to continue their study of the manuals.

The morning of that day dawned brightly and the tired pilots were so relieved that after the three days of virtually non-stop intensive flying they could enjoy a lie-in, most of them missed breakfast. Wojdat, who never seemed to get tired, had volunteered to fly the Spitfire patrol. And Elmore, who never missed breakfast no matter what, was another of the exceptions. He was detailed to be Wojdat's wingman.

The noise, when it came, startled the dozing pilots awake and they rushed to their respective windows to check, primed to head to the nearest shelters, expecting an attack. The multiple sound of powerful engines approaching seemed to fill the world.

'Who's on patrol?' someone yelled.

'Must be Elmore and Wojdat,' came an answer. 'They're not here. Mason-Dixon never passes up a chance to eat, and Wojdat won't stop flying until he gets every Jerry, or they get him.'

'An attack?'

'We'd better get out of here if it is.'

But when they rushed outside, an astonishing sight greeted them.

Six black Typhoons, in perfect echelon starboard formation and trailed by two Spitfires, were approaching the airfield. When the first aircraft reached a point roughly halfway along the runway, it broke smartly left and up into a crisp ninety-degree bank to curve across on to a reciprocal heading. The mighty Napier was throttled back, the aircraft banked once more, wheels coming down. With exact precision, each following aircraft performed the same manoeuvre, including the Spitfires, giving the impression of a vast fan spreading in the air across the airfield.

'Wow!' exclaimed Kelly. 'They look beautiful. Those guys handle those planes like aces. Somebody must like us. The CO's got his extra Tiffies.'

'Those Spits are extra too,' a voice said. 'That's not Wojdat and Elmore.'

'You're right,' Mackenzie said. He was staring upwards at two small shapes. 'They're up top.'

'So now we've gotten *four* Spits as well.' Kelly sounded pleased. 'Great! Wonder who's bringing them in. Did you see those peel-offs? Beautiful, beautiful.'

'For an air show,' a cautionary voice put in. 'But can they fight?'

The first Typhoon landed. It was a classic three-point touchdown. The remaining aircraft followed precisely in its wake.

'God,' Kelly said. 'Don't those landings make you feel sick with envy? Hey, you don't think the CO's so cheesed with us,' he went on to them all, expressing a sudden worry, 'he's asked for new pilots, do you? I mean, after what he said when Benson . . .'

'He gave us a day off. He wouldn't do that unless he felt we were getting things right,' Keane said from a doorway. Instinctively, he rubbed at his right shoulder.

'One way to find out,' Mackenzie said. 'Let's get dressed and see who they are.'

'Now why didn't you think of that, Kelly?' a new voice, the New Zealander, Knowles, demanded.

They all laughed and hurried back inside, but Kelly's words had sounded ominous.

A second surprise awaited the Cobra Squadron pilots when they'd made it to Dispersal. The new aircraft were being marshalled to a stop, and one by one the engines were cut. The abrupt, relative silence appeared to leave the echo of their arrival hanging in the March air.

Kelly, Dodson and Mackenzie were the first to reach the lead aircraft. As they did so, the patrol Spitfires swept low along the runway then broke into their own rather spectacular peel-off, to come curving in to land. Wojdat had always been a superb practitioner of the art, but Elmore was catching up. Both made excellent landings.

However, not many people were watching. Nearly all attention was focused on the new Typhoons and Spitfires.

Kelly, Dodson and Mackenzie watched agape as the pilot of the lead Typhoon, goggles still on, slid back the hood, then picked up something from within the cockpit and began applying it carefully.

'What the hell?' Kelly began softly, astonished. '*Lipstick?*'

The helmet came off, and a mass of blonde hair tumbled down.

'Oh . . . my . . . God,' Dodson whispered in reverence. 'A blonde job. How . . . how . . .?'

'How are you?' Mackenzie called, stealing a march and hurrying up to the cockpit. 'Here, let me help you out of there.'

'Why thank you,' she said, smiling prettily at him. Her green eyes sparkled with amusement.

Male consternation was repeated at each of the other aircraft, including the Spitfires. All were 'blonde jobs', though they were not all blonde. They came in different heights, sizes, and hair colours. All were astonishingly attractive. The pilots, having witnessed the women's professional flying abilities, found themselves trying to balance their damaged egos with their desire to entertain their female guests. One of the female pilots was so small that they wondered how she managed to see over the nose of the huge Typhoon at all. Yet her flying had been impeccable.

'Kind of makes us look pretty silly, don't it?' Kelly murmured to Dodson as Mackenzie helped the blonde pilot out.

It was obvious she was quite capable of climbing out of cockpits, but chose to humour the Canadian. At the other aircraft, the rest of the squadron were also rediscovering the pleasures of chivalry.

'I have a feeling,' Dodson said, 'the CO's going to have a few stinging comments to make to us.'

'Funny. I've got the same feeling.'

Mackenzie dropped to the ground and helped his charge off the aircraft. 'Flying Officers Kelly and Dodson, Miss Amanda Treven of the Air Transport Auxiliary.'

She shook hands with each man, her green eyes amused by their confusion. 'Don't looked so shocked. I've been doing this for some time, you know.' Her voice was full of warm laughter. 'I've delivered many different aircraft, including Lancaster bombers. Mike Pendrake's the CO here, isn't he?'

'You know the CO?' Mackenzie asked.

'Oh yes. We're old friends,' she added mysteriously.

'Wouldn't you just know it?' a disappointed Mackenzie began. 'Just my luck.'

The ATA pilot gave him one of her best smiles. 'We're just good friends.'

'I've heard that one before.'

'Come on. Take me to him. I've got to deliver these aeroplanes officially.'

'Yes, ma'am,' he said, giving in gracefully. He turned to

see Kelly and Dodson hurrying towards the other aircraft. 'Hey. Where are you two going?'

'Pastures new!' they called back.

Pendrake's car, on the way to Dispersal, pulled up when they were halfway to the squadron buildings. He got out, eyes full of surprise. '*Amanda?*'

She gave him a great hug, while Mackenzie looked on ruefully. 'Hullo, Mike,' she greeted him warmly. 'Nice new rank, I see. How does it feel.'

'That would take hours to tell.' Pendrake looked at Mackenzie. 'Thank you, Mac. I'll take it from here.'

'Yes, sir,' Mackenzie said with his wistful smile. 'Oh to be a CO.' He turned and hurried back to where the new aircraft were parked. 'Leave some for me!' he shouted at the others.

Pendrake looked at Amanda Treven. 'What's this? You're here for a few seconds and you're already breaking my pilots' hearts?'

'I'm the one with the broken heart.'

'Amanda . . . you know that's not true.'

'Megan and I were best friends, Mike. It hurt me too when she was killed. And I'll even admit I was jealous when you married her instead of me. But you can't grieve for ever . . .'

'Let's do the hand-over,' he interrupted tersely.

She gave him a world-weary smile. 'I'll let you change the subject. For now.' She kissed him quickly where the scar marked his cheek.

'I'd heard you had taken up flying,' he began as they got into the car and headed back to the squadron, 'with the intention of getting into the ATA. But it never occurred to me you'd one day wind up on a station where I'd be, *and* flying a monster like the Tiffie, of all things. You were so . . .'

'Ladylike?'

'Not quite that . . . but you know what I'm getting at.'

She nodded. 'People used to think I was just an empty-headed blonde, waiting for the right moment to snare an indolent young man with inherited wealth . . . but war changes many things.'

'I never believed that about you.'

'I know,' she told him fondly. 'That was why I thought Megan was so lucky . . .' She stopped suddenly. 'Oh my God, Mike. I'm . . . I'm so sorry. That was quite stupid of me.'

'Not to worry,' he assured her; but his eyes had briefly lost their welcoming warmth as the memory of Megan's death once more assailed him. 'And here we are. My first squadron.'

Lewis was standing outside, near the entrance. She looked interestedly at the car as it drew up.

'And who's that pretty thing waiting so patiently for you?' Amanda Treven enquired pointedly, eyes sharpening. 'My word. She's even wearing nylons.'

'Section Officer Karen Lewis, my adjutant. And I haven't noticed the nylons.'

'Your adjutant, in nylons, and you haven't noticed. She looks frightfully possessive. Should be an interesting evening.'

He glanced at her as he parked in his slot. 'Evening? You're staying the night?'

'But of course. All of us. The Ansons will be picking us up tomorrow, to take us back to HQ at WW.'

'This will make the boys happy. I gave them the day off.'

'And you? Will you be happy? Will I see you in the mess later?'

'You will.'

'And Section Officer Lewis?'

'What of her?'

She gave a private smile of mystery. 'We shall see what we shall see.'

'Behave yourself, Amanda.'

'I always behave myself . . . according to my own lights.'

Pendrake's own tiny smile betrayed memories of times that seemed centuries ago. How innocent we all were, he thought.

'I know how you behave,' he told her.

'Forewarned is forearmed,' she said unrepentantly.

As they climbed out, she saw that Karen Lewis's blue eyes were riveted on her.

'If that isn't a challenge,' she murmured to herself, 'I don't know what is.'

They were having a rare old time in the mess that evening. Outside, a light flurry of snow eddied about. It didn't settle. The ATA pilots, some of whom had not seen each other for several days and even weeks before the ferry flight, were catching up on horror stories about particular aeroplanes they'd previously delivered to other units. The squadron pilots, meanwhile, danced attendance on them. For the evening, Pendrake had invited the sergeant pilots as guests of the mess.

Wojdat was in his element, having discovered to his joy that not only was one of the ATA pilots a Pole, but her family happened to come from a small town close to his own home. They were conversing with each other in a torrent of animated Polish, each glad to have someone with whom to share the language. Roza Licyzyk was so petite that she looked tiny by comparison with all the other women pilots. Yet she had brought in a hulking Typhoon.

Over in a cosy corner, Michel Montcarneau was holding court to an attentive statuesque, black-haired beauty and three squadron pilots who dearly wished he would go away and leave her to them.

The barman had turned on the speakers that were part

of the station's radio diffusion system. Glenn Miller's *Moonlight Serenade* was softly playing.

Observing Wojdat talking to little Roza at one end of the room, Elmore said, 'I can hear the old man tomorrow. "If a slip of a girl like that can fly the Typhoon",' he continued in an atrocious imitation of an English accent, '"you should be ashamed if you cannot".'

'He'll never say that, Mason-Dixon,' Dodson said, going past with two beers. 'And that was a wretched accent.' He handed one to an elegant redhead at a nearby table, and sat down.

They'd brought two tables together. Four of them had managed to secure the company of two of the ATA pilots, of whom the redhead was one. The other was a sultry but very self-contained brunette with eyes that looked out upon the world with clinical detachment as she swayed very slightly to the music. Her husband, a lieutenant commander on a destroyer, had been torpedoed in the Atlantic two years before. His body was never found.

'You wait,' Elmore said with baleful promise. 'Where is he, anyway?'

'Entertaining our leader,' the redhead, Marcia Torrance, informed him. 'They know each other from way back.'

'Oh ho!' Elmore said.

'Leave it,' Mackenzie said to him sternly.

The brunette, Eileen Taft, gave him one of her less detached looks. 'You're always quick to defend him. Your CO, I mean.' It was a question as well as a statement.

'He has a tough job,' Mackenzie told her. 'He needs all the breaks he can get.'

'Well, he's sure got a break tonight,' the irrepressible Elmore announced brightly. 'Not one, but two. Take a look, guys.'

They all looked and saw Pendrake enter with both Amanda Treven and Karen Lewis.

'Who is she?' Eileen asked in a voice heavy with meaning.

'That is Section Officer Lewis,' the fourth squadron pilot in the group replied. He was a sergeant named Williams, who came from Newport in Wales. 'Our adjutant.'

'She's very pretty and despite that pleasant smile trapped on her face, I'd say she's not happy to have our Amanda hovering around your CO. Not happy at all. Wouldn't you say so, Marcia?'

'Oh, I would. I would. To a woman, it's very obvious. Mind you, he's rather nice. That scar suits him. The battle-hardened warrior. Sends a woman weak at the knees.'

'Hey,' Elmore began in an aggrieved tone. 'Hold it. We're nice too. We're warriors as well. I was with an Eagle Squadron. Gotten me a couple of 109s and a 110. And Dodson, Mac and Taff Williams have . . .'

She patted him on the knee. 'Of course you're all warriors.' She glanced in Pendrake's direction. 'Strange, though, he doesn't seem really interested in either of them.'

'His wife died,' a voice said evenly from above.

They looked up, startled, and saw Bingo Wilson.

'Two days after they were married,' he continued in the same calm voice. 'Blown to bits by a bomb. He was there at the time. Not a scratch on him.'

Both women paled.

'How terrible!' Marcia said.

'He's handling it,' Wilson said in the same unruffled voice. 'He can take care of himself. Go easy on the liquids, gentlemen,' he went on to the pilots. 'You fly tomorrow. You will not be allowed to fly if, in the MO's opinion, your blood's changed places with alcohol. Not being able to fly will count very badly against you indeed. Within those parameters, enjoy yourselves.' He moved on.

Watching as Wilson stopped at another table to pass on his warning, Elmore said, 'He must have been a nice guy, once. I remember when . . .'

'Oh come on,' Mackenzie said. 'You know he's right.'

In the silence that descended, the music came to an end. The voice on the radio said, 'And here is another popular number.'

The upbeat of *Tuxedo Junction* flowed from the speakers.

Eileen, tapping a finger lightly to the rhythm, was looking in Pendrake's direction.

'He's still in love with his wife,' she observed quietly.

'A challenge to any woman, something like that,' Marcia remarked shrewdly. 'And irresistible.'

'Hey,' Elmore pleaded. 'Ladies. We're still here.'

'Of course you are, darling,' she said. She lit a cigarette and looked at him through the smoke that she blew. She smiled at them all, a little sadly. 'Isn't war hell?'

They had found a quiet table. As the women sat down, Pendrake said, 'What's it to be?' He looked at each of them in turn.

'Can your mess barman run to mixing a Martini, if you've got the stocks?'

'I think he can manage. As you can see by the unit badges, the Americans were here and they left quite a few things. And we've got a shaker.'

'You remembered.'

'I've not been on another planet, Amanda. Karen?'

She'd been listening to their banter, feeling a little out of it. 'Er . . . a beer, please, sir.'

'Let's dispense with the "sir", shall we?'

'Yes, s . . .' She stopped, and gave a quick nod.

'Share a Martini with me,' Amanda said to her unexpectedly.

'But I . . .'

'Get her a Martini, Mike.'

Pendrake looked at Karen. 'Is that all right?'

After a pause, she gave another quick nod.

'A little protective of you, isn't he?' Amanda said as Pendrake went up to the bar. 'Nice to see. But take my advice. Don't fall in love with him.'

A bright flush appeared briefly along Karen's jawline and upper neck. 'I . . . I don't know what you mean,' she said quickly.

'My dear, you've just betrayed yourself with those simple words. And I won't mention your blushes. He's still in mourning. Believe me. I know. She was my best friend and after it happened I tried to snap him out of it. I confess to having a personal interest. But it didn't work. We lost touch for nearly two years. It's the first time I've seen him since.'

Amanda paused, then went on reflectively, 'I wanted him to choose me instead of Megan. Of course, there was not the slightest chance. He was absolutely mad about her. And yet, if he had chosen me, I'd be the one who was dead. I wouldn't have flown that aircraft in today; and I wouldn't be here, trying to talk you out of falling for him. Bit of a thought, isn't it?' She gave a slight shiver.

Karen glanced to where Pendrake was waiting as the barman mixed the drinks. Amanda studied her expression closely.

'God,' the ATA pilot said softly, resignation in her voice. 'You have got it bad. Does he know? And please don't deny it – not to a . . . veteran like me, anyway.'

Karen shook her head, not trusting herself to speak.

'Just as well,' Amanda said. 'But please bear in mind what I said. When he does come out of it, you may not like the man that emerges.'

'And you?'

'If I loved him, I wouldn't care what he was like.'

'And do you love him?'

Amanda looked sideways at Karen, her head tilted

slightly, glanced to where Pendrake was collecting the drinks and putting them on a small tray, then back to Karen again.

'Who knows?' she said.

10

There was no snow on the ground the next day.

Two Ansons arrived an hour after breakfast for the ATA pilots, who gave addresses and telephone num- bers to the squadron aircrew who were in turn forbidden to make contact until after the mission. Bingo Wilson's warning had been taken very seriously and the medical officer had passed everyone fit to fly.

Pendrake accompanied Amanda to the waiting aircraft.

'Let's not allow another two years to pass,' she said to him, her green eyes searching his face. 'In fact, let's not even wait two months. How about dinner in town?'

'Don't say the Ritz,' he said. 'Everyone planning to meet in London always says the Ritz, or the Savoy.'

'Did you plan to take Megan to either?'

'Both,' he admitted reluctantly.

'All right. Not the Ritz, or the Savoy. I know a nice little place. Guaranteed not to be crowded by every uniform in the country.' She kissed him quickly on the mouth. 'Do look after yourself, Mike.' She glanced about her and saw the rest of her pilots saying their goodbyes. 'Most of your young men appear to have come to see my girls off. A few budding romances, perhaps?'

'Does that happen everywhere they go?'

'Not always. We don't often go to one destination in such a large group. Roza seems to have taken to your Polish friend.' She smiled at him. 'I like Karen. She's nice.'

He looked at her questioningly. 'I thought I detected a slight . . . edginess between the two of you last night.'

'I wouldn't pay much attention to that. Woman's stuff.'

'Don't quite know what I'd have done without her,' he said. 'I'm fortunate she was assigned to me. She's rather a find. A treasure, really.'

'A treasure,' she repeated. 'I suppose so.' She turned and walked towards the waiting Anson. She didn't tell him she thought Karen reminded her very strongly of Megan.

The Ansons began to taxi towards the runway.

'That was some lady.'

Pendrake whirled to see Halloran standing behind him.

'Jack Halloran!' he exclaimed. 'No one warned us you were coming. Where did you spring from? I didn't see you come off the aircraft.'

Halloran, carrying the familiar briefcase, grinned at him. 'That's because you were so busy saying goodbye. I got told the Ansons were coming from White Waltham to pick up your ferry pilots, so I got there fast and hitched a ride. Very, very nice,' he added, looking at the aircraft Amanda Treven had boarded.

'An old friend.'

'Very, very nice,' Halloran repeated. He held out a hand.

'How do, Mike?' They shook hands.

'Doing all right.'

'Like your new airplanes?' Halloran continued as they paused to watch the Ansons line up for take-off. 'Got your Spitfires too, I see.'

'Thanks for getting that through.'

'Anything to help.'

'Well, yes. The price might be a bit steep.'

'I'm sorry. I . . . heard about young Benson.'

The Ansons revved up for take-off then began their sedate run. As the squadron pilots, already kitted out, waved furiously, Pendrake could see answering waves coming from both aircraft.

Halloran said, 'Your boys made new friends?'

'Perhaps. But you never can tell, with a war on, how long that might last.'

'I guess.'

The Ansons drifted primly into the air and Pendrake headed back to his car, followed by Halloran.

As they got in, Halloran saw the pilots hurrying towards their Typhoons. 'Keeping them busy.'

Pendrake started the car and moved off. 'They're coming along. Benson's accident taught them a harsh lesson.'

'I hear you got two Messerschmitts.'

Pendrake glanced at him. 'So you know.'

'You made a report. Anything to do with this outfit gets passed on to me.'

'I want to talk to you about that.'

'Oh?'

'Those 109s weren't just wandering around looking for trouble. They were on a definite mission. They were looking for this place . . . for us.'

Halloran stared at Pendrake. 'What do you mean?'

'What I did not mention in the report I sent in, was the fact that they were armed PR jobs with long-range tanks. I decided to wait until I'd spoken to you. We retrieved one of their cameras. The pilot had already taken some shots . . . of the airfield, and even very detailed close-ups of the new Typhoons. How was it, I asked myself, that the enemy seemed able to mount a photo-recce so soon after our own arrival here?'

'You tell me,' Halloran said quietly.

'Someone's been talking.'

'Are you suggesting *my* people . . .'

'I'm suggesting nothing. Bend your mind to it and see what you come up with. Because they were able to penetrate so deeply, I've assumed they maintained strict radio silence. This means, I hope, their base has no idea of the circumstances under which they were shot down. So we're still unknown, for the moment.

'The pilot who took the photographs would only fight long enough in order to gain sufficient breathing space, to enable him to carry out his mission: taking the photos. That was such a priority, he was prepared to risk being shot down. He was a pretty good pilot too. Every time I went into the attack, he evaded, and would only counter when hard-pressed. In the end, I boxed him into a corner. He overcooked it, and went in. Just over there, beyond the perimeter.'

'Where's the camera?'

'Safe.'

'May I see the film?'

'Of course.'

'Has Michel seen it?'

'No. He knows nothing of the camera.'

Halloran was staring at him again. '*What?* You didn't tell Michel? Why?' Halloran paused. 'Oh come *on*. You can't suspect *him*. Do you know how long I've worked with that guy on the other side of the water? When I first started, he kept me alive and prevented me from making an asshole of myself. I could have gotten killed lots of times if Michel hadn't been there to see I didn't get my fool butt shot off. I was the original eager American who thinks he knows it all. Michel was very patient with me. Not him, Mike. He's got his wife inside that goddam place, for Pete's sake!'

'He could be under pressure. The Gestapo are past masters at emotional blackmail. They know how to turn the screw. If anyone knows about that, you do.'

'You're wrong about Michel.'

'I hope so. I like the man. But you've got to accept we've got a problem. I do not expect another intrusion up here. But when we move to the forward airfield, we'll be within easy range for a night bomber assault. If that happens, our aircraft may be destroyed and your mission sunk without trace. I'd suggest you get your people to seal off all potential sources of leaks; and do it quickly. Time's running out, if you want to keep to the original schedule.'

Halloran was silent as they drove on to the squadron.

'I'll see what I can do.'

'That's all I ask. My pilots have a dangerous enough task as it is.'

By the time Pendrake had pulled into his parking slot, four Typhoons were up in the air.

Halloran watched the short film in silence. Michel Montcarneau had not been asked to attend.

When it had flickered to the end of its run, he gave a deep sigh. 'No doubt about it. They came hunting for you. I'll get word to my people about it. Damn it!' He sounded very upset.

'Thank you, Sergeant,' Pendrake called to the Photo Intelligence WAAF NCO at the projector. 'Seal both the film and the camera, and keep them handy for the major for when he's ready to leave the station.'

'Yes, sir.'

'Well?' Pendrake said to Halloran as they left the small room. 'What now?'

Halloran tapped his briefcase. 'It so happens that I've gotten some new information from the château. New gun emplacements and troop positions.'

'*New* emplacements . . .'

'Not really new. Just ones that were always there but we haven't put on the model, and new positioning. Better get Michel to handle that.'

'What will you tell him about the camera and the film?'

Halloran gave a tight smile. 'Nothing. See? You've got me at it.'

'I am sorry. I don't want you to fall out with the man who's looked after you since this madness began.'

'Hell, there must be things he hasn't told me about . . .

in case I got caught one day. If he ever gets to know of this, I'll use that excuse.'

'Would he accept that?'

Halloran shrugged.

At the Château de St Sauveur, Mariette went for one of her restricted strolls in the grounds, under the stony gaze of the SS guards. There were wisps of cloud high in the otherwise clear sky. She heard a faint sound and looked up. Two fast-moving specks traversed the air directly above. She wondered whether one of them was piloted by Karl-Heinz Ketelheim.

'The Luftwaffe maintaining its constant patrol, madame.'

The suddenness of the voice made her jump and she turned to look into the vulpine features of Grüber. His smart turnout, his hair slicked to his scalp, only served to increase her feeling of revulsion. She gave no outward sign of this.

'I do apologize for startling you,' he told her smoothly. But there was no contrition upon the hated face. 'Not harbouring a guilty conscience, I hope?'

'What have I got to be guilty about?' she snapped.

'Now, now, madame. No hostility, please. You've always been so . . . cooperative. I would not like to have to revise my opinion of you.' Though he was softly spoken, there was an undisguised promise of the menace to come, should such a change of opinion actually take place. 'That would indeed be so unfortunate.'

'You . . . you startled me, Herr Grüber.'

'Again, I apologize most humbly.'

Having deposited his poison, Grüber walked silently away.

She looked about her and noticed a couple of the SS guards smirking openly. She decided to go back inside, her walk in the gardens now completely ruined.

* * *

Ketelheim was indeed piloting one of the pair of highly manoeuvrable and powerful late-model Focke-Wulf Fw-190Ds – specially designated Ta152Cs to honour the aircraft's designer, Kurt Tank – that Mariette had spotted flying high above her. He had deliberately altered his course so that his patrol track would cross directly over the château. He wondered what she was doing.

On the left side of the nose of the 190, he sported an emblem that had, from his early career as a fighter pilot, earned him the name 'Goldener Ritter' – Golden Knight. It was of a golden armoured knight mounted upon a golden charger at full gallop, lance held ready, surrounded by a black border. The pilots of his new unit had copied it and inevitably, they were known as the Golden Knights. He was quite touched by this mark of respect.

His thoughts lingered upon Mariette as the day for the invited return approached. He knew that Franz Meckler was virtually pawing the ground in his eagerness to get Odile into bed. But his own feelings about Mariette were ambivalent. After the shock of Trudi, he was not sure that he could feel any real warmth for a woman any more. A visit to a knocking shop seemed to him a far more honest form of distraction.

Yet, in a country where the invaders were heartily despised by a vast section of the populace, it was a welcome relief to be able to spend some time in the company of someone as pleasant and as sophisticated as Mariette.

'Black Two,' he called.

'Black Two,' came the crisp acknowledgement.

'Come in closer.'

'Coming in.'

He watched approvingly as Oberfeldwebel Jürgen Prinz tucked smoothly in. The boy was a good pilot.

Strange how life changed in so many confusing ways.

Jürgen Prinz, son of a local chemist, came from his own home town and had lived only a few streets away. He wondered if the old chemist's shop was still standing.

Before I was sent to the Eastern Front, he reminisced, *he was just a child. Now he's a senior sergeant, flying on my wing.*

Prinz was a recent addition to his forces and had not yet been blooded, having not had a kill. The boy was eager to put that right. Ketelheim had taken responsibility for introducing him into the complexities of aerial warfare, and had made him his personal wingman.

He spotted a column of smoke in the distance. It was a good thirty kilometres away, and outside his patrol area. Other units would be engaged.

Prinz had also seen it. 'Black One! Some action?'

'I feel as you do, Jürgen,' Ketelheim said. In the air, he sometimes used the familiar '*du*' with the younger pilot. 'But we will not stray outside the patrol area. Some Tommies and Amis will come into our net. Have patience.'

He was as frustrated as Prinz felt. He, too, wanted action. But it did not come that day.

They were lucky with the weather and although the forecast was for rain the next day, it was as if spring had arrived. Meckler picked Ketelheim up in the Mercedes 540K. Each was in a spotless uniform and wearing a side-arm.

As he climbed in, Ketelheim was amused to see a bunch of flowers behind the seats. He had also brought one. Meckler watched as he placed it next to the other.

'So. I persuaded you.'

'Don't read too much into it,' Ketelheim said as the Mercedes roared off. 'I'm going for a restful afternoon.'

'You might be,' Meckler remarked. He wasn't smirking, but there was no disguising his intentions.

'Do you really believe a French noblewoman, admittedly very . . . er . . . physical, is going to let you sleep with her, in her invaded country, and in her own invaded home? Especially a member of the Waffen-SS, no matter how apparently cultured?'

'"Apparently"?' Meckler pretended to be insulted. 'Smile when you say that. I am not wrong about her, Karl-Heinz,' Meckler continued more seriously. 'There's a spark.'

'Don't get burned. That's all I'm saying.'

Meckler sniffed loudly at the air. 'Away with gloomy thoughts, my Golden Knight! Enjoy that air. My blood tingles.'

'I'd check lower down,' Ketelheim suggested with a smile.

'Even though spring's not here yet,' Meckler continued, undeterred, 'summer's soon coming.'

Ketelheim looked up at the sky. No movement interrupted the cool blue of its canopy.

'And something else too.'

At the château, Mariette said, 'I don't like that look in your eye, Odile. This is not just some man you have taken a fancy to. Remember what I told you before. This is Waffen-SS. Play him for all you're worth to help the Resistance, but please don't get too close. I don't want anything to happen to you.'

'You fret too much,' Odile told her nonchalantly. 'As I've also said before, I can take care of it.' She had put on a dress that showed plenty of bare leg. She performed a brief pirouette that caused the light material of the skirt to flare and rise well above her buttocks. 'What do you think? Will this do?'

'It will certainly make him want to take it off. It may be a nice day, but you'll freeze.'

'Oh Mariette! Be serious! I'll put a light coat over it.'

Mariette sighed. 'It will have to do, I suppose. Nothing I say will make you change it.'

'That's true enough.'

*   *   *

Agnès Grappin was hurrying along a corridor towards the baron's quarters when Grüber caught up with her on silent feet.

'Hello, Fräulein.'

She jumped and gave a frightened little squeal at the same time. 'Monsieur!'

For the moment, there was no one else in the corridor.

Grüber gave a wolfish smile. 'I seem to be startling all the women in this place lately. I'm beginning to get worried. You must all be hiding guilty secrets of one kind or another.' He raised a hand briefly to stifle her protests. 'Calm yourself. I am not trying to trap you. I am more interested in the . . . nobility.' His mouth turned down at the corners as he spoke the word. 'Have you heard anything of interest?'

She gave a nervous shake of the head. 'No, monsieur.'

'No matter. Keep at it. I have a policy of believing that no one is ever what he – or she – seems, no matter how outwardly convincing. Take you, for instance. You would like to kill me, wouldn't you?'

'Oh no, monsieur! No!'

'Oh yes, monsieur! Yes!' he mimicked contemptuously. 'It is what I would expect.' He reached for one of her full breasts. She flinched, but he held on to it and squeezed.

She gasped in pain. 'You're hurting me!'

He let go of her and she hunched herself against the lingering throb of his grip, half-expecting him to reach for her once more.

'Just remember,' he snarled softly at her. 'I can *really* hurt you, and your family . . . not forgetting your brother, for whom we can devise some very special treatment. Today the Malzey sisters are entertaining two German officers. See to it that you serve them, and listen to everything they say. *Everything*. No matter how frivolous. I will decide what is, or what is not, important. Understood?'

She nodded wordlessly. She knew just how much he could

really hurt her and all her family. Everyone knew what went on in the cellars. Everyone knew what had happened to Jeanne-Anne from the Resistance. Her eyes were filming over, but she did not break into tears.

Despite the rigours of the Occupation, her body still carried the remains of teenage puppy-fat – a ripeness that excited Grüber. His eyes roved lingeringly over her.

'Now on your way,' he ordered curtly, as if her presence had suddenly begun to disturb him. 'Come and see me tonight. I need to relax.'

Again she nodded, and hurried away. It was only when she'd locked herself in her small room that she allowed the terrible fear to overwhelm her, and at last let the tears flow.

Meckler did not slow down as they approached the barrier, and Ketelheim knew exactly why.

'Don't goad them,' he cautioned. 'They'd be quite happy to shoot us and hang the consequences.'

Meckler appeared not to have heard.

Ketelheim could see the Totenkopf guards beginning to ready their Schmeisser sub-machine-guns, despite the fact that they must have recognized the car.

'Franz!' he said, drawing out the name warningly.

Meckler still said nothing, then at the last moment, it seemed, slowed down and stamped on the brakes. The big sports car squealed to a halt, almost touching the barrier.

He grinned cheerfully. 'I can almost smell spring in the air,' he said to the guards.

For reply, they scowled at the two officers and clicked to attention. Their right arms shot out.

'*Heil Hitler!*' they barked in unison.

'The Oberstleutnant should not drive so quickly on this road,' one remonstrated as the other went to raise the barrier. 'There could be . . . accidents.' It was a barely veiled warning.

Ketelheim gave the usual Luftwaffe salute, while Meckler waved a vague hand as they drove through.

''Hitler!' he said in his deliberate mumble.

'One day, Franz,' Ketelheim muttered at him. 'One day.'

But Meckler was about to let nothing spoil his mood. 'Forget those humourless fanatics. Let us instead look forward to a most pleasant few hours.'

From an upper window that overlooked the front garden, Odile saw the Mercedes arrive and smiled to herself.

Pendrake was leading a flight of four Typhoons on a low-level training mission. Every pilot had come up to standard and despite a few rough edges, there had been no further accidents. All in all, he now thought, it hadn't been bad going. The schedule was being maintained.

'This is Cobra One,' he said to them. 'Remember what I said before take-off. I don't want to see anyone above me.'

He took a quick look round and was pleased to note that not a single aircraft was flying higher than he was. They looked good.

'All right,' he continued. 'Line astern. Now!'

They manoeuvred smoothly into the new formation, forming a neat line behind him. In the other three aircraft were Keane, Elmore and Williams. Keane's arm no longer appeared to give him trouble.

Pendrake looked ahead and saw the deep Cotswold valley he'd chosen for the exercise. He brought his goggles down.

'Follow me!'

He flipped the big aircraft on to its back and plunged downwards into the valley. He rolled upright, pulled the stick gently and was hurtling along at barely a hundred feet. One by one, with exquisite precision, the others followed him down. Their multiple bellow, amplified by the natural depression, echoed around it and pummelled the air.

Pendrake stood the Typhoon on a wingtip and hauled round a bend in the valley. A quick rearward glance showed the next aircraft right there, hanging on to his tail. Then the valley was coming to an end, a tree-lined slope fast approaching. There was space between the trees. He headed for the slot and rocketed up the hill through the screen of trees.

That ought to sort the men out from the boys, he thought as he breasted the rise and pulled into a steep climb.

He glanced back once more. No. There they were, slicing their way through the trees and pulling up in his wake.

He felt a smile of satisfaction stretching his lips in his oxygen mask. The fire was in their bellies.

But there was more to come. They would have to learn to use the aircraft as a weapon in all weathers, day or night. They would have to learn to attack in coordinated pairs, with split-second timing. And they would have to get it right in a very short space of time.

He took them through a punishing routine, forcing them to remain low throughout. There were times when he led them through spaces among the trees that would not allow passage of an aircraft unless it was tilted over on a wing. On one occasion it was like a slalom course where one mistake would result in a terminal collision with an unyielding tree trunk, or an embrace of branches. But they had to learn to use the trees. The trees were protection. A flitting dip behind a screen of them could mean the only difference between being hit and getting away.

Nobody panicked. Nobody made a mistake.

On their way back to the airfield, Pendrake saw another four Typhoons in the distance, low down, heading in the opposite direction. It was Bingo Wilson leading his bunch out.

Pendrake led the flight into an impressive peel-off for landing. Each aircraft landed perfectly.

'Keep this up,' he said to them afterwards, 'and you might be able to hit the target. Well done.'

He walked away, not letting them see the look of satisfaction on his face.

Elmore, feeling as if he'd just come from a gruelling session with a malevolent boxer, watched the receding form and said to no one in particular, 'I'm wrecked, but pinch me, somebody. I think I just heard a compliment.' Then he yelled, 'Hey!' And looked round.

Williams, the imprint of his oxygen mask etched on his face, was grinning at him. 'You said pinch you.'

'Well . . . well . . . not literally! And not so hard!'

'Oh. Sorry.' Williams kept grinning.

'You Limeys are crazy. You know that?'

'I'm Welsh.'

At the Château de St Sauveur, Agnès Grappin followed the Malzey sisters out of the building with a large picnic basket. Accompanying her, and carrying another basket and a couple of light rugs, was a young man who worked with her.

Meckler and Ketelheim were on either side of Mariette and Odile. As the party moved some distance from the château and were about to turn a corner past the family wing, they were confronted by a pair of Totenkopf guards.

Everyone came to an uncertain halt.

'We are your escort,' one of the guards said flatly. He was a Scharführer with exceedingly cold eyes.

The other carried a man-pack radio, the headphones pressed down over his peaked cap. He stared at them blankly. Both carried Schmeissers, with Luger automatics in black holsters at their hips.

Meckler immediately decided to take the initiative.

'Thank you for your concern,' he said to the guards, 'but the Oberstleutnant and I can offer the ladies every protection necessary. In fact, I was about to suggest that he and I carry the baskets and rugs, so that these good people can return to their duties in the house.'

The Scharführer, whose equivalent rank was that of sergeant, looked at the two officers as if they were the subordinates.

'That is not allowed, Herr Oberstleutnant. German officers should not carry baskets and . . .things for these people.'

Meckler ignored him and turned to Agnès. 'Can you understand German?' And when she had looked at him uncomprehendingly, said in French, 'We'll take the baskets and the rugs. You two can go back inside.' He reached for the one she carried.

But she would not let him have it. 'I must stay.'

He smiled disbelievingly at her. 'What's this? A chaperone? Surely not.'

Uncertain of what to say to that and fearful of Grüber's reaction if she did not remain, she stayed silent.

The Scharführer smirked. 'We'll accompany you,' he said in his native language.

'You will not!' Meckler countered. 'This is unnecessary.'

'Herr Oberstleutnant, I have my orders.'

'And *I'm* giving you an order, *Sergeant*,' Meckler snapped. 'I will tolerate no insubordination from you! You are not to accompany us. Do you understand?'

The SS NCO did not back down. 'I have my orders, sir!'

'Who gave them?'

The man did not reply.

'I see,' Meckler said stiffly. He turned to his companions. 'Please wait here,' he said in French, and strode back to the building.

His heels cracked rhythmically along the corridor as he went in search of one of the senior Gestapo men. He caught up with Grüber as the man was about to enter an office.

'*Herr Grüber!*'

The Gestapo deputy district chief paused. He did not appear surprised to see the furious Meckler.

'Did you order those men to watch us?' Meckler demanded sharply.

'Not to watch you, my dear Meckler. To escort . . .'

'To escort? Here? The entire area is saturated with my Panzer troops. Are you mad? Do you expect the Resistance to suddenly attack us while we're having a picnic in the grounds?'

'One can never be certain where an attack may come from.'

Meckler stared at him. 'You are now a combat strategist?'

Grüber stared pointedly at Meckler's decorations. 'I am aware of your prowess in battle, Meckler. I am also aware that your troops provide the area's security. However, within the bounds of this château, the Gestapo takes precedence over *all* considerations. Do not make an enemy of me, Herr Oberstleutnant.'

'You are threatening *me*? Who wants to make an enemy of anyone? I am asking for privacy, man! As a senior officer of the Waffen-SS, I will not stand for insubordinate behaviour by one of your sergeants. Would you like me to make a report of this lack of cooperation *and* insolence by one of your guards, to Gruppenführer Herrenbach?'

Grüber blinked slyly, and appeared to back down. 'Let us not make this something more than it is. I shall return the men to their other duties. Will that do?'

'Yes,' Meckler snapped. 'Thank you.' He turned brusquely, and walked away.

Grüber's eyes were venomous as they watched Meckler leave.

Meckler strode up to the waiting Totenkopf guards. 'You are relieved of this duty,' he said to the Scharführer.

The man hesitated, his expression giving no hint of what he was actually thinking. Then the radio crackled. The radioman stiffened as he listened.

'*Jawohl, Oberscharführer!*' he acknowledged. He glanced at his superior NCO who gave an almost imperceptible nod. 'The Oberscharführer has been ordered to tell us it is no longer necessary to escort your party, Herr Oberstleutnant,' he announced to Meckler. He didn't look annoyed, but his voice betrayed him.

'Very well. You are dismissed.'

They stood there just long enough to register the fact that they did not consider they had lost the encounter, then clicked their heels, gave a 'Heil Hitler' and marched off without a backwards glance.

Both Mariette and Odile had watched the entire incident with apparent indifference, but in reality were most interested in this display of latent antipathy between these two branches of the SS. It was something that might well be of use later.

'Come,' Meckler said cheerfully in French. 'After this minor unpleasantness, let us continue with our afternoon.' He turned to Agnès's male colleague. 'I'll take that basket and your rugs. No need for you to come and sit around. We can manage.'

The man looked uncertain.

'Do not be afraid. Those guards are gone. I have had them dismissed. Here. Give me the basket. Karl-Heinz, you take one of the rugs and Agnès's basket.'

After further hesitation and a look at Mariette, the man handed it over. Agnès, however, refused when Ketelheim reached for hers.

'No, monsieur,' she insisted. 'I will accompany madame and . . .'

'All right, Agnès,' Mariette said. 'You can come. You

can go back in, Philippe,' she went on to the young man. 'No need for both of you to wait on us. Thank you.'

Philippe gave a courteous nod. 'Thank you, madame.' He left them and returned to the château.

Odile gave Meckler a surreptitious look of resignation; but he was still cheered by the prospect of being with her. Perhaps Agnès would leave them after a while.

'Shall we speak German?' he asked. 'English? Or French?'

'Ladies' choice,' Mariette said, joining the spirit of his game. 'German, in honour of you two gentlemen and for bringing us such beautiful flowers.'

'We're most flattered,' he said to her, adding, 'Are we not, Karl-Heinz?'

'We are,' Ketelheim replied gallantly, 'and the flowers were a pleasure.'

Odile gave one of her more girlish giggles.

11

Each couple was lying on a rug, with Agnès sitting on the edge of the bigger of the two, upon which Mariette and Ketelheim lay.

'It's so peaceful here,' Mariette remarked in a lazy voice, 'it's hard to believe people are fighting a war.' She was leaning on an elbow as she looked about her. 'I cannot even see your soldiers, Franz,' she added to Meckler. 'Apart from those by the château.'

This was not strictly true, for she had spotted several in other places, and had noted their positions. Yet the silence was uncanny. There was none of the expected clanking of tank tracks, nor the surreptitious roar of an engine being tested; no practice firing of guns; no distant and disembodied shouting of orders. It was as if their part of the world were inhabited by ghosts of field-grey.

Perhaps we are ghosts too, she found herself thinking in the gentle warmth of the March sunshine.

Then Meckler's voice broke the momentary spell.

'They are there,' he assured her. 'Among the trees, on the slopes, in the vineyards, at the sides of the roads. All the way out for at least thirty kilometres from the château, in all directions. And with Karl-Heinz's aeroplanes up above, you should feel very safe.'

'I do,' she said. She looked at Ketelheim, who was lying on his back, eyes closed, cap partially obscuring his face. 'You've eaten too much and had more than your fair share of wine, Karl-Heinz. Are you asleep?'

'No,' he replied. 'I may have eaten well, but only sparingly taken wine. It's because it is so peaceful here, as you have said, that I feel so relaxed. I also have wonderful company. It's a beautiful pause in the dirty business of war.'

She smiled at his words. 'Then you are glad you came?'

'Yes.'

They had picnicked near a small stream that ran at the back of the château, some distance from it. In the strange silence, even the low murmur of the water seemed to make their own voices sound louder. Near the château, the flak guns on their special platforms could be clearly seen. These were manned constantly.

Odile and Meckler were lying close together – although because of the presence of Agnès, she restricted herself to tracing a finger lightly along his cheek and jawline. Her light coat had fallen open and the dress had ridden up, showing plenty of glorious leg and thigh.

'It's strange that we can't even hear the sounds of war,' she said.

'War, my dear,' he told her, 'is ninety-nine per cent waiting around for something to happen, and one per cent wishing it hadn't. Others may put it differently, but essentially it's the same thing.'

'It feels like the calm . . .'

'Before the storm,' Ketelheim finished for her. 'And the storm *is* coming.'

'You are certain?' Mariette asked.

'It must,' he replied. 'This whole thing must be resolved, one way or the other.' He moved his cap so he could look up at her. 'Either we win, or we lose – but it must be resolved.'

'And will you?'

'Will I what?'

'Will you win? How about you, Franz? What do you think?'

There was a long silence. Odile looked at Meckler keenly, while Mariette alternated her glances between him and

Ketelheim. Agnès, not understanding a word that was being spoken, watched them all, knowing that something important was being discussed.

'If I were Daggenau, or Grüber,' Meckler at last replied, 'I would say we are bound to win. But I'm a realist. If we do win, it will be at such cost that I do not believe Germany can survive as a viable state. If we lose, the price will still be high, but not as much. But Germany *will* survive.'

'And Hitler?'

'He won't survive.'

Ketelheim had now turned his head briefly to glance at Meckler, astonished that his friend had spoken so openly to non-Germans.

'I am surprised to hear a member of the Waffen-SS say that,' Mariette said.

'I am a soldier and, I repeat, a realist. Do not believe this means my Panzer troops will not fight. They will fight, and very, very hard for every centimetre of ground. The Allies will also pay dearly for their victory, if they do eventually achieve it.'

'Karl-Heinz?'

'I agree. My pilots will also fight hard. The Tommies and Amis will not find it easy.'

'Oh, do let's stop talking about the war,' Odile put in brightly. 'Let us enjoy the afternoon.'

'I agree,' Meckler said.

'So do I,' Ketelheim concurred.

Odile looked at Agnès and switched to French. 'You don't have to stay, Agnès. You've been very helpful. You can go back to the château. I'm sure Philippe would like that.'

'Philippe?' Agnes said uncertainly.

'Why yes. I thought you two were . . .?'

'No. No. There is nothing between us.'

'But Agnès,' Mariette began. 'Everyone knows he is very attracted to you. He is also a very handsome young man.'

'There . . . there is nothing, madame. I do not find him . . . attractive.'

'Oh,' Mariette said, as if she had made a dreadful mistake. 'It just goes to show how mistaken one can be about certain things.'

But Odile was looking at Agnès, a slight frown creasing her forehead.

On the other side of the Channel, Pendrake was continuing to push his pilots hard. Immediately after breakfast, he'd hauled them into the briefing room to give them their tasks for the day. In pairs, they were to carry out simulated attacks on a target building in wooded country at precise times, and from different directions. Gun cameras would record the action, and no one would be able to talk their way out of a mistake.

'Timing is of paramount importance,' he'd told them, 'if you are not to collide with each other. In the real thing, you'll have plenty to worry about, without wondering whether an aircraft coming in from another direction is going to keep you company in the cockpit. Only thing, you won't have much to say about it.'

It was now 1500 hours, and Pendrake was leading his second sortie of the day. Tucked in close was Williams, as Cobra One-Two. Over to the right was another pair, Wilson and Knowles, who would be attacking within twenty seconds of the first. The third pair of the black Typhoons, flown by Elmore and Wojdat, would attack from the left twenty seconds later. Simulated release of all eight rockets in a single burst was to be carried out by each of the six aircraft.

In the attack on the château, the concentrated barrage of forty-eight ultra-high-explosive warheads delivered by six aircraft would virtually reduce to rubble the section of building attacked. However, Pendrake had decided to split the flight so that at least two aircraft would attack the gun emplacements, first with rockets, then with cannon fire. When the attack on the château was complete, all aircraft would concentrate on the ground forces.

Pendrake reached forward to turn on the gun-sight reflector switch. Next was the weapons selector box against the left cockpit wall just aft of the supercharger lever, and rockets selected. He then swiftly reached to his right to flick on the camera master switch. It was all done within a fleeting moment with practised, instinctive skill.

'All Cobra One aircraft,' he now called. 'Target in sight. Take positions. Going down. Follow me, One-Two.'

'Roger.'

Pendrake rolled the aircraft steeply and plunged towards the woods. Williams followed close behind.

Pendrake took his Typhoon to fifty feet, below the treetops, as he hurtled towards the ruined manor house that was serving as the target. He had his gun-sight lined up on the gaping maw of a long-vanished window. The building rushed towards him. He pressed the gun button. The camera recorded his 'release' and he was hauling on the stick just long enough to clear the building before going back down again, hugging a slope as he made his escape. He glanced behind to see Williams right there with him.

He climbed for height, better to observe the progress of the other aircraft. They came in bang on time, from different directions. None came close to hitting the other.

He waited for them to format on his aircraft.

'Well done,' he said to them. 'Now, to see how well you *did* do, all film will be viewed on our return to base. The camera cannot lie.'

Says who? thought Elmore. He had a feeling he'd messed up his attack.

The next daylight attack would be done with practice rockets which had concrete rather than high-explosive heads.

When the films were studied, everyone had scored including Elmore, much to his relief.

'Sir,' he said, when they'd seen Pendrake's film, 'that pile of stone looks like it was *in* your cockpit!'

'Just an illusion, Captain,' Pendrake told him. 'Take comfort. On the night, the target will be shooting back and you'll have neither the time nor the inclination to see it like this.'

'Thank you, sir. That sure cheers me up.'

On the next trip out, Pendrake was again leading the same pilots, and again repeating the heart-stopping manoeuvre as he dived towards the derelict manor house. After the attack, target-range personnel – who were positioned well out of danger – went to check the results. The concrete rockets, even without their explosive charges, had knocked huge chunks out of the ruined building with the sheer kinetic energy of the impact. Pendrake's window had become larger. All rockets from each subsequent aircraft had landed inside.

The intensive training for Cobra Squadron continued throughout the afternoon. They would also be flying an attack sortie for the first time that night, with weak lights placed in the ruins, to give them an aiming point.

'That ought to be fun,' Mackenzie said when he heard.

While Cobra Squadron was continuing its work-up for the mission, the picnickers at the Château de St Sauveur had decided that the day was at last no longer warm and were reluctantly making their way back. As they approached the main entrance, a big black saloon, preceded by two motorcycle outriders in black SS uniforms, powered up the drive. The motorcade swept past them in a crunch of gravel and came to a halt at the entrance.

They paused to watch.

Boucheron, accompanied by his wife, climbed out self-importantly. Daggenau was with him. Two guards at the tall, ornate doors snapped to attention as the party went inside. The saloon and the outriders pulled away to park near the pool of staff cars and other military transport. Boucheron had studiously ignored Mariette's waiting group.

Then Daggenau reappeared, and approached them. 'Ladies,' he greeted them politely in French, before switching to German, 'Gentlemen. Ah . . . Meckler, may I have a quick word with you?'

'Certainly,' Meckler said, wondering what it was all about. 'Please excuse me,' he said to the others and followed Daggenau a short distance.

Daggenau stopped. 'There is to be a meeting here,' he began, 'of some high-ranking officers of both the Wehrmacht and the Waffen-SS, to discuss tactical responses to the possible Allied invasion. As commander of the château defence area, you are required to attend.'

'When is this to be?'

'One week from today. The meeting is at 1600 hours. Be on time. You may consider that a direct order from Gruppenführer Herrenbach who will not be attending, though Obergruppenführer Schlierhof will be. You may also, therefore, consider yourself Herrenbach's deputy in this instance. Feather in your cap, Meckler. You are being groomed. It will be a long session, and you may have to stay the night.' Daggenau glanced in the direction of Odile. 'However, I do not expect you will find that too great a hardship.' He did not smile.

'And what about Ketelheim? He's in command of the Luftwaffe element here.'

'He is not required for this. We will not be discussing air combat.'

'I see. If this is a direct order from my commander, I shall of course be there. When I return to my command, I shall check with him.'

Daggenau's eyes were hooded. 'I expect you to.'

'Thank you, Herr Daggenau.'

'Thank *you*, Herr Oberstleutnant.'

Daggenau then went back inside.

Meckler returned to the others.

'What did he want?' Ketelheim asked in German.

'It appears I must attend a meeting here next week.'

'Just you?'

Meckler nodded. 'It's a meeting of all ground forces. Senior staff officers. Schlierhof's coming.' He glanced at Mariette. 'It's not a dinner.'

She looked relieved.

'I'll be staying the night,' he went on to Odile, 'so perhaps we can share a coffee afterwards.'

The disappointment he'd felt at not being able to have her to himself for even a short while had evaporated as soon as Daggenau had told him about the meeting. He now eagerly anticipated returning.

Her smile warmed him. 'I shall look forward to it.'

In Mariette's room later that evening, after Ketelheim and Meckler had gone, Odile said, 'We must send news about the meeting. Our people will know what to do.'

Mariette nodded. 'Some new gun positions too. They're always changing around. It's becoming difficult to keep up.'

There was a slight pause, then Odile said, 'Did you notice anything strange about Agnès today?'

'What do you mean exactly?'

'I thought she looked very nervous. I'd even go as far as to say terrified of something. She was afraid to leave us this afternoon. And that story about Philippe sounded unbelievable. She actually told *me* once how much she liked him. She seemed to have forgotten all about that today. I'm going to her room tonight to find out what's going on.'

Mariette looked at her in alarm. 'Grüber's pigs patrol the entire house. You know what they'll do – what *he'll* do to you – if you're caught. He just wants an excuse.'

'Mariette,' Odile began dismissively, 'I know every secret passage and hiding-place in this old pile of bricks, stone and mortar. Have you forgotten how we used to play tricks on our brothers?'

Mention of her brothers brought a shadow of sadness to Mariette's features. 'I haven't forgotten. I also have not forgotten that of the four of us you were the best at finding hiding-places.' Her eyes now looked at her sister fixedly. 'You've being going out during the night, haven't you? You've been taking some of those messages to the Resistance. Odile . . . do you realize what those troops out there would do to you if you were caught?'

'We ask those who work for us to take risks,' Odile said unrepentantly. 'Why shouldn't we? What you're doing is very dangerous. I can't just play the man-eater all the time.'

'It protects you! We've lost our brothers. I don't want to lose you too. I know you've been going on raids.'

'What? Don't be ridiculous!'

'I've found your gun.'

Odile stared at her and said nothing.

'I followed you one night,' Mariette said. 'I came to talk to you and you were not in your room. I know the passage you used. It's the same one you used to go into when hiding from us when we were children. I found the gun in one of the places you used to hide your treasure when we played pirates. It's an American automatic. Where did that come from?'

After these revelations, Odile decided there was little point in useless denials.

'I found it near one of the tracks. It was in tall grass. I was hiding from a patrol one night, when I felt this thing hurting my elbow. At first, I thought it was a mine and I was terrified that if I moved I would blow myself up.

Then I worked up the courage to feel for it. There was ammunition too. I think it's Jeanne-Anne's gun. It was near there that they caught her. She threw it away when she saw the patrol, hoping perhaps that would be enough to save her. But of course, as we now know, she had those papers on her. So she might as well have kept the gun. I'll use it on one of those pigs one day.'

'Even on Franz Meckler?'

The question brought Odile up short. She had not considered that. 'If he tries to kill me,' she said at last, 'yes.'

Agnès was making her way to her room when the silent feet caught up with her and a firm hand grasped the soft flesh of her upper arm. As before, she jumped with a squeal of fear.

'You are very, very nervous, *Fraulein*,' Grüber said in his revoltingly silky voice. 'I am sorry I have not been able to see you sooner, my dear Agnès, but I have had a busy day. So many people to . . . interrogate. Come with me to my room. You can tell me what happened this afternoon.'

'But . . . but, monsieur. Not much! I . . .'

'Come with me!'

There was no choice.

The room was far more luxurious and elegant than any in which Grüber had ever slept in his life. It was also one in which he would have been most unlikely to, but for the war. He pushed Agnès in before him and shut the door, locking it. The force of his shove caused her to stumble forward, so that she fell untidily against the large bed. The heavy curtains were drawn, sealing in the soft lighting in the room. He began to remove his clothes.

'Get undressed,' he ordered.

'Please, monsieur!' she pleaded.

'Oh, do stop whining. Take off your clothes and talk. What happened out there today?'

Miserably, she began to undress.

'Talk!' he snapped at her. 'What did you hear.'

'I don't know, monsieur. I did . . . not understand. They spoke your tongue.'

He stared at her. 'You mean *German*?'

She nodded.

'Strange. Did they suspect you might have had an interest in what they would be saying and spoke German to prevent you?'

The implications of what he was saying served to terrify her even more. '*No, no*, monsieur. They just began to talk like that from the very start.'

'I see. Did you recognize anything? Names perhaps?'

'They did mention names.'

'Ah! Tell me.'

'Your . . . your name . . .'

'*My name?*'

She nodded, staring at him fearfully.

'And whose else? Speak!'

'Monsieur Daggenau . . .'

'And? Come on, girl! Are there more?'

She was practically speechless with fear now, dreading to say the hated name. 'Hi . . . Hitler . . .' She cringed, expecting him to strike at her.

His reaction was totally the opposite. 'They mentioned my name alongside the Führer's?' He spoke reverently, totally ignoring the fact that Daggenau's had also been mentioned. Then he looked at her suspiciously. 'Were they respectful? Or were they laughing?'

'Their . . . their voices were ordinary, monsieur.' She was so relieved that he hadn't struck her, she initially missed the fact that her naked body was now beginning to excite him.

'All right,' he said. 'We shall leave the subject for now. You have not really brought me anything. This means you will now have to please me.'

He reached for the cringing girl and turned her roughly

over on to her stomach. He licked his lips as the hint of plumpness about the back of her thighs sent him into a compelling arousal.

'Oh please!' she begged, her voice now muffled. 'No! *No!*' But she did not struggle, fearing he might hit her.

He grabbed her at the hips and entered her savagely, pulling at her yet pushing her down at the same time. She screamed into the bedclothes. Ignoring her cries of pain, he reached beneath her to grab at her breasts and continued to abuse her until he was finally satisfied, straining and shuddering against her with a loud groan of release. At long last, he collapsed upon her violated young body.

The subdued lighting of the elegant room bathed them in a gentle glow; but there was no love in this brutal place. Her muted whimperings, punctuated by the harsh breathing of a spent Grüber, were those of a small wounded and trapped animal. He lay on her naked back exhausted, a thin stream of saliva leaking out of his open mouth and on to her skin.

Odile, her dressing gown over her nightdress, made her way along a dark passageway that was unknown to any others but the Malzey family. She reached its end and paused to listen. All was quiet. She waited, remaining absolutely silent and after a while, let herself out and into a cupboard beneath a small staircase. She waited again. Nothing.

Slowly, she shut the entrance to the passage, then pushed at the false panel within the cupboard. The panel effectively hid the hatch that sealed the entrance. Once she had manoeuvred herself past the panel and into the cupboard properly, she pushed the panel back into place, then opened the cupboard door slightly. Through the crack, she could see the dimly lit length of a short corridor. She cautiously stuck her head out to look the other way. Empty. The distance to Agnès's door was a mere four metres.

Odile got out quickly and hurried to the door on bare feet. She knocked softly.

'Agnès!' she whispered. 'Agnès! It's Odile. Let me in before I'm seen out here!'

There was a pause, then hesitant shuffling.

'Agnès! *Hurry!*'

There was the sound of a key turning and at last the door opened. Odile slipped in quickly.

'Close it and lock it!' she hissed. 'Then put on a light.'

Agnès did as she was told, then as the bedside lamp came on, Odile looked at her in shock. Agnès was naked, her body drenched in sweat, her face marked by continuing tears. She stood there, slightly hunched, knees and thighs locked tightly together, feet turned in, with the toes touching, arms hugging herself so fiercely it was as if she thought letting go would allow her body to fall apart.

'My God!' Odile said softly. 'What's happened to you?'

Agnès remained as she was and wept silent tears, body shaking, but no sounds came out of her. Odile went close and put out a hand gently. Agnès flinched away. Odile persisted until at last Agnès allowed herself to be embraced. She continued to hug herself and wept for a full ten minutes before haltingly, then in a torrent of words spoken in hushed tones, told Odile all about Grüber.

'I'll kill him,' Odile snarled.

'Please! No! Do nothing!' Agnès said frantically, pulling away in fright.

'It's all right. I didn't mean I was going out there right now to do it.'

'I'm so sorry I spied on your family. You have been so good to me . . . but my family . . .'

'It's all right, Agnès,' Odile repeated. 'You haven't told him anything as yet. But one thing I don't understand. You say he's threatened to arrest your brother?'

Agnès nodded.

'But, according to you, your brother Armand's in the Resistance and Grüber already knows this.'

Again, Agnès nodded.

'And Grüber claims he knows what he looks like.'

Agnès nodded for a third time. 'Yes.'

'I see. All right,' Odile said gently. 'Put something on and try and get some sleep. Come. I'll help you.'

After she'd helped Agnès to get ready, she said, 'You must not let Grüber suspect that you have spoken about this to *anyone*. He'd certainly arrest your family, and you with them. Continue as before and take courage. He won't touch you again. We'll look after you. I'll say my mother needs you constantly. Now lock your door after I've gone, and try to sleep.'

Agnès, looking like a lost child, eyes mirroring the hurt that had been done to her, nodded wordlessly.

Odile slipped out and made her way back to the cupboard. She was none too soon, for as she pulled the door shut booted feet echoed at one end of the corridor, where they paused.

Odile remained perfectly still.

After what seemed like years, the footsteps continued but did not get closer, and after a while they faded.

Odile went through the connecting door to Mariette's bedroom and gently woke her sister.

'Odile!' Mariette said in a sharp whisper, staring at her in the weak light she'd turned on. 'What are you doing?'

Odile told her about Agnès and Grüber. 'I know his little game,' she continued in distaste. 'I think Grüber's managed to get Armand to work for him, but hasn't told Agnès. He's using his threat of arrest to blackmail Agnès into having sex with him. *The bastard!* When the time comes . . .'

'Don't do anything foolish, Odile.'

'I'm not going to use the automatic on him . . . yet. In better times, I would have asked Dr Norbert to examine her. God knows what damage that Nazi bastard has done. But if we have her examined, he'll know she talked.'

'His time will come,' Mariette said in a hard voice.

'Do you think I'm right about Armand?' Odile asked. 'Is he working for Grüber, do you think?'

'We can't know for certain, but we can find out. We'll send someone out . . .'

'I'll go.'

'Odile . . . no. There are others . . .'

'I'm the best person, and you know it. If Armand is being run by Grüber, he mustn't be alerted. You know I won't do that. And don't worry, I'll get back all right.'

Mariette hated the idea, but gave in reluctantly. Odile would still go, irrespective of her objections. 'When were you thinking of going?'

'Now, if I'm to be back by morning. And don't try to make me put it off. We've got to make sure Armand doesn't find out who's really in the cellars, in case he passes the information on to Grüber. I'll use the passage that comes out in the south vineyard.'

'That's two kilometres long! There could be all sorts of things in there. Rats, snakes . . .'

Odile smiled. 'They know me, I know them. We keep out of each other's way.'

Mariette gave a sigh of resignation. 'You've used it before.'

'But of course.' Odile kissed her elder sister quickly on the forehead. 'I'd better be going.'

She left before Mariette could say anything in protest.

Odile crawled out of the dark hole and into more darkness. A huge, half-buried boulder on a slope that had for centuries formed a perfect barrier, hid the overgrown entrance from the world. Her eyes had already adjusted themselves to the gloom within the secret passage so that to her the darkness outside was relatively light.

As she made her way past the boulder she heard the

drone of aircraft engines. She wondered what they were and hoped they would not drop any bombs near where she was. The thick clothes she wore could not have been more different from those with which she normally attired herself for the likes of Franz Meckler, and for those who saw her in the persona she liked to flaunt.

It took her an hour of careful progress, avoiding the SS patrols, to reach the point where she normally made contact with the Resistance. What she subsequently learned sent her hurrying back to the château.

Two and a half hours later, she was back in Mariette's bedroom, having first hidden the clothes she'd worn and quietly washed the dirt off herself. She'd made sure she used only just enough water, turning on the tap slowly so as to minimize the sounds of it going through the pipes.

'Are you awake?' she called softly in the dark.

'I haven't been asleep since you left,' came the reply. 'Well? Did you find out anything?'

They did not put on a light.

'News from England. Someone *has* been talking. The Germans sent two planes to look for the base, but they were shot down. If it's Armand, the Resistance will kill him later. We are to be ready for the attack in one week. I've given them the new information about the guns. I have also told them about the meeting of all those officers here next week, so they'll get word to England to make the attack on that night.'

'Then we must be ready for when it comes,' Mariette said.

'This poor old place will be destroyed.'

'It will be deloused,' Mariette corrected her. 'We'll build it again. Now you'd better get some sleep. You must be tired and I feel worn out, waiting for you to get back safely. Imagine what would have happened if your body had been found out there.'

'But it wasn't,' Odile said and went back in the dark to her own room.

12

The morning weather at the airfield was gloomy. Cloud cover began at a thousand feet and seemed to go up for ever. The Spitfire patrol had returned to report that clear air was at 25,000 feet.

The weather matched Pendrake's mood as he sat at his desk, staring at a blank sheet of paper. It was to be his second letter of condolence.

The night-time training had been a limited success. For though there would be no lights showing during the attack on the château itself, he had allowed navigation lights as an aid to the maintenance of formation during the first night-attack practice.

All had gone well until the time had come for the final pair. The last man in, a pilot officer named Farrand, perhaps excessively worried about hitting his companion, had moved out of the approach line. He became disorientated and misjudged his angle of bank.

Had he kept his nerve, he would have made it. But he over-corrected and his wingtip brushed some branches. Again, the speed of the aircraft would normally have caused the tough Typhoon wing to slice away at the relatively thin branches of the upper foliage, enabling Farrand to haul the lightly damaged aircraft out. Such incidents had occurred several times during combat. Lancasters had returned with sprouts of leaves on their wings, Mosquitoes with foliage in their cockpits, and so on.

Unfortunately for Farrand, among the branches was a particularly sturdy one that had survived just long enough to jerk at the wing. The Typhoon had pivoted into the trees and exploded in a night-searing ball of fire.

Dear Mr & Mrs Farrand

It is with great regret that I must inform you that your son . . .

Pendrake stopped with a sigh. He laid down the pen. This one was going to be no easier than with Benson. It would never get easier, no matter how many times he might have to do it. There would be more after the attack on the château. If he didn't return, it would be Bingo Wilson's job. At least they were all unmarried. Small mercies.

The sharp bark of engines starting, followed by a multiple bellow, told him that six Typhoons were getting ready for a sortie. He had not called a halt to the flying. The thousand-foot cloud base meant that if they remained below that altitude they would have a clear run to the target range. They would be into cloud at the pull-up, but could easily limit the gain in height and be back out of cloud for the return to base. Besides, flying in cloud held no terrors for them.

He knew they would see the spot where Farrand had gone in; but they'd be witnessing far worse over the Channel. They would simply have to get used to it.

He listened as the aircraft took off, all engines running smoothly. He listened until the sounds faded.

A soft knock preceded Lewis's entry into the room. Her eyes, full of sympathy, seemed extra large and dark as she looked at him. She had brought a thin folder, which she placed gently on the desk.

'Pilot Officer Farrand's particulars, sir.'

Pendrake looked at it. 'Is this what we all come down to in the end, Lewis? A few sheets of paper? Surely we're more than that?'

Unable to give him the answer he needed, she could only look on, wishing she could put her arms about him.

He looked up at her. 'No clever words for me today?'

'It's . . . it's not an easy one, sir. There are many answers to . . .'

There was another knock.

'In!' Pendrake called.

An aircraftwoman came through with an envelope. 'Sir . . . ma'am.' She handed the envelope to Lewis, who opened it, took out a single sheet and read swiftly. 'Thank you, Hilary.'

'Ma'am.' The WAAF left the room.

Lewis passed the signal to Pendrake. He began to read.

ATTACK ONE WEEK FROM TODAY. TIME OVER TARGET 0330 HOURS. TAKE-OFF 0300 HOURS. MOVE TO FORWARD BASE ABLE THREE 19 HOURS PRIOR. LEAK FOUND. H.

So they had discovered the leak. Pendrake was glad it was someone on the other side and not Montcarneau. He returned the signal to her.

'No turning back now,' he said.

'No, sir.' She folded the signal with exaggerated care and placed it back in the envelope. She looked paler. 'Sir.'

'Yes?'

'I'd like to move to the forward airfield . . .'

'Out of the question. You've got to hold the fort until we return. I have a feeling this will be our permanent home.'

'But sir . . .'

'We'll be there for twenty-four hours, perhaps forty-eight. Besides, we'll be within reach of hit-and-run night bombers, and the accommodation will be rather less salubrious. Hardly worth your being there.'

He didn't tell her he also harboured a nightmare vision of seeing her blown up by a bomb, just like Megan.

'Now don't force me to make that an order,' he said to her kindly.

'No, sir,' she said and went out quickly.

He sighed, and swiftly read through the thin file on Farrand before going back to his letter-writing, starting afresh.

Dear Mr & Mrs Farrand

It is with the deepest regret . . .

Ably supported by Wilson, Pendrake continued to push his pilots hard, not giving them time to dwell upon Farrand's death. Taking turns with Wilson and the flight leaders, he led various attacks into the target-range area, pressing them to surpass their own best performance. His methods achieved results, and two days after the signal from Halloran he began to feel they were at last turning into the precision-honed killers he wanted.

As for the pilots themselves, they discovered that their daily routines were split between flying, eating and sleeping. Even Elmore had developed into a finely tuned fighting machine. He hadn't lost his crazy sense of humour, but he had reined in many of the less-endearing aspects of his bravado.

Pendrake was again at his desk on the morning of the third day after the signal, when he heard the unmistakable sound of an Anson flying overhead. He picked up his cap and went into Lewis's office.

'Where's Montcarneau?' he asked as she looked up.

'Making a few last-minute changes to the target model.'

'I'll get him. I think his flight out just came in. If you need me in a hurry I'll either be in there, or at Dispersal.'

'Very well, sir.' Her eyes followed him out.

In the model room, Montcarneau was standing to one side looking at his handiwork, when Pendrake entered.

'Hullo, Michel. Finished?'

'Ah, Mike. My plane?' he said, and when Pendrake had nodded, 'Well, I am as finished with this as it is possible to be under the circumstances. Take a look here. Do you see those tracks which lead to the château?'

Pendrake looked, then nodded. The tracks, three of them, radiated in different directions.

'I suggest they are your best points of entry. You can get between the trees, and very low. Mark them on your maps. If you look here, here and here, you will see that you can be relatively free from the guns until you are near the château. Perhaps by then your rockets will be doing some damage before the gunners wake up. Two of the tracks are across vineyards, and the one in the south goes up that slope here, before flattening out to the château. That route is OK, I think.'

Pendrake studied the model closely. 'It was a possibility I had considered. Now you've recommended it, you've confirmed my hunch.'

Montcarneau looked pleased. 'I am glad I have been of help to you. And we are grateful for what you and your brave men are doing for us.'

'I'd rather be up in the air, Michel, than taking my chances with the Waffen-SS in those woods.'

'Ah well, see how different we are. I like to know I am on the ground. I can hide. In the air . . .' Montcarneau gave an eloquent shrug.

Pendrake grinned. 'I can hide too. But each to his own. Are you packed?'

'I didn't bring much. May I say my goodbye to the charming Miss Lewis?'

'Certainly. I'll wait outside by the car.'

'Thank you.'

In Lewis's office, Montcarneau said, 'He needs you, but does not realize it. Look after him, my dear.'

'I will,' she promised. 'And you, Michel, don't take any chances. Good people like you must survive this.'

'Thank you, my dear. I shall do my very best. Perhaps we shall meet again and if not before, then certainly after the end of the war, when we have won. You must both come to the château .... you and the brave squadron leader. It will be rebuilt after this. You must come,' he repeated.

'I will, and I'll make sure he's with me. It's a promise.'

Pendrake had a surprise as he approached the Anson with Montcarneau. Halloran climbed out, holding on to his cap against the propwash, and came towards them. For once, he did not have the briefcase. The aircraft's engines continued running, in preparation for take-off. This was clearly a very short stay.

'Thought I'd come over to say goodbye,' Halloran said over the noise of the Anson, holding out his hand, 'and to wish you and the guys luck. A Lysander's taking us over tonight. Got to be with my people when they go in.'

They shook hands firmly.

'You take care out there, Mike,' Halloran said.

'And you, Jack. As I said to Michel, I don't envy your mixing it in those woods with the SS.'

'Unfinished business.'

Pendrake nodded. 'I understand.'

Halloran gave a tight-lipped smile. 'Some heavy-duty brass are going to be in the château when you hit. Give 'em hell.'

'You too.'

A final handshake from Montcarneau, and Pendrake stood back as both men hurried to the Anson.

Soon, the aircraft was taxiing back to the runway, and in a short while it was lifting into the air, taking Halloran and Montcarneau on their way to whatever destiny awaited them on the other side of the Channel.

The day before the move to the forward airfield, Pendrake called all his pilots to the model room.

'Arrange yourselves as best as you can around the platform,' he said to them, 'and take a long, hard look.

You won't be seeing it again before the mission. At the forward airfield, you will receive a full briefing, prior to take-off. Your flight commanders are already well versed on the target. However, the briefing will cover in detail the purpose of our task.

'There are now twenty of us instead of our original twenty-two, and as a result there will be a slight reassignment of pilots for the attack. We shall have two flights of seven aircraft each, and one of six. One Flight, led by Keane, will go for the airfield. Two Flight, Dodson, the guns and tanks in the immediate area of the château are yours. Begin inwards and work your way outwards. I will lead Three Flight, comprising Wilson, Kelly, Mackenzie, Williams and Hargreaves, to attack the château itself.

'Your respective flight commanders will furnish you with the necessary information for the move to the forward airfield. Remain in here as long as you need to, for a maximum of two hours. Study the layout well. If you do get separated, you'll not want to waste time wondering where you are. Nothing gunners like more than a lost pilot stooging around trying to get his bearings.

'The flying programme continues today. There will be at least one sortie for each pilot to the target range, then you may all stand down. Prepare only your essential kit for the move. We won't be setting up home there and shall be returning after the mission, once we have landed at the forward airfield and rearmed and refuelled. Flight commanders' meeting at 1700 hours. Thank you, gentlemen.'

No one made any mistakes. Every pilot put his practice warheads right on target, and cannon firing at board targets placed near the ruined manor to simulate gun positions were shredded. By the time 1700 hours came round and the flight commanders filed into Pendrake's office, Wilson was looking pleased with himself.

'By the look on your face, Bingo,' Pendrake said, 'I take it we've still got all our remaining pilots.'

'Alive and kicking and ready to go, and the targets pulverized.'

Pendrake looked at them in turn. 'Well, we do seem to have managed it. Thank you all.' He waved a hand at them as he sat on the edge of his desk. 'Perch anywhere . . .'

Lewis knocked and entered. 'Just wondering if any one would like some tea. It's good stuff.'

All hands went up.

She smiled at them. 'Hilary will bring it in.'

'Take-off will be at 0800 tomorrow,' Pendrake said to his flight commanders as she went out. 'You've already got the route details. From now on you fly in pairs, the same leaders and wingmen as for the attack itself. We'll take off by flight, One Flight leading. Bingo and I will go on ahead, so your flight will seem a little undermanned, Mr Kelly.'

Kelly gave a quick grin. 'Undermanned, but just as mean, sir.'

'Be as mean as you like over the target and you shan't hear any complaints from me. For some time now,' Pendrake continued, 'various attacks have been mounted all along the coast of occupied Europe from Denmark to France. Tiffy 1Bs have been doing pretty much what I was, hitting at everything in sight. There has been an escalation of these attacks, to keep Jerry guessing. He'll not be expecting us at the château when we come knocking. We were nearly compromised . . .' He paused as the WAAF aircraftwoman came in with the mugs of tea on a tray.

Kelly sprang to his feet to take it off her.

'Thank you, sir,' she said with a shy smile at him.

'My pleasure.'

She hurried out, after giving him a glance that was certainly daring.

'All right, Sean,' Pendrake said. 'You can stop fraternizing with my staff and pass the tea around. Thank you,' he continued as Kelly handed him the mug upon which an anonymous artist had stencilled 'COBRA ONE'. 'We were very nearly compromised,' he went on. 'Hence those two 109s. They were searching us out. That particular leak, I've been assured, has now been plugged. But this does not mean we should take any chances at the forward airfield.

'The aircraft will be dispersed, with their pilots close by. Sleeping arrangements will no doubt be quite primitive, when compared with our current luxurious situation. As I've never been to Able Three, I can't tell you what to expect. So make the most of your time and have a good long sleep tonight. Tell your pilots.'

Pendrake stopped. They were all looking at him solemnly and he wondered if each was thinking the same thing.

How many would be coming back?

After they'd gone, he stood reflectively before his desk and looked at the aviation cartoon Wilson had given him. It was then that he sensed Lewis had entered the room.

He turned slowly to face her.

'Karen . . .' he began.

'No. Don't ask me to.' Her eyes, wide and dark, looked at him for the first time without deference for rank. 'Don't ask me to make arrangements for you. You're coming back.'

'It's a simple request.'

'No! You're coming back!' she repeated vehemently.

He tried again. 'No one knows what might happen. I want you to have the cartoon . . .'

'I won't listen!' She had stopped about three feet from him, her eyes never leaving his face. 'You can't make me.'

'Look, Karen . . .'

'No!' She turned away, to quickly leave the room.

He stared helplessly at the closing door.

In her own office, she tried to hold back her tears. It wouldn't do to be seen to be crying. She'd handled it all wrongly. That was not how she'd wanted to say goodbye to him. What if something did happen and he did not return? His last memory of her would be her refusal of his request.

There was a vivid picture of him in her mind: the scar suddenly glowing in a face made pale by the thought of what was to come and of the men he might lose. He'd looked so alone.

How could she do that to him?

Her entire body ached. What she really wanted was to have him deep and safe within her. She carefully dabbed at her eyes, composed herself and went back in.

He watched as she re-entered. He thought she looked a little strained, but that was to be expected. The great blue eyes were unnaturally luminous.

'I'll do it,' she said.

'Thank you. I've written a few letters. Send them off for me if . . .'

She nodded. 'I know.'

'I meant it about the cartoon.'

'I know you did, and it . . . it's very good of you to think of me.' A slight tremor had entered her voice. 'But I shan't have to take it because you'll be back.'

'Thank you for the vote of confidence.'

'Yes.' She seemed to be trembling just perceptibly, as if on the edge of control.

'Thank you, Karen.' he said again.

'Sir.' She turned, and went out once more.

Again he found himself staring at the closing door. Why hadn't he told her about the changes that had begun to occur within him? It was the first time since Megan's death that he'd started to . . .

He halted in mid-thought. He hadn't yet finished taking his revenge for what they had done. The scorched wood was still there in his mind, with bits of her all over the place. The nightmare was alive within him. There was still plenty to do.

That night, he slept soundly.

*   *   *

Punctually at 0800 the next morning, Pendrake lifted the black Typhoon cleanly and tucked in the wheels. Over to his right and a little to the rear, Bingo Wilson kept perfect station.

They banked sharply while still at only a hundred feet and curved round the airfield to head south for Able Three. As they turned, he saw that One Flight was moving on to the runway for take-off. The other aircraft were also all on the move. Soon, One Flight was taking to the air.

As he settled into a shallow climb with Cobra Two fixed in place on his wing as if glued there, he glanced behind to see the rest of his brood climbing in a series of pairs spread out over a great expanse of sky. It was, he thought, an impressive sight.

He felt proud of them.

Lewis heard the multitudinous bellow of the twenty aircraft and remained at her desk. She did not want to see them leave. The aching she'd felt the day before had pursued her into the night and was still with her. If anything, it was stronger.

I need him inside of me, she found herself thinking. But now he was gone, and might not come back.

She caressed the mug with 'COBRA ONE' on it. One of the ground crew had originally brought it to her, saying it was for the CO. She refused to allow herself to contemplate the possibility that Mike Pendrake would not return.

Karl-Heinz Ketelheim walked out to his Focke-Wulf 190 with a jaunty Jürgen Prinz at his side.

'Think we'll have some more action today, sir?' Prinz asked. He'd been blooded, had got his first kill, and was eager for more.

'Hoping for a repeat of our little sortie the other day, eh?' They had caught two Typhoons 1Bs that had strayed into their area.

'Yes, sir!'

'We might, Jürgen. Then again, we might not. Have patience. More will come. Believe me. Now let's see if today the Tommies or Amis might decide to wander our way again.'

But although they patrolled extensively and even saw smoke rising at several points in the distance, nothing came within their area.

Frustrated, they returned to base.

At the château, Odile had accosted Grüber. She was wearing a long, body-hugging dress with a split on either side that reached the upper thigh. As she walked, her legs were displayed in fleeting, sensuous flashes.

Grüber had observed her approach with undisguised longing.

'Good morning, Herr Grüber,' she began in French.

'Good morning, Mademoiselle Malzey,' he replied, his bad French making him sound even more unctuous than usual. 'To what do I owe the pleasure?'

'It's Agnès.'

'Oh?' His expression gave absolutely nothing away. 'And what about her?'

'You may have noticed that she's been on our side of the château for the past days.'

'I haven't,' he lied smoothly. 'Are you having a problem with her?'

'Oh no. It's just that my mother, as you know, is not too well and she wanted Agnès to tend to her. I felt that as Herr Daggenau and yourself are in charge here, you should know if we've changed any of the staffing arrangements. As Agnès will be spending this extra time with us, I felt it would be best to let you know. If you have any objections . . .'

'No objections at all. Of course, you do realize that if the Reich has need of her, we do have the right to demand her presence.'

'Of course.'

'However, I am certain the new arrangements will be perfectly in order.'

Odile gave him a melting smile she did not feel. 'Thank you, Herr Grüber.'

'My absolute pleasure.'

Talking to Mariette later in the family wing, Odile looked as if she wanted to vomit.

'"If the Reich has need of her",' she repeated his words with contempt. 'For "Reich" substitute Grüber. All the time I was talking to him, he was undressing me. It's what I was playing for, but even so . . .' She paused; the idea nauseated her.

Mariette waited silently for her to continue giving vent to her feelings.

'Horrible little man!' Odile went on. 'He showed no emotion when I mentioned Agnès. It was as if nothing at all had happened, but I could sense he was wondering whether she'd talked. I'm certain he thinks she didn't. The way his mind works, he can't believe I would know and say nothing. I didn't look as if I was hiding his dirty secret. I also think he feels he's done me a favour which he hopes to be able to call in later. Ugh!'

'Don't be complacent,' Mariette cautioned, 'even if he seems to believe it. That kind always suspects everyone. It's the trademark of the Gestapo, which is why he's part of it. If he even thinks she might have talked . . .'

'Soon it won't matter if he does know,' Odile said coldly. 'His time is coming. We must make sure,' she continued, the warmth returning to her voice, 'that the parents are safe before the raid begins.'

Mariette nodded. 'They're getting ready to go underground with us tonight. I'm glad we managed to get Agnès here in time. It's a pity about her brother. We'll never really know why he did it.'

'When this war is finally over,' Odile said, 'there will be

a lot of this kind of pain for many families.' She looked about her, as if saying goodbye to the room. There was no telling how much of the building would be left standing. 'The Resistance know which passages to use to get in and they'll be in place by the time the air raid begins. To think we could have all got out a long time ago.'

'You know why we couldn't. We couldn't leave our St Sauveur to those pigs and we're of far greater help to the Resistance, even as prisoners in our own home.'

But they knew there was an added, harsher and more horrific reason. Their compliance had been secured with the lives of the people of the district. Both Daggenau and Grüber had let the family know in no uncertain terms that an escape attempt, successful or otherwise, would have had dire consequences for the populace.

The decision to remain had not been difficult after that, despite the horrors being perpetrated in the cellars.

Franz Meckler was greatly anticipating his return to the château. Once the tedious business of the tactical conference was over, it would be a private coffee in his room with Odile. Who knew where the rest of the evening might lead?

He walked out of the small hotel that served as his headquarters, with his second in command, Major Udo Sonnenberg.

'Well, Udo, I'll leave it all in your capable hands when I go to see the big chiefs this afternoon.'

Sonnenberg gave him a sideways look. 'And the beauteous Odile, no doubt.'

'Aah, my good friend. There's a body! Magnificent. A true goddess.'

Sonnenberg smiled briefly. 'After the hell of the Eastern Front, you need something to bring a little cheer into your life. It's the first time I've seen you so worked up about a woman since . . . oh, let me see . . . Leni, Ludmila, Magda . . . Shall I go on?'

Meckler took no offence. 'This is very different. Leni was a boyhood crush back home. Magda . . . well, Magda was Magda. I hear she's now got a general in tow. In Russia, I helped Ludmila bury her child. She couldn't believe there was any humanity in a Waffen-SS soldier and perhaps got a little too grateful, then that bastard Major Kramer shot her when she wouldn't service him. Being a captain under the command of that Nazi shit was no joke.'

'I remember,' Sonnenberg said with feeling. 'It was even worse being a very scared lieutenant.'

'Well, the Russkis got him in the end. And very good riddance. I can still see the people we butchered in the name of warfare and ideology.' Meckler gave his colleague a brief pat on the shoulder. 'They took a piece of you too.'

Sonnenberg, a married man in his early thirties, had lost an arm. He hadn't seen his wife and boy for years. The last time, the child had been an infant. At least they were still alive.

'But you saved my life,' he now said. 'To this day, I cannot understand why you weren't killed. I'll always remember lying there looking up at you through a red haze while you stood over me firing that heavy machine-gun like some kind of Aryan hero from a bad opera. I hate to make your head even bigger, but you were magnificent.' Then Sonnenberg grinned. 'Especially as it meant I was going to live, after all.'

'Just stay alive, Udo. Just stay alive till this whole nasty business is all over. Germany will need men like you.'

Cobra Squadron swept in to land at Able Three near the south coast of England, in an impressive display of ultra-sharp flying. On approach to the well-camouflaged forward airfield, Pendrake had instructed all three flights to join up in line astern. Like a great black tail, the twenty aircraft roared in at minimum height to sweep into the break and peel off in a continuing, shifting ballet as Typhoon after

Typhoon stood on its wingtip to curve round for the landing. The pattern spread itself over a great area of sky. Those on the ground watched with awe and a surge of pride.

They landed one after another, with a regularity that the spectators would later claim was at precise intervals that could be measured to the nanosecond.

The first person Pendrake saw as he climbed down from his aircraft brought a huge grin to his face.

'Spy!' he exclaimed happily. 'How the devil did you get here? What did they have to bribe Foxy with to let you go?'

The Intelligence officer from his old unit looked at him gravely. 'So you don't know.'

Pendrake felt a knot in his stomach. 'Know what?' And as Stanley's silence confirmed his worst fears, he continued, 'Oh no. Not Foxy. It's some mistake, Spy. It must be!'

Stanley shook his head slowly. 'I'm afraid not, old boy. It's been confirmed. Foxy took a new boy out on a rhubarb. You know what he's . . . was . . . like. Hated not being up in the air. So he took this new chappie out to show him the works.

'They got bounced just south-east of Caen, by two Me-109s. There was a heavy flak battery nearby and it put up a ferocious barrage. The Jerry gunners didn't seem to care if they hit their own aircraft. The new boy caught a packet from the flak, but was only damaged. Foxy sorted out the two 109s and got them both. But his wingman, a kid named Patterson, had suffered mild engine damage and had lost some speed. Naturally, Foxy began to shepherd him out of the area and headed for home.

'The battle had taken them away from the flak, but they were not out of the woods yet. As they made their way back, two Fw-190s came flashing down from up high. Patterson went down on that first pass. The poor blighter never knew what hit him. And Foxy himself got peppered, but he was still able to fight. The Tiffy's a tough old bird, as you well know. But something strange was happening. One of the 190s seemed to take little part in the proceedings, except to herd poor Foxy into the guns of the other. There were Golden Knight emblems on the 190s.

'The Resistance saw those when the fight came low enough. Said it reminded them of a hunt where the skilled hunter would initiate the recruit, helping him with his first kill. It was murder, Mike. According to the people on the ground, Foxy outwitted the unskilled pilot every time, but each time he went in for the kill, the ace came down to chase him off. It went on like that for ages. I think they just wore old Foxy down, and he must have been distracted by his diminishing fuel by then.'

Pendrake, listening to the tale with a simmering anger, took time to reflect how he himself had driven the pilot of the photo-recce Messerschmitt 109 to distraction over the home airfield. The pilot had been very good, and he'd simply used all his own skill to eventually gain the upper hand. It was war. But this had been a cold-blooded game.

'In the end,' Stanley was saying, 'the ace virtually set it up for his comrade, who took the shot. And that was it. Foxy never got out. There was no chute.'

Pendrake had listened to the harrowing tale benumbed, his fury growing by the second. He felt a powerful heat behind his eyes.

'I'll bet he's the same one who got Braddock,' he said tightly. 'I hope I meet that bastard one day.'

'You well might,' Stanley told him. 'The area where Foxy went down is right in your target area. That 190 may well come from the airfield.'

'It's Keane's job to attack the field. But I hope he misses that sod. I want him up in the air.' Pendrake removed his helmet and gripped at it, as if squeezing the life out of the unknown Focke-Wulf pilot. '*I want him!*'

13

While Able Three could not be described as a luxurious airfield, it was not as bad as the pilots had feared. The runway was steel matting on a bed of hard-packed earth. There was no mess, and sleeping accommodation was a series of four-man wooden huts with basic metal beds, not far from each group of dispersed aircraft. This arrangement suited Pendrake, for it meant the pilots of the Typhoon pairs could be reasonably close to their aeroplanes if they needed to take off in a hurry.

Everyone ate in the same building, another wooden hut, long and low-lying. Ops and Briefing were in a similar structure. The control tower was hidden among tall trees and was virtually invisible from the air. All other airfield services were similarly concealed. Even the dispersal areas were beneath camouflaged canopies. It was obvious to the Cobra Squadron pilots that Able Three had not been set up just for them and that the forward airfield had many other, clandestine uses.

The briefing began at 1700 hours. At the end of the briefing room was a huge map, with coloured tracks leading to and from the various sections of the target area.

First to speak was Stanley. As the Spy launched into a very detailed briefing of the mission, it dawned on an astonished Pendrake that the Intelligence officer had known far more about the matter than he had previously disclosed. By the time Stanley was drawing his brief to its conclusion, every pilot was fully conversant with the detailed aspects of the target area, and the true purpose of the mission.

'One other thing to watch for,' Stanley now said. 'There is the possibility that a specialized night fighter *Staffel* or squadron, using the twin-engined Junkers Ju-88, may be in your area. This is not hard information, but you'd be wise to keep a sharp lookout. If they are there, it's because of the damage that has been done to the coastal radars. These aircraft are obviously gap-pluggers.

'As you do not carry radar warning for them to home in on, they must rely on visual identification and other radar acquisition. Your black finish will make it more difficult for visual ID. And I happen to know that some of the Fw-190s have also been modified as single-seat night fighters. The pilots of these are fighter aces who were previously on bombers. At first, this sounds crazy; but when you consider that a bomber pilot spends long hours flying on instruments, it begins to make sense. A pilot with such high skill at night flying who is also an ace in fighter combat . . . Well, you don't need me to elaborate. So watch your backs. Squadron Leader Pendrake will now take over.'

Pendrake nodded to Stanley and went straight in. 'First thing I want to say is that I am proud to lead you all on this mission. When we began, with the short time allowed, I must confess I didn't think we'd make it this far. But you've proved me wrong and that's one instance when I'm glad to be. I was even wrong about you, Captain Elmore.'

'Well, sir, don't count your chickens.'

The room exploded into laughter that was at once relief and genuine enjoyment of Elmore's remark. Even the Spy smiled appreciatively.

Pendrake waited patiently for the laughter to die down. 'We'll cross the water,' he continued, 'as low as we dare, to avoid any coastal radars that may be operational, and any of those night fighters that the Spy has just mentioned. Try and remember that the windmill in front of your nose is not an outboard motor. A Tiffy can do many things, but she won't swim. Hit that water, and you're fish food. So it's instruments, instruments, *instruments*.

'Time over the target is 0330 hours, which equates with 0430 local and is thirty minutes before sunrise over there, at 0500. We shall therefore be arriving with the dawn, but in sufficient gloom to catch them by surprise. It also means you should have enough light to see what you're doing. Turn your instrument lighting as far down as is necessary for you to still be able to read them. You will experience less out-of-cockpit momentary blindness.

'A cruise at 380mph will give us twenty-five minutes to target. This will leave us with plenty of fuel, plus a wide power margin to our top speed of 460. At low to medium levels, we can eat 190s for breakfast, so we keep them there. Your aircraft will be equipped with special armament for both rockets and cannon. The rounds for both carry greater explosive force than is normal. I'm not sure whether we can dent any Tiger Panzers we may see, with the cannon; but Panthers, and armoured vehicles and anything else will die, especially 190s.' He paused for the resultant chuckles, then carried on, 'The rockets will take care of the rest. Choose how you wish to fire them . . . in a full salvo of eight, or in pairs. Prime rule, don't hang about.

'That's it, gentlemen. Make all the final checks you need, then have yourselves a good rest. Take-off is at 0300 hours. You will be called half an hour before. Good luck, and let's see you all back here when it's over. Met will give you the weather. Thank you.'

Pendrake was standing by his aircraft in the twilight, when Bingo Wilson came up to him.

'Terrible thing about Foxy,' Wilson began.

Pendrake nodded. 'I never expected it. Foxy seemed indestructible. I owed him a lot.'

'Yes.' Wilson paused to take a deep breath of the cool

evening air. 'Do you really think it was the same 190 that got Braddock?'

'From what Spy has said, it sounds suspiciously like it.'

'I'd like to get the sod.'

'I have first claim,' Pendrake said.

'If you miss him, he's mine.'

'I won't miss.'

There was another pause as both men, deep within their own private thoughts, watched the sky grow dark.

'Look, Mike, if . . .'

'Don't say it, Bingo. You're coming back.'

In the Château de St Sauveur, Meckler smiled with pleasure as he saw Odile walking towards him. She was dressed in a flowing black dress that came sharply in at the waist, then curved snugly down the hips to fall in soft folds to her ankles. The top showed a discreet but teasing roundness of breasts which promised a fullness he found intoxicating. He hardly dared believe his luck that she had come to him. As she walked, he saw that there were multiple slits in the folds of the dress and every so often, her bare, unstockinged legs gleamed at him. On her feet were golden sandals, and her golden hair shone past her shoulders like an extra piece of raiment, matching perfectly the dark texture of her dress.

'So you kept your word,' he said to her in French as she stopped before him.

'I kept my word.'

'I did order the coffee . . . the real thing. It's . . . it's in my room.' He smiled sheepishly. 'Look at me. I'm like a schoolboy on his first date. Is that any way for a Waffen-SS lieutenant colonel to behave?'

'I don't know,' she said, smiling at him. 'How do Waffen-SS lieutenant colonels behave?'

'Some,' he began seriously, 'you would not like to know. My God, you are beautiful. Come. We should not be standing here like a pair of statues. Please come in.'

He stood back for her to enter, then shut the door. The smell of the coffee pervaded the room.

'Lock it,' she said. 'We would not like to be disturbed, would we?'

'No . . . No,' he replied quickly and did as she had requested.

She looked about her, eyes lingering upon the big bed that was the centrepiece of all the furnishings. 'So they gave you this room. It was one of my favourites.'

'Was it? Oh, I'm sorry,' he said sympathetically. 'Of course. You'll know every room in this place.'

'Yes.'

'The . . . the bed is very big.'

'All our beds are very big.' Her eyes wandered to where the coffee waited. There was a small, unopened bottle of Asbach brandy with it. 'Are you trying to get me drunk?'

'What?' He seemed genuinely startled. 'Oh. No. That bottle has travelled with me throughout the war. I promised myself I would only open it if something very special happened to me. I have seen many things . . . done many . . . but until tonight, nothing was worth opening it for.'

Despite her reasons for being there, she was touched and almost hated herself for the deceitful role she was playing. Then she remembered the cellars, and Agnès, and all the things that had happened to France, and all doubts vanished. Keeping him here, no matter how accomplished whoever was second in command might be, would slow down the response time of the Waffen-SS units. That might just be enough to make the difference between success and failure. At least, she thought, what she was about to do was with someone she did honestly find attractive.

Outside, a pair of silent feet walked past Meckler's door. Grüber continued walking, a foul look of jealousy on his pinched features.

'They didn't mind you leaving?' Odile asked.

'No. I had served my function as the most junior officer

there. They're still talking . . . Schlierhof, Daggenau, the revolting Grüber and a few others, including a couple of Wehrmacht brigadier generals.

They were sitting at the table and Meckler had poured the coffee. He now poured the Asbach into two small glasses he'd brought with him.

'Don't tell me the glasses travelled too.'

'Oh yes. They're my father's.'

She gave her familiar giggle. 'You carried that all through your battles?'

'Yes. You think it is strange?' He put a cup and a glass before her. 'Let me tell you something even more strange. On the Eastern Front, we once captured a Russian general. He had a complete samovar with him, all highly polished.'

She giggled again. 'What happened to him?'

'He tried to escape of course and was shot.'

The giggles went. 'That sounds familiar.'

'No, no. It was a genuine escape. He killed ten of our troops. I was almost sorry he was killed. A very brave man.'

'Who killed him. You?'

'No. A one-armed friend of mine.'

'I see.'

'Well,' Meckler said brightly, raising his glass. 'To you, a goddess.'

'I'm no goddess, Franz.'

'To me, you are. Raise your glass. Please.'

She raised the glass.

'Now you must drink at one go. That's how I would like to do it tonight.'

'All right.'

'To you,' he said.

'To the end of the war,' she said.

He looked at her steadily. 'Yes. I would like that.'

They drank together.

'Wooo!' she said, as the Asbach went down.

He grinned. 'Good?'

She nodded, not yet ready to speak, a hand against her chest.

'Coffee, perhaps?' he suggested.

She nodded quickly and took a swallow.

'You own vineyards,' he said. 'You must have drunk a variety of . . .'

'This . . . this one was something special,' she interrupted.

He picked up the bottle, studied it, then put it back down.

'Yes. It was, wasn't it?'

She did something to her dress and stood up suddenly. The dress tumbled away from her like a slow waterfall. She had nothing on underneath.

He stared at her, his eyes nearly popping. 'My drink has done this to you?'

She shook her head slowly, her own eyes fastened upon him. She said nothing.

'You are a goddess,' he said hoarsely as she walked slowly over to the bed and sat upon it, her legs slightly apart.

She still said nothing.

Meckler stood up and slowly unbuttoned his tunic. 'Are you sure of this?'

She nodded silently.

'For days and days I have been dreaming of being able to . . .'

He stopped as he threw the tunic to the floor. He sat down again and hauled off his jackboots while she continued to watch him. Then, rapidly, he removed the rest of his clothing. He came towards the bed and stood before her.

No words passed between them.

He got to his knees and began to kiss her on the ankle, moving slowly up her inner leg all the way to the top of her thigh. A *frisson* of pleasure caused her body to tremble slightly, and a sharp intake of breath came from her.

He continued to work upwards until he reached her breasts, his body sliding itself over her. She lowered herself slowly as he did so until her entire upper body, propped by her buttocks on the edge of the bed, lay upon the large duvet.

He kissed her body in adoration for several minutes, until she felt she must squeal for release. And still he continued to kiss her. When at last he came into her, it was a powerful entry that made her gasp out loud as she brought her legs about him, trapping him within her.

And yet, for all his vigour, he was strangely gentle.

'I shall have to go back,' she said. 'It's nearly midnight.'

'I know,' he said regretfully.

They were lying in close embrace. Their lovemaking had made the bed look as if there had been a wrestling contest.

'Odile, this was . . .'

'Shhh! Say nothing.'

'But . . .'

'Please, Franz. Nothing.'

'All right. But I want to see you again.'

'You will.'

'All right,' he repeated. 'With such a promise, I will let you go.'

She got out of bed and dressed quickly. He also climbed out and began to dress.

'What are you doing?' she asked.

'I'm escorting you back. Do you think I'll let you walk back alone?'

'I am in my own house.'

'Your house, but not controlled by you.'

'There really is no need, Franz. I'll be fine.' She went to the door, unlocked it and opened it.

And looked straight into Grüber's face.

She gave a start of surprise. Meckler, his tunic not quite

buttoned, came to see what it was all about, then grew angry when he saw Grüber.

'My God, man!' he snapped. 'Must you always be creeping around? Haven't you got your own bed to go to?'

'I was going to my room when your door opened. I was quite startled. Perhaps I can escort the lady to her quarters.'

'I shall do that, thank you, Herr Grüber!' Meckler said roughly as he finished buttoning his tunic. 'Come, Odile.' Taking her arm, he brushed roughly past Grüber.

The Gestapo man watched them go, his villainous eyes blank. They all knew his own room was a long way from there.

Back in her bedroom, Odile got undressed and washed herself. She then set an alarm clock, which she muffled by putting a folded handkerchief between the knocker and the bell; but she did not put on her nightdress. Instead, she put on totally unfeminine clothes and leaving a pair of soft boots under the bed got in beneath the first layer of bedclothes.

She lay in the darkness and waited.

In his own room, Meckler got fully undressed and climbed into bed a very happy man. The Asbach, he thought, before he fell asleep, had been worth keeping for the right moment.

Grüber was not having a good night of it. The raging jealousy he felt drove him to an arousal for which he had no immediate female body to give him relief. In the morning, he decided, he would demand the return of Agnès. The Malzeys did not control what went on in the château.

When Agnès returned, he would revel in that young

body for all the days he'd not had her. He would find new and inventive ways to make up for the lost time. The Malzeys would not be getting her back; ever. As for that aristocratic tart Odile, she would soon know what it was like to have Helmut Grüber inside her, whether she wanted him there or not.

And Meckler. Meckler was no doubt feeling smug. Well, Meckler would be pulled off his high horse one day soon, Knight's Cross notwithstanding. Heroes could fall.

Two kilometres from the château, silent, armed people were converging on the secret entrances to some of the hidden passages that led into the building itself. They would enter the dark labyrinths and there they would wait, until the time was right.

Several other small bands were taking up positions well away from the Waffen-SS troops that formed the defensive screen of the château, but close enough for when the time came to mount their own attack.

A third group, to the west, were preparing for their assault upon the airfield.

Then suddenly all movement in all the locations stopped. The waiting had begun.

Ketelheim woke up with a start. He switched on his bedside lamp: 0200 hours. He listened. There was nothing untoward. Then why had he woken? He turned off the light, waited for his eyes to become accustomed to the dark, then drew open his curtain slightly. All was quiet on the airfield. Must have been a dream, he thought.

He closed the curtain, sensing unease, but not understanding why. After a while, he lay back in the bed.

He still had no idea why he had woken so suddenly.

At precisely the same time that Ketelheim had been startled out of sleep, Pendrake lay on the hard bed at Able Three, his eyes wide open in the dark. Everything he could possibly have done in the time allowed had been done. The men had come through. It was now up to them. No point worrying now.

He drifted off to sleep, listening to Bingo Wilson frequently shifting position on his own bed.

It seemed only seconds later that someone was shaking him.

'Time, sir,' the unknown voice said, shining a torch in his face.

'All right. I'm awake.'

The torch moved on.

'Turn that bloody thing off!' Bingo Wilson said.

'Yes, sir,' the aircraftman said and proceeded to shine it on Kelly.

'Hey! Hey!' Kelly said. 'OK, OK. You can turn off the sun.'

In the next hut Mackenzie, Williams and Hargreaves were undergoing the same treatment, as well as all those in the aircrew huts dotted about the place.

They moved without haste but purposefully, as they got ready. No one spoke. There was no need to. They ate the prepared sandwiches and drank the hot tea that had been brought to them; then they went out to their aircraft.

Stanley appeared at Pendrake's hut just as he was leaving. He hung back for the others to move on ahead.

'I should tell you,' Stanley began, 'do this well, and there could be more Cobra Squadron missions. You never know with these things.'

'Glad you came, Spy,' Pendrake said. 'Here.'

'What's this?'

'A letter to Section Officer Lewis at the Cobra station. It says a few things.'

Stanley took the envelope and put it in one of the pouch pockets of his tunic. 'I'll hang on to it till you get back, then you can give it to her yourself if it's still appropriate. See you later.'

They didn't shake hands.

One by one, the black Typhoons ripped apart the night as they burst into life. All engines started smoothly. Twenty aircraft would be going. Subdued lighting came on to illuminate the flare path; despite its deliberately low intensity, the whole place seemed unnaturally bright. Take-off would have to be rapid so that the airfield could be shrouded once more in darkness in as short a time as possible.

The aircraft would lift off in pairs by flight in reverse order, with Pendrake going off first, leading Three Flight. He taxied out to the runway, instrument lighting dimmed as far as he dared. A dark shape following told him Bingo Wilson was right there with him. Then they were on the runway.

He pushed the throttle to its full travel. The Typhoon with the mangled hand gathered speed swiftly. The tail inched off the ground. He held it for a brief moment. The aircraft wanted to fly. A gentle backwards pressure and she was off. He bought the wheels up, and banked gently on to the heading for the track to target.

He glanced back. The airfield was nowhere to be seen. All the aircraft had got into the air and the lights immediately turned off. When airspeed reached 380mph, he throttled back and held it there. To his right, a shape that was Bingo Wilson in Cobra Two was keeping station.

They were on their way.

In Odile's room at the château, the muffled alarm went off. She stopped it quickly and got out of bed, grabbed at her boots and put them on. Next to where she'd placed the boots was a powerful torch. She picked it up and went to the connecting door to Mariette's room.

'Mariette!' she whispered.

'We're coming!'

Odile went to the entrance to the secret passage, which was at the back of a false wardrobe attached to the real one. She waited as her parents, Mariette, Agnès and Philippe, whom they had managed to warn in time, entered her bedroom.

They all trooped through to the passage, Odile leading the way. Mariette brought up the rear and shut the wardrobe, then the entrance. No one who entered the room would know where they'd gone. They went far enough to be well away from the building. Odile retrieved her automatic pistol, surprising everyone except Mariette, who already knew. They settled down in the dark to wait.

Soon they saw a pinprick of light approaching. It was the first of the Resistance fighters, a woman.

In his room, Grüber slept fitfully. Every so often, he would jerk awake, thinking of revenge on Odile, on Agnès, on Meckler.

Meckler slept soundly, dreaming of Odile, while in the other bedrooms the senior officers who had attended the tactical meeting had put away their logistical, strategic and political worries to sleep equally soundly, lulled by the château's excellent wines.

Ketelheim was awake again. This was ridiculous. He was as jumpy as a rookie pilot about to go on his first mission. Something was itching at him, but what?

He decided it was pointless going back to sleep and began to dress. He picked up the phone and called the duty officer.

'Wake my mechanics,' he ordered. 'I want my plane made ready.'

'*Now*, sir?' came the startled reaction.

'Of course now! Do you think I'm in the habit of making funny calls in the middle of the night?'

'No. No, Herr Oberstleutnant!'

'And wake Oberfeldwebel Prinz. Get his plane ready too.'

'Yes, sir!'

The duty officer will be thinking the old man's finally gone mad, Ketelheim thought as he put the phone down.

'Old,' he said to himself. 'I'm twenty-seven. Perhaps I have indeed gone mad.'

They made it to the coast of France without alerting any radars that might have been searching. No night fighters came probing. They gained height on instruments to clear high ground, but maintained low altitude across the sleeping countryside. To remain undetected as long as possible, they neither made nor received any radio transmissions. In any case, there was little need at this stage, as each flight knew precisely what to do, without further instructions.

It wouldn't be long now, Pendrake thought, before the thunder of twenty Napier engines woke someone up.

A sudden flash over to the right told him someone was indeed awake. A flak battery missing by a wide margin. Probably fired long after the squadron had passed. But the phones would be ringing and radio traffic hotting up. It was time for Keane's flight to go.

Right on schedule, One Flight curved away from the invisible formation to head for the airfield. The others forged on.

The phone rang in Ketelheim's bedroom. It was the duty officer, sounding astonished and clearly wondering whether his CO had second sight.

'Message just came through, sir! A large formation of aircraft has crossed the coast and is heading this way! A battery fired, but hit nothing.'

Ketelheim was galvanized. He had *known* something was about to happen. 'Did you wake Prinz?'

'Yes, sir. He's on his way to his aircraft.'

'Good. I'll join him. Wake up every pilot. Hurry!'

He slammed the phone down and rushed out of the room.

Pendrake felt warm. He reached to his right for the cockpit heating lever to reduce the temperature slightly. He glanced at the watch in its holder, on the left-hand section of the instrument panel. Time soon for Two Flight to break away.

A minute later, Dodson led his flight out of formation to make for the hell of the flak-infested woods.

Ketelheim spoke rapidly to Prinz. 'Keep your cockpit lighting low and follow my instructions. Keep your nerve *at all times*. We're going high to see what the radars have for us. You know how to use your equipment. It will soon be dawn and we'll be able to see them and hit them like fish in a barrel. OK, Jürgen?'

'Yes, sir.'

'Good. Get in and let's go.'

They were on their take-off run when Keane's group arrived.

The rockets came off the Typhoons like emissaries from Hades. The air was filled with the roar of their powerful engines, the whoosh of the rockets, the enormous explosions when they hit. A salvo ripped apart a section of the runway.

Then the cannons started a deadly, coughing stutter. The ultra-high-explosive shells began their own murderous accompaniment as they impacted against aircraft, buildings, trucks and gun emplacements. They mowed down running people, sleeping people, mechanics, pilots, drivers. The duty officer to whom Ketelheim had spoken was hit while he was still on the phone. He never finished what he'd been saying.

Astoundingly, the surprise had been so complete that not a single flak gun had so far opened up. Ketelheim and Prinz had managed, against all odds, to get off the ground.

Ketelheim watched in mounting despair as he banked his aircraft steeply to get out of the way, seeing the great explosions and widening blaze of fires spreading about the airfield.

He wondered whether any of the other pilots had managed to get off, perhaps using the emergency runway, or even the grass, if it was not too soft. The Fw-190 had a nasty habit of flipping over on indifferent ground and smashing its canopy on your head. At least in the 109, the weak landing-gear would snap, leaving you with an enforced belly landing. You'd be the right way up, which was a lot better than being trapped upside down with fuel leaking all around you.

Ketelheim thought he saw something flit across the fires like a great bat, then it was gone. What the hell was it?

He was beginning to feel angry.

For three terrible minutes, the Typhoons wreaked havoc, then, saving ammunition, One Flight headed for the woods to help Dodson and the others.

'This is Night Owl,' Ketelheim called. 'Did anyone get up?'

'Schiller,' came a voice.

'Neumann.'

'Hartz.'

'Möhn.'

'Anyone else?'

Silence greeted him.

Six, he thought bitterly. *Six out of twenty-five.*

He didn't know how many of those attacking aircraft there had been, but he would pursue with his six. Perhaps some 109s would come looking when the light got better.

What had happened to those wretched coastal radars? Didn't any of them work any more?

'Night Owl,' he called to his other pilots. 'Form on me. Let's go after them.' He contacted various ground-control stations and radars to get a lead on the enemy aircraft. None came up with anything. '*They're here*!' he shouted. '*Do something!*'

Meanwhile, he trusted his own instincts and headed towards the château.

Pendrake had arrived at the back of the château, with Wilson close behind. The flak platforms were his first priority. Pulling up slightly from his low altitude, he released a salvo of rockets and broke sharply just as Wilson fired.

The gunners barely had time to assimilate the direction of the swelling noise of the approach, the sudden dark apparitions, and the streams of white hurtling towards them, before their world turned into fire.

Eight rockets tore into the gun platforms, ripping them apart in great gouts of flame that slashed through the paling darkness. Ammunition exploded in sympathy, adding to the destruction. Bodies flew through the air.

Pendrake wheeled away in preparation for another run as the second pair of Kelly and Mackenzie unleashed a total salvo of sixteen rockets at the château itself. They had to haul away quickly as great catapulting lumps seemed to fly past them. The third pair roasted gun emplacements in the grounds.

All six repeated the attack, leaving that part of the château a crackling, burning shell. The Malzey apartments were not hit by a single round.

But the flak was waking up in the woods, over which

Dodson had now been joined by Keane's flight. All over the wooded expanse, Meckler's men were taking a beating. Rockets lit up the gloom like something out of Dante. Tracers streamed from the diving, wheeling aircraft, still barely distinguishable, lacing the air with red-gold pulses that seared earthwards like demented lightning. Explosions erupted as men died where they slept or were consumed within their vehicles. Anti-aircraft ammunition exploded while gunners tried to load, turning them into burning lumps of flesh that mixed with their disintegrating weaponry.

But now, something exploded in the air as some flak gunners, out in one of the vineyards, scored a kill.

The château grounds had been pulverized, and Pendrake's Typhoons headed for the woods.

It was up to Halloran's people now.

Of the nineteen remaining Typhoons, those still carrying rockets were wheeling in the still weak approaching light, and unleashing into the woods. They were like a flock of huge bats, flitting between the spouts of fire that came at them as they hunted. Then the flak claimed another. It spiralled into the trees. Even if the pilot had still been alive, he would not have had time to bail out.

'Cobra Squadron,' Pendrake called, 'let's go home.'

And then he saw the fighters.

14

'Break! Break!' he heard someone call urgently. Not to him, for in the distance something flamed silently.

'109s!' another voice called.

'And 190s! Gawd! Look at them!' It was Elmore.

When the first rockets hit, Grüber, with the instincts of a born survivor, had leapt out of bed and rolled away from any flimsy barriers like windows. In desperation, he hid in the bathroom. It saved his life. A rocket had entered a window and exploded on the bed. All that was left of the room was the bathroom, whose solid door had somehow contained the by then dissipating blast. For a while, Grüber was totally deaf.

In a daze, he at last moved cautiously out of the bathroom, and stopped. There was no floor. Choking dust was everywhere. Then he saw that he could creep along a narrow ledge to the now non-existent door to the bedroom. Some of his clothes lay in the still-intact corridor.

He eventually made it, chose some, and put them on. Then he saw something he needed.

His gun. He picked it up. It was fully loaded. Someone was going to pay for this.

Meckler was thrown out of bed by the first explosions. Instincts of the battlefield taking over, he got dressed swiftly when he realized he was still alive and unhurt. Although there was plenty of dust in the room, it was intact; but he could smell burning.

He rushed out of the room gun in hand, tunic open and bare-headed. His booted feet crunched on broken glass. Several paintings lay in untidy heaps along the masonry-strewn corridor. He'd heard the departing aircraft, but no answering sounds of anti-aircraft guns close by, although the distant crump of his flak batteries in the woods could be distinguished.

Surprise had been total, he thought clinically. He had failed. He knew whose head would roll.

He wondered what had happened to Odile and her family.

'Cobra Squadron!' Pendrake called. 'Take them!'

He moved the throttle to the 'wall and then slid the supercharger lever forward. The Typhoon leapt for altitude. But he did not intend to go high. He was going to drag them down into his arena. He cut the supercharger and found himself curving behind a darting 190 that seemed unsure which of the Typhoons to go for. At last, its pilot picked one. Pendrake stayed glued to him.

The range closed quickly. The 190 pilot was not checking his tail. The Focke-Wulf looked like a ghostly moth in the dawn light.

Pendrake went in closer until the 190, still intent on its own prey, seemed to fill his windscreen.

He fired.

The high-explosive shells tore into the unsuspecting aircraft. It jerked upright as if it had itself felt the blow and slowly turned over on to its back, streaming dark smoke. Then it suddenly changed into a puff of flame, a metamorphosis that was as sudden as it was spectacular.

Ketelheim had seen Jürgen Prinz go after one of the black aircraft which he himself had belatedly recognized as a special mark of Typhoon, a type he'd never come across before.

He had called to his eager wingman, who, perhaps incensed by the unexpected attack on the airfield and mesmerized by what he'd mistakenly believed were plenty of easy targets, had plunged in without thinking. In that single moment of unreason, all the discipline that had marked Prinz's flying career so far had disappeared.

Then Ketelheim had seen the ominous black shadow lining up precisely behind the 190, and knew his young wingman was being stalked by a highly skilled practitioner of the art of air combat. He had recognized something of himself in the implacable way in which the Typhoon seemed fixed to Prinz's 190.

'Jürgen!' he'd called. 'Break! Break!'

But he'd been far too late. With an awe-inspiring economy, the black Typhoon had fired the shortest of bursts. But it had been enough. Jürgen Prinz's young life was over.

Ketelheim looked for the black aircraft that had done the deed, determined to take his revenge. But it had gone, and was somewhere among the others. There had been no distinguishable marking on it and even when the light got better, he knew that all he would see would be its faded national insignia.

But he would know it when he saw it again. He would recognize the flying skill.

Pendrake had broken swiftly away after his kill and gone after another 190 that seemed to be pursuing a Typhoon low down. But the Typhoon pilot was well aware that someone was on his tail. It broke sharply left, disappearing momentarily in the gloom below. When Pendrake saw it again it was curving to the right, while the 190, outmanoeuvred, was desperately trying to recover the situation.

But the Typhoon had hauled itself tightly round and was now pulling in behind its erstwhile pursuer. A brief flash of tracer and the 190 exploded, going straight into the trees.

'How do you like *that*?' a disembodied voice exclaimed.

Elmore had made the kill.

Pendrake smiled grimly and went looking for more prey.

Keane, with Wojdat close in, spotted another Typhoon; it appeared to be dancing in a wall of fire coming up from the ground. The light was getting better and better, and the blackbirds of the night were beginning to gain visibility.

'Josef, do something about that flak. I'll watch your back.'

'Roger.'

Wojdat flung the Typhoon on to its back, rolled upright and hurtled towards the flak battery. He had laid down a ferocious fire at the airfield and it had been his cannon shell, though he could have had no way of knowing, that had cut short the life of the duty officer in mid-phone conversation.

The gunners were still intent on downing their target and so were quite surprised when the hellish cannon fire began ripping them apart. The gunfire stopped reaching skywards.

'Many thanks!' someone called with relief. It was Knowles, the New Zealander from Two Flight.

'You are OK?'

'Josef?'

'Yes.'

'Thanks, mate. A few holes in the wings, but otherwise OK.' Knowles brought his aircraft close. The 'few holes' made a section of his left wing look like netting.

He tucked in on Wojdat and together they went to rejoin Keane, who was waiting up top.

Ketelheim had spotted a solitary Typhoon streaking just above the treetops. As the light got better, he was able to see it quite clearly. High above him, some 109s that had come to join the fight were having a fracas of their own. He had now lost Prinz, Möhn and Hartz. That left just himself, Schiller and Neumann. He couldn't see them anywhere, although he'd heard Schiller exclaim loudly, using foul language. Schiller had scored.

Three out of twenty-five.

It was a disaster of monumental proportions.

He felt a cold anger as he dived on the Typhoon like an avenging hawk. The black aircraft drew swiftly closer. The pilot was obviously not keeping a good lookout. Perhaps he was wounded. Ketelheim felt no mercy.

Had she been there to observe him, Mariette would not have recognized the charming man with whom she'd picnicked.

Ketelheim had no intention of letting the Typhoon escape.

Hargreaves was trying to make it back to base. His left arm, hit by a flak splinter, would not move. His radio was out, so he could warn no one of his predicament. When he'd been hit, he had just been pulling out of a dive and had eased the throttle back. It now gave him a power setting that allowed a good turn of speed, with fuel economy, so there had been no need to try to reach it with his good right hand. The aircraft handled perfectly. He was low down, and the trees still screened him.

But the pain had dulled his instincts, for though enough remained to make him check behind, it was just as the first shells from the pursuing 190 struck the aircraft.

A savage bang on the armour-plating behind him threw him forward, causing him to shove at the stick. The Typhoon toppled into a steep dive as more shells exploded viciously against it.

Hargreaves never saw the trees that claimed him.

* * *

'That was for Jürgen,' Ketelheim said in his mask as he hauled the 190 upwards. He had to jink suddenly as the tumbling, flaming carcass of a 109 fell past on its way to earth.

The Messerschmitts were not having a good time of it. The fight had now gone out of reach of Meckler's flak batteries. Briefly, he wondered what had happened to Franz. The château had been successfully attacked. Was Franz even still alive?

But where was the man who had shot down the boy from the chemist's shop with such clinical skill?

The man was right behind him.

Pendrake had seen the Typhoon go down before the swiftly diving Focke-Wulf and felt a strange recognition. He knew he had never met this pilot in combat before; but there seemed to be an inevitability about the approaching confrontation.

Just as he was about to fire his first shells, the pilot of the 190 spotted him and rolled swiftly, pulling sharply away in a dive.

Pendrake did not follow. Instead, he pulled up slightly, then banked hard right, almost on the canopy, to pull down to where he judged the 190 would be. And there it was, curving hard to come back at him.

Pendrake rolled upright and turned into the incoming aircraft. They flashed past each other. Neither fired.

No point wasting ammunition, Pendrake thought grimly. This pilot was no novice. He knew he had met the ace.

Ketelheim was also certain he had met Jürgen's killer. It took nerve to face an oncoming aircraft and to hold fire.

'You are a cold one,' Ketelheim said quietly.

He looked swiftly about him. There was no one in sight. The sky seemed to be theirs alone.

'All right, my friend,' he murmured at the black aircraft as he watched it flash past above him, knowing its pilot was about to pull down on to his tail. 'May the best man win.'

He felt a sense of admiration for the other pilot, who was as implacable as he was. The Typhoon looked beautiful as it danced with him, never once allowing itself to become vulnerable.

They used up great segments of sky as they fought for advantage. The crew of an isolated flak battery were so mesmerized when the ballet arrived above them that they chose not to fire and instead paused to watch. The whirling aircraft moved on.

Pendrake watched as the 190 curved above him upside down, then stood on its wingtip trying to turn into him, coming in close from the starboard quarter. He saw the golden emblem clearly.

Marvelling at the fantastic view out that the canopy afforded him, he rolled into the approaching Focke-Wulf, then pulled on the stick. As he fell towards the ground, he was aware that the 190 had missed again. Again no shots were fired.

He kept low down, forcing the other pilot to come after him, leading him towards a large expanse of wood.

Ketelheim could not believe it when he saw the Typhoon roll into a ninety-degree bank, to slip between a colony of trees. Instinctively, he pulled up to avoid colliding with the branches. But where was the Typhoon?

The sudden slamming on his aircraft gave him the answer he did not want. As the shells exploded about him, he felt an unbearable pain savaging his body. His hands let go of the controls. The 190, still in the climb, lost speed, stalled and fell back upon itself.

Just before it exploded among the trees, Ketelheim whispered one word.

'Trudi,' he said.

* * *

Pendrake had known exactly what he intended to do when he'd entered the wood. There had been an exit to his right and he'd taken it, just as the 190 had baulked upwards to avoid the trees. He'd then continued his turn and had again begun to climb, nicely on the tail of the fleeing 190.

Choosing the moment well, he'd made sure that every shell counted. This enemy pilot had not been the sort of man to be given a second chance.

Pendrake circled the place of dying once, then went to look for his squadron.

In and around the château, the sound of small-arms fire was a chilling dawn chorus.

Odile, leaving her parents with Mariette, had returned to her home. She was followed by Agnès, who refused to remain, and Philippe, who had been given a weapon by one of the Resistance, some of whom had followed too. They streamed through the building. Odile became separated and turned a corner, to find herself face to face with a dishevelled Meckler. He stared at the clothes she wore, and at the gun in her hand. He pointed his own gun at her.

'*You! You fooled me! You used me!* And now, look what you have done. I am finished.'

She stood before him, completely unafraid. 'What did I do to you? You came to my country and occupied it. You took my house from me. *Your* people abused *my* people in *my* home. You abused *my* country. What did you expect?'

He continued to stare at her. 'And last night? Did you also pretend? Did I share my special drink with you for nothing?'

'If you believe that . . . and if you believe that I am wrong to fight for my own beliefs, then . . .' She lowered her automatic. 'Shoot me.'

For long moments, he just looked at her, remembering how she had felt in his arms. Outside, and within other parts of the building, the ferocious rattle of small-arms fire continued.

Then Meckler lowered his own pistol.

'Oh, Odile,' he said. 'Why couldn't we have met . . .'

'*Veräter!*' someone screamed. 'Traitor! They are all dead, Meckler. It is your fault!'

Two shots barked from behind him and Franz Meckler's eyes opened wide as he pitched forwards, falling almost at Odile's feet.

Shocked by the suddenness of it, she looked up to see the venomous eyes of a bedraggled Grüber, glaring at her.

'And as for you,' he hissed, gun zeroed upon her as he came forward. 'I will have my revenge upon you until you scream for death.'

She backed away from him as he continued to approach, stepping over Meckler's body with total indifference.

'*Stand still!*' he barked.

She stopped.

'Drop the gun. *Drop it!*'

She did so.

'Now,' he said. 'I shall teach you a lesson you will remember until the moment of your death. Remove your clothes.'

She stared at him in disbelief.

'*Remove them!*' he screamed.

Slowly, she began to unbutton the rough, workman's jacket she was wearing. Then she saw movement behind Grüber. *Agnès. Agnès with a long, wicked-looking knife.*

Odile did not pause, so as not to warn him. He licked at his lips as he waited for her to bare her body to him.

But now, Agnès was rushing forward. Grüber began to turn. Agnès gave an inhuman scream of rage and hatred as she launched herself upon the man who had tormented her for so long. The knife plunged deep into his chest, came out, and went in again repeatedly. He screamed, a high-pitched wail that seemed to echo for ever. Blood gushed all over him, and upon Agnès. She kept plunging the knife in as if that was all that mattered to her in all the world. As Grüber began to collapse, the gun fired. Once.

Agnès reeled away, a great wound just below her left breast.

'*Agnès!*' Odile shouted in horror, and ran to help the stricken girl. But it was of little use. Agnès was dying. 'Oh, Agnès,' she said softly.

Odile cradled her in her arms. Agnès never spoke as she died. Odile laid her down gently, then turned to where Grüber lay dead, looking like a butchered carcass.

She spat upon the body. 'For Agnès, and for Jeanne-Anne.'

A slight movement made her look. 'Franz! You're all right! Here. Let me help.' She crouched to attempt to prop him up.

'No, no,' he said weakly. 'I am not all right.' He coughed, and a great stream of blood came out of his mouth. 'See?' he gasped. 'I have seen many such wound . . . wounds before. Go, Odile. Let me . . . let me die. I've . . . I've been waiting a long time.'

'No, Franz. I cannot . . .'

'Go, my love. Go and save your country. Mine is finished.'

She kissed his forehead gently as he died, and stood up to move away. She turned, and gave a start. Michel Montcarneau was standing there, a sub-machine-gun in his hand. The sounds of small-arms fire came more sporadically now.

'Michel! You're safe!'

He nodded slowly then turned as a man, wearing two pistols in shoulder holsters and also carrying a sub-machine-gun, approached. 'Fer de Lance,' Montcarneau said.

Odile and Halloran nodded at each other.

'Boucheron's dead,' Montcarneau continued, 'and that

o-called wife of his. Our people in the cellars are safe.' He ooked at each of the bodies. 'What happened here?'

She told them about Agnès and the Gestapo deputy, vatching as the faces of the two men registered disgust ınd outrage.

'And this one?' Montcarneau pointed with the gun at Meckler and looked at her keenly.

She wiped the beginnings of tears from her eyes. 'Some-one who should not have come here,' she said. 'Not at this time.'

'And Mariette? Is she all right?'

'I'll take you to her. Come, Monsieur Fer de Lance.'

As Halloran went with them, he briefly touched the small crucifix Jeanne-Anne had given him.

'Cobra One,' Pendrake called. 'Heading home. On me.'

No one replied. There was no need to. Those still alive would all be heading towards the homeward track, marked out on the map at Able Three.

Soon, he could see them arriving. It was a glorious sight in the new day. Of the twenty aircraft that had set out, sixteen were returning. A lot better than he had feared. They had acquitted themselves well. Hargreaves and Williams had gone. As had Charlton, who would now never wear his officer's rank.

Pendrake looked about him with a pride tinged with sadness for those he'd lost, as his flock followed him home. There would be more letters to write. Then a new feeling came to him; one that gave him an immense rush of well-being. He would be seeing Karen Lewis again.

In his mind's eye, he saw her running towards him as he landed back at the home airfield.

Only Theo Neumann survived to make it back in his battered Focke-Wulf 190. He was forced to use the emergency strip, but landed badly. The plane hit a bump, turned over on to its back, settling down on the cockpit. Fuel began to leak from ruptured pipes. It exploded while he was still vainly trying to get out.

The Golden Knights had ceased to exist.

YVERT & TELLIER

CATALOGUE
DE TIMBRES-POSTE

CENT QUATORZIÈME ANNÉE

TOME I

FRANCE

ÉMISSIONS GÉNÉRALES DES COLONIES

2010

ASCAT

YVERT&TELLIER

2, rue de l'Étoile - 80094 AMIENS cedex 3
http://www.yvert.com

Le catalogue Mondial de Cotation

Le Tome de Référence des Catalogues - *(Outil pour l'identification et le classement des Timbres-Poste)*

I. - FRANCE, Émissions Générales des Colonies - *(En couleurs. Parution annuelle)*

Ibis. - TOM - Monaco - Andorre - Europa - Nations Unies - *(En couleurs. Parution annuelle)*

II. - COLONIES FRANÇAISES - *(1re partie en couleurs)*

II. - PAYS INDÉPENDANTS D'AFRIQUE

(2e partie **Algérie à Haute-Volta + Cambodge et Laos**).
(3e partie **Madagascar à Tunisie + Vanuatu - Vietnam**).

III. - EUROPE de l'Ouest

(1re partie **Allemagne à Epire**).
(2e partie **Espagne à Luxembourg**).
(3e partie **Macédoine à Yougoslavie**).

IV. - EUROPE de l'Est

(1re partie **Albanie à Pologne**).
(2e partie **Roumanie à Ukraine**).

OUTRE-MER

(Volume 1 **Aden à Burundi**).
(Volume 2 **Caïmanes à Dominicaine**).
(Volume 3 **Dominique à Guatemala**).
(Volume 4 **Guinée-Bissau à Lesotho**).
(Volume 5 **Liban à Nyassaland**).
(Volume 6 **Océan Indien à Samoa**).
(Volume 7 **Seychelles à Zoulouland**).

Les Classiques du Monde (1840-1940)

Le Catalogue Mondial des nouveautés

1998 - 1999 - 2000 - 2001 - 2002 - 2003 - 2004 - 2005 - 2006 - 2007 - 2008

Le Catalogue des Timbres Fiscaux et Socio-Postaux

de France et de Monaco.

AVERTISSEMENT

Yvert & Tellier attire l'attention des utilisateurs du présent catalogue sur le fait que les cotations qui y figurent ne constituent pas des indications de prix conseillés, et que les prix effectivement pratiqués résultent d'un accord librement conclu entre les vendeurs et les acheteurs. La responsabilité d'Yvert & Tellier ne saurait donc en aucun cas être recherchée sur le fondement d'un quelconque écart entre le prix indiqué et le prix effectif.

Yvert & Tellier draw users' attention of the present catalogue to the fact that quotes given in it are not an indication of recommended prices and that prices effectively applied are the result of agreements reached freely between sellers and buyers. Therefore, Yvert & Tellier's responsibility cannot be implicated on the basis of any discrepancy between the price indicated and the price applied in practice.

ISBN13 978-2-86814-195-8 Publication annuelle

INDEX ALPHABÉTIQUE

FRANCE

INDEX ALPHABÉTIQUE DES ANNONCEURS

AVERTISSEMENT

Les Etats Généraux de la Philatélie qui se sont tenus le 2 avril 2008 ont débouché sur la Charte de la Philatélie signée conjointement par la Poste, la FFAP (Associations de collectionneurs) et la CNEP (Négociants) le 24 juin 2009.

Cette charte distingue plusieurs catégories de timbres : le timbre d'usage courant, traditionnellement représenté par la Marianne - le timbre commémoratif - le timbre d'écriture, souvent autoadhésif - le timbre personnalisé.

Cela aura pour conséquence certaines modifications dans les rubriques de notre Tome 1.

La traditionnelle rubrique Poste qui débute avec la Cérès de 1849 est désormais constituée des timbres du programme philatélique et une nouvelle rubrique rassemble tous les timbres autoadhésifs.

A l'avenir si un timbre n'est émis qu'en version autoadhésive, il ne figurera que dans cette rubrique. Par contre s'il est émis dans les deux versions - gommée et autoadhésive - il figurera dans les deux rubriques.

Notre livret de l'Expert a pour but de vous proposer des sujets passionnants mais demeurés confidentiels : cette année vous découvrirez les porte-timbres, qui connurent leur heure de gloire au début du 20ème siècle. Thématistes, régionalistes, amateurs d'Histoire y trouveront, nous en sommes certains, leur bonheur.

Que les deux auteurs de ce livret, Lucien Coutan et André Métayer, trouvent ici l'expression de notre gratitude.

Bonne année philatélique à tous.

Benoît GERVAIS
Christophe YVERT

Millésime

Légende

1949. - *Exposition philatélique internationale de Paris (CITEX). Type de 1849. Taille-douce. Non dentelé (bordure dentelée 13).* BF *n° 5.*

Sujet repris à la rubrique Blocs et Feuillets

Numéro Yvert

841 10 f. (+100 f.) vermil. 6 50 40 » 54 »
a. (Non dent. complet) 1600 »

Surtaxe

Valeur faciale

Variété ou autre état (ex : Non dentelé)

1949. - *Congrès international de Télégraphie et Téléphonie, à Paris. Taille-douce. Dentelés 13.* ✈

Sujets repris à la rubrique Avion

Claude Chappe.

F. Arago et Ampère.

Dentelure

Couleur

844	10 f. rouge	1 10	0 65	1 10
845	15 f. brun-noir	1 25	0 65	1 25

Modes d'impression

Emile Baudot. Général Ferrié.

Couleur en italique = Non émis

Sujet

Cote du timbre oblitéré

846	25 f. lie de vin	3 »	2 »	2 75
846A	25 f. *lie de vin*	4000 »	3000 »	
847	50 f. bleu	5 65	3 »	4 90

Prix de la série

Nos 844 à 847 sans le 846A (4 val.) 11 » 6 30 10 »

La série (sans le 846A), non dentelée 215 »

Chiffre de tirage du ou des timbres

Note

Le n° 846A, portant une erreur de date (1848 au lieu de 1845), n'a pas été émis.

Tirages : 844 : 2 900 000 - 845 : 3 340 000 - 846 : 2 700 000 - 847 : 2 585 000.

Cote du timbre avec charnière

Cote du timbre neuf sans charnière

CLEF DU CATALOGUE

Afin de ne pas alourdir le texte par la constante et fastidieuse répétition de notes explicatives, les auteurs ont adopté certaines conventions IMMUABLES, simples, peu nombreuses. Leur connaissance étant indispensable pour une parfaite utilisation du catalogue, nous les exposons ici aussi clairement que possible.

COMPLÉMENTS RELATIFS AUX TOMES I ET I BIS

Pour les timbres antérieurs à 1900, les cotes s'entendent pour des exemplaires sans défaut de papier, avec des marges correctes et filets visibles pour les timbres non dentelés et une dentelure normale pour les timbres dentelés ; une gomme d'origine pour les timbres neufs et une oblitération n'altérant pas le sujet du timbre pour les timbres oblitérés.

Les exemplaires avec défauts, clair dans le papier, marge courte, dents irrégulières, oblitération lourde ne sont pas sans valeur. On peut leur attribuer, suivant l'importance du défaut de 40 à 10% de la cote. Inversement, pour les exemplaires dits « de luxe » la cote doit être augmentée.

Dès l'origine à 1899, les cotes sont disposées sur deux colonnes : les cotes de la colonne de gauche concernent les timbres neufs avec charnière, celles de la colonne de droite les timbres oblitérés.

De 1900 à 1959, les cotes sont disposées sur trois colonnes : les cotes de la colonne de gauche concernent les timbres neufs avec gomme d'origine intacte et sans charnière **, celles de la colonne centrale les timbres neufs avec charnière légère *, celles de la colonne de droite les timbres oblitérés ⊙.

A partir de 1960, les cotes de la colonne de gauche concernent les timbres neufs sans charnière.

Les cotes des timbres sur lettres s'entendent pour un affranchissement et des cachets oblitérants normaux. Dans le cas d'affranchissements composés, il conviendra de prendre la cote du principal timbre ***sur lettre*** *et d'y ajouter les cotes des autres timbres* ***oblitérés****. Pour certains timbres, nous avons indiqué une seconde cote qui s'applique à l'affranchissement comportant un timbre unique ; cette cote est signalée par l'abréviation* ***(id. seul)****. Les affranchissements préparés philatéliquement valent moins.*

Centrage des timbres : les cotes s'entendent pour des timbres *bien centrés*. Lorsque le « très bon centrage » mérite une plus-value, nous indiquons entre parenthèses le pourcentage à appliquer à la cote pour obtenir le prix du timbre *très bien centré*. Pour un *centrage moyen*, il convient de diminuer la cote du même pourcentage, sans jamais excéder 50 %.

CLASSEMENT. - Dans chacun des volumes qui constituent le catalogue, nous avons suivi *l'ordre alphabétique*. Cette règle n'a souffert d'exceptions que lorsqu'il s'agissait de ne pas séparer certains départements d'un même pays, certaines régions géographiques, certains anciens États autrefois indépendants et plus tard groupés pour ne former qu'un seul État. En cas de doute, se reporter à **l'index alphabétique**.

Dans chaque pays, nous avons suivi autant que possible *l'ordre chronologique*. Pour faciliter les classements nous avons souvent groupé plusieurs émissions du même type ; nous avons alors indiqué les dates extrêmes d'émission. Lorsqu'un type ancien a été repris après un temps trop long pour qu'une telle réunion puisse être logiquement effectuée, nous avons indiqué, à la suite de la première émission à ce type, la référence des émissions successives.

COTES. - Les cotes sont disposées dans deux colonnes ; celle de gauche concerne les timbres **neufs** sans charnière ; celle de droite concerne les timbres **oblitérés**. (Voir ci-dessus les compléments relatifs aux tomes 1 et 1bis).

En général, les variétés valent plus cher que les timbres-types. Cependant, ce n'est pas une règle absolue. Pour faire connaître, tout de suite, s'il existe une variété moins chère que le timbre-type, nous avons mis les cotes de ce dernier en *chiffres italiques* (sauf dans le cas où les cotes sont à côté les unes des autres ou immédiatement l'une au-dessus de l'autre).

Remarque concernant les cotes des timbres oblitérés du 20e siècle, les cotes s'appliquent pour des exemplaires oblitérés proprement, durant la période de vente aux guichets et avec une tolérance de une à deux années, les oblitérés avec cachets tardifs lisibles ou non valent beaucoup moins. En revanche les timbres avec oblitération centrale lisible se rapportant à la période de vente valent beaucoup plus.

COULEURS. - La désignation des couleurs, difficile, a été cependant faite méthodiquement et permet un classement rationnel des variétés de nuances.

Pour les timbres imprimés en plusieurs couleurs nous avons toujours décrit celles-ci en partant des bords extérieurs du timbre de la droite vers la gauche. Pour les timbres à quatre ou cinq couleurs ou plus, nous mettons polychrome lorsque les couleurs sont confondues et multicolore lorsqu'elles sont côte à côte. - Lorsque la couleur d'une surcharge n'est pas spécifiée entre parenthèses, c'est que cette surcharge est noire.

Les couleurs en *italiques* signalent un timbre qui n'a pas été mis en cours, un « non émis ». De tels timbres ne sont naturellement cotés qu'à l'état neuf.

NUMÉROTAGE. - En principe nous avons donné un numéro différent - suivi parfois d'une lettre majuscule (toutefois les lettres i et o ne sont pas utilisées) - à chaque *timbre-type*, et aux *variétés* de ce timbre une lettre minuscule de l'alphabet. Toutes ces variétés sont imprimées en petits caractères. De plus elles sont mises en retrait afin que, à gauche de la composition, la suite normale des timbres-types saute à l'oeil du premier coup.

REPRODUCTIONS. - Tous les clichés utiles à connaître pour classer rapidement une collection figurent à leur place. Nous avons jugé superflue la reproduction entière de quelques séries sur le classement desquelles il est impossible d'hésiter un instant et, dans ce cas, nous avons remplacé les clichés par la désignation des sujets de chaque timbre.

L'expression *cadres variés* signifie que tous les timbres d'une émission ne sont pas exactement semblables au type reproduit, mais n'en diffèrent que par le détail des encadrements.

Les clichés des *timbres* sont réduits aux trois-quarts de leur grandeur réelle. Les *surcharges* ont été gravées en grandeur réelle et reproduites aussi fidèlement que possible. Il en est de même pour les *filigranes*.

[ ] - Deux crochets encadrant la couleur d'un timbre indiquent que ce timbre n'a pas été émis sans la surcharge qu'il porte.

( ) - Deux parenthèses encadrant la valeur nominale d'un timbre indiquent que cette valeur n'est pas portée sur le timbre ; s'agissant de timbres de bienfaisance, elles indiquent, accompagnées du signe +, la plus-value avec laquelle étaient vendus ces timbres, lorsque celle-ci n'est pas exprimée sur la vignette.

- Nous employons aussi les parenthèses pour faire connaître le numéro de certains timbres surchargés, lorsque nous n'avons pas la place de les décrire complètement ou lorsqu'une confusion peut se produire.

▯ - Un petit rectangle à la suite de la désignation de la couleur d'un timbre signifie que ce timbre existe *non dentelé*. Le même rectangle placé immédiatement après la légende, signifie que tous les timbres de la série existent *non dentelés*, ce qui ne veut pas dire que le prix en soit le même.

◺ - Un triangle indique que le timbre a été employé, *coupé en deux*, pour la moitié de sa valeur, soit obliquement, soit verticalement ou horizontalement.

✈ - Ce signe renvoie à la rubrique « Poste aérienne » où l'on trouvera une émission soit de même type, soit commémorant le même événement.

[BF] - Ce signe, lorsqu'il est suivi d'un numéro, renvoie à la rubrique « Blocs et feuillets ». Sous cette rubrique nous cataloguons les timbres imprimés en bloc, en bande, en paire ou même par unité sur des feuillets de dimensions variables, et nous donnons les cotes de ces pièces munies de toutes leurs marges.

- Lorsque le signe [BF] n'est pas suivi d'un numéro, c'est que le timbre existe en feuillet, mais que le caractère ou les conditions d'émission de ce feuillet ne nous ont pas paru justifier son homologation dans le catalogue.

[C] - Ce signe renvoie à la rubrique « Carnet ».

PETIT LEXIQUE PHILATÉLIQUE

Avec le concours de l'Académie de Philatélie et de l'Académie Européenne de Philatélie. Les termes précédés d'un astérisque sont extraits du dictionnaire philatélique et postal édité conjointement par les deux Académies.

*** AFFRANCHISSEMENT.** - Acquittement préalable de la totalité des frais de port, représenté, selon les époques et les cas, par des mentions, des marques spécifiques, des timbres-poste, des empreintes de machines à affranchir ou autres valeurs fiduciaires.

AMINCISSEMENT. - Diminution plus ou moins légère de l'épaisseur du papier, en un ou plusieurs endroits. Un timbre aminci perd beaucoup de sa valeur, laquelle est réduite proportionnellement à l'importance de l'amincissement.

BANDE. - Ensemble horizontal de plus de deux timbres qui n'ont pas été séparés. Les bandes de timbres non dentelés, lorsque les exemplaires qui les composent sont en parfait état, présentent de grosses plus-values. Les bandes verticales répondent à la même définition, mais leur plus-value est comparativement moins grande.

BIENFAISANCE (Timbres de). - Un grand nombre d'États ont pris l'habitude d'émettre des timbres qu'ils vendent à un prix supérieur à celui de la valeur d'affranchissement ; la différence est généralement versée à des oeuvres de bienfaisance. D'autres obligent à ajouter, certains jours, au prix normal du port de la lettre, un timbre n'ayant aucune valeur d'affranchissement et dont le montant intégral est remis à des oeuvres charitables. Ce sont seulement ces derniers que nous classons sous la rubrique « *Timbres de bienfaisance* ».

BLOC. - Ensemble de timbres qui n'ont pas été séparés. Le plus petit est le bloc de quatre, qui se présente ainsi : ⊞ ; ceux des timbres anciens sont très recherchés, surtout à l'état neuf, et présentent souvent de très importantes plus-values.

BURELAGE. - Fond formé de lignes légère entrecroisées ou parallèles, sur lequel se détache le dessin principal d'un timbre.

CADRES VARIÉS. - Ces mots signifient que les timbres d'une même émission représentent un même type entouré d'ornements différents. - Nous les employons lorsque nous croyons pouvoir nous dispenser, sans nuire à la clarté, de reproduire plusieurs timbres ne différant que par des détails d'encadrement.

CARACTÈRES. - Voici un modèle des caractères typographiques les plus employés et les noms sous lesquels on les désigne :

ANTIQUES — **ÉGYPTIENNES**
ROMAINS – *ITALIQUES*
NORMANDES

CENTRÉ. - Un timbre bien centré est celui dont les marges sont égales les unes aux autres, qu'il soit dentelé ou non.

CHARNIÈRES. - Petits morceaux de papier pelure gommé, à l'aide desquels on fixe les timbres dans les albums.

CHOIX. - Premier choix, second choix, expressions qui indiquent respectivement qu'un timbre est parfait ou imparfait. Nos cotes s'appliquent à des exemplaires de premier choix ; un amincissement, une petite fente, une dentelure incomplète, une oblitération trop forte, même un défaut de fraîcheur, sont autant de tares qui en diminuent plus ou moins la valeur.

COINS DATÉS. - De nombreuses feuilles de timbres de France, des Colonies françaises, de Monaco, etc., portent dans la marge inférieure de droite, depuis 1922, l'indication de la date de l'impression. Nos cotes s'entendent pour des blocs de quatre, neufs, attachés à la marge où figure la date.

COMMÉMORATIFS. - Timbres émis pour commémorer un événement. Ces émissions ont été mises à la mode en 1892 par les États d'Amérique qui ont presque tous émis des timbres à l'occasion du quatrième centenaire de la découverte de l'Amérique. La plupart de ces émissions sont faites pour être vendues aux collectionneurs plutôt que pour affranchir les lettres.

COUCHÉ. - Se dit d'un papier dont la surface est très glacée et brillante ; c'est le *chalky paper* des Anglais. Les séries jubilaires d'Autriche, quelques émissions des Colonies anglaises et françaises ainsi que de nombreuses séries modernes, ont été imprimées sur ce papier, qui constitue un support très mauvais pour les couleurs. Il ne faut pas mettre ces timbres dans l'eau et si on ne les protège pas, dans l'album, par une feuille de papier cristal, les couleurs se fanent et se rayent rapidement.

*** DÉCENTRÉ**. - Se dit d'un timbre-poste dont la partie imprimée n'est pas à égale distance des limites du papier ou de la dentelure, c'est-à-dire dont le centrage est défectueux.

*** DÉFECTUEUX.** - Se dit d'un timbre, ou d'une lettre, dont l'état est mauvais. L'appellation " troisième choix " est parfois utilisée dans ce sens. Les timbres défectueux n'ont, en règle générale, qu'une faible valeur.

DÉMONÉTISÉ. - Se dit d'un timbre qui n'est plus valable pour l'affranchissement des correspondances, à la suite d'un décret le retirant de la circulation.

DENTELÉ. - Se dit d'un timbre dont les bords ont été perforés ; cette perforation a pour but de faciliter la séparation des timbres d'une même feuille. — Lorsque ce mot n'est pas inscrit en tête d'une émission, les timbres de cette émission sont *non dentelés*. Le mot « dentelé » est toujours suivi d'un chiffre qui indique le nombre de dents contenues dans une longueur de deux centimètres et qu'on peut immédiatement évaluer à l'aide d'un *odontomètre* (voir ce mot).

Dentelés 13 signifie que les timbres d'une émission sont tous dentelés 13 sur les quatre côtés.

Dentelés 13x14 signifie que le côté horizontal a 13 dents et le côté vertical 14.

Dentelés 13-14 signifie que les timbres d'une émission sont indifféremment dentelés 13, 13x14, 14x13 ou 14.

Dentelés 12, 12x12½ signifie que chaque timbre de la série existe sous deux formes de dentelure différentes 12 et 12x12½.

*** DOUBLE IMPRESSION.** - Impression résultant de deux passages successifs sous la presse. Cela ne peut concerner que des presses imprimant feuille à feuille. Il peut aussi s'agir de feuilles de réglage de machine, utilisées successivement afin d'économiser le papier.

ÉMIS (NON). - Timbre préparé et dont une circonstance politique, économique ou financière n'a pas permis la mise en cours. Dans le catalogue, la couleur des timbres non émis est indiquée en caractères *italiques*.

EMPATTEMENT. - Forme donnée à la terminaison des jambages verticaux des lettres :

M : sans empattement (antiques) ;

M : empattement rectangulaire (égyptiennes) ;

M : empattement triangulaire (elzévir) ;

M : empattement à trait fin (romain).

ENTIER. - Mot qui sert à désigner les enveloppes, cartes postales, cartes-lettre, bandes, etc., portant un timbre imprimé.

*** EPREUVE.** - Empreinte sur papier d'un outil destiné à fabriquer le matériel d'impression des timbres-poste. Le mot " outil " est pris dans son sens large, il peut s'agir d'un poinçon métallique ou d'une pierre lithographique. Les épreuves sont imprimées à partir d'un poinçon sur petits feuillets avec marges, à l'unité. Grâce à elles, le graveur peut contrôler l'avancement de son travail. Elles permettent également de s'assurer de la mise en place des goujons ou de vérifier les poinçons de service. Le plus souvent elles sont imprimées en noir.

*** EPREUVE D'ARTISTE.** - Epreuve prise par le graveur sur le poinçon, soit en cours de gravure soit lorsqu'il est achevé. Les philatélistes l'appelle épreuve d'état lorsque le poinçon n'est pas terminé et épreuve terminale lorsque le poinçon est terminé. Pendant de nombreuses années, les artistes ont eu le droit de tirer des épreuves dont ils avaient la libre disposition.

ERREUR. - Timbre imprimé dans une couleur autre que celle qu'il aurait dû avoir, ou comportant une ou plusieurs fautes de composition, d'impression ou de disposition. Voir aussi **Tête-bêche**. Les erreurs sont trés recherchées par les spécialistes.

ESSAIS. - Épreuves tirées en diverses couleurs ou sur divers papiers avant l'adoption définitive d'un type de timbre.

*** EXPERTISE.** - Ensemble des opérations permettant de donner l'état civil d'un timbre ou d'une pièce, et de ce fait déterminer son numéro suivant un catalogue, son état, sa couleur, son authenticité.

EXPRÈS (Timbres). - Timbres émis par certains pays pour l'affranchissement des lettres qui doivent être délivrées par exprès dès leur arrivée au lieu de destination.

FAC-SIMILÉ. - Ces mots, imprimés au recto ou au verso des timbres, indiquent que ceux-ci sont faux. Cette mention est malheureusement exceptionnelle et les timbres faux se présentent en général sous les aspects les plus trompeurs.

FEUILLET. - Petite feuille sur laquelle sont imprimés un ou plusieurs timbres, dentelés ou non, et dont les marges portent souvent des inscriptions.

FIL DE SOIE. - Quelques timbres sont imprimés sur un papier contenant, dans la pâte, un fil de soie qu'on voit plus ou moins nettement en regardant le verso ; c'était un moyen d'empêcher la contrefaçon des timbres lorsque ce procédé de fabrication était secret. — Le papier mélangé de fils de soie est celui dans la pâte duquel se trouvent des multitudes de petits bouts de fils qui donnent au papier l'aspect de papier chiné. C'est aussi au verso qu'on les voit le mieux.

FILIGRANE. - Marque qui se trouve dans la pâte du papier et qui apparaît lorsqu'on regarde le timbre par transparence. Il y a cependant bien des cas où cet examen ne suffit pas à déceler le filigrane ; on a recours alors à la benzine ; on place le timbre, verso en l'air, sur une surface noire ou dans un *filigranoscope*, et on le recouvre de quelques gouttes de benzine. La plupart des filigranes apparaissent alors. Malheureusement un grand nombre de timbres sont imprimés avec des couleurs qui filent dans la benzine et, pour tous les timbres émis en ces dernières années, nous ne saurions recommander trop de circonspection.

Lorsque nous n'indiquons pas de filigrane en tête d'une émission, c'est qu'il s'agit de timbres *sans filigrane* ; dans le cas contraire, un cliché donne presque toujours l'aspect du filigrane tel qu'on le voit par transparence, c'est-à-dire le recto tourné vers soi. Pour les Colonies cependant, nous n'avons pas reproduit les filigranes employés dans les métropoles ; c'est, par exemple, au Danemark qu'on pourra voir le filigrane des Antilles danoises.

Nous reproduisons ici les quatre filigranes qui ont été employés successivement dans les Colonies anglaises :

CC ♔

CA ♔

CA *multiple*

𝒞𝒜 *multiple*

FISCAUX-POSTAUX. - Les timbres fiscaux sont ceux qui sont émis uniquement pour les besoins du fisc (enregistrement, contributions directes et indirectes, etc.). Quelques pays ont admis des timbres fiscaux à l'affranchissement des correspondances ; ce sont ces timbres que nous appelons *fiscaux-postaux*.

FORMAT. - Lorsque nous indiquons le format d'un timbre, les dimensions sont exprimées en millimètres et ne comprennent que le dessin, à l'exclusion des marges. La dimension horizontale est toujours indiquée la première.

GAUFRÉ. - Se dit d'un papier qui a passé à sec entre deux cylindres gravés et qui montre, en un léger relief, l'empreinte de cette gravure.

GOMME. - La plupart des collectionneurs attachent une grande importance à ce que les timbres neufs aient encore au verso la *gomme d'origine*, c'est-à-dire soient encore gommés comme ils l'étaient au moment où ils ont été émis. C'est souvent un premier indice qu'ils n'ont été ni lavés ni truqués.

GRAVÉ. - Se dit d'un timbre imprimé en taille-douce. Les timbres gravés se reconnaissent à la finesse de leur impression et à la légère saillie de l'encre sur le papier. Ils figurent parmi les plus beaux qui aient été émis et la France, qui avait été longtemps rebelle à l'emploi de ce procédé, lui a fait faire par la suite des progrès remarquables.

GRILLES EN RELIEF. - Léger burelage appliqué à sec en relief sur certains timbres anciens des États-Unis et du Pérou et qui avait pour but d'empêcher le lavage de l'oblitération.

GUILLOCHÉ. - Gravure formée d'un réseau d'entrelacs gravé par un moyen mécanique et d'une finesse remarquable.

HÉLIOGRAVÉ. - Nous appelons ainsi les timbres imprimés sur des planches obtenues par des moyens chimiques, après insolation naturelle ou artificielle. Ce procédé a fait son apparition philatélique en Bavière avec la série de 1914 à l'effigie du prince Louis III, alors régnant.

IDEM. - Ce mot, placé en tête d'une émission, signifie que toutes les indications de l'émission précédente, papier, filigrane, dentelure, etc., sont les mêmes, sauf contre-indication pour l'une ou plusieurs d'entre elles.

LÉGENDE. - Nous appelons ainsi les inscriptions qui figurent sur un timbre.

LETTRES EN RETARD (Timbres pour). - Dans certains pays, les lettres mises à la poste après l'heure normale de la dernière levée doivent être munies d'un timbre spécial pour être acheminées le jour même vers leur destination.

LITHOGRAPHIÉ. - Imprimé sur pierre. Nous indiquons, lorsque cela est possible, le moyen de distinguer les timbres lithographiés des gravés ou des typographiés. En général, la couleur est moins vive, l'impression est moins nette et ne laisse au verso aucune trace de foulage.

LOCAUX. - Timbres émis dans une ville ou dans un territoire quelconque et n'ayant pouvoir d'affranchir que les correspondances à destination de cette ville ou de ce territoire. La tradition seule a déterminé quels étaient ceux de ces timbres qui devaient faire partie de la collection générale (par ex. les cantonaux de Suisse) et ceux qui en étaient exclus (par ex. les ruraux de Russie), exclusion qui n'empêche pas ces derniers d'être recherchés par les spécialistes et d'être parfois excessivement rares et chers.

MANCOLISTE. - Liste des timbres qui manquent à un collectionneur.

MARGE. - Espace non imprimé qui encadre un timbre non dentelé. On dit « court de marge d'un côté » un timbre qui n'a pas de marge de ce côté, et cela diminue sa valeur.

MILLÉSIME. - Chiffre indiquant l'année dans laquelle un timbre a été émis ou imprimé. Certains millésimes ne sont pas indiqués sur le timbre, mais sur une marge de feuille, et souvent alors d'une façon conventionnelle.

* **MODERNE.** - Dans le langage philatélique, concerne les timbres-poste émis après 1945.

NETTOYAGE. - Nous ne saurions trop conseiller aux collectionneurs de ne jamais coller un timbre oblitéré dans leur album avant de l'avoir soigneusement nettoyé. Le meilleur moyen pour cela est de le laisser tremper un quart d'heure dans l'eau froide et de le faire sécher ensuite entre deux morceaux de buvard blanc et bien propre. — Il y a des timbres dont la couleur se dissout ou se dénature dans l'eau et que l'usage apprendra à connaître. Citons parmi eux : les premières émissions de Cachemire, de Russie, du Levant russe, certains timbres verts de Grande-Bretagne et tous les timbres des États malais, de Johore, de Maurice, de Sarawak, etc., imprimés en vert tendre (émissions postérieures à 1890). Il en est de même des timbres imprimés sur papier très glacé (dit couché). Le meilleur moyen de les nettoyer est de les placer sur un feutre dont on maintient l'humidité.

NEUF. - Ce n'est pas assez de dire qu'un timbre neuf n'est pas oblitéré : il faut aussi qu'il soit frais et de tout premier choix. La présence de la gomme d'origine doit être exigée quand un timbre est beaucoup plus cher à l'état neuf qu'à l'état oblitéré. Elle est d'ailleurs un premier indice qu'il n'a été ni tripoté ni lavuré.

NOIR SUR COULEUR. - Nous employons cette expression lorsqu'il s'agit d'une émission imprimée en noir sur papiers de couleur. La couleur indiquée est alors celle du papier.

* **NON DENTELÉ.** - Timbre-poste dépourvu de dents. Il peut s'agir :

- des premiers timbres-poste émis avant l'utilisation des machines à denteler (1849-1862).

- de timbres ayant échappé accidentellement à la dentelure : " non dentelé accidentel ".

- de timbres volontairement laissés sans dentelure, généralement pour des collections officielles (Empire Lauré) ou de timbres-poste destinés à être offerts.

* **NON ÉMIS.** - Il s'agit de vignettes dont la création fut décidée, l'effigie, la valeur faciale et les couleurs choisies, et qui reçurent un commencement de fabrication mais ne furent pas livrées au public par suite d'une décision de l'Administration des Postes, ou qui ne figurèrent que dans des collections officielles.

OBLITÉRATION. - Cachet ou marque quelconque qui indique qu'un timbre a servi et ne peut plus être utilisé. Certaines oblitérations donnent une grande valeur à certains timbres, mais ne sont guère collectionnées que dans les pays d'origine de ces timbres ; on ne saurait trop conseiller l'expertise avant l'acquisition de pièces de ce genre, qui ne prennent d'ailleurs tout leur intérêt que quand elles sont sur lettre, sur enveloppe ou sur grand fragment. — Les oblitérations à la plume sont les moins recherchées. Cependant, lorsqu'on ne trouve pas un prix spécial pour les timbres O P, on pourra admettre qu'ils ont la même valeur que les timbres oblitérés poste. L'oblitération fiscale consiste généralement en un cachet violet ; l'oblitération télégraphique, en un ! à l'emporte-pièce.

* **OBLITÉRATION TYPOGRAPHIQUE.** - Annulation des timbres mobiles par les caractères d'imprimerie des journaux. Réglementairement apposés en haut et à droite de la première page du journal avant impression, ils étaient annulés par celle-ci. Cette forme de préoblitération répond au désir des éditeurs, soucieux de la fraîcheur de leurs informations, de remettre les journaux en dernière minute, sans perdre de temps pour l'oblitération.

En dehors de quelques précurseurs, l'annulation typographique se rencontre sur les timbres pour journaux (timbres fiscaux ou fiscaux-postaux) dès 1869. Sur les timbres-poste, l'annulation typographique se rencontre normalement à partir de septembre 1870 (suppression du droit fiscal pour les journaux le 5 septembre 1870) et jusqu'en novembre 1893 avec quelques rares cas tardifs (dernière date connue 1931).

ODONTOMÈTRE. - Petit instrument en carton ou en celluloïd, portant un graphique qui sert à mesurer les dentelures.

OFFICIEL. - Apposé en surcharge sur un timbre-poste, ce mot le transforme presque toujours en timbre de service.

OFFSET. - Procédé lithographique dans lequel la pierre est remplacée par une plaque de métal, du zinc le plus souvent. L'impression sur le papier se fait par décalquage sur un cylindre plastique, ce qui permet l'emploi de papiers très peu satinés.

PAIRE. - Ensemble de deux timbres se tenant. La paire horizontale est davantage recherchée que la paire verticale. Voir **Bande.**

* **PAPIER GC** *(Grande Consommation).* - Qualité médiocre du papier utilisé entre 1916 et 1920 pour l'impression de certains timbres d'usage courant.

* **PELURAGE.** - Synonyme d'aminci. On emploie le mot pelurage lorsque l'aminci est de faible surface et de faible profondeur. Certains timbres, imprimés dans des conditions précaires sur des papiers de mauvaise qualité présentent généralement des pelurages (vignettes lithographiées de Diego Suarez). Certains papiers, tels les papiers de Chine ou de Japon, généralement utilisés pour l'impression d'épreuves, ne supportent que difficilement l'enlèvement de charnière qui provoque souvent un pelurage.

PERCÉS EN LIGNES. - Se dit d'un timbre dont les bords ont reçu légèrement l'empreinte d'une lame coupante ; cette empreinte a pour but de faciliter la séparation des timbres. Elle est quelquefois colorée et on dit alors que les timbres sont *percés en lignes colorées*. Les mots *percés en scie, en arc,* etc., indiquent des variantes du même procédé, désignées d'après la forme des empreintes.

* **PIQUAGE A CHEVAL.** - Résultat d'un dérèglement de l'unité de perforation lors de la fabrication des timbres-poste. La dentelure se trouve plus ou moins décalée, soit verticalement soit horizontalement. Il faut se défier des faux piquages à cheval appliqués sur des timbres modernes non dentelés.

PIQUÉ. - Synonyme de *dentelé*. De même, *piquage* est employé dans le même sens que *dentelure*.

PLANCHE. - Ensemble des clichés, généralement d'une même valeur, sur lesquels on imprime les timbres par feuilles entières. Lorsque ces planches sont numérotées, le même numéro est reproduit sur tous les timbres de la feuille.

* **PLI.** - Papier replié formant enveloppe, d'où l'expression courante de " lettre sous pli cacheté ". Par extension, lettre ou message. Jusqu'à la généralisation de l'enveloppe industrielle, en seconde partie du XIXe siècle, les lettres se présentent le plus souvent sous forme de pli.

POINTILLÉ. - Se dit d'un papier qui présente une impression plus ou moins visible de petits points rapprochés, formant une espèce de semis grisâtre.

POREUX. - Se dit d'un papier à trame apparente, mou et généralement assez épais.

PROVISOIRE. - Timbre ou émission faite occasionnellement par suite du manque d'une ou plusieurs valeurs postales. La brièveté de leur existence leur confère souvent une certaine rareté.

* **RARETE.** - Caractère de ce qui est peu courant et dont le nombre d'exemplaires connus est faible. En philatélie, il n'y a pas de lien systématique entre la rareté et la valeur marchande.

RECTO VERSO (Impression). - Se dit d'un timbre imprimé à l'endroit au recto et à l'envers, par décalque, au verso.

RECTO ET VERSO (Impression). - Se dit d'un timbre imprimé à l'endroit, au recto comme au verso.

RE-ENTRY. - Mot anglais qui s'applique à un timbre présentant quelques traces d'un report mal effacé et qui doublent certaines parties de l'image obtenue par un nouveau report.

RÉIMPRESSION. - Tirage fait, alors qu'un timbre n'est plus en cours, sur la planche qui a servi à imprimer ce timbre.

REPORT. - Opération qui consiste :

— soit à décalquer l'image d'une gravure pour la reproduire sur une pierre lithographique ou sur un bloc de métal ;

— soit à reporter sur zinc (pour l'impression *offset*), par un procédé photographique, le texte et les clichés qui ont été préalablement imprimés — ou montés (*typons*) — sur cellophane.

SERVICE (Timbres de). - Timbres avec lesquels sont affranchies dans certains pays les correspondances des fonctionnaires admises en franchise.

SERVICE INTÉRIEUR (Timbres pour le). - Timbres qui n'ont pas eu cours dans l'Union Postale Universelle ; on devrait logiquement faire entrer dans cette catégorie les premiers timbres d'un grand nombre de pays (Réunion, Cap de Bonne-Espérence, Suisse, etc.) et tous les timbres de certains autres (les petits États indiens, Shanghai, etc.).

SIGNATURE. - Mention faite, au bas d'un timbre, du nom du dessinateur, du graveur ou de l'imprimeur.

SPÉCIALISTE. - Collectionneur qui limite sa collection à un ou quelques pays, voire à une émission, dont il recherche alors les moindres variétés.

*** SPECIMEN.** - Mention enlevant toute valeur fiduciaire aux timbres-poste.

1) Surcharge apposée sur des timbres-poste non destinés à la vente.

2) Surcharge apposée sur diverses valeurs destinées à être exposées dans des bureaux de poste (2e série des Orphelins).

3) Surcharge apposée sur des timbres, carnets et entiers utilisés dans des cours pratiques des PTT de 1921 à 1931.

4) Surcharge apposée sur les timbres-poste d'une série des "Chômeurs intellectuels" de 1936, collés sur une présentation exposée chez les buralistes.

SPÉCIMEN. - Cette mention fut également apposée sur certains timbres qui ont été remis comme échantillons au bureau de l'Union Postale Universelle, à Berne, ou offerts par un gouvernement à des particuliers. Ces timbres sont admis dans beaucoup de collections ; nous en cotons d'ailleurs quelques-uns parmi ceux qu'on rencontre le plus souvent. Ceux des fortes valeurs de quelques colonies anglaises sont de véritables raretés.

SURCHARGE. - Inscription apposée sur un timbre et qui a pour objet d'en modifier la valeur ou la destination. — Nous indiquons toujours la couleur de la surcharge (voir aux **abréviations**) lorsqu'elle n'est pas noire ; et sa position lorsqu'elle n'est pas horizontale. Il n'est pas inutile de faire remarquer que, dans l'exemple ci-dessous, les surcharges I et II sont verticales et les surcharges III et IV horizontales :

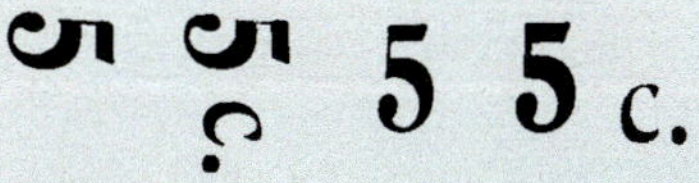

I II III IV

*** SURTAXE. -** 1) TIMBRES-POSTE : taxe supplémentaire, sans valeur d'affranchissement, s'ajoutant à la valeur fiduciaire d'un timbre-poste et collectée par l'administration postale au profit d'une œuvre (Croix-Rouge, Chômeurs intellectuels, etc.).

2) TARIFS : taxe supplémentaire s'ajoutant à l'affranchissement principal pour donner droit à un service particulier (surtaxe aérienne, de levée exceptionnelle, etc.).

TAXE (Timbres-). - Vignettes apposées sur les correspondances non ou insuffisamment affranchies.

TEINTÉ. - Se dit d'un papier qui à reçu une teinte de fond avant l'impression de la vignette-timbre. — Nous employons les mots *papier teinté*, — lorsque les timbres, sont imprimés sur un papier ayant reçu une teinte de fond de la même couleur que le timbre lui-même, mais dans un ton beaucoup plus pâle.

TÊTE-BÊCHE. - État de deux timbres tenant l'un à l'autre, dont l'un est à l'envers par rapport à l'autre. Le tête-bêche est dit horizontal lorsque les timbres sont à côté l'un de l'autre ; vertical lorsque l'un est au-dessus de l'autre. — Les amateurs préfèrent le tête-bêche horizontal ; c'est ce dernier que nous entendons coter lorsque nous indiquons un prix.

TÊTE D'IVOIRE. - Timbre au verso duquel se détache, en blanc sur azuré, le contour plus ou moins flou de l'effigie du recto.

*** TIRAGE.** - En philatélie, le mot désigne la quantité de timbres qui ont été imprimés. La date de tirage correspond donc à celle de l'impression des timbres.

TYPOGRAPHIÉ. - Se dit d'un timbre imprimé en typographie, c'est-à-dire sur des caractères ou des clichés en relief. Le signe distinctif de cette impression est le *foulage*, empreinte légère qu'on remarque souvent au verso.

USÉ. - Se dit (à tort) d'un timbre qui a servi et qui est oblitéré.

VERGÉ. - Se dit d'un papier bâtonné dans la pâte (comme le sont les papiers dits *anglais* du commerce). - A défaut d'indications contraires, la vergeure est horizontale.

SIGNES ET ABRÉVIATIONS

A. C.	Amérique Centrale
Af.	Afrique
A. N.	Amérique du Nord
ann.	Anniversaire
ard.	Ardoise
A. S.	Amérique du Sud
As.	Asie
Av.	Poste aérienne
B.	Annulé par barres
B.	Surcharge bleue
bienf.	Bienfaisance
briq.	Brique
C.	Surch. CANCELLED
C.	Surcharge carmin
cath.	Cathédrale
cent.	Centenaire
chs	Chamois
chaudr.	Chaudron
c^{in}	Carmin
$c^{né}$	Carminé
cl.	Clair
c^{net}	Carnet
Com.	Commémoratif
D.	Dentelé
Dble	Double
Eff.	Effigie
Eg.	Église
Eu.	Europe
F.	Fond
fcé	Foncé
Fil.	Filigrane
Fig.	Figure
fve	Fauve
gr.	Gris
imp.	Impression
J.	Surcharge jaune
jne	Jaune
L.	Surcharge lilas
l.d.v.	Lie-de-vin
Lég.	Légende
M. T.	Même type
Mill.	Millésime
N.	Surcharge noire
Non d.	Non dentelé
n^{r}	Noir
Obl.	Oblitéré
Oc.	Océanie
O. E.	Oblitéré entier
O. F.	Oblitéré fiscalement
O. P.	Oblitéré plume
O. T.	Oblitéré télégraphe
ol.	Olive
or^{ge}	Orange
outr.	Outremer
P.	Papier
P. en l.	Percé en lignes
Pl.	Planche
Quad.	Quadrillé
R.	Réimpression
R.	Surcharge rouge
renv.	Renversé(e)
rge	Rouge
s.	Sur
S. ou Surch.	Surcharge
sép.	Sépia
Sign.	Signature
SP.	Surch. SPÉCIMEN
T.	Timbre
T.-P.	Timbre-poste
V.	Surcharge verte
Val.	Valeur
v^{on}	Vermillon
v^{rt}	Vert
Vte	Surcharge violette
£	Livre sterling
$	Dollar, Peso ou Yuan
○	Perforé d'un cercle

INDEX

Le présent index renvoie le numéro des timbres correspondants aux sujets, précédé de "PA" pour les aériens, ou de "L" pour les vignettes LISA.

YVERT&TELLIER
Partenaires de vos passions...
LILLE
AMIENS
LE HAVRE
PARIS
LYON
MARSEILLE
espaces YVERT&TELLIER
6 magasins dédiés à toutes vos collections
Achat - Vente de Timbres
Catalogues de cotations
Materiel toutes marques
Monnaies - Cartes postales - Telecartes
Des professionnels au service de vos loisirs
LILLE
54, rue Molinel 59000 LILLE 03 20 44 22 22
AMIENS
26, rue au Lin 80000 AMIENS 03 22 92 33 32
PARIS
10, rue Châteaudun 75009 PARIS 01 40 82 74 70
LE HAVRE
72, avenue Foch 76600 LE HAVRE 02 35 41 22 22
LYON
48/50, rue de la Charité 69002 LYON 04 78 42 22 22
MARSEILLE
263, rue Paradis 13006 MARSEILLE 04 91 58 22 22

Type "Cérès"

1c.

39 A, B et C
(non dentelés)

39A

39B et C

50
(dentelé)

39A- Ombres sous l'oeil formées par des points. Les impressions usées présentent un léger contour blanc derrière la tête.
39B - Ombres sous l'oeil formées par des traits. Une ligne blanche derrière la tête souligne le contour des cheveux.
39C - Ombres sous l'oeil formées par des traits. Pas de contour blanc derrière la tête.

2c.

40 A et B
(non dentelés)

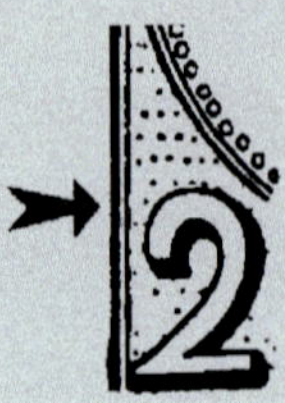

40 A

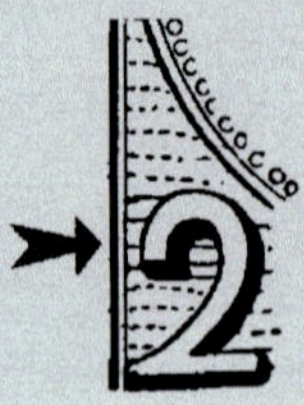

40 B

51
(dentelé)

40A - Toutes les lignes ondulées sont formées par des points, notamment celles entre le cadre et la boucle du 2 qui sont peu visibles.
40B - La plupart des lignes ondulées sont formées par des traits. Trois lignes horizontales séparées se trouvent entre le cadre et la boucle du 2.

4c.

41 A et B
(non dentelés)

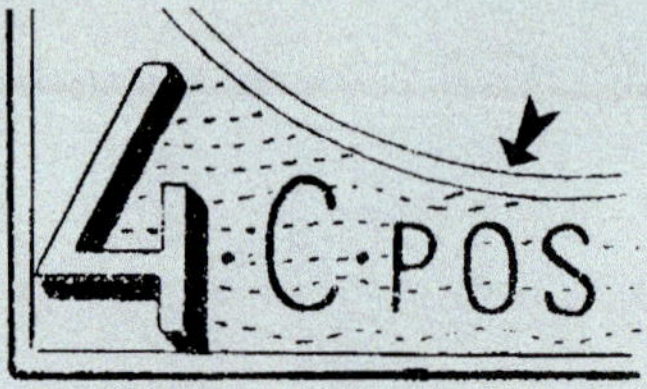

41 A

52
(dentelé)

41A - Impression fine du burelage constitué par des points. Les traits formant les ombres sous l'oeil sont plus ou moins reliés entre eux.
41B - Impression plus lourde. Le burelage est constitué de traits irréguliers dont certains se touchent.

5c.

42 A et B
(non dentelés)

42 A

42 B

53
(dentelé)

348
(dentelé)

42A - Pas de ligne blanche derrière la tête. L'iris de l'oeil est fait d'un trait et d'un point qui ne touche que la paupière supérieure. Menton en retrait de la lèvre inférieure. Impression très fine donnant aspect dépouillé.
42B - Ligne blanche derrière la tête plus ou moins marquée. L'iris de l'oeil est fait d'une seule grosse tache ovale. Menton fuyant en avant de la lèvre inférieure. Impression générale plus lourde.

10c.

1
(non dentelé)
imp. typo

36
(dentelé)
imp. typo

43A et B
(non dentelés)
imp. litho

54
gros chiffres
papier teinté

58
petits chiffres
papier teinté

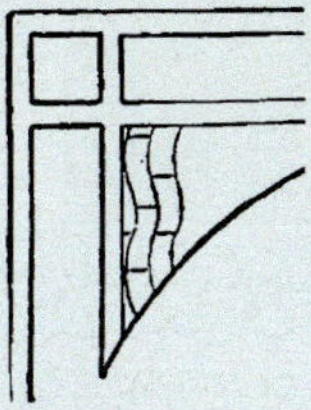

43 A

43A - Le cadre triangulaire intérieur est formé de traits égaux en épaisseur.
43B - Le filet intérieur du cadre est plus épais.

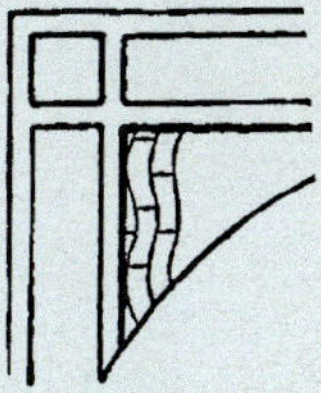

43 B

15c.

2

55
gros chiffres

59
petits chiffres

349

20c.

3

8
imp. typo

37
(dentelé)

44 A, B
45 A, B et C
46 A,B
imp. litho

Type I

Type I. - L'ombre du cou est formée par des points, les inscriptions sont petites.

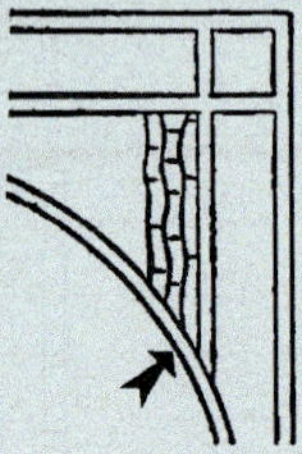

44A
Type I, Report 1

Report. 1. - Imbriquement normal.

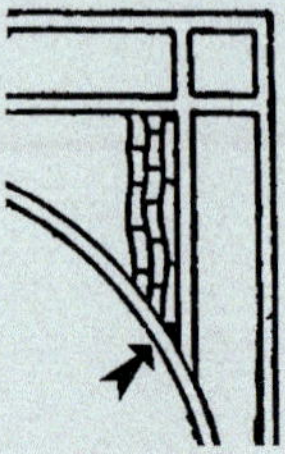

44B
Type I, Report 2

Report 2. - Dans la partie supérieure droite du timbre, un point de couleur réunit la ligne intérieure du cadre au premier trait horizontal de l'imbriquement.

Type II

Type II. L'ombre du cou est formée par des traits, les inscriptions sont petites comme dans le type I. La grecque supérieure gauche est prolongée à sa base par un trait blanc de forme triangulaire.

45A
Type II, Report 1

45B
Type II, Report 2

45C
Type II, Report 3

Report 1.
Les seconds grains de raisin des 1re et 3e rangées de la grappe sont blancs. Le premier lobe de la feuille de vigne de droite est à peine indiqué.

Report 2.
Les seconds grains de raisins des 1re et 3e rangées de la grappe sont ombrés par un trait courbe. La feuille de vigne est franchement découpée. Il y a un point ou un trait parasite dans le cinquième intervalle de l'imbriquement à gauche en bas.

Report 3.
Mêmes caractéristiques que le report 2. De plus le contour des cheveux est souligné par une ligne blanche.

Type III

Type III. - Les inscriptions sont plus grandes.

46A
Type III, Report 1

46B
Type III, Report 2

Report 1.
Le cadre est formé de traits égaux en épaisseur (voir R. 1 du 10 c.). Le contour des cheveux est souligné par une légère ligne blanche.

Report 2.
Le filet intérieur du cadre triangulaire est plus épais (voir R. 2 du 10 c.). Pas de contour blanc derrière la tête.

4
(non dentelé)

60A
(dentelé)

47
(non dentelé)

56
(dentelé)

350

← 25 c. → ← 30 c. →

5
(non dentelé)

38
(dentelé)

48
(non dentelé)

351

← 50 c. →

49

57

6

7

← 80 c. → ← 1 F. →

372

373

374

375

375A

Type “Louis-Napoléon Bonaparte”

11

19

25

26

12

20

35

27

9

13 A ou B

21

28A

34

14A ou B

22

29 A ou B

10

15

30

16

23

31

17A

17B

24

32

18

33

Type “Sage”

Pour identifier les timbres du type Sage, il convient de regarder en bas à gauche sous la légende “République Française”, la signature “J.A. SAGE INV”.
Dans le type I, le N de “INV” se trouve sous le B de “République”.
Dans le type II le N se trouve sous le U.

61

83
noir sur azuré

Préo 11

84
noir sur bleu de prusse

62
Type I

74
Type II

85

Préo 1

Préo 12

86

87

Préo 13

63

88

Préo 2

Préo 14

64
Type I

75
Type II

Préo 3

Préo 15

102
Type III

106
Type II

le N° 102 a une nuance différente de celle du N° 64, de plus le chiffre 5 est plus large

65
Type I

76
Type II

89
Type II

Préo 4

Préo 16

103
Type I

66
Type I

77
Type II

90
Type II

Préo 5

Préo 17

67
Type I

73

96
Type II

Préo 6

Préo 18

68
outremer Type I

78
outremer Type II

79
bleu Type II

91

92

Préo 7

Préo 19

69
Type I

80
Type II

Préo 8

Préo 20

93

70
Type I

94
Type II

Préo 9

Préo 21

98
Type II

Préo 10

Préo 22

104
Type I

71
Type I

81
Type II

99
Type II

Préo 10A

Préo 23

72
Type I

82
Type II

Préo 23A

105

95

Type “Blanc”

107

157

108

109

Préo 39

110

Préo 40

111

Préo 41

Préo 42

233

Préo 43

Type “Merson”

119

143

Préo 44

120

144

121

182

122

145

257A

PA 1

206

240

123

PA 2

207

208

Type “semeuse lignée”

129 FM 4 130 Préo 25 Préo 28 Préo 31 Préo 34

Préo 37 Préo 45 FM 3 131 132 133 197

Préo 46 161 Préo 47 247 199 FM 6 250

198 362 254 267 276 200 223

201 Préo 48 234 224 Préo 49 202 203

220 204 221 205 1233 1234A 3619-adhésif 36

Type "semeuse fond plein"

277A 279A 277B 279B 278 278A 137

Préo 24 Préo 26 158 Préo 27 Préo 30 Préo 33

Préo 36 Préo 50 278B 134 135 138 159

Préo 51 188B 279 Préo 52 FM 5 146 147

189 Préo 53 139 Préo 54 190 Préo 55 140

Préo 56 235 141 Préo 29 Préo 35 160 Préo 32

Préo 38

Préo 58

191

Préo 59

192

Préo 60

217

360

Préo 61

136

142

Préo 62

218

361

Préo 63

476

193

194

Préo 64

236

237

246

249

253

266

275

195

225

227

238

196

228

268

277

239

241

242

Type "Paix"

280 Préo 69 281 Préo 70 282 Préo 71 283

FM 7 363 478 364 Préo 72 284 Préo 73

365 FM 8 479 284A 480 366 Préo 74

Préo 75 481 285 367 368 FM 9 FM 10

482 286 359 369 Préo 76 287 298

370 483 371 Préo 77 484 288

485 289

Type "Iris"

431 649 432 433 650 651 434

435 652 653 654 655 656

Marianne de Gandon

712 713 Préo 94 714 Préo 95 715

716 Préo 96 716A 806 716B 717

718 807 Préo 98 808 Préo 99

725 Préo 97 718A 719 719A 719B

809 883 720 721 Préo 100 721A

827

884

810

Préo 101

722

723

811

Préo 102

726

812

Préo 103

885

Préo 103A

724

813

Préo 104

886

727

832

887

968

728

730

729

833

731

732

733

3977-adhésif 96

Type "Marianne de Cheffer"

1535

1536

1536A

1611

1536B

1643

4109-adhésif 139

4291-adhésif 229

Type "Marianne de Béquet"

1663 (sans signature)

1664

4292-adhésif 230

1815

1814 (sans signature)

1816

1893

1894

1891 (sans signature)

1892

1895

Sabine de Gandon

1962

1963

1964

1965

1966

1967

1968

1969

4292-adhésif 231

1970

1971

2120

1972

1981

1973

1981A

2057

2058

2062

1974

1981B

2101

2103

2059

2063

1975

2102

2104

2154

2157

2060

2155

2158

1976

2061

1977

1978

2156

1979

2121

2122

2123

Liberté de Gandon

2178

2179

2180

2181

2182

2183

2184

2239 2240 2241 2242 2185 2186 2191

2187 2192 2219 2222 2318 2321 2220

2223 2375 2378 2424 2426 2188 2274

2277 2484 2487 2319 2322 2376 2379

2427 2461 2524 2530 4294-adhésif 232

2189 2221 2275 2243 2320 2377

2425 2485 2486 2244 2190 2276

2423 2483 2615 2616

Marianne du Bicentenaire

2617 | 2618 | 2619 | 2824-adhésif 5 | 2873-adhésif 6 | 2620 | 3009-adhésif 8

2621 | 2906 | 2622 | 2627 | 2714 | 2718 | 2790

2614 | 2628 | 2629 | 2630-adhésif 1 | 2820 | 2823 | 2715

2719 | 2720-adhésif 3 | 3005 | 3008 | 2623 | 2716

2821 | 2624 | 3006 | 2717 | 2770 | 2822

3007 | 2625 | 2626 | 2711 | 2712 | 2713-adhésif 2

2806 | 2807-adhésif 4 | 2819 | 2874-adhésif 7 | 4295-adhésif 233

Marianne du 14 Juillet

3086

3087

3088

3089

3101-adhésif 16

3090

3091

3100

3127

3092

3093

3094

3095

3096

3097

3098

3099

3083

3084

3085-adhésif 15

3689

3417

3418

3419-adhésif 30

Personnalisé 3688H

Personnalisé 3587A

Personnalisé 3729A

4296-adhésif 234

3443

Personnalisé 3688B

3444

Personnalisé 3688C

Personnalisé 3688D

3445

3446

Personnalisé 3688E

3447

Personnalisé 3688F

3448

3458

3449

3450

3451

Personnalisé 3688J

3570

3452

3453

3454

3571

Personnalisé 3688K

Personnalisé 3688L

3572

Personnalisé 3729B

3573

Personnalisé 3688M

3455

Personnalisé 3688N

3456

3574

Personnalisé 3729C

Personnalisé 3688P

Personnalisé 3729D

3575

Personnalisé 3688Q

3457

Personnalisé 3688R

3535A

Personnalisé 3688G

3535B

Marianne de Lamouche

3731 — Personnalisé 4048A ou 4048P — Personnalisé 3925A — Personnalisé 4048B ou 4048Q

3754 — Personnalisé 3925B — Personnalisé 4048Cou 4048R — 3965

Personnalisé 3925C — Personnalisé 3916A — 3732 — 3733

3742 — Personnalisé 3925D — Personnalisé 4048Dou 4048S — 3734

Personnalisé 3925E — Personnalisé 4048Eou 4048T — 3743 — 3743a — 3744-adhésif 49 — 4297-adhésif 235

Personnalisé 3802A — 3744b — Personnalisé 3745 — 3755

3807

4127-adhésif 147

4153

Personnalisé 3925F

Personnalisé 3802D

4159

3735

3973

Personnalisé 3966A

Personnalisé 4048Fou 4048U

3966

3742a

3756

Personnalisé 3925G

3967

3736

4154

3737

Personnalisé 3925H

Personnalisé 4048Gou 4048V

3757

Personnalisé 3925J

Personnalisé 3802B

Personnalisé 3969A

3968

Personnalisé 4048Hou 4048W

3969

Personnalisé 4048Jou 4048X

4155

3738

Personnalisé 3925K

3739

Personnalisé 3925L

Personnalisé 4048Kou 4048Y

3740

3970

Personnalisé 4048Lou 4048Z

3758

Personnalisé 3925M

Personnalisé 3802C

4156

3971

Personnalisé 4048Mou 4048AA

4157

3741

3759

Personnalisé 3925N

3972

Personnalisé 4048Nou 4048AB

4158

3925-adhésif 85

Marianne à la nef

1216

1229

1234

4287-adhésif 225

Marianne de Cocteau

1282

4289-adhésif 227

Marianne de Decaris

1263

4288-adhésif 226

Coq de Decaris

1331

1331A

4290-adhésif 228

Marianne de Beaujard

4197-adhésif 175

4230

4240-adhésif 220

4298-adhésif 236

4201-adhésif 179

4231

4241-adhésif 221

4236-adhésif 216

4344-adhésif 288

4229-adhésif 211

4239-adhésif 219

4226-adhésif 208

4227-adhésif 209

4228-adhésif 210

4232-adhésif 212

4342-adhésif 286

4233-adhésif 213

4345-adhésif 289

4234-adhésif 214

4343-adhésif 287

4235-adhésif 215

4237-adhésif 217

4238-adhésif 218

4346-adhésif 290

4242-adhésif 193

PRINCIPALES OBLITERATIONS SE RENCONTRANT SUR LES PREMIÈRES ÉMISSIONS DE FRANCE

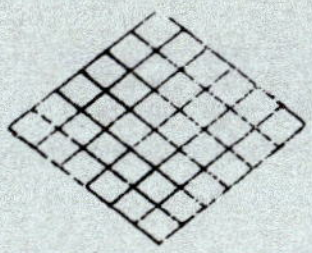

Grille de 1849

Gros points

Grille sans fin

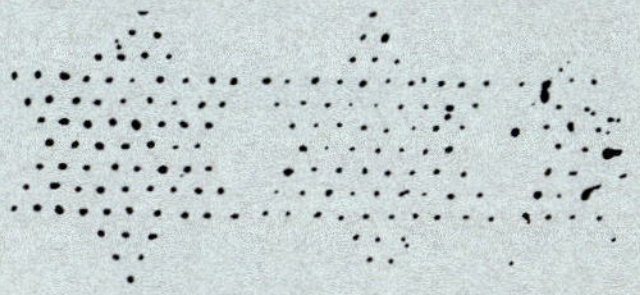

Roulette d'étoiles

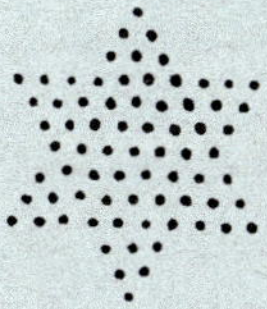

Etoile

Pontillé

Cercle de points

Losange petits chiffres

Losange gros chiffres

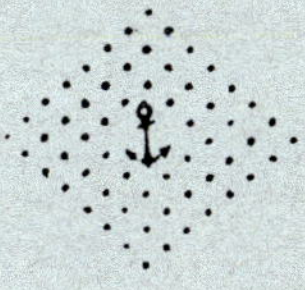

Ancre

Petit cachet à date

Grand cachet à date

Moyen cachet à date

Cachet à date à cercle pointillé

OR dans un cercle (Origine Rurale)

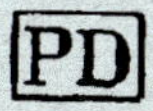

PD dans un rectangle (Payé jusqu'à destination)

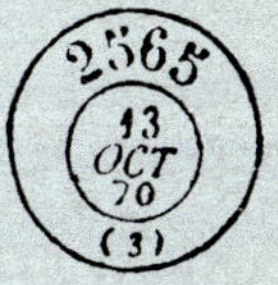

Cachet à date de bureau de Passe

Cachet à date rouge des Imprimés

Annulation typographique des journaux.

Assemblée Nationale

Lorsque la couleur n'est pas précisée, il s'agit d'une oblitération noire.

CERES Philatélie
France - Colonies Françaises
Europe et Outre-Mer
Depuis 60 ans au service des collectionneurs
EMPIRE FRANC
POSTES
COLONIES
POSTES
REPUBLIQUE FRANÇAISE
PAQUEBOT PASTEUR
70c
POSTES
RF
VENTES SUR OFFRES et A PRIX NETS
vente par correspondance et en magasin
27
AOUT
1851
Arzew
ALGÉRIE
POSTE AERIENNE
500F
RÉPUBLIQUE FRANÇAISE
Retrouvez-nous sur
www.ceres.fr
Timbres neufs, Lettres, Carnets, Variétés, Epreuves, Spéciali
EXPERTISE . ESTIMATION . ACHAT
Déplacement possible
23, rue du Louvre 75001 PARIS
Tél 01 42 33 31 91 - Fax 01 42 33 61 67 - www.ceres.fr

FRANCE

100 c(entimes) =1 f(ranc)

Depuis le 1er Janvier 2002 : 1 €(uro) =100 c(entimes).

IIe République

Pour les timbres (sur lettre) voir rubrique "Clef du catalogue".

La cote des timbres oblitérés des nos 1 à 106 varie en fonction du type d'oblitération.

En règle générale, la cote figurant dans la colonne de droite correspond à l'oblitération la plus commune.

Voir également nos éditions spécialisées.

TÊTE-BÊCHE DANS UN BLOC

Pour évaluer la cote d'un tête-bêche dans un bloc de quatre, ajouter la cote du tête-bêche à celle du bloc de quatre.

Type Cérès

Ce type a été repris en 1870-71 pour la France et les Colonies générales : en 1937 à l'occasion de l'Exposition philatélique de Paris (nos 348 à 351), en 1949, à l'occasion de l'Exposition du Centenaire du Timbre (nos 830, 831 et 841) et en 1999 pour le cent cinquantième anniversaire (nos 3211 et 3212 et entier no 3094).

1850. – *Typographie. Papier teinté. non dentelé.*

N°	Désignation	Neuf	Oblitéré
1	**10 c. bistre-jaune**	**2 200 »**	**330 »**
	(Sur lettre)		700 »
	(Neuf sans gomme)	900 »	
	d. (la paire, tête-bêche)	90 000 »	18 000 »
	(Sur lettre)		35 000 »
	⊞	10 000 »	12 000 »
	⊞ annulation rouleau de gros points		4 000 »
	a. bistre-brun	2 700 »	425 »
	b. bistre verdâtre	3 500 »	500 »
	e. (la paire, tête bêche)	110 000 »	27 500 »
	(Sur lettre)		42 500 »
	⊞	18 000 »	16 000 »
	⊞ annulation rouleau de gros points		6 500 »
	c. bistre verdâtre foncé	5 500 »	1 000 »
	f. bistre clair (réimpression)	600 »	

Oblitérations	⊙	🖂
Grille sans fin	500 »	1 200 »
Grille (rouge)	2 300 »	
Gros points	385 »	1 250 »
Etoile de points	460 »	900 »
Losange petits chiffres	340 »	650 »
Petit cachet à date	900 »	3 700 »
Moyen cachet date	1 110 »	7 800 »
Grand cachet à date	1 400 »	11 000 »
O.R. dans un cercle	700 »	2 200 »

1850. – *Typographie. Papier teinté. non dentelé.*

N°	Désignation	Neuf	Oblitéré
2	**15 c. vert**	**25 000 »**	**1 000 »**
	(Sur lettre)		1 750 »
	⊞	140 000 »	80 000 »
	(Neuf sans gomme)	10 000 »	
	d. (la paire, tête-bêche, sur lettre)		325 000 »

On ne connaît qu'un exemplaire oblitéré et défectueux du n° 2d (sur devant de lettre).

Désignation	Neuf	Oblitéré
a. vert clair	26 500 »	1 100 »
b. vert foncé	30 000 »	1 200 »
⊞	160 000 »	100 000 »
c. vert très foncé	35 000 »	2 500 »
e. vert vif clair (réimpression)	800 »	

Oblitérations	⊙	🖂
Grille sans fin	1 000 »	2 500 »
Grille (rouge)	4 600 »	
Gros points	1 300 »	2 800 »
Etoile de points	1 100 »	1 600 »
Losange petits chiffres	4 600 »	25 000 »
Petit cachet à date	3 500 »	
Moyen cachet date	3 850 »	

1849. – *Typographie. Papier teinté. non dentelé.*

N°	Désignation	Neuf	Oblitéré
3	**20 c. noir s. jaune**	**500 »**	**60 »**
	(Sur lettre)		100 »
	⊞	2 350 »	5 000 »
	(Neuf sans gomme)	200 »	
	d. (la paire, tête-bêche)	12 000 »	7 500 »
	(Sur lettre)		15 000 »
	a. noir s. blanc	550 »	65 »
	⊞	2 750 »	5 500 »
	e. (la paire, tête-bêche)	13 000 »	8 500 »
	(Sur lettre)		17 500 »
	b. noir s. chamois	1 100 »	200 »
	c. gris-noir	2 300 »	500 »
	f. (réimpression)	500 »	
	i. Gris souris	3 700 »	1 000 »

Oblitérations	⊙	🖂
Grille sans fin	950 »	15 000 »
Grille (rouge)	1 000 »	12 000 »
Etoile de points	600 »	14 000 »
Losange petits chiffres	800 »	5 350 »
Petit cachet à date	200 »	700 »
Moyen cachet date	400 »	2 000 »
Grand cachet à date	800 »	4 800 »

NOTA : les oblitérations provisoires des premiers jours de janvier 1849, jusqu'à l'apparition de la grille (à partir du 10 janvier) sont particulièrement recherchées (voir notre catalogue spécialisé, tome 1, éd. 1975).

1850. – *Typographie. Papier teinté. non dentelé.*

4	**25 c. bleu**	**7 500** »	**45** »
	(Sur lettre)		70 »
	(Neuf sans gomme)	2 500 »	
	c. (la paire, tête-bêche)	160 000 »	15 000 »
	(Sur lettre)		30 000 »
	⊞	40 000 »	5 750 »
	a. bleu foncé	8 500 »	70 »
	b. bleu s. jaune	8 000 »	55 »
	h. bleu-noir	9 500 »	110 »
	d. (réimpression)	550 »	

Oblitérations	⊙	🖂
Grille sans fin	110 »	170 »
Grille (rouge)	2 300 »	
Gros points	85 »	400 »
Etoile de points	45 »	90 »
Losange petits chiffres	40 »	60 »
Petit cachet à date	600 »	3 200 »

1850. – *Typographie. Papier teinté. non dentelé*

5	**40 c. orange**	**4 750** »	**500** »
	(Sur lettre)		800 »
	(Coupé sur lettre)		150 000 »
	(Neuf sans gomme)	2 000 »	
	⊞ (gomme blanche)	27 000 »	20 000 »
	a. orange vif	5 500 »	575 »
	b. orange foncé	5 500 »	650 »
	c. (Gomme brunâtre)	2 700 »	
	g. (réimpression)	750 »	

Oblitérations	⊙	🖂
Grille sans fin	575 »	840 »
Grille (rouge)	3 850 »	
Gros points	500 »	800 »
Etoile de points	500 »	750 »
Losange petits chiffres	500 »	750 »
Petit cachet à date	1 000 »	3 850 »

Coupés sur lettre : On connaît deux lettres affranchies de cette façon, dont une avec la moitié gauche d'un timbre de 40 c. ayant servi de timbre de 20 c. ; oblitération losange de points avec 851 en petits chiffres (Le Cheylard).

4 retouchés (plus larges).

normal

retouché

Par erreur, on avait placé deux clichés du 20 c. dans une planche du 40 c. Cette erreur fut corrigée en modifiant individuellement les chiffres 2.

5d	40 c. ("4" retouché)	30 000 »	7 000 »
	(Sur lettre)		15 000 »
5h	("4" retouché, réimpression)	14 000 »	
5e	(Paire avec un normal)	47 500 »	16 000 »
5j	(Paire avec un normal, réimpression)	20 000 »	
5f	(Paire des deux timbres retouchés)	125 000 »	65 000 »
5k	(Paire des 2 retouchés, réimpression)	35 000 »	

1849. – *Typographie. Papier teinté. non dentelé.*

carmin foncé

6	**1 f. carmin foncé**	**14 000** »	**900** »
	(Sur lettre)		1 600 »
	(Neuf sans gomme)	5 000 »	
	e. (la paire, tête-bêche)	200 000 »	28 000 »
	(Sur lettre)		75 000 »
	⊞	70 000 »	16 500 »
	a. carmin clair	16 000 »	1 200 »
	d. carmin cerise		3 250 »
	f. (réimpression)	800 »	

Oblitérations	⊙	🖂
Grille sans fin	1 150 »	1 700 »
Gros points	1 100 »	1 800 »
Etoile de points	1 050 »	1 600 »
Losange petits chiffres	950 »	1 600 »
Petit cachet à date	3 100 »	
Moyen cachet date	3 200 »	
Grand cachet à date	3 200 »	

1849. – *Typographie. Papier teinté. non dentelé.*

rouge-brun

6A	**1 f. rouge-brun**	**24 000** »	**2 700** »
	(Neuf sans gomme)	8 000 »	
	a. (tête-bêche, sur lettre)		140 000 »
	⊞	120 000 »	

1849. – *Typographie. Papier teinté. non dentelé.*

carmin-brun

6B	**1 f. carmin-brun**	**14 000**	**» 1 000**	**»**
	(Neuf sans gomme)	5 000	»	
	⊞	75 000	» 40 000	»
	a. (la paire, tête-bêche)	220 000	» 45 000	»
	(Sur lettre)		75 000	»

1849. – *Typographie. Papier teinté. non dentelé.*

vermillon

7	**1 f. vermillon**	**95 000**	**»20 000**	**»**
	(Sur lettre)		32 500	»
	⊞	450 000	»135 000	»
	(Neuf sans gomme)	60 000	»	
	a. vermillon vif	120 000	» 26 500	»
	⊞	500 000	»160 000	»
	d. (la paire, tête-bêche)	1 000 000	»200 000	»
	b. vermillon terne	60 000	» 17 000	»
	⊞	275 000	» 95 000	»
	e. (la paire, tête-bêche)		200 000	»

Oblitérations	⊙		✉	
Grille sans fin	23 000	»		
Gros points	20 000	»		
Etoile de points	22 000	»		
Losange petits chiffres	23 000	»	34 000	»
Petit cachet à date	24 000	»	40 000	»
Moyen cachet date	27 500	»	50 000	»
Grand cachet à date	28 000	»	90 000	»

NOTA : Comme pour le N°3, les oblitérations provisoires des premiers jours de janvier 1849, jusqu'à l'apparition de la grille (à partir du 10 janvier) sont particulièrement recherchées (voir notre catalogue spécialisé, tome 1, éd. 1975).

1850. – *Typographie. Papier teinté. non dentelé.*

vermillon pâle

7A	**1 f.** ***vermillon pâle (Vervelle)***	**28 000**	**»**
	f. (la paire, tête-bêche)	400 000	»
	⊞	200 000	»

Le n° 7A, toujours sans gomme, est généralement aminci. Il n'existe qu'à l'état neuf. Il est appelé Vervelle du nom du négociant qui le découvrit, à la fin du XIXème siècle.

DOCUMENT POSTAL

Le 1er décembre 1849, une circulaire portant une moitié de 1 f. vermillon et une moitié de 1 f. carmin fut envoyée aux bureaux de poste, afin de procéder au retrait des timbres vermillon dont la couleur était proche de celle des 40 c. orange, imprimés depuis avril 1849, mais qui ne furent émis qu'en 1850.

sur circulaire entière	70 000	»
sur fragment	10 000	»

NON ÉMIS

1849. – *Typographie. non dentelé.*

8	**20 c.** ***bleu s. jaunâtre***	**4 000**	**»**
	⊞	18 000	»
	c. (la paire, tête-bêche)	100 000	»
	a. *bleu foncé*	3 400	»
	⊞	15 000	»
	d. (la paire, tête-bêche)	85 000	»
	b. *bleu s. azuré*	3 200	»
	⊞	16 000	»
	e. (la paire, tête-bêche)	75 000	»
	f. (réimpression)	600	»

Le n° 8 est toujours sans gomme, les n°s 8a et 8b sont avec ou sans gomme

N°8 Surchargé.

8A	**25 c. s. 20 c.** ***bleu*** **(R)**	**22 000**	**»**

On connaît un exemplaire d'un n° 8 original avec une surcharge voisine qui ne comprend ni le point sous le c ni les barres ornementales

1852. – *Prince-président Louis-Napoléon. Légende REPUB. FRANC. B sous le cou. Typographie. Papier teinté. non dentelé.*

9	**10 c. bistre-jaune**	**42 000**	**»**	**700**	**»**
	(Sur lettre)			1 000	»
	(Neuf sans gomme)	12 000	»		
	⊞	230 000	»	50 000	»
	a. bistre-brun	45 000	»	900	»
	b. (avec lignes d'encadrement)	60 000	»	8 500	»
	c. bistre clair (réimpression, 1862)	750	»		

Oblitérations	⊙		✉	
Gros points	765	»	2 200	»
Grille sans fin	1 100	»	4 000	»
Petit cachet à date	1 300	»	11 500	»
O.R. dans un cercle	1 300	»	6 500	»
Grille	1 500	»	15 000	»

1852. – *Prince-président Louis-Napoléon. Légende REPUB. FRANC. B sous le cou. Typographie. Papier teinté. non dentelé.*

10	**25 c. bleu**	**3 650**	**»**	**40**	**»**
	(Sur lettre)			100	»
	⊞	16 500	»	2 300	»
	(Neuf sans gomme)	1 300	»		
	a. bleu foncé	4 200	»	80	»
	b. (avec lignes d'encadrement)	6 000	»	1 700	»
	c. bleu (réimpression, 1862)	500	»		

Oblitérations	⊙	✉
Gros points	130 »	700 »
Grille sans fin	200 »	800 »
Petit cachet à date	900 »	3 850 »
Grille	800 »	5 000 »

Second Empire

1853-60. – *Napoléon III. Idem. Légende EMPIRE FRANC.*

Le 1 c. n'a existé qu'au type II, les 5, 25, 40, 80 c. et 1 f., qu'au type I.

Type I : La mèche temporale présente trois cheveux : celui du milieu est formé par un double trait plus épais, dont le trait de droite est légèrement plus long que celui de gauche qui a sensiblement la même longueur que les autres cheveux de la mèche

Type II : La mèche est formée par quatre cheveux, nettement séparés, et toujours d'égale longueur.

Les 1 c. et 25 c. ont subi certaines retouches qu'on reconnaît aux raccords des filets des cadres ou à des lettres déformées.

Il a été fait un tirage spécial, dit des *"Arts & Métiers"* : ces timbres sont sans gomme et d'une impression très soignée.

TIMBRES AVEC LIGNES D'ENCADREMENT.

Une partie des planches est, comme toutes celles de la Présidence, entourée par un filet d'encadrement situé à 7 ou 8 mm des timbres, selon les panneaux.

Les timbres avec ligne d'encadrement formant coin de feuille valent le double des cotes ci-dessous.

Piquages.

Nous référençons dans ce catalogue 7 types de piquages :

Piquage Susse, consistant en larges trous (7¼ x 7)

Percés en lignes, percés en scie (ou en arc), et les piquages de Clamecy (dents en pointes allongées), Cosne (dents en triangle), Chéroy et Sancerre. Voir nos éditions spécialisées.

1860. – ***Type II.***

11	**1 c. olive**	**250 »**	**100 »**
	⊞	1 200 »	1 250 »
	(Neuf sans gomme)	120 »	
	a. bronze	250 »	110 »

Oblitérations	⊙	✉
Grille	320 »	
Etoile (bleue)	280 »	1 600 »
Etoile (rouge)	300 »	2 500 »
Roulette d'étoiles	210 »	1 250 »
Pointillé	200 »	600 »
Losange petits chiffres	125 »	400 »
Losange petits chiffres (bleu)	300 »	
Losange petits chiffres (rouge)	320 »	
Losange grands chiffres	125 »	380 »
Ancre	385 »	
Petit cachet à date	100 »	230 »
Cachet à date à cercle pointillé	120 »	320 »
Cachet à date des imprimés (rouge)	150 »	725 »
PD dans un rectangle	275 »	
O.R. dans un cercle	220 »	
Cachet des facteurs (autres lettres que OR)	250 »	

Piquages	sur fragment	✉
Piquage Susse	500 »	6 000 »
Percé en lignes	120 »	750 »
Percés en scie (ou en arc)	120 »	725 »

1854. – ***Type I.***

12	**5 c. vert**	**1 000 »**	**100 »**
	(Neuf sans gomme)	400 »	
	a. vert-jaune	1 000 »	100 »
	⊞	4 750 »	1 250 »
	b. vert foncé	1 500 »	185 »
	c. vert foncé s. vert	2 750 »	325 »
	d. (Avec lignes d'encadrement)	7 500 »	2 850 »
	e. *vert clair* (tirage des Arts & Métiers)	800 »	

Oblitérations	⊙	✉
Grille	270 »	1 000 »
Gros points	140 »	650 »
Cercle de points	150 »	400 »
Etoile (bleue)	230 »	1 200 »
Etoile (rouge)	280 »	1 200 »
Roulette d'étoiles	185 »	700 »
Pointillé	140 »	450 »
Losange petits chiffres	100 »	200 »
Losange petits chiffres (bleu)	280 »	1 000 »
Losange petits chiffres (rouge)	300 »	840 »
Losange grands chiffres	115 »	200 »
Ancre	270 »	900 »
Petit cachet à date	100 »	200 »
Cachet à date à cercle pointillé	110 »	250 »
Cachet à date des imprimés (rouge)	170 »	725 »
PD dans un rectangle	250 »	
O.R. dans un cercle	200 »	800 »
Cachet des facteurs (autres lettres que OR)	220 »	850 »

Piquages	sur fragment	✉
Piquage Susse	250 »	2 400 »
Percé en lignes	100 »	400 »
Percés en scie (ou en arc)	100 »	575 »
Piquage de Clamecy	2 000 »	20 000 »

1853. – ***Type I.***

13A	**10 c. bistre (I)**	**700 »**	**12 »**
	(Sur lettre)		25 »
	(Coupé sur lettre)		
	⊞	3 000 »	350 »
	(Neuf sans gomme)	250 »	
	a. jaune-citron	2 300 »	80 »
	b. bistre-orange	800 »	25 »
	c. bistre-brun	700 »	35 »
	d. (Avec lignes d'encadrement)(I)	1 500 »	650 »
	e. *bistre-jaune* (tirage des Arts & Métiers)	700 »	

Oblitérations	⊙	✉
Grille	70 »	300 »
Gros points	50 »	220 »
Grille sans fin	220 »	
Cercle de points	30 »	70 »
Etoile (bleue)	160 »	750 »
Etoile (rouge)	180 »	1 000 »
Roulette d'étoiles	70 »	320 »
Pointillé	25 »	80 »
Losange petits chiffres	12 »	25 »
Losange petits chiffres (bleu)	130 »	400 »
Losange petits chiffres (rouge)	140 »	480 »
Losange grands chiffres	20 »	40 »
Ancre	45 »	100 »
Petit cachet à date	20 »	80 »
Cachet à date à cercle pointillé	25 »	100 »
Cachet à date des imprimés (rouge)	130 »	650 »
PD dans un rectangle	150 »	800 »
O.R. dans un cercle	80 »	300 »
Cachet des facteurs (autres lettres que OR)	120 »	535 »

Piquages	sur fragment	✉
Piquage Susse	60 »	385 »
Percé en lignes	25 »	140 »
Percés en scie (ou en arc)	35 »	300 »
Piquage de Clamecy	1 000 »	8 000 »
Piquage de Chéroy	2 500 »	20 000 »

1854. – *Type II.*

13B	**10 c. brun clair (II)**	**800**	**»**	**30**	**»**
	(Sur lettre)			50	»
	⊞	3 600	»	450	»
	(Neuf sans gomme)	300	»		
	a. bistre-brun	800	»	45	»
	b. brun	1 000	»	70	»

Oblitérations	⊙		✉	
Grille	70	»	300	»
Gros points	50	»	220	»
Grille sans fin	220	»		
Cercle de points	30	»	70	»
Etoile (bleue)	160	»	750	»
Etoile (rouge)	180	»	1 000	»
Roulette d'étoiles	70	»	320	»
Pointillé	25	»	80	»
Losange petits chiffres	12	»	25	»
Losange petits chiffres (bleu)	130	»	400	»
Losange petits chiffres (rouge)	140	»	480	»
Losange grands chiffres	20	»	40	»
Ancre	45	»	100	»
Petit cachet à date	20	»	80	»
Cachet à date à cercle pointillé	25	»	100	»
Cachet à date des imprimés (rouge)	130	»	650	»
PD dans un rectangle	150	»	800	»
O.R. dans un cercle	80	»	300	»
Cachet des facteurs (autres lettres que OR)	120	»	535	»

Piquages	**sur fragment**		✉	
Piquage Susse	50	»	285	»
Percé en lignes	25	»	140	»
Percés en scie (ou en arc)	35	»	300	»
Piquage de Clamecy	1 000	»	8 000	»
Piquage de Chéroy	2 500	»	20 000	»

1854. – *Type I.*

14A	**20 c. bleu (I)**	**300**	**»**	**2**	**»**
	(Sur lettre)			3	»
	⊞	1 350	»	90	»
	(Coupé sur lettre)			25 000	»
	(Neuf sans gomme)	150	»		
	a. bleu foncé	400	»	2	»
	(Sur lettre)			4	»
	b. bleu-noir	1 700	»	40	»
	c. bleu s. azuré	500	»	12	»
	d. bleu s. vert	7 500	»	180	»
	e. bleu s. lilas	6 000	»	80	»
	f. bleu laiteux	350	»	12	»
	g. bleu s. rose			4 500	»
	h. (POSTFS)	1 350	»	75	»
	j. (Avec lignes d'encadrement)(I)	850	»	400	»
	k. *bleu laiteux* (tirage des Arts & Métiers)	750	»		
	m. bleu laiteux sur vert	10 000	»	250	»

Oblitérations	⊙		✉	
Grille	50	»	300	»
Gros points	55	»	220	»
Grille sans fin	110	»		
Cercle de points	12	»	35	»
Etoile (bleue)	125	»	550	»
Etoile (rouge)	180	»	1 500	»
Roulette d'étoiles	60	»	200	»
Pointillé	20	»	75	»
Losange petits chiffres	2	»	3	»
Losange petits chiffres (bleu)	120	»	550	»
Losange petits chiffres (rouge)	180	»	600	»
Losange grands chiffres	10	»	30	»
Ancre	40	»	100	»
Petit cachet à date	20	»	60	»
Cachet à date à cercle pointillé	30	»	120	»
Cachet à date des imprimés (rouge)	170	»	800	»
PD dans un rectangle	150	»	750	»
O.R. dans un cercle	130	»	800	»
Cachet des facteurs (autres lettres que OR)	160	»	800	»

Piquages	**sur fragment**		✉	
Piquage Susse	30	»	180	»
Piquage Susse sur bleu s. vert	200	»	800	»
Percé en lignes	10	»	110	»
Percés en lignes, bleu s. vert	200	»	700	»
Percés en scie (ou en arc)	10	»	140	»
Percés en scie, bleu s. vert	200	»	750	»
Piquage de Clamecy	700	»	7 500	»
Piquage de Clamecy, bleu s. vert	1 000	»	8 500	»
Piquage de Cosne	2 000	»	20 000	»
Piquage de Chéroy	2 000	»	20 000	»
Piquage de Sancerre	1 500	»	12 500	»

1860. – *Type II.*

14B	**20 c. bleu (II)**	**450**	**»**	**6**	**»**
	(Sur lettre)			8	»
	(Neuf sans gomme)	200	»		
	⊞	2 000	»	450	»
	c. (la paire, tête-bêche)(II)	200 000	»		

Le n° 14Bc est en réalité le n° 22b non dentelé

a. bleu s. vert	7 000	»	200	»
b. bleu s. lilas	6 000	»	450	»

Oblitérations	⊙		✉	
Grille	50	»	300	»
Gros points	55	»	220	»
Grille sans fin	110	»		
Cercle de points	12	»	35	»
Etoile (bleue)	125	»	500	»
Etoile (rouge)	180	»	1 300	»
Roulette d'étoiles	60	»	200	»
Pointillé	20	»	75	»
Losange petits chiffres	2	»	3	»
Losange petits chiffres (bleu)	120	»	450	»
Losange petits chiffres (rouge)	180	»	550	»
Losange grands chiffres	10	»	30	»
Ancre	40	»	100	»
Petit cachet à date	20	»	60	»
Cachet à date à cercle pointillé	30	»	120	»
Cachet à date des imprimés (rouge)	170	»	800	»
PD dans un rectangle	150	»	750	»
O.R. dans un cercle	130	»	800	»
Cachet des facteurs (autres lettres que OR)	160	»	800	»

Piquages	sur fragment	⊠
Piquage Susse	30 »	150 »
Percé en lignes	10 »	110 »
Percés en scie (ou en arc)	10 »	140 »
Piquage de Clamecy	700 »	7 500 »
Piquage de Cosne	2 000 »	20 000 »
Piquage de Chéroy	2 000 »	20 000 »
Piquage de Sancerre	1 500 »	12 500 »

1853. – *Type I.*

15	**25 c. bleu**	**2 800 »**	**285 »**
	(Sur lettre)		500 »
	⊞	13 500 »	2 500 »
	(Neuf sans gomme)	1 200 »	
	a. bleu laiteux	2 850 »	300 »
	b. (Avec lignes d'encadrement)	5 500 »	3 000 »
	c. bleu clair (Réimpression)	600 »	

Oblitérations	⊙	⊠
Grille	600 »	
Gros points	280 »	920 »
Grille sans fin	300 »	725 »
Losange petits chiffres	270 »	500 »
Losange petits chiffres (bleu)	420 »	
Losange grands chiffres	400 »	
Petit cachet à date	450 »	

1853. – *Type I.*

16	**40 c. jaune-orange**	**2 750 »**	**18 »**
	(Sur lettre)		30 »
	(Coupé sur lettre)		85 000 »
	⊞	13 500 »	950 »
	(Neuf sans gomme)	1 100 »	
	a. orange vif	3 500 »	25 »
	b. orange s. paille	3 500 »	30 »
	c. (Avec lignes d'encadrement)	7 750 »	1 300 »
	d. *orange vif* (tirage des Arts & Métiers)	2 250 »	

Oblitérations	⊙	⊠
Grille	120 »	700 »
Gros points	30 »	120 »
Grille sans fin	130 »	
Cercle de points	60 »	280 »
Etoile (bleue)	250 »	1 300 »
Etoile (rouge)	270 »	4 000 »
Roulette d'étoiles	80 »	850 »
Pointillé	30 »	100 »
Losange petits chiffres	18 »	30 »
Losange petits chiffres (rouge)	230 »	850 »
Losange grands chiffres	20 »	50 »
Ancre	25 »	70 »
Petit cachet à date	75 »	230 »
Cachet à date à cercle pointillé	100 »	350 »
Cachet à date des imprimés (rouge)	160 »	1 000 »
PD dans un rectangle	170 »	1 000 »

Piquages	sur fragment	⊠
Piquage Susse	100 »	480 »
Percé en lignes	30 »	150 »
Percés en scie (ou en arc)	35 »	230 »
Piquage de Clamecy	1 800 »	25 000 »

1854. – *Type I.*

17A	**80 c. carmin foncé**	**7 000 »**	**120 »**
	(Sur lettre)		200 »
	(Coupé sur lettre)		30 000 »
	⊞	35 000 »	1 500 »
	(Neuf sans gomme)	3 000 »	
	f. (la paire, tête-bêche)	320 000 »	25 000 »
	(Sur lettre)		35 000 »
	tête-bêche, sur lettre		35 000 »

On ne connaît qu'un exemplaire neuf du n° 17Af et La moitié de 80 c. n'est connue que sur fragment.

a. carmin clair	2 800 »	60 »
(Neuf sans gomme)	1 100 »	
⊞	11 000 »	650 »
b. carmin-rose	2 800 »	60 »
(Neuf sans gomme)	1 000 »	
c. carmin foncé s. paille	7 500 »	150 »
d. vermillonné	20 000 »	600 »
e. *carmin terne* (tirage des Arts & Métiers)	2 000 »	
g. (Avec lignes d'encadrement)	15 000 »	4 000 »
h. carmin-rose (Réimpression)	2 400 »	

Oblitérations	⊙	⊠
Grille	300 »	1 300 »
Gros points	90 »	500 »
Cercle de points	120 »	480 »
Etoile (bleue)	300 »	2 000 »
Roulette d'étoiles	120 »	1 000 »
Pointillé	80 »	250 »
Losange petits chiffres	70 »	130 »
Losange petits chiffres (rouge)	280 »	1 000 »
Losange grands chiffres	80 »	150 »
Ancre	85 »	230 »
Petit cachet à date	185 »	700 »
Cachet à date à cercle pointillé	200 »	
Cachet à date des imprimés (rouge)	220 »	1 250 »
PD dans un rectangle	220 »	1 300 »

Piquages	sur fragment	⊠
Percé en lignes	80 »	280 »
Percés en scie (ou en arc)	100 »	550 »

1859. – *Type I.*

17B	**80 c. rose**	**2 500 »**	**55 »**
	(Sur lettre)		120 »
	⊞	12 000 »	650 »
	(Neuf sans gomme)	1 000 »	
	c. (la paire, tête-bêche)	65 000 »	15 000 »
	(Sur lettre)		27 000 »
	a. rose vif	2 800 »	80 »
	b. rose pâle	2 400 »	60 »

Oblitérations	⊙	✉
Grille	250 »	1 100 »
Gros points	100 »	600 »
Cercle de points	130 »	500 »
Roulette d'étoiles	120 »	1 000 »
Pointillé	80 »	250 »
Losange petits chiffres	90 »	280 »
Losange petits chiffres (rouge)		
Losange grands chiffres	55 »	120 »
Ancre	80 »	200 »
Petit cachet à date	150 »	600 »
Cachet à date des imprimés (rouge)	200 »	1 000 »
PD dans un rectangle		

Piquages	**sur fragment**	✉
Piquage Susse	200 »	1 600 »
Percé en lignes	70 »	300 »
Piquage de Clamecy	1 750 »	27 500 »

1853. – *Type I.*

18	**1 f. carmin**	**8 000 »**	**3 250 »**
	(Sur lettre)		6 500 »
	(Seul sur lettre)		7 500 »
	⊞	40 000 »	32 000 »
	(Neuf sans gomme)	4 000 »	
	b. (la paire, tête-bêche)	350 000 »	145 000 »
	(Sur lettre)		250 000 »

On ne connaît que deux exemplaires neufs du n° 18b

	a. carmin foncé	11 000 »	4 200 »
	(Neuf sans gomme)	4 500 »	
	c. (Avec lignes d'encadrement)	15 000 »	11 000 »
	d. (Réimpression)	1 700 »	
	e. (Tête-bêche, Réimpression)	30 000 »	

Oblitérations	⊙	✉
Grille	5 400 »	
Gros points	3 500 »	6 000 »
Grille sans fin	3 800 »	7 800 »
Etoile (bleue)	4 000 »	
Losange petits chiffres	3 250 »	5 500 »
Petit cachet à date	4 300 »	8 500 »

1862. – *Napoléon III. Légende EMPIRE FRANC. Typographie. Papier teinté. Dentelé 14 x 13½.*

19	**1 c. olive**	**220 »**	**45 »**
	⊞	1 000 »	500 »
	(Neuf sans gomme)	70 »	
	a. bronze	230 »	50 »
	b. Mordoré	450 »	
	c. Mordoré (non dentelé)	550 »	
	d. (Grand C dans le cartouche supérieur)	1 400 »	1 100 »

Oblitérations	⊙	✉
Gros points	170 »	
Losange petits chiffres	65 »	250 »
Ancre	200 »	600 »
Petit cachet à date	45 »	160 »
Cachet à date à cercle pointillé	60 »	420 »
Cachet à date des imprimés (rouge)	65 »	350 »
Cachet à date de Bureau de Passe	100 »	
O.R. dans un cercle	120 »	
Annulation typographique des journaux	160 »	2 850 »

1862. – *Napoléon III. Légende EMPIRE FRANC. Typographie. Papier teinté. Dentelé 14 x 13½.*

20	**5 c. vert**	**275**	**»**	**12**	**»**
	⊞	1 350	»	275	»
	(Neuf sans gomme)	100	»		
	a. vert foncé	325	»	17	»

Oblitérations	⊙		✉	
Gros points	170	»	1 200	»
Pointillé	100	»		
Etoile (rouge)	150	»	2 500	»
Losange petits chiffres	25	»	70	»
Ancre	170	»	550	»
Petit cachet à date	13	»	45	»
Cachet à date à cercle pointillé	40	»	230	»
Cachet à date des imprimés (rouge)	30	»	150	»
Cachet à date de Bureau de Passe	90	»	500	»
O.R. dans un cercle	75	»	575	»
Annulation typographique des journaux	270	»		

Ce timbre a été réimprimé vert pâle sur bleu en novembre 1871, voir N° 35

1862. – *Napoléon III. Légende EMPIRE FRANC. Typographie. Papier teinté. Dentelé 14 x 13½.*

21	**10 c. bistre**	**1 900**	**»**	**3**	**»**
	(Sur lettre)			10	»
	⊞	9 250	»	175	»
	(Neuf sans gomme)	450	»		
	a. bistre-jaune	2 000	»	3	»
	b. bistre-brun	2 500	»	12	»

Oblitérations	⊙		✉	
Grille	60	»	500	»
Gros points	50	»	700	»
Pointillé	30	»	100	»
Etoile (rouge)	120	»	1 500	»
Losange petits chiffres	15	»	35	»
Ancre	18	»	60	»
Petit cachet à date	10	»	15	»
Cachet à date à cercle pointillé	15	25	85	»
Cachet à date des imprimés (rouge)	30	»	320	»
Cachet à date de Bureau de Passe	40	»	230	»
O.R. dans un cercle	35	»	230	»

1862. – *Napoléon III. Légende EMPIRE FRANC. Typographie. Papier teinté. Dentelé 14 x 13½.*

22	**20 c. bleu**	**310**	**»**	**1**	**»**
	(Sur lettre)			2	»
	⊞	1 350	»	100	»
	(Neuf sans gomme)	100	»		
	b. (la paire, tête bêche)	4 500	»	1 300	»
	(Sur lettre)			3 000	»
	a. bleu foncé	350	»	2	»

Oblitérations	⊙		✉	
Grille	50	»	350	»
Gros points	50	»	500	»
Pointillé	20	»	70	»
Etoile (rouge)	100	»	1 000	»
Losange petits chiffres	5	»	10	»
Ancre	17	»	70	»
Petit cachet à date	5	»	10	»
Cachet à date à cercle pointillé	11	50	70	»
Cachet à date des imprimés (rouge)	40	»	340	»
Cachet à date de Bureau de Passe	30	»	90	»
O.R. dans un cercle	50	»	535	»

1862. – *Napoléon III. Légende EMPIRE FRANC. Typographie. Papier teinté. Dentelé 14 x 13½.*

23	**40 c. orange**	**1 900**	**»**	**7**	**»**
	(Sur lettre)			15	»
	⊞	8 250	»	300	»
	(Neuf sans gomme)	500	»		
	a. orange pâle	1 700	»	6	»
	b. orange vif	2 400	»	13	»

Oblitérations	⊙		✉	
Grille	120	»	1 000	»
Gros points	70	»	700	»
Pointillé	25	»	90	»
Etoile (rouge)	140	»	1 500	»
Losange petits chiffres	15	»	35	»
Ancre	16	»	40	»
Petit cachet à date	15	»	45	»
Cachet à date à cercle pointillé	35	»	185	»
Cachet à date des imprimés (rouge)	55	»	480	»
Cachet à date de Bureau de Passe	60	»	250	»

1862. – *Napoléon III. Légende EMPIRE FRANC. Typographie. Papier teinté. Dentelé 14 x 13½.*

24	**80 c. rose**	**1 700 »**	**40 »**
	(Sur lettre)		80 »
	⊞	8 000 »	500 »
	(Neuf sans gomme)	500 »	
	b. (la paire, tête-bêche)	25 000 »	10 000 »
	(Sur lettre)		37 500 »
	a. rose foncé	1 900 »	65 »

Le 24b est généralement décentré.

Une plus-value est à ajouter pour tout exemplaire très bien centré.

Oblitérations	⊙	✉
Gros points	120 »	1 200 »
Pointillé	80 »	250 »
Etoile (rouge)	180 »	2 200 »
Losange petits chiffres	70 »	120 »
Ancre	55 »	185 »
Petit cachet à date	60 »	130 »
Cachet à date à cercle pointillé	92 »	450 »
Cachet à date des imprimés (rouge)	130 »	1 100 »
Cachet à date de Bureau de Passe	90 »	700 »

Napoléon III lauré

Types des 10 c. et 20 c.

Type I : petits points

Type II : gros points

Le 30 c. est au type I, les 40 c. et 80 c. sont au type II. Il existe également deux types pour les 2 c. et 4 c. (voir catalogue spécialisé Volume I édition 1975).

Émission Rothschild : Impression très fine. Non dentelés.

Réimpressions Granet : voir avant le n°61.

1870. – *Typographie. Papier teinté. Dentelé 14 x 13½.*

25	**1 c. bronze**	**65 »**	**20 »**
	(Seul sur lettre)		100 »
	⊞	285 »	175 »
	(Neuf sans gomme)	20 »	
	a. olive	70 »	20 »
	b. (à la cigarette)	3 250 »	1 200 »
	c. (Émission Rothschild)	1 500 »	
	d. bronze (réimpression Granet, sans gomme)	1 350 »	

Oblitérations	⊙	✉
Losange petits chiffres	40 »	120 »
Ancre	140	»
Petit cachet à date	15 »	40 »
Cachet à date à cercle pointillé	30 »	120 »
Cachet à date de Bureau de Passe	60 »	500 »
Cachet à date des imprimés (rouge)	30 »	150 »
O.R. dans un cercle	70 »	400 »
Annulation typographique des journaux	20 »	100 »

1862. – *Typographie. Papier teinté. Dentelé 14 x 13½.*

26	**2 c. rouge-brun**	**170 »**	**35 »**
	(Seul sur lettre)		130 »
	(Coupé sur lettre)		42 000 »
	⊞	800 »	400 »
	(Neuf sans gomme)	50 »	
	a. rouge-brun foncé	185 »	75 »
	b. (Boule blanche sous le cou)	2 200 »	1 600 »
	c. (Émission Rothschild)	250 »	

Oblitérations	⊙	✉
Losange petits chiffres	50 »	130 »
Ancre	170	»
Petit cachet à date	30 »	70 »
Cachet à date à cercle pointillé	35 »	150 »
Cachet à date de Bureau de Passe	70 »	650 »
Cachet à date des imprimés (rouge)	40 »	250 »
O.R. dans un cercle	75 »	400 »
Annulation typographique des journaux	35 »	180 »

Tirage : 117 708 900.

1863. – *Typographie. Papier teinté. Dentelé 14 x 13½.*

27	**4 c. gris**	**300 »**	**65 »**
	(Seul sur lettre)		450 »
	(Coupé sur lettre)		55 000 »
	⊞	1 400 »	750 »
	(Neuf sans gomme)	120 »	
	la paire, tête-bêche	28 000 »	17 000 »
	tête-bêche, sur lettre		48 000 »
	a. gris jaunâtre	300 »	65 »
	b. gris-lilas	375 »	90 »
	c. gris foncé	400 »	90 »
	d. (Émission Rothschild)	200 »	

Oblitérations	⊙	✉
Losange petits chiffres	75 »	200 »
Ancre	180	»
Petit cachet à date	65 »	130 »
Cachet à date à cercle pointillé	70 »	200 »
Cachet à date de Bureau de Passe	250 »	2 000 »
Cachet à date des imprimés (rouge)	80 »	450 »
O.R. dans un cercle	120 »	450 »
Annulation typographique des journaux	180 »	1 250 »

Tirage : 20 909 100.

1867. – *Typographie. Papier teinté. Dentelé 14 x 13½.*

28A	**10 c. bistre (I)**	**700 »**	**10 »**
	(Sur lettre)		10 »
	(Coupé sur lettre)		4 200 »
	⊞	3 250 »	125 »
	(Neuf sans gomme)	200 »	

Oblitérations	⊙	✉
Gros points	80 »	450 »
Losange petits chiffres	10 »	20 »
Ancre	18 »	50 »
Petit cachet à date	10 »	15 »
Cachet à date à cercle pointillé	15 »	40 »
Cachet à date de Bureau de Passe	20 »	100 »
Cachet à date des imprimés (rouge)	40 »	385 »
O.R. dans un cercle	50 »	200 »

Tirage : 253 000 000.

1868. – *Typographie. Papier teinté. Dentelé 14 x 13½.*

28B	**10 c. bistre (II)**	**340 »**	**4 »**
	(Sur lettre)		8 »
	(Neuf sans gomme)	130 »	
	⊞	1 800 »	100 »
	a. bistre foncé	375 »	8 »

1867. – *Typographie. Papier teinté. Dentelé 14 x 13½.*

29A	**20 c. bleu (I)**	**425 »**	**2 »**
	(Sur lettre)		3 »
	(Coupé sur lettre)		45 000 »
	⊞	2 000 »	75 »
	(Neuf sans gomme)	140 »	
	a. bleu foncé	500 »	3 »
	b. (Émission Rothschild)(I)	350 »	
	c. bleu laiteux (Non dentelé, dit Lebaudy, sur lettre)		22 000 »

Oblitérations	⊙	✉
Gros points	75 »	450 »
Losange petits chiffres	7 »	15 »
Ancre	17 »	50 »
Petit cachet à date	5 »	15 »
Cachet à date à cercle pointillé	10 »	42 »
Cachet à date de Bureau de Passe	10 »	40 »
Cachet à date des imprimés (rouge)	40 »	385 »
O.R. dans un cercle	70 »	385 »

1868. – *Typographie. Papier teinté. Dentelé 14 x 13½.*

29B	**20 c. bleu (II)**	**250 »**	**2 »**
	(Sur lettre)		3 »
	⊞	1 350 »	65 »
	(Neuf sans gomme)	100 »	
	a. bleu foncé	300 »	3 »
	b. (à la corne)	2 500 »	125 »
	c. (aux abeilles)	3 800 »	300 »
	d. (à la pipe)		1 250 »
	Le timbre détaché, oblitéré vaut		4 600 »

1867. – *Typographie. Papier teinté. Dentelé 14 x 13½.*

30	**30 c. brun**	**1 000 »**	**20 »**
	(Sur lettre)		35 »
	⊞	4 750 »	375 »
	(Neuf sans gomme)	300 »	
	a. brun clair	1 000 »	25 »
	b. brun-noir	1 500 »	50 »
	c. (Émission Rothschild)	250 »	

Oblitérations	⊙	✉
Gros points	85 »	500 »
Losange petits chiffres	23 »	60 »
Ancre	35 »	90 »
Petit cachet à date	30 »	80 »
Cachet à date à cercle pointillé	35 »	100 »
Cachet à date de Bureau de Passe	40 »	370 »
Cachet à date des imprimés (rouge)	70 »	480 »
O.R. dans un cercle		

1868. – *Typographie. Papier teinté. Dentelé 14 x 13½.*

31	**40 c. orange**	**1 100**	**»**	**10**	**»**
	(Sur lettre)			20	»
	(Coupé sur lettre)			45 000	»
	⊞	5 000	»	400	»
	(Neuf sans gomme)	320	»		
	a. orange pâle	950	»	10	»
	b. orange vif	1 750	»	15	»
	c. (Émission Rothschild)	250	»		

Oblitérations	⊙		✉	
Gros points	80	»	500	»
Losange petits chiffres	20	»	40	»
Ancre	20	»	45	»
Petit cachet à date	28	»	70	»
Cachet à date à cercle pointillé	35	»	110	»
Cachet à date de Bureau de Passe	40	»	300	»
Cachet à date des imprimés (rouge)	70	»	550	»

1867. – *Typographie. Papier teinté. Dentelé 14 x 13½.*

32	**80 c. rose**	**1 300**	**»**	**20**	**»**
	(Sur lettre)			60	»
	(Coupé sur lettre)			50 000	»
	(Coupé sur lettre (1/4))			60 000	»
	⊞	6 250	»	300	»
	(Neuf sans gomme)	380	»		
	a. rose carminé	1 750	»	45	»
	b. (Émission Rothschild)	550	»		

Oblitérations	⊙		✉	
Gros points	90	»	600	»
Losange petits chiffres	30	»	85	»
Ancre	40	»	90	»
Petit cachet à date	35	»	120	»
Cachet à date à cercle pointillé	40	»	185	»
Cachet à date de Bureau de Passe	70	»	650	»
Cachet à date des imprimés (rouge)	90	»	850	»

Typographie. Papier teinté.

33	**5 f. violet-gris**	**8 000**	**»**	**1 100**	**»**
	(Sur lettre)			2 500	»
	(Seul sur lettre)			2 500	»
	⊞	37 500	»	10 000	»
	(Neuf sans gomme)	2 500	»		
	a. gris-bleu	8 500	»	1 100	»
	b. (5 et F en bleu)	9 500	»	1 350	»
	c. (Non dentelé)	11 000	»		

Oblitérations	⊙		✉	
Gros points	1 450	»		
Losange petits chiffres	1 400	»	2 700	»
Ancre	1 450	»	3 200	»
Petit cachet à date	1 000	»	2 200	»
Cachet à date à cercle pointillé	1 200	»	2 500	»
Cachet à date des imprimés (rouge)	1 600	»	6 500	»

Grand chiffre "5"

Grand chiffre 5

Chiffre 5 normal

33d	(grand chiffre 5)	8 500	»	1 350	»

Le "grand chiffre 5" mesure 4,3 mm de haut.

ERREUR Sans "5" et "F".

33e	violet-gris (Sans "5" et "F")	110 000	»

On ne connaît que quelques exemplaires oblitérés, plus ou moins défectueux, de cette rarissime variété.

On connaît également un exemplaire de la variété sans "5" mais avec "F" tenant à la variété sans "5" et sans "F" dans un bloc de 6 oblitérés.

1871. – *Non émis. Timbre de 1863 surchargé.*

34	**10 s.10 c. *bistre* (B)**	**2 350**	**»**
	(Neuf sans gomme)	1 200	»
	⊞	12 500	»
	a. (bleu pâle)	2 350	»

Le changement de tarif du 1er septembre 1871 avait porté de 5 à 10 c. l'affranchissement des cartes du Nouvel An. Comme la pénurie de timbres était grande, on songea à utiliser le stock restant du 10 c. Empire lauré. Pour éviter la confusion avec le 15 c. (n° 59) on apposa la surcharge 10 en bleu. Il ne fut jamais mis officiellement en cours. Il peut se rencontrer oblitéré tardivement par complaisance.

1871. – *(Novembre) Type de 1862. Typographie. Dentelé 14 x 13½.*

35	**5 c. vert pâle s. bleu (20)**	**2 900 »**	**160 »**
	(Seul sur lettre)		370 »
	⊞	20 000 »	1 200 »
	(Neuf sans gomme)	700 »	

Oblitérations	⊙	⊠
Losange petits chiffres	200 »	250 »
Ancre	200	»
Cachet à date des imprimés (rouge)	200 »	650 »

Émission dite du Siège de Paris.
Type de 1849 (Cérès)

1870. – *Typographie. Dentelé 14 x 13½.*

36	**10 c. bistre-jaune**	**875 »**	**85 »**
	(Seul sur lettre)		220 »
	⊞	4 250 »	1 300 »
	(Coupé sur lettre)		6 000 »
	(Neuf sans gomme)	300 »	
	b. (la paire, tête-bêche)	8 000 »	3 000 »
	(Sur lettre)		7 000 »
	a. bistre-brun	1 000 »	120 »
	c. bistre-jaune (Réimpression Granet, non dentelé, papier teinté, avec ou sans gomme)	450 »	

Oblitérations	⊙	⊠
Gros points	125 »	800 »
Losange petits chiffres	100 »	150 »
Ancre	170 »	850 »
AS. NA.	180 »	1 400 »
Cachet à date des imprimés (rouge)	125 »	900 »
O.R. dans un cercle	150 »	

1870. – *Typographie. Dentelé 14 x 13½.*

37	**20 c. bleu**	**350 »**	**8 »**
	(Sur lettre)		12 »
	⊞	1 700 »	130 »
	(Neuf sans gomme)	120 »	
	c. (la paire, tête-bêche)	5 250 »	2 000 »
	(Sur lettre)		5 000 »
	a. bleu foncé	475 »	10 »
	b. (Papier jaunâtre)	600 »	20 »
	d. (papier jaunâtre, la paire, tête-bêche)	6 500 »	2 250 »
	(Sur lettre)		5 000 »
	f. bleu clair (Réimpression Granet, non dentelé, papier teinté, avec ou sans gomme)	500 »	

Oblitérations	⊙	⊠
Gros points	80 »	600 »
Losange petits chiffres	14 »	40 »
Ancre	80 »	500 »
AS. NA.	70 »	700 »
Cachet à date des imprimés (rouge)	75 »	700 »

1870. – *Typographie. Dentelé 14 x 13½.*

38	**40 c. orange**	**725 »**	**8 »**
	(Sur lettre)		15 »
	⊞	3 600 »	125 »
	(Coupé sur lettre)		60 000 »
	(Neuf sans gomme)	250 »	
	a. jaune-orange	800 »	10 »
	b. orange terne	725 »	10 »
	c. (Coin inférieur gauche absent)	1 100 »	100 »
	d. (4 retouchés)	4 350 »	200 »
	e. (4 retouchés, paire avec un normal)	9 000 »	650 »
	f. (Paire de deux 4 retouchés)	27 500 »	4 000 »

Oblitérations	⊙	⊠
Gros points	65 »	500 »
Losange petits chiffres	12 »	30 »
Ancre	40 »	85 »
AS. NA.	80 »	800 »
Cachet à date des imprimés (rouge)	55 »	450 »

Gouvernement provisoire

On distingue les timbres lithographiés de cette émission des timbres au même type, typographiés (qui servirent non dentelés, en France en 1849-50 et aux Colonies en 1871-76), par la couronne d'épis qui fait beaucoup moins saillie au sommet de la tête sur les timbres imprimés à Bordeaux que sur les autres (cette observation ne s'applique pas au premier type du 20 c. bleu).

1870. – *Cérès. Émission dite de Bordeaux. Lithographie. Papier teinté. non dentelés.*

Reports du 1 centime.

Report 1

Reports 2 et 3

Report 3 (2e état)

R. 1. Ombres sous l'oeil formées par des points. Les impressions usées présentent un léger contour blanc derrière la tête.

R. 2. - Ombres sous l'oeil formées par des traits. Une ligne blanche derrière la tête souligne le contour des cheveux.

R. 3. - Pas de contour blanc derrière la tête.

1er état : ombres sous l'oeil formées par des traits.

2e état : les traits formant les ombres de l'oeil sont reliés entre eux.

39A	**1 c. olive *impression fine, Report I (1er état)***	**200**	**»**	**180**	**»**
	(Neuf sans gomme)	120	»		
	⊞	950	»	1 100	»
	(Bloc de 15)	3 500	»		
	a. olive (2ème étatimpression usée)	200	»	180	»
	b. olive très foncé (2ème état)	300	»	300	»
39B	**1 c. olive *Report 2***	**175**	**»**	**175**	**»**
	(Neuf sans gomme)	100	»		
	⊞	850	»	1 000	»
	(Bloc de 15)	2 500	»		
	a. olive foncé	190	»	190	»

39C	**1 c. olive *Report 3 (1er état)***	**160**	**»**	**160**	**»**
	(Seul sur lettre)			1 250	»
	(Neuf sans gomme)	100	»		
	⊞	750	»	900	»
	(Bloc de 15)	2 600	»		
	a. olive clair (2ème état)	190	»	190	»
	b. olive foncé	210	»	210	»
	c. olive bronze	280	»	280	»

Oblitérations	⊙		✉	
Losange petits chiffres	180	»	500	»
Cachet à date	150	»	300	»
étoile	200	»		
Ancre	385	»		
O.R. dans un cercle	200	»		
Annulation typographique des journaux	180	»	2 000	»

Piquages	**sur fragment**	✉	
Percé en lignes		1 700	»

1870. – *Cérès. Émission dite de Bordeaux. Lithographie. Papier teinté. non dentelés.*

Reports du 2 centimes.

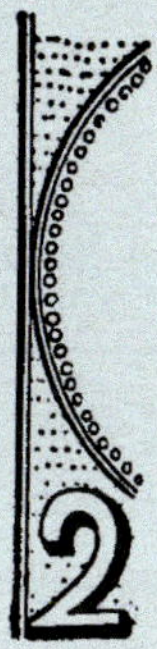

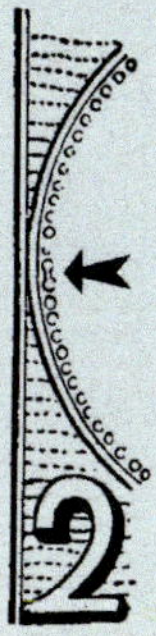

R. 1. - Toutes les lignes ondulées sont formées par des points, notamment celles entre le cadre et la boucle du 2 qui sont peu visibles.

R. 2. - La plupart des lignes ondulées sont formées par des traits. Trois lignes horizontales séparées se trouvent entre le cadre et la boucle du 2.

40A	**2 c. chocolat clair (Report 1)**	**1 100**	**»**	**1 100**	**»**
	(Neuf sans gomme)	40 000	»		
	⊞	5 200	»	9 000	»
	(Bloc de 15)	32 000	»		
	(Coupé sur lettre)				
	a. chocolat	1 400	»	1 200	»
	b. brun-rouge	7 000	»	8 000	»
	c. (impression très fine dite de Tours)	1 900	»	5 500	»
	⊞			12 000	»
40B	**2 c. brun-rouge (Report 2)**	**350**	**»**	**325**	**»**
	(Seul sur lettre)			1 800	»
	(Neuf sans gomme)	200	»		
	⊞	1 700	»	2 400	»
	(Bloc de 15)	5 300	»		
	a. rouge-brique	1 300	»	900	»
	b. marron	1 800	»	1 100	»
	c. chocolat foncé	6 500	»	4 250	»
	f. rouge-brique foncé	2 400	»	1 500	»

Oblitérations	⊙		✉	
Losange petits chiffres	350	»	840	»
Cachet à date	300	»	420	»
Etoile	350	»	2 300	»
Ancre	420	»		
O.R. dans un cercle	400	»	2 400	»
Annulation typographique des journaux	385	»	1 800	»

Piquages	**sur fragment**	✉	
Percé en lignes		1 700	»

1870. – *Cérès. Émission dite de Bordeaux. Lithographie. Papier teinté. non dentelés.*

Reports du 4 centimes.

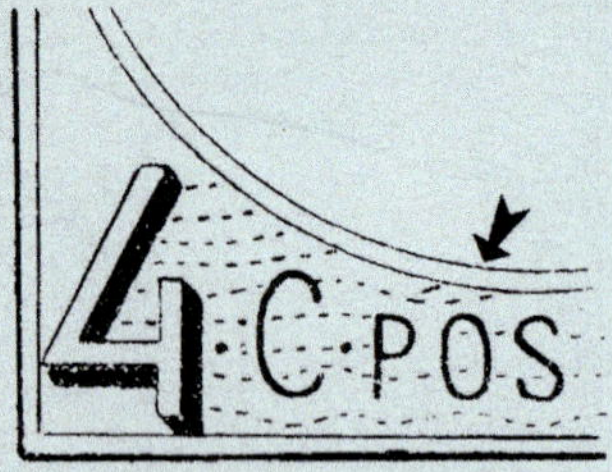

R. 1. - Impression fine du burelage constitué par des points. Les traits formant les ombres sous l'oeil sont plus ou moins reliés entre eux.

R. 2. - Impression plus lourde. Le burelage est constitué de traits irréguliers dont certains se touchent.

41A	**4 c. gris (Report 1)**	**2 500 »**	**2 500 »**
	(Neuf sans gomme)	1 500 »	
	⊞	12 500 »	17 500 »
	(Bloc de 15)	60 000 »	
	a. gris jaunâtre	2 700 »	2 700 »
41B	**4 c. gris (Report 2)**	**375 »**	**325 »**
	(Sur lettre)		750 »
	(Seul sur lettre)		17 000 »
	(Neuf sans gomme)	200 »	
	⊞	1 850 »	2 250 »
	(Bloc de 15)	7 000 »	
	a. gris jaunâtre	400 »	325 »
	b. gris-lilas	550 »	450 »
	c. gris-noir	3 000 »	2 600 »

Oblitérations	⊙	🖂
Losange petits chiffres	350 »	1 100 »
Cachet à date	280 »	650 »
Etoile	400 »	9 000 »
Ancre	460 »	
O.R. dans un cercle	450 »	4 000 »
Annulation typographique des journaux	535 »	

Piquages	**sur fragment**	🖂
Percé en lignes		1 600 »

1871. – *Cérès. Émission dite de Bordeaux. Lithographie. Papier teinté. non dentelés.*

Reports du 5 centimes.

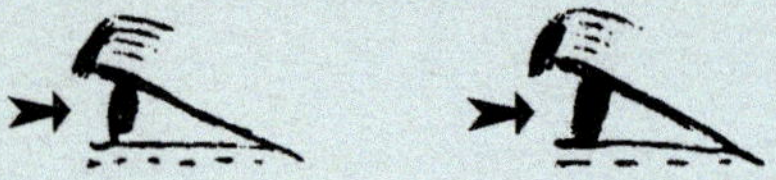

Report 1 *Report 2*

R. 1. - Pas de ligne blanche derrière la tête. L'iris de l'oeil est fait d'un trait et d'un point qui ne touche que la paupière supérieure. Menton en retrait de la lèvre inférieure. Impression très fine donnant aspect dépouillé.

R. 2. - Ligne blanche derrière la tête plus ou moins marquée. L'iris de l'oeil est fait d'une seule grosse tache ovale. Menton fuyant en avant de la lèvre inférieure. Impression générale plus lourde.

42A	**5 c. vert-jaune**	**4 000 »**	**4 750 »**
	(Neuf sans gomme)	2 300 »	
	⊞	19 000 »	
	(Bloc de 15)	85 000 »	
42B	**5 c. vert-jaune**	**350 »**	**225 »**
	(Seul sur lettre)		5 000 »
	(Neuf sans gomme)	220 »	
	⊞	1 750 »	2 250 »
	(Bloc de 15)	7 000 »	
	a. vert-jaune foncé	450 »	280 »
	b. vert-émeraude foncé	5 250 »	1 650 »
	c. vert-gris	1 000 »	550 »
	d. vert-sauge	1 600 »	600 »
	e. vert très foncé	3 000 »	1 000 »

Oblitérations	⊙	🖂
Losange petits chiffres	230 »	700 »
Cachet à date	200 »	350 »
étoile	270 »	650 »
Ancre	360 »	
O.R. dans un cercle	300 »	2 000 »
Annulation typographique des journaux	575 »	

Piquages	**sur fragment**	🖂
Percé en lignes		700 »

1870. – *Cérès. Émission dite de Bordeaux. Lithographie. Papier teinté. non dentelés.*

Reports du 10 centimes.

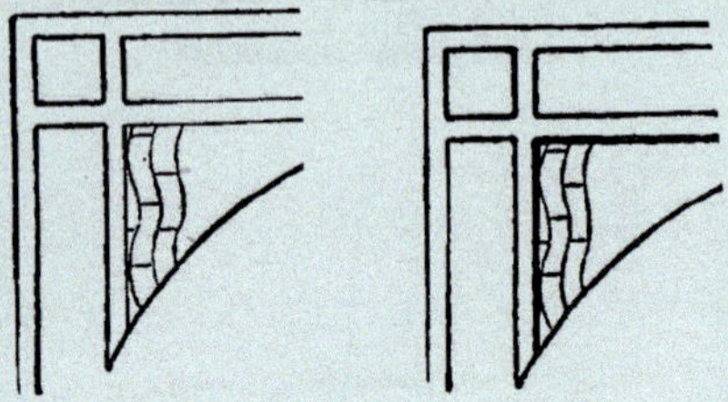

Report 1 *Report 2*

R. 1. - Le cadre triangulaire intérieur est formé de traits égaux en épaisseur.

R. 2. - Le filet intérieur du cadre est plus épais.

43A	**10 c. bistre (Report 1)**	**1 100 »**	**80 »**
	(Sur lettre)		130 »
	(Neuf sans gomme)	450 »	
	⊞	5 200 »	2 000 »
	(Bloc de 15)	28 500 »	
	(Coupé sur lettre)		16 500 »
	a. brun clair	1 100 »	90 »
	b. bistre verdâtre	2 000 »	700 »
43B	**10 c. bistre-jaune (Report 2)**	**1 100 »**	**100 »**
	(Neuf sans gomme)	450 »	
	⊞	5 200 »	2 000 »
	(Bloc de 15)	31 000 »	
	a. bistre orangé	1 600 »	140 »
	b. bistre verdâtre	1 700 »	600 »
	c. citron	2 750 »	850 »

Oblitérations	⊙	✉
Losange petits chiffres	120 »	200 »
Cachet à date	100 »	130 »
Etoile	120 »	450 »
Ancre	160 »	500 »
O.R. dans un cercle	180 »	1 200 »
Annulation typographique des journaux		

Piquages	**sur fragment**	✉
Percé en lignes		500 »
Piquage d'Avallon	1 300 »	22 500 »

43A coupé sur lettre

Types et reports du 20 centimes

Type I. - L'ombre du cou est formée par des points, les inscriptions sont petites.

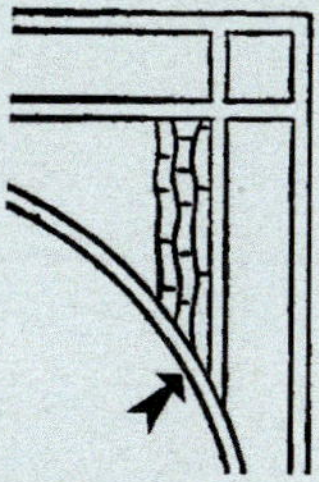

Report 1

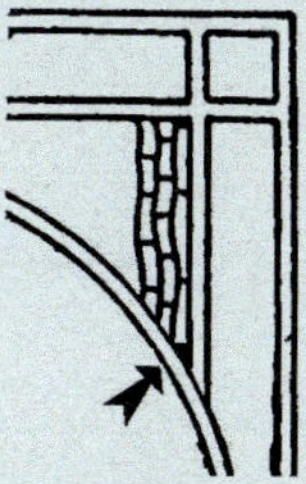

Report 2

R. 1. - Imbriquement normal.

R. 2. - Dans la partie supérieure droite du timbre, un point de couleur réunit la ligne intérieure du cadre au premier trait horizontal de l'imbriquement.

Type II. L'ombre du cou est formée par des traits, les inscriptions sont petites comme dans le type I.

La grecque supérieure gauche est prolongée à sa base par un trait blanc de forme triangulaire.

Report 1

Report 2

R. 1. Les seconds grains de raisin des 1re et 3e rangées de la grappe sont blancs. Le premier lobe de la feuille de vigne de droite est à peine indiqué.

R. 2. - Les seconds grains de raisins des 1re et 3e rangées de la grappe sont ombrés par un trait courbe. La feuille de vigne est franchement découpée. Il y a un point ou un trait parasite dans le cinquième intervalle de l'imbriquement à gauche en bas.

R. 3. - Mêmes caractéristiques que le report 2. De plus le contour des cheveux est souligné par une ligne blanche.

Type III. - Les inscriptions sont plus grandes.

R. 1. - Le cadre est formé de traits égaux en épaisseur (voir R. 1 du 10 c.). Le contour des cheveux est souligné par une légère ligne blanche.

R. 2. - Le filet intérieur du cadre triangulaire est plus épais (voir R. 2 du 10 c.). Pas de contour blanc derrière la tête.

1870. – ***Cérès. Émission dite de Bordeaux. Lithographie. Papier teinté. non dentelés.***

Type I.

44A	**20 c. bleu (I, Report 1)**	**25 000**	**»**	**700**	**»**
	(Sur lettre)			1 000	»
	(Neuf sans gomme)	12 000	»		
	⊞	135 000	»		
	(Bloc de 15)	500 000	»		
	a. bleu foncé	30 000	»	1 100	»
	b. bleu outremer	32 500	»	1 500	»
44B	**20 c. bleu (I, Report 2)**	**25 000**	**»**	**800**	**»**
	(Neuf sans gomme)	12 000	»		
	a. bleu foncé	32 000	»	1 300	»
	⊞			45 000	»
	Faux pour servir (Lyon)				
	Faux pour servir, sur lettre			20 000	»

Oblitérations	⊙		✉	
Losange petits chiffres	900	»	2 300	»
Cachet à date	1 200	»	2 600	»
Etoile	1 400	»	2 100	»
Ancre	1 000	»		

Piquages	sur fragment		✉	
Percé en lignes			2 850	»
Piquage d'Avallon	1 000	»	18 000	»

1870. – ***Cérès. Émission dite de Bordeaux. Lithographie. Papier teinté. non dentelés.***

Type II.

45A	**20 c. bleu (II, Report 1)**	**1 300**	**»**	**65**	**»**
	(Neuf sans gomme)	450	»		
	⊞	6 200	»	1 900	»
	(Bloc de 15)	60 000	»		
	a. bleu foncé	1 500	»	120	»
	b. bleu-noir	4 000	»	1 200	»
	c. (Impression fine)	2 200	»	350	»
45B	**20 c. bleu (II, Report 2)**	**1 300**	**»**	**65**	**»**
	(Neuf sans gomme)	450	»		
	⊞	6 200	»	1 900	»
	(Bloc de 15)	60 000	»		
	a. bleu foncé	1 500	»	120	»

45C	**20 c. bleu (II, Report 3)**	**1 300**	**»**	**65**	**»**
	(Sur lettre)			75	»
	(Neuf sans gomme)	450	»		
	⊞	6 200	»	1 900	»
	(Bloc de 15)	60 000	»		
	a. bleu foncé	1 600	»	120	»
	b. outremer	27 520	»	4 500	»
	Faux pour servir (Marseille)			2 800	»
	Faux pour servir, sur lettre				

Oblitérations	⊙		✉	
Losange petits chiffres	70	»	170	»
Cachet à date	100	»	285	»
Etoile	100	»	450	»
Ancre	160	»	385	»

Piquages	sur fragment	✉	
Percé en lignes		200	»

1871. – ***Cérès. Émission dite de Bordeaux. Lithographie. Papier teinté. non dentelés.***

Type III.

46A	**20 c. bleu (III, Report 1)**	**1 300**	**»**	**70**	**»**
	(Neuf sans gomme)	500	»		
	⊞	6 750	»	1 800	»
	(Bloc de 15)	54 000	»		
	a. bleu pâle	1 400	»	70	»
	b. bleu foncé	1 600	»	175	»
	c. gris-bleu	1 750	»	275	»
	d. outremer	3 500	»	850	»
46B	**20 c. bleu (III, Report 2)**	**1 200**	**»**	**25**	**»**
	(Sur lettre)			35	»
	(Neuf sans gomme)	450	»		
	⊞	6 000	»	1 900	»
	(Bloc de 15)	50 000	»		
	a. bleu foncé	1 500	»	70	»
	b. gris-bleu	1 400	»	100	»
	Faux pour servir (Marseille)	550	»	1 800	»
	Faux pour servir, sur lettre			5 500	»

Oblitérations	⊙		✉	
Losange petits chiffres	30	»	80	»
Cachet à date	100	»	340	»
Etoile	60	»	270	»
Ancre	125	»	340	»

Piquages	sur fragment	✉	
Percé en lignes		185	»

1870. – ***Cérès. Émission dite de Bordeaux. Lithographie. Papier teinté. non dentelé.***

47	**30 c. brun**	**450 »**	**250 »**
	(Sur lettre)		400 »
	(Bloc de 15)	11 000 »	
	⊞	2 250 »	3 500 »
	(Neuf sans gomme)	280 »	
	a. brun pâle	480 »	270 »
	b. brun-noir	2 400 »	1 100 »
	c. brun verdâtre	3 200 »	1 700 »
	d. brun foncé	700 »	350 »
	e. (R. relié au cadre)	700 »	450 »

Oblitérations	⊙	✉
Losange petits chiffres	340 »	840 »
Cachet à date	370 »	1 300 »
Etoile	385 »	1 300 »
Ancre	420 »	800 »

Piquages	**sur fragment**	✉
Percé en lignes		1 850 »

1870. – ***Cérès. Émission dite de Bordeaux. Lithographie. Papier teinté. non dentelé.***

48	**40 c. orange**	**575 »**	**130 »**
	(Sur lettre)		280 »
	(Coupé sur lettre)		60 000 »
	(Bloc de 15)	15 000 »	
	⊞	2 800 »	3 750 »
	(Neuf sans gomme)	300 »	
	a. orange vif	800 »	220 »
	b. jaune citron	13 000 »	2 700 »
	c. rouge-orange	850 »	220 »
	d. rouge sang clair	1 500 »	900 »
	e. rouge sang foncé	6 500 »	2 200 »
	f. ocre	10 000 »	2 000 »
	g. vermillon très vif	5 000 »	2 000 »

Oblitérations	⊙	✉
Losange petits chiffres	160 »	385 »
Cachet à date	180 »	780 »
Etoile	200 »	1 300 »
Ancre	160 »	400 »

Piquages	**sur fragment**	✉
Percé en lignes		600 »

1870. – ***Cérès. Émission dite de Bordeaux. Lithographie. Papier teinté. non dentelé.***

49	**80 c. rose**	**700 »**	**320 »**
	(Sur lettre)		900 »
	(Coupé sur lettre)		100 000 »
	(Coupé sur lettre (1/4))		75 000 »
	(Bloc de 15)	16 500 »	
	⊞	3 500 »	3 900 »
	(Neuf sans gomme)	320 »	
	a. rose pâle	650 »	320 »
	b. rose vif	1 000 »	350 »
	c. rose carminé	1 100 »	450 »
	d. groseille	2 500 »	1 200 »
	e. saumon	5 000 »	2 200 »
	f. (88 au lieu de 80)	20 000 »	8 000 »
	g. (Boule blanche sous le cou)	26 000 »	8 000 »

Oblitérations	⊙	✉
Losange petits chiffres	385 »	950 »
Cachet à date	400 »	1 100 »
Etoile	500 »	1 700 »
Ancre	370 »	900 »

Piquages	**sur fragment**	✉
Percé en lignes		2 200 »

IIIe République

Type Cérès

a. - Grands chiffres dans les angles inférieurs.

1872. – ***Cérès. Typographie. Papier teinté. Dentelé 14 x 13½.***

50	**1 c. vert-olive**	**90 »**	**20 »**
	(Seul sur lettre)		120 »
	⊞	400 »	225 »
	(Neuf sans gomme)	30 »	
	a. vert-bronze	90 »	25 »
	b. (Trait inférieur du cadre brisé)	160 »	65 »
	c. (non dentelé)	350 »	
	d. (Fond ligné)	95 »	35 »

Oblitérations	⊙	✉
Losange grands chiffres (bleu)	80 »	600 »
Losange petits chiffres	25 »	100 »
Ancre	140 »	
Cachet à date des imprimés (rouge)	25 »	150 »
O.R. dans un cercle	50 »	
Annulation typographique des journaux	30 »	100 »

1872. – ***Cérès. Typographie. Papier teinté. Dentelé 14 x 13½.***

N°	Désignation	Neuf	Oblitéré
51	**2 c. rouge-brun**	**170 »**	**18 »**
	(Seul sur lettre)		100 »
	(Neuf sans gomme)	50 »	
	⊞	850 »	250 »
	a. brun-rouge foncé	180 »	20 »
	b. (Trait inférieur du cadre brisé)	325 »	150 »
	c. (non dentelé)	450 »	
	d. (Fond ligné)	200 »	23 »

Oblitérations	⊙	✉
Losange grands chiffres (bleu)	80 »	60 »
Losange petits chiffres	20 »	100 »
Ancre	120	»
Cachet à date des imprimés (rouge)	25 »	120 »
O.R. dans un cercle	50 »	
Annulation typographique des journaux	20 »	100 »

1872. – ***Cérès. Typographie. Papier teinté. Dentelé 14 x 13½.***

N°	Désignation	Neuf	Oblitéré
52	**4 c. gris**	**400 »**	**50 »**
	(Seul sur lettre)		340 »
	⊞	1 900 »	700 »
	(Neuf sans gomme)	150 »	
	a. gris-jaunâtre	425 »	50 »
	b. (non dentelé)	500 »	
	c. (Fond ligné)	550 »	70 »

Oblitérations	⊙	✉
Losange grands chiffres (bleu)	100 »	750 »
Losange petits chiffres	50 »	250 »
Ancre	170	»
AS. NA.	220 »	
Cachet à date des imprimés (rouge)	70 »	400 »
O.R. dans un cercle	90 »	
Annulation typographique des journaux	150 »	1 400 »

1872. – ***Cérès. Typographie. Papier teinté. Dentelé 14 x 13½.***

N°	Désignation	Neuf	Oblitéré
53	**5 c. vert-jaune s. azuré**	**260 »**	**10 »**
	(Seul sur lettre)		40 »
	⊞	1 250 »	150 »
	(Neuf sans gomme)	100 »	
	a. vert s. blanc	265 »	10 »
	b. (Trait inférieur du cadre brisé)	325 »	90 »
	c. (Trait mince sous le cadre inférieur)	350 »	120 »
	d. (non dentelé)	300 »	
	e. (Papier filigrané)	1 400 »	450 »
	f. (Fond ligné)	340 »	85 »

Oblitérations	⊙	✉
Gros points	200 »	850 »
Losange grands chiffres (bleu)	70 »	400 »
Losange petits chiffres	12 »	50 »
Ancre	70 »	300 »
AS. NA.	120 »	1 100 »
Cachet à date des imprimés (rouge)	15 »	125 »
O.R. dans un cercle	60 »	350 »
Annulation typographique des journaux	230 »	

Le filigrane "LACROIX FRÈRES" porte sur la surface de 12 timbres d'un tirage.

b. - Type de 1849-50. Gros chiffres.

1875. – ***Cérès. Typographie. Papier teinté. Dentelé 14 x 13½.***

N°	Désignation	Neuf	Oblitéré
54	**10 c. brun s. rose**	**550 »**	**12 »**
	(Sur lettre)		30 »
	⊞	2 750 »	200 »
	(Neuf sans gomme)	180 »	
	a. brun foncé s. rose	625 »	15 »
	b. (Fond ligné)	600 »	25 »

Oblitérations	⊙	✉
Gros points	80 »	600 »
Losange grands chiffres (bleu)	50 »	300 »
Losange petits chiffres	13 »	35 »
Ancre	45 »	150 »
AS. NA.	110 »	780 »
Cachet à date des imprimés (rouge)	20 »	120 »
O.R. dans un cercle	50 »	220 »

1873. – ***Cérès. Typographie. Papier teinté. Dentelé 14 x 13½***

N°	Désignation	Neuf	Oblitéré
55	**15 c. bistre**	**550 »**	**5 »**
	(Sur lettre)		30 »
	⊞	2 750 »	200 »
	(Neuf sans gomme)	180 »	
	a. bistre-jaune	600 »	5 »

Oblitérations	⊙	✉
Gros points	80 »	600 »
Losange grands chiffres (bleu)	50 »	300 »
Losange petits chiffres	6 »	35 »
Ancre	45 »	150 »
AS. NA.	80 »	780 »
Cachet à date des imprimés (rouge)	20 »	130 »
O.R. dans un cercle	50 »	230 »

ERREUR

55b	15 c. brun s. rose	6 000 »	6 500 »
	(Sur lettre)		35 000 »
55c	15 c. et 10 c. (se tenant)	12 000 »	15 000 »
	(Sur lettre)		40 000 »

L'erreur provient de ce qu'un cliché de 15 c. s'est glissé dans une planche de 10 c.

1872. – *Cérès. Typographie. Papier teinté. Dentelé 14 x 13½.*

56	**30 c. brun**	**850 »**	**7 »**
	(Sur lettre)		15 »
	⊞	4 200 »	225 »
	(Neuf sans gomme)	250 »	
	a. brun foncé	1 000 »	10 »
	b. (non dentelé)	700 »	
	c. (Fond ligné)	1 000 »	20 »

Oblitérations	⊙	✉
Gros points	70 »	600 »
Losange grands chiffres (bleu)	60 »	350 »
Losange petits chiffres	10 »	30 »
Ancre	45 »	120 »
AS. NA.	125 »	1 100 »
Cachet à date des imprimés (rouge)	40 »	280 »

1872. – *Cérès. Typographie. Papier teinté. Dentelé 14 x 13½.*

57	**80 c. rose**	**1 000 »**	**12 »**
	(Sur lettre)		50 »
	⊞	4 750 »	225 »
	(Neuf sans gomme)	300 »	
	a. carmin-rose	1 100 »	15 »
	b. carmin vif	1 300 »	25 »
	c. (non dentelé)	1 000 »	
	d. (Fond ligné)	1 100 »	35 »

Oblitérations	⊙	✉
Gros points	70 »	700 »
Losange grands chiffres (bleu)	70 »	400 »
Losange petits chiffres	15 »	50 »
Ancre	30 »	80 »
AS. NA.	170 »	1 400 »
Cachet à date des imprimés (rouge)	60 »	380 »

c. - Même type. Petits chiffres.

1873. – *Cérès. Typographie. Papier teinté. Dentelé 14 x 13½.*

58	**10 c. brun s. rose**	**425 »**	**12 »**
	(Sur lettre)		30 »
	⊞	2 100 »	175 »
	(Neuf sans gomme)	150 »	
	c. (la paire, tête-bêche)	6 000 »	2 500 »
	(Sur lettre)		4 750 »
	a. brun foncé s. rose	475 »	15 »
	b. (non dentelé)	600 »	
	d. (Fond ligné)	525 »	20 »

Oblitérations	⊙	✉
Gros points	70 »	650 »
Losange grands chiffres (bleu)	50 »	280 »
Losange petits chiffres	13 »	30 »
Ancre	45 »	140 »
AS. NA.	80 »	780 »
Cachet à date des imprimés (rouge)	20 »	100 »
O.R. dans un cercle	50 »	220 »

1871. – *Cérès. Typographie. Papier teinté. Dentelé 14 x 13½.*

59	**15 c. bistre**	**525 »**	**5 »**
	(Sur lettre)		15 »
	⊞	2 500 »	175 »
	(Neuf sans gomme)	150 »	
	b. (la paire, tête-bêche)	65 000 »	22 000 »
	(Sur lettre)		50 000 »
	a. bistre-brun	550 »	6 »
	c. (non dentelé)	500 »	

Oblitérations	⊙	✉
Gros points	70 »	650 »
Losange grands chiffres (bleu)	50 »	250 »
Losange petits chiffres	6 »	25 »
Ancre	40 »	140 »
AS. NA.	80 »	765 »
Cachet à date des imprimés (rouge)	20 »	130 »
O.R. dans un cercle	50 »	230 »

1871. – ***Cérès. Typographie. Papier teinté. Dentelés 14 x 13½.***

Le 25 c. a été tiré sur plusieurs planches différentes. Trois planches du type **I** et deux planches au type **II** ont été complètement reconstituées. Le nombre de planches au type **III** n'est pas encore déterminé avec certitude.

I. - Type normal (1er état, sans les signes ci-après).

II (2e état).

II. - Point de couleur à gauche du fleuron supérieur droit et point blanc sous le fleuron inférieur droit.

III (3e état).

III. - Trois points de couleur, un dans le coin supérieur gauche, branche supérieure gauche, les deux chacun sur une des branches supérieures, coin supérieur droit.

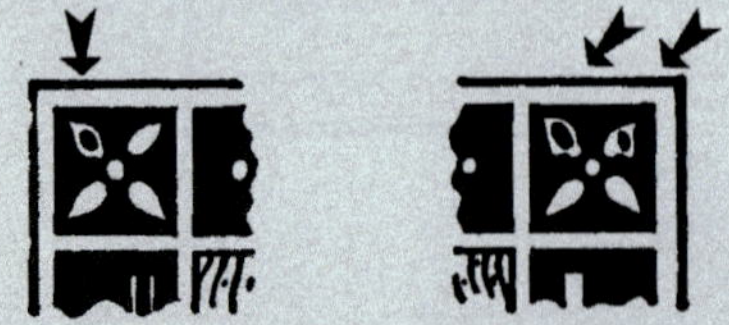

60A	**25 c. bleu (I)**	**180 »**	**2 »**
	(Sur lettre)		3 »
	(Neuf sans gomme)	60 »	
	⊞	900 »	50 »
	b. (la paire, tête-bêche)	10 000 »	4 500 »
	(Sur lettre)		12 000 »
	a. bleu foncé	225 »	2 »
60B	**25 c. bleu (II)**	**3 000 »**	**30 »**
	(Sur lettre)		40 »
	(Neuf sans gomme)	800 »	
	⊞	15 000 »	650 »

60C	**25 c. bleu (III)**	**180 »**	**2 »**
	(Sur lettre)		3 »
	(Neuf sans gomme)	70 »	
	⊞	900 »	50 »
	a. (25 c. (II) et 25 c. (III) se tenant)	8 500 »	2 350 »

Oblitérations	⊙	✉
Gros points	60 »	600 »
Losange grands chiffres (bleu)	50 »	180 »
Losange petits chiffres	4 »	10 »
Ancre	25 »	80 »
AS. NA.	40 »	250 »
Cachet à date des imprimés (rouge)	20 »	250 »
O.R. dans un cercle		400 »

RÉIMPRESSION (Granet). (1887)

25 c. bleu laiteux 600 »

réimpressions Granet, voir note avant le n° 61.

Groupe allégorique Paix et Commerce dit Type Sage

Les n°s 61 à 106 trés bien centrés méritent une plus-value de 60% environ.

En outre les timbres neufs avec gomme d'origine intacte et sans charnière méritent une plus-value de 50%.

Le coin (plaque gravée) se fendit pendant une trempe et le graveur dut refaire tout l'angle inférieur gauche du timbre ; la signature J. A. SAGE INV. ne fut pas disposée exactement de la même façon que sur le cliché original et ceci donna naissance aux deux types ci-dessous :

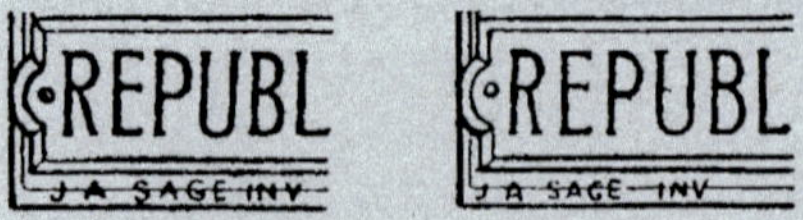

I. N sous B. *II. N sous U.*

En 1897 on utilisa un troisième poinçon peu différent du Type I.

Note concernant l'émission dite "des Régents"

Ce tirage de luxe a été fait officiellement, alors que les timbres français étaient imprimés par la Banque de France.

Les timbres, tous non dentelés et au type **II**, se distinguent par la perfection de l'impression et la texture du papier, qui est épais.

La série complète (19 valeurs) 5 500 »

Une deuxième série des mêmes timbres existe, dans les mêmes couleurs, mais sans teinte de fond (même valeur).

Voir les réimpressions Granet après le n° 99.

RÉIMPRESSIONS (Granet 1887).

Ces réimpressions sont connues sous le nom du Ministre des Postes. Leurs nuances et la structure du papier, ainsi que leur réaction sous la lumière de Wood, où elles prennent une teinte jaune caractéristique, permettent de les distinguer.

Elles sont toutes au type **II** et non dentelées et souvent sans gomme (même prix).

La série complète (27 valeurs) 5 600 »

1876-78. – ***Type Sage. Typographie. Papier teinté. Dentelés 14 x 13½.***

Type **I.**

61	**1 c. vert**	**200 »**	**90 »**
	(Sur lettre)		300 »
	(Seul sur lettre)		800 »
	⊞	1 000 »	420 »
	a. (non dentelé)	200 »	
	réimp. Granet, non dentelé (II)	80 »	

Oblitérations	⊙	✉
Petit cachet à date (bleu)	130 »	350 »
Cachet à date des imprimés (rouge)	120 »	350 »
Annulation typographique des journaux	150 »	2 000 »

62	**2 c. vert**	**1 900 »**	**300 »**
	(Sur lettre)		400 »
	(Seul sur lettre)		600 »
	⊞	10 000 »	2 800 »
	a. (non dentelé)	2 000 »	
	Oblitérations	⊙	✉
	Petit cachet à date (bleu)	385 »	900 »
	Cachet à date des imprimés (rouge)	340 »	1 000 »
	Annulation typographique des journaux	350 »	2 000 »
63	**4 c. vert**	**220 »**	**70 »**
	(Sur lettre)		280 »
	(Seul sur lettre)		750 »
	⊞	975 »	500 »
	a. (non dentelé)	200 »	
	réimp. Granet, non dentelé (II)	80 »	
	Oblitérations	⊙	✉
	Petit cachet à date (bleu)	100 »	300 »
	Cachet à date des imprimés (rouge)	90 »	300 »
	Annulation typographique des journaux	220 »	1 700 »
64	**5 c. vert**	**950 »**	**45 »**
	(Sur lettre)		70 »
	(Seul sur lettre)		85 »
	⊞	5 000 »	400 »
	a. (non dentelé)	800 »	
	Oblitérations	⊙	✉
	Petit cachet à date (bleu)	75 »	150 »
	Cachet à date des imprimés (rouge)	70 »	130 »
	Annulation typographique des journaux	240 »	

65	**10 c. vert**	**1 200 »**	**20 »**
	(Sur lettre)		35 »
	(Seul sur lettre)		45 »
	⊞	5 900 »	350 »
	a. (non dentelé)	900 »	
	Oblitérations	⊙	✉
	Petit cachet à date (bleu)	60 »	120 »
	Cachet à date des imprimés (rouge)	40 »	100 »
66	**15 c. gris**	**1 100 »**	**12 »**
	(Sur lettre)		30 »
	(Seul sur lettre)		45 »
	⊞	6 000 »	350 »
	a. (non dentelé)	900 »	
	Oblitérations	⊙	✉
	Petit cachet à date (bleu)	35 »	65 »
	Cachet à date des imprimés (rouge)	40 »	90 »
67	**20 c. brun-lilas**	**825 »**	**15 »**
	(Sur lettre)		40 »
	(Seul sur lettre)		85 »
	⊞	4 000 »	350 »
	a. (non dentelé)	650 »	
	émission des Régents, non dent. (II)	270 »	
	réimp. Granet, non dentelé (II)	70 »	
	Oblitérations	⊙	✉
	Petit cachet à date (bleu)	40 »	130 »
	Cachet à date des imprimés (rouge)	40 »	90 »
68	**25 c. outremer**	**11 000 »**	**60 »**
	(Sur lettre)		85 »
	⊞	75 000 »	3 000 »
	(Neuf sans gomme)	2 500 »	
	Oblitérations	⊙	✉
	Petit cachet à date (bleu)	150 »	400 »
	Cachet à date des imprimés (rouge)	140 »	400 »

69	**30 c. brun clair**	**600 »**	**8 »**
	(Sur lettre)		15 »
	⊞	3 000 »	150 »
	a. (non dentelé)	300 »	
	Oblitérations	⊙	✉
	Petit cachet à date (bleu)	25 »	40 »
	Cachet à date des imprimés (rouge)	15 »	70 »
70	**40 c. rouge-orange**	**800 »**	**30 »**
	(Sur lettre)		50 »
	⊞	4 000 »	285 »
	a. (non dentelé)	300 »	
	Oblitérations	⊙	✉
	Petit cachet à date (bleu)	55 »	140 »
	Cachet à date des imprimés (rouge)	45 »	
71	**75 c. carmin**	**1 400 »**	**8 »**
	(Sur lettre)		50 »
	(Seul sur lettre)		40 »
	⊞	6 500 »	170 »
	a. (non dentelé)	700 »	
	Oblitérations	⊙	✉
	Petit cachet à date (bleu)	50 »	150 »
	Cachet à date des imprimés (rouge)	45 »	
72	**1 f. bronze**	**1 300 »**	**10 »**
	(Sur lettre)		70 »
	(Seul sur lettre)		100 »
	⊞	6 000 »	130 »
	a. (non dentelé)	450 »	
	Oblitérations	⊙	✉
	Petit cachet à date (bleu)	35 »	140 »
	Cachet à date des imprimés (rouge)	45 »	

Non émis.

73	**20 c. *bleu***	**47 500 »**	

le n° 73 est souvent sans gomme

Type **II**.

74	**2 c. vert**	**165 »**	**20 »**
	(Sur lettre)		60 »
	(Seul sur lettre)		100 »
	⊞	800 »	170 »
	réimp. Granet, non dentelé (II)	80 »	
	Oblitérations	⊙	✉
	Petit cachet à date (bleu)	35 »	120 »
	Cachet à date des imprimés (rouge)	40 »	120 »
	Ancre	35 »	200 »
75	**5 c. vert**	**40 »**	**0 50**
	(Sur lettre)		1 »
	⊞	170 »	10 »
	a. (non dentelé)	200 »	
	émission des Régents, non dent. (II)	80 »	
	réimp. Granet, non dentelé (II)	70 »	

Oblitérations	⊙	✉
Petit cachet à date (bleu)	10 »	40 »
Cachet à date des imprimés (rouge)	5 »	50 »
Ancre	15 »	10 75
Annulation typographique des journaux	100 »	

76	**10 c. vert**	**1 400 »**	**280 »**
	(Sur lettre)		320 »
	(Seul sur lettre)		400 »
	⊞	8 400 »	2 500 »
	réimp. Granet, non dentelé (II)	80 »	

Oblitérations	⊙	✉
Petit cachet à date (bleu)	340 »	750 »
Cachet à date des imprimés (rouge)	350 »	850 »
Ancre	370 »	

77	**15 c. gris**	**900 »**	**2 »**
	(Sur lettre)		3 »
	⊞	4 500 »	60 »
	jaune clair, émission dite "des Régents", non dentelé, type II	80 »	
	réimp. Granet, non dentelé (II)	90 »	

Oblitérations	⊙	✉
Petit cachet à date (bleu)	15 »	60 »
Cachet à date des imprimés (rouge)	15 »	70 »

78	**25 c. outremer**	**600 »**	**1 »**
	(Sur lettre)		1 50
	⊞	2 700 »	75 »
	b. outremer sur vert clair		850 »
	c. (non dentelé)	350 »	
	réimp. Granet, non dentelé (II)	65 »	

Oblitérations	⊙	✉
Petit cachet à date (bleu)	10 »	40 »
Cachet à date des imprimés (rouge)	10 »	60 »

79	**25 c. bleu**	**675 »**	**2 »**
	(Sur lettre)		2 50
	⊞	3 000 »	110 »
	réimp. Granet, non dentelé (II)	75 »	

Oblitérations	⊙	✉
Petit cachet à date (bleu)	10 »	40 »
Cachet à date des imprimés (rouge)	10 »	60 »

80	**30 c. brun-jaune**	**130 »**	**1 50**
	(Sur lettre)		3 »
	(Seul sur lettre)		5 »
	⊞	600 »	100 »
	a. brun	140 »	2 »
	b. (non dentelé)	600 »	
	émission des Régents, non dent. (II)	80 »	
	réimp. Granet, non dentelé (II)	80 »	

Oblitérations	⊙	✉
Petit cachet à date (bleu)	15 »	40 »
Cachet à date des imprimés (rouge)	20 »	100 »

81	**75 c. rose**	**2 500 »**	**120 »**
	(Sur lettre)		250 »
	(Seul sur lettre)		500 »
	⊞	12 000 »	1 000 »
	a. (non dentelé)		
	émission des Régents, non dent. (II)	80 »	
	réimp. Granet, non dentelé (II)	180 »	

Oblitérations	⊙	✉
Petit cachet à date (bleu)	140 »	450 »

82	**1 f. olive clair**	**225 »**	**8 »**
	(Sur lettre)		60 »
	(Seul sur lettre)		100 »
	⊞	1 100 »	70 »
	a. (non dentelé)	1 400 »	
	émission des Régents, non dent. (II)	80 »	
	réimp. Granet, non dentelé (II)	150 »	

Oblitérations	⊙	✉
Petit cachet à date (bleu)	20 »	80 »

Types **I** *et* **II** *se tenant.*

78a	25 c. et 25 c.	100 000 »	23 000 »
	(Sur lettre)		80 000 »

Non émis.

73a	20 c. (non dentelé)	800 »	
	émission des Régents, non dent. (II)	925 »	
	réimp. Granet, non dentelé (II)	700 »	

1877-80. – ***Type Sage (type II). Typographie. Papier teinté. Dentelés 14 × 13½.***

Noir sur azuré — *Noir sur bleu de Prusse*

83	**1 c. noir s. azuré**	**10 »**	**1 »**
	(Sur lettre)		5 »
	(Seul sur lettre)		3 »
	⊞	50 »	20 »
	a. noir s. bleu	11 »	1 25
	b. noir s. gris	10 »	1 »
	c. noir sur cobalt	2 500 »	1 000 »
	d. (non dentelé)	80 »	
	émission des Régents, non dent. (II)	80 »	
	réimp. Granet, non dentelé (II)	70 »	

Oblitérations	⊙	✉
Petit cachet à date (bleu)	10 »	50 »
Cachet à date des imprimés (rouge)	5 »	50 »
Annulation typographique des journaux	5 »	40 »

84	**1 c. noir s. bleu de Prusse**	**15 000 »**	**6 000 »**
	(Seul sur lettre)		30 000 »
	⊞	110 000 »	
	(Neuf sans gomme)	8 500 »	

Oblitérations	⊙	✉
Cachet à date des imprimés (rouge)	7 800 »	
Annulation typographique des journaux	8 000 »	

85	**2 c. brun-rouge**	**12 »**	**2 »**
	(Sur lettre)		5 »
	(Seul sur lettre)		10 »
	⊞	55 »	25 »
	a. brun foncé	14 »	3 »
	b. (non dentelé)	80 »	
	émission des Régents, non dent. (II)	80 »	
	réimp. Granet, non dentelé (II)	70 »	

Oblitérations	⊙	✉
Petit cachet à date (bleu)	10 »	50 »
Cachet à date des imprimés (rouge)	10 »	50 »
Annulation typographique des journaux	10 »	60 »

86	**3 c. bistre s. jaune**	**300 »**	**50 »**
	(Sur lettre)		450 »
	(Seul sur lettre)		900 »
	⊞	1 400 »	400 »
	a. bistre s. jaune (non dentelé)	280 »	
	réimp. Granet, non dentelé (II)	80 »	

Oblitérations	⊙	✉
Petit cachet à date (bleu)	80 »	70 »
Cachet à date des imprimés (rouge)	70 »	50 »
Annulation typographique des journaux	100 »	2 600 »

N°			
87	**3 c. gris**	**10 »**	**2 »**
	(Sur lettre)		20 »
	(Seul sur lettre)		20 »
	⊞	40 »	20 »
	a. gris clair	10 »	2 »
	b. gris-jaunâtre	9 »	2 »
	c. gris (non dentelé)	80 »	
	émission des Régents, non dent. (II)	275 »	
	réimp. Granet, non dentelé (II)	80 »	

Oblitérations	⊙	✉
Petit cachet à date (bleu)	15 »	70 »
Cachet à date des imprimés (rouge)	10 »	50 »
Annulation typographique des journaux	70 »	2 600 »

N°			
88	**4 c. lilas-brun**	**13 »**	**2 »**
	(Sur lettre)		20 »
	(Seul sur lettre)		110 »
	⊞	55 »	23 »
	a. lilas s. azuré	13 »	3 »
	b. lilas foncé s. azuré	17 »	4 »
	c. (non dentelé)	80 »	
	émission des Régents, non dent. (II)	80 »	

Oblitérations	⊙	✉
Petit cachet à date (bleu)	15 »	70 »
Cachet à date des imprimés (rouge)	10 »	50 »
Annulation typographique des journaux	80 »	3 500 »

N°			
89	**10 c. noir s. lilas**	**60 »**	**1 »**
	(Sur lettre)		2 »
	⊞	275 »	15 »
	a. noir s. violet	65 »	2 »
	b. (non dentelé)	130 »	
	émission des Régents, non dent. (II)	80 »	
	réimp. Granet, non dentelé (II)	150 »	

Oblitérations	⊙	✉
Petit cachet à date (bleu)	10 »	60 »
Cachet à date des imprimés (rouge)	10 »	50 »

N°			
90	**15 c. bleu**	**50 »**	**0 50**
	(Sur lettre)		1 »
	⊞	225 »	12 »
	a. bleu sur bleu	675 »	5 »
	b. (non dentelé)	110 »	
	émission des Régents, non dent. (II)	700 »	
	réimp. Granet, non dentelé (II)	70 »	

Oblitérations	⊙	✉
Petit cachet à date (bleu)	10 »	50 »
Cachet à date des imprimés (rouge)	15 »	50 »

Il existe un certain nombre de timbres de 15 c. faux, ayant servi à l'affranchissement des lettres ; les plus connus sont, entre autres, ceux de Chalon-sur-Saône.

valeur neuf	100 »	
oblitéré sur lettre		2 000 »

Ces faux se reconnaissent à la dentelure, qui n'est pas rectangulaire mais linéaire, et montre, par conséquent, des irrégularités aux quatre angles.

N°			
91	**25 c. noir s. rouge**	**1 500 »**	**25 »**
	(Sur lettre)		45 »
	⊞	7 000 »	600 »
	a. noir s. rouge foncé	1 600 »	30 »
	b. noir s. rouge (non dentelé)	750 »	
	émission des Régents, non dent. (II)	275 »	
	noir s. rouge-brique, réimp. Granet, non dentelé (II)	600 »	

Oblitérations	⊙	✉
Petit cachet à date (bleu)	50 »	150 »
Cachet à date des imprimés (rouge)	35 »	120 »

N°			
92	**25 c. bistre s. jaune**	**500 »**	**5 »**
	(Sur lettre)		13 »
	⊞	2 250 »	300 »
	a. jaune s. bistre-jaune	480 »	6 »
	b. bistre s. jaune (non dentelé)	400 »	
	jaune clair, émission dite "des Régents", non dentelé, type II	775 »	
	réimp. Granet, non dentelé (II)	80 »	

Oblitérations	⊙	✉
Petit cachet à date (bleu)	20 »	50 »
Cachet à date des imprimés (rouge)	15 »	60 »

N°			
93	**35 c. violet-noir s. jaune**	**750 »**	**35 »**
	(Sur lettre)		100 »
	(Seul sur lettre)		140 »
	⊞	3 350 »	400 »
	a. violet-noir s. orange	800 »	40 »
	b. (non dentelé)	320 »	
	émission des Régents, non dent. (II)	80 »	

Oblitérations	⊙	✉
Petit cachet à date (bleu)	75 »	350 »
Cachet à date des imprimés (rouge)	60 »	280 »

N°			
94	**40 c. rouge-orange**	**160 »**	**2 »**
	(Sur lettre)		10 »
	⊞	700 »	50 »
	a. vermillon	160 »	3 »
	b. (non dentelé)	350 »	
	émission des Régents, non dent. (II)	80 »	

Oblitérations	⊙	✉
Petit cachet à date (bleu)	25 »	85 »
Cachet à date des imprimés (rouge)	50 »	

N°			
95	**5 f. violet s. lilas**	**600 »**	**90 »**
	(Sur lettre)		500 »
	(Seul sur lettre)		3 500 »
	⊞	3 000 »	500 »
	a. lilas-rose s. lilas pâle	750 »	100 »
	émission des Régents, non dent. (II)	425 »	
	réimp. Granet, non dentelé (II)	2 300 »	

Oblitérations	⊙	✉
Petit cachet à date (bleu)	140 »	500 »
Cachet à date des imprimés (rouge)	200 »	

Voir le 5 f. carmin sous le n° 216.

1884-90. – *Type Sage (type II). Typographie. Papier teinté. Dentelés 14 x 13½.*

96	**20 c. brique s. vert**	**75 »**	**4 »**
	(Sur lettre)		30 »
	(Seul sur lettre)		130 »
	⊞	350 »	40 »
	a. garance s. vert	75 »	5 »
	b. (non dentelé)	120 »	
	émission des Régents, non dent. (II)	775 »	
	réimp. Granet, non dentelé (II)	100 »	

Oblitérations	⊙	✉
Petit cachet à date (bleu)	20 »	80 »
Cachet à date des imprimés (rouge)	20 »	90 »

97	**25 c. noir s. rose**	**120 »**	**1 »**
	(Sur lettre)		4 »
	⊞	500 »	30 »
	a. noir s. rose foncé	130 »	1 50
	b. (non dentelé)	200 »	
	noir s. rose, réimp. Granet, non dentelé (II)	80 »	

Oblitérations	⊙	✉
Petit cachet à date (bleu)	17 »	60 »
Cachet à date des imprimés (rouge)	15 »	80 »

98	**50 c. rose**	**275 »**	**3 »**
	(Sur lettre)		25 »
	(Seul sur lettre)		30 »
	⊞	1 350 »	45 »
	a. rose pâle	275 »	3 »

Oblitérations	⊙	✉
Petit cachet à date (bleu)	20 »	80 »
Cachet à date des imprimés (rouge)	20 »	80 »

99	**75 c. violet s. orange**	**300 »**	**35 »**
	(Sur lettre)		150 »
	(Seul sur lettre)		280 »
	⊞	1 400 »	300 »
	a. violet s. jaune	325 »	45 »

Oblitérations	⊙	✉
Petit cachet à date (bleu)	60 »	300 »
Cachet à date des imprimés (rouge)	60 »	

Type Sage (type II). Papier quadrillé. Dentelé 14 x 13½.

101	**15 c. bleu**	**28 »**	**0 50**
	(Sur lettre)		2 »
	⊞	125 »	
	a. bleu foncé	25 »	1 »
	b. (Non dentelé)	250 »	

Oblitérations	⊙	✉
Petit cachet à date (bleu)	8 »	25 »
Cachet à date des imprimés (rouge)	8 »	50 »
O.R. dans un cercle	15 »	100 »

Il s'agit d'un quadrillé de vernis gras incolore, qui forme sur le recto un réseau de petits carrés de 31 mm de côté. Il s'aperçoit plus ou moins visiblement.

1898-1900. – *Type Sage. Typographie. Dentelés 14 x 13½.*

Type **III**.

Pour les n°s 102 à 105 on utilisa un troisième poinçon, gravé dès 1876. Ce poinçon est peu différent du type **I** (N sous B).

102	**5 c. vert-jaune**	**30 »**	**2 »**
	(Sur lettre)		3 »
	⊞	140 »	12 »
	a. (non dentelé)	700 »	
103	**10 c. noir s. lilas**	**40 »**	**3 »**
	(Sur lettre)		5 »
	⊞	190 »	20 »
	c. (non dentelé)	300 »	
104	**50 c. rose**	**325 »**	**35 »**
	(Sur lettre)		70 »
	(Seul sur lettre)		100 »
	⊞	1 400 »	300 »
105	**2 f. bistre s. azuré**	**185 »**	**40 »**
	(Sur lettre)		500 »
	(Seul sur lettre)		5 500 »
	⊞	850 »	400 »
	a. (non dentelé)	3 000 »	

Type **II**.

106	**5 c. vert-jaune**	**35 »**	**2 »**
	(Sur lettre)		3 »
	⊞	170 »	20 »
	b. (non dentelé)	100 »	

Types **III** *et* **II** *se tenant verticalement.*

106a	5 c. et 5 c.	175 »
103a	10 c. (II) et 10 c. (III)	275 »
103b	10 c. (III) et 10 c. (II)	500 »

Les n°s 61 à 106 très bien centrés méritent une plus-value de 60 % environ.

En outre les timbres neufs avec gomme d'origine intacte et sans charnière méritent une plus-value de 50 %.

Récapitulatif des Réimpressions des timbres classiques

1862. – ***Cérès. Ces réimpressions ont été faites en 1862 dans les couleurs employées à cette époque, qui sont généralement plus claires que celles de 1849-50.***

1f	10 c. bistre clair (réimpression)	600	»
2e	15 c. vert vif clair (réimpression)	800	»
3f	20 c. (réimpression)	500	»
4d	25 c. (réimpression)	550	»
5g	40 c. (réimpression)	750	»
5h	40 c. ("4" retouché, réimpression)	14 000	»
5j	40 c. (Paire avec un normal, réimpression)	20 000	»
5k	40 c. (Paire des 2 retouchés, réimpression)	35 000	»
6f	1 F. (réimpression)	800	»
8f	20 c. (réimpression)	600	»

1862. – ***Prince-président Louis-Napoléon. Légende REPUB. FRANC.***

9c	10 c. bistre clair (réimpression, 1862)	750	»
10c	25 c. bleu (réimpression, 1862)	500	»

1862-63. – ***Napoléon III. Légende EMPIRE FRANC.***

15c	25 c. bleu clair (Réimpression)	600	»
17Ah	80 c. carmin-rose (Réimpression)	2 400	»
18d	1 F. (Réimpression)	1 700	»
18e	1 F. (Tête-bêche, Réimpression)	30 000	»

Emission Rothschild. Impression très fine. Non dentelés.

25c	1 c. bronze	1 500	»
26c	2 c. rouge-brun	250	»
27d	4 c. gris	200	»
28Aa	10 c. bistre	200	»
29Ab	20 c. bleu	350	»
30c	30 c. brun	250	»
31c	40 c. orange	250	»
32b	80 c. rose	550	»

1887. – ***RÉIMPRESSION (Granet).***

25d	1 c. bronze (réimpression Granet, sans gomme)	1 350	»

1887. – ***RÉIMPRESSIONS (Granet). Non dentelés. Papier teinté. Avec ou sans gomme.***

36c	10 c. bistre-jaune (Réimpression Granet, non dentelé, papier teinté, avec ou sans gomme)	450	»
37f	20 c. bleu clair (Réimpression Granet, non dentelé, papier teinté, avec ou sans gomme)	500	»

1887. – ***Réimpression GRANET.***

60Ac	25 c. bleu laiteux (Granet)	600	»

Ces réimpressions sont connues sous le nom du Ministre des Postes. Leurs nuances et la structure du papier, ainsi que leur réaction sous la lumière de Wood, où elles prennent une teinte jaune caractéristique, permettent de les distinguer.

Elles sont toutes au type **II** et non dentelées et souvent sans gomme (même prix).

61c	1 c. vert foncé s. vert (Granet, N.D.) (II)	80	»
83f	1 c. noir s. azuré (Granet, N.D.) (II)	70	»
74a	2 c. vert foncé s. vert (Granet, N.D.) (II)	80	»
85d	2 c. brun sur jaune (Granet, N.D.) (II)	70	»
86b	3 c. jaune (Granet, N.D.) (II)	80	»
87e	3 c. gris (Granet, N.D.) (II)	80	»
63b	4 c. vert foncé s. vert (Granet, N.D.) (II)	80	»
88e	4 c. lilas-brun s. azuré (Granet, N.D.) (II)	100	»
75c	5 c. vert foncé s. vert (Granet, N.D.) (II)	70	»
76a	10 c. vert foncé s. vert (Granet, N.D.) (II)	80	»
89d	10 c. noir s. lilas (Granet, N.D.) (II)	150	»
77a	15 c. gris (Granet, N.D.) (II)	90	»
77Ab	15 c. jaune clair (Granet, N.D.) (II)	600	»
90d	15 c. bleu (Granet, N.D.) (II)	70	»
96d	20 c. brun s. jaune (Granet, N.D.) (II)	70	»
73c	20 c. bleu foncé (Granet, N.D.) (II)	700	»
96e	20 c. rouge s. vert (Granet, N.D.) (II)	100	»
78d	25 c. outremer (Granet, N.D.) (II)	65	»
79a	25 c. bleu (Granet, N.D.) (II)	75	»
91d	25 c. noir s. rouge brique (Granet, N.D.) (II)	600	»
92d	25 c. bistre s. jaune (Granet, N.D.) (II)	80	»
91e	25 c. noir s. rose (Granet, N.D.) (II)	80	»
80c	30 c. brun (Granet, N.D.) (II)	80	»
93d	35 c. violet s. orange (Granet, N.D.) (II)	85	»
94d	40 c. vermillon s. paille (Granet, N.D.) (II)	85	»
81c	75 c. rose vif (Granet, N.D.) (II)	180	»
82b	1 f. vert-bronze (Granet, N.D.) (II)	150	»
95c	5 f. violet (Granet, N.D.) (II)	2 200	»

La série complète (28 valeurs) 6 250 »

Emission dite "des Régents". Non dentelés, Type II papier épais.

Ce tirage de luxe a été fait officiellement, alors que les timbres français étaient imprimés par la Banque de France.

Les timbres, tous non dentelés et au type **II**, se distinguent par la perfection de l'impression et la texture du papier, qui est épais.

83e	1 c. noir sur azuré (Régents, N.D.) (II)	80	»
85c	2 c. brun-rouge (Régents, N.D.) (II)	80	»
87d	3 c. gris (Régents, N.D.) (II)	270	»
88d	4 c. lilas-brun (Régents, N.D.) (II)	80	»
75b	5 c. vert (Régents, N.D.) (II)	80	»
89c	10 c. noir s. lilas (Régents, N.D.) (II)	80	»
77Aa	15 c. jaune clair (Régents, N.D.) (II)	500	»
90c	15 c. bleu (Régents, N.D.) (II)	700	»
73b	20 c. bleu (Régents, N.D.) (II)	925	»
67b	20 c. brun-lilas s. paille (Régents, N.D.) (II)	270	»
96c	20 c. brique sur vert (Régents, N.D.) (II)	775	»
91c	25 c. noir s. rouge (Régents, N.D.) (II)	275	»
92c	25 c. jaune clair (Régents, N.D.) (II)	80	»
69b	30 c. brun clair (Régents, N.D.) (II)	80	»
93c	35 c. violet s. jaune (Régents, N.D.) (II)	80	»
93aa	violet sur orange (Régents, N.D.) (II)	80	»
94c	40 c. rouge-orange (Régents, N.D.) (II)	80	»
81b	75 c. rose (Régents, N.D.) (II)	80	»
72b	1 f. vert-bronze (Régents, N.D.) (II)	80	»
95b	5 f. violet sur lilas (Régents, N.D.) (II)	425	»

La série complète (20 valeurs) 5 100 »

Une deuxième série des mêmes timbres existe, dans les mêmes couleurs, mais sans teinte de fond (même valeur).

A partir de 1900 et jusqu'en 1959 les cotes de la colonne de gauche concernent les timbres neufs avec gomme d'origine intacte et sans charnière, celles de la colonne centrale les timbres neufs avec charnière légère, celles de la colonne de droite les timbres oblitérés.

1900-24. – ***Type Blanc. Typographie. Dentelés 14 x 13½.*** ©

Type I

Type II

Type I. - A la bordure de la draperie qui se trouve sous la lettre E de FRANÇAISE, il n'y a qu'un seul trait d'ombre.

Type II. - A cet endroit, il y a deux traits d'ombre.

Type IIB (roulette). - Comme II mais trait cassé à droite du gros orteil du pied droit.

Un type II existe pour le 4 c. mais seulement en préoblitérés.

Type IA

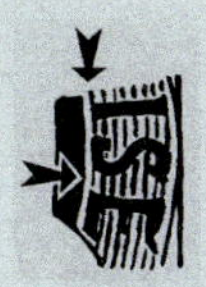

Type IB

Types du 1 c.

Type IA. - Ligne blanche allant en se rétrécissant sous ISE de FRANÇAISE. Trait épais reliant le pied du S à celui du E.

Type IB. - Ligne blanche de largeur régulière. Trait mince ou ne se marquant pas, ou très peu entre S et E.

107	**1 c. gris (IB)**	1 25	0 80	0 50
	(Sur lettre)			0 80
	a. ardoise (IB)	1 40	0 80	0 80
	b. ardoise (II)	1 25	0 80	0 80
	c. (non dentelé)		70 »	
	d. gris (Papier GC) (IB)	1 55	1 »	1 »
	e. ardoise (Papier GC) (IB)	1 85	1 10	1 10
	f. gris (IA)	3 »	1 85	0 80
	g. ardoise (IA)	2 30	1 55	0 80
	h. (double impression) (IB)			6 000 »
	j. ardoise (Papier GC) (IA)			

Type IA

Type IB

Types du 2 c.

Type IA. - Tache reliant deux lignes.

Type IB. - Tache à cheval sur une ligne.

108	**2 c. brun-lilas (IB)**	1 55	1 »	0 30
	(Sur lettre)			0 80
	a. brun-lilas foncé (IB)	3 35	2 »	0 50
	b. brun-lilas (II)	1 55	1 »	0 50
	c. (non dentelé)		70 »	
	d. (Papier GC) (IA)	4 »	1 85	1 10

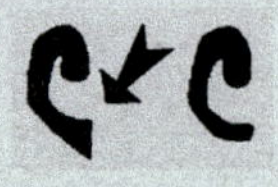

Types du 3 c.

Type IA. - La boucle inférieure du C se termine par un triangle.

Type IB. - Boucle inférieure du C ramenée à une simple pointe par retaille au burin.

109	**3 c. orange (IB)**	1 »	0 65	0 65
	(Sur lettre)			3 »
	(Seul sur lettre)			9 15
	a. rouge-orange (IB)	1 10	0 65	0 80
	b. rouge (IB)	30 »	23 »	7 65
	c. rouge-orange (II)	3 »	2 30	0 80
	d. (Non dentelé)		70 »	
	e. (Papier GC) (IB)	1 »	0 80	1 10
	f. rouge-orange (IA)	4 60	3 »	1 55
	g. rouge (IA)	40 »	30 »	12 50

110	**4 c. brun-jaune (I)**	5 »	3 »	2 »
	(Sur lettre)			4 60
	(Seul sur lettre)			61 »
	a. brun (I)	10 »	6 10	2 30
	b. brun foncé (I)	15 50	9 15	3 85
	c. (Non dentelé)		210 »	

Type IA *Type IB*

Types du 5 c.

Type IA. - Dans le coin supérieur gauche, l'extrémité de la plume est ronde et éloignée de l'angle ; dans le coin supérieur droit, l'extrémité est rapprochée du cadre, ou le touche.

Type IB. - Dans le coin supérieur gauche, l'extrémité est pointue et se dirige vers l'angle du cadre ; dans le coin supérieur droit, l'extremité est éloignée du cadre. Ce type n'a existé qu'en carnets.

Type IIA *Type IIB*

Trait sous le pied (zone inférieure droite du timbre).

IIA - Trait continu (feuilles rotatives).

IIB - Trait interrompu un peu à droite du gros orteil (roulettes rotatives).

111	**5 c. vert (IIA (1925)**	5 »	2 30	0 30
	(Sur lettre)			0 80
	a. vert (IIB)	100 »	77 »	30 »
	b. vert-jaune (IA)	5 35	2 60	0 50
	c. vert-bleu (IA)	7 65	4 15	0 65
	d. vert (IA)	11 50	7 65	1 55
	e. vert (IB)	42 »	35 »	13 »
	f. (id. paire verticale de carnet (IB))	88 »	77 »	
	g. (Non dentelé)		92 »	
	h. vert sur fond jaune (IA)		5 500 »	

Paire verticale de carnet :

Les cotes s'appliquent à des paires avec marges blanches supérieure et inférieure.

A ce type ont paru en 1919, un ½ c. sur 1 c. (157), en 1926, un 7½ c. lilas (Préoblitérés, n° 42) et, en 1929, un 10 c. violet (233).

1900-01. – *Types Mouchon. Typographie. Dentelés 14* x *13½.*

Type I *Type I*

Type I : les premiers tirages étaient faits en deux fois : on imprimait tout d'abord la vignette, ensuite le chiffre de la valeur, et il arriva que celui-ci occupait dans le cartouche des places variables ou n'était pas exactement de la même couleur que la vignette.

Type II *Type II*

Type II : ces timbres furent par la suite imprimés en une seule fois. Les 10 c. et 25 c. existent seuls dans les deux types. Dans le premier type du 10 c., la barre inférieure du 1 est droite, tandis qu'elle est courbe dans le type II.

Dans le deuxième type du 25 c., les traits du cadre inférieur du cartouche sont interrompus.

Chiffres déplacés.

Un des chiffres doit sortir du cartouche blanc, soit à gauche ou à droite, soit en bas ou en haut.

Type **I**.

N°				
112	**10 c. rose**	90 »	27 »	11 50
	(Sur lettre)			13 »
	a. (Chiffres déplacés)	225 »	130 »	45 »
	b. (Sans chiffres)		9 500 »	
	c. (Non dentelé)		425 »	275 »
113	**20 c. brun-lilas**	200 »	61 »	10 »
	(Sur lettre)			15 50
	(Seul sur lettre)			40 »
	a. (Chiffres déplacés)	300 »	215 »	50 »
	b. (Chiffres doubles)		3 850 »	
	c. (Sans chiffres)		12 500 »	
	d. (Impression recto-verso)	325 »	180 »	40 »
	e. (Non dentelé)		600 »	425 »
114	**25 c. bleu**	375 »	135 »	10 »
	(Sur lettre)			11 »
	(Seul sur lettre)			15 50
	a. (Chiffres déplacés)	1 400 »	950 »	190 »
	b. (Sans chiffres)		13 500 »	
	c. (Impression recto-verso)	500 »	300 »	60 »
	d. (Non dentelé)		750 »	550 »
115	**30 c. violet**	315 »	90 »	6 »
	(Sur lettre)			15 50
	(Seul sur lettre)			40 »
	a. (Chiffres déplacés)	500 »	300 »	45 »
	b. (Chiffres doubles)		15 500 »	
	c. (Impression recto-verso)	425 »	250 »	50 »
	d. (Non dentelé)			385 »

Type **II**.

N°				
116	**10 c. rouge**	130 »	33 »	2 »
	(Sur lettre)			11 50
	(Seul sur lettre)			15 50
	a. (Non dentelé)		375 »	250 »
117	**15 c. orange**	32 »	9 »	0 50
	(Sur lettre)			0 80
	a. (Chiffre 1 touchant le cadre)	100 »	70 »	15 »
	b. (Impression recto-verso)	40 »	23 »	10 »
	c. (Non dentelé)		275 »	50 »
118	**25 c. bleu**	485 »	150 »	2 15
	(Sur lettre)			4 60
	(Seul sur lettre)			8 »
	a. (Non dentelé)		800 »	525 »

Très bon centrage (+125 %). Voir note Clef du catalogue.

Pour les non dentelés, la colonne de droite concerne les timbres sans gomme.

1900. – *Type Merson. Typographie. Dentelés 13½ x 14.*

N°				
119	**40 c. rouge et bleu**	65 »	16 »	0 80
	(Sur lettre)			1 55
	(Seul sur lettre)			2 30
	a. (non dentelé)		350 »	225 »
	b. (Centre déplacé)	140 »	80 »	17 »
	c. (Sans teinte de fond)	800 »	600 »	100 »
	d. (Papier GC)	75 »	30 »	1 40

N°				
120	**50 c. brun et gris**	375 »	115 »	1 60
	(Sur lettre)			2 30
	(Seul sur lettre)			3 85
	a. (non dentelé)		750 »	450 »
	b. (Centre déplacé)	700 »	450 »	85 »
	c. (Sans teinte de fond)	875 »	550 »	115 »
	d. (Papier GC)	450 »	225 »	2 30

N°				
121	**1 f. lie-de-vin et olive**	110 »	31 »	0 80
	(Sur lettre)			2 30
	(Seul sur lettre)			4 60
	a. (non dentelé)		325 »	225 »
	b. (Centre déplacé)	350 »	250 »	25 »
	c. (Sans teinte de fond)	850 »	550 »	100 »
	d. (Double teinte de fond)	750 »	500 »	200 »
	e. (Double teinte de fond, dont une renversée)		1 250 »	800 »
	f. (Papier GC)	150 »	55 »	1 40
122	**2 f. violet et jaune**	2 350 »	950 »	90 »
	(Sur lettre)			305 »
	(Seul sur lettre)			2 300 »
	a. (non dentelé)			1 750 »

123	**5 f. bleu et chamois**	325 »	100 »	5 »
	(Sur lettre)			40 »
	(Seul sur lettre)			155 »
	a. bleu et olive	425 »	200 »	20 »
	b. (non dentelé)		1 500 »	900 »
	c. (Centre déplacé)	575 »	375 »	85 »
	d. (Sans teinte de fond)	1 150 »	800 »	175 »

Très bon centrage (+100 %).

Pour les non dentelés, la colonne de droite concerne les timbres sans gomme.

1902. – ***Type Mouchon retouché. Typographie. Dentelés 14* x *13½.***

124	**10 c. rose**	190 »	50 »	1 25
	(Sur lettre)			1 55
	a. (Non dentelé)		800 »	375 »
	b. (Impression recto-verso)	275 »	110 »	
125	**15 c. vermillon**	45 »	12 »	0 50
	(Sur lettre)			0 65
	a. (Queue du 5 touchant le cadre)	175 »	110 »	45 »
	b. (Non dentelé)		800 »	450 »
	c. (Impression recto-verso)	100 »	40 »	
126	**20 c. brun-lilas**	315 »	95 »	16 »
	(Sur lettre)			23 »
	(Seul sur lettre)			46 »
	a. (Non dentelé)			650 »

127	**25 c. bleu**	400 »	100 »	2 30
	(Sur lettre)			4 60
	(Seul sur lettre)			8 »
	a. (Impression recto-verso)	600 »	300 »	
128	**30 c. violet**	930 »	275 »	17 »
	(Sur lettre)			23 »
	(Seul sur lettre)			45 »
	a. (Non dentelé)			1 000 »

Très bon centrage (+125 %).

Pour les non dentelés, la colonne de droite concerne les timbres sans gomme.

1903. – ***Type Semeuse lignée de Roty (gravée par Mouchon). Dentelés 14* x *13½.*** C

Types du 10 c.

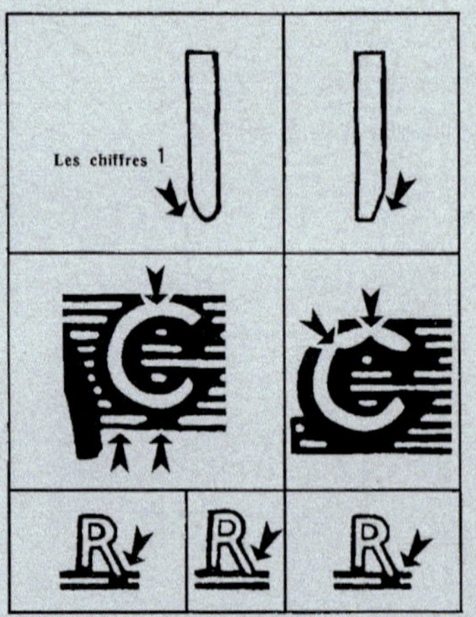

Type I. - Deuxième jambage du R de République avec ombre pied du chiffre 1 arrondi et courbe inférieure du C de 10 c. régulière.

Type II. - Semblable au type I mais le deuxième jambage du R est sans ombre.

Type III. - Pied du chiffre 1 avec méplat à droite, courbe inférieure du C irrégulière et deuxième jambage du R avec ombre.

129	**10 c. rose (type I)**	28 »	9 »	0 30
	(Sur lettre)			0 65
	a. rose (II)	120 »	61 »	3 »
	b. rose (III)	28 »	9 »	0 30
	c. rose foncé (III)	40 »	15 50	1 »
	d. (Non dentelé)	350 »	210 »	90 »
	e. (Impression recto-verso)	70 »	35 »	7 »

Types du 15 c.

Types I, II, III, IV *Types I et II* *Type II* *Type III*

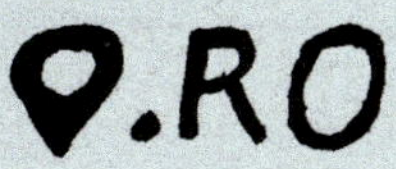

Types III, IV, V et VI *Types V et VI* *Type V*

Les types I à V sont difficilement identifiables lorsque les timbres sont décentrés vers le bas.

Type I. - Ligne de lumière en deux tronçons sur la partie postérieure de la Semeuse. Lettre M de MOUCHON normale.

Type II. - Comme type I mais les deux premières lettres de MOUCHON sont brisées, notamment la lettre M.

Type III. - Ligne de lumière en un seul tronçon ; lettre H de MOUCHON avec boule au pied du deuxième jambage.

Type IV. - Ligne de lumière en un seul tronçon, mais lettre H sans boule. La lettre M de Mouchon est dissymétrique.

Types I à IV. - Deuxième jambage du R de République avec ombre ; ces types sont ceux des timbres des feuilles et roulettes à plat.

Type V. - R de République sans ombre. Le premier O de O. ROTY est en forme de toupie. C'est le type propre aux timbres des carnets.

Type VI. - R de République sans ombre, format plus grand 22,5 mm de filet à filet (c'est le seul type du 15 c. imprimé sur rotative pour roulettes). Dentelures latérales avec coupe mécanique rectiligne et nette, 4 hachures dans le bras qui tient le sac.

Pour les non dentelés, la colonne de droite concerne les timbres sans gomme.

130	**15 c. vert-gris ((I) (1903-06)**	10 »	4 50	0 30
	(Sur lettre)			0 50
	a. vert-gris (II)	38 »	19 »	0 80
	b. vert-gris (III)	61 »	30 »	2 30
	c. (id., à olive (IV) (1904-06, 1916-24))	9 »	4 50	0 30
	d. vert (V)	60 »	30 »	5 »
	e. (id., paire verticale de carnet à partir de)	155 »	77 »	
	f. vert-gris (VI)		6 100 »	210 »
	g. (Non dentelé)	425 »	170 »	80 »
	h. (Impression recto-verso)	54 »	27 »	8 »
	j. (Papier GC) (IV)	11 »	5 »	0 80
	k. (Papier GC) (V)	35 »	16 »	2 »
	l. (paire vertic. de carnet Papier GC)	75 »	35 »	

131	**20 c. brun-lilas**	190 »	77 »	2 »
	(Sur lettre)			8 »
	(Seul sur lettre)			30 »
	a. brun-lilas foncé	220 »	95 »	3 »
	b. (Non dentelé)	675 »	325 »	130 »
132	**25 c. bleu**	225 »	84 »	1 55
	(Sur lettre)			3 85
	(Seul sur lettre)			5 35
	a. bleu foncé	240 »	110 »	2 30
	b. bleu-noir	550 »	305 »	70 »
	c. (Non dentelé)	650 »	385 »	125 »
	d. (Impression recto-verso)	350 »	200 »	15 »
133	**30 c. lilas**	550 »	200 »	6 50
	(Sur lettre)			12 50
	(Seul sur lettre)			28 25
	a. violet foncé	600 »	230 »	7 »
	b. violet très foncé	850 »	500 »	25 »
	c. (Non dentelé)	1 000 »	765 »	305 »
	d. (Impression recto-verso)	805 »	420 »	77 »

Très bon centrage (+100 %).

1906. – *Type Semeuse fond plein avec sol. Typographie. Dentelé 14 x 13½.*

134	**10 c. rouge (I)**	4 60	3 »	2 »
	(Sur lettre)			6 10

Type I. - La figure et le bras droit de la "Semeuse", ainsi que le sol, sont fortement ombrés.

Type II. - La figure et le bras droit, ainsi que le sol, sont moins ombrés et apparaissent beaucoup plus blancs et plus contrastés.

a. rouge clair (I)	7 65	4 60	2 »
b. (Non dentelé avec gomme)		300 »	
c. (Non dentelé sans gomme)		200 »	
d. rouge (II)	6 75	3 »	2 »
e. rouge clair (II)	8 40	4 60	2 30
f. rouge sombre (II)	13 »	6 »	3 »
g. (Non dentelé sans gomme)		200 »	

1906. – *Type Semeuse fond plein sans sol, à inscriptions maigres. Typographie. Dentelés 14* x *13½.* 🄲

Types du 10 c.

Types I et II

Type III

Type I des 10 c. et 35 c. - Le contour de la Semeuse et du sac se confond avec le fond plein.

Type IIA. - Des lignes de lumière dessinent le contour et détachent le sujet du fond uni. Sur ces 2 types la dernière lettre de RÉPUBLIQUE a la forme d'un F.

Type IIB (particulier aux entiers postaux). - Accentuation des lignes de lumière, notamment celle de la partie postérieure.

Type III du 10 c. - Comme type IIA mais la lettre finale de RÉPUBLIQUE ressemble à un E. C'est le type des timbres de carnets, les deux autres étant ceux des timbres de feuilles.

135	**10 c. rouge (I)**	35 »	9 »	1 10
	(Sur lettre)			3 »
	a. rouge foncé (IIA)	50 »	20 »	1 50
	b. rouge (IIA)	45 »	17 »	1 25
	c. rouge (III)	38 »	15 »	5 »
	d. (id. paire verticale de carnet)	90 »	60 »	
	e. (Non dentelé)		385 »	
	f. (Impression recto verso) (IIA)	100 »	50 »	11 »
136	**35 c. violet clair (IIA)**	425 »	170 »	8 »
	(Sur lettre)			23 »
	a. violet (I)	700 »	305 »	30 »
	b. (Non dentelé sans gomme)		500 »	

Très bon centrage (+40 %).

A ce type est paru, en 1926, un 10 c. vert (n°s 188 à 188B).

1907. – *Type Semeuse fond plein sans sol, à inscriptions grasses. Dentelés 14* x *13½.*

Les inscriptions sont plus fortes et rappellent celles du n° 134.

Types du 5 c.

On distingue 2 types principaux pour le 5 c.

I

II

Type I. - Le bas de la lettre Q est formé par un point (timbres des feuilles, des roulettes à plat et des premiers carnets).

Type IIA. - La lettre Q est normale (timbres des seconds carnets).

137	**5 c. vert foncé (I)**	3 50	1 80	0 15
	(Sur lettre)			0 50
	a. vert clair	4 60	2 30	0 50
	b. vert	4 30	2 30	0 30
	c. (id. paire verticale de carnet)	37 »	18 50	
	d. vert (IIA)	7 »	4 »	2 »
	e. (id. paire verticale de carnet)	17 »	10 »	
	f. (Non dentelé)(I)		23 »	
	g. (Non dentelé)(IIA)		210 »	
	h. (Papier GC)(I)	5 »	3 »	0 80
	j. (Papier GC)(IIA)	18 50	9 »	3 »
	k. (Papier GC, paire verticale de carnet)	32 »	20 »	
	l. (Impression recto-verso)(I)	15 »	10 »	5 »

Types du 10 c.

Il existe 2 types et 1 sous-type du 10 c. rouge.

Type IA. - Timbres des feuilles et des roulettes à plat : lettre Q avec un trait, barre médiane du B de RÉPUBLIQUE horizontale, hachures régulières dans la main qui sème.

Type IC. - Timbres des carnets de 20 : la barre médiane du B est oblique et la troisième hachure est brisée dans la main qui sème. Le type IB appartient au 10 c. vert n° 159.

Type IA

Type IC

Type II (carnets de 30 timbres et feuilles de 144 pour les dits carnets). - Lettre Q avec un gros point. R de RÉPUBLIQUE avec 2 jambages égaux.

138	**10 c. rouge (IA)**	3 35	1 80	0 15
	(Sur lettre)			0 50
	a. rouge foncé	8 »	4 60	0 50
	b. rouge-orange	3 35	1 80	0 15
	c. écarlate	345 »	230 »	54 »
	d. rouge (1910)(IC)	25 »	15 »	5 »
	e. (id. paire verticale de carnet)	60 »	30 »	
	f. rouge (II)	130 »	65 »	55 »
	g. (Non dentelé)(IA)		23 »	
	h. (Non dentelé)(IC)		230 »	
	j. (Papier GC)(IA)	23 »	14 »	2 30
	k. (Papier GC)(IC)	185 »	115 »	15 50
	l. (Papier GC, paire verticale de carnet)	380 »	230 »	
	m. (Impression recto-verso) (IA)	15 »	10 »	5 »

Types du 20 c.

Il est connu 3 types du 20 c. (hormis les entiers postaux).

Type I. - Timbres des feuilles à plat dont les mesures du cadre sont 18 x 22 mm. Les 20 c. sur papiers GC sont à ce type.

Type III. - Timbres des feuilles rotatives. Dimensions du cadre 18½ x 22½ mm.

Type IV. - Timbres des roulettes rotatives ; mêmes dimensions que type III.

Type III

Type IV

Bon repère entre types III et IV : présence ou absence de point et hachure à l'endroit indiqué par la flèche supérieure.

139	**20 c. brun-rouge (III)**	11 »	3 »	0 65
	(Sur lettre)			1 55
	a. lilas-brun (I)	11 »	4 »	0 65
	b. brun très foncé (I)	15 »	6 50	1 60
	c. brun-rouge (IV)	32 »	17 »	10 »
	d. (Non dentelé)(I)		30 »	
	e. (Papier GC)(I)	14 »	5 »	1 25
	f. (Impression recto-verso) (I)	55 »	30 »	12 50

Types du 25 c.

Il est connu 4 types principaux et 5 sous-types pour le 25 c.

Type I

Type II

Type III

Type IV

Type I (feuilles, roulettes à plat et carnets). - La branche supérieure du C n'est pas barrée et présente un tracé caractéristique presque horizontal. - Le chiffre 2 a la tête moins creusée que dans les autres types. La pointe inférieure gauche est distante de 1 mm du cadre extérieur. La base du chiffre 2 est mince et bien déliée.

Type IA. - Chiffre 2 avec tête la moins creusée et boule la plus grosse dont l'axe est en biais.

Type IB. - Boule du 2 plus creusée, base de ce chiffre bien déliée.

Type II (carnets). - La branche supérieure du C est nettement courbe et a son extrémité barrée. Le chiffre 2 a la tête plus creuse que dans le type 1. Sa pointe est à 3/4 de mm du cadre extérieur. La base du 2 est épaisse et beaucoup moins déliée que dans les autres types.

Type III. - La branche supérieure du C est courbe mais moins nettement barrée que dans le type II. Le chiffre 2 a la tête creuse. Sa pointe inférieure forme presque angle droit et est à moins de 3/4 de mm du cadre extérieur. La base du 2 est épaisse mais bien déliée sa partie droite descend plus bas que sa partie gauche qui se divise en :

Type IIIA (feuilles à plat). - Le filet intérieur blanc du cadre gauche est important et d'épaisseur irrégulière.

Type IIIB (feuilles rotatives). - Comme le type IIIA, mais le filet est très mince et le cadre plus haut.

Type IIIC (roulettes). - Comme le type IIIB, mais la rencontre des boucles du R de FRANÇAISE forme un angle aigu.

Type IV (carnets). - La lettre C a le même aspect que dans le type I. Le chiffre 2 a la tête creuse ; sa pointe est à un peu plus de 3/4 de mm du cadre extérieur. La base du chiffre est plus épaisse que dans le type I, mais est cependant bien déliée.

Timbre avec bande publicitaire.

140	**25 c. bleu (IA)**	6 »	3 »	0 15
	(Sur lettre)			0 50
	a. bleu foncé (IA)	8 »	3 »	0 80
	b. bleu-noir (IA)	35 »	15 »	5 50
	c. bleu (IB)	325 »	200 »	50 »
	d. (id. paire verticale de carnet)	675 »	425 »	
	e. bleu (II)	25 »	16 »	3 »
	f. (id. paire verticale de carnet)	130 »	80 »	
	g. (id. unité (avec bande publ.)	25 »	18 50	6 10
	h. bleu (IIIA)	34 »	18 50	3 »
	j. bleu (IIIB)	5 50	2 30	0 15
	k. bleu (IIIC)	60 »	40 »	15 »
	l. bleu (IV)	175 »	100 »	10 »
	m. (id. paire verticale de carnet)	425 »	300 »	
	n. (Non dentelé) (IA)		27 »	
	p. (Non dentelé) (II)		92 »	
	q. (Non dentelé) (IIIA)		170 »	
	r. (Papier GC) (IA)	14 »	6 »	1 25
	s. (Impression recto-verso) (IA)	17 »	9 »	4 60
141	**30 c. orange (I)**	35 »	15 »	1 55
	(Sur lettre)			2 30
	(Seul sur lettre)			6 90
	a. jaune foncé	38 »	20 »	2 60
	b. (Non dentelé)		92 »	
	c. (Papier GC)	40 »	20 »	2 15
	d. (Impression recto-verso)	72 »	46 »	12 50

Types du 35 c.

Enfin on distingue 2 types pour le 35 c. :

Type I (feuilles à plat). Le premier S de POSTES est ouvert dans le bas.

Type II (feuilles rotatives). La boucle inférieure du S remonte fortement.

Type I

Type II

142	**35 c. violet (I)**	16 »	9 »	1 »
	(Sur lettre)			1 85
	a. violet foncé	18 50	10 »	1 25
	b. (1926)(II)	105 »	65 »	40 »
	c. (Non dentelé)		92 »	
	d. (Papier GC)(I)	30 »	14 »	1 85
	e. (Impression recto-verso)(I)	72 »	46 »	12 50

1907. – *Type Merson. Dentelés 13½ x 14.*

143	**45 c. vert et bleu**	120 »	35 »	2 50
	(Sur lettre)			4 60
	(Seul sur lettre)			6 10
	a. (sans teinte de fond)		1 100 »	765 »
	b. (Non dentelé)		425 »	275 »
	c. (Centre très déplacé)	250 »	150 »	35 »
	d. (Papier GC)	120 »	45 »	4 »
	e. (Impression recto-verso)	200 »	140 »	77 »
144	**60 c. violet et bleu**	2 »	1 »	1 »
	(Sur lettre)			4 60
	a. (sans teinte de fond)		1 600 »	1 200 »
	b. (Non dentelé)		900 »	650 »
	c. (Impression recto-verso)	225 »	140 »	85 »

Nº 145

Nº 145c

145	**2 f. orange et vert-bleu**	150 »	55 »	0 50
	(Sur lettre)			7 65
	(Seul sur lettre)			30 »
	a. (double teinte de fond)	800 »	550 »	100 »
	b. (triple teinte de fond)	1 100 »	750 »	
	c. (cassure dans le bas de l'écusson)	1 800 »	1 250 »	305 »
	d. (sans teinte de fond)	525 »	350 »	175 »
	e. (Non dentelé)		850 »	600 »
	f. (Centre très déplacé)	350 »	225 »	35 »

Nos 143 à 145, très bon centrage (+75 %).

Pour les nos 143b à 145e, la colonne de droite concerne les timbres sans gomme.

1914. – *Au profit de la Croix-Rouge. Semeuse fond plein avec surtaxe carmin.*

146	**+ 5 c. s. 10 c. rouge foncé**	7 50	6 »	6 »
	(Sur lettre)			11 50
	(Seul sur lettre)			15 50
	a. (sur 10 c. rouge-orange)	10 »	7 »	7 »

Premier timbre de France avec surtaxe.

1914. – *Au profit de la Croix-Rouge. Semeuse fond plein avec surtaxe carmin. Typographie. Dentelé 14 x 13½.* [C]

147	**10 c. +5 c. rouge**	100 »	40 »	4 »
	(Sur lettre)			12 50
	(Seul sur lettre)			16 »
	a. rouge-orange	130 »	55 »	8 »
	b. (paire verticale de carnet)	280 »	160 »	

Très bon centrage (+50 %).

1917-18. – *Au profit des Orphelins de la guerre. Typographie. Dentelés 13½ x 14.*

148	2 c. +3 c. brun-lilas	25 »	5 »	5 »
149	5 c. +5 c. vert	75 »	25 »	12 »

150	15 c. +10 c. gris-vert	100 »	35 »	28 »
151	25 c. +15 c. bleu	225 »	90 »	65 »

Tranchée et drapeau.

Le Lion de Belfort (réplique de Paris).

152	35 c. +25 c. ardoise et violet	400 »	170 »	140 »
153	50 c. +50 c. brun et brun clair ▯	825 »	285 »	210 »

La Marseillaise (haut-relief de Rude, Arc de Triomphe de l'Etoile), à Paris.

La Marseillaise (haut-relief de Rude, Arc de Triomphe de l'Etoile), à Paris.

154	1 f. +1 f. carmin	1 350 »	490 »	440 »
155	5 f. +5 f. noir et bleu	5 000 »	2 000 »	2 000 »
	N°s 148 à 155 (8 val.)	**8 000 »**	**3 100 »**	**2 900 »**

Très bon centrage (+25 %).

Ces timbres ont été surchargés en 1922 (n°s 162 à 169), puis ont reparu en 1926-27 avec réduction de la surtaxe (n°s 229 à 232).

1918. – *Au profit de la Croix-Rouge. Typographie. Dentelé 13½ x 14.*

156	15 c. +5 c. noir et rouge	300 »	140 »	70 »
	(Sur lettre)			92 »
	a. (Non dentelé)	2 750 »	2 000 »	

Très bon centrage (+50 %).

1919-26. – *Timbre de 1900 (nº 107) surchargé. Dentelé*

157	**½ c. s. 1 c. gris-noir (R) (IA)**	1 »	0 30	0 30
	(Sur lettre)			40 »
	(Seul sur lettre)			765 »
	a. ardoise (II)	1 »	0 30	0 30
	e. gris-noir (R)	1 55	0 65	0 30

Papier GC.

157b	½ c. s. 1 c. (IA)	0 50	0 30	0 30
157c	½ c. s. 1 c. (Surch. renv)		1 400 »	1 150 »
157d	½ c. s. 1 c. (Double surcharge)			
157f	½ ▯. s. 1 ▯. gris-noir (IBR)	1 55	0 65	0 30

Voir note au nº 107d.

Il existe deux types de surcharges : la première, de 14½ mm de haut, nette (surcharge à plat), la seconde de 15 mm, moins nette (surcharge rotative).

1921-22. – *Typographie. Dentelés 14 x 13½.* 🄲

Type Semeuse fond plein, inscriptions grasses.

Types du 5 c.

Type I (feuilles et roulettes à plat) et type IIA (carnets). - Se reporter au nº 137 mêmes types.

Type IIB (roulette rotative). - Dimensions du cadre 18¼ x 22½ contre 18 x 22 pour les types IA et IIA. Le trait signalé par la flèche est absent.

158	**5 c. orange (I)**	2 80	1 40	0 30
	(Sur lettre)			0 80
	(Seul sur lettre)			3 »
	a. orange (IIA)	3 70	2 30	0 30
	b. (id. paire verticale de carnet)	9 »	5 35	
	c. orange (IIB)	27 »	20 »	9 15
	d. (Non dentelé)		54 »	

Types du 10 c.

Type IB

Type III

Type IV

Type IA. - Lettre Q avec un trait ; lettre C de 10 c. à dos plat (feuilles et roulettes à plat) voir au nº 138.

Type IB. - Lettre Q avec un point ; C à dos plat (premières feuilles rotatives de France).

Type IC. - Voir au nº 138 (carnets).

Type III. - C de 10 c. à dos rond avec boucle inférieure courte (deuxièmes feuilles rotatives).

Type IV. - C à dos rond avec longue boucle inférieure (roulettes rotatives).

159	**10 c. vert (III)**	1 25	0 65	0 50
	(Sur lettre)			0 80
	a. vert (IA)	2 »	1 10	0 65
	b. vert (IB)	2 90	1 55	0 65
	c. vert (IC)	11 »	7 »	2 »
	d. (id. paire verticale de carnet)	24 »	15 »	
	e. vert (IV)	8 40	5 35	3 85
	f. (Non dentelé) (IA)		185 »	
	g. (Non dentelé) (III)		305 »	
	h. (Premier s de Postes retouché)		155 »	92 »

160	**30 c. rouge (I)**	17 »	8 »	2 »
	(Sur lettre)			4 60

Type Semeuse lignée.

161	**50 c. bleu (I)**	80 »	30 »	1 25
	(Sur lettre)			3 »
	(Seul sur lettre)			4 60
	a. (Non dentelé)		155 »	

Très bon centrage (+50 %).

1922. – *Au profit des Orphelins de la guerre. Timbres de 1917 surchargés. Dentelés.*

162	**+1 c. s. 2+3 c. (148)**	1 »	0 50	0 50
163	**+2½ c. s. 5+5 c. (149)**	1 50	0 80	0 80

164	**+5 c. s. 15+10 c. (150)**	3 »	1 40	1 40
165	**+5 c. s. 25+15 c. (151)**	4 50	2 80	2 80

166	**+5 c. s. 35+25 c. (152)**	35 »	16 50	16 50
167	**+10 c. s. 50+50 c. ▯ (153)**	65 »	27 »	27 »

168	**+25 c. s. 1+1 f. (154)**	70 »	36 »	36 »
169	**+1 f. s. 5+5 f. [noir et bleu-gris] (155)**	350 »	170 »	170 »
	a. (+ 1f. s. 5+5 f. noir et bleu)	385 »	220 »	220 »
	N°s 162 à 169 (8 val.)	**530 »**	**255 »**	**255 »**

Très bon centrage (+25 %).

La surcharge est différente sur chaque valeur.

1923-26. – ***Type Pasteur. Typographie. Dentelés 14 x 13½.*** Ⓒ

170	**10 c. vert**	1 60	0 80	0 30
	(Sur lettre)			0 80
	(Seul sur lettre)			2 30
	a. (paire verticale de carnet)	7 »	3 50	
171	**15 c. vert**	3 70	1 85	0 30
	(Sur lettre)			0 80
	(Seul sur lettre)			2 30
172	**20 c. vert**	5 70	3 35	1 »
	(Sur lettre)			2 30
	(Seul sur lettre)			4 60
173	**30 c. rouge**	1 70	1 »	1 85
	(Sur lettre)			3 85
	(Seul sur lettre)			6 10

Louis Pasteur (1822-1895)

174	**30 c. vert**	1 55	0 80	0 50
	(Sur lettre)			3 85
	(Seul sur lettre)			6 10
175	**45 c. rouge**	4 30	2 30	2 50
	(Sur lettre)			6 10
176	**50 c. bleu**	9 30	5 20	0 50
	(Sur lettre)			5 35
	a. (roulette)	420 »	305 »	155 »
	b. (imp. recto verso)	70 »		
177	**75 c. bleu**	7 65	4 60	1 25
	(Sur lettre)			3 85
	(Seul sur lettre)			5 35
	a. (Non dentelé)		155 »	

178	**90 c. rouge**	23 50	13 »	4 »
	(Sur lettre)			5 35
	(Seul sur lettre)			7 65
179	**1 f. bleu**	50 »	25 »	0 50
	(Sur lettre)			5 35
	(Seul sur lettre)			40 »
180	**1 f. 25 bleu**	51 »	31 »	10 »
	(Sur lettre)			23 »
	(Seul sur lettre)			46 »
	a. bleu-noir	285 »	200 »	21 »
181	**1 f. 50 bleu**	25 »	6 10	0 30
	(Sur lettre)			1 55
	(Seul sur lettre)			2 30
	N°s 170 à 181 (12 val.)	**185 »**	**95 »**	**23 »**

Très bon centrage (+25 %).

Le 50 c. provenant de roulettes a son format plus haut (22 mm).

Les valeurs suivantes ont également donné lieu à l'impression de timbres sur bandes sans fin pour roulettes : 10 c., 15 c., 30 c. vert, 75 c., 1 f. et 1 f. 50. Leur identification n'est pas toujours aisée. Se reporter au tableau "ROULETTES".

Le 1 f. 50 a été surchargé 10 f. en 1928 (voir Poste aérienne N° 4). Il a également été surchargé CONGRES DU B.I.T. 1930 (n° 265).

1923. – ***Congrès philatélique de Bordeaux. Timbre de 1900 (n° 121) surchargé en bleu. Typographie.***

182	**1 f. (+2 f.) lie-de-vin et olive (B) (121)**	925 »	575 »	625 »
	a. (BORDFAUX)		4 500 »	4 500 »

Très bon centrage (+50 %).

Le prix indiqué pour le timbre oblitéré s'entend pour oblitération apposée à Bordeaux à l'époque du Congrès (15 au 24 juin).

Ce timbre n'était vendu que contre le ticket d'entrée à l'exposition, qui valait 2 f.

1924. – ***Jeux olympiques de Paris. Typographie. Dentelés 13½ x 14.***

183	**10 c. vert-jaune et vert-gris**	8 »	2 50	1 10
	(Sur lettre)			2 30
	(Seul sur lettre)			4 60
	a. (Non dentelé)		1 600 »	
	b. (Bague au doigt)	70 »	50 »	35 »
184	**25 c. rouge carminé et rouge**	10 »	3 50	0 90
	(Sur lettre)			2 30
	(Seul sur lettre)			5 35
	b. (centre très déplacé)	225 »	185 »	125 »
	a. (Non dentelé)		1 600 »	

Milon de Crotone (Louvre).

185	**30 c. noir et rouge-brun**	25 »	10 »	13 »
	(Sur lettre)			23 »
	(Seul sur lettre)			58 »
	a. (Non dentelé)		1 600 »	
186	**50 c. bleu et outremer**	115 »	29 »	5 »
	(Sur lettre)			40 »
	(Seul sur lettre)			100 »
	a. (Non dentelé)		1 600 »	
	N°s 183 à 186 (4 val.)	**158 »**	**45 »**	**20 »**

Voir également à la rubrique des Entiers postaux (n° 185-CP1).

On trouvera au n° 42 des Préoblitérés le timbre précédemment catalogué sous le n° 187.

1924-26. – ***Type Semeuse fond plein, inscriptions maigres (type III) avec bandelette supérieure ou inférieure au timbre. Dentelés 14 x 13½.*** [C]

188	**10 c. *Phéna***	65 »	45 »	50 »
188A	**10 c. *Minéraline***	725 »	500 »	600 »
188B	**10 c. vert *Sans bandelette***	60 »	40 »	45 »

Très bon centrage (+40 %).

N'ont été émis qu'en carnets pour les produits pharmaceutiques des laboratoires Phéna ou du laboratoire Mauchant (Minéraline).

1924-26. – ***Type Semeuse fond plein, inscriptions grasses. Dentelés** 14 x 13½.* Ⓒ

Types du 15 c.

Type I

Type II

15 c. Type I. - Le chiffre 1 est élancé et mince, le trait horizontal du 5 se termine par un triangle pointe en bas.

Type II. - Le chiffre 1 est plus épais, la barre horizontale du 5 se termine par un trait vertical.

189	**15 c. brun-lilas (I)**	0 50	0 30	0 15
	(Sur lettre)			0 50
	a. (avec bande publ)	21 50	15 50	11 50
	b. (Type II)	1 »	0 50	0 15

Types du 20 c.

Types III, IV et VI

Type V

Type III (premières feuilles rotatives). - Le chiffre 2 a le graphisme de celui des timbres brun-lilas n° 139.

Type IV (roulettes). - Se reporter au n° 139 pour distinction entre les types III et IV.

Type V (deuxième feuilles rotatives). - Chiffre 2 à pointe effilée.

Type VI (carnets). - Graphisme semblable au type IV ; le timbre est grand ; marges réduites.

190	**20 c. lilas-rose (III)**	0 50	0 30	0 30
	(Sur lettre)			0 65
	a. (Type IV)	26 »	18 50	5 35
	b. (Type V)	1 »	0 50	0 50
	c. (Type VI)	1 70	1 10	0 30
	d. (Id. avec bande publ)	2 »	1 55	0 65
	e. (Paire des types III et V se tenant verticalement)		385 »	270 »

Types du 30 c.

Type I (feuilles à plat). - La barre du chiffre 3 mesure 1¾ de mm (les n°s 141 et 160 sont à ce type).

Type II. - La barre du 3 mesure 2¼ de mm. Ce type se divise en :

Type IIA (feuilles rotatives). - Avec la boucle supérieure du S de FRANÇAISE ouverte, courte et horizontale.

Type I

Type II

Type IIA

Type IIB

Type IIB (carnets). - Avec la boucle du S plongeante.

Type IIC (roulette). - Comme le type IIA, mais il manque la deuxième hachure à la partie antérieure du pied droit.

191	**30 c. rose (I)**	2 50	1 30	0 80
	(Sur lettre)			3 »
	(Seul sur lettre)			7 65
	a. (Type IIA)	5 »	3 85	1 10
	b. (Type IIB)	7 65	3 85	1 85
	c. (Id. avec bande publ)	8 40	6 10	3 35
	d. (Non dentelé)		305 »	
192	**30 c. bleu (IIA)**	7 30	4 60	0 50
	(Sur lettre)			1 55
	a. (Type IIB)	7 65	4 60	0 65
	b. (Id. avec bande publ)	8 40	5 35	1 85
	c. (Type IIC)	340 »	245 »	46 »

Types du 40 c.

Type I

Type II

Type I (feuilles et carnets à plat). - Les 2 extrémités du c de la valeur se trouvent sur une même verticale. Le trait gauche du 4 est incurvé.

Type II (feuilles rotatives). - L'extrémité inférieure du c est plus arrondie et dépasse la verticale correspondante à la tête de la lettre. Le trait gauche du 4 est droit.

193	**40 c. brun-olive (I)**	3 70	1 50	0 50
	(Sur lettre)			1 55
	a. (avec bande publ)	13 50	8 40	4 60
	b. (Type II)	3 70	2 30	0 65
	c. (Non dentelé)		610 »	
194	**40 c. vermillon (II)**	6 »	3 »	0 50
	(Sur lettre)			1 55
	a. (Type I)	5 »	3 »	0 80
	b. (avec bande publ)	6 75	4 60	2 75

195	**1 f. 05 vermillon**	21 50	10 »	5 25
	(Sur lettre)			11 »
	(Seul sur lettre)			40 »
196	**1 f. 40 rose**	48 »	21 »	23 »
	(Sur lettre)			77 »
	Nos 189 à 196 (8 val.)	**90 »**	**42 »**	**31 »**

Très bon centrage (+20 %).

1924-32. – ***Type Semeuse lignée. Typographie. Dentelés 14 x 13½.*** Ⓒ

Types du 50 c.

On distingue pour le 50 c. :

Type I (feuilles et premiers carnets à plat). - Seul type avec point dans le bonnet. Les oeilletons des deux R sont égaux ; les oeilletons des A de FRANCAISE sont normaux et les deux du B sont à peu près égaux.

Type II (feuilles rotatives IIA, seconds carnets IIB et seconds carnets rotatifs IIA). - L'oeilleton du premier R est plus grand que celui du deuxième. L'oeilleton supérieur du B est plus petit que l'inférieur. Ceux des A sont minuscules.

Type III (roulettes). - Comme le type II, mais sans ombre sous le R de RÉPUBLIQUE.

Type IV (premiers carnets rotatifs sans, puis avec publicité sur marges des timbres). - R de RÉPUBLIQUE sans ombre ; le cadre intérieur de gauche est très épais. Le fond apparaît plein derrière les lettres de RÉPUBLIQUE ; ligne large du fond ligné.

Types du 75 c.

Type I

Type II

Type I. - Une ligne blanche entre le c de centimes et la pointe de la retombée de la ceinture.

Type II. - Au même endroit, deux lignes blanches, l'aspect du chiffre de la valeur est différent du type I, 7 plus cambré ; pas d'ombre sous le c.

197	**45 c. lilas**	13 »	7 »	2 15
	(Sur lettre)			8 40
	(Seul sur lettre)			40 »
	a. violet clair	15 50	8 40	1 25
198	**50 c. olive (I)**	13 »	7 50	1 25
	(Sur lettre)			3 »
	(Seul sur lettre)			12 50
	a. vert (IIA)	15 50	9 15	1 10
	b. (c. fermé : 50c)	240 »	180 »	85 »
	c. (Non dentelé)		140 »	

199	**50 c. rouge (IIA)**	2 30	1 50	0 15
	(Sur lettre)			0 50
	a. (Avec bande publ)	6 10	4 60	1 85
	b. (Type I)	4 30	2 30	0 65
	c. (Avec bande publ)	5 35	3 85	1 55
	d. (Type IIB)	3 35	2 30	0 50
	e. (Avec bande publ)	5 »	3 »	1 55
	f. (Type III)	35 »	22 »	7 65
	g. (Type IV)	7 65	4 60	2 »
	h. (Id. paire verticale de carnet)	17 »	11 »	
	j. (Avec bande publ)	6 75	4 60	1 85
	k. (c fermé : 50°)	65 »	40 »	16 »
	l. (Non dentelé)		92 »	
	m. (avec bande publicitaire Non dentelé)		125 »	
200	**60 c. lilas**	13 50	6 90	1 85
	(Sur lettre)			3 85
	(Seul sur lettre)			7 65
201	**65 c. rose**	6 »	3 »	1 55
	(Sur lettre)			5 35
	(Seul sur lettre)			30 »
	a. (Non dentelé)		385 »	
202	**75 c. lilas-rose (I)**	11 70	6 10	0 65
	(Sur lettre)			1 55
	(Seul sur lettre)			3 85
	a. (Type II)	1 250 »	880 »	155 »
	b. (Non dentelé)		575 »	
203	**80 c. rouge**	60 »	30 »	9 »
	(Sur lettre)			11 50
	(Seul sur lettre)			46 »
204	**85 c. rouge**	27 »	15 »	2 60
	(Sur lettre)			3 85
	(Seul sur lettre)			7 65
205	**1 f. bleu**	14 50	7 »	0 80
	(Sur lettre)			3 »
	(Seul sur lettre)			10 »
	a. bleu-noir	155 »	100 »	20 »
	b. (Non dentelé)		1 150 »	
	N°s 197 à 205 (9 val.)	**161 »**	**84 »**	**20 »**

Très bon centrage (+20 %) ; n° 203 : (+50 %).

1925-26. – ***Type Merson. Typographie. Dentelés 13½ x 14.***

206	**3 f. violet et bleu**	60 »	30 »	8 »
	(Sur lettre)			15 50
	(Seul sur lettre)			46 »
	a. (sans teinte de fond)	1 500 »	900 »	
	b. (Non dentelé)		1 250 »	
	c. (Centre déplacé)	375 »	225 »	
207	**10 f. vert et rouge**	340 »	145 »	17 »
	(Sur lettre)			30 »
	(Seul sur lettre)			92 »
208	**20 f. lilas-rose et vert-bleu**	550 »	230 »	40 »
	(Sur lettre)			125 »
	(Seul sur lettre)			385 »

Très bon centrage (+50 %).

1924. – ***4e centenaire de la naissance du poète Pierre de Ronsard (1524-1585). Typographie. Dentelé 14 x 13½.***

209	**75 c. bleu s. azuré**	3 50	2 30	1 85
	(Sur lettre)			11 50
	(Seul sur lettre)			20 »
	a. (Impression recto-verso)	130 »		

1924-25. – ***Exposition internationale des Arts décoratifs, à Paris. Typographie. Dentelés 13½ x 14.***

210	**10 c. vert-noir et jaune**	1 40	0 80	1 »
	(Sur lettre)			1 85
	(Seul sur lettre)			4 60
	a. (Centre déplacé)	200 »	170 »	140 »
211	**15 c. bleu-vert et vert**	1 70	0 80	1 10
	(Sur lettre)			1 85
	(Seul sur lettre)			5 35
	a. (Non dentelé)		1 100 »	

212	**25 c. violet-brun et lilas-brun**	2 »	0 80	0 50
	(Sur lettre)			1 55
	(Seul sur lettre)			5 35
213	**25 c. gris-bleu et violet**	2 90	1 75	1 »
	(Sur lettre)			1 55
	(Seul sur lettre)			2 »
	a. (Non dentelé)		1 100 »	
214	**75 c. gris et outremer (212)**	8 »	3 85	2 75
	(Sur lettre)			3 85
	(Seul sur lettre)			14 »
215	**75 c. bleu foncé et bleu (210)**	44 »	20 »	7 65
	(Sur lettre)			12 50
	(Seul sur lettre)			25 »
	a. (Non dentelé)		840 »	
	b. (Tenant à dentelé)	1 100 »	900 »	
	N°s 210 à 215 (6 val.)	**60 »**	**28 »**	**14 »**

Très bon centrage (+50 %).

Voir également à la rubrique des Entiers postaux (n° 213-CP1).

1925. – *Exposition philatélique internationale de Paris. Type de 1876-77 (II). Typographie. Dentelé 14 x 13½.* BF n° 1.

216	**5 f. carmin**	275 »	160 »	160 »
	a. (Non dentelé)		1 300 »	

Le prix indiqué pour le timbre oblitéré s'entend pour une oblitération apposée à Paris. (2 au 12 mai).

1926-27. – *Timbres de 1906-26 surchargés. Avec double bande publicitaire. Dentelés.*

Avec double bande publicitaire.

217	**25 c. s. 30 c. bleu (IIA) (192)**	0 50	0 30	0 50
	(Sur lettre)			3 85
	a. ((192 IIB))	3 35	2 30	1 55
	b. (Avec bde publ. Gibbs)	6 75	3 85	2 30
	c. (Avec bde publ. autre)	275 »	200 »	200 »
	d. (Avec double publ. Gibbs)	15 50	9 15	
	e. (Boucle du 5 fermée)	84 »	61 »	
218	**25 c. s. 35 c. violet (142)**	0 50	0 30	0 50
	(Sur lettre)			3 85
	a. (Double surcharge)	725 »	675 »	
	b. (Boucle du 5 fermée)	60 »	40 »	

219	**50 c. s. 75 c. bleu (177)**	6 »	3 75	2 »
	(Sur lettre)			5 35
220	**50 c. s. 80 c. rouge (203)**	2 50	1 40	1 25
	(Sur lettre)			4 60
221	**50 c. s. 85 c. rouge (204)**	7 »	2 30	1 10
	(Sur lettre)			4 60
222	**50 c. s. 1 f. 25 bleu (180)**	6 »	3 »	2 60
	(Sur lettre)			5 35
223	**50 c. s. 60 c. violet (200)**	2 90	1 40	1 25
	(Sur lettre)			5 35
224	**50 c. s. 65 c. rose (201)**	1 70	0 80	0 80
	(Sur lettre)			4 60
	a. (Surch. renversée)	2 200 »	1 600 »	1 600 »
225	**50 c. s. 1 f. 05 vermillon (195)**	2 60	1 40	0 80
	(Sur lettre)			4 60
	a. (Double surcharge)	» »	» »	

227	**90 c. s. 1 f. 05 vermillon (195)**	4 30	2 75	3 10
	(Sur lettre)			4 60
228	**1 f. 10 s. 1 f. 40 rose (196)**	2 »	1 10	1 10
	(Sur lettre)			7 »
	(Seul sur lettre)			23 »
	N°s 217 à 228 (11 val.)	**36 »**	**18 50**	**15 »**

Le 55 c. s. 60 c. lilas (n° 200), précédemment répertorié sous le n° 226, n'existe qu'avec surcharge Affr. Postes (voir Préoblitérés, n° 47).

1926-27. – *Au profit des Orphelins de la guerre. Types de 1917 avec surtaxe modifiée. Typographie. Dentelés 13½-14.*

229	**2 c. +1 c. brun-lilas (148)**	5 »	2 »	1 50
230	**50 c. +10 c. brun foncé et brun (153)**	95 »	25 »	15 50
231	**1 f. +25 c. carmin (154)**	190 »	63 »	48 »
232	**5 f. +1 f. noir et bleu (155)**	300 »	120 »	110 »
	N°s 229 à 232 (4 val.)	**590 »**	**210 »**	**175 »**

Très bon centrage (+50 %).

1927-31. – *Typographie. Dentelés 14 x 13½.* C

Type Blanc.

233	**10 c. violet (II)**	7 65	4 60	0 50
	(Sur lettre)			3 »
	(Seul sur lettre)			46 »

Type Semeuse lignée.

234	**65 c. olive**	16 »	8 »	2 30
	(Sur lettre)			9 15
	(Seul sur lettre)			54 »

Type Semeuse fond plein, inscriptions grasses.

235	**25 c. jaune-brun (IIIB)**	0 30	0 15	0 15
	(Sur lettre)			0 65
	a. jaune-brun (IIIC)	80 »	55 »	20 »

236	**40 c. violet (II)**	4 30	2 30	1 »
	(Sur lettre)			1 10
	a. (Non dentelé)			
237	**40 c. outremer (II)**	2 60	1 55	0 50
	(Sur lettre)			0 80
	a. gris-bleu	3 35	1 85	0 80
	b. (Sans le chiffre 4)	100 »	70 »	50 »
238	**1 f. 10 rose**	25 »	12 50	2 60
	(Sur lettre)			8 40
	(Seul sur lettre)			19 25
239	**2 f. vert-bleu**	27 »	16 »	1 60
	(Sur lettre)			15 50
	(Seul sur lettre)			54 »
	a. (Sans nom du graveur)		27 50	4 60

Type Merson. Dentelé 13½ x 14.

240	**3 f. lilas et carmin**	170 »	61 »	2 30
	(Sur lettre)			11 50
	(Seul sur lettre)			40 »
	a. (Non dentelé)	850 »	600 »	

Très bon centrage (+50 %).

1927. – *Exposition philatélique de Strasbourg. Semeuse sur fond plein. Typographie. Dentelés 14 x 13½.* BF n° 2.

241	**5 f. bleu**	500 »	300 »	300 »
242	**10 f. rouge**	500 »	300 »	300 »
242A	***Paire avec intervalle***	1 200 »	800 »	800 »

Les prix indiqués pour les timbres oblitérés s'entendent pour des oblitérations apposées à Strasbourg (4 au 12 Juin).

1927. – *Centenaire de la naissance de Marcelin Berthelot (1827-1907). Typographie. Dentelé 14 x 13½.*

243	**90 c. rouge**	3 80	2 30	0 65
	(Sur lettre)			2 30

A été surchargé 10 f. en 1928 (voir Poste aérienne n° 3).

Voir également à la rubrique des Entiers Postaux (n° 243-CP1).

1927. – *Visite de la Légion Américaine. Bustes de Marie-Joseph Motier, marquis de La Fayette (1757-1834), et Washington. Le "Spirit of Saint-Louis"survolant le "Paris". Typographie. Dentelés 13½ x 14.*

244	**90 c. rouge**	3 »	1 40	1 85
	(Sur lettre)			4 60
	(Seul sur lettre)			9 15
	a. (Non dentelé)	13 000 »	11 000 »	
	d. (Tenant à dentelé)	24 000 »	20 000 »	
245	**1 f. 50 outremer**	9 »	4 60	2 30
	(Sur lettre)			5 35
	(Seul sur lettre)			9 15
	a. (Non dentelé)		1 050 »	

Sans valeur dans le cartouche.

244b	(sans val.) rouge ▯	3 500 »	2 750 »	
245b	(sans val.) outremer ▯	2 500 »	1 850 »	

Valeur déplacée.

244c	90 c.	2 500 »	1 850 »	1 850 »

"90 c." se trouve dans le coin supérieur gauche du timbre.

Vendus durant un mois seulement.

1927. – *Au profit de la Caisse d'Amortissement. Types anciens surchargés. Typographie. Dentelés 14 x 13½.*

246	**+10 c. s. 40 c. [bleu] (C)**	10 »	6 »	6 »
247	**+25 c. s. 50 c. [vert-bleu] (B)**	15 »	9 »	9 »
248	**+50 c. s. 1 f. 50 [rouge-orange]**	45 »	18 »	15 »

Très bon centrage (+20 %).

Sans le premier e d'Amortissement.

246a	+10 c. s. 40 c.	160 »	100 »	100 »

Sans point sur le i d'Amortissement.

247a	+25 c. s. 50 c.	100 »	60 »	50 »

Avec les mêmes surcharges, ont paru de 1928 à 1931 :

Au type Semeuse sur fond plein :

+10 c. sur 40 c. violet-gris (nº 249)

+10 c. sur 40 c. vert (nº 253)

+10 c. sur 40 c. rose (nº 266)

+10 c. sur 40 c. olive (nº 275)

+50 c. sur 1 f. 50, violet (nº 268)

+50 c. sur 1 f. 50, rouge (nº 277)

Au type Semeuse sur fond ligné :

+25 c. sur 50 c. rouge-brun (nº 250)

+25 c. sur 50 c. rose-lilas (nº 254)

+25 c. sur 50 c. brun (nº 267)

+25 c. sur 50 c. violet (nº 276)

Au type Pasteur :

+50 c. sur 1 f. 50, lilas (nº 251)

+50 c. sur 1 f. 50, rouge-brun (nº 255)

1928. – *Au profit de la Caisse d'Amortissement. Types anciens surchargés. Typographie. Dentelés 14 x 13½.*

249	**+10 c. s. 40 c. [violet-gris] (C)**	40 »	12 »	10 »
250	**+25 c. s. 50 c. [rouge-brun] (B)**	75 »	35 »	30 »
251	**+50 c. s. 1 f. 50 [lilas]**	120 »	60 »	45 »

Très bon centrage (+20 %).

Sans le premier e d'Amortissement.

249a	+10 c. s. 40 c.	150 »	85 »	85 »

Sans point sur le i d'Amortissement.

250a	+25 c. s. 50 c.	130 »	85 »	85 »

1928. – *Au Profit de la Caisse d'Amortissement. Taille-douce. Dentelé 13½.*

Le Travail.

I

II

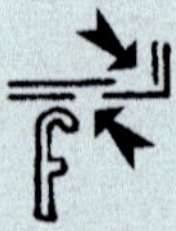
III

252	**1 f. 50 + 8 f. 50 bleu**	260 »	180 »	180 »
	(Sur lettre)			250 »
	(Seul sur lettre)			325 »
	a. (Etat II)	425 »	250 »	250 »
	b. (Etat III)	260 »	180 »	180 »
	c. bleu-vert (I, II ou III)	840 »	610 »	610 »
	d. (Non dentelé)	700 »	550 »	
	Les trois états (III+II+I) se tenant	1 400 »	1 000 »	

Très bon centrage (+20 %).

1929. – *Au profit de la Caisse d'Amortissement. Types anciens surchargés. Typographie. Dentelés 14 x 13½.*

253	**+10 c. s. 40 c. [vert]**	50 »	20 »	17 »
254	**+25 c. s. 50 c. [rose-lilas]**	75 »	35 »	30 »
255	**+ 50 c. s. 1 f. 50 [rouge-brun]**	150 »	65 »	65 »

Très bon centrage (+20 %).

Sans le premier e d'Amortissement.

253a	+10 c. s. 40 c.	150 »	100 »	100 »

Sans point sur le i d'Amortissement.

254a	+25 c. s. 50 c.	140 »	100 »	100 »

1930. – ***Au profit de la Caisse d'Amortissement. Taille-douce. Dentelé 13.*** Ⓒ

Détail de "l'Ange au Sourire",
de la Cathédrale de Reims.

256	**1 f. 50+3 f. 50 lilas**	160 »	100 »	100 »
	(Sur lettre)			140 »
	(Seul sur lettre)			230 »
	a. (Paire verticale de carnet)	330 »		

La cote de la paire s'applique à une paire avec marges blanches supérieure et inférieure.

Ce timbre a été présenté en feuilles de 25 et en carnets de 8 (Deux blocs de 4 entourés chacun de marges blanches).

1929. – ***5e centenaire de la délivrance d'Orléans par Jeanne d'Arc. Typographie. Dentelé 14 x 13½.***

257	**50 c. bleu (I)**	3 50	2 30	0 30
	(Sur lettre)			0 80
	a. (avec bande publ)	5 »	3 85	1 55
	b. (avec bande publicitaire)(II)	6 75	4 60	2 30
	c. (Non dentelé)		230 »	
	d. (avec bande publ.)		275 »	

Le type II est celui des timbres des carnets tirés sur rotative. La ligne à la base des lettres de ORLÉANS est fine, interrompue ou absente entre les lettres O et R ; le cadre du cartouche est aminci au-dessus des lettres AN ; le timbre est légèrement plus haut que le 257a, tiré à plat.

1929. – ***Exposition philatélique du Havre. Timbre de 1906, Type Merson, surchargé.***

257A	**2 f. (+5 f.) orange et vert-bleu (B) (145)**	1 600 »	875 »	875 »

Très bon centrage (+60 %).

Le prix oblitéré s'entend avec l'oblitération de l'Exposition (18 au 26 mai).

Ce timbre n'était vendu que contre le ticket d'entrée à l'exposition qui valait 5 f.

1929-31. – ***Monuments et sites. Taille-douce. Dentelés 13.***

Arc de Triomphe de l'Etoile.

258	**2 f. brun-rouge**	95 »	42 »	1 »
	(Sur lettre)			3 85
	(Seul sur lettre)			9 15

3 FRANCS

Cathédrale de Reims.

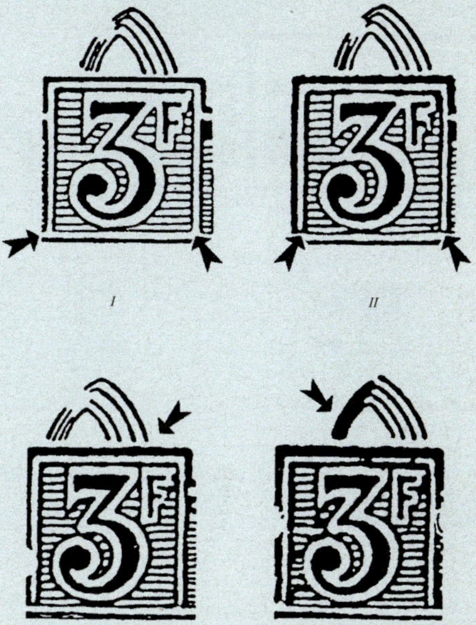

I II III IV

I. - Ogive brisée à gauche, 3 et F non séparés, ligne du bas interrompue.

II. - Ogive brisée à gauche, 3 et F non séparés, ligne du bas continue.

III. - Ogive brisée à gauche, 3 et F séparés, pas de pointillé sous le porche central, ligne du bas continue. (Le type III est, en fait, un état de molette du type II).

IV. - Ogive intacte, 3 et F séparés, ligne du bas continue.

259	**3 f. ardoise (I)**	135 »	77 »	3 »
	(Sur lettre)			5 35
	(Seul sur lettre)			23 »
	a. (Type II)	325 »	160 »	5 »
	b. (Type III)	800 »	460 »	27 »
	c. (Type IV)	135 »	77 »	3 »
	d. (Non dentelé)(III)		5 000 »	

Un 65 c. + 35 c. outremer au type Cathédrale de Reims modifié, a paru en 1938 (n° 399).

5 FRANCS

Mont-Saint-Michel.

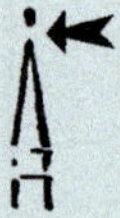

I

II

I. - Trait interrompu en haut du clocher.

260	**5 f. brun (II)**	45 »	25 »	0 80
	(Sur lettre)			3 »
	(Seul sur lettre)			11 »
	a. brun (I)	50 »	27 50	5 35

Le millénaire du Mont-Saint-Michel a été célébré en 1966 (n° 1482).

10 FRANCS

Port de La Rochelle.

I

II et III

I. - Le E de POSTES montre un petit trait vertical en haut à droite.

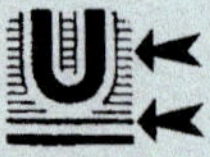

II

III

II. - Pas de trait vertical au E de POSTES. L'ovale allongé qui se trouve à l'intérieur du chiffre zéro est ouvert dans le bas et le filet d'encadrement du même chiffre est brisé à la partie inférieure.

III. - Pas de trait vertical au E de POSTES. L'ovale intérieur du zéro est fermé dans le bas et le filet qui encadre ce chiffre est intact.

261	**10 f. bleu (III)**	170 »	84 »	7 65
	(Sur lettre)			17 »
	(Seul sur lettre)			35 »
	a. outremer vif (III)		15 500 »	
	b. outremer pâle (I)	185 »	125 »	18 50
	c. bleu (II)	285 »	180 »	30 »
	d. outremer (II)	425 »	280 »	45 »

261A	**10 f. *chaudron clair* (I)**	6 500 »	5 000 »
	a. (Non dentelé)	5 000 »	4 250 »

261B	**10 f. *brun-noir* (I)**	6 000 »	5 000 »
	a. (Non dentelé)	4 750 »	4 000 »
261C	**10 f. *outremer vif* (III)**	21 000 »	15 500 »

20 FRANCS

Pont du Gard.

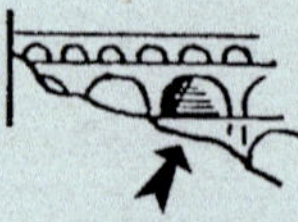

I

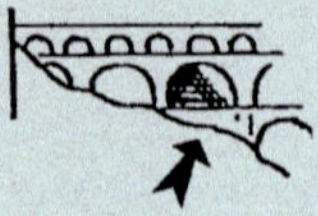

IIA, IIB

I. - L'ombre sous la seconde arcade gauche moyenne du pont est terminée par des lignes horizontales (tirage à plat).

IIA-IIB. - Le relief de la même arcade est limité par 3 traits obliques qui coupent les horizontales à leurs extrémités droites.

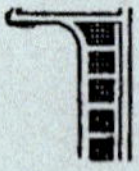

I et IIA

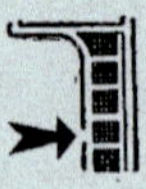

IIB

I - IIA. - Le filet du cadre intérieur, à droite, est intact.

IIB. - Le filet de ce cadre est brisé.

Papier transparent (tirage rotatif) (1931).

Dentelure rectangulaire 13.

262	**20 f. chaudron (IIB)**	550 »	325 »	42 »
	(Sur lettre)			92 »
	(Seul sur lettre)			345 »
	a. chaudron foncé	575 »	375 »	45 »
	b. chaudron clair	625 »	400 »	45 »
	c. chaudron (IIA)	625 »	400 »	45 »
	d. chaudron foncé	610 »	420 »	55 »
	e. chaudron clair	765 »	535 »	61 »
	f. (Types se tenant (IIA+IIB) verticalement)	1 400 »	915 »	305 »
	g. (Types se tenant (IIA+IIB) horizontalement)	2 000 »	1 400 »	450 »
	h. (Types se tenant (IIB+IIA) horizontalement)	3 500 »	2 800 »	1 000 »

Papier opaque (tirage à plat) (1929).

Dentelure rectangulaire 13½ x 13.

262A	**20 f. chaudron (I)**	575 »	350 »	45 »
	a. chaudron clair	2 300 »	1 400 »	385 »

Dentelure linéaire 11 (1930).

Pont du Gard.

262B	**20 f. chaudron clair (I)**	2 250 »	1 250 »	425 »
	a. (sur 3 côtés)	12 500 »	10 000 »	

1930. – *Centenaire de l'Algérie Française. Vue prise de Mustapha supérieur, à Alger. Typographie. Dentelé 13½ x 14.*

263	**50 c. bleu et rose**	7 »	3 »	0 50
	(Sur lettre)			1 55
	(Seul sur lettre)			3 85
	a. (Non dentelé)		305 »	
	b. (ALCERIE)	200 »	120 »	75 »

1930. – *Réunion du conseil d'administration du Bureau International du Travail, à Paris. Timbres de 1923-24 surchargés. Dentelés.*

264	**50 c. rouge (199)**	7 »	2 75	2 30
	(Sur lettre)			7 65
	(Seul sur lettre)			11 50
265	**1 f. 50 bleu (181)**	48 »	21 »	15 50
	(Sur lettre)			27 »
	(Seul sur lettre)			40 »

Sans accent grave sur le E de CONGRES.

264a	50 c.	125 »	70 »	70 »
265a	1 f. 50	225 »	150 »	150 »

1930. – *Au profit de la Caisse d'Amortissement. Types anciens surchargés. Dentelés 14 x 13½.*

266	**+10 c. s. 40 c. [rose]**	85 »	25 »	25 »
267	**+25 c. s. 50 c. brun**	135 »	45 »	40 »
268	**+50 c. s. 1 f. 50 [violet]**	200 »	80 »	80 »

Très bon centrage (+20 %).

Sans point sur le i d'Amortissement.

267a	+25 c. s. 50 c.	150 »	100 »	80 »

Surcharge déplacée.

C de Caisse au-dessus du premier t d'Amortissement.

268a	+50 c. s. 1 f. 50	220 »	155 »	155 »

1931. – *Au profit de la Caisse d'Amortissement. Taille-douce. Dentelé 13.*

Les coiffes des provinces françaises (Arlésienne, Boulonnaise, Alsacienne et Bretonne).

269	**1 f. 50+3 f. 50 vert-jaune**	350 »	175 »	175 »
	(Sur lettre)			245 »
	(Seul sur lettre)			300 »

1930-31. – ***Exposition coloniale internationale de Paris (1931). Typographie, sauf n° 274 : héliogravure. Dentelure 14 x 13½, sauf n° 274 : Dentelé 13½.*** ©

Femme Fachi.

270	**15 c. gris**	2 60	1 40	0 50
	(Sur lettre)			1 »
	(Seul sur lettre)			3 85
271	**40 c. sépia**	5 50	2 60	0 50
	(Sur lettre)			1 »
	(Seul sur lettre)			1 85

Types du 50 c.

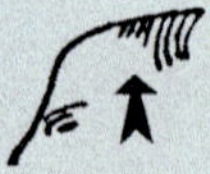

Type I

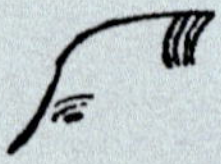

Type II

Type I. - Cheveux en haut du front ; profil du menton peu visible flou dans le feuillage (timbres des premières feuilles).

Type II. - Front dégagé ; menton souligné par un trait ; lignes de lumière dans le feuillage (timbres des deuxièmes feuilles et des carnets).

272	**50 c. rouge (I)**	1 40	1 »	0 15
	(Sur lettre)			0 80
	(Seul sur lettre)			1 55
	a. (Id. II)	1 55	1 »	0 30
	b. (Avec bande publicitaire)	6 75	3 85	1 85
	c. (Non dentelé)		92 »	
	d. (Avec bande publicitaire non dentelé)		155 »	

273	**1 f. 50 bleu**	25 50	11 »	0 65
	(Sur lettre)			1 25
	(Seul sur lettre)			2 30
274	**1 f. 50 bleu**	110 »	50 »	2 20
	(Sur lettre)			3 85
	(Seul sur lettre)			5 35
	a. (sans point après le F de RF)	900 »	600 »	225 »
	Nos 270 à 274 (5 val.)	**145 »**	**66 »**	**4 »**

Très bon centrage (+50 %).

1931. – ***Au profit de la Caisse d'Amortissement. Types anciens surchargés. Dentelés 14 x 13½.***

275	**+10 c. s. 40 c. [olive]**	140 »	60 »	40 »
276	**+25 c. s. 50 c. [violet]**	300 »	140 »	110 »
277	**+50 c. s. 1 f. 50 [rouge sombre]**	235 »	125 »	110 »

Très bon centrage (+20 %).

Sans point sur le i d'Amortissement.

276a	+25 c. s. 50 c.	400 »	200 »	200 »

Surchage déplacée.

C de Caisse au-dessus du premier t d'Amortissement.

277a	+50 c. s. 1 f. 50	350 »	240 »	225 »

1932-37. – ***Type Semeuse fond plein, inscriptions grasses. Dentelés 14 x 13½.***

277A	**1 c. bistre-olive**	0 30	0 15	0 30
	(Sur lettre)			3 »
	(Seul sur lettre)			46 »
	a. (retouche STE de POSTES)	90 »	60 »	50 »
277B	**1 c. bistre-brun**	0 30	0 15	0 30
	(Sur lettre)			3 »
	(Seul sur lettre)			46 »
278	**2 c. vert foncé**	0 30	0 15	0 30
	(Sur lettre)			3 »
	(Seul sur lettre)			46 »
278A	**3 c. rouge-orange**	0 30	0 15	0 30
	(Sur lettre)			3 »
	(Seul sur lettre)			77 »

278B	**5 c. rose (III)**	0 80	0 15	0 30
	(Sur lettre)			3 85
	(Seul sur lettre)			140 »

Le graphisme au type III du 5 c. rose est particulier à ce timbre.

279	**10 c. outremer (III)**	3 »	1 85	0 30
	(Sur lettre)			1 55
	(Seul sur lettre)			15 50
	a. (Id. IV)	10 50	6 90	3 »

Surchargés.

279A	**½ c. s. 1 c. bistre-olive**	0 65	0 30	0 50
	a. (retouche 1er S de POSTES)	100 »	60 »	50 »

279B	**½ c. s. 1 c. bistre-brun**	2 »	1 »	1 50

Sur ce dernier, le tirage de la surcharge a été défectueux et presque tous les exemplaires présentent un doublage des caractères et de la barre de fraction.

1932-33. – *Type Paix. Typographie. Dentelés 14 x 13½.* [C]

On distingue les types suivants :

Pour le 40 c. :

Type I. - La barre horizontale formant la base de la boucle du R de FRANÇAISE est mince par rapport à l'ensemble des traits de la lettre.

Type II (roulette). - La barre du R est d'épaisseur normale.

Pour le 50 c., il existe 4 types et 1 sous-type du type II :

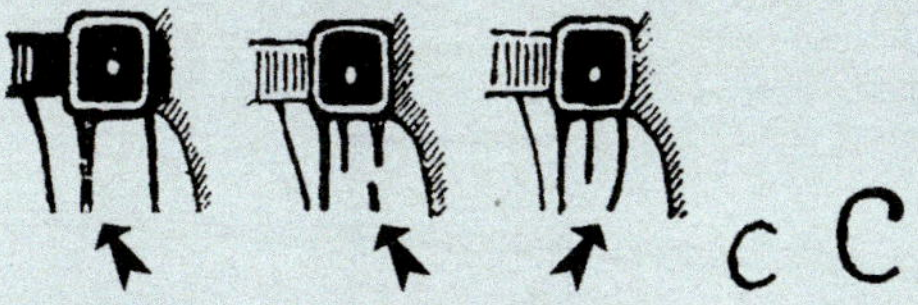

I et II *III* *IV* *A* *B*

Type I. - Petit c (A) ; sous la boucle de la ceinture, lignes comme en (I).

Type IIA. - c plus grand et avec boule (B) ; sous la boucle de la ceinture, lignes comme en (II).

Type IIB (roulette). - Comme le type IIA, mais le filet inférieur est plus épais dans sa partie centrale, entre les 2 signatures.

Type IIB

Type III. - Petit c (A) ; sous la boucle de la ceinture, lignes comme en (III).

Type IV. - Petit c (A) sous la boucle de la ceinture, lignes comme en (IV). (La ceinture est fortement ombrée sur les types I et II ; elle est plus aérée sur les types III et IV).

Pour le 1 F :

Type I. - Ceinture unie à gauche de la boucle.

Type II. - Ceinture avec traits blancs.

Type I

Type II

280	**30 c. vert**	2 60	1 »	0 65
	(Sur lettre)			1 55
	(Seul sur lettre)			4 60
281	**40 c. lilas (I)**	0 50	0 30	0 30
	(Sur lettre)			1 »
	(Seul sur lettre)			2 30
	a. (Type II)	» »	» »	
282	**45 c. bistre**	4 20	2 »	1 30
	(Sur lettre)			15 50
	(Seul sur lettre)			46 »
283	**50 c. rose-rouge (I)**	0 30	0 15	0 15
	(Sur lettre)			0 30
	(Seul sur lettre)			0 65
	a. (Avec bande publ)	3 35	1 85	0 80
	b. (Type IIA)	5 »	3 »	0 50
	c. (Avec bande publ)	6 »	4 »	1 85
	d. (Type IIB)	155 »	92 »	9 15
	e. (Type III)	0 30	0 15	0 15
	f. (Avec bande publ)	3 70	2 30	1 »
	g. (Type IV)	35 »	18 50	2 30
	h. (Avec bande publ)	40 »	23 »	3 85
	i. (Non dentelé)(I)		70 »	
	k. (avec bande publNon dentelé)		115 »	
	l. (Non dentelé)(IA)		140 »	

284	**65 c. violet-brun**	1 10	0 50	0 50
	(Sur lettre)			1 »
	(Seul sur lettre)			3 85
284A	**75 c. olive**	0 30	0 15	0 30
	(Sur lettre)			0 65
	(Seul sur lettre)			2 30
285	**90 c. rouge carminé**	75 »	42 »	2 30
	(Sur lettre)			6 10
	(Seul sur lettre)			10 »
286	**1 f. orange (II)**	7 50	3 60	0 30
	(Sur lettre)			3 »
	(Seul sur lettre)			6 10
	a. (Type I)	9 30	5 »	0 50

287	**1 f. 25 olive**	215 »	85 »	5 40
	(Sur lettre)			7 65
	(Seul sur lettre)			40 »
288	**1 f. 50 bleu**	0 50	0 30	0 30
	(Sur lettre)			1 55
	(Seul sur lettre)			3 »
289	**1 f. 75 rose-lilas**	18 »	5 »	0 50
	(Sur lettre)			1 »
	(Seul sur lettre)			3 »
	N°s 280 à 289 (11 val.)	**325 »**	**140 »**	**12 »**

N°s 285 et 287. Très bon centrage (+30 %).

Timbres se tenant verticalement.

283m	50 c. (I)+50 c. (III)	37 »
283n	50 c. (III)+50 c. (I)	61 »

Timbres se tenant horizontalement.

283p	50 c. (I)+50 c. (IIA)	77 »
283q	50 c. (IIA)+50 c. (III)	175 »
283r	50 c. (I)+50 c. (III)	115 »

Pour les timbres émis à ce type, de 1937 à 1939, voir Tableau par Types et Genres.

1933. – *Taille-douce. Dentelé 13.*

Le Puy-en-Velay.

290	**90 c. rose-lilas**	7 »	4 »	1 10
	(Sur lettre)			2 15
	(Seul sur lettre)			3 »

Tirage : 12 000 000.

1933. – *Célébrités. Typographie. Dentelés 14 x 13½.*

Aristide Briand (1862-1932).

Paul Doumer (1857-1932).

Victor Hugo (1802-1885).

291	**30 c. bleu-vert**	42 »	20 »	9 15
	(Sur lettre)			11 »
	(Seul sur lettre)			15 50
292	**75 c. lilas** ▯	85 »	30 »	1 55
	(Sur lettre)			3 »
	(Seul sur lettre)			9 15
293	**1 f. 25 lilas-rose**	13 »	7 »	2 30
	(Sur lettre)			4 60
	(Seul sur lettre)			23 »

Très bon centrage (+30 %).

1934. – *Colombe de la Paix, de Daragnès. Typographie. Dentelé 14 x 13½.*

294	**1 f. 50 outremer**	120 »	61 »	17 »
	(Sur lettre)			27 »
	(Seul sur lettre)			46 »

Tirage : 6 000 000.

1934. – *Centenaire de la mort du tisseur Joseph Marie Jacquard (1752-1834). Taille-douce. Dentelé 14 x 13.*

295	**40 c. bleu-gris**	6 »	4 »	1 »
	(Sur lettre)			1 55
	(Seul sur lettre)			2 30

Tirage : 10 000 000.

1934. – *4e centenaire de l'arrivée de Jacques Cartier (1491-1557) au Canada. Taille-douce. Dentelés 13.*

296	**75 c. lilas**	110 »	30 »	2 30
	(Sur lettre)			4 60
	(Seul sur lettre)			15 50
297	**1 f. 50 bleu**	190 »	52 »	4 60
	(Sur lettre)			7 65
	(Seul sur lettre)			11 50

1934. – *Timbre de 1932-33 (n° 287) surchargé.*

298	**50 c. s. 1 f. 25 olive (287)**	8 »	4 60	0 65
	(Sur lettre)			3 »
	(Seul sur lettre)			11 »

1935-36. – *Paquebot "Normandie". Taille-douce. Dentelés 13.*

299	**1 f. 50 bleu** ▯	32 »	15 »	2 30
	(Sur lettre)			3 »
	(Seul sur lettre)			5 35
300	**1 f. 50 bleu clair** ▯	190 »	70 »	20 »
	(Sur lettre)			40 »
	(Seul sur lettre)			61 »
	b. turquoise	460 »	300 »	40 »
300A	**1 f. 50 *bleu-vert***	32 500 »	26 500 »	

Le 1 f. 50 bleu clair a été émis lorsque "Normandie" a obtenu le "Ruban bleu".

Voir également à la rubrique des Entiers postaux (n° 299-CP1).

1935. – *Taille-douce. Dentelés 13.*

Rivière bretonne.

Cloître de St-Trophime à Arles.

301	**2 f. vert**	85 »	40 »	1 »
	(Sur lettre)			3 »
	(Seul sur lettre)			15 50
301A	**2 f. *ardoise***	10 000 »	8 000 »	
302	**3 f. 50 brun**	90 »	32 »	4 60
	(Sur lettre)			8 50
	(Seul sur lettre)			20 »

Tirages : 20 000 000, (nc) et 8 000 000.

1935. – ***Congrès international des Caisses d'épargne, à Paris et centenaire de leur création. Taille-douce. Dentelé 13.***

Benjamin, baron Delessert (1773-1847).

303 **75 c. vert** 60 » 21 50 1 50
(Sur lettre) 3 »
(Seul sur lettre) 7 65

Tirage : 10 000 000.

1935. – ***Cinquantenaire de la mort de Victor Hugo (1802-1885). Taille-douce. Dentelé 14 x 13.***

304 **1 f. 25 lilas-rose** 9 » 5 35 2 30
(Sur lettre) 6 10
(Seul sur lettre) 30 »

Tirage : 5 000 000.

1935. – ***Tricentenaire de l'Académie Française. Effigie d'Armand-Jean Du Plessis, cardinal de Richelieu (1585-1642). Taille-douce. Dentelé 13.***

305 **1 f. 50 rose** 90 » 25 » 1 50
(Sur lettre) 3 »
(Seul sur lettre) 6 10

Tirage : 10 000 000.

1935. – ***Tricentenaire de la mort du graveur Jacques Callot (1592-1635) (d'après le tableau de Van Dyck, 1599-1641). Taille-douce. Dentelé 14 x 13.***

306 **75 c. rouge-brique** 22 » 12 » 0 65
(Sur lettre) 1 55
(Seul sur lettre) 6 »

Tirage : 8 000 000.

1935. – ***Au profit des Chômeurs intellectuels. Taille-douce. Dentelés 13.***

307 **50 c. +10 c. bleu** 5 50 3 » 3 »
(Sur lettre) 4 60
(Seul sur lettre) 7 65

308 **50 c. +2 f. rouge-brique** 135 » 65 » 55 »
(Sur lettre) 61 »
(Seul sur lettre) 100 »

Le 50 c. +2 f. est reparu, surchargé +20 c. en 1936 (n° 329).

1936. – ***Au profit des réfugiés politiques. Statue de la Liberté, par Frédéric-Auguste Bartholdi (1834-1904). Taille-douce. Dentelé 13.***

309 **75 c. +50 c. violet** 25 » 11 » 11 »
(Sur lettre) 15 »
(Seul sur lettre) 27 50

Au même type a paru, en 1937, un 50 c. +25 c. bleu-gris (n° 352).

1936. – ***Centenaire de la mort d'André-Marie Ampère (1775-1836). Taille-douce. Dentelé 13.***

310 **75 c. brun** 45 » 20 » 2 30
(Sur lettre) 3 »
(Seul sur lettre) 8 »

1936. – ***Le moulin d'Alphonse Daudet. Taille-douce. Dentelé 13.***

311 **2 f. outremer** 6 » 4 50 0 50
(Sur lettre) 1 55
(Seul sur lettre) 5 50
a. (fond blanc) 135 » 100 » 30 »

Tirage : 8 000 000.

1936. – *Au profit des enfants des Chômeurs. Taille-douce. Dentelé 13.*

312	**50 c. +10 c. rouge-brique**	8 »	5 35	5 35
	(Sur lettre)			8 »
	(Seul sur lettre)			11 »

1936. – *150e anniversaire de la mort de l'aéronaute François Pilâtre de Rozier (1756-1785). Taille-douce. Dentelé 13.*

Cathédrale de Metz et montgolfière.

313	**75 c. bleu-vert**	45 »	20 »	3 »
	(Sur lettre)			6 »
	(Seul sur lettre)			9 15

Tirage : 8 100 000.

1936. – *Centenaire de la mort de Claude Rouget de Lisle (1760-1836). Taille-douce. Dentelés 13.*

Sa statue, à Lons-le-Saunier.

La Marseillaise de Rude (haut-relief de l'Arc de Triomphe).

314	**20 c. vert**	6 50	3 85	2 30
	(Sur lettre)			3 »
	(Seul sur lettre)			4 60
315	**40 c. brun**	13 »	6 »	3 85
	(Sur lettre)			4 60
	(Seul sur lettre)			5 35

Tirages : 16 000 000 et 15 000 000.

La gravure du 40 c. a été utilisé en 1940 pour une enveloppe. Voir à la rubrique des Entiers postaux (nº 315-E1).

1936. – *Inauguration du monument de Vimy à la mémoire des Canadiens tombés au cours de la guerre 1914-1918. Taille-douce. Dentelés 13.*

316	**75 c. rouge-brun**	35 »	10 »	2 30
	(Sur lettre)			4 60
	(Seul sur lettre)			23 »
317	**1 f. 50 bleu**	37 »	18 »	10 »
	(Sur lettre)			12 50
	(Seul sur lettre)			20 »

Tirages : 7 000 000 et 5 000 000.

1936. – *22e anniversaire de la mort de Jean Jaurès (1859-1914). Taille-douce. Dentelés 13.*

318	**40 c. brun-rouge**	6 50	4 »	1 60
	(Sur lettre)			1 60
	(Seul sur lettre)			4 »
319	**1 f. 50 outremer**	42 »	15 »	4 »
	(Sur lettre)			4 60
	(Seul sur lettre)			7 65

Tirages : 15 000 000 et 8 000 000.

1936. – *100e traversée aérienne de l'Atlantique-Sud par les avions postaux français. Taille-douce. Dentelés 13.*

320	**1 f. 50 bleu-violet**	40 »	20 »	5 50
	(Sur lettre)			7 65
	(Seul sur lettre)			23 »
321	**10 f. vert foncé**	800 »	375 »	150 »
	(Sur lettre)			160 »
	(Seul sur lettre)			210 »

Tirages : 8 000 000 et 500 000.

1936. – *Propagande pour l'Exposition internationale de Paris, 1937. Typographie. Dentelés 13½ x 14.*

322	**20 c. lilas**	1 »	0 50	0 65
	(Sur lettre)			1 60
	(Seul sur lettre)			4 60
323	**30 c. vert-bleu**	4 50	3 »	1 85
	(Sur lettre)			3 85
	(Seul sur lettre)			23 »
324	**40 c. outremer**	3 50	1 60	0 80
	(Sur lettre)			1 85
	(Seul sur lettre)			3 »

325	**50 c. rouge-orange**	3 »	1 40	0 40
	(Sur lettre)			0 80
	(Seul sur lettre)			1 60
325A	**50 c.** ***rouge carminé***	12 500 »	10 000 »	

326	**90 c. rose carminé**	30 »	13 50	8 70
	(Sur lettre)			14 »
	(Seul sur lettre)			27 »
327	**1 f. 50 outremer**	78 »	37 »	4 60
	(Sur lettre)			9 15
	(Seul sur lettre)			20 »
	N°s 322 à 327 (sauf nº 325A) (6 val.)	**120 »**	**57 »**	**17 »**

Très bon centrage (+20 %).

Voir également le nº 336, émis l'année suivante.

1936. – ***Rassemblement universel pour la paix, à Paris. Taille-douce. Dentelé 13.***

328	**1 f. 50 bleu**	40 »	17 »	4 60
	(Sur lettre)			6 »
	(Seul sur lettre)			12 50

Tirage : 6 000 000.

1936. – ***Au profit des Chômeurs intellectuels. Timbre de 1935 (nº 308) surchargé.***

329	**+20 c. s. 50 c. +2 f. rouge-brique (308)**	5 50	4 »	4 »
	(Sur lettre)			5 50
	(Seul sur lettre)			10 »

La surcharge recouvre entièrement l'ancienne surtaxe.

1936. – ***Au profit des Chômeurs intellectuels. Taille-douce. Dentelés 13.***

Jacques Callot (1592-1635).

Louis-Hector Berlioz (1802-1869).

330	**20 c. +10 c. brun carminé**	5 »	3 »	3 »
	(Sur lettre)			4 60
	(Seul sur lettre)			10 »
331	**40 c. +10 c. vert**	6 »	3 »	4 »
	(Sur lettre)			5 50
	(Seul sur lettre)			10 »

Victor Hugo (1802-1885).

Louis Pasteur (1822-1895).

332	**50 c. +10 c. rouge-brique**	12 »	5 »	4 »
	(Sur lettre)			5 50
	(Seul sur lettre)			7 »
333	**1 f. 50+50 c. outremer**	47 »	23 »	22 »
	(Sur lettre)			26 »
	(Seul sur lettre)			35 »
	N°s 330 à 333 (4 val.)	**70 »**	**34 »**	**33 »**

Tirages : 1 600 000, 1 600 000, 1 600 000 et 1 300 000.

De nouvelles valeurs à ces types ont paru en 1938 (n°s 380 à 385).

Voir également les n°s 343 et 344 (1937), 436 à 439 (1939) et 462 à 464 (1940).

1937. – ***Championnats internationaux de ski, à Chamonix. Taille-douce. Dentelé 13.***

334	**1 f. 50 bleu-violet**	16 »	7 65	1 85
	(Sur lettre)			4 »
	(Seul sur lettre)			5 50

Tirage : 4 000 000.

1937. – ***Tricentenaire de la tragédie "Le Cid". Taille-douce. Dentelé 13.***

Pierre Corneille (1606-1684), par Lebrun.

335	**75 c. brun carminé**	4 30	2 30	1 60
	(Sur lettre)			2 30
	(Seul sur lettre)			5 50

Tirage : 6 000 000.

1937. – ***Propagande pour l'Exposition internationale de Paris. Taille-douce. Dentelé 13.***

336	**1 f. 50 bleu-vert**	4 75	2 75	1 25
	(Sur lettre)			2 »
	(Seul sur lettre)			4 60

Tirage : 30 000 000.

1937. – *En souvenir de l'aviateur Jean Mermoz (1901-1936) et de ses compagnons de l'hydravion "Croix du Sud". Taille-douce. Dentelés 13.*

337	**30 c. vert-gris**	1 »	0 50	0 80
	(Sur lettre)			4 60
	(Seul sur lettre)			6 »
337A	**30 c. *vert-jaune***	15 000 »	10 000 »	
338	**3 f. lilas**	15 »	6 »	4 »
	(Sur lettre)			11 50
	(Seul sur lettre)			27 »
	a. violet	15 »	7 »	4 60
	b. violet-gris	400 »	200 »	60 »

Tirages : 8 900 000, (nc) et 5 750 000.

1937. – *13e Congrès international des chemins de fer, à Paris. Taille-douce. Dentelés 13.*

Locomotive électrique.

"Pacific"carénée.

339	**30 c. vert**	1 70	1 »	1 60
	(Sur lettre)			4 »
	(Seul sur lettre)			6 »
340	**1 f. 50 outremer**	17 »	8 50	8 50
	(Sur lettre)			11 50
	(Seul sur lettre)			30 »

Tirages : 3 000 000 et 2 400 000.

1937. – *Tricentenaire du Discours de la méthode. Effigie de René Descartes, dit "Cartesius"(1596-1650), Portrait, d'après Frans Hals. Taille-douce. Dentelés 13.*

Discours "sur" la méthode.

Discours "de" la méthode.

341	**90 c. rouge-brique**	4 30	2 30	1 60
	(Sur lettre)			2 30
	(Seul sur lettre)			4 60
342	**90 c. rouge-brique**	12 »	7 »	2 »
	(Sur lettre)			3 »
	(Seul sur lettre)			4 60

Tirages : 5 000 000 et 4 500 000.

Le n° 341 porte l'inscription erronée : Discours sur la méthode.

1937. – *Au profit des Chômeurs intellectuels. Taille-douce. Dentelés 13.*

Anatole France (1844-1924).

Auguste Rodin (1840-1917), et "le Penseur".

343	**30 c. +10 c. vert**	5 »	2 30	3 »
	(Sur lettre)			4 60
	(Seul sur lettre)			8 »
344	**90 c. +10 c. rose carminé**	16 »	7 »	7 »
	(Sur lettre)			7 »
	(Seul sur lettre)			8 »

De nouvelles valeurs à ces types ont paru en 1938 (nos 380 et 384).

1937. – *Au profit des oeuvres sociales et sportives des P.T.T. Légende P.T.T. SPORTS ET LOISIRS. Taille-douce. Dentelés 13.*

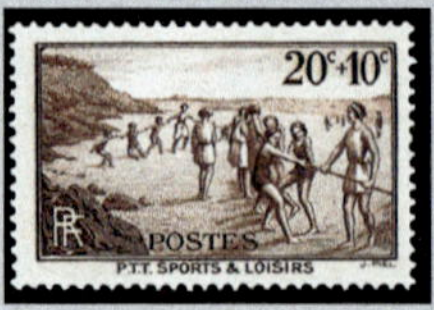

Plaisirs de la plage.

345	**20 c. +10 c. brun**	3 35	1 85	2 30
	(Sur lettre)			3 »
	(Seul sur lettre)			4 60

Sports.

346	**40 c. +10 c. brun-rouge**	3 35	1 85	2 30
	(Sur lettre)			3 »
	(Seul sur lettre)			4 60

L'auberge des loisirs.

347	**50 c. +10 c. brun-violet**	3 35	1 85	2 30
	(Sur lettre)			3 »
	(Seul sur lettre)			4 60

1937. – Exposition philatélique de Paris (PEXIP). Type Cérès de 1849-50. Typographie. Dentelés 14 x 13½. **BF n° 3.**

348	**5 c. outremer et brun**	100 »	60 »	60 »
349	**15 c. rouge-brun et rose**	100 »	60 »	60 »
350	**30 c. outremer et rose**	100 »	60 »	60 »
351	**50 c. rouge-brun et brun**	100 »	60 »	60 »
	N°s 348 à 351 (4 val.)	**400 »**	**240 »**	**240 »**
	La série, non dentelée	300 »	2 400 »	

Les prix oblitérés s'entendent avec l'oblitération de l'exposition (18 au 27 juin 1937).

1937. – Au profit des réfugiés politiques. Type de 1936. Taille-douce. Dentelé 13.

352	**50 c. +25 c. bleu-gris (309)**	8 »	4 »	4 60
	(Sur lettre)			6 »
	(Seul sur lettre)			12 50

Tirage : 1 500 000, ventes : 800 000

1937. – Pour le fonds d'érection d'un monument à Pierre Loti (1850-1923). Taille-douce. Dentelé 13.

Buste de Pierre Loti et vue de Constantinople.

353	**50 c. +20 c. rose carminé**	8 »	4 »	4 60
	(Sur lettre)			7 65
	(Seul sur lettre)			23 »

Tirage : 1 300 000, ventes : 800 000

1937. – Pour les musées nationaux, Victoire de Samothrace (Musée du Louvre). Taille-douce. Dentelés 13.

354	**30 c. vert**	210 »	85 »	50 »
	(Sur lettre)			65 »
	(Seul sur lettre)			110 »
354A	**30 c.** ***rouge***	» »	» »	
355	**55 c. rouge**	210 »	85 »	50 »
	(Sur lettre)			65 »
	(Seul sur lettre)			110 »

Très bon centrage (+50 %).

Vendus avec plus-value de 70 c., représentant le coût de la carte illustrée qu'on était obligé d'acheter en même temps que chacun de ces timbres.

Les cotes, sur lettres, s'entendent pour affranchissement non philatélique.

1937. – Au profit de la Société de prophylaxie sanitaire et morale. Taille-douce. Dentelé 13.

356	**65 c. +25 c. brun-lilas**	6 »	3 85	3 »
	(Sur lettre)			4 60
	(Seul sur lettre)			6 »
	a. (Non dentelé)		385 »	

Un 90 c. +30 c. bleu-vert au même type a paru en 1939 (n° 419).

Tirage : 2 000 000.

1937. – Sesquicentenaire de la Constitution des Etats-Unis. Taille-douce. Dentelé 13½.

357	**1 f. 75 outremer**	5 »	3 »	2 30
	(Sur lettre)			4 »
	(Seul sur lettre)			4 60

Tirage : 10 600 000.

1937. – Ouverture de la route du col de l'Iseran. Taille-douce. Dentelé 13½.

358	**90 c. vert foncé**	4 30	2 30	0 30
	(Sur lettre)			0 80
	(Seul sur lettre)			2 30
	a. (Non dentelé)	4 250 »	3 500 »	

Tirage : 30 000 000.

1937. – *Timbre de 1932-33 (nº 286) avec surcharge rouge.*

359	**80 c. s. 1 f. orange (R) (II) (286)**	0 65	0 50	0 65
	(Sur lettre)			4 »
	(Seul sur lettre)			54 »
	a. (80 c. s. 1 f. Type I)	2 »	1 10	1 10
	b. (Surch. renv)	1 350 »	1 000 »	
	c. (Tenant à non surchargé)	1 650 »	1 250 »	

Voir aux "Préoblitérés" nº 74a.

Il existe deux types de surcharge : la première a les barres, épaisses, écartées de 1¼ mm (surcharge à plat), la seconde a les barres, moins épaisses, écartées de 1½ mm (surcharge rotative).

1937-39. – *Timbres d'usage courant. Typographie. Dentelés 14 x 13½.* ⓒ

Type Semeuse fond plein, inscriptions grasses.

IIA

III

Le type III spécial au nº 360 n'a été émis qu'en carnet. (Boucle du 3 remontant haut et 0 étroit).

360	**30 c. rouge sombre (IIA)**	1 »	0 50	0 30
	(Sur lettre)			0 80
	(Seul sur lettre)			1 60
	a. (Type III)	2 »	1 »	0 50
	b. (avec bande publ)	2 60	1 25	1 10
361	**35 c. vert (II)**	1 40	0 80	0 65
	(Sur lettre)			1 60
	(Seul sur lettre)			6 »
	a. (Non dentelé)		460 »	

Type Semeuse lignée (1938).

362	**50 c. turquoise**	2 60	1 60	0 50
	(Sur lettre)			1 60
	(Seul sur lettre)			4 60
	a. (Non dentelé)		77 »	

Type Paix.

On distingue les types suivants :

Pour le 65 c. :

Type I (feuilles). - La ligne blanche sous l'avant-bras gauche est mal venue ou manquante. Deux points de couleur dans la robe, à la verticale du Q de RÉPUBLIQUE.

Type II (carnets). - Comme le type 1, mais un seul point de couleur dans la robe.

Type III (roulettes). - Forte ligne blanche sous l'avant-bras gauche et un seul point à la robe.

Toutefois, dans certains tirages, la différenciation de ce type peut être difficilement repérable.

Pour le 90 c. :

Type I (feuilles et carnets). - La barre du L. de LAURENS touche le A.

LAU

Type I

LAU

Type II

Type II (roulettes). - La barre du L ne touche pas le A.

363	**55 c. violet**	1 40	0 80	0 30
	(Sur lettre)			0 80
	(Seul sur lettre)			1 60
364	**60 c. bistre**	0 50	0 30	0 50
	(Sur lettre)			4 »
	(Seul sur lettre)			20 »
365	**65 c. outremer (I)**	0 65	0 30	0 15
	(Sur lettre)			0 50
	(Seul sur lettre)			0 80
	a. (Type II)	3 »	1 60	0 50
	b. (Avec bande publ)	3 70	2 30	1 25
	c. (Type III)	47 »	30 »	6 »
366	**80 c. orange**	0 30	0 15	0 30
	(Sur lettre)			0 80
	(Seul sur lettre)			3 »
367	**90 c. vert (I)**	0 15	0 15	0 15
	(Sur lettre)			0 80
	(Seul sur lettre)			3 85
368	**90 c. outremer (I)**	1 70	1 »	0 15
	(Sur lettre)			0 50
	(Seul sur lettre)			0 80
	a. (Avec bande publ)	3 70	2 30	1 25
	b. (Type II)	84 »	70 »	15 50
	c. (Id. avec bde publicitNon dentelé)		420 »	
369	**1 f. rose (II)**	7 »	4 40	0 50
	(Sur lettre)			1 »
	(Seul sur lettre)			2 30
370	**1 f. 25 rose**	4 30	2 »	2 50
	(Sur lettre)			4 »
	(Seul sur lettre)			8 »
371	**1 f. 40 lilas**	14 »	7 »	6 »
	(Sur lettre)			15 50
	(Seul sur lettre)			77 »
	Nºs 360 à 371 (12 val.)	**35 »**	**19 »**	**12 »**

Le nºs 365a, émis en carnets, existe avec variété sans C (timbre supérieur droit).

1938-41. – *Type Cérès. Typographie. Dentelés 14 x 13½.*

372	**1 f. 75 bleu**	1 50	0 80	0 60
	(Sur lettre)			1 »
	(Seul sur lettre)			5 50
373	**2 f. rose-rouge**	0 30	0 20	0 30
	(Sur lettre)			1 »
	(Seul sur lettre)			12 50
374	**2 f. 25 outremer**	20 »	10 »	1 »
	(Sur lettre)			1 60
	(Seul sur lettre)			4 60

375	**2 f. 50 vert**	3 50	1 70	0 80
	(Sur lettre)			1 60
	(Seul sur lettre)			4 »
375A	**2 f. 50 outremer**	1 40	0 65	0 80
	(Sur lettre)			1 »
	(Seul sur lettre)			4 60

376	**3 f. lilas-rose**	1 30	0 65	0 50
	(Sur lettre)			1 25
	(Seul sur lettre)			3 »
	N°s 372 à 376 (6 val.)	**28 »**	**14 »**	**4 »**

1938-39. – *Au profit de la Société des oeuvres de mer. Effigie de Charcot (1867-1936). Taille-douce. Dentelés 13.*

377	**65 c. +35 c. vert-bleu**	3 20	1 60	3 »
	(Sur lettre)			4 60
	(Seul sur lettre)			6 »
377A	**90 c. +35 c. lilas-rose**	34 »	13 »	13 »
	(Sur lettre)			17 »
	(Seul sur lettre)			40 »

Tirages : 2 000 000 et 1 200 000.

1938. – *Centenaire de la naissance de Léon Gambetta (1838-1882). Taille-douce. Dentelé 13.*

378	**55 c. lilas**	0 65	0 50	0 65
	(Sur lettre)			1 60
	(Seul sur lettre)			3 »

Tirage : 4 500 000.

1938. – *Au profit des "Saisons nationales d'Art français". Taille-douce. Dentelé 13.*

Cour d'honneur du château de Versailles.

379	**1 f. 75+75 c. bleu**	45 »	23 »	21 50
	(Sur lettre)			25 »
	(Seul sur lettre)			35 »

Tirage : 1 500 000, ventes : 500 000

1938. – *Au profit des Chômeurs intellectuels. Types de 1936-37. Taille-douce. Dentelés 13.*

380	**30 c. +10 c. brun-rouge (343)**	3 50	2 »	2 »
	(Sur lettre)			4 60
	(Seul sur lettre)			8 »
381	**35 c. +10 c. vert-bleu (330)**	4 50	3 »	3 »
	(Sur lettre)			5 50
	(Seul sur lettre)			8 »

382	**55 c. +10 c. lilas (331)**	14 »	7 »	4 50
	(Sur lettre)			6 »
	(Seul sur lettre)			7 65
383	**65 c. +10 c. outremer (332)**	15 »	7 »	4 50
	(Sur lettre)			6 »
	(Seul sur lettre)			7 65

384	**1 f. +10 c. carmin (344)**	10 »	6 »	6 »
	(Sur lettre)			6 »
	(Seul sur lettre)			8 »
385	**1 f. 75+25 c. bleu (333)**	43 »	20 »	20 »
	(Sur lettre)			25 »
	(Seul sur lettre)			30 »
	N°s 380 à 385 (6 val.)	**90 »**	**45 »**	**40 »**

Tirages : 1 500 000, 1 500 000, 1 400 000, 1 400 000, 1 250 000 et 1 250 000.

1938. – *Pour l'érection d'un monument à la gloire de l'infanterie. Taille-douce. Dentelés 13.*

386	**55 c. +70 c. brun-violet**	10 »	5 35	5 35
	(Sur lettre)			8 »
	(Seul sur lettre)			23 »
387	**65 c. +1 f. 10 bleu-vert**	7 »	5 35	5 35
	(Sur lettre)			8 »
	(Seul sur lettre)			23 »

1938. – *Taille-douce. Dentelés 13.*

Champenoise coiffée du toquat.

Arc de Triomphe d'Orange.

388	**1 f. 75 outremer**	10 »	4 »	4 60
	(Sur lettre)			5 50
	(Seul sur lettre)			8 »
389	**2 f. brun-gris**	1 50	0 70	1 30
	(Sur lettre)			3 »
	(Seul sur lettre)			15 50

Mineurs.

Avignon : le château des Papes et le pont Benazet.

390	**2 f. 15 brun-lilas**	13 »	5 »	1 »
	(Sur lettre)			1 25
	(Seul sur lettre)			2 30
391	**3 f. brun-rouge**	33 »	15 »	4 60
	(Sur lettre)			6 90
	(Seul sur lettre)			23 »

Remparts de la cité de Carcassonne.

Donjon du château de Vincennes.

392	**5 f. outremer**	1 50	0 80	0 50
	(Sur lettre)			3 »
	(Seul sur lettre)			15 50
	a. (Non dentelé)		535 »	
393	**10 f. brun sur azuré**	6 »	1 50	2 »
	(Sur lettre)			4 60
	(Seul sur lettre)			30 »

Port de Saint-Malo.

394	**20 f. vert foncé**	100 »	45 »	21 »
	(Sur lettre)			27 »
	(Seul sur lettre)			42 »
	a. (Papier épais)	115 »	63 »	26 »
	N°s 388 à 394 (7 val.)	**165 »**	**72 »**	**35 »**

Tirages : 3 500 000, 10 000 000, 14 000 000, 8 000 000, 50 000 000, 15 500 000 et 1 500 000.

Les 2 f. 15, 5 f., 10 f. et 20 f. ont été surchargés d'une nouvelle valeur en 1940-41 (nos 489 à 492).

1938. – *Pour l'érection du monument à la gloire du Service de Santé militaire, à Lyon. Taille-douce. Dentelé 13.*

395	**55 c. +45 c. rouge**	25 »	13 »	13 »
	(Sur lettre)			18 50
	(Seul sur lettre)			46 »

Tirage : 1 000 000, ventes : 500 000

1938. – *3e Coupe mondiale de football, à Paris. Taille-douce. Dentelé 13.*

396	**1 f. 75 outremer**	35 »	15 »	15 »
	(Sur lettre)			30 »
	(Seul sur lettre)			61 »

Tirage : 3 500 000.

1938. – *En l'honneur du fabuliste Jean de La Fontaine (1621-1695). Taille-douce. Dentelé 13.*

La Fontaine et scène du loup et de l'agneau.

397	**55 c. vert**	1 40	0 65	1 25
	(Sur lettre)			1 60
	(Seul sur lettre)			2 30

Tirage : 6 000 000.

1938. – *En souvenir de Clément Ader (1841-1925), pionnier de l'aviation. Ader et son "Avion N° 3". Taille-douce. Dentelé 13.*

398	**50 f. outremer**	180 »	110 »	80 »
	(Sur lettre)			185 »
	(Seul sur lettre)			305 »
	a. outremer foncé (Papier épais)	190 »	110 »	92 »

Les nos 398 et 398a ont été surchargés d'une nouvelle valeur en 1940-41 (nos 493 et 493a).

Tirage : 570 000.

1938. – ***Fêtes de la restauration de la cathédrale de Reims. Type du n° 259 modifié. Taille-douce. Dentelé 13.***

399	**65 c. +35 c. outremer (259)**	20 »	10 »	12 50
	(Sur lettre)			17 »
	(Seul sur lettre)			23 »

Tirage : 1 500 000, ventes : 700 000

1938. – ***Visite des souverains britanniques. Taille-douce. Dentelé 13.***

Tour du Palais de Wesminster et Arc de Triomphe.

400	**1 f. 75 outremer**	1 40	0 65	1 25
	(Sur lettre)			2 30
	(Seul sur lettre)			4 »

Voir également à la rubrique des Entiers postaux (n°s 400-CP1 et 400-CP2).

Tirage : 4 000 000.

1938. – ***Au profit du Comité d'assistance aux Français rapatriés d'Espagne. Taille-douce. Dentelé 13.***

401	**65 c. +60 c. rose**	9 50	4 50	6 »
	(Sur lettre)			8 »
	(Seul sur lettre)			15 50

Tirage : 1 100 000, ventes : 750 000

1938. – ***40e anniversaire de la découverte du radium. Taille-douce. Dentelé 13.***

Pierre (1859-1906) et Marie Curie (1867-1934).

402	**1 f. 75+50 c. outremer**	27 »	10 »	12 50
	(Sur lettre)			15 50
	(Seul sur lettre)			23 »

Dans 21 colonies, a paru un timbre similaire de même couleur. Ce dessin a également été utilisé en Afghanistan et à Cuba (Voir les tomes 5 1re et 2e parties).

Tirage : 1 500 000, ventes : 850 000

1938. – ***20e anniversaire de la Victoire. Taille-douce. Dentelé 13.***

Défilé du 11 Novembre.

403	**65 c. +35 c. rouge carminé**	6 50	3 70	4 50
	(Sur lettre)			7 »
	(Seul sur lettre)			8 50

Voir également à la rubrique des Entiers postaux (n°s 403-CP1 et 403-CP2).

Tirage : 1 700 000, ventes : 1 000 000

1938-41. – ***Type Mercure. Typographie. Dentelés 14 x 13½.***

Timbres de roulettes :

30 c. type II. - La barre oblique du chiffre 3 descend plus bas et sa boucle est plus fermée que sur le type I ; le dos du C est rond et plus rapproché du zéro. La différenciation de ce type peut être difficilement repérable.

70 c. type II. - Les traits de l'aile entre le caducée et le serpent sont détachés les uns des autres. Ils sont en partie comme soudés entre eux sur le type I.

404	**1 c. sépia**	0 15	0 15	0 15
	(Sur lettre)			4 60
	(Seul sur lettre)			55 »
405	**2 c. vert foncé**	0 15	0 15	0 15
	(Sur lettre)			4 60
	(Seul sur lettre)			54 »
406	**5 c. rose**	0 15	0 15	0 15
	(Sur lettre)			4 60
	(Seul sur lettre)			61 »
407	**10 c. outremer**	0 15	0 15	0 15
	(Sur lettre)			3 »
	(Seul sur lettre)			23 »
408	**15 c. vermillon**	0 30	0 15	0 30
	(Sur lettre)			3 »
	(Seul sur lettre)			46 »
	a. orange pâle	0 50	0 30	0 30
409	**15 c. brun-orange**	1 25	0 75	0 80
	(Sur lettre)			3 »
	(Seul sur lettre)			46 »
410	**20 c. lilas**	0 15	0 15	0 15
	(Sur lettre)			2 30
	(Seul sur lettre)			8 »
411	**25 c. vert**	0 15	0 15	0 15
	(Sur lettre)			2 30
	(Seul sur lettre)			8 »
412	**30 c. rouge (I)**	0 15	0 15	0 15
	(Sur lettre)			0 80
	(Seul sur lettre)			2 30
	a. (Type II)	60 »	40 »	20 »
413	**40 c. violet**	0 15	0 15	0 15
	(Sur lettre)			0 80
	(Seul sur lettre)			2 »
414	**45 c. vert-jaune**	1 10	0 50	0 80
	(Sur lettre)			4 60
	(Seul sur lettre)			15 50
414A	**50 c. bleu**	5 »	3 »	0 65
	(Sur lettre)			3 »
	(Seul sur lettre)			15 50
414B	**50 c. vert**	1 »	0 50	0 65
	(Sur lettre)			3 »
	(Seul sur lettre)			23 »
415	**60 c. rouge-orange**	0 30	0 15	0 30
	(Sur lettre)			1 60
	(Seul sur lettre)			6 »

416	**70 c. lilas-rose (I)**	0 35	0 15	0 30
	(Sur lettre)			0 80
	(Seul sur lettre)			2 30
	a. (Type II)	125 »	90 »	35 »
416A	**75 c. brun-rouge**	9 50	4 60	2 75
	(Sur lettre)			30 »
	(Seul sur lettre)			92 »
	N°s 404 à 416A (16 val.)	**20 »**	**11 »**	**7 75**

Un 50 c. turquoise au même type a paru en 1942 (n° 538).

- Les 10, 30, 40 et 50 c. ont paru en 1942 avec légende POSTES FRANÇAISES (n°s 546 à 549) ; ces derniers ont été surchargés RF en 1944 (n°s 657 à 660).

1938. – ***Au profit des oeuvres sociales en faveur des étudiants. Taille-douce. Dentelé 13.***

417	**65 c. +60 c. bleu-vert**	20 »	9 15	9 15
	(Sur lettre)			11 50
	(Seul sur lettre)			18 50

Tirage : 1 500 000, ventes : 657 800

1938. – ***Au profit de l'oeuvre "La radio aux aveugles". Taille-douce. Dentelé 13.***

418	**90 c. +25 c. brun-lilas**	20 »	9 »	10 »
	(Sur lettre)			11 50
	(Seul sur lettre)			18 50

Tirage : 1 500 000, ventes : 751 500

1938

Du n° 372 au n° 418 :

52 timbres ****749** ***376** **⊙301**

1939. – ***Au profit de la Société de prophylaxie sanitaire et morale. Type de 1937. Taille-douce. Dentelé 13.***

419	**90 c. +30 c. bleu-vert (356)**	4 50	2 50	3 »
	(Sur lettre)			5 50
	(Seul sur lettre)			15 »
	a. (Non dentelé)		305 »	

Tirage : 1 511 700.

1939. – ***Pour l'érection du monument aux victimes civiles de la guerre de 1914-1918. Taille-douce. Dentelé 13.***

Maquette du monument au jeune Léon Trulin qui devait être érigé à Lille.

420	**90 c. +35 c. brun-gris**	21 »	10 »	11 »
	(Sur lettre)			14 »
	(Seul sur lettre)			18 50

Tirage : 1 200 000, ventes : 729 780

1939. – ***Centenaire de la naissance du peintre Paul Cézanne (1839-1906). Taille-douce. Dentelés 13.***

421	**2 f. 25 bleu-vert**	11 »	4 »	4 »
	(Sur lettre)			5 »
	(Seul sur lettre)			8 »
421A	**2 f. 25** ***bleu foncé***	5 750 »	4 250 »	
421B	**2 f. 25** ***bleu-vert***	6 250 »	4 500 »	

Les n°s 421A et 421B se distinguent du n° 421 non seulement par leurs couleurs mais aussi par de sensibles différences dans la gravure : traits du paysage du fond plus accentués, sourcil droit en angle aigu, quadrillé du veston moins distinct et hachures dans la lettre R.

1939. – ***75e anniversaire de la Croix-Rouge internationale. Croix en rouge. Taille-douce. Dentelés 13.***

422	**90 c. +35 c. noir et turquoise**	17 »	8 »	8 50
	(Sur lettre)			10 »
	(Seul sur lettre)			14 »
422A	**90 c. +35 c.** ***noir et outremer***	17 500 »		

Tirages du n° 422 : 1 200 000. Ventes du n° 422 : 720 000.

1939. – ***A la gloire du génie militaire. Taille-douce. Dentelé 13.***

423	**70 c. +50 c. rouge**	16 »	7 »	7 65
	(Sur lettre)			11 50
	(Seul sur lettre)			46 »

Tirage : 1 200 000, ventes : 725 650

1939. – ***Au profit de l'oeuvre des Orphelins des P.T.T. Taille-douce. Dentelé 13.***

Paris, le ministère des P.T.T.

424	**90 c. +35 c. bleu-vert**	50 »	22 50	22 50
	(Sur lettre)			25 »
	(Seul sur lettre)			40 »

Tirage : 1 260 000, ventes : 667 300

1939. – ***Mise sur cale du cuirassé "Clemenceau". Taille-douce. Dentelé 13.***

Cuirassé "Clemenceau".

425	**90 c. outremer**	1 »	0 65	0 80
	(Sur lettre)			2 30
	(Seul sur lettre)			4 60

Tirage : 4 000 000.

1939. – ***Exposition internationale de New York. Taille-douce. Dentelé 13.***

Le pavillon de la France et la statue de la Liberté.

426	**2 f. 25 outremer**	20 »	9 »	7 »
	(Sur lettre)			8 »
	(Seul sur lettre)			11 50
	a. (Non dentelé)		285 »	

Un 2 f. 50 à ce type a paru en 1940 (n° 458).

Voir également à la rubrique des Entiers postaux (n° 426-CP1).

Tirage : 4 000 000, ventes : 2 000 000

1939. – ***Centenaire de la photographie. Effigies de J. -N. Niepce (1765-1833) et Louis Daguerre (1787-1851). Taille-douce. Dentelé 13.***

François Arago annonçant la découverte à l'Académie des Sciences.

427	**2 f. 25 bleu**	18 »	8 »	7 »
	(Sur lettre)			8 »
	(Seul sur lettre)			12 50

Tirage : 4 000 000, ventes : 2 000 000

1939. – ***Au profit de l'oeuvre des enfants des chômeurs. Taille-douce. Dentelé 13.***

428	**90 c. +35 c. rouge-brique**	4 30	2 75	2 75
	(Sur lettre)			4 60
	(Seul sur lettre)			10 »

Tirage : 1 250 000.

1939. – ***Fêtes du cinquantenaire de la tour Eiffel. Taille-douce. Dentelé 13.***

429	**90 c. +50 c. lilas-rose**	17 »	9 15	9 15
	(Sur lettre)			11 50

En 1982, une carte postale a utilisé cette gravure de la tour Eiffel.

Voir à la rubrique des Entiers postaux (n° 429-CP1).

Tirage : 1 140 000, ventes : 875 000

1939. – ***Exposition de l'eau, à Liège (Belgique). Taille-douce. Dentelé 13.***

"La machine de Marly", à Bougival (démolie).

430	**2 f. 25 outremer**	37 »	13 »	5 50
	(Sur lettre)			7 »
	(Seul sur lettre)			10 »

Tirage : 4 000 000.

1939-41. – ***Type Iris. Typographie. Dentelés 14 x 13½.*** [C]

431	**80 c. brun-carmin**	0 30	0 15	0 30
	(Sur lettre)			0 80
	(Seul sur lettre)			11 »
432	**1 f. vert**	1 40	0 80	0 30
	(Sur lettre)			0 80
	(Seul sur lettre)			1 60
433	**1 f. rouge**	0 70	0 30	0 30
	(Sur lettre)			0 80
	(Seul sur lettre)			1 60
	a. (Paire verticale de carnets non confectionnés)	8 40	5 35	

434	**1 f. 30 outremer**	0 30	0 15	0 30
	(Sur lettre)			4 »
	(Seul sur lettre)			15 50
435	**1 f. 50 orange**	0 30	0 15	0 30
	(Sur lettre)			1 60
	(Seul sur lettre)			11 »
	N°s 431 à 435 (5 val.)	**3 »**	**1 55**	**1 50**

Le n° 434 existe sans nom du graveur.

Le n° 433a a été émis en feuilles de 80 sans publicité marginale (voir chapitre des carnets).

Les 80 c., 1 f. et 1 f. 50 ont reparu en d'autres couleurs en 1944, en même temps que d'autres valeurs (n°s 649 à 656).

1939. – ***Au profit des Chômeurs intellectuels. Taille-douce. Dentelés 13.***

Pierre Puvis de Chavannes (1824-1898).

Claude Debussy (1862-1918) et évocation du "Prélude à l'après-midi d'un faune".

436	**40 c. +10 c. rouge**	2 »	0 90	1 25
	(Sur lettre)			3 »
	(Seul sur lettre)			6 »
437	**70 c. +10 c. brun-lilas**	12 »	4 60	2 75
	(Sur lettre)			4 60
	(Seul sur lettre)			10 »

Honoré de Balzac (1799-1850).

Claude Bernard (1813-1878).

438	**90 c. +10 c. lilas-rose**	9 »	4 »	3 »
	(Sur lettre)			4 60
	(Seul sur lettre)			8 »
439	**2 f. 25+25 c. outremer**	32 »	17 »	13 »
	(Sur lettre)			15 50
	(Seul sur lettre)			20 »
	N°s 436 à 439 (4 val.)	**55 »**	**26 50**	**20 »**

Tirage : 1 200 000 séries.

Ces trois derniers types ont été remis en cours en 1940 (n°s 462 à 464).

1939. – ***Propagande en faveur de la natalité. Taille-douce. Dentelés 13.***

440 **70 c. +80 c. bleu, vert et violet** 6 » 3 85 4 50
(Sur lettre) 6 »
(Seul sur lettre) 15 »

441 **90 c. +60 c. brun, lilas et brun-rouge** 10 » 5 15 6 »
(Sur lettre) 6 »
(Seul sur lettre) 9 »

La paire, non dentelée 185 »
Vente : 673 000 paires.

1939. – ***14e centenaire de la naissance de Grégoire de Tours (v. 538-v. 594). Taille-douce. Dentelé 13.***

Effigie de Grégoire de Tours et vue de Clermont-Ferrand.

442 **90 c. rouge** 1 » 0 50 0 80
(Sur lettre) 1 60
(Seul sur lettre) 2 30
Tirage : 4 000 000.

1939. – ***5e centenaire de l'achèvement de la flèche de la cathédrale de Strasbourg. Taille-douce. Dentelé 13.***

Cathédrale de Strasbourg.

443 **70 c. brun-rouge** 1 70 1 » 1 50
(Sur lettre) 2 »
(Seul sur lettre) 3 »
Tirage : 4 000 000.

1939. – ***Sesquicentenaire de la Révolution. Taille-douce. Dentelé 13.***

Le Serment du Jeu de Paume, d'après David.

444 **90 c. ardoise** 4 30 2 15 2 15
(Sur lettre) 3 »
(Seul sur lettre) 4 60
Tirage : 4 000 000.

1939. – ***23e anniversaire de la victoire de Verdun. Taille-douce. Dentelé 13.***

Verdun : la Porte Chaussée.

445 **90 c. gris-brun** 1 40 0 65 1 10
(Sur lettre) 1 60
(Seul sur lettre) 4 60
Tirage : 4 000 000.

1939. – ***Au profit du Musée postal. Taille-douce. Dentelé 13.***

L'inspiration favorable (de Fragonard).

446 **40 c. +60 c. brun-lilas, brun et sépia** 5 » 2 75 3 85
(Sur lettre) 5 50
(Seul sur lettre) 7 65
a. (Non dentelé) 270 »
Tirage : 1 000 000, ventes : 954 500

1939. – ***Pour l'érection du monument national "Aux Marins perdus en mer", à Boulogne-sur-Mer. Taille-douce. Dentelé 13.***

Statue de Desruelles.

447 **70 c. +30 c. lilas-brun** 35 » 14 » 14 »
(Sur lettre) 15 50
(Seul sur lettre) 25 »
Tirage : 730 000.

1939. – ***Sites et paysages. Taille-douce. Dentelés 13.***

Languedocienne et cathédrale de Béziers.

448	**70 c. noir sur azuré**	0 65	0 50	0 65
	(Sur lettre)			4 60
	(Seul sur lettre)			23 »

Château de Pau.

Pont de la Guillotière, à Lyon.

449	**90 c. carmin sur azuré**	1 70	1 »	1 25
	(Sur lettre)			4 60
	(Seul sur lettre)			10 »
450	**90 c. brun-violet**	1 25	0 65	1 »
	(Sur lettre)			4 60
	(Seul sur lettre)			16 »

1939

Du n° 419 au n° 450
(sauf n° 421A et 421B) :
32 timbres ****343** ***157** **⊙147**

1940. – ***Pour nos soldats. Taille-douce. Dentelés 13.***

Fantassin et Strasbourg.

Marsouin et village africain.

451	**40 c. +60 c. brun**	5 50	2 30	3 »
	(Sur lettre)			5 50
	(Seul sur lettre)			12 50
452	**1 f. +50 c. vert-bleu**	5 »	2 30	3 »
	(Sur lettre)			5 50
	(Seul sur lettre)			12 50

Tirages : 1 700 000 et 2 000 000.

1940. – ***Pour la France d'Outre-Mer. Taille-douce. Dentelé 13.***

Carte de l'Empire français.

453	**1 f. +25 c. rouge**	3 35	2 »	2 75
	(Sur lettre)			4 60
	(Seul sur lettre)			6 »

A reparu en 1941 avec mill. 1941 (n° 503) et en 1945 avec mill. 1945 et croix de Lorraine (n° 741).

Tirage : 1 700 000, ventes : 920 000

1940. – ***Au profit des oeuvres de guerre. Taille-douce. Dentelés 13.***

Joseph Joffre (1852-1931), Maréchal de France.

Ferdinand Foch (1851-1929), Maréchal de France, de Grande-Bretagne et de Pologne.

454	**80 c. +45 c. brun-rouge**	11 »	5 »	7 »
	(Sur lettre)			10 »
	(Seul sur lettre)			15 50
455	**1 f. +50 c. violet**	10 »	8 50	7 »
	(Sur lettre)			10 »
	(Seul sur lettre)			15 50

Joseph-Simon Galliéni (1849-1916).

La femme au labour.

456	**1 f. 50+50 c. rouge-brun**	9 »	4 50	4 50
	(Sur lettre)			10 »
	(Seul sur lettre)			15 50
457	**2 f. 50+50 c. bleu**	22 »	9 »	12 50
	(Sur lettre)			15 50
	(Seul sur lettre)			46 »
	N°s 454 à 457 (4 val.)	**52 »**	**27 »**	**31 »**
	La série, non dentelée		340 »	

Tirage : 1 700 000 séries.

1940. – ***Exposition internationale de New York. Type de 1939. Taille-douce. Dentelé 13.***

458	**2 f. 50 outremer (426)**	35 »	11 »	11 »
	(Sur lettre)			11 »
	(Seul sur lettre)			14 »

Tirage : 2 000 000, ventes : 1 000 000

1940. – ***Au profit des blessés. Croix rouge en surchage typographique. Taille-douce. Dentelés 13.***

459	**80 c. +1 f. vert**	11 »	5 50	7 »
	(Sur lettre)			12 50
	(Seul sur lettre)			80 »
460	**1 f. +2 f. brun-lilas**	15 »	7 »	7 »
	(Sur lettre)			11 »
	(Seul sur lettre)			16 »

1940. – *Capitaine aviateur Georges Guynemer (1894-1917), par Lawrence (Musée de l'Armée, Paris). Taille-douce. Dentelé 13.*

461	**50 f. bleu**	20 »	10 »	10 »
	(Sur lettre)			92 »
	(Seul sur lettre)			230 »
	a. outremer	24 »	12 »	12 »
	b. (Non dentelé)		230 »	

Tirage : 937 500.

1940. – *Au profit des Chômeurs intellectuels. Types de 1939. Taille-douce. Dentelés 13.*

462	**80 c. +10 c. brun-lilas (437)**	12 50	5 50	9 »
	(Sur lettre)			10 »
	(Seul sur lettre)			12 50
463	**1 f. +10 c. lilas-rose (438)**	12 50	5 50	9 »
	(Sur lettre)			10 »
	(Seul sur lettre)			12 50

464	**2 f. 50+25 c. outremer (439)**	12 50	5 50	9 »
	(Sur lettre)			10 »
	(Seul sur lettre)			12 50
	a. (Papier carton)	14 »	5 50	8 50

1940. – *Au profit des victimes de la guerre. Taille-douce. Dentelé 13.*

465	**1 f. +2 f. brun-lilas**	1 70	1 10	1 25
	(Sur lettre)			3 »
	(Seul sur lettre)			10 »
	a. (Double signature)	50 »	40 »	25 »

Tirage : 1 500 000, ventes : 1 430 000.

1940. – *Au profit du Secours national. Taille-douce. Dentelés 13.*

Moisson.

Semailles.

466	**80 c. +2 f. brun**	4 80	1 85	2 50
	(Sur lettre)			4 60
	(Seul sur lettre)			80 »
467	**1 f. +2 f. brun-rouge**	4 20	1 85	2 50
	(Sur lettre)			4 60
	(Seul sur lettre)			23 »

Vendanges.

Elevage.

468	**1 f. 50+2 f. violet**	4 80	2 »	2 50
	(Sur lettre)			4 60
	(Seul sur lettre)			40 »
469	**2 f. 50+2 f. vert**	5 70	2 80	2 50
	(Sur lettre)			4 60
	(Seul sur lettre)			46 »
	N°s 466 à 469 (4 val.)	**19 50**	**8 50**	**10 »**

1940

Du n° 451 au n° 469 :

19 timbres ****206** ***93** **⊙113**

État Français

1940-41. – *Effigie du Maréchal Pétain. Taille-douce. Dentelés 13.*

470	**40 c. brun-rouge**	0 50	0 30	0 50
	(Sur lettre)			8 »
	(Seul sur lettre)			40 »
471	**80 c. vert-bleu**	0 65	0 30	0 65
	(Sur lettre)			8 »
	(Seul sur lettre)			30 »

472	**1 f. rouge**	0 30	0 15	0 30
	(Sur lettre)			1 60
	(Seul sur lettre)			3 »
473	**2 f. 50 outremer**	1 85	1 10	1 40
	(Sur lettre)			10 »
	(Seul sur lettre)			30 »
	N°s 470 à 473 (4 val.)	**3 30**	**1 85**	**2 85**
	La série, non dentelée		185 »	

Tirages : 1 930 000, 1 950 000, 4 000 000 et 2 000 000.

Le 1 f. est reparu surchargé + 10 c. (n° 494).

Ce type a été repris en 1943 pour deux timbres de 2 f. + 12 f. (n°s 570 et 571).

1941. – *Au profit des prisonniers de guerre. Taille-douce. Dentelés 13.*

474	**80 c. +5 f. vert**	2 »	1 10	1 90
	(Sur lettre)			4 60
	(Seul sur lettre)			46 »
475	**1 f. +5 f. brun carminé**	2 15	1 25	2 »
	(Sur lettre)			4 60
	(Seul sur lettre)			30 »

1940-41. – *Timbres de 1932-38 avec nouvelle valeur en surcharge rouge (noire sur le n° 483). Dentelés.*

Type Semeuse fond plein.

476	**30 sur 35 c. vert (361)**	0 35	0 15	0 35
	(Sur lettre)			1 70
	(Seul sur lettre)			11 50
	a. (Double surcharge)	1 100 »	825 »	

Type Mercure.

477	**50 sur 75 c. brun-rouge (416A)**	0 35	0 15	0 35
	(Sur lettre)			1 70
	(Seul sur lettre)			23 »

Type Paix.

478	**50 sur 55 c. violet (363)**	0 35	0 15	0 35
	(Sur lettre)			1 »
	(Seul sur lettre)			11 50
	a. (Surcharge renversée)	1 250 »	1 000 »	
479	**50 sur 65 c. outremer (365)**	0 15	0 15	0 15
	(Sur lettre)			1 »
	(Seul sur lettre)			11 50
	a. (Surcharge renversée)	700 »	550 »	
	b. (Double surcharge dont une verticale)	1 100 »	915 »	
480	**50 sur 75 c. olive (284A)**	0 35	0 15	0 35
	(Sur lettre)			1 »
	(Seul sur lettre)			11 50
481	**50 sur 80 c. orange (366)**	0 35	0 15	0 35
	(Sur lettre)			1 »
	(Seul sur lettre)			11 50

482	**50 sur 90 c. outremer (368)**	0 15	0 15	0 15
	(Sur lettre)			1 »
	(Seul sur lettre)			11 50
	a. (Surcharge renversée)	650 »	475 »	
	b. (Sans surcharge tenant à normal)	1 300 »	1 000 »	
	c. (05 sur 90 c)	10 000 »	8 000 »	
483	**1 F. sur 1 f. 25 rose (370)**	0 35	0 15	0 35
	(Sur lettre)			1 »
	(Seul sur lettre)			3 »
484	**1 F. sur 1 f. 40 lilas (371)**	0 50	0 15	0 50
	(Sur lettre)			1 70
	(Seul sur lettre)			4 60
	a. (Double surcharge)	1 600 »	1 250 »	
485	**1 F. sur 1 f. 50 bleu (288)**	1 40	1 »	1 40
	(Sur lettre)			1 70
	(Seul sur lettre)			3 »
	a. (tenant à non surchargé)	1 700 »	1 250 »	

Type Cérès.

486	**1 F. sur 1 f. 75 bleu (372)**	0 35	0 20	0 35
	(Sur lettre)			0 80
	(Seul sur lettre)			3 »
487	**1 F. sur 2 f. 25 outremer (374)**	0 35	0 20	0 35
	(Sur lettre)			0 80
	(Seul sur lettre)			3 »
	a. (Sans surcharge tenant à normal)	1 650 »	1 300 »	
488	**1 F. sur 2 f. 50 vert (375)**	1 70	1 »	1 70
	(Sur lettre)			1 70
	(Seul sur lettre)			3 »
	a. (tenant à non surchargé)	2 000 »	1 450 »	

Timbres grand format en taille-douce, avec nouvelle valeur et traits sur l'ancienne en surcharge rouge.

489	**1 F. sur 2 f. 15 brun-lilas (390)**	0 50	0 35	0 50
	(Sur lettre)			0 80
	(Seul sur lettre)			3 »
	a. (Surcharge renversée)	13 500 »	6 100 »	
490	**2 f. 50 s. 5 f. outremer (392)**	0 50	0 35	0 50
	(Sur lettre)			8 »
	(Seul sur lettre)			23 »
	a. (Double surcharge)	385 »	170 »	

491	**5 F. sur 10 f. brun s. azuré (393)**	2 30	1 45	2 30
	(Sur lettre)			8 »
	(Seul sur lettre)			30 »
492	**10 F. sur 20 f. vert foncé (394)**	2 »	1 10	2 »
	(Sur lettre)			15 50
	(Seul sur lettre)			61 »

493	**20 f. s. 50 f. outremer foncé *(Pap. épais)* (398a)**	85 »	40 »	45 »
	(Sur lettre)			92 »
	(Seul sur lettre)			275 »
	a. (Papier mince)	90 »	55 »	62 »
	b. (Double surcharge)	3 500 »	2 800 »	
	N°s 476 à 493 (18 val.)	**97 »**	**47 »**	**57 »**

1941. – ***Au profit du Secours national. Timbre précédent (n° 472), avec surcharge violette.***

494	**+10 c. sur 1 f. rose carminé (violette) (472)**	0 30	0 15	0 15
	(Sur lettre)			3 »
	(Seul sur lettre)			5 50
	a. (Non dentelé)		23 »	

Tirage : 2 000 000.

1941. – ***Frédéric Mistral (1830-1914), poète. Taille-douce. Dentelé 14 x 13.***

495	**1 f. brun carminé**	0 30	0 15	0 30
	(Sur lettre)			1 60
	(Seul sur lettre)			6 »
	a. (Non dentelé)		40 »	

Tirage : 3 070 000.

1941. – ***Lutte contre le cancer. Taille-douce. Dentelé 13.***

496	**2 f. 50+50 c. ardoise et brun**	2 »	1 10	1 70
	(Sur lettre)			6 »
	(Seul sur lettre)			30 »
	a. (Non dentelé)		110 »	

Tirage : 1 235 000.

1941. – ***Au profit du Secours national. Taille-douce. Dentelés 13.***

497	**1 f. +2 f. brun-violet**	3 35	1 85	1 60
	(Sur lettre)			3 »
	(Seul sur lettre)			15 50
498	**2 f. 50+7 f. 50 bleu**	11 »	5 80	3 »
	(Sur lettre)			4 »
	(Seul sur lettre)			30 »
	La paire, non dentelée		155 »	

1941. – ***Monuments et sites. Taille-douce. Dentelés 13.***

Hôtel-Dieu de Beaune Cour intérieure.

Angers.

499	**5 f. brun-noir**	0 50	0 30	0 30
	(Sur lettre)			3 »
	(Seul sur lettre)			15 50
	a. brun	0 65	0 50	0 30
	b. (Non dentelé)		30 »	
500	**10 f. violet foncé**	1 10	0 50	0 65
	(Sur lettre)			3 »
	(Seul sur lettre)			23 »
	a. (Non dentelé)		30 »	

Remparts d'Aigues-Mortes.

501	**20 f. brun-noir**	1 70	0 80	1 25
	(Sur lettre)			6 »
	(Seul sur lettre)			40 »
	a. brun-gris	2 15	1 25	1 85
	b. (Non dentelé)		140 »	

Tirages : 52 850 000, 35 000 000 et 7 140 000.

Au type du 5 f., a été émis en 1942 un 15 f. (n° 539). La légende a été modifiée.

1941. – ***Au profit des oeuvres de mer. Lancement du paquebot "Pasteur". (Non émis) surchargé en rouge. Taille-douce. Dentelé 13.***

502	**1 f. +1 f. sur 70 c. [vert foncé] (R)**	0 50	0 30	0 50
	(Sur lettre)			1 60
	(Seul sur lettre)			4 60
	a. (Non dentelé)		40 »	
	b. (Sans surcharge)	» »	» »	

Tirage : 3 350 000.

Des exemplaires de ce timbre sans surcharge sont régulièrement offerts à la vente sur internet. Il s'agit en général de timbres transformés au moyen d'un procédé chimique.

1941. – ***"Pour la France d'Outre-Mer". Type de 1940 avec millésime 1941. Taille-douce. Dentelé 13.***

503	**1 f. +1 f. vert, lilas et bleu**	1 »	0 50	0 65
	(Sur lettre)			1 60
	(Seul sur lettre)			4 »
	a. (Non dentelé)		35 »	

Ce timbre ne porte plus la mention R. F.

Tirage : 1 260 000.

1941. – *Au profit des oeuvres de mer. Taille-douce. Dentelé 13.*

504	**1 f. +9 f. vert**	1 25	0 65	1 10
	(Sur lettre)			4 »
	(Seul sur lettre)			23 »
	a. (Non dentelé)		77 »	

Tirage : 1 200 000.

1941-42. – *Effigies du Maréchal Pétain. Typographie, sauf n° 522, 523, 524, 525 : taille-douce. Dentelé 14 x 13½.*

505	**20 c. lilas-rose (Type Prost) 14 x 13½**	0 15	0 15	0 15
	(Sur lettre)			8 »
506	**30 c. rouge (Type Prost) 14 x 13½**	0 15	0 15	0 15
	(Sur lettre)			4 60
	(Seul sur lettre)			27 »
507	**40 c. outremer (Type Prost) 14 x 13½**	0 15	0 15	0 15
	(Sur lettre)			4 60
	(Seul sur lettre)			30 »

508	**50 c. vert (Type Hourriez) 14 x 13½**	0 15	0 15	0 15
	(Sur lettre)			2 30
	(Seul sur lettre)			8 »
509	**60 c. violet (Type Hourriez) 14 x 13½**	0 15	0 15	0 15
	(Sur lettre)			1 60
	(Seul sur lettre)			3 »
510	**70 c. bleu (Type Hourriez) 14 x 13½**	0 15	0 15	0 15
	(Sur lettre)			1 60
	(Seul sur lettre)			40 »
	a. bleu foncé	0 50	0 30	0 50
511	**70 c. orange (Type Hourriez) 14 x 13½**	0 15	0 15	0 15
	(Sur lettre)			1 60
	(Seul sur lettre)			23 »

512	**80 c. brun (Type Hourriez) 14 x 13½**	0 30	0 15	0 30
	(Sur lettre)			1 60
	(Seul sur lettre)			40 »
513	**80 c. vert-jaune (Type Hourriez) 14 x 13½**	0 15	0 15	0 15
	(Sur lettre)			1 60
	(Seul sur lettre)			23 »
514	**1 f. rouge (Type Hourriez) 14 x 13½**	0 15	0 15	0 15
	(Sur lettre)			1 »
	(Seul sur lettre)			1 60
515	**1 f. 20 brun-rouge (Type Hourriez) 14 x 13½**	0 15	0 15	0 15
	(Sur lettre)			1 25
	(Seul sur lettre)			1 60

516	**1 f. 50 rose (Type Bersier) 14 x 13½**	0 15	0 15	0 15
	(Sur lettre)			0 65
	(Seul sur lettre)			1 25
517	**1 f. 50 brun-rouge (Type Bersier) 14 x 13½**	0 15	0 15	0 15
	(Sur lettre)			0 50
	(Seul sur lettre)			0 80
	a. (Avec bande publ)	1 25	0 80	0 50
	b. (avec bande publ non dentelé)		115 »	
	c. (Paire verticale de carnets avec barres)	8 »	5 »	5 »
	d. (Faux FFI : sans gomme dentelé 11½)	5 »		
518	**2 f. vert (Type Bersier) 14 x 13½**	0 15	0 15	0 15
	(Sur lettre)			0 65
	(Seul sur lettre)			2 30
519	**2 f. 40 rouge (Type Bersier) 14 x 13½**	0 30	0 15	0 30
	(Sur lettre)			8 »
	(Seul sur lettre)			115 »

520	**2 f. 50 outremer (Type Bersier) 14 x 13½**	1 »	0 30	1 »
	(Sur lettre)			8 »
	(Seul sur lettre)			30 »
521	**3 f. orange (Type Bersier) 14 x 13½**	0 15	0 15	0 15
	(Sur lettre)			3 »
	(Seul sur lettre)			12 50

521A	**4 f. bleu (Type Hourriez) 14 x 13½**	0 30	0 15	0 30
	(Sur lettre)			1 60
	(Seul sur lettre)			3 »
521B	**4 f. 50 vert-jaune (Type Hourriez) 14 x 13½**	1 20	0 50	0 80
	(Sur lettre)			1 60
	(Seul sur lettre)			4 »

Taille-douce. Format 18 x 21. Dentelés 14 x 13.

522	**4 f. outremer (Type Hourriez) Dentelé 14 x 13**	0 30	0 15	0 30
	(Sur lettre)			2 30
	(Seul sur lettre)			5 50
523	**4 f. 50 vert foncé (Type Hourriez) Dentelé 14 x 13**	0 30	0 15	0 30
	(Sur lettre)			1 60
	(Seul sur lettre)			5 50

524	**5 f. vert-bleu (Types Mazelin) 14 x 13½**	0 30	0 15	0 30
	(Sur lettre)			8 »
	(Seul sur lettre)			23 »
525	**50 f. noir (Types Mazelin) Dentelé 13**	5 40	3 20	5 »
	(Sur lettre)			46 »
	(Seul sur lettre)			92 »
	a. (Papier jaunâtre)	7 65	4 60	6 »
	b. (Non dentelé)		100 »	
	N°s 505 à 525 (23 val.)	**11 50**	**7 »**	**10 70**

Le type du 50 f. a été repris en 1943 pour deux timbres de 1 f. + 10 f. (n°s 568 et 569).

Pour les timbres aux types Pétain surchargés R. F., voir à la rubrique Libération.

La série, non dentelée, sauf n° 525 (23 valeurs) 130 »

1941. – *Au profit du Secours national. Armoiries de ville (I). Taille-douce. Dentelés 14 x 13.*

Nancy.

Lille.

Rouen.

526	**20 c. +30 c. noir**	3 »	2 »	3 »
527	**40 c. +60 c. brun-rouge**	3 »	2 »	3 »
528	**50 c. +70 c. bleu-vert**	3 »	2 »	3 »

Bordeaux.

Toulouse.

Clermont-Ferrand.

529	**70 c. +80 c. lilas-rose**	3 »	2 »	3 »
530	**80 c. +1 f. rose**	3 »	2 »	3 »
531	**1 f. +1 f. noir**	3 »	2 »	3 »

Marseille.

Lyon.

Rennes.

532	**1 f. 50+2 f. bleu**	3 »	2 »	3 »
533	**2 f. +2 f. violet**	3 40	2 »	3 40
534	**2 f. 50+3 f. vert-jaune**	3 40	2 »	3 40

Reims.

Montpellier.

Paris.

535	**3 f. +5 f. brun-rouge**	3 40	2 »	3 40
536	**5 f. +6 f. outremer**	3 40	2 »	3 40
537	**10 f. +10 f. rouge**	3 40	2 »	3 40
	N°s 526 à 537 (12 val.)	**38 »**	**24 »**	**38 »**
	La série, non dentelée		185 »	

1941

Du n° 470 au n° 537 :

70 timbres ****177** ***94** **⊙124**

1942. – *Type Mercure. Typographie. Dentelé 14 x 13½.*

538	**50 c. turquoise**	0 15	0 15	0 15
	(Sur lettre)			0 80
	(Seul sur lettre)			4 »
	a. (Non dentelé)		4 60	

A reparu avec inscriptions modifiées (n° 549).

1942. – *Hôtel-Dieu de Beaune. Type de 1941. Lég. : POSTES FRANÇAISES. Taille-douce. Dentelé 13.*

539	**15 f. brun carminé**	0 80	0 30	0 65
	(Sur lettre)			3 »
	(Seul sur lettre)			10 »
	a. (Non dentelé)		27 »	
	b. (Papier carton)	9 15	6 »	4 60

1942. – ***Au profit des oeuvres de l'air. Taille-douce. Dentelé 13.***

540	**1 f. 50+3 f. 50 violet**	3 »	1 85	3 »
	(Sur lettre)			3 »
	(Seul sur lettre)			10 »
	a. (Non dentelé)		155 »	

Tirage : 1 560 000, ventes : 1 210 000

Ce timbre existe en bleu-gris (Voir Tome II, 1ère partie, Algérie n°245c)

1942. – ***Au profit du Secours national. Bicentenaire de la naissance de Jean-François de Galaup, comte de La Pérouse (1741-1788). Taille-douce. Dentelé 13.***

La Boussole et l'Astrolabe.

541	**2 f. 50+7 f. 50 bleu**	1 85	1 10	1 85
	(Sur lettre)			2 30
	(Seul sur lettre)			15 50
	a. (Non dentelé)		140 »	

Tirage : 1 225 000.

1942. – ***Au profit des oeuvres d'entraide des musiciens. Centenaire de la naissance d'Emmanuel Chabrier (1841-1894). Taille-douce. Dentelé 13.***

Chabrier au piano (extrait du tableau de Fantin-Latour).

542	**2 f. +3 f. brun-gris**	1 70	0 80	1 60
	(Sur lettre)			2 30
	(Seul sur lettre)			15 50
	a. (Non dentelé)		140 »	

Tirage : 1 225 000.

1942. – ***Au profit du comité de propagande de la Quinzaine impériale. Taille-douce. Dentelé 13.***

543	**1 f. 50+8 f. 50 noir**	1 40	0 80	1 40
	(Sur lettre)			2 30
	(Seul sur lettre)			15 50
	a. (Non dentelé)		110 »	

Tirage : 1 275 000.

1942. – ***Sixième centenaire de la naissance de Jean de Vienne (1341-1396), amiral de France. Au profit des oeuvres de la marine. Taille-douce. Dentelé 13.***

544	**1 f. 50+8 f. 50 brun-violet**	1 60	0 80	1 60
	(Sur lettre)			2 30
	(Seul sur lettre)			8 »
	a. (Non dentelé)		110 »	

Tirage : 1 250 000.

1942. – ***Centenaire de la naissance du compositeur Jules Massenet (1842-1912). Taille-douce. Dentelé 14 x 13.***

545	**4 f. vert-bleu**	0 30	0 15	0 30
	(Sur lettre)			1 60
	(Seul sur lettre)			12 50
	a. (Non dentelé)		18 50	

Tirage : 2 150 000.

1942. – ***Type Mercure modifié avec légende POSTES FRANÇAISES. Typographie. Dentelés 14 x 13½.***

546	**10 c. outremer**	0 15	0 15	0 15
	(Sur lettre)			2 30
	(Seul sur lettre)			15 50
547	**30 c. rouge**	0 15	0 15	0 15
	(Sur lettre)			2 30
	(Seul sur lettre)			6 »
548	**40 c. violet**	0 30	0 15	0 30
	(Sur lettre)			1 60
	(Seul sur lettre)			6 »
549	**50 c. turquoise**	0 15	0 15	0 15
	(Sur lettre)			1 60
	(Seul sur lettre)			3 »
	a. (Bord de feuille filigrané)	60 »	50 »	
	Nos 546 à 549 (4 val.)	**0 75**	**0 60**	**0 75**
	La série, non dentelée		30 »	

Ces timbres ont reparu, surchargés R F en 1944 (nos 657 à 660).

1942. – ***Centenaire de la mort de l'écrivain Henri Beyle, dit Stendhal (1783-1842). Taille-douce. Dentelé 13.***

Henri Beyle, dit Stendhal, par Alfred de Dreux-Dorcy (Musée de Grenoble).

550	**4 f. brun-noir et carmin**	0 65	0 50	0 65
	(Sur lettre)			3 »
	(Seul sur lettre)			23 »
	a. (Non dentelé)		61 »	
	b. (Ligne du bas en rouge)	8 »	5 »	2 »

Tirage : 2 060 000.

1942. – ***En souvenir du physicien André Blondel (1863-1938). Taille-douce. Dentelé 13.***

André Blondel.

551	**4 f. bleu**	0 65	0 50	0 65
	(Sur lettre)			3 »
	(Seul sur lettre)			15 50
	a. (Non dentelé)		61 »	

Tirage : 2 060 000.

1942. – ***Secours national. Type Bersier de 1941-42, avec surcharge. Dentelé 14 x 13½.***

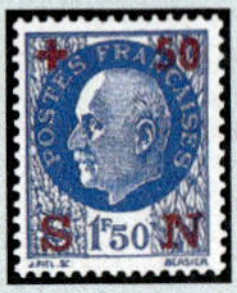

552	**+50 sur 1 f. 50 [outremer] (carmin)**	0 15	0 15	0 15
	(Sur lettre)			1 60
	(Seul sur lettre)			4 »
	a. (Non dentelé)		15 50	
	b. (Sans surch)		200 »	
	c. (Sans surcharge, non dentelé)		200 »	
	d. brun (N)		2 200 »	

Tirage : 5 100 000, ventes : 5 050 000

1942. – ***Au profit du Secours national. Armoiries de villes (II). Taille-douce. Dentelés 14 x 13.***

Chambéry.

La Rochelle.

Poitiers.

553	**50 c. +60 c. noir**	6 »	3 »	4 65
554	**60 c. +70 c. bleu-vert**	4 50	2 30	3 90
555	**80 c. +1 f. rose**	4 50	2 30	3 90

Orléans.

Grenoble.

Angers.

556	**1 f. +1 f. 30 vert**	4 50	2 30	3 90
557	**1 f. 20+1 f. 50 lie-de-vin**	4 50	2 30	4 20
558	**1 f. 50+1 f. 80 bleu foncé**	5 »	2 30	4 30

Dijon.

Limoges.

Le Havre.

559	**2 f. +2 f. 30 rouge**	5 »	2 30	4 30
560	**2 f. 40+2 f. 80 vert-gris**	5 »	2 60	4 30
561	**3 f. +3 f. 50 violet**	5 »	2 60	4 30

Nantes.

Nice.

Saint-Étienne.

562	**4 f. +5 f. outremer**	5 »	3 »	4 30
563	**4 f. 50+6 f. orange**	5 »	3 »	4 30
564	**5 f. +7 f. lilas-rose**	6 »	3 »	4 65
	Nos **553 à 564 (12 val.)**	**60 »**	**31 »**	**51 »**
	La série, non dentelée		185 »	

1942. – ***Pour la Légion tricolore. Taille-douce. Dentelés 13.***

565	**1 f. 20+8 f. 80 bleu**	12 50	6 90	12 50
566	**1 f. 20+8 f. 80 rouge**	12 50	6 90	12 50
	a. (La paire avec intervalle, impr. en relief)	27 50	15 50	26 »
	b. (La bande complète avec intervalle)	55 »	35 »	54 »
	c. (La bande complète avec intervalle, non dentelée)		1 300 »	

Ces timbres ont été imprimés par feuilles de 20 exemplaires (10 timbres bleus dans le haut, 10 rouges dans le bas).

La bande blanche qui les sépare porte une impression du timbre à sec.

1942. – *Beffroi d'Arras. Taille-douce. Dentelé 13.*

567	**10 f. vert**	0 30	0 15	0 30
	(Sur lettre)			1 60
	(Seul sur lettre)			4 60
	a. (Non dentelé)		55 »	
	b. (Double légende inférieure)	50 »	40 »	25 »

Tirage : 17 400 000.

1942			
Du n° 538 au n° 567 :			
30 timbres	****98**	***53**	**⊙89**

1943. – *Au profit du Secours national. Types de 1940-42. Taille-douce. Dentelés 13.*

568	**1 f. +10 f. bleu**	3 »	1 60	3 »
569	**1 f. +10 f. rouge**	3 »	1 60	3 »
570	**2 f. +12 f. bleu**	3 »	1 60	3 »
571	**2 f. +12 f. rouge**	3 »	1 60	3 »
	N°s 568 à 571 (4 val.)	**12 »**	**6 40**	**12 »**
	La bande de quatre timbres avec francisque			
571A	La bande	18 »	10 »	18 »
	a. Non dentelée		1 250 »	

Tirés par feuilles de cinq bandes.

1943. – *Armoiries de provinces (I). Typographie. Dentelés 14 x 13½.*

Lyonnais.

Bretagne.

572	**5 f. outremer, rouge et jaune**	0 50	0 30	0 50
	(Sur lettre)			0 80
	(Seul sur lettre)			7 65
	a. outremer et jaune (Sans impression rouge dans l'écusson)		125 »	
573	**10 f. noir et jaune-brun**	0 80	0 50	0 65
	(Sur lettre)			0 80
	(Seul sur lettre)			15 50
	a. (Signature EL au lieu de PIEL)	25 »	14 »	14 »

Provence.

Ile-de-France.

574	**15 f. outremer, rouge et jaune**	2 30	1 40	1 70
	(Sur lettre)			3 »
	(Seul sur lettre)			23 »
575	**20 f. brun, outremer et jaune**	1 90	1 »	1 90
	(Sur lettre)			4 »
	(Seul sur lettre)			23 »
	N°s 572 à 575 (4 val.)	**5 50**	**3 20**	**4 75**
	La série, non dentelée		46 »	

Tirages : 39 500 000, 45 350 000, 12 000 000 et 10 600 000.

1943. – *Au profit du Secours national. ("Travail, Famille, Patrie"). Taille-douce. Dentelés 13.*

576	**1 f. 20+1 f. 40 violet-brun**	20 »	12 »	18 50
577	**1 f. 50+2 f. 50 rouge**	20 »	12 »	18 50
578	**2 f. 40+7 f. brun**	20 »	12 »	18 50
579	**4 f. +10 f. violet-brun**	20 »	12 »	18 50
580	**5 f. +15 f. rouge-brun**	20 »	12 »	18 50
	N°s 576 à 580 (5 val.)	**100 »**	**60 »**	**92 50**
	La bande de cinq timbres			
580A	La bande	155 »	95 »	140 »
	a. Non dentelée		1 250 »	

Tirés par feuilles de cinq bandes.

1943. – *Antoine Laurent de Lavoisier (1743-1794) (d'après David). Taille-douce. Dentelé 14 x 13.*

581	**4 f. bleu**	0 30	0 15	0 30
	(Sur lettre)			3 »
	(Seul sur lettre)			15 50
	a. (Non dentelé)		15 50	

Tirage : 2 610 000.

1943. – *Paysage du Dauphiné. Taille-douce. Dentelé 13.*

Le lac Lérié et la Meije.

582	**20 f. vert foncé**	1 10	0 80	1 10
	(Sur lettre)			3 »
	(Seul sur lettre)			30 »
	a. (Non dentelé)		70 »	

Tirage : 1 675 000.

1943. – ***Cinquième centenaire de l'Hôtel-Dieu de Beaune. Taille-douce. Dentelé 13.***

Nicolas Rolin (1380-1461) et Guigone de Salins, d'après Roger de La Pasture (Van der Weyden), et porche de l'Hôtel-Dieu.

583	**4 f. bleu**	0 30	0 15	0 30
	(Sur lettre)			2 30
	(Seul sur lettre)			15 50
	a. bleu-gris	2 30	1 40	2 30
	b. bleu-gris (impression très défectueuse)		420 »	
	c. bleu-noir	1 25	0 80	0 80
	d. (Non dentelé)		46 »	

Tirage : 2 450 000.

1943. – ***Au profit du Secours national. Taille-douce. Dentelé 13.***

584	**1 f. 50+3 f. 50 noir**	0 65	0 50	0 65
	(Sur lettre)			1 60
	(Seul sur lettre)			15 50
	a. (Non dentelé)		61 »	

Tirage : 1 150 000.

1943. – ***Au profit de la famille du prisonnier. Taille-douce. Dentelés 13.***

585	**1 f. 50+8 f. 50 gris-brun**	1 10	0 80	1 10
	(Sur lettre)			4 »
	(Seul sur lettre)			15 50
586	**2 f. 40+7 f. 60 vert**	1 25	0 80	1 25
	(Sur lettre)			4 »
	(Seul sur lettre)			77 »

La paire, non dentelée 125 »

1943. – ***Célébrités du XVIe siècle. Taille-douce. Dentelés 13.***

Michel Eyquem de Montaigne (1533-1592), moraliste. François Clouet (1520-1572), peintre, Autoportrait. Ambroise Paré (1510-1590), chirurgien.

587	**60 c. +80 c. vert-bleu**	2 40	1 40	2 40
588	**1 f. 20+1 f. 50 noir**	2 40	1 40	2 40
589	**1 f. 50+3 f. outremer**	2 40	1 40	2 40

Pierre Terrail, seigneur de Bayard (1476-1524). Maximilien de Béthune, baron de Rosny, duc de Sully (1560-1641). Henri IV (1553-1610).

590	**2 f. 40+4 f. rouge**	2 40	1 40	2 40
591	**4 f. +6 f. brun-rouge**	2 65	1 40	2 65
592	**5 f. +10 f. vert**	2 75	1 60	2 75
	Nos 587 à 592 (6 val.)	**15 »**	**8 60**	**15 »**
	La série, non dentelée		230 »	

1943. – ***Coiffes régionales. Au profit du Secours national. Taille-douce. Dentelés 13.***

Picardie. Bretagne. Ile-de-France.

593	**60 c. +1 f. 30 brun**	2 45	1 75	2 45
594	**1 f. 20+2 f. violet**	2 45	1 75	2 45
595	**1 f. 50+4 f. bleu-vert**	2 45	1 75	2 45

Bourgogne.

Auvergne.

Provence.

596	**2 f. 40+5 f. carmin**	2 45	1 75	2 45
597	**4 f. +6 f. bleu**	3 60	2 »	3 60
598	**5 f. +7 f. rouge**	3 60	2 »	3 60
	N°s 593 à 598 (6 val.)	**17 »**	**11 »**	**17 »**
	La série, non dentelée		230 »	

1943

Du n° 568 au n° 598 :

Soit I : sauf 571A et 580A :

31 timbres ****154** ***92** **⊙146**

Soit I I : sauf 568-71 et 576-80 :

24 timbres ****215** ***131** **⊙199**

1944. – ***Centenaire de la naissance du physicien Édouard Branly (1844-1940). Taille-douce. Dentelé 14 x 13.***

599	**4 f. outremer**	0 30	0 15	0 30
	(Sur lettre)			4 »
	(Seul sur lettre)			15 50
	a. (Non dentelé)		23 »	

Tirage : 2 500 000.

1944. – ***Tricentenaire de la naissance du maréchal Anne-Hilarion de Cotentin, comte de Tourville (1642-1701). Taille-douce. Dentelé 13.***

600	**4 f. +6 f. rouge-brun**	1 »	0 65	1 »
	(Sur lettre)			3 »
	(Seul sur lettre)			15 50
	a. fond teinté	3 »	1 85	1 60
	b. (Non dentelé)		54 »	

Tirage : 1 185 000.

1944. – ***Cinquantenaire de la mort du compositeur Charles Gounod (1818-1893). Taille-douce. Dentelé 14 x 13.***

601	**1 f. 50+3 f. 50 sépia**	1 25	0 65	1 »
	(Sur lettre)			3 »
	(Seul sur lettre)			23 »
	a. (Non dentelé)		46 »	

Tirage : 1 350 000, ventes : 1 200 000

1944. – ***Armoiries de provinces (II). Typographie. Dentelés 14 x 13½.***

Flandre.

Languedoc.

602	**5 f. rouge, noir et orange**	0 30	0 15	0 30
	(Sur lettre)			0 80
	(Seul sur lettre)			15 50
603	**10 f. noir, carmin et jaune**	0 30	0 15	0 30
	(Sur lettre)			0 80
	(Seul sur lettre)			15 50

Orléanais.

Normandie.

604	**15 f. brun, bleu et jaune**	1 »	0 70	1 »
	(Sur lettre)			1 10
	(Seul sur lettre)			15 50
605	**20 f. outremer, rouge et jaune**	1 60	1 »	1 25
	(Sur lettre)			1 60
	(Seul sur lettre)			15 50
	N°s 602 à 605 (4 val.)	**3 20**	**2 »**	**2 85**
	La série, non dentelée		61 »	

Tirages : 35 400 000, 28 900 000, 13 500 000 et 9 100 000.

1944. – ***88e anniversaire du maréchal Pétain. Taille-douce. Dentelés 13.***

Buste du maréchal (médaille, par Lavrillier).

606	**1 f. 50+3 f. 50 brun-noir**	4 60	2 75	4 60
	a. brun rosé	11 »	6 40	11 »
	b. (Non dentelé)		115 »	

Corporation paysanne.

Charte du travail.

607	**2 f. +3 f. bleu**	0 80	0 50	0 80
608	**4 f. +6 f. rose**	0 80	0 50	0 80
	La série, non dentelée		92 »	

Tirages : 1 100 000, 1 200 000 et 1 200 000.

1944. – ***Centenaire du service postal ambulant. Taille-douce. Dentelé 13.***

609	**1 f. 50 vert**	1 »	0 50	0 80
	(Sur lettre)			1 60
	(Seul sur lettre)			8 »
	a. (Non dentelé)		46 »	

Tirage : 3 070 000.

1944. – ***Château de Chenonceaux. Taille-douce. Dentelés 13.***

610	**15 f. brun-lilas**	0 80	0 30	0 65
	(Sur lettre)			1 60
	(Seul sur lettre)			8 »
	a. brun-noir	11 »	6 90	2 30
	b. (Non dentelé)		30 »	
	c. gris-noir	65 »	50 »	46 »
611	**25 f. noir**	1 »	0 50	0 80
	(Sur lettre)			1 60
	(Seul sur lettre)			8 »
	a. (Non dentelé)		61 »	

Tirages : 2 500 000 et 4 000 000.

Le n° 611, paru en octobre 1944, porte R F dans le coin supérieur droit.

1944. – ***Célébrités du XVIIe siècle. Taille-douce. Dentelés 13.***

J.-B. Poquelin, dit Molière (1622-1673).

Jules Hardouin dit Hardouin-Mansart (1646-1708).

Blaise Pascal (1623-1662).

612	**50 c. +1 f. 50 rouge carminé**	2 50	1 60	2 50
613	**80 c. +2 f. 20 vert foncé**	1 90	1 10	1 90
614	**1 f. 20+2 f. 80 noir**	1 90	1 10	1 90

Louis II, prince de Condé (1621-1686).

J.-B. Colbert (1619-1683).

Louis XIV (1638-1715), par Rigaud.

615	**1 f. 50+3 f. 50 outremer**	1 90	1 10	1 90
616	**2 f. +4 f. brun-rouge**	1 90	1 10	1 90
617	**4 f. +6 f. vermillon**	1 90	1 10	1 90
	N°s 612 à 617 (6 val.)	**12 »**	**7 10**	**12 »**
	La série, non dentelée		245 »	

1944. – ***Centenaire des lignes de chemin de fer Paris-Orléans et Paris-Rouen. Au profit du Secours national. Taille-douce. Dentelé 13.***

618	**4 f. +6 f. noir**	2 60	1 60	2 30
	(Sur lettre)			8 »
	(Seul sur lettre)			30 »
	a. (Non dentelé)		61 »	

Tirage : 1 160 000.

1944. – ***Sesquicentenaire du télégraphe optique. Taille-douce. Dentelé 14 x 13.***

Claude Chappe (1763-1805), ingénieur.

619	**4 f. bleu**	0 30	0 15	0 30
	(Sur lettre)			3 »
	(Seul sur lettre)			15 50
	a. (Non dentelé)		23 »	

Tirage : 2 725 000.

Gouvernement Provisoire

1944. – ***Arc de Triomphe de l'Étoile. 1re série. Lithographié. Dentelés 11.***

620	**5 c. lilas-rose**	0 15	0 15	0 15
	(Sur lettre)			8 »
	(Seul sur lettre)			» »

621	**10 c. gris**	0 15	0 15	0 15
	(Sur lettre)			8 »
	(Seul sur lettre)			77 »
622	**25 c. brun-jaune**	0 15	0 15	0 15
	(Sur lettre)			8 »
	(Seul sur lettre)			61 »
623	**50 c. jaune-olive**	0 15	0 15	0 15
	(Sur lettre)			8 »
	(Seul sur lettre)			77 »
624	**1 f. vert**	0 15	0 15	0 15
	(Sur lettre)			8 »
	(Seul sur lettre)			77 »
625	**1 f. 50 rose**	0 15	0 15	0 15
	(Sur lettre)			8 »
	(Seul sur lettre)			15 50
	a. (Auréolé)	30 »	30 »	30 »
626	**2 f. 50 violet**	0 15	0 15	0 15
	(Sur lettre)			15 50
	(Seul sur lettre)			110 »
627	**4 f. bleu**	0 15	0 15	0 15
	(Sur lettre)			9 15
	(Seul sur lettre)			15 50
628	**5 f. gris-noir**	0 30	0 30	0 30
	(Sur lettre)			30 »
	(Seul sur lettre)			110 »
629	**10 f. orange**	38 50	21 50	27 50
	(Sur lettre)			155 »
	(Seul sur lettre)			460 »
	N°s 620 à 629 (10 val.)	**40 »**	**23 »**	**29 »**

Cette série a été imprimée aux États-Unis.

Les 50 c. et 1 f. 50 ont reparu en 1945, mais avec chiffres en noir, en même temps que d'autres valeurs (n°s 702 à 711).

1944. – ***Série d'Alger. Coq et Marianne (d'Alger). Lithographié. Dentelés 12.***

630	**10 c. vert-jaune**	0 15	0 15	0 15
	(Sur lettre)			23 »
	(Seul sur lettre)			» »
631	**30 c. lilas foncé**	0 50	0 30	0 50
	(Sur lettre)			23 »
	(Seul sur lettre)			125 »
632	**40 c. bleu**	0 15	0 15	0 15
	(Sur lettre)			23 »
	(Seul sur lettre)			125 »
633	**50 c. rouge**	0 15	0 15	0 15
	(Sur lettre)			23 »
	(Seul sur lettre)			230 »

Nº 635a

634	**60 c. sépia**	0 15	0 15	0 15
	(Sur lettre)			30 »
	(Seul sur lettre)			230 »
635	**70 c. lilas-rose**	0 15	0 15	0 15
	(Sur lettre)			23 »
	(Seul sur lettre)			125 »
	a. (bonnet à pointe)	30 »	30 »	30 »
636	**80 c. vert-jaune**	1 40	0 80	1 40
	(Sur lettre)			23 »
	(Seul sur lettre)			155 »

637	**1 f. violet**	0 30	0 15	0 30
	(Sur lettre)			15 50
	(Seul sur lettre)			155 »
638	**1 f. 20 rouge carminé**	0 30	0 15	0 30
	(Sur lettre)			15 50
	(Seul sur lettre)			185 »
639	**1 f. 50 bleu**	0 15	0 15	0 15
	(Sur lettre)			8 »
	(Seul sur lettre)			15 50
640	**2 f. gris-bleu**	0 15	0 15	0 15
	(Sur lettre)			15 50
	(Seul sur lettre)			230 »

641	**2 f. 40 vermillon**	1 85	1 10	1 85
	(Sur lettre)			40 »
	(Seul sur lettre)			915 »
642	**3 f. vert foncé**	0 30	0 15	0 30
	(Sur lettre)			23 »
	(Seul sur lettre)			125 »
643	**4 f. bleu clair**	0 30	0 15	0 30
	(Sur lettre)			15 50
	(Seul sur lettre)			61 »
644	**4 f. 50 noir**	0 15	0 15	0 15
	(Sur lettre)			15 50
	(Seul sur lettre)			46 »

645	**5 f. bleu-violet**	5 50	3 35	5 50
	(Sur lettre)			77 »
	(Seul sur lettre)			230 »
646	**10 f. violet**	6 »	3 85	6 »
	(Sur lettre)			77 »
	(Seul sur lettre)			» »
647	**15 f. sépia**	6 »	3 90	6 »
	(Sur lettre)			77 »
	(Seul sur lettre)			» »
648	**20 f. vert-noir**	5 35	3 40	5 35
	(Sur lettre)			77 »
	(Seul sur lettre)			305 »
	N°s 630 à 648 (19 val.)	**29 »**	**18 50**	**29 »**
	La série, non dentelée		500 »	

Les timbres au type Coq ont une gomme mate, peu visible.

1944. – ***Type Iris. Typographie. Dentelés 14 x 13½.***

N°				
649	**80 c. vert-jaune**	0 30	0 15	0 30
	(Sur lettre)			4 60
	(Seul sur lettre)			15 50
650	**1 f. bleu clair**	0 15	0 15	0 15
	(Sur lettre)			1 60
	(Seul sur lettre)			4 60
	a. (Bord de feuille filigrané)	30 »		
651	**1 f. 20 violet**	0 15	0 15	0 15
	(Sur lettre)			0 80
	(Seul sur lettre)			1 60
652	**1 f. 50 rouge-brun**	0 15	0 15	0 15
	(Sur lettre)			0 80
	a. bistre	0 15	0 15	0 15

N°				
653	**2 f. brun**	0 15	0 15	0 15
	(Sur lettre)			0 80
	(Seul sur lettre)			1 60
	a. (Bord de feuille filigrané)	120 »		
654	**2 f. 40 rose carminé**	0 30	0 15	0 30
	(Sur lettre)			3 »
	(Seul sur lettre)			46 »
655	**3 f. rouge-orange**	0 30	0 15	0 15
	(Sur lettre)			3 »
	(Seul sur lettre)			6 »
	a. (Bord de feuille filigrané)	30 »		
656	**4 f. bleu**	0 30	0 15	0 30
	(Sur lettre)			4 60
	(Seul sur lettre)			10 »
	N°s 649 à 656 (8 val.)	**1 80**	**1 20**	**1 65**
	La série, non dentelée		77 »	

1944. – ***Type Mercure. Timbres de 1942 (n°s 546 à 549) surchargés RF. Dentelés.***

N°				
657	**10 c. outremer**	0 15	0 15	0 15
	(Sur lettre)			1 60
	(Seul sur lettre)			8 »
658	**30 c. rouge**	0 15	0 15	0 15
	(Sur lettre)			1 60
	(Seul sur lettre)			4 60
659	**40 c. violet**	0 15	0 15	0 15
	(Sur lettre)			1 60
	(Seul sur lettre)			3 »
660	**50 c. turquoise**	0 15	0 15	0 15
	(Sur lettre)			0 80
	(Seul sur lettre)			1 60
	N°s 657 à 660 (4 val.)	**0 60**	**0 60**	**0 60**

1944. – ***Huitième centenaire de la basilique de Saint-Denis. Taille-douce. Dentelé 13.***

Tombeaux des rois de France dans la crypte.

N°				
661	**2 f. 40 brun-rouge**	0 50	0 30	0 50
	(Sur lettre)			4 60
	(Seul sur lettre)			155 »
	a. (Non dentelé)		40 »	

Tirage : 2 400 000.

1944. – ***Centenaire de la bataille de l'Isly (Algérie). Effigie du maréchal Bugeaud (1784-1849). Taille-douce. Dentelé 13.***

Thomas Robert Bugeaud, marquis de la Piconnerie.

N°				
662	**4 f. gris-vert**	0 30	0 15	0 30
	(Sur lettre)			4 60
	(Seul sur lettre)			23 »
	a. (Non dentelé)		40 »	

Tirage : 2 400 000.

1944. – ***Cathédrales. Au profit de l'Entraide française. Taille-douce. Dentelés 13.***

Angoulême.

Chartres.

Amiens.

N°				
663	**50 c. +1 f. 50 noir**	1 »	0 65	1 »
664	**80 c. +2 f. 20 lie-de-vin**	1 »	0 65	1 »
665	**1 f. 20+2 f. 80 brun-rouge**	1 »	0 65	1 »

Beauvais.

Albi.

N°				
666	**1 f. 50+3 f. 50 bleu**	1 »	0 65	1 »
667	**4 f. +6 f. orange**	1 »	0 65	1 »
	N°s 663 à 667 (5 val.)	**5 »**	**3 25**	**5 »**
	La série, non dentelée		345 »	

1944. – ***Journée du Timbre. Au profit de l'Entraide française. Taille-douce. Dentelé 13.***

Ecusson de Renouard de Villayer, créateur de la Petite Poste.

668	**1 f. 50+3 f. 50 brun**	0 30	0 15	0 30
	(Sur lettre)			4 60
	(Seul sur lettre)			16 »
	a. (Non dentelé)		46 »	

Tirage : 2 700 000.

1944

Du n° 599 au n° 668 :

70 timbres ****107** ***65** **⊙95**

1945. – ***Libération. Taille-douce. Dentelé 13.***

669	**4 f. bleu**	0 50	0 30	0 50
	(Sur lettre)			3 »
	(Seul sur lettre)			15 50
	a. (Non dentelé)		54 »	

Tirage : 7 500 000.

IVe République

1945-47. – ***Typographie. Dentelés 14 x 13½.***

Type Chaînes brisées.

670	**10 c. brun-noir**	0 15	0 15	0 15
	(Sur lettre)			3 »
	(Seul sur lettre)			40 »
671	**30 c. vert**	0 15	0 15	0 15
	(Sur lettre)			3 »
	(Seul sur lettre)			23 »
672	**40 c. lilas-rose**	0 35	0 15	0 35
	(Sur lettre)			3 »
	(Seul sur lettre)			23 »
673	**50 c. violet foncé**	0 15	0 15	0 15
	(Sur lettre)			3 »
	(Seul sur lettre)			15 50

Type Cérès de Mazelin.

674	**60 c. outremer**	0 15	0 15	0 15
	(Sur lettre)			3 »
	(Seul sur lettre)			23 »
675	**80 c. vert-jaune**	0 15	0 15	0 15
	(Sur lettre)			3 »
	(Seul sur lettre)			15 50
676	**1 f. rose-rouge**	0 15	0 15	0 15
	(Sur lettre)			3 »
	(Seul sur lettre)			4 60
677	**1 f. 20 brun-noir**	0 15	0 15	0 15
	(Sur lettre)			3 »
	(Seul sur lettre)			61 »

678	**1 f. 30 bleu**	0 15	0 15	0 15
	(Sur lettre)			3 »
	(Seul sur lettre)			11 »
679	**1 f. 50 lilas**	0 15	0 15	0 15
	(Sur lettre)			3 »
	(Seul sur lettre)			4 60
680	**2 f. vert-jaune**	0 15	0 15	0 15
	(Sur lettre)			3 »
	(Seul sur lettre)			4 60
681	**2 f. 50 brun**	0 15	0 15	0 15
	(Sur lettre)			3 »
	(Seul sur lettre)			4 60
	N°s 670 à 681 (12 val.)	**2 »**	**1 80**	**2 »**
	N°s 670 à 681, sauf 678 et 680, ▯, chaque		9	15

Le 90 c. vert au type Cérès de Mazelin n'existe qu'avec préoblitération (voir Préoblitérés n° 89).

1945. – ***Série de Londres. Marianne de Dulac. Taille-douce. Dentelés 11½ x 12½.***

682	**10 c. bleu**	0 15	0 15	0 15
	(Sur lettre)			3 »
	(Seul sur lettre)			46 »
683	**30 c. jaune-bistre**	0 15	0 15	0 15
	(Sur lettre)			3 »
	(Seul sur lettre)			30 »
684	**40 c. bleu-noir**	0 15	0 15	0 15
	(Sur lettre)			3 »
	(Seul sur lettre)			30 »

685	**50 c. vermillon**	0 15	0 15	0 15
	(Sur lettre)			3 »
	(Seul sur lettre)			92 »

686 **60 c. bleu-gris** 0 15 0 15 0 15
(Sur lettre) 3 »
(Seul sur lettre) 92 »

687 **70 c. brun-violet** 0 15 0 15 0 15
(Sur lettre) 3 »
(Seul sur lettre) 46 »

688 **80 c. vert** 0 15 0 15 0 15
(Sur lettre) 3 »
(Seul sur lettre) 15 50

689 **1 f. lilas** 0 15 0 15 0 15
(Sur lettre) 3 »
(Seul sur lettre) 6 »

690 **1 f. 20 noir-olive** 0 15 0 15 0 15
(Sur lettre) 3 »
(Seul sur lettre) 40 »

691 **1 f. 50 groseille** 0 15 0 15 0 15
(Sur lettre) 3 »
(Seul sur lettre) 4 60

692 **2 f. brun** 0 15 0 15 0 15
(Sur lettre) 3 »
(Seul sur lettre) 4 60

693 **2 f. 40 rouge** 0 15 0 15 0 15
(Sur lettre) 3 »
(Seul sur lettre) 305 »
a. (Non dentelé) 900 » 750 »

694 **3 f. olive** 0 15 0 15 0 15
(Sur lettre) 3 »
(Seul sur lettre) 8 »

695 **4 f. outremer** 0 30 0 15 0 30
(Sur lettre) 3 »
(Seul sur lettre) 15 50

696 **4 f. 50 gris foncé** 0 30 0 15 0 30
(Sur lettre) 3 »
(Seul sur lettre) 23 »

697 **5 f. orange** 0 30 0 15 0 30
(Sur lettre) 8 »
(Seul sur lettre) 46 »

698 **10 f. vert clair** 0 30 0 15 0 30
(Sur lettre) 8 »
(Seul sur lettre) 46 »

699 **15 f. lie-de-vin** 0 50 0 15 0 30
(Sur lettre) 15 50
(Seul sur lettre) 77 »

700 **20 f. brun-orange** 2 15 1 10 1 85
(Sur lettre) 15 50
(Seul sur lettre) 61 »

701 **50 f. violet foncé** 4 20 2 30 3 »
(Sur lettre) 23 »
(Seul sur lettre) 77 »

Nos 682 à 701 (20 val.) **10 »** **6 10** **8 30**

Imprimés à Londres chez De La Rue.

Toutes les valeurs existent, non dentelées, souvent collées sur les feuilles de De La Rue. (valeur : 460 » chaque).

1942. – *Marianne de Dulac. Dentelés 15 x 14.*

Dès 1942 deux séries de trois valeurs chacune, portant la même effigie mais avec encadrement différent avaient été imprimées en héliogravure chez Harrison and Sons et livrées au gouvernement de la France Libre du Général de Gaulle. Ces deux séries ne furent pas mises en cours.

Type **I**.

701A **25 c. *vert* (Type I)** 225 » 130 »
701B **1 f. *rose-rouge* (Type I)** 225 » 130 »
701C **2 f.50 *outremer* (Type I)** 225 » 130 »

Type **II**.

701D **25 c. *vert* (Type II)** 40 » 27 »
701E **1 f. *rose-rouge* (Type II)** 40 » 27 »
701F **2 f.50 *outremer* (Type II)** 40 » 27 »

1945. – *Type Arc de Triomphe de 1944. 2e série. Chiffres de la valeur en noir. Lithographié. Dentelés 11.*

702 **30 c. orange** 0 15 0 15 0 15
(Sur lettre) 3 »
(Seul sur lettre) 30 »

703 **40 c. gris** 0 15 0 15 0 15
(Sur lettre) 3 »
(Seul sur lettre) 40 »

704 **50 c. jaune-olive** 0 15 0 15 0 15
(Sur lettre) 3 »
(Seul sur lettre) 46 »

705 **60 c. violet** 0 15 0 15 0 15
(Sur lettre) 3 »
(Seul sur lettre) 46 »

706	**80 c. vert-jaune**	0 15	0 15	0 15
	(Sur lettre)			3 »
	(Seul sur lettre)			30 »
707	**1 f. 20 brun**	0 15	0 15	0 15
	(Sur lettre)			3 »
	(Seul sur lettre)			30 »
708	**1 f. 50 rouge**	0 15	0 15	0 15
	(Sur lettre)			3 »
	(Seul sur lettre)			30 »
709	**2 f. jaune-orange**	0 15	0 15	0 15
	(Sur lettre)			3 »
	(Seul sur lettre)			30 »
710	**2 f. 40 rose carminé**	0 15	0 15	0 15
	(Sur lettre)			6 »
	(Seul sur lettre)			385 »
711	**3 f. lilas**	0 15	0 15	0 15
	(Sur lettre)			6 »
	(Seul sur lettre)			46 »
	Nos 702 à 711 (10 val.)	**1 50**	**1 50**	**1 50**

Série imprimée aux États-Unis.

1945-47. – *Marianne de Gandon. Format 17* x *21. Typographie. Dentelés 14* x *13½.*

N° 712

N° 722a

712	**1 f. 50 rose carminé**	0 15	0 15	0 15
	(Seul sur lettre)			8 »
	a. (Sans f après 1)	12 50	8 »	4 »
713	**2 f. vert**	0 15	0 15	0 15
	(Seul sur lettre)			1 60
	a. vert foncé	0 30	0 15	0 15
	b. (2 sans f)	14 »	8 40	5 50
714	**2 f. 40 rouge**	0 50	0 15	0 50
	(Seul sur lettre)			460 »
715	**3 f. brun foncé**	0 15	0 15	0 15
	(Seul sur lettre)			1 60
	a. brun-noir	0 30	0 15	0 30
716	**3 f. rose**	0 15	0 15	0 15
	(Seul sur lettre)			1 60
	a. rose carminé	0 30	0 15	0 15
716A	**3 f. vert**	2 30	1 10	0 50
	(Seul sur lettre)			3 »
716B	**3 f. 50 rouge-brun**	1 »	0 50	0 65
	(Seul sur lettre)			4 60
717	**4 f. outremer**	0 15	0 15	0 15
	(Seul sur lettre)			30 »
	a. bleu	0 30	0 15	0 30
718	**4 f. violet clair**	0 15	0 15	0 15
	(Seul sur lettre)			15 50
	a. violet vif	0 30	0 15	0 30
718A	**4 f. 50 bleu**			0 15
	(Seul sur lettre)			15 50
	(Non dentelé)		305 »	
719	**5 f. vert**	0 30	0 15	0 15
	(Seul sur lettre)			8 »
719A	**5 f. rose**	0 15	0 15	0 15
	(Sur lettre)			8 »
	(Sur lettre des 1 ou 2/1/47)			460 »

Le no 719A, vendu à la poste avec un rabais de 10 %, n'affranchissait que pour 4 f. 50.

719B	**5 f. bleu**	0 30	0 15	0 30
	(Seul sur lettre)			3 »
	(Non dentelé)		305 »	

Mèches reliées.

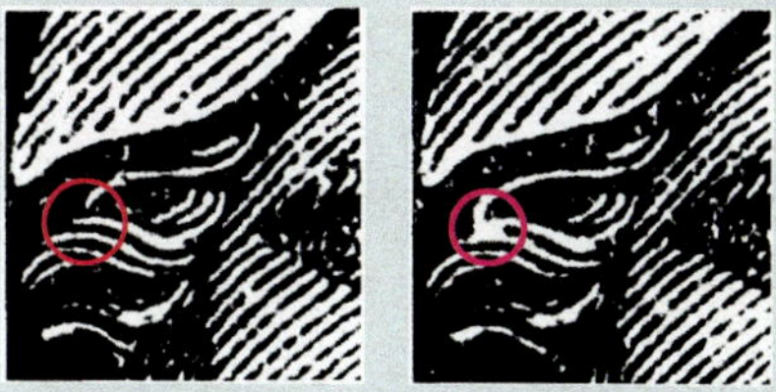

Cette variété existant sur les cases 44 et 94 a été retouchée au cours des tirages du 6 f. rose.

Mèches croisées.

Cette variété existe sur les cases 15 et 65.

720	**6 f. bleu-violet**	0 30	0 15	0 30
	(Seul sur lettre)			1 60
	a. (Mèches reliées)	28 »	20 »	11 50
	b. (Mèches croisées)	28 »	20 »	11 50
721	**6 f. rouge**	2 »	1 10	1 30
	(Seul sur lettre)			30 »
	a. (Mèches reliées)	28 »	20 »	14 »
	b. (Mèches croisées)	28 »	20 »	14 »
721A	**6 f. rose carminé**	0 30	0 15	0 15
	(Seul sur lettre)			3 »
	a. (Mèches reliées)	28 »	20 »	11 50
	b. (Mèches reliées, retouché)	54 »	40 »	17 »
	c. (Mèches croisées)	28 »	20 »	11 50
722	**10 f. orange**	0 80	0 45	0 65
	(Seul sur lettre)			30 »
	a. (Boucle d'oreille)	50 »	40 »	25 »
723	**10 f. bleu**	2 »	1 10	1 »
	(Seul sur lettre)			125 »
724	**15 f. lilas-rose**	4 »	2 30	2 30
	(Seul sur lettre)			30 »
	Nos 712 à 724 (19 val.)	**14 85**	**8 35**	**9 »**

Nos 712, 713, 714, 715, 716, 717, 719, 720, 721, 722, 723 et 724 (12 valeurs), non dentelés 215 »

Voir, de 1948 à 1953, les valeurs au même type parues dans d'autres couleurs (nos 806 à 813, 827, 883 à 887, 968 et Préoblitérés n° 95) et celles émises en 1949 à l'occasion de l'Exposition du centenaire du Timbre (nos 832 et 833).

1945-47. – *Marianne de Gandon. Taille douce. Dentelure 14* x *13, sauf n° 730, 731, 732, 733 : 13.*

Format 18 x *22.*

725	**4 f. bleu**	0 30	0 15	0 30
	(Seul sur lettre)			8 »
726	**10 f. bleu**	1 60	0 80	0 65
	(Seul sur lettre)			46 »
727	**15 f. lilas-rose**	11 »	6 »	2 50
	(Seul sur lettre)			77 »
	a. lilas-rose pâle	12 50	6 90	2 30

728	**20 f. vert**	1 60	0 80	0 65
	(Seul sur lettre)			46 »
	a. vert pâle	1 85	1 10	0 80
729	**25 f. orange**	11 »	5 80	1 85
	(Seul sur lettre)			92 »

Format 22 x 36.

730	**20 f. vert**	1 60	1 »	1 40
	(Seul sur lettre)			92 »
	(Non dentelé)		115 »	
731	**25 f. violet**	2 »	1 10	1 60
	(Seul sur lettre)			54 »
	(Non dentelé)		115 »	
	a. lilas-gris	3 85	2 30	2 »
732	**50 f. brun-rouge**	2 40	1 25	2 40
	(Seul sur lettre)			54 »
	(Non dentelé)		535 »	

" à la bretetelle "

733	**100 f. carmin**	15 50	9 10	7 65
	(Seul sur lettre)			230 »
	(Non dentelé)		535 »	
	a. rose	17 »	11 »	8 40
	b. (à la bretelle)	150 »	90 »	50 »
	Nos 725 à 733 (9 val.)	**47 »**	**26 »**	**19 »**
	Nos 725 à 729 (5 valeurs), non dentelés		110 »	

1945. – *Libération de Metz et de Strasbourg. Armoiries. Taille-douce. Dentelés 14 x 13.*

Metz.

Strasbourg.

734	**2 f. 40 bleu**	0 30	0 15	0 30
	(Sur lettre)			8 »
	(seul sur carte postale pour l'étranger)			155 »
735	**4 f. brun-noir**	0 30	0 15	0 30
	(Sur lettre)			8 »
	(Seul sur lettre)			30 »
	La paire, non dentelée		70 »	

Tirages : 5 035 000 et 5 040 000.

1945. – *Au profit des tuberculeux. Typographie. Dentelé 14 x 13½.*

736	**2 f. +1 f. orange**	0 30	0 15	0 30
	a. (Non dentelé)		20 »	

Est reparu surchargé en 1945 (n° 750).

Tirage : 38 000 000.

1945. – *Au profit des victimes de guerre des P.T.T. Taille-douce. Dentelé 13.*

737	**4 f. +6 f. brun-lilas**	0 30	0 15	0 30
	a. (Non dentelé)		42 »	

Tirage : 5 050 000.

1945. – *Centenaire de la naissance de Sarah Bernhardt (1844-1923). Au profit de la fondation Coquelin. Taille-douce. Dentelé 13.*

Rosine Bernard dite Sarah Bernhardt par Bastien-Lepage.

738	**4 f. +1 f. brun-lilas**	0 50	0 30	0 50
	a. (Non dentelé)		77 »	

Tirage : 4 500 000.

1945. – *Libération de l'Alsace et de la Lorraine. Taille-douce. Dentelé 13.*

Alsacienne et Lorraine, Cathédrales de Strasbourg et de Metz.

739	**4 f. rouge-brun**	0 30	0 15	0 30
	a. (Non dentelé)		54 »	

Tirage : 4 950 000.

1945. – ***Au profit de la Croisade de l'air pur. Taille-douce. Dentelé 13.***

740	**4 f. +2 f. vert-bleu**	0 30	0 15	0 30
	a. (Non dentelé)		46 »	

Tirage : 3 500 000.

1945. – ***La France d'Outre-mer. Type de 1940 avec millésime 1945 et Croix de Lorraine. Taille-douce. Dentelé 13.***

741	**2 f. bleu-vert (453)**	0 30	0 15	0 30
	a. (Non dentelé)		30 »	

Tirage : 4 250 000.

1945. – ***Anniversaire de la destruction d'Oradour-sur-Glane. Au profit de l'Entraide française. Taille-douce. Dentelé 13.***

L'incendie de l'Église.

742	**4 f. +2 f. gris**	0 30	0 15	0 30
	a. (Non dentelé)		40 »	

Tirage : 4 500 000.

1945. – ***Journée du Timbre. Effigie de Louis XI. Au profit de l'Entraide française. Taille-douce. Dentelé 13.***

Louis XI (1423-1483).

743	**2 f. +3 f. bleu**	0 65	0 30	0 65
	a. (Non dentelé)		50 »	

Tirage : 3 530 000.

1945. – ***Au profit de l'Entraide française. Taille-douce. Dentelés 13.***

Place Jean Bart, à Dunkerque.

Cathédrale et quais de Rouen.

744	**1 f. 50+1 f. 50 rouge-brun**	0 65	0 50	0 65
745	**2 f. +2 f. violet**	0 65	0 50	0 65

Eglise Saint-Jean, à Caen.

Les remparts, à Saint-Malo.

746	**2 f. 40+2 f. 60 bleu**	0 65	0 50	0 65
747	**4 f. +4 f. noir**	0 65	0 50	0 65
	N°s 744 à 747 (4 val.)	**2 60**	**2 »**	**2 60**
	La série, non dentelée		185 »	

1945

Du n° 669 au n° 747

(sauf n° 701A à 701F) :

85 timbres ****82** ***48** **⊙46**

1946. – ***Propagande sanitaire. Taille-douce. Dentelés 13.***

Alfred Fournier (1839-1914), médecin.

Henri Becquerel (1852-1908), prix Nobel de Physique, 1903.

748	**2 f. +3 f. rouge-brun**	0 50	0 30	0 50
749	**2 f. +3 f. violet**	0 50	0 30	0 50
	La paire, non dentelée		110 »	

Le n° 748 a été émis en bleu-noir en 1947 (n° 789).

1946. – ***Timbre de 1945 (n° 736) surchargé :***

750	**3 f. s. 2 f. +1 f. orange (736)**	0 30	0 15	0 30

Tirage : 11 700 000.

1946. – *Pour les plus grands invalides de guerre. Taille-douce. Dentelé 13.*

Chapelle des Invalides, à Paris.

751	**4 f. +6 f. rouge-brun**	0 50	0 30	0 50
	a. (Non dentelé)		40 »	

Tirage : 2 300 000.

1946. – *Pour les oeuvres de la marine. Taille-douce. Dentelé 13.*

Bâtiments de ligne.

752	**2 f. +3 f. noir**	1 »	0 65	1 »
	a. (Papier mince)	1 85	1 »	1 10
	b. (Non dentelé)		125 »	

Tirage : 2 525 000.

1946. – *Pour le Musée postal. Taille-douce. Dentelé 13.*

"Le cachet de cire", d'après J.-B. Chardin (1699-1779).

753	**2 f. +3 f. rouge-brun**	0 65	0 30	0 65
	a. (Papier mince)	1 60	1 »	1 10
	b. (Non dentelé)		155 »	

Tirage : 2 640 000.

1946. – *Journée du Timbre. Taille-douce. Dentelé 13.*

Guillaume Fouquet, marquis de La Varane (1560-1616), et chapelle du Prytanée de la Flèche.

754	**3 f. +2 f. brun-noir**	0 80	0 50	0 80
	a. (Non dentelé)		84 »	

Tirage : 3 100 000.

1946. – *Armoiries de Provinces (III). Typographie. Dentelés 14* x *13½.*

Corse.

Alsace.

755	**10 c. outremer et noir**	0 15	0 15	0 15
	a. bleu-gris et noir	0 30	0 15	0 30
756	**30 c. noir, rouge et jaune**	0 15	0 15	0 15

Lorraine.

Nice.

757	**50 c. brun, jaune et rouge**	0 15	0 15	0 15
758	**60 c. noir, rouge et outremer**	0 15	0 15	0 15
	N°s 755 à 758 (4 val.)	**0 60**	**0 60**	**0 60**
	La série, non dentelée		61 »	

Tirages : 71 900 000, 129 900 000, 244 500 000 et 64 600 000.

1946. – *Monuments et sites. Taille-douce. Dentelés 13.*

Vézelay.

Palais du Luxembourg, oeuvre de Salomon de Brosse (1571-1626).

759	**5 f. lilas**	0 30	0 15	0 30
760	**10 f. bleu**	0 30	0 15	0 30
	a. bleu clair	0 30	0 15	0 30
	b. (Non dentelé)		840 »	

Tirages : 34 500 000 et 124 300 000.

Un 12 f. rose carminé et un 15 f. rouge, Palais du Luxembourg, ont paru en 1948 (n°s 803 et 804).

1946. – *Conférence de la paix, à Paris. Taille-douce. Dentelés 13.*

761	**3 f. vert foncé**	0 30	0 15	0 30
762	**10 f. bleu**	0 30	0 15	0 30
	La paire, non dentelée		110 »	

Tirages : 15 000 000 et 10 000 000.

1946. – ***Monuments et sites. Taille-douce. Dentelés 13.***

Rocamadour.

Pointe du Raz.

763	**15 f. brun-lilas**	5 35	3 »	0 65
764	**20 f. bleu-noir**	1 60	0 80	0 30
	a. (Non dentelé)	840 »		

Tirages : 46 850 000 et 185 300 000.

1946. – ***Célébrités du XVe siècle. Taille-douce. Dentelés 13.***

Villon.

Fouquet.

Commynes.

765	**2 f. +1 f. vert foncé**	1 90	1 25	1 90
766	**3 f. +1 f. noir**	1 90	1 25	1 90
	a. (Bonnet à pointe)	40 »	25 »	30 »
	b. (Non dentelé)		500 »	
767	**4 f. +3 f. brun-rouge**	1 90	1 25	1 90

Jeanne d'Arc.

Jean Charlier, dit Jean de Gerson.

Charles VII.

768	**5 f. +4 f. outremer**	2 10	1 25	2 10
769	**6 f. +5 f. sépia**	2 10	1 50	2 10
770	**10 f. +6 f. rouge**	2 10	1 50	2 10
	a. (Papier mince)	14 »	9 15	14 »
N°s 765 à 770 (6 val.)		**12 »**	**8 »**	**12 »**

1946. – ***Conférence générale de l'U.N.E.S.C.O. (Organisation pour le développement de l'éducation, des sciences et de la culture dans les Nations Unies), à Paris. Taille-douce. Dentelé 13.***

771	**10 f. bleu**	0 30	0 15	0 30

Tirage : 5 000 000.

> **1946**
>
> **Du n° 748 au n° 771 :**
>
> **24 timbres** ****25** ***16** **⊙19**

1947. – ***Cathédrales et Basiliques. Taille-douce. Dentelés 13.***

Basilique romane Saint-Sernin, de Toulouse.

Basilique Notre-Dame du Port, à Clermont-Ferrand.

772	**1 f. +1 f. rose**	1 30	0 80	1 30
773	**3 f. +2 f. bleu-noir**	3 70	2 15	3 70

Saint-Front, de Périgueux.

Saint-Julien, Le Mans.

774	**4 f. +3 f. brun-rouge**	1 90	1 10	1 90
775	**6 f. +4 f. bleu**	1 90	1 10	1 90

Notre-Dame de Paris.

776	**10 f. +6 f. vert**	3 70	2 15	3 70
N°s 772 à 776 (5 val.)		**12 50**	**7 30**	**12 50**

1947. – *Monuments et sites. Taille-douce. Dentelés 13.*

La Croisette, à Cannes.

Place Stanislas, à Nancy.

777	**6 f. rouge**	1 85	1 10	0 80
778	**25 f. brun-noir**	5 35	3 »	0 50

Tirages : 16 350 000 et 72 800 000.

Ce dernier a reparu en bleu en 1948 (nº 822).

1947. – *Journée du Timbre. Michel Le Tellier, marquis de Louvois. Taille-douce. Dentelé 13.*

779	**4 f. 50+5 f. 50 rose carminé**	1 85	1 10	1 85
	a. (Papier mince)	10 »	6 »	10 »

Tirage : 2 200 000.

1947. – *12e Congrès de l'Union Postale Universelle, à Paris. Taille-douce. Dentelés 13.* ✈

Colonnade du Louvre.

La Conciergerie.

780	**3 f. 50 brun-lilas**	0 50	0 30	0 50
781	**4 f. 50 bleu-gris**	0 70	0 50	0 50

La Cité.

Place de la Concorde.

782	**6 f. rouge**	1 40	0 80	1 25
783	**10 f. outremer**	1 40	0 80	1 25
	a. bleu	2 60	1 70	2 60
	Nos 780 à 783 (4 val.)	**4 »**	**2 40**	**3 50**

Tirages : 2 500 000, 4 500 000, 2 500 000 et 3 500 000.

La série, non dentelée

1947. – *Centenaire de la naissance de l'explorateur Auguste Pavie. Taille-douce. Dentelé 13.*

784	**4 f. 50 brun foncé**	0 50	0 30	0 50

Tirage : 2 000 000.

1947. – *En l'honneur de Fénelon. Taille-douce. Dentelé 13.*

François de Salignac de la Mothe-Fénélon.

785	**4 f. 50 brun-lilas**	0 50	0 30	0 50

Tirage : 2 000 000.

1947. – *5e anniversaire du débarquement britannique à Saint-Nazaire. Taille-douce. Dentelé 13.*

Monument commémoratif.

786	**6 f. +4 f. bleu-noir**	0 80	0 50	0 80

Tirage : 1 800 000.

1947. – *Jamboree mondial, à Moisson. Taille-douce. Dentelé 13.*

Emblème scout.

787	**5 f. brun**	0 50	0 30	0 50

Tirage : 2 875 000.

1947. – *Voie de la Liberté. Taille-douce. Dentelé 13.*

Une des bornes de la Voie de la Liberté, à Ste-Mère-Église.

788	**6 f. +4 f. vert-bleu**	1 25	0 80	1 25
	a. (anneau sur la flamme)	30 »	20 »	28 »

Tirage : 1 900 000.

1947. – *Alfred Fournier. Type de 1946 (n° 748). Taille-douce. Dentelé 13.*

789	**2 f. +3 f. bleu-noir (748)**	0 50	0 30	0 50

Tirage : 1 970 000.

1947. – *Résistance. Taille-douce. Dentelé 13.*

790	**5 f. sépia**	0 80	0 50	0 80

Tirage : 2 500 000.

1947. – *Timbre de 1945-47 (Cérès, n° 678) surchargé :*

791	**1 f. s. 1 f. 30 bleu (R) (678)**	0 15	0 15	0 15

Tirage : 18 300 000.

1947. – *Abbaye de Conques. Taille-douce. Dentelé 13.*

792	**15 f. brun-orange**	5 35	3 »	1 25

Voir au n° 805 un 18 f. bleu au même type.

Tirage : 22 700 000.

> **1947**
>
> **Du n° 772 au n° 792 :**
>
> **21 timbres** ****36** ***21** **⊙25**

1948. – *Au bénéfice de l'Entraide française. Effigie de Louis Braille. Taille-douce. Dentelé 13.*

793	**6 f. +4 f. violet**	0 50	0 30	0 50

Tirage : 1 900 000.

1948. – *Journée du Timbre et centenaire de l'institution du Timbre-poste par Étienne Arago. Taille-douce. Dentelé 13.*

794	**6 f. +4 f. sépia**	0 80	0 50	0 80

Tirage : 2 160 000.

1948. – ***Centenaire de la Révolution de 1848. Taille-douce. Dentelés 13.***

Alphonse Marie-Louis de Prat de Lamartine (1790-1869).

Alexandre-Auguste Ledru-Rollin (1807-1874).

Louis Blanc (1811-1882).

795	**1 f. +1 f. vert**	1 60	1 »	1 60
796	**3 f. +2 f. rouge-brun**	1 60	1 »	1 60
797	**4 f. +3 f. brun-lilas**	1 60	1 »	1 60

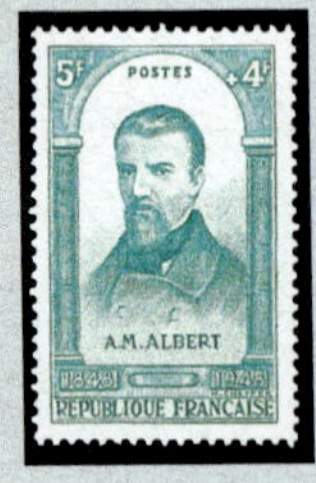

A.-M. Albert (1815-1895).

Pierre Joseph Proudhon (1809-1865).

Louis-Auguste Blanqui (1805-1881).

798	**5 f. +4 f. émeraude**	4 »	2 50	4 »
799	**6 f. +5 f. bleu-noir**	3 10	1 85	3 10
800	**10 f. +6 f. carmin**	3 10	1 85	3 10

Armand Barbès (1809-1870).

Mgr Denis-Auguste Affre (1793-1848).

801	**15 f. +7 f. bleu-vert**	4 »	2 15	4 »
802	**20 f. +8 f. violet**	4 »	2 15	4 »
	N°s 795 à 802 (8 val.)	**23 »**	**13 50**	**23 »**
	La série, non dentelée		185 »	

1948. – ***Palais du Luxembourg. Type de 1946 (n° 760). Légende FRANCE au lieu de R.F. Taille-douce. Dentelés 13.***

803	**12 f. rose carminé**	3 85	2 30	0 80
804	**15 f. rouge**	1 »	0 50	1 »

Tirages : 25 300 000 et 8 000 000.

1948. – ***Abbaye de Conques. Type de 1947 (n° 792). Légende FRANCE au lieu de RÉPUBLIQUE FRANÇAISE. Taille-douce. Dentelé 13.***

805	**18 f. bleu (792)**	5 35	2 75	0 50

Tirage : 44 000 000.

1948. – ***Type Marianne de Gandon. Format 17 x 21. Typographie. Dentelés 14 x 13½.*** [C]

806	**3 f. rose-lilas**	0 30	0 15	0 30
807	**4 f. émeraude**	0 30	0 15	0 30
808	**4 f. orange**	3 70	2 15	1 10

809	**5 f. vert clair**	1 »	0 65	0 30
810	**8 f. bleu clair**	0 50	0 30	0 30

811	**10 f. lilas**	0 30	0 15	0 15
	a. (Sans le "F" après le 10)	60 »	60 »	60 »
812	**12 f. outremer**	3 70	2 15	0 50
	a. (Non dentelé)	30 »		

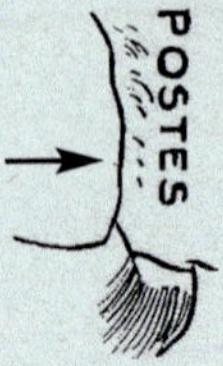

Type I

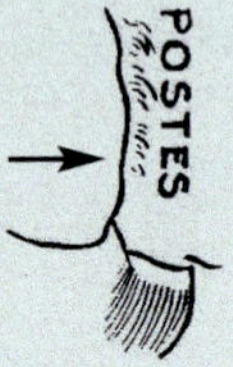

Type II

813	**15 f. rouge (I)**	1 20	0 50	0 15
	a. (Type II)	20 »	13 »	5 »
	b. (avec band. publ.) (II)	20 »	13 »	6 »
	c. (Non dentelé) (I)		20 »	
	N°s 806 à 813 (8 val.)	**11 »**	**6 20**	**3 10**

Voir au n° 95 des Préoblitérés, le 2 f. 50, brun, au même type.

1948. – ***1er Congrès international du B. C. G. (Bacille, Calmette-Guérin). Taille-douce. Dentelé 13.***

Calmette dans son laboratoire.

814	**6 f. +4 f. bleu-vert**	1 »	0 50	0 80

Tirage : 1 800 000.

1948. – ***Anniversaire de la mort du général Leclerc de Hauteclocque (1902-1947). Taille-douce. Dentelé 13.***

Leclerc et cathédrale de Strasbourg.

815	**6 f. noir**	0 50	0 30	0 50
	a. (Non dentelé)		40 »	

Un 8 f. brun-rouge et un 12 f. olive et bleu-gris au même type ont été émis en 1953-54 avec la légende GÉNÉRAL LECLERC, MARÉCHAL DE FRANCE (nos 942 et 984).

Tirage : 8 100 000.

1948. – ***Centenaire de la mort de François-René, Vicomte de Chateaubriand. Taille-douce. Dentelé 13.***

Chateaubriand et le château de Combourg.

816	**18 f. bleu**	0 50	0 30	0 50
	a. (Non dentelé)		40 »	

Tirage : 2 480 000.

1948. – ***Barrage de Génissiat. Taille-douce. Dentelé 13.***

Barrage de Génissiat.

817	**12 f. rose carminé**	1 »	0 50	1 »
	a. (Non dentelé)		40 »	

Tirage : 2 000 000.

1948. – ***Assemblée générale des Nations Unies, à Paris, Palais de Chaillot. Taille-douce. Dentelés 13.***

Palais de Chaillot. — Palais de Chaillot.

818	**12 f. rouge carminé**	0 65	0 30	0 65
819	**18 f. bleu-noir**	0 65	0 50	0 65
	La paire, non dentelée	305 »		

Tirages : 3 000 000 et 3 500 000.

1948. – ***Transfert, au Panthéon des cendres de célébrités. Taille-douce. Dentelés 14 x 13.***

Paul Langevin. — Jean Perrin.

820	**5 f. brun-rouge**	0 50	0 30	0 30
821	**8 f. bleu-vert**	0 50	0 30	0 30
	La paire, non dentelée		50 »	

1948. – ***Place Stanislas, à Nancy. Type de 1947 (n° 778). Taille-douce. Dentelé 13.***

822	**25 f. bleu (778)**	14 »	7 65	1 60

Tirage : 8 000 000.

> **1948**
>
> **Du n° 793 au n° 822 :**
>
> **30 timbres** ****65 *37 ⊙36**

1949. – ***Série des métiers. Taille-douce. Dentelés 13.***

Agriculteur. — Marin pêcheur.

823	**3 f. +1 f. lilas-brun**	1 20	0 65	0 80
824	**5 f. +3 f. bleu**	1 20	0 65	1 »
	a. (Double galon sur la manche)	40 »	23 »	9 15

Mineur. Métallurgiste.

825	**8 f. +4 f. bleu-noir**	1 20	0 65	1 »
826	**10 f. +6 f. rouge**	1 40	1 05	1 20
	N°s 823 à 826 (4 val.)	**5 »**	**3 »**	**4 »**
	La série, non dentelée		92 »	

Tirage : 1 600 000 séries.

1949. – ***Timbre de 1945-47 (Marianne de Gandon, n° 721A) surchargé :***

827	**5 f. s. 6 f. rose (721A)**	0 30	0 15	0 30
	a. (mèches reliées)	230 »	125 »	29 »
	b. (mèches reliées, retouché)	17 »	11 »	8 40
	c. (mèches croisées)	15 50	9 15	7 65

Pour explication des n°s 827a, b et c voir après le n° 733.

Tirage : 32 500 000.

1949. – ***Journée du Timbre. Portrait d'Étienne-François, duc de Choiseul (1719-1785) et malle-poste. Taille-douce. Dentelé 13.***

828	**15 f. +5 f. vert**	1 40	0 65	1 40
	a. (Non dentelé)		77 »	

Tirage : 1 800 000.

1949. – ***Expéditions polaires de Paul-Emile Victor. Taille-douce. Dentelé 13.***

829	**15 f. bleu-noir**	0 50	0 30	0 50
	a. (Non dentelé)		77 »	

Tirage : 3 450 000.

1949. – ***Centenaire du Timbre. Non dentelé, sauf n° 832, 833 : 14 x 13.***

Type de 1849-50 (Cérès).

Taille-douce. Non dentelés.

830	**15 f. rouge**	4 »	2 30	4 »
831	**25 f. bleu**	4 »	2 30	4 »

Type de 1945 (Marianne de Gandon).

Taille-douce. Dentelés 14 x 13.

832	**15 f. rouge**	4 »	2 30	4 »
833	**25 f. bleu**	4 »	2 30	4 »

Ces quatre timbres ont été imprimés par bandes verticales, les deux paires étant séparées par un intervalle portant la mention CENTENAIRE 1849-1949 DU TIMBRE-POSTE, imprimée en rouge-brun.

833A	La bande	20 »		20 »
	Idem, avec dentelure inversée	2 700 »		

Tirage : 2 520 000.

Le 10 f., émis à l'occasion de la CITEX, est catalogué sous le n° 841. Voir aussi la rubrique BF n° 5.

1949. – ***Armoiries de provinces (IV). Typographie. Dentelés 14 x 13½.***

Bourgogne. Guyenne. Savoie.

834	**10 c. outremer, rouge, jaune et noir**	0 15	0 15	0 15
835	**50 c. outremer, rouge, jaune et noir**	0 15	0 15	0 15
836	**1 f. brun et rouge**	0 65	0 30	0 50

Auvergne.

Anjou.

837	**2 f. vert, jaune et rouge**	0 65	0 30	0 30
838	**4 f. outremer, rouge et jaune**	0 50	0 15	0 50
	N°s 834 à 838 (5 val.)	**2 10**	**1 05**	**1 60**

Tirages : 145 010 000, 58 990 000, 94 060 000, 64 000 000 et 36 040 000.

La série, non dentelée

1949. – ***6e centenaire du rattachement du Dauphiné. Taille-douce. Dentelé 13.***

Collégiale St Barnard, à Romans et armoiries du Dauphiné.

839	**12 f. brun-rouge**	0 50	0 30	0 50
	a. (Non dentelé)		30 »	

Tirage : 2 550 000.

1949. – ***Amitié franco-américaine. Taille-douce. Dentelé 13.***

Ecussons des États-Unis et de la France.

840	**25 f. bleu et rouge**	0 80	0 50	0 80
	a. (Non dentelé)		92 »	

Tirage : 2 575 000.

1949. – ***Exposition philatélique internationale de Paris (CITEX). Type de 1849. Taille-douce. Non dentelé (bordure dentelée 13).*** BF ***n° 5.***

841	**10 f. (+100 f.) vermillon**	65 »	40 »	54 »
	a. (Non dentelé complet)	1 850 »	1 600 »	

Imprimés sur feuilles de 10 comme ci-dessous (voir bloc feuillet n° 5).

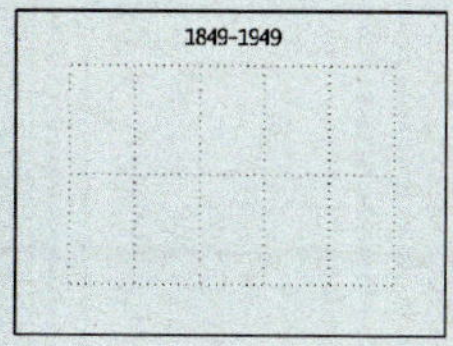

841b	(La bande horizontale de 3 timbres avec marge supérieure portant 1849-1949)	245 »	185 »	245 »

Le prix d'entrée à l'exposition (100 francs) donnait droit à l'achat d'un timbre (10 francs).

1949. – ***Monuments et sites. Taille-douce. Dentelés 13.***

Saint-Bertrand-de-Comminges.

Abbaye de Saint-Wandrille.

841A	**20 f. rouge-brique**	0 30	0 15	0 30
842	**25 f. outremer**	0 50	0 30	0 30

Vallée de la Meuse.

Mont Gerbier de Jonc.

842A	**40 f. vert-noir**	18 50	10 »	0 50
843	**50 f. brun violacé**	3 »	1 85	0 30
	a. brun-noir	28 »	20 »	12 »
	N°s 841A à 843 (4 val.)	**22 30**	**12 30**	**1 40**
	La série, non dentelée		100 »	

Tirages : 132 185 000, 133 345 000, 74 450 000 et 126 750 000.

Un 30 f. bleu clair, Abbaye St-Wandrille a paru en 1951 (n° 888).

1949. – ***Congrès international de Télégraphie et Téléphonie, à Paris. Taille-douce. Dentelés 13.*** ✈

Claude Chappe.

F. Arago et Ampère.

844	**10 f. rouge**	1 10	0 65	1 10
845	**15 f. brun-noir**	1 25	0 65	1 25

Emile Baudot.

Emile Baudot, erreur de date (1848 au lieu de 1845).

Général Ferrié.

846	**25 f. lie-de-vin**	3 »	2 »	2 75
846A	**25 f. *lie-de-vin***	4 200 »	3 200 »	
847	**50 f. bleu**	5 65	3 »	4 90
	N°s 844 à 847 (sauf n° 846A) (4 val.)	**11 »**	**6 30**	**10 »**

Tirages : 2 900 000, 3 390 000, 2 700 000, (nc) et 2 585 000.

La série (sans le 846A), non dentelée 215 »

Le n° 846A, portant une erreur de date (1848 au lieu de 1845), n'a pas été émis.

1949. – *250e anniversaire de la mort de Jean Racine (1639-1699). Taille-douce. Dentelé 13.*

848	**12 f. brun violacé**	0 50	0 30	0 50
	a. (Non dentelé)		27 »	

Tirage : 2 580 000.

1949. – *Assemblée des présidents de Chambres de Commerce de l'Union française, à Paris. Taille-douce. Dentelé 13.*

849	**15 f. rouge carminé**	0 30	0 15	0 30
	a. (Non dentelé)		27 »	

Tirage : 2 800 000.

1949. – *75e anniversaire de l'U.P.U. Taille-douce. Dentelés 13.*

850	**5 f. vert**	0 30	0 15	0 30
851	**15 f. rouge**	0 50	0 30	0 30
852	**25 f. bleu**	1 60	1 10	1 10

La série, non dentelée 690 »

Tirages : 2 000 000, 3 000 000 et 2 000 000.

1949. – *Célébrités du XVIIIe siècle (I). Taille-douce. Dentelés 13.*

Charles de Secondat, baron de La Brède et de Montesquieu.

François Marie Arouet, dit Voltaire.

Antoine Watteau.

853	**5 f. +1 f. vert**	4 »	2 30	4 »
854	**8 f. +2 f. bleu-noir**	4 »	2 30	4 »
855	**10 f. +3 f. brun-rouge**	4 60	2 70	4 60

George Louis Leclerc, comte de Buffon.

Joseph François, marquis Dupleix.

Anne Robert Jacques Turgot, baron de l'Aulne.

856	**12 f. +4 f. violet**	4 60	2 70	4 60
857	**15 f. +5 f. rouge**	6 »	4 »	6 »
858	**25 f. +10 f. bleu**	7 80	5 »	7 80
	N°s 853 à 858 (6 val.)	**31 »**	**19 »**	**31 »**

La série, non dentelée 305 »

1949. – *Série des saisons. Bas-reliefs de la Fontaine de Bouchardon, rue de Grenelle, à Paris. Taille-douce. Dentelés 13.*

Printemps.

Eté.

859	**5 f. +1 f. vert**	2 20	1 10	2 15
860	**8 f. +2 f. jaune et brun**	2 80	1 60	2 75

Automne.

Hiver.

861	**12 f. +3 f. violet**	3 »	1 60	2 75
862	**15 f. +4 f. bleu**	5 »	2 70	4 60
	N°s 859 à 862 (4 val.)	**13 »**	**7 »**	**12 25**

La série, non dentelée 305 »

1949			
Du n° 823 au n° 862			
(sauf n° 833A et 846A) :			
42 timbres	****172**	***102**	**⊙136**

1950. – *Journée du Timbre. Taille-douce. Dentelé 13.*

Facteur rural.

863	**12 f. +3 f. bleu**	4 60	2 75	3 55
	a. (Non dentelé)		84 »	

Tirage : 1 275 000.

1950. – *Raymond Poincaré. Taille-douce. Dentelé 13.*

864	**15 f. bleu-noir**	0 50	0 30	0 50
	a. (Non dentelé)		30 »	

Tirage : 3 825 000.

1950. – *Charles Péguy et cathédrale de Chartres. Taille-douce. Dentelé 13.*

865	**12 f. brun-noir**	0 50	0 30	0 50
	a. (Non dentelé)		40 »	

Tirage : 2 950 000.

1950. – *François Rabelais (1494-1553). Taille-douce. Dentelé 13.*

866	**12 f. brun-rouge**	1 »	0 65	1 »
	a. (Non dentelé)		30 »	

Tirage : 2 800 000.

1950. – *Célébrités du XVIII*^{e} *siècle (II) (Révolution de 1789). Cadre bleu-noir. Taille-douce. Dentelés 13.*

André-Marie de Chénier, par J.-B. Suvée.

Jacques-Louis David, d'après son autoportrait.

Lazare Carnot.

867	**5 f. +2 f. lilas**	13 »	7 »	13 »
868	**8 f. +3 f. sépia**	13 »	7 »	13 »
869	**10 f. +4 f. lie-de-vin**	14 »	9 »	14 »

Georges Jacques Danton.

Maximilien de Robespierre.

Lazare Hoche.

870	**12 f. +5 f. brun-rouge**	16 »	10 »	16 »
871	**15 f. +6 f. vert**	17 »	10 »	17 »
872	**20 f. +10 f. bleu**	17 »	10 »	17 »
	N°s 867 à 872 (6 val.)	**90 »**	**53 »**	**90 »**
	La série, non dentelée		305 »	

1950. – *Taille-douce. Dentelés 13.*

Château de Châteaudun.

Madame de Sévigné, par Nanteuil.

873	**8 f. brun-violet et brun**	1 »	0 60	0 70
	a. (Non dentelé)		30 »	
874	**15 f. bleu clair**	0 80	0 40	0 70
	a. (Non dentelé)		30 »	

Tirages : 2 895 000 et 3 000 000.

1950. – ***Madame Récamier (1777-1849) (détail), d'après Gérard. Taille-douce. Dentelé 13.***

875 **12 f. vert** 0 80 0 40 0 70

a. (Non dentelé) 30 »

Tirage : 2 960 000.

1950. – ***Au profit de la Croix-Rouge. Croix en rouge. Taille-douce. Dentelés 13.***

Portrait de Brongniart enfant (1739-1813), par Houdon (1741-1828).

L'Amour, par Falconet (1716-1791).

876 **8 f. +2 f. bleu-gris** 2 75 1 60 2 75

877 **15 f. +3 f. brun-rouge** 3 35 1 85 3 »

La paire, non dentelée 275 »

1950			
Du n° 863 au n° 877 :			
15 timbres	****105**	***62**	**⊙103**

1951. – ***Château de Fontainebleau. Taille-douce. Dentelé 13.***

La Cour des Adieux.

878 **12 f. brun violacé** 1 30 0 70 1 »

a. (Non dentelé) 40 »

Tirage : 2 895 000.

1951. – ***Journée du Timbre. Taille-douce. Dentelé 13.***

Intérieur d'un wagon-poste.

879 **12 f. +3 f. gris-violet** 4 60 3 » 4 60

a. (Non dentelé) 77 »

Tirage : 1 625 000.

1951. – ***Jules Ferry. Taille-douce. Dentelé 13.***

880 **15 f. vermillon** 0 65 0 30 0 65

a. (Non dentelé) 50 »

Tirage : 3 010 000.

1951. – ***Exposition textile internationale de Lille. Taille-douce. Dentelé 13.***

Navette de métier à tisser.

881 **25 f. bleu-violet** 1 25 0 65 0 80

a. (Non dentelé) 30 »

Tirage : 2 800 000.

1951. – ***Tricentenaire de la naissance de Saint Jean-Baptiste de La Salle (1651-1719). Taille-douce. Dentelé 13.***

882 **15 f. brun-lilas** 0 80 0 50 0 65

a. (Non dentelé) 40 »

Tirage : 3 115 000.

1951. – ***Type Marianne de Gandon. Format 17 x 21. Typographie. Dentelés 14 x 13½.*** Ⓒ

Pour le type II du 886b se reporter au cliché du 813a.

Dans le type III du 886d, la dernière lettre (C) suivant le nom du graveur (CORTOT SC) dépasse nettement à droite la verticale du cadre du timbre.

883	**5 f. violet**	0 60	0 15	0 15
884	**6 f. vert**	8 »	4 70	0 70
	a. (mèches reliées, retouché)	130 »	54 »	4 60
	b. (mèches croisées)	100 »	52 »	5 50
885	**12 f. orange**	1 »	0 50	0 30

886	**15 f. outremer (Type I)**	0 40	0 15	0 15
	a. (avec bande publ)	6 »	4 »	2 »
	b. (Avec bande publ.) (Type II)	8 40	5 35	1 85
	c. (avec bande publ)	10 »	6 »	2 75
	d. (Avec bande publ, roulette) (Type III)	46 »	30 »	8 40
887	**18 f. rose carminé**	20 »	11 50	1 70
	N°s 883 à 887 (5 val.)	**30 »**	**17 »**	**3 »**
	La série, non dentelée		77 »	

1951. – ***Abbaye de St-Wandrille. Type de 1949 (n° 842). Taille-douce. Dentelé 13.***

888	**30 f. bleu clair (842)**	6 »	3 85	5 »
	a. (Non dentelé)		35 »	

Tirage : 6 160 000.

1951. – ***Cinquantenaire des troupes coloniales. Taille-douce. Dentelé 13.***

889	**15 f. bleu**	1 »	0 60	0 70
	a. (Non dentelé)		40 »	

Tirage : 3 000 000.

1951. – ***Centenaire de la naissance du compositeur Vincent d'Indy (1851-1931). Taille-douce. Dentelé 13.***

890	**25 f. vert foncé**	2 30	1 40	2 30
	a. (Non dentelé)		54 »	

Tirage : 2 000 000.

1951. – ***Célébrités du XIXe siècle (I). Cadres brun-violet. Taille-douce. Dentelés 13.***

Alfred de Musset, par Landelle.

Eugène Delacroix (autoportrait).

Louis-Joseph Gay-Lussac.

891	**5 f. +1 f. vert**	8 »	4 50	8 »
892	**8 f. +2 f. lie-de-vin**	9 50	5 50	9 50
893	**10 f. +3 f. bleu-vert**	8 »	4 50	8 »

Robert, baron Surcouf, par Alaux.

Charles-Maurice de Talleyrand-Périgord, par Prud'hon (1758-1823).

Napoléon, par Gros (détail) (1771-1835).

894	**12 f. +4 f. violet-brun**	9 50	5 50	9 50
895	**15 f. +5 f. brun carminé**	9 50	6 »	9 50
896	**30 f. +10 f. bleu**	15 50	10 »	15 50
	N°s 891 à 896 (6 val.)	**60 »**	**36 »**	**60 »**
	La série, non dentelée		275 »	

1951. – ***Hommage à la médecine vétérinaire et à la médecine militaire. Taille-douce. Dentelés 13.***

Docteurs Nocard, Bouley, Chauveau et péristyle de l'École vétérinaire de Lyon.

Docteurs Picqué, Roussin, Villemin et chapelle du Val-de-Grâce, à Paris.

897	**12 f. lilas-rose**	0 70	0 50	0 65
	a. (Non dentelé)		46 »	
898	**15 f. brun-lilas**	0 90	0 50	0 65
	a. (Non dentelé)		54 »	

Tirages : 2 550 000 et 3 055 000.

1951. – *Armoiries de provinces (V). Typographie. Dentelés 14 x 13½.*

Artois.

Limousin.

899	**10 c. carmin, outremer, noir et jaune**	0 15	0 15	0 15
900	**50 c. olive, noir et carmin**	0 15	0 15	0 15

Béarn.

Touraine.

Franche-Comté.

901	**1 f. outemer, carmin et jaune foncé**	0 30	0 15	0 30
902	**2 f. outremer, carmin, noir et jaune**	1 10	0 65	0 50
903	**3 f. carmin, outremer et jaune foncé**	1 »	0 65	0 50
	N°s 899 à 903 (5 val.)	**2 70**	**1 75**	**1 60**
	La série, non dentelée		77 »	

1951. – *Inauguration du musée de l'imagerie française, à Epinal. Taille-douce. Dentelé 13.*

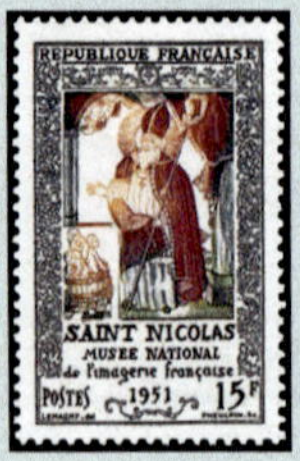

La légende de saint Nicolas.

904	**15 f. bleu-noir, lie-de-vin, vert et orange**	1 70	0 90	1 30
	a. (Non dentelé)		77 »	

Tirage : 3 265 000.

1951. – *Vue d'Arbois. Taille-douce. Dentelé 13.*

905	**30 f. bleu-noir**	1 25	0 65	0 30
	a. (Non dentelé)		40 »	

Tirage : 69 615 000.

1951. – *Bimillénaire de Paris. Taille-douce. Dentelé 13.*

Sceau de la corporation des bateliers.

906	**15 f. rouge, sépia et bleu**	0 80	0 50	0 50
	a. (Non dentelé)		70 »	

Tirage : 3 570 000.

1951. – *A la mémoire de l'aviateur Maurice Noguès (1889-1934) et 20e anniversaire de la ligne aérienne France-Indochine. Taille-douce. Dentelé 13.*

907	**12 f. bleu-noir et bleu clair**	1 10	0 65	1 »
	a. (Non dentelé)		77 »	

Tirage : 2 935 000.

1951. – *Poètes symbolistes. Taille-douce. Dentelés 13.*

Charles Baudelaire (1821-1867) et évocation des "Fleurs du Mal".

Paul Verlaine (1844-1896) et évocation de l'"Après-midi d'un faune", par Carrière.

908	**8 f. violet**	1 »	0 60	0 90
909	**12 f. gris**	1 »	0 60	0 90

Arthur Rimbaud (1854-1891) et évocation du "Bateau ivre", par Fantin-Latour.

910	**15 f. vert foncé**	1 »	0 60	0 90
	La série, non dentelée		92 »	

1951. – *6ᵉ session des Nations Unies, à Paris. Taille-douce. Dentelés 13.*

Tour Eiffel et palais de Chaillot.

911	**18 f. rouge**	1 40	1 »	1 »
912	**30 f. bleu**	2 45	1 40	1 40
	La paire, non dentelée		305 »	

1951. – *4ᵉ Centenaire du château du Clos de Vougeot. Taille-douce. Dentelé 13.*

Château du Clos de Vougeot.

913	**30 f. brun et violet-brun**	7 65	3 85	3 »
	a. brun-jaune et violet-brun	20 »	11 50	6 »
	b. (Non dentelé)		77 »	

Tirage : 2 997 000.

1951. – *Au profit de la Croix-Rouge. Croix en rouge. Taille-douce. Dentelés 13.*

Enfant royal en prière (portrait présumé du dauphin Charles), par le Maître de Moulins.

Portrait de Nicole Ricard, par Quentin de La Tour.

914	**12 f. +3 f. brun-rouge**	3 85	2 30	3 85
915	**15 f. +5 f. bleu**	4 60	3 »	4 60
	La paire, non dentelée		230 »	

1951. – *Monuments et sites. Taille-douce. Dentelés 13.*

Pic du Midi de Bigorre et observatoire.

Abbaye aux Hommes, Caen.

916	**40 f. violet foncé**	6 90	3 85	0 30
	a. (Non dentelé)		77 »	
917	**50 f. brun-noir**	6 »	3 »	0 30
	a. (Papier carton)	12 50	8 »	1 60

Tirages : 57 780 000 et 113 000 000.

1951. – *33ᵉ anniversaire de l'armistice. Taille-douce. Dentelé 13.*

Georges Clemenceau.

918	**15 f. brun-noir**	0 65	0 50	0 65
	a. (Non dentelé)		30 »	

Tirage : 3 500 000.

1951

Du n° 878 au n° 918 :

41 timbres ****154** ***90** **⊙103**

1952. – *Journée du Timbre. Taille-douce. Dentelé 13.*

Malle-poste.

919	**12 f. +3 f. vert**	5 50	3 50	5 50
	a. (Non dentelé)		77 »	
	b. (RepublTque : "T" au lieu de "I")	60 »	40 »	20 »

Tirage : 1 575 000.

1952. – *Maréchal de Lattre de Tassigny (1889-1952). Taille-douce. Dentelé 13.*

Vue de Colmar et piton de Ninh-Binh.

920	**15 f. brun-lilas**	1 25	0 80	0 80
	a. (Non dentelé)		40 »	

Un 12 f. à ce type a paru en 1954 (nº 982).

Tirage : 5 120 000.

1952. – *Porte de France, à Vaucouleurs. Taille-douce. Dentelé 13.*

921	**12 f. noir violacé**	1 60	1 »	1 25
	a. (Non dentelé)		70 »	

Tirage : 2 800 000.

1952. – *12e anniversaire de la bataille de Narvik (Norvège). Taille-douce. Dentelé 13.*

Le Monument aux soldats et marins français.

922 **30 f. bleu-violet** 4 » 2 30 2 75
a. (Non dentelé) 77 »

Tirage : 2 500 000.

1952. – *Réunion du Conseil de l'Europe, à Strasbourg. Taille-douce. Dentelé 13.*

Siège du Conseil et cathédrale de Strasbourg.

923 **30 f. vert** 9 50 5 50 7 »
a. (Non dentelé) 575 »

Tirage : 2 450 000.

1952. – *Château de Chambord et premier spectacle "Son et Lumière". Taille-douce. Dentelé 13.*

924 **20 f. violet foncé** 0 65 0 30 0 30
a. (Non dentelé) 35 »

Tirage : 66 500 000.

1952. – *10e anniversaire de la victoire de Bir Hakeim (Libye). Taille-douce. Dentelé 13.*

Le monument érigé dans le désert.

925 **30 f. brun carminé** 4 50 2 80 2 50
a. (Non dentelé) 77 »

Tirage : 2 000 000.

1952. – *14e centenaire de l'abbaye Sainte-Croix de Poitiers. Taille-douce. Dentelé 13.*

926 **15 f. vermillon** 0 65 0 50 0 65
a. (Non dentelé) 35 »

Tirage : 4 280 000.

1952. – *Centenaire de la Médaille militaire. Taille-douce. Dentelé 13.*

927 **15 f. marron, vert et jaune** 0 80 0 60 0 70
a. (Non dentelé) 95 »

Tirage : 4 500 000.

1952. – *Viaduc de Garabit. Taille-douce. Dentelé 13.*

928 **15 f. bleu foncé** 0 80 0 50 0 65
a. (Non dentelé) 40 »

Tirage : 4 080 000.

1952. – *5e centenaire de la naissance de Léonard de Vinci (1452-1519). Taille-douce. Dentelé 13.*

Autoportrait, château d'Amboise, et vue de Florence.

929 **30 f. bleu-violet** 10 » 6 » 8 40
a. (Non dentelé) 130 »

Tirage : 2 250 000.

1952. – *Célébrité du XIXe siècle (II). Cadres sépia. Taille-douce. Dentelés 13.*

Gustave Flaubert, écrivain. Edouard Manet, peintre. Camille St-Saëns, compositeur.

930	**8 f. +2 f. bleu-noir**	8 50	5 »	8 50
	a. (Papier carton)	25 »	16 »	16 »
931	**12 f. +3 f. outremer**	8 50	5 »	8 50
932	**15 f. +4 f. vert foncé**	8 50	5 »	8 50

Jules-Henri Poincaré, physicien. Georges Eugène baron Haussmann, urbaniste. Adolphe Thiers, homme d'État.

933	**18 f. +5 f. brun-violet**	11 50	7 »	11 50
934	**20 f. +6 f. carmin**	11 50	7 »	11 50
935	**30 f. +7 f. violet**	11 50	7 »	11 50
	N°s 930 à 935 (6 val.)	**60 »**	**36 »**	**60 »**
	La série, non dentelée		230 »	

1952. – *Dr René Laennec, inventeur du stéthoscope. Taille-douce. Dentelé 13.*

936	**12 f. vert foncé**	1 »	0 60	0 75
	a. (Non dentelé)		77 »	

Tirage : 2 825 000.

1952. – *Au profit de la Croix-Rouge. Motifs du bassin de Diane, à Versailles. Croix en rouge. Taille-douce. Dentelés 13.* C

937	**12 f. +3 f. vert**	6 »	4 »	6 »
938	**15 f. +5 f. bleu foncé**	6 »	4 »	6 »
	a. (avec bande publ)	16 »	10 »	16 »
	La paire, non dentelée		230 »	

Le 15+5 f. a également été émis en carnet de 10.

1952. – *Grille d'entrée du château de Versailles (d'après une gouache de Maurice Utrillo (1883-1955). Taille-douce. Dentelé 13.*

939	**18 f. brun**	3 50	2 »	2 30
	a. (Non dentelé)		77 »	

Ce timbre a reparu dans d'autres couleurs en 1954 (n° 988).

Tirage : 2 600 000.

1952

Du n° 919 au n° 939 :

21 timbres ****116** ***70** **⊙106**

1953. – *Journée du Timbre. Taille-douce. Dentelé 13.*

Marc-Pierre, comte d'Argenson (1696-1764), surintendant général des Postes.

940	**12 f. +3 f. bleu**	4 »	2 »	4 »
	a. (Non dentelé)		77 »	

Tirage : 1 570 000.

1953. – *Haute couture parisienne. Taille-douce. Dentelé 13.*

Mannequin en robe de soirée et place Vendôme, à Paris.

941	**30 f. violet et bleu-noir**	1 20	0 65	0 50
	a. (Non dentelé)		42 »	

Voir également les n°s 970 à 974 et 1020.

Tirage : 29 950 000.

1953. – ***Maréchalat posthume de Philippe de Hautecloque, dit Leclerc (1902-1947). Type de 1948 (n° 815) modifié. Légende GÉNÉRAL LECLERC, MARÉCHAL DE FRANCE. Taille-douce. Dentelé 13.***

Le Maréchal Leclerc. Cathédrale de Strasbourg.

942	**8 f. brun-rouge (815)**	1 25	0 65	1 10
	a. (Non dentelé)		40 »	

Un 12 f. à ce type a paru en 1954 (n° 984).

Tirage : 2 540 000.

1953. – ***Théâtre français. Taille-douce. Dentelés 13.***

Gargantua. Hernani.

943	**6 f. rose-rouge et lilas**	0 40	0 30	0 30
944	**18 f. violet-brun et brun-noir**	0 75	0 30	0 50
	La paire, non dentelée		70 »	

Tirages : 32 600 000 et 20 350 000.

Voir également les n°s 956 et 957.

1953. – ***Célébrités du XIIe au XXe siècles. Taille-douce. Dentelés 13.***

Saint Bernard, 8e centenaire de sa mort. Olivier de Serres, agronome. Jean-Philippe Rameau, compositeur.

Gaspard Monge, comte de Peluse, mathématicien. Jules Michelet, historien. Maréchal Hubert Lyautey.

945	**8 f. +2 f. outremer**	8 »	5 »	8 »
946	**12 f. +3 f. vert foncé**	8 »	5 »	8 »
947	**15 f. +4 f. brun carminé**	13 »	8 »	13 »
948	**18 f. +5 f. bleu**	13 50	8 »	13 50
949	**20 f. +6 f. violet**	13 50	8 »	13 50
950	**30 f. +7 f. brun-lilas**	14 »	10 »	14 »
	N°s 945 à 950 (6 val.)	**70 »**	**44 »**	**70 »**
	La série, non dentelée		200 »	

1953. – ***Armoiries de provinces (VI). Typographie. Dentelés 14 x 13½.***

Picardie. Poitou.

951	**50 c. outremer, rouge et jaune**	0 30	0 15	0 30
952	**1 f. noir, rouge et jaune**	0 30	0 15	0 30

Champagne. Dauphiné.

953	**2 f. brun-rouge, outremer et jaune**	0 60	0 15	0 50
954	**3 f. rouge, outremer et jaune**	0 80	0 55	0 50
	N°s 951 à 954 (4 val.)	**2 »**	**1 »**	**1 60**
	La série, non dentelée		61 »	

Tirages : 22 500 000, 53 450 000, 73 000 000 et 39 000 000.

1953. – ***Cinquantenaire du Tour de France cycliste. Taille-douce. Dentelé 13.***

Cyclistes de 1903 et 1953.

955	**12 f. rouge-brun, outremer et noir**	2 75	1 60	1 60
	a. (Non dentelé)		54 »	

Tirage : 3 075 000.

1953. – ***Théâtre français. Taille-douce. Dentelés 13.***

Célimène.

Figaro.

956	**8 f. bleu-noir et outremer**	0 40	0 15	0 30
957	**12 f. brun-lilas et vert-bleu**	0 40	0 15	0 30

La paire, non dentelée 70 »

Tirages : 42 285 000 et 84 125 000.

Voir également les n°s 943 et 944.

1953. – ***Armoiries de provinces (VI). Typographie. Dentelés 14 x 13½.***

Gascogne.

Berri.

958	**70 c. rouge, outremer et jaune**	0 30	0 15	0 30
959	**80 c. outremer, rouge et jaune**	0 30	0 15	0 30

La paire, non dentelée 30 »

Tirages : 10 600 000 et 10 250 000.

1953. – ***Jeux olympiques d'Helsinki (1952). Taille-douce. Dentelés 13.***

Natation.

Athlétisme.

960	**20 f. rose-carmin et bistre**	3 »	1 85	0 30
961	**25 f. vert foncé et bistre**	16 »	9 50	0 70

Escrime.

Canoë.

962	**30 f. bleu-violet et bistre**	3 »	2 »	0 50
963	**40 f. bistre et bleu-violet**	14 »	7 65	0 70

Aviron.

Hippisme.

964	**50 f. émeraude et bistre**	10 »	6 »	0 30
965	**75 f. orange et brun carminé**	44 »	26 »	15 50
	N°s 960 à 965 (6 val.)	**90 »**	**53 »**	**18 »**

La série, non dentelée 275 »

Tirages : 26 650 000, 13 950 000, 16 850 000, 17 000 000, 21 200 000 et 6 650 000.

Série émise en l'honneur des athlètes français médaillés d'or : Boiteux, Mimoun (argent sur 5000 et 10000 m), D'Oriola, Turller et Laudet, Salles et Mercier barré par Mallvoire, et Jonquères d'Oriola.

1953. – ***Au profit de la Croix-Rouge. Croix en rouge. Taille-douce. Dentelés 13.*** [C]

Marie-Louise Elisabeth Vigée-Le Brun et sa fille, par elle-même (1755-1842).

"Le retour du baptême", par Louis Le Nain (détail), (1593-1648).

966	**12 f. +3 f. brun**	10 »	5 50	8 50
967	**15 f. +5 f. bleu-noir**	13 50	8 »	12 »

La paire, non dentelée 230 »

Ont été émis aussi en carnets (tirage : 127 000).

1953

Du n° 940 au n° 967 :

28 timbres ****197** ***118** **⊙119**

1954. – ***Timbre de 1951 (Marianne de Gandon, n° 887) surchargé.***

968	**15 f. s. 18 f. rose-carmin (887)**	0 65	0 30	0 65

Tirage : 21 750 000.

1954. – ***Journée du timbre. Taille-douce. Dentelé 13.***

Comte de La Valette.

969	**12 f. +3 f. vert et sépia**	5 50	3 »	4 60
	a. (Non dentelé)		77 »	

Tirage : 1 507 000.

1954. – ***Productions de luxe. Métiers d'Art. Taille-douce. Dentelés 13.***

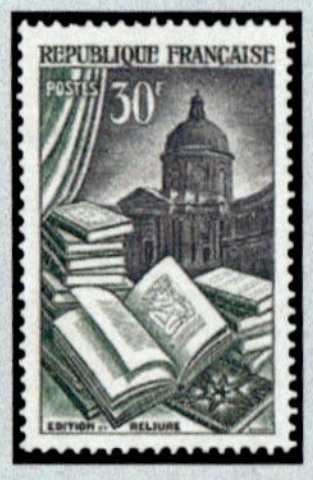

Tapisserie et cour des Gobelins. Edition, reliure et Institut de France. Porcelaine, cristaux et le Louvre.

970	**25 f. brun-rouge, rose et noir**	17 »	10 »	0 65
971	**30 f. violet-gris et vert-bleu**	3 »	1 50	0 30
972	**40 f. brun, violet et brun-jaune**	5 »	3 »	0 50

Joaillerie, orfèvrerie et la Madeleine. Fleurs, parfums et l'Opéra.

973	**50 f. bleu-violet, vert et brun clair**	3 »	1 50	0 30
974	**75 f. rouge-carmin et lie-de-vin**	17 »	10 »	1 40
	N°s 970 à 974 (5 val.)	**45 »**	**26 »**	**3 15**
	La série, non dentelée		130 »	

Tirages : 31 160 000, 90 525 000, 63 325 000, 134 195 000 et 19 295 000.

Voir également les n°s 941 et 1020.

1954. – ***Cinquantenaire de la foire de Paris. Taille-douce. Dentelé 13.***

Entrée de la Foire à la Porte de Versailles.

975	**15 f. rouge et bleu**	0 50	0 30	0 50
	a. (Non dentelé)		30 »	

Tirage : 3 880 000.

1954. – ***Série touristique. Taille-douce. Dentelés 13.***

Lourdes. La vallée de la Seine aux Andelys et le château Gaillard.

976	**6 f. bleu-noir, outremer et olive**	0 60	0 40	0 50
977	**8 f. bleu et olive**	0 40	0 20	0 30
	a. noir et bleu	2 850 »	2 300 »	

Royan. Quimper, la rue Kéréon.

978	**10 f. brun-rouge et bleu clair**	0 40	0 20	0 15
979	**12 f. lilas et violet**	0 60	0 40	0 15
	a. violet	130 »	80 »	45 »

Château de Cheverny (1630), oeuvre de Hurault et Boyer. Baie d'Ajaccio (Corse).

980	**18 f. vert foncé et bleu-noir**	4 »	2 30	1 10
981	**20 f. brun foncé, brun-rouge et bleu-vert**	3 50	2 50	0 30
	N°s 976 à 981 (6 val.)	**9 50**	**6 »**	**2 50**
	La série, non dentelée		140 »	

Tirages : 48 750 000, 116 600 000, 110 000 000, 194 750 000, 23 500 000 et 61 250 000.

Le type du 6 f. (Lourdes) a été repris en 1958 pour un 20 f. olive et bleu-vert (n° 1150).

1954. – *Maréchal de Lattre de Tassigny. Type de 1952 (n° 920). Taille-douce. Dentelé 13.*

982 **12 f. bleu-violet et bleu-noir (920)** 2 30 1 60 1 60
a. (Non dentelé) 30 »
Tirage : 3 080 000.

1954. – *10e anniversaire de la Libération. Taille-douce. Dentelé 13.*

983 **15 f. rouge et bleu** 2 50 1 50 1 70
a. (Non dentelé) 50 »
Tirage : 5 215 000.

1954. – *Maréchal Leclerc. Type de 1953 (n° 942). Taille-douce. Dentelé 13.*

984 **12 f. olive et bleu-gris (942)** 3 70 2 15 2 30
a. (Non dentelé) 30 »
Tirage : 3 085 000.

1954. – *13e centenaire de l'abbaye de Jumièges. Taille-douce. Dentelé 13.*

Ruines de l'abbaye.

985 **12 f. outremer, vert foncé et bleu-noir** 2 » 1 20 1 50
a. (Non dentelé) 23 »
Tirage : 2 970 000.

1954. – *1er colloque du Centre international d'études romanes, à Tournus. Taille-douce. Dentelé 13.*

Eglise St-Philibert, vue du cloître.

986 **30 f. bleu-noir et bleu clair** 6 » 4 » 5 50
a. (Non dentelé) 25 »
Tirage : 2 450 000.

1954. – *Tricentenaire du rattachement de Stenay. Taille-douce. Dentelé 13.*

Place de la République et armoiries.

987 **15 f. brun-noir et brun-rouge** 1 » 0 50 0 80
a. (Non dentelé) 23 »
Tirage : 3 810 000.

1954. – *Grille d'entrée du château de Versailles. Type de 1952 (n° 939). Taille-douce. Dentelé 13.*

988 **18 f. brun-lilas, bleu-noir et bleu (939)** 11 » 7 » 7 65
a. (Non dentelé) 70 »
Tirage : 2 515 000.

1954. – *Célébrités du XIIIe au XXe siècles. Taille-douce. Dentelés 13.*

Louis IX, dit Saint-Louis. Roi de France de 1226 à 1270.

Jacques-Bénigne Bossuet. 250e anniversaire de sa mort.

Marie-François Sadi Carnot. Président de la République de 1887 à 1894.

989 **12 f. +4 f. bleu** 26 » 15 » 26 »
990 **15 f. +5 f. violet** 26 » 15 » 26 »
991 **18 f. +6 f. brun foncé** 26 » 15 » 26 »

Bourdelle.

Dr Émile Roux.

Paul Valéry.

992	**20 f. +7 f. rouge**	36 »	22 »	36 »
993	**25 f. +8 f. bleu-noir**	36 »	22 »	36 »
994	**30 f. +10 f. lilas-brun**	36 »	21 »	36 »
	N°s 989 à 994 (6 val.)	**186 »**	**110 »**	**186 »**
	La série, non dentelée		230 »	

1954. – *Château de Villandry (Touraine). Taille-douce. Dentelé 13.*

995	**18 f. bleu et vert**	6 »	3 50	5 »
	a. (Non dentelé)		25 »	

Tirage : 2 385 000.

1954. – *150e anniversaire de l'École spéciale militaire de Saint-Cyr. Taille-douce. Dentelé 13.*

St-Cyrien et porche de l'École.

996	**15 f. bleu, gris-bleu et rouge**	1 60	1 »	1 60
	a. (Non dentelé)		46 »	

Tirage : 3 550 000.

1954. – *150e anniversaire de la Légion d'honneur. Taille-douce. Dentelé 13.*

Napoléon 1er au camp de Boulogne.

997	**12 f. rouge**	2 »	1 50	1 50
	a. (Non dentelé)		61 »	

Tirage : 3 000 000.

1954. – *10e conférence internationale des Poids et Mesures, à Paris. Le Système métrique. Taille-douce. Dentelé 13.*

998	**30 f. bleu-noir et brun-lilas**	6 »	3 50	5 50
	a. (Non dentelé)		35 »	

Tirage : 1 800 000.

1954. – *Armoiries de provinces (VII). Typographie. Dentelés 14 x 13½.*

Maine.

Navarre.

999	**50 c. brun-noir, rouge, outremer et jaune**	0 30	0 15	0 30
1000	**70 c. vert, rouge et jaune**	0 30	0 15	0 30

Nivernais.

Bourbonnais.

Angoûmois.

1001	**80 c. outremer, rouge et jaune**	0 30	0 15	0 30
1002	**1 f. rouge, outremer et jaune**	0 15	0 15	0 15
1003	**2 f. noir, rouge et jaune**	0 15	0 15	0 15

Aunis.

Saintonge.

1004	**3 f. brun, rouge et jaune**	0 15	0 15	0 15
1005	**5 f. outremer et jaune**	0 15	0 15	0 15
	N°s 999 à 1005 (7 val.)	**1 50**	**1 05**	**1 50**
	La série, non dentelée		77 »	

Tirages : 16 600 000, 9 500 000, 5 320 000, 40 060 000, 273 420 000, 130 690 000 et 1 104 660 000.

1954. – *Au profit de la Croix-Rouge. Croix en rouge. Taille-douce. Dentelés 13.* [C]

Maternité, par Eugène Carrière (1849-1906).

Jeune fille aux colombes, par J.-B. Greuze (1725-1805).

1006	**12 f. +3 f. bleu-gris et bleu-noir**	14 50	8 »	12 50
1007	**15 f. +5 f. brun et sépia**	16 »	10 »	14 »
	La paire, non dentelée		230 »	

Ont été émis aussi en carnets (tirage : 135 000).

1954

Du n° 968 au n° 1007 :

40 timbres ****323** ***192** **⊙260**

1955. – *Bicentenaire de la mort de Louis de Rouvroy, duc de Saint-Simon. Taille-douce. Dentelé 13.*

1008	**12 f. brun et lie-de-vin**	0 80	0 50	0 80
	a. (Non dentelé)		23 »	

Tirage : 2 500 000.

1955. – *Cinquantenaire du Rotary international. Taille-douce. Dentelé 13.*

1009	**30 f. bleu et jaune**	3 30	2 »	2 »
	a. (Non dentelé)		125 »	

Tirage : 2 500 000.

1955-59. – *Marianne de Muller. Typographie. Dentelés 14 x 13½.* [C]

1009A	**6 f. brun-orange**	3 50	1 60	2 30
	a. (Non dentelé)		270 »	
1010	**12 f. vert-jaune**	4 »	1 70	1 60
	a. (Feuillet de 10)	55 »	40 »	
	b. (Non dentelé)		270 »	
	c. (feuillet de 10, non dentelé)		2 700 »	
1011	**15 f. rose carminé**	0 30	0 15	0 15
	a. (Avec bande publicitaire)	1 85	1 25	0 65
	b. (Non dentelé)		30 »	

Type I.

Type II.

1011A	**18 f. vert foncé (II)**	0 30	0 15	0 30
	a. (Type I)	1 50	1 »	1 »
	b. (Non dentelé)		30 »	

Type I.

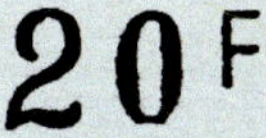

Type II.

1011B	**20 f. bleu (I)**	0 60	0 30	0 15
	b. (Avec bande pub.) (I)	2 30	1 40	1 »
	c. (Type II)	19 »	12 »	6 »
	d. (Avec bande pub.) (II)	19 »	12 »	6 »
	e. (Non dentelé) (I)		30 »	
	f. (avec pub non dentelé)		385 »	

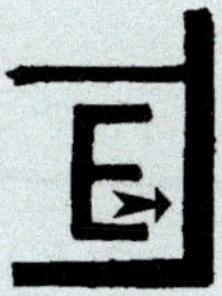

Type I.

Type II (carnet de 8).

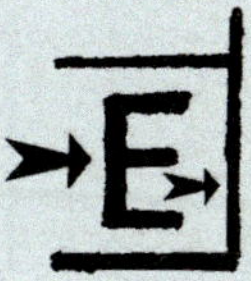

Type II (carnet de 8).

1011C	**25 f. rouge (I)**	1 80	0 80	0 15
	a. (Paire verticale de carnet avec barres, Type I)	6 »	4 »	
	b. (Type II)	3 50	2 50	0 70
	c. (Avec bandelette inférieure blanche) (II)	16 »	10 »	6 »
	d. (Non dentelé)		30 »	
	N°s 1009A à 1011C (6 val.)	**10 50**	**4 70**	**4 65**

Le n° 1009A n'a été émis qu'en roulettes. La coupe des dentelures verticales des roulettes rotatives est toujours nette et rectiligne, parfois rognée. Il en est de même des timbres provenant des carnets pour distributeurs (Exemple : 1011Cb).

Deux textes et dessins différents se rencontrent sur les feuillets de 10 timbres de 12 F n° 1010a.

Les timbres au type II du n° 1011C sont ceux des carnets de 8.

1955. – *Inventeurs célèbres. Taille-douce. Dentelés 13.*

Philippe Le Bon (gaz d'éclairage).

Barthélémy Thimonnier (machine à coudre).

1012	**5 f. Bleu et bleu clair**	0 90	0 50	0 90
1013	**10 f. brun foncé et brun-rouge**	1 10	0 70	1 10

Nicolas Appert (conserve alimentaire).

Sainte-Claire Deville (aluminium).

1014	**12 f. vert-bleu**	1 50	0 80	1 50
1015	**18 f. bleu et bleu-gris**	3 50	1 70	3 50

Pierre Martin (fabrication de l'acier) (40[e] anniv. de sa mort).

Louis-Maurice-Hilaire de Bernigaud, comte de Chardonnet (soie artificielle).

1016	**25 f. brun-violet et violet-noir**	4 »	2 »	3 »
1017	**30 f. carmin et vermillon**	4 »	2 30	3 »
	N°s 1012 à 1017 (6 val.)	**15 »**	**8 »**	**13 »**
	La série, non dentelée		125 »	

Tirage : 2 500 000 séries.

1955. – *Journée du Timbre et 85e anniversaire de la poste aérienne. Taille-douce. Dentelé 13.*

Départ d'un ballon-poste pendant le Siège de Paris.

1018	**12 f. +3 f. bleu-olive et brun-rouge**	6 »	3 60	5 50
	a. (Non dentelé)		61 »	

Tirage : 1 470 000.

1955. – *Vue de Limoges (le pont Saint-Étienne et la cathédrale). Taille-douce. Dentelé 13.*

1019	**12 f. brun-jaune et brun-lilas**	2 »	1 20	1 80
	a. (Non dentelé)		23 »	

Tirage : 2 540 000.

1955. – *La ganterie. Taille-douce. Dentelé 13.*

Elégante devant les fontaines de l'Obélisque de la place de la Concorde.

1020	**25 f. noir violacé et bleu-violet**	1 25	0 50	0 30
	a. (Non dentelé)		23 »	

Voir également les n°s 941 et 970 à 974.

Tirage : 31 500 000.

1955. – *Bicentenaire de la naissance du fabuliste Jean-Pierre Claris de Florian (1755-1794). Taille-douce. Dentelé 13.*

Florian et scène de "Estelle et Nemorin".

1021	**12 f. bleu-vert**	1 »	0 65	0 80
	a. (Non dentelé)		23 »	

Tirage : 2 545 000.

1955. – *La Télévision. Taille-douce. Dentelé 13.*

La Tour Eiffel et antennes, au-dessus des toits de Paris.

1022	**15 f. bleu-noir et outremer**	1 25	0 80	1 10
	a. (Non dentelé)		35 »	

Tirage : 3 500 000.

1955. – *10e anniversaire de la libération des camps de déportation. Taille-douce. Dentelé 13.*

1023	**12 f. brun-noir et gris-bleu**	1 25	0 80	1 10
	a. (Non dentelé)		30 »	

Tirage : 2 500 000.

1955. – *Électrification de la ligne Valenciennes-Thionville. Taille-douce. Dentelé 13.*

Locomotive Alsthom.

1024	**12 f. sépia et gris-bleu**	2 60	1 60	1 60
	a. (Non dentelé)		40 »	

Tirage : 2 500 000.

1955. – *5ᵉ centenaire du Jacquemart de Moulins. Taille-douce. Dentelé 13.*

Moulins : le Jacquemart.

1025	**12 f. brun-gris**	1 85	1 10	1 60
	a. (Non dentelé)		23 »	

Tirage : 2 600 000.

1955. – *Cinquantenaire de la mort de Jules Verne (1828-1905). Taille-douce. Dentelé 13.*

Jules Verne et le "Nautilus".

1026	**30 f. bleu-noir**	9 »	4 50	6 »
	a. (Non dentelé)		80 »	

Tirage : 2 200 000.

1955. – *Célébrités du XIIᵉ au XXᵉ siècles. Taille-douce. Dentelés 13.*

Philippe-Auguste, roi de France de 1180 à 1223.

François de Malherbe, poète.

Sébastien Le Prestre de Vauban, par Rigaud.

1027	**12 f. +5 f. violet**	20 »	12 »	19 »
1028	**15 f. +6 f. bleu**	20 »	12 »	19 »
1029	**18 f. +7 f. vert**	22 »	12 50	21 »

Charles Gravier, comte de Vergennes.

Pierre Simon, marquis de Laplace.

Pierre-Auguste Renoir.

1030	**25 f. +8 f. violet-gris**	30 »	15 50	26 »
1031	**30 f. +9 f. lie-de-vin**	32 »	17 »	30 »
1032	**50 f. +15 f. bleu-vert**	36 »	21 »	35 »
	Nᵒˢ 1027 à 1032 (6 val.)	**160 »**	**90 »**	**150 »**
	La série, non dentelée		245 »	

Tirage : 1 050 000 séries.

1955. – *60ᵉ anniversaire de l'invention du cinématographe par les frères Lumière. Taille-douce. Dentelé 13.*

Auguste (1862-1954) et Louis (1864-1948) Lumière.

1033	**30 f. brun-rouge**	7 50	4 »	5 50
	a. (Non dentelé)		40 »	

Tirage : 2 200 000.

1955. – *5ᵉ centenaire de la mort de Jacques Coeur (1395-1456). Taille-douce. Dentelé 13.*

Jacques Coeur et son palais de Bourges.

1034	**12 f. violet foncé**	2 80	1 50	1 90
	a. (Non dentelé)		23 »	

Tirage : 2 535 000.

1955. – *Centenaire de l'amitié franco-canadienne. Frégate "La Capricieuse". Taille-douce. Dentelé 13.*

1035	**30 f. bleu-vert et bleu**	6 »	3 60	5 50
	a. (Non dentelé)		30 »	

Tirage : 2 200 000.

1955. – ***Série touristique. Taille-douce. Dentelés 13.***

Région bordelaise (la Gironde et puits de pétrole de Parentis).

Marseille, le vieux port et N. D. de la Garde.

1036	6 f. rouge carminé	0 40	0 15	0 30
1037	8 f. ardoise	0 80	0 30	0 30

Le port de Nice.

Pont Valentré, à Cahors.

1038	10 f. bleu	0 40	0 15	0 30
1039	12 f. sépia et gris-bleu	0 40	0 15	0 30

Uzerche (Limousin).

Le Mont Pelé, Martinique.

1040	18 f. vert et bleu-noir	1 »	0 70	0 30
1041	20 f. violet et lilas	4 »	2 30	0 30

Remparts de Brouage (Aunis) (16e siècle).

1042	25 f. brun-rouge et brun-lilas	1 50	1 »	0 30
	Nos 1036 à 1042 (7 val.)	**8 50**	**4 75**	**2 10**
	La série, non dentelée		125 »	

Tirages : 53 830 000, 115 050 000, 169 885 000, 38 483 500, 60 370 000, 75 080 000 et 114 595 000.

Les types des 6 f. et 12 f. ont été repris en 1957 pour des 35 f. et 70 f. (nos 1118 et 1119).

1955. – ***Centenaire de la mort de l'écrivain Gérard Labrunie, dit de Nerval. Taille-douce. Dentelé 13.***

Médaillon, par Ichan Duseigneur.

1043	12 f. brun carminé et brun-noir	0 70	0 50	0 50
	a. (Non dentelé)		23 »	

Tirage : 2 500 000.

1955. – ***Armoiries de provinces (VIII). Typographie. Dentelés 14 x 13½.***

Comté de Foix.

Marche.

1044	50 c. noir, vert, jaune et rouge	0 20	0 20	0 20
1045	70 c. rouge, bleu et jaune	0 20	0 20	0 20

Roussillon.

Comtat Venaissin.

1046	80 c. bistre, jaune et rouge	0 20	0 20	0 20
1047	1 f. outremer, rouge et jaune	0 20	0 20	0 20
	Nos 1044 à 1047 (4 val.)	**0 80**	**0 80**	**0 80**
	La série, non dentelée		46 »	

Tirages : 35 920 000, 26 240 000, 8 240 000 et 102 230 000.

1955. – ***Au profit de la Croix-Rouge. Croix en rouge. Taille-douce. Dentelés 13.*** [C]

L'enfant à la cage, par J.-B. Pigalle (1714-1785).

L'enfant à l'oie (statue grecque).

1048	12 f. +3 f. lie-de-vin	10 »	5 »	10 »
1049	15 f. +5 f. bleu-gris	6 50	4 50	6 50
	a. (paire verticale de carnet)		52 »	
	La paire, non dentelée		160 »	

Tirage : 1 500 000 paires.

Le 15 f. +5 f. a aussi été émis en carnets de 10 (tirage : 150 000).

La cote du no 1049a s'applique à une paire avec marges blanches supérieure et inférieure.

1955

Du n° 1008 au n° 1049 :

46 timbres ****259** ***145** **⊙223**

1956. – *Mémorial national de la déportation, à Struthof (Alsace). Taille-douce. Dentelé 13.*

1050	**15 f. brun-carmin et brun-noir**	0 80	0 50	0 65
	a. (Non dentelé)		30 »	

Tirage : 2 600 000.

1956. – *Beffroi de Douai. Taille-douce. Dentelé 13.*

1051	**15 f. bleu foncé et bleu clair**	0 70	0 50	0 65
	a. (Non dentelé)		23 »	

Tirage : 3 000 000.

1956. – *40e anniversaire de la mort du colonel Émile A. -C. Driant (1855-1916) à Verdun. Taille-douce. Dentelé 13.*

Le colonel Driant et son poste de commandement du bois des Caures.

1052	**15 f. bleu**	0 55	0 30	0 50
	a. (Non dentelé)		23 »	

Tirage : 3 130 000.

1956. – *40e anniversaire de la victoire de Verdun. Taille-douce. Dentelé 13.*

Fantassins dans la tranchée.

1053	**30 f. bleu-violet et brun-olive**	2 40	1 40	1 85
	a. (Non dentelé)		30 »	

Tirage : 2 350 000.

1956. – *Journée du Timbre. Taille-douce. Dentelé 13.*

François de Tassis et courrier à cheval, gravure de Dürer.

1054	**12 f. +3 f. vert, outremer et brun-lilas**	3 50	2 »	3 50
	a. (Non dentelé)		40 »	

Tirage : 1 400 000.

1956. – *Inventeurs et chercheurs célèbres. Taille-douce. Dentelés 13.*

J-H. Fabre et insectes.

Charles Tellier et navire frigorifique.

1055	**12 f. brun-violet et brun-orange**	1 25	0 50	0 80
1056	**15 f. noir et violet-noir**	1 25	0 50	0 80

Camille Flammarion et observatoire de Juvisy.

Paul Sabatier et catalyseur.

1057	**18 f. outremer**	2 25	1 30	2 »
1058	**30 f. vert-noir et vert-bleu**	5 75	3 20	3 50
	Nos 1055 à 1058 (4 val.)	**10 50**	**5 50**	**7 10**
	La série, non dentelée		110 »	

Tirage : 2 300 000 séries.

1956. – *Grand Trianon de Versailles. Taille-douce. Dentelé 13.*

Oeuvre d'Hardouin-Mansart (1646-1708).

1059	**12 f. vert foncé et brun**	1 90	1 10	1 25
	a. (Non dentelé)		23 »	

Tirage : 2 800 000.

1956. – ***Amitié France-Amérique latine. Taille-douce. Dentelé 13.***

Sculpture péruvienne du XVIe siècle (guerrier Ataviado et tête de "La Prudence"(XVIe siècle), par Michel Colombe (1431-1512).

1060	**30 f. brun et brun-rouge**	2 50	1 60	2 »
	a. (Non dentelé)		30 »	

Tirage : 2 075 000.

1956. – ***Jumelage Reims-Florence. Taille-douce. Dentelé 13.***

Détail de "l'Ange au Sourire", cathédrale de Reims. Palais de la Seigneurie à Florence et détail du "Printemps", de Botticelli.

1061	**12 f. noir et vert**	1 »	0 65	1 »
	a. (Non dentelé)		42 »	

Tirage : 2 550 000.

1956. – ***Ordre de Malte. Taille-douce. Dentelé 13.***

Léproserie en A.E.F.

1062	**12 f. sépia, rouge et brun-rouge**	0 70	0 50	0 65
	a. (Non dentelé)		35 »	

Tirage : 2 450 000.

1956. – ***Saint Yves, patron des hommes de loi. Taille-douce. Dentelé 13.***

St Yves entre le pauvre et le riche.

1063	**15 f. gris et noir**	0 55	0 30	0 50
	a. (Non dentelé)		27 »	

Tirage : 2 900 000.

1956. – ***Centenaire de la naissance du maréchal Franchet d'Esperey. Taille-douce. Dentelé 13.***

Maréchal Franchet d'Esperey.

1064	**30 f. lilas-brun**	3 25	1 85	2 30
	a. (Non dentelé)		23 »	

Tirage : 2 200 000.

1956. – ***Centenaire de l'érection en commune de Montceau-les-Mines. Taille-douce. Dentelé 13.***

Monument aux mineurs de Montceau-les-Mines.

1065	**12 f. brun-violet**	0 70	0 50	0 65
	a. (Non dentelé)		23 »	

Tirage : 2 730 000.

1956. – ***Célébrités du XVe au XXe siècles. Taille-douce. Dentelés 13.***

Guillaume Budé, humaniste. Jean Goujon, sculpteur. Samuel de Champlain, explorateur.

1066	**12 f. +3 f. bleu**	7 »	4 »	7 »
1067	**12 f. +3 f. gris-violet**	7 »	4 »	7 »
1068	**12 f. +3 f. vermillon**	7 »	4 »	7 »

Jean-Baptiste Siméon Chardin (autoportrait).

Maurice Barrés, écrivain.

Maurice Ravel, compositeur.

1069	**15 f. +5 f. vert**	10 »	6 »	10 »
1070	**15 f. +5 f. bistre**	10 »	6 »	10 »
1071	**15 f. +5 f. violet**	10 »	6 »	10 »
	N°s 1066 à 1071 (6 val.)	**51 »**	**30 »**	**51 »**
	La série, non dentelée	185 »		

Tirage : 1 100 000 séries.

1956. – *Série sportive. Taille-douce. Dentelés 13.*

Basket-ball.

Pelote basque.

1072	**30 f. gris et noir**	1 80	0 80	0 30
1073	**40 f. brun foncé et lilas**	7 20	4 50	0 50

Rugby.

Alpinisme.

1074	**50 f. lilas et violet**	2 50	1 20	0 30
1075	**75 f. bleu ardoise et vert**	14 50	9 50	2 90
	N°s 1072 à 1075 (4 val.)	**26 »**	**16 »**	**4 »**
	La série, non dentelée	155 »		

Tirages : 53 475 000, 35 575 000, 101 575 000 et 13 590 000.

1956. – *Europa. Format 21 x 35½. Typographie. Dentelés 13½ x 14.*

1076	**15 f. rose et grenat**	1 25	0 80	0 30

Taille-douce. Format 22 x 36. Dentelé 13.

1077	**30 f. bleu foncé et bleu**	7 20	4 »	1 25
	La paire, non dentelée	500 »		

Tirage : 13 300 000 paires.

1956. – *Réalisations techniques (I). Taille-douce. Dentelés 13.*

Barrage de Donzère-Mondragon.

Téléphérique de l'Aiguille du Midi.

1078	**12 f. ardoise et brun**	2 »	1 10	1 40
1079	**18 f. bleu-noir**	4 »	2 30	2 75

Port de Strasbourg.

1080	**30 f. bleu-noir et bleu**	17 »	9 50	7 65
	La série, non dentelée	80 »		

Tirages : 2 590 000, 2 200 000 et (nc).

1956. – *Antoine-Augustin, baron Parmentier, créateur de la chimie alimentaire (1737-1803). Taille-douce. Dentelé 13.*

1081	**12 f. brun-rouge et brun-lilas**	1 10	0 60	0 80
	a. (Non dentelé)	23 »		

Tirage : 2 600 000.

1956. – ***Personnages étrangers ayant participé à la vie française. Taille-douce. Dentelés 13.***

Pétrarque, poète italien.

J.-B. Lulli, musicien italien.

J.-J. Rousseau, littérateur suisse.

1082	**8 f. vert**	1 »	0 50	0 80
1083	**12 f. lie-de-vin**	1 »	0 50	0 80
1084	**15 f. rouge**	1 50	0 65	0 80

Benjamin Franklin, homme d'État et physicien américain.

Frédéric Chopin, musicien polonais.

Vincent van Gogh, peintre néerlandais (autoportrait).

1085	**18 f. outremer**	3 30	1 75	2 80
1086	**20 f. violet**	4 70	2 60	2 20
1087	**30 f. turquoise**	7 »	4 »	3 60
	Nos 1082 à 1087 (6 val.)	**18 50**	**10 »**	**11 »**
	La série, non dentelée	155 »		

Tirage : 2 500 000 séries.

1956. – ***60e anniversaire de la rénovation des Jeux Olympiques. Baron Pierre de Coubertin, rénovateur. Taille-douce. Dentelé 13.***

1088	**30 f. gris et lilas**	2 50	1 50	1 80
	a. (Non dentelé)	185 »		

Tirage : 2 500 000.

1956. – ***Surtaxe au profit de la Croix-Rouge. Croix en rouge. Taille-douce. Dentelés 13.*** [C]

Jeune paysan. Détail de "Famille de paysans dans un intérieur", par Le Nain.

"Gilles", par Watteau.

1089	**12 f. +3 f. brun-olive**	3 50	1 85	3 50
1090	**15 f. +5 f. carmin**	3 60	2 »	3 60
	La paire, non dentelée		155 »	

Tirage : 1 600 000 paires.

Ont été émis aussi en carnets (tirage : 155 700).

1956			
Du n° 1050 au n° 1090 :			
41 timbres	****167**	***96**	**⊙112**

1957. – ***En l'honneur de la colombophilie. Taille-douce. Dentelé 13.***

Pigeon "Bleu-Sion-Lamotte".

1091	**15 f. bleu-noir, bleu et rose**	0 55	0 30	0 50
	a. (Non dentelé)		30 »	

Tirage : 4 550 000.

1957. – ***A la mémoire de Victor Schoelcher (1804-1893). Taille-douce. Dentelé 13.***

1092	**18 f. rose**	0 80	0 50	0 80
	a. (Non dentelé)		23 »	

Tirage : 2 645 000.

1957. – *Journée du Timbre. Taille-douce. Dentelé 13.*

Felouque du XVIIIe siècle.

1093	**12 f. +3 f. gris-bleu et brun-noir**	2 40	1 50	1 90
	a. (Non dentelé)		27 »	

Tirage : 1 900 000.

1957. – *Bicentenaire de la manufacture nationale de Sèvres. Biscuit "La Baigneuse", d'après Falconet. Taille-douce. Dentelé 13.*

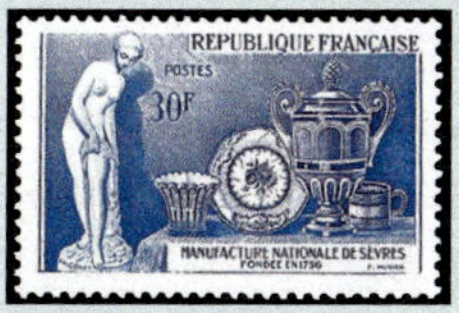

1094	**30 f. outremer et bleu foncé**	1 »	0 65	0 80
	a. (Non dentelé)		27 »	

Tirage : 2 595 000.

1957. – *Savants et inventeurs. Taille-douce. Dentelés 13.*

Gaston Planté, inventeur de l'accumulateur électrique.

Antoine Béclère, fondateur de la radiologie.

1095	**8 f. gris-olive et brun-lilas**	0 60	0 30	0 60
1096	**12 f. bleu, vert et noir**	0 70	0 30	0 70

Octave Terrillon, créateur de l'asepsie.

Etienne Oehhmichen, inventeur de l'hélicoptère.

1097	**18 f. rose et lie-de-vin**	1 70	0 80	1 70
1098	**30 f. vert et vert-noir**	3 »	1 70	3 »
	N°s 1095 à 1098 (4 val.)	**6 »**	**3 10**	**6 »**
	La série, non dentelée		125 »	

Tirage : 2 500 000 séries.

1957. – *Château d'Uzès. Taille-douce. Dentelé 13.*

1099	**12 f. bleu-vert et bistre**	0 50	0 30	0 50
	a. (Non dentelé)		23 »	

Tirage : 2 980 000.

1957. – *Héros de la Résistance (I). Taille-douce. Dentelés 13.*

Jean Moulin.

Honoré d'Estienne d'Orves.

1100	**8 f. brun-lilas**	1 30	0 80	0 65
1101	**10 f. noir et outremer**	1 30	0 80	0 65

Robert Keller.

Pierre Brossolette.

Jean-Baptiste Lebas.

1102	**12 f. bistre et vert foncé**	1 30	0 80	1 10
1103	**18 f. violet et noir**	2 30	1 25	1 85
1104	**20 f. bleu-vert et bleu**	2 »	1 10	1 25
	N°s 1100 à 1104 (5 val.)	**8 20**	**4 75**	**5 50**
	La série, non dentelée		115 »	

Tirage : 2 570 000 séries.

1957. – *Le Quesnoy. Taille-douce. Dentelés 13.*

Remparts, lac Vauban et porte fortifiée de Fauroeulx.

1105	**8 f. vert foncé**	0 15	0 15	0 15
1106	**15 f. sépia et vert-bleu**	0 15	0 15	0 15
	La paire, non dentelée		40 »	

Tirages : (nc) et 244 255 000.

1957. – *Sesquicentenaire de la Cour des Comptes. Taille-douce. Dentelé 13.*

1107	**12 f. brun-olive, noir et bleu**	0 30	0 15	0 30
	a. (Non dentelé)		17 »	

Tirage : 2 800 000.

1957. – *Célébrités du XIIIe au XIXe siècles. Taille-douce. Dentelés 13.*

Jean de Joinville. Bernard Palissy. Quentin de La Tour. Autoportrait.

1108	**12 f. +3 f. brun-olive et olive**	3 30	1 85	3 30
1109	**12 f. +3 f. vert-noir et bleu**	3 30	1 85	3 30
1110	**15 f. +5 f. lie-de-vin et rouge**	4 50	2 50	4 50

Félicité Robert de Lamennais. George Sand. Jules Guesde.

1111	**15 f. +5 f. outremer et bleu-noir**	4 40	2 30	4 40
1112	**18 f. +7 f. vert-noir et vert-gris**	5 25	2 75	5 25
1113	**18 f. +7 f. brun-lilas et brun**	5 25	2 75	5 25
	N°s 1108 à 1113 (6 val.)	**26 »**	**14 »**	**26 »**
	La série, non dentelée		140 »	

Tirage : 1 100 000 séries.

1957. – *Travaux publics. Taille-douce. Dentelé 13.*

1114	**30 f. vert-noir, violet-brun et bistre**	2 50	1 40	1 60
	a. (Non dentelé)		20 »	

Tirage : 2 320 000.

1957-59. – *Type Moissonneuse. Typographie. Dentelés 14 x 13½.*

1115	**6 f. brun-jaune**	0 15	0 15	0 15
1115A	**10 f. vert**	1 »	0 30	0 15
1116	**12 f. lilas-rose**	0 30	0 15	0 30

Tirages : 390 910 000, 303 740 000 et 148 980 000.

Chaque, non dentelé 15 50

Plusieurs timbres à ce type ont été émis avec préoblitération (voir Préoblitérés n°s 106 et suivants).

Un 10 c. vert a paru en 1960 (n° 1231).

1957. – *Port de Brest. Taille-douce. Dentelé 13.*

1117	**12 f. brun et vert foncé**	1 40	0 80	1 40
	a. (Non dentelé)		23 »	

Tirage : 2 500 000.

1957. – *Série touristique. Types de 1955. Taille-douce. Dentelés 13.*

1118	**35 f. vert-noir et vert-bleu (1036)**	4 60	3 »	1 10
1119	**70 f. noir et vert (1039)**	24 »	13 »	2 30
	La paire, non dentelée		50 »	

Tirages : 14 345 000 et 9 635 000.

1957. – *Jeux universitaires mondiaux, à Paris. Taille-douce. Dentelé 13.*

Léo Lagrange (1900-1940) et stade.

1120 **18 f. gris et noir** 0 65 0 50 0 65
a. (Non dentelé) 46 »

Tirage : 2 200 000.

1957. – *Centenaire de la mort d'Auguste Comte. Taille-douce. Dentelé 13.*

Auguste Comte.

1121 **35 f. brun-rouge et sépia** 0 50 0 30 0 50
a. (Non dentelé) 23 »

Tirage : 3 000 000.

1957. – *Europa. Taille-douce. Dentelés 13.*

1122 **20 f. brun et vert** 0 75 0 35 0 35
1123 **35 f. brun-noir et bleu** 1 40 1 10 1 10

La paire, non dentelée 230 »

Tirages : 12 630 000 et 9 335 000.

1957. – *Bimillénaire de Lyon. Taille-douce. Dentelé 13.*

Théâtre antique de Fourvière.

1124 **20 f. lilas-brun et orange** 0 50 0 30 0 50
a. (Non dentelé) 27 »

Tirage : 4 400 000.

1957. – *Série touristique. Taille-douce. Dentelés 13.*

Rivière Sens, à la Guadeloupe.

1125 **8 f. vert et ocre** 0 20 0 15 0 15
a. vert-jaune et ocre 0 30 0 15 0 15

Palais de l'Élysée, à Paris. *Sans légende ni faciale*

1126 **10 f. violet-gris et bistre** 0 20 0 15 0 15
a. (Sans légende ni faciale) 500 »

Beynac-Cazenac.

1127 **18 f. bleu et brun-lilas** 0 35 0 15 0 30

Château de Valençay. Cathédrale de Rouen.

1128 **25 f. brun-rouge et gris-bleu** 0 85 0 50 0 30
1129 **35 f. rose et lie-de-vin** 0 35 0 15 0 15

St-Rémy-les-Antiques. Evian-les-Bains.

1130 **50 f. bistre et vert** 0 70 0 30 0 15
1131 **65 f. bleu-noir et bleu** 0 85 0 50 0 50

Nos 1125 à 1131 (7 val.) **3 50** **1 90** **1 70**

La série, non dentelée 170 »

Tirages : 63 840 000, 67 850 000, 92 855 000, 55 335 000, 121 900 000, 190 615 000 et 110 430 000.

Les types des 8 f., 10 f. et 65 f. ont été repris en 1959 (nos 1192 à 1194).

Le 35 f. a été surchargé CONSEIL DE L'EUROPE en janvier 1958, pour les besoins de cette institution (voir Timbres de Service, no 16).

1957. – ***Célébrités étrangères. Taille-douce. Dentelés 13.***

Nicolas Copernic.

Michelangelo Buonarroti, dit Michel-Ange.

1132	**8 f. brun-violet**	1 10	0 70	0 80
1133	**10 f. vert-bleu**	1 10	0 70	0 80

Miguel Cervantès de Saavedra.

Rembrandt (autoportrait).

Newton.

1134	**12 f. violet foncé**	1 10	0 70	1 »
1135	**15 f. bistre et brun**	1 40	1 »	1 10
1136	**18 f. bleu**	2 »	1 10	1 30

Wolfgang Amadeus Mozart.

Johann Wolfgang Von Goethe.

1137	**25 f. violet et brun-violet**	2 »	1 60	1 30
1138	**35 f. bleu**	2 30	1 60	1 70
	N°s 1132 à 1138 (7 val.)	**11 »**	**7 40**	**8 »**
	La série, non dentelée		170 »	

Tirage : 2 700 000 séries.

1957. – ***Centenaire de la mort du chimiste L. -J. Thénard et de la fondation de la Société de secours des amis des sciences. Taille-douce. Dentelé 13.***

1139	**15 f. jaune-olive et vert foncé**	0 50	0 30	0 50
	a. (Non dentelé)		20 »	

Tirage : 3 000 000.

1957. – ***Au profit de la Croix-Rouge. Croix en rouge. Gravures de Jacques Callot (1592-1635) (musée de Nancy). Taille-douce. Dentelés 13.*** [C]

L'aveugle et le mendiant.

La mendiante et la borgnesse.

1140	**15 f. +7 f. outremer**	5 »	2 50	5 »
1141	**20 f. +8 f. brun-lilas**	6 50	3 80	6 50
	La paire, non dentelée		115 »	

Tirage : 1 350 000 paires.

Ont été émis aussi en carnets (tirage : 180 000).

1957			
Du n° 1091 au n° 1141 :			
52 timbres	****110**	***63**	**⊙74**

1958. – ***Grands médecins. Taille-douce. Dentelés 13.***

Philippe Pinel.

Fernand Widal.

1142	**8 f. olive**	1 10	0 65	0 80
1143	**12 f. violet**	1 10	0 65	0 80

Charles Nicolle.

René Leriche.

1144	**15 f. bleu**	1 70	0 80	1 »
1145	**35 f. noir**	2 10	1 10	1 40
	N°s 1142 à 1145 (4 val.)	**6 »**	**3 20**	**4 »**
	La série, non dentelée		95 »	

Tirage : 2 600 000 séries.

1958. – ***Grands savants. Taille-douce. Dentelés 13.***

Joseph-Louis Lagrange.

Urbain Le Verrier.

1146	**8 f. bleu-vert et bleu-violet**	1 10	0 50	0 80
1147	**12 f. brun-noir et violet-gris**	1 30	0 65	0 80
	a. brun-noir	185 »	125 »	

Léon Foucault.

Claude-Louis Berthollet.

1148	**15 f. vert-noir et vert**	2 20	1 25	1 10
1149	**35 f. carmin et brun-carmin**	2 90	1 60	1 60
	N°s 1146 à 1149 (4 val.)	**7 50**	**4 »**	**4 30**
	La série, non dentelée		100 »	

Tirage : 2 400 000 séries.

1958. – ***Série touristique. Type de 1954 (976). Taille-douce. Dentelé 13.***

1150	**20 f. olive et bleu**	0 50	0 30	0 30
	a. (Non dentelé)		23 »	

1958. – ***Journée du Timbre. Taille-douce. Dentelé 13.***

Mécanisation de la distribution rurale.

1151	**15 f. +5 f. vert-brun et olive foncé**	2 20	1 25	1 60
	a. (Non dentelé)		35 »	

Tirage : 1 900 000.

1958. – ***Villes reconstruites. Taille-douce. Dentelés 13.***

Le Havre.

Maubeuge.

1152	**12 f. olive et rose-rouge**	0 80	0 50	0 65
1153	**15 f. bistre, lilas et violet-brun**	0 80	0 50	0 65

Saint-Dié.

Sète.

1154	**18 f. vert-noir et outremer**	1 30	0 80	1 »
1155	**25 f. bistre, vert-bleu et bleu foncé**	1 60	1 »	1 »
	N°s 1152 à 1155 (4 val.)	**4 50**	**2 80**	**3 30**
	La série, non dentelée		95 »	

Tirage : 2 700 000 séries.

1958. – ***Exposition de Bruxelles. Taille-douce. Dentelé 13.***

1156	**35 f. vert foncé et bleu**	0 30	0 15	0 30
	a. (Non dentelé)		46 »	

Tirage : 3 600 000.

1958. – *Héros de la Résistance (II). Taille-douce. Dentelés 13.*

Jean Cavaillès.

Fred Scamaroni.

1157	**8 f. violet et brun-noir**	0 90	0 50	0 90
1158	**12 f. bleu clair et vert-bleu**	0 90	0 50	0 90

Simone Michel-Lévy.

Jacques Bingen.

1159	**15 f. brun et gris**	2 40	1 25	1 25
1160	**20 f. olive et bleu foncé**	1 80	1 25	1 40
	N°s 1157 à 1160 (4 val.)	**6 »**	**3 50**	**4 45**
	La série, non dentelée		95 »	

Tirage : 2 450 000 séries.

1958. – *Jeux traditionnels. Taille-douce. Dentelés 13.*

Boules.

Joutes nautiques.

1161	**12 f. rouge et brun-orange**	1 25	0 80	1 10
1162	**15 f. vert foncé, bleu et vert**	1 60	1 »	1 20
	a. (FFRANÇAISE)	230 »	185 »	130 »
	b. (FFRANÇAISE, non dent.)		2 000 »	

Tir à l'arc.

Lutte bretonne.

1163	**18 f. vert et brun-orange**	3 »	1 60	1 60
1164	**25 f. brun et vert-noir**	4 15	3 »	2 50
	N°s 1161 à 1164 (4 val.)	**10 »**	**6 40**	**6 40**
	La série, non dentelée		115 »	

Tirages : 2 350 000, 2 685 000, 2 585 000 et 2 350 000.

1958. – *Cathédrale de Senlis. Taille-douce. Dentelé 13.*

1165	**15 f. gris-bleu et bleu**	0 50	0 30	0 50
	a. (Non dentelé)		20 »	

Tirage : 2 800 000.

1958. – *Célébrités. Taille-douce. Dentelés 13.*

Joachim du Bellay.

Jean Bart.

Denis Diderot.

1166	**12 f. +4 f. vert**	2 20	1 25	2 20
1167	**12 f. +4 f. bleu**	2 20	1 25	2 20
1168	**15 f. +5 f. lilas-brun**	2 40	1 60	2 40

Gustave Courbet.

J.-B. Carpeaux (autoportrait).

Toulouse-Lautrec.

1169	**15 f. +5 f. outremer**	2 50	1 70	2 50
1170	**20 f. +8 f. rouge**	2 50	1 70	2 50
1171	**35 f. +15 f. vert-bleu**	3 20	2 »	3 20
	N°s 1166 à 1171 (6 val.)	**15 »**	**9 50**	**15 »**
	La série, non dentelée		130 »	

Tirages : 1 250 000, 1 300 000, 1 100 000, 1 200 000, 1 200 000 et 1 100 000.

1958. – *Fragment de la tapisserie de la reine Mathilde, à Bayeux. Taille-douce. Dentelé 13.*

1172	**15 f. rouge et bleu**	0 55	0 30	0 55
	a. (Non dentelé)		40 »	

Tirage : 2 900 000.

1958. – *Europa. Taille-douce. Dentelés 13.*

1173	**20 f. rouge**	0 50	0 20	0 40
1174	**35 f. outremer**	1 50	0 70	1 15
	La paire, non dentelée	155 »		

Tirages : 19 805 000 et 9 210 000.

1958. – *Château de Foix. Taille-douce. Dentelé 13.*

Château de Foix.

1175	**15 f. outremer, gris, brun et vert**	0 50	0 30	0 50
	a. (Non dentelé)	20 »		

Tirage : 3 285 000.

1958. – *Jumelage Paris-Rome. Taille-douce. Dentelé 13.*

Hôtels de Ville des deux capitales.

1176	**35 f. gris, rouge et bleu clair**	0 50	0 30	0 50
	a. (Non dentelé)	30 »		

Tirage : 3 335 000.

1958. – *Inauguration du palais de l'U.N.E.S.C.O., à Paris. Taille-douce. Dentelés 13.*

1177	**20 f. bistre et bleu-vert**	0 15	0 15	0 15
1178	**35 f. orange et vert-noir**	0 30	0 15	0 30
	La paire, non dentelée	125 »		

Tirages : 5 350 000 et 4 400 000.

1958. – *40e anniversaire de l'armistice. Taille-douce. Dentelé 13.*

1179	**15 f. vert et bleu**	0 70	0 30	0 50
	a. (Non dentelé)	23 »		

Tirage : 4 050 000.

1958. – *Armoiries de villes (III). Typographie. Dentelés 14 x 13½.*

Marseille.

Lyon.

1180	**50 c. bleu et outremer**	0 15	0 15	0 15
1181	**70 c. brun-rouge, rouge, bleu et jaune**	0 15	0 15	0 15

Toulouse.

Bordeaux.

1182	**80 c. rouge, bleu et jaune**	0 15	0 15	0 15
	a. Bleu et jaune très décalés	200 »		
1183	**1 f. bleu, rouge et jaune**	0 15	0 15	0 15

Nice.

Nantes.

Lille.

1184	**2 f. bleu foncé, rouge et vert**	0 15	0 15	0 15
1185	**3 f. noir, rouge, jaune et vert**	0 15	0 15	0 15
1186	**5 f. brun-noir et rouge**	0 15	0 15	0 15
	Nos 1180 à 1186 (7 val.)	**1 05**	**1 05**	**1 05**
	La série, non dentelée	95 »		

Tirages : 11 790 000, 13 930 000, 8 160 000, 92 560 000, 41 850 000, 35 540 000 et 473 320 000.

Un 5 c. au type du 5 f. Lille a paru en 1960 (n° 1230).

1958. – *Au profit de la Croix-Rouge. Croix en rouge. Taille-douce. Dentelés 13.* [C]

Saint Vincent de Paul.

J. Henri Dunant.

1187	**15 f. +7 f. vert foncé**	1 60	1 »	1 60
1188	**20 f. +8 f. violet**	1 60	1 »	1 60
	La paire, non dentelée		115 »	

Tirage : 1 700 000 paires.

Ont été émis aussi en carnets (tirage : 199 300).

> **1958**
> **Du n° 1142 au n° 1188 :**
> **47 timbres** ****61** ***37** **⊙48**

Vᵉ République

1959. – *Floralies parisiennes. Taille-douce. Dentelé 13.*

Arc de Triomphe du Carrousel, à Paris.

1189	**15 f. polychrome**	0 65	0 50	0 50
	a. (Non dentelé)		30 »	

Tirage : 6 360 000.

1959. – *Sesquicentenaire des Palmes académiques. Taille-douce. Dentelé 13.*

1190	**20 f. grenat, violet et sépia**	0 30	0 15	0 30
	a. (Non dentelé)		20 »	

Tirage : 3 325 000.

1959. – *Centenaire de la naissance de Charles de Foucauld, apôtre du Sahara (1858-1916). Taille-douce. Dentelé 13.*

Le Père de Foucauld devant son ermitage, à Tamanrasset.

1191	**50 f. bleu, brun-rouge et brun-lilas**	0 65	0 30	0 65
	a. (Non dentelé)		30 »	

Tirage : 3 060 000.

1959. – *Série touristique. Types de 1957. Taille-douce. Dentelés 13.*

Palais de l'Elysée, à Paris.

Evian-les-Bains.

1192	**30 f. vert foncé (1126)**	3 20	1 60	0 30
1193	**85 f. lilas-brun (1131)**	4 70	2 75	0 50

Rivière Sens, à la Guadeloupe.

1194	**100 f. violet (1125)**	38 »	21 »	0 50
	La série, non dentelée		110 »	

Tirages : 67 095 000, 46 445 000 et 59 775 000.

1959. – *Blason d'Alger. Typographie. Dentelé 14 x 13½.*

1195	**15 f. polychrome**	0 30	0 15	0 15
	a. (Non dentelé)		15 50	

Un 15 c. à ce type a paru en 1960 (nᵒ 1232).

Tirage : 96 490 000.

1959. – *Journée du Timbre et 20ᵉ anniversaire du service aéropostal de nuit. Taille-douce. Dentelé 13.*

1196	**20 f. +5 f. polychrome**	0 80	0 50	0 80
	a. (Non dentelé)		61 »	

Ce type a été repris, modifié, en 1964 (nᵒ 1418).

Tirage : 2 500 000.

1959. – ***175ᵉ anniversaire de l'École des Mines à Paris. Taille-douce. Dentelé 13.***

Façade de l'École et lampe de mineur.

1197	**20 f. carmin, noir et bleu-vert**	0 30	0 15	0 30
	a. (Non dentelé)		23 »	

Tirage : 2 950 000.

1959. – ***Héros de la Résistance (III). Taille-douce. Dentelés 13.***

Les 5 martyrs du lycée Buffon.

Yvonne Le Roux.

Médéric Védy.

1198	**15 f. violet et gris-noir**	0 55	0 30	0 30
1199	**15 f. lilas-rose et lilas**	0 55	0 30	0 55
1200	**20 f. vert et bleu-vert**	0 55	0 30	0 55

Louis-Martin Bret.

Gaston Moutardier.

1201	**20 f. brun-orange et brun clair**	0 75	0 30	0 75
1202	**30 f. lilas-rose et violet foncé**	0 90	0 30	0 75
	Nos 1198 à 1202 (5 val.)	**3 30**	**1 50**	**2 90**
	La série, non dentelée		95 »	

Tirages : 3 085 000, 3 150 000, 3 000 000, 3 100 000 et 3 100 000.

1959. – ***Réalisations techniques (II). Taille-douce. Dentelés 13.***

Barrage de Foum el Gherza, en Algérie.

Centre atomique de Marcoule.

1203	**15 f. olive et bleu-vert**	0 50	0 20	0 30
1204	**20 f. carmin et brun-rouge**	0 70	0 30	0 70

Hassi-Messaoud, Sahara.

Palais du C.N.I.T (Centre National des Industries et des Techniques).

1205	**30 f. brun-olive, bleu et bleu-vert**	0 70	0 30	0 70
1206	**50 f. vert terne et bleu-gris**	1 10	0 80	0 80
	N°ˢ 1203 à 1206 (4 val.)	**3 »**	**1 60**	**2 50**
	La série, non dentelée		100 »	

Tirages : 4 140 000, 4 550 000, 4 110 000 et 4 085 000.

1959. – *Célébrités. Taille-douce. Dentelés 13.*

Geoffroi de La Villehardouin.

André Le Nôtre et vue du parc de Versailles.

1207	**15 f. +5 f. bleu-violet**	1 60	1 »	1 60
1208	**15 f. +5 f. vert foncé**	1 60	1 »	1 60

Jean d'Alembert.

David d'Angers, sa statue et le château du roi René, à Angers.

1209	**20 f. +10 f. brun-jaune**	1 60	1 »	1 60
1210	**20 f. +10 f. gris**	1 80	1 »	1 80

Xavier Bichat.

Frédéric-Auguste Bartholdi et ses oeuvres : la statue de la Liberté, à New York et le Lion de Belfort.

1211	**30 f. +10 f. carmin**	1 60	1 25	1 60
1212	**30 f. +10 f. brun-rouge**	2 »	1 25	1 80
	N°ˢ 1207 à 1212 (6 val.)	**10 20**	**6 50**	**10 »**
	La série, non dentelée		140 »	

Tirage : 1 500 000 séries.

1959. – *Hommage aux pilotes d'essai. Taille-douce. Dentelé 13.*

Charles Goujon et colonel Rozanoff.

1213	**20 f. bleu et brun-orange**	0 65	0 30	0 65
	a. (Non dentelé)		54 »	

Tirage : 4 380 000.

1959. – *Centenaire de la mort de Marceline Desbordes-Valmore. Taille-douce. Dentelé 13.*

Marceline Desbordes-Valmore et église N.-D. de Douai.

1214	**30 f. vert-bleu, brun-lilas et bleu**	0 30	0 15	0 30
	a. (Non dentelé)		27 »	

Tirage : 4 200 000.

1959. – *Inauguration du pont de Tancarville. Taille-douce. Dentelé 13.*

1215	**30 f. bistre, vert et bleu**	0 50	0 15	0 50
	a. (Non dentelé)		30 »	
	b. (inscript. en bleu clair)	46 »	30 »	15 50

Tirage : 4 930 000.

1959. – *Marianne à la nef. Typographie. Dentelé 14* x *13½.*

1216	**25 f. vert-gris et rouge**	0 50	0 30	0 15
	a. (Non dentelé)		20 »	

Un 25 c. bleu et rouge à ce type a paru en 1960 (n° 1234).

Tirage : 714 710 000.

1959. – ***Centenaire de la naissance de Jean Jaurès. Taille-douce. Dentelé 13.***

1217 50 f. brun-violet 0 50 0 30 0 50
a. (Non dentelé) 23 »

Tirage : 4 630 000.

1959. – ***Europa. Taille-douce. Dentelés 13.***

1218 25 f. vert 0 50 0 20 0 20
1219 50 f. violet 2 » 1 » 1 40

La paire, non dentelée 155 »

Tirages : 10 000 000 et 8 500 000.

1959. – ***Hommage aux donneurs de sang. Taille-douce. Dentelé 13.***

1220 20 f. lilas-rose et gris 0 30 0 15 0 30
a. (Non dentelé) 42 »

Tirage : 4 890 000.

1959. – ***Tricentenaire du traité des Pyrénées. Taille-douce. Dentelés 13.***

Avesnes-s-Helpe (la place Guillemin). Perpignan (le Castillet).

1221 20 f. bleu et bistre 0 50 0 30 0 30
1222 30 f. lilas-brun et bleu 0 50 0 30 0 50

Symbole du traité (détail du revers de la médaille frappée à cette occasion).

1223 50 f. bleu, orange et rose 0 65 0 30 0 50

La série, non dentelée 77 »

Tirages : 4 475 000, 4 990 000 et 4 730 000.

1959. – ***Pour vaincre la poliomyélite. Taille-douce. Dentelé 13.***

1224 20 f. bleu foncé 0 30 0 15 0 30
a. (Non dentelé) 35 »

Tirage : 4 500 000.

1959. – ***Centenaire de la naissance du philosophe Henri Bergson. Taille-douce. Dentelé 13.***

1225 50 f. brun-orange 0 50 0 30 0 50
a. (Non dentelé) 27 »

Tirage : 4 600 000.

1959. – ***Au profit de la Croix-Rouge. Croix en rouge. Taille-douce. Dentelés 13.*** 🄲

Abbé de L'Épée. Valentin Haüy.

1226 20 f. +10 f. noir et brun-violet 2 60 1 60 2 60
1227 25 f. +10 f. bleu et noir 3 » 1 60 3 »

La paire, non dentelée 110 »

Tirage : 1 700 000 paires.

ont été émis aussi en carnets tirage : 132 000.

1959. – ***10e anniversaire de l'O.T.A.N. et inauguration de son palais, à Paris. Taille-douce. Dentelé 13.***

Le Palais de l'O.T.A.N., porte Dauphine.

1228	**50 f. vert, outremer et brun-lilas**	0 65	0 30	0 65
	a. (Non dentelé)		77 »	

Tirage : 4 325 000.

1959. – ***Au profit des sinistrés de Fréjus. Timbre de même date (Marianne à la nef, n° 1216) surchargé.***

1229	**+5 f. s. 25 f. vert-gris et rouge (1216)**	0 30	0 15	0 30
	a. (Non dentelé)		23 »	
	b. (Surch. renv)		2 700 »	
	c. (tenant à non surchargé)		2 250 »	

Tirage : 12 420 000.

> **1959**
>
> **Du n° 1189 au n° 1229 :**
>
> **41 timbres** ****80** ***44** **⊙32**

A partir de 1960 : 100 c(entimes) = 1 NF.

1 (nouveau) f(ranc) = 100 f. anciens.

Avec le "nouveau franc", les mentions c (centimes) et f (franc) n'apparaissent plus sur les timbres : pour garder l'homogénéité du catalogue nous avons préféré indiquer comme avant 1960, les valeurs inférieures au franc en centimes (Exemple : N° 1230 : 5 c. et 0,05 sur le timbre).

A partir de 1960 les cotes de la colonne de gauche concernent les timbres neufs, sans charnière, celles de la colonne de droite les timbres oblitérés.

1960-61. – ***Types de 1957-59 (nouveaux pour les nos 1230A, 1233 et 1234A) avec valeur en nouveau franc. Typographie. Dentelés 14 x 13½.*** [C]

20 c. Type I : Présence de deux taches parasites entre 0 et 2.

20 c. Type II : Taches parasites absentes (roulettes).

Voir note après le n°181

25 c. Type I : Présence de petites taches en bout des hachures.

25 c. Type II : Taches supprimées (carnets de 8).

Armoiries d'Oran.

1230	**5 c. brun-noir et rouge**	5 »	0 20
1230A	**5 c. polychrome**	0 30	0 15
1231	**10 c. vert**	0 65	0 15

La semeuse de Piel, d'après Roty.

1232	**15 c. polychrome**	1 »	0 20
1233	**20 c. turquoise et rose (I)**	0 30	0 15
	a. (roulette) (II)	25 »	6 »

1234	**25 c. bleu et rouge (I)**	2 75	0 15
	a. (paire verticale de carnet avec barres)	12 »	
	b. (type II)	8 »	2 »
	c. (avec bandelette inférieure blanche)	22 »	
1234A	**30 c. noir et outremer (1233)**	2 »	0 50
	Nos 1230 à 1234A (7 val.)	**12 »**	**1 50**
	La série, non dentelée	115 »	

Tirages : 143 580 000, 255 500 000, (nc), 143 760 000, (nc), 390 300 000 et (nc).

Le n° 1231 a été surchargé "E.A. " en 1962 (voir tome II Algérie nos 354 et 359).

1960. – ***Série touristique. Taille-douce. Dentelés 13.***

Cathédrale de Laon.

1235	**15 c. bleu-noir et bleu**	0 50	0 30

Château de Fougères.

Gorges de Kerrata, en Algérie.

1236	**30 c. brun, vert et bleu**	3 »	0 40
1237	**45 c. olive et violet**	1 »	0 30

Mosquée de Tlemcen, en Algérie.

Vallée de la Sioule.

1238	**50 c. vert foncé et lie-de-vin**	2 »	0 15
1239	**65 c. bistre-olive, brun et bleu**	1 50	0 30

Viaduc de Chaumont.

Massif du Grand Bénard et église de Cilaos, à La Réunion.

1240	**85 c. vert, sépia et bleu**	3 »	0 30
1241	**1 f. violet, vert et bleu**	3 »	0 25
	N°s 1235 à 1241 (7 val.)	**14 »**	**2 »**
	La série, non dentelée	170 »	

Tirages : 32 680 000, 37 360 000, 63 670 000, 87 050 000, 36 965 000, 55 365 000 et 87 130 000.

Les n°s 1237 et 1238 ont été surchargés "E.A. " en 1962 (voir tome II 2e partie Algérie n°s 356, 357, 361 et 362).

1960. – *Centenaire de la naissance de l'historien Pierre Girauld de Nolhac. Taille-douce. Dentelé 13.*

Effigie de l'historien, château de Versailles et St-Pierre de Rome.

1242	**20 c. noir et gris**	0 65	0 50
	a. (Non dentelé)	30 »	

Tirage : 4 500 000.

1960. – *Musée d'art et d'industrie de Saint-Étienne. Taille-douce. Dentelé 13.*

1243	**30 c. brun-lilas, vert-bleu et rouge**	0 65	0 50
	a. (Non dentelé)	23 »	

Tirage : 4 500 000.

1960. – *5e session des États généraux des communes d'Europe, à Cannes. Taille-douce. Dentelé 13.*

Vue de Cannes.

1244	**50 c. rouge-orange et vert**	1 »	0 80
	a. (Non dentelé)	77 »	

Tirage : 4 500 000.

1960. – *Journée du Timbre. Taille-douce. Dentelé 13.*

Navire câblier "Ampère".

1245	**20 c. +5 c. bleu, bleu-vert et bleu-noir**	1 85	1 50
	a. (Non dentelé)	30 »	
	b. (nuages bleus)	23 »	

Tirage : 2 600 000.

1960. – *Centenaire du rattachement du duché de Savoie et du comté de Nice. Taille-douce. Dentelés 13.*

Savoyarde et glaciers de l'Homme.

Niçoise et plage.

1246	**30 c. vert foncé**	0 80	0 70
1247	**50 c. brun-rouge, rouge et jaune**	0 80	0 50
	La paire, non dentelée	77 »	

Tirages : 4 500 000 et 5 000 000.

1960. – *Héros de la Résistance (4e série). Taille-douce. Dentelés 13.*

Edmond Debeaumarché.

Pierre Masse.

Maurice Ripoche.

1248	**20 c. jaune-olive et noir**	2 »	1 50
1249	**20 c. rose et lilas-rose**	2 »	1 50
1250	**30 c. violet et lilas**	3 »	2 »

Léonce Vieljeux.

Abbé René Bonpain.

1251	**30 c. bleu-gris et bleu**	3 »	2 »
1252	**50 c. olive et brun-rouge**	4 »	3 »
	N°s 1248 à 1252 (5 val.)	**14 »**	**10 »**
	La série, non dentelée	95 »	

Tirage : 3 300 000 séries.

1960. – *Année mondiale du réfugié. Taille-douce. Dentelé 13.*

1253	**25 c. +10 c. vert, brun-olive et bleu-noir**	0 50	0 50
	a. (Non dentelé)	70 »	

Tirage : 3 030 000.

1960. – *Sesquicentenaire de l'École Normale de Strasbourg. Taille-douce. Dentelé 13.*

1254	**20 c. rose-lilas, violet et noir**	0 30	0 30
	a. (Non dentelé)	23 »	

Tirage : 4 500 000.

1960. – *Château de Blois. Taille-douce. Dentelé 13.*

1255	**30 c. bleu, sépia et vert-bleu**	1 »	0 80
	a. (Non dentelé)	23 »	

Tirage : 4 500 000.

1960. – *Station thermale de La Bourboule. Taille-douce. Dentelé 13.*

1256	**50 c. brun foncé, carmin et vert-bleu**	0 80	0 80
	a. (Non dentelé)	27 »	

Tirage : 4 500 000.

1960. – *Célébrités. Taille-douce. Dentelés 13.*

Michel de l'Hospital et château de La Roche les Aigueperse.

Henri de La Tour d'Auvergne, vicomte de Turenne et la ferme de Turenne, à Bazeille.

1257	**10 c. +5 c. lilas-rose et violet**	2 »	2 »
1258	**20 c. +10 c. olive et lilas-brun**	3 »	3 »

Nicolas Boileau et sa maison, à Auteuil.

Jean-Martin Charcot et hôpital de la Salpétrière, à Paris.

1259	**20 c. +10 c. vert et vert-bleu**	3 »	3 »
1260	**30 c. +10 c. lie-de-vin et rouge**	4 »	4 »

Georges Bizet et évocation de l'Arlésienne et de Carmen.

Edgar Degas et ses oeuvres : Danseuse au bouquet, Femme se baignant, La Ballerine.

1261	**30 c. +10 c. violet et bleu**	4 »	4 »
1262	**50 c. +15 c. ardoise**	5 »	5 »
	N°s 1257 à 1262 (6 val.)	**21 »**	**21 »**
	La série, non dentelée	130 »	

Tirage : 1 600 000 séries.

1960. – *Type Marianne de Decaris. Typographie. Dentelé 14 x 13½.*

Type II : présence d'une ligne épaisse (carnets de 8), à la base du menton, dentelures verticales souvent rognée sur 1 coté.

1263	**25 c. gris clair et carmin foncé (I)**	0 30	0 15
	a. rose et carm. foncé (I)	20 »	8 »
	b. (Non dentelé)	30 »	
	c. (avec bande publicit) (I)	5 »	3 »
	d. (paire verticale de carnets avec barres)	5 »	
	e. gris et carmin (II)	2 »	1 »
	f. (avec bandelette inférieure blanche) (II)	15 »	
	g. gris omis	200 »	
	h. rouge omis	150 »	

Ce timbre a été surchargé "E.A. " en 1962 (voir Algérie Tome II 2e partie nos 355 et 360).

1960. – *20e anniversaire de l'Appel du général de Gaulle (18 juin 1940). Taille-douce. Dentelé 13.*

1264	**20 c. brun-rouge, vert et sépia**	0 80	0 50
	a. (Non dentelé)	77 »	

Tirage : 10 000 000.

1960. – *Jeux olympiques de Rome. Taille-douce. Dentelé 13.*

Jean Bouin (1888-1914).

1265	**20 c. noir, lie-de-vin et bleu**	0 50	0 50
	a. (Non dentelé)	125 »	

Tirage : 5 500 000.

1960. – *Europa. Taille-douce. Dentelés 13.*

1266	**25 c. vert et bleu-vert**	0 25	0 15
1267	**50 c. carmin et lilas**	0 75	0 50
	a. (centre de la rosace rose pâle)	15 »	
	La paire, non dentelée	140 »	

Tirages : 17 050 000 et 11 735 000.

1960. – *Basilique de Lisieux. Taille-douce. Dentelé 13.*

Statue de sainte Thérèse et la basilique.

1268	**15 c. bleu, gris et sépia**	0 50	0 50
	a. (Non dentelé)	30 »	

Tirage : 4 795 000.

1960. – *Madame de Staël (Précurseur de l'Idée Européenne). Taille-douce. Dentelé 13.*

Corrine au Cap Misène, par Gérard (détail).

1269	**30 c. lilas et brun-jaune**	0 50	0 50
	a. (Non dentelé)	54 »	

Tirage : 5 200 000.

1960. – *Centenaire de la naissance du général Estienne. Taille-douce. Dentelé 13.*

Portrait, char Renault et avion d'observation.

1270	**15 c. lilas et gris-olive**	0 50	0 50
	a. (Non dentelé)	40 »	

Tirage : 4 750 000.

1960. – *10e anniversaire de la mort de Marc Sangnier. Taille-douce. Dentelé 13.*

Marc Sangnier et auberge de la jeunesse.

1271	**20 c. bleu, lilas et noir**	0 30	0 30
	a. (Non dentelé)	30 »	

Tirage : 5 025 000.

1960. – *20e anniversaire de l'Ordre de la Libération. Taille-douce. Dentelé 13.*

1272	**20 c. noir et vert**	0 50	0 50
	a. (Non dentelé)	35 »	

Tirage : 4 990 000.

1960. – *Oiseaux. Taille-douce. Dentelés 13.*

Vanneaux.

1273	**20 c. multicolore**	0 30	0 30

Macareux-moines.

1274	**30 c. multicolore**	0 30	0 30
	a. (Houppe prononcée sur le 4e Macareux)	2 »	1 »

Sarcelles. Guêpiers.

1275	**45 c. multicolore**	0 80	1 »
1276	**50 c. multicolore**	1 »	0 50
	Nos 1273 à 1276 (4 val.)	**2 40**	**2 10**
	La série, non dentelée	125 »	

Tirages : 5 000 000, 5 350 000, 3 600 000 et 5 250 000.

1960. – *10e anniversaire de la mort d'André Honnorat. Taille-douce. Dentelé 13.*

André Honnorat et entrée de la Cité Universitaire de Paris.

1277	**30 c. noir, vert et bleu**	0 30	0 30
	a. (Non dentelé)	19	25

Tirage : 4 835 000.

1960. – *Au profit de la Croix-Rouge. Croix en rouge. Taille-douce. Dentelés 13.* ©

Bâton de Confrérie de St-Martin (bois doré).

Bois sculpté de l'église St-Martin (Oise, XVIe siècle).

1278	**20 c. +10 c. grenat**	4 »	4 »
1279	**25 c. +10 c. bleu**	4 »	4 »
	La paire, non dentelée	110 »	

Tirages : 1 480 000 et 1 435 000.

Ont été émis aussi en carnets (tirage : 110 200).

1960. – *5e centenaire du collège Sainte-Barbe, à Paris. Taille-douce. Denielé 13.*

Statuette de Ste Barbe et ancien plan du quartier du Collège.

1280	**30 c. brun-olive, bleu, olive et rouge**	0 50	0 50
	a. (Non dentelé)	23 »	

Tirage : 5 145 000.

1960

Du n° 1230 au n° 1280 :

53 timbres ****85** **⊙56**

Autres rubriques de l'année :

Poste aérienne 38 à 41

Préoblitérés 119 à 122

Service 22 à 26

Taxe 90 à 94

1961. – *Centenaire de la naissance du sculpteur Aristide Maillol. Taille-douce. Dentelé 13.*

"La Pensée", de Maillol (Hôtel de Ville de Perpignan).

1281	**20 c. rouge et vert-noir**	0 30	0 30
	a. (Non dentelé)	30 »	

Tirage : 5 445 000.

1961. – *Type Marianne de Cocteau. Taille-douce. Dentelé 13.*

I

II

1282	**20 c. bleu et rouge (I)**	0 30	0 15
	a. (Type II)	4 »	0 80
	b. (Non dentelé) (I)	46 »	

1961. – *Inauguration de l'aéroport de Paris-Orly. Taille-douce. Dentelé 13.*

Aérogare-Sud.

1283	**50 c. bleu, bleu clair et sépia**	0 65	0 50
	a. (Non dentelé)	46 »	

Tirage : 5 175 000.

1961. – *Centenaire de la naissance de Georges Méliès. Taille-douce. Dentelé 13.*

Georges Méliès et son film "Le voyage dans la Lune".

1284	**50 c. violet, olive et vert foncé**	1 »	0 80
	a. (Non dentelé)	65 »	

Tirage : 5 270 000.

1961. – *Journée du Timbre. Taille-douce. Dentelé 13.*

Facteur de la Petite Poste de Paris, 1760.

1285	**20 c. +5 c. vert foncé, rouge et bistre**	1 »	0 80
	a. (Non dentelé)	30 »	

Tirage : 2 200 000.

1961. – *4e centenaire de l'introduction du tabac. Taille-douce. Dentelé 13.*

J. Nicot, feuilles et fleurs de tabac.

1286	**30 c. vert, brun-orange et rouge**	0 30	0 30
	a. (Non dentelé)	30 »	

Tirage : 5 440 000.

1961. – *Centenaire de la mort de Jean-Baptiste Henri de Lacordaire. Taille-douce. Dentelé 13.*

Portrait, par Chasseriau.

1287	**30 c. brun et sépia**	0 50	0 50
	a. (Non dentelé)	23 »	

Tirage : 5 080 000.

1961. – *Héros de la Résistance (5e série). Taille-douce. Dentelés 13.*

Jacques Renouvin.

Lionel Dubray.

1288	**20 c. bleu et lilas**	1 20	0 80
1289	**20 c. olive et bleu**	1 20	0 80

Paul Gateaud.

Mère Elisabeth.

1290	**30 c. brun-orange et noir**	2 »	1 10
1291	**30 c. outremer et gris-vert**	1 60	1 30
	Nos 1288 à 1291 (4 val.)	**6 »**	**4 »**
	La série, non dentelée	77 »	

Tirages : 3 400 000, 3 115 000, 3 315 000 et 3 565 000.

1961. – ***Réunion à Paris de la fédération mondiale des anciens combattants. Taille-douce. Dentelé 13.***

1292	**50 c. bleu, vert et grenat**	0 50	0 50
	a. (Non dentelé)	20 »	

Tirage : 4 800 000.

1961. – ***Bagnoles-de-l'Orne. Taille-douce. Dentelé 13.***

Le lac de la Vée.

1293	**20 c. vert, bleu et ocre**	0 30	0 30
	a. (Non dentelé)	20 »	

Tirage : 5 135 000.

1961. – ***Centenaire de Deauville. Taille-douce. Dentelé 13.***

Deauville en 1861.

1294	**50 c. rose-lilas**	2 30	1 70
	a. (Non dentelé)	30 »	

Tirage : 4 750 000.

1961. – ***Célébrités. Taille-douce. Dentelés 13.***

Du Guesclin et scène de la bataille de Cocherel.

Pierre Puget et ses oeuvres Milon de Crotone cariatides de l'Hôtel de Ville de Toulon, figure de proue.

1295	**15 c. +5 c. lilas-brun et noir**	2 »	2 »
1296	**20 c. +10 c. vert foncé et bleu**	3 »	3 »

Coulomb et sa balance de torsion.

Général Drouot et les grilles de Lamour, place Stanislas, à Nancy.

1297	**20 c. +10 c. orange et carmin**	3 »	3 »
1298	**30 c. +10 c. brun-orange et noir**	3 »	3 »

Honoré Daumier et ses oeuvres : laveuses, le drame, Ratapoil.

Guillaume Apollinaire et évocation de ses oeuvres.

1299	**45 c. +10 c. violet-brun et vert foncé**	4 »	4 »
1300	**50 c. +15 c. lilas-rose et violet**	4 »	4 »
	N°s 1295 à 1300 (6 val.)	**19 »**	**19 »**
	La série, non dentelée	130 »	

Tirages : 1 600 000, 1 600 000, 1 500 000, 1 550 000, 1 600 000 et 1 600 000.

1961. – ***Comédiens français. Encadrement grenat. Taille-douce. Dentelés 13.***

La Champmeslé, dans le rôle de Roxane.

Talma, dans le rôle d'Oreste.

Rachel, dans Phèdre.

1301	**20 c. vert et brun-violet**	1 20	0 50
1302	**30 c. brun-jaune et rouge**	1 25	0 65
1303	**30 c. vert-jaune et vert-noir**	1 25	0 65

Raimu, dans le rôle de César (Marius).

Gérard Philipe, dans Le Cid.

1304	**50 c. bleu-vert et brun-orange**	1 70	1 »
1305	**50 c. olive et brun-violet**	1 60	0 80
	N°s 1301 à 1305 (5 val.)	**7 »**	**3 60**
	La série, non dentelée	115 »	

Tirages : 5 200 000, 4 745 000, 4 580 000, 5 650 000 et 5 650 000.

1961. – ***Le Mont-Dore. Taille-douce. Dentelé 13.***

Téléphérique du Puy de Sancy.

1306	**20 c. orange et lilas**	0 30	0 30
	a. (Non dentelé)	35 »	

Tirage : 10 390 000.

1961. – ***Bicentenaire de la mort de Pierre Fauchard. Taille-douce. Dentelé 13.***

Gravure, par J. Le Bel.

1307	**50 c. vert et noir**	0 65	0 65
	a. (Non dentelé)	20 »	

Tirage : 4 300 000.

1961. – ***8ᵉ centenaire de la ville de Thann. Taille-douce. Dentelé 13.***

Thann.

1308	**20 c. vert foncé, brun-lilas et violet**	0 80	0 65
	a. (Non dentelé)	23 »	

Tirage : 4 835 000.

1961. – ***Europa. Taille-douce. Dentelés 13.***

1309	**25 c. rouge**	0 25	0 15
1310	**50 c. outremer**	0 75	0 50
	La paire, non dentelée	140 »	

Tirages : 19 725 000 et 14 395 000.

1961-62. – ***Série touristique. Taille-douce. Dentelés 13.***

Saint-Paul-de-Vence.

1311	**15 c. violet, bleu et gris**	0 15	0 15

Arcachon.

1312	**30 c. vert-gris, outremer et bistre**	0 30	0 30
	a. (Sans "Postes")	300 »	

Sully-sur-Loire.

1313	**45 c. bleu, vert et brun-orange**	0 30	0 15
	a. (Château blanc)	350 »	

Cognac.

1314	**50 c. vert, vert foncé et bleu-vert**	1 60	0 30
	a. (2 péniches absentes)	5 »	1 »
	b. (3 péniches et digue absentes)	20 »	5 »

Dinan.

Calais.

1315	**65 c. vert foncé, brun-orange et bleu**	0 50	0 30
1316	**85 c. vert foncé, bleu-gris et brun-orange**	0 65	0 50

Dunkerque. 3ᵉ centenaire du port.

Médéa (Algérie).

1317	**95 c. bistre, lilas et vert**	1 50	0 80
1318	**1 f. bistre, vert foncé et bleu**	5 »	0 50
	Nᵒˢ 1311 à 1318 (8 val.)	**10 »**	**3 »**
	La série, non dentelée	170 »	

Tirages : 22 625 000, 63 025 000, 123 325 000, 93 125 000, 58 980 000, 44 190 000, 22 900 000 et 46 950 000.

Voir également le nº 1355.

Le nº 1318 a été surchargé "E.A. " en 1962 (voir Tome II Algérie nᵒˢ 358 et 363).

1961. – ***Tableaux de peintres modernes. Taille-douce. Dentelés 13*** x ***12½.***

Le Messager, de Braque (1882-1963).

1319	**50 c. polychrome**	4 »	2 »
	a. (Liseré blanc très prononcé au dessus de la couleur noir)	30 »	10 »

Les Nus bleus, d'Henri Matisse (1869-1954).

1320	**65 c. vert, bleu foncé et violet-noir**	6 »	3 »
	a. Vert, bleu ciel, violet-noir	10 »	5 »

Les Joueurs de cartes, de Paul Cézanne (1839-1906).

1321	**85 c. polychrome**	3 »	2 »

"14 juillet", de R. de La Fresnaye (1885-1925).

1322	**1 f. polychrome**	5 »	3 »
	N°s 1319 à 1322 (4 val.)	**18 »**	**10 »**
	La série, non dentelée	420 »	

Tirages : 4 252 500, 3 315 000, 4 137 000 et 3 520 000.

1961. – ***Au profit de la Croix-Rouge. Reproductions d'oeuvres de Rouault (1871-1958). Croix en rouge. Taille-douce. Dentelés 13.*** [C]

"Il serait si doux d'aimer".

"L'aveugle a parfois consolé le voyant".

1323	**20 c. +10 c. noir et sépia**	2 75	2 75
1324	**25 c. +10 c. noir et sépia**	3 50	3 50
	La paire, non dentelée	155 »	

Tirages : 1 575 000 et 1 610 000.

Ont été émis aussi en carnets (tirage : 242 800).

> **1961**
>
> **Du n° 1281 au n° 1324 :**
>
> **44 timbres** ****76** **⊙54**

1962. – ***Premier voyage du paquebot "France". Taille-douce. Dentelé 13.***

1325	**30 c. bleu foncé, noir et rouge**	1 »	0 65
	a. (Non dentelé)	40 »	
	b. (Cheminée noire)	95 »	

Tirage : 6 230 000.

1962. – ***Championnats du monde de ski, à Chamonix. Taille-douce. Dentelés 13.***

Descente.

Slalom.

1326	**30 c. outremer et violet foncé**	0 30	0 30
	a. (Ski court)	15 »	5 »
1327	**50 c. vert foncé, violet et bleu-vert**	0 65	0 50
	La paire, non dentelée	155 »	

Tirages : 5 545 000 et 6 800 000.

1962. – *Centenaire de la mort du docteur Pierre-Fidèle Bretonneau. Taille-douce. Dentelé 13.*

Vue de Tours.

1328 **50 c. violet et bleu** 0 50 0 50
a. (Non dentelé) 23 »
Tirage : 6 375 000.

1962. – *60e anniversaire de la naissance du journaliste Maurice Bourdet (1902-1944). Taille-douce. Dentelé 13.*

1329 **30 c. gris** 0 30 0 30
a. (Non dentelé) 19 25
Tirage : 5 970 000.

1962. – *Vue de Laval. Taille-douce. Dentelé 13.*

Château et Pont-Vieux
sur la Mayenne.

1330 **20 c. brun et vert** 0 30 0 30
a. (Non dentelé) 19 25
Tirage : 6 650 000.

1962-65. – *Type Coq de Decaris. Taille-douce. Dentelés 13.* [C]

1331 **25 c. outremer, carmin et brun** 0 30 0 15
a. (Non dentelé) 61 »
b. (no rouge au verso) 80 »
c. (no vert au verso) 265 »
d. (Papier spécial fluor. jaune vif aux U. V) 900 » 65 »

1331A **30 c. vert, rouge et bistre** 1 » 0 15
a. (Non dentelé) 40 »
b. (no rouge au verso) 13 50

Depuis 1962, les timbres des roulettes destinés aux distributeurs portent tous les 10 exemplaires, un numéro inscrit au verso. C'est ce timbre que nous cotons sous l'appellation : (no rouge au verso). A partir de 1986, les numéros apparaissent tous les 5 timbres.

1962. – *Journée du Timbre. Taille-douce. Dentelé 13.*

Messager royal de la fin
du Moyen Age.

1332 **20 c. +5 c. rose-rouge, violet-brun et bleu** 1 » 1 »
a. (Non dentelé) 30 »
Tirage : 2 200 000.

1962. – *Remparts illuminés de Vannes. Taille-douce. Dentelé 13.*

Vannes.

1333 **30 c. bleu foncé** 1 » 1 »
a. (Non dentelé) 23 »
Tirage : 5 150 000.

1962. – *Journée mondiale du théâtre. Taille-douce. Dentelé 13.*

1334 **50 c. vert foncé, jaune et carmin** 0 65 0 50
a. (Non dentelé) 23 »
Tirage : 5 810 000.

1962. – *Hauts lieux de la Résistance. Taille-douce. Dentelés 13.*

Mont Valérien.

1335 **20 c. vert foncé et olive** 1 » 0 80

Vercors.

Ile de Sein.

1336	**30 c. ardoise**	1 »	0 80
1337	**50 c. bleu et bleu-noir**	1 25	1 »
	La série, non dentelée	100 »	

Tirages : 4 300 000, 4 870 000 et 4 870 000.

Voir également les n°s 1380 et 1381.

1962. – ***Eradication du paludisme. Taille-douce. Dentelé 13.***

1338	**50 c. bleu, vert foncé et rouge**	0 50	0 40
	a. (Non dentelé)	61 »	

Tirage : 5 995 000.

1962. – ***Semaine nationale des hôpitaux. Taille-douce. Dentelé 13.***

1339	**30 c. vert, gris et rouge-brun**	0 30	0 30
	a. (Non dentelé)	27 »	

Tirage : 5 240 000.

1962. – ***Aviation légère et sportive. Taille-douce. Dentelés 13.***

Vol à voile.

Aviation de tourisme.

1340	**15 c. brun-orange et violet-brun**	0 65	0 50
1341	**20 c. lilas-rose et lie-de-vin**	0 65	0 50
	La paire, non dentelée	125 »	

Tirages : 5 560 000 et 5 120 000.

1962. – ***Centenaire de l'école d'horlogerie de Besançon. Taille-douce. Dentelé 13.***

1342	**50 c. brun-lilas, violet foncé et ocre**	0 65	0 50
	a. (Non dentelé)	23 »	

Tirage : 4 745 000.

1962. – ***Tricentenaire de la manufacture des Gobelins. Taille-douce. Dentelé 13.***

Louis XIV visitant la manufacture.
Tapis de Ch. Le Brun et tapis moderne.

1343	**50 c. vert, rose et vert-bleu**	0 65	0 50
	a. (Non dentelé)	23 »	

Tirage : 6 050 000.

1962. – ***Tricentenaire de la mort de Blaise Pascal. Taille-douce. Dentelé 13.***

1344	**50 c. vert-noir et orange**	0 65	0 50
	a. (Non dentelé)	27 »	

Tirage : 5 825 000.

1962. – ***Célébrités. Taille-douce. Dentelés 13.***

Denis Papin.

Edmé Bouchardon.

Joseph Lakanal.

1345	**15 c. + 5 c. vert-bleu et sépia**	2 »	2 »
1346	**20 c. +10 c. lilas-brun et brun**	3 »	3 »
1347	**20 c. +10 c. gris et bleu-gris**	3 »	3 »

Gustave Charpentier.

Edouard Estaunié.

Hyacinthe Vincent.

1348	**30 c. +10 c. bleu et bleu-noir**	3 »	3 »
1349	**45 c. +15 c. brun-rouge et violet-brun**	3 »	3 »
1350	**50 c. +20 c. bleu-vert et noir**	3 »	3 »
	N°s 1345 à 1350 (6 val.)	**17 »**	**17 »**
	La série, non dentelée	125 »	

Tirage : 1 600 000 séries.

1962. – *Palais de justice de Rennes. Taille-douce. Dentelé 13.*

Palais de Justice.

1351	**30 c. noir, vert et gris-bleu**	1 50	1 »
	a. (Non dentelé)	27 »	

Tirage : 5 645 000.

1962-65. – *Armoiries de villes (IV). Typographie. Dentelés 14 x 13½.* 🄲

Niort.

Guéret.

Amiens.

1351A	**1 c. bleu et jaune**	0 15	0 15
1351B	**2 c. vert, outremer et jaune**	0 15	0 15
1352	**5 c. rouge, bleu et jaune**	0 15	0 15

Troyes.

Agen.

Nevers.

1353	**10 c. brun, outremer et jaune**	0 15	0 15
	a. (Trois bandes de phosphore)	0 20	0 15
1353A	**12 c. rouge, jaune et noir**	0 15	0 15
1354	**15 c. rouge, bleu foncé et jaune**	0 15	0 15

Saint-Denis de La Réunion.

Paris.

1354A	**18 c. bleu, vert, rouge et jaune**	0 50	0 50
1354B	**30 c. bleu et rouge**	0 60	0 15
	a. (Paire verticale de carnet, avec barres)	8 »	
	N°s 1351A à 1354B (8 val.)	**2 »**	**1 55**
	La série, non dentelée	95 »	

1962. – *Le Touquet-Paris-Plage. Taille-douce. Dentelé 13.*

1355	**1 f. bleu, vert-bleu et brun-rouge**	0 65	0 15
	a. (Non dentelé)	70 »	
	b. (plage verte)	70 »	30 »

Fait partie de la série touristique n°s 1311 à 1318.

Tirage : 193 700 000.

1962. – *Roses. Taille-douce. Dentelés 13.*

1356	**20 c. olive, rose-rouge et vert**	0 80	0 50
1357	**30 c. olive, vert-noir et rose**	0 80	0 65
	La paire, non dentelée	140 »	

Tirages : 7 940 000 et 5 800 000.

1962. – *Europa. Taille-douce. Dentelés 13.*

1358	**25 c. lilas**	0 25	0 15
1359	**50 c. rouge-brique**	0 75	0 50
	La paire, non dentelée	140 »	

Tirages : 18 975 000 et 10 380 000.

1962-63. – ***Télécommunications spatiales. Taille-douce. Dentelés 13.***

Centre de télécommunications spatiales
de Pleumeur-Bodou.

1360 **25 c. gris, vert-bleu et jaune** 0 30 0 30

Première liaison de télévision par satellite "Telstar".

1361 **50 c. bleu foncé, outremer et vert pâle** 0 65 0 50

Radiotélescope de Nançay.

1362 **50 c. bleu et brun-violet** 0 65 0 50

La série, non dentelée 275 »

Tirages : 11 212 500, 10 650 000 et 6 457 500.

Afin de commémorer les premières liaisons de télécommunications spatiales et à l'intention de tous ceux qui furent les artisans de cette réussite, il a été émis un bloc-feuillet spécial comportant les n°s 1360 et 1361 (tirage : 400), valeur 765 ».

1962. – ***Tableaux de Maîtres. Taille-douce. Dentelés 12½-13.***

Bonjour, M. Courbet ! de Courbet (1819-1877).

1363 **50 c. polychrome** 4 » 2 »
a. (Double baton) 10 » 5 »

Madame Manet au canapé bleu, de Manet (1832-1883).

1364 **65 c. polychrome** 4 » 2 »
a. (Liseré blanc très prononcé entre haut de la robe et canapé) 30 » 15 »

Officier de chasseurs de la Garde,
de Théodore Géricault (1791-1824).

1365 **1 f. polychrome** 6 » 3 »
a. (Sabre et chiffre rouge) 10 » 5 »

La série, non dentelée 305 »

Tirages : 3 365 000, 3 962 500 et 3 900 000.

1962. – ***Au profit de la Croix-Rouge. Reproductions d'oeuvres de Fragonard (1732-1806). Croix en rouge. Taille-douce. Dentelés 13.*** [C]

Rosalie Fragonard.

L'enfant en Pierrot.

1366 **20 c. +10 c. lilas-brun** 1 50 1 50
a. lilas-brun foncé 100 » 100 »

1367 **25 c. +10 c. vert** 2 50 2 50
a. gris 100 » 100 »

La paire, non dentelée 125 »

Tirages : 2 110 000 et 2 100 000.

Ont été émis aussi en carnets (tirage : 242 600).

Les n°s 1366a et 1367a proviennent du 2e tirage des carnets.

1962

Du n° 1325 au n° 1367 :

49 timbres ****58** **⊙45**

A compter de 1963 la plupart des timbres portent le millésime de l'année de parution.

1963. – ***Bathyscaphe "Archimède". Taille-douce. Dentelé 13.***

1368 30 c. bleu et noir 0 30 0 30
a. (Non dentelé) 40 »
Tirage : 5 400 000.

1963. – ***Floralies nantaises. Taille-douce. Dentelé 13.***

1369 30 c. polychrome 0 30 0 30
a. (Non dentelé) 46 »
Tirage : 5 450 000.

1963. – ***Célébrités. Taille-douce. Dentelés 13.***

Jacques Amyot (écrivain, 450e anniversaire de sa naissance).

Etienne Méhul (compositeur, bicentenaire de sa naissance).

1370 20 c. +10 c. brun-lilas, gris et violet 1 25 1 25
1371 20 c. +10 c. rouge, bleu et brun-rouge 1 50 1 50

Pierre de Marivaux (écrivain, bicentenaire de sa mort).

Nicolas Vauquelin (chimiste, bicentenaire de sa naissance).

1372 30 c. +10 c. vert-bleu et lie-de-vin 1 25 1 25
1373 30 c. +10 c. lilas-brun olive et sépia 1 50 1 50

Jacques Daviel (chirurgien, bicentenaire de sa mort).

Alfred de Vigny (poète, centenaire de sa mort).

1374 50 c. +20 c. bleu, jaune-brun et olive 1 50 1 50
1375 50 c. +20 c. brun-noir, bleu-gris et sépia 2 » 2 »

Nos 1370 à 1375 (6 val.) **9 »** **9 »**
La série, non dentelée 125 »

Tirages : 1 950 000, 1 900 000, 1 950 000, 1 900 000, 1 950 000 et 1 900 000.

1963. – ***Oeuvres d'art. Taille-douce. Dentelés 12½ x 13.***

Lutte de Jacob avec l'Ange, de Delacroix.

1376 50 c. polychrome 4 » 3 »

Vitrail de l'Église Sainte-Foy, à Conches.

1377 1 f. polychrome 5 » 4 »
La paire, non dentelée 215 »
Tirages : 4 290 000 et 3 622 500.

1963. – ***Journée du Timbre. Taille-douce. Dentelé 13.***

Char de poste gallo-romain.

1378 20 c. +5 c. lilas-brun et bistre 0 30 0 30
a. (Non dentelé) 35 »
Tirage : 3 000 000.

1963. – ***Campagne mondiale contre la faim. Taille-douce. Dentelé 13.***

1379 50 c. vert-noir et brun-rouge 0 50 0 50
a. (Non dentelé) 46 »
Tirage : 5 050 000.

1963. – ***Hauts lieux de la Résistance. Taille-douce. Dentelés 13.***

A la mémoire des résistants des Glières (Haute-Savoie).

A la mémoire des déportés, monument de Paris.

1380	**30 c. brun-violet et olive**	0 65	0 65
1381	**50 c. bleu-noir**	0 65	0 65
	La paire, non dentelée	54 »	

Tirages : 5 460 000 et 5 655 000.

Voir également les n°s 1335 à 1337.

1963. – ***Grands hommes de la Communauté Economique Européenne. Taille-douce. Dentelés 13.***

Ludwig van Beethoven, musicien allemand (1770-1827).

Emile Verhaeren, poète belge (1855-1916).

1382	**20 c. vert, bleu-noir et brun-jaune**	0 50	0 50
1383	**20 c. grenat, noir et violet**	0 50	0 50

F. Mazzini, homme d'État italien.

Emile Mayrisch, diplomate luxembourgeois.

1384	**20 c. olive, bleu-noir et brun carminé**	0 50	0 50
1385	**20 c. brun-jaune, sépia et brun carminé**	0 50	0 50

Hugo de Groot, homme d'État néerlandais.

1386	**30 c. brun-jaune, violet et sépia**	0 50	0 50
	N°s 1382 à 1386 (5 val.)	**2 50**	**2 50**
	La série, non dentelée	125 »	

Tirages : 6 000 000, 6 250 000, 6 600 000, 6 100 000 et 5 150 000.

1963. – ***Centenaire de la 1re Conférence postale internationale, à Paris. Taille-douce. Dentelé 13.***

Hôtel des Postes, en 1863.

1387	**50 c. sépia**	0 50	0 50
	a. (Non dentelé)	58 »	

Tirage : 5 580 000.

1963. – ***4e centenaire du Lycée Louis le Grand, à Paris. Taille-douce. Dentelé 13.***

Lycée Louis le Grand.

1388	**30 c. vert foncé**	0 30	0 30
	a. (Non dentelé)	30 »	

Tirage : 7 295 000.

1963. – ***36e Congrès de la Fédération des sociétés philatéliques françaises, à Caen. Taille-douce. Dentelé 13.***

Eglise Saint-Pierre et donjon du château.

1389	**30 c. gris-bleu et brun**	0 30	0 30
	a. (Non dentelé)	23 »	

Tirage : 6 620 000.

1963-65. – ***Série touristique. Taille-douce. Dentelés 13.***

Château d'Amboise.

Côte d'Azur varoise.

1390	**30 c. bleu-gris, vert et ocre**	0 50	0 20
1391	**50 c. bleu-noir, rouge-brun et vert**	0 50	0 15

Saint-Flour.

Tour de César, à Provins.

1392	60 c. bleu, vert et rouge-brun	0 80	0 40
1392A	70 c. gris, vert-bleu et rose	0 50	0 15

Vittel.

Abbaye de Moissac.

1393	85 c. vert-jaune, vert et violet-brun	1 70	0 40
1394	95 c. sépia et gris	1 »	0 30

Chapelle de Notre-Dame du Haut, à Ronchamp.

1394A	1 f. 25 bleu, vert-noir et olive	1 »	0 40
	N°s 1390 à 1394A (7 val.)	**6 »**	**2 »**
	La série, non dentelée	155 »	

Tirages : 82 250 000, 74 250 000, 47 690 000, 279 535 000, 29 240 000, 19 830 000 et 19 650 000.

Un 40 c. au type du 1 f. 25 a été émis en 1965 (nº 1435).

1963. – *Championnats du monde de ski nautique, à Vichy. Taille-douce. Dentelé 13.*

1395	30 c. vert foncé, noir et rouge	0 30	0 30
	a. (Non dentelé)	70 »	

Tirage : 6 515 000.

1963. – *Europa. Taille-douce. Dentelés 13.*

1396	25 c. brun-rouge	0 40	0 30
1397	50 c. vert-bleu	0 60	0 50
	La paire, non dentelée	140 »	

Tirages : 19 435 000 et 10 765 000.

1963. – *Oeuvres d'art. Taille-douce. Dentelés 12½ x 13.*

Les mariés de la Tour Eiffel, de Chagall.

1398	85 c. polychrome	2 20	1 60

Les marchands de fourrures, vitrail de la cathédrale de Chartres.

1399	95 c. polychrome	0 80	0 80
	La paire, non dentelée	230 »	

Tirages : 4 435 000 et 4 292 500.

1963. – *Au profit de la Croix-Rouge. Centenaire de la Croix-Rouge internationale. Croix en rouge. Taille-douce. Dentelés 13.* [C]

L'enfant à la grappe, par David d'Angers (1788-1856).

Le fifre, par Manet (1832-1883).

1400	**20 c. +10 c. noir**	1 »	1 »
1401	**25 c. +10 c. vert foncé**	1 »	1 »
	La paire, non dentelée	155 »	

Tirage : 2 100 000 paires.

Ont été aussi émis en carnets (tirage : 300 700).

1963. – *Maison de la Radiodiffusion-Télévision à Paris. Taille-douce. Dentelé 13.*

1402	**20 c. bleu, bistre, vert et rouge**	0 30	0 30
	a. (Non dentelé)	23 »	

Tirage : 9 660 000.

1963. – *Exposition philatélique internationale "PHILATEC 1964", à Paris (Prélude). Taille-douce. Dentelé 13.*

Le Grand Palais. Cheval de Marly, aux Champs-Élysées.

1403	**25 c. gris, rouge et vert**	0 30	0 30
	a. (Non dentelé)	40 »	

Des timbres à ce type ont été émis dans les différents Territoires d'Outre-Mer, à l'exception des T.A.A.F. (voir Tome 1bis).

Voir également les n°s 1414 à 1417 et le n° 1422 émis en 1964.

Tirage : 52 525 000.

> **1963**
>
> **Du n° 1368 au n° 1403 :**
>
> **38 timbres** ****37** **⊙30**
>
> Autre rubrique de l'année :
>
> Service 27 à 35

1964. – *Protection civile (sapeurs-pompiers). Taille-douce. Dentelé 13.*

1404	**30 c. jaune-orange, carmin et outremer**	0 50	0 50
	a. (Non dentelé)	30 »	

Tirage : 6 735 000.

1964. – *Reclassement professionnel des paralysés. Taille-douce. Dentelé 13.*

1405	**30 c. brun-olive, orange et vert**	0 30	0 30
	a. (Non dentelé)	23 »	

Tirage : 6 370 000.

1964. – *Journée du Timbre. Taille-douce. Dentelé 13.*

Courrier à cheval (18e s.). Gravure de Parrocel.

1406	**20 c. +5 c. vert**	0 30	0 30
	a. (Non dentelé)	30 »	

Tirage : 3 690 000.

1964. – *20e anniversaire de la Libération. Taille-douce. Dentelure 13, sauf n° 1408 : 13 x 12½.*

Déportation.

L'affiche "A tous les Français".

1407	**20 c. +5 c. gris foncé**	0 80	0 80
1408	**25 c. +5 c. carmin, bleu, rouge et noir**	1 20	1 20
	a. (Papier bleuté)	8 »	8 »

Vingtième anniversaire des débarquements de Normandie et de Provence.

1409 **30 c. +5 c. brun-orange, gris-bleu et sépia** 1 » 1 »

Libération de Paris et de Strasbourg. Résistance.

1410 **30 c. +5 c. lie-de-vin, noir et rouge** 1 » 1 »

1411 **50 c. +5 c. vert foncé** 1 » 1 »

N°s 1407 à 1411 (5 val.) **5 »** **5 »**

La série, non dentelée 155 »

Tirages : 2 500 000, 5 975 000, 3 300 000, 3 800 000 et 2 500 000.

1964. – *2e anniversaire de la mort du président René Coty. Taille-douce. Dentelé 13.*

1412 **30 c. +10 c. lilas-brun et noir** 0 50 0 50

a. (Non dentelé) 23 »

Tirage : 2 875 000.

1964. – *6e centenaire de la mort de Jean II le Bon, roi de France (1319-1364). Taille-douce. Dentelé 12½ x 13.*

1413 **1 f. polychrome** 2 » 1 60

a. (Non dentelé) 100 »

Tirage : 4 325 000.

1964. – *Exposition philatélique internationale PHILATEC, à Paris (Interlude). Taille-douce. Dentelés 13.*

1414 **25 c. brun-jaune et brun-lilas *Type Blanc*** 0 50 0 50

1415 **25 c. brun-jaune et bleu *Type Mouchon*** 0 50 0 50

1416 **30 c. noir, bleu et brun-orange *Poste*** 0 50 0 50

1417 **30 c. sépia, rose et vert-bleu *Télécommunications. Tour hertzienne de Meudon*** 0 50 0 50

N°s 1414 à 1417 (4 val.) **2 »** **2 »**

Tirage : 4 500 000 séries.

La bande de quatre avec emblème PHILATEC

1417A La bande 2 20 2 20

a. non dentelée 305 »

1964. – *25e anniversaire du service aéropostal de nuit. Taille-douce. Dentelé 13.*

Douglas DC-3.

1418 **25 c. polychrome** 0 30 0 30

a. (Non dentelé) 58 »

Tirage : 20 155 000.

1964. – *8e centenaire de Notre-Dame de Paris. Taille-douce. Dentelé 12½ x 13.*

Rose Ouest de la Cathédrale.

1419 **60 c. polychrome** 0 65 0 65

a. (Non dentelé) 100 »

Tirage : 5 675 000.

1964. – *Personnages célèbres. Taille-douce. Dentelés 13.*

Jean Calvin, réformateur (4ᵉ centenaire de sa mort).

Gerbert (pape sous le nom de Sylvestre II).

1420	**30 c. +10 c. vert, noir et bistre**	0 50	0 50
1421	**30 c. +10 c. gris et lilas-brun**	0 50	0 50
	La paire, non dentelée	61 »	

Tirages : 2 755 000 et 2 790 000.

1964. – ***Exposition philatélique internationale PHILATEC à Paris (Ouverture). Taille-douce. Dentelé 13.*** **BF n° 6.**

1422	**1 f. (+3 f.) brun, bleu foncé et carmin**	30 »	25 »
	a. (Non dentelé)	305 »	
	b. (Sans vignette attenante)	15 »	10 »

Le prix d'entrée de l'Exposition (3 f.) donnait droit à l'achat d'un timbre (1 f.).

Tirage : 2 400 000 feuillets de 8 timbres.

1964. – ***20ᵉ anniversaire de la mort de Georges Mandel. Taille-douce. Dentelé 13.***

1423	**30 c. lilas-brun**	0 30	0 30
	a. (Non dentelé)	18 50	

Tirage : 6 450 000.

1964-65. – *Oeuvres d'art. Taille-douce. Dentelés 12½ x 13.*

Plaque tombale Email champlevé limousin (XIIᵉ s.), de Geoffroi IV le Bel, dit Plantagenet (1113-1151), comte d'Anjou et du Maine.

1424	**1 f. polychrome**	1 50	1 20
	a. (Non dentelé)	95 »	

La Dame à la licorne. Tapisserie (15ᵉ s.). Musée de Cluny.

1425	**1 f. polychrome**	0 80	0 80
	a. (Non dentelé)	95 »	

La serveuse anglaise du "Star", au Havre, par Toulouse-Lautrec.

1426	**1 f. polychrome**	0 60	0 50
	a. (Non dentelé)	95 »	

Saint Paul sur le chemin de Damas. Vitrail de la cathédrale de Sens.

1427 **1 f. polychrome** 0 60 0 50
a. (Non dentelé) 95 »

N°s 1424 à 1427 (4 val.) **3 50** **3 »**

Tirages : 4 385 000, 4 770 000, 6 917 500 et 7 182 500.

Ce dernier timbre commémore le 8e centenaire de la cathédrale.

1964. – *Jeux olympiques de Tokyo. Taille-douce. Dentelé 13.*

1428 **50 c. bleu et brun-lilas** 0 50 0 50
a. (Non dentelé) 115 »

Tirage : 9 360 000.

1964. – *Cinquantenaire de la Victoire de la Marne. Taille-douce. Dentelé 13.*

Le rassemblement des "Taxis de la Marne".

1429 **30 c. noir, rouge et bleu** 0 30 0 30
a. (Non dentelé) 30 »

Tirage : 6 500 000.

1964. – *Europa. Taille-douce. Dentelés 13.*

1430 **25 c. carmin, ocre et vert** 0 25 0 15
1431 **50 c. violet, vert et carmin** 0 75 0 30

La paire, non dentelée 140 »

Tirages : 28 990 000 et 10 225 000.

1964. – *Coopération avec l'Afrique et Madagascar. Taille-douce. Dentelé 13.*

1432 **25 c. brun-rouge et bleu** 0 30 0 30
a. (Non dentelé) 27 »

Treize pays africains ont émis simultanément une valeur à ce type (voir au tome II, 2e partie).

Tirage : 15 175 000.

1964. – *Au profit de la Croix-Rouge. Croix en rouge. Taille-douce. Dentelés 13.* [C]

Jean-Nicolas baron Corvisart.

Dominique baron Larrey.

1433 **20 c. +10 c. noir** 0 50 0 50
1434 **25 c. +10 c. noir** 0 50 0 50

La paire, non dentelée 125 »

Tirages : 2 790 000 et 2 810 000.

Ont été aussi émis en carnets (tirage : 345 000).

1964	
Du n° 1404 au n° 1434	
(sauf 1417A) :	
31 timbres	****49 ⊙43**
Autres rubriques de l'année :	
Blocs et feuillets 6	
Préoblirérés 123 à 129	
Taxe 95 à 102	

1965. – *Série touristique. Type de 1963-64 pour le 40 c. Taille-douce. Dentelés 13.*

Chapelle de Notre-Dame du Haut, à Ronchamp.

Moustiers-Sainte-Marie.

1435 **40 c. vert, ocre et violet-brun (1394A)** 0 40 0 30
a. vert-olive foncé, bistre-jaune et violet-brun (Provenant de roulette) 0 50 0 50
b. (2 n^os^ rouges au verso) 5 »

1436 **50 c. vert, bleu-gris et ocre** 0 50 0 20
a. (neige sur le bourg) 25 » 10 »

Aix-les-Bains.

Gorges du Tarn.

1437	**60 c. bleu et brun**	1 »	0 35
1438	**75 c. brun violacé, bleu et vert**	1 60	1 20

Paysage vendéen.

Alignements de Carnac.

1439	**95 c. bistre, vert et bleu**	5 »	1 20
1440	**1 f. gris, vert et bistre**	1 75	0 25

Château de Joux (Doubs).

1441	**1 f. 30 ocre, violet-brun et brun-orange**	1 75	0 50
	N°s 1435 à 1441 (7 val.)	**12 »**	**4 »**
	La série, non dentelée	155 »	

Tirages : 64 000 000, 108 600 000, 36 290 000, 14 915 000, 19 355 000, 129 840 000 et 20 000 000.

Pour les n°s 1435a et b, voir note après le n° 1331Ab.

1965. – ***Célébrités. Taille-douce. Dentelés 13.***

François VI, prince de Marcillac, duc de La Rochefoucauld (1613-1680), moraliste, tricentenaire de la publication de ses "Maximes".

Nicolas Poussin (1594-1665), peintre, tricentenaire de sa mort (autoportrait), détail.

1442	**30 c. +10 c. bleu foncé et brun-orange**	0 50	0 50
1443	**30 c. +10 c. brun foncé et rouge**	0 65	0 65

Paul Dukas (1865-1955), compositeur, centenaire de sa naissance.

Charles d'Orléans (1391-1465), poète, 5e centenaire de sa mort.

1444	**40 c. +10 c. gris-bleu et brun-lilas**	0 65	0 65
1445	**40 c. +10 c. rouge-brique, brun foncé et bleu-vert**	0 65	0 65
	N°s 1442 à 1445 (4 val.)	**2 45**	**2 45**
	La série, non dentelée	115 »	

Tirages : 2 600 000, 2 750 000, 2 500 000 et 2 950 000.

1965. – ***Journée du Timbre. Taille-douce. Dentelé 13.***

Paquebot-poste "La Guienne".

1446	**25 c. +10 c. bleu, vert foncé et sépia**	1 »	1 »
	a. (Non dentelé)	30 »	

Tirage : 4 300 000.

1965. – ***20e anniversaire du retour des déportés. Taille-douce. Dentelé 13.***

1447	**40 c. bleu-vert et vert**	0 65	0 50
	a. (Non dentelé)	30 »	

Tirage : 7 250 000.

1965. – ***Maisons des Jeunes et de la Culture. Taille-douce. Dentelé 13.***

Troyes : Maison des Jeunes et de la Culture.

1448	**25 c. noir, vert foncé et brun-lilas**	0 30	0 30
	a. (Non dentelé)	18 50	

Tirage : 11 240 000.

1965. – *Campagne de l'accueil et de l'amabilité. Taille-douce. Dentelé 13.*

1449	**60 c. vert foncé, bistre et rouge**	0 50	0 50
	a. (Non dentelé)	23 »	

Tirage : 10 650 000.

1965. – *20e anniversaire de la Victoire. Taille-douce. Dentelé 13.*

1450	**40 c. bleu, rouge et noir**	0 50	0 30
	a. (Non dentelé)	30 »	

Tirage : 8 285 000.

1965. – *Centenaire de l'Union Internationale des Télécommunications. Taille-douce. Dentelé 13.*

1451	**60 c. bleu, bistre et noir**	0 65	0 65
	a. (Non dentelé)	95 »	

A l'intention des personnalités invitées à assister à la Commémoration du Centenaire de l'Union Internationale des Télécommunications, dans le Salon de l'Horloge du Ministère des Affaires Étrangères où fut signée le 17 mai 1865 la première Convention Télégraphique Internationale, il a été émis un feuillet spécial dentelé et gommé comportant un bloc de quatre du n° 1451 (tirage : 300)

Le feuillet spécial 950 »

Tirage : 7 000 000.

1965. – *Cinquantenaire de la Croix de guerre. Taille-douce. Dentelé 13.*

1452	**40 c. vert, brun et rouge**	0 65	0 65
	a. (Non dentelé)	30 »	

Tirage : 7 760 000.

1965. – *Cathédrale de Bourges. Taille-douce. Dentelé 13.*

1453	**40 c. brun-rouge et gris-bleu**	0 50	0 50
	a. (Non dentelé)	23 »	

Tirage : 7 780 000.

1965. – *Inauguration du tunnel routier sous le Mont-Blanc. Taille-douce. Dentelé 13.*

1454	**30 c. turquoise, bleu et violet**	0 30	0 30
	a. (Non dentelé)	30 »	

Tirage : 19 550 000.

1965. – *Europa. Taille-douce. Dentelés 13.*

1455	**30 c. rouge**	0 75	0 30
1456	**60 c. bleu-gris**	1 25	0 75
	La paire, non dentelée	140 »	

Tirages : 23 890 000 et 11 225 000.

1965. – *Oeuvres d'art. Taille-douce. Dentelés 12½-13.*

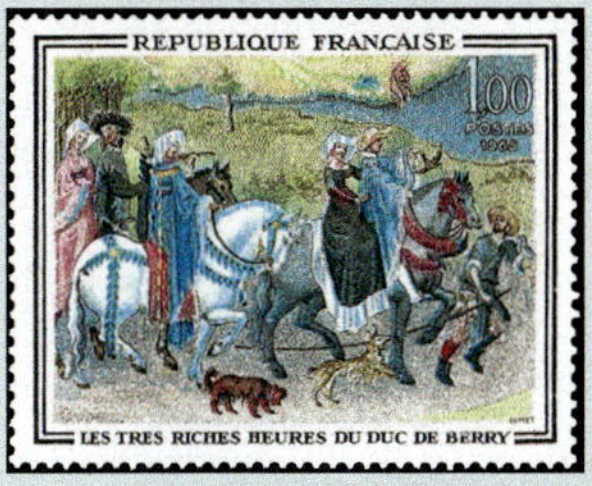

Les très riches heures du duc de Berry.

1457	**1 f. polychrome**	0 50	0 50
	a. (Non dentelé)	100 »	
	b. (Sans le jaune)	150 »	

L'Apocalypse (tapisserie du XIVe s., à Angers).

1458	**1 f. polychrome**	0 50	0 50
	a. (Non dentelé)	95 »	

Le violon rouge, de Raoul Dufy.

1459	**1 f. noir, rose et rouge**	0 50	0 50
	a. (Non dentelé)	95 »	

Tirages : 7 647 000, 7 275 000 et 7 275 000.

1965. – *Millionième hectare reboisé. Taille-douce. Dentelé 13.*

1460	**25 c. vert foncé, vert et bistre**	0 30	0 30
	a. (Non dentelé)	30 »	

Tirage : 12 460 000.

1965. – *Tricentenaire du peuplement de l'île Bourbon (La Réunion). Taille-douce. Dentelé 13.*

1461	**30 c. carmin et bleu-noir**	0 30	0 30
	a. (Non dentelé)	23 »	

A paru avec valeur exprimée en francs CFA. Voir tome II 1re partie à département de La Réunion (no 365).

Tirage : 17 565 000.

1965. – *20e anniversaire du Commissariat à l'énergie atomique. Taille-douce. Dentelé 13.*

Centre d'étude nucléaire de Cadarache (Bouches-du-Rhône), la pile Rapsodie.

1462	**60 c. outremer et bleu foncé**	0 65	0 65
	a. (Non dentelé)	70 »	

Tirage : 7 800 000.

1965. – *30e anniversaire de l'École de l'Air, à Salon-de-Provence. Taille-douce. Dentelé 13.*

1463	**25 c. bleu foncé et vert**	0 50	0 30
	a. (Non dentelé)	70 »	
	b. (sans les toits)	200 »	100 »

Tirage : 8 505 000.

1965. – *Lancement du premier satellite national, à Hammaguir (Sahara). Taille-douce. Dentelés 13.*

1464	**30 c. bleu-vert, bleu-noir et bleu**		
	Fusée Diamant	0 30	0 30
1465	**60 c. bleu-noir, bleu et bleu-vert**		
	Satellite A1	0 50	0 30
1465a	(La paire se tenant)	1 20	1 20

Les deux timbres sont émis sous forme de triptyque avec, au centre, une vignette bleue MISE SUR ORBITE DU PREMIER SATELLITE FRANÇAIS 26 NOVEMBRE 1965.

1465A	*Le triptyque*	1 »	1 »
	a. (non dentelé)	230 »	

Tirage : 8 052 800 paires.

BF voir note après le no 1476.

1965. – ***Au profit de la Croix-rouge. Oeuvres de Renoir (1841-1919). Croix en rouge. Taille-douce. Dentelés 13.*** 🄲

Bébé à la cuiller.

Coco écrivant.

1466	**25 c. +10 c. gris-bleu**	0 30	0 30
1467	**30 c. +10 c. brun-lilas**	0 50	0 50
	La paire, non dentelée	140 »	

Tirages : 3 350 000 et 3 450 000.

Ont été aussi émis en carnets (tirage : 524 000).

1965

Du n° 1435 au n° 1467

(sauf 1465A) :

33 timbres ****26** **⊙17**

Autre rubrique de l'année :

Poste aérienne 42

1966. – ***Armoiries de ville (V). Typographie. Dentelés 14 x 13½.***

Auch.

Mont-de-Marsan.

1468	**5 c. bleu et rouge**	0 15	0 15
	a. (roulette, Dentelé 13)	0 15	0 15
	b. (n° rouge au verso)	2 50	
1469	**25 c. brun-rouge et bleu**	1 10	0 30
	a. (n° rouge au verso)	100 »	
	La paire, non dentelée	30 »	

Voir note après le 1331Ab.

1966. – ***Célébrités. Taille-douce. Dentelés 13.***

Saint Pierre Fourier, éducateur (1565-1640) et basilique St-Pierre Fourier, à Mattaincourt (Vosges).

François Mansart architecte (1598-1666) et hôtel Carnavalet, à Paris.

1470	**30 c. +10 c. vert et sépia**	0 50	0 50
1471	**30 c. +10 c. vert et violet-brun**	0 50	0 50

Marcel Proust, écrivain (1871-1922), et pont St-Hilaire, à Illiers (Eure-et-Loire).

Gabriel Faure et "Ulysse et Pénélope", pour le Prématice.

1472	**30 c. +10 c. bleu-noir, vert et brun-olive**	0 50	0 50
1473	**30 c. +10 c. gris-bleu et ocre**	0 50	0 50

Elie Metchnikoff, biologiste.

Hippolyte Taine, philosophe.

1474	**30 c. +10 c. noir et sépia**	0 50	0 50
1475	**30 c. +10 c. brun et vert**	0 50	0 50
	N°s 1470 à 1475 (6 val.)	**3 »**	**3 »**
	La série, non dentelée	155 »	

Tirages : 3 350 000, 3 320 000, 3 485 000, 3 825 000, 3 760 000 et 3 300 000.

1966. – ***Lancement du satellite D1, à Hammaguir (Algérie). Taille-douce. Dentelé 13.***

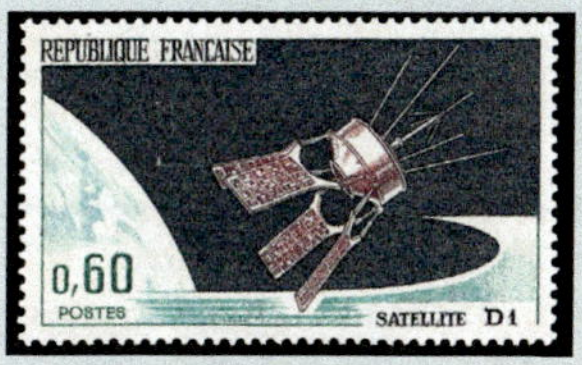

1476	**60 c. bleu-noir, lilas et émeraude**	0 30	0 30
	a. (Non dentelé)	77 »	

Afin de commémorer le lancement, par la fusée Diamant, des Satellites A1 et D1 et à l'intention de tous ceux qui furent les artisans de cette réussite, il a été émis un bloc-feuillet spécial comportant les n°s 1464, 1465 et 1476 (tirage : 400).

Le feuillet	925 »

Tirage : 9 807 500.

1966. – ***Journée du Timbre. Taille-douce. Dentelé 13.***

Gravure d'un poinçon.

1477	**25 c. +10 c. brun-lilas, bistre et ardoise**	0 30	0 30
	a. (Non dentelé)	23 »	

Tirage : 3 400 000.

1966. – *Oeuvres d'art. Taille-douce. Dentelés 12½-13.*

Vase "Cratère de Vix".

1478	**1 f. lilas, noir et vert**	0 50	0 50
	a. (Non dentelé)	84 »	

"Le Nouveau-Né", de Georges de La Tour.

1479	**1 f. polychrome**	0 50	0 50
	a. (Non dentelé)	100 »	

Tirages : 6 957 075 et 802 457.

Un feuillet spécial a été émis fin 1966 au profit du Musée Postal :

Document philatélique de 92 x 185 reproduisant les phases d'impression du timbre-poste "Le Nouveau Né", de Georges de la Tour (n° 1479). De gauche à droite, impression taille-douce report (jaune, jaune-orange et rouge), impression taille-douce (noir et blanc) et impression définitive (polychrome). Avec - POUR LE MUSEE POSTAL -, Phases d'impression du Timbre-poste "Le Nouveau-Né", de Georges de La tour. Sans pouvoir d'affranchissement. Sans gomme. Non dentelé.

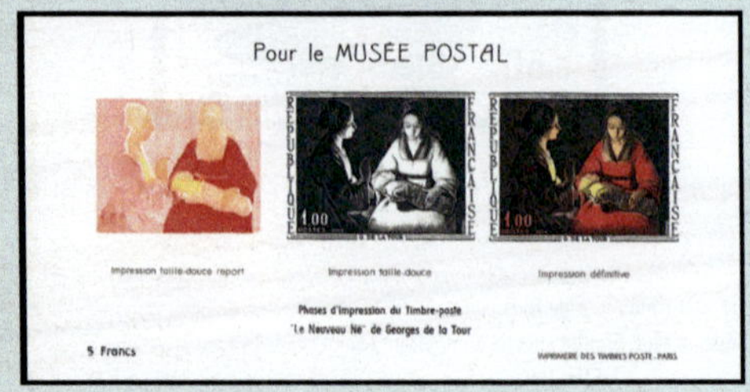

1479b polychrome 2 30

1966. – *Festival international d'échecs, au Havre. Taille-douce. Dentelé 13.*

1480	**60 c. outremer, gris-bleu, ocre et noir**	0 80	0 80
	a. (Non dentelé)	200 »	

Tirage : 6 470 000.

1966. – *7e centenaire du pont de Pont-Saint-Esprit. Taille-douce. Dentelé 13.*

1481	**25 c. noir et bleu**	0 30	0 30
	a. (Non dentelé)	23 »	

Tirage : 9 795 000.

1966. – *Millénaire du Mont-Saint-Michel. Taille-douce. Dentelé 13.*

1482	**25 c. noir, vert et rouge s. paille**	0 30	0 30
	a. (Non dentelé)	30 »	
	b. (Colonnes gris-vert)	5 »	1 »

Tirage : 10 160 000.

1966. – *Bicentenaire de l'intégration de la Lorraine et du Barrois. Taille-douce. Dentelé 13.*

Stanislas Leczinski (1677-1766) et château de Lunéville.

1483	**25 c. vert, bleu et brun-rouge**	0 30	0 30
	a. (Non dentelé)	23 »	

Tirage : 9 610 000.

1966. – *Cinquantenaire de la Victoire de Verdun. Taille-douce. Dentelé 13.*

Porte de la Chaussée, à Verdun.

1484	**30 c. +5 c. outremer, bleu-vert et vert**	0 30	0 30
	a. (Non dentelé)	23 »	

Tirage : 5 600 000.

1966. – ***39e Congrès de la Fédération des sociétés philatéliques françaises, à Niort. Taille-douce. Dentelé 13.***

Eglise Saint-André.

1485 **40 c. bleu, gris-bleu et vert** 0 50 0 30
a. (Non dentelé) 23 »
Tirage : 9 595 000.

1966. – ***9e centenaire de la bataille d'Hastings. Taille-douce. Dentelé 13.***

Le château de Falaise, la statue de Guillaume le Conquérant.

1486 **60 c. outremer et brun-orange** 0 65 0 50
a. (Non dentelé) 46 »
Tirage : 5 700 000.

1966. – ***Tricentenaire de l'Académie des Sciences, à Paris. Taille-douce. Dentelé 13.***

Bernard Le Bovier de Fontenelle (1657-1757), écrivain, Secrétaire perpétuel de l'Académie des Sciences (1699-1740).

1487 **60 c. carmin et violet-brun** 0 50 0 50
a. (Non dentelé) 23 »
Tirage : 6 380 000.

1966. – ***19e congrès international des chemins de fer, à Paris. Taille-douce. Dentelé 13.***

1488 **60 c. carmin, bleu et violet-brun** 1 » 0 80
a. (Non dentelé) 46 »
Tirage : 6 510 000.

1966. – ***Inauguration du pont d'Oléron. Taille-douce. Dentelé 13.***

1489 **25 c. bleu-vert, bleu, brun et vert** 0 30 0 30
a. (Non dentelé) 27 »
Tirage : 10 805 000.

1966. – ***Europa. Taille-douce. Dentelés 13.***

1490 **30 c. bleu et bleu foncé** 0 50 0 30
1491 **60 c. rouge et rouge foncé** 1 » 0 50
La paire, non dentelée 140 »
Tirages : 31 310 000 et 8 200 000.

1966. – ***Oeuvres d'art. Taille-douce. Dentelés 12½-13.***

Vitrail de la Sainte-Chapelle (le baptême de Judas).

1492 **1 f. polychrome** 0 50 0 50
a. (Non dentelé) 84 »

Tapisserie de Lurçat (lunes et toros).

1493 **1 f. polychrome** 0 50 0 50
a. (Non dentelé) 84 »

Crispin et Scapin, de Daumier.

1494	**1 f. polychrome**	0 50	0 50
	a. (Non dentelé)	95 »	

Tirages : 7 665 000, 7 537 000 et 7 610 000.

1966. – *Grands noms de l'Histoire. Taille-douce. Dentelés 13.*

Vercingétorix (82-46 av. J.-C.).

1495	**40 c. brun-rouge et sépia**	0 50	0 50

Clovis (455-511).

Charlemagne (742-814).

1496	**40 c. vert, bleu et violet-brun**	0 50	0 50
1497	**60 c. brun-violet, rose et violet**	0 65	0 50
	La série, non dentelée	95 »	

Tirages : 6 550 000, 6 545 000 et 6 232 000.

1966. – *Centenaire de la poste pneumatique, à Paris. Taille-douce. Dentelé 13.*

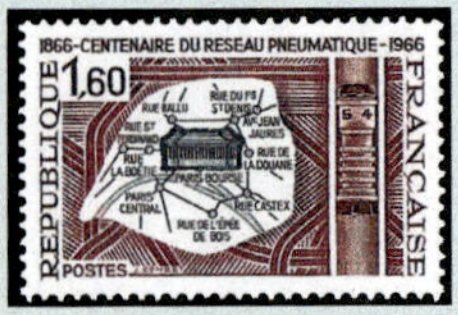

1498	**1 f. 60 violet-brun et gris-bleu foncé**	1 »	0 80
	a. (Non dentelé)	23 »	

Tirage : 6 323 650.

1966-67. – *Monuments et sites. Taille-douce. Dentelés 13.*

Hôtel de Ville de St-Quentin.

Porte de l'Horloge à Vire.

1499	**50 c. bistre, bleu-noir et bleu clair**	0 50	0 30
1500	**60 c. bleu clair, bleu foncé et bistre**	0 70	0 70

Château de St-Germain-en-Laye.

La Baule.

1501	**70 c. brun, carmin et bleu**	0 50	0 15
1502	**75 c. bleu-vert, bistre et rouge**	1 50	1 10

Boulogne-sur-Mer.

Cathédrale de Rodez.

1503	**95 c. vert, violet et bleu**	1 50	1 60
1504	**1 f. gris-bleu**	0 80	0 15

Morlaix.

Château de Val, à Lanobre (Cantal) et lac de Bort-les-Orgues (Corrèze).

1505	**1 f. 50 rouge, outremer et vert-jaune**	1 50	0 50
1506	**2 f. 30 bleu, violet, brun et vert foncé**	2 »	0 50
	Nos 1499 à 1506 (8 val.)	**9 »**	**5 »**
	La série, non dentelée	170 »	

1966. – *Usine marémotrice de la Rance. Taille-douce. Dentelé 13.*

1507	60 c. gris-bleu, brun et vert	0 65	0 65
	a. (Non dentelé)	27 »	

Tirage : 7 610 000.

1966. – *Au profit de la Croix-Rouge. Croix en rouge. Taille-douce. Dentelés 13.* ▣

Ambulancière (1859).

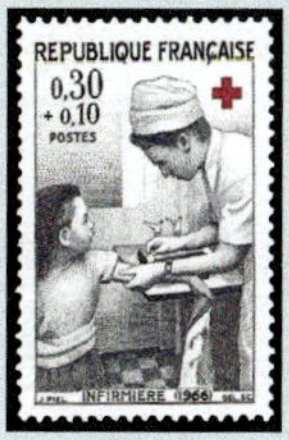

Infirmière (1966).

1508	25 c. +10 c. vert-gris et rouge	0 65	0 65
1509	30 c. +10 c. gris-bleu et rouge	0 65	0 65
	La paire, non dentelée	125 »	

Tirages : 3 500 000 et 4 100 000.

Ont été émis aussi en carnets (tirage : 538 800).

1966. – *Armoiries de ville (VI). Héliogravure. Dentelé 13.*

Blason de Saint-Lô.

1510	20 c. multicolore	0 15	0 15
	a. (Non dentelé)	27 »	
	b. (n° rge au verso (1971)	18 »	
	c. (Trois bandes de phosphore)	0 15	0 15
	d. (1510 et 1510c en paire verticale)	170 »	

Pour le n° 1510b, voir note après le n° 1331Ab.

1966

Du n° 1468 au n° 1510 :

43 timbres **28 ⊙21

Autre rubrique de l'année :

Service 36 à 38

1967. – *Célébrités. Taille-douce. Dentelés 13.*

Emile Zola.

Beaumarchais.

1511	30 c. +10 c. noir et bleu-vert	0 50	0 50
1512	30 c. +10 c. rouge-brique et violet	0 50	0 50

Saint François de Sales.

Albert Camus.

1513	30 c. +10 c. bleu-violet et violet	0 50	0 50
1514	30 c. +10 c. bistre-brun et lilas	0 50	0 50
	N°s 1511 à 1514 (4 val.)	**2 »**	**2 »**
	La série, non dentelée	115 »	

Tirages : 3 850 000, 3 870 000, 4 080 000 et 4 160 000.

1967. – *3ᵉ congrès international de l'Union Européenne de Radiodiffusion, à Paris. Taille-douce. Dentelé 13.*

1515	40 c. violet et rouge-brun	0 30	0 30
	a. (Non dentelé)	30 »	

Tirage : 6 810 000.

1967. – *Journée du Timbre. Taille-douce. Dentelé 13.*

Facteur du Second Empire.

1516	25 c. +10 c. gris-bleu, vert et rouge	0 30	0 30
	a. (Non dentelé)	30 »	

Tirage : 5 120 000.

1967. – ***Oeuvres d'art. Taille-douce. Dentelés 12½-13.***

La carriole du pére Juniet, du douanier Henri Rousseau (1844-1910).

1517	**1 f. polychrome**	0 50	0 50
	a. (Non dentelé)	100 »	
	b. (Coté droit de la roue entièrement blanc)	3 »	1 »

Portrait de François Ier (1494-1547), par Jean Clouet (1475-1541).

1518	**1 f. polychrome**	0 50	0 50
	a. (Non dentelé)	100 »	

Tirages : 8 142 500 et 8 092 500.

1967. – ***Exposition internationale de Montréal (Canada). Taille-douce. Dentelé 13.***

Pavillon français.

1519	**60 c. bleu et vert-bleu**	0 50	0 50
	a. (Non dentelé)	50 »	

Tirage : 8 730 000.

1967. – ***Prélude aux Jeux Olympiques d'hiver, à Grenoble. Héliogravure. Dentelé 13.***

1520	**60 c. bleu, bleu clair et rouge**	0 50	0 50
	a. (Non dentelé)	130 »	

Tirage : 20 000 000.

1967. – ***Europa. Taille-douce. Dentelés 13.***

1521	**30 c. bleu, gris et bleu foncé**	0 50	0 30
1522	**60 c. brun, bleu et sépia**	1 25	0 80
	La paire, non dentelée	125 »	

Tirages : 40 600 000 et 10 310 000.

1967. – ***40e anniversaire de la tentative de traversée aérienne de l'Atlantique-Nord. Taille-douce. Dentelé 13.***

Nungesser, Coli et avion Levasseur "L'Oiseau blanc".

1523	**40 c. violet-brun, brun-jaune et bleu-noir**	0 65	0 50
	a. (Non dentelé)	61 »	

Tirage : 7 300 000.

1967. – ***Inauguration du grand pont de Bordeaux. Taille-douce. Dentelé 13.***

1524	**25 c. noir et brun**	0 30	0 30
	a. (Non dentelé)	23 »	

Tirage : 15 485 000.

1967. – ***40e Congrès de la Fédération des Sociétés philatéliques françaises, à Tours. Taille-douce. Dentelé 13.***

Hôtel Goüin à Tours.

1525	**40 c. brun-rouge, rouge et violet**	0 65	0 65
	a. (Non dentelé)	23 »	

Tirage : 8 000 000.

1967. – ***10e anniversaire de la mort de Robert Esnault-Pelterie (1881-1957). Taille-douce. Dentelé 13.***

1526 **60 c. outremer foncé, bleu-gris et gris-vert** 0 65 0 65
a. (Non dentelé) 70 »

Tirage : 7 325 000.

1967. – ***Bicentenaire de l'École Vétérinaire d'Alfort. Taille-douce. Dentelé 13.***

Professeur Gaston Ramon (1886-1953).

1527 **25 c. vert, bleu et brun** 0 30 0 30
a. (Non dentelé) 30 »

Tirage : 13 165 000.

1967. – ***Floralies d'Orléans. Taille-douce. Dentelé 13.***

Orchidées.

1528 **40 c. rouge, rose et violet** 1 » 0 80
a. (Non dentelé) 40 »

1967. – ***9e congrès international de comptabilité, à Paris. Taille-douce. Dentelé 13.***

1529 **60 c. violet, gris-vert et ocre** 0 80 0 80
a. (Non dentelé) 18 50

Tirage : 6 610 000.

1967. – ***Oeuvres d'art. Taille-douce. Dentelés 12½-13.***

La Baigneuse, de Dominique Ingres (1780-1867).

1530 **1 f. polychrome** 0 50 0 50
a. (Non dentelé) 100 »

Vitrail de l'église Sainte-Madeleine de Troyes (Aube).

1531 **1 f. polychrome** 0 50 0 50
a. (Non dentelé) 95 »

1967. – ***25e anniversaire de la Victoire de Bir-Hakeim. Taille-douce. Dentelé 13.***

1532 **25 c. bleu-violet, bleu et brun** 0 30 0 30
a. (Non dentelé) 30 »

Tirage : 8 810 000.

1967. – ***Centenaire de la naissance de Marie Sklodowska-Curie (1867-1934). Taille-douce. Dentelé 13.***

1533 **60 c. bleu et outremer** 0 50 0 50
a. (Non dentelé) 77 »

Tirage : 7 040 000.

1967. – *Cinquantenaire du Lions international. Taille-douce. Dentelé 13.*

1534	**40 c. violet-brun et bleu foncé**	1 »	0 65
	a. (Non dentelé)	95 »	

Tirage : 10 000 000.

1967-69. – *Type Marianne de Cheffer (I). Taille-douce. Dentelés 13.* [C] [BF]

1535	**25 c. bleu**	0 50	0 50
	a. (n° rouge au verso)	75 »	
1536	**30 c. lilas**	0 50	0 15
	a. (Gomme tropicale)	2 »	
	b. (n° rouge au verso)	15 »	
1536A	**30 c. vert**	0 50	0 15
	a. (Gomme tropicale)	1 »	
	b. (n° rouge au verso)	4 50	
1536B	**40 c. rouge carminé**	0 50	0 20
	a. (Deux bandes de phosphore)	4 »	2 30
	b. (Gomme tropicale)	1 50	
	c. (n° rouge au verso)	17 50	
	N°s 1535 à 1536B (4 val.)	**2 »**	**1 »**
	La série, non dentelée	77 »	

Les timbres avec gomme tropicale (gomme mate) proviennent de roulettes.

Voir note après le n°1331Ab.

Afin de commémorer la parution des deux premières valeurs à l'effigie de Marianne (de Cheffer), un bloc-feuillet a été émis, comportant les n°s 1535-1536 en bloc de quatre (tirage : 300)

Le feuillet 1 250 »

Le 30 c. vert a été réimprimé en typographie en 1969 (n° 1611).

Le 40 c. a été réimprimé en 1970 avec vignette attenante à l'occasion de l'inauguration de l'Imprimerie des timbres-poste à Périgueux (n° 1643).

1967. – *Grands noms de l'Histoire. Taille-douce. Dentelés 13.*

Hugues Capet (938-996).

Philippe II Auguste (1165-1222).

Louis IX (Saint Louis) (1214-1270).

1537	**40 c. bleu-vert foncé et outremer**	0 50	0 50
1538	**40 c. gris et noir**	0 50	0 50
1539	**60 c. brun-rouge et vert foncé**	0 65	0 50
	La série, non dentelée	125 »	

Tirages : 7 212 000, 7 450 000 et 6 300 000.

1967. – *Au profit de la Croix-Rouge. Ivoires du musée de Dieppe. Croix en rouge. Taille-douce. Dentelés 13.* [C]

Joueur de flûte.

Violoneux.

1540	**25 c. +10 c. violet et brun carminé**	0 65	0 65
1541	**30 c. +10 c. vert foncé et brun carminé**	0 65	0 65
	La paire, non dentelée	125 »	

Tirages : 3 735 000 et 4 280 000.

Ont été émis aussi en carnets (tirage : 525 000).

1967

Du n° 1511 au n° 1541 :

33 timbres ****18** **⊙16**

1968. – *Cinquantenaire des Comptes courants postaux (chèques postaux). Taille-douce. Dentelé 13.*

1542	**40 c. vert foncé et brun pâle**	0 30	0 30
	a. (Non dentelé)	23 »	

Afin de commémorer le cinquantenaire de l'établissement des chèques postaux, un bloc-feuillet a été émis comportant le n° 1542 en bloc de quatre (tirage : 300), valeur : 420 ».

Tirage : 11 670 000.

1968. – *Jeux Olympiques d'hiver, à Grenoble. Taille-douce. Dentelés 13.*

Ski (saut et fond).

Hockey sur glace.

Flamme.

1543	**30 c. +10 c. gris, brun et rouge**	0 50	0 50
1544	**40 c. +10 c. jaune-olive, lilas et violet**	0 50	0 50
1545	**60 c. +20 c. violet, rouge et vert**	0 65	0 65

Patinage artistique.

Ski (slalom).

1546	**75 c. +25 c. vert-jaune, brun-violet et rose-lilas**	0 65	0 65
1547	**95 c. +35 c. rose-lilas, brun-rouge et turquoise**	0 70	0 70
	Nos 1543 à 1547 (5 val.)	**3 »**	**3 »**
	La série, non dentelée	230 »	

Tirages : 6 330 000, 6 515 000, 6 000 000, 5 030 000 et 5 005 000.

1968. – *Prévention routière. Taille-douce. Dentelé 13.*

1548	**25 c. lilas, carmin et bleu-vert**	0 30	0 30
	a. (Non dentelé)	23 »	

Tirage : 9 555 000.

1968. – *Journée du Timbre. Taille-douce. Dentelé 13.*

Facteur rural de 1830.

1549	**25 c. +10 c. ardoise, bleu, rouge et noir**	0 30	0 30
	a. (Non dentelé)	30 »	

Tirage : 5 210 000.

1968. – *Célébrités. Taille-douce. Dentelés 13.*

François Couperin, compositeur (1668-1733).

Général Louis-Charles-Antoine Desaix de Veygoux (1768-1800).

1550	**30 c. +10 c. violet et lilas**	0 30	0 30
1551	**30 c. +10 c. vert et brun-carmin**	0 30	0 30

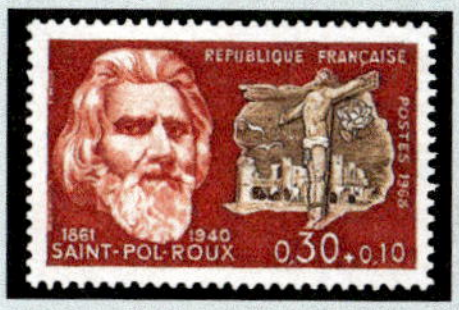

Paul-Pierre Roux, dit Saint-Pol-Roux, et "Golgotha".

Paul-Louis-Charles Claudel et "Jeanne au bûcher".

1552	**30 c. +10 c. bistre-rouge et sépia**	0 30	0 30
1553	**30 c. +10 c. brun et violet**	0 30	0 30
	Nos 1550 à 1553 (4 val.)	**1 20**	**1 20**
	La série, non dentelée	95 »	

Tirages : 4 980 000, 4 400 000, 4 150 000 et 4 550 000.

1968. – *5e conférence de Coopération mondiale pour l'enseignement audiovisuel des langues vivantes, à Royan. Taille-douce. Dentelé 13.*

1554	**40 c. sépia, vert foncé et bleu**	0 50	0 50
	a. (Non dentelé)	23 »	

Tirage : 8 855 000.

1968. – *Oeuvre d'art. Taille-douce. Dentelé 13 × 12½.*

Peinture rupestre de la grotte de Lascaux à Montignac (Dordogne).

1555	**1 f. polychrome**	0 65	0 65
	a. (Non dentelé)	95 »	

Tirage : 7 747 500.

1968. – *Europa. Taille-douce. Dentelés 13.*

1556	**30 c. lilas et brun-orange**	0 50	0 15
1557	**60 c. brun et violet**	1 25	0 80
	La paire, non dentelée	125 »	

Tirages : 30 290 000 et 11 165 000.

1968. – *Tricentenaire de la naissance de l'écrivain Alain René Lesage (1668-1747). Taille-douce. Dentelé 13.*

1558	**40 c. violet et bleu**	0 30	0 30
	a. (Non dentelé)	23 »	

Tirage : 14 535 000.

1968. – *Château de Langeais. Taille-douce. Dentelé 13.*

Construction de Jean Bourré de 1450 à 1460.

1559	**60 c. vert, bleu et brun**	0 75	0 65
	a. (Non dentelé)	23 »	

Tirage : 7 555 000.

1968. – *Sesquicentenaire de la naissance du grammairien Pierre Larousse (1817-1875). Taille-douce. Dentelé 13.*

1560	**40 c. violet et bistre**	0 50	0 50
	a. (Non dentelé)	23 »	

Tirage : 17 905 000.

1968. – *Jumelage de la forêt de Rambouillet et de la Forêt Noire. Taille-douce. Dentelé 13.*

1561	**25 c. bleu-vert, vert et brun**	0 50	0 50
	a. (Non dentelé)	30 »	

Tirage : 9 630 000.

1968. – *650e anniversaire de l'enclave papale de Valréas. Taille-douce. Dentelé 13.*

1562	**60 c. brun-lilas, olive et violet**	0 65	0 65
	a. (Non dentelé)	27 »	

Tirage : 7 215 000.

1968. – *Tricentenaire du rattachement de la Flandre (traité d'Aix-la-Chapelle). Taille-douce. Dentelé 13.*

Louis XIV.

1563	**40 c. gris, olive et carmin**	0 30	0 30
	a. (Non dentelé)	30 »	

Tirage : 7 665 000.

1968. – ***Pont de Martrou, à Rochefort. Taille-douce. Dentelé 13.***

1564 25 c. bleu, noir et rose 0 30 0 30
a. (Non dentelé) 27 »

Tirage : 9 615 000.

1968. – ***50e anniversaire de la première liaison postale régulière par avion (Paris - Le Mans - Saint-Nazaire). Taille-douce. Dentelé 13.***

1565 25 c. bleu foncé, bleu et rouge 0 65 0 50
a. (Non dentelé) 77 »

Tirage : 9 750 000.

1968. – ***Bicentenaire de la libération des prisonnières huguenotes de la tour de Constance, à Aigues-Mortes. Taille-douce. Dentelé 13.***

1566 25 c. bleu, olive et brun-carmin 0 30 0 30
a. (Non dentelé) 30 »

Tirage : 7 400 000.

1968. – ***41e Congrès de la Fédération des Sociétés philatéliques françaises, à Béziers. Taille-douce. Dentelé 13.***

Cathédrale Saint-Nazaire et Pont-Vieux de Béziers.

1567 40 c. bistre, vert et bleu 1 » 0 65
a. (Non dentelé) 23 »

Tirage : 10 620 000.

1968. – ***Oeuvres d'art. Taille-douce. Dentelés 12½-13.***

L'arearea, de Paul Gauguin (1848-1903).

1568 1 f. polychrome 0 80 0 65
a. (Non dentelé) 115 »

La Danse, d'Antoine Bourdelle (1861-1929).

1569 1 f. olive et rouge 0 80 0 50
a. (Non dentelé) 95 »

Modèle, d'Auguste Renoir (1841-1919).

1570 1 f. polychrome 1 » 0 65
a. (Non dentelé) 110 »

Tirages : 8 567 000, 8 270 000 et 7 950 000.

1968. – ***Cinquantenaire de l'Armistice sur le front d'Orient. Taille-douce. Dentelé 13.***

La Tour Blanche de Salonique (Grèce).

1571 40 c. violet foncé et violet 0 30 0 30
a. (non dentelé) 27 »

Tirage : 7 300 000.

1968. – *Bicentenaire du rattachement de la Corse. Taille-douce. Dentelé 13.*

Louis XV.

1572	**25 c. vert, noir et bleu**	0 30	0 30
	a. (Non dentelé)	27	»

Tirage : 17 000 000.

1968. – *Jeux Olympiques de Mexico. Taille-douce. Dentelé 13.*

1573	**40 c. bleu, brun et vert**	0 65	0 65
	a. (Non dentelé)	115	»

Tirage : 6 285 000.

1968. – *20e anniversaire des Expéditions polaires françaises. Taille-douce. Dentelé 13.*

1574	**40 c. bleu-vert et brun-rouge**	0 50	0 50
	a. (Non dentelé)	110	»

Tirage : 6 917 500.

1968. – *Cinquantenaire du bal des Petits Lits Blancs. Taille-douce. Dentelé 13.*

Léon Bailby (1867-1954).

1575	**40 c. rouge, brun-orange et brun**	0 30	0 30
	a. (Non dentelé)	19	25

Tirage : 7 760 000.

1968. – *Cinquantenaire de l'Armistice du 11 novembre. Taille-douce. Dentelé 13.*

1576	**25 c. carmin et bleu**	0 30	0 30
	a. (Non dentelé)	27	»

Tirage : 8 120 000.

1968. – *Grands noms de l'Histoire. Taille-douce. Dentelés 13.*

Philippe IV le Bel (1268-1314), États Généraux de 1302.

1577	**40 c. gris, rouge-brun et vert**	0 50	0 50

Mort de Bertrand du Guesclin (1320-1380), devant Châteauneuf-de-Randon (Lozère).

Jeanne d'Arc (1412-1431), départ de Vaucouleurs (1429).

1578	**40 c. vert, bleu et brun**	0 50	0 50
1579	**60 c. gris-bleu, bleu et brun**	0 80	0 65
	La série, non dentelée	95	»

Tirages : 6 675 000, 6 950 000 et 6 817 000.

1968. – *Au profit de la Croix-Rouge. Tableaux de Nicolas Mignard (1606-1668). Croix en rouge. Taille-douce. Dentelés 13.* Ⓒ

Le Printemps.

L'Automne.

1580	**25 c. +10 c. bleu, violet et rouge**	0 50	0 50
1581	**30 c. +10 c. carmin, rouge et brun**	0 50	0 50
	La paire, non dentelée	125 »	

Tirages : 4 025 000 et 4 750 000.

Ont été émis aussi en carnets (tirage : 554 000).

1968

Du n° 1542 au n° 1581 :

40 timbres ****21** **⊙19**

1969. – *Série touristique. Taille-douce. Dentelés 13.*

Eglise de Brou, à Bourg-en-Bresse (Ain).

Barrage de Vouglans (Jura).

1582	**45 c. polychrome**	0 30	0 20
1583	**80 c. brun-violet, rouge, brun et jaune**	0 50	0 15

Château de Chantilly (Oise).

Port de La Trinité-sur-Mer (Morbihan).

1584	**85 c. gris-bleu, vert foncé et bleu**	1 »	0 90
1585	**1 f. 15 bleu, brun-rouge et brun**	1 »	0 75
	a. brun-rouge omis	115 »	45 »
	N°s 1582 à 1585 (4 val.)	**2 80**	**2 »**
	La série, non dentelée	110 »	

1969. – *Oeuvres d'art. Taille-douce. Dentelés 12½-13.*

Bas-relief de la cathédrale d'Amiens (Quatre-feuilles de Février, paysan au coin du feu).

1586	**1 f. brun-olive et vert foncé**	0 80	0 65
	a. (Non dentelé)	77 »	

Philippe le Bon, duc de Bourgogne, (1396-1467), par Rogier de La Pasture.

1587	**1 f. polychrome**	0 80	0 65
	a. (Non dentelé)	100 »	

Fresque de l'Abbaye de Saint-Savin (Vienne).

1588	**1 f. polychrome**	0 80	0 65
	a. (Non dentelé)	95 »	

"Le Cirque", de G. Seurat (1859-1891).

1588A	**1 f. polychrome**	0 80	0 65
	a. (Non dentelé)	100 »	
	N°s 1586 à 1588A (4 val.)	**3 20**	**2 60**

Tirages : 7 830 000, 7 920 000, 7 622 500 et 7 700 000.

1969. – *Journée du Timbre. Taille-douce. Dentelé 13.*

Omnibus de transport des facteurs (1890).

1589	**30 c. +10 c. violet-brun, noir et vert**	0 30	0 30
	a. (Non dentelé)	30 »	

Tirage : 5 000 000.

1969. – *Célébrités du XVIIIe au XXe siècles. Taille-douce. Dentelés 13.*

Albert-Charles-Paul, Marie Roussel, compositeur (1869-1937).

Général François, Séverin, Marceau Desgravier, dit Marceau (1769-1796).

Charles, Augustin Sainte-Beuve, poète (1804-1869).

1590	**50 c. +10 c. bleu-gris**	0 50	0 50
1591	**50 c. +10 c. brun-rouge**	0 50	0 50
1592	**50 c. +10 c. gris**	0 50	0 50

Maréchal Jean, Lannes (1769-1809), duc de Montebello.

André Gide (1869-1951), écrivain.

Georges, baron Cuvier (1769-1832), naturaliste.

1593	**50 c. +10 c. brun-violet**	0 50	0 50
1594	**50 c. +10 c. émeraude**	0 50	0 50
1595	**50 c. +10 c. lie-de-vin**	0 50	0 50
	N°s 1590 à 1595 (6 val.)	**3 »**	**3 »**
	La série, non dentelée	155 »	

Tirages : 4 350 000, 4 200 000, 4 290 000, 5 025 000, 5 045 000 et 4 630 000.

1969. – *Château de Hautefort (Dordogne). Taille-douce. Dentelé 13.*

1596	**70 c. bistre, bleu et bleu foncé**	0 50	0 50
	a. (Non dentelé)	23 »	

Tirage : 10 530 000.

1969. – *Floralies internationales de Paris. Héliogravure. Dentelé 13.*

1597	**45 c. polychrome**	0 50	0 50
	a. (Non dentelé)	40 »	

Tirage : 8 980 000.

1969. – *Europa. 10e anniversaire de la Conférence Européenne des Postes et Télécommunications. Taille-douce. Dentelés 13.*

1598	**40 c. rouge carminé**	0 50	0 15
1599	**70 c. bleu-vert**	0 75	0 50
	La paire, non dentelée	125 »	

Tirages : 24 920 000 et 11 925 000.

1969. – *Cinquantenaire de l'Organisation Internationale du Travail. Taille-douce. Dentelé 13.*

Albert Thomas (1878-1932).

1600	**70 c. brun-olive, brun-rouge et gris-bleu**	0 50	0 50
	a. (Non dentelé)	40 »	

Tirage : 9 265 000.

1969. – *25e anniversaire de la victoire du Garigliano. Taille-douce. Dentelé 13.*

Victoire du Maréchal Alphonse Juin (1888-1967).

1601	**45 c. violet-gris et gris**	0 65	0 65
	a. (Non dentelé)	40 »	

Tirage : 7 920 000.

1969. – *42e Congrès national de la Fédération des Sociétés philatéliques françaises. Taille-douce. Dentelé 13.*

Ancien pont des Archers, à Châlons-sur-Marne (Marne).

1602	**45 c. vert, brun-olive et bleu-gris**	0 50	0 50
	a. (Non dentelé)	23 »	

Tirage : 8 850 000.

1969. – *25ᵉ anniversaire de la Libération. Taille-douce. Dentelés 13.*

Débarquement en Normandie.

Combats du mont Mouchet.

1603 **45 c. bleu-violet, gris et gris-vert** 1 50 0 65
a. (Non dentelé) 40 »

1604 **45 c. gris-bleu, vert et gris** 1 » 0 80
a. (Non dentelé) 30 »

Débarquement en Provence.

1605 **45 c. bistre foncé, gris et bleu foncé** 1 25 0 80
a. (Non dentelé) 30 »

Escadrille Normandie-Niemen.

1606 **45 c. ardoise, bleu et rouge** 1 » 1 »
a. (Non dentelé) 54 »

Libération de Paris et Maréchal Leclerc.

1607 **45 c. +10 c. gris-bleu et brun-olive** 1 25 1 25
a. (Non dentelé) 40 »

Libération de Strasbourg et Maréchal Leclerc.

1608 **70 c. +10 c. brun-rouge, lilas-brun et brun-olive** 3 » 3 »
a. (Non dentelé) 40 »

Nᵒˢ 1603 à 1608 (6 val.) **9 »** **7 50**

Tirages : 8 440 000, 8 520 000, 8 370 000, 7 975 000, 4 870 000 et 4 100 000.

1969. – *Championnats du monde de canoë-kayak, à Bourg-Saint-Maurice (Savoie). Taille-douce. Dentelé 13.*

1609 **70 c. bistre, bleu et gris-olive** 0 50 0 50
a. (Non dentelé) 77 »

Tirage : 9 150 000.

1969. – *Bicentenaire de la naissance de Napoléon Bonaparte. Taille-douce. Dentelé 13.*

1610 **70 c. violet, turquoise et olive** 0 50 0 50
a. (Non dentelé) 95 »

Tirage : 8 880 000.

1969. – *Type Marianne de Cheffer. Typographie. Dentelé 14 x 13.*

1611 **30 c. vert** 0 30 0 15
a. (Non dentelé) 15 50
b. (Une bande de phosphore) (1970) 0 40 0 15

1969. – *Charte européenne de l'eau. Taille-douce. Dentelé 13.*

1612 **70 c. bleu, émeraude et noir** 0 50 0 50
a. (Non dentelé) 46 »

Tirage : 8 415 000.

1969. – *Fonds mondial pour la Nature. Taille-douce. Dentelé 13.*

Mouflon méditerranéen.

1613	**45 c. olive, brun-rouge et noir**	0 80	0 65
	a. (Non dentelé)	95	»

Tirage : 8 855 000.

1969. – *École centrale des Arts et Manufactures, à Châtenay-Malabry. Taille-douce. Dentelé 13.*

1614	**70 c. vert et orange**	0 50	0 50
	a. (Non dentelé)	61	»

Tirage : 8 775 000.

1969. – *Sous-marin "Le Redoutable", à propulsion nucléaire. Taille-douce. Dentelé 13.*

1615	**70 c. vert clair, vert foncé et bleu**	0 50	0 50
	a. (Non dentelé)	30	»

Tirage : 8 590 000.

1969. – *Grands noms de l'Histoire. Taille-douce. Dentelés 13.*

Louis XI et Charles le Téméraire.

1616	**80 c. vert, brun et sépia**	0 65	0 50

Le chevalier Bayard à la bataille de Brescia.

1617	**80 c. bistre, noir et sépia**	0 65	0 50

Henri IV (1553-1610) et l'Edit de Nantes.

1618	**80 c. bleu, noir et violet**	0 65	0 50
	La série, non dentelée	77	»

Tirages : 6 300 000, 7 500 000 et 7 500 000.

1969. – *Au profit de la Croix-Rouge. Croix en rouge. Tableaux de Nicolas Mignard (1606-1668). Taille-douce. Dentelés 13.* Ⓒ

L'Été.

L'Hiver.

1619	**40 c. +15 c. brun-jaune**	0 65	0 65
1620	**40 c. +15 c. bleu-vert et violet**	0 65	0 65
	La paire, non dentelée	125	»

Tirages : 4 475 000 et 4 195 000.

Ont été émis aussi en carnets. (Tirage : 550 000).

1969

Du n° 1582 au n° 1620 :

40 timbres ****29** **⊙25**

Autres rubriques de l'année :

Poste aérienne 43

Service 39 à 42

1970. – *Tour du monde par Alain Gerbault (1923-1929). Taille-douce. Dentelé 13.*

1621	**70 c. bleu et ardoise**	0 80	0 65
	a. (Non dentelé)	46 »	

Tirage : 7 527 500.

1970. – *Gendarmerie nationale. Taille-douce. Dentelé 13.*

Ses différentes activités.

1622	**45 c. outremer, vert foncé et brun**	1 20	0 65
	a. (Non dentelé)	30 »	

Tirage : 7 250 000.

1970. – *Personnages célèbres. Taille-douce. Dentelés 13.*

Louis Le Vau, architecte (1612-1670).

Prosper Mérimée, écrivain (1803-1870).

1623	**40 c. +10 c. brun-rouge**	0 50	0 50
1624	**40 c. +10 c. vert-bleu**	0 50	0 50

Philibert de l'Orme, architecte (1515-1570).

Edouard Branly, physicien et chimiste (1844-1940).

1625	**40 c. +10 c. olive foncé**	0 50	0 50
1626	**40 c. +10 c. brun-lilas**	0 50	0 50

Maurice de Broglie, physicien (1875-1960).

Alexandre Dumas, écrivain (1803-1870).

1627	**40 c. +10 c. gris**	0 50	0 50
1628	**40 c. +10 c. bleu foncé**	0 50	0 50
	N°s 1623 à 1628 (6 val.)	**3 »**	**3 »**
	La série, non dentelée	140 »	

Tirages : 4 205 000, 4 500 000, 4 440 000, 4 750 000, 5 000 000 et 5 350 000.

1970. – *7e championnat du monde de handball. Taille-douce. Dentelé 13.*

1629	**80 c. vert**	0 65	0 60
	a. (Non dentelé)	40 »	

Tirage : 7 545 000.

1970. – *Maréchal Juin. Taille-douce. Dentelé 13.*

La chapelle des Invalides.

1630	**45 c. bleu et violet-brun**	0 50	0 30
	a. (Non dentelé)	35 »	

Tirage : 7 337 500.

1970. – *Aérotrain. Taille-douce. Dentelé 13.*

1631	**80 c. violet et bistre**	0 80	0 60
	a. (Non dentelé)	46 »	

Tirage : 7 600 000.

1970. – ***Journée du Timbre. Taille-douce. Dentelé 13.***

Facteur de ville en 1830.

1632	**40 c. +10 c. bleu, carmin et noir**	0 50	0 50
	a. (Non dentelé)	23 »	

Tirage : 6 250 000.

1970. – ***150ᵉ anniversaire de la découverte de la quinine. Taille-douce. Dentelé 13.***

Pelletier et Caventou.

1633	**50 c. vert foncé, bleu clair et carmin**	0 50	0 50
	a. (Non dentelé)	42 »	

Tirage : 7 000 000.

1970. – ***Année européenne de la Nature. Taille-douce. Dentelé 13.***

Flamant rose.

1634	**45 c. olive, rose et gris**	0 50	0 30
	a. (Non dentelé)	40 »	

Tirage : 9 280 000.

1970. – ***Premier lancement de la fusée "Diamant B". Taille-douce. Dentelé 13.***

1635	**45 c. émeraude**	0 80	0 65
	a. (Non dentelé)	70 »	

Tirage : 7 300 000.

1970. – ***Journée mondiale de lutte contre le cancer. Taille-douce. Dentelé 13.***

1636	**40 c. +10 c. bleu, sépia et rose carminé**	0 30	0 30
	a. (Non dentelé)	30 »	

Tirage : 6 750 000.

1970. – ***Europa. Taille-douce. Dentelés 13.***

Symbole en forme de soleil.

1637	**40 c. rouge**	0 50	0 30
1638	**80 c. turquoise**	0 75	0 65
	La paire, non dentelée	125 »	

Tirages : 20 375 000 et 15 900 000.

1970. – ***25ᵉ anniversaire de l'Armistice du 8 mai 1945. Taille-douce. Dentelé 13.***

Maréchal de Lattre de Tassigny (Berlin 8 mai 1945).

1639	**40 c. +10 c. gris-vert et violet**	0 80	0 80
	a. (Non dentelé)	35 »	

Tirage : 4 325 000.

1970. – ***Oeuvres d'art. Taille-douce. Dentelés 12½-13.***

"L'Annonciation". Primitif de Savoie (15ᵉ siècle).

1640	**1 f. polychrome**	0 65	0 65
	a. (Non dentelé)	95 »	

Sculpture "Le Triomphe de Flore", de J.-B. Carpeaux (1827-1875).

1641	**1 f. polychrome**	0 65	0 65
	a. (Non dentelé)	77 »	

Tirages : 7 700 000 et 7 700 000.

1970. – ***43e Congrès national de la Fédération des Sociétés Philatéliques françaises, à Lens. Taille-douce. Dentelé 13.***

1642	**40 c. carmin**	0 30	0 30
	a. (Non dentelé)	23 »	

Tirage : 10 455 000.

1970. – ***Inauguration de l'Imprimerie des timbres-poste de Périgueux. Type Marianne de Cheffer. Taille-douce. Dentelé 13.***

1643	**40 c. rouge carminé**	0 50	0 30

Ce timbre a été émis en feuilles de 50 figurines, chacune de ces figurines étant jumelée avec une vignette portant l'inscription JUIN 1970 PÉRIGUEUX 1re ÉMISSION.

La vignette peut, bien entendu, être attenante à l'un quelconque des quatre côtés du timbre.

Tirage : 20 330 000.

1970. – ***Série touristique. Taille-douce. Dentelés 13.***

Rocher du Diamant (Martinique).

Abbaye de Chancelade (Dordogne).

1644	**50 c. vert foncé, bleu foncé et lie-de-vin**	0 50	0 15
	a. bleu omis	230 »	
1645	**95 c. olive, violet-brun et rouge-brun**	1 20	1 »

Ilet du Gosier (Guadeloupe).

Observatoire de Haute-Provence.

1646	**1 f. vert foncé, bleu foncé et rouge-brun**	0 80	0 15
1647	**1 f. 30 bleu foncé, bleu-violet et vert**	1 50	1 20
	Nos 1644 à 1647 (4 val.)	**4 »**	**2 50**
	La série, non dentelée	125 »	

1970. – ***25e anniversaire de la libération des camps de concentration. Taille-douce. Dentelé 13.***

1648	**45 c. bistre, bleu-violet et bleu ciel**	0 65	0 50
	a. (Non dentelé)	40 »	

Tirage : 7 235 000.

1970. – ***Jeux mondiaux des handicapés physiques, à Saint-Etienne. Taille-douce. Dentelé 13.***

1649	**45 c. lilas foncé, vert et bleu**	0 55	0 50
	a. (Non dentelé)	42 »	

Tirage : 7 340 000.

1970. – ***1ers championnats d'Europe d'athlétisme des Juniors. Taille-douce. Dentelé 13.***

1650	**45 c. lilas-rose, bleu et gris-bleu**	0 60	0 50
	a. (Non dentelé)	40 »	

Tirage : 7 300 000.

1970. – ***Salines de Chaux - Nicolas Ledoux, Centre du futur à Arc-et-Senans (Doubs). Taille-douce. Dentelé 13.***

1651 **80 c. bleu, violet-brun et vert-noir** 0 70 0 60
a. (Non dentelé) 30 »

Tirage : 6 800 000.

1970-71. – ***Oeuvres d'art. Taille-douce. Dentelés 12½-13.***

"Diane au retour de la chasse", de Boucher (1703-1770).

1652 **1 f. polychrome** 1 » 0 80
a. (Non dentelé) 100 »

"Danseuse au bouquet saluant", de Degas (1834-1917).

1653 **1 f. polychrome** 1 » 0 80
a. (Non dentelé) 100 »

Sculpture de la cathédrale de Strasbourg.

1654 **1 f. violet-brun** 1 » 0 80
a. (Non dentelé) 77 »

Tirages : 7 600 000, 6 800 000 et 6 600 000.

1970. – ***Histoire de France. Taille-douce. Dentelés 13.***

Richelieu (1575-1642).

1655 **45 c. gris-bleu, sépia et carmin** 0 80 0 65

Louis XIV (1637-1715).

1656 **45 c. vert foncé, ocre et rouge-brun** 0 80 0 65

Bataille de Fontenoy (1745).

1657 **45 c. rouge-brun, gris-bleu et violet-brun** 0 80 0 80

La série, non dentelée 95 »

Tirages : 7 100 000, 7 200 000 et 7 200 000.

1970. – ***25ᵉ anniversaire de l'O.N.U. Taille-douce. Dentelé 13.***

1658 **80 c. violet-brun, bleu et olive** 0 65 0 50
a. (Non dentelé) 54 »

Tirage : 7 200 000.

1970. – ***Centenaire de l'"Émission de Bordeaux". Taille-douce. Dentelé 13.***

Vue générale de Bordeaux.

1659 **80 c. violet et gris-bleu** 0 65 0 50
a. (Non dentelé) 46 »

Tirage : 730 000.

1970. – *100e anniversaire du Siège de Belfort. Taille-douce. Dentelé 13.*

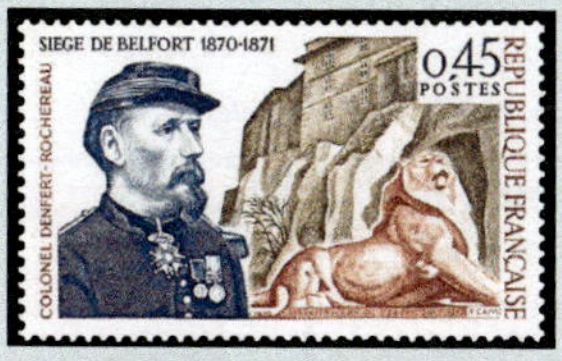

Colonel Denfert-Rochereau.

1660 **45 c. rouge-brun, gris-olive et bleu foncé** 0 50 0 50
a. (Non dentelé) 40 »
Tirage : 7 200 000.

1970. – *Au profit de la Croix-Rouge. Croix en rouge. Fresques de la chapelle de Dissay (Vienne). Taille-douce. Dentelés 13.* [C]

Seigneurs.

L'ange au fouet.

1661 **40 c. +15 c. vert** 0 80 0 80
1662 **40 c. +15 c. rouge-brun** 0 80 0 80
La paire, non dentelée 125 »
Tirages : 4 600 000 et 4 900 000.
Ont été émis aussi en carnets. (Tirage : 613 000).

> **1970**
>
> **Du n° 1621 au n° 1662 :**
>
> **42 timbres** ****29** **⊙24**
>
> Autre rubrique de l'année :
>
> Poste aérienne 44

1971. – *Type Marianne de Béquet. 1re série. Dentelés 14 x 13.* [C]

Typographie.

Taille-douce.

Les timbres typographiés ne portent pas la signature BÉQUET en bas à gauche.

1663 **45 c. bleu** 0 50 0 15
a. (sans "postes") 30 » 15 »
1664 **50 c. carmin-rose** 0 30 0 15
a. (Gomme tropicale) 1 25
b. (n° rouge au verso) 28 »
c. (Trois bandes de phosphore) 0 50 0 15
d. (Gomme tropicale 3 bandes de phosphore) 1 25
e. (n° rouge au verso, Gomme tropicale) 27 »
La paire, non dentelée 61 »

Ce type a été repris avec de nouvelles valeurs en 1974-75 (nos 1814 à 1816) et en 1976 (nos 1891 à 1895).

Voir note après le n°1331Ab.

1971. – *Championnats du monde de patinage sur glace. Taille-douce. Dentelé 13.*

1665 **80 c. noir, bleu pâle et violet** 0 65 0 65
a. (Non dentelé) 61 »
Tirage : 7 500 000.

1971. – *OCÉANEXPO. Bordeaux 1971. Taille-douce. Dentelé 13.*

1666 **80 c. bleu-vert et bleu foncé** 0 65 0 50
a. (Non dentelé) 23 »
Tirage : 7 400 000.

1971. – *Personnages célèbres. Taille-douce. Dentelés 13.*

Esprit Auber (1782-1871).

Général Diégo Brosset (1898-1944).

1667 **50 c. +10 c. lilas-brun et bistre** 0 60 0 60
1668 **50 c. +10 c. vert foncé et réséda** 0 65 0 65

Victor Grignard (1872-1935).

Henri Farman (1874-1958).

1669 **50 c. +10 c. brique et bistre** 0 60 0 60
1670 **50 c. +10 c. violet et lilas** 0 65 0 65
Nos 1667 à 1670 (4 val.) **2 50** **2 50**
La série, non dentelée 110 »
Tirages : 4 200 000, 4 300 000, 4 840 000 et 3 645 000.
Cette série est complétée par deux timbres émis en 1971 (nos 1689 et 1690).

1971. – *Journée du Timbre. Taille-douce. Dentelé 13.*

La poste aux Armées, 1914-1918.

1671 **50 c. +10 c. bistre, bleu foncé et brun-orange** 0 65 0 50
a. (Non dentelé) 23 »
Tirage : 5 900 000.

1971. – ***Oeuvres d'art. Taille-douce. Dentelés 12½ x 13.***

"Le Vanneur", de Millet (1814-1875).

1672	**1 f. polychrome**	0 80	0 65
	a. (Non dentelé)	95 »	

"Songe creux", oeuvre de Rouault (1871-1958).

1673	**1 f. polychrome**	0 80	0 65
	a. (Non dentelé)	95 »	

Tirages : 6 600 000 et 6 948 000.

1971. – ***Quatre-mâts. Cap-hornier "Antoinette". Taille-douce. Dentelé 13.***

1674	**80 c. gris-vert, bleu et violet pâle**	1 20	0 80
	a. (Non dentelé)	30 »	

Tirage : 7 297 000.

1971. – ***Protection de la nature. Taille-douce. Dentelé 13.***

Isard.

1675	**65 c. bleu, ocre et violet**	0 70	0 65
	a. (Non dentelé)	27 »	

Voir également les n°s 1692 à 1694 émis en 1971-72.

Tirage : 15 400 000.

1971. – ***Europa. Taille-douce. Dentelés 13.***

Basilique de la Salute, à Venise.

1676	**50 c. gris-bleu et bistre**	0 75	0 30
1677	**80 c. lilas-rose**	1 »	0 70
	La paire, non dentelée	125 »	

Tirages : 20 000 000 et 10 100 000.

1971. – ***Histoire de France. Taille-douce. Dentelés 13.***

Salle des États Généraux et représentants des trois ordres.

1678	**45 c. brun-orange, bleu et violet**	0 65	0 50

Bataille de Valmy.

1679	**45 c. bistre, bleu et brun-orange**	0 80	0 60

Prise de la Bastille.

1680	**65 c. violet-brun, bleu-gris et lilas**	1 »	0 80
	La série, non dentelée	125 »	

Tirages : 8 045 000, 6 800 000 et 6 880 000.

1971. – ***44e congrès national de la Fédération des sociétés philatéliques françaises, à Grenoble. Taille-douce. Dentelé 13.***

1681	**50 c. ocre-orange, rouge et lilas**	0 50	0 30
	a. (Non dentelé)	20 »	

Tirage : 13 900 000.

1971. – *Aide familiale rurale. Taille-douce. Dentelé 13.*

1682	**40 c. violet foncé et vert foncé**	0 30	0 30
	a. (Non dentelé)	18 50	

Tirage : 23 800 000.

1971. – *Série touristique. Taille-douce. Dentelés 13.*

Sainte-Chapelle de Riom.

Dôle.

Riquewihr.

1683	**60 c. vert, gris et bleu**	0 60	0 30
1684	**65 c. noir, ocre-jaune et lilas**	0 80	0 30
1685	**90 c. violet-brun, ocre-orange et vert**	0 80	0 30

Château fort de Sedan.

Gorges de l'Ardèche.

1686	**1 f. 10 vert foncé, brun et bleu**	0 80	0 80
1687	**1 f. 40 vert, violet-brun et bleu**	1 »	0 30
	N°s 1683 à 1687 (5 val.)	**4 »**	**2 »**
	La série, non dentelée	95 »	

1971. – *59e conférence de l'Union interparlementaire. Taille-douce. Dentelé 13.*

L'Assemblée Nationale.

1688	**90 c. bleu-violet**	0 80	0 80
	a. (Non dentelé)	27 »	

Tirage : 10 550 000.

1971. – *Personnages célèbres. Taille-douce. Dentelés 13.*

Général Delestraint.

Robert Houdin.

1689	**50 c. +10 c. violet foncé et lilas**	1 »	1 »
1690	**50 c. +10 c. bleu foncé et bleu-vert**	0 60	0 60
	La paire, non dentelée	46 »	

Tirages : 4 600 000 et 4 050 000.

Voir également les n°s 1667 à 1670.

1971. – *40e anniversaire de l'assemblée permanente des Chambres de métiers. Taille-douce. Dentelé 13.*

1691	**90 c. rouge et lilas**	0 80	0 50
	a. (Non dentelé)	17 »	

Tirage : 8 900 000.

1971-72. – *Protection de la nature. Dentelés 13.*

Caméléon (Ile de la Réunion).

1692	**60 c. polychrome**	1 »	0 80

Saumon.

Grand-duc.

1693	**60 c. vert, outremer et bleu-gris**	1 »	0 80
1694	**65 c. bleu-gris, brun foncé et brun**	1 »	0 80
	La série, non dentelée	77 »	

Tirages : 8 408 000, 7 450 000 et 7 600 000.

Voir également le n° 1675.

1971. – *Anniversaire de la mort du général de Gaulle. Taille-douce. Dentelés 13.*

1695	**50 c. sépia** *Le général de Gaulle en juin 1940*	0 75	0 75
1696	**50 c. outremer** *Le général de Gaulle à Brazzaville en 1944*	0 75	0 75
1697	**50 c. rouge** *La descente des Champs Elysées en 1944*	0 75	0 75
1698	**50 c. sépia** *Portrait officiel du président de la République*	0 75	0 75
	Nos 1695 à 1698 (4 val.)	**3 »**	**3 »**

Tirage : 14 140 000 séries.

Imprimés en bandes horizontales de quatre timbres avec une vignette centrale sans valeur représentant une croix de Lorraine.

1698A	La bande	3 50	3 25
	a. Non dentelée	305 »	

1971. – *Sesquicentenaire de l'Académie nationale de Médecine. Taille-douce. Dentelé 13.*

Baron Antoine Portal (1742-1832).

1699	**45 c. violet et lilas**	0 50	0 50
	a. (Non dentelé)	27 »	

Tirage : 8 728 000.

1971. – *Au profit de la Croix-Rouge. Croix en rouge. "Oeuvres de Greuze (1725-1805)". Taille-douce. Dentelés 13.* [C]

Jeune fille au petit chien.

L'oiseau mort.

1700	**30 c. +10 c. outremer**	0 80	0 80
1701	**50 c. +10 c. rouge-brique**	0 80	0 80
	La paire, non dentelée	77 »	

Tirages : 5 007 000 et 4 503 000.

Ont été émis aussi en carnets (tirage : 641 000).

1971

Du n° 1663 au n° 1701

(sauf 1698A) :

39 timbres **29 ⊙23

Autres rubriques de l'année :

Poste aérienne 45, 46

Préoblitérés 130 à 133

1972. – *Oeuvres d'art. Taille-douce. Dentelés 12½ x 13.*

L'Étude, de Fragonard (1732-1806).

1702	**1 f. polychrome**	1 »	0 80
	a. (Non dentelé)	100 »	

Femmes au Jardin, de Monet (1840-1926).

1703	**1 f. polychrome**	1 20	0 80
	a. (Non dentelé)	100 »	

Tirages : 6 625 000 et 6 775 000.

1972. – *200e anniversaire de la découverte des îles Crozet et Kerguelen. Taille-douce. Dentelé 13.*

1704 **90 c. noir, bleu et bistre** 0 80 0 65
a. (Non dentelé) 84 »
Tirage : 7 750 000.

1972. – ***Jeux olympiques d'hiver de Sapporo. Taille-douce. Dentelé 13.***

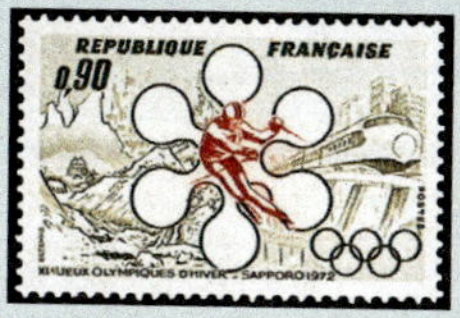

1705 **90 c. olive et rouge** 0 65 0 50
a. (Non dentelé) 84 »
Tirage : 7 750 000.

1972. – ***Personnages célèbres. Surtaxe au profit de la Croix-Rouge. Taille-douce. Dentelés 13.***

Paul de Chomedey, sieur de Maisonneuve.

Aristide Bergés.

1706 **50 c. +10 c. bleu-noir, noir et bleu pâle** 0 60 0 60
1707 **50 c. +10 c. vert foncé, noir et vert** 0 60 0 60

Edouard Belin.

Louis Blériot.

1708 **50 c. +10 c. lilas et gris** 0 60 0 60
1709 **50 c. +10 c. rouge et gris** 0 70 0 70

N°s 1706 à 1709 (4 val.) **2 50** **2 50**
La série, non dentelée 95 »

Tirages : 4 300 000, 4 250 000, 4 650 000 et 4 500 000.

Voir également les n°s 1727 et 1728.

1972. – ***Journée du Timbre. Taille-douce. Dentelé 13.***

Facteur rural et église de Champignelles (Yonne).

1710 **50 c. +10 c. gris-olive, bleu et jaune** 0 80 0 80
a. (Non dentelé) 23 »
Tirage : 5 800 000.

1972. – ***Mois mondial du coeur. Taille-douce. Dentelé 13.***

1711 **45 c. gris, orange et carmin** 0 50 0 50
a. (Non dentelé) 19 25
Tirage : 7 750 000.

1972. – ***Série touristique. Taille-douce. Dentelés 13.***

Abbaye de Charlieu.

Narbonne, Cathédrale Saint-Just.

1712 **1 f. 20 bistre et bleu** 0 80 0 30
a. (Non dentelé) 18 50
1713 **3 f. 50 turquoise, carmin et olive** 2 » 0 65
a. (Non dentelé) 18 50

1972. – ***Europa. Taille douce, sauf n° 1715 : héliogravure. Dentelés 13.***

Cathédrale d'Aix-la-Chapelle.

1714 **50 c. jaune, olive et brun-violet** 0 75 0 30
1715 **90 c. multicolore** 1 » 0 70
La paire, non dentelée 110 »

Tirages : 21 550 000 et 10 500 000.

1972. – ***20e anniversaire des donneurs de sang bénévoles des P.T.T. Taille-douce. Dentelé 13.***

1716 **40 c. rouge-orange** 0 30 0 30
a. (Non dentelé) 19 25
Tirage : 13 100 000.

1972. – *Trois-mâts, terre-neuvas "Côte d'Emeraude". Taille-douce. Dentelé 13.*

1717 **90 c. saumon, vert foncé et bleu** 1 » 0 80
a. (Non dentelé) 23 »
Tirage : 8 275 000.

1972. – *45ᵉ congrès national de la Fédération des sociétés philatéliques françaises, à Saint-Brieuc. Taille-douce. Dentelé 13.*

1718 **50 c. rouge** 0 30 0 30
a. (Non dentelé) 17 »
Tirage : 8 500 000.

1972. – *Code postal. Typographie. Dentelés 13.*

1719 **30 c. vert et rouge** 0 15 0 15
1720 **50 c. rouge et jaune** 0 50 0 30
La paire, non dentelée 35 »

1972. – *XXIᵉ congrès mondial de l'Internationale P.T.T. Taille-douce. Dentelé 13.*

Tour du Télégraphe Chappe de Saverne.

1721 **45 c. gris-bleu et bleu foncé** 0 50 0 30
a. (Non dentelé) 23 »
Tirage : 7 500 000.

1972. – *Jeux olympiques de Munich. Taille-douce. Dentelé 13.*

1722 **1 f. brun-olive** 0 65 0 50
a. (Non dentelé) 77 »
Tirage : 17 900 000.

1972. – *Année du tourisme pédestre. Héliogravure. Dentelé 13.*

1723 **40 c. polychrome** 0 60 0 50
a. (Non dentelé) 18 50
Tirage : 7 500 000.

1972. – *Championnats du monde cyclistes. Taille-douce. Dentelé 13.*

1724 **1 f. gris-bleu, brun-olive et lilas** 1 50 0 60
a. (Non dentelé) 65 »
Tirage : 7 500 000.

1972. – *Série touristique. Taille-douce. Dentelés 13.*

Sologne.

Château de Bazoches-du-Morvand.

1725 **1 f. ocre et brun** 0 75 0 30
a. (Non dentelé) 27 »
1726 **2 f. vert-noir et brun-lilas** 1 25 0 30
a. (Non dentelé) 15 50

1972. – ***Personnages célèbres. Taille-douce. Dentelés 13.***

Amiral de Grasse.

Théophile Gautier.

1727	**50 c. +10 c. orange et noir**	0 60	0 60
1728	**50 c. +10 c. brun-jaune et noir**	0 60	0 60
	La paire, non dentelée	30 »	

Tirages : 3 700 000 et 3 850 000.

Voir également les n°s 1706 à 1709.

1972. – ***Histoire de France. Taille-douce. Dentelés 13.***

"Incroyables et Merveilleuses".

1729	**45 c. olive, vert foncé et carmin**	0 50	0 50

Bonaparte au pont d'Arcole.

Expédition d'Égypte.

1730	**60 c. rouge, gris et bleu-noir**	1 »	0 65
1731	**65 c. ocre, outremer et brun-violet**	1 »	0 80
	La série, non dentelée	95 »	

Tirages : 6 700 000, 6 800 000 et 6 625 000.

1972. – ***Oeuvres d'art. Taille-douce. Dentelés 12½-13.***

Pierre de Bourbon présenté par saint Pierre, oeuvre du maître de Moulins.

1732	**2 f. polychrome**	1 80	1 20
	a. (Non dentelé)	95 »	

"Les Péniches", de Derain (1880-1954).

1733	**2 f. polychrome**	2 20	1 30
	a. (Non dentelé)	95 »	

Tirages : 6 750 000 et 6 625 000.

1972. – ***150e anniversaire du déchiffrement des hiéroglyphes par Jean-François Champollion. Taille-douce. Dentelé 13.***

1734	**90 c. outremer et rouge-brun**	0 65	0 50
	a. (Non dentelé)	30 »	

Tirage : 7 500 000.

1972. – ***Au profit de la Croix-Rouge. Croix en rouge. Taille-douce. Dentelés 13.*** C

N. Desgenettes.

F. Broussais.

1735	**30 c. +10 c. vert**	0 80	0 80
1736	**50 c. +10 c. rouge**	0 80	0 80
	La paire, non dentelée	84 »	

Tirage : 4 300 000 paires.

Ont été émis aussi en carnets (tirage : 617 000).

1972

Du n° 1702 au n° 1736 :

35 timbres **29 ⊙21

Autre rubrique de l'année :

Poste aérienne 47

1973. – ***Centenaire de la naissance de Sainte Thérèse de l'Enfant-Jésus. Taille-douce. Dentelé 13.***

1737	**1 f. turquoise et gris-bleu**	0 80	0 65
	a. (Non dentelé)	23	»

Tirage : 8 350 000.

1973. – ***L'Anthurium de la Martinique. Héliogravure. Dentelé 13.***

1738	**50 c. polychrome**	0 50	0 50
	a. (Non dentelé)	23	»

Tirage : 15 150 000.

1973. – ***X[e] anniversaire du traité sur la coopération franco-allemande. Héliogravure. Dentelé 13.***

1739	**50 c. multicolore**	0 50	0 50
	a. (Non dentelé)	46	»
	b. bleu omis		

La République Fédérale Allemande a émis simultanément une figurine au même type, de 40 p. (N° 603 ; cotes : 1,70 0,40).

Tirage : 9 650 000.

1973. – ***Immigration polonaise de 1921-23. Taille-douce. Dentelé 13.***

1740	**40 c. carmin, violet et vert**	0 30	0 30
	a. (Non dentelé)	15 50	

Tirage : 8 000 000.

1973. – ***Oeuvres d'art. Taille-douce. Dentelés 12½ x 13.***

Le chapiteau de la Cène de l'église Saint-Austremoine d'Issoire.

1741	**2 f. polychrome**	1 50	1 20
	a. (Non dentelé)	77	»

"Étude de femme à genoux", de Charles Le Brun.

1742	**2 f. jaune-orange et rouge**	1 50	1 20
	a. (Non dentelé)	77	»

Boiseries du Moutier d'Ahun.

1743	**2 f. ocre et lilas-brun foncé**	1 50	1 20
	a. (Non dentelé)	77	»

Tirages : 6 375 000, 6 875 000 et 6 700 000.

1973. – ***Personnages célèbres. Taille-douce. Dentelés 13.***

Amiral de Coligny.

Ernest Renan.

Santos-Dumont.

1744	**50 c. +10 c. olive, violet et gris-bleu**	0 60	0 60
1745	**50 c. +10 c. orange, carmin et gris**	0 80	0 60
1746	**50 c. +10 c. gris-olive, jaune et lilas**	0 60	0 60

Colette.

Duguay-Trouin.

1747	**50 c. +10 c. lilas, rouge-brun et ocre**	0 60	0 60
1748	**50 c. +10 c. lilas, ocre et gris-bleu**	0 60	0 60
	N°s 1744 à 1748 (5 val.)	**3 20**	**3 »**
	La série, non dentelée	100 »	

Tirages : 4 250 000, 4 100 000, 4 150 000, 4 000 000 et 4 350 000.

Voir également les n°s 1768 et 1769.

1973. – ***Journée du Timbre. Taille-douce. Dentelé 13.***

Relais de Poste.

1749	**50 c. +10 c. turquoise**	0 50	0 50
	a. (Non dentelé)	23 »	

Tirage : 5 550 000.

1973. – ***Série "Grandes réalisations". Taille-douce. Dentelés 13.***

Centre téléphonique "Tuileries".

A 300 B Airbus.

1750	**45 c. outremer, olive et vert**	0 30	0 30
	a. (Non dentelé)	15 50	
1751	**3 f. noir et bleu clair**	2 »	1 60
	a. (Non dentelé)	61 »	

Tirages : 8 100 000 et 8 050 000.

Voir également le n° 1772.

1973. – ***Europa. Taille douce, sauf n° 1753 : héliogravure. Dentelés 13.***

Grand place de Bruxelles : l'Hôtel de Ville.

Cor postal.

1752	**50 c. lilas-rose et brun-violet**	0 75	0 30
1753	**90 c. vert foncé, rouge, ocre-orange et jaune**	1 75	1 10
	La paire, non dentelée	95 »	

Tirages : 20 000 000 et 10 200 000.

1973. – ***Protection de la nature. Taille-douce. Dentelés 13.***

Raton laveur de la Guadeloupe.

Cigognes d'Alsace.

1754	**40 c. lilas, olive et violet-brun**	0 50	0 30
	a. (Non dentelé)	23 »	
1755	**60 c. gris, turquoise et rose**	0 65	0 65
	a. (Non dentelé)	23 »	

Tirages : 21 900 000 et 8 250 000.

1973. – ***Bicentenaire du Grand-Orient de France. Taille-douce. Dentelé 13.***

1756	**90 c. violet et carmin**	0 65	0 50
	a. (Non dentelé)	27 »	

Tirage : 8 250 000.

1973. – ***Série touristique. Taille-douce. Dentelés 13.***

Palais des Ducs de Bourgogne, à Dijon.

1757	**65 c. violet et rouge**	0 50	0 30
	a. (Non dentelé)	17 »	

Château de Gien.

Le Clos-Lucé, à Amboise.

1758	**90 c. gris-bleu et brun carminé**	0 65	0 15
	a. (Non dentelé)	15 50	
	b. gris-bleu		
1759	**1 f. ocre-orange, vert et bleu clair**	0 65	0 15
	a. (Non dentelé)	15 50	

1973. – ***50e anniversaire de l'Académie des Sciences d'Outre-Mer. Taille-douce. Dentelé 13.***

1760	**1 f. lilas, vert-noir et rouge**	0 65	0 50
	a. (Non dentelé)	15 50	

Tirage : 7 650 000.

1973. – ***50e anniversaire des 24 heures du Mans. Taille-douce. Dentelé 13.***

1761	**60 c. violet et outremer**	0 80	0 65
	a. (Non dentelé)	42 »	

Tirage : 8 250 000.

1973. – ***Cinq-mâts "France II". Taille-douce. Dentelé 13.***

1762	**90 c. bleu et gris-bleu**	1 20	0 80
	a. (Non dentelé)	23 »	

Tirage : 7 600 000.

1973. – ***46e congrès national de la Fédération des sociétés philatéliques françaises, à Toulouse. Taille-douce. Dentelé 13.***

1763	**50 c. violet et rouge-brun**	0 50	0 30
	a. (Non dentelé)	15 50	

Tirage : 11 500 000.

1973. – ***Série touristique. Taille-douce. Dentelé 13.***

Le saut du Doubs.

1764	**60 c. turquoise, vert foncé et bleu-noir**	0 50	0 30
	a. (Non dentelé)	15 50	

Voir également les n°s 1757 à 1759.

1973-74. – ***Oeuvres d'art. Taille-douce. Dentelure 12½ x 13, sauf n° 1766 : 12 x 13.***

1765	**2 f. *"La Finette", de Watteau (1684-1721)***	1 50	1 20
	a. (Non dentelé)	84 »	

1766	**2 f. *Cardinal de Richelieu, tableau de Philippe de Champaigne (1602-1674)***	1 50	1 25
	a. (Non dentelé)	84 »	

Tirages : 6 500 000 et 6 700 000.

Ce dernier timbre est imprimé attenant à une vignette portant la mention "ARPHILA 1975", qui ne fait pas partie du timbre, mais qui est comprise avec le non dentelé.

1973. – ***Centenaire de la découverte du bacille de la lèpre par Hansen (1841-1912). Taille-douce. Dentelé 13.***

1767 **45 c. vert-olive, brun-jaune et vert** 0 50 0 30
a. (Non dentelé) 46 »

Tirage : 8 750 000.

1973. – ***Personnages célèbres. Taille-douce. Dentelés 13.***

Pasteur.

Tony Garnier (La cité industrielle).

1768 **50 c. +10 c. brun-olive, lilas et violet** 0 60 0 60
1769 **50 c. +10 c. lilas-rose, noir et gris-bleu** 0 60 0 60

La paire, non dentelée 40 »

Tirages : 4 050 000 et 3 550 000.

Voir également les n°s 1744 à 1748.

1973. – ***75ᵉ anniversaire de la liaison T.S.F. "Tour Eiffel-Panthéon (E. Ducretet)". Taille-douce. Dentelé 13.***

1770 **1 f. vert et grenat** 0 65 0 65
a. (Non dentelé) 18 50

Tirage : 8 150 000.

1973. – ***Tricentenaire de la mort de Molière. Taille-douce. Dentelé 13.***

1771 **1 f. brun et rouge** 0 65 0 50
a. (Non dentelé) 18 50
Tirage : 8 250 000.

1973. – ***Série "Grandes réalisations". Taille-douce. Dentelé 13.***

Le Havre, écluse François 1er.

1772 **90 c. noir, bleu et lilas foncé** 0 65 0 65
a. (Non dentelé) 18 50
Voir également les n°s 1750 et 1751.
Tirage : 8 000 000.

1973. – ***Pierre Bourgoin et Philippe Kieffer. Héros des parachutistes S.A.S. et commandos F.F.L. Compagnons de la Libération. Taille-douce. Dentelé 13.***

1773 **1 f. rouge, carmin et bleu** 0 65 0 50
a. (Non dentelé) 30 »
Tirage : 8 050 000.

1973. – ***Histoire de France. Taille-douce. Dentelés 13.***

Bonaparte. Jean Portalis. Préparation du Code Civil, 1800-1804.

1774 **45 c. bleu, brun-violet et gris** 0 65 0 50

Encouragement à l'industrie, 1806.

1775 **60 c. brun-jaune, vert-bleu et brun** 0 65 0 65

Sacre de Napoléon.

1776 **1 f. vert-noir, olive et carmin** 0 80 0 65

La série, non dentelée 100 »

Tirages : 7 575 000, 7 575 000 et 7 525 000.

1973. – ***50e anniversaire de la flamme sous l'Arc de Triomphe. Taille-douce. Dentelé 13.***

1777 **40 c. lilas, rouge et bleu** 0 50 0 30
a. (Non dentelé) 18 50

Tirage : 8 150 000.

1973. – ***50e anniversaire de la création des chambres d'agriculture. Taille-douce. Dentelé 13.***

1778 **65 c. outremer, noir et vert** 0 50 0 50
a. (Non dentelé) 15 50

Tirage : 8 050 000.

1973. – ***Au profit de la Croix-Rouge. Taille-douce. Dentelés 13.*** Ⓒ

Sépulcre de Tonnerre. (Marie-Madeleine).

Sépulcre de Tonnerre. (Femme avec vase aux aromates).

1779 **30 c. +10 c. vert foncé et rouge** 0 65 0 65

1780 **50 c. +10 c. noir et rouge** 0 65 0 65

La paire, non dentelée 84 »

Tirage : 4 000 000 paires.

Ont été émis aussi en carnets (tirage : 616 000).

1973. – ***25e anniversaire de la déclaration des Droits de l'Homme. Taille-douce. Dentelé 13.***

1781 **45 c. orange, brun-rouge et brun** 0 30 0 30
a. (Non dentelé) 23 »

Tirage : 7 700 000.

1973. – ***Musée Postal. Maison de la poste et de la philatélie. Taille-douce. Dentelé 13.***

1782 **50 c. brun carminé et ocre** 0 30 0 30
a. (Non dentelé) 15 50

Tirage : 6 900 000.

1973

Du n° 1737 au n° 1782 :

46 timbres ****35** **⊙28**

Autre rubrique de l'année :

Poste aérienne 48

1974. – ***Arphila 75. Paris. Taille-douce. Dentelé 13.***

1783 **50 c. lilas foncé, brun et bleu** 0 30 0 30
a. (Non dentelé) 21 »

Tirage : 16 350 000.

1974. – *Personnages célèbres. Taille-douce. Dentelés 13.*

Saint-Louis Marie Grignon de Montfort (1673-1716).

Francis Poulenc (1899-1963).

1784	**50 c. +10 c. sépia, carmin et vert foncé**	0 60	0 60
1785	**50 c. +10 c. brun carminé et lilas foncé**	0 60	0 60
	La paire, non dentelée	35 »	

Tirages : 3 800 000 et 3 600 000.

Voir également les n°s 1822 et 1823.

1974. – *Journée du Timbre. Taille-douce. Dentelé 13.*

Centre de tri automatique d'Orléans la Source.

1786	**50 c. +10 c. rouge-brique et sépia**	0 50	0 50
	a. (Non dentelé)	17 »	

Tirage : 5 655 000.

1974. – *Série "Grandes réalisations". Taille-douce. Dentelé 13.*

Aéroport Charles de Gaulle.

1787	**60 c. olive et violet**	0 50	0 50
	a. (Non dentelé)	100 »	

Tirage : 8 200 000.

1974. – *Centenaire du club alpin français. Taille-douce. Dentelé 13.*

Gentiane et glacier.

1788	**65 c. bleu-noir et violet**	0 50	0 50
	a. (Non dentelé)	30 »	

Tirage : 7 750 000.

1974. – *Europa. Sculptures. Taille-douce. Dentelés 13.*

"L'Age d'Airain", de Rodin (1840-1917).

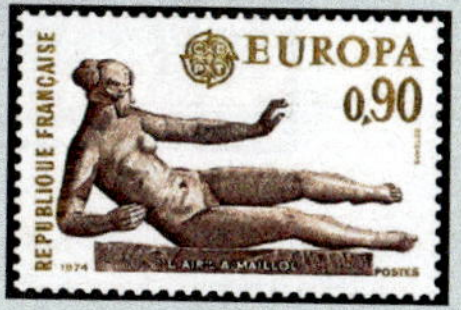

"L'Air", Maillol (1861-1944).

1789	**50 c. lilas et noir**	0 75	0 30
1790	**90 c. violet-brun et ocre**	1 25	0 70
	La paire, non dentelée	95 »	

Tirages : 20 300 000 et 10 200 000.

1974. – *Sauvetage en mer. Taille-douce. Dentelé 13.*

1791	**90 c. gris, bleu foncé, ocre et rouge**	0 65	0 50
	a. (Non dentelé)	18 50	

Tirage : 7 575 000.

1974. – *25e anniversaire du Conseil de l'Europe. Taille-douce. Dentelé 13.*

1792	**45 c. ocre, bleu et gris-bleu**	0 50	0 50
	a. (Non dentelé)	46 »	

Tirage : 7 675 000.

1974. – *Série touristique. Taille-douce. Dentelés 13.*

Salers.

Golfe de Saint-Florent (Corse).

1793	**65 c. vert-jaune et violet-brun**	0 50	0 50
	a. (Non dentelé)	15 50	
1794	**3 f. bleu, rouge et vert-jaune**	1 60	0 65
	a. (Non dentelé)	21 50	

1974. – *Protection de la nature. Taille-douce. Dentelé 13.*

Bison d'Europe.

1795 **40 c. ocre, bleu et violet-brun** 0 50 0 30
a. (Non dentelé) 23 »

Tirage : 10 350 000.

1974. – *30e anniversaire de la Libération. Taille-douce. Dentelés 13.*

Général Koenig.

1796 **1 f. lilas, lilas-rose et brun-jaune** 0 65 0 50
a. (Non dentelé) 21 »

Villes "Compagnons de la Libération".

1797 **1 f. +10 c. vert-émeraude, noir et sépia** 0 80 0 80
a. (Non dentelé) 27 »

Tirages : 7 725 000 et 4 200 000.

1974. – *47e congrès national de la Fédération des sociétés philatéliques françaises, à Colmar. Taille-douce. Dentelé 13.*

La maison Pfister.

1798 **50 c. rouge-brique et lilas** 0 30 0 30
a. (Non dentelé) 15 50

Tirage : 8 450 000.

1974. – *30e anniversaire du débarquement en Normandie. Taille-douce. Dentelé 13.*

1799 **45 c. vert, gris-bleu et rouge pâle** 1 » 0 80
a. (Non dentelé) 27 »

Tirage : 7 750 000.

1974. – *XXIe Jeux olympiques échiquéens. Taille-douce. Dentelé 13.*

1800 **1 f. brun, outremer et rouge** 0 80 0 50
a. (Non dentelé) 155 »

Tirage : 8 050 000.

1974. – *Tricentenaire de la fondation de l'Hôtel des Invalides. Taille-douce. Dentelé 13.*

1801 **40 c. bleu, brun-jaune et gris-bleu foncé** 0 30 0 30
a. (Non dentelé) 18 50

Tirage : 7 765 000.

1974-75. – *Série "Grandes réalisations". Taille-douce. Dentelés 13.*

Turbotrain TGV 001.

Surrégénérateur Phénix.

1802 **60 c. bleu-gris, rouge et sépia** 1 10 0 80
a. (Non dentelé) 61 »
b. (Barbouillé de rouge) 250 »

1803 **65 c. rouge-orange, lilas et noir** 0 50 0 50
a. (Non dentelé) 30 »

Réseau Express Régional.

Hélicoptère Gazelle.

1804	1 f. gris-bleu et bleu	0 80	0 50
	a. (Non dentelé)	46 »	
1805	1 f. 30 violet et vert-olive	0 80	0 65
	a. (Non dentelé)	70 »	
	Nos 1802 à 1805 (4 val.)	**3 20**	**2 45**

Tirages : 7 800 000, 7 700 000, 10 000 000 et 6 000 000.

1974-75. – *Série touristique. Taille-douce. Dentelés 13.*

Palais de Justice de Rouen.

La vallée du Lot.

1806	85 c. bistre et bleu	0 65	0 50
1807	1 f. 10 brun et olive	0 65	0 50

Saint-Pol-de-Léon.

Château de Rochechouart.

1808	1 f. 20 brun-olive, bleu et bistre	0 65	0 30
1809	1 f. 40 bleu-gris, vert-jaune et brun	0 80	0 30

Basilique de Saint-Nicolas de Port.

1810	2 f. gris et lilas-rose	1 25	0 30
	Nos 1806 à 1810 (5 val.)	**4 »**	**1 90**
	La série, non dentelée	77 »	

1974. – *"Arphila'75". Héliogravure, sauf n° 1812 : taille douce. Dentelés 12-13.*

Tableau de Miro.

1811	2 f. bleu, rouge, vert, jaune et noir	1 50	1 10
	a. (Non dentelé)	84 »	

"Canal du Loing". Tableau de A. Sisley.

1812	2 f. polychrome	1 50	1 10
	a. (Non dentelé)	84 »	

Tapisserie de la manufacture nationale des Gobelins, par Mathieu. "Hommage à Nicolas Fouquet".

1813	2 f. polychrome	1 50	1 10
	a. (Non dentelé)	84 »	

Tirages : 6 800 000, 5 825 000 et 5 950 000.

Timbres imprimés attenant à une vignette portant la mention "ARPHILA 75 Paris", qui ne fait pas partie du timbre, mais qui est comprise avec le non dentelé.

1974. – *Type Marianne de Béquet. Taille douce, sauf n° 1814 : typographie. Une bande de phosphore, sauf n° 1816 : trois bandes de phosphore. Dentelure 13, sauf n° 1814 : 14 x 13.* [C]

Typographie.

Taille-douce.

Taille-douce.

Les timbres typographiés ne portent pas la signature BÉQUET en bas à gauche.

1814	**60 c. vert**	0 80	0 15
	a. (sans bande de phosphore)	4 »	1 »
	b. (Non dentelé)	30 »	
1815	**60 c. vert**	5 »	0 70
	a. (Gomme tropicale)	8 »	
	b. (n° rouge au verso, Gomme tropicale)	25 »	
	c. (sans bande de phosphore)	25 »	20 »
1816	**80 c. rouge**	0 80	0 15
	a. (sans bandes de phosphore, gomme brillante)	22 »	2 »
	b. (Gomme tropicale)	2 »	
	c. (n° rouge au verso, Gomme tropicale)	25 »	
	d. (Gomme tropicale, sans bande de phosphore)	9 »	2 »
	e. (Non dentelé)	35 »	

Les n°s 1815 et 1815c proviennent de carnets ; le 1815c est avec gomme tropicale, la dentelure est souvent rognée.

1974. – *Centenaire de l'U.P.U. Taille-douce. Dentelé 13.*

1817	**1 f. 20 outremer, carmin et vert-olive**	0 65	0 50
	a. (Non dentelé)	95 »	

Tirage : 7 525 000.

1974. – *500e anniversaire de la naissance de Nicolas Copernic. Taille-douce. Dentelé 13.*

1818	**1 f. 20 bleu-gris, brun et lilas-rose**	0 65	0 50
	a. (Non dentelé)	46 »	

Tirage : 6 825 000.

1974-75. – *Protection de la nature. Taille-douce. Dentelés 13.*

Tatou géant de la Guyane.

Aigrette Garzette.

1819	**65 c. bleu-gris, bistre et vert-jaune**	0 50	0 50
	a. (Non dentelé)	27 »	
1820	**70 c. bleu et bistre**	0 50	0 50
	a. (Gomme tropicale)	20 »	
	b. (Non dentelé)	27 »	

Tirages : 9 050 000 et 6 750 000.

1974. – *XXXe anniversaire de la Libération, médaille de la Résistance française. Taille-douce. Dentelé 13.*

1821	**1 f. rouge, bistre et noir**	0 80	0 65
	a. (Non dentelé)	40 »	

Tirage : 5 100 000.

1974. – *Personnages célèbres. Légende RÉPUBLIQUE FRANÇAISE. Taille-douce. Dentelés 13.*

Jean Giraudoux.

Barbey d'Aurevilly.

1822	**80 c. +15 c. bleu, lilas et violet-brun**	0 65	0 65
1823	**80 c. +15 c. bleu-gris, lilas et noir**	0 65	0 65
	La paire, non dentelée	30 »	

Tirages : 3 100 000 et 3 050 000.

Voir également les n°s 1784 et 1785.

1974. – ***Personnages célèbres avec légende FRANCE. Taille-douce. Dentelés 13.***

Docteur A. Schweitzer.

Edmond Michelet.

1824	**80 c. +20 c. vert-noir, brun-rouge et rouge**	0 70	0 70
1825	**80 c. +20 c. gris-bleu et bleu**	0 65	0 65

Robert Schuman.

Eugène Thomas.

1826	**80 c. +20 c. bleu-noir et noir**	1 »	1 »
1827	**80 c. +20 c. gris-bleu et gris**	0 65	0 65
	N°s 1824 à 1827 (4 val.)	**3 »**	**3 »**
	La série, non dentelée	95 »	

Tirages : 3 050 000, 3 300 000, 3 750 000 et 3 500 000.

Ces timbres ont paru en 1975.

1974. – ***Au profit de la Croix-Rouge. "Les saisons". Taille-douce. Dentelés 13.*** [C]

L'été.

L'hiver.

1828	**60 c. +15 c. bleu, brun-lilas et rouge**	0 65	0 65
1829	**80 c. +15 c. gris-bleu et bistre**	0 80	0 80
	La paire, non dentelée	84 »	

Tirages : 3 400 000 et 3 050 000.

Ont été émis aussi en carnets (tirage : 600 000).

> **1974**
> **Du n° 1783 au n° 1829 :**
> **47 timbres** ****40** **⊙27**

1975. – ***Arphila'75. Paris. Taille-douce. Dentelés 13.***

"L'oeil".

1830	**1 f. violet foncé, jaune-orange et rouge**	0 50	0 50

Le Chapiteau.

1831	**2 f. carmin, vert-olive et vert-noir**	1 »	0 80

Graphisme.

1832	**3 f. vert et brun carminé**	1 50	1 10

Cérès.

1833	**4 f. vert-noir, bistre et rouge**	2 »	1 60
	N°s 1830 à 1833 (4 val.)	**5 »**	**4 »**
	La série, non dentelée	185 »	

Tirage : 7 500 000 séries.

1975. – ***Idem. Valeurs et couleurs différentes. Taille-douce. Dentelés 13 x 13½.*** [BF] n° 7.

1834	**2 f. gris-vert et rouge-brique**	1 50	1 50

1835 **3 f. rouge, bleu et gris-bleu** 2 » 2 »

1836 **4 f. bleu, rouge-brique et vert-noir** 2 30 2 30

1837 **6 f. gris-vert, rouge et bleu** 3 20 3 20

N°s 1834 à 1837 (4 val.) 9 » 9 »

Tirage : 2 300 000 séries.

Émis seulement en feuillet.

1975. – *Journée du Timbre. Héliogravure. Dentelé 13.*

Plaque de facteur de Paris sous la IIe République.

1838 **80 c. +20 c. bleu, noir et jaune** 0 65 0 65
a. (Non dentelé) 17 »

Tirage : 4 150 000.

1975. – *Président Georges Pompidou (1911-1974). Taille-douce. Dentelé 13.*

Georges Pompidou.

1839 **80 c. gris-bleu et gris** 0 50 0 30
a. (Non dentelé) 17 »

A partir du n° 1840 les timbres portent la légende FRANCE, pour reprendre la légende REPUBLIQUE FRANÇAISE en septembre 1981.

1975. – *Europa. Tableaux. Héliogravure. Dentelés 13.*

Paul en Arlequin, de Picasso (1881-1973).

1840 **80 c. polychrome** 0 75 0 35
a. (marron omis : sans valeur ni logo CEPT) » » » »

En la plaza, femme à la balustrade, de Van Dongen (1877-1968).

1841 **1 f. 20 polychrome** 1 10 0 90

La paire, non dentelée 125 »

Tirages : 20 000 000 et 10 000 000.

1975. – *Exposition mondiale de la machine-outil. Taille-douce. Dentelé 13.*

1842 **1 f. 20 turquoise, noir et brun-rouge** 1 25 0 50
a. (Non dentelé) 15 50

Tirage : 6 100 000.

1975. – *Centenaire du Sénat de la République. Taille-douce. Dentelé 13.*

1843 **1 f. 20 gris-olive et carmin** 0 80 0 65
a. (Non dentelé) 15 50

Tirage : 7 500 000.

1975. – *Convention du mètre. Taille-douce. Dentelé 13.*

1844	**1 f. violet et lilas**	0 65	0 50
	a. (Non dentelé)	18 50	

Tirage : 6 000 000.

1975. – *Fondation santé des étudiants de France. Taille-douce. Dentelé 13.*

1845	**70 c. noir, lilas et rouge**	0 50	0 50
	a. (Non dentelé)	15 50	

Tirage : 10 000 000.

1975. – *Théâtre du peuple de Bussang. Taille-douce. Dentelé 13.*

1846	**85 c. bleu, olive et violet**	0 50	0 50
	a. (Non dentelé)	15 50	

Tirage : 7 000 000.

1975. – *Régions. Taille-douce. Dentelés 13.*

Picardie.

Bourgogne.

Pays de la Loire.

1847	**85 c. bleu, vert-bleu et orange**	0 80	0 50
1848	**1 f. brun, rouge et jaune**	0 80	0 50
1849	**1 f. 15 bistre-olive, turquoise et émeraude**	0 80	0 50

Auvergne.

Poitou-Charentes.

1850	**1 f. 30 bleu-gris, noir et rouge**	1 »	0 65
1851	**1 f. 90 gris, olive et bleu-gris**	1 25	0 50

Nord - Pas-de-Calais.

1852	**2 f. 80 carmin, gris et bleu**	1 70	1 25
	N°s 1847 à 1852 (6 val.)	**6 35**	**3 90**
	La série, non dentelée	77 »	

1975. – *30e anniversaire de la libération des camps de concentration. Taille-douce. Dentelé 13.*

Pierre Kaan. F. H. Manhes et le général Jean Verneau.

1853	**1 f. bleu, olive et rouge**	0 65	0 50
	a. (Non dentelé)	30 »	

Tirage : 7 000 000.

1975. – *30e anniversaire de la création du service de déminage. Taille-douce. Dentelé 13.*

1854	**70 c. bleu, olive et bistre-olive**	0 50	0 30
	a. (Non dentelé)	15 50	

Tirage : 10 000 000.

1975. – *Villes nouvelles. Taille-douce. Dentelé 13.*

1855	**1 f. 70 brun-jaune, vert et bleu**	1 »	0 80
	a. (Non dentelé)	15 50	

Tirage : 7 000 000.

1975. – *Pont de Saint-Nazaire. Taille-douce. Dentelé 13.*

1856	**1 f. 40 turquoise, vert-bleu et noir**	0 80	0 50
	a. (Non dentelé)	15 50	

Tirage : 10 000 000.

1975. – *Année internationale de la Femme. Héliogravure. Dentelé 13.*

1857	**1 f. 20 polychrome et argent**	0 65	0 50
	a. (Non dentelé)	40 »	

Tirage : 7 500 000.

1975. – *Personnage célèbre. André Siegfried (1875-1959). Taille-douce. Dentelé 13.*

1858	**80 c. +20 c. noir et turquoise**	0 65	0 65
	a. (Non dentelé)	15 50	

Tirage : 3 500 000.

1975. – *50e anniversaire des relations diplomatiques franco-soviétiques. Taille-douce. Dentelé 13.*

1859	**1 f. 20 bleu, rouge et bistre-jaune**	0 65	0 50
	a. (Non dentelé)	18 50	

Tirage : 7 000 000.

1975. – *Au profit de la Croix-Rouge. "Les saisons". Taille-douce. Dentelés 13.* [C]

Le printemps.

L'automne.

1860	**60 c. +15 c. olive, rouge et brun-rouge**	0 65	0 65
1861	**80 c. +20 c. brun-olive, rouge et orange**	0 80	0 80
	La paire, non dentelée	100 »	

Tirage : 3 500 000 paires.

Ont été émis aussi en carnets (tirage : 600 000).

1975. – *Bateau-école. Frégate "La Melpomène". Taille-douce. Dentelé 13.*

1862	**90 c. rouge, orange et vert-noir**	1 10	0 60
	a. (Non dentelé)	23 »	

Tirage : 8 000 000.

1975

Du n° 1830 au n° 1862 :

33 timbres ****35** **⊙28**

Autres rubriques de l'année :

Blocs et feuillets 7

Préoblitérés 134 à 137

Service 43 à 48

1976. – ***Régions. Taille douce, sauf n° 1866 : héliogravure. Dentelés 13.***

Centre.

1863	**25 c. bleu, vert-jaune et vert**	0 30	0 30
	a. (Non dentelé)	15 50	

Aquitaine.

Limousin.

1864	**60 c. brun carminé, vert foncé et outremer**	0 30	0 30
	a. (Non dentelé)	15 50	
1865	**70 c. noir, vert foncé et bleu**	0 70	0 50
	a. (Non dentelé)	15 50	

Guyane.

Midi-Pyrénées.

1865A	**1 f. 25 vert, orange et turquoise**	0 80	0 80
	a. (Non dentelé)	54 »	
1866	**2 f. 20 multicolore**	1 40	1 25
	a. ("France"omis)	3 450 »	1 700 »
	b. (Non dentelé)	70 »	
	Nos 1863 à 1866 (5 val.)	**3 50**	**3 15**

1976. – ***Oeuvres d'art. Taille douce, sauf n° 1869 : héliogravure. Dentelés 13.***

Linteau de l'église de Saint-Genis-des-Fontaines.

1867	**2 f. gris-bleu et bleu**	1 40	1 10
	a. (Non dentelé)	70 »	

La Vénus de Brassempouy.

1868	**2 f. sépia et bistre**	1 25	1 10
	a. (Non dentelé)	70 »	

La joie de vivre de Robert Delaunay (1885-1941).

1869	**2 f. polychrome**	1 40	1 25
	a. (Non dentelé)	77 »	

Tirage : 6 000 000 séries.

1976. – ***Journée du Timbre. Centenaire du Timbre-poste au type Sage. Taille-douce. Dentelé 13.***

1870	**80 c. +20 c. noir et lilas**	0 50	0 50
	a. (Non dentelé)	23 »	

Tirage : 4 000 000.

1976. – *Série touristique. Taille-douce. Dentelés 13.*

Château fort de Bonaguil.

1871 1 f. vert foncé, bistre et brun-rouge 0 50 0 30

Ussel. Château de Malmaison.

1872 2 f. lilas, brun-jaune et ocre 1 10 0 30

1873 3 f. bleu-gris, vert-jaune et bistre 1 40 0 30

La série, non dentelée 35 »

1976. – *Cinquantenaire de l'Association Centrale des Officiers de Réserve de l'Armée de Mer (A.C.O.R.A.M.). Taille-douce. Dentelé 13.*

1874 1 f. outremer, carmin et bistre-jaune 0 65 0 50

a. (Non dentelé) 15 50

Tirage : 7 000 000.

1976. – *49e congrès national de la Fédération des sociétés philatéliques françaises à Rouen. Taille-douce. Dentelé 13.*

1875 80 c. brun-olive et brun-orange 0 50 0 30

a. (Non dentelé) 14 »

Tirage : 10 000 000.

1976. – *Exposition philatélique mondiale de la jeunesse "JUVAROUEN". Taille-douce. Dentelé 13.*

1876 60 c. bleu-vert, carmin et gris-bleu 0 50 0 30

a. (Non dentelé) 15 50

Voir également à la rubrique "Entiers Postaux (n° 1876-CP1)".

Tirage : 10 000 000.

1976. – *Europa. Héliogravure. Polychrome. Dentelés 13.*

Faïence de Strasbourg. Porcelaine de Sèvres.

1877 80 c. polychrome 0 75 0 30

1878 1 f. 20 polychrome 1 25 0 75

La paire, non dentelée 100 »

Tirages : 20 000 000 et 10 000 000.

1976. – *Bicentenaire de l'indépendance des États-Unis. Taille-douce. Dentelé 13.*

Charles Gravier de Vergennes (1719-1787), et Benjamin Franklin (1706-1790).

1879 1 f. 20 gris-bleu, bleu et carmin 0 65 0 50

a. (Non dentelé) 77 »

Tirage : 8 000 000.

1976. – *Personnages célèbres. Taille-douce. Dentelés 13.*

Maréchal Moncey. Max Jacob. Mounet-Sully.

1880	**80 c. +20 c. lilas et brun-jaune**	0 65	0 65
1881	**80 c. +20 c. brun-rouge et brun-olive**	0 65	0 65
1882	**80 c. +20 c. vert-olive et carmin**	0 65	0 65
	La série, non dentelée	40 »	

Tirage : 3 000 000 séries.

Voir également les n°s 1896 à 1898.

1976. – ***Verdun. Taille-douce. Dentelé 13.***

1883	**1 f. vert foncé, rouge et brun carminé**	0 65	0 50
	a. (Non dentelé)	14 »	

Tirage : 8 000 000.

1976. – ***La Communication. Héliogravure. Dentelé 13.***

1884	**1 f. 20 polychrome**	0 65	0 65
	a. (Non dentelé)	14 »	

Tirage : 6 500 000.

1976. – ***30e anniversaire de l'Association des Français libres. Taille-douce. Dentelé 13.***

1885	**1 f. bleu, rouge et outremer**	0 80	0 50
	a. (Non dentelé)	30 »	

Tirage : 8 000 000.

1976. – ***Protection de la nature et de l'environnement. Taille-douce. Dentelé 13.***

Forêt de Tronçais.

1886	**70 c. vert foncé, bistre et bleu**	0 50	0 30
	a. (Non dentelé)	18 50	

Tirage : 8 000 000.

1976. – ***Satellite "Symphonie". Taille-douce. Dentelé 13.***

1887	**1 f. 40 violet et brun-violet**	0 80	0 65
	a. (Non dentelé)	54 »	

Tirage : 7 000 000.

1976. – ***La Fête. Taille-douce. Dentelé 13.***

1888	**1 f. bleu-nuit, rouge et vert-jaune**	0 65	0 50
	a. (Non dentelé)	12 50	

Tirage : 8 000 000.

1976. – ***Jeux Olympiques de Montréal. Taille-douce. Dentelé 13.***

1889	**1 f. 20 bleu, outremer et noir**	0 80	0 50
	a. (Non dentelé)	77 »	

Tirage : 6 500 000.

1976. – *Centenaire du Corps des officiers de réserve. Taille-douce. Dentelé 13.*

1890	**1 f. noir, bleu et carmin**	0 65	0 30
	a. (Non dentelé)	12 50	

Tirage : 8 000 000.

1976. – *Type Marianne de Béquet. Taille douce, sauf n° 1891 : typographie. 1 bande de phosphore, sauf n° 1892, 1895 : 3 bandes de phosphore. Dentelure 13, sauf n° 1891 : 14 x 13.*

Les timbres typographiés ne portent pas la signature BÉQUET en bas à gauche.

Pour ces 3 timbres, la 1re colonne de prix concerne les timbres neufs avec gomme brillante, la 2e les oblitérés.

1891	**80 c. vert**	0 65	0 15
	a. (Non dentelé)	21 »	
	b. (sans bande de phosphore) (1977)	2 »	1 »
	c. (Gomme tropicale)	1 »	
1892	**1 f. rouge**	0 65	0 15
	a. (Non dentelé)	21 »	
	b. (sans bande de phosphore) (1977)	3 »	1 »
	c. (Gomme tropicale)	1 25	

Provenant de carnet.

1893	**80 c. vert**	1 50	0 70
	a. (sans bande de phosphore)	230 »	
	b. (Gomme tropicale)	1 75	

Émis seulement en carnets de 20, une des dentelures horizontales de ce timbre est coupée ou rognée.

Provenant de roulettes. Non dentelés verticalement

1894	**80 c. vert**	0 80	0 70
	a. (n° rouge au verso)	3 »	
1895	**1 f. rouge**	0 80	0 70
	a. (n° rouge au verso)	3 »	

Voir note après le n° 1331Ab.

1976. – *Marianne d'Excoffon. Taille douce. 2 bandes de phosphore.*

1895A	**1 f.** ***rouge***	»	»

Ce timbre, destiné à remplacer la marianne de Béquet, n'a pu voir le jour en raison de difficultés d'impression : les cylindres d'impression s'usant trop vite, le projet a été abandonné.

1976. – *Personnages célèbres. Au profit de la Croix-Rouge. Taille-douce. Dentelés 13.*

Général Daumesnil. Eugène Fromentin. Anna de Noailles.

1896	**1 f. +20 c. bleu-vert, bleu et turquoise**	0 70	0 70
1897	**1 f. +20 c. outremer, violet-brun et lilas-rose**	0 70	0 70
1898	**1 f. +20 c. gris-bleu et brique**	0 70	0 70
	La série, non dentelée	40 »	

Tirage : 3 000 000 séries.

Voir également les nos 1880 à 1882.

1976. – *Oeuvres d'art. Taille-douce. Dentelés 13 x 12½.*

Ramsés (fresque d'Abu-Simbel).

1899	**2 f. polychrome**	1 25	1 »
	a. (Non dentelé)	77 »	

Oeuvre de Carzou.

1900	**2 f. polychrome**	1 25	1 »
	a. (Non dentelé)	77 »	

Nature morte, de Maurice de Vlaminck (1876-1958).

1901	**2 f. polychrome**	1 25	1 »
	a. (Non dentelé)	84 »	

Tirage : 6 000 000 séries.

1976. – ***Série touristique. Taille-douce. Dentelés 13.***

Cathédrale de Lodève.

Biarritz-Côte basque.

1902 **1 f. 10 outremer** 0 65 0 50
a. (Non dentelé) 15 50

1903 **1 f. 40 brun, bleu et olive** 0 80 0 30
a. (Non dentelé) 15 50

Thiers.

1904 **1 f. 70 bleu, vert-olive et lilas-brun** 1 » 0 30
a. (Non dentelé) 15 50

1976. – ***Centenaire de la première liaison téléphonique. Taille-douce. Dentelé 13.***

1905 **1 f. gris, bleu et brique** 0 65 0 30
a. (Non dentelé) 23 »
Tirage : 12 000 000.

1976. – ***X*** ***e*** ***festival international du film de tourisme, Tarbes 1976. Taille-douce. Dentelé 13.***

1906 **1 f. 40 vert-noir, orange et brun-olive** 0 80 0 65
a. (Non dentelé) 17 »
Tirage : 6 000 000.

1976. – ***Police nationale. Taille-douce. Dentelé 13.***

1907 **1 f. 10 bleu, olive et rouge** 0 65 0 50
a. (Non dentelé) 15 50
Tirage : 6 000 000.

1976. – ***Accélérateur européen de particules. Héliogravure. Dentelé 13.***

1908 **1 f. 40 multicolore** 1 » 0 80
a. (Non dentelé) 50 »
Tirage : 6 000 000.

1976. – ***Foires expositions. Taille-douce. Dentelé 13.***

1909 **1 f. 50 bleu-noir, vert-bleu et ocre** 1 » 0 65
a. (Non dentelé) 12 50
Tirage : 8 000 000.

1976. – ***Au profit de la Croix-Rouge. Sculptures religieuses de l'église de Brou. Croix en rouge. Taille-douce. Dentelés 13.*** C

Sainte Barbe.

Sibylle cimmérienne.

1910 **80 c. +20 c. lilas** 0 65 0 65
1911 **1 f. +25 c. sépia** 1 » 1 »
La paire, non dentelée 61 »
Tirage : 3 500 000 paires.
Ont été émis aussi en carnets.

1976. – ***Douane. Héliogravure. Dentelé 13.***

1912	**1 f. 10 polychrome et or**	0 65	0 65
	a. (Non dentelé)	18 50	

Tirage : 6 000 000.

1976. – ***Port-Louis (Morbihan). Musée de l'Atlantique. Taille-douce. Dentelé 13½ x 13.***

Vue aérienne et trois-mâts "Duchesse Anne".

1913	**1 f. 45 bleu-vert et olive**	0 80	0 65
	a. (Non dentelé)	18 50	

Tirage : 6 000 000.

> **1976**
>
> **Du n° 1863 au n° 1913 :**
>
> **52 timbres (sauf 1895A)** ****43** **⊙31**
>
> Autres rubriques de l'année :
>
> Poste aérienne 49
>
> Préoblitérés 138 à 145
>
> Service 49 à 52

1977. – ***Régions. Taille douce, sauf n° 1914, 1915, 1918 : héliogravure. Dentelés 13.***

Réunion.

Martinique.

1914	**1 f. 45 vert et rose carminé**	0 80	0 50
1915	**1 f. 50 multicolore**	0 80	0 65

Franche-Comté.

Bretagne.

1916	**2 f. 10 turquoise, bleu et jaune**	1 25	1 »
1917	**2 f. 40 olive, brun et outremer**	1 40	0 50

Languedoc-Roussillon.

Rhône-Alpes.

1918	**2 f. 50 multicolore**	1 40	1 »
1919	**2 f. 75 bleu-vert foncé**	1 75	1 »

Champagne-Ardenne.

Alsace.

1920	**3 f. 20 bleu, vert-noir et bistre**	2 »	1 10
1921	**3 f. 90 bleu, lilas-brun et bistre**	2 60	1 75
	N°s 1914 à 1921 (8 val.)	**12 »**	**7 50**
	La série, non dentelée	95 »	

1977. – ***Centre national d'Art et de Culture Georges Pompidou. Taille-douce. Dentelé 13.***

1922	**1 f. vert foncé, bleu et rouge**	0 50	0 30
	a. (Non dentelé)	19 25	

Tirage : 6 500 000.

1977. – ***Oeuvres d'art. Taille-douce. Dentelés 12½-13.***

Le "Pont de Mantes", de Camille Corot (1796 1875).

1923 2 f. polychrome 1 25 1 »
a. (Non dentelé) 84 »

"Hommage à l'hexagone". Oeuvre de Vasarely.

1924 3 f. lilas pâle et vert-noir 1 85 1 »
a. (Non dentelé) 77 »

Tirage : 6 000 000 paires.

1977. – ***Extensions portuaires de Dunkerque. Taille-douce. Dentelé 13.***

1925 50 c. lilas-brun, bleu-noir et bleu 0 30 0 30
a. (Non dentelé) 14 »

Tirage : 10 000 000.

1977. – ***Le Souvenir français. Taille-douce. Dentelé 13.***

1926 80 c. bleu, rouge et brun-olive 0 65 0 50
a. (Non dentelé) 15 50

Tirage : 8 000 000.

1977. – ***Journée du Timbre. Taille-douce. Dentelé 13.***

Enseigne du relais de poste à Marckolsheim (Bas-Rhin).

1927 1 f. +20 c. bleu et bleu-noir 0 65 0 65
a. (Non dentelé) 15 50

Tirage : 4 500 000.

1977. – ***Europa. Taille-douce. Dentelés 13.***

Village provençal. Port breton.

1928 1 f. bleu, olive et brique 0 75 0 25
1929 1 f. 40 vert-olive, brun-olive et noir 1 25 0 45

La paire, non dentelée 95 »

Tirages : 20 000 000 et 10 000 000.

1977. – ***150e anniversaire de la Société nationale d'horticulture. Taille-douce. Dentelé 13.***

1930 1 f. 70 vert-olive et carmin-brun 1 » 0 65
a. (Non dentelé) 27 »

Tirage : 8 000 000.

1977. – ***Floralies internationales de Nantes. Taille-douce. Dentelé 13.***

1931 1 f. 40 lilas, jaune et bleu-vert 1 » 0 80
a. (Non dentelé) 23 »

Tirage : 8 000 000.

1977. – *Rattachement du Cambrésis. Taille-douce. Dentelé 13.*

1932	**80 c. bleu, brun-lilas et lilas-rouge**	0 50	0 50
	a. (Non dentelé)	15 50	

Tirage : 7 000 000.

1977. – *Instituts catholiques de France. Taille-douce. Dentelé 13.*

1933	**1 f. 10 gris-bleu, brun et brun-olive**	0 65	0 65
	a. (Non dentelé)	15 50	

Tirage : 7 000 000.

1977. – *Fédération européenne de la construction. Taille-douce. Dentelé 13.*

1934	**1 f. 10 outremer, rouge et bistre**	0 65	0 50
	a. (Non dentelé)	19 25	

Tirage : 7 000 000.

1977. – *50ᵉ congrès national de la Fédération des sociétés philatéliques françaises à Annecy. Taille-douce. Dentelé 13.*

1935	**1 f. brun-olive et brun-lilas**	0 65	0 50
	a. (Non dentelé)	15 50	

Tirage : 10 000 000.

1977. – *École polytechnique de Palaiseau. Taille-douce. Dentelé 13.*

1936	**1 f. 70 vert-noir, outremer et rouge**	1 »	0 50
	a. (Non dentelé)	19 25	

Tirage : 7 000 000.

1977. – *Série touristique. Taille-douce. Dentelés 13.*

Collégiale du Dorat (XIIᵉ s.).

1937	**1 f. 45 gris-bleu et brun-olive**	0 80	0 50

Abbaye de Fontenay (XIIᵉ s.) Côte d'Or.

Cathédrale de Bayeux (XIIᵉ-XVᵉ siècles).

1938	**1 f. 50 brun-rouge, rouge et brun-olive**	0 80	0 50
1939	**1 f. 90 jaune et sépia**	1 10	0 50
	La série, non dentelée	42 »	

1977. – *60ᵉ anniversaire de la coupe de France de football. Taille-douce. Dentelé 13.*

1940	**80 c. rouge, bleu et brun-olive**	1 »	0 65
	a. (Non dentelé)	46 »	

Tirage : 6 000 000.

1977. – ***5e anniversaire du Mémorial au général de Gaulle. Héliogravure. Dentelé 13.***

1941 1 f. polychrome et or 1 » 0 80

a. (Non dentelé) 77 »

Tirage : 15 000 000.

1977. – ***Jeune Chambre économique française. Taille-douce. Dentelé 13.***

1942 1 f. 10 outremer et rouge 0 65 0 50

a. (Non dentelé) 14 »

Tirage : 7 000 000.

1977. – ***5e centenaire de la bataille de Nancy. Taille-douce. Dentelé 13.***

1943 1 f. 10 bleu et gris 1 » 0 65

a. (Non dentelé) 18 50

Tirage : 6 000 000.

1977. – ***5e centenaire du rattachement de la Bourgogne (1477). Taille-douce. Dentelé 13.***

1944 1 f. 25 bistre et vert-noir 0 65 0 50

a. (Non dentelé) 14 »

Tirage : 7 000 000.

1977. – ***10e anniversaire de l'Association internationale des parlementaires de langue française. Taille-douce. Dentelé 13.***

1945 1 f. 40 bleu, rouge et bistre clair 0 80 0 50

a. (Non dentelé) 12 50

Tirage : 7 000 000.

1977. – ***La cigale rouge. Héliogravure. Dentelé 13.***

1946 80 c. polychrome 0 65 0 50

a. (Non dentelé) 42 »

b. (Inscriptions omises) 5 000 »

Tirage : 10 000 000.

1977. – ***Série touristique. Taille-douce. Dentelés 13.***

Abbaye des Prémontrés à Pont-à-Mousson.

1947 1 f. 25 sépia, rouge et gris 0 65 0 50

Tour abbatiale de Saint-Amand-les-Eaux.

Château de Vitré.

1948	**1 f. 40 lilas-brun, lilas-rouge et vert-bleu**	0 80	0 50
1949	**2 f. 40 gris, vert et brun**	1 25	0 50
	La série, non dentelée	46 »	

1977. – *Oeuvres d'art. Dentelés 12½-13.*

Oeuvre originale de Trémois.

1950	**3 f. noir et rouge-brun**	2 »	1 60
	a. (Non dentelé)	77 »	

Oeuvre originale d'Excoffon.

1951	**3 f. bleu et bistre-rouge**	2 »	1 60
	a. (Non dentelé)	77 »	

Tirage : 6 000 000 paires.

1977. – *Meilleurs ouvriers de France. Taille-douce. Dentelé 13.*

1952	**1 f. 40 brun-rouge et olive**	1 »	0 65
	a. (Non dentelé)	12 50	

Tirage : 7 000 000.

1977. – *Personnages célèbres. Taille-douce. Dentelés 13.*

Edouard Herriot.

Abbé Breuil.

1953	**1 f. +20 c. noir**	0 75	0 75
1954	**1 f. +20 c. vert-bleu et olive**	0 75	0 75

Guillaume de Machault.

Charles Cros.

1955	**1 f. +20 c. brun, vert-noir et brun-lilas**	0 75	0 75
1956	**1 f. +20 c. grenat, bleu-vert et bleu-noir**	0 75	0 75
	N°s 1953 à 1956 (4 val.)	**3 »**	**3 »**
	La série, non dentelée	61 »	

Tirage : 3 000 000 séries.

1977. – *30ᵉ anniversaire du Conseil économique et social. Taille-douce. Dentelé 13.*

1957	**80 c. brun foncé, brun-olive et bistre-olive**	0 50	0 30
	a. (Non dentelé)	12 50	

Tirage : 10 000 000.

1977. – ***400**^e^ **anniversaire de la naissance de P. P. Rubens. Tableau. Détail du tableau "La Vierge à l'Enfant et deux donateurs Alexandre Goubeau et sa femme". Taille-douce. Dentelé 12½ x 13.***

1958	**2 f. polychrome**	1 50	1 »
	a. (Non dentelé)	84 »	

Tirage : 6 000 000.

1977. – ***Au profit de la Croix-Rouge. "Santons" de Provence. Taille-douce. Dentelés 13.*** [C]

Chemineau.

Guérisseuse.

1959	**80 c. +20 c. rouge et bleu-gris foncé**	0 65	0 65
1960	**1 f. +25 c. rouge et vert-noir**	0 80	0 80
	La paire, non dentelée	95 »	

Tirage : 4 000 000 paires.

Ont été émis aussi en carnets.

1977. – ***Tournoi du cinquantenaire de la Fédération française de tennis de table. Taille-douce. Dentelé 13.***

1961	**1 f. 10 orange, lilas-rouge et vert-bleu**	2 »	1 »
	a. (Non dentelé)	95 »	

Tirage : 7 000 000.

1977

Du n° 1914 au n° 1961 :

48 timbres **49 ⊙34

Autres rubriques de l'année :

Poste aérienne 50

Préoblitérés 146 à 149

Service 53 à 55

1977-78. – ***Type Sabine, tirée d'une oeuvre du peintre Louis David. 1**^re^ **série. Taille-douce. Dentelés 13.*** [C]

Les n°s 1970 (80 c. vert) et 1972 (1 f. rouge) ont été seuls émis en 1977.

La 1re colonne concerne les neufs avec gomme métropolitaine (brillante), la 2e les oblitérés.

1962	**1 c. gris foncé**	0 15	0 15
	a. (Gomme tropicale)	0 15	
1963	**2 c. bleu-violet**	0 15	0 15
	a. (Gomme tropicale)	0 15	
1964	**5 c. vert-noir**	0 15	0 15
	a. (Gomme tropicale)	0 15	
1965	**10 c. rouge-brun**	0 15	0 15
	a. (Gomme tropicale)	0 15	

1966	**15 c. vert-bleu**	0 50	0 50
	a. (Deux bandes de phosphore)	155 »	
	b. (Gomme tropicale)	0 50	
1967	**20 c. émeraude**	0 15	0 15
	a. (Bande de phosphore à gauche)	0 50	0 15
	b. (Gomme tropicale)	0 30	
1968	**30 c. orange**	0 15	0 15
	a. (Gomme tropicale)	0 30	
1969	**50 c. violet**	0 30	0 15
	a. (Gomme tropicale)	0 30	

1970	**80 c. vert**	1 »	0 30
	a. (Sans phosphore gomme brillante)	90 »	
	b. (Gomme tropicale)	1 25	
	c. (Gomme tropicale, sans bande de phosphore)	2 »	
1971	**80 c. jaune-olive**	0 30	0 30
	a. (Gomme tropicale)	0 50	
1972	**1 f. rouge**	1 »	0 15
	a. (Sans phosphore gomme brillante)	90 »	
	b. (Gomme tropicale)	1 60	
	c. (Gomme tropicale, sans bande de phosphore)	5 »	
1973	**1 f. vert**	0 80	0 15
	a. (Gomme tropicale)	1 10	

1974	**1 f. 20 rouge**	0 80	0 15
	a. (Gomme tropicale)	1 10	
1975	**1 f. 40 bleu**	1 80	0 80
	a. (Gomme tropicale)	2 15	
1976	**1 f. 70 bleu clair**	1 10	0 65
	a. (Gomme tropicale)	1 25	
1977	**2 f. vert-jaune**	1 »	0 15
	a. (Gomme tropicale)	1 25	

1978	**2 f. 10 rose carminé**	1 10	0 30
	a. (Gomme tropicale)	1 25	
1979	**3 f. brun**	1 40	0 50
	a. (Gomme tropicale)	1 60	
	N°ˢ 1962 à 1979 (18 val.)	**12 »**	**5 »**
	La série, non dentelée	305 »	

Les 1 c., 2 c. et 5 c. sont sans phosphore. - Les 10 c., 15 c., 20 c., 30 c., 50 c., les deux 80 c. et le 1 f. vert, avec une bande de phosphore à droite (sauf n° 1967a). - Les autres valeurs avec deux bandes de phosphore.

Les n°ˢ 1965 à 1979, avec gomme métropolitaine (brillante), sont connus sans bande de phosphore.

La série de 15 val.	400 »

De nouvelles valeurs à ce type ont paru en 1979 (n°ˢ 2056 à 2063), en 1980 (n°ˢ 2101 à 2104) et en 1981 (n°ˢ 2118 à 2123 et n°ˢ 2154 à 2158).

1977-78. – ***Type Sabine, provenant de roulettes. 1 bande de phosphore, sauf n° 1981, 1981 : 2 bandes de phosphore. non dentelés verticalement et dentelés 13 horizontalement.***

1980	**80 c. vert**	1 60	1 40
	a. (n° rouge au verso)	4 »	
1981	**1 f. rouge**	1 60	1 20
	a. (n° rouge au verso)	4 »	
1981A	**1 f. vert**	1 25	1 »
	a. (n° rouge au verso)	4 »	
1981B	**1 f. 20 rouge**	1 25	1 »
	a. (n° rouge au verso)	4 »	
	N°ˢ 1980 à 1981B (4 val.)	**5 70**	**4 60**

Voir note après le n° 1331Ab.

1978. – ***Tableau de Jacques Birr. Héliogravure. Dentelé 13.***

Percheron.

1982	**1 f. 70 polychrome**	1 25	1 »
	a. (Non dentelé)	46 »	

Tirage : 8 000 000.

1978. – ***Les Tuileries, 1662. Dessin du "Cabinet du Roy". Taille-douce. Dentelé 12.***

Carrousel sous Louis XIV.

1983	**2 f. noir**	2 »	1 50
	a. (Non dentelé)	77 »	

Tirage : 6 000 000.

1978. – ***Centenaire de l'École Nationale Supérieure des Télécommunications. Taille-douce. Dentelé 13.***

1984	**80 c. bleu-vert foncé**	0 50	0 30
	a. (Non dentelé)	15 50	

Tirage : 10 000 000.

1978. – ***Rattachement de l'île de Saint-Barthélemy à la France (1878-1978). Taille-douce. Dentelé 13.***

1985	**1 f. 10 carmin, rouge-brun et brun**	0 65	0 50
	a. (Non dentelé)	14 »	

Tirage : 7 000 000.

1978. – ***Personnages célèbres. Taille-douce. Dentelés 13.***

Marie Noël.

Georges Bernanos.

Leconte de Lisle.

1986	**1 f. +20 c. bleu-noir et bleu**	0 75	0 75
1987	**1 f. +20 c. olive, brun-jaune et bleu-gris**	0 75	0 75
1988	**1 f. +20 c. lilas-rouge et bleu-violet**	0 75	0 75

Léon Tolstoi.

Voltaire et Rousseau.

Claude Bernard.

1989	1 f. +20 c. vert foncé et vert-olive	0 75	0 75
1990	1 f. +20 c. grenat et lilas	0 75	0 75
1990A	1 f. +20 c. bistre, brun, rouge et noir	0 75	0 75
	Nos 1986 à 1990A (6 val.)	**4 50**	**4 50**
	La série, non dentelée	77 »	

Tirage : 3 000 000 séries.

1978. – *"Régions". Héliogravure, sauf n° 1992 : taille douce. Dentelés 13.*

Ile-de-France.

Haute-Normandie.

1991	1 f. noir, bleu et rouge	0 65	0 30
1992	1 f. 40 vert, outremer et orange	1 »	0 65

Basse-Normandie.

1993	1 f. 70 noir, grenat et or	1 40	0 80
	La série, non dentelée	46 »	

1978. – *Oeuvre d'art. Taille-douce. Dentelé 13 x 12½.*

Oeuvre originale de Bernard Buffet.

1994	3 f. bleu pâle, vert pâle, jaune et noir	2 50	1 60
	a. (Non dentelé)	77 »	

Tirage : 6 000 000.

1978. – *15e anniversaire de la délégation à l'aménagement du territoire et à l'action régionale (DATAR). Taille-douce. Dentelé 13.*

1995	1 f. 10 violet et vert	0 65	0 30
	a. (Non dentelé)	14 »	

Tirage : 7 000 000.

1978. – *Série touristique. Taille-douce. Dentelés 13.*

Les gorges du Verdon.

Le Pont-Neuf de Paris.

1996	50 c. bleu, vert-noir et turquoise	0 30	0 30
1997	80 c. vert-noir et bleu-vert	0 50	0 30

Eglise de St-Saturnin.

Abbaye Notre-Dame du Bec-Hellouin.

1998	1 f. noir	0 50	0 30
1999	1 f. 10 brun-olive, bleu et lilas	0 80	0 50

Château d'Esquelbecq.

Eglise abbatiale Aubazine.

2000	1 f. 10 brun, gris-bleu et vert	0 70	0 50
2001	1 f. 25 carmin et brun-rouge	1 »	0 50

Abbaye de Fontevraud.

2002 **1 f. 70 brun-rouge et noir** 1 20 0 80

N°s 1996 à 2002 (7 val.) **5 »** **3 20**

La série, non dentelée 95 »

1978. – ***"Juvexniort". Taille-douce. Dentelé 13.***

2003 **80 c. brun foncé, carmin et bistre** 0 50 0 30
a. (Non dentelé) 14 »

Tirage : 10 000 000.

1978. – ***Journée du Timbre. Taille-douce. Dentelé 13.***

Facteur parisien de 1900.

2004 **1 f. +20 c. olive et gris-bleu** 0 65 0 65
a. (Gomme tropicale) 20 »
b. (Non dentelé) 14 »

Tirage : 4 500 000.

1978. – ***Parc national de Port-Cros. Héliogravure. Dentelé 13.***

2005 **1 f. 25 polychrome** 1 25 1 25
a. (Non dentelé) 27 »

Tirage : 8 000 000.

1978. – ***Fleurir la France. Taille-douce. Dentelé 13.***

2006 **1 f. 70 vert-olive, bleu et carmin** 1 50 0 65
a. (Non dentelé) 27 »

Tirage : 8 000 000.

1978. – ***Économies d'énergie. Taille-douce. Dentelé 13.***

2007 **1 f. bistre, brun et ocre** 0 65 0 50
a. (Non dentelé) 15 50

Tirage : 10 000 000.

1978. – ***Europa. Monuments. Taille-douce. Dentelés 13.***

Fontaine des Innocents à Paris.

Fontaine du Parc floral de Paris.

2008 **1 f. outremer, bistre et noir** 1 » 0 35
a. (Gomme tropicale) 20 »

2009 **1 f. 40 bleu, vert et brun** 1 25 0 60

La paire, non dentelée 95 »

Tirages : 20 000 000 et 10 000 000.

1978. – ***Colline Notre-Dame de Lorette. Taille-douce. Dentelé 13.***

2010 **2 f. bistre-olive et lilas-rouge** 1 25 0 50
a. (Non dentelé) 14 »

Tirage : 7 000 000.

1978. – *51e Congrès national de la Fédération des Sociétés Philatéliques Françaises, à Troyes. Taille-douce. Dentelé 13.*

2011 **1 f. bleu, carmin, brun et noir** 0 65 0 50
a. (Non dentelé) 14 »

Tirage : 10 000 000.

1978. – *Cinquantenaire du stade Roland Garros. Taille-douce. Dentelé 13.*

2012 **1 f. bleu-noir, bleu et brique** 2 50 0 50
a. (Gomme tropicale) 10 »
b. (Non dentelé) 61 »

Tirage : 10 000 000.

1978. – *Métiers d'Art. Taille-douce. Dentelé 13.*

2013 **1 f. 30 brun foncé, carmin et vert-olive** 0 65 0 50
a. (Non dentelé) 12 25

Tirage : 7 000 000.

1978. – *Imprimerie nationale. Taille-douce. Dentelé 13.*

2014 **1 f. vert-bleu, bleu et noir** 0 50 0 30
a. (Non dentelé) 12 25

Tirage : 7 000 000.

1978. – *Réunion de la Franche-Comté à la Couronne par la Paix de Nimègue (1678-1978). Taille-douce. Dentelé 13.*

2015 **1 f. 20 bleu-vert et vert foncé** 0 65 0 30
a. (Gomme tropicale) 20 »
b. (Non dentelé) 15 »

Tirage : 10 000 000.

1978. – *300e anniversaire du rattachement de Valenciennes et Maubeuge. Taille-douce. Dentelé 13.*

2016 **1 f. 20 gris-brun, rouge et violet** 0 65 0 50
a. (Non dentelé) 15 »

Tirage : 7 000 000.

1978. – *Cinquantenaire de l'Académie de Philatélie. Taille-douce. Dentelé 13.*

2017 **1 f. outremer, lilas-rouge et turquoise** 0 65 0 50
a. (Non dentelé) 23 »

Tirage : 8 000 000.

1978. – *Série nature. Taille-douce. Dentelé 13.*

Balbuzard.

2018 **1 f. 80 vert-jaune, olive et brun** 1 10 0 65
a. (Non dentelé) 30 »

Tirage : 7 000 000.

1978. – *XIX*[es] *championnats du monde de gymnastique, à Strasbourg. Taille-douce. Dentelé 13.*

2019 1 f. brun, orange et brun carminé 0 65 0 50
a. (Non dentelé) 70 »
Tirage : 7 000 000.

1978. – *Sport pour tous. Taille-douce. Dentelé 13.*

2020 1 f. violet, turquoise et rose 1 » 0 80
a. (Non dentelé) 46 »
Tirage : 7 000 000.

1978. – *Monument aux Combattants Polonais 1939-1945. Taille-douce. Dentelé 13.*

2021 1 f. 70 rouge, vert-bleu et carmin-brun 1 » 0 80
a. (Non dentelé) 14 »
Tirage : 7 000 000.

1978. – *60*[e] *anniversaire de l'Armistice à Rethondes. Taille-douce. Dentelé 13.*

Le wagon de l'Armistice.

2022 1 f. 20 noir 1 » 0 50
a. (Non dentelé) 40 »
Tirage : 8 000 000.

1978. – *Aide à la réadaptation. Taille-douce. Dentelé 13.*

2023 1 f. ocre, brun et rouge 0 65 0 50
a. (Non dentelé) 14 »
Tirage : 7 000 000.

1978. – *Au profit de la Croix-Rouge. Fables de La Fontaine. Taille-douce. Dentelés 13.* [C]

Le lièvre et la tortue.

Le rat de ville et le rat des champs.

2024 1 f. +25 c. brun-olive, olive et rouge 1 » 0 80
2025 1 f. 20+30 c. olive, brun-olive et rouge 1 » 1 »
La paire, non dentelée 80 »
Tirage : 3 000 000 paires.
Ont été émis aussi en carnets (Tirage : 550 000).

1978. – *Oeuvre d'art. Taille-douce. Dentelé 13 x 12½.*

"Chevaux de Camargue", oeuvre originale d'Yves Brayer.

2026 3 f. polychrome 2 » 1 40
a. (Non dentelé) 85 »
Tirage : 6 000 000.

1978. – *30*[e] *anniversaire de la Déclaration universelle des Droits de l'Homme. Taille-douce. Dentelé 13.*

2027 1 f. 70 brun et bleu 1 » 0 50
a. (Non dentelé) 54 »
Tirage : 7 000 000.

1978

Du n° 1962 au n° 2027 :

69 timbres ****63** ⊙**40**

Autres rubriques de l'année :

Poste aérienne 51

Préoblitérés 150 à 157

Service 56 à 59

1979. – *Année internationale de l'Enfant. Taille-douce. Dentelé 13.*

2028	**1 f. 70 brun-rouge, violet et rouge**	2 50	2 »
	a. (Non dentelé)	80 »	

Tirage : 7 000 000.

1979. – *Personnages célèbres. Taille-douce. Dentelés 13.*

Ladislas de Bercheny.

Léon Jouhaux.

Pierre Abélard.

2029	**1 f. 20+30 c. brun, bleu vif et bleu-vert**	1 »	1 »
2030	**1 f. 20+30 c. gris-noir et ocre**	1 »	1 »
2031	**1 f. 20+30 c. brun-rose, orange, et brun**	0 80	0 80

G. Moineaux, dit Courteline.

Simone Weil.

André Malraux.

2032	**1 f. 20+30 c. rouge, lilas-rouge et bleu-gris**	1 »	1 »
2032A	**1 f. 30+30 c. carmin et brun-rouge**	1 »	1 »
2032B	**1 f. 30+30 c. bleu et outremer**	1 »	1 »
	N°s 2029 à 2032B (6 val.)	**5 80**	**5 80**
	La série, non dentelée	80 »	

Tirage : 3 000 000 séries.

1979. – *Miniature du XVe siècle sur la musique. Taille-douce. Dentelé 13 x 12.*

2033	**2 f. polychrome**	1 50	1 »
	a. (Non dentelé)	85 »	

Tirage : 6 000 000.

1979. – *100e anniversaire de la naissance de Victor Segalen (1878-1919). Ecrivain. Taille-douce. Dentelé 13.*

2034	**1 f. 50 brun, vert-bleu et carmin**	0 80	0 50
	a. (Non dentelé)	23 »	

Tirage : 7 000 000.

1979. – *Floralies internationales de la Martinique. Taille-douce. Dentelé 13.*

2035	**35 c. vert, carmin et violet-brun**	0 30	0 30
	a. (Non dentelé)	23 »	

Tirage : 7 000 000.

1979. – *Temple de Borobudur à Java. Taille-douce. Dentelé 13.*

2036	**1 f. 80 brun clair et vert-bleu**	1 10	0 50
	a. (Non dentelé)	46 »	

Tirage : 7 000 000.

1979. – *Journée du Timbre. Taille-douce. Dentelé 13.*

Hôtel des Postes de Paris sur carte postale.

2037 **1 f. 20+30 c. gris-bleu, rouge et bistre clair** 0 80 0 65
a. (Non dentelé) 23 »

Tirage : 4 500 000.

1979. – *100e anniversaire de la naissance de Francisque Poulbot (1879-1946), dessinateur. Héliogravure. Dentelé 13.*

2038 **1 f. 30 rose, orange, bleu ciel, jaune et noir** 0 80 0 50
a. (Non dentelé) 18 50

Tirage : 10 000 000.

1979. – *Protection de la nature. L'abeille (apis mellifica). Taille-douce. Dentelé 13.*

2039 **1 f. sépia, olive et ocre** 1 » 0 50
a. (Non dentelé) 50 »

Tirage : 8 000 000.

1979. – *Série touristique. Taille-douce. Dentelés 13.*

Abbayes normandes.

Auray (Morbihan).

Moulin de Steenvoorde (Nord).

2040 **1 f. vert-bleu, vert-olive et vert** 0 50 0 50
2041 **1 f. brun, bistre et violet** 0 50 0 30
2042 **1 f. 20 turquoise, olive et brun-lilas** 0 65 0 30

Grotte de Niaux.

Palais des Rois de Majorque.

2043 **1 f. 50 brun-jaune, rouge et brun** 0 80 0 50
2044 **1 f. 70 brun-rouge et gris-bleu** 0 80 0 80
a. (Gomme tropicale) 20 »

Nos 2040 à 2044 (5 val.) **3 25** **2 40**

La série, non dentelée 110 »

1979. – *Abbaye de Saint-Germain-des-Prés. Taille-douce. Dentelé 13.*

2045 **1 f. 40 bleu, carmin et gris-bleu** 0 80 0 50
a. (Non dentelé) 15 »

Tirage : 7 000 000.

1979. – *Europa. Taille-douce. Dentelés 13.*

"Simoun", aviation postale intérieure.

Boule de Moulins.

2046 **1 f. 20 bleu, bleu-turquoise et vert** 1 » 0 30
2047 **1 f. 70 vert foncé, rouge et bleu-turquoise** 2 » 0 70

La paire, non dentelée 125 »

Tirage : 10 000 000 paires.

1979. – *52e Congrès national de la Fédération des Sociétés Philatéliques Françaises, à Nantes. Taille-douce. Dentelé 13.*

2048 **1 f. 20 violet, bleu et gris** 0 65 0 50
a. (Non dentelé) 15 »

Tirage : 10 000 000.

1979. – ***Palais Royal. Taille-douce. Dentelé 13.***

2049 1 f. grenat et carmin 0 50 0 30
a. (Non dentelé) 15 »

Tirage : 7 000 000.

1979. – ***Élection de l'Assemblée des Communautés Européennes. Héliogravure. Dentelé 13.***

2050 1 f. 20 multicolore 0 65 0 30
a. (Non dentelé) 70 »

Tirage : 15 000 000.

1979. – ***Hommage à Jeanne d'Arc. Monument national. Taille-douce. Dentelé 13.***

2051 1 f. 70 carmin 1 » 0 65
a. (Non dentelé) 30 »

Tirage : 7 000 000.

1979. – ***Félix Guyon (1831-1920), chirurgien français. Maître de l'école urologique française. Taille-douce. Dentelé 13.***

2052 1 f. 80 brun et vert-bleu 1 » 0 50
a. (Non dentelé) 14 »

Tirage : 7 000 000.

1979. – ***Série artistique. Taille douce, sauf n° 2054 : héliogravure. Dentelés 12½ x 13.***

Diane au bain. Château d'Écouen.

2053 2 f. bistre-orange et noir 1 50 1 25
a. (Non dentelé) 80 »

L'église d'Auvers-sur-Oise, de Vincent van Gogh (1853-1890).

2054 2 f. polychrome 2 50 1 50
a. (Non dentelé) 85 »

Tirage : 6 000 000 paires.

1979. – ***3e exposition mondiale des télécommunications "TELECOM 79". Genève 20-26 sept. 1979. Taille-douce. Dentelé 13.***

2055 1 f. 10 olive, bleu-vert et brun 0 65 0 30
a. (Non dentelé) 23 »

Tirage : 7 000 000.

1979. – *Type Sabine. Taille-douce. Dentelés 13.* Ⓒ

La 1re colonne concerne les neufs avec gomme métropolitaine (brillante), la 2e les oblitérés.

2056	**70 c. bleu-violet**	0 30	0 30
	a. (sans bande de phosphore)	300 »	
	b. (Gomme tropicale)	0 50	
2057	**1 f. olive**	0 50	0 15
	a. (sans bande de phosphore)	15 »	
	b. (Gomme tropicale)	0 50	
2058	**1 f. 10 vert**	0 80	0 30
	a. (sans bande de phosphore)	12 50	
	b. (Gomme tropicale)	1 85	

2059	**1 f. 30 rouge**	0 80	0 15
	a. (sans bande de phosphore)	130 »	
	b. (Gomme tropicale)	2 30	
2060	**1 f. 60 violet**	1 25	0 50
	a. (sans bande de phosphore)	185 »	
	b. (Gomme tropicale)	1 55	
2061	**1 f. 80 ocre orangé**	1 10	0 80
	a. (sans bande de phosphore)	54 »	
	b. (Gomme tropicale)	1 10	
	Nos 2056 à 2061 (6 val.)	**4 75**	**2 20**
	La série, non dentelée	110 »	

Les 70 c., 1 f. et 1 f. 10, sont avec une bande de phosphore à droite, les autres valeurs avec deux bandes de phosphore.

1979. – *Type Sabine, provenant de roulette. Taille douce. 1 bande de phosphore, sauf n° 2063 : 2 bandes de phosphore. non dentelés verticalement et dentelés 13 horizontalement.*

2062	**1 f. 10 vert**	2 »	1 »
	a. (n° rouge au verso)	4 »	
2063	**1 f. 30 rouge**	2 »	1 »
	a. (n° rouge au verso)	4 »	

1979. – *Série touristique. Taille-douce. Dentelé 13.*

Château de Maisons-Laffitte.

2064	**45 c. bleu, turquoise et violet**	0 30	0 30
	a. (Non dentelé)	15 »	

1979. – *Région. Héliogravure. Dentelé 13.*

Lorraine.

2065	**2 f. 30 rouge, noir et jaune**	1 25	0 50
	a. (Non dentelé)	15 »	

1979. – *150e anniversaire de la fondation de l'École Centrale des Arts et Manufactures. Héliogravure. Dentelé 13.*

2066	**1 f. 80 vert, noir et jaune**	1 »	0 80
	a. (Non dentelé)	15 »	

Tirage : 7 000 000.

1979. – *Série "Création philatélique". Tableaux. Taille-douce. Dentelés 12½ x 13.*

Oeuvre originale de Salvador Dali.

2067	**3 f. brun, noir, rouge, outremer et jaune**	1 75	1 25
	a. (Non dentelé)	85 »	

"Danseur du feu, la flûte enchantée", de Chapelain-Midy.

2068	**3 f. olive et brun**	1 85	1 25
	a. (Non dentelé)	80 »	

Tirage : 6 000 000 paires.

1979. – *Championnats du monde de judo. Taille-douce. Dentelé 13.*

2069	**1 f. 60 vert et noir**	0 80	0 50
	a. (Non dentelé)	80 »	

Tirage : 7 000 000.

1979. – *Au profit de la Croix-Rouge. Vitraux de l'église Jeanne d'Arc à Rouen (détails). Taille-douce. Dentelés 13.* [C]

"Hérodiade".

"Simon le Magicien".

2070	**1 f. 10+30 c. polychrome**	0 65	0 65
	a. (Dentelé 12½ x 13)	1 »	0 80
2071	**1 f. 30+30 c. polychrome**	1 »	0 80
	a. (Dentelé 12½ x 13)	1 »	1 »
	La paire, non dentelée	92 »	

Tirage : 4 000 000 paires.

Ont été aussi émis en carnets (tirage : 550 000). Les n°s 2070a et 2071a proviennent des carnets.

1979. – *Métiers d'Art. "La Lutherie". Taille-douce. Dentelé 13.*

2072	**1 f. 30 brun-rouge et sépia**	0 80	0 50
	a. (Non dentelé)	20 »	

Tirage : 10 000 000.

1979

Du n° 2028 au n° 2072 :

47 timbres ****48** **⊙32**

Autres rubriques de l'année :

Poste aérienne 52

Préoblitérés 158 à 165

1980. – *Eurovision. Taille-douce. Dentelé 13.*

2073	**1 f. 80 gris, bleu et bleu-vert**	1 10	1 »
	a. (Non dentelé)	46 »	

Tirage : 7 000 000.

1980. – *Série artistique. Taille-douce. Dentelés 12½-13.*

Femme à l'éventail de Zadkine (1890-1967).

2074	**3 f. bistre, vert et brun**	1 85	1 25
	a. (Non dentelé)	80 »	

Oeuvre de Raoul Ubac.

2075	**3 f. bleu-noir, bleu-gris et beige**	1 85	1 25
	a. (Non dentelé)	80 »	
	b. couleur beige omise	650 »	

Tirage : 6 000 000 paires.

1980. – *Les Géants du Nord. Taille-douce. Dentelé 13.*

2076	**1 f. 60 vert, rouge et bleu**	0 80	0 50
	a. (Non dentelé)	12 50	

Tirage : 7 000 000.

1980. – *Gastronomie française. Taille-douce. Dentelé 13.*

2077 **90 c. rouge et brun** 1 » 0 80
a. (Non dentelé) 12 50

Tirage : 7 000 000.

1980. – *Journée du Timbre. Héliogravure. Dentelé 13.*

La Lettre à Mélie, d'Avati.

2078 **1 f. 30+30 c. noir, rose-lilas et bleu-gris** 0 80 0 80
a. (Non dentelé) 15 »

Tirage : 4 500 000.

1980. – *Métiers d'Art. "La Broderie", d'après une oeuvre de Toffoli. Taille-douce. Dentelé 13.*

2079 **1 f. 10 bleu foncé, jaune clair et orange** 0 65 0 50
a. (Non dentelé) 15 »

Tirage : 8 000 000.

1980. – *Lutte contre le tabagisme. Héliogravure. Dentelé 13.*

2080 **1 f. 30 multicolore** 0 65 0 30
a. (non dentelé) 15 »

1980. – *Série touristique. Taille-douce. Dentelés 13.*

Bastide (1222) Cordes (Tarn).

Château de Maintenon.

2081 **1 f. 50 orange, brun et bleu** 0 80 0 30
a. (Non dentelé) 14 »
2082 **2 f. noir, brun et rouge-brun** 1 » 0 50
a. (Non dentelé) 14 »

Montauban.

Cathédrale du Puy.

2083 **2 f. 30 brun, vert et bleu** 1 25 0 50
a. (Non dentelé) 14 »
2084 **3 f. 20 bleu et brun-rouge** 1 70 0 70
a. (Non dentelé) 15 »

N°s 2081 à 2084 (4 val.) **4 75** **2 »**

1980. – *Europa. Personnages célèbres. Taille-douce. Dentelés 13.*

Aristide Briand (1862-1932).

Saint Benoît (v. 480-547). Patron de l'Europe.

2085 **1 f. 30 brun-rouge, rouge, bleu et jaune** 0 75 0 35
2086 **1 f. 80 brun-rouge et rouge** 1 25 0 75

La paire, non dentelée 115 »

Tirages : 10 000 000 et 8 000 000.

1980. – *200e anniversaire de l'École nationale supérieure d'Arts et Métiers. Taille-douce. Dentelé 13.*

2087 **2 f. vert foncé et lie-de-vin** 1 » 0 50
a. (Non dentelé) 15 »

Tirage : 7 000 000.

1980. – *53e Congrès national de la Fédération des Sociétés Philatéliques Françaises, à Dunkerque. Taille-douce. Dentelé 13.*

2088	**1 f. 30 bleu-vert, violet et bleu**	0 65	0 30
	a. (Non dentelé)	15 »	

Tirage : 10 000 000.

1980. – *Série nature. Papillon. Héliogravure. Dentelé 13.*

Graellsia isabellae gr.

2089	**1 f. 10 vert-olive, brun foncé, jaune et bleu-vert**	1 »	0 65
	a. (Non dentelé)	61 »	

Tirage : 8 000 000.

1980. – *"Philexfrance'82". Exposition philatélique internationale. Taille-douce. Dentelé 12½ x 13.*

Autoportrait, d'Albrecht Dürer (1471-1528).

2090	**2 f. noir, rose carminé, brun, vert-olive et bistre**	1 25	1 »
	a. (Avec marge attenante (logo))	2 »	1 85
	b. (Non dentelé)	92 »	
	c. (avec marge attenante, Non dentelé)	155 »	

Les marges, à gauche et à droite de chaque rangée horizontale de 5 timbres, comportent, imprimés en noir, le logo de Philexfrance 82 et la légende : EXPOSITION PHILATELIQUE INTERNATIONALE PARIS-LA DEFENSE 10-24 JUIN 1982.

Tirage : 12 000 000.

1980. – *25e anniversaire de l'Association internationale des relations publiques. Héliogravure. Dentelé 13.*

2091	**1 f. 30 rouge-brun et bleu**	0 80	0 50
	a. (Non dentelé)	20 75	

Tirage : 9 000 000.

1980. – *Année du Patrimoine. Taille-douce. Dentelé 13.*

2092	**1 f. 50 gris et noir**	0 80	0 50
	a. (Non dentelé)	20 »	

Tirage : 12 000 000.

1980. – *Sciences de la Terre. Taille-douce. Dentelé 13.*

2093	**1 f. 60 rouge, brun-vert et brun**	1 »	0 65
	a. (Non dentelé)	14 »	

Tirage : 8 000 000.

1980. – *Rochambeau. 2e centenaire de l'arrivée à Newport. Taille-douce. Dentelé 13.*

2094	**2 f. 50 violet, rouge orangé et gris**	1 50	1 »
	a. (Non dentelé)	46 »	

Tirage : 8 000 000.

1980. – *Personnages célèbres. Taille-douce. Dentelés 13.*

Viollet-le-Duc. (1814-1879).

Jean Monnet (1888-1979).

2095	**1 f. 30+30 c. noir**	1 »	0 80
2096	**1 f. 30+30 c. brun-rouge et vert**	1 60	1 60

Jean-Marie de La Mennais (1780-1860).

Frédéric Mistral (1830-1914).

2097	**1 f. 40+30 c. bleu et bleu-gris**	1 »	0 80
2098	**1 f. 40+30 c. noir**	1 »	0 80

Saint-John Perse (1887-1975).

Pierre Paul de Riquet (1604-1680).

2099	**1 f. 40+30 c. vert foncé et vert-olive**	1 »	0 80
2100	**1 f. 40+30 c. gris et noir**	1 »	0 80
	N°s 2095 à 2100 (6 val.)	**6 60**	**5 60**
	La série, non dentelée	92 »	

Tirage : 3 000 000 séries.

1980. – *Type Sabine. Taille-douce. Dentelés 13.* ©

La 1re colonne concerne les neufs avec gomme métropolitaine (brillante), la 2e les oblitérés.

2101	**1 f. 20 vert**	0 65	0 15
	a. (sans bande de phosphore)	8 »	
	b. (Gomme tropicale)	1 »	
2102	**1 f. 40 rouge**	0 80	0 15
	a. (sans bande de phosphore)	17 »	
	b. (Gomme tropicale)	1 »	

Timbres non dentelés verticalement et dentelés 13 horizontalement, provenant de roulettes.

2103	**1 f. 20 vert**	0 80	0 65
	a. (n° rouge au verso)	2 »	
2104	**1 f. 40 rouge**	1 »	0 50
	a. (n° rouge au verso)	2 »	
	La série, non dentelée	35 »	

Le n° 2103 est connu sans bande de phosphore.

1980. – *Fédération française de golf. Taille-douce. Dentelé 13.*

2105	**1 f. 40 brun et vert**	0 80	0 50
	a. (Non dentelé)	61 »	

Tirage : 10 000 000.

1980. – *300e anniversaire de la Comédie Française. Taille-douce. Dentelé 13.*

2106	**2 f. gris foncé, bleu foncé et carmin**	1 10	0 65
	a. (Non dentelé)	20 »	

Tirage : 8 000 000.

1980. – *Série artistique. Héliogravure, sauf n° 2108, 2109 : taille-douce. Dentelés 12½-13.*

"Hommage à J.-S. Bach", Tapisserie de Jean Picart Le Doux.

2107	**3 f. noir, rouge, jaune, gris et brun clair**	2 »	1 30
	a. (Non dentelé)	80 »	

"La famille de paysans" (détail), de Louis Le Nain (1593-1648).

2108	**3 f. brun foncé, brun-rouge, brun clair et gris**	2 »	1 30
	a. (Non dentelé)	85 »	

"Femme aux yeux bleus", oeuvre d'Amedeo Modigliani (1884-1920).

2109	**4 f. noir, vert, sépia, rose et bleu**	2 50	1 40
	a. (Non dentelé)	85	»

Oeuvre de Hans Hartung.

2110	**4 f. gris-bleu, noir et bleu-gris**	2 50	1 50
	a. (Non dentelé)	85	»
	b. (Sans la valeur)	»	»

N°s 2107 à 2110 (4 val.)	**9 »**	**5 50**

Tirages : 6 000 000, 5 500 000, 5 000 000 et 5 500 000.

1980. – ***Série touristique. Taille-douce. Dentelés 13.***

Le château de Rambouillet.

L'Abbaye Saint-Pierre de Solesmes.

2111	**2 f. 20 bleu, vert et brun-rouge**	1 10	0 50
2112	**2 f. 50 violet, bleu et lilas-rose**	1 25	0 30
	La paire, non dentelée	30	»

1980. – ***Série "Création philatélique". Héliogravure. Dentelé 13.***

"Message de Paix", oeuvre de Yaacov Agam.

2113	**4 f. multicolore**	2 50	1 50
	a. (Non dentelé)	80	»
	b. (couleur noire omise)	2 850	»

Tirage : 5 000 000.

1980. – ***Charles de Gaulle. 40e anniversaire de l'Appel du 18 juin 1940 et 10e anniversaire de la mort du général de Gaulle. Oeuvre de G. Mathieu. Héliogravure. Dentelé 13.***

2114	**1 f. 40 noir, gris, jaune, bleu et rouge**	1 40	0 65
	a. (Non dentelé)	140	»

Tirage : 10 000 000.

1980. – ***Garde Républicaine. Taille-douce. Dentelé 13.***

Trompette de la Garde.

2115	**1 f. 70 rouge, bleu et rouge carminé**	1 10	0 65
	a. (Non dentelé)	15	»

Tirage : 8 000 000.

1980. – *Au profit de la Croix-Rouge. Stalles de la cathédrale d'Amiens (détails). Taille-douce. Dentelés 13.* [c]

Remplissage des greniers.

Le raisin de la terre promise.

2116	**1 f. 20+30 c. rouge et brun-rouge**	0 80	0 80
	a. (Dentelé 12½ x 13)	1 25	1 25
2117	**1 f. 40+30 c. rouge et brun-rouge**	1 »	1 »
	a. (Dentelé 12½ x 13)	1 25	1 25
	La paire, non dentelée	80 »	

Tirage : 4 000 000 paires.

Ont été émis aussi en carnets. (Tirage : 550 000). Les n°s 2116a et 2117a proviennent des carnets.

1980

Du n° 2073 au n° 2117 :

45 timbres ****53** **⊙34**

Autres rubriques de l'année :

Poste aérienne 53

Préoblitérés 166 à 169

Service 60 à 64

Depuis 1981 les bandes-carnets, les paires et les triptyques ne figurent plus dans les années complètes.

1981. – *Type Sabine. Taille-douce. Une bande de phosphore à droite, sauf n° 2121, 2122, 2123 : deux bandes de phosphore. Dentelés 13.* ▯

voir note au n°1962

2118	**40 c. brun foncé**	0 30	0 30
	a. (Sans bande de phosphore)	7 65	
	b. (Gomme tropicale)	0 40	
2119	**60 c. brun-rose**	0 30	0 30
	a. (Sans bande de phosphore)	40 »	
	b. (Gomme tropicale)	0 40	
2120	**90 c. lilas-rose**	0 50	0 50
	a. (Gomme tropicale)	0 60	

2121	**3 f. 50 vert-olive**	1 70	0 80
	a. (Gomme tropicale)	2 »	
2122	**4 f. carmin**	2 15	0 70
	a. (Sans bandes de phosphore)	42 »	
	b. (Gomme tropicale)	2 50	
2123	**5 f. bleu**	2 75	0 30
	a. (Sans bandes de phosphore)	» »	
	b. (Gomme tropicale)	3 »	
	N°s 2118 à 2123 (6 val.)	**7 70**	**2 90**
	La série, non dentelée	100 »	

1981. – *Journée du Timbre. Oeuvre de Goya (1746-1828). Taille-douce. Dentelé 13 x 12½.*

"La lettre d'amour".

2124	**1 f. 40+30 c. multicolore**	1 »	1 »
	a. (Non dentelé)	70 »	

Tirage : 4 500 000.

1981. – *"L'Eau". Concours de dessins d'enfants. Taille-douce. Dentelé 13.*

Dessin de Virginie Saura.

2125	**1 f. 40 bleu, noir et rouge**	0 80	0 50
	a. (Non dentelé)	20 75	

Tirage : 8 000 000.

1981. – *Série "Grandes réalisations". Héliogravure. Dentelés 13.*

La microélectronique du C.N.E.T. (Microprocesseurs).

Biologie (micro-organisme en évolution).

2126	**1 f. 20 multicolore**	0 65	0 50
2127	**1 f. 20 vert-jaune, bleu-gris, vert et brun**	0 65	0 50

Energies nouvelles ("Dialogue"stylisé entre la terre et le Soleil).

Fonds marins (Recherche des dépôts pélagiques).

2128	**1 f. 40 jaune, noir, bleu et bleu foncé**	0 80	0 50
2129	**1 f. 80 bleu, bleu foncé et jaune**	1 »	0 80

2130	**2 f. bleu clair, noir et rouge**	1 25	1 »
	a. (Sans rayures horizontales dans le cercle)	3 050 »	2 150 »
	N°s 2126 à 2130 (5 val.)	**4 35**	**3 30**
	La série, non dentelée	85 »	

Tirages : 8 000 000, 8 000 000, 8 000 000, 7 000 000 et 7 000 000.

1981. – ***Série "Métiers d'Art". La Reliure. Taille-douce. Dentelé 13.***

Relieur à sa presse.

2131	**1 f. 50 brun-olive, gris et rouge-carmin**	1 »	0 65
	a. (Non dentelé)	14 »	

Tirage : 7 000 000.

1981. – ***Série touristique. Taille-douce. Dentelés 13.***

Cathédrale Saint-Jean de Lyon, "Primatiale des Gaules".

La Maison Carrée, à Nîmes.

2132	**1 f. 40 carmin et brun**	0 80	0 30
2133	**1 f. 70 bleu, brun-rouge et olive**	1 10	0 65

Basilique de Sainte-Anne d'Auray.

Château de Sully, à Rosny-sur-Seine.

2134	**2 f. 20 noir et bleu**	1 25	0 65
2135	**2 f. 50 brun, bleu et vert-olive**	1 25	0 50
	N°s 2132 à 2135 (4 val.)	**4 40**	**2 10**
	La série, non dentelée	80 »	

1981. – ***Série artistique. Taille douce. Dentelés 12½-13.***

"La sente du chou", oeuvre de Camille Pissarro (1830-1903).

2136	**2 f. multicolore**	1 25	1 10
	a. (Non dentelé)	85 »	

2136b	(Arbres du milieu vert - Héliogravure)	12 »	5 »

"Composition 1920-23", oeuvre d'Albert Gleizes (1881-1953).

2137	**4 f. multicolore**	2 30	1 10
	a. (Non dentelé)	80 »	

Tirage : 5 500 000 paires.

1981. – ***Europa. Folklore. Danses traditionnelles. Taille-douce. Dentelés 13.***

La Bourrée croisée (Berry).

La Sardane (Pays Catalans).

2138	**1 f. 40 noir, brun et vert**	0 80	0 30
2139	**2 f. brun, bleu et noir**	1 50	0 50
	La paire, non dentelée	92 »	

Tirages : 20 000 000 et 10 000 000.

1981. – ***Centenaire de l'École militaire de Saint-Maixent. Taille-douce. Dentelé 13.***

Formations militaires et sportives
(croquis juxtaposés).

2140 **2 f. 50 lilas-rose, bleu et violet** 1 25 0 50
a. (Non dentelé) 15 »

Tirage : 7 000 000.

1981. – ***"Philexfrance'82". Exposition philatélique internationale. Dessins symboliques de Trémois. Héliogravure. Dentelés 13.***

2141 **2 f.** ***"La France"*** 1 40 1 10
2142 **2 f.** ***"Paris"*** 1 40 1 10
2142A ***La paire attenant au logo*** 3 » 3 »
a. (non dentelée) 230 »
b. (or omis) » »

Tirage : 8 000 000 séries.

Imprimés en bande horizontale de 2 paires disposées ainsi :

Logo	2141	2142	2141	2142	Logo

1981. – ***Presse. Anniversaires : Centenaire des lois sur la liberté de la presse. 350e anniversaire de la fondation du journal : "La Gazette", par Théophraste Renaudot et centenaire de la mort d'Emile de Girardin, créateur du journalisme moderne. Taille-douce. Dentelé 13.***

Portraits de T. Renaudot
(1586-1653) et d'Émile de Girardin
(1806-1884).

2143 **2 f. 20 noir et rouge** 1 25 0 80
a. (Non dentelé) 15 »

Tirage : 7 000 000.

1981. – ***54e Congrès national de la Fédération des Sociétés Philatéliques Françaises, à Vichy. Taille-douce. Dentelé 13.***

Loisirs, sports et station thermale
de Vichy.

2144 **1 f. 40 brun, bleu et olive** 0 80 0 50
a. (Non dentelé) 20 »

Tirage : 10 000 000.

1981. – ***Centenaire de la fondation de l'École des hautes études commerciales. Taille-douce. Dentelé 13.***

H.E.C., sigle de l'École.

2145 **1 f. 40 rouge, vert-olive et bleu** 0 80 0 50
a. (Non dentelé) 20 »

Tirage : 8 000 000.

1981. – ***Conservatoire de l'espace littoral et des rivages marécageux. Taille-douce. Dentelé 13.***

Héron, symbole de la vie protégée et côte
de la Palissade.

2146 **1 f. 60 vert, brun et rouge** 1 10 0 80
a. (Non dentelé) 26 75

Tirage : 8 000 000.

1981. – ***Championnats du monde d'escrime. Taille-douce. Dentelé 13.***

Restitution de l'assaut fulgurant.

2147 **1 f. 80 noir et brique** 1 10 0 80
a. (Non dentelé) 46 »

Tirage : 7 000 000.

1981. – *Personnages célèbres. Taille-douce. Dentelés 13.*

Louis Armand (1905-1971), académicien.

Louis Jouvet (1887-1951), artiste et directeur de théâtre.

2148	**1 f. 20+30 c. olive et vert-olive**	0 80	0 80
2149	**1 f. 20+30 c. gris-noir et vermillon**	0 80	0 80

Soeur Anne-Marie Javouhey (1779-1851), fondatrice de la congrégation Saint-Joseph de Cluny.

Jacques Offenbach (1819-1880), compositeur.

2150	**1 f. 40+30 c. brun clair et vert-olive**	1 »	1 »
2151	**1 f. 40+30 c. noir et bleu-gris**	1 »	1 »

Révérend-Père Pierre Teilhard de Chardin (1881-1955), théologien et savant.

Pasteur Marc Boegner (1881-1970), penseur et écrivain.

2152	**1 f. 40+30 c. bleu foncé et violet**	1 15	1 15
2153	**1 f. 40+30 c. olive et brun**	1 25	1 25
	Nos 2148 à 2153 (6 val.)	**6 »**	**6 »**
	La série, non dentelée	92 »	

Tirages : 3 000 000, 3 200 000, 2 500 000, 2 500 000, 3 000 000 et 3 200 000.

1981. – *Type Sabine. Légende "République Française". Taille-douce. Deux bandes de phosphore, sauf n° 2154 : une bande de phosphore. Dentelés 13.* Ⓒ

La 1re colonne concerne les neufs avec gomme métropolitaine (brillante), la 2e les oblitérés.

2154	**1 f. 40 vert**	0 80	0 15
	a. (Gomme tropicale)	1 »	
2155	**1 f. 60 rouge**	0 80	0 15
	a. (Sans bandes de phosphore)	» »	
	b. (Gomme tropicale)	1 »	
2156	**2 f. 30 bleu**	2 30	1 10
	a. (Sans bandes de phosphore)	11 »	
	b. (Gomme tropicale)	4 »	
	La série, non dentelée	54 »	

1981. – *Type Sabine. Légende "République Française", provenant de roulettes. Une bande de phosphore à droite, sauf n° 2158 : deux bandes de phosphore. Dentelés 13 horizontalement.*

2157	**1 f. 40 vert**	0 80	0 65
	a. (N° rouge au verso)	2 »	
2158	**1 f. 60 rouge**	0 80	0 50
	a. (N° rouge au verso)	2 »	

1981. – *Campagne pour la sécurité routière : "Boire ou conduire, à vous de choisir". Taille-douce. Dentelé 13.*

2159	**1 f. 60 brun, rouge et olive**	1 10	0 50
	a. (Non dentelé)	17 »	

Tirage : 8 000 000.

1981. – *Série touristique. Taille-douce. Dentelés 13.*

Abbaye de Vaucelles (Nord).

Notre-Dame de Louviers.

2160	**2 f. noir et rouge**	1 25	0 65
2161	**2 f. 20 brun et carmin**	1 25	0 65

Saint-Émilion (Gironde).

Crest (Drôme).

2162	**2 f. 60 olive et carmin**	1 40	0 50
2163	**2 f. 90 vert-noir**	1 60	0 30
	a. (Gomme tropicale)	40 »	
	Nos 2160 à 2163 (4 val.)	**5 50**	**2 10**
	La série, non dentelée	61 »	

1981. – ***45ᵉ congrès international du "P.E.N. Club". Poètes, Essayistes et Romanciers. Taille-douce. Dentelé 13.***

"La plume" (Pen en anglais).

2164 2 f. vert, violet et noir 1 10 0 50
a. (Non dentelé) 15 »
Tirage : 7 000 000.

1981. – ***Centenaire de la Caisse nationale d'épargne. Héliogravure. Dentelés 13.***

2165 1 f. 40 vert, bleu et rouge 0 80 0 30
2166 1 f. 60 carmin, bleu et rouge 1 » 0 30
La paire, non dentelée 30 »
Tirages : 10 000 000 et 12 000 000.

1981. – ***Centenaire de l'École publique. Taille-douce. Dentelé 13.***

Portrait de Jules Ferry (1832-1893).

2167 1 f. 60 brun foncé, violet et noir 1 » 0 50
a. (Non dentelé) 15 »
Tirage : 8 000 000.

1981. – ***Série "Création philatélique". Tableaux. Héliogravure. Dentelés 12½-13.***

"Les Plongeurs", oeuvre d'Edouard Pignon.

2168 4 f. polychrome 2 30 1 10
a. (Non dentelé) 80 »

"Alléluia", d'Alfred Manessier.

2169 4 f. polychrome 2 30 1 10
a. (Non dentelé) 80 »
Tirages : 5 500 000 et 11 000 000.

1981. – ***150ᵉ anniversaire de l'École navale. Taille-douce. Dentelé 13.***

Bateau "Borda" et bâtiments de la nouvelle École navale.

2170 1 f. 40 bleu-gris, rouge et brun 1 » 0 50
a. (Non dentelé) 15 »
Tirage : 8 000 000.

1981. – ***Maison de la chasse et de la nature. Hôtel de Guénégaud. Taille-douce. Dentelé 13.***

Saint Hubert devant le "cerf", sculpture sur pierre du 15ᵉ siècle.

2171 1 f. 60 brun foncé et beige 1 10 0 50
a. (Non dentelé) 15 »
Tirage : 10 000 000.

1981. – *"Panthéon - 21 mai 1981". Visite du Président de la République. Hommage à trois grandes figures de la Nation. Portraits. Taille-douce. Dentelé 13.*

J. Moulin (1899-1943), J. Jaurès (1859-1914) et V. Schoelcher (1804-1893).

2172	**1 f. 60 violet et bleu**	1 »	0 30
	a. (Non dentelé)	23 »	

Tirage : 8 000 000.

1981. – *Année internationale des personnes handicapées. Taille-douce. Dentelé 13.*

Réadaptation professionnelle.

2173	**1 f. 60 rouge, gris-bleu et noir**	0 80	0 50
	a. (Non dentelé)	15 »	

Tirage : 9 000 000.

1981. – *Hommage à Virgile (70 av. J.-C. - 19 av. J.-C.). Taille-douce. Dentelé 13 x 12½.*

Mosaïque du 2e siècle (Musée de Saint-Germain-en-Laye).

2174	**2 f. brun, gris, rose-brun et brun foncé**	1 50	1 10
	a. (Non dentelé)	80 »	

Tirage : 7 000 000.

1981. – *Au profit de la Croix-Rouge. Église du Sacré-Coeur d'Audincourt. Vitraux de Fernand Léger. Héliogravure. Dentelés 13.* ©

"Les fouets de la Passion".

"La paix".

2175	**1 f. 40+30 c. multicolore**	1 »	1 »
2176	**1 f. 60+30 c. multicolore**	1 10	1 »
	La paire, non dentelée	115 »	

Tirage : 4 000 000 paires.

Ont été émis aussi en carnets (tirage : 550 000).

1981. – *Hommage aux martyrs de Châteaubriant. Taille-douce. Dentelé 13.*

Mémorial national de la Résistance Française, oeuvre de Antoine Rohal.

2177	**1 f. 40 violet, noir et bleu**	0 80	0 50
	a. (Non dentelé)	15 »	

Tirage : 8 000 000.

1981

Du n° 2118 au n° 2177

(sauf bandes-carnet, paires et triptyques) :

60 timbres ****69** **⊙40**

Autres rubriques de l'année :

Poste aérienne 54 et 55

Préoblitérés 170 à 173

Service 65 à 70

1982. – *Type Liberté, d'après le tableau "La Liberté guidant le peuple", de Delacroix. Taille-douce. Une bande de phosphore à droite, sauf n° 2178 : sans bande de phosphore ; n° 2187, 2188, 2189, 2190 : deux bandes de phosphore. Dentelés 13.* ©

2178	**0,05 c. vert-noir**	0 30	0 30
2179	**10 c. rouge-brun**	0 15	0 15
	b. (sans bande de phosphore)	80 »	
	c. (Papier couché)	110 »	
2180	**15 c. rose**	0 50	0 50
2181	**20 c. émeraude**	0 15	0 15
	a. (sans bande de phosphore)	60 »	

2182	**30 c. orange**	0 15	0 15
	a. (sans bande de phosphore)	70 »	
	b. (Papier couché)	110 »	
2183	**40 c. brun foncé**	0 30	0 30
	a. (Papier couché)	5 »	
	b. (sans bande de phosphore)	54 »	
2184	**50 c. violet**	0 30	0 15
	a. (Papier couché)	7 »	
	b. (sans bande de phosphore)	42 »	
2185	**1 f. olive foncé**	0 50	0 30
	a. (Papier couché)	10 »	
	b. (sans bande de phosphore)	8 »	

2186	**1 f. 40 vert**	1 »	0 15
2187	**1 f. 60 rouge**	0 80	0 15
2188	**2 f. vert-jaune**	1 10	0 15
	a. (Une bande de phosphore)	1 50	0 30
	b. (sans bande de phosphore)	42 »	
2189	**2 f. 30 bleu**	2 30	1 40
	a. (sans bande de phosphore)	25 »	

2190	**5 f. bleu-vert foncé**	2 70	0 15
	a. (sans bande de phosphore)	10 »	
	N°s 2178 à 2190 (13 val.)	**10 25**	**4 »**
	La série, non dentelée	200 »	

De nouvelles valeurs ont paru à ce type en 1982 (n°s 2219 à 2223 et 2239 à 2244), en 1983 (n°s 2274 à 2277) en 1984 (n°s 2318 à 2322), en 1985 (n°s 2375 à 2379) en 1986 (n°s 2423 et 2424 à 2427) et en 1987 (n°s 2483 et 2484 à 2487).

Un 2 f. 20 a été imprimé, avec vignette attenante pour annoncer l'Exposition philatélique mondiale "Philexfrance'89" (n° 2461), puis sur un timbre grand format (n° 2524).

Le 2 f. 20 est paru en 1988, avec surcharge en ÉCU (n° 2530).

1982. – *Type "Liberté" de Delacroix, provenant du carnet n° 1501. Paire se tenant horizontalement. Dentelure horizontale souvent rognée.* C

2179a	La Paire (10 c. + 40 c. (n° 2183)	2 »	1 70

1982. – *Type "Liberté" de Delacroix, provenant de roulettes. Une bande de phosphore, sauf n° 2192 : deux bandes de phosphore. Dentelés 13 horizontalement.*

2191	**1 f. 40 vert**	1 50	1 25
	a. (N° rouge au verso)	5 »	
2192	**1 f. 60 rouge**	1 50	1 25
	a. (N° rouge au verso)	5 »	

1982. – *Série touristique. Taille-douce. Dentelés 13.*

Saint-Pierre-et-Miquelon.

Aix-en-Provence.

2193	**1 f. 60 bleu foncé, vert et noir**	1 »	0 30
2194	**2 f. rouge et violet**	1 »	0 50

Pau - Château Henri IV.

Collonges-la-Rouge.

2195	**3 f. bleu foncé, bleu et noir**	1 40	0 65
2196	**3 f. rouge, jaune et bleu foncé**	1 40	0 50
	N°s 2193 à 2196 (4 val.)	**4 80**	**1 95**
	La série, non dentelée	80 »	

Tirages : 12 000 000, 8 000 000, 8 000 000 et 8 000 000.

1982. – *Région. Taille-douce. Dentelé 13.*

Corse.

2197	**1 f. 90 bleu et rouge-brique**	1 »	0 50
	a. (Non dentelé)	17 »	

Tirage : 10 000 000.

1982. – *800e anniversaire de la naissance de saint François d'Assise. Taille-douce. Dentelé 13.*

Saint François d'Assise.

2198	**2 f. bleu et noir**	1 10	0 65
	a. (Non dentelé)	18 50	

Tirage : 7 000 000.

1982. – ***"Philexfrance'82". Exposition philatélique internationale. Dessins de Jean-Michel Folon. Héliogravure. Dentelés 13.***

2199	**2 f. "La Poste et les Hommes"**	3 »	2 50
2200	**2 f. "La Poste et les Techniques"**	3 »	2 50

Tirage : 7 000 000 paires.

2200A	La paire attenant au logo	6 »	5 »
	a. (La paire, non dentelée)	170 »	

Imprimés en bande horizontale de 2 paires disposées ainsi :

Logo	2199	2200	2199	2200	Logo

1982. – ***125e anniversaire de la naissance de Lord Baden-Powell et 75e anniversaire du Mouvement scout. Taille-douce. Dentelé 13.***

Portrait de Baden-Powell et scouts.

2201	**2 f. 30 noir et vert**	1 10	0 50
	a. (Non dentelé)	85 »	

Tirage : 6 000 000.

1982. – ***Recensement de la population. Héliogravure. Dentelé 13.***

"Une belle moisson de chiffres".

2202	**1 f. 60 multicolore**	0 80	0 30
	a. (Chiffre 7 vert manquant sur la Corse)	25 »	20 »
	b. (Couleur verte manquante)	535 »	345 »
	c. (Non dentelé)	23 »	
	d. (sans le chiffre 7, non dentelé)	» »	

Il existe deux n° 2202a par planche de 50 timbres (29e et 39e cases).

Tirage : 10 000 000.

1982. – ***Aéroport Bâle-Mulhouse. Taille-douce. Dentelé 13.***

Aérogare, passerelle "Swissair"
et avion "Air-France".

2203	**1 f. 90 bleu, rouge et brun**	1 25	0 65
	a. (Non dentelé)	40 »	

Tirage : 5 000 000.

1982. – ***Lutte contre le racisme. Taille-douce. Dentelé 13.***

Fraternité des races.

2204	**2 f. 30 orange et brun foncé**	1 25	0 65
	a. (Non dentelé)	14 »	

Tirage : 6 000 000.

1982. – ***Journée du Timbre. Oeuvre de Pablo Picasso. Taille-douce. Dentelé 13 x 12½.***

"Femme lisant".

2205	**1 f. 60+40 c. multicolore**	1 10	0 80
	a. (Non dentelé)	61 »	

Tirage : 4 500 000.

1982. – ***Série "Métiers d'art". La ferronnerie. Taille-douce. Dentelé 13.***

Ferronnier à son ouvrage.

2206	**1 f. 40 multicolore**	0 80	0 65
	a. (Non dentelé)	14 »	

Tirage : 10 000 000.

1982. – ***Europa. Faits historiques. Taille-douce. Dentelés 13.***

Traité de Rome de 1957.

Traité de Verdun de 843.

2207	**1 f. 60 bleu foncé**	1 25	0 65
2208	**2 f. 30 noir, brun et brun-vert**	1 50	0 65
	La paire, non dentelée	110 »	

Tirages : 12 000 000 et 8 000 000.

1982. – *Coupe du monde de football. Taille-douce. Dentelé 13.*

Gardien de but et stade.

2209 1 f. 80 bleu foncé, olive et rouge 1 85 0 50
a. (Non dentelé) 70 »
Tirage : 8 000 000.

1982. – *Série artistique. Taille douce. Dentelés 12½-13.*

"L'Éphèbe d'Agde", chef-d'oeuvre de la statuaire hellénistique.

2210 4 f. brun foncé, brun et bleu pâle 2 30 1 10
a. (Non dentelé) 80 »

"Embarquement à Ostic", oeuvre de Claude Gellée, dit Le Lorrain.

2211 4 f. bleu-vert, ocre, noir, bleu et rose 2 30 1 10
a. (Non dentelé) 80 »
Tirages : 5 500 000 et 5 500 000.

1982. – *35ᵉ festival international du film, à Cannes. Héliogravure. Dentelé 13.*

Affiche du festival, illustration du film "Amarcord".

2212 2 f. 30 polychrome 1 25 1 »
a. (Non dentelé) 30 »
Tirage : 6 000 000.

1982. – *20ᵉ anniversaire du Centre national d'études spatiales (C.N.E.S.). Taille-douce. Dentelé 13.*

Satellite "Éole", fusée "Ariane" et antenne terrestre.

2213 2 f. 60 bleu, bleu-violet et rouge-brun 1 25 0 80
a. (Non dentelé) 42 »
Tirage : 7 000 000.

1982. – *Sommet des Pays industrialisés. Château de Versailles. Héliogravure. Dentelé 13.*

Synthèse graphique.

2214 2 f. 60 multicolore 1 25 0 80
a. (Non dentelé) 23 »
Tirage : 6 000 000.

1982. – *150ᵉ anniversaire de la naissance de Jules Vallès (1832-1885), écrivain et journaliste. Taille-douce. Dentelé 13.*

2215 1 f. 60 olive, vert et noir 1 » 0 30
a. (Non dentelé) 15 »
Tirage : 10 000 000.

1982. – *"Philexfrance'82". Exposition philatélique internationale. La "Marianne" de Jean Cocteau. Type de 1961. Taille-douce. Dentelés 13.* BF *n° 8.*

2216 4 f. rouge et bleu 7 » 7 »
2217 6 f. bleu et rouge 7 » 7 »
Vente : 1 252 652 paires.
Émis seulement en feuillet vendu 30 f. (10 f. de valeur faciale et 20 f. de droit d'entrée permanente à l'exposition).
Voir également à la rubrique "Entiers postaux (nᵒ 2216-CP1)".

1982. – *Hommage à Frédéric et Irène Joliot - Curie, physiciens. Taille-douce. Dentelé 13.*

2218	**1 f. 80 rose, violet et bleu**	1 »	0 50
	a. (Non dentelé)	35 »	

Tirage : 10 000 000.

1982. – *Type "Liberté" de Delacroix. Taille-douce. Deux bandes de phosphore, sauf n° 2219 : une bande de phosphore. Dentelés 13.* [C]

2219	**1 f. 60 vert**	1 »	0 15
	a. (sans bande de phosphore)	100 »	
2220	**1 f. 80 rouge**	1 »	0 15
	a. (sans bande de phosphore)	110 »	
2221	**2 f. 60 bleu clair**	2 »	1 25
	La série, non dentelée	46 »	

1982. – *Type "Liberté" de Delacroix, provenant de roulettes. Une bande de phosphore, sauf n° 2223 : deux bandes de phosphore. Multicolore. Dentelés 13 horizontalement.*

2222	**1 f. 60 vert**	1 »	0 50
	a. (N° rouge au verso)	2 »	
	b. (sans bande de phosphore)	85 »	
	c. (N° Rouge au verso, sans bande de phosphore)	115 »	
2223	**1 f. 80 rouge**	1 10	0 50
	a. (N° rouge au verso)	2 »	

1982. – *Première réalisation d'un éclairage public à l'électricité - Grenoble 14 juillet 1882. Taille-douce. Dentelé 13.*

Évocation.

2224	**1 f. 80 violet, bleu-gris et bleu**	1 »	0 30
	a. (Non dentelé)	15 »	

Tirage : 10 000 000.

1982. – *Personnages célèbres. Taille-douce. Dentelés 13.*

Guillaume Postel (1510-1581), érudit. Henri Mondor (1885-1962), chirurgien et écrivain.

2225	**1 f. 40+30 c. brun-rouge et noir**	1 10	1 10
2226	**1 f. 40+30 c. bleu-noir et brun**	1 10	1 10

Louis Pergaud (1882-1915), écrivain. Robert Debré (1882-1978), pédiatre.

2227	**1 f. 60+40 c. bleu et brun foncé**	1 10	1 10
2228	**1 f. 60+40 c. vert-bleu foncé et noir**	1 10	1 10

André Chantemesse (1851-1919), médecin, bactériologiste. Gustave Eiffel (1832-1923), ingénieur.

2229	**1 f. 60+30 c. bleu, brun-violet et violet**	1 20	1 20
2230	**1 f. 80+40 c. brun**	1 40	1 40
	N°s 2225 à 2230 (6 val.)	**7 »**	**7 »**
	La série, non dentelée	92 »	

Tirage : 3 000 000 séries.

1982. – *Série artistique. Héliogravure. Dentelé 12½ x 13.*

"La Dentellière", de Vermeer.

2231	**4 f. polychrome**	2 30	1 25
	a. (Non dentelé)	80 »	

Tirage : 6 000 000.

1982. – *Série touristique. Taille-douce. Dentelé 13.*

Château de Ripaille (Haute-Savoie).

2232	**2 f. 90 brun-rouge et brun**	1 55	1 »
	a. (Non dentelé)	15 »	

Tirage : 10 000 000.

1982. – *100e anniversaire de la Fédération nationale des Sapeurs-Pompiers. Taille-douce. Dentelé 13.*

Sapeurs-Pompiers au combat.

2233	**3 f. 30 brun et rouge**	1 85	0 50
	a. (Non dentelé)	26 75	

Tirage : 8 000 000.

1982. – *Sculpture de Marc Boyan. Taille-douce. Dentelé 12½ x 13.*

"La Famille".

2234	**4 f. bleu-gris foncé et brun clair**	2 30	1 25
	a. (Non dentelé)	80 »	

Tirage : 8 000 000.

1982. – *Marionnettes. Taille-douce. Dentelé 13.*

Marionnettes à tige, fils et gaine.

2235	**1 f. 80 carmin, bleu et violet**	1 »	0 50
	a. (Non dentelé)	15 »	

Tirage : 10 000 000.

1982. – *Rugby. Taille-douce. Dentelé 13.*

Phase de jeu.

2236	**1 f. 60 bleu foncé, rouge et olive**	2 »	0 50
	a. (Non dentelé)	58 »	

Tirage : 8 000 000.

1982. – *Écoles Normales supérieures. Taille-douce. Dentelé 13.*

Hémicycle.

2237	**1 f. 80 rouge-brique et gris-bleu**	1 »	0 50
	a. (Non dentelé)	17 »	

Tirage : 10 000 000.

1982. – *Lille. Année du Beffroi. Taille-douce. Dentelé 13.*

2238	**1 f. 80 olive et rouge-brique**	1 »	0 50
	a. (Non dentelé)	15 »	

Tirage : 12 000 000.

1982. – *Type "Liberté" de Delacroix. Taille-douce. Une bande de phosphore à droite, sauf n° 2243, 2244 : deux bandes de phosphore. Dentelés 13.*

2239	**60 c. brun-rose**	0 30	0 15
	a. (sans bande de phosphore)	42 »	
2240	**70 c. bleu-violet**	0 50	0 30
	a. (Double frappe)	15 »	
	b. (sans bande de phosphore)	5 »	
2241	**80 c. brun-olive**	0 50	0 15
	a. (Bande de phosphore à gauche)	3 50	
	b. (sans bande de phosphore)	30 »	

2242	**90 c. violet clair**	0 50	0 30
	a. (sans bande de phosphore)	54 »	
2243	**3 f. brun-violet**	1 40	0 30
	a. (sans bande de phosphore)	27 50	
2244	**4 f. rouge-carmin**	1 80	0 30
	a. (sans bande de phosphore)	185 »	
	N°s 2239 à 2244 (6 val.)	**5 »**	**1 50**
	La série, non dentelée	70 »	

1982. – ***Série "Création philatélique". Tableau. Héliogravure. Dentelé 13 x 12½.***

"La chambre turque", oeuvre de Balthus.

2245	**4 f. polychrome**	2 30	1 25
	a. (Non dentelé)	80 »	
	b. (Dominante rose)	25 »	

Tirage : 5 500 000.

1982. – ***Centenaire de la découverte du bacille de la tuberculose par Robert Koch. Taille-douce. Dentelé 13.***

Microscope, R. Koch et évolutions bacillaires.

2246	**2 f. 60 noir et rouge**	1 25	0 65
	a. (Non dentelé)	18 50	

Tirage : 7 000 000.

1982. – ***Au profit de la Croix-Rouge. Hommage à Jules Verne. Illustrations de romans. Taille-douce. Dentelés 13.*** [C]

"Cinq semaines en ballon".

"Vingt mille lieues sous les mers".

2247	**1 f. 60+30 c. brun et rouge**	1 10	0 80
	a. (Dentelé 12½ x 13)	1 25	1 »
2248	**1 f. 80+40 c. vert et rouge**	1 10	0 80
	a. (Dentelé 12½ x 13)	1 25	1 »
	La paire, non dentelée	110 »	

Tirage : 4 500 000 paires.

Ont été aussi émis en carnets (tirage : 500 000). Les n°s 2247a et 2248a proviennent des carnets.

1982. – ***4e centenaire de la mort de sainte Thérèse d'Avila. Taille-douce. Dentelé 13.***

Portrait et remparts d'Avila.

2249	**2 f. 10 vert, brun et noir**	1 10	0 65
	a. (Non dentelé)	18 50	

Tirage : 6 000 000.

1982. – ***Cavelier de La Salle. Découverte de la Louisiane, 1682. Taille-douce. Dentelé 13.***

Portrait et carte avec tracé du Mississippi.

2250	**3 f. 25 vert, rose et brun-rouge**	1 50	0 65
	a. (Non dentelé)	18 50	

Tirage : 5 500 000.

1982. – ***Hommage à Léon Blum (1872-1950), écrivain et homme politique. Taille-douce. Dentelé 13.***

2251	**1 f. 80 brun et brun-rouge**	1 »	0 30
	a. (Non dentelé)	14 »	

Tirage : 10 000 000.

1982

Du n° 2178 au n° 2251

(sauf bandes-carnets, paires et triptyques) :

74 timbres ****103** **⊙62**

Autres rubriques de l'année :

Poste aérienne 56

Bloc-feuillet 8

Préoblitérés 174 à 177

Service 71 à 74

Taxe 103 à 108

1983. – ***Région. Héliogravure. Dentelé 13.***

Provence-Alpes-Côte d'Azur.

2252	**1 f. multicolore**	0 65	0 30
	a. (Non dentelé)	15 »	

Tirage : 10 000 000.

1983. – ***Série touristique. Taille-douce. Dentelés 13.***

Brantôme en Périgord.

Concarneau, remparts de la Ville-close.

2253	**1 f. 80 vert foncé, bleu foncé et brun-rouge**	1 »	0 30
2254	**3 f. brun foncé et bleu-vert**	1 40	0 80

Abbaye de Noirlac, Bruère Allichamps (Cher).

2255	**3 f. 60 bleu, noir et brun**	1 85	0 50
	La série, non dentelée	46 »	

Tirages : 10 000 000, 8 000 000 et 8 000 000.

1983. – ***500e anniversaire de la naissance de Martin Luther (1483-1546), théologien et réformateur. Taille-douce. Dentelé 13 x 12½.***

Portrait, d'après Lucas Cranach.

2256	**3 f. 30 bistre et brun**	1 70	0 65
	a. (Non dentelé)	40 »	

Tirage : 8 000 000.

1983. – ***Centenaire de l'Alliance française. Taille-douce. Dentelé 13.***

Symboles.

2257	**1 f. 80 bleu, brun et rouge**	1 »	0 50
	a. (Non dentelé)	18 50	

Tirage : 10 000 000.

1983. – ***Journée du timbre. Oeuvre de Rembrandt. Taille-douce. Dentelé 13.***

"Homme dictant une lettre".

2258	**1 f. 80+40 c. sépia et bistre**	1 25	1 »
	a. (Non dentelé)	61 »	

Tirage : 4 500 000.

1983. – ***Hommage à la femme. Journée internationale de la femme. Taille-douce. Dentelé 13.***

Danielle Casanova, résistante morte en déportation.

2259	**3 f. noir et brun-rouge**	1 40	0 50
	a. (Non dentelé)	15 »	

Tirage : 7 000 000.

1983. – ***Année mondiale des communications. Héliogravure. Dentelé 13.***

2260	**2 f. 60 multicolore**	1 25	1 »
	a. (Non dentelé)	15 »	

Tirage : 8 000 000.

1983. – *Bicentenaire de l'air et de l'espace. Premières ascensions de l'homme dans l'atmosphère. Polychrome et or. Héliogravure. Dentelés 13.*

2261	2 f. *1re ascension en montgolfière à air chaud par Pilâtre de Rozier et le marquis d'Arlandes*	1 25	0 80
2262	3 f. *2e ascension en ballon à hydrogène par J. Charles et M.N. Robert*	1 50	1 »

Tirage : 6 000 000 paires.

2262A	La paire attenant au logo	3 »	2 50
	a. (La paire non dentelée)	170 »	

Imprimés en bande horizontale de 2 paires disposées ainsi :

*	2261	2262	2261	2262	*

* Emblème des manifestations du bicentenaire.

Émis en feuille de 10 paires.

1983. – *Série "Création philatélique". Héliogravure. Dentelé 13.*

"Aurora-Set", oeuvre de Dewasne.

2263	**4 f. multicolore**	2 30	1 25
	a. (Non dentelé)	80 »	

Tirage : 6 000 000.

1983. – *Série artistique. Taille-douce. Dentelés 12½ x 13.*

"Vénus et Psyché", oeuvre de Raphaël.

2264	**4 f. brun-orange et brun clair**	2 30	1 25
	a. (Non dentelé)	85 »	

Illustration des Contes de Perrault, oeuvre de Gustave Doré.

2265	**4 f. multicolore**	2 30	1 25
	a. (Non dentelé)	80 »	

Tirage : 6 000 000 paires.

1983. – *Flore et faune de France (I). Fleurs de montagne. Taille-douce. Dentelés 12½.*

Carline (Carlina flore rubente).

Martagon (Lilium montanum).

2266	**1 f. multicolore**	0 50	0 30
2267	**2 f. multicolore**	1 10	0 30

Aster (Aster montanus coeruleus).

Aconit (Aconitum pyrenaicum).

2268	**3 f. multicolore**	1 60	0 70
2269	**4 f. multicolore**	2 30	0 70
	N°s 2266 à 2269 (4 val.)	**5 50**	**2 »**
	La série, non dentelée	125 »	

Tirage : 8 000 000 séries.

1983. – *Europa. Les grandes oeuvres du génie humain. Taille-douce. Dentelés 13.*

La photographie.

Le cinéma.

2270	**1 f. 80 brun foncé et brun-rouge**	1 50	0 50
2271	**2 f. 60 brun foncé et brun-rouge**	2 »	1 »
	La paire, non dentelée	115 »	

Tirages : 12 000 000 et 8 000 000.

1983. – *Convention de Paris pour la protection de la propriété industrielle. Héliogravure. Dentelé 13.*

2272	**2 f. multicolore**	1 »	0 30
	a. (Non dentelé)	12 50	

Tirage : 8 000 000.

1983. – *56e Congrès national de la Fédération des Sociétés Philatéliques Françaises, à Marseille. Taille-douce. Dentelé 13.*

Vieux-Port et Notre-Dame-de-la-Garde.

2273	**1 f. 80 bleu et rouge**	1 »	0 50
	a. (Non dentelé)	15 »	

Tirage : 8 000 000.

1983. – *Type "Liberté" de Delacroix. Taille-douce. Deux bandes de phosphore. Dentelés 13.* [C]

2274	**2 f. rouge**	1 »	0 15
	a. (sans bande de phosphore)	70 »	
2275	**2 f. 80 bleu**	2 »	1 10
2276	**10 f. violet**	4 »	0 15
	a. (Papier couché)	23 »	
	b. (sans bande de phosphore)	20 »	
	La série, non dentelée	40 »	

1983. – *Type "Liberté" de Delacroix, provenant de roulettes. Deux bandes de phosphore. Multicolore. Dentelé 13 horizontalement.*

2277	**2 f. rouge**	1 10	0 30
	a. (N° rouge au verso)	2 30	

1983. – *50e anniversaire de la création de la Compagnie Air-France. Héliogravure. Dentelé 13.*

2278	**3 f. 45 *Logo d'Air France***	1 85	1 10
	a. (Non dentelé)	30 »	

Tirage : 6 500 000.

1983. – *Personnages célèbres. Taille-douce. Multicolore. Dentelés 13.*

André Messager (1852-1929), compositeur et chef d'orchestre.

Jacques-Ange Gabriel (1698-1782), architecte.

Hector Berlioz (1803-1869), compositeur.

2279	**1 f. 60+30 c. noir et bleu**	1 10	1 10
2280	**1 f. 60+30 c. orange et noir**	1 »	1 »
2281	**1 f. 80+40 c. noir et violet**	1 20	1 20

Max-Pol Fouchet (1913-1980), écrivain.

René Cassin (1887-1976), juriste. (Prix Nobel de la paix, 1968).

Stendhal (Henri Beyle, dit), (1783-1842), écrivain.

2282	**1 f. 80+40 c. rouge et noir**	1 20	1 20
2283	**2 f. +40 c. vert et noir**	1 25	1 25
2284	**2 f. +40 c. noir et outremer**	1 25	1 25
	N°s 2279 à 2284 (6 val.)	**7 »**	**7 »**
	La série, non dentelée	92 »	

Tirage : 3 000 000 séries.

1983. – *Indépendance américaine 1783. Traités de Versailles et de Paris. Dentelé 13 x 12½.*

"La jeune Amérique défendue par la France contre l'Angleterre". médaille du 18e siècle.

2285 **2 f. 80 noir et gris-olive** 1 40 0 80
a. (Non dentelé) 46 »

Les Etats-Unis ont émis simultanément sur ce sujet une figurine de 20 c. (no 1494 cotes : 1,20 0,30).

Tirage : 7 000 000.

1983. – *Série "Métiers d'art". Art du bijou. Héliogravure. Dentelé 13.*

Fabrication d'une bague.

2286 **2 f. 20 multicolore** 1 » 0 50
a. (Non dentelé) 20 »

Tirage : 8 000 000.

1983. – *Série touristique. Taille-douce. Dentelure 13, sauf n° 2288 : 13 x 12½.*

Jarnac (Charente).

2287 **2 f. bistre-orange et noir** 1 » 0 50

Charleville-Mézières (Ardennes).

2288 **3 f. 10 rose foncé et brun** 1 60 1 »
La paire, non dentelée 30 »

Tirages : 10 000 000 et 8 000 000.

1983. – *30e anniversaire du Conseil de coopération douanière. Taille-douce. Dentelé 13.*

Musée des Douanes à Bordeaux et emblème du C.C.D.

2289 **2 f. 30 vert, brun-olive et noir** 1 » 0 65
a. (Non dentelé) 14 »

Tirage : 10 000 000.

1983. – *Vélocipède. Pierre et Ernest Michaux. Taille-douce. Dentelé 13.*

Ancêtres de la bicyclette.

2290 **1 f. 60 carmin, brun-olive et outremer** 1 50 0 50
a. (Non dentelé) 20 »

Tirage : 8 000 000.

1983. – *Série "Création philatélique". Hommage à Jean Effel. Héliogravure. Dentelé 13.*

Lettre de Marianne, dessin humoristique du caricaturiste.

2291 **4 f. bleu pâle, noir, rouge et rose** 2 30 1 25
a. (Non dentelé) 80 »

Tirage : 6 000 000.

1983. – *Météorologie nationale. Taille-douce. Dentelé 13.*

Satellite et carte de météorologie sur globe.

2292 **1 f. 50 bleu foncé, bleu et brun foncé** 0 80 0 30
a. (Non dentelé) 46 »
b. bleu foncé omis 155 »

Tirage : 8 000 000.

1983. – ***Héroïnes de la Résistance. Taille-douce. Dentelés 13.***

Renée Lévy (1906-1943). Berthie Albrecht (1893-1943).

2293	**1 f. 60 brun foncé et bleu**	0 80	0 50
2294	**1 f. 60 brun foncé et olive**	0 80	0 50
	La paire, non dentelée	40 »	

Tirage : 7 000 000 paires.

1983. – ***Au Profit de la Croix-Rouge. Sculptures en bois polychrome. Taille-douce. Dentelés 13.*** 🄲

Vierge à l'Enfant, Baillon, 16e siècle. Vierge à l'Enfant, Genainville, 16e siècle.

2295	**1 f. 60+40 c. rouge et brun**	1 »	0 80
	a. (Dentelé 12½ x 13)	1 25	1 »
2296	**2 f. +40 c. rouge et bleu**	1 10	0 80
	a. (Dentelé 12½ x 13)	1 25	1 10
	La paire, non dentelée	80 »	

Tirage : 3 500 000 paires.

Ont été aussi émis en carnets (tirage : 450 000). Les nos 2295a et 2296a proviennent des carnets.

1983. – ***Série artistique. Taille-douce. Dentelé 13 x 12½.***

"Le Lapin Agile", de Maurice Utrillo (1883-1955).

2297	**4 f. multicolore**	2 30	1 10
	a. (Non dentelé)	80 »	

Tirage : 6 000 000.

1983. – ***Hommage à Pierre Mendès France (1907-1982). Taille-douce. Dentelé 13.***

Portrait de l'homme d'État.

2298	**2 f. bleu et carmin**	1 »	0 30
	a. (Non dentelé)	14 »	

Tirage : 12 000 000.

1983

Du n° 2252 au n° 2298

(sauf bandes carnets, paires et triptyques) :

47 timbres ****67** **⊙35**

Autres rubriques de l'année :

Préoblitérés 178 à 181

Service 75 à 78

Taxe 109 à 112

1984. – ***Série artistique. Taille douce, sauf n° 2300 : héliogravure. Dentelés 12½-13.***

"Hommage au Cinéma", sculpture de César (César Baldaccini, dit).

2299	**4 f. brun foncé et brun-orange**	2 30	1 10
	a. (Non dentelé)	80 »	

"Les 4 coins du ciel", de Jean Messagier.

2300	**4 f. polychrome**	2 30	1 25
	a. (Non dentelé)	70 »	

"Coin de salle à manger au Cannet", de Pierre Bonnard (1867-1947).

2301 **4 f. multicolore** 2 30 1 25
a. (Non dentelé) 80 »

Tirage : 6 000 000 séries.

1984. – ***Région. Taille-douce. Dentelé 13.***

La Guadeloupe.

2302 **2 f. 30 brun-rouge, rose foncé et violet** 1 » 0 50
a. (Non dentelé) 14 »

Tirage : 10 000 000.

1984. – ***Hommage aux Femmes. Taille-douce. Dentelé 13.***

Flora Tristan (Flore Tristan-Morcoso, dite Flora) (1803-1844), femme de lettres et initiatrice du féminisme en France.

2303 **2 f. 80 lilas-rose et noir** 1 40 0 65
a. (Non dentelé) 14 »

Tirage : 7 000 000.

1984. – ***Journée du Timbre. Oeuvre de L.M. Van Loo. Taille-douce. Dentelé 12½ x 13.***

"Diderot".

2304 **2 f. +40 c. bleu et noir** 1 25 1 10
a. (Non dentelé) 61 »

Tirage : 4 500 000.

1984. – ***Centenaire de la création des Syndicats professionnels par la loi du 21 mars 1884. Taille-douce. Dentelé 13.***

Pierre Waldeck-Rousseau (1846-1904), promoteur de la loi.

2305 **3 f. 60 noir et bleu** 1 70 0 50
a. (Non dentelé) 14 »

Tirage : 8 000 000.

1984. – ***2ᵉˢ élections au Parlement Européen - 17 juin 1984. Héliogravure. Dentelé 13.***

Emblème du Parlement.

2306 **2 f. multicolore** 1 » 0 30
a. (Non dentelé) 30 »

Tirage : 12 000 000.

1984. – ***Jacques Cartier. 450ᵉ anniversaire de son 1ᵉʳ voyage au Canada. Emission commune franco-canadienne. Taille-douce. Deux bandes de phosphore. Dentelé 13.***

Evocation symbolique.

2307 **2 f. multicolore** 1 » 0 30
a. (sans bande de phosphore) 300 »
b. (Non dentelé) 30 »

Imprimé au Canada.

Le Canada a émis simultanément une figurine au même type de 32 c. (nº 869 cotes : 1,60 0,80).

Tirage : 15 000 000.

1984. – ***"Philex-Jeunes'84". Exposition philatélique de la jeunesse, à Dunkerque. Taille-douce. Dentelé 13.***

Eveil philatélique de la jeunesse et semeuse des timbres de France.

2308 **1 f. 60 violet, brun et rouge-brique** 0 80 0 50
a. (Non dentelé) 14 »

Voir également à la rubrique "Entiers postaux, (nº 2308-CP1)".

Tirage : 8 000 000.

1984. – *Europa. 25e anniversaire de la Conférence européenne des administrations des postes et télécommunications (C.E.P.T.). Taille-douce. Dentelés 13.*

Pont de la coopération européenne (thème commun).

Pont de la coopération européenne (thème commun).

2309	**2 f. rouge-brique**	1 50	0 50
2310	**2 f. 80 bleu**	2 »	0 85
	La paire, non dentelée	80 »	

Tirages : 10 000 000 et 8 000 000.

Voir également à la rubrique "Entiers postaux (n° 2309-CP1)".

1984. – *Légion étrangère. Taille-douce. Dentelé 13.*

Le serment de Camerone et uniforme actuel.

2311	**3 f. 10 vert, rouge et noir**	1 50	0 65
	a. (Non dentelé)	15 »	

Tirage : 7 000 000.

1984. – *40e anniversaire de la Libération : Résistance et débarquements. Taille-douce. Dentelés 13.*

Imprimés se tenant avec vignette centrale "Croix de la Libération".

2312	**2 f. *Résistance au combat***	1 »	0 65
2313	**3 f. *Débarquements des armées***	1 60	0 80
	Tirage : 10 000 000 paires.		
2313A	Le triptyque	2 75	2 50
	a. (Non dentelé)	92 »	

Imprimés en bande horizontale de 2 triptyques disposés ainsi :

2312	*	2313	2312	*	2313

* : Croix de la Libération.

1984. – *Jeux olympiques d'été, à Los Angeles. 90e anniversaire du Comité international olympique (C.I.O.). Taille-douce. Dentelé 13.*

Mouvements de différentes disciplines.

2314	**4 f. violet pâle, olive et bleu**	2 »	1 10
	a. (Non dentelé)	70 »	

Tirage : 7 000 000.

1984. – *Série "Métiers d'art". Art de la gravure. Taille-douce. Dentelé 13.*

Exécution d'une gravure ancienne.

2315	**2 f. noir, vert et bistre**	1 »	0 30
	a. (Non dentelé)	14 »	

Tirage : 8 000 000.

1984. – *57e Congrès national de la Fédération des Sociétés philatéliques françaises, à Bordeaux. Taille-douce. Dentelé 13.*

Monuments, édifices et croissant de lune de la ville.

2316	**2 f. rouge-brique**	1 »	0 30
	a. (Non dentelé)	14 »	

Tirage : 8 000 000.

1984. – *40e anniversaire du Centre national d'études des télécommunications (CNET). Héliogravure. Dentelé 13.*

Moyens modernes de télécommunications.

2317	**3 f. bleu-noir et bleu**	1 40	0 50
	a. (Non dentelé)	20 »	

Tirage : 8 000 000.

1984. – *Type "Liberté" de Delacroix. Taille-douce. Deux bandes de phosphore, sauf n° 2318 : une bande de phosphore. Dentelés 13.* [C]

2318	**1 f. 70 vert**	1 »	0 15
	a. (sans bande de phosphore)	55 »	
2319	**2 f. 10 rouge**	1 »	0 15
	a. (sans bande de phosphore)	30 »	
2320	**3 f. bleu**	2 »	0 80
	La série, non dentelée	40 »	

1984. – *Type "Liberté" de Delacroix, provenant de roulettes. Une bande de phosphore, sauf n° 2322 : deux bandes de phosphore. Dentelés 13 horizontalement.*

2321	**1 f. 70 vert**	1 »	0 65
	a. (N° rouge au verso)	1 85	
	b. (Gomme brillante)	5 »	
	c. (N° rouge au verso, Gomme brillante)	20 »	
2322	**2 f. 10 rouge**	1 10	0 50
	a. (N° rouge au verso)	2 30	
	b. (Gomme brillante)	7 »	
	c. (N° rouge au verso, Gomme brillante)	25 »	

1984. – *Série touristique. Taille-douce. Dentelés 13.*

Monastère de la Grande Chartreuse (Isère).

Palais idéal du Facteur Cheval, à Hauterives (Drôme).

2323	**1 f. 70 gris-bleu et rose violacé**	1 »	0 30
2324	**2 f. 10 brun, vert et brun-rouge**	1 10	0 30

La citadelle de Vauban. Belle-Ile-en-Mer (Morbihan).

Phare de Cordouan (16e siècle), Gironde.

2325	**2 f. 50 olive, bleu et brun**	1 25	0 50
2326	**3 f. 50 violet et noir**	2 15	0 50
	N°s 2323 à 2326 (4 val.)	**5 50**	**1 60**
	La série, non dentelée	61 »	

Tirages : 10 000 000, 12 000 000, 10 000 000 et 7 000 000.

1984. – *25e Congrès international de géographie. Dentelé 13.*

2327	**3 f. jaune orangé, noir et gris**	1 40	0 65
	a. (Non dentelé)	23 »	

Tirage : 6 000 000.

1984. – *Personnages célèbres. Taille-douce. Dentelés 13.*

Emile Littré (1801-1881), lexicographe.

Jean Zay (1904-1944), homme politique.

2328	**1 f. 60+40 c. violet clair et noir**	1 »	1 »
2329	**1 f. 60+40 c. vert et noir**	1 »	1 »

Pierre Corneille (1606-1684), auteur dramatique.

Gaston Bachelard (1884-1962), philosophe.

2329A	**1 f. 70+40 c. violet et noir**	1 10	1 10
2330	**2 f. +40 c. gris et noir**	1 10	1 10

Jean Paulhan (1884-1968), critique et essayiste.

Evariste Galois (1811-1832), mathématicien.

2331	**2 f. 10+40 c. brun et noir**	1 10	1 10
2332	**2 f. 10+40 c. bleu et noir**	1 10	1 10
	N°s 2328 à 2332 (6 val.)	**6 40**	**6 40**
	La série, non dentelée	80 »	

Tirage : 3 000 000 séries.

1984. – *Lancement du satellite TELECOM 1. Héliogravure. Dentelé 13.*

Télécom 1 en service.

2333	**3 f. 20 multicolore**	1 70	0 65
	a. (Non dentelé)	35 »	

Tirage : 7 000 000.

1984. – *Mise en service du TGV postal. Héliogravure. Dentelé 13.*

2334	**2 f. 10 multicolore**	1 55	0 30
	a. (Non dentelé)	50 »	

Tirage : 12 000 000.

1984. – *Série touristique. Taille-douce. Dentelé 13.*

Château de Montségur (Ariège).

2335	**3 f. 70 violet, violet-rouge et rouge**	1 70	0 50
	a. (Non dentelé)	15 »	

Tirage : 8 000 000.

1984. – *Hommage à Marx Dormoy (1888-1941). Taille-douce. Dentelé 13.*

2336	**2 f. 40 noir et bleu**	1 25	0 50
	a. (Non dentelé)	12 50	

Tirage : 7 000 000.

1984. – *Faune et flore de France (II). Rapaces diurnes. Taille-douce. Dentelés 13.*

Gypaète barbu (Gypaetus barbatus aureus).

Circaète Jean le Blanc (Circaetus G. Gallicus).

2337	**1 f. multicolore**	0 50	0 30
2338	**2 f. multicolore**	1 25	0 50

Epervier d'Europe (Accipiter N. Nisus).

Faucon pèlerin (Falco P. Peregrinus).

2339	**3 f. multicolore**	1 70	1 »
2340	**5 f. multicolore**	2 75	0 70
	N°s 2337 à 2340 (4 val.)	**6 20**	**2 50**
	La série, non dentelée	110 »	

Tirage : 8 000 000 séries.

1984. – *Centenaire de l'automobile. Taille-douce. Dentelé 13.*

Plans du véhicule de MM. Delamare, Deboutteville et Malandin.

2341	**3 f. brun, rouge et bleu**	1 85	0 50
	a. (Non dentelé)	26 75	

Tirage : 7 000 000.

1984. – *Série artistique. Héliogravure. Dentelés 12 x 13.*

"La Pythie", oeuvre d'André Masson.

2342	**5 f. multicolore**	3 »	1 25
	a. (Non dentelé)	70 »	

"Le peintre piétiné par son modèle", oeuvre de Jean Hélion.

2343	**5 f. multicolore**	3 »	1 25
	a. (Non dentelé)	70 »	

Tirage : 6 000 000 paires.

1984. – *Hommage à Vincent Auriol (1884-1966). Taille-douce. Dentelé 13.*

Portrait du Président.

2344	**2 f. 10 brun et vert**	1 »	0 30
	a. (Non dentelé)	14 »	

Tirage : 8 000 000.

1984. – *Au profit de la Croix-Rouge. "La corbeille rose", d'après une oeuvre de Caly. Héliogravure. Dentelé 12½ x 13.*

2345	**2 f. 10+50 c. multicolore**	1 25	1 10
	a. (Dentelé 13½ x 13)	1 40	1 25
	b. (Non dentelé)	46 »	

A été aussi émis en carnets (tirage : 500 000 carnets). Le n° 2345a provient des carnets.

Tirage : 4 000 000.

1984. – *9e Plan. Moderniser la France. Héliogravure. Dentelé 13.*

Symbole du 9e Plan.

2346	**2 f. 10 bleu, rouge et noir**	1 10	0 30
	a. (Non dentelé)	15 »	

Tirage : 10 000 000.

> **1984**
>
> **Du n° 2299 au n° 2346**
>
> **(sauf bandes carnets, paires et triptyques) :**
>
> **49 timbres** ****71** **⊙33**
>
> Autres rubriques de l'année :
>
> Poste aérienne 57
>
> Préoblitérés 182 à 185
>
> Service 79 à 84

1985. – *La Francophonie. Taille-douce. Dentelé 13.*

Symbolique de l'égalité et de l'union entre peuples différents.

2347	**3 f. bleu foncé et bleu clair**	1 40	0 50
	a. (Non dentelé)	14 »	

Tirage : 7 000 000.

1985. – *Série touristique. Taille-douce. Dentelés 13.*

Vienne (Isère).

Abbaye de Landévennec (1500e anniversaire).

2348	**1 f. 70 vert, brun clair et brun foncé**	1 »	0 30
2349	**1 f. 70 vert et violet**	1 »	0 30

Millénaire de la fondation de Montpellier (985).

Abbaye Saint-Michel-de-Cuxa.

2350	**2 f. 10 brun et jaune**	1 10	0 50
2351	**2 f. 20 beige, brun, bleu et rouge**	1 10	0 30
	a. (198 au lieu de 1985)	80 »	40 »

Saintonge Romane : l'Église de Talmont.

2352	**3 f. brun, rouge et bleu**	1 40	0 70
	Nos 2348 à 2352 (5 val.)	**5 60**	**2 10**
	La série, non dentelée	70 »	

Tirages : 10 000 000, 7 000 000, 10 000 000, 10 000 000 et 7 000 000.

1985. – ***50e anniversaire de la Télévision. Héliogravure. Dentelé 13.***

Représentation schématique du balayage de l'écran par le "spot" électronique.

2353	**2 f. 50 multicolore**	1 25	0 65
	a. (Non dentelé)	17 »	

Tirage : 6 000 000.

1985. – ***La Saint-Valentin. Héliogravure. Dentelé 13.***

"Les amoureux", de Peynet.

2354	**2 f. 10 multicolore**	1 10	0 30
	a. (Non dentelé)	50 »	
	b. (Valeur omise)	17 500 »	
	c. (Oiseau dans la branche)	15 »	

Tirage : 12 000 000.

1985. – ***Personnages célèbres. Écrivains. Taille-douce. Dent. 13.*** [C]

Romain Rolland (1866-1944). Jules Romains (1885-1972).

2355	**1 f. 70+40 c. rouge violacé et violet foncé**	1 50	1 50
	a. (Dentelé 15 x 15½)	3 »	3 »
2356	**1 f. 70+40 c. violet clair et violet foncé**	1 50	1 50
	a. (Dentelé 15 x 15½)	3 »	3 »

Jean-Paul Sartre (1905-1980). Victor Hugo (1802-1885).

2357	**1 f. 70+40 c. violet foncé et rouge violacé**	1 50	1 50
	a. (Dentelé 15 x 15½)	3 »	3 »
	b. (point sur le I de FRANCAISE)	20 »	15 »
2358	**2 f. 10+50 c. violet clair et rouge violacé**	1 50	1 50
	a. (Dentelé 15 x 15½)	3 »	3 »

Roland Dorgelès (1885-1973). François Mauriac (1885-1970).

2359	**2 f. 10+50 c. rouge violacé et violet foncé**	1 50	1 50
	a. (Dentelé 15 x 15½)	3 »	3 »
2360	**2 f. 10+50 c. violet clair et violet foncé**	1 50	1 50
	a. (Dentelé 15 x 15½)	3 »	3 »
	Nos 2355 à 2360 (6 val.)	**9 »**	**9 »**
	La série, non dentelée	110 »	

Tirage : 2 500 000 séries.

2360A	La bande carnet, non pliée	30 »	25 »

1985. – ***Hommage aux femmes. Taille-douce. Dentelé 13.***

Pauline Kergomard. Portrait de l'inspiratrice de l'école maternelle.

2361	**1 f. 70 bleu-gris et rouge**	1 »	0 30
	a. (Non dentelé)	14 »	

Tirage : 7 000 000.

1985. – *Journée du Timbre. Machine à oblitérer Daguin. Taille-douce. Dentelé 13.*

Vue de la machine et cachets.

2362	**2 f. 10+50 c. bistre foncé, gris et noir**	1 25	1 10
	a. (Non dentelé)	18 50	

Tirage : 4 500 000.

1985. – *Série artistique. Taille douce, sauf n° 2364 : héliogravure. Dentelés 12½-13.*

Vitrail de la cathédrale de Strasbourg.

2363	**5 f. multicolore**	3 »	1 25
	a. (Non dentelé)	70 »	
	b. (Vitrail jaune au lieu de vert)	500 »	

"Nature morte au chandelier", de Nicolas de Staël.

2364	**5 f. multicolore**	3 »	1 25
	a. (Non dentelé)	70 »	

Tirage : 6 000 000 paires.

1985. – *L'architecture contemporaine. Taille-douce. Dentelé 13.*

Vue de Givors.

2365	**2 f. 40 noir, vert et orange**	1 25	0 65
	a. (Non dentelé)	15 »	

Tirage : 6 000 000.

1985. – *Europa. Année européenne de la Musique. Taille-douce. Dentelés 13.*

Adam de la Halle (1240-1285), trouvère.

Darius Milhaud (1892-1974), compositeur.

2366	**2 f. 10 bleu, bleu clair et noir**	1 30	0 65
2367	**3 f. noir, bleu et bleu clair**	2 »	1 »
	La paire, non dentelée	92 »	

Tirages : 10 000 000 et 6 000 000.

1985. – *40e anniversaire de la Victoire. Taille-douce. Bleu, rouge, noir et or. Dentelés 13.*

2368	**2 f. *"Retour à la Paix"***	1 »	0 65
2369	**3 f. *"Retour à la Liberté"***	1 40	0 65

Tirage : 8 000 000 paires.

2369A	Le triptyque	2 45	2 15
	a. (Non dentelé)	80 »	

Imprimés attenant à une vignette centrale sans valeur en bande horizontale de 3 triptyques n° 2369B.

1985. – *58e Congrès national de la Fédération des Sociétés philatéliques françaises, à Tours. Taille-douce. Dentelé 13.*

La cathédrale de Tours.

2370	**2 f. 10 bleu-noir et turquoise**	1 10	0 50
	a. (Non dentelé)	14 »	

Tirage : 8 000 000.

1985. – *Centenaire de la découverte du vaccin contre la rage. Taille-douce. Dentelé 13.*

Vaccination d'un patient (gravure d'époque).

2371	**1 f. 50 vert foncé et rouge sur beige**	0 80	0 30
	a. (Non dentelé)	20 »	
	b. (sans point sur le "i" de "française")	10 »	3 »

Tirage : 10 000 000.

1985. – *Série "Grandes réalisations". Taille-douce. Dentelé 13.*

Mystère Falcon 900.

2372	**10 f. bleu**	4 60	2 30
	a. (Non dentelé)	54 »	

Tirage : 6 000 000.

1985. – *Centenaire de la Société internationale de sauvetage du Lac Léman. Taille-douce. Dentelé 13.*

Canot de sauvetage en action.

2373	**2 f. 50 bleu-gris, rouge et bleu**	1 25	0 65
	a. (Non dentelé)	23 »	

La Suisse a émis simultanément sur ce sujet une figurine de 70 c. (n° 1221 cotes : 1,35 1 »).

Tirage : 8 000 000.

1985. – *40e anniversaire de l'Organisation des Nations Unies. Taille-douce. Dentelé 13.*

Emblème de l'O.N.U.

2374	**3 f. bleu clair, bleu et gris**	1 40	0 50
	a. (Non dentelé)	23 »	

Tirage : 7 000 000.

1985. – *Type "Liberté" de Delacroix. Taille-douce. Deux bandes de phosphore, sauf n° 2375 : une bande de phosphore à droite. Dentelés 13.* ©

2375	**1 f. 80 vert**	1 »	0 15
	a. (sans bande de phosphore)	11 »	

Type I.

Type II. Barre du grand 2 plus droite et plus épaisse.

2376	**2 f. 20 rouge (I)**	1 »	0 15
	a. (Type II)	4 »	1 »
	c. (Type II, Papier couché)	100 »	
	d. (Type I, Papier couché)	5 »	
	e. (Type I, double frappe tenant à normal)	11 50	
	f. (sans bande de phosphore) (I)	4 »	
	g. (sans bande de phosphore) (II)	40 »	
2377	**3 f. 20 bleu**	3 »	1 »
	La série, non dentelée	40 »	

Le papier couché glacé fait apparaître une gravure plus fine et précise. Sur le 2376c les bandes de phosphore semblent jaunes.

1985. – *Type "Liberté" de Delacroix, provenant du carnet n° 1501. Paire se tenant horizontalement. Dentelure horizontale souvent rognée.* ©

2376b	2 f. 20+40 c. (n° 2183)	5 »	4 »

Pour le 2 f. 20 rouge dentelé sur 3 côtés voir au n° 2427.

Le 2 f. 20 a été imprimé en 1987, avec vignette attenante pour annoncer l'exposition philatélique mondiale "Philexfrance'89" (n° 2461), puis en 1988, sur un timbre de grand format horizontal (n° 2524).

Le 2 f. 20 a en outre été surchargé, en 1988, en ÉCU (n° 2530).

2005. – *Type "Liberté" de Delacroix, provenant de roulettes. Une bande de phosphore, sauf n° 2379 : deux bandes de phosphore. Dentelés 13 horizontalement.*

a

b

Depuis le mois de mars 1986, la numérotation des figurines a été modifiée. Les numéros rouges apparaissant au verso sont désormais apposés tous les cinq timbres. Les chiffres composant ces numéros sont également légèrement différents.

2378 **1 f. 80 vert** 1 » 0 50
a. (N° rouge au verso) 2 »
b. (N° rouge au verso) 3 »
c. (Gomme brillante) 25 »
d. (n° rouge type *b* au verso, Gomme brillante) (b) 70 »

2379 **2 f. 20 rouge** 1 » 0 30
a. (N° rouge au verso) 3 »
b. (N° rouge au verso) 2 »
c. (Gomme jaunâtre brillante, 1988) 3 »
d. (n° rouge type *b* au verso, gomme jaunâtre brillante, 1988) 7 »
e. (sans bande de phosphore) 10 »
f. (n° rouge au verso, sans bande de phosphore) 20 »

1985. – ***Tricentenaire de la révocation de l'Édit de Nantes : accueil des Huguenots. Taille-douce. Dentelé 13.***

La croix huguenote, emblème des Huguenots accueillis en tous pays du "Refuge".

2380 **2 f. 50 brun, rouge et bleu** 1 25 0 65
a. (Non dentelé) 20 »

Tirage : 10 000 000.

1985. – ***Série artistique. Taille douce, sauf n° 2381 : héliogravure. Dentelés 12½-13.***

"L'égaré", Oeuvre de Dubuffet.

2381 **5 f. polychrome** 3 » 1 25
a. (Non dentelé) 70 »

Oeuvre de Pierre Alechinsky.

2382 **5 f. vert clair, rouge et noir** 3 » 1 25
a. (Non dentelé) 70 »

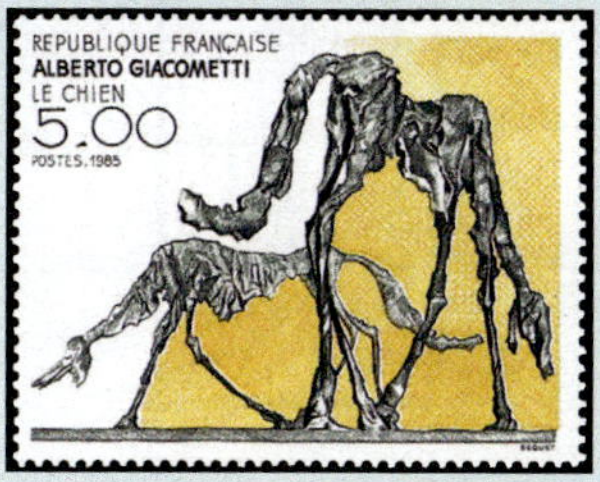

"Le chien", sculpture par Alberto Giacometti.

2383 **5 f. olive clair et noir** 3 » 1 25
a. (Non dentelé) 80 »

Tirage : 6 000 000 séries.

1985. – ***Flore et faune de France (III). Arbres. Dentelés 13.***

Fagus sylvatica.

Ulmus montana.

2384 **1 f. multicolore** 0 65 0 30
2385 **2 f. multicolore** 1 25 0 30

Quercus pedunculata.

Picea abies.

2386 **3 f. multicolore** 1 60 0 80
2387 **5 f. multicolore** 2 50 0 60

N°s 2384 à 2387 (4 val.) **6 »** **2 »**
La série, non dentelée 110 »

Tirage : 8 000 000 séries.

1985. – *Série touristique. Dentelé 13.*

Solutré.

2388	**3 f. 90 brun, bleu et rouge**	2 »	0 50
	a. (Non dentelé)	15 »	

Tirage : 12 000 000.

1985. – *La France à ses morts. 65e anniversaire de l'inhumation du Soldat inconnu sous l'Arc de Triomphe. Dentelé 13.*

Allégorie.

2389	**1 f. 80 rouge violacé, brun clair et noir**	1 »	0 30
	a. (Non dentelé)	14 »	

Tirage : 12 000 000.

1985. – *Hommage à Charles Dullin. Dentelé 13.*

Portrait.

2390	**3 f. 20 noir et bleu**	1 50	0 65
	a. (Non dentelé)	14 »	

Tirage : 7 000 000.

1985. – *La documentation française. Dentelé 13.*

Livre et planisphère, clavier d'ordinateur.

2391	**2 f. 20 noir et rouge**	1 »	0 30
	a. (Non dentelé)	15 »	

Tirage : 15 000 000.

1985. – *Au profit de la Croix-rouge. Retable d'Issenheim Colmar. Dentelé 12½ x 13.*

2392	**2 f. 20+50 c multicolore**	1 25	1 »
	a. (Dentelé 13½ x 13)	1 25	1 »
	b. (Non dentelé)	40 »	

A été aussi émis en carnets (tirage : 600 000 carnets). Le n° 2392a provient des carnets.

Tirage : 3 500 000.

1985

Du n° 2347 au n° 2392

(sauf bandes-carnets, paires et triptyques) :

46 timbres ****73** **⊙36**

Autres rubriques de l'année :

Poste aérienne 58

Préoblitérés 186 à 189

Service 85 à 90

A compter du 1-1-1986, nous indiquons sous "Tirage" les chiffres de vente.

1986. – *Tricentenaire des relations diplomatiques avec la Thaïlande. Emission conjointe France-Thaïlande. Taille-douce. Dentelé 13.*

Les émissaires du Roi de Siam présentant à Louis XIV leurs lettres de créance.

2393	**3 f. 20 rouge violacé et noir**	1 70	0 80
	a. (Non dentelé)	17 »	

La Thaïlande a émis simultanément sur ce sujet deux figurines de 2 b. et 8 b. 50 (n° 1131/32 cotes : 4,60 2,50).

Tirage : 5 658 008.

1986. – *Cinquantenaire du Front populaire. Héliogravure. Dentelé 13.*

"Les Loisirs", d'après Fernand Léger.

2394	**2 f. 20 multicolore**	1 »	0 30
	a. (Non dentelé)	30 »	

Tirage : 15 465 238.

1986. – *Carnaval. Venise à Paris. Héliogravure. Dentelé 12½ x 13.*

Tour Eiffel et masques.

2395	**2 f. 20 multicolore et or**	1 »	0 30
	a. (Non dentelé)	25 »	
	b. (Tour Eiffel jaune au lieu de vert)	20 »	

Tirage : 14 456 244.

1986. – *Personnages célèbres. Physicien, chimistes et ingénieurs. Taille-douce. Dentelés 13.* [C]

François Arago, physicien (1786-1853).

Henri Moissan, chimiste (1852-1907).

2396	**1 f. 80+40 c. gris, bleu et vert**	1 »	1 »
2397	**1 f. 80+40 c. gris, bleu et vert**	1 »	1 »

Henri Fabre, ingénieur (1882-1984).

Marc Seguin, ingénieur (1786-1875).

Paul Héroult, chimiste (1863-1914).

2398	**1 f. 80+40 c. gris, bleu et vert**	1 »	1 »
2399	**2 f. 20+50 c. gris, vert et bleu**	1 25	1 25
2400	**2 f. 20+50 c. gris, vert et bleu**	1 25	1 25
	N°s 2396 à 2400 (5 val.)	**5 50**	**5 50**
	La série, non dentelée	92 »	

Tirages : 1 727 727, 1 705 385, 1 737 701, 1 727 204 et 1 677 350.

Ont été aussi émis en carnets (tirage : 1 224 392).

La bande (format horizontal) destinée à la confection de carnets et comprenant les timbres 2396 à 2400 est disposée comme suit (de gauche à droite) : guillochis, vignette, 2396, 2399, 2397, 2400, 2398, vignette.

BC2400A	La bande-carnet non pliée	6 »	6 »

Voir après le n° 2360 la présentation de la bande.

1986. – *Série touristique. Taille-douce. Dentelés 13.*

Monument mégalithique de Filitosa (Corse du Sud).

Château de Loches.

2401	**1 f. 80 multicolore**	1 »	0 30
2402	**2 f. bleu-gris et noir**	1 10	0 70

Manoir normand, à Saint-Germain de Livet.

Cloître de Notre-Dame-en-Vaux, à Châlons-sur-Marne.

2403	**2 f. 20 brun, bleu-gris et vert**	1 10	0 50
2404	**2 f. 50 brun et rouge**	1 40	0 50
	a. (Double frappe)	11 50	

Bastide de Monpazier (Dordogne).

2405	**3 f. 90 ocre-jaune et noir**	2 40	1 »
	N°s 2401 à 2405 (5 val.)	**7 »**	**3 »**
	La série, non dentelée	80 »	

Tirages : 9 690 496, 5 749 800, 12 197 138, 6 800 730 et 4 862 657.

1986. – *Hommage à Pierre Cot (1895-1977). Surtaxe. Taille-douce. Dentelé 13.*

Portrait de l'homme politique.

2406	**2 f. 20+50 c. brun et noir**	1 50	1 50
	a. (Non dentelé)	17 »	

Tirage : 1 750 000.

1986. – *La Typographie. Taille-douce. Dentelé 12½ x 13.*

Figure allégorique.

2407	**5 f. noir et rouge**	3 »	1 25
	a. (Non dentelé)	70 »	

Tirage : 5 014 497.

1986. – *Hommage aux Femmes. Taille-douce. Dentelé 13.*

Louise Michel (1830-1905).

2408	**1 f. 80 noir et rouge**	1 »	0 30
	a. (Non dentelé)	14 »	

Tirage : 13 258 357.

1986. – *La Villette, cité des Sciences et de l'Industrie. Dentelé 13.*

Vue d'une partie des aménagements.

2409	**3 f. 90 multicolore**	2 »	0 65
	a. (Non dentelé)	21 50	
	b. bleu foncé omis	800 »	

Tirage : 7 191 188.

1986. – *Journée du Timbre. Taille-douce. Dentelé 13.*

Malle-poste Briska.

2410	**2 f. 20+60 c. marron sur beige**	1 40	1 25
	a. (Non dentelé)	23 »	

Tirage : 2 241 433.

1986. – *Idem. Timbre provenant de carnet. Dentelé.* 🄲

2411	**2 f. 20+60 c. brun foncé sur jaune clair**	1 50	1 40

Tirage : 1 011 328 séries.

La bande (format vertical) destinée à la confection de carnets comprend six n° 2411 plus deux vignettes.

BC2411A	La bande-carnet	9 »	9 »

Voir après le n° 2360 la présentation de la bande.

1986. – *Centre des Hautes Etudes sur l'Afrique et l'Asie Modernes. Héliogravure. Dentelé 13.*

Carte des deux continents.

2412	**3 f. 20 rouge, vert et noir**	1 50	0 50
	a. (Non dentelé)	17 »	

Tirage : 5 744 816.

1986. – *Série artistique. Héliogravure. Dentelés 13 x 12½.*

"Skibet", de Maurice Estève.

2413	**5 f. multicolore**	3 »	1 25
	a. (Non dentelé)	70 »	

"Virginia", d'Alberto Magnelli.

2414	**5 f. multicolore**	3 »	1 40
	a. (Non dentelé)	70 »	
	b. (Légende absente)	2 850 »	

Tirages : 4 658 187 et 4 830 517.

1986. – *Année internationale de la Paix. Taille-douce. Dentelé 13.*

Portrait de Victor Basch (1863-1944), et emblème de l'année.

2415 **2 f. 50 noir et vert clair** 1 25 0 50
a. (Non dentelé) 21 »

Tirage : 7 101 440.

1986. – *Europa. Protection de la nature et de l'environnement. Mammifères. Taille-douce. Dentelés 13.*

Genette. Petit rhinolophe.

2416 **2 f. 20 noir et rouge** 1 50 0 40
2417 **3 f. 20 noir et rouge** 2 » 0 80

La paire, non dentelée 92 »

Tirages : 12 106 214 et 6 187 592.

1986. – *Bicentenaire de la naissance de saint J.M.B. Vianney (1786-1859), curé d'Ars. Taille-douce. Dentelé 13.*

Portrait du Saint, vue de l'église.

2418 **1 f. 80 brun, brun foncé et brun clair** 1 » 0 30
a. (Non dentelé) 23 »

Tirage : 12 118 058.

1986. – *59e Congrès national de la Fédération des Sociétés philatéliques françaises, à Nancy. Taille-douce. Dentelé 13.*

La porte de la Craffe.

2419 **2 f. 20 bleu-gris et vert** 1 » 0 30
a. (Non dentelé) 14 »

Tirage : 11 889 017.

1986. – *Championnat du monde masculin de volley-ball. Taille-douce. Dentelé 13.*

2420 **2 f. 20 violet, brun-lilas et rouge** 1 » 0 50
a. (Non dentelé) 23 »

Tirage : 11 378 250.

1986. – *Centenaire de l'érection de la statue de la Liberté, à New York. Emission conjointe France-États-Unis. Taille-douce. Dentelé 13.*

Tête de la Statue.

2421 **2 f. 20 bleu et rouge** 1 » 0 30
a. (Non dentelé) 58 »

Les Etats-Unis ont émis simultanément une figurine au même type de 22 c. (n° 1672 cotes : 1 » 0,40).

Voir également à la rubrique "Entiers postaux" (n° 2421-CP1).

Tirage : 21 562 605.

1986. – *Bicentenaire de la première ascension du Mont-Blanc (8 août 1786), par le guide Balmat et le Dr Paccard. Taille-douce. Dentelé 13.*

2422 **2 f. bleu, bleu-vert et brun** 1 » 0 65
a. (Non dentelé) 23 »

Tirage : 6 316 152.

1986. – *Type Liberté avec lettre A (valeur du tarif postal pour P.N.U. de 20 gr maximum : 1 f. 90 à compter du 1.8.86). Taille-douce. Une bande de phosphore. Dentelé 13.*

2423 **A = (1 f. 90) vert** 1 » 0 30
a. (Non dentelé) 11 50
b. (sans bande de phosphore) 4 »
c. (Antenne sur le front) 30 » 15 »

1986. – *Type "Liberté" de Delacroix.. Taille-douce. Une bande de phosphore à droite, sauf n° 2425 : deux bandes de phosphore. Dentelés 13.* [C]

2424	**1 f. 90 vert**	1 50	0 15
	a. (sans bande de phosphore)	14 »	
2425	**3 f. 40 bleu**	2 »	1 »
	La paire, non dentelée	23 »	

1986. – *Type "Liberté" de Delacroix, provenant de roulettes. Dentelé 13 horizontalement.*

2426	**1 f. 90 vert**	1 50	0 50
	a. (N° rouge au verso)	3 »	
	b. (sans bande de phosphore)	61 »	

1986. – *Type "Liberté" de Delacroix, provenant de carnets. Deux bandes de phosphore. Dentelé 13 sur 3 côtés.* [C]

2427	**2 f. 20 rouge**	1 25	0 30
	a. (Paire verticale)	3 »	2 30

1986. – *250ᵉ anniversaire des mesures d'arcs de méridien par Maupertuis, en Laponie. Emission conjointe franco-finnoise. Taille-douce. Dentelé 13.*

Compas ; effigies de Maupertuis et La Condamine.

2428	**3 f. bleu et gris foncé**	1 50	0 65
	a. (Non dentelé)	23 »	

La Finlande a émis simultanément une figurine au même type de 1 m. 60 (n° 966 cotes : 1,50 0,45).

L'Équateur a de son côté commémoré la partie équatoriale de cet événement scientifique.

Tirage : 6 185 949.

1986. – *Série "Nature de France" (IV). Minéraux. Taille-douce. Dentelés 13.*

Marcassite.

Quartz.

2429	**2 f. jaune, noir et lilas**	1 10	0 30
2430	**3 f. bleu clair, noir et lilas**	1 40	0 30

Calcite.

Fluorite.

2431	**4 f. brun clair, noir et lilas**	2 »	1 »
2432	**5 f. turquoise, noir et lilas**	2 50	0 80
	N°s 2429 à 2432 (4 val.)	**7 »**	**2 40**
	La série, non dentelée	125 »	

Tirages : 6 589 906, 5 803 786, 4 787 581 et 5 014 583.

1986. – *Cinquantenaire de la cinémathèque française. Héliogravure. Dentelés 13 x 13½.* [BF] *n° 9.*

Louis Feuillade - "Les vampires".

Max Linder.

2433	**2 f. 20 noir et gris**	1 50	1 25
2434	**2 f. 20 noir et gris**	1 50	1 25

Sacha Guitry - "Le roman d'un tricheur".

Jean Renoir - "La grande illusion".

2435	**2 f. 20 noir et gris**	1 50	1 25
2436	**2 f. 20 noir et gris**	1 50	1 25

Marcel Pagnol - "La femme du boulanger".

Jean Epstein - "La glace à trois faces".

2437	**2 f. 20 noir et gris**	1 50	1 25
2438	**2 f. 20 noir et gris**	1 50	1 25

René Clair - "Les belles de nuit".

Jean Grémillon - "Gueule d'amour".

2439	**2 f. 20 noir et gris**	1 50	1 25
2440	**2 f. 20 noir et gris**	1 50	1 25

Jacques Becker - "Casque d'or".

François Truffaut - "L'enfant sauvage".

2441	**2 f. 20 noir et gris**	1 50	1 25
2442	**2 f. 20 noir et gris**	1 50	1 25

N°s 2433 à 2442 (10 val.) **15 »** **12 50**

Tirage : 2 364 800 séries.

Emis uniquement en feuillet.

1986. – *Centenaire de la naissance d'Henri Alain-Fournier (1886-1914). Taille-douce. Dentelé 13.*

Illustration du livre "Le Grand Meaulnes".

2443	**2 f. 20 noir et rouge**	1 »	0 50
	a. (Non dentelé)	18 50	

Tirage : 14 854 238.

1986. – *Centenaire de l'enseignement technique. Taille-douce. Dentelé 13.*

Circuit imprimé, profil féminin, équerre et rapporteur.

2444	**1 f. 90 violet et rose carminé**	1 »	0 30
	a. (Non dentelé)	14 »	

Tirage : 14 645 588.

1986. – *Conférence mondiale de l'énergie, à Cannes. Héliogravure. Dentelé 13.*

Symbole.

2445	**3 f. 40 bleu foncé, rose et rouge**	1 70	0 80
	a. (Gomme tropicale)	3 »	
	b. (Non dentelé)	15 »	

Tirage : 6 990 654.

1986. – *Série artistique. Dentelés 12½-13.*

"Portrait d'Isabelle d'Este", de Léonard de Vinci.

2446	**5 f. jaune clair et brun**	3 »	1 10
	a. (Non dentelé)	80 »	

"La danseuse", de Jean Arp.

2447 **5 f. multicolore** 3 » 1 10
a. (Non dentelé) 70 »

Oeuvre de Pierre Soulages.

2448 **5 f. violet, gris et noir** 3 » 1 10
a. (Non dentelé) 70 »

Tirages : 4 743 992, 4 751 615 et 4 839 227.

1986. – ***Au profit de la Croix-Rouge. Vitrail de Vieira da Silva (église Saint-Jacques de Reims, Marne). Héliogravure. Dentelé 12½ x 13.*** [C]

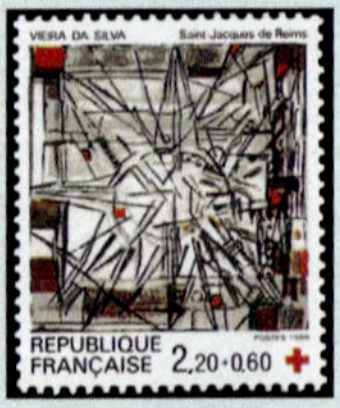

2449 **2 f. 20+60 c. gris, noir et rouge** 1 40 1 10
a. (Dentelé 13 x 13½) 1 60 1 25
b. (Non dentelé) 46 »

A été aussi émis en carnets (tirage : 637 434). Le n° 2449a provient des carnets.

Tirage : 1 900 058.

1986. – ***Les Musées techniques de Mulhouse. Taille-douce. Dentelé 13.*** [C]

Automobile, locomotive
et étoffe imprimée.

2450 **2 f. 20 noir, rouge et bleu** 1 25 0 50
a. (Non dentelé) 30 »

Tirage : 15 696 071.

1986. – ***Inauguration du Musée d'Orsay. Héliogravure. Dentelé 13.***

Façade du bâtiment.

2451 **3 f. 70 bleu clair sur bleu foncé** 1 70 0 80
a. (Non dentelé) 27 »

Ce timbre porte le millésime "1987".

Tirage : 8 715 853.

1986

Du n° 2393 au n° 2451

(sauf bandes-carnets, paires et triptyques) :

59 timbres ****92** **⊙48**

Autres rubriques de l'année :

Poste aérienne 59

Bloc-feuillet 9

Préoblitérés 190 à 193

Service 91 à 95

1987. – ***Hommage à Fulgence Bienvenue (1852-1936), créateur du métropolitain de Paris. Taille-douce. Dentelé 13.***

Portrait, et rame de métro.

2452 **2 f. 50 brun, vert et violet** 1 25 0 50
a. (Non dentelé) 30 »

Tirage : 6 898 795.

1987. – ***Hommage à Raoul Follereau (1903-1977), "père" des lépreux. Taille-douce. Dentelé 13.***

Portrait.

2453 **1 f. 90 vert foncé et vert clair** 1 » 0 30
a. (Non dentelé) 15 »

Tirage : 13 187 607.

1987. – ***Personnages célèbres médecins et biologistes. Taille-douce. Gomme tropicale. Dentelés 13.*** 🄲

Charles Richet, physiologiste (1850-1935). Prix Nobel 1913.

Eugène Jamot, médecin (1879-1937).

2454 **1 f. 90+50 c. bleu-gris** 1 » 1 »
2455 **1 f. 90+50 c. violet-brun** 1 » 1 »

Bernard Halpern, immunologiste (1804-1978).

Alexandre Yersin, microbiologiste (1863-1943).

2456 **1 f. 90+50 c. gris-vert** 1 » 1 »
2457 **2 f. 20+50 c. gris-vert** 1 10 1 10

Jean Rostand, biologiste et écrivain (1894-1977).

Jacques Monod, biologiste (1910-1976). Prix Nobel 1965.

2458 **2 f. 20+50 c. bleu-gris** 1 10 1 10
2459 **2 f. 20+50 c. violet-brun** 1 10 1 10

Nos 2454 à 2459 (6 val.) **6 30** **6 30**

La série, non dentelée 80 »

Tirages : 1 597 149, 1 588 002, 1 599 507, 1 593 116, 1 600 228 et 1 599 816.

Gomme brillante.

Nos 2454a à 2459a (6 val.) 10 »

Ont été aussi émis en carnets (tirage : 1 112 598). Les 2454a à 2459a proviennent des carnets.

La bande (format vertical), destinée à la confection de carnets et comprenant les timbres nos 2454a à 2459a est disposée comme suit (de haut en bas).

Vignette, 2454a, 2457a, 2455a, 2458a, 2456a, 2459a, vignette.

Voir après le no 2360 la présentation de la bande.

BC2460 La bande carnet, non pliée 10 » 10 »

1987. – ***"Philexfrance'89" : exposition philatélique mondiale, à Paris, du 7 au 17 juillet 1989. T.-P. de 1985 émis attenant à une vignette sans valeur comportant une adaptation du logotype de l'exposition. Dentelé 13.***

2461 **2 f. 20 rouge (2376)** 1 » 0 30
a. (Non dentelé) 46 »

Ce timbre a été émis en feuilles de 50 figurines, attenant chacune à une vignette.

Est connu sans bandes de phosphore.

Tirage : 19 866 306.

1987. – ***Série touristique. Dentelure 13, sauf n° 2465 : 13 x 12½.***

Redon. Clocher de l'abbatiale.

Vue d'Étretat, d'après E. Delacroix.

2462 **2 f. 20 noir, brun et violet** 1 » 0 30
2463 **2 f. 20 multicolore** 1 » 0 65

Château d'Azay-le-Rideau.

Les Baux de Provence.

2464 **2 f. 50 turquoise et olive** 1 40 0 65
2465 **3 f. brun et violet** 1 60 0 50

Les Côtes de Meuse.

2466 **3 f. 70 brun-rouge, violet et bleu-gris** 2 » 1 90

Nos 2462 à 2466 (5 val.) **7 »** **4 »**

La série, non dentelée 80 »

Tirages : 10 372 259, 15 214 784, 6 734 412, 5 472 387 et 6 020 150.

1987. – ***Série "Métiers d'art". La coutellerie Thiers. Taille-douce. Dentelé 13.***

Emouleur au travail.

2467 **1 f. 90 noir et rouge foncé** 1 » 0 30
a. (Non dentelé) 14 »

Tirage : 11 314 323.

1987. – ***Journée du Timbre. Taille-douce. Dentelé 13.***

Berline.

2468 **2 f. 20+60 c. brun sur beige clair** 1 40 1 10
a. (Non dentelé) 23 »

Tirage : 2 165 203.

1987. – ***Idem. Timbre provenant de carnet. Dentelé 13.*** [C]

2469 2 f. 20+60 c. bleu sur bleu clair 1 50 1 25

Tirage : 972 323 séries.

La bande (format vertical) destinée à la confection de carnets comprend six n° 2469 plus deux vignettes.

Voir après le n° 2360 la présentation de la bande.

BC2469A La bande carnet, non pliée 9 » 9 »

1987. – ***Centenaire de la naissance de Le Corbusier (1887-1965), architecte et urbaniste. Héliogravure. Dentelé 13 x 12½.***

Le "Modulor".

2470 3 f. 70 noir, rouge, bleu et brun clair 1 50 0 65
a. (Non dentelé) 25 »

Tirage : 6 522 477.

1987. – ***Europa. Architecture moderne. Taille-douce. Dentelés 13.***

"57 métal" Boulogne-Billancourt. Rue Mallet-Stevens Paris 16ᵉ.

2471 2 f. 20 bleu et vert 1 50 0 70
2472 3 f. 40 brun et vert 2 » 0 90

La paire, non dentelée 80 »

Tirages : 10 649 881 et 5 344 668.

1987. – ***Série artistique. Dentelés 13 x 12½.***

Oeuvre de Bram Van Velde (1895-1981).

2473 5 f. multicolore 3 » 1 25
a. (Non dentelé) 70 »

"Femme à l'ombrelle", d'Eugène Boudin (1824-1898).

2474 5 f. multicolore 3 » 1 85
a. (Non dentelé) 70 »

Tirages : 4 855 255 et 4 472 074.

1987. – ***Centenaire de la naissance de l'écrivain Henri Pourrat (1887-1959). Taille-douce. Dentelé 13.***

Illustration de "Gaspard des Montagnes".

2475 1 f. 90 brun et vert 1 » 0 30
a. (Non dentelé) 14 »

Tirage : 9 194 800.

1987. – ***60ᵉ Congrès national de la Fédération des Sociétés philatéliques françaises, à Lens. Taille-douce. Dentelé 13.***

2476 2 f. 20 rouge et brun 1 » 0 50
a. (Non dentelé) 14 »

Tirage : 9 072 088.

1987. – ***70ᵉ anniversaire de l'entrée en guerre des États-Unis, lors de la 1ʳᵉ Guerre mondiale. Taille-douce. Dentelé 13.***

Général Pershing, soldats, drapeau.

2477 3 f. 40 vert, rouge et bleu 1 70 1 »
a. (Non dentelé) 40 »

Tirage : 5 632 166.

1987. – ***Millénaire de l'avènement d'Hugues Capet. Offset. Dentelé 13.***

Sceau et cathédrale de Noyon.

2478 **1 f. 90 bleu clair et noir** 1 » 0 65

a. (Non dentelé) 15 »

Tirage : 6 365 174.

1987. – ***Le Prytanée national militaire de la Flèche (Sarthe). Taille-douce. Dentelé 13.***

Bâtiment principal et portail d'entrée.

2479 **2 f. 20 vert, turquoise et brun clair** 1 » 0 50

a. (Non dentelé) 15 »

Tirage : 9 121 641.

1987. – ***6e Congrès international des transports à câbles, à Grenoble. Héliogravure. Dentelé 13.***

Chaîne de nacelles sur fond montagneux.

2480 **2 f. bleu, noir et vert** 1 » 0 80

a. (Non dentelé) 15 »

b. (vert omis) 4 200 »

Tirage : 7 225 043.

1987. – ***Rassemblement mondial des "Pieds-Noirs" : Nice 25 ans après. Héliogravure. Dentelé 13.***

2481 **1 f. 90 bleu, rouge, noir et gris** 1 » 0 65

a. (Non dentelé) 17 »

Tirage : 5 582 608.

1987. – ***Championnats du monde de lutte, à Clermont-Ferrand. Dentelé 13.***

Mappemonde et lutteurs.

2482 **3 f. brun clair, gris et violet** 1 50 0 80

a. (Non dentelé) 30 »

Tirage : 5 514 618.

1987. – ***Type Liberté avec lettre B. (Valeur du tarif postal pour P.N.U. de 20 g maximum : 2 F à compter du 1.8.87). Taille-douce. Une bande de phosphore. Dentelé 13.***

2483 **B = (2 f.) vert** 1 » 0 30

a. (Non dentelé) 11 50

b. (sans bande de phosphore) 25 »

1987. – ***Type "Liberté" de Delacroix. Taille-douce. Deux bandes de phosphore, sauf n° 2484 : une bande de phosphore à droite. Dentelés 13.***

2484 **2 f. vert** 1 » 0 15

a. (sans bande de phosphore) 46 »

2485 **3 f. 60 bleu** 1 50 0 65

a. (Papier couché) 15 »

2486 **3 f. 70 rose** 1 50 0 50

a. (Une bande de phosphore à droite) 4 » 0 80

La série, non dentelée 35 »

1987. – ***Type "Liberté" de Delacroix, provenant de roulettes. Une bande de phosphore à droite. Dentelé 13 horizontalement.***

2487	**2 f. vert**	1 25	0 60
	a. (N° rouge au verso)	1 60	
	b. (gomme brillante jaunâtre, 1988)	4 »	
	c. (n° rouge au verso, gomme brillante jaunâtre, 1988)	8 »	
	d. (sans bande de phosphore)	12 50	

1987. – ***Flore et faune de France (V). Champignons. Taille-douce. Dentelés 12½.***

Indigotier (Gyroporus cyanescens).

Chanterelle violette (Gomphus clavatus).

2488	**2 f. bleu, jaune et brun**	1 10	0 30
2489	**3 f. violet, jaune et bistre**	1 40	0 50

Morille conique (Morchella conica).

Palomet (Russula virescens).

2490	**4 f. brun, jaune et noir**	2 »	1 40
2491	**5 f. vert, brun et noir**	2 50	1 »
	N°s 2488 à 2491 (4 val.)	**7 »**	**3 20**
	La série, non dentelée	125 »	

Tirages : 7 898 588, 6 173 011, 4 947 838 et 6 074 754.

1987. – ***900e anniversaire de la mort de Guillaume le Conquérant. Taille-douce. Dentelé 13.***

Guillaume et ses frères (d'après la tapisserie de Bayeux).

2492	**2 f. brun, rouge et vert**	1 »	0 50
	a. (Non dentelé)	20 »	

Tirage : 6 985 275.

1987. – ***Série artistique. Dentelés 12½-13.***

Oeuvre de Camille Bryen, "Précambrien".

2493	**5 f. multicolore**	3 »	1 25
	a. (Non dentelé)	70 »	

Oeuvre d'Antoine Pevsner, "Monde".

2494	**5 f. brun, beige rosé et noir**	3 »	1 25
	a. (Non dentelé)	70 »	

Tirages : 5 126 658 et 5 175 365.

1987. – ***Montbenoît, "capitale" de la "République" du Saugeais. Taille-douce. Dentelé 13.***

Les fondateurs ; chapiteaux du cloître ; les 24 heures des neiges.

2495	**2 f. 50 bleu, rouge et bleu-noir**	1 25	0 65
	a. (Non dentelé)	14 »	

Tirage : 6 633 075.

1987. – ***Centenaire de l'Institut Pasteur. Taille-douce. Dentelé 13.***

L'entrée principale.

2496	**2 f. 20 rouge et bleu**	1 »	0 30
	a. (Non dentelé)	15 »	

Voir également à la rubrique "Entiers postaux" (n° 2496-CP1).

Tirage : 14 197 436.

1987. – ***Centenaire de la naissance de Blaise Cendrars (1887-1961). Taille-douce. Dentelé 12½.***

Portrait du poète et écrivain, d'après Modigliani.

2497	**2 f. gris, vert et jaune**	1 »	0 50
	a. (Non dentelé)	30 »	

Tirage : 13 691 216.

1987. – ***Au profit de la Croix-Rouge. Retable de la Chartreuse de Champmol. Héliogravure. Dentelé 12½ x 13.***

"La fuite en Égypte", de Melchior Broederlam.

2498	**2 f. 20+60 c. multicolore**	1 25	1 »
	a. (Dentelé 13½ x 13)	1 40	1 10
	b. (Non dentelé)	42 »	

A été aussi émis en carnets (tirage : 728 126). Le n° 2498a provient des carnets.

Tirage : 2 098 021.

1987. – ***40e anniversaire de la mort du Général Leclerc, Maréchal de France (1902-1947). Taille-douce. Dentelé 13.***

Portrait, char et monuments.

2499	**2 f. 20 brun, brun clair et gris**	1 25	0 30
	a. (Non dentelé)	20 »	

Tirage : 13 961 416.

1987. – ***1400e anniversaire du Traité d'Andelot. Taille-douce. Dentelé 13.***

Gontran, Chilpéric II et Brunehaut, sur fond de parchemin.

2500	**3 f. 70 bleu foncé, gris et bleu clair**	1 85	0 65
	a. (Non dentelé)	15 »	

Tirage : 6 526 313.

1987

Du n° 2452 au n° 2500

(sauf bandes-carnets, paires et triptyques) :

48 timbres ****69** **⊙36**

Autres rubriques de l'année :

Poste aérienne 60

Préoblitérés 194 à 197

Service 96 à 99

1988. – ***25e anniversaire du traité sur la coopération franco-allemande. Émission conjointe France-R.F.A. Taille-douce. Dentelé 13.***

Portraits du Chancelier Adenauer et du Général De Gaulle.

2501	**2 f. 20 noir et violet-brun**	1 50	0 50
	a. (Non dentelé)	30 »	

La R.F.A. a émis simultanément une figurine au même type de 80 p. (n° 1183 cotes : 2,50 0,75).

Tirage : 19 736 659.

1988. – *Hommage à Marcel Dassault (1892-1986). Taille-douce. Dentelé 13.*

Portrait de l'avionneur et avions.

2502	**3 f. 60 bleu-rouge et brun**	2 »	0 80
	a. (Non dentelé)	28 »	

Tirage : 5 129 018.

1988. – *"La Communication", vue par 12 auteurs de bandes dessinées français, lauréats du "Grand Prix"du Festival d'Angoulême. Héliogravure. Multicolores. Dentelés 13½ x 13.* C

Pellos. Reiser.

2503	**2 f. 20 multicolore**	1 »	0 80
2504	**2 f. 20 multicolore**	1 »	0 80

Marijac. Fred.

2505	**2 f. 20 multicolore**	1 »	0 80
2506	**2 f. 20 multicolore**	1 »	0 80

Giraud-Moebius. Gillon.

2507	**2 f. 20 multicolore**	1 »	0 80
2508	**2 f. 20 multicolore**	1 »	0 80

Brétécher. Forest.

2509	**2 f. 20 multicolore**	1 »	0 80
2510	**2 f. 20 multicolore**	1 »	0 80

Mezières. Tardi.

2511	**2 f. 20 multicolore**	1 »	0 80
2512	**2 f. 20 multicolore**	1 »	0 80

Lob. Bilal.

2513	**2 f. 20 multicolore**	1 »	0 80
2514	**2 f. 20 multicolore**	1 »	0 80
	Nos 2503 à 2514 (12 val.)	**12 »**	**9 60**

Tirage : 3 252 778 séries.

Emis uniquement en carnets.

Voir également à la rubrique "Prêt-à-Poster" (no 2514-E1).

La bande (format vertical) destinée à la confection de carnets.

BC2515	La bande carnet, non pliée	12 »	10 »
	a. non dentelée	275 »	

1988. – *La Grande Synagogue de la rue de la Victoire, à Paris. Offset. Dentelé 13.*

2516	**2 f. noir et or**	1 »	0 50
	a. (Non dentelé)	23 »	
	b. (Double impression)	270 »	

Tirage : 13 680 577.

1988. – ***Personnages célèbres. Grands navigateurs français. Buste et carte de leurs périples. Taille-douce. Dentelés 13.*** [C]

Duquesne (1610-1688). Suffren (1729-1788).

2517	**2 f. +50 c. noir, bleu clair et marron clair**	1 »	1 »
2518	**2 f. +50 c. noir, bleu clair et marron clair**	1 »	1 »

La Pérouse (1741-1788). La Bourdonnais (1699-1753).

2519	**2 f. +50 c. noir, bleu clair et marron clair**	1 »	1 »
2520	**2 f. 20+50 c. noir, bleu clair et marron clair**	1 »	1 »

Bougainville (1729-1811). Dumont d'Urville (1790-1842).

2521	**2 f. 20+50 c. noir, bleu clair et marron clair**	1 »	1 »
2522	**2 f. 20+50 c. noir, bleu clair et marron clair**	1 »	1 »
	Nos 2517 à 2522 (6 val.)	**6 »**	**6 »**
	La série, non dentelée	110 »	

Tirages : 1 720 946, 1 771 611, 1 742 590, 1 731 475, 1 788 790 et 1 758 714.

Ont été aussi émis en carnets (tirage : 1 505 898).

La bande (format vertical) destinée à la confection de carnets et comprenant les timbres nos 2517 à 2522 est disposée comme suit (de haut en bas).

Vignette, 2517, 2520, 2518, 2521, 2519, 2522, vignette.

BC2523	La bande carnet, non pliée	6 »	6 »
	a. Méridiens estompés	15 »	15 »

1988. – ***"Philexfrance'89". Exposition philatélique mondiale, à Paris, du 7 au 17 juillet 1989 (II). Taille-douce. Dentelé 13.***

"Liberté de Gandon" et logotype de l'exposition.

2524	**2 f. 20 rouge, bleu et noir**	1 »	0 30
	a. (Non dentelé)	46 »	

Tirage : 20 275 130.

1988. – ***Journée du Timbre. Taille-douce. Dentelé 13.***

Voiture montée.

2525	**2 f. 20+60 c. violet sur mauve clair**	1 40	1 25
	a. (Non dentelé)	23 »	

Tirage : 2 122 028.

1988. – ***Idem. Timbre provenant de carnet. Dentelé.*** [C]

2526	**2 f. 20+60 c. brun sur beige clair**	1 40	1 25

Tirage : 1 049 374 séries.

La bande (format vertical) destinée à la confection de carnets comprend six nº 2526 plus deux vignettes.

Voir après le no 2360 la présentation de la bande.

BC2526A	La bande carnet, non pliée	8 »	8 »

1988. – ***Centenaire de l'École nationale supérieure des P.T.T. Taille-douce. Dentelé 13.***

Mappemonde et enveloppe.

2527	**3 f. 60 bleu, bleu-vert et brun**	1 70	0 50
	a. (Non dentelé)	17 »	

Tirage : 4 752 194.

1988. – ***En faveur du don du sang. Héliogravure. Dentelé 13.***

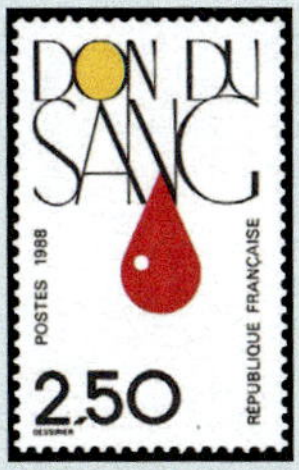

Goutte de sang.

2528	**2 f. 50 noir, rouge et jaune**	1 25	0 50
	a. (Non dentelé)	23 »	

Tirage : 5 649 234.

1988. – ***"Philex-Jeunes 88". Exposition philatélique des jeunes, à Nevers. Taille-douce. Dentelé 13.***

"Timbres" représentant de jeunes collectionneurs et une vue de Nevers.

2529	**2 f. rose, rouge, violet et bleu clair**	1 »	0 30
	a. (Non dentelé)	15 »	

Tirage : 14 244 013.

1988. – ***Série courante. Type Liberté. T.-P. de 1985 avec en surcharge valeur convertie en monnaie européenne (ECU).***

2530	**0,31 ECU s. 2 f. 20 rouge (2376)**	1 50	0 30
	a. (Non dentelé)	14 »	

1988. – ***Europa. Transports et communication. Taille-douce. Dentelés 13.***

Câbles et Satellites.

Transports urbains de demain.

2531	**2 f. 20 bleu-vert et gris**	1 50	0 40
2532	**3 f. 60 violet et noir**	2 »	0 65
	La paire, non dentelée	92 »	

Tirages : 12 047 695 et 5 167 380.

1988. – ***Centenaire de la naissance de Jean Monnet (1888-1979). Taille-douce. Dentelé 13.***

Portrait du "Père" de l'Europe.

2533	**2 f. 20 gris-bleu, noir et brun**	1 25	0 30
	a. (Non dentelé)	28 »	

Tirage : 13 676 133.

1988. – ***61ᵉ Congrès de la Fédération des Sociétés philatéliques françaises, à Valence. Taille-douce. Dentelé 13.***

Sculptures, et vue de l'Hôtel de Ville.

2534	**2 f. 20 ocre, bleu et bleu clair**	1 »	0 50
	a. (Non dentelé)	15 »	

Tirage : 8 919 789.

1988. – ***Assistance médicale internationale. Héliogravure. Dentelé 13.***

Arc-en-ciel, caducée et globe.

2535	**3 f. 60 bleu, bleu clair, jaune et rouge**	1 70	0 65
	a. (Non dentelé)	15 »	
	b. (sans le jaune sur l'Asie)	» »	

Tirage : 5 469 681.

1988. – ***Accessibilité aux handicapés. Héliogravure. Dentelé 13.***

Illustration des difficultés d'accès pour les handicapés.

2536	**3 f. 70 bleu-gris, bleu, vert et jaune**	1 70	0 65
	a. (Non dentelé)	15 »	

Tirage : 5 375 689.

1988. – ***Bicentenaire de la Révolution. "Philexfrance'89". Exposition philatélique mondiale, à Paris. Taille-douce. Dentelés 13 x 12½.***

Tableaux d'Alexandre Debelle.

2537	**3 f. bleu, noir et rouge** ***"L'Assemblée des 3 Ordres, à Vizille, en 1788"***	1 40	1 25
2538	**4 f. bleu, noir et rouge** ***"La journée des Tuiles, à Grenoble, en 1788"***	1 70	1 40

Tirage : 4 192 961 paires.

2538A	Le triptyque	3 35	3 »
	a. (Non dentelé)	170 »	

1988. – ***Série "Nature de France" (VI). Animaux de l'"Histoire naturelle", de Buffon. Taille-douce. Dentelés 13.***

Loutre.

Cerf.

2539	**2 f. vert et noir**	1 »	0 30
2540	**3 f. rouge et noir**	1 40	0 50

Renard.

Blaireau.

2541	**4 f. violet et noir**	1 90	1 »
2542	**5 f. bleu et noir**	2 30	0 70
	N°s 2539 à 2542 (4 val.)	**6 60**	**2 50**
	La série, non dentelée	92 »	

Tirages : 10 335 162, 5 731 452, 4 700 949 et 5 639 184.

1988. – ***Centenaire des Troupes alpines. Taille-douce. Dentelé 13.***

Soldats en tenues de 1888 et 1988.

2543	**2 f. 50 bleu-gris, rouge et bleu**	1 50	0 80
	a. (Non dentelé)	15 »	

Tirage : 6 429 637.

1988. – ***Centenaire de la naissance de Roland Garros (1888-1918). Taille-douce. Dentelé 13.***

Monoplan d'époque (vue et schémas).

2544	**2 f. vert clair, vert et bleu**	1 25	0 30
	a. (Non dentelé)	30 »	

Tirage : 11 033 695.

1988. – ***Série touristique. Taille-douce. Dentelure 13, sauf n° 2548 : 13 x 12½.***

Musée du Bateau, à Douarnenez.

Château de Sedières.

2545	**2 f. multicolore**	1 »	0 30
2546	**2 f. 20 brun, ardoise et bleu clair**	1 »	0 50

Cirque de Gavarnie.

2547	**3 f. violet, vert et brun**	1 40	0 50

Hermès dicéphale (Haut Empire romain) Fréjus.

2548	**3 f. 70 gris, bleu et rouge**	1 60	1 »
	N°s 2545 à 2548 (4 val.)	**5 »**	**2 30**
	La série, non dentelée	85 »	

Tirages : 12 879 594, 11 838 961, 5 510 097 et 5 832 492.

1988. – ***70e anniversaire de l'Armistice du 11 novembre 1918. Taille-douce. Dentelé 13.***

Soldats souriants sortant des tranchées.

2549	**2 f. 20 gris clair, bleu et noir**	1 25	0 30
	a. (Non dentelé)	23 »	

Tirage : 14 959 414.

1988. – ***Série touristique. Taille-douce. Dentelé 13.***

Vue de Pérouges (Ain).

2550	**2 f. 20 bleu-violet, vert et vert clair**	1 »	0 30
	a. (Non dentelé)	15 »	

Tirage : 12 026 633.

1988. – ***Série artistique. Année culturelle France-Danemark. Émission conjointe franco-danoise. Taille-douce. Dentelé 12½ x 13.***

"Hommage à Léon Degand", sculpture de Robert Jacobsen.

2551 **5 f. noir et brun-rouge sur bleuté** 3 » 1 55
a. (Non dentelé) 70 »

Le Danemark a émis simultanément une figurine au même type de 4 k. 10 (nº 931 cotes : 3,75 3 »).

Tirage : 4 283 267.

1988. – ***Bimillénaire de Strasbourg. Taille-douce. Dentelé 13.***

Armoiries.

2552 **2 f. 20 bleu, or, rouge, gris et noir** 1 » 0 30
a. (Non dentelé) 20 »

Tirage : 14 085 946.

1988. – ***Série artistique. Taille douce, sauf n° 2554 : héliogravure. Dentelés 13 x 12½.***

Le Sépulcre Saint-Mihiel de Ligier-Richier.

2553 **5 f. brun foncé** 3 » 1 25
a. (Non dentelé) 70 »

"Composition", de Serge Poliakoff.

2554 **5 f. multicolore** 3 » 1 25
a. (Non dentelé) 70 »
Tirages : 4 046 917 et 4 124 399.

1988. – ***Au profit de la Croix-rouge. 125ᵉ anniversaire de la Croix-Rouge. Taille-douce. Dentelé 12½ x 13.*** [C]

Emblème.

2555 **2 f. 20+60 c. noir, rouge et bleu** 1 25 1 »
a. (Dentelé 13½ x 13) 1 40 1 25
b. (Non dentelé) 30 »
A été aussi émis en carnets (tirage : 806 609). Le nº 2555a provient des carnets.
Tirage : 1 891 561.

1988. – ***Le thermalisme. Taille-douce. Dentelé 13.***

Source stylisée ; curistes.

2556 **2 f. 20 bleu, rouge et vert** 1 » 0 30
a. (2 f. 20, rouge au lieu de bleu) 600 »
b. ("aux doigts coupés") 60 »
c. (Non dentelé) 23 »
Nº 2556a est sur papier couché.
Tirage : 11 973 844.

1988. – ***Série artistique. Émission conjointe franco-suisse. Oeuvre de Tinguely. Héliogravure. Dentelé 13 x 12½.***

"Meta".

2557 **5 f. multicolore** 3 » 1 50
a. (Non dentelé) 80 »
La Suisse a émis simultanément une figurine au même type de 90 c. (nº 1308 cotes : 4 » 4 »).
Tirage : 4 430 027.

1988. – *Série artistique. Héliogravure. Dentelé 13 x 12½.*

2558 **5 f. multicolore et or** ***Pietà de Villeneuve-lès-Avignon, par Enguerrand Quarton*** 3 » 1 50
a. (Non dentelé) 80 »

Tirage : 4 753 456.

1988. – ***40e anniversaire de la Déclaration universelle des Droits de l'Homme. Offset. Dentelé 13.***

Article 1er de la Déclaration.

2559 **2 f. 20 bleu et turquoise** 1 » 0 30
a. (Non dentelé) 28 »

Tirage : 7 655 416.

> **1988**
>
> **Du n° 2501 au n° 2559**
>
> **(sauf bandes-carnets, paires et triptyques) :**
>
> **57 timbres** ****80** **⊙43**
>
> Autre rubrique de l'année :
>
> Préoblitérés 198 à 201

1989. – ***Bicentenaire de la Révolution. Héliogravure. Dentelé 13.***

Logotype de J.-M. Folon (Liberté, Égalité, Fraternité).

2560 **2 f. 20 bleu et rouge** 1 » 0 50
a. (sans signature FOLON) 185 » 100 »
b. (Non dentelé) 61 »

Voir également à la rubrique des Entiers Postaux (Aérogramme n° 1017).

Tirage : 42 232 940.

1989. – ***Série artistique. Oeuvre d'Yves Klein. Héliogravure. Dentelé 13 x 12½.***

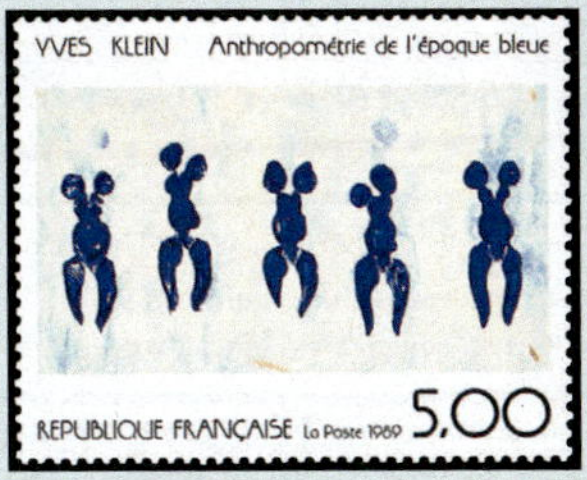

"Anthropométrie de l'époque bleue".

2561 **5 f. bleu, noir et jaune clair** 2 75 1 25
a. (Non dentelé) 61 »

Tirage : 4 410 474.

1989. – ***Pour le bien des aveugles. Héliogravure. Dentelé 13.***

Texte en braille (V. Haüy).

2562 **2 f. 20 orange, gris et bleu** 1 » 0 50
a. (Non dentelé) 23 »
b. (sans l'inscription en relief du braille) 3 500 »

Tirage : 14 250 009.

1989. – ***Centenaire de l'École Estienne (École supérieure des Arts et industries graphiques). Taille-douce. Dentelé 12½.***

2563 **2 f. 20 noir et rouge sur gris** 1 » 0 50
a. (Non dentelé) 18 50

Tirage : 9 765 711.

1989. – ***Personnages célèbres de la Révolution. Taille-douce. Dentelés 13.*** 🄲

Sieyès (1748-1836). Mirabeau (1749-1791).

2564 **2 f. 20+50 c. rouge, bleu, noir et rose** 1 10 1 10
2565 **2 f. 20+50 c. rouge, bleu, noir et rose** 1 10 1 10

Vicomte de Noailles (1756-1804). La Fayette (1757-1834).

2566 **2 f. 20+50 c. rouge, bleu, noir et rose** 1 10 1 10
2567 **2 f. 20+50 c. rouge, bleu, noir et rose** 1 10 1 10

Barnave (1761-1793). Drouet (1763-1824).

2568 **2 f. 20+50 c. rouge, bleu, noir et rose** 1 10 1 10
2569 **2 f. 20+50 c. rouge, bleu, noir et rose** 1 10 1 10

N°s 2564 à 2569 (6 val.) **6 60** **6 60**

La série, non dentelée 125 »

Tirages : 2 120 770, 2 036 369, 1 964 055, 1 983 435, 1 975 224 et 2 070 210.

Ont été aussi émis en carnets (tirage : 1 648 703).

La bande (format vertical) destinée à la confection de carnets comprend les timbres n°s 2564 à 2569, dans l'ordre des numéros de haut en bas, encadrés de deux vignettes.

Voir après le n° 2360 la présentation de la bande.

BC2570 La bande carnet, non pliée 7 » 7 »

1989. – ***Vol franco-soviétique "C.N.E.S. -Glavcosmos-Intercosmos". Offset. Dentelé 13.***

Spationaute, engins spatiaux.

2571 **3 f. 60 multicolore** 2 » 0 80
a. (Non dentelé) 42 »

La Russie a émis simultanément un timbre (n° 5567 cotes : 0,80 0,30).

Tirage : 6 191 638.

1989. – ***3es élections au Parlement européen. Offset. Dentelé 13.***

Symbole.

2572 **2 f. 20 multicolore** 1 » 0 30
a. (Non dentelé) 42 »

Tirage : 11 100 939.

1989. – ***Bicentenaire de la Révolution et de la Déclaration des Droits de l'Homme et du Citoyen. Taille-douce. Dentelés 12½ x 13.***

La Liberté. L'Égalité.

2573 **2 f. 20 multicolore** 1 » 0 50
2574 **2 f. 20 multicolore** 1 » 0 50

La Fraternité.

2575 **2 f. 20 multicolore** 1 » 0 50

La série, non dentelée 155 »

Tirage : 4 899 857 séries.

Idem - imprimés en bande horizontale de deux triptyques, attenant chacun à une vignette sans valeur (logo de "Philexfrance'89", Liberté, Egalité, Fraternité).

2576 Le triptyque, avec vignette 3 » 2 50
a. (Non dentelé) 185 »

1989. – ***Journée du Timbre. Taille-douce. Dentelé 13.***

Diligence Paris-Lyon.

2577 **2 f. 20+60 c. bleu-gris sur bleu clair** 1 40 1 10
a. (Non dentelé) 30 »

Tirage : 2 329 828.

1989. – *Idem. Timbre provenant de carnet. Dentelé* [C]

2578	**2 f. 20+60 c. violet sur mauve**	1 40	1 10

Tirage : 1 145 898 séries.

La bande (format vertical) destinée à la confection de carnets comprend six n° 2578 plus deux vignettes.

Voir après le no 2360 la présentation de la bande.

BC2578A	La bande carnet, non pliée	8 »	8 »

1989. – *Panorama de Paris. Monuments de la Capitale. Taille-douce. Multicolores. Dentelés 13 x 12½.*

Imprimés se tenant horizontalement.

2579	**2 f. 20 *Arche de la Défense***	1 25	1 »
2580	**2 f. 20 *Centenaire de la tour Eiffel***	1 25	1 »
2581	**2 f. 20 *Pyramide du Grand Louvre***	1 25	1 »
2582	**2 f. 20 *Notre-Dame***	1 25	1 »
2583	**2 f. 20 *Opéra Bastille***	1 25	1 »
	N°s 2579 à 2583 (5 val.)	**6 25**	**5 »**

Tirage : 4 154 665 séries.

Voir également à la rubrique "Entiers Postaux" (n°s 2579-CP1 à 2583-CP1).

La bande entière

2583A	La bande	6 25	6 »
	a. Non dentelée	185 »	

1989. – *Europa. Jeux d'enfants. Taille-douce. Dentelés 13.*

La marelle.

2584	**2 f. 20 multicolore**	2 »	0 45

Jeu de balle.

2585	**3 f. 60 multicolore**	3 »	1 »
	La paire, non dentelée	80 »	

Tirages : 13 302 761 et 5 939 388.

1989. – *Série touristique. Taille-douce. Dentelure 13, sauf n° 2587 :* 13 x 12½.

Forêt de Fontainebleau.

2586	**2 f. 20 vert, brun et orange**	1 10	0 30

Château de Vaux-le-Vicomte.

2587	**3 f. 70 olive et noir**	1 85	0 80

Malestroit.

2588	**3 f. 70 rouge et noir**	1 85	0 65
	La série, non dentelée	50 »	

Tirages : 10 282 672, 5 581 100 et 6 602 565.

1989. – *Conférence des plénipotentiaires de l'U.I.T. (Union Internationale des Télécommunications), à Nice. Offset. Dentelé 13.*

Bâtiment et emblème.

2589	**3 f. 70 bleu, orangé et rouge**	1 70	0 50
	a. (Non dentelé)	42 »	

Tirage : 6 277 192.

1989. – *Championnats du monde de cyclisme. Offset. Dentelé 13.*

2590	**2 f. 20 multicolore**	1 40	0 30
	a. (Non dentelé)	42 »	

Tirage : 13 442 328.

1989. – *Bicentenaire de la Révolution et de la Déclaration des Droits de l'Homme et du Citoyen. Héliogravure. Dentelé 13 x 12½.*

"Le serment du Jeu de Paume"par David.

2591	**5 f. multicolore**	2 75	1 25
	a. (Non dentelé)	61	»

Tirage : 5 459 534.

1989. – *Personnages célèbres de la Révolution. Taille-douce. Dentelés 13.* BF *n° 10.*

Antoine Caritat, marquis de Condorcet (1743-1794) ; philosophe et mathématicien.

Mme Roland (1754-1793).

2592	**2 f. 20 multicolore**	1 10	0 80
2593	**2 f. 20 multicolore**	1 10	0 80

Camille Desmoulins (1760-1794) ; avocat et journaliste.

François-Christophe Kellermann, Maréchal de France, Duc de Valmy (1735-1820).

2594	**2 f. 20 multicolore**	1 10	0 80
2595	**2 f. 20 multicolore**	1 10	0 80
	N°s 2592 à 2595 (4 val.)	**4 40**	**3 20**

Tirage : 3 616 296 séries.

Emis uniquement en feuillet.

1989. – *Bicentenaire de la Révolution et de la Déclaration des Droits de l'Homme et du Citoyen. Taille-douce et offset. Multicolores. Dentelés 13 x 12½.* BF *n° 11.*

Préambule et texte de la Déclaration, d'après peinture et gravure conservées au Musée Carnavalet.

2596	**5 f.** ***préambule ; article 1er***	4 50	4 50
2597	**5 f.** ***articles II à VI***	4 50	4 50
2598	**5 f.** ***articles VII à XI***	4 50	4 50
2599	**5 f.** ***articles XII à XVII***	4 50	4 50
	N°s 2596 à 2599 (4 val.)	**18 »**	**18 »**

Tirage : 1 440 114 séries.

Émis uniquement en feuillet, vendu 50 f. (20 f. de valeur faciale et 30 f. de droit d'entrée permanent à l'Exposition "Philexfrance'89").

1989. – *Sommet des pays industrialisés, à l'Arche de la Défense. Héliogravure. Dentelé 13.*

Logo de la Conférence.

2600	**2 f. 20 multicolore**	1 »	0 65
	a. (Non dentelé)	27 »	
	b. (ligne verte omise)	2 700 »	2 000 »

Tirage : 12 322 901.

1989. – *Série touristique. Taille-douce. Dentelé 13 x 12½.*

La Brenne.

2601	**4 f. bleu**	2 »	0 80
	a. (Non dentelé)	17 »	

Tirage : 4 666 010.

1989. – ***Bicentenaire de la Déclaration des Droits de l'Homme et du Citoyen. Taille-douce. Dentelés 13 x 12½.***

Faisceau de licteur et texte de la Déclaration.

Pour les textes des n°s 2603 à 2605 se reporter aux clichés des n°s 2597 à 2599.

2602	**2 f. 50** ***Préambule et article premier***	1 10	1 »
2603	**2 f. 50** ***Articles II à VI***	1 10	1 »
2604	**2 f. 50** ***Articles VII à XI***	1 10	1 »
2605	**2 f. 50** ***Articles XII à XVII***	1 10	1 »
	N°s 2602 à 2605 (4 val.)	**4 40**	**4 »**

Tirage : 2 505 756 séries.

Imprimés se tenant horizontalement, et attenant à une vignette sans valeur (illustration et date de la Déclaration).

La bande, avec vignette

2605A	La bande	4 40	4 40
	a. non dentelée	155 »	

1989. – ***Série artistique. Héliogravure. Dentelé 12½ x 13.***

"Régates vent arrière", de Lapicque.

2606	**5 f. multicolore**	2 75	1 25
	a. (Non dentelé)	61 »	

Tirage : 4 791 363.

1989. – ***Le TGV atlantique. Héliogravure. Dentelé 13.***

2607	**2 f. 50 bleu, argent et rouge**	2 »	0 50
	a. (Non dentelé)	46 »	

Tirage : 6 588 053.

1989. – ***Centenaire du 1er tramway électrique, à Clermont-Ferrand. Taille-douce. Dentelé 13.***

2608	**3 f. 70 marron clair et noir**	2 »	0 50
	a. (Non dentelé)	30 »	

Tirage : 6 737 815.

1989. – ***450e anniversaire de l'Ordonnance de Villers-Cotterêts sur le traitement des archives. Taille-douce. Dentelé 13.***

2609	**2 f. 20 noir et rouge**	1 »	0 50
	a. (Non dentelé)	15 »	

Tirage : 14 631 414.

1989. – ***Bicentenaire de la naissance d'Augustin Cauchy (1789-1857), mathématicien. Taille-douce. Dentelé 13.***

Portrait, formule et courbes.

2610	**3 f. 60 bleu-vert, rouge et noir**	1 70	0 65
	a. (Non dentelé)	15 »	

Tirage : 5 332 706.

1989. – ***Centenaire de la naissance du Maréchal de Lattre de Tassigny (1889-1952). Taille-douce. Dentelé 13.***

Portrait et devise.

2611	**2 f. 20 rouge, noir et bleu**	1 25	0 65
	a. (Non dentelé)	20 »	

Tirage : 14 188 987.

1989. – ***Au profit de la Croix-Rouge. Motif d'une soierie de Lyon (XVIIIe siècle). Héliogravure. Dentelé 12½ x 13.*** [C]

Oiseau ; nid avec oisillons.

2612	**2 f. 20+60 c. multicolore**	1 25	1 10
	a. (Dentelé 13½ x 13)	1 40	1 25
	b. (Non dentelé)	35 »	

A été aussi émis en carnets (tirage : 935 167). Le n° 2612a provient des carnets.

Tirage : 2 137 931.

1989. – ***Hommage aux Harkis, soldats de la France. Héliogravure. Dentelé 13.***

Profil d'un harki.

2613	**2 f. 20 multicolore**	1 25	0 30
	a. (Non dentelé)	18 50	

Tirage : 11 084 185.

1989. – ***Type Marianne du Bicentenaire. Taille-douce. Deux bandes de phosphore. Dentelé 13*** [C]

2614	**2 f. 30 rouge**	1 »	0 15
	b. (Non dentelé)	12 50	
	c. (Sans bandes de phosphore)	20 »	

Pour le 2 f. 30, provenant de carnets et de roulettes, voir ci-dessous après le n° 2626.

De nouvelles valeurs à ce type sont parues en 1990 (n°s 2617 à 2630), 1991 (n°s 2711 à 2720), 1992 (n° 2770), 1993 (n°s 2790, 2806 et 2807), 1994 (2873, 2874 et 2906).

1989

Du n° 2560 au n° 2614

(sauf bandes-carnets, paires et triptyques) :

53 timbres ****90** **⊙59**

Autre rubrique de l'année :

Blocs et feuillets 10 à 11

Préoblitérés 198 à 201

Service 100 à 101

1990. – *Type "Liberté" avec lettre C (valeur du tarif postal pour plis de 20 g maximum, à compter du 1er janvier 1990 : P.N.U. = 2 f. 10 ; Lettre = 2 f. 30). Une bande de phosphore à droite pour le timbre "C" vert, deux bandes pour le "C" rouge. Taille-douce. Dentelés 13.*

2615	**C = (2 f. 10) vert**	1 »	0 50
2616	**C = (2 f. 30) rouge**	1 »	0 50
	La paire, non dentelée	23 »	

1990. – *Type Marianne du Bicentenaire. Taille-douce. Une bande de phosphore à droite, sauf n° 2623, 2624, 2625, 2626 : deux bandes de phosphore. Dentelés 13.* 🄲

2617	**10 c. bistre-noir**	0 15	0 15
2618	**20 c. émeraude**	0 15	0 15
	a. (sans bande de phosphore)	15 »	
2619	**50 c. violet-rouge**	0 15	0 15
	a. (sans bande de phosphore)	12 »	
2620	**1 f. orange**	0 50	0 30
	a. (sans bande de phosphore)	10 »	

2621	**2 f. vert clair**	1 »	0 15
2622	**2 f. 10 vert**	1 »	0 15
2623	**3 f. 20 bleu**	1 70	1 »
2624	**3 f. 80 rose**	1 85	0 30
	a. (sans bande de phosphore)	40 »	

2625	**5 f. bleu-vert**	2 20	0 15
2626	**10 f. violet**	4 30	0 30
	Nos 2617 à 2626 (10 val.)	**13 »**	**2 80**
	La série, non dentelée	92 »	

1990. – *Type Marianne du Bicentenaire. Provenant de carnets. Paires se tenant horizontalement. Dentelure horizontale souvent rognée.*

2614a	2 f. 30+20 c.	13 »	11 »
2617a	10 c.+20 c.	7 »	6 »

1990. – *Type Marianne du Bicentenaire. Provenant de roulettes. Une bande de phosphore à droite, sauf n° 2628 : deux bandes de phosphore. Dentelés 13 horizontalement.*

2627	**2 f. 10 vert**	1 25	0 40
	a. (N° rouge au verso)	2 »	
2628	**2 f. 30 rouge**	1 50	0 40
	a. (N° rouge au verso)	2 »	

1990. – *Type Marianne du Bicentenaire. Provenant de carnets. Deux bandes de phosphore. Dentelé 13 sur 3 côtés.*

2629	**2 f. 30 rouge**	2 30	0 30
	a. (Paire verticale)	5 »	3 »

1990. – *Type Marianne du Bicentenaire. Provenant de carnets. Deux bandes de phosphore. Autoadhésifs. Non dentelé.* 🄲

2630	**2 f. 30 rouge**	1 25	0 15

Ce numéro ainsi que les nos 2713, 2720, 2807 et 2824 sont non dentelés par précoupe droite entre les timbres.

Les timbres adhésifs doivent être conservés sur leur support papier.

1990. – *Métiers d'art. La dentelle. Taille-douce. Dentelé 13.*

Dentelle réalisée à la main.

2631	**2 f. 50 rouge et rose**	1 25	0 50
	a. (Non dentelé)	15 »	

Tirage : 6 793 697.

1990. – ***"Albertville'92". Jeux olympiques d'hiver 1992, à Albertville (I). Héliogravure. Dentelé 13.***

Logo des jeux.

2632	**2 f. 50 multicolore**	1 25	0 30
	a. (Non dentelé)	46 »	

Tirage : 22 822 844.

1990. – ***"Albertville'92" (II). Patinage artistique. Taille-douce. Dentelé 13.***

Logo, et couple de patineurs.

2633	**2 f. 30+20 c. rouge, gris et bleu**	1 25	1 »
	a. (Non dentelé)	46 »	

A ce type est paru en 1992 un 2 f. 50+20 c. (n° 2737).

Tirage : 3 110 831.

1990. – ***Centenaire de la naissance du Général de Gaulle (1890-1970). Taille-douce. Dentelé 13.***

Portrait.

2634	**2 f. 30 bleu, violet et noir**	1 50	0 50
	a. bleu, violet-rose et noir	2 »	0 80
	b. (Non dentelé)	50 »	

Tirage : 27 279 272.

1990. – ***Série artistique. Taille douce, sauf n° 2635 : offset. Dentelés 12½ x 13.***

"Profil de femme", d'Odilon Redon.

2635	**5 f. multicolore**	2 75	1 25
	a. (Non dentelé)	61 »	

"Cambodgienne assise", d'Auguste Rodin.

2636	**5 f. bleu et ocre**	2 75	1 25
	a. (Non dentelé)	61 »	

Tête de Christ de Wissembourg.

2637	**5 f. jaune, bleu et rouge**	2 75	1 25
	a. (Non dentelé)	61 »	

Tirages : 3 564 206, 4 991 667 et 4 625 323.

1990. – *Hommage à Max Hymans (1900-1961), résistant, homme d'Etat, organisateur d'Air-France. Dentelé 13.*

Portrait, avions, emblème d'Air-France.

2638 **2 f. 30 lilas, olive et bleu** 1 » 0 30
a. (Non dentelé) 28 »

Tirage : 11 295 930.

1990. – *Journée du Timbre. Les Métiers de la Poste. Héliogravure. Dentelé 13.*

Les services financiers. Chiffres, clavier, et regard d'un employé.

2639 **2 f. 30+60 c. bleu et jaune** 1 40 1 10
a. (Non dentelé) 17 »

Tirage : 1 974 379.

1990. – *Idem. Timbre provenant de carnet. Dentelé.* ©

2640 **2 f. 30+60 c. bleu, jaune et vert** 1 40 1 25

Tirage : 1 069 529 séries.

La bande (format vertical), destinée à la confection de carnets comprend six n° 2640 plus deux vignettes.

Voir après le n° 2360 la présentation de la bande.

BC2640A La bande carnet, non pliée 8 » 8 »

1990. – *Centenaire de la naissance de Jean Guéhenno (1890-1978), écrivain, critique et polémiste. Taille-douce. Dentelé 13.*

2641 **3 f. 20 brun sur crème** 1 50 0 50
a. (Non dentelé) 15 »

Tirage : 5 873 958.

1990. – *Europa. Bâtiments postaux d'hier et d'aujourd'hui. Taille-douce. Dentelés 13.*

Bâtiment postal historique : Mâcon. Bâtiment postal moderne : Cerizay.

2642 **2 f. 30 brun, noir et bleu clair** 1 50 0 90
2643 **3 f. 20 brun, jaune et bleu** 2 » 1 40

La paire, non dentelée 80 »

Tirages : 13 711 930 et 5 524 562.

1990. – *Centenaire du 1er Mai. Héliogravure. Dentelé 13.*

Manifestants avec banderoles.

2644 **2 f. 30 multicolore** 1 » 0 30
a. (Non dentelé) 23 »

Tirage : 15 915 063.

1990. – *L'Institut du Monde arabe. Taille-douce. Dentelé 13.*

Institut et "Tour des Livres".

2645 **3 f. 80 bleu et rouge** 1 85 0 65
a. (Non dentelé) 15 »

Tirage : 6 419 141.

1990. – *Au profit de la Croix-Rouge. Faïence de Quimper. Héliogravure. Dentelé 12½ x 13.* ©

Assiette avec bretonne en costume régional.

2646 **2 f. 30+60 c. multicolore** 1 40 1 10
a. (Dentelé 13½ x 13) 1 60 1 25
b. (Non dentelé) 30 »

A été aussi émis en carnets (tirage : 942 429). Le n° 2646a provient de carnets.

Tirage : 2 152 858.

1990. – ***63*****e** ***Congrès de la Fédération des Sociétés philatéliques françaises, à Villefranche sur Saône. Taille-douce. Dentelé 13.***

Frises gothiques de Notre-Dame des Marais.

2647	**2 f. 30 rouge, vert et noir**	1 »	0 50
	a. (Non dentelé)	15 »	

Tirage : 14 582 552.

1990. – ***Course autour du monde 1989-1990. Taille-douce. Dentelé 13.***

"La Poste" en course.

2648	**2 f. 30 vert, bleu et jaune**	1 »	0 30
	a. (Non dentelé)	30 »	

Voir également à la rubrique "Entiers postaux" (n° 2648-CP1).

Tirage : 15 038 805.

1990. – ***Personnages célèbres. Grands noms de la chanson française. Héliogravure. Dentelés 13.*** [C]

Aristide Bruant.

Maurice Chevalier.

2649	**2 f. 30+50 c. noir et rouge sur or**	1 25	1 25
2650	**2 f. 30+50 c. rose et noir sur or**	1 25	1 25

Tino Rossi.

Edith Piaf.

2651	**2 f. 30+50 c. bleu, rouge et jaune sur or**	1 25	1 25
2652	**2 f. 30+50 c. noir et rouge sur or**	1 25	1 25

Jacques Brel.

Georges Brassens.

2653	**2 f. 30+50 c. multicolore sur or**	1 25	1 25
2654	**2 f. 30+50 c. rouge, bleu et noir sur or**	1 25	1 25
	N°s 2649 à 2654 (6 val.)	**7 50**	**7 50**
	La série, non dentelée	125 »	

Tirages : 2 103 508, 2 123 638, 2 052 815, 2 164 172, 2 136 464 et 2 093 868.

Ont été aussi émis en carnets (tirage : 1 650 476).

La bande (format horizontal) destinée à la confection de carnets est disposée comme suit, de gauche à droite : deux vignettes (effigies des 6 personnages, réparties sur les 2 vignettes), timbres n°s 2649 à 2654, dans l'ordre des numéros.

Voir après le n° 2360 la présentation de la bande.

BC2655	La bande carnet, non pliée	8 »	8 »

1990. – ***Cinquantenaire de l'Appel à la Résistance (Appel du 18 juin 1940). Taille-douce. Dentelé 13.***

Croix de Lorraine sur Marianne symbolique.

2656	**2 f. 30 noir, rouge et bleu**	1 25	0 30
	a. (Non dentelé)	42 »	

Tirage : 14 447 618.

1990. – ***Série touristique. Taille-douce. Dentelés 13.***

Abbaye de Cluny.

Pont-canal de Briare.

2657	**2 f. 30 bleu, orange et noir**	1 »	0 50
2658	**2 f. 30 bleu, noir et vert**	1 »	0 50

Abbaye de Flaran (Gers).

Cap Canaille à Cassis.

2659	**3 f. 80 brun et vert**	2 »	0 65
2660	**3 f. 80 bleu, violet et rouge-brique**	2 »	0 65
	N°s 2657 à 2660 (4 val.)	**6 »**	**2 30**
	La série, non dentelée	61 »	

Tirages : 12 048 208, 15 818 595, 6 885 399 et 6 868 558.

1990. – *La Maison France-Brésil à Rio de Janeiro. Taille-douce. Dentelé 13.*

Vue aérienne.

2661	**3 f. 20 multicolore**	1 60	1 »
	a. (Non dentelé)	23 »	

Ce timbre porte le millésime "1989".

Le Brésil a émis simultanément une figurine de 50 C. sur ce sujet (nº 1973 : cotes 3 » 1,35).

Tirage : 5 211 605.

1990. – *Cinquantenaire de l'Institut Géographique National. Héliogravure. Dentelé 13.*

Carte de France.

2662	**2 f. 30 multicolore**	1 25	0 65
	a. (Non dentelé)	28 »	

Tirage : 15 176 965.

1990. – *Série "Nature de France" (VII). Poissons d'eau douce. Taille-douce. Dentelés 13.*

Gardon.

Perche.

2663	**2 f. multicolore**	1 »	0 15
2664	**3 f. multicolore**	1 40	0 25

Saumon.

Brochet.

2665	**4 f. multicolore**	2 30	0 80
2666	**5 f. multicolore**	2 30	0 80
	Nos 2663 à 2666 (4 val.)	**7 »**	**2 »**
	La série, non dentelée	110 »	

Tirages : 7 187 192, 5 755 146, 5 284 988 et 5 455 607.

1990. – *Bicentenaire de la Révolution. Taille-douce. Dentelés 13.* BF *n° 12.*

Gaspard Monge, comte de Péluse (1746-1818), mathématicien.

Abbé Grégoire (Henri) (1750-1831).

2667	**2 f. 50 multicolore**	1 25	1 »
2668	**2 f. 50 multicolore**	1 25	1 »

Création du drapeau tricolore (allégorie).

Création des départements français.

2669	**2 f. 50 multicolore**	1 25	1 »
2670	**2 f. 50 multicolore**	1 25	1 »
	Nos 2667 à 2670 (4 val.)	**5 »**	**4 »**

Tirage : 2 539 176 séries.

Emis uniquement en feuillet.

1990. – *Centenaire de la naissance de Maurice Genevoix (1890-1980). Taille-douce. Dentelé 13.*

Portrait de l'écrivain.

2671	**2 f. 30 noir sur jaune verdâtre**	1 »	0 30
	a. (Non dentelé)	15 »	

Tirage : 15 293 317.

1990. – ***Série artistique. Héliogravure. Dentelé 12½ x 13.***

"Jaune et gris", de Roger Bissière.

2672	**5 f. multicolore**	2 75	1 25
	a. (Non dentelé)	61	»

Tirage : 4 707 417.

1990. – ***30ᵉ anniversaire de l'O.C.D.E. (Organisation de Coopération et de Développement Economiques). Offset. Dentelé 13.***

Sigle et dates sur planisphère.

2673	**3 f. 20 bleu et bleu clair**	1 50	0 80
	a. (Non dentelé)	42	»

Tirage : 6 312 668.

1990. – ***"Albertville'92". Jeux olympiques d'hiver (III). Logo et disciplines sportives. Taille-douce. Dentelés 13.***

Saut à skis (Courchevel). Ski de vitesse-démonstration (Les Arcs).

2674	**2 f. 30+20 c. rouge, gris et bleu**	1 25	0 80
2675	**2 f. 30+20 c. rouge, gris et bleu**	1 25	0 80
	La paire, non dentelée	92	»

Tirages : 2 946 636 et 2 694 522.

A ces types ont parus en 1992 des 2 f. 50 + 20 c. (nᵒˢ 2738 et 2739).

1990

Du n° 2615 au n° 2675 :

(sauf bandes-carnets, paires et triptyques) :

60 timbres	****87**	**⊙41**

Autres rubriques de l'année :

Bloc-feuillet 12

Préoblitérés 206 à 212

Service 102 à 105

1991. – ***"Albertville'92". Jeux olympiques d'hiver (IV). Logo et disciplines sportives. Taille-douce. Dentelés 13.***

Slalom (Les Ménuires). Hockey (Méribel).

2676	**2 f. 30+20 c. rouge, gris et bleu**	1 25	1 »
2677	**2 f. 30+20 c. rouge, gris et bleu**	1 25	1 »

Ski de fond (Les Saisies).

2678	**2 f. 30+20 c. rouge, gris et bleu**	1 25	1 »

Luge (La Plagne). Curling-démonstration (Pralognan).

2679	**2 f. 50+20 c. rouge, gris et bleu**	1 25	1 »
	a. (Papier blanc brillant)	2 »	2 »
2680	**2 f. 50+20 c. rouge, gris et bleu**	1 25	1 »
	a. (Papier blanc brillant)	2 »	2 »
	Nᵒˢ 2676 à 2680 (5 val.)	**6 25**	**5 »**
	La série, non dentelée	230 »	

Tirages : 2 709 745, 2 587 163, 2 689 257, 2 285 528 et 2 198 160.

Le nᵒ 2678 porte le millésime 1992.

Les nᵒˢ 2679a et 2680a proviennent du BF nᵒ 14.

Aux types des nᵒˢ 2676 à 2678 sont parus en 1992 des 2 f. 50+20 c. (nᵒˢ 2740 à 2742).

1991. – ***Personnages célèbres. Poètes français du 20ᵉ siècle. Taille-douce. Dentelés 13.*** C

Paul Eluard (1895-1952). André Breton (1896-1966).

2681	**2 f. 50+50 c. gris, noir et bleu**	1 30	1 30
2682	**2 f. 50+50 c. gris, noir et bleu**	1 30	1 30

Louis Aragon (1897-1982). Francis Ponge (1899-1988).

2683	**2 f. 50+50 c. gris, noir et bleu**	1 30	1 30
2684	**2 f. 50+50 c. gris, noir et bleu**	1 30	1 30

Jacques Prévert (1900-1977).

René Char (1907-1988).

2685	**2 f. 50+50 c. gris, noir et bleu**	1 30	1 30
2686	**2 f. 50+50 c. gris, noir et bleu**	1 30	1 30
	N°s 2681 à 2686 (6 val.)	**7 80**	**7 80**
	La série, non dentelée	110 »	

Tirages : 1 450 778, 1 587 752, 1 460 619, 1 541 987, 1 579 234 et 1 556 674.

Ont été aussi émis en carnets (tirage : 1 196 527).

Réalisés à partir de dessins originaux de Pablo Picasso pour P. Eluard et J. Prévert ; Man Ray pour A. Breton ; Henri Matisse pour L. Aragon ; Stella Martens pour F. Ponge ; Valentine Hugo pour R. Char.

La bande, destinée à la confection de carnets est disposée comme suit, de haut en bas : vignette avec noms des poètes des 3 premiers timbres et des artistes ayant réalisé le dessin original, timbres n°s 2681 à 2686, vignettes avec noms des poètes et dessinateurs des 3 derniers timbres.

Voir après le n° 2360 la présentation de la bande.

BC2687 La bande carnet, non pliée 8 » 8 »

1991. – *Journée du Timbre. Les Métiers de la Poste. Héliogravure. Dentelé 13.*

Le Tri postal.

2688	**2 f. 50+60 c. bleu clair, lilas, jne et rge**	1 40	1 25
	a. (Non dentelé)	18 50	

Tirage : 1 915 789.

1991. – *Idem. Timbre provenant de carnet. Dentelé.* C

2689	**2 f. 50+60 c. lilas, bleu, jaune et rouge**	1 50	1 40

Tirage : 1 030 310 séries.

La bande (format vertical) destinée à la confection de carnets comprend six n°s 2689 plus deux vignettes.

Voir après le n° 2360 la présentation de la bande.

BC2689A La bande carnet, non pliée 9 » 9 »

1991. – *"Philexjeunes'91". Exposition philatélique des Jeunes, à Cholet. Offset. Dentelé 13.*

Garçon avec bicyclette, fillette au cerceau, oiseau et lettres.

2690	**2 f. 50 multicolore**	1 25	0 50
	a. (Non dentelé)	15 »	
	b. (Vélo sans cadre inférieur)	15 »	5 »

1991. – *350e anniversaire de l'Imprimerie Nationale. Héliogravure. Dentelé 13.*

Portrait de Gutenberg réalisé en caractères.

2691	**4 f. multicolore**	1 85	0 80
	a. (Non dentelé)	15 »	

Tirage : 6 823 246.

1991. – *Série artistique. Taille-douce. Dentelés 12½ x 13.*

"La balançoire", d'Auguste Renoir.

2692	**5 f. multicolore**	2 75	1 25
	a. (Non dentelé)	61 »	

"Le Noeud noir", de Georges Seurat.

2693	**5 f. jaune clair et gris foncé**	2 75	1 25
	a. (Non dentelé)	61 »	

Tirage : 4 522 541 paires.

1991. – *90e anniversaire du Concours Lépine. Taille-douce. Dent. 13.*

Affiche du 13e Concours Lépine.

2694	**4 f. multicolore**	1 85	1 »
	a. (Non dentelé)	15 »	

Tirage : 7 160 543.

1991. – *Bicentenaire de la mort de Mozart (1756-1791). Héliogravure. Dentelé 13.*

Allégorie.

2695 **2 f. 50 bleu, noir, rouge et bleu foncé** 1 25 0 80

a. (Non dentelé) 54 »

Tirage : 9 769 188.

1991. – *Europa. L'Europe et l'espace. Taille-douce. Dentelés 13.*

Espace et Guyane.

Satellite de télévision directe.

2696 **2 f. 50 bleu, rouge et vert** 1 50 0 45

2697 **3 f. 50 bleu, vert et rouge** 2 50 1 »

La paire, non dentelée 85 »

Tirages : 21 313 540 et 5 429 361.

Un 2 f. 80 est paru en 1995 au type du 2 f. 50, avec inscriptions modifiées et sans le sigle de la C.E.P. T. (n° 2948).

1991. – *Congrès de la Fédération des Sociétés Philatéliques françaises, à Perpignan. Taille-douce. Dentelé 13.*

Monuments perpignanais.

2698 **2 f. 50 rouge, gris et bleu** 1 25 0 30

a. (Non dentelé) 15 »

Tirage : 10 319 163.

1991. – *"Roland Garros 1991". Tournoi du centenaire. Taille-douce. Dentelé 13.*

Oeuvre originale de Miro.

2699 **3 f. 50 multicolore** 1 85 0 65

a. (Non dentelé) 46 »

Tirage : 6 042 117.

1991. – *Bicentenaire de la Révolution française. Taille-douce. Dentelés 13.* BF *n° 13.*

La Tour d'Auvergne (1743-1800).

Plantation de l'Arbre de la Liberté.

2700 **2 f. 50 multicolore** 1 25 1 »

2701 **2 f. 50 multicolore** 1 25 1 »

Bicentenaire de la Gendarmerie Nationale.

Saint-Just (1767-1794).

2702 **2 f. 50 multicolore** 1 25 1 »

2703 **2 f. 50 multicolore** 1 25 1 »

N°s 2700 à 2703 (4 val.) **5 »** **4 »**

Tirage : 2 451 507 séries.

Emis uniquement en feuillet.

1991. – *Série touristique. Taille-douce. Dentelés 13.*

Le pont de Cheviré, à Nantes.

Carennac (Lot).

2704 **2 f. 50 gris, orange et bleu clair** 1 25 0 30

2705 **2 f. 50 brun-rouge, brun et vert foncé** 1 60 0 50

Wasquehal (Nord) ; le buffet d'orgue.

Vallée de Munster.

2706	**4 f. crème et noir**	2 »	0 65
2707	**4 f. mauve**	1 85	0 65
	N°s 2704 à 2707 (4 val.)	**6 70**	**2 10**
	La série, non dentelée	110 »	

Tirages : 10 104 448, 7 348 981, 6 788 360 et 6 765 129.

1991. – ***Sixième centenaire de la mort de Gaston Fébus (1331-1391). Héliogravure. Dentelé 13.***

2708	**2 f. 50 multicolore**	1 25	0 65
	a. (Non dentelé)	23 »	

Tirage : 7 582 438.

1991. – ***"Albertville'92". Jeux olympiques d'hiver (V). Disciplines sportives. Taille-douce. Dentelés 13.***

Ski artistique (Tignes).

Ski alpin (Val d'Isère).

2709	**2 f. 50+20 c. rouge, gris et bleu**	1 25	1 »
	a. (Papier blanc brillant)	2 »	2 »
2710	**2 f. 50+20 c. rouge, gris et bleu**	1 25	1 »
	a. (Papier blanc brillant)	2 »	2 »
	La paire, non dentelée	92 »	

Tirages : 2 084 907 et 1 999 543.

Les n°s 2709a et 2710a proviennent du BF n° 14.

1991. – ***Type Marianne du Bicentenaire avec lettre D (valeur du tarif postal pour plis de 20 g maximum, à compter du 19 août 1991 : ECOPLI : 2 f. 20, lettre : 2 f. 50). Une bande de phosphore à droite pour le timbre "D" vert, deux bandes pour le "D" rouge. Taille douce. Dentelés 13.*** Ⓒ

2711	**D = (2 f. 20) vert**	1 25	0 30
2712	**D = (2 f. 50) rouge**	1 25	0 30
	La paire, non dentelée	23 »	

1991. – ***Type Marianne du Bicentenaire avec lettre D. Provenant de carnet. Deux bandes de phosphore. Autoadhésifs. Non dentelé.*** Ⓒ

2713	**D = (2 f. 50) rouge**	1 50	0 40

1991. – ***Type Marianne du Bicentenaire. Taille-douce. Deux bandes de phosphore, sauf n° 2714 : une bande de phosphore à droite. Dentelés 13.*** Ⓒ

2714	**2 f. 20 vert**	1 40	0 15
	a. (sans bande de phosphore)	15 »	
2715	**2 f. 50 rouge**	1 25	0 15
	b. (sans bande de phosphore)	20 »	
2716	**3 f. 40 bleu**	1 60	0 65
2717	**4 f. rose**	2 25	0 30
	a. (sans bande de phosphore)	40 »	
	N°s 2714 à 2717 (4 val.)	**6 50**	**1 25**
	La série, non dentelée	46 »	

1991. – ***Type Marianne du Bicentenaire. Provenant du carnet n° 2715-C1. Dentelure souvent rognée.*** Ⓒ

2715a	**2 f. 50 rouge**	6 »	4 »

Provenant du carnet n°2715-C1

1991. – ***Type Marianne du Bicentenaire. Provenant de roulettes. Une bande de phosphore à droite, sauf n° 2719 : deux bandes de phosphore. Dentelés 13 horizontalement.***

2718	**2 f. 20 vert**	1 50	0 65
	a. (N° rouge au verso)	2 »	
	b. (sans bande de phosphore)	230 »	
2719	**2 f. 50 rouge**	1 50	0 50
	a. (N° rouge au verso)	2 »	
	b. (sans bande de phosphore)	230 »	
	c. (Gomme brillante)	5 »	
	d. (N° rouge au verso, Gomme brillante)	10 »	

1991. – *Type Marianne du Bicentenaire. Provenant de carnet. Deux bandes de phosphore. Autoadhésifs. Non dentelé.* 🄲

2720 **2 f. 50 rouge** 1 40 0 15

1991. – *Série "Nature de France" (VIII). Espèces protégées. Taille-douce. Dentelés 13.*

Ours des Pyrénées.

Tortue terrestre.

2721 **2 f. marron, violet et vert** 1 10 0 50

2722 **3 f. marron clair, rouge et noir** 1 40 0 50

Castor.

Martin pêcheur.

2723 **4 f. marron, lilas et noir** 2 » 1 10

2724 **5 f. bleu clair, jaune et noir** 2 50 1 10

Nos 2721 à 2724 (4 val.) **7 »** **3 20**

La série, non dentelée 110 »

Tirages : 6 552 732, 5 651 069, 7 884 441 et 5 103 792.

1991. – *10e Congrès forestier mondial, à Paris. Taille-douce. Dentelé 13.*

Composition symbolique.

2725 **2 f. 50 vert foncé, bleu-vert et noir** 1 25 0 30

a. (Non dentelé) 18 50

Tirage : 11 948 802.

1991. – *Centenaire de l'École Spéciale des Travaux Publics. Taille-douce et offset. Dentelé 13.*

Têtes casquées, engin, réalisations.

2726 **2 f. 50 multicolore** 1 25 0 65

a. (Non dentelé) 15 »

Tirage : 5 629 966.

1991. – *Centenaire de la naissance de Max Ernst (1891-1976). Émission conjointe franco-allemande. Oeuvre de l'artiste. Héliogravure. Dentelé 13.*

"Après nous la maternité".

2727 **2 f. 50 multicolore** 1 50 1 »

a. (Non dentelé) 54 »

La R.F.A. a émis simultanément sur ce sujet une figurine de 100 p. (n° 1401 cotes 2,20 - 0,90).

Tirage : 7 495 036.

1991. – *30e anniversaire d'"Amnesty International". Héliogravure. Dentelé 13.*

2728 **3 f. 40 rose, bleu et noir** 1 70 0 65

a. (Non dentelé) 28 »

Tirage : 6 304 294.

1991. – *75e anniversaire de la naissance de Marcel Cerdan (1916-1949). Héliogravure. Dentelé 13.*

Un combat de Cerdan.

2729 **2 f. 50 noir, rouge et gris** 1 25 0 50

a. (Non dentelé) 28 »

Tirage : 7 928 177.

1991. – ***Série artistique. Taille douce, sauf n° 2731 : héliogravure. Dentelés 12½-13.***

Oeuvre de François Rouan. "Volta faccia".

2730 **5 f. noir** 2 75 1 10
a. (Non dentelé) 61 »

Oeuvre de Roberto Matta. "Ô tableau noir".

2731 **5 f. multicolore** 2 75 1 25
a. (Non dentelé) 61 »

Tirages : 4 099 831 et 4 206 186.

1991. – ***Parcours de la flamme olympique (VI). Taille-douce. Dentelé 13.***

Logo officiel.

2732 **2 f. 50 bleu, rouge et noir** 1 25 0 30
a. (Non dentelé) 46 »

Tirage : 27 928 695.

1991. – ***Au profit de la Croix-Rouge. Toulon, d'après l'oeuvre de François Nardi. Héliogravure. Dentelé 13 x 12½.*** [C]

Vue du port.

2733 **2 f. 50+60 c. multicolore** 1 40 1 10
a. (Dentelé 13 x 13½) 1 60 1 40
b. (Non dentelé) 30 »

A été aussi émis en carnets. Tirage : 957 135. Le n° 2733a provient des carnets.

Tirage : 1 819 292.

1991. – ***Ves Jeux paralympiques, à Tignes. Héliogravure. Dentelé 13.***

Oiseau aux ailes brisées de Folon.

2734 **2 f. 50 bleu foncé et bleu clair** 1 25 0 65
a. (Non dentelé) 40 »

Porte le millésime 1992.

Tirage : 14 882 599.

1991. – ***150e anniversaire du rattachement volontaire de Mayotte à la France. Taille-douce. Dentelé 13.***

Paysage et logo.

2735 **2 f. 50 brun, vert, jaune et bleu clair** 1 25 0 30
a. (Non dentelé) 15 »

Porte le millésime 1992.

Tirage : 12 176 397.

1991

Du n° 2676 au n° 2735 :

(sauf bandes-carnets, paires et triptyques) :

59 timbres ****91** **⊙47**

Autres rubriques de l'année :

Timbres Autoadhésifs 2

Bloc-feuillet 13

Service 106 à 109

1992. – ***"Expo'92". Exposition universelle de 1992, à Séville (Espagne). Taille-douce et offset. Dentelé 13.***

Croquis sommaire du pavillon français.

2736 **2 f. 50 bleu, noir et vert clair** 1 25 0 30
a. (Non dentelé) 30 »

Tirage : 15 659 136.

1992. – *"Albertville'92". Jeux olympiques d'hiver (VII). Types des T.-P. de 1990 et 1991, avec valeur faciale différente. Taille-douce. Dentelés 13.* BF *n° 14.*

2737	**2 f. 50+20 c. rouge, gris et bleu (2633)**	2 »	2 »
2738	**2 f. 50+20 c. rouge, gris et bleu (2674)**	2 »	2 »
2739	**2 f. 50+20 c. rouge, gris et bleu (2675)**	2 »	2 »
2740	**2 f. 50+20 c. rouge, gris et bleu (2676)**	2 »	2 »
2741	**2 f. 50+20 c. rouge, gris et bleu (2677)**	2 »	2 »
2742	**2 f. 50+20 c. rouge, gris et bleu (2678)**	2 »	2 »
	N°s 2737 à 2742 (6 val.)	**12 »**	**12 »**

Tirage : 1 777 996 séries.

Ces timbres portent le millésime 1990 (2737, 2738, 2739), 1991 (2740, 2741) ou 1992 (2742).

Émis uniquement en feuillet.

1992. – *Journée du Timbre. Les Métiers de la Poste. Offset. Dentelé 13.*

L'accueil des usagers.

2743	**2 f. 50+60 c. bleu, gris et jaune**	1 40	1 10
	a. (Non dentelé)	18 50	

Tirage : 1 816 225.

1992. – *Idem. Timbre provenant de carnet. Héliogravure. Dentelé 13.* C

2744	**2 f. 50+60 c. bleu, rouge et jaune**	1 50	1 10

Tirage : 1 023 174 séries.

La bande (format vertical) destinée à la confection de carnets comprend 6 n°s 2744 et deux vignettes.

Voir après le n° 2360 la présentation de la bande.

BC2744A	La bande carnet, non pliée	9 »	9 »

1992. – *Jeux olympiques d'été 1992, à Barcelone (Espagne). Émission conjointe franco-grecque. Offset. Dentelé 13.*

Silhouette de coureur.

2745	**2 f. 50 rouge, ocre, noir et bleu**	1 50	0 30
	a. (Non dentelé)	42 »	

La Grèce a émis simultanément une figurine au même type de 90 d. (n° 1781 cotes : 2,50 - 0,60).

Tirage : 13 193 419.

1992. – *500e anniversaire de la naissance de Marguerite d'Angoulême, Reine de Navarre (1492-1549). Offset. Dentelé 13.*

Portrait, d'après l'oeuvre de Clouet.

2746	**3 f. 40 multicolore**	1 70	1 10
	a. (Non dentelé)	20 »	

Tirage : 7 560 069.

1992. – *Personnages célèbres. Musiciens. Héliogravure. Dentelés 13.* C

César Franck (1822-1890). Erik Satie (1866-1925). Florent Schmitt (1870-1958).

2747	**2 f. 50+50 c. multicolore**	1 40	1 40
2748	**2 f. 50+50 c. multicolore**	1 40	1 40
2749	**2 f. 50+50 c. multicolore**	1 40	1 40

Arthur Honegger (1892-1955). Georges Auric (1899-1983). Germaine Tailleferre (1892-1983).

2750	**2 f. 50+50 c. multicolore**	1 40	1 40
2751	**2 f. 50+50 c. multicolore**	1 40	1 40
2752	**2 f. 50+50 c. multicolore**	1 40	1 40
	N°s 2747 à 2752 (6 val.)	**8 40**	**8 40**
	La série, non dentelée	110 »	

Tirages : 155 305, 1 573 526, 1 534 763, 1 558 541, 1 554 152 et 1 560 581.

Ont été aussi émis en carnets (tirage : 1 171 197).

La bande (format horizontal) destinée à la confection de carnets comprend les timbres n°s 2747 à 2752, dans l'ordre des numéros de gauche à droite, encadrés de deux vignettes.

Voir après le n° 2360 la présentation de la bande.

BC2753	La bande carnet, non pliée	9 »	9 »

1992. – *500ᵉ anniversaire de la fondation d'Ajaccio. Détail d'une oeuvre de Sandro Botticelli. Héliogravure. Dentelé 13.*

2754	**4 f. multicolore sur bistre *"La Vierge et l'Enfant soutenus par un ange, sous une guirlande"***	1 85	0 65
	a. (Non dentelé)	23 »	

Tirage : 4 872 476.

1992. – *Europa. 500ᵉ anniversaire de la découverte de l'Amérique par Christophe Colomb. Taille-douce. Dentelés 13.*

1493. Christophe Colomb. Carte avec trajet ; instruments de navigation.

1507. America. Carte, caravelle, rose des vents.

2755	**2 f. 50 rouge, jaune, brun, bleu et noir**	1 50	0 50
2756	**3 f. 40 rouge, noir, jaune et vert-bleu**	2 50	1 »
	La paire, non dentelée	85 »	

Tirages : 12 128 142 et 5 634 125.

Voir également à la rubrique des "Entiers Postaux" (nᵒˢ 2755-CP1 et 2756-CP1).

1992. – *Congrès international des céréales et du pain. Offset. Dentelé 13.*

Pains, épis et coquelicots.

2757	**3 f. 40 multicolore**	1 70	1 25
	a. (Non dentelé)	18 50	

Tirage : 6 823 504.

1992. – *Congrès des Sociétés philatéliques françaises, à Niort. "L'Europe d'Art". Héliogravure. Dentelé 13.*

Personnages allégoriques sur timbre triangulaire.

2758	**2 f. 50 multicolore**	1 25	0 30
	a. (Non dentelé)	28 »	

Tirage : 12 484 695.

1992. – *L'Homme de Tautavel. Héliogravure. Dentelé 13.*

Homme préhistorique avec javelot ; grotte.

2759	**3 f. 40 multicolore**	1 70	0 80
	a. (Non dentelé)	18 50	

Tirage : 4 906 292.

1992. – *La France et l'Espagne pays olympiques 1992. Émission conjointe franco-espagnole. Héliogravure. Dentelé 13.*

Anneaux olympiques sur noms "Albertville" et "Barcelone" répétés.

2760	**2 f. 50 multicolore**	1 50	0 50
	a. (Non dentelé)	46 »	

L'Espagne à émis simultanément une figurine au même type de 45 ptas (nᵒ 2808 cotes 1,35 - 0,50).

Tirage : 17 063 210.

1992. – *Série artistique. Gravure de Jacques Callot. Taille-douce. Dentelé 12½ x 13.*

"Portrait de Claude Deruet".

2761	**5 f. noir sur crème**	2 75	0 80
	a. (Non dentelé)	61 »	

Tirage : 3 972 272.

1992. – *500ᵉ anniversaire de la 1ʳᵉ ascension du Mont Aiguille (Isère). Taille-douce. Dentelé 13.*

Vue du Mont.

2762	**3 f. 40 brun, vert et bleu**	1 70	0 80
	a. (Non dentelé)	23 »	

Tirage : 5 203 910.

1992. – ***Série touristique. Taille-douce. Dentelés 13.***

Château de Biron (Dordogne).

2763	**2 f. 50 vert, bleu foncé et brun**	1 25	0 30

Le canal de l'Ourcq. Lorient.

2764	**4 f. vert, noir et bleu**	1 85	0 65
2765	**4 f. ocre, vert clair et vert foncé**	1 85	0 80
	La série, non dentelée	61 »	

Tirages : 13 680 272, 6 647 681 et 5 556 441.

1992. – ***Série "Nature de France" (IX). Fleurs des étangs et marais. Taille-douce. Dentelés 12½.***

Lys de mer. Rossolis.

2766	**2 f. multicolore**	1 »	0 30
2767	**3 f. multicolore**	1 40	0 50

Orchis des marais. Nénuphar jaune.

2768	**4 f. multicolore**	1 80	0 80
2769	**5 f. multicolore**	2 30	1 40
	Nos 2766 à 2769 (4 val.)	**6 50**	**3 »**
	La série, non dentelée	92 »	

Tirages : 5 567 941, 5 105 801, 5 528 486 et 4 235 364.

1992. – ***Type Marianne du Bicentenaire. Taille-douce. Deux bandes de phosphore. Dentelé 13.***

2770	**4 f. 20 rose**	2 »	0 30
	a. (Non dentelé)	11 50	
	b. (sans bande de phosphore)	30 »	

1992. – ***1792, An I de la République Française. Taille-douce. Dentelé 13.***

Allégorie de la République et texte.

2771	**2 f. 50 multicolore**	1 25	0 30
	a. (Non dentelé)	42 »	

Tirage : 14 734 220.

1992. – ***Bicentenaire de la proclamation de la République. Oeuvres d'artistes contemporains. Taille-douce. Dentelés 13.***

Oeuvre d'Alechinsky. Oeuvre de M. Raysse.

2772	**2 f. 50 rouge**	1 25	0 15
2773	**2 f. 50 rouge**	1 25	0 15

Oeuvre de G. Garrouste. Oeuvre de J.-C. Blais.

2774	**2 f. 50 rouge**	1 25	0 15
2775	**2 f. 50 rouge**	1 25	0 15
	Nos 2772 à 2775 (4 val.)	**5 »**	**0 60**
	La série, non dentelée	110 »	

Tirages : 102 877 017, 102 877 017, 108 017 074 et 108 017 074.

2772c à 2775c, la série avec sigle 1792-1992	10 »	4 »

Imprimés par feuilles de 100 avec interpanneaux comportant des inscriptions (50 exemplaires du n° 2772 à gauche et 50 du n° 2773 à droite ; idem pour les nos 2774 et 2775).

Paires se tenant.

2772a	2 f. 50 (2772+2773)	7 »	5 »
2774a	2 f. 50 (2774+2775)	7 »	5 »

Sans bandes de phosphore.

2772b 2 f. 50 25 »

2773a 2 f. 50 25 »

1992. – *Mise en vigueur du Marché unique européen. Héliogravure. Dentelé 13.*

Composition de N. de Saint-Phalle.

2776 2 f. 50 multicolore 1 25 0 50

a. (Sans le vert, sur maillot et coeur) 200 »

b. (Non dentelé) 46 »

Tirage : 15 238 156.

1992. – *10e anniversaire de la mort de Marcel Paul (1900-1982), ancien Ministre (1945). Taille-douce. Dentelé 13.*

Portrait, et pylône électrique, conduite de gaz.

2777 4 f. 20 lilas-brun et bleu 2 30 0 65

a. (Non dentelé) 23 »

Tirage : 6 565 323.

1992. – *80e anniversaire de la 1re liaison postale aérienne, Nancy-Lunéville. Héliogravure. Dentelé 13.*

Avions ancien et moderne en vol.

2778 2 f. 50 multicolore 1 25 0 65

a. (Non dentelé) 23 »

Voir également à la rubrique des "Entiers postaux" (n° 2778-CP1).

Tirage : 24 520 065.

1992. – *Série européenne d'art contemporain. Héliogravure. Dentelés 13 x 12½.*

"Étude pour le portrait de John Edward", de F. Bacon (Grande-Bretagne).

2779 5 f. multicolore 2 30 1 10

Création pour la Poste d'Alberto Burri (Italie).

2780 5 f. multicolore 2 30 1 10

"Le rendez-vous d'Ephèse", de P. Delvaux (Belgique).

2781 5 f. multicolore 2 30 1 10

Création pour la Poste d'Antoni Tapies (Espagne).

2782 5 f. multicolore 2 30 1 10

Nos 2779 à 2782 (4 val.) **9 20** **4 40**

La série, non dentelée 230 »

Tirages : 3 834 334, 3 786 880, 3 922 429 et 3 861 977.

Voir également les nos 2834, 2835, 2858, 2914, 2969, 2986 et 2987 ainsi que le n° 2797.

1992. – *Au profit de la Croix-Rouge. L'Entraide, Strasbourg. Héliogravure. Dentelé 13½ x 13.* [C]

Illustration de l'entraide.

2783 2 f. 50+60 c. multicolore 1 40 1 10

a. (Non dentelé) 35 »

A été aussi émis en carnets. (Tirage : 880 680).

Tirage : 1 709 276.

1992. – ***Les gens du voyage. Taille-douce. Dentelé 13.***

Composition symbolique.

2784	**2 f. 50 multicolore**	1 25	0 50
	a. (Non dentelé)	28 »	

Tirage : 13 151 767.

1992

Du n° 2736 au n° 2784 :

(sauf bandes-carnets, paires et triptyques) :

48 timbres ****81** **⊙45**

Autres rubriques de l'année :

Bloc-feuillet 14

Préoblitérés 213 à 227

1993. – ***Série "Nature de France" (X). Espèces protégées de canards. Taille-douce. Dentelés 13.***

Harle Piette.

Fuligule Nyroca.

2785	**2 f. multicolore**	1 »	0 30
2786	**3 f. multicolore**	1 50	0 30

Tadorne de Belon.

Harle huppé.

2787	**4 f. multicolore**	2 »	1 »
2788	**5 f. multicolore**	2 50	0 80
	Nos 2785 à 2788 (4 val.)	**7 »**	**2 40**
	La série, non dentelée	92 »	

Tirages : 5 934 372, 5 162 410, 6 036 310 et 4 581 175.

1993. – ***Les Postiers autour du monde dans la "Whitbread". Taille-douce. Dentelé 13.***

Mappemonde et voilier en course.

2789	**2 f. 50 multicolore**	1 60	0 50
	a. (Non dentelé)	35 »	

Au même type est paru un 2 f. 80 (n° 2831).

Voir également à la rubrique "Entiers postaux" (n° 2789-E1).

Tirage : 16 512 108.

1993. – ***Type Marianne du Bicentenaire. Taille-douce. Une bande de phosphore. Dentelé 13.***

2790	**2 f. 20 vert clair**	1 50	0 30
	a. (Non dentelé)	15 »	
	Sans bandes de phosphore.		
2790b	2 f. 20 (sans bande de phosphore)	20 »	

1993. – ***Mémorial des guerres en Indochine (Nécropole de Fréjus). Taille-douce. Dentelé 13.***

Motif symbolique.

2791	**4 f. multicolore**	1 85	0 65
	a. (Non dentelé)	23 »	

Ce timbre porte le millésime 1992.

Tirage : 5 371 957.

1993. – ***Journée du Timbre. Les métiers de la Poste. "La distribution du courrier", d'après une affiche dessinée pour le film "Jour de Fête". Héliogravure. Dentelé 12½ x 13.***

Le facteur et son vélo.

2792	**2 f. 50+60 c. multicolore sur rouge**	1 40	1 10
	a. (Non dentelé)	23 »	

Tirage : 1 942 284.

1993. – ***Idem, sans surtaxe. Émis en carnet. Héliogravure. Dentelé 12½ x 13.*** 🄲

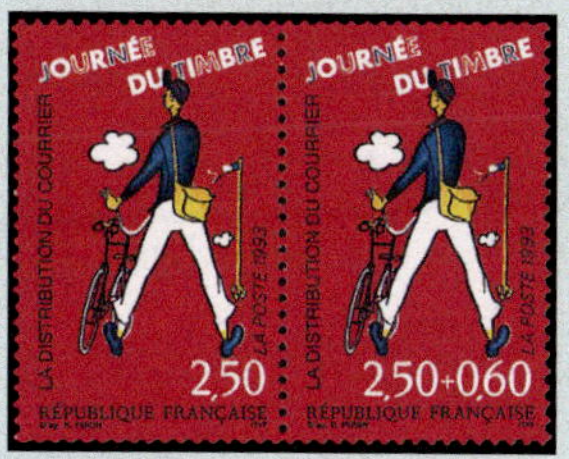

2793 **2 f. 50 multicolore sur rouge** 1 50 0 80

Tirage : 1 196 978 séries.

2793A La paire 2793+2792 3 » 2 50

a. (La paire, avec vignette) 5 » 4 »

La bande (format horizontal) destinée à la confection de carnets comprend 1 vignette, 4 timbres n° 2793 et 3 timbres n° 2792 intercalés entre les précédents.

BC2794 La bande carnet, non pliée 10 » 10 »

1993. – ***Jeux méditerranéens 93. Agde Languedoc Roussillon. Héliogravure. Dentelé 13 x 12½.***

Coureur en action.

2795 **2 f. 50 multicolore** 1 25 0 30

a. (Non dentelé) 35 »

b. (Cicatrice au bras) 25 » » »

Tirage : 15 291 910.

1993. – ***Centenaire du "Droit Humain", Ordre maçonnique mixte international. Taille-douce. Dentelé 13.***

Emblèmes : couple en médaillon.

2796 **3 f. 40 bleu et noir** 1 70 0 65

a. (Non dentelé) 35 »

Tirage : 4 569 906.

1993. – ***Europa. Art contemporain. Héliogravure. Dent. 12½-13.***

Oeuvre d'Olivier Debré, "Rouge rythme bleu".

2797 **2 f. 50 rouge, bleu, vert et violet** 1 25 0 50

Oeuvre de Germaine Richier, "Le griffu".

2798 **3 f. 40 gris clair, gris foncé et bronze** 1 80 0 90

La paire, non dentelée 110 »

Tirages : 16 455 095 et 4 376 647.

Le n° 2797 fait également partie de la série européenne d'art contemporain.

1993. – ***Personnages célèbres. Ecrivains français. Taille-douce. Dentelés 13.*** 🄲

Guy de Maupassant (1850-1893).

Emile Chartier, dit Alain (1868-1951).

2799 **2 f. 50+50 c. bleu, vert et noir** 1 40 1 40

2800 **2 f. 50+50 c. bleu, vert et noir** 1 40 1 40

Jean Cocteau (1889-1963).

Marcel Pagnol (1895-1974).

2801 **2 f. 50+50 c. bleu, vert et noir** 1 40 1 40

2802 **2 f. 50+50 c. bleu, vert et noir** 1 40 1 40

André Chamson (1909-1983).

Marguerite Yourcenar (1903-1987).

2803 **2 f. 50+50 c. bleu, rouge et noir** 1 40 1 40

2804 **2 f. 50+50 c. bleu, vert et noir** 1 40 1 40

N°s 2799 à 2804 (6 val.) **8 40** **8 40**

La série, non dentelée 110 »

Tirages : 1 389 269, 1 401 390, 1 394 740, 1 404 071, 1 382 329 et 1 437 729.

Ont été aussi émis en carnets (tirage : 1 058 740).

La bande (format vertical) destinée à la confection de carnets comprend de haut en bas : une vignette sans valeur (titre de l'émission), une seconde vignette (signatures des écrivains), les timbres n°s 2799 à 2804, dans l'ordre des numéros.

Voir après le n° 2360 la présentation de la bande.

BC2805 La bande carnet, non pliée 9 » 9 »

1993. – ***Type Marianne du Bicentenaire. Sans valeur indiquée (validité permanente). Taille douce. Deux bandes de phosphore. Dentelé 13.*** [C]

2806 **(sans val.) rouge** 1 40 0 15
a. (Non dentelé) 15 »
b. (sans bande de phosphore) 11 »

1993. – ***Type Marianne du Bicentenaire. Sans valeur indiquée (validité permanente). Émis en carnet. Gommage adhésif. Non dentelé.*** [C]

2807 **(sans val.) rouge** 1 50 0 15

Imprimé attenant horizontalement à la gauche d'une vignette sans valeur ("l'enveloppe à cases. Elle facilite votre courrier"). Provenant du carnet n° 1503.
2807a ((sans val.) + vignette) 3 »

Ce timbre non dentelé a été remplacé en 1994 par un timbre comportant une dentelure verticale en lignes ondulées (n° 2874).

1993. – ***IXe Conférence des Cours Constitutionnelles européennes. Protection des Droits de l'Homme. Taille-douce. Dentelé 13.***

Allégorie.

2808 **2 f. 50 multicolore** 1 25 0 30
a. (Non dentelé) 30 »
Tirage : 9 434 623.

1993. – ***Centenaire de la naissance et 10e anniversaire de la mort de Louise Weiss (1893-1983), écrivain et femme politique. Taille-douce. Dentelé 13.***

Portrait : logo européen, main et crayon.

2809 **2 f. 50 noir, crème et rouge** 1 25 0 50
a. (Non dentelé) 30 »
Tirage : 9 778 832.

1993. – ***40e anniversaire de la mort du compositeur et guitariste Django Reinhardt (1910-1953). Héliogravure. Dentelé 13 x 12½.***

Tête vue de face, Reinhardt à la guitare.

2810 **4 f. 20 multicolore** 2 » 0 80
a. (Non dentelé) 23 »
Tirage : 5 438 585.

1993. – ***Congrès de la Fédération des Sociétés Philatéliques françaises, à Lille. Taille-douce. Dentelé 13.***

TGV et bâtiments.

2811 **2 f. 50 multicolore** 1 25 0 50
a. (Non dentelé) 30 »
Tirage : 9 827 621.

1993. – ***Bicentenaire du Muséum national d'Histoire naturelle. Taille-douce et offset. Dentelé 13.***

Sceau, avec rappel des 3 ordres (minéral, végétal, animal).

2812 **2 f. 50 multicolore** 1 25 0 30
a. (Non dentelé) 23 »
Tirage : 9 204 339.

1993. – ***Martyrs et Héros de la Résistance. Héliogravure. Dentelés 13.***

2813 **2 f. 50 noir et gris sur rouge *Martyrs*** 1 40 0 80
2814 **4 f. 20 noir et gris sur rouge *Héros.*** 2 » 1 10
Tirage : 5 676 802 paires.
2813A La paire se tenant 3 50 3 »
a. (La paire, non dentelée) 61 »

Imprimés se tenant horizontalement.

1993. – ***Bicentenaire de la mise en service du télégraphe optique Chappe (1794). Taille-douce. Dentelé 13.***

2815	**2 f. 50 bleu clair, jaune et noir**	1 25	0 30
	a. (Non dentelé)	28 »	

Tirage : 7 550 119.

1993. – ***Série touristique. Taille-douce. Dentelure 13, sauf n° 2817 : 13 x 12½.***

Le petit train d'Artouste (Pyrénées-Atlantiques).

2816	**3 f. 40 bleu, vert et rouge**	1 85	1 »

Chinon, Indre-et-Loire.

2817	**4 f. 20 multicolore**	2 »	1 »

Minerve.

2818	**4 f. 20 brun et vert**	2 »	0 50
	La série, non dentelée	70 »	

Tirages : 3 890 852, 5 451 297 et 4 701 486.

1993. – ***Type Marianne du Bicentenaire. Sans valeur indiquée. Émis en roulettes. Taille-douce. Deux bandes de phosphore. Dentelé 13 horizontalement.***

2819	**(sans val.) rouge**	2 »	0 30
	a. (N° rouge au verso)	2 50	

1993. – ***Type Marianne du Bicentenaire. Taille-douce. Deux bandes de phosphore, sauf n° 2820 : une bande de phosphore à droite. Dentelés 13.***

2820	**2 f. 40 vert**	1 25	0 15
	a. (sans bande de phosphore)	17 »	
2821	**3 f. 50 vert-jaune**	1 70	0 30
	a. (Une bande de phosphore)	2 50	0 30
2822	**4 f. 40 bleu**	2 »	0 65
	La série, non dentelée	54 »	

1993. – ***Type Marianne du Bicentenaire. Provenant de roulettes. Une bande de phosphore à droite. Dentelé 13 horizontalement.***

2823	**2 f. 40 vert**	2 »	1 »
	a. (N° rouge au verso)	2 50	

1993. – ***Type Marianne du Bicentenaire. Provenant du carnet n°1503. Taille douce. Autoadhésif. Une bande de phosphore à droite. Non dentelé.*** C

Imprimé attenant horizontalement à la gauche d'une vignette sans valeur ("L'enveloppe à cases. Elle facilite votre courrier").

2824	**70 c. brun**	13 »	7 »
	a. (70 c. +vignette)	13 »	8 »
	b. ((sans val.) + 70c. + vignette)	18 »	12 »

Remplacé en 1994 par un timbre comportant une dentelure verticale en lignes ondulées (n° 2873)

1993. – *Série touristique. Taille-douce. Dentelés 13.*

Abbaye de la Chaise-Dieu (Haute-Loire).

2825 2 f. 80 brun, bleu et vert 1 40 0 50

Palais et temple de Montbéliard (Doubs).

Le Jacquemard de Lambesc (Bouches-du-Rhône).

2826 4 f. 40 vert, ardoise et brun-rouge 2 » 0 80
2827 4 f. 40 multicolore 2 » 0 80
La série, non dentelée 61 »

Tirages : 15 277 579, 6 210 973 et 6 330 234.

1993. – *Série artistique. 400ᵉ anniversaire de la naissance de Georges de la Tour (1593-1652). Héliogravure. Dentelé 12½ x 13.*

"Saint Thomas".

2828 5 f. multicolore 2 75 1 10
a. (Non dentelé) 61 »

Tirage : 3 880 322.

1993. – *Cinquantenaire de la libération de la Corse. Taille-douce. Dentelé 13.*

Carte de l'île, sous-marin "Casabianca".

2829 2 f. 80 noir, brun-rouge et bleu 1 50 0 30
a. (Non dentelé) 30 »

Tirage : 13 746 395.

1993. – *Bicentenaire de l'implantation du Service de Santé des Armées au Val de Grâce. Taille-douce. Dentelé 13.*

Le Dôme.

2830 3 f. 70 noir et vert 1 70 0 50
a. (Non dentelé) 23 »

Tirage : 8 211 384.

1993. – *Les Postiers autour du monde dans la "Withbread". Type du nº 2789. Taille-douce. Dentelé 13.*

2831 2 f. 80 bleu et jaune (2789) 2 » 0 50
a. (Non dentelé) 23 »

Voir également à la rubrique des "Entiers postaux" (nᵒˢ 2831-CP1 et 2831-CP2).

Tirage : 14 301 047.

1993. – *Série artistique. Cinquantième anniversaire de la mort de Maurice Denis (1870-1943). Héliogravure. Dentelé 12½ x 13.*

"Les Muses".

2832 5 f. multicolore 2 60 1 »
a. (Non dentelé) 61 »

Tirage : 4 092 500.

1993. – *Centre National des Arts du Cirque, à Châlons-sur-Marne. Héliogravure. Dentelé 13.*

"Les Clowns", d'après Albert Gleizes.

2833	**2 f. 80 multicolore**	1 40	0 30
	a. (Non dentelé)	23	»

Tirage : 14 927 518.

1993. – *Série européenne d'art contemporain. Héliogravure. Dentelés 13 x 12½.*

Oeuvre originale de Takis (Grèce).

2834	**5 f. rouge et noir**	2 30	0 80
	a. (Non dentelé)	61	»

"Gravure rehaussée", oeuvre de Marie Hélène Vieira da Silva (1909-1992).

2835	**5 f. multicolore**	2 30	0 80
	a. (Non dentelé)	61	»

Tirages : 3 815 619 et 3 906 369.

1993. – *"Le plaisir d'écrire", vu par 12 auteurs de bandes dessinées. Héliogravure. Dentelés 13½ x 13.* ©

"Bonne Fête", de C. Wendling.

"Bonne Fête", de B. Olivié.

2836	**2 f. 80 multicolore**	1 25	0 50
2837	**2 f. 80 multicolore**	1 25	0 50

"Joyeux anniversaire", de S. Colman.

"Joyeux anniversaire", de G. Sorel.

2838	**2 f. 80 multicolore**	1 25	0 50
2839	**2 f. 80 multicolore**	1 25	0 50

"Avec flamme", de J.-M. Thiriet.

"Plaisir d'écrire", d'E. Davodeau.

2840	**2 f. 80 multicolore**	1 25	0 50
	b. (accent sur le "e" de "avec")	10 »	5 »
2841	**2 f. 80 multicolore**	1 25	0 50

"Félicitations", de J. de Moor.

"Bonne chance", de Mezzo.

2842	**2 f. 80 multicolore**	1 25	0 50
2843	**2 f. 80 multicolore**	1 25	0 50

"Meilleurs voeux", de N. de Crécy.

"Meilleurs voeux", de F. Magnin.

2844	**2 f. 80 multicolore**	1 25	0 50
2845	**2 f. 80 multicolore**	1 25	0 50

"Joyeux Noël", de T. Robin. "Joyeux Noël", de P. Prugne.

2846 **2 f. 80 multicolore** 1 25 0 50
2847 **2 f. 80 multicolore** 1 25 0 50

N°s 2836 à 2847 (12 val.) **15 »** **6 »**

Dentelés 12½.

N°s 2836a à 2847a (12 val.) 17 » 5 50

Émis en carnets ces timbres ont également été émis en feuilles composées de 4 bandes verticales des 12 timbres, séparées les unes des autres par un perçage en lignes et avec inscription dans la marge supérieure ("Feuille de 4 bandes de 12 timbres à 2,80 F : 33,60 F x 4 = 134,40").

Voir également à la rubrique des "Prêt-à-Poster" (n°s 2841-E1, 2844-E1 à 2846-E1).

La bande (format vertical) destinée à la confection de carnets comprend six paires horizontales superposées, entourées de marges blanches.

BC2848 La bande carnet, non pliée 15 » 13 »
a. (Dentelée 12½) 17 » 15 »
b. (Non dentelée) 275 » 275 »
c. (Avec accent sur le "e" de "avec") 25 » 20 »

1993. – ***Salon du Timbre. 1er Salon européen des Loisirs du Timbre (I). Héliogravure. Dentelés 13.*** BF ***n° 15.***

Rhododendrons. Parc floral de Paris.

2849 **2 f. 40 multicolore** 9 » 9 »
2850 **2 f. 40 multicolore** 9 » 9 »

Emis uniquement en feuillet.

1993. – ***Bicentenaire de la création du Musée du Louvre. Héliogravure. Dentelés 13.***

1793 Le Palais devient Musée. 1993 Le Grand Louvre.

2851 **2 f. 80 multicolore** 1 40 1 »
2852 **4 f. 40 multicolore et or** 2 » 1 25

Imprimés se tenant horizontalement pour former panorama. Les diptyques sont imprimés attenant horizontalement de part et d'autre d'une vignette centrale sans valeur (regard de la "Joconde"). Emis en feuille de 20 diptyques, vendus en bande de 2 diptyques et 1 vignette.

2852A **Le diptyque avec vignette** 8 » 7 »
2852B **La bande de 2 diptyques et 1 vignette** 8 » 7 »
a. non dentelée 170 »

Tirage : 2 199 329.

1993. – ***Au profit de la Croix-Rouge. L'imagerie de Metz. Taille-douce. Dentelé 12½ x 13.***

Saint Nicolas.

2853 **2 f. 80+60 c. multicolore** 1 70 1 25
a. (Dentelé 13½ x 13) 1 70 1 25
b. (Non dentelé) 40 »

A été aussi émis en carnets (tirage : 898 823). Le n° 2853a provient de carnets.

Tirage : 1 749 138.

1993

Du n° 2785 au n° 2853 (sauf bandes-carnets, paires et triptyques) :

66 timbres ****132** **⊙68**

Autres rubriques de l'année :

Timbres Autoadhésifs 3 à 5

Bloc-feuillet 15

Préoblitérés 228 à 231

Service 110 et 111

1994. – ***Série "Arts décoratifs". Héliogravure. Dentelés 12½ x 13.***

Verrerie de Gallé (1901). Fonte de Guimard (vers 1900).

2854 **2 f. 80 multicolore** 1 25 0 30
2855 **2 f. 80 multicolore** 1 25 0 30

Ebénisterie de Majorelle (vers 1902). Théière en céramique de Dalpayrat (vers 1898).

2856 **4 f. 40 multicolore** 1 75 0 65
2857 **4 f. 40 multicolore** 1 75 0 65

N°s 2854 à 2857 (4 val.) **6 »** **1 90**

La série, non dentelée 85 »

Tirages : 12 246 349, 13 348 130, 4 987 910 et 5 077 513.

1994. – *Série européenne d'art contemporain. Héliogravure. Dentelé 13 x 12½.*

Oeuvre originale de Sean Scully (Irlande).

2858	**6 f. 70 multicolore**	3 »	1 10
	a. (Non dentelé)	61 »	

Tirage : 5 265 258.

1994. – *Série artistique. Vitrail roman de la cathédrale du Mans. Taille-douce. Dentelé 12½ x 13.*

"La légende de Saint Étienne"(XIIe siècle)

2859	**6 f. 70 multicolore sur bleu**	3 »	1 25
	a. (Non dentelé)	61 »	

Tirage : 5 844 468.

1994. – *4e élections au Parlement Européen. Offset. Dentelé 13.*

Drapeau européen.

2860	**2 f. 80 gris-bleu et jaune**	1 25	0 30
	a. (Non dentelé)	40 »	

Tirage : 11 237 249.

1994. – *150e anniversaire de la mort de Laurent Mourguet (1769-1844), créateur de Guignol. Héliogravure. Dentelé 13.*

Portrait ; la marionnette.

2861	**2 f. 80 multicolore**	1 25	0 50
	a. (Non dentelé)	23 »	

Tirage : 14 489 257.

1994. – *Bicentenaire de la création de l'École Polytechnique. Héliogravure. Dentelé 13.*

"X" allégorique.

2862	**2 f. 80 multicolore**	1 25	0 50
	a. (Non dentelé)	23 »	

Tirage : 8 112 308.

1994. – *Journée du Timbre. Cinquantenaire de la Marianne de Dulac. Timbre sur timbre. Taille-douce. Dentelé 13.*

2863	**2 f. 80+60 c. rouge et bleu**	1 40	1 40
	a. (Id. timbre de carnet, dentelé 13½ x 13)	1 50	1 60
	b. (Non dentelé)	30 »	

Tirage : 1 651 056.

1994. – *Idem, sans surtaxe. Émis en carnet. Taille-douce. Dentelé 13½ x 13* [C]

2864	**2 f. 80 rouge et bleu**	4 »	2 »

Tirage : 974 324 séries.

2864A	La paire 2864+2863a	5 »	4 60
	a. (La paire avec vignette)	7 »	6 »

La bande (format vertical) destinée à la confection de carnets comprend 1 vignette sans valeur, 4 timbres n° 2864 et 3 timbres n° 2863a intercalés entre les précédents (voir au n° 2794).

BC2865	**La bande carnet, non pliée**	**16 »**	**15 »**
	a. non dentelée	305 »	

1994. – *Relations culturelles France-Suède. Émission conjointe franco-suédoise. Émis en carnet. Taille-douce. Dentelés 13.* [C]

"Les Vikings"; détails de la tapisserie de Bayeux.

"Les Vikings"; détails de la tapisserie de Bayeux.

2866	**2 f. 80 multicolore**	2 25	1 10
2867	**2 f. 80 multicolore**	2 25	1 10

Costumes de Fernand Léger pour les Ballets Suédois ("Skating Rink") : "Un marin".

Costumes de Fernand Léger pour les Ballets Suédois ("Skating Rink") : "Monsieur en haut-de-forme".

2868	**2 f. 80 multicolore**	2 25	1 10
2869	**2 f. 80 multicolore**	2 25	1 10

"Fête au Trianon pour Gustave III" (1784), de Niclas Lafrensen le jeune.

2870	**3 f. 70 multicolore**	4 50	1 80

"Relations France-Suède", composition de René Dessirier.

2871	**3 f. 70 multicolore**	4 50	1 80
	N°s 2866 à 2871 (6 val.)	**18 »**	**8 »**

Tirage : 1 505 086 séries.

La Suède a émis simultanément sur ce sujet un carnet de 30 k., de 6 timbres dont 2 sont identiques aux n°s 2870 et 2871 (carnet C1794 cote : 12 »).

La bande (format horizontal) destinée à la confection de carnets comprend les six timbres ci-dessus dans l'ordre de gauche à droite : 2866, 2867, 2870, 2871, 2868, 2869, entourés de marges blanches.

BC2872	La bande carnet, non pliée	18 »	15 »
	a. non dentelée	200 »	

1994. – *Type Marianne du Bicentenaire. Émis en carnets. Gommage adhésif. Dentelés. Précoupé vertical en lignes ondulées.* [C]

Type I

Type II

Type I : lettres plus épaisses, cadre du bas interrompu au milieu et base de l'échancrure du cou arrondie

Type II : lettres plus fines, cadre du bas continu et base de l'échancrure du cou en points

2873	**70 c. brun**	11 »	6 »
2874	**(sans val.) rouge (I)**	1 25	0 15
	a. (Type II)	9 »	4 »

Une bande de phosphore pour le 70 c., deux bandes pour le timbre sans valeur indiquée.

Le n° 2874a provient du carnet 2874-C9.

Imprimé attenant horizontalement à une vignette sans valeur ("l'enveloppe à cases, elle facilite votre courrier"), provenant des carnets n°s 1504 à 1506.

2873a	70 c. +vignette	13 »	8 »

2873b	70 c. (+vignette caractères maigres)	15 »	9 »
2874b	(sans val.) (+vignette)	3 »	1 50
2874ba	(sans val.) (+vignette caractères maigres)	4 »	2 »
2874c	(sans val.) (+70 c. +vignette)	16 »	12 »
2874ca	(sans val.) (+70 c. +vignette caractères maigres)	20 »	15 »

1994. – *20e anniversaire de la mort du Président Georges Pompidou. Taille-douce. Dentelé 13.*

Esquisse du portrait.

2875	**2 f. 80 brun sur verdâtre**	1 25	0 50
	a. (Non dentelé)	30 »	

Tirage : 8 963 204.

1994. – *Hommage aux Maquis. Taille-douce. Dentelé 13.*

Maquisards en embuscade, et convoi ennemi.

2876	**2 f. 80 noir, vert, jaune et bleu**	1 25	0 30
	a. (Non dentelé)	46 »	

Tirage : 7 683 096.

1994. – *"Philexjeunes'94". Exposition philatélique des Jeunes, à Grenoble. Héliogravure. Dentelé 13 x 12½.*

"La chasse aux timbres".

2877	**2 f. 80 multicolore**	1 25	0 30
	a. (Non dentelé)	20 »	

Tirage : 14 189 093.

1994. – *Europa. L'Europe et les découvertes. Taille-douce et offset. Dentelés 13.*

Le virus du SIDA. L'onde de Louis de Broglie.

2878	**2 f. 80 multicolore**	1 40	0 30
2879	**3 f. 70 multicolore**	1 65	1 25
	La paire, non dentelée	80 »	

Tirages : 11 040 316 et 6 960 223.

Le n° 2878 a été réimprimé attenant à une vignette sans valeur à l'occasion de la journée mondiale de lutte contre le SIDA (n° 2916).

1994. – *Inauguration du tunnel sous la Manche. Emission commune franco-britannique. Héliogravure. Dentelés 13½.*

2880	**2 f. 80** ***Lion britannique et coq gaulois se serrant la "main" par-dessus la Manche***	1 25	0 50

2881	**2 f. 80** ***Mains britannique et française (cocardes) sous la mer et au-dessus du TGV***	1 25	0 50

2882	**4 f. 30** ***Lion britannique et coq gaulois se serrant la "main" par-dessus la Manche***	2 »	1 10

2883	**4 f. 30** ***Mains britannique et française (cocardes) sous la mer et au-dessus du TGV***	2 »	1 10
	N°s 2880 à 2883 (4 val.)	**6 50**	**3 20**
	La série, non dentelée	170 »	

Tirages : 8 973 307, 8 973 307, 3 677 868 et 3 677 868.

Imprimés se tenant horizontalement par valeurs faciales identiques.

La Grande-Bretagne a émis simultanément 4 timbres identiques de 25 p. (x 2) et 41 p. (x 2), (n°s 1758 à 1761).

1994. – *Banque asiatique de développement. Offset. Dentelé 13.*

Logo de l'établissement.

2884	**2 f. 80 multicolore**	1 25	0 30
	a. (Non dentelé)	18 50	

Tirage : 7 851 171.

1994. – *67e Congrès de la Fédération des Sociétés Philatéliques Françaises, à Martigues. Taille-douce. Dentelé 13.*

Poisson englobant une vue de la ville.

2885	**2 f. 80 multicolore**	1 25	0 30
	a. (Non dentelé)	18 50	

Tirage : 8 087 369.

1994. – *La Cour de Cassation. Taille-douce et offset. Dentelé 12½ x 13.*

Vue du monument.

2886	**2 f. 80 bleu, noir et jaune**	1 25	0 30
	a. (Non dentelé)	18 50	

Tirage : 7 606 174.

1994. – *50e anniversaire du débarquement des troupes alliées en Normandie. Taille-douce. Dentelés 13.*

Le débarquement.

Hommage aux libérateurs.

2887	**4 f. 30 bleu, rouge et gris**	2 »	0 80
2888	**4 f. 30 multicolore**	2 »	0 80
	La paire, non dentelée	92 »	

Tirages : 7 800 256 et 7 795 045.

1994. – *Centenaire de la création du C.I.O. (Comité International Olympique). Offset. Dentelé 13.*

Visage de P. de Coubertin, coupole de la Sorbonne, anneaux olympiques.

2889	**2 f. 80 multicolore**	1 85	0 50
	a. (Non dentelé)	46 »	

Tirage : 7 823 574.

1994. – *Bicentenaire de l'orgue de la cathédrale de Poitiers. Dentelé 13½.*

Vue du buffet.

2890	**4 f. 40 noir, jaune, lilas et brun-rouge**	2 »	0 65
	a. (Non dentelé)	18 50	

Tirage : 6 000 720.

1994. – *Série touristique. Taille douce, sauf n° 2891 : héliogravure. Dentelés 13.*

La montagne Sainte-Victoire, d'après une aquarelle de Cézanne.

Pays de la Saulx (Meuse). Le pont de Rupt-aux-Nonains.

2891	**2 f. 80 multicolore**	1 25	0 30
2892	**2 f. 80 bleu nuit**	1 25	0 30

Bastia. Le vieux port et l'église Saint-Jean-Baptiste.

Argentat (Corrèze).

2893	**4 f. 40 brun et bleu**	1 85	0 65
2894	**4 f. 40 rouge et brun**	1 85	0 65
	Nos 2891 à 2894 (4 val.)	**6 20**	**1 90**
	La série, non dentelée	80 »	

Tirages : 9 781 660, 11 712 066, 5 912 166 et 5 460 779.

1994. – *Débarquement et bataille de Provence-Août 1944. Taille-douce. Dentelé 13.*

Emblème, tracé des côtes, soldat débarquant, dans la mer.

2895	**2 f. 80 noir, bleu, jaune et rouge**	1 25	0 30
	a. (Non dentelé)	46 »	

Tirage : 11 955 533.

1994. – ***400*[e] *anniversaire de la naissance de Nicolas Poussin (1594-1665). Oeuvre de l'artiste. Taille-douce. Dentelé 13.***

"Moïse et les filles de Jethro".

2896	**4 f. 40 noir et brun-jaune**	2 »	1 »
	a. (Non dentelé)	35 »	

Tirage : 5 068 456.

1994. – ***Personnages célèbres. "De la scène à l'écran". Héliogravure. Dentelés 13.*** [c]

Yvonne Printemps (1894-1977). Fernandel (1903-1971). Joséphine Baker (1906-1975).

2897	**2 f. 80+60 c. multicolore**	1 50	1 50
2898	**2 f. 80+60 c. multicolore**	1 50	1 50
2899	**2 f. 80+60 c. multicolore**	1 50	1 50

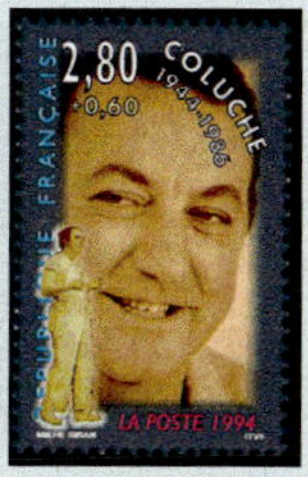

Bourvil (1917-1970). Yves Montand (1921-1991). Coluche (1944-1986).

2900	**2 f. 80+60 c. multicolore**	1 50	1 50
2901	**2 f. 80+60 c. multicolore**	1 50	1 50
2902	**2 f. 80+60 c. multicolore**	1 50	1 50
	N°s 2897 à 2902 (6 val.)	**9 »**	**9 »**
	La série, non dentelée	125 »	

Voir également à la rubrique "Entiers postaux" (N° 2902-CP1).

La bande (format horizontal) destinée à la confection de carnets comprend, de gauche à droite, deux vignettes reproduisant le rideau de scène à l'Olympia, puis les timbres n°s 2897 à 2902, dans l'ordre des numéros.

BC2903	La bande carnet, non pliée	9 »	9 »
	a. (Non dentelée)	230 »	

Tirage : 1 416 202 carnets.

1994. – ***Bicentenaire du Conservatoire National des Arts et Métiers. Taille-douce. Dentelé 13.***

Pendule de Foucault ; carte de France.

2904	**2 f. 80 rouge, noir et bleu**	1 25	0 30
	a. (Non dentelé)	20 »	

Tirage : 7 630 288.

1994. – ***Série touristique. La Grande Cascade du Parc de Saint-Cloud. Taille-douce. Dentelé 13.***

Vue de la cascade.

2905	**3 f. 70 vert-bleu, vert clair et noir**	1 70	0 65
	a. (Non dentelé)	20 »	

Tirage : 5 697 830.

1994. – ***Type Marianne du Bicentenaire. Une fine bande de phosphore à droite. Dentelé 13.***

2906	**2 f. bleu**	1 »	0 15
	a. (Non dentelé)	12 50	

1994. – ***Bicentenaire de l'École Normale Supérieure. Taille-douce. Dentelé 13.***

Porche d'entrée, rue d'Ulm à Paris.

2907	**2 f. 80 lilas et brun-rouge**	1 25	0 30
	a. (Non dentelé)	18 50	

Tirage : 7 923 636.

1994. – *Journée mondiale de prévention des toxicomanies. Héliogravure. Dentelé 13.*

Oeuvre symbolique de V. Velikovic.

2908	**2 f. 80 multicolore**	1 25	0 50
	a. (Non dentelé)	18 50	

Tirage : 7 877 313.

1994. – *Salon du Timbre. 1er Salon européen des Loisirs du Timbre (II). Héliogravure. Dentelés 13. BF n° 16.*

Parc floral de Paris.

Dahlias.

2909	**2 f. 80 multicolore**	9 »	9 »
2910	**2 f. 80 multicolore**	9 »	9 »

Emis uniquement en feuillet.

1994. – *Hommage à Georges Simenon (1903-1989). Émission conjointe Belgo-Franco-Suisse. Taille-douce et offset. Dentelé 13.*

Portrait du romancier ; vue du Quai des Orfèvres.

2911	**2 f. 80 multicolore**	1 40	0 30
	a. (Non dentelé)	28 »	

La Belgique et la Suisse ont chacune émis simultanément un timbre de présentation identique, la vue en arrière-plan étant différente Belgique 16 f. (nº 2579), Suisse 100 c. (nº 1463).

Tirage : 17 064 208.

1994. – *Centenaire de la Grande Loge de France. Taille-douce. Dentelé 13.*

Symboles maçonniques.

2912	**2 f. 80 bleu-vert, rouge et ocre**	1 25	0 30
	a. (Non dentelé)	35 »	

Tirage : 8 703 799.

1994. – *Hommage à Alain Colas (1943-1978). Taille-douce. Dentelé 13.*

Portrait ; mer déchaînée.

2913	**3 f. 70 vert clair, noir et vert foncé**	1 85	0 80
	a. (Non dentelé)	28 »	

Tirage : 5 805 738.

1994. – *Série européenne d'art contemporain. Héliogravure. Dentelé 13 x 12½.*

Oeuvre originale de Georg Baselitz.

2914	**6 f. 70 multicolore**	3 »	1 25
	a. (Non dentelé)	61 »	

Vous désirez voir les personnages ? tournez votre catalogue.

Tirage : 4 573 902.

1994. – *Au profit de la Croix-Rouge. Tapisserie d'Arras (XVe siècle). Héliogravure. Dentelé 12½ x 13.*

Saint Vaast.

2915	**2 f. 80+60 c. multicolore**	1 70	1 25
	a. (Dentelé 13½ x 13)	1 70	1 40
	b. (Non dentelé)	40 »	

A été aussi émis en carnets (tirage : 913 860). Le nº 2915a provient des carnets.

Tirage : 1 767 018.

1994. – *Journée mondiale de lutte contre le SIDA. T.-P. précédent réimprimé attenant à une vignette sans valeur. Taille-douce et offset. Dentelé.*

2916	**2 f. 80 multicolore (2878)**	1 40	0 80
	a. (valeur faciale et légende omises)	7 500 »	

Tirage : 7 857 312.

1994. – *Cinquantenaire de la Fédération nationale de la Presse française. Héliogravure. Dentelé 13.*

2917 **2 f. 80 lilas et jaune** 1 25 0 30
a. (Non dentelé) 15 »

Le n° 2917 porte le millésime 1995.
Tirage : 8 219 584.

1994

Du n° 2854 au n° 2917 :

(sauf bandes-carnets, paires et triptyques) :

61 timbres ****131 ⊙70**

Autres rubriques de l'année :

Timbres Autoadhésifs 6 et 7

Bloc-feuillet 16

Préoblitérés 232 à 235

1995. – *Série touristique. Taille-douce. Dentelé 13.*

Avenue des Champs-Élysées.

2918 **4 f. 40 multicolore** 2 30 0 80
a. (Non dentelé) 28 »

Imprimé attenant à une vignette sans valeur ("Bonne Année 1995-Happy New Year").
Tirage : 5 837 023.

1995. – *1er siècle du cinéma. Héliogravure. Dent. 13.* BF *n° 17.*

Tête d'acteur, projecteur.

Projecteur, tête avec casquette.

2919 **2 f. 80 multicolore** 1 75 1 50
2920 **2 f. 80 multicolore** 1 75 1 50

Projecteur, tête grimée, style "La Bête".

Bobines et tête d'Indien.

2921 **2 f. 80 multicolore** 1 75 1 50
2922 **2 f. 80 multicolore** 1 75 1 50

Nos 2919 à 2922 (4 val.) **7 »** **6 »**
Tirage : 2 334 341 séries.

Emis uniquement en feuillet.

1995. – *Inauguration du pont de Normandie. Taille-douce. Dentelé 13.*

Vue de l'ouvrage d'art.

2923 **4 f. 40 bleu et vert** 2 30 0 65
23 »

Tirage : 5 247 073.

1995. – *Le Notariat européen. Taille-douce. Dentelé 13.*

Drapeau européen, emblème, devise.

2924 **2 f. 80 bleu clair, jaune et bleu foncé** 1 25 0 30
a. (Non dentelé) 23 »

Tirage : 8 372 272.

1995. – *Centenaire de la mort de Louis Pasteur (1822-1895). Héliogravure. Dentelé 13.*

Portrait.

2925 **3 f. 70 multicolore** 1 70 1 10
a. (Non dentelé) 23 »

Tirage : 5 413 259.

1995. – *Série artistique. Dentelés 12½-13.*

La châsse de Saint-Taurin, à Evreux.

2926 **6 f. 70 jaune, brun-rouge et noir** 3 » 1 10
a. (Non dentelé) 54 »

"Etude pour le rêve du bonheur". Oeuvre de Pierre Prud'hon (1758-1823).

2927	**6 f. 70 gris foncé, beu clair et bleu**	3 »	1 10
	a. (Non dentelé)	61 »	

Oeuvre originale de Zao Wou-Ki.

2928	**6 f. 70 bleu fcé, bleu clair, vert et brun**	3 »	1 10
	a. (Non dentelé)	61 »	

Tirages : 4 694 480, 4 912 561 et 4 781 970.

1995. – ***Série "Arts décoratifs". Les oiseaux de J.-J. Audubon. Héliogravure. Dentelés 12½.*** **BF** ***n° 18.***

Aigrette neigeuse.

Pigeons à queue rayée.

2929	**2 f. 80 multicolore**	1 25	0 50
	a. (Dentelé 13½)	1 50	1 50
2930	**2 f. 80 multicolore**	1 25	0 50
	a. (Dentelé 13½)	1 50	1 50

Sterne Pierre-Garin.

Buse pattue.

2931	**4 f. 30 multicolore**	1 75	1 »
	a. (Dentelé 13½)	2 »	2 »
2932	**4 f. 40 multicolore**	1 75	1 »
	a. (Dentelé 13½)	2 »	2 »
	N°s 2929 à 2932 (4 val.)	**6 »**	**3 »**
	La série, non dentelée	92 »	

Tirage : 1 517 342 séries.

Les timbres dentelés 13½ sont issus du bloc.

1995. – ***Journée du Timbre. Cinquantenaire de la Marianne de Gandon. Timbre sur timbre. Taille-douce. Dentelé 13.***

2933	**2 f. 80+60 c. rouge, lilas et vert-gris**	1 75	1 25
	a. (timbre de carnet, longueur 39 mm (au lieu de 40), dentelé 13½ x 13)	2 »	1 50
	b. (Non dentelé)	23 »	

Tirage : 1 656 110.

1995. – ***Idem, sans surtaxe. Émis en carnet. Taille-douce. Dentelé 13½ x 13*** **C**

2934	**2 f. 80 rouge, lilas et vert-gris**	4 »	2 50

Tirage : 958 276 séries.

2934A	La paire 2933a+2934	5 »	4 60
	a. (La paire avec vignette)	7 »	6 »

La bande (format vertical) destinée à la confection de carnets comprend 1 vignette sans valeur, 4 timbres n° 2934, et 3 timbres n° 2933a intercalés entre les précédents.

BC2935	La bande carnet, non pliée	16 »	15 »
	a. (Non dentelée)	305 »	

1995. – ***50e anniversaire de la création des Comités d'Entreprise. Taille-douce. Dentelé 13.***

Composition avec sablier.

2936	**2 f. 80 bleu et brun-jaune**	1 25	0 30
	a. (Non dentelé)	15 »	

Tirage : 8 787 316.

1995. – ***Centenaire de l'École Supérieure d'Électricité. Héliogravure. Dentelé 13.***

Logotype, train, antenne.

2937	**3 f. 70 bleu foncé, bleu clair et rouge**	1 70	1 25
	a. (Non dentelé)	23 »	

Tirage : 4 882 277.

1995. – ***Bicentenaire de l'École des Langues Orientales. Héliogravure. Dentelé 13.***

Lettres : arabe, hébreu, chinois, cyrillique.

2938 **2 f. 80 bleu-vert, bleu, rouge et jaune** 1 25 0 50
a. (Non dentelé) 23 »

Tirage : 9 479 147.

1995. – ***Centenaire de la naissance de Jean Giono (1895-1970). Taille-douce. Dentelé 13.***

Portrait de l'écrivain, paysage.

2939 **3 f. 70 bleu clair, bleu et jaune-brun** 1 85 1 25
a. (Non dentelé) 15 »

Tirage : 4 858 508.

1995. – ***La sidérurgie lorraine. Taille-douce. Dentelé 13 x 12½.***

Acier laminé, câble, ouvrier fondeur, haut fourneau, coulée de métal.

2940 **2 f. 80 multicolore** 1 25 0 30
a. (Non dentelé) 15 »

Tirage : 8 397 847.

1995. – ***Europa. Paix et Liberté. Héliogravure. Dentelés 13.***

2941 **2 f. 80 multicolore sur gris** 1 25 0 30
2942 **3 f. 70 multicolore sur gris** 1 80 1 »

La paire, non dentelée 80 »

Tirages : 9 232 583 et 5 477 765.

1995. – ***Métier de la forêt. Taille-douce. Dentelé 13 x 12½.***

Bûcheron des Ardennes.

2943 **4 f. 40 multicolore** 1 85 0 80
a. (Non dentelé) 15 »

Tirage : 5 246 485.

1995. – ***"8 mai 1945 - La Victoire". Héliogravure. Dentelé 13.***

Portrait du Général de Gaulle et monuments de Paris.

2944 **2 f. 80 bleu, brun-jaune, jaune et rouge** 1 70 0 50
a. (Non dentelé) 46 »

Tirage : 14 923 903.

1995. – ***L'Assemblée Nationale. Héliogravure. Dentelé 13.***

Vue du bâtiment ; Liberté avec drapeau.

2945 **2 f. 80 multicolore** 1 25 0 65
a. (Non dentelé) 20 »

Tirage : 9 342 688.

1995. – ***Au profit de la Croix-Rouge. Tapisserie de Saumur (XVIIe siècle). Héliogravure. Dentelé 12½ x 13.*** [C]

Louis XIII à cheval.

2946 **2 f. 80+60 c. multicolore** 1 70 1 40
a. (Dentelé 13½ x 13) 1 70 1 55
b. (Non dentelé) 40 »

A été aussi émis en carnets (tirage : 827 924). Le n° 2946a provient des carnets.

Tirage : 1 583 020.

1995. – *Cinquantenaire du Secours Populaire Français. Taille-douce. Dentelé 13.*

Logo du mouvement humanitaire.

2947	**2 f. 80 jaune, noir, rouge et bleu**	1 25	0 30
	a. (Non dentelé)	15 »	

Tirage : 8 979 423.

1995. – *Espace et Guyane ; Ariane. Type du n° 2696, sans "EUROPA" ni le sigle C.E.P.T. Taille-douce. Dentelé 12½ x 13.*

2948	**2 f. 80 bleu, rouge et vert (2696)**	1 60	0 30
	a. (Non dentelé)	35 »	

Tirage : 7 757 322.

1995. – *Série courante. Les régions françaises. Taille-douce. Dentelés 13.*

Bretagne.

Vosges.

2949	**2 f. 40 vert**	1 »	0 15
2950	**2 f. 40 vert**	1 »	0 15

Auvergne.

Camargue.

2951	**2 f. 80 rouge**	1 25	0 15
2952	**2 f. 80 rouge**	1 25	0 15
	N°s 2949 à 2952 (4 val.)	**4 50**	**0 60**
	La série, non dentelée	40 »	

Tirages : 27 385 699, 27 177 146, 37 800 566 et 37 710 695.

Les 2 f. 40 sont avec une bande de phosphore à droite, les 2 f. 80 avec deux bandes de phosphore.

1995. – *68e Congrès de la Fédération Française des Associations Philatéliques à Orléans. Taille-douce. Dentelé 13.*

Pont George V et Cathédrale Sainte-Croix.

2953	**2 f. 80 brun, brun-orange et bleu**	1 25	0 30
	a. (Non dentelé)	17 »	

Tirage : 8 270 701.

1995. – *Série touristique. Taille-douce. Dentelés 13.*

La malterie de Stenay (Meuse).

Remiremont (Vosges).

2954	**2 f. 80 vert foncé et olive clair**	1 25	0 30
2955	**2 f. 80 bleu, brun et vert**	1 25	0 30

Le pont de Nyons (Drôme).

Corrèze.

2956	**4 f. 40 multicolore**	2 »	0 80
2957	**4 f. 40 vert, mauve et ardoise**	2 »	0 80
	N°s 2954 à 2957 (4 val.)	**6 50**	**2 20**
	La série, non dentelée	61 »	

Tirages : 8 833 489, 8 790 960, 6 144 929 et 5 885 635.

1995. – *Tricentenaire de la mort de Jean de la Fontaine (1621-1695). Illustrations de fables. Héliogravure. Dentelés.*

2958	**2 f. 80 multicolore sur crème** *La cigale et la fourmi*	1 60	0 80
2959	**2 f. 80 multicolore sur crème** *La grenouille qui veut se faire aussi grosse que le boeuf*	1 60	0 80
2960	**2 f. 80 multicolore sur crème** *Le loup et l'agneau*	1 60	0 80

2961	**2 f. 80 multicolore sur crème**		
	Le corbeau et le renard	1 60	0 80
2962	**2 f. 80 multicolore sur crème**		
	Le chat, la belette et le petit lapin	1 60	0 80
2963	**2 f. 80 multicolore sur crème**		
	Le lièvre et la tortue	1 60	0 80
	N°s 2958 à 2963 (6 val.)	**9 60**	**4 80**

Tirage : 5 171 225 séries.

Imprimés se tenant horizontalement, avec 2 vignettes sans valeur (titres des fables illustrées, portrait du fabuliste).

Voir également à la rubrique des "Prêt-à-Poster" (n°s 2958-E1 à 2963-CP1).

BC2964 La bande		10 »	9 »
	a. (Non dentelée)	170 »	

1995. – *Commémoration de la rafle du 16 juillet 1942 dite "Rafle du Vel d'Hiv"(vélodrome d'hiver). Héliogravure. Dentelé 13.*

Barbelés, étoile, fleur symbolique.

2965	**2 f. 80 multicolore**	1 25	0 50
	a. (Non dentelé)	23 »	

1995. – *Hommage à André Maginot (1877-1932). Taille-douce. Dentelé 13.*

Portrait de l'homme politique et Ministère de la Guerre.

2966	**2 f. 80 brun-jaune et vert**	1 25	0 30
	a. (Non dentelé)	17 »	

Tirage : 7 850 944.

1995. – *50e anniversaire de la Grande Loge Féminine de France. Taille-douce. Dentelé 13.*

Emblème ; colonnes à chapiteau.

2967	**2 f. 80 multicolore**	1 25	0 30
	a. (Non dentelé)	20 »	

Tirage : 9 169 607.

1995. – *500e anniversaire de la Pharmacie hospitalière. Taille-douce. Dentelé 13.*

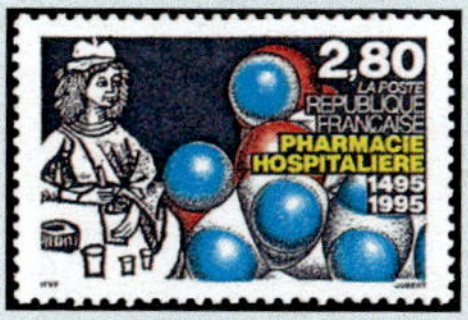

Préparateur d'antan ; gélules.

2968	**2 f. 80 multicolore**	1 25	0 30
	a. (Non dentelé)	17 »	

Tirage : 8 168 174.

1995. – *Série européenne d'art contemporain. Héliogravure. Dentelé 13 x 12½.*

Oeuvre originale de Kirkeby.

2969	**6 f. 70 marron, vert et noir**	3 »	1 25
	a. (Non dentelé)	58 »	

Tirage : 5 117 729.

1995. – *Série touristique. Barbizon. Héliogravure. Dentelé 13.*

"Les chaumières de Barbizon vers 1838-1839". Détail d'un tableau de Diaz de la Peña.

2970	**4 f. 40 multicolore**	2 »	0 80
	a. (Non dentelé)	20 »	

Tirage : 5 557 198.

1995. – *50e anniversaire de l'Ecole Nationale d'Administration. Héliogravure. Dentelé 13.*

Couleurs nationales.

2971	**2 f. 80 bleu, rouge et noir**	1 25	0 30
	a. (Non dentelé)	17 »	

Tirage : 8 354 551.

1995. – *Série artistique. Oeuvre de Berthe Morisot (1841-1895). Offset. Dentelé 12½ x 13.*

"Le Berceau".

2972	**6 f. 70 multicolore**	3 »	1 10
	a. (Non dentelé)	60 »	

Tirage : 4 669 866.

1995. – *Bicentenaire de l'Institut de France. Taille-douce. Dentelé 13.*

Vue aérienne.

2973	**2 f. 80 noir, vert et brun-orange**	1 25	0 30
	a. (Non dentelé)	17 »	

Tirage : 8 685 711.

1995. – *Centenaire de l'Automobile Club de France. Taille-douce. Dentelé 13.*

Parties avant et arrière de voitures ancienne et moderne ; logo et siège du Club, Place de la Concorde à Paris.

2974	**4 f. 40 gris, rouge et bleu**	2 »	0 80
	a. (Non dentelé)	20 »	

Tirage : 5 649 914.

1995. – *Cinquantenaire de l'Organisation des Nations Unies. Héliogravure. Dentelé 13.*

Emblème et nombre 50 ; colombe et casque stylisés.

2975	**4 f. 30 multicolore**	2 »	1 25
	a. (Non dentelé)	20 »	

Tirage : 5 378 159.

1995. – *Personnages célèbres. "Les santons de Provence". Taille-douce. Dentelés 13.* [C]

Le berger. Le meunier. Le tambourinaire et le ravi.

2976	**2 f. 80+60 c. multicolore**	1 50	1 50
2977	**2 f. 80+60 c. multicolore**	1 50	1 50
2978	**2 f. 80+60 c. multicolore**	1 50	1 50

La poissonnière. Le rémouleur. Les vieux.

2979	**2 f. 80+60 c. multicolore**	1 50	1 50
2980	**2 f. 80+60 c. multicolore**	1 50	1 50
2981	**2 f. 80+60 c. multicolore**	1 50	1 50
	Nos 2976 à 2981 (6 val.)	**9 »**	**9 »**
	La série, non dentelée	110 »	

Tirage : 1 388 014 séries.

La bande (format horizontal) destinée à la confection de carnets, comprend, de gauche à droite, deux vignettes représentant un village provençal stylisé, puis les timbres 2976 à 2981, dans l'ordre des numéros.

BC2982 La bande carnet, non pliée 9 » 9 »
a. (Non dentelée) 140 »

1995. – *Hommage à Francis Jammes (1868-1938). Taille-douce. Dentelé 13.*

Portrait de l'écrivain.

2983 3 f. 70 bleu et noir 1 70 1 25
a. (Non dentelé) 17 »

Tirage : 5 048 195.

1995. – *La Cathédrale d'Evry. Taille-douce. Dentelé 13.*

2984 2 f. 80 multicolore 1 40 0 30
a. (Non dentelé) 17 »

Tirage : 7 137 652.

1995. – *"France 98". Coupe du monde de Football (I). Dentelé 13.*

Logo sur terrain stylisé.

2985 2 f. 80 multicolore 1 25 0 30
a. (Non dentelé) 23 »

Voir également à la rubrique "Prêt-à-Poster" (n°s 2985-E1 à 2985-CP1).

1995		
Du n° 2918 au n° 2985		
(sauf bandes-carnets, paires et triptyques) :		
65 timbres	****110**	**⊙54**
Autre rubrique de l'année :		
Blocs et feuillets 17 et 18		

1996. – *Série européenne d'art contemporain. Héliogravure. Dentelés 13 x 12½.*

Oeuvre originale de Wercollier (Luxembourg).

2986 6 f. 70 noir, rouge et bleu 3 » 1 10

"Horizon". Oeuvre originale de Dibbets (Pays-Bas).

2987 6 f. 70 bleu, rouge et noir 3 » 1 10

Tirages : 6 165 090 et 5 758 829.

1996. – *Civilisation des Arawaks (Guadeloupe). Taille-douce. Dentelé 13.*

Chien en céramique.

2988 2 f. 80 multicolore 1 25 0 50

Tirage : 7 071 771.

1996. – *Série artistique. Bicentenaire de la naissance de Jean-Baptiste Corot (1796-1875). Offset. Dentelé 13 x 12½.*

"Le pont de Narni".

2989 6 f. 70 multicolore 3 » 1 10

Tirage : 5 234 438.

1996. – *Journée du Timbre. "Semeuse 1903". Taille-douce. Dentelé 13½.*

2990 2 f. 80+60 c. bleu et rose violacé 1 70 1 50
a. (timbre de carnet, dentelé 13½ x 13) 2 » 1 70
Tirage : 1 864 530.

1996. – *Idem, sans surtaxe. Emis en carnet. Taille-douce. Dentelé 13½ x 13.* 🄲

2991 2 f. 80 bleu et rose violacé 4 » 2 50
a. (Timbre avec vignette) 5 » 3 »
2991A La paire 2991+2990a 6 » 4 60
Tirage : 1 154 867 paires.

La bande (format vertical) destinée à la confection de carnets comprend 1 vignette sans valeur, 4 timbres n° 2991 et 3 timbres n° 2990a.

BC2992 La bande carnet, non pliée 18 » 16 »

1996. – *"L'imaginaire irlandais". Emission conjointe avec l'Irlande. Héliogravure. Dentelé 13½.*

Saint Patrick (d'après l'oeuvre d'Evie Hone).

2993 2 f. 80 multicolore 1 25 0 50

L'Irlande a émis simultanément sur ce sujet une figurine de 32 p. (n° 937 cotes 1,50 1 »).

Tirage : 5 960 508.

1996. – *Centenaire de la naissance de Jacques Rueff (1896-1978). Taille-douce. Dentelé 13.*

Portrait de l'économiste.

2994 2 f. 80 noir, bleu et jaune 1 25 0 50
Tirage : 5 490 049.

1996. – *400e anniversaire de la naissance de René Descartes (1596-1650). Taille-douce. Dentelé 13.*

Portrait du philosophe et savant (d'après Frans Hals).

2995 4 f. 40 rouge-brique 2 » 1 40
Tirage : 5 969 830.

1996. – *Cinquantenaire de Electricité de France-Gaz de France. Héliogravure. Dentelé 13.*

Incandescence d'une ampoule électrique.

2996 3 f. multicolore 1 50 0 50
Tirage : 9 413 295.

1996. – *Série "Nature de France"(XI). Parcs naturels nationaux. Héliogravure. Dentelés 13 x 13½.*

Parc des Cévennes (Marmotte et ancolie). Parc de la Vanoise (Bouquetin et gentiane bleue).

2997 3 f. multicolore 1 40 0 65
2998 4 f. 40 multicolore 2 15 0 80

Parc du Mercantour (Gypaète barbu et saxifrage).

2999 4 f. 40 multicolore 2 15 1 25
Tirages : 10 516 008, 6 332 455 et 5 705 200.

1996. – *50e Salon philatélique d'Automne. Dentelé 13.*

3000 3 f. multicolore 1 40 0 30

A l'exemple de cette sympathique Tour Eiffel, nous avons légèrement joué avec la chronologie pour affecter le n° 3000 au timbre commémorant cet évènement philatélique. Nos amis lecteurs apprécieront certainement ce geste.

Tirage : 10 280 525.

1996. – *Europa. Les femmes célèbres. Héliogravure. Dentelé 13.*

Madame de Sévigné.

3000A 3 f. multicolore 1 40 0 50

Tirage : 11 857 721.

1996. – *Cinquantenaire de l'Institut National de la Recherche Agronomique. Héliogravure. Dentelé 13.*

Pinces saisissant une fleur, et jeunes pousses.

3001 3 f. 80 multicolore 1 90 1 25

Tirage : 6 772 467.

1996. – *Maison de Jeanne d'Arc à Domrémy-la-Pucelle (Vosges). Héliogravure. Dentelé 13.*

3002 4 f. 50 multicolore 2 15 0 65

Tirage : 6 297 310.

1996. – *20e anniversaire de l'Accord RAMOGE. Emission conjointe avec l'Italie et Monaco. Taille-douce. Dentelé 13.*

Poissons, navire, phare et littoral.

3003 3 f. multicolore 1 90 0 50

L'Italie et Monaco ont chacune émis simultanément un timbre de présentation identique :

Italie 750 lires (n° 2167 cotes 1,50 0,50)

Monaco 3 f. (n° 2038 cotes 2 » 0,80).

Tirage : 11 241 200.

1996. – *69e Congrès de la Fédération Française des Associations Philatéliques, à Clermont-Ferrand. Taille-douce. Dentelé 13.*

Flèches de la cathédrale et horloge avec personnages sculptés.

3004 3 f. brun, rouge et vert 1 40 0 50

Tirage : 10 020 590.

1996. – *Type Marianne du Bicentenaire. Taille-douce. Dentelés 13.*

Une bande de phosphore pour le 2 f. 70 et deux bandes de phosphore pour les 3 f. 80 et 4 f. 50.

3005	**2 f. 70 vert**	1 40	0 15
	a. (sans bande de phosphore)	8 »	
3006	**3 f. 80 bleu**	1 70	0 80
3007	**4 f. 50 rose**	2 »	0 30
	a. (sans bande de phosphore)	28 »	

Provenant de roulettes. Une bande de phosphore à droite. Dentelé 13 horizontalement.

3008	**2 f. 70 vert**	2 75	1 50
	a. (N° rouge au verso)	3 »	

Provenant de carnet. Une bande de phosphore. Gommage adhésif précoupé vertical en lignes ondulées.

3009 1 f. orange 5 » 3 »

Imprimé attenant horizontalement à une vignette sans valeur ("Simplifiez vous la vie ! essayez l'enveloppe timbrée"), provenant du carnet 1507.

3009a	1 f. (+vignette)	5 »	3 50
3009b	(2874 (sans val.)+1 f. +vignette)	9 »	7 »

1996. – *"France 98". Coupe du Monde de Football (II). Héliogravure. Dentelés 13.* BF *n° 19.*

Logo, joueurs en action stylisés et mentions.

3010	**3 f. *Lens***	1 40	0 50
3011	**3 f. *Montpellier***	1 40	0 50

3012	**3 f. *Saint-Etienne***	1 40	0 50
3013	**3 f. *Toulouse***	1 40	0 50
	N°s 3010 à 3013 (4 val.)	**5 60**	**2 »**

Voir également à la rubrique des "Prêt-à-Poster" (n°s 3010-E1 à 3013-E1).

1996. – *Série artistique. Le trésor de Neuvy-en-Sullias. Taille-douce. Dentelé 12½ x 13.*

Bronze gallo-romain (Cheval).

3014	**6 f. 70 beige rosé, bronze, vert et marron**	3 »	1 10

Tirage : 5 874 691.

1996. – *Hommage à Jacques Marette (1922-1984). Taille-douce. Dentelé 13.*

Portrait de l'homme politique.

3015	**4 f. 40 violet foncé**	2 »	1 25

Tirage : 5 257 104.

1996. – *Centenaire des Jeux olympiques. Héliogravure. Dent. 13.*

Lanceur de disque.

3016	**3 f. multicolore**	1 40	0 65

Tirage : 11 589 444.

1996. – *Centenaire de la mise en service du train Ajaccio-Vizzavona. Héliogravure. Dentelé 13.*

3017	**3 f. multicolore**	1 40	0 65

Tirage : 10 356 590.

1996. – *Série touristique. Dentelure 13, sauf n° 3020 : 12½ x 13.*

Bitche (Moselle).

Vue des îles Sanguinaires.

3018	**3 f. multicolore**	1 40	0 50
3019	**3 f. multicolore**	1 40	0 50

Abbaye du Thoronet (Var).

Cathédrale de Chambéry.

3020	**3 f. 80 brun et violet**	1 60	1 »
3021	**4 f. 50 multicolore**	1 90	0 80
	N°s 3018 à 3021 (4 val.)	**6 30**	**2 80**

Tirages : 9 269 186, 9 906 847, 4 780 232 et 6 163 979.

1996. – *Centenaire de la consécration de la Basilique Notre-Dame de Fourvière, à Lyon. Taille-douce. Dentelé 13 x 12½.*

3022	**3 f. multicolore**	1 40	0 30

Tirage : 8 804 801.

1996. – *Série artistique. Oeuvre originale d'Arman. Héliogravure. Dentelé 13 x 13½.*

3023 **6 f. 70 noir, or rouge et or jaune** 3 35 1 25
Tirage : 5 861 609.

1996. – *De la Gaule à la France (I) (496-1996). Taille-douce. Dentelé 13.*

Le baptême de Clovis.

3024 **3 f. multicolore** 1 40 0 30
a. (Sans la couleur violette) 600 »
Tirage : 15 260 439.

1996. – *Personnages célèbres. Héros français du roman policier. Héliogravure. Dentelés 13.* 🄲

Rocambole.

Arsène Lupin.

Rouletabille.

3025 **3 f.+60 c. multicolore** 1 60 1 60
3026 **3 f.+60 c. multicolore** 1 60 1 60
3027 **3 f.+60 c. multicolore** 1 60 1 60

Fantômas.

Maigret.

Nestor Burma.

3028 **3 f.+60 c. multicolore** 1 60 1 60
3029 **3 f.+60 c. multicolore** 1 60 1 60
3030 **3 f.+60 c. multicolore** 1 60 1 60

N°s 3025 à 3030 (6 val.) **9 60** **9 60**
Tirage : 1 124 832 séries.

La bande (format vertical) destinée à la confection de carnets comprend de haut en bas, deux vignettes et les timbres n°s 3025 à 3030.

BC3031 La bande carnet, non pliée 10 » 10 »

1996. – *Bicentenaire du Lycée Henri IV. Taille-douce. Dentelé 12½ x 13.*

Vue de la Tour Clovis.

3032 **4 f. 50 multicolore** 2 » 0 80
Tirage : 5 988 255.

1996. – *Cinquantenaire de l'U.N.I.C.E.F. (Fonds des Nations Unies pour l'enfance). Héliogravure. Dentelé 13½.*

3033 **4 f. 50 multicolore** 2 » 0 80
Tirage : 6 679 565.

1996. – *Cinquantenaire du Conseil Economique et Social. Taille-douce. Dentelé 13.*

Façade et hémicycle du Palais d'Iéna.

3034 **3 f. multicolore** 1 40 0 30
Tirage : 8 474 373.

1996. – *Cinquantenaire de l'UNESCO (Organisation des Nations Unies pour l'éducation, la science et la culture). Offset. Dentelé 13.*

Oeuvre du sculpteur Calder et bâtiment de la salle plénière.

3035 **3 f. 80 multicolore** 1 70 1 »
Tirage : 4 569 832.

1996. – *Cinquantenaire de la création des Départements d'Outre-Mer. Héliogravure. Dentelé 13.*

Silhouette avec mention du nom des D.O.M.

3036	**3 f. multicolore**	1 40	0 50

Tirage : 10 409 941.

1996. – *150*ᵉ *anniversaire de l'Ecole Française d'Athènes. Héliogravure. Dentelé 13.*

La tholos (Delphes).

3037	**3 f. multicolore**	1 40	0 50

Tirage : 8 941 394.

1996. – *20*ᵉ *anniversaire de la mort d'André Malraux (1901-1976). Taille-douce. Dentelé 13* x *12½.*

Portrait et signature.

3038	**3 f. multicolore**	1 40	0 50

Tirage : 11 483 713.

1996. – *Au profit de la Croix-Rouge. Fêtes de fin d'année. Héliogravure. Dentelé 12½* x *13.* [C]

Ours blanc et bonhomme de neige en ballon.

3039	**3 f.+60 c. multicolore**	1 70	1 40
	a. (Dentelé 13½ x 13)	1 70	1 60

A été aussi émis en carnets (tirage : 880 602).

Le nᵒ 3039a provient des carnets.

Voir également à la rubrique des "Prêt-à-Poster" (nᵒˢ 3039-E1 à 3039-E5).

Tirage : 1 561 945.

1996. – *50*ᵉ *Festival international du Film de Cannes. Héliogravure. Dentelé 13.*

Clap, caméra et tige de laurier.

3040	**3 f. multicolore**	1 40	0 30

Tirage : 9 687 483.

1996. – *Bibliothèque Nationale de France. Héliogravure. Dentelé 13½.*

3041	**3 f. bleu, rouge et jaune**	1 40	0 30

Tirage : 9 759 120.

1996		
Du n° 2986 au n° 3041		
(sauf bandes-carnets, paires et triptyques) :		
55 timbres	****102**	**⊙49**
Autres rubriques de l'année :		
Timbres Autoadhésifs 8		
Préoblitérés 236 à 239		
Service 114 à 117		

1997. – *1*ᵉʳ *anniversaire de la mort du Président François Mitterrand (1916-1996). Héliogravure. Dentelé 13.*

Portrait.

3042	**3 f. multicolore**	1 40	0 30

Tirage : 17 227 298.

1997. – *Innovation participative. Héliogravure. Dentelé 13½.*

3043 3 f. multicolore 1 40 0 30
Tirage : 11 519 528.

1997. – *20*[e] *anniversaire du Centre Georges Pompidou. Taille-douce. Dentelé 12½ x 13.*

Détail de la façade : escaliers mécaniques.

3044 3 f. vert, bleu et rouge 1 40 0 30
Tirage : 8 325 294.

1997. – *Timbres de souhaits. Héliogravure. Dentelés 13.*

"Bonne fête".

"Joyeux anniversaire".

3045 3 f. multicolore 1 40 0 30
3046 3 f. multicolore 1 40 0 30
Tirages : 9 214 065 et 8 736 199.
Voir également à la rubrique des "Prêt-à-Poster" (n°s 3045-E1, 3046-E1).

1997. – *250*[e] *anniversaire de l'École Nationale des Ponts et Chaussées. Taille-douce. Dentelé 12½ x 13.*

Partie de la façade de la nouvelle École.

3047 3 f. multicolore 1 40 0 30
Tirage : 8 262 928.

1997. – *Patrimoine guyanais. Saint-Laurent-du-Maroni. Taille-douce. Dentelé 12½ x 13.*

Le Camp de la Transportation.

3048 3 f. multicolore 1 40 0 30
Tirage : 8 528 668.

1997. – *Série artistique. Dentelés 13-13½.*

Fresques de Tavant (Indre-et-Loire).
Scènes avec deux personnages.

3049 6 f. 70 multicolore 3 » 1 »

Oeuvre originale de Bernard Moninot.

3050 6 f. 70 multicolore 3 » 1 »
Tirages : 5 858 074 et 6 055 830.

1997. – *Journée du Timbre "Mouchon 1902". Taille-douce. Dentelé 13½.*

3051 3 f.+60 c. violet, gris clair et bleu foncé 1 70 1 25
a. (timbre de carnet, dentelé 13½ x 13) 2 » 1 50
Tirage : 1 454 012.

1997. – *Idem. Sans surtaxe. Emis en carnet. Taille-douce. Dentelé 13½ x 13.* [C]

3052 3 f. violet, gris clair et bleu foncé 4 » 2 50
a. (Timbre avec vignette) 5 » 3 »
3052A La paire 3052+3051a 6 » 4 60
Tirage : 909 689 séries.

La bande (format vertical) destinée à la confection de carnets comprend 1 vignette sans valeur, 4 timbres verticaux n° 3052 et 3 timbres verticaux n° 3051a.

BC3053 La bande carnet, non pliée	19 »	17 »

1997. – *Série "Nature de France"(XII). Parcs naturels nationaux. Héliogravure. Dentelés 13½.*

Parc des Ecrins (Barre des Ecrins, aigle royal et chardon bleu).

Parc de la Guadeloupe (Volcan de la Soufrière, fleur de balisier et racoon (raton laveur).

3054	**3 f. multicolore**	1 40	0 50
3055	**3 f. multicolore**	1 40	0 50

Parc des Pyrénées (Isard et lis jaune).

Parc de Port-Cros (Tête de puffin et lavande maritime).

3056	**4 f. 50 multicolore**	1 90	1 25
3057	**4 f. 50 multicolore**	1 90	1 25
	N°s 3054 à 3057 (4 val.)	**6 60**	**3 50**

Tirages : 11 521 101, 13 354 630, 6 424 678 et 6 298 394.

1997. – *Europa. Contes et légendes. Taille-douce. Dentelé 13.*

"Le chat Botté"de Charles Perrault (d'après illustration de Gustave Doré).

3058	**3 f. bleu**	1 40	0 30

Tirage : 12 255 013.

1997. – *"Philexjeunes'97". Exposition philatélique de jeunes collectionneurs, à Nantes. Offset. Dentelé 13.*

3059	**3 f. multicolore**	1 40	0 30

Tirage : 10 573 301.

1997. – *Les Journées de la Lettre. Le voyage d'une lettre. Héliogravure. Dentelés 13* x *13½.* ©

Enveloppe personnage écrivant une lettre.

Pli grimpant à l'échelle pour accéder à la boîte aux lettres.

3060	**3 f. multicolore**	2 50	1 »
3061	**3 f. multicolore**	2 50	1 »

Pli roulant à toute vitesse.

Facteur portant du courrier et deux plis le suivant.

3062	**3 f. multicolore**	2 50	1 »
3063	**3 f. multicolore**	2 50	1 »

La réception de la lettre.

Sa longue et captivante lecture.

3064	**3 f. multicolore**	2 50	1 »
3065	**3 f. multicolore**	2 50	1 »
	N°s 3060 à 3065 (6 val.)	**15 »**	**6 »**

Tirage : 7 439 291 séries.

Imprimés se tenant verticalement avec mini-vignette supérieure sans valeur.

3065A La bande	15 »	10 »

Tirage : 434 636.

Idem. Emis en carnet de 2 séries. Autoadhésifs Dentelés 11. ©

3066	**3 f. (3060)**	2 »	1 50
3067	**3 f. (3061)**	2 »	1 50
3068	**3 f. (3062)**	2 »	1 50
3069	**3 f. (3063)**	2 »	1 50
3070	**3 f. (3064)**	2 »	1 50
3071	**3 f. (3065)**	2 »	1 50
	N°s 3066 à 3071 (6 val.)	**12 »**	**9 »**

Voir également à la rubrique des "Prêt-à-Poster" (n°s 3060-E1 à 3065-E1).

BC3071A La bande carnet, non pliée	24 »	20 »

Tirage : 7 439 291.

1997. – *Hommage aux combattants français en Afrique du Nord (1952-1962). Dentelé 13.*

Soldat ; carte de l'Afrique du Nord.

3072 **3 f. multicolore** 1 40 0 30

Tirage : 8 323 352.

1997. – *70ᵉ Congrès de la Fédération Française des Associations Philatéliques, à Versailles. Héliogravure. Dentelé 13.*

Façade du château, sculptures du bassin d' Apollon.

3073 **3 f. multicolore** 1 40 0 30

Imprimé attenant à une vignette sans valeur (Logo du 75ᵉ anniversaire de la Fédération des Associations Philatéliques).

1997. – *"France 98". Coupe du Monde de Football (III). Héliogravure. Dentelés 13.* BF *n° 19.*

Logo, joueurs en action stylisés et mentions.

3074 **3 f. *Lyon*** 1 40 0 50

3075 **3 f. *Marseille*** 1 40 0 50

3076 **3 f. *Nantes*** 1 40 0 50

3077 **3 f. *Paris*** 1 40 0 50

Nᵒˢ 3074 à 3077 (4 val.) **5 60** **2 »**

Tirages : 8 354 710, 8 516 834, 8 479 289 et 8 209 295.

Voir également à la rubrique des "Prêt-à-Poster" (nᵒˢ 3074-E1 à 3077-E1).

1997. – *De la Gaule à la France (II) (397-1997). Taille-douce. Dentelé 13½.*

Saint Martin (320-397).

3078 **4 f. 50 multicolore** 2 » 0 80

Tirage : 6 317 371.

1997. – *Série touristique. Taille douce, sauf n° 3081 : taille-douce et offset ; n° 3082 : héliogravure. Dentelés 12½-13½.*

Millau (Aveyron).

Guimiliau (Finistère).

3079 **3 f. vert clair et vert foncé** 1 40 0 30

3080 **3 f. gris-noir et brun clair** 1 40 0 30

Château du Plessis-Bourré (Maine et Loire).

Les Salles-Lavauguyon (Hte-Vienne). ("La Création"fresque de l'église Saint-Eutrope).

3081 **4 f. 40 multicolore** 1 90 1 20

3082 **4 f. 50 multicolore** 1 90 0 70

Nᵒˢ 3079 à 3082 (4 val.) **6 60** **2 50**

Tirages : 9 078 785, (nc), 5 499 206 et 5 770 482.

1997. – *Type Marianne du 14 Juillet. Sans valeur indiquée (validité permanente). Taille-douce. Deux bandes de phosphore. Dentelés 13.*

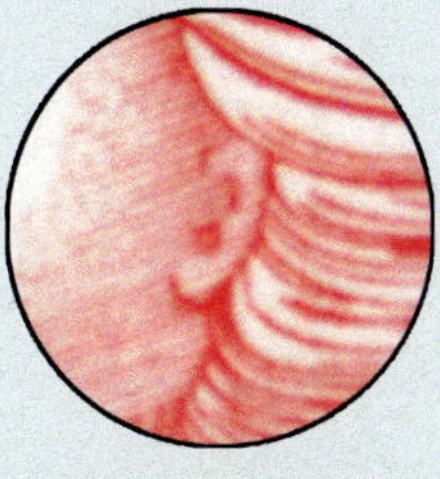

Type I, gravure mécanique, "Oreille intacte".

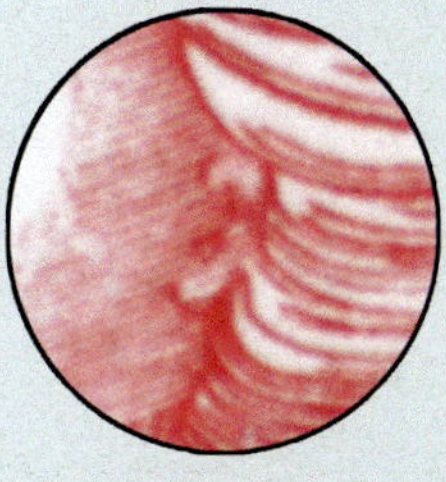

Type II, gravure numérique "Oreille cassée".

3083	**(sans val.) rouge**	1 »	0 15

Provenant de roulette. Dentelé 13 horizontalement.

3084	(sans val.) rouge	2 »	0 50
	a. (N° rouge au verso)	2 50	

Provenant de carnet. Gommage adhésif. Précoupé vertical en lignes ondulées. C

3085	(sans val.) rouge	1 »	0 15
	a. (gravure numérique) (II)	4 »	0 50

Sans bande de phosphore.

3083a	(sans val.)	12 »	
3084b	(sans val.)	» »	

1997. – *Type Marianne du 14 Juillet. Taille-douce. Dentelés 13.* BF *n° 41.* BF *n° 42.*

3086	**10 c. bistre-noir**	0 15	0 15
3087	**20 c. émeraude**	0 15	0 15
3088	50 c. violet-rouge	0 15	0 15
3089	**1 f. orange**	0 40	0 15

3090	**2 f. bleu**	0 65	0 30
3091	**2 f. 70 vert**	1 »	0 15
3092	**3 f. 50 vert-jaune**	1 50	0 30
3093	**3 f. 80 bleu**	2 »	1 30

3094	**4 f. 20 orange foncé**	2 »	0 90
3095	**4 f. 40 bleu**	2 »	1 30
3096	**4 f. 50 rose**	1 50	0 30
3097	**5 f. bleu-vert**	1 50	0 30

3098	**6 f. 70 vert foncé**	2 »	0 30
3099	**10 f. violet**	3 »	0 30

Une bande de phosphore à droite pour les 10 c., 20 c., 50 c., 1 f., 2 f. et 2 f. 70, une bande à gauche pour le 3 f. 50 et deux bandes pour les autres valeurs.

Les timbres sans phosphore proviennent des blocs et feuillets 41 et 42.

Sans bande de phosphore.

3086a	10 c.	14 »	
3091a	2 f. 70	12 »	

Provenant de roulette, une bande de phosphore à droite. Dentelé 13 horizontalement.

3100	**2 f. 70 vert**	2 »	1 25
	a. (N° rouge au verso)	2 50	

Provenant de carnet, une bande de phosphore. Gommage adhésif. Précoupé vertical en lignes ondulées.

3101	**1 f. orange**	4 »	2 »
	c. (gravure numérique) (II)	10 »	7 »
	N°s 3086 à 3101 (16 val.)	**24 »**	**9 30**

Imprimés attenant horizontalement à une vignette sans valeur ("simplifiez vous la vie ! essayez l'enveloppe timbrée") provenant du carnet 1508.

3101a	1 f. +vignette	4 »	2 50
3101aa	(Type II)	10 »	8 »
3101b	3084 (sans val.)+1 f. +vignette	7 »	5 »
3101bc	(Type II)	15 »	12 »

1997. – *Championnats du monde d'Aviron-Savoie. Taille-douce. Dentelé 13 x 13½.*

3102	**3 f. bleu, violet et brun**	1 40	0 30

Tirage : 8 099 187.

1997. – *Corsaires basques. Taille-douce. Dentelé 13½ x 13.*

Corsaires, navire, fort de Socoa et la Rhune.

3103	**3 f. multicolore**	1 40	0 30

Tirage : 8 496 509.

1997. – ***Série artistique. Héliogravure. Dentelés 13½ x 13.***

"Le Pouce". Oeuvre de César.

3104 6 f. 70 multicolore 3 » 1 25

"Raisins et grenades". Oeuvre de Chardin (1699-1779).

3105 6 f. 70 multicolore 3 » 1 25

Tirages : 5 188 850 et 5 684 074.

1997. – ***Voiturier de marée - Port de Boulogne. Taille-douce. Dentelé 13½ x 13.***

3106 3 f. gris, bleu et violet 1 40 0 30

Tirage : 8 008 670.

1997. – ***Série touristique. Taille-douce. Dentelé 12 x 13 (n° 3107), 13 x 12½ (n° 3108) et 13 (n° 3109).***

Sablé-sur-Sarthe.

Basilique Saint-Maurice, à Epinal (Vosges).

3107 3 f. vert, brun et bleu 1 40 0 30

3108 3 f. brun, rouge et vert 1 40 0 30

Les cascades Domaine de Sceaux.

3109 3 f. jaune, vert et bleu 1 40 0 30

Tirages : 8 558 587, 8 494 246 et 8 579 494.

1997. – ***Année du Japon. Taille-douce. Dentelé 13½.***

Kudara Kannon, bodhisattva (statue du VIIe s.) et façade de la Maison de la Culture du Japon à Paris.

3110 4 f. 90 bleu, orange et noir 2 15 1 25

Tirage : 4 205 274.

1997. – ***Championnats du monde de Judo 1997. Héliogravure. Dentelé 13.***

Composition avec judokas.

3111 3 f. multicolore 1 40 0 50

Tirage : 8 131 763.

1997. – ***Espace européen SAR. LOR. LUX (Sarre, Lorraine et Luxembourg). Héliogravure. Dentelé 13.***

Motif symbolique.

3112 3 f. multicolore 1 40 0 50

L'Allemagne et le Luxembourg ont chacun émis simultanément un timbre de présentation identique (respectivement n° 1789 cote : 2 » 1 » et n° 1375 cote : 1,50 0,75).

Tirage : 9 431 280.

1997. – *La Qualité. Héliogravure. Dentelé 13.*

Motif symbolique.

3113	**4 f. 50 multicolore**	1 90	0 65

Tirage : 6 746 187.

1997. – *Le Collège de France. Taille-douce. Dentelé 13.*

Vue du bâtiment ; effigie de François 1er.

3114	**4 f. 40 vert, brun et noir**	1 90	1 »

Tirage : 4 497 468.

1997. – *Personnages célèbres. Héros d'aventures. Héliogravure. Dentelés 13.* 🄲

Lancelot.

Pardaillan.

3115	**3 f.+60 c. multicolore**	1 60	1 60
3116	**3 f.+60 c. multicolore**	1 60	1 60

D'Artagnan.

Cyrano.

3117	**3 f.+60 c. multicolore**	1 60	1 60
3118	**3 f.+60 c. multicolore**	1 60	1 60

Le capitaine Fracasse.

Le Bossu.

3119	**3 f.+60 c. multicolore**	1 60	1 60
3120	**3 f.+60 c. multicolore**	1 60	1 60
	Nos 3115 à 3120 (6 val.)	**9 60**	**9 60**

Tirage : 1 070 219 séries.

La bande (format horizontal) destinée à la confection de carnets comprend de gauche à droite, deux vignettes et les timbres nos 3115 à 3120.

BC3121	La bande carnet, non pliée	10 »	10 »

1997. – *Au profit de la Croix-Rouge. Fêtes de fin d'année. Héliogravure. Dentelé 12½ x 13.* 🄲

Ourson en peluche aux commandes d'une étoile.

3122	**3 f. +60 c. multicolore**	1 70	1 40
	a. (Dentelé 13½ x 13)	1 70	1 60

A été aussi émis en carnets (Tirage : 831 825).

Le no 3122a provient des carnets.

Tirage : 1 453 692.

1997. – *"Meilleurs voeux"du facteur. Héliogravure. Dentelé 13.*

Souris présentant un paquet cadeau à un chat.

3123	**3 f. multicolore**	1 40	0 50

Tirage : 9 996 949.

1997. – *Protection de l'enfance maltraitée. Héliogravure. Dentelé 13½.*

Ours en peluche tenant un moulinet.

3124	**3 f. multicolore**	1 40	0 50

Tirage : 9 035 408.

1997. – *"Meilleurs voeux"du facteur. Héliogravure. Dentelé 13.*

Oeuvre originale du facteur Michel Trani.

3125	**3 f. multicolore**	1 40	0 50

Tirage : 9 261 945.

1997. – ***Cinquantenaire de la mort du Maréchal Leclerc. Héliogravure. Dentelé 13.***

Portrait : Croix de Lorraine sur carte de France.

3126 3 f. vert, noir et bleu 1 40 0 50

Tirage : 9 229 374.

1997. – ***"Philexfrance'99". Exposition philatélique mondiale, à Paris, du 2 au 11 juillet 1999. Taille-douce. Dentelé 13½ x 13.***

Marianne du 14 Juillet et logo de l'exposition.

3127 3 f. bleu et rouge 1 40 0 30

1997. – ***Millénaire de l'abbaye de Moutier d'Ahun (Creuse). Taille-douce. Dentelé 13½ x 13.***

Eglise Notre-Dame ; détail d'une sculpture sur bois (XVIIe s.).

3128 4 f. 40 multicolore 2 » 1 »

Tirage : 5 078 452.

1997		
Du n° 3042 au n° 3128		
(sauf bandes-carnets, paires, triptyques) :		
85 timbres	****146**	**⊙65**
Autres rubriques de l'année :		
Poste aérienne 61		
Timbres Autoadhésifs 9 à 16		

1998. – ***Hommage à Michel Debré (1912-1996). Héliogravure. Dentelé 13.***

Portrait de l'homme politique.

3129 3 f. multicolore 1 40 0 50

Tirage : 7 664 200.

1998. – ***"France'98". Coupe du Monde de Football (IV). Héliogravure. Dentelés 13½. BF n° 19.***

Logo, joueurs en action stylisés et mentions.

3130 3 f. ***Bordeaux*** 1 40 0 50

3131 3 f. ***Saint-Denis*** 1 40 0 50

Tirages : 8 085 858 et 8 122 324.

Voir également à la rubrique des "Prêt-à-Poster" (n°s 3130-E1 et 3131-E1).

1998. – ***Bicentenaire de l'Assemblée Nationale. Héliogravure. Dentelé 13.***

Composition avec façade du bâtiment stylisée.

3132 3 f. rouge sur bleu 1 40 0 50

1998. – ***Timbres de souhaits. "Bonne fête". Héliogravure. Dentelé 13.***

Petite fille tenant un bouquet et un pli avec coeur.

3133 3 f. multicolore 1 40 0 30

Tirage : 8 557 976.

1998. – ***25e anniversaire de la fonction de Médiateur de la République. Offset. Dentelé 13.***

Composition symbolique.

3134 3 f. multicolore 1 40 0 50

Tirage : 8 012 534.

1998. – *Journée du Timbre. "Blanc 1900". Taille-douce. Dentelé 13½.*

3135	**3 f.+60 c. orange sur vert**	1 50	1 25
	a. (timbre de carnet, Dentelé 13½ x 13)	2 »	1 50

Les caractères des noms du dessinateur et du graveur sont légèrement plus grands sur le n° 3135a.

Tirage : 1 704 748.

1998. – *Idem. Sans surtaxe. Emis en carnet. Taille-douce. Dentelé 13½ x 13.* [C]

3136	**3 f. orange sur vert**	4 »	2 50
	a. (Timbre avec vignette)	5 »	3 »

Tirage : 966 459 séries.

3136A	La paire 3136+3135a	6 »	4 60

La bande (format vertical) destinée à la confection de carnets comprend 4 timbres verticaux n° 3136, 1 vignette et 3 timbres verticaux n° 3135a.

BC3137 La bande carnet, non pliée	20 »	18 »

Tirage : 966 459.

1998. – *50e anniversaire de la mort de l'Abbé Franz Stock (1904-1948), aumônier des prisons. Taille-douce. Dentelé 13.*

Portrait.

3138	**4 f. 50 bleu**	1 90	1 »

Tirage : 5 020 920.

1998. – *"France'98". Coupe du Monde de Football (V). Héliogravure. Dentelé.*

Ballon.

3139	**3 f. multicolore**	1 40	0 30

Un timbre à ce type a ensuite été émis avec la mention "Champion du Monde FRANCE" (n° 3170).

Tirage : 35 714 414.

1998. – *Idem. Emis en carnet. Héliogravure. Auto-adhésif. Dentelé.* [C]

3140	**3 f. multicolore**	1 50	0 80

Tirage : 7 969 653 séries.

Un exemplaire de ce timbre figure également sur un feuillet de 286 x 210, comportant 7 vignettes auto-adhésives représentant la mascotte "Footix" au cours de 7 actions de jeu (tête, passe, shoot, etc).

3140a (Le feuillet)	12 »	
BC3140 La bande carnet, non pliée	15 »	

Tirage : 7 969 653.

1998. – *Timbre de souhaits. "Joyeux anniversaire". Héliogravure. Dentelé 13.*

Composition avec bougie.

3141	**3 f. multicolore**	1 40	0 30

Tirage : 7 506 204.

1998. – *Bicentenaire de la réunion de la République de Mulhouse à la France. Héliogravure. Dentelé 13½.*

Mulhousiens célébrant l'événement devant l'Hôtel de Ville.

3142	**3 f. multicolore**	1 40	0 50

Tirage : 9 074 549.

1998. – *900e anniversaire de la fondation de l'abbaye de Cîteaux - Côte d'Or. Taille-douce. Dentelé 13.*

Aile de la bibliothèque entre deux enluminures (un scribe et un lecteur).

3143 3 f. multicolore 1 40 0 50

Tirage : 9 470 807.

1998. – *Patrimoine réunionnais. Saint-Pierre. Taille-douce. Dentelé 13.*

La Sous-Préfecture.

3144 3 f. multicolore 1 40 0 50

Tirage : 8 333 329.

1998. – *Centenaire de la naissance du peintre René Magritte (1898-1967). Emission commune avec la Belgique. Héliogravure. Dentelé 13.*

"Le Retour".

3145 3 f. multicolore 1 50 0 65

La Belgique a émis simultanément un timbre du même type de 17 f. belges (n° 2755).

Tirage : 9 167 913.

1998. – *400e anniversaire de la signature de l'Edit de Nantes. Offset. Dentelé 13.*

Portrait d'Henri IV.

3146 4 f. 50 multicolore 2 » 0 80

Tirage : 5 367 150.

1998. – *Série artistique. Bicentenaire de la naissance du peintre Eugène Delacroix (1798-1863). Taille-douce. Dentelé 12½ x 13.*

"Entrée des Croisés dans Constantinople".

3147 6 f. 70 multicolore 3 » 1 25

Tirage : 4 820 310.

1998. – *150e anniversaire de l'Abolition de l'esclavage. Offset. Dentelé 13.*

Composition symbolique.

3148 3 f. multicolore 1 40 0 50

Tirage : 8 399 615.

1998. – *Centenaire de la Ligue des Droits de l'Homme. Héliogravure. Dentelé 13.*

Composition symbolique.

3149 4 f. 40 multicolore 1 90 1 »

Tirage : 4 628 216.

1998. – *Les Journées de la Lettre. La lettre au fil du temps. Héliogravure. Multicolores. Dentelés 13 x 13½.*

Colombe tenant un pli et l'arche de Noé.

Scribe égyptien.

3150 3 f. multicolore 2 50 1 »

3151 3 f. multicolore 2 50 1 »

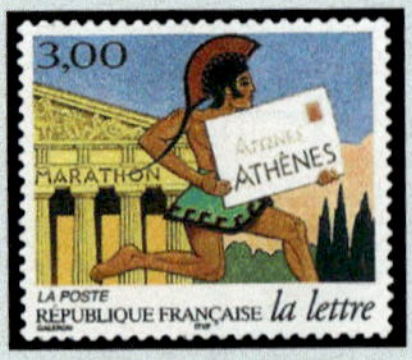

Messager de Marathon portant un pli destiné à Athènes.

Chevalier avec pli et porte-plume géants.

3152	**3 f. multicolore**	2 50	1 »
3153	**3 f. multicolore**	2 50	1 »

L'écrivain Voltaire.

Cosmonaute avec une lettre.

3154	**3 f. multicolore**	2 50	1 »
3155	**3 f. multicolore**	2 50	1 »
	N°s 3150 à 3155 (6 val.)	**15 »**	**6 »**

Imprimés se tenant verticalement avec mini-vignette supérieure sans valeur.

3155A	La bande carnet, non pliée	15 »	10 »

Tirage : 2 342 104.

Idem. Emis en carnet de 2 séries. Autoadhésifs. Multicolores. [C]

3156	**3 f. multicolores (3150)**	2 »	1 50
3157	**3 f. multicolores (3151)**	2 »	1 50
3158	**3 f. multicolores (3152)**	2 »	1 50
3159	**3 f. multicolores (3153)**	2 »	1 50
3160	**3 f. multicolores (3154)**	2 »	1 50
3161	**3 f. multicolores (3155)**	2 »	1 50
	N°s 3156 à 3161 (6 val.)	**12 »**	**9 »**

Tirage : 2 905 848 séries.

BC3161A	La bande carnet, non pliée	24 »	

1998. – *Série artistique. Oeuvre de Pablo Picasso (1881-1973). Offset. Dentelé 13 x 13½.*

"Le Printemps". © Succession Picasso 98.

3162	**6 f. 70 multicolore**	3 »	1 25

Tirage : 6 609 416.

1998. – *Hommage au compositeur Henri Collet (1885-1951). Taille-douce. Dentelé 12½ x 13.*

Portrait ; extrait de la partition de la "Symphonie de l'Alhambra".

3163	**4 f. 50 gris, jaune et noir**	2 »	1 »

Tirage : 5 457 567.

1998. – *71e Congrès de la Fédération Française des Associations Philatéliques, à Dunkerque. Taille-douce. Dentelé 13½.*

Géant, Bateau feu de France, église Saint-Eloi.

3164	**3 f. multicolore**	1 40	0 30

Tirage : 9 748 106.

1998. – *Le Mont Saint-Michel. Héliogravure. Dentelé 13.*

3165	**3 f. multicolore**	1 90	0 65

Tirage : 12 982 187.

1998. – *Europa. Festivals nationaux. Fêtes nationales. La Fête de la Musique le 21 juin. Héliogravure. Dentelé 13.*

Le dieu Pan.

3166 **3 f. multicolore** 1 40 0 50

Tirage : 10 872 487.

1998. – *Série touristique. Héliogravure, sauf n° 3169 : taille douce. Dentelés 13.*

Le Gois - Ile de Noirmoutier (Vendée).

La Baie de Somme.

3167 **3 f. multicolore** 1 40 1 »

3168 **3 f. multicolore** 1 40 0 50

Le château de Crussol (Ardèche).

3169 **3 f. multicolore** 1 40 0 30

Tirages : 8 367 789, 9 473 425 et 10 039 684.

1998. – *"France'98". Coupe du Monde de Football (VI). T.-P. de même date avec la mention "Champion du Monde FRANCE". Héliogravure.*

3170 **3 f. multicolore** 1 40 0 30

Tirage : 12 440 852.

1998. – *Centenaire de la mort du poète Stéphane Mallarmé (1842-1898). Taille-douce et offset. Dentelé 13.*

Portrait.

3171 **4 f. 40 multicolore** 1 90 1 »

Tirage : 3 509 890.

1998. – *Centenaire de l'Aéro-Club de France. Héliogravure. Dentelé 13.*

Composition avec avions, ballon.

3172 **3 f. multicolore** 1 40 0 50

Tirage : 9 192 284.

1998. – *Emission commune France-Chine. Patrimoine culturel. Héliogravure. Dentelés 13½.*

Palais impérial.

Palais du Louvre - Paris.

3173 **3 f. multicolore** 1 60 0 50

3174 **4 f. 90 multicolore** 2 30 1 20

Tirages : 9 441 381 et 4 493 139.

La Chine a émis simultanément deux timbres aux mêmes types (n°s 3609 et 3610 cote 1,25).

1998. – *"Philexfrance 99". Exposition philatélique internationale (II). Emis en feuillet et en bande se tenant. "Le Petit Prince"d'Antoine de Saint-Exupéry (1900-1944). © Fondation Saint-Exupéry 1998. Héliogravure. Dentelés 13.* **BF** *n° 20.*

3175 **3 f.** ***Portrait du petit Prince*** 1 40 0 80

3176 **3 f.** ***Le petit Prince avec le renard*** 1 40 0 80

3177	**3 f.** ***Le petit Prince sur sa planète***	1 40	0 80
3178	**3 f.** ***Le petit Prince assis sur un mur, et le serpent***	1 40	0 80
3179	**3 f.** ***Le petit Prince arrosant la fleur***	1 40	0 80
	Nos 3175 à 3179 (5 val.)	**7 »**	**4 »**

Tirage : 3 520 868 séries.

3179A	La bande	7 »	5 »

1998. – ***Série touristique. La Collégiale de Mantes-la-Jolie. Taille-douce. Dentelé 13½.***

3180	**4 f. 40 multicolore**	1 90	1 »

Tirage : 3 926 212.

1998. – ***L'Opéra de Paris - Palais Garnier. Héliogravure. Dentelé 13½.***

Détail du rideau d'avant-scène, silhouette de danseuse.

3181	**4 f. 50 multicolore**	1 90	0 80

Tirage : 6 397 059.

1998. – ***Série "Nature de France"(XIII). Chevaux. Héliogravure. Multicolores. Dentelés 13½.***

3182	**2 f. 70** ***Le camarguais***	1 40	0 50
3183	**3 f.** ***Le trotteur***	1 40	0 50

3184	**3 f.** ***Le Pottok***	1 40	0 50
3185	**4 f. 50** ***L'ardennais***	2 »	1 »
	Nos 3182 à 3185 (4 val.)	**6 20**	**2 50**

Tirages : 19 365 376, 10 068 500, 10 701 081 et 6 916 359.

1998. – ***Centenaire du Salon de l'Auto. Héliogravure. Dentelé 12½.***

Dessins d'un bolide et d'une de Dion-Bouton.

3186	**3 f. multicolore**	1 40	0 50
	a. (rouge omis)	5 000 »	

Tirage : 8 854 016.

1998. – ***Personnages célèbres. Acteurs du cinéma français. Héliogravure. Dentelés 13.*** 🄲

Romy Schneider (1938-1982). Simone Signoret (1921-1985). Jean Gabin (1904-1976).

3187	**3 f.+60 c. multicolore**	2 »	2 »
3188	**3 f.+60 c. multicolore**	2 »	2 »
3189	**3 f.+60 c. multicolore**	2 »	2 »

Louis de Funès (1914-1983). Bernard Blier (1916-1989). Lino Ventura (1919-1987).

3190	**3 f.+60 c. multicolore**	2 »	2 »
3191	**3 f.+60 c. multicolore**	2 »	2 »
3192	**3 f.+60 c. multicolore**	2 »	2 »
	Nos 3187 à 3192 (6 val.)	**12 »**	**12 »**

Tirage : 944 798 séries.

La bande (format vertical) destinée à la confection de carnets comprend de haut en bas, une vignette et les timbres n°s 3187 à 3192.

BC3193 La bande carnet, non pliée	12 »	12 »

1998. – *Série touristique. Saint-Dié (Vosges). Taille-douce. Dentelé 13.*

La Tour de la Liberté.

3194	**3 f. multicolore**	1 40	0 30

Tirage : 9 361 812.

1998. – *40e anniversaire de la Constitution de la Ve République. Héliogravure. Dentelé 13.*

Composition symbolique.

3195	**3 f. multicolore**	1 40	0 50

Tirage : 9 594 822.

1998. – *80e anniversaire de l'Armistice. Héliogravure. Dentelé 13 x 13½.*

Composition avec drapeaux des pays belligérants.

3196	**3 f. multicolore**	1 40	0 50

Tirage : 7 235 949.

1998. – *Série artistique. Oeuvre de Marcel Duchamp. Héliogravure. Dentelé 13 x 13½.*

Les neufs moules Malic.

3197	**6 f. 70 multicolore**	3 »	1 25

Tirage : 3 990 450.

1998. – *Cinquantenaire de l'Union Mondiale pour la Nature (UICN). Offset. Dentelé 13 x 13½.*

Composition avec logo, visage d'enfant, macareux, étoile de mer, fleur.

3198	**3 f. multicolore**	1 40	0 50

Tirage : 3 965 129.

1998. – *Au profit de la Croix-Rouge. Fêtes de fin d'année. Héliogravure. Dentelé 12½ x 13.* [C]

Lutin marchant sur une boule dorée.

3199	**3 f. +60 c. multicolore**	1 60	1 10
	a. (Dentelé 13½ x 13)	1 60	1 40

A été aussi émis en carnets (Tirage : 790 756).

Le n° 3199a provient des carnets.

Tirage : 1 333 983.

1998. – *"Meilleurs Voeux". Emis uniquement en feuillet. Héliogravure. Dentelés 13 x 13½.* [BF] ***n° 21.***

Père Noël sur surf des neiges ; collines jaunes. — Maison décorée, aux volets verts. — Père Noël sur surf et cimes de sapins.

3200	**3 f. multicolore**	2 »	0 80
3201	**3 f. multicolore**	2 »	0 80
3202	**3 f. multicolore**	2 »	0 80

Maison décorée, aux volets rouges.

Père Noël sur surf et collines enneigées.

3203 **3 f. multicolore** 2 » 0 80
3204 **3 f. multicolore** 2 » 0 80

N°s 3200 à 3204 (5 val.) **10 »** **4 »**

Tirage : 3 998 825 séries.

Sur les timbres n°s 3200, 3202 et 3204 figure "Bonne Année" ; sur ceux n°s 3201 et 3203 figure "Meilleurs Voeux".

1998. – ***Médecins Sans Frontières. Héliogravure. Dentelé 13½.***

Logo et dessin de Plantu.

3205 **3 f. multicolore** 1 40 0 50

Tirage : 8 424 894.

1998. – ***Nouvel hémicycle du Parlement Européen. Héliogravure. Dentelé 13.***

3206 **3 f. multicolore** 1 40 0 50

Tirage : 9 017 758.

1998. – ***150e anniversaire de la naissance du peintre Paul Gauguin (1848-1903). Héliogravure. Dentelé 13 x 13½.***

D'après "Vision après le sermon".

3207 **6 f. 70 multicolore** 3 » 1 60

Tirage : 4 911 908.

1998. – ***Cinquantenaire de la Déclaration Universelle des Droits de l'Homme. Offset. Dentelés 13½ x 13.***

Globe et 4 visages.

3208 **3 f. multicolore** 1 40 0 50

Portraits de R. Cassin et E. Roosevelt.
Palais de Chaillot.

3209 **3 f. multicolore** 1 40 0 50

Tirages : 7 847 308 et 5 531 456.

1998. – ***Centenaire de la découverte du radium par Pierre et Marie Curie. Héliogravure. Dentelé 13.***

Composition symbolique.

3210 **3 f. multicolore** 1 40 0 50

Tirage : 6 387 286.

1998

Du n° 3129 au n° 3210

(sauf bandes-carnets, paires et triptyques)

80 timbres ****144** **⊙72**

Autres rubriques de l'année :

Poste aérienne 62

Timbres Autoadhésifs 17 à 23

Blocs et feuillets 19 à 21

Service 118 et 119

1999. – ***150e anniversaire du premier timbre-poste français. Emis en carnet. Timbres sur timbres. Taille-douce. Dentelés 13.*** **C**

"Cérès noir"de 1849 sur timbre. "Cérès rouge"de 1849 sur timbre.

3211 **3 f. noir et rouge** 7 » 5 »
3212 **3 f. rouge et noir** 1 25 0 50

Tirage : 2 166 956 paires.

3212A La paire 3211+3212+vignette 8 50 5 »

La bande (format vertical) destinée à la confection de carnets comprend de haut en bas, une vignette avec le logo et les dates de l'Exposition philatélique mondiale "Philexfrance 99", le timbre n°3211 et 4 timbres n°3212.

BC3213 La bande carnet, non pliée 12 » 12 »

1999. – *Le timbre Euro. Taille-douce. Dentelés 13.*

Symbole de l'euro.

3214 3 f. rouge et bleu 1 » 0 15

Idem. Emis en carnet. Auto-adhésif. Précoupé vertical en lignes ondulées. Ⓒ

3215 3 f. rouge et bleu 1 50 0 50

BC3215A La bande carnet, non pliée 12 » 12 »

1999. – *150ᵉ anniversaire de l'Assistance publique - Hôpitaux de Paris. Héliogravure. Dentelé 13½.*

3216 3 f. multicolore sur rose 1 40 0 50

Tirage : 7 869 628.

1999. – *50 ans de relations diplomatiques France-Israël. Héliogravure. Dentelé 13.*

Composition avec drapeaux des deux Etats.

3217 4 f. 40 multicolore 2 » 1 »

Tirage : 3 661 337.

1999. – *Saint-Valentin. Héliogravure. Dentelés.*

Coeur avec "Je t'aime". Rose dans un coeur.

3218 3 f. multicolore 1 50 0 50

3219 3 f. multicolore 1 50 0 50

Tirages : 7 844 196 et 8 534 935.

1999. – *Saint-Valentin. Héliogravure. Autoadhésif. Multicolore. Dentelés.* Ⓒ

3220 3 f. *Cœur avec "Je t'aime"* (3218) 2 50 0 80

3221 3 f. *Rose dans un coeur* (3219) 2 50 0 80

Tirage : 2 453 722 paires.

BC3221A La bande carnet, non pliée 20 » 15 »

1999. – *Série artistique. Jean Goujon, architecte et sculpteur (v. 1510-v. 1566). Taille-douce. Dentelé 13½ x 13.*

3222 6 f. 70 multicolore 2 75 1 25

Tirage : 3 711 475.

1999. – *Recensement de la Population. Héliogravure. Dent. 13½.*

Composition symbolique.

3223 3 f. multicolore 1 40 0 50

Tirage : 8 969 556.

1999. – *Patrimoine culturel du Liban. Héliogravure. Dentelé 12½.*

D'après mosaïque de pavement "L'Enlèvement d'Europe".

3224 4 f. 40 multicolore 1 50 0 80

Tirage : 5 039 001.

1999. – ***Journée du Timbre. Astérix. © 1999 Les Editions Albert René/Goscinny-Uderzo. Héliogravure. Dentelés 13½.*** [C]

Oeuvre originale d'Albert Uderzo.

3225	**3 f. multicolore**	1 40	0 50
3225a	3 f. (provenant de carnet, dentelé 13½)	1 50	0 80
3225b	3 f. (timbre 3225a avec vignette)	3 »	1 50

Idem. Emis en carnet. Dentelé 13½ x 13. [C]

3226	**3 f.+60 c. multicolore**	4 »	2 50
3226A	**La paire 3226+3225a**	5 50	4 »

Idem. Emis uniquement en feuillet. Sans réserve blanche autour de l'image. Dentelé 13½ x 13. [BF] *n° 22.*

3228	**3 f. +60 c. multicolore**	2 75	2 50

Tirage : 1 471 430.

La bande (format vertical) destinée à la confection de carnets comprend 4 timbres verticaux no 3225a, 1 vignette et 3 timbres verticaux n° 3226.

BC3227 La bande carnet, non pliée — 18 » — 16 »

1999. – ***Timbre pour Mariages. Héliogravure. Dentelé 13.***

Couple de tourterelles, coeurs, "Oui".

3229	**3 f. multicolore**	1 »	0 50

Tirage : 15 785 596.

1999. – ***Timbre pour Remerciements. Héliogravure. Dentelé 13.***

"merci"en plusieurs langues.

3230	**3 f. multicolore**	1 »	0 50

Tirage : 10 246 896.

1999. – ***Timbres pour Naissances. Héliogravure. Dentelés 13.***

Cigogne avec petit paquet et "c'est une fille".

Idem et "c'est un garçon".

3231	**3 f. rose, noir et bleu**	1 »	0 50
3232	**3 f. bleu, noir et rose**	1 »	0 50

Tirages : 12 069 478 et 12 353 144.

1999. – ***Cinquantenaire du Conseil de l'Europe. Héliogravure. Dentelé 13.***

Carte du monde et étoiles européennes.

3233	**3 f. multicolore**	1 40	0 50

Tirage : 8 749 529.

1999. – ***"Philexfrance'99". Exposition philatélique internationale (III). Emis uniquement en feuillet. Chefs-d'oeuvre de l'Art. Taille-douce pour le n° 3234, offset pour les autres valeurs. Dentelure 13, sauf n° 3234 : 13½ x 13.*** [BF] ***n° 23.***

La Vénus de Milo (2ᵉ s. av. J.-C.).

La Joconde, de Léonard de Vinci (1452-1519).

3234	**5 f. multicolore**	15 »	15 »
3235	**5 f. multicolore**	30 »	30 »

Détail de "La Liberté guidant le peuple" d'Eugène Delacroix (1798-1863).

3236 **10 f. multicolore** 20 » 20 »

Emis uniquement en feuillet vendu 50 f. dont 30 f. reversés à l'Association pour le Développement de la Philatélie.

1999. – ***13 juin 1999, élections au Parlement européen. Héliogravure. Dentelé 13.***

Oeuvre originale de Jean-Michel Folon.

3237 **3 f. multicolore** 1 40 0 50

Tirage : 7 506 444.

1999. – ***800ᵉ anniversaire de la mort du Roi d'Angleterre Richard Iᵉʳ Coeur de Lion (1157-1199). Taille-douce. Dentelé 13 x 12.***

Détail de l'"Historia Anglorus"(d'après photo).

3238 **3 f. multicolore** 1 40 0 50

Tirage : 6 791 259.

1999. – ***Série touristique. Dieppe. Taille-douce. Dentelé 13½.***

3239 **3 f. multicolore** 1 40 0 30

Tirage : 7 944 627.

1999. – ***Europa. Réserves et parc naturels. La Camargue. Héliogravure. Dentelé 13 x 13½.***

Flamants roses en vol, cheval s'abreuvant, coucher de soleil.

3240 **3 f. multicolore** 1 40 0 50

Tirage : 8 759 012.

1999. – ***Timbre "Bonne vacances". Héliogravure. Dentelé 13.***

Soleil avec lunettes.

3241 **3 f. multicolore** 1 25 0 50

Tirage : 12 201 066.

1999. – ***Timbre "Joyeux anniversaire". Héliogravure. Dentelé 13.***

Gâteau avec bougie.

3242 **3 f. multicolore** 1 25 0 50

Tirage : 8 737 064.

1999. – ***Timbre "Vive les vacances". Héliogravure. Dentelé 13.***

Bouchon flottant.

3243 **3 f. multicolore** 1 25 0 50

Tirage : 11 991 541.

1999. – ***Saint-Pierre, patrimoine martiniquais. Héliogravure. Dentelé 13.***

Maison de la Bourse, hibiscus, barque, volcan, mer.

3244 **3 f. multicolore** 1 40 0 50

Tirage : 7 493 091.

1999. – *Série touristique. Château du Haut-Koenigsbourg (Bas-Rhin). Taille-douce et offset. Dentelé 13.*

3245	**3 f. multicolore**	1 25	0 60

Tirage : 5 995 562.

1999. – *Centenaire de l'Ecole de Nancy. Offset. Dentelé 13.*

Détail de la coupe "Noctuelles"d'Emile Gallé.

3246	**3 f. multicolore**	1 40	0 50
	a. (Non dentelé)	150 »	

Tirage : 9 297 921.

1999. – *Série artistique. Claude Monet (1840-1926). Offset. Dentelé 13.*

"Nymphéas, effet du soir".

3247	**6 f. 70 multicolore**	3 »	1 25

Tirage : 4 992 635.

1999. – *Congrès mondial de Roses anciennes, à Lyon. Emis uniquement en feuillet. Héliogravure. Dentelés 13½ x 13.* BF *n° 24.*

Rose "Madame Alfred Carrière" (1879).

Rose "Madame Caroline Testout" (1890).

3248	**3 f. multicolore**	4 »	3 »
3249	**4 f. 50 multicolore**	4 »	3 »

Rose "La France" (1867).

3250	**4 f. 50 multicolore**	4 »	3 »

Tirage : 1 902 214 séries.

1999. – *800ᵉ anniversaire de la Jurade de Saint-Emilion. Taille-douce. Dentelé 13½ x 13.*

Sceau d'origine et vignes de "la grande muraille".

3251	**3 f. 80 multicolore**	1 70	1 20

Tirage : 3 663 727.

1999. – *Hôtel de la Monnaie, à Paris. Taille-douce. Dentelé 13.*

3252	**4 f. 50 multicolore**	2 »	0 80

Tirage : 5 994 382.

1999. – *Bicentenaire de la naissance de la Comtesse de Ségur (1799-1874). Héliogravure. Dentelé 13½.*

"Les Petites Filles modèles"(1858).

3253	**3 f. multicolore**	1 40	0 50

Tirage : 8 884 221.

1999. – *Série artistique. Vitrail de la cathédrale d'Auch. Taille-douce. Dentelé 13½ x 13.*

Détail de vitrail réalisé par Arnaud de Moles.

3254 6 f. 70 multicolore 3 » 1 25
Tirage : 3 907 372.

1999. – *Timbre "Aimer accueillir". Héliogravure. Dentelé 13.*

Mosaïque avec soleil, colombes, fleurs.

3255 3 f. multicolore 1 40 0 50
Tirage : 8 967 013.

1999. – *Série touristique. Figeac (Lot). Taille-douce. Dentelé 13½.*

3256 3 f. multicolore 1 40 0 30
Tirage : 8 348 183.

1999. – *Bicentenaire de la naissance de l'explorateur René Caillié (1799-1838). Taille-douce. Dentelé 13½ x 13.*

Portrait.

3257 4 f. 50 multicolore 2 » 0 80
Tirage : 5 606 640.

1999. – ***"Philexfrance'99". Exposition philatélique internationale (III). 150e anniversaire du premier timbre-poste français. Héliogravure. Dentelé 12 x 13.***

Composition avec le timbre n° 3 sur timbre et le visage de Cérès en hologramme.

3258 6 f. 70 multicolore 4 » 2 »

Imprimé avec petite vignette attenant horizontalement comportant la mention "Philexfrance'99" - Paris et le logo de l'Exposition.

Ce timbre fût le dernier timbre en francs.

Tirage : 3 360 554.

1999. – ***Célébration de l'an 2000. Héliogravure. Dentelé 13½.***

Composition symbolique.

3259 3 f. (0,46 €) multicolore 1 40 0 50

Tirage : 8 596 121.

1999. – ***"Dessine-moi l'an 2000". Héliogravure. Dent. 13 x 12½.***

Oeuvre de Morgane Toulouse (9 ans).

3260 3 f. (0,46 €) multicolore 1 40 0 50

Tirage : 8 730 690.

1999. – ***Eclipse de soleil, le 11 août 1999. Héliogravure. Dentelé 12½.***

La Lune occultant le disque solaire.

3261 3 f. (0,46 €) multicolore 1 40 0 50

Tirage : 9 701 481.

1999. – ***Personnages célèbres. Les oeuvres des grands photographes français. Héliogravure. Dentelés 13.*** [C]

Robert Doisneau.

Braissaï.

3262 3 f.+60 c. (0,46+0,09 €) multicolore 1 90 1 90

3263 3 f.+60 c. (0,46+0,09 €) multicolore 1 90 1 90

Jacques-Henri Lartigue.

Henri Cartier-Bresson.

3264 3 f.+60 c. (0,46+0,09 €) multicolore 1 90 1 90

3265 3 f.+60 c. (0,46+0,09 €) multicolore 1 90 1 90

Atget.

Nadar.

3266 3 f.+60 c. (0,46+0,09 €) multicolore 1 90 1 90

3267 3 f.+60 c. (0,46+0,09 €) multicolore 1 90 1 90

Nos 3262 à 3267 (6 val.) **11 40** **11 40**

Tirage : 963 790 séries.

La bande (format horizontal) destinée à la confection de carnets comprend de gauche à droite, une vignette et les timbres nos 3262 à 3267.

BC3268 La bande carnet, non pliée 12 » 12 »

1999. – ***Série "Collection Jeunesse". Armada du siècle - Rouen 1999. Grands voiliers. Héliogravure. Multicolores. Dentelés 13.*** [BF] ***n° 25.***

3269 1 f. (0,15 €) ***"Simón Bolivar"*** 0 60 0 50

3270 1 f. (0,15 €) ***"Iskra"*** 0 60 0 50

3271 1 f. (0,15 €) ***"Statsraad Lehmkuhl"*** 0 60 0 50

3272 1 f. (0,15 €) ***"Asgard II"*** 0 60 0 50

3273 **1 f. (0,15 €) *"Belle-Poule"*** 0 60 0 50
3274 **1 f. (0,15 €) *"Belem"*** 0 60 0 50

3275 **1 f. (0,15 €) *"Amérigo Vespucci"*** 0 60 0 50
3276 **1 f. (0,15 €) *"Sagres"*** 0 60 0 50

3277 **1 f. (0,15 €) *"Europa"*** 0 60 0 50
3278 **1 f. (0,15 €) *"Cuauhtemoc"*** 0 60 0 50

Nos 3269 à 3278 (10 val.) **6 »** **5 »**

Tirage : 3 277 294 séries.

1999. – *Série touristique. Arnac-Pompadour (Corrèze). Taille-douce. Dentelé 13 x 13½.*

Le château.

3279 **3 f. (0,46 €) multicolore** 1 40 0 50

Tirage : 8 900 801.

1999. – *Coupe du monde de Rugby 1999. Héliogravure. Dentelé.* BF *n° 26.*

Plaquage.

3280 **3 f. (0,46 €) multicolore** 1 10 0 50
a. (Sans le "F"de "ITVF") 6 »

Tirage : 11 812 584.

1999. – *Hommage à Frédéric Ozanam (1813-1853). Taille-douce. Dentelé 13.*

Portrait de l'historien.

3281 **4 f. 50, (0,69 €) multicolore** 1 90 0 80

Tirage : 4 950 197.

1999. – *Cinquantenaire du Mouvement Emmaüs. Héliogravure. Dentelé 13.*

Silhouettes d'hommes et de femmes se tenant par la main ; logo.

3282 **3 f. (0,46 €) multicolore** 1 40 0 50

Tirage : 8 516 890.

1999. – *Série "Nature de France"(XIV). Chats et chiens. Héliogravure. Dentelés 13½.*

Le chartreux.

L'européen.

3283 **2 f. 70, (0,41 €) multicolore** 1 25 0 50
3284 **3 f. (0,46 €) multicolore** 1 25 0 50

Le montagne des Pyrénées.

L'épagneul breton.

3285 **3 f. (0,46 €) multicolore** 1 25 0 50
3286 **4 f. 50, (0,69 €) multicolore** 1 90 1 »

Nos 3283 à 3286 (4 val.) **5 65** **2 50**

Tirages : 16 937 307, 10 891 595, 11 206 547 et 6 655 178.

1999. – ***150e anniversaire de la mort du compositeur Frédéric Chopin (1810-1849). Emission commune Pologne - France. Taille-douce. Dentelé 13½.***

Portrait de profil ; bâtiment de la Bibliothèque de l'Université, à Varsovie.

3287	**3 f. 80, (0,58 €) bleu, violet et orange**	1 25	1 »

La Pologne a émis simultanément une figurine au même type de 1 z. 40, (n° 3564 cotes : 1,50 1 »).

Tirage : 4 401 778.

1999. – ***Au profit de la Croix-Rouge. Fêtes de fin d'année. Héliogravure. Dentelé 12½ x 13.*** 🄲

Etoile s'apprêtant à frapper les douze coups de minuit sur un tambour-horloge.

3288	**3 f. +60 c. (0,46+0,09 €) multicolore**	1 60	1 10
	a. (Dentelé 13½ x 13)	1 60	1 40

A été aussi émis en carnets (Tirage : 756 536).

Le n° 3288a provient des carnets.

Tirage : 1 287 089.

1999. – ***400e anniversaire de la naissance du peintre flamand Antoon Van Dyck (1599-1641). Héliogravure. Dentelé 13½ x 13.***

Détail du portrait de Charles à la chasse.

3289	**6 f. 70, (1,02 €) multicolore**	3 »	1 40

Tirage : 4 834 869.

1999. – ***"Meilleurs Voeux 2000". Héliogravure. Dentelé 13 x 13½ (n° 3290) et 13 (n° 3291).***

Paquet cadeau dont le papier déchiré fait découvrir un morceau de ciel.

3290	**3 f. (0,46 €) multicolore**	1 25	0 50

Composition avec le nombre 2000.

3291	**3 f. (0,46 €) multicolore**	1 25	0 65

Le timbre n° 3291 est imprimé attenant horizontalement à une vignette sans valeur (mention "Vive l'An 2000" en plusieurs langues).

1999. – ***Centenaire du Métro. Héliogravure. Dentelé 13.***

Panneaux anciens et modernes.

3292	**3 f. (0,46 €) multicolore**	1 25	0 50

Tirage : 9 336 704.

1999. – ***Bicentenaire du Conseil d'Etat. Héliogravure. Dentelé 13 x 12½.***

Dessin d'entablement.

3293	**3 f. (0,46 €) multicolore**	1 25	0 50

Tirage : 6 329 612.

1999

Du n° 3211 au n° 3293 (sauf bandes-carnets, paires et triptyques) :

80 timbres ****196** **⊙137**

Autres rubriques de l'année :

Poste aérienne 63

Timbres Autoadhésifs 24 à 26

Blocs et feuillets 22 à 26

Service 120 et 121

2000. – *Le phare du bout du monde. Héliogravure. Dentelé 13 x 12½.*

Le phare de San Juan de Salvamento (Cap Horn) et sa réplique à la Rochelle achevée le 1er janvier 2000.

3294 **3 f. (0,46 €) multicolore** 1 25 0 50

Tirage : 19 295 891.

2000. – *Saint-Valentin. Coeurs 2000 du couturier Yves Saint Laurent. Héliogravure. Dentelés.* BF *n° 27.*

Coeurs entourés de deux serpents. Coeur avec profil féminin.

3295 **3 f. (0,46 €) multicolore** 1 50 0 60

3296 **3 f. (0,46 €) multicolore** 1 50 0 60

2000. – *Saint-Valentin. Coeurs 2000 du couturier Yves Saint Laurent. Héliogravure. Autoadhésif. Dentelés.* C

3297 **3 f. (0,46 €)** ***Cœurs entourés de deux serpents*** **(3295)** 2 50 1 »

3298 **3 f. (0,46 €)** ***Cœur avec profil féminin*** **(3296)** 2 50 1 »

Tirage : 1 719 608 paires.

BC3298A La bande carnet, non pliée 20 » 15 »

2000. – *Bicentenaire de la Banque de France. Offset. Dentelé 13.*

Portail, parties de billets.

3299 **3 f. (0,46 €) multicolore** 1 » 0 30

Tirage : 9 151 038.

2000. – *Bicentenaire de la création du Corps préfectoral. Héliogravure. Dentelé 13 x 12½.*

Allégorie.

3300 **3 f. (0,46 €) multicolore** 1 » 0 50

Tirage : 8 578 997.

2000. – *Série artistique. Sandro Botticelli (1445-1510). Héliogravure. Dentelé 13.*

"Vénus et les Grâces offrant des présents à une jeune fille"(détail de fresque).

3301 **6 f. 70, (1,02 €) multicolore** 2 75 1 90

Tirage : 4 910 543.

2000. – *Série touristique. La cité de Carcassonne (Aude). Héliogravure. Dentelé 13.*

3302 **3 f. (0,46 €) multicolore** 1 » 0 60

Tirage : 9 963 764.

2000. – *Fête du Timbre. © Hergé/Moulinsart 2000. Héliogravure. Dentelés 13½.*

Tintin et Milou (d'après l'oeuvre de Hergé).

3303	**3 f. (0,46 €) multicolore**	1 40	0 50
3303a	(provenant de carnet, Dentelé 13½ x 13)	1 50	0 70
3303b	(timbre 3303a avec vignette)	3 »	1 50

Idem. Emis en carnet. Dentelés 13½ x 13. C BF *n° 28.*

3304	**3 f. +60 c. (0,55 €) multicolore**	2 50	1 80

Tirage : 1 054 591 paires.

3304A	La paire 3304+3303a	4 »	3 »

La bande (format vertical) destinée à la confection de carnets comprend 1 timbre n° 3303a et 1 vignette, et 3 paires successives n°s 3303a+3304.

BC3305	La bande carnet, non pliée	16 »	16 »

2000. – *Flore. Pervenche de Madagascar. Offset. Dentelé 13 x 13½.*

3306	**4 f. 50, (0,69 €) multicolore**	1 40	0 80

Tirage : 6 780 877.

2000. – *Le Parlement de Bretagne (Rennes). Héliogravure. Dentelé 13½.*

3307	**3 f. (0,46 €) multicolore**	1 »	0 30

Tirage : 9 495 807.

2000. – *Timbre "Félicitations". Héliogravure. Dentelé 13.*

Composition avec "Félicitations", fleur stylisée.

3308	**3 f. (0,46 €) multicolore**	1 »	0 30

2000. – *Série artistique. Camille Claudel (1864-1943). Héliogravure. Dentelé 13½ x 13.*

Sculpture "La Valse".

3309	**6 f. 70, (1,02 €) multicolore**	2 75	1 40

Tirage : 4 468 344.

2000. – *Série touristique. Saint-Guilhem-le-Désert (Hérault). Taille-douce. Dentelé 13½.*

3310	**3 f. (0,46 €) multicolore**	1 »	0 30

Tirage : 9 690 478.

2000. – *Série touristique. Gérardmer - Vallée des lacs (Vosges). Taille-douce. Dentelé 13½.*

3311	**3 f. (0,46 €) multicolore**	1 »	0 30

Tirage : 10 024 180.

2000. – ***Le siècle au fil du timbre (I). Le sport. Héliogravure. Dentelure 13½ x 13, sauf n° 3312, 3316 : 13.*** **BF** ***n° 29.***

Portrait du boxeur Marcel Cerdan et détail ceinture (champion du monde des poids moyens en 1948).

L'athlète américain Carl Lewis (4 médailles d'or aux Jeux olympiques de Los Angeles, en 1984).

3312	**3 f. (0,46 €) multicolore**	1 »	0 50
	a. (3312+3316 la paire verticale se tenant)	2 50	1 80
3313	**3 f. (0,46 €) multicolore**	1 »	0 50

La France, championne du monde de football en 1998 (coupe et supporters en fond).

Le skieur Jean-Claude Killy (3 médailles d'or aux Jeux olympiques de Grenoble en 1968).

3314	**3 f. (0,46 €) multicolore**	1 »	0 50
3315	**3 f. (0,46 €) multicolore**	1 »	0 50

L'aviateur Charles Lindbergh et partie avant de son avion le "Spirit of Saint Louis" (1ère traversée sans escale de l'Atlantique les 20-21 mai 1927).

3316	**3 f. (0,46 €) multicolore**	1 »	0 50
	Nos 3312 à 3316 (5 val.)	**5 »**	**2 50**

Tirage : 5 895 439 séries.

Le feuillet comprend deux séries, la première dans la partie supérieure est sur un format photographique illustrant l'équipe de France victorieuse de la coupe du monde de football, Jean-Claude Killy et Charles Lindbergh à son arrivée au Bourget ; la seconde, dans la partie inférieure est une bande se tenant des cinq timbres.

3316A	La bande	6 »	4 »

2000. – ***Série "Collection Jeunesse". Voitures anciennes. "Philexjeunes 2000"- Annecy. Héliogravure. Multicolores. Dentelés 13½ x 13.*** **BF** ***n° 30.***

3317	**1 f. (0,15 €)** ***Bugatti 35***	0 40	0 35
3318	**1 f. (0,15 €)** ***Citroën Traction***	0 40	0 35

3319	**1 f. (0,15 €)** ***Renault 4 CV***	0 40	0 35
3320	**1 f. (0,15 €)** ***Simca Chambord***	0 40	0 35

3321	**1 f. (0,15 €)** ***Hispano-Suiza K6***	0 40	0 35
3322	**2 f. (0,30 €)** ***Coccinelle Volkswagen***	0 80	0 60

3323	**2 f. (0,30 €)** ***Cadillac 62***	0 80	0 60
3324	**2 f. (0,30 €)** ***Peugeot 203***	0 80	0 60

3325	**2 f. (0,30 €)** ***Citroën DS19***	0 80	0 60
3326	**2 f. (0,30 €)** ***Ferrari 250 GTO***	0 80	0 60
	Nos 3317 à 3326 (10 val.)	**6 »**	**4 75**

Tirage : 3 065 089 séries.

2000. – *Europa 2000. Héliogravure. Dentelé 13½.*

Colonne d'étoiles européennes et enfants cueillant de nouvelles étoiles.

3327 **3 f. (0,46 €) multicolore** 1 » 0 50

Tirage : 8 948 921.

2000. – ***300**^e^ **anniversaire de la naissance de l'ingénieur et agronome Henri-Louis Duhamel du Monceau (1700-1782). Taille-douce. Dentelé 13.***

Portrait sur fond de forêt.

3328 **4 f. 50, (0,69 €) multicolore** 1 40 0 80
a. (bleu omis)

Tirage : 5 290 745.

2000. – *73e Congrès de la Fédération Française des Associations Philatéliques, à Nevers. Taille-douce. Dentelé 13½.*

Aiguière en faïence, du 17e s. et la Porte de Croux.

3329 **3 f. (0,46 €) multicolore** 1 » 0 30

Tirage : 9 413 848.

2000. – *Timbre "Bonnes vacances". Héliogravure. Dentelé 13.*

Composition symbolique.

3330 **3 f. (0,46 €) multicolore** 1 » 0 30

Tirage : 1 687 497.

2000. – *Cinquantenaire de la conquête de l'Annapurna. Taille-douce. Dentelé 13 x 12½.*

Alpinistes en cordée et montagne en fond.

3331 **3 f. (0,46 €) multicolore** 1 » 0 50

Tirage : 9 434 075.

2000. – *Série "Nature de France" (XV). Faune et flore. Héliogravure. Dentelés 13½.* **BF** *n° 31.*

Papillon sardanapale.

Girafe réticulée.

3332 **2 f. 70, (0,41 €) multicolore** 1 » 0 50
3333 **3 f. (0,46 €) multicolore** 1 » 0 50

Allosaure.

Tulipa lutea.

3334 **3 f. (0,46 €) multicolore** 1 » 0 50
3335 **4 f. 50, (0,69 €) multicolore** 1 40 1 »

N°s 3332 à 3335 (4 val.) **4 40** **2 50**

Tirages : 9 610 899, 2 103 922, 11 100 790 et 6 715 091.

Pour les timbres n°s 3332 à 3335, en juxtaposant à droite ou à gauche, au-dessus ou en-dessous de chaque timbre, un autre exemplaire du même timbre, on obtient l'image de l'animal en entier.

2000. – *Série touristique. Abbatiale d'Ottmarsheim (Haut-Rhin). Taille-douce. Dentelé 12½ x 13.*

3336 **3 f. (0,46 €) multicolore** 1 » 0 30

Tirage : 10 852 927.

2000. – ***Centenaire de la naissance d'Antoine de Saint-Exupéry (1900-1944). Héliogravure. Dentelé 13.***

Portrait, avion.

3337 3 f. (0,46 €) multicolore 1 » 0 50

Tirage : 11 869 655.

2000. – ***Le Train jaune de Cerdagne. Héliogravure. Dentelé 13.***

Le train de face et sur un viaduc.

3338 3 f. (0,46 €) multicolore 1 » 0 50

Tirage : 9 963 430.

2000. – ***Folklores. Héliogravure. Dentelé 13.***

Silhouettes de danseurs, musicien, instruments de musique.

3339 4 f. 50, (0,69 €) multicolore 1 40 0 80

Tirage : 5 548 595.

2000. – ***Jeux olympiques de Sydney (Australie). Disciplines. Héliogravure. Dentelés 13.*** BF ***n° 31A.***

3340 3 f. (0,46 €) ***Cyclisme, escrime, relais*** 1 » 0 50

3341 3 f. (0,46 €) ***Relais, judo, plongeon*** 1 » 0 50

Tirage : 3 409 172 paires.

3340A La paire 3340+3341 2 » 1 50

a. (La paire, avec vignette Henri Didon) 6 » 5 »

2000. – ***Personnages célèbres. Les grands aventuriers français. Héliogravure. Dentelés 13.*** C

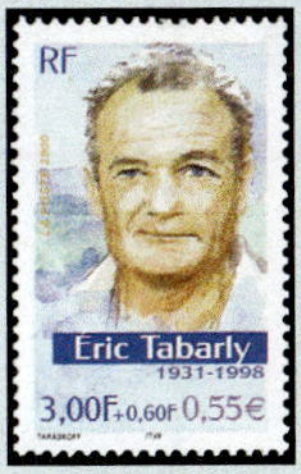

Eric Tabarly (1931-1998).

Alexandra David-Néel (1868-1969).

3342 3 f. +0.60 f. (0,55 €) multicolore 1 25 0 80

3343 3 f. +0.60 f. (0,55 €) multicolore 1 25 0 80

Haroun Tazieff (1914-1998).

Paul-Emile Victor (1907-1995).

3344 3 f. +0.60 f. (0,55 €) multicolore 1 25 0 80

3345 3 f. +0.60 f. (0,55 €) multicolore 1 25 0 80

Jacques-Yves Cousteau (1910-1997).

Norbert Casteret (1897-1987).

3346 3 f. +0.60 f. (0,55 €) multicolore 1 25 0 80

3347 3 f. +0.60 f. (0,55 €) multicolore 1 25 0 80

Nos 3342 à 3347 (6 val.) **7 50** **4 80**

Tirage : 2 562 396 séries.

La bande (format vertical) destinée à la confection de carnets comprend une vignette et les timbres nos 3342 à 3347.

BC3348 La bande carnet, non pliée 10 »

2000. – ***25e anniversaire de la mort du Frère Alfred Stanke (1904-1975). Taille-douce. Dentelé 13.***

Portrait et cathédrale de Bourges.

3349 4 f. 40 (0,67 €) bleu-noir, bleu et brun 1 50 1 »

Tirage : 3 139 953.

2000. – *Série artistique. Gaston Chaissac (1910-1964). Héliogravure. Dentelé 13½ x 13.*

Tableau "Visage rouge".

3350	**6 f. 70 (1,02 €) multicolore**	2 50	1 40

Tirage : 10 395 270.

2000. – *Le siècle au fil du timbre (II). Société. Emis uniquement en feuillet. Héliogravure. Dentelés 13½-13.* BF *n° 32.*

1901, le lave-linge.

1936, les congés payés (famille se baignant d'après photo d'époque).

3351	**3 f. (0,46 €) multicolore**	1 »	0 50
3352	**3 f. (0,46 €) multicolore**	1 »	0 50

1944, le droit de vote des femmes (femmes votant).

1948, la Déclaration universelle des Droits de l'Homme (mentions : dignité, droits de l'homme, libres, égaux, et mur en brique en fond).

3353	**3 f. (0,46 €) multicolore**	1 »	0 50
3354	**3 f. (0,46 €) multicolore**	1 »	0 50

1969, le premier pas sur la Lune (astronaute sur la Lune).

3355	**3 f. (0,46 €) multicolore**	1 »	0 50
Nos 3351 à 3355 (5 val.)		**5 »**	**2 50**
3355A	La bande issue du BF n° 32	5 »	3 50

Tirage : 5 895 439.

2000. – *40e anniversaire de S.O.S. amitié. Offset. Dentelé 13.*

3356	**3 f. (0,46 €) multicolore**	1 »	0 50

2000. – *2001 nouveau millénaire. Offset. Dentelé 13.*

3357	**3 f. (0,46 €) multicolore**	1 »	0 30

Tirage : 4 933 796.

2000. – *Série artistique. Mosaïque (9e siècle) de Germigny-des-Prés (Loiret). Héliogravure. Dentelé 13½ x 13.*

Détail (ange).

3358	**6 f. 70 (1,02 €) multicolore**	2 50	1 40

Tirage : 12 870 664.

2000. – *Hommage au dessinateur Raymond Peynet (1908-1999). Taille-douce. Dentelé 13½ x 13.*

"Le kiosque des amoureux - Valence".

3359	**3 f. (0,46 €) multicolore**	2 »	0 60

Tirage : 8 743 795.

2000. – *Faune en voie de disparition. Emission commune avec la Nouvelle-Zélande. Héliogravure. Dentelés 13½.*

Kiwi austral (Nouvelle-Zélande).

3360 **3 f. (0,46 €) multicolore** 1 20 0 50

Faucon crécerellette (France).

3361 **5 f. 20 (0,79 €) multicolore** 1 80 1 20

Tirages : 9 281 120 et 3 007 257.

La Nouvelle-Zélande a émis simultanément deux timbres aux mêmes types (nos 1793 et 1798).

2000. – *Au profit de la Croix-Rouge. Fêtes de fin d'année. Héliogravure. Dentelé 13½ x 13.*

Avion en bois avec pilote larguant des cadeaux.

3362 **3 f. +60 c. (0,55 €) multicolore** 1 25 1 »

2000. – *"Bonne année" et "Meilleurs voeux". Héliogravure. Dentelé 12½ x 13 (n° 3363) et 13½ x 13 (n° 3364).*

Cristaux de neige et feuille de houx.

3363 **3 f. (0,46 €) multicolore** 1 » 0 30

Boule de neige - Terre avec bonnet rouge.

3364 **3 f. (0,46 €) multicolore** 1 » 0 30

Tirages : 13 737 871 et 13 737 871.

2000. – 3ème *millénaire. Héliogravure. Dentelé 13 x 13½.*

3365 **3 f. (0,46 €) *Pli avec carte du monde et @*** 1 20 0 50

Imprimé attenant horizontalement à une vignette sans valeur (symboles @ et "Meilleurs voeux"). Emis en petite feuille de 10 timbres+vignettes avec marges illustrées de nuages.

F3365 La feuille 12 » 8 »

2000. – *Métallurgie - 1900-2000. Taille-douce. Dentelé 13 x 13½.*

3366 **4 f. 50 (0,69 €) multicolore et argent *Silhouette de tour Eiffel et de fusée Ariane*** 1 60 1 »

Tirage : 4 046 406.

2000

Du n° 3294 au n° 3366 :

(sauf bandes-carnets, paires et triptyques) :

71 timbres ****86** **⊙45**

Autres rubriques de l'année :

Poste aérienne 64

Timbres Autoadhésifs 27 et 28

Blocs et feuillets 27 à 32

2001. – *Championnat du monde de Handball, à Nantes. Héliogravure. Dentelé 13½.*

Joueur stylisé.

3367 **3 f. (0,46 €) multicolore** 1 » 0 50

Tirage : 14 994 651.

2001. – ***Saint-Valentin. Coeur 2001 du couturier Christian Lacroix. Héliogravure.*** BF ***n° 33.***

3368 3 f. (0,46 €) multicolore 1 » 0 50

Tirage : 12 451 763.

2001. – ***Série artistique. Pieter Bruegel l'Ancien (v. 1525-1569). Taille-douce. Dentelé 13 x 13½.***

"La danse des paysans".

3369 6 f. 70 (1,02 €) multicolore 2 50 1 40

2001. – ***Fête du Timbre, Gaston Lagaffe (d'André Franquin). © 2001 Marsu by Franquin. Héliogravure. Dentelure 13½, sauf n° 3371 : 13½ x 13.***

Gaston Lagaffe.

3370 3 f. (0,46 €) ***Gaston Lagaffe*** 1 » 0 50

a. (Timbre de carnet, Dentelé 13½ x 13) 1 » 0 65

Idem. Emis en carnet. Héliogravure.

Dentelé 13½ x 13. C BF *n° 34.*

Avec surtaxe. Emis en carnet et en feuillet.

3371 3 f. +0 f. 60 (0,55 €) ***Gaston Lagaffe*** 2 50 1 50

3371A La paire 4 » 3 »

La bande (format vertical) destinée à la confection de carnets comprend 1 paire horizontale du n° 3370a et 3 paires horizontales n° 3370a+3371.

BC3370a La bande carnet, non pliée 14 » 14 »

2001. – ***Le siècle au fil du timbre (III). Communication. Emis uniquement en feuillet. Héliogravure. Dentelés 13.*** BF ***n° 35.***

La télévision : personnages de "Bonne nuit les petits".

La publicité au cinéma : le Petit Mineur.

3372 3 f. (0,46 €) multicolore 1 » 0 60

3373 3 f. (0,46 €) multicolore 1 » 0 60

Le téléphone portable.

La radio : "Salut les copains".

3374 3 f. (0,46 €) multicolore 1 » 0 60

3375 3 f. (0,46 €) multicolore 1 » 0 60

Le disque compact.

3376 3 f. (0,46 €) multicolore 1 » 0 60

N°s 3372 à 3376 (5 val.) **5 » 3 »**

Tirage : 5 923 089 séries.

B3372 La bande issue du BF n° 35 6 » 4 »

2001. – ***Timbres pour naissances. Héliogravure. Dentelés 13.***

"C'est un garçon".

"C'est une fille".

3377 3 f. (0,46 €) multicolore 1 » 0 50

3378 3 f. (0,46 €) multicolore 1 » 0 50

Tirages : 9 397 791 et 9 282 655.

2001. – *Timbres de messages. Héliogravure. Dentelés 13.*

"merci".

"oui".

3379	**3 f. (0,46 €) multicolore**	1 »	0 50
	a. (Sans "ITVF")	100 »	50 »
3380	**4 f. 50 (0,69 €) multicolore**	1 40	0 80

Tirages : 7 473 798 et 10 899 004.

2001. – *Série "Nature de France" (XVI). Faune. Héliogravure. Dentelés 13½.* BF *n° 36.*

Ecureuil.

Chevreuil.

3381	**2 f. 70 (0,41 €) multicolore**	1 »	0 50
3382	**3 f. (0,46 €) multicolore**	1 »	0 50

Hérisson.

Hermine.

3383	**3 f. (0,46 €) multicolore**	1 »	0 50
3384	**4 f. 50 (0,69 €) multicolore**	1 50	1 »
	N°s 3381 à 3384 (4 val.)	**4 50**	**2 50**

Tirages : 3 382, 10 748 348, 3 383 et 10 748 348.

2001. – *Série artistique. Hôtel des Chevaliers de Saint-Jean-de-Jérusalem, à Toulouse. Taille-douce. Dentelé 13.*

Détail peinture murale (13e s.).

3385	**6 f. 70 (1,02 €) multicolore**	2 50	1 40

Tirage : 4 494 886.

2001. – *Série touristique. Nogent-le-Rotrou (Eure-et-Loir). Taille-douce et offset. Dentelé 13½ x 13.*

Château.

3386	**3 f. (0,46 €) multicolore**	1 »	0 50

Tirage : 7 558 383.

2001. – *Série touristique. Besançon (Doubs). Taille-douce. Dentelé 13.*

La citadelle de Vauban et fontaine.

3387	**3 f. (0,46 €) multicolore**	1 »	0 50

Tirage : 10 144 364.

2001. – *Europa. L'eau, richesse naturelle. Héliogravure. Dentelé 13.*

Globe dans une goutte d'eau.

3388	**3 f. (0,46 €) multicolore**	1 »	0 30

Tirage : 12 414 392.

2001. – *Les Jardins de Versailles. Hommage au jardinier Le Nôtre (1613-1700). Héliogravure. Dentelé 13.*

3389	**4 f. 40 (0,67 €) multicolore**	1 50	1 »

Tirage : 4 426 885.

2001. – *Le Vieux-Lyon (Rhône). Taille-douce. Dentelé 13½ x 13.*

Les traboules.

3390 3 f. (0,46 €) multicolore 1 » 0 50

Tirage : 7 723 398.

2001. – *Les personnages célèbres. Artistes de la chanson. Héliogravure. Dentelés 13.* BF *n° 37.*

3391 3 f. (0,46 €) *Claude François (1939-1978)* 1 » 0 60
3392 3 f. (0,46 €) *Léo Ferré (1916-1993)* 1 » 0 60

3393 3 f. (0,46 €) *Serge Gainsbourg (1928-1991)* 1 » 0 60
3394 3 f. (0,46 €) *Dalida (1933-1987)* 1 » 0 60

3395 3 f. (0,46 €) *Michel Berger (1947-1992)* 1 » 0 60
3396 3 f. (0,46 €) *Barbara (1930-1997)* 1 » 0 60

Nos 3391 à 3396 (6 val.) 6 » 3 60

Tirages : 10 265 425, 7 607 564, 7 825 407, 10 157 601, 7 748 031 et 7 736 323.

2001. – *74e Congrès de la Fédération Française des Associations Philatéliques, à Tours. Taille-douce. Dentelé 13½.*

Statuette de compagnon (de Jean Bourreau), pont et cathédrale.

3397 3 f. (0,46 €) multicolore 1 » 0 50

Tirage : 7 306 979.

2001. – *30e anniversaire de la mort de Jean Vilar (1912-1971). Taille-douce et offset. Dentelé 13.*

Portrait de l'acteur et metteur en scène de théâtre ; Palais des Papes à Avignon.

3398 3 f. (0,46 €) multicolore 1 » 0 50

Tirage : 7 488 028.

2001. – *"Bonnes Vacances". Offset. Deux bandes de phosphore. Dentelé 13.*

Empreinte de pied sur une plage.

3399 3 f. (0,46 €) multicolore 1 » 0 50

Tirage : 9 719 579.

2001. – *"Bonnes Vacances". Type du T.-P. de même date. Emis en carnet. Offset. Auto-adhésif. Deux bandes de phosphore. Dentelé 11.* C

3400 3 f. (0,46 €) multicolore (3399) 1 50 0 60

Tirage : 2 109 534 séries.

BC3400A La bande carnet, non pliée 15 » 12 »

2001. – *Série touristique. Calais (Pas-de-Calais). Taille-douce. Dentelé 13.*

Jetée, Hôtel de ville et ferry.

3401 3 f. (0,46 €) multicolore 1 » 0 50

Tirage : 6 521 947.

2001. – *"Demain l'Euro". Héliogravure. Dentelé.*

Composition avec pièce de 1 euro et étoiles du drapeau européen

3402 3 f. (0,46 €) multicolore 1 40 0 50

Tirage : 14 377 621.

2001. – *120ᵉ anniversaire de la naissance de l'ingénieur Albert Caquot (1881-1976). Taille-douce. Dentelé 13½.*

Portrait ; pont ; ballon "saucisse".

3403 4 f. 50 (0,69 €) multicolore 1 40 1 »

Tirage : 4 374 880.

2001. – *Centenaire de la Loi du 1er Juillet 1901 sur la liberté d'association. Héliogravure. Dentelé 13.*

Composition avec pièces de puzzle et mention "Liberté d'association".

3404 3 f. (0,46 €) multicolore 1 » 0 50

2001. – *Série "Collection Jeunesse". Les légendes du rail. Locomotives. Héliogravure. Multicolores. Dentelés 13½ x 13.* BF *n° 38.*

3405 1 f. 50 (0,23 €) *Eurostar* 0 60 0 50
3406 1 f. 50 (0,23 €) *American 220* 0 60 0 50

3407 1 f. 50 (0,23 €) *Crocodile* 0 60 0 50
3408 1 f. 50 (0,23 €) *Crampton* 0 60 0 50

3409 1 f. 50 (0,23 €) *Garratt 59* 0 60 0 50
3410 1 f. 50 (0,23 €) *Pacific Chapelon* 0 60 0 50

3411 1 f. 50 (0,23 €) *Mallard* 0 60 0 50
3412 1 f. 50 (0,23 €) *Capitole* 0 60 0 50

3413 1 f. 50 (0,23 €) *Autorail panoramique* 0 60 0 50
3414 1 f. 50 (0,23 €) *230 Classe P8* 0 60 0 50

Nos 3405 à 3414 (10 val.) **6 »** **5 »**

Emis uniquement en feuillet.

2001. – *Série touristique. Château de Grignan (Drôme). Taille-douce. Dentelé 13.*

3415 3 f. (0,46 €) multicolore 1 » 0 30

2001. – ***Cinquantenaire de la Convention de Genève relative aux Réfugiés. Héliogravure. Dentelé 13.***

Emblème.

3416	**4 f. 50 (0,69 €) multicolore**	1 40	1 »

Tirage : 4 298 032.

2001. – ***Type Marianne du 14 Juillet. Type du T.-P. de 1997. Mention RF (au lieu de République Française). Sans valeur indiquée (validité permanente). Taille-douce. Deux bandes de phosphore. Dentelés 13.***

3417	**(sans val.) rouge (3083)**	1 »	0 15
	a. (Avec vignette personnalisée attenante)	5 »	4 »

Ce timbre personnalisé a été mis en vente en feuillets de 10 au 76ᵉ Congrès de la FFAP à Mulhouse du 6 au 9 juin 2003.

Papier fluorescent aux U.V., gomme blanche et mate à ne pas confondre avec le n°3587A.

Provenant de roulette. Deux bandes de phosphore. Taille-douce. Dentelé 13 horizontalement.

3418	**(sans val.) rouge (3084)**	2 »	0 50
	a. (N° rouge au verso)	2 50	
	b. (N° noir au verso)	1 50	

le n° 3418b existe sans bande de phosphore

Provenant de carnet. Deux bandes de phosphore. Gommage adhésif. Taille-douce. Précoupé vertical en lignes ondulées. Ⓒ

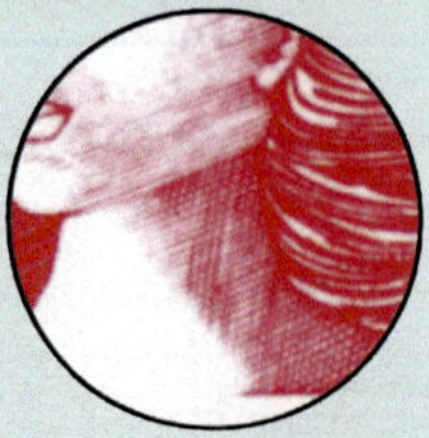

Type I, gravure mécanique, impression fine, oreille intacte

Type II, gravure numérique, impression floue, oreille cassée

3419	**(sans val.) rouge (Type II gravure numérique) (3085)**	1 »	0 15
	a. (Type I, transfert mécanique du poinçon)	2 »	0 50

Le timbre 3419a a été émis, en 2003, en carnet "Centenaire de la Semeuse de Roty".

2001. – ***400ᵉ anniversaire de la naissance du mathématicien Pierre de Fermat (1601-1665). Taille-douce. Dentelé 13½ x 13.***

Portrait.

3420	**4 f. 50 (0,69 €) multicolore**	1 40	1 »

Tirage : 5 236 779.

2001. – ***Série artistique. Centenaire de la mort du peintre Henri de Toulouse-Lautrec (1864-1901). Héliogravure. Dentelé 13½ x 13.***

"Yvette Guilbert chantant "Linger, Longer, Loo".

3421	**6 f. 70 (1,02 €) multicolore**	2 50	1 40

Tirage : 4 955 125.

2001. – ***Le siècle au fil du timbre (IV). Sciences. Héliogravure. Dentelés 13½ x 13.*** BF ***n° 39.***

La pénicilline.

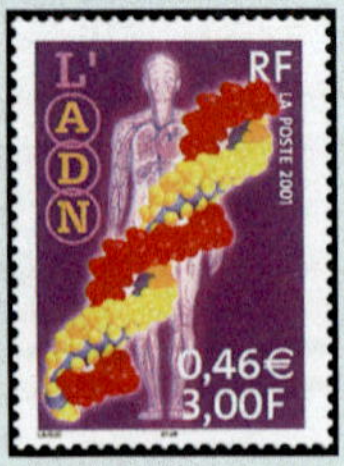

L'ADN.

3422	**3 f. (0,46 €) multicolore**	1 »	0 50
3423	**3 f. (0,46 €) multicolore**	1 »	0 50

Le laser.

Le 1ᵉʳ homme dans l'espace.

3424	**3 f. (0,46 €) multicolore**	1 »	0 50
3425	**3 f. (0,46 €) multicolore**	1 »	0 50

La carte à puce.

3426 3 f. (0,46 €) multicolore 1 » 0 50

N°s 3422 à 3426 (5 val.) **5 »** **2 50**

3422B La bande issue du BF n° 39 6 » 4 »

2001. – ***Val-de-Reuil (Eure). Héliogravure. Dentelé 13.***

"L'Astrolabe", sculpture d'Alain Le Boucher.

3427 3 f. (0,46 €) multicolore 1 » 0 30

Tirage : 6 883 497.

2001. – ***Halloween. Héliogravure. Phosphorescence. Dentelé 13.*** BF ***n° 40.***

Citrouille.

3428 3 f. (0,46 €) multicolore 1 » 0 30

2001. – ***Série artistique. Johan Barthold Jongkind (1819-1891). Offset. Dentelé 13 x 13½.***

"Honfleur à marée basse".

3429 6,70 f. (1,02 €) multicolore 2 50 1 40

Tirage : 4 499 423.

2001. – ***Hommage à Jacques Chaban-Delmas (1915-2000). Taille-douce. Deux bandes de phosphore. Dentelé 13 x 13½.***

Portrait de l'homme politique.

3430 3 f. (0,46 €) multicolore 1 » 0 40

Tirage : 6 701 813.

Les n°s 3431 à 3433 se trouvent à la rubrique Timbres-Poste avec vignette personnalisée.

2001. – ***Hommage à Jean Pierre-Bloch (1905-1999). Taille-douce. Deux bandes de phosphore. Dentelé 13.***

Portrait de l'homme politique.

3434 4,50 f. (0,69 €) bleu 1 40 1 »

Tirage : 5 096 745.

2001. – ***Centenaire de la naissance du dessinateur et graveur Albert Decaris (1901-1988). Taille-douce. Dentelé 13½ x 13.***

3435 3 f. (0,46 €) multicolore 1 25 0 50

Tirage : 6 756 951.

2001. – *Au profit de la Croix-Rouge. Fêtes de fin d'année. Héliogravure. Deux bandes de phosphore. Dentelé 12½ x 13.* ⓒ

Boule-Père Noël.

3436	**3 f. +0,60 f. (0,46+0,09 €) multicolore**	1 10	0 70
	a. (Dentelé 13½ x 13)	1 10	0 70

A été aussi émis en carnets (Tirage : 769 786).

Le n° 3436a provient de carnets.

Tirage : 1 208 513.

2001. – *"Bonne Année" et "Meilleurs Voeux". Offset. Deux bandes de phosphore. Dentelure 13, sauf n° 3439, 3440 : 11.*

Enfants et bonhomme de neige.

Enfants transportant du houx et un paquet cadeau dans une brouette.

3437	**3 f. (0,46 €) multicolore**	1 »	0 50
3438	**3 f. (0,46 €) multicolore**	1 »	0 50

Emis en carnet. Auto-adhésifs. Deux bandes de phosphore. Offset. Dentelés 11. ⓒ

3439	**3 f. (0,46 €) (3437)**	1 50	0 50
3440	**3 f. (0,46 €) (3438)**	1 50	0 50
	La paire	3 »	1 50

Existe sans phosphore.

BC3440A La bande carnet, non pliée	15 »	12 »

2001. – *Fontaines. Emission commune avec le Maroc. Héliogravure. Dentelés 13½.*

Fontaine Nejjarine (Maroc).

Fontaine Wallace (France).

3441	**3,00 f. (0,46 €) multicolore**	1 »	0 50
3442	**3,80 f. (0,58 €) multicolore**	2 »	1 50

Le Maroc a émis simultanément deux timbres aux mêmes types (n°s 1298 et 1299).

2001

Du n° 3367 au n° 3442

(sauf bandes-carnets, paires et triptyques) :

72 timbres	****82**	**⊙45**

Autres rubriques de l'année :

Timbres Autoadhésifs 29 à 32

Blocs et feuillet 33 à 42

Service 122 à 125

2002. – *Type Marianne du 14 Juillet. Types des T.-P. de 1997. Mention RF (au lieu de République Française). Taille-douce. Dentelés 13.* BF *n° 44.* BF *n° 45.*

3443	**0,01 € jaune**	0 15	0 15
3444	**0,02 € bistre-noir**	0 15	0 15
3445	**0,05 € vert-émeraude**	0 15	0 15
3446	**0,10 € violet-rouge**	0 30	0 15

3447	**0,20 € orange**	0 50	0 20
3448	**0,41 € vert**	1 25	0 40
3449	**0,50 € bleu nuit**	1 50	0 50
3450	**0,53 € vert-jaune**	1 50	0 80

3451	**0,58 € bleu**	1 50	1 25
3452	**0,64 € orange foncé**	2 »	1 »
3453	**0,67 € bleu outremer**	2 »	1 25
3454	**0,69 € rose**	2 »	1 »

3455	**1,00 € bleu-vert**	3 »	1 »
3456	**1,02 € vert foncé**	3 »	1 »
3457	**2,00 € violet**	5 »	1 »
	N°s 3443 à 3457 (15 val.)	**24 »**	**10 »**

Une bande de phosphore à droite pour les 0,01 €, 0,02 €, 0,05 €, 0,10 €, 0,20 €, 0,41 €, 0,53 € et 0,64 € et deux bandes de phosphore pour les autres valeurs. Les timbres sans phosphore proviennent des blocs et feuillets 44 et 45.

2002. – *Type de même date, provenant de roulette. Taille-douce. Une bande de phosphore à droite. Dentelé 13 horizontalement.*

3458 **0,41 € vert** 2 » 1 »
a. (N° rouge au verso) 3 »
b. (N° noir au verso) 2 »

2002. – *Saint-Valentin. Coeur 2002, du photographe Yann Arthus-Bertrand. Héliogravure. Dentelé.* BF *n° 43.*

Photo aérienne de Voh (Nouvelle-Calédonie).

3459 **0,46 € multicolore** 0 90 0 50

2002. – *Jeux olympiques d'hiver de Salt Lake City (Etats-Unis). Héliogravure. Deux bandes de phosphore. Dentelé 13.*

Snowboard.

3460 **0,46 € multicolore** 0 90 0 50
Tirage : 10 850 252.

2002. – *Série artistique. Gustav Klimt (1862-1918). Héliogravure. Dentelé 13½* x *13.*

"Le Baiser".

3461 **1,02 € multicolore** 2 50 1 20
a. (valeur faciale et légende omises) 5 000 »
Tirage : 5 424 594.

2002. – *Hommage à l'écrivain Alain Bosquet (1919-1998). Taille-douce. Deux bandes de phosphore. Dentelé 13.*

Portrait.

3462 **0,58 € multicolore** 1 20 1 »

Existe sans phosphore.

Tirage : 2 565 780.

2002. – *Timbres pour naissances. Héliogravure. Deux bandes de phosphore. Dentelés 13.*

"C'est une fille". "C'est un garçon".

3463 **0,46 € multicolore** 1 » 0 50
3464 **0,46 € multicolore** 1 » 0 50

Tirage : 8 766 030 et 8 840 973.

2002. – *Timbre pour mariages. Héliogravure. Deux bandes de phosphore. Dentelé 13.*

"Oui".

3465 **0,69 € multicolore** 1 40 1 »

Tirage : 9 580 698.

2002. – *Europa. Le cirque. Héliogravure. Deux bandes de phosphore. Dentelé 13½.*

3466 **0,46 € multicolore** 1 25 0 50

Tirage : 9 988 558.

2002. – ***Fête du timbre. © Boule et Bill ®, international s.a. 2002. Héliogravure. Deux bandes de phosphore. Dentelure 13½ x 13, sauf n° 3467 : 13½.***

Boule et Bill (de Jean Roba).

3467	**0,46 € multicolore**	1 »	0 50
	a. (provenant de carnet, Dent. 13½ x 13)	1 40	0 60

Idem. Emis en carnet. Sans bandes de phosphore. Héliogravure. Dentelés 13½ x 13. [C]

3468	***0,46 €+0,09 € Boule et Bill, croix rouge et ballon (de Jean Roba)***	3 »	2 »
P3467a	La paire 3467a+3468	4 »	3 »

Idem. Emis uniquement en feuillet. Sans réserve blanche autour de l'image. Sans bandes de phosphore. Dentelé 13½ x 13. [BF] *n° 46.*

3469	***0,46 €+0,09 € Boule et Bill, croix rouge et ballon (de Jean Roba). Sans réserve blanche autour de l'image*** **(3468)**	3 »	2 50

Tirages : 10 470 356, (nc) et 896 131.

La bande (format vertical) destinée à la confection de carnets comprend 1 paire 3468+3467a, 1 paire 3467a+3468, 1 paire 3468+3467a et 1 paire du n° 3467a.

BC3467a La bande carnet, non pliée	14 »	14 »

Tirage : 749 464.

2002. – ***Les arènes de Nîmes. Taille-douce et offset. Dentelé 13.***

3470	**0,46 € multicolore**	1 »	0 50
	a. (Valeur faciale et légende omises)	7 500 »	

Tirage : 7 760 279.

2002. – ***Le siècle au fil du timbre (V). Transports. Héliogravure. Dentelure 13, sauf n° 3472, 3473, 3474 : 13½ x 13.*** [BF] ***n° 47.***

Concorde.

La mobylette.

3471	**0,46 € multicolore**	2 »	1 »
3472	**0,46 € multicolore**	1 »	0 60

Le France.

La 2 CV.

3473	**0,46 € multicolore**	1 »	0 60
3474	**0,46 € multicolore**	1 »	0 60

Le TGV.

3475	**0,46 € multicolore**	1 »	0 60
	N°s 3471 à 3475 (5 val.)	**6 »**	**3 40**
B3471	La bande issue du [BF] n° 47	6 »	5 »

2002. – *Bicentenaire de la rencontre des deux navigateurs et explorateurs Nicolas Baudin (1754-1803) et Matthew Flinders (1774-1814). Emission commune avec l'Australie. Héliogravure. Deux bandes de phosphore. Dentelés 13½.*

Portrait de M. Flinders et l'"Investigator".

Portrait de N. Baudin et le "Géographe".

3476	**0,46 € multicolore**	1 »	0 50
3477	**0,79 € multicolore**	2 »	1 50

L'Australie à émis simultanément deux timbres (n°s 2026 et 2027).

Tirage : 9 232 578 et 2 869 308.

2002. – *Série touristique. La Charité-sur-Loire (Nièvre). Taille-douce. Deux bandes de phosphore. Dentelé 13½.*

3478	**0,46 € multicolore**	1 »	0 50

Tirage : 7 131 747.

2002. – *Timbre pour invitations. Héliogravure. Deux bandes de phosphore. Dentelé 13.*

3479	**0,46 € or et multicolore**	1 »	0 50

2002. – *Timbre pour anniversaires. Héliogravure. Deux bandes de phosphore. Dentelé 13.*

3480	**0,46 € multicolore**	1 »	0 50

2002. – *100e Paris-Roubaix. Héliogravure. Deux bandes de phosphore. Dentelé 13.*

Coureurs sur les pavés.

3481	**0,46 € multicolore**	1 25	0 50

Tirage : 8 155 496.

2002. – *Série artistique. Fernando Botero. Héliogravure. Dentelé 13.*

"Les Danseurs".

3482	**1,02 € multicolore**	2 50	1 50

Tirage : 4 460 886.

2002. – *Champions du monde de Football. Emission commune avec l'Allemagne, l'Argentine, le Brésil, l'Italie et l'Uruguay. Héliogravure. Dentelure (12½ pour le n° 3484).* BF *n° 49.*

3483	**0,46 €** ***Ballon, terrain et drapeaux de 6 des 7 pays ayant remporté la coupe du monde***	1 25	0 60
3484	**0,46 €** ***Drapeau français, 1998, image floue de joueurs***	1 25	0 60

Tirage : 3 315 684 paires.

Imprimés se tenant horizontalement.

La paire	2 75	2 »

2002. – ***Série "Nature de France" (XVII). Faune marine. Héliogravure. Dentelés 13½.*** BF ***n° 48.***

Tortue luth.

Grand dauphin.

3485 0,41 € multicolore 1 » 0 50
3486 0,46 € multicolore 1 » 0 50

Orque.

Phoque veau marin.

3487 0,46 € multicolore 1 » 0 50
3488 0,69 € multicolore 1 50 1 »

N°s 3485 à 3488 (4 val.) **4 50** **2 50**

Tirages : 16 956 056, 9 864 176, 9 230 761 et 6 131 148.

2002. – ***75e Congrès de la Fédération Française des Associations Philatéliques, à Marseille. Taille-douce. Deux bandes de phosphore. Dentelé 13.***

Vue panoramique de la ville.

3489 0,46 € multicolore 1 » 0 60

Tirage : 7 585 080.

2002. – ***Bicentenaire de la Légion d'honneur. Héliogravure. Dentelé 13.***

Croix.

3490 0,46 € multicolore 1 » 0 50

Tirage : 7 340 695.

2002. – ***Bicentenaire de la mort de Louis Delgrès (1766-1802), défenseur de l'abolition de l'esclavage. Héliogravure. Deux bandes de phosphore. Dentelé 13½.***

Portrait de l'officier.

3491 0,46 € multicolore 1 » 0 50

Tirage : 6 850 070.

2002. – ***Rocamadour (Lot). Héliogravure. Deux bandes de phosphore. Dentelé 13½.***

3492 0,46 € multicolore 1 » 0 50

Tirage : 8 859 244.

2002. – ***Timbre pour vacances. Offset. Deux bandes de phosphore. Dentelé 13.***

3493 0,46 € multicolore 1 » 0 50

Tirage : 9 719 579.

2002. – ***Timbre pour vacances. Type de même date. Emis en carnet. Offset. Auto-adhésif. Deux bandes de phosphore. Dent. 11.*** C

3494 0,46 € (3493) multicolore 1 50 0 60

Tirage : 2 109 534 séries.

BC3494A La bande carnet, non pliée 15 » 12 »

2002. – *Championnat du monde d'Athlétisme Handisport, au stadium Lille-Métropole. Héliogravure. Deux bandes de phosphore. Dentelé 13½.*

Course en fauteuils roulants.

3495 0,46 €multicolore 1 » 0 50

Tirage : 7 703 234.

2002. – *Chapelle de Saint-Ser (Bouches-du-Rhône). Taille-douce. Deux bandes de phosphore. Dentelé 13 x 13½.*

3496 0,46 € multicolore 1 » 0 50

Tirage : 9 148 078.

2002. – *Série touristique. Collioure (Pyrénées-Orientales). Héliogravure. Deux bandes de phosphore. Dentelé 13½.*

"Le phare de Collioure", d'André Derain.

3497 0,46 € multicolore 1 » 0 50

Tirage : 11 169 114.

2002. – *Cathédrale de Metz. Taille-douce. Dentelé 13½ x 13.*

Détail vitrail "Eve et le serpent, La Création" (1963-64), de Marc Chagall.

3498 0,46 € multicolore 1 20 0 60

Tirage : 8 011 300.

2002. – *Série touristique. Locronan (Finistère). Taille-douce. Deux bandes de phosphore. Dentelé 13.*

Eglise Saint-Ronan et chapelle du Pénity.

3499 0,46 € multicolore 1 » 0 50

2002. – *Les personnages célèbres. Grands interprètes de jazz. Héliogravure. Deux bandes de phosphore. Dentelés 13.*

3500 0,46 € multicolore et or ***Louis Armstrong (1901-1971)*** 1 » 0 60

3501 0,46 € multicolore et or ***Sidney Bechet (1897-1959)*** 1 » 0 60

3502 0,46 € multicolore et or ***Duke Ellington (1899-1974)*** 1 » 0 60

3503 0,46 € multicolore et or ***Ella Fitzgerald (1918-1996)*** 1 » 0 60

3504 0,46 € multicolore et or ***Stéphane Grappelli (1908-1997)*** 1 » 0 60

3505 0,46 € multicolore et or ***Michel Petrucciani (1962-1999)*** 1 » 0 60

N°s 3500 à 3505 (6 val.) **6 » 3 60**

Idem. Emis en feuillet. Sans bandes de phosphore. Héliogravure.
Dentelés 13. BF n° 50.

3500a	0,46 € multicolore et or	2 »	1 »
3501a	0,46 € multicolore et or	2 »	1 »
3502a	0,46 € multicolore et or	2 »	1 »
3503a	0,46 € multicolore et or	2 »	1 »
3504a	0,46 € multicolore et or	2 »	1 »
3505a	0,46 € multicolore et or	2 »	1 »

2002. – *Notre-Dame de La Salette (Isère). Taille-douce. Deux bandes de phosphore. Dentelé 13½ x 13.*

Basilique.

3506 **0,46 € multicolore** 1 » 0 50

Tirage : 8 387 189.

2002. – *L'Art chorégraphique. Héliogravure. Deux bandes de phosphore. Dentelé 13.*

3507 **0,53 € multicolore** 1 50 0 80

Existe sans bande de phosphore.

2002. – *Série "Collection Jeunesse". Cylindrées et carénages. Motos. Emis uniquement en feuillet. Héliogravure. Multicolores. Dentelés 13½ x 13.* BF *n° 51.*

3508	**0,16 € *Honda 750 Four***	0 40	0 30
3509	**0,16 € *Terrot 500 RGST***	0 40	0 30

3510	**0,16 € *Majestic***	0 40	0 30
3511	**0,16 € *Norton Commando 750***	0 40	0 30

3512	**0,16 € *Voxan 1000 Café Racer***	0 40	0 30
3513	**0,30 € *BMW R90S***	0 80	0 50

3514	**0,30 € *Harley Davidson Hydra glide***	0 80	0 50
3515	**0,30 € *Triumph Bonneville 650***	0 80	0 50

3516	**0,30 € *Ducati 916***	0 80	0 50
3517	**0,30 € *Yamaha 500XT***	0 80	0 50
	N°s 3508 à 3517 (10 val.)	**6 »**	**4 »**

Tirage : 2 313 645 feuillets.

2002. – *20e anniversaire de la mort de l'écrivain Georges Perec (1936-1982). Taille-douce. Deux bandes de phosphore. Dentelé 13½.*

Portrait avec chat.

3518 **0,46 € multicolore** 1 » 0 50

Tirage : 7 338 386.

2002. – *Le siècle au fil du timbre (VI). Vie quotidienne. Emis uniquement en feuillet. Héliogravure. Dentelure 13½ x 13, sauf n° 3519, 3523 : 13.* BF *n° 52.*

"Pêcheur de sable", Plage de Capbreton, 1947.

"Enfant à la fontaine", Avignon, 1950.

3519	**0,46 € multicolore**	1 »	0 60
3520	**0,46 € multicolore**	1 »	0 60

"Un superbe été", Saint-Brévin-les-Pins, 1955.

"Sur les bancs de l'école", Paris, 1965.

3521	**0,46 € multicolore**	1 »	0 60
3522	**0,46 € multicolore**	1 »	0 60

"Louise la repasseuse", La Pommeraye, 1950.

3523	**0,46 € multicolore**	1 »	0 60
	N°s 3519 à 3523 (5 val.)	**5 »**	**3 »**
	3519B La bande issue du BF n° 52	6 »	3 »

Tirage : 4 487 837 feuillets.

2002. – ***Centenaire de la mort de l'écrivain Emile Zola (1840-1902). Héliogravure. Deux bandes de phosphore. Dentelé 13.***

Portrait.

3524	**0,46 € multicolore**	1 »	0 50

2002. – ***Série touristique. Neufchâteau (Vosges). Taille-douce. Deux bandes de phosphore. Dentelé 13½ x 13.***

Pavillon des Goncourt.

3525	**0,46 € multicolore**	1 »	0 50

Existe sans bande de phosphore.

Tirage : 8 308 032.

2002. – ***Série artistique. Elisabeth Vigée-Lebrun (1755-1842). Taille-douce. Dentelé 13½ x 13.***

Autoportrait.

3526	**1,02 € multicolore**	2 50	1 20

2002. – ***Capitales européennes. Rome. Emis uniquement en feuillet. Héliogravure. Dentelés 13-13½.*** BF ***n° 53.***

Le Colisée.

La Fontaine de Trevi.

3527	**0,46 € multicolore**	1 50	1 »
3528	**0,46 € multicolore**	1 50	1 »

L'Eglise de la Trinité-des-Monts.

La Basilique Saint-Pierre.

3529	**0,46 € multicolore**	1 50	1 »
3530	**0,46 € multicolore**	1 50	1 »
	N°s 3527 à 3530 (4 val.)	**6 »**	**4 »**

Tirage : 1 607 976 feuillets.

2002. – ***Au profit de la Croix-Rouge. Fêtes de fin d'année. Héliogravure. Deux bandes de phosphore. Dentelé 12½ x 13.***

"Le sommeil de l'Enfant Jésus", du peintre Giovanni Battista Salvi.

3531	**0,46 €+0,09 € multicolore**	1 20	0 80
	a. (Dentelé 13½ x 13)	1 20	0 50

A été aussi émis en carnets (tirages : 673 850)

Le n° 3531a provient de carnets.

2002. – ***"Le Monde en réseau". Timbre destiné au courrier des Entreprises. Héliogravure. Deux bandes de phosphore. Dentelé 13.***

3532	**0,46 € multicolore**	1 »	0 50

Tirage : 7 798 200.

2002. – ***"Meilleurs Voeux". Offset. Deux bandes de phosphore. Dentelé 13.***

Chalet sous la neige.

3533	**0,46 € multicolore**	1 »	0 50

Tirage : 7 609 695.

2002. – ***"Meilleurs Voeux". Type du T.-P. de même date. Emis en carnet. Offset. Auto-adhésif. Deux bandes de phosphore. Dentelé 11.*** [C]

3534	**0,46 €** ***Chalet sous la neige***	1 50	0 60
BC3534A	La bande carnet, non pliée	15 »	12 »

2002. – ***Série artistique. Jesus Rafael Soto. Héliogravure. Dentelé 13½ x 13.***

"Sphère Concorde" (art cinétique).

3535	**0,75 € multicolore**	2 »	1 »

Tirage : 3 616 978.

2002. – ***Type Marianne du 14 Juillet. Type de 2002. Sans valeur indiquée (validité permanente) (pour les écoplis). Une bande de phosphore à droite. Dentelés 13.***

3535A	**(sans val.) vert**	1 50	0 20

Provenant de roulette. N° noir au verso. Une bande de phosphore à droite. Dentelé 13 horizontalement.

3535B	**(sans val.) vert**	2 »	1 »

2002. – ***Bicentenaire de la naissance de l'écrivain Alexandre Dumas (1802-1870). Héliogravure. Deux bandes de phosphore. Dentelé 13.***

Portrait, dessin du Panthéon.

3536	**0,46 € multicolore**	1 »	0 50

Tirage : 6 944 786.

2002. – ***1er anniversaire de la mort de Léopold Sédar Senghor (1906-2001), homme d'Etat et poète sénégalais. Héliogravure. Deux bandes de phosphore. Dentelé 13.***

Portrait.

3537	**0,46 € multicolore**	1 »	0 50

2002

Du n° 3443 au n° 3537

(Sauf bandes-carnets, paires et triptyques) :

97 timbres	****122**	**⊙65**

Autres rubriques de l'année :

Aérien 65

Timbres Autoadhésifs 33 et 34

Blocs et feuillet 43 à 53

Préoblitérés 244 et 245

2003. – ***Saint-Valentin. Coeurs 2003 du couturier Torrente. Emis également en feuillet pour le n° 3538. Héliogravure. Dentelés.*** **BF** ***n° 54.***

3538	**0,46 € multicolore et or** ***Coeur avec trèfle à quatre feuilles et signature***	1 25	0 50
3539	**0,69 € multicolore** ***Coeur avec roses et signature***	1 75	1 »

Tirage : 5 327 743 et 5 102 376.

2003. – ***Timbre de message. "Merci". Héliogravure. Deux bandes de phosphore. Dentelé 13.***

3540 **0,46 € multicolore** 1 » 0 50

2003. – ***Timbre pour naissances. Héliogravure. Deux bandes de phosphore. Dentelé 13.***

3541 **0,46 € bleu et orange** 1 » 0 50

2003. – ***40e anniversaire du Traité sur la Coopération franco-allemande. Emission conjointe avec l'Allemagne. Héliogravure. Deux bandes de phosphore. Dentelé 13.***

3542 **0,46 € multicolore** 1 25 0 50

2003. – ***40 ans d'aménagement du territoire. Héliogravure. Deux bandes de phosphore. Dentelé 13.***

Composition avec carte de France.

3543 **0,46 € multicolore** 1 » 0 50

2003. – ***Hommage à Geneviève de Gaulle Anthonioz (1920-2002). Héliogravure. Deux bandes de phosphore. Dentelé 13.***

Portrait de la résistante, ancienne Présidente d'ATD Quart Monde, grand-croix de la Légion d'honneur.

3544 **0,46 € brun et noir** 1 » 0 50

2003. – ***Bicentenaire de la Chambre de commerce et d'industrie de Paris. Héliogravure. Deux bandes de phosphore. Dentelé 13½.***

Tour Eiffel composée par des silhouettes.

3545 **0,46 € multicolore** 1 » 0 50

2003. – ***Fête du timbre. © Lucky Comics 2003. Héliogravure. Deux bandes de phosphore. Dentelé 13½.***

Lucky Luke (de Morris).

3546	**0,46 € multicolore**	1 »	0 50
	a. (provenant de carnet, dentelé 13½ x 13)	1 »	0 50

La bande (format vertical) destinée à la confection de carnets comprend 1 paire 3547+3546a, 1 paire 3546a+3547, 1 paire 3547+3546a et 1 paire du n° 3546a.

BC3546a La bande carnet, non pliée 14 » 12 »

2003. – ***Fête du timbre. Héliogravure. Deux bandes de phosphore. Dentelé 13½ x 13.*** BF ***n° 55.***

Lucky Luke (de Morris).

3547	**0,46 €+0,09 € multicolore**	2 50	2 »
P3547	La paire (3546a+3547)	4 »	3 »

2003. – ***Série "Nature de France" (XVIII). Oiseaux d'outre-mer. Héliogravure. Dentelés 13½.*** BF ***n° 56.***

Colibri à tête bleue.

Toucan ariel.

3548	**0,41 € multicolore**	1 »	0 50
3549	**0,46 € multicolore**	1 »	0 50

Colibri grenat.

Terpsiphone de Bourbon.

3550	**0,46 € multicolore**	1 »	0 50
3551	**0,69 € multicolore**	1 50	1 »
	N°s 3548 à 3551 (4 val.)	**4 50**	**2 50**

2003. – ***Série touristique. Nantes (Loire-Atlantique). Taille-douce. Deux bandes de phosphore. Dentelé 13½.***

Tramway TAN et tour LU (Lefèvre-Utile).

3552	**0,46 € multicolore**	1 »	0 50

2003. – ***Hommage à Pierre Bérégovoy (1925-1993). Taille-douce. Deux bandes de phosphore. Dentelé 13 x 13½.***

Portrait de l'homme politique.

3553	**0,46 € multicolore**	1 »	0 50

Existe sans bande de phosphore.

2003. – ***Hommage à Milan Rastislav Stefanik (1880-1919), astronome, diplomate, Général de brigade de l'Armée de l'Air française, nommé ministre de la Défense de la République tchécoslovaque en 1918. Emission commune avec la Slovaquie. Taille-douce. Deux bandes de phosphore. Dentelé 13 x 13½.***

Portrait, Observatoire de Meudon.

3554	**0,50 € multicolore**	1 »	0 50

2003. – ***Charte des droits fondamentaux de l'Union européenne. Héliogravure. Deux bandes de phosphore. Dentelé 13½.***

3555	**0,50 € multicolore**	1 »	0 50

2003. – ***Europa. Art de l'affiche. Héliogravure. Deux bandes de phosphore. Dentelé 13½.***

"Bal des affiches" (1986), oeuvre de Raymond Savignac.

3556	**0,50 € multicolore**	1 »	0 50

2003. – *Bâtiment de guerre. Porte-avions Charles de Gaulle. Taille-douce. Dentelé 13½.*

3557	**0,50 € multicolore**	1 25	0 50

2003. – *Série artistique. Michel-Ange (1475-1564). Taille-douce. Dentelé 13½ x 13.*

"Esclave rebelle", "Esclave mourant", sculptures.

3558	**0,75 € multicolore**	1 75	1 »

2003. – *Portraits de régions. La France à vivre. Emis uniquement en feuillet. Héliogravure. Deux bandes de phosphore. Dentelés 13.* **BF** *n° 57.*

Les cabines de bain.

La pêche au carrelet.

3559	**0,50 € multicolore**	1 20	0 60
3560	**0,50 € multicolore**	1 20	0 60

Les vignobles de Champagne.

Le camembert.

3561	**0,50 € multicolore**	1 20	0 60
3562	**0,50 € multicolore**	1 20	0 60

Le foie gras.

La pétanque.

3563	**0,50 € multicolore**	1 20	0 60
3564	**0,50 € multicolore**	1 20	0 60

Guignol.

La crêpe.

3565	**0,50 € multicolore**	1 20	0 60
3566	**0,50 € multicolore**	1 20	0 60

Le cassoulet.

La porcelaine.

3567	**0,50 € multicolore**	1 20	0 60
3568	**0,50 € multicolore**	1 20	0 60
	N°s 3559 à 3568 (10 val.)	**12 »**	**6 »**

2003. – *Timbre pour anniversaires. Personnage de bande dessinée. © André Franquin & BATEM Marsu 2003. Héliogravure. Deux bandes de phosphore. Dentelé 13.*

Marsupilami portant un gâteau, d'André Franquin et Batem.

3569	**0,50 € multicolore**	1 »	0 50

2003. – *Type Marianne du 14 juillet. Type de 2002. Taille-douce. Dentelés 13.*

3570	**0,58 € jaune-olive**	1 50	0 50
3571	**0,70 € vert-olive**	2 »	0 70
3572	**0,75 € bleu ciel**	2 »	0 70

3573	**0,90 € bleu foncé**	2 50	1 50
3574	**1,11 € lilas**	3 »	1 10
3575	**1,90 € brun-prune**	5 »	2 »
	N°s 3570 à 3575 (6 val.)	**16 »**	**6 50**

Une bande de phosphore à droite pour les n°s 3570 et 3571 et deux bandes pour les n°s 3572 à 3575.

2003. – *76e Congrès de la Fédération Française des Associations Philatéliques, à Mulhouse. Taille-douce. Deux bandes de phosphore. Dentelé 13½ x 13.*

La Tour du Bolwerk et automobile Bugatti coupé cabriolet d'Esders.

3576	**0,50 € multicolore**	1 »	0 50

2003. – *Timbre pour vacances. Offset. Deux bandes de phosphore. Dentelé 13 x 13½.*

Mère et enfants sur leur serviette de plage.

3577	**0,50 € multicolore**	1 25	0 50

2003. – *Timbre pour vacances. Type de même date. Emis en carnet. Offset. Auto-adhésif. Deux bandes de phosphore. Dentelé 11.* Ⓒ

3578	**0,50 € (3577) multicolore**	1 50	0 60
BC3578A	La bande carnet, non pliée	15 »	12 »

2003. – *Basilique Notre-Dame de l'Epine (Marne). Taille-douce. Dentelé 13 x 13½.*

3579	**0,50 € multicolore**	1 »	0 50

2003. – *Série touristique. Tulle (Corrèze). Taille-douce. Deux bandes de phosphore. Dentelé 13½.*

Cathédrale.

3580	**0,50 € multicolore**	1 »	0 50

2003. – *275e anniversaire de la Franc-maçonnerie française. Taille-douce. Dentelé 13½ x 13.*

Symboles : compas et équerre.

3581	**0,50 € multicolore**	1 »	0 50

2003. – ***Cyclisme. Centenaire du Tour de France. Emis uniquement en feuillet. Héliogravure. Dentelés 13.*** **BF** ***n° 59.***

Le coureur Maurice Garin, vainqueur du Tour de 1903.

Coureur de 2003 à l'arrivée.

3582	**0,50 € multicolore**	1 50	0 75
3583	**0,50 € multicolore**	1 60	0 75
P3582	La paire 3582+3583	3 »	1 50

2003. – ***Série artistique. Paul Signac (1863-1935). Héliogravure. Dentelé 13½ x 13.***

"La Bouée Rouge", tableau du peintre.

3584	**0,75 € multicolore**	2 »	1 »

2003. – ***Série artistique. Wassily Kandinsky (1866-1944). Offset. Dentelé 13½ x 13.***

Tableau du peintre.

3585	**1,11 € multicolore**	2 50	1 25
	a. (Valeur faciale omise)	5 000 »	

Un feuillet de 3 timbres accompagnés de la décomposition des 4 phases d'impression était intégré dans l'ouvrage "Impressions Expressions" édité par La Poste début 2004 (voir paragraphe "Carnets & ouvrages de luxe" à la fin de la rubrique Carnets)

2003. – ***Eglise de Saint-Père (Yonne). Deux bandes de phosphore. Dentelé 13½.***

3586	**0,50 € multicolore**	1 »	0 50

2003. – ***Championnats du monde d'Athlétisme Paris 2003 Saint-Denis. Héliogravure. Deux bandes de phosphore. Dentelé 13.***

Lancer du javelot, course, saut en hauteur.

3587	**0,50 € multicolore**	1 »	0 60

2003. – ***Les personnages célèbres. Personnages de la littérature française. Héliogravure. Deux bandes de phosphore. Dentelés 13.*** **BF** ***n° 60.***

Vidocq.

Esmeralda.

3588	**0,50 € multicolore**	1 »	0 60
3589	**0,50 € multicolore**	1 »	0 60

Claudine.

Nana.

3590	**0,50 € multicolore**	1 »	0 60
3591	**0,50 € multicolore**	1 »	0 60

Le comte de Monte-Cristo.

Gavroche.

3592	**0,50 € multicolore**	1 »	0 60
3593	**0,50 € multicolore**	1 »	0 60
	Nos 3588 à 3593 (6 val.)	**6 »**	**3 60**

2003. – *Cinquantenaire de la naissance du Commandant afghan Ahmad Shah Massoud (1953-2001). Héliogravure. Deux bandes de phosphore. Dentelé 13.*

Portrait.

3594	**0,50 € multicolore**	1 »	0 50

2003. – *Portraits de régions. La France à voir. Emis uniquement en feuillet. Héliogravure. Deux bandes de phosphore. Dentelés 13.* BF *n° 61.*

Le château de Chenonceau.

Maison alsacienne.

3595	**0,50 € multicolore**	1 20	0 60
3596	**0,50 € multicolore**	1 20	0 60

Toits de Bourgogne.

Tour génoise en Corse.

3597	**0,50 € multicolore**	1 20	0 60
3598	**0,50 € multicolore**	1 20	0 60

L'Arc de Triomphe.

Mas provençal.

3599	**0,50 €multicolore**	1 20	0 60
3600	**0,50 € multicolore**	1 20	0 60

La pointe du Raz.

Le mont Blanc.

3601	**0,50 € multicolore**	1 20	0 60
3602	**0,50 € multicolore**	1 20	0 60

Maison basque.

Le pont du Gard.

3603	**0,50 € multicolore**	1 20	0 60
3604	**0,50 € multicolore**	1 20	0 60
	Nos 3595 à 3604 (10 val.)	**12 »**	**6 »**

2003. – *Série touristique. Arras (Pas-de-Calais). Taille-douce. Deux bandes de phosphore. Dentelé 13.*

Le beffroi et les maisons de la Grand'Place.

3605	**0,50 € multicolore**	1 »	0 50

Tirage : 4 238 591.

2003. – *Jardins de France. Emis uniquement en feuillet. Héliogravure. Dentelés 13½ x 13.* BF *n° 62.*

Parc des Buttes-Chaumont (détail falaise avec le temple de la Sibylle).

Jardin du Luxembourg (détail avec le bâtiment du Sénat en fond).

3606	**1,90 € multicolore**	5 »	4 »
3607	**1,90 € multicolore**	5 »	4 »

2003. – *Série touristique. Pontarlier (Doubs). Papier GPW non phosphorescent. Deux bandes de phosphore. Dentelé 13½.*

La Porte Saint-Pierre.

3608	**0,50 € multicolore**	1 »	0 50

2003. – *Série "Collection Jeunesse". Véhicules utilitaires et grande échelle. Emis uniquement en feuillet. Multicolores. Dentelés 13½ x 13.* BF *n° 63.*

3609	**0,20 € *Autocar***	0 50	0 40
3610	**0,20 € *Tracteur***	0 50	0 40

3611	**0,20 € *Camion de pompiers à échelle***	0 50	0 40
3612	**0,20 € *Voiture postale***	0 50	0 40

3613	**0,20 € *Autobus parisien***	0 50	0 40
3614	**0,30 € *Véhicule de livraison***	0 70	0 50

3615	**0,30 € *Camion de chantier***	0 70	0 50
3616	**0,30 € *Véhicule de Police***	0 70	0 50

3617	**0,30 € *Ambulance***	0 70	0 50
3618	**0,30 € *Véhicule de Premiers secours***	0 70	0 50
	N°s 3609 à 3618 (10 val.)	**6 »**	**4 50**

2003. – *Centenaire de la Semeuse de Roty. Emis en carnet. Taille-douce. Autoadhésif. Deux bandes de phosphore. Précoupé vertical en lignes ondulées. Dentelé.* C

3619	**0,50 € rouge**	2 50	2 »
P3619	La paire 3619+3419a	4 »	3 »

2003. – *Au profit de la Croix-Rouge. Fêtes de fin d'année. Timbre avec surtaxe. Héliogravure. Deux bandes de phosphore. Dentelé 13½ x 13.*

"La Vierge à la grappe", du peintre Pierre Mignard.

3620	**0,50 € multicolore**	2 »	1 »

2003. – *"Meilleurs Voeux". Offset. Deux bandes de phosphore. Dentelé 13.* BF *n° 65.*

Rouge-gorge.

3621	**0,50 € multicolore**	1 »	0 50
	a. (sans bandes de phosphore, gomme brillante)	160 »	160 »
	b. (Gomme mate sans bande de phosphore)	5 »	5 »

Le n° 3621a est issu du BF n° 65.

2003. – *"Meilleurs Voeux". Type du T.-P. de même date. Emis en carnet. Offset. Auto-adhésif. Deux bandes de phosphore. Dentelé 11.* [C]

3622 0,50 € (3621) multicolore 1 50 0 60
BC3622 La bande carnet, non pliée 15 » 12 »

2003. – *"Meilleurs Voeux". Héliogravure. Deux bandes de phosphore. Dentelé 13.*

3623 0,50 € multicolore 1 » 0 50

Emis en 2 feuilles de 10 timbres avec vignettes attenantes personnalisées avec "Cérès - Service Philatélique de la Poste - Paris France" pour l'une, avec le logo "Les timbres personnalisés" pour l'autre.

2003. – *Capitales européennes. Luxembourg. Emis uniquement en feuillet. Héliogravure. Dentelés 13-13½.* [BF] ***n° 64.***

Cathédrale Notre-Dame.

Citadelle Saint-Esprit.

3624 0,50 € multicolore 1 50 1 »
3625 0,50 € multicolore 1 50 1 »

Palais grand-ducal.

Pont Adolphe.

3626 0,50 € multicolore 1 50 1 »
3627 0,50 € multicolore 1 50 1 »

N°s 3624 à 3627 (4 val.) **6 »** **4 »**

2003. – *Série artistique. Andy Warhol (1928-1987). Héliogravure. Dentelé 13½ x 13.*

"Marilyn", 1967, sérigraphie du peintre.

3628 1,11 € multicolore 2 50 1 25

2003. – *Art. Emission commune avec l'Inde. Taille-douce. Dentelés 13½ x 13.*

Enluminure française du 15e s. extraite du livre des Heures à l'usage de Rome (coq).

Joaillerie indienne du 19e s. (paon).

3629 0,50 € multicolore 1 » 0 50
3630 0,90 € multicolore 2 » 1 50

2003. – *Paquebot. Le "Queen Mary 2". Héliogravure. Deux bandes de phosphore. Dentelé 13½.*

3631 0,50 € multicolore 1 50 0 50

2003

Du n° 3538 au n° 3631 :

(sauf bandes-carnets, paires et triptyques) :

94 timbres ****129** **⊙70**

Autres rubriques de l'année :

Aérien 66

Timbres Autoadhésifs 35 à 37

Blocs et feuillet 54 à 65

Blocs Souvenirs 1

Service 126 à 129

2004. – ***Saint-Valentin. Coeurs 2004 du couturier Karl Lagerfeld. Emis également en feuillet pour le n° 3632. Héliogravure. Dentelés.*** BF ***n° 66.***

Flacon de parfum Chanel n° 5 dans un coeur.

Le tailleur Chanel sur fond avec Tour Eiffel dans un coeur.

3632 **0,50 € multicolore** 1 50 0 50

3633 **0,75 € multicolore** 2 » 1 »

2004. – ***Saint-Valentin. Coeurs 2004 du couturier Karl Lagerfeld. Types des T.-P. de même date. Autoadhésifs. Multicolore. Dentelés.***

3632B **0,50 €** ***Flacon de parfum Chanel n° 5 dans un cœur*** 3 50 3 »

3633B **0,75 €** ***Le tailleur Chanel sur fond avec Tour Eiffel dans un cœur*** 4 50 4 »

2004. – ***Saint-Valentin. Coeurs 2004 du couturier Karl Lagerfeld. Type des T. -P. de même date, provenant de roulettes, numéro noir au verso.. Autoadhésifs. Dentelés.***

3632C **0,50 €** ***Flacon de parfum Chanel n° 5 dans un coeur*** 200 »

3633C **0,75 €** ***Le tailleur Chanel sur fond avec Tour Eiffel dans un coeur*** 200 »

2004. – ***Timbres pour naissances. "C'est une fille", "c'est un garçon". Emis en carnets. © Anne Geddes. Offset. Autoadhésifs. Deux bandes de phosphore. Dentelés 11.*** C

Bébé-abeille.

Bébé-papillon.

3634 **0,50 € multicolore** 1 50 0 60

3635 **0,50 € multicolore** 1 50 0 60

Bande-carnet Timbres pour naissances. "C'est une fille"

BC3634 La bande carnet, non pliée 15 » 10 »

Bande-carnet Timbres pour naissances. "C'est un garçon"

BC3635 La bande carnet, non pliée 15 » 10 »

2004. – ***Timbres de messages. Héliogravure. Deux bandes de phosphore. Dentelés 13.***

"Ceci est une invitation"avec point des "i"perforé.

"Un grand merci"avec point du "i"perforé.

3636 **0,50 € multicolore** 1 » 0 50

3637 **0,50 € multicolore** 1 » 0 50

2004. – ***Lille, capitale européenne de la Culture en 2004. Héliogravure. Deux bandes de phosphore. Dentelé 13.***

Les Maisons Folies.

3638 **0,50 € multicolore** 1 10 0 50

2004. – ***Personnalité. Centenaire de la mort du sculpteur Auguste Bartholdi (1834-1904). Taille-douce. Dentelé 13½*** x ***13.***

Statue de la Liberté.

3639 **0,90 € multicolore** 2 » 1 20

2004. – *Personnalité. 800e anniversaire de la mort de la reine Aliénor d'Aquitaine (v. 1122-1204). Taille-douce. Deux bandes de phosphore. Dentelé 13 x 13½.*

Portrait d'après un détail d'une miniature.

3640 0,50 € multicolore 1 » 0 50

2004. – *Fête du timbre. © Disney. Héliogravure. Deux bandes de phosphore. Dentelé 13½.* [C]

Mickey.

3641 0,50 € multicolore 1 » 0 50
a. (provenant de carnet, dentelé 13½ x 13) 1 » 0 50

La bande (format horizontal) destinée à la confection de carnets comprend 2 rangées composées chacune de 1 n° 3879, 1 n° 3877a, 1 n° 3878, 1 n° 3877a et 1 n° 3879.

BC3641a La bande carnet, non pliée 14 » 12 »

2004. – *Fête du timbre. Héliogravure. Type du T.-P. de même date pour le n° 3641a. Emis en carnet. Deux bandes de phosphore. Dentelés 13½ x 13.*

Donald.

Minnie.

3642 0,45 € multicolore 2 50 2 »
3643 0,75 € multicolore 1 50 1 »
T3641a Le triptyque 3641a+3643+3642 5 » 4 »

2004. – *Bicentenaire du Code Civil. Taille-douce. Deux bandes de phosphore. Dentelé 13½ x 13.*

3644 0,50 € multicolore 1 » 0 50

2004. – *Personnalité. Bicentenaire de la naissance de l'écrivain George Sand (1804-1876). Taille-douce. Deux bandes de phosphore. Dentelé 13½ x 13.*

Portrait, maison à Nohant.

3645 0,50 € multicolore 1 » 0 50

2004. – *Portraits de régions. La France à vivre. Emis uniquement en feuillet. Héliogravure. Deux bandes de phosphore. Dentelés 13.* [BF] *n° 68.*

La coutellerie.

Le marché de Provence.

3646 0,50 € multicolore 1 20 0 60
3647 0,50 € multicolore 1 20 0 60

Les vignobles du Beaujolais.

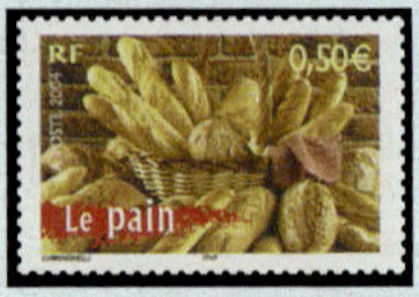

Le pain.

3648 0,50 € multicolore 1 20 0 60
3649 0,50 € multicolore 1 20 0 60

Coiffe madras.

Les huîtres.

3650 0,50 € multicolore 1 20 0 60
3651 0,50 € multicolore 1 20 0 60

La quiche lorraine.

La course landaise.

3652 0,50 € multicolore 1 20 0 60
3653 0,50 € multicolore 1 20 0 60

Le clafoutis. Le bagad.

3654	**0,50 € multicolore**	1 20	0 60
3655	**0,50 € multicolore**	1 20	0 60
	N°s 3646 à 3655 (10 val.)	**12 »**	**6 »**

2004. – *Série touristique. Clermont-Ferrand (Puy-de-Dôme). Taille-douce. Deux bandes de phosphore. Dentelé 13½.*

Statue équestre de Vercingétorix (oeuvre de Bartholdi), cathédrale, le puy de Dôme.

3656	**0,50 € multicolore**	1 »	0 50

2004. – *Centenaire de l'Entente cordiale. Emission commune avec la Grande-Bretagne. Héliogravure. Deux bandes de phosphore. Dentelés 13½.*

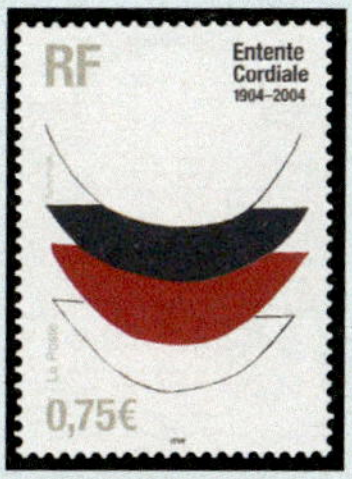

"Coccinelle", aquarelle du peintre Sonia Delaunay (1885-1979).

"Lace I (Trial Proof)", 1968, lithographie du peintre abstrait Terry Frost (1915-2003).

3657	**0,50 € multicolore**	1 »	0 50
	a. (Valeur faciale et "RF" omises)	150 »	
3658	**0,75 € multicolore**	1 50	1 »

2004. – *Sécurité routière. Héliogravure. Deux bandes de phosphore. Dentelé 13½.*

Composition avec ceinture de sécurité.

3659	**0,50 € multicolore**	1 »	0 50

2004. – *Série artistique. Jean-Léon Gérôme (1824-1904). Héliogravure. Dentelé 13 x 13½.*

"Un combat de coqs", détail tableau du peintre.

3660	**1,11 € multicolore**	2 50	1 25

2004. – *Série touristique. Bordeaux (Gironde). Taille-douce. Deux bandes de phosphore. Dentelé 13.*

Tramway et pont.

3661	**0,50 € multicolore**	1 »	0 60

2004. – *Série "Nature de France" (XIX). Animaux de la ferme. Héliogravure. Dentelés 13½.* BF *n° 69.*

Le lapin. La poule.

3662	**0,45 € multicolore**	0 90	0 50
3663	**0,50 € multicolore**	1 »	0 50

La vache. Le baudet.

3664	**0,50 € multicolore**	1 »	0 50
3665	**0,75 € multicolore**	1 50	1 »
	N°s 3662 à 3665 (4 val.)	**4 40**	**2 50**

2004. – ***1er mai 2004, élargissement de l'Union Européenne. Héliogravure. Deux bandes de phosphore. Dentelé 13½.***

Carte avec drapeaux des pays membres, étoiles européennes.

3666 0,50 € multicolore 1 » 0 50

2004. – ***Cinquantenaire de la bataille de Diên Biên Phu (Vietnam). Hommage aux combattants. Héliogravure. Deux bandes de phosphore. Dentelé 13.***

Soldats, parachutage.

3667 0,50 € multicolore 1 » 0 50

2004. – ***Europa. Les vacances. © Raoul Dufy, ADAGP, Paris 2004. Héliogravure. Deux bandes de phosphore. Dent. 13 x 13½.***

Détail d'une œuvre originale du peintre Raoul Dufy (1877-1953).

3668 0,50 € multicolore 1 » 0 50

2004. – ***Bande dessinée. "Blake et Mortimer", du dessinateur Edgar-Pierre Jacobs (1904-1987). Emission commune avec la Belgique. Héliogravure. Deux bandes de phosphore. Dentelés 13½-13.***

"La Marque Jaune".

Blake et Mortimer.

3669 0,50 € multicolore 1 » 0 50

3670 1,00 € multicolore 2 » 1 50

La Belgique a émis simultanément une figurine au même type (n° 3270), émis également en bloc dans un format différent.

2004. – ***Centenaire de la FIFA (Fédération Internationale de Football Association). © 2004 FIFA TM. Héliogravure. Deux bandes de phosphore. Dentelé 13.***

Logo.

3671 0,50 € multicolore 1 » 0 50

2004. – ***Europa. Les vacances. Type du T.-P. de 2004. Emis en carnet. Offset. Autoadhésif. Deux bandes de phosphore. Dent. 11.*** [C]

3672 0,50 € (3668) multicolore 1 50 0 50

BC3672 La bande carnet, non pliée 15 » 12 »

2004. – ***Jardins de France. Emis uniquement en feuillet. Héliogravure. Dentelés 13½ x 13.*** [BF] ***n° 70.***

Le Jardin des Tuileries (perspective sur les bassins, l'Obélisque de la place de la Concorde et l'Arc de Triomphe).

Le Parc floral de Paris.

3673 1,90 € multicolore 5 » 4 »

3674 1,90 € multicolore 5 » 4 »

2004. – ***60e anniversaire des Débarquements des troupes alliées et de la Libération. Héliogravure. Deux bandes de phosphore. Dentelé 13.***

3675 0,50 € multicolore 1 25 0 50

2004. – *Série artistique. Salvador Dali (1904-1989). Dentelé 13½ x 13. © Salvador Dali, Fondation Gala-Salvador Dali/ADAGP Paris 2004.*

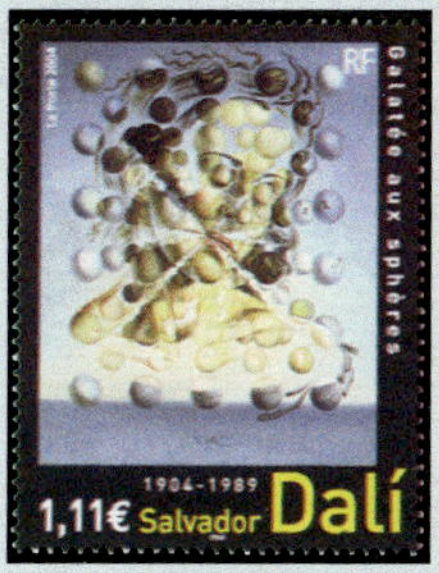

"Galatée aux sphères", tableau du peintre.

3676	1,11 € multicolore	2 50	1 25

2004. – *Le don d'organes. Héliogravure. Deux bandes de phosphore.Dentelé 13½.*

3677	0,50 € multicolore	1 »	0 50

2004. – *400ᵉ anniversaire de la fondation de la colonie de l'île Sainte-Croix par Pierre Dugua de Mons. Emission commune avec le Canada. Taille-douce et offset. Deux bandes de phosphore. Dentelé 13.*

Portrait de l'explorateur et marchand de fourrures.

3678	0,90 € multicolore	2 »	1 20

Le Canada a émis simultanément une figurine au même type (n°2086).

2004. – *Personnages célèbres. Napoléon 1ᵉʳ et la garde impériale. Héliogravure. Deux bandes de phosphore. Dentelé 13.* BF *n° 72.*

Chasseur à cheval.

Artilleur à pied.

3679	0,50 € multicolore	1 »	0 60
3680	0,50 € multicolore	1 »	0 60

Dragon.

Mameluk.

3681	0,50 € multicolore	1 »	0 60
3682	0,50 € multicolore	1 »	0 60

Napoléon 1ᵉʳ à cheval.

Grenadier à pied.

3683	0,50 € multicolore	1 »	0 60
3684	0,50 € multicolore	1 »	0 60
	Nᵒˢ 3679 à 3684 (6 val.)	**6 »**	**3 60**

2004. – *77ᵉ Congrès de la Fédération Française des Associations Philatéliques, à Paris. Taille-douce et offset. Deux bandes de phosphore. Dentelé 13½ x 13.*

Composition avec la Tour Eiffel.

3685	0,50 € multicolore	1 »	0 50

2004. – *Jeux olympiques d'Athènes (Grèce). Emis uniquement en feuillet. Héliogravure. Dentelés.* BF *n° 73.*

Kayak, tennis, saut d'obstacles.

Athlète antique portant la flamme olympique et relayeur.

3686	**0,50 € multicolore**	1 50	1 »
3687	**0,50 € multicolore**	1 50	1 »
P3686	La paire 3686+3687	3 »	2 20

2004. – ***Timbre pour Anniversaires. Héliogravure. Dentelé 13.*** BF ***n° 75.***

Maître d'hôtel portant un énorme gâteau (Oeuvre originale du dessinateur humoriste Jean-Jacques Sempé).

3688	**0,50 € multicolore**	1 »	0 50

2004. – ***Fonds mondial de lutte contre le SIDA, la Tuberculose et le Paludisme. Timbre sur timbre. Sans valeur indiquée (Validité permanente). Taille-douce. Dentelé 13.***

Timbre n° 3417 de la Marianne du 14 Juillet sur timbre et composition avec le logo de l'Organisme.

3689	**(sans val.) rouge**	1 »	0 50

2004. – ***Série artistique. Vincent Van Gogh (1853-1890). © AKG/E. Lessing (d'après photo). Héliogravure. Dentelé 13×13½.***

"La méridienne"d'après Millet, tableau du peintre Vincent Van Gogh.

3690	**0,75 € multicolore**	2 »	1 »

2004. – ***Série "Collection Jeunesse". Les sports de glisse. Héliogravure. Emis uniquement en feuillet. Dentelé 13½×13.***

BF ***n° 76.***

Skateboard.

Parachutisme.

3691	**0,20 € multicolore**	0 50	0 40
3692	**0,20 € multicolore**	0 50	0 40

Planche à voile.

Surf.

3693	**0,20 € multicolore**	0 50	0 40
3694	**0,20 € multicolore**	0 50	0 40

Luge.

Bicross.

3695	**0,20 € multicolore**	0 50	0 40
3696	**0,30 € multicolore**	0 70	0 50

Parapente.

Jet-ski.

3697	**0,30 € multicolore**	0 70	0 50
3698	**0,30 € multicolore**	0 70	0 50

Snowboard.

Roller.

3699	**0,30 € multicolore**	0 70	0 50
3700	**0,30 € multicolore**	0 70	0 50
	N°s 3691 à 3700 (10 val.)	**6 »**	**4 50**

2004. – *Série touristique. Vaux-sur-Mer (Charente-Maritime). Taille-douce. Deux bandes de phosphore. Dentelé 13½ .*

Eglise Saint-Etienne du 12e s.

3701 **0,50 € multicolore** 1 » 0 50
a. (Bleu clair omis) » »

Existe sans phosphore

2004. – *Portraits de régions. La France à voir. Emis uniquement en feuillet. Héliogravure. Deux bandes de phosphore. Dentelés 13.* BF *n° 77.*

3702 **0,50 €** ***Maison normande*** 1 20 0 60
3703 **0,50 €** ***Le château de Chambord*** 1 20 0 60

3704 **0,50 €** ***Les gorges du Tarn*** 1 20 0 60
3705 **0,50 €** ***Notre-Dame de Paris*** 1 20 0 60

3706 **0,50 €** ***Moulin du Nord*** 1 20 0 60
3707 **0,50 €** ***Maison troglodytique*** 1 20 0 60

3708 **0,50 €** ***Les calanques de Cassis*** 1 20 0 60
3709 **0,50 €** ***Le phare du Cap-Ferret*** 1 20 0 60

3710 **0,50 €** ***Château cathare*** 1 20 0 60
3711 **0,50 €** ***Chalet des Alpes*** 1 20 0 60

Nos 3702 à 3711 (10 val.) **12 »** **6 »**

2004. – *Cathédrale de Luçon (Vendée). Taille-douce. Deux bandes de phosphore. Dentelé 13 x 13½.*

3712 **0,50 €** ***Edifice et portrait du cardinal de Richelieu*** 1 » 0 50
a. (Rose omis) 750 »

2004. – *Halloween. Offset. Deux bandes de phosphore. Encres phosphorescentes. Zones recouvertes de vernis. Dentelé 13.*

3713 **0,50 €** ***Composition avec citrouille, sorcière, araignée*** 1 » 0 50

2004. – *Personnalité. 60 ans de la mort de Félix Eboué (1884-1944). Héliogravure. Deux bandes de phosphore. Dentelé 13.*

3714 **0,50 €** ***Portrait de l'administrateur des colonies et portrait du Général de Gaulle*** 1 » 0 50

2004. – ***Le phare d'Ouistreham. Héliogravure. Deux bandes de phosphore. Dentelé 13½.***

3715 0,50 € multicolore 1 » 0 50

2004. – ***60e anniversaire de la Marianne d'Alger. Emis en carnet. Taille-douce. Autoadhésif. Deux bandes de phosphore. Précoupé vertical en lignes ondulées.*** [C]

3716 0,50 € rouge 3 » 1 75

P3716 La paire 3716+3419 4 50 3 50

2004. – ***Au profit de la Croix-Rouge. Fêtes de fin d'année. Timbre avec surtaxe de 0,16 €. Emis en carnet. Héliogravure. Deux bandes de phosphore. Dentelé 13½ x 13.*** [C]

3717 0,50 € *"Vierge à l'Enfant", icône de l'Ecole crétoise (fin XVe siècle)* 2 » 1 »

2004. – ***Capitales européennes. Athènes. Emis uniquement en feuillet. Héliogravure. Dentelés 13-13½.*** [BF] ***n° 78.***

3718 0,50 € *L'Académie* 1 50 1 »

3719 0,50 € *Le Parthénon* 1 50 1 »

3720 0,50 € *L'Odéon d'Hérode Atticus* 1 50 1 »

3721 0,50 € *L'Eglise des Saints-Apôtres* 1 50 1 »

Nos 3718 à 3721 (4 val.) **6 » 4 »**

2004. – ***"Meilleurs Voeux". Emis en carnet de 2 séries. Offset. Autoadhésif. Deux bandes de phosphore. Dent. 11.*** [BF] ***n° 79 et blocs souvenir n°3.*** [C]

3722 0,50 € *Etoiles personnages avec chapeaux* 2 » 1 »

3723 0,50 € *Etoiles, oiseau et sapins stylisés* 2 » 1 »

3724 0,50 € *Etoile personnage tenant une fleur* 2 » 1 »

a. (papier gommé, sans bande de phosphore) 18 » 18 »

3725 0,50 € *Guirlande avec sujets décoratifs* 2 » 1 »

3726 0,50 € *Etoiles personnages* 2 » 1 »

Nos 3722 à 3726 (5 val.) **10 » 5 »**

BC3722 La bande carnet, non pliée 15 » 12 »

Tirage : 2 722 019 carnets.

Le n° 3727 a été supprimé. Il porte le n° 3724a (papier gommé). Issu du bloc souvenir n° 3

2004. – ***"Meilleurs Voeux"(Pour entreprises). Héliogravure. Deux bandes de phosphore. Dentelé 13.***

3728 0,50 € *Composition avec étoile* 1 25 0 50

2004. – *Personnalité. Centenaire de la mort d'Henri Wallon (1812-1904), historien et homme politique. Héliogravure. Deux bandes de phosphore. Dentelé 13.*

3729	**0,50 €** *Portrait*	1 »	0 50

2004. – *Inauguration du viaduc de Millau. Héliogravure. Deux bandes de phosphore. Dentelé 13 x 13¼.*

3730	**0,50 €** *Vue de l'ouvrage*	3 »	1 »

2004

Du n° 3632 au n° 3730 (sauf n° 3632C, 3633C, bandes-carnets, paires et triptyques) :

102 timbres ****541** **⊙81**

Autres rubriques de l'année :

Poste aérienne 67

Timbres Autoadhésifs 38 à 48

Blocs et feuillets 66 à 79

Blocs Souvenirs 2 et 3

Préoblitéré 248

2005. – *Type Marianne de Lamouche. Sans valeur indiquée (validité permanente) pour les nos 3733 (Ecopli 20 g) et 3734 (Lettre 20 g). Taille-douce. Une bande de phosphore, sauf n° 3732, 3733, 3735, 3736 : une bande de phosphore à droite ; n° 3734, 3737, 3738, 3739, 3740, 3741 : deux bandes de phosphore. Dentelés 13.*

3731	**0,01 € jaune**	0 20	0 15
	a. (Légende ITVF, gravure assistée par ordinateur)	0 20	0 15
	b. (Légende Phil@poste, gravure assistée par ordinateur)	0 15	0 15
3732	**0,10 € violet-rouge**	0 30	0 15
	a. (Légende ITVF, gravure assistée par ordinateur)	0 50	0 20
3733	**(sans val.) vert**	1 »	0 15
	a. (Légende ITVF, gravure assistée par ordinateur)	1 »	0 15
	b. (Légende Phil@poste, gravure assistée par ordinateur)	1 »	0 15
3734	**(sans val.) rouge**	1 20	0 15
	a. (Légende ITVF, gravure assistée par ordinateur)	1 20	0 15
	b. (Légende Phil@poste, gravure assistée par ordinateur)	1 »	0 15

3735	**0,58 € jaune-olive**	1 50	0 85
3736	**0,70 € vert-olive**	2 »	1 »
3737	**0,75 € bleu ciel**	1 50	0 75
3738	**0,90 € bleu foncé**	2 »	1 50

3739	**1,00 € orange**	3 »	1 »
	a. (Légende ITVF, gravure assistée par ordinateur)	3 »	1 »
	b. (Légende Phil@poste, gravure assistée par ordinateur)	2 »	0 30
3740	**1,11 € lilas**	3 50	2 »
3741	**1,90 € brun-prune**	3 80	1 80
	Nos 3731 à 3741 (11 val.)	**20 »**	**9 50**

Le timbre n° 3736 a été réimprimé en 2006 avec la légende Phil@poste (en gravure assistée par ordinateur) (n° 3967)

Les n° 3731 à 3734, 3739 et 3741 existent sans phosphore légende de ITVF

Les timbres avec signature Phil@poste à la place d'ITVF sont parus fin 2006

Taille-douce numérique (ou gravure électromécanique - GEM) : flou et couleur plus foncée. Gravure assistée par ordinateur (GAO) : net, couleur plus claire

2005. – *Type Marianne de Lamouche. Sans valeur indiquée (validité permanente) pour le n° 3742 (Ecopli 20 g) et 3743 (Lettre 20 g). Provenant de roulette. N° noir au verso. Taille-douce numérique. Une bande de phosphore à droite, sauf n° 3743 : deux bandes de phosphore. Dentelés 13 horizontalement.*

3742	**(sans val.) vert (3733)**	2 25	0 60
	a. vert (Légende Phil@poste, gravure assistée par ordinateur)	2 25	0 60
3743	**(sans val.) rouge (3734)**	2 25	0 50
	a. rouge (Légende Phil@poste, gravure assistée par ordinateur)	2 25	0 50

Taille-douce numérique (ou gravure assistée par ordinateur - **GEM**) : flou et couleur plus foncée.

Gravure assistée par ordinateur (**GAO**): net, couleur plus claire.

Provenant de carnet. Taille-douce. Autoadhésif. Deux bandes de phosphore. Précoupé vertical en lignes ondulées. [C]

Type I, gravure mécanique, noms plus fins du dessinateur, de l'imprimeur et du graveur (boucle du J remontant plus haute).

Type II, gravure numérique.

3744 (sans val.) rouge (Type II), *gravure numérique* (3734) 1 25 0 15
a. (Type I transfert mécanique du poinçon) 2 » 1 »
b. (Légende Phil@poste au lieu d'ITVF) 1 25 0 30

Le timbre n° 3744a a été émis, en 2005, en carnet "60e anniversaire de la Marianne de Dulac".

Le timbre n° 3744b est émis en carnets (à partir de 2006) (gravure numérique)

Le timbre n° 3744c est émis en carnets pour distributeurs Sagem (à partir de septembre 2007)

2005. – ***Solidarité Asie. Croix-Rouge Française. Timbre avec surtaxe au profit des sinistrés du tsunami. Timbre sur timbre. Timbre sans valeur indiquée (Validité permanente). Taille-douce. Deux bandes de phosphore. Dentelé 13.***

Timbre n° 3734 de la Marianne de Lamouche sur timbre, logo de la Croix-Rouge Française et mention "Solidarité Asie - 0,20 € de don".

3745 (sans val.) rouge 1 40 1 »

2005. – ***Personnalité. Rachi (1040-1105), rabbin, commentateur de la Bible et du Talmud. Taille-douce. Deux bandes de phosphore. Dentelé 13¼.***

3746 0,50 € ***Portrait*** 1 » 0 50

2005. – ***Saint-Valentin. Coeurs 2005 du couturier Cacharel. Héliogravure. Dentelés.*** [BF] ***n° 80.***

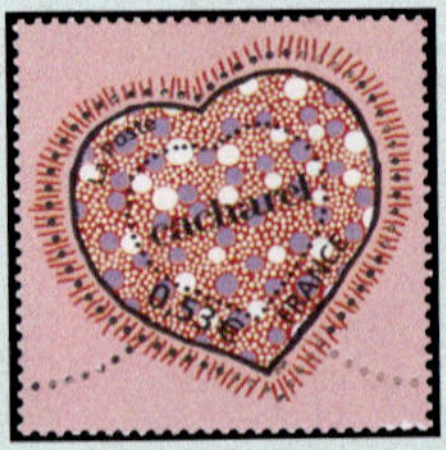

3747 0,53 € ***Coeur en tissu Liberty*** 1 80 0 75
3748 0,82 € ***Coeur au motif d'un cacharel, oiseau de Camargue*** 3 » 1 75
a. (sans "Poste") 150 » 100 »

2005. – ***Saint-Valentin. Coeurs 2005 du couturier Cacharel. Types des T.-P. de même date. Autoadhésifs. Dentelés.***

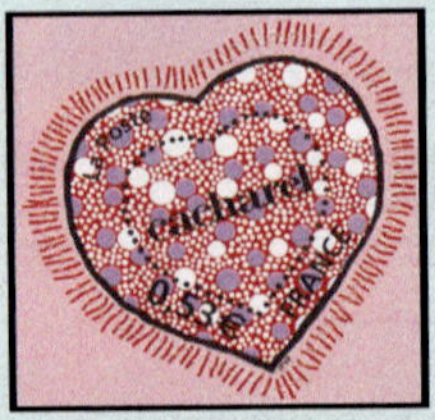

3747B 0,53 € multicolore 4 » 3 »
3748B 0,82 € multicolore 5 » 4 »
a. (sans "Poste") 50 » 30 »

2005. – ***Année lunaire chinoise du coq. Sans valeur indiquée (Lettre 20 g). Héliogravure. Papier gaufré. Dentelé 13½ x 13.***

3749 (sans val.) ***Coq stylisé*** 1 50 0 50

Emis en petite feuille composée de 10 timbres n° 3749 avec marge centrale illustrée par des idéogrammes et des dessins des animaux du zodiaque chinois.

F3749 La feuille 15 »

2005-06. – ***Centenaire du Rotary Club International. Héliogravure. Deux bandes de phosphore. Dentelure 13¼.***

3750 0,53 € ***Emblème sur carte de France*** 1 25 0 50
3750A ***Emis en 2006, Autoadhésif, dentelé 11*** 3 » 2 »

2005. – *Fête du Timbre. Bande dessinée. Titeuf, du dessinateur Zep. Sans valeur indiquée (validité permanente) (Lettre 20 g). Héliogravure. Deux bandes de phosphore. Dentelé 13¼.*

3751	(sans val.) *Le personnage*	1 10	0 50
	a. (provenant de carnetDentelé 13¼ x 13)	1 10	0 50

La bande (format horizontal) destinée à la confection de carnets comprend 2 rangées composées chacune de 1 n° 3879, 1 n° 3877a, 1 n° 3878, 1 n° 3877a et 1 n° 3879.

BC3751a La bande carnet, non pliée	15 »	14 »

2005. – *Fête du Timbre. Bande dessinée. Titeuf, du dessinateur Zep. Sans valeur indiquée (validité permanente) (Ecopli 20 g pour le n° 3752) (Monde 20 g pour le n° 3753). Type du T. -P. de même date pour le n° 3751a. Emis en carnet. Héliogravure. Deux bandes de phosphore. Dentelés 13¼ x 13.* C

3752	(sans val.) *Manu*	2 »	1 50
3753	(sans val.) *Nadia*	1 80	0 90
T3751a Le triptyque 3753+3751a+3752		5 »	4 »

2005. – *Type Marianne de Lamouche. Taille-douce. Une bande de phosphore à droite, sauf n° 3755, 3757, 3758, 3759 : deux bandes de phosphore. Dentelés 13.*

3754	**0,05 € bistre-noir**	0 20	0 15
	a. (Légende ITVF, gravure assistée par ordinateur)	0 20	0 15
	b. (Légende Phil@poste, gravure assistée par ordinateur)	0 15	0 15
3755	**0,55 € bleu**	1 50	0 50
3756	**0,64 € vert-olive**	1 50	0 60
	a. (Légende ITVF, gravure assistée par ordinateur)	1 50	0 60

3757	**0,82 € lilas-brun clair**	2 »	0 75
	a. (Légende ITVF, gravure assistée par ordinateur)	2 »	0 75
3758	**1,22 € lilas**	3 »	1 25
3759	**1,98 € brun-prune**	4 80	1 75
	a. (Légende ITVF, gravure assistée par ordinateur)	4 80	1 75
	N°s 3754 à 3759 (6 val.)	**13 »**	**5 »**

2005. – *Timbres de messages. Sans valeur indiquée (validité permanente) (Lettre 20 g). Héliogravure. Deux bandes de phosphore. Dentelés 13.*

3760	(sans val.) *"ceci est une invitation"avec point des "i"perforé*	1 10	0 50
3761	(sans val.) *"un grand merci"*	1 10	0 50

2005. – *Série artistique. Nicolas de Staël (1914-1955). Héliogravure. Dentelé 13 x 13¼.*

3762	**1,22 €** *"Sicile", tableau du peintre*	2 40	1 20

2005. – *Série "Nature"(XX). Flore. Fleurs. Orchidées. Héliogravure. Dentelés 13¼.* BF *n° 81.*

3763	0,53 € *Orchidée "Mabel Sanders"*	1 10	0 50
3764	0,53 € *Sabot de Vénus*	1 10	0 50

3765	0,55 € *Orchidée papillon*	1 10	0 50
3766	0,82 € *Orchidée d'Aphrodite*	1 70	1 »
	Nos 3763 à 3766 (4 val.)	5 »	2 50

2005. – *Portraits de régions. La France à vivre. Emis uniquement en feuillet. Héliogravure. Deux bandes de phosphore. Dentelés 13.* BF *n° 82.*

3767	0,53 € *Les joutes nautiques*	1 20	0 60
3768	0,53 € *L'horlogerie comtoise*	1 20	0 60

3769	0,53 € *Le cantal*	1 20	0 60
3770	0,53 € *Les guinguettes*	1 20	0 60

3771	0,53 € *La bouillabaisse*	1 20	0 60
3772	0,53 € *Le P'tit Quinquin (sculpture)*	1 20	0 60

3773	0,53 € *Les rillettes*	1 20	0 60
3774	0,53 € *La choucroute*	1 20	0 60

3775	0,53 € *La pelote basque*	1 20	0 60
3776	0,53 € *La canne à sucre*	1 20	0 60
	Nos 3767 à 3776 (10 val.)	12 »	6 »

2005. – *Série touristique. Aix-en-Provence. Taille-douce. Deux bandes de phosphore. Dentelé 13¼.*

3777	0,53 € *Fontaine des Quatre-Dauphins et montagne Sainte-Victoire*	1 10	0 50

2005. – ***Timbre pour Anniversaires. Bande dessinée. Centenaire de Bécassine, du dessinateur Joseph Porphyre Pinchon. Héliogravure. Deux bandes de phosphore. Dentelé 13¼. Caumery Pinchon © Hachette Livre/GL 2005.*** **BF** ***n°83.***

3778 **(Lettre 20g)** ***Bécassine portant un gâteau d'anniversaire*** 1 10 0 50

2005. – ***Personnalité. Cinquantenaire de la mort d'Albert Einstein (1879-1955), physicien. Héliogravure. Deux bandes de phosphore. Dentelé 13¼.***

3779 **0,53 €** ***Portrait du Prix Nobel de physique en 1921, formule E=mc2*** 1 10 0 50

2005. – ***Personnalité. Alexis de Tocqueville (1805-1859), historien et homme politique. Taille-douce. Deux bandes de phosphore. Dentelé 13 x 13¼.***

3780 **0,90 €** ***Portrait*** 1 80 1 40

2005. – ***60ᵉ anniversaire de la Libération des camps. Héliogravure. Deux bandes de phosphore. Dentelé 13¼.***

3781 **0,53 €** ***Soldats américain et soviétique libérant un déporté (dessin de Plantu)*** 1 10 0 50

2005. – ***Bicentenaire de la bataille d'Austerlitz. Emission commune avec la République tchèque. Taille-douce et offset. Deux bandes de phosphore. Dentelé 13¼.***

3782 **0,55 €** ***L'empereur Napoléon 1ᵉʳ, monument de la Paix à Austerlitz, soleil*** 1 10 0 80

La République Tchèque a émis une figurine au même type de 19 K (nº 399).

2005. – ***Série touristique. Golfe du Morbihan. Héliogravure. Deux bandes de phosphore. Dentelé 13.***

3783 **0,53 €** ***Paysage avec voiliers, sinagot, maisons sur une île*** 1 10 0 60

2005. – ***Europa. La gastronomie. Héliogravure. Deux bandes de phosphore. Dentelé 13½ x 13¼.***

3784 **0,53 €** ***Chef cuisinier présentant des plats dont un avec homard*** 1 10 0 50

2005. – ***78ᵉ Congrès de la Fédération française des associations philatéliques, à Nancy. Taille-douce. Deux bandes de phosphore. Dentelé 13.***

3785 **0,53 €** ***La place Stanislas avec la statue de Stanislas 1ᵉʳ Leszczynski, duc de Lorraine, et ses édifices du XVIIIᵉ siècle réalisés par l'architecte Emmanuel Héré de Corny*** 1 10 0 60

a. multicolore (Légende Phil@poste (au lieu d'ITVF), sans vignette attenante) 8 » 8 »

Le nº 3785a est issu du bloc souvenir nº 14.

Imprimé attenant horizontalement à une vignette sans valeur.

2005. – *Jardins de France. Emis uniquement en feuillet. Héliogravure. Dentelés 13½ x 13.* BF *n° 84.*

3786	1,98 € *Jardin de la Fontaine à Nîmes ("La nymphe de la source"(1746), sculpture de Dominique Raché)*	5 »	4 »
	a. (Légende Phil@poste (au lieu d'ITVF), couleur des arbres dans les tons violets)	5 »	4 »
3787	1,98 € *Jardin de la fontaine à Nîmes (sculpture du bassin du Nymphée)*	5 »	4 »
	a. (Légende Phil@poste (au lieu d'ITVF), couleur des arbres dans les tons violets)	5 »	4 »

Les timbres n°s 3786a et 3787a sont issus du BF n° 99.

2005. – *Timbre pour vacances. Sans valeur indiquée (validité permanente) (Lettre de 20 g). Emis en carnet. Offset. Autoadhésif. Deux bandes de phosphore. Dentelé 11.* C

3788	(sans val.) *Cabines de plage*	1 50	0 50
BC3788	La bande carnet, non pliée	15 »	12 »

2005. – *Personnages célèbres. Héros de romans de l'écrivain Jules Verne (1828-1905). Héliogravure. Deux bandes de phosphore. Dentelés 13.* BF *n° 85.*

3789	0,53 € *"Cinq semaines en ballon"(1863) (montgolfière et éléphant)*	1 25	0 60
3790	0,53 € *"De la Terre à la Lune"(1865) (fusée)*	1 25	0 60

3791	0,53 € *"Voyage au centre de la Terre"(1864) (faune préhistorique, radeau)*	1 25	0 60
3792	0,53 € *"Michel Strogoff"(1876) (scène avec le héros, courrier du tsar, à cheval)*	1 25	0 60

3793	0,53 € *"Le Tour du monde en 80 jours"(1873) (locomotive, bisons)*	1 25	0 60
3794	0,53 € *"Vingt mille lieues sous les mers"(1870) (combat contre une pieuvre géante)*	1 25	0 60
	N°s 3789 à 3794 (6 val.)	**7 50**	**3 60**

Chacun de ces timbres figure sur une page gommée intégrée dans l'ouvrage "Jules Verne, aventures et légendes". Voir paragraphe Carnets et ouvrages de luxe à la fin de la rubrique carnets.

2005. – *Sport automobile. Coupe Gordon Bennett. Emis uniquement en feuillet. Héliogravure. Dentelés.* BF *n°s 86 et n° 87.*

3795	0,53 € *Coupe Gordon Bennett (voiture de course Richard Brasier vainqueur en 1905)*	2 50	1 50

3796	0,53 € *Coupe Gordon Bennett (voiture de course Richard Brasier vainqueur en 1905, représentée sur partie de route protégée par une palissade)*	2 50	1 50

3797	0,53 € *Voiture de course d'endurance*	1 25	1 »

3798 **0,53 €** ***Voiture de rallye*** 1 25 1 »

3799 **0,53 €** ***Voiture de rallye-raid*** 1 25 1 »
3800 **0,53 €** ***Voiture de Formule 1*** 1 25 1 »

N°s 3795 à 3800 (6 val.) **10 »** **7 »**

2005. – Charte de l'environnement. Héliogravure. Papier recyclé alga carta naturale verde. Deux bandes de phosphore. Dentelé 13.

3801 **0,53 €** ***Mains d'adulte tenant un parchemin sur lequel des mains d'enfant sont posées sur l'image d'un paysage verdoyant avec cascade, rivière et hirondelle rousseline*** 1 10 0 60

2005. – Série touristique. Villefranche-sur-Mer (Alpes-Maritimes). Héliogravure. Dentelé 13¼.

3802 **0,53 €** ***Vue de la rade*** 1 10 0 50

2005. – 30ᵉ anniversaire de la Loi pour les personnes handicapées. Héliogravure. Deux bandes de phosphore. Dentelé 13¼.

3803 **0,53 €** ***Composition symbolique*** 1 10 0 50

2005. – Timbres de naissances. "C'est une fille", "C'est un garçon". Sans valeur indiquée (validité permanente) (Lettre 20 g). Emis en carnets. Offset. Autoadhésifs. Deux bandes de phos-phore. Dentelés 11. [C]

3804 **(sans val.)** ***"C'est un fille"(nouveau-né sur une pivoine) (d'après photographie d'Anne Geddes, Australienne)*** 1 50 0 50
BC3804 La bande carnet, non pliée 12 » 10 »
3805 **(sans val.)** ***"C'est un garçon"(nouveau-né sur un lotus) (d'après photographie d'Anne Geddes, Australienne)*** 1 50 0 50
BC3805 La bande carnet, non pliée 12 » 10 »

2005. – Série artistique. François Pompon (1855-1933), sculpteur. Héliogravure. Dentelé 13 x 13¼.

3806 **0,90 €** ***"L'Ours blanc", sculpture de 1929*** 2 50 1 40

2005. – Type Marianne de Lamouche. Type du T.-P. de 2005. Taille-douce. Deux bandes de phosphore. Dentelé 13 horizontalement.

3807 **0,55 € bleu (3755)** 2 50 1 »

2005. – ***Le Haras du Pin. Héliogravure. Deux bandes de phosphore. Dentelé 13 x 13¼.***

3808	**0,53 €** *Entrée du haras, tête de cheval*	1 10	0 50

2005. – ***Série touristique. La Roque-Gageac (Dordogne). Taille-douce. Deux bandes de phosphore. Dentelé 13¼.***

3809	**0,53 €** *Maisons au pied de la falaise*	1 10	0 50

2005. – ***Capitales européennes. Berlin. Emis uniquement en feuillet. Héliogravure. Dentelés 13½ x 13⅜. BF n° 88.***

3810	**0,53 €** *La Porte de Brandebourg*	1 50	1 25
3811	**0,53 €** *L'église du Souvenir*	1 50	1 25

3812	**0,53 €** *La Philharmonie*	1 50	1 25
3813	**0,53 €** *Le Reichstag*	1 50	1 25
	Nos 3810 à 3813 (4 val.)	**6 »**	**5 »**

2005. – ***Portraits de régions. La France à voir. Emis uniquement en feuillet. Héliogravure. Deux bandes de phosphore. Dentelés 13. BF n° 89.***

3814	**0,53 €** *Le Lac d'Annecy*	1 20	0 60
3815	**0,53 €** *Les falaises d'Etretat*	1 20	0 60

3816	**0,53 €** *Pigeonnier*	1 20	0 60
3817	**0,53 €** *Lavoir*	1 20	0 60

3818	**0,53 €** *Quais de Seine*	1 20	0 60
3819	**0,53 €** *Les mégalithes de Carnac*	1 20	0 60

3820	**0,53 €** *Maison solognote*	1 20	0 60
3821	**0,53 €** *La dune du Pilat*	1 20	0 60

3822	**0,53 €** *Le phare du Stiff*	1 20	0 60
3823	**0,53 €** *Borie*	1 20	0 60
	Nos 3814 à 3823 (10 val.)	**12 »**	**6 »**

2005. – *Personnalité. Victor Baltard (1805-1874), architecte en chef de la Ville de Paris. Taille-douce. Deux bandes de phos-phore. Dentelé 13 x 13¼.*

3824	1,22 € *Le Pavillon Baltard n° 8, remonté à Nogent-sur-Marne en 1976*	2 50	1 20

2005. – *"Sourires"avec le Chat du dessinateur et humoriste Philippe Geluck. Créations originales du dessinateur. Emis en carnet. Sans valeur indiquée (validité permanente) (Lettre 20 g). Offset. Autoadhésifs. Deux bandes de phosphore. Dentelés 11.* ©

3825	(sans val.) *"L'envers d'un timbre autocollant est un excellent attrape-mouche"*	1 30	0 60
3826	(sans val.) *"Une seule lettre vous manque""et tout est épeuplé"*	1 30	0 60

3827	(sans val.) *"Envoyer une lettre""est un jeu d'adresse"*	1 30	0 60
3828	(sans val.) *"J'écris""donc tu lis"*	1 30	0 60

3829	(sans val.) *"Vous avez un joli timbre""J 'aime votre enveloppe"*	1 30	0 60
3830	(sans val.) *"Homme de lettres vu de dos"*	1 30	0 60

3831	(sans val.) *"Ecrire ou ne pas écrire""Lettre ou le néant ? "*	1 30	0 60
3832	(sans val.) *"C'est l'histoire d'un timbre""qui colle une enveloppe pour l'emmener en boîte"*	1 30	0 60

3833 (sans val.) *"Le mot enveloppe" "contient neuf lettres"* 1 30 0 60

3834 (sans val.) *"Entre nous""ça colle"* 1 30 0 60

N°s 3825 à 3834 (10 val.) **13 »** **6 »**

BC3825 La bande carnet, non pliée 13 »

2005. – ***Série artistique. Jean-Baptiste Greuze (1725-1805). Héliogravure. Dentelé 13¼ x 13.***

3835 **0,82 €** ***"Le guitariste", détail du tableau du peintre*** 2 » 1 »

2005. – ***Dépistage du cancer du sein. Héliogravure. Deux bandes de phosphore. Dentelé 13¼.***

3836 **0,53 € multicolore** 1 10 0 50

2005. – ***Personnalité. Raymond Aron (1905-1983), philosophe et sociologue. Taille-douce. Deux bandes de phosphore. Dent. 13¼.***

Portrait.

3837 **0,53 € bleu et noir** 1 10 0 50

2005. – ***Art. "L'Annonciation", oeuvre du peintre italien Raphaël (1483-1520). Emission commune avec le Vatican. Emis uniquement en feuillet. Taille-douce et offset. Dent. 13 x 13½.*** BF ***n° 90.***

Détails de "L'Annonciation", panneau de la prédelle du retable du "Couronnement de la Vierge"(v. 1502-1504) peint pour la chapelle Oddi de l'église Saint-François du Prato de Pérouse (Pinacothèque du Vatican).

3838 **0,53 €** ***Dessin préparatoire de l'ange Gabriel (Musée du Louvre) et peinture de la Vierge Marie*** 1 20 0 80

3839 **0,55 €** ***Peinture de l'ange Gabriel et dessin de préparatoire de la Vierge Marie (Musée du Louvre)*** 1 30 1 »

2005. – ***Au profit de la Croix-Rouge. Fêtes de fin d'année. Emis uniquement en carnet. Héliogravure. Deux bandes de phosphore. Dentelé 13½ x 13.*** C

Timbre avec surtaxe de 0,17 €.

3840 **0,53 €** ***Détail du diptyque "Vierge à l'Enfant et Martin Van Nieuwenhoven"(1487), du peintre flamand Hans Memling (v. 1433-1494)*** 2 » 0 80

2005. – ***60ᵉ anniversaire de la Marianne de Dulac. Emis en carnet. Taille-douce. Autoadhésif. Deux bandes de phosphore. Précoupé vertical en lignes ondulées. Dentelé*** C

3841 **0,53 € rouge** 2 50 1 50

P3841 La paire 3841+3744a 3 50 2 50

2005. – ***Série "Collection jeunesse". Héros des jeux vidéo. Emis uniquement en feuillet. Héliogravure. Dent. 13¼ x 13.*** BF ***n° 91.***

3842 **0,20 €** ***Link avec son bouclier et son épée Excalibur*** 0 50 0 30

3843 **0,20 €** ***Pac-Man*** 0 50 0 30

3844	**0,20 €** ***Prince of Persia***	0 50	0 30
3845	**0,20 €** ***Spyro le petit dragon***	0 50	0 30

3846	**0,20 €** ***Donkey Kong le gorille***	0 50	0 30
3847	**0,33 €** ***Mario le plombier***	0 70	0 50

3848	**0,33 €** ***Adibou***	0 70	0 50
3849	**0,33 €** ***Rayman***	0 70	0 50

3850	**0,33 €** ***Lara Croft***	0 70	0 50
3851	**0,33 €** ***Les Sims***	0 70	0 50
	N°s 3842 à 3851 (10 val.)	**6 »**	**4 »**

2005. – ***Personnalité. Avicenne (980-1037), médecin et philosophe. Taille-douce. Deux bandes de phosphore. Dentelé 13 x 13¼.***

3852	**0,53 €** ***Portrait***	1 10	0 50

2005. – ***"Meilleurs voeux". Sans valeur indiquée (validité permanente) (Lettre 20 g). Emis en carnet de 2 séries. Offset. Autoadhésifs. Deux bandes de phosphore. Dentelés 11.*** **BF** ***n° 92 et bloc souvenir n° 5.*** **C**

3853	**(sans val.)** ***Ours blanc et manchot sur patins à glace et deux jeunes manchots sur une luge***	2 »	0 60
3854	**(sans val.)** ***Manchots, renne et bonhomme de neige***	2 »	0 60
	a. multicolore (Dentelé 13 Héliogravure Papier gommé sans bande de phosphore)	18 »	18 »

3855	**(sans val.)** ***Renne et manchot sur une luge***	2 »	0 60
3856	**(sans val.)** ***Manchots avec boules de neige***	2 »	0 60

3857	**(sans val.)** ***Ours blanc sur une luge et manchots skiant ou glissant***	2 »	0 60
	N°s 3853 à 3857 (5 val.)	**10 »**	**3 »**
	BC3853 La bande carnet, non pliée	20 »	12 »

Le n° 3858 a été supprimé, il porte le n°3854a (papier gommé). Issu du bloc souvenir n°5.

Tous ces timbres existent sans bande de phosphore.

2005. – ***Personnalité. Jacob Kaplan (1895-1994), grand rabbin de France. Taille-douce. Deux bandes de phosphore. Dentelé 13.***

3859	**0,53 €** ***Portrait du grand rabbin de France de 1955 à 1981***	1 10	0 50

2005. – *Centenaire de la loi relative à la séparation des Eglises et de l'Etat. Héliogravure. Deux bandes de phosphore. Dentelé 13¼ x 13.*

3860 **0,53 €** ***Eglise et extrait du Journal officiel*** 1 10 0 50

2005
Du n° 3731 au n° 3860
(sauf bandes-carnets, paires et triptyques) :
132 timbres ****204** **⊙107**
Autres rubriques de l'année :
Aériens 68
Timbres Autoadhésifs 49 à 71
Blocs et feuillet 80 à 92
Blocs Souvenirs 4 et 5
Préoblitéré 249
Service 130 à 133
Timbres Personnalisés

2006. – *Saint-Valentin. Coeurs 2006 du couturier Stéphane Rolland de la Maison Jean-Louis Scherrer. Sans valeur indiquée (validité permanente). Héliogravure. Dentelés.* BF *n° 93.*

3861	**(Lettre 20 g)** ***Coeur***	1 10	0 50
3862	**(Lettre 50 g)** ***Coeur***	1 60	0 80

2006. – *Saint-Valentin. Coeurs 2006 du couturier Stéphane Rolland de la Maison Jean-Louis Scherrer. Types des T.-P. de même date. Autoadhésifs. Multicolore. Dentelés.*

3863	**(Lettre 20 g) multicolore (3861)**	3 »	2 »
3864	**(Lettre 50 g) multicolore (3862)**	4 »	3 »

Emis chacun en feuille de 30 timbres.

2006. – *Année lunaire chinoise du chien. Sans valeur indiquée (validité permanente) (Lettre 20 g). Héliogravure. Deux bandes de phosphore. Dentelé 13½ x 13.*

Chien, oeuvre originale de Li Zhongyao, peintre et calligraphe.

3865	**(Lettre 20 g) multicolore**	1 50	0 50
F3865	**La feuille**	15 »	

Emis en petite feuille de 10 timbres n° 3865 avec marge centrale illustrée par les animaux du zodiaque chinois.

2006. – *Art. Peinture. Les impressionnistes. Sans valeur indiquée (validité permanente). Emis en carnet. Offset. Autoadhésifs. Deux bandes de phosphore. Multicolore. Dentelés 11.* C

3866	**(Lettre 20 g)** ***"Portraits à la campagne"(1876), détail de tableau du peintre Gustave Caillebotte (1848-1894)***	1 50	0 60
3867	**(Lettre 20 g)** ***"La chasse aux papillons"(1874), détail de tableau du peintre Berthe Morisot (1841-1895)***	1 50	0 60

3868	**(Lettre 20 g)** ***"Mère et enfant"(1886), détail de tableau du peintre Mary Cassatt (1845-1926)***	1 50	0 60
3869	**(Lettre 20 g)** ***"Jeunes filles au piano"(1892), détail de tableau du peintre Auguste Renoir (1841-1919)***	1 50	0 60

3870	**(Lettre 20 g)** ***"La bergère"ou "Jeune fille à la baguette"(1881), détail de tableau du peintre Camille Pissarro (1830-1903)***	1 50	0 60
3871	**(Lettre 20 g)** ***"Mademoiselle Gachet dans son jardin"(1890), détail de tableau du peintre Vincent Van Gogh (1853-1890)***	1 50	0 60

3872	(Lettre 20 g) *"L'air du soir"(1893-1894), détail de tableau du peintre Henri-Edmond Cross (1856-1910)*	1 50	0 60
3873	(Lettre 20 g) *"Danseuses"(1884-1885), détail de tableau du peintre Edgar Degas (1834-1917)*	1 50	0 60

3874	(Lettre 20 g) *"Le déjeuner sur l'herbe"(1863), détail de tableau du peintre Edouard Manet (1832-1883)*	1 50	0 60
3875	(Lettre 20 g) *"Femmes de Tahiti"ou "Sur la plage"(1891), détail de tableau du peintre Paul Gauguin (1848-1903)*	1 50	0 60
	N°s 3866 à 3875 (10 val.)	**15 »**	**6 »**
	BC3866 La bande carnet, non pliée	13 »	7 »

2006. – ***Jeux olympiques d'hiver 2006 à Turin (Italie). Héliogravure. Deux bandes de phosphore. Dentelé 13.***

3876	0,53 € *Biathlon, ski de fond*	1 25	0 50

2006. – ***Fête du timbre. Bande dessinée. Spirou, du dessinateur José Luis Munuera. Sans valeur indiquée (validité permanente). Héliogravure. Deux bandes de phosphore. Dentelé 13¼.***

3877	(Lettre 20 g) *Spirou*	1 20	0 50
	a. (provenant de carnet, Dentelé 13¼ x 13)	1 20	0 50

2006. – ***Fête du timbre. Bande dessinée. Spirou, du dessinateur José Luis Munuera. Sans valeur indiquée (validité permanente) (Ecopli 20 g pour le n° 3878) (Monde 20 g pour le n° 3879). Type du T.-P. de même date pour le n° 3877a. Emis en carnet. Héliogravure. Deux bandes de phosphore. Dentelés 13¼ x 13.***

3878	(Ecopli 20 g) *Spirou, Fantasio et Spip, l'écureuil*	2 »	1 »
3879	(Monde 20 g) *Fantasio*	2 50	1 »
T3877a	Le triptyque 3879+3877a+3878	6 »	4 »

La bande (format horizontal) destinée à la confection de carnets comprend 2 rangées composées chacune de 1 n° 3879, 1 n° 3877a, 1 n° 3878, 1 n° 3877a et 1 n° 3879.

BC3877Ba	La bande carnet, non pliée	15 »	12 »

2006. – ***Hommage aux mineurs victimes de la catastrophe de Courrières (Pas-de-Calais) en 1906. Héliogravure. Deux bandes de phosphore. Dentelé 13½ x 13¼.***

3880	0,53 € *Mineur de l'époque*	1 10	0 55

2006. – ***Ossuaire de Douaumont (Meuse). Taille-douce. Deux bandes de phosphore. Dentelé 13¼.***

3881	0,53 € multicolore	1 10	0 55

2006. – ***Portraits de régions. La France à vivre. Emis uniquement en feuillet. Héliogravure. Deux bandes de phosphore. Dentelés 13.*** **BF** *n° 94.*

3882	0,53 € *La mirabelle*	1 20	0 60
3883	0,53 € *Les marais salants*	1 20	0 60

3884 0,53 € *Le beurre* 1 20 0 60
3885 0,53 € *Le roquefort* 1 20 0 60

3886 0,53 € *L'huile d'olive* 1 20 0 60
3887 0,53 € *Le carnaval* 1 20 0 60

3888 0,53 € *Les vendanges* 1 20 0 60
3889 0,53 € *Le café* 1 20 0 60

3890 0,53 € *La transhumance* 1 20 0 60
3891 0,53 € *Les hortillonnages* 1 20 0 60

N°s 3882 à 3891 (10 val.) 12 » 6 »

2006. – *Série touristique. Yvoire (Haute-Savoie). Héliogravure. Deux bandes de phosphore. Dentelé 13.*

3892 0,53 € *Le village au bord du Lac Léman* 1 10 0 50

2006. – *Série touristique. Dijon (Côte-d'Or). Taille-douce. Deux bandes de phosphore. Dentelé 13¼.*

3893 0,53 € *Détails statues du Puits de Moïse (1396-1406), du sculpteur hollandais Claus Sluter et l'église Saint-Bégnine* 1 10 0 50

2006. – *Série artistique. Paul Cézanne (1839-1906), peintre. Héliogravure. Dentelé 13 x 13¼.*

3894 0,82 € *"Baigneuses", tableau du peintre* 2 50 1 25

2006. – *Jardins de France. Emis uniquement en feuillet. Héliogravure. Dentelés 13½ x 13.* BF *n° 95.*

3895 1,98 € *Arboretum du Parc de la Vallée-aux-Loups, à Châtenay-Malabry (Hauts-de-Seine)* 4 » 3 »
a. (Légende Phil@poste (au lieu d'ITVF)) 5 » 4 »
3896 1,98 € *Jardin Albert Kahn, à Boulogne-Billancourt (Hauts-de-Seine) (pont japonais)* 4 » 3 »
a. (Légende Phil@poste (au lieu d'ITVF)) 5 » 4 »

Les timbres n°s 3895a et 3896a sont issus du BF n° 99.

2006. – *Série "Nature"(XXI). Faune. Les jeunes animaux domestiques. Héliogravure. Dentelés 13¼.* BF *n° 96.*

3897 **0,53 €** ***Le chaton*** 1 10 0 50

3898 **0,53 €** ***Le chiot*** 1 10 0 50

3899 **0,55 €** ***Le poulain*** 1 10 0 50

3900 **0,82 €** ***L'agneau*** 1 70 0 80

Nos 3897 à 3900 (4 val.) **5 »** **2 30**

2006. – *Personnalité. Littérature. Pierre Bayle (1647-1706), écrivain et philosophe. Taille-douce. Deux bandes de phosphore. Dentelé 13 x 13¼.*

Portrait.

3901 **0,53 € noir et brun foncé** 1 10 0 55

2006. – *Europa. L'intégration. Héliogravure. Deux bandes de phosphore. Dentelé 13¼.*

3902 **0,53 €** ***Oeuvre originale de l'auteur de bandes dessinées Enki Bilal*** 1 10 0 55

2006. – *Mémoires de l'esclavage et de son abolition. Héliogravure. Deux bandes de phosphore. Dentelé 13¼ x 13½.*

3903 **0,53 € multicolore** 1 10 0 55

2006. – *Timbre pour vacances. Sans valeur indiquée (validité permanente) (Lettre 20 g). Emis en carnet. Offset. Autoadhésif. Deux bandes de phosphore. Dentelé 11.* C

3904 **(sans val.)** ***Oeuvre originale du dessinateur de bandes dessinées Jean Giraud*** 1 20 0 55

BC3904 La bande carnet, non pliée 15 » 10 »

2006. – *Série artistique. Grotte de Rouffignac (Dordogne). Taille-douce. Dentelé 13 x 13¼.*

3905 **0,55 €** ***Peinture rupestre d'animaux*** 1 50 0 75

2006. – *Coupe du monde de football 2006 en Allemagne. Emis uniquement en feuillet. Héliogravure. Multicolores. Dentelés.* BF *n° 97.*

3906 **0,53 €** ***Les remplaçants*** 1 30 1 »

3907 **0,53 €** ***Les supporters*** 1 30 1 »

3908 **0,53 €** ***L'entraîneur*** 1 30 1 »

3909 **0,53 €** ***Les journalistes*** 1 30 1 »

3910 0,53 € *Le dégagement* 1 30 1 »
3911 0,53 € *Le contrôle* 1 30 1 »

3912 0,53 € *Le centre* 1 30 1 »
3913 0,53 € *Le retourné* 1 30 1 »

3914 0,53 € *La feinte de corps* 1 30 1 »
3915 0,53 € *L'arbitre* 1 30 1 »

Nos 3906 à 3915 (10 val.) 13 » 10 »

2006. – ***Série artistique. Claude Viallat, peintre. Héliogravure. Dentelé 13¼ x 13.***

3916 1,22 € *Oeuvre originale sur cape de torero* 3 » 1 20

2006. – ***Personnages célèbres. Les opéras de Mozart. Héliogravure. Deux bandes de phosphore. Dent. 13.*** **BF** ***n° 98.***

3917 0,53 € *L'Enlèvement au sérail (1782) (costume de Varona)* 1 10 0 55
3918 0,53 € *Les Noces de Figaro (1786) (costume d'Ezio Frigerio)* 1 10 0 55

3919 0,53 € *Don Giovanni (1787) (costume de Marillier)* 1 10 0 55
3920 0,53 € *Cosi fan tutte (1790) (costume d'Erté)* 1 10 0 55

3921 0,53 € *La Clémence de Titus (1791) (costume de Graf)* 1 10 0 55
3922 0,53 € *La Flûte enchantée (1791) (costume de Chapelain-Midy)* 1 10 0 55

Nos 3917 à 3922 (6 val.) 6 60 3 30

2006. – ***Monuments. Patrimoine mondial. Emission commune avec les Nations Unies à Genève (n° 554 à 1,00 F et 555 à 1,30 F). Héliogravure. Deux bandes de phosphore. Dentelés 13¼.***

3923 0,53 € *La tour César (XIIe siècle), à Provins (Seine-et-Marne)* 1 10 0 55
3924 0,90 € *Le Mont-Saint-Michel et son abbaye (Manche)* 1 80 0 90

2006. – ***Type Marianne de Lamouche. Autoadhésif. Gravure à chaud argent. Dentelé 13.***

3925	**5,00 € argent**	10 »	8 »

Timbre (en argent 999 millièmes) présenté sous blister sur un support cartonné.

2006. – ***79e Congrès de la Fédération française des associations philatéliques, à Paris. Taille-douce. Deux bandes de phosphore. Dentelé 13 x 13¼.***

3926	**0,53 €** ***Edifice de l'Opéra Garnier, à Paris***	1 10	0 70

Imprimé attenant horizontalement à une vignette sans valeur (Apollon élevant sa lyre (dôme), du sculpteur Millet).

2006. – ***Timbre pour Anniversaires. Bande dessinée. 75 ans de l'éléphant Babar par l'auteur et dessinateur Laurent de Brunhoff. Sans valeur indiquée (timbre à validité permanente) (Lettre 20 g). Héliogravure. Deux bandes de phosphore. Dentelé 13¼. Babar ™ and © Nelvana Jointly Licensed by Nelvana Rosse.*** **BF** ***n° 100.***

3927	**(sans val.)** ***Babar portant un gâteau d'anniversaire***	1 10	0 55

2006. – ***Capitales européennes. Nicosie (Chypre). Emis uniquement en feuillet. Héliogravure. Multicolore. Dentelés 13 x 13¼.*** **BF** ***n° 101.***

3928	**0,53 €** ***Le Musée archéologique***	1 50	1 »
3929	**0,53 €** ***L'église byzantine de Chrysaliniotissa (1450)***	1 50	1 »

3930	**0,53 €** ***La Porte de Famagouste***	1 50	1 »
3931	**0,53 €** ***Le palais de l'Archevêché***	1 50	1 »
	Nos 3928 à 3931 (4 val.)	**6 »**	**4 »**

2006. – ***Musique et danse. Le tango. Emission commune avec l'Argentine (n° 2614 à 75 c et 2615 à 4 P). Oeuvres originales du peintre argentin Antonio Segui. Héliogravure. Deux bandes de phosphore. Dentelés 12¼.***

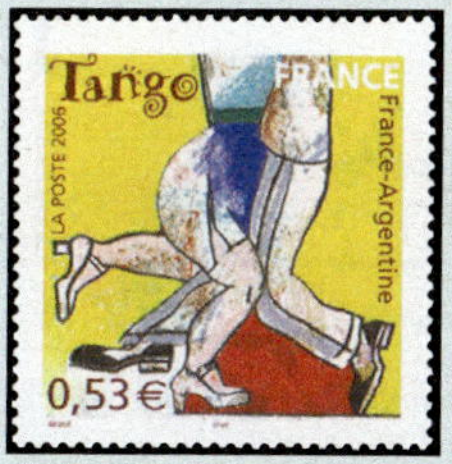

3932	**0,53 €** ***Danseurs de tango***	1 10	0 55
3933	**0,90 €** ***Joueur de bandonéon***	1 80	0 90

2006. – ***10e anniversaire de la Fondation d'entreprise La Poste. Sans valeur indiquée (timbre à validité permanente) (Lettre 20 g). Offset. Papier de type kraft. Deux bandes de phosphore. Dentelé 13.***

3934	**(sans val.)** ***Clé de sol, arobase et écriture manuscrite***	1 10	0 55

2006. – ***Sport. Golf. Centenaire de l'Open de France. Héliogravure. Papier gaufré. Deux bandes de phosphore. Dentelé 13¼.***

3935	**0,53 €** ***Silhouettes de joueurs de 1906 et de 2006***	1 10	0 55
	a. (Sans phosphore)	8 »	8 »

Le n° 3935a est issu du bloc souvenir n° 13.

2006. – *Sport. Football. "Merci les Bleus". Héliogravure. Deux bandes de phosphore. Multicolore. Dentelé 13¼.*

3936 **0,53 €** *Mains et ballon* 1 25 0 60

2006. – *Inauguration du Musée du Quai Branly. Héliogravure. Deux bandes de phosphore. Dentelé 13*

3937 **0,53 €** *Statuette, édifice, tour Eiffel* 1 10 0 60

2006. – *Personnalité. Réhabilitation du capitaine Alfred Dreyfus (1859-1935). Taille-douce. Deux bandes de phosphore. Dentelé 13 x 13¼.*

3938 **0,53 € multicolore** 1 10 0 50

2006. – *Personnalité. Capitaine Claude Joseph Rouget de Lisle (1760-1836). Héliogravure. Deux bandes de phosphore. Dentelé 13¼.*

3939 **0,53 €** *"Rouget de Lisle chantant la Marseillaise" (d'après tableau du peintre Isidore Pils), village de Montaigu à gauche, ville natale de Lons-le-Saunier à droite* 1 10 0 50

2006. – *Série touristique. Antibes Juan les Pins (Alpes-Maritimes). Taille-douce. Deux bandes de phosphore. Dentelé 13 x 13½.*

3940 **0,53 €** *Vue du Vieil Antibes* 1 10 0 50

2006. – *Personnalité. Musique. Pablo Casals (1876-1973), violoncelliste et chef d'orchestre espagnol. Héliogravure. Deux bandes de phosphore. Dentelé 13¼.*

3941 **0,53 €** *Portrait, manche de violoncelle* 1 10 0 50

2006. – *Portraits de régions. La France à voir. Héliogravure. Deux bandes de phosphore. Multicolore. Dentelés 13.* BF *n° 102.*

Emis uniquement en feuillet.

3942 **0,54 €** *Tours catalanes* 1 10 0 50
3943 **0,54 €** *La Croisette à Cannes (Alpes-Maritimes)* 1 10 0 50

3944 **0,54 €** *La forêt de Brocéliande* 1 10 0 50
3945 **0,54 €** *Les volcans d'Auvergne* 1 10 0 50

3946 **0,54 €** *Les Invalides, à Paris (l'édifice illuminé)* 1 10 0 50
3947 **0,54 €** *Le château de Chaumont-sur-Loire* 1 10 0 50

3948 **0,54 €** ***Les gorges de l'Ardèche*** 1 10 0 50
3949 **0,54 €** ***Le moulin de Valmy*** 1 10 0 50

3950 **0,54 €** ***La grotte de Lourdes*** 1 10 0 50
3951 **0,54 €** ***Calanche de Piana (Corse)*** 1 10 0 50

N°s 3942 à 3951 (10 val.) **11 »** **5 »**

2006. – ***Série touristique. Thionville (Moselle). Taille-douce. Deux bandes de phosphore. Dentelé 13.***

3952 **0,54 €** ***Le pont-écluse sud, œuvre de Louis de Cormontaigne (XVIIIe siècle)*** 1 10 0 50

2006. – ***"Sourires" avec le chien Cubitus du dessinateur Michel Rodrigue et scénariste Pierre Aucaigne. © Rodrigue & Aucaigne Dupa/Le Lombard 2006. Offset. Autoadhésifs. Deux bandes de phosphore. Multicolore. Dentelés 11.*** 🄲

Sans valeur indiquée (timbre à validité permanente).

Emis en carnet.

3953 **(Lettre 20 g)** ***Tête de Cubitus sur un timbre affranchissant un pli destiné au chat Sénéchal*** 1 30 0 60
3954 **(Lettre 20 g)** ***Tête de Cubitus avec un timbre collé sur la truffe*** 1 30 0 60

3955 **(Lettre 20 g)** ***"Oh ! le timbre a une dent de plus ! " (Cubitus et son neveu Bidule montrant sa nouvelle dent en riant)*** 1 30 0 60

3956 **(Lettre 20 g)** ***"Youhou ! il y a quelqu'un ? " (Cubitus, Sémaphore, Sénéchal et Bidule)*** 1 30 0 60

3957 **(Lettre 20 g)** ***"Ouf ! ce n'est pas une facture ! " (Cubitus ouvrant son courrier)*** 1 30 0 60
3958 **(Lettre 20 g)** ***Cubitus avec bonnet phrygien et fleur violette*** 1 30 0 60

3959 **(Lettre 20 g)** ***Cubitus tenant un pli d'où s'échappent des cœurs*** 1 30 0 60
3960 **(Lettre 20 g)** ***Cubitus : "Ce sont de bonnes nouvelles", Sénéchal : "C'est bon ! vous pouvez ouvrir ! "*** 1 30 0 60

3961 **(Lettre 20 g)** ***"Je suis le seul timbre au monde qu'on caresse dans le sens du poil ! " (Cubitus et l'escargot)*** 1 30 0 60
3962 **(Lettre 20 g)** ***"Je suis un timbre qui adore les papouilles ! " (main chatouillant Cubitus)*** 1 30 0 60

N°s 3953 à 3962 (10 val.) **13 »** **6 »**

BC3953 La bande carnet, non pliée 11 »

2006. – ***Art. Œuvres de Constantin Brancusi (1876-1957), sculpteur. © Brancusi, Adagp Paris 2006. Héliogravure. Deux bandes de phosphore. Multicolore. Dentelés 13¼.***

Emission conjointe avec la Roumanie.

3963 **0,54 €** ***"Muse endormie", sculpture*** 1 10 0 50
3964 **0,85 €** ***"Le sommeil" (1908), sculpture*** 1 70 1 »

La Roumanie a émis deux timbres aux mêmes types n° 5147 de 2,10 L et n° 5148 de 3,10 L.

2006. – ***Type Marianne de Lamouche. Gravure assistée par ordinateur, sauf n° 3966 : taille-douce numérique. Une bande de phosphore à droite, sauf n° 3966, 3968, 3969, 3970, 3971, 3972 : deux bandes de phosphore. Dentelés 13.***

3965	**0,10 € gris**	0 30	0 15
3966	**0,60 € bleu**	1 30	0 30

Type du T. -P. n° 3736 de 2005

3967	**0,70 € vert-olive**	1 50	0 40
3968	**0,85 € violet rouge**	2 »	0 50
3969	**0,86 € lilas-brun clair**	2 »	0 50
	a. (sans bande de phosphore)		

3970	**1,15 € bleu ciel**	2 30	0 50
3971	**1,30 € lilas**	2 50	0 65
3972	**2,11 € brun-prune**	4 20	1 »
	N°s 3965 à 3972 (8 val.)	**16 10**	**4 »**

Taille-douce numérique (ou gravure électromécanique - GEM) : flou et couleur plus foncée.

Gravure assistée par ordinateur (GAO) : net, couleur plus claire.

2006. – ***Type Marianne de Lamouche. Taille-douce numérique. Deux bandes de phosphore. Dentelé 13 horizontalement.***

Provenant de roulette. N° noir au verso de 1 à 500.

3973	**0,60 € bleu (Type du T.-P. de même date) (3966)**	2 »	1 »

Taille-douce numérique (ou gravure électromécanique - GEM) : flou et couleur plus foncée.

2006. – ***25e anniversaire d'Aviation Sans Frontières (ASF) association humanitaire. Héliogravure. Deux bandes de phosphore. Dentelé 13.***

3974	**0,54 €** ***Avion, enfant avec colis***	1 10	0 50

2006. – ***Personnalité. Henri Moissan (1852-1907), pharmacien et chimiste. Taille-douce. Deux bandes de phosphore. Dentelé 13¼ x 13.***

3975	**0,54 €** ***Portrait du prix Nobel de chimie en 1906***	1 10	0 50

2006. – ***Premières rencontres internationales sur la mémoire partagée, à Paris. Héliogravure. Deux bandes de phosphore. Dentelé 13¼.***

3976	**0,54 €** ***Rencontres sur la mémoire combattante***	1 10	0 50

2006. – ***60e anniversaire de la Marianne de Gandon. Taille-douce. Autoadhésif. Deux bandes de phosphore. Dent. : précoupé vertical en lignes ondulées. Ⓒ (carnets de timbres à composition variable).***

Emis en carnet.

3977	**0,54 € rouge**	2 50	1 50
P3977	La paire 3977+3744b	3 50	2 »

2006. – *Aviation. Les machines volantes. Taille-douce. Deux bandes de phosphore. Multicolore. Dentelés 13.* BF *n° 103.*

Emis uniquement en feuillet.

3978	**0,54 €** *L' "Hélicoptère" du vicomte Ponton d'Amécourt*	1 30	1 »
3979	**0,54 €** *La "Demoiselle" d'Alberto Santos-Dumont*	1 30	1 »

3980	**0,54 €** *La "Barque ailée" de Jean-Marie Le Bris*	1 30	1 »
3981	**0,54 €** *L'Avion III de Clément Ader*	1 30	1 »

3982	**0,54 €** *L' "Hydravion" d'Henri Fabre*	1 30	1 »
3983	**0,54 €** *Le "Ballon à rames" de Jean-Pierre Blanchard*	1 30	1 »
	N°s 3978 à 3983 (6 val.)	**7 80**	**6 »**

2006. – *Série artistique. Rembrandt (1606-1669), peintre et graveur hollandais. Taille-douce. Dentelé 13¼ x 13.*

3984	**1,30 €** *"Mendiants à la porte d'une maison" (1648), eau-forte*	3 »	1 40

2006. – *Tram-train. Héliogravure. Deux bandes de phosphore. Dentelé 13 x 13¼.*

3985	**0,54 €** *Rame du tramway Trancilien de la ligne Bondy-Aulnay-sous-Bois (93) inauguré le 18 novembre 2006*	1 10	0 50

2006. – *"Meilleurs Vœux". Offset. Autoadhésifs. Deux bandes de phosphore. Multicolore. Dentelés 11.* C

Sans valeur indiquée (validité permanente).

Emis en carnet de 2 séries.

3986	**(Lettre 20 g)** *Manchots et renne en traîneau*	1 50	0 60
3987	**(Lettre 20 g)** *Renne pêchant et manchots se baignant*	1 50	0 60

3988	**(Lettre 20 g)** *Renne et manchots décorant un sapin*	1 50	0 60
3989	**(Lettre 20 g)** *Manchots regardant le renne patiner*	1 50	0 60

3990	**(Lettre 20 g)** *Renne avec paquet cadeau et manchots dans des paquets cadeaux*	1 50	0 60
	a. (provenant du bloc souvenir n° 15, dentelé 13. Papier gommé 2 bandes de phosphore)	18 »	18 »
	N°s 3986 à 3990 (5 val.)	**7 50**	**3 »**
BC3986	La bande carnet, non pliée	15 »	10 »

2006. – ***Au profit de la Croix-Rouge. "Dessine ton vœu pour les enfants du monde". Héliogravure. Deux bandes de phosphore. Multicolore. Dentelés 13¼ x 12¾.*** **[C]** ***(Croix-Rouge sans publicité)***

Sans valeur indiquée (validité permanente).

Timbre avec surtaxe de 0,17 €.

Emis en carnet.

3991	**(Lettre 20 g)** ***"Fleur", dessin de Yacine Lorafy, élève de CM2***	1 60	0 70
3992	**(Lettre 20 g)** ***"Jouons ensemble ! ", dessin de Margot Deram, élève de CM2***	1 60	0 70
P3991	La Paire 3991+3992	3 25	2 25

La bande (format vertical) destinée à la confection de carnets comprend 5 paires n° 3991+3992

BC3991 La bande carnet, non pliée 14 »

2006. – ***Grande Loge Nationale Française. Héliogravure. Deux bandes de phosphore. Dentelé 13.***

3993 **0,54 €** ***Emblème de l'ordre maçonnique*** 1 25 0 50

2006. – ***Personnalité. Alain Poher (1909-1996), homme politique. Taille-douce. Deux bandes de phosphore. Dentelé 13¼.***

3994 **0,54 €** ***Portrait, le Sénat (Palais du Luxembourg)*** 1 25 0 50

2006. – ***Le tramway à Paris. Héliogravure. Deux bandes de phosphore. Dentelé 13¼.***

3995 **0,54 €** ***Rame du tramway parisien dont la ligne n° 3 a été inaugurée le 16 décembre 2006*** 1 25 0 50

2006

Du n° 3861 au n° 3995

(sauf bandes-carnets, paire et triptyques) :

136 timbres ****205** **⊙106**

Autres rubriques de l'année :

Aériens 69

Timbres Autoadhésifs 72 à 101

Blocs et feuillet 81 à 103

Blocs Souvenirs 6 à 15

Service 134 à 135

Timbres Personnalisés

2007. – ***Saint-Valentin. Cœurs 2007 de la Maison de couture Givenchy. Héliogravure. Dentelés.*** **BF** ***n° 104.***

Sans valeur indiquée (validité permanente).

3996	**(Lettre 20 g) noir sur rouge** ***Cœur rouge***	1 25	0 50
3997	**(Lettre 50 g) noir et rouge** ***Cœur blanc***	2 »	1 »

2007. – ***Saint-Valentin. Cœurs 2007 de la Maison de couture Givenchy. Héliogravure. Autoadhésifs. Dentelés.***

Types des T. -P. de même date.

Sans valeur indiquée (validité permanente).

3998	**(Lettre 20 g) noir sur rouge** ***Cœur rouge*** **(3996)**	10 »	6 »
3999	**(Lettre 50 g) noir et rouge** ***Cœur blanc*** **(3997)**	5 »	4 »

Emis chacun en feuilles de 30 timbres.

2007. – ***Hommage aux Justes de France. Deux bandes de phosphore. Dentelé 13¼ x 12½.***

4000 **0.54 €** ***Le Panthéon*** 1 50 0 50

2007. – ***Année lunaire chinoise du Cochon. Héliogravure. Deux bandes de phosphore. Dentelé 13½ x 13.***

Sans valeur indiquée (validité permanente).

4001 **(Lettre 20 g)** ***Cochon, œuvre originale de Li Zhongyao, peintre et calligraphe*** 1 50 0 55

Emis en petite feuille de 10 timbres n° 4001 avec marge centrale illustrée par les animaux du zodiaque chinois.

F4001 **La feuille** 15 » 10 »

2007. – ***Art. Antiquités. Offset. Autoadhésifs. Deux bandes de phosphore. Multicolore. Dentelés 11.*** [C]

Sans valeur indiquée (validité permanente). Emis en carnet.

4002 **(Lettre 20 g)** ***Hippopotame égyptien en faïence*** 1 30 0 60

4003 **(Lettre 20 g)** ***Tête de la déesse grecque Aphrodite*** 1 30 0 60

4004 **(Lettre 20 g)** ***Statue grecque de la Victoire de Samothrace*** 1 30 0 60

4005 **(Lettre 20 g)** ***Fresque romaine de Pompéi*** 1 30 0 60

4006 **(Lettre 20 g)** ***Le pharaon Amenemhat III*** 1 30 0 60

4007 **(Lettre 20 g)** ***Statue de la déesse romaine Junon*** 1 30 0 60

4008 **(Lettre 20 g)** ***Harpiste égyptien*** 1 30 0 60

4009 **(Lettre 20 g)** ***Le sarcophage des époux, antiquité étrusque*** 1 30 0 60

4010 **(Lettre 20 g)** ***Statue égyptienne de scribe accroupi*** 1 30 0 60

4011 **(Lettre 20 g)** ***Tête de Périclès, antiquité grecque*** 1 30 0 60

N°s 4002 à 4011 (10 val.) **13 »** **6 »**

BC4002 La bande carnet, non pliée 13 » 8 »

2007. – ***Série touristique. Valenciennes (Nord). Taille-douce. Deux bandes de phosphore. Dentelé 13¼.***

4012 **0.54 €** ***Détails de la fontaine Watteau, œuvre du sculpteur Jean-Baptiste Carpeaux (1827-1875)*** 1 10 0 50

2007. – ***Bibliothèque humaniste de Sélestat. Taille-douce. Deux bandes de phosphore. Dentelé 12¼ x 13.***

4013 **0,60 €** ***Lettrine enluminée extraite du manuscrit "Livre des Miracles de sainte Foy", 11e s.*** 1 20 0 60

2007. – ***Portraits de régions. La France à voir. Héliogravure. Deux bandes de phosphore. Multicolore. Dentelés 13.*** [BF] ***n° 105.***

Emis uniquement en feuillet.

4014 **0,54 €** ***Les Baux-de-Provence*** 1 10 0 50

4015 **0,54 €** ***Cascade dans le Doubs*** 1 10 0 50

4016	0,54 € *La forêt de Fontainebleau*	1 10	0 50
4017	0,54 € *Les bords de Loire*	1 10	0 50

4018	0,54 € *Le château de Chantilly*	1 10	0 50
4019	0,54 € *Le massif de la Grande-Chartreuse*	1 10	0 50

4020	0,54 € *Saint-Malo*	1 10	0 50
4021	0,54 € *Saint-Tropez*	1 10	0 50

4022	0,54 € *Le ballon d'Alsace*	1 10	0 50
4023	0,54 € *Le canal du Midi*	1 10	0 50
	Nos 4014 à 4023 (10 val.)	11 »	5 »

2007. – ***Fête du timbre. « Harry Potter », héros de la série de l'écrivain britannique Joanne Kathleen Rowling. © TM & © Warner Bros. Entertainment Inc. (s07). Héliogravure. Deux bandes de phosphore. Multicolore. Dentelé 13¼.*** **BF** ***n° 106.***

Sans valeur indiquée.

4024	**(Lettre prioritaire 20 g)** ***Harry Potter***	1 10	0 60
	a. (Dentelé 13¼ x 13 provenant de carnet)	1 10	0 60

2007. – ***Fête du timbre. « Harry Potter », héros de la série de l'écrivain britannique Joanne Kathleen Rowling. © TM & © Warner Bros. Entertainment Inc. (s07). Héliogravure. Deux bandes de phosphore. Multicolore. Dentelés 13¼ x 13.*** **C (carnets journée du timbre)**

Sans valeur indiquée. Emis en carnet.

4025	**(Ecopli 20 g)** ***Ron Weasley***	1 40	0 70
4026	**(Monde 20 g)** ***Hermione Granger***	2 »	0 85

La bande (format horizontal) destinée à la confection de carnets comprend deux rangées composées pour la première de : 1 n° 4026, 1 n° 4024a, 1 n°4026, 1 n° 4024a et 1 n° 4026, pour la seconde de : 1 n° 4025, 1 n° 4024a, 1 n° 4025, 1 n° 4024a et 1 n° 4025

BC4024a	La bande carnet, non pliée	13 »	12 »

2007. – ***Fête du timbre. « Harry Potter », héros de la série de l'écrivain britannique Joanne Kathleen Rowling. © TM & © Warner Bros. Entertainment Inc. (s07). Héliogravure. Autoadhésifs. Deux bandes de phosphore. Multicolore. Dentelés 11.***

Types des T. -P. de même date.

Sans valeur indiquée.

4024A	**(Lettre prioritaire 20 g)** ***Harry Potter***	5 »	3 »
4025A	**(Ecopli 20 g)** ***Ron Weasley***	5 »	3 »
4026A	**(Monde 20 g)** ***Hermione Granger***	9 »	5 »

Emis chacun en petite feuille de 5 timbres attenant chacun à une vignette illustrée différente.

Feuilles Harry Potter avec vignettes illustrées (Autoadhésifs)

F4024A	**La feuille**	**25 »**
F4025A	**La feuille**	**45 »**
F4026A	**La feuille**	**35 »**

2007. – ***Personnalité. Albert Londres (1884-1932), journaliste. Taille-douce. Deux bandes de phosphore. Dentelé 13 x 13¼.***

4027	**0,54 € brun et bleu** ***Portrait du reporter, scène d'arrivée de bagnards en Guyane***	1 10	0 50

2007. – ***Bicentenaire de la Cour des Comptes. Taille-douce. Deux bandes de phosphore. Dentelés 13¼.***

Emission conjointe avec la France et les collectivités territoriales et les territoires d'Outre-Mer.

4028 **0,54 €** ***Façade du Palais Cambon à Paris*** 1 10 0 50

4028A ***Idem, Autoadhésif*** 3 » 1 50

2007. – ***Série touristique. Limoges (Haute-Vienne). Taille-douce. Deux bandes de phosphore. Dentelé 13¼.***

4029 **0,54 €** ***La gare des Bénédictins et détail d'une porcelaine*** 1 50 0 50

2007. – ***Cinquantenaire du traité de Rome. Héliogravure. Deux bandes de phosphore. Dentelé 13¼.***

4030 **0,54 €** ***Composition avec silhouettes-étoiles sur texte avec signatures sur fond bleu*** 1 10 0 50

2007. – ***Personnalité. Sébastien Le Prestre de Vauban (1633-1707), maréchal de France. Taille-douce. Deux bandes de phosphore. Dentelé 13¼.***

4031 **0,54 €** ***Portrait et citadelle de Mont-Louis dans les Pyrénées-Orientales*** 1 10 0 50

2007. – ***"Allez les petits". Timbre annonce de la VIe Coupe du monde de Rugby en France en 2007. Héliogravure. Deux bandes de phosphore. Dentelé 13¼.***

4032 **0,54 €** ***Encouragement du commentateur sportif Roger Couderc (1918-1984) et joueurs*** 1 10 0 50

2007. – ***Série "Nature" (XXII). Faune en voie de disparition dans les départements d'outre-mer. Héliogravure. Multicolore. Dentelés 13¼.*** BF ***n° 107.***

4033 **0,54 €** ***Iguane des Antilles (Iguana delicatissima)*** 1 10 0 50

4034 **0,54 €** ***Le racoon de la Guadeloupe*** 1 10 0 50

4035 **0,60 €** ***Le jaguar de Guyane*** 1 20 0 60

4036 **0,86 €** ***Le pétrel de Barau à La Réunion*** 1 70 0 85

N°s 4033 à 4036 (4 val.) **5 10** **2 45**

2007. – ***Timbres pour vacances. Offset. Autoadhésifs. Deux bandes de phosphore. Multicolore. Dentelés 11.*** C

Sans valeur indiquée (validité permanente).

Emis en carnet.

4037 **(Lettre prioritaire 20 g)** ***Détail d'une porte peinte en bleue et roses trémières*** 1 30 0 60

4038 **(Lettre prioritaire 20 g)** ***Poisson-chirurgien à poitrine blanche*** 1 30 0 60

4039 (Lettre prioritaire 20 g) *Gentiane bleue* 1 30 0 60

4040 (Lettre prioritaire 20 g) *Myrtilles* 1 30 0 60

4041 (Lettre prioritaire 20 g) *Détails de barques peintes en bleu* 1 30 0 60

4042 (Lettre prioritaire 20 g) *Echeveaux teints en bleu séchant* 1 30 0 60

4043 (Lettre prioritaire 20 g) *Glacier* 1 30 0 60

4044 (Lettre prioritaire 20 g) *Cocotier et ciel bleu* 1 30 0 60

4045 (Lettre prioritaire 20 g) *Parasols bleus* 1 30 0 60

4046 (Lettre prioritaire 20 g) *Pigments de différentes couleurs* 1 30 0 60

N°s 4037 à 4046 (10 val.) **13 »** **6 »**

BC4037 La bande carnet, non pliée 13 » 8 »

2007. – *Jardins de France. Le Parc de la Tête d'Or à Lyon (Rhône). Héliogravure. Multicolore. Dent. 13½ x 13.* BF *n° 108.*

Emis uniquement en feuillet.

4047 **2,11 €** ***Détail vue du Parc de la Tête d'Or à Lyon*** 4 20 3 »

4048 **2,11 €** ***Détail vue des serres du Parc de la Tête d'Or à Lyon*** 4 20 3 »

2007. – *Europa. Le scoutisme. Héliogravure. Deux bandes de phosphore. Dentelé 13¼.*

4049 **0,60 €** ***Scout réalisant un brélage*** 1 20 0 60

2007. – *Centenaire de la Fédération internationale de voile. Héliogravure. Deux bandes de phosphore. Dentelé 13.*

4050 **0,85 €** ***Voiliers en compétition*** 1 70 0 85

2007. – *Personnages célèbres. Les voyages de Tintin. © Hergé/Moulinsart 2007. Héliogravure. Deux bandes de phos-phore. Multicolore. Dentelés 13.* BF *n° 109.*

4051 **0,54 €** ***Tintin et Milou*** 1 10 0 50

4052 **0,54 €** ***Le professeur Tournesol avec ses jumelles*** 1 10 0 50

4053 **0,54 €** ***La capitaine Haddock utilisant un sextant*** 1 10 0 50

4054 **0,54 €** ***Dupond et Dupont en voiture*** 1 10 0 50

4055 **0,54 €** ***Bianca Castafiore, la diva*** 1 10 0 50

4056 **0,54 €** ***Le Chinois Tchang*** 1 10 0 50

N°s 4051 à 4056 (6 val.) **6 60** **3 »**

2007. – *Série touristique. Arcachon (Gironde). Héliogravure. Deux bandes de phosphore. Dentelé 13¼.*

4057	**0,54 €** ***Le bassin d'Arcachon, villa, bateau***	1 10	0 50

2007. – *Art. Œuvres religieuses. Héliogravure. Deux bandes de phosphore. Multicolore. Dentelés 13¼.*

Emission conjointe avec l'Arménie (n° 542 et 543).

4058	**0,54 €** ***"Nativité", miniature d'un manuscrit liturgique du XVe siècle (collection du Matenadaran)***	1 10	0 50
4059	**0,85 €** ***"L'Ange au Sourire", détail d'une statue du portail nord de la cathédrale de Reims***	1 70	0 85

2007. – *Série artistique. Sanglier-enseigne gaulois (Musée archéologique de Soulac-sur-Mer en Gironde). Taille-douce. Dentelé 13 x 13¼.*

4060	**1,30 € multicolore**	3 »	1 40

2007. – *Inauguration du TGV Est Européen. Héliogravure. Deux bandes de phosphore. Dentelé 13.*

4061	**0,54 €** ***Nez du TGV, trajet avec le nom des villes desservies***	1 10	0 50

2007. – *80e congrès de la Fédération française des associations philatéliques, à Poitiers (Vienne). Taille-douce. Deux bandes de phosphore. Dentelé 13 x 13¼.*

4062	**0,54 € brun foncé et ocre jaune** ***Eglise Notre-Dame la Grande, collégiale du XIe siècle, et détail de la frise biblique de sa façade (l'Annonciation et l'arbre de Jessé)***	1 10	0 50

Imprimé attenant à une vignette sans valeur (mandorle avec le Christ, sculpture figurant tout en haut du fronton).

2007. – *VIe coupe du monde de Rugby organisée par la France en 2007. Héliogravure. Multicolore. Dentelés 13 x 13½.* BF *n° 110.*

Emis uniquement en feuillet.

4063	**0,54 €** ***La mêlée***	1 30	1 »
4064	**0,54 €** ***L'attaque***	1 30	1 »

4065	**0,54 €** ***L'essai***	1 30	1 »
4066	**0,54 €** ***La touche***	1 30	1 »

4067	**0,54 €** ***La transformation***	1 30	1 »
4068	**0,54 €** ***La passe***	1 30	1 »

4069	0,54 € *Le raffut*	1 30	1 »
4070	0,54 € *Le haka*	1 30	1 »

4071	0,54 € *Le plaquage*	1 30	1 »
4072	0,54 € *Les supporters*	1 30	1 »
	Nos 4063 à 4072 (10 val.)	13 »	10 »

2007. – ***Capitales européennes. Bruxelles (Belgique). Héliogravure. Multicolore. Dentelure 13 x 13½, sauf n° 4074, 4075 : 13½ x 13.*** **BF** ***n° 111.***

Emis uniquement en feuillet.

4073	0,54 € *La Maison du Roi*	1 50	1 »
4074	0,54 € *L'Hôtel de Ville*	1 50	1 »

4075	0,54 € *Le Manneken Pis*	1 50	1 »
4076	0,54 € *L'Atomium*	1 50	1 »

2007. – ***Centenaire de l'Association des Maires de France. Héliogravure. Deux bandes de phosphore. Dentelé 13½.***

4077	0,54 € *Profil de Marianne et devise de la République française*	1 10	0 50

2007. – ***Personnalité. Pierre Pflimlin (1907-2000), homme politique. Héliogravure. Deux bandes de phosphore. Dentelé 13¼.***

4078	0,60 € *Portrait, étoiles européennes et clocher de la cathédrale de Strasbourg*	1 20	0 60

2007. – ***Série touristique. Castres (Tarn). Taille-douce. Deux bandes de phosphore. Dentelé 13¼.***

4079	0,54 € *Le jardin de l'Evêché, dessiné par André Le Nôtre (1613-1700)*	1 10	0 50

2007. – ***Coupe du monde de Rugby 2007 en France. Offset. Autoadhésif. Procédé lenticulaire. Dentelé 11.***

4080	3,00 € *Image animée du passage du ballon entre les poteaux*	6 »	4 »

2007. – ***Timbre pour Anniversaires. Sylvain et Sylvette, héros de bandes dessinées de Jean-Louis Pesch. © Dargaud 2007. Héliogravure. Deux bandes de phosphore. Dentelé 13¼.*** **BF** ***n° 112.***

Sans valeur indiquée. Lettre prioritaire 20 g.

Emis uniquement en feuillet.

4081	(sans val.) *Sylvain et Sylvette portant un gâteau*	1 50	0 7

2007. – *Timbres de messages. "Invitation", "Merci". Offset. Autoadhésifs. Deux bandes de phosphore. Multicolore. Dentelés 11.* 🄲 (carnets commémoratifs).

Sans valeur indiquée. Lettre prioritaire 20 g.

Emis en carnet d'1 série.

4082	(sans val.) *Boîte d'où s'échappent des papillons*	1 30	0 60
4083	(sans val.) *Boîte d'où s'échappent des cœurs*	1 30	0 60
4084	(sans val.) *Boîte remplie de fleurs*	1 30	0 60

4085	(sans val.) *Boîte d'où s'échappent des bulles*	1 30	0 60
4086	(sans val.) *Boîte d'où s'échappent des notes de musique*	1 30	0 60
	N°s 4082 à 4086 (5 val.)	**6 50**	**3 »**
	BC4082 La bande carnet, non pliée	6 50	4 »

2007. – *Série touristique. Firminy (Loire). Taille-douce. Deux bandes de phosphore. Dentelé 13¼.*

4087	**0,54 €** *Eglise Saint-Pierre, œuvre de l'architecte Le Corbusier (1887-1965)*	1 10	0 50

2007. – *Personnalité. Sully Prudhomme (1839-1907), poète. Taille-douce. Deux bandes de phosphore. Dentelé 13¼.*

4088	**1,30 €** *Portrait*	2 60	1 30

2007. – *"Sourires" avec les vaches humoristiques du dessinateur Alexis Nesmes. Offset. Autoadhésifs. Deux bandes de phosphore. Multicolore. Dentelés 11.* 🄲 (carnets commémoratifs).

Sans valeur indiquée. Lettre prioritaire 20 g.

Emis en carnet de 2 séries.

4089	(sans val.) *Vache humectant des timbres*	1 30	0 60
4090	(sans val.) *Vache affranchie avec des timbres " Encore 1 ou 2 et je peux partir "*	1 30	0 60

4091	(sans val.) *Vache postant son courrier*	1 30	0 60
4092	(sans val.) *Vache avec oblitération sur la tête*	1 30	0 60

4093	(sans val.) *Vache chantant " Ne meuuh quitte pas… "*	1 30	0 60
	N°s 4089 à 4093 (5 val.)	**6 50**	**3 »**
	BC4089 La bande carnet, non pliée	13 »	8 »

2007. – *Portraits de régions. La France à vivre. Héliogravure. Deux bandes de phosphore. Multicolore. Dentelés 13.* BF *n° 113.*

Emis uniquement en feuillet.

4094	0,54 € *La porcelaine de Sèvres*	1 10	0 50
4095	0,54 € *Les géants*	1 10	0 50

4096	0,54 € *Le béret basque*	1 10	0 50
4097	0,54 € *Le parfum de Grasse*	1 10	0 50

4098	0,54 € *Les tapisseries d'Aubusson*	1 10	0 50
4099	0,54 € *Le marché de Noël*	1 10	0 50

4100	0,54 € *Le bouchon lyonnais*	1 10	0 50
4101	0,54 € *Le savon de Marseille*	1 10	0 50

4102	0,54 € *Les charentaises*	1 10	0 50
4103	0,54 € *Le melon*	1 10	0 50
	N°s 4094 à 4103 (10 val.)	**11 »**	**5 »**

2007. – *Conquête de l'espace 1957-2007. Héliogravure. Deux bandes de phosphore. Dentelé 13 x 12¾.*

4104	0,85 € *Spoutnik 1, vaisseau Apollo 11, satellite SPOT 5, fusée russe Soyouz lançant le satellite français Corot et la fusée Ariane 5 transportant l'ATV*	1 70	0 85

2007. – *Série artistique. Paul Sérusier (1865-1927), peintre. Héliogravure. Dentelé 13¼ x 13.*

4105	0,86 € *"La Barrière fleurie", tableau de 1889*	1 70	0 85

2007. – *60ᵉ anniversaire de la Fondation Recherche Médicale. Héliogravure. Deux bandes de phosphore. Dentelé 13¼.*

4106	0,54 € *Mains de chercheur tenant une éprouvette avec soleil stylisé*	1 10	0 50

2007. – *Personnalité. Guy Môquet (1924-1941), résistant. Taille-douce. Deux bandes de phosphore. Dentelé 13¼.*

4107	0,54 € *Portrait*	1 10	0 50

2007. – ***Série touristique. Dole (Jura). Taille-douce. Deux bandes de phosphore. Dentelé 13¼.***

4108 **0,54 €** ***La collégiale du XVI*** ***siècle et le vieux Dole*** 1 10 0 50

2007. – ***40e anniversaire de la Marianne de Cheffer. Taille-douce. Autoadhésif. Deux bandes de phosphore. Dent : précoupé vertical en lignes ondulées.*** **[C] (carnets de timbres à composition variable).**

Emis en carnet.

4109 **0,54 € rouge** 2 50 1 50
P4109 La paire 4109+3744b 3 50 2 »

2007. – ***Personnalité. Jean-Baptiste Charcot (1867-1936), scientifique et explorateur des régions polaires. Taille-douce, sauf n° 4111 : taille-douce et offset. Deux bandes de phosphore. Multicolore. Dentelés 13¼ x 12¾.***

Emission conjointe avec le Groenland (n° 475 et 476, BF n° 38).

4110 **0,54 €** ***Portrait du navigateur*** 1 10 0 50
4111 **0,60 €** ***Voilier le " Pourquoi-pas ? "*** 1 20 0 60
P4110 La paire 4110+4111 2 30 1 10

Imprimés se tenant.

2007. – ***Les phares. Taille-douce et offset. Deux bandes de phosphore. Multicolore. Dentelés 13¹⁄₄ x 13.*** **[BF]** ***n° 114.***

Emis uniquement en feuillet.

4112 **0,54 €** ***Phare du Cap Fréhel (1846-1950), Côtes-d'Armor*** 1 30 1 »
4113 **0,54 €** ***Phare de l'Espiguette (1869), Grau-du-Roi (Gard)*** 1 30 1 »

4114 **0,54 €** ***Phare d'Ar-Men (1867-1881), Chaussée de Sein*** 1 30 1 »
4115 **0,54 €** ***Phare du Grand-Léjon (1881), au large de Saint-Quay-Portrieux (Côtes-d'Armor)*** 1 30 1 »

4116 **0,54 €** ***Phare du Cap d'Arme (1830) (île de Porquerolles)*** 1 30 1 »
4117 **0,54 €** ***Phare de Chassiron (1836), île d'Oléron*** 1 30 1 »

Nos 4112 à 4117 (6 val.) **7 80** **6 »**

2007. – ***Sport. XVIII*** ***championnat du monde de handball féminin, en France. Héliogravure. Deux bandes de phosphore. Dentelé 13¼.***

4118 **0,54 €** ***Silhouettes de joueuses*** 1 10 0 50

2007. – ***Série artistique. La galerie des Glaces du château de Versailles (Yvelines). Héliogravure. Dentelé 13 x 13¼.***

4119 **0,85 €** ***Lustres et miroirs de la galerie*** 2 » 0 85

2007. – *"Meilleurs Voeux". Offset. Autoadhésifs. Deux bandes de phosphore. Multicolore. Dentelés 11.* **[C] (carnets commémoratifs).** *Blocs souvenir n° 25.*

Sans valeur indiquée (validité permanente).

Emis en carnet de 2 séries.

4120 **(Lettre prioritaire 20 g)**
Ecureuil avec bonnet vert 1 30 0 60
4121 **(Lettre prioritaire 20 g)**
Oiseau avec chapeau de fête 1 30 0 60

4122 **(Lettre prioritaire 20 g)**
Faon sur une luge 1 30 0 60
4123 **(Lettre prioritaire 20 g)**
Hérisson avec chapeau de fête 1 30 0 60

4124 **(Lettre prioritaire 20 g)**
Chien avec bonnet rouge 1 30 0 60

N°s 4120 à 4124 (5 val.) **6 50** **3 »**
BC4120 La bande carnet, non pliée 13 » 8 »

2007. – *Au profit de la Croix-Rouge. "Dessine ton voeu pour les enfants du monde" 2007. Héliogravure. Deux bandes de phosphore. Autoadhésifs. Multicolore. Dentelés 11.* **[C] (Croix-Rouge sans publicité).**

Sans valeur indiquée (validité permanente). Timbre avec surtaxe de 0,17 €.

Emis en carnet de 5 paires.

4125 **(Lettre prioritaire 20 g)** ***" Les enfants = Amour ", dessin de Chloé Hilbrunner, élève de CP*** 1 75 0 70
4126 **(Lettre prioritaire 20 g)** ***" Que tous les enfants du monde soient heureux ", dessin de Maya Thieulle, élève de CE1*** 1 75 0 70
P4125 La paire 4125+4126 3 » 2 »

Imprimés se tenant.

BC4125 La bande carnet, non pliée 17 50 12 »

2007

Du n° 3996 au n° 4126

(sauf bandes-carnets, paires et triptyques) :

135 timbres ****216** **⊙116**

Autres rubriques de l'année :

Aériens 70

Timbres Autoadhésifs 102 à 146

Blocs et feuillet 104 à 124

Blocs Souvenirs 17 à 25

Préoblitérés 250 à 252

Service 136 à 137

Timbres Personnalisés

2008. – *Type Marianne de Lamouche. Taille-douce. Autoadhésif. Deux bandes de phosphore. Dent. : précoupé vertical en lignes ondulées.* **[C]**

Type du T.-P. n° 3966 de 2006.
Sans valeur indiquée (validité permanente).
Lettre prioritaire 20 g vers l'Union Européenne et la Suisse.
Emis en carnet.
4127 **(sans val.) bleu (3966)** 2 » 0 60

2008. – *Saint-Valentin. Cœur 2008 du couturier Franck Sorbier. Héliogravure. Multicolore. Dentelés.* **[BF]** *n° 115.*

Sans valeur indiquée (validité permanente).

4128 **(Lettre prioritaire 20 g)**
Visages formant un cœur 1 30 0 55
4129 **(Lettre prioritaire 50 g)**
Arbre aux feuilles-cœurs 2 » 1 »

2008. – *Saint-Valentin. Cœur 2008 du couturier Franck Sorbier. Héliogravure. Autoadhésif.*
Type du T.-P. de même date.
Sans valeur indiquée (validité permanente).

4130 **(Lettre prioritaire 20 g)**
Visages formant un cœur **(4128)** 3 » 1 50

Emis en feuilles de 30 timbres.

Un "lettre 50g" est paru fin 2008 (voir rubrique "autoadhésif" n° 149).

YVERT&TELLIER
Partenaires de vos passions...
LILLE
AMIENS
LE HAVRE
PARIS
LYON
MARSEILLE
espaces YVERT&TELLIER
6 magasins dédiés à toutes vos collections
Achat - Vente de Timbres
Catalogues de cotations
Matériel toutes marques
Monnaies - Cartes postales - Télécartes
Des professionnels au service de vos loisirs.
LILLE
54, rue Molinel 59000 LILLE 03 20 44 22 22
AMIENS
26, rue au Lin 80000 AMIENS 03 22 92 33 32
PARIS
10, rue Châteaudun 75009 PARIS 01 40 82 74 70
LE HAVRE
72, avenue Foch 76600 LE HAVRE 02 35 41 22 22
LYON
48/50, rue de la Charité 69002 LYON 04 78 42 22 22
MARSEILLE
263, rue Paradis 13006 MARSEILLE 04 91 58 22 22

2008. – *Année lunaire chinoise du Rat. Deux bandes de phosphore. Dentelé 13¼ x 13.*

4131 **(Lettre prioritaire 20 g)** ***Rat mangeant des grains de raisin*** 1 50 0 55

Emis en petite feuille de 5 timbres

F4131 **La feuille** 7 50 6 »

2008. – *Art. Chefs d'œuvre de la peinture. Offset. Deux bandes de phosphore. Multicolore. Dentelés 11.* **(carnets commémoratifs).**

Sans valeur indiquée (validité permanente).

Emis en carnet.

4132 **(Lettre prioritaire 20 g)** ***"Scènes de la vie de saint François", du peintre italien Giotto di Bondone (1266-1337)*** 1 30 0 60

4133 **(Lettre prioritaire 20 g)** ***"Port de mer au soleil couchant", du peintre français Le Lorrain (1600-1682)*** 1 30 0 60

4134 **(Lettre prioritaire 20 g)** ***"La jeune fille à la perle", du peintre hollandais Jan Vermeer (1632-1675)*** 1 30 0 60

4135 **(Lettre prioritaire 20 g)** ***"La Joconde" (1503-1505), du peintre italien Léonard de Vinci (1452-1519)*** 1 30 0 60

4136 **(Lettre prioritaire 20 g)** ***"Le prêteur et sa femme", du peintre flamand Quentin Metsys (1465-1530)*** 1 30 0 60

4137 **(Lettre prioritaire 20 g)** ***"La naissance de Vénus", du peintre italien Sandro Botticelli (1445-1510)*** 1 30 0 60

4138 **(Lettre prioritaire 20 g)** ***"Bonaparte, Premier consul", du peintre français Jacques Louis David (1748-1825)*** 1 30 0 60

4139 **(Lettre prioritaire 20 g)** ***"La belle jardinière", du peintre italien Raphaël (Raffaello Sanzio, dit) (1483-1520)*** 1 30 0 60

4140 **(Lettre prioritaire 20 g)** ***"L'été", du peintre italien Guiseppe Arcimboldo (v. 1527-1593)*** 1 30 0 60

4141 **(Lettre prioritaire 20 g)** ***"L'Infante Marie Marguerite", du peintre espagnol Diego Velasquez (1599-1660)*** 1 30 0 60

N°s 4132 à 4141 (10 val.) **13 »** **6 »**

BC4132 La bande carnet, non pliée 13 » 8 »

2008. – ***10e anniversaire du Stade de France. Héliogravure. Deux bandes de phosphore. Dentelé 13¼.***

4142 **0,54 €** ***Détail vue du toit illuminé*** 1 10 0 50

2008. – ***Série touristique. Vendôme (Loir-et-Cher). Taille-douce. Deux bandes de phosphore. Dentelé 13¼.***

4143 **0,54 €** ***Eglise de la Trinité*** 1 10 0 50

2008. – *Série artistique. Les globes de Coronelli. Taille-douce et offset. Dentelé 13¼ x 13.*

4144 **0,85 €** ***Globes terrestre et céleste, réalisés par Vincenzo Coronelli et offerts au roi Louis XIV, grue figurant sur le globe céleste*** 1 70 0 85

2008. – *Personnalité. L'émir Abd el-Kader (1808-1883). Taille-douce. Deux bandes de phosphore. Dentelé 13¼.*

4145 **0,54 €** ***Portrait de l'émir d'Algérie*** 1 10 0 55

2008. – *Fête du timbre. Personnages des dessins animés de Tex Avery (1907-1980), réalisateur américain. TM & © Turner Entertainment Co WB Shield, TM & © Warner Bros. Entertainment Inc. (s08). Héliogravure. Deux bandes de phosphore. Multicolore. Dentelés 13 x 13¼.*

4146 **0,55 €** ***Droopy et le loup*** 1 10 0 55

4147 **0,55 €** ***La girl et le loup*** 1 10 0 55

4148 **0,55 €** ***Le loup et la girl*** 1 10 0 55

Imprimés se tenant. Emis en feuille de 20 paires.

2008. – *Fête du timbre. Personnages des dessins animés de Tex Avery (1907-1980), réalisateur américain. TM & © Turner Entertainment Co WB Shield, TM & © Warner Bros. Entertainment Inc. (s08). Offset. Autoadhésifs. Deux bandes de phosphore. Multicolore. Dentelés 11.* **[C] (carnets journée du timbre).**

Types des T.-P. de même date.

Sans valeur indiquée (validité permanente).

Emis en carnet de 3 séries + 1 n° 160.

4149 **(Lettre prioritaire 20 g)** ***Droopy et le loup*** **(4146)** 1 50 0 55

4150 **(Lettre prioritaire 20 g)** ***La girl et le loup*** **(4147)** 1 50 0 55

4151 **(Lettre prioritaire 20 g)** ***Le loup et la girl*** **(4148)** 1 50 0 55

Bande-carnet "Fête du timbre. Tex Avery" composée de 4 timbres n° 4149, 3 timbres n° 4150 et 3 timbres n° 4151

BC4149 La bande carnet, non pliée 14 » 8 »

2008. – *Fête du timbre. Personnages des dessins animés de Tex Avery (1907-1980), réalisateur américain. TM & © Turner Entertainment Co WB Shield, TM & © Warner Bros. Entertainment Inc. (s08). Héliogravure. Autoadhésifs. Deux bandes de phosphore. Multicolore. Dentelés 11.*

Types des T.-P. de même date.

Sans valeur indiquée (validité permanente).

4149A **(Lettre prioritaire 20 g)** ***Le chien Droopy et le loup*** 4 »

4150A **(Lettre prioritaire 20 g)** ***La girl et le loup*** 4 »

4151A **(Lettre prioritaire 20 g)** ***Le loup et la girl*** 4 »

Emis chacun en petite feuille de 5 timbres attenant chacun à une vignette illustrée différente.

F4149A La feuille 20 »
F4150A La feuille 20 »
F4151A La feuille 20 »

2008. – ***Fête du timbre. Droopy, personnage des dessins animés de Tex Avery (1907-1980). © TM & Turner Entertainment Co WB Shield, TM & Warner Bros. Entertainment Inc. (s08). Héliogravure. Deux bandes de phosphore. Encre thermochrome. Dentelé 13 x 13¼. BF n° 116.***

Emis uniquement en feuillet.

4152 2,18 € ***Le chien Droopy*** 5 » 4 40

En posant un doigt sur la bulle d'encre thermochrome on découvre ce que dit Droopy.

2008. – ***Type Marianne de Lamouche. Gravure assistée par ordinateur. Deux bandes de phosphore, sauf n° 4154 : une bande de phosphore à droite. Dentelés 13.***

Types des T.-P. de 2006 pour les n° 4154 à 4158.

Sans valeur indiquée (validité permanente).

4153 (sans val.) bleu (Type du T.-P. n° 4127) (4127) (147) 1 50 0 20
4154 0,72 € vert-olive (3967) 1 50 0 40
4155 0,88 € lilas-brun clair (3969) 2 » 0 40

4156 1,25 € bleu ciel (3970) 2 50 0 55
4157 1,33 € lilas (3971) 3 » 0 60
4158 2,18 € brun-prune (3972) 4 50 0 85

N°s 4153 à 4158 (6 val.) **15 » 3 »**

2008. – ***Type Marianne de Lamouche. Taille-douce numérique. Deux bandes de phosphore. Dentelé 13 horizontalement.***

Type du T.-P. de 2008.
Provenant de roulette. N° noir au verso de 1 à 500.
Sans valeur indiquée (validité permanente). Lettre prioritaire 20 g vers l'Union Européenne et la Suisse.

4159 (sans val.) bleu (4153) 2 » 1 »

Existe sans phosphore.

2008. – ***Les Bibliothèques sonores. Héliogravure. Deux bandes de phosphore. Dentelé 13¼.***

4160 0,55 € multicolore 1 10 0 55

2008. – ***Portraits de régions. La France à voir. Héliogravure. Deux bandes de phosphore. Multicolore. Dentelés 13. BF n° 117.***

Emis uniquement en feuillet.

4161 0,55 € ***Le château d'Ussé (Indre et Loire)*** 1 10 0 55
4162 0,55 € ***Le moulin de Cugarel*** 1 10 0 55

4163 0,55 € ***La côte de granit rose (phare)*** 1 10 0 55
4164 0,55 € ***Vézelay*** 1 10 0 55

4165 0,55 € ***Honfleur*** 1 10 0 55
4166 0,55 € ***Le Marais (Paris)*** 1 10 0 55

4167 0,55 € ***La Petite France (Strasbourg)*** 1 10 0 55
4168 0,55 € ***Le Marais poitevin*** 1 10 0 55

4169	0,55 € *Sarlat-la-Canéda*	1 10	0 55
4170	0,55 € *Le cirque de Mafate (La Réunion)*	1 10	0 55
	N°s 4161 à 4170 (10 val.)	**11 »**	**5 50**

2008. – *Série touristique. Lyon (Rhône). Taille-douce et offset. Deux bandes de phosphore. Dentelé 13.*

4171	0,55 € *Passerelle de Saint-Georges et immeubles*	1 10	0 55

2008. – *Série touristique. La Rochelle (Charente-Maritime). Taille-douce. Deux bandes de phosphore. Dentelé 13.*

4172	0,55 € *Le Vieux-Port, les tours Saint-Nicolas et de la Chaîne*	1 10	0 55

2008. – *Jardins de France. Héliogravure. Multicolore. Dentelés 13½* x *13.* BF *n° 118.*

Emis uniquement en feuillet.

4173	2,18 € *Le Parc Longchamp à Marseille*	4 40	3 »
4174	2,18 € *Le Parc Borély à Marseille (gloriette)*	4 40	3 »

2008. – *Faune préhistorique. Héliogravure. Multicolore. Dentelés 13¼.* BF *n° 119.*

Smilodon.

Phorusrhacos.

4175	**0,55 € multicolore**	1 10	0 55
4176	**0,55 € multicolore**	1 10	0 55

Megaloceros.

Mammouth.

4177	**0,65 € multicolore**	1 30	0 65
4178	**0,88 € multicolore**	1 80	0 85
	N°s 4175 à 4178 (4 val.)	**5 30**	**2 60**

2008. – *40e anniversaire de la première greffe du cœur en Europe. Héliogravure. Deux bandes de phosphore. Dentelé 13.*

4179	0,55 € *Composition avec cœur*	1 10	0 55

2008. – *700e anniversaire du Pont Valentré de Cahors. Taille-douce. Deux bandes de phosphore. Dentelé 13¼.*

4180	0,55 € *Le pont et ses tours*	1 10	0 55

2008. – *Europa. L'écriture d'une lettre. Héliogravure. Deux bandes de phosphore. Dentelé 13 x 13¼.*

4181	0,55 € *Composition avec plume d'oie et de stylo*	1 10	0 55

2008. – *400ᵉ anniversaire de la fondation de la ville de Québec. Taille-douce. Deux bandes de phosphore. Dentelé 13.*

Emission conjointe avec le Canada (n° 2351).

4182	0,85 € *L'explorateur et cartographe Samuel de Champlain (1567-1635) saluant les autochtones en canot depuis son navire, forteresse en construction*	1 70	0 85

2008. – *Timbre pour anniversaires. © CRL Oui-Oui™ Hachette Livre. Héliogravure. Deux bandes de phosphore. Dentelé 13¼.*

Sans valeur indiquée (validité permanente).

4183	(Lettre prioritaire 20 g) *Oui-Oui portant un gâteau*	1 50	0 55

Emis en petite feuille de 5 timbres.

2008. – *Timbre de naissances "C'est une fille". Héliogravure. Autoadhésif. Deux bandes de phosphore. Dentelé 11.* 🄲 **(carnets commémoratifs)**

Sans valeur indiquée (validité permanente).
Emis en carnet.

4184	(Lettre prioritaire 20 g) *Poussin en tissu, chien sur roulettes, et cubes*	1 10	0 55

Quand on gratte le timbre il apparaît "C'est une fille"

BC4184	La bande carnet, non pliée	11 »	7 »

2008. – *Timbre de naissances "C'est une garçon". Héliogravure. Autoadhésif. Deux bandes de phosphore. Dentelé 11.* 🄲 **(carnets commémoratifs)**

Sans valeur indiquée (validité permanente).

Emis en carnet.

4185	(Lettre prioritaire 20 g) *Nounours avec biberon, poussin sur roulettes, cubes*	1 10	0 55

Quand on gratte le timbre il apparaît "C'est un garçon"

BC4185	La bande carnet, non pliée	11 »	7 »

2008. – *Timbres pour vacances. Héliogravure. Autoadhésifs. Deux bandes de phosphore. Multicolore. Dentelés 11.* 🄲 **(carnets commémoratifs)**

Sans valeur indiquée (validité permanente).

Emis en carnet.

4186	(Lettre prioritaire 20 g) *Fougères*	1 30	0 60
4187	(Lettre prioritaire 20 g) *Papillon*	1 30	0 60

4188	(Lettre prioritaire 20 g) *Feuilles de thé*	1 30	0 60
4189	(Lettre prioritaire 20 g) *Cocotier*	1 30	0 60

4190	(Lettre prioritaire 20 g) *Jardin avec plan d'eau*	1 30	0 60
4191	(Lettre prioritaire 20 g) *Golf*	1 30	0 60

4192	(Lettre prioritaire 20 g) *Fleur de lotus blanche*	1 30	0 60
4193	(Lettre prioritaire 20 g) *Arrosoirs*	1 30	0 60

4194 (Lettre prioritaire 20 g) *Kiwis coupés en deux* 1 30 0 60
4195 (Lettre prioritaire 20 g) *Petits pois* 1 30 0 60

Nos 4186 à 4195 (10 val.) 13 » 6 »

Bande-carnet "Vacances" (2008)
BC4186 La bande carnet, non pliée 13 » 8 »

2008. – ***Beffroi d'Evreux. Taille-douce. Deux bandes de phosphore. Dentelé 13.***

4196 0,55 € *Partie supérieure de la tour* 1 10 0 55

2008. – ***Marianne et les valeurs de l'Europe. Taille-douce. Autoadhésifs. Deux bandes de phosphore. Rouge. Dent. : précoupé vertical en lignes ondulées.*** **[C] (carnets de timbres à composition variable)**

Emis en carnet.

4197 (sans val.) rouge *Marianne de Beaujard* 1 20 0 25
4198 0,55 € rouge *Démocratie (main glissant un bulletin de vote dans une urne)* 1 60 0 65
4199 0,55 € rouge *Environnement (arbre dans la paume d'une main)* 1 60 0 65
4200 0,55 € rouge *Paix (colombe avec rameau d'olivier)* 1 60 0 65

Nos 4197 à 4200 (4 val.) 6 » 2 20

La bande 4197+4198+4197+4199+4197+4200
B4197 La bande 9 »

Peut aussi se présenter en mini-bloc de 6 timbres.

2008. – ***Marianne et les valeurs de l'Europe. Taille-douce. Autoadhésifs. Deux bandes de phosphore. Bleu. Dent. : précoupé vertical en lignes ondulées.*** **[C] (carnets de timbres à composition variable)**

Emis en carnet.

4201 (sans val.) bleu *Marianne de Beaujard* 1 50 0 35
4202 0,65 € bleu *Démocratie (main glissant un bulletin de vote dans une urne)* 2 » 0 75
4203 0,65 € bleu *Environnement (arbre dans la paume d'une main)* 2 » 0 75
4204 0,65 € bleu *Paix (colombe avec rameau d'olivier)* 2 » 0 75

Nos 4201 à 4204 (4 val.) 7 50 2 60

La bande 4201+4202+4201+4203+4201+4204
B4201 La bande 10 » 6 »

Peut aussi se présenter en mini-bloc de 6 timbres.

2008. – ***Environnement. Développement durable. "Timbrez des idées durables ! ". Héliogravure. Autoadhésifs. Deux bandes de phosphore. Multicolore. Dentelés 11.*** **[C] (carnets commémo-ratifs)**

Sans valeur indiquée (validité permanente).

Emis en carnet.

4205 (Lettre prioritaire 20 g) *"Bureau durable - papier à protéger" (arbre)* 1 30 0 60
4206 (Lettre prioritaire 20 g) *"Déplacement durable - Transport du futur" (bicyclette)* 1 30 0 60

4207 (Lettre prioritaire 20 g) *"Tourisme durable - Site à préserver" (carte du monde)* 1 30 0 60
4208 (Lettre prioritaire 20 g) *"Electronique durable - Bon à recycler" (ordinateur)* 1 30 0 60

4209 (Lettre prioritaire 20 g) *"Eau durable - Ceci est un trésor" (gouttes d'eau)* 1 30 0 60
4210 (Lettre prioritaire 20 g) *"Energie durable - Ceci est un radiateur" (soleil)* 1 30 0 60

4211 (Lettre prioritaire 20 g) *"Lavage durable - A la bonne dose" (récipients en plastique)* 1 30 0 60
4212 (Lettre prioritaire 20 g) *"Mode durable - Recyclage en pull" (bouteilles d'eau en plastique)* 1 30 0 60

4213	(Lettre prioritaire 20 g) *"Jardinage durable - Ceci est un engrais" (trognon de pomme)*	1 30	0 60
4214	(Lettre prioritaire 20 g) *"Alimentation durable - Inconnue en hiver" (fraise)*	1 30	0 60
	N°s 4205 à 4214 (10 val.)	**13 »**	**6 »**

Bande-carnet "Timbrez des idées durables ! " (2008)

BC4205	La bande carnet, non pliée	13 »	8 »

2008. – *81e congrès de la Fédération française des associations philatéliques, à Paris. Taille-douce. Deux bandes de phosphore. Dentelé 13 x 13½.*

4215	**0,55 €** *Le Grand Palais et le pont Alexandre III à Paris*	1 10	0 70

Imprimé attenant à une vignette sans valeur (détail escalier)

2008. – *Personnages célèbres. Le cirque. Héliogravure. Deux bandes de phosphore. Multicolore. Dentelés 13.* BF *n° 121.*

4216	**0,55 €** *Le trapéziste*	1 10	0 55
4217	**0,55 €** *L'écuyère*	1 10	0 55

4218	**0,55 €** *L'auguste*	1 10	0 55
4219	**0,55 €** *Le dompteur (numéro avec lion)*	1 10	0 55

4220	**0,55 €** *Le clown blanc*	1 10	0 55
4221	**0,55 €** *Le jongleur*	1 10	0 55
	N°s 4216 à 4221 (6 val.)	**6 60**	**3 30**

2008. – *Jeux olympiques d'été à Pékin (Chine) en 2008. Héliogravure. Deux bandes de phosphore. Multicolore. Dentelure 13¼ x 13, sauf n° 4224, 4225 : 13 x 13¼.* BF *n° 122.*

Emis uniquement en feuillet.

4222	**0,55 €** *Equitation et cyclisme*	1 60	0 80
4223	**0,55 €** *Tennis et course à pied*	1 60	0 80

4224	**0,55 €** *Natation et aviron*	1 40	0 70
4225	**0,55 €** *Judo et escrime*	1 40	0 70
	N°s 4222 à 4225 (4 val.)	**6 »**	**3 »**

2008. – *Type Marianne de Beaujard. Gravure assistée par ordinateur. Papier gommé. Une bande de phosphore à droite, sauf n° 4230, 4233, 4234, 4235, 4236, 4237, 4238 : deux bandes de phosphore. Dentelés 13.*

Marianne et l'Europe.

4226	**0,01 € jaune**	0 20	0 15
4227	**0,05 € bistre-noir**	0 20	0 15
4228	**0,10 € gris**	0 30	0 15
4229	**(sans val.) vert**	1 10	0 20

4230	(sans val.) rouge (4197) (175)	1 10	0 20
4231	(sans val.) [bleu] (4201) (179)	1 30	0 25
4232	0,72 € vert-olive	1 50	0 40
4233	0,85 € violet-rouge	1 70	0 40

4234	0,88 € lilas-brun clair	2 »	0 60
4235	1,00 € orange	2 »	0 50
4236	1,25 € bleu ciel	2 60	0 70

4237	1,33 € lilas	2 50	0 50
4238	2,18 € brun-prune	4 50	0 80

N°s 4226 à 4238 (13 val.) 21 » 5 »

2008. – *Type Marianne de Beaujard. Gravure assistée par ordinateur. Papier gommé. Une bande de phosphore à droite, sauf n° 4240 : deux bandes de phosphore. Dent. 13 horizontalement.*

Marianne et l'Europe.

Types des T.-P. de même date.

Provenant de roulette. N° noir au verso de 1 à 500.

4239	(sans val.) vert (4229)	1 20	0 40
4240	(sans val.) rouge (4230)	1 20	0 40
4241	(sans val.) bleu (4231)	1 50	0 50

2008. – *Type Marianne de Beaujard. Gravure à chaud argent. Autoadhésif. Dentelé 13.*

4242	5,00 € argent *Marianne et l'Europe*	10 »	8 »

Timbre (en argent 999 millièmes) présenté sous blister sur un support cartonné.

2008. – *Mémorial Charles de Gaulle, à Colombey-les-Deux-Eglises (Haute-Marne). Taille-douce. Deux bandes de phosphore. Dentelé 13¼.*

4243	0,55 € *Portraits du général et président de la République Charles de Gaulle (1890-1970), Mémorial au pied de la Croix de Lorraine*	1 10	0 55

2008. – *Série artistique. Gérard Garouste, peintre. Héliogravure. Dentelé 13¼ x 13.*

4244	1,33 € *Œuvre de l'artiste*	3 »	1 30

2008. – *Grands projets européens. Héliogravure. Multicolore. Dentelés 13.* BF *n° 123.*

Emis uniquement en feuillet.

4245	0,55 € *L'euro*	1 25	0 70
4246	0,55 € *Présidence française du Conseil de l'Union européenne durant le 2e semestre 2008 (drapeaux français et européen)*	1 25	0 70

4247	0,55 € *Satellite Galileo*	1 25	0 70
4248	0,55 € *Erasmus (étudiants, drapeaux)*	1 25	0 70

N°s 4245 à 4248 (4 val.) 5 » 2 80

2008. – *Voiliers célèbres. Héliogravure. Multicolore. Dentelés 13.* BF *n° 124.*

Emis uniquement en feuillet.

La Confiance. La Grande Hermine.

4249	**0,55 € multicolore**	1 25	0 70
4250	**0,55 € multicolore**	1 25	0 70

La Boudeuse. L'Astrolabe.

4251	**0,55 € multicolore**	1 25	0 70
4252	**0,55 € multicolore**	1 25	0 70

L'Hermione. La Boussole.

4253	**0,55 € multicolore**	1 25	0 70
4254	**0,55 € multicolore**	1 25	0 70
	N°s 4249 à 4254 (6 val.)	**7 50**	**4 20**

2008. – *Paysages de France et du Brésil. Héliogravure. Multicolore. Dentelés 13.*

Emission conjointe avec le Brésil (n° 3026 et 3027).

4255 **0,55 €** ***La forêt amazonienne au Brésil*** 1 10 0 55

4256 **0,85 €** ***La mer de Glace, vallée de Chamonix (Haute-Savoie)*** 1 70 0 85

P4255 La paire, se tenant 3 » 1 50

Imprimés se tenant pour former une seule image.

2008. – *Série touristique. Toulon (Var). Taille-douce. Deux bandes de phosphore. Dentelé 13¼.*

4257 **0,55 €** ***Le port du Levant et sa rade, atlante du sculpteur Pierre Puget*** 1 10 0 55

2008. – *Série touristique. Richelieu (Indre-et-Loire). Taille-douce. Deux bandes de phosphore. Dentelé 13¼.*

4258 **0,55 €** ***Porte monumentale et statue du cardinal de Richelieu (1696-1788)*** 1 10 0 55

2008. – *Sommet de Paris pour la Méditerranée. Héliogravure. Deux bandes de phosphore. Dentelé 13¼.*

4259 **0,55 €** ***Olivier*** 1 50 0 55

2008. – *Portraits de régions. La France à vivre. Héliogravure. Deux bandes de phosphore. Multicolore. Dentelés 13¼ × 13.* BF *n° 125.*

Emis uniquement en feuillet.

4260	**0,55 €** ***Les espadrilles du Pays-Basque***	1 10	0 55
4261	**0,55 €** ***L'image d'Epinal (Le Chat botté)***	1 10	0 55

4262 0,55 € *La lentille* 1 10 0 55

4263 0,55 € *Le pot au feu* 1 10 0 55

4264 0,55 € *Le reblochon* 1 10 0 55

4265 0,55 € *La chataîgne* 1 10 0 55

4266 0,55 € *Le calisson* 1 10 0 55

4267 0,55 € *Les feux d'artifice* 1 10 0 55

4268 0,55 € *Les échasses* 1 10 0 55

4269 0,55 € *La moutarde* 1 10 0 55

Nos 4260 à 4269 (10 val.) 11 » 5 50

2008. – ***Série touristique. Le Havre (Seine-Maritime). Taille-douce et offset. Deux bandes de phosphore. Dentelé 13¼.***

4270 0,55 € ***L'hôtel de ville (1958), œuvre des architectes Auguste Perret et Jacques Tournant*** 1 10 0 55

2008. – ***"Sourires" avec le chat Garfield du dessinateur américain Jim Davis. Offset. Autoadhésifs. Deux bandes de phosphore. Multicolore. Dentelés 11.*** **(carnets commémoratifs)**

Sans valeur indiquée (validité permanente).

Emis en carnet.

4271 **(Lettre prioritaire 20 g)** ***"Vous saisissez ?"*** 1 10 0 55

4272 **(Lettre prioritaire 20 g)** ***"Tu veux une bonne nouvelle ?"*** 1 10 0 55

4273 **(Lettre prioritaire 20 g)** ***"Ecris-moi ou la pizza y passe"*** 1 10 0 55

4274 **(Lettre prioritaire 20 g)** ***"Slurp !"*** 1 10 0 55

4275 **(Lettre prioritaire 20 g)** ***"J'aime le courrier"*** 1 10 0 55

4276 **(Lettre prioritaire 20 g)** ***"Pour toi"*** 1 10 0 55

4277 **(Lettre prioritaire 20 g)** ***"Livraison urgente"*** 1 10 0 55

4278 **(Lettre prioritaire 20 g)** ***"Juste pour toi !"*** 1 10 0 55

4279 **(Lettre prioritaire 20 g)** ***"Réponse attendue"*** 1 10 0 55

4280 **(Lettre prioritaire 20 g)** ***"J'arrive dans ta boîte aux lettres"*** 1 10 0 55

Nos 4271 à 4280 (10 val.) 11 » 5 50

Bande-carnet "Sourires" (2008) avec Garfield

BC4271 La bande carnet, non pliée 11 » 7 »

2008. – *Série touristique. Josselin (Morbihan). Taille-douce. Deux bandes de phosphore. Dentelé 13¼.*

4281 0,55 € *Château de la famille de Rohan (XIe siècle)* 1 10 0 55

2008. – *Cinquantenaire de la Ve République. Héliogravure. Deux bandes de phosphore. Dentelé 13¼.*

4282 0,55 € *Général Charles de Gaulle (1890-1970), ancien président, préambule de la Constitution et le Grand Sceau de France* 1 10 0 55

2008. – *"Je suis sport". Héliogravure.*

4283 0,55 € multicolore 1 10 0 55

2008. – *Paysages de France et du Vietnam. Héliogravure. Deux bandes de phosphore. Multicolore. Dentelés 13 x 12¾.*

Emission conjointe avec le Vietnam (n° 2311 et n° 2312).

4284 0,55 € *La baie d'Along (Vietnam)* 1 10 0 55

4285 0,85 € *Maisons surplombant les Bouches de Bonifacio (Corse)* 1 70 0 85

2008. – *Série artistique. Jean-Jacques Henner (1829-1905), peintre. Héliogravure. Dentelé 13¼ x 13.*

4286 0,88 € *"Jeune fille se chauffant les mains à un grand poêle", tableau* 2 » 0 85

2008. – *Les visages de la Ve République. Héliogravure. Autoadhésifs. Deux bandes de phosphore. Dent. : précoupé vertical en lignes ondulées.* [C] (carnets de timbres à composition variable)

Emis en carnet.

4287 0,55 € vert-gris et rouge *Marianne à la nef* 1 25 0 55

4288 0,55 € gris clair et carmin foncé *Marianne de Decaris* 1 25 0 55

4289 0,55 € bleu et rouge *Marianne de Cocteau* 1 25 0 55

4290 0,55 € outremer, carmin et brun *Coq de Decaris* 1 25 0 55

4291 0,55 € rouge carminé *Marianne de Cheffer* 1 25 0 55

4292 0,55 € carmin-rose *Marianne de Béquet* 1 25 0 55

4293 0,55 € rouge *Sabine de Gandon* 1 25 0 55

4294 0,55 € rouge *La Liberté de Gandon* 1 25 0 55

4295 0,55 € rouge *La Marianne du Bicentenaire, de Louis Briat* 1 25 0 55

4296 0,55 € rouge *La Marianne du 14 Juillet, d'Eve Luquet* 1 25 0 55

4297	0,55 € rouge *Marianne et l'environnement, de Thierry Lamouche*	1 25	0 55
4298	0,55 € rouge *Marianne et l'Europe, d'Yves Beaujard*	1 25	0 55
	N°s 4287 à 4298 (12 val.)	**15 »**	**6 60**

Tirages : 700 000 carnets

Bande-carnet "Les visages de la Ve République"

BC4287 La bande carnet, non pliée — 15 » — 7 »

2008. – *60e anniversaire du premier vol Etat d'Israël-France. Héliogravure. Multicolore. Dentelés 13¼ x 13.*

Emission conjointe avec Israël (n° 1936 et 1937).

4299	0,55 € *Pli d'époque, avion en vol, vue aérienne de Tel-Aviv*	1 10	0 55

4300	0,85 € *Pli d'époque, avion en vol, vue aérienne de Paris avec la tour Eiffel*	1 70	0 85

Tirage : 2 300 000 paires.

2008. – *Capitales européennes. Prague (République tchèque). Héliogravure. Multicolore. Dentelés 13¼ x 13.* BF *n° 126.*

Emis uniquement en feuillet.

4301	0,55 € *Tour du Petit Côté*	1 25	0 70
4302	0,55 € *Hôtel de ville (horloge astronomique et calendrier)*	1 25	0 70

4303	0,55 € *Eglise Notre-Dame de Tyn*	1 25	0 70
4304	0,55 € *Le château*	1 25	0 70
	N°s 4301 à 4304 (4 val.)	**5 »**	**2 80**

2008. – *Série artistique. Honoré Daumier (1808-1879), dessinateur et peintre. Taille-douce. Dentelé 13¼ x 13.*

4305	1,33 € *"Un guichet de théâtre", gravure*	3 »	1 30

Tirage : 2 500 000.

2008. – *Au profit de la Croix-Rouge. "Dessine la planète aux couleurs de la vie ! ". Offset. Autoadhésifs. Deux bandes de phosphore. Multicolore. Dentelés 11.* **(Croix-Rouge sans publicité)**

Sans valeur indiquée (validité permanente).

Emis en carnet.

4306	(Lettre prioritaire 20 g) *"La Couleur, la Vie" (globe et animaux), dessin d'Inès Scharff*	1 50	0 70
4307	(Lettre prioritaire 20 g) *Globe avec animaux et arbres, dessin d'Elise Boulay*	1 50	0 70

Tirages : 1 200 000 carnets

BC4306 La bande carnet, non pliée — 15 » — 7 »

2008. – *"Bonnes fêtes". Offset. Autoadhésifs. Deux bandes de phosphore. Multicolore. Dentelés 11.*

Sans valeur indiquée (validité permanente).

Emis en carnet.

4308	(Lettre prioritaire 20 g) *Composition avec planètes* (21 x 27)	1 10	0 55
4309	(Lettre prioritaire 20 g) *Personnage volant sur le dos d'un oiseau* (21 x 27)	1 10	0 55
4310	(Lettre prioritaire 20 g) *Silhouette en fil* (21 x 27)	1 10	0 55

4311 (Lettre prioritaire 20 g) *Bouche* (21 x 27) 1 10 0 55

4312 (Lettre prioritaire 20 g) *Cœur fleuri* (21 x 27) 1 10 0 55

4313 (Lettre prioritaire 20 g) *Composition avec étoiles* (21 x 27) 1 10 0 55

4314 (Lettre prioritaire 20 g) *Jambes de danseurs* (39 x 25) 1 10 0 55

4315 (Lettre prioritaire 20 g) *Cœur* (39 x 25) 1 10 0 55

4316 (Lettre prioritaire 20 g) *Composition avec caméléon* (39 x 25) 1 10 0 55

4317 (Lettre prioritaire 20 g) *Composition avec ballons* (39 x 25) 1 10 0 55

4318 (Lettre prioritaire 20 g) *Composition avec étoiles, lune, silhouette de fillette se balançant* (39 x 25) 1 10 0 55

4319 (Lettre prioritaire 20 g) *Composition sur fond vert* (39 x 25) 1 10 0 55

4320 (Lettre prioritaire 20 g) *Composition sur fond fuchsia* (39 x 25) 1 10 0 55

4321 (Lettre prioritaire 20 g) *Composition avec silhouette d'un couple avec enfant* (39 x 25) 1 10 0 55

N°s 4308 à 4321 (14 val.) 15 40 7 70

Tirages : 3 200 000 carnets

BC4308 La bande carnet, non pliée 15 40 8 »

2008. – *90e anniversaire de la signature de l'Armistice 1914-1918. Taille-douce. Deux bandes de phosphore. Dentelé 13¼.*

4322 0,55 € *Soldats dans une tranchée, soldat sonnant du clairon pour annoncer la victoire et les retrouvailles* 1 10 0 55

Tirage : 2 000 000.

2008. – *France - Liban. Héliogravure. Deux bandes de phosphore. Dentelé 13 x 12¾.*

Emission conjointe avec le Liban (n° 444).

4323 0,85 € *Chêne de France, carte du pourtour méditerranéen, cèdre du Liban* 1 70 0 85

Tirage : 2 300 000.

2008

Du n° 4127 au n° 4323 :

200 timbres ****293 ⊙132**

Autres rubriques de l'année:

Aérien 1

Timbres Autoadhésifs 147 à 252

Blocs et feuillet 115 à 126

Blocs Souvenirs 26 à 35

Préoblitérés 253 à 258

Service 140 et 141

A partir de 2009, les timbres autoadhésifs sont isolés dans la rubrique des adhésifs (voir pages 485 à 510) et ne figurent plus dans les années complétes des timbres de France.

2009. – *Personnalité. Louis Braille (1809-1852), inventeur du système d'écriture en points saillants. Taille-douce. Deux bandes de phosphore. Papier gaufré. Dentelé 13 x 12¾.*

4324 **0,55 € noir et violet** ***Portrait, faciale en braille*** 1 10 0 55

Tirage : 2 900 000.

2009. – *Année lunaire chinoise du Buffle. Héliogravure. Deux bandes de phosphore. Dentelé 13¼ x 13.*

4325 **(Lettre prioritaire 20 g)** ***Buffle*** 1 25 0 55

Tirage : 9 000 000.

Emis en petite feuille de 5 timbres avec marge centrale illustrée.

F4325 **La feuille** 6 25 5 »

2009. – *Personnalité. René Ier d'Anjou (1409-1480). Taille-douce. Deux bandes de phosphore. Dentelé 13¼.*

4326 **0,55 €** ***Statue du roi René à Aix-en-Provence et château d'Angers*** 1 10 0 55

Tirage : 3 000 000.

2009. – *Saint-Valentin. Cœur 2009 de la Maison de couture Emanuel Ungaro. Héliogravure. Multicolore. Dent.* BF *n° 127.*

Sans valeur indiquée (validité permanente).

4327 **(Lettre prioritaire 20 g)** ***Perroquet et fleurs roses*** 1 10 0 55

4328 **(Lettre prioritaire 50 g)** ***Couple de perroquets et fleurs roses*** 1 80 0 90

Tirages : 4 500 000 et 3 750 000.

2009. – *Championnats du monde FIS de ski alpin 2009 à Val d'Isère. Héliogravure. Deux bandes de phosphore. Multicolore. Dentelés 13 x 13¼.*

4329 **0,55 €** ***Super combiné*** 1 25 0 70

4330 **0,55 €** ***Slalom*** 1 25 0 70

4331 **0,55 €** ***Descente*** 1 25 0 70

4332 **0,55 €** ***Slalom géant*** 1 25 0 70

4333 **0,55 €** ***Val d'Isère (équipe de skieurs)*** 1 25 0 70

Nos 4329 à 4333 (5 val.) **6 25** **3 50**

Tirage : 2 100 000 séries.

Emis en feuillet.

F4329 **La feuille** 6 25 5 »

2009. – *Série touristique. Les Sables-d'Olonne (Vendée). Héliogravure. Deux bandes de phosphore. Dentelé 13¼.*

4334 **0,55 €** ***Voiliers, maisons le long des quais*** 1 10 0 55

Tirage : 2 700 000.

2009. – *40e anniversaire de la Fondation de France. Héliogravure. Deux bandes de phosphore. Dentelé 13¼.*

4335 **0,55 €** ***Mains-arbre*** 1 10 0 55

Tirage : 2 400 000.

2009. – ***Série artistique. Cathédrale Sainte-Cécile (Albi). Offset. Dentelé 13.***

4336 **0,85 €** ***Ange avec trompette, détail peinture de la voûte*** 1 70 0 85

Tirage : 2 400 000.

2009. – ***Série touristique. Menton (Alpes-Maritimes). Taille-douce. Deux bandes de phosphore. Dentelé 13¼.***

4337 **0,56 €** ***Vue de la vieille ville, citrons*** 1 10 0 55

Tirage : 2 650 000.

2009. – ***Fête du timbre. Personnages de dessins animés des Looney Tunes des studios Warner Bros. © Warner Bros. Entertainment Inc. (s09). Héliogravure. Deux bandes de phosphore. Multicolore. Dentelés 13¼ x 13½.***

4338 **0,56 €** ***Vil Coyote sur une planche à surf et Bip-Bip*** 1 10 0 55

4339 **0,56 €** ***Grosminet jouant au tennis de table avec Titi*** 1 10 0 55

4340 **0,56 €** ***Bugs Bunny et Daffy Duck en randonnée*** 1 10 0 55

Tirage : 18 000 000 séries.

Imprimés se tenant.

2009. – ***Fête du timbre. Personnages de dessins animés des Looney. © Warner Bros. Enternainment Inc. (s09). Héliogravure. Deux bandes de phosphore. Dentelé 13.***

4341 **1,00 €** ***Jeu de tir à la corde par les personnages des Looney Tunes*** 2 » 1 »

Tirage : 1 900 000.

Emis en feuillet.

F4341 **La feuille** 2 » 1 »

2009. – ***Type Marianne de Beaujard. Gravure assistée par ordinateur. Papier gommé. Une bande de phosphore à droite, sauf n° 4343, 4344, 4345, 4346 : deux bandes de phosphore. Dent. 13.***

Marianne et l'Europe.

Types des T.-P. de 2008.

4342 **0,73 € vert-olive (4232)** 1 45 0 35
4343 **0,90 € lilas-brun clair (4234)** 1 80 0 40
4344 **1,30 € bleu ciel (4236)** 2 60 0 55

4345 **1,35 € lilas (4237)** 2 70 0 55
4346 **2,22 € brun-prune (4238)** 4 40 0 70

N°s 4342 à 4346 (5 val.) **12 95** **2 55**

2009. – ***Cinquantenaire du Conseil constitutionnel. Héliogravure. Deux bandes de phosphore. Dentelé 13¼ x 13½.***

4347 **0,56 €** ***Logo*** 1 10 0 55

Tirage : 2 350 000.

2009. – ***Série touristique. Le Palais des Papes à Avignon (Vaucluse). Taille-douce. Deux bandes de phosphore. Dentelé 13 x 12¾.***

4348 **0,70 €** ***Vue de l'ensemble architectural*** 1 40 0 70

Tirage : 2 500 000.

2009. – ***Série touristique. Mâcon (Saône-et-Loire). Taille-douce. Deux bandes de phosphore. Dentelé 13 x 12¾.***

4349 **0,56 €** ***Statue de l'écrivain Alphonse de Lamartine né à Mâcon en 1790, pont et vue de la ville*** 1 10 0 55

Tirage : 2 800 000.

2009. – ***Protection des zones polaires et des glaciers. Taille-douce et offset. Multicolore. Dentelure 13 x 13¼, sauf n° 4351 : 13¼ x 13.***

4350 **0,56 €** ***Paysage polaire avec albatros en vol*** 1 10 0 55

4351 **0,85 €** ***Manchots empereurs avec poussins*** 1 70 0 85

Tirage : 1 800 000 paires.

Emis en feuillet.

F4350 **La feuille** 2 80 2 »

2009. – ***Personnalité. Aimé Césaire (1913-2008), poète et homme politique. Héliogravure. Deux bandes de phosphore. Dentelé 13¼.***

4352 **0,56 €** ***Portrait*** 1 10 0 55

Tirage : 2 000 000.

2009. – ***Europa. L'astronomie. Offset. Multicolore. Dentelés 13½ x 13.***

4353 **0,70 €** ***Planète Saturne*** 1 40 0 70

4354 **0,70 €** ***Exoplanète*** 1 40 0 70

Tirage : 2 300 000 paires.

Emis en feuillet.

F4353 **La feuille** 2 80 2 »

2009. – ***Série touristique. Chaumont (Haute-Marne). Héliogravure. Deux bandes de phosphore. Dentelé 13¼.***

4355 **0,56 €** ***Graphisme réalisé par Frank Vriens*** 1 10 0 55

Tirage : 5 000 000.

2009. – ***Personnalité. Jean Calvin (1509-1564), réformateur religieux français. Taille-douce. Deux bandes de phosphore. Dentelé 13¼.***

4356 **0,56 €** ***Portrait, extrait d'une lettre*** 1 10 0 55

Tirage : 2 500 000.

2009. – ***Le chocolat. Héliogravure. Timbre parfumé au chocolat. Dentelés 13.***

4357 **0,56 € chocolat** ***Cabosse et fèves*** 1 10 0 60

4358 **0,56 € chocolat** ***Personnage aztèque*** 1 10 0 60

4359 **0,56 € chocolat** ***Silhouette de conquistador*** 1 10 0 60

4360	0,56 € chocolat *Silhouette de l'Alhambra à Grenade (Espagne)*	1 10	0 60
4361	0,56 € chocolat *Carte de France mentionnant Bayonne, 1609*	1 10	0 60
4362	0,56 € chocolat *Personnages d'époque*	1 10	0 60

4363	0,56 € chocolat *Fabrication*	1 10	0 60
4364	0,56 € chocolat *Plaque de chocolat*	1 10	0 60

4365	0,56 € chocolat *Chocolatière, tasse*	1 10	0 60
4366	0,56 € chocolat *Visage croquant du chocolat*	1 10	0 60
	Nos 4357 à 4366 (10 val.)	11 »	6 »

Tirage : 2 500 000 séries.

Emis en petite feuille.

F4357	La feuille	11 »	7 »

2009. – ***Série touristique. Château de la Bâtie d'Urfé (Loire). Taille-douce. Deux bandes de phosphore. Dentelé 13¼.***

4367	0,56 € *Château et décor de la salle des Rocailles*	1 10	0 55

Tirage : 2 600 000.

2009. – ***82e Congrès de la Fédération Française des Associations Philatéliques, à Tarbes (Hautes-Pyrénées). Taille-douce. Deux bandes de phosphore. Dentelé 13 x 13½.***

4368	0,56 € *Le Jardin public Massey (pavillon du Musée d'histoire naturelle, statue l'Ouragan d'Edmond Desca (1855-1918)*	1 10	0 55

Tirage : 2 850 000.

Imprimé attenant à une vignette sans valeur (tête de cheval).

2009. – ***Série artistique. Le Pont-Neuf à Paris, empaqueté par Christo et Jeanne-Claude. Héliogravure. Dentelé 13¼ x 13.***

4369	1,35 € *Vue du pont en 1985*	2 70	1 35

Tirage : 2 800 000.

2009. – ***Série touristique. Bordeaux (Gironde). Taille-douce. Deux bandes de phosphore. Dentelé 13.***

4370	0,56 € *Bâtiments du Port de la Lune*	1 10	0 55

Tirage : 2 750 000.

2009. – *Mémorial Jean Moulin à Caluire (Rhône). Taille-douce. Deux bandes de phosphore. Dentelé 13¼.*

4371	0,56 € *Edifice et portrait de Jean Moulin (1899-1943), résistant*	1 10	0 55

Tirage : 2 900 000.

2009. – *Série "Nature" (XXIII). Animaux disparus ou menacés d'extinction. Héliogravure. Multicolore. Dent. 13¼.* BF *n° 128.*

4372	0,56 € *Panda géant (Ailuropoda melanoleuca)*	1 10	0 55
4373	0,56 € *Rhinocéros*	1 10	0 55
4374	0,70 € *Aurochs*	1 40	0 70
4375	0,90 € *Condor de Californie (Gymnogyps californianus)*	1 80	0 90
	N°s 4372 à 4375 (4 val.)	**5 40**	**2 70**

Tirages : 5 500 000, 5 500 000, 5 000 000 et 6 500 000.

2009. – *Centenaire de la Coupe Gordon-Bennett d'aviation. Taille-douce. Deux bandes de phosphore. Dentelé 13¼.*

4376	0,56 € *Avion biplan piloté par l'américain Glenn Curtiss, vainqueur en 1909*	1 10	0 55

Tirage : 2 600 000.

ANNÉES COMPLÈTES

TIMBRES-POSTE

	**	*	⊙			
1938	749	376	301	Du N° 372 au N° 418	*52 timbres*	
1939	343	157	147	Du N° 419 au N° 450	*32 timbres*	*(sauf n° 421A et B)*
1940	206	93	113	Du N° 451 au N° 469	*19 timbres*	
1941	177	94	124	Du N° 470 au N° 537	*70 timbres*	
1942	98	53	89	Du N° 538 au N° 567	*30 timbres*	
1943 (1)	154	92	146	Du N° 568 au N° 598	*31 timbres*	*(sauf 571A et 580A)*
1943 (2)	215	131	199		*24 timbres*	*(sauf 568-71 et 576-80)*
1944	107	65	95	Du N° 599 au N° 668	*70 timbres*	
1945	82	48	46	Du N° 669 au N° 747	*85 timbres*	*(sauf 701A à F)*
1946	25	16	19	Du N° 748 au N° 771	*24 timbres*	
1947	36	21	25	Du N° 772 au N° 792	*21 timbres*	
1948	65	37	36	Du N° 793 au N° 822	*30 timbres*	
1949	172	102	136	Du N° 823 au N° 862	*42 timbres*	*(sauf N° 833A et 846A)*
1950	105	62	103	Du N° 863 au N° 877	*15 timbres*	
1951	154	90	103	Du N° 878 au N° 918	*41 timbres*	
1952	116	70	106	Du N° 919 au N° 939	*21 timbres*	
1953	197	118	119	Du N° 940 au N° 967	*28 timbres*	
1954	323	192	260	Du N° 968 au N° 1007	*40 timbres*	
1955	259	145	223	Du N° 1008 au N° 1049	*46 timbres*	
1956	167	96	112	Du N° 1050 au N° 1090	*41 timbres*	
1957	110	63	74	Du N° 1091 au N° 1141	*52 timbres*	
1958	61	37	48	Du N° 1142 au N° 1188	*47 timbres*	
1959	80	44	32	Du N° 1189 au N° 1229	*41 timbres*	
1960	85		56	Du N° 1230 au N° 1280	*53 timbres*	
1961	76		54	Du N° 1281 au N° 1324	*44 timbres*	
1962	58		45	Du N° 1325 au N° 1367	*49 timbres*	
1963	37		30	Du N° 1368 au N° 1403	*38 timbres*	
1964	49		43	Du N° 1404 au N° 1434	*31 timbres*	*(sauf 1417A)*
1965	26		17	Du N° 1435 au N° 1467	*33 timbres*	*(sauf 1465A)*
1966	28		21	Du N° 1468 au N° 1510	*43 timbres*	
1967	18		16	Du N° 1511 au N° 1541	*33 timbres*	
1968	21		19	Du N° 1542 au N° 1581	*40 timbres*	
1969	29		25	Du N° 1582 au N° 1620	*40 timbres*	
1970	29		24	Du N° 1621 au N° 1662	*42 timbres*	
1971	29		23	Du N° 1663 au N° 1701	*39 timbres*	*(sauf 1698A)*
1972	29		21	Du N° 1702 au N° 1736	*35 timbres*	
1973	35		28	Du N° 1737 au N° 1782	*46 timbres*	
1974	40		27	Du N° 1783 au N° 1829	*47 timbres*	
1975	35		28	Du N° 1830 au N° 1862	*33 timbres*	
1976	43		31	Du N° 1863 au N° 1913	*52 timbres*	*(sauf 1895A)*
1977	49		34	Du N° 1914 au N° 1961	*48 timbres*	
1978	63		40	Du N° 1962 au N° 2027	*69 timbres*	
1979	48		32	Du N° 2028 au N° 2072	*47 timbres*	
1980	53		34	Du N° 2073 au N° 2117	*45 timbres*	
1981	69		40	Du N° 2118 au N° 2177	*60 timbres*	***A partir de 1981 sauf : bandes-carnets, paires***
1982	103		62	Du N° 2178 au N° 2251	*74 timbres*	***et triptyques***
1983	67		35	Du N° 2252 au N° 2298	*47 timbres*	
1984	71		33	Du N° 2299 au N° 2346	*49 timbres*	
1985	73		36	Du N° 2347 au N° 2392	*46 timbres*	
1986	92		48	Du N° 2393 au N° 2451	*59 timbres*	
1987	69		36	Du N° 2452 au N° 2500	*48 timbres*	
1988	80		43	Du N° 2501 au N° 2559	*57 timbres*	
1989	90		59	Du N° 2560 au N° 2614	*53 timbres*	
1990	87		41	Du N° 2615 au N° 2675	*60 timbres*	
1991	91		47	Du N° 2676 au N° 2735	*59 timbres*	
1992	81		45	Du N° 2736 au N° 2784	*48 timbres*	
1993	132		68	Du N° 2785 au N° 2853	*66 timbres*	
1994	131		70	Du N° 2854 au N° 2917	*61 timbres*	
1995	110		54	Du N° 2918 au N° 2985	*65 timbres*	
1996	102		49	Du N° 2986 au N° 3041	*55 timbres*	
1997	146		65	Du N° 3042 au N° 3128	*85 timbres*	
1998	144		72	Du N° 3129 au N° 3210	*80 timbres*	
1999	196		137	Du N° 3211 au N° 3293	*80 timbres*	
2000	86		45	Du N° 3294 au N° 3366	*71 timbres*	
2001	82		45	Du N° 3367 au N° 3442	*72 timbres*	
2002	122		65	Du N° 3443 au N° 3537	*97 timbres*	
2003	129		70	Du N° 3538 au N° 3631	*94 timbres*	
2004	140		81	Du N° 3632 au N° 3730	*100 timbres*	*(sauf nos 3632C et 3633C)*
2005	204		107	Du N° 3731 au N° 3860	*132 timbres*	
2006	205		106	Du N° 3861 au N° 3995	*135 timbres*	
2007	216		116	Du N° 3996 au N° 4126	*135 timbres*	
2008	293		132	Du N° 4127 au N° 4323	*200 timbres*	

TIMBRES-POSTE AUTOADHÉSIFS

1990. – *Type Marianne du Bicentenaire. Taille-douce. Deux bandes de phosphore. Autoadhésif. Non dentelé.* ©

Provenant de carnets.

1 2 f. 30 rouge (2630) 1 25 0 15

Ce numéro ainsi que les n° 2, 3, 4 et 5 sont non dentelés par précoupe droite entre les timbres.

Les timbres adhésifs doivent être conservés sur leur support papier.

1991. – *Type Marianne du Bicentenaire avec lettre D. Taille-douce. Deux bandes de phosphore. Autoadhésif. Non dentelé.* ©

Provenant de carnet.

2 D = (2 f. 50) rouge (2713) 1 50 0 40

1991. – *Type Marianne du Bicentenaire. Taille-douce. Deux bandes de phosphore. Autoadhésif. Non dentelé.* ©

Provenant de carnet.

3 2 f. 50 rouge (2720) 1 40 0 15

1993. – *Type Marianne du Bicentenaire. Taille-douce. Autoadhésif. Deux bandes de phosphore. Non dentelé.* ©

Sans valeur indiquée (validité permanente).

Émis en carnet.

4 (sans val) rouge (2807) 1 50 0 15

Imprimé attenant horizontalement à la gauche d'une vignette sans valeur ("l'enveloppe à cases. Elle facilite votre courrier"). Provenant du carnet n° 1503

4a ((sans val.)+vignette) 3 »

Ce timbre non dentelé a été remplacé en 1994 par un timbre comportant une dentelure verticale en lignes ondulées (n° 7).

1993. – *Type Marianne du Bicentenaire. Taille-douce. Autoadhésif. Une bande de phosphore à droite. Non dentelé.* ©

Provenant du carnet n° 1503

Imprimé attenant horizontalement à la gauche d'une vignette sans valeur ("L'enveloppe à cases. Elle facilite votre courrier").

5 70 c brun (2824) 13 » 7 »

a. (70 c. +vignette) 13 » 8 »

b. (sans val.) + 70 c. + vignette) 18 » 12 »

Remplacé en 1994 par un timbre comportant une dentelure verticale en lignes ondulées (n° 6)

1994. – *Type Marianne du Bicentenaire. Taille-douce. Autoadhésifs. Dent. : précoupé vertical en lignes ondulées.* ©

Émis en carnets.

Type I

Type II

Type I : lettres plus épaisses, cadre du bas interrompu au milieu et base de l'échancrure du cou arrondie

Type II : lettres plus fines, cadre du bas continu et base de l'échancrure du cou en points

6 70 c brun (2873) 13 » 8 »

7 (sans val.) rouge) (I) (2874) 1 25 0 15

a. (Type II) 9 » 4 »

Une bande de phosphore pour le 70 c., deux bandes pour le timbre sans valeur indiquée.

Le n° 7a provient du carnet 2874-C9. (Trait ininterrompu au milieu du bas).

Imprimé attenant horizontalement à une vignette sans valeur ("l'enveloppe à cases, elle facilite votre courrier"), provenant des carnets n°s 1504 à 1506.

6a 70 c. +vignette 13 » 8 »

6b	70 c (+vignette caractères maigres)	15 »	9 »
7b	(sans val.) (+vignette)	3 »	1 50
7ba	(sans val.) (+vignette caractères maigres)	4 »	2 »
7c	(sans val.) (+70 c. +vignette)	16 »	12 »
7ca	(sans val.) (+70 c. +vignette caractères maigres)	20 »	15 »

1996. – *Type Marianne du Bicentenaire. Taille-douce. Autoadhésif. Une bande de phosphore. Dent. : précoupé vertical en lignes ondulées.* [C]

Provenant de carnet.

8	**1 f orange (3009)**	5 »	3 »

Imprimé attenant horizontalement à une vignette sans valeur ("Simplifiez vous la vie ! essayez l'enveloppe timbrée"), provenant du carnet 1507

a. orange (+vignette)	5 »	3 50
b. orange (n° 7 (sans val.)+1 f. +vignette)	9 »	7 »

1997. – *Les Journées de la Lettre. Le voyage d'une lettre. Autoadhésifs. Dentelés 11.* [C]

Emis en carnet de 2 séries.

9	**3 f. multicolore (3066) (3060)**	2 »	1 50
10	**3 f. multicolore (3067) (3061)**	2 »	1 50

11	**3 f. multicolore (3068) (3062)**	2 »	1 50
12	**3 f. multicolore (3069) (3063)**	2 »	1 50

13	**3 f. multicolore (3070) (3064)**	2 »	1 50
14	**3 f. multicolore (3071) (3065)**	2 »	1 50
Nos 9 à 14 (6 val.)		**12 »**	**9 »**
BC9	**La bande**	24 »	20 »

Tirage : 7 439 291.

1997. – *Type Marianne du 14 Juillet. Taille-douce. Autoadhésif. Deux bandes de phosphore. Dent. : précoupé vertical en lignes ondulées.* [C]

Sans valeur indiquée (validité permanente).

Provenant de carnet.

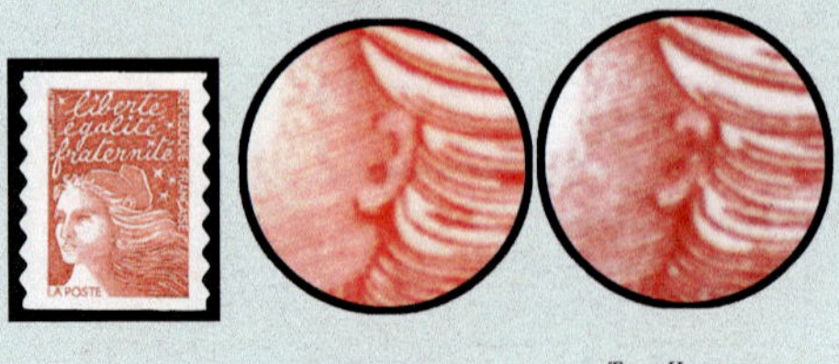

Type I, gravure mécanique, "Oreille intacte". *Type II, gravure numérique "Oreille cassée".*

15	**(sans val.) rouge (Type I gravure mécanique) (3085)**	1 »	0 15
	a. (gravure numérique) (II)	4 »	0 30

1997. – *Type Marianne du 14 Juillet. Taille-douce. Autoadhésif. Une bande de phosphore. Dent. : précoupé vertical en lignes ondulées.* [C]

Provenant de carnet.

16	**1 f orange (3101)**	4 »	2 50
	c. (gravure numérique) (II)	10 »	7 »

Imprimés attenant horizontalement à une vignette sans valeur ("simplifiez vous la vie ! essayez l'enveloppe timbrée") provenant du carnet 1508

a. (1 f. +vignette)	4 »	2 »
aa. (avec vignette II)	10 »	8 »
b. (n° 3084 (sans val.)+1 f. +vignette)	7 »	5 »
bc. (Type II) 15+16+vignette (II)	15 »	12 »

1998. – *"France 98". Coupe du Monde de Football (V). Héliogravure. Autoadhésif. Dentelé.* [C]

Type du T.-P. de même date.

Emis en carnet.

17	**3 f multicolore (3140) (3139)**	1 50	0 80

Tirage : 7 969 653 séries.

Un exemplaire de ce timbre figure également sur un feuillet de 286 x 210, comportant 7 vignettes auto-adhésives représentant la mascotte "Footix" au cours de 7 actions de jeu (tête, passe, shoot, etc).

17a	(Le feuillet)	12 »	
BC17	La bande carnet, non pliée	15 »	

Tirage : 7 969 653.

1998. – *Les Journées de la Lettre. La lettre au fil du temps. Héliogravure. Autoadhésifs. Multicolore. Dentelés 11.* C

Types des T.-P. de même date.

Emis en carnet de 2 séries.

18	**3 f multicolore (3150) (3156)**	2 »	1 50
19	**3 f multicolore (3151) (3157)**	2 »	1 50
20	**3 f multicolore (3152) (3158)**	2 »	1 50
21	**3 f multicolore (3153) (3159)**	2 »	1 50
22	**3 f multicolore (3154) (3160)**	2 »	1 50
23	**3 f multicolore (3155) (3161)**	2 »	1 50
	N°s 18 à 23 (6 val.)	**12 »**	**9 »**

Tirage : 2 905 848 séries.

BC18	**La bande carnet, non pliée**	24 »	

1999. – *Le timbre Euro. Taille-douce. Autoadhésif. Dent. : précoupé vertical en lignes ondulées.* C

Type du T.-P. de même date.

Emis en carnet.

24	**3 f rouge et bleu (3214) (3215)**	1 50	0 50
BC24	**La bande carnet, non pliée**	12 »	

1999. – *Saint-Valentin. Héliogravure. Autoadhésifs. Dentelés.* C

Types des T.-P. de même date.

Emis en carnet.

Cœur avec "Je t'aime".

Rose dans un coeur.

25	**3 f multicolore (3220) (3218)**	2 50	0 80
26	**3 f multicolore (3221) (3219)**	2 50	0 80

Tirage : 2 453 722 paires.

BC25	**La bande carnet, non pliée**	20 »	15 »

2000. – *Saint-Valentin. Cœurs 2000 du couturier Yves Saint Laurent. Héliogravure. Autoadhésifs. Dentelés.* C

Types des T.-P. de même date.

Emis en carnet.

Cœurs entourés de deux serpents.

Cœur avec profil féminin.

27	**3 f. (0,46 €) multicolore (3297) (3295)**	2 50	1 »
28	**3 f. (0,46 €) multicolore (3298) (3296)**	2 50	1 »

Tirage : 1 719 608 paires.

BC27	**La bande carnet, non pliée**	20 »	15 »

2001. – *"Bonnes vacances". Offset. Autoadhésif. Deux bandes de phosphore. Dentelé 11.* [C]

Type du T.-P. de même date.
Emis en carnet.

29 **3 f. (0,46 €) multicolore (3399) (3400)** 1 50 0 60

Tirage : 2 109 534.

BC29 **La bande carnet, non pliée** 15 » 12 »

2001. – *Type Marianne du 14 Juillet. Taille-douce. Autoadhésif. Deux bandes de phosphore. Dent. : précoupé vertical en lignes ondulées.*

Provenant de carnet.

Type I, gravure mécanique, impression fine, oreille intacte.

Type II, gravure numérique, impression floue, oreille cassée.

30 **(sans val.) rouge (Type II gravure numérique) (3419) (15)** 1 » 0 15

a. (Type I transfert mécanique du poinçon) 2 » 0 50

Le timbre 30a a été émis, en 2003, en carnet "Centenaire de la Semeuse de Roty".

2001. – *"Bonne Année" et "Meilleurs Vœux". Offset. Deux bandes de phosphore. Dentelés 11.* [C]

Types des T.-P. de même date.
Emis en carnet.

31 **3 f. (0,46 €) multicolore (3437) (3439)** 1 50 0 50

32 **3 f. (0,46 €) multicolore (3438) (3440)** 1 50 0 50

Tirages : 9 898 933 et 9 970 853.

La paire 3 » 1 50

BC31 **La bande carnet, non pliée** 15 » 12 »

Existe sans phosphore.

2002. – *Timbre pour vacances. Offset. Autoadhésif. Deux bandes de phosphore. Dentelé 11.* [C]

Type du T.-P. de même date.
Emis en carnet.

33 **0,46 € multicolore (3493) (3494)** 1 50 0 60

Tirage : 2 109 534 carnets

BC33 **La bande carnet, non pliée** 15 » 12 »

2002. – *"Meilleurs Vœux". Offset. Autoadhésif. Deux bandes de phosphore. Dentelé 11.* [C]

Chalet sous la neige.

Type du T.-P. de même date.
Emis en carnet.

34 **0,46 € multicolore (3533) (3534)** 1 50 0 60

Tirage : 2 084 425 carnets

BC34 **La bande carnet, non pliée** 15 » 12 »

2003. – *Timbre pour vacances. Offset. Autoadhésif. Deux bandes de phosphore. Dentelé 11.* [C]

Mère et enfants sur leur serviette de plage.

Type du T.-P. de même date.
Emis en carnet.

35 **0,50 € multicolore (3577) (3578)** 1 50 0 60

Tirages : 2 620 381 carnets

BC35 **La bande carnet, non pliée** 15 » 12 »

2003. – *Centenaire de la Semeuse de Roty. Taille-douce. Autoadhésif. Deux bandes de phosphore. Précoupé vertical en lignes ondulées.* [C]

Emis en carnet.

36 **0,50 € rouge (3619)** 2 50 2 »

P36 **La paire 36+30** 4 » 3 »

2003. – *"Meilleurs Vœux". Offset. Autoadhésif. Deux bandes de phosphore. Dentelé 11.* [C]

Type du T.-P. de même date.
Emis en carnet.

37 **0,50 € multicolore (3621) (3622)** 1 50 0 60

Tirages : 3292833 carnets

BC37 **La bande carnet, non pliée** 15 » 12 »

2004. – ***Saint-Valentin. Cœurs 2004 du couturier Karl Lagerfeld. Autoadhésifs. Dentelés.***

Types des T.-P. de même date.

Flacon de parfum Chanel n° 5 dans un cœur.

Le tailleur Chanel sur fond avec Tour Eiffel dans un cœur.

38	**0,50 € multicolore (3632B) (3632)**	4 »	3 »
39	**0,75 € multicolore (3633B) (3633)**	5 »	4 »

Emis chacun en feuilles.

2004. – ***Saint-Valentin. Cœurs 2004 du couturier Karl Lagerfeld. Autoadhésifs. Multicolore. Dentelés.***

Types des T.-P. de même date.

provenant de roulettes, numéro noir au verso.

38A	**0,50 € multicolore (38) (3632C)**	400 »	
39A	**0,75 € multicolore (39) (3633C)**	400 »	

2004. – ***Timbres pour naissances. "C'est une fille", "c'est un garçon". Offset. Autoadhésifs. Deux bandes de phosphore. Dentelés 11.*** [C]

Emis en carnets.

Bébé-abeille.

Bébé-papillon.

40	**0,50 € multicolore (3634)**	1 50	0 60
41	**0,50 € multicolore (3635)**	1 50	0 60
BC40	**La bande carnet, non pliée**	12 »	10 »
BC41	**La bande carnet, non pliée**	12 »	10 »

2004. – ***Europa. Les vacances. © Raoul Dufy, ADAGP, Paris 2004. Offset. Autoadhésif. Deux bandes de phosphore. Dentelé 11.*** [C]

Détail d'une œuvre originale du peintre Raoul Dufy (1877-1953).

Type du T.-P. de 2004.

Emis en carnet.

42	**0,50 € multicolore (3668) (3672)**	1 50	0 50
BC42	**La bande carnet, non pliée**	15 »	10 »

2004. – ***60e anniversaire de la Marianne d'Alger. Taille-douce. Autoadhésif. Deux bandes de phosphore. Dent. : précoupé vertical en lignes ondulées.*** [C]

Emis en carnet.

43	**0,50 € rouge (3716)**	3 »	1 75

P43	**La paire 43+30**	4 50	3 50

2004. – ***"Meilleurs Vœux". Offset. Autoadhésifs. Deux bandes de phosphore. Dentelés 11.*** [BF] ***n° 79.*** [C]

Emis en carnet de 2 séries.

Etoiles personnages avec chapeaux.

Etoiles, oiseau et sapins stylisés.

44	**0,50 € multicolore (3722)**	2 »	1 »
45	**0,50 € multicolore (3723)**	2 »	1 »

Etoile personnage tenant une fleur.

Guirlande avec sujets décoratifs.

46	**0,50 € multicolore (3724)**	2 »	1 »
	a. (papier gommé, sans bande de phosphore)	2 »	1 »
47	**0,50 € multicolore (3725)**	2 »	1 »

Etoiles personnages.

48	**0,50 € multicolore (3726)**	2 »	1 »
Nos 44 à 48 (5 val.)		**10 »**	**5 »**

Tirage : 2 722 019 séries.

BC44	**La bande carnet, non pliée**	20 »	15 »

2005. – *Type Marianne de Lamouche. Taille-douce. Autoadhésif. Deux bandes de phosphore. Dent. : précoupé vertical en lignes ondulées.* [C]

Type I, gravure mécanique, noms plus fins du dessinateur, de l'imprimeur et du graveur.

Type II, gravure numérique.

Type II, gravure numérique.

Sans valeur indiquée (validité permanente).
Type II, gravure numérique.
Provenant de carnet.

49	**(sans val.) rouge (3744)**	1 25	0 15
	a. (Type I transfert mécanique du poinçon)	2 »	1 »
	b. (Légende Phil@poste au lieu d'ITVF)	1 25	0 30

Le timbre n° 49a a été émis, en 2005, en carnet "60e anniversaire de la Marianne de Dulac".

Le timbre n° 49b est émis en carnets (à partir de 2006) (gravure numérique).

Le timbre n° 49c est émis en carnets pour distributeurs Sagem (à partir de septembre 2007).

2005. – *Saint-Valentin. Cœurs 2005 du couturier Cacharel. Autoadhésifs. Dentelés.*

Types des T.-P. de même date.

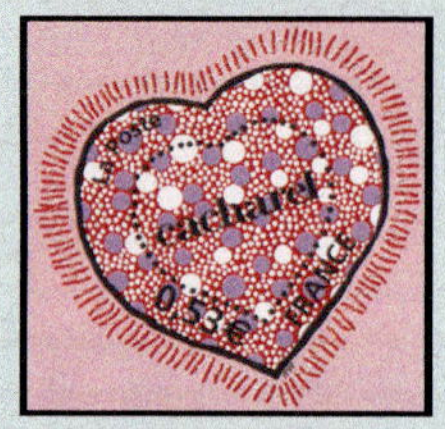

50	**0,53 € multicolore (3747B) (3747)**	4 »	3 »
51	**0,82 € multicolore (3748B) (3748)**	5 »	4 »
	a. (sans "Poste")	50 »	30 »

Emis chacun en feuilles.

2005. – *Centenaire du Rotary Club International. Autoadhésif. Deux bandes de phosphore. Dentelé 11.*

Emblème sur carte de France.

Type du T.-P. de 2005.
Emis en 2006 en autoadhésif.

52	**0,53 € multicolore (3750) (3750A)**	3 »	2 »

Emis en feuilles

2005. – *Timbre pour vacances. Offset. Autoadhésif. Deux bandes de phosphore. Dentelé 11.* [C]

Cabines de plage.

Sans valeur indiquée (validité permanente).
Emis en carnet.

53	**(Lettre 20 g) multicolore (3788)**	1 50	0 50
BC53	**La bande carnet, non pliée**	15 »	10 »

2005. – *Timbres de naissances. "C'est une fille", "C'est un garcon". Offset. Autoadhésifs. Deux bandes de phosphore. Dentelés 11.* [C]

Sans valeur indiquée (validité permanente).
Emis en carnets.

"C'est un fille" (nouveau-né sur une pivoine) (d'après photographie d'Anne Geddes, Australienne).

"C'est un garçon" (nouveau-né sur un lotus) (d'après photographie d'Anne Geddes, Australienne).

54	**(Lettre 20 g) multicolore (3804)**	1 50	0 50
55	**(Lettre 20 g) multicolore (3805)**	1 50	0 50
BC54	**La bande carnet, non pliée**	15 »	10 »
BC55	**La bande carnet, non pliée**	15 »	10 »

2005. – *"Sourires" avec le chat du dessinateur et humoriste Philippe Geluck. Offset. Autoadhésifs. Deux bandes de phosphore. Dentelés 11.* [C]

Créations originales du dessinateur.
Sans valeur indiquée (validité permanente).
Emis en carnet.

"L'envers d'un timbre autocollant est un excellent attrape-mouche".

"Une seule lettre vous manque" "et tout est épeuplé".

56	**(Lettre 20 g) multicolore (3825)**	1 30	0 60
57	**(Lettre 20 g) multicolore (3826)**	1 30	0 60

"Envoyer une lettre" "est un jeu d'adresse".

"J'écris" "donc tu lis".

58	**(Lettre 20 g) multicolore (3827)**	1 30	0 60
59	**(Lettre 20 g) multicolore (3828)**	1 30	0 60

"Vous avez un joli timbre" "J 'aime votre enveloppe". "Homme de lettres vu de dos".

60 **(Lettre 20 g) multicolore (3829)** 1 30 0 60

61 **(Lettre 20 g) multicolore (3830)** 1 30 0 60

"Ecrire ou ne pas écrire" "Lettre ou le néant ?". "C'est l'histoire d'un timbre" "qui colle une enveloppe pour l'emmener en boîte".

62 **(Lettre 20 g) multicolore (3831)** 1 30 0 60

63 **(Lettre 20 g) multicolore (3832)** 1 30 0 60

"Le mot enveloppe" "contient neuf lettres". "Entre nous" "ça colle".

64 **(Lettre 20 g) multicolore (3833)** 1 30 0 60

65 **(Lettre 20 g) multicolore (3834)** 1 30 0 60

Nos 56 à 65 (10 val.) **13 »** **6 »**

BC56 **La bande carnet, non pliée** 13 » 6 »

2005. – *60e anniversaire de la Marianne de Dulac. Taille-douce. Autoadhésif. Deux bandes de phosphore. Dent. : précoupé vertical en lignes ondulées.* Ⓒ

Emis en carnet.

66 **0,53 € rouge (3841)** 2 50 1 50

P66 **La paire 66+3744a** 3 50 2 »

2005. – *"Meilleurs Vœux". Offset. Autoadhésifs. Deux bandes de phosphore. Multicolore. Dentelés 11.* BF ***n° 92.*** Ⓒ

Sans valeur indiquée (validité permanente).

Emis en carnet de 2 séries.

Ours blanc et manchot sur patins à glace et deux jeunes manchots sur une luge. Manchots, renne et bonhomme de neige.

67 **(Lettre 20 g) multicolore (3853)** 2 » 0 60

68 **(Lettre 20 g) multicolore (3854)** 2 » 0 60

Renne et manchot sur une luge. Manchots avec boules de neige.

69 **(Lettre 20 g) multicolore (3855)** 2 » 0 60

70 **(Lettre 20 g) multicolore (3856)** 2 » 0 60

Ours blanc sur une luge et manchots skiant ou glissant.

71 **(Lettre 20 g) multicolore (3857)** 2 » 0 60

Nos 67 à 71 (5 val.) **10 »** **3 »**

BC67 **La bande carnet, non pliée** 20 » 10 »

2006. – *Saint-Valentin. Cœurs 2006 du couturier Stéphane Rolland de la Maison Jean-Louis Scherrer. Autoadhésifs. Multicolore. Dentelés.*

Types des T.-P. de même date.

72 **(Lettre 20 g) multicolore (3863) (3861)** 3 » 2 »

73 **(Lettre 50 g) multicolore (3864) (3862)** 4 » 3 »

Emis chacun en feuille de 30 timbres.

2006. – *Art. Peinture. Les impressionnistes. Offset. Autoadhésifs. Deux bandes de phosphore. Dentelés 11.* ⓒ
Sans valeur indiquée (validité permanente).
Emis en carnet.

"Portraits à la campagne" (1876), détail de tableau du peintre Gustave Caillebotte (1848-1894).

"La chasse aux papillons" (1874), détail de tableau du peintre Berthe Morisot (1841-1895).

74	**(Lettre 20 g) multicolore (3866)**	1 50	0 60
75	**(Lettre 20 g) multicolore (3867)**	1 50	0 60

"Mère et enfant" (1886), détail de tableau du peintre Mary Cassatt (1845-1926).

"Jeunes filles au piano" (1892), détail de tableau du peintre Auguste Renoir (1841-1919).

76	**(Lettre 20 g) multicolore (3868)**	1 50	0 60
77	**(Lettre 20 g) multicolore (3869)**	1 50	0 60

"La bergère" ou "Jeune fille à la baguette" (1881), détail de tableau du peintre Camille Pissarro (1830-1903).

"Mademoiselle Gachet dans son jardin" (1890), détail de tableau du peintre Vincent Van Gogh (1853-1890).

78	**(Lettre 20 g) multicolore (3870)**	1 50	0 60
79	**(Lettre 20 g) multicolore (3871)**	1 50	0 60

"L'air du soir" (1893-1894), détail de tableau du peintre Henri-Edmond Cross (1856-1910).

"Danseuses" (1884-1885), détail de tableau du peintre Edgar Degas (1834-1917).

80	**(Lettre 20 g) multicolore (3872)**	1 50	0 60
81	**(Lettre 20 g) multicolore (3873)**	1 50	0 60

"Le déjeuner sur l'herbe" (1863), détail de tableau du peintre Edouard Manet (1832-1883).

"Femmes de Tahiti"ou "Sur la plage" (1891), détail de tableau du peintre Paul Gauguin (1848-1903).

82	**(Lettre 20 g) multicolore (3874)**	1 50	0 60
83	**(Lettre 20 g) multicolore (3875)**	1 50	0 60
	Nos 74 à 83 (10 val.)	**15 »**	**6 »**
BC74	**La bande carnet, non pliée**	15 »	6 »

2006. – *Timbre pour vacances. Offset. Autoadhésif. Deux bandes de phosphore. Dentelé 11.* ⓒ

Œuvre originale du dessinateur de bandes dessinées Jean Giraud.

Sans valeur indiquée (validité permanente).
Emis en carnet.

84	**(Lettre 20 g) multicolore (3904)**	1 50	0 55
BC84	**La bande carnet, non pliée**	15 »	10 »

2006. – *Type Marianne de Lamouche. Autoadhésif. Gravure à chaud argent. Dentelé 13.*

85	**5,00 € argent (3925)**	10 »	8 »

Timbre (en argent 999 millièmes) présenté sous blister sur un support cartonné

2006. – *"Sourires" avec le chien Cubitus du dessinateur Michel Rodrigue et scénariste Pierre Aucaigne. © Rodrigue & Aucaigne Dupa/Le Lombard 2006. Offset. Autoadhésifs. Deux bandes de phosphore. Dentelés 11.* ⓒ **(carnets commémoratifs).**
Sans valeur indiquée (timbre à validité permanente).
Emis en carnet.

Tête de Cubitus sur un timbre affranchissant un pli destiné au chat Sénéchal.

Tête de Cubitus avec un timbre collé sur la truffe.

86	**(Lettre 20 g) multicolore (3953)**	1 30	0 60
87	**(Lettre 20 g) multicolore (3954)**	1 30	0 60

"Oh ! le timbre a une dent de plus !" (Cubitus et son neveu Bidule montrant sa nouvelle dent en riant).

"Youhou ! il y a quelqu'un ?" (Cubitus, Sémaphore, Sénéchal et Bidule) .

88	**(Lettre 20 g) multicolore (3955)**	1 30	0 60
89	**(Lettre 20 g) multicolore (3956)**	1 30	0 60

"Ouf ! ce n'est pas une facture !" (Cubitus ouvrant son courrier) .

Cubitus avec bonnet phrygien et fleur violette.

90	**(Lettre 20 g) multicolore (3957)**	1 30	0 60
91	**(Lettre 20 g) multicolore (3958)**	1 30	0 60

Cubitus tenant un pli d'où s'échappent des cœurs.

Cubitus : "Ce sont de bonnes nouvelles", Sénéchal : "C'est bon ! vous pouvez ouvrir !".

92	**(Lettre 20 g) multicolore (3959)**	1 30	0 60
93	**(Lettre 20 g) multicolore (3960)**	1 30	0 60

"Je suis le seul timbre au monde qu'on caresse dans le sens du poil !" (Cubitus et l'escargot).

"Je suis un timbre qui adore les papouilles !" (main chatouillant Cubitus).

94	**(Lettre 20 g) multicolore (3961)**	1 30	0 60
95	**(Lettre 20 g) multicolore (3962)**	1 30	0 60
	N°s 86 à 95 (10 val.)	**13 »**	**6 »**
BC86	**La bande carnet, non pliée**	13 »	6 »

2006. – *60e anniversaire de la Marianne de Gandon. Taille-douce. Autoadhésif. Deux bandes de phosphore. Dent. : précoupé vertical en lignes ondulées.* Ⓒ (carnets de timbres à composition variable).

Emis en carnet.

96	**0,54 € rouge (3977)**	2 50	1 50
P96	**La paire 96+3744b**	3 50	2 »

2006. – *"Meilleurs Vœux". Offset. Autoadhésifs. Deux bandes de phosphore. Dentelés 11.* Ⓒ (carnets commémoratifs).

Sans valeur indiquée (validité permanente).

Emis en carnet de 2 séries.

Manchots et renne en traîneau.

Renne pêchant et manchots se baignant.

97	**(Lettre 20 g) multicolore (3986)**	1 50	0 60
98	**(Lettre 20 g) multicolore (3987)**	1 50	0 60

Renne et manchots décorant un sapin.

Manchots regardant le renne patiner.

99	**(Lettre 20 g) multicolore (3988)**	1 50	0 60
100	**(Lettre 20 g) multicolore (3989)**	1 50	0 60

Renne avec paquet cadeau et manchots dans des paquets cadeaux.

101	**(Lettre 20 g) multicolore (3990)**	1 50	0 60
	N°s 97 à 101 (5 val.)	**7 50**	**3 »**
BC97	**La bande carnet, non pliée**	15 »	10 »

2007. – *Saint-Valentin. Cœurs 2007 de la Maison de couture Givenchy. Héliogravure. Autoadhésifs. Dentelés.*

Types des T.-P. de même date.

Sans valeur indiquée (validité permanente).

Cœur rouge.

Cœur blanc.

102	**(Lettre 20 g) noir sur rouge (3998) (3996)**	10 »	6 »
103	**(Lettre 50 g) noir et rouge (3999) (3997)**	5 »	4 »

Emis chacun en feuilles de 30 timbres.

2007. – *Art. Antiquités. Offset. Autoadhésifs. Deux bandes de phosphore. Dentelés 11.* Ⓒ (carnets commémoratifs).

Sans valeur indiquée (validité permanente). Emis en carnet.

Hippopotame égyptien en faïence.

Tête de la déesse grecque Aphrodite.

104	**(Lettre 20 g) multicolore (4002)**	1 30	0 60
105	**(Lettre 20 g) multicolore (4003)**	1 30	0 60

Statue grecque de la Victoire de Samothrace.

Fresque romaine de Pompéi.

106	**(Lettre 20 g) multicolore (4004)**	1 30	0 60
107	**(Lettre 20 g) multicolore (4005)**	1 30	0 60

Le pharaon Amenemhat III.

Statue de la déesse romaine Junon.

108 **(Lettre 20 g) multicolore (4006)** 1 30 0 60

109 **(Lettre 20 g) multicolore (4007)** 1 30 0 60

Harpiste égyptien.

Le sarcophage des époux, antiquité étrusque.

110 **(Lettre 20 g) multicolore (4008)** 1 30 0 60

111 **(Lettre 20 g) multicolore (4009)** 1 30 0 60

Statue égyptienne de scribe accroupi.

Tête de Périclès, antiquité grecque.

112 **(Lettre 20 g) multicolore (4010)** 1 30 0 60

113 **(Lettre 20 g) multicolore (4011)** 1 30 0 60

N°s 104 à 113 (10 val.) **13 »** **6 »**

BC104 La bande carnet, non pliée 13 » 7 »

2007. – ***Fête du timbre. "Harry Potter", héros de la série de l'écrivain britannique Joanne Rowling. © TM & © Warner Bros. Entertainment Inc. (s07). Héliogravure. Autoadhésifs. Deux bandes de phosphore. Multicolore. Dentelés 11.***

Types des T.-P. de même date.

Sans valeur indiquée.

114 **(Lettre prioritaire 20 g) multicolore (4024A) (4024)** 5 » 4 »

115 **(Ecopli 20 g) multicolore (4025A) (4025)** 5 » 4 »

116 **(Monde 20 g) multicolore (4026) (4026A)** 9 » 8 »

Emis chacun en petite feuille de 5 timbres attenant chacun à une vignette illustrée différente.

Feuilles Harry Potter avec vignettes illustrées (Autoadhésifs).

F114 La feuille **25 »**

F115 La feuille **25 »**

F116 La feuille **45 »**

2007. – ***Bicentenaire de la Cour des Comptes. Taille-douce. Autoadhésif. Deux bandes de phosphore. Dentelé 11.***

Façade du Palais Cambon à Paris.

Type du T.-P. de 2007.

117 **0,54 € multicolore (4028) (4028A)** 3 » 1 50

2007. – ***Timbres pour vacances. Offset. Autoadhésifs. Deux bandes de phosphore. Dentelés 11.*** **Ⓒ (carnets commémoratifs).**

Sans valeur indiquée (validité permanente).

Emis en carnet.

Détail d'une porte peinte en bleue et roses trémières.

Poisson-chirurgien à poitrine blanche.

118 **(Lettre prioritaire 20 g) multicolore (4037)** 1 30 0 60

119 **(Lettre prioritaire 20 g) multicolore (4038)** 1 30 0 60

Gentiane bleue.

Myrtilles.

120 **(Lettre prioritaire 20 g) multicolore (4039)** 1 30 0 60

121 **(Lettre prioritaire 20 g) multicolore (4040)** 1 30 0 60

Détails de barques peintes en bleu.

Echeveaux teints en bleu séchant.

122 **(Lettre prioritaire 20 g) multicolore (4041)** 1 30 0 60

123 **(Lettre prioritaire 20 g) multicolore (4042)** 1 30 0 60

Glacier.

Cocotier et ciel bleu.

124 **(Lettre prioritaire 20 g) multicolore (4043)** 1 30 0 60

125 **(Lettre prioritaire 20 g) multicolore (4044)** 1 30 0 60

Parasols bleus.

Pigments de différentes couleurs.

126 **(Lettre prioritaire 20 g) multicolore (4045)** 1 30 0 60

127 **(Lettre prioritaire 20 g) multicolore (4046)** 1 30 0 60

N°s 118 à 127 (10 val.) **13 » 6 »**

BC118 **La bande carnet, non pliée** 13 » 8 »

2007. – ***Coupe du monde de Rugby 2007 en France. Offset. Autoadhésif. Procédé lenticulaire. Dentelé 11.***

Image animée du passage du ballon entre les poteaux.

128 **3,00 € multicolore (4080)** 6 » 4 »

2007. – ***Timbres de messages. "Invitation", "Merci". Offset. Autoadhésifs. Deux bandes de phosphore. Multicolore. Dentelés 11.*** **[C] (carnets commémoratifs).**

Sans valeur indiquée. Lettre prioritaire 20 g.

Emis en carnet d'1 série.

Boîte d'où s'échappent des papillons.

Boîte d'où s'échappent des cœurs.

129 **(sans val.) multicolore (4082)** 1 30 0 60

130 **(sans val.) multicolore (4083)** 1 30 0 60

Boîte remplie de fleurs.

Boîte d'où s'échappent des bulles.

131 **(sans val.) multicolore (4084)** 1 30 0 60

132 **(sans val.) multicolore (4085)** 1 30 0 60

Boîte d'où s'échappent des notes de musique.

133 **(sans val.) multicolore (4086)** 1 30 0 60

N°s 129 à 133 (5 val.) **6 50 3 »**

BC129 **La bande carnet, non pliée** 6 50 4 »

2007. – ***"Sourires" avec les vaches humoristiques du dessinateur Alexis Nesmes. Offset. Autoadhésifs. Deux bandes de phosphore. Dentelés 11.*** **[C] (carnets commémoratifs)**

Sans valeur indiquée. Lettre prioritaire 20 g.

Emis en carnet de 2 séries.

Vache humectant des timbres.

Vache affranchie avec des timbres " Encore 1 ou 2 et je peux partir ".

134 **(sans val.) multicolore (4089)** 1 30 0 50

135 **(sans val.) multicolore (4090)** 1 30 0 50

Vache postant son courrier.

Vache avec oblitération sur la tête.

136 **(sans val.) multicolore (4091)** 1 30 0 50

137 **(sans val.) multicolore (4092)** 1 30 0 50

Vache chantant "Ne meuuh quitte pas…".

138 **(sans val.) multicolore (4093)** 1 30 0 50

N°s 134 à 138 (5 val.) **6 50 2 50**

BC134 **La bande carnet, non pliée** 13 » 8 »

2007. – ***40e anniversaire de la Marianne de Cheffer. Taille-douce. Autoadhésif. Deux bandes de phosphore. Dent : précoupé vertical en lignes ondulées.*** **[C] (carnets de timbres à composition variable).**

Emis en carnet.

139 **0,54 € rouge (4109)** 2 50 1 50

2007. – ***La paire 139+49b.***

P139 La paire 139+49b 3 50 2 »

2007. – ***"Meilleurs Vœux". Offset. Autoadhésifs. Deux bandes de phosphore. Multicolore. Dentelés 11.*** BF ***n° 25.*** C **(carnets commémoratifs).**

Sans valeur indiquée (validité permanente).

Emis en carnet.

Ecureuil avec bonnet vert.

Oiseau avec chapeau de fête.

140 (Lettre prioritaire 20 g) multicolore (4120) 1 30 0 60

141 (Lettre prioritaire 20 g) multicolore (4121) 1 30 0 60

Faon sur une luge.

Hérisson avec chapeau de fête.

142 (Lettre prioritaire 20 g) multicolore (4122) 1 30 0 60

143 (Lettre prioritaire 20 g) multicolore (4123) 1 30 0 60

Chien avec bonnet rouge.

144 (Lettre prioritaire 20 g) multicolore (4124) 1 30 0 60

Nos 140 à 144 (5 val.) **6 50** **3 »**

La bande-carnet non pliée

BC140 La bande carnet, non pliée 13 » 8 »

2007. – ***Au profit de la Croix-Rouge. "Dessine ton vœu pour les enfants du monde" 2007. Héliogravure. Autoadhésifs. Deux bandes de phosphore. Multicolore. Dentelés 11.*** C **(Croix-Rouge sans publicité)**

Sans valeur indiquée (validité permanente). Timbre avec surtaxe de 0,17 €.

Emis en carnet de 5 paires.

"Que tous les enfants du monde soient heureux", dessin de Maya Thieulle, élève de CE1.

"Les enfants = Amour", dessin de Chloé Hilbrunner, élève de CP.

145 (Lettre prioritaire 20 g) multicolore (4125) 1 75 0 70

146 (Lettre prioritaire 20 g) multicolore (4126) 1 75 0 70

P145 La paire 145+146 3 50 2 »

Imprimés se tenant.

BC145 La bande carnet, non pliée 17 50 12 »

2008. – ***Type Marianne de Lamouche. Taille-douce. Autoadhésif. Deux bandes de phosphore. Dent. : précoupé vertical en lignes ondulées.*** C

Type du T.-P. n° 3966 de 2006.

Sans valeur indiquée (validité permanente).

Lettre prioritaire 20 g vers l'Union Européenne et la Suisse.

Emis en carnet.

147 (sans val.) bleu (3966) (4127) 2 » 0 60

2008. – ***Saint-Valentin. Cœurs 2008 du couturier Franck Sorbier. Héliogravure. Autoadhésifs. Multicolore. Dentelés.***

Types des T.-P. de 2008.

Sans valeur indiquée (validité permanente).

Visages formant un cœur.

Arbre aux feuilles-cœurs.

148 (Lettre prioritaire 20 g) multicolore (4130) (4128) 3 » 1 50

149 (Lettre prioritaire 50 g) multicolore (4129) 5 » 2 50

Emis chacun en feuilles de 30 timbres.

2008. – ***Art. Chefs d'œuvre de la peinture. Offset. Deux bandes de phosphore. Dentelés 11.*** **Ⓒ (carnets commémoratifs).**

Sans valeur indiquée (validité permanente).

Emis en carnet.

"Scènes de la vie de saint François", du peintre italien Giotto di Bondone (1266-1337).

"Port de mer au soleil couchant", du peintre français Le Lorrain (1600-1682).

150	**(Lettre prioritaire 20 g) multicolore (4132)**	1 30	0 60
151	**(Lettre prioritaire 20 g) multicolore (4133)**	1 30	0 60

"La jeune fille à la perle", du peintre hollandais Jan Vermeer (1632-1675).

"La Joconde" (1503-1505), du peintre italien Léonard de Vinci (1452-1519).

152	**(Lettre prioritaire 20 g) multicolore (4134)**	1 30	0 60
153	**(Lettre prioritaire 20 g) multicolore (4135)**	1 30	0 60

"Le prêteur et sa femme", du peintre flamand Quentin Metsys (1465-1530).

"La naissance de Vénus", du peintre italien Sandro Botticelli (1445-1510).

154	**(Lettre prioritaire 20 g) multicolore (4136)**	1 30	0 60
155	**(Lettre prioritaire 20 g) multicolore (4137)**	1 30	0 60

"Bonaparte, Premier consul", du peintre français Jacques Louis David (1748-1825).

"La belle jardinière", du peintre italien Raphaël (Raffaello Sanzio, dit) (1483-1520).

156	**(Lettre prioritaire 20 g) multicolore (4138)**	1 30	0 60
157	**(Lettre prioritaire 20 g) multicolore (4139)**	1 30	0 60

"L'été", du peintre italien Guiseppe Arcimboldo (v. 1527-1593).

"L'Infante Marie Marguerite", du peintre espagnol Diego Velasquez (1599-1660).

158	**(Lettre prioritaire 20 g) multicolore (4140)**	1 30	0 60
159	**(Lettre prioritaire 20 g) multicolore (4141)**	1 30	0 60
	N°s 150 à 159 (10 val.)	**13 »**	**6 »**
BC150	**La bande carnet, non pliée**	13 »	8 »

2008. – ***Fête du timbre. Personnages des dessins animés de Tex Avery (1907-1980), réalisateur américain. © TM & Turner Entertainment Co WB Shield, TM & Warner Bros. Entertainment Inc. (s08). Offset. Autoadhésifs. Deux bandes de phosphore. Dentelés 11.*** **Ⓒ (carnets journée du timbre).**

Types des T.-P. de même date.

Sans valeur indiquée (validité permanente).

Emis en carnet de 3 séries + 1 n° 160.

Droopy et le loup.

La girl et le loup.

160	**(Lettre prioritaire 20 g) multicolore (4149) (4146)**	1 30	0 55
161	**(Lettre prioritaire 20 g) multicolore (4150) (4147)**	1 30	0 55

Le loup et la girl.

162	**(Lettre prioritaire 20 g) multicolore (4151) (4148)**	1 30	0 55

Bande-carnet "Fête du timbre. Tex Avery" composée de 4 timbres n° 160, 3 timbres n° 161 et 3 timbres n° 162.

BC160	**La bande carnet, non pliée**	13 »	8 »

2008. – ***Fête du timbre. Personnages des dessins animés de Tex Avery (1907-1980), réalisateur américain. © TM & Turner Entertainment Co WB Shield, TM & Warner Bros. Entertainment Inc. (s08). Héliogravure. Autoadhésifs. Deux bandes de phosphore. Multicolore. Dentelés 11.***

Types des T.-P. de même date.

Sans valeur indiquée (validité permanente).

Le chien Droopy et le loup.

160A (Lettre prioritaire 20 g) multicolore (4149A) 3 »

La girl et le loup.

161A (Lettre prioritaire 20 g) multicolore (4150A) 3 »

Le loup et la girl.

162A (Lettre prioritaire 20 g) multicolore (4151A) 3 »

Emis chacun en petite feuille de 5 timbres attenant chacun à une vignette illustrée différente.

F160A	**La feuille**	**15 »**
F161A	**La feuille**	**15 »**
F162A	**La feuille**	**15 »**

2008. – ***Timbre de naissances "C'est une fille". Héliogravure. Autoadhésif. Deux bandes de phosphore. Dentelé 11.*** **[C] (carnets commémoratifs).**

Poussin en tissu, chien sur roulettes, et cubes.

Sans valeur indiquée (validité permanente).

Emis en carnet.

163 (Lettre prioritaire 20 g) multicolore (4184) 1 10 0 55

Quant on gratte le timbre il apparaît "C'est une fille"

BC163 La bande carnet, non pliée 11 » 7 »

2008. – ***Timbre de naissances "C'est un garçon". Héliogravure. Autoadhésif. Deux bandes de phosphore. Dentelé 11.*** **[C] (carnets commémoratifs).**

Nounours avec biberon, poussin sur roulettes, cubes.

Sans valeur indiquée (validité permanente).

Emis en carnet.

164 (Lettre prioritaire 20 g) multicolore (4185) 1 10 0 55

Quant on gratte le timbre il apparaît "C'est un garçon"

BC164 La bande carnet, non pliée 11 » 7 »

2008. – ***Timbres pour vacances. Héliogravure. Autoadhésifs. Deux bandes de phosphore. Dentelés 11.*** **[C] (carnets commémoratifs).**

Sans valeur indiquée (validité permanente).

Emis en carnet.

Fougères. Papillon.

165 (Lettre prioritaire 20 g) multicolore (4186) 1 30 0 60

166 (Lettre prioritaire 20 g) multicolore (4187) 1 30 0 60

Feuilles de thé. Cocotier.

167 (Lettre prioritaire 20 g) multicolore (4188) 1 30 0 60

168 (Lettre prioritaire 20 g) multicolore (4189) 1 30 0 60

Jardin avec plan d'eau. Golf.

169 (Lettre prioritaire 20 g) multicolore (4190) 1 30 0 60

170 (Lettre prioritaire 20 g) multicolore (4191) 1 30 0 60

171	**(Lettre prioritaire 20 g) multicolore (4192)**	1 30	0 60
172	**(Lettre prioritaire 20 g) multicolore (4193)**	1 30	0 60

Kiwis coupés en deux.

Petits pois.

173	**(Lettre prioritaire 20 g) multicolore (4194)**	1 30	0 60
174	**(Lettre prioritaire 20 g) multicolore (4195)**	1 30	0 60
	N°s 165 à 174 (10 val.)	**13 »**	**6 »**
BC165	**La bande carnet, non pliée**	13 »	8 »

2008. – *Marianne et les valeurs de l'Europe. Taille-douce. Autoadhésifs. Deux bandes de phosphore. Rouge. Dent. : précoupé vertical en lignes ondulées.* **[C] (carnets de timbres à composition variable).**

Emis en carnet.

Marianne de Beaujard. — Démocratie (main glissant un bulletin de vote dans une urne). — Environnement (arbre dans la paume d'une main). — Paix (colombe avec rameau d'olivier).

175	**(sans val.) rouge (4197)**	1 20	0 25
	a. (Emis en feuilles de 100 timbres avec la série n° 208 à 218)	1 20	0 25
176	**0,55 € rouge (4198)**	1 60	0 65
177	**0,55 € rouge (4199)**	1 60	0 65
178	**0,55 € rouge (4200)**	1 60	0 65
	N°s 175 à 178 (4 val.)	**6 »**	**2 20**
	La bande 175+176+175+177+175+178		
B175	**La bande**	9 »	5 »

2008. – *Marianne et les valeurs de l'Europe. Taille-douce. Autoadhésifs. Deux bandes de phosphore. Bleu. Dent. : précoupé vertical en lignes ondulées.* **[C] (carnets de timbres à composition variable).**

Emis en carnet.

Marianne de Beaujard. — Démocratie (main glissant un bulletin de vote dans une urne). — Environnement (arbre dans la paume d'une main). — Paix (colombe avec rameau d'olivier).

179	**(sans val.) bleu (4201)**	1 50	0 35
	a. (Emis en feuilles de 100 timbres avec la série n° 208 à 218)	2 »	0 75
180	**0,65 € bleu (4202)**	2 »	0 75
181	**0,65 € bleu (4203)**	2 »	0 75
182	**0,65 € bleu *Paix* (4204)**	2 »	0 75
	N°s 179 à 182 (4 val.)	**7 50**	**2 60**
	La bande 179+180+179+181+179+182		
B179	**La bande**	10 »	6 »

2008. – *Environnement. Développement durable. Héliogravure. Autoadhésifs. Deux bandes de phosphore. Multicolore. Dentelés 11.* **[C] (carnets commémoratifs).**

"Timbrez des idées durables ! ".

Sans valeur indiquée (validité permanente).

Emis en carnet.

"Bureau durable - papier à protéger" (arbre).

"Déplacement durable - Transport du futur" (bicyclette).

183	**(Lettre prioritaire 20 g) multicolore (4205)**	1 30	0 60
184	**(Lettre prioritaire 20 g) multicolore (4206)**	1 30	0 60

"Tourisme durable - Site à préserver" (carte du monde).

"Electronique durable - Bon à recycler" (ordinateur).

185	**(Lettre prioritaire 20 g) multicolore (4207)**	1 30	0 60
186	**(Lettre prioritaire 20 g) multicolore (4208)**	1 30	0 60

"Eau durable - Ceci est un trésor" (gouttes d'eau).

"Energie durable - Ceci est un radiateur" (soleil).

187 **(Lettre prioritaire 20 g) multicolore**
(4209) 1 30 0 60

188 **(Lettre prioritaire 20 g) multicolore**
(4210) 1 30 0 60

"Lavage durable - A la bonne dose" (récipients en plastique).

"Mode durable - Recyclable en pull" (bouteilles d'eau en plastique).

189 **(Lettre prioritaire 20 g) multicolore**
(4211) 1 30 0 60

190 **(Lettre prioritaire 20 g) multicolore**
(4212) 1 30 0 60

"Jardinage durable - Ceci est un engrais" (trognon de pomme).

"Alimentation durable - Inconnue en hiver" (fraise).

191 **(Lettre prioritaire 20 g) multicolore**
(4213) 1 30 0 60

192 **(Lettre prioritaire 20 g) multicolore**
(4214) 1 30 0 60

N°s 183 à 192 (10 val.) **13 »** **6 »**

BC183 **La bande carnet, non pliée** 13 » 6 »

2008. – *Type Marianne de Beaujard. Gravure à chaud argent. Autoadhésif. Dentelé 13.*

Marianne et l'Europe

193 **5,00 € argent (4242)** 10 » 8 »

Timbre (en argent 999 millièmes) présenté sous blister sur un suport cartonné.

2008. – *"Sourires" avec le chat Garfield du dessinateur américain Jim Davis. Offset. Autoadhésifs. Deux bandes de phosphore. Dentelés 11.* 🄲 **(carnets commémoratifs).**

Sans valeur indiquée (validité permanente).

Emis en carnet.

"Vous saisissez ?".

"Tu veux une bonne nouvelle ?".

194 **(Lettre prioritaire 20 g) multicolore**
(4271) 1 10 0 55

195 **(Lettre prioritaire 20 g) multicolore**
(4272) 1 10 0 55

"Ecris-moi ou la pizza y passe".

"Slurp !".

196 **(Lettre prioritaire 20 g) multicolore**
(4273) 1 10 0 55

197 **(Lettre prioritaire 20 g) multicolore**
(4274) 1 10 0 55

"J'aime le courrier".

"Pour toi".

198 **(Lettre prioritaire 20 g) multicolore**
(4275) 1 10 0 55

199 **(Lettre prioritaire 20 g) multicolore**
(4276) 1 10 0 55

"Livraison urgente".

"Juste pour toi !".

200 **(Lettre prioritaire 20 g) multicolore**
(4277) 1 10 0 55

201 **(Lettre prioritaire 20 g) multicolore**
(4278) 1 10 0 55

"Réponse attendue".

"J'arrive dans ta boîte aux lettres".

202 **(Lettre prioritaire 20 g) multicolore**
(4279) 1 10 0 55

203 **(Lettre prioritaire 20 g) multicolore**
(4280) 1 10 0 55

N°s 194 à 203 (10 val.) **11 »** **5 50**

BC194 **La bande carnet, non pliée** 11 » 7 »

2008. – ***Timbre de message "ceci est une invitation". Héliogravure. Autoadhésif. Deux bandes de phosphore. Dentelé 11.***

Type du T.-P. de 2005.
Sans valeur indiquée (validité permanente).

204 (Lettre prioritaire 20 g) multicolore (3760) 3 » 2 »

Emis en feuilles de 50 timbres.

2008. – ***Timbre de message "un grand merci". Héliogravure. Autoadhésif. Deux bandes de phosphore. Dentelé 11.***

Type du T.-P. de 2005.
Sans valeur indiquée (validité permanente).

205 (Lettre prioritaire 20 g) multicolore (3761) 3 » 2 »

Emis en feuilles de 50 timbres.

2008. – ***Série artistique. La galerie des Glaces du château de Versailles (Yvelines). Héliogravure. Autoadhésif. Dentelé 11.***

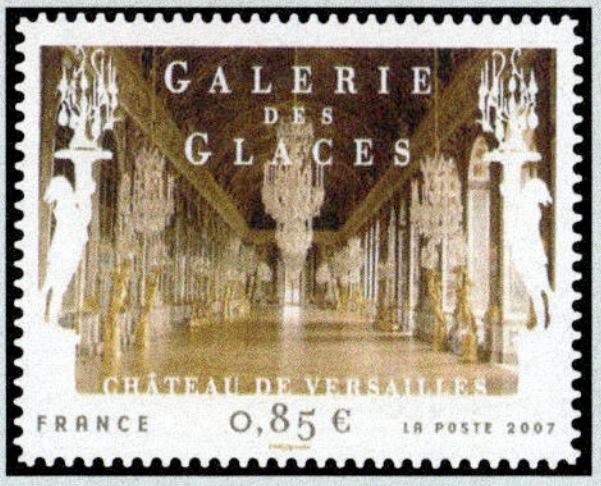

Lustres et miroirs de la galerie.

Type du T.-P. de 2007.

206 0,85 € multicolore (4119) 6 » 4 »

Emis en feuilles de 30 timbres.

2008. – ***Europa. L'écriture d'une lettre. Héliogravure. Autoadhésif. Deux bandes de phosphore. Dentelé 11.***

Composition avec plume d'oie et de stylo.

Type du T.-P. de 2008.

207 0,55 € multicolore (4181) 3 » 2 »

Emis en feuilles de 48 timbres.

2008. – ***Type Marianne de Beaujard. Gravure assistée par ordinateur. Autoadhésifs. Une bande de phosphore à droite, sauf n° 213, 214, 215, 216, 217, 218 : deux bandes de phosphore. Dent. : précoupé vertical en lignes ondulées.***

Types des T.-P. de 2008.

208	**0,01 € jaune (4226)**	0 15	0 15
209	**0,05 € bistre-noir (4227)**	0 20	0 15
210	**0,10 € gris (4228)**	0 30	0 20
211	**(sans val.) vert (4229)**	1 50	0 50

212	**0,72 € vert-olive (4232)**	4 »	3 »
213	**0,85 € violet-rouge (4233)**	3 »	2 »
214	**0,88 € lilas-brun clair (4234)**	4 »	3 »
215	**1,00 € orange (4235)**	3 »	1 50

216	**1,25 € bleu ciel (4236)**	3 »	2 »
217	**1,33 € lilas (4237)**	5 »	4 »
218	**2,18 € brun-prune (4238)**	8 »	6 »

Emis chacun en feuilles de 100 timbres.

Les n°s 175a (rouge, sans valeur) et 179a (bleu sans valeur) sont intégrés dans cette série et sont présentés sous les n°s 175 et 175.

2008. – ***Type Marianne de Beaujard. Gravure assistée par ordinateur. Autoadhésifs. Une bande de phosphore à droite, sauf n° 220 : deux bandes de phosphore. Dent. : précoupé vertical en lignes ondulées.***

Types des T.-P. de 2008.
Emis en roulettes. N° noir au verso.

219	**(sans val.) vert (4239)**	1 40	0 50
220	**(sans val.) rouge (4240)**	1 60	0 50
221	**(sans val.) bleu (4241)**	2 »	0 80

2008. – ***Série artistique. Gérard Garouste, peintre. Héliogravure. Autoadhésif. Dentelé 11.***

Œuvre de l'artiste.

Type du T.-P. de 2008.

222	**1,33 € multicolore (4244)**	20 »	10 »

Emis en feuilles de 30 timbres.

2008. – ***Série artistique. Jean-Jacques Henner (1829-1905), peintre. Héliogravure. Autoadhésif. Dentelé 11.***

"Jeune fille se chauffant les mains à un grand poêle", tableau.

Type du T.-P. de 2008.

223	**0,88 € multicolore (4286)**	4 »	3 »

Emis en feuilles de 30 timbres.

2008. – ***Série artistique. Honoré Daumier (1808-1879), dessinateur et peintre. Autoadhésif. Dentelé 11.***

"Un guichet de théâtre", gravure.

Type du T.-P. de 2008.

224	**1,33 € multicolore (4305)**	20 »	10 »

Emis en feuilles de 30 timbres.

2008. – ***Les visages de la Vᵉ République. Héliogravure. Autoadhésifs. Deux bandes de phosphore. Dent. : précoupé vertical en lignes ondulées.*** **[C] (carnets de timbres à composition variable).**
Emis en carnet.

Marianne à la nef. — Marianne de Decaris. — Marianne de Cocteau. — Coq de Decaris.

225	**0,55 € vert-gris et rouge (4287)**	1 25	0 65
226	**0,55 € gris clair et carmin foncé (4288)**	1 25	0 65
227	**0,55 € bleu et rouge (4289)**	1 25	0 65
228	**0,55 € outremer, carmin et brun (4290)**	1 25	0 65

Marianne de Cheffer. — Marianne de Béquet. — Sabine de Gandon. — La Liberté de Gandon.

229	**0,55 € rouge carminé (4291)**	1 25	0 65
230	**0,55 € carmin-rose (4292)**	1 25	0 65
231	**0,55 € rouge (4293)**	1 25	0 65
232	**0,55 € rouge (4294)**	1 25	0 65

La Marianne du Bicentenaire, de Louis Briat. — La Marianne du 14 Juillet, d'Eve Luquet. — Marianne et l'environnement, de Thierry Lamouche. — Marianne et l'Europe, d'Yves Beaujard.

233	**0,55 € rouge (4295)**	1 25	0 65
234	**0,55 € rouge (4296)**	1 25	0 65
235	**0,55 € rouge (4297)**	1 25	0 65
236	**0,55 € rouge (4298)**	1 25	0 65
	Nos 225 à 236 (12 val.)	**15 »**	**7 80**

Tirages : 700 000 carnets.

BC225	**La bande carnet, non pliée**	15 »	9 »

2008. – ***Au profit de la Croix-Rouge. "Dessine la planète aux couleurs de la vie !". Offset. Autoadhésifs. Deux bandes de phosphore. Multicolore. Dentelés 11.*** **[C] (Croix-Rouge sans publicité).**
Sans valeur indiquée (validité permanente).
Emis en carnet de 5 paires.

"La Couleur, la Vie" (globe et animaux), dessin d'Inès Scharff.

Globe avec animaux et arbres, dessin d'Elise Boulay.

237 **(Lettre prioritaire 20 g) multicolore (4306)** 1 45 0 70
238 **(Lettre prioritaire 20 g) multicolore (4307)** 1 45 0 70

Tirages : 1 200 000 carnets.

BC237 **La bande carnet, non pliée** 14 50

2008. – *"Bonnes fêtes". Offset. Autoadhésifs. Deux bandes de phosphore. Multicolore. Dentelés 11.* **Ⓒ (carnets commémoratifs).**

Sans valeur indiquée (validité permanente).
Emis en carnet.

Composition avec planètes.

Personnage volant sur le dos d'un oiseau.

Silhouette en fil.

239 **(Lettre prioritaire 20 g) multicolore (21 x 27) (4308)** 1 10 0 55
240 **(Lettre prioritaire 20 g) multicolore (21 x 27) (4309)** 1 10 0 55
241 **(Lettre prioritaire 20 g) multicolore (21 x 27) (4310)** 1 10 0 55

Bouche.

Cœur fleuri.

Composition avec étoiles.

242 **(Lettre prioritaire 20 g) multicolore (21 x 27) (4311)** 1 10 0 55
243 **(Lettre prioritaire 20 g) multicolore (21 x 27) (4312)** 1 10 0 55
244 **(Lettre prioritaire 20 g) multicolore (21 x 27) (4313)** 1 10 0 55

Jambes de danseurs.

Cœur.

245 **(Lettre prioritaire 20 g) multicolore (39 x 25) (4314)** 1 10 0 55
246 **(Lettre prioritaire 20 g) multicolore (39 x 25) (4315)** 1 10 0 55

Composition avec caméléon.

Composition avec ballons.

247 **(Lettre prioritaire 20 g) multicolore (39 x 25) (4316)** 1 10 0 55
248 **(Lettre prioritaire 20 g) multicolore (39 x 25) (4317)** 1 10 0 55

Composition avec étoiles, lune, silhouette de fillette se balançant.

Composition sur fond vert.

249 **(Lettre prioritaire 20 g) multicolore (39 x 25) (4318)** 1 10 0 55
250 **(Lettre prioritaire 20 g) multicolore (39 x 25) (4319)** 1 10 0 55

Composition sur fond fuchsia.

Composition avec silhouette d'un couple avec enfant.

251 **(Lettre prioritaire 20 g) multicolore (39 x 25) (4320)** 1 10 0 55
252 **(Lettre prioritaire 20 g) multicolore (39 x 25) (4321)** 1 10 0 55

N°s 239 à 252 (14 val.) **15 40** **7 70**

Tirages : 3 200 000 carnets.

BC239 **La bande carnet, non pliée** 15 40

2009. – *Métiers d'art. Héliogravure. Autoadhésifs. Deux bandes de phosphore. Multicolore. Dentelés 11.* **Ⓒ (carnets commémoratifs)**

Sans valeur indiquée (validité permanente).
Emis en carnet.

Verre (détail pièce de collection du Musée de Nancy).

Horlogerie (détail horloge des collections du Musée du Louvre).

253 **(Lettre prioritaire 20 g) multicolore** 1 10 0 55
254 **(Lettre prioritaire 20 g) multicolore** 1 10 0 55

Vitrail (détail vitrail de l'église Sainte-Jeanne d'Arc à Rouen).

Ebénisterie (détail décor de meuble des collections du Musée du Louvre).

255 **(Lettre prioritaire 20 g) multicolore** 1 10 0 55
256 **(Lettre prioritaire 20 g) multicolore** 1 10 0 55

Marqueterie (détail décor du château de Valençay).

Faïence de Quimper (détail décor d'assiette - Musée de Sèvres).

257	**(Lettre prioritaire 20 g) multicolore**	1 10	0 55
258	**(Lettre prioritaire 20 g) multicolore**	1 10	0 55

Ferronnerie (détail ornement - Musée de l'Armée, à Paris).

Mosaïque (détail décor avec oiseaux - château de Versailles).

259	**(Lettre prioritaire 20 g) multicolore**	1 10	0 55
260	**(Lettre prioritaire 20 g) multicolore**	1 10	0 55

Email (détail ornement - cathédrale d'Apt).

Tapisserie (détai motifs de roses - château de Malmaison).

261	**(Lettre prioritaire 20 g) multicolore**	1 10	0 55
262	**(Lettre prioritaire 20 g) multicolore**	1 10	0 55

Joaillerie (détail pierres précieuses - château de Malmaison).

Cristal (motifs de fleurs - Cristallerie de Clichy).

263	**(Lettre prioritaire 20 g) multicolore**	1 10	0 55
264	**(Lettre prioritaire 20 g) multicolore**	1 10	0 55
	N°s 253 à 264 (12 val.)	**13 20**	**6 60**

Tirages : 7 000 000 de carnets

BC253	**La bande carnet, non pliée**	13 »	7 »

2009. – ***Saint-Valentin. Cœur 2009 de la Maison de couture Emanuel Ungaro. Héliogravure. Autoadhésif.***

Perroquet et fleurs roses.

Type du T.-P. de même date.

Sans valeur indiquée (validité permanente).

265	**(Lettre prioritaire 20 g) multicolore (4327)**	1 50	0 75

Emis en feuilles de 30 timbres.

2009. – ***Saint-Valentin. Cœur 2009 de la Maison de couture Emanuel Ungaro. Héliogravure. Autoadhésif.*** **Ⓒ (carnets commémoratifs).**

Couple de perroquets et fleurs roses.

Type du T.-P. de même date.

Sans valeur indiquée (validité permanente).

266	**(Lettre prioritaire 50 g) multicolore (4328)**	2 50	1 25

Tirages : 2 500 000 carnets.

Emis en feuilles de 30 timbres et en carnet.

BC266	**La bande carnet, non pliée**	21 »	10 »

2009. – ***Série artistique. Cathédrale Sainte-Cécile (Albi). Offset. Autoadhésif. Dentelé 11.***

Ange avec trompette, détail peinture de la voûte.

Type du T.-P. de 2009.

267	**0,85 € multicolore (4336)**	3 »	1 50

Emis en feuilles de 30 timbres.

2009. – ***Fête du timbre. Personnages de dessins animés des Looney Tunes des studios Warner Bros. © Warner Bros. Enternainment Inc. (s09). Offset. Autoadhésifs. Deux bandes de phosphore. Multicolore. Dentelés 11.*** **Ⓒ (carnets journée du timbre).**

Types des T.-P. de même date.

Sans valeur indiquée (validité permanente).

Emis en carnet de 4 séries.

Vil Coyote sur une planche à surf et Bip-Bip.

Gosminet jouant au tennis de table avec Titi.

268	**(Lettre prioritaire 20 g) multicolore (4338)**	1 10	0 55
269	**(Lettre prioritaire 20 g) multicolore (4339)**	1 10	0 55

Bugs Bunny et Daffy Duck en randonnée.

270 **(Lettre prioritaire 20 g) multicolore (4340)** 1 10 0 55

Tirages : 7 000 000 de carnets.

BC268 **La bande carnet, non pliée** 13 40

2009. – ***Fête du timbre. Personnages de dessins animés des Looney Tunes des studios Warner Bros. © Warner Bros. Entertainment Inc. (s09). Héliogravure. Autoadhésifs. Deux bandes de phosphore. Dentelés 11.***

Types des T.-P. de même date.

Vil Coyote sur une planche à surf et Bip-Bip.

Gosminet jouant au tennis de table avec Titi.

271 **0,56 € multicolore (4338) (268)** 3 » 2 »

272 **0,56 € multicolore (4339) (269)** 3 » 2 »

Bugs Bunny et Daffy Duck en randonnée.

273 **0,56 € multicolore (4340) (270)** 3 » 2 »

Tirage : 500 000 séries.

Emis chacun en petite feuille de 5 timbres attenant chacun à une vignette illustrée différente.

F271 **La feuille** **15 »** **8 »**

F272 **La feuille** **15 »** **8 »**

F273 **La feuille** **15 »** **8 »**

2009. – ***Art. "Femmes du Monde" par l'artiste Titouan Lamazou. Héliogravure. Autoadhésifs. Deux bandes de phosphore. Dentelés 11.*** **🄲 (carnets commémoratifs).**

Sans valeur indiquée (validité permanente).

Emis en carnet.

Helena (Etats-Unis).

Dayu (Indonésie).

274 **(Lettre prioritaire 20 g) multicolore** 1 10 0 55

275 **(Lettre prioritaire 20 g) multicolore** 1 10 0 55

Deborah (France).

Kabari (Bangladesh).

276 **(Lettre prioritaire 20 g) multicolore** 1 10 0 55

277 **(Lettre prioritaire 20 g) multicolore** 1 10 0 55

Mei Mei (Chine).

Malika (Maroc).

278 **(Lettre prioritaire 20 g) multicolore** 1 10 0 55

279 **(Lettre prioritaire 20 g) multicolore** 1 10 0 55

Dayan (Colombie).

Francine (Rwanda).

280 **(Lettre prioritaire 20 g) multicolore** 1 10 0 55

281 **(Lettre prioritaire 20 g) multicolore** 1 10 0 55

Blessing (Nigeria).

Nandita (Inde).

282 **(Lettre prioritaire 20 g) multicolore** 1 10 0 55

283 **(Lettre prioritaire 20 g) multicolore** 1 10 0 55

Elmas (Turquie).

Nadia (Brésil).

284 **(Lettre prioritaire 20 g) multicolore** 1 10 0 55

285 **(Lettre prioritaire 20 g) multicolore** 1 10 0 55

N°s 274 à 285 (12 val.) **13 20** **6 60**

Tirages : 4 150 000 carnets

BC274 **La bande carnet, non pliée** 13 20

2009. – ***Type Marianne de Beaujard. Gravure assistée par ordinateur. Autoadhésifs. Une bande de phosphore à droite, sauf n° 287, 288, 289, 290 : deux bandes de phosphore. Dent. : précoupé vertical en lignes ondulées.***

Marianne et l'Europe.

Types des T.-P. de 2009.

286	**0,73 € vert-olive (4342)**	2 »	1 »
287	**0,90 € lilas-brun clair (4343)**	3 »	1 50
288	**1,30 € bleu ciel (4344)**	3 »	1 50

289	**1,35 € lilas (4345)**	3 »	1 50
290	**2,22 € brun-prune (4346)**	5 »	2 »
	N°s 286 à 290 (5 val.)	**16 »**	**7 50**

Emis en feuilles de 100 timbres.

2009. – ***Flore des régions. La flore du Nord. Héliogravure. Autoadhésifs. Deux bandes de phosphore. Multicolore. Dentelés 11.*** **[C] (carnets commémoratifs).**

Sans valeur indiquée (validité permanente).

Emis en carnet.

La quetsche (Alsace).

La mirabelle (Lorraine).

291	**(Lettre prioritaire 20 g) multicolore**	1 10	0 55
292	**(Lettre prioritaire 20 g) multicolore**	1 10	0 55

Le bouleau (Centre).

L'ophrys abeille (Champagne-Ardenne).

293	**(Lettre prioritaire 20 g) multicolore**	1 10	0 55
294	**(Lettre prioritaire 20 g) multicolore**	1 10	0 55

Le lys (Paris).

La jacinthe des bois (Ile de France).

295	**(Lettre prioritaire 20 g) multicolore**	1 10	0 55
296	**(Lettre prioritaire 20 g) multicolore**	1 10	0 55

L'ajonc (Bretagne).

Le muguet (Pays de la Loire).

297	**(Lettre prioritaire 20 g) multicolore**	1 10	0 55
298	**(Lettre prioritaire 20 g) multicolore**	1 10	0 55

La pomme (Basse Normandie).

Le hêtre (Haute Normandie).

299	**(Lettre prioritaire 20 g) multicolore**	1 10	0 55
300	**(Lettre prioritaire 20 g) multicolore**	1 10	0 55

La rose (Picardie).

La pomme de terre (Nord-Pas de Calais).

301	**(Lettre prioritaire 20 g) multicolore**	1 10	0 55
302	**(Lettre prioritaire 20 g) multicolore**	1 10	0 55
	N°s 291 à 302 (12 val.)	**13 20**	**6 60**

Tirages : 5 000 000 de carnets.

2009. – *Flore des régions. La flore du Sud. Héliogravure. Autoadhésifs. Deux bandes de phosphore. Multicolore. Dentelés 11.* [C] (carnets commémoratifs).

Sans valeur indiquée (validité permanente).

Emis en carnet.

L'olivier (Provence-Alpes-Côte d'Azur) et champ de lavande. La châtaigne (Corse).

303	(Lettre prioritaire 20 g) multicolore	1 10	0 55
304	(Lettre prioritaire 20 g) multicolore	1 10	0 55

Le thym sauvage (Languedoc-Rousillon). La gentiane jaune (Auvergne).

305	(Lettre prioritaire 20 g) multicolore	1 10	0 55
306	(Lettre prioritaire 20 g) multicolore	1 10	0 55

Le cèpe (Limousin). La salicorne (Poitou-Charentes).

307	(Lettre prioritaire 20 g) multicolore	1 10	0 55
308	(Lettre prioritaire 20 g) multicolore	1 10	0 55

Le pin maritime (Aquitaine). L'épicéa (Franche-Comté).

309	(Lettre prioritaire 20 g) multicolore	1 10	0 55
310	(Lettre prioritaire 20 g) multicolore	1 10	0 55

L'awara (Guyane). La violette de Toulouse (Midi-Pyrénées).

311	(Lettre prioritaire 20 g) multicolore	1 10	0 55
312	(Lettre prioritaire 20 g) multicolore	1 10	0 55

La myrtille (Rhône-Alpes). Le cassis (Bourgogne) et vignobles.

313	(Lettre prioritaire 20 g) multicolore	1 10	0 55
314	(Lettre prioritaire 20 g) multicolore	1 10	0 55
	N°s 303 à 314 (12 val.)	**13 20**	**6 60**

Tirages : 5 000 000 de carnets.

2009. – *Timbres pour vacances. Offset. Autoadhésifs. Deux bandes de phosphore. Multicolore. Dentelés 11.* [C] (carnets commémoratifs).

Format 27 x 21 pour les n° 315 à 320.

Format 39 x 25 pour les n° 321 à 328.

Sans valeur indiquée (validité permanente).

Emis en carnet.

Balle de tennis sur un court. Fauteuil en toile. Coccinelle.

315	(Lettre prioritaire 20 g) multicolore	1 10	0 55
316	(Lettre prioritaire 20 g) multicolore	1 10	0 55
317	(Lettre prioritaire 20 g) multicolore	1 10	0 55

Turban rouge. Matelas pneumatique rouge. Tomates en grappe.

318	(Lettre prioritaire 20 g) multicolore	1 10	0 55
319	(Lettre prioritaire 20 g) multicolore	1 10	0 55
320	(Lettre prioritaire 20 g) multicolore	1 10	0 55

Tête de coq.

Coquelicot.

321	**(Lettre prioritaire 20 g) multicolore**	1 10	0 55
322	**(Lettre prioritaire 20 g) multicolore**	1 10	0 55

Plaque d'immatriculation de Bonaire (Antilles néerlandaises).

Papillon aux ailes rouges.

323	**(Lettre prioritaire 20 g) multicolore**	1 10	0 55
324	**(Lettre prioritaire 20 g) multicolore**	1 10	0 55

Framboises.

Heurtoir de porte.

325	**(Lettre prioritaire 20 g) multicolore**	1 10	0 55
326	**(Lettre prioritaire 20 g) multicolore**	1 10	0 55

Mur rouge avec fleurs.

Détail coque de bateau rouge à quai.

327	**(Lettre prioritaire 20 g) multicolore**	1 10	0 55
328	**(Lettre prioritaire 20 g) multicolore**	1 10	0 55
	N°s 315 à 328 (14 val.)	**15 40**	**7 70**

Tirages : 7 000 000 de carnets.

BC315 La bande carnet, non pliée 15 70

2009. – ***La France en timbres. Offset. Autoadhésifs. Deux bandes de phosphore. Multicolore. Dentelés 11.*** **[C] (carnets commémoratifs).**

Sans valeur indiquée (validité permanente).
Emis en carnet.

329	**(Monde 20 g)** *Maisons à colombages (Maison des tanneurs à Strasbourg)*	1 70	0 85
330	**(Monde 20 g)** *Château d'Azay-le-Rideau*	1 70	0 85

331	**(Monde 20 g)** *Cathédrale Notre Dame de Paris*	1 70	0 85
332	**(Monde 20 g)** *Vignobles du Bordelais*	1 70	0 85

333	**(Monde 20 g)** *La promenade des Anglais à Nice avec l'hotel Negresco*	1 70	0 85
334	**(Monde 20 g)** *Le Mont Saint-Michel*	1 70	0 85

335	**(Monde 20 g)** *La Tour Eiffel*	1 70	0 85
336	**(Monde 20 g)** *Saint-Paul-de-Vence (Alpes Maritimes)*	1 70	0 85
	N°s 329 à 336 (8 val.)	**13 60**	**6 80**

Tirages : 1 500 000 carnets

BC329 La bande carnet, non pliée 13 60

2009. – ***Cinquantenaire du Conseil constitutionnel. Héliogravure. Autoadhésif. Deux bandes de phosphore. Dentelé 11.***

Logo.

Type du T.-P. de 2009.

337	**0,56 € multicolore (4347)**	» »	» »

Emis en feuilles de 48 timbres

2009. – *Série artistique. Le Pont-Neuf à Paris, empaqueté par Christo et Jeanne-Claude. Héliogravure. Autoadhésif. Dentelé 11.*

Vue du pont en 1985.

Type du T.-P. de 2009.

338 **1,35 € multicolore (4369)** 3 » 1 50

Emis en feuilles de 30 timbres.

2009. – *Série touristique. Bordeaux (Gironde). Taille-douce. Autoadhésif. Deux bandes de phosphore. Dentelé 11.*

Bâtiments du Port de la Lune.

Type du T.-P. de 2009.

339 **0,56 € multicolore (4370)** 1 50 0 75

Emis en feuilles de 40 timbres.

2009. – *Mémorial Jean Moulin à Caluire (Rhône). Taille-douce. Autoadhésif. Deux bandes de phosphore. Dentelé 11.*

Edifice et portrait de Jean Moulin (1899-1943), résistant.

Type du T.-P. de 2009.

340 **0,56 € multicolore (4371)** 1 50 0 75

Emis en feuilles de 48 timbres.

TIMBRES POUR LA POSTE AERIENNE

Jusqu'en 1959 les cotes de la colonne de gauche concernent les timbres neufs avec gomme d'origine intacte et sans charnière, celles de la colonne centrale les timbres neufs avec charnière légère, celles de la colonne de droite les timbres oblitérés.

1927. – ***Premier Salon international de l'Aviation et de la Navigation, à Marseille. Timbres-poste de 1900-06 (Merson, n°s 145 et 123) surchargés. Dentelés 13½ x 14.***

1	**2 f. orange et vert-bleu (B) (145)**	475 »	250 »	250 »
	a. (Coin de l'écusson cassé)	2 100 »	1 400 »	1 400 »
2	**5 f. bleu et chamois (123)**	475 »	250 »	250 »

Tirage : 90 000 paires. Vente : 65 000 paires.

Très bon centrage (+100 %).

1928. – ***Timbres-poste de 1923-27 (Berthelot, n° 243 et Pasteur, n° 181) surchargés. Dentelés.***

3	**10 f. sur 90 c. rouge (243)**	4 500 »	3 000 »	3 000 »
	a. (Surch. renv)	27 000 »	20 000 »	20 000 »
4	**10 f. s. 1 f. 50 bleu (181)**	17 500 »	12 500 »	12 500 »

Tirages : 2 700 et 900.

Surcharge espacée (8 mm au lieu de 6 mm entre la base du 1 et le second trait).

3b	10 f. s. 90 c.	6 500 »	4 750 »	4 750 »
3c	(Surch. renv)		47 500 »	
4a	10 f. s. 1 f. 50	21 500 »	14 500 »	14 500 »

Surcharge espacée tenant à non espacée.

3d	10 f. s. 90 c.	12 500 »	9 750 »	9 750 »
3e	10 f. s. 90 c. (Surcharge renversée)		90 000 »	
4b	10 f. s. 1 f. 50	48 000 »	33 000 »	

Ces timbres ont été émis à bord du paquebot Ile-de-France et servaient uniquement pour la surtaxe aérienne.

1930. – ***Avion survolant Marseille. Taille-douce. Dentelés 13.***

5	**1 f. 50 carmin**	47 »	26 »	4 60
	(Sur lettre)			6 10
6	**1 f. 50 bleu**	47 »	26 »	2 30
	(Sur lettre)			4 60
	a. outremer	150 »	70 »	25 »
	b. outremer vif	805 »	575 »	460 »

Tirages : 6 000 000 et 36 800 000.

Le n° 6a fut émis à l'occasion de l'Exposition Internationale de la Poste Aérienne, à Paris ; pendant la durée de celle-ci, un certain nombre d'exemplaires ont été perforés comme ci-dessous :

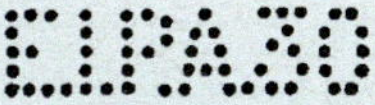

6c	1 f. 50 (+5 f.) outremer	875 »	580 »	450 »
6d	1 f. 50 (+5 f.) carmin	5 000 »	3 850 »	5 350 »

1934. – ***25e anniversaire de la traversée de la Manche par Louis Blériot. Taille-douce. Dentelé 13.***

Monoplan de Blériot.

7	**2 f. 25 lilas**	47 »	25 »	7 »
	(Sur lettre)			11 50
	(Seul sur lettre)			20 »

Tirage : 8 100 000.

1936. – ***Avion survolant Paris. Taille-douce. Dentelés 13.***

8	**85 c. vert foncé**	10 »	3 »	3 »
	(Sur lettre)			6 10
	(Seul sur lettre)			11 50
	a. vert clair	40 »	25 »	5 »
9	**1 f. 50 bleu**	25 »	13 »	6 »
	(Sur lettre)			9 20
	(Seul sur lettre)			15 50

10	**2 f. 25 violet**	40 »	24 »	7 50
	(Sur lettre)			12 25
	(Seul sur lettre)			23 »
11	**2 f. 50 rose**	51 »	30 »	9 20
	(Sur lettre)			15 50
	(Seul sur lettre)			23 »

12	**3 f. outremer**	44 »	25 »	2 30
	(Sur lettre)			6 10
	(Seul sur lettre)			23 »
13	**3 f. 50 brun-jaune**	120 »	75 »	27 »
	(Sur lettre)			30 »
	(Seul sur lettre)			46 »
	N°s 8 à 13 (6 val.)	**290 »**	**170 »**	**55 »**

Tirages : 2 400 000, 5 000 000, 1 100 000, 1 400 000, 6 000 000 et 1 000 000.

14	**50 f. vert-jaune**	2 000 »	1 100 »	420 »
	(Sur lettre)			610 »
	(Seul sur lettre)			1 250 »
	a. vert	2 100 »	1 200 »	450 »
	b. vert foncé	2 400 »	1 400 »	700 »

Tirage : 118 000.

1936. – *Avion survolant Paris. Taille-douce. Burelage rose. Dentelé 12½ x 13.*

Caudron "Simoun", sur Paris.

15	**50 f. outremer**	1 500 »	800 »	400 »
	(Sur lettre)			610 »
	(Seul sur lettre)			1 150 »
	a. (Spécimen)	7 000 »	5 500 »	

Imprimé par l'Institut de Gravure à Paris.

Tirage : 210 000.

1946-47. – *Série mythologique. Taille-douce. Dentelés 13.*

Sagittaire.

Iris.

16	**40 f. vert foncé**	1 »	0 50	0 50
17	**50 f. rouge**	1 »	0 50	0 30
	a. rose	1 »	0 50	0 50

Egine enlevée par Jupiter.

Char du Soleil.

18	**100 f. bleu foncé**	9 »	6 »	1 30
	a. bleu-noir	11 »	7 65	1 55
19	**200 f. vermillon**	7 »	4 »	1 90
	a. rge-sang (pap. carton)	60 »	30 »	8 50
	b. rge fcé (pap. normal)	12 »	9 20	1 85
	N°s 16 à 19 (4 val.)	**18 »**	**11 »**	**4 »**
	La série, non dentelée		460 »	

Tirages : 51 970 775, 67 757 250, 19 505 000 et 7 656 975.

1947. – *12e Congrès de l'Union Postale Universelle à Paris. Vue de Paris. Taille-douce. Dentelé 13.*

Les ponts de Paris.

20	**500 f. vert foncé**	65 »	42 »	54 »

Tirage : 520 000.

F20	**La feuille de 10 timbres**	700 »

1947. – *Surtaxe au profit de l'Entraide française. Taille-douce. Dentelés 13.*

Antoine de Saint-Exupéry (1900-1944).

Jean Dagnaux (1891-1940).

21	**50 f. +30 f. brun-lilas**	4 »	2 30	3 85
22	**100 f. +70 f. bleu**	5 »	3 »	4 60
	La paire, non dentelée		230 »	

Tirage : 975 000 paires.

Le n° 21 a été repris en 1994 pour un aérogramme. Voir à la rubrique des "Entiers postaux" (n° 1021).

1948. – *Surtaxe au profit de l'Entraide française. Cinquantenaire du premier vol de l'avion d'Ader (1897). Taille-douce. Dentelé 13.*

23	**40 f. +10 f. bleu foncé**	2 »	1 25	1 85
	a. (Non dentelé)		115 »	
	b. (hachures sur "FRANCE")	16 »	10 »	5 »

Tirage : 1 500 000.

1949. – *Vues stylisées de grandes villes. Taille-douce. Dentelés 13.*

24	100 f. brun-violet *Lille*	1 50	1 »	0 50
25	200 f. vert *Bordeaux*	17 50	10 »	1 »
	a. (Papier épais)	60 »	33 »	23 »

26	300 f. violet *Lyon*	20 »	14 »	13 »
27	500 f. rouge *Marseille*	77 »	45 »	7 »
	N°s 24 à 27 (4 val.)	**116 »**	**70 »**	**21 50**
	La série, non dentelée		460 »	

Tirages : 85 152 500, 8 207 500, 3 212 500 et 2 827 500.

1949. – *Congrès international de Télégraphie et Téléphonie. Vue de Paris. Taille-douce. Dentelé 13.*

Grand Palais et pont Alexandre III.

28	**100 f. rouge-brun**	9 »	6 »	7 »
	a. (Non dentelé)		230 »	

Tirage : 1 625 000.

1950. – *Vue de Paris. Papier bleuté. Dentelé 13.*

29	**1000 f. noir et brun violacé**	165 »	95 »	30 »
	a. (Non dentelé)		690 »	

Tirage : 1 137 500.

F29	**La feuille de 10 timbres**		1 800 »	

1954. – *Prototypes. Taille-douce. Dentelés 13.*

Dassault "Mystère IV".

Nord-Aviation "Noratlas".

30	**100 f. bleu et brun-rouge**	3 50	3 »	0 30
31	**200 f. brun-noir et outremer**	11 50	7 »	0 50

Fouga "Magister".

Bréguet "Provence"et vue générale du port d'Alger.

32	**500 f. jaune-orange et rouge**	250 »	110 »	16 »
33	**1000 f. bleu-vert, bleu-noir et brun-rouge**	135 »	80 »	20 »
	N°s 30 à 33 (4 val.)	**400 »**	**200 »**	**36 80**
	La série, non dentelée		500 »	

Un 2 f. au type du 200 f. a paru en 1960 (n° 38).

1955. – *Troisième anniversaire de la mort de l'aviatrice Maryse Bastié (1898-1952). Taille-douce. Dentelé 13.*

34	**50 f. rose et brun-violet**	8 »	5 »	5 »
	a. (Non dentelé)		92 »	

Tirage : 1 485 000.

1957-59. – *Prototypes. Taille-douce. Dentelés 13.*

Morane-Saulnier 760 "Paris".

35	**300 f. vert foncé, olive et bleu-vert**	8 »	4 60	3 85
	a. (Non dentelé)		61 »	

Sud-Aviation "Caravelle".

Hélicoptère "Alouette".

36	**500 f. bleu foncé et noir**	35 »	23 »	4 60
	a. (Non dentelé)		140 »	
37	**1000 f. olive, lilas et noir**	77 »	46 »	27 »
	a. (Non dentelé)		170 »	

A partir de 1960 les cotes de la colonne de gauche concernent les timbres neufs sans charnière, celles de la colonne de droite, les timbres oblitérés.

1960-64. – *Prototypes. Types de 1954-59 avec valeur en nouveau franc. Taille-douce. Dentelés 13.*

38	**2 f. brun-noir et outremer (31)**	2 »	0 30
	a. outremer	3 85	0 50
39	**3 f. vert foncé, olive et bleu-vert (35)**	2 »	0 20
	a. vert foncé et bleu-vert	3 »	0 30

40	**5 f. bleu foncé et noir (36)**	4 »	1 »
41	**10 f. olive, lilas et noir (37)**	16 »	2 50
	a. olive, rose et noir	30 »	3 »
	Nos 38 à 41 (4 val.)	**24 »**	**4 »**
	La série, non dentelée	305 »	

1965. – *Dassault "Mystère 20". Taille-douce. Dentelé 13.*

"Mystère 20".

42	**2 f. bleu-vert et bleu**	1 »	0 30
	a. (Non dentelé)	61 »	

1969. – *Premier vol de l'avion supersonique "Concorde". Taille-douce. Dentelé 13.*

43	**1 f. bleu et bleu-noir**	1 »	0 65
	a. (Non dentelé)	200 »	

Voir également à la rubrique des Entiers postaux (Aérogramme 1001).

Des timbres à ce type ont été émis dans les différents Territoires d'Outre-Mer (Voir Tome 2, 1re partie).

1970. – *Mermoz (1901-1936) et Saint-Exupéry (1900-1944). Pionniers de la Poste Aérienne. Taille-douce. Dentelé 13.*

44	**20 f. bleu et gris-bleu**	12 50	0 65
	a. (Non dentelé)	140 »	
	b. (Paire horizontale)	30 »	
	c. (Paire horizontale avec intervalle blanc)	35 »	

Le 44b provient du tirage de 1970 (feuilles de 25), le 44c de feuilles de 10.

1971. – *Centenaire de la poste par ballons montés. Taille-douce. Dentelé 13.*

45	**95 c. multicolore**	1 »	0 80
	a. (Non dentelé)	100 »	

1971. – *Didier Daurat (1891-1969) et Raymond Vanier. Pionniers de la Poste Aérienne. Taille-douce. Dentelé 13.*

46	**5 f. bleu-nuit, sépia et vert**	3 »	0 30
	a. (Non dentelé)	77 »	

1972. – *Hélène Boucher (1908-1934) et Maryse Hilsz (1903-1946). Pionniers de la Poste Aérienne. Taille-douce. Dentelé 13.*

47	**10 f. violet et noir**	6 »	0 50
	a. (Non dentelé)	61 »	

1973. – *Guillaumet et Codos (1896-1960). Pionniers de la Poste Aérienne. Taille-douce. Dentelé 13.*

48 **15 f. gris-bleu, carmin et violet-brun** 9 » 0 80
a. (Non dentelé) 77 »

1976. – *Mise en service commercial de "Concorde" Paris-Rio de Janeiro 1976. Taille-douce. Dentelé 13.*

49 **1 f. 70 rouge, bleu et noir** 1 » 0 65
a. (Non dentelé) 155 »

1977. – *Cinquantenaire de la traversée de l'Atlantique-Nord par Charles Lindbergh (1902-1974) et de la disparition de Nungesser (1892-1927) et Coli (1881-1927). Taille-douce. Dentelé 13.*

50 **1 f. 90 bleu-vert, olive et bleu-noir** 1 » 0 80
a. (Non dentelé) 77 »

1978. – *65ᵉ anniversaire de la première liaison postale aérienne officielle entre Villacoublay et Pauillac. Taille-douce. Dentelé 13.*

51 **1 f. 50 bleu, vert foncé et brun-rouge** 1 » 0 65
a. (Non dentelé) 77 »

1979. – *Salon international de l'Aéronautique et de l'Espace. Taille-douce. Dentelé 13.*

52 **1 f. 70 outremer, brun-rouge et orange** 1 25 1 10
a. (Non dentelé) 110 »

1980. – *Cinquantenaire de la première traversée Paris-New York sans escale, par Costes (1892-1973) et Bellonte. Taille-douce. Dentelé 13.*

Avion "Point d'interrogation".

53 **2 f. 50 bleu et rouge-brun** 1 40 0 50
a. (Non dentelé) 84 »

1981. – *34ᵉ Salon international de l'Aéronautique et de l'Espace. Taille-douce. Dentelé 13.*

Avions "Mirage 2000".

54 **2 f. bleu, violet et rose** 2 » 0 65
a. (Non dentelé) 84 »

1981. – *Hommages aux aviateurs Dieudonné Costes (1892-1973) et Joseph Le Brix (1899-1931). Première traversée de l'Atlantique-Sud sans escale, 1927. Taille-douce. Dentelé 13.*

Portraits et avion Bréguet XIX GR "Nungesser-Coli".

55 **10 f. noir et rouge** 5 » 0 50
a. (Non dentelé) 70 »

1982. – *Hydravion Laté 300 "Croix du Sud". Taille-douce. Dentelé 13.*

L'hydravion au décollage et noms de son équipage.

56 **1 f. 60 bleu et violet** 1 » 1 »
a. (Non dentelé) 61 »

Tirage : 8 000 000.

1984. – ***Avion bimoteur Farman F 60 Goliath. Taille-douce. Dentelé 13.***

57 **15 f. bleu foncé** 6 » 0 80
a. (Non dentelé) 61 »

Impression fine. Papier couché azurant (1987).

57b 15 f. bleu-gris 10 » 1 »

1985. – ***Hydravion CAMS 53. Taille-douce. Dentelé 13.***

58 **20 f. orange** 8 » 0 80
a. (Non dentelé) 61 »

Impression fine. Papier couché azurant (1987).

58b 20 f. orange 15 » 1 50

1986. – ***Trimoteur Wibault 283. Taille-douce. Dentelé 13.***

Profil et face de l'appareil.

59 **30 f. violet** 12 » 2 »
a. (Non dentelé) 61 »

Impression fine. Papier couché azurant (1992).

59b 30 f. violet 26 » 3 »

1987. – ***Trimoteur Dewoitine 338. Taille-douce. Dentelé 13.***

60 **50 f. vert** 16 » 6 »
a. (Non dentelé) 61 »

1997. – ***Biplan Breguet XIV. Héliogravure. Dentelé 13 x 12½.***

61 **20 f. multicolore** 10 » 2 »
a. (avec bord de feuille illustré)
(Dentelé 13 x 13½) 20 » 5 »
b. (Sans bord de feuille illustré)
(Dentelé 13 x 13½) 10 » 2 »

Le timbre "a" a été émis en petite feuille de 10 timbres avec marges illustrées.

F61a **La feuille** 150 »

1998. – ***Biplan Potez 25. Héliogravure. Dentelé 13 x 12½.***

62 **30 f. multicolore** 10 » 3 »
a. (Dentelé 13 x 13½) 18 » 8 »
b. (Sans "Poste Aérienne 1998", sans valeur faciale et ITVF) 10 000 »

Le timbre "a" a été émis en petite feuille de 10 timbres avec marges illustrées.

F62a **La feuille** 180 »

1999. – ***Airbus A300-B4. Héliogravure. Dentelé 13 x 12½.***

63 **15 f. multicolore** 8 » 1 »
a. (Dentelé 13 x 13½) 20 » 7 »

Le timbre "a" a été émis en petite feuille de 10 timbres avec marges illustrées.

F63 **La feuille** 200 »

2000. – ***Couzinet 70. Héliogravure. Dentelé 13 x 12½.***

64 **50 f. (7,62 €) multicolore** 18 » 7 »
a. (Dentelé 13 x 13½) 25 » 12 »

Le timbre "a" a été émis en petite feuille de 10 timbres avec marges illustrées..

F64a **La feuille** 250 »

2002. – ***30e anniversaire du premier vol de l'Airbus A300. Héliogravure. Deux bandes de phosphore. Dentelé 13 x 13½.***

65 **3,00 € multicolore** 7 » 3 »
a. (Papier mat) 12 » 7 »

Emis également en petite feuille de 10 timbres avec marges illustrées.

F65 **La feuille** 120 »

2003. – ***Hommage à l'aviatrice Jacqueline Auriol (1917-2000). Taille-douce et offset. Deux bandes de phosphore. Dentelé 13.***

Portrait, avion.

66 **4,00 € multicolore** 10 » 4 »
a. (Légende et noir omis) » »

Emis également en petite feuille de 10 timbres avec marges illustrées.

F66 **La feuille** 110 »

2004. – ***Personnalité. Hommage à Marie Marvingt (1875-1963), aviatrice, créatrice de l'avion sanitaire. Taille-douce et offset. Dentelé 13.***

Portrait de l'infirmière et assistante en chirurgie, avion.

67 **5,00 € multicolore** 11 » 5 »

Le timbre "a" a été émis en petite feuille de 10 timbres avec marges illustrées.

F67a **La feuille** 120 »

2005. – ***Personnalité. Hommage à Adrienne Bolland (1895-1975), aviatrice. Taille-douce et offset. Deux bandes de phosphore. Multicolore. Dentelé 13.***

68 **2,00 €** ***Portrait du premier pilote à avoir traversé la cordillère des Andes le 1er avril 1921 à bord d'un Caudron G3 (dessin de l'avion)*** 4 » 2 »

Emis également en petite feuille de 10 timbres avec marges illustrées.

F68 **La feuille** 50 »

2006. – ***Avion Airbus A380. Héliogravure. Deux bandes de phosphore. Dentelé 13 x 13¼.***

69 **3,00 € multicolore** 6 » 3 »

Emis également en petite feuille de 10 timbres avec marges illustrées.

F69 **La feuille** 70 »

2007. – ***Centenaire de l'hélicoptère. Héliogravure. Deux bandes de phosphore. Dentelé 13 x 12¾.***

70 **3,00 €** ***Dessin de l'engin de Paul Cornu et hélicoptère EC 130*** 6 » 3 »
a. (Dentelé 13 x 13¼) 7 » 3 »

Le n° 70a provient d'une petite feuille de 10 timbres avec marges illustrées

F70a **La feuille** 70 »

2008. – ***La Patrouille de France. Taille-douce et offset. Deux bandes de phosphore. Dentelé 13.***

71 **3,00 €** ***Avions Alphajet, Arc de triomphe de l'Etoile (Paris)*** 6 » 3 »

Emis également en petite feuille de 10 timbres avec marges illustrées

F71 **La feuille** 70 »

POSTE AERIENNE MILITAIRE

1943. – ***Timbres-poste de 1940-41 surchargés. Dentelés.***

1	**50 c. s. 75 c. brun-rouge (477)**	1 300 »	1 100 »	1 400 »
2	**1 f. rouge (514)**	1 100 »	840 »	1 100 »
3	**1 f. 50 brun-rouge (517)**	240 »	185 »	270 »

Idem, sur timbres de Mauritanie de 1938.

4	**2 f. lilas-rose (90)**	535 »	460 »	535 »
5	**3 f. vert (91)**	535 »	460 »	535 »

Idem, sur timbres de Sénégal de 1938-40.

6	**1 f. brun-rouge (164)**	650 »	535 »	535 »
7	**1 f. 75 outremer (148)**	765 »	645 »	645 »

Il existe quelques exemplaires d'autres timbres de France (n°s 491, 499, 500 et 512) d'Algérie (n° 133) et du Sénégal (n°s 121, 127 et 165) et revêtus de la même surcharge. (Les timbres se trouvant à bord, à l'agence postale embarquée, ont été utilisés).

Les lettres connues sont adressées aux États-Unis, au Sénégal et en Algérie lors du séjour du RICHELIEU à New York en 1943 (février à octobre) (*Valeur... à partir de* 2300 »).

Le RICHELIEU séjourna ensuite en Grande-Bretagne où il fut incorporé à la Royal Navy de novembre 1943 à mars 1944. Pendant cette période furent utilisés à bord les timbres et entiers postaux de Grande-Bretagne (*Valeur... à partir de* 2450 »).

Après diverses missions dans le Pacifique, le bâtiment a séjourné à Casablanca d'octobre 1944 à février 1945. Pendant cette période furent utilisés à bord les timbres et entiers des Etats-Unis avec la surcharge RF de Casablanca (voir ci-dessous).

1944-45. – *Timbre de poste aérienne n° 26 des États-Unis surchargés. Dentelés.*

I

II

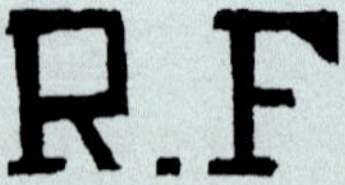

III

IV

8	**6 c. *rouge* (Type I) *(Casablanca)***	88 »	500 »
9	**6 c. *rouge* (Type II) *(Oran)***	100 »	535 »
10	**6 c. *rouge* (Type III) *(Alger)***	88 »	500 »
11	**6 c. *rouge* (Type IV) *(Marseille)***	215 »	840 »

La colonne de droite concerne les timbres oblitérés sur lettre.

En France métropolitaine ces cachets furent utilisés en 1945 et 1946.

Les plis avec marque de censure américaine sont rares.

6 cents rouge... à partir de 1250 ».

Entier postal, 6 cents orange à partir de 1850 ».

ALSACE-LORRAINE

Guerre de 1870-71

TIMBRES DITS D'ALSACE-LORRAINE

1870. – *Typographie. Dentelés 13½ x 14½.*

1	**1 c. vert-bronze**	**120 »**	**120 »**
	(Sur lettre)		230 »
	a. vert-olive	115 »	115 »
2	**2 c. brun-rouge**	**225 »**	**240 »**
	(Sur lettre)		345 »
	(Seul sur lettre)		1 100 »
	a. brun-lilas	210 »	225 »
3	**4 c. gris-lilas**	**250 »**	**135 »**
	(Sur lettre)		210 »
	(Seul sur lettre)		690 »
	a. gris-noir	275 »	150 »
4	**5 c. vert-jaune**	**250 »**	**20 »**
	(Sur lettre)		46 »
	(Seul sur lettre)		155 »
	a. vert foncé	275 »	20 »
5	**10 c. bistre-brun**	**200 »**	**8 »**
	(Sur lettre)		23 »
	a. bistre-orange (Burelage citron)	225 »	12 »
6	**20 c. bleu**	**225 »**	**20 »**
	(Sur lettre)		30 »
	a. bleu laiteux	250 »	20 »
7	**25 c. brun-noir**	**270 »**	**135 »**
	(Sur lettre)		305 »
	(Seul sur lettre)		385 »
	a. brun clair	300 »	135 »

Ces timbres furent émis le 6 septembre 1870 par les armées allemandes occupant le territoire français : ils eurent cours forcé dans les départements envahis et n'ont pas été réimprimés.

Burelage renversé.

Ces timbres étant imprimés en deux fois, les feuilles qui se trouvaient à l'envers, au second passage, produisirent des timbres avec burelage renversé.

La distinction des burelages droits et renversés est aisée à faire : le fond des timbres est couvert d'arcs de cercle qui se coupent ; la convexité est tournée vers le bas dans les burelages droits (︶︶), vers le haut dans les burelages renversés (︵︵).

1b	1 c.	625 »	850 »
2b	2 c.	315 »	800 »
3b	4 c.	315 »	260 »
4b	5 c.	8 050 »	805 »
5b	10 c.	315 »	25 »
6b	20 c.	400 »	125 »
7b	25 c.	900 »	400 »

Guerre de 1939-1945

Jusqu'en 1953, les cotes de la colonne de gauche concernent les timbres neufs avec gomme d'origine intacte et sans charnière, celles de la colonne centrale les timbres neufs avec charnière légère, celles de la colonne de droite les timbres oblitérés.

1940. – *Timbres d'Allemagne de 1933-36 (Hindenburg) surchargés. Dentelés.*

8	**3 p. bistre-brun**	0 80	0 50	0 50
9	**4 p. bleu-ardoise**	0 80	0 50	0 50

10	**5 p. vert vif**	0 80	0 50	0 50
11	**6 p. vert foncé**	0 80	0 50	0 50
	a. (Surch. renversée)		1 000 »	
12	**8 p. rouge-orange**	0 80	0 50	0 50
	a. (Surch. renversée)		1 000 »	
13	**10 p. marron**	0 80	0 50	0 50
14	**12 p. rouge carminé**	1 25	0 65	0 65
15	**15 p. lilas**	1 25	0 65	0 65
16	**20 p. bleu**	1 85	0 80	0 80
17	**25 p. outremer**	1 85	0 80	0 80
18	**30 p. brun-olive**	1 85	0 80	0 80
19	**40 p. lilas-rose**	2 75	1 20	1 20
20	**50 p. vert et noir**	9 20	3 55	3 55
21	**60 p. lie-de-vin et noir**	9 20	3 55	3 55
22	**80 p. bleu et noir**	23 »	9 »	9 »
23	**100 p. jaune-orange et noir**	23 »	8 »	8 »
	N°s 8 à 23 (16 val.)	**80 »**	**32 »**	**32 »**

24	**3 p. bistre-brun**	1 25	0 65	0 65
25	**4 p. bleu-ardoise**	1 25	0 65	0 65
26	**5 p. vert vif**	1 25	0 65	0 65
27	**6 p. vert foncé**	1 25	0 65	0 65
28	**8 p. rouge-orange**	1 25	0 65	0 65
29	**10 p. marron**	1 50	0 80	0 80
30	**12 p. rouge carminé**	1 50	0 80	0 80
31	**15 p. lilas**	1 50	0 80	0 80
32	**20 p. bleu**	2 »	1 »	1 »
33	**25 p. outremer**	2 »	1 »	1 »
34	**30 p. brun-olive**	2 75	1 15	1 15
35	**40 p. lilas-rose**	3 »	1 50	1 50
36	**50 p. vert et noir**	8 »	3 55	3 55
37	**60 p. lie-de-vin et noir**	8 »	3 55	3 55
38	**80 p. bleu et noir**	23 50	9 20	9 20
39	**100 p. jaune-orange et noir**	23 »	8 40	8 40
	N°s 24 à 39 (16 val.)	**83 »**	**35 »**	**35 »**

une qualité irréprochable pour transmettre
le meilleur
Yvert & Tellier - 2 rue de l'Étoile
80094 Amiens cedex 3 - www.yvert.com
YVERT&TELLIER

CORRESPONDANCES TRANSPORTÉES PAR

BALLONS MONTÉS

PENDANT LE SIÈGE DE PARIS

(18 septembre 1870 - 27 janvier 1871)

Pendant le Siège, le transport du courrier à destination de l'extérieur fut assuré par aérostats. Au total, 67 ballons quittèrent la capitale, parmi lesquels on distingue : les ballons de la Compagnie des Aérostiers puis de la Compagnie des Aéronautes (dont les plis, à elles confiés portent leur cachet au dos) ; les ballons de l'Administration des Postes et les ballons privés, lesquels ne pouvaient, officiellement emporter de la correspondance.

Il est à peu près établi que, sur les 67 ballons, 56 seulement ont transporté officiellement des plis.

Le plus souvent, il est malaisé de déterminer le ballon ayant transporté le pli ; dans ce cas, il est alors dénommé « pli ordinaire » (§ A). Par contre, l'identification certaine du ballon donne une plus-value très nette au pli, qui est alors dénommé « ballon identifié » (§ B).

D'autres plus-values peuvent intervenir ; elles proviennent :

a) des timbres utilisés pour l'affranchissement (§ C) ;
b) de la destination (§ D) ;
c) de la nature du pli : Lettres-Journaux (§ E) ;
Journaux (§ F) ;
Correspondance de Presse (§ G) ;
Circulaires officielles ou privées (§ H) ;
d) des marques de départ, de transit ou d'arrivée (§ J).

A - PLIS ORDINAIRES

Les cotes s'entendent pour un affranchissement normal constitué :

soit avec deux 10 c. de l'Empire lauré (n° 28)
soit avec un 20 c. de l'Empire lauré (n° 29) ;
soit avec un 20 c. du Siège de Paris (n° 37) ;
soit (cartes postales) un 10 c. de l'Empire lauré (n° 28).

Le pli, à partir de ...... 300 ».

B - BALLONS IDENTIFIÉS

Les ballons dont le nom est suivi de la lettre A ont été affrêtés par la Compagnie des Aérostiers, ou par la Compagnie des Aéronautes.

20 c. Siège oblitéré Etoile 1 ; Cachet à date de Paris : Place de la Bourse - 19 Nov. 70 - 6e Levée
à destination de la Côte St André (Isère). Arrivée au verso : cachet à date du 27 Nov. 70.
Voyagé par le Ballon L'ARCHIMÈDE

Nom des ballons	*Cachets de départ*	*Cachets d'arrivée*	*Valeur*
Le Neptune ....A	19 au 22-9-70	23 au 25-9-70	13 000 »
La Ville de Florence	23 et 24-9-70	27 et 28-9-70	995 »
Les États-Unis	25 au 28-9-70	29-9 au 3-10-70	765 »
Le Céleste	28 et 29-9-70	antérieurs au 7-10-70	535 »

Nom des ballons	*Cachets de départ*	*Cachets d'arrivée*	*Valeur*
Le non dénommé n° 1	27 au 29-9-70	sans ou du 15 au 22-10-70	385 »
L'Armand Barbès A	30-9 au 6-10-70	antérieurs au 11-10-70	305 »
Le non dénommé n° 2	30-9 au 8-10-70	Trouvé à La Courneuve le 10-10-70	4 600 »
Le Washington	7 au 11-10-70	12 au 14-10-70	305 »
Le Louis Blanc A	7 au 11-10-70	12 au 14-10-70	305 »
Le Godefroy Cavaignac	12 et 13-10-70	15 au 18-10-70	305 »
Le Jean-Bart n° 1	11 au 14-10-70 (1re levée)	15 au 17-10-70	305 »
Le Jules Favre n° 1	14 et 15-10-70	17 au 19-10-70	305 »
Le Jean-Bart n° 2	14 et 15-10-70	17 au 19-10-70	305 »
Le Victor Hugo A	16 au 18 (1re levée)10-70	20 au 22-10-70	400 »
Le Lafayette	18 (autres levées) 10-70	19 au 23-10-70	430 »
Le Garibaldi A	19 au 21-10-70	23-10 au 3-11-70	400 »
Le Montgolfier	22 et 23-10-70	sans	800 »
Le Vauban	24 au 26-10-70	27-10 au 4-11-70	360 »
Le Colonel Charras A	27 au 29 (2e levée) 10-70	30-10 au 3-11-70	360 »
Le Fulton	29 (autres levées) 10 au 1-11-70	3-4-11-70	345 »
Le Ferdinand Flocon A	2, 3-11-70	5, 6 au 8-11-70	360 »
Le Galilée	2 au 4 (1re levée) 11-70	sans ou 5, 6-11-70	575 »
La Ville de Châteaudun A	4 (autres levées),		
....	5 et 6-11 (1re levée)	5 au 10-11-70	325 »
La Gironde	6 au 8 (1re levée), 11-70	9 au 11-11-70	360 »
Le Daguerre	8 (autres levées) au 11-11-70 .	sans arrivée	765 »
....	....	20 au 29-11-70	550 »
Le Général Uhrich A	12 au 18-11-70	20 au 27-11-70	305 »
L'Archimède	19 et 20-11-70	antérieurs au 30-11-70	360 »
La Ville d'Orléans A	12 au 24-11-70	10-12-70 et 1-71 accidenté	1 700 »
....	....	non accid.	800 »
Le Jacquard	24 au 28-11-70	3 au 28-12-70	2 600 »
Le Jules Favre n° 2 A	28 au 30-11-70	antérieurs au 5-12-70.	305 »
Le Franklin	1er au 4-12-70	5 et 6-12-70	385 »
Le Denis-Papin	5 et 6-12-70	7-12-70	450 »
L'Armée de Bretagne A	5 et 6-12-70	8 au 10-12-70	305 »
Le Général Renault A	7 au 10-12-70	antérieurs au 15-12-70	490 »
La Ville de Paris A	10 (7e levée) au 13-12-70	sans ou 26-7-71	475 »
Le Parmentier	14, 15 et 16-12-70	22 au 31-12-70	360 »
Le Davy	17-12-70	18 au 21-12-70	610 »
Le Général Chanzy A	18 (1re à 6e levée), 12-70	sans	2 000 »
Le Lavoisier	18 (7e levée) au 21-12-70	22 au 26-12-70	370 »
La Délivrance A	22-12-70	23 au 26-12-70	385 »
Le Tourville	23 au 26-12-70	27 à 29-12-70	370 »
Le Bayard	27 et 28-12-70	30-12-70 au 3-1-71	385 »
L'Armée de la Loire A	29 au 30-12-70	1er au 3-1-71	385 »
Le Newton	31-12-70 au 3-1-71	antérieurs au 9-1-71	385 »
Le Duquesne	4 au 8-1-71	10 au 18-1-71	385 »
Le Gambetta A	9-1-71	11 au 17-1-71	385 »
Le Kepler	10-1-71	11, 12 et 13-1-71	500 »
Le Général Faidherbe A	11 et 12-1-71	13, 14, 15-1-71	385 »
Le Vaucanson	13 et 14-1-71	15, 16 et 17-1-71	375 »
La Poste de Paris A	15 au 17-1-71	21 au 29-1-71	450 »
Le Général Bourbaki A	18 et 19-1-71	23 au 29-1-71	385 »
Le Général Daumesnil	20 et 21-1-71	22, 23-1-71	370 »
Le Torricelli	22 et 23-1-71	25 au 30-1-71	560 »
Le Richard Wallace A	24 au 26-1-71	à partir du 7-2-71	5 750 »
Le Général Cambronne	27-1-71	28-1 au 4-2-71	1 550 »

Les cotes s'entendent pour affranchissement normal constitué comme décrit au paragraphe A.

C - AFFRANCHISSEMENTS

10 c. Empire, non dentelé		
20 c.	3 450	»
40 c.	6 000	»
1 c. Empire, dentelé		
5 c.	1 500	»
10 c.	535	»
20 c. Empire, dentelé	385	»
40 c.	840	»
80 c.	2 200	»
1 c. Empire lauré		
2 c.		
4 c. Empire lauré		
30 c.	125	»
40 c.	230	»
80 c.	765	»
10 c. Siège	275	»
10 c. Sage Tête-bêche	15 000	»
40 c.	245	»

D - DESTINATIONS

Certaines lettres transportées étaient à destination de pays lointains (voir ci-dessous) ; elles sont relativement rares. Le chiffre ( ) suivant le nom du pays indique le montant de l'affranchissement courant :

France, territ. occupés (20)
cachet arrivée franç. . . . 1 250 »
allem . . . . 2 850 »
France (Corse) (20) . . . 1 300 »
Allemagne (40 ou 50),
sans cachet d'arrivée 1 000 »
avec cachet d'arrivée . 2 750 »

Algérie (20) . . . . 1 550 »
Autriche (60) . . . . 3 400 »
Antilles (70) . . . . 10 000 »
Argentine (80) . . . . 16 500 »
Belgique (30) . . . . 340 »
Brésil (80) . . . . 12 000 »
Cap de Bonne Esp. (80) 40 000 »
Chili (80) . . . . 15 000 »

Danemark (50) . . . . 5 000 »
Égypte (40) . . . . 7 000 »
Espagne (40) . . . . 2 450 »
États-Unis (70 ou 80) . . 4 000 »
Grande-Bretagne (30) . . . 340 »
Haïti (80) . . . . 15 000 »
Indes (80) . . . . 21 000 »
Italie (40) . . . . 2 300 »

80 c. Empire Lauré oblitéré Etoile 16 sur formule imprimée ;
Paris rue de Palestro du 25 Octobre 70 à destination d'Osaka Japon (par Marseille).
Pli ayant voyagé par le Ballon Monté le Vauban le 27 Octobre.
Cachet de Transit de Marseille du 2 Novembre 70 et Arrivée au
bureau français de Yokohama le 25 Décembre 70.

Gabon (80) . . . . .30 000 »
Japon (80) . . . . .40 000 »
Luxembourg (25) . . . . . 10 000 »
Malaisie (80) . . . . 25 000 »
Maurice (80) . . . . 20 000 »
Monaco (20) . . . . 10 000 »
Mexique (80) . . . . 14 000 »
Norvège (70) . . . . 7 000 »

Pays-Bas (40) . . . . 1 300 »
Pérou (1 f.) . . . . 15 000 »
Philippines (80) . . . . . . 22 000 »
Portugal (40) . . . . 3 500 »
Puerto Rico (80) . . . . . 22 000 »
Réunion (50) . . . . 16 500 »
Roumanie (40) . . . . 14 000 »
Russie (80) ss cach. arr. 3 050 »

Russie (80) av. cach. arr.12 500 »
Russie du Sud (1 f.)
sans cachet d'arrivée . 4 000 »
Sénégal (50) . . . . 15 000 »
Suède (70) . . . . 7 000 »
Suisse (30) . . . . 300 »
Turquie (40) (voie marit.) 3 050 »
Turquie (80) (voie de terre)6 500 »

E. - LETTRES-JOURNAUX

Ces plis comportent une partie imprimée, donnant des nouvelles de Paris assiégé, et une partie réservée à la correspondance.

a) *LA GAZETTE DES ABSENTS* (32 numéros).

N° 1, par Le Montgolfier (22 et 23-10-70) . . . . 1 500 »
N° 1, autres dates . . . . 425 »
N° 10, par La Ville d'Orléans, non accidentée . . . . 1 200 »
N° 10, par La Ville d'Orléans, accidentée avec cachet PP . . . . 4 000 »
N° 11, par Le Jacquard (25 au 28-11-70) . . . . 2 600 »
N° 11, autres dates . . . . 1 400 »
N° 31, par Le Richard Wallace . . . . 3 000 »
N° 31, par Le Cambronne (arrivée jusqu'au 4 février) . . . . 1 950 »
N° 32, par Le Richard Wallace . . . . 3 000 »
N° 32, par Le Général Cambronne (arrivée jusqu'au 4 février) . . . . 1 850 »
Autres numéros, chaque . . . . de 385 » à 460 »
N°s 4, 7, 13, 14, 15 et 20, avec supplément imprimé, chaque . . . . 690 »
Les n°s 13, 14 et 19 avec griffe « Le Figaro », chaque . . . . 3 850 »
Chaque numéro à l'état neuf, depuis . . . . 60 »
Plan de Paris, en couleurs (2 différents), neuf, chaque . . . . 610 »
Plan de Paris, en noir, neuf . . . . 765 »
Suppléments illustrés à la Gazette des Absents
(4 différents), neufs, chaque . . . . 690 »

(Un supplément illustré est connu ayant volé).

b) *LA DÉPÊCHE-BALLON* (27 numéros).

N° 1 . . . . 1 850 »
N° 8, par La Ville d'Orléans, non accidentée . . . . 1 550 »
N° 8, par La Ville d'Orléans, accidentée avec cachet PP . . . . 2 200 »
N° 9, par Le Jacquard . . . . 3 500 »

N° 26, par Le Richard Wallace	3 200 »
N° 27, par Le Général Cambronne	2 200 »
Autres numéros, chaque	de 460 » à 690 »
Chaque numéro à l'état neuf, depuis	75 »

c) *AUTRES JOURNAUX-LETTRES.*

Le Ballon-Poste, sur papier rose (21 numéros).	
Nos 1 à 4, chaque	1 850 »
N° 8, par Le Jacquard	4 350 »
Autres numéros, chaque	de 600 » à 765 »
Chaque numéro, à l'état neuf	75 »
Le Ballon-Poste, sur papier saumon, 31 octobre	3 850 »
La Cloche, 26 et 30 novembre, chaque	3 000 »
L'Echo des Étrangers (5 numéros), chaque	6 500 »
L'Électeur Libre, 29 novembre	6 000 »
L'Enveloppe-Gazette, du 7 au 19 décembre (13 numéros), chaque	6 000 »
Le Journal-Ballon (4 numéros), chaque	3 000 »
Le Moniteur Aérien, 27 octobre	8 000 »
Le Montgolfier, 15 novembre	12 000 »
Le Soir (17 numéros), chaque	3 000 »
Pour tous ces journaux, chaque numéro à l'état neuf,	depuis 155 »
Le Journal-Poste (17 numéros),	
Nos 12, 13, 14, 16, sous enveloppe avec griffe du journal, chaque	3 850 »
Autres numéros, chaque	1 100 »
Nos 3 et 7 avec supplément, chaque	2 300 »
A l'état neuf, chaque	80 »

F - JOURNAUX

Certains journaux parisiens ont imprimé, durant le Siège, des éditions spéciales, généralement sur papier pelure, destinées à être expédiées par ballons. Ils n'ont aucune place réservée à la correspondance.

L'Ami de la France, 15 décembre	
La Chronique Illustrée, 21 décembre sous enveloppe	6 300 »
Le Gaulois, grand format : (13 numéros), chaque	7 000 »
petit format : (2 numéros), chaque	6 800 »
Le Journal des Débats (5 numéros), chaque	8 000 »
Journal Le Français, sous enveloppe (2 numéros), chaque	9 000 »
Le Journal Officiel, 7 numéros connus ayant volé (sous bande)	9 000 »
Le Journal d'Outre-Mer (2 numéros connus)	
La Liberté, 2 novembre (sous enveloppe)	7 000 »
Le Moniteur des Communes	
Le National, sous enveloppe (un numéro)	3 800 »
Les Nouvelles, 17 décembre	
Les Nouvelles du Matin, 3 décembre	3 800 »
Les Nouvelles du Midi, 31 décembre, sous enveloppe	4 200 »
Les Nouvelles du Soir, 24 octobre	3 800 »
Le Petit Journal (7 numéros sous enveloppe), chaque	3 300 »
Le Petit Journal, reproduction photo, sous enveloppe (4 numéros), chaque	4 400 »
La Revue des Deux Mondes (1 numéro sous enveloppe)	4 600 »
Le Siècle (2 numéros sous enveloppe), chaque	4 600 »
Paris-Journal	5 500 »
Chaque numéros, à l'état neuf,	depuis 250 »

D'autres journaux sont connus, mais seulement à l'état neuf.

G. - CORRESPONDANCES DE PRESSE

Agence Fournier, sous enveloppe	5 000 »
Dernières Nouvelles (Havas), sous enveloppe, 20, 23, 26, septembre, chaque	4 200 »
Correspondance Havas, édition française	1 000 »
Correspondance Havas, édition allemande, sans arrivée	1 500 »
Correspondance Havas, édition allemande, avec arrivée	3 700 »
Gazette de Francfort	4 600 »
Nouvelle Presse Libre de Vienne	5 200 »

H - CIRCULAIRES

a) *CIRCULAIRES OFFICIELLES.*

Circulaire de la Compagnie du Chemin de fer P. L. M.	5 150 »
Conseil Général des Hospices	5 600 »
Ministère des Finances aux Directeurs des Manufactures	5 000 »
Circulaire du Directeur général des Manufactures de l'État	5 000 »

Circulaire de l'Assistance Publique .... 5 050 »
Circulaire de la Direction Générale des Domaines .... 4 800 »
Chacune de ces circulaires, à l'état neuf, ... depuis 300 »

b) *CIRCULAIRES PRIVÉES*

Circulaire du Directeur de l'École Albert-le-Grand .... 5 600 »
Circulaire de la Banque Vernes (sur Gazette n° 7) .... 6 300 »
Circulaire de la Banque Vernes (sur papier libre) .... 6 300 »
Circulaire de la Société Générale .... 4 800 »
Circulaire de « La Nationale » .... 3 500 »
Circulaire de « L'Union » .... 4 800 »
Circulaire de la Maison Paul Dupont .... 7 250 »
Circulaire de « La Providence » .... 4 800 »
Circulaire de L'Illustration .... 5 600 »
Circulaire de l'Alliance Républicaine .... 5 250 »
Crédit Viager .... 5 250 »
Compagnie des Courriers .... 7 250 »
Lettre aux Électeurs .... 5 250 »
Lettre aux Électeurs de l'Aisne .... 5 250 »
Lettre aux Électeurs de la Corrèze .... 5 250 »
Lettre aux Électeurs de la Dordogne .... 5 250 »
Lettre du Comité Vendéen de Paris .... 5 250 »
Lettre des Convoyeurs de Paris .... 6 400 »
Circulaire de la Maison Decugis .... 6 500 »
Manifeste des Loges .... 31 500 »
Circulaire de la Société Fraternelle des Enfants de la Drôme .... 6 800 »
Chacune de ces circulaires, à l'état neuf, ... depuis 290 »

J - MARQUES DE DÉPART

A. - Bureaux de Paris : Bureau central, étoile pleine ; bureaux de quartier ; étoile avec chiffre. Les plus rares sont ➔ 23 (rue d'Aligre) et ☆ 28 (Cardinal Lemoine) (le cachet à date y a servi habituellement) ; ☆ 29 (rue Pascal) ; ☆ 33 (boulevard de l'Hôpital) ; ☆ 36 (boulevard Voltaire).

Cachet à date Paris S. C. rouge .... à partir de 1 000 »

B. - Bureaux intra-muros et banlieue : Losanges GC les plus rares : 904 Paris-Charonne, 1625 Paris-Gare d'Ivry, 3180 Les Lilas, 3240 Rueil, 4097 Vanves, 4290 Vincennes (cachet à date simple cercle). Les losanges P. C. sont rares ; on connaît 432, 2170, 2523, 3739.

C. - Cachets avec taxe à payer 15 et 30 c .... à partir de 1 400 »

D. - Poste militaire :
a) Armée du Rhin 13e Corps : griffes AR 13e C, ARAL, ARAM, ARAN, avec cachet à date
Armée du Rhin .... à partir de 2 700 »
b) 14e Corps (le cachet à date sert d'oblitération) .... 3 000 »
c) Armée française : griffe AFA à AFM, en noir, parfois en rouge .... à partir de 2 500 »

K. - PLIS CONFIÉS AUX AÉRONAUTES

Monsieur Juhel
Docteur médecin
à Questembert
(Morbihan)

Lettre manuscrite de Paris du 16 Oct.70 affranchie à l'aide d'un 20 c. Siège.
Lettre confiée aux Aérostiers de Paris qui ont apposé leur cachet rouge.
REPUBLIQUE FRANÇAISE
1
AEROSTIERS
NADAR - DARTOIS
DURUOF

Ce pli quitta Paris le 18 Oct par le Ballon le Victor Hugo. Les aérostiers ont atterri dans l'Aisne le même jour et ont gagné Tours le 20 Oct. pour déposer le courrier. Le timbre fut annulé par le cachet à date de Tours du 21 Oct. et le pli distribué les jours suivants dans le Morbihan

a) Compagnie des Aérostiers
Grand cachet Nadar, Dartois, Duruof, rouge .... 9 000 »

b) Compagnie des Aéronautes
Grand cachet Dartois et Yon, bleu .... 12 500 »
rouge (Ballon Général Uhrich) .... 30 000 »

c) Plis sans cachet de départ, oblitérés en cours de route ou à l'arrivée ; le plus souvent :
Tours simple cercle, double cercle ou 3997 .... à partir de 2 000 »
Cachet à date avec PP .... à partir de 2 750 »
Bordeaux GC 532 .... à partir de 2 150 »

Autres cachets apposés en cours de route, soit griffe GC, PC, ambulant, soit cachet à date, permettant d'identifier le ballon .... à partir de 1 950 »
Le cachet des Aérostiers peut se trouver sur ces plis.

L. - AUTRES MARQUES DE TRANSIT OU D'ARRIVÉE

Certains cachets apposés en cours de route, ou à l'atterrissage, permettent d'identifier plus sûrement le ballon transporteur et donnent une plus-value aux plis. Certains sont forts rares.

L'identification de certains ballons est parfois difficile, par exemple lorsque deux de ceux-ci ont quitté Paris le même jour, ou bien lorsque le cachet d'arrivée est plus tardif que celui indiqué dans le tableau A. Il est recommandé, dans ce cas, de se reporter au Catalogue Spécialisé des Timbres de France (Volume I).

M. - PLIS TRANSPORTÉS PENDANT LE SIÈGE DE PARIS PAR D'AUTRES VOIES

Les plis sortis de Paris par passeur officiel ou par passeur privé sont très rares.
Les plis sortis ou entrés par la voie diplomatique sont rarissimes.

N. - AUTRES VILLES ASSIÉGÉES

Plusieurs villes de province, assiégées pendant la guerre, ont utilisé divers moyens officiels et privés pour assurer le transport du courrier.

CORRESPONDANCES TRANSPORTÉES PAR BOULES DE MOULINS

Pendant le Siège, dans le sens province-Paris, l'envoi de ballons montés, qui n'étaient pas dirigeables et dont le lieu d'atterrissage était donc parfaitement aléatoire, n'étant pas envisageable, trois inventeurs, ROBERT, DELORT et VONOVEN, firent adopter un système connu sous le nom de Boules de Moulins.

Les plis devaient initialement être centralisés à Clermont-Ferrand mais l'on opta très vite pour Moulins sur Allier.

Les lettres, après avoir été centralisées au bureau de Poste de Moulins, furent insérées dans 55 sphères de zinc contenant 500 à 800 missives. Chaque lettre était affranchie au tarif spécial de 1 franc et portait la mention manuscrite « Paris par Moulins-sur-Allier ». Au cours du mois de janvier 1871 les boules furent immergées dans la Seine en amont de Paris. Malheureusement, les filets installés dans Paris assiégé pour intercepter les boules, furent emportés par les blocs de glace que charriait la Seine.

Tandis qu'une partie des boules s'enlisèrent avant d'arriver à Paris, les autres traversèrent la capitale et allèrent se perdre jusque dans l'estuaire de la Seine, si bien que les premiers repêchages n'intervinrent qu'après la fin du Siège.

AFFRANCHISSEMENTS

- Affranchissement absent pour cause d'immersion .... 200 »
- Affranchissement incomplet pour cause d'immersion........ 400 »

Les affranchissements les plus habituels sont composés des timbres de l'émission Empire lauré (E.L.) et de ceux de l'émission de Bordeaux (B).

- 20 c. (E.L.) + 80 c. (E.L.) .... 1 000 »
- 20 c. (E.L.) x 5 .... 1 250 »
- 20 c. (E.L.) + 40 c. (E.L.) x 2........ 1 500 »
- 20 c. (E.L.) + 80 c. (B)........ 1 500 »
- 40 c. (E.L.) x 2 + 20 c. (B)........ 1 800 »
- 80 c. (E.L.) + 20 c. (B)........ 1 750 »
- 20 c. (B) + 80 c. (B)........ 1 500 »

A partir des timbres-poste de ces deux émissions, d'autres compositions sont possibles ; certaines sont très rares.

Ainsi on connaît des plis affranchis avec 5 pièces du 20 c. (I) Bordeaux .... 15 000 »

L'importance du tarif et l'exiguïté des lettres (qui ne devaient pas peser plus de 4 grammes) interdisaient totalement l'emploi de petites valeurs à 1, 2 et 4 centimes et rendaient difficile l'emploi de timbres à 5 ou 10 centimes :

Sont connus :

5 c. (B) .... 8 000 »
10 c. (B) .... 4 000 »
10 c. (E.L.)........ 4 000 »

Exceptionnellement des timbres des émissions antérieures ont été utilisés :

Sont connus :

5 c. Empire dentelé .... 20 000 »
10 c. Empire dentelé .... 7 500 »
20 c. + 80 c. Empire dentelé .... 7 500 »
40 c. Empire dentelé + 20 c. (B) .... 5 000 »
80 c. Empire dentelé + 20 c. (E.L.) .... 2 500 »
ainsi que les 20 c. et 80 c. Empire non dentelés.... 20 000 »

Dans les localités dépourvues de timbres, les lettres recevaient une griffe « PP » encadrée, accompagnée d'une mention manuscrite « Perçu 1 F en numéraire ».

LETTRES EN PROVENANCE DE L'ÉTRANGER

La plupart des plis en provenance de l'étranger étaient centralisés à Bordeaux (oblitération GC 532) mais certains parvinrent directement à Moulins (GC 2565) et quelques autres sont oblitérés de Marseille (GC 2240).

On connaît des lettres originaires des pays suivants : BELGIQUE, PAYS-BAS, GRANDE-BRETAGNE, SUISSE et PORTUGAL.

GC 532........ 2 000 »
GC 2565........ 3 000 »
GC 2240........ 4 000 »

(Ces cotes s'entendent pour des plis contenant une correspondance établissant la provenance étrangère de la lettre).

Certaines lettres étrangères étaient postées en France près de la frontière : on connaît ainsi des plis de Belgique ou de Grande-Bretagne postés à Lille, de Suisse postés à Saint-Julien en Genevois ou Fernex : .... 3 000 »

• Plis de Grande-Bretagne affranchis en timbres anglais .... 25 000 »

• Plis avec double affranchissement (Suisse + France, Belgique + France)........ 45 000 »

LES « SACS DE RIZ »

Après la fin du Siège des lettres en souffrance à Moulins furent acheminées sur Paris, cachées dans des sacs de ravitaillement, d'où leur surnom de « Sacs de riz ». Elles portent un cachet d'arrivée à Paris du 12 février 1871.

• Lettre avec cachet d'arrivée à Paris le 12 février 1871 .... 3 000 »

Peu après, d'autres lettres en souffrance furent acheminées officiellement à Paris (cachet d'arrivée du 17, 18 ou 22 février 1871).

• Lettres avec cachet d'arrivée à Paris le 17, 18 ou 22 Février 1871........ 3 000 »

LES REPÊCHAGES TARDIFS

Aucune lettre ne parvint à son destinataire pendant le Siège mais à partir de 1871 eurent lieu des repêchages suivis d'une distribution officielle par l'Administration avec cachet d'arrivée : 6 mars 1871, 26 mars 1871, 15 mai 1871, 2 et 5 juin 1871, 8 juin 1871, 23 juin 1871, 2, 26, 27 août 1871, 13 janvier 1872, 18 mars 1872, 2, 3 mai 1872, 29 août 1872, 29 novembre 1872, 11 décembre 1872, 13 mai 1873, 16 mai 1873, 5 juin 1873, 25 juin 1873, 25 juillet 1873, 6 juillet 1874, 10 décembre 1875, 7 juillet 1876, 18 avril 1882, 6 août 1968, 14 avril 1982 à partir de 6 000 »

Trois de ces repêchages donnèrent lieu à l'apposition d'une griffe spéciale :

- « Trouvée dans une boîte échouée sur les bords de la Seine à Quillebeuf (Eure), le 26 mars 1871 » .... 15 000 »
- « Corresp[ce] contenue dans une boule « de Moulins » repêchée prés de St-Wandrille, le 6 août 1968 » .... 30 000 »
- « Pli contenu dans une boule de Moulins découverte à Vatteville la Rue, le 14 avril 1982 »........ » »

BLOCS ET FEUILLETS

Jusqu'en 1949 les cotes de la colonne de gauche concernent les blocs neufs avec gomme d'origine intacte et sans charnière, celles de la colonne centrale les blocs neufs avec charnière légère, celles de la colonne de droite les blocs oblitérés.

1925. – ***Exposition philatélique internationale de Paris. T.-P. imprimé par bloc de quatre sur feuillets de 140 x 220, avec cadre et EXPOSITION INTERNATIONALE DE TIMBRES-POSTE - Émission spéciale - PARIS - 1925. Dentelé.***

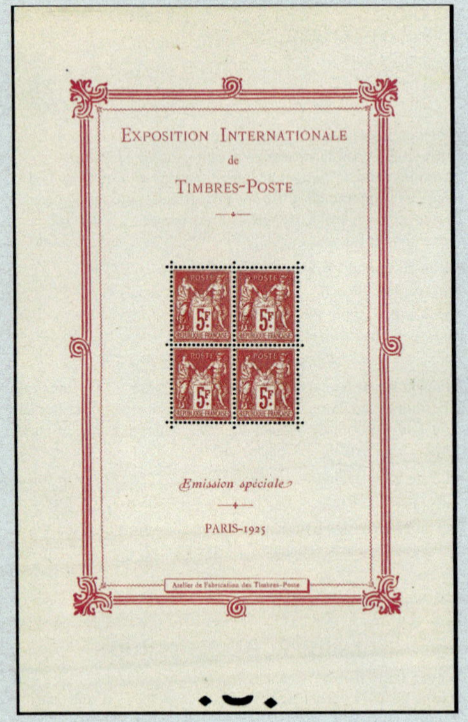

1	4 x 5 f. carmin (216)	4 750 »	1 500 »	1 500 »
	a. (Non dentelé)		6 000 »	
	b. (Avec cachet témoin de l'exposition hors timbre)	2 850 »	1 400 »	1 400 »

Pour acheter ce bloc, il fallait présenter un ticket d'entrée à l'exposition vendu 5 f. Il en a été de même pour les blocs suivants n°s 2 et 3.

1927. – ***Exposition philatélique internationale de Strasbourg. T.-P. au type Semeuse réunis sur feuillets de 110 x 140 et séparés par un intervalle blanc avec inscription bleue STRASBOURG - 1927. Dentelé.***

2	5 f. bleu (241)			
	10 f. rouge (242)			
	Le feuillet	3 000 »	1 350 »	1 350 »
	a. (Avec cachet témoin de l'exposition hors timbre)	1 900 »	135 »	1 350 »

1937. – ***Exposition philatélique internationale de Paris. (PEXIP). Timbres au type des T.-P. de 1849 imprimés en paires verticales séparées par un intervalle et les mots PEXIP - PARIS - 1937, sur feuillets de 150 x 220. Dentelé.***

3	5 c. outremer et brun (348)			
	15 c. rouge-brun et rose (349)			
	30 c. outremer et rose (350)			
	50 c. rouge-brun et brun (351)			
	Le feuillet	800 »	450 »	400 »
	a. (Non dentelé)		3 500 »	
	b. (Avec cachet témoin de l'exposition hors timbre)	500 »	420 »	385 »
	c. (Sans perforation)	850 »	550 »	450 »

1945. – ***Non émis. Marianne de Dulac. T.-P. de même date réunis en bloc de quatre sur feuillets de 121 x 172. Non dentelé.***

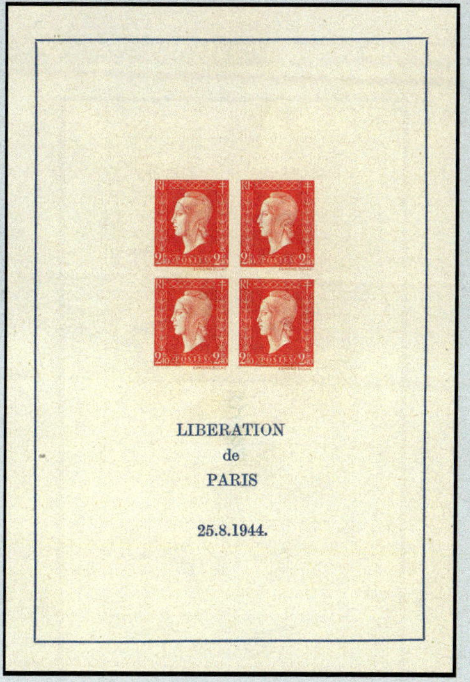

4	4 x 2 f. 40 rouge (693)	8 000 »	5 250 »

Imprimé pendant la guerre sur papier de très mauvaise qualité.

1949. – ***Exposition du centenaire du Timbre (Paris CITEX). Timbre non dentelé (avec dentelure extérieure pour découpage), imprimé par feuilles de dix de 154 x 279. Chaque feuille porte dans la marge supérieure les millésimes 1849-1949 (format d'un timbre : 40 x 52). Dentelé.***

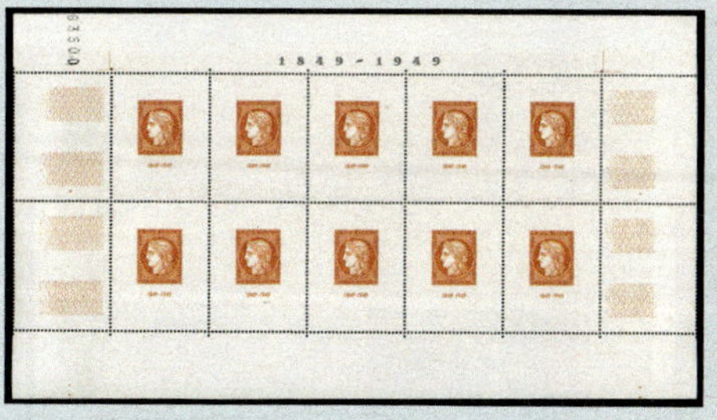

5	10 x 10 f. (+100 f.) vermillon (841)	875 »	600 »	600 »
	a. (Non dentelée)			16 500 »

A partir de 1960 les cotes de la colonne de gauche concernent les blocs neufs sans charnière, celles de la colonne de droite les blocs oblitérés.

1964. – ***Exposition philatélique internationale "Philatec", à Paris. T.-P. de même date imprimé par huit sur feuillets de 145 x 285 avec EXPOSITION INTERNATIONALE PHILATEC PARIS 1964. Dentelé.***

6	8 x 1 f. (+3 f.) brun, bleu foncé et carmin (1422)	300 »	230 »
	a. (Non dentelé)	3 000 »	
	b. (Numéroté)	330 »	
	c. (Coin daté)	2 250 »	

1975. – ***Exposition philatélique internationale "Arphila'75". T.-P. de même date réunis sur feuillets de 150 x 143. Dentelé.***

7 2 f. gris-vert et rouge-brique (1834)
3 f. rouge, bleu et gris-bleu (1835)
4 f. bleu, rouge-brique et vert-noir (1836)
6 f. gris-vert, rouge et bleu (1837)

Le feuillet	10 »	10 »
a. (Non dentelé)	500 »	

1982. – ***"Philexfrance'82". Exposition philatélique internationale. T.-P. de même date réunis sur feuillets de 100 x 71,5, avec une vignette centrale sans valeur, sur laquelle figure le logo de l'exposition. Vendu 30 f. Dentelé.***

8 4 f. rouge et bleu (2216)
6 f. bleu et rouge (2217)

Le feuillet	14 »	14 »
a. (Non dentelé)	300 »	

Épreuve en noir insérée dans le catalogue de l'exposition : 55 ».

1986. – ***Cinquantenaire de la cinémathèque française. T.-P. de même date réunis sur feuillet de 143 x 180. Dentelé.***

9 2 f. 20 noir et gris *Louis Feuillade - "Les vampires"* (2433)
2 f. 20 noir et gris *Max Linder* (2434)
2 f. 20 noir et gris *Sacha Guitry - "Le roman d'un tricheur"* (2435)
2 f. 20 noir et gris *Jean Renoir - "La grande illusion"* (2436)
2 f. 20 noir et gris *Marcel Pagnol - "La femme du boulanger"* (2437)
2 f. 20 noir et gris *Jean Epstein - "La glace à trois faces"* (2438)
2 f. 20 noir et gris *René Clair - "Les belles de nuit"* (2439)
2 f. 20 noir et gris *Jean Grémillon - "Gueule d'amour"* (2440)
2 f. 20 noir et gris *Jacques Becker - "Casque d'or"* (2441)
2 f. 20 noir et gris *François Truffaut - "L'enfant sauvage"* (2442)

Le feuillet	15 »	15 »
a. (Non dentelé)	300 »	

1989. – ***Personnages célèbres de la Révolution. T.-P. de même date réunis sur feuillet de 78 x 105. Dentelé.***

10 2 f. 20 *Antoine Caritat, marquis de Condorcet (1743-1794) ; philosophe et mathématicien* (2592)
2 f. 20 *Mme Roland (1754-1793)* (2593)
2 f. 20 *Camille Desmoulins (1760-1794) ; avocat et journaliste* (2594)
2 f. 20 *François-Christophe Kellermann, Maréchal de France, Duc de Valmy (1735-1820)* (2595)

Le feuillet	5 »	5 »
a. (Non dentelé)	270 »	

1989. – ***Bicentenaire de la Révolution et de la Déclaration des Droits de l'Homme et du Citoyen. T.-P. de même date réunis sur feuillet de 130 x 143. Vendu 50 f. Dentelé.***

11 5 f. *Préambule ; article 1ᵉʳ* (2596)
5 f. *Articles II à VI* (2597)
5 f. *Articles VII à XI* (2598)
5 f. *Articles XII à XVII* (2599)

Le feuillet	18 »	18 »
a. (Non dentelé)	400 »	
b. (En noir)	150 »	
c. (Papier fluorescent)	300 »	

Le N° 11b accompagnait les deux tomes du catalogue de l'exposition "Philexfrance'89".

1990. – ***Bicentenaire de la Révolution. T.-P. de même date réunis sur feuillet de 78 x 105. Taille-douce. Dentelé.***

12 2 f. 50 *Gaspard Monge, comte de Péluse (1746-1818), mathématicien* (2667)
2 f. 50 *Abbé Grégoire (Henri) (1750-1831)* (2668)
2 f. 50 *Création du drapeau tricolore (allégorie)* (2669)
2 f. 50 *Création des départements français* (2670)

Le feuillet	5 »	5 »
a. (Non dentelé)	300 »	

1991. – ***Bicentenaire de la Révolution française. T.-P. de même date réunis sur feuillet de 106 x 80. Dentelé.***

13 2 f. 50 *La Tour d'Auvergne (1743-1800)* (2700)
2 f. 50 *Plantation de l'Arbre de la Liberté* (2701)
2 f. 50 *Bicentenaire de la Gendarmerie Nationale* (2702)
2 f. 50 *Saint-Just (1767-1794)* (2703)

Le feuillet	5 »	5 »
a. (Non dentelé)	300 »	

1992. – *"Albertville'92". Jeux olympiques d'hiver. T.-P. de 1991 et 1992 réunis sur feuillet de 143 x 27 avec vignette centrale sans valeur (logo des Jeux, impression offset). Dentelé.*

14 2 f. 50+20 c. rouge, gris et bleu (2737)
2 f. 50+20 c. rouge, gris et bleu (2738)
2 f. 50+20 c. rouge, gris et bleu (2739)
2 f. 50+20 c. rouge, gris et bleu (2740)
2 f. 50+20 c. rouge, gris et bleu (2742)
2 f. 50+20 c. rouge, gris et bleu (2741)
2 f. 50+20 c. multicolore (2679a)
2 f. 50+20 c. multicolore (2680a)
2 f. 50+20 c. multicolore (2709a)
2 f. 50+20 c. multicolore (2710a)

Le feuillet	15 »	15 »
a. (Non dentelé)	500 »	
b. (En noir)	500 »	
c. (Vignette centrale brillante)	18 »	18 »

1993. – *Salon du Timbre. 1er Salon européen des Loisirs du Timbre. T.-P. de même date réunis sur feuillet de 105 x 78, vendu 15 f. avec deux vignettes sans valeur. Dentelé.*

15 2 f. 40 *Rhododendrons* (2849)
2 f. 40 *Parc floral de Paris* (2850)

Le feuillet	18 »	18 »
a. (Non dentelé)	200 »	

1994. – *Salon du Timbre. 1er Salon européen des Loisirs du Timbre. T.-P. de même date réunis sur feuillet de 106 x 78, vendu 16 f. Dentelé.*

16 2 f. 80 *Parc floral de Paris* (2909)
2 f. 80 *Dahlias* (2910)

Le feuillet	18 »	18 »
a. (Non dentelé)	200 »	

1995. – *1er siècle du cinéma. T.-P. de même date réunis sur feuillet de 105 x 78. Dentelé.*

17 2 f. 80 *Tête d'acteur, projecteur* (2919)
2 f. 80 *Projecteur, tête avec casquette* (2920)
2 f. 80 *Projecteur, tête grimée, style "La Bête"* (2921)
2 f. 80 *Bobines et tête d'Indien* (2922)

Le feuillet	7 »	7 »
a. (Non dentelé)	185 »	

1995. – *Série Arts décoratifs. Hommage au peintre ornithologue J.-J. Audubon (1785-1851). T.-P. de même date réunis sur feuillet de 121 x 113. Dentelé.*

18 2 f. 80 *Aigrette neigeuse* (2929a)
2 f. 80 *Pigeons à queue rayée* (2930a)
4 f. 30 *Sterne Pierre-Garin* (2931a)
4 f. 40 *Buse pattue* (2932a)
Le feuillet 7 » 7 »

1998. – "France'98". *Coupe du Monde de Football. Types des T.-P. de 1996, 1997 et 1998 réunis avec vignette centrale sans valeur (le Stade de France) sur feuillet de 148 x 140. Dentelé.*

19 3 f. *Saint-Etienne* (3012)
3 f. *Lyon* (3074)
3 f. *Montpellier* (3011)
3 f. *Lens* (3010)
3 f. *Paris* (3077)
3 f. *Bordeaux* (3130)
3 f. *Nantes* (3076)
3 f. *Marseille* (3075)
3 f. *Toulouse* (3013)
3 f. *Saint-Denis* (3131)
Le feuillet 14 » 14 »

Les caractères des noms du graveur et de l'imprimeur sont légèrement plus serrés, et les espaces de "République française La Poste" un peu plus grands que sur les timbres de feuilles.

1998. – "Philexfrance 99". *Exposition philatélique internationale. © Fondation Saint-Exupéry 1998. T.-P. de même date réunis sur feuillet de 112 x 158 vendu 25 f. dont 10 f. au profit de l'Exposition.. © Fondation Saint-Exupéry 1998.*

20 3 f. *Portrait du petit Prince* (3175)
3 f. *Le petit Prince avec le renard* (3176)
3 f. *Le petit Prince sur sa planète* (3177)
3 f. *Le petit Prince assis sur un mur, et le serpent* (3178)
3 f. *Le petit Prince arrosant la fleur* (3179)
Le feuillet 9 » 9 »

Le logo de l'Exposition figure hors timbres.

1998. – "Meilleurs Voeux". *T.-P. de même date réunis sur feuillet. Dentelé.*

21 2 x 3 f. *Père Noël sur surf des neiges ; collines jaunes* (3200)
2 x 3 f. *Maison décorée, aux volets verts* (3201)
2 x 3 f. *Père Noël sur surf et cimes de sapins* (3202)
2 x 3 f. *Maison décorée, aux volets rouges* (3203)
2 x 3 f. *Père Noël sur surf et collines enneigées* (3204)
Le feuillet 20 » 20 »

1999. – *Journée du Timbre. Astérix. T.-P. de même date imprimé sur feuillet de 102 x 77. © Les Editions Albert René/Goscinny-Uderzo.*

22	3 f.+60 c. multicolore (3228)	2 75	2 50

1999. – *"Philexfrance'99". Exposition philatélique internationale (III). Chefs d'oeuvre de l'Art. T.-P. de même date réunis sur feuillet de 158 x 112, vendu 50 f. dont 30 f. reversés à l'Association pour le Développement de la Philatélie. Dentelé.*

23 5 f. *La Vénus de Milo (2e s. av. J.-C.)* (3234)
5 f. *La Joconde, de Léonard de Vinci (1452-1519)* (3235)
10 f. *Détail de "La Liberté guidant le peuple" d'Eugène Delacroix (1798-1863)* (3236)

Le feuillet	70 »	70 »

Le logo de l'Exposition figure hors timbres.

Vendu sous bande plastique dans une présentation illustrée (2 versions), avec laissez-passer pour l'Exposition.

1999. – *Congrès mondial de Roses anciennes, à Lyon. T.-P. de même date réunis sur feuillet de 110 x 160. Dentelé.*

24 3 f. *Rose "Madame Alfred Carrière" (1879)* (3248)
4 f. 50 *Rose "Madame Caroline Testout" (1890)* (3249)
4 f. 50 *Rose "La France" (1867)* (3250)

Le feuillet	12 »	12 »

1999. – *Série "Collection Jeunesse". Armada du siècle - Rouen 1999. Grands voiliers. T.-P. de même date réunis sur feuillet de 108 x 183. Dentelé.*

25 1 f. (0,15 €) *"Simón Bolivar"* (3269)
1 f. (0,15 €) *"Iskra"* (3270)
1 f. (0,15 €) *"Statsraad Lehmkuhl"* (3271)
1 f. (0,15 €) *"Asgard II"* (3272)
1 f. (0,15 €) *"Belle-Poule"* (3273)
1 f. (0,15 €) *"Belem"* (3274)
1 f. (0,15 €) *"Amérigo Vespucci"* (3275)
1 f. (0,15 €) *"Sagres"* (3276)
1 f. (0,15 €) *"Europa"* (3277)
1 f. (0,15 €) *"Cuauhtemoc"* (3278)

Le feuillet 6 » 6 »

1999. – *Coupe du monde de Rugby 1999. T.-P. de même date imprimé sur feuillet de 143 x 210 avec vignette centrale sans valeur (coupe Webb-Ellis). Dentelé.*

26 10 x 3 f. (0,46 €) *Plaquage* (3280) 12 » 12 »

2000. – *Saint-Valentin. Coeurs 2000 du couturier Yves Saint Laurent. T.-P. de même date réunis sur feuillet de 95 x 150. Dentelé.*

27 3 x 3 f. (0,46 €) *Coeurs entourés de deux serpents* (3295)
2 x 3 f. (0,46 €) *Coeur avec profil féminin* (3296)

Le feuillet 9 » 9 »

2000. – *Fête du Timbre "Tintin". T.-P. de même date imprimé sur feuillet de 100 x 75. Héliogravure.. © Hergé/Moulinsart 2000.*

28 3 f.+60 c. (0,55 €) multicolore (3304) 2 75 2 75

2000. – *Le siècle au fil du timbre (I). Le sport. T.-P. de même date imprimés sur feuillet de 185 x 245. Héliogravure. Dentelé.*

29 2 x 3 f. (0,46 €) *Portrait du boxeur Marcel Cerdan et détail ceinture (champion du monde des poids moyens en 1948)* (3312)
2 x 3 f. (0,46 €) *L'athlète américain Carl Lewis (4 médailles d'or aux Jeux olympiques de Los Angeles, en 1984)* (3313)
2 x 3 f. (0,46 €) *La France, championne du monde de football en 1998 (coupe et supporters en fond)* (3314)
2 x 3 f. (0,46 €) *Le skieur Jean-Claude Killy (3 médailles d'or aux Jeux olympiques de Grenoble en 1968)* (3315)
2 x 3 f. (0,46 €) *L'aviateur Charles Lindbergh et partie avant de son avion le "Spirit of Saint Louis" (1ère traversée sans escale de l'Atlantique les 20-21 mai 1927)* (3316)

Le feuillet 12 » 12 »

Vendu dans une pochette illustrée.

2000. – *Série "Collection Jeunesse". Voitures anciennes. "Philexjeunes 2000"-Annecy. T.-P. de même date imprimés sur feuillet de 108* x *183. Héliogravure. Dentelé.*

30 1 f. (0,15 €) *Bugatti 35* (3317)
1 f. (0,15 €) *Citroën Traction* (3318)
1 f. (0,15 €) *Renault 4 CV* (3319)
1 f. (0,15 €) *Simca Chambord* (3320)
1 f. (0,15 €) *Hispano-Suiza K6* (3321)
2 f. (0,30 €) *Coccinelle Volkswagen* (3322)
2 f. (0,30 €) *Cadillac 62* (3323)
2 f. (0,30 €) *Peugeot 203* (3324)
2 f. (0,30 €) *Citroën DS19* (3325)
2 f. (0,30 €) *Ferrari 250 GTO* (3326)

Le feuillet 6 » 6 »

La mention de l'exposition "Philexjeunes 2000-Annecy" figure hors timbres.

2000. – *Série "Nature de France" (XV). Faune et flore. T.-P. de même date imprimés sur feuillet de 110* x *160. Dentelé.*

31 2 f. 70, (0,41 €) *Papillon sardanapale* (3332)
3 f. (0,46 €) *Girafe réticulée* (3333)
3 f. (0,46 €) *Allosaure* (3334)
4 f. 50, (0,69 €) *Tulipa lutea* (3335)

Le feuillet 5 » 5 »

2000. – *Jeux olympiques de Sydney (Australie). Disciplines. T.-P. de même date imprimés sur feuillet de 210* x *143. Héliogravure. Dentelé.*

31A 5 x 3 f. (0,46 €) *Cyclisme, escrime, relais* (3340)
5 x 3 f. (0,46 €) *Relais, judo, plongeon* (3341)

Le feuillet 12 » 12 »

2000. – *Le siècle au fil du timbre (II). Société. T.-P. de même date imprimés sur feuillet de 185* x *245. Héliogravure. Dentelé.*

32 2 x 3 f. (0,46 €) *1901, le lave-linge* (3351)
2 x 3 f. (0,46 €) *1936, les congés payés (famille se baignant d'après photo d'époque)* (3352)
2 x 3 f. (0,46 €) *1944, le droit de vote des femmes (femmes votant)* (3353)
2 x 3 f. (0,46 €) *1948, la Déclaration universelle des Droits de l'Homme (mentions : dignité, droits de l'homme, libres, égaux, et mur en brique en fond)* (3354)
2 x 3 f. (0,46 €) *1969, le premier pas sur la Lune (astronaute sur la Lune)* (3355)

Le feuillet 12 » 12 »

2001. – *Saint-Valentin. Coeur 2001 du couturier Christian Lacroix. T.-P. de même date imprimé sur feuillet de 137 x 143. Dentelé.*

33 5 x 3 f. (0,46 €) multicolore (3368) 6 » 6 »

2001. – *Fête du Timbre. T.-P. de même date imprimé sur feuillet de 100 x 75. Dentelé.*

34 3 f. +0 f. 60 (0,55 €) *Gaston Lagaffe* (3371) 2 50 2 50

2001. – *Le siècle au fil du timbre (III). Communication. T.-P. de même date imprimés sur feuillet de 185 x 245. Héliogravure. Dentelé.*

35 2 x 3 f. (0,46 €) *La télévision : personnages de "Bonne nuit les petits"* (3372)
2 x 3 f. (0,46 €) *La publicité au cinéma : le Petit Mineur* (3373)
2 x 3 f. (0,46 €) *Le téléphone portable* (3374)
2 x 3 f. (0,46 €) *La radio : "Salut les copains"* (3375)
2 x 3 f. (0,46 €) *Le disque compact* (3376)

Le feuillet 12 » 12 »

2001. – *Série "Nature de France" (XVI). Faune. T.-P. de même date imprimés sur feuillet de 160 x 110. Dentelé.*

36 2 f. 70 (0,41 €) *Ecureuil* (3381)
3 f. (0,46 €) *Chevreuil* (3382)
3 f. (0,46 €) *Hérisson* (3383)
4 f. 50 (0,69 €) *Hermine* (3384)

Le feuillet 5 » 5 »

2001. – *Personnages célèbres. Artistes de la chanson. T.-P. de même date imprimés sur feuillet de 135 x 143, vendu 28 f. (4,27 €) (faciale 18 f. (2,76 €) dont 10 f. reversés à la Croix-Rouge Française. Dentelé.*

37 3 f. (0,46 €) *Claude François (1939-1978)* (3391)
3 f. (0,46 €) *Léo Ferré (1916-1993)* (3392)
3 f. (0,46 €) *Serge Gainsbourg (1928-1991)* (3393)
3 f. (0,46 €) *Dalida (1933-1987)* (3394)
3 f. (0,46 €) *Michel Berger (1947-1992)* (3395)
3 f. (0,46 €) *Barbara (1930-1997)* (3396)

Le feuillet 12 » 12 »

2001. – Série "Collection Jeunesse". Les légendes du rail. Locomotives. T.-P. de même date imprimés sur feuillet de 108 x 183. Dentelé.

38 1 f. 50 (0,23 €) *Eurostar* (3405)
1 f. 50 (0,23 €) *American 220* (3406)
1 f. 50 (0,23 €) *Crocodile* (3407)
1 f. 50 (0,23 €) *Crampton* (3408)
1 f. 50 (0,23 €) *Garratt 59* (3409)
1 f. 50 (0,23 €) *Pacific Chapelon* (3410)
1 f. 50 (0,23 €) *Mallard* (3411)
1 f. 50 (0,23 €) *Capitole* (3412)
1 f. 50 (0,23 €) *Autorail panoramique* (3413)
1 f. 50 (0,23 €) *230 Classe P8* (3414)

Le feuillet 6 » 6 »

2001. – Le siècle au fil du timbre (IV). Sciences. T.-P. de même date imprimés sur feuillet de 185 x 245. Héliogravure. Dentelé.

39 2 x 3 f. (0,46 €) *La pénicilline* (3422)
2 x 3 f. (0,46 €) *L'ADN* (3423)
2 x 3 f. (0,46 €) *Le laser* (3424)
2 x 3 f. (0,46 €) *Le 1er homme dans l'espace* (3425)
2 x 3 f. (0,46 €) *La carte à puce* (3426)

Le feuillet 12 » 12 »

2001. – Halloween. T.-P. de même date imprimé sur feuillet de 135 x 143, avec 4 vignettes sans valeur. Dentelé.

40 5 x 3 f. (0,46 €) *Citrouille* (3428) 5 » 5 »

2001. – Les couleurs de Marianne en Francs. Les valeurs de la monnaie et les valeurs de la lettre. Types des T.-P. de 1997 imprimés sur feuillets de 145 x 143. Taille-douce. Sans bandes de phosphore. Dentelés 13.

41 10 c. bistre-noir (3086)
20 c. émeraude (3087)
50 c. violet-rouge (3088)
1 f. orange (3089)
2 f. bleu (3090)
5 f. bleu-vert (3097)
10 f. violet (3099)

Le feuillet 7 » 7 »

42 2 f. 70 vert (3091)
(sans val.) rouge (3083)
3 f. 50 vert-jaune (3092)
3 f. 80 bleu (3093)
4 f. 20 orange foncé (3094)
4 f. 40 bleu (3095)
4 f. 50 rose (3096)
6 f. 70 vert foncé (3098)

Le feuillet 13 » 13 »

2002. – ***Saint-Valentin. Coeur 2002, du photographe Yann Arthus-Bertrand. T.-P. de même date imprimé sur feuillet de 135 x 143. Dentelé.***

43 5 x 0,46 € *Photo aérienne de Voh (Nouvelle-Calédonie)* (3459) 5 » 5 »

2002. – ***Les couleurs de Marianne en Euros. Les valeurs de la monnaie et les valeurs de la lettre. Types des T.-P. de 2001 et 2002 imprimés sur feuillets de 145 x 143. Taille-douce. Sans bandes de phosphore. Dentelé 13.***

44 0,01 € jaune (3443)
0,02 € bistre-noir (3444)
0,05 € vert-émeraude (3445)
0,10 € violet-rouge (3446)
0,20 € orange (3447)
0,50 € bleu nuit (3449)
1,00 € bleu-vert (3455)
2,00 € violet (3457)

Le feuillet 12 » 12 »

45 0,41 € vert (3448)
(sans val.) rouge (3417)
0,53 € vert-jaune (3450)
0,58 € bleu (3451)
0,64 € orange foncé (3452)
0,67 € bleu outremer (3453)
0,69 € rose (3454)
1,02 € vert foncé (3456)

Le feuillet 15 » 15 »

2002. – *Fête du timbre. T.-P. de même date imprimé sur feuillet de 100 x 75. Dentelé.*

46 0,46 €+0,09 € *Boule et Bill, croix rouge et ballon (de Jean Roba). Sans réserve blanche autour de l'image* (3469) 3 » 3 »

2002. – *Le siècle au fil du timbre (V). Transports. T.-P. de même date imprimés sur feuillet de 185 x 245. Héliogravure. Dentelé.*

47 2 x 0,46 € *Concorde* (3471)
2 x 0,46 € *La mobylette* (3472)
2 x 0,46 € *Le France* (3473)
2 x 0,46 € *La 2 CV* (3474)
2 x 0,46 € *Le TGV* (3475)

Le feuillet 12 » 12 »

2002. – *Série "Nature de France" (XVII). Faune marine. T.-P. de même date imprimés sur feuillet de 110 x 160. Dentelé.*

48 0,41 € *Tortue luth* (3485)
0,46 € *Grand dauphin* (3486)
0,46 € *Orque* (3487)
0,69 € *Phoque veau marin* (3488)

Le feuillet 5 » 5 »

L'emblème du WWF figure hors timbres.

2002. – *Champions du monde de Football. Emission commune avec l'Allemagne, l'Argentine, le Brésil et l'Uruguay. T.-P. de même date imprimés sur feuillet de 143 x 210. Dentelé.*

49 5 x 0,46 € *Ballon, terrain et drapeaux de 6 des 7 pays ayant remporté la coupe du monde* (3483)
5 x 0,46 € *Drapeau français, 1998, image floue de joueurs* (3484)

Le feuillet 12 » 12 »

Impression au verso du feuillet permettant d'inscrire le nom des pays sélectionnés depuis les quarts de finale jusqu'à la finale.

2002. – ***Les personnages célèbres. Grands interprètes de jazz. T.-P. de même date imprimés sur feuillet de 135 x 143, vendu 4,36 € dont 1,60 € reversés à la Croix-Rouge Française. Dentelé.***

50 0,46 € multicolore et or (3500a)
0,46 € multicolore et or (3501a)
0,46 € multicolore et or (3502a)
0,46 € multicolore et or (3503a)
0,46 € multicolore et or (3504a)
0,46 € multicolore et or (3505a)
Le feuillet 12 » 12 »

2002. – ***Série "Collection Jeunesse". Cylindrées et carénages. Motos. T.-P. de même date imprimés sur feuillet de 107 x 183. Dentelé.***

51 0,16 € *Honda 750 Four* (3508)
0,16 € *Terrot 500 RGST* (3509)
0,16 € *Majestic* (3510)
0,16 € *Norton Commando 750* (3511)
0,16 € *Voxan 1000 Café Racer* (3512)
0,30 € *BMW R90S* (3513)
0,30 € *Harley Davidson Hydra glide* (3514)
0,30 € *Triumph Bonneville 650* (3515)
0,30 € *Ducati 916* (3516)
0,30 € *Yamaha 500XT* (3517)
Le feuillet 6 » 6 »

2002. – ***Le siècle au fil du timbre (VI). Vie quotidienne. T.-P. de même date imprimés sur feuillet de 185 x 245. Héliogravure. Dentelé.***

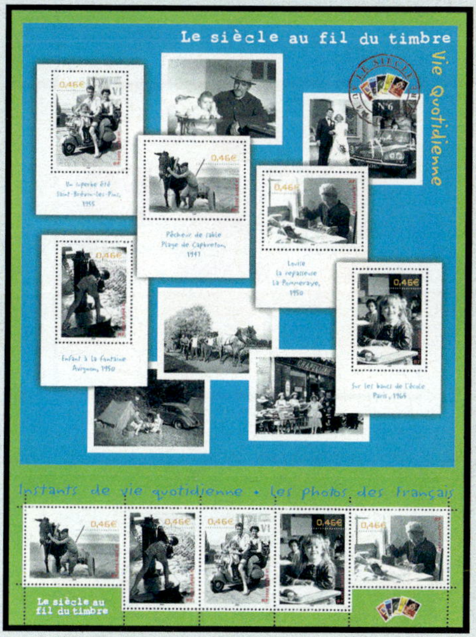

52 2 x 0,46 € *"Pêcheur de sable", Plage de Capbreton, 1947* (3519)
2 x 0,46 € *"Enfant à la fontaine", Avignon, 1950* (3520)
2 x 0,46 € *"Un superbe été", Saint-Brévin-les-Pins, 1955* (3521)
2 x 0,46 € *"Sur les bancs de l'école", Paris, 1965* (3522)
2 x 0,46 € *"Louise la repasseuse", La Pommeraye, 1950* (3523)
Le feuillet 12 » 12 »

2002. – ***Capitales européennes. Rome. T.-P. de même date imprimés sur feuillet de 143 x 135. Multicolore. Dentelé.***

53 0,46 € *Le Colisée* (3527)
0,46 € *La Fontaine de Trevi* (3528)
0,46 € *L'Eglise de la Trinité-des-Monts* (3529)
0,46 € *La Basilique Saint-Pierre* (3530)
Le feuillet 6 » 6 »

2003. – Saint-Valentin. Coeurs 2003 du couturier Torrente. T.-P. de même date imprimé sur feuillet de 135 x 143. Dentelé.

54 5 x 0,46 € multicolore et or *Coeur avec trèfle à quatre feuilles et signature* (3538) 5 » 5 »

2003. – Fête du timbre. Lucky Luke (de Morris). T.-P. de même date imprimé sur feuillet de 100 x 75. © Lucky Comics 2003.

55 0,46 €+0,09 € *Lucky Luke (de Morris)* (3547) 2 50 2 50

2003. – Série "Nature de France" (XVIII). Oiseaux d'outre-mer. T.-P. de même date imprimés sur feuillet de 110 x 160. Dentelé.

56 0,41 € *Colibri à tête bleue* (3548)

0,46 € *Toucan ariel* (3549)

0,46 € *Colibri grenat* (3550)

0,69 € *Terpsiphone de Bourbon* (3551)

Le feuillet 5 » 5 »

2003. – Portraits de régions. La France à vivre n° 1. T.-P. de même date imprimés sur feuillet de 285 x 110. Héliogravure. Dentelé.

57 0,50 € *Les cabines de bain* (3559)

0,50 € *La pêche au carrelet* (3560)

0,50 € *Les vignobles de Champagne* (3561)

0,50 € *Le camembert* (3562)

0,50 € *Le foie gras* (3563)

0,50 € *La pétanque* (3564)

0,50 € *Guignol* (3565)

0,50 € *La crêpe* (3566)

0,50 € *Le cassoulet* (3567)

0,50 € *La porcelaine* (3568)

Le feuillet 12 » 12 »

2003. – Timbre pour anniversaires. Personnage de bande dessinée. T.-P. de même date imprimé sur feuillet de 135 x 143, avec 4 vignettes sans valeur. Héliogravure. André Franquin & BATEM © Marsu 2003.

58 5 x 0,50 € *Marsupilami portant un gâteau, d'André Franquin et Batem* (3569) 5 » 5 »

2003. – ***Cyclisme. Centenaire du Tour de France. T.-P. de même date imprimés sur feuillet de 210 x 143. Héliogravure. Dentelé.***

59 5 x 0,50 € *Le coureur Maurice Garin, vainqueur du Tour de 1903* (3582)
5 x 0,50 € *Coureur de 2003 à l'arrivée* (3583)

Le feuillet 15 » 15 »

2003. – ***Les personnages célèbres. Personnages de la littérature française. T.-P. de même date imprimés sur feuillet de 135 x 142, vendu 4,60 € dont 1,60 € reversés à la Croix-Rouge Française. Héliogravure. Dentelé.***

60 0,50 € *Vidocq* (3588)
0,50 € *Esmeralda* (3589)
0,50 € *Claudine* (3590)
0,50 € *Nana* (3591)
0,50 € *Le comte de Monte-Cristo* (3592)
0,50 € *Gavroche* (3593)

Le feuillet 10 » 10 »

2003. – ***Portraits de régions. La France à voir n° 2. T.-P. de même date imprimés sur feuillet de 285 x 110. Héliogravure. Dentelé.***

61 0,50 € *Le château de Chenonceau* (3595)
0,50 € *Maison alsacienne* (3596)
0,50 € *Toits de Bourgogne* (3597)
0,50 € *Tour génoise en Corse* (3598)
0,50 € *L'Arc de Triomphe* (3599)
0,50 € *Mas provençal* (3600)
0,50 € *La pointe du Raz* (3601)
0,50 € *Le mont Blanc* (3602)
0,50 € *Maison basque* (3603)
0,50 € *Le pont du Gard* (3604)

Le feuillet 12 » 12 »

2003. – ***Jardins de France. T.-P. de même date imprimés sur feuillet de 286 x 109. Héliogravure. Dentelé.***

62 1,90 € *Parc des Buttes-Chaumont (détail falaise avec le temple de la Sibylle)* (3606)
1,90 € *Jardin du Luxembourg (détail avec le bâtiment du Sénat en fond)* (3607)

Le feuillet 10 » 10 »

La mention "Le Salon du Timbre 2004" figure hors timbres.

BF conçu pour être plié de façon à évoquer l'ouverture d'un portail sur un jardin.

2003. – ***Série "Collection Jeunesse". Véhicules utilitaires et grande échelle. T.-P. de même date imprimés sur feuillet de 108 x 183. Héliogravure. Dentelé.***

63 0,20 € *Autocar* (3609)
0,20 € *Tracteur* (3610)
0,20 € *Camion de pompiers à échelle* (3611)
0,20 € *Voiture postale* (3612)
0,20 € *Autobus parisien* (3613)
0,30 € *Véhicule de livraison* (3614)
0,30 € *Camion de chantier* (3615)
0,30 € *Véhicule de Police* (3616)
0,30 € *Ambulance* (3617)
0,30 € *Véhicule de Premiers secours* (3618)

Le feuillet 6 » 6 »

2003. – *Capitales européennes. Luxembourg. T.-P. de même date imprimés sur feuillet de 142 x 135. Héliogravure. Dentelé.*

64 0,50 € *Cathédrale Notre-Dame* (3624)
0,50 € *Citadelle Saint-Esprit* (3625)
0,50 € *Palais grand-ducal* (3626)
0,50 € *Pont Adolphe* (3627)

Le feuillet 6 » 6 »

2003. – *"Meilleurs Voeux" (Rouge-gorge). Type du T.-P. de même date imprimé sur feuillet de 205 x 95. Sans bandes de phosphore. Dentelé.*

65 0,50 € *Rouge-gorge* (3621a) 225 » 225 »

BF inséré dans une carte de voeux 2004.

2004. – *Saint-Valentin. Coeurs 2004 du couturier Karl Lagerfeld. T.-P. de même date imprimé sur feuillet de 135 x 143. Héliogravure. Dentelé.*

66 5 x 0,50 € *Flacon de parfum Chanel n° 5 dans un coeur* (3632) 5 » 5 »

2004. – *Les couleurs de Marianne en Euros. Les valeurs de la lettre. Types des T.-P. de 2001, 2002 et 2003 imprimés sur feuillet de 145 x 143, vendu 6,89 €. Taille-douce. Sans bandes de phosphore. Dentelé 13.*

67 (sans val.) vert (3535A)
(sans val.) rouge (3417)
0,58 € jaune-olive (3570)
0,70 € vert-olive (3571)
0,75 € bleu ciel (3572)
0,90 € bleu foncé (3573)
1,11 € lilas (3574)
1,90 € brun-prune (3575)

Le feuillet 18 » 18 »

2004. – Portraits de régions. La France à vivre n° 3. T.-P. de même date imprimés sur feuillet de 286 x 110. Héliogravure. Dentelé.

68 0,50 € *La coutellerie* (3646)
0,50 € *Le marché de Provence* (3647)
0,50 € *Les vignobles du Beaujolais* (3648)
0,50 € *Le pain* (3649)
0,50 € *Coiffe madras* (3650)
0,50 € *Les huîtres* (3651)
0,50 € *La quiche lorraine* (3652)
0,50 € *La course landaise* (3653)
0,50 € *Le clafoutis* (3654)
0,50 € *Le bagad* (3655)

Le feuillet 12 » 12 »

2004. – Série "Nature de France" (XIX). Animaux de la ferme. T.-P. de même date imprimés sur feuillet de160 x 110. Héliogravure. Dentelé.

69 0,45 € *Le lapin* (3662)
0,50 € *La poule* (3663)
0,50 € *La vache* (3664)
0,75 € *Le baudet* (3665)

Le feuillet 5 » 5 »

2004. – Jardins de France. T.-P. de même date imprimés sur feuillet de 286 x 110. Héliogravure. Dentelé.

70 1,90 € *Le Jardin des Tuileries (perspective sur les bassins, l'Obélisque de la place de la Concorde et l'Arc de Triomphe)* (3673)
1,90 € *Le Parc floral de Paris* (3674)

Le feuillet 10 » 10 »

La mention "Le Salon du Timbre 2004" figure hors timbres.

2004. – Jardins de France. T.-P. de 2003 et 2004 imprimés sur feuillet de 144 x 210. Héliogravure. Dentelé.

71 1,90 € *Parc des Buttes-Chaumont (détail falaise avec le temple de la Sibylle)* (3606)
1,90 € *Jardin du Luxembourg (détail avec le bâtiment du Sénat en fond)* (3607)
1,90 € *Le Jardin des Tuileries (perspective sur les bassins, l'Obélisque de la place de la Concorde et l'Arc de Triomphe)* (3673)
1,90 € *Le Parc floral de Paris* (3674)

Le feuillet 25 » 25 »

2004. – Personnages célèbres. Napoléon 1er et la garde impériale. T.-P. de même date imprimés sur feuillet de 135 x 143, vendu 4,60 € dont 1,60 € reversés à la Croix-Rouge Française. Héliogravure. Dentelé.

72 0,50 € *Chasseur à cheval* (3679)
0,50 € *Artilleur à pied* (3680)
0,50 € *Dragon* (3681)
0,50 € *Mameluk* (3682)
0,50 € *Napoléon 1er à cheval* (3683)
0,50 € *Grenadier à pied* (3684)

Le feuillet 10 » 10 »

2004. – *Jeux olympiques d'Athènes (Grèce). T.-P. de même date imprimés sur feuillet de 183 x 108. Héliogravure. Dentelé.*

73 5 x 0,50 € *Kayak, tennis, saut d'obstacles* (3686)
5 x 0,50 € *Athlète antique portant la flamme olympique et relayeur* (3687)

Le feuillet 15 » 15 »

2004. – *Jeux olympiques d'Athènes (Grèce). Passage de la flamme olympique à Paris. T.-P. de même date imprimé sur feuillet de 205 x 95. Héliogravure. Dentelé.*

74 0,50 € *Athlète antique portant la flamme olympique et relayeur* (3687) 15 » 15 »

BF inséré dans une carte "Athènes".

2004. – *Timbre "Anniversaire". T.-P. de même date imprimé sur feuillet de 135 x 143. Héliogravure. Dentelé.*

75 5 x 0,50 € *Maître d'hôtel portant un énorme gâteau (Oeuvre originale du dessinateur humoriste Jean-Jacques Sempé)* (3688) 5 » 5 »

2004. – *Série "Collection Jeunesse". Les sports de glisse. T.-P. de même date imprimés sur feuillet de 108 x 183. Héliogravure. Dentelé.*

76 0,20 € *Skateboard* (3691)
0,20 € *Parachutisme* (3692)
0,20 € *Planche à voile* (3693)
0,20 € *Surf* (3694)
0,20 € *Luge* (3695)
0,30 € *Bicross* (3696)
0,30 € *Parapente* (3697)
0,30 € *Jet-ski* (3698)
0,30 € *Snowboard* (3699)
0,30 € *Roller* (3700)

Le feuillet 6 » 6 »

2004. – *Portraits de régions. La France à voir n° 4. T.-P. de même date imprimés sur feuillet de 286 x 110. Dentelé.*

77 0,50 € *Maison normande* (3702)
0,50 € *Le château de Chambord* (3703)
0,50 € *Les gorges du Tarn* (3704)
0,50 € *Notre-Dame de Paris* (3705)
0,50 € *Moulin du Nord* (3706)
0,50 € *Maison troglodytique* (3707)
0,50 € *Les calanques de Cassis* (3708)
0,50 € *Le phare du Cap-Ferret* (3709)
0,50 € *Château cathare* (3710)
0,50 € *Chalet des Alpes* (3711)

Le feuillet 12 » 12 »

2004. – ***Capitales européennes. Athènes. T.-P. de même date imprimés sur feuillet de 142 x 134. Dentelé.***

78 0,50 € *L'Académie* (3718)
0,50 € *Le Parthénon* (3719)
0,50 € *L'Odéon d'Hérode Atticus* (3720)
0,50 € *L'Eglise des Saints-Apôtres* (3721)

Le feuillet 6 » 6 »

2004. – ***"Meilleurs Voeux" (étoile personnage avec fleur). Type du T.-P. de même date imprimé sur feuillet de 205 x 95. Dentelé.***

79 0,50 € *Etoile personnage tenant une fleur* (3724a) 35 » 35 »

BF inséré dans une carte de voeux 2005 vendue 3 €. Voir Blocs souvenirs n° 3.

2005. – ***Saint-Valentin. Coeurs 2005 du couturier Cacharel. T.-P. de même date imprimé sur feuillet de 135 x 143. Dentelé.***

80 5 x 0,53 € *Coeur en tissu Liberty* (3747) 6 » 6 »

2005. – ***Série "Nature" (XX). T.-P. de même date imprimés sur feuillet de 110 x 160. Dentelé.***

81 0,53 € *Orchidée "Mabel Sanders"* (3763)
0,53 € *Sabot de Vénus* (3764)
0,55 € *Orchidée papillon* (3765)
0,82 € *Orchidée d'Aphrodite* (3766)

Le feuillet 6 » 6 »

Certaines parties d'images du bloc sont recouvertes d'un vernis parfumé à la vanille.

2005. – ***Portraits de régions. La France à vivre n° 5. T.-P. de même date imprimés sur feuillet de 251 x 110. Dentelé.***

82 0,53 € *Les joutes nautiques* (3767)
0,53 € *L'horlogerie comtoise* (3768)
0,53 € *Le cantal* (3769)
0,53 € *Les guinguettes* (3770)
0,53 € *La bouillabaisse* (3771)
0,53 € *Le P'tit Quinquin (sculpture)* (3772)
0,53 € *Les rillettes* (3773)
0,53 € *La choucroute* (3774)
0,53 € *La pelote basque* (3775)
0,53 € *La canne à sucre* (3776)
Le feuillet 12 » 12 »

2005. – ***Timbre pour Anniversaires. Bande dessinée. Centenaire de Bécassine, du dessinateur Joseph Porphyre Pinchon. T.-P. de même date imprimé sur feuillet de 135 x 143.***

83 5 x Lettre 20g *Bécassine portant un gâteau d'anniversaire* (3778) 6 » 6 »

2005. – ***Jardins de France. T.-P. de même date imprimés sur feuillet de 286 x 110. Dentelé.***

84 1,98 € *Jardin de la Fontaine à Nîmes ("La nymphe de la source " (1746), sculpture de Dominique Raché)* (3786)
1,98 € *Jardin de la fontaine à Nîmes (sculpture du bassin du Nymphée)* (3787)
Le feuillet 10 » 10 »

La mention "Le Salon du Timbre 2006" figure hors timbres.

2005. – ***Personnages célèbres. Héros de romans de l'écrivain Jules Verne (1828-1905). T.-P. de même date imprimés sur feuillet de 135 x 144, vendu 4,80 €, dont 1,62 € de don reversé à la Croix-Rouge Française. Dentelé.***

85 0,53 € *"Cinq semaines en ballon" (1863) (montgolfière et éléphant)* (3789)
0,53 € *"De la Terre à la Lune" (1865) (fusée)* (3790)
0,53 € *"Voyage au centre de la Terre" (1864) (faune préhistorique, radeau)* (3791)
0,53 € *"Michel Strogoff" (1876) (scène avec le héros, courrier du tsar, à cheval)* (3792)
0,53 € *"Le Tour du monde en 80 jours" (1873) (locomotive, bisons)* (3793)
0,53 € *"Vingt mille lieues sous les mers" (1870) (combat contre une pieuvre géante)* (3794)
Le feuillet 10 » 10 »

2005. – ***Sport automobile. Coupe Gordon Bennett. T.-P. de même date imprimés sur feuillet de 210 x 142. Dentelé.***

86 0,53 € *Coupe Gordon Bennett (voiture de course Richard Brasier vainqueur en 1905)* (3795)
0,53 € *Coupe Gordon Bennett (voiture de course Richard Brasier vainqueur en 1905, représentée sur partie de route protégée par une palissade)* (3796)
2 x 0,53 € *Voiture de course d'endurance* (3797)
2 x 0,53 € *Voiture de rallye* (3798)
2 x 0,53 € *Voiture de rallye-raid* (3799)
2 x 0,53 € *Voiture de Formule 1* (3800)
Le feuillet 14 » 14 »

2005. – *Sport automobile. Coupe Gordon Bennett. T.-P. de même date imprimé sur feuillet de 205 x 95. Dentelé.*

87 0,53 € *Coupe Gordon Bennett (voiture de course Richard Brasier vainqueur en 1905)* (3795) 110 » 110 »

BF inséré dans une carte "Coupe Gordon Bennett" vendue 3 €. Voir Blocs souvenirs n° 4.

2005. – *Capitales européennes. Berlin. T.-P. de même date imprimés sur feuillet de 143 x 136. Dentelé.*

88 0,53 € *La Porte de Brandebourg* (3810)
0,53 € *L'église du Souvenir* (3811)
0,53 € *La Philharmonie* (3812)
0,53 € *Le Reichstag* (3813)
Le feuillet 6 » 6 »

2005. – *Portraits de régions. La France à voir n° 6. T.-P. de même date imprimés sur feuillet de 252 x 110. Dentelé.*

89 0,53 € *Le Lac d'Annecy* (3814)
0,53 € *Les falaises d'Etretat* (3815)
0,53 € *Pigeonnier* (3816)
0,53 € *Lavoir* (3817)
0,53 € *Quais de Seine* (3818)
0,53 € *Les mégalithes de Carnac* (3819)
0,53 € *Maison solognote* (3820)
0,53 € *La dune du Pilat* (3821)
0,53 € *Le phare du Stiff* (3822)
0,53 € *Borie* (3823)
Le feuillet 12 » 12 »

2005. – *Art. "L'Annonciation", oeuvre du peintre italien Raphaël (1483-1520). Emission commune avec le Vatican. T.-P. de même date imprimés sur feuillet de 130 x 85. Dentelé.*

90 0,53 € *Dessin préparatoire de l'ange Gabriel (Musée du Louvre) et peinture de la Vierge Marie* (3838)
0,55 € *Peinture de l'ange Gabriel et dessin de préparatoire de la Vierge Marie (Musée du Louvre)* (3839)
Le feuillet 2 50 2 50

2005. – *Série "Collection jeunesse". Héros des jeux vidéo. T.-P. de même date imprimés sur feuillet de 108 x 183. Dentelé.*

91 0,20 € *Link avec son bouclier et son épée Excalibur* (3842)
0,20 € *Pac-Man* (3843)
0,20 € *Prince of Persia* (3844)
0,20 € *Spyro le petit dragon* (3845)
0,20 € *Donkey Kong le gorille* (3846)
0,33 € *Mario le plombier* (3847)
0,33 € *Adibou* (3848)
0,33 € *Rayman* (3849)
0,33 € *Lara Croft* (3850)
0,33 € *Les Sims* (3851)
Le feuillet 6 » 6 »

2005. – "Meilleurs voeux" (manchots, renne et bonhomme de neige). Type du T.-P. de même date imprimé sur feuillet de 206 x 96. Dentelé.

92 (sans val.) *Manchots, renne et bonhomme de neige* (3854a) 30 » 30 »

BF inséré dans une carte de voeux 2006 vendue 3 €. Voir Blocs souvenirs n° 5.

2006. – Saint-Valentin. Coeurs 2006 du couturier Stéphane Rolland de la Maison Jean-Louis Scherrer. T.-P. de même date imprimé sur feuillet de 135 x 142. Dentelé.

93 5 x Lettre 20 g *Coeur* (3861) 6 » 6 »

2006. – Portraits de régions. La France à vivre n° 7. T.-P. de même date imprimés sur feuillet de 251 x 110. Dentelé.

94 0,53 € *La mirabelle* (3882)
0,53 € *Les marais salants* (3883)
0,53 € *Le beurre* (3884)
0,53 € *Le roquefort* (3885)
0,53 € *L'huile d'olive* (3886)
0,53 € *Le carnaval* (3887)
0,53 € *Les vendanges* (3888)
0,53 € *Le café* (3889)
0,53 € *La transhumance* (3890)
0,53 € *Les hortillonnages* (3891)

Le feuillet 12 » 12 »

2006. – Jardins de France. T.-P. de même date imprimés sur feuillet de 286 x 110. Dentelé.

95 1,98 € *Arboretum du Parc de la Vallée-aux-Loups, à Châtenay-Malabry (Hauts-de-Seine)* (3895)
1,98 € *Jardin Albert Kahn, à Boulogne-Billancourt (Hauts-de-Seine) (pont japonais)* (3896)

Le feuillet 10 » 10 »

2006. – Série "Nature" (XXI). Faune. Les jeunes animaux domestiques. T.-P. de même date imprimés sur feuillet de 110 x 160. Dentelé.

96 0,53 € *Le chaton* (3897)
0,53 € *Le chiot* (3898)
0,55 € *Le poulain* (3899)
0,82 € *L'agneau* (3900)

Le feuillet 6 » 6 »

2006. – *Coupe du monde de football 2006 en Allemagne. T.-P. de même date imprimés sur feuillet de 210 x 142. Dentelé.*

97 0,53 € *Les remplaçants* (3906)
0,53 € *Les supporters* (3907)
0,53 € *L'entraîneur* (3908)
0,53 € *Les journalistes* (3909)
0,53 € *Le dégagement* (3910)
0,53 € *Le contrôle* (3911)
0,53 € *Le centre* (3912)
0,53 € *Le retourné* (3913)
0,53 € *La feinte de corps* (3914)
0,53 € *L'arbitre* (3915)

Le feuillet 13 » 13 »

2006. – *Personnages célèbres. Les opéras de Mozart. T.-P. de même date imprimés sur feuillet de 135 x 143, vendu 4,80 € dont 1,62 € de don reversé à la Croix-Rouge Française. Dentelé.*

98 0,53 € *L'Enlèvement au sérail (1782) (costume de Varona)* (3917)
0,53 € *Les Noces de Figaro (1786) (costume d'Ezio Frigerio)* (3918)
0,53 € *Don Giovanni (1787) (costume de Marillier)* (3919)
0,53 € *Cosi fan tutte (1790) (costume d'Erté)* (3920)
0,53 € *La Clémence de Titus (1791) (costume de Graf)* (3921)
0,53 € *La Flûte enchantée (1791) (costume de Chapelain-Midy)* (3922)

Le feuillet 10 » 8 »

2006. – *"Salon du timbre 2006". Jardins de France. Types des T.-P. de 2005 et 2006 imprimés sur feuillet de 210 x 143. Légende Phil@poste (au lieu d'ITVF). Dentelé.*

99 1,98 € *Jardin de la Fontaine à Nîmes ("La nymphe de la source" (1746), sculpture de Dominique Raché)* (3786a)
1,98 € *Jardin de la fontaine à Nîmes (sculpture du bassin du Nymphée)* (3787a)
1,98 € *Arboretum du Parc de la Vallée-aux-Loups, à Châtenay-Malabry (Hauts-de-Seine)* (3895a)
1,98 € *Jardin Albert Kahn, à Boulogne-Billancourt (Hauts-de-Seine) (pont japonais)* (3896a)

Le feuillet 25 » 25 »

2006. – *Timbre pour Anniversaires. Bande dessinée. 75 ans de l'éléphant Babar par l'auteur et dessinateur Laurent de Brunhoff. T.-P. de même date imprimé sur feuillet de 135 x 143.*

100 5 x (sans val.) *Babar portant un gâteau d'anniversaire* (3927) 6 » 6 »

2006. – *Capitales européennes. Nicosie (Chypre). T.-P. de même date imprimés sur feuillet de 143 x 135. Dentelé.*

101 0,53 € *Le Musée archéologique* (3928)
0,53 € *L'église byzantine de Chrysaliniotissa (1450)* (3929)
0,53 € *La Porte de Famagouste* (3930)
0,53 € *Le palais de l'Archevêché* (3931)

Le feuillet 6 » 6 »

2006. – *Portraits de régions. La France à voir n° 8. T.-P. de même date imprimés sur feuillet de 251 x 110. Dentelé.*

102 0,54 € *Tours catalanes* (3942)
0,54 € *La Croisette à Cannes (Alpes-Maritimes)* (3943)
0,54 € *La forêt de Brocéliande* (3944)
0,54 € *Les volcans d'Auvergne* (3945)
0,54 € *Les Invalides, à Paris (l'édifice illuminé)* (3946)
0,54 € *Le château de Chaumont-sur-Loire* (3947)
0,54 € *Les gorges de l'Ardèche* (3948)
0,54 € *Le moulin de Valmy* (3949)
0,54 € *La grotte de Lourdes* (3950)
0,54 € *Calanche de Piana (Corse)* (3951)

Le feuillet 12 » 12 »

2006. – *Aviation. Les machines volantes. T.-P. de même date imprimés sur feuillet de 143 x 105. Dentelé.*

103 0,54 € *L' "Hélicoptère" du vicomte Ponton d'Amécourt* (3978)
0,54 € *La "Demoiselle" d'Alberto Santos-Dumont* (3979)
0,54 € *La "Barque ailée" de Jean-Marie Le Bris* (3980)
0,54 € *L'Avion III de Clément Ader* (3981)
0,54 € *L' "Hydravion" d'Henri Fabre* (3982)
0,54 € *Le "Ballon à rames" de Jean-Pierre Blanchard* (3983)

Le feuillet 6 50 6 50

2007. – *Saint-Valentin. Coeurs 2007 de la Maison de couture Givenchy. T.-P. de même date imprimé sur feuillet de 135 x 143. Dentelé.*

104 5 x Lettre 20 g noir sur rouge
Cœur rouge (3996) 5 40 5 40

2007. – *Portraits de régions. La France à voir n° 9. T.-P. de même date imprimés sur feuillet de 250 x 110. Multicolore. Dentelé.*

105 0,54 € *Les Baux-de-Provence* (4014)
0,54 € *Cascade dans le Doubs* (4015)
0,54 € *La forêt de Fontainebleau* (4016)
0,54 € *Les bords de Loire* (4017)
0,54 € *Le château de Chantilly* (4018)
0,54 € *Le massif de la Grande-Chartreuse* (4019)
0,54 € *Saint-Malo* (4020)
0,54 € *Saint-Tropez* (4021)
0,54 € *Le ballon d'Alsace* (4022)
0,54 € *Le canal du Midi* (4023)

Le feuillet 11 » 11 »

2007. – *Fête du timbre. "Harry Potter", héros de la série de l'écrivain britannique Joanne Kathleen Rowling. T.-P. de même date imprimé sur feuillet de 105* x *70. Dentelé.*

106 Lettre prioritaire 20 g *Harry Potter* (4024) 1 50 1 50

2007. – *Série "Nature" (XXII). Faune en voie de disparition dans les départements d'outre-mer. T.-P. de même date imprimés sur feuillet de 110×160. Multicolore. Dentelé.*

107 0,54 € *Iguane des Antilles (Iguana delicatissima)* (4033)
0,54 € *Le racoon de la Guadeloupe* (4034)
0,60 € *Le jaguar de Guyane* (4035)
0,86 € *Le pétrel de Barau à La Réunion* (4036)

Le feuillet 5 10 5 10

2007. – *Jardins de France. Le Parc de la Tête d'Or à Lyon (Rhône). T.-P. de même date imprimés sur feuillet de 285* x *110. Multicolore. Dentelé.*

108 2,11 € *Détail vue du Parc de la Tête d'Or à Lyon* (4047)
2,11 € *Détail vue des serres du Parc de la Tête d'Or à Lyon* (4048)

Le feuillet 8 40 8 40

2007. – *Personnages célèbres. Les voyages de Tintin. T.-P. de même date imprimés sur feuillet de 135* x *143. Multicolore. Dentelé.*

109 0,54 € *Tintin et Milou* (4051)
0,54 € *Le professeur Tournesol avec ses jumelles* (4052)
0,54 € *La capitaine Haddock utilisant un sextant* (4053)
0,54 € *Dupond et Dupont en voiture* (4054)
0,54 € *Bianca Castafiore, la diva* (4055)
0,54 € *Le Chinois Tchang* (4056)

Le feuillet 10 » 10 »

Vendu 5,00 € dont 1,76 € de don reversé à la Croix-Rouge Française.

2007. – *VIᵉ coupe du monde de Rugby organisée par la France en 2007. T.-P. de même date imprimés sur feuillet de 210 x 143. Multicolore. Dentelé.*

110 0,54 € *La mêlée* (4063)
0,54 € *L'attaque* (4064)
0,54 € *L'essai* (4065)
0,54 € *La touche* (4066)
0,54 € *La transformation* (4067)
0,54 € *La passe* (4068)
0,54 € *Le raffut* (4069)
0,54 € *Le haka* (4070)
0,54 € *Le plaquage* (4071)
0,54 € *Les supporters* (4072)

Le feuillet	10 80	10 80

2007. – *Capitales européennes. Bruxelles (Belgique). T.-P. de même date imprimés sur feuillet de 143 x 136. Multicolore. Dentelé.*

111 0,54 € *La Maison du Roi* (4073)
0,54 € *L'Hôtel de Ville* (4074)
0,54 € *Le Manneken Pis* (4075)
0,54 € *L'Atomium* (4076)

Le feuillet	6 »	6 »

2007. – *Timbre pour Anniversaires. Sylvain et Sylvette, héros de bandes dessinées de Jean-Louis Pesch. T.-P. de même date imprimé sur feuillet de 135 x 142. Multicolore. Dentelé.*

112 5 x (sans val.) *Sylvain et Sylvette portant un gâteau* (4081) 7 50 7 50

2007. – *Portraits de régions. La France à vivre n° 10. T.-P. de même date imprimés sur feuillet de 252 x 110. Multicolore. Dentelé.*

113 0,54 € *La porcelaine de Sèvres* (4094)
0,54 € *Les géants* (4095)
0,54 € *Le béret basque* (4096)
0,54 € *Le parfum de Grasse* (4097)
0,54 € *Les tapisseries d'Aubusson* (4098)
0,54 € *Le marché de Noël* (4099)
0,54 € *Le bouchon lyonnais* (4100)
0,54 € *Le savon de Marseille* (4101)
0,54 € *Les charentaises* (4102)
0,54 € *Le melon* (4103)

Le feuillet	11 »	11 »

2007. – *Les phares. T.-P. de même date imprimés sur feuillet de 143 x 105. Multicolore. Dentelé.*

114 0,54 € *Phare du Cap Fréhel (1846-1950), Côtes-d'Armor* (4112)

0,54 € *Phare de l'Espiguette (1869), Grau-du-Roi (Gard)* (4113)

0,54 € *Phare d'Ar-Men (1867-1881), Chaussée de Sein* (4114)

0,54 € *Phare du Grand-Léjon (1881), au large de Saint-Quay-Portrieux (Côtes-d'Armor)* (4115)

0,54 € *Phare du Cap d'Arme (1830) (île de Porquerolles)* (4116)

0,54 € *Phare de Chassiron (1836), île d'Oléron* (4117)

Le feuillet 7 80 7 80

2008. – *Saint-Valentin. Coeur 2008 du couturier Franck Sorbier. T.-P. de même date imprimé sur feuillet de 135 x 143. Multicolore. Dentelé.*

115 5 x Lettre prioritaire 20 g *Visages formant un cœur* (4128) 6 » 6 »

2008. – *Fête du timbre. Droopy, personnage des dessins animés de Tex Avery (1907-1980). T.-P. de même date imprimé sur feuillet de 106 x 72.*

116 2,18 € *Le chien Droopy* (4152) 5 » 5 »

"Frottez la zone bleue du timbre pour voir apparaître ce que dit Droopy".

2008. – *Portraits de régions. La France à voir n° 11. T.-P. de même date imprimés sur feuillet de 250 x 110.*

117 0,55 € *Le château d'Ussé (Indre et Loire)* (4161)

0,55 € *Le moulin de Cugarel* (4162)

0,55 € *La côte de granit rose (phare)* (4163)

0,55 € *Vézelay* (4164)

0,55 € *Honfleur* (4165)

0,55 € *Le Marais (Paris)* (4166)

0,55 € *La Petite France (Strasbourg)* (4167)

0,55 € *Le Marais poitevin* (4168)

0,55 € *Sarlat-la-Canéda* (4169)

0,55 € *Le cirque de Mafate (La Réunion)* (4170)

Le feuillet 11 » 11 »

2008. – *Jardins de France. T.-P. de même date imprimés sur feuillet de 286 x 100.*

118 2,18 € *Le Parc Longchamp à Marseille* (4173)

2,18 € *Le Parc Borély à Marseille (gloriette)* (4174)

Le feuillet 8 80 8 80

2008. – *Faune préhistorique. T.-P. de même date imprimés sur feuillet de 110* x *160.*

119 0,55 € *Smilodon* (4175)

0,55 € *Phorusrhacos* (4176)

0,65 € *Megaloceros* (4177)

0,88 € *Mammouth* (4178)

Le feuillet 5 30 5 30

2008. – *"Salon du Timbre 2008". Jardins de France. T.-P. de 2007 et 2008 imprimés sur feuillet de 210* x *142.*

120 2,11 € *Détail vue du Parc de la Tête d'Or à Lyon* (4047)

2,11 € *Détail vue des serres du Parc de la Tête d'Or à Lyon* (4048)

2,18 € *Le Parc Longchamp à Marseille* (4173)

2,18 € *Le Parc Borély à Marseille (gloriette)* (4174)

Le feuillet 25 » 25 »

2008. – *Personnages célèbres. Le cirque. T.-P. de même date imprimés sur feuillet de 136* x *142.*

121 0,55 € *Le trapéziste* (4216)

0,55 € *L'écuyère* (4217)

0,55 € *L'auguste* (4218)

0,55 € *Le dompteur (numéro avec lion)* (4219)

0,55 € *Le clown blanc* (4220)

0,55 € *Le jongleur* (4221)

Le feuillet 10 25 10 25

Vendu 5,10 € dont 1,80 € reversés à la Croix-Rouge Française.

2008. – *Jeux olympiques d'été à Pékin (Chine) en 2008. T.-P. de même date imprimés sur feuillet de 210* x *143.*

122 2 x 0,55 € *Equitation et cyclisme* (4222)

2 x 0,55 € *Tennis et course à pied* (4223)

3 x 0,55 € *Natation et aviron* (4224)

3 x 0,55 € *Judo et escrime* (4225)

Le feuillet 11 » 11 »

2008. – *Grands projets européens. T.-P. de même date imprimés sur feuillet de 142* x *105.*

123 0,55 € *L'euro* (4245)
0,55 € *Présidence française du Conseil de l'Union européenne durant le 2e semestre 2008 (drapeaux français et européen)* (4246)
0,55 € *Satellite Galileo* (4247)
0,55 € *Erasmus (étudiants, drapeaux)* (4248)

Le feuillet 5 » 5 »

2008. – *Voiliers célèbres. T.-P. de même date imprimés sur feuillet de 143* x *105.*

124 0,55 € *La Confiance* (4249)
0,55 € *La Grande Hermine* (4250)
0,55 € *La Boudeuse* (4251)
0,55 € *L'Astrolabe* (4252)
0,55 € *L'Hermione* (4253)
0,55 € *La Boussole* (4254)

Le feuillet 7 50 7 50

2008. – *Portraits de régions. La France à vivre. T.-P. de même date imprimés sur feuillet de 252* x *110.*

125 0,55 € *Les espadrilles du Pays-Basque* (4260)
0,55 € *L'image d'Epinal (Le Chat botté)* (4261)
0,55 € *La lentille* (4262)
0,55 € *Le pot au feu* (4263)
0,55 € *Le reblochon* (4264)
0,55 € *La chataîgne* (4265)
0,55 € *Le calisson* (4266)
0,55 € *Les feux d'artifice* (4267)
0,55 € *Les échasses* (4268)
0,55 € *La moutarde* (4269)

Le feuillet 11 » 11 »

2008. – *Capitales européennes. Prague (République tchèque). T.-P. de même date imprimés sur feuillet de 144* x *134.*

126 0,55 € *Tour du Petit Côté* (4301)
0,55 € *Hôtel de ville (horloge astronomique et calendrier)* (4302)
0,55 € *Eglise Notre-Dame de Tyn* (4303)
0,55 € *Le château* (4304)

Le feuillet 5 » 5 »

Tirage : 2 200 000.

2009. – ***Saint-Valentin. Cœur 2009 de la Maison de couture Emanuel Ungaro. T.-P. de même date imprimé sur feuillet de 143 x 135.***

127	5 x Lettre prioritaire 20 g *Perroquet et fleurs roses* (4327)	5 50	5 50

Tirage : 2 200 000.

2009. – ***Série "Nature" (XXIII). Animaux disparus ou menacés d'extinction. T.-P. de même date imprimés sur feuillet de 160 x 110.***

128 0,56 € *Panda géant (Ailuropoda melanoleuca)* (4372)
0,56 € *Rhinocéros* (4373)
0,70 € *Aurochs* (4374)
0,90 € *Condor de Californie (Gymnogyps californianus)* (4375)

Le feuillet 5 40 5 40

BLOCS SOUVENIRS

2003. – ***"Meilleurs Vœux" (Rouge-gorge). Type du T.-P. de même date imprimé sur feuillet de 205 x 95. Sans bandes de phosphore.*** BF ***n° 65.***

1	0,50 € *Rouge-gorge* (3621a)	225 »	225 »

Bloc inséré dans une carte de vœux 2004.

2004. – ***Jeux olympiques d'Athènes (Grèce). Passage de la flamme olympique à Paris. T.-P. de même date imprimé sur feuillet de 205 x 95.*** BF ***n° 74.***

2	0,50 € *Athlète antique portant la flamme olympique et relayeur* (3687)	15 »	15 »

Bloc inséré dans une carte "Athènes" vendue 3 €.

2004. – ***"Meilleurs Voeux" (étoile personnage avec fleur). Type du T.-P. de même date imprimé sur feuillet de 205 x 95.*** BF ***n° 79.***

3	0,50 € *Etoile personnage tenant une fleur* (3724a)	35 »	35 »

Bloc inséré dans une carte de vœux 2005 vendue 3 €.

2005. – ***Sport automobile. Coupe Gordon Bennett. T.-P. de même date imprimé sur feuillet de 205 x 95.*** BF ***n° 87.***

4	0,53 € *Coupe Gordon Bennett (voiture de course Richard Brasier vainqueur en 1905)* (3795)	110 »	110 »

Bloc inséré dans une carte "Coupe Gordon Bennett" vendue 3 €.

2005. – *"Meilleurs voeux" (manchots, renne et bonhomme de neige). Type du T.-P. de même date imprimé sur feuillet de 206 x 96.* BF *n° 92.*

5 (sans val.) *Manchots, renne et bonhomme de neige* (3854a) 30 » 30 »

Bloc inséré dans une carte de vœux 2006 vendue 3 €.

2006. – *Année lunaire chinoise du chien. T.-P. de même date imprimé sur feuillet de 206 x 96.*

6 Lettre 20 g *Chien, oeuvre originale de Li Zhongyao, peintre et calligraphe* (3865) 8 » 8 »

Bloc inséré dans une carte "Nouvel An chinois" vendue 3 €.

2006. – *Personnages célèbres. Les opéras de Mozart. T.-P. de même date imprimé sur feuillet de 205 x 95.*

7 0,53 € *L'Enlèvement au sérail (1782) (costume de Varona)* (3917) 8 » 8 »

Bloc inséré dans une carte "L'Enlèvement au sérail", Mozart.

2006. – *Personnages célèbres. Les opéras de Mozart. T.-P. de même date imprimé sur feuillet de 205 x 95.*

8 0,53 € *Les Noces de Figaro (1786) (costume d'Ezio Frigerio)* (3918) 8 » 8 »

Bloc inséré dans une carte "Les Noces de Figaro", Mozart.

2006. – *Personnages célèbres. Les opéras de Mozart. T.-P. de même date imprimé sur feuillet de 205 x 95.*

9 0,53 € *Don Giovanni (1787) (costume de Marillier)* (3919) 8 » 8 »

Bloc inséré dans une carte "Don Giovanni", Mozart.

2006. – *Personnages célèbres. Les opéras de Mozart. T.-P. de même date imprimé sur feuillet de 205 x 95.*

10 0,53 € *Cosi fan tutte (1790) (costume d'Erté)* (3920) 8 » 8 »

Bloc inséré dans une carte "Cosi fan tutte", Mozart.

2006. – *Personnages célèbres. Les opéras de Mozart. T.-P. de même date imprimé sur feuillet de 205 x 95.*

11 0,53 € *La Clémence de Titus (1791) (costume de Graf)* (3921) 8 » 8 »

Bloc inséré dans une carte "La Clémence de Titus", Mozart.

2006. – *Personnages célèbres. Les opéras de Mozart. T.-P. de même date imprimé sur feuillet de 205 x 95.*

12 0,53 € *La Flûte enchantée (1791) (costume de Chapelain-Midy)* (3922) 8 » 8 »

Bloc inséré dans une carte "La Flûte enchantée", Mozart.

2007. – *Sport. Golf. Centenaire de l'Open de France. Type du T.-P. de même date imprimé sur feuillet de 205 x 95. Sans bandes de phosphore.*

13 0,53 € *Silhouettes de joueurs de 1906 et de 2006* (3935a) 8 » 8 »

Bloc inséré dans une carte "Centenaire de l'Open de France de golf", vendue 3 €.

2006. – *"Nancy 2005", le plus beau timbre de l'année 2005. Type du T.-P. de 2005 imprimé sur feuillet de 207 x 95. Légende Phil@poste (au lieu d'ITVF).*

14 (sans val.) *La place Stanislas avec la statue de Stanislas 1er Leszczynski, duc de Lorraine* (3785a) 8 » 8 »

Bloc inséré dans une carte "Nancy 2005", vendue 3 €.

2006. – *"Meilleurs Voeux " (Renne et paquets cadeaux). Type du T.-P. de même date imprimé sur feuillet de 205 x 95. Papier gommé.*

15 Lettre 20 g *Renne avec paquet cadeau et manchots dans des paquets cadeaux* (3990a) 18 » 18 »

Bloc inséré dans une carte "Meilleurs vœux", vendue 3 €.

2007. – *Année lunaire chinoise du Cochon. T.-P. de même date imprimé sur feuillet de 205 x 95.*

16 Lettre 20 g *Cochon, œuvre originale de Li Zhongyao, peintre et calligraphe* (4001) 8 » 8 »

Bloc inséré dans une carte "Nouvel An chinois" vendue 3 €.

2007. – *Personnalité. Albert Londres (1884-1932), journaliste. T.-P. imprimé sur feuillet de 205 x 95.*

17 0,54 € brun et bleu *Portrait du reporter, scène d'arrivée de bagnards en Guyane* (4027) 9 » 9 »

Bloc avec marge illustrée "Tianjin 1922, les troupes de Zhang Zuolin" inséré dans une carte" Pékin 1922".

2007. – *Personnalité. Albert Londres (1884-1932), journaliste. T.-P. imprimé sur feuillet de 205 x 95.*

18 0,54 € brun et bleu *Portrait du reporter, scène d'arrivée de bagnards en Guyane* (4027) 9 » 9 »

Bloc avec marge illustrée "Cayenne, l'îlet de l'enfant perdu" inséré dans une carte "Cayenne 1923, le bagne".

2007. – *Personnalité. Albert Londres (1884-1932), journaliste. T.-P. imprimé sur feuillet de 205 x 95.*

19 0,54 € brun et bleu *Portrait du reporter, scène d'arrivée de bagnards en Guyane* (4027) 9 » 9 »

Bloc avec marge illustrée "Les Flandres 1917" inséré dans une carte "La Ruhr 1923".

2007. – *Personnalité. Albert Londres (1884-1932), journaliste. T.-P. imprimé sur feuillet de 205 x 95.*

20 0,54 € brun et bleu *Portrait du reporter, scène d'arrivée de bagnards en Guyane* (4027) 9 » 9 »

Bloc avec marge illustrée "Marseille 1926" inséré dans une carte " Marseille 1926".

2007. – *Personnalité. Albert Londres (1884-1932), journaliste. T.-P. imprimé sur feuillet de 205 x 95.*

21 0,54 € brun et bleu *Portrait du reporter, scène d'arrivée de bagnards en Guyane* (4027) 9 » 9 »

Bloc avec marge illustrée "Les galériens de Bahreïn 1930" inséré dans une carte "Golfe persique 1930, Sambouk des pêcheurs de perles".

2007. – *Personnalité. Albert Londres (1884-1932), journaliste. T.-P. imprimé sur feuillet de 205 x 95.*

22 0,54 € brun et bleu *Portrait du reporter, scène d'arrivée de bagnards en Guyane* (4027) 9 » 9 »

Bloc avec marge illustrée "Reims 1914" inséré dans une carte "Shanghai 1932, Le Georges-Philippar".

2007. – *Centenaire de la Fédération internationale de voile. T.-P. de même date imprimé sur feuillet de 206 x 95.*

23 0,85 € *Voiliers en compétition* (4050) 12 » 12 »

Bloc inséré dans une carte vendue 3 €.

2007. – *"Opéra Garnier 2006", le plus beau timbre de l'année 2006. Type du T.-P. de 2006 imprimé sur feuillet de 205 x 95. Sans vignette attenante.*

24 0,53 € *Edifice de l'Opéra Garnier, à Paris* (3926a) 6 » 6 »

Bloc inséré dans une carte "Opéra Garnier 2006", vendue 3 €.

2007. – *"Meilleurs Voeux" (hérisson). Type du T.-P. de même date imprimé sur feuillet de 205 x 95. Papier gommé.*

25 Lettre prioritaire 20 g *Hérisson avec chapeau de fête* (4123a) 6 » 6 »

Bloc inséré dans une carte "Meilleurs voeux" vendue 3 €.

2008. – *Les globes de Coronelli. T.-P. de même date imprimé sur feuillet de 205 x 95.*

26 0,85 € *Globes terrestre et céleste, réalisés par Vincenzo Coronelli et offerts au roi Louis XIV, grue figurant sur le globe céleste* (4144) 6 » 6 »

Bloc inséré dans une carte "Les globes de Coronelli" vendue 3 €.

2008. – *400e anniversaire de la fondation de la ville de Québec. T.-P. de même date imprimé sur feuillet de 205 x 95.*

27 0,85 € *L'explorateur et cartographe Samuel de Champlain (1567-1635) saluant les autochtones en canot depuis son navire, forteresse en construction* (4182) 6 » 6 »

Bloc avec marge illustrée par un détail d'une carte ancienne de l'estuaire du Saint-Laurent, inséré dans une carte "Jacques Cartier".

2008. – *400e anniversaire de la fondation de la ville de Québec. T.-P. de même date imprimé sur feuillet de 205* x *95.*

28 0,85 € *L'explorateur et cartographe Samuel de Champlain (1567-1635) saluant les autochtones en canot depuis son navire, forteresse en construction* (4182) 6 » 6 »

Bloc avec marge illustrée par un détail d'une carte ancienne avec l'île de Sainte-Croix, inséré dans une carte "Samuel de Champlain".

2008. – *400e anniversaire de la fondation de la ville de Québec. T.-P. de même date imprimé sur feuillet de 205* x *95.*

29 0,85 € *L'explorateur et cartographe Samuel de Champlain (1567-1635) saluant les autochtones en canot depuis son navire, forteresse en construction* (4182) 6 » 6 »

Bloc avec marge illustrée d'un détail d'une carte ancienne avec l'habitation du capitaine Champlain, inséré dans une carte "Etienne Brûlé" (A partir de 1610 Etienne Brûlé vivra dans une tribu algonquienne pour apprendre la langue et les mœurs. Il séjournera parmi les Amérindiens durant plus de vingt ans).

2008. – *400e anniversaire de la fondation de la ville de Québec. T.-P. de même date imprimé sur feuillet de 205* x *95.*

30 2 x 0,85 € *L'explorateur et cartographe Samuel de Champlain (1567-1635) saluant les autochtones en canot depuis son navire, forteresse en construction* (4182) 6 » 6 »

Bloc avec marge illustrée par un détail d'une carte ancienne, inséré dans une carte "Savignon" (jeune Huron/Wendat qui en 1610 séjourna en France pendant un an).

2008. – *400e anniversaire de la fondation de la ville de Québec. T.-P. de même date imprimé sur feuillet de 205* x *95.*

31 0,85 € *L'explorateur et cartographe Samuel de Champlain (1567-1635) saluant les autochtones en canot depuis son navire, forteresse en construction* (4182) 6 » 6 »

Bloc avec marge illustrée d'un détail d'une carte ancienne avec habitations et tête d'une baleine rejetant de l'eau, inséré dans une carte "Le Cardinal de Richelieu" (A l'origine de la fondation de la Compagnie des Cent-Associés en 1627 pour le monopole du commerce des fourrures canadiennes).

2008. – *400e anniversaire de la fondation de la ville de Québec. T.-P. de même date imprimé sur feuillet de 205* x *95.*

32 0,85 € *L'explorateur et cartographe Samuel de Champlain (1567-1635) saluant les autochtones en canot depuis son navire, forteresse en construction* (4182) 6 » 6 »

Bloc avec marge illustrée par le portrait d'autochtones, inséré dans une carte "La foire des fourrures".

2008. – *Année lunaire chinoise du Rat. T.-P. de même date imprimé sur feuillet de 205* x *95.*

33 Lettre prioritaire 20 g *Rat mangeant des grains de raisin* (4131) 6 » 6 »

Bloc inséré dans une carte "Année du Rat" vendue 3 €.

2008. – *"Jean-Baptiste Charcot (1867-1936)", le plus beau timbre de l'année 2007. T.-P. de même date imprimés sur feuillet de 205 x 95.*

34 0,54 € *Portrait du navigateur* (4110)
0,60 € *Voilier le "Pourquoi-pas ?"* (4111)

Le feuillet 8 » 8 »

Bloc inséré dans une carte "Emission commune France-Groenland 2007" vendue 4 €.

2008. – *"Bonnes fêtes" (coeur). Type du T.-P. de même date imprimé sur feuillet de 205 x 95. Papier gommé.*

35 Lettre prioritaire 20 g *Cœur* (4315a) 6 » 6 »

Bloc inséré dans une carte "Bonnes fêtes" vendue 3 €.

Tirage : 100 000.

2009. – *Année lunaire chinoise du Buffle. T.-P. de même date imprimé sur feuillet de 206 x 96.*

36 Lettre prioritaire 20 g *Buffle* (4325) 6 » 6 »

Bloc inséré dans une carte "Année chinoise du buffle" vendue 3 €.

Tirage : 120 000.

2009. – *Série artistique. Cathédrale Sainte-Cécile (Albi). T.-P. de même date imprimé sur feuillet de 205 x 95.*

37 0,85 € *Ange avec trompette, détail peinture de la voûte* (4336) 6 » 6 »

Bloc inséré dans une carte "Cathédrale Sainte-Cécile d'Albi" vendue 3 €.

Tirage : 120 000.

BLOCS SPÉCIAUX SUR PAPIER GOMMÉ

Ces blocs-feuillets ont pouvoir d'affranchissement et, à l'exception de Av. n° 20, sont dentelés.

N[os]		
446 et 753,	Lettre de Fragonard et Musée Postal (sans gomme)	3 500 »
748 et 789,	Fournier (2 f. + 3 f. rouge-brun 2 f. + 3 f. bleu-noir)	1 250 »
755 à 758,	Armoiries (Corse 10 c., Alsace 30 c., Lorraine 50 c., Nice 60 c.)	1 250 »
761 et 762,	Conférence de la Paix (3 et 10 f.)	610 »
765 à 770,	Célébrités du XVe siècle (2 f. + 1 f., 3 f. + 1 f., 4 f. + 3 f., 5 f. + 4 f., 6 f. + 5 f., 10 f. + 6 f.)	1 700 »
772 à 776,	Cathédrales (1 f . + 1 f., 3 f. + 2 f., 4 f. + 3 f., 6 f. + 4 f., 10 f. + 6 f.)	1 700 »
759, 760, 763, 764, 777 et 778	(5, 10, 15, 20, 6 et 25 f.)	1 350 »
780 à 783,	12e Congrès de l'Union Postale (3,50, 4,50, 6 et 10 f.)	1 700 »
	Idem, non dentelés	1 250 »
795 à 802,	Centenaire de la Révolution de 1848	1 700 »
792, 803 et 805	(15, 12, 18 f.)	1 250 »
818 et 819,	Palais de Chaillot (12 f. et 18 f.)	610 »
820 et 821,	Paul Langevin (5 f.) et Jean Perrin (8 f.)	1 350 »
823 à 826,	Série des métiers (3 f. + 1 f., 5 f. + 3 f., 8 f. + 4 f., 10 f. + 6 f.)	1 350 »
830 à 833,	Centenaire du Timbre	4 000 »
834 à 838,	Armoiries (Bourgogne 10 c., Guyenne 50 c., Savoie 1 f., Auvergne 2 f., Anjou 4 f.)	1 250 »
841A, 842, 842A et 843	(St-Bertrand de Comminges 20 f., St-Wandrille 25 f., Vallée de la Meuse 40 f., Gerbier de Jonc 50 f.)	1 250 »
844 à 847,	Congrès international de télégraphie et téléphonie	1 700 »
850 à 852,	75e anniversaire de l'U.P.U	2 450 »
853 à 858,	Célébrités du XVIIIe siècle (1re série) (5 f. + 1 f., 8 f. + 2 f., 10 f. + 3 f., 12 f. + 4 f., 15 f. + 5 f., 25 f.+ 10 f.)	1 400 »
859 à 862,	Les saisons (5 f. + 1 f., 8 f. + 2 f., 12 f. + 3 f., 15 f. + 4 f.)	1 400 »
867 à 872,	Célébrités du XVIIIe siècle (2e série) (5 f. + 2 f., 8 f. + 3 f., 10 f. + 4 f., 12 f. + 5 f., 15 f. + 6 f., 20 f. + 10 f.)	1 400 »
874 et 875,	Mme de Sévigné (15 f.), Mme Récamier (12 f.)	1 200 »
876 et 877,	Croix-Rouge, 8 f. + 2 f., 15 f. + 3 f.	1 850 »
873 et 878,	Châteaudun 8 f., Fontainebleau 12 f.	1 200 »
891 à 896,	Célébrités du XIXe siècle (1re série) (5 f. + 1 f., 8 f. + 2 f., 10 f. + 3 f., 12 f. + 4 f., 15 f. + 5 f., 30 f. + 10 f.)	1 400 »
899 à 903,	Armoiries	1 250 »
908 à 910,	Poètes symbolistes	1 350 »
911 et 912,	Nations Unies	1 650 »
914 et 915,	Croix-Rouge	1 750 »
905, 916, 917 et 924,	Arbois (30 f.), Pic du Midi (40 f.), Abbaye aux Hommes (50 f.), Château de Chambord (20 f.)	1 250 »
922 et 925,	Narvik (30 f.), Bir Hakeim (30 f.)	1 250 »
921 et 928,	Vaucouleurs (12 f.), Viaduc de Garabit (15 f.)	1 400 »
930 à 935,	Célébrités du XIXe siècle (2e série) (8 f. + 2 f., 12 f. + 3 f., 15 f. + 4 f., 18 f. + 5 f., 20 f. + 6 f., 30 f. + 7 f.)	1 400 »
937 et 938,	Croix-Rouge	1 700 »
815 et 942,	Leclerc (6 f.), Maréchal Leclerc (8 f.)	1 350 »
945 à 950,	Célébrités du XIIe au XXe siècles (8 f. + 2 f., 12 f. + 3 f., 15 f. + 4 f., 18 f. + 5 f., 20 f. + 6 f., 30 f. + 7 f.)	1 400 »
951 à 954,	Armoiries	1 250 »
943, 944, 956 et 957,	Gargantua (6 f.), Hernani (18 f.), Célimène (8 f.), Figaro (12 f.)	1 250 »
958 et 959,	Armoiries	1 200 »
960 à 965,	Jeux Olympiques sur 2 feuillets	2 450 »
966 et 967,	Croix-Rouge	2 100 »
941 et 970 à 974,	Productions, sur 2 feuillets	1 950 »
976 à 981,	sur 2 feuillets, Lourdes (6 f.), Les Andelys (8 f.), Royan (10 f.), Quimper (12 f.), Cheverny (18 f.), Ajaccio (20 f.)	1 950 »

Partie centrale du bloc.

982 à 984,	Maréchal de Lattre (12 f.), Libération (15 f.), Maréchal Leclerc (12 f.)	1 350 »

Nos	
939 et 988, Versailles (18 f.)	1 200 »
989 et 994, Célébrités du XIIIe au XXe siècles	1 350 »
999 à 1005, Armoiries	1 200 »
1006 et 1007, Croix-Rouge	1 700 »
1009A, 1010, 1011 et 1011B, Marianne (de Muller)	1 500 »
1012 à 1017, Inventeurs, sur 2 feuillets	1 650 »
1027 à 1032, Célébrités diverses	1 350 »
1036 à 1042, Série touristique, sur 2 feuillets	1 700 »
1044 à 1047, Armoiries	1 200 »
1048 et 1049, Croix-Rouge	1 700 »
1052 et 1053, Driant, Verdun	1 100 »
1055 à 1058, Fabre, Tellier, Flammarion, Sabatier	1 200 »
1066 à 1071, Célébrités du XVe au XXe siècles	1 350 »
1072 à 1075, Sports	1 700 »
1076 et 1077, Europa	6 000 »
1078 à 1080, Réalisations techniques	1 200 »
1082 à 1087, Personnages étrangers	1 500 »
1089 et 1090, Croix-Rouge	1 650 »
1095 à 1098, Savants et inventeurs	950 »
1100 à 1104, Héros de la Résistance (1re série)	1 200 »
1108 à 1113, Célébrités diverses du XIIIe au XXe siècles, sur 2 feuillets	1 350 »
1115 et 1116, Moissonneuse	1 200 »
1105, 1118 et 1119, Le Quesnoy, Région bordelaise, Cahors	1 100 »
1122 et 1123, Europa	2 250 »
1106 et 1125 à 1131, Série touristique, sur 3 feuillets	1 650 »
1132 à 1138, Célébrités étrangères, sur 2 feuillets	1 850 »
1140 et 1141, Croix-Rouge	1 350 »
1142 à 1145, Grands médecins	1 250 »
1146 à 1149, Grands savants	1 250 »
1152 à 1155, Villes reconstruites	1 200 »
1157 à 1160, Héros de la Résistance (2e série)	1 200 »
1161 à 1164, Jeux traditionnels	1 350 »
1166 à 1171, Célébrités diverses	1 200 »
1173 et 1174, Europa	1 800 »
1177 et 1178, U.N.E.S.C.O.	1 500 »
1180 à 1186, Armoiries	1 250 »
1187 et 1188, Croix-Rouge	1 500 »
1198 à 1202, Héros de la Résistance (3e série)	1 200 »
1203 à 1206, Réalisations techniques (2e série)	1 050 »
1207 à 1212, Célébrités diverses	1 200 »
1218 et 1219, Europa	1 500 »
1226 et 1227, Croix-Rouge	1 500 »

POSTE AÉRIENNE.

Nos	
16 à 19, Série mythologique	2 100 »
20, Congrès de l'Union Postale	2 300 »
Idem, non dentelé	1 100 »
21 et 22, Saint-Exupéry, Dagnaux	1 800 »
21, 22 et 23, Saint-Exupéry, Dagnaux, Ader	1 800 »
24 à 27, Lille, Bordeaux, Lyon, Marseille	2 000 »
28, Congrès international de télégraphie et téléphonie	2 000 »
30 à 33, Prototypes	2 300 »
36, Caravelle	2 000 »

TIMBRES DE SERVICE.

Nos	
17, 18 et 20, Conseil de l'Europe	1 800 »

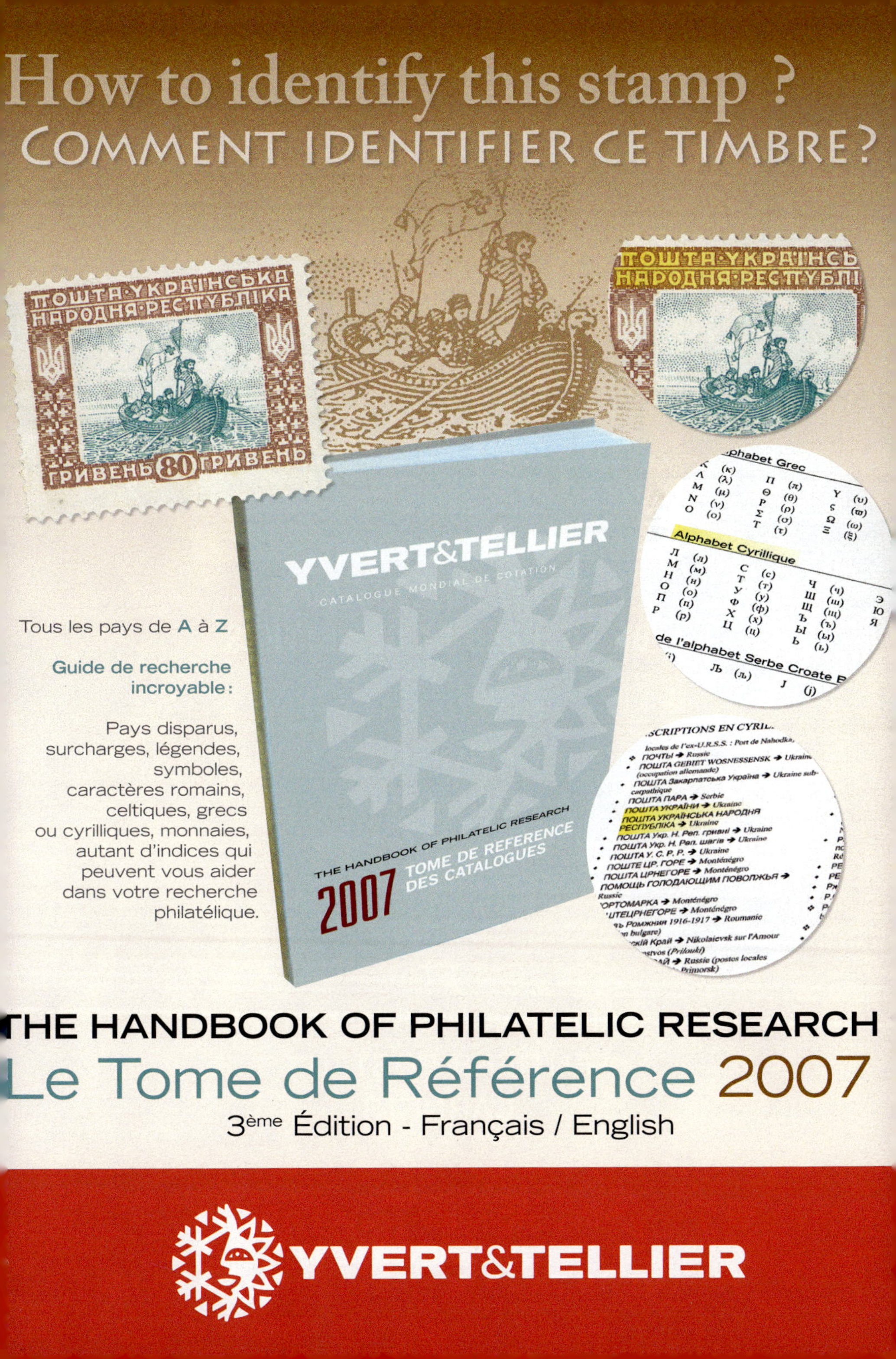
How to identify this stamp ?
COMMENT IDENTIFIER CE TIMBRE?
ПОШТА·УКРАЇНСЬКА
НАРОДНЯ·РЕСПУБЛІКА
ГРИВЕНЬ 80 ГРИВЕНЬ
YVERT&TELLIER
CATALOGUE MONDIAL DE COTATION
THE HANDBOOK OF PHILATELIC RESEARCH
2007 TOME DE REFERENCE DES CATALOGUES
Alphabet Grec
Alphabet Cyrillique
Tous les pays de A à Z
Guide de recherche incroyable :
Pays disparus, surcharges, légendes, symboles, caractères romains, celtiques, grecs ou cyrilliques, monnaies, autant d'indices qui peuvent vous aider dans votre recherche philatélique.
THE HANDBOOK OF PHILATELIC RESEARCH
Le Tome de Référence 2007
3ème Édition - Français / English
YVERT&TELLIER

I. - CARNETS ANCIENS

* **Nouveauté 2010 :**

Cette rubrique est complétée avec les carnets annulés par l'agence comptable.

* **Nombre de timbres**

Les carnets contiennent généralement 20 timbres - les exceptions sont signalées.

* **Formats**

De l'origine (1906) à 1922 le format des carnets est de 110 x 60

De 1923 à 1965 le format passe à 115 x 72 puis de 120 x 72

Les formats différents sont précisés.

* **Couvertures**

De 1906 à 1921 les couvertures sont postales

De 1922 à 1965 (sauf exceptions précisées) les couvertures sont avec publicité

* **Séries**

A partir de 1922 les carnets se rencontrent avec une ou plusieurs couvertures différentes. Les cotes indiquées correspondent aux carnets neufs et complets avec **les couvertures les plus courantes**.

* **NB**

Cette rubrique ne reprend que les carnets de "base" ; elle exclue les carnets particuliers tels que :

carnets "spécimen"

carnets des cours d'instruction

carnets non dentelés

carnets avec variété d'impression ou de piquage

Les collectionneurs ont maintenant à leur disposition les spécialisés "CARNETS de FRANCE" Volume I et II dans lesquels ils trouveront pour la période 1906-1932 la reproduction de tous les carnets et de toutes les couvertures actuellement connues.

Des ouvrages que tous les collectionneurs de carnets doivent posséder comme documentation.

Le volume III en cours de préparation sera consacré aux carnets PAIX - 1932-1939.

-*-*-*-*-

111 TYPE BLANC - 5c. vert (type I B) - n° 111 e

111-C1

111-C 1	Carnet de 40 figurines à 0f.05 - Prix : 2f.05	....................1 800 »
111-C 2	Carnet C1 - surchargé : Prix réduit : 2 Fr	....................1 900 »

111 TYPE BLANC - 5c. vert (type I B) - n° 111

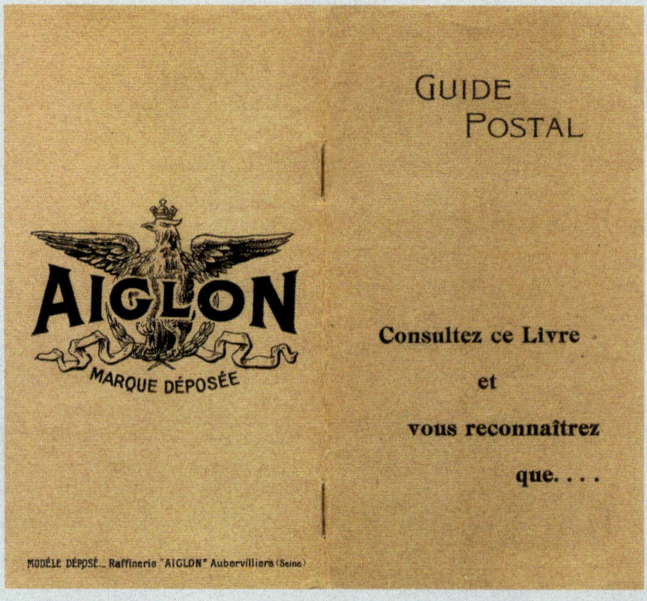

111-CP1

111-CP 1 Aiglon - 8 timbres sur porte-timbre - carnet de 16 pages (format 160x87)..........3 350 »

129 TYPE SEMEUSE LIGNÉE - 10c. rose - n° 129

129-CP2

129-CP 1 MANCHON HELLA - 6 timbres sur porte-timbre (format 121x72) 3 400 »
129-CP 2 MIGNON - 6 timbres sur porte-timbre (format 121x72) ....3 500 »

130 TYPE SEMEUSE LIGNEE - 15c. vert olive (type V) - n° 130 d

130-C1

130-C 1	Couverture avec texte sur la 1re page de la couverture - papier GC	950 »
130-C 2	Couverture avec en 2e page : loi du 30 décembre 1916 - papier GC	750 »
130-C 3	Carnet C2 - papier et gomme blancs	1 450 »
130-C 3a	Carnet C2 - isolé au Type IV case 1	2 300 »
130-C 4	Carnet C2 - papier X (gomme striée)	15 000 »
130-C 5	Couverture avec en 2e page : taxes révisées le 12 août 1919 - papier GC	850 »
130-C 6	Carnet C5 - papier blanc	1 100 »
130-C 7	Couverture avec bandes striées - papier GC (40 timbres)	7 000 »

135 TYPE SEMEUSE CAMEE chiffres maigres - 10c. rouge (Type III) - n° 135 c

135-C1a

135-C 1	Carnet de 20 figurines à 0f.10 - Prix : 2f.05	600 »
135-C 1a	Carnet C1 - variété semeuse blanche	750 »
135-C 2	Carnet C1 - surchargé : Prix réduit : 2 Fr	700 »
135-C 2a	Carnet C2 - variété semeuse blanche	800 »

135 TYPE SEMEUSE CAMEE chiffres maigres - 10c. rouge (Type III) - n° 135

135-CP3

135-CP1	LA BELLE JARDINIERE - 6 t. sur porte-timbre - pub sur pardessus (format 121x72)	4 500 »
135-CP2	MANCHON HELLA - 6 timbres sur porte-timbre (format 121x72)	3 250 »
135-CP3	MIGNON - 6 timbres sur porte-timbre - le timbre poste économique (format 121x72)	3 500 »

137 TYPE SEMEUSE CAMEE chiffres gras - 5c. vert (type I) - n° 137

137-C 1	Carnet de 40 figurines à 0f.05 - Prix : 2f.05 850	»
137-C 2	Carnet C1 - surchargé: Prix réduit : 2 Fr 1 000	»

137 TYPE SEMEUSE CAMEE chiffres gras - 5c. vert (type II) - n° 137 d

137-C3

137-C 3	Carnet de 40 Timbres-Poste à 0f.05 - Prix : 2 francs. 370	»
137-C 3a	Demi feuille de 3 carnets n° 137C3 non dentelée 35 000	»
137-C 3b	Paire de 2 carnets n° 137C3 dentelée 37 000	»
137-C 3ac	idem C3. Surchargé ANNULE cachet à main VIOLET 3 500	»
137-C 4	Carnet C3 - couverture grisâtre - papier brouillé 380	»
137-C 5	Carnet C3 - papier GC 500	»
137-C 5a	Carnet C3 - papier GC blanc 750	»
137-C 6	Carnet C3 ou C4 - papier X (gomme striée) 14 600	»
137-C 7	Couverture avec en 2e page : taxes révisées le 12 août 1919 (40 timbres) 360	»
137-C 8	Carnet C7 - papier GC 950	»
137-C 9	Couverture avec en 2e page : loi du 29 mars 1920 (40 timbres) 370	»

Il existe que 3 exemplaires des 2 paires ci-dessus, ils proviennent de feuilles non dentelées et dentelées préparées pour la fabrication du carnet 137 C3.

137 TYPE SEMEUSE CAMEE chiffres gras - 5c. vert (type II) - n° 137

137-CP1

137-CP1	BUSSANG - 16 timbres sur porte-timbre bleu-noir (format 136x80) 4 900	»
137-CP2	BUSSANG - 8 timbres sur porte-timbre bleu-noir (format 136x80) 3 800	»

138 TYPE SEMEUSE CAMEE chiffres gras - 10c. rouge (type I C) - n° 138 d

138-C5

138-C 1	Carnet de 20 Timbres-Poste à 0f.10 - Prix : 2 francs 600	»
138-C 1a	Demi feuille de 3 carnets n° 138C1 non dentelée 40 000	»

138 TYPE SEMEUSE CAMEE chiffres gras - 10c. rouge (type I C) - n° 138 d (suite)

138-C 1b	Paire de 2 carnets n° 138C1 dentelée	42 000 »
138-C 1ac	idem 138 C1. ANNULE EN VIOLET par cachet à main	3 000 »
138-C 2	Carnet C1 - papier X (gomme striée)	15 500 »
138-C 3	Carnet C1 - avec 1 timbre isolé au type 1a (case 13)	630 »
138-C 3ac	idem 138 C3. ANNULE EN VIOLET par cachet à main	3 200 »
138-C 4	Carnet C3 - papier X (gomme striée)	16 200 »
138-C 5	Carnet C1 - papier GC	4 000 »
138-C 6	Carnet C5 - papier GC - avec 1 timbre isolé au type 1a (case 13)	4 200 »

Il existe que 3 exemplaires des 2 paires ci-dessus, ils proviennent de feuilles non dentelées et dentelées préparées pour la fabrication du carnet 138 C1.

138 TYPE SEMEUSE CAMEE chiffres gras - 10c. rouge (type II) - n° 138 f

138-C7

138-C 7	Carnet de 30 timbres - 5 feuillets de 6 sur papier X (format 74x48)	3 300 »
138-C 8	Carnet C7 - 5 feuillets de 6 sur papiers mélangés (X et normal)	2 700 »
138-C 9	Carnet C7 - 5 feuillets de 6 sur papier normal (gomme lisse).	2 900 »
138-C 10	Feuille de 144 t. - sur papier X (pour fabrication du carnet C7)	17 000 »

138 TYPE SEMEUSE CAMEE chiffres gras - 10c. rouge - n°138

138-CP1	AIGLON - 8 timbres sur porte-timbre - carnet de 16 pages (format 160x87)...	1 520 »
138-CP2	LA BELLE JARDINIERE - 6 t. sur porte-timbre - pub sur veston (format 121x72)	4 600 »
138-CP3	MANCHON HELLA - 6 timbres sur porte-timbre (format 121x72)	3 200 »

138-CP4

138-CP4	MENTHE-PASTILLES - 6 timbres sur porte-timbre (format 121x72)	3 600 »
138-CP5	MIGNON - 6 timbres sur porte-timbre - le timbre poste économique (format 121x72)	3 500 »

138 TYPE SEMEUSE CAMEE chiffres gras - 10c. rouge - n°138 (suite)

138-CP6

138-CP6 TISANE du LABOUREUR - 6 timbres sur porte-timbre (format 121x72) » »

140 TYPE SEMEUSE CAMEE chiffres gras - 25c. bleu (type IV) - n°140 L

140-C1

140-C 1	Carnet de 20 Timbres à 0f.25 - Prix : 5 francs (couv. postale) 4 900	»
140-C 2	Carnet C1 - papier GC ....»	»

140 TYPE SEMEUSE CAMEE chiffres gras - 25c. bleu (type IB) - n°140 c

140-C 3	Carnet de 20 Timbres à 0f.25 - Prix : 5 francs (couv. postale) 7 000	»

140 TYPE SEMEUSE CAMEE chiffres gras - 25c. bleu (type II) - n°140 e

140-C5 Série 12-G

140-C 4	Carnet de 20 Timbres à 0f.25 - Prix : 5 francs (couv. postale) 19 000	»
140-C 5	Carnet avec publicité privée sur couverture (format 110x60)	
	séries : SA - 1 à 4 - 6 à 10 - 12 à 25 - 27 ....2 300	»

140 TYPE SEMEUSE CAMEE chiffres gras - 25c. bleu (type II) - n°140 e (suite)

Série 40

140-C 6 Carnet avec publicité privée sur couverture (format 115x72)
séries : 29 à 42 ....2 700 »

140 TYPE SEMEUSE CAMEE chiffres gras - 25c. bleu (type II) - n°140 g

Série 71

140-C 7 ANNALES - ANNALES - ROZAN - ROZAN - série : 45 ....3 300 »
140-C 8 ANNALES - GREY POUPON - OLIBET - VICHY
séries : 68 à 72 - 74 - 77 - 78 ....2 750 »
140-C 9 BERNOT - BERNOT - KOTO - JIF - série : 76 ....14 500 »
140-C 10 BISQUIT - BISQUIT - BISQUIT - BISQUIT
séries : 75 - 78 - 79 - 81 - 82 ....950 »
140-C 11 ECO - ECO - OLIBET - OLIBET - séries : 45 - 46 ....5 300 »
140-C 12 EVIAN - EVIAN - EVIAN - EVIAN
séries : 43 - 47 - 48 - 50 - 51 à 54 - 56 - 58 - 62 - 63 - 67 -
75 - 79 - 81 à 89 - 89B ....700 »
140-C 13 LOUVRE - LOUVRE - LOUVRE - LOUVRE - série 73..................5 900 »
140-C 14 LOUVRE - LOUVRE - 10 timbres - série : 73 ....32 000 »
140-C 15 SECOURS - GREY POUPON - SECOURS - AMOURETTE
séries : 79 à 82 ....3 100 »
140-C 16 SECOURS - GUYOT - SECOURS - JIF - séries 75 à 77 - 80 à 82 ......2 750 »
140-C 17 SECOURS - SECOURS - SECOURS - SECOURS
séries : 50 - 55 - 56 - 57 - 61 - 64 à 66 - 68 ....2 750 »
140-C 18 SOULAC - GREY POUPON - OLIBET - VICHY
séries : 63 à 65 - 68 - 69 ....2 750 »
140-C 19 VICHY - SECOURS - OLIBET - SECOURS
séries : 55 à 57 - 59 à 61 ....2 750 »

147 TYPE SEMEUSE CAMEE avec surtaxe - 10c.+ 5c. (type II) - n°147

147-C1

147-C 1 Couverture avec inscriptions postales sur la 1re page ....2 300 »

158 TYPE SEMEUSE CAMEE chiffres gras - 5c. orange (type IIA) - n° 158 a

158-C1

158-C 1 Carnet de 40 Timbres-Poste à 0f.05 - Prix : 2 francs (couv. postale) ......260 »

158-C 2 Carnet avec publicité privée sur couverture (format 110x60)
séries : 5 - 11 ....155 »

159 TYPE SEMEUSE CAMEE chiffres gras - 10c. vert (type IC) - n° 159 c

Série 26-A

159-C 1 Carnet avec publicité privée sur couverture (format 110x60)
séries : SSB - 26 ....360 »

159-C 2 Carnet C1 - avec 1 timbre isolé au type 1a (case 13) ....380 »

159-C3ac

159-C 3 Carnet avec publicité privée sur couverture (format 115X72)
séries : 28 - 44...330 »

159-C 3ac idem C3 - Surchargé ANNULE. Série 28 ....1 300 »

159-C 4 Carnet C3 - avec 1 timbre isolé au type 1a (case 13) ....350 »

159-C 4ac idem C4 - Surchargé ANNULE Avec ISOLE type 1a Case 13 ....1 400 »

159-C 5 Carnet C3 - avec couverture cartonnée (Pasteur à l'écran) série : 28 ......870 »

159 TYPE SEMEUSE CAMEE chiffres gras - 10c. vert (type IC) - n° 159 c (suite)

159-CP1

159-CP1 Idem C3 - MAURICE DIGEAUX - pub privée sur marge des timbres
séries : 28 et 44 ....8 200 »

170 TYPE PASTEUR - 10c. vert (type II) - n° 170

170-C1

170-C 1 Carnet avec publicité privée sur couverture (format 115x72)
séries : 44 - 49 - 93 ....65 »

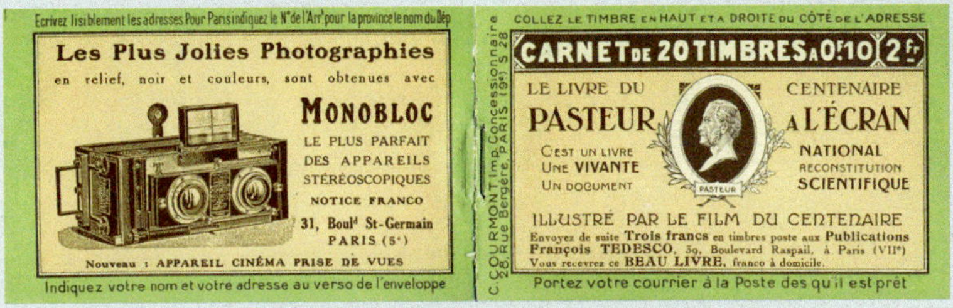

Série 28-B (cartonnée) RARE qu'il ne faut pas confondre (comme c'est souvent le cas !)
avec la couverture 28-A associée avec le timbre n° 159.
Voir pages 390 et 402 "Carnets de France" volume 1.

170-C 2 Carnet C1 - avec couverture cartonnée (Pasteur à l'écran) série : 28 ......720 »

170-CP4

170-CP 1 Idem C1 - VILLES du DOUBS - pub privée sur marge des timbres
série : 93 ....1 300 »

170 TYPE PASTEUR - 10c. vert (type II) - n° 170 (suite)

170-CP 2 Idem C1 - VILLES de NORMANDIE - pub privée sur marge des timbres - série : 93 ....1 300 »

170-CP 3 Idem C1 - MAURICE DIGEAUX - pub privée sur marge des timbres série : 93 ....4 900 »

170-CP 4 Idem C1 - CYCLES CHANTECLER - pub privée sur marge des timbres - couverture privée - 10 timbres........2 900 »

170-CP 5 Idem C1 - CYCLES CHANTECLER - pub privée sur marge des timbres - couverture privée - 20 timbres .... 6 000 »
On ne connait qu'un seul exemplaire de ce carnet.

170-CP 6 Idem C1 - HUILE AIGLON - pub privée sur marge des timbres couverture privée - 10 timbres ....2 800 »

170-CP7

170-CP 7 Idem C1 - HUILE AIGLON - pub privée sur marge des timbres couverture privée - 20 timbres ....5 400 »

188 TYPE SEMEUSE CAMEE chiffres maigres - 10c. Vert (type III) - n° 188

188-C1

188-C 1 MINERALINE - 10 timbres - (1926) ....6 000 »

188-C 1a MINERALINE - variété case 5 ....6 200 »

188-C 2 PHENA - 10 timbres - (1927) ....550 »

188-C 2a PHENA - variété case 5 ....600 »

189 TYPE SEMEUSE CAMEE chiffres gras - 15c. Brun (type I) - n° 189 a

Couverture du 189-C1

189-C 1 VIRGILE CHAREYRE X 2 - 10 timbres - (1928) ....200 »

189-C 2 ROLLAND laboratoires - 20 timbres - (1929) ....400 »

189 TYPE SEMEUSE CAMEE chiffres gras - 15c. Brun (type I) - n° 189

une des couvertures du 189-CP1

189-CP 1 LE PHILOPODE - 4 timbres (format 108x50) ....1 530 »

190 TYPE SEMEUSE CAMEE chiffres gras - 20c. lilas-rose (type VI) - n° 190 d

190-C1

190-C 1 POSTE - BYRRH - BYRRH - POSTE série : 9 ....50 »

191 TYPE SEMEUSE CAMEE chiffres gras - 30c. rose (type IIB) - n° 191 c

191-C2

191-C 1 EVIAN - EVIAN - EVIAN - EVIAN séries : 88S - 89S - 90..................220 »

191-C 2 SECOURS - AEQUITAS - SECOURS - OXYMENTOL
séries : 88S - 89S - 90 ....220 »

191-C 3 SECOURS - GREY POUPON - SECOURS - PIVOLO
séries : 88S - 89S - 90 - 91 ....220 »

192 TYPE SEMEUSE CAMEE chiffres gras - 30c. bleu (type IIB) - n° 192 b

192-C5ac

192-C 1 EVIAN - EVIAN - EVIAN - EVIAN
séries : 88S - 89S - 90 à 92 - 94 - 95 ....300 »
192-C 2 GIBBS - GIBBS - GIBBS - GIBBS
séries : 97 - 99 - 101 - 102 - LILOR ....180 »
192-C 2ac idem C2 - ANNULE Agence Comptable - cachet rond ....700 »
192-C 3 SECOURS - AEQUITAS - SECOURS - OXYMENTOL
séries : 88S - 89S - 90 - 91 - 95 - 96 ....320 »
192-C 4 SECOURS - GREY POUPON - SECOURS - PIVOLO
séries : 88S - 89S - 90 - 91 - 95 - 96 ....320 »
192-C 5 SECOURS - MENIER - SECOURS - FLORENT
séries : 97 à 101 - LILOR ....230 »
192-C 5ac idem C5 - ANNULE Agence Comptable ....700 »
192-C 5as idem C5 - surchargé SPECIMEN ....1 050 »

193 TYPE SEMEUSE CAMEE chiffres gras - 40c. brun-olive (type I) - n° 193 a

193-C 1 GREY POUPON - URODONAL - GUYOT - GYRALDOSE
séries : 103 - 104 ....270 »

série SLA

193-C 1a Carnet C1 - série : SLA ....1 900 »
193-C 1ac idem C1 - ANNULE Agence Comptable ....900 »

194 TYPE SEMEUSE CAMEE chiffres gras - 40c. vermillon (type I) - n° 194 b

couverture "Tête de Mercure" du 194-C6am

194-C 1 EVIAN - EVIAN - EVIAN - EVIAN séries : 108 à 110 ....200 »

194 TYPE SEMEUSE CAMEE chiffres gras - 40c. vermillon (type I) - n° 194 b (suite)

194-C 1a Carnet C1 - série : SLA ....1 900 »
194-C 1ac idem C1 - ANNULE Agence Comptable ....750 »
194-C 2 Feuille de 120 timbres pour la confection de 6 carnets C1 ....5 500 »
194-C 3 GIBBS - GIBBS - GIBBS - GIBBS séries : 104 à 107 ....200 »
194-C 3ac idem C3 - ANNULE Agence Comptable ....850 »

194-C 4 GREY POUPON - VITTEL - SECOURS - SECOURS
séries : 107 à 110 ....200 »
194-C 5 Feuille de 120 timbres pour la confection de 6 carnets C4 ....5 500 »
194-C 6 LESIEUR - LESIEUR - LESIEUR - LESIEUR séries : 107 - 109 ......250 »
194-C 6ac idem C6 - ANNULE Agence Comptable ....850 »
194-C 6am idem C6 - ANNULE Agence Comptable couverture tête de Mercure 1 100 »
194-C 7 Feuille de 120 timbres pour la confection de 6 carnets C6 ....2 650 »

199 TYPE SEMEUSE LIGNEE - 50c. rouge (type I) - n° 199 c
"carnets imprimés à plat et agrafés à la couverture"

199-C1ac

199-C 1 CHEVAL VERT - CHEVAL VERT - CHEVAL VERT
CHEVAL VERT séries : 120 à 123 ....740 »
199-C 1ac idem C1 - ANNULE Agence Comptable ....1 550 »
199-C 2 COQ - COQ - COQ - COQ séries : 143 - 144 - 144 Hérault
145 - 145 Belfort - 146 à 149 - Le Mans II - Rouen I
Versailles II - Vichy II ....225 »
199-C 2ac idem C2 - ANNULE Agence Comptable ....900 »
199-C 3 EVIAN - EVIAN - EVIAN - EVIAN séries : 108s - 110s - 111 à 115
130 à 142 - Dijon I - Le Mans I - Lourdes A - Reims I
Versailles I - S V Y ....225 »
199-C 3ac idem C3 - ANNULE Agence Comptable ....900 »
199-C 3am Couverture tête de Mercure ....1 500 »
199-C 4 EVIAN - DELFT - EVIAN - LESIEUR séries : 126 à 129 ....430 »
199-C 5 EVIAN - GIBBS (Barbe) - EVIAN - GIBBS (Beauté)
séries : 128 à 133 - 137 - Carcassonne....................360 »
199-C 5ac idem C5 - ANNULE Agence Comptable ....900 »
199-C 5am idem C5 - ANNULE Agence Comptable - couverture tête de Mercure 1 500 »
199-C 6 EVIAN - GIBBS (Beauté) - EVIAN - GIBBS (Barbe)
séries : 128 à 133 - Carcassonne - Le Mans I - Reims I - Versailles I ......360 »
199-C 6ac idem C6 - ANNULE Agence Comptable ....900 »
199-C 6am idem C6 - ANNULE Agence Comptable - couverture tête de Mercure 1 500 »
199-C 7 EVIAN - GOA - EVIAN - R et C séries : 126 à 129 - Reims I ....360 »
199-C 7ac idem C7 - ANNULE Agence Comptable ....900 »
199-C 7am idem C7 - ANNULE Agence Comptable - couverture tête de Mercure 1 500 »
199-C 8 EVIAN - GREY POUPON - EVIAN - SECOURS
séries : 141 à 143 ....330 »
199-C 8ac idem C8 - ANNULE Agence Comptable ....900 »
199-C 9 EVIAN - RADIUM - EVIAN - LESIEUR séries : 126 à 129 ....540 »
199-C 9ac idem C9 - ANNULE Agence Comptable ....1 300 »
199-C 9am idem C9 - ANNULE Agence Comptable - couverture tête de Mercure 1 700 »
199-C 10 EVIAN - VOUVRAY - EVIAN - SANGLIER
séries : 119 - 120 à 124 ....460 »
199-C 10ac idem C10 - ANNULE Agence Comptable ....1 000 »
199-C 10am idem C10 - ANNULE Agence Comptable - couverture tête
de Mercure ....1 700 »
199-C 11 EVIAN - VOUVRAY - EVIAN - SANS RIVALE séries : 119 à 123
Toile d'avion - Dijon I - Le Mans I - Versailles I - S V Y ....410 »

199 TYPE SEMEUSE LIGNEE - 50c. rouge (type I) - n° 199 c (suite)

199-C 12 GIBBS - GIBBS - GIBBS - GIBBS séries : 120 à 122 - 124 à 126 ......410 »
199-C 12ac idem C12 - ANNULE Agence Comptable ......1 000 »
199-C 12am idem C12 - ANNULE Agence Comptable - couverture tête de Mercure ......1 600 »
199-C 13 GREY POUPON - URODONAL - GUYOT - GYRALDOSE séries : 115 à 118......1 850 »
199-C 14 GREY POUPON - VITTEL - SECOURS - SECOURS séries : 110 surchargée - 111 ......3 600 »
199-C 14ac idem C14 - ANNULE Agence Comptable ......4 800 »
199-C 14am idem C14 - ANNULE Agence Comptable - couverture tête de Mercure ......5 500 »
199-C 15 LESIEUR - LESIEUR - LESIEUR - LESIEUR séries : 111 - 115 - 118 ......1 170 »
199-C 15ac idem C15 - ANNULE Agence Comptable ......2 050 »
199-C 15am idem C15 - ANNULE Agence Comptable - couverture tête de Mercure ......2 400 »
199-C 16 SECOURS - URODONAL - SECOURS - GYRALDOSE séries : 108S - 111 - 113 à 119 ......380 »
199-C 16ac idem C16 - ANNULE Agence Comptable ......950 »
199-C 16am idem C16 - ANNULE Agence Comptable - couverture tête de Mercure ......1 500 »

199 TYPE SEMEUSE LIGNEE - 50c. rouge (type IIB) - n° 199 e
"carnets imprimés à plat et agrafés à la couverture"

199-C27ac

199-C 17 MONTPEYROUX - 10 timbres - feuillet de gauche perforé ......1 800 »
199-C 18 Carnet C17 - feuillet de gauche non perforé ......170 »
199-C 19 PROVINS - 10 timbres ......130 »
199-C 20 VIRGILE CHAREYRE - 10 timbres ......110 »
199-C 21 BUSSANG - BUSSANG - BUSSANG - BUSSANG série : Nancy ......335 »
199-C 22 Carnet C21 - feuillet gauche : 10 timbres au type IV série : Nancy ......1 000 »
199-C 23 COQ - COQ - COQ - COQ séries : 157 à 160 - 165 Orléans 166 Allier - Clermont Ferrand - Lille - Marseille ......170 »
199-C 24 COQ - COQ - FALIERES - MIREILLE séries : 172 à 174 - 174 Paris - 180 - Vichy II ......250 »
199-C 25 DU - DU - DU - DU séries : 189 - 192 à 194 - (192 n° int - Blois Orléans - Saumur) - 197 à 200 - (200 n° int - Amiens Beauvais - Chartres Cognac - Gironde - Haut Rhin - Loire inf - Rennes - Strasbourg - Tours) Toile d'avion - 212 - 217 - 218 - 221 ......180 »
199-C 25ac idem C25 - ANNULE Agence Comptable ......850 »
199-C 26 DU - DU - CALVET - KWATTA séries : 189 - 192 à 194 - (192 n° int Orléans - Saumur - Blois) - Toile d'avion - 197 à 200 - (200 n° int Amiens - Beauvais - Chartres - Gironde - Loire inf) ......235 »
199-C 27 Carnet C26 - feuillet gauche : 10 timbres au type IV séries : 193 RP 194 RP - 197SA - Toile d'avion ......1 550 »
199-C 27ac idem C27 - ANNULE Agence Comptable ......2 450 »
199-C 28 FALIERES - SHYB - ANNALES - SHYB séries : 172 à 174 - 174 Paris - 180 - Vichy II ......325 »
199-C 29 FALIERES - SHYB - GREY POUPON - SHYB séries : 172 à 174 174 Paris - Vichy II - 175 ......320 »
199-C 30 FLORENT - FLORENT - VACHE QUI RIT - MIREILLE séries : 154 à 157 - Histoire de la chemise - 157 Hérault - Le Mans II 220 »
199-C 31 GITANES - GREY POUPON - REDOUTE - PHENIX séries : 183 - 185 à 189 - (192 n° int - Amiens - Chaumont - Laval Lyon - St Brieuc - Troyes) ......210 »
199-C 31ac idem C31 - ANNULE Agence Comptable ......900 »

199 TYPE SEMEUSE LIGNEE - 50c. rouge (type IIB) - n° 199 e (suite)

199-C 32 GREY POUPON - MOET - CALVET - GUYOT séries : 205 (Chartres Loire inférieure - Saumur) - 206 - 207 - 212 - 212 Paris - Toile d'avion 300 »

199-C 33 GREY POUPON - SHYB - PHENIX - SHYB séries : 174 - 175 - 177 - 180 ....310 »

199-C 33ac idem C33 - ANNULE Agence Comptable ....1 000 »

199-C 34 GUILHON - SHYB - PHENIX - SHYB séries : 174 - 175 - 177 - 180 ......290 »

199-C 34ac idem C34 - ANNULE Agence Comptable ....950 »

199-C 35 GUYOT - MOET - SPHERE - SPHERE séries : 198 - 199 - 202 206 - 207 - 212 - Toile d'avion - S205 (Chartres - Loire inférieure Orléans - Saumur)....220 »

199-C 36 MADON - REDOUTE - ORSAM - PHENIX séries : 181 - 183 - 185 Beauvais - Gironde - Haut Rhin - Lille - Loire inférieure - Lyon ....230 »

199-C 36ac idem C36 - ANNULE Agence Comptable ....900 »

199-C 37 PHENIX - OSRAM - REDOUTE - REDOUTE séries : 180 - 181 ......300 »

199-C 37ac idem C37 - ANNULE Agence Comptable ....900 »

199-C 38 PHENIX - PHENIX - PHENIX - PHENIX série : Nogent en Bassigny 160 »

199-C 39 PLOMBIERES - SANGLIER - JAFFELIN - JAFFELIN séries : 147 à 149 - 151 - Le Mans II - Rouen I - Versailles II - Vichy II 230 »

199-C 39ac idem C39 - ANNULE Agence Comptable ....900 »

199-C 40 QUINZAINE PHILATELIQUE X 4 série : Provins....240 »

199-C 41 REDOUTE - SPHERE - SPHERE - REDOUTE séries : 212 - 212 Paris 217 - 218 - 221 ....410 »

199-C 41ac idem C41 - ANNULE Agence Comptable ....1 100 »

199-C 42 REDOUTE - PHENIX - PHENIX - REDOUTE séries : 187 à 189 192 n° int & ext (Amiens - Chaumont - Laval - Lyon - Saint Brieuc Troyes) ....230 »

199-C 43 SPHERE - SPHERE - SPHERE - SPHERE séries : 198 - 199 - 202 Toile d'avion - 205 (Blois - Chaumont - Laval - Lyon - Saint Brieuc Troyes) ....310 »

199-C 44 TOILE D'AVION X 4 - séries : 149 à 155 - 153 (Hérault - Le Havre Orléans) - 154 Belfort - 155 Allier - 157 - 157 Hérault - Histoire de la chemise - Clermont-Fer. - Lille I - Lyon I - Rouen I ....155 »

199-C 44ac idem C44 - ANNULE Agence Comptable ....900 »

199-C 45 TOILE D 'AVION X 2 - LAINES st EPIN X 2 - séries : 149 à 152 Clermont-Ferrand - Lyon I ....235 »

199-C 46 TOURING - FLORENT - FLORENT - QUINZAINE PHILATELIQUE séries : 157 à 160 - Histoire de la chemise ....230 »

199-C 46ac idem C46 - ANNULE Agence Comptable ....1 000 »

199-C 47 carnet C46 - 1 seul "e" à "ARMEE " (case 5) séries : 157 à 160 - Histoire de la chemise ....290 »

199 TYPE SEMEUSE LIGNEE - 50c. rouge (type IV) - n° 199 h - sans publicité "carnets imprimés sur rotative et collés à la couverture"

199-C48ac

199-C 48 Carnet avec inscriptions postales sur couverture : 1re et 4e page ....165 »

199-C 48ac idem C48 - ANNULE Agence Comptable ....3 000 »

199-C 49 Carnet avec publicité privée sur couverture (format 115x72) séries : 161 - 167 à 169 ....165 »

199 TYPE SEMEUSE LIGNEE - 50c. rouge (type IV) - n° 199 j - avec publicités

199-C56ac

199-C 50 BLEDINE - MAZDA - BENJAMIN - BENJAMIN
séries : 228 - 228 Rhône - 233 - 234 - 236 à 239 .... 290 »

199-C 51 Carnet C50 avec 1 timbre isolé au type IIB (case 11)
séries : 234 - 236 - S228 .... 1 500 »

199-C 52 DU - DU - DU - DU séries : 191 - 195 - 196 - S190 .... 225 »

199-C 53 GITANES - GREY POUPON - REDOUTE - PHENIX
séries : 182 - 184 .... 650 »

199-C 54 GREY POUPON - MOET - CALVET - GUYOT séries : 203 - 204 .... 475 »

199-C 55 GREY POUPON - SHYB - PHENIX - SHYB
séries : 167 à 169 - 176 - 178 .... 215 »

199-C 56 PHENIX - DU - CALVET - DU séries : 182 - 184 - 190 - 191 .... 240 »

199-C 56ac idem C56 - ANNULE Agence Comptable .... 1 000 »

199-C 57 PHENIX - OSRAM - REDOUTE - REDOUTE
séries : 176 - 178 - 179 .... 425 »

199-C 57ac idem C57 - ANNULE Agence Comptable .... 950 »

199-C 58 PHENIX - SHYB - ORSAM - SHYB séries : 178 - 179 - 182 - 184 .... 325 »

199-C 58ac idem C58 - ANNULE Agence Comptable .... 950 »

199-C 59 REDOUTE - MAZDA - BENJAMIN - BENJAMIN
séries : 242 à 246 .... 540 »

199-C 60 Carnet C59 avec 1 timbre isolé au type IIA (cases 1 et 14)
séries : 242 à 243 .... 1 250 »

199-C 61 REDOUTE - MOET - SPHERE - SPHERE séries : 208 à 211
213 à 216 .... 325 »

199-C 62 REMA - GUILHON - CALVET - REDOUTE
séries : 208 à 211 - 213 - 215 - 216 .... 390 »

199-C 62ac idem C62 - ANNULE Agence Comptable .... 2 000 »

199-C 63 Carnet C62 avec 1 timbre isolé au type IIA (case 1)
séries : 208 - 213 .... 1 500 »

199-C 64 Carnet C62 avec pont perforé horizontalement séries : 203 - 204 .... 1 050 »

199-C 65 Carnet C64 avec 1 timbre isolé au type IIA (case 1)
séries : 203 - 204 .... 3 400 »

199-C 66 SPHERE - SPHERE - SPHERE - SPHERE
séries : 182 - 184 - 195 - 196 - 201 - 203 - 204 .... 225 »

199 TYPE SEMEUSE LIGNEE - 50c. rouge (type IIA) - n° 199 a
"carnets imprimés sur rotative et collés à la couverture"

Série 257 - Clermond Ferrand

199-C 67 BENJAMIN - MOET - GREY POUPON - BENJAMIN
séries : 257 (Limoges - Sud-Ouest) - Vosges - 259 - 261 à 263 ....330 »
199-C 68 BLECAO - MAZDA - BENJAMIN - BENJAMIN
séries : 236 - 238 à 241 ....730 »
199-C 69 BLEDINE - MAZDA - BENJAMIN - BENJAMIN
série : 240 ....3 850 »
199-C 70 GREY POUPON - MAZDA - REDOUTE - BENJAMIN
séries : 238 - 239 - 241 à 245..340 »
199-C 71 MOET - BENJAMIN - BENJAMIN - BENJAMIN
séries : 246 - 249 à 256 - 258..300 »
199-C 72 MOET - VICHY - REDOUTE - BENJAMIN séries : 251 à 256
257 Clermont-Ferrand - 258 - 260 ....340 »
199-C 73 PUPIER - MOET - BENJAMIN - BENJAMIN séries : 244 - 245
257 Limoges - 257 Sud-Ouest - 257 Vosges - 258 à 262 - Lyon ....310 »
199-C 74 REDOUTE - MAZDA - BENJAMIN - BENJAMIN séries : 244 à 248 500 »
199-C 75 VICHY - MAZDA - BENJAMIN - REDOUTE
séries : 244 à 252 - 256 RP ....330 »

199 TYPE SEMEUSE LIGNEE - 50c. rouge - n° 199

199-CP2

199-CP 1 LE PHILOPODE - 4 timbres (format 108x50) ....410 »
199-CP 2 Idem C48 - MAURICE DIGEAUX - pub privée sur marges
des timbres - couverture postale .... 4 200 »
199-CP 3 Idem C49 - MAURICE DIGEAUX - pub privée sur marges
des timbres - séries : 167 à 169 .... 4 200 »
199-CP 4 Idem C48 - CYCLES CHANTECLER - pub privée sur marges
des timbres - couverture privée - 10 timbres .... 2 950 »
199-CP 5 Idem C48 - CYCLES CHANTECLER - pub privée sur marges
des timbres - couverture privée - 20 timbres .... 5 000 »

217 TYPE SEMEUSE CAMEE chiffres gras - 25c. sur 30c. bleu (type IIB) - n° 217 a

217-C 1 GIBBS - GIBBS - GIBBS - GIBBS -
feuille de 120 timbres (pour la confection de 6 carnets non émis) ......1 600 »

217-C 2 GIBBS - GIBBS - GIBBS - GIBBS -
bloc de 20 t. de la feuille C1 ....260 »

217-C 3 SECOURS - MENIER - SECOURS - FLORENT -
feuille de 120 timbres (pour confection de 6 carnets non émis) ......30 000 »

217-C 4 SECOURS - MENIER - SECOURS - FLORENT -
bloc de 20 t. de la feuille C3 ....4 600 »

235 TYPE SEMEUSE CAMEE chiffres gras - 25c brun-jaune - n° 235

235-CP 1 LE PHILOPODE - 4 timbres (format 108x50) ....460 »

235-CP2

235-CP 2 LAFLEUR - 12 timbres sur porte-timbre (format 120x93)..................4 200 »

256 TYPE SOURIRE DE REIMS - n° 256

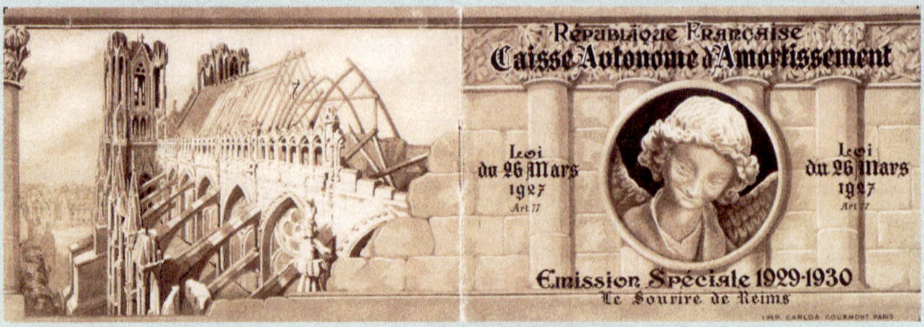

256-C1

256-C 1 Carnet de 8 timbres, émis pour la caisse d'amortissement ....1 000 »

257 TYPE JEANNE D'ARC - 50c. bleu (type I) - n° 257 a

257-C8ac

257-C 1 BUSSANG - BUSSANG - BUSSANG - BUSSANG - série : Nancy ......270 »

257 TYPE JEANNE D'ARC - 50c. bleu (type I) - n° 257 a (suite)

257-C 2 CHAMPIGNEULLES X 4 - série : Nancy ....250 »
257-C 3 COQ - COQ - FALIERES - MIREILLE séries : 162 à 166 - 171 à 173
Histoire de la chemise - Dijon - Gironde - Haut-Rhin - Le Mans II
Lille - Loire inf - Marseille - Strasbourg - Vichy II ....140 »
257-C 4 FALIERES - BENEDICTINS - FLORENT - FLORENT
séries : 162 à 166 - 171 - Histoire de la chemise - Doubs - Le Havre
Le Mans II - Rouen I - Vichy II ....135 »
257-C 4ac idem C4 - ANNULE Agence Comptable ....1 250 »
257-C 5 FALIERES - BENEDICTINS - VACHE QUI RIT - VIN
séries : 162 à 166 - 171 - Histoire de la chemise - Dijon - Doubs
Le Havre - Le Mans II - Rouen I - Strasbourg..................................110 »
257-C 6 Carnet C5 - R de RF brisé (case 5) - séries : 162 à 166 - 171 -
Histoire de la chemise - Le Havre - Le Mans II - Rouen I ....160 »
257-C 7 FALIERES - SHYB - ANNALES - SHYB séries : 171 à 173
Histoire de la chemise - Gironde - Haut-Rhin - Le Mans II
Lille - Loire inf - Marseille ....225 »
257-C 8 FALIERES - TOURING-CLUB - FLORENT - FLORENT
séries : 162 à 166 - 171 - Histoire de la chemise - Dijon - Doubs
Le Havre - Le Mans II - Rouen I - Strasbourg - Vichy II ....150 »
257-C 8ac idem C8 - ANNULE Agence Comptable ....1 300 »
257-C 9 Carnet C8 - 1 seul "e" à "Armée" (case 10) séries : 162 à 166 - 171
Histoire de la chemise - Le Havre - Le Mans II - Rouen I - Vichy II ......175 »
257-C 10 FLORAVENE X 4 - série : Bordeaux ....270 »
257-C 11 GALLIA X 4 - série : Provins III ....420 »
257-C 12 LE HAVRE X 4 - série : Le Havre ....160 »
257-C 13 LUX RADIO X 4 - série : Lourdes ....220 »
257-C 14 PHILA GALLIA X 4 - série : Provins II ....410 »

257 TYPE JEANNE D'ARC - 50c. bleu (type II) - n° 257 b

257-C 15 VALS - SHYB - FALIERES - SHYB - séries : 167 à 169 ....155 »
257-C 16 VALS - SHYB - PROVINS - SHYB - séries : 167 à 169 ....145 »

272 TYPE FACHI - 50c. rouge (type II) - n° 272 b

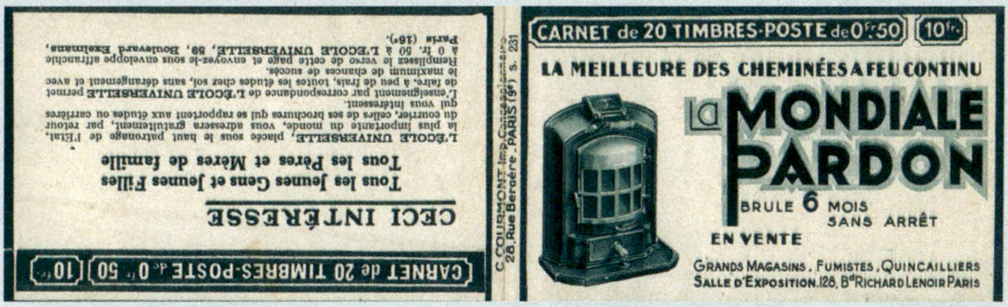

Série 231

272-C 1 BENJAMIN - BENJAMIN - BENJAMIN - BENJAMIN
séries : 208 à 211 - 213 à 215 - 219 - 220 - 222 à 226 - 229 ....340 »
272-C 2 Carnet C1 - avec 1 timbre isolé au type I (case 14)
séries : 214 - 219 - 220 - 222 - 223 ....1 350 »
272-C 3 BENJAMIN - MAZDA - BENJAMIN - BENJAMIN
séries : 228 - 233 à 235 ....320 »
272-C 4 BLEDINE - MAZDA - BENJAMIN - BENJAMIN séries : 233 - 234 4 550 »
272-C 5 Carnet C4 - avec 1 timbre isolé au type I (case 4) série : 234 ....» »
272-C 6 DU - DU - DU - DU séries : 208 à 211 - 213 à 216 ....350 »
272-C 7 Carnet C6 - avec 1 timbre isolé au type I (case 14) séries : 213 ....1 250 »
272-C 8 GREY POUPON - BENJAMIN - REDOUTE - BENJAMIN
séries : 219 - 220 - 222 à 225..390 »
272-C 9 Carnet C8 - avec 1 timbre isolé au type I (case 19)
séries : 219 - 220 - 222 - 223 - 225 ....1 350 »
272-C 10 LA CROIX MIR - GREY POUPON - BENJAMIN - BENJAMIN
séries : 224 à 227 - 229 ....350 »
272-C 11 LA CROIX MIR - MAZDA - BENJAMIN - BENJAMIN
séries : 228 - 228 Orléans - 230 à 235 ....350 »

272 TYPE FACHI - 50c. rouge (type II) - n° 272 b (suite)

272-C 12 REDOUTE - MOET - SPHERE - SPHERE
séries : 208 à 211 - 213 à 216 ....340 »

272-C 13 REDOUTE - SPHERE - SPHERE - REDOUTE
séries : 209 à 211 - 213 à 216 - 219 - 220 ....440 »

272-C 14 Carnet C13 - avec 1 timbre isolé au type I (case 19) série : 215 - 216 1 450 »

272-C 15 RIPOLIN - BENJAMIN - BENJAMIN - BENJAMIN
séries : 227 - 229 à 232 ....340 »

283 TYPE PAIX - 50c. rouge (type I) - n° 283 a

Série 266 - Cote d'Or - C

283-C 1 ARC EN CIEL - ART VIVANT - PARIZOT - BENJAMIN
séries : 274 à 277 - 279 - 280 - 281 Nord ....295 »

283-C 2 ARC EN CIEL - PRUD'HOMME - PARIZOT - BENJAMIN
séries : 274 à 277 - 279 - 280 - 281 Nord ....295 »

283-C 3 ART VIVANT - BENJAMIN - BENJAMIN - ART VIVANT
séries : 266 Lyon - 269 Nord - 270 à 273 - Paris ....200 »

283-C 4 ART VIVANT - BON SEL - POISSON DIEPPE - BENJAMIN
séries : 268 - 269 (Est - Nord) - Paris ....560 »

283-C 5 ART VIVANT - MAZDA - GALERIES BARBES - LEDUN
séries : 296 à 299 - 300 (Paris - Rouen) - 301 - 302 ....480 »

283-C 6 BENJAMIN - ART VIVANT - BLEDINE - MAZDA
séries : 300 (Paris - Rouen) - 301 à 304 ....360 »

283-C 7 BLEDINE - MAZDA - BENJAMIN - ART VIVANT
séries : 293 à 299 et 300 Paris ....480 »

283-C 8 FER A CHEVAL - REDOUTE - BENJAMIN - ART VIVANT
séries : 285 - 285 Paris - 287 à 295 ....245 »

283-C 9 MOET - BENJAMIN - BENJAMIN - BENJAMIN
séries : 264 - 265 - 266 Côte-d'Or - 267 - 268..........250 »

283-C 10 MONLEON - NELOMBO - MONLEON - BON SEL
séries : 271 - 272 ....760 »

283-C 10ac idem C10 - annulé 9-11-32 ....1 560 »

283-C 11 PARIZOT - ART VIVANT - ART VIVANT - BENJAMIN
séries : 264 - 267 - 268 - 269 (Nord - Est) - 270 - Paris ....245 »

283-C 11ac idem C11 - annulé 2 AOUT 32 ondulé violet ....1 100 »

283-C 12 REDOUTE - ART VIVANT - ART VIVANT - BENJAMIN
séries : 273 à 278 ....280 »

283-C 13 REDOUTE - HAHN - ART VIVANT - BENJAMIN
séries : 280 - 281 Nord - 282 à 284 - 285 (Ouest - Sud)
286 à 291 - 293 ....245 »

283-C 13ac idem C13 - ANNULE Agence Comptable ....1 100 »

283-C 14 REMA - ART VIVANT - ART VIVANT - BENJAMIN
séries : 274 à 278 ....280 »

283-C 15 RICQLES - HAHN - BLECAO - ART VIVANT
séries : 292 - 293 - 295 ....1 650 »

283-C 16 RICQLES - HAHN - BLECAO - NUPTIA
séries : 287 à 295 ....350 »

283-C 16ac idem C16 - ondulé violet 8 juin 33
ANNULE Agence Comptable ....1 250 »

283 TYPE PAIX - 50c. rouge (type I) - n° 283 a (suite)

283-C 17 RICQLES - MAZDA - GALERIES BARBES - BLECAO
séries : 296 - 298 - 299 - 300 (Paris - Rouen) - 301 - 302 ....560 »

283-C 17ac idem C17 - ondulé violet 30 août 33 ANNULE.........................1 600 »

283-C 18 RICQLES - MAZDA - BLEDINE - POUGUES
séries : 285 Paris - 285 - 289 - 290 - 292 à 298 ....480 »

283-C 19 VERAMINT - HAHN - BLECAO - ART VIVANT
séries : 287 à 295 ....410 »

283-C 20 VERAMINT - HAHN - BLECAO - NUPTIA séries : 290 à 295 770 »

283-C 21 VERAMINT - MAZDA - BLEDINE - GREBEL LA PERLE
séries : 285 Paris - 285 - 289 - 290 - 292 à 298 ....390 »

283 TYPE PAIX - 50c. rouge (type IIA) - n° 283 c

Série 300-C Paris

283-C 22 ART VIVANT - ART VIVANT - ART VIVANT - ART VIVANT
séries : 354 à 359 ....400 »

283-C 23 ART VIVANT - HAHN - ART VIVANT - ART VIVANT
séries : 338 à 344 - 346 à 351 - 353 à 356 - Lille..............................250 »

283-C 23ac idem C23 - ANNULE Agence Comptable ....1 050 »

283-C 24 ART VIVANT - MAZDA - BENJAMIN - BENJAMIN
séries : 299 - 304 à 310 ....360 »

283-C 25 BERNARD - ART VIVANT - ART VIVANT - CALVADOS
séries : 318 - 320 à 329 - 321 Rennes et Sud-Ouest ....330 »

283-C 26 BERNARD - BLEDINE - ART VIVANT - ART VIVANT
séries : 321 - 324 à 334 ....330 »

283-C 27 Carnet C26 - avec 1 timbre isolé au type I (cases 1 - 5 ou 19)
séries : 321 - 324 à 327 - 330 - 334 ....1 150 »

283-C 28 BERNARD - FAUROY - ART VIVANT - ART VIVANT
séries : 318 à 320 - 322 à 325 ....310 »

283-C 29 Carnet C28 - avec 1 timbre isolé au type I (cases 1 ou 5)
séries : 318 à 320 - 322 ....1 160 »

283-C 30 BERNARD - RISBAN - DU - DU
séries : 306 à 311 - 312 Lyon - 313 à 317 - 319 - 320 ....330 »

283-C 31 COURTOIS - MAZDA - BENJAMIN - BLEDINE
séries : 306 à 311 - 312 Dijon - 313 - 314 - 316 ....260 »

283-C 32 D U - GONDOLO - DU - CONORD séries : 315 à 320 - 312 Lyon ......310 »

283-C 33 GALERIES BARBES - MAZDA - BLEDINE - BENJAMIN
séries : 299 - 300 Paris - 304 à 308 ....390 »

283-C 34 MOET - GITANE - BLEDINE - MOET séries 367 à 372 ....770 »

283-C 35 RICQLES - BLEDINE - ART VIVANT - ART VIVANT
séries : 328 à 335 ....450 »

283-C 36 RICQLES - BLEDINE - ART VIVANT - CONORD
séries : 328 à 333 - 335 ....550 »

283-C 37 Carnet C36 - avec 1 timbre isolé au type I (case 20)
séries : 328 à 333..1 050 »

283-C 38 RICQLES - FER A CHEVAL - BLEDINE - MOET
séries : 358 à 364 - 366 - 367...350 »

283-C 39 RICQLES - GITANE - BLEDINE - MOET séries : 367 à 372 ....620 »

283 TYPE PAIX - 50c. rouge (type IIA) - n° 283 c (suite)

283-C 40 RICQLES - HAHN - FAUROY - ART VIVANT
séries : 346 à 348 ....780 »

283-C 41 RICQLES - HERCULE - FAUROY - ART VIVANT
séries : 330 - 331 à 333 - 336 à 338 ....580 »

283-C 42 RICQLES - MOET - BLEDINE - DU séries : 356 à 363 - Lyon ....380 »

283-C 43 RICQLES - POMMADE F. M - FAUROY - BLECAO
séries : 331 à 333 - 336 à 338 ....430 »

283-C 43ac idem C43 - annulé 7-9-34 série 330 ....1 550 »

283-C 44 RIPOLIN - HAHN - ART VIVANT - TETRA
séries : 338 - 339 à 344 - 346 à 348 - Lyon ....400 »

283-C 44ac idem C44 - ondulé violet 12 décembre 34 ....1 300 »

283-C 45 TETRA - HAHN - ART VIVANT - ART VIVANT
séries : 346 à 351 - 353 ....460 »

283-C 45ac idem C45 - ANNULE Agence Comptable ....1 250 »

283-C 46 VALISERE - VALISERE - VALISERE - VALISERE
séries : 343 - 345 - 365 - 368 - 370 ....310 »

283 TYPE PAIX - 50c. rouge (type IV) - n° 283 h

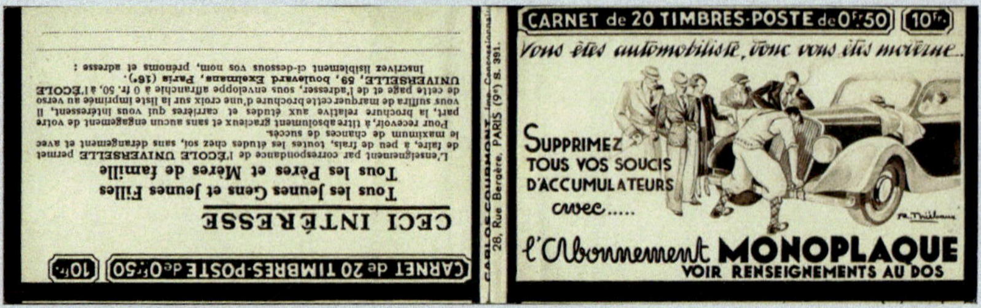

Série 391

283-C 47 BLEDINE - HAHN - BLEDINE - BLEDINE
séries : 393 à 399....................1 300 »

283-C 48 MOET - BLEDINE - RICQLES - HAHN séries : 377 à 380 - 382 ......640 »

283-C 49 MOET - FER A CHEVAL - BLEDINE - BLEDINE
séries : 373 à 378 ....650 »

283-C 50 MOET - GITANE - BLEDINE - MOET séries : 367 à 378 ....650 »

283-C 51 MOET - HAHN - BLEDINE - MOET séries : 386 à 393 ....670 »

283-C 51ac idem C51 - ANNULE Agence Comptable ....1 550 »

283-C 52 RICQLES - GITANE - BLEDINE - MOET séries : 367 à 372 ....900 »

283-C 53 RICQLES - HAHN - BLEDINE - MOET séries : 385 à 393 ....850 »

283-C 54 RICQLES - HAHN - MOET - BLEDINE séries : 383 à 385 ....950 »

283-C 54ac idem C54 - ondulé violet 5 mai 36
ANNULE Agence Comptable ....1 550 »

283-C 55 RICQLES - HAHN - MOET - FER A CHEVAL séries : 383 à 388 ......700 »

283-C 56 RICQLES - JIL - FER A CHEVAL - JIL
séries : 379 - 380 - 382 à 384....................840 »

283-C 57 VALISERE - VALISERE - VALISERE - VALISERE série : 381 ......760 »

283 TYPE PAIX - 50c. rouge (type III) - n° 283 f

Série 414-A

283-C 58	BLEDINE - BLEDINE - BLEDINE - BLEDINE séries : 396 - 398 - 400 - 401 - 404 - 405	330 »
283-C 59	BLEDINE - HAHN - BLEDINE - BLEDINE séries : 393 à 395 - 397 à 399	340 »
283-C 60	FER A CHEVAL - BYRRH - BYRRH - TETRA série : 2	275 »
283-C 61	GALERIES BARBES - HAHN - BLEDINE - BLEDINE séries : 406 à 408	490 »
283-C 62	GALERIES BARBES - HAHN - MOET - BLEDINE séries : 387 à 392 - 395 à 397	350 »
283-C 63	MOET - HAHN - MOET - BLEDINE séries : 387 à 392 - 395 à 397	410 »
283-C 64	P. AERIENNE - BYRRH (Gin) - BYRRH (Zeste) - C.C.P. séries : 2 - (5-7) - (8-9)	190 »
283-C 65	P. AERIENNE - BYRRH (Santé) - BYRRH (Fatigués) - C.C.P. séries : (5-7) - (8-9)	1 000 »
283-C 66	P. AERIENNE - BYRRH (Naturel) - BYRRH (Noble) - TETRA séries : 2 - 4 - (5-7)	250 »
283-C 67	TETRA - HAHN - BLEDINE - BLEDINE séries : 401 à 414	160 »

360 TYPE SEMEUSE CAMEE chiffres gras - 30c. rouge sombre (type III) - n° 360 b

360-C 1	POSTE AERIENNE - BYRRH - BYRRH - C.C.POSTAL série : 21	45 »

365 TYPE PAIX - 65c. outremer (type II) - n° 365 b

Série 18

365-C 1	FER A CHEVAL - BYRRH (Gin) - BYRRH (Zeste) - P.A. séries : 27 à 29 - 33 à 36	260 »
365-C 2	FER A CHEVAL - BYRRH (Naturel) - BYRRH (Noble) - TETRA séries : 27 à 32	215 »
365-C 3	FER A CHEVAL - BYRRH (Velouté) - BYRRH (Fameux) - TETRA séries : 14 - 16 /21 - 18 - 19 - 20/21	260 »
365-C 4	HAHN - BYRRH (Naturel) - BYRRH (Noble) - C.C.P. séries : 28 à 30 - 32 - 36 à 40 - 46	230 »
365-C 5	HAHN - BYRRH (Gin) - BYRRH (Zeste) - C.C.P. séries : 25 - 30 à 32 - 34 - 37 à 42 - 46	220 »
365-C 6	HAHN - BYRRH (Naturel) - BYRRH (Noble) - P.A. séries : 25 - 27 à 32	280 »

365 TYPE PAIX - 65c. outremer (type II) - n° 365 b (suite)

365-C 7 HAHN - BYRRH (Virilise) - BYRRH (Stimule) - P.A.
séries : 26 à 29 - 33 à 38 - 41 - 42 ....215 »
365-C 8 HAHN - BYRRH - BYRRH - TETRA séries : 22 - 23/21 - 24 - 26 ......250 »
365-C 9 P. AERIENNE - BYRRH (Santé) - BYRRH (Fatigués) - C.C.P.
séries : (5-7) - 12 - 13/1 - 15/1 - 16/21 - 17/1 ....180 »
365-C 10 P. AERIENNE - BYRRH (Virilise) - BYRRH (Stimule) - C.C.P.
séries : 17/1 - 19 - 20/21 - 22 - 23/21 - 24 à 26 ....215 »
365-C 11 P. AERIENNE - BYRRH (Velouté) - BYRRH (Fameux) - C.C.P.
séries : 13/1 - 14 - 15/1 - 16/21 - 17/1 - 18 - 19 - 20/21 ....220 »
365-C 12 TELEA - BYRRH (Velouté) - BYRRH (Fameux) - C.C.P.
séries : 12 - 13/1 - 14 - 15/1 - 16/21 - 17/1 ....340 »
365-C 13 TELEA - BYRRH (Gin) - BYRRH (Zeste) - C.C.P.
séries : 25 - 26 - 30 - 32 ....360 »

368 TYPE PAIX - 90c. outremer (type I) - n° 368 a

Série 62-B

368-C 1 FER A CHEVAL - BYRRH - BYRRH - C.C.POSTAL
séries : 43 à 45 - 47 à 54 ....170 »
368-C 2 HAHN - BYRRH (Naturel) - BYRRH (Noble) - C.C.POSTAL
séries : 43 à 45 - 47 - 48 - 51 à 62 ....170 »
368-C 3 HAHN - BYRRH (Virilise) - BYRRH (Stimule) - C.C.POSTAL
séries : 51 - 52 - 55 à 61 ....170 »
368-C 4 HAHN - BYRRH (Velouté) - BYRRH (Fameux) - C.C.POSTAL
séries : 45 - 47 à 54 - 58 ....160 »

433 TYPE IRIS - 1fr. rouge - n° 433 a

433-C 1 Feuille de 80 timbres (pour la confection de 4 carnets non émis) ....450 »
433-C 2 Bloc de 20 timbres de la feuille C1 ....100 »

517 TYPE PETAIN - 1fr.50 brun rouge - n° 517 c et 517 a

517-C1 - série 63 - 8 points sous le timbre case 20

517-C 1 Carnet avec barres sur la marge des timbres
(1 à 8 points sous le 20e timbre) ....110 »
517-C 2 SECOURS NATIONAL X 4 - séries : 63 à 67 ....52 »

813 TYPE GANDON - 15fr. rouge (type II) - n° 813 b

Série 2

813-C 1 HAHN - POSTE - POSTE - POSTE - séries : 1 - 2 ....400 »
813-C 2 HAHN - POSTE - SECCOTINE - POSTE - série : 3 ....380 »

Pour les types voir les explications à la rubrique Poste au 813 et 886.

886 TYPE GANDON - 15fr. bleu (type II) - n° 886 c

Série INF (sans numéro)

886-C 1 BIC - BIC - BIC - BIC - série : 5 ....250 »
886-C 2 BIC - HAHN - BIC - HAHN - série : 8 ....260 »
886-C 3 EXCEL - BIC - EXCEL - BIC - série : 10 ....250 »
886-C 4 HAHN - BIC - HAHN - BIC - série : 4 ....250 »

Pour les types I et II des "Marianne de Gandon (813 et 816)" voir les notes à la rubrique Poste.

886-C 5 KANGOUROU - BIC - POSTE - BIC - série : 6 ....290 »
886-C 6 PERNOT - PERNOT - PERNOT - PERNOT
sans n°- couvertures INF 1 et loterie ....230 »
886-C 7 POSTE - BIC - POSTE - BIC - série : 6........................1 220 »
886-C 8 POSTE - BIC - POSTE - BIC - série : 7 ....260 »
886-C 9 SECCOTINE - POSTE - BIC - BIC
sans n° - couverture revue des PTT ....265 »

886 TYPE GANDON - 15fr. bleu (type I) - n° 886 a

Couverture série 12

886-C 10 EXCEL - BIC - EXCEL - BIC séries : 9 - 11 ....155 »

886 TYPE GANDON - 15fr. bleu (type I) - n° 886 a (suite)

886-C 11 EXCEL - BIC - EXCEL - BIC série : 10 ....655 »
886-C 12 EXCEL - BIC - EXCEL - BIC série : 14 ....160 »
886-C 13 EXCEL - BIC - EXCEL - BIC série : 15 ....190 »
886-C 14 EXCEL - BIC - EXCEL - BIC série : 16 ....160 »
886-C 15 HAHN - BIC - HAHN - BIC série : 4 ....750 »
886-C 16 HAHN (barres E et H hautes) - BIC
HAHN (barres E et H hautes) - BIC - série : 13 ....560 »
886-C 17 HAHN (barres E et H centrées) - BIC
HAHN (barres E et H centrées) - BIC - série : 13 ....1 000 »
886-C 18 HAHN (barres E et H centrées) - BIC
HAHN (barres E et H hautes) - BIC - série : 13 ....610 »
886-C 19 KANGOUROU - BIC - POSTE - BIC série : 6 ....1 380 »
886-C 20 POSTE - BIC - POSTE - BIC série : 7 ....1 050 »
886-C 21 PROVINS - BIC - POSTE - BIC série : 12 ....215 »
886-C 22 SECCOTINE - POSTE - BIC - BIC sans n° - couv. revue des PTT ......670 »
886-CP 1 VILLES de PROVINS - 10 timbres - série 12 ....780 »

886-CP2

886-CP 2 VILLES de PROVINS - 10 timbres - couverture PROVINS ....830 »

1010 TYPE MULLER - 12fr. vert - n° 1010 (feuillet de 10 timbres)

1010-C 1 Couverture (mains pliant le feuillet) gomme jaunâtre - 10 timbres............50 »
1010-C 1a Carnet C1 non dentelé ....3 700 »
1010-C 2 Couverture (mains pliant le feuillet) gomme blanche - 10 timbres............125 »
1010-C 3 Couverture (voyageurs) gomme blanche - 10 timbres ....85 »

1011 TYPE MULLER - 15fr. rouge - n° 1011 a

Couverture série 2-55 du carnet 1011-C3

1011-C 1 A.G.VIE - SATAM - A.G.VIE - GRAMMONT
série : 5-57 ....90 »
1011-C 2 EXCEL - BIC - EXCEL - BIC séries : (3-56) ....95 »
1011-C 2 EXCEL - BIC - EXCEL - BIC séries : (4-56) ....110 »

1011 TYPE MULLER - 15fr. rouge - n° 1011 a (suite)

1011-C 3 EXCEL - BIC CLIC - EXCEL - BIC CLIC séries : (2-55) ....95 »
1011-C 3 EXCEL - BIC CLIC - EXCEL - BIC CLIC séries : (8-55) ....95 »
1011-C 3 EXCEL - BIC CLIC - EXCEL - BIC CLIC séries : (16-55) ....95 »
1011-C 3 EXCEL - BIC CLIC - EXCEL - BIC CLIC séries : (2-56) ....105 »
1011-C 4 EXCEL - GRAMMONT - EXCEL - GRAMMONT
série : 4-57 ....90 »
1011-C 5 EXCEL - HAHN (cheveux) - EXCEL - HAHN (cheveux)
série : 1-57 ....350 »
1011-C 6 EXCEL - HAHN (cheveux) - EXCEL - HAHN (pellicules)
série : 1-57 ....130 »
1011-C 7 EXCEL - LINCOLN - EXCEL - LINCOLN séries : (14-56) ....85 »
1011-C 7 EXCEL - LINCOLN - EXCEL - LINCOLN séries : (3-57) ....85 »
1011-C 8 EXCEL - SATAM - EXCEL - GRAMMONT - série : 2-57 ....90 »
1011-C 9 GRAMMONT - BIC CLIC - GRAMMONT - BIC CLIC série : 7-55 ......85 »
1011-C 10 HAHN (barres E-H-A- centrées) - BIC - HAHN - BIC série : 5-56 ......175 »
1011-C 11 HAHN (barres E-H-A- hautes) - BIC - HAHN - BIC séries 5-56 ......470 »
1011-C 12 HAHN - BIC CLIC - HAHN - BIC CLIC séries : (4-55)........................85 »
1011-C 12 HAHN - BIC CLIC - HAHN - BIC CLIC séries : (1-56) ....105 »
1011-C 13 HAHN - SLAVIA (5 cases) - HAHN - SLAVIA (case 4) série : 13-56 480 »
1011-C 14 HAHN - SLAVIA (case 4) - HAHN - SLAVIA (case 4) série : 13-56......320 »
1011-C 15 HAHN - SLAVIA (5 cases) - HAHN - SLAVIA (5 cases) série : 13-56 480 »
1011-C 16 JIF - SLAVIA (5 cases) - JIF - SLAVIA (5 cases) série : 12-56 ....280 »
1011-C 17 JIF - SLAVIA (5 cases) - JIF - SLAVIA (case 4) série : 12-56 ....540 »
1011-C 18 JIF - SLAVIA (case 4) - JIF - SLAVIA (case 4) série : 12-56 ....540 »
1011-C 19 JIF - SLAVIA (case 4) - JIF - SLAVIA (5 cases) série : 12-56 ....670 »
1011-C 20 LIEBIG - BIC CLIC - LIEBIG - BIC CLIC
séries : (3-55) - (5-55) - (6-55) ....90 »
1011-C 21 POSTE (Barres) - BIC - PROVINS - BIC série : 6-56 ....85 »
1011-C 22 POSTE - POSTE - POSTE - POSTE séries : (10-56) ....100 »
1011-C 22 POSTE - POSTE - POSTE - POSTE séries : (11-56) ....100 »
1011-C 23 PRIMAGAZ - GRAMMONT - WHYP - PROVINS série : 8-56 ....95 »
1011-C 24 ROLLA - AVIA - POSTE - POSTE série 9-56 ....100 »
1011-C 25 SLAVIA (5 cases) - A.G VIE - SLAVIA (5 cases) - A.G VIE
série : 6-57 ....420 »
1011-C 26 SLAVIA (5 cases) - A.G VIE - SLAVIA (case 4) - A.G VIE
série : 6-57 ....180 »
1011-C 27 SLAVIA (case 4) - A.G VIE - SLAVIA (case 4) - A.G VIE
série : 6-57 ....340 »
1011-C 28 SLAVIA - SLAVIA - SLAVIA - SLAVIA série 7-56 ....135 »

1011-CP1 - série 6-56

1011-CP 1 VILLES de PROVINS - 10 timbres - série 6-56 ....760 »
1011-CP 2 VILLES de PROVINS - 10 timbres - couverture PROVINS ....800 »

1011B TYPE MULLER - 20fr. bleu (type I) - n° 1011Bb

Carnet 1011B-C8 (avec petit F) RARE

1011B-C 1 A.G VIE - GRAMMONT - A.G VIE - GRAMMONT
série : 12-57 ....95 »
1011B-C 2 A.G VIE - GRAMMONT - A.G VIE - PROVINS série : 5-58 ....95 »
1011B-C 3 A.G VIE - GRAMMONT - A.G VIE - SATAM série : 15-57 ....85 »
1011B-C 4 AKYLON - GRAMMONT - AKYLON - GRAMMONT
série : 12-58 ....100 »
1011B-C 5 CALBERSON - GRAMMONT - CALBERSON - SATAM
série : 16-57 ....90 »
1011B-C 6 COMPTOIR ELECTRIQUE - GRAMMONT - SATAM - SATAM
série : 11-57 ....85 »
1011B-C 7 ELAUL - GRAMMONT - ELAUL - THIAUDE série : 1-58 ....95 »
1011B-C 8 ELCO - GRAMMONT - ELCO - GRAMMONT série : 13-57 ....450 »
1011B-C 9 EXCEL - A.G VIE - EXCEL - A.G VIE série : 14-58 ....85 »
1011B-C 10 EXCEL - GRAMMONT - EXCEL - GRAMMONT séries : (3-58) ......90 »
1011B-C 10 EXCEL - GRAMMONT - EXCEL - GRAMMONT séries : (4-58) ......85 »
1011B-C 10 EXCEL - GRAMMONT - EXCEL - GRAMMONT séries : (15-58) ......90 »
1011B-C 11 FRIMATIC - A.G VIE - HAHN - A.G VIE série : 10-58 ....180 »
1011B-C 12 Carnet C11 - 2e I de FRIMATIC cassé (point sur le i)
série : 10-58 ....410 »
1011B-C 13 FRIMATIC - GRAMMONT - FRIMATIC - ROLLA
ssérie : 8-58 ....95 »
1011B-C 14 FRIMATIC - GRAMMONT - FRIMATIC - THIAUDE
série : 16-58 ....135 »
1011B-C 15 Carnet C14 - 2e I de FRIMATIC (supérieur) cassé (point sur le i)
série : 16-58 ....220 »
1011B-C 16 Carnet C14 - 2e I de FRIMATIC (inférieur) cassé (point sur le i)
série : 16-58 ....600 »
1011B-C 17 GUEULES CASSEES - GRAMMONT - A.G VIE - GRAMMONT
série : 11-58 ....100 »
1011B-C 18 HAHN - GRAMMONT - HAHN - SATAM série : 6-58 ....100 »
1011B-C 19 HAHN - PRIMAGAZ - HAHN - GUEULES CASSEES
série : 13-58 ....95 »
1011B-C 20 HAHN - SATAM - HAHN (pellicules) - SATAM série : 14-57 ....135 »
1011B-C 21 HAHN - SATAM - HAHN (cheveux) - SATAM série : 14-57 ....340 »
1011B-C 22 ROLLA - GRAMMONT - FRIMATIC - CHÂTEAU THIERRY
série : 7-58 ....95 »
1011B-C 23 ROLLA - SATAM - GRAMMONT - GRAMONT
série : 7-57 ....100 »
1011B-C 24 SLAVIA (5 cases) - ELAUL - SLAVIA (case 4) THIAUDE
série : 2-58 ....210 »
1011B-C 25 SLAVIA (5 cases) - ELAUL - SLAVIA (5 cases) THIAUDE
série : 2-58 ....340 »
1011B-C 26 SLAVIA (case 4) - ELAUL - SLAVIA (case 4) THIAUDE
série : 2-58 ....340 »
1011B-C 27 SLAVIA (5 cases) - GRAMMONT - SLAVIA (5 cases) GRAMMONT
série : 10-57 ....245 »
1011B-C 28 SLAVIA (5 cases) - GRAMMONT - SLAVIA (case 4) GRAMMONT
série : 10-57 ....310 »

1011B TYPE MULLER - 20fr. bleu (type I) - n° 1011Bb (suite)

1011B-C 29 SLAVIA (4) - GRAMMONT - SLAVIA (case 4) GRAMMONT
série : 10-57 ....300 »

1011B-C 30 SLAVIA (4) - GRAMMONT - SLAVIA (5 cases) GRAMMONT
série : 10-57 ....400 »

1011B-C 31 SLAVIA (5 cases) - SLAVIA (case 4) - SLAVIA (case 4) SLAVIA (5 cases)
série : 9-58 ....520 »

1011B-C 32 SLAVIA (case 4) - SLAVIA (5 cases) - SLAVIA (case 4) SLAVIA (case 4)
série : 9-58 ....360 »

1011B-C 33 SLAVIA (5 cases) - SLAVIA (5 cases) - SLAVIA (4) SLAVIA (5 cases)
série : 9-58 ....430 »

1011B-C 34 SLAVIA (5 cases) - SLAVIA (case 4) - SLAVIA (5 cases) SLAVIA (5 cases)
série : 9-58 ....580 »

1011B-C 35 SLAVIA (5 cases) - SLAVIA (case 4) - SLAVIA (case 4) SLAVIA (case 4)
série : 9-58 ....520 »

1011B-C 36 SLAVIA (case 4) - SLAVIA (case 4) - SLAVIA (5 cases) SLAVIA (5 cases)
série : 9-58 ....550 »

Les carnets du type MULLER 15F rouge et 20F bleu avec pub SLAVIA comportent dans certaines compositions, le 2ème A de SLAVIA ouvert à la base. Celles-ci sont repérées par les n° de cases indiqués.

1011B TYPE MULLER - 20fr. bleu (type II) - n° 1011Bd

1011B-C 37 ELCO - GRAMMONT - ELCO - GRAMMONT série : 13-57 ....340 »

1011B-C 38 PROVINS - GRAMMONT - GRAMMONT - ROLLA
série : 8-57 ....340 »

1011B-C 39 SATAM - A.G VIE - SATAM - A.G VIE série : 9-57 ....360 »

1011C TYPE MULLER - 25fr. rouge (type II) - n° 1011Cc

1011C-C 1 Carnet de 8 timbres - (format 40x75) série : 1-59 ....65 »

1011C TYPE MULLER - 25fr. rouge (type I) - n° 1011Ca

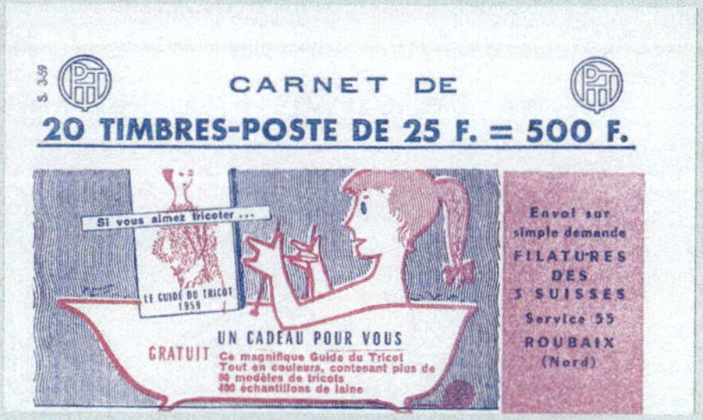

Série 3-59

1011C-C 2 Carnet de 20 timbres - avec barres sur les marges
séries : 1-59 à 14-59 ....75 »

1234 TYPE MARIANNE A LA NEF - 0,25fr. bleu et rouge (type II) - n° 1234 b

1234-C 1 Carnet de 8 timbres - (format 40x75) séries : 01-60 - 02-60 ....90 »

1234 TYPE MARIANNE A LA NEF - 0,25fr. bleu et rouge (type I) - n° 1234 a

Série 4-60

1234-C 2 Carnet de 20 timbres - avec barres sur les marges
séries : 1-60 à 8-60 .... 110 »

1263 TYPE MARIANNE de DECARIS - 0,25fr. gris et carmin (type II) - n° 1263 e

1263-C 1 Carnet de 8 timbres - (format 40x75) - n° de série sur 8 mm.
séries : 03-60 à 05-60 - 01-61 à 05-61
01-62 à 05-62 - 01-63 à 04-63 .... 50 »

1263-C 2 Carnet C1 - n° de série sur 6 mm. série : 04-63 .... 80 »

1263 TYPE MARIANNE de DECARIS - 0,25fr. gris et carmin (type I) - n° 1263 d et 1263 c

Série 11-61

1263-C 3 Carnet de 20 timbres - avec barres sur les marges
séries : 9-60 à 15-60 - 1-61 à 22-61
1-62 à 24-62 - 1-63 à 25-63 - 1 à 5-64 - 9-64 à 24-64 .... 85 »

1263-C 4 Carnet C3 avec pubs PHILATEC sur marges
séries : 6 à 8-64 .... 100 »

1354 TYPE BLASON de PARIS - 0,30fr. bleu et rouge - n° 1354B

Série 9-65

1354-C 1 Carnet de 20 timbres - avec barres sur les marges
séries : 1-65 à 10-65 .... 80 »

YVERT&TELLIER
Partenaires de vos passions...
LILLE
AMIENS
LE HAVRE
PARIS
LYON
MARSEILLE
espaces YVERT&TELLIER
6 magasins dédiés à toutes vos collections
Achat - Vente de Timbres
Catalogues de cotations
Matériel toutes marques
Monnaies - Cartes postales - Télécartes
Des professionnels au service de vos loisirs.
LILLE
54, rue Molinel 59000 LILLE 03 20 44 22 22
AMIENS
26, rue au Lin 80000 AMIENS 03 22 92 33 32
PARIS
10, rue Châteaudun 75009 PARIS 01 40 82 74 70
LE HAVRE
72, avenue Foch 76600 LE HAVRE 02 35 41 22 22
LYON
48/50, rue de la Charité 69002 LYON 04 78 42 22 22
MARSEILLE
263, rue Paradis 13006 MARSEILLE 04 91 58 22 22

II. - CARNETS MODERNES

Les carnets modernes comprennent deux grandes catégories :
- carnets fermés
- carnets ouverts

* **Carnets fermés :**

Ces carnets contiennent 5,10 ou 20 timbres (exceptionnellement 8 ou 9)
Sur la couverture est indiqué (ou non) un n° de confectionneuse
Format 72x26 pour les carnets de 5 à 10 timbres (sauf confectionneuse 9)
Format 78x26 pour la confectionneuse 9 - toujours avec gomme brillante
Format 72x52 pour les carnets de 20 timbres
Pendant toute la période allant du n° 1331 A (coq 0,30fr) au n° 2424 (liberté 1,90fr vert) les couvertures comportent 3 types de publicité :

* Caisse d'épargne postale

* Code postal

* Philexfrance 82

Toutes les autres couvertures sont représentées

* **Carnets ouverts (3 formes)**

Carnet pour guichets (avec ou sans pont) - (format : 125x52)

Carnet pour distributeurs - (format 120x57)

Carnet pour distributeurs automatiques de billets - (DAB) - (format : 143x96)

* **Carnets avec carré noir**

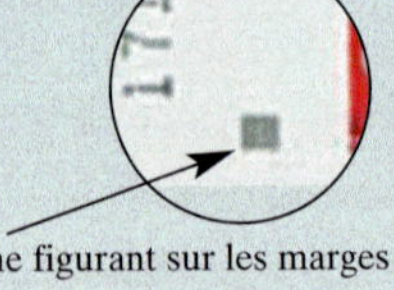

Signe figurant sur les marges de certaines feuilles de carnet RGR-2.

Ce repère, utilisé pour préparer l'enliassage des carnets, ne se rencontre que sur des carnets avec n° de liasse égal à 100 (ou 99 mais il est alors tronqué) / fréquence d'1 carnet sur 500 produits.

1331 TYPE COQ de DECARIS - 0,25 Fr. outremer et carmin-brun - n° 1331

1331-C 1 8 timbres - couverture CALBERSON (diagonal) - série : 101 - 62 ......150 »
1331-C 1a Carnet C1 - sans n° de série..320 »

1331-C 2 8 timbres - couverture CALBERSON (horizontal)
séries : (101 - 63) - (102 - 63)- (103 - 63) ....40 »

1331-C 3 8 timbres - couverture PHILATEC - série : 101 - 64 ....100 »
1331-C 3a 8 timbres - couverture PHILATEC - série : 102 - 64 ....35 »

1331-C 4 8 timbres - caisse d'épargne postale - sans n° ....45 »

1331-C 5 8 timbres - imprimerie - 7 couleurs différentes - série : PHILATEC - 64 35 »
1331-C 5 A Carnets C5 - série complète des 7 couleurs - série : PHILATEC - 64 ......300 »

1331A TYPE COQ de DECARIS - 0,30 Fr. vert,rouge et bistre - n° 1331 A

1331A-C 1 10 timbres - caisse d'épargne postale - sans n° ....23 »
1331A-C 2 20 timbres - caisse d'épargne postale - sans n° ....45 »

1536 TYPE CHEFFER - 0,30 Fr. lilas - n° 1536

1536-C 1 10 timbres - caisse d'épargne postale - conf. 1 - 2 - 3 - 7
ouvrir ici (avec trait) ....15 »
1536-C 2 10 timbres - caisse d'épargne postale - sans n° - ouvrir ici (sans trait) ......200 »
1536-C 3 20 timbres - caisse d'épargne postale - conf. 4 - 5 - 6
ouvrir ici (avec trait) ....30 »
1536-C 4 20 timbres - caisse d'épargne postale - sans n° - ouvrir ici (sans trait) ......250 »

1536 A TYPE CHEFFER - 0,30 Fr. vert - n° 1536 A

1536 A-C 1 20 timbres - caisse d'épargne postale - conf. 5 - 6 ....17 »

1536 B TYPE CHEFFER - 0,40 Fr. rose - n° 1536 B

1536 B-C 1 10 timbres - caisse d'épargne postale - conf. 1 à 3 - 7 ....15 »
1536 B-C 2 20 timbres - caisse d'épargne postale - conf. 4 - 5 - 6..............................17 »

1664 TYPE MARIANNE de BEQUET - 0,50 Fr. rouge - n° 1664

1664-C 1 10 timbres - caisse d'épargne postale - conf. 1 à 5 - 7 - 8 ....14 »
1664-C 2 20 timbres - caisse d'épargne postale - conf. 6 à 8 ....23 »
1664-C 3 10 timbres - code postal - ouvrir ici - (sans trait) - conf. 3 à 5 - 7 ....17 »
1664-C 4 10 timbres - code postal - ouvrir ici - (avec trait) - conf. 1 - 2..................120 »
1664-C 5 20 timbres - code postal - ouvrir ici - (sans trait) - conf. 6 à 8 ....22 »
1664-C 5a Carnet C5 avec plusieurs timbres-poste non imprimés ....520 »
1664-C 6 20 timbres - code postal - ouvrir ici - (avec trait) - conf. 8 ....150 »

1664 TYPE MARIANNE de BEQUET - 0,50 Fr. rouge - n° 1664 c - 3 bandes de phosphore

1664-C 7 10 timbres - code postal - ouvrir ici - (sans trait) - conf. 3 à 5 - 7 et sans n° 13 »
1664-C 8 10 timbres - code postal - ouvrir ici - (avec trait) - conf. 1 - 2 et sans n°......28 »
1664-C 9 20 timbres - code postal - ouvrir ici - (sans trait) - conf. 6 - 8 et sans n° ......21 »
1664-C 10 20 timbres - code postal - ouvrir ici - (avec trait) - conf. 6 ....75 »

1815 TYPE MARIANNE de BEQUET - 0,60 Fr. vert - n° 1815

1815-C 1 20 timbres - code postal - conf. 6 et sans n° ....140 »

1815 TYPE MARIANNE de BEQUET - 0,60 Fr. vert - n° 1815 c - sans phosphore

1815-C 2 20 timbres - code postal - conf. 6 ....400 »

1816 TYPE MARIANNE de BEQUET - 0,80 Fr. rouge - n° 1816

1816-C 1 5 timbres - code postal - conf. 2 et sans n° ....11 »
1816-C 2 10 timbres - code postal - conf. 3 à 5 - 7 et sans n° ....12 »
1816-C 3 20 timbres - code postal - conf. 6 - 8 ....21 »

1816 TYPE MARIANNE de BEQUET - 0,80 Fr. rouge - n° 1816 d - sans phosphore

1816-C 4 10 timbres - code postal - conf. 4 ....100 »
1816-C 5 20 timbres - code postal - conf. 4 - 6 ....160 »

1892 TYPE MARIANNE de BEQUET - 1 Fr. rouge - n° 1892

1892-C 1 5 timbres - code postal - gomme brillante - sans n° de confectionneuse 13 »
1892-C 1a 5 timbres - code postal - gomme mate - sans n° de confectionneuse ......38 »
1892-C 2 10 timbres - code postal - gomme brillante - conf. 3 à 5 - 7 - 8 et sans n° 14 »
1892-C 2a 10 timbres - code postal - gomme mate - conf. 4 et sans n° ....38 »
1892-C 3 20 timbres - code postal - gomme brillante - conf. 6 - 8 et sans n° ....23 »
1892-C 3a 20 timbres - code postal - gomme mate - conf. 6 ....50 »

1893 TYPE MARIANNE de BEQUET - 0,80 Fr. vert - n° 1893

1893-C 1 20 timbres - code postal - gomme brillante - conf. 6 - 8 ....46 »
1893-C 1a 20 timbres - code postal - gomme mate - conf. 8 ....54 »

1970 TYPE SABINE - 0,80 Fr. vert - n° 1970

1970-C 1 20 timbres - code postal - gomme brillante - conf. 6 ....45 »
1970-C 1a 20 timbres - code postal - gomme mate - conf. 6 ....62 »

1972 TYPE SABINE - 1 Fr. rouge - n° 1972

1972-C 1 5 timbres - code postal - gomme brillante
sans n° de confectionneuse ....16 »
1972-C 1a 5 timbres - code postal - gomme mate
sans n° de confectionneuse ....44 »
1972-C 2 10 timbres - code postal - gomme brillante - conf. 3 à 7 ....23 »
1972-C 2a 10 timbres - code postal - gomme mate - conf. 6 ....67 »
1972-C 3 20 timbres - code postal - gomme brillante - conf. 6 - 8 ....45 »
1972-C 3a 20 timbres - code postal - gomme mate - conf. 8 ....133 »

1973 TYPE SABINE - 1 Fr. vert - n° 1973

1973-C 1 20 timbres - code postal - gomme brillante - conf. 6 - 8 ....23 »
1973-C 1a 20 timbres - code postal - gomme mate - conf. 8 ....39 »

1974 TYPE SABINE - 1,20 Fr. rouge - n° 1974

1974-C 1 5 timbres - code postal - gomme brillante
sans n° de confectionneuse ....9 »
1974-C 1a 5 timbres - code postal - gomme mate
sans n° de confectionneuse ....15 »
1974-C 2 10 timbres - code postal - gomme brillante - conf. 3 à 8 et sans n° ....12 »
1974-C 2a 10 timbres - code postal - gomme mate - conf. 3 à 5 - 7 ....25 »
1974-C 2b 10 timbres - code postal - conf. 7 plusieurs Timbres-Poste à sec ....180 »
1974-C 3 10 timbres - code postal - conf. 9 ....15 »
1974-C 4 20 timbres - code postal - gomme brillante - conf. 8 et sans n° ....24 »
1974-C 4a 20 timbres - code postal - gomme mate - conf. 8 ....46 »

2058 TYPE SABINE - 1,10 Fr. vert - n° 2058

2058-C 1 20 timbres - code postal - gomme brillante - conf. 8 et sans n° ....23 »
2058-C 1a 20 timbres - code postal - gomme mate - sans n° de confectionneuse ......63 »

2059 TYPE SABINE - 1,30 Fr . Rouge - n° 2059

2059-C 1 5 timbres - code postal - gomme brillante
sans n° de confectionneuse ....8 »
2059-C 1a 5 timbres - code postal - gomme mate
sans n° de confectionneuse ....24 »
2059-C 2 10 timbres - code postal - gomme brillante - conf. 3 à 7 ....13 »
2059-C 2a 10 timbres - code postal - gomme mate - conf. 3 à 5 -7 ....39 »
2059-C 2b 10 timbres - code postal - gomme brillante - conf. 3 - TP sans phosphore 350 »
2059-C 3 10 timbres - code postal - conf. 9 ....17 »
2059-C 4 20 timbres - code postal - gomme brillante - conf. 8 ....23 »
2059-C 4a 20 timbres - code postal - gomme mate - conf. 8 ....75 »

2101 TYPE SABINE - 1,20 Fr. vert - n° 2101

2101-C 1 20 timbres - code postal - gomme brillante - conf. 8 ....17 »

2101-C 1a 20 timbres - code postal - gomme mate - conf. 8 ....32 »

2101-C 1b 20 timbres - code postal - gomme brillante - couverture avec nouveau logo de La Poste ....70 »

2101-C 2 20 timbres - philexfrance 82 - gomme brillante - conf. 8 ....43 »

2102 TYPE SABINE - 1,40 Fr. Rouge - n° 2102

2102-C 1 5 timbres - code postal - gomme brillante sans n° de confectionneuse ....16 »

2102-C 1a 5 timbres - code postal - gomme mate - sans n° de confectionneuse ......26 »

2102-C 2 5 timbres - philexfrance 82 - gomme brillante sans n° de confectionneuse ....31 »

2102-C 2a 5 timbres - philexfrance 82 - gomme mate sans n° de confectionneuse ....11 »

2102-C 3 10 timbres - code postal - gomme brillante - conf. 3 à 7 ....13 »

2102-C 3a 10 timbres - code postal - gomme mate - conf. 4 ....23 »

2102-C 4 10 timbres - code postal - conf. 9 ....14 »

2102-C 5 10 timbres - philexfrance 82 - gomme brillante - conf. 3 à 7 et sans n° ......9 »

2102-C 5a 10 timbres - philexfrance 82 - gomme mate - conf. 6 ....11 »

2102-C 6 10 timbres - philexfrance 82 - conf. 9 ....11 »

2102-C 7 20 timbres - code postal - gomme brillante - conf. 8 ....22 »

2102-C 7a 20 timbres - code postal - gomme mate - conf. 8 ....38 »

2102-C 8 20 timbres - philexfrance 82 - gomme brillante - conf. 8 ....17 »

2102-C 8a 20 timbres - philexfrance 82 - gomme mate - conf. 8 ....30 »

2154 TYPE SABINE - 1,40 Fr. vert - n° 2154

2154-C 1 20 timbres - philexfrance 82 - gomme brillante - conf. 8 ....22 »

2154-C 1a 20 timbres - philexfrance 82 - gomme mate - conf. 8 ....34 »

2155 TYPE SABINE - 1,60 Fr . Rouge - n° 2155

2155-C 1 5 timbres - philexfrance 82 - gomme brillante sans n° de confectionneuse ....13 »

2155-C 1a 5 timbres - philexfrance 82 - gomme mate - sans n° de confectionneuse 16 »

2155-C 2 10 timbres - philexfrance 82 - gomme brillante - conf. 3 à 7 ....11 »

2155-C 2a 10 timbres - philexfrance 82 - gomme mate - conf. 4 - 6 ....17 »

2155-C 3 10 timbres - philexfrance 82 - conf .9 ....14 »

2155-C 4 20 timbres - philexfrance 82 - gomme brillante - conf. 8 et sans n° ....22 »

2155-C 4a 20 timbres - philexfrance 82 - gomme mate - conf. 8 et sans n° ....26 »

2186 TYPE LIBERTE de DELACROIX - 1,40 Fr. vert - n° 2186

2186-C 1 20 timbres - philexfrance 82 - gomme brillante - conf. 8 ....20 »

2186-C 1a 20 timbres - philexfrance 82 - gomme mate - conf. 8 ....75 »

2187 TYPE LIBERTE de DELACROIX - 1,60 Fr. rouge - n° 2187

2187-C 1 5 timbres - philexfrance 82 - gomme brillante
sans n° de confectionneuse ....8 »
2187-C 2 10 timbres - philexfrance 82 - gomme brillante - conf. 3 à 7 ....13 »
2187-C 2a 10 timbres - philexfrance 82 - gomme mate - conf. 4 - 5 - 6 ....32 »
2187-C 3 10 timbres - philexfrance 82 - conf. 9 ....17 »
2187-C 4 20 timbres - philexfrance 82 - gomme brillante - conf. 8 ....23 »
2187-C 4a 20 timbres - philexfrance 82 - gomme mate - conf. 8 ....50 »

2219 TYPE LIBERTE de DELACROIX - 1,60 Fr. vert - n° 2219

2219-C 1 20 timbres - philexfrance 82 - gomme mate - conf. 8 ....55 »
2219-C 2 20 timbres - code postal - gomme brillante - conf. 8 ....20 »
2219-C 2a 20 timbres - code postal - gomme mate - conf. 8 ....150 »

2220 TYPE LIBERTE de DELACROIX - 1,80 Fr. rouge - n° 2220

2220-C 1 5 timbres - code postal - gomme brillante
sans n° de confectionneuse ....7 »
2220-C 1a 5 timbres - code postal - gomme mate - sans n° de confectionneuse ......10 »
2220-C 2 10 timbres - philexfrance 82 - gomme brillante - conf. 5 à 7 ....38 »

2220-C 3 10 timbres - CNIT philexfrance 82 - conf. 9 ....11 »
2220-C 3A Carnets C3 - série complète des 11 carnets de couleurs
différentes - conf. 9 ....120 »
2220-C 4 10 timbres - philexfbrance 82 - conf. 9 ....16 »
2220-C 5 10 timbres - code postal - gomme brillante - conf. 3 à 7 ....11 »
2220-C 5a 10 timbres - code postal - gomme mate - conf. 6 ....80 »
2220-C 6 10 timbres - code postal - conf. 9 ....12 »
2220-C 7 20 timbres - philexfrance 82 - gomme brillante - conf. 8 ....60 »
2220-C 7a 20 timbres - philexfrance 82 - gomme mate - conf. 8 ....70 »
2220-C 8 20 timbres - code postal - gomme brillante - conf. 8 ....19 »
2220-C 8a 20 timbres - code postal - gomme mate - conf. 8 ....75 »

2274 TYPE LIBERTE de DELACROIX - 2 Fr. rouge - n° 2274

2274-C 1 5 timbres - code postal - gomme brillante
sans n° de confectionneuse ....28 »
2274-C 1a 5 timbres - code postal - gomme mate - sans n° de confectionneuse ......10 »
2274-C 1b Carnet C 1 - date imprimée à gauche ....40 »
2274-C 2 10 timbres - code postal - gomme brillante- conf. 3 à 7 ....15 »
2274-C 2a 10 timbres - code postal - gomme mate - conf. 5 à 7 ....20 »
2274-C 3 10 timbres - code postal - conf. 9 ....16 »
2274-C 4 20 timbres - code postal - gomme brillante - conf. 8 ....20 »
2274-C 4a 20 timbres - code postal - gomme mate - conf. 8 ....50 »

2318 TYPE LIBERTE de DELACROIX - 1,70 Fr. vert - n° 2318

2318-C 1 20 timbres - code postal - gomme brillante - conf. 8 ....23 »
2318-C 1a 20 timbres - code postal - gomme mate - conf. 8 ....100 »

2319 TYPE LIBERTE de DELACROIX - 2,10 Fr. rouge - n° 2319

2319-C 1 10 timbres - code postal - gomme brillante - couverture rouge sur crème - conf. 4 à 8 .... 13 »
2319-C 1a 10 timbres - code postal - gomme mate - couverture rouge sur crème - conf. 4 à 8 .... 20 »
2319-C 1b 10 timbres - code postal - sans phosphore .... 200 »
2319-C 2 10 timbres - code postal - conf. 9 .... 14 »
2319-C 3 10 timbres - code postal - gomme mate - couverture bleu sur crème sans n° de confectionneuse .... 12 »
2319-C 4 20 timbres - code postal - gomme brillante - couverture rouge sur crème - conf. 8 .... 23 »
2319-C 4a 20 timbres - code postal - gomme mate - couverture rouge sur crème - conf. 8 .... 60 »

2375 TYPE LIBERTE de DELACROIX - 1,80 Fr. vert - n° 2375

2375-C 1 10 timbres - code postal - gomme brillante - conf. 6 .... 14 »
2375-C 1a 10 timbres - code postal - gomme mate - conf. 6 .... 70 »

2376 TYPE LIBERTE de DELACROIX - 2,20 Fr. rouge - n° 2376

2376-C 1 10 timbres - code postal - gomme mate - couverture bleu sur crème sans n° de confectionneuse .... 14 »

2376-C 2 10 timbres - code postal - gomme brillante - couverture rouge sur crème - conf. 4 à 8 .... 14 »
2376-C 2a 10 timbres - code postal - gomme mate - couverture rouge sur crème - conf. 6 - 7 .... 25 »

2376-C 3 10 timbres - code postal - conf. 9 .... 14 »

2376-C 4 10 timbres - POUR OFFRIR DES TIMBRES - la pochette trimestrielle conf. 9 .... 18 »

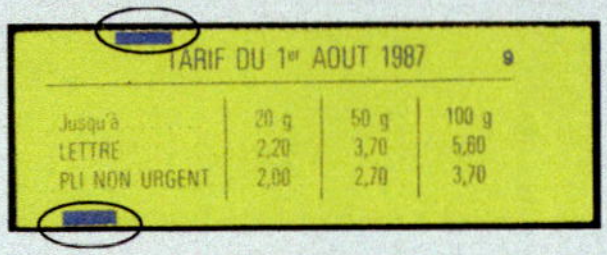

2376-C 5 10 timbres - POUR OFFRIR DES TIMBRES - la pochette semestrielle conf. 9 .... 17 »
2376-C 5a Carnet C 5 - sans phosphore .... 180 »

2376 TYPE LIBERTE de DELACROIX - 2,20 Fr. rouge - n° 2376 (suite)

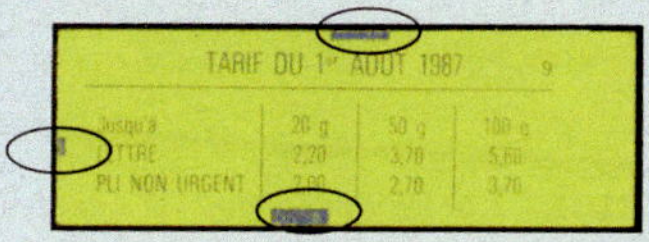

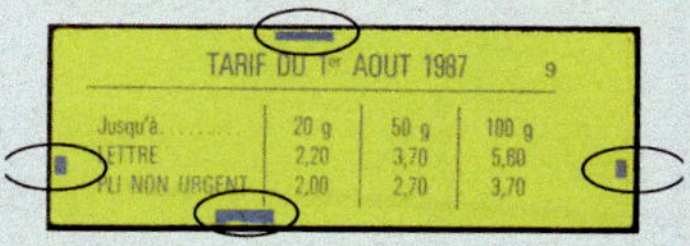

2376-C 5b Carnet C 5 - avec 3 cavaliers (2 sur grands cotés et 1 sur petit coté) ......70 »
2376-C 5c Carnet C 5 - avec cavaliers sur 4 cotés..15 »

2376-C 6 10 timbres - POUR OFFRIR DES TIMBRES - la pochette semestrielle - conf. 6 ....25 »
2376-C 6a Carnet C 6 - conf. 6 - Plusieurs timbres-poste mal imprimés ....130 »
2376-C 6b 10 timbres - POUR OFFRIR DES TIMBRES - la pochette semestrielle - conf. 7 ....40 »
2376-C 6c 10 timbres - POUR OFFRIR DES TIMBRES - la pochette semestrielle - conf. 8 ....80 »

2376-C 7 10 timbres - POUR OFFRIR DES TIMBRES - la pochette semestrielle - (plus lettre D) - conf. 8 ....45 »

2376-C 8 10 timbres 2376d - Faites de la MUSIQUE - conf. 9..............................40 »

2376-C 9 10 timbres - LA RESERVATION GRATUITE DES TIMBRES conf. 6 - 7 ....42 »

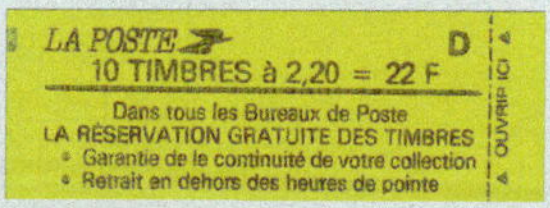

2376-C 10 10 timbres - LA RESERVATION GRATUITE DES TIMBRES - (plus lettre D) - conf. 8 ....42 »

2376-C11

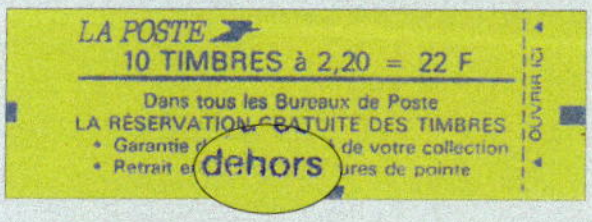

2376-C11a

2376-C 11 10 timbres - LA RESERVATION GRATUITE DES TIMBRES conf. 9 ....17 »
2376-C 11a Carnet C11 sans “S” à dehors ....35 »
2376-C 11b Carnet C11 - sans phosphore ....150 »

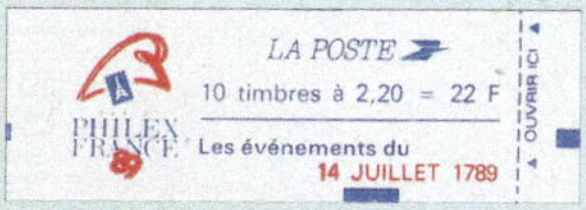

2376-C 12 10 timbres - philexfrance 89 - évenements de juillet 1789 - conf. 9............15 »
2376-C 12A Carnets C12 - série complète des 11 carnets différents ....170 »

2424 TYPE LIBERTE de DELACROIX - 1,90 Fr. vert - n° 2424

2 424-C 1 10 timbres - code postal - conf. 8 ....45 »

2427 TYPE LIBERTE de DELACROIX - 2,20 Fr. rouge - n° 2427 - dentelé 3 côtés

2427-C 1 10 timbres - code postal - couverture rouge sur blanc - format 140x52 ......18 »

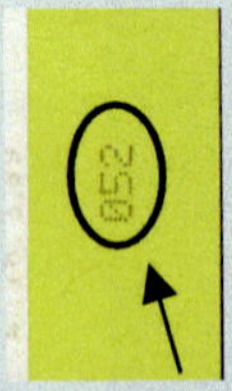

2427-C 2 10 timbres - RESERVEZ VOS TIMBRES DE COLLECTION
bleu sur jaune - (format 140x52) ....15 »

2427-C 2a Idem C2 avec N° ordre de 4,5 mm de hauteur ....25 »

2614 TYPE MARIANNE de BRIAT - 2,30 Fr. rouge - n° 2614

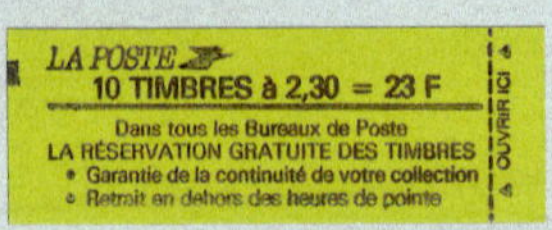

2614-C 1 10 timbres - LA RESERVATION GRATUITE DES TIMBRES
conf. 6 - 7 ....32 »

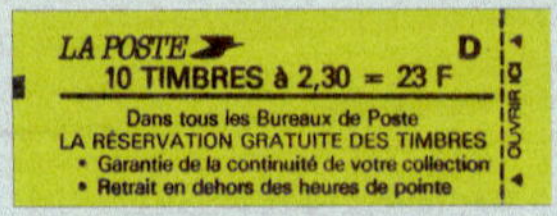

2614-C 2 10 timbres - LA RESERVATION GRATUITE DES TIMBRES
(plus lettre D) - conf. 8 ....32 »

2614-C 3 10 timbres - LA RESERVATION GRATUITE DES TIMBRES
conf. 9 ....18 »

2614-C 3a Idem C3 avec découpe des timbres-poste à cheval ....300 »

2614-C 4 10 timbres - LA RESERVATION GRATUITE DES TIMBRES
schweppes (au verso) - conf. 9 ....14 »

2614 TYPE MARIANNE de BRIAT - 2,30 Fr. rouge - n° 2614 (suite)

2614-C 5 10 timbres - JEUX OLYMPIQUES D'HIVER - conf. 6 ....600 »
2614-C 5a 10 timbres - JEUX OLYMPIQUES D'HIVER - conf. 7 ....500 »
2614-C 5b 10 timbres - JEUX OLYMPIQUES D'HIVER - conf. 8 ....650 »

2614-C 6 10 timbres - JEUX OLYMPIQUES D'HIVER - plus lettre D - conf. 8 90 »
2614-C 6a 10 timbres - JEUX OLYMPIQUES D'HIVER - plus lettre D - conf. 6 400 »

2614-C 7 10 timbres - JEUX OLYMPIQUES D'HIVER - conf. 9 ....20 »
2614-C 7a Idem C7 avec erreur de date 01.05.90 ....80 »
2614-C 7b Idem C7 avec plusieurs timbres-poste à sec ....350 »

2614-C 8 9 timbres à 2,30 —20 F - lettre D - JEUX OLYMPIQUES D'HIVER - conf. 9 ....17 »

2614-C 9 10 timbres - Faites de la MUSIQUE - sacem - conf. 9 - 1........................14 »

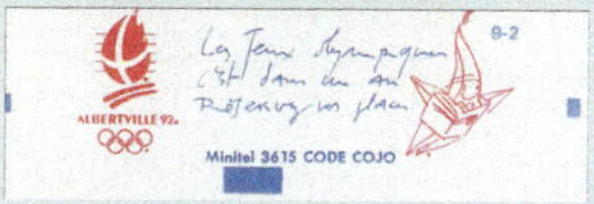

2614-C 10 10 timbres - JEUX OLYMPIQUES D'HIVER - couverture blanche conf. 9 - 2 ....14 »
2614-C 10a 10 timbres - JEUX OLYMPIQUES D'HIVER - couverture blanche sans n° de confectionneuse..50 »

2614-C11a 

 2614-C11

2614-C 11 10 timbres - la poste avec le train MOZART - conf. 9 - 3 ....14 »
2614-C 11a Carnet C 11 sans point après Blois ....45 »

2614-CP 1 10 timbres - la poste figeac - (format 125x54) ....520 »

2629 TYPE MARIANNE de BRIAT - 2,30 Fr. rouge - n° 2629 - dentelé 3 côtés

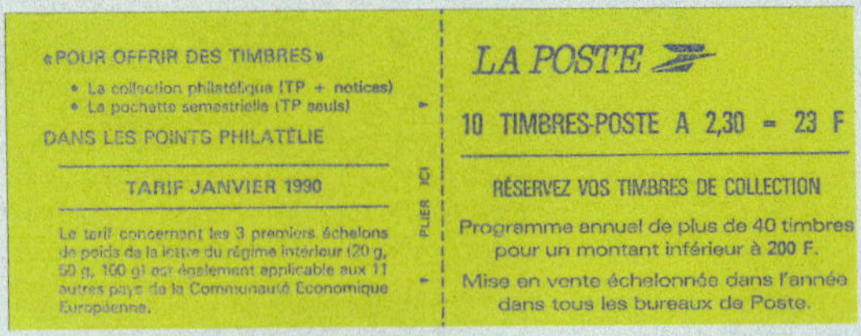

2629-C 1 10 timbres - RESERVEZ VOS TIMBRES DE COLLECTION
bleu sur jaune - (format 140x52) ....34 »
2629-C 1a Carnet C1 avec n° d'ordre supérieur à 100 ....110 »

2630 TYPE MARIANNE de BRIAT - 2,30 Fr. rouge - n° 2630 - non dentelé adhésif

2630-C 1 10 timbres - RESERVEZ VOS TIMBRES DE COLLECTION
bleu sur jaune ....25 »

2630-C 2 10 timbres - JEUX OLYMPIQUES D'HIVER - bleu sur jaune ....17 »
2630-C 2a Carnet C2 erreur de date 1999 au lieu de 1990...................................130 »

2712 TYPE MARIANNE de BRIAT - lettre D - rouge - n° 2712 - dentelé

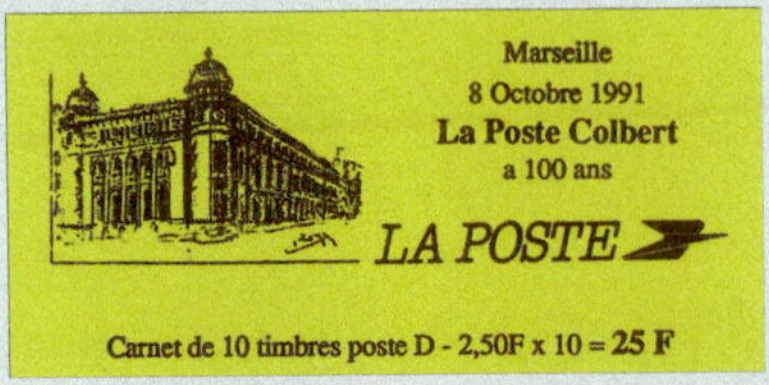

2712-CP 1

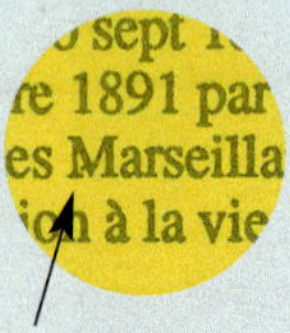

2712-C 1

2712-CP 1 10 timbres - Marseille La Poste Colbert - format 114x54 - tirage local
"en page 4 : M de Marseillais sans trait parasite sur
la branche inclinée gauche ....230 »
2712-C 1 10 timbres - Marseille La Poste Colbert - format 114x54 - tirage officiel
"en page 4 : M de Marseillais avec trait parasite sur
la branche inclinée gauche ....14 »

2713 TYPE MARIANNE de BRIAT - lettre D - rouge - n° 2713 - non dentelé adhésif

2713-C 1 10 timbres - CHANGEMENT DE TARIF (LETTRE D) ....14 »

2715 TYPE MARIANNE de BRIAT - 2,50 Fr. rouge - n° 2715 - dentelé

2715-C 1 8 timbres - Albertville 92 - lettre D - conf. 9 ....17 »

2715-C 2 10 timbres - Albertville 92 - lettre G - conf. 9 ....15 »

2715-C 3 10 timbres - loisirs culture passion - lettre G - conf. 9 ....16 »

2715-C 4 10 timbres - Albertville 92 - lettre D - conf. 6 ....18 »

2715-C 4a 10 timbres - Albertville 92 - lettre D - conf. 8 ....60 »

2715-C 5 10 timbres - Albertville 92 - lettre G - conf. 7 ....17 »

2715-C 5a 10 timbres - Albertville 92 - lettre G - conf. 6 ....600 »

2715-C 6 10 timbres - loisirs culture passion - lettre G - conf. 6 ....21 »

2715-C 6a Carnet C 6 - sans la lettre “g” de 100 g sur la couverture ....40 »

2715 TYPE MARIANNE de BRIAT - 2,50 Fr. rouge - n° 2715 - dentelé (suite)

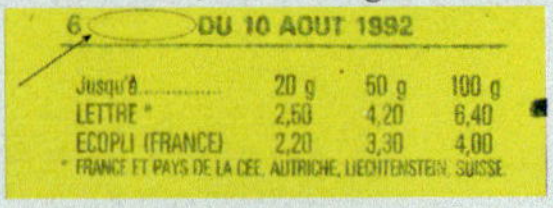

2715-C 6b Carnet C 6 - sans le mot "tarif" sur la couverture ....50 »

2715-C 7 10 timbres - publicité M&M's - sans n° de confectionneuse ....14 »

2720 TYPE MARIANNE de BRIAT - 2,50 Fr. rouge - n° 2720 - non dentelé adhésif

2720-C 1 10 timbres - Albertville 92 - format 125X52 ....14 »

2720-C 1a Idem C1 avec papier timbres-poste phosphorescent ....20 »

2720-C 1b Idem C1 avec papier timbres-poste et couverture phosphorescent............30 »

2720-C 2 10 timbres - loisir,culture,passion - format 125 X 52 ....14 »

2720-C 2a Carnet C2 - absence de prédécoupe des timbres ....120 »

2720-C 3 10 timbres - médiamétrie - sans n° de confectionneuse ....15 »

2806 TYPE MARIANNE de BRIAT - TVP - rouge - n° 2806 - dentelé

2806-C 1 10 timbres à validité permanente - lettre D - conf. 6 ....16 »

2806-C 1a Idem C1 avec date à gauche ....40 »

2807 TYPE MARIANNE de BRIAT - TVP - rouge - n° 2807 - non dentelé adhésif

2807-C 1 10 timbres - carnet pour distributeur sagem - format 120x57 ....34 »
2807-C 1a Carnet C 1 - paire de 2 carnets se tenant ....100 »
2807-C 1b Roulette de 5 carnets se tenant ....300 »

2807-C 2 10 timbres - carnet pour guichets ....15 »

2874 TYPE MARIANNE de BRIAT - TVP - rouge - n° 2874 (type I) - cisaillés en ligne

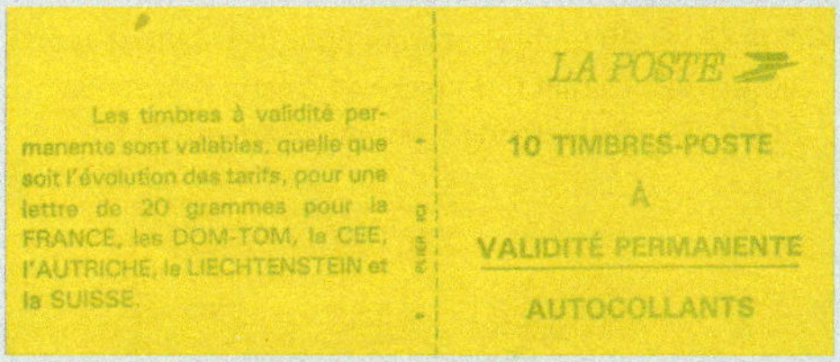

2874-C 1 10 timbres - carnet pour guichets - sans pont ....14 »
2874-C 1a Carnet C 1 avec carré noir ....100 »

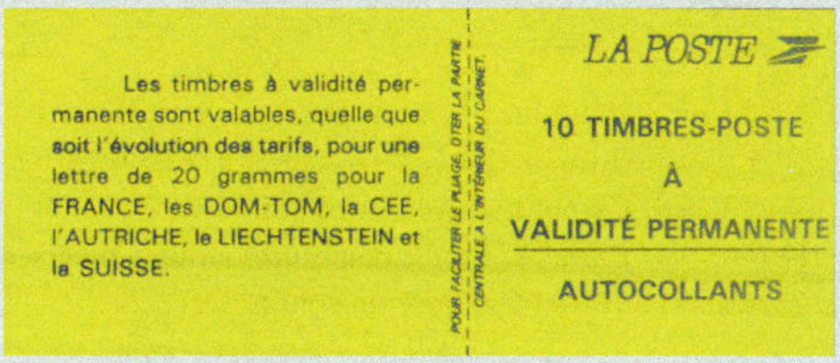

2874-C 2 10 timbres - carnet pour guichets - avec pont ....14 »
2874-C 2a Carnet C 2 avec carré noir ....80 »
2874-C 2b Idem C 2 - sans phosphore ....90 »
2874-C 2c Idem C 2 - papier phosphorescent ....90 »

2874-C 3 Carnet C2 - texte modifié : DOM/TOM...(zone 1 export.....Vatican) ......14 »
2874-C 3a Carnet C3 avec carré noir ....40 »
2874-C 3b Idem C 3 - papier phosphorescent ....40 »

2874 TYPE MARIANNE de BRIAT - TVP - rouge - n° 2874 (type I) - cisaillés en ligne (suite)

2874-C 4 10 timbres - carnet pour distributeur sagem - (pointillé entre les 2 lignes) 22 »
2874-C 4a Carnet C 4 - paire de 2 carnets se tenant ....60 »
2874-C 4b Roulette de 5 carnets se tenant ....200 »

2874-C 5 10 timbres - carnet pour distributeur sagem - (pointillé sous les 2 lignes) 49 »
2874-C 5a Carnet C 5 - paire de 2 carnets se tenant ....140 »
2874-C 5b Roulette de 5 carnets se tenant ....350 »

2874-C 6 10 timbres - carnet pour guichets - Essayez l'enveloppe timbrée
(format 125x52) ....14 »
2874-C 6a Carnet C 6 avec carré noir ....65 »
2874-C 6b Carnet C 6 avec dentelure ondulée inversée ....45 »
2874-C 6c Carnet C 6 sans phosphore ....400 »

2874-C 7 10 timbres - carnet pour distributeur sagem - Essayez l'enveloppe timbrée 15 »
2874-C 7a Carnet C 7 - paire de 2 carnets se tenant ....50 »
2874-C 7b Roulette de 5 carnets se tenant ....150 »

2874 TYPE MARIANNE de BRIAT - TVP - rouge - n° 2874 (type I) - cisaillés en ligne (suite)

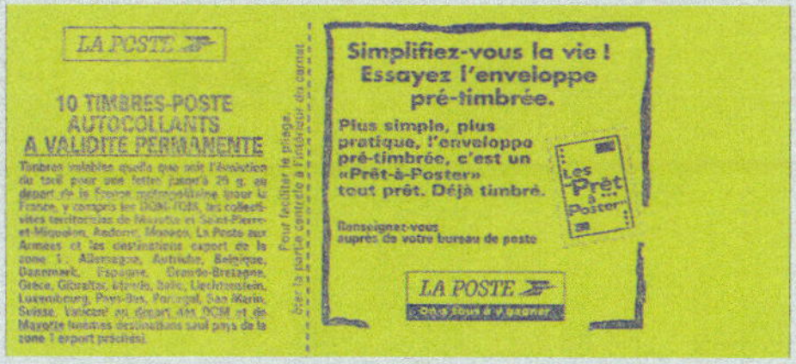

2874-C 8 10 timbres - carnet pour distributeur sagem - Essayez l'enveloppe pré-timbrée ....30 »

2874-C 8a Carnet C 8 - paire de 2 carnets se tenant ....90 »

2874-C 8b Roulette de 5 carnets se tenant ....240 »

2874-C 8c Carnet C 8 - erreur de date 91.12.96 ....110 »

2874a TYPE MARIANNE de BRIAT - TVP - rouge - n° 2874a (type II) - cisaillés en ligne

2874-C 9 20 timbres - carnet pour distributeurs de billets (DAB) Essayez l'enveloppe pré-timbrée ....150 »

3085 TYPE MARIANNE "du 14 juillet" - TVP - rouge - n° 3085 (type I) cisaillés en ligne

3085-C 1 10 timbres - carnet pour guichets - essayez l'enveloppe timbrée format 125x52 ....13 »

3085-C 1a Carnet C 1 avec carré noir ....40 »

3085-C 1b Roulette de 5 carnets se tenant ....100 »

3085-C 2 20 timbres - carnet pour distributeurs de billets (DAB) - Essayez l'enveloppe pré-timbrée ....25 »

3085 TYPE MARIANNE "du 14 juillet" - TVP - rouge - n° 3085 (type I) cisaillés en ligne (suite)

3085-C 3 10 timbres - carnet pour guichets - LE TIMBRE , UN PLAISIR QUI SE COMMUNIQUE ....13 »
(Ce carnet existe au Type II voir n°3085a-C2)
3085-C 3a Carnet C 3 avec carré noir ....40 »
3085-C 3b Carnet C 3 - sans phosphore ....1 000 »
3085-C 3c Carnet C 3 - avec prédécoupe à cheval sur timbres ....350 »

3085-C 4 10 timbres - carnet pour guichets - le mondial du timbre - PHILEX France 99....................12 »
3085-C 4a Carnet C 4 avec carré noir ....40 »
3085-C 4b Carnet C 4 - dentelure inversée ....300 »
3085-C 4c Carnet C 4 - n° d'ordre à gauche au lieu de droite ....30 »

3085-C 5 20 timbres - carnet pour distributeur (DAB) - LE TIMBRE , UN PLAISIR QUI SE COMMUNIQUE ....22 »
(Ce carnet existe au Type II voir n°3085a-C4)

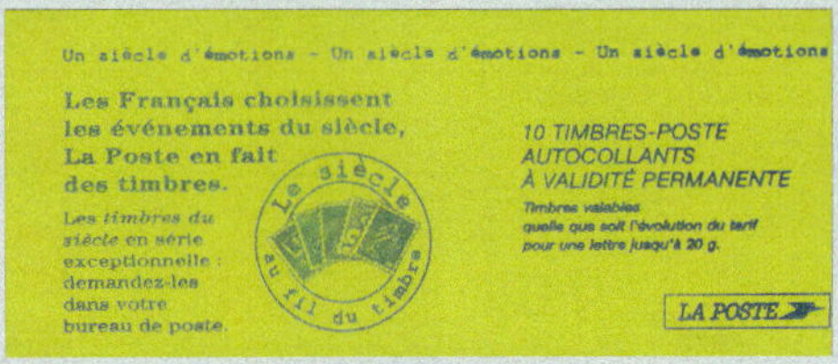

3085-C 6 10 timbres - carnet pour guichets - Un siècle d'émotions ....12 »
3085-C 6a Carnet C 6 avec carré noir ....35 »
3085-C 6b Carnet C 6 - papier phosphorescent ....45 »

3085 TYPE MARIANNE "du 14 juillet" - TVP - rouge - n° 3085 (type I) cisaillés en ligne (suite)

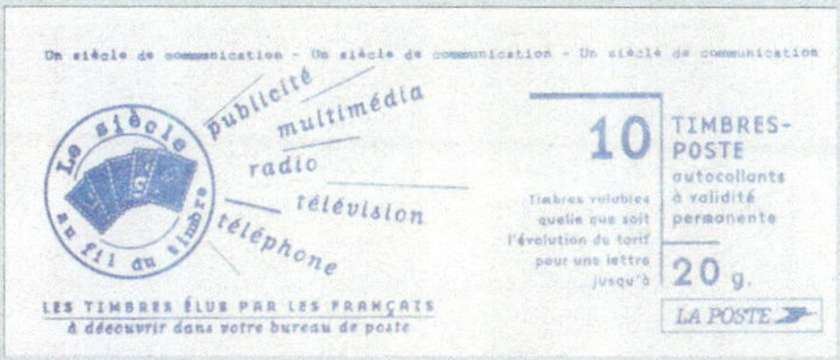

3085-C 7 10 timbres - carnet pour guichets - Un siècle de communication ....12 »

(Ce carnet existe au Type II voir n°3085a-C5)

3085-C 7a Carnet C 7 avec carré noir ....30 »

3085a TYPE MARIANNE "du 14 juillet" - TVP - rouge - n° 3085a (type II) cisaillés en ligne

3085a-C 1 10 timbres - carnet pour distributeur sagem - Essayez l'enveloppe pré-timbrée ....17 »

3085a-C 1a Carnet C 1 - paire de 2 carnets se tenant ....40 »

3085a-C 1b Roulette de 5 carnets se tenant ....100 »

3085a-C 2 10 timbres - carnet pour guichets - LE TIMBRE , UN PLAISIR QUI SE COMMUNIQUE ....35 »

(Ce carnet existe au Type I voir n° 3085-C3)

3085a-C 2a Carnet C 2 avec carré noir ....60 »

3085a-C 3 10 timbres - carnet pour distributeur sagem - LE TIMBRE, UN PLAISIR QUI SE COMMUNIQUE ....32 »

3085a-C 3a Carnet C 3 - paire de 2 carnets se tenant ....65 »

3085a-C 3b Carnet C 3 - sans phosphore ....50 »

3085a-C 3c Roulette de 5 carnets se tenant ....160 »

3085a TYPE MARIANNE "du 14 juillet" - TVP - rouge - n° 3085a (type II) cisaillés en ligne (suite)

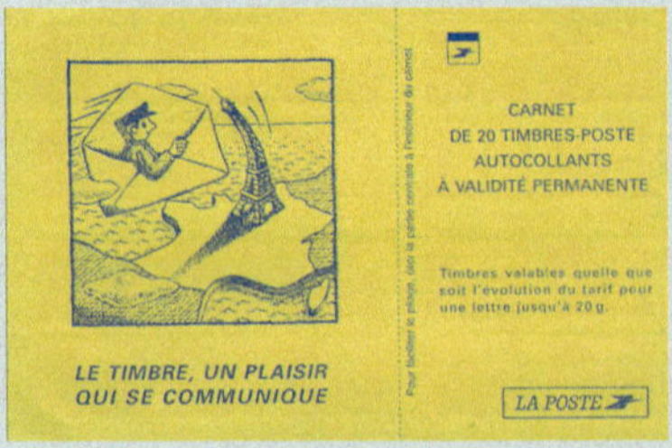

3085a-C 4 20 timbres - carnet pour distributeur (DAB) - LE TIMBRE , UN PLAISIR QUI SE COMMUNIQUE ....60 »
(Ce carnet existe au Type I voir n°3085-C5)

3085a-C 5 10 timbres - carnet pour guichets - Un siècle de communication ....35 »
(Ce carnet existe au Type I voir n°3085-C7)

3085a-C 5a Carnet C 5 avec carré noir ....60 »

3215 TIMBRE "EURO" - 3 Fr - 0,46 Euro - n° 3215 - cisaillés en ligne

3215-C 1 10 timbres - sigle EURO ....12 »

3215-C 1a Carnet C 1 avec carré noir à droite en haut ....100 »

3215-C 1b Carnet C 1 - Timbres imprimés sur le papier de la couverture et couverture imprimée sur le papier des timbres ....70 »

3215-C 1c Carnet C 1 - sans ITVF et sans signature ....200 »

3419 TYPE MARIANNE "du 14 juillet" avec RF - TVP - rouge - n° 3419 type II cisaillés en ligne

3419-C 1 10 timbres - carnet pour guichets - Un siècle de sciences ....12 »

3419-C 1a Carnet C 1 avec carré noir ....25 »

3419 TYPE MARIANNE "du 14 juillet" avec RF - TVP - rouge - n° 3419 type II cisaillés en ligne (suite)

3419-C 2 10 timbres - carnet pour guichets - la poste vous facilite l'Euro ....12 »
3419-C 2a Carnet C 2 avec carré noir ....25 »

3419-C 3 10 timbres - carnet pour distributeur sagem - LE TIMBRE ,
UN PLAISIR QUI SE COMMUNIQUE ....12 »
3419-C 3a Carnet C 3 - paire de 2 carnets se tenant ....25 »
3419-C 3b Carnet C 3 - erreur de date 5.12.91 ....120 »
3419-C 3c Roulette de 5 carnets se tenant ....60 »

3419-C 4 20 timbres - carnet pour distributeur (DAB) - LE TIMBRE ,
UN PLAISIR QUI SE COMMUNIQUE ....21 »

3419-C 5 10 timbres - carnet pour guichets - Un siècle de transport ....12 »
3419-C 5a Carnet C 5 avec carré noir ....25 »

3419-C 6 10 timbres - carnet pour guichets - la boutique du timbre ....12 »
3419-C 6a Carnet C 6 avec carré noir ....25 »
3419-C 6b Carnet C 6 - erreur de date 71.02.03 ....60 »

3419 TYPE MARIANNE "du 14 juillet" avec RF - TVP - rouge - n° 3419 type II cisaillés en ligne (suite)

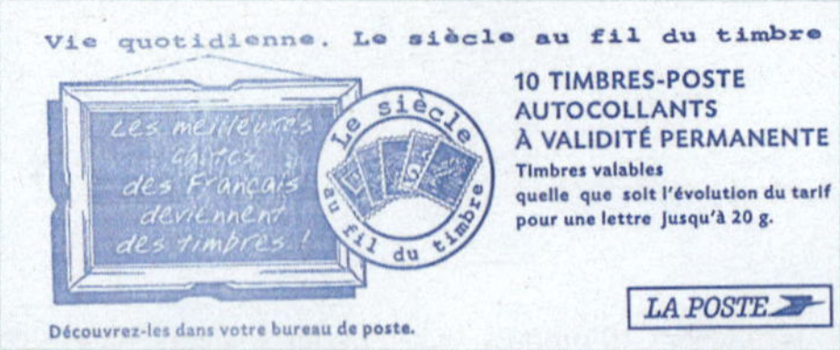

3419-C 7 10 timbres - carnet pour guichets - Vie quotidienne ....12 »

3419-C 7a Carnet C 7 avec carré noir ....25 »

3419-C 7b Carnet C 7 - sans bande de phosphore ....110 »

3419-C 7c Carnet C 7 - sans prédécoupe ....900 »

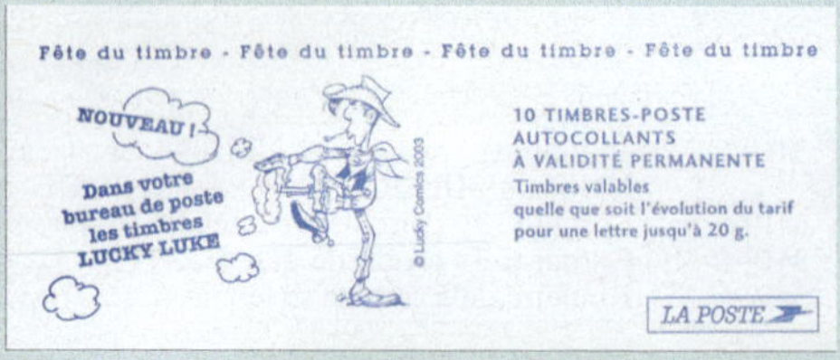

3419-C 8 10 timbres - carnet pour guichets - Lucky Luke ....12 »

3419-C 8a Carnet C 8 avec carré noir ....25 »

3419-C 8b Carnet C 8 - erreur de date 31.03.02 et 01.04.02............................70 »

3419-C 9 10 timbres - carnet pour guichets - La France à vivre. Les spécialités de nos régions ....12 »

3419-C 9a Carnet C 9 avec carré noir ....25 »

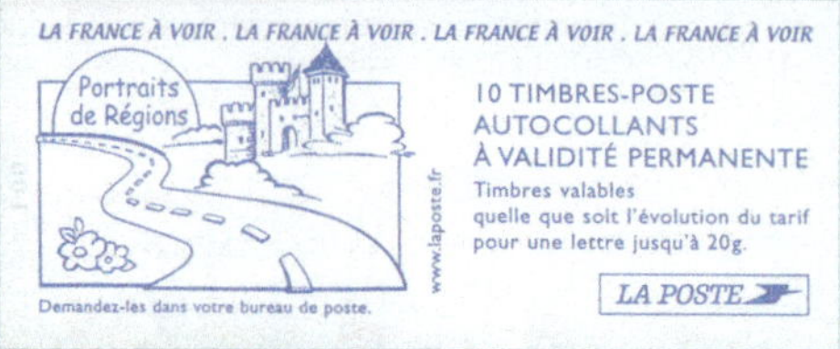

3419-C 10 10 timbres - carnet pour guichets - La France à voir. Portraits de régions............................12 »

3419-C 10a Carnet C 10 avec carré noir ....25 »

3419 TYPE MARIANNE "du 14 juillet" avec RF - TVP - rouge - n° 3419 type II cisaillés en ligne (suite)

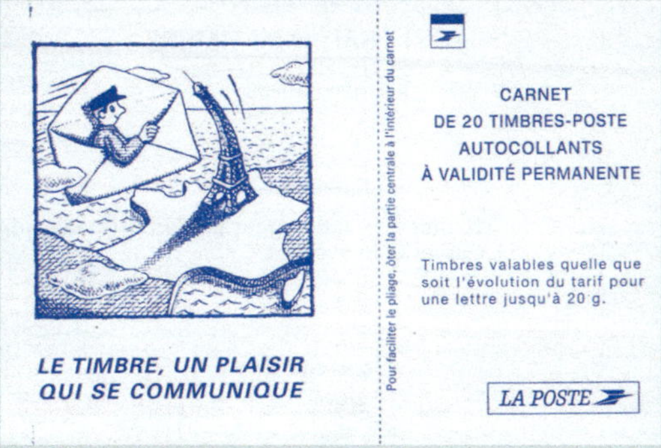

3419-C 11 20 timbres - carnet pour distributeur (DAB) - LE TIMBRE, UN PLAISIR QUI SE COMMUNIQUE
Idem 3419-C 4 sauf couverture papier blanc ....21 »

3419-C 12 Idem 3419-C 3 sauf papier de la couverture "blanchâtre" du côté des timbres ....12 »
3419-C 12a Carnet C 12 - paire de 2 carnets se tenant ....25 »
3419-C 12b Roulette de 5 carnets se tenant ....60 »

3419-C 13 10 timbres - carnet pour guichets - Dessinez la nouvelle Marianne ......12 »
3419-C 13a Carnet C 13 avec carré noir ....25 »

3419-C 14 10 timbres - carnet pour guichets
La France à vivre. Portraits de régions ....12 »
3419-C 14a Carnet C 14 avec carré noir ....25 »

3419 TYPE MARIANNE "du 14 juillet" avec RF - TVP - rouge - n° 3419 type II cisaillés en ligne (suite)

3419-C 15 10 timbres - carnet pour guichets - Le salon du Timbre ....12 »
3419-C 15a Carnet C 15 avec carré noir ....25 »

3419-C 16 10 timbres - carnet pour guichets - La boutique Web du timbre ....12 »
3419-C 16a Carnet C 16 avec carré noir ....25 »

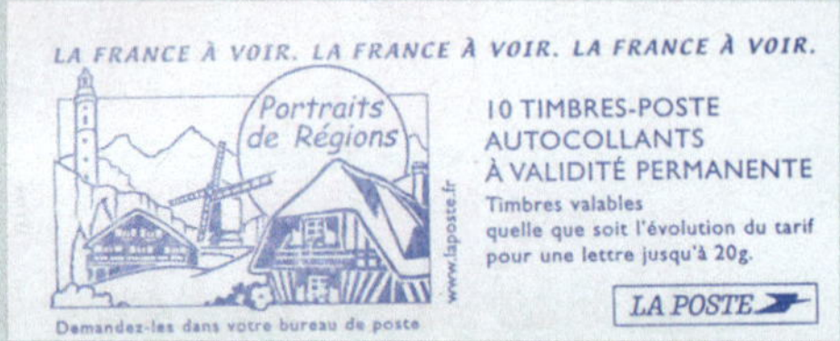

3419-C 17 10 timbres - carnet pour guichets - La France à voir. Portraits de régions 15 »
3419-C 17a Carnet C 17 avec carré noir ....30 »

3744 TYPE MARIANNE de LAMOUCHE - TVP - rouge - n° 3744 type II cisaillés en ligne

3744-C 1 10 timbres - carnet pour guichets - L'amour des jeux - Paris 2012 - ville candidate ....11 »
3744-C 1a Carnet C 1 avec carré noir ....25 »

3744-C 2 10 timbres - carnet pour distributeur sagem - La boutique Web du timbre 11 »
Couverture jaune - papier blanc côté timbres
3744-C 2a Carnet C 2 - paire de 2 carnets se tenant ....22 »
3744-C 2b Roulette de 5 carnets se tenant ....55 »

3744 TYPE MARIANNE de LAMOUCHE - TVP - rouge - n° 3744 type II cisaillés en ligne (suite)

3744-C 3 20 timbres - carnet pour distributeur (DAB) - La boutique Web du timbre ....20 »

3744-C 4 10 timbres - carnet pour guichets - La France à vivre. Portraits de régions 11 »
3744-C 4a Carnet C 4 avec carré noir ....25 »

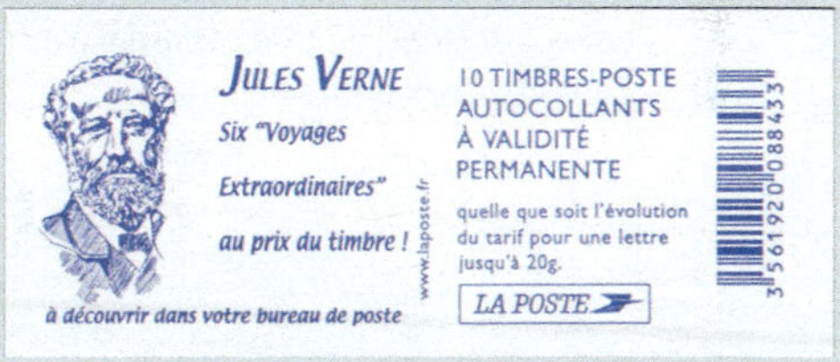

3744-C 5 10 timbres - carnet pour guichets - Jules Verne - Six "Voyages extraordinaires" au prix du timbre ! ....11 »
3744-C 5a Carnet C 5 avec carré noir ....25 »

3744-C 6 10 timbres – carnet pour guichets – La France à voir. Portraits de région 11 »
3744-C 6a Carnet C 6 avec carré noir ....25 »

3744 TYPE MARIANNE de LAMOUCHE - TVP - rouge - n° 3744 type II cisaillé en ligne (suite)

3744-C 7 10 timbres – carnet pour guichets – " Vous aimez les beaux timbres, La Poste vous les réserve " ....11 »

3744-C 7a Carnet C 7 avec carré noir ....25 »

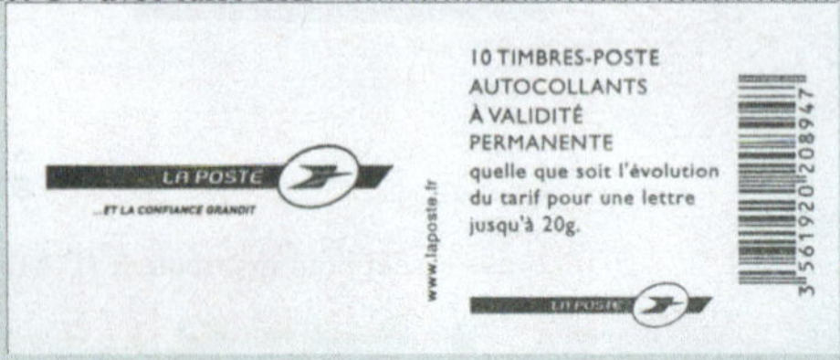

3744-C 8 10 timbres – carnet pour guichets – " La Poste ...et la confiance grandit " ....11 »

3744-C 8a Carnet C 8 avec carré noir ....25 »

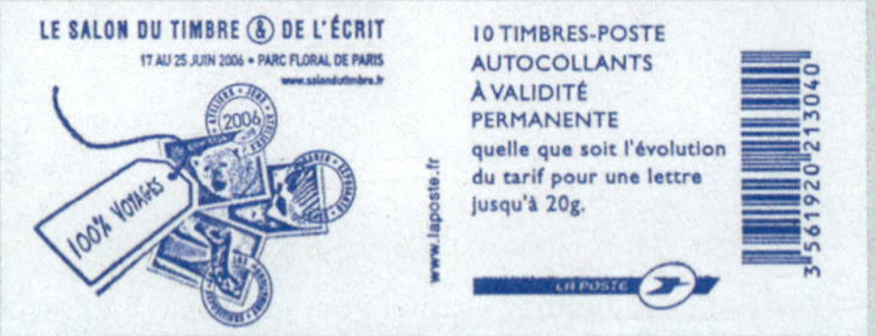

3744-C 9 10 timbres – carnet pour guichets – "Le Salon du Timbre & de l'Ecrit – 17 au 25 juin 2006 – Parc floral de Paris " ....11 »

3744-C 9a Carnet C 9 avec carré noir ....25 »

3744-C 10 10 timbres – carnet pour guichets – La France à vivre. Portraits de région ....11 »

3744-C 10a Carnet C 10 avec carré noir ....25 »

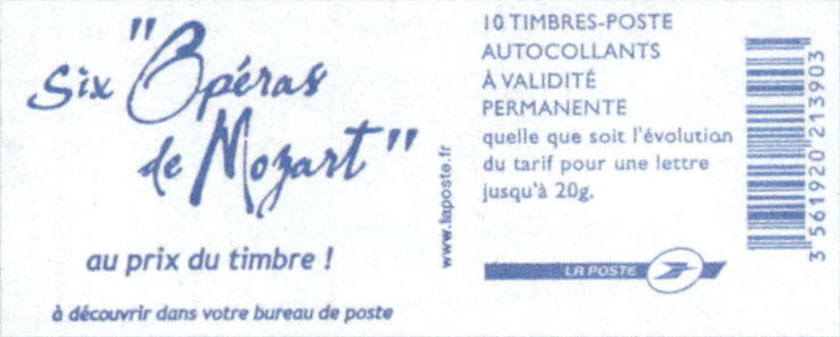

3744-C 11 10 timbres – carnet pour guichets – Six "Opéras de Mozart" au prix du timbre ! ....10 »

3744-C 11a Carnet C 11 avec carré noir ....15 »

3744 TYPE MARIANNE de LAMOUCHE - TVP - rouge - n° 3744b - PHIL@POSTE en bas au centre

3744b-C 1 10 timbres - carnet pour guichets - la boutique du web du timbre nouveau logo ....10 »

3744b-C 1a Carnet C 1 avec carré noir ....15 »

3744b-C 2 10 timbres - carnet pour distributeur sagem - la boutique du web du timbre nouveau logo ....10 »

3744b-C 2a Paire de 2 carnets se tenant ....22 »

3744b-C 2b Roulette de 5 carnets se tenant ....55 »

3744b-C 3 20 timbres - carnet pour distributeur (DAB) - la boutique du web nouveau logo ....20 »

3744 TYPE MARIANNE de LAMOUCHE - TVP - rouge - n° 3744b - PHIL@POSTE en bas au centre (suite)

3744b-C 4 10 timbres - carnet pour guichets - la France à voir. Portraits de régions 10 »

3744b-C 4a Carnet C 4 avec carré noir ....15 »

3744b-C 5 12 timbres - carnet pour guichets - l'éco carnet pour la planète
papier kraft au verso ....15 »

3744b-C 5a Carnet C 5 avec carré noir ....20 »

3744b-C 6 12 timbres - carnet pour guichets - la France à voir. Portraits de régions
papier kraft au verso ....15 »

3744b-C 6a Carnet C avec carré noir ....20 »

3744 TYPE MARIANNE de LAMOUCHE - TVP - rouge - n° 3744b - PHIL@POSTE en bas au centre (suite)

3744b-C 7 12 timbres - carnet pour guichets - Timbres Plus ....15 »

3744b-C 7a Idem avec carré noir ....20 »

3744b-C 8 12 timbres - carnet pour guichets - la France à vivre. Portraits de régions 15 »

3744b-C 8a Idem avec carré noir ....20 »

3744b-C 9 12 timbres - carnet pour guichets - Guy Moquet ....15 »

3744b-C 9a Idem avec carré noir ....20 »

3744b-C 10 12 timbres - carnet pour guichets - la France à voir. Portraits de régions 15 »

3744b-C 10a Idem avec carré noir ....20 »

3744 TYPE MARIANNE de LAMOUCHE - TVP - rouge - n° 3744b - PHIL@POSTE en bas au centre (suite)

3744b-C 11 12 timbres - carnet pour guichets - Les mots de la rencontre ....15 »
3744b-C 11a Idem avec carré noir ....20 »

3744b-C 12 12 timbres - carnet pour guichets - Le salon du Timbre et de l'Ecrit ......15 »
3744b-C 12a Idem avec carré noir ....20 »

4127 TYPE MARIANNE de LAMOUCHE - TVP - bleu pour affranchissement

CEE + Suisse - n° 4127 - PHIL@POSTE en bas au centre

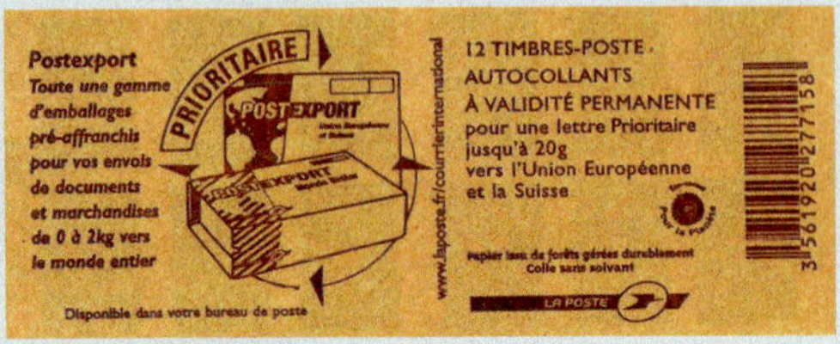

4127-C 1 12 timbres - carnet pour guichets - Postexport ....18 »
4127-C 1a Idem avec carré noir ....22 »

4197 TYPE MARIANNE de BEAUJARD - TVP - rouge – n° 4197

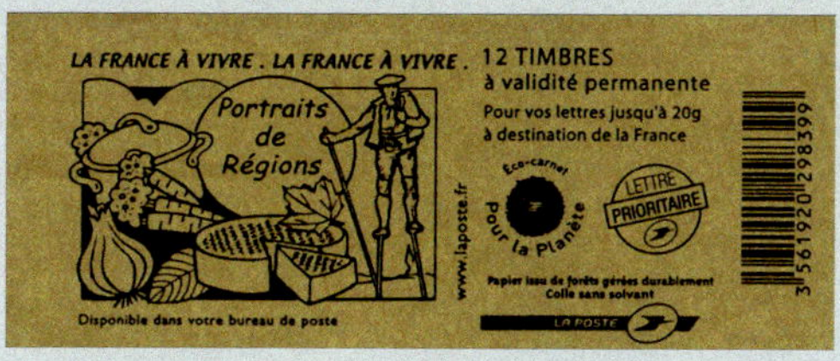

4197-C 1 12 timbres – carnet pour guichets « La France à Vivre » - Portraits de régions ....15 »

4197-C 1a Idem avec carré noir ....20 »

4197-C 2 20 timbres – carnet pour distributeur (DAB) « La France à Vivre » - Portraits de régions ....20 »

4197-C 3 12 timbres – carnet pour guichets « Les droits de l'Homme Universels et Indivisibles ....15 »

4197-C 3a Idem avec carré noir .... 20 »

4197 TYPE MARIANNE de BEAUJARD - TVP - rouge - n° 4197 (suite)

4197-C 4	10 timbres – carnet pour distributeur Sagem « La France à Vivre ». Portraits de régions	12 »
4197-C 4a	Paire de 2 carnets se tenant	25 »
4197-C 4b	Roulette de 5 carnets se tenant	80 »

4197-C 5	12 timbres – carnet pour guichets « MonTimbreaMoi »	15 »
4197-C 5a	Idem avec carré noir	20 »

4197-C 6	12 timbres – carnet pour guichets « La Boutique Web du Timbre »	15 »
4197-C 6a	Idem avec carré noir	20 »

4197-C 7	20 timbres – carnet pour distributeur (DAB) « MonTimbreaMoi »	20 »

4197 TYPE MARIANNE de BEAUJARD - TVP - rouge - n° 4197 (suite)

4197-C 8	12 timbres – carnet pour guichets « La Boutique du courrier pour les Pros »	15 »
4197-C 8a	Idem avec carré noir	20 »

4201 TYPE MARIANNE DE BEAUJARD – TVP bleu pour affranchissement CEE + Suisse

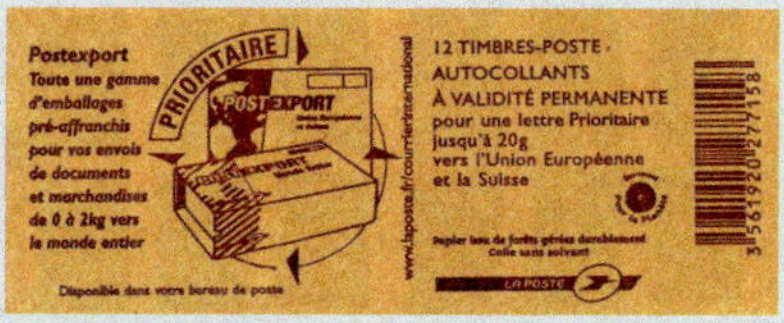

4201-C 1	12 timbres – carnet pour guichets « Postexport »	18 »
4201-C 1a	Idem avec carré noir	22 »

III. - CARNETS DE TIMBRES A COMPOSITION VARIABLE

Type Liberté de Delacroix

Carnet à 10 f., contenant deux bandes horizontales de 5 timbres.

1 bande avec 4 timbres n° 2376 et 1 timbre n° 2183
1 bande avec 4 timbres n° 2179 et 1 timbre n° 2183

1501 Le carnet 12 »

Dentelures horizontales souvent défectueuses.

Type Marianne de BRIAT

Carnet à 10 f., contenant deux bandes horizontales de 5 timbres.

1 bande avec 4 timbres n° 2614 et 1 timbre n° 2618
1 bande avec 4 timbres n° 2617 et 1 timbre n° 2618

1502 Le carnet 32 »

Dentelures horizontales souvent défectueuses.

—

Carnet à 20 f., contenant deux bandes horizontales de 4 timbres et une vignette.

1 bande avec 4 timbres n° 2807 et 1 vignette
1 bande avec 3 timbres n° 2807, 1 timbre n° 2824 et 1 vignette

1503 Le carnet 35 »

Il existe deux modalités de fixation des bandes sur la couverture.

Idem, couverture modifiée.

1504 Le carnet 30 »

Idem, couverture modifiée.

1505 Le carnet 40 »

Idem, couverture blanche.

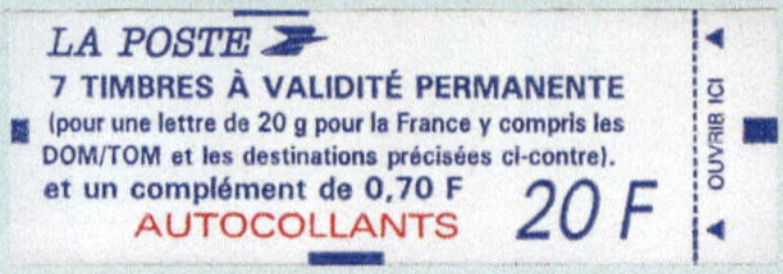

1506 Le carnet 40 »

Il existe deux types de vignettes à caractères différents.

—

Carnet à 20 f., contenant deux bandes identiques de 4 timbres et une vignette.

Bandes de 3 timbres n° 2874 avec 1 timbre n° 3009 et 1 vignette

1507 Le carnet 20 »

Type Marianne du 14 Juillet (Type I)

Carnet à 20 f., contenant deux bandes identiques de 4 timbres et une vignette.

Bandes de 3 timbres n° 3085 avec 1 timbre n° 3101 et 1 vignette

1508 Le carnet 17 »

Idem. Couverture modifiée.

Idem. Couverture modifiée.

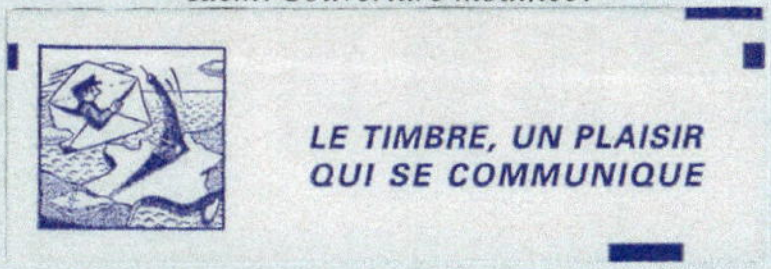

1509 Le carnet 16 »

Ce carnet existe au Type II voir n° 1510.

Type Marianne du 14 Juillet (Type II)

Carnet à 20 f., contenant deux bandes identiques de 4 timbres et une vignette

Bandes de 3 timbres n°3085a avec 1 timbre n° 3101c.

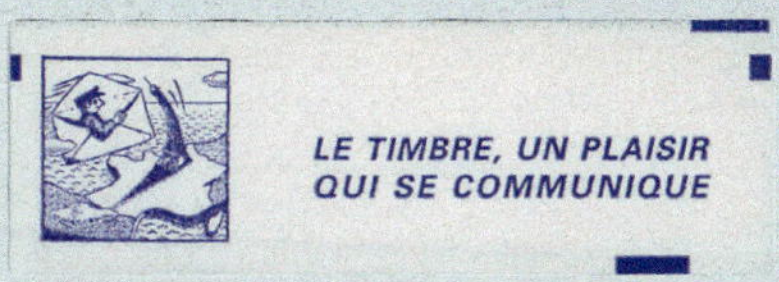

1510 Le carnet 40 »

Ce carnet existe au Type I voir n° 1509.

Type I = oreille intacte + pas d'accent sur "Timbree".

Type II = oreille cassée + accent sur "Timbrée".

Les cent ans de la semeuse de Roty

Carnet à 5 €., contenant : 5 timbres Marianne du 14 Juillet n° 3419a et 5 timbres semeuse de Roty n° 3619.

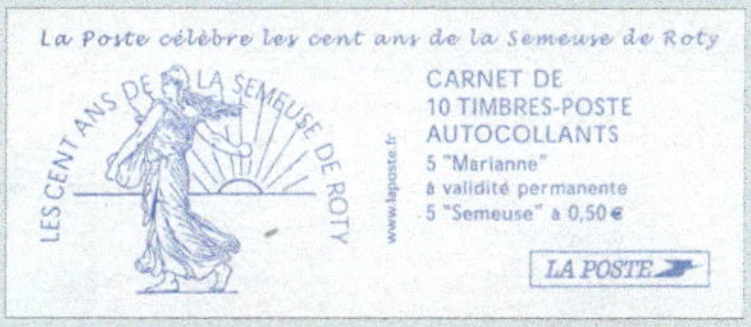

1511 Le carnet 23 »

1511a Idem 1511 avec carré noir 100 »

Les soixante ans de la Marianne d'Alger

Carnet à 5 €., contenant : 5 timbres Marianne du 14 Juillet n° 3419 et 5 timbres Marianne d'Alger n° 3716.

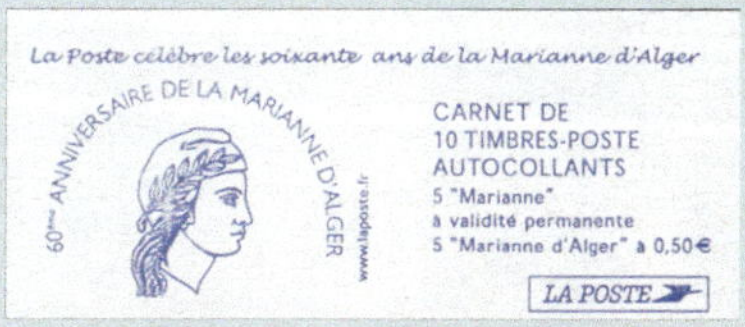

1512 Le carnet 17 »

1512a Idem 1512 avec carré noir 60 »

Les soixante ans de la Marianne de Dulac

Carnet à 5,30 €, contenant : 5 timbres Marianne de Lamouche n° 3744a et 5 timbres Marianne de Dulac n° 3841.

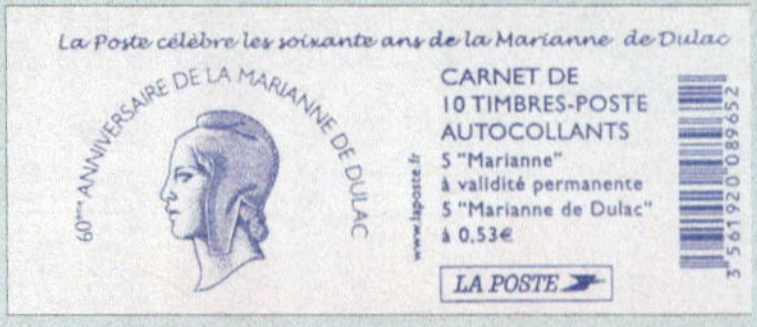

1513	Le carnet	17 »
1513a	Idem 1513 avec carré noir	35 »

Les soixante ans de la Marianne de Gandon

Carnet à 5,40 €., contenant : 5 timbres Marianne de Lamouche n° 3744b et 5 timbres Marianne de Gandon n° 3977.

1514	Le carnet	17 »
1514a	Idem 1514 avec carré noir	23 »

Les quarante ans de la Marianne de Cheffer

Carnet à 6,48 €., contenant : 6 timbres Marianne de Lamouche n° 3744b et 6 timbres Marianne de Cheffer n° 4109.

1515	Le carnet	17 »
1515a	Idem 1515 avec carré noir	23 »

Présidence Française de l'Union Européenne

Carnet à 6,60 €. pour affranchissement en France, contenant : 6 timbres Marianne de Beaujard n° 4197 et 3 x 2 timbres à 0,55 €. pour les 3 valeurs de l'Europe : La Paix n° 4200, la Démocratie n° 4198, l'Environnement n°4199.

1516	Le carnet	18 »
1516a	Idem 1516 avec carré noir	24 »

Présidence Française de l'Union Européenne

Carnet à 7,80 €. pour affranchissement en CEE et Suisse, contenant : 6 timbres Marianne de Beaujard n° 4201 et 3 x 2 timbres à 0,65 €. pour les 3 valeurs de l'Europe : La Paix n° 4204, la Démocratie n° 4202, l'Environnement n° 4203.

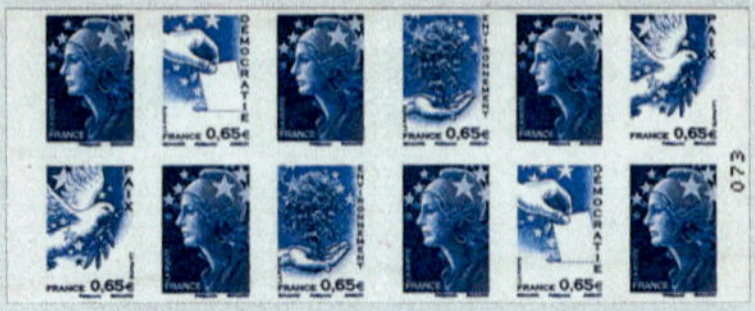

1517	Le carnet	20 »
1517a	Idem 1517 avec carré noir	26 »

Les Visages de la Vème République

Carnet à 6,60 €. contenant 12 timbres autocollants à 0,55 €.

1518 Le carnet 15 »

Les carnets des rubriques IV à VII existent oblitérés souvent du 1er jour de l'émission. (Mêmes cotes que pour le carnet à l'état neuf).

IV. - CROIX-ROUGE AVEC PUBLICITÉ (1952)

2001 15 f. + 5 f. bleu foncé et rouge (938a) 550 »

V. - CROIX-ROUGE SANS PUBLICITÉ

2002 12 f. + 3 f. et 15 f. + 5 f. (966-967), 4 timbres de chaque (1953) 160 »

2003 12 f. + 3 f. et 15 f. + 5 f. (1006-1007), 4 timbres de chaque (1954) 180 »

2004 15 f. + 5 f. bleu et rouge (1049) (1955) 450 »

2005 12 f. + 3 f. et 15 f. + 5 f. (1089-1090), 4 timbres de chaque (1956) 90 »

2006 15 f. + 7 f. et 20 f. + 8 f. (1140 et 1141), 4 timbres de chaque (1957) 90 »

2007 15 f. + 7 f. et 20 f. + 8 f. (1187 et 1188), 4 timbres de chaque (1958) 38 »

2008 20 f. + 10 f. et 25 f. + 10 f. (1226 et 1227), 4 t. de chaque (1959) 50 »

2009 20 c. + 10 c. et 25 c. + 10 c. (1278 et 1279), 4 t. de chaque (1960) 57 »

2010 20 c. + 10 c. et 25 c. + 10 c. (1323 et 1324), 4 t. de chaque (1961) 47 »

2011 20 c. + 10 c. et 25 c. + 10 c. (1366 et 1367), 4 t. de chaque (1962) 47 »

a. (2e tirage) avec 1366a et 1367a 925 »

2012 20 c. + 10 c. et 25 c. + 10 c. (1400 et 1401), 4 t. de chaque (1963) 16 »

2013 20 c. + 10 c. et 25 c. + 10 c. (1433 et 1434), 4 t. de chaque (1964) 9 »

2014 25 c. + 10 c. et 30 c. + 10 c. (1466 et 1467), 4 t. de chaque (1965) 8 »

2015 25 c. + 10 c. et 30 c. + 10 c. (1508 et 1509), 4 t. de chaque (1966) 8 »

2016 25 c. + 10 c. et 30 c. + 10 c. (1540 et1541), 4 timbres de chaque (1967) 8 »

2017 25 c. + 10 c. et 30 c. + 10 c. (1580 et 1581) 4 timbres de chaque (1968) 8 »

2018 40 c. + 15 c. et 40 c. + 15 c. (1619 et 1620), 4 timbres de chaque (1969) 8 »

2019 40 c. + 15 c. et 40 c. + 15 c. (1661 et 1662), 4 timbres de chaque (1970) 16 »

a. (Sur la couverture l'inscription « Croix-Rouge » à 27 mm (au lieu de 32) 88 »

2020 30 c. + 10 c. et 50 c. + 10 c. (1700 et 1701), 4 timbres de chaque (1971) 10 »

2021 30 c. + 10 c. et 50 c. + 10 c. (1735 et 1736), 4 timbres de chaque (1972) 10 »

2022 30 c. + 10 c. et 50 c. + 10 c. (1779 et 1780), 4 timbres de chaque (1973) 10 »

2023 60 c. + 15 c. et 80 c. + 15 c. (1828 et 1829), 4 timbres de chaque (1974) 9 »

2024 60 c. + 15 c. et 80 c. + 20 c. (1860 et 1861) 4 timbres de chaque (1975) 9 »

2025 80 c. + 20 c. et 1 f. + 25 c. (1910 et 1911), 4 timbres de chaque (1976) 9 »

2026 80 c. + 20 c. et 1 f. + 25 c. (1959 et 1960), 4 timbres de chaque (1977) 9 »

2027 1 f. + 25 c. et 1 f. 20 + 30 c. (2024 et 2025), 4 timbres de chaque (1978) 9 »

2028 1 f. 10 + 30 c. et 1 f. 30 + 30 c. (2070a et 2071a), 4 timbres de chaque (1979) 10 »

2029 1 f. 20 + 30 c. et 1 f. 40 + 30 c. (2116a et 2117a), 4 timbres de chaque (1980) 9 »

2030 1 f. 40 + 30 c. et 1 f. 60 + 30 c. (2175 et 2176), 4 timbres de chaque (1981) 9 »

2031 1 f. 60 + 30 c. et 1 f. 80 + 40 c. (2247a et 2248a), 4 timbres de chaque (1982) 11 »

2032 1 f. 60 + 40 c. et 2 f. + 40 c. (2295a et 2296a) 4 timbres de chaque (1983) 11 »

Imprimés en feuillet de 10 timbres et deux vignettes sans valeur « Affranchissez Croix-Rouge » :

2033 2 f. 10 + 50 c. multicolore (2345a) (1984) 15 »

2034 2 f. 20 + 50 c. multicolore (2392a) (1985) 13 »

2035 2 f. 20 + 60 c. gris, noir et rouge (2449a) (1986) 15 »

2036 2 f. 20 + 60 c. multicolore (2498a) (1987) 13 »

2037 2 f. 20 + 60 c. noir, rouge et bleu (2555a) (1988) 13 »

Imprimés en feuillet de 10 timbres et deux vignettes sans valeur (motif du timbre, sans valeur faciale, teintes différentes et légende « Affranchissez votre coeur ») :

2038 2 f. 20 + 60 c. multicolore (2612a) (1989) 13 »

2039 2 f. 30 + 60 c. multicolore (2646a) (1990) 15 »

Imprimé en feuillet de 10 timbres et 2 vignettes sans valeur (« Tous les jours une preuve d'amour ») :

2040 2 f. 50 + 60 c. multicolore (2733a) (1991) 15 »

Imprimé en feuillet de 10 timbres et 2 vignettes sans valeur (« Soyons fidèles, continuons l'histoire ») :

2041 2 f. 50 + 60 c. multicolore (2783) (1992) 14 »

Imprimé en feuillet de 10 timbres et 2 vignettes sans valeur (« Avec la Croix-Rouge, soyons plus près de ceux qui ont besoin ») :

2042 2 f. 80 + 60 c. multicolore (2853a) (1993) 17 »
a. (Non dentelé) 385 »

Imprimés en feuillet de 10 timbres et 2 vignettes sans valeur (« L'intégralité des surtaxes de 0,60 F par timbre est réservée à la Croix-Rouge française. LA POSTE »).

2043 2 f. 80 + 60 c. multicolore (2915a) (1994) 15 »
a. (Non dentelé) 385 »

2044 2 f. 80 + 60 c. multicolore (2946a) (1995) 15 »
a. (Non dentelé) 385 »

2045 3 f.+60 c. multicolore (3039a) (1996) 15 »

2046 3 f.+60 c. multicolore (3122a) (1997) 15 »

2047 3 f.+60 c. multicolore (3199a) (1998) 15 »

2048 3 f.+60 c. (0,46+0.09) multicolore (3288a) (1999) 15 »

2049 3 f.+60 c. (0,55 €) multicolore (3362) (2000) 15 »

2050 3 f.+60 c. (0,46+0.09 €) multicolore (3436a) (2001) 14 »

2051 0,46 €+0,09 € multicolore (3531a) (2002) 14 »

2052 0,50 € multicolore (3620) (2003), 1,60 € reversés à la Croix-Rouge Française 20 »

2053 0,50 € multicolore (3717) (2004), 1,60 € reversés à la Croix-Rouge Française 20 »

2054 0,53 € multicolore (3840) (2005), 1,70 € reversés à la Croix-Rouge Française 20 »

2055 (sans val.) multicolores (3991+3992) (2006), 1,70 € reversés à la Croix-Rouge Française 15 »

2056 (sans val.) multicolores (4125+4126) (2007), 1,70 € reversés à la Croix-Rouge Française 15 »

2057 (sans val.) multicolores (4306+4307) (2008), 1,80 € reversés à la Croix-Rouge Française 14 60

VI. - CARNETS COMMÉMORATIFS

BC2360A Personnages célèbres (1985) 35 »

BC2400A Personnages célèbres (1986) 6 »

BC2460 Personnages célèbres (1987) 10 »

BC2515 La Communication en bandes dessinées(1988) 12 »

BC2523 Personnages célèbres (1988) 6 »

BC2570 Personnages célèbres (1989) 7 »

BC2655 Personnages célèbres (1990) 8 »

BC2687 Personnages célèbres (1991) 8 »

BC2753 Personnages célèbres (1992) 9 »

BC2805 Personnages célèbres (1993) 9 »

BC2848 Le plaisir d'écrire (1993) 15 »

BC2872 Relations culturellesFrance-Suède (1994) 20 »

BC2903 Personnages célèbres (1994) 9 »

BC2982 Personnages célèbres (1995) 9 »

BC3031 Personnages célèbres (1996) 10 »

BC3071A Les Journées de la Lettre (1997) 24 »

BC3121 Personnages célèbres (1997) 10 »

BC3140 "France 98" (1998) 15 »

BC3161A La lettre au fil du temps (1998) 24 »

BC3193 Personnages célèbres(1998) 12 »

BC3213 150e anniversaire du premier timbre-poste Français(1999) 12 »

BC3215A Timbre Euro (1999) 12 »

BC3221A Saint Valentin (1999) 18 »

BC3268 Personnages célèbres (1999) 12 »

BC3298A Cœurs 2000 d'Yves Saint Laurent (2000) 20 »

BC3348 Personnages célèbres (2000) 10 »

BC3400A "Bonnes Vacances" (2001) 15 »

BC3440A "Bonnes Année" et " Meilleurs vœux" (2001) 15 »

BC3494A "Vacances" (2002) 15 »

BC3534A "Meilleurs Vœux" (2002) 15 »

BC3578A "Vacances" (2003) 15 »

BC3622 "Meilleurs Vœux" (2003) 15 »

BC3634 "C'est une fille" (2004) 15 »

BC3635	"C'est un garçon" (2004)	15 »
BC3672	Europa "Les vacances" (2004)	15 »
BC3722	"Meilleurs Vœux" (2004)	20 »
BC3788	"Vacances" (2005)	12 »
BC3804	"C'est une fille" (2005)	15 »
BC3805	"C'est un garçon" (2005)	15 »
BC3825	"Sourires" (2005)	13 »
BC3853	"Meilleurs voeux" (2005)	20 »
BC3866	Art. Peinture. Les impressionnistes (2006)	15 »
BC3904	"Vacances" (2006)	15 »
BC3953	"Sourires" avec Cubitus (2006)	13 »
BC3986	"Meilleurs voeux" (2006)	15 »
BC4002	"Art. Antiquités" (2006)	13 »
BC4037	"Vacances" (2006)	13 »
BC4082	"Invitations" "Merci"	6 50
BC4089	"Sourires" avec les vaches	13 »
BC4120	"Meilleurs voeux" (2007)	13 »
BC4132	"Chefs d'oeuvre de la peinture (2008)	13 »
BC4184	"C'est une fille"	11 »
BC4185	"C'est un garçon"	11 »
BC4186	"Vacances" (2008)	13 »
BC4205	"Timbres des idées durables"	13 »
BC4271	"Sourires" avec Garfield (2008)	11 »
BC4308	"Bonnes Fêtes" (2008)	15 50
BC253	"Métiers d'Art" (2009)	13 »
BC266	"Coeurs 2009" Emanuel Ungaro	21 »
BC274	"Femmes du Monde"	13 20
BC291	"Flore des Régions du Nord"	13 40
BC303	"Flore des Régions du Sud"	13 40
BC315	"Vacances"	15 70
BC329	"La France en timbres"	13 60

VII. - CARNETS « JOURNÉE DU TIMBRE »

Imprimés en carnet de 6 timbres et deux vignettes sans valeur.

BC2411A	Journée du Timbre 1986	9 »
BC2469A	Journée du Timbre 1987	9 »
BC2526A	Journée du Timbre 1988	8 »
BC2578A	Journée du Timbre 1989	8 »
BC2640A	Journée du Timbre 1990	8 »
BC2689A	Journée du Timbre 1991	9 »
BC2744A	Journée du Timbre 1992	9 »
BC2794	Journée du Timbre 1993	10 »

BC2865	Journée du Timbre 1994	16 »
BC2935	Journée du Timbre 1995	16 »
BC2992	Journée du Timbre 1996	18 »
BC3053	Journée du Timbre 1997	19 »
BC3137	Journée du Timbre 1998	20 »
BC3227	Journée du Timbre 1999	18 »
BC3305	Fête du Timbre 2000	16 »
BC3370a	Fête du Timbre 2001	14 »
BC3467a	Fête du Timbre 2002	14 »
BC3546a	Fête du Timbre 2003	14 »
BC3641a	Fête du Timbre 2004	14 »
BC3751a	Fête du Timbre 2005	15 »
BC3877a	Fête du Timbre 2006	15 »
BC4024a	Fête du Timbre 2007	13 »
BC4149	Fête du Timbre 2008	11 »
BC268	Fête du Timbre 2009	13 20

VIII. - CARNETS ET OUVRAGES DE LUXE

4001 Portraits de régions "La France à vivre" (2003) 38 »

Carnet de 19,00 € composé de 24 pages de textes, illustrations, et de 10 feuillets de timbres, chaque feuillet reprenant un des 10 timbres nos 3559 à 3568 du BF n° 57.

4002 Portraits de régions "La France à voir" (2003) 38 »

Carnet de 19,00 € composé de 24 pages de textes, illustrations, et de 10 feuillets de timbres, chaque feuillet reprenant un des 10 timbres nos 3595 à 3604 du BF n° 61.

4003 "Impressions & expressions" (2004) 100 »

Livre de 196 pages, vendu 60 €, contenant 1 feuillet gommé de 250x235 montrant, avec l'exemple du timbre n° 3585 "Kandinsky", les phases d'impression en héliogravure en quadrichromie (pour ces 3 timbres, la valeur faciale, "La Poste 2003" et le logo "RF" ont été imprimés à partir de plusieurs couleurs, alors que pour le timbre émis en feuilles une seule encre a été utilisée : brun-rouge pour "1,11 €" et orange pour "La Poste 2003" et le logo "RF".

4004 Portraits de régions "La France à vivre" (2004) 38 »

Carnet de 19 € composé de 24 pages de textes, illustrations, et de 10 feuillets de timbres, chaque feuillet reprenant un des 10 timbres nos 3646 à 3655 du BF n° 68.

4005 Portraits de régions "La France à voir" (2004) 38 »

Carnet de 19 € composé de 24 pages de textes, illustrations, et de 10 feuillets de timbres, chaque feuillet reprenant un des 10 timbres nos 3702 à 3711 du BF n° 77.

4006 Portraits de régions "La France à vivre" (2005) 38 »

Carnet de 19 € composé de 24 pages de textes, illustrations, et de 10 feuillets de timbres, chaque feuillet reprenant un des 10 timbres nos 3767 à 3776 du BF n° 82

4007 "Jules Verne - Aventures et légendes" (2005) 58 »

Livre de 85 pages, vendu 29 €, contenant 6 feuillets gommés et illustrés de 250x235, composés chacun d'1 des 6 timbres de la série nos 3789 à 3794 (feuillets imprimés en offset. Gomme brillante). 1 BF n° 85 est inséré dans le livre, présenté dans une pochette transparente.

4008 Portraits de régions "La France à voir" (2005) 38 »

Carnet de 19 € composé de 58 pages de textes, illustrations, et de 10 feuillets de timbres, chaque feuillet reprenant un des 10 timbres nos 3814 à 3823 du BF n° 89.

4009 Portraits de régions "La France à vivre" (2006) 38 »

Carnet de 19 € composé de 58 pages de textes, illustrations, et de 10 feuillets de timbres, chaque feuillet reprenant un des 10 timbres nos 3882 à 3891 du BF n° 94.

4010 Le timbre voyage avec...Mozart (2006) 38 »

Livre de 85 pages, vendu 19 €, contenant 6 feuillets gommés et illustrés de 265x202, composés chacun d'1 des 6 timbres de la série nos 3917 à 3922.

4011 Portraits de régions "La France à voir" (2006) 38 »

Carnet de 19 € composé de 48 pages de textes et illustrations et de 10 feuillets de timbres, chaque feuillet reprenant un des 10 timbres nos 3942 à 3951 du BF n° 102.

4012 Portraits de régions “La France à voir” (2007) 38 »

Carnet de 19 € composé de 48 pages de textes et illustrations et de 10 feuillets de timbres, chaque feuillet reprenant un des 10 timbres n°s 4014 à 4023 du BF n° 105.

4013 Le timbre voyage avec ...Tintin 38 »

Livre de 85 pages, vendu 19,80 €, contenant 6 feuillets gommés et illustrés de 265x202, composés chacun d'un des 6 timbres de la série n°s 4051 à 4056.

4014 Portraits de régions “La France à vivre” (2007) 38 »

Carnet de 19 € composé de 60 pages de textes et illustrations et de 10 feuillets de timbres, chaque feuillet reprenant un des 10 timbres n°s 4094 à 4103 du BF n° 113.

4015 Le timbre voyage avec...le Cirque 38 »

Livre de 85 pages, vendu 19,80 €, contenant 6 feuillets gommés et illustrés de 265x202, composés chacun d'1 des 6 timbres de la série n° 4216 à 4221.

4016 Voiliers célèbres, figures de proue 39 60

Livre de 82 pages, vendu 14,99 €, contenant 6 feuillets gommés et illustrés de 270x210, composés chacun d'1 des 6 timbres de la série n° 4249 à 4254.

4017 Portraits de régions “La France à vivre” (2007) 30 »

Carnet de 19 € composé de 60 pages de textes et illustrations et de 10 feuillets de timbres, chaque feuillet reprenant un des 10 timbres n°s 4094 à 4103 du BF n° 113.

4018 Portraits de régions “La France à vivre” (2008) 38 »

Carnet de 19 € composé de 84 pages de textes et illustrations et de 10 feuillets de timbres, chaque feuillet reprenant un des 10 timbres n°s 4260 à 4269 du BF n° 125.

COINS DATÉS

On trouve en général les blocs de quatre timbres avec coin daté comportant deux timbres avec charnière et deux timbres sans charnière.

Entre 1900 et 1959 nos cotes s'entendent pour ce cas de figure ; lorsque les quatre timbres sont sans charnière, avec gomme d'origine intacte, on ajoute, à la cote indiquée pour le coin daté, la cote d'un timbre sans charnière.

A partir de 1960 les prix s'entendent pour des blocs de quatre timbres sans charnière.

A partir de 1975, pour certains timbres sur la rotative à grand rendement (R.G.R.), les prix s'entendent pour un bloc de six timbres (date complète). Ces timbres sont indiqués **[6]**.

On tiendra compte, le cas échéant, des % pour très bon centrage.

Coin daté avec date à gauche (provenant de bandes sans fin pour roulettes).

Le mot erreur est utilisé pour signaler :

1° que la date indiquée n'est pas celle de l'impression (cas n° 175) ;

2° que la date ne devait pas être portée sur la feuille (cas des commémoratifs modernes comme le n° 1060).

L'année n'est pas indiquée pour les timbres qui n'ont duré que l'année d'émission.

107 Blanc (II)	*1 c.*	
26	45	»
27	8	»
28	8	»
29	9	»
30	8	»
31	10	»
32	100	»
108 idem (II)	*2 c.*	
24	15	»
25	75	»
26	10	»
28	10	»
30	10	»
31	12	50
109 idem (II)	*3 c.*	
30	35	»
32	40	»
111 idem	*5 c.*	
25 (IIA)	40	»
25 (à gauche IIB)	1000	»
26 (IIA)	25	»
27 (IIA)	25	»
28 (IIA)	25	»
29 (IIA)	25	»
31 (IIA)	25	»
32 (IIA)	30	»
139 Semeuse	*20 c.*	
23 (III)	35	»
24 (III)	40	»
25 (III)	45	»
25 (à gauche IV)	700	»
140 idem (IIIB)	*25 c.*	
24	45	»
25	90	»
26	25	»

27	25	»
142 idem (II)	*35 c.*	
26	600	»
157 Blanc surchargé (II)	*½ s. 1 c.*	
26	15	»
27	7	»
28	7	»
30	35	»
31	35	»
32	45	»
159 Semeuse	*10 c.*	
22 (IB)	15	»
23 (III)	9	»
24 (III)	180	»
25 (III)	25	»
25 (à gauche IV)	750	»
26 (III)	8	»
26 (à gauche IV)	750	»
27 (III)	8	»
28 (III)	8	»
29 (III)	8	»
170 Pasteur	*10 c.*	
23	8	»
24	125	»
25 (erreur)	200	»
171 idem	*15 c.*	
24	17	50
25	25	»
172 idem	*20 c.*	
26	25	»
174 idem	*30 c.*	
26	10	»
27	9	»
28	9	»
29	9	»

30	9	»
31	9	»
175 Pasteur	*45 c.*	
24	22	50
34 (erreur)	500	»
176 idem	*50 c.*	
24 (à gauche)	7000	»
177 idem	*75 c.*	
24 (à gauche)	6000	»
178 idem	*90 c.*	
26	110	»
179 idem	*1 f.*	
25	225	»
25 (à gauche)	1000	»
26	250	»
180 idem	*1 f. 25*	
26	250	»
181 idem	*1 f. 50*	
26	90	»
27	75	»
28	75	»
29	75	»
32	75	»
189 Semeuse	*15 c.*	
25 (I)	10	»
26 (I)	6	»
27 (I)	4	»
28 (I)	5	»
29 (I)	4	»
30 (I)	4	»
31 (I)	5	»
32 (I)	5	»
33 (I)	4	»
34 (I)	4	»
35 (I)	4	»
36 (I)	4	»
35 (II)	9	»

36 (II)	9	»
37 (II)	6	»
38 (II)	7	»
190 idem	*20 c.*	
26 (III)	4	»
27 (III)	4	»
29 (III)	4	»
30 (III)	4	»
31 (III)	7	»
32 (III)	4	»
33 (III)	4	»
34 (III)	4	»
35 (III)	4	»
35 (V)	7	»
36 (V)	7	»
37 (V)	7	»
38 (V)	7	»
191 idem (IIA)	*30 c.*	
25	40	»
192 idem	*30 c.*	
25 (IIA)	40	»
26 (IIA)	40	»
26 (à gauche IIC)	6000	»
193 idem (II)	*40 c.*	
26	40	»
194 idem (II)	*40 c.*	
26	25	»
195 idem	*1 f. 05*	
25	100	»
196 idem	*1 f. 40*	
26	200	»
197 idem	*45 c.*	
26	50	»
27	50	»
28	50	»

29	50	»
31	65	»
32	65	»
198 idem (IIA)	*50 c.*	
26	80	»
199 Semeuse (IIA)	*50 c.*	
26	20	»
27	12	»
28	12	»
29	12	»
30	12	»
31	12	»
32	12	»
200 idem	*60 c.*	
24	65	»
25	75	»
201 idem	*65 c.*	
24	30	»
202 idem	*75 c.*	
26 (I)	60	»
28 (I)	60	»
29 (I)	60	»
30 (I)	65	»
31 (I)	65	»
32 (II)	6000	»
203 idem	*80 c.*	
25	350	»
204 idem	*85 c.*	
24	135	»
205 idem	*1 f.*	
26	80	»
27	75	»
28	75	»
29	80	»
30	80	»

TIMBRES-POSTE (suite)

31 90 »
32 100 »

217 Surch. 25/30 c.
25 (IIA) 150 »
26 (IIA) 6 »

218 idem (II) 25/35 c.
26 8 »

220 idem 50/80 c.
25 17 50

221 idem 50/85 c.
24 35 »

222 idem 50/1 f. 25
26 40 »

223 idem 50/60 c.
24 25 »
25 17 50

224 idem 50/65 c.
24 12 50

225 idem 50/1 f. 05
25 17 50

227 idem 90/1 f. 05
25 35 »

228 idem 1 f.10/1 f. 40
26 15 »

233 Blanc (II) 10 c.
29 45 »
30 55 »
31 45 »

234 Semeuse 65 c.
26 80 »
28 100 »
29 90 »
31 90 »

235 idem (IIIB) 25 c.
27 4 »
28 3 »
29 3 »
30 4 »
31 3 »
32 3 »
33 3 »
34 3 50
35 3 »
36 3 »
37 3 »
38 3 »

236 idem (II) 40 c.
27 25 »
28 25 »

237 idem (II) 40 c.
28 15 »
29 18 »
30 15 »
31 18 »
32 15 »

238 idem 1 f. 10
27 115 »
28 130 »
30 145 »

239 Semeuse 2 f.
30 140 »
31 175 »

243 Berthelot
27 20 »
28 20 »
29 20 »
31 22 50
32 55 »

246 Caisse d'Amort. 50 »
247 » 70 »
248 » 95 »
249 » 90 »
250 » 275 »
251 » 450 »
253 » 175 »
254 » 250 »
255 » 500 »
256 » 700 »

257 Jeanne d'Arc 20 »

258 Arc de Triomphe
30 350 »
31 350 »
33 350 »
34 400 »

259 Cath. de Reims
30 (I) 600 »
30 (II) 900 »
30 (III) 3000 »
31 (IV) 575 »
32 (IV) 575 »

260 Mont-St-Michel
28 (erreur) 375 »
29 (I) 225 »
30 (I) 225 »
30 (II) 175 »
31 (II) 165 »
32 (II) 175 »
33 (II) 175 »
34 (II) 175 »
35 (II) 165 »
36 (II) 165 »
37 (II) 165 »

261 La Rochelle
29 (I) 900 »
29 (à droite) 1000 »
30 (II) 1300 »
31 (II) 1450 »
31 (III) 700 »
32 (III) 750 »
35 (III) 725 »
36 (III) 725 »
37 (III) 725 »
38 (III) 700 »

262 Pont du Gard (IIB)
31 2500 »
36 2500 »
37 2250 »

264 B.I.T. 50 c.
30 30 »

265 idem 1 f. 50
29 190 »

266 Caisse d'Amort. 225
267 » 450 »
268 » 700 »
269 » 1600 »

270 Expo. Colon. 15 c.
30 12 50
31 12 50

271 idem 40 c.
30 30 »
31 30 »

272 idem 50 c.
30 (I) 8 »
30 (II) 9 »
31 (I) 9 »
31 (II) 10 »
32 (erreur) 40 »

273 idem 1 f. 50
30 150 »
31 150 »

275 Caisse d'Amort. 400
276 » 1250 »
277 » 1200 »

277A Semeuse 1 c.
33 2 75
34 3 50
35 2 75
36 3 50

277B idem 1 c.
36 3 50
37 3 50
38 4 50

278 idem 2 c.
32 2 75
33 2 75
34 3 50
35 2 75
36 2 75
37 2 75
38 3 »
43 (erreur) 30 »

278A idem 3 c.
33 3 »
34 4 50
35 3 »
36 3 »
37 3 »

278B idem (III) 5 c.
34 2 75
35 2 75
36 2 75
37 4 »
38 4 »

279 idem 10 c.
32 (III) 20 »
33 (à gauche IV) 125 »
34 (III) 20 »
34 (à gauche IV) 125 »
35 (III) 20 »
36 (III) 20 »
37 (III) 20 »
38 (III) 20 »

279A idem ½ s. 1 c.
33 5 »
34 4 50
35 4 50
36 6 »

279B idem ½ s. 1 c.
37 10 »

280 Paix 30 c.
32 12 50
33 12 50
34 20 »
35 12 50
36 12 50
37 12 50

281 idem (I) 40 c.
32 3 »
33 3 »
34 3 »
35 3 »
36 3 »
37 3 »

282 idem 45 c.
33 20 »
34 25 »
35 22 50
36 20 »
37 20 »

283 idem 50 c.
32 (I) 2 50
33 (I) 2 50
34 (I) 2 50
35 (I) 2 50
35 (III) 3 »
36 (III) 3 »
37 (III) 3 »

284 idem 65 c.
33 7 »
35 5 »
36 5 »
37 5 »

284A idem 75 c.
32 2 50
33 4 »
34 2 50
35 2 50
36 2 50
37 2 50
38 2 50
39 2 50

285 idem 90 c.
32 375 »
33 400 »

286 idem 1 f.
33 (I) 45 »
34 (I) 45 »
35 (II) 35 »
36 (II) 35 »
37 (II) 35 »

287 idem 1 f. 25
32 950 »

288 idem 1 f. 50
32 3 »
33 3 50
34 3 75
35 3 »
36 3 75
37 5 »
38 9 »

289 idem 1 f. 75
32 60 »
34 55 »
35 60 »
36 65 »
37 60 »

290 Le Puy 90 c.
33 35 »
34 35 »
35 35 »
36 55 »
37 35 »

291 Briand 30 c.
33 175 »
34 185 »

292 Doumer 325 »

293 Victor Hugo 1 f. 25
33 60 »
34 60 »
35 70 »

294 Colombe 600 »

295 Jacquard 33 »

296 Cartier 500 »
297 » 750 »

298 Paix 50 c./1 f. 25
32 35 »

299 Normandie 1 f. 50
35 150 »
36 (erreur) 275 »

300 idem
36 650 »

301 Rivière bretonne 2 f.
34 375 »
35 375 »

302 St-Trophine 3 f. 50
35 400 »

TIMBRES-POSTE (suite)

303 Delessert 225 »

304 Victor Hugo 1 f. 25
35 45 »
36 65 »
37 45 »

305 Richelieu 350 »

306 Callot 100 »

307 Chômeurs intellectuels 50 c.+10 c.
35 30 »
36 30 »

308 idem 50 c.+2 f.
35 600 »

309 Aide aux réfugiés 75 c.+50 c.
36 125 »
26 (erreur) 250 »

310 Ampère 200 »

311 Moulin de Daudet 2 f.
36 30 »
37 30 »
38 30 »

312 Enfants de chômeurs 50 c.+10 c.
36 40 »

313 Pilâtre de Rozier 75 c.
36 200 »

314 Rouget de l'Isle 20 c.
36 35 »

315 Marseillaise 75 »

316 Vimy 125 »
317 » 175 »

318 Jaurès 30 »
319 » 175 »

320 Atlantique 200 »
321 » 3500 »

322 Exposition 5 »
323 » 22 50
324 » 15 »
325 » 15 »
326 » 145 »
327 » 350 »

328 Rassemblement pour la Paix 160 »

329 Chômeurs 30 »

330 Chômeurs
36 » 25 »
37 (erreur) 200 »

331 Chômeurs 25
332 » 40 »
333 » 235 »

334 Chamonix 1 f. 50
36 80 »
37 100 »

335 Corneille 20 »

336 Exposition 25 »

337 Mermoz 6 »

338 idem 3 f.
37 70 »
38 85 »

339 Chemins de fer 12 50
340 » 80 »

341 Descartes 22 50
342 » 65 »

343 A. France 25 »

344 Rodin 85 »

345 Œuvres des P.T.T. 18 »
346 » 18 »
347 » 18 »

352 Réfugiés 45 »

353 Loti 45 »

354 Samothrace
37 800 »
42 (erreur) 1500 »
355 » 800 »

356 Pour sauver la race
37 30 »
38 40 »

357 États-Unis 1 f. 75
37 27 50
38 35 »

358 Col de l'Iseran
37 25 »
38 25 »

359 Paix 80 c./1 f.
34 (I) 12 50
35 (II) 5 »
37 (II) 5 »
38 (II) 4 50

360 Semeuse (IIA) 30 c.
37 5 »
38 6 50

361 idem (II) 35 c.
37 9 »
38 10 »

362 idem 50 c.
38 17 50
39 (erreur) 100 »

363 Paix 55 c.
37 9 »
38 11 »

364 idem 60 c.
37 3 50
38 4 »

365 idem 65 c.
36 (erreur) 75 »
37 6 »
38 6 »
39 (erreur) 65 »

366 idem 80 c.
38 2 75
39 2 75
40 5 »

367 idem 90 c.
38 2 »

368 idem (I) 90 c.
38 10 »
39 10 »

369 idem (II) 1 f.
37 35 »
38 35 »
39 35 »

370 idem (I) 1 f. 25
39 25 »

371 idem 1 f.
39 70 »

372 idem 1 f. 75
38 8 »

373 idem 2 f.
39 2 50
40 2 50
41 (erreur) 30 »

374 idem 2 f. 25
39 100 »

375 idem 2 f. 50
39 17 50

375A idem (I) 2 f. 50
40 8 »
41 8 »

376 idem (I) 3 f.
39 9 »
40 9 »
41 9 »

377 Charcot 18 »
377A » 145 »

378 Gambetta 4 »

379 Versailles 175 »

380 Chômeurs 20 »
381 » 25 »
382 » 70 »
383 » 75 »

384 Chômeurs
38 60 »
39 60 »

385 Chômeurs 200 »

386 Infanterie 50 »
387 » 35 »

388 Champenoise 45 »

389 Orange 10 »

390 Mineurs 45 »

391 Avignon 150 »

392 Carcassonne
38 7 »
39 7 »
40 9 »

393 Vincennes
38 17 50
39 17 50

394 Saint-Malo
38 425 »
39 425 »
40 425 »

395 Santé 110 »

396 Football 160 »

397 La Fontaine 8 »

398 Ader
38 850 »
39 850 »
40 900 »

399 Reims 100 »

400 Souverains anglais 8 »

401 Rapatriés 50 »

402 Curie 130 »

403 Armistice 35 »

404 Mercure 1 c.
38 1 »
39 1 »
41 1 »

405 idem 2 c.
38 1 »
39 1 »

406 idem 5 c.
38 1 »
39 1 »
40 1 »

407 idem 10 c.
38 1 »
39 1 »
40 1 »
42 1 50

408 idem 15 c.
38 1 50

409 idem 15 c.
39 8 50

410 idem (I) 20 c.
37 (erreur) 35 »
38 1 »
39 1 »
41 1 »

411 idem 25 c.
38 1 25
39 1 25
40 2 »

412 idem (II) 30 c.
39 1 »
40 1 »
41 1 »
42 1 »

413 Mercure 40 c.
39 1 »
40 1 »
41 1 »
42 1 50

414 idem 45 c.
39 7 »

414A idem 50 c.
39 25 »

414B idem 50 c.
40 6 »
41 6 »

415 idem 60 c.
39 2 »

416 idem (II) 70 c.
38 2 50
39 2 50
40 2 50

416A idem 75 c.
39 60 »

417 Étudiant 100 »

418 Radio aveugles 100 »

419 Race 22 50

420 Trulin 100 »

421 Cézanne 50 »

422 Croix-Rouge 85 »

TIMBRES-POSTE (suite)

423 Génie 80 »
424 Orphelins 250 »
425 Clémenceau 6 »
426 New York 100 »
427 Niepce-Daguerre
38 (erreur) 150 »
39 85 »
428 Enfants chômeurs 20 »
429 Tour Eiffel 85 »
430 Liège 125 »
431 Iris *80 c.*
40 2 »
432 idem *1 f.*
39 8 »
40 8 »
433 idem *1 f.*
39 3 »
40 3 »
41 3 »
434 idem *1 f. 30*
39 2 »
40 2 »
435 idem *1 f. 50*
40 2 »
41 3 »
436 Puvis de Chavanne 10 »
437 Debussy 50 »
438 Balzac 45 »
439 Claude Bernard 175 »
440 Natalité 30 »
441 » 50 »
442 Grégoire de Tours 6 »
443 Strasbourg 10 »
444 Révolution 22 50
445 Verdun 8 »
446 Musée Postal 25 »
447 Marins 160 »
448 Languedoc 4 »
449 Pau 8 »
450 Lyon 6 »
451 Soldats 25 »
452 » 25 »

453 France d'Outre-mer 20 »
454 Joffre 50 »
455 Foch 50 »
456 Galliéni 40 »
457 Paysanne 90 »
458 New York 135 »
459 Blessés 50 »
460 » 60 »
461 Guynemer
40 100 »
41 100 »
462 Debussy 55 »
463 Balzac 55 »
464 Claude Bernard 55 »
465 Victimes de la guerre 8 »
466 Secours national 20 »
467 » 20 »
468 » 20 »
469 » 27 50
470 Pétain
40 2 50
471 Pétain
40 3 50
472 Pétain
40 1 50
473 Pétain
40 9 »
474 Prisonniers 9 »
475 » 9 »
476 Surch. *30/35 c.*
38 (II) 1 50
477 idem *50/75 c.*
39 1 80
478 idem *50/55 c.*
37 12 50
38 1 50
479 idem *50/65 c.*
38 1 25
480 idem *50/75 c.*
34 7 »
35 1 50
38 2 25
481 idem *50/80 c.*
38 15 »
39 1 50
40 110 »

482 idem *50/90 c.*
38 2 »
39 1 25
483 idem *1 f./1 f. 25*
39 2 »
484 idem *1 f./1 f. 40*
39 3 »
485 idem *1 f./1 f. 50*
34 12 50
35 7 50
36 15 »
38 8 »
486 idem *1 f./1 f. 75*
38 2 »
487 idem *1 f./2 f. 25*
39 2 »
488 idem *1 f./2 f. 50*
39 8 »
489 idem *1 f./2 f. 15*
38 3 »
490 idem *2 f. 50/5 f.*
39 8 »
40 3 »
491 idem *5 f./10 f.*
39 14 »
492 idem *10 f./20 f.*
39 11 »
40 11 »
493 idem *20 f./50 f.*
40 400 »
40 papier mince 450 »
494 idem *10 f./1 f.*
41 1 50
495 Mistral 2 »
496 Cancer
40 10 »
41 12 50
497 Secours national 16 »
498 » 60 »
499 Beaune *5 f.*
41 3 »
42 3 25
500 Angers *10 f.*
41 5 »
42 5 »
501 Aigues-Mortes
41 8 »
42 8 »
43 15 »
502 Paquebot Pasteur 3 »

505 Pétain *20 c.*
41 1 »
506 idem *30 c.*
41 1 »
507 idem *40 c.*
41 1 25
508 idem *50 c.*
40 (erreur) 45 »
41 1 »
42 1 »
509 idem *60 c.*
42 1 »
43 1 »
44 12 »
510 idem *70 c.*
41 1 50
42 3 »
511 idem *70 c.*
42 1 50
512 idem *80 c.*
41 2 »
513 idem *80 c.*
42 1 »
514 idem *1 f.*
41 1 »
42 1 »
43 1 »
44 8 »
515 idem *1 f. 20*
42 1 »
43 1 »
44 4 »
516 idem *1 f. 50*
41 1 25
42 1 25
517 idem *1 f. 50*
42 1 »
43 1 »
44 1 50
518 idem *2 f.*
41 1 »
42 1 »
43 1 »
44 2 »
519 idem *2 f. 40*
42 1 50
520 idem *2 f. 50*
41 6 »
521 idem *3 f.*
41 1 »
42 1 »
43 1 »
44 2
521A idem *4 f.*
42 1 50
43 1 50
44 2 75
521B idem *4 f. 50*
42 7 »
43 7 »
44 12 50
522 idem *4 f.*
42 2 »
43 2 25
523 idem *4 f. 50*
42 2 »
524 idem *5 f.*
42 2 »
525 Pétain *50 f.*
42 27 50
43 40 »
538 Mercure *50 c.*
42 1 25
539 Beaune 5 »
546 Mercure *10 c.*
42 1 25
43 1 25
44 1 25
45 1 25
547 idem *30 c.*
42 1 25
43 1 25
44 1 25
45 1 50
548 idem *40 c.*
42 1 50
43 1 50
44 1 50
549 idem *50 c.*
42 1 50
43 1 50
44 1 50
45 5 »
552 Secours national
42 2 »
567 Beffroi d'Arras
42 2 »
43 2 75
572 Armoiries *5 f.*
43 2 75
44 4 50
573 idem *10 f.*
43 4 »
574 idem *15 f.*
43 12 50
575 idem *20 f.*
43 9 »
582 Dauphiné *20 f.*
43 6 »

TIMBRES-POSTE (suite)

602 Armoiries *5 f.*
44 2 »

603 idem 10 f. 2 »
604 idem 15 f. 6 »
605 idem 20 f. 8 »

610 Chenonceaux *15 f.*
44 4 »

611 idem *25 f.*
44 4 50

630 à 648 Coq et Marianne
44, la série 225 »

649 Iris *80 c.*
44 1 75

650 idem *1 f.*
44 1 25
45 2 75

651 idem *1 f. 20*
44 1 25
45 1 50

652 idem *1 f. 50*
44 1 25
45 1 25

653 idem *2 f.*
44 1 25
45 1 35

654 idem *2 f. 40*
44 1 50

655 idem *3 f.*
44 1 50
45 3 »

656 idem *4 f.*
44 2 »
45 9 »

657 Surch. R.F. *10 c.*
42 3 »
43 7 »
44 1 25

658 idem *30 c.*
42 1 25
43 1 25

659 idem *40 c.*
44 1 25

660 idem *60 c.*
43 7 »
44 1 25

670 Écusson *10 c.*
45 1 25
46 1 25

671 idem *30 c.*
45 1 25
46 1 25

672 idem *40 c.*
44 4 »
45 1 75

673 idem *50 c.*
45 1 25
46 1 25

674 Cérès *60 c.*
45 1 25
46 1 35

675 idem *80 c.*
45 1 25

676 idem *1 f.*
45 1 25
46 1 25
47 1 25
48 1 50

677 idem *1 f. 20*
45 2 »

678 idem *1 f. 30*
47 2 »

679 idem *1 f. 50*
45 1 25
46 1 25
47 1 25

680 idem *2 f.*
46 1 35
47 1 35
48 1 50
49 6 »

681 idem *2 f. 50*
46 1 35
47 1 35

712 Marianne, Gandon *1 f. 50*
44 35 »
45 1 50

713 idem *2 f.*
45 1 25

714 idem *2 f. 40*
45 2 50

715 idem *3 f.*
45 1 25
46 1 25

716 idem *3 f.*
46 1 25

716A idem *3 f.*
47 9 15
48 10 »

716B idem *3 f. 50*
47 4 15

717 idem *4 f.*
45 1 25

718 idem *4 f.*
46 1 »
47 1 »
48 9 15

718A idem *4 f. 50*
47 1 »

719 idem *5 f.*
45 1 10
46 1 10

719A idem *5 f.*
46 1 »
47 1 »

719B idem *5 f.*
47 1 60
48 1 60

720 idem *6 f.*
45 2 30

721 idem *6 f.*
46 8 »

721A idem *6 f.*
47 1 40
48 1 40

722 idem *10 f.*
45 3 »
46 3 85

723 idem *10 f.*
46 7 35

724 idem *15 f.*
45 15 50

725 idem *4 f.*
44 4 60
45 1 40

726 idem *10 f.*
46 6 10

727 idem *15 f.*
46 50 »

728 idem *20 f.*
46 5 60
48 (erreur) 200 »

729 idem *25 f.*
46 40 »

730 idem *20 f.*
45 10 »
46 9 »

731 idem *25 f.*
45 10 »
46 12 50

732 idem *50 f.*
45 12 50

733 idem *100 f.*
45 80 »

736 Tuberculeux
45 1 50

750 idem *3 f./2 f.+1 f.*
45 1 50

755 Armoiries *10 c.*
46 1 25
47 1 25
48 1 50

756 idem *30 c.*
46 1 25
47 1 25
48 2 »

757 idem *50 c.*
46 1 25
47 1 25
48 3 »

758 idem *60 c.*
46 1 25
47 1 25
48 1 50

759 Vézelay *5 f.*
46 2 »
47 2 50

760 Luxembourg *10 f.*
46 1 50
47 1 50
48 2 »

763 Rocamadour *15 f.*
46 25 »
47 25 »

764 Pointe du Raz *20 f.*
46 8 »
47 8 »
48 8 »
49 15 »

777 Cannes 9 »

778 Nancy *25 f.*
47 25 »
48 25 »

791 Surchargé 1 50

792 Conques *15 f.*
47 25 »
48 25 »

803 Luxembourg *12 f.*
48 17 50

804 idem *15 f.*
48 5 »

805 Conques 27 50

806 Marianne, Gandon *3 f.*
48 1 50

807 idem *4 f.*
48 2 »

808 idem *4 f.*
48 20 »
49 28 »

809 idem *5 f.*
48 5 50
49 5 50
50 5 50
51 5 50

810 idem *8 f.*
48 2 50
49 2 50
50 2 50
51 2 50
52 3 »
53 4 »

811 idem *10 f.*
48 1 50
50 1 75
51 1 75
52 1 50
53 1 75
54 2 50

812 idem *12 f.*
49 20 »
50 20 »
51 20 »

813 idem (I) *15 f.*
49 7 »
50 7 »
51 9 »

822 Nancy *25 f.*
48 80 »
49 100 »

827 Surchargé *5 f./6 f.*
48 1 50

834 Armoiries *10 c.*
49 1 25
50 1 25
51 1 25

835 idem *50 c.*
49 1 25
50 1 25
51 1 50

836 idem *1 f.*
49 4 50
50 6 »
51 7 »

837 idem *2 f.*
49 5 »
50 7 »
51 10 »

838 idem *4 f.*
49 3 »

841A St-Bertrand-de-Comminges *20 f.*
49 2 »
50 2 »
51 2 »
52 3 »

842 St-Wandrille *25 f.*
49 3 »
50 3 »
51 3 »

842A Vallée de la Meuse *40 f.*
49 90 »
50 90 »
51 90 »

843 Gerbier-de-Jonc *50 f.*
49 15 »
50 15 »

TIMBRES-POSTE (suite)

51 15 »

883 Marianne, Gandon *5 f.*
51 3 »
52 3 50
53 3 50
54 3 50

884 idem *6 f.*
51 40 »
52 40 »
53 70 »

885 idem *12 f.*
51 6 »
52 6 »
53 6 »

886 idem (I) *15 f.*
51 1 50
52 1 50
53 1 50
54 1 50
55 1 50

887 idem *18 f.*
51 100 »

888 St-Wandrille *30 f.*
51 35 »

899 Armoiries *10 c.*
51 1 25

900 idem *50 c.*
51 1 35
53 16 »

901 idem *1 f.*
51 2 »
52 2 »
53 3 »

902 idem *2 f.*
51 5 »
52 5 »
53 5 »

903 idem *3 f.*
51 6 »

905 Arbois *30 f.*
51 7 »
52 8 »
53 10 »

916 Pic du Midi *40 f.*
51 40 »
52 40 »
53 40 »

917 Abbaye aux Hommes *50 f.*
51 30 »
52 30 »
53 30 »

924 Chambord *20 f.*
52 3 »
53 3 »

941 Haute couture *30 f.*
53 6 »

943 Gargantua *6 f.*
53 2 50
54 3 50

944 Hernani *18 f.*
53 3 50

951 Armoiries *50 c.*
53 2 »

952 idem *1 f.*
53 2 »
54 2 »

953 idem *2 f.*
53 2 50
54 2 50

954 idem *3 f.*
53 3 50
54 3 50

956 Célimène *8 f.*
53 2 »
54 3 »

957 Figaro *12 f.*
53 1 50
54 2 »

958 Armoiries *70 c.*
53 2 »

959 idem *80 c.*
53 2 »

960 Sports *20 f.*
53 15 »
54 17 50

961 idem *25 f.*
53 85 »
54 90 »

962 idem *30 f.*
53 15 »
54 17 50

963 idem *40 f.*
53 85 »
54 90 »

964 idem *50 f.*
53 37 50
54 42 50

965 idem *75 f.*
53 225 »
54 250 »

968 Gandon *15 f./18 f.*
51 4 »

970 Productions de luxe *25 f.*
54 85 »

971 idem *30 f.*
54 9 »
55 10 »
56 12 50

972 idem *40 f.*
54 25 »
55 30 »
56 30 »

973 idem *50 f.*
54 9 »
55 10 »
56 11 »

974 idem *75 f.*
54 85 »
55 90 »
56 110 »

976 Lourdes *6 f.*
54 2 50
55 2 50

977 Les Andelys *8 f.*
54 2 25
55 2 25

978 Royan *10 f.*
54 2 50
55 3 »

979 Quimper *12 f.*
53 (erreur) 45 »
54 3 »
55 3 »

980 Cheverny *18 f.*
54 18 »
55 22 50

981 Ajaccio *20 f.*
54 20 »
55 21 »

999 Armoiries *50 c.*
54 2 »
55 (en jaune) 3 »

1000 idem *70 c.*
54 2 »
55 3 »

1001 idem *80 c.*
54 2 »
55 3 »

1002 idem *1 f.*
54 1 75
55 2 25

1003 idem *2 f.*
54 1 25
55 1 25
56 1 35
57 1 35
58 1 35

1004 idem *3 f.*
54 1 25
55 1 25
56 1 25
57 1 25
58 1 50

1005 idem *5 f.*
54 1 »
55 1 »
56 1 »
57 1 25
58 1 35

1011 Marianne, Muller *15 f.*
55 2 »
56 2 »
57 2 50

1011A idem *18 f.*
58 (I) 9 »
58 (II) 2 50

1011B idem (II) *20 f.*
57 3 »
58 3 »
59 3 »
62 (erreur) 100 »

1011C idem (I) *25 f.*
59 8 »

1020 Ganterie *25 f.*
55 6 »

1036 Bordelais *6 f.*
55 2 »
56 2 50
57 3 »

1037 Marseille *8 f.*
55 3 »
56 3 »
57 15 »

1038 Nice *10 f.*
55 2 »
56 2 »
57 2 »

1039 Cahors *12 f.*
55 2 »
56 2 »
57 2 »

1040 Uzerche *18 f.*
55 5 »
56 5 »
57 7 »

1041 Martinique *20 f.*
55 20 »
56 20 »
57 27 50

1042 Brouage *25 f.*
55 7 »
56 7 »
57 11 »

1044 Foix *50 c.*
55 1 »
56 1 35
57 1 35
58 1 75

1045 Marche *70 c.*
55 1 »
56 1 »
57 1 25
58 2 »

1046 Roussillon *80 c.*
55 1 »
56 1 »
57 2 »
58 2 »

1047 Comtat-Venaissin *1 f.*
55 1 »
56 1 35
57 1 35
58 1 75

1060 France-Amérique *30 f.*
56 (erreur) 200 »

1072 Basket *30 f.*
56-57 7 50

1073 Pelote *40 f.*
56-57 35 »

1074 Rugby *50 f.*
56-57 12 50

1075 Alpinisme *75 f.*
56-57 75 »

1105 Le Quesnoy 1 50
1106 (57-58) 1 35

1115 Moissonn. *6 f.*
57 1 »
58 1 25

1115A idem *10 f.*
59 4 »
61 100 »
62 75 »

1116 idem *12 f.*
57 1 50
58 1 50

1118 Bordelais 22 50

1119 Cahors 125 »

1125 Guadeloupe *8 f.*
57 1 25
58 1 25

1126 Élysée *10 f.*
57 1 25
58 1 25
59 8 50

1127 Beynac-Cazenac *18 f.*
57 2 »
58 12 50

1128 Valençay *25 f.*
57 4 »
58 4 »
59 8 »

1129 Rouen *35 f.*
57 2 »
58 2 »
59 3 »

1130 St-Rémy *50 f.*
57 3 »

TIMBRES-POSTE (suite)

58 3 »
59 4 »

1131 Évian 65 f.
57 5 »
58 6 »

1181 Marseille 1 »

1181 Lyon 1 »

1182 Toulouse 1 »

1183 Bordeaux 1 »

1184 Nice 1 »

1185 Nantes 1 »

1186 Lille
58 1 50
59 1 50

1192 Élysée 15 »

1193 Évian 22 50

1194 Guadeloupe 100 f.
59 175 »
62 275 »

1195 Alger 15 f. 1 50

1216 Marianne, Nef (I) 25 f.
59 2 75
61 60 »
62 60 »

1229 Fréjus 2 »

1230 Lille 5 c.
59 45 »
60 45 »

1230A Oran 5 c.
60 2 »
61 2 »
62 2 »

1231 Moissonn. 10 c.
59 4 »
60 4 »
61 4 »
62 4 »

1232 Alger 15 c.
59 6 »
60 6 »
61 6 »
62 7 »

1233 Semeuse 20 c.
59 2 »
60 2 »
61 2 »
62 2 »
63 2 25
64 3 »

1234 Marianne, Nef 25 c.
59 15 »
60 15 »

1234A Semeuse 30 c.
61 14 »

1235 Laon 15 c.
59 2 50
60 2 50

1236 Fougères 30 c.
59 25 »
60 25 »
61 25 »

1237 Kerrata 45 c.
59 5 »
60 5 »
61 5 50

1238 Tlemcen 50 c.
59 17 50
60 17 50
61 25 »

1239 Sioule 65 c.
59 9 »
60 9 »
61 14 »
63 (erreur) 84 »

1240 Chaumont 85 c.
59 18 50
60 18 50
61 18 50

1241 Cilaos 1 f.
59 18 »
60 18 »
61 18 »

1263 Marianne, Decaris (I) 25 c.
60 1 60
61 1 60
62 1 60
63 1 60
64 1 85
65 50 »

1282 Marianne, Cocteau 20 c.
61 (I) 1 60
62 (I) 1 60
63 (I) 1 60
64 (I) 1 60
65 (I) 1 60
66 (II) 22 50

1311 Saint-Paul 15 c.
61 1 »
62 1 »

1312 Arcachon 30 c.
61 1 60
62 1 60
63 1 60

1313 Sully-sur-Loire 45 c.
61 1 60
62 1 60
63 2 30
64 2 30

1314 Cognac 50 c.
61 8 40
62 8 40
63 11 50

1315 Dinan 65 c.
61 2 30
62 2 30
63 2 30
64 3 85

1316 Calais 85 c.
61 3 »
62 3 »
63 3 »

1317 Dunkerque 95 c.
62 6 10

1318 Medéa 1 f.
61 27 50
62 27 50

1331 Coq 25 c.
62 2 »
63 2 »
64 2 »
65 4 50

1331A idem 30 c.
63 4 60
64 4 60
65 4 60
66 4 60
67 7 65

1351A Armoiries, Niort 1 c.
63, 64 1 »
74 1 »
75 1 »
77 1 10

1351B idem Guéret 2 c.
63 1 »
64 1 »
76 1 25

1352 idem Amiens 5 c.
62 1 »
63 1 »
64 1 »
65 1 »

1353 idem Troyes 10 c.
62 1 »
63 1 »
64 1 »
65 1 »
66 1 »
67, 68, 69 1 »
70 1 »
71 1 »
72, 74 1 25
75, 76 1 25
77, 78 1 »

1353a (avec bandes de phosphore)
70 3 »
71 1 60
73, 76 1 »

1353A idem Agen 12 c.
63 1 »
64 1 »
65 1 »
66 1 »

1354 idem Nevers 15 c.
62 1 »
63 1 »
64 1 »
69 1 25
70 1 25
71 1 25
72, 73 1 »
75, 76, 77 1 »

1354A idem La Réunion 18 c.
63 2 50
64 2 50
65 2 50

1354B idem Paris 30 c.
63 4 »
64 4 »
65 4 »
66 4 »
67 4 »
68 6 »

1355 Le Touquet 1 f.
62 3 85
63 3 85
64 3 85
65 3 85

1390 Amboise 30 c.
63 2 30
64 2 30
65 3 35

1391 Côte d'Azur varoise 50 c.
63 2 30
64 2 30
65 2 30

1392 St-Flour 60 c.
63 3 85
64 3 85
65 3 85

1392A Provins 70 c.
64 2 30
65 2 30
66 2 30
67 2 30

1393 Vittel 85 c.
63 10 »
64 14 50

1394 Moissac 95 c.
63 4 60
65 6 10

1394A Ronchamp 1 f. 25
64 4 60

1433 Croix-Rouge 20 c.+10 c.
64 (erreur) 100 »

1434 idem25 c.+10 c.
64 (erreur) 100 »

1435 Ronchamp 40 c.
64 1 60
65 1 60
66 1 60
67 1 60

1436 Moustiers 50 c.
65 2 30
66 2 30
67 2 30

1437 Aix-les-Bains 60 c.
65 4 60
66 4 60
67 4 60

1438 Gorges du Tarn 75 c.
65 6 90
66 10 »

1439 Vendée 95 c.
65 30 50

1440 Carnac 1 f.
65 7 65
66 7 65
67 9 15

1441 Joux 1 f. 30
64 7 65
65 7 65

1468 Armoiries, Auch 5 c.
66 0 80
67, 68 0 80
69 4 60
70, 71, 72, 73 0 80
74 0 80
75 0 80
76, 77 0 80

1469 idem Mont-de-Marsan 25 c.
66 5 35
67 5 35

1499 Saint-Quentin 50 c.
67, 68 2 30
69 2 30
70 2 30

1500 Vire 60 c.
67 3 »
69 3 85

1501 Saint-Germain 70 c.
67 2 30
68, 69 2 30

1502 La Baule 75 c.
67 11 50

TIMBRES-POSTE (suite)

1503 Boulogne 95 c.
67 7 65

1504 Rodez 1 f.
67, 68, 69 3 85
70 3 85

1505 Morlaix 1 f. 50
67 7 65

1506 Château de Val 2 f. 30
66 11 50
67 11 50
68 17 »

1510 Saint-Lô 20 c.
66, 67 1 25
68, 70 1 25
71, 72 1 25
73, 74 1 85

1510c (avec bandes de phosphore) 40 c.
71 4 60
73, 74, 75, 76 1 25
77, 78 1 25

1535 Marianne, Cheffer 25 c.
67 3 »

1536 idem 30 c.
67 2 45
68 2 45

1536A idem 30 c.
68 3 »
69 3 »
75 3 »

1536B idem 40 c.
68 3 »
69 3 »
70 3 »

1536Ba (2 bdes phos.)
70 21 50

1546 Grenoble 75 c.+25 c.
67 (erreur) 77 »

1582 Brou 45 c.
69 1 60

1583 Vouglans 80 c.
69, 70 3 »

1584 Chantilly 85 c.
69 5 35
70 17 »

1585 Trinité 1 f. 15
69 5 35

1611 Républ. Cheffer 30 c.
69, 70, 71 1 60
72, 73, 74, 75 1 60
76, 77 2 30

1611b (avec bande de phosphore
70 3 85
71, 72, 73, 74, 75 1 60

1644 Martinique 50 c.
70, 71 2 30

1645 Chancelade 95 c.
70 7 65

1646 Ilet du Gosier 1 f.
70, 71, 72 3 »

1647 Observatoire de Haute-Provence 1 f. 30
70 11 50

1663 Marianne de Béquet 45 c.
71, 72 2 30
73, 74 2 30
77 3 »

1664 Marianne de Béquet 50 c.
70, 71, 72, 73 2 30
74 2 30
71, coin à gauche (TD.3) 765 »

1664c (avec bandes de phosphore)
70 3 85
71, 72, 73 3 »
74, 75, 76, 77 2 30

1683 Riom 60 c.
71, 72 2 50
73 4 »

1684 Dole 65 c.
71, 72 3 85
73 13 75

1685 Riquewihr 90 c.
71, 72, 73 3 85

1686 Sedan 1 f. 10
71 3 85
73 6 10

1687 Gorges de l'Ardèche 1 f. 40
71 4 60
74 4 60

1692 Caméléon 60 c.
71 6 10

1712 Charlieu 1 f. 20
72, 73, 74 3 85

1713 Narbonne 3 f. 50
72, 73 12 25

1719 Code postal 30 c.
72 0 80

1720 idem 50 c.
72 2 30

1725 Sologne 1 f.
72 3 85
73 6 10

1726 Bazoches 2 f.
72, 73, 74 6 10

1757 Dijon 65 c.
73 2 60
74 2 30

1758 Gien 90 c.
73 2 75
74 2 75

1759 Amboise (Clos-Lucé) 1 f.
73 3 85
74 5 35
75 3 »
76 4 60

1764 Saut du Doubs 60 c.
73 2 30
74 2 30

1793 Salers 65 c.
74 3 »

1794 St-Florent 3 f. 74
8 40
75 8 40

1806 Rouen (Palais de Justice) 35 c.
75 3 »

1807 Vallée du Lot 1 f. 10
74 3 »
76 6 90

1808 Saint-Pol-de-Léon 1 f. 20
74 4 60
75 3 »
76 3 »

1809 Rochechouart 1 f. 40
74 3 85
75 3 85
76 3 85

1810 Saint-Nicolas de Port 2 f.
74 6 10
75 6 10
76 6 10

1814 Marianne de Béquet 60 c.
74 4 60
75 4 60
76 4 60

1814a (sans bande de phosphore)
74, 75 13 »

1816 idem 80 c.
74 4 30
75 3 85
76 3 85
75, 76 **[6]** 7 65

1816a (sans bande de phosphore)
74 65 »

G.T. = gomme tropicale

1816b G.T.
75 35 »

1816d G.T. (sans bande de phosphore)
74 35 »

1871 Bonaguil 1 f.
76 2 30

1872 Ussel 2 f.
76 5 35
77, 78 5 35

1873 Malmaison 3 f.
76 7 »
77 7 65

1891 Marianne de Béquet 80 c.
76 3 »
77 3 »

1891 idem G.T.
76 6 10
77 6 10

1891b idem (sans bde de phosphore)
77 10 »

1892 idem 1 f.
76 3 »
77 3 »

1892 idem G.T.
76 9 15
77 10 75

1892b idem (sans bde de phosphore)
77 9 15

1902 Lodève 1 f. 10
76 3 »

1903 Biarritz 1 f. 40
76, 77 3 85

1904 Thiers 1 f. 70
76, 77, 78 4 60

1937 Dorat 1 f. 45
77 3 85

1938 Fontenay 1 f. 50
77, 78 3 85

1939 Bayeux 1 f. 90
77 5 35

1947 Pont-à-Mousson 1 f. 25
77 3 »

1948 St-Amand-les-Eaux 1 f. 40
77 3 85

1949 Vitré 2 f. 40
77, 78 6 10

1951 Excoffon 3 f.
77 (erreur) 150 »

1962 Sabine 1 c.
78, 79, 80, 81 0 80

1962 idem G.T.
78 1 »

1963 idem 2 c.
78, 79 0 80

1963 idem G.T.
78 1 »

1964 idem 5 c.
78, 79, 80 0 80

1964 idem G.T.
78, 79, 80 1 »

1965 idem 10 c.
78, 79, 80, 81 0 80

1965 idem G.T.
78, 79, 80 1 »

1966 idem 15 c.
78, 79, 80 2 30

1966 idem G.T.
78, 79, 80 2 30

1967 idem 20 c.
78, 79, 80, 81 0 80

1967 idem G.T.
78, 79, 80 1 85

1967a idem (bande à gauche)
79 3 »

1968 idem 30 c.
78, 79, 80, 81 0 80
78, coin à gauche (TD.3) 23 »

1968 idem G.T.
78, 79 1 60

1969 idem 50 c.
78, 79, 80, 81 1 60

1969 idem G.T.
79, 80, 81 1 85

1970 idem 80 c. vert
77 6 90

1970 idem G.T.
78 15 50

1970a (sans bande de phosphore) G.T.
77 10 75

1971 id. 80 c. jne-ol.
78, 79, 80, 81 2 30
78, coin à gauche (TD.3) 12 25

TIMBRES-POSTE (suite)

1971 idem G.T.
78 2 30

1972 idem 1 f. rouge
77 7 65
78 15 50

1972 idem G.T.
77,78 30 50

1972a (sans bande de phosphore) G.T.
77 29 »

1973 idem 1 f. vert
78, 79 3 85
78, coin à gauche (TD.3) » »

1973 idem G.T.
78, 79 5 35

1974 idem 1 f. 20
78, 79 3 85

1974 idem G.T.
78, 79 6 90

1975 idem 1 f. 40
78, 79 9 15

1975 idem G.T.
79 13 75

1976 idem 1 f. 70
78, 79, 80 5 35

1976 idem G.T.
78, 80 6 90

1977 idem 2 f.
78, 79, 80, 81 4 60

1977 idem G.T.
78, 79 5 35

1978 idem 2 f. 10
78, 79 5 35
80 8 40

1978 idem G.T.
78 7 65

1979 idem 3 f.
78, 79, 80, 81 6 90

1979 idem G.T.
78, 80 9 15

1996 Verdon 50 c.
77 1 60

1998 Saint-Saturnin 1 f.
78 2 30

1999 Bec-Hellouin 1 f. 10
78 3 85

2000 Esquelbecq 1 f. 10
78 3 »

2001 Église Aubazine 1 f. 25
77 6 90
78 4 60

2002 Abbaye de Fontevraud 1 f. 70
78 5 35

2040 Abbayes Normandes 1 f. 79
2 30
80 11 50

2041 Auray 1 f.
79 2 30
80 11 50

2042 Moulin de Steenvoorde 1 f. 20
79 3 »

2043 Grotte de Niaux 1 f. 50
78 3 85
79 3 85
80 4 60

2044 Palais des Rois Majorque 1 f. 70
79 3 85

2056 Sabine 70 c.
79 1 60
80 3 »

2056 idem G.T.
79 2 30

2057 idem 1 f. olive
79, 80, 81 2 30

2057 idem G.T.
79, 80 2 30

2058 idem 1 f. 10
79, 80 4 60

2058 idem G.T.
79 12 25

2059 idem 1 f. 30
78, 79 4 60

2059 idem G.T.
79, 80 12 25

2060 idem 1 f. 60
78, 79 6 10

2060 idem G.T.
79 10 »

2060a (sans bande de phosphore)
79 » »

2061 idem 1 f. 80
79 5 35

2061 idem G.T.
79 6 10

2064 Maisons-Laffitte 45 c.
79 1 60
80 2 30

2081 Cordes 1 f. 50
79, 80 3 85

2082 Maintenon 2 f. 80
4 50

2083 Montauban 2 f. 30
79, 80 6 10

2084 Le Puy 3 f. 20
80 3 84

2101 Sabine 1 f. 20
80, 81 3 »

2101 idem G.T.
80 4 60

2102 idem 1 f. 40
80, 81 3 85

2102 idem G.T.
80, 81 4 60

2111 Rambouillet 2 f. 20
80 5 35
81 6 90

2112 Solesmes 2 f. 50
80, 81 6 10

2118 Sabine 40 c.
80 2 30

2118 idem G.T.
80 1 60

2119 idem 60 c.
80 1 60

2119 idem G.T.
80 2 30

2120 idem 90 c.
80 2 30

2120 idem G.T.
80 3 »

2121 idem 3 f. 50
80 8 40

2121 idem G.T.
80 8 40

2122 idem 4 f.
80 10 75

2122 idem G.T.
80 11 50

2123 idem 5 f.
80, 81 13 75

2123 idem G.T.
80, 81 15 50

2132 Cathédrale Saint-Jean de Lyon 1 f. 40
81 3 85

2133 Nîmes 1 f. 70
80 5 35

2134 Ste-Anne d'Auray 2 f. 20
81 6 10

2135 Sully 2 f. 50
81 6 10

2154 Sabine 1 f. 40
81 3 85

2154 idem G.T.
81 4 50

2155 idem 1 f. 60
81 3 85

2155 idem G.T.
81 5 35

2156 idem 2 f. 30
81 11 50

2156 idem G.T.
81 20 »

2160 Abbaye de Vaucelles 2 f.
81 6 10

2161 N.-D. de Louviers 2 f. 20
81 6 10

2162 Saint-Émillion 2 f. 60
81, 82 6 90

2163 Crest 2 f. 90
81, 82 7 65

2178 Liberté 5 c.
81, 82, 83 1 60
84, 85, 86 1 60

2179 idem 10 c.
81, 82, 83, 84, 85 1 »
85, 86, 87, 88
89, 90 **[6]** 1 40

2180 idem 15 c.
81, 82, 84 2 30

2181 idem 20 c.
81, 82, 83, 84, 85 1 »
85, 86, 87, 88
89, 90 **[6]** 1 40

2182 idem 30 c.
81, 82, 83, 84, 85
86, 87, 88, 89, 1 »

2183 idem 40 c.
81, 82, 83, 84, 85
86, 87, 88, 89, 1 60

2184 idem 50 c.
81, 82, 83, 84, 85
86, 87, 88, 89 ,90 1 60

2185 idem 1 f.
81, 82, 83, 84, 85
86, 87, 88, 89, 90 2 30

2186 idem 1 f. 40
81, 82, 4 60

2187 idem 1 f. 60
81, 82, 3 85

2188 idem 2 f.
81, 82, 5 35

2188a idem 2 f.
84, 86 5 35

2189 idem 2 f. 30
81 12 25

2190 idem 5 f.
81, 82, 83, 84,
85, 86, 87, 88,
89, 90 13 »

2193 Saint-Pierre-et-Miquelon 1 f. 60
81, 82, 4 60

2194 Aix-en-Provence 2 f.
82, 4 60

2195 Château de Pau 3 f.
82, 6 90

2196 Collonges-la-Rouge 3 f.
82, 6 90

2219 Liberté 1 f. 60
82, 83, 84 4 60

2220 idem 1 f. 80
82, 83 4 60

2221 idem 2 f. 60
82 15 50

2232 Château de Ripaille 2 f. 90
82 7 65

2239 Liberté 60 c.
82, 83, 84, 85,
87, 88, 89, 90 1 60

2240 idem 70 c.
82, 83, 84, 85,
86, 87, 88, 89 2 30

2241 idem 80 c.
82, 83, 85, 87,
88 2 30

2242 idem 90 c.
82, 83, 84, 86,
87 2 30

2243 idem 3 f.
82, 83, 85, 86,
87, 88, 89 6 90

2244 idem 4 f.
82, 83, 84, 85,
87, 88, 9 15

2274 idem 2 f.
83, 84 4 60

2275 idem 2 f. 80
83 14 50

TIMBRES-POSTE (suite)

2276 idem *10 f.*
82, 84, 85, 86,
87, 88, 89, 90 23 »

2311 Légion étrangère *3 f. 10*
84 (erreur) 9 15

2318 Liberté *1 f. 70*
84, 85 4 60

2319 idem *2 f. 10*
84, 85 5 35

2320 idem *3 f.*
84, 85 13 »

2375 Liberté *1 f. 80*
85 5 35
85, 86 **[6]** 8 40

2376 idem *2 f. 20*
85, 86, 89 5 35
85, 86, 87, 88,
89 **[6]** 8 40

2376a idem (Type II) *1 f. 60*
85 19 50
86, 87, 89 15 50
85, 86 **[6]** 27 »

2377 idem *3 f. 20*
85 18 »

2423 idem A=*(1 f. 90)*
86 **[6]** 7 65

2424 idem *1 f. 90*
86, 87 **[6]** 17 »

2425 idem *3 f. 40*
86 14 50
87 23 »

2483 idem B = *(2 f.)*
87 **[6]** 6 90

2484 idem *2 f.*
87, 88, 89 **[6]** 7 65

2485 idem *3 f. 60*
87, 89 9 15

2486 idem *3 f. 70*
87, 88, 89 9 15

2486a idem (1 bande phosphore)
88 17 »

2530 idem surch. 0,31 écu s. 2 f. 20
88 7 65

2614 Marianne du Bicentenaire 2 f. 30
89, 90, 91 5 35
89, 90, 91 **[6]** 9 15

2615 Liberté
C = *(2 f. 10) vert*
89 **[6]** 8 40

2616 idem
C = *(2 f. 30) rouge*
89 **[6]** 9 15

2617 Marianne du Bicentenaire 10 c.
90, 91, 92, 93,
94, 96 **[6]** 1 25

2618 idem *20 c.*
90, 91, 92, 93,
94, 95, 96,
97 **[6]** 9 15

2619 idem *50 c.*
90, 91, 92, 93,
94, 95, 96, 97 1 »

2620 idem *1 f.*
90, 91, 92, 93,
94, 95, 96, 97 2 30

2621 idem *2 f.*
90, 91, 92 4 60

2622 idem *2 f. 10*
89, 90, 91 5 35
89, 90 **[6]** 7 65

2623 idem *3 f. 20*
90 9 15

2624 idem *3 f. 80*
90, 91 9 15

2625 idem *5 f.*
90, 91, 92, 93,
94, 95, 96, 97 11 50

2626 idem *10 f.*
90, 91, 92, 93,
94, 95, 96, 97 21 50

2711 idem
D = *(2 f. 20) vert*
90, 91 **[6]** 8 »

2712 idem
D = *(2 f. 50) rouge*
90, 91 **[6]** 8 »

2714 idem *2 f. 20*
91, 92 **[6]** 9 15

2715 idem *2 f. 50*
91, 92, 93 **[6]** 10 »

2716 idem *3 f. 40*
91, 92 8 40

2717 idem *4 f.*
91, 92 11 50

2770 idem *4 f. 20*
92, 93, 94 10 »

2773 Bicentenaire de la République (M. Raysse)
93 **[6]** 10 »

2775 idem (J.-C. Blais) *2 f. 50*
93 **[6]** 10 »

2790 Marianne du Bicentenaire *2 f. 20*
92, 93 **[6]** 10 75

2806 idem (*sans val.*)
93, 94, 95, 96,
97 **[6]** 10 75

2820 idem *2 f. 40*
93, 94, 95 **[6]** 9 15

2821 idem *3 f. 50*
93 8 40

2821a idem *3 f. 50*
93, 95, 97 10 75

2822 idem *4 f. 40*
93, 94, 95 10 »

2906 idem *2 f.*
94, 95, 96, 97 4 60

2949 Bretagne *2 f. 40*
95 **[6]** 8 40

2950 Vosges *2 f. 40*
95 **[6]** 8 40

2951 Auvergne *2 f. 80*
95 **[6]** 10 »

2952 Camargue *2 f. 80*
95 **[6]** 10 »

3005 Marianne du Bicentenaire *2 f. 70*
96, 97 **[6]** 9 15

3006 idem *3 f. 80*
96 8 40

3007 idem *4 f. 50*
96, 97 10 »

3081 Château du Plessis-Bourré *4 f. 40*
97 (erreur) 11 50

3083 Marianne du 14 Juillet *(Sans val.)*
97, 98, 99,
00 **[6]** 7 65

3086 idem *10 c*
97, 98, 99,
00 **[6]** 1 25

3087 idem *20 c.*
97, 98, 99 **[6]** 1 25

3088 idem *50 c.*
97, 98, 99, 00 1 »

3089 idem *1 f.*
97, 98, 99, 00 1 60

3090 idem *2 f.*
97, 98, 99 3 »

3091 idem *2 f. 70*
97, 98, 99,
00 **[6]** 7 65

3092 idem *3 f. 50*
97, 98, 99, 00 5 35

3093 idem *3 f. 80*
97, 98, 99 6 10

3094 idem *4 f. 20*
97, 98 6 90

3095 idem *4 f. 40*
97, 98 6 90

3096 idem *4 f. 50*
97, 98, 99, 00 6 90

3097 idem *5 f.*
97, 98, 99 7 65

3098 idem *6 f. 70*
97, 98, 99, 00 10 »

3099 idem *10 f.*
97, 98, 99, 00 15 50

3417 Marianne du 14 Juillet avec mention RF *(sans val.)*
01, 02, 03, 04 5 »

3443 idem *0,01 €*
01, 02, 03, 04 0 75

3444 idem *0,02 €*
01, 02, 03, 04 0 75

3445 idem *0,05 €*
01, 02, 03, 04 0 75

3446 idem *0,10 €*
01, 02, 03, 04 1 »

3447 idem *0,20 €*
01, 02, 03, 04 2 »

3448 idem *0,41 €*
01, 02, 03 3 50

3449 idem *0,50 €*
01, 02, 03, 04 5 50

3450 idem *0,53 €*
01, 02, 03 6 »

3451 idem *0,58 €*
01, 02, 03, 04 7 »

3452 idem *0,64 €*
01, 02, 03 8 »

3453 idem *0,67 €*
01, 02, 03 8 »

3454 idem *0,69 €*
01, 02, 03 8 »

3455 idem *1,00 €*
01, 02, 03, 04 10 »

3456 idem *1,02 €*
01, 02, 03 10 »

3457 idem *2,00 €*
01, 02, 03, 04 20 »

3535A Marianne du 14 Juillet avec mention RF *(sans val.)*
02, 03, 04 5 »

3570 idem *0,58 €*
03, 04 5 »

3571 idem *0,70 €*
03, 04 7 »

3572 idem *0,75 €*
03, 04 7 »

3573 idem *0,90 €*
03, 04 9 »

3574 idem *1,11 €*
03, 04 11 »

3575 idem *1,90 €*
03, 04 20 »

3594 Massoud *0,50 €*
03 5 »

3676 Salvatore Dali *1,11 €*
(21.04.04) » »

3731 Marianne de Lamouche *0,01 €*
04 0 75

3732 idem *0,10 €*
04 1 »

3733 idem vert *(sans val.)*
04 5 »

3734 idem rouge *(sans val.)*
04 6 »

3735 idem *0,58 €*
04 6 »

3736 idem *0,70 €*
04 7 »

3737 idem *0,75 €*
04 7 »

3738 idem *0,90 €*
04 10 »

3739 idem *1,00 €*
04 10 »

3740 idem *1,11 €*
04 11 »

3741 idem *1,90 €*
04 20 »

3754 idem *0,05 €*
05 0 75

3755 idem *0,55 €*
05 6 »

3756 idem *0,64 €*
05 6 50

3757 idem *0,82 €*
05 8 »

3758 idem *1,22 €*
05 12 »

3759 idem *1,98 €*
05 20 »

POSTE AÉRIENNE

5 Marseille *1 f. 50*
28 (erreur) 275 »
29 225 »
30 225 »
31 (erreur) 275 »

6 Marseille *1 f. 50*
30 225 »
30, outremer 450 »
30, outr. vif 3500 »
31 225 »
32 225 »

6c perf. EIPA *1 f. 50+5 f.*
30 4500 »

7 Blériot *2 f. 25*
34 225 »

8 Avion s. Paris *85 c.*
35 (8a) 125 »
36 30 »
37 30 »

9 idem *1 f. 50*
35 100 »

10 idem *2 f. 25*
35 200 »
37 200 »

11 idem *2 f. 50*
35 250 »
36 250 »

12 idem *3 f.*
35 225 »

13 idem *3 f. 50*
35 600 »

14 idem *50 f.*
35 9000 »
35, vert fcé 10000 »

15 Burelé *50 f.*
7000 »

16 Sagittaire *40 f.*
46 5 »
47 6 »
48 5 »
49 5 »

17 Iris *50 f.*
46 5 »
47 5 »
48 5 »
49 5 »

18 Egine *100 f.*
46 45 »
47 60 »
48 50 »
49 50 »

19 Soleil *200 f.*
46 35 »
48 35 »
49 50 »

24 Lille *100 f.*
49 7 50
50 7 50
51 7 50
52 7 50
53 7 50

25 Bordeaux *200 f.*
49 80 »
50 80 »
51 80 »
52 80 »
53 80 »

26 Lyon *300 f.*
49 100 »

27 Marseille *500 f.*
49 400 »
53 450 »

29 Paris *1000 f.*
49 900 »
51 1000 »
52 900 »
53 900 »

30 Mystère IV *100 f.*
53 17 50
54 17 50
55 17 50
56 17 50
57 17 50
58 17 50

31 Noratlas *200 f.*
53 60 »
54 60 »
55 60 »
56 60 »
57 60 »
58 60 »
59 75 »

32 Magister *500 f.*
53 1000 »
54 1000 »
55 1100 »

33 Provence *100 f.*
53 650 »
54 650 »

35 Morane *300 f.*
59 40 »

36 Caravelle *500 f.*
57 175 »
59 175 »

37 Alouette *1000 f.*
57 385 »
58 385 »
59 385 »

38 Noratlas *2 f.*
59 10 »
60 10 »
61 10 »
62 10 »
63 10 »
64 10 »
65 10 »

38a Noratlas
63 20 »
64 20 »

39 Morane *3 f.*
59 10 »
61 10 »
62 à 69 10 »
70 10 »
71 10 »
72 à 73 10 »
74 30 »

40 Caravelle
59 à 68 20 »
69 20 »
sans date 30 »

41 Alouette *10 f.*
59 à 65, 67, 68 80 »
70 110 »

42 Mystère 20 *2 f.*
65 à 69 5 »
70 5 »
71, 72 7 50

44 Mermoz et Saint-Exupéry *20 f.*
70 90 »
76, 78, 79, 80, 81, 82, 83, 84 70 »

46 Daurat et Vanier *5 f.*
76 16 »
77 16 »
78, 79 16 »
80, 81 20 »

47 Boucher et Hilsz *10 f.*
72 30 »
74 30 »
75, 76 30 »
77, 78, 79 30 »
80, 81 30 »

48 Guillaumet et Codos *15 f.*
72 80 »
73, 79 50 »
80, 81
82, 84 45 »
83 80 »

55 Costes et Le Brix *10 f.*
81, 82, 83 30 »

57 Farman Goliath *15 f.*
84, 85, 86 42 »

57b 87, 88, 89, 90, 91, 92, 94 45 »

58 Hydravion CAMS 53 *20 f.*
84, 85, 86 50 »

58b 87, 88, 89, 90, 91, 92, 93, 94, 95, 96 60 »

59 Trimoteur Wibault 283 *30 f.*
85, 86 70 »

59b, 92 80 »

62 Biplan Potez 25 *30 f.*
98 50 »

64 Couzinet 70 *50 f.*
99, 00 75 »

65 Airbus A300 *3,00 €*
04, 05 30 »

66 Jacqueline Auriol *4,00 €*
03 40 »

67 Marie Marvingt *5,00 €*
04 50 »

TIMBRES DES COURS D'INSTRUCTION

ANNULÉ

Semeuse camée

139CI 2 — *20 c.*
23 — 125 »

SPÉCIMEN

Type Blanc

108CI 3 — *2 c.*
25 — 400 »

111CI 1 — *5 c.*
25 — 400 »

Semeuse lignée

200CI 1 — *60 c.*
25 — 125 »
203CI 1 — *80 c.*
25 — 250 »

Semeuse camée

159CI 3 — *10 c.*
25 — 150 »
26 — 150 »
189CI 1 — *15 c.*
25 — 200 »

Semeuse camée

139CI 3 — *20 c.*
25 — 200 »
140CI 4 — *25 c.*
25 — 200 »
192CI 1 — *30 c.*
25 — 150 »
195CI 1 — *1 f. 05*
25 — 225 »

Pasteur

175CI 1 — *45 c.*
24 — 275 »
179CI 1 — *1 f.*
25 — 275 »

Préoblitérés

41CI 1 — *5 c.*
25 — 2500 »
51CI 1 — *10 c.*
25 — 2250 »
53CI 1 — *15 c.*
25 — 2250 »
54CI 2 — *20 c.*
24 — 2250 »
67CI 1 — *45 c.*
24 — 2250 »

TIMBRES DE FRANCHISE

6 Semeuse (IIA) — *50 c.*
28 — 100 »
31 — 85 »

7 Paix — *50 c.*
33 (I) — 60 »
34 (I) — 45 »
35 (I) — 45 »
35 (III) — 42 50
36 (III) — 42 50
37 (III) — 50 »

8 Paix (I) — *65 c.*
36 (erreur) — 6 »
37 — 7 »
38 — 7 »

9 Paix (I) — *90 c.*
39 — 6 »

10 Paix (I) — *90 c.*
39 — 20 »

11 Emblème Vert
46 — 12 50

12 Emblème Rouge
46 — 3 50
47 — 4 »
48 — 3 50
49 — 4 »
50 — 4 »
51 — 4 »
52 — 3 50
53 — 3 50
54 — 4 »
55 — 3 50
56 — 3 50
57 — 4 »
58 — 4 »
59 — 4 »
60 — 4 »
61 — 4 »
62 — 3 50
63 — 3 50
64 — 10 »

13 Drapeau
64 — 3 »
67 — 3 »
68 — 3 »
69 — 3 »
70 — 5 »
71 — 5 »

TIMBRES DE SERVICE

1 (42) — 400 »
2 (42) — 400 »
3 (42) — 500 »
4 (42) — 500 »
5 (42) — 4500 »
6 (42) — 2500 »
7 (42) — 1250 »
8 (42) — 500 »
9 (42) — 200 »
10 (42) — 550 »
11 (42) — 1250 »
12 (42) — 100 »
13 (42) — 500 »
14 (42) — 200 »
15 (42) — 250 »
1 à 15 (42) — 14000 »
16 (57,58) — 12 50
17 (58) — 2 »
18 (58) — 2 50
19 (59) — 6 »
20 (58) — 5 »
21 (59) — 10 »
22 (61) — 2 50
23 (61) — 3 50
25 (61) — 10 »
27 (62, 63) — 7 »
28 (62, 63) — 17 »
29 (63, 65) — 7 »
30 (63, 65) — 7 »
31 (69) — 9 »
32 (62, 63) — 17 »
33 (71) — 20 »
34 (63, 65) — 8 »
35 (69) — 27 50
39 (69) — 4 »
40 (69) — 6 »
41 (71) — 15 »
42 (69) — 20 »
43 (75) — 10 »
44 (75) — 15 »
45 (75) — 30 »
46 (75) — 8 »
47 (75) — 12 50
48 (75) — 42 »
49 (76) — 30 »
50 (76) — 7 »
51 (76) — 4 50
52 (76) — 15 »
53 (76) — 7 50
54 (76) — 5 »
55 (76) — 17 »
56 (78) — 4 10
57 (78) — 5 50
58 (78) — 4 »
59 (78) — 5 50
60 (80) — 4 50
61 (80) — 5 50
62 (80) — 7 »
63 (80) — 5 50
64 (80) — 7 »
65 (81) — 5 »
66 (81) — 5 »
67 (81) — 6 »
68 (81) — 6 »
69 (81) — 6 »
70 (81) — 6 »
71 (82) — 6 »
72 (82) — 7 »
73 (82) — 6 »
74 (82) — 7 »
75 (83) — 5 50
76 (83) — 8 »
77 (83) — 6 »
78 (83) — 8 »
79 (84) — 6 »
80 (84) — 7 »
81 (84) — 11 »
82 (84) — 5 50
83 (84) — 6 »
84 (84) — 9 50
85 (85) — 6 »
86 (85) — 8 »
87 (85) — 11 50
88 (85) — 8 50
89 (85) — 8 50
90 (85) — 17 50
91 (86) — 7 65
92 (86) — 15 »
93 (86) — 10 »
94 (86) — 10 »
95 (86) — 17 »
96 (87) — 8 »
97 (87) — 15 »
98 (87) — 8 »
99 (87) — 15 »
100 (89) — 11 »
101 (89) — 18 50
102 (90) — 9 »
103 (90) — 11 »
104 (90) — 9 »
105 (90) — 13 75
106 (91) — 9 »
107 (91) — 11 »
108 (91) — 9 »
109 (91) — 11 »
110 (93) — 9 »
111 (93) — 9 »
112 (93) — 9 »
113 (93) — 9 »
114 (96) — 7 »
115 (96) — 10 »
116 (96) — 7 »
117 (96) — 10 »
118 (98) — 7 »
119 (98) — 8 50
120 (99) — 8 50
121 (99) — 8 50
122 (01) — 8 50
123 (01) — 8 50
124 (01) — 8 50
125 (01) — 8 50

TIMBRES-PRÉOBLITÉRÉS

40 Blanc (II)	*4 c.*
24 (à gauche)	4000 »
41 idem	*5 c.*
25 (IIA)	50 »
25 (41a)	575 »
25 (à gauche IIB)	1100 »
26 (IIA)	50 »
42 idem (II)	*7½ c.*
26	10 »
43 idem (II)	*10 c.*
29	15 »
30	15 »
31	15 »
32	40 »
46 Semeuse	*45 c.*
27	75 »
28	50 »
29	50 »
30	65 »
31	50 »
47 idem	*55 c. s. 60 c.*
25	1250 »
48 idem	*65 c.*
24	70 »
49 idem	*65 c.*
27	100 »
28	175 »
29	100 »
30	110 »
32	125 »
51 idem (III)	*10 c.*
25	60 »
25 (51a)	450 »
26	11 »
27	5 »
28	5 »
29	5 »
52 idem (III)	*10 c.*
32	7 50
33	7 50
34	7 50
35	7 50
36	7 50
37	30 »
53 idem	*15 c.*
25 (I)	20 »
25 (I) (53a)	450 »
26 (I)	5 »
27 (I)	5 »
28 (I)	4 »
30 (I)	4 »
31 (I)	4 »
32 (I)	4 »
33 (I)	4 »
34 (I)	5 »
35 (I)	4 »
35 (II)	6 »
36 (I)	4 »

36 (II)	25 »
37 (II)	6 »
38 (II)	6 »
54 idem (III)	*20 c.*
23	650 »
24	600 »
25	650 »
55 idem	*20 c.*
32 (III)	25 »
33 (III)	25 »
35 (III)	30 »
35 (V)	32 50
36 (V)	30 »
37 (V)	30 »
56 idem (IIIB)	*25 c.*
24	325 »
26	100 »
27	100 »
57 idem (IIIB)	*25 c.*
27	30 »
28	20 »
29	20 »
30	20 »
31	20 »
31 (à gauche IIIC)	600 »
32	20 »
33	30 »
34	20 »
35	30 »
36	20 »
37	30 »
38	20 »
60 idem (IIA)	*30 c.*
25	2000 »
61 idem (IIA)	*30 c.*
38	12 50
63 idem (II)	*35 c.*
37	60 »
38	75 »
64 idem (II)	*40 c.*
26	200 »
65 Pasteur	*15 c.*
24	300 »
25	400 »
66 idem	*30 c.*
32	300 »
67 Pasteur	*45 c.*
24	200 »
69 Paix	*30 c.*
33	32500 »
70 idem (I)	*40 c.*
34	75 »
35	75 »
37	90 »

71 idem	*45 c.*
32	175 »
34	200 »
35	180 »
36	180 »
72 idem	*60 c.*
37	65 »
38	65 »
73 idem	*65 c.*
33	450 »
35	400 »
36	400 »
74 idem (II)	*80 c./1 f.*
37	8 »
75 idem	*80 c.*
38	700 »
76 idem	*1 f.*
38	100 »
77 idem	*1 f. 40*
39	100 »
78 Mercure (I)	*20 c.*
38	6 »
39	6 »
40	6 »
41	7 »
79 idem (I)	*30 c.*
41	20 »
80 idem	*40 c.*
39	9 »
40	9 »
42	11 »
81 idem	*40 c.*
43	5 »
44	5 »
82 idem	*50 c.*
42	5 »
83 idem	*60 c.*
40	225 »
84 Pétain	*70 c.*
42	12 50
85 idem	*1 f. 20*
42	15 »
86 idem	*2 f.*
42	30 »
87 Mazelin	*60 c.*
45	4 »
88 idem	*80 c.*
45	4 »
89 idem	*90 c.*
46	5 »
90 idem	*1 f.*
46	4 »
47	4 »

91 idem	*1 f. 20*
45	5 »
91A idem	*1 f. 50*
47	4 »
48	5 »
92 idem	*2 f.*
46	5 »
93 idem	*2 f. 50*
47	7 »
94 Marianne	*2 f.*
45	4 »
95 idem	*2 f. 50*
48	15 »
96 idem	*3 f.*
46	4 »
97 idem	*4 f.*
47	4 »
98 idem	*4 f.*
48	4 »
99 idem	*4 f.*
49	8 »
100 idem	*6 f.*
47	8 »
48	35 »
101 idem	*8 f.*
49	6 »
50	6 »
51	6 »
52	7 50
53	7 50
102 idem	*10 f.*
48	4 »
103 idem	*12 f.*
49	7 »
50	7 »
51	9 »
103A idem	*12 f.*
51	45 »
52	45 »
53	47 50
104 idem (I)	*15 f.*
49	5 »
105 Armoiries, Anjou	*4 f.*
49 (105a)	250 »
49	3 »
50	3 »
51	3 »
52	4 »
53	4 »
106 Moissonneuse	*4 f.*
54	2 50

55	2 50
56	2 50
57	2 50
107 Coq	*5 f.*
57	2 50
58	3 50
108 Moissonneuse	*8 f.*
54	35 »
55	40 »
56	35 »
57	40 »
109 Coq	*8 f.*
59	5 »
110 idem	*10 f.*
57	12 50
58	15 »
111 idem	*12 f.*
54	22 50
55	25 »
56	25 »
57	25 »
112 idem	*15 f.*
57	17 50
58	22 50
113 idem	*20 f.*
59	12 50
114 idem	*24 f.*
54	125 »
55	150 »
56	150 »
57	150 »
115 idem	*30 f.*
57	60 »
58	75 »
116 idem	*40 f.*
59	30 »
117 Coq	*45 f.*
57	140 »
118 idem	*55 f.*
59	110 »
119 idem	*8 c.*
59	7 »
60	7 »
61	7 »
62	8 »
63	8 »
64	13 »
120 idem	*20 c.*
59	20 »
60	22 »
61	22 »
62	22 »
63	30 »

TIMBRES-PRÉOBLITÉRÉS (suite)

121 idem	*40 c.*
59	65 »
60	75 »
61	75 »
62	75 »
63	75 »
64	100 »
122 idem	*55 c.*
59	200 »
61	230 »
62	230 »
63	230 »
123 Monnaie	*10 c.*
63	6 »
64	6 »
65	7 »
66	7 »
124 idem	*15 c.*
66, 67	3 »
68	3 »
125 idem	*22 c.*
69	6 »
70	6 »
126 idem	*25 c.*
63	5 »
64	5 »
66	5 »
67	5 »
68	7 »
127 idem	*35 c.*
69	10 »
70	17 »
128 idem	*50 c.*
63, 64	8 »
66, 67	8 »
68	10 »
129 idem	*70 c.*
69	40 »
130 idem	*26 c.*
71	5 »
131 idem	*30 c.*
71	6 »
74	10 »
132 idem	*45 c.*
71	12 »
133 idem	*90 c.*
71	15 »
72	18 »
134 idem	*42 c.*
75	8 »
135 idem	*48 c.*
75	9 »
136 idem	*70 c.*
75	17 »
137 idem	*1 f. 35*
75	22 »
138 idem	*50 c.*
75	9 »
139 idem	*52 c.*
76	5 »
140 idem	*60 c.*
75	13 »
141 idem	*62 c.*
76	9 »
142 idem	*90 c.*
75	17 »
143 idem	*95 c.*
76	11 »
144 idem	*1 f. 60*
75	35 »
145 idem	*1 f. 70*
76	23 »
146 Zodiaque	*54 c.*
76	6 »
77	8 »
147 idem	*68 c.*
77	8 »
148 idem	*1 f. 05*
76	12 »
149 idem	*1 f. 85*
76	46 »
77	23 »
150 idem	*58 c.*
77, 78	9 »
151 idem	*73 c.*
78	12 »
152 idem	*1 f. 15*
78	19 »
153 idem	*2 f.*
78	23 »
154 idem	*61 c.*
78	7 »
155 idem	*78 c.*
78	7 »
156 idem	*1 f. 25*
78	9 »
157 idem	*2 f. 10*
78	12 »
158 Champignon	*64 c.*
78	8 »
79	7 »
159 idem	*83 c.*
78	8 »
79	7 »
160 idem	*1 f. 30*
78	11 »
79	9 »
161 idem	*2 f. 25*
78	12 »
79	11 »
162 Tours	*68 c.*
79	5 »
163 idem	*88 c.*
79	5 »
164 idem	*1 f. 40*
79	7 »
165 idem	*2 f. 35*
79	9 »
166 Châteaux	*76 c.*
80	4 »
167 idem	*99 c.*
80	4 »
168 idem	*1 f. 60*
80	5 »
169 idem	*2 f. 65*
80	9 »
170 idem	*88c.*
81	4 »
171 idem	*1 f. 14*
81	4 »
172 idem	*1 f. 84*
81	6 »
173 idem	*3 f. 05*
81	11 »
174 Monuments	*97 c.*
82	4 »
175 idem	*1 f. 25*
81, 82	4 »
176 idem	*2 f. 03*
82	6 »
177 idem	*3 f. 36*
82	10 »
178 Saisons	*1 f. 05*
83	4 »
179 idem	*1 f. 35*
83	5 »
180 idem	*2 f. 19*
82, 83	6 »
181 idem	*3 f. 63*
83	11 »
182 Cartes à jouer	*1 f. 14*
84	3 »
183 idem	*1 f. 47*
84	4 »
184 idem	*2 f. 38*
84	7 »
185 idem	*3 f. 95*
84	12 »
186 Mois de l'année	*1 f. 22*
85	8 »
187 idem	*1 f. 57*
85	10 »
188 idem	*2 f. 55*
85	12 »
189 idem	*4 f. 23*
85	19 »
190 idem	*1 f. 28*
86	8 »
191 idem	*1 f. 65*
86	10 »
192 idem	*2 f. 67*
86	12 »
193 idem	*4 f. 44*
86	20 »
194 idem	*1 f. 31*
87	9 »
195 idem	*1 f. 69*
87	12 »
196 idem	*2 f. 74*
87	15 »
197 idem	*4 f. 56*
87	22 »
198 Les quatre éléments	*1 f. 36*
88	8 »
199 idem	*1 f. 75*
88	12 »
200 idem	*2 f. 83*
88	12 »
201 idem	*4 f. 75*
88	22 »
202 Instruments de musique	*1 f. 39*
89	8 »
203 idem	*1 f. 79*
89	9 »
204 idem	*2 f. 90*
89	15 »
204a idem	*2 f. 90*
90	1050 »
205 idem	*4 f. 84*
89	21 »
206 idem	*1 f. 46*
90	7 »
207 idem	*1 f. 89*
90	9 »
208 idem	*3 f. 06*
90	17 »
209 idem	*5 f. 10*
90	23 »
210 idem	*1 f. 93*
90	9 »
211 idem	*2 f. 39*
90	12 »
212 idem	*2 f. 74*
90	17 »
213 idem	*1 f. 60*
91	260 »
213a idem	*1 f. 60*
91	38 »
214 idem	*1 f. 98*
91	23 »
92	46 »
214a idem	*1 f. 98*
92	765 »
215 idem	*2 f. 08*
91	15 »
215a idem	*2 f. 08*
91	195 »
216 idem	*2 f. 46*
91	15 »
216a idem	*2 f. 46*
91	54 »
217 idem	*2 f. 98*
91	15 »
218 idem	*3 f. 08*
91, 92	37 »
218a idem	*3 f. 08*
91, 92	54 »
219 idem	*3 f. 14*
91	31 »
219a idem	*3 f. 14*
91	305 »
220 idem	*3 f. 19*
91	37 »
220a idem	*3 f. 19*
91, 92	43 »
221 idem	*5 f. 28*
91	31 »
221a idem	*5 f. 28*
91	140 »
222 idem	*5 f. 3*
91	19 »
222a idem	*5 f. 30*
91	385 »
223 idem	*5 f. 32*
91	20 »
223a idem	*5 f. 32*
91	115 »
224 idem	*1 f. 73*
92	5 »
225 idem	*2 f. 25*
92	7 »
226 idem	*3 f. 51*
92	13 »
227 idem	*5 f. 40*
92	17 »
228 idem	*1 f. 82*
93	5 »
229 idem	*2 f. 34*
93	6 »
230 idem	*3 f. 86*
32	12 »
231 idem	*5 f. 93*
93	17 »

TIMBRES-PRÉOBLITÉRÉS (suite)

232 Feuilles d'arbres *1 f. 91*
94 5 »
233 idem *2 f. 46*
94 7 »
234 idem *4 f. 24*
94 12 »
235 idem *6 f. 51*
94 19 »
236 idem *1 f. 87*
96 5 »
237 idem *2 f. 18*
96 6 »
238 idem *4 f. 66*
96 12 »
239 idem *7 f. 11*
96 17 »
240 Fleurs sauvages *1 f. 87*
98 5 »
241 idem *2 f. 18*
98 6 »
242 idem *4 f. 66*
98 11 »
243 idem *7 f. 11*
98 15 »
244 Orchidées *0,29 €*
02 6 »
245 idem *0,33 €*
02 10 »
246 idem *0,30 €*
03 6 »
247 idem *0,35 €*
03 7 50
248 idem *0,39 €*
04 10 »
249 idem *0,42 €*
05 10 »

TIMBRES-TAXE

28 Banderole *5 c.*
34 5 »
35 5 »
36 5 »
37 5 »
38 7 »
29 Banderole *10 c.*
34 6 »
35 5 »
36 5 »
37 5 »
38 5 »
40 5 »
42 5 »
33 Banderole *30 c.*
34 6 »
35 6 »
36 6 »
37 5 »
38 5 »
39 5 »
40 5 »
42 5 »
37 Banderole *50 c.*
34 7 »
35 7 »
36 7 »
37 6 »
38 6 »
39 6 »
40 6 »
42 6 »
38 Banderole *60 c.*
35 10 »
36 12 »
37 9 »
38 9 »
39 9 »
40A Banderole *1 f.*
35 15 »
36 15 »
37 15 »
38 15 »
39 15 »
40 15 »
41 25 »
42 15 »
42 Banderole *2 f.*
34 8 »
35 7 »
37 7 »
40 7 »
42 7 »
42A Banderole *3 f.*
26 7 50
36 25 »
37 7 50
38 7 50
39 7 50
40 7 50
42 7 50
55 Recouvrem. *1 c.*
27 12 50
28 40 »
56 Recouvrem. *10 c.*
30 20 »
31 20 »
57 Recouvrem. *30 c.*
26 60 »
28 50 »
29 50 »
58 Recouvrem. *60 c.*
26 55 »
27 50 »
28 45 »
30 45 »
31 45 »
59 Recouvrem. *1 f.*
26 175 »
60 Recouvrem. *1 f.*
31 190 »
32 190 »
33 190 »
34 190 »
35 190 »
61 Recouvrem. *2 f.*
27 800 »
62 Recouvrem. *2 f.*
31 1500 »
63 Recouvrem. *1/60 c.*
31 275 »
64 Recouvrem. *1 f. 20/2 f.*
27 450 »
65 Recouvrem. *5 f./1 f.*
26 600 »
66 Banderole *5 f.*
40 15 »
42 17 50
67 Gerbes Chiffre-Taxe *10 c.*
43 1 »
45 1 25
68 Gerbes *30 c.*
43 1 »
69 Gerbes *50 c.*
43 1 »
44 1 »
45 1 »
46 1 25
70 Gerbes *1 f.*
43 1 »
45 1 25
46 1 25
71 Gerbes *1 f. 50*
43 1 75
44 2 50
45 3 »
72 Gerbes *2 f.*
43 1 75
45 2 50
46 2 50
73 Gerbes *3 f.*
43 2 50
45 3 50
17 3 50
74 Gerbes *4 f.*
45 35 »
75 Gerbes *5 f.*
43 3 »
76 Gerbes *10 f.*
45 22 50
77 Gerbes *20 f.*
46 60 »
78 Gerbes Timbre-Taxe *10 c.*
47 9 »
79 Gerbes *30 c.*
47 9 »
80 Gerbes *50 c.*
47 150 »
81 Gerbes *1 f.*
47 1 75
48 1 75
49 1 75
50 1 75
51 1 75
52 1 75
53 3 »
55 1 75
56 3 »
57 3 »
58 4 »
82 Gerbes *2 f.*
46 1 75
47 1 75
48 1 75
51 1 75
52 1 75
53 1 75
54 1 75
55 1 75
56 1 75
58 4 »
83 Gerbes *3 f.*
46 3 »
47 3 »
48 2 30
50 1 75
51 1 75
54 3 »
84 Gerbes *4 f.*
46 1 75
47 2 »
48 2 »
52 2 »
53 2 50
85 Gerbes *5 f.*
47 1 75
48 1 75
49 1 75
50 3 »
51 1 75
52 1 75
53 1 75
54 1 75
55 1 75
56 1 75
57 1 75
58 1 75
59 17 50
86 Gerbes *10 f.*
47 1 75
48 1 75
49 1 75
50 1 75
51 1 75
52 1 75
53 1 75
54 1 75
55 1 75
56 1 75
57 1 75
58 1 75
59 1 75
61 20 »
87 Gerbes *20 f.*
47 10 »
49 10 »
50 10 »
51 10 »
52 10 »
53 10 »
54 10 »
55 10 »
56 10 »
57 10 »
58 10 »
59 10 »
88 Gerbes *50 f.*
50 140 »
51 140 »
52 140 »
53 140 »
54 140 »
55 140 »
57 140 »
59 140 »
61 175 »
89 Gerbes *100 f.*
53 425 »
55 425 »
57 425 »
90 Gerbes *5 c.*
59 20 »
60 20 »
61 20 »
62 22 50
63 22 50
64 25 »
91 Gerbes *10 c.*
59 35 »
60 35 »
61 35 »
62 35 »
63 35 »
92 Gerbes *20 c.*
59 30 »
60 30 »
61 30 »
62 30 »
63 30 »
64 30 »
93 Gerbes *50 c.*
60 85 »
61 100 »
62 85 »
63 65 »
64 85 »
94 Gerbes *1 f.*
60 325 »
61 325 »
62 325 »
63 400 »
64 325 »
95 Centaurée *5 c.*
64 0 80
65 0 80

TIMBRES-TAXE (suite)

66, 68	0 80
70, 71	0 80
76, 79	0 80
96 Gentiane	*10 c.*
65	0 80
66	0 80
67	0 80
69	0 80
70, 71	0 80
75, 76	0 80
78, 79	0 80
80, 81	0 80
97 Coquelicot	*15 c.*
64	1 55
98 Pervenche	*20 c.*
71	0 80
74	0 80
75	0 80
76, 78	0 80
79, 81	0 80
99 Myosotis	*30 c.*
64	1 10
66	1 10
67	1 10
68	1 10
69	1 10
70	1 10
71	1 10
72	1 55
74, 75, 76, 77, 78	1 10
79, 80, 81	1 10
100 Ancolie	*40 c.*
71	2 30
74	1 85
75	1 85
76, 77, 78	1 85
79, 81	1 85
101 Trèfles	*5 c.*
64	1 85
65	1 85
66	3 05
67	1 85
68	1 85
69	1 85
71	1 85
73	1 85
74	1 85
75	1 85
76, 77, 78, 79	1 85
80	1 85
102 Soldanelle	*1 f.*
64	3 85
65	3 85
66	3 85
67	3 85
68	3 85
69	3 85
70	3 85
71	3 85
73	3 85
74	3 85
75, 76	3 85
78, 79, 80, 81	3 85
103 Coléoptères	*10 c.*
81, 82, 84, 86	1 55
104 idem	*20 c.*
81, 82, 83	1 55
105 idem	*50 c.*
81, 82, 83, 85, 87	1 55
106 idem	*1 f.*
81, 83, 84, 86	4 20
87	5 85
107 idem	*2 f.*
81, 86	6 90
108 idem	*4 f.*
81, 82, 83, 84, 85	13 75
109 idem	*30 c.*
82, 83, 85, 87	2 30
110 idem	*40 c.*
82, 83, 85, 86	2 50
111 idem	*3 f.*
82, 83, 84, 85	10 »
87	20 »
112 idem	*5 f.*
82, 83	15 25
87	18 50

TIMBRES POUR COLIS POSTAUX

Jusqu'en 1939 les cotes de la colonne de gauche concernent les timbres neufs avec charnière légère, et celles de la colonne de droite les timbres oblitérés.

1892. – *Lithographie. Dentelés.*

II - VALEUR DÉCLARÉE. I - APPORT A LA GARE. III - LIVRAISON PAR EXPRÈS.

a

Non dentelé.

1	**10 c. rouge sombre (II)**	23 »	18 50

Dentelés 13½.

2	**10 c. rouge (II)**	1 200 »	300 »
3	**25 c. brun s. jaune (I)**	950 »	300 »
4	**25 c. vert (III)**	60 »	30 »

Dentelé 10 x 13½.

5	**10 c. rouge (II)**	1 000 »	360 »

Dentelés 11.

6	**10 c. rouge-orange (II)**	32 »	14 »
	a. rose foncé	38 »	15 »
7	**25 c. brun s. jaune (I)**	32 »	23 »
8	**25 c. vert-jaune (III)**	50 »	25 »

De nouvelles valeurs à ce type ont paru en 1918-23 (nos 28 à 32). Les 10 c. noir, 25 c. bleu sur azuré et 25 c. lilas, appartiennent à l'Algérie, ainsi que le même type à valeur encadrée.

1901. – *Typographie. Dentelés 14 x 13½.*

9	**5 c. *gris***	3 »	
10	**10 c. *vert pâle***	4 »	
11	**20 c. *rose pâle***	22 »	
	a. (Non dentelé)	170 »	
12	**50 c. *bleu***	9 »	
13	**1 f. *brun***	10 »	
14	**2 f. *rouge-brun***	46 »	
	Nos 9 à 14 (6 val.)	**94 »**	

1918. – *Typographie. Dentelés 11.*

b

15	**5 c. noir**	1 25	1 »
16	**15 c. lilas-brun**	1 25	1 »

Non dentelés.

17	**5 c. noir**	3 85	2 30
18	**15 c. violet**	10 »	4 60
	a. lilas-brun	11 50	6 10

1918-20. – *Impression plus fine. Typographie. Dentelés 11-11½.*

c

19	**5 c. noir**	115 »	42 »
20	**35 c. rouge**	4 »	2 30
21	**50 c. violet foncé**	5 »	1 55
22	**1 f. jaune-orange**	4 »	1 55

Non dentelés.

23	**5 c. noir**	115 »	42 »
24	**15 c. lilas**	30 »	18 50
25	**35 c. rouge**	3 85	2 30
26	**50 c. violet-bleu**	26 »	14 »
27	**1 f. jaune**	20 »	14 »

De nouvelles valeurs à ce type ont paru en 1926 (nos 77 à 80) et en 1938 (nos 155 à 159).

Les mêmes timbres avec indication de monnaie (fr.) appartiennent à l'Algérie.

1918-23. – *Type a. Lithographie. Dentelés 10½-11.*

I. - Apport à la gare.

28	**30 c. brun s. jaune**	50 »	15 50
29	**60 c. brun s. jaune**	60 »	30 »

II - Valeur déclarée.

30	**15 c. vermillon**	20 »	11 50

III. - Livraison par exprès.

31	**30 c. vert**	50 »	23 »
32	**60 c. vert**	95 »	55 »

1924. – *Type Daussy. Valeur et COLIS POSTAUX en bleu. Typographie. Dentelé 13½.*

33	**15 c. rouge**		4 60
	Sur document		300 »
	a. (Valeur et COLIS POSTAUX renversés)	800 »	500 »
	b. (Valeur en rouge)	1 100 »	
	c. (Sans légende)	1 100 »	
	d. (Non dentelé)	1 300 »	

1926. – *Types de 1918-20 (dentelés 11) surchargés. Dentelés.*

Les cotes de la 1re colonne concernent les timbres avec gomme, la 2e colonne sans gomme et la 3e colonne oblitérés.

34	**0 F. 20 s. 2 f. rose (c)**	2 50	1 25	1 25
35	**0 F. 30 s. 2 f. jaune (c)**	2 50	1 25	1 25
	a. (Sans 0,30 mais avec les traits)	50 »		
36	**0 F. 40 s. 3 f. gris (c)**	2 50	1 25	1 55
37	**0 F. 45 s. 3 f. orange (c)**	2 50	1 25	0 80
	a. (Ss point après F)	12 25	6 10	6 10
38	**0 F. 95 s. 1 f. jaune (c)**	10 »	3 85	3 »
	a. (Non dentelé)	70 »		
39	**1 F. 35 s. 3 f. violet (c)**	14 »	7 65	5 35
40	**1 F. 45 s. 5 c. noir (R) (b)**	2 50	1 25	1 25
41	**1 F. 75 s. 2 f. bleu (c)**	14 »	7 »	5 35
42	**1 F. 85 s. 10 c. orange**	2 50	1 25	1 55
43	**1 F. 95 s. 15 c. lilas-brun (b)**	3 »	1 85	1 55
	a. (Non dentelé)	85 »		
44	**2 F. 35 s. 25 c. vert (c)**	3 »	1 10	1 10
	a. (Non dentelé)	85 »		
45	**2 F. 90 s. 35 c. rouge (c)**	4 »	1 25	0 80
	a. (Point avant et après F)	15 »		6 10
	b. (Non dentelé)	95 »		
46	**3 F. 30 s. 50 c. violet foncé (R) (c)**	4 50	2 »	1 85
	(Non dentelé)	65 »		
	a. (Double Surcharge)	130 »		

Les cotes de la 1re colonne concernent les timbres avec gomme, la 2e colonne sans gomme et la 3e colonne oblitérés.

1926. – *Fond formé des mots COLIS POSTAL répétés à l'infini. Format 18 x 21,5. Typographie. Dentelés 11.*

d

e

f

I. - Apport à la gare.

47	**1 F. 00, s. 60 c. brun s. jaune (d)**	17 »	12 25
48	**1 f. 00 brun s. jaune (e)**	20 »	14 »
49	**1 F. 30, s. 1 f. brun s. jaune**	20 »	13 »
50	**1 f. 50 brun s. jaune (e)**	22 »	12 25
51	**1 f. 65 brun s. jaune (e)**	17 »	13 »
52	**1 F. 90 s. 1 f. 50 brun s. jaune**	20 »	13 »
53	**2 F. 10 s. 1 f. 65 brun s. jaune**	20 »	13 »

I bis. - Apport à la gare d'un colis déposé dans un bureau de Paris.

I

II

III

54	**15 c. brun s. jaune (I) (f)**	9 »	3 »
	a. brun foncé s. jaune vif (II)	230 »	
	b. (Non dentelé)	260 »	

Le type III concerne le no 95.

II. - Valeur déclarée.

55	**0 F. 50 s. 15 c. rouge (d)**	3 20	1 55
56	**50 c. rouge (e)**	950 »	
57	**50 c. rouge (1)**		2 30
	a. (Double impression du chiffre 1)	245 »	
	b. (Non dentelé)	200 »	
58	**0 F. 55 s. 15 c. rouge (d) (1)**	7 »	3 85
59	**0 F. 55 s. 50 c. rouge (1)**	7 »	4 60
60	**0 F. 65 s. 50 c. rouge**	3 »	2 30
61	**0 F. 65 s. 50 c. rouge (1)**	17 »	9 95
62	**1 F. 50 s. 50 c. rouge □ (3)**	7 »	5 35
63	**2 F. 00 s. 50 c. rouge (4)**	9 »	3 »
64	**2 F. 50 s. 50 c. rouge (5)**	17 »	9 15

Les chiffres entre ( ) sont ceux qui ont été imprimés en haut et à gauche du timbre, pour rappeler au personnel combien de fois la taxe initiale de 50 centimes devait être perçue.

III. - Livraison par exprès.

65	**1 F. 00 s. 60 c. vert (d)**	10 »	6 10
66	**1 f. 00 vert (e)**	90 »	49 »
67	**1 F. 30 s. 1 f. vert**	18 »	14 »
68	**1 f. 50 vert (e)**	18 »	15 50
69	**1 f. 65 vert (e)**	18 »	14 »
70	**1 F. 90 s. 1 f. 50 vert**	18 »	14 »
71	**2 F. 10 s. 1 f. 65 vert**	37 »	20 »

IV. - Intérêt à la livraison.

72	**50 c. lilas (d)**	3 »	1 55
73	**50 c. lilas (e) (1)**	7 50	4 60
74	**1 F. 50 s. 50 c. lilas (e) (3)**	9 »	5 35
75	**2 F. s. 50 c. lilas (e) (4)**	11 »	7 65
76	**2 F. 50 s. 50 c. lilas (e) (5)**	11 »	7 65

Le type **d** a reparu en 1933 (nos 96 à 100), en 1937 (nos 119 à 126), en 1938 (nos 147 à 154) et en 1939 (no 164) ; il a été ensuite légèrement retouché (nos 165 à 173).

1926. – *Type c. Typographie. Dentelés 11.*

77	**10 c. orange**	3 »	1 55
78	**25 c. vert**	3 »	1 55
79	**2 f. bleu**	33 »	18 50
80	**3 f. violet**	135 »	77 »

1928. – *Timbres de 1926 surchargés. Dentelés.*

Les chiffres entre ( ) indiquent les prix auxquels étaient vendus ces timbres provisoires.

I. - Apport à la gare.

81	1 f. 00 brun s. jaune (1,45)	18 »	15 50
82	1 f. 50 brun s. jaune (2,15)	18 »	12 25
83	1 f. 65 brun s. jaune (2,35)	18 »	12 25

II. - Valeur déclarée.

84	**50 c. rouge □ (nº 56) (0,75)**	7 »	4 60
	a. (Surcharge renversée)	190 »	185 »

III. - Livraison par exprès.

85	1 f. 00 vert (1,45)	20 »	15 50
86	1 f. 50 vert (2,15)	20 »	15 50
87	1 f. 65 vert (2,35)	20 »	15 50

1928-29. – *Type d (nº 88) et type e (nºs 88A à 94) avec nouvelle valeur en surcharge. Dentelés 11.*

I. - Apport à la gare.

88	1 F. 45 s. 60 c. brun s. jaune	8 »	7 »
88A	1 F. 45 s. 1 f. brun s. jaune	50 »	30 »
89	2 F. 15 s. 1 f. 50 brun s. jaune	75 »	46 »
90	2 F. 35 s. 1 f. 65 brun s. jaune	75 »	46 »

II. - Valeur déclarée.

91	0 F. 75 s. 50 c. rouge	3 »	1 55

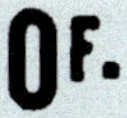

au lieu de

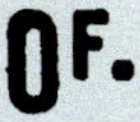

91a	(Lettre F plus petite)	15 50	3 85

III. - Livraison par exprès.

92	1 F. 45 s. 1 f. vert	75 »	42 »
93	2 F. 15 s. 1 f. 50 vert	75 »	42 »
94	2 F. 35 s. 1 f. 65 vert	75 »	42 »

1932. – *Type f modifié. Dentelé 11.*

95	15 c. brun s. jaune (III)	10 »	4 60

(Voir différence des types avant le nº 54).

1933-34. – *Type d. Dentelés 11.*

I. - Apport à la gare.

96	1 f. 45 brun s. jaune	50 »	20 »
97	2 f. 35 brun clair s. jaune	1 800 »	

II. - Valeur déclarée.

98	75 c. rouge	20 »	3 »

III. - Livraison par exprès.

99	1 f. 45 vert	550 »	325 »

V. - Colis encombrant.

100	2 f. bleu	50 »	21 »

Voir à Algérie les timbres à ce type avec la surcharge CONTROLE REPARTITEUR (nºs 38 à 43) ou CONTROLE (nºs 62 et 63).

1936. – *Timbres de 1926 (type e) surchargés B. Dentelés.*

I. - Apport à la gare.

101	1 f. 00 *brun s. jaune* (48)	115 »
102	1 f. 50 *brun s. jaune* (50)	115 »
103	1 f. 65 *brun s. jaune* (51)	115 »

II. - Valeur déclarée.

104	50 c. *rouge* (56)	115 »

III. - Livraison par exprès.

105	1 f. 00 *vert* (66)	115 »
106	1 f. 50 *vert* (68)	115 »
107	1 f. 65 *vert* (69)	115 »

Les nºs 101 à 107, préparés en vue d'une augmentation des tarifs, n'ont pas été émis.

1937. – *Timbres de 1928-33 (type e pour les nºs 109, 114 et 116, type d pour les autres, surchargés. Dentelés.*

Les chiffres entre ( ) indiquent les prix auxquels étaient vendus ces timbres :

Les crochets [ ] encadrant la couleur d'un timbre indiquent que ce timbre n'a pas été émis sans surcharge.

I. - Apport à la gare.

108	1 f. 45 brun s. jaune (96)	7 »	7 »
109	2 F. 15 s. 1 f. 50 brun s. jaune (89)	45 »	30 »
110	2 f. 15 [brun s. jaune] (2 f. 75)	30 »	20 »
111	2 f. 35 brun s. jaune (3 f. 05) (97)	30 »	20 »

II - Valeur déclarée.

112	75 c. rouge (0 f. 95) (98)	20 »	17 »
	a. (Surch. renversée)	115 »	
	b. (Paire dont un sans surcharge)	280 »	
	c. (Double surcharge)	130 »	

III. - Livraison par exprès.

113	1 f. 45 vert (1 f. 85) (99)	20 »	15 50
114	2 F. 15 s. 1 f. 50 (2f.75) (93)	20 »	15 50
115	2 f. 15 [vert] (2 f. 75)	50 »	30 »
116	2 F. 35 s. 1 f. 65 (3 f. 05) (94)	300 »	100 »
117	2 f. 35 [vert] (3 f. 05)	20 »	15 50

V. - Colis encombrant.

118	2 f. bleu (2 f. 60) (100)	45 »	35 »

1937. – *Timbres de 1933-34 (type d) avec nouvelle valeur en surcharge. Dentelés.*

Les crochets [ ] encadrant la couleur d'un timbre indiquent que ce timbre n'a pas été émis sans surcharge.

I. - Apport à la gare.

119	1 F. 85 s. 1 f. 45 brun s. jaune (96)	17 »	10 »
120	2 F. 75 s. 2 f. 15 [brun s. jaune]	33 »	20 »
121	3 F. 05 s. 2 f. 35 brun s. jaune (97)	60 »	28 »

II - Valeur déclarée.

122	0 F. 95 s. 75 c. rouge (98)	50 »	25 »

III. - Livraison par exprès.

123	1 F. 85 s. 1 f. 45 vert (99)	80 »	45 »
124	2 F. 75 s. 2 f. 15 [vert]	80 »	45 »
125	3 F. 05 s. 2 f. 35 [vert]	80 »	45 »

V. - Colis encombrant.

126	2 F. 60 s. 2 f. bleu (100)	20 »	14 »

Le tarif des colis postaux ayant été augmenté, ces timbres, émis en remplacement des provisoires surchargés C, ont été remplacés à leur tour par les suivants avec surcharge D.

1938. – *Timbres de 1928-37 (type e pour les nos 129, 139 et 141, type d pour les autres) surchargés. Dentelés.*

Les chiffres entre ( ) indiquent les prix auxquels étaient vendus ces timbres provisoires.

Les crochets [ ] encadrant la couleur d'un timbre indiquent que ce timbre n'a pas été émis sans surcharge.

I. - Apport à la gare.

127	1 f. 45 brun s. jaune (2 f. 30) (96)	3 »	2 30
128	1 F. 85 s. 1 f. 45 brun s. jaune (2 f. 30) (119)	3 »	2 30
129	2 F. 15 s. 1 f. 50 brun s. jaune (3 f. 45) (89)	3 »	2 30
130	2 f. 15 [brun s. jaune] (3 f. 45)	45 »	35 »
131	2 F. 35 s. 1 f. 65 brun s. jaune (3 f. 85) (90)	750 »	550 »
132	2 f. 35 brun s. jaune (3 f. 85) (97)	3 »	2 30
133	2 F. 75 s. 2 f. 15 brun s. jaune (3 f. 45) (120)	3 »	2 30
134	3 F. 05 s. 2 f. 35 brun s. jaune (3 f.85) (121)	6 50	5 35

II. - Valeur déclarée.

135	75 c. rouge (1 f. 15) (98)	4 »	3 »
	a. (Paire dont un sans surcharge)	160 »	
136	0 F. 95 s. 75 c. rouge (1 f. 15) (122)	3 »	3 »

III. - Livraison par exprès.

137	1 f. 45 vert (2 f. 30) (99)	5 »	3 85
138	1 F. 85 s. 1 f.45 (2 f. 30) (123)	7 50	3 85
139	2 F. 15 s. 1 f. 50 (3 f. 45) (93)	325 »	370 »
140	2 f. 15 [vert] (3 f. 45)	20 »	18 50
141	2 F. 35 s. 1 f. 65 (3 f. 45) (94)	850 »	800 »
142	2 f. 35 [vert] (3 f. 85)	12 50	12 50
143	2 F. 75 s. 2 f. 15 (3 f. 45) (124)	4 50	3 »
144	3 F. 05 s. 2 f. 35 (3 f. 85) (125)	6 »	3 85

V - Colis encombrant.

145	2 f. bleu (3 f. 25) (100)	3 »	2 30
146	2 F. 60 s. 2 f. bleu (3 f. 25) (126)	3 »	2 30

1938. – *Timbres de 1933-34 (type d) avec nouvelle valeur en surcharge. Dentelés.*

Les crochets [ ] encadrant la couleur d'un timbre indiquent que ce timbre n'a pas été émis sans surcharge.

I. - Apport à la gare.

147	2 F. 30 s. 1 f. 45 brun s. jaune (96)	4 50	3 »
148	3 F. 45 s. 2 f. 15 [brun s. jaune]	4 50	3 »
149	3 F. 85 s. 2 f. 35 brun s. jaune (97)	4 50	3 »

II. - Valeur déclarée.

150	1 F. 15 s. 75 c. rouge (98)	2 »	1 55

III. - Livraison par exprès.

151	2 F. 30 s. 1 f. 45 vert (99)	4 50	3 »
152	3 F. 45 s. 2 f. 15 [vert]	4 50	3 »
153	3 F. 85 s. 2 f. 35 [vert]	4 50	3 »

V. - Colis encombrant.

154	3 F. 25 s. 2 f. bleu (100)	1 55	1 55

Cette série a été émise en remplacement des provisoires surchargés D.

1938. – *Type c. Typographie. Dentelés 11.*

155	10 c. noir	20 »	18 50
156	10 c. lilas-rose	100 »	100 »
	a. (Non dentelé)	110 »	110 »
157	15 c. outremer	100 »	100 »
	a. (Non dentelé)	110 »	110 »
158	20 c. lilas-brun	20 »	18 50

Percé en lignes.

159	**20 c. lilas-brun**	12 »	11 50	

1938. – ***Timbres de 1938 (surchargés D.) avec nouvelle surcharge 10 kg = 2 f. 30. Dentelés.***

160	**2 F. 30 s. 2 f. 15 vert (140)**	80 »	70 »	
161	**2 F. 30 s. 2 f. 35 vert (142)**	80 »	70 »	
162	**2 F. 30 s. 2 F. 75 s. 2 f. 15 (143)**	160 »	110 »	
163	**2 F. 30 s. 3 F. 05 s. 2 f. 35 (144)**	160 »	110 »	

A partir de 1939 et jusqu'en 1945, les cotes de la colonne de gauche concernent les timbres neufs avec gomme d'origine intacte et sans charnière, celles de la colonne centrale les timbres neufs avec charnière légère, celles de la colonne de droite les timbres oblitérés.

1939. – ***Type d. Valeur déclarée. Typographie. Dentelé 11.***

164	**1 f. 15 rouge**	3 »	1 55	1 55

1939. – ***Format 17,5 x 21. Typographie. Dentelés 11.***

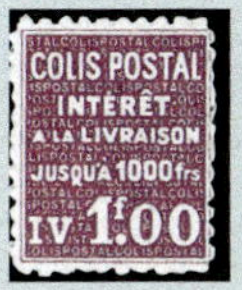

I. - Domicile.

165	**2 f. 40 brun s. jaune**	5 »	3 »	3 »
166	**3 f. 50 brun s. jaune**	5 »	3 »	3 »
167	**3 f. 80 brun s. jaune**	5 »	3 »	3 »

II. - Valeur déclarée.

168	**1 f. rouge**	5 »	3 »	2 30
169	**5 f. rouge**	5 »	3 »	3 »

III. Remboursement.

170	**2 f. 50 vert-jaune**	5 »	3 »	2 30
171	**7 f. 50 vert-jaune**	5 »	3 »	2 30

IV - Intérêt à la livraison.

172	**1 f. lilas**	17 »	10 75	7 65

V. - Colis encombrant.

173	**3 f. 20 bleu**	20 »	12 25	8 40

1941. – ***Taille-douce. Dentelés 12-12½.***

i

k

Viaduc de Garabit.
l

Viaduc de Fontpedrouse.
m

Lorsque le cartouche ne porte pas la valeur, nous indiquons entre ( ) le prix auquel était vendu le timbre.

*I. - Livraison à domicile (**i**).*

174	**(2 f. 70) brun**	10 75	6 10	5 35
175	**(3 f. 90) bleu**	10 75	6 10	5 35
176	**(4 f. 20) vert foncé**	10 75	6 10	5 35
	a. (Non dentelé)		100 »	

*II. - Valeur déclarée (**k**).*

177	**1 f. brun**	4 60	2 75	1 55
	a. (Valeur omise)		77 »	
	b. (Id. non dentelé)		155 »	
178	**5 f. carmin**	2 30	1 55	1 85
	a. (Valeur omise)		77 »	
	b. (Id. non dentelé)		155 »	

*III. - Remboursement (**l**).*

179	**2 f. 50 bleu**	2 30	1 55	1 85
	a. (Valeur omise)		77 »	
	b. (Double impression de la valeur dont une à l'envers)		115 »	
180	**7 f. 50 vert-jaune**	2 30	1 55	3 85
	a. (Non dentelé)		77 »	
	b. (Valeur omise)		385 »	

*IV. - Intérêt à la livraison (**m**).*

181	**1 f. violet**	1 55	1 »	1 10
	a. (Valeur omise)		140 »	
	b. (Id. non dentelé)		200 »	

*V. - Colis encombrant (**n**).*

n

182	**(3 f. 50) bleu**	15 50	12 25	11 50

Le cartouche des nos 174, 175, 176 et 182 ne porte pas l'indication de la valeur.

1941. – ***Types précédents avec valeur dans le cartouche. Taille-douce. Dentelés 12-12½.***

*I. - Livraison à domicile (**i**).*

183	**2 f. 70 brun**	12 25	7 65	6 10
184	**3 f. 90 bleu**	12 25	7 65	6 10
185	**4 f. 20 vert foncé**	12 25	7 65	6 10

*V. - Colis encombrant (**n**).*

186	**3 f. 50 bleu**	55 »	40 »	18 50

De nouvelles valeurs au type **i** ont paru en 1943 (n°s 208 à 210) et en 1944 (n°s 212 à 214). Le type **n** a également été repris en 1944 (n° 215).

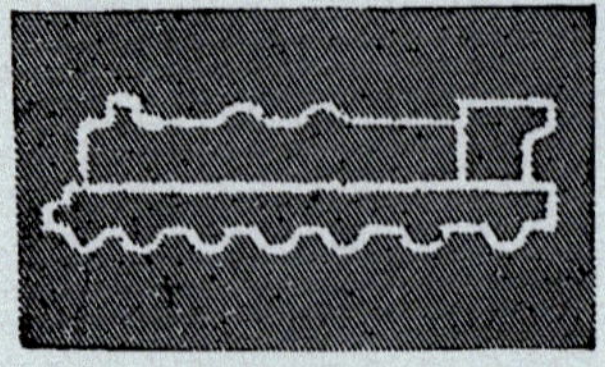

A

1942-43. – *Idem, avec chiffres de la valeur plus forts. Taille-douce. Filigrane A.. Dentelés 12½.*

au lieu de

II. - Valeur déclarée.

Avec filigrane A.

187A	**1 f. brun (k)**	10 75	7 65	7 65
188A	**5 f. carmin (k)**	21 50	15 50	12 25

Sans filigrane.

187B	**1 f. brun (k)**	2 30	1 55	1 55
188B	**5 f. carmin (k)**	7 65	6 10	6 10

III. - Remboursement.

Avec filigrane A.

189A	**2 f. 50 bleu (l)**	14 »	9 15	6 10
190A	**7 f. 50 vert-jaune (l)**	23 »	17 »	12 25

Sans filigrane.

189B	**2 f. 50 bleu (l)**	2 30	1 55	1 55
190B	**7 f. 50 vert-jaune (l)**	11 50	7 65	7 65

Un 20 f. rouge au type **l** a été émis en 1943 (n° 211).

1942. – *Surtaxe au profit du Comité national de solidarité des cheminots. Timbres de 1941-42 surchargés. Dentelés.*

Les lignes de la surcharge sont moins espacées sur les timbres du petit format.

I. - Livraison à domicile.

191	**+3 F s. 2 f. 70 brun (V) (183)**	20 »	15 »
192	**+3 F s. 3 f. 90 bleu (B) (184)**	20 »	15 »
193	**+3 F s. 4 f. 20 vert foncé (V) (185)**	20 »	15 »

II. - Valeur déclarée.

194	**+3 F s. 1 f. brun (Br) (187)**	21 »	15 »
195	**+3 F s. 5 f. carmin (V) (178)**	21 »	15 »

III. - Remboursement

196	**+3 F s. 2 f. 50 bleu (B) (189)**	21 »	15 »
197	**+3 F s. 7 f. 50 vert (V) (190)**	21 »	15 »

IV - Intérêt à la livraison.

198	**+3 F s. 1 f. violet (R) (181)**	23 »	15 »

V. - Colis encombrant.

199	**+3 F s. 3 f. 50 bleu (B) (186)**	23 »	15 »
	N°s 191 à 199 (9 val.)	**190 »**	**135 »**

Les n°s 194 à 198 existent sans point après N.

1943. – *Timbres de 1941 avec lettre F dans le cartouche réservé à la valeur. Taille-douce. Dentelés.*

*I. - Livraison à domicile (n°s 174 à 176, type **i**).*

200	**(3 f.) brun (B)**	4 60	3 »	3 »
201	**(4 f. 30) bleu (R)**	4 60	3 »	3 »
202	**(4 f. 70) vert foncé (R)**	4 60	3 »	3 »

*V. - Colis encombrant (n° 182, type **n**).*

203	**(3 f. 90) bleu (R)**	11 50	7 »	7 »

1943. – *Timbres de 1941 avec nouvelle valeur en surcharge. Dentelés.*

I. - Livraison à domicile.

o

204	**3 F 0 s. 2 f. 70 brun (B)**	7 65	6 10	4 60
205	**4 F 3 s. 3 f. 90 bleu (R)**	4 60	3 »	3 »
206	**4 F 7 s. 4 f. 20 vert foncé (R)**	5 35	3 85	3 »

V. - Colis encombrant.

207	**3 F 9 s. 3 f. 50 bleu (R)**	5 35	3 85	3 »

1943. – *Types de 1941 avec valeur dans le cartouche. Taille-douce. Dentelés.*

*I. - Livraison à domicile (***l***). Dentelé 12 x 12½.*

208	**3 f. 0 brun et bleu**	6 10	4 60	3 »
	a. brun-rouge et bleu	7 »	5 35	3 85
209	**4 f. 3 bleu et rouge**	15 50	10 75	6 10
210	**4 f. 7 vert foncé et rouge**	17 »	12 25	2 30

Ont reparu avec filigrane A en 1944 (Nos 212 à 214).

*III. - Remboursement (***l***). Filigrane A. Dentelé 12½ x 13.*

211	**20 f. rouge**	7 65	5 35	4 60

1944. – *Types de 1941 avec valeur dans le cartouche. Taille-douce. Filigrane A. Dentelés 12-12½.*

*I. - Livraison à domicile (***l***).*

212	**3 f. 0 brun et bleu**	22 »	14 »	10 »
213	**4 f. 3 bleu et rouge**	35 »	22 »	14 »
214	**4 f. 7 vert et rouge**	35 »	22 »	14 »

*V. - Colis encombrant (***n***).*

215	**3 f. 9 bleu et rouge**	22 »	14 »	12 25
	a. (Sans filigrane)		77 »	

1944-45. – *Taille-douce. Dentelés 12 x 12½.*

Barrage de Marèges.
p

Caténaires.
q

Ligne à haute tension.
r

*II. - Valeur déclarée (***p***).*

Avec filigrane A.

216A	**1 f. lie-de-vin**	8 40	6 10	6 10
217A	**5 f. carmin**	10 »	7 »	7 »

Sans filigrane.

216B	**1 f. lie-de-vin**	400 »	300 »
217B	**5 f. carmin**	400 »	300 »

*III. - Remboursement (***q***).*

Avec filigrane A.

218A	**2 f. 5 bleu**	10 »	7 »
219A	**7 f. 5 vert**	10 »	7 »

Sans filigrane.

218B	**2 f. 5 bleu**	400 »	300 »
219B	**7 f. 5 vert**	400 »	300 »

*IV. - Intérêt à la livraison (***r***).*

Avec filigrane A.

220A	**1 f. violet**	10 »	7 »

Sans filigrane.

220B	**1 f. violet**	400 »	300 »

1945. – *Timbres de 1941 avec lettre G dans le cartouche réservé à la valeur. Dentelés.*

*I. - Livraison à domicile (***l***).*

Avec filigrane A.

221A	**(5 f.) brun**	23 »	18 50	20 »
222A	**(7 f. 2) bleu (Vte)**	20 »	14 »	14 »
223A	**(7 f. 8) vert foncé (Vte)**	20 »	14 »	14 »

Sans filigrane.

221B	**(5 f.) brun**	7 65	6 10	6 10
222B	**(7 f. 2) bleu (Vte)**	7 65	6 10	6 10
223B	**(7 f. 8) vert foncé (Vte)**	7 65	6 10	6 10

*V. - Colis encombrant (***n***).*

224	**(6 f. 6) bleu (Vte)**	9 15	7 »	7 »

L'ancien no 225 est catalogué sous le no 187B.

1945. – *Timbres de 1943 avec nouvelle valeur en surcharge. Dentelés.*

I. - Livraison à domicile.

Avec filigrane A.

226A	**5 F. 0 s. 3 f. 0**	9 15	7 »	7 »
227A	**7 F. 2 s. 4 f. 3**	9 15	7 »	7 »
228A	**7 F. 8 s. 4 f. 7**	9 15	7 »	7 »

Sans filigrane.

226B	**5 F. 0 s. 3 f. 0**	65 »	46 »
227B	**7 F. 2 s. 4 f. 3**	65 »	46 »
228B	**7 F. 8 s. 4 f. 7**	65 »	46 »

V. - Colis encombrant.

Avec filigrane A.

229A	**6 F. 6 s. 3 f. 9**	11 50	7 65

Sans filigrane.

229B	**6 F. 6 s. 3 f. 9**	65 »	46 »

1945. – ***Taille-douce. Dentelés 12 x 12½.***

s

t

*I. - Livraison à domicile (***s***).*

Avec filigrane A.

230A	**5 f. lie-de-vin et noir**	23 »	17 »
231A	**7 f. 2 bleu et violet**	23 »	17 »
232A	**7 f. 8 vert et violet**	23 »	17 »

Sans filigrane.

230B	**5 f. lie-de-vin et noir**	12 25	7 65
231B	**7 f. 2 bleu et violet**	46 »	30 »
232B	**7 f. 8 vert et violet**	30 »	20 »

*V. - Colis encombrant (***t***).*

Avec filigrane A.

233	**6 f. 6 outremer et violet**	9 15	7 »

TIMBRES POUR COLIS POSTAUX ET AUTRES (DE 0 À 50 KILOS)

Dits Timbres pour "Petits Colis".

Émis par la S.N.C.F., ces timbres n'ont pas été vendus à l'état neuf. Leur dentelure est de qualité médiocre.

1944-47. – ***Lithographié. Filigrane A. Dentelés 12½.***

1	**1 f. vert**	1 50
2	**2 f. violet**	1 85
3	**3 f. gris**	1 85
3A	**4 f. gris-noir**	2 50

Taille-douce. Format 18,5 x 22.

4	**5 f. bleu**	2 30
4A	**5 f. outremer**	1 50
5	**6 f. lilas-rose**	1 50
6	**7 f. violet**	3 35
7	**7 f. mauve**	20 »
8	**8 f. vert-olive**	2 50
9	**9 f. bleu-vert**	5 35
10	**10 f. rose**	1 70
11	**20 f. vert-jaune**	1 50
	a. (Non dentelé, sans filigrane)	230 »
12	**30 f. violet-rouge**	1 50
13	**30 f. gris**	1 50
14	**40 f. ocre**	1 50
15	**50 f. orange**	1 40
16	**60 f. lilas-rose**	1 50
17	**70 f. violet**	28 »
18	**70 f. mauve**	7 65
19	**80 f. olive**	2 »
20	**90 f. bleu-vert**	29 »
21	**90 f. turquoise**	2 45
22	**100 f. gris-brun**	1 50
23	**100 f. jaune clair**	2 30
23A	**100 f. rouge**	2 »
24	**200 f. vert-jaune**	2 »
25	**500 f. jaune-orange**	2 30
26	**1000 f. jaune**	16 »
	Nos 1 à 26 (29 val.)	150 »

Seul le 1er tirage des nos 1, 2, 4, 10, 11, 15 et 22 est sans filigrane.

1948-54. – ***Type de 1944-47. Taille-douce. Filigrane A. Dentelés 13 x 13½.***

27	**9 f. bleu clair**	17 »
28	**10 f. vert**	10 »
29	**20 f. lilas**	17 »
30	**50 f. bleu**	11 »
	Nos 27 à 30 (4 val.)	55 »

Des séries des nos 1 à 30 existent neuves.
Valeur : 3 050 »

1960. – ***Taille-douce. Filigrane A. Dentelés 13.***

31	**5 c. orange**	2 »
32	**10 c. rouge**	10 »
33	**20 c. rouge**	4 »
34	**30 c. rouge**	4 »
35	**40 c. rouge**	9 »
36	**50 c. rouge**	4 50
37	**60 c. rouge**	4 50
38	**70 c. rouge**	4 50
39	**80 c. rouge**	4 50
40	**90 c. rouge**	4 50
41	**1 f. bleu**	2 50
42	**2 f. bleu**	2 »
43	**3 f. bleu**	2 »
44	**4 f. bleu**	2 »
45	**5 f. bleu**	2 »
46	**10 f. jaune**	3 »
47	**20 f. vert**	20 »
	Nos 31 à 47 (17 val.)	85 »

Des séries des nos 31 à 47 existent neuves.
Valeur : 500 »
Ces timbres existent avec surcharge SPECIMEN.
La série 250 »

Seul le dernier tirage (sur papier très blanc) est sans filigrane. Il comporte toute la série sauf les nos 31, 32, 36 et 37.

COLIS POSTAUX D'ALSACE-LORRAINE

(Timbres-Pré-Perforés)

Entre les deux guerres mondiales, le Service des Colis-Postaux a été directement assuré, en Alsace-Lorraine, par la Poste.

L'affranchissement consistait en timbres-poste apposés sur des récépissés. Les timbres des valeurs faciales supérieures à 2 F devaient réglementairement posséder une perforation centrale.

Cette dernière fut souvent obtenue, après affranchissement et oblitération, par un coup de poinçon ou d'emporte-pièce traversant le récépissé. Mais dans certains bureaux, les fortes valeurs étaient vendues pré-perforées aux usagers. Les perforations étaient de forme variable, mais le plus souvent circulaire.

Il est actuellement connu, sur récépissé, les pré-perforés suivants : Merson : nos 123, 206, 207 et 240 et Monuments : nos 259, 260 et 261. D'autres valeurs ont pu être pré-perforées occasionnellement. Par suite d'une mauvaise application des directives postales, le 2 F Merson no 145 fut pré-perforé en 1927 par le Bureau de Strasbourg-Tanneries.

Valeur sur récépissé.

1919-31. – ***Type Merson. Dentelés.***

1	**3 f. violet et bleu (206)**	45 »
2	**3 f. lilas et carmin (240)**	95 »
3	**5 f. bleu et chamois (123)**	30 »
4	**10 f. vert et rouge (207)**	77 »

Erreur.

5	**2 f. orange et vert-bleu (145)**	340 »

1929-31. – ***Sites et Monuments. Dentelés.***

6	**3 f. ardoise (259)**	50 »
7	**5 f. brun (260)**	23 »
8	**10 f. bleu (261)**	77 »

Timbres de Port-payé d'Entreprises.

Au début des années 30, certaines entreprises, grandes utilisatrices du service des colis-postaux d'Alsace-Lorraine, furent autorisées à remplacer, sur leurs bulletins d'expédition, les timbres-poste normaux par une étiquette numérotée portant la mention "P.P." et l'indication de chaque entreprise expéditrice (une cinquantaine de connues). Ces étiquettes étaient imprimées en noir pour les colis normaux et en rouge pour les envois de colis contre remboursement.

(Val. des timbres de port-payé d'entreprise, sur bull. d'expéd. : Noirs, à partir de 61 » Rouges, à partir de 140 »).

TIMBRES DES COURS D'INSTRUCTION

En 1911, un arrêté du 9 mai publié au Bulletin mensuel des postes et des Télégraphes daté du 15 octobre institue et organise des ***cours d'instruction*** pour les surnuméraires. Parmi le matériel dont doivent être pourvues les salles de cours, on relève notamment des timbres-poste nécessaires aux exercices pratiques. Pour leur ôter toute valeur fiduciaire, ces timbres-poste sont préalablement annulés d'une mention spécifique décrite ci-après.

Les cotes de la colonne de gauche concernent les timbres neufs avec gomme d'origine intacte et sans charnière, celles de la colonne de droite, les timbres avec charnière légère. Les timbres oblitérés proprement avec un cachet de COURS PRATIQUES valent plus que les timbres avec charnière.

Emission de 1911

Surcharge ANNULE en noir, apposée en typographie "à plat" sur toutes les valeurs ayant cours à l'époque. Cette surcharge est dite "basse" puisque l'écart entre le bas de la surcharge et celui du timbre est généralement compris entre 8 et 9 millimètres.

ANNULÉ

Surcharge A

Une surcharge similaire de couleur violette sera également utilisée individuellement et manuellement sur les timbres de carnets et les entiers.

ANNULÉ

Surcharge B

Emission de 1923

La même surcharge A est réutilisée pour un nouveau tirage sur des timbres re-émis. Cette surcharge est dite "haute" car l'écart entre le bas de la surcharge et celui du timbre est plus constant à 11 millimètres. Pour les timbres de grand format (type Merson) la surcharge est répétée 2 fois dans le sens horizontal.

Emission de 1925

La précédente mention est abandonnée et fait place à la surcharge SPECIMEN dont on connaît 2 types selon qu'il s'agisse de timbre au petit format (Surcharge C) ou au grand format (Surcharge D).

SPÉCIMEN
Surcharge C

Spécimen
Surcharge D

Variétés

Toutes les surcharges (notamment les ANNULE) comportent de nombreuses variétés de positionnement (décalages importants) ou d'impressions multiples (surcharges doubles ou triples). Au regard des abus possibles, nous recommandons aux collectionneurs de ne leur consentir qu'une faible plus-value sur la cote.

La surcharge C comporte une variété constante avec une fréquence de deux par feuille : **absence d'accent**. Le prix est de 2 fois la cote du timbre sans variété correspondant.

Type Blanc

107-CI 1 1 c. gris (Surcharge A) (Type I) tirage de 1911 40 » 27 »
107a-CI 2 1 c. ardoise (Surcharge A) (Type I) tirage de 1923 20 » 15 »
107a-CI 3 1 c. ardoise (Surcharge C) (Type I) tirage de 1925 55 » 40 »
157-CI 4 ½ sur 1 c. ardoise (Surcharge C) (Type I) tirage de 1925 1 100 » 770 »

108-CI 1 2 c. brun-lilas (Surcharge A) (Type I) tirage de 1911 25 » 18 »
108a-CI 2 2 c. brun-lilas foncé Type I Surcharge A tirage de 1923 20 » 15 »
108-CI 3 2 c. brun-lilas (Surcharge C) (Type II) 60 » 42 »

109-CI 1 3 c. orange (Surcharge A) (Type I) tirage de 1911 28 » 20 »
109a-CI 2 3 c. rouge-orange Type I Surcharge A tirage de 1923 20 » 15 »
109-CI 3 3 c. orange (Surcharge C) (Type I) 60 » 42 »
111-CI 1 5 c. vert (Surcharge C) (Type II A) 60 » 42 »

Type Merson

119-CI 1 40 c. rouge et bleu (Surcharge A) tirage de 1911 1 600 » 1 050 »
119-CI 2 40 c. rouge et bleu (Deux surcharges A) tirage de 1923 60 » 42 »

143-CI 1 45 c. vert et bleu (Surcharge A) tirage de 1911 1 600 » 1 050 »
143-CI 2 45 c. vert et bleu (Deux surcharges A) tirage de 1923 160 » 112 »

120-CI 1 50 c. brun et gris (Surcharge A) tirage de 1911 1 600 » 1 050 »

144-CI 1 60 c. violet et bleu (Deux surcharges A) tirage de 1923 20 » 14 »

121-CI 1 1 f. lie-de-vin et olive (Surcharge A) tirage de 1911 — 1 600 » 1 050 »

121-CI 2 1 f. lie-de-vin et olive (Deux surcharges A) tirage de 1923 — 140 » 98 »

122-CI 1 2 f. violet et jaune (Surcharge A) tirage de 1911 — 3 400 » 2 380 »

145-CI 1 2 f. orange et vert-bleu (Deux surcharges A) tirage de 1923 — 200 » 140 »

145-CI 2 2 f. orange et vert-bleu (Surcharge D) — 220 » 154 »

206-CI 1 3 f. violet et bleu (Surcharge D) — 220 » 140 »

123-CI 1 5 f. bleu et chamois (Surcharge A) tirage de 1911 — 1 600 » 1 100 »

123-CI 2 5 f. bleu et chamois (Deux surcharges A) tirage de 1923 — 500 » 350 »

123-CI 3 5 f. bleu et chamois (Surcharge D) — 400 » 275 »

Type Semeuse Lignée

130-CI 1 15 c. vert-olive (Surcharge A) (Type IV) (feuille de 1906) tirage de 1911 — 22 » 15 »

130-CI 2 15 c. vert-olive (Surcharge A) (Type IV) (feuille de 1923) tirage de 1923 — 22 » 15 »

161-CI 2 50 c. bleu (Surcharge A) tirage de 1923 — 100 » 70 »

198-CI 2 50 c. vert-olive (Surcharge C) (Type I) — 37 » 25 »

200-CI 1 60 c. violet (Surcharge C) — 37 » 25 »

203-CI 1 80 c. rouge (Surcharge C) — 70 » 50 »

Type Semeuse Fond plein

137-CI 1 5 c. vert foncé (Surcharge A) (Type I) tirage de 1911 — 70 » 46 »

137-CI 2 5 c. vert foncé (Surcharge B) (Type II A) — 260 » 182 »

158-CI 1 5 c. orange (Surcharge A) (Type I) tirage de 1911 — 9 » 6 »

138-CI 1 10 c. rouge (Surcharge A) (Type IA) tirage de 1911 — 80 » 55 »

138-CI 2 10 c. rouge (Surcharge B) (Type IC) — 260 » 182 »

159-CI 1 10 c. vert (Surcharge A) (Type IA) tirage de 1911 — 12 » 8 »

159-CI 2 10 c. vert (Surcharge A) (Type IC) tirage de 1923 — 100 » 65 »

159-CI 3 10 c. vert (Surcharge C) (Type III) — 22 » 15 »

189-CI 1 15 c. brun-lilas (Surcharge C) (Type I) 36 » 24 »

139a-CI 1 20 c. brun-lilas (Surcharge A) (Type I) tirage de 1911 22 » 14 »
139-CI 2 20 c. brun-lilas (Surcharge A) (Type III) tirage de 1923 22 » 14 »
139-CI 3 20 c. brun-lilas (Surcharge C) (Type III) 32 » 22 »

140a-CI 1 25 c. bleu foncé (Surcharge A) (Type IA) tirage de 1911 20 » 13 »
140a-CI 2 25 c. bleu clair (Surcharge A) (Type IA) tirage de 1923 15 » 9 »
140-CI 3 25 c. bleu (Surcharge A) (Type II de carnet) tirage de 1923 220 » 154 »
140-CI 4 25 c. bleu (Surcharge C) (Type IIB) 30 » 20 »

141-CI 1 30 c. orange (Surcharge A) tirage de 1911 76 » 55 »
160-CI 1 30 c. rouge (Surcharge A) tirage de 1923 16 » 11 »

192-CI 30 c. bleu (Surcharge C) (Type IIA) 20 » 13 »
192-CI 30 c. bleu (Surcharge C) (Type IIB de carnet) 130 » 91 »

142a-CI 1 35 c. violet (Surcharge A) (Type I) tirage de 1911 40 » 28 »
142-CI 1 35 c. violet foncé (Surcharge A) (Type I) tirage de 1923 70 » 49 »
142-CI 2 35 c. violet (Surcharge C) (Type I) 80 » 56 »

193-CI 1 40 c. brun olive (Surcharge C) (Type I) 26 » 16 »
195-CI 1 1 f. 05 vermillon (Surcharge C) 34 » 23 »

Type Pasteur

170-CI 1 10 c. vert (Surcharge C) 330 » 220 »
175-CI 1 45 c. rouge (Surcharge C) 37 » 25 »
177-CI 1 75 c. bleu (Surcharge C) 37 » 25 »
179-CI 1 1 f. bleu (Surcharge C) 37 » 25 »

TAXE

10-CI 1 1 c. noir (Surcharge A) 45 » 30 »
28-CI 1 5 c. bleu (Surcharge A) 45 » 30 »
28-CI 2 5 c. bleu (Surcharge C) 45 » 30 »

29-CI 1 10 c. brun (Surcharge A) 45 » 30 »
29-CI 2 10 c. brun (Surcharge C) 45 » 30 »
31-CI 1 20 c. olive (Surcharge A) 45 » 30 »
31-CI 2 20 c. olive (Surcharge C) 45 » 30 »

32-CI 1 25 c. rose (Surcharge A) 45 » 30 »
33-CI 1 30 c. rouge carminé (Surcharge A) 45 » 30 »
33-CI 2 30 c. rouge carminé (Surcharge C) 45 » 30 »
35-CI 1 40 c. rose (Surcharge C) 45 » 30 »

37-CI 1 50 c. lilas (Surcharge A) 45 » 30 »
37-CI 2 50 c. lilas (Surcharge C) 45 » 30 »
40-CI 1 1 f. lilas-brun sur paille (Surcharge A) 90 » 60 »
40-CI 2 1 f. lilas-brun sur paille (Surcharge C) 45 » 30 »

41-CI 1	**2 f. rouge-orange (Surcharge A)**	800	»	560	»

Il existe, pour tous les taxes, deux tirages avec la surcharge A : l'un en 1911, l'autre en 1923. Les surcharges et les timbres support étant identiques, seule la hauteur de la surcharge permet de les distinguer, ce qui est parfois difficile. Nous n'avons pas jugé utile de leur attribuer une numérotation différente et nous laissons le soin aux collectionneurs de juger.

SURCHARGE LOCALE de CAEN

Surcharge réalisée localement sur des timbres au type blanc (N° 109a-CI 2) par l'ajout de la mention CH-T (CHiffre-Taxe) en violet et d'une nouvelle valeur.

CH-T

50

Surcharge E

109a-CI 4	"5" sur 3 c. orange type I	200	»	140	»
109a-CI 5	"10" sur 3 c. orange type I	200	»	140	»
109a-CI 6	"30" sur 3 c. orange type I	200	»	140	»
109a-CI 7	"50" sur 3 c. orange type I	200	»	140	»
109a-CI 8	"60" sur 3 c. orange type I	200	»	140	»
109a-CI 9	"1 F" sur 3 c. orange type I	200	»	140	»
109a-CI 10	"2 F" sur 3 c. orange type I	200	»	140	»

RECOUVREMENTS

43-CI 1	**1 c. olive (Surcharge A)**	45	»	30	»
43-CI 2	**1 c. olive (Surcharge C)**	90	»	60	»
44-CI 1	**10 c. violet (Surcharge A)**	45	»	30	»
44-CI 2	**10 c. violet (Surcharge C)**	90	»	60	»

46-CI 1	**30 c. bistre (Surcharge A)**	45	»	30	»
46-CI 2	**30 c. bistre (Surcharge C)**	90	»	60	»
47-CI 1	**50 c. rouge (Surcharge A)**	700	»	460	»
48-CI 1	**60 c. rouge (Surcharge C)**	90	»	60	»

Même remarque que pour les timbres TAXE.

PREOBLITERES

41-CI 1	**5 c. vert (Surcharge C) (Type IIA)**	485	»	325	»
44-CI 1	**45 c. vert et bleu (Surcharge A) tirage de 1923**	435	»	290	»
45-CI 1	**15 c. vert type IV (Surcharge A) tirage de 1923**	125	»	85	»

50-CI 1	**5 c. orange (Surcharge A) (Type I) tirage de 1923**	150	»	105	»
51-CI 1	**10 c. vert (Surcharge C) (Type III)**	400	»	270	»
53-CI 1	**15 c. brun (Surcharge C) (Type II)**	400	»	270	»

54-CI 1	**20 c. lilas-brun (Surcharge A) (Type I) tirage de 1923**	145	»	95	»
54-CI 2	**20 c. lilas-brun (Surcharge C) (Type III)**	400	»	270	»
58-CI 1	**30 c. rouge (Surcharge A) tirage de 1923**	320	»	200	»
59-CI 1	**30 c. rose (Surcharge C) (Type I)**	400	»	270	»

62-CI 1	**35 c. violet (Surcharge A) (Type I) tirage de 1923**	300	»	190	»
62-CI 2	**35 c. violet (Surcharge C) (Type I)**	400	»	270	»
67-CI 1	**45 c. rouge (Surcharge C)**	400	»	270	»
68-CI 1	**50 c. bleu (Surcharge C)**	400	»	270	»

Pour les carnets et les entiers postaux utilisés dans les cours d'instruction on se reportera aux rubriques correspondantes.

Attention : il existe de nombreuses surcharges ANNULÉ SPÉCIMEN avec différentes typographies et couleurs non-destinées aux Cours d'Instruction. Les plus connues sont répertoriées à la rubrique "Timbres-Spécimens" du présent catalogue.

TIMBRES DE DISTRIBUTEURS

En 1969, l'Administration postale a mis en service à titre expérimental, une machine automatique avec laquelle il était possible d'obtenir, entre autres, des vignettes d'affranchissement. Ces dernières, imprimées par le distributeur, étaient traitées comme des timbres-poste ordinaires, donc régulièrement oblitérées. L'appareil, installé dans le centre commercial de MONTGERON (91230 Essonne), a fonctionné pendant une quinzaine de mois.

1969. - *Timbre de distributeur. Impression rouge. Papier blanc. Gommé.*

A droite, valeur dans un cadre, avec indicatif BAA-001 (Bureau Affranchissement Automatique).

A gauche, origine 91 MONTGERON 1 ESSONNE dans un cercle.

1 –.–	*(Valeur selon affranchissement usuel - 0,10 à 0,50, particulièrement)*	500 »
	(Sur lettre)	350 »
1A –.–	*(Trait d'union à mi-hauteur)*	1 850 »
	(Sur lettre)	1 200 »

Type 1

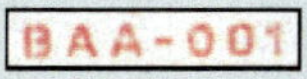

Type 1A

1969. -

A droite, valeur dans un cadre, avec indicatif SA 0001 (Service Automatique).

A gauche, origine 91 MONTGERON AUT. 1 ESSONNE sur trois lignes.

2 –.–	*(Valeur selon affranchissement usuel 0,10 à 0,50, particulièrement)*	350 »
	(Sur lettre)	310 »
	2,90 (Sur lettre recommandée)	1 400 »

2a	000 (pour démonstration)	300 »

Cette dernière vignette existe en papier rose.

1969. - *Idem. Papier jaunâtre.*

Le point entre AUT et 1 est placé prés du .1

2A –.–	*(Valeur selon affranchissement usuel - 0,10 à 0,50, particulièrement)*	200 »
	(Sur lettre)	150 »
2Aa	000 (pour démonstration)	100 »

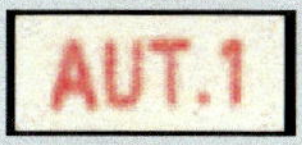

Type 2

Type 2A

NOTE. - Le n° 1 a été délivré en mai et juin 1969, le n° 2, dès juillet 1969, et le n° 2A d'avril 1970 jusqu'à la fin de l'exploitation (juillet 1970).

Dès 1981, de nouveaux distributeurs (9 maquettes non définitives) ont été mis en service. Ces appareils effectuent en totalité l'impression des timbres, sur papier adhésif, avec, à la demande de l'usager, l'une des 40 valeurs tarifaires du régime intérieur en vigueur (LETTRES ET PLIS NON URGENTS - PNU - PAQUETS POSTE ORDINAIRES et URGENTS), à l'exclusion des envois recommandés.

1981. - *Timbres de distributeurs. Papier adhésif. Impression lilas-rose, carmin, rouge ou rouge-orange. Valeur selon tarif en vigueur. Avec inscriptions LS ou LSA (Libre Service Affranchissement), n° de l'appareil et code comptable du bureau d'exploitation (les valeurs indiquées s'entendent pour l'unité inférieure de chaque tarif concerné).*

Type 1. Distributeur C.G.A. (LSA 04)
(sans support papier).

Type 2. Distributeur EMD-CAMP (LS 1, 2, 3)
(sans support papier).

Type 3. Distributeur C.G.A. (PNU sans point)
(LSA 05 et 06) (avec support papier).

Type 4. Distributeur CROUZET (LS 07, 08, 09)
(sans trait d'union entre LS 07 et le n° comptable)
(avec support papier).

Type 4a. Distributeur CROUZET (LS 07)
(avec trait d'union entre LS 07 et le n° comptable)
(avec support papier).

—

P.N.U. ou PNU = Pli non urgent.
LETTRE = Courrier rapide.
– = Paquet poste ordinaire.
URGENT = Paquet poste urgent.

—

Dès 1988,
– = Paquet poste départemental.

Les cotes indiquées concernent les vignettes neuves les plus courantes. Les supports papier existent en blanc ou en jaune.

—

Type 1. LSA 04 - 75649 (rue Molière, PARIS).

3 1 f. 20 (P.N.U.) 75 »
4 1 f. 40 (LETTRE) 75 »
a. sans indication LETTRE 200 »
5 2 f. 20 (–) 90 »
6 3 f. 50 (URGENT) 90 »

Type 2. LS 1 PC - 75652 (bd du Montparnasse, PARIS)
LS 2 PC - 93048 (MONTREUIL Ppal)
LS 3 PC - 75508 (rue La Boétie, PARIS)

7 1 f. 20 (P.N.U.) 65 »
8 1 f. 40 (LETTRE) 65 »
9 2 f. 20 (–) 75 »
10 3 f. 50 (URGENT) 75 »
7a à 10a (LS1) 4 val. 540 »
7b à 10b (LS2) 4 val. 310 »

Type 3. LSA 05 - 75724 (bd Bonne-Nouvelle, PARIS)
LSA 06 - 94022 (CHOISY-LE-ROI)

11 1 f. 20 (P.N.U.) 65 »
12 1 f. 40 (LETTRE) 65 »
13 2 f. 20 (–) 75 »
14 3 f. 50 (URGENT) 75 »
11a à 14a (LSA 06) 4 val. 500 »

Type 4. LS 07 - 92050 (NANTERRE R.P.)
LS 08 - 75628 (rue des Ecoles, PARIS)
LS 09 - 75513 (avenue d'Italie, PARIS)

15 1 f. 20 (P.N.U.) 65 »
16 1 f. 40 (LETTRE) 65 »
17 2 f. 20 (–) 65 »
18 3 f. 50 (URGENT) 65 »
15a à 18a (LS 07) 4 val. 460 »
15b à 18b (LS 08) 4 val. 310 »

1981. - *Idem. Tarif postal au 01.09.81.*

Type 1. LSA 04 - 75747 (avenue du Général Leclerc, PARIS)

19 1 f. 40 (P.N.U.) 45 »
20 1 f. 60 (LETTRE) 45 »
21 2 f. 60 (–) 45 »
22 4 f. (URGENT) 45 »

Type 2. LS 1 PC - 75652 (bd du Montparnasse, PARIS)
LS 2 PC - 93048 (MONTREUIL Ppal)
LS 3 PC - 75508 (rue La Boétie, PARIS)

23 1 f. 40 (P.N.U.) 65 »
24 1 f. 60 (LETTRE) 65 »
25 2 f. 60 (–) 65 »
26 4 f. (URGENT) 65 »
23a à 26a (LS 1) 4 val. 700 »
23b à 26b (LS 2) 4 val. 310 »

Type 3. LSA 05 - 75724 (bd Bonne-Nouvelle, PARIS)
LSA 06 - 92184 (NEUILLY-SABLONS)

27 1 f. 40 (P.N.U.) 25 »
28 1 f. 60 (LETTRE) 25 »
29 2 f. 60 (–) 25 »
30 4 f. (URGENT) 25 »
27a à 30a (LSA 06) 160 »

Type 4. LS 07 - 92962 (BOULOGNE-BILLANCOURT)
LS 08 - 75628 (rue des Ecoles, PARIS)
LS 09 - 75513 (avenue d'Italie, PARIS)

31 1 f. 40 (P.N.U.) 25 »
32 1 f. 60 (LETTRE) 25 »
33 2 f. 60 (–) 25 »
34 4 f. (URGENT) 25 »

1982. - *Idem. Tarif postal au 01.06.82.*

Type 2. LS 3 PC - 75508 (rue La Boétie, PARIS)

35 1 f. 60 (P.N.U.) 17 50
36 1 f. 80 (LETTRE) 17 50
37 2 f. 90 (–) 17 50
38 4 f. 50 (URGENT) 17 50

Type 3. LSA 05 - 75724 (bd Bonne Nouvelle, PARIS)
LSA 06 - 92184 (NEUILLY-SABLONS)
LSA 06 - 75747 (av. du Général Leclerc, PARIS)

39 1 f. 60 (P.N.U.) 17 50
40 1 f. 80 (LETTRE) 17 50
41 2 f. 90 (–) 17 50
42 4 f. 50 (URGENT) 17 50
39a à 42a (LSA 05) 4 val. 100 »

Type 4. LS 07 - 92962 (BOULOGNE-BILLANCOURT)
LS 08 - 75628 (rue des Ecoles, PARIS)
LS 09 - 75513 (avenue d'Italie, PARIS)

43	1 f. 60 (P.N.U.)	15 »
44	1 f. 80 (LETTRE)	15 »
45	2 f. 90 (–)	15 »
46	4 f. 50 (URGENT)	15 »
43a à 46a	(LS 07) 4 val.	65 »

Type 4a. LS 07 - 75747 (avenue du Général Leclerc, PARIS)

47	1 f. 60 (P.N.U.)	17 50
48	1 f. 80 (LETTRE)	17 50
49	2 f. 90 (–)	25 »
50	4 f.50 (URGENT)	25 »

1982. - *Idem. Philexfrance 1982. Exposition philatélique internationale, à Paris.*

Type 1. PHILEXFRANCE 1982 (texte 36 mm).

51	1 f. 60 (P.N.U.)	25 »
52	1 f. 80 (LETTRE)	25 »
53	2 f. 90 (–)	32 50
54	4 f. 50 (URGENT)	32 50

Type 2. PHILEXFRANCE 1982 (texte 39 mm).

55	1 f. 60 (P.N.U.)	20 »
56	1 f. 80 (LETTRE)	20 »
57	2 f. 90 (–)	25 »
58	4 f. 50 (URGENT)	25 »

1982. - *Idem. SICOB 1982.*

59	1 f. 60 (P.N.U.)	20 »
60	1 f. 80 (LETTRE)	20 »
61	2 f. 90 (–)	25 »
62	4 f. 50 (URGENT)	25 »

NOTE. - Majoration 100 % pour timbres avec impression parfaitement lisible. En effet, cette impression a tendance à disparaître au contact de certaines matières (cristal ou plastique) ou à une exposition prolongée à la lumière. Conservation difficile.

1983. - *Idem. Tarif postal au 01.06.83.*

Type 2. LS 3 PC - 75508 (rue La Boétie, PARIS)

63	2 f. (LETTRE)	8 50
64	3 f. 10 (–)	8 50
65	4 f. 90 (URGENT)	8 50

Type 4. LS 09 - 75513 (avenue d'Italie, PARIS)

66	2 f. (LETTRE)	8 50
67	3 f. 10 (–)	8 50
68	4 f. 90 (URGENT)	8 50

Type 4a. LS 07 - 75747 (avenue du Général Leclerc, PARIS)

69	2 f. (LETTRE)	8 50
70	3 f. 10 (–)	8 50
71	4 f. 90 (URGENT)	8 50

1983. - *Idem. Bourg-en-Bresse (28 au 30.10). Congrès du Parti socialiste. LSO 01053.*

72	1 f. 60 (P.N.U.)	115 »
73	2 f. (LETTRE)	115 »
74	3 f. 10 (–)	115 »
75	4 f. 90 (URGENT)	115 »

1984. - *Idem. Valence : 10e exposition du Cercle Philatélique Crouzet (21 et 22.01) et Foire-Exposition (27.04-06.05). LSO 26362.*

76	1 f. 60 (P.N.U.)	25 »
77	2 f. (LETTRE)	25 »
78	3 f. 10 (–)	25 »
79	4 f. 90 (URGENT)	25 »

1984. - *Idem. Tarif postal au 01.07.84.*

Type 4. LS 09 - 75513 (avenue d'Italie, PARIS)

80	1 f. 70 (P.N.U.)	8 50
81	2 f. 10 (LETTRE)	8 50
82	3 f. 20 (–)	8 50
83	5 f. (URGENT)	8 50

Type 4a. LS 07 - 75747 (avenue du Général Leclerc, PARIS)

84	1 f. 70 (P.N.U.)	8 50
85	2 f. 10 (LETTRE)	8 50
86	3 f. 20 (–)	8 50
87	5 f. (URGENT)	8 50

NOTE. - Les timbres de distributeurs avec mention SPECIMEN proviennent d'appareils placés en démonstration dans certaines expositions. Exemples : LS 1, à la Foire internationale de NANCY (juin 1981), LS 07, au SICOB, Paris - La Défense (octobre 1981).

Les vignettes portant les mentions. TSTPTT, JOUR, PERP, etc. n'ont aucune valeur fiducaire. Il s'agit de vignettes de service des P.T.T.

Fonctionnement des appareils :

LS 1	Du 04. 02.81 au 23.09.81	Bd de Montparnasse, PARIS 52 (14e arr.)
LS 2	Du 18.02.81 au 07.05.82	MONTREUIL PRINCIPAL (93)
LS3	Du 26.01.81 à 11-1983	Rue La Boétie, PARIS 8 (8e arrondissement)

LSA 04	Du 13.01.81 au 31.07.81	Rue Molière, PARIS 49 (1er arrondissement)
	Du 17.11.81 à février 82	Avenue du Général Leclerc, PARIS (14e arr.)
LSA 05	Du 06.03.81 au 07.06.82	Bd Bonne-Nouvelle, PARIS 124 (10e arr.)

NOTE. - Cet appareil a fonctionné avec la référence LSA 06, du 09.06.82 à février 1983, avenue du Général Leclerc, PARIS 147 (14e arr.).

LSA 06	Du 26.02.81 au 06.06.81	CHOISY-LE-ROI (94)
	Du 12.11.81 au 17.12.82 (92)	NEUILLY-SABLONS

NOTE. - Pendant un court laps de temps (fin avril 82), le distributeur de Neuilly-Sablons a délivré, par erreur, des étiquettes portant la référence

LSA 05	- 75724 (Paris Bonne-Nouvelle).	
LS 07	Du 29.04.81 au 18.09.81	NANTERRE R.P. (92)
	Du 17.03.82 au 15.02.83	BOULOGNE-BILLANCOURT (Hôtel de Ville) (92)
	Dès le 16.03.83	Avenue du Général Leclerc, PARIS 147 (14e arr.)
LS 08	Du 13.05.81 au 07.03.83	Rue des Écoles, PARIS 28 (5e arr.)
LS 09	Dès le 11.06.81	Avenue d'Italie, PARIS 13 (13e arr.)

Ces maquettes (prototypes) très sensibles, sont l'objet de fréquents arrêts de marche dus à leur réglage et leur mise au point.

A l'issue de la période d'essai précédente, dix distributeurs identiques aux appareils LSA 07, 08, 09 sont commandés à la firme CROUZET. Ils seront mis en place dans les bureaux à partir de 1985. Tout comme les appareils prototypes, ils effectuent en totalité l'impression des timbres. Au numéro de machine près qui est exprimé sous la forme "C0001", le cliché utilisé est identique à celui des appareils prototypes de la firme.

1985. - *Timbres de distributeurs. Papier adhésif bleu ciel. Impression lilas-rose. Valeur selon tarif en vigueur (1.07.84). Avec n° de l'appareil et code comptable du bureau d'exploitation. Papier support jaune ou gris-bleu.*

Type A (papier Carrier)

88	1 f. 70 (P.N.U.)	11 50
89	2 f. 10 (LETTRE)	11 50
90	3 f. 20 (–)	15 25
91	5 f. (URGENT)	15 25
88a à 91a	C 007 75628 (R. des Ecoles, PARIS) (4 val.)	77 »
88b à 91b	C 001 - 69123) (R.P. LYON) (4 val.)	115 »
88c et 89c	C 001 - 69264) (VILLEFRANCHE-SUR-SAONE) (2 val.)	125 »

NOTE. - Le Service Philatélique des P.T.T. a vendu ces timbres sous forme de plaquette comprenant 1.70 (P.N.U.), 3 f. 70 (LETTRE), 2 f. 10 (–) et 5 f. (URGENT).

La plaquette	11 50
La plaquette (Code erroné 75951)	77 »

Fonctionnement des appareils :

C 001 - 01249 (25.02.85) (MIRIBEL (Ain)
C 004 - 75961 (04.85) (Service Philatélique des P.T.T., PARIS)
C 007 - 75628 (24.06.85 au 31.07.85) (Rue des Ecoles, PARIS 28)
C 001 - 69920 (02.07.85) (LYON-BROTTEAUX)
C 001 - 75508 (05.07.85) (Rue La Boétie, PARIS 8)
C 001 - 75513 (05.07.85) (Av. d'Italie, PARIS 13)
C 001 - 75747 (05.07.85) (Av. du Général Leclerc, PARIS 147)
C 001 - 69123 (29.07.85) (Recette Principale, LYON)
C 001 - 69264 (31.07.85) (VILLEFRANCHE-SUR-SA0NE)

NOTE. - Début 1985, le type A a été utilisé à titre d'essai sur les appareils L 07-75747 et LS 09 75513.

1985. - *Timbres de distributeurs FRAMA/SATAS. Papier blanc fluorescent. Gomme invisible. Impression lilas-rose. L'usager a le choix d'une valeur de taxe de 0 f. 10 à 80 f. Les deux valeurs courantes du tarif peuvent être obtenues directement en poussant une touche correspondant à ces valeurs. Ce sont celles que nous mentionnons (ce type d'appareil ne rend pas la monnaie en pièces, comme les précédents, mais en vignette).*

92	1 f. 70, lilas-rose	1 40
92A	0 f. 10 à 80 f.	Valeur faciale x 5
	Avec minimum de 3	
93	2 f. 10, lilas-rose	1 70

Appareils

S 01 45234 ORLÉANS (dès le 26.02.85)
S 01 92184 NEUILLY-SABLONS (dès le 26.03.85) (retirés en 1989).

NOTE. - Les rouleaux de papier placés dans ces appareils annonçaient la fin du tirage par l'impression d'une, deux voire trois bandes verticales roses (valeur de chaque timbre ainsi marqués : 16 €).

1985. - *Timbres de distributeurs. Type A. Tarif postal au 1er 08.85.*

94	1 f. 80 (P.N.U.)	8 50
95	2 f. 20 (LETTRE)	8 50
96	3 f. 20 (–)	8 50
97	5 f. (URGENT)	8 50
94a à 97a	C 001 - 010201 (ARS) (4 val.)	40 »

NOTE. - En 1985 et 1986, le Service Philatélique des P.T.T. a vendu ces timbres sous forme de plaquette comprenant les nos 94 à 97.

La plaquette (C 004 - 75961)	54 »
La plaquette (C 004 - 75951) (code erroné)	15 25
La plaquette (C 034 - 34001) (code erroné)	45 75

Fonctionnement des appareils (du 01.08.85 au 31.07.86, sauf indications contraires)

C 001 - 01249 MIRIBEL (Ain)
C 001 - 69123 (LYON R.P.)
C 001 - 69264 (VILLEFRANCHE-SUR-SA0NE)
C 001 - 69920 (01.08.85 à juillet 86) (LYON BROTTEAUX) (cet appareil a été transféré à ARS-SUR-FORMANS)
C 001 - 75508 PARIS 8)
C 001 - 75513 PARIS 13)
C 001 - 75628 PARIS 28) (code modifié)
C 001 - 75747 PARIS 147)
C 001 - 75500 (26.09.85) (PARIS R.P.)
C 001 - 75505 (27.10.85) (PARIS 5 - rue de l'Epée de Bois)
C 001 - 01021 (16.07.86) (ARS-SUR-FORMANS)

1985. - *Idem. Exposition « FESTIVAL INDUSTRIE et TECHNOLOGIE » La Villette, PARIS (27.10.85 au 19.01.86).*

98 1 f. 80 (P.N.U.) 8 50
99 2 f. 20 (LETTRE) 8 50
100 3 f. 20 (-) 8 50
101 5 f. (URGENT) 8 50
98a à 101a (avec support jaune) (4 val.) 47 50

Appareil C 001 - 75900.

1985. - *Timbres de distributeurs FRAMA/SATAS. Type précédent (n° 92). Tarif postal au 1er.08.85.*

102 1 f. 80, lilas-rose 1 75
103 2 f. 20, lilas-rose 2 »

Voir au n° 92A Appareil en service du 21.02.86 au 28.06.89 :

S 01 29039 CONCARNEAU, Finistère

1986. - *Timbres de distributeurs. Type A. Tarif postal au 01.08.1986.*

104 1 f. 90 (P.N.U.) 4 50
105 2 f. 20 (LETTRE) 4 50
106 3 f. 50 (-) 4 50
107 5 f. 40 (URGENT) 4 50
104a à 107a C 001 - 01021 (ARS) (4 val.) 25 »

Fonctionnement des appareils.

Modifications :

C 001 - 01021 (ARS-SUR-FORMANS du 01.08.86 au 11.10.86)

(Cet appareil a fonctionné le 15.10.86 par erreur avec ce code à LYON BROTTEAUX où il était de retour).

C 001 - 69920 (16.10.86) (LYON BROTTEAUX)

1986. - *Timbres de distributeurs FRAMA/SATAS. Type précédent (n° 92). Tarif postal au 01.08.86.*

108 1 f. 90, rose-lilas 2 »

1986. - *Timbres de distributeurs IIe Congrès philatélique régional du Dauphiné et cinquantenaire de la Société Philatélique de Valence (25 et 26.10.1986), à Valence. Types de 1984 (nos 76 à 79).*

109 1 f. 90 (P.N.U.) 16 50
110 2 f. 20 (LETTRE) 16 50
111 3 f. 50 (-) 16 50
112 5 f. 40 (URGENT) 16 50

1987. - *Timbres de distributeurs. Type A. Tarif postal au 01.08.1987.*

113 2 f. (P.N.U.) 4 60
114 2 f. 20 (LETTRE) 4 60
115 3 f. 70 (-) 4 60
116 5 f. 60 (URGENT) 4 60

Codes A à G (voir fonctionnement des appareils).

1987. - *Timbre de distributeurs FRAMA/SATAS. Type précédent (n° 92). Tarif postal au 01.08.87.*

117 2 f. lilas-rose 1 55

1988.- *Idem. Type A. Valence. Congrès national de la Fédération des Sociétés philatéliques françaises. N° de Code C. 000 26362.*

118 2 f. (P.N.U.) 15 25
119 2 f. 20 (LETTRE) 15 25
120 3 f. 70 (–) 15 25
121 5 f. 60 (URGENT) 15 25

Type B

1988. - *Timbres de distributeurs. Type B. Support papier jaune.*

122 2 f. (P.N.U.) 4 60
123 2 f. 20 (LETTRE) 4 60
124 3 f. 70 (–) 9 15

Codes A à I (1988) et J (1989).

1988. - *Idem. Type B.*

125 5 f. 60 (–) 23 »
126 5 f. 60 (URGENT) 15 25

Codes A à F.
Le n° 125, Code E, n'existe pas.

1988. - *Tarif postal au 16.08.88. Timbres de distributeurs. Type A.*

127 6 f. 20 (–) 23 »
128 6 f. 20 (URGENT) 15 25

Codes A, B, C, F, G et H.

Idem. Type B.

129 6 f. 20 (–) 23 »
130 6 f. 20 (URGENT) 15 25

Codes A à I.

Fonctionnement des appareils (références) :

A) C 001 - 01249 (MIRIBEL)
B) C 001 - 75500 (PARIS LOUVRE RP)
C) C 001 - 75505 (PARIS MOUFFETARD)
D) C 001 - 75508 (PARIS LA BOETIE)
E) C 001 - 75513 (PARIS ITALIE)
F) C 001 - 75628 (PARIS JUSSIEU)
G) C 001 - 75747 (PARIS DENFERT ROCHEREAU)

Mise en place de 1988 à 1990 :

H) C 001 - 75702 (PARIS BIENVENUE) (15.11.88)
I) C 001 - 77468 (TORCY) (14.11.88)
J) C 001 - 75724 (PARIS BONNE NOUVELLE) (01.08.89)
K) C 001 - 75663 (PARIS JEANNE D'ARC) (17.01.90)
L) C 002 - 75500 (PARIS LOUVRE RP) (12.07.90)

NOTES. - A sa mise en service, l'appareil (code H) placé à PARIS BIENVENUE a distribué les vignettes n° 113 à 115 et 127, 128 (valeur : 40 €).

De même l'appareil (code J) a distribué les vignettes nos 113 à 115 et 143-144 (valeur : 35 €) et, idem, avec support publicitaire Fassroll (valeur : 47 50 €).

En août 1988, un nouvel échelon de tarif est introduit d'où une nouvelle nomenclature :

(–) Paquet-poste départemental à délai garanti (URGENT) - idem, extra départemental

Fin juin 1989, est introduit le service "COLISSIMO" qui entraîne peu à peu l'émission de nouveaux timbres :
(J + 1) Colissimo départemental
(J + 2) Colissimo extra-départemental

1989. - *Tarif postal modifié. Type B.*

131	11 f. (URGENT)	30 50

Codes A, I et G.

1989. - *PHILEXFRANCE 89. Exposition mondiale de philatélie à Paris (07-17.07). Timbres de distributeurs type B. Code C 001 75900.*

132	1 f. 90 cerise	385 »
133	2 f. cerise	25 »
134	2 f. 20 cerise	25 »
135	3 f. 70 cerise	32 50
136	6 f. 20 cerise	32 50
137	11 f. cerise	32 50
133a à 137a	brun-rouge (5 val.)	100 »

En 1990, à la faveur d'une réparation de l'appareil à PARIS ITALIE (Code E), ces vignettes ont été émises par erreur avec le code du bureau C 001 75513 (Valeur de chaque timbre : 80 €).

NOTE. - Le n° 132, à la suite d'une erreur, n'a été disponible que le 07.07 de 14 h à 20 h. (Nbre de timbres : 599).

1989. - *Sommet des pays industrialisés, à l'Arche de la Défense, à Puteaux (14.17.07). Timbres de distributeurs. Type B.*

138	2 f	77 »
139	2 f. 20	77 »
140	3 f. 70	115 »
141	6 f. 20	115 »
142	11 f.	115 »

NOTE. - A la mise en service, les timbres étaient du type A (Valeur : 305 € la vignette).

1989. - *Timbres de distributeurs. Type A.*

143	6 f. 20 (J+1)	11 50
144	11 f. (J+2)	11 50

Codes J et K (1991).

1989. - *Idem. Type B.*

145	6 f. 20 (J+1)	11 50
146	11 f. (J+2)	11 50

Codes A, B, C, E, G, H, I, J (1989), K et L (1990).

NOTE. - A sa mise en service l'appareil Code K, placé à PARIS JEANNE D'ARC a délivré des timbres avec valeurs inversées 6,20 (J+2) et 11,00 (J+1) valeur de chaque timbre : 200 €.

1989. - *Modernité et LA POSTE. Exposition de la Poste à l'Assemblée nationale (05.07.12). Timbre de distributeur. Type B.*

147	2 f.	125 »
148	2 f. 20	125 »
149	3 f. 70	125 »
150	6 f. 20	125 »
151	11 f.	125 »

1989. - *Idem. Exposition de la Poste au Sénat (12.14.12). Timbres de distributeurs. Type B.*

152	2 f.	92 »
153	2 f. 20	92 »
154	3 f. 70	92 »
155	6 f. 20	92 »
156	11 f.	92 »

1990. - *Tarif postal du 11.01.90. Timbres de distributeurs. Type B.*

157	2 f. 10 (P.N.U.)	3 85
158	2 f. 30 (LETTRE)	3 85
159	4 f. 20 (–)	7 65

Codes A, B, C, E, G, H, I, J, K et L.

Type A.

157A	2 f. 10 (P.N.U.)	3 85
158A	2 f. 30 (LETTRE)	3 85
159A	4 f. 20 (–)	7 65

Code K (1991).

En 1990, deux nouveaux types de distributeurs sont mis en service dans les bureaux :

- le DIVA (Distributeur de Vignettes d'Affranchissement).

- le LISA (Libre Service Affranchissement).

Fabriqué par la firme CERSEM, le DIVA délivre des timbres dont la valeur d'affranchissement correspond exactement aux sommes introduites dans l'équipement.

Les timbres délivrés se caractérisent par :

- une hauteur des chiffres de la valeur d'affranchissement de 6 mm ;

- 2 grosses étoiles à 6 branches placées de part et d'autre de cette valeur d'affranchissement.

Par contre aucune inscription ne caractérise :

- le tarif utilisé pour l'objet à affranchir,
- le numéro de l'appareil,
- le code comptable du bureau d'implantation

Le LISA est fabriqué par la firme MONETEL. Il délivre des timbres dont la valeur d'affranchissement peut être soit précisée par l'utilisateur soit calculée automatiquement par l'équipement. Le calcul effectué tient compte de la catégorie de courrier sélectionnée par l'utilisateur et du poids de l'objet à affranchir.

Les timbres délivrés se caractérisent par :

- une hauteur des chiffres da la valeur d'affranchissement de 5 mm ;
- 2 petites étoiles à 8 branches placées de part et d'autre de cette valeur d'affranchissement ;
- l'inscription d'une mention tarifaire complémentaire ajoutée pour certaines catégories de courriers (LETTRE, J+1, J+2) ;

Par contre aucune inscription ne caractérise le numéro de l'appareil ni le code comptable du bureau d'implantation.

DIVA

LISA

1990. - *Timbres de distributeurs. Papier adhésif gris-bleu. Impression de la valeur en rouge. Papier support jaune.*

Type C (DIVA). Gros chiffres avec étoiles à 6 branches.

160	0 f. 10 à 200 f. avec minimum de 3	Valeur faciale x 3

Type C (LISA). Chiffres maigres avec étoiles à 8 branches. Impression rouge-orange.

- = valeur à la demande, pli non urgent, lettre ordinaire au premier échelon de poids et colis au tarif économique,

LETTRE = lettre ordinaire à partir du deuxième échelon de poids

J+1 = Colis intradépartementaux à délais garanti J+1

J+2 = Colis extradépartementaux à délais garanti J+2

—

A partir de août 1993

J+1 = Colis intradépartementaux et colis régionaux à délais garanti J+1

J+2 = Colis nationaux à délais garanti J+2

161	0 f. 10 à 99 f. 90 avec minimum de 3 (avec mention)	Valeur faciale x 5
162	3 f. 80 (LETTRE)	3 05
163	6 f. 20 (J+1)	4 60
164	11 f. (J+2)	7 65

Idem. Impression violet-rose.

(sans mention) (rare)

161a	0 f. 10 à 99 f. 90 avec minimum de 10 (avec mention)	Valeur faciale x 30
162a	3 f. 80 (LETTRE)	23 »
163a	6 f. 20 (J+1)	34 50
164a	11 f. (J+2)	45 75

NOTE. - Pour information, nous donnons les mises en place des premiers appareils seulement, les timbres étant désormais partout identiques.

1 DIVA PARIS ÉTOILE (12.03.90)
RAMBOUILLET (13.03.90)
LA DÉFENSE PUTEAUX (14.03.90)

2 LISA PARIS ST LAZARE (19.04.90)
PARIS MONTMARTRE (19.04.90)

Le distributeur LISA de PARIS ST LAZARE a délivré le 19.04.90, un timbre erroné 2 f. 80 (LETTRE) valeur : 95 €.

NOTE. – Les vignettes portant les mention : TEST IMPRIMANTE, TEST de valeur, Table de tarifs (LISA), AUTOTEST (Diva), ANNULÉ (centres d'instruction disposant d'appareils), sont des vignettes de service des P.T.T. sans valeur fiduciaire ; elles complètent agréablement une collection.

Type C (LSA)

165	2 f. 10 (P.N.U.)	23 »
166	2 f. 30 (LETTRE)	23 »
167	4 f. 20 (–)	23 »
168	6 f. 20 (J+1)	23 »
169	11 f. (J+2)	23 »

Codes B et L. (Août 1990 et février 1991).
(Émission due à un manque de papier de type B)

1991. - *Tarif postal au 19.08.91. Timbres de distributeur. Type B (L.S.A.).*

170	2 f. 20 (P.N.U.)	1 55
171	2 f. 50 (LETTRE)	1 55
172	6 f. (–)	4 60
173	9 f. (J+1)	7 65
174	12 f. (J+2)	7 65

Codes B, C, E, G, H, J, K et L.

NOTE. - Les distributeurs Codes C, E, H, K et L ont délivré des timbres 000,00 (possibilité technique erronée). Valeur de chaque timbre : 80 € Code H 160 €.

170a à 174a (5 val.) 305 »

Code I (TORCY).

1991. - *Idem. Type C (LISA). Impression rouge-orange.*
(avec mention)

175 4 f. (LETTRE) 3 05
176 9 f. (J+1) 4 60
177 12 f. (J+2) 7 65

NOTE. - En janvier 1992, le distributeur mis en service rue Duhesmes à Paris 18e a délivré des timbres 0,00 (valeur : 40 € la vignette).

1991. - *Idem. Type C (LISA). Impression violet-rose.*

175a 4 f. (LETTRE) 23 »
176a 9 f. (J+1) 34 50
177a 12 f. (J+2) 45 75

NOTE. - La rupture de stock, soit du papier, soit du ruban de l'imprimante, est à l'origine d'emissions provisoires d'une durée de quelques heures à quelques semaines (Nos 189 à 196).

En particulier, l'utilisation de papier du type A de 1985 (Carrier) a été constatée fin 1992 et début 1993 sur distributeurs DIVA (Saint-André de Cubzac) ou LISA (Rue Duc, Paris 18e) (valeur d'un timbre 50 €. Puis dès le 05.07.93, selon nouveau tarif postal.

Par ailleurs un rouleau de timbres avec impression décalée (suppression des mots République Française) a été utilisé au bureau R. de la Boétie, à Paris. Valeur de chaque vignette : 25 €.

1991. - *Idem. Type B (L.S.A.) Impression en noir.*

178 2 f. 20 (P.N.U.) 19 25
179 2 f. 50 (LETTRE) 19 25
180 6 f. (–) 19 25
181 9 f. (J+1) 19 25
182 12 f. (J+2) 19 25

Code I (TORCY).

1991. - *Idem. Type C (LSA). Impression en noir.*

183 2 f. 20 (P.N.U.) 19 25
184 2 f. 50 (LETTRE) 19 25
185 6 f. (–) 19 25
186 9 f. (J+1) 19 25
187 12 f. (J+2) 19 25

Code I (TORCY).

1991. - *Idem. Type B (LSA). Valeur erronée. 19.08.*

188 14 f. (P.N.U.) 38 25

Code B, J et L (impression rouge).
Code I (impression en noir).

Idem. Type C (LSA)

188a 14 f. (P.N.U.) 38 25

Code I (Impression en noir)

1991. - *Idem. Type B (LISA).*

(sans mention)

189 0 f. 10 à 99 f. 90 Valeur faciale x 10 avec minimum de 10

(avec mention)

190 4 f. (LETTRE) 6 10
191 9 f. (J+1) 15 25
192 12 f. (J+2) 15 25

NOTE. - A Bandol, du 13 au 20.08.93, le distributeur a délivré par erreur un timbre LETTRE à 1 f. 30 (valeur : 100 €).

1992. - *Idem. Type C (LISA). Impression en noir.*
(sans mention)

193 0 f. 10 à 99 f. 90 Valeur faciale x 40 avec minimum de 10

(avec mention)

194 4 f. (LETTRE) 30 50
195 9 f. (J+1) 38 25
196 12 f. (J+2) 38 25

Origine : PARIS MOUFFETARD (25.02)

1992. - *Timbres de distributeurs. Papier adhésif TURQUOISE. Impression de la valeur en rouge. Type C de 1990 (DIVA) (n° 160).*

197 0 f. 10 à 200 f. Valeur faciale x 3 avec minimum de 3

1992. - *Idem. Type C de 1990 (LISA) (n° 161). Papier adhésif turquoise.*

(sans mention)

198 0 f. 10 à 99 f. 90 Valeur faciale x 3
avec minimum de 3

(avec mention)

199 4 f. (LETTRE) 3 05
200 9 f. (J+1) 7 65
201 12 f. (J+2) 9 15

L'usager peut obtenir du distributeur, avec chaque timbre du type LISA, une vignette "Reçu" libellée en français, en allemand, en anglais, en italien ou en espagnol, au choix.

1993. - *Idem. Impression de la valeur en noir.*

198a 0 f. 10 à 99 f. 90 Valeur faciale x 20
avec minimum de 13

Impression de la valeur en lilas (Nantes).

198b 0 f. 10 à 99 f. 90 Valeur faciale x 50
avec minimum de 100

1992. - *Tarif postal au 10.08.92. Timbres de distributeurs. Type C. (LISA) avec mentions. Papier adhésif gris-bleu. Impression de la valeur en rouge.*

202 4 f. 20 (LETTRE) 3 05
203 11 f. (J+1) 7 65
204 14 f. (J+2) 9 15

Par erreur de programmation : on peut trouver 2 f. 50 (LETTRE) (valeur 32 50 €) (1993) (PARIS 9-ROCHECHOUART).

1992. - *Idem. Papier adhésif turquoise. Impression de la valeur en rouge.*

205 4 f. 20 (LETTRE) 3 05
206 11 f. (J+1) 7 65
207 14 f. (J+2) 9 15

1993. - *Erreurs : 11 f. (J+2), 14 f. (J+1) : valeur de chaque timbre 100 € (PARIS-Gare de Lyon) ; 2 f. 50 (LETTRE) valeur 32 50 € (Paris 9 - Rochechouart)*

1993. - *Impression de la valeur en noir.*

205a 4 f. 20 (LETTRE) 45 75
206a 11 f. (J+1) 45 75
207a 14 f. (J+2) 61 »

Origine : PARIS POPINCOURT (05.93)

1993. - *Papier Type B (LISA).*

(avec mention)

205b 4 f. 20 (LETTRE) 23 »
206b 11 f. (J+1) 23 »
207b 14 f. (J+2) 23 »

1993. - *Papier Type A (LISA). Montage à l'endroit (PARIS MONTMARTRE) ou à l'envers.*

(avec mention)

205c 4 f. 20 (LETTRE) 45 75
206c 11 f. (J+1) 45 75
207c 14 f. (J+2) 45 75

1993. - *Idem. Type C (LISA). Papier adhésif bleu. Impression de la valeur en rouge.*

2080 f. 10 à 99 f. 90 Valeur faciale x 3
avec minimum de 3

209 4 f. 20 (LETTRE) 4 60
210 11 f. (J+1) 7 65
211 14 f. (J+2) 9 15

1993. - *Idem. Type C (DIVA). Papier adhésif bleu. Impression de la valeur en rouge.*

212 0 f. 10 à 200 f. Valeur faciale x 3
avec minimum de 3

1993. - *Idem. Type C (DIVA). Papier adhésif turquoise. Impression de la valeur en noir.*

213 0 f. 10 à 200 f. Valeur faciale x 20
avec minimum de 50

Origine : PARIS-PATAY (10-93)

1993. - *Tarif postal au 05.07.93. Timbres de distributeur, appareil LISA. Impression en rouge.*

(avec mention)

Papier adhésif Type C, turquoise.

214 4 f. 40 (LETTRE) 3 05
215 13 f. (J+1) 7 65
216 17 f. (J+1) * 9 95
217 17 f. (J+2) 9 95

* NOTE : Nouveau tarif colissimo avec délai garanti en 24 heures pour les départements de proximité.

Papier adhésif Type C, bleu.

214a 4 f. 40 (LETTRE) 3 05
215a 13 f. (J+1) 7 65
216a 17 f. (J+1) 9 95
217a 17 f. (J+2) 9 95

Papier adhésif Type C, gris-bleu.

214b 4 f. 40 (LETTRE) 3 05
215b 13 f. (J+1) 7 65
216b 17 f. (J+1) 9 95
217b 17 f. (J+2) 9 95

Papier adhésif Type B.

214c 4 f. 40 (LETTRE) 3 05
215c 13 f. (J+1) 7 65
216c 17 f. (J+1) 9 95
217c 17 f. (J+2) 9 95

Papier adhésif Type A, (Carrier). Support jaune, avec publicité. Montage à l'envers.

214d 4 f. 40 (LETTRE) 23 »
215d 13 f. (J+1) 23 »
217d 17 f. (J+2) 23 »

Origine : LE PERREUX

Papier adhésif Type A, (Carrier). Support jaune. Montage à l'endroit.

214e 4 f. 40 (LETTRE) 23 »
215e 13 f. (J+1) 23 »
216e 17 f. (J+1) 23 »
217e 17 f. (J+2) 23 »

Origine : STRASBOURG

Papier adhésif Type A, (Carrier). Support bleu.

214f 4 f. 40 (LETTRE) 23 »
215f 13 f. (J+1) 23 »
217f 17 f. (J+2) 23 »

Origine : SAINT-QUENTIN

Papier adhésif Type C, turquoise. Impression en noir.

214g	4 f. 40 (LETTRE)	15 25
215g	13 f. (J+1)	15 25
216g	17 f. (J+1)	15 25
217g	17 f. (J+2)	15 25

Papier adhésif Type C, turquoise. Impression en lilas.

214h	4 f. 40 (LETTRE)	23 »
215h	13 f. (J+1)	23 »
216h	17 f. (J+1)	23 »
217h	17 f. (J+2)	23 »

Papier adhésif Type C, bleu. Impression en noir (Mégève).

214j	4 f. 40 (LETTRE)	30 50
215j	13 f. (J+1)	30 50
216j	17 f. (J+1)	30 50
217j	17 f. (J+2)	30 50

1996. - *Tarif postal au 18 Mars. Type C (Lisa). Papier adhésif turquoise (avec mentions). Impression en rouge.*

218	4 f. 50 (LETTRE)	7 65
219	19 f. (J+1)	15 25
220	19 f. (J+2)	15 25

Papier adhésif Type C, turquoise. Impression en noir.

218a	4 f. 50 (LETTRE)	23 »
219a	19 f. (J+1)	23 »
220a	19 f. (J+2)	23 »

Papier adhésif Type C, gris-bleu. Impression en noir.

218b	4 f. 50 (LETTRE)	30 50
219b	19 f. (J+1)	30 50
220b	19 f. (J+2)	30 50

Papier adhésif Type B, (Comète). Impression en rouge.

218c	4 f. 50 (LETTRE)	23 »
219c	19 f. (J+1)	23 »
220c	19 f. (J+2)	23 »

Papier adhésif Type C, gris-bleu. Impression en rouge.

218d	4 f. 50 (LETTRE)	23 »

1996. - *Modification de logiciel, les vignettes portent de nouveaux codes (mise en service échelonnée) afin d'identifier le tarif choisi.*

E = Ecopli
C = Colieco
J+1D = Colissimo Départemental (délai 24 h.)
J+1R = Colissimo Régional (délai 24 h.)
J+2N = Colissimo National (délai 48 h.)

221	2 f. 70 (E)	3 05
222	13 f. (C)	7 65
223	13 f. (J+1D)	7 65
224	19 f. (J+1R)	10 75
225	19 f. (J+2N)	10 75

Papier adhésif Type C, turquoise. Impression en noir.

221a	2 f. 70 (E)	7 65
222a	13 f. (C)	7 65
223a	13 f. (J+1D)	7 65
224a	19 f. (J+1R)	10 75
225a	19 f. (J+2N)	10 75

Papier adhésif Type C, gris-bleu. Impression en rouge.

221b	2 f. 70 (E)	23 »
222b	13 f. (C)	23 »
223b	13 f. (J+1D)	23 »
224b	19 f. (J+1R)	23 »
225b	19 f. (J+2N)	23 »

Papier adhésif Type B, (Comète). Impression en rouge.

221c	2 f. 70 (E)	15 25
222c	13 f. (C)	15 25
223c	13 f. (J+1D)	15 25
224c	19 f. (J+1R)	15 25
225c	19 f. (J+2N)	15 25

La vignette "Reçu" que l'usager peut obtenir (voir après N° 201) porte la mention complémentaire : "SANS VALEUR D'AFFRANCHISSEMENT". A noter une erreur dans le libellé anglais : "WHITOUT au lieu de WITHOUT" (SANS...), erreur rectifiée par la suite.

De nombreuses variétés de toutes sortes apparaissent, telles que : Montage du papier à l'envers, impression sur support, impression du reçu sur la vignette, massicotage à cheval, erreurs de programmation (ex : 0,00, J+1 1.70 (1994) etc., nouvelles erreurs de ruban encreur : impression en NOIR ou en VIOLET.
Valeur de chaque pièce : 20 €

1996. - *Tarif de 1993 avec nouveaux codes, le basculement sur le tarif 1996 n'ayant pas été effectué sur certains appareils.*

221A	2 f. 40 (E)	» »
222A	13 f. (C)	» »
223A	13 f. (J+1D)	» »
224A	17 f. (J+1R)	» »
225A	17 f. (J+2N)	» »

1998. - *Tarif postal du 07.09.98. Type C (Lisa) turquoise. Impression en rouge.*

226	13 f. 50 (C)	7 65
227	13 f. 50 (J+1D)	7 65
228	19 f. 50 (J+1R)	10 75
229	19 f. 50 (J+2N)	10 75

Idem. Impression en noir (Stains).

226a	13 f. 50 (C)	15 25
227a	13 f. 50 (J+1D)	15 25
228a	19 f. 50 (J+1R)	23 »
229a	19 f. 50 (J+2N)	23 »

Idem. Papier gris-bleu. Impression en rouge (Perpignan).

226b	13 f. 50 (C)	23 »
227b	13 f. 50 (J+1D)	23 »
228b	19 f. 50 (J+1R)	30 50
229b	19 f. 50 (J+2N)	30 50

Type B (Comète). Impression en rouge (Eure).

226c	13 f. 50 (C)	15 25
227c	13 f. 50 (J+1D)	15 25
228c	19 f. 50 (J+1R)	23 »
229c	19 f. 50 (J+2N)	23 »

1998. - *Nouveau logiciel (préparation à l'introduction à l'Euro). Type C (Lisa) papier turquoise. Impression en rouge. L'étoile placée derrière la valeur faciale est supprimée, remplacée par les lettres FRF (franc français).*

230 0 f. 10 à 99 f. 90 Valeur faciale x 10 avec minimum de 15

231	2 f. 70 FRF (E)	2 30
232	4 f. 50 FRF (LETTRE)	2 30
233	13 f. 50 FRF (C)	6 10
234	13 f. 50 FRF (J+1D)	6 10
235	19 f. 50 FRF (J+1R)	9 15
236	19 f. 50 FRF (J+2N)	9 15

Par suite de basculement non effectué, il existe :

231a	2 f. 40 FRF (E)	
232a	4 f. 40 FRF (LETTRE)	

Origine : AUBERVILLIERS et PANTIN
(le jour de la mise en service).

1998/99. - *Type C (Lisa) modifié comme précédemment avec mention de la parité Euro* **(€)**. *Les règles précises de l'arrondi ne sont parfois pas respectées.*

237	0 f. 10 FRF à 99 f. 90 FRF avec valeur en € avec minimum de 0 50	Valeur faciale x 3	

Note : Le 0 f. 10 FRF sort avec la parité € 0 01 EUR valeur 0 50 €.

238	2 f.70 FRF (E)	0,41 EUR	1 25
239	4 f. 50 FRF (LETTRE)	0,68 EUR	3 »
240	13 f. 50 FRF (C)	2,06 EUR	4 50
241	13 f. 50 FRF (J+1D)	2,06 EUR	4 50
242	19 f. 50 FRF (J+1R)	2,97 (ou 2,98) EUR	6 25
243	19 f. 50 FRF (J+2N)	2,97 (ou 2,98) EUR	6 25

Idem. Impression en noir

237a	0 f.10 FRF à 99 f. 90 FRF (avec val. en €) avec minimum de 7 50	Valeur faciale x 5	
238a	2 f. 70 FRF (E)	0,41 EUR	7 50
239a	4 f. 50 FRF (LETTRE)	0,68 EUR	7 50
240a	13 f. 50 FRF (C)	2,06 EUR	12 50
241a	13 f. 50 FRF (J+1D)	2,06 EUR	12 50
242a	19 f. 50 FRF (J+1R)	2,97 (ou 2,98) EUR	16 50
243a	19 f. 50 FRF (J+2N)	2,97 (ou 2,98) EUR	16 50

Idem. Impression en violet-bleu

237b	0 f. 10 FRF à 99 f. 90 FRF (avec val. en €) avec minimum de 7 50	Valeur faciale x 10	
238b	2 f. 70 FRF (E)	0,41 EUR	7 50
239b	4 f. 50 FRF (LETTRE)	0,68 EUR	7 50
240b	13 f. 50 FRF (C)	2,06 EUR	20 »
241b	13 f. 50 FRF (J+1D)	2,06 EUR	20 »
242b	19 f. 50 FRF (J+1R)	2,97 (ou 2,98) EUR	30 »
243b	19 f. 50 FRF (J+2N)	2,97 (ou 2,98) EUR	30 »

La parité FRF/EUR est introduite manuellement par les postiers, entraînant de nombreuses erreurs, telles que :

Paris Champs Elysées 3 f. FRF donne 20 EUR

Chassieu 0 f. 10 FRF donne 0,00 EUR, 3 f. FRF donne 0 04 EUR

1999. - *Type C (Lisa), comme précedemment avec mention de la parité EURO (€). Logiciel corrigé. La parité FRF/EUR est intégrée directement, les règles de l'arrondi sont respectées.*

244	0 f. 10 FRF	0,02 EUR	0 50

Pour les autres valeurs sans mention, voir le n° 237.

245	4 f. 50 FRF (LETTRE)	0,69 EUR	3 »
246	19 f. 50 FRF (J+1R)	2,97 EUR	6 25
247	19 f. 50 FRF (J+2N)	2,97 EUR	6 25

Note : Les n°s 237 à 247 existent sur papier Type B (Comète) avec impression rouge ou en noir.

1999. - *PHILEXFRANCE 99. Exposition philatélique internationale « Mondial du Timbre » Paris (2-11.07). Timbre de distributeur Type D (Lisa) ; papier bleu-turquoise, adhésif.*

A. Avec parité FRF-EUR. Paiement en numéraire.

Type D (LISA). Monuments de Paris.

248	2 f. 70 FRF à 130 f. FRF avec valeur en € avec minimum de 2 30 avec mentions :	Valeur faciale x 5	
249	2 f. 70 FRF (E)	0,41 EUR	2 30
250	4 f. 50 FRF (LETTRE)	0,69 EUR	3 50
251	13 f. 50 FRF (C)	2,06 EUR	10 »
252	13 f. 50 FRF (J+1D)	2,06 EUR	10 »
253	19 f. 50 FRF (J+1R)	2,97 EUR	15 »
254	19 f. 50 FRF (J+2N)	2,97 EUR	15 »

Impossible d'obtenir des valeurs inférieures à 2 f. 70.

B. Sans parité EUR. Paiement par carte à puce (porte-monnaie électronique) MODEUS à 50 f. (vendue 60 f.) ou à 100 f. (vendue 120 f.)

259	2 f. 70 à 105 f. avec minimum de 7 50	Valeur faciale x 10	
260	4 f. 50 (LETTRE)		7 50
261	13 f. 50 (J+1)		22 50
262	19 f. 50 (J+2)		30 »

Note : Le 0 f. 10, bien qu'interdit, a pu être obtenu (valeur 15 €).

En 1999, un nouveau type de distributeur fabriqué par la firme IER est mis en service dans les bureaux : le LISA 2 (Libre Service Affranchissement de 2e génération).

Le procédé d'impression employé par l'équipement nécessite l'utilisation de vignettes thermosensibles.

Tout comme les distributeurs fabriqués par MONETEL, il délivre des timbres dont la valeur d'affranchissement peut être soit précisée par l'utilisateur soit calculée automatiquement par l'équipement.

Pourvu d'un écran tactile, il accepte les paiements soit en numéraire, soit par carte bancaire.

Les timbres délivrés se caractérisent par :

- une valeur d'affranchissement exprimée en francs et en euros ;

- une hauteur des chiffres de la valeur d'affranchissement de 5 mm ;

- 3 petites étoiles à 8 branches placées devant cette valeur d'affranchissement ;

- l'inscription d'une mention tarifaire complémentaire ajoutée devant les étoiles pour certaines catégories de courrier (E, LETTRE, C, J+1D, J+1R, J+2N).

Par contre, aucune inscription ne caractérise le numéro de l'appareil, ni le code comptable du bureau d'implantation.

Deux prototypes sont mis en place à Saint-Germain des Prés et à la Défense le 22 octobre, d'autres appareils seront ensuite mis en place progressivement.

1999. - *Timbre de distributeurs Type E (Lisa 2) Société IER. Papier adhésif thermosensible turquoise. Impression en noir, avec parité €.*

Type E (Lisa 2) Sté IER.

263	0 f. 10 FRF à 130 f. FRF avec parité € avec minimum de 0 50	Valeur faciale x 3	
264	2 f. 70 FRF (E)	0,41 EUR	1 25
265	4 f. 50 FRF (LETTRE)	0,69 EUR	3 »
266	13 f. 50 FRF (C)	2,06 EUR	4 50
267	13 f. 50 FRF (J+1D)	2,06 EUR	4 50
268	19 f. 50 FRF (J+1R)	2,97 EUR	6 25
269	19 f. 50 FRF (J+2N)	2,97 EUR	6 25

A la mise en service, une valeur 3 f. FRF (LETTRE) a été émise (valeur 120 €).

Note : Le reçu délivré n'est pas semblable au timbre mais imprimé sur papier blanc thermosensible. Par ailleurs du papier thermosensible du type E a également été utilisé sur un appareil LISA de la première génération.

Comme pour les machines de type Lisa 1, ces machines de type LISA 2 délivrent des vignettes TEST qui peuvent agrémenter une collection

Vignette TEST LISA 2 type 1

2000. - *Timbre de distributeur. Type C (Lisa 1). Papier adhésif turquoise thermosensible analogue à celui utilisé sur les appareils LISA 2 ci-dessus. Impression en rouge. (PARIS-LA DEFENSE).*

263a	0 f. 10 FRF à 130 f. FRF avec parité € avec minimum de 7 50	Valeur faciale x 5	
264a	2 f. 70 FRF (E)	0,41 EUR	7 50
265a	4 f. 50 FRF (LETTRE)	0,69 EUR	7 50
266a	13 f. 50 FRF (C)	2,06 EUR	10 »
267a	13 f. 50 FRF (J+1D)	2,06 EUR	10 »
268a	19 f. 50 FRF (J+1R)	2,97 EUR	15 »
269a	19 f. 50 FRF (J+2N)	2,97 EUR	15 »

Note : Plus lisse et acceptant difficilement l'impression, le papier thermosensible est néanmoins souvent introduit dans tous les appareils en usage (Lisa 1 et Diva).

2000. - *2e Biennale philatélique de Paris (25-27.02). Timbre de distributeur. Type F (Lisa). Papier adhésif bleu clair. Impression rouge, avec parité €.*

Type F (Lisa)

270	2 f. 70 FRF à 130 f. FRF avec valeur en € avec minimum de 7 50	Valeur faciale x 5	
271	2 f. 70 FRF (E)	0,41 EUR	7 50
272	4 f. 50 FRF (LETTRE)	0,69 EUR	7 50
273	13 f. 50 FRF (C)	2,06 EUR	10 »
274	13 f. 50 FRF (J+1D)	2,06 EUR	10 »
275	19 f. 50 FRF (J+1R)	2,97 EUR	15 »
276	19 f. 50 FRF (J+2N)	2,97 EUR	15 »

Impossible d'obtenir des valeurs inférieures à 2 f. 70.

2000. - *Tarif postal au 01.06. Timbre de distributeur Type C (Lisa). Papier adhésif turquoise. Sans parité €. Impression en noir.*

277	14 f. 50 (C)	6 75
278	14 f. 50 (J+1D)	6 75
279	20 f. 50 (J+1R)	10 »
280	20 f. 50 (J+2N)	10 »

2000. - *Idem avec parité €. Impression en rouge.*

281	14 f. 50 FRF (C)	2,21 EUR	6 75
282	14 f. 50 FRF (J+1D)	2,21 EUR	6 75
283	20 f. 50 FRF (J+1R)	3,13 EUR	10 »
284	20 f. 50 FRF (J+2N)	3,13 EUR	10 »

Idem. Impression en noir.

285	14 f. 50 FRF (C)	2,21 EUR	6 75
286	14 f. 50 FRF (J+1D)	2,21 EUR	6 75
287	20 f. 50 FRF (J+1R)	3,13 EUR	10 »
288	20 f. 50 FRF (J+2N)	3,13 EUR	10 »

Idem. Impression en violet.

285a	14 f. 50 FRF (C)	2,21 EUR	6 75
286a	14 f. 50 FRF (J+1D)	2,21 EUR	6 75
287a	20 f. 50 FRF (J+1R)	3,13 EUR	10 »
288a	20 f. 50 FRF (J+2N)	3,13 EUR	10 »

Idem. Papier thermosensible. Impression en rouge.

281a	14 f. 50 FRF (C)	2,21 EUR	6 75
282a	14 f. 50 FRF (J+1D)	2,21 EUR	6 75
283a	20 f. 50 FRF (J+1R)	3,13 EUR	10 »
284a	20 f. 50 FRF (J+2N)	3,13 EUR	10 »

Idem. Papier thermosensible. Impression en noir.

285b	14 f. 50 FRF (C)	2,21 EUR	6 75
286b	14 f. 50 FRF (J+1D)	2,21 EUR	6 75
287b	20 f. 50 FRF (J+1R)	3,13 EUR	10 »
288b	20 f. 50 FRF (J+2N)	3,13 EUR	10 »

Idem. Type E (Lisa 2) Sté IER. Papier thermosensible. Impression en noir.

289	14 f. 50 FRF (C)	2,21 EUR	6 75
290	14 f. 50 FRF (J+1D)	2,21 EUR	6 75
291	20 f. 50 FRF (J+1R)	3,13 EUR	10 »
292	20 f. 50 FRF (J+2N)	3,13 EUR	10 »

2000. - *Timbre de distributeur. Type G (Diva). Papier adhésif bleu clair et jeune clair. Impression de la valeur en rouge. Sans parité €.*

Type G (Diva). Avions en papier plié.

293	0 f. 10 à 200 f. avec minimum de 1 40	Valeur faciale x 5

2001. - *Idem. Avec une barre de phosphore à gauche et à droite (barres de sécurité).*

293a 0 f. 10 à 200 f. Valeur faciale
avec minimum de 1 40 x 5

2000. - *Idem. Impression de la valeur en noir.*

294 0 f. 10 à 200 f. Valeur faciale
avec minimum de 1 40 x 5

2001. - *Idem. Avec une barre de phosphore à gauche et à droite (barres de sécurité).*

294a 0 f. 10 à 200 f. Valeur faciale
avec minimum de 1 40 x 5

2001. - *Idem. Type G (Diva). Papier thermosensible. Impression de la valeur en rouge.*

294A 0 f. 10 à 200 f. Valeur faciale
avec minimum de 1 40 x 5

Note. L'exploitation des appareils DIVA a cessé le 31 décembre 2001, avec la disparition du franc.

2000. - *Idem. Type G (Lisa). Impression en rouge, avec parité €.*

Type G (Lisa 1). Avions en papier plié.

295 0 f. 10 à 200 f. Valeur faciale
avec parite € x 3
avec minimum de 1 40

296	2 f. 70 FRF (E)	0,41 EUR	1 40
297	4 f. 50 FRF (LETTRE)	0,69 EUR	2 25
298	14 f. 50 FRF (C)	2,21 EUR	6 75
299	14 f. 50 FRF (J+1D)	2,21 EUR	6 75
300	20 f. 50 FRF (J+1R)	3,13 EUR	9 50
301	20 f. 50 FRF (J+2N)	3,13 EUR	9 50

Ancien tarif maintenu par erreur.

298a	13 f. 50 FRF (C)	2,06 EUR	10 »
299a	13 f. 50 FRF (J+1D)	2,06 EUR	10 »
300a	19 f. 50 FRF (J+1R)	2,97 EUR	15 »
301a	19 f. 50 FRF (J+2N)	2,97 EUR	15 »

2000. - *Idem. Type G (Lisa 1). Impression en noir, avec parité €.*

Type G (Lisa 1). Avions en papier plié.

302 0 f. 10 à 130 f. Valeur faciale
avec parite € x 3
avec minimum de 1 40

303	2 f. 70 FRF (E)	0,41 EUR	1 40
304	4 f. 50 FRF (LETTRE)	0,69 EUR	2 25
305	14 f. 50 FRF (C)	2,21 EUR	6 75
306	14 f. 50 FRF (J+1D)	2,21 EUR	6 75
307	20 f. 50 FRF (J+1R)	3,13 EUR	9 50
308	20 f. 50 FRF (J+2N)	3,13 EUR	9 50

Idem. Impression en violet (Région de Nantes et à Nanterre).

302a 0 f. 10 à 130 f. Valeur faciale
avec parite € x 3
avec minimum de 1 40

303a	2 f. 70 FRF (E)	0,41 EUR	1 40
304a	4 f. 50 FRF (LETTRE)	0,69 EUR	2 25
305a	14 f. 50 FRF (C)	2,21 EUR	6 75
306a	14 f. 50 FRF (J+1D)	2,21 EUR	6 75
307a	20 f. 50 FRF (J+1R)	3,13 EUR	9 50
308a	20 f. 50 FRF (J+2N)	3,13 EUR	9 50

Ancien tarif maintenu à Nanterre par erreur.

305b	13 f. 50 FRF (C)	2,06 EUR	6 75
306b	13 f. 50 FRF (J+1D)	2,06 EUR	6 75
307b	19 f. 50 FRF (J+1R)	2,97 EUR	9 50
308b	19 f. 50 FRF (J+2N)	2,97 EUR	9 50

2000. - *Timbre de distributeur. Type I (Lisa 1). Papier bleu clair et jaune clair. Impression en noir. Sans parité €. (Gennevilliers).*

Type I (Lisa 1). Sans parité €.

309 0 f. 10 à 130 f. Valeur faciale
avec minimum de 1 40 x 3

310	2 f. 70 (E)	1 40
311	4 f. 50 (LETTRE)	2 25
312	14 f. 50 (C)	6 75
313	14 f. 50 (J+1D)	6 75
314	20 f. 50 (J+1R)	9 50
315	20 f. 50 (J+2N)	9 50

2000. - *Timbre de distributeur. Type H (Lisa 2). Société IER. Parpier thermosensible bleu clair et jaune clair. Impression en noir, avec parité €.*

Type H (Lisa 2). S[té] IER

316 0 f. 10 à 130 f. Valeur faciale
avec parité € x 3
avec minimum de 1 40

317	2 f. 70 FRF (E)	0,41 EUR	1 40
318	4 f. 50 FRF (LETTRE)	0,69 EUR	2 25
319	14 f. 50 FRF (C)	2,21 EUR	6 75
320	14 f. 50 FRF (J+1D)	2,21 EUR	6 75
321	20 f. 50 FRF (J+1R)	3,13 EUR	9 50
322	20 f. 50 FRF (J+2N)	3,13 EUR	9 50

2000. - *Idem. Type G (Lisa 1). Papier thermosensible. Impression en noir. Avec parité €.*

Type G (Lisa 1). Avions en papier plié. Lisse.

323	0 f. 10 à 130 f. avec parité € avec minimum de 1 40	Valeur faciale x 3	
324	2 f. 70 FRF (E)	0,41 EUR	1 40
325	4 f. 50 FRF (LETTRE)	0,69 EUR	2 25
326	14 f. 50 FRF (C)	2,21 EUR	6 75
327	14 f. 50 FRF (J+1D)	2,21 EUR	6 75
328	20 f. 50 FRF (J+1R)	3,13 EUR	9 50
329	20 f. 50 FRF (J+2N)	3,13 EUR	9 50

2000. - *Idem. Papier thermosensible. Impression en rouge.*

330	0 f. 10 à 130 f. avec parité € avec minimum de 1 40	Valeur faciale x 3	
331	2 f. 70 FRF (E)	0,41 EUR	1 40
332	4 f. 50 FRF (LETTRE)	0,69 EUR	2 25
333	14 f. 50 FRF (C)	2,21 EUR	6 75
334	14 f. 50 FRF (J+1D)	2,21 EUR	6 75
335	20 f. 50 FRF (J+1R)	3,13 EUR	9 50
336	20 f. 50 FRF (J+2N)	3,13 EUR	9 50

2000-01. - *Timbre de distributeur. Type B (Comète). Impression en noir, avec parité €. (Deville-les-Rouen).*

330A	0 f. 10 à 130 f. avec parité € avec minimum de 1 40	Valeur faciale x 3	
331A	2 f. 70 FRF (E)	0,41 EUR	1 40
332A	4 f. 50 FRF (LETTRE)	0,69 EUR	2 25
333A	14 f. 50 FRF (C)	2,21 EUR	6 75
334A	14 f. 50 FRF (J+1D)	2,21 EUR	6 75
335A	20 f. 50 FRF (J+1R)	3,13 EUR	9 50
336A	20 f. 50 FRF (J+2N)	3,13 EUR	9 50

2000-01. - *Idem. Impression en rouge, avec parité €. (Vanves).*

330B	0 f. 10 à 130 f. avec parité € avec minimum de 1 40	Valeur faciale x 3	
331B	2 f. 70 FRF (E)	0,41 EUR	1 40
332B	4 f. 50 FRF (LETTRE)	0,69 EUR	2 25
333B	14 f. 50 FRF (C)	2,21 EUR	6 75
334B	14 f. 50 FRF (J+1D)	2,21 EUR	6 75
335B	20 f. 50 FRF (J+1R)	3,13 EUR	9 50
336B	20 f. 50 FRF (J+2N)	3,13 EUR	9 50

1999-2000. - *Expérimentation du porte-monnaie électronique MODEUS, à NOISY LE GRAND, avec utilisation d'un ancien programme analogue à celui implanté sur les appareils de type Lisa, en 1996. (N°s 218 à 220).*

1999. - *Timbre de distributeur. Type C (Lisa). Papier adhésif turquoise. Impression en rouge.*

337	13 f. 50 (J+1)	9 »
338	19 f. 50 (J+2)	15 »

2000. - *Idem. Tarif au 01.06. Impression en rouge.*

339	14 f. 50 (J+1)	9 »
340	20 f. 50 (J+2)	15 »

Idem. Impression en noir.

341	14 f. 50 (J+1)	9 »
342	20 f. 50 (J+2)	15 »

2000. - *Timbre de distributeur. Type I (Lisa). Papier adhésif bleu clair et jaune clair. Impression en rouge. Sans parité €.*

Type I (Lisa 1). Sans parité € (en rouge).

343	0 f. 10 à 130 f. avec minimum de 1 40	Valeur faciale x 3	
344	4 f. 50 (LETTRE)		2 50
345	14 f. 50 (J+1)		7 50
346	20 f. 50 (J+2)		10 »

NB. Seules mentions existantes.

Idem. Impression en noir.

Type I (Lisa 1). Sans parité € (en noir).

	0 f. 10 à 130 f. avec minimum de 1 40 (voir n° 309)	Valeur faciale x 3	
	4 f. 50 (LETTRE) (voir n° 311)		
347	14 f. 50 (J+1)		7 50
348	20 f. 50 (J+2)		10 »

NB. Idem. Seule mentions existantes.

2001. - *Idem. Tarif au 01.06. Impression en noir, sans parité €.*

348A	15 f. 50 (J+1)	50 »
348B	21 f. 70 (J+2)	50 »

Note : L'expérience MODEUS a cessé en juillet 2001.

2000. - *54e Salon philatélique d'automne. Paris (9-12-11). Timbre de distributeur. Type K (Lisa). Papier adhésif orangé. Impression en noir, avec parité €.*

Type K (Lisa). Feuilles d'automne et Tour Eiffel stylisées.

349	2 f. 70 FRF à 130 f. FRF avec parité € avec minimum de 7 50	Valeur faciale x 5	
350	2 f. 70 FRF (E)	0,41 EUR	7 50
351	4 f. 50 FRF (LETTRE)	0,69 EUR	7 50
352	14 f. 50 FRF (C)	2,21 EUR	10 »
353	14 f. 50 FRF (J+1D)	2,21 EUR	10 »
354	20 f. 50 FRF (J+1R)	3,13 EUR	15 »
355	20 f. 50 FRF (J+2N)	3,13 EUR	15 »

2001. - *Salon philatélique, Nancy (23-25.03). Timbre de distributeur. Type L (Lisa). Papier adhésif gris-beige. Impression en noir, avec parité €.*

Type L (Lisa). Place Stanislas et 50e anniversaire du 1er jour.

356	0 f. 10 FRF à 130 f. FRF avec parité € avec minimum de 7 50	Valeur faciale x 5	
357	2 f. 70 FRF (E)	0,41 EUR	7 50
358	4 f. 50 FRF (LETTRE)	0,69 EUR	7 50
359	14 f. 50 FRF (C)	2,21 EUR	10 »
360	14 f. 50 FRF (J+1D)	2,21 EUR	10 »
361	20 f. 50 FRF (J+1R)	3,13 EUR	15 »
362	20 f. 50 FRF (J+2N)	3,13 EUR	15 »

L'un des appareils a délivré des timbres à l'ancien tarif.

359a	13 f. 50 FRF (C)	2,06 EUR	12 »
360a	13 f. 50 FRF (J+1D)	2,06 EUR	12 »
361a	19 f. 50 FRF (J+1R)	2,97 EUR	18 »
362a	19 f. 50 FRF (J+2N)	2,97 EUR	18 »

Par ailleurs, reçus obtenus datés des 23 et 24.03.2000... De l'un des deux autres distributeurs mis en place.

2001. - *74e Congrès de la F.F.A.P. (1-4 juin), Tours. Timbre de distributeur. Type M (Lisa). Papier adhésif vert pâle. Impression en noir, avec parité €. Deux bandes de phosphore à droite (barre de sécurité).*

Type M (Lisa). La gare de Tours.

363	0 f. 10 FRF à 130 f. FRF avec parité € avec minimum de 7 50	Valeur faciale x 5	
364	2 f. 70 FRF (E)	0,41 EUR	7 50
365	4 f. 50 FRF (LETTRE)	0,69 EUR	7 50
366	15 f. 50 FRF (C)	2,36 EUR	12 »
367	15 f. 50 FRF (J+1D)	2,36 EUR	12 »
368	21 f. 70 FRF (J+1R)	3,31 EUR	16 50
369	21 f. 70 FRF (J+2N)	3,31 EUR	16 50

2001. - *Modifications tarifaires du 01.06. Timbre de distributeur. Type G (Lisa 1). Avions en papier plié. Impression en rouge, avec parité €.*

370	15 f. 50 FRF (C)	2,36 EUR	6 75
371	15 f. 50 FRF (J+1D)	2,36 EUR	6 75
372	21 f. 70 FRF (J+1R)	3,31 EUR	9 50
373	21 f. 70 FRF (J+2N)	3,31 EUR	9 50

2001. - *Idem. Papier thermosensible. Impression en rouge.*

370a à 373a — Mêmes prix

2001. - *Idem. Impression en noir.*

374	15 f. 50 FRF (C)	2,36 EUR	6 75
375	15 f. 50 FRF (J+1D)	2,36 EUR	6 75
376	21 f. 70 FRF (J+1R)	3,31 EUR	9 50
377	21 f. 70 FRF (J+2N)	3,31 EUR	9 50

2001. - *Idem. Papier thermosensible. Impression en noir.*

374a à 377a — Mêmes prix

2001. - *Idem. Type I (Lisa 1). Impression en noir, sans parité €. (Gennevilliers).*

378	15 f. 50 (C)	25 »
379	15 f. 50 (J+1D)	25 »
380	21 f. 70 (J+1R)	25 »
381	21 f. 70 (J+2N)	25 »

2001. - *Idem. Type H (Lisa 2). Sté IER. Impression en noir, avec parité €.*

382	15 f. 50 FRF (C)	2,36 EUR	6 75
383	15 f. 50 FRF (J+1D)	2,36 EUR	6 75
384	21 f. 70 FRF (J+1R)	3,31 EUR	9 50
385	21 f. 70 FRF (J+2N)	3,31 EUR	9 50

2001. - *Timbre de distributeur. Type C (Lisa 1). Oiseaux papier turquoise. Impression en noir, sans parité €.*

386	15 f. 50 FRF (C)	2,36 EUR	6 75
387	15 f. 50 FRF (J+1D)	2,36 EUR	6 75
387A	21 f. 70 FRF (J+1R)	3,31 EUR	9 50
387B	21 f. 70 FRF (J+2N)	3,31 EUR	9 50

2001. - *Idem. Type C (Lisa 1). Impression en rouge, avec parité €.*

386a	15 f. 50 FRF (C)	2,36 EUR	6 75
387a	15 f. 50 FRF (J+1D)	2,36 EUR	6 75
387Aa	21 f. 70 FRF (J+1R)	3,31 EUR	9 50
387Ba	21 f. 70 FRF (J+2N)	3,31 EUR	9 50

2001. - *Timbre de distributeur. Type E (Lisa 2). Sté IER. Oiseaux papier turquoise thermosensible. Impression en noir, avec parité €.*

387C	15 f. 50 FRF (C)	2,36 EUR	6 75
387D	15 f. 50 FRF (J+1D)	2,36 EUR	6 75
387E	21 f. 70 FRF (J+1R)	3,31 EUR	9 50
387F	21 f. 70 FRF (J+2N)	3,31 EUR	9 50

Au cours du 2e trimestre 2001, l'utilisation du papier avec bandes de phosphore se généralise (barres de sécurité). Ces bandes peuvent se trouver à cheval sur deux timbres.

2001. - *Timbre de distributeur. Type G (Lisa 1). Impression en noir, avec parité € et 2 bandes de phosphore à gauche et à droite (barres de sécurité).*

Type G (Lisa 1). Avec barres de sécurité.

388	0 f. 10 FRF à 130 f. FRF avec parité € avec minimum de 1 40	Valeur faciale x 3	
389	2 f. 70 FRF (E)	0,41 EUR	1 40
390	4 f. 50 FRF (LETTRE)	0,69 EUR	2 25
391	15 f. 50 FRF (C)	2,36 EUR	6 75
392	15 f. 50 FRF (J+1D)	2,36 EUR	6 75
393	21 f. 70 FRF (J+1R)	3,31 EUR	9 50
394	21 f. 70 FRF (J+2N)	3,31 EUR	9 50

2001. - *Idem. Impression en rouge.*

394A	0 f. 10 FRF à 130 f. FRF avec parité € avec minimum de 1 40	Valeur faciale x 3	
394B	2 f. 70 FRF (E)	0,41 EUR	1 40
394C	4 f. 50 FRF (LETTRE)	0,69 EUR	2 25
394D	15 f. 50 (C)	2,36 EUR	6 75
394E	15 f. 50 (J+1D)	2,36 EUR	6 75
394F	21 f. 70 (J+1R)	3,31 EUR	9 50
394G	21 f. 70 (J+2N)	3,31 EUR	9 50

Voir également le type G (Diva) n°s 293a, 294a et 294A.

2001. - *Idem. Type G (Lisa 1). Papier thermosensible, impression en noir, avec parité € et barres de sécurité.*

395	0 f. 10 FRF à 130 f. FRF avec parité € avec minimum de 1 40	Valeur faciale x 3	
396	2 f. 70 FRF (E)	0,41 EUR	1 40
397	4 f. 50 FRF (LETTRE)	0,69 EUR	2 25
398	15 f. 50 FRF (C)	2,36 EUR	6 75
399	15 f. 50 FRF (J+1D)	2,36 EUR	6 75
400	21 f. 70 FRF (J+1R)	3,31 EUR	9 50
401	21 f. 70 FRF (J+2N)	3,31 EUR	9 50

2001. - *Idem. Papier thermosensible, impression en rouge.*

402	0 f. 10 FRF à 130 f. FRF avec parité € avec minimum de 1 40	Valeur faciale x 3	
403	2 f. 70 FRF (E)	0,41 EUR	1 40
404	4 f. 50 FRF (LETTRE)	0,69 EUR	2 25
405	15 f. 50 FRF (C)	2,36 EUR	6 75
406	15 f. 50 FRF (J+1D)	2,36 EUR	6 75
407	21 f. 70 FRF (J+1R)	3,31 EUR	9 50
408	21 f. 70 FRF (J+2N)	3,31 EUR	9 50

2001. - *Timbre de distributeur. Type H (Lisa 2). S[té] IER. Impression en noir, avec parité € et barres de sécurité.*

409	0 f. 10 FRF à 130 f. FRF avec parité € avec minimum de 1 40	Valeur faciale x 3	
410	2 f. 70 FRF (E)	0,41 EUR	1 40
411	4 f. 50 FRF (LETTRE)	0,69 EUR	2 25
412	15 f. 50 FRF (C)	2,36 EUR	6 75
413	15 f. 50 FRF (J+1D)	2,36 EUR	6 75
414	21 f. 70 FRF (J+1R)	3,31 EUR	9 50
415	21 f. 70 FRF (J+2N)	3,31 EUR	9 50

2001. - *55e Salon philatélique d'automne. Paris (8-11.11). Timbre de distributeur. Type N (Lisa). Papier adhésif gris. Impression en noir, avec parité €.*

Type N (Lisa). Hommage au graveur Albert Decaris, Paris et la Tour Eiffel.

416	2 f. 70 FRF à 130 f. FRF avec parité € avec minimum de 7 50	Val. fac. en € x 5	
417	2 f. 70 FRF (E)	0,41 EUR	7 50
418	4 f. 50 FRF (LETTRE)	0,69 EUR	7 50
419	15 f. 50 FRF (C)	2,36 EUR	12 »
420	15 f. 50 FRF (J+1D)	2,36 EUR	12 »
421	21 f. 70 FRF (J+1R)	3,31 EUR	16 50
422	21 f. 70 FRF (J+2N)	3,31 EUR	16 50

A partir du 1er janvier 2002
100 centimes d'euro = 1 EURO (€)
1 EURO = 6 f. 55957.

2002. - *(01 et 02.01). Timbre de distributeur. Types précédents G (Lisa 1) et H (Lisa 2).*

Type G (Lisa 1). Impression en noir.

423	0,01 EUR à 99,99 EUR avec minimum de 1 40	Valeur faciale x 3
424	0,41 EUR (E)	1 40
425	0,69 EUR (LETTRE)	2 25
426	2,35 EUR (C)	6 75
427	2,35 EUR (J+1D)	6 75
428	3,30 EUR (J+1R)	9 50
429	3,30 EUR (J+2N)	9 50

Idem. Impression en rouge.

423a à 429a — Mêmes prix

Idem. Impression en noir, avec une bande de phosphore à gauche et à droite (barres de sécurité).

430 à 436 — Mêmes prix

Idem. Impression en rouge.

430a à 436a — Mêmes prix

Idem. Impression en noir. Papier thermosensible.

437 à 443 — Mêmes prix

Idem. Impression en rouge.

437a à 443a — Mêmes prix

Idem. Impression en noir. Papier thermosensible, avec une bande de phosphore à gauche et à droite (barres de sécurité).

444 à 450 — Mêmes prix

Idem. Impression en violet (région de Nantes).

Type G (Lisa 1). Impression en violet.

450A à 450G		Mêmes prix

Type H (Lisa 2). S[té] IER. Papier thermosensible.

451	0,01 EUR à 99,99 EUR avec minimum de 1 40	Valeur faciale x 3
452	0,41 EUR (E)	1 40
453	0,69 EUR (LETTRE)	2 25
454	2,35 EUR (C)	6 75
455	2,35 EUR (J+1D)	6 75
456	3,30 EUR (J+1R)	9 50
457	3,30 EUR (J+2N)	9 50

Idem. Avec une bande de phosphore à gauche et à droite (barres de sécurité).

458 à 464		Mêmes prix

Type H (Lisa 2). Avec trait diagonal et bande de phosphore à gauche et à droite.

(Origine : PARIS RP rue du Louvre, en particulier).

465	0,01 EUR à 99,99 EUR avec minimum de 7 50	Valeur faciale x 5
466	0,41 EUR (E)	7 50
467	0,69 EUR (LETTRE)	7 50
468	2,36 EUR (C)	12 »
469	2,36 EUR (J+1D)	12 »
470	3,31 EUR (J+1R)	16 50
471	3,31 EUR (J+2N)	16 50

(Les n°s 468 à 479 ont des valeurs non réajustées avant la mise en service 01.01.2002).

2002. - *Timbre de distributeur. Type B (Lisa 1). Papier adhésif bleu clair "Comète". Impression en noir.*

Type B (LISA 1). Impression en noir.

471A	0,01 EUR à 99,99 EUR avec minimum de 1 40	Valeur faciale x 3
471B	0,41 EUR (E)	1 40
471C	0,69 EUR (LETTRE)	2 25
471D	2,35 EUR (C)	6 75
471E	2,35 EUR (J+1D)	6 75
471F	3,30 EUR (J+1R)	9 50
471G	3,30 EUR (J+2N)	9 50

Idem. Impression en rouge.

471Aa à 471Ga		Mêmes prix

2002. - *Timbre de distributeur. Type C (Lisa 1). Oiseaux papier turquoise. Impression en rouge.*

Type C (Lisa 1). (EURO).

472	0,01 EUR à 99,99 EUR avec minimum de 1 40	Valeur faciale x 3
473	0,41 EUR (E)	1 40
474	0,69 EUR (LETTRE)	2 25
475	2,35 EUR (C)	6 75
476	2,35 EUR (J+1D)	6 75
477	3,30 EUR (J+1R)	9 50
478	3,30 EUR (J+2N)	9 50

Idem. Impression en noir.

Type C (Lisa 1). Impression en noir.

479 à 485		Mêmes prix

2002. - *Timbre de distributeur. Type E (Lisa 2). S[té] IER. Oiseaux papier turquoise thermosensible. Impression en noir.*

486	0,01 EUR à 99,99 EUR avec minimum de 1 40	Valeur faciale x 3
487	0,41 EUR (E)	1 40
488	0,69 EUR (LETTRE)	2 25
489	2,35 EUR (C)	6 75
490	2,35 EUR (J+1D)	6 75
491	3,30 EUR (J+1R)	9 50
492	3,30 EUR (J+2N)	9 50

2002. - *3e Biennale philatélique de Paris (08-10.02). Timbre de distributeur. Type P (Lisa). Papier adhésif bleu clair. Impression en noir.*

Type P (Lisa). Avénement de l'Euro (sigles €).

493	0,01 EUR à 99,99 EUR avec minimum de 7 50	Valeur faciale x 5
494	0,41 EUR (E)	7 50
495	0,69 EUR (LETTRE)	7 50
496	2,35 EUR (C)	12 »
497	2,35 EUR (J+1D)	12 »
498	3,30 EUR (J+1R)	16 50
499	3,30 EUR (J+2N)	16 50

2002. - *Salon philatélique de printemps. Les arènes de Nîmes (22-24.03). Timbre de distributeur. Type Q (Lisa). Papier adhésif orange. Impression en noir.*

Type Q (Lisa). Le Pont du Gard.

500	0,01 EUR à 99,99 EUR avec minimum de 7 50	Valeur faciale x 5
501	0,41 EUR (E)	7 50
502	0,69 EUR (LETTRE)	7 50
503	2,35 EUR (C)	12 »
504	2,35 EUR (J+1D)	12 »
505	3,30 EUR (J+1R)	16 50
506	*3,30 EUR (J+2N)*	16 50

2002. - *75e Congrès de la FFAP (17-20-05), Marseille. Timbre de distributeur. Type R. (Lisa). Papier adhésif bleu clair, impression en noir. Bandes de phosphore à gauche et à droite.*

Type R (Lisa). Le port de Marseille.

507	0,01 EUR à 99,99 EUR avec minimum de 7 50	Valeur faciale x 5
508	0,41 EUR (E)	7 50
509	0,69 EUR (LETTRE)	7 50
510	2,35 EUR (C)	15 »
511	2,35 EUR (J+1D)	15 »
512	3,30 EUR (J+1R)	20 »
513	3,30 EUR (J+2N)	20 »

Idem. Nouveau tarif minimum des colis (Voir ci-après n°s 514 à 517).

510A	3,40 EUR (C)	15 »
511A	3,40 EUR (J+1D)	15 »
512A	4,60 EUR (J+1R)	20 »
513A	4,60 EUR (J+2N)	20 »

2002. - *Timbre de distributeur. Nouveau tarif minimum des colis (dès le 2.04 - mise en place échelonnée) dû à la suppression de la première tranche de poids (1gr à 250 gr devient 1 gr à 500 gr.) Types précédents G (Lisa 1) et H (Lisa 2).*

Type G (Lisa 1). Impression en noir.

514	3,40 EUR (C)	15 »
515	3,40 EUR (J+1D)	15 »
516	4,60 EUR (J+1R)	20 »
517	4,60 EUR (J+2N)	20 »

Idem. Impression en rouge.

514a à 517a — Mêmes prix

Idem. Impression en violet (Nantes Degré).

514b	3,40 EUR (C)	18 »
515b	3,40 EUR (J+1D)	18 »
516b	4,60 EUR (J+1R)	25 »
517b	4,60 EUR (J+2N)	25 »

Idem. Impression en noir avec une bande de phosphore à gauche et à droite (barres de sécurité).

514A	3,40 EUR (C)	15 »
515A	3,40 EUR (J+1D)	15 »
516A	4,60 EUR (J+1R)	20 »
517A	4,60 EUR (J+2N)	20 »

Idem. Impression en rouge.

514Aa à 517Aa — Mêmes prix

Idem. Papier thermique. Impression en noir.

514B à 517B — Mêmes prix

Idem. Papier thermique. Impression en rouge.

514Ba	3,40 EUR (C)	18 »
515Ba	3,40 EUR (J+1D)	18 »
516Ba	4,60 EUR (J+1R)	25 »
517Ba	4,60 EUR (J+2N)	25 »

Idem. Type H (LISA 2). Papier thermique avec ou sans bandes de phosphore. Impression de la valeur en noir en bas des vignettes.

514C	3,40 EUR (C)	15 »
515C	3,40 EUR (J+1D)	15 »
516C	4,60 EUR (J+1R)	20 »
517C	4,60 EUR (J+2N)	20 »

Idem. Type B (LISA 1). Papier adhésif bleu clair "Comète". Impression en noir (ou en rouge vraisemblablement).

514D	3,40 EUR (C)	18 »
515D	3,40 EUR (J+1D)	18 »
516D	4,60 EUR (J+1R)	25 »
517D	4,60 EUR (J+2N)	25 »

Idem. Type C (LISA 1). Papier Oiseaux turquoise. Impression en noir.

514E	3,40 EUR (C)	15 »
515E	3,40 EUR (J+1D)	15 »
516E	4,60 EUR (J+1R)	20 »
517E	4,60 EUR (J+2N)	20 »

Idem. Type C (LISA 1). Impression en rouge.

514Ea	3,40 EUR (C)	18 »
515Ea	3,40 EUR (J+1D)	18 »
516Ea	4,60 EUR (J+1R)	25 »
517Ea	4,60 EUR (J+2N)	25 »

Idem. Type E (LISA 2). Papier thermique. Oiseaux turquoise. Impression de la valeur en noir.

514F à 517F	Mêmes prix

2002. - *56ᵉ Salon philatélique d'automne, Paris (7-11.11). Timbre de distributeur. Type S (Lisa). Thème Paris-Rome. Papier adhésif multicolore. Impression en noir.*

Type S (Lisa). Paris (Tour Eiffel - Sacré-Coeur) et Rome (Colisée).

518	0,01 EUR à 99,99 EUR avec minimum de 4 »	Valeur faciale x 4
519	0,41 EUR (E)	4 »
520	0,69 EUR (LETTRE)	4 »
521	3,40 EUR (C)	13 50
522	3,40 EUR (J+1D)	13 50
523	4,60 EUR (J+1R)	18 50
524	4,60 EUR (J+2N)	18 50

2003. - *Tarif du 02.04.02. Timbre de distributeur. Type H (LISA 2). Papier thermique. Impression de la valeur en noir à mi-hauteur des vignettes.*
(0.01 EUR à 99,99 EUR (voir n° 532).

519A	0,41 EUR (E)	1 50
520A	0,69 EUR (LETTRE)	2 25
521A	3,40 EUR (C)	18 »
522A	3,40 EUR (J+1D)	18 »
523A	4,60 EUR (J+1R)	25 »
524A	4,60 EUR (J+2N)	25 »

Idem. Impression en noir avec une bande de phosphore à gauche et à droite.

519Aa à 524Aa	Mêmes prix

Note : les vignettes TEST subissent également la même modification

Vignette TEST LISA 2 type2 impression à mi-hauteur.

2003. - *Salon philatélique de printemps, Nantes (4-6.04). Timbre de distributeur. Type T (Lisa). Papier adhésif multicolore. Bandes de phosphore à gauche et à droite. Impression en noir.*

Type T (Lisa). Nantes, Cité des Congrès.

525	0,41 EUR à 99,99 EUR avec minimum de 4 »	Valeur faciale x 4
525a	0,01 EUR à 0,40	10 »
526	0,41 EUR (E)	4 »
527	0,69 EUR (LETTRE)	4 »
528	3,40 EUR (C)	13 50
529	3,40 EUR (J+1D)	13 50
530	4,60 EUR (J+1R)	18 50
531	4,60 EUR (J+2N)	18 50
528a	4,00 EUR (C)	» »
529a	4,00 EUR (J+1D)	» »
530a	4,80 EUR (J+1R)	» »
531a	4,80 EUR (J+2N)	» »
528b	2,35 EUR (C)	» »
529b	2,35 EUR (J+1D)	» »
530b	3,30 EUR (J+1R)	» »
531b	3,30 EUR (J+2N)	» »

Remarque : Cette émission a été réalisée dans la confusion. Pour éviter le tirage de petites valeurs, la Poste avait bridé les appareils, ce qui a eu pour résultat de ne pouvoir obtenir dans l'enceinte du Salon
- des vignettes au tarif colis pour la France
- des vignettes au tarif réduit (ECOPLI)
- des vignettes au tarif international

Dès lors, la Poste a proposé la vente des vignettes par commande sur place, exécutée par courrier recommandé ultérieur.
Aucun reçu n'a été délivré.
Cependant pour permettre l'intervention sur les machines, le technicien pouvait les débrider. Lors de changements de rouleaux l'opération inverse fut omise, autorisant ainsi l'émission de petites valeurs (0,01 EUR - une centaine) et quelques séries complètes avec ou sans reçu (une trentaine au tarif d'avril 2003, une dizaine à celui de janvier 2002).

2003. - *(01.04) Modification du tarif des colis Timbre de distributeur. Types G (LISA 1). Impression en noir.*

528A	4,00 EUR (C)	12 »
529A	4,00 EUR (J+1D)	16 »
530A	4,80 EUR (J+1R)	20 »
531A	4,80 EUR (J+2N)	14 50

Idem. Impression en rouge.

528Aa à 531Aa	Mêmes prix

Idem. Impression en noir avec une bande de phosphore à gauche et à droite.

528B	4,00 EUR (C)	12 »
529B	4,00 EUR (J+1D)	16 »
530B	4,80 EUR (J+1R)	20 »
531B	4,80 EUR (J+2N)	14 50

Idem. Impression en rouge.

528Ba à 531Ba	Mêmes prix

Idem. Impression en violet (Nantes Degré).

528Bb	4,00 EUR (C)	20 »
529Bb	4,00 EUR (J+1D)	20 »
530Bb	4,80 EUR (J+1R)	25 »
531Bb	4,80 EUR (J+2N)	25 »

Idem. Papier thermique. Impression en noir.

528C	4,00 EUR (C)	12 »
529C	4,00 EUR (J+1D)	20 »
530C	4,80 EUR (J+1R)	25 »

531C 4,80 EUR (J+2N) 14 50

Idem. Papier thermique. Impression en violet (Nantes Degré).

525Ca 0,01 EUR à 99,99 EUR avec minimum de 2 » Valeur faciale x 5
526Ca 0,41 EUR (E) 2 25
527Ca 0,69 EUR (LETTRE) 3 50
528Ca 4,00 EUR (C) 20 »
529Ca 4,00 EUR (J+1D) 20 »
530Ca 4,80 EUR (J+1R) 25 »
531Ca 4,80 EUR (J+2N) 25 »

Idem. Type C (LISA 1). Papier Oiseaux turquoise. Impression en noir.

Type C (LISA 1). Impression en noir.

528D 4,00 EUR (C) 12 »
529D 4,00 EUR (J+1D) 20 »
530D 4,80 EUR (J+1R) 25 »
531D 4,80 EUR (J+2N) 14 50

Idem. Type C (LISA 1). Impression en rouge.

528Da à 531Da Mêmes prix

2003. - *Timbre de distributeur. Type H (LISA 2). Papier thermique. Impression de la valeur en noir à mi-hauteur des vignettes.*

529E 4,00 EUR (J+1D) 12 »
530E 4,80 EUR (J+1R) 14 50

Idem. Impression en noir avec une bande de phosphore à gauche et à droite.

529F et 530F Mêmes prix

Note : Les n°s 529E, 530E, 529F et 530F existent vraisemblablement avec impression de la valeur en bas des vignettes.

2003. - *Timbre de distributeur. Type précédent (H Lisa 2). Tarif au 01.06. Impression de la valeur en noir à mi-hauteur.*

Type H (Lisa 2). Papier thermosensible.

532 0,01 EUR à 99,99 EUR avec minimum de 1 50 Valeur faciale x 3
533 0,45 EUR (E) 1 50
534 0,50 EUR (P) 1 50
535 0,75 EUR (LETTRE) 2 25
536 4,00 EUR (C) 12 »
537 4,00 EUR (J+2D) 12 »
538 4,80 EUR (J+2N) 14 40

Remarques : Nouvelle mention P (PRIORITY) pour lettre à destination de l'étranger ; par contre l'indication J+1R est supprimée.

Lorsqu'un timbre à valeur à choix (0,01 EUR à 99,99 EUR) est demandé en cumul de service après une lettre prioritaire pour l'étranger, la valeur faciale de cette vignette est également précédée de la lettre P.

534a 0,01 EUR à 99,99 EUR (P) avec minimum de 3 » Valeur faciale x 4

Type H (LISA 2). Papier thermique édité en cumul. (P).

2003. - *Timbre de distributeur. Tarif au 01.06. Types G (LISA 1). Impression en noir.*

533A 0,45 EUR (E) 1 50
534A 0,50 EUR (P) 1 50
535A 0,75 EUR (LETTRE) 2 25
537A 4,00 EUR (J+2D) 12 »

Idem. Impression en rouge.

533Aa à 537Aa Mêmes prix

Idem. Impression en noir avec une bande de phosphore à gauche et à droite.

533B à 537B Mêmes prix

Idem. Impression en rouge.

533Ba à 537Ba Mêmes prix

Idem. Papier thermique. Impression en noir.

533C 0,45 EUR (E) 2 »
534C 0,50 EUR (P) 2 »
535C 0,75 EUR (LETTRE) 3 »
537C 4,00 EUR (J+2D) 15 »

Idem. Papier thermique. Impression en rouge.

533Ca 0,45 EUR (E) 4 »
534Ca 0,50 EUR (P) 4 »
535Ca 0,75 EUR (LETTRE) 5 »
536Ca 4,00 EUR (C) 20 »
537Ca 4,00 EUR (J+2D) 20 »
538Ca 4,80 EUR (J+2N) 25 »

Idem. Type C (LISA 1). Papier Oiseaux turquoise. Impression en noir.

533D 0,45 EUR (E) 1 50
534D 0,50 EUR (P) 1 50
535D 0,75 EUR (LETTRE) 2 25
537D 4,00 EUR (J+2D) 12 »

Idem. Type C (LISA 1). Impression en rouge.

533Da 0,45 EUR (E) 2 »
534Da 0,50 EUR (P) 2 »
535Da 0,75 EUR (LETTRE) 3 »
537Da 4,00 EUR (J+2D) 15 »

Idem. Type E (LISA 2). Papier thermique. Oiseaux turquoise. Impression de la valeur en noir à mi-hauteur de la vignette.

Type E (LISA 2). Papier thermique.
Impression en noir.

532E	0,01 EUR à 99,99 EUR avec minimum de 3 »	Valeur faciale x 4
533E	0,45 EUR (E)	4 »
534E	0,50 EUR (P)	4 »
535E	0,75 EUR (LETTRE)	6 »
536E	4,00 EUR (C)	20 »
537E	4,00 EUR (J+2D)	20 »
538E	4,80 EUR (J+2N)	25 »
534Ea	0,01 EUR à 99,99 EUR (P) avec minimum de 4 »	Valeur faciale x 5

Note : voir remarque concernant le 534a.

Idem. Type B (LISA 1). Papier "Comète".
Impression en noir.

533F	0,45 EUR (E)	4 »
534F	0,50 EUR (P)	4 »
535F	0,75 EUR (LETTRE)	6 »
536F	4,00 EUR (C)	20 »
537F	4,00 EUR (J+2D)	20 »
538F	4,80 EUR (J+2N)	25 »

Idem. Type B (LISA 1). Existe vraisemblablement avec impression en rouge.

533Fa à 538Fa — Mêmes prix

2003. - *76e Congrès de la FFAP (06-09.06), Mulhouse. Timbre de distributeur. Type U. (Lisa 2). Papier adhésif quadrichromie, impression de la valeur en noir. Bandes de phosphore à gauche et à droite.*

Type U (Lisa 2). Mairie et armoiries de Mulhouse.

539	0,45 EUR à 99,99 EUR avec minimum de 3 »	Valeur faciale x 4
539A	0,01 EUR à 0,44 EUR	3 »
540	0,45 EUR (E)	3 »
541	0,50 EUR (P)	3 »
542	0,75 EUR (LETTRE)	3 »
543	4,00 EUR (C)	16 »
544	4,00 EUR (J+2D)	16 »
545	4,80 EUR (J+2N)	19 20

Note : Afin de terminer les rouleaux invendus, la Poste décida de les utiliser sur les appareils de Mulhouse Principal. Ces derniers n'étant pas bridés comme ceux du Congrès, il fut possible d'obtenir des petites valeurs (n° 539A - 0,01 EUR à 0,44 EUR).

541a	0,01 EUR à 99,99 EUR (P) avec minimum de 10 »	Valeur faciale x 4

Note : voir remarque concernant le 534a

2003. - *Foire européenne de Strasbourg (5-15.09). Timbre de distributeur. Type V (LISA 2). Papier adhésif thermique, quadrichromie. Impression de la valeur en noir. Bandes de phosphore à gauche et à droite.*

Type V (LISA 2). Strasbourg.
L'Ill et "La Petite France".

546	0,45 EUR à 99,99 EUR avec minimum de 3 »	Valeur faciale x 4
546A	0,01 EUR à 0,44 EUR	3 »
547	0,45 EUR (E)	3 »
548	0,50 EUR (P)	3 »
549	0,75 EUR (LETTRE)	3 »
550	4,00 EUR (C)	16 »
551	4,00 EUR (J+2D)	16 »
552	4,80 EUR (J+2N)	19 20

Note : Les timbres de petites valeurs n'ont pu être obtenus qu'en début de service le premier jour de la Foire (05.09), les machines étant ensuite bridées, ou après l'exposition au bureau de Strasbourg Marseillaise (utilisation normale du reste des rouleaux).

548a	0,01 EUR à 99,99 EUR (P) avec minimum de 4 »	Valeur faciale x 5

Note : voir remarque concernant le 534a.

2003. - *57e Salon Philatélique d'automne, Paris (06-10.11). Timbre de distributeur. Type W (LISA 1). Thème Paris-Luxembourg. Papier adhésif, quadrichromie. Impression de la valeur en noir. Bandes de phosphore à gauche et à droite.*

Type W (LISA 1). Luxembourg : Palais Grand Ducal, Cathédrale Notre-Dame, Citadelle Saint-Esprit et Pont Adolphe. Paris : Notre-Dame, la Cité et le Pont Neuf.

553	0,45 EUR à 99,99 EUR avec minimum de 1 50	Valeur faciale x 3
554	0,45 EUR (E)	1 50
555	0,50 EUR (P)	1 50
556	0,75 EUR (LETTRE)	1 50
557	4,00 EUR (C)	12 »
558	4,00 EUR (J+2D)	12 »
559	4,80 EUR (J+2N)	14 50

2004. - *Salon Philatélique de printemps, Clermont-Ferrand (26-28.03). Timbre de distributeur. Type X (LISA 2). Papier adhésif thermique, quadrichromie. Impression de la valeur en noir. Une bande de phosphore à gauche et à droite.*

Type X (LISA 2). Clermont-Ferrand : monuments anciens et modernes.

560 0,01 EUR à 99,99 EUR avec minimum de 3 » — Valeur faciale x 4
561 0,45 EUR (E) — 3 »
562 0,50 EUR (P) — 3 »
563 0,75 EUR (LETTRE) — 3 »
564 4,00 EUR (C) — 16 »
565 4,00 EUR (J+2D) — 16 »
566 4,80 EUR (J+2N) — 19 20
562a 0,01 EUR à 99,99 EUR (P) avec minimum de 10 » — Valeur faciale x 4

Note : Voir remarque concernant le n° 534a.

Note : Dès le 01.04, par suite de la réforme tarifaire des colis, les distributeurs LISA ne délivrent plus de timbres J+2D et J+2N.

2004. - *Le Salon du timbre 2004 - Paris (26.6-4.7.04). Timbre de distributeur. Type Y (LISA). Papier adhésif, multicolore. Impression en noir. Bandes de phosphore à gauche et à droite.*

Type Y (LISA). Dahlia, fleur de Lotus et coin du parc floral de Paris.

567 0,45 EUR à 99,99 EUR avec minimum de 1 50 — Valeur faciale x 3
568 0,45 EUR (E) — 1 50
569 0,50 EUR (P) — 1 50
570 0,75 EUR (LETTRE) — 2 50
571 4,00 EUR (C) — 12 »

2004. - *77ᵉ Congrès de la FFAP - Paris (26.6-4.7.04). Timbre de distributeur. Type Z (LISA). Papier adhésif, multicolore. Impression en noir. Bandes de phosphore à gauche et à droite.*

Type Z (LISA). Vue générale de Paris.

572 0,45 EUR à 99,99 EUR avec minimum de 1 50 — Valeur faciale x 3
573 0,45 EUR (E) — 1 50
574 0,50 EUR (P) — 1 50
575 0,75 EUR (LETTRE) — 2 50
576 4,00 EUR (C) — 12 »

2004. – *Timbre de distributeur LISA2. Papier thermique adhésif "avion papier plié" Type AA, marges latérales larges, bandes de phosphore larges à gauche et à droite (type 1). Impression en noir.*

Type AA (LISA 2). Avions en papier plié, marges latérales larges

577 0,01 EUR à 99,99EUR avec un minimum de 1,50 — Valeur faciale x 3
578 0,45 EUR (E) — 1 50
579 0,50 EUR (P) — 1 50
580 0,75 EUR (LETTRE) — 2 50
581 4,00 EUR (C) — 12 »
577a 0,01 EUR à 99,99EUR (P) avec un minimum de 2,50 — Valeur faciale x 5

Note : voir remarque concernant le 534a

Bandes de phosphore larges, type 1

Bandes de phosphore étroites, type 2

Idem LISA 2, papier thermique type AA, bandes de phosphore étroites à gauche et à droite (type 2).

Impression en noir

577A à 581A — Même prix
577a 0,01 EUR à 99,99EUR (P) avec un minimum de 2,50 — Valeur faciale x 5

Note : voir remarque concernant le 534a

2004. – *SALON PHILATELIQUE – ANGERS 2004, Angers (9 – 10.10). Timbre de distributeur LISA 2. Papier adhésif, quadrichromie Type AB. Bandes de phosphore à gauche et à droite. Impression en noir.*

Type AB (LISA 2) Angers : le château.

582 0,01 EUR à 99,99EUR avec minimum de 1,50 — Valeur faciale x 4
583 0,45 EUR (E) — 2 »
584 0,50 EUR (P) — 2 »

585 0,75 EUR (LETTRE) 3 »
586 4,00 EUR (C) 16 »

2004. – *Timbre de distributeur LISA 1. Tarif du 01.06.02. Type G. Impression en violet (Nantes)*

587 0,45 EUR (E) 2 50
588 0,50 EUR (P) 2 50
589 0,75 EUR (LETTRE) 3 75
590 4,00 EUR (C) 20 »

2004. – *Timbre de distributeur LISA 1. Papier thermique Type AA marges latérales larges, bandes de phosphore larges à gauche et à droite (type 1). Impression en noir*

591 0,01 EUR à 99,99EUR avec minimum de 1,50 — Valeur faciale x 4
592 0,45 EUR (E) 2 »
593 0,50 EUR (P) 2 »
594 0,75 EUR (LETTRE) 3 »
595 4,00 EUR (C) 16 »
582 0,01 EUR à 99,99EUR avec minimum de 1,50 — Valeur faciale x 4
583 0,45 EUR (E) 2 »
584 0,50 EUR (P) 2 »
585 0,75 EUR (LETTRE) 3 »
586 4,00 EUR (C) 16 »

2004. – *Timbre de distributeur LISA 1. Tarif du 01.06.02. Type G. Impression en violet (Nantes)*

587 0,45 EUR (E) 2 50
588 0,50 EUR (P) 2 50
589 0,75 EUR (LETTRE) 3 75
590 4,00 EUR (C) 20 »

2004. – *Timbre de distributeur LISA 1. Papier thermique Type AA marges latérales larges, bandes de phosphore larges à gauche et à droite (type 1). Impression en noir.*

Type AA (LISA 1). Avions en papier plié, marges latérales larges

591 0,01 EUR à 99,99EUR avec minimum de 1,50 — Valeur faciale x 4
592 0,45 EUR (E) 2 »
593 0,50 EUR (P) 2 »
594 0,75 EUR (LETTRE) 3 »
595 4,00 EUR (C) 16 »

2004. – *58ᵉ Salon philatélique d'automne, Paris (29.10 – 1.11). Timbre de distributeur LISA 1. Thème Paris - Athènes. Papier adhésif, quadrichromie Type AC. Bandes de phosphore à gauche et à droite. Impression en noir.*

Type AC (LISA 2) Athènes : Parthénon ; Paris : église de la Madeleine, colonne de la Bastille

596 0,45 EUR à 99,99EUR avec minimum de 1,50 — Valeur faciale x 4
597 0,45 EUR (E) 2 »
598 0,50 EUR (P) 2 »
599 0,75 EUR (LETTRE) 3 »
600 4,00 EUR (C) 16 »

2005. – *Timbre de distributeur LISA 2. Tarif du 01/03/05. Papier thermique Type AA, marges latérales larges, bandes de phosphore larges type 1. Impression en noir.*

601 0,48 EUR (E) 1 50
602 0,55 EUR (P) 2 »
603 0,82 EUR (LETTRE) 2 50
604 4,05 EUR (C) 12 »

Idem. LISA 2, papier thermique Type AA, bandes de phosphore étroites type 2. Impression en noir.

601A à 604A Même prix

Note : Pendant quelques jours la date de fabrication des rouleaux de vignettes est imprimée au dos des vignettes (toutes les 23 vignettes). Cette date s'étale sur 3 ou 4 vignettes. Les dates connues actuellement vont du 9 au 14/06/2005. (valeur = valeur des vignettes correspondantes + 10,00 €).

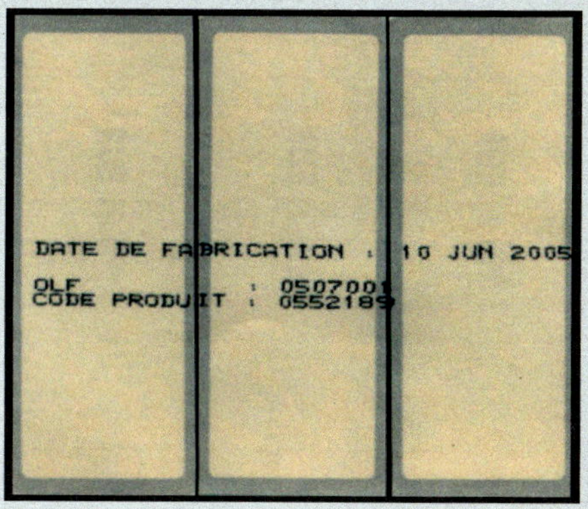

2005. - *Timbre de distributeur LISA 2. Papier thermique Type AA, marges latérales larges, sans bandes de phosphore. Impression en noir.*

601B 0,48 EUR (E) 2 50
602B 0,55 EUR (P) 2 75
603B 0,82 EUR (LETTRE) 4 »
604B 4,05 EUR (C) 20 »

Idem. LISA 2. Papier thermique Type H. Bandes de phosphore à gauche et à droite. Impression en noir.

601C à 604C Même prix

2005. – *Timbre de distributeur LISA1. Tarif du 01/03/05. Papier Type G. Bandes de phosphore à gauche et à droite. Impression en noir.*

605 0,48 EUR (E) 1 50
606 0,55 EUR (P) 2 »
607 0,82 EUR (LETTRE) 2 50
608 4,05 EUR (C) 12 »

Idem. Impression en rouge

605a à 608a Même prix

Idem. Sans bande phosphore. Impression en noir

605A à 608A Même prix

Idem. Papier thermique marges étroites. Bandes de phosphore à gauche et à droite. Impression en noir

605B à 608B Même prix

Idem. Impression en rouge

605Ba à 608Ba Même prix

Idem. Papier thermique marges étroites. Sans bande de phosphore. Impression en noir

605Bb à 608Bb Même prix

2005. - *Timbre de distributeur LISA 1. Papier thermique type AA marges latérales larges, bandes de phosphore larges (type 1). Impression en noir.*

609 0,48 EUR (E) 1 50
610 0,55 EUR (P) 2 »
611 0,82 EUR (LETTRE) 2 50
612 4,05 EUR (C) 12 »

Idem. Impression en rouge

609a à 612a Même prix

Idem. Papier thermique type AA marges latérales larges, bandes de phosphore étroites (type 2). Impression en noir

609A à 612A Même prix

Idem. Papier thermique type AA marges latérales larges, sans bande de phosphore. Impression en noir

609B à 612B » »

2005. – *Timbre de distributeur LISA 1. Papier "Oiseaux turquoise" Type C. Impression en rouge (Toulon).*

613 0,48 EUR (E) 2 50
614 0,55 EUR (P) 3 »
615 0,82 EUR (LETTRE) 4 »
616 4,05 EUR (C) 20 »

Idem. Papier thermique. Impression en rouge (Poste de Paris Musée du Louvre - mai 2005)

613A à 616A » »

Idem. Papier thermique. Impression en noir (Poste de Paris Musée du Louvre - mai 2005)

613Aa à 616Aa » »

2005. – *Timbre de distributeur LISA 1. Papier "Comète" Type B. Impression en noir.*

617 0,48 EUR (E) 3 »
618 0,55 EUR (P) 3 50
619 0,82 EUR (LETTRE) 5 »
620 4,05 EUR (C) 25 »

2005. – *SALON PHILATELIQUE DE PRINTEMPS - AIX-EN-PROVENCE 2005, Aix-en-Provence (01- 03.04). Timbre de distributeur LISA 2. Papier adhésif, quadrichromie Type AD. Bandes de phosphore à gauche et à droite. Impression en noir.*

Type AD (LISA 2) Aix-en-Provence : Fontaine de la Rotonde et Montagne Ste Victoire.

621 0,48 EUR à 99,99EUR avec minimum de 1,50 Valeur faciale x 4
622 0,48 EUR (E) 2 »
623 0,55 EUR (P) 2 »
624 0,82 EUR (LETTRE) 3 »
625 4,05 EUR (C) 16 »

Note : des vignettes à 0,01 EUR ont pu être obtenues hors salon

621a 0,01 EUR 5 »

2005. - *FÉDÉRATION FRANÇAISE DES ASSOCIATIONS PHILATÉLIQUES - 78e CONGRÈS - NANCY 2005 (05-08.05). Timbre de distributeur LISA 1. Papier adhésif, quadrichromie Type AE. Bandes de phosphore à gauche et à doite. Impression en noir.*

Type AE (LISA 1) Nancy : place Stanislas - fontaine et grille en fer forgé de Jean Lamour.

626 0,48 EUR à 99,99EUR avec minimum de 2,00 Valeur faciale x 4
627 0,48 EUR (E) 2 »
628 0,55 EUR (P) 2 »
629 0,82 EUR (LETTRE) 3 »
630 4,05 EUR (C) 16 »

Note : des vignettes à 0,01 EUR ont pu être obtenues en tout début de service le premier jour à l'ouverture du Congrès.

626a 0,01 EUR 5 »

2005. – *Timbre de distributeur LISA 1. Papier non thermique Type AA, marges latérales larges, bandes de phosphore étroite type 2. Impression en noir.*

631 0,48 EUR (E) 1 50
632 0,55 EUR (P) 2 »
633 0,82 EUR (LETTRE) 2 50
634 4,05 EUR (C) 12 »

2005. - *MAXIFRANCE 2005 CORBEIL ESSONNES - Corbeil Essonnes (23-25.09.05). Timbre de distributeur Lisa1. Papier adhésif, quadrichromie Type AF. . Impression en noir. Bandes de phosphore à gauche et à droite.*

Type AF (LISA1) : Mairie, église et monuments divers de Corbeil Essonnes.

636 0,48 EUR à 99,99EUR avec minimum de 2,00 Valeur faciale x 4
637 0,48 EUR (E) 2 »
638 0,55 EUR (P) 2 »
639 0,82 EUR (LETTRE) 3 »
640 4,05 EUR (C) 16 »

2005. – *59e Salon philatélique d'automne, Paris (10.11 – 13.11). Timbre de distributeur LISA1. Thème Paris – Stockholm. Papier adhésif, quadrichromie Type AG. Bandes de phosphore à gauche et à droite. Impression en noir.*

Type AG (LISA 1) Stocholm : Hôtel de ville ; Paris : Mairie de Paris.

641	0,48 EUR à 99,99EUR avec minimum de 2,00	Valeur faciale x 4	
642	0,48 EUR (E)		2 »
643	0,55 EUR (P)		2 »
644	0,82 EUR (LETTRE)		3 »
645	4,05 EUR (C)		16 »

Note : A partir du 01/03/2006 les distributeurs de type LISA1 et LISA2 ne délivrent plus de timbres C (COLIECO).

2006. – *SALON PHILATELIQUE DE PRINTEMPS - DIJON 2006, Dijon (07- 09.04). Timbre de distributeur LISA 2. Papier adhésif, quadrichromie Type AH. Bandes de phosphore à gauche et à droite. Impression en noir.*

Type AH (LISA 2) : Place de la libération à Dijon.

646	0,01 EUR à 99,99EUR avec minimum de 1,50	Valeur faciale x 4	
647	0,48 EUR (E)		2 »
648	0,55 EUR (P)		2 50
649	0,82 EUR (LETTRE)		3 50

2006. – *LE SALON DU TIMBRE & DE L'ECRIT 2006, Parc floral de Paris (17-25.06). Timbre de distributeur LISA 1. Papier adhésif, quadrichromie Type AI. Bandes de phosphore à gauche et à droite. Impression en noir.*

Type AI (LISA 1), Hommage à Mozart : piano et violon sur fond de partition.

650	0,48 EUR à 99,99EUR avec minimum de 2,00	Valeur faciale x 4	
651	0,48 EUR (E)		2 »
652	0,55 EUR (P)		2 50
653	0,82 EUR (LETTRE)		3 50

2006. – *LE SALON DU TIMBRE & DE L'ECRIT 2006, Parc floral de Paris (17-25.06). Timbre de distributeur LISA 1. Papier adhésif, quadrichromie Type AJ. Bandes de phosphore à gauche et à droite. Impression en noir.*

Type AJ (LISA 1) : fruits exotiques divers (banane, mangue, pastèque…).

654	0,48 EUR à 99,99EUR avec minimum de 2,00	Valeur faciale x 4	
655	0,48 EUR (E)		2 »
656	0,55 EUR (P)		2 50
657	0,82 EUR (LETTRE)		3 50

2006. – *FEDERATION FRANÇAISE DES ASSOCIATIONS PHILATELIQUES – 79e CONGRES – PARIS 2006, Parc floral de Paris (18-25.06). Timbre de distributeur LISA 1. Papier adhésif, quadrichromie Type AK. Bandes de phosphore à gauche et à droite. Impression en noir.*

Type AK (LISA 1) : Paris : fronton de l'Opéra Garnier.

658	0,48 EUR à 99,99EUR avec minimum de 2,00	Valeur faciale x 4	
659	0,48 EUR (E)		2 »
660	0,55 EUR (P)		2 50
661	0,82 EUR (LETTRE)		3 50

Note : Contrairement aux deux autres timbres émis lors du salon du timbre et de l'écrit, le timbre commémorant le 79e Congrès de la Fédération n'a été utilisé qu'à partir du 18 juin.

2006 – *BILATÉRALE FRANCE-ALLEMAGNE – NEVERS 2006 (15.09 – 17.09). Timbre de distributeur LISA 2. Papier adhésif, quadrichromie Type AL. Bandes de phosphore à gauche et à droite. Impression en noir.*

Type AL (LISA 2) vues diverses de Nevers.

662	0,01 EUR à 99,99EUR avec minimum de 2,00	Valeur faciale x 4	
663	0,48 EUR (E)		2 50
664	0,55 EUR (P)		2 50
665	0,82 EUR (LETTRE)		3 50

Note : Après le 1er octobre (date de changement de tarif) La Poste de Nevers confectionna par correspondance des vignettes au nouveau tarif et correspondant aux nouvelles inscriptions portées sur les vignettes par les LISA 2.

Type AL (LISA 2) vues diverses de Nevers. nouvelle présentation

662A	0,01 EUR à 99,99EUR avec minimum de 2,00	Valeur faciale x 10
664A	0,60 EUR (PRIORITAIRE)	6 »
665A	0,86 EUR (LETTRE)	8 50

2006 – *Timbre de distributeur LISA 2. Tarif du 01/10/06 Papier thermique Type AA, marges latérales larges, bandes de phosphore type 1 ou 2. Impression en noir. La valeur faciale est maintenant centre horizontalement sure le timbre La mention tarifaire E (ECOPLI) n'est plus inscrite sur les timbres, la mention PRIORITAIRE est inscrite en toute lettre sous la valeur faciale du timbre comme la mention tarifaire LETTRE.*

Type AA (LISA 2) nouvelle présentation.

666	0,01 EUR à 99,99EUR avec minimum de 1,50	Valeur faciale x 3
667	0,60 EUR (PRIORITAIRE)	2 »
668	0,86 EUR (LETTRE)	2 50

Note: existe sans bande de phosphore.

Note : les vignettes TEST délivrées par les LISA 2 subissent également une modification.

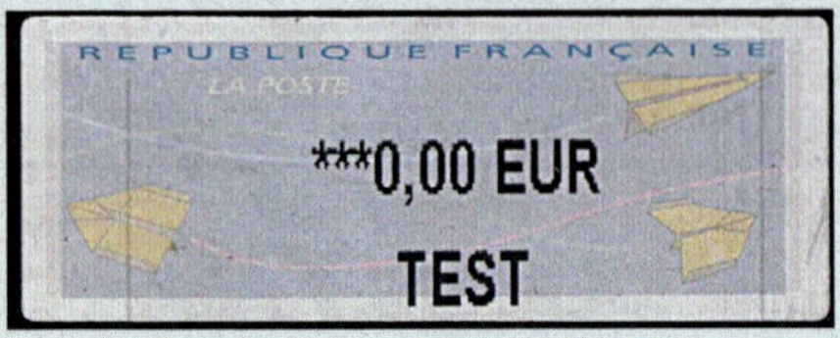

Vignette TEST LISA 2 type 3

Idem. LISA 2. Papier thermique Type H. Bandes de phosphore à gauche et à droite Impression en noir.

666B et 667B — Même prix

2006 – *Timbre de distributeur LISA1. Tarif du 01/10/06. Papier Type G. Bandes de phosphore à gauche et à droite. Impression en noir.*

669	0,49EUR (E)	1 50
670	0,60EUR (P)	2 »
671	0,86 EUR (LETTRE)	2 50

Note : Contrairement aux LISA 2, les LISA 1 ne subirent pas de modification dans l'inscription des mentions tarifaires.

Idem. Impression en rouge

605a à 608a — Même prix

2006 - *Timbre de distributeur LISA 1. Papier thermique type AA marges latérales larges, bandes de phosphore type 1 ou 2). Impression en noir.*

672	0,49 EUR (E)	1 50
673	0,60 EUR (P)	2 »
674	0,86 EUR (LETTRE)	2 50

2006 – *60e Salon philatélique d'automne, Paris (08.11 – 11.11). Timbre de distributeur LISA1. Thème Paris - Vienne. Papier adhésif, quadrichromie Type AM. Bandes de phosphore à gauche et à droite. Impression en noir.*

Type AM (LISA 1) Vienne : Paris : l'Opéra Garnier.

675	0,49 EUR à 99,99EUR avec minimum de 2,00	Valeur faciale x 4
676	0,49 EUR (E)	2 »
677	0,60 EUR (P)	2 50
678	0,86 EUR (LETTRE)	3 50

2007 – *FÊTE DU TIMBRE 2007 (10.3 – 11.03) -Timbre de distributeur LISA1. Thème Harry Potter. Papier adhésif nonthermique, quadrichromie Type AN. Bandes de phosphore à gauche et à droite. Impression en noir.*

Type AN (LISA 1) Harry Potter.

679	0,49 EUR à 99,99EUR avec minimum de 2,50	Valeur faciale x 5
680	0,49 EUR (E)	2 50
681	0,60 EUR (P)	3 »
682	0,86 EUR (LETTRE)	4 50

Note : Vu la dispersion des sites où il était possible d'obtenir ces timbres, des vignettes à 0,01 EUR ont pu être obtenues.

679a	0,01 EUR	4 »

Idem. Papier thermique. Impression en noir (bureau de Poste de Valbonne Village 06)

679A	0,49 EUR à 99,99EUR avec minimum de 5,00	Valeur faciale x 10
680A	0,49 EUR (E)	5 »
681A	0,60 EUR (P)	6 »
682A	0,86 EUR (LETTRE)	9 »

Idem. Timbre de distributeur LISA 2. Papier thermique, Type AN

Type AN (LISA 2) Harry Potter, papier thermique.

683	0,01 EUR à 99,99EUR avec minimum de 2,00	Valeur faciale x 4
684	0,60 EUR (PRIORITAIRE)	2 50
685	0,86 EUR (LETTRE)	3 50

2007 – *Salon philatélique de printemps – LIMOGES 2007 (23.03 – 25.03). Timbre de distributeur LISA 2. Papier adhésif, quadrichromie Type AO. Bandes de phosphore à gauche et à droite. Impression en noir.*

Type AO (LISA 2) Gare et mairie de limoges.

686	0,49 EUR à 99,99EUR avec minimum de 2,00	Valeurfaciale x 4
687	0,60 EUR (PRIORITAIRE)	2 50
688	0,86 EUR (LETTRE)	3 50

2007 – *Fédération française des associations philatéliques - 80e Congrès – Poitiers (15.06 – 17.06). Timbre de distributeur LISA 2. Papier adhésif, quadrichromie Type AP. Bandes de phosphore à gauche et à droite. Impression en noir.*

Type AP (LISA 2) : Notre-Dame La Grande et mairie de Poitiers.

689	0,01 EUR à 99,99EU avec minimum de 2,00	Valeur faciale x 4
690	0,60 EUR (PRIORITAIRE)	2 50
691	0,86 EUR (LETTRE)	3 50

2007 – *Timbres Pasion 2007 DOLE (02.11 - 04.11). Timbre de distributeur LISA 2. Papier adhésif, quadrichromie Type AQ. Bandes de phosphore à gauche et à droite. Impression en noir.*

Type AQ (LISA 2) : Effigie de Pasteur, sa maison natale, Hôtel-dieu de Dôle.

692	0,01 EUR à 99,99EU avec minimum de 2,00	Valeur faciale x 4
693	0,60 EUR (PRIORITAIRE)	2 50
694	0,86 EUR (LETTRE)	3 50

2007 – *61e Salon philatélique d'automne, PARIS (08.11 – 11.11). Timbre de distributeur LISA 1. Papier adhésif, quadrichromie Type AR. Bandes de phosphore. à gauche et à droite. Impression en noir.*

Type AR (LISA 1) Paris : Arc de Triomphe, Tour Eiffel, .Pont Neuf et Notre Dame.

695	0,49 EUR à 99,99EUR avec minimum de 2,00	Valeur faciale x 4
696	0,49 EUR (E)	2 »
697	0,60 EUR (P)	2 50
698	0,86 EUR (LETTRE)	3 50

2007 – *MACON 2007 – Championnat Philatélique Interrégional (16.11 - 18.11). Timbre de distributeur LISA 1, Papier adhésif, quadrichromie Type AS. Bandes phosphore à gauche et à droite. Impression en noir.*

Type AS (LISA 1) Maçon : Statue de Lamartine, cathédrale du vieux Saint-Vincent, Pont Saint-Laurent.

699	0,49 EUR à 99,99EUR avec minimum de 2,00	Valeur faciale x 4
700	0,49 EUR (E)	2 »
701	0,60 EUR (P)	2 50
702	0,86 EUR (LETTRE)	3 50

2008 – *Timbre de distributeur LISA 2. Tarif du 01/03/08 Papier thermique Type AA, marges latérales larges, bandes de phosphore type 1 ou 2. Impression en noir. La mention tarifaire LETTRE est remplacée par la mention LETTRE PRIORITAIRE toujours inscrite sous la valeur faciale du timbre, mais en plus petits caractères. Cette mention apparaît maintenant sur les timbres dés le premier gramme. La mention tarifaire PRIORITAIRE apparaît toujours sur les timbres au tarif pour l'étranger mais en plus petit caractère comme pour la mention LETTRE PRIORITAIRE. Les mentions ne sont plus centrées sous la valeur faciale du timbre.*

Type AA (LISA 2). Nouvelle présentation.

703	0,01 EUR à 99,99EUR avec minimum de 1,50	Valeur faciale x 3
704	0,55 EUR (LETTRE PRIORITAIRE)	2 »
705	0,60 EUR (PRIORITAIRE)	2 »

Coins à angle à petit arrondi, type 1

Coins à angle à grand arrondi, type 2

Idem LISA2, papier thermique type AA, Coins à angle à grand arrondi, type 2 - Impression en noir.

703A à 705A *même prix*

Note : les vignettes TEST délivrées par les LISA 2 subissent également une modification.

Vignette TEST LISA 2 type 4

2008 – *Bicentenaire de Guignol – LYON 2008 (23.03 – 25.03). Timbre de distributeur LISA 2. Papier adhésif, quadrichromie Type AR. Bandes de phosphore à gauche et à droite. Impression en noir.*

Type AR (LISA 2). Guignol et statue du buste de Laurent Mourguet, son créateur.

706	0,50 EUR à 99,99EUR avec minimum de 2,00	Valeur faciale x 4
707	0,55 EUR (LETTRE PRIORITAIRE)	2 50
708	0,65 EUR (PRIORITAIRE)	3 50

2008 – *Le Salon du Timbre et de l'Ecrit - PARIS 2008, Parc floral de Paris (14-22.06). Timbre de distributeur LISA 1. Papier adhésif, quadrichromie Type AS. Bandes de phosphore à gauche et à droite. Impression en noir.*

Type AS (LISA 1), Monuments de Paris (Notre Dame, le Sacré Cœur, la Fontaine des Innocents....).

709	0,50 EUR à 99,99EUR avec minimum de 2,00	Valeur faciale x 4
710	0,50 EUR (E)	2 »
711	0,65 EUR (P)	250
712	0,88 EUR (LETTRE)	3 50

2008 – *Le Salon du Timbre et de l'Ecrit - PARIS 2008, Parc floral de Paris (14-22.06). Timbre de distributeur LISA 1. Papier adhésif, quadrichromie Type AT. Bandes de phosphore à gauche et à droite. Impression en noir.*

Type AT (LISA 1) : Le Cirque (Clown, tigre, chapiteau...).

713	0,50 EUR à 99,99EUR avec minimum de 2,00	Valeur faciale x 4
714	0,50 EUR (E)	2 »
715	0,65 EUR (P)	250
716	0,88 EUR (LETTRE)	3 50

2008 – *Fédération Française des Associations Philatéliques – 81e Congrès – PARIS 2008, Parc floral de Paris (14-22.06). Timbre de distributeur LISA 1. Papier adhésif, quadrichromie Type AU. Bandes de phosphore à gauche et à droite. Impression en noir.*

Type AU (LISA 1) : Paris : Le Grand Palais.

717	0,50 EUR à 99,99EUR avec minimum de 2,00	Valeur faciale x 4	
718	0,50 EUR (E)		2 »
719	0,65 EUR (P)		2 50
720	0,88 EUR (LETTRE)		3 50

Note : Malgré l'ouverture officielle du salon au public prévue pour le 14 juin, les machines furent mises en service le 13 lors de l'inauguration officielle du salon. Seules les personnes invitées pouvaient y entrer et obtenir des vignettes avec chacun des trois visuels décrits ci-dessus accompagnées de reçus datés du13/06/2008. Elles purent également faire oblitérer les vignettes avec les cachets prévus pour chaque visuel à la date du 13 juin 2008.

Vignettes accompagnées d'un reçu daté du 13/06/2008 — *cote vignette correspondante x 5*

Pli oblitéré du 13 juin 2088 avec cachet correspondant à la vignette — *cote vignette correspondante x 3*

2008 – *62e Salon philatélique d'automne, PARIS (06.11 – 09.11). Timbre de distributeur LISA1. Papier adhésif, quadrichromie Type AV. Bandes de phosphore à gauche et à droite. Impression en noir.*

Type AV (LISA 1) Paris : sortie du métro Porte Dauphine, une fontaine Wallace, pont du canal St Martin.

721	0,50 EUR à 99,99EUR avec minimum de 2,00	Valeur faciale x 4	
722	0,50 EUR (E)		2 »
723	0,65 EUR (P)		2 50
724	0,88 EUR (LETTRE)		3 »

Note 1 : Suite à un problème de batterie sur une machine il fut possible d'obtenir des vignettes au tarif du 01/10/2006.

721A	0,50 EUR à 99,99EUR avec minimum de 5,00	Valeur faciale x 10	
722A	0,50 EUR (E)		5 »
723A	0,65 EUR (P)		6 50
724A	0,88 EUR (LETTRE)		9 »

Note 2 : suite à un défaut dans l'embobinage des rouleaux de vignettes lors de leur confection à Périgueux décelé quelques temps avant l'ouverture du salon et retiré de la vente, un ou deux rouleaux ont échappé au retrait et ont été utilisés pendant le salon.

Vignettes imprimées à l'envers — *cote vignette correspondante x 3*

2009 – *Timbre de distributeur LISA 2. Tarif du 02/03/09 Papier thermique Type AA, marges latérales larges, bandes de phosphore type 1 ou 2. Coins à angle arrondi, type 1 ou 2 Impression en noir.*

La Poste profite du changement de tarif pour compléter les mentions inscrites sur les vignettes :
- *MINI MAX : nouveau tarif de la Poste dédié à l'envoi de petites marchandises de faible valeur,*
- *R L1 AR : Tarif de la lettre recommandée avec accusé de réception, régime indemnitaire type 1,*
- *R L2 AR : Tarif de la lettre recommandée avec accusé de réception, régime indemnitaire type 2,*
- *R L3 AR : Tarif de la lettre recommandée avec accusé de réception, régime indemnitaire type 3,*

Note : Les tarifs correspondant aux lettres recommandées avec accusé de réception peuvent être armés ou non selon le bon vouloir du chef d'établissement du bureau dans lequel est installé la LISA 2.

Type AA (LISA 2). coins au grand arrondi (type 2) Tarif de la lettre recommandée avec accusé de réception, régime indemnitaire type 1.

725	0,56 EUR (LETTRE PRIORITAIRE)	2 »
726	0,70 EUR (PRIORITAIRE)	2 50
727	1,50 EUR (MINI MAX)	4 50
728	4,36 EUR (R L1 AR)	13 »
729	4,96 EUR (R L2 AR)	15 »
730	5,86 EUR (R L3 AR)	18 »

2009 - *SALON PHILATELIQUE DE PRINTEMPS-MACON 2009 (27-29.03) - Timbre de distributeur LISA1. Papier adhésif, quadrichromie Type AW. Bandes de phosphore à gauche et à droite. Impression en noir.*

Type AW (LISA 1) Macon : Pont Saint-Laurent, carte du département, vestige de l'ancienne cathédrale Saint-Vincent.

731	0,51 EUR à 99,99EUR avec minimum de 2,00	Valeur faciale x 4	
732	0,51 EUR (E)		2 »
733	0,70 EUR (P)		3 »
734	0,90 EUR (LETTRE)		3 50

2009 - *EXPOSITION PHILATELIQUE INTERREGIONALE - RAEDERSHEIM (04-05.04) Timbre de distributeur LISA 2. Papier thermique Type AX, bandes de phosphore à gauche et à droite. Coins à angle à grand arrondi, Impression en noir.*

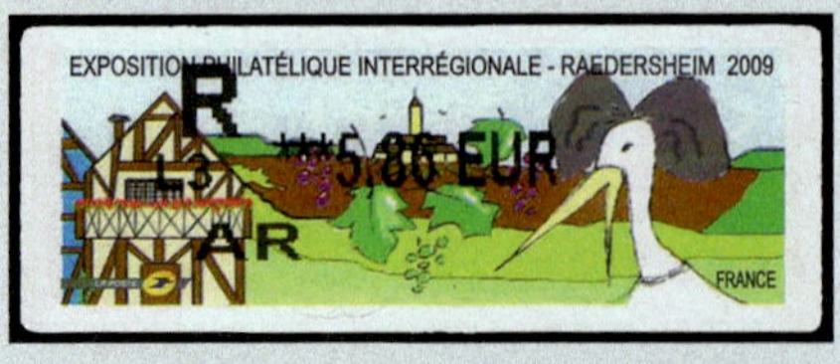

Type AX (LISA 2) : symboles alsaciens : maison, campagne, cigogne avec coiffe alsacienne.

735	0,01 EUR à 99,99EUR avec minimum de 2,00	Valeur faciale x 4
736	0,56 EUR (LETTRE PRIORITAIRE)	2 50
737	0,70 EUR (PRIORITAIRE)	3 »
738	1,50 EUR (MINI MAX)	6 »
739	4,36 EUR (R L1 AR)	17 50
740	4,96 EUR (R L2 AR)	20 »
741	5,86 EUR (R L3 AR)	30 »

2009 – *FEDERATION FRANÇAISE DES ASSOCIATIONS PHILATELIQUES – 82e CONGRES – TARBES 2009 - Timbre de distributeur LISA1. Papier adhésif, quadrichromie Type AY. Bandes de phosphore à gauche et à droite. Impression en noir.*

Type AY (LISA 1) : vues diverses du jardin Massey de Tarbes : conifères et cèdres, un des bustes du jardin, la serre et le Musée Massey, végétation luxuriante.

742	0,51 EUR à 99,99EUR avec minimum de 2,00	Valeur faciale x 4
743	0,51 EUR (E)	2 »
744	0,70 EUR (P)	3 »
745	0,90 EUR (LETTRE)	3 50

2009 - *PARIS TOUR EIFFEL (08.06) - Timbre de distributeur LISA 2. Papier thermique Type AZ, bandes de phosphore à gauche et à droite. Coins à angle à grand arrondi, Impression en noir.*

Type AZ (LISA 2) : 1ère étage de la Tour Eiffel, Tour Eiffel sur pied, statues du Trocadéro.

703	0,01 EUR à 99,99EUR avec minimum de 2,00	Valeur faciale x 4
704	0,56 EUR (LETTRE PRIORITAIRE)	2 50
705	0,70 EUR (PRIORITAIRE)	3 »
704	1,50 EUR (MINI MAX)	4 50

Note : Les tarifs correspondant aux lettres recommandées avec accusé de réception n'ont pas été armés par le chef d'établissement du bureau dans lequel a été installé la LISA 2.

TIMBRES FISCAUX

Voir catalogue des Timbres Fiscaux et Socio-postaux de France - 2004, Yvert & Tellier, Amiens, 1er catalogue de Fiscaux en couleurs.

ENTIERS POSTAUX

Tout support tel que carte postale, carte-lettre, enveloppe ou bande pour journaux, sur lequel un timbre-poste est imprimé est un « ENTIER POSTAL ».

La nomenclature donnée ci-après est celle des entiers émis par le Service des Postes et diffuses auprès du public, augmentée de quelques entiers timbrés sur commande à des types qui n'existent pas en entiers postaux usuels. Timbrés sur commande (TSC) : il s'agit d'entiers postaux fabriqués sur mesure pour une entreprise, une association, une manifestation qui en commande une certaine quantité à l'administration.

Pour les entiers postaux TSC dont le timbre imprimé existe déjà en entier postal usuel vendu au public on se reportera aux catalogues spécialisés : « Les entiers postaux de France et de Monaco » par Robert Françon et Jean Storch et « Catalogue des entiers postaux de France » édité par l'Association des Collectionneurs d'Entiers Postaux (ACEP).

Par contre, nous avons jugé utile de mentionner dans ce chapitre les entiers TSC dont le timbre imprimé n'existe pas en entier postal usuel (exemple : 10 c Pasteur vert, 4 F 50 Gandon bleu…).

Repiquages : il s'agit de surimpressions effectuées sur des entiers postaux usuels existants. Les repiquages n'apportent pas de plus-value, sauf dans quelques cas particuliers comme les annonces publicitaires permettant de vendre l'entier repiqué à un prix réduit (voir catalogues spécialisés).

ABRÉVIATIONS

AER- Aérogramme.

BJ- Bande pour journaux.

CL- Carte-lettre.

CLPM- Carte-lettre pneumatique pour Marseille.

CLPMRP- Idem, avec réponse payée.

CP- Carte postale

CPP- Carte pneumatique pour Paris.

CPRP- Carte postale pour réponse payée.

D- Date, avec date.

E- Enveloppe.

EPM- Enveloppe pneumatique pour Marseille.

EPP- Idem, pour Paris.

LI- Livret d'identité.

MC- Maxicarte

RPCE- Pneu avec réponse payée de la Caisse d'Epargne

SD- Sans date.

NOTES EXPLICATIVES

Les chiffres romains entre parenthèses sont ceux des « TYPES » des timbres.

Dates des « ENTIERS » : Assez nombreux sont les entiers postaux datés.

La date dont ils sont porteurs est constituée de trois chiffres : le premier indique le millésime de l'année et les deux autres la énième semaine au cours de laquelle l'entier a été imprimé dans la dite année.

Il existe des dates obliques et renversées.

Cotations : les cotes des entiers postaux avec réponse payée, oblitérés, s'appliquent à chacun des éléments de ceux-ci. Cependant, il faut admettre que la partie « réponse » mérite une majoration de 100 % et davantage si le timbre est oblitéré de l'étranger.

1878-1906 TYPE SAGE

83-BJ1	1 c. noir	6 50	2 50
83-BJ2	1 c. noir avec date (801 à 108)	6 50	2 50

85-BJ1	2 c. brun-rouge	6 50	2 50
85-BJ2	2 c. brun rouge- avec date (806 à 032)	6 50	2 50

BJ1	3 c. vermillon	18 50	11 50

75-E1	5 c. vert (107x70 mm)	8 »	4 75
75-E2	5 c. vert sur vert (116x76 mm)	8 »	4 75
75-E3	5 c. vert sur blanc (116x76 mm)	6 50	3 »
75-E4	5 c. vert sur bulle (152x117 mm)	25 »	12 50

102-E1	5 c. vert-jaune (107x70 mm)	11 »	5 »

89-CP1	10 c. noir sur lilas (sans « République Française » et avec « réservé exclusivement »)	25 »	5 »
89-CP2	10 c. noir sur lilas (sans « République Française » et avec « exclusivement réservé »)	8 »	2 50
89-CP3	10 c. noir sur chamois (sans « République Française » et avec « exclusivement réservé »)	8 »	1 75
89-CP4	10 c. noir sur vert (sans « République Française » et avec « exclusivement réservé »)	6 50	1 »
89-CP5	10 c. noir sur vert (avec « République Française » et « exclusivement réservé »)	5 »	1 »
89-CPRP1	10 c. noir sur bleu (sans « République Française » et avec « réservé exclusivement »)	25 »	10 »
89-CPRP2	10 c. noir sur bleu (sans « République Française » et avec « exclusivement réservé »)	16 »	9 50
89-CPRP3	10 c. noir sur bleu (avec « République Française »)	16 »	9 50

90-CP1	15 c. bleu sur bleu (2 lignes pour l'adresse)	37 50	25 »
90-CP2	15 c. bleu sur bleu (3 lignes pour l'adresse)	37 50	26 »

CARTES-LETTRES

Trois piquages ont été successivement utilisés.

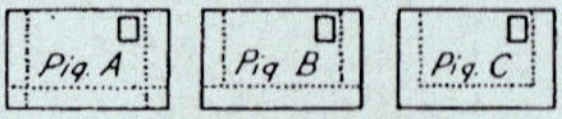

90-CL1	15 c. bleu sur paille (piquage A sans « avis » sur bandelette inférieure)	47 50	16 »

90-CL2	Idem, avec surcharge « Taxe réduite à 0f10 » de 1906	47 50	30 »
90-CL3	15 c. bleu sur paille (piquage A avec « Avis : pour ouvrir… » sur bandelette inférieure)	47 50	16 »
90-CL4	Idem, avec surcharge « Taxe réduite à 0f10 » de 1906	47 50	30 »
90-CL5	15 c. bleu sur gris, piquage A	65 »	40 »
90-CL6	Idem, avec surcharge « Taxe réduite à 0f10 » de 1906	20 »	15 »
90-CL7	15 c. bleu sur paille (piquage B)	31 »	13 »
90-CL8	Idem, avec surcharge « Taxe réduite à 0f10 » de 1906	40 »	31 »
90-CL9	15 c. bleu sur gris (piquage B)	11 »	5 50
90-CL10	Idem, avec surcharge « Taxe réduite à 0f10 » de 1906	25 »	16 »

90-CL11	15 c. bleu sur verdâtre (piquage B)	220 »	110 »
90-CL12	15 c. bleu sur gris (sans République Française, sans date)	9 50	4 75
90-CL13	Idem, avec surcharge « Taxe réduite à 0f10 » de 1906	20 »	13 50
90-CL14	15 c. bleu sur gris (sans République Française, dates 602 à 608)	16 »	8 »
90-CL15	Idem, avec surcharge « Taxe réduite à 0f10 » de 1906	16 »	8 »
90-CL16	15 c. bleu sur gris (sans République Française, dates 624 ou 625	16 »	8 »
90-CL17	15 c. bleu sur gris foncé ou clair (avec République Française)	6 50	1 75
90-CL18	Idem, avec surcharge « Taxe réduite à 0f10 » de 1906	8 »	2 50
90-CLRP1	15 c. + 15 c. bleu sur gris (sans République Française)	32 »	25 »
90-CLRP2	Idem, avec surcharge « Taxe réduite à 0f10 » de 1906	» »	» »
90-CLRP3	15 c. bleu sur chamois (avec République Française – sans date)	32 »	25 »
90-CLRP4	Idem, avec surcharge « Taxe réduite à 0f10 » de 1906	115 »	
90-CLRP5	15 c. bleu sur chamois (avec République Française, date 926)	45 »	31 »
90-CLRP6	Idem, avec surcharge « Taxe réduite à 0f10 » de 1906	115 »	
90-E1	15 c. bleu sur azuré (116x76 mm)	31 »	16 »
90-E2	15 c. bleu sur bleu gris ou bleu vert	15 »	8 »
90-E3	15 c. bleu sur azuré (123x96 mm)	31 »	16 »
90-E4	Idem, avec surcharge « Taxe réduite à 0f10 » de 1906	27 »	13 »
90-E5	15 c. bleu sur bleu-gris (123x96 mm)	16 »	8 »
90-E6	Idem avec surcharge « Taxe réduite à 0f10 »	9 50	6 50
90-E7	15 c. bleu sur bleu-vert (123x96 mm)	11 »	6 50
90-E8	Idem, avec surcharge « Taxe réduite à 0f10 » de 1906	5 »	3 »
90-E9	15 c. bleu sur verdâtre (123x96 mm – avec date au verso 808 à 022)	6 50	3 »
90-E10	Idem, avec surcharge « Taxe réduite à 0f10 » de 1906	5 »	3 »
90-E11	15 c. bleu sur azuré (147x112 mm)	32 50	16 »
90-E12	Idem – surcharge « Taxe réduite à 0f10 » de 1906	26 »	12 50
90-E13	15 c. bleu sur bleu-gris (format 147x112 mm)	16 »	8 »
90-E14	Idem avec surcharge « Taxe réduite à 0f10 » de 1906	9 50	6 50
90-E15	15 c. bleu sur bleu vert (format 147x112 mm)	12 »	6 50
90-E16	Idem avec surcharge « Taxe réduite à 0f10 » de 1906	5 »	3 »
90-E17	15 c. bleu sur vert clair, date 813 à 027	45 »	25 »
90-E18	Idem avec surcharge « Taxe réduite à 0f10 » de 1906	5 »	3 »

90-CPRP1	15 C. + 15 C. noir sur vert	250 »	120 »

97-CL1	25 c. noir sur rose (sans « République Française », sans « avis », piquage A)	32 »	16 »
97-CL2	25 c. noir sur rose (sans « République Française », sans « avis », piquage B)	32 »	16 »
97-CL3	25 c. noir sur rose (sans « République Française », sans « avis », piquage B ou C)	25 »	17 50
97-CL4	25 c. noir sur rose (avec « République Française », sans date ou date 806 à 110)	20 »	17 50

98-CPP1	50 c. rose sur chamois	160 »	100 »

98-CPP2	Idem, avec surcharge « Taxe réduite 30 c. » de 1880	150 »	100 »
98-LI1	Livret d'identité postal de 36 pages	4000 »	4000 »

81-CLPP1	75 c. noir sur bleu	160 »	100 »

81-CLPP2	Idem avec surcharge « Taxe réduite 50 c. » de 1880	160 »	100 »

1901-1924 TYPE BLANC

107-BJ1	1 c. gris (n° 107-I)	7 »	4 »

107a-BJ2	1 c. ardoise (n° 107a-I) avec date	7 »	4 »
	a) avec surcharge « Annulé » en violet	65 »	
107a-BJ3	1 c. ardoise, (n° 107a-I) sans date	16 »	8 »
107a-BJ4	1 c. ardoise (n° 107b-II) dates 217 à 222	175 »	125 »

108-BJ5	2 c. brun rouge (n°108-I) avec date	5 50	4 »
	a) avec surcharge « annulé » en noir ou violet	60 »	
108-BJ6	2 c. brun rouge (n° 108-I) sans date	20 »	9 50
108-BJ7	2 c. brun rouge (n° 108b-II), dates 921 à 937 ou 115 à 139	80 »	55 »
108-BJ8	2 c. brun rouge (n° 108b-II) sans date	47 50	31 »

109-BJ9	3 c. brun orange	25 »	12 50

111-E1	5 c. vert-jaune (107x70 mm), dates 113 à 226	18 »	10 »
111-E2	5 c. vert-bleu (107x70 mm) (n° 111a-I) dates 237 à 617	12 50	3 »

111-E3	5 c. vert (107x70 mm) (n° 111b-I), dates 635 à 649	25 »	10 »
111-BJ1	5 c. vert (n° 111-Ic), dates 437 à 531	95 »	31 »

1901-1906 TYPE MOUCHON

112-CP1	10 c. rouge (dates 114 à 212)	15 »	2 »
112-CPRP1	10 c. + 10 c. rouge (date 131)	60 »	20 »

117-CL1	15 c. orange sur gris (dates 115 à 123)	13 »	11 »
117-CL2	15 c. orange sur gris (sans date)	16 »	12 »
117-CL3	Idem avec surcharge « Taxe réduite à 0f10 » de 1906	12 50	7 »
117-CLRP1	15 C. + 15 C. orange sur chamois	55 »	32 »

117-CLRP2	Idem avec surcharge « Taxe réduite à 0f10 » de 1906	225 »	
117-E1	15 c. orange sur vert-gris (123x96 mm) (sans inscriptions pour l'expéditeur)	17 50	7 50
117-E2	Idem avec surcharge « Taxe réduite à 0f10 » de 1906	6 »	5 »
117-E3	15 c. orange sur vert-gris (147x112 mm) (sans inscriptions pour l'expéditeur)	17 50	7 50
117-E4	Idem, avec surcharge « Taxe réduite à 0f10 » de 1906	7 »	5 »
117-E5	15 c. orange sur vert-gris (123x96 mm) (avec inscriptions pour l'expéditeur)	12 »	6 50
117-E6	Idem, avec surcharge « Taxe réduite à 0f10 » de 1906	5 »	2 50
117-E7	15 c. orange sur vert-gris (147x112 mm) (avec inscriptions pour l'expéditeur)	12 »	6 50

1902-1906 MOUCHON RETOUCHE

124-CP1	10 c. rose sur vert (dates 211 à 347)	15 »	2 »
124-CPRP1	10 c. + 10 c. rose sur bleu (dates 221 et 324)	47 50	16 »

125-CL1	15 c. vermillon sur gris (dates 244 à 342)	9 50	5 »
125-CL2	Idem avec surcharge « Taxe réduite à 0f10 » de 1906	4 »	3 »

125-CLRP1	15 c. + 15 c. vermillon sur chamois	55 »	31 »
125-CLRP2	Idem avec surcharge « Taxe réduite à 0f10 » de 1906	275 »	
125-E1	15 c. Vermillon sur vert-gris (123x96 mm) (dates 313 et 314 ou sans date)	9 50	4 50
125-E2	Idem avec surcharge « Taxe réduite à 0f10 » de 1906	5 »	3 50
125-E3	15 c. vermillon sur vert-gris (147x112 mm) (dates 313 et 314 ou sans date)	9 50	3 50
125-E4	Idem avec surcharge « Taxe réduite à 0f10 » de 1906	3 50	2 50

127-CL1	25 c. bleu sur rose	120 »	65 »

1910 TYPE MERSON

120-LI1	Livret d'identité postal de 36 pages	7500 »	

1904-1944 SEMEUSE LIGNEE

129-CP1	10 c. rose sur vert (dates 344 à 647)	9 50	1 50
129-CPRP1	10 c. + 10 c. rose sur bleu (dates 414 et 513)	30 »	11 »
129-CPRP2	10 c. + 10 c. rose sur bleu (sans date)	30 »	11 »
129-CL1	10 c. rose sur chamois ou gris	12 »	6 50
129-E1	10 c. rose sur blanc (123x96 mm) (intérieur bleu clair) (dates 533 et 534)	16 »	6 50
129-E2	10 c. rose sur blanc (123x96 mm) (intérieur violet-noir) (date 646)	19 50	8 »
129-E3	10 c. rose sur gris-vert (123x96 mm) (dates 610 à 613 et 645 ou sans date)	13 »	5 »
129-E4	10 c. rose sur blanc (147x112 mm) (intérieur bleu clair) (dates 533 et 534 ou sans date)	16 »	6 50
129-E5	10 c. rose sur blanc (147x112 mm) (intérieur violet noir) (date 646)	22 50	8 »
129-E6	10 c. rose sur gris-vert (147x112 mm) (dates 610 à 613 et 645 ou sans date)	13 »	5 »

130-CP1	15 c. vert sur vert ou gris (dates 727 à 742)	10 »	5 »

Mention de l'expéditeur sur 6 lignes : inscriptions sur marge inférieure, papier gris épais, avec date

130-CL1	15 c. vert sur gris (timbre au type 1) (dates 404 à 601)	9 50	4 »
130-CL2	Idem, avec surcharge « Taxe réduite à 0f10 » de 1906	3 25	1 75
130-CL3	15 c. vert sur gris (timbre au type 2) (dates 432 à 505)	13 »	6 50
130-CL4	Idem avec surcharge « Taxe réduite à 0f10 » de 1906	5 »	3 50

Papier mou gris-chamois, inscriptions sur marge inférieure seulement

130-CL5	15 c. vert sur gris chamois (timbre au type 1)	16 »	6 50
130-CL6	15 c. vert sur gris chamois (timbre au type 4)	12 50	5 »

Inscriptions sur les 3 marges

130-CL7 15 c. vert sur bulle (timbre au type 5) 15 » 6 50

Avec mention pour l'expéditeur, papier vert-gris.

130-E1 15 c. vert sur vert gris (123x96 mm) (timbre au type 1) (dates 412 et 507) 9 50 4 »
130-E2 Idem, avec surcharge « Taxe réduite à 0f10 » de 1906 4 75 1 60
130-E3 15 c. vert sur vert gris (147x112 mm) (timbre au type 1) (dates 410, 411, 507 et 510) 9 50 4 »
130-E4 Idem avec surcharge « Taxe réduite à 0f10 » de 1906 4 75 1 60

Sans mention de l'expéditeur, papier vergé crème

130-E5 15 c. vert sur papier vergé crème (123x96 mm) (dates 751, 752 et 754) 47 50 20 »
130-E6 15 c. vert sur papier vergé crème (147x112 mm) (date 747) 47 50 20 »
130-E7 15 c. vert sur papier vergé crème (147x112 mm) (sans date) 55 » 20 »

Mention de l'expéditeur sur 4 lignes

130-E8 15 c. vert sur papier vergé crème (147x112 mm) (dates 841 et 842) 55 » 20 »
130-E9 15 c. vert sur papier jaunâtre ou blanchâtre (147x112 mm) (intérieur lilas) (dates 912 à 943) 16 » 8 »

132-CL1 25 c. bleu sur rose ou saumon 125 » 40 »

199-CL1 50 c. rouge sur chamois gris (timbre au type IIA à 4,5) mm à droite du mot lettre) 15 » 6 50
199-CL2 50 c. rouge sur chamois gris (timbre au type IIB à 7 mm à droite du mot lettre) 25 » 10 »
199-CL3 50 c. rouge sur chamois gris (timbre au type IV à 7 mm à droite du mot lettre) 20 » 8 »

CP 1f20 brun sur chamois 92 » 92 »
CP 1f20 brun sur jaune 92 » 92 »

Ces deux cartes postales ont été imprimées à Rennes à l'automne 1944 pour les départements libérés de l'Ouest à partir d'un poinçon réalisé localement par l'Imprimerie Oberthur.

1906 - TYPE SEMEUSE FOND PLEIN À INSCRIPTIONS MAIGRES.

135-CP1 10 c. rouge sur vert (dates 646 à 727) 32 » 16 »
135-CL1 10 c. rouge (timbre au type I) (dates 628, 629 et 630) 45 » 20 »
135-CL2 10 c. rouge (timbre au type IIA) (dates 632 à 651) 16 » 8 »
135-CL3 10 c. rouge (timbre au type IIB) (dates 652 à 710) 12 50 6 25
135-CL4 10 c. rouge (timbre au type III) (dates 702 et 703) 80 » 32 »

1907-1939 TYPE SEMEUSE CAMÉE

277A-BJ1 1 c. bistre-olive sur chamois (dates 425 à 745 ou sans date) 4 » 1 75

278-BJ1 2 c. vert foncé sur chamois (dates 224 à 721) 4 » 1 75

137-E1 5 c. vert sur papier blanc vergé (107x70 mm) (dates 736 à 419 ou sans date) 4 » 1 75
a) avec surcharge « annulé » en noir ou en violet 32 50

158-BJ1	5 c. orange sur chamois	55 »	32 »

138-CP1	10 c rouge sur vert-bleu (dates 749 à 611)	6 50	3 »
138-CPRP1	10 c + 10 c. rouge sur vert-bleu (timbre au type 1C) sans date	20 »	9 50
138-CPRP2	10 c. + 10 c. rouge sur vert-clair (même date sur les 2 volets)	25 »	9 50
138-CPRP3	10 c. + 10 c. rouge sur azuré (dates diverses et date 537 sur le volet réponse)	32 »	12 50
	a) avec surcharge « annulé » en violet	40 »	
138-CL1	10 c. rouge sur chamois clair à gris (timbre au type 1A) (dates 711 à 629)	3 25	1 75
	a) avec surcharge « annulé » en violet	30 »	
138-E1	10 c. rouge sur vert-gris (123x96 mm) (avec inscriptions pour l'expéditeur)	6 50	3 »
	a) avec surcharge « annulé » en violet	32 50	
138-E2	10 c. rouge sur blanc (123x96 mm) (avec inscriptions pour l'expéditeur)	14 »	5 »
	a) avec surcharge « annulé » en violet	32 50	
138-E3	10 c. rouge sur vert-gris (147x112 mm) (avec inscriptions pour l'expéditeur)	6 50	2 50
	a) avec surcharge « annulé » en violet	32 50	
138-E4	10 c. rouge sur blanc (147x112 mm) (avec inscriptions pour l'expéditeur)	18 »	6 50
	a) avec surcharge « annulé » en violet	32 50	
138-E5	10 c. rouge sur blanc (123x96 mm) (sans inscriptions pour l'expéditeur) (dates 815 à 419)	8 »	3 50
	a) avec surcharge « annulé » en violet	32 50	
138-E6	10 c. rouge sur blanc (123x96 mm) (sans inscriptions pour l'expéditeur) (sans date)	9 50	2 50
	a) avec surcharge « annulé » en violet	32 50	
138-E7	10 c. rouge sur blanc (147x112 mm) (sans inscriptions pour l'expéditeur) (dates 815 à 601)	12 50	4 »
	a) avec surcharge « annulé » en violet	32 50	
138-E8	10 c. rouge sur papier vergé crème (147x112 mm) (dates 640 et 641)	55 »	16 »
	a) avec surcharge « annulé » en violet	32 50	

279-BJ1	10 c. outremer sur chamois-brun (dates 726 à 949)	7 »	3 50

189-BJ1	15 c. brun sur papier bulle chamois clair (dates 650 à 004 et 037 à 828)	47 50	16 »
189-BJ2	15 c. brun sur papier bulle chamois clair (sans date)	47 50	16 »

139-CP1	20 c. lilas-brun (timbre au type IIA) (dates 015 à 035 ou sans date)	9 50	2 50
139-CP2	20 c. lilas-brun (timbre au type IIB)	9 50	2 50
139-CPRP1	20 c. + 20 c. lilas brun sur bleuté (dans date ou avec date 431 sur la réponse)	80 »	25 »

190-BJ1	20 c. lilas-rose sur chamois (dates 737 à 806)	130 »	55 »

140-CL1	25 c. bleu sur chamois clair (timbre au type 3) (dates 447 à 452 et 502)	32 50	25 »
140-CL2	25 c. bleu sur chamois clair (timbre au type 4) (dates 017 à 502)	8 50	8 50

140-E1	25 c. bleu (147x112 mm) (avec inscriptions pour l'expéditeur) (dates 015 017 ou sans date)	20 »	8 »
140-E2	25 c. bleu (147x112 mm) (sans inscriptions pour l'expéditeur) (sans date)	15 »	6 50

TYPE 1 : Se reporter aux Timbres-poste (émission de 1924-26).

TYPE IV.

Boule du chiffre 3 plus haute que dans le type 1.

Dans République, la lettre B est plus haute que les autres et le i petit. La signature O. Roty est tronquée près du cadre.

CLPP1	30 c. violet (Type 1) (1907), 14 lignes au verso, 19 localités desservies	85 »	16 »
CLPP2	30 c. idem, 16 lignes au verso, 20 localités desservies (1908) (dates 733 à 735)	85 »	16 »
CLPP3	30 c. idem (sans date	80 »	20 »
CLPP4	30 c. idem, 17 lignes au verso et 3 lignes de texte ajoutées au bas du recto (1910) (dates obliques 010 à 026)	85 »	16 »
	a) avec surcharge « annulé » en noir ou violet	70 »	
CLPP5	30 c. violet (type IV) (1911), 17 lignes au verso, petits caractères, 42 localités desservies (dates 128 à 516)	85 »	16 »
CLPP6	30 c. idem (1916), 3 lignes consacrées aux tarifs au verso (dates 629 à 636)	85 »	16 »
CLPPRP1	30 c. violet (Type I) (1908), (sans date) 16 lignes au verso, 20 localités desservies	120 »	32 »
CLPPRP2	30 c. Idem (1910), même recto que CLPP4	120 »	32 »
	a) avec surcharge « annulé » en noir ou violet	160 »	
CLPPRP3	30 c. violet (Type IV) (1911), 17 lignes au verso, petits caractères, 42 localités desservies	120 »	32 »
EPP1	30 c. violet (Type I) (1907) au verso : 19 villes desservies	67 50	16 »
EPP2	30 c. Idem (1908), 20 villes desservies	67 50	16 »
EPP3	30 c. violet (Type IV) (1911), tarifs au recto et 42 villes desservies au verso	67 50	16 »
	a) avec surcharge « annulé »	110 »	
CLPM	30 c. violet (Type IV) (1910)	310 »	240 »
CLPMRP	30 c. Id. (id.)	550 »	275 »
EPM	30 c. Idem (idem)	385 »	240 »

PRPCE1	30 c. + 30 c. noir sur verdâtre (270x230 mm) (timbre au type I) (date 190)	500 »	550 »
PRPCE2	30 c. + 30 c. noir sur bleuté (261x223 mm) (timbre au type I) (date 190)	500 »	550 »
PRCPE3	30 c. + 30 c. noir sur lilacé (261x223 mm)	500 »	550 »
PRCPE4	30 c. + 30 c. noir sur gris verdâtre (270x228 mm) (timbre au type I)	500 »	550 »
PRCPE5	30 c. + 30 c. noir sur papier gris verdâtre glacé (avec mention « remboursement par tube pneumatique ») (timbre au type IV)	525 »	550 »

160-CP1	Rouge sur vert (timbre au type IV) (dates 128 et 129 ou sans date)	47 »	16 »

Types du 30 c.

HA

HD

Type HD : Boucle inférieure de l's de Française qui remonte.

Type HA : Boucle plus horizontale, donc plus ouverte.

192-CP1	30 c. bleu sur verdâtre (timbre au type IID) (dates 631 à 635 ou sans date)	32 »	11 »
192-CPRP1	30 c. + 30 c. bleu sur vert (timbre au type IID) (sans date ou date 631 sur la réponse)	80 »	27 50
192-E1	30 c. bleu (147x112 mm) (timbre au type IIA)	95 »	40 »

360-BJ1 30 c. rouge sombre sur chamois (timbre au type IIA) (dates 917 à 919) 150 » 95 »

Types du 40 c.

II III

Type II : pas de point à l'endroit d'une flèche. Boucle supérieure de l's de Française « fermée ».

Type III : Présence constante d'un point à l'endroit précité. Boucle supérieure de l's « ouverte ». N'existe que sur entiers.

194-CL1 40 c. vermillon sur chamois gris (timbre au type II) (dates 619 à 627) 12 50 3 »

194-CL2 Idem, mais timbre au type III 15 50 4 »

236-CP1 40 c. violet sur gris vert (137x88 mm) (timbre au type II) (dates horizontales 637 à 649) 5 » 1 60

236-CP2 40 c. violet sur gris vert (147x104 mm) (timbre au type II) (dates verticales à droite 701 à 735 ou à gauche 813 à 823) 5 » 1 60

236-CPRP1 40 c. + 40 c. violet sur gris vert (sans date) 65 » 25 »

237-CP1 40 c. outremer sur gris (timbre au type II) (dates 848 à 218) 4 » 1 »

237-CP2 40 c. outremer sur gris vert (timbre au type II) (sans date) 40 » 20 »

237-CPRP1 40 c + 40 c outremer sur gris-vert (147x104 mm) (sans date) 62 50 20 »

237-CPRP2 40 c. + '0 c. outremer sur gris-vert (147x104 mm) (date 047) 62 50 20 »

NB : sur les entiers du n° 237 la couleur du timbre varie de l'outremer au gris à peine bleuté.

CP1 90 c rouge (dates 021, 026, 124 ou sans date) 95 » 47 50

CPRP1 90 c. + 90 c. rouge (dates 021, 124 ou sans date) 145 » 62 50

1924 – JEUX OLYMPIQUES DE PARIS

185-CP1 30 c. noir et rouge sur vert 125 » 200 »

1925 – EXPOSITION INTERNATIONALE DES ARTS DECORATIFS DE PARIS

213-CP1 45 c. lilas et carmin 50 » 32 50

1923-1927 – TYPE PASTEUR

170-CP1 10 c. vert entrepôt d'Ivry 1500 » 1500 »

170-CP2 10 c. vert savon Lecat 4000 » » »

171-CP1	15 c. vert jeux olympiques de Paris 1924 avec illustration au verso (aviron, boxe, course à pied, javelot, lutte, rugby, saut, tennis) chaque	275 »	275 »
	a) la série complète dans sa pochette	2500 »	
171-CP2	15 c. vert expo philatélique de Paris	45 »	30 »

172-CP1	20 c. vert, dates 541 à 543	15 »	5 »
172-CP2	20 c. vert, sans date	15 »	5 »

173-CP1	30 c. rouge, date 318	30 »	8 »
173-CPRP1	30 c. + 30 c. rouge, date 324	125 »	35 »
	a) Surcharge « Annulé »	100 »	

174-CP1	45 c. rouge expo philatélique de Paris	45 »	35 »

CPRP1	60 c. + 60 c. rouge	200 »	85 »

CP1	75 c. rouge	200 »	100 »

CPRP1	90 c + 90 c. rouge	400 »	175 »

1927 – CENTENAIRE DE LA NAISSANCE DE MARCELIN BERTHELOT

243-CP1	90 c. rouge	200 »	150 »

TYPE PAIX

281-CP1	40 c. lilas sur gris ou gris vert (type 1, dates 241 à 710, pas de lignes sous « adresse »)	5 »	0 90
281-CP2	40 c. lilas sur crème (type 3, dates 706 à 711, 4 lignes sous « adresse »)	25 »	6 50
281-CPRP1	40 c. + 40 c. lilas (sans date ou date 546)	140 »	40 »

283-CL1	50 c. rouge sur chamois gris (dates 235 à 721)	32 »	10 »
283-E1	50 c. rouge sur blanc	25 »	10 »

363-CP1	55 c. violet	13 »	3 »
363-CPRP1	55 c. + 55 c. violet	1600 »	600 »

365-CL1	65 c outremer (type 1)	32 »	9 50
365-E1	65 c. outremer (type 2)	47 50	20 »

285-CP-CP1	90 c. rouge (sans date ou date 540)	130 »	32 »
285-CPRP1	90 c. + 90 c. rouge (sans date ou date 540)	150 »	50 »

368-CL1 90 c. outremer sur chamois clair (date 916 ou sans date) (type 3) 115 » 40 »

368-CL2 90 c. outremer sur gris bleu (type 3) (dates 916 à 929) 55 » 20 »

363-CP1 1 f. rose sur crème (dates 828, 848 ou sans date) (type 2) 130 » 60 »

1938 – MEMORIAL AUSTRALIEN DE VILLERS-BRETONNEUX

400-CP1 55 c. vert 16 » 12 50

400-CP2 1 f. carmin 16 » 12 50

(vendus en pochettes de 5 cartes postales avec vues différentes en sépia au verso).

1939-1940 – DEFILE DU 11 NOVEMBRE

403-CP1 70 c. bleu 8 » 2 50
a) oblitéré sans timbre complémentaire 16 »

403-CP2 80 c. bleu 15 » 6 50

1939 – EXPOSITION INTERNATIONALE DE NEW-YORK

426-CP1 70 c. vert 17 50 11 »
a) avec repiquage « Coupe internationale du philatéliste » 15 » 10 »

1939- PAQUEBOT NORMANDIE

299-CP1 1f25 vermillon 25 » 14 »
a) avec repiquage « Coupe internationale du philatéliste » 22 50 12 50

1939-1940 – TYPE MERCURE

416-CP1 70 c. lilas-rose 32 » 9 »

SPE-CL1 1 f. bleu 35 » 12 »

1940 – LA MARSEILLAISE DE RUDE

315-E1 50 c. carmin 32 » 27 50

Cette enveloppe, imprimée en 1937 n'a été mise en vente qu'en 1940.

On connaît des essais (cartes postales et enveloppes) à 40 c. (valeur 750 »).

1940 – 1944 – TYPE IRIS

431-CP1 80 c. brun sur crème ou chamois (sans mention d'expéditeur) 6 50 1 75

431-CP2 80 c. brun sur chamois (avec mentions » expéditeur » et « destinataire ») 6 50 1 75

431-CPRP1 80 c. + 80 c. brun sur crème 1600 » 625 »

433-CL1 1 f. rouge sur gris bleu ou gris-jaunâtre 32 » 15 »

433-E1 1 f. rouge 40 » 14 »

651-CP1 1 f. 20 violet sur blanc couché 4 » 1 50

SPE-CP1 1 f. 25 carmin sur crème 100 » 50 »

ESSAI-CP1 1 f. 30 noir sur 1 f. 20 Pétain brun-rouge 2500 »

(Cet essai, dont on connaît quatre modèles, fut réalisé à l'automne 1944 dans l'espoir de recycler les entiers 1 f. 20 Pétain démonétisés le 1er novembre 1944).

435-CP1 1 f. 50 orange sur crème 70 » 46 »

654-CP1 2 f. 40 rose carminé sur blanc couché 25 » 8 »

SANS VALEUR-CP1 brun sur carton de couleur variable 6 » 1 »

Cette carte, comportant au verso 4 lignes d'instructions et 14 lignes de texte à compléter fut mise en vente à partir du 26 septembre 1940 pour assurer la correspondance familiale entre zone occupée et zone libre. Elle se rencontre sur carton beige, chamois, brun, blanc, rouge, gris-bleu, vert-clair ou jaune.

Elle fut aussi utilisée hors de France : Algérie, Maroc, Tunisie (à partir de 10 »), Côte des Somalis (225 »), Côte d'Ivoire (120 »), Dahomey (250 »), Guadeloupe (350 »), Guinée (75 »), Guyane (400 »), Indochine (350 »), Liban (200 »), Madagascar (400 »), Réunion (500 ») Sénégal (45 »), Soudan (125 »), Syrie (300 »), Togo (300 »).

SANS VALEUR-CP2 Brun sur chamois 8 » 1 »

Cette carte comporte au verso 8 lignes d'instructions et 7 lignes pointillées. Elle fut aussi utilisée hors de France (voir carte précédente).

SANS VALEUR-CP3 Brun sur gris ou chamois, correspondance commerciale avis de commande 120 » 75 »

SANS VALEUR-CP4 Brun sur rose, correspondance commerciale accusé de réception d'avis de commande 150 » 85 »

1941-1943 – TYPE PETAIN

512-CP1 80 c. brun rouge sur chamois 3 » 0 90

512-CP2 80 c. brun sur blanc couché 1 » 0 50

512 CPRP1 80 c. + 80 c. br. sur blanc couché 120 » 60 »

512-CP3 80 c. brun sur blanc couché avec surcharge encadrée « complément de taxe perçu » en haut à gauche de la carte 3 » 0 75

Les cartes postales CP1, CP2 et CP3 ont été utilisées hors de France en Algérie, Maroc, Tunisie (10 »), Côte des Somalis (225 »), Côte d'Ivoire (150 »), Dahomey (225 »), Guinée (100 »), Sénégal (45 »), Togo (300 »), Monaco (60 »).

512-CP4 80 c. rouge sur vert « correspondance commerciale » 80 » 45 »

512-CP5 80 c. rouge sur vert avec surcharge encadrée « complément de taxe perçu » 80 » 45 »

514-CL1 1 f. rouge sur gris bleuté 40 » 12 50

514-E1 1 f. rouge sur blanc 40 » 15 »

515-CP1 1 f. 20 brun rouge sur blanc couché 1 » 0 50

Cette carte postale a été utilisée hors de France en Algérie, Maroc, Tunisie (10 »), Côte des Somalis (225 »), Côte d'Ivoire (75 »), Dahomey (225 »), Guinée (75 »), Sénégal (45 »).

Cette carte postale a été surchargée RF à Orléans et Blois au moment de la libération (40 » 40 »).

515-CP2 1 f. 20 rouge-brun sur bleu « correspondance commerciale » 110 » 65 »

515-CPRP1 1 f. 20 + 1 f. 20 brun rouge sur blanc couché 125 » 50 »

515-CPRP2 1 f. 20 + 1 f.20 brun sur chamois « demande d'extrait de mariage » 400 » 60 »

515-CPRP3 1 f. 20 + 1 f. 20 brun sur chamois « demande d'extrait de naissance » 400 » 60 »

515-CPRP4 1 f. 20 + 1 f. 20 brun sur blanc « demande d'extrait de mariage » 750 » 200 »

515-CP 5 f. bleu « Salon du prisonnier » 40 » 40 »

FRANCE FRANCE

Etat 1 Etat 2

Deux états de cet entier existent selon que sous « France » le trait commence à gauche du « F » (Etat 1) ou à droite du « F » (Etat 2).

Des essais de couleurs numérotés 1 à 18 (sauf n° 13 adopté) ou non numérotés furent réalisés (750 » chaque)

Des essais de CPRP 5 f. + FM furent réalisés fin 1942 en vert foncé, vert vif, marron, rouge, noir (1500 » chaque) mais les allemands n'en autorisèrent pas la mise en circulation.

517-E1 1 f. 50 brun sur grisâtre « L'urbaine et la Seine » (caractères ornés) 750 » 750 »

517-E2 1 f. 50 brun sur blanc « L'urbaine et la Seine » (caractères bâtons) 750 » 750 »

519-CP1 2 f. 40 rouge sur blanc couché 50 » 40 »

521-CLPP1 3 f. orange sur vert jaune ou gris azuré 50 » 12 »

521-PRCPE 3 f. + 3 f. noir Caisse d'Epargne 6500 » 2750 »

1945 – 1946 – TYPE CERES DE MAZELIN

Essai-CP1 1 f. 20 noir sur 1 f. 20 Pétain brun-rouge 2500 »

679-CP1 1 f. 50 lilas 8 » 2 50

679-CPRP 1 f.50 + 1 f. 50 lilas 135 » 80 »

681-CP2 2 f. 50 brun 8 50 2 50

1945 – 1954 – TYPE MARIANNE DE GANDON

713-E1 2 f. vert foncé L'urbaine et la Seine 750 » 750 »

715-E1 3 f. brun foncé L'urbaine et la Seine 600 » 600 »

716-E1 3 f. rose chemin de fer métropolitain de Paris 3000 » » »

716A-CP1 3 f. vert expo philatélique de Nancy – Blason de Nancy 45 » 40 »

716A-CP2 3 f. vert expo philatélique de Nancy – Porterie du palais ducal 45 » 40 »

716B-CP1 3 f. 50 rouge-brun sur blanc couché 35 » 7 »

716B-CP2 3 f. 50 rouge-brun sur gris 50 » 8 »

718A-ENV1 4 f. 50 bleu L'urbaine et la Seine 700 » 700 »

719B-CP1 5 f. bleu sur chamois 12 » 3 »

721-CP1 6 f. rouge-orange sur blanc couché 130 » 50 »

810-CP1 8 f. bleu clair sur chamois 52 » 8 »

812-CP1 12 f. outremer sur chamois clair (3 lignes pour l'expéditeur) 30 » 8 »

812-CP2 12 f. outremer sur chamois clair (4 lignes pour l'expéditeur) 30 » 8 »

885-CP1 12 f. orange sur chamois clair (format 148x104 mm) ou 140x100 mm) 17 » 3 »

813-CP1 15 f. rouge sur chamois clair (trois lignes pour l'expéditeur) 95 » 40 »

813-CP2 15 f. rouge sur chamois clair (quatre lignes pour l'expéditeur) 85 » 30 »

886-CL1 15 f. bleu sur chamois carte-lettre annonces les panneaux bleus 1250 » 2000 »

886-E1 15 f. bleu sur chamois RATP 300 » 300 »

D'autres enveloppes 15 f. bleu TSC existent : Banque Populaire Montrouge, Crédit du Nord Paris, Crédit de l'Ouest Paris, Général Motors Frigidaire, I.N.S.E.E., Urbaine-Seine Paris, Banque Industrielle et Commerciale Montrouge (300 » chaque) et Henri Doré Chartres (750 »).

887-CP1 18 f. rose carminé (148x104mm ou 140x100mm) 190 » 115 »

1955 – 1961 – TYPE MARIANNE DE MULLER

1010-CP1 12 f. vert-jaune sur chamois ou jaune 20 » 5 »

1011-CP1 15 f. rose 12 » 3 »

1011A-CP1 18 f. bleu sur chamois ou jaune 145 » 65 »

1011B-CP1 20 f. bleu sur chamois ou rosé 16 » 2 50

1011C-E1 25 f. rouge TSC Crédit Français60 » 45 »

D'autres enveloppes 25 f. rouge TSC existent : Crédit Lyonnais, Général Motors Frigidaire, R.A.T.P., Statistiques Laitières, Crédit du Nord, O'Cédar, Diffusion Industrielle Nouvelle (60 » 45 » chaque)

0,20 bleu CP1 Laboratoire Bellon 100 » 75 »

D'autres cartes postales 0,20 bleu TSC existent : Cinéma publicité, Duburcq, Ford, Pied-Selle, Société Coopérative… (100 » 75 »)

0,25 rouge sur blanc E1 (utilisateur R. Bloch, Metz) 45 » 30 »

D'autres enveloppes 0,25 rouge TSC existent : Ancienne Mutuelle, Cie Générale d'Assurances, La Confiance, Crédit Français, Crédit Lyonnais (Paris, Toulouse), Crédit du Nord, Formation Professionnelle des Adultes, etc…

1960 – TYPE SEMEUSE LIGNEE DE PIEL

1233-CP1		16 »	2 50

1965 – TYPE MARIANNE DE DECARIS

1263-CP1	25 c. lie de vin et gris sur chamois ou blanc crème	4 50	1 75

1969-1973 – TYPE MARIANNE DE CHEFFER

1611-CP1	30 c. vert sur beige clair (recto divisé par un trait vertical	5 »	1 50
1611-CP2	30 c. vert sur beige clair (recto non divisé. Destinataire en rouge)	3 25	1 75

1975-1976 – *Type MARIANNE DE BEQUET . Typographie.*

Bande de phosphore sur REPUBLIQUE FRANCAISE

1814-CP1	60 c. vert	3 25	1 60
1891-CP1	80 c. vert	3 25	1 60

1976. - *Exposition philatélique JUVAROUEN. Taille-douce.*

1876-CP1	60 c. Ardoise	2 50	1 25

1978-80 – *Type SABINE – Taille-douce.*

Bande de phosphore sur le timbre, à droite.

1970-CP1	80 c. vert	4 75	3 »
1973-CP1	1 f. vert	3 25	1 »
2058-CP1	1 f. 10 vert	3 25	0 90
2101-CP1	1 f. 20 vert	4 »	0 90

1981 – *Idem légende REPUBLIQUE FRANCAISE.*

2154-CP1	1 f. 40 vert	2 50	1 60

1982 – *Exposition philatélique internationale PHILEX-FRANCE 82. Taille-douce.*

2216-CP1	1 f. 60 brun-rouge	2 »	1 »

1982 – *Inauguration du bureau de poste de Paris-Tour Eiffel. Taille-douce.*

429-CP1	1 f 60 vert-jaune	2 50	1 25

1982-88 – *Type LIBERTE DE GANDON.*

2186-CP1	1 f 40 vert	1 60	0 80
2219-CP1	1 f. 60 vert	1 90	0 75
2318-CP1	1 f. 70 vert	1 60	0 75
2375-CP1	1 f. 80 vert	1 60	0 75
2424-CP1	1 f. 90 vert	1 60	0 75
2484-CP1	2 f. vert	1 60	0 75

1984. - *Liberté de Gandon. Nouveaux types, sans valeurs faciales indiquées. Carton ou papier jaune.*

2484A-CP	(1 f. 70), vert	1 60	0 80
CL	(2 f. 10), rouge	1 60	1 »
E	(2 f. 10), rouge	1 60	1 »

Ces entiers expérimentaux ont été vendus dans le département de l'Isère ; leur validité n'a pas été affectée par les changements de tarifs postaux.

1984. - *"Philex-Jeunes'84". Exposition philatélique de la jeunesse, à Dunkerque. Taille-douce.*

2308-CP1	2 f. rouge	2 40	1 »

1984. - *Europa. 25e anniversaire de la Conférence européenne des administrations des postes et télécommunications (C.E.P.T.). Taille-douce.*

2309-CP1	2 f. 20 bleu	2 40	1 »

1986. - *Centenaire de l'érection de la Statue de la Liberté, à New York. Taille-douce.*

2421-CP1	2 f. 50 bleu et rouge	2 40	1 30

1987. - *Centenaire de l'Institut Pasteur. Taille-douce.*

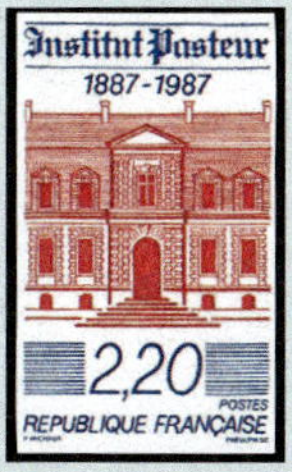

2496-CP1	2 f. 20 rouge et bleu	1 60	0 80

1989. - *Liberté de Gandon. "Carte Postale électronique". Valeur imprimée à l'Exposition "Philexfrance'89". La valeur imprimée dans le timbre varie selon le pays de destination. L'illustration au verso reproduit l'affiche de l'exposition.*

2496A-CP	bleu, rouge et noir, valeur imprimée : 2 f. 20	12 50
	a. autre valeur, à destination de l'étranger	21 50

1989. - *Panorama de Paris. Multicolores. Taille-douce.*

2579-CP1	2 f. 20 *(Arche de la Défense)*	1 55	0 80
2580-CP1	2 f. 20 *(Centenaire de la tour Eiffel)*	1 55	0 80
2581-CP1	2 f. 20 *(Pyramide du Grand Louvre)*	1 55	0 80
2582-CP1	2 f. 20 *(Notre-Dame)*	1 55	0 80
2583-CP1	2 f. 20 *(Opéra Bastille)*	1 55	0 80
	La série de 5 cartes postales	7 75	4 »

1990-91. - *Type MARIANNE DU BICENTENAIRE.*

2622-CP1	2 f. 10, vert	1 25	0 75

2715-CP1	2 f. 50, rouge	1 »	0 75

1990. - *Course autour du monde 1989-1990. Offset. Au recto : "La Poste".*

2648-CP1 2 f. 30, vert, bleu et jaune 1 85 1 10

1992. - *Course autour du monde à la voile en équipage. Au recto, le voilier "La Poste".*

2755-CP1 2 f. 50, multicolore (2755) 2 30 1 55
2756-CP1 3 f. 40, multicolore (2756) 3 05 2 30

1992. - *80e anniversaire de la 1re liaison postale aérienne, Nancy-Lunéville. Offset.*

2778-CP1 2 f. 50, multicolore (2778) 1 85 1 10

1993. - *Les Postiers autour du monde. Offset. Dentelure figurée.*

2789-E1 2 f. 50, multicolore 1 25 0 80
2831-CP1 2 f. 80, multicolore 2 » 1 »
2831-CP2 2 f. 80, multicolore 2 » 1 »

Texte de la CP2 : « Whitbread 1993-94 ». Le Maxi-Yacht « La Poste » à Fremantle (Australie).

Date d'impression : Fév. 94 (au lieu de Sept. 93).

1994. - *Les restaurants du coeur. Offset. Dentelures figurées.*

2902-CP1 2 f. 80 + 0,60 multicolore 4 » 2 50

1994. - *Marianne du Bicentenaire. Sans valeur indiquée (validité permanente). Timbre sur fond de sécurité bleu.*

2806-CP1 (sans val.) rouge 1 25 0 65
2806-E1 (sans val.) rouge (162x114) 1 25 0 50
2806-E2 (sans val.) rouge (220x110) 1 25 0 50

Il existe de nombreuses variétés des n°s 442 et 443.

Idem. Fond de sécurité modifié.

2806-E3 (sans val.) rouge (162x114) 1 25 0 30
2806-E4 (sans val.) rouge (220x110) 1 25 0 30
2806-E5 (sans val.) rouge (220x110) (à fenêtre, autocollante) 1 25 0 30
2806-E6 (sans val.) rouge(225x115) (à fenêtre, patte gommée) 1 25 0 30

1997. - *Marianne du Bicentenaire. Sans valeur indiquée (Validité permanente pour l'envoi en "Lettre" en Métropole, à destination d'Andorre et Monaco ou à l'intérieur des DOM, de documents jusqu'à 100 g (I) et jusqu'à 500 g (II). Deux barres de phosphore à gauche du timbre dans la partie fluorescente entourant le timbre.*

2806-E7 (sans val.) rouge Enveloppe cartonnée (I) (229x162) 3 05 1 »
2806-E8 (sans val.) rouge Enveloppe cartonnée (II) (328x248) 6 10 2 30

Timbre agrandi sur le 449.

Idem. Sans valeur indiquée (Validité permanente pour l'envoi en "Prioritaire" de documents à destination des DOM-TOM ou en provenance des DOM, jusqu'à 100 g (I) et jusqu'à 500 g (II). Deux barres de phosphore à gauche du timbre dans la partie fluorescente entourant le timbre.

2806-E9 (sans val.) bleu turquoise Enveloppe cartonnée (I) (229x162) 3 85 1 85

2806-E10 (sans val.) bleu turquoise Envel. cartonnée (II) (328x248) 10 75 3 85

Timbre agrandi sur le 451.

1997. - *Type MARIANNE DU 14 JUILLET. Sans valeur indiquée (validité permanente). Timbre sur fond de sécurité bleu avec tête de la Marianne.*

3083-E1 (sans val.) rouge (162x115) 1 25 0 30
3083-E2 (sans val.) rouge (220x110) 1 25 0 30
3083-CP1 (sans val.) rouge (150x105) 2 » 1 »

1999. - *Type Marianne du 14 Juillet. Sans valeur indiquée . Validité permanente pour l'envoi en "Lettre" en Métropole, à destination d'Andorre et Monaco ou à l'intérieur des DOM, de documents jusqu'à 100 g. (I) et jusqu'à 500 g. (II). Deux barres de phosphore à gauche du timbre.*

3083-E3 (sans val.) rouge Enveloppe cartonnée (I) (229x162) 3 05 1 25
3083-E4 (sans val.) rouge Enveloppe cartonnée (II) (328x248) 6 10 2 30

2000. - *Type Marianne du 14 Juillet. Sans valeur indiquée (validité permanente). Enveloppes réservées à la réexpédition temporaire ou définitive des correspondances ordinaires dont le destinataire a changé d'adresse en France. Deux barres de phosphore à gauche du timbre.*

3083-E5 (sans val.) rouge 1 55 » »
3083-E6 (sans val.) rouge 2 30 » »

2001. - *Type Marianne du 14 Juillet. Sans valeur indiquée (validité permanente). Lettre recommandée suivie R1 avec avis de réception. Deux barres de phosphore à gauche du timbre. Se présente comme une carte-lettre.*

3083-CL1 (sans val.) rouge 7 » 5 »

2002. - *Type Marianne du 14 Juillet avec mention RF. Sans valeur indiquée (validité permanente pour l'envoi en "Lettre" en Métropole, à destination d'Andorre et Monaco ou à l'intérieur des DOM). Deux barres de phosphore.*

3417-E1 (sans val.) rouge (170x114) 1 » 0 30
3417-E2 (sans val.) rouge (220x110) 1 » 0 30
3417-E3 (sans val.) rouge lettre jusqu'à 50 g (229x162) 1 50 0 40
3417-E4 (sans val.) rouge lettre jusqu'à 100 g (324x229) 2 50 0 50

2002. - *Type Marianne du 14 Juillet avec mention RF. Sans valeur indiquée. Validité permanente pour l'envoi en « Lettre » en Métropole, à destination d'Andorre et Monaco ou à l'intérieur des DOM, de documents jusqu'à 100 g (I) et jusqu'à 500 g (II). Deux barres de phosphore à gauche du timbre.*

3417-E5 (sans val.) rouge Enveloppe cartonnée(I) (229x162) 3 » 1 »
3417-E6 (sans val.) rouge Enveloppe cartonnée (II) (328x248) 6 » 2 »
3417-E7 (sans val.) bleue Enveloppe cartonnée utilisée aux DOM (II) (328x248) 7 » 3 »

2002. - *Type Marianne du 14 Juillet avec mention RF. Sans valeur indiquée (validité permanente). Enveloppes réservées à la réexpédition temporaire ou définitive des correspondances ordinaires dont le destinataire a changé d'adresse en France. Deux barres de phosphore à gauche du timbre.*

3417-E8 (sans val.) rouge (230x163) 1 50 » »
3417-E9 (sans val.) rouge (328x248) 2 25 » »

2002. - *Type Marianne du 14 Juillet. Sans valeur indiquée (validité permanente). Lettre recommandée suivie R1 avec avis de réception. Deux barres de phosphore à gauche du timbre. Se présente comme une carte-lettre.*

3417-CL1 (sans val.) rouge 7 » 5 »

AÉROGRAMMES

1969. - *Avion Concorde. Offset. Timbre au type du n° 43 de poste aérienne.*

1001-AER 1 f. bleu et noir 20 » 12 »

1970-75. - *Timbre « Emblème » des P.T.T. (oiseau stylisé). Offset.*

1002-AER 1 f. 15, jaune et bleu-violet 15 » 8 »
a. ocre-jaune et bleu-violet 16 » 8 »
1003-AER 1 f. 40, jaune et bleu-violet 14 » 7 »

1977-80. - *Avion Concorde survolant Paris. Offset.*

1004-AER 1 f. 60, noir et polychrome 8 » 4 »
1005-AER 1 f. 90, noir et polychrome 8 » 4 »
1006-AER 2 f. 10, noir et polychrome 9 » 4 »
1007-AER 2 f. 35, noir et polychrome 9 » 4 »

1982. - *Idem. Légende RÉPUBLIQUE FRANÇAISE.*

1008-AER 2 f. 70, noir et polychrome 6 » 3 »
1009-AER 3 f. 10, noir et polychrome 6 » 3 »

1983. - *Bicentenaire de l'air et de l'espace et type Liberté de Gandon. Offset.*

1010-AER 3 f. 10, bleu, rouge et noir 4 » 2 »

1984. - *Type de 1982.*

1011-AER 3 f. 30, noir et polychrome 4 » 2 »
1012-AER 3 f. 50, noir et multicolore 3 » 2 »

1984. - *Avion survolant Paris. Offset.*

1013-AER 3 f. 50, bleu et outremer 3 » 2 »

1985-87. - *Type de 1982.*

1014-AER 3 f. 70, multicolore 3 » 2 »
1015-AER 3 f. 90, multicolore 3 » 2 »
1016-AER 4 f. 20, multicolore 3 » 2 »

1989. - *Bicentenaire de la Révolution. Timbre au type du n° 2560. Offset.*

1017-AER 4 f. 20, bleu et rouge 3 » 2 »

1990. - *Avion ATR 72 en vol. Offset.*

1018-AER 4 f. 20, bleu clair et bleu 3 » 2 »

1992. - *Hélicoptère Dauphin 2 en vol. Offset.*

1019-AER 4 f. 50, multicolore 3 » 2 »

1993. - *Airbus A 340 en vol, sur planisphère. Offset.*

1020-AER 5 f. multicolore 3 » 2 »

1994. - *50e anniversaire de la disparition d'Antoine de Saint-Exupéry. Type du T. aérien de 1947. Offset.*

1021-AER 5 f. brun-lilas 3 » 2 »

1996-2002. - *Hélicoptère Eurocopter EC 135. Héliogravure.*

1022-AER 5 f. multicolore 3 » 2 »
1023-AER 0,76 e. multicolore 2 » 1 »

La cote des aérogrammes oblitérés s'entend pour des plis ayant voyagé au tarif.

ENVELOPPES « DISTINGO »

1991. - *Enveloppes "Distingo", pour envoi de documents importants. Imperméables et indéchirables.*

Composition géométrique.

Au verso : « La Poste organisateur officiel » et logotypes des jeux olympiques d'hiver et du parcours de la flamme olympique.

2001-E ( ) multicolore, format de l'enveloppe 229x162 15 25 10 »
2002-E ( ) multicolore, format de l'enveloppe 326x229 15 25 12 25

Idem, sans les mentions olympiques

2003-E ( ) format 229x162 11 50 3 85
2004-E ( ) format 326x229 13 75 4 60

Des N°s 2001, 2002 et 2003 ont été surchargés : Envoi intra-départemental pour les D.O.M. et inter D.F.A.

Idem, validité étendue pour les D.O.M.

Bandeau « La Poste » réduit.

2005-E ( ) format 229x162 9 95 6 90

2006-E ( ) format 326x229 8 40 5 35

Existent avec et sans précasage ; ces derniers font souvent l'objet d'une personnalisation pour l'entreprise utilisatrice.

Idem. Logo « La Poste » plus petit et encadré.

2007-E ( ) format 229x162 6 10 3 85
2008-E ( ) format 326x229 7 65 4 60

Idem. Mention ronde « Courrier suivi » en haut à gauche et étiquette de suivi collée sur l'enveloppe.

2009-E ( ) format 221x110 2 30 1 55
2010-E ( ) format 221x121 2 30 1 55
2011-E ( ) format 230x162 3 05 2 30

Le n° 2009 possède une fenêtre ; les mentions : "Distingo 20" figure sur les n°s 2009 et 2010 et "Distingo 50" sur le n° 2011.

EMBALLAGES PRÉAFFRANCHIS « DILIGO »

Depuis 1992 La Poste commercialise divers emballages préaffranchis comportant des vignettes autocollantes. Il ne s'agit pas d'entiers postaux. Ces pièces postales ont été placées dans ce chapitre par commodité.

2101 « Flèches entrecroisées »

1996. -

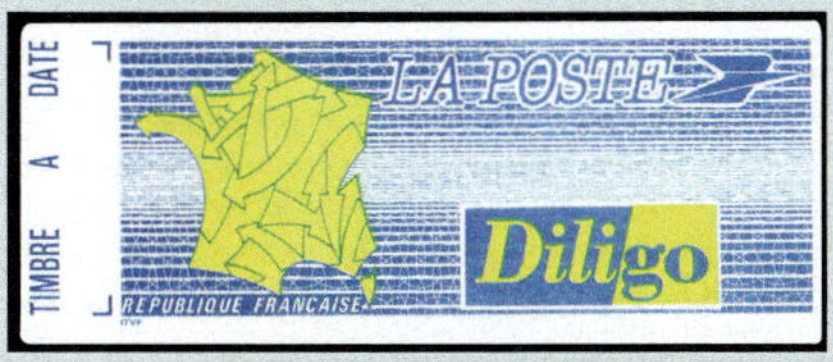

2102 « Carte de France avec flèches »

1997. - *Avec fond de sûreté. Dentelé.*

2103

Ces objets ont été placés dans la rubrique « Entiers Postaux », La Poste ne vendant pas les vignettes séparément.

TYPE CHAPLAIN

30 c. rose.

2501 CPP 30 c. (1880) 15 25 4 60
2502 CPRP 30 c. (1882) 38 25 7 65
2504 CPRP 30 c. surchargée « valable pour tout Paris » (1885) 69 » 15 25

30 c. carmin.

Légende « République Française » et « carte pneumatique ». Six lignes d'avis au verso.

2594 CLPP 30 c. (1902) 15 25 4 60
2595 CLPPRP 30 c. (1903) 33 75 15 25

Quatorze lignes d'avis au verso.

2596 CLPP 30 c. (1907) 15 25 6 10
2597 CLPPRP 30 c. (1907) 61 » 17 »
2763 EPP 30 c. (1902) 15 25 6 10

30 c. noir.
Plan de Paris, teinté foncé à l'ouest.

2505 CPP 30 c. (1882) 12 25 3 85

Idem, à l'ouest et au nord.

2506 CPP 30 c. (1883) 13 75 3 85

Plan de Paris, sans teinte rose.

2507 CPP 30 c. (1884) 13 75 3 85

Idem, avec surcharge « valable pour tout Paris ».

2508 CPP 30 c. (1885), à partir de 13 75 3 85

Texte vertical simplifié. Sans plan. Avec et sans date.

2511 CPP 30 c. (1885-1894), à partir de 10 75 3 »
2512 CPRP 30 c. (1887-1896), à partir de 70 » 21 50

Nouvelle légende : « République Française » et « Carte pneumatique ». Avec date.

2521 CPP 30 c. (1897-1898) 15 25 3 »

Idem. Avec ou sans date.

2523	CPRP	30 c. (1897-1899)	62 50	15 25
2593	CLPP	30 c. (1902)	15 25	7 65

Caisse d'épargne.

2780	PRPCE	30 c.+30 c. noir	110 »	250 »

Existe avec à l'intérieur date "188" ou "190".

2783	PRPCE	30 c.+30 c. noir	120 »	225 »

Formule 265x140 mm sur papier jaune paille.

40 c. rouge-brique.

2598	CLPP	40 c. (1919)	30 50	9 15
2750	CLPM	40 c. (1919)	275 »	175 »
2773	EPP	40 c. (1919)	38 25	12 25

50 c. rose.

2516	CPP	50 c. (1880)	61 »	38 25
2519	CPRP	50 c. (1880)	460 »	305 »

Idem, surcharge « Taxe réduite 30 c. ».

2517	CPP	30 c. s. 50 c. (1880)	45 75	15 25
2520	CPRP	30 c. s. 50 c. (1880)	77 »	45 75

50 c. carmin.

Format 145x85 mm.

2764	EPP	50 c. (1897),à partir de	30 50	7 65
2765	EPP	30 c. s. 50 c. (1902), à partir de	54 »	23 »

Format 123x95 mm.

2766	EPP	50 c. (1897)	15 25	6 10

Surcharge à la main.

2767	EPP	30 c. s. 50 c. (1902), à partir de	10 75	6 10

Surcharge typographique.

2768	EPP	30 c. s. 50 c. (1902)	10 »	5 35

50 c. noir.
Papier bleu. Légende : « Télégramme ».
Cinq lignes d'avis au verso. Piquage AA 10½.

N.B. : AA, BB, CC désignent les piquages A, B et C à l'envers.

2526	CLPP	50 c. (1881)	38 25	12 25

Plan de Paris, teinté violet à l'ouest.

2527	CLPP	50 c. (1882)	30 50	9 15

Plan de Paris, teinté violet à l'ouest et au nord.

2528	CLPP	50 c. (1883)	23 »	9 15

Plan de Paris, sans teinte violette.

2529	CLPP	50 c. (1884)	26 75	9 15

Idem, surcharge « valable pour tout Paris ».

2530	CLPP	50 c. (1885)	38 25	10 75

Neuf lignes d'avis au verso.
Piquage AA 13½. ou 10½.

2531	CLPP	50 c. (1885) à partir de	30 50	9 15
2533	CLPP	30 c. s. 50 c. (1902)	15 25	7 65

Idem. Piquage CC. Avec ou sans date.

2534	CLPP	50 c. (1890)	10 75	7 65
2535	CLPP	30 c. s. 50 c. (1902)	19 25	4 60

Légende : «Carte pneumatique fermée»
et « République Française ».
Six lignes d'avis au verso. Piquage CC.

2550	CLPP	50 c. (1897)	9 15	6 10
2551	CLPP	30 c. s. 50 c. (1902), à partir de	15 25	4 60

Trois lignes d'avis du verso sont barrées de six traits.

2553	CLPP	50 c. (1898), à partir de	15 25	4 60
2554	CLPP	30 c. s. 50 c. (1902), à partir de	45 75	15 25

Cinq lignes d'avis au verso. Piquage CC.

2563	CLPP	50 c. (1899)	9 15	5 35

Surcharge faite à la presse.

2564	CLPP	30 c. s. 50 c. (1902), à partir de	15 25	3 85

Surcharge faite à la main.

2567	CLPP	30 c. s. 50 c. (1902), à partir de	15 25	4 60

60 c. carmin.

2756	EPP 60 c. (1889)	45 75	10 75

2757	EPP 50 c. s. 60 c. (1896), à partir de	15 25	7 65

60 c. violet.

2599	CLPP 60 c. (1921)	30 50	7 65
2751	CLPM 60 c. (1921)	305 »	275 »
2774	EPP 60 c. (1921)	38 25	7 65

Caisse d'Epargne.

2787	PRCPE 60 c.+60 c. noir	175 »	» »

Format 270x230 mm sur papier gris verdâtre.
Existe avec à l'intérieur dates "19", "191" ou "192".

2787	PRCPE 60 c. + 60 c.noir	175 »	» »

Format 120x230 mm sur papier paille.

75 c. carmin.

2759	EPP 75 c. (1885)	33 75	23 »
2760	EPP 60 c. s. 75 c. (1887)	20 »	10 75

75 c. violet.

2600	CLPP 75 c. (1924)	30 50	12 25

1 f. noir.

Papier rose avec « Bon de réponse » sur côté droit. Légende: « Télégramme ». Piquage AA 13½.

2540	CLPPRP 1 f. (1884)	45 75	30 50
2541	CLPPRP 60 c. s. 1 f. (1902), à partir de	77 »	45 75

Inscription « Pour ouvrir... » de 69 mm. Piquage AA 10½.

2543	CLPPRP 1 f. (1884)	45 75	30 50
2544	CLPPRP 60 c. s. 1 f. (1902)	77 »	38 25

Inscription « Pour ouvrir...» de 73 mm.

2545	CLPPRP 1 f. (1884)	45 75	30 50
2546	CLPPRP 60 c. s. 1 f. (1902)	77 »	23 »

Idem. Piquage CC.

2547	CLPPRP 1 f. (1890)	54 »	30 50
2548	CLPPRP 60 c. s. 1 f. (1902), à partir de	110 »	30 50

Légende : « Carte pneumatique fermée » et « République Française ». Piquage AA. Neuf lignes d'avis au verso.

2574	CLPPRP 1 f. (1898)	61 »	45 75
2575	CLPPRP 60 c. s. 1 f. (1902)	110 »	45 75

Idem. Trois lignes du verso sont barrées de six gros traits.

2576	CLPPRP 1 f. (1899)	61 »	36 75
2577	CLPPRP 60 c. s. 1 f. (1902), à partir de	77 »	30 50

Bon de réponse tenant en plein. Cinq lignes d'avis au verso. Piquage AA 13½ ou AA 13½ sur 10 ½.

2580	CLPPRP 1 f. (1899), à partir de	45 75	30 50
2581	CLPPRP 60 c. s. 1 f. (1902), à partir de	38 25	19 25

Idem. Bon de réponse perforé. Piquage AA 13½.

2588	CLPPRP 1 f. (1899)	61 »	38 25
2589	CLPPRP 60 c. s. 1 f. (1902), à partir de	38 25	26 75

1 f. violet.

2601	CLPP 1 f. (1926)	38 25	9 15
2752	CLPM 1 f. (1926)	305 »	255 »
2775	EPP 1 f. (1925)	38 25	7 65

1 f. noir
Caisse d'Epargne.

2790	PRCPE	1 f.+1 f. noir	225 »	350 »

1 f. 50, violet.

2603	CLPP	1 f. 50 (1929), à partir de	38 25	9 15
2776	EPP	1 f. 50 (1928)	38 25	9 15

1 f. 50, rouge.
Papier bleu-vert foncé.

2604	CLPP	1 f. 50 (1929)	38 25	9 15
2753	CLPM	1 f. 50 (1929)	345 »	270 »
2777	EPP	1 f. 50 (1930)	23 »	9 15

Papier azuré clair.

2605	CLPP	1 f. 50 (1930)	13 75	4 60
2754	CLPM	1 f. 50 (1934)	305 »	270 »
2778	EPP	1 f. 50 (1931)	26 75	6 10

Une carte-lettre à 1 f. 50 a été émise en 1964 (n° 2617).

1 f. 50 noir
Caisse d'Epargne.

2791	PRCPE	1 f. 50+1 f. 50 noir	175 »	350 »

Existe avec à l'intérieur date "192" ou "193", et en plusieurs formats (276x235 mm - 260x220 mm - 268x226 mm - 280x240 mm).

2 f. rouge.

2606	CLPP	2 f. (1938)	69 »	5 35
2755	CLPM	2 f. (1938)	610 »	385 »
2779	EPP	2 f. (1938)	45 75	12 25

2 f. noir.
Caisse d'Epargne.

2794	PRCPE	2 f.+2 f. noir	200 »	400 »

3 f. rouge.
Papier épais avec fils de soie.

2607	CLPP	3 f. (1944)	23 »	7 65

6 f. rouge.

2608	CLPP	6 f. (1946)	30 50	7 65

6 f. noir.
Caisse d'Epargne

2795	PRCPE	6 f.+6 f. noir	225 »	300 »

19 f. rouge.

2609	CLPP	19 f. (1947)	45 75	10 75

30 f. rouge.

2610	CLPP	30 f. (1949)	38 25	10 75

45 f. rouge.

2611 CLPP 45 f. (1950-1951), à partir de 45 75 10 75

100 f. rouge.

2613 CLPP 100 f. (1958) 45 75 15 25

125 f. rouge.

2614 CLPP 125 f. (1959) 45 75 15 25

Nouveau franc.
1 f. 25, rouge.
Papier vert-jaune clair.

2615 CLPP 1 f. 25 (1960) 38 25 12 25

Papier bleu.

2616 CLPP 1 f. 25 (1963) 30 50 13 »

1 f. 50, rouge.

2617 CLPP 1 f. 50 (1964) 30 50 10 75

1 f. 60, rouge.
Papier gris-bleu, au verso liste des communes Seine et Seine-et-Oise.
Dimensions maxima 155x125 mm.

2618 CLPP 1 f. 60 (1965) 24 50 7 65

Papier azuré. Suppression de la liste du verso.
Dimensions maxima 155x125 mm.

2619 CLPP 1 f. 60 (1968) 23 » 7 65

Papier gris-bleu. Idem. Dimensions maxima 225x125 mm.

2620 CLPP 1 f. 60 (1970) 23 » 7 65

Idem. Papier azuré.

2621 CLPP 1 f. 60 (1971) 24 50 7 65

3 f. rouge.
Papier azuré.

2622 CLPP 3 f. (1971) 12 25 5 35

8 f. 40, rouge.

2623 CLPP 8 f. 40 (1977) 9 15 6 10

12 f. rouge.

2624 CLPP 12 f. (1981) 9 15 6 10

Le Service Pneumatique a été suspendu le 30 mars 1984.

ENTIERS A TYPES SPÉCIAUX.

1935-36. - *Vues de Paris. Illustrations au recto. Héliogravure.*

a) Notre-Dame, Champs Élysées, Concorde. Tombeau de Napoléon, La Madeleine, soit 5 cartes dans chacune des couleurs noire, verte et sépia.

Sans la légende RÉPUBLIQUE FRANÇAISE.

1 CP 90 c. rouge 23 » 12 25

Avec la légende RÉPUBLIQUE FRANÇAISE. *

2 CP 90 c. rouge 42 » 19 25

b) La Conciergerie : 5 cartes avec illustrations différentes dans chacune des couleurs verte, prune, sanguine, brune, sépia et noire.

Sans la légende RÉPUBLIQUE FRANÇAISE.

3 CP 90 c. rouge 23 » 15 25

Avec la légende RÉPUBLIQUE FRANÇAISE. *

4 CP 90 c. rouge 42 » 20 »

c) Le lac du Bois de Boulogne : 5 cartes avec illustrations différentes en vert.

Sans la légende RÉPUBLIQUE FRANÇAISE.

5 CP 90 c. rouge 25 25 15 25

Avec la légende RÉPUBLIQUE FRANÇAISE. *

6 CP 90 c. rouge 42 » 26 75

* Pour les n°s 2, 4 et 6 « REPUBLIQUE FRANÇAISE » se situe sur la C. P. au dessus de « CARTE POSTALE ».

1936. - *Mémorial de Vimy. Héliogravure.*

Dix illustrations au verso de chacune des CP n°s 7 et 8.

7 CP 50 c. vert sur chamois ou crème 20 » 12 25

8 CP 90 c. rouge 20 » 12 25

Cinq illustrations au verso de chacune des CP n°s 9 à 13

1937. - *Mémorial de Montfaucon. Héliogravure.*

CP 9/10.

CP 11.

9 CP 1 f. brun-noir 20 » 12 50

10 CP 1 f. sépia 20 » 12 50

1937. - *Mémorial de Château-Thierry. Héliogravure.*

11 CP 1 f. brun-noir 36 » 18 50

1938. - *Mémorial de la Pointe de Grave. Héliogravure.*

12 CP 55 c. bleu 20 » 11 50

13 CP 1 f. rouge 20 » 11 50

1938. - *Armoiries de l'Ile-de-France. Héliogravure.*

Dix illustrations en noir ou brun.

14 CL 65 c. bleu 32 50 35 »

1939. - *Éclaireurs de France.*

15 CP 40 c.+60 c. bleu 60 » 47 50

ÉPREUVES DE LUXE

Depuis 1923, l'Administration des Postes fait imprimer des épreuves de luxe de la plupart des timbres émis. Ces épreuves sont constituées, en général, par un feuillet mesurant 150 x 120 mm, au centre duquel le ou les timbres sont imprimés dans leur couleur exacte, mais *non dentelés.* Ces feuilles, *officiellement* réservées aux titulaires des hautes charges de l'État et à quelques hauts fonctionnaires des Postes, sont recherchées par les collectionneurs.

Sans indication de valeur ; celle-ci (10 c., 30 c., 50 c.) est imprimée en petits chiffres au-dessous de chaque timbre :

N^{os}			
170	Pasteur, vert		
173	“ rouge		
174	“ bleu		
	Épreuve collective	2000	»
	Avec chiffres de la valeur :		
170	Pasteur, 10 c. vert		
173	“ 30 c. rouge		
176	“ 50 c. bleu		
	Épreuve collective	2000	»
183	Jeux Olympiques, 10 c.		
184	“ “ 25 c.		
185	“ “ 30 c.		
186	“ “ 50 c.		
	Épreuve collective	5500	»
209	Ronsard, 75 c.	130	»
210	Arts décoratifs, 10 c.		
211	“ “ 15 c.		
212	“ “ 25 c.		
213	“ “ 25 c.		
214	“ “ 75 c.		
215	“ “ 75 c.		
	Entier 38. 45 c. rouge		
	Épreuve collective	1200	»
216	Exposition philatélique de Paris, 5 f., en bloc de 4 (BF n° 1)	3000	»
241, 242,	Exposition philatélique de Strasbourg, 5 f. et 10 f. (BF n° 2)	3000	»
243	Berthelot, 90 c.	130	»
244	Légion américaine, 90 c.		
245	“ “ 1 f. 50		
	Épreuve collective	700	»
246	Caisse d'Amortissement, + 10, bleu		
247	“ “ + 25, vert-olive		
248	“ “ + 50, rge-orange		
	Épreuve collective	900	»
249	Caisse d'Amortissement, + 10, violet-gris		
250	“ “ + 25, rouge-br.		
251	“ “ + 50, lilas		
	Épreuve collective	1000	»
252	Le Travail, 1 f. 50+8 f. 50	700	»
253	Caisse d'Amortissement, + 10, vert		
254	“ “ + 25, roses-lilas		
255	“ “ + 50, rouge-br.		
	Épreuve collective	1000	»
256	Sourire de Reims, 1 f. 50 + 3 f. 50	700	»
257	Jeanne d'Arc, 50 c.	200	»
257A	Exposition philatélique du Havre, 2 f.	1850	»
258	Arc de Triomphe, 2 f.	280	»
259	Cathédrale de Reims, 3 f.	400	»
260	Mont-Saint-Michel, 5 f.	250	»
261	Port de la Rochelle, 10 f.	380	»
262	Pont du Gard, 20 f.	1000	»
263	Centenaire de l'Algérie, 50 c.	135	»
264	Congrès du B.I.T., 50 c.		
265	“ 1 f. 50		
	Épreuve collective	700	»
266	Caisse d'Amortissement, + 10, rose		
267	“ “ + 25, brun		
268	“ “ + 50, violet		
	Épreuve collective	1000	»
269	Provinces françaises, 1 f. 50 + 3 f. 50	700	»
270	Femme Fachi, 15 c.		
271	“ “ 40 c.		
272	“ “ 50 c.		
273	“ “ 1 f. 50		
	Épreuve collective	375	»
274	Exposition coloniale, 1 f. 50	250	
275	Caisse d'Amortissement, + 10, vert-olive		
276	“ “ + 25, violet		
277	“ “ + 50, rouge		
	Épreuve collective	1000	»

277A	Semeuse, 1c.		
278	“ 2 c.		
278A	“ 3 c.		
278B	“ 5 c.		
279	“ 10 c.		
	Épreuve collective	450	»
280	Type Paix, 30 c.		
281	“ “ 40 c.		
282	“ “ 45 c.		
283	“ “ 50 c.		
284	“ “ 65 c.		
284A	“ “ 75 c.		
285	“ “ 90 c.		
369	“ “ 1 f.		
288	“ “ 1 f. 50		
	Épreuve collective	850	»
286	Type Paix, 1 f.		
287	“ “ 1 f. 25		
289	“ “ 1 f. 75		
	Épreuve collective	600	»
290	Le puy-en-Velay, 90 c.	120	»
291	Briand, 30 c.	140	»
292	Doumer, 75 c.	140	»
293	Victor Hugo, 1 f. 25	160	»
294	Colombe, 1 f. 50	240	»
295	Jacquard, 40 c.	100	»
296	Jacques Cartier, 75 c.		
297	“ “ 1 f. 50 les 2 épreuves	550	»
	Épreuve collective	550	»
299	Normandie, 1 f. 50, bleu	150	»
299	“ *petit format*	400	»
300	“ 1 f. 50, bleu clair	350	»
300	“ *petit format*	600	»
301	Rivière Bretonne, 2 f.	160	»
302	Saint-Trophime, 3 f. 50	140	»
303	Delessert, 75 c.	140	»
304	Victor Hugo, 1 f. 25	160	»
305	Richelieu, 1 f. 50	140	»
306	Jacques Callot, 75 c.	140	»
307	Chômeurs intellectuels, 50 + 10 c.	110	»
308	“ “ 50 + 2 f.	175	»
308	“ “ petit format	275	»
309	Aide aux réfugiés, 75 + 50 c	180	»
310	Ampère, 75 c.	135	»
311	Moulin de Daudet, 2 f.	100	»
312	Enfants de Chômeurs, 50 + 10 c.	100	»
313	Pilâtre de Rozier, 75 c.	350	»
314	Rouget de l'Isle, 20 c.	135	»
315	La Marseillaise, 40 c.	135	»
316	Vimy, 75 c.	100	»
316	“ 75 c., *petit format*	140	»
317	“ 1 f. 50	100	»
317	“ 1 f. 50, *petit format*	140	»
318	Jaurès, 40 c.	130	»
319	“ 1 f. 50	130	»
320	Conquête de l'Atlantique, 1 f. 50	325	»
32	“ “ 10 f.	1400	»
322	Exposition de Paris, 20 c.		
323	“ “ 30 c.		
324	“ “ 40 c.		
325	“ “ 50 c.		
326	“ “ 90 c.		
327	“ “ 1 f. 50		
	Deux épreuves collectives	575	»
328	Rassemblement pour la Paix, 1 f. 50	100	»
329	Chômeurs intellectuels, 50 + 20 c.	90	»
329	“ “ *petit format*	175	»
330	Jacques Callot, 20 + 10 c.	110	»
331	Berlioz, 40 + 10 c.	120	»
332	Victor Hugo, 50 + 10 c.	150	»
333	Pasteur, 1 f. 50 + 50 c.	150	»
334	Chamonix, 1 f. 50	375	»
335	Corneille, 75 c.	90	»
336	Exposition de Paris, 1 f. 50	90	»
337	Mermoz, 30 c.	175	»
338	“ 3 f.	225	»
339	Chemins de fer, 30 c.	275	»
340	“ “ 1 f. 50	300	»
341	Discours *sur* la méthode, 90 c.	90	»
342	Discours de la méthode, 90 c.	90	»
343	Anatole France, 30 + 10 c.	90	»
344	Rodin, 90 + 10 c.	90	»
345	Sports et Loisirs, 20 + 10 c.		
346	Sports et Loisirs 40 + 10 c.		
347	“ “ 50 + 10 c.		
	Les trois	240	»

N°	Désignation	Prix	
348 à 351	PEXIP , 5c., 15 c., 30 c., 50 c. (*B.-F.* 3)	1300	»
352	Réfugiés politiques, 50 + 25 c.	140	»
353	Pierre Loti, 50 + 20 c.	90	»
354	Samothrace, 30 c.		
355	" 55 c.		
	Les deux	725	»
356	Pour sauver la race, 65 + 25 c.	90	»
357	Constitution des États-Unis, 1 f. 75	110	»
358	Col de l'Iseran, 90 c.	85	»
360	Semeuse, 30 c.		
361	" 35 c.		
362	" 50 c.		
	Épreuve collective	350	»
363	Type Paix, 55 c.		
364	" " 60 c.		
365	" " 65 c.		
	Épreuve collective	350	»
366	Type Paix, 80 c.	50	»
367	" " 90 c. vert	50	»
368	" " 90 c. bleu	50	»
369	" " 1 f.	50	»
370	" " 1 f. 25	50	»
371	" " 1 f. 40	50	»
372	Cérès, 1 f. 75	50	»
373	" 2 f.	50	»
374	" 2 f. 25	50	»
375	" 2 f. 50, vert	50	»
375A	" 2 f. 50, outremer	50	»
376	" 3 f.	50	»
377	Charcot, 65 + 35 c.		
377A	" 90 + 35 c.		
	Les deux	350	»
378	Gambetta, 55 c.	70	»
379	Château de Versailles, 1 f. 75 + 75 c.	100	»
380	Anatole France, 30 + 10 c.	70	»
381	Jacques Callot, 35 + 10 c.	70	»
382	Berlioz, 55 + 10 c.	90	»
383	Victor Hugo, 65 + 10 c.	145	»
384	Rodin, 1 f. + 10 c.	90	»
385	Pasteur, 1 f. 75 + 25 c.	160	»
386	Infanterie, 55 + 70 c.		
387	" 65 + 1 f. 10		
	Les deux	140	»
388	Champagne, 1 f. 75	70	»
389	Arc de Triomphe d'Orange, 2 f.	70	»
390	Mineurs, 2 f. 15	70	»
391	Avignon, 3 f.	75	»
392	Carcassone, 5 f.	75	»
393	Donjon de Vincennes, 10 f.	80	»
394	Saint-Malo, 20 f.	150	»
395	Service de Santé, 55 + 45 c.	90	»
396	Football, 1 f. 75	400	»
397	La Fontaine, 55 c.	60	»
398	Ader, 50 f.	375	»
399	Cathédrale de Reims, 65 + 35 c.	75	»
400	Souvenirs anglais, 1 f. 75	60	»
400	" " 1 f. 75, *petit format*	115	»
401	Rapatriés d'Espagne, 65 + 60 c.	70	»
402	Pierre et Marie Curie, 1 f. 75 + 50 c.	200	»
403	Armistice, 65 + 35 c.	60	»
404	Mercure, 1 c.	30	»
405	" 2 c.	30	»
406	" 5 c.	30	»
407	" 10 c.	30	»
408	" 15 c. vermillon	30	»
409	" 15 c. brun-orange	30	»
410	Mercure, 20 c.	30	»
411	" 25 c.	30	»
412	" 30 c.	30	»
413	" 40 c.	30	»
414	" 45 c.	30	»
414A	" 50 c. bleu	30	»
414B	" 50 c. vert	30	»
415	" 60 c.	30	»
416	" 70 c.	30	»
416A	" 75 c.	30	»
417	Oeuvres des Étudiants, 65 + 60 c.	65	»
418	Radio aux Aveugles, 90 + 25 c.	65	»
419	Prophylaxie, 90 + 30 c.	65	»
420	Le jeune Trulin, 90 + 35 c.	75	»
421	Cézanne, 2 f. 25	200	»
422	75e anniversaire de la Croix-Rouge 90 + 35 c.	260	»
423	Génie Militaire, 70 + 50 c.	70	»
424	Orphelins des P.T.T., 90 + 35 c.	85	»
425	Clémenceau, 90 c.	65	»
426	Exposition de New York, 2 f. 25	140	»

N°	Désignation	Prix	
427	Niepce et Daguerre, 2 f. 25	95	»
428	Enfants des Chômeurs, 90 + 35 c.	60	»
429	Tour Eiffel, 90 + 50 c.	120	»
430	Exposition de Liège, 2 f. 25	65	»
431	Iris, 80 c.	50	»
432	" 1 f. vert	50	»
433	" 1 f. rouge	50	»
434	" 1 f. 30	50	»
435	" 1 f. 50	50	»
436	Puvis de Chavannes, 40 + 10 c.	80	»
437	Debussy, 70 + 10 c.	90	»
438	Balzac, 90 + 10 c.	70	»
439	Claude bernard, 2 f. 25 + 25 c.	70	»
440	Pour la Natalité, 70 + 80 c.		
441	" " 90 + 60 c.		
	Les deux	200	»
442	Grégoire de Tours, 90 c.	80	»
443	Cathédrale de Strasbouirg, 70 c.	90	»
444	150e aniversaire de la Révolution, 90 c.	90	»
445	Verdun,90 c.	70	»
446	La lettre de Fragonard, 40 + 60 c.	125	»
446	" *Petit format*	325	»
446	" *Petit format avec remarque*	350	»
446	" 40 + 60 c. violet, *Petit format*	350	»
447	Marins perdus en mer, 70 + 30 c.	70	»
448	Languedoc, 70 c.	65	»
449	Château de Pau, 90 c.	65	»
450	Pont de la Guillotière, 90 C.	65	»
451	Pour nos Soldats, 40 + 60 c.		
452	" " 1 f. + 50 c.		
	Les deux	125	»
453	France d'Outre-Mer, 1 f. + 25 c.	80	»
454	Joffe, 80 c. + 45 c.		
455	Foch, 1 f. + 50 c.		
456	Galliéni, 1 f. 50 + 50 c.		
457	Paysanne à la charrue, 2 f. 50 + 50 c.		
	Les quatre	325	»
458	Exposition de New York, 2 f. 50	140	»
459	Croix-Rouge, 80 c. + 1 f.		
460	" " 1 f. + 2 f.		
	Les deux	400	»
461	Guynemer, 50 f.	250	»
462	Debussy, 80 + 10 c.	70	»
463	Balzac, 1 f. + 10 c.	70	»
464	Claude Bernard, 2 f. 50 + 25 c.	70	»
465	Pour les victimes de la guerre, 1 f. + 2 f.	70	»
466	Secours national, 80 c. + 2 f.		
467	" " 1 f. + 2 f.		
468	" " 1 f. 50 + 2 f.		
469	" " 2 f. 50 + 2 f.		
	Les quatre	180	»
470	Maréchal Pétain, 40 c.		
471	" " 80 c.		
472	" " 1 f.		
473	" " 2 f. 50		
	Les quatre	240	»
	Les 4 valeurs, épreuve collective	475	»
474	Pour nos Prisonniers, 80 c. + 5 f.		
475	" " 1 f. + 5 f.		
	Les deux	100	»
476	Semeuse, 30 s. 35 c.	40	»
477	Mercure, 50 s. 75 c.	40	»
478	Paix, 50 s. 55 c.	40	»
479	" 50 s. 65 c.	40	»
480	" 50 s. 75 c.	40	»
481	" 50 s. 80 c.	40	»
482	" 50 s. 90 c.	40	»
483	" 1 f. s. 1 f. 25	40	»
484	" 1 f. s. 1 f. 40	40	»
485	" 1 f. s. 1 f. 50	40	»
486	Cérès, 1 f. s. 1 f. 75	40	»
487	" 1 f. s. 2 f. 25	40	»
488	" 1 f. s. 2 f. 50	40	»
489	Mineurs, 1 f. s. 2 f. 15	80	»
490	Carcassonne, 2 f. 50 s. 5 f.	80	»
491	Vincennes, 5 f. s. 10 f.	80	»
492	Saint-Malo, 10 f. s. 20 f.	80	»
493	Ader, 20 f. s. 50 f.	250	»
494	Maréchal Pétain, + 10 s. 1 f.	80	»
495	Mistral, 1 f.	80	»
495	" 1 f., *grand format vertical, avec remarque*	110	»
495	" sur papier rose	130	»
496	Contre la cancer, 2 f. 50 + 50 c.	135	»
497	Secours national, 1 f. + 2 f.		
498	" " 2 f. 50 + 7 f. 50		
	Les deux	225	»
	1 f. + 2 f. et 2 f. 50 + 7 f. 50, Épreuve collective	350	»

499 Hôtel-Dieu de Beaume, 5 f. 80 »
500 Angers, 10 f. 80 »
501 Aigues-Mortes, 20 f. 80 »
502 Paquebot Pasteur, 1 f. + 1f. s. 70 c. 100 »
503 Pour la France d'Outre-Mer, 1 f. + 1 f. 80 »
504 Société des œuvres de mer, 1 f. + 9 f. 80 »
505 à 524 (+ 521A-B), Maréchal Pétain
Les 22 épreuves 450 »
505 à 507 (20 c., 30 c., 40 c.,),
Les 3 valeurs, épreuve collective 500 »
508 à 515 (50 c., 60 c., 70 c. bleu, 70 c., orange, 80 c. brun, 80 c. vert-jaune, 1 f., 1 f. 20)
Les 8 valeurs, épreuve collective 500 »
516 à 521 (1 f. 50, rose, 1 f. 50, brun-rouge, 2 f., 2 f. 40, 2 f. 50, 3 f.).
Les 6 valeurs, épreuve collective 550 »
521A + B (4 f. bleu-violet, 4 f. 50, vert-jaune).
Les 2 valeurs, épreuve collective 550 »
522 à 524 (4 f. outremer, 4 f. 50, vert foncé, 5 f.).
Les 3 valeurs, épreuve collective 550 »
525 Maréchal Pétain, 50 f. 150 »
526 à 537, Armoiries de villes, 20 c. + 30 c., 40 c. + 60 c., 50 c. + 70 c., 70 c + 80 c., 80 c. + 1 f., 1 f. + 1 f., 1 f. 50 + 2 f., 2 f. + 2 f., 2 f. 50 + 3 f., 3 f. + 5 f., 5 f. + 6 f., 10 f. + 10 f.
Les 12 épreuves 480 »
Les 12 valeurs, épreuve collective 1000 »
538 Mercure, 50 c. turquoise 45 »
539 Hôtel-Dieu de Beaume, 15 f. 50 »
540 Œuvres de l'air, 1 f. 50 + 3 f. 50 200 »
541 La Pérouse, 2 f. 50 + 7 f. 50 150 »
542 Chabrier, 2 f. + 3 f. 170 »
543 Qinzaine impériale, 1 f. 50 + 8 f. 50 150 »
544 Jean de Vienne, 1 f. 50 + 8 f. 50 150 »
545 Massenet, 4 f. 80 »
546 Mercure, 10 c.
547 " 30 c.
548 " 40 c.
549 " 50 c.
Les quatre 140 »
550 Stendhal, 4 f. 85 »
551 Blondel, 4 f. 85 »
552 Secours national, + 50 c. sur 1 f. 50 50 »
553 à 564, Armoiries de villes, 50 c. + 60 c. 60 c. + 70 c., 80 c. + 1 f., 1 f. + 1 f. 30, 1 f. 20 + 1 f. 50, 1 f. 50 + 1 f. 80, 2 f. + 2 f. 30, 2 f. 40 + 2 f. 80, 3 f. + 3 f. 50, 4 f. + 5 f., 4 f. 50 + 6 f., 5 f. + 7 f.
La série des 12 valeurs 480 »
Les 12 valeurs, épreuve collective 1000 »
565 à 566, Légion tricolore, 1 f. 20 + 8 f. 80, bleu et 1 f. 20 + 8 f. 80, rouge.
Les 2 valeurs, sur même feuillet 250 »
567 Beffroi d'Arras, 10 f. vert 70 »
568 à 571, Secours national, 1 f. + 10 f. bleu, 1 f. + 10 f. rouge, 2 f. + 12 f. bleu et 2 f. + 12 f. rouge 300 »
Les 4 valeurs, sur même feuillet 700 »
572 Armoiries du Lyonnais, 5 f.
573 Armoiries de la Bretagne, 10 f.
574 Armoiries de la Provence, 15 f.
575 Armoiries de l'Ile-de-France, 20 f.
Les quatre 125 »
Les 4 valeurs, épreuve collective 300 »
576 à 580, Secours national, 1 f. 20 + 1 f. 40, 1 f. 50 + 2 f. 50, 2 f. 40 + 7 f., 4 f. + 10 f., 5 f. + 15 f.
Les 5 épreuves 300 »
Les 5 valeurs, épreuve collective 700 »
Épreuve collective en violet 800 »
581 Lavoisier, 4 f. 50 »
582 Paysage du Dauphiné, 20 f. 80 »
583 Hôtel-Dieu de Beaune, 4 f. 80 »
584 Secours national, 1 f. 50 + 3 f. 50 90 »
585 Famille du prisonnier, 1 f. 50 + 8 f. 50
586 " " 2 f. 40 + 7 f. 60
Les deux 150 »
Les 2 valeurs, épreuve collective 375 »
587 à 592, Célébrités du XVIe siècle, 60 c. + 80 c., 1 f. 20 + 1 f. 50, 1 f. 50 + 3 f., 2 f. 40 + 4 f., 4 f. + 6 f., 5 f. + 10 f.
Les 6 épreuves 250 »
Les 6 valeurs, épreuve collective 525 »
593 à 598, Costumes régionaux, 60 c. + 1 f. 30, 1 f. 20 + 2 f., 1 f. 50 + 4 f., 2 f. 40 + 5 f., 4 f. + 6 f., 5 f. + 7 f.
Les 6 épreuves 250 »
Les 6 valeurs, épreuve collective 525 »
599 Branly, 4 f. 60 »
600 Tourville, 4 f. + 6 f. 90 »
601 Gounod, 1 f. 50 + 3 f. 50 65 »
602 Armoires de Flandre, 5 f.
603 " du Languedoc, 10 f.
604 " de l'Orléannais, 15 f.
605 " de la Normandie, 20 f.
Les quatre 160 »
Les 4 valeurs, épreuve collective 300 »
606 Maréchal Pétain, 1 f. 50 + 3 f. 50
607 Corporation payasanne, 2 f. + 3 f.
608 Charte du travail, 4 f. + 6 f.
Les trois 275 »
Les 3 valeurs, épreuve collective 500 »
609 Création du service ambulant, 1 f. 50 80 »
610 Château de Chenonceaux, 15 f. 70 »
611 " " 25 f. 80 »
612 à 617, Célébrités du XVIIe siècle, 50 c. + 1 f. 50, 80 c. + 2 f. 20, 1 f. 20 + 2 f. 80, 1 f. 50 + 3 f. 50, 2 f. + 4 f., 4 f. + 6 f.
Les 6 épreuves 250 »
Les 6 valeurs, épreuve collective 525 »
618 Paris-Orléans, 4 f. + 6 f. 90 »
619 Claude Chappe, 4 f. 65 »
649 Iris, 80 c. vert-jaune
650 " 1 f. bleu clair
651 " 1 f. 20, violet
652 " 1 f. 50, rouge-brun
653 " 2 f. brun
654 " 2 f. 40, rose carminé
655 " 3 f. rouge-orange
656 " 4 f. bleu
Les huit 250 »
Les 8 valeurs, épreuve collective 650 »
661 Basilique de Saint-Denis, 2 f. 40 60 »
662 Maréchal Bugeaud, 4 f. 60 »
663 à 667, Cathédrales, 50 c. + 1 f. 50, 80 c. + 2 f. 20, 1 f. 20 + 2 f. 80, 1 f. 50 + 3 f. 50, 4 f. + 6 f. 350 »
Les 5 valeurs, épreuve collective 525 »
668 Journée du Timbre (1944) 60 »
669 Libération, 4 f. bleu 65 »
670 Chaîne brisée, 10 c.
671 " " 30 c.
672 " " 40 c.
673 " " 50 c.
Les quatre 130 »
Les 4 valeurs, épreuve collective 450 »
674 Cérès (de Mazelin), 60 c. 40 »
675 " " 80 c. 40 »
677 " " 1 f. 40 »
678 " " 1 f. 20 40 »
678A " " 1 f. 30 40 »
679 " " 1 f. 50 40 »
674, 675 et 677 à 679, 60 et 80 c., 1 f., 1 f. 20 et 1 f. 50
Les 5 valeurs, épreuve collective 375 »
680 Cérès (de Mazelin), 2 f. vert-jaune 40 »
68 1 " " 2 f. 50, brun 40 »
Les 2 valeurs, épreuve collective 350 »

Marianne (de Gandon), typographiés

712 1 f. 50, rose carminé 50 »
713 2 f. vert 50 »
714 2 f. 40, rouge 50 »
715 3 f. brun 50 »
716 3 f. rose 50 »
716A 3 f. vert 50 »
716B 3 f. 50, rouge-brun 50 »
717 4 f. bleu 50 »
718 4 f. violet 50 »
718B 4 f. 50, bleu 50 »
719 5 f. vert 50 »
719A 5 f. rose 50 »
719B 5 f. bleu 50 »
720 6 f. bleu-violet 50 »
721 6 f. rouge 50 »
721A 6 f. rose 50 »
722 10 f. orange 50 »
723 10 f. bleu 45 »
716B, 718A et 719A : 3 f. 50, 4 f. 50 et 5 f. rose
Les 3 valeurs, épreuve collective 525 »
716, 718, 721, 723 : 3 f. rose, 4 f. violet, 6 f. rouge et 10 f. bleu
Les 4 valeurs, épreuve collective 525 »
716A, 719B et 721 : 3 f. vert, 5 f. bleu et 6 f. rouge
Les 3 valeurs, épreuve collective 525 »

N°	Désignation	Prix
724 : 15 f. lilas-rose		45 »
712, 713, 714, 715, 717, 719, 720, 722, 724 :		
	1 f. 50, 2 f., 2 f. 40, 3 f. brun,	
	4 f. bleu, 5 f., 6 f. bleu-violet,	
	10 f. orange et 15 f.	
	Les 9 valeurs, épreuve collective	700 »
	Marianne (de Gandon), gravés	
725	4 f. bleu	
726	10 f. bleu	
727	15 f. lilas-rose	
728	20 f. vert	
729	25 f. orange	
	Les cinq	275 »
	Les 5 valeurs, épreuve collective	600 »
	Grand format	
730	20 f. vert	
731	25 f. violet	
732	50 f. brun-rouge	
733	100 f. carmin	
	Les quatre	300 »
	Les 4 valeurs, épreuve collective	600 »
734	Metz, 2 f. 40	
735	Strasbourg, 4 f.	
	Les deux	120 »
736	Ligue anti-tuberculeuse, 2 f. + 1 f.	60 »
737	Semaine des P.T.T., 4 f. + 6 f.	60 »
738	Sarah Bernhardt, 4 f. + 1f.	90 »
739	Libération, 4 f. brun-rouge	60 »
740	Croisade. Air pur, 4 f. + 2 f.	60 »
741	France d'Outre-Mer, 2 f.	60 »
742	Oradour, 4 f. + 2 f.	65 »
743	Journée du Timbre (1945)	80 »
744	Dunkerque, 1 f. 50 + 1 f. 50	
745	Rouen, 2 f. + 2 f.	
746	Caen, 2 f. 40 + 2 f. 60	
747	Saint-Malo, 4 f. + 4 f.	
	Les quatre	240 »
	Les 4 valeurs, épreuve collective	500 »
748	Fournier, 2 f. + 3 f.	80 »
749	Becquerel, 2 f. + 3 f.	80 »
750	3 f. s. 2 f. + 1 f. orange	60 »
751	Invalides de guerre, 4 f. + 6 f.	70 »
752	Œuvres de la Marine, 2 f. + 3 f.	80 »
753	Musée Postal, 2 f.+ 3 f.	175 »
753	" " *petit format*	300 »
753	" " *petit format*	
	" " *avec remarque*	400 »
753	" " *petit format*	
	" " *papier bleuté*	400 »
446 et 753, Lettre de Fragonard et le cachet de cire.		
	Les 2 valeurs, épreuve collective	1500 »
754	Journée du Timbre (1946)	120 »
755	Armoiries, Corse, 10 c.	
756	" Alsace, 30 c.	
757	" Lorraine, 50 c.	
758	" Nice, 60 c.	
	Les quatre	180 »
755 à 758. Les 4 valeurs, épreuve collective		350 »
759	Vézelay, 5 f.	65 »
760	Palais du Luxembourg, 10 f.	65 »
761	Conférence de la Paix, 3 f.	
762	" " 10 f.	
	Les deux	140 »
761 et 762. Les 2 valeurs, épreuve collective		225 »
763	Rocamadour, 15 f.	60 »
764	Pointe du Raz, 20 f.	60 »
765 à 770. Célébrités du XVe siècle :		
	2 f. + 1 f. ; 3 f. + 1 f. ; 4 f. + 3 f. ;	
	5 f. + 4 f. ; 6 f. + 5 f. ; 10 f. + 6 f.	250 »
	Les 6 valeurs, épreuve collective	525 »
771	U.N.E.S.C.O., 10 f. bleu	180 »
772 à 776. Cathédrales : 1 f. + 1 f. ; 3 f. + 2 f. ;		
	4 f. + 3 f. ; 6 f. + 4 f. ; 10 f. + 6 f.	
	Les 5 épreuves	225 »
	Les 5 valeurs, épreuve collective	525 »
777	Cannes, 6 f.	65 »
778	Nancy, 25 f.	65 »
759, 760, 763, 764, 777 et 778 : 5, 6, 10,		
	15, 20 et 25 f.	
	Les 6 valeurs, épreuve collective	500 »
779	Louvois, Journée du Timbre (1947)	60 »
780 à 783. 12e Congrès de l'Union Postale :		
	3,50, 4,50, 6 et 10 f.	525 »
780 à 783. *Petit format*, les 4 épreuves		600 »
780 à 783 et *Av.* 20		
	Les 5 valeurs, épreuve collective	2800 »

N°	Désignation	Prix
784	Pavie, 4 f. 50	60 »
785	Fénelon, 4 f. 50	60 »
786	Saint-Nazaire, 6 f. + 4 f.	65 »
787	Jamboree, 5 f.	500 »
788	Voie de la Liberté, 6 f. + 4 f.	60 »
789	Fournier, 2 f. + 3 f. bleu-noir	50 »
748 et 789. Fournier, 2 f. + 3 f. rouge-brun		
	et Fournier, 2 f. + 3 f. bleu-noir.	
	Les 2 valeurs, épreuve collective	450 »
790	Résistance, 5 f.	65 »
790	Id., épr. collect. en bleu et en rouge	725 »
791	Cérès, 1 f. sur 1 f. 30, bleu	50 »
678 et 791 : 1 f. 30, bl. et 1 f. sur 1 f. 30		
	Les 2 valeurs, épreuve collective	450 »
792	Abbaye de Conques, 15 f.	60 »
793	Braille, 6 f. + 4 f.	65 »
794	Arago. Journée du Timbre (1948)	80 »
795 à 802. Centenaire de la Révolution		
	de 1848. Les 8 épreuves	325 »
795 à 802. Les 8 valeurs, épreuve collective		750 »
803	Palais du Luxembourg, 12 f.	60 »
804	" " 15 f.	60 »
805	Conques, 18 f.	60 »
792, 803, 805. Les 3 val., épreuve collective		450 »
806	Marianne (de Gandon), 3 f.	55 »
807	" " 4 f.	55 »
808	" " 4 f.	55 »
809	" " 5 f.	55 »
810	" " 8 f.	55 »
811	" " 10 f.	55 »
806, 807, 811. Marianne (de Gandon)		
	Les 3 valeurs, sur même feuillet	500 »
812	Marianne (de Gandon), 12 f.	55 »
813	" " 15 f.	55 »
814	Calmette, 6 f. + 4 f.	60 »
815	Leclerc, 6 f.	60 »
816	Chateaubriand, 18 f.	60 »
817	Barrage de Génissiat, 12 f.	60 »
818	Palais de Chaillot, 12 f.	
819	" " 18 f. Les deux	350 »
	Idem. Les 2 valeurs, épreuve collective	525 »
820	Paul Langevin, 5 f.	
821	Jean Perrin, 8 f. Les deux	110 »
	Les 2 valeurs, épreuve collective	150 »
822	Nancy, 25 f.	60 »
823 à 826. Série des métiers, 3 f. + 1 f. ; 5 f.		
	+ 3 f. ; 8 f. +4 f. ; 10 f. + 6 f.	240 »
	Les 4 valeurs, épreuve collective	450 »
827	Marianne (de Gandon), 5 f. s. 6 f.	60 »
828	Choiseul. Journée du Timbre (1949)	100 »
829	Expéditions polaires, 15 f.	200 »
	Centenaire du Timbre.	
830	Cérès, 15 f	
831	" 25 f.	
832	Marianne, 15 f.	
833	" 25 f. Les quatre	300 »
830 à 833. Épreuve collective		1100 »
830 à 833. *Petit format,*		
	avec remarque. Les quatre	1100 »
834	Armoiries, Bourgogne, 10 c.	
835	" Guyenne, 50 c.	
836	" Savoie, 1 f.	
837	" Auvergne, 2 f.	
838	" Anjou, 4 f. Les cinq	200 »
	Les cinq valeurs, épreuve collective	400 »
839	6e centenaire du rattachement du	
	Dauphiné, 12 f.	65 »
840	Amitié franco-américaine, 25 f.	110 »
841	Exposition philatélique de Paris	
	(Citex), 10 f.	425 »
841	Id. *Petit format, avec remarque*	700 »
830 à 833 et 841. Les 5 valeurs, épreuve collective		1350 »
841A	Saint-Bertrand de Comminges, 20 f.	
842	Saint-Wandrille, 25 f.	
842A	Vallée de la Meuse, 40 f.	
843	Gerbier de Jonc, 50 f. Les quatre	200 »
841A à 843. Les 4 valeurs, épreuve collective		450 »
	Congrès International de Télégraphie et Téléphonie.	
844 à 847 : 10, 15, 25 et 50 f. Les 4 épreuves		250 »
844 à 847 et P.A. 28. *Grand format.*		
	Les 5 valeurs, épreuve collective, distance	
	entre les timbres : 2 cm	1000 »
	Petit format.	
	Les 5 valeurs, épreuve collective, distance	
	entre les timbres : 1 cm	800 »
848	Racine, 12 f.	65 »

> A partir du n° 849, toutes les épreuves simples sont de petit format, à peu près 130x110 mm.

849 Chambres de Commerce, 15 f. 50 »

75e anniversaire de l'U.P.U. :

850 à 852 : 5, 15 et 25 f. Les 3 épreuves 850 »
Les 3 valeurs, épreuve collective 1600 »

Célébrités du XVIIIe siècle (première série) :

853 à 858 : 5 f. + 1 f. ; 8 f. + 2 f. ; 10 f. + 3 f. ; 12 f. + 4 f. ; 15 f. + 5 f. ; 25 f. + 10 f.
Les 6 épreuves 360 »
Les 6 valeurs, épreuve collective 725 »

Les saisons :

859 à 862 : 5 f. + 1 f. ; 8 f. + 2 f. ; 12 f. + 3 f. ; 15 f. + 4 f. Les 4 épreuves 325 »
Les 4 valeurs, épreuve collective 550 »
863 Facteur, 12 f. + 3 f. 100 »
864 Poincarré, 15 f. 60 »
865 Péguy, 12 f. 60 »
866 Rabelais, 12 f. 60 »

Célébrités du XVIIIe siècle (deuxième série) :

867 à 872 : 5 f. + 2 f. ; 8 f. + 3 f. ; 10 f. + 4 f. ; 12 f. + 5 f. ; 15 f. + 6 f. ; 20 f. + 10 f.
Les 6 épreuves 360 »
Les 6 valeurs, épreuve collective 700 »
873 Châteaudun, 8 f. 60 »
874 Madame de Sévigné, 15 f. 60 »
875 Madame de Récamier, 12 f. 65 »
874-875. Épreuve collective 200 »
876-877. Croix-Rouge (1950). La paire 325 »
876-877. *Idem*, épreuve collective 550 »
878 Fontainebleau, 12 f. 60 »
873 et 878. Épreuve collective 200 »
879 Journée du Timbre (1951) 90 »
880 Jules Ferry, 15 f. 60 »
881 Textile, 25 f. 60 »
882 Saint Jean-Baptiste de la Salle, 15 f. 60 »
883 à 887. *Gandon*, 5 f., 6 f., 12 f., 15 f. et 18 f.
Les 5 épreuves 200 »
883-887. Épreuve collective 400 »
888 Saint-Wandrille, 30 f. 60 »
889 Troupes coloniales, 15 f. 60 »
890 Vincent d'Indy, 25 f. 90 »

Célébrités du XIXe siècle (première série) :

891 à 896 : 5 f. + 1 f. ; 8 f. + 2 f. ; 10 f. + 3 f. ; 12 f. + 4 f. ; 15 f. + 5 f. ; 30 f. + 10 f.
Les 6 épreuves 360 »
Les mêmes, épreuve collective 700 »
897 Médecine vétérinaire, 12 f. 60 »
898 Médecine militaire, 15 f. 60 »

Armoiries des provinces françaises (5e série) :

899 à 903. Les 5 épreuves 125 »
Les mêmes, épreuve collective 225 »
904 Saint Nicolas, 15 f. 100 »
905 Arbois, 30 f. 60 »
906 Bimillénaire de Paris, 15 f. 80 »
907 Noguès, 12 f. 90 »
908 à 910. Symbolistes. Les 3 épreuves 150 »
Les mêmes, épreuve collective 450 »
911, 912. Nations Unies. Les deux 500 »
Les mêmes, épreuve collective 650 »
913 Clos de Vougeot, 30 f. 90 »
914-15. Croix-Rouge (1951). La paire 300 »
Les mêmes, épreuve collective 500 »
916 Pic du Midi, 40 f. 85 »
917 Abbaye aux Hommes, 50 f. 65 »
918 Clémenceau, 15 f. 60 »
919 Journée du Timbre (1952) 90 »
920 Maréchal de Lattre, 15 f. 60 »
921 aucouleurs, 12 f. 70 »
922 Narvik, 30 f. 70 »
923 Conseil de l'Europe, 30 f. 600 »
924 Château de Chambord, 20 f. 60 »
924, 905, 916, 917. Épreuve collective 225 »
925 Bir Hakeim, 30 f. 70 »
922 et 925. Épreuve collective 200 »
926 Sainte-Croix de Poitiers, 15 f. 60 »
927 Médaille, militaire, 15 f. 70 »
921 et 928. Épreuve collective 200 »
928 Viaduc de Garabit, 15 f. 70 »
929 Léonard de Vinci, 30 f. 180 »

Célébrités du XIXe siècle (deuxième série) :

930 à 935 : 8 f. + 2 f. ; 12 f. + 3 f. ; 15 f. + 4 f. ; 18 f. + 5 f. ; 20 f. + 6 f. ; 30 f. + 7 f.
Les 6 épreuves 360 »
Les mêmes, épreuve collective 700 »
936 Laennec, 12 f. 70 »
937-38. Croix-Rouge (1952). La paire 250 »
Les mêmes, épreuve collective 450 »
939 Versailles, 18 f. (voir aussi 988) 90 »
940 Comte d'Argenson. Journée du Timbre (1953) 80 »
668, 743, 754, 779, 794, 828, 863, 879, 919 et 940. Épreuve collective 1000 »
941 Haute Couture, 30 f. 70 »
942 Maréchal Leclerc, 8 f. 60 »
815 et 942. Épreuve collective 200 »
943 Gargantua, 6 f. 65 »
944 Hernani, 18 f. 65 »

Célébrités du XIIe au XXe siècles :

945 à 950 : 8 f. + 2 f. ; 12 f. + 3 f. ; 15 f. + 4 f. ; 18 f. + 5 f. ; 20 f. + 6 f. ; 30 f. + 7 f.
Les 6 épreuves 360 »
Les mêmes, épreuve collective 700 »
951 à 954. Armoiries. Les 4 épreuves 160 »
Les mêmes, épreuve collective 300 »
955 Tour de France, 12 f. 90 »
956 Célimène, 8 f. 65 »
957 Figaro, 12 f. 65 »
943, 944, 956, 957. Épreuve collective 250 »
958, 959. Armoiries. Les deux 90 »
Les mêmes, épreuve collective 175 »
960 à 965. Sports. Les 6 épreuves 450 »
Les mêmes, épreuve collective, sur deux épreuves. Les deux 1000 »
966-67. Croix-Rouge (1953). La paire 250 »
Les mêmes, épreuve collective 450 »
968 15 f. s. 18 f. 60 »
969 La Valette. Journée du Timbre (1954) 90 »
970 à 974. Productions. Les 5 épreuves 250 »
970 à 974, 941. Épreuve collective sur deux épreuves. Les deux 450 »
975 Foire de Paris, 15 f. 65 »
976 Lourdes, 6 f.
977 LesAndelys, 8 f.
978 Royan, 10 f.
979 Quimper, 12 f.
980 Cheverny, 18 f.
981 Ajaccio, 20 f. Les six 250 »
976 à 981. Épreuve collective, sur deux épreuves. Les deux 475 »
982 Maréchal de Lattre, 12 f. 65 »
983 Libération, 15 f. 65 »
984 Maréchal Leclerc, 12 f. 65 »
982 à 984. Épreuve collective 275 »
985 Jumièges, 12 f. 60 »
986 Tournus, 30 f. 60 »
987 Stenay 60 »
988 Versailles 90 »
939, 988; Épreuve collective 225 »

Célébrités du XIIe au XXe siècles :

989 à 994. Les 6 épreuves 390 »
Les mêmes, épreuve collective 750 »
995 Villandry 65 »
996 Saint-Cyr 90 »
997 Légion d'Honneur 75 »
998 Système métrique 65 »
999 à 1005. Armoiries. Les 7 épreuves 245 »
Les mêmes, épreuve collective 380 »
1006-07. Croix-Rouge (1954). La paire 350 »
Les mêmes, épreuve collective 500 »
1008 Saint-Simon 60 »
1009 Rotary 250 »
1009A Marianne (Muller) 150 »
1010A Marianne (Muller) 150 »
1011 Marianne (Muller) 80 »
1011A Marianne (Muller) 80 »
1001B Marianne (Muller) 80 »
1009A, 1010, 1011 1011B. En épreuve collective 725 »
1011C Marianne (Muller) 80 »
1012-1017. Les six 240 »
Inventeurs, sur 2 épreuves collectives 475 »
1018 Journée du Timbre (1955) 80 »
1019 Limoges 60 »
1020 Ganterie 65 »
1021 Florian 60 »
1022 Télévision 65 »
1023 Déportation 60 »
1024 Électrification 65 »

N°	Désignation	Prix
1025	Jacquemart	60 »
1026	Jules Verne	125 »
1027 à 1032.	Les six	390 »
	Épreuve collective	750 »
1033	Lumière	65 »
1034	Jacques Cœur	60 »
1035	Canada	70 »
1036 à 1042.	Les sept	300 »
	Idem. Sur 2 épreuves collectives	450 »
1043	Gérard de Nerval	65 »
1044 à 1047.	Les 4 armoiries	160 »
	Id. Épreuve collective	300 »
1048-49.	Croix Rouge (1955). La paire	250 »
	Idem. Épreuve collective	400 »
1050	Déportation	60 »
1051	Douai	60 »
1052	Driant	60 »
1053	Verdun	60 »
	Les 2, en épreuve collective	150 »
1054	F. de Tassis. J. du T. (1956)	65 »
1055	J.-H. Fabre	
1056	Charles Tellier	
1057	Camille Flammarion	
1058	Paul Sabatier. Les quatre	200 »
	Idem. Épreuve collective	325 »
1059	Grand Trianon	60 »
1060	France-Amérique Latine	65 »
1061	Reims-Florence	70 »
1062	Malte	65 »
1063	Saint Yves	60 »
1064	Franchet d'Esperey	60 »
1065	Montceau-les-Mines	60 »
1066 à 1071.	Les six	240 »
	Épreuve collective	450 »
1072 à 1075.	Les quatre	240 »
	Épreuve collective	500 »
1076 et 1077.	Europa (1956). La paire	700 »
	Épreuve collective	1100 »
1078 à 1080.	Les trois	150 »
	Épreuve collective	250 »
1081	Parmentier	60 »
1082 à 1087.	Les six	240 »
	Épreuve collective	400 »
1088	Coubertin	220 »
1089-90.	Croix-Rouge (1956). La paire	200 »
	Épreuve collective	325 »
1091	Colombophilie	65 »
1092	Schœlcher	60 »
1093	Felouque. J. du Timbre (1957)	65 »
1094	Sièvres	60 »
1095 à 1098.	Les quatre	160 »
	Épreuve collective	325 »
1099	Uzès	60 »
1100 à 1104.	Les cinq	200 »
	Épreuve collective	350 »
1105, 1106.	Le Quesnoy. Les deux	80 »
1107	Cour des Comptes	60 »
1108 à 1113.	Les six	200 »
	Deux Épreuves collectives	425 »
1114	Travaux publics	60 »
1115, 1115A, 1116.	Moissonneuse. Les trois	120 »
1115, 1116.	Épreuve collective	200 »
1117	Brest	60 »
1118	Région bordelaise	60 »
1119	Cahors	60 »
1118, 1119 et 1105.	Épreuve collective	250 »
1120	Jeux anniversaires	60 »
1121	Auguste Comte	60 »
1122-23.	Europa (1957). La paire	420 »
	Épreuve collective	600 »
1124	Bimillénaire de Lyon	60 »
1125 à 1131.	Les sept	200 »
	Les sept, sur trois épreuves collectives	400 »
1132 à 1138.	Les sept	210 »
	Les sept, sur deux épreuves collectives	400 »
1139	Thénard	60 »
1140-41.	Croix-Rouge (1957). La paire	170 »
	Épreuve collective	350 »
1142 à 1145.	Les quatre	160 »
	Épreuve collective	275 »
1146 à 1149.	Les quatre	160 »
	Épreuve collective	300 »
1150	Lourdes	50 »
1151	Journée du Timbre (1958)	60 »
1152 à 1155.	Les quatre	160 »
	Épreuve collective	300 »
1156	Exposition de Bruxelles	60 »
1157 à 1160.	Les quatre	160 »
	Épreuve collective	300 »
1161 à 1164.	Les quatre	160 »
	Épreuve collective	300 »
1165	Cathédrale de Senlis	60 »
1166 à 1171.	Les six	200 »
	Épreuve collective	325 »
1172	Tapisserie	60 »
1173-74.	Europa (1958). La paire	225 »
	Épreuve collective	400 »
1175	Château de Foix	50 »
1176	Jumelage Paris-Rome	65 »
1177, 1178.	U.N.E.S.C.O. Les deux	130 »
	Épreuve collective	250 »
1179	Armistice	60 »
1180 à 1186.	Armoiries. Les sept	200 »
	Épreuve collective	350 »
1187-1188.	Croix-Rouge. La paire	180 »
	Épreuve collective	325 »
1189	Floralies	60 »
1190	Palmes académiques	50 »
1191	Charles de Foucauld	50 »
1192 à 1194.	Les trois	120 »
1195	Blason d'Alger	50 »
1196	Journée du Timbre (1959)	70 »
1197	Écoles des Mines	50 »
1198 à 1202.	Les cinq	200 »
	Épreuve collective	325 »
1203 à 1206.	Les quatre	160 »
	Épreuve collective	275 »
1207 à 1212.	Les six	200 »
	Épreuve collective	325 »
1213	Goujon et Rozanoff	70 »
1214	Marceline Desbordes-Valmore	50 »
1215	Pont de Tancarville	60 »
1216	Marianne à la Nef	50 »
1217	Jaurès	50 »
1218-19.	Europa (1959). La paire	225 »
	Épreuve collective	375 »
1220	Donneurs de sang	50 »
1221 à 1223.	Tricentenaire du traité des Pyrénées	80 »
1224	Poliomyélite	50 »
1225	Bergson	50 »
1226-27.	Croix-Rouge (1959). la paire	150 »
	Épreuve collective	300 »
1228	O.T.A.N.	110 »
1229	Fréjus	60 »
1230 à 1234.	Les cinq	325 »
	Épreuve collective	550 »
1230A	5 c. Oran	60 »
1234A	30 c. Semeuse	100 »
1235 à 1241.	Les sept	225 »
	Sur 2 épreuves collectives	375 »
1242	Nolhac	50 »
1243	Musée d'Art et d'Industrie	60 »
1244	États Généraux	90 »
1245	Journée du Timbre (1960)	60 »
1246-1247.	Savoie et Nice. Les deux	100 »
	Épreuve collective	225 »
1248 à 1252.	Résistance. Les cinq	200 »
	Épreuve collective	325 »
1253	Réfugiés	80 »
1254	Strasbourg	50 »
1255	Blois	50 »
1256	La Bourboule	50 »
1257 à 1262.	Célébrités. Les six	200 »
	Épreuve collective	325 »
1263	Marianne de Decaris	80 »
1264	18 juin	175 »
1265	Jeux olympiques	175 »
1266-67.	Europa (1960). La paire	225 »
	Épreuve collective	350 »
1268	Lisieux	50 »
1269	Madame de Staël	60 »
1270	Estienne	50 »
1271	Sangnier	50 »
1272	Libération	55 »
1273 à 1276.	Oiseaux. Les quatre	200 »
1277	Honnorat	50 »
1278-79.	Croix-Rouge (1960). La paire	125 »
	Épreuve collective	250 »
1280	Sainte-Barbe	50 »
1281	Maillol	50 »
1282	20 c.Cocteau	60 »
1283	Orly	50 »
1284	Méliès	100 »
1285	Journée du Timbre (1961)	50 »

1286	Nicot	60	»
1287	Lacordaire	50	»
1288 à 1291.	Résistance. Les quatre	160	»
	Épreuve collective	280	»
1292	Anciens Combattants	50	»
1293	Bagnoles-de-l'Orne	50	»
1294	Deauville	50	»
1295 à 1300.	Célébrités. Les six	200	»
	Épreuve collective	350	»
1301 à 1305.	Comédiens. Les cinq	200	»
	Épreuve collective	350	»
1306	Mont-Dore	50	»
1307	Fauchard	50	»
1308	Thann	50	»
1309-10.	Europa (1961). La paire	225	»
	Épreuve collective	350	»
1311-18.	Série touristique. Les huit	250	»
	(sauf 1317), sur 2 épreuves collectives	450	»
1319-22.	Tableaux. Les quatre	800	»
1323-24.	Croix-Rouge (1961). La paire	180	»
	Épreuve collective	350	»
1325	Paquebot France	90	»
1326-27.	Ski	180	»
	Épreuve collective	375	»
1328	Bretonneau	40	»
1329	Bourdet	40	»
1330	Laval	50	»
1331	Coq	80	»
1331A	Coq	80	»
1332	Journée du Timbre (1962)	50	»
1333	Vannes	50	»
1334	Journée de Théâtre	40	»
1335-37.	Résistance. Les trois	100	»
	Épreuve collective	225	»
1338	Paludisme	110	»
1339	Semaine national des hôpitaux	40	»
1340-41.	Aviation. La paire	160	»
	Épreuve collective	350	»
1342	Besançon	40	»
1343	Gobelins	40	»
1344	Pascal	40	»
1345-50.	Célébrités. Les six	180	»
	Sur deux épreuves collectives	350	»
1351	Rennes	40	»
1351A-54B.	Armoiries. Les huit	250	»
1355	Touquet	80	»
1356-57.	Roses. Les deux	110	»
	Épreuve collective	250	»
1358-59.	Europa (1962). La paire	200	»
	Épreuve collective	350	»
1360-61	Télécommunications. Les deux	250	»
	Épreuve collective	550	»
1362	Radiotéléscope de Nançay	110	»
1363-65	Tableaux. Les trois	550	»
1366-67	Croix-Rouge (1962). La paire	180	»
	Épreuve collective	350	»
1368	Bathyscaphe	60	»
1369	Floralies nantaises	60	»
1370-75	Célébrités. Les six	180	»
	Les deux épreuves collectives	350	»
1376	Tableau de Delacroix	175	»
1377	Vitrail Sainte-Foy	175	»
1378	Journée du Timbre (1963)	50	»
1379	Campagne mondiale contre la faim	60	»
1380-81	Résistants. Les deux	80	»
	Épreuve collective	200	»
1382-86	Grands hommes. Les cinq	160	»
	Épreuve collective	350	»
1387	Première Conférence postale	90	»
1388	Lycée Louis-le-Grand	50	»
1389	Caen	50	»
1390-94A	Série touristique. Les sept	200	»
1390-94	Épreuve collective	380	»
1395	Ski nautique	70	»
1396-97	Europa (1963). La paire	200	»
	Épreuve collective	380	»
1398-99	Tableaux. Les deux	350	»
1400-01	Croix-Rouge (1963). La paire	180	»
	Épreuve collective	350	»
1402	Maison de la Radio	50	»
1403	PHILATEC	90	»
1404	Sapeurs-Pompiers	50	»
1405	Paralysés	50	»
1406	Journée du Timbre (1964)	50	»
1407-11.	Libération. Les cinq	185	»
1412	Coty	40	»
1413	Jean le Bon	150	»

1414-17	PHILATEC - Les quatre	450	»
	+ *emblème Philatec,* épreuve coll.	750	»
	En noir, grand format, épreuve coll.	1200	»
1418	Postale de nuit	60	»
1419	Notre-Dame de Paris	150	»
1420	Calvin	50	»
1421	Gerbet	50	»
1422	PHITALEC	500	»
1423	Mandel	40	»
1424-25	Champlevé, Licorne. Les deux	300	»
1426	La serveuse anglaise «du Star»	150	»
1427	Vitrail de Sens	150	»
1428	Tokyo	200	»
1429	Bataille de la Marne	60	»
1430-31	Europa (1964). La paire	200	»
	Épreuve collective	350	»
1432	Coopération	40	»
1433-34	Croix-Rouge (1964). La paire	150	»
	Épreuve collective	275	»
1435 à 1441.	Les 7 épreuves	200	»
	Idem + 1392A. Épreuves collectives (2)	380	»
1442 à 1445.	Célébrités 1965. Les 4 épreuves	150	»
	Idem. Épreuve collective	250	»
1446	«La Guienne» J. du T. (1965)	50	»
1447	Retour des Déportés	50	»
1448	Maison des Jeunes	40	»
1449	Campagne d'accueil	40	»
1450	20e anniversaire de la Victoire	50	»
1451	U.I.T.	60	»
1452	Croix de guerre	50	»
1453	Bourges	50	»
1454	Tunnel Mont-Blanc	55	»
1455-56	Europa (1965). La paire	200	»
	Idem. Épreuve collective	380	»
1457	Duc de Berry	130	»
1458	Apocalypse	130	»
1459	Violon rouge, de Dufy	130	»
1460	Reboisement	40	»
1461	Ile Bourbon	50	»
1462	Énergie atomique	60	»
1463	École de l'Air	60	»
1464-65	Diamant/A 1. Les deux	300	»
	Idem. Épreuve collective	550	»
1466-67	Croix-Rouge (1965). La paire	140	»
	Idem. Épreuve collective	300	»
1468-69	5 + 25 c. Blasons. Les deux	80	»
1470 à 1475.	Célébrités (1966) (6)	180	»
	Idem. Épreuve collective	300	»
1476	Satellite D 1	120	»
1477	Journée du Timbre (1966)	40	»
1478	Cratère de Vix	130	»
1479	Nouveau-Né	130	»
1480	Échecs	450	»
1481	Pont-Saint-Esprit	50	»
1482	Millénaire du Mont-Saint-Michel	50	»
1483	Bicentenaire de la Lorraine	40	»
1484	Verdun	50	»
1485	Niort	50	»
1486	Hastings	50	»
1487	Académie	40	»
1488	Chemins de fer	50	»
1489	Oléron	50	»
1490-91	Europa (1966). La paire	200	»
	Idem. Épreuve collective	380	»
1492	Sainte-Chapelle	130	»
1493	Lurçat	130	»
1494	Daumier	130	»
1495 à 1497.	Sujets historiques (3)	120	»
	Idem. Épreuve collective	280	»
1498	Pneumatique	50	»
1499 à 1506.	Sites (8)	225	»
	Idem. Deux Épreuves collectives	425	»
1507	Rance	50	»
1508-09	Croix-Rouge (1966). La paire	140	»
	Idem. Épreuve collective	300	»
1510	Blason de Saint-Lô	60	»
1511-14	Célébrités (4)	130	»
	Idem. Épreuve collective	225	»
1515	Radio européenne	50	»
1516	Journée du Timbre (1967)	50	»
1517	Rousseau	130	»
1518	François 1er	130	»
1519	Montréal	50	»
1520	Grenoble	150	»
1521-22	Europa (1967). La paire	160	»
	Idem. Épreuve collective	350	»
1523	Nungesser-Coli	60	»

N°	Désignation	Prix	
1524	Bordeaux	50	»
1525	Tours	50	»
1526	Esnault-Pelterie	100	»
1527	Vétérinaire	50	»
1528	Floralies	60	»
1529	Comptablité	50	»
1530	Ingres	140	»
1531	Troyes	140	»
1532	Bir-Hakeim	50	»
1533	Curie	150	»
1534	Lions international	225	»
1535-36	Marianne Cheffer (2)	120	»
	Idem. Épreuve collective	325	»
1536A/B	2 val. Cheffer (30 et 40 c.)	120	»
	Idem. Épreuve collective	425	»
1537 à 1539.	Histoire	120	»
	Idem. Épreuve collective	250	»
1540-41	Croix-Rouge (1967). La paire	140	»
	Idem. Épreuve collective	280	»
1542	Chèque postaux	35	»
1543-47	Grenoble (5)	380	»
	Idem. Épreuve collective	600	»
1548	Prévention routière	30	»
1549	Journée du Timbre (1968)	35	»
1550 à 1553	Personnages (4)	100	»
	Idem. Épreuve collective	185	»
1554	5e Conférence de l'audiovisuel	30	»
1555	Lascaux	130	»
1556-57	Europa (1968). La paire	150	»
	Idem. Épreuve collective	275	»
1558	Lesage	35	»
1559	Langeais	35	»
1560	Larousse	35	»
1561	Rambouillet	35	»
1562	Valreas	35	»
1563	Flandre	35	»
1564	Pont de Martrou	35	»
1565	Liaison Paris-Saint-Nazaire	150	»
1566	Prisonnières Huguenottes	40	»
1567	Béziers	40	»
1568	Arearea	130	»
1569	La Danse	125	»
1570	Modèle	130	»
1571	Armistice en Orient	35	»
1572	Corse	35	»
1573	Jeux de Mexico	175	»
1574	Expéditions polaires	110	»
1575	Petits lits blancs	35	»
1576	Armistice	35	»
1571 + 1576	Épreuve collective	160	»
1577 à 1579	Histoire	150	»
	Idem. Épreuve collective	275	»
1580-81	Croix-Rouge (1968). La paire	140	»
	Idem. ÉPreuve collective	250	»
1582 à 1585	Sites (4)	140	»
	Idem. Épreuve collective	225	»
1586	Amiens	120	»
1587	Philippe le Bon	120	»
1588	Abbaye de Saint-Savin	120	»
1588A	Le Cirque	130	»
1589	Journée du Timbre (1969)	40	»
1590 à 1595.	Célébrités (6)	180	»
	Idem. Épreuve collective	275	»
1596	Hautefort	35	»
1597	Floralies	40	»
1598-99	Europa (1969). La paire	140	»
	Idem. Épreuve collective	250	»
1600	Albert Thomas	40	»
1601	Garigliano	40	»
1602	Châlons-sur-Marne	40	»
1603	Libération	40	»
1604	Libération	40	»
1605	Libération	40	»
1606	Normandie-Niémen	50	»
1607	Libération de Paris	40	»
1608	Libération de Strasbourg	40	»
1609	Canoë-kayak	100	»
1610	Bonaparte	125	»
1611	Marianne (Cheffer)	50	»
1612	Charte européenne de l'eau	50	»
1613	Année de la nature	40	»
1614	Châtenay-Malabry	40	»
1615	« Le Redoutable »	50	»
1616 à 1618.	Histoire (3)	110	»
	Idem. Épreuve collective	220	»
1619-20	Croix-Rouge (1969). La paire	120	»
	Idem. Épreuve collective	225	»

N°	Désignation	Prix	
1621	Tour du monde	50	»
1622	Gendarmerie nationale	40	»
1623 à 1628.	Personnages célèbres (6)	180	»
	Idem. Épreuve collective	275	»
1629	Handball	60	»
1630	Maréchal Juin	50	»
1631	Aérotrain	70	»
1632	Journée du Timbre (1970)	40	»
1633	Quinine	50	»
1634	Protection de la nature	80	»
1635	Diamant B.	80	»
1636	Lutte contre le cancer	50	»
1637-38	Europa (1970). La paire	130	»
	Idem. Épreuve collective	275	»
1639	De Lattre de Tassigny	50	»
1640	Primitif de Savoie	110	»
1641	Triomphe de Flore	110	»
1642	Lens	35	»
1644	Rochers du diamant	35	»
1645	Chancelade	35	»
1646	Ilet du Gosier	35	»
1647	Observatoire de Haute-Provence	50	»
1648	Camp de concentration	35	»
1649	Jeux des handicapés	35	»
1650	Athlétisme	50	»
1651	Salines de chaux	40	»
1652	Diane, de Boucher	110	»
1653	Degas	110	»
1654	Cathédrale de Strasbourg	110	»
1655 à 1657.	Histoire (1970) (3)	110	»
	Idem. Épreuve collective	200	»
1658	25e anniversaire de l'O.N.U.	40	»
1659	Bordeaux	50	»
1660	Belfort	35	»
1661-62	Croix-Rouge (1970). La paire	120	»
	Idem. Épreuve collective	200	»
1663	45 c. Béquet	70	»
1664	50 c. Béquet	70	»
1665	Patinage	70	»
1666	Océanexpo	40	»
1667-70	Célébrités (4)	120	»
1671	Journée du Timbre (1971)	35	»
1672	Millet	110	»
1673	« Songe creux »	110	»
1674	« Cap-Hornier »	40	»
1675	Isard	40	»
1676-77	Europa 71. La paire	125	»
	Idem. Épreuve collective	250	»
1678-80	Histoire	160	»
	Idem. Épreuve collective	250	»
1681	Grenoble	35	»
1682	Famille rurale	35	»
1683-87	Sites 71 (5)	150	»
1688	Union interparlementaire	35	»
1689-90	Célébrités 71 (2 val. suppl.)	60	»
	Idem. Épreuve collective	200	»
1691	Chambre des Métiers	35	»
1692	Caméléon	40	»
1693	Saumon	40	»
1694	Grand-duc	40	»
1695 à 1698.	De Gaulle (4)	400	»
	Idem. Épreuve collect. (la bande compl.)	750	»
1699	Académie de Médecine	35	»
1700-01	Croix-Rouge (1971). La paire	120	»
	Idem. Épreuve collective	200	»
1702	Fragonard	110	»
1703	Monet	110	»
1704	Crozet et Kerguelen	80	»
1705	Sapporo	100	»
1706-09	Célébrités (4)	130	»
1710	Journée du Timbre (1972)	40	»
1711	Mois du cœur	40	»
1712	Charlieu	35	»
1713	Narbonne	35	»
1714-15	Europa 72. La paire	130	»
1716	Donneurs de sang	40	»
1717	Voilier Terre-Neuvas	40	»
1718	Saint-Brieuc	35	»
1719-20	Code postal	70	»
	Idem. Épreuve collective	100	»
1721	Internationale P.T.T.	35	»
1722	J.O. de Munich	110	»
1723	Tourisme pédestre	35	»
1724	Championnats cyclistes	80	»
1725	Sologne	40	»
1726	Bazoches du Morvand	35	»
1727-28	Célébrités	65	»

1729-31	Histoire (3)	150	»
	Idem. Épreuve collective	200	»
1732	Maître de Moulins	100	»
1733	Derain	100	»
1734	Champollion	50	»
1735-36	Croix-Rouge (1972). La paire	110	»
	Idem. Épreuve collective	200	»
1737	Sainte-Thérèse	40	»
1738	Anthurium	50	»
1739	Traité Franco-Allemand	80	»
1740	Immigration Polonaise	35	»
1741	Chapiteau d'Issoire	100	»
1742	Le Brun	100	»
1743	Moutier d'Ahun	100	»
1744-48	Célébrités (5)	150	»
1749	Journée du Timbre (1973)	40	»
1750	Centre téléph. Tuileries	35	»
1751	Airbus	80	»
1752-53	Europa (1973). La paire	120	»
1754	Raton laveur	40	»
1755	Cigognes	40	»
1756	Bicentenaire du Grand-Orient	50	»
1757	Dijon	35	»
1758	Gien	35	»
1759	Amboise	35	»
1760	Académie des Sciences d'Outre-Mer	35	»
1761	24 heures du Mans	60	»
1762	5 mâts « France »	40	»
1763	Toulouse	35	»
1764	Saut du Doubs	35	»
1765	Watteau	110	»
1766	Cardinal de Richelieu	125	»
1767	Hansen	35	»
1768	Pasteur	40	»
1769	Tony Garnier	35	»
1770	Ducretet	35	»
1771	Molière	40	»
1772	Écluse «François 1er»	35	»
1773	Bourgoin et Kieffer	40	»
1774-76	Histoire (3)	130	»
	Idem. Épreuve collective	200	»
1777	Flamme de l'Arc de Triomphe	35	»
1778	Chambre d'Agriculture	35	»
1779-80	Croix-Rouge (1973). La paire	110	»
	Idem. Épreuve collective	200	»
1781	Déclaration des Droits de l'Homme	35	»
1782	Musée Postal	35	»
1783	Exposition «Arphila»	40	»
1784	Saint-Grignon de Montfort	35	»
1785	Poulenc	35	»
1786	Journée du Timbre (1974)	35	»
1787	Aéroport «Charles de Gaulle»	110	»
1788	Centenaire du Club Alpin	40	»
1789-90	Europa (1974). la paire	120	»
	Idem. Épreuve collective	200	»
1791	Sauvetage en mer	35	»
1792	Conseil de l'Europe	60	»
1793	Salers	35	»
1794	Saint-Florent	35	»
1795	Bison	40	»
1796	Général Kœning	35	»
1797	Villes Compagnons de la Libération	35	»
1798	Colmar	35	»
1799	Débarquement en Normandie	40	»
1800	J.O. échiquéens	325	»
1801	Tricentenaire l'Hôtel des Invalides	35	»
1802	Turbotrain TGV 001	60	»
1803	Surrégénérateur Phénix	40	»
1804	Réseau Exprès Régional	50	»
1805	Hélicoptère Gazelle	70	»
1806-10	Sites (5)	100	»
1811	Tableau de Miro	120	»
1812	Tableau de Sisley	120	»
1812 et 1766.	Épreuve collective en noir	500	»
1813	Tapisserie, par Mathieu	120	»
1814	60 c. Béquet (*Typo)*	60	»
1816	80 c. Béquet	60	»
1817	Centenaire de l'U.P.U.	200	»
1818	Naissance de Copernic	60	»
1819	Tatou géant de la Guyane	40	»
1820	Aigrette Garzette	40	»
1821	Libération et médaille de la Libération	40	»
1822	Jean Giraudoux	35	»
1823	Barbey d'Aurevilly	35	»
1824	Docteur Schweitzer	60	»
1825	Edmond Michelet	35	»
1826	Robert Schuman	40	»
1827	Eugène Thomas	35	»
1828-29.	Croix-Rouge (1974). La paire	110	»
	Idem. Épreuve collective	200	»
1830-33.	Arphila (4)	300	»
	Idem. Épreuve collective	650	»
	Idem. En noir	1100	»
1834-37.	Arphila (4). Voir BF n° 7		
1838	Journée du Timbre (1975)	35	»
1839	Président Georges Pompidou	35	»
1840-41.	Europa (1975). La paire	140	»
1842	Exposition de la machine-outil	35	»
1843	Centenaire du Sénat	35	»
1844	Convention du mètre	40	»
1845	Fondation Santé des étudiants	35	»
1846	Théâtre du peuple du Bussang	35	»
1847	Région de Picardie	35	»
1848	Région de Bourgogne	35	»
1849	Région des Pays de la Loire	35	»
1850	Région d'Auvergne	35	»
1851	Région Poitou-Charentes	35	»
1852	Région Nord-Pas-de-Calais	35	»
1853	Libération des camps de concentration	35	»
1854	Création du Service de Déminage	35	»
1855	Villes nouvelles	35	»
1856	Pont de Saint-Nazaire	35	»
1857	Année internationale de la Femme	50	»
1858	André Siegfried	35	»
1859	Relations franco-sociétiques	35	»
1860-61.	Croix-Rouge (1975). La paire	110	»
	Idem. Épreuve collective	200	»
1862	Frégate «La Melpomène»	35	»
1863	Région du Centre	35	»
1864	Région Aquitaine	35	»
1865	Région Limousin	35	»
1865A	Région Guyane	35	»
1866	Région Midi-Pyrénées	40	»
1867	Linteau de Saint-Genis des Fontaines	100	»
1868	Vénus de Brassempouy	100	»
1869	Delaunay	100	»
1870	Journée du Timbre (1976)	40	»
1871-73.	Sites (3)	80	»
1874	Cinquantenaire ACORAM	35	»
1875	Rouen	35	»
1876	Juvarouen	35	»
1877-78.	Europa (1976). La paire	140	»
1879	Bicentenaire des États-Unis	100	»
1880	Maréchal Moncey	35	»
1881	Max Jacob, par Picasso	35	»
1882	Mounet-Sully	35	»
1883	Verdun	35	»
1884	Communication	35	»
1885	Associaition France-Libre	35	»
1886	Protection de la nature (Tronçais)	35	»
1887	Satellite Symphonie	50	»
1888	La Fête	35	»
1889	J.O. Montréal	100	»
1890	Officiers de réserve	35	»
1891	80 c. Béquet (*Typo*)	40	»
1892	1 f. Béquet (*Gravé*)	40	»
1896	Général Daumesnil	35	»
1897	Eugène Fromentin	35	»
1898	Anna de Noailles	35	»
1899	Ramsès	100	»
1900	Carzou	100	»
1901	Vlaminck	100	»
1902	Lodève	35	»
1903	Biarritz	35	»
1904	Thiers	35	»
1905	Centenaire du Téléphone	50	»
1906	10e festival du film de Tarbes	35	»
1907	Police nationale	35	»
1908	Accélérateur CERN	80	»
1909	Foires Expositions	35	»
1910-11.	Croix-Rouge (1976). La paire	100	»
	Idem. Épreuve collective	200	»
1912	Douane	35	»
1913	Musée de l'Atlantique (Port-Louis)	40	»
1914-21.	Régions (8 valeurs)	180	»
1922	Centre Pompidou	50	»
1923	Corot	110	»
1924	Vasarely	100	»
1925	Dunkerque	35	»
1926	Souvenir Français	35	»
1927	Journée du Timbre (1977)	35	»
1928-29.	Europa (1977). La paire	130	»
	Idem. Épreuve collective	225	»
1930	Horticulture	40	»

1931	Floralies Internationales de Nantes	40	»
1932	Rattachement du Cambrésis	35	»
1933	Instituts catholiques	35	»
1934	Fédération Europ. de la Construction	35	»
1935	Annecy	35	»
1936	École Polytechnique de Palaiseau	45	»
1937	Dorat	35	»
1938	Abbaye de Fontenay	35	»
1939	Bayeux	35	»
1940	60e anniv. Coupe de France de football	70	»
1941	Mémorial au Général de Gaulle	100	»
1942	Chambre économique	35	»
1943	5e anniv. de la bataille de Nancy	35	»
1944	Rattachement de la Bourgogne	35	»
1945	Assoc. Internat. des Parlementaires de langue française	35	»
1946	Cigale rouge	40	»
1947	Pont-à-Mousson	35	»
1948	Saint-Amand-les-Eaux	35	»
1949	Vitré	35	»
1950	Trémois	120	»
1951	Excoffon	110	»
1952	Meilleurs ouvriers de France	35	»
1953	Édouard Herriot	35	»
1954	Abbé Breuil	35	»
1955	Guillaume de Machault	35	»
1956	Charles Cros	35	»
1957	Conseil Économique et Social	35	»
1958	4e centenaire de la naissance de Rubens	120	»
1959-60.	Croix-Rouge (1977). La paire	100	»
	Idem. Épreuve collective	200	»
1961	Tennis de Table	100	»
1962 à 1979.	Sabine (18)	650	»
1970 et 1972.	Épreuve collective	500	»
1982	Birr (Percheron)	50	»
1983	Carrousel sous Louis XIV	120	»
1984	École Nationale Supérieure des Télécommunications	35	»
1985	Ile Saint-Barthélémy	35	»
1986-90A.	Célébrités (6)	150	»
1991-93.	Régions (3)	80	»
1994	Buffet	110	»
1195	Aménagement du Territoire (DATAR)	35	»
1996 à 2002.	Sites (7)	200	»
2003	Juvexniort	35	»
2004	Journée du Timbre (1978)	35	»
2005	Port Cros	40	»
2006	Fleurir la France	35	»
2007	Économies d'Énergie	35	»
2008-09.	Europa (1978). La paire	100	»
	Idem. Épreuve collective	200	»
2010	Notre-Dame de Lorette	35	»
2011	Troyes	35	»
2012	Stade Roland Garros	110	»
2013	Métiers d'Art	35	»
2014	Imprimerie Nationale	35	»
2015	Réunion de la Franche-Comté	35	»
2016	Rattachement de Valenciennes et Maubeuge	35	»
2017	Académie de Philatélie	50	»
2018	Balbuzard	40	»
2019	Championnat européen de gymnastique, à Strasbourg	100	»
2020	Sport pour Tous	50	»
2021	Monument aux Combattants polonais	35	»
2022	60e anniversaire de l'Armistice	35	»
2023	Aide à la réadaptation	35	»
2024-25.	Croix-Rouge (1978). La paire	110	»
	Idem. Épreuve collective	200	»
2026	Brayer	100	»
2027	Droits de l'Homme	70	»
2028	Année de l'Enfant	70	»
2029	Maréchal de Bercheny	35	»
2030	Léon Jouhaux	35	»
2031	Pierre Abélard	35	»
2032	Courteline	35	»
2032A	Simone Weil	35	»
2032B	André Malraux	35	»
2033	Miniature sur la musique	110	»
2034	Victor Segalen	35	»
2035	Floralies de la Martinique	40	»
2036	Temple de Borobudur	70	»
2037	Journée du Timbre (1979)	35	»
2038	Francisque Poulbot	35	»
2039	Abeille	80	»
2040-44.	Sites (5)	150	»
2045	Saint-Germain-des-Prés	35	»
2046-47.	Europa (1979). La paire	130	»
	Idem. Épreuve collective	200	»
2048	Nantes	35	»
2049	Palais Royal	35	»
2050	Élection Assemblée des Communautés Européennes	85	»
2051	Jeanne d'Arc	35	»
2052	Félix Guyon	35	»
2053	Diane au bain	110	»
2054	Van Gogh	120	»
2055	Télécom 79	35	»
2056-61.	Sabine (6)	200	»
2064	Maisons-Laffitte	35	»
2065	Lorraine	35	»
2066	École Centrale	35	»
2067	Dali	110	»
2068	Chapelain-Midy	100	»
2069	Championnats de judo	90	»
2070-71.	Croix-Rouge (1979). La paire	100	»
	Idem. Épreuve collective	200	»
2072	La Lutherie	35	»
2073	Eurovision	60	»
2074	Zadkine	100	»
2075	Ubac	100	»
2076	Géants du Nord	35	»
2077	Gastronomie française	35	»
2078	Journée du Timbre (1980)	50	»
2079	La Broderie	35	»
2080	Lutte contre le tabagisme	35	»
2081	Cordes	35	»
2082	Maintenon	35	»
2083	Montauban	35	»
2084	Le Puy	35	»
2085-86.	Europa (1980). La paire	120	»
	Idem. Épreuve collective	200	»
2087	École d'Arts et Métiers	35	»
2088	Dunkerque	35	»
2089	Papillon	40	»
2090	Dürer (Philexfrance)	150	»
	Idem. Noir. *Grand format*	400	»
2091	Assoc. des Relations publiques	35	»
2092	Année du Patrimoine	35	»
2093	Sciences de la Terre	35	»
2094	Rochambeau	80	»
2095	Viollet-le-Duc	35	»
2096	Jean Monnet	50	»
2097	Jean-Marie de La Mennais	35	»
2098	Frédéric Mistral	35	»
2099	Saint-John Perse	35	»
2100	Pierre Paul de Riquet	35	»
2101	Sabine 1 f. 20, vert	50	»
2102	Sabine 1 f. 40, rouge	50	»
2105	Fédération française de Golf	80	»
2106	Comédie Française (Tricentenaire)	35	»
2107	Picart Le Doux	100	»
2108	Le Nain	110	»
2109	Modigliani	110	»
2110	Hartung	100	»
2111	Rambouillet	35	»
2112	Abbaye de Solesmes	35	»
2113	Agam	100	»
2114	40e anniversaire du 18 juin 1940	150	»
2115	Garde Républicaine	35	»
2116-17.	Croix-Rouge (1980). La paire	100	»
	Idem. Épreuve collective	200	»
2118-23.	Sabine (6)	180	»
2124	Journée du Timbre (1981)	70	»
2125	L'eau	35	»
2126 à 30.	Grandes réalisations (5)	180	»
2131	La Reliure	35	»
2132	Saint-Jean de Lyon	35	»
2133	Maison Carrée, Nîmes	35	»
2134	Sainte-Anne d'Auray	35	»
2135	Château de Rosny	35	»
2136	Pissarro	110	»
2137	Gleizes	100	»
2138-39.	Europa (1981). La paire	110	»
	Idem. Épreuve collective	200	»
2140	École Saint-Maixent	35	»
2141-42	Philexfrance'82 - Trémois	280	»
	Idem. Épreuve collective	500	»
2143	Presse	35	»
2144	Vichy	35	»
2145	H.E.C.	35	»
2146	Espace littoral	40	»
2147	Escrime	70	»
2148	Louis Armand	35	»
2149	Louis Jouvet	35	»
2150	Sœur Javouhey	35	»
2151	Offenbach	50	»
2152	Theillard de Chardin	35	»
2153	Pasteur Boegner	35	»

2154-56	Sabine R.F. (3)	130 »
	Idem. Épreuve collective	300 »
2159	Boire ou conduire	35 »
2160	Abbaye de Vaucelles	35 »
2161	Notre-Dame de Louviers	35 »
2162	Saint-Émilion	35 »
2163	Crest	35 »
2164	Pen Club	35 »
2165-66	Caisse Nationale d'Épargne	50 »
	Idem. Épreuve collective	150 »
2167	École publique	35 »
2168	Pignon	100 »
2169	Manessier	100 »
2170	École navale	35 »
2171	Maison de la Chasse	35 »
2172	Panthéon	40 »
2173	Année Internationale des personnes handicapées	35 »
2174	Virgile	100 »
2175-76	Croix-Rouge (1981). La paire	130 »
	Idem. Épreuve collective	200 »
2177	Châteaubriant	35 »
2178-90	Liberté (13)	400 »
	Idem. Épreuve collective (N°s 2186, 2187, 2189)	350 »
2193	Saint-Pierre-et-Miquelon	35 »
2194	Aix-en-Provence	35 »
2195	Pau. Château Henri IV	35 »
2196	Collonges-la-Rouge	35 »
2197	Région. Corse	35 »
2198	Saint François d'Assise	35 »
2199-2200	Philexfranc'82. Folon	250 »
	Idem. Épreuve collective	600 »
2201	Lord Baden-Powell	110 »
2202	Recensement	40 »
2203	Aéroport Bâle-Mulhouse	40 »
2204	Lutte contre le racisme	35 »
2205	Journée du Timbre (1982)	80 »
2206	La Ferronnerie	35 »
2207-08	Europa (1982). La paire	120 »
	Idem. Épreuve collective	200 »
2209	Coupe du monde de football	80 »
2210	« L'éphèbe d'Agde »	110 »
2211	Claude Gelée, dit Le Lorrain	110 »
2212	Festival international du film. Cannes	35 »
2213	Centre National d'Études Spatiales	50 »
2214	Sommet des Pays industrialisés	35 »
2215	Jules Vallès	35 »
2216-17	Philexfrance'82. Voir BF n°8	
2218	F. et I. Joliot-Curie	50 »
2219-21	Liberté (3)	110 »
2224	Éclairage public, Grenoble 1882	35 »
2225	Guillaume Postel	35 »
2226	Henri Mondor	35 »
2227	Louis Pergaud	35 »
2228	Robert Debré	35 »
2229	André Chantemesse	35 »
2230	Gustave Eiffel	40 »
2231	«Le Dentellière», de Vermeer	110 »
2232	Château de Ripaille	35 »
2233	Sapeurs-Pompiers	35 »
2234	«La Famille», de Marc Boyan	100 »
2235	Marionnettes	35 »
2236	Rugby	80 »
2237	Écoles Normales Supérieures	35 »
2238	Lille	35 »
2239-44	Liberté (6)	200 »
2245	«Chambre turque», de Balthus	100 »
2246	Bacille de Koch	30 »
2247-48	Croix-Rouge 1982. La paire	120 »
	Idem. Épreuve collective	200 »
2249	Sainte Thérèse d'Avila	35 »
2250	Cavelier de La Salle	40 »
2251	Léon Blum	35 »
2252	Région. Provence-Alpes-Côte d'Azur	35 »
2253	Brantôme en Périgord	35 »
2254	Concarneau	35 »
2255	Noirlac	35 »
2256	Martin Luther	50 »
2257	Alliance Française	35 »
2258	Journée du Timbre (1983)	80 »
2259	Danielle Casanova	35 »
2260	Année mondiale des communications	35 »
2261-62	Bicentenaire de l'air et de l'espace (2)	225 »
2263	Dewasne	100 »
2264	Raphaël	110 »
2265	Gustave Doré	100 »
2266-69	Flore et Faune de France (4)	180 »
2270-71	Europa (1983). La paire	110 »
	Idem. Épreuve collective	200 »
2272	Propriété industrielle	35 »
2273	Marseille	35 »
2274-76	Liberté (3)	130 »
	Idem. Épreuve collective	250 »
2278	Air France	50 »
2279	André Messager	35 »
2280	Jacques-Ange Gabriel	35 »
2281	Hector Berlioz	50 »
2282	Max-Pol Fouchet	35 »
2283	René Cassin	35 »
2284	Stendhal	35 »
2285	Traités de Paris et de Versailles	80 »
2286	Art du Bijou	35 »
2287	Jarnac	35 »
2288	Charleville-Mézières	35 »
2289	Conseil de Coopération douanière	35 »
2290	Vélocipède P. et E. Michaux	50 »
2291	Jean Effel	110 »
2292	Météorologie nationale	50 »
2293	Renée Lévy	35 »
2294	Berthie Albrecht	35 »
2295-96	Croix-Rouge 1983. La paire	100 »
	Idem. Épreuve collective	180 »
2297	Utrillo	110 »
2298	Pierre Mendès France	35 »
2299	César	100 »
2300	Messagier	100 »
2301	Bonnard	100 »
2302	Guadeloupe	35 »
2303	Flora-Tristan	35 »
2304	Journée du Timbre (1984)	80 »
2305	Syndicats professionnels	35 »
2306	Élections Parlement Européen	40 »
2307	Jacques Cartier	80 »
2308	Philex-Jeunes'84	35 »
2309-10	Europa (1984). La paire	100 »
	Idem. Épreuve collective	200 »
2311	Légion Étrangère	35 »
2312-13	40e anniv. Libération (2)	120 »
	Idem Le Triptyque	200 »
2314	Jeux Olympiques	120 »
2315	La Gravure	35 »
2316	Bordeaux	35 »
2317	CNET	35 »
2318-20	Liberté (3)	120 »
	Idem. Épreuve collective	400 »
2323	Grande Chartreuse	35 »
2324	Palais Facteur Cheval	35 »
2325	Belle-Ile-en-Mer	35 »
2326	Phare de Cordouan	35 »
2327	Congrès de géographie	70 »
2328	Émile Littré	35 »
2329	Jean Zay	35 »
2329A	Pierre Corneille	35 »
2330	Gaston Bachelard	35 »
2331	Jean Paulhan	35 »
2332	Evariste Galois	35 »
2333	Télécom 1	70 »
2334	TGV Postal	70 »
2335	Château de Montségur	35 »
2336	Marx Dormoy	35 »
2337-40	Faune et Flore de Ffrance (Rapaces)-(4)	200 »
2341	Centenaire de l'automobile	50 »
2342	Masson	100 »
2343	Hélion	100 »
2344	Vincent Auriol	35 »
2345	Croix-Rouge (1984)	80 »
2346	9e Plan	35 »
2347	La Francophonie	35 »
2348	Vienne (Isère)	35 »
2349	Abbaye de Landévennec	35 »
2350	Cathédrale de Montpellier	35 »
2351	Saint-Michel-de-Cuxa	35 »
2352	Saintonge romane (Talmont)	35 »
2353	50e anniversaire de la Télévision	40 »
2354	La Saint-Valentin	80 »
2355	Romain Rolland	30 »
2356	Jules Romains	30 »
2357	Jean-Paul Sartre	30 »
2358	Victor Hugo	30 »
2359	Roland Dorgelès	30 »
2360	François Mauriac	30 »
2355-60	Personnages célèbres	
	Épreuve collective	400 »
2361	Pauline Kergomard	35 »

N°	Désignation	Prix	
2362	Journée du Timbre (1985)	40	»
2363	Vitrail de Strasbourg	100	»
2364	Nicolas de Staël	100	»
2365	Architecture contemporaine (Givors)	35	»
2366-67	Europa (1985). La paire	110	»
	Idem. Épreuve collective	200	»
2368-69	40e anniv. de la Victoire (2)	100	»
	Idem. Le triptyque	200	»
2370	Tours	35	»
2371	Vaccin contre la rage	40	»
2372	Mystère Falcon 900	80	»
2373	Société sauvetage du Lac Léman	40	»
2374	40e anniversaire des Nations Unies	35	»
2375-77	Liberté (3)	80	»
	Idem. Épreuve collective	1000	»
2380	Accueil des Huguenots	35	»
2381	Dubuffet	100	»
2382	Alechinski	100	»
2383	«Le chien», de Giacometti	100	»
2384-87	Faune et Flore de France (Arbres) (4)	150	»
2388	Solutré	35	»
2389	La France à ses morts	35	»
2390	Charles Dullin	35	»
2391	Documentation française	35	»
2392	Croix-Rouge (1985)	50	»
2393	Tricentenaire France-Thaïlande	35	»
2394	Front populaire	80	»
2395	Carnaval - Venise à Paris	60	»
2396	François Arago	35	»
2397	Henri Moissan	35	»
2398	Henri Fabre	35	»
2399	Marc Seguin	35	»
2400	Paul Héroult	35	»
2396-2400	Personnages célèbres (5 épreuves)	150	
	Épreuve collective	400	»
2401	Filitosa	35	»
2402	Château de Loches	35	»
2403	Saint-Germain de Livet	35	»
2404	Notre-Dame-en-Vaux	35	»
2405	Monpazier	50	»
2406	Pierre Cot	35	»
2407	La Typographie	90	»
2408	Louise Michel	35	»
2409	La Villette, Cité des Sciences et de l'Industrie	50	»
2410	Journée du Timbre (1986)	40	»
2411	Idem. Timbre du carnet	40	»
2412	Hautes Études Afrique et Asie modernes	35	»
2413	Estève	100	»
2414	Magnelli	100	»
2415	Année internationale de la Paix	35	»
2416-17	Europa (1986). La paire	110	»
	Idem. Épreuve collective	180	»
2418	Curé d'Ars	40	»
2419	Nancy	35	»
2420	Championnats de volley-ball	50	»
2421	Statue de la Liberté	60	»
2422	Bicentenaire ascension Mont-Blanc	35	»
2423	Liberté «A»	40	»
2424-25	Libert (2)	80	»
2423-25	Idem. Épreuve collective	400	»
2428	Mesures arcs de méridien	35	»
2429-32	Nature de France (Minéraux) (4)	180	»
2443	Henri Alain-Fournier	35	»
2444	Enseignement technique	35	»
2445	Conférence énergie, à Cannes	35	»
2446	Léonard de Vinci	100	»
2447	Arp	100	»
2448	Soulages	100	»
2449	Croix-Rouge (1986)	70	»
2450	Musées techniques de Mulhouse	50	»
2451	Musée d'Orsay	45	»
2452	Fulgence Bienvenüe	40	»
2453	Raoul Follereau	35	»
2454	Charles Richet	35	»
2455	Eugène Jamot	35	»
2456	Bernard Halpern	35	»
2457	Alexandre Yersin	35	»
2458	Jean Rostand	35	»
2459	Jacques Monod	35	»
2454-59	Personnages célèbres 6 épreuves	150	»
	Épreuve collective	475	»
2461	«Philexfrance'89»	80	»
2462	Redon	35	»
2463	Étretat	35	»
2464	Azay-le-Rideau	35	»
2465	Les Baux de Provence	35	»
2466	Côtes de Meuse	35	»
2467	Coutellerie de Thiers	35	»
2468	Journée du Timbre (1987)	40	»
2469	Idem. Timbre du carnet	40	»
2470	Le Corbusier	40	»
2471-72	Europa (1987). La paire	110	»
	Idem. Épreuve collective	180	»
2473	Bram Van Velde	100	»
2474	Eugène Boudin	100	»
2475	Henri Pourrat	35	»
2476	Lens	35	»
2477	Entrée en guerre des États-Unis	60	»
2478	Millénaire Hugues Capet	35	»
2479	La Flèche	35	»
2480	Congrès transports à câbles	35	»
2481	Nice 25 ans après	35	»
2482	Championnats de lutte	50	»
2483	Liberté «B»	40	»
2484-85	Libert (2)	120	»
	Idem. Épreuve collective	400	»
2486	Liberté	60	»
2488-91	Nature de France (Champignons) (4)	200	»
2492	Guillaume le Conquérant	40	»
2493	Camille Bryen	100	»
2494	Antoine Pevsner	100	»
2495	Montbenoît, Le Saugeais	35	»
2496	Institut Pasteur	40	»
2497	Blaise Cendrars	50	»
2498	Croix-Rouge (1987)	60	»
2499	Maréchal Leclerc	35	»
2500	Traité d'Andelot	35	»
2501	Coopération franco-allemande	50	»
2502	Marcel Dassault	50	»
2515	La Communication en bandes dessinées	500	»
2516	Synagogue Victoire	35	»
2517	Duquesne	35	»
2518	Suffren	35	»
2519	La Pérouse	35	»
2520	La Bourdonnais	35	»
2521	Bougainville	35	»
2522	Dumont d'Urville	35	»
2517-22	Personnages célèbres 6 épreuves	180	»
	Épreuve collective	475	»
2524	Liberté «Philexfrance'89»	80	»
2525	Journée du Timbre (1988)	40	»
2526	Idem. Timbre du carnet	40	»
2527	École Nationale Supérieure P.T.T.	35	»
2528	Don du sang	35	»
2529	«Philex-Jeunes 88»	35	»
2530	Liberté surchargé en ÉCU	50	»
2531-32	Europa (1988). La paire	130	»
	Idem. Épreuve collective	200	»
2533	Jean Monnet	40	»
2534	Valence	35	»
2535	Assistance médicale internationale	35	»
2536	Handicapés	35	»
2537-38	Bicentenaire de la Révolution (2)	225	»
2537-38	Épreuve collective, couleur	600	»
2537-38	Épreuve collective, noire	500	»
2539-42	Nature de Ffrance («Histoire naturelle» de Buffon) (4)	160	»
2543	Troupes alpines	35	»
2544	Roland Garros	60	»
2545	Douarnenez	35	»
2546	Sédières	35	»
2547	Cirque de Gavarnie	35	»
2548	Hermès dicéphale	45	»
2549	Armistice de 1918	35	»
2550	Pérouges	35	»
2551	Jacobsen	100	»
2552	Bimillénaire de Strasbourg	35	»
2553	Sépulcre de Ligier-Richier	100	»
2554	Serge Poliakoff	100	»
2555	Croix-Rouge (1988)	60	»
2556	Le thermalisme	70	»
2557	Tinguely	120	»
2558	Pietà de Villeneuve-lés-Avignon	100	»
2559	Droits de l'Homme	50	»
2560	Bicentenaire de la Révolution - Folon	90	»
2561	Yves Klein	100	»
2562	Pour le bien des aveugles	35	»
2563	École Estienne	40	»
2564	Sieyes	35	»
2565	Mirabeau	35	»
2566	Vicomte de Noailles	35	»
2567	La Fayette	35	»
2568	Barnave	35	»
2569	Drouet	35	»

2564-69	Personnages célèbres. 6 épreuves	180 »
	Épreuve collective	575 »
2571	Vol franco-soviétique	70 »
2572	Élections Parlement européen	80 »
2573	La Liberté	60 »
2574	L'Égalité	60 »
2575	La Fraternité	60 »
2576	Liberté, Égalité, Fraternité (triptyque)	350 »
2577	Journée du Timbre (1989)	50 »
2578	Idem. Timbre de carnet	50 »
2579-83	Panorama de Paris (bande)	275 »
2584-85	Europa (1989) La paire	180 »
	Idem. Épreuve collective	400 »
2586	Forêt de Fontainebleau	35 »
2587	Château de Vaux-le-Vicomte	40 »
2588	Malestroit	35 »
2589	U-I-T	90 »
2590	Championnats du monde de cyclisme	100 »
2591	«Le Serment du Jeu de Paume» par David	100 »
2600	Sommet des pays industrialisés	60 »
2601	La Brenne	40 »
2602-05	Bicentenaire de la Déclaration des Droits de l'Homme et du Citoyen (bande)	275 »
2606	Lapicque	100 »
2607	TGV Atlantique	90 »
2608	Tramway électrique	50 »
2609	Ordonnance de Villers-Cotterêts	35 »
2610	Cauchy	35 »
2611	Maréchal de Lattre de Tassigny	40 »
2612	Croix-Rouge (1989)	50 »
2613	Harkis	40 »
2614	Marianne du Bicentenaire	35 »
2615-16	Liberté «C» (2)	100 »
2617-26	Marianne du Bicentenaire : 10 valeurs	450 »
	Épreuve collective (11 valeurs) 10 valeurs + le 2F30 rouge	1000 »
2631	La dentelle	35 »
2632	«Albertville'92»	110 »
2633	«Albertville'92» Patinage artistique	110 »
2634	Centenaire de la naissance du Général de Gaulle	100 »
2635	Odilon Redon	100 »
2636	Odilon Redon	100 »
2637	Odilon Redon	100 »
2638	Max Hymans	50 »
2639	Journée du Timbre (1990)	35 »
2640	Idem. Timbre de carnet	35 »
2641	Jean Guehenno	35 »
2642-43	Europa (1990). La paire	130 »
	Idem. Épreuve collective	550 »
2644	Centenaire du 1er Mai	35 »
2645	Institut du Monde arabe	35 »
2646	Croix-Rouge (1990)	60 »
2647	Villefrance-sur-Saône	35 »
2648	Course autour du monde «La Poste»	50 »
2649	Aristide Bruant	35 »
2650	Maurice Chevalier	35 »
2651	Tino Rossi	35 »
2652	Édith Piaf	35 »
2653	Jacques Brel	35 »
2654	Georges Brassens	35 »
2649-51	Personnages célèbres. Épreuve collective	600 »
2656	Cinquantenaire Appel du 18 juin 1940	100 »
2657	Abbaye de Cluny	35 »
2658	Pont-canal de Briare	35 »
2659	Abbaye de Flaran	35 »
2660	Cap Canaille	35 »
2661	Maison France-Brésil	40 »
2662	Institut Géographique National	40 »
2663-66	Nature de France : Poissons d'eau douce (4)	150 »
2671	Maurice Genevoix	35 »
2672	Roger Bissière	100 »
2673	O-C-D-E	80 »
2674	«Albertville'92» Saut à skis	90 »
2675	«Albertville'92» Ski de vitesse	90 »
2676	«Albertville'92» Slalom	90 »
2677	«Albertville'92» Hockey	90 »
2678	«Albertville'92» Ski de fond	90 »
2679	«Albertville'92» Luge	90 »
2680	«Albertville'92» Curling	90 »
2681	Paul Éluard	35 »
2682	André Breton	35 »
2683	Louis Aragon	35 »
2684	Francis Ponge	35 »
2685	Jacques Prévert	35 »
2686	René Char	35 »
2681-86	Personnages célèbres. Épreuve collective	525 »
2688	Journée du Timbre (1991)	35 »
2689	Idem. Timbre de carnet	35 »
2690	«Philexjeunes'91». Cholet	35 »
2691	Imprimerie Nationale	35 »
2692	Auguste Renoir	100 »
2693	Georges Seurat	100 »
2694	Concours Lépine	35 »
2695	Mozart	100 »
2696-97	Europa (1991) La paire	180 »
	Idem. Épreuve collective	600 »
2698	Perpignan	35 »
2699	Tournoi de Roland Garros	100 »
2700-03	Bicentenaire Révolution (bloc)	380 »
2704	Pont de Cheviré	50 »
2705	Carennac	50 »
2706	Wasquehal	50 »
2707	Munster	50 »
2708	Gaston Febus	40 »
2709	«Albertville'92» Ski artistique	100 »
2710	«Albertville'92» Ski alpin	100 »
2711-12	«Albertville'92»	90 »
2714-17	«Albertville'92»	240 »
	Série épreuves collectives	700 »
2721-24	Nature de France (espèces protégées)	180 »
2725	Congrès Forestier	40 »
2726	École Spéciale des Travaux Publics	35 »
2727	Max Ernst	60 »
2728	Amnesty International	35 »
2729	Marcel Cerdan	35 »
2730	François Rouan	100 »
2731	Roberto Matta	100 »
2732	Parcours de la Flamme Olympique	70 »
2733	Croix-Rouge (1991)	60 »
2734	Jeux Paralympiques à Tignes	50 »
2737-42	«Albertville'92» Épreuve collective	50 »

De 1992 à 1998 (N° 3210 - Le Radium), les épreuves de luxe furent remplacées par des feuillets non dentelés avec gomme. Ces feuillets, outre le verso gommé se distinguent des épreuves de luxe par la présence d'une légende imprimée sous la figurine.

PRÉOBLITÉRÉS

89	Cérès, 90 c.	30 »
95	Marianne (de Gandon), 2 f. 50	50 »
106 à 118	(13 val.)	275 »
119 à 122	(4 val.)	110 »
123 à 133.	Monnaie gauloise (11 val.)	200 »
134 à 137.	Monnaie gauloise (4 val.)	80 »
138 à 145.	Monnaie gauloise (8 val.)	125 »
146 à 149.	Zodiaque (4 val.)	80 »
150 à 153.	Zodiaque (4 val.)	80 »
154 à 157.	Zodiaque (4 val.)	80 »
158 à 161	Champignons (4 val.)	200 »
162 à 165.	Cathédrales (4 val.)	75 »
166 à 169.	Châteaux (4 val.)	75 »
170 à 173.	Monuments (4 val.)	75 »
174 à 177.	Monuments (4 val.)	75 »
178 à 181.	Les quatre saisons (4 val.)	75 »
182 à 185.	Cartes à jouer (4 val.)	75 »
186 à 189.	Les mois de l'année (4 val.)	75 »
190 à 193.	Les mois de l'année (4 val.)	75 »
194 à 197.	Les mois de l'année (4 val.)	75 »
198 à 201.	Les quatre éléments (4 val.)	75 »
202 à 205.	Instruments de musique (4 val.)	75 »
206 à 209.	Instruments de musique (4 val.)	75 »
210 à 212.	Instruments de musique (3 val.)	75 »

POSTE AÉRIENNE

1	Premier Salon de l'Aviation, 2 f.	
2	» » 5 f.	
	Les 2 sur même feuillet	3000 »
5	Port de Marseille, 1 f. 50, carmin	550 »
6	» 1 f. 50, bleu	550 »
7	Blériot, 2 f. 25	400 »
8	Vues de Paris, 85 c.	275 »
9	» 1 f. 50	275 »
10	» 2 f. 25	275 »
11	» 2 f. 50	275 »
12	» 3 f.	275 »
13	» 3 f. 50	275 »
14	» 50 f. vert	2750 »

15	Vues de Paris, 50 f. outremer et rose	3250	»
16	Mythologie, 40 f. vert foncé		
17	» 50 f. rose carminé		
18	» 100 f. bleu foncé		
19	» 200 f. vermillon. Les quatre	900	»
16 à 19.	Les 4 valeurs. Épreuve collective	1800	»
20	Congrès de l'U.P.U., 500 f. vert foncé	550	»
20	*Petit format*	700	»
21	Saint-Exupéry, 50 f. + 30 f.		
22	Dagnaux, 100 f. + 70 f. Les deux	450	»
21 et 22.	Les 2 valeurs. Épreuve collective	700	»
23	Premier vol Ader, 40 f. + 10 f., bl. fcé	160	»
21, 22, 23.	Les 3 val. Épreuve collective	750	»
24	Lille, 100 f.		
25	Bordeaux, 200 f.		
26	Lyon, 300 f.		
27	Marseille, 500 f. Les quatre	650	»
24 à 27	*Grand format*. Les 4 valeurs Épreuve collective	1100	»
28	Congrès international de Télégraphie et Téléphonie, 100 f.	400	»
29	Paris, 1000 f.	900	»
30 à 33	Les 4 valeurs	700	»
	Épreuve collective	1100	»
34	Maryse Bastié	100	»
35	Morane Saulnier	90	»
36	Caravelle	200	»
37	Alouette	250	»
38 à 41.	Les quatre valeurs	500	»
	Idem. Épreuve collective	900	»
42	Mystère 20	90	»
43	Concorde	275	»
44	20 f. Mermoz et Saint-Exupéry	200	»
45	Ballon monté	125	»
46	5 f. Daurat et Vanier	100	»
47	10 f. Boucher et Hilsz	100	»
48	15 f. Guillaumet et Codos	100	»
49	Concorde	200	»
50	Traversée Atlantique-Nord	100	»
51	Liaison Villacoublay et Pauillac	100	»
52	Salon Aéronautique	150	»
53	Anniversaire Paris-New-York	100	»
54	Salon Aéronautique (1981)	100	»
55	Costes et Le Brix	100	»
56	Hydravion Laté 300	90	»
57	Avion bimoteur Farman F 60 Goliath	90	»
58	Hydravion CAMS 53	90	»
59	Trimoteur Wibault 283	90	»
60	Trimoteur Dewoitine 338	90	»

BLOCS ET FEUILLETS

7	Arphila'75	700	»
8	Philexfrance'82	500	»
	Idem. En noir (insérée dans le catalogue de l'exposition). *Format* 140 x 200 mm. Avec inscriptions «EXPOSITION PHILATÉLIQUE INTERNATIONALE - PARIS - La Défense - 11-21 Juin 1982»	50	»
	Idem. En noir. *Format* 200 x 290 Sans inscriptions	1000	»
9	Cinémathèque française	275	»
10	Personnages célèbres de la Révolution	250	»
11	Bicentenaire de la Révolution et de la Déclaration des Droits de l'Homme et du Citoyen	325	»
12	Bicentenaire de la Révolution	375	»
13	Bicentenaire de la Révolution	375	»
14	«Albertville'92» Jeux olympiques	800	»

FRANCHISE MILITAIRE

11	Vert	40	»
12	Rouge	40	»
13	Bleu, blanc, rouge	40	»

TIMBRES DE SERVICE

16	Conseil de l'Europe	700	»
17 à 21	Conseil de l'Europe. Les cinq val.	750	»
17-18-20	Idem. Épreuve collective	900	»
22 à 26	UNESCO. Les cinq val.	600	»
	Idem. Épreuve collective (22, 24, 25)	750	»
27 à 35	Conseil de l'Europe, 9 épreuves	700	»
27-28-32	Épreuve collective	600	»
36 à 38	UNESCO (3 val.)	220	»
	Idem. Épreuve collective	400	»
39 à 42	UNESCO (4 val.)	200	»
39-40-42	Épreuve collective	300	»
43 à 45	UNESCO (3 val.)	150	»
	Idem. Épreuve collective	200	»
46 à 49	Conseil de l'Europe (4 val.)	250	»
50 à 52	UNESCO (3 val.)	160	»
	Idem. Épreuve collective	220	»
53 à 55	Bâtiment du Conseil (3 val.)	200	»
	Idem. Épreuve collective	220	»
56-57	UNESCO (2 val.)	110	»
	Idem. Épreuve collective	200	»
58-59	Anniversaire des Droits de l'Homme (Conseil de l'Europe) (2 val.)	120	»
	Idem. Épreuve collective	240	»
60-62	UNESCO (Patrimoine universel) (3 val.)	110	»
	Idem. Épreuve collective	175	»
63-64	Conseil de l'Europe (2 val.)	90	»
65-67	Conseil de l'Europe (3 val.)	120	»
	Idem. Épreuve collective	240	»
68-70	UNESCO (Patrimoine universel) (3 val.)	110	»
	Idem. Épreuve collective	200	»
71-72	UNESCO (Patrimoine universel) (2 val.)	80	»
	Idem. Épreuve collective	180	»
73-74	Conseil de l'Europe (2 val.)	90	»
75-76	UNESCO (Patrimoine universel) (2 val.)	60	»
	Idem. Épreuve collective	180	»
77-78	Conseil de l'Europe (2 val.)	80	»
79-81	UNESCO (Patrimoine universel) (3 val.)	110	»
	Idem. Épreuve collective	200	»
82-84	Conseil de l'Europe (3 val.)	110	»
85-87	Conseil de l'Europe (3 val.)	110	»
	Idem. Épreuve collective	180	»
88-90	UNESCO (Patrimoine universel) (3 val.)	110	»
	Idem. Épreuve collective	180	»
91-92	UNESCO (Patrimoine universel) (2 val.)	80	»
	Idem. Épreuve collective	170	»
93-95	Conseil de l'Europe (3 val.)	90	»
	Idem. Épreuve collective	180	»
96-97	Conseil de l'Europe (2 val.)	80	»
	Idem. Épreuve collective	180	»
98-99	UNESCO (Patrimoine universel) (2 val.)	80	»
	Idem. Épreuve collective	180	»
100-101	Conseil de l'Europe (2 val.)	100	»
	Idem. Épreuve collective	200	»
102-103	UNESCO (Patrimoine universel) (2 val.)	100	»
	Idem. Épreuve collective	250	»
104-105	Conseil de l'Europe (2 val.)	100	»
106-107	Conseil de l'Europe (2 val.)	80	»
108-109	UNESCO (Patrimoine universel) (2 val.)	80	»
	Idem. Épreuve collective	300	»

TIMBRES-TAXE

67 à 77	10, 30, 50 c., 1, 1,50, 2, 3, 4, 5 10 et 20 f. Les 10 val.	250	»
67 à 73 et 75	Les 8 val. Épreuve collective	500	»
74, 76 et 77	4, 10 et 20 f. Les 3 valeurs Épreuve collective	275	»
78 à 87	Lég. timbre-taxe : 10, 30, 50 c. 1, 2, 3, 4, 5, 10 et 20 f. Les dix val.	225	»
78 à 87	Les 10 valeurs. Épreuve collective	500	»
88	*Petit format*, 50 f.	40	»
89	100 f.	90	»
90 à 94	Les cinq val.	140	»
95 à 102	Les huit val.	140	»
103-108	Coléoptères (6 val.)	150	»
109-112	Coléoptères (4 val.)	100	»

ENTIERS POSTAUX

39 et 40	Les deux val.	400	»

BLOCS ET FEUILLETS NON DENTELES AVEC GOMME

De 1992 à 1998 (N° 3210 – Le Radium), les épreuves de luxe furent remplacées par des feuillets non dentelés avec gomme. Ces feuillets, outre le verso gommé se distinguent des épreuves de luxe par la présence d'une légende imprimée sous la figurine.

N°	Sujet	Prix	
2735	Rattachement de Mayotte	125	»
2736	Exposition Universelle de Séville	125	»
2743	Journée du Timbre (1992)	150	»
2744	Idem. Timbre de carnet	150	»
2745	Jeux olympiques de Barcelone	200	»
2746	Marguerite d'Angoulême	100	»
2747-52	Personnages célèbres (6)	600	»
2754	Sandro Botticelli	100	»
2755-56	Europa (1992) La paire	250	»
	Idem. Feuillet collectif	500	»
2757	Congrès des céréales et du pain	100	»
2758	Niort	125	»
2759	L'Homme de Tautavel	100	»
2760	Pays olympiques 1992	200	»
2761	Gravure de Jacques Callot	150	»
2762	Ascension du Mont Aiguille	100	»
2763	Château de Biron	100	»
2764	Canal de l'Ourcq	100	»
2765	Lorient	100	»
2766-69	Nature de France : Fleurs des étangs et des marais (4)	500	»
2770	4 f. 20 Marianne de Briat	150	»
2771	An 1 de la République	100	»
2772-75	Proclamation de la République	400	»
2776	Marché unique européen	150	»
2777	Marcel Paul	125	»
2778	Liaison aérienne Nancy-Lunéville	150	»
2779	Francis Bacon	200	»
2780	Alberto Burri	200	»
2781	Paul Delvaux	200	»
2782	Antoni Tapies	200	»
2783	Croix-Rouge (1992)	150	»
2784	Les gens du voyage	125	»
2785-88	Nature de France : Canards (4)	500	»
2789	Postiers autour du monde	125	»
2790	2 f. 20 Marianne de Briat	150	»
2791	Mémorial des guerres en Indochine	125	»
2792	Journée du Timbre (1993)	150	»
2793	Idem. Timbre de carnet	150	»
2795	Jeux méditerranéens 93	150	»
2796	Ordre maçonnique " Droit humain "	150	»
2797-98	Europa (1993) La paire	250	»
	Idem. Feuillet collectif	500	»
2799-2804	Personnages célèbres (6)	600	»
	Idem. Feuillet collectif	1200	»
2806	T.V.P. Marianne de Briat	150	»
2808	Cours constitutionnelles européennes	125	»
2809	Louise Weiss	125	»
2810	Django Reinhardt	150	»
2811	Lille	150	»
2812	Museum d'Histoire naturelle	125	»
2813-14	Martyrs et héros de la Résistance	250	»
2815	Télégraphe Chappe	125	»
2816	Train d'Artouste	125	»
2817	Chinon	100	»
2818	Minerve	100	»
2820	2 f. 40 Marianne de Briat	150	»
2821	3 f. 50 Marianne de Briat	150	»
	Idem. Feuillet collectif 2824-2820-2821-2822	1000	»
2825	Abbaye de la Chaise-Dieu	100	»
2826	Montbéliard	100	»
2827	Jacquemard de Lambesc	100	»
2828	Georges de la Tour	200	»
2829	Libération de la Corse	125	»
2830	Service de santé	100	»
2831	Postiers autour du monde	125	»
2832	Maurice Denis	200	»
2833	Arts du cirque	150	»
2834	Takis	200	»
2835	Vieira da Silva	200	"
2836-47	Le plaisir d'écrire	750	»
2849-50	Salon du Timbre	600	»
2851-52	Musée du Louvre	200	»
	Idem. Feuillet collectif	400	»
2853	Croix-Rouge (1993)	150	»
2854-57	Arts décoratifs (4)	400	»
2858	Sean Scully	200	»
2859	Vitrail de la cathédrale du Mans	200	»
2860	Elections au Parlement Européen	150	»
2861	Guignol	125	»
2862	Ecole Polytechnique	125	»
2863	Journée du Timbre (1994)	150	»
2864	Idem. Timbre de carnet	150	»
2866-71	Relations France-Suède	300	»
2875	Georges Pompidou	125	»
2876	Hommage aux Maquis	150	»
2877	Philexjeunes 94	125	»
2878-79	Europa (1994) La paire	300	»
	Idem. Feuillet collectif	600	»
2880-81	Tunnel sous la Manche, feuillet collectif	200	»
2882-83	Tunnel sous la Manche, feuillet collectif	200	»
2884	Banque asiatique	100	»
2885	Martigues	125	»
2886	Cour de cassation	100	»
2887-88	Débarquement (2)	300	»
2889	Centenaire du C.I.O.	200	»
2890	Orgue de Poitiers	125	»
2891	Montagne Sainte-Victoire	100	»
2892	Pays de la Saulx	100	»
2893	Bastia	100	»
2894	Argentat	100	»
2895	Débarquement de Provence	125	»
2896	Nicolas Poussin	150	»
2897-2902	Personnages célèbres (6)	600	»
	Idem. Feuillet collectif	1200	»
2904	Conservatoire des Arts et Métiers	125	»
2905	Parc de Saint-Cloud	125	»
2906	2 f. Marianne de Briat	150	»
2907	Ecole Normale Supérieure	125	»
2908	Prévention des toxicomanies	100	»
2909-10	Salon du Timbre	600	»
2911	Georges Simenon	125	»
2912	Grande Loge de France	125	»
2913	Alain Colas	125	»
2914	Georg Baselitz	200	»
2915	Croix-Rouge (1994)	150	»
2917	La Presse	125	»
2918	Champs-Elysées	150	»
2919-22	1er siècle du cinéma	500	»
2923	Pont de Normandie	150	»
2924	Notariat européen	125	»
2925	Louis Pasteur	150	»
2926	Chasse Saint-Taurin, Evreux	200	»
2927	Prud'hon	200	»
2928	Zao Wou Ki	200	»
2929-32	Oiseaux de J.J. Audubon (4)	500	»
2933	Journée du Timbre (1995)	150	»
2934	Idem. Tirage de carnet	150	»
2936	Comités d'entreprise	125	»
2937	Ecole Supérieure d'Electricité	125	»
2938	Ecole de Langues Orientales	125	»
2939	Jean Giono	125	»
2940	Sidérurgie Lorraine	125	»
2941-42	Europa (1995) La paire	300	»
	Idem. Feuillet collectif	600	»
2943	Métier de la forêt	125	»
2944	8 mai 1945. La Victoire	150	»
2945	Assemblée Nationale	150	»
2946	Croix-Rouge (1995)	150	»
2947	Secours Populaire Français	125	»
2948	Espace et Guyane	150	»

2949-52	Les régions françaises (4)	450	»
2953	Orléans	125	»
2954	Malterie de Stenay	100	»
2955	Remiremont	100	»
2956	Pont de Nyons	100	»
2957	Corrèze en Corrèze	100	»
2958-2963	Fables de la Fontaine (6)	600	»
2965	Rafle de Vel d'Hiv	100	»
2966	André Maginot	125	»
2967	Grande Loge Féminine	125	»
2968	Pharmacie hospitalière	125	»
2969	Kirkeby	200	»
2970	Barbizon	150	»
2971	Ecole Nationale d'Administration	125	»
2972	Berthe Morisot	200	»
2973	Institut de France	150	»
2974	Automobile Club de France	200	»
2975	Organisation des Nations Unies	150	»
2976-81	Santons de Provence (6)	700	»
2983	Francis Jammes	125	»
2984	Cathédrale d'Evry	125	»
2985	Coupe du Monde de Football	150	»
2986	Wercollier	200	»
2987	Dibbets	200	»
2988	Civilisations des Arawaks (Guadeloupe)	125	»
2989	Corot	200	»
2990	Journée du Timbre (1996)	150	»
2991	Idem. Timbre de carnet	150	»
2993	L'Imaginaire irlandais	125	»
2994	Jacques Rueff	125	»
2995	René Descartes	125	»
2996	E.D.F. – G.D.F.	125	»
2997-99	Nature de France (3)	375	»
3000	50e Salon Philatélique d'Automne	150	»
3000A	Europa (1996)	200	»
3001	Institut National de la Recherche Agronomique	125	»
3002	Maison de Jeanne d'Arc	125	»
3003	Accord Ramoge	125	»
3004	Clermont-Ferrand	125	»
3005-3007	Marianne de Briat (3)	500	»
	Idem. Feuillet collectif	1000	»
3010-13	Coupe du Monde de Football (4)	600	»
3014	Trésor de Neuvy en Sullias	200	»
3015	Jacques Marette	150	»
3016	Centenaire des Jeux Olympiques	200	»
3017	Train Ajaccio-Vizzavona	125	»
3018	Bitche	100	»
3019	Iles Sanguinaires	100	»
3020	Abbaye du Thoronet	100	»
3021	Cathédrale de Chambéry	100	»
3022	Basilique Notre-Dame de Fourvière	100	»
3023	Arman	200	»
3024-30	Héros français du roman policier (6)	600	»
	Idem. Feuillet collectif	1200	»
3032	Lycée Henri IV	125	»
3033	U.N.I.C.E.F.	125	»
3034	Conseil Economique et Social	100	»
3035	Cinquantenaire de l'UNESCO	125	»
3036	Départements d'Outre-Mer	100	»
3037	Ecole Française d'Athènes	100	»
3038	André Malraux	100	»
3039	Croix-Rouge (1996)	150	»
3040	50e Festival de Cannes	150	»
3041	Bibliothèque Nationale de France	100	»
3042	François Mitterrand	125	»
3043	Innovation participative	100	»
3044	Centre Georges Pompidou	125	»
3045-46	Timbres de souhaits (2)	250	»
3047	Ecole Nationale des Ponts et Chaussées	125	»
3048	Patrimoine guyanais	125	»
3049	Tavant	200	»
3050	Bernard Moninot	200	»
3051	Journée du Timbre (1997)	150	»
3052	Idem. Timbre de carnet	150	»
3053-57	Nature de France : Parcs naturels (4)	500	»
3058	Europa (1997)	200	»
3059	Philexjeunes 97	150	»
3060-65	Les Journées de la Lettre (6)	600	»
3072	Combattants français en Afrique du Nord	150	»
3073	Versailles	125	»
3074-77	Coupe du Monde de Football (4)	600	»
3078	De la Gaule à la France	125	»
3079	Millau	100	»
3080	Guimiliau	100	»
3081	Château de Plessis-Bourré	100	»
3082	Les Salles Lavauguyon	100	»
3083-3091-3093	Marianne du 14 Juillet, feuillet collectif	500	»
3086-99	(sauf 3091 et 3093) (12)	1000	»
	Idem. Feuillet collectif	1500	»
3102	Championnat du Monde d'Aviron	125	»
3103	Corsaires basques	125	»
3104	César	200	»
3105	Chardin	200	»
3106	Voiturier de marée	125	»
3107	Sablé sur Sarthe	125	»
3108	Basilique d'Epinal	125	»
3109	Domaine de Sceaux	125	»
3110	Année du Japon	125	»
3111	Championnats du Monde de Judo	125	»
3112	Espace européen SAR.LOR.LUX	125	»
3113	La Qualité	125	»
3114	Le Collège de France	125	»
3115-20	Héros d'Aventures (6)	600	»
	Idem. Feuillet collectif	1200	»
3122	Croix-Rouge (1997)	150	»
3123	Meilleurs vœux	150	»
3124	Protection de l'enfance maltraitée	125	»
3125	Meilleurs vœux du facteur	150	»
3126	Maréchal Leclerc	150	»
3127	Philexfrance 99	150	»
3128	Abbaye du Moutier d'Ahun	125	»
3129	Michel Debré	100	»
3130-31	Coupe du Monde de Football (2)	300	»
3132	Bicentenaire de l'Assemblée Nationale	100	»
3133	Bonne fête	150	»
3134	Le Médiateur de la République	125	»
3135	Journée du Timbre (1998)	150	»
3136	Idem. Timbre de carnet	150	»
3138	Abbé Franz Stock	125	»
3139	Coupe du Monde de Football	150	»
3141	Joyeux anniversaire	150	»
3142	Réunion de Mulhouse à la France	125	»
3143	Abbaye de Citeaux	125	»
3144	Patrimoine réunionnais	125	»
3145	Magritte	200	»
3146	Edit de Nantes	125	»
3147	Delacroix	200	»
3148	Abolition de l'esclavage	125	»
3149	Ligue des Droits de l'Homme	125	»
3150-55	Les Journées de la Lettre (bande de 6)	500	»
3162	Pablo Picasso	200	»
3163	Henri Collet	100	»
3164	Dunkerque	125	»
3165	Mont Saint Michel	120	»
3166	Europa (1998)	150	»
3167	Le Gois – Ile de Noirmoutier	100	»
3168	Baie de Somme	100	»
3169	Château de Crussol	100	»
3171	Stéphane Mallarmé	125	»
3172	Aéro-Club de France	125	»
3173-74	Emission commune France-Chine (2)	250	»
3180	Collégiale de Mantes-la-Jolie	100	»
3181	Opéra de Paris – Palais Garnier	100	»
3182-85	Nature de France chevaux (4)	500	»
3186	Salon de l'Auto	125	»
3194	Saint-Dié	100	»
3195	La Constitution 1958-1998	125	»
3196	80e Anniversaire de l'Armistice	125	»
3197	Marcel Duchamp	200	»
3198	Union Mondiale pour la Nature	125	»
3199	Croix-Rouge (1998)	150	»
3205	Médecins sans frontières	125	»
3206	Parlement Européen	125	»
3207	Paul Gauguin	200	»
3208-09	Déclaration Universelle des Droits de l'Homme (2)	300	»
3210	Le Radium	150	»

TIMBRES FICTIFS

En 1932, l'Administration a cessé d'utiliser des timbres-poste surchargés. Elle les a remplacés par des simili-timbres appelés par les collectionneurs "FICTIFS". Il s'agit d'un cadre entourant la mention "SANS VALEUR" et un chiffre fixant la valeur. Les couleurs sont, jusqu'en 1964, celles des timbres en cours au moment de l'impression. Cette concordance est signalée par le N° du timbre correspondant entre parenthèses.

Les cotes de la colonne de gauche concernent les timbres neufs avec gomme d'origine intacte et sans charnière, celles de la colonne de droite, les timbres avec charnière légère. Les timbres oblitérés proprement avec un cachet de COURS PRATIQUES valent plus que les timbres avec charnière.

A partir de 1960, une unique colonne indique la valeur des timbres sans charnière. Les timbres oblitérés, sur documents d'exercices pratiques authentiques, sont très recherchés. Les oblitérations de complaisance, communes dans cette période, valent beaucoup moins.

Emission de 1932

Impression par presse "à plat" par feuilles de 150 pour les petits formats, de 75 pour les grands formats.

F1	0,01 ardoise (107)	15 »	12 »
F2	0,02 brun-lilas (108)	15 »	12 »
F3	0,03 orange (109)	15 »	12 »
F4	0,05 vert (111)	6 »	4 80

F5	0,10 violet (233)	50 »	40 »
F6	0,15 brun-violet (189)	6 »	4 80
F7	0,20 lilas-rose (190)	6 »	4 80
F8	0,25 jaune-brun (235)	6 »	4 80

F9	0,30 vert (174)	6 »	4 80
F10	0,40 outremer (237)	6 »	4 80
F11	0,45 violet (197)	6 »	4 80
F12	0,50 rouge-orange (199)	4 »	3 20

F13	0,65 vert-olive (234)	6 »	4 80
F14	0,75 lilas-rose (202)	6 »	4 80
F15	0,90 rouge vif (243)	6 »	4 80
F16	1,00 bleu (205)	13 »	10 40

F17	1,50 bleu clair (181)	13 »	10 40
F18	2 brun-rouge (258)	15 »	12 »

F19	3 ardoise (259)	15 »	12 »
F20	5 brun (260)	15 »	12 »

F21	10 outremer (261b)	30 »	24 »
F22	20 chaudron (262)	30 »	24 »

Année 1932 **290 *232

Emission de 1935

De 1935 à 1976, on distingue 2 cas : d'une part les *petits formats* qui sont entièrement imprimés sur presse typograpgique par rotative, d'autre part les *grands formats* pour lesquels la rotative est inadaptée au format et qui sont réalisés en deux temps : tirage de feuilles blanches sur presses taille-douce avec perforations et indications de service, puis impression des timbres "feuille à feuille" par presse à platine.

F23	0,01 bistre-olive (277A)	25 »	20 »
F24	0,02 vert-olive (278)	25 »	20 »
F25	0,03 vermillon (278A)	20 »	16 »
F26	0,05 rose (278B)	2 »	1 60

F27	0,10 outremer (279)	2 »	1 60
F28	0,15 brun-lilas (189)	12 »	9 60
F29	0,20 lilas-rose (190)	3 »	2 40
F30	0,25 brun-jaune (235)	3 »	2 40

F31	0,30 vert (280)	2 »	1 60
F32	0,40 lilas (281)	2 »	1 60
F33	0,45 bistre (282)	15 »	12 »
F34	0,50 rose-rouge (283)	2 »	1 60

F35	0,65 violet-brun (284)	3 »	2 40
F36	0,75 olive (284A)	3 »	2 40
F37	1,00 orange (286)	3 »	2 40
F38	1,25 lilas-rose (293)	5 »	4 »

F39	1,50 bleu (288)	2 »	1 60
F40	1,75 lilas-rose (289)	3 »	2 40
F41	0,90 carmin (290)	6 »	4 80

F42	2 vert foncé (301)	6 »	4 80
F43	3,50 brun foncé (302)	23 »	18 40

F44	5 brun (260) Papier jaune	5 »	4 »
F45	10 bleu foncé (261)	4 »	3 20

F46	20 bleu	4 »	3 20

Année 1935 **180 *144

Emission de 1945

F47	0,60 outremer (674)	2 »	1 60
F48	0,80 vert-jaune (675)	2 »	1 60
F49	1,00 rose-rouge (676)	3 »	2 40
F50	1,20 brun-noir (677)	2 »	1 60

F51	1,50 lilas (679)	32 »	25 60
F52	2,00 vert foncé (713)	2 »	1 60
F53	3,00 brun foncé (715)	30 »	24 »

F54	4,00 outremer (717)	2 »	1 60
F55	5,00 vert (719)	5 »	4 »

F56	6,00 outremer (720)	2 »	1 60
F57	15 lilas-rose (724)	13 »	10 40
F58	25 violet (731)	5 »	4 »

F59	50 brun-rouge (732)	280 »	224 »
F60	100 carmin (733)	40 »	32 »

Année 1945 **420 *336

Emission de 1946 et 1949

F61	2,50 brun sur 1,25 N° F38 (681)	3 »	2 40
F62	3 carmin sur 0,15 N° F28 (716)	5 »	4 »
F63	3 carmin sur 0,20 N° F29 (716)	3 »	2 40
F64	*3 carmin sur 0,25 N° F30 Non émis*	» »	» »

Seule deux feuilles-témoins sont conservées au Musée de la Poste à Paris

F65	10 bleu sur 0,45 N° F33 (723)	3 »	2 40

F66	25 rouge sur 1,75 N° F40 (729)	3 »	2 40
F67	5 vert sur 0,10 N° F27 (719)	3 »	2 40
F68	5 vert sur 0,30 N° F31 (719)	5 »	4 »
F69	10 lilas sur 0,40 N° F32 (811)	3 »	2 40

F70	12 bleu sur 0,80 N° F48 (812)	3 »	2 40
F71	15 rouge sur 0,50 N° F34 (813)	3 »	2 40
F72	15 rouge sur 0,60 N° F47 (813)	60 »	48 »
F73	20 bleu-violet sur 1,50 N° F51 (764)	3 »	2 40

F74	25 bleu sur 1,20 N° F50 (822)	10 »	8 »
F75	200 rouge sur 6,00 N° F56 (PA 19)	200 »	160 »
F76	100 bleu sans surcharge (PA 18)	10 »	8 »

Année 1946 et 1949 **313 *250

Emission de 1950

F77	0,10 rouge et bleu (834)	5 »	4 »
F78	0,50 vermillon (835)	1 »	0 80
	Papier mince et gomme striée		
F79	1 brun (836)	1 »	0 80
F80	2 vert (837)	1 »	0 80

F81	4 outremer et rouge (838)	4 »	3 20
F82	5 vert-jaune (809)	1 »	0 80
F83	8 bleu-turquoise (810)	1 »	0 80

F84	10 lilas (811)	2 »	1 60
F85	12 outremer (812)	1 »	0 80
F86	15 rouge (813)	1 »	0 80

F87	20 rouge-orange (841A)	3 »	2 40
F88	25 outremer (842)	3 »	2 40

F89	40 vert-noir (842A)	3 »	2 40
F90	50 brun-violet (843)	3 »	2 40

F91	100 brun-noir (PA 24)	3 »	2 40
F92	200 vert (PA 25)	3 »	2 40

F93	300 violet (PA 26)	4 »	3 20
F94	500 vermillon (PA 27)	5 »	4 »

F95	1000 noir et gris (PA 29)	6 »	4 20

Année 1950 **51 *40,80

Emissions de 1951 et 1952

F96	3 jaune et outremer (903)	1 50	1 20
F97	6 vert (884)	5 »	4 »
F98	18 rose carminé (887)	2 »	1 60

F99	30 bleu-noir (905)	3 »	2 40
F100	1 outremer et rouge (901)	1 »	0 80

F101	20 violet foncé (924)	2 50	2 »

Année 1951 et 1952 **15 *12

Emission de 1954

F102	2 outremer et jaune (953)	2 »	1 60
F103	5 violet (883)	1 »	0 80
F104	15 bleu (886)	1 »	0 80

F105	6 ardoise et bleu (976)	3 »	2 40
F106	8 bleu et vert (977)	3 »	2 40

F107	10 brun-rouge et bleu clair (978)	3 »	2 40
F108	12 violet (979)	3 »	2 40

F109	18 vert foncé et ardoise (980)	3 »	2 40
F110	20 brun foncé et turquoise (981)	3 »	2 40

F111	30 gris et vert (971)	3 »	2 40
F112	40 brun et brun foncé (972)	3 »	2 40
F113	50 bleu foncé et brun-rouge (973)	6 »	4 80

F114	100 brun-rouge et bleu (PA 30)	5 »	4 »
F115	500 vermillon et jaune (PA 32)	6 »	4 80

Année 1954 **45 *36

Emission de 1956

F116	0,70 bleu et rouge (1045)	6 »	4 80
F117	0,80 brun et rouge (1046)	4 »	3 20
F118	1 bleu foncé et rouge (1047)	1 50	1 20
F119	3 vermillon et brun foncé (1004)	4 »	3 20

F120	10 bleu clair (1038)	2 »	1 60
F121	12 ardoise et brun-noir (1039)	10 »	8 »

F122	25 brun et brun foncé (1042)	7 »	5 60
F123	50 violet et lilas (1074)	5 »	4 »

F124	75 vert et vert-noir (1075)	40 »	32 »
F125	100 bleu et brun-rouge (PA 30)	3 »	2 40

F126	200 bleu et bleu-violet (PA 31)	3 »	2 40
F127	500 jaune et rouge (PA 32)	40 »	28 »

F128	1000 noir et brun (PA 33)	12 »	9 60

Année 1956 **138 *110

Emission de 1957

F129	6 brun-jaune (1115)	12 »	9 60
F130	12 lilas (1116)	12 »	9 60
F131	20 outremer (1111C)	1 »	0 80

F132	15 vert et noir (1106)	2 50	2 »
F133	35 carmin et lilas (1129)	2 50	2 »

F134	50 vert-gris et brun-noir (1130)	15 »	12 »
F135	65 bleu et vert-noir (1131)	65 »	52 »

Année 1957 **110 *88

Emission de 1958

F136	8 ocre et vert-jaune (1125)	60 »	48 »
F137	25 brun foncé et gris-ardoise (1128)	6 »	4 80

F138	500 bleu et noir (PA 36)	6 »	4 80
F139	1000 lilas et noir (PA 37)	8 »	6 40

Année 1958 **100 *80

Emissions de 1961 et 1962

F140 0,05 outremer et rouge (1230A) 1 »

F141 0,10 vert (1231) 1 »

F142 0,15 vert et rouge (1232) 1 »

F143 0,20 turquoise et rose (1233) 1 50

F144 0,20 bleu et carmin (1282) 1 »

F145 0,25 carmin foncé et gris (1263) 1 »

F146 0,15 bleu et bleu-noir (1235) 1 50

F147 0,30 bleu et brun foncé (1236) 1 50

F148 0,45 violet et noir (1237) 1 50

F149 0,50 olive et lilas (1238) 1 50

F150 0,65 bleu-noir et sépia (1239) 1 »

F151 0,85 vert-noir et sépia (1240) 1 50

F152 1 violet et vert (1241) 2 »

F153 2 noir et violet (PA 38) 2 »

F154 3 bleu-vert et olive (PA 39) 5 »

F155 5 bleu foncé et noir (PA 40) 4 »

F156 10 lilas et noir (PA 41) 5 »

F157 0,95 vert et carmin (1317) 2 »

Emissions de 1964 et 1965

F158 0,01 bleu et jaune (1351A) 1 »

F159 0,02 vert et jaune (1351B) 1 »

F160 0,12 brun foncé et rouge (1353A) 1 »

F161 0,18 vert et bleu (1354A) 1 50

F162 0,40 brun et vert foncé (1435) 1 50

F163 0,60 vert foncé et lilas-brun (1437) 1 »
F164 0,70 vert foncé et ardoise (1392A) 1 »

F165 1 brun et vert (1440) 1 »
F166 1,30 brun foncé et lilas (1441) 1 »

F167 2,30 brun et turquoise (1506) 1 »
F168 3 brun et bleu clair (PA 39) 1 »

F169 5 brun et noir (PA 40) 1 »
F170 0,30 bleu et rouge (1354B) 1 »

Emission de 1966

F171 0,05 vert et rouge 1 »
F172 0,10 vert et orange 1 50
F173 0,20 vert et bleu foncé 1 50

Emission de 1967

F174 0,05 vert et noir 2 »
F175 0,30 vert (1536A) 2 »

F176 0,45 brun et bleu 1 »
F177 0,50 brun et carmin 1 »

F178 0,80 brun et brun-rouge 1 »
F179 2 brun et bleu 2 »

F180 10 brun et violet 1 »

Emissions de 1969 et 1971

F181 0,40 brun et ver 1 »
F182 1,00 brun et vert-olive 1 »

F183 2 brun et orange 1 50
F184 3 brun et vert 1 »

F185 5 brun et gris 1 50
F186 5,00 brun et gris-noir 1 »

F187 10 brun clair et orange 1 »
F188 10 brun et orange foncé 1 »

Emission de 1972

F189 0,01 brun et jaune 1 »
F190 0,02 brun et jaune 1 »
F191 0,05 brun et noir 1 »

F192 0,10 brun et orange 1 »
F193 0,20 brun et outremer 1 »
F194 0,30 brun et vert 1 »

F195 0,15 brun foncé 1 »
F196 0,40 brun foncé et carmin 1 »

F197 0,50 sépia et carmin 1 »
F198 0,85 brun et vert clair 1 »

F199 0,90 brun et bleu-violet 1 »
F200 20 brun et vert (PA 44) 1 »

Emission de 1974

F201 0,60 brun clair et violet 1 »
F202 2,00 brun clair et orange 1 »

F203 3,00 brun clair et lilas 1 »

Emission de 1976

D'octobre 1976 à 1987, les vignettes fictives sont toujours imprimées en ***typographie*** mais sur ***rotative 2 couleurs*** en une seule passe. Les petits formats (limités à la valeur 0,50) se présentent en feuilles de 100. Les grands formats (correspondants aux valeurs supérieures) se présentent en feuilles de 50.

F204 0,40 brun clair et carmin 1 »
F205 1 vert et orange 1 »

F206 1,40 bleu foncé et orange 1 »

Emission de 1978

F207 0,05 rouge et bleu 1 »
F208 0,20 vert foncé et vert clair 1 »
F209 0,45 violet et bleu 2 »
F210 0,50 brun et orange 1 »

F211 0,70 orange et rouge 1 »
F212 1 vert et orange foncé 1 »

F213 1,20 vert et bleu foncé 1 »
F214 1,70 violet et vert foncé 1 »

F215 2 violet 1 »
F216 3 bleu clair et vert 1 »

F217 5 bleu clair et brun foncé 1 »
F218 15 brun et vert (PA 48) 1 »

Emissions de 1979 et 1980

F219 1,10 vert et vert foncé (2058) 1 »
F220 1,30 vert et violet (2059) 1 »

F221 0,10 orange clair 1 »
F222 0,15 orange et brun 1 »
F223 0,20 vert-gris 1 »

F224 0,30 vert et bleu 1 »
F225 0,50 brun clair et orange 1 »
F226 20 brun et bleu (valeur de P A) 1 »

Emission de 1981

F227 1,40 bleu et jaune d'or (2154) 1 »
F228 1,60 violet et vert (2155) 1 »

F229 1,80 violet et bleu 1 »
F230 2,10 bleu et marron 1 »

Emission de 1982

F231 0,05 rouge et bleu 1 »
F232 0,10 orange-rouge 1 »

F233 0,60 rouge et vert-gris 1 »
F234 0,80 orange et violet 1 »

F235 1,20 vert et bleu pâle 2 »
F236 10 brun et vert-gris (PA 55) 1 »

Emissions de 1984 et 1985

F237 50 vert et lilas (précurseur du PA 60) 1 »
F238 0,40 bleu-violet et violet 3 »

Emission de 1987

Impression en *taille-douce* sur presse T.D. 3 - 13. C'est le seul FICTIF gravé.

F239 vert (Valeur du tarif postal pour P.N.U. de 20 g maximum) 1 50

F240 rouge (Valeur du tarif postal pour la Lettre de 20 g maximum) 1 50

Emission de 1989

Impression en héliogravure pour le cadre et en typographie pour la valeur. Les N°s 250 et 251 sont imprimés uniquement en héliogravure.

F241 0,10 jaune citron et rouge 1 50

F242 0,20 rouge cerise et turquoise 1 50

F243 0,50 outremer foncé et bleu 1 50

F244 1 jaune citron vif et turquoise 2 »

F245 2 orange vif et lilas 2 »

F246 4 rouge cerise et turquoise 2 »

F247 5 lilas-rose vif et rouge carmin 2 »

F248 10 bleu vif et orange 2 »

F249 20 bleu violet et outremer 2 »

F250 vert (Valeur du tarif postal pour P.N.U. de 20 g maximum) 12 »

F251 rouge (Valeur du tarif postal pour la Lettre de 20 g maximum) 12 »

Emission tardive de 1991

Même mode d'impression que la série précédente.

F252-50 Bleu et vert » »

TIMBRES-TAXE

Emissions de 1949 à 1956

FT1 1 outremer (81) 1 »

FT2 2 turquoise (82) 1 »

FT3 3 brun-rouge (83) 1 »

FT4 4 violet (84) 1 »

FT5 5 rose-lilas (85) 1 »

FT6 10 orange (86) 1 »

FT7 20 brun-olive (87) 1 »

FT8 50 vert foncé (88) 2 »

FT9 100 vert (89) 5 »

Emission de 1961

FT10 0,05 rose-lilas (90) 1 »

FT11 0,10 rouge-orange (91) 1 »

FT12 0,20 bistre-olive (92) 1 »

FT13 0,50 vert-noir (93) 1 »
FT14 1 vert (94) 1 »

Emissions de 1965 et 1968

FT15 0,15 brun et rouge (97) 1 »
FT16 0,30 brun et bleu (99) 1 »
FT17 0,05 outremer et rouge (95) 1 »
FT18 0,10 outremer et bleu (96) 1 »

FT19 0,30 outremer et bleu (99) 1 »
FT20 0,50 outremer et rouge (101) 1 »
FT21 1,00 outremer et lilas (102) 1 »

Emissions de 1972 à 1985

FT22 0,15 brun et violet (97) 1 »
FT23 0,20 brun et outremer (98) 1 »
FT24 0,40 brun et rouge (100) 1 »
FT25 0,05 brun et noir (95) 1 »

FT26 0,30 brun et vert (99) 1 »
FT27 0,50 brun et lilas (101) 1 »
FT28 1,00 brun et vert (102) 1 »
FT29 0,20 brun et outremer (98) 1 »

FT30 0,10 orange 1 »
FT31 0,15 orange et brun 60 »
FT32 0,30 vert et bleu 1 »

FT33 0,50 brun et orange 1 »
FT34 1 vert et orange 1 »

FT35 0,20 vert foncé et vert-jaune (104) 8 »
FT36 0,40 bleu-violet et violet (100) 8 »
FT37 2 bleu-violet (107) 1 50

FT38 3 bleu et vert-jaune (111) 1 50
FT39 4 bleu (108) 1 50
FT40 5 bleu et brun (112) 1 50

Il existe d'autres valeurs dont la faciale est exprimée en Francs CFA. Ces timbres destinés aux Cours pour l'Outre-Mer sont répertoriés dans le Tome 2 troisième partie.

Pour faire face à l'évolution des tarifs postaux, à la défection des approvisionnements, ou à l'absence de certains produits, de nombreux cours d'instruction fabriquèrent leurs propres "timbres" pour compenser ces insuffisances. Les surcharges les plus diverses confectionnées localement ne sauraient manquer d'intéresser les collectionneurs mais ne peuvent être répertoriées.

Enfin, certaines valeurs des années 60 sont également surchargées EA par le Cours de LAGHOUAT en Algérie.

CARTE POSTALE

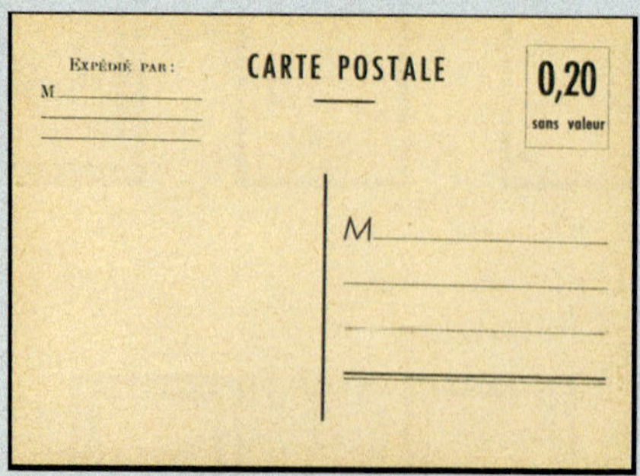

FCP1 0,20 SANS VALEUR Impression en noir sur carton crème 400 »

CARNETS

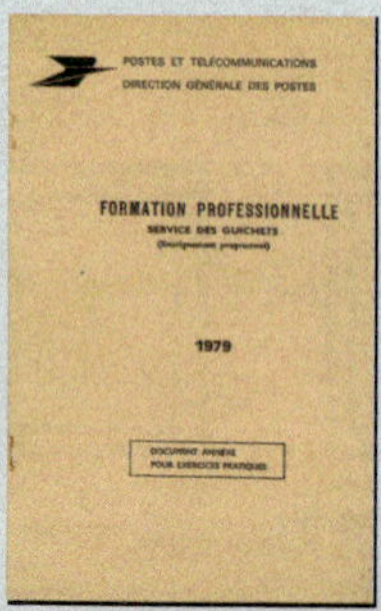

Carnets pour l'enseignement programmé - service des guichets. Ils se présentent dans un format de cahiers (160 x 250 mm) et comportent plusieurs vignettes détachables de même facture que les FICTIFS avec mention "SANS VALEUR". Ils sont destinés aux travaux pratiques des cours de guichetiers organisés au niveau départemental.

FC1 1971 avec N° de série 510.0 111.51081 - 7 valeurs différentes de 0,15 à 10 800 »

FC2 1972 avec N° de série 510.111.51101 - 8 valeurs différentes de 0,15 à 10 500 »

FC3 1973 avec N° de série 510.211.510710 - 11 valeurs différentes de 0,05 à 10 200 »

FC4 1973 avec N° de série 510.IN3.11508910F - Idem FC3 avec date moins large : 12 mm au lieu de 16 mm 85 »

FC5 1976 avec N° de série 510.IN3.11508910F - 14 valeurs différentes de 0,05 à 20 65 »

FC6 1979 sans N° de série - 15 valeurs différentes de 0,05 à 20 54 »

FC7 1985 sans N° de série - 15 valeurs différentes de 0,05 à 20 54 »

FC8 1986 sans N° de série - Idem FC7 avec couverture saumon 43 »

La dernière émission de timbres FICTIFS date de 1989. A partir de 1993, par la volonté de l'administration, les centres d'instruction ferment leurs portes les uns après les autres. Ils sont quasiment tous fermés aujourd'hui, ainsi l'usage des timbres FICTIFS s'est éteint progressivement.

TIMBRE DE FRANCHISE

Jusqu'en 1964 les cotes de la colonne de gauche concernent les timbres neufs avec gomme d'origine intacte et sans charnière, celles de la colonne centrale les timbres neufs avec charnière légère, celles de la colonne de droite les timbres oblitérés.

1901-04. – *Timbres-poste surchargés. Dentelés.*

Les lettres F.M. sont les initiales des mots "Franchise Militaire".

1	**15 c. orange (117)**	230 »	85 »	8 »
	(Sur lettre)			17 »
	a. (Surch. renversée)	600 »	400 »	150 »
	b. (Chiffre 1 touchant le cadre)	325 »	200 »	40 »
	c. (Non dentelé)		250 »	
2	**15 c. vermillon (125)**	315 »	100 »	7 »
	(Sur lettre)			14 »
3	**15 c. vert-olive (IV) (130c)**	210 »	80 »	7 »
	(Sur lettre)			13 75
	a. (Sans point après M)	350 »	175 »	50 »
	b. (Non dentelé)		200 »	

Très bon centrage (+50 %).

1906-07. – *Idem. Dentelés.*

4	**10 c. rose (III) (129b)**	130 »	45 »	9 »
	(Sur lettre)			17 »
	a. (Sans point après M)	275 »	165 »	50 »
	b. (Non dentelé)		200 »	
5	**10 c. rouge (IA) (138)**	4 »	2 »	1 »
	(Sur lettre)			5 35
	a. (Surch. renversée)	165 »	125 »	55 »
	b. (Non dentelé)		110 »	

Très bon centrage (+50 %).

1929. – *Timbre-poste surchargé.*

6	**50 c. rouge (IIA) (199)**	18 »	6 »	1 »
	(Sur lettre)			4 60
	a. (Sans point après M)	70 »	40 »	15 »
	b. (Point avant et après F)	70 »	40 »	15 »
	c. (M rapproché)	25 »	15 »	11 »

1933. – *Timbre-poste surchargé.*

7	**50 c. rose-rouge (I) (283)**	14 »	4 »	0 80
	(Sur lettre)			4 60
	a. (Type III)	14 »	4 »	0 80
	b. (Surch. renversée)		225 »	125 »

1937. – *Timbre-poste surchargé.*

8	**65 c. outremer (C) (I) (365)**	0 80	0 50	0 50
	(Sur lettre)			3 85
	a. (Sans point après M)		35 »	25 »

1939. – *Timbre-poste surchargé.*

9	**90 c. outremer (C) (I) (368)**	1 »	0 65	0 65
	(Sur lettre)			3 85

1939. – *Pour la correspondance des réfugiés espagnols. Timbre-poste de 1937-39 surchargé.*

10	**90 c. outremer (C) (I) (368)**	3 40	2 30	3 »
	(Sur lettre)			9 15
	a. (Avec point après F)	60 »	30 »	25 »

1946-58. – *Typographie. Dentelés 14 x 13½.*

11	**(sans val.) vert**	1 85	1 50	1 50
	(Sur lettre)			23 »
	a. (Non dentelé)		23 »	
12	**(sans val.) rouge**	0 50	0 30	0 30
	(Sur lettre)			2 30
	a. rouge carminé	0 65	0 30	0 65

1964. - *Drapeau. Typographie. Dentelé 12 x 14.*

13	**(sans val.) Bleu, blanc, rouge**		0 50	0 50
	(Sur lettre)			1 »
	a. (Non dentelé)		19 25	

1991. – *Etiquettes "Daguet Armées" (Guerre du golfe). Autoadhésif.*

13A	**vert *Etiquettes "Daguet Armées"***		35 »	35 »
	(Sur lettre)			100 »

Timbres de Franchise Militaire pour colis

En 1952, les P.T.T. ont mis en service une formule illustrée destinée aux paquets militaires bénéficiant de la Franchise Postale. La partie supérieure était conservée par le Bureau de Poste recevant le colis ; la partie inférieure était une étiquette à coller sur l'envoi. Elle était gommée et dentelée.

MINISTÈRE DES POSTES, TÉLÉGRAPHES & TÉLÉPHONES

Cachet de l'Unité

Régiment et Cie
Bâtiment ou Formation

BON POUR UN PAQUET
en FRANCHISE POSTALE

Délivré le (1)
Bénéficiaire (1)
Nom et grade
(1) Partie à remplir par l'autorité militaire.

Timbre à date de la Poste

Paquet expédié par M
Nom et adresse

Bon valable pendant **trois mois** seulement à compter de sa délivrance.
L'imitation et la contrefaçon de la présente formule exposent les contrevenants aux sanctions prévues par le Code pénal.

Étiquette à coller sur le paquet

FRANCHISE POSTALE
(Loi du 24 Mai 1951.)

14 **noir *FRANCHISE POSTALE***
(Loi du 24 mai 1951) 60 »

Le texte de la partie inférieure a été modifié en 1964 :

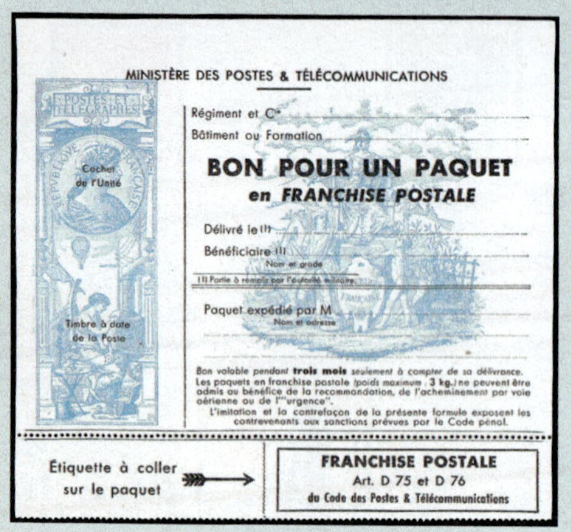
MINISTÈRE DES POSTES & TÉLÉCOMMUNICATIONS

Cachet de l'Unité

Régiment et Cie
Bâtiment ou Formation

BON POUR UN PAQUET
en FRANCHISE POSTALE

Délivré le (1)
Bénéficiaire (1)
Nom et grade
(1) Partie à remplir par l'autorité militaire.

Timbre à date de la Poste

Paquet expédié par M
Nom et adresse

Bon valable pendant **trois mois** seulement à compter de sa délivrance.
Les paquets en franchise postale (poids maximum : 3 kg.) ne peuvent être admis au bénéfice de la recommandation, de l'acheminement par voie aérienne ou de l'"urgence".
L'imitation et la contrefaçon de la présente formule exposent les contrevenants aux sanctions prévues par le Code pénal.

Étiquette à coller sur le paquet

FRANCHISE POSTALE
Art. D 75 et D 76
du Code des Postes & Télécommunications

15 **noir *FRANCHISE POSTALE***
(Art. D 75 et D 76) 10 »

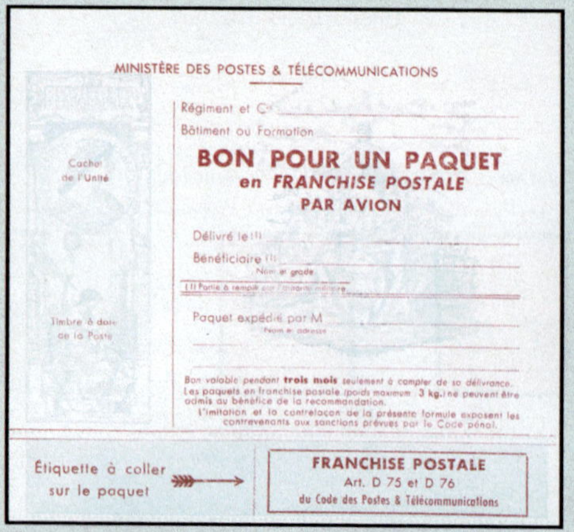
MINISTÈRE DES POSTES & TÉLÉCOMMUNICATIONS

Cachet de l'Unité

Régiment et Cie
Bâtiment ou Formation

BON POUR UN PAQUET
en FRANCHISE POSTALE
PAR AVION

Délivré le (1)
Bénéficiaire (1)
Nom et grade
(1) Partie à remplir par l'autorité militaire.

Timbre à date de la Poste

Paquet expédié par M
Nom et adresse

Bon valable pendant **trois mois** seulement à compter de sa délivrance.
Les paquets en franchise postale (poids maximum : 3 kg.) ne peuvent être admis au bénéfice de la recommandation.
L'imitation et la contrefaçon de la présente formule exposent les contrevenants aux sanctions prévues par le Code pénal.

Étiquette à coller sur le paquet

FRANCHISE POSTALE
Art. D 75 et D 76
du Code des Postes & Télécommunications

16 **rouge sur bleu *FRANCHISE POSTALE***
(Art. D 75 et D 76) 640 »

TIMBRES DE GRÈVE

Dans cette rubrique figurent les timbres de grève postale, c'est-à-dire uniquement les figurines émanant d'organismes auxiliaires de transport de courrier ayant effectivement fonctionné.

Jusqu'en 1953, les cotes de la colonne de gauche concernent les timbres neufs avec gomme d'origine intacte et sans charnière, celles de la colonne centrale les timbres neufs avec charnière légère, celles de la colonne de droite les timbres oblitérés.

1909. – *Emis en lithographie par la Chambre de Commerce d'Amiens, du 13 au 19 mai 1909.. Lithographié. Dentelure défectueuse 11½.*

1	**10 c. vert et outremer**	35 »	20 »	30 »
	a. (10 sans c)	90 »	60 »	80 »
	b. (Tête-bêche)	130 »	90 »	130 »
	c. (Non dentelé)			
	d. vert (sans teinte de fond)		120 »	
	e. (10 sans c)		350 »	
	f. (Tête-bêchesans teinte de fond)		1 000 »	
	La feuille de 25, avec les variétés 6a et 6b		1 100 »	

Documents : Ce timbre de grève a eu cours à Amiens pendant la grève des postiers, du 13 au 19 mai : il était apposé conjointement avec un timbre normal, et oblitéré du cachet postal d'Amiens.

1953. – *Emis par la Chambre de Commerce d'Orléans, du 11 au 25 août. Typographie. Dentelés 11½.*

2	**10 f. rouge-brun sur bleu**	250 »	200 »	200 »
	(Sur lettre)			305 »
3	**10 f. rouge-brique sur jaune**	400 »	305 »	275 »
	(Sur lettre)			385 »

3A **10 f. surchargé + 5** ***rouge-brun sur bleu*** 550 »

Documents : Ces timbres de grève étaient apposés sur les plis conjointement à un timbre poste normal et oblitérés par un cachet de la Chambre émettrice. Certaines lettres à en-tête de cette chambre, ont été confectionnées après coup avec le n°2, et ne méritent donc que la cote de ce timbre détaché.

A partir de 1968 les cotes de la colonne de gauche concernent les timbres neufs, sans charnière, celles de la colonne de droite les timbres oblitérés.

1968. – ***Emis par diverses Chambre de Commerce, lors de la grève postale de mai-juin. Typographie. Dentelure percés en ligne, sauf n° 7 : partiellement dentelé.***

4	**0,20 F noir s. paille** ***Epinal***	120	»	120	»
	(Sur lettre)			220	»
	a. (Fond ocre au lieu de jaune)	400	»	400	»
	(Sur lettre)			600	»
5	**0,50 F noir** ***Libourne***	40	»	40	»
	(Sur lettre)			70	»
	a. (Double impression)	80	»	»	»
	b. (Point à la place de la virgule)	50	»	»	»
	c. (absence de perçage vertical)	45	»	»	»
	d. (double perçage)	70	»	»	»
6	**1 F. rouge** ***Libourne***	40	»	40	»
	(Sur lettre)			70	»
	a. (Double impression)	80	»	»	»
	b. (Point à la place de la virgule)	50	»	»	»
	c. (absence de perçage vertical)	45	»	»	»
	d. (double perçage)	60	»	»	»

7	**0,10 F. bleu** ***Saint-Dié***	70	»	60	»
	(Sur lettre)			120	»
	a. (tête-bêche)	150	»	150	»
	(Sur lettre)			220	»
8	**10 c. noir s. jaune** ***Saint-Dizier***	100	»	100	»
	(Sur lettre)			400	»

Documents : Les timbres de grève n°s 4 à 8 se rencontrent sur les plis transportés par les Chambres concernées, avec les oblitérations de ces organismes, ou éventuellement avec certains cachets postaux.

1968. – ***Emis par la Chambre de Commerce de Tarbes, lors de la grève postale de mai-juin 1968 : Vignettes touristiques surchargées "1968 Taxe d'Acheminement". Dentelés.***

9	**0,50 f. rouge** ***statue du Maréchal Foch***	100	»	100	»
	(Sur lettre)			400	»
10	**1 f. bleu-gris** ***Sainte Bernadette***	100	»	100	»
	(Sur lettre)			400	»

Documents : Ces timbres de grève n°s 9 et 10 se rencontrent apposés sur les plis transportés par la Chambre de commerce émettrice et y sont oblitérés des cachets de cet organisme. Les plis comportant les 2 timbres à la fois sont de complaisance et leur valeur se limite donc à celle de ces 2 figurines détachées.

1971. – ***Timbres-taxe de Grève dits "de l'office Lainé", destinés à payer le transport en France du courrier international de Jersey bloqué par la Grève postale britannique (4 liaisons connues, avec dépôts à 3 bureaux de postes français) : Payables à Paris 28 par les destinataires, après réception des envois. Imprimés au cachet à main. Dentelés percés en ligne.***

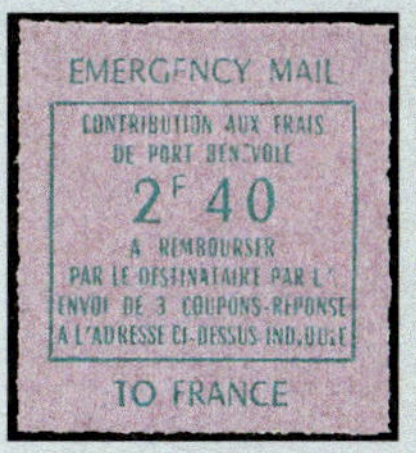

11	**2,40 f. rouge s. jaune**	150	»	100	»
	(Sur lettre)			200	»
	sur lettre avec timbre jersiais			250	»
12	**2,40 f. vert s. violet**	180	»	120	»
	(Sur lettre)			200	»
	sur lettre avec timbre jersiais			250	»
	a. (double impression)	250	»	»	»
	b. vert s. bleu-pâle (Erreur, tirage : 96 ex.)	650	»	450	»

13	**9,60 f. vert s. bleu-pâle**	220	»	200	»
	Sur fragment (de colis)			400	»
	sur fragment, colis, avec cachet retour			350	»
	a. (double impression)	300	»	»	»

Documents : Les timbres n°s 11 et 12 ont servi sur des lettres, accompagnés, suivant les liaisons (cinq), de timbres jersiais ou français oblitérés à Paris de l'un des bureaux postaux français de dépôt. Les n[os]13 et 12b, destinés au colis, doivent être considérés comme sur document, quand ils sont sur fragments d'emballage. avec cachet postal de départ ou de retour.

En fin de la grève, les exemplaires restants des n°s 11 à 13 furent détruits ou surchargés "C. S" aux fins d'annulation : Mêmes cotes.

1974. – ***Timbres de Paris-Orly dits "du Courrier Familial", destinés à acquitter le transport via Jersey ou Bruxelles, du courrier français pour l'étranger bloqué par la Grève (4 liaisons connues) : Vente des timbres et dépôts des envois à Orly, à des dates annoncées par circulaire. Imprimés au cachet à main, par feuilles de 12. non dentelés, sauf n° 17 : 11.***

14	**5 f. violet s. rouge-orangé**	90	»	90	»
	(Sur lettre)			300	»
	(Seul sur lettre)			200	»
	a. (double impression)	200	»	300	»
15	**10 f. s. 5 f. violet s. orange**	120	»	120	»
	(Sur lettre)			300	»
	a. (surcharge omise)	140	»	»	»
16	**10 f. sur 5 f. violet s. jaune**	140	»	130	»
	(Sur lettre)			350	»
	a. (double impression)	250	»	»	»

17	**5 f. noir sur vert**	90 »	90 »
	(Sur lettre)		350 »
	s. lettre obl. Paris-Invalides		220 »
	a. (double impression)	200 »	» »
	(Sur lettre)		400 »
	b. (non dentelé)	120 »	120 »
	(Sur lettre)		250 »
	c. (perforation à cheval)	150 »	» »
	(Sur lettre)		350 »

Documents : Les timbres de grève n°s 14 et 17 ont servi sur lettres, accompagnés, selon les liaisons, de timbres français et jersiais, ou français et belges, oblitérés soit par un cachet de l'Aéroport de Jersey, soit par la flamme belge de dépôt. La grève ayant pris fin au cours de la 5ème liaison, les plis collectés le 30 novembre ont été remis sans délai à la poste de Paris-Invalides (terminal aérien d'Orly) qui les a frappés de ses griffes d'annulation.

Les n°s 15 ou 16 n'ont été employés que sur des entiers-reçus d'envois encombrants, accompagnés de 0F30 en timbres fiscaux et oblitérés du cachet à date du transporteur. Ces entiers-reçus étaient remis aux expéditeurs.

Surcharge "Jersey-Paris" Deux timbres de cette émission, le 5F sur fond rose et le 10F sur 5F sur fond jaune, ont été surchargés " Jersey-Paris" (n°17A et 17B) pour affranchir les réponses éventuelles des destinataires jersiais. Mais ils n'ont pu être émis, de par la carence de la société pressentie pour distribuer ces réponses en France. (Valeur : 100 et 150).

Les figurines au type des n°s 14 à 17B, mais en d'autres couleurs, avec ou sans surcharge, sont des essais..

TIMBRES DE GUERRE

Pour le n° 1 et les n°s 26 à 37 les cotes de la colonne de gauche concernent les timbres neufs avec gomme d'origine intacte et sans charnière, celles de la colonne centrale les timbres neufs avec charnière légère, celles de la colonne de droite les timbres oblitérés.

1914. – ***Dentelé 11½.***

1	**10 c. vermillon**	900 »	500 »	480 »
	(Sur lettre)			650 »

Émis le 3 septembre 1914 par la Chambre de Commerce de Valenciennes pendant l'occupation allemande. A été en cours jusqu'au 30 octobre.

a. (Non dentelé) 1 600 »

1940. – ***Timbres de France de 1932-38 aux types Mercure et Paix (n°s 3 et 6) surchargés à la main. Dentelés.***

Dunkerque (paires).

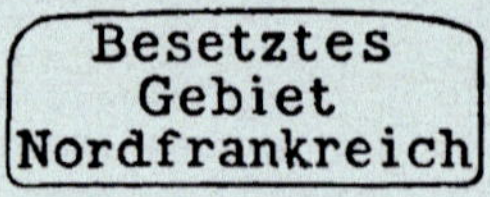

2	**40 c. violet (413)**	2 800 »	3 200 »
3	**50 c. rose-rouge (283)**	150 »	140 »
4	**50 c. bleu (414A)**	150 »	140 »

Coudekerque (paires).

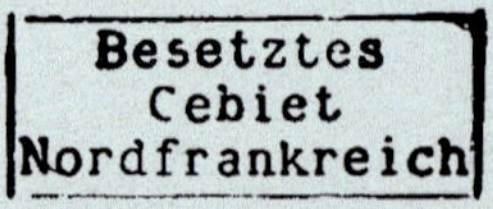

5	**40 c. violet (413)**	620 »	850 »
6	**50 c. rose-rouge (283)**	1 200 »	1 250 »
7	**50 c. bleu (414A)**	260 »	255 »

Les prix des timbres oblitérés s'appliquent à des paires sur lettres.

En dehors des timbres n°s 2 à 7, qui ont été vendus aux guichets de la poste en paires neuves surchargées, il existe, tant pour Dunkerque que pour Coudekerque, diverses autres valeurs dans les types *Semeuse, Paix, Cérès, Mercure et Iris,* ainsi que certains timbres de grand format (n°s 392 à 394, 419,

421, 428, 436 à 441, 446, 451 à 457). Des enveloppes et des cartes, jetées dans des boîtes postales et affranchies au moyen de ces timbres et dont la valeur totale ne dépassait pas 1 franc pour les lettres et 80 c. pour les cartes ont été en effet régulièrement acheminées par la poste après avoir été munies de la surcharge qui, dans ce cas, doit être à cheval sur le ou les timbres et l'enveloppe ou la carte. Les différentes valeurs ainsi utilisées pour l'affranchissement normal d'une lettre ou d'une carte peuvent être considérées comme régulières, à la condition toutefois d'être sur les enveloppes ou cartes originales et de porter les cachets à date du départ et de l'arrivée.

Les autres valeurs que l'on peut rencontrer revêtues de l'un des deux cachets, et qui constituent un affranchissement supérieur à 1 f., doivent être considérées comme ayant été surchargées par complaisance.

1945. – *Lithographié. sans gomme. Dentelés 11½.*

8	**50 c. vert foncé s. vert pâle**	185 »	210 »
	Non dentelé	1 000 »	
	Sur lettre		225 »
	a. (Tête-bêche)	700 »	
	b. (Surchargé libération en noir)	200 »	220 »
9	**2 f. brun-lilas s. vert pâle**	185 »	210 »
	Non dentelé	1 000 »	
	Sur lettre		225 »
	a. (Tête-bêche)	700 »	
	b. (Surchargé libération en noir)	200 »	220 »

Ces timbres furent émis par la Chambre de Commerce de Saint-Nazaire pour pallier la pénurie de timbres-poste dans les bureaux de la "poche" allemande de Saint-Nazaire.

Le sujet du timbre représente les armes de la ville de Saint-Nazaire : une galère avec rameurs, voile déployée brodée d'une clef. Tirage : 30000 pour le 50 c. (dont 19000 vendus) et 20000 pour le 2 f. (dont 16000 vendus). Du 9 au 15 mai ces timbres reçurent une surcharge manuelle "Libération" (même valeur).

Interdits sur le reste du territoire à partir du 1.11.1944, les timbres au type Pétain continuèrent à affranchir le courrier de la "poche" jusqu'au 8.5.1945 (valeur 300 »). De février-mars à mai 1945, les bureaux de La Turballe, Batz-sur-Mer, Guérande et Piriac sur Mer, dépourvus de timbres ont apposé une griffe "taxe perçue" sur les plis non affranchis (valeur : 400 »). A partir du 8.1.1945 le bureau de La Baule a apposé l'empreinte de machine à affranchir rouge C0443 des Chantiers navals de Penhöet - Saint-Nazaire sur le courrier.

Il n'y a pas de n°s 10 à 25, pour conserver à la série suivante la même numérotation qu'en Belgique. En effet cette série servait aux Postes d'étapes, tant dans la partie envahie du Nord de la France qu'en Belgique (voir Tome III).

1916-17. – *Timbres d'Allemagne de 1905-16 surchargés. Dent.*

26	**3 c. sur 3 p. brun**	2 30	0 80	0 80
27	**5 c. sur 5 p. vert**	2 30	0 80	0 80
28	**8 c. sur 7½ p. orange**	3 85	1 40	1 40
29	**10 c. sur 10 p. rouge**	2 30	0 80	0 80
30	**15 c. sur 15 p. bistre**	3 05	1 »	1 »
31	**25 c. sur 20 p. bleu-violet**	3 05	1 »	1 »
	a. outremer	6 10	1 85	1 85
32	**40 c. sur 30 p. rouge et noir sur chamois**	6 50	2 20	2 20
33	**50 c. sur 40 p. carmin et noir**	7 65	3 »	3 »
34	**75 c. sur 60 p. lilas**	39 50	11 50	11 50
35	**1 F. sur 80 p. rouge et noir sur rose**	39 50	11 50	11 50
36	**1 F. 25 cent. sur 1 m. carmin**	170 »	52 »	52 »
37	**2 F. 50 cent. sur 2 m. bleu**	170 »	54 »	54 »
	N°s 26 à 37 (12 val.)	**450 »**	**140 »**	**140 »**

POSTES MONTÉNÉGRINES EN EXIL À BORDEAUX

(Émissions privées)

L'inscription S.P. du M. est l'abréviation des mots "Service Postal du Monténégro". - Les timbres ci-dessous ont été ainsi surchargés par le gouvernement monténégrin durant son séjour à Bordeaux. Ils ont affranchi pendant trois semaines un nombre restreint de correspondances simples ou recommandées.

1916. – *Timbres de France de 1900-06 surchargés. Dentelés.*

1	**5 c. (137)**
2	**10 c. (138)**
3	**15 c. (130)**
4	**20 c. (139)**
5	**25 c. (140)**
6	**30 c. (141)**
7	**35 c. (142)**
8	**40 c. (119)**
9	**45 c. (143)**
10	**50 c. (120)**
11	**1 f. (121)**

Existent tous avec surcharge renversée et les n°s 8, 9 et 11 avec surcharge verticale.

TIMBRES DE RETOUR

1916. – *Dentelés.*

1	**noir sur bleu**	10 »

Idem Légende : Le destinataire n'a pu être atteint.

2	**noir sur rouge**	10 »

3	**bleu sur blanc**	40 »

Le cliché du n° 3 est réduit de moitié.

POSTES SERBES À CORFOU

1917. – *Timbres de France de 1900-06 revêtus de la griffe postale apposée pour donner l'origine des plis en langue française. Dentelés.*

1	**1 c. gris (107)**
2	**2 c. brun-lilas (108)**
3	**3 c. orange (109)**
4	**5 c. vert foncé (137)**
5	**10 c. rouge (138)**
6	**15 c. vert-olive (130)**

7	**20 c. lilas-brun (139)**			
8	**25 c. bleu (140)**			
9	**30 c. orange (141)**			
10	**35 c. violet (142)**			
11	**40 c. rouge et bleu (119)**			
12	**45 c. vert et bleu (143)**			
13	**50 c. brun et gris (120)**			
14	**1 f. lie-de-vin et olive (121)**			

Cette marque a été utilisée par les employés du bureau serbe à Corfou, pour pallier l'absence momentanée de timbres de Serbie.

Trois timbres de Grèce (5, 10 et 20 l.) ont été employés dans les mêmes conditions.

BASE NAVALE ITALIENNE DE BORDEAUX

Jusqu'en 1953, les cotes de la colonne de gauche concernent les timbres neufs avec gomme d'origine intacte et sans charnière, celles de la colonne centrale les timbres neufs avec charnière légère, celles de la colonne de droite les timbres oblitérés.

1943-44. – *Timbres d'Italie de 1929-30 surchargés. Dentelés.*

1	**10 c. sépia (226)**	12 50	8 50	12 50
2	**15 c. vert-gris (227)**	17 000 »	11 500 »	11 500 »
3	**20 c. rose-rouge *Jules César* (228)**	47 50	35 »	47 50
4	**25 c. vert *Victor-Emmanuel III de profil* (229)**	140 »	77 »	115 »
5	**30 c. sépia *Victor-Emmanuel III de face* (230)**	17 »	9 15	17 »
6	**50 c. violet *Victor-Emmanuel III de face* (232)**	50 »	30 50	50 »

Sans T à FASCISTA.

1a	10 c.		77 »	110 »
3a	20 c.		385 »	535 »
4a	25 c.		460 »	690 »
5a	30 c.		385 »	535 »
6a	50 c.		535 »	690 »

Tenant à non surchargé.

1b	10 c. +10 c.		230 »	305 »
3b	20 c. +20 c.		535 »	690 »
4b	25 c. +25 c.		535 »	690 »
5b	30 c. +30 c.		535 »	690 »
6b	50 c. +50 c.		535 »	690 »

7	**5 c. sépia *la louve allaitant Romulus et Remus* (224)**	9 250 »	5 750 »	6 100 »
8	**10 c. sépia *Auguste* (226)**	305 »	255 »	270 »
9	**15 c. vert-gris *"Italia"* (227)**	1 400 »	1 100 »	1 400 »
10	**25 c. vert *Victor-Emmanuel III de profil* (229)**	25 »	15 25	25 »
11	**30 c. sépia *Victor-Emmanuel III de face* (230)**	35 »	23 »	31 »
12	**50 c. violet *Victor-Emmanuel III de face* (232)**	20 »	11 50	17 »
	a. (Impression recto verso)		270 »	

Existent sans le second b à Répubblica.

Ces émissions ont été faites à Bordeaux pour les équipages des sous-marins stationnés dans cette ville.

TIMBRES POUR JOURNAUX

1868. – *Typographie. Non dentelés.*

Le 2 c. lilas acquittait une taxe purement fiscale ; les timbres bleus de 2 c. étaient vendus 4 c., dont 2 pour la poste et 2 pour le fisc ; les timbres roses de 2 c. étaient vendus 6 c., dont 4 pour la poste et 2 pour le fisc. - Il existe des essais sur fond moiré. - Les n°s 3 à 6 sont généralement sans gomme.

1	**2 c. lilas**	**350 »**	**85 »**
2	**2 c. bleu**	**700 »**	**350 »**
3	**2 c. rose carminé**	**1 550 »**	
4	**5 c. *lilas***	**21 500 »**	
5	**5 c. *bleu***	**10 000 »**	
6	**5 c. *rose carminé***	**10 000 »**	

Les réimpressions, dentelées ou non dentelées, faites à l'occasion de l'exposition du Gand (1913), ont été tirées sur les papiers les plus divers au moyen du coin original. Il y a une très grande variété de teintes. Quelques exemplaires portent la surcharge ÉPREUVE.

Une nouvelle réimpression des n°s 1 à 6 a été faite à l'occasion de l'exposition de Paris (PEXIP, 1937) tirée avec soin sur papier blanc, timbre par timbre, celle-ci se rapproche beaucoup plus des originaux.

1869. – *Même type. Typographie. Dentelés 11½-12½.*

7	**2 c. violet**	**60 »**	**25 »**
8	**2 c. bleu**	**90 »**	**40 »**
9	**2 c. rose**	**300 »**	**115 »**
10	**5 c. lilas**	**1 500 »**	**725 »**
11	**5 c. *bleu***	**2 750 »**	
12	**5 c. *rose***	**2 750 »**	

Les n°s 10, 11 et 12 sont sur papier teinté.

LEGION DES VOLONTAIRES FRANCAIS CONTRE LE BOLCHEVISME (L.V.F.)

Après l'invasion de l'U.R.S.S. par l'armée allemande le 22 juin 1941, la L.V.F. fut créée le 7 juillet, à l'instigation des mouvements collaborateurs. La L.V.F. procéda à plusieurs émissions de timbres de bienfaisance qui, bien que vendus exclusivement à Paris, peuvent se rencontrer sur des lettres de soldats du Front de l'Est (valeur : à partir de 150 »).

Jusqu'en 1953, les cotes de la colonne de gauche concernent les timbres neufs avec gomme d'origine intacte et sans charnière, celles de la colonne centrale les timbres neufs avec charnière légère, celles de la colonne de droite les timbres oblitérés.

1941. – *Bloc-feuillet de l'Ours. Taille-douce. Dentelé 12½.*

1	**F+100F bleu et rouge**	575 »	325 »	600 »
	a. (Non dentelé)	1 250 »	750 »	

1941. – *Timbres pour le courrier. Taille-douce. Dent. 12 x 12½.*

2	**F vert foncé et rouge**	17 50	10 »	50 »

3	**F+10F carmin et bleu**	17 50	10 »	50 »

Tirage : 450.000 paires dont 141.000 vendues par souscription du 10 au 20 novembre 1941 puis au public du 12 au 15 décembre.

1942. – *Timbres précédents surchargés "Front de l'Est - Ostfront". Dentelés.*

4	**F vert foncé et rouge**	22 50	12 »	60 »

5	**F+10F carmin et bleu**	22 50	12 »	60 »

Tirage : 300.000 paires dont 137.000 vendus par souscription le 15 janvier 1942 puis au public du 20 janvier au 7 février.

1942. – *Série "Borodino". Héliogravure. Dentelés 13.*

Guetteur devant un village russe.

Artillerie.

6	**F+1F violet et rouge**	5 »	2 »	12 »
7	**F+1F vert et noir**	5 »	2 »	12 »

Char d'assaut.

Soldats de la L.V.F. et grenadiers du 1er empire.

8	**F+1F sépia et bleu**	5 »	2 »	12 »
9	**F+1F outremer et rouge**	5 »	2 »	12 »

Cavalerie.

10	**F+1F carmin et vert**	5 »	2 »	12 »
	Nos 6 à 10 (5 val.)	**25 »**	**10 »**	**60 »**
	La série avec vignette	30 »	12 50	

Tirage : 1.000.000 séries dont 450.000 vendues par souscription close le 20 avril 1942 et au public à partir du 30 avril.

La L.V.F. envisagea ensuite l'émission d'une série de timbres sur les rapprochements Franco-Allemands depuis Charlemagne mais le projet n'eut pas de suite.

TIMBRES DE LA LIBÉRATION

Nous décrivons, sous cette rubrique, les seules émissions authentifiées par le ministère des Postes après la libération du territoire. Certaines de ces émissions (Bordeaux, Lille, Lyon) ont eu cours dans une région. Les autres ont eu un emploi plus restreint, à l'échelon départemental, voire local. Pour tous ces timbres, le prix est le même à l'état neuf ou oblitéré, mais les exemplaires sur lettre bénéficient d'une plus-value parfois importante.

D'autres surcharges ont été faites à la même époque dans un certain nombre de localités plus ou moins importantes, dont nous donnons la liste en fin de rubrique ; elle n'est pas limitative.

L'ordonnance N° 45-2458 du 19 octobre 1945 parue dans le Journal officiel de la République Française ordonne l'arrêt des surcharges sur Timbres-Poste et la validité d'affranchissement.
Précise, dans son article 2, que cet arrêté du gouvernement signé par le Général de Gaulle, le garde des Sceaux, les Ministres des Postes et des Colonies, n'est pas applicable aux Timbres-Poste surchargés antérieurement. Ce qui constitue une reconnaissance de fait de toutes les surcharges de la Libération.

Aveyron (DECAZEVILLE).

1944. - ***Timbres de 1941-42 surchargés en bleu.***

I II

		I	II
1	**10 c. outremer *(Mercure)***	400 »	400 »

Maréchal Pétain.

		I	II
2	**60 c. violet**	190 »	190 »
3	**70 c. rouge-orange**	180 »	180 »
4	**1 f. rouge**	130 »	130 »
5	**1 f. 20, brun-rouge**	190 »	190 »
6	**1 f. 50, brun-rouge**	110 »	110 »
7	**2 f. vert**	200 »	200 »
8	**3 f. rouge-orange**	200 »	200 »
9	**4 f. bleu-violet**	200 »	200 »
10	**4 f. 50, vert**	200 »	200 »
	Nos 1 à 10 (10 val.)	**2 000 »**	**2 000 »**

Il existe un 40 c. violet (Mercure) et 80 c. vert (Pétain) non émis.
Il existe un type III.

Charente-Maritime (PONS).

1944. - ***Timbres de 1941-42 (Maréchal Pétain) surchargés.***

I II

		I	II
1	**60 c. violet**	15 »	20 »
2	**70 c. rouge-orange**	15 »	20 »
3	**80 c. vert-jaune**	20 »	25 »
4	**1 f. rouge**	10 »	15 »
5	**1 f. 20, brun-rouge**	15 »	20 »
6	**1 f. 50, brun-rouge**	10 »	15 »
7	**2 f. vert**	15 »	20 »
8	**2 f. 40, rouge**	60 »	200 »
9	**3 f. rouge-orange**	15 »	25 »
10	**4 f. bleu-violet**	20 »	25 »
11	**4 f. 50, vert**	20 »	25 »
12	**4 f. 50, vert *(gravé)***	85 »	300 »
	Nos 1 à 12 (12 val.)	**300 »**	**700 »**

Creuse (MEASNES).

1944. - ***Timbres de 1941-42 (Maréchal Pétain) surchargés.***

1	**1 f. rouge**	50 »
2	**1 f. 50, brun-rouge**	50 »
3	**2 f. vert**	50 »
4	**3 f. rouge-orange**	50 »
5	**4 f. bleu**	50 »
6	**4 f. 50, vert-jaune**	150 »
	Nos 1 à 6 (6 val.)	**400 »**

Deux-Sèvres (NIORT).

1944. - ***Timbres de 1941-42 (Maréchal Pétain) surchargés en rouge.***

I II

		I	II
1	**60 c. violet**	20 »	20 »
2	**70 c. rouge-orange**	20 »	20 »
3	**80 c. vert-jaune**	20 »	20 »
4	**1 f. rouge**	20 »	20 »
5	**1 f. 20, brun-rouge**	20 »	20 »
6	**1 f. 50, brun-rouge**	20 »	20 »
7	**2 f. vert**	20 »	20 »
8	**2 f. 40, rouge**	100 »	100 »
9	**3 f. rouge-orange**	30 »	30 »
10	**4 f. bleu-violet**	20 »	20 »
11	**4 f. 50, vert**	40 »	40 »
	Nos 1 à 11 (11 val.)	**330 »**	**330 »**
12	**4 f. 50, vert *(gravé)***	900 »	900 »
13	**5 f. vert-bleu**	1 100 »	1 100 »
14	**1 f. 50 + 3 f. 50, brun (n° 606)**	3 200 »	4 000 »

Gironde (BORDEAUX).

1944. - ***Timbres de 1941-42 (Maréchal Pétain) surchargés.***

R. F.   **R. F.**   **R. F.**

I II III

		I	II	III
1	**60 c. violet**	70 »	95 »	180 »
2	**70 c. rouge-orange**	4 »	5 »	6 »
3	**80 c. vert**	8 »	12 »	16 »
4	**1 f. rouge**	3 »	4 »	5 »
	a. (Dble surch.)	100 »	125 »	170 »
	b. (Surch. renv.)	100 »	140 »	200 »
5	**1 f. 20, brun-rouge**	3 »	4 »	5 »
6	**1 f. 50, brun-rouge**	2 »	3 »	4 »
	a. (Dble surch.)	110 »	140 »	200 »
	b. (Surch. renv.)	110 »	140 »	200 »
7	**2 f. vert**	3 »	4 »	5 »
8	**2 f. 40, rouge**	8 »	11 »	13 »
9	**3 f. rouge-orange**	3 »	4 »	5 »
10	**4 f. bleu-violet**	3 »	4 »	6 »
	a. (Surch. renv.)	100 »	140 »	170 »
11	**4 f. 50, vert**	3 »	4 »	5 »
N°s 1 à 11 (11 val.)		**110 »**	**150 »**	**250 »**

Timbres-taxe de 1943 avec les mêmes surcharges.

		I	II	III
12	**30 c. lilas-rose**	90 »	135 »	270 »
13	**50 c. vert**	8 »	10 »	15 »
14	**1 f. outremer**	8 »	10 »	15 »
15	**1 f. 50, rouge**	8 »	10 »	15 »
16	**2 f. bleu-vert**	12 »	18 »	25 »
	a. (Dble surch.)	140 »	200 »	255 »
17	**3 f. rouge-brun**	9 »	12 »	25 »
18	**5 f. rose-lilas**	15 »	25 »	35 »
N°s 12 à 18 (7 val.)		**150 »**	**220 »**	**400 »**

La série complète (poste et taxe),
54 valeurs : 1 280 »

La feuille de 100 timbres contenait 50 surcharges au type I, 30 au type II et 20 au type III.

Indre (AIGURANDE).

1944. - *Timbres de 1941-42 (Maréchal Pétain) surchargés.*

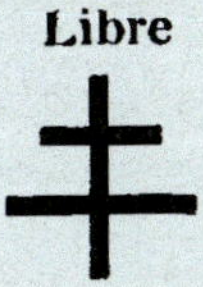

1	**60 c. violet**	20 »
2	**70 c. rouge-orange**	25 »
3	**80 c. vert-jaune**	25 »
4	**1 f. rouge**	20 »
5	**1 f. 20, brun-rouge**	50 »
6	**1 f. 50, brun-rouge**	40 »
7	**2 f. vert**	20 »
8	**2 f. 40, rouge**	80 »
9	**3 f. rouge-orange**	40 »
10	**4 f. bleu-violet**	65 »
11	**4 f. 50, vert**	65 »
N°s 1 à 11 (11 val.)		**450 »**

Indre-et-Loire (TOURS-GARE).

1944. - *Timbres de 1941-42 (Maréchal Pétain) surchargés.*

1	**70 c. rouge-orange**	38 »
2	**1 f. rouge**	38 »
3	**1 f. 20, brun-rouge**	38 »
4	**1 f. 50, brun-rouge**	38 »
5	**2 f. vert**	38 »
6	**4 f. outremer *(gravé)***	550 »
7	**4 f. 50, vert *(gravé)***	170 »
8	**5 f. vert-bleu**	185 »
N°s 1 à 8 (8 val.)		**1 100 »**

Il existe d'autres valeurs et d'autres surcharges de Tours (Tours-Mairie - Tours-Halles - Tours gare transit - Tours Ravenel).

(LOCHES).

1944. - *Timbre de 1941-42 surchargé.*

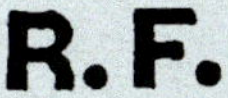

1	**40 c. violet *(Mercure n° 548)***	100 »
2	**1 f. 50, brun-rouge *(Pétain n° 517)***	200 »

D'autres valeurs en surcharge de Loches existent.

Loir et Cher (BLOIS) *et Loiret* (ORLÉANS).

Surcharge d'une carte postale valeur 375.

Voir rubrique des Entiers Postaux (n° 389).

Manche (CHERBOURG).

1944. - *Timbres de 1941-42 (Maréchal Pétain) surchargés.*

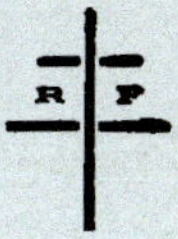

1	**60 c. violet**	15 »
2	**70 c. rouge-orange**	15 »
3	**80 c. vert-jaune**	15 »
4	**1 f. rouge**	15 »
5	**1 f. 20, brun-rouge**	25 »
6	**1 f. 50, brun-rouge**	25 »
7	**2 f. vert**	20 »
8	**2 f. 40, rouge**	25 »
9	**3 f. rouge-orange**	15 »
10	**4 f. bleu-violet**	15 »
11	**4 f. outremer *(gravé)***	115 »
12	**4 f. 50, vert**	15 »
13	**4 f. 50, vert *(gravé)***	115 »
14	**5 f. vert-bleu**	100 »
15	**50 f. noir**	720 »
N°s 1 à 15 (15 val.)		**1 250 »**

Marne (CHALONS, REIMS).

1944. - *Timbre de 1941-42 surchargé.*

R.F.

1	**1 f. 50, brun-rouge (517)**	35 »

Nord (LILLE).

1944. - *Timbre de 1941-42 surchargé.*

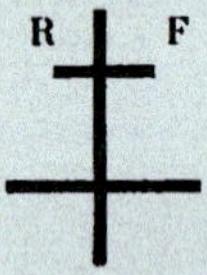

1	**1 f. 50, brun-rouge (517)**	3 »
	a. (Surch. renv.)	45 »
	b. Petite cassure	5 »
	c. Grande cassure	20 »
	d. Sa,ns F (case 50)	25 »
	e. R et F rapprochés	15 »

Il exite d'autres valeurs LILLE mais non émises.

Rhône-Alpes (LYON).

1944. - *Timbres de 1941-42 surchargés.*

R. F.

Mercure.

1	**10 c. outremer**	0 80
2	**30 c. rouge**	0 80
3	**40 c. violet**	0 80
4	**50 c. turquoise**	0 70

Maréchal Pétain.

5	**60 c. violet**	1 25
6	**70 c. rouge-orange**	1 75
7	**80 c. vert-jaune**	1 75
8	**1 f. rouge**	0 80
9	**1 f. 20, brun-rouge**	0 80
10	**1 f. 50, brun-rouge**	0 80
11	**2 f. vert**	1 »
12	**2 f. 40, rouge**	14 50
13	**3 f. rouge-orange**	1 25
14	**4 f. bleu-violet**	1 25
15	**4 f. 50, vert**	1 75

N°s 1 à 15 (15 val.) **30 »**

Ces timbres ont été utilisés simultanément et pendant deux mois dans huit départements de la région Rhône-Alpes : Rhône, Ain, Isère, Loire, Savoie, Haute-Savoie, Drôme, Ardèche.

On note l'exitence de 3 timbres BLASONS (N°s 603 à 60) LYON vendus un seul jour et retirés de la vente. (Valeur 800).

Savoie (CHAMBÉRY).

1944. - *Timbres de 1941-44 surchargés.*

F. F. I.
SAVOIE
+ 1F50

Timbres de 1941-42.

1	**+ 1 f.50 s. 1 f. 50, brun-rouge (517)**	20 »
2	**+ 10 f. s. 5 f. vert-bleu (524)**	20 »

Timbres de 1944.

3	**+ 15 f. s. 10 f. (603)**	20 »
4	**+ 20 f. s. 15 f. (604)**	20 »
5	**+ 25 f. s. 20 f. (605)**	25 »

F. F. I.
SAVOIE
25-8-1944
+ 20F

Timbres de 1944 (Célébrités du XVIIe siècle).

6	**+ 6 f. s. 50 c. + 1 f. 50**	150 »
7	**+ 6 f. s. 80 c. + 2 f. 20**	150 »
8	**+ 6 f. s. 1 f. 20 + 2 f. 80, noir**	150 »
9	**+ 6 f. s. 1 f. 50 + 3 f. 50, outremer**	150 »
10	**+ 6 f. s. 2 f. + 4 f. bruit-rouge**	150 »
11	**+ 6 f. s. 4 f. + 6 f. rouge-orange**	150 »

Timbre de 1944 (Centenaire des chemins de fer).

12	**+ 20 f. s. 4 f. + 6 f. noir**	150 »

+ 6F
F. F. I.
SAVOIE

Timbre de 1944 (Claude Chappe).

13	**+ 6 f. s. 4 f. bleu**	765 »

F F I. SAVOIE
25 Août 1944
+ 30F

Timbre de 1943 (Paysage du Dauphiné).

14	**+ 30 f. s. 20 f. vert foncé**	80 »

N°s 1 à 14 (14 val.) **2 000 »**

Vienne (CHATELLERAULT).

1944. - *Timbres de 1941-42 (Maréchal Pétain) surchargés.*

1	**60 c. violet (R)**	50 »
	a. (Surcharge rouge)	92 »
2	**70 c. rouge-orange**	20 »
3	**80 c. vert-jaune**	20 »
4	**1 f. rouge**	20 »
5	**1 f. 20, brun-rouge**	20 »
6	**1 f. 50, brun-rouge**	20 »
7	**2 f. vert**	30 »
8	**2 f. 40, rouge**	100 »
9	**3 f. rouge-orange**	20 »
10	**4 f. bleu-violet**	20 »
	a. (Surcharge rouge)	77 »
11	**4 f. outremer *(gravé)***	170 »
12	**4 f. 50, vert**	20 »
13	**4 f. 50, vert *(gravé)***	170 »
14	**5 f. vert-bleu**	220 »
15	**50 f. noir**	900 »
	Nos 1 à 15 (15 val.)	**1 800 »**

*Vienne (*POITIERS).

1944. - *Timbres de 1941-42 (Maréchal Pétain) surchargés.*

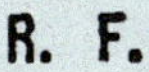

I

16	**1 f. 50, brun-rouge**	36 »

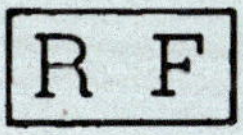

II

III

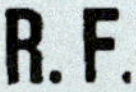

IV

		II	III	IV
17	**60 c. violet**	40 »	110 »	8 »
18	**70 c. rouge-orange**	50 »	160 »	12 »
19	**80 c. vert-jaune**	80 »	130 »	10 »
20	**1 f. rouge**	30 »	100 »	7 »
21	**1 f. 20, brun-rouge**	25 »	100 »	7 »
22	**1 f. 50, brun-rouge**	20 »	400 »	7 »
23	**2 f. vert**	30 »	2 300 »	10 »
24	**2 f. 40, rouge**	30 »	2 100 »	15 »
25	**3 f. rouge-orange**	55 »	150 »	7 »
26	**4 f. bleu-violet**	80 »	200 »	7 »
27	**4 f. 50, vert**	80 »	3 250 »	8 »
	Nos 17 à 27 (11 val.)	**520 »**	**9 000 »**	**100 »**
28	**50 f. noir**	1 150 »	2 550 »	1 700 »

Surchargé avec la planche des petits formats, le n° 28, type IV, porte des doubles ou parties de doubles surcharges. On ne connaît que quelques exemplaires portant une seule surcharge. (Valeur 16500).

AUTRES SURCHARGES LOCALES

Annecy (1 val.)	54 »
Annemasse (Poste 11 val., type I ou II (Type I)	610 »
et taxe 8 val., type I ou II) : (Type II)	1 550 »
Baccarat (10 val., type I ou II)	275 »
Badonviller (11 val.)	275 »
Bellegarde (6 val.)	305 »
Bourg d'Oisans (3 val.) sur cartes	460 »
Chouzé-sur-Loire (12 val.)	385 »
Cinq-Mars-la-Pile (16 val.)	1 850 »
Collonges (20 val.)	1 100 »
Curzay (16 val.)	8 800 »
Lignères (12 val.)	275 »
Montreuil-Bellay (14 val.)	185 »
Sainte-Foy-la-Grande (1 val.)	140 »
Thorens (4 val.)	305 »

Saverne.

Nos 1 à 20, 1 p. à 1 m. (type I) effigie d'Hitler	805 »
Nos 1a à 20a, 1 p. à 1 m. (type II)	
effigie d'Hitler	1 200 »
Les 2 séries se tenant	2 150 »

Haguenau.

Effigie d'Hitler surchargée (6 val.)	500 »

Région parisienne.

Pendant l'interruption du service postal, entre le 19 et le 26 août 1944, les services F.F.I. de la région parisienne ont utilisé pour leur service personnel intérieur des enveloppes sur lesquelles étaient apposés un timbre de 1 f. 50 (Maréchal Pétain) surchargé d'une croix de Lorraine et une vignette bleue à l'effigie du Général de Gaulle.

L'enveloppe (griffe FFI du 19 au 25 Août)	25 »
L'enveloppe du 26 Août griffe PARIS LIBRE	30 »

Pour plus de renseignements sur les autres émissions locales et les cotations des timbres à l'unité voir catalogue spécialisé LIBERATION.

MILLESIMES

A partir d'octobre 1891, les 3 panneaux de 50 timbres constituants la feuille de vente de 150, ont reçu chacun sur leur 2e rangée, un chiffre correspondant au millésime de l'année de fabrication (1 pour 1901, 5 pour 1915 etc…). C'est ce chiffre encadré de 2 timbres que nous côtons. (Il y en a 3 par feuille).

Seul 1 bloc de quatre surmonté d'un haut de feuille ou d'un interpanneau prouve l'absence sur la 2e rangée de ce millésime. C'est ce bloc de 4 sans chiffre que nous cataloguons. (Il peut en exister 3 par feuille).

Durant la guerre, un papier GC, dit de grande consommation, fut utilisé. Il peut être blanc, gris, chamois, jaunâtre etc… Sur la feuille de 150 timbres l'inscription GC (dans la couleur du timbre) était apposée au centre et en haut de feuille. C'est ce bloc de 4 avec "manchette" GC qui est catalogué. (Il en existe 1 par feuille).

Les feuilles émises pour la confection des roulettes ont une disposition différente. Elles sont aussi de 150 timbres, mais d'un seul tenant sans interpanneaux. Pour les différencier avec certitude, il suffit d'un bloc de 6 avec le Millésime surmonté de 2 rangées blanches ou bien d'un bloc de 12 montrant 6 timbres verticaux se tenant (par opposition aux 5 timbres verticaux maximum des feuilles normales).

Les côtes indiquées ci-dessous s'entendent pour des millésimes encadrés de 2 timbres neufs avec charnières légères. Un timbre, voire les deux, pouvant avoir une gomme d'origine intacte sans charnière, on ajoutera dans ce cas aux côtes ci-dessous la différence entre les côtes respectives des deux qualités et ceci pour chaque timbre concerné. Pour cette qualité (sans charnière) ont peut néanmoins admettre une trace sur le pont interpanneau.

Les Millésimes suivis d'un (*) correspondent à une impression sur papier GC.

Millésime sur la 2e rangée

Sans millésime sur la 2e rangée

Millésime roulette avec 2 rangées au dessus

Millésime 6 (1916) - N° 137
Bloc de 4 avec manchette GC

Millésime 8 (1918) - N° 140
Bloc de 4 avec manchette GC

Millésime 8 (1918) - N° 142
Bloc de 4 avec manchette GC

TYPE SAGE

N^{os}	Sans Mill.	**1** (1891)	**2** (1892)	**3** (1893)	**4** (1894)	**5** (1895)	**6** (1896)	**7** (1897)	**8** (1898)	**9** (1899)	**0** (1900)
75 (5 c. vert)	220 »	380 »	185 »	200 »	180 »	130 »	120 »	100 »	90 »		
80 (30 c. brun-jaune)	550 »	800 »	500 »	400 »	380 »	350 »	330 »	330 »	320 »	320 »	300 »
82 (1 f. olive clair)	950 »	1500 »	875 »	825 »	550 »	550 »	525 »	500 »	475 »	450 »	450 »
83 (1 c. noir s. azuré)	110 »	200 »	100 »	80 »	40 »	35 »	25 »	22 »	20 »	20 »	20 »
85 (2 c. brun-rouge)	110 »	130 »	85 »	50 »	50 »	45 »	40 »	35 »	30 »	30 »	25 »
87 (3 c. gris)	90 »	130 »	45 »	35 »	40 »	40 »	30 »	22 »	22 »	20 »	20 »
88 (4 c. lilas-brun)	110 »	150 »	55 »	45 »	45 »	40 »	35 »	40 »	25 »	30 »	25 »
89 (10 c. noir s. lilas)	250 »	400 »	250 »	250 »	180 »	170 »	150 »	130 »	120 »	120 »	
94 (40 c. rouge-orange)	800 »	1200 »	650 »	600 »	500 »	500 »	400 »	370 »	340 »	340 »	340 »
95 (5 f. violet s. lilas)	3400 »	3800 »	1700 »		1800 »				1700 »	1600 »	
95 (Non encadré)		1000 »	800 »		850 »				750 »	700 »	

Le n° 83 (1 c. noir) existe avec le chiffre 8 renversé (valeur : 50 »)

N^{os}	Sans Mill.	**1** (1891)	**2** (1892)	**3** (1893)	**4** (1894)	**5** (1895)	**6** (1896)	**7** (1897)	**8** (1898)	**9** (1899)	**0** (1900)
96 (20 c. brique s. vert)	300 »	450 »	250 »	250 »	230 »	200 »	180 »	150 »	150 »	140 »	140 »
97 (25 c. noir s. rose)	550 »	700 »	350 »	375 »	350 »	350 »	300 »	280 »	280 »	270 »	270 »
98 (50 c. rose)	1300 »	1650 »	1000 »	1500 »	770 »	800 »	700 »	650 »	675 »	650 »	
99 (75 c. violet s. orange)	1750 »	1650 »	700 »	700 »	700 »	650 »	900 »				
101 (15 c. bleu)	320 »	45 »	40 »	240 »	160 »	240 »	55 »	50 »	45 »	50 »	45 »
102 (5 c. vert-jaune III)									100 »	65 »	60 »
103 (10 c. noir s. lilas)									90 »	100 »	80 »
104 (50 c. rose)											700 »
105 (2 f. bistre s. azuré)											400 »
106 (5 c. vert-jaune II)									75 »	70 »	

Le n° 106 (5 c. vert-jaune II) existe avec chiffre 8 renversé (valeur : 150 »)

TYPE BLANC

Nos	Sans Mill.	0 (1900)	1 (1901)	2 (1902)	3 (1903)	4 (1904)	5 (1905)	6 (1906)	7 (1907)	8 (1908)
107 (1 c. gris IA)		10 »	12 »							
107 (1 c. gris IB)	230 »		7 »	6 »	6 »	17 »	15 »	13 »	15 »	
108 (2 c. brun-lilas IA)		12 »	8 »	7 »						
108 (2 c. brun-lilas IB)	300 »				7 »	7 »	7 »	9 »	18 »	7 »
109 (3 c. orange IA)	340 »	9 »						110 »	110 »	25 »
109 (3 c. orange IB)									150 »	25 »
110 (4 c. brun-jaune)	370 »	27 »	25 »	32 »	25 »	17 »	27 »	27 »	20 »	
111 (5 c. vert IA)	330 »	16 »	13 »	24 »	18 »	18 »	18 »	18 »	30 »	

Les timbres sans millésime proviennent :

- 107 IB (Mill. 5 à sec en 1905)
- 108 IB (Mill. 6 omis ou cassé en 1906)
- 109 IA (Mill. omis sur papier GC)
- 110 (Mill. 4 omis ou cassé en 1924)
- 111 (Mill. 2 omis ou cassé en 1902)

Nos	9 (1909)	0 (1910)	1 (1911)	2 (1912)	3 (1913)	4 (1914)	5 (1915)	6 (1916)	6* (1916)	7* (1917)
107 (1 c. gris IA)					240 »	15 »	840 »	22 »		30 »
107 (1 c. gris IB)	25 »	11 »	10 »	15 »	12 »	12 »		22 »	26 »	
108 (2 c. brun-lilas IB)	7 »	7 »	7 »	14 »	14 »	7 »				24 »
109 (3 c. orange IB)	8 »	8 »	8 »	7 »			7 »	7 »		7 »

Nos	8* (1918)	9* (1919)	0 (1920)	0* (1920)	1 (1921)	2 (1922)	3 (1923)	4 (1924)	5 (1925)	6 (1926)
107 (1 c. gris IA)	27 »	30 »								
107 (1 c. ardoise IA)		12 »		25 »	9 »	11 »	8 »			
107 (1 c. ardoise IB)		12 »		25 »		11 »	8 »	7 »	7 »	18 »
108 (2 c. brun-lilas IA)				29 »		12 »	12 »			
108 (2 c. brun lilas IB)		45 »		28 »	9 »	12 »	12 »			
109 (3 c. orange IB)		9 »	9 »		9 »		9 »			
110 (4 c. brun-jaune)								15 »		

- 107 IA ou IB sur papier x en 1916 (300 ») - 108 IB est connu en 1908 avec le Mill. 8 renversé (35 »)

On connaît les Mill. suivants avec timbres non dentelés :

- 107 (Tous les Mill. sauf le 8) - 108 (Mill. 0,2,5 et 8) - 109 (Tous les Mill.) - 111 (Mill. 3)

Pour déterminer l'année d'un millésime on devra se référencer à la qualité du papier et/ou à la nuance du timbre.

TYPE BLANC (suite)

Mill. 7 (1917) avec Manchette GC (n° 109)

Nos	6*	7*	8*	9*	0*
Bloc de 4 avec manchette GC	(1916)	(1917)	(1918)	(1919)	(1920)
107 (1 c. gris IA)		50 »	50 »	80 »	
107 (1 c. gris IB)	80 »				
107 (1 c. ardoise IA)				40 »	70 »
107 (1 c. ardoise IB)				40 »	70 »
108 (2 c. brun-lilas IA)					80 »
108 (2 c. brun-lilas IB)		65 »		100 »	75 »
109 (3 c. orange IB)		27 »		27 »	

On trouve des papiers GC gris - jaune - blanc ou chamois.

TYPE MOUCHON

Nos	Sans Mill.	0 (1900)	1 (1901)	2 (1902)	3 (1903)
112 (10 c. rose)		120 »			
113 (20 c. brun-lilas)		250 »			
114 (25 c. bleu)	» »	400 »			
115 (30 c. violet)		370 »			
116 (10 c. rouge II)		120 »	100 »		
117 (15 c. orange II)	500 »	35 »	35 »	40 »	
118 (25 c. bleu II)		450 »	500 »		
124 (10 c. rose)				120 »	125 »
125 (15 c. vermillon)				45 »	50 »
126 (20 c. brun-lilas)				325 »	
127 (25 c. bleu)				325 »	450 »
128 (30 c. violet)				850 »	

SEMEUSE LIGNEE

Nos	Sans Mill.	3 (1903)	4 (1904)	5 (1905)	6 (1906)	7 (1907)
129 (10 c. rose I)		33 »				
129 (10 c. rose II)			180 »			
129 (10 c. rose III)			32 »	32 »	37 »	
130 (15 c. vert I)		20 »	35 »	25 »	35 »	
130 (15 c. vert II)		65 »	90 »			
130 (15 c. vert III)			110 »			
130 (15 c. vert IV)			50 »	15 »	17 »	
131 (20 c. brun-lilas)		265 »	320 »	300 »	275 »	
132 (25 c. bleu)		280 »	300 »	310 »	300 »	
133 (30 c. lilas)		620 »	670 »	700 »	725 »	
134 (10 c. rouge I)	90 »					
134 (10 c. rouge II)	200 »				13 »	
135 (10 c. rouge I)					36 »	
135 (10 c. rouge IIA)					72 »	100 »
136 (35 c. violet I)					900 »	
136 (35 c. violet clair II)					550 »	

Nos	6 (1916)	6* (1916)	7* (1917)	8* (1918)	9* (1919)	0 (1920)	1 (1921)	2 (1922)	3 (1923)	4 (1924)
130 (15 c. vert IV)	22 »	50 »	20 »	22 »	28 »	28 »	17 »	17 »	17 »	17 »
130 (bloc de 4 + Manchette GC)		100 »	60 »	65 »	70 »					

- Il existe des blocs avec manchette GC, non dentelés avec le Mill. 8

- Le 130 Type IV est connu sur papier x Mill. 7 en 1917 (120 »)

SEMEUSE CAMEE

Nos	Sans Mill.	7 (1907)	8 (1908)	9 (1909)	0 (1910)	1 (1911)	2 (1912)	3 (1913)	4 (1914)	5 (1915)
137 (5 c. vert foncé)	200 »	7 »	7 »	7 »	10 »	9 »	9 »	9 »	10 »	
138 (10 c. rouge)	300 »	9 »	8 »	8 »	9 »	9 »	9 »	8 »	9 »	8 »
139 (20 c. brun-rouge)		14 »	14 »	14 »	14 »		17 »	17 »	17 »	
140 (25 c. bleu) IA	» »	10 »	12 »	12 »	10 »	15 »	15 »	19 »	15 »	45 »
141 (30 c. orange)		50 »	50 »	50 »	60 »	75 »	60 »	70 »	70 »	70 »
142 (35 c. violet)		32 »	35 »		35 »	35 »	38 »	38 »	48 »	32 »

SEMEUSE CAMEE (suite)

Nos	6 (1916)	6* (1916)	7* (1917)	8* (1918)	9* (1919)	0* (1920)	0 (1920)	1 (1921)	2 (1922)	3 (1923)	4 (1924)
137 (5 c. vert foncé)	9 »	11 »	16 »	16 »	20 »	130 »	15 »	20 »			
138 (10 c. rouge)	8 »	130 »					14 »	11 »			
139 (20 c. brun-rouge)	19 »		19 »	22 »	24 »	24 »		14 »			
140 (25 c. bleu) IA	14 »		25 »	30 »	45 »	55 »	12 »	12 »	12 »	12 »	
140 (25 c. bleu IIIA)										70 »	62 »
141 (30 c. orange)	85 »	75 »	75 »	70 »	70 »	80 »	55 »				
142 (35 c. violet)	35 »			40 »	45 »		30 »	30 »	30 »		32 »

137 : Mill. 8 renversé (25 »)
Sans Mill. en vert-clair 1920 (250 »)
Tous les Mill. existent non dentelés sauf le 8.

138 : Mill. 5 penché (20 ») - Mill. 7 "écarlate" (650 ») - Mill. 7 "rouge sang" (175 »)
Mill. 6 (1916) sur papier x (140 »)
Tous les Mill. existent non dentelés sauf 3 et 4

139 : Est connu en non dentelé avec Mill. 2-8-9

140 : Mill. 7 (1907) bleu-noir (70 ») - Mill. 5 (1915) sur papier x (60 ») - Mill. 6 (1916) sur papier x (40 »)
Les Mill. 0-2-8 sont connus non dentelés.

141 : Mill. 6 (1916) sur papier x (120 »)
Les Mill. 0-2-6-7-9 sont connus non dentelés.

142 : Les Mill. 2-7-8 sont connus non dentelés.

137 Mill. 7 (1917) avec manchette GC

Nos Bloc de 4 avec manchette GC	6* (1916)	7* (1917)	8* (1918)	9* (1919)	0* (1920)
137 (5 c. vert foncé)	37 »	45 »	55 »	50 »	280 »
138 (10 c. rouge)	325 »				
139 (20 c. brun-rouge)		80 »	85 »	85 »	70 »
140 (25 c. bleu) IA		90 »	100 »	130 »	150 »
141 (30 c. orange)	190 »	190 »	175 »	175 »	200 »
142 (35 c. violet)			130 »	140 »	

Les 137 Mill. 6* - 139 Mill. 8* et 142 Mill. 8* et 9* existent en non dentelés.

Les papiers GC existent en blanc, gris, gris jaunâtre et chamois.

TIMBRES COMMEMORATIFS ET DIVERS

Nos	4 (1914)	5 (1915)	6 (1916)	7 (1917)	9 (1919)
146 (+ 5 c. s. 10 c. rouge)	23 »				
147 (10 c. + 5 c. rouge)	140 »	190 »	400 »		
148 (2 c. + 3 c. brun-lilas)				20 »	
149 (5 c. + 5 c. vert)					80 »
150 (15 c. + 10 c. gris-vert)				120 »	
151 (25 c. + 15 c. bleu)				360 »	
162 (+1 c. s. 2 + 3 c.)				6 »	
163 (+ 2½ c. s. 5 + 5 c.)					11 »
164 (+ 5 c. s. 15 + 10 c.)				11 »	
165 (+ 5 c. s. 25 + 15 c.)				80 »	
229 (2 c. + 1 c. brun-lilas)				10 »	

Nos	9* (1919)	0* (1920)	0 (1920)	1 (1921)	2 (1922)
151 (25 c. + 15 c.bleu)			400 »		
157 (1 c. s. 1 c. gris IA)	5 »	65 »			6 »
157 (1 c. s. 1 c. gris IB)	8 »	90 »			
157 (bloc de 4 + manch. GC IA)	40 »	160 »			
157 (bloc de 4 + manch. GC IB)	50 »	225 »			
158 (5 c. orange I)				7 »	7 »
159 (10 c. vert IA)				9 »	7 »
160 (30 c. rouge)				28 »	
161 (50 c. bleu)				115 »	
162 (+ 1 c. s. 2 + 3 c.)					8 »
163 (+ 2½ c. s. 5 + 5 c.)					10 »
165 (+ 5 c. s. 25 + 15 c.)			14 »		12 »

Nos	3 (1923)	4 (1924)	5 (1925)	6 (1926)
157 (1 c. s. 1 c. gris IB)		6"	10"	13"
158 (5 c. orange I)	12 »	15 »		
159 (10 c. vert IA)	25 »			
173 (30 c. Pasteur rouge)	6 »			
176 (50 c. Pasteur bleu)	25 »	90 »		
177 (75 c. Pasteur bleu)		19 »		
191 (30 c. rose I)		7 »	50 »	
193 (40 c. brun-olive I)			15 »	9 »
198 (50 c. olive I)			35 »	
209 (75 c. Ronsard bleu)		12 »		
219 (50 c. s. 75 c. bleu)		20 »		

- 157 IA avec Mill. 9* est connu avec surcharge renversée (très rare)
- 158 existe sans Mill. 2 (omis ou cassé) (200 »)
- 159 avec Mill. 1 existe non dentelé.
- 177 avec Mill. 4, dentelé tenant à non dentelé (7000 »)

TIMBRES PREOBLITERES

Nos	3 (1893)	6 (1916)	7* (1917)	9* (1919)	0 (1920)	1 (1921)
13 (3 c. gris "Sage")	2000 »					
24 (5 c. vert)				1500 »	1750 »	
25 (15 c. vert-olive)				1200 »	1200 »	
26 (5 c. vert)		1200 »	1300 »			1200 »
27 (5 c. orange)						2800 »
28 (15 c. vert-olive)					2500 »	2500 »
29 (30 c. orange)					2000 »	
30 (5 c. orange)					800 »	
32 (30 c. rouge)						2750 »
33 (5 c. orange)						920 »
34 (15 c. vert-olive)						6500 »

Nos	9* (1919)	1 (1921)	2 (1922)	3 (1923)	4 (1924)	5 (1925)
36 (5 c. orange)			720 »			
37 (15 c. olive)	2750 »					
39 (3 c. orange I)		120 »		47 »		
40 (4 c. brun I)					11 »	135 »
45 (15 c. olive IV)		10 »	15 »	10 »	10 »	
50 (5 c. orange I)		160 »	140 »	140 »	140 »	
54 (20 c. lilas-brun I)		325 »				
58 (30 c. rouge I)		500 »				
59 (30 c. rose I)					130 »	
62 (35 c. violet I)			300 »		275 »	
68 (50 c. bleu)				465 »	640 »	

TIMBRES FM

Nos	1 (1901)	2 (1902)	4 (1904)	5 (1905)	6 (1906)
1 (15 c. orange "Mouchon")	220 »	450 »			
2 (15 c. vermillon "Mouchon")			250 »		
3 (15 c. vert-olive IV)			180 »	210 »	
4 (10 c. rose III)				120 »	110 »

Nos	7 (1907)	8 (1908)	0 (1910)	1 (1911)	2 (1912)	3 (1913)	4 (1914)	5 (1915)	6 (1916)
5 (10 c. rouge IA)	8 »	12 »	10 »	13 »	13 »	14 »	16 »	13 »	14 »

On connaît le n° 1 avec surch. renversée Mill. 1 (1350 »), le n° 4 avec Mill. 5 penché (150 »), et le n° 5 Mill. 2 non dentelé (450 »), Mill. 5 surch. renversée (600 »), Mill. 7 surch. renversée (500 »).

TIMBRES-TAXE

Nos	Sans Mill.	8 (1898)	9 (1899)	0 (1900)	1 (1901)	2 (1902)	3 (1903)	4 (1904)	5 (1905)	6 (1906)	7 (1907)
10 (1 c. noir)	250 »	12 »	14 »	12 »	10 »	11 »	10 »	12 »	12 »	14 »	10 »

Nos	Sans Mill.	1 (1891)	2 (1892)
14 (5 c. noir)	750 »		375 »
15 (10 c. noir)	700 »		350 »
16 (15 c. noir)	650 »	300 »	260 »
18 (30 c. noir)	1350 »	850 »	780 »
20 (50 c. noir)	3500 »	2000 »	2200 »
22 (1 f. noir)	4200 »	2250 »	2300 »

Nos	3 (1893)	4 (1894)	5 (1895)	6 (1896)	7 (1897)	8 (1898)	9 (1899)	0 (1900)	1 (1901)	2 (1902)	3 (1903)
28 (5 c. bleu)	9 »	9 »	7 »	7 »	8 »	7 »	7 »	7 »	7 »	7 »	7 »
29 (10 c. brun)	7 »	7 »	7 »	7 »	7 »	6 »	6 »	6 »	6 »	6 »	6 »
30 (15 c. vert-jaune)	125 »			125 »	125 »	105 »	105 »	105 »	105 »		125 »
33 (30 c. rouge carminé)	6 »	6 »		6 »	6 »	6 »	6 »	6 »	6 »	6 »	6 »
34 (30 c. rouge-orange)		2000 »									
37 (50 c. lilas)		9 »	8 »	6 »	6 »	6 »	6 »	6 »	6 »	6 »	6 »
39 (1 f. rose s. paille)				2000 »							

Nos	4 (1904)	5 (1905)	6 (1906)	7 (1907)	8 (1908)	9 (1909)	1 (1911)	2 (1912)	3 (1913)	4 (1914)
28 (5 c. bleu)	7 »	7 »	7 »	7 »	7 »	7 »	7 »	7 »	7 »	7 »
29 (10 c. brun)		6 »	6 »	6 »	6 »	6 »	6 »	6 »	6 »	6 »
30 (15 c. vert-jaune)	125 »	140 »								
31 (20 c. olive)			32 »	32 »	32 »	32 »	32 »	32 »	32 »	
33 (30 c. rouge carminé)	6 »	6 »								
37 (50 c. lilas)	6 »		6 »							

TIMBRES-TAXE (suite)

Nos	5 (1915)	7* (1917)	8* (1918)	9 (1919)	9* (1919)	0 (1920)	0* (1920)	1 (1921)	2 (1922)	3 (1923)
28 (5 c. bleu)	6 »	7 »	7 »	6 »		6 »	6 »	6 »	6 »	
29 (10 c. brun)	6 »	7 »	7 »	6 »		6 »		6 »	6 »	
30 (15 c. vert-jaune)		120 »								
31 (20 c. olive)	32 »		40 »			32 »		32 »	32 »	32 »
32 (25 c. rose)										40 »
33 (30 c. rouge carminé)		7 »			8 »			6 »	6 »	6 »
37 (50 c. lilas)			20 »			6 »	22 »		6 »	6 »
40 (1 f. lilas-brun s. paille)						50 »				

Nos	7*	8*	9*	0*
Bloc de 4 avec manchette GC	(1917)	(1918)	(1919)	(1920)
28 (5 c. bleu)	20 »	20 »		
29 (10 c . brun)	20 »	25 »		
30 (15 c. vert-jaune)	240 »			
31 (20 c. olive)		75 »		
33 (30 c. rouge carminé)	20 »		22 »	
37 (50 c. lilas)		37 »		47 »

Nos	4 (1924)	5 (1925)	6 (1926)	7 (1927)	8 (1928)	9 (1929)	0 (1930)	1 (1931)	2 (1932)	3 (1933)	4 (1934)
28 (5 c. bleu)	6 »		6 »	6 »	6 »	6 »	6 »		6 »	6 »	
29 (10 c. brun)	6 »		6 »	6 »	6 »	6 »	6 »	6 »		6 »	
31 (20 c. olive)	32 »		32 »								
33 (30 c. rouge carminé)	6 »		6 »	6 »	6 »	6 »	6 »	6 »	6 »		
35 (40 c. rose)		55 »									
36 (45 c. vert)	50 »										
37 (50 c. lilas)	6 »		6 »	6 »	6 »		6 »	6 »	6 »	6 »	
38 (60 c. vert)		7 »			7 »	8 »		7 »	7 »		
40 (1 f. lilas-brun s. paille)			70 »	50 »	50 »	50 »	50 »	50 »		50 »	50 »
42 (2 f. violet)			6 »				6 »		6 »		

Le n° 31 est connu sans Mill. (80 »)

Le n° 41 (2 f. vermillon) est connu sans Mill. (1450 »)

TIMBRES-TAXE (Recouvrements)

Nos	8 (1908)	9 (1909)	0 (1910)	1 (1911)	2 (1912)	6 (1916)	7* (1917)	8* (1918)	9* (1919)
43 (1 c. olive)	9 »							12 »	
44 (10 c. violet)	12 »	10 »	10 »	10 »	10 »	10 »	12 »		
45 (20 c. bistre)									200 »
46 (30 c. bistre)		80 »	80 »		80 »				
47 (50 c. rouge)		950 »	950 »						
49 (20 c. s. 30 c. bistre)		85 »	80 »		85 »				
50 (40 c. s. 50 c. rouge)		40 »	40 »						
52 (60 c. s. 1 c. olive)								40 »	

Nos	0 (1920)	2 (1922)	3 (1923)	4 (1924)	5 (1925)	6 (1926)
44 (10 c. violet)	8 »	8 »	8 »		8 »	8 »
45 (20 c. bistre)	160 »					
46 (30 c. bistre)			80 »	80 »	80 »	80 »
48 (60 c. rouge)					17 »	
51 (50 c. s. 10 c. violet)					13 »	13 »
53 (1 f. s. 60 c. rouge)					65 »	
54 (2 f. s. 60 c. rouge)					65 »	

Nos	7*	8*	9*
Bloc de 4 avec manchette GC	(1917)	(1918)	(1919)
43 (1 c. olive)		25 »	
44 (10 c. violet)	45 »		
45 (20 c. bistre)			380 »
52 (60 c. s. 1 c. olive)		85 »	

TIMBRES "ANNULE"

Nos	6 (1906)	0 (1910)	1 (1911)
1 (1 c. gris IB)			100 »
3 (2 c. brun-lilas IB)		55 »	
5 (3 c. orange IB)			60 »
13 (15 c. vert-olive IV)	60 »		
16 (5 c. vert foncé IA)		160 »	
18 (10 c. rouge IA)			175 »
20 (20 c. brun-lilas I)		45 »	
21 (25 c. bleu IA)			45 »
22 (30 c. orange)			160 »
24 (35 c. violet foncé I)			75 »

Nos	1 (1921)	2 (1922)	3 (1923)
2 (1 c. ardoise IA)		47 »	
2 (1 c. ardoise IB)		47 »	47 »
3 (2 c. brun-lilas IA)			47 »
3 (2 c. brun-lilas IB)			47 »
5 (3 c. orange IB)	50 »		50 »
13 (15 c. vert-olive IV)			50 »
15 (50 c. bleu I)	100 »		
17 (5 c. orange IA)		23 »	20 »
19 (10 c. vert IA)		27 »	
21 (25 c. bleu IA)			20 »
23 (30 c. rouge I)	38 »		
24 (35 c. violet foncé I)		38 »	

Nos	**Sans** Mill.	**6** (1906)	**7** (1907)	**1** (1911)	**0** (1920)	**1** (1921)	**2** (1922)	**3** (1923)
25 (1 c. noir)			80 »					
26 (5 c. bleu)				80 »			80 »	
27 (10 c. brun)				80 »			80 »	
28 (20 c. olive)				80 »		80 »		
29 (25 c. rose)								85 »
30 (30 c. rouge carminé)							80 »	
31 (50 c. lilas)		80 »					80 »	
32 (1 f. lilas-brun s. paille)					160 »			
33 (2 f. rouge-orange)	1400 »							

Nos	**8** (1908)	**9** (1909)	**0** (1910)	**8*** (1918)	**1** (1921)	**2** (1922)	**3** (1923)
34 (1 c. olive)	110 »			100 »			
34 (bloc de 4 + manch. GC)				230 »			
35 (10 c. violet)			100 »				100 »
36 (30 c. bistre)			100 »				100 »
37 (50 c. rouge)		1200 »					
38 (15 c. vert-olive IV)							320 »
39 (5 c. orange)						320 »	
40 (20 c. lilas-brun)					320 »		
41 (30 c. rouge)					320 »		
42 (35 c. violet)						310 »	

TIMBRES "SPECIMEN"

Nos	3 (1923)	4 (1924)	5 (1925)
50 (1/2 c. 1 c. ardoise IB)		1700 »	
51 (1 c. ardoise IB)			130 »
53 (3 c. orange IB)	130 »		
58 (50 c. vert-olive I)			100 »
66 (35 c. violet I)		130 »	
67 (40 c. brun-olive I)			60 »
71 (1 f. bleu Pasteur)		90 »	
73 (5 c. bleu Taxe)		65 »	
74 (10 c. brun Taxe)		90 »	
75 (20 c. olive Taxe)		90 »	

Nos	8 (1908)	0 (1920)	4 (1924)	5 (1925)
76 (30 c. rouge carminé Taxe)			90 »	
77 (40 c. rose Taxe)				90 »
78 (50 c. lilas Taxe)			140 »	
79 (1 f. brun-lilas s. paille Taxe)		90 »		
80 (1 c. olive Recouvrement)	200 »			
81 (10 c. violet Recouvrement)				150 »
82 (30 c. bistre Recouvrement)				150 »
83 (60 c. rouge Recouvrement)				150 »
88 (30 c. rose I)			1000 »	
89 (35 c. violet I)			1000 »	
91 (50 c. bleu Pasteur)			1000 »	

TIMBRES DE ROULETTES

Nos (Bloc de 6)	Sans Mill.	8 (1908)	0 (1910)	2 (1912)	3 (1913)	4 (1914)	5 (1915)	7 (1917)	8 (1918)
130 (15 c. vert-gris) IV								1600 »	1600 »
137 (5 c. vert I)	3750 »		750 »		750 »	750 »			
138 (10 c. rouge IA)	7000 »	375 »	375 »	375 »		375 »	375 »		
140 (25 c. bleu I)	»								

- Afin de différencier avec certitude les Sans Mill. de feuilles pour roulettes, il faut constater leur absence dans un bloc de 12 timbres (voir début de rubrique).

- On ne connaît actuellement qu'une feuille de 150 timbres (sans mill.) du 25 c. bleu. Elle se trouve au musée postal.

TIMBRES-POSTE AVEC VIGNETTES PERSONNALISÉES OU PERSONNALISABLES

Il convient de distinguer deux sortes de timbres:

- Les timbres avec vignette **personnalisée** par La Poste tels que le logo "Cérès", "Les timbres personnalisés", "Meilleurs voeux"...

- Les timbres avec vignette **personnalisable** à la demande des particuliers ou d'entreprises. Ces logos sont très variables.

Impression Offset : La trame est nettement visible à la loupe

Impression Hélio : pas de trame visible dans les aplats de couleur.

2000. – ***3e millénaire. Type du T.-P. de même date. Offset ou hélio. Dentelés 13 x 13½.***

3365A 3 f. (0,46 €) ***avec logo personnalisé*** **(3365)** 10 » 9 »

Imprimé attenant horizontalement à une vignette sans valeur, personnalisée par un portrait d'après photo, pendant toute la durée du 54e Salon philatélique d'Automne. Cette possibilité de personnalisation a été renouvelée et élargie pendant l'année 2001. (Musée de la Poste et Salons de Tours et Nancy).

Ce timbre a également été vendu par correspondance à partir de juillet 2002 avec vignette attenante "Cérès" ou "Les Timbres personnalisés" (voir note après les nos 3431 et 3432).

3365B 3 f. (0,46 €) ***Logo Cérès ou Timbres personnalisés*** 5 » 4 »

2001. – ***Timbres pour naissances. Types des T.-P. de même date. Avec vignette "Cérès" ou "Les timbres personnalisés". Offset ou hélio. Dentelés 13.***

3431 3 f. (0,46 €) ***"C'est un garçon"*** **(3377)** 5 » 4 »

3432 3 f. (0,46 €) ***"Cest une fille"*** **(3378)** 5 » 4 »

Ces timbres personnalisés (3431 et 3432), en offset, furent proposés lors du 55e Salon Philatélique d'Automne (8 au 11 novembre 2001), mais par suite d'une panne informatique, peu d'exemplaires furent réalisés. Ils furent proposés à nouveau à Bordeaux du 5 au 13 mai. Finalement ils furent mis en vente par correspondance à partir de juillet 2002 avec vignette personnalisée "Cérès - Service Philatélique de la Poste - Paris France" ou "Les Timbres personnalisés".

Emis en feuille de 10.

2001. – ***Timbre de message. "merci". Type du T.-P. de même date. Avec vignette personnalisée "Cérès" ou "Les timbres personnalisés". Offset ou hélio. Dentelé 13.***

3433 3 f. (0,46 €) ***"merci"*** **(3379)** 5 » 4 »

Voir note après le no 3432.

2002. – ***Timbre pour invitations. Type du T.-P. de même date. Avec vignette "Cérès" ou "Les timbres personnalisés" ou personnalisable. Impression offset. Sans bandes de phosphore. Dentelé 13.***

3479A 0,46 € or et multicolore 5 » 4 »

Emis en feuilles de 10 timbres avec vignettes attenantes personnalisées avec "Cérès - Service Philatélique de la Poste - Paris France" ou avec le logo "Les timbres personnalisés" ou personnalisables.

2002. – ***Timbre pour anniversaires. Type du T.-P. de même date. Avec vignette "Cérès" ou "Les timbres personnalisés" ou personnalisable. Impression offset. Sans bandes de phosphore. Dentelé 13.***

3480A 0,46 € multicolore 5 » 4 »

Emis en feuilles de 10 timbres avec vignettes attenantes personnalisées avec "Cérès - Service Philatélique de la Poste - Paris France" ou avec le logo "Les timbres personnalisés" ou personnalisables.

2002. – ***"Le Monde en réseau". Timbre destiné au courrier des Entreprises. Type du T.-P. de même date. Avec vignette "Cérès" ou "Les timbres personnalisés" ou personnalisable. Impression offset. Sans bandes de phosphore. Dentelé 13.***

3532A 0,46 € multicolore 6 » 4 »

Emis en 2 feuilles de 10 timbres avec vignettes attenantes personnalisées avec "Cérès - Service Philatélique de la Poste - Paris France" pour l'une, avec le logo "Les timbres personnalisés" pour l'autre.

2002. – *"Meilleurs Voeux". Type du T.-P. de même date. Avec vignette "Cérès" ou "Les timbres personnalisés" ou personnalisable. Impression offset. Sans bandes de phosphore. Dentelé 13.*

3533A 0,46 € multicolore 6 » 4 »

Emis en feuilles de 10 timbres avec vignettes attenantes personnalisées avec "Cérès - Service Philatélique de la Poste - Paris France" ou avec le logo "Les timbres personnalisés" ou personnalisables.

2003. – *Timbre pour anniversaires. Personnage de bande dessinée. Marsupilami, d'André Franquin et Batem. Type du T.-P. de même date. Avec vignette "Cérès" ou "Les timbres personnalisés" ou personnalisable. © André Franquin & BATEM Marsu 2003. Impression offset. Sans bandes de phosphore.. Dentelé 13.*

3569A 0,50 € multicolore 5 » 4 »

Emis en feuilles de 10 timbres avec vignettes attenantes personnalisées avec "Cérès - Service Philatélique de la Poste - Paris France" ou avec le logo "Les timbres personnalisés" ou personnalisables.

2003. – *Type Marianne du 14 Juillet. Type du T.-P. de 2001. Avec vignette "Cérès", "Les timbres personnalisés" ou personnalisable. Impression offset. Deux bandes de phosphore. Dentelé 13.*

3587A (0,46 €) rouge (3417a) 5 » 4 »

Emis en feuilles de 15 timbres avec vignettes attenantes personnalisées avec "Cérès - Service Philatélique de la Poste - Paris France" pour l'une, avec le logo "Les timbres personnalisés" ou personnalisables.

Papier jaunâtre aux U.V., gomme jaunâtre et brillante ne pas confondre avec le n° 3417a.

Le timbre n° 3417a (papier fluorescent aux U.V., gomme blanche et mate) a été personnalisé et mis en vente en feuillets de 15 au 76e Congrès de la FFAP à Mulhouse du 6 au 9 juin 2003.

2003. – *"Meilleurs Voeux". Rouge-gorge. Avec vignette "Cérès" ou "Les timbres personnalisés" ou personnalisable. Impression offset. Gomme mate. Sans bandes de phosphore. Dentelé 13.*

3621A 0,50 € *Rouge-gorge* 5 » 4 »

Emis en feuilles de 10 timbres avec vignettes attenantes personnalisées avec "Cérès - Service Philatélique de la Poste - Paris France" ou avec le logo "Les timbres personnalisés" ou personnalisables.

2003. – *"Meilleurs Voeux" (pour entreprises). Avec vignette "Cérès" (2 types) ou "Les timbres personnalisés" ou personnalisable. Impression offset. Deux bandes de phosphore. Dentelé 13.*

3623A 0,50 € multicolore 6 » 4 »

Types des vignettes "Cérès" :

- France
- Paris France

a. (Vignette "France") 12 » 8 »

Emis en feuilles de 10 timbres avec vignettes attenantes personnalisées avec "Cérès - Service Philatélique de la Poste - Paris France", "Cérès - Service Philatélique de la Poste - France" ou avec le logo "Les timbres personnalisés" ou personnalisables.

2004. – *Saint-Valentin. Coeurs 2004 du courturier Karl Lagerfeld. Type des T.-P. de même date. Avec vignette "Cérès" ou "Les timbres personnalisés" ou personnalisable. Impression offset. Gomme brillante ou mate. Multicolore. Dentelés.*

3632A 0,50 € *Flacon de parfum Chanel n° 5 dans un coeur* (3632) 5 » 4 »

3633A 0,75 € *Le tailleur Chanel sur fond avec Tour Eiffel dans un coeur* (3633) 6 » 5 »

Emis chacun en feuilles de 10 timbres avec vignettes attenantes personnalisées avec "Cérès - Service Philatélique de la Poste - Paris France" ou avec le logo "Les timbres personnalisés" ou personnalisables.

2004. – *Timbre pour naissances. "C'est une fille". Type du T.-P. de même date. Avec vignette "Cérès" ou "Les timbres personnalisés" ou personnalisable. Impression offset. Gomme brillante ou mate. Deux bandes de phosphore. Dentelé 13.*

3634A 0,50 € *"C'est une fille"* 5 » 4 »

Emis en feuilles de 10 timbres avec vignettes attenantes personnalisées avec "Cérès - Service Philatélique de la Poste - Paris France" ou avec le logo "Les timbres personnalisés" ou personnalisables.

2004. – *Timbre pour naissances. "C'est un garçon". Type du T.-P. de même date. Avec vignette "Cérès" ou "Les timbres personnalisés" ou personnalisable. Impression offset. Gomme brillante ou mate. Deux bandes de phosphore. Dentelé 13.*

3635A 0,50 € *"C'est un garçon"* 5 » 4 »

Emis en feuilles de 10 timbres avec vignettes attenantes personnalisées avec "Cérès - Service Philatélique de la Poste - Paris France" ou avec le logo "Les timbres personnalisés" ou personnalisables.

2004. – *Timbre de message. "Ceci est une invitation". Type du T.-P. de même date. Avec vignette "Cérès" ou "Les timbres personnalisés" ou personnalisable. Impression offset. Gomme brillante ou mate. Deux bandes de phosphore. "ī" non perforés. Dentelé 13.*

3636A 0,50 € multicolore 5 » 4 »

Emis en feuilles de 10 timbres avec vignettes attenantes personnalisées avec "Cérès - Service Philatélique de la Poste - Paris France" ou avec le logo "Les timbres personnalisés" ou personnalisables.

2004. – *Timbre de message. "Un grand merci". Type du T.-P. de même date. Avec vignette "Cérès" ou "Les timbres personnalisés" ou personnalisable. Impression offset. Gomme brillante ou mate. Deux bandes de phosphore. "ī" non perforé. Dentelé 13.*

3637A 0,50 € multicolore 5 » 4 »

Emis en feuilles de 10 timbres avec vignettes attenantes personnalisées avec "Cérès - Service Philatélique de la Poste - Paris France" ou avec le logo "Les timbres personnalisés" ou personnalisables.

2004. – *Timbre pour Anniversaires. Type du T.-P. de même date. Avec vignette "Cérès", "Les timbres personnalisés" ou personnalisable. Impression offset. Gomme brillante ou mate. Deux bandes de phosphore. Dentelé 13.*

3688A 0,50 € multicolore (3688) 5 » 4 »

Emis en feuilles de 10 timbres avec vignettes attenantes personnalisées avec "Cérès - Service Philatélique de la Poste - Paris France" ou avec le logo "Les timbres personnalisés" ou personnalisables.

2004. – *Type Marianne du 14 juillet. Types des T.-P. 2002 et 2003. Avec vignette "Cérès" ou "Les timbres personnalisés" ou personnalisable. Sans valeur indiquée pour les nos 3688G et 3688H (validité permanente). Impression offset. Gomme mate ou brillante. Couche de vernis. Deux bandes de phosphore. Dentelés 13.*

3688B 0,01 € jaune (3443)
3688C 0,02 € bistre-noir (3444)
3688D 0,05 € vert-émeraude (3445)
3688E 0,10 € violet-rouge (3446)
3688F 0,20 € orange (3447)
3688G (sans val.) vert (3535A)
3688H (sans val.) rouge (3417)
3688J 0,58 € jaune-olive (3570)
3688K 0,70 € vert-olive (3571)
3688L 0,75 € bleu ciel (3572)
3688M 0,90 € bleu foncé (3573)
3688N 1,00 € bleu-vert (3455)
3688P 1,11 € lilas (3574)
3688Q 1,90 € brun-prune (3575)
3688R 2,00 € violet (3457)

La série 48 » 42 »

Emis en feuilles composées chacune de 15 timbres avec vignettes attenantes personnalisées avec "Cérès - Service Philatélique de la Poste - Paris France" ou avec le logo "Les timbres personnalisés" ou personnalisables.

F3688B La feuille 48 » 42 »

2004. – *"Meilleurs Voeux". Types des T.-P. de même date. Avec vignette "Cérès" ou "Les timbres personnalisés" ou personnalisable. Impression offset. Gomme brillante ou mate. Deux bandes de phosphore. Multicolore. Dentelés 13.*

3722A 0,50 € multicolore 5 » 4 »
3723A 0,50 € multicolore 5 » 4 »
3724A 0,50 € multicolore 5 » 4 »
3725A 0,50 € multicolore 5 » 4 »
3726A 0,50 € multicolore 5 » 4 »

N°s 3722A à 3726A (5 val.) **25 » 20 »**

Emis en feuilles composées chacune de 2 séries n°s 3722A à 3726A avec vignettes attenantes personnalisées avec "Cérès - Service Philatélique de la Poste - Paris France" ou avec le logo "Les timbres personnalisés" ou personnalisables.

F3722A La feuille 50 » 40 »

2004. – *Type Marianne du 14 Juillet. Type du T.-P. de 2001. Avec petite ou grande vignette personnalisable. Sans valeur indiquée (validité permanente). Autoadhésif. Deux bandes de phosphore. Précoupé vertical en lignes ondulées.*

3729A (sans val.) rouge (3419) (30) 8 » 6 »

Emis en roulettes sur support jaune avec petite ou grande vignette attenante personnalisable à destination des entreprises.

Emis également en feuilles de 50 timbres avec petites vignettes attenantes personnalisables (support blanc) à destination des entreprises ou en feuilles de 30 timbres avec grandes vignettes attenantes personnalisables (support blanc) à destination des entreprises.

a. (Petite vignette) 6 » 5 »

2004. – *Type Marianne du 14 Juillet. Type du T.-P. de 2003. Impression avec grande vignette personnalisable. Autoadhésif. Deux bandes de phosphore. Précoupé vertical en lignes ondulées.*

3729B 0,75 € bleu ciel (3572) 12 » 10 »

Emis en feuilles de 30 timbres avec grandes vignettes attenantes personnalisables à destination des entreprises.

2004. – *Type Marianne du 14 Juillet. Type du T.-P. de 2003. Impression avec grande vignette "Cérès" ou "Les timbres personnalisés". Autoadhésif. Deux bandes de phosphore. Précoupé vertical en lignes ondulées.*

3729C 1,11 € brun-prune (3574) 8 » 6 »

Emis en feuilles de 30 timbres avec grandes vignettes attenantes personnalisées soit avec "Cérès - Service Philatélique de la Poste - Paris France", soit avec le logo "Les timbres personnalisés". Existe par erreur avec logo privé et également avec faciale de 1,90 €.

2004. – *Type Marianne du 14 Juillet. Type du T.-P. de 2003. Impression avec grande vignette personnalisable. Autoadhésif. Deux bandes de phosphore. Précoupé vertical en lignes ondulées.*

3729D 1,11 € lilas (3574) 12 » 10 »

Emis en feuilles de 30 timbres avec grandes vignettes attenantes personnalisables à destination des entreprises.

2005. – *Type Marianne de Lamouche. Type du T.-P. de 2005. Sans valeur indiquée (validité permanente). Avec vignette "Cérès" ou "Les timbres personnalisés" ou personnalisable. Légende ITVF. Impression offset. Deux bandes de phosphore. Dentelé 13.*

3741A (sans val.) rouge (3734) 4 » 3 »

Emis en feuilles de 15 timbres avec vignettes attenantes personnalisées avec "Cérès - Service Philatélique de la Poste - Paris France" ou avec le logo "Les timbres personnalisés" ou personnalisables.

2005-06. – *Type Marianne de Lamouche. Type du T.-P. de 2005. Emis en feuilles avec vignette personnalisable. Sans valeur indiquée (validité permanente) (Lettre 20 g). Légende ITVF. Autoadhésif. Deux bandes de phosphore. Dentelé 11 sur 4 côtés.*

3744A (sans val.) rouge 10 » 8 »

Emis en feuilles de 15 timbres avec vignettes attenantes personnalisables.

2005. – *Saint-Valentin. Coeurs 2005 du couturier Cacharel. Types des T.-P. de même date. Avec vignette "Cérès" ou "Les timbres personnalisés" ou "Bonne fête maman" ou "Bonne fête papa" ou personnalisable. Impression offset. Gomme brillante ou mate. Dentelés.*

3747A 0,53 € ***Coeur en tissu Liberty*** 4 » 3 »

Le timbre no 3747A a été émis en feuilles de 10 timbres avec vignettes attenantes personnalisées avec "Cérès - Service Philatélique de la Poste - Paris France" ou avec le logo "Les timbres personnalisés" ou avec "Bonne fête maman" ou avec "Bonne fête papa" ou personnalisables.

3748A 0,82 € ***Coeur au motif d'un cacharel, oiseau de Camargue*** 6 » 5 »

Le timbre no 3748A a été émis en feuilles de 10 timbres avec vignettes attenantes personnalisées avec "Cérès - Service Philatélique de la Poste - Paris France" ou avec le logo "Les timbres personnalisés" ou personnalisables.

2005. – *Timbre de message. "Ceci est une invitation". Type du T.-P. de même date. Avec vignette "Cérès" ou "Les timbres personnalisés" ou personnalisable. Impression offset. Deux bandes de phosphore. "i" non perforés. Dentelé 13.*

3760A (Lettre 20 g.) multicolore 4 » 3 »

Emis en feuilles de 10 timbres avec vignettes attenantes personnalisées avec "Cérès - Service Philatélique de la Poste - Paris France" ou avec le logo "Les timbres personnalisés" ou personnalisables.

2005-06. – *Timbre de message. "Ceci est une invitation". Type du T.-P. de même date. Avec vignette personnalisable. Deux bandes de phosphore. Impression offset. Autoadhésif. Deux bandes de phosphore. Dentelé 11.*

3760B (Lettre 20 g.) multicolore 10 » 8 »

Emis en feuilles de 10 timbres avec vignettes attenantes personnalisables.

2005. – *Timbre de message. "Un grand merci". Type du T.-P. de même date. Avec vignette "Cérès" ou "Les timbres personnalisés" ou personnalisable. Impression offset. Deux bandes de phosphore. "i" non perforé. Dentelé 13.*

3761A (Lettre 20 g.) multicolore 4 » 3 »

Emis en feuilles de 10 timbres avec vignettes attenantes personnalisées avec "Cérès - Service Philatélique de la Poste - Paris France" ou avec le logo "Les timbres personnalisés" ou personnalisables.

2005-06. – *Timbre de message. "Un grand merci". Type du T.-P. de même date. Avec vignette personnalisable. Deux bandes de phosphore. Impression offset. Autoadhésif. Deux bandes de phosphore. Dentelé 11.*

3761B (Lettre 20 g.) multicolore 10 » 8 »

Emis en feuilles de 10 timbres avec vignettes attenantes personnalisables.

2005. – *Timbre pour Anniversaires. Bande dessinée. Centenaire de Bécassine, du dessinateur Joseph Porphyre Pinchon. Type du T.-P. de même date. Avec vignette "Cérès" ou "Les timbres personnalisés" ou personnalisable. Impression offset. Gomme brillante ou mate. Deux bandes de phosphore. Dentelé 13¼.*

3778A (Lettre 20 g.) multicolore 6 » 5 »

Emis en feuilles de 10 timbres avec vignettes attenantes personnalisées avec "Cérès - Service Philatélique de la Poste - Paris France" et "ANS" pour l'une, avec le logo "Les timbres personnalisés" et "ANS" pour l'autre, ou personnalisables.

2005-06. – ***Timbre pour Anniversaires. Bande dessinée. Centenaire de Bécassine, du dessinateur Joseph Porphyre Pinchon. Type du T.-P. de même date. Avec vignette personnalisable. Impression offset. Autoadhésif. Deux bandes de phosphore. Dentelé 11.***

3778B (Lettre 20 g.) multicolore 35 » 30 »

Emis en feuilles de 10 timbres avec vignettes attenantes personnalisables.

2005-06. – ***Type Marianne de Lamouche. Type du T.-P. de 2005. Emis en roulettes et feuilles avec petite ou grande vignette personnalisable. Sans valeur indiquée (validité permanente) (Lettre 20 g). Autoadhésif. Deux bandes de phosphore. Précoupé vertical en lignes ondulées.***

3802A (Lettre 20 g.) rouge *Légende ITVF* (3744) (49) 6 » 5 »
a. (Petite vignette) 5 » 4 »
b. (Dentelé sur 4 côtés, légende Phil@poste, grande vignette) 6 » 5 »
c. (Dentelé sur 4 côtés, légende Phil@poste, petite vignette) 5 » 4 »

Emis en roulettes sur support jaune au verso avec petite ou grande vignette attenante personnalisable à destinations des entreprises.

Emis également en feuilles de 30 timbres avec grandes vignettes attenantes personnalisables à destination des entreprises (n° 3802A - légende ITVF) ou en feuilles de 50 timbres avec petites vignettes attenantes personnalisables à destination des entreprises (n° 3802Aa - légente ITVF).

Emis en feuilles de 10 timbres avec grandes vignettes attenantes personnalisables (n° 3802Ab - légende Phil@poste) ou en feuilles de 15 timbres avec petites vignettes attenantes personnalisables (n° 3802Ac - légende Phil@poste).

2005-06. – ***Type Marianne de Lamouche. Type du T.-P. de 2005. Impression avec petite ou grande vignette personnalisable. Autoadhésif. Deux bandes de phosphore. Précoupé vertical en lignes ondulées.***

3802B 0,82 € lilas-brun clair *Légende ITVF* (3757) 12 » 10 »
a. (Dentelé sur 4 côtés, légende Phil@poste, grande vignette) 10 » 8 »
b. (Dentelé sur 4 côtés, légende Phil@poste, petite vignette) 10 » 8 »

Emis en feuilles de 30 timbres avec grandes vignettes attenantes personnalisable à destination des entreprises.

Emis en feuilles de 10 timbres avec grandes vignettes attenantes personnalisables (n° 3802Ba - légende Phil@poste) ou en feuilles de 15 timbres avec petites vignettes attenantes personnalisables (n° 3802Bb - légende Phil@poste).

2005. – ***Type Marianne de Lamouche. Type du T.-P. de 2005. Impression avec grande vignette personnalisable. Autoadhésif. Deux bandes de phosphore. Précoupé vertical en lignes ondulées.***

3802C 1,22 € lilas *Légende ITVF* (3758) 14 » 12 »

Emis en feuilles de 30 timbres avec grandes vignettes attenantes personnalisables à destination des entreprises.

2005-06. – ***Type Marianne de Lamouche. Type du T.-P. de 2005. Légende Phil@poste. Impression avec grande ou petite vignette personnalisable. Autoadhésif. Deux bandes de phosphore. Dentelé sur 4 côtés.***

3802D 0,55 € bleu *(grande vignette)* (3755) 35 » 30 »
a. (Petite vignette) 25 » 20 »

Emis en feuuilles de 10 timbres avec grandes vignettes attenantes personnalisables (n° 3802D - légende Phil@poste) ou en feuilles de 15 timbres avec petites vignettes attenantes personnalisables (n° 3802Da - légende Phil@poste).

2005. – ***Timbre pour naissances. "C'est une fille". Type du T.-P. de même date. Avec vignette "Cérès" ou "Les timbres personnalisés" ou personnalisable. Impression offset. Gomme brillante ou mate. Deux bandes de phosphore. Dentelé 13.***

3804A (Lettre 20 g.) *"C'est une fille"* 4 » 3 »

Emis en feuilles de 10 timbres avec vignettes attenantes personnalisées avec "Cérès - Service Philatélique de la Poste - Paris France" ou avec le logo "Les timbres personnalisés" ou personnalisables.

2005-06. – ***Timbre pour naissances. "C'est une fille". Type du T.-P. de même date. Avec vignette personnalisable. Impression offset. Autoadhésif. Deux bandes de phosphore. Dentelé 11.***

3804B (Lettre 20 g.) *"C'est une fille"* 10 » 8 »

Emis en feuilles de 10 timbres avec vignettes attenantes personnalisables.

2005. – *Timbre pour naissances. "C'est un garçon". Type du T.-P. de même date. Avec vignette "Cérès" ou "Les timbres personnalisés" ou personnalisable. Impression offset. Gomme brillante ou mate. Deux bandes de phosphore. Dentelé 13.*

3805A (Lettre 20 g.) *"C'est un garçon"* 4 » 3 »

Emis en feuilles de 10 timbres avec vignettes attenantes personnalisées avec "Cérès - Service Philatélique de la Poste - Paris France" ou avec le logo "Les timbres personnalisés" ou personnalisables.

2005-06. – *Timbre pour naissances. "C'est un garçon". Type du T.-P. de même date. Avec vignette parsonnalisable. Impression offset. Autoadhésif. Deux bandes de phosphore. Dentelé 11.*

3805B (Lettre 20 g.) *"C'est un garçon"* 10 » 8 »

Emis en feuilles de 10 timbres avec vignettes attenantes personnalisables.

2005. – *"Meilleurs Voeux". Types des T.-P. de même date. Avec vignette "Cérès" ou "Les timbres personnalisés" ou personnalisable. Impression offset. Gomme brillante ou mate. Deux bandes de phosphore. Dentelés 13.*

3853A	**(Lettre 20 g.) multicolore**	9 »	8 »
3854A	**(Lettre 20 g.) multicolore**	9 »	8 »
3855A	**(Lettre 20 g.) multicolore**	9 »	8 »
3856A	**(Lettre 20 g.) multicolore**	9 »	8 »
3857A	**(Lettre 20 g.) multicolore**	9 »	8 »
	N°s 3853A à 3857A (5 val.)	**45 »**	**40 »**

Emis en feuilles composées chacune de 2 séries n°s 3853A à 3857A avec vignettes attenantes personnalisées avec "Cérès - Service Philatélique de la Poste - Paris France" ou avec le logo "Les timbres personnalisés" ou personnalisables.

F3853A La feuille 90 » 80 »

2006. – *Saint-Valentin. Coeurs 2006 du couturier Stéphane Rolland de la Maison Jean-Louis Scherrer. Type du T.-P. de même date. Avec vignette "Cérès", "Les timbres personnalisés", "Je t'aime" ou "Bonne fête maman" en 10 langues ou personnalisable. Impression offset. Gomme brillante ou mate. Dentelé.*

3861A (sans val.) *coeur* 4 » 3 »

Emis en feuilles de 10 timbres avec vignettes attenantes personnalisées avec "Cérès - Service Philatélique de la Poste - Paris France" ou avec le logo "Les timbres personnalisés" ou "Je t'aime" ou "Bonne fête maman" en 10 langues ou personnalisables.

F3861A La feuille "Je t'aime" en 10 langues 25 » 20 »

F3861B La feuille "Bonne fête maman" 25 » 20 »

2006. – *Saint-Valentin. Coeurs 2006 du couturier Stéphane Rolland de la Maison Jean-Louis Scherrer. Type du T.-P. de même date. Avec vignette "Cérès", "Les timbres personnalisés" ou personnalisable. Impression offset. Gomme brillante ou mate. Dentelé.*

3862A (sans val.) *Coeur* 6 » 5 »

Emis en feuilles de 10 timbres avec vignettes attenantes personnalisées avec "Cérès - Service Philatélique de la Poste - Paris France", avec le logo "Les timbres personnalisés" ou personnalisables.

2005-06. – *Saint-Valentin. Coeurs 2006 du couturier Stéphane Rolland de la Maison Jean-Louis Scherrer. Type du T.-P. de même date. Avec vignette personnalisable. Impression offset. Autoadhésif.*

3863A (sans val.) *Coeur* 10 » 8 »

Emis en feuilles de 10 timbres avec vignettes attenantes personnalisables.

2005-06. – *Saint-Valentin. Coeurs 2006 du couturier Stéphane Rolland de la Maison Jean-Louis Scherrer. Type du T.-P. de même date. Avec vignette personnalisable. Impression offset. Autoadhésif.*

3864A (sans val.) *Coeur* 12 » 10 »

Emis en feuilles de 10 timbres avec vignettes attenantes personnalisables.

2006. – ***Art. Peinture. Les impressionnistes. Sans valeur indiquée (validité permanente) (Lettre 20 g). Types des T.-P. de même date. Avec vignette "Cérès" ou "Les timbres personnalisés" ou personnalisable. Impression offset. Papier gommé. Deux bandes de phosphore. Dentelés.***

3866A	**(sans val.)** ***"Portraits à la campagne" (1876), détail de tableau du peintre Gustave Caillebotte (1848-1894)***	2 50	2 »
3867A	**(sans val.)** ***"La chasse aux papillons" (1874), détail de tableau du peintre Berthe Morisot (1841-1895)***	2 50	2 »
3868A	**(sans val.)** ***"Mère et enfant" (1886), détail de tableau du peintre Mary Cassatt (1845-1926)***	2 50	2 »
3869A	**(sans val.)** ***"Jeunes filles au piano" (1892), détail de tableau du peintre Auguste Renoir (1841-1919)***	2 50	2 »
3870A	**(sans val.)** ***"La bergère" ou "Jeune fille à la baguette" (1881), détail de tableau du peintre Camille Pissarro (1830-1903)***	2 50	2 »
3871A	**(sans val.)** ***"Mademoiselle Gachet dans son jardin" (1890), détail de tableau du peintre Vincent Van Gogh (1853-1890)***	2 50	2 »
3872A	**(sans val.)** ***"L'air du soir" (1893-1894), détail de tableau du peintre Henri-Edmond Cross (1856-1910)***	2 50	2 »
3873A	**(sans val.)** ***"Danseuses" (1884-1885), détail de tableau du peintre Edgar Degas (1834-1917)***	2 50	2 »
3874A	**(sans val.)** ***"Le déjeuner sur l'herbe" (1863), détail de tableau du peintre Edouard Manet (1832-1883)***	2 50	2 »
3875A	**(sans val.)** ***"Femmes de Tahiti" ou "Sur la plage" (1891), détail de tableau du peintre Paul Gauguin (1848-1903)***	2 50	2 »
	N°s 3866A à 3875A (10 val.)	**25 »**	**20 »**

Emis en feuilles, soit avec chacun des 10 timbres attenant à une vignette personnalisée avec "Cérès - Service Philatélique de la Poste", soit avec chacun des 10 timbres attenant à une vignette personnalisée avec le logo "Les timbres personnalisés" ou personnalisables.

F3866A	**La feuille**	25 »	20 »
F3866B	**La feuille (10 val. autoadhésifs)**	40 »	30 »

2006. – ***Type Marianne de Lamouche. Type du T.-P. de 2005. Gomme mate. Héliogravure. Papier blanc brillant. Sans bande de phosphore. Dentelé 13 (2 diamètres de trous).***

3916A	**(0,10 €) violet (3732)**	2 »	1 50

émis en feuilles de 10 timbres attenant chacun à une vignette "Timbres Plus" (cadeau de La Poste aux réservataires).

2006. – ***Type Marianne de La mouche. Types des T.-P. de 2005. Légende Phil@poste (au lieu d'ITVF). Sans valeur indiquée pour les n°s 3925D et 3925E (validité permanente). Avec vignette "Cérès" ou "Les timbres personnalisés" ou personnalisable. Impression offset. Gomme mate ou brillante. Couche de vernis. Deux bandes de phosphore. Dentelés 13.***

3925A	**0,01 € jaune (3731)**	0 35	0 20
3925B	**0,05 € bistre-noir (3754)**	0 35	0 20
3925C	**0,10 € violet-rouge (3732)**	0 40	0 30
3925D	**(sans val.) vert (3733)**	2 70	2 »
3925E	**(sans val.) rouge (3734)**	2 70	2 »
3925F	**0,55 € bleu (3755)**	3 25	2 »
3925G	**0,64 € vert-olive (3756)**	3 25	2 »
3925H	**0,75 € bleu ciel (3737)**	3 25	2 50
3925J	**0,82 € lilas-brun clair (3757)**	3 25	2 50
3925K	**0,90 € bleu foncé (3738)**	4 30	3 »
3925L	**1,00 € orange (3739)**	4 30	3 »
3925M	**1,22 € lilas (3758)**	5 40	3 30
3925N	**1,98 € brun-prune (3759)**	8 50	7 »
	N°s 3925A à 3925N (13 val.)	**42 »**	**30 »**

Emis en feuille de 15 timbres attenant chacun à une vignette personnalisée avec "Cérès - Service Philatélique de la Poste" ou en feuille de 15 timbres attenant chacun à une vignette personnalisée avec le logo "Les timbres personnalisés" ou en feuille de 15 timbres attenant chacun à une vignette personnalisable, les timbres n°s 3925D et 3925E figurant deux fois dans les feuilles.

F3925A	**La feuille (15 val. papier gommé)**	50 »
F3925P	**La feuille (15 val. autoadhésifs)**	100 »

2006. – *Timbre pour Anniversaires. Bande dessinée. 75 ans de l'éléphant Babar par l'auteur et dessinateur Laurent de Brunhoff. Type du T.-P. de même date. Avec vignette "Cérès" ou "Les timbres personnalisés". Impression offset. Deux bandes de phosphore. Dentelé 13¼.*

3927A (sans val.) multicolore 4 » 3 »

Emis en feuilles de 10 timbres, soit avec chacun des 10 timbres attenant à une vignette personnalisée avec "Cérès - Service Philatélique de la Poste", soit avec chacun des 10 timbres attenant à une vignette personnalisée avec le logo "Les timbres personnalisés" ou personnalisable.

2006. – *Timbre pour Anniversaires. Bande dessinée. 75 ans de l'éléphant Babar par l'auteur et dessinateur Laurent de Brunhoff. Type du T.-P. de même date. Avec vignette personnalisable. Impression offset. Autoadhésif. Deux bandes de phosphore.*

3927B (sans val.) multicolore 10 » 8 »

Emis en feuille de 10 timbres avec vignettes attenantes personnalisables.

2006. – *Sport. Football. "Merci les Bleus". Offset. Papier gommé. Deux bandes de phosphore. Dentelé 13.*

Type du T.-P. de même date.

3936A 0,53 € *Mains et ballon* (3936) 5 » 4 »

Impression avec vignette "Cérès" ou "Les timbres personnalisés".

Emis en feuilles de 10 timbres, soit avec chacun des 10 timbres attenant à une vignette personnalisée avec "Cérès - Service Philatélique de la Poste", soit avec chacun des 10 timbres attenant à une vignette personnalisée avec le logo "Les timbres personnalisés".

2006. – *Sport. Football. "Merci les Bleus". Offset. Autoadhésif. Deux bandes de phosphore. Dentelé 11.*

Type du T.-P. de 2006.

3936B 0,53 € *Mains et ballon* (3936A) 10 » 8 »

Impression avec vignette personnalisable.

Emis en feuilles de 10 timbres avec vignettes attenantes personnalisables.

2006. – *Type Marianne de Lamouche. Taille-douce numérique. Autoadhésif. Deux bandes de phosphore. Dentelé 11 sur 4 côtés.*

Type du T.-P. de 2006.

3966A 0,60 € bleu (3966) 10 » 8 »
a. (Petite vignette) 8 » 7 »

Impression avec grande vignette personnalisable.

Le timbre n° 3966A est émis en feuilles de 10 timbres avec grandes vignettes attenantes personnalisables.

Le timbre n° 3966Aa est émis en feuilles de 15 timbres avec petites vignettes attenantes personnalisables.

2006. – *Type Marianne de Lamouche. Taille-douce numérique. Autoadhésif. Deux bandes de phosphore. Dentelé 11 sur 4 côtés.*

Type du T.-P. de 2006.

3969A 0,86 € lilas-brun clair (3969) 11 » 9 »
a. (Petite vignette) 9 » 7 »

Impression avec grande vignette personnalisable.

Le timbre n° 3969A est émis en feuilles de 10 timbres avec grandes vignettes attenantes personnalisables.

Le timbre n° 3969Aa est émis en feuilles de 15 timbres avec petites vignettes attenantes personnalisables.

2006. – *"Meilleurs Vœux". Offset. Papier gommé. Deux bandes de phosphore. Multicolore. Dentelés.*

Types des T.-P. de même date. Impression avec vignette "Cérès" ou "Les timbres personnalisés".

Sans valeur indiquée (validité permanente).

3986A	**(Lettre 20 g)** ***Manchots et renne en traîneau***	4 »	3 »
3986Aa	**(Lettre 20 g)** ***Manchots et renne en traîneau***	2 50	2 »
3987A	**(Lettre 20 g)** ***Renne pêchant et manchots se baignant***	4 »	3 »
3988A	**(Lettre 20 g)** ***Renne et manchots décorant un sapin***	4 »	3 »
3989A	**(Lettre 20 g)** ***Manchots regardant le renne patiner***	4 »	3 »
3990A	**(Lettre 20 g)** ***Renne avec paquet cadeau et manchots dans des paquets cadeaux***	4 »	3 »
	N° 3986A à 3990A (5 val.)	**20 »**	**15 »**
F3986A	**La feuille**	40 »	30 »
F3986Aa	**La feuille**	12 »	10 »

Emis en feuilles composées chacune de 2 séries n° 3986A à 3990A avec vignettes attenantes personnalisées avec "Cérès – Service Philatélique de la Poste – Paris France" ou avec le logo "Les timbres personnalisés".

Le timbre n° 3986A a également été émis en feuille de 5 timbres attenant chacun à une vignette personnalisée notamment par "Meilleurs vœux pour 2007" (cadeaux de la Poste).

2006. – *"Meilleurs Vœux". Offset. Autoadhésifs. Deux bandes de phosphore. Multicolore. Dentelés 11.*

Types des T.-P. de même date. Impression avec vignette personnalisable.

Sans valeur indiquée (validité permanente).

3986B	**(Lettre 20 g)** ***Manchots et renne en traîneau*** **(3986A)**	10 »	9 »
3987B	**(Lettre 20 g)** ***Renne pêchant et manchots se baignant*** **(3987A)**	10 »	9 »
3988B	**(Lettre 20 g)** ***Renne et manchots décorant un sapin*** **(3988A)**	10 »	9 »
3989B	**(Lettre 20 g)** ***Manchots regardant le renne patiner*** **(3989A)**	10 »	9 »
3990B	**(Lettre 20 g)** ***Renne avec paquet cadeau et manchots dans des paquets cadeaux*** **(3990A)**	10 »	9 »

Emis en feuilles composées chacune de 2 séries n° 3986B à 3990B avec vignettes attenantes personnalisables.

F3986B	**La feuille**	100 »	90 »
F3986C	**La feuille**	50 »	45 »

2007. – *Année lunaire chinoise du Cochon. Offset. Papier gommé. Deux bandes de phosphore. Dentelé 13½ x 13*

Type du T.-P. de même date.

Sans valeur indiquée (validité permanente).

4001A	**(Lettre 20 g)** ***Cochon, œuvre originale de Li Zhongyao, peintre et calligraphe***	6 »	5 »

Impression avec vignette "Cérès" ou "Les timbres personnalisés"

Emis en feuilles de 5 timbres avec vignettes attenantes personnalisées soit avec "Cérès - Service Philatélique de la Poste - Paris France", soit avec le logo "Les timbres personnalisés"

2007. – *Année lunaire chinoise du Cochon. Offset. Autoadhésif. Deux bandes de phosphore. Dentelé 11.*

Type du T.-P. de même date.

Sans valeur indiquée (validité permanente).

4001B	**(Lettre 20 g)** ***Cochon, œuvre originale de Li Zhongyao, peintre et calligraphe*** **(4001A)**	12 »	10 »

Impression avec vignette personnalisable.

Emis en feuille de 10 timbres avec vignettes attenantes personnalisables.

2007. – *L'Arc de Triomphe. Papier gommé. Deux bandes de phosphore. Multicolore. Dentelé 13.*

Type du T.-P. de même date.

Sans valeur indiquée (validité permanente).

3599A	**(Lettre prioritaire 20 g)** ***L'Arc de Triomphe illuminé*** **(3599)**	4 »	3 »

Impression avec vignettes personnalisées "J'aime Paris" en 10 langues (Ancien n° 4027A).

Emis en feuilles de 10 timbres attenant chacun à une vignette personnalisée par "J'aime Paris" en 10 langues".

F3599A La feuille 40 » 30 »

2007. – ***L'Arc de Triomphe. Type du T.-P. de même date. Autoadhésif. Deux bandes de phosphore. Dentelé 11.***

Sans valeur indiquée (validité permanente).

3599B (Lettre prioritaire 20 g) ***L'Arc de Triomphe illuminé*** **(3599A)** 20 » 15 »

Impression avec vignette personnalisable.

(Ancien n° 4027B).

Emis en feuille de 10 timbres avec vignettes attenantes personnalisables.

2007. – ***"Allez les petits". Timbre annonce de la VIe Coupe du monde de Rugby en France en 2007. Offset. Papier gommé. Deux bandes de phosphore. Dentelé 13 x 13¼.***

Type du T.-P. de même date.

4032A 0,54 € ***Encouragement du commentateur sportif Roger Couderc (1918-1984) et joueurs*** 5 » 4 »

Impression avec vignette "Cérès" ou "Les timbres personnalisés".

Emis en feuilles de 5 timbres avec vignettes attenantes personnalisées soit avec "Cérès - Service Philatélique de la Poste - Paris France", soit avec le logo "Les timbres personnalisés".

2007. – ***"Allez les petits". Timbre annonce de la VIe Coupe du monde de Rugby en France en 2007. Offset. Autoadhésif. Deux bandes de phosphore. Dentelé 11.***

Type du T.-P. de même date.

4032B 0,54 € ***Encouragement du commentateur sportif Roger Couderc (1918-1984) et joueurs*** **(4032A)** 10 » 9 »

Impression avec vignette personnalisable.

Emis en feuille de 10 timbres avec vignettes attenantes personnalisables.

2007. – ***Type Marianne de Lamouche. Offset. Papier gommé. Deux bandes de phosphore. Dentelés 13.***

Types des T.-P. de 2006. Impression avec vignettes "Cérès" ou "Les timbres personnalisés".

4048A 0,01 € jaune (Type du T.-P. n° 3731b)
4048B 0,05 € bistre-noir (Type du T.-P. n° 3754b)
4048C 0,10 € gris (3965)
4048D (sans val.) vert (Type du T.-P. n° 3733b)
4048E (sans val.) rouge (Type du T.-P. n° 3734b)
4048F 0,60 € bleu (3966)
4048G 0,70 € vert-olive (3967)
4048H 0,85 € violet-rouge (3968)
4048J 0,86 € lilas-brun clair (3969)
4048K 1,00 € orange (Type du T.-P. n° 3739b)
4048L 1,15 € bleu ciel (3970)
4048M 1,30 € lilas (3971)
4048N 2,11 € brun-prune (3972)

Emis en feuille de 15 timbres attenant chacun à une vignette personnalisée avec "Cérès -Service Philatélique de la Poste" ou en feuille de 15 timbres attenant chacun à une vignette personnalisée avec le logo "Les timbres personnalisés", les timbres n° 4048D et 4048E figurant deux fois dans la feuille.

F4048A La feuille 70 »

2007. – ***Type Marianne de Lamouche. Offset. Autoadhésifs. Deux bandes de phosphore. Dentelés 11.***

Types des T.-P. de même date. Impression avec vignettes personnalisables.

4048P 0,01 € jaune (4048A)
4048Q 0,05 € bistre-noir (4048B)
4048R 0,10 € gris (4048C)
4048S (sans val.) vert (4048D)
4048T (sans val.) rouge (4048E)
4048U 0,60 € bleu (4048F)
4048V 0,70 € vert-olive (4048G)
4048W 0,85 € violet-rouge (4048H)

4048X 0,86 € lilas-brun clair (4048J)
4048Y 1,00 € orange (4048K)
4048Z 1,15 € bleu ciel (4048L)
4048AA 1,30 € lilas (4048M)
4048AB 2,11 € brun-prune (4048N)

Nos 4048P à 4048AB (13 val.)

Emis en feuille de 15 timbres attenant chacun à une vignette personnalisable, les timbres n° 4048S et 4048T figurant deux fois dans la feuille.

F4048P La feuille 110 »
a. (non personnalisée) » »

2007. – ***Timbre pour Anniversaires. Sylvain et Sylvette, héros de bandes dessinées de Jean-Louis Pesch. Type du T.-P. de même date. © Dargaud 2007. Offset. Deux bandes de phosphore. Dentelé 13¼.***

Sans valeur indiquée. Lettre prioritaire 20 g.

4081A (sans val.) ***Sylvain et Sylvette portant un gâteau*** **(4081)** 3 » 2 »

Impression avec vignette "Cérès" ou "Les timbres personnalisés".

Emis en feuilles de 5 timbres avec vignettes attenantes personnalisées soit avec "Cérès - Service Philatélique de la Poste - Paris France", soit avec le logo "Les timbres personnalisés".

2007. – ***Timbres de messages. "Invitation", "Merci". Héliogravure. Papier gommé. Deux bandes de phosphore. Multicolore. Dentelés 13¼ x 13.***

Sans valeur indiquée. Lettre prioritaire 20 g.

4082A (sans val.) ***Boîte d'où s'échappent des papillons*** **(4082) (129)** 2 » 1 50
4083A (sans val.) ***Boîte d'où s'échappent des cœurs*** **(4083) (130)** 2 » 1 50
4084A (sans val.) ***Boîte remplie de fleurs*** **(4084) (131)** 2 » 1 50
4085A (sans val.) ***Boîte d'où s'échappent des bulles*** **(4085) (132)** 2 » 1 50
4086A (sans val.) ***Boîte d'où s'échappent des notes de musique*** **(4086) (133)** 2 » 1 50

Nos 4082A à 4086A (5 val.) **10 » 7 50**

Impression avec vignette "Cérès" ou "Les timbres personnalisés".

Emis en feuilles composées de la série avec vignettes attenantes personnalisées soit avec "Cérès - Service Philatélique de la Poste - Paris France", soit avec le logo "Les timbres personnalisés".

F4082A La feuille 10 »

2007. – ***« Meilleurs Vœux ». Offset. Papier gommé. Deux bandes de phosphore. Multicolore. Dentelés.***

Sans valeur indiquée (validité permanente).

4120A (Lettre prioritaire 20 g) ***Ecureuil avec bonnet vert*** 2 » 1 50
4121A (Lettre prioritaire 20 g) ***Oiseau avec chapeau de fête*** 2 » 1 50
4122A (Lettre prioritaire 20 g) ***Faon sur une luge*** 2 » 1 50
4123A (Lettre prioritaire 20 g) ***Hérisson avec chapeau de fête*** 2 » 1 50
4124A (Lettre prioritaire 20 g) ***Chien avec bonnet rouge*** 2 » 1 50

Nos 4120A à 4124A (5 val.) **10 » 7 50**

Impression avec vignette "Cérès" ou "Les timbres personnalisés".

Emis en feuilles composées de la série avec vignettes attenantes personnalisées soit avec "Cérès - Service Philatélique de la Poste - Paris France", soit avec le logo "Les timbres personnalisés".

F4120A La feuille 10 »

2008. – ***Saint-Valentin. Cœur 2008 du couturier Franck Sorbier. Offset.***

Type du T.-P. de même date.

Sans valeur indiquée (validité permanente)..

4128A (Lettre prioritaire 20 g) ***Visages formant un cœur*** **(4128)** 2 50 2 »

Impression avec vignettes "Je t'aime" en 10 langues.

Emis en feuille de 10 timbres avec vignettes attenantes personnalisées par "Je t'aime" en 10 langues.

F4128A La feuille 25 »

2008. – *Type Marianne de Beaujard. Offset. Papier gommé. Une bande de phosphore à droite, sauf n° 4230, 4233, 4234, 4235, 4236, 4237, 4238 : deux bandes de phosphore. Dentelés 13.*

Marianne et l'Europe.

Types des T.-P. de même date. Impression avec vignettes "Cérès".

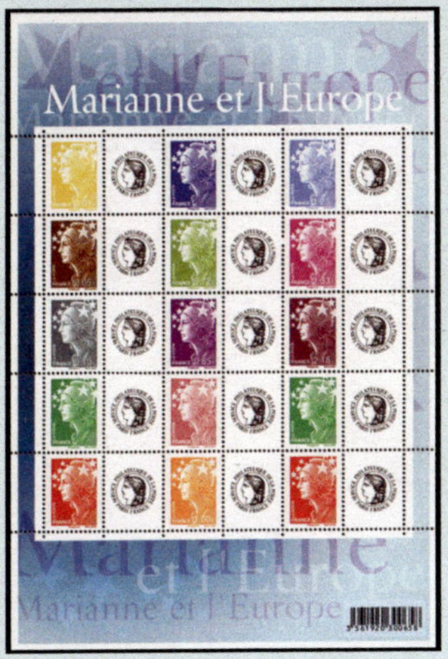

4226A 0,01 € jaune (4226)
4227A 0,05 € bistre-noir (4227)
4228A 0,10 € gris (4228)
4229A (sans val.) vert (4229)
4230A (sans val.) rouge (4230)
4231A (sans val.) bleu (4232) (4231)
4232A 0,72 € vert-olive
4233A 0,85 € violet-rouge (4233)
4234A 0,88 € lilas-brun clair (4234)
4235A 1,00 € orange (4235)
4236A 1,25 € bleu ciel (4236)
4237A 1,33 € lilas (4237)
4238A 2,18 € brun-prune (4238)

Emis en feuille de 15 timbres attenant chacun à une vignette personnalisée avec "Cérès -Service Philatélique de la Poste - Paris France", les timbres n° 4229A et 4230A figurant deux fois dans la feuille.

F4226A La feuille 35 »

TIMBRES-POSTE PERSONNALISES MONTIMBRAMOI®

(Également appelés "ID timbres" et "Collector")

2007. – *Timbres-poste personnalisés MonTimbraMoi®. Visuel principal variable. Offset. Autoadhésifs. Dentelés 11.*

Sans valeur indiquée (validité permanente).

Format Horizontal

1 **(Lettre prioritaire 20 g)** 3 » 2 »

2 **(Lettre 50 g)** 4 » 3 »

3 **(Monde 20 g)** 4 » 3 »

Format Vertical

4 **(Lettre prioritaire 20 g)** 3 » 2 »
5 **(Lettre 50 g)** 4 » 3 »

6 **(Monde 20 g)** 4 » 3 »

N°s 1 à 6 (6 val.) **22 »** **16 »**

Cadres gris, bleu, rose ou vert-olive.

Emis en feuilles de 10 ou 30 timbres

Valeur postale "Lettre prioritaire 20 g" : 0,55 €

Valeur postale "Lettre prioritaire 50 g" : 0,88 €

Valeur postale "Monde 20 g" : 0,85 €.

2008. – *Timbres-poste personnalisés réédition de 6 valeurs.*

Lettre prioritaire 20g, 50g, 100g, 250g, 500g, 1kg.

La série de 6 valeurs

N°s 7 à 12 (6 val.) 40 »

Idem légende Monde

Lettre prioritaire 20g, 50g, 100g, 250g, 500g, 1kg.

La série de 6 valeurs

N°s 13 à 18 (6 val.) 70 »

VOTRE PASSION EN UN CLIC
LE TIMBRE SUR INTERNET
Découvrez notre sélection de timbres de France, Monaco, Andorre, Nouvelle Calédonie, Polynésie, Wallis et Futuna, TAAF et St-Pierre-et-Miquelon, Thématiques, en vente au détail.
YVERT.COM

DOCUMENTS OFFICIELS (Doc)

Collection historique réalisée par l'Administration.

De 1973 à 1992, l'Administration des Postes et Télécommunications a réalisé pour le « Musée Postal », à l'occasion de chaque parution de timbre, un Document mis en vente pendant 8 semaines.

De format 22 x 29,7, tiré sur les presses de l'Imprimerie des Timbres-Poste à Périgueux, ce Document, qui est sur velin pur chiffon d'Arches, comporte :

- le texte de la notice officielle
- l'impression du poinçon original
- une illustration gravée
- le timbre oblitéré du cachet Premier Jour
- la marque à sec de l'Imprimerie du Timbre
- le n° d'ordre de parution (que nous indiquons avant le sujet).

Depuis 1993, le « Document Philatélique Officiel édité par la Poste et tiré sur les presses de l'Imprimerie des Timbres-Poste et des Valeurs Fiduciaires » ne comporte plus de numéro d'ordre de parution ; la période de mise en vente a été portée à un an.

A compter de 2000 le papier utilisé est un Montevrain Lana Vélin.

OBLITÉRATIONS « PREMIER JOUR » (1er j.)

Le premier timbre ayant fait l'objet d'une mise en vente anticipée régulière fut le 20 c. Rouget de l'Isle, disponible à Lons-le-Saunier et à Paris R.P. dès le 27 juin 1936. Cette exception devint une règle à peu près constante à partir du timbre Péguy (juin 1950) ; une oblitération spéciale dite « Premier Jour » l'a sanctionnée à partir du timbre Fontainebleau (février 1951) ; avec le 15 f. Jules Ferry (mars 1951), un modèle standard d'oblitération fut adopté, qui au début de 1966 (voir pages suivantes), a été modifié.

Ce type de marque n'a cependant pas l'exclusivité de la qualification « Premier Jour ». Un certain nombre d'oblitérations spéciales, illustrées ou non, de grand ou de petit format, ont pleine valeur de « Premiers Jours ». Il en est de même de quelques oblitérations ordinaires, sous réserve d'origine et de date déterminées.

Premier Jour (PJ)

Grand Format (GF)

Petit Format spécial (PF)

Ordinaire (O)

Grand Format - Premier Jour (GF-PJ)

SUR ENVELOPPES illustrées ou non

La plupart des enveloppes émises avant 1950 se présentent non illustrées.

1936	(Doc)	(1er j)
20 c. Rouget de l'Isle (O), Lons-le-Saunier, 27/6		90 »
75 c. et 1 f. Vimy (PF), Vimy, 26/7		125 »

1938	(Doc)	(1er j)
Journée du Timbre, oblit. format ord.		45 »

1939	(Doc)	(1er j)
Journée du Timbre, oblit. format ord. 5/3		25 »

1940	(Doc)	(1er j)
Journée du Timbre		35 »

1941	(Doc)	(1er j)
Journée du Timbre		35 »

1942	(Doc)	(1er j)
Journée du Timbre, oblit. (GF), ill. 19/4		12 »

1943	(Doc)	(1er j)
Journée du Timbre, oblit. (GF), ill. 10/10		15 »
4 f. Beaune (GF), Beaune, 21/7		25 »

1944	(Doc)	(1er j)
1 f. 50+3 f. 50, Journée du Timbre (GF), 9/12		38 »

1945	(Doc)	(1er j)
4 f. + 2 f. Oradour (GF), Oradour, 13/10		30 »
2 f. + 3 f. Journée du Timbre (GF), 13/10		35 »

1946	(Doc)	(1er j)
2 f. + 3 f. Musée Postal (GF), Paris-Salon de la Philatélie, 25/5		5 50
3 f. + 2 f. Journée du Timbre (GF), 29/6		25 »
5 f. Vézelay (GF), Vézelay, 21/7		35 »
3 f. et 10 f. Conférence de Paris (PF), Paris 29/7		10 »
10 f. U.N.E.S.C.O. (PF), Paris, 19/11		20 »

1947	(Doc)	(1er j)
4 f. 50+5 f. 50, Journée du Timbre (GF), 15/3		30 »
3 f. 50, 4 f. 50, 6 f., 10 f., U.P.U. (PF), Paris, 7/5		125 »
500 f. U.P.U. (PF), Paris, 7/5		350 »
4 f. 50, Pavie (PF), Dinan, 1/6		18 »
4 f. 50, Fénelon (GF), Cambrai, 12/7		18 »
6 f. + 4 f. Saint-Nazaire (GF), Saint-Nazaire, 2/8		40 »
5 f. Jamboree (PF), Moisson (S.-et-O.), 2/8		35 »

1948	(Doc)	(1er j)
6 f. +4 f. Journée du Timbre (GF), 6/3		30 »
12 f. et 18 f. Nations Unies (PF),		
bureau temporaire de Chaillot, 21/9		35 »

1949	(Doc)	(1er j)
15 f.+5 f. Journée du Timbre Choiseul (GF), 26/3		27 »
12 f. Dauphiné (GF), Grenoble et Romans, 14/5		55 »
Bloc CITEX (GF et grille), Paris-Grand Palais, 1/6		85 »
Série C.I.T.T. (PF), Paris, bureau temporaire du		
Congrès, 13/6,		400 »

1950	(Doc)	(1er j)
12 f. + 3 f. Journée du Timbre (GF), 11/3		38 »
12 f. Péguy (O). Toutes oblitérations de l'Eure-et-Loir		
et du Loiret du 10/6		110 »
12 f. Rabelais (O), Chinon et Meudon, 24/6		110 »
Révolutionnaires de 1789 (CD), Paris, 10/7		1000 »
8 f. Châteaudun (PF), Châteaudun, 25/11		85 »
15 f. Madame de Sévigné (O), Grignan, 25/11		450 »
(PF), Hôtel Carnavalet, 25/11		85 »
15 f. Madame Récamier (O), Lyon, 9/12		85 »
Paire Croix-Rouge (GF), Paris-Musée Postal, 22/12 (2 env.)		450 »

1951	(Doc)	(1er j)
12 f. Fontainebleau (PJ), Fontainebleau, 20/1		250 »
12 f. + 3 f. Journée du Timbre (GF), 10/3		160 »
15 f. Jules Ferry (PJ), Saint-Dié, 17/3		225 »
25 f. Textile (Lille) (O), 9/4		140 »
15 f. Saint J.-B. de La Salle (GF) Reims, 28/4		90 »
15 f. Troupes coloniales (GF), Paris, 12/5		70 »
15 f. Idem. Bordeaux - Congrès fédéral, 12/5		125 »
25 f. D'Indy (PJ), Paris, 15/5		75 »
5 f. + 1 f. A. de Musset (PJ), Paris, 2/6		125 »
8 f. + 2 f. Delacroix (PJ), Saint-Maurice, 2/6		125 »
10 f. + 5 f. Gay-Lussac (PJ),		
Saint-Léonard-de-Noblat, 2/6		160 »
12 f. + 14 f. Surcouf (PJ), Saint-Malo, 12/6		160 »
15 f. + 5 f. Talleyrand (PJ), Paris, 12/6		125 »
30 f. + 10 f. Napoléon (PJ), Ajaccio, 2/6		170 »
La série, Musset à Napoléon (sur 1 enveloppe)		850 »
12 f. Médecine vétérinaire (PF), Journée vétérinaire		
d'Alfort, 8/6		60 »
15 f. Médecine militaire (GF), Paris - Val-de-Grâce, 17/6		60 »
15 f. Saint-Nicolas (GF), Epinal - Imagerie, 23/6		60 »
30 f. Arbois (PJ), Arbois, 23/6		60 »
15 f. Bimillénaire de Paris (GF), Paris - Musée de Cluny, 7/7		40 »
12 f. Noguès (PJ), Rennes, 13/10		65 »
(GF), Paris exposition philatélique, 13/10		100 »
8 f. Baudelaire (PJ), Paris, 27/10		50 »
12 f. Verlaine (PJ), Metz, 27/10		50 »
15 f. Raimbaud (PJ), Charleville, 27/10		50 »
18 f. et 30 f. Nations Unies (PF),		
Paris - Palais de Chaillot, 6/11		100 »
15 f. Clemenceau (PJ), Paris, 11/11		18 »
(O), St-Vincent-sur-Jard, 11/11		30 »
30 f. Clos-Vougeot (PJ), Vougeot, 17/11		38 »
Paire Croix-Rouge (GF), Paris, 15/12		50 »
40 f. Pic du Midi (PJ), Bagnères-de-Bigorre, 22/12		35 »
50 f. Caen (PJ), Caen, 22/12		35 »

1952	(Doc)	(1er j)
12 f. + 3 f. Journée du Timbre (GF), 8/3		35 »
15 f. De Lattre (PJ), Paris, 8/5		15 »
(O), Mouilleron-en-Pareds, 8/5		125 »
12 f. Vaucouleurs (PJ), Vaucouleurs, 11/5		25 »
30 f. Narvik (PJ), Paris, 28/5		30 »
20 f. Chambord (PJ), Chambord, 30/5		45 »
30 f. Conseil de l'Europe (PJ), Strasbourg, 31/5		60 »
30 f. Bir Hakeim (PJ), Paris, 14/6		30 »
15 f. Poitiers (PJ), Poitiers, 21/6		35 »
15 f. Médaille militaire (PJ), Paris, 5/7		25 »
15 f. Viaduc de Garabit (PJ), Saint-Flour, 5/7		45 »
30 f. Léonard de Vinci (PJ), Amboise, 9/7		45 »
(GF), Congrès d'Amboise, 9/7		850 »
8 f. + 2 f. Flaubert (PJ), Rouen, 18/10		25 »
12 f. + 3 f. Manet (PJ), Paris, 18/10		25 »
15 f. + 4 f. Saint-Saëns (PJ), Paris, 18/10		30 »
18 f. + 5 f. Henri Poincaré (PJ), Nancy, 18/10		25 »
20 f. + 6 f. Haussmann (PJ), Paris, 18/10		25 »
30 f. + 7 f. Thiers (PJ), Marseille, 18/10		25 »
12 f. Laennec (PJ), Quimper, 7/11		14 »
(GF), Paris-Salon Philatélique d'Automne, 7/11		17 »
Paire Croix-Rouge (GF), Metz, 13/12		25 »
(GF), Paris, 13/12		25 »
18 f. Versailles (PJ), Versailles, 20/12		35 »
(O), Château de Versailles, 20/12		850 »

1953	(Doc)	(1er j)
12 f. + 3 f. Journée du Timbre (GF), 14/3		20 »
30 f. Haute Couture (PJ), Paris, 24/4		13 »
6 f. Gargantua (PJ), Paris, 27/5		13 »
18 f. Hernani (PJ), Paris, 6/6		13 »
8 f. Leclerc (GF), Paris-Kermesse aux étoiles, 13/6		15 »
8 f . + 2 f. Saint Bernard (PJ), Citeaux, 9/7		15 »
12 f. +3 f. Olivier de Serres (PJ), Le Pradel, 9/7		15 »
15 f.+ 4 f. Rameau (PJ), Dijon, 9/7		18 »
18 f. + 5 f. Monge (PJ), Beaune, 9/7		15 »
20 f. + 6 f. Michelet (PJ), Paris, 9/7		15 »
30 f. + 7 f. Lyautey (PJ), Nancy, 9/7		16 »
12 f. Tour de France cycliste (PJ), Paris, 26/7		20 »
(GF), Paris, 26/7		150 »
8 f. Célimène (PJ), Paris, 19/9		13 »
12 f. Figaro (PJ), Paris, 19/9		13 »
20 f., 25 f., 30 f., 40 f., 50 f., 75 f. Sports (PJ), Paris, 28/11		100 »
Paire Croix-Rouge (GF), Le Havre, 12/12		40 »

1954	(Doc)	(1er j)
100 f., 200 f., 500 f., 1000 f. Avion (PJ), Paris, 16/1		1200 »
12 f. + 3 f. Journée du Timbre (GF), 20/3		22 »
25 f., 30 f., 40 f., 50 f., 75 f. Métiers d'Art (PJ), Paris, 6/5		90 »
15 f. Foire de Paris (PJ), Paris, 22/5		10 »
(GF), Paris, 22/5		95 »
15 f. Débarquement (PJ), Arromanches, 5/6		32 »
Deuxième Jour : (GF), Lion-sur-Mer, 6/6		110 »
(GF), Sainte-Marie-du-Mont, 6/6		110 »
(GF), Paris, 6/6		50 »
8 f. Les Andelys (PJ), Les Andelys, 5/6		5 »
12 f. De Lattre (GF), Paris, 5/6		20 »
12 f. Leclerc (GF), Paris-Kermesse aux étoiles, 12/6		7 »
12 f. Quimper (PJ), Quimper, 12/6		5 »
6 f. Lourdes (PJ), Lourdes, 12/6		7 »
12 f. Jumièges (PJ), Jumièges, 13/6		7 »
30 f. Tournus (PJ), Tournus, 18/6		15 »
18 f. Cheverny (PJ), Cour-Cheverny, 19/6		10 »
15 f. Stenay (PJ), Stenay, 26/6		5 »
10 f. Royan (PJ), Royan, 3/7		6 »
20 f. Ajaccio (PJ), Ajaccio, 3/7		7 »
18 f. Versailles (obl. hexagone du château), 10/7		18 »
12 f. + 4 f. Saint-Louis (PJ), Poissy, 10/7		35 »
15 f. + 5 f. Bossuet (PJ), Dijon, 10/7		30 »
18 f. + 6 f. Sadi Carnot (PJ), Limoges, 10/7		30 »
20 f. + 7 f. Bourdelle (PJ), Montauban, 10/7		30 »
25 f. + 8 f. Dr Roux (PJ), Confolens, 10/7		32 »
30 f. + 10 f. Paul Valéry (PJ), Sète, 10/7		35 »
18 f. Villandry (PJ), Villandry, 17/7		15 »
15 f. Saint-Cyr (PJ), Coetquidan 1/8		10 »
12 f. Légion d'Honneur (PJ), Boulogne-sur-Mer, 14/8		35 »
30 f. Système métrique (PJ), Paris, 4/10		16 »
50 c. Maine, 70 c. Navarre, 80 c. Bourbonnais,		
1 f. Nivernais (PJ), Paris, 3/11		6 »
(GF), Paris-Enfance, 3/11		30 »
2 f. Aunis, 3 f. Angoumois, 5 f. Saintonge (PJ), Paris, 11/11		6 »
(GF), Paris-Salon Philatélique d'Automne, 11/11		60 »
Paire Croix-Rouge (GF), Mulhouse, 13/12		35 »

1955	(Doc)	(1er j)
12 f. Saint-Simon (PJ), Paris, 5/2	7 »	
30 f. Rotary (PJ), Paris, 23/2	8 »	
5 f. Le Bon (PJ), Brachay, 5/3	3 »	
10 f. Thimonnier (PJ), L'Arbresle, 5/3	3 »	
12 f. Appert (PJ), Châlons-s/-Marne, 5/3	3 »	
18 f. Sainte-Claire-Deville (PJ), Paris, 5/3	4 »	
25 f. Martin (PJ), Bourges, 5/3	4 »	
30 f. Chardonnet (PJ), Besançon, 5/3	4 »	
12 f. +3 f. Journée du Timbre (GF), 19/3	18 »	
25 f. Ganterie (PJ), Saint-Junien, 26/3	4 »	
12 f. Limoges (PJ), Limoges, 26/3	5 »	
12 f. Florian (PJ), Sauves, 2/4	5 »	
15 f. Télévision (PJ), Paris, 16/4	4 »	
12 f. Camp de déportés (PJ), Paris, 23/4	4 »	
12 f. Électrification Chemin de fer (PJ), Lille, 11/5	7 »	
12 f. Jacquemart de Moulins (PJ), Moulins, 28/5	4 »	
(GF), Congr. féd. de Vichy, 28/5	35 »	
30 f. Jules Verne (PJ), Nantes, 3/6	20 »	
(GF), Paris, 3/6	60 »	
(O), Amiens, 3/6	525 »	
50 f. Maryse Bastié (PJ), Limoges, 4/6	45 »	
(GF), Paris, 4/6	70 »	
12 f. + 5 f. Philippe-Auguste (PJ), Gonesse, 11/6	20 »	
15 f. + 6 f. Malherbe (PJ), Caen, 11/6	20 »	
18 f. + 7 f. Vauban (PJ), St-Léger-Vauban, 11/6	20 »	
25 f. + 8 f. Vergennes (PJ), Dijon, 11/6	20 »	
30 f. + 9 f. Laplace (PJ), Beaumont (Calvados). 11/6	20 »	
50 f. + 15 f. Renoir (PJ), Limoges, 11/6	30 »	
30 f. Lumière (PJ), Besançon, 12/6	18 »	
(GF), Lyon, 12/6	270 »	
12 f. Jacques Coeur (PJ), Bourges, 18/6	8 »	
30 f. France-Canada (PJ), La Rochelle, 9/7	20 »	
6 f. Bordeaux (PJ), Bordeaux, 15/10	3 »	
8 f. Marseille (PJ), Marseille, 15/10	3 »	
10 f. Nice (PJ), Nice, 15/10	3 »	
12 f. Cahors (PJ), Cahors, 15/10	3 »	
18 f. Uzerche (PJ), Uzerche, 15/10	4 50	
25 f. Remparts de Brouage (PJ), Brouage, 15/10	3 50	
20 f. Martinique (GF), Paris-Salon de l'enfance + griffe, 1/11	3 »	
12 f. G. de Nerval (PJ), Paris, 11/11	4 »	
(GF), Paris-Salon Philatélique d'Automne, 11/11	22 »	
50 f. Comté de Foix (PJ), Foix, 19/11	1 80	
70 f. Marche (PJ), Guéret, 19/11	1 80	
80 f. Roussillon (PJ), Perpignan, 19/11	1 80	
1 f. Comtat Venaissin (PJ), Carpentras, 19/11	1 80	
Paire Croix-Rouge (GF), Angers, 17/12	30 »	
6 f. Marianne de Muller obl. Service Pub. P.T.T., 24/11	30 »	

1956	(Doc)	(1er j)
15 f. Struthof (PJ), Natzwillers, 14/1	30 »	
(GF), Paris, 14/1	25 »	
15 f. Douai (PJ), Douai, 11/2	6 »	
15 f. Colonel Driant (PJ), Neufchâtel-sur-Aisne, 21/2	6 »	
30 f. Verdun (PJ), Verdun, 3/3	13 »	
(GF), Paris 3/3	15 »	
12 f. +3 f. Journée du Timbre (GF), 17/3	12 »	
12 f. Fabre (PJ), Saint-Léons (Aveyron), 7/4	7 50	
(O), Sérignan, 7/4	12 »	
15 f. Charles Tellier (PJ), Amiens, 7/4	4 »	
(GF), Paris, 7/4	5 »	
18 f. Flammarion (PJ), Montigny-le-Roi, 7/4	7 50	
(GF), Juvisy, 7/4	8 »	
30 f. Sabatier (PJ), Carcassonne, 7/4	6 »	
12 f. Trianon (PJ), Versailles, 14/4	6 »	
30 f. France-Amérique Latine (PJ), Paris, 21/4	6 »	
12 f. Reims-Florence (PJ), Reims, 5/5	7 »	
12 f. Ordre de Malte (PJ), Paris, 12/5	5 »	
15 f. Saint-Yves (PJ), Tréguier, 19/5	4 »	
30 f. Franchet d'Esperey (PJ), Paris, 26/5	2 50	
12 f. Montceau les Mines (PJ), Montceau-les-Mines, 2/6	2 50	
(GF), Montceau-les-Mines, 2/6	5 50	
12 f. + 3 f. Jean Goujon (PJ), Paris, 9/6	7 50	
12 f. + 3 f. G. Budé (PJ), Paris, 9/6	7 50	
12 f. + 3 f. Champlain (PJ), Brouage, 9/6	10 »	
(GF), Paris, 9/6	15 »	
15 f. + 5 f. Chardin (PJ), Paris, 9/6	9 »	
15 f. + 5 f. M. Barrés (PJ), Charmes, 9/6	9 »	
15 f. + 5 f. M. Ravel (PJ), Ciboure, 9/6	12 »	
30 f. Basket (PJ), Mulhouse, 7/7	6 »	
40 f. Pelote basque (PJ), Hasparren, 7/7	6 »	
50 f. Rugby (PJ), Toulouse, 7/7	7 »	
75 f. Alpinisme (PJ), Grenoble, 7/7	8 »	
15 f. et 30 f. Europa 56 (GF), Paris, 15/9	50 »	
(GF), Strasbourg, 15/9	65 »	
12 f. Donzère-Mondragon (PJ), Bollène-Ecluse, 6/10	9 »	
18 f. Téléphérique (PJ), Chamonix, 6/10	9 »	
30 f. Port de Strasbourg (PJ), Strasbourg, 6/10	9 »	
12 f. Parmentier (PJ), Montdidier, 27/10	3 »	
8 f. Pétrarque (PJ), Fontaine-de-Vaucluse, 10/11	3 »	
12 f. Lulli (PJ), Paris, 10/11	6 »	
(GF), Paris-Salon Philatélique d'Automne, 10/11	8 »	
15 f. J.-J. Rousseau (PJ), Montmorency, 10/11	6 »	
18 f. Franklin (PJ), Paris, 10/11	4 50	
(GF), Paris-Salon de l'enfance, 10/11	3 »	
20 f. Chopin (PJ), Paris, 10/11	10 »	
(GF), Paris-Salon Philatélique d'Automne, 10/11	10 »	
30 f. Van Gogh (PJ), Paris, 10/11	12 »	
(GF), Paris, 10/11	22 »	
30 f. Coubertin (PJ), Paris, 24/11	15 »	
Paire Croix-Rouge (GF), Epinal, 8/12	13 »	

1957	(Doc)	(1er j)
15 f. Colombophilie (PJ), Vincennes, 12/1	10 »	
(PF), Vincennes, 12/1	11 »	
500 f. Caravelle (PJ), Toulouse, 26/1	135 »	
18 f. Schoelcher (PJ), Paris, 16/2	8 »	
12 f. + 3 f. Journée du Timbre (GF), 16/3	12 »	
30 f. Sèvres (PJ), Sèvres, 23/3	8 »	
8 f. Planté (PJ), Orthez, 13/4	3 »	
12 f. Beclère (PJ), Paris, 13/4	3 »	
18 f. Terrillon (PJ), Oigny-s/-Seine, 13/4	3 »	
30 f. Oehmichen (PJ), Châlons-sur-Marne, 13/4	12 »	
(GF), Valentigney, 13/4	15 »	
12 f. Uzès (PJ), Uzès, 27/4	4 »	
8 f. Jean Moulin (PJ), Béziers, 18/5	12 »	
10 f. D'Estienne d'Orves (PJ), Verrières-le-Buisson, 18/5	7 »	
12 f. Keller (PJ), Petit-Quevilly, 18/5	7 »	
18 f. Brossolette (PJ), Paris, 18/5	7 »	
20 f. Lebas (PJ), Roubaix, 18/5	7 »	
8 f. Le Quesnoy (PJ), Le Quesnoy, 1/6	2 50	
12 f. Cour des Comptes (PJ), Paris, 1/6	2 50	
12 f. + 3 f. Joinville (PJ), Joinville (Hte-Mne), 15/6	4 50	
12 f. + 3 f. B. Palissy (PJ), Agen, 15/6	4 50	
15 f. + 5 f. Lamennais (PJ), Saint-Malo, 15/6	4 50	
15 f. + 5 f. Quentin de la Tour (PJ), Saint-Quentin, 15/6	7 50	
18 f. + 7 f. George Sand (PJ), Paris, 15/6	6 »	
18 f. + 7 f. J. Guesde (PJ), Paris, 15/6	6 »	
(GF), Roubaix, 15/6	6 »	
30 f. Travaux publics (PJ), Paris, 20/6	2 20	
12 f. Brest (PJ), Brest, 6/7	3 »	
18 f. Jeux universitaires (PJ), Paris, 31/8	4 »	
(GF), Antony, 31/8	5 50	
35 f. Aug. Comte (PJ), Montpellier, 14/9	2 70	
(GF), Paris, 14/9	2 70	
20 f. et 35 f. Europa 57 (GF), Paris, 16/9	22 »	
(GF), Strasbourg, 16/9	22 »	
20 f. Lyon (PJ), Lyon, 5/10	3 »	
8 f. Guadeloupe (PJ), Basse-Terre et Pointe-à-Pitre, 19/10	3 »	
10 f. Elysée (PJ), Paris, 19/10	3 »	
12 f. Beynac (PJ), Beynac-Cazenac, 19/10	3 »	
25 f. Valençay (PJ), Valençay, 19/10	4 »	
35 f. Rouen (PJ), Rouen, 19/10	3 »	
50 f. Saint-Rémy (PJ), Saint-Rémy, 19/10	2 »	
65 f. Evian (PJ), Evian, 19/10	2 »	
8 f. Copernic (PJ), Paris, 9/11	7 50	
10 f. Michel-Ange (PJ), Paris, 9/11	3 »	
12 f. Cervantès (PJ), Paris, 9/11	2 50	
(GF), Paris-Salon de l'enfance, 9/11	2 50	
15 f. Rembrandt (PJ), Paris, 9/11	3 »	
(GF), Paris-Salon Philatélique d'Automne, 9/11	4 »	
18 f. Newton (PJ), Paris, 9/11	3 50	
25 f. Mozart (PJ), Paris, 9/11	10 »	
35 f. Goethe (PJ), Paris, 9/11	3 50	
15 f. Thénard (PJ), La Louptière (Aube), 30/11	1 80	
Paire Croix-Rouge (GF), Niort, 7/12	12 »	

1958	(Doc)	(1er j)
1000 f. Alouette (PJ), Paris, 11/1	135 »	
8 f. Pinel (PJ), Jonquière 25/1	5 »	
12 f. Widal(PJ), Paris, 25/1	5 »	
15 f. Nicolle (PJ), Rouen, 25/1	5 »	
35 f. Leriche (PJ), Roanne, 25/1	5 »	
35 f. Surchargé Conseil de l'Europe (flamme PJ du Conseil), 14/1	24 »	
8 f. Lagrange (PJ), Paris, 15/2	3 »	

12 f. Le Verrier (PJ), Saint-Lô, 15/2	3 »
15 f. Foucault (PJ), Paris, 15/2	3 »
35 f. Berthollet (PJ), Talloires, 15/2	4 »
20 f. Lourdes obl. flamme, 28/2	9 »
12 f. Le Havre (PJ), Le Havre, 29/3	3 »
15 f. Maubeuge (PJ), Maubeuge, 29/3	3 »
18 f. Saint-Dié (PJ), Saint-Dié, 29/3	3 »
25 f. Sète (PJ), Sète, 29/3	4 »
15 f. + 5 f. Journée du Timbre (GF), 17/3	8 »
35 f. Expo. Bruxelles (PJ), 12/4	4 »
8 f. Cavaillès (PJ), Saint-Maixent, 19/4	5 »
12 f. Scamaroni (PJ), Ajaccio, 19/4	5 »
15 f. Simone Lévy (PJ), Chaussin, 19/4	5 »
20 f. Bingen (PJ), Paris, 19/4	5 »
12 f. Boules (PJ), Valence, 26/4	4 »
15 f. Joutes (PJ), Givors, 26/4	4 »
18 f. Arc (PJ), Soissons, 26/4	5 »
25 f. Lutte bretonne (PJ), Quimper, 26/4	4 »
15 f. Senlis (PJ), Senlis, 17/5	2 70
12 f. + 4 f. J. du Bellay (PJ), Liré, 7/6	4 »
12 f. + 4 f. Jean Bart (PJ) Dunkerque, 7/6	6 »
(GF), Paris, 7/6	7 »
15 f. + 5 f. Diderot (PJ), Langres, 7/6	4 »
15 f. + 5 f. Courbet (PJ), Ornans, 7/6	8 »
20 f. + 8 f. Carpeaux (PJ), Valenciennes, 7/6	6 »
(GF) Courbevoie, 7/6	5 »
35 f. + l5 f. Toulouse-Lautrec (PJ), Albi, 7/6	11 »
15 f. Bayeux (PJ), Bayeux, 21/6	3 50
20 f. Marianne de Muller, mise en service des timbres de métropole en Algérie, Alger 22/7	40 »
20 f. et 25 f. Europa 58 (GF), Paris, 13/9	5 »
(GF), Strasbourg, 13/9	6 »
Cachet de Bruxelles	6 »
8 f. Conseil de l'Europe sur fragment (PF), 11/10	4 50
Flamme sur lettre	37 50
20 f. Conseil de l'Europe sur fragment (PF), 12/10	4 50
Flamme sur lettre	37 50
35 f. Conseil de l'Europe sur fragment (PF), 13/10	4 50
Flamme sur lettre	37 50
Les 3 fragments réunis sur une enveloppe 11-12-13/10	12 »
15 f. Foix (PJ), Foix, 11/10	3 50
35 f. Paris-Rome (PJ), Paris, 11/10	7 »
20 f. et 35 f. U.N.E.S.C.O. (PJ), Paris, 1/11	3 »
15 f. Armistice (PJ), Compiègne-Rethondes, 11/11	7 »
50 c. Blason Marseille (PJ), Marseille, 15/11	2 »
70 c. Blason Lyon (PJ), Lyon, 15/11	2 »
80 c. Blason Toulouse (PJ), Toulouse, 15/11	2 »
1 f. Blason Bordeaux (PJ), Bordeaux, 15/11	2 »
2 f. Blason Nice (PJ), Nice, 15/11	2 »
3 f. Blason Nantes (PJ), Nantes, 15/11	2 »
5 f. Blason Lille (PJ), Lille, 15/11	2 »
15 f. + 7 f. Saint Vincent de Paul (PJ), Saint-Vincent-de-Paul (Landes), 6/12	4 »
20 f.+ 8 f. Dunant (PJ), Paris, 6/12	4 »
Les deux précédents (GF), Toulouse, 6/12	10 »

1959

	(Doc)	(1er j)
25 f. Marianne de Muller, obl. Musée Postal, 5/1		3 »
10 f. Moissonneuse, obl. Paris R.P. 12/1		3 »
15 f. Floralies (PJ), Paris, 17/1		3 »
20 f. Palmes académiques (PJ), Paris, 24/1		5 »
300 f. Avion (PJ), Paris, 14/2		25 »
50 f. Père de Foucauld (PJ), Strasbourg, 31/1		8 »
30 f. Palais de l'Élysée, obl. Musée Postal, 10/2		4 »
65 f. Évian obl. Musée Postal, 10/2		4 50
100 f. Guadeloupe obl. Musée Postal, 10/2		7 50
15 f. Blason d'Alger (PJ), Alger, 7/3		2 »
20 f. + 5 f. Journée du Timbre (GF), 21/3		15 »
20 f. École des Mines (PJ), Paris, 11/4		2 50
15 f. Yvonne Le Roux (PJ), Toulon, 25/4		3 »
15 f. Martyrs du Lycée Buffon (PJ), Paris, 25/4		3 »
20 f. Martin-Bret (PJ), Marseille, 25/4		3 »
20 f. Médéric (PJ), Paris, 25/4		3 »
30 f. Moutardier (PJ), Comines, 25/4		3 »
15 f. Foum et Guerza (PJ), Biskra, 23/5		3 »
20 f. Marcoule (PJ), Chusclan, 23/5		4 »
30 f. Hassi Messaoud (PJ), Hassi-Messaoud, 23/5		3 »
50 f. Palais du C.N.I.T. (PJ), Puteaux, 23/5		4 50
20 f. Pilotes d'essai (PJ), Le Bourget, 13/6		7 50
20 f. + 5 f. Villehardouin (PJ), Piney (Aube), 13/6		4 »
15 f. + 5 f. Le Notre (PJ), Paris, 13/6		4 50
15 f. + 10 f. D'Alembert (PJ), Paris, 13/6		4 »
20 f. + 10 f. David d'Angers (PJ), Angers, 13/6		4 50
30 f. + 10 f. Bichat (PJ), Thoirette, 13/6		4 50
30 f. + 10 f. Bartholdi (PJ), Colmar, 13/6		8 »
30 f. Desbordes-Valmore (PJ), Douai, 20/6		2 »
30 f. Tancarville (PJ), Tancarville, 1/8		3 »
50 f. Jaurès (PJ), Castres, 12/9		2 50
25 f. et 50 f. Europa 59 (GF), Paris, 19/9		4 »
(GF), Strasbourg, 19/9		4 »
20 f. Donneurs de sang (PJ), Paris, 17/10		3 »
(GF), Paris, 17/10		3 50
50 f. Traité des Pyrénées (PJ), Behobie, 24/10		3 »
20 f. Poliomyélite (PJ), Paris, 31/10		2 »
(GF), Paris-Salon de l'enfant, 31/10		2 »
50 f. Bergson (PJ), Paris, 7/11		2 »
20 f. Avesnes (PJ), Avesnes, 14/11		2 »
30 f. Castillet de Perpignan (PJ), Perpignan, 14/11		2 »
20 f. + 10 f. Abbé de l'Epée (PJ), Versailles, 5/12		4 »
25 f. + 10 f. Valentin Hauy (PJ), Saint-Just-en-Chaussée, 5/12		4 »
La paire des précédents (GF), Châlons-s/-M., 5/12		6 »
25 f.+ 5 f. Fréjus (O), Paris, 11/12		3 »
50 f. O.T.A.N. (PJ), Paris, 12/12		3 50
Conférence De Gaulle - Eisenhower (O) Paris 14/12		5 »
Session Ministérielle (O) Paris 15/12		5 »

1960

	(Doc)	(1er j)
20 c. Semeuse de Piel obl. Paris R.P., 2/1		3 »
15 c. Laon (PJ), Laon, 16/1		3 »
30 c. Fougères (PJ), Fougères, 16/1		3 »
45 c. Gorges de Kerrata (PJ), Kerrata, 16/1		3 »
50 c. Tlemcen (PJ), Tlemcen, 16/1		3 »
65 c. Vallée de la Sioule (PJ), Ebreuil, 16/1		3 »
(GF), Menat, 16/1		4 »
85 c. Chaumont (PJ), 16/1		3 »
1 f. Réunion (PJ), Paris, 16/1		2 »
20 c. Nolhac (PJ), Ambert, 13/2		2 »
30 c. Saint-Etienne (PJ), Saint-Etienne, 20/2		2 »
50 c. Communes d'Europe (PJ), Cannes, 5/3		2 50
(GF), Cannes, 5/3		3 »
20 c. + 5 c. Journée du Timbre (GF), 12/3		5 »
30 c. Savoie (PJ), Chambéry, 24/3		3 »
50 c. Nice (PJ), 24/3		2 50
20 c. Debeaumarché (PJ), Dijon, 26/3		3 »
20 c. Masse (PJ), Ribérac, 26/3		3 »
30 c. Ripoche (PJ), Paris, 26/3		4 »
30 c. Vieljeux (PJ), Les Vans (Ardèche), 26/3		4 50
(GF), La Rochelle, 26/3		4 »
50 c. Abbé Bonpain (PJ), Dunkerque, 26/3		5 »
25 c. + 10 c. Réfugié (PJ), Paris, 7/4		2 »
(GF), Paris, 7/4		2 »
20 c. Strasbourg (PJ), Strasbourg, 21/5		2 »
30 c. Blois (PJ), Blois, 21/5		3 »
50 c. La Bourboule (PJ), La Bourboule, 28/5		4 »
10 c. + 5 c. L 'Hospital (PJ), Aigueperse, 11/6		4 »
20 c. + 10 c. Turenne (PJ) Sedan, 11/6		4 »
(GF), Paris, 11/6		4 »
20 c. + 10 c. Boileau (PJ), Paris, 11/6		4 »
30 c. + 10 c. Dr Charcot (PJ), Paris, 11/6		5 50
30 c. + 10 c. Bizet (PJ), Paris, 11/6		8 »
50 c. + 15 c. Degas (PJ), Paris, 11/6		8 »
25 c. Marianne de Decaris (GF), Paris, 15/6		5 »
20 c. 18 Juin (PJ), Paris, 18/6		11 »
20 c. Jeux olympiques (PJ), Paris, 9/7		7 »
25 c. et 50 c. Europa 60 (GF), Paris, 17/9		3 »
(GF), Strasbourg, 17/9		3 »
15 c. Basilique de Lisieux (PJ), Lisieux, 24/9		2 »
5 c. Blason d'Oran (PJ), Oran, 15/10		1 50
30 c. Madame de Staël (PJ), Paris, 22/10		2 20
15 c. Général Estienne (PJ), Condé-en-Barrois, 5/11		2 20
(GF), Paris, 5/11		2 20
20 c. Marc Sangnier (PJ), Paris, 5/11		2 20
(GF), Paris Salon de l'Enfant, 5/11		1 80
20 c. Ordre de la Libération (PJ), Paris, 11/11		8 »
30 c . Macareux (PJ), Paris, 12/11		10 »
50 c. Guêpier (PJ), Paris, 12/11		8 »
30 c. André Honnorat (PJ), Paris, 19/11		2 »
30 c. Collège Sainte-Barbe (PJ), Paris, 3/12		2 »
20 c. + 10 c. et 25 c. + 10 c. Saint-Martin (PJ), Tours 3/12		8 »
(GF), Marseille, 3/12		8 »
20 c. Vanneau (PJ), Paris, 17/12		8 »
45 c. Sarcelle (PJ), Paris, 17/12		8 »

1961

	(Doc)	(1er j)
20 c., 25 c., 50 c. U.N.E.S.C.O. (PJ), Paris, 21/1		8 »
20 c. Aristide Maillol (PJ), Banyuls-sur-Mer, 18/2		3 »
30 c. Semeuse de Piel obl. Musée Postal, 23/2		3 »

20 c. Marianne de Cocteau, obl. Musée Postal, 23/2	4 »
50 c. Aéroport de Paris (PJ), Paris, 25/2	5 50
50 c. Georges Méliès (PJ), Paris, 11/3	7 »
20 c. + 5 c. Journée du Timbre (GF), 18/3	5 20
30 c. Jean Nicot (PJ), Nîmes, 25/3	3 »
30 c. Lacordaire (PJ), Recey-sur-Ource, 25/3	3 50
20 c. Jacques Renouvin (PJ), Paris, 22/4	3 »
(GF), Paris, 22/4	3 »
20 c. Lionel Dubray (PJ), Joinville-le-Pont, 22/4	3 »
30 c. Paul Gateaud (PJ), Ozolles, 22/4	3 »
(GF), Mâcon, 22/4	3 »
30 c. Mère Elisabeth (PJ), Draria (Algérie), 22/4	3 »
(GF), Lyon, 22/4	3 »
50 c. Fédération mondiale des Anciens Combattants	
(PJ), Paris, 6/5	3 50
20 c. Bagnoles de l'Orne (PJ), Bagnoles-de-l'Orne, 6/5	2 50
50 c. Deauville (PJ), Deauville, 13/5	3 »
15 c. + 5 c. Du Guesclin (PJ), Broons, 20/5	4 »
20 c. + 10 c. Pierre Puget (PJ), Marseille, 20/5	4 »
20 c. + 10 c. Coulomb (PJ), Angoulême, 20/5	4 »
30 c. + 10 c. Général Drouot (PJ), Nancy, 20/5	4 »
(GF), Nancy, 20/5	4 »
45 c. + 10 c. Daumier (PJ), Marseille, 20/5	6 »
(GF), Paris, 20/5	6 »
50 c. + 15 c. Guillaume Apolinaire (PJ), Paris, 20/5	5 »
20 c. La Champmeslé (PJ), Rouen, 10/6	3 »
30 c. Talma (PJ), Paris, 10/6	3 »
30 c. Rachel (PJ), Paris, 10/6	3 »
50 c. Raimu (PJ), Toulon, 10/6	5 »
50 c. Gérard Philippe (PJ), Cannes, 10/6	5 »
20 c. Le Mont-Dore (PJ), Mont-Dore, 1/7	4 50
50 c. Pierre Fauchard (PJ), Paris, 1/7	3 »
20 c. Thann (PJ), Thann, 1/7	2 50
25 c. + 50 c. Europa (GF), Paris, 16/9	3 »
(GF), Strasbourg, 16/9	3 »
(GF), Lens 16/9	3 »
(GF), Charleville 16/9	3 »
15 c. Saint-Paul (PJ), Saint-Paul, 7/10	4 »
30 c. Arcachon (PJ), Arcachon, 7/10	4 »
45 c. Sully-sur-Loire (PJ), Sully-sur-Loire, 7/10	5 »
50 c. Cognac (PJ), Cognac, 7/10	4 »
65 c. Dinan (PJ), Dinan, 7/10	4 »
85 c. Calais (PJ), Calais, 7/10	4 »
1 f. Médéa (PJ), Médéa (Algérie), 7/10	4 »
50 c. Le Messager (PJ), Paris, 10/11	35 »
65 c. Nus bleus (PJ), Paris, 10/11	35 »
85 c. Joueurs de cartes (PJ), Aix-en-Provence, 10/11	65 »
1 f. 14 Juillet (PJ), Paris, 10/11	60 »
20 c. + 10 c. et 25 c. + 10 c. Croix-Rouge (PJ), Bourges, 2/12	20 »

1962

(Doc)	(1er j)
30 c. Paquebot France (PJ), Le Havre, 11/1	11 »
Traversée Le Havre - U.S.A 3/2 (O)	11 »
30 c. et 50 c. Championnats du monde de ski	
(PJ), Chamonix, 27/1	17 »
50 c. Pierre - Fidèle Bretonneau (PJ),	
Saint-Georges-sur-Cher, 17/2	3 50
(GF), Tours, 17/2	3 50
30 c. Maurice Bourdet (PJ), Marseille, 17/2	3 50
(GF), Paris, 17/2	3 50
20 c. Laval (PJ), Laval, 24/2	4 »
25 c. Coq Gaulois (PJ), Paris, 10/3	6 50
20 c. + 5 c. Journée du Timbre (GF), 17/3	6 »
50 c. Journée mondiale du Théâtre (PJ), Paris, 24/3	4 »
30 c. Vannes (PJ), Vannes, 24/3	5 »
95 c. Dunkerque (PJ), Dunkerque, 24/3	6 50
20 c. Mont-Valérien (PJ), Mont-Valérien, 7/4	7 50
30 c. Vercors (PJ), La Chapelle-en-Vercors, 7/4	7 50
50 c. Ile de Sein (PJ), Ile de Sein, 7/4	7 50
50 c. Lutte contre le paludisme (PJ), Paris, 14/4	2 20
30 c. Semaine nationale des hôpitaux (PJ), Paris, 5/5	3 »
15 c. Vol à voile (PJ) - Toussus le Noble 12/5	3 50
20 c. Aviation légère et sportive (PJ), Toussus-le-Noble, 12/5	3 50
(GF), Paris, 12/5 (2 env.)	6 »
50 c. Ecole d'horlogerie de Besançon (PJ), Besançon, 19/54	»
50 c. Tricentenaire des Gobelins (PJ), Paris, 26/5	4 »
50 c. Pascal (PJ), Clermont-Ferrand, 26/5	4 50
15 c. + 5 c. Denis Papin (PJ), Blois, 2/6	6 »
20 c. + 10 c. Edmé Bouchardon (GF), Chaumont, 2/6	5 20
20 c. + 10 c. Joseph Lakanal (PJ), Serres-sur- Arget, 2/6	5 20
30 c. + 10 c. Gustave Charpentier (PJ), Dieuze, 2/6	7 50
45 c. + 15 c. Edouord Esraunier (PJ), Dijon, 2/6	5 20
50 c.+ 20 c. Hyacinthe Vincent (PJ), Bordeaux, 2/6	6 »
30 c. Rennes (PJ), Rennes, 9/6	3 50
(GF), Rennes, 9/6	3 50
5 c. Blason d'Amiens (PJ), Amiens, 21/7	2 20
15 c. Blason de Nevers (PJ), Nevers, 21/7	2 20
1 f. Le Touquet-Paris-Plage (PJ), Touquet-Paris Plage,1/9	2 20
20 c. et 30 c. Roses (PJ), Orléans, 8/9 (2 envel.)	7 »
Idem "Vertolaye" (GF) (2 envel.)	8 »
25 c. et 50 c. Europa (GF), Paris, 15/9	2 20
(GF), Strasbourg, 15/9	2 50
(GF), Aix-en-Provence, 15/9	3 »
25 c. et 50 c. Télécommunications spatiales (PJ),	
Pleumeur-Bodou, 29/9 (2 envel.)	4 50
50 c. "Bonjour, Monsieur Courbet" (PJ), Ornans, 9/11	40 »
65 c. "Madame Manet au canapé bleu" (PJ), Paris, 9/11	40 »
1 f. "Officier de chasseurs à cheval" (PJ), Rouen, 9/11	40 »
(GF), Paris, 9/11	20 »
20 c. + 10 c. et 25 c. + 10 c. "Croix-Rouge"	
(PJ), Angoulême, 8/12	20 »

1963

(Doc)	(1er j)
20 c., 25 c. et 50 c. Conseil de l'Europe (PJ),Strasbourg, 3/1	10 »
10 c. Blason de Troyes (PJ), Troyes, 12/1	2 »
30 c. Bathyscaphe "Archimède" (PJ), Paris, 26/1	2 »
30 c. Floralies nantaises (PJ), Nantes, 9/2	2 50
20 c. + 10 c. Amyot (PJ), Melun, 23/2	3 »
30 c. + 10 c. Marivaux (PJ), Paris, 23/2	3 »
50 c. + 20 c. Daviel (PJ), Barre-en-Ouche, 23/2	3 »
50 c. "La lutte de Jacob avec l'ange" (PJ), St-Maurice, 2/3	12 »
1 f. "Vitrail de l'église Sainte-Foy de Conches"	
(PJ), Conches-en-Ouche, 2/3	12 »
20 c. + 5 c. Journée du Timbre (GF), 16/3	4 »
50 c. Campagne mondiale contre la faim (PJ), Paris, 22/3	2 »
30 c. Plateau des Glières (PJ), Thônes, 23/3	4 »
(GF), Thorens-Glières 23/3	4 »
50 c. Déportés, Paris (PJ), Paris, 23/3	3 »
Déportés (idem) (GF), Paris, 23/3	3 »
20 c. Beethoven, 20 c. Verhaeren, 20 c. Mazzini,	
20 c. Mayrish, 30 c. De Groot (PJ), Paris, 27/4	10 »
50 c. 1re Conférence postale internationale (PJ), Paris, 4/5	2 »
30 c. Lycée Louis-le-Grand (PJ), Paris, 18/5	2 »
20 c. + 10 c. Etienne Méhul (PJ), Givet, 25/5	3 »
30 c. + 10 c. Nicolas Vauquelin (PJ),	
Saint-André-d'Hébertot, 25/5	2 20
(GF), Paris, 25/5	2 20
50 c. + 20 c. Alfred de Vigny (PJ), Loches, 25/5	3 70
30 c. Caen (PJ), Caen, 1/6	3 »
(GF), Caen, 1/6	3 50
50 c. Radiotélescope de Nançay (PJ), Nançay, 8/6	3 50
(GF), Le Bourget, 8/6	10 »
30 c. Château d'Amboise (PJ), Amboise, 15/6	3 »
50 c. Côte d'Azur varoise (PJ), Saint-Raphaël, 15/6	2 50
60 c. Saint-Flour (PJ), Saint-Flour, 15/6	2 50
85 c. Vittel (PJ), Vittel, 15/6	2 50
95 c. Abbaye de Moissac (PJ), Moissac, 15/6	2 50
30 c. Ski nautique (PJ), Vichy, 31/8	2 »
25 c. et 50 c. Europa (GF), Paris, 14/9	2 »
(GF), Strasbourg, 14/9	3 »
85 c. Les Mariés de la Tour Eiffel (PJ), Paris, 9/11	10 »
(GF), Vence, 9/11	7 50
(GF), Paris, 9/11	7 50
95 c. Vitrail de la cathédrale de Chartres (PJ), Chartres, 9/11	15 »
20 c. + 10 c. et 25 c. + 10 c. Croix-Rouge	
(GF-PJ), Bordeaux, 7/12	5 »
25 c. Philatec (PJ), Paris, 14/12	1 50
20 c. Maison de la radio-télévision (PJ), Paris, 15/12	1 50

1964

(Doc)	(1er j)
1 c. Blason de Niort (GF), Niort, 25/1	2 »
2 c. Blason de Guéret (PJ), Guéret, 25/1	2 »
30 c. Protection civile (PJ), Paris, 8/2	4 »
30 c. Reclassement professionnel des paralysés (PJ),	
Paris, 22/2	2 »
20 c. + 5 c. Journée du Timbre (GF), 14/3	4 »
20 c. + 5 c. Déportation (PJ), Paris, 21/3	3 50
50 c. + 5 c. Résistance (PJ), Paris, 21/3	3 50
30 c. + 10 c. Président Coty (PJ), Le Havre, 25/4	2 »
1 f. Jean le Bon (PJ), Le Mans, 25/4	12 »
25 c., 25 c., 30 c. et 30 c. Bande Philatec (PJ), Paris, 9/5	4 50
25 c. Aéropostale de Nuit (PJ), Le Bourget, 9/5	3 »
12 c. Blason d'Agen (PJ), Agen, 16/5	2 »
18 c. Saint-Denis de la Réunion (PJ), Paris, 16/5	2 »
30 c. + 10 c. Calvin (PJ), Noyon, 23/5	2 »
60 c. Notre-Dame de Paris (PJ), Paris, 23/5	9 »
30 c. + 10 c. Gerbert (PJ), Aurillac, 30/5	1 60
(GF), Reims, 30/5	1 60

1 f. Philatec (PJ), Paris, 5/6 30 »
(GF), Paris, 8/6 30 »
idem, en bloc de quatre sur grande enveloppe 100 »
30 c. + 5 c. Débarquements de Normandie et de Provence
(GF-PJ), Caen, Bayeux, Saint-Lô, Cherbourg,
Valognes, Sainte-Mère-Eglise, 6/6 (6 enveloppes) 22 50
70 c. Tour de César (PJ), Provins, 13/6 2 »
1 f. 25, Chapelle de Notre-Dame-du-Haut (PJ),
Ronchamp, 13/6 3 »
15 c.+ 5 c. Appel du 18 Juin (PJ), Paris, 18/6 10 »
30 c. Georges Mandel (PJ), Chatou, 4/7 1 50
50 c. Jeux Olympiques de Tokyo (PJ), Paris, 4/7 2 »
1 f. Email champlevé limousin (PJ), Limoges, 4/7 7 50
(GF), Le Mans, 4/7 7 »
30 c. + 5 c. Libération de Paris et de Strasbourg
(GF-PJ), Paris, 22/8 4 »
30 c. 50e anniversaire de la victoire de la Marne
(PJ), Gagny, 5/9 3 »
(GF), Sézanne, 5/9 3 »
25 c. et 50 c. Europa (PJ), Paris, 12/9 2 60
(GF), Strasbourg, 12/9 2 60
1 f. "La Dame à la licorne" (PJ), Paris, 31/10 8 »
25 c. Coopération (PJ), Paris, 6/11 2 »
20 c. + 10 c. Jean Nicolas Corvisart (PJ), Dricourt, 12/12 6 »
25 c. + 10 c. Dominique Larrey (PJ), Baudéan, 12/12 6 »

1965 (Doc) (1er j)

30 c. Coq gaulois (PJ), Paris, 15/1 3 50
30 c. Blason de Paris (PJ), Paris, 16/1 3 50
25, 30 et 60 c. Conseil de l'Europe (PJ), Paris, 16/1 9 »
30 et 60 c. U.N.E.S.C.O. (PJ), Paris, 23/1 4 50
40 c. Chapelle Notre-Dame-du-Haut, à Ronchamp
(PJ), Ronchamp, 6/2 3 »
1 f. 30, Château de Joux (PJ), Pontarlier, 6/2 3 »
30 c. + 10 c. La Rochefoucauld (PJ), Paris, 13/2 2 »
40 c. + 10 c. Paul Dukas (PJ), Paris, 13/2 2 50
30 c. + 10 c. Nicolas Poussin (PJ), Les Andelys, 20/2 3 »
40 c. + 10 c. Charles d'Orléans (PJ), Paris, 20/2 3 »
(GF), Blois, 20/2 2 »
1 f. "L'anglaise du Star au Havre" (PJ), Albi, 12/3 10 »
(GF), Paris, 12/3 9 »
25 c. + 5 c. Journée du Timbre (GF), 27/3 4 »
40 c. Retour des déportés (PJ), Paris, 1/4 3 »
(GF), Paris, 2-3/4 3 »
25 c. Maison des Jeunes et de la Culture (PJ), Paris, 10/4 3 »
60 c. "Campagne de l'accueil et de l'amabilité"
(PJ), Paris, 24/4 2 »
40 c. 20e anniversaire de la Victoire de 1945 (PJ), Reims, 8/5 3 70
(GF), Paris, 8/5 3 50
60 c. U.I.T. (PJ), Paris, 17/5 2 20
40 c. Croix de Guerre (PJ), Paris, 22/5 3 »
40 c. Cathédrale de Bourges (PJ), Bourges, 5/6 3 »
(GF), Bourges, 5/6 3 »
1 f. Cathédrale de Sens (PJ), Sens, 5/6 6 »
(GF), Sens, 7/6 14 »
2 f. Mystère 20 (PJ), Le Bourget, 12/6 12 »
(GF), Le Bourget, 12/6 14 »
50 c. Moustiers-Sainte-Marie (PJ), Moustiers, 19/6 3 »
75 c. Gorges du Tarn (PJ), Sainte-Enimie, 10/7 3 »
95 c. Paysage vendéen (PJ), Saint-Jean-de-Monts, 10/7 3 »
1 f. Alignements de Carnac (PJ), Carnac, 10/7 3 »
30 c. Tunnel routier sous le Mont-Blanc (PJ), Chamonix, 17/7 3 »
60 c. Aix-les-Bains (PJ), Aix-les-Bains, 17/7 3 »
30 c. et 60 c. Europa (PJ), Paris, 25/9 1 50
(GF), Strasbourg, 25/9 2 »
1 f. Les très riches heures du duc de Berry
(PJ), Chantilly, 25/9 5 50
25 c. 1 000 000 ha reboisés (PJ), Paris, 2/10 2 »
30 c. Tricentenaire du repeuplement de l'Ile
Bourbon (PJ), Paris, 2/10 2 »
60 c. 20e anniversaire du Commissariat à
l'énergie atomique (PJ), Paris, 9/10 2 20
1 f. L'apocalypse (PJ), Angers, 30/10 5 50
(GF), Paris, 31/10 3 20
25 c. 30e anniversaire de l'École de l'Air (PJ),
Salon-de-Provence, 6/11 2 20
(GF), Paris, 6/11 3 »
1 f. Le violon rouge (PJ), Le Havre, 6/11 4 »
(GF), Paris, 6/11 2 50
30 et 60 c. Fusée Diamant et Satellite A I (PJ), Paris, 30/11 2 »
25 c. + 10 c. et 30 c. + 10 c. Croix-Rouge
(GF-PJ), Strasbourg, 11/12 3 »
(GF), Cagnes-sur-Mer, 11/12 3 »

1966 (Doc) (1er j)

La plupart des oblitérations Premier Jour sont désormais à l'un des trois types ci-dessous :
I. Grand format illustré avec la mention Premier Jour.
II. Grand format illustré sans mention Premier Jour.
III. Grand format ordinaire avec mention Premier jour.
Il y a de très rares exceptions, telle l'oblitération accompagnant le satellite D1
Les clichés sont réduits d'1/3.

I

II

III

5 c. Armoiries d'Auch (I), Auch, 22/1 2 20
25 c. Armoiries de Mont-de-Marsan (I),
Mont-de-Marsan, 22/1 2 20
30 c. Marcel Proust (I), Paris, 12/2 2 50
(II), Illiers, 12/2 2 20
30 c. Saint Pierre Fourier (I), Mirecourt, 12/2 3 »
30 c. François Mansart (I), Paris, 12/2 3 »
60 c. Satellite D I (PJ), Paris, 18/2 1 80
25 c. + 10 c. Journée du Timbre (II), 19/3 3 50
1 f. Cratère de Vix (I), Châtillon-sur-Seine, 26/3 10 »
60 c. Jeu d'échecs (I), Le Havre, 2/4 4 »
25 c. Pont de Pont-Saint-Esprit (I), Pont-Saint-Esprit, 23/4 2 20
25 c. Millénaire du Mont-Saint-Michel (I),
Le Mont-Saint-Michel, 30/4 4 »
25 c. Bicentenaire de la réunion de la Lorraine et
du Barrois à la France (I), Nancy, 6/5 2 20
(II), Bar-le-Duc, 6/5 2 20
30 c. + 5 c. 50e anniversaire de la victoire de Verdun (I), 28/5 3 50
(II), Paris, 28/5 3 50
40 c. Niort (III), Niort, 28/5 2 20
60 c. 9e centenaire de la bataille d'Hastings (I), Falaise, 4/6 3 »
(II), Bayeux, 4/6 3 »
60 c. Tricentenaire de l'académie des Sciences (I), Paris, 4/6 2 »
60 c. 19e Congrès international des Chemins de fer
(I), Paris, 11/6 2 20
25 c. Pont d'Oléron (I), Château d'Oléron et
Bourcefranc, 18/6, chaque 2 »
1 f. Le Nouveau-Né (I), Rennes, 25/6 4 »
30 c. + 10 c. Gabriel Fauré (1), Pamiers, 25/6 2 50
30 c. + 10 c. Elie Metchnikoff (I), Paris, 9/7 2 »
30 c. + 10 c. Hippolyte Taine (I), Vouziers, 9/7 2 »
30 c. et 60 c. Europa (I), Paris, 24/9 2 »
(II), Strasbourg, 24/9 2 »
1 f. Vitrail de la Sainte-Chapelle à Paris (I), Paris, 22/10 4 »
40 c. Vercingétorix (I), Clermont-Ferrand, 5/11 2 »
(II), Alésia, 5/11 2 »
40 c. Clovis (I), Reims, 5/11 2 »
60 c. Charlemagne (I), Noyon, 5/11 2 »
(II), Paris, 5/11 2 »
1 f. 60, Centenaire du réseau pneumatique (I), Paris, 11/11 4 50
2 f. 30, Château de Val (I), Lanobre, 19/11 8 50
1 f. Tapisserie de Lurçat (I), Aubusson, 19/11 3 »
(II), St-Céré, 19/11 2 20
60 c. Usine marémotrice de la Rance (I), Saint-Servan, 3/12 2 »
La Richardais, 3/12 2 »
1 f. Crispin et Scapin (I), Marseille, 10/12 2 20
25 c. + 10 c. et 30 c. + 10 c. Croix-Rouge
(I), Saint-Étienne, 10/12 3 »
20 c. Blason de Saint-Lô (I), Saint-Lô, 17/12 2 »
25, 30 et 60 c. U.N.E.S.C.O. (I), Paris, 17/12 4 50

1967	(Doc)	(1er j)
30 c. + 10 c. Émile Zola (I) Paris, 4/2		3 »
(II), Paris		2 »
30 c. +10 c. Beaumarchais (I), Paris, 4/2		3 »
(II), Paris, 4/2		2 »
40 c. 3e Congrès international de l'U.E.R. (I) Paris, 4/3		1 50
25 c. +10 c. Journée du Timbre (II), 8/4		3 50
1 f. "La carriole du Père Juniet" (I), Laval, 15/4		5 »
60 c. Exposition internationale de Montréal (I), Paris, 22/4		1 80
60 c. 10es Jeux olympiques d'hiver (I), Grenoble, 22/4		2 »
30 c. et 60 c. Europa (I), Paris, 29/4		2 20
(II), Strasbourg, 29/4		2 20
40 c. Nungesser et Coli (I), Paris, 6/5		3 »
25 c. Pont de Bordeaux (I), Bordeaux, 6/5		2 20
40 c. Tours (III), Tours, 13/5		2 50
60 c. Esnault-Pelterie (I), Le Bourget, 27/5		2 50
25 c. Ecole vétérinaire (I), Maisons-Alfort, 27/5		1 80
1 f. Cathédrale de Rodez (I), Rodez, 10/6		2 50
1 f. 50, Morlaix (I), Morlaix, 10/6		2 50
70 c. Saint-Germain-en-Laye		
(I), Saint-Germain-en-Laye, 17/6		3 »
30 c. +10 c. Saint François de Sales (I), Thorens-Glières, 24/6		2 »
30 c. +10 c. Camus (I), Lourmarin, 24/6		2 »
1 f. François 1er (I), Cognac, 1/7		4 »
95 c. Boulogne-sur-Mer (I), Boulogne-sur-Mer, 8/7		2 20
60 c. Vire (I), Vire, 8/7		2 20
50 c. Saint-Quentin (I), Saint-Quentin, 8/7		2 20
75 c. La Baule (I), La Baule, 22/7		2 20
40 c. Floralies d'Orléans (I), Orléans, 29/7		2 50
40 c. 9e Congrès international de la Comptabilité (I), Paris, 2/9		2 »
Ingres "La Baigneuse" (I), Montauban, 9/9		7 »
Bir Hakeim, 25e anniversaire (I), Paris, 7/10		3 »
Eglise Sainte-Madeleine (I), Troyes, 7/10		4 »
Marie Curie (I), Paris, 21/10		3 »
Cinquantenaire du Lions international, Paris, 28/10		2 50
République, nouvelles valeurs 0,25, 0,30 (I), Paris, 4/11		2 50
Hugues Capet (I), Senlis, 10/11		2 »
Hugues Capet (II), Paris, 10/11		2 »
Philippe-Auguste (I), Bouvines, 10/11		2 »
Saint Louis (I), Paris, 10/11		2 »
Croix-Rouge (I), Dieppe, 16/12		4 »

1968	(Doc)	(1er j)
Cinquantenaire des Chèques Postaux (I), Paris, 6/1		1 50
Xes Jeux Olympiques d'hiver,		
sur 5 env. différentes (I), Grenoble, 27/1		7 50
Idem, cachet "Inauguration",		
sur 5 env. différentes (II), Grenoble, 6/2		7 50
La Prévention routière (I), Paris, 24/2		2 »
Journée du Timbre 1968 (II), 16/3		3 »
François Couperin (I), Paris, 23/3		2 »
Général Desaix (I), Ayat-sur-Sioule (23-3)		1 50
5e Conférence de coopération mondiale 'Cités Unies'		
(I), Royan, 13/4		1 80
Grotte préhistorique de Lascaux-Montignac (I), 13/4		25 »
Europa (I), Paris, 27/4		1 80
"Conseil de l'Europe" (II), Strasbourg, 27/4		2 »
Alain René Lesage (I), Sarzeau, 4/5		1 50
Château de Langeais (I), Langeais, 4/5		2 50
Pierre Larousse (I), Toucy, 11/5		1 80
Jumelage Forêt de Rambouillet-Forêt Noire,		
Rambouillet, 18/5		2 »
650e anniversaire de l'Enclave des Papes, Valréas (I), 25/5		2 »
Tricentenaire du traité d'Aix-la-Chapelle, Paris (I), 29/6		1 50
Paul Claudel, Villeneuve-sur-Fère (I), 6/7		2 »
Paris (II), 6/7		1 80
Saint-Pol-Roux, Marseille (I), 6/7		1 80
Camaret (II), 6/7		1 80
Le Pont de Martrou, Rochefort (I), 20/7		3 »
1re liaison postale par avion, Saint-Nazaire (I), 17/8		2 »
1re liaison postale par avion, Paris (I), 17/8		2 »
Bicentenaire de la Libération des prisonnières		
huguenotes, Aigues-Mortes (I), 31/8		3 50
Béziers, Béziers (I), 7/9		1 80
Arearea, Paris (I), 21/9		4 »
50e anniversaire de l'Armistice sur le front d'Orient,		
Paris (I), 28/9		2 20
Bicentenaire du rattachement de la Corse à la France,		
Ajaccio (I), 5/10		2 20
Jeux olympiques de Mexico, Paris (I), 12/10		2 »
20e anniversaire des Expéditions polaires françaises,		
Paris (I), 19/10		3 »
La Danse, Paris (I), 26/10		3 »
50e anniversaire du bal des Petits Lits Blancs,		
Paris (I), 26/10		1 50
50e anniversaire de l'Armistice, Paris (I), 9/11		2 20
50e anniversaire de l'Armistice, La Capelle (I), 9/11		4 50
Portrait de modèle, Paris (I), 9/11		3 »
Philippe IV le Bel, Paris (I), 16/11		1 80
Du Guesclin, Châteauneuf-les-Randon (I), 16/1		1 80
Jeanne-d'Arc, Vaucouleurs (I), 16/11		2 »
Croix-Rouge, Troyes (I), 14/12		4 »

1969	(Doc)	(1er j)
Marianne de Cheffer, Paris (I et II), 11/1		2 50
Eglise de Brou, Bourg-en-Bresse (I), 15/2		1 80
Barrage de Vouglans, Vouglans (I), 15/2		2 20
La Trinité-sur-Mer, La Trinité-s/Mer (I), 15/2		3 »
Cathédrale d'Amiens, Amiens (I), 22/2		3 »
Avion " Concorde ", Toulouse (I), 2/3		9 »
U.N.E.S.C.O. Paris (I), 8/3		8 »
Journée du Timbre, Paris (I), 15/3		3 »
Albert Roussel, Tourcoing (I), 22/3		2 »
Général Marceau, Chartres (I), 22/3		2 »
Sainte-Beuve, Boulogne-sur-Mer (I), 22/3		1 80
Conseil de l'Europe, Strasbourg (I), 22/3		7 »
Château de Hautefort, Hautefort (I), 5/4		2 50
Floralies de Paris, Paris (I), 12/4		2 50
Floralies de Paris, "Inauguration" (I), 23/4		6 »
Europa, Paris (I), 26/4		1 80
Europa, Strasbourg (II), 26/4		4 »
Philippe le Bon, Dijon (I), 3/5		3 »
Victoire du Garigliano, Paris (I), 10/5		2 »
50e anniversaire de l'O.I.T., Paris (I), 10/5		1 50
Maréchal Lannes, Lectoure (I), 10/5		1 80
André Gide, Paris (I), 17/5		1 80
Georges Cuvier, Montbéliard (I), 17/5		1 80
Châlons-sur-Marne, Châlons-s.-Marne (I), 24/5		1 80
25e anniversaire du débarquement de Normandie,		
Paris (I), 31/5		4 »
Combats du Mont Mouchet, St-Flour (I), 7/6		3 »
Chantilly, Chantilly (I), 21/6		1 50
Saint-Savin-sur-Gartempe, St-Savin (I), 28/6		2 70
Canoë-Kayak, Bourg-Saint-Maurice (I), 2/8		1 80
Bicentenaire de Napoléon, Ajaccio (I), 16/8		3 50
Débarquement de Provence, St-Raphaël (I), 23/8		3 »
Maréchal Leclerc, Paris (I), 23/8		3 50
Charte de l'Eau, Paris (I), 27/9		1 80
Charte de l'Eau, Strasbourg (II), 27/9		1 80
Mouflon, Paris (I), 11/10		2 80
Normandie-Niemen, Paris (I), 18/10		3 50
Ecole Centrale, Châtenay-Malabry (I), 18/10		2 »
Le Redoutable, Cherbourg (I), 25/10		2 »
Le Redoutable, Paris (II), 25/10		2 20
Louis XI, Paris (I), 8/11		2 »
Idem, Charles le Téméraire, Dijon (II)		2 »
Bayard, Poncharra (I), 8/11		2 »
Henri IV, Nantes (I), 8/11		2 50
"Le Cirque", de Seurat, Paris (I), 8/11		4 »
Maréchal Leclerc Strasbourg (I), 22/11		3 50
Croix-Rouge, Avignon (I), 13/12		5 50

1970	(Doc)	(1er j)
Alain Gerbault, Laval (I), 10/1		4 »
Alain Gerbault, Puteaux (II), 10/1		6 »
Gendarmerie, Paris (I), 31/1		6 »
Philibert de l'Orme, Lyon (I), 14/2		1 80
Le Vau, Paris (I), 14/2		1 50
Prosper Mérimée, Paris (I), 14/2		2 »
Handball, Paris (I), 21/2		2 »
Maréchal Juin, Paris (I), 28/2		2 50
Aérotrain, Orléans (I), 7/3		2 50
Journée du Timbre, (II), 14/3		3 »
Flamant rose, Paris (I), 21/3		2 20
Caventou, Saint-Omer (I), 21/3		1 50
Pelletier, Paris (I), 21/3		1 50
Fusée Diamant, Kourou Guyane (I), 28/3		3 »
Lutte contre le cancer, Paris (I), 4/4		2 50
Alexandre Dumas, Villers-Cotterets (I), 11/4		2 »
Edouard Branly, Amiens (I), 11/4		2 »
Maurice de Broglie, Paris (I), 11/4		2 »
Europa, Paris (I), 2/5		1 80
Europa, Strasbourg (II), 2/5		3 »
Armistice de Berlin, Paris (I), 8/5		2 50
Primitif de Savoie, Chambéry (I), 9/5		4 50
Lens, Lens (I), 16/5		1 50

Périgueux, Périgueux (II), 13/6	2 »
Martinique, Diamant (I), 20/6	1 50
Chancelade, Chancelade (I), 20/6	2 20
Guadeloupe, Le Gosier (I), 20/6	1 80
Retour des Déportés, Strasbourg (I), 27/6	2 »
Handicapés physiques, Saint-Étienne (I), 27/6	1 80
"Flore" de Carpeaux, Valenciennes (I), 4/7	4 50
Observatoire de Haute-Provence,	
Saint-Michel-l'Observatoire (I), 4/7	2 50
Mermoz, Aubenton (I), 19/9	60 »
Saint-Exupéry, Lyon (I), 19/9	70 »
Athlétisme, Paris (I), 11/9	1 80
Salines Royales, Arc et Senans (I), 26/9	1 80
Diane (Boucher), Paris (I), 10/10	3 50
Richelieu, La Rochelle (I), 17/10	2 »
Louis XIV, Versailles (I), 17/10	4 »
Fontenoy, Paris (I), 17/10	2 »
O.N.U., Paris (I), 24/10	1 80
Bordeaux, Bordeaux (I), 7/11	3 50
Denfert-Rochereau, Belfort (I), 14/11	2 70
Degas, Paris (I), 14/11	4 »
Fresque de Dissay, Poitiers	
Croix-Rouge (I), 12/12	4 50

1971	(Doc)	(1er j)
Marianne de Béquet, Paris (I), 2/1		2 »
Ballons montés, Paris (I), 16/1		5 »
Musée Postal, (III), 16/1		3 »
Saint Mathieu, Strasbourg (I), 23/1		3 30
Marianne 0,45, Paris (I), 6/2		2 »
U.N.E.S.C.O., Paris (I), 13/2		3 »
Conseil de l'Europe, Strasbourg (I), 20/2		3 »
Patinage artistique, Lyon (I), 20/2		2 »
Auber, Caen (I), 6/3		2 70
Général Brosset, Paris (I), 6/3		2 20
Lyon (III), 6/3		2 20
Océanexpo, Bordeaux (I), 6/3		2 »
Journée du Timbre (III), 27/3		2 50
Millet, Paris (I), 3/4		4 »
Cap Hornier, Saint-Malo (I), 10/4		5 »
Didier Daurat, Paris (I), 17/4		15 »
Raymond Vanier, Orléans (I), 17/4		15 »
Isard, Tarbes (I), 24/4		2 »
Etats Généraux, Versailles (I), 8/5		3 »
Grignard, Cherbourg (I), 8/5		1 80
Lyon (III), 8/5		1 80
Europa (2 enveloppes), Paris (I), 8/5		3 »
Strasbourg (III), 8/5		3 »
Grenoble "Congrès", Grenoble (I), 29/5		2 »
Farman, Le Bourget (I), 29/5		3 »
A.F.R., Angers (I), 5/6		1 50
Rouault, Paris (I), 5/6		3 »
Sedan "Château", Sedan (I), 12/6		2 20
Pont d'Arc, Vallon Pont d'Arc (I), 12/6		2 20
Sainte-Chapelle, Riom (I), 19/6		1 50
Place aux Fleurs, Dole (I), 3/7		1 50
Le Dolder, Riquewihr (I), 3/7		1 80
La Bastille, Paris (I), 10/7		3 »
U.I. Interparlementaire, Paris (I), 28/8		1 80
Valmy, Valmy (I), 18/9		4 »
Général Delestraint, Saint-Vaast (I), 16/10		2 50
Bourg-en-Bresse (II), 16/10		2 50
Robert Houdin, Blois (I), 16/10		4 50
Chambre des Métiers, Paris (I), 16/10		1 50
Caméléon, Paris (I), 6/11		1 80
Général de Gaulle, Lille (O), 9/11		5 »
Entrevue de Brazza, Lille (O), 9/11		5 »
Arc de Triomphe, Lille (O), 9/11		5 »
Président de la République, Lille (O), 9/11		5 »
La bande complète, Lille (O), 9/11		15 »
Existe avec oblitération de Colombey-les-Deux-Eglises		15 »
Académie de Médecine, Paris (I), 13/11		2 »
Croix-Rouge (2 env.), Tournus (I), 11/12, R		4 »
(2 env.), Royan (II), 11/12, R		6 »

1972	(Doc)	(1er j)
Fragonard, Paris (I), 22/1		4 »
Crozet, Paris (I), 29/1		3 »
J.O. Sapporo, Paris (I), 5/2		2 20
Chomedey de Maisonneuve, Neuville-s.-Vanne (I)		1 80
Troyes (O)		2 20
Bergès, Lorp-Sentaraille (I), 19/2		1 80
Lancey (II)		2 20
Journée du Timbre 1972 (I), 18/3		2 50
Mois du coeur, Paris (I), 8/4		1 80
Cathédrale de Saint-Just, Narbonne (I), 8/4		3 70
Grand-duc, Paris (I), 15/4		3 »
Europa (2 enveloppes), Paris (I), 22/4		3 »
(2 enveloppes), Strasbourg (II), 22/4		4 50
Abbaye de Charlieu, Charlieu (I), 29/415		2 50
Donneurs de sang, Nantes (I), 5/5		2 »
Terre-Neuvas, Dinard (I), 6/5		3 »
45e Congrès Société phil., Saint-Brieuc (I), 20/5		1 50
Saumon, Paris (I), 27/5		2 20
Code Postal, Paris (I), 3/6		2 »
Aviatrices, H. Boucher, Paris (I), 10/6		11 »
M. Hilsz, Levallois (I), 10/6		11 »
Claude Monet, Paris (I), 17/6		3 »
Edouard Belin, Vesoul (I), 24/6		1 80
I.P.T.T., Paris (I), 1/7		1 50
Louis Blériot, Cambrai (I), 1/7		2 50
J.O. Munich, Paris (I), 8/7		2 »
Randonnée pédestre, Florac (I), 15/7		2 20
Championnats du monde cyclistes, Gap (I), 22/7		3 »
Marseille (I), 22/7		3 »
Château de Bazoches, Bazoches (I), 2/9		2 50
Amiral de Grasse, Le Bar-sur-Loup (I), 9/9		2 »
Idem, Toulon (II), 9/9		2 »
Théophile Gautier, Tarbes (I), 9/9		2 70
La Sologne, Romorantin (I), 30/9		1 80
Incroyables, Paris (I), 7/10		2 »
Le Maître de Moulins, Paris (I), 14/10		3 50
Champollion, Paris (I), 14/10		3 50
Idem, Figeac (II), 14/10		3 50
Pont d'Arcole, Paris (I), 11/11		3 50
Bonaparte en Egypte, Paris (I), 11/11		3 50
Desgenettes, Luxeuil (I), 16/12		3 »
Broussais, Luxeuil (I), 16/12		3 »
Derain, Paris (I), 16/12		6 »

"A partir de la fin de l'année 1973 les cotes de la colonne de gauche concernent les Documents Officiels et celles de droite les Premiers Jours".

1973	(Doc)	(1er j)
Sainte Thérèse, Alençon (I), 6/1		3 »
Anthurium, Fort-de-France (I), 20/1		2 20
Coopération Franco-Allemande, Paris (I), 22/1		2 50
Amiral Coligny, Châtillon-Coligny (I), 17/2		1 80
Idem, Paris (II), 17/2		1 80
Immigration polonaise, Auchel (I), 3/2		1 80
Eglise Saint-Austremoine, Issoire (I), 10/2		6 »
Codos, Ivier, 24/2		35 »
Guillaumet, Bouy, 24/2		35 »
Journée du Timbre (II), 24/3		3 »
Airbus, Toulouse (I), 7/4		12 »
Europa (2 enveloppes), Paris (I), 14/4		3 »
Idem Strasbourg (II), 14/4		3 »
Ernest Renan, Tréguier (I), 28/4		1 80
Lebrun, "Etude", Paris (I), 28/4		3 70
Cigogne, Strasbourg (I), 12/5		2 20
Grand-Orient de France, Paris (I), 12/5		3 »
Centre "Tuileries", Paris (I), 15/5		1 50
Palais des Ducs de Bourgogne, Dijon (I), 19/5		2 »
(Le cachet n'est pas illustré, avec texte au centre)		
Santos-Dumont, Le Bourget (I), 26/5		3 »
Boiseries, "Le Moutier d'Ahun" (I), 26/5 +		3 50
Cinquantenaire de l'Académie des Sciences		
d'Outre-Mer, Paris (I), 26/5		1 50
Colette, Saint-Sauveur-en-Puisaye (I), 2/6		3 70
Cinquantenaire des 24 heures du Mans, Le Mans (I), 2/6		2 30
Congrès des sociétés philatéliques, Toulouse (I), 9/6		1 80
Duguay-Trouin, Saint-Malo (I), 9/6		5 »
5 mâts "France II", La Rochelle (I), 9/6		5 »
Raton laveur, Basse-Terre (I), 23/6		2 »
Le Clos-Lucé, Amboise (I), 23/6		2 »
Château de Gien, Gien (I), 18/8		2 »
Saut du Doubs, Villers-le-Lac (I), 8/9		1 80
Watteau "La Finette", Paris (I), 22/9		3 »
Hansen, "Lèpre", Paris (I), 29/9		1 80
Pasteur, Dole (I), 6/10		2 50
Idem, Paris (II), 6/10		2 50
E. Ducretet, Paris (I), 6/10		1 80
Molière, Paris (I), 20/10		2 20
Idem, Pezenas (II), 20/10		2 20
Ecluse "François 1er", Le Havre (I), 27/10		2 20
Bourgoin-Kieffer, Paris (I), 27/10		2 50

	(Doc)	(1er j)
Code Civil, Paris (I), 3/11		1 80
Anniversaire de la flamme, Paris (I), 10/11		2 20
Sacre de l'Empereur, Paris (I), 10/11		3 20
Tony Garnier, Lyon (I), 17/11		2 »
Industrie, Paris (I), 24/11		1 50
Agriculture, Paris (I), 1/12		1 50
Croix-Rouge, Cognac (I) R, 1/12		4 »
Idem, Tonnerre (II), 1/12		4 »
Droits de l'Homme, Paris (I), 8/12		3 »
Musée Postal, Paris (I), 19/12	10 »	1 50

1974

	(Doc)	(1er j)
Arphila, Paris (I), 19/1	7 »	2 20
St-Louis Grignion de Montfort, Montfort (I), 23/2	23 »	2 50
Journée du Timbre, (II), 9/3	20 »	3 70
Aéroport Charles de Gaulle, Paris (I), 16/3	30 »	3 »
Richelieu, Paris (I), 23/3	30 »	5 »
Club Alpin Français, Paris (I), 30/3	8 »	3 »
Europa, "Rodin Maillol", Paris (I), 20/4	15 »	2 20
Idem, Strasbourg (II), 20/4		2 20
Sauvetage en mer, Paris (I), 27/4	15 »	2 »
Conseil de l'Europe, Strasbourg (I), 4/5	15 »	1 80
Saint-Florent, Saint-Florent (I), 11/5	12 »	6 »
Bison, Mouzon (I), 25/5	20 »	2 20
Général Koenig, Caen (I), 25/5	12 »	2 »
Idem, Paris (II), 25/5		2 »
Colmar, Colmar (I), 1/6	8 »	1 50
Débarquement, Arromanches (I), 8/6	23 »	4 50
XXes J.O. Echecs, Nice (I), 8/6	30 »	3 »
Hôtel des Invalides Paris (I), 15/6	9 »	1 80
Villes Compagnons de la Libération (III), 15/6	7 »	2 50
Musée Postal, Koenig, Villes Compagnons de la Libération ont été oblitérés avec cachet sans cercle.		
Salers, Salers (I), 22/6	9 »	1 80
Francis Poulenc, Paris (I), 20/7	9 »	2 »
Turbotrain 001, Tours (I), 31/8	33 »	4 »
Turbotrain 001, Tours (II), 1/9		15 »
Vallée du Lot, Decazeville (I), 7/9	6 »	1 50
Oeuvre de Miro, Paris (III), 14/9	14 »	3 30
Phenix, Bagnols-sur-Cèze (I), 21/9	11 »	1 80
U.P.U. Paris (I), 5/10	13 »	2 70
0,60/0,80, Marianne, Paris (I), 5/10	13 »	6 »
Saint-Nicolas-de-Port, (I), 12/10	7 »	2 »
Copernic, Paris (I), 12/10	10 »	3 »
Tatou, Cayenne (I), 19/10	15 »	3 »
Oeuvre de Sisley, Paris (I), 9/11	18 »	3 »
Barbey d'Aurevilly, Saint-Sauveur-le-Vicomte (I), 16/11	9 »	2 20
Jean Giraudoux, Bellac (I), 16/11	9 »	2 20
Tapisserie de Mathieu, Créteil (I), 16/11	10 »	3 50
Médaille Résistance, Paris (I), 23/11	10 «	3 50
Croix-Rouge, Pau (I), 30/11	10 »	6 »
Mulhouse (II), 30/11		6 50

1975

	(Doc)	(1er j)
A. Schweitzer, Kaysersberg (I), 11/1	20 »	4 »
Château de Rochechouart (I), 11/1	20 »	2 50
Église de Saint-Paul-de-Léon (I), 18/1	15 »	2 »
Palais de Justice, Rouen (I), 25/1	13 »	2 »
Aigrette, Villars-les-Dombes (I), 15/2	15 »	3 »
Edmond Michelet, Paris/Brives (I), 22/2	7 »	2 20
Arphila, "Oeil", Paris (I), 1/3	8 »	1 60
Journée du Timbre, Paris (II), 8/3	20 »	3 »
Arphila, " Chapiteau ", Paris (I), 22/3	8 »	2 »
Georges Pompidou, Aurillac-Saint-Flour (III), 2/4	11 »	4 50
Paris (III), 2/4		4 50
Arphila, " Graphisme ", Paris (I), 19/4	9 »	2 »
Europa, Paris (I), 26/4 (2 enveloppes)	10 »	8 »
Strasbourg (II), 26/4 (2 enveloppes)		8 »
Exposition Machine-Outil, Paris (I), 3/5	11 »	2 20
Robert Schuman, Paris-Scy-Chazelles (III), 10/5	11 »	2 »
Arphila, "Cérès", Paris (I), 17/5	9 »	2 50
Sénat, Paris (I), 24/5	7 »	2 »
Convention du Mètre, Paris (I), 31/5	9 »	2 »
Hélicoptère Gazelle, Le Bourget (I), 31/5	10 »	4 50
Arphila (4 enveloppes), Paris (I), 9/6		45 »
Bloc entier, Paris (I), 6/6		25 »
(4 enveloppes), Paris (II)		45 »
Bloc entier, Paris (II), 9/6	19 »	30 »
Santé des Etudiants, Paris (I), 21/6	7 »	2 »
Métro régional, Puteaux (I), 21/6	23 »	4 »
Paris (I), 21/6		8 »
Eugène Thomas, Vieux-Condé-Le Quesnoy (I), 28/6	4 »	2 »
Théâtre du Peuple, Bussang (I), 9/8	6 »	1 50
Pays de la Loire, Nantes (I), 6/9	6 »	1 80
Libération des Camps, Besançon (I), 27/9	7 »	1 80
Auvergne, Clermont-Ferrand (I), 4/10	6 »	1 80
Déminage, Lepuix (I), 11/10	4 »	1 50
Villes-Nouvelles, Evry, Cergny, l'Isle d'Abeau (I), 18/10	6 »	2 »
Bourgogne, Dijon (I), 25/10	6 »	2 »
Année de la Femme, Paris, 8/11 (cachet sans cercle).	7 »	2 »
Pont de Saint-Nazaire, Saint-Nazaire, Saint-Brevin (cachet sans cercle), 8/11	6 »	2 »
Picardie, Noyon (I), 15/11	6 »	2 »
Siegfried André, Le Havre (I), 15/11	4 »	1 80
U.N.E.S.C.O. Paris (I), 15/11		10 »
Franco-Russe (50e anniversaire) (III), 22/11	7 »	2 »
Conseil de l'Europe, Strasbourg, 22/11		10 »
Croix-Rouge, Le Creusot (I), 29/11	9 »	5 50
Croix-Rouge, Fort-de-France (I), 29/11		6 »
La Melpomène , Paris (I), 6/12	9 »	3 »
Poitou-Charentes, Poitiers (I), 6/12	6 »	2 70
Nord-Pas-de-Calais, Lille (I), 13/12	7 »	5 »

1976

	(Doc)	(1er j)
Concorde Paris/Rio, Paris (I), 10/1	24 »	8 »
Midi-Pyrénées, Toulouse (I), 10/1	6 »	3 70
Art Roman, St-Genis-des-Fontaines (I), 24/1	9 »	5 »
Centre, Orléans (I), 31/1	5 »	2 »
Vénus de Brassempuy, St-Germain-en-Laye, 6/3	9 »	5 »
Journée du Timbre (II), 13/3	8 »	3 »
Château, Rueil-Malmaison (I), 10/4	6 »	3 »
A.C.O.R.A.M., Paris (I), 24/4	5 »	1 50
Le Gros Horloge, Rouen (I), 24/4	6 »	1 50
Juvarouen, Rouen (I), 27/4	6 »	2 »
Europa (céramique), Paris (I), 8/5	9 »	3 »
Europa (céramique), Strasbourg (I) 8/5		4 50
Bicentenaire des États-Unis, Versailles (I), 15/5	9 »	2 20
Aquitaine, Bordeaux (I), 22/5	3 »	1 50
Maréchal Moncey, Paris Palise (I), 22/5	5 »	1 80
Limousin, Limoges (I), 29/5	5 »	1 50
Verdun, Paris, Verdun (I), 12/6	6 »	3 »
La Communication, Paris (I), 12/6	5 »	1 50
Forêt de Tronçais, Montluçon (I), 19/6	6 »	2 »
France Libre, Paris (I), 19/6	5 »	2 »
Symphonie, Toulouse, Issy-les-Moulineaux, 26/6	6 »	3 »
Bonaguil, Saint-Flour-sur-Lémance (I), 10/7	6 »	2 »
La Fête, Paris (I), 10/7	5 »	1 50
Ussel, Ussel (I), 10/7	6 »	2 20
J.O. Montréal, Paris (I), 17/7	6 »	1 80
Officiers de Réserve, Saint-Denis de la Réunion (I), 17/7	5 »	2 »
Oeuvre de Delaunay, Paris (III), 24/7	7 »	5 »
Max Jacob, Quimper (I), 22/7	7 »	1 80
Marianne 76, Paris (I), 31/7	23 »	3 »
Mounet-Sully, Bergerac (I), 28/8	5 »	2 »
Général Daumesnil, Périgueux et Vincennes (I), 4/9	5 »	2 20
Ramsès, Paris (I), 4/9	9 »	6 50
Oeuvre de Carzou, Vence, Paris (III), 18/9	9 »	4 50
Fromentin, La Rochelle (I), 25/9	5 »	1 80
Côte Basque, Biarritz (I), 25/9	6 »	1 80
Centenaire Téléphone, Paris et Riquewihr (I), 25/9	5 »	1 50
Film de tourisme, Tarbes (I), 2/10	6 »	2 »
Police nationale, Paris (I), 9/10	5 »	2 »
Thiers, Thiers (I), 9/10	6 »	2 »
Conseil de l'Europe, Strasbourg (I), 16/10		5 »
Guyane, Cayenne (I), 16/10	5 »	1 80
C.E.R.N., Pressevin (I), 22/10	8 »	2 50
U.N.E.S.C.O. Paris (I), 23/10		6 »
Anna de Noailles, Paris (I), 6/11	5 »	1 80
Cathédrale de Lodève, Lodève (I), 13/11	6 »	1 50
Croix-Rouge, Bourg-en-Bresse et Saint-Denis de la Réunion (I), 20/11	6 »	3 70
Foire Exposition, Paris (I), 20/11	5 »	1 50
Douane, Paris (I), 27/11	6 »	1 50
Musée de l'Atlantique, Port-Louis et Paris (I), 4/12	6 »	3 »
Oeuvre de de Vlaminck, Paris (I), 18/12	7 »	3 »

1977

	(Doc)	(1er j)
Franche-Comté, Besançon (I), 8/1	8 »	2 »
Languedoc-Roussillon, Montpellier (I), 15/1	8 »	2 »
Rhône-Alpes, Lyon (I), 22/1	6 »	2 50
Conseil de l'Europe, Strasbourg (I), 22/1		5 »
Martinique, Fort-de-France (I), 29/1	6 »	1 80

Réunion, Saint-Denis (I), 5/2	7 »	1 80
Centre Pompidou, Paris (I), 5/2	9 »	3 »
Oeuvre de Corot, Paris (I), 12/2	9 »	4 »
Dunkerque, Dunkerque (I), 12/2	5 »	1 50
Bretagne, Rennes (I), 19/2	6 »	2 70
Alsace, Strasbourg (I), 26/2	5 »	3 20
Souvenir français, Lille (I), 5/3	6 »	3 »
Journée du Timbre (II), 26/3	7 »	3 »
Oeuvre de Vasarely, Paris (III), 7/4	9 »	3 »
Champagne-Ardenne, Châlons-s.-Marne (I), 16/4	5 »	3 »
Europa, Paris (I), 23/4	7 »	2 20
Europa, Strasbourg (I), 23/4		2 20
Horticulture, Paris (I), 23/4	5 »	2 »
Floralies, Nantes (I), 7/5	5 »	2 »
Rattachement du Cambrésis, Cambrai (I), 14/5	5 »	1 50
Instituts catholiques, Paris-Lille-Lyon (I), 14/5	5 »	1 80
Fédérat. Europ. construct., Paris (I), 21/5	5 »	1 50
Congrès Philatélique, Annecy (I), 28/5	4 »	2 »
Abbaye de Fontenay, Marmagne (I), 4/6	5 »	1 80
Ecole Polytechnique, Palaiseau (I), 4/6	5 »	2 »
Traversée Atlantique Nord, Le Bourget et Nogent-sur-Marne (I), 4/6	9 »	4 50
Coupe de France de football, Paris (I), 11/6	21 »	3 50
Mémorial de Gaulle, Colombey-Paris (I), 18/6	20 »	5 50
Jeune Chambre économique, Paris-Lyon (I), 18/6	5 »	1 50
Bataille de Nancy, Nancy (I), 25/6	5 »	1 80
Rattachement de la Bourgogne, Dijon (I), 2/7	5 »	1 80
Parlementaires de langue française, Paris (I), 8/7	5 »	1 80
Cathédrale de Bayeux, Bayeux (I), 9/7	5 »	2 50
Collégiale de Dorat, Le Dorat (I), 16/7	5 »	1 80
Cigale Rouge, Paris-Serignan (I), 10/9	5 »	3 »
Saint-Amand-les-Eaux, Saint-Amand (I), 17/9	5 »	1 80
Oeuvre de Trémois, Paris (III), 17/9	24 »	4 »
Château de Vitré, Vitré (I), 24/9	5 »	2 »
Les Prémontrés, Pont-à-Mousson (I), 1/10	5 »	1 50
Meilleurs ouvriers, Paris (I), 1/10	5 »	1 50
Éd. Herriot, Troyes et Lyon (I), 8/10	5 »	2 »
Abbé Breuil, Mortain (I), 15/10	5 »	2 20
Conseil Economique, Paris (I), 22/10	5 »	1 50
Oeuvre de Rubens, Tours-Paris (I), 5/11	18 »	6 »
Guillaume de Machault, Machault et Paris (I), 12/11	4 »	2 50
Croix-Rouge, Marseille (I), 26/11	7 »	4 »
Charles Cros, Fabrezan-Paris (I), 3/12	4 »	1 80
Tennis de table, Paris-Annecy (I), 17/12	13 »	4 »
Art contemporain-Excoffon, Paris (III), 17/12	8 »	3 20
Sabine, Lille (I), 17/12	41 »	6 »

1978	(Doc)	(1er j)
Percheron, Paris (I), 7/1	9 »	3 70
Carrousel, Versailles (I), 14/1	9 »	7 »
École de Communications, Paris (I), 19/1	8 »	1 50
Saint-Barthélémy, Saint-Barthélémy (I), 19/1	8 »	1 50
Haute-Normandie, Rouen (I), 21/1	8 »	2 »
Oeuvre de Buffet, Paris (I), 4/2	22 »	5 »
Aménagement du territoire, Paris (I), 11/2	6 »	1 50
Marie Noël, Auxerre (I), 11/2	5 »	1 50
Bernanos, Paris (I), 18/2	5 »	1 80
Aubazine, Aubazine (I), 18/2	7 »	1 80
Juvexniort, Niort (I), 25/2	5 »	2 50
Gorges du Verdon, La Palud (I), 4/3	5 »	1 50
Ile-de-France, Paris (I), 4/3	5 »	1 80
Bec-Hellouin, Bec-Hellouin (I), 25/3	5 »	2 20
Lecomte de l'Isle, Saint-Paul (I), 25/3	5 »	1 80
Basse-Normandie, Caen (I), 1/4	5 »	2 40
Sabine (11 val.), Paris (I), 31/3 (3 enveloppes)	21 »	18 »
Journée du Timbre (II), 8/4	5 »	3 »
Tolstoï Paris (I), 15/4	5 »	2 »
Port Cros, Hyères (I), 15/4	5 »	3 »
Économies d'Énergie, Paris (I), 22/4	5 »	1 50
Fleurir la France, Nice-Colmar (I), 22/4	5 »	2 50
Notre-Dame de Lorette, Ablain St-Nazaire (I), 6/5	5 »	2 »
Europa, Paris (I), 6/5	6 »	2 70
Europa, Strasbourg (II), 6/5		2 70
Congrès Philatélique, Troyes (I), 13/5	6 »	2 »
Pont-Neuf, Paris (I), 27/5	5 »	1 80
Stade Roland Garros, Paris (I), 27/5	6 »	3 »
Abbaye de Fontevraud, Fontevraud (I), 3/6	5 »	1 80
Saint-Saturnin, Saint-Saturnin (I), 10/6	5 »	1 80
Sabine (5 val.), Paris (I), 3/6 (2 env.)	21 »	9 »
Château d'Esquelbecq, Esquelbecq (I), 17/6	6 »	2 »
Voltaire, J.-J. Rousseau, Ferney-Voltaire-Montmorency (I), 1/7	7 »	2 »
Métiers d'Art, Paris (I), 9/9	5 »	1 80
Claude Bernard Saint-Julien (I), 16/9	5 »	2 »
Imprimerie Nationale, Paris (I), 23/9	5 »	1 50
Franche-Comté, Besançon (I), 23/9	5 »	1 50
Rattachement de Valenciennes et Maubeuge, (I), 30/9	5 »	1 50
Académie de Philatélie, Paris (I), 7/10	5 »	2 »
Balbuzard, Bastia (I), 14/10	9 »	2 50
1re liaison, Villacoublay-Pauillac (I), 14/10	9 »	2 70
Conseil de l'Europe, Strasbourg (I), 14/10		2 30
U.N.E.S.C.O., Paris (I), 14/10		2 30
Gymnastique, Strasbourg (I), 21/10	9 »	1 80
Sport pour Tous, Blanzac (I), 21/10	7 »	1 80
Armistice 1918/1978, Compiègne et la Flamengrie (I), 11/11	5 »	2 20
Combattants Polonais, Paris (I), 11/11	5 »	2 »
Réadaptation, Paris (I), 18/11	5 »	1 80
Croix-Rouge, Château-Thierry (I), 26/12	9 »	3 »
Droits de l'Homme, Paris (I), 9/12	6 »	3 »
Yves Brayer, Paris (I), 9/12	9 »	3 »

1979	(Doc)	(1er j)
Année de l'Enfant, Paris (I), 6/1	10 »	5 »
Maréchal de Bercheny, Tarbes (I), 13/1	6 »	2 »
Miniature sur la musique, Paris (I), 13/1	10 »	3 50
Victor Segalen, Brest-Paris (I), 20/1	8 »	1 80
Floralies internationales, Les Trois Ilets (I), 3/2	8 »	1 50
Borobudur, Paris (1), 24/2	8 »	2 20
Journée du Timbre (I), 10/3	8 »	2 50
Poulbot, Paris (I), 24/3	8 »	2 50
Abeille, Paris-Evian (I), 31/3	8 »	3 »
Abbaye de Saint-Germain-des-Prés, Paris (I), 21/4	8 »	2 »
Palais des Rois, Perpignan (I), 21/4	8 »	1 80
Europa (2 envel.), Paris (I), 28/4	8 »	2 20
Idem (2 envel.), Strasbourg (II), 28/4		2 20
Congrès Fédération, Nantes (I), 5/5	7 »	1 50
Léon Jouhaux, Paris (I), 12/5	8 »	2 »
Moulin de Steenvoorde (I), 12/5	8 »	2 »
Palais Royal, Paris (I), 19/5	8 »	2 50
Elections Européennes, Strasbourg (I), 19/5	8 »	3 »
Hommage à Jeanne d'Arc, Rouen (I), 24/5	8 »	2 »
Abélard, Le Pallet (I), 9/6	8 »	2 »
Salon Aéronautique, Le Bourget (I), 9/6	8 »	5 »
Abbayes Normandes, Bernay, Saint-Pierre-sur-Dives (I), 16/6	8 »	2 »
Courteline, Tours (I), 23/6	8 »	2 »
Félix Guyon, Paris (I), 23/6	8 »	1 80
Auray, Auray (I), 30/6	8 »	1 50
Grotte de Niaux, Niaux (I), 7/7	8 »	2 »
Télécom 79, Paris (I), 22/9	8 »	1 80
Diane au Bain, Ecouen (I), 22/9	8 »	4 »
Sabine (6 val.) (2 envel.), Paris (II), 1/10	23 »	15 »
Château de Maisons-Laffitte (I), 6/10	6 »	1 80
L'église d'Auvers-sur-Oise, Paris (I), 27/10	25 »	11 »
"Lorraine", Nancy-Metz (I), 10/11	5 »	2 »
Simone Weil, Paris (I), 10/11	5 »	2 »
École Centrale des Arts et Manufactures, Paris (I), 17/11	6 »	1 80
Oeuvre de Salvador Dali, Paris (III), 17/11	12 »	4 »
André Malraux, Paris (I), 24/11	5 »	2 »
Championnats du monde de judo, Paris (I), 24/11	5 »	2 »
Oeuvre de Chapelain-Midy, Paris (III), 1/12	8 »	3 »
Croix-Rouge, "Vitrail", de Rouen (I), 1/12	6 »	3 »
La Lutherie, Paris-Mirecourt (I), 8/12	3 »	3 »

1980	(Doc)	(1er j)
Eurovision, Paris (I), 12/1	5 »	2 50
"Femme à l'Eventail", Paris (I), 19/1	6 »	2 50
Oeuvre de Ubac, Paris (III), 2/2	6 »	2 50
Viollet-le-Duc, Paris (I), 16/2	3 »	2 20
Géants du Nord, Douai-Lille, 16/2	3 »	1 80
Gastronomie française, Paris (I), 23/2	3 »	1 80
Journée du Timbre, Paris (I), 8/3	6 »	3 50
Jean Monnet, Cognac (I), 15/3	11 »	2 50
La Broderie, Paris (I), 29/3	4 »	2 20
Cité médiévale de Cordes (I), 5/4	4 »	1 80
Tabac ou Santé, Paris (I), 5/4	4 »	1 80
A. Briand, "Europa", Paris (I), 26/4	7 »	2 20
Saint Benoît, "Europa", Paris (I), 26/4		3 »
A. Briand, Europa 80, Strasbourg (I), 26/4		2 20
Saint Benoît, Europa 80, Strasbourg (I), 26/4		2 50
Cathédrale du Puy, Le Puy (I), 10/5	4 »	2 50
Montauban, Montauban (I), 17/5	4 »	3 »
École Normale Supérieure d'Arts et Métiers Liancourt (I), 17/5	3 »	1 50
Congrès S.P.F., Dunkerque (1), 24/5	3 »	1 50
Papillon ; Gap (I), 31/5	6 »	2 50

Château de Maintenon (I), 7/6	4 »	2 »
Albrecht Dürer, Paris (I), 7/6	18 »	2 20
Relations Publiques, Paris (I), 10/6	3 »	1 50
Patrimoine National, Paris (I), 21/6	3 »	1 80
Congrès géologique, Paris (1), 5/7	3 »	1 80
Bicentenaire du débarquement à Newport, Paris (I), 12/7	5 »	2 50
Sabine, 2 valeurs, Paris (I), 1/8	10 »	5 »
Traversée Paris-New York, Le Bourget (I), 30/8	10 »	3 50
De La Mennais, Saint-Malo (I), 6/9	4 »	2 »
Mistral, Maillane (I), 6/9	4 »	2 »
Abbaye de Solesmes (I), 20/9	4 »	2 »
Jean Picart Le Doux, Paris (I), 20/9	6 »	4 50
Agam. Message de Paix, Paris et Pérouges (I), 4/10	7 »	4 50
Saint-John Perse, Point-à-Pitre et Aix-en-Provence (I), 11/10	4 »	2 »
Pierre-Paul de Riquet, Béziers (I), 11/10	4 »	2 »
Le golf, Paris (I), 18/10	10 »	3 »
Comédie Française, Paris (I), 18/10	3 »	2 »
Modigliani, Creil (I), 25/10	10 »	3 »
Hommage à Charles de Gaulle, Paris (I), 8/11	11 »	5 »
Louis Le Nain, Paris (I), 8/11	10 »	3 »
U.N.E.S.C.O. (I), 15/11		4 »
Garde Républicaine, Paris (I), 22/11	4 »	3 50
Conseil de l'Europe, Strasbourg (I), 22/11		3 20
Croix-Rouge, "Stalles", Amiens (I), 6/12	4 »	3 20
Château de Rambouillet, Rambouillet (I), 6/12	4 »	2 50
Oeuvre de Hans Hartung, Paris (I), 20/12	10 »	3 20

1981	(Doc)	(1er j)
"Sabine", 6 val. (2 enveloppes), Paris (I), 10/1	30 »	38 »
Microélectronique, Meylan (I), 5/2	7 »	2 20
A.-M. Javouhey, Jallanges et Paris (I), 7/2	5 »	2 »
Jacques Offenbach, Paris (I), 14/2	7 »	2 70
Albert Gleizes, Paris (I), 28/2	6 »	3 »
Journée du Timbre, "Goya", Paris (II), 7/3	6 »	5 »
L'Eau, Paris et Châteauneuf-les-Martigues (I), 14/3	5 »	2 20
Château de Sully, Rosny-sur-Seine (I), 21/3	5 »	2 50
Biologie, Paris (1), 28/3	4 »	1 80
Energies nouvelles, Odeillo et Nandy (I), 28/3	6 »	2 »
Fonds marins, Dunkerque (I), 28/3	6 »	2 »
Télématique, Rennes (I), 28/3	7 »	2 »
La Reliure, Paris (I), 4/4	5 »	2 »
La maison carrée, Nîmes (I), 11/4	5 »	2 »
Oeuvre de Pissarro, Perpignan (1), 18/4	9 »	6 »
Europa, Paris (I), 2/5	7 »	3 »
Europa, Strasbourg (I), 2/5		3 »
Centen. de l'École Militaire, Saint-Maixent (I), 16/5	6 »	2 »
Teilhard de Chardin, Orcines (I), 23/5	6 »	2 »
Louis Armand, Cruseilles (I), 23/5	6 »	2 20
Philexfrance, 3 enveloppes (I), 23/5	20 »	10 »
Saint-Jean de Lyon (I), 30/5	4 »	1 50
La Presse. Th. Renaudot, Loudun et Paris (I), 30/5	5 »	2 »
Congrès S.P.F., Vichy (I), 6/6	4 »	1 80
Salon de l'aéronautique, Le Bourget (I), 6/6	9 »	5 20
Louis Jouvet, Crozon (I), 13/6	5 »	2 20
Hautes Etudes commerciales, Jouy-en-Josas (I), 19/6	6 »	1 80
Conservatoire de l'espace littoral, Rochefort (I), 20/6	5 »	2 20
Championnats du monde d'escrime, Clermont-Ferrand (I), 27/6	6 »	2 20
Basilique, Sainte-Anne d'Auray (I), 4/7	5 »	2 »
"Sabine", 3 val., Paris (I), 1/9	16 »	10 »
Boire ou conduire, Paris (I), 5/9	5 »	2 20
Costes et Le Brix, Baden/Septfonds (I), 12/9	10 »	12 »
Abbaye de Vaucelles, Les Rues des Vignes (1), 19/9	5 »	1 80
Pen Club, Paris (I), 19/9	5 »	1 80
Caisse Nationale d'Epargne, Paris (I), 21/9	5 »	2 »
Centenaire École publique, Saint-Dié-Paris (I), 26/9	5 »	1 80
Notre-Dame de Louviers, Louviers (I), 26/9	5 »	1 80
Pignon. "Les Plongeurs", Paris (I), 3/10	8 »	3 »
Saint-Émilion, Saint-Émilion (I), 10/10	5 »	2 »
École Navale, Lanvéoc-Paris (I), 17/10	4 »	1 80
Chasse et nature, Paris (I), 24/10	4 »	1 80
Panthéon, Paris (I), 2/11	8 »	2 »
Handicapés, Paris (I), 7/11	5 »	1 80
Pasteur Boegner, Epinal (I), 14/11	6 »	2 »
Virgile, Paris (I), 14/11	13 »	2 30
Conseil de l'Europe, Strasbourg (I), 21/11		3 »
Crest, Crest (I), 28/11	5 »	2 »
Croix-Rouge, Audincourt-Argentan (1), 5/12	10 »	4 »
U.N.E.S.C.O., Paris (I), 12/12		3 »
Martyrs de Châteaubriant (I), 12/12	5 »	2 20
Manessier. "Alléluia", Paris (I), 19/12	7 »	3 50

1982	(Doc)	(1er j)
"Liberté", 13 val., Paris (I), 4 envelop., 4/1	35 »	45 »
Corse, Ajaccio-Bastia (I), 9/1	5 »	2 20
Saint-Pierre-et-Miquelon, Saint-Pierre (I), 9/1	5 »	3 »
Guillaume Postel, Barenton (I), 23/1	4 »	1 80
Louis Pergaud, Belmont (I), 23/1	4 »	1 80
Saint François d'Assise, Paris (I), 6/2	9 »	1 80
Philexfrance, Folon, Paris (I), 13/2	35 »	12 »
Lord Baden-Powell, Lille (I), 20/2	7 »	3 »
Recensement, Paris (I), 27/2	7 »	2 20
Idem, sans chiffre 7		140 »
Aéroport Bâle-Mulhouse, Mulhouse (I), 13/2	7 »	4 »
Lutte contre le racisme, Paris (I), 20/3	6 »	1 80
Clichy (II), 20/3		1 80
Journée du Timbre, Paris (II), 27/3	6 »	4 »
La Ferronnerie, Paris (I), 17/4	6 »	2 50
Europa, Paris (I), 24/4	7 »	2 70
Europa, Strasbourg (II), 24/4		2 70
Coupe du monde de football, Paris (I), 28/4	15 »	2 50
Robert Debré, Sedan (I), 15/5	6 »	2 »
Paris (II), 15/5		2 »
Ephèbe d'Agde, Agde (I), 15/5	9 »	5 »
Château Henri IV, Pau (I), 15/5	6 »	3 50
Festival de Cannes, Cannes (I), 15/5	10 »	2 20
C.N.E.S., Toulouse (I), 15/5	6 »	3 70
Henri Mondor, Saint-Cernin (I), 22/5	6 »	2 20
Aurillac (II), 22/5		2 50
Créteil (II), 22/5		2 50
"Liberté", 3 val., Paris (I), 1/6	21 »	5 »
Sommet pays industrialisés, Versailles (I), 4/6	6 »	2 »
Jules Vallès, Le Puy (I), 5/6	6 »	1 50
Philexfrance-Bloc Cocteau, Paris-La-Défense (I), 11/6	40 »	34 »
Philexfrance-Bloc Cocteau, Paris-La-Défense (II), 14/6		30 »
Cl. Gellée, dit Le Lorrain, Charme (I), 19/6	10 »	5 »
Aix-en-Provence, Aix-en-Provence (I), 19/6	5 »	1 80
Frédéric et Irène Joliot-Curie, Paris (I), 26/6	10 »	1 80
Collonges-la-Rouge, Collonges (I), 3/7	3 »	2 »
Eclairage Public, Grenoble (I), 10/7	3 »	1 80
Château de Ripaille, Thonon-les-Bains (I), 4/9	3 »	2 50
"La dentelière", de Vermeer, Paris (I), 4/9	10 »	6 50
Sapeurs-Pompiers, Reims (I), 18/9	10 »	6 50
"La Famille", de Boyan, Paris (I), 18/9	3 »	6 50
Marionnettes, Charleville (I), 25/9	3 »	3 »
Marionnettes, Lyon (II), 25/9		3 »
Rugby, Bordeaux (I), 9/10	10 »	3 20
Écoles Normales Supérieures (III), 16/10	3 »	1 50
Beffroi de Lille, Lille (I), 16/10	3 »	1 50
Chantemesse, Le Puy (I), 23/10	3 »	1 80
U.N.E.S.C.O., Paris (I), 23/10		3 »
"Liberté", 6 val., Paris (I), 3/11 (2 env.)	20 »	10 »
La "chambre turque", de Balthus, Paris (III), 6/11	9 »	4 50
Robert Koch, Paris (I), 13/11	6 »	2 50
Conseil de l'Europe, Strasbourg (I), 13/11		3 30
Croix-Rouge, Nantes (I), 20/11	6 »	11 »
Sainte Thérèse d'Avila, Paris (I), 20/11	6 »	2 »
Croix du Sud, Biscarrosse (I), 4/12	7 »	5 »
Croix du Sud, Les Mureaux (II), 4/12		5 »
Léon Blum, Paris (I), 18/12	7 »	1 80
Gustave Eiffel, Dijon (I) 18/12	7 »	2 20
Gustave Eiffel, Paris (II), 18/12		2 20
Cavelier de la Salle, Paris (1), 18/12	16 »	3 »

1983	(Doc)	(1er j)
Provence-Alpes-Côte d'Azur, Marseille (I), 8/1	6 »	1 50
André Messager, Montluçon (I), 15/1	6 »	3 »
Hector Berlioz, La Côte-Saint-André (I), 22/1	6 »	3 »
Brantôme, Brantôme (I), 5/2	6 »	1 50
Martin Luther, Paris (I), 12/2	7 »	2 »
Alliance Française, Paris (I), 19/2	6 »	1 50
Journée du Timbre, Paris (II), 26/2	6 »	3 »
Hommage à la Femme, Paris (I), 8/3	6 »	2 »
Année des communications, Paris (I), 12/3	6 »	1 80
Bicentenaire de l'air et de l'espace, 3 enveloppes, Le Bourget (I), 19/3	19 »	8 »
Bicentenaire de l'air et de l'espace, Annonay (II), 19/3		5 »
"Aurora-Set", de Dewasne, Paris (III), 19/3	8 »	3 »
Oeuvre de Raphaël, Paris (I), 9/4	19 »	3 »
Jacques-Ange Gabriel, Paris (I), 16/4	6 »	2 »
Flore et Faune de France, 4 val. Toulouse (I), 23/4	15 »	8 »
Europa, Paris (I), 29/4	7 »	5 20
Europa, Strasbourg (II), 29/4		5 20
Max-Pol Fouchet, St-Vaast-la-Hougue (1), 30/4	6 »	2 »
Max-Pol Fouchet, Vézelay (II), 30/4		2 »

Propriété industrielle, Paris (I), 14/5	4 »	1 50
Congrès S.P.F., Marseille (I), 21/5	5 »	1 50
Idem, P.T.T. France (II), 21/5		2 »
"Liberté", 3 val., Paris (I), 1/6	22 »	16 »
Concarneau, Concarneau (I), 11/6	6 »	2 20
Air-France, Paris (I), 18/6	15 »	3 »
Gustave Doré, Strasbourg (I), 18/6	10 »	3 »
René Cassin, Bayonne (I), 25/6	6 »	2 »
René Cassin, Nice (II), 25/6		2 »
Abbaye de Noirlac, Bruère-Allichamps (I), 2/7	6 »	2 40
Traités de Versailles, Versailles (III), 2/9	7 »	3 50
Traités de Versailles, Paris (II), 2/9		3 50
Traités de Versailles (obl. Washington), 2/9		4 50
Art du Bijou, Paris (I), 10/9	6 »	2 20
Charleville-Mézières, Charleville-Mézières (I), 17/9	6 »	2 50
Coopération douanière, Bordeaux (1), 22/9	6 »	1 60
Vélocipède, Bar-le-Duc (I), 1/10	10 »	2 50
Vélocipède, Paris (II), 1/10		2 50
Jarnac, Jarnac (1), 8/10	10 »	2 »
U.N.E.S.C.O. Paris (I), 8/10		3 »
Hommage à Jean Effel, Paris (I), 15/10	17 »	5 »
Météorologie Nationale, Paris (I), 22/10	4 »	1 50
Renée Lévy, Auxerre (I), 5/11	6 »	2 »
Berthie Albrecht, Marseille (I), 5/11	6 »	2 »
Stendhal, Grenoble (I), 12/11	6 »	2 »
Stendhal, Paris (II), 12/11		2 »
Conseil de l'Europe, Strasbourg (I), 19/11		3 »
Croix-Rouge, Enghien-les-Bains (I), 26/11	7 »	3 »
Utrillo, Paris (I), 3/12	9 »	3 »
Pierre Mendès France, Paris (I), 16/12	6 »	1 80
Pierre Mendès France, Louviers (II), 17/12		1 80

1984	(Doc)	(1er j)
Émile Littré, Paris (I), 14/1	6 »	2 »
César, Paris (1), 4/2	16 »	5 »
Jean Zay, Orléans (I), 18/2	6 »	2 »
Guadeloupe, Basse-Terre, Pointe-à-Pitre (I), 25/2	6 »	1 80
Farman F 60 Goliath, Toulouse (I), 3/3	15 »	7 50
Farman F 60 Goliath, Toulouse (II), 3/3		9 »
Flora Tristan, Paris (I), 8/3	6 »	1 80
Journée du Timbre, Paris (II), 17/3	6 »	3 »
Centenaire des syndicats, Paris (I), 22/3	6 »	2 »
Élections au Parlement Européen, Strasbourg (I), 24/3	7 »	2 20
Messagier, Paris (I), 31/3	9 »	6 »
Colombier Fontaine (II) 1/4		6 »
Pierre Bonnard, Paris (I), 14/4	10 »	6 »
Jacques Cartier, Saint-Malo (I), 20/4	7 »	4 50
Jacques Cartier (Canada n° 869), Saint-Malo (I), 20/4		4 50
Philex-Jeunes, Dunkerque (I), 21/4	5 »	2 »
Europa, Paris (I), 28/4	7 »	3 »
Europa, Strasbourg (II), 28/4		3 »
Légion Étrangère, Aubagne (1), 30/4	10 »	2 »
Légion Etrangère, Paris (II), 30/4		2 20
40e anniversaire de la Libération, Paris (I), 8/5	10 »	4 »
Belle-Ile-en-Mer, Belle-Ile-en-Mer (I), 26/5	6 »	2 »
Jeux Olympiques, Paris (I), 2/6	13 »	2 50
La Gravure, Versailles (I), 8/6	6 »	1 80
Bordeaux, Bordeaux (I), 9/6	6 »	1 80
CNET, Paris (I), 18/6	5 »	2 »
Phare de Cordouan, Verdon (I), 23/6	10 »	2 »
Gaston Bachelard, Bar-sur-Aube (I), 23/6	5 »	2 »
Palais idéal du Facteur Cheval, Hauterives (I), 30/6	9 »	5 »
"Liberté", 3 valeurs, Paris (I), 2/7	15 »	8 »
Grande Chartreuse, St-Pierre-de-Chartreuse (I), 7/7	8 »	1 80
Congrès de géographie, Paris (I), 25/8	7 »	2 »
Télécom I, Paris (1), 1/9	10 »	3 »
TGV Postal, Lyon (I), 8/9		5 »
TGV 1re rame postale (C.D.), 1/10	21 »	5 »
Château de Montségur (Lavelanet) (I), 15/9	7 »	2 30
Les Rapaces, Paris (I), 22/9	30 »	8 »
Marx Dormoy, Montluçon (I), 22/9	7 »	1 80
Pierre Corneille, Rouen (I), 29/9	6 »	2 »
Centenaire Automobile, Paris (1), 6/10	10 »	2 50
La Pythie (A. Masson), Paris (I), 13/10	7 »	4 »
U.N.E.S.C.O. (3 P.J.), Paris (I), 20/10		4 »
Jean Paulhan, Nîmes (I), 27/10	6 »	2 »
Vincent Auriol, Revel (I), 3/11	6 »	1 80
Conseil de l'Europe, Strasbourg (I), 10/11		4 »
Evariste Galois, Bourg-la-Reine (I), 10/11	6 »	2 »
Croix-Rouge, Grasse (I), 24/11	9 »	4 »
Jean Hélion, Amiens (I), 1/12	9 »	3 »
9e Plan, Paris (I), 8/12	7 »	1 80

1985	(Doc)	(1er j)
La Francophonie, Paris (I), 15/1	6 »	2 »
Vienne (Isère), Vienne (1), 19/1	6 »	2 »
Télévision (50e anniversaire), Paris (I), 26/1	6 »	2 »
Peynet, Saint-Amour (I), 14/2	23 »	4 »
Idem, avec oiseau blanc sur branche		60 »
Peynet, Saint-Valentin (I), 14/2		4 »
Idem, avec oiseau blanc sur branche		60 »
Victor Hugo, Besançon (1), 23/2	10 »	5 »
Roland Dorgelès, Amiens (I), 23/2	9 »	4 50
François Mauriac, Bordeaux (I), 23/2	9 »	4 50
Romain Rolland, Clamecy (I), 23/2	9 »	4 50
Jules Romains, Saint-Julien-Chapteuil (I), 23/2	9 »	4 50
Jean-Paul Sartre, Paris (I), 23/2	10 »	4 50
Idem, avec point sur i de française		75 »
Personnages Célèbres (bande carnet) (III), 23/2	51 »	70 »
Hydravion CAMS 53, Marseille (I), 2/3	15 »	20 »
Hydravion CAMS 53, Marseille (II), 2/3		22 »
Pauline Kergomard, Paris (I), 8/3	7 »	1 50
Journée du Timbre, Paris (II), 16/3	7 »	3 »
Millénaire de la fondation de Montpellier (I), 30/3	10 »	1 80
Vitrail Cathédrale, Strasbourg (I), 13/4	10 »	4 50
Architecture contemporaine, Givors (I), 20/4	7 »	2 »
Abbaye de Landévennec (I), 20/4	7 »	1 70
Europa "Musiciens", Paris (2 P.J.) (I), 27/4	6 »	3 70
Europa "Musiciens", Strasbourg (2 P.J.) (II), 27/4		3 70
40e anniversaire de la Victoire, Paris (I), 8/5	9 »	3 50
Congrès Fédération, Tours (I), 25/5	6 »	1 50
Vaccin contre la rage, Paris (I), 1/6	7 »	2 »
Nicolas de Staël, Antibes (I), 1/6	9 »	5 »
Mystère Falcon 900, Le Bourget (I), 1/6	9 »	6 »
Saintonge Romane, Talmont (I), 15/6	7 »	2 »
Société Internationale de Sauvetage du Lac Léman, Saint-Gingolph (I), 15/6	10 »	3 »
Idem, Jumelage Franco/Suisse, 15/6		3 »
40e anniversaire de l'O.N.U., Paris (I), 26/6	6 »	2 »
Abbaye Saint-Michel-de-Cuxa, Codalet (I), 6/7	6 »	2 »
"Liberté", 3 valeurs, Paris (I), 1/8	17 »	7 »
Accueil des Huguenots, Anduze (I), 31/8	10 »	3 »
Conseil de l'Europe, Strasbourg (I), 31/8	10 »	6 »
Jean Dubuffet, Le Havre (I), 14/9	10 »	3 »
Les Arbres, Orléans (I), 21/9	30 »	8 »
Solutré, Solutré (I), 28/9	11 »	3 »
P. Alechinsky, Paris (I), 12/10	10 »	3 50
U.N.E.S.C.O. (3 P.J.), Paris (I) B, 26/10	9 »	4 »
La France à ses Morts, Paris (I), 2/11	7 »	2 »
Charles Dullin, Yenne (I), 9/11	6 »	2 »
Charles Dullin, Puteaux (II), 9/11		2 50
Documentation Française, Paris (I), 16/11	5 »	1 50
Croix-Rouge, Colmar (I) R, 23/11	9 »	3 »
Croix-Rouge-P.T.T. France, New York (II) R, 23/11		3 »
Giacometti, Paris (I), 7/12	11 »	4 »
Giacometti-P.T.T. France, Monaco (II), 7/12		4 »

1986	(Doc)	(1er j)
Franco-Thaïlandaise, Paris (I), 25/1	10 »	2 »
Franco-Thaïlandaise, Brest (II), 25/1		2 »
Front Populaire, Paris (I), 1/2	9 »	2 40
Carnaval. Venise à Paris, Paris (I), 11/2	9 »	2 »
François Arago, Estagel (I), 22/2	7 »	2 20
Henri Moissan, Paris (I), 22/2	7 »	2 20
Henri Fabre, Marseille (I), 22/2	7 »	2 20
Henri Fabre, La Terrasse (II), 22/2		2 20
Marc Seguin, Annonay (I), 22/2	7 »	2 20
Paul Héroult, Thury-Harcourt (I), 22/2	7 »	2 20
Personnages célèbres (feuille du carnet) (III), 22/2	15 »	15 »
Raymond Gid. Typographie, Paris (I), 1/3	15 »	3 »
Raymond Gid. Typographie, Rennes (II), 1/3		3 70
Pierre Cot, Coise (I), 1/3	9 »	4 »
Saint-Germain-de-Livet, Saint-Germain (I), 1/3	7 »	2 »
Louise Michel, Paris (I), 8/3	7 »	2 »
La Villette, Paris (I), 14/3	9 »	2 50
Journée du Timbre. "La Briska" (II), 5/4	10 »	3 »
Journée du Timbre (timbre du carnet) (II), 5/4		3 »
Journée du Timbre (feuille du carnet) (II), 5/4	15 »	35 »
C.H.E.A.M., Paris (I), 12/4	4 »	1 80
Estève, Culan (I), 12/4	9 »	4 »
Victor Basch, La Rochelle (I), 26/4	8 »	1 80
Europa, Paris (I), 26/4	8 »	3 »
Europa, Strasbourg (II), 26/4		4 50
Curé d'Ars, Ars-sur-Formans (I), 3/5	4 »	1 80
Curé d'Ars, Dardilly (I), 3/5		1 80
Congrès Fédération, Nancy (I), 17/5	6 »	2 »
Volley-ball, Paris (I), 24/5	9 »	2 »

Notre-Dame-en-Vaux, Châlons-sur-Marne (I), 7/6	8 »	1 80
Château de Loches, Loches (I), 14/6	8 »	2 »
Château de Loches. "Stamplink'86",		
P.T.T. France (II), 14/6		2 50
Magnelli, Paris (I), 25/6	11 »	3 30
Magnelli, Vallauris (II), 25/6		3 »
Statue de la Liberté, Paris (I), 4/7	16 »	4 »
Statue de la Liberté, obl. New York, 4/7		4 »
Statue de la Liberté, sur grande envel. cachet		
PARIS-NEW YORK, 4/7		
Filitosa, Filitosa (Corse) (I), 5/7	8 »	2 »
Monpazier, Monpazier (I), 5/7	10 »	2 50
"Liberté" "A", Paris (I), 1/8	11 »	3 »
"Liberté" "3 f. 40", Paris (II), 1/8		3 50
Bicentenaire Mont-Blanc, Chamonix (I), 8/8	10 »	2 »
Mesures d'arcs de méridien, Paris (I), 5/9	10 »	2 50
Mesures d'arcs de méridien "Stockholmia 86",		
P.T.T. France (II), 5/9		2 50
"Liberté" "1 f 90", Paris (II), 13/9		2 20
Minéraux, Paris (I), 13/9	30 »	10 »
Cinémathèque (5 PJ), Paris (I), 20/9		12 »
Cinémathèque (Bloc), Paris (I), 20/9	30 »	23 »
H. Alain Fournier, La Chapelle d'Angillon (I), 4/10,	9 »	1 80
Épineuil le Fleuriel (I), 4/10		1 80
Enseignement technique, Voiron (I), 4/10	7 »	1 50
Conférence énergie, Cannes (I), 5/10	7 »	2 40
Trimoteur Wibault 283, Le Bourget (I), 11/10	15 »	30 »
"La danseuse" d'Arp, Strasbourg (I), 8/11	9 »	4 »
"Isabelle d'Esté" de Léonard de Vinci,		
Puteaux (I), 8/ 11	10 »	4 »
Croix-Rouge, Reims (I) R, 22/11	9 »	2 20
Musées techniques de Mulhouse, Mulhouse (I), 22/11	15 »	3 »
U.N.E.S.C.O. (2 P.J.), Paris (I) B, 6/12	9 »	3 »
Musée d'Orsay, Paris (I), 9/12	10 »	3 »
Conseil de l'Europe, Strasbourg (I), 13/12	9 »	4 »
Pierre Soulages, Paris (I), 20/12	9 »	4 »

1987	(Doc)	(1er j)
F. Bienvenüe, métropolitain, Paris (I), 17/1	9 »	2 20
Uzel près l'Oust (I), 17/1		2 20
Raoul Follereau, Nevers (I) 24/1	8 »	2 »
Charles Richet Paris (I), 21/2	8 »	3 »
Eugène Jamot St Sulpice les champs (I), 21/2	8 »	3 »
Bernard Halpern, Paris (I), 21/2	8 »	3 »
Alexandre Yersin, Paris (I), 21/2	8 »	3 »
Jean Rostand, Paris (I), 21/2	8 »	3 »
Jacques Monod, Paris (I), 21/2	8 »	3 »
Personnages célèbres, (bande-carnet), (I), 21/2	20 »	30 »
"Philexfrance'89", Dijon (I), 7/3	9 »	2 20
Redon, Redon (I) (I), 7/3	7 »	1 80
Coutellerie, Thiers (I), 7/3	7 »	3 »
Journée du Timbre, "La Berline", (II), 14/3	9 »	3 »
Journée du Timbre, (timbre de carnet), (II), 14/3		3 »
Journée du Timbre, (bande-carnet), (II), 14/3	9 »	20 »
Le Corbusier, Paris (I), 11/420	9 »	2 50
Dewoitine 338, Toulouse (I), 11/4	23 »	40 »
Bram Van Velde, Paris (I), 25/4	9 »	5 »
Europa, Paris (I), 25/4	9 »	3 50
Europa, Strasbourg (II), 25/4		3 50
Henri Pourrat Ambert (I), 9/5	8 »	1 80
Château d'Azay le Rideau, Azay le Rideau (I), 9/5	9 »	2 50
Eugène Boudin, Honfleur (I), 23/5	10 »	6 »
Côtes de Meuse, Vigneulles les Hattonchatel		
(I), 30/5	10 »	3 »
Congrès Fédération, Lens (I), 6/6	6 »	1 80
Congrès Exposition Philatélique, Lens (II), 6/6		2 »
Vue d'Étretat d'après Delacroix, Étretat (I), 12/6	10 »	2 70
Entrée en guerre des États-Unis, Paris (I), 13/6	10 »	2 30
Transports à câbles, Grenoble (I), 17/6	9 »	2 »
Millénaire Hugues Capet, Noyon (I), 20/6	9 »	2 »
Prytanée national de La Flèche, La Flèche (I), 20/6	9 »	2 »
Les Baux de Provence, Baux de Provence (I), 27/6	7 »	2 »
Rassemblement mondial des "Pieds-noirs",		
Nice (I), 27/6	10 »	1 80
"Liberté" "B", Paris (I), 1/8	12 »	4 »
"Liberté" "3f. 60", Paris (II), 1/8		4 »
Championnats de lutte, Clermont-Ferrand (I), 21/8	9 »	3 »
Champignons (4 P.J.), Paris (I), 5/9	29 »	10 »
Guillaume le Conquérant, Caen (I), 5/9	9 »	2 20
Rouen (I), 5/9		2 20
Camille Bryen, Paris (I), 12/9	9 »	3 »
Le Saugeais, Montbenoît (I), 19/9	9 »	2 »
Institut Pasteur, Paris (I), 3/10	10 »	1 80
Conseil de l'Europe, Strasbourg, 10/10	9 »	3 »
"Liberté" "2f", Paris (II), 15/10		2 20
Blaise Cendrars, Courbevoie (II), 6/11	9 »	1 80
Antoine Pevsner Paris (I), 14/11	9 »	3 »
Monaco (II), 14/11		3 20
"Liberté" "f. 70", Paris (II), 16/11		3 »
Croix-Rouge, Dijon (I), 21/11	9 »	3 »
Maréchal Leclerc, Paris (I), 28/11	9 »	2 50
Strasbourg (I), 28/11		2 50
Traité d'Andelot, Andelot-Blancheville (I), 28/11	9 »	2 20
U.N.E.S.C.O. (2 P.J.), Paris (I), 5/12	9 »	3 50

1988	(Doc)	(1er j)
Coopération franco-allemande, Paris (I), 14/1	10 »	3 »
Idem, timbre allemand, Bonn, 14/1		3 »
Idem, les 2 timbres, Paris et Bonn, 14/1		3 »
Marcel Dassault, Suresnes (I), 23/1	10 »	3 »
"La communication" en bandes dessinées, (6 envel.),		
Angoulême (I), 29/1	23 »	15 »
Idem, bande-carnet Angoulême (I) 29/1		30 »
Synagogue, Paris (I), 7/2	10 »	1 80
Duquesne, Dieppe (I), 20/2	9 »	2 20
Suffren, St-Cannat (I), 20/2	9 »	2 20
St-Tropez (II), 20/2		2 20
La Pérouse, Albi (I), 20/2	9 »	2 20
La Bourdonnais, St-Malo (I), 20/2	9 »	2 20
Bougainville, Paris (I), 20/2	9 »	2 20
Dumont d'Urville, Condé-sur-Noireau (I), 20/2	9 »	2 20
Personnages célèbres, (bande-carnet) (I), 20/2	10 »	22 »
"Philexfrance'89", Metz (I), 4/3	9 »	2 20
Paris (I), 4/3		2 20
Journée du Timbre, "Voiture montée", (II), 12/3	9 »	3 »
Journée du Timbre, (timbre de carnet), (II), 12/3		3 »
Journée du Timbre, (bande-carnet), (II), 12/3	30 »	15 »
Ecole Nationale Supérieure P.T.T., Paris (I), 21/3	8 »	2 20
"Philex-Jeunes 88", Nevers (I), 5/4	5 »	1 80
Don du sang, Metz (I), 9/4	15 »	2 »
"Liberté" surcharge en Ecu, Paris (I), 16/4	15 »	6 »
Europa (2 P.J.), Paris (I), 30/4	9 »	3 50
Europa (2 P.J.), Strasbourg (II), 30/4		3 70
Jean Monnet, Cognac (I), 9/5	11 »	2 »
Congrès Fédération, Valence (I), 21/5	6 »	2 »
Assistance médicale, Paris (I), 23/5	8 »	2 10
Handicapés, Lyon (I), 28/5	9 »	2 20
Hermès dicéphale, Fréjus (I), 11/6	9 »	3 »
Bicentenaire de la Révolution (2 P.J.),		
Vizille-Grenoble (I), 18/6	15 »	6 »
Idem, le triptyque sur grande enveloppe,		
Vizille-Grenoble (I), 18/6		8 »
Animaux de Buffon, (4 PJ), Montbard (I), 18/6	30 »	5 »
Paris (I), 18/6		5 »
Troupes alpines, Grenoble (I), 27/6	6 »	1 80
Roland Garros, Saint-Denis de la Réunion (I), 2/7	10 »	2 »
Vouziers (II), 2/7		2 »
Château de Sédières, Clergoux (I), 2/7	9 »	3 50
Cirque de Gavarnie, Gavarnie (I), 25/7	9 »	2 20
Musée du Bateau, Douarnenez (I), 25/7		1 80
Armistice de 1918, Paris (I), 10/9	9 »	2 »
Pérouges, Pérouges (I) 10/9	6 »	1 80
Jacobsen Paris (I), 22/9	10 »	3 »
Copenhague, 22/9		4 »
Bimillénaire de Strasbourg, Strasbourg, 24/9	9 »	2 20
Sépulcre Saint-Mihiel, St-Mihiel, 15/10,	9 »	4 »
Poliakoff, Lille (I), 22/10	11 »	3 50
Thermalisme, Paris (I), 22/10	9 »	2 »
Idem, main coupée		75 »
Croix-Rouge, Le Bourget (I), 19/11	11 »	3 »
Tinguely, Paris (I), 25/11	10 »	5 »
Bâle, 25/11		5 20
Pietà de Villeneuve-lès-Avignon,		
Villeneuve-les-Avignon (II), 10/12	10 »	4 »
Paris (I), 10/12		4 »
Droits de l'Homme, Paris (I), 10/12	11 »	2 50

1989	(Doc)	(1er j)
Bicent. de la Révolution Française, Paris (I), 1/1	10 »	3 »
Idem. 100 enveloppes avec cachets		
des 100 départements (II), 1/1		375 »
Yves Klein Paris (I), 21/1	9 »	4 »
Pour le bien des aveugles, Paris (I), 27/1	9 »	2 »
École Estienne, Paris (I), 4/2	8 »	2 »
Conseil de l'Europe, Strasbourg (I), 4/2	9 »	3 »
Sieyès, Fréjus (I), 25/2	8 »	3 »
Mirabeau, Bignon/Mir., 25/2	8 »	3 »
Mirabeau (II), 25/2		3 »

Vicomte de Noailles, Maintenon (I), 25/2	8 »	3 »
La Fayette, Chavaniac (I), 25/2	8 »	3 »
Barnave, St-Egreve (I), 25/2	8 »	3 »
Drouet, St-Menehould (I), 25/2	8 »	3 »
Varennes (II), 25/2		3 »
Personnages célèbres (bande-carnet) (II), 25/2	10 »	12 »
Élections Parlement Européen, Strasbourg (I), 4/3	9 »	2 »
Vol Franco-soviétique, Paris (I), 4/3	11 »	3 »
La Liberté, Villeurbanne (I), 18/3	9 »	3 »
Journée du Timbre, (II), 15/4	9 »	3 »
Journée du Timbre (timbre de carnet) (II), 15/4		3 »
Journée du Timbre (bande-carnet) (II), 15/4	11 »	12 »
L'Égalité, Ermenonville (I), 22/4	9 »	2 50
Panorama de Paris (5 P.J.), Puteaux (I), 21/4		11 50
Idem bande entière, Puteaux (I), 21/4	10 »	9 »
Europa, Paris (I), 29/4	9 »	3 »
Europa, Strasbourg (II), 29/4		3 »
Forêt de Fontainebleau, Fontainebleau (I), 20/5	6 »	2 »
U.I.T., Nice (I), 23/5	8 »	2 20
La Fraternité, Champagney (I), 27/5	9 »	2 50
Champ. du monde de cyclisme, Chambéry (I), 3/6	9 »	2 50
Malestroit, Malestroit (I), 10/6	8 »	2 20
Serment du Jeu de Paume, Paris (I), 20/6	9 »	4 »
Serment du Jeu de Paume, Versailles (I), 20/6		4 »
Mme Roland, Paris (I), 24/6		2 70
Camille Desmoulins, Guise (I), 24/6		2 70
Condorcet, Ribemont (I), 24/6		2 70
Bourg la Reine (II), 24/6		3 »
Clamart (II), 24/6		3 »
Kellermann, Strasbourg (I), 24/6		2 70
Personnages célèbres, Bloc (Bloc-Feuillet), 24/6	12 »	12 »
Philexfrance'89, Bloc (I), Paris 7/7	15 »	30 »
Idem. (4 P.J.) avec bloc découpé (I) Paris, 7/7		40 »
Liberté, Egalité, Fraternité, tryptique avec vignette, Paris (II), 14/7	13 »	5 »
Sommet de l'Arche, Puteaux (I), 14/7	9 »	2 50
Sommet Puteaux (II), 14/7		5 »
Château de Vaux-le-Vicomte, Maincy (I), 14/7	9 »	5 »
La Brenne, Rosnay (I), 25/8	9 »	2 50
Droits de l'Homme, (4 P.J.), Versailles (I), 26/8	15 »	10 »
Idem bande sur grande enveloppe, Versailles (I), 26/8		10 »
TGV Atlantique, Nantes (I), 23/9	11 »	5 »
Paris (II), 23/9		5 »
Charles Lapicque, Dijon (I), 23/9	10 »	3 50
Villers-Cotterêts, Villers-Cotterêts (I), 28/10	9 »	2 »
Tramway électrique, Clermont-Ferrand (I), 28/10	9 »	3 50
Augustin Cauchy, Paris (I), 10/11	7 »	2 20
Sceaux (II), 10/11		2 20
Maréchal de Lattre, Belfort (I), 18/11	7 »	2 20
Mouilleron (I), 18/11		2 20
Croix-Rouge, Lyon (I), 18/11	7 »	2 50
Washington (II), 18/11		2 50
Harkis, Paris (I), 9/12	10 »	2 »
Marseille (II), 9/12		2 »
Marianne du Bicentenaire, 2 f. 30, Paris (I), 31/12	11 »	3 50

1990	(Doc)	(1er j)
"Liberté" " C", Paris (I), 2/1	15 »	3 »
Marianne du Bicentenaire, 2 f. 10, Paris (I), 22/1		3 »
2 f. 30 adhésif, Paris (II), 29/1		6 »
La Dentelle, Paris (I), 3/2	9 »	2 50
Jeux d'Albertville'92, Albertville (I), 8/2	13 »	2 20
Jeux olympiques, Patinage (I) Albertville, 8/2	13 »	3 »
Gal de Gaulle, Lille (I), 24/2	11 »	4 »
Paris (II), 24/2		4 »
Max Hymans, Paris (I), 3/3	9 »	2 »
Odilon Redon, Bordeaux (I) 3/3	13 »	3 20
Journée du Timbre, (II) 17/3	9 »	3 »
(Timbre du carnet) (II) 17/3		3 »
(Bande carnet) (II) 17/3	12 »	12 »
Jean Guehenno, Fougères (I), 24/3	9 »	2 50
Marianne du Bicentenaire, 0,10, 0,20, 0,50, 3,20 et 3,80. (2 P.J.), Paris (I), 26/3		8 »
U.N.E.S.C.O., Paris (I), 7/4	9 »	3 »
Abbaye de Flaran, Valence s/Baïse, (I) 21/4	9 »	3 »
Europa, (2 P.J), Strasbourg (I), 28/4	9 »	4 50
Macon (II), 28/4		2 20
Cerizay (II), 28/4		2 20
1er Mai, Paris (I) 1/5	9 »	2 20
Institut du Monde Arabe, Paris (I), 5/5	9 »	3 »
Croix-Rouge, Quimper (I), 5/5	9 »	3 50
Marianne du Bicentenaire 1, 2, 5 et 10 f. (2 P.J.), Paris (I) 21/5	15 »	12 »
Conseil de l'Europe, Strasbourg (I), 26/5	9 »	3 50
Congrès Fédération, Villefranche sur Saône (I), 2/6	6 »	2 20
Course autour du monde, Paris (I), 6/6	11 »	2 20
Lorient (II), 9/6		2 20
Auguste Rodin, Paris (I), 9/6	10 »	4 »
Aristide Bruant, Courtenay (I), 16/6	11 »	4 »
Maurice Chevalier, Paris (I), 16/6	11 »	4 »
Tino Rossi, Ajaccio (I), 16/6	11 »	4 »
Édith Piaf, Paris (I), 16/6	11 »	4 »
Jacques Brel, Paris (I), 16/6	11 »	4 »
Georges Brassens, Sète (I), 16/6	11 »	4 »
Personnages célèbres, (bande-carnet) (II), 16/6	18 »	20 »
Christ de Wissembourg, Wissembourg (I), 16/6	10 »	4 »
Appel du 18 Juin 40, Paris (I), 17-18/6	11 »	3 50
Lille (II), 17-18/6		3 50
Abbaye de Cluny, Cluny (I), 23/6	7 »	2 20
Pont-Canal de Briare, Briare (I), 7/7	9 »	2 20
Maison France-Brésil, Paris (I), 14/7	9 »	2 70
Cap Canaille, Cassis (I), 14/7	7 »	2 70
Institut Géographique National, St-Mandé (I), 29/9	10 »	2 20
Nature : les Poissons, (2 P.J.), Neuilly s/S. (I), 6/10	30 »	10 »
Création du Drapeau Tricolore, Paris (I), 13/10		3 »
Création des Départements Français, Port s/Saône (I), 13/10		3 »
G. Monge, Beaune (I), 13/10		3 »
Abbé Grégoire, Vého-Embermenil (I), 13/10		3 »
Bicentenaire de la Révolution Française, Paris (II), 13/10		
Bloc-feuillet (II), 13/10	15 »	12 »
Maurice Genevoix, Decize (I), 10/11	7 »	2 20
Châteauneuf s/Loire (II), 10/11		2 70
Verdun (II), 10/11		2 70
Roger Bissière, Paris (I), 8/12	9 »	3 »
O.C.D.E., Paris (I), 15/12	10 »	2 70
Jeux olympiques, Saut, Courchevel (I), 22/12	13 »	3 »
Ski de vitesse, Les Arcs (I), 29/12	13 »	3 »

1991	(Doc)	(1er j)
Jeux olympiques, Slalom, Les Ménuires (I), 19/1	13 »	2 50
Ski de fond, Les Saisies (I), 2/2	13 »	2 50
Hockey, Méribel (I), 9/2	13 »	2 50
Auguste Renoir, Limoges (I), 23/2	13 »	4 »
Jacques Prévert, Neuilly s/S (I), 23/2	11 »	3 »
Paul Éluard, St-Denis (I), 23/2	11 »	3 »
Louis Aragon, St-Arnoult en Y. (I), 23/2	11 »	3 »
André Breton, Tinchebray (I), 23/2	11 »	3 »
Francis Ponge, Montpellier (I), 23/2	11 »	3 »
René Char, L'Isle s/La Sorgue (I), 23/2	11 »	3 »
Personnages célèbres, (bande-carnet) (II), 23/2	12 »	22 50
Jeux olympiques, Luge, Macot, La Plagne (I), 2/3	13 »	2 50
Journée du Timbre, (II) 16/3	11 »	3 »
(Timbre de carnet) (II), 16/3		3 »
(Bande-carnet) (II), 16/3	10 »	12 »
Philexjeunes'9I, Cholet (I), 30/3	9 »	2 50
Mozart, Paris (I), 9/4	15 »	3 20
Imprimerie Nationale, Paris (I), 13/4	13 »	3 »
Georges Seurat, Mulhouse (I), 13/4	13 »	3 70
Jeux olympiques, Curling, Pralognan (I), 20/4	13 »	2 80
Concours Lépine, Paris (I), 27/4	12 »	3 »
Pont de Cheviré, Nantes (I), 27/4	12 »	2 50
Europa. Espace, Strasbourg (I), 27/4	10 »	4 »
Kourou (I), 27/4		4 »
Congrès Fédération, Perpignan (I), 18/5	9 »	2 20
Roland Garros'9I, Paris (I), 24/5	14 »	3 »
Paris (II), 26/5		3 »
L'Arbre de La Liberté, Paris (I), 1/6	6 »	3 »
Gendarmerie Nationale, Paris (I), 1/6	10 »	3 »
La Tour d'Auvergne, Carhaix Plouguer (I), 1/6	7 »	3 »
Saint-Just, Decize (I), 1/6	6 »	3 »
Blérancourt (II), 1/6 Blérancourt		3 »
Bloc-Feuillet, Révolution (I), 1/6	15 »	12 »
Orgues de Wasquehal, Wasquehal (I), 22/6	13 »	3 »
Carennac, Carennac (I), 6/7	9 »	2 20
Vallée de Munster, Munster (I), 6/7	9 »	2 70
Gaston Fébus, l'Hôpital d'Orion-Orthez (I), 13/7	12 »	4 »
Foix (II), 13/7		4 »
Jeux Olympiques, ski artistique, Tignes (I), 3/8	13 »	3 »
Jeux Olympiques, ski alpin, Val d'Isère (I), 17/8	13 »	3 »
Marianne du Bicentenaire "D", Paris (I), 19/8		3 »
Idem, "D" adhésif, Paris (I), 19/8		3 »
Ours des Pyrénées, St-Lory-Soulan (I), 14/9	10 »	3 »
Tortue terrestre, Gonfaron (I), 14/9	9 »	3 »
Castor, Ste-Marie-de-la-Mer (I), 16/9	9 »	3 »
Martin-pêcheur, Dole (I), 14/9	9 »	3 »
Congrès forestier mondial, Paris (I), 22/9	9 »	2 50
Langeac (II), 22/9		2 50
Marianne du Bicentenaire, 2 f. 20, 2 f. 50, 3 f. 40 et 4 f., Paris (I), 30/9 (2 PJ)	16 »	10 »

Marianne du Bicentenaire, 2 f. 50, Rge adhésif, Paris (I), 30/9	10 »	3 »
École Spéciale Travaux Publics, Paris (I), 5/10	12 »	2 20
Max Ernst, Sceaux (I), 10/10	12 »	3 »
Bonn 1 (I), 10/10		3 »
Marcel Cerdan, Paris (I), 19/10	12 »	2 50
Amnesty International, Paris (I), 19/10	9 »	3 »
François Rouan, Paris (I), 9/11	10 »	3 50
Flamme Olympique, Paris (I), 14/11	11 »	2 50
Idem, parcours de la Flamme :		
Départ, Paris (II), 14/12/91		4 »
Arrivée, Albertville (II), 8/2/92		4 »
U.N.E.S.C.O., Paris (I), 13/11	11 »	4 »
Conseil de l'Europe, Strasbourg (I), 23/11	11 »	4 »
Roberto Matta, Paris (I), 30/11	10 »	3 70
Croix-Rouge, Toulon (I), 30/11	10 »	3 »
Montréal (II), 30/11		3 »
Idem, Carnet, Toulon (I), 30/11		20 »
Jeux Paralympiques, Paris (I), 6/12	12 »	2 50
Lyon (II), 7/12		2 50
Ratt. volontaire Mayotte, Paris (I), 20/12	9 »	2 20

1992	(Doc)	(1er j)
Expo 92 Séville, Paris (I), 18/1	11 »	2 70
Bloc Jeux Olympiques, Albertville (II), 8/2	17 »	25 »
Journée du Timbre (II), 7/3	10 »	3 »
(Timbre du Carnet) (II), 7/3		3 »
(Bande Carnet) (II), 7/3	9 »	15 »
Jeux Olympiques, émission franco-grecque, Tours (I), 3/4	13 »	3 »
Idem, Timbre grec, Athènes-Tours (I), 3/4		3 20
César Franck, Paris (I), 11/4	9 »	3 »
Germaine Tailleferre, St-Maur-des-Fossés (I), 11/4	9 »	3 »
Érik Satie, Honfleur (I), 11/4	9 »	3 »
Arcueil (II), 11/4		3 »
Arthur Honegger, Le Havre (I), 11/4	9 »	3 »
Florent Schmitt, Blamont (I), 11/4	9 »	3 »
Georges Auric, Lodère (I), 11/4	9 »	3 »
Personnages célèbres, (Bande-carnet) (I), 11/4	11 »	15 »
Marguerite d'Angoulême, Angoulême (I), 11/4	9 »	3 50
Fondation d'Ajaccio, Ajaccio (I), 30/4	11 »	3 50
Europa. Christophe Colomb, Strasbourg (I), 9/5	13 »	4 »
St-Dié (I), 9/5		4 »
Essen (I), 9/5		4 »
Canal de l'Ourcq, Bondy (I), 30/5	11 »	2 50
Congrès des céréales et du pain, Paris (I), 30/5	11 »	2 70
Congrès Fédération, Niort (I), 6/6	9 »	2 20
France et Espagne, Pays olympiques, Paris (I), 19/6	13 »	3 »
Madrid (II),		3 20
L'Homme de Tautavel, Tautavel (I), 20/6	11 »	3 »
Jacques Callot, Nancy (I), 27/6	11 »	4 50
Metz (II), 27/6		4 50
Mont Aiguille, Clelles en Trièves, 27/6	11 »	2 70
Château de Biron, Biron, 4/7	11 »	2 70
Lorient, Lorient, 4/7	11 »	3 »
Fleurs des étangs et marais, Nantes (I), 12/9 (4 PJ)	30 »	12 »
Marianne du Bicentenaire, 4 f. 20, Paris (I), 14/9		3 70
1792, An I de la République, Paris (I), 26/9	12 »	4 »
Bicentenaire de la proclamation de la République, Paris (I), 26/9 (4 PJ)	15 »	16 »
Marché unique européen, Paris (I), 6/11	13 »	3 50
Idem Strasbourg (II), 6/11		3 »
Liaison postale aérienne Nancy-Lunéville, Roissy (I), 12/11	9 »	3 »
Lunéville (II), 12/11		4 »
Nancy (II), 12/11		4 »
Marcel Paul, Paris (I), 13/11	9 »	3 »
"Philateg", Paris (II), 13/11		6 50
Francis Bacon, Paris (I), 20/11	10 »	5 50
Alberto Burri, Paris (I), 20/11	10 »	5 50
Paul Delvaux, Paris (I), 20/11	10 »	5 50
Antoni Tapies, Paris (I), 20/11	10 »	5 50
Croix-Rouge, Strasbourg (I), 28/11	10 »	3 »
Stockholm (II), 28/11		3 »
Idem, Carnet, Strasbourg (I), 28/11		21 »
Les Gens du voyage, Paris (I), 5/12	9 »	3 »

1993	(Doc)	(1er j)
Les Postiers autour du monde, Port Camargue (I), 6/2	9 »	3 50
Espèces protégées de canards, Villars-les-Dombes (I), 6/2 (4 PJ)	27 »	15 »
Marianne du Bicentenaire, 2 f. 20, vert clair, Paris (II), 8/2		3 20
Mémorial des guerres en Indochine, Fréjus (I), 16/2	11 »	2 70
Journée du Timbre, (II) 6/3	10 »	3 50
(Paire du carnet) (II) 6/3		4 »
(Bande carnet) (II) 6/3	10 »	20 »
Jeux méditerranéens 93, Montpellier (I), 13/3	9 »	2 20
Centenaire du "Droit Humain", Paris (I), 3/4	10 »	3 50
Europa, art contemporain, Strasbourg (I), 17/4 (2 PJ)	10 »	6 »
Idem Paris (II), 17/4 (2 PJ)	10 »	6 »
Marianne du Bicentenaire "à validité permanente", Boulogne sur Seine (I), 19/4	11 »	4 »
Guy de Maupassant, Tourville sur Arques (I), 24/4	10 »	3 »
Alain, Mortagne au Perche (I), 24/4	10 »	3 »
Jean Cocteau, Maisons Lafitte (I), 24/4	10 »	3 »
Marcel Pagnol, Aubagne (I), 24/4	10 »	3 »
André Chamson, Nîmes (I), 24/4	10 »	3 »
Marguerite Yourcenar, Paris (I), 24/4	10 »	3 »
Bailleul (II), 24/4		3 »
Personnages célèbres, (Bande-carnet) (I), 24/4	10 »	20 »
Chinon, Chinon (I), 24/4	10 »	3 20
Conférence des Cours Constitutionnelles, Paris (I), 8/5	10 »	2 20
Django Reinhardt, Boulogne sur Seine (I), 14/5	10 »	3 »
Louise Weiss, Paris, (I) 15/5	10 »	2 20
Congrès Fédération, Lille (I), 29/5	9 »	3 20
Muséum national d'Histoire naturelle, Paris (I), 5/6	10 »	2 20
Martyrs et Héros de la Résistance, Lyon (I), 18/6	10 »	5 20
Télégraphe optique de Chappe, Saint-Martin-du-Tertre (I), 10/7	10 »	3 »
Petit train d'Artouste, Laruns (I), 10/7	10 »	3 20
Minerve, Minerve (I), 17/7	9 »	3 »
Marianne du Bicentenaire, 2 f. 40 vert, Paris (I), 12/7	13 »	2 50
4 f. 40 bleu, Paris (I), 26/7		3 »
70 c. adhésif avec timbre adhésif "à validité permanente", Paris (II), 2/8		15 »
3 f. 50 vert-jaune, Paris (I), 9/8		3 »
Abbaye de La Chaise-Dieu, La Chaise-Dieu (I), 4/9	10 »	2 50
Georges de la Tour, Vic sur Seille (I), 9/9	10 »	4 50
Libération de la Corse, Ajaccio ou Bastia (I), 9 et 10/9	10 »	2 70
Montbéliard, Montbéliard (I), 11/9	10 »	3 »
Le Val de Grâce, Paris (I), 25/9	10 »	3 »
Les Postiers autour du monde, Cherbourg (II), 25/9		3 »
Maurice Denis, Saint Germain en Laye (I), 2/10	10 »	4 50
Arts du cirque, Châlons sur Marne (I), 2/10	10 »	3 »
Takis, Paris (I), 9/10	10 »	4 50
Le Jacquemard de Lambesc, Lambesc (I), 9/10	10 »	3 »
"Le plaisir d'écrire", Paris (I), 21/10 (7 PJ)	9 »	22 50
La bande-carnet, sur grande enveloppe		22 50
U.N.E.S.C.O., Paris (I), 23/10	10 »	5 25
Salon du Timbre, (2 env.), Paris (I), 10/11		12 »
Bloc sur grande enveloppe, Paris (I) 10/11	11 »	12 »
Musée du Louvre, diptyque, Paris (I), 20/11	11 »	4 50
Musée du Louvre, bande de deux diptyques, grande enveloppe, Paris (II), 20/11		11 »
Croix-Rouge, Metz (I), 27/11	9 »	3 »
Montréal (II), 27/11		3 »
Idem, carnet, Metz (I)		20 »
Marie-Hélène Vieira da Silva, Paris (I), 11/12	9 »	5 »

1994	(Doc)	(1er j)
Conseil de l'Europe, Strasbourg (I), 15/1	10 »	6 50
Arts décoratifs, Nancy (I), 22/1 (4 PJ)	30 »	12 »
Bourg la Reine (II), 22/1 (4 PJ)		12 »
Sean Scully, Paris (I), 29/1	10 »	4 50
Cathédrale du Mans, Le Mans (I), 12/2	10 »	4 50
Marianne du Bicentenaire, timbre adhésif "à validité permanente" avec dentelure verticale en lignes ondulées, Paris (II), 16/2		5 »
Bastia, Bastia (I), 19/2	13 »	2 70
Élections au Parlement Européen, Paris (I), 26/2	10 »	2 40
Strasbourg (II), 26/2		2 40
Laurent Mourguet, créateur de Guignol, Villeurbanne (I), 4/3	9 »	2 70
Salon Lugdunum (II), 4/3		5 »
École Polytechnique, Palaiseau (I), 11/3	10 »	2 40
Journée du Timbre, (II) 12/3	10 »	4 »
Paire du carnet (II) 12/3		5 »
Bande carnet	9 »	22 »

Relations culturelles France-Suède, Paris (I), 18/3 (4 PJ)	23 »	18 »
Bande carnet, grande enveloppe		25 »
Bande carnet et carnet suédois sur grande enveloppe, Paris et Stockholm (I et II), 18/3		28 »
Président Georges Pompidou, Paris (I), 9/4	10 »	2 40
Hommage aux Maquis, Thones (I), 9/4	10 »	2 70
Petit Bornand (II), 9/4		3 »
Thorens-Glières (II), 9/4		3 »
Philexjeunes'94, Grenoble (I), 22/4	9 »	2 40
Europa, l'Europe et les découvertes, Strasbourg (I), 30/4	10 »	5 50
Paris (II), 30/4	10 »	5 50
Inauguration du Tunnel sous la Manche, Coquelles (I), 3/5 (2 PJ)	15 »	8 »
Calais (II), 3/5 (2 PJ)		10 »
Timbres français et britanniques sur grande enveloppe (I) et (II), 3/5		24 »
Banque asiatique de développement, Nice (I), 3/5	10 »	2 20
Congrès Fédération, Martigues (I), 20/5	9 »	2 20
Cour de Cassation, Paris (I), 3/6	10 »	2 40
Cinquantenaire du Débarquement, Bayeux (I), 4/6	10 »	4 »
Caen (II), 4/6		4 »
Hommage aux libérateurs, Bayeux (I), 4/6	10 »	4 »
Montagne Sainte Victoire, Aix en Provence (I), 18/6	10 »	3 »
Argentat (Corrèze), Argentat (I), 18/6	10 »	3 »
Centenaire du C.I.O., Paris (I), 23/6	10 »	3 »
Pays de la Saulx (Meuse), Haironville (I), 2/7	10 »	2 50
Orgues de Poitiers, Poitiers (I), 5/7	10 »	3 »
Marianne du Bicentenaire 2 f., Paris (I), 5/7	7 »	2 70
50e anniversaire du Débarquement en Provence La Croix Valmer (I), 13/8	12 »	3 »
Draguignan (II), 13/8		3 50
Saint-Raphaël (II), 13/8		3 50
Toulon (II), 13/8		3 50
Nicolas Poussin, Les Andelys (I), 10/9	10 »	3 50
Fernandel, Marseille (I), 17/9	10 »	3 70
Yvonne Printemps, Ermont (I), 17/9	10 »	3 70
Joséphine Baker, Castelnaud (I), 17/9	10 »	3 70
Bourvil, Pretot-Vicquemare (I), 17/9	10 »	3 70
Yves Montand, Marseille (I), 17/9	10 »	3 70
Coluche, Paris (I), 17/9	10 »	4 »
Personnages célèbres (Bande carnet) (I), 17/9	13 »	22 »
Conservatoire des Arts et Métiers, Paris (I), 24/9	10 »	2 70
Cascade du Parc de Saint Cloud Saint Cloud (I), 24/9	10 »	3 »
Ecole Normale Supérieure, Paris (I), 8/10	10 »	2 70
Toxicomanie, Paris (I), 15/10		2 70
Georges Simenon, Paris (I), 15/10	9 »	3 »
Parc Floral de Paris - Salon du Timbre Paris (I), 15/10 (2 env.)		14 »
Bloc sur grande enveloppe, Paris (I), 15/10	12 »	16 »
Grande loge de France, Paris (I), 5/11	10 »	3 50
Baselitz, Paris (I), 19/11	10 »	5 »
Alain Colas, Clamecy (I), 19/11	10 »	3 »
Croix Rouge, Arras (I), 26/11	9 »	3 70
Montreal (II), 26/11		3 70
Idem. Carnet Arras (I), 26/11		20 »
Contre le Sida, Paris (I), 1/12		2 50
Fédération Nationale de la Presse, Paris (I), 1/12	10 »	2 70
Les Champs Elysées, Paris (I), 31/12	15 »	5 »

1995	(Doc)	(1er j)
Les Champs Elysées, Paris (II), 1/1		6 »
Centenaire du Cinéma (4 env.), Paris (I), 14/1		12 »
(4 env.), Lyon (II), 14/1		12 »
Bloc sur 1 grande enveloppe, Paris (I), Lyon (II), Besançon (II) et La Ciotat (II), 14/1	15 »	14 »
Pont de Normandie,, Le Havre (I), 20/1	17 »	5 50
Honfleur (II), 20/1		5 50
Notariat Européen, Paris (I), 21/1	10 »	2 70
Louis Pasteur, Dole (I), 18/2	9 »	3 »
Paris (II), 18/2		3 »
Châsse de Saint Taurin, Evreux (I), 25/2	10 »	5 »
Audubon, Les Oiseaux (4 PJ), Paris (I), 25/2		14 »
Idem (4 PJ) Nantes (II), 25/2		16 »
Bloc oiseaux, Paris (I), 25/2	10 »	18 »
Nantes (II), 25/2		32 »
Malterie, Stenay (I), 25/2	10 »	2 70
Journée du Timbre (II), 4/3	9 »	4 50
Paire du Carnet, 4/3		5 »
Bande-carnet sur grande env., 4/3	10 »	20 »
Comités d'Entreprise, Paris (I), 7/3	10 »	2 70
Ecole supérieure d'Electricité, Gif/Yvette (I), 11/3	10 »	4 »
Institut langues Orientales, Paris (I), 25/3	10 »	3 »
Jean Giono, Manosque (I), 25/3	10 »	3 »
Ariane - 100e satellite, Kourou (I), 28/3		3 »
Sidérurgie lorraine, Hayange (I) 1/4	10 »	3 »
Europa, Paix et Liberté (2 env.), Strasbourg (I), 29/4	10 »	6 »
Paris (II), 29/4		6 »
Métier de la Forêt (I), Renwez, 29/4	9 »	3 30
De Gaulle - La Victoire, Paris (I), 8/5	10 »	5 »
Pierre Prud'hon, Toulouse (I), 12/5	10 »	7 »
Remiremont, Remiremont (I), 13/5	10 »	2 70
Assemblée Nationale, Paris (I), 13/5	10 »	3 »
Croix Rouge, Saumur (I), 13/5	10 »	5 »
Helsinki (II), 13/5		7 »
Carnet, Saumur (I), 13/5		20 »
Secours populaire, Paris (I), 20/5	10 »	2 20
Metz (II), 20/5		2 20
Pont de Nyons, Nyons (I), 20/5	11 »	3 30
La Bretagne, Rennes (I), 27/5	(les 4) 11 »	3 »
Les Vosges, Epinal (I), 27/5		3 »
L'Auvergne, Clermont-Ferrand (I), 27/5		3 »
La Camargue, Arles (I), 27/5		3 »
Congrès Fédération, Orléans (I), 2/6	9 »	3 »
Orléans (II), 2/6		6 »
Village de Corrèze, Corrèze (I), 3/6	10 »	3 »
Zao Wou-Ki, Paris (I), 10/6	12 »	7 »
Fables de La Fontaine (6 env.) (I), Château-Thierry 24/6	10 »	20 »
Bande de 6 T.-P., Château-Thierry 24/6		15 »
Rafle du Vel d'Hiv, Paris (I) 9/7	10 »	3 »
André Maginot, Paris (I), 9/9	10 »	3 »
Revigny (II),9/9		3 »
Grande Loge Féminine, Paris (I)	10 »	3 »
Kirkeby, Paris (I) 23/9	10 »	7 »
La pharmacie hospitalière, Paris (I), 23/9	10 »	3 »
Lyon (II), 23/9		4 »
Congrès, Paris (II), 26/9		10 »
Barbizon, Barbizon (I), 30/9	10 »	4 »
Ecole Nationale d'Administration, Paris (I), 5/10	10 »	3 »
Ecole Nationale d'Administration, Strasbourg (I), 5/10		3 »
Berthe Morisot, Paris (I), 7/10	10 »	6 »
Institut de France, Paris (I), 14/10	10 »	3 »
Automobile Club de France, Paris (I), 4/11	10 »	3 50
50e anniversaire de l'O.N.U., Paris (I), 16/11	10 »	3 50
50e anniversaire de l'O.N.U., enveloppe mixte France - O.N.U. - Paris 16/11		5 »
Les santons de Provence (6 env.)	chaque 11 »	
Marseille (I), 25/11		25 »
Sceaux (II), 25/11		27 »
Carnet santons (I), 25/11		17 »
Montréal (II), 25/11		30 »
Francis James, Orthez (I), 2/12	10 »	5 »
Tournay (II), 2/12		5 »
Cathédrale d'Evry, Evry (I), 9/12	10 »	4 »
Coupe du Monde de Football 98, Paris (1), 12/12	9 »	4 »

1996	(Doc)	(1er j)
Wercollier, Strasbourg (I), 20/1	9 »	6 »
Dibbets, Paris (I) 10/2	10 »	6 »
Civilisation des Arawaks, St Martin (I), 10/2	10 »	3 »
Corot, Ville d'Avray (I), 2/3	10 »	7 »
L'Imaginaire Irlandais, Paris (I) 16/3	10 »	3 »
Journée du Timbre (II), 16/3	10 »	4 »
Paire du Carnet (II), 16/3		6 »
Bande-carnet (II) 16/3		18 »
Jacques Rueff, Paris (I), 23/3	9 »	3 50
Marianne du Bicentenaire (2 70-3 80-4 50) Paris (I), 18/3	12 »	6 50
René Descartes, Descartes (I), 30/3	10 »	4 »
50 ans d'EDF-GDF, Paris (I) 6/4	10 »	3 »
Toulouse (II) 6/4		3 »
Grenoble (II) 6/4		3 »
Parc des Cévennes, Florac (I), 20/4	(les 3) 15 »	3 50
Parc du Mercantour, St Etienne de Tinée (I) 20/4		4 »
Parc de la Vanoise, Planay (I) 20/4		4 »
I.N.R.A., Paris (I) 4/5	10 »	3 »
Europa, Madame de Sévigné, Strasbourg (I) 27/4	10 »	4 »
Paris (II) 27/4		4 »
Maison de Jeanne d'Arc - Domrémy 11/5	10 »	5 »
Accord Ramoge, Marseille 14/5	7 »	4 »
Monaco 14/5		6 »
Gênes 14/5		7 »
Congrès Fédération, Clermont Ferrand (I) 26/5	9 »	3 »
Aulnat (II) 26/5		3 50

Bitche, Bitche (I), 25/5	7 »	2 70
Coupe du Monde de Football, Lens, Montpellier, Saint-Etienne, Toulouse (I), 1/6 (4 env.)	9 »	12 »
U.N.E.S.C.O., Paris (I), 1/6 (2 env.)		6 50
Conseil de l'Europe, Strasbourg (I), 1/6		6 50
Iles Sanguinaires, Ajaccio (I), 1/6	10 »	3 50
Cathédrale de Chambéry, Chambéry (I), 8/6	10 »	3 70
Trésor de Neuvy-en-Sullias, Orléans (I), 8/6	9 »	5 »
Jacques Marette, Paris (I), 15/6	9 »	3 »
Centenaire des Jeux olympiques, Lille (I), 15/6	10 »	3 »
Train Ajaccio-Vizzavona, Ajaccio (I), 29/6	10 »	4 »
Abbaye du Thoronet, Le Thoronet (I), 6/7	10 »	3 70
Notre-Dame de Fourvière, Lyon (I), 6/9	10 »	3 »
Baptême de Clovis, Reims (I), 14/9	9 »	3 50
Arman, Marseille (I), 21/9	10 »	5 50
Héros français du roman policier (6 env.)		
Paris (I), 5/10	12 »	22 »
Saint-Nazaire (II), 5/10		23 »
bande carnet (I) Paris 5/10		22 »
Lycée Henri IV, Paris (I), 12/10	10 »	3 »
U.N.I.C.E.F., Paris (I), 19/10	10 »	3 »
Conseil Economique et Social, Paris (I), 26/10	10 »	2 70
Cinquantenaire de l'U.N.E.S.C.O., Paris (I), 2/11	10 »	3 »
Salon Philatélique d'Automne, Paris (I), 7/11	10 »	5 »
Croix-Rouge, Paris (I) 16/11	10 »	5 »
Bande carnet, Paris (I) 16/11		20 »
Départements d'Outre-Mer, Paris (I), 16/11	10 »	3 »
Basse Terre (II), 16/11		3 »
Cayenne (II), 16/11		3 »
Fort de France (II), 16/11		3 »
Saint Denis de la Réunion (II), 16/11		3 »
Ecole Française d'Athènes, Paris (I), 23/11	10 »	3 »
André Malraux, Paris (I), 23/11	10 »	3 »
Festival de Cannes, Paris (I), 30/11	12 »	3 »
Cannes (II), 30/11		3 »
Bibliothèque Nationale de France, Paris (I), 14/12	10 »	4 50

1997	(Doc)	(1er j)
François Mitterrand, Château Chinon (I), 4/1	18 »	4 50
Paris (II), 4/1		4 50
Innovation participative, Paris (I), 24/1	9 »	2 70
Centre Pompidou, Paris (I), 31/1	10 »	3 »
Timbres de souhaits, Chessy (I), 8/2	10 »	2 70
Saint Valentin (I), 8/2		2 70
Ecole Nationale des Ponts et Chaussées, Paris (I), 14/2	10 »	2 70
Patrimoine guyanais, Saint-Laurent-du Maroni (I) 22/2	10 »	2 70
Fresques de Tavant, Tavant (I), 1/3	10 »	5 »
Journée du Timbre, (II), 15/3	10 »	3 50
Paire du carnet (II), 15/3		5 »
Bande-carnet (II), 15/3		20 »
Millau, Millau (I), 15/3	8 »	3 50
Bernard Moninot, Paris (I), 29/3	10 »	6 »
Parc des Ecrins, Briançon (I), 12/4		3 »
Parc de la Guadeloupe, Petit Bourg (I), 12/4		3 »
Parc des Pyrénées, 12/4		3 70
Parc de Port-Cros, Hyères (I) 12/4		3 70
Les 4 Parcs ci-dessus, Mulhouse (II) 12/4	12 »	15 »
Europa "Le Chat Botté", Strasbourg (I), 26/4	10 »	3 50
Philexjeunes'97, Nantes (I), 2/5	9 »	2 70
Les Journées de la Lettre, Paris (I) 8/5 (6 env.)		17 »
Idem. Timbres auto-adhésifs du carnet Paris (I), 8/5	13 »	20 »
Idem. Enveloppe grand format (avec oblitérations de 8 villes : Lille, Strasbourg, Bordeaux, Lyon, Rennes, Marseille, Clermont Ferrand, Paris) (II)		30 »
Hommage aux combattants en A.F.N., Paris (I) 10/5	10 »	3 »
Congrès Fédération, Versailles (I), 17/5	9 »	6 »
Versailles (O), 17/5		6 »
75e anniversaire de la Fédération, Versailles (II) 17/5		6 »
Château du Plessis-Bourré, Ecuillé (I) 24/5	11 »	4 »
Coupe du Monde de Football, Lyon, Marseille, Nantes, Paris (I) 31/5 (4 env.)	10 »	12 »
Fresque Les Salles Lavauguyon, Les Salles Lavauguyon (I) 14/6	10 »	4 »
Saint Martin, Tours (I) 5/7	10 »	4 »
Amiens, Ligugé, St Martin Lacaussade (II) 5/7 (3 env.)		12 »
Enclos Paroissial, Guimiliau (I) 12/7	10 »	3 »
Marianne du 14 Juillet (4 val.), Paris (I) 14/7 (2 env.)	10 »	8 20
Championnats du monde d'aviron, Novalaise (I) 30/8	10 »	3 »
César, Paris (I) 13/9	10 »	5 »
Corsaires Basques, St Jean de Luz (I) 13/9	10 »	2 70
Marianne du 14 Juillet (12 val.) Paris (I) 15/9 (4 env.)	15 »	22 »
Sablé sur Sarthe, Sablé (I) 20/9	9 »	2 70
Basilique St Maurice, Epinal (I) 20/9	10 »	2 70
Voiturier de Marée, Boulogne s/mer (I) 26/9	10 »	2 70
J. B. Chardin, Paris (I) 27/9	10 »	5 »
Année du Japon, Paris (I) 4/10	10 »	4 »
Judo, Paris (I) 9/10	10 »	3 »
Domaine de Sceaux, Sceaux (I) 11/10	10 »	2 70
SAR.LOR.LUX Metz (I) 16/10	10 »	2 70
Luxembourg 16/10		3 »
Bonn 16/10		3 »
La Qualité, St Dié (I) 18/10	8 »	3 »
Abbeville et Dijon (II) 18/10 (2 env.)		6 70
Collège de France, Paris (I) 18/10	8 »	3 70
Héros d'aventures, Paris (I) 25/10 (6 env.)		20 »
Lancelot, Rennes (II) 25/10		3 50
Le Bossu, Nevers (II) 25/10		3 50
Cyrano, Bergerac (II) 25/10		3 50
Héros d'aventures (bande-carnet) (I) 25/10	12 »	20 »
Croix-Rouge, Paris (I) 6/11	10 »	5 »
Idem carnet, Paris (I) 6/11		20 »
Meilleurs Voeux ; chat et souris, Paris (I) 8/11	10 »	3 »
Breguet XIV, Paris (I) 15/11	20 »	20 »
Enfance maltraitée, Paris (I) 20/11	10 »	2 70
Meilleurs Voeux du Facteur, Paris (I) 22/11	10 »	3 »
Maréchal Leclerc, Paris (I) 28/11	11 »	3 »
Amiens, Strasbourg (II) 28/11 (2 env.)		6 »
"Philexfrance 99" Paris (I) 6/12	15 »	3 »
Moutier d'Ahun, Moutier d'Ahun (I) 13/12	10 »	3 »

1998	(Doc)	(1er j)
Michel Debré, Paris (I) 15/1	6 »	3 »
Amboise, St Denis Réunion (II) 15/1 (2 env.)		6 50
Assemblée Nationale, Paris (I) 24/1	7 »	2 70
Coupe du Monde de Football, Bordeaux, St Denis (I) 24/1 (2 env.)	11 »	6 »
Idem bloc 10 villes (I) 24/1	15 »	25 »
"Bonne Fête" St Valentin (I) (31/1)	11 »	2 70
Médiateur de la République Paris (I) 5/2	11 »	2 70
Journée du Timbre, Paris (II) 21/2	12 »	3 »
Paire du carnet (II) 21/2		5 »
Bande carnet (II) 21/2		16 »
Coupe du Monde de Football (timbre rond gommé), St Denis (I) 28/2	7 »	3 »
Idem (timbre rond auto-adhésif), Paris (I) 28/2		3 »
Abbé Franz Stock, Paris (I) 28/2	9 »	4 »
Chartres (II) 28/2		4 »
"Joyeux anniversaire", Paris (I) 13/3	11 »	2 70
Réunion Mulhouse à la France, Mulhouse (I) 14/3	11 »	4 »
Abbaye de Cîteaux, St Nicolas les Cîteaux (I) 14/3	11 »	4 »
Patrimoine réunionnais, St Pierre (I) 4/4	11 »	4 »
Magritte, Paris (I) 18/4	13 »	8 »
Bruxelles 18/4		8 »
Edit de Nantes, Nantes (I) 18/4	11 »	4 »
Pau (II) 18/4		5 »
Delacroix, St Maurice (I) 25/4	13 »	8 »
Abolition esclavage, Paris (I) 25/4	11 »	2 70
Nantes, Champagney, Basse Terre, Cayenne, St Denis, Fort de France (II) 25/4 (6 env.)		18 »
Gois de Noirmoutiers, Barbâtre (I) 2/5	11 »	3 »
Beauvoir s/mer (II) 2/5		3 »
Les Journées de la Lettre, Paris (I) 9/5 (6 env.)	20 »	20 »
Idem, auto-adhésifs, Lille, Lyon, Rennes, Marseille, Strabourg, Chateauroux (II) 9/5 (6 env.)		21 »
Idem env . G. F. avec la bande+1 carnet oblit. des 7 villes 9/5		30 »
Ligue des Droits de l'Homme, Paris (I) 9/5	9 »	4 »
Pablo Picasso, Villeurbanne (I) 15/5	12 »	7 »
Henri Collet, Bordeaux (I) 15/5	9 »	4 »
Congrès Fédération Dunkerque, Dunkerque (I) 29/5	7 »	3 »
71e Congrès (II) 30/5		4 »
Le Mont Saint-Michel, Mont Saint-Michel (I) 6/6	11 »	6 »
Europa, Fête de la Musique, Strasbourg (I) 13/6	9 »	3 50
Paris (II) 13/6		3 50
La Baie de Somme, St Valéry s/Somme (I) 27/6	11 »	3 »
Château de Crusol, St Péray (I) 4/7	7 »	3 »
"Champion du Monde FRANCE", St Denis (II) 12/7		5 »
Potez 25, Evreux (I) 13/7	16 »	25 »
Stéphane Mallarmé, Vulaines s/Seine (I) 5/9	9 »	3 »
Sens (II) 5/9		3 50
Aéro-Club de France, Paris (I) 12/9	9 »	3 »
avec griffe spéciale Transport par ballon, oblitération ordinaire d'arrivée, Matougues 14/9		5 »
Saint-Exupéry, (5 env.), Paris (I) 12/9		20 »
Bloc entier, env. G.F. 12/9	15 »	16 »

France-Chine (2 env.), Paris (I) 12/9	12 »	6 »
Pékin (II) 12/9		4 50
Collégiale de Mantes-la-Jolie, Mantes-la-Jolie		
(I) 19/9	9 »	3 50
Opéra de Paris, Paris (I) 19/9	9 »	4 50
Chevaux, (4 env.) Paris (I) 27/9	8 »	13 »
(4 env.) Argentan, Arles, Charleville,		
Espelette (II) 27/9		14 »
(3 env.) St Lo, La Glacerie,		
Marcq en Baroeul (II) 27/9		10 »
Salon de l'Auto, Paris (I) 1/10	10 »	3 »
Paris, Salon (II) 1/10		4 »
Acteurs de Cinéma Français (6 env.) Paris (I) 3/10	12 »	20 »
Bande-carnet (I) 3/10		20 »
Saint-Dié, Saint-Dié (I) 3/10	10 »	3 »
Constitution de la Ve République, Reims (I) 3/10	10 »	3 »
Armistice 1914-1918, Paris (I) 17/10	10 »	3 »
Marcel Duchamp, Rouen (I) 17/10	10 »	5 »
UNESCO (2 env.), Paris (I) 24/10	10 »	6 70
Union Mondiale pour la Nature, Fontainebleau		
(I) 3/11	10 »	3 »
Croix-Rouge, Paris (I) 5/11	10 »	4 »
Carnet, Paris (I) 5/11		20 »
"Meilleurs voeux", Paris (I) 7/11	13 »	5 »
"Bonne année", Paris (I) 7/11		5 »
Bloc-feuillet, Paris, (I) 7/11		22 »
Médecins Sans Frontières, Paris (I) 21/11	10 »	3 »
Paul Gauguin, Pont Aven (I) 5/12	10 »	7 »
Parlement européen, Strasbourg (I) 5/12	10 »	3 »
Déclaration Universelle des Droits de l'Homme		
(2 env), Paris, (I) 10/12	10 »	6 »
Dijon (II), Manosque (II) 10/12		6 »
Le radium, Fontenay-aux-Roses (I) (15/12	9 »	3 »
Paris (II) 15/12		3 »

1999	(Doc)	(1er j)
150e anniversaire du timbre-poste français, (2 env.)		
Paris (I) 1/1	11 »	8 »
Bande-carnet, Paris (I) 1/1		14 »
Timbre Euro, Paris (I) 1/1	10 »	5 »
Assistance Publique - Hôpitaux de Paris, Paris (I) 9/1	9 »	2 70
Relations diplomatiques France-Israël, Paris (I) 24/1	11 »	3 »
(4 env.), Lyon (II), Marseille (II), Strasbourg (II),		
Toulouse (II)		15 »
Timbres de souhaits (2 env.), Paris (I) 6/2	11 »	7 50
Timbre Euro auto-adhésif, Paris (I) 6/2		5 »
Jean Goujon, Paris (I) 13/2	10 »	5 50
Recensement de la population, Paris (I) 20/2	10 »	2 70
Patrimoine culturel du Liban, Paris (I) 27/2	10 »	4 »
Journée du Timbre - Astérix, Paris (II) 6/3	16 »	5 »
Paire du carnet, Paris (II) 6/3		7 »
Bande-carnet, Paris (II) 6/3		30 »
Bloc et paire du carnet, Paris (II) 6/3		18 »
Cinquantenaire du Conseil de l'Europe, Strasbourg		
(I) 19/3	10 »	3 »
Mariages, remerciements, naissance (4 env.),		
Strasbourg (I) 20/3	10 »	12 »
Elections au Parlement Européen, Paris (I) 27/3	10 »	2 70
Strasbourg (II) 27/3		2 70
Philexfrance'99, oeuvres d'art (3 env.), timbres du bloc		
Paris (I) 26/3		65 »
Bloc-feuillet, Paris (I) 26/3	25 »	35 »
Richard Coeur de Lion, Chalus (I) 10/4	10 »	3 »
Les Andelys, Fontevraud (II) 10/4		7 50
Airbus A300-B4, Blagnac (I) 10/4	27 »	18 »
Dieppe, Dieppe (I) 17/4	15 »	3 »
Europa, la Camargue, Strasbourg (I) 24/4	10 »	3 50
Arles (II) 24/4		3 50
Bonnes vacances, Joyeux anniversaire (2 env.)		
Paris (I) 13/5	11 »	6 70
Betton (II) 13/5		7 50
Patrimoine martiniquais, St Pierre (I) 15/5	10 »	3 »
Château du Haut Koenigsbourg, Sélestat (I) 15/5	10 »	4 50
Ecole de Nancy - Emile Gallé, Nancy (I) 22/5	10 »	3 50
Claude Monet, Giverny (I) 29/5	10 »	7 »
Roses anciennes (3 env.), Lyon (I) 28/5		10 »
Bloc feuillet, Lyon (I) 28/5	13 »	12 »
Jurade de St Emilion, St Emilion (I) 29/5	9 »	3 30
Hôtel de la Monnaie, Paris (I) 5/6	9 »	3 70
La Comtesse de Ségur, Aube (I) 12/6	9 »	3 »
Pluneret (II) 12/6		3 50
Aimer accueillir, Paris (I) 19/6	9 »	3 »
Vitrail de la Cathédrale d'Auch, Auch (I) 19/6	9 »	5 »
René Caillié, Mauzé sur le Mignon (I) 26/6	9 »	3 70
Figeac - Hommage à Champollion,		
Figeac (I) 26/6	8 »	3 50
"Philexfrance'99" - Cérès avec hologramme,		
Paris (I) 2/7	9 »	65 »
Célébration de l'An 2000, Paris (I) 5/7	9 »	6 20
Dessine-moi l'An 2000, Paris (I) 6/7	9 »	3 »
Laubert (II) 6/7		6 »
Eclipse de Soleil, Paris (I) 8/7	9 »	4 »
Photographes français (6 env.), Paris (I) 10/7	10 »	25 »
Bande carnet, Paris (I) 10/7		22 »
Armada du Siècle (5 env.), Rouen (I) 10/7		18 »
Bloc, Rouen (I) 10/7	10 »	14 »
Arnac-Pompadour, Arnac-Pompadour (I) 10/7	9 »	3 »
Frédéric Ozanam, Paris (I) 11/9	8 »	3 70
Coupe du Monde de Rugby, St Denis (I) 11/9	8 »	3 50
Toulouse, Béziers, Montpellier, Lens (4 env.) (I) 11/9		18 »
Conseil de l'Europe - Art (2 env.), Strasbourg (I) 18/9	9 »	7 »
Mouvement Emmaüs, Orléans (I) 26/9	9 »	3 »
Chats et chiens, (4 env.), Gennevilliers (I) 2/10		16 »
(les 2 doc.)	20 »	
Laon, Brignais, Laruns, Rennes (II) 2/10		16 »
Frédéric Chopin, Paris (I) 17/10	12 »	4 »
Pologne (I) 17/10		4 »
Croix-Rouge, Paris (I) 10/11	7 »	4 »
Bande carnet, Paris (I) 10/11		20 »
Van Dyck, Paris (I) 11/11	11 »	5 »
Salon Automne (II) 11/11		6 »
Meilleurs Vœux 2000, Melun (I) 20/11	9 »	6 »
Paris (II) 31/12/99 et 1/01/2000		8 »
Le métro parisien, Paris (I) 4/12	7 »	3 50
Conseil d'Etat, Paris (I) 11/12	9 »	3 »

2000	(Doc)	(1er j)
Le phare du bout du monde, Paris (I) 1/1/2000	9 »	3 50
Le phare du bout du monde, La Rochelle (I) 1/1		3 50
Nantes (II) 1/1		4 »
Cœurs 2000 (2 env.), Paris (I) 8/1	10 »	9 »
Bloc, St Valentin (II) 14/2		11 »
Banque de France, Paris (I) 15/1	8 »	3 20
Chamalières (II) 15/1		3 50
Avion Couzinet 70, Paris (I) 12/2	20 »	25 »
Corps Préfectoral, Paris (I) 17/2	9 »	3 »
Sandro Botticelli, Paris (I) 25/2	9 »	6 »
Carcassonne, Carcassonne (I) 3/3	9 »	6 »
Fête du Timbre, Tintin et Milou (TP feuille),		
Paris (II) 11/3	12 »	7 »
Paire carnet, Paris (II) 11/3		8 »
Bande carnet, Paris (II) 11/3		25 »
Bloc + paire carnet, Paris (II) 11/3		17 »
Parlement de Bretagne, Rennes (I) 25/3	9 »	3 »
Pervenche de Madagascar, Castres (I) 25/3	9 »	4 »
Félicitations, Villeurbanne (I) 7/4	9 »	3 »
Camille Claudel, Paris (I) 8/4	9 »	5 50
Fère en Tardenois (II) 8/4		6 »
St-Guilhem-le-Désert, St-Guilhem-le-Désert (I) 8/4	9 »	3 »
Le Siècle au fil du Timbre, N° 1 Sport (5 env.)		
Clermont-Ferrand, Lens, Paris, Marseille,		
St Etienne (I) 15/4	16 »	17 »
Bande, Bordeaux, Reims, Vannes, Paris (I) 15/4		13 »
Gérardmer, vallée des lacs, Gérardmer (I) 15/4	9 »	3 »
Voitures anciennes " Philexjeunes 2000 ", (5 env.),		
Annecy (I) 5/5		20 »
Sochaux, Mulhouse, Puteaux (II) 5/5		20 »
Bloc, Annecy (I) 5/5	10 »	13 »
Europa 2000, Strasbourg (I) 9/5	8 »	3 50
Paris (II) 9/5		3 50
Henri-Louis Duhamel du Monceau, Orléans (I) 13/5	9 »	4 »
73e Congrès F.F.A.P Nevers, Nevers (I) 19/5	7 »	3 »
Bonnes Vacances, Paris (I) 1/6	9 »	3 »
Conquète Annapurna - Premier 8000, Chamonix		
Mt-Blanc (I) 3/6	9 »	3 »
Abbatiale d'Ottmarsheim, Ottmarsheim (I) 17/6	9 »	3 50
Papillon sardanapale, Paris (I) 17/6		4 »
Allosaure, Paris (I) 17/6		3 50
Girafe reticulée, Paris (I) 17/6		3 50
Tulipe lutea, Paris (I) 17/6		4 »
Bloc regard sur la nature, Paris (I) 17/6	13 »	17 »
Antoine de Saint-Exupéry, Lyon (I) 24/6	11 »	4 »
Agay (II) - St Maurice de Remens (II) 24/6 sur 1 envel.		5 »
Le Train Jaune, Villefranche de Conflent (I) 14/7	15 »	3 50
Ste Léocadie (II) 14/7		3 50
Folklores de France, Confolens (I) 12/8	10 »	3 80
Biarritz (II) 12/8		3 80
J.O Sydney 2000, Arcueil (I) 9/9 (2 P.J)		6 »
Bloc J.O Sydney 2000, Arcueil (I) 9/9	13 »	20 »
Paul-Emile-Victor, Paris (I) 16/9		4 »
Prémanon (II) 16/9		4 50

Haroun Tazieff, Paris (I) 16/9		4 »
Eric Tabarly, La Trinité (I) 16/9		4 »
Nantes (II) 16/9		4 50
Jacques-Yves Cousteau, St André de Cubzac (I) 16/9		4 »
Norbert Casteret, St Martory (I) 16/9		4 »
Aramits (II) 16/9		4 50
Alexandra David-Néel, Digne les Bains (I) 16/9		4 »
Saint-Mandé (II) 16/9		4 50
Carnet Aventuriers célèbres, (I) 16/9	30 »	20 »
Gaston Chaissac, Paris (I) 23/9	9 »	6 »
Les Sables d'Olonnes (II) 23/9		6 »
Frère Alfred Stanke, Bourges (I) 23/9	7 »	4 »
Dijon (II) 23/9		4 »
S.O.S amitié, Paris (I) 30/9	9 »	3 »
Le Siècle au fil du timbre, N° 2 Société (5 P.J)		
Paris, Rouen, Pleumeur Bodou, Toulouse,		
Nice (I) 30/9	15 »	17 »
Bande entière Paris (I) 30/9		13 »
Nouveau Millenaire 2001, Paris (I) 14/10	9 »	3 »
Mosaïque Carolingienne, Germigny-des-Prés (I) 21/10	11 »	5 »
France/Nouvelle Zélande, Paris (I) 4/11 (2 P.J)	11 »	8 »
Stamps Centre Wanganui (II) 4/11 (2 P.J)		8 »
Raymond Peynet, Valence (I) 4/11	13 »	6 »
Saint Valentin (II) 4/11		6 »
Croix-Rouge, Paris (I) 9/11	9 »	4 »
Bande carnet, Paris (I) 9/11		20 »
3e Millenaire, Paris (I) 9/11	9 »	3 »
Timbre personnalisé, Paris (II) 9/11		6 »
Bonne Année - Meilleurs vœux, Paris (I) 11/11	9 »	4 50
La Métallurgie, Paris (I) 9/12	9 »	4 50
Le Creusot (II) 9/12		4 50

2001

	(Doc)	(1er j)
Championnat du Monde de Handball, Nantes (I) 20/1	7 »	3 »
Dunkerque, Montpellier, Besançon (II)		
3 envel. 20/1		15 »
Cœur 2001- Christian Lacroix, Paris (I) 27/1	7 »	3 »
Bloc Cœur 2001, Paris (I) 27/1		11 »
Pieter Bruegel l'ancien, Paris (I) 3/2	10 »	7 »
Fête du Timbre, Gaston Lagaffe, (TP feuille), Paris		
(II) 24/2	11 »	5 »
Paire carnet, Paris (II) 24/2		6 »
Bande carnet, Paris (II) 24/2		18 »
Bloc seul, Paris (II) 24/2		11 »
Le siècle au fil du Timbre, N° 3 Communication, Paris		
(I) 17/3 (5 P.J)	15 »	17 »
Bande entière, Paris (I) 17/3		13 »
Garçon - Fille - Oui - Merci, Nancy (I) 23/3 (3 P.J)		11 50
(les 2 doc.)	19 »	
L'écureuil, Paris (I) 21/4		3 50
Le Hérisson, Paris (I) 21/4		3 »
Le Chevreuil, Paris (I) 21/4		3 »
L' hermine, Paris (I) 21/4		3 50
Bloc Animaux des bois, Paris (I) 21/4	10 »	13 »
Hôtel des Chevaliers St Jean de Jerusalem, Toulouse		
(I) 21/4	9 »	5 »
Nogent le Retrou, le château, Nogent le Retrou (I) 28/4	9 »	4 »
Besançon, la citadelle, Besançon (I) 5/5	9 »	3 »
Europa 2001, l' eau, Strasbourg (I) 8/5	9 »	3 »
St Jean de Luz (II) 8/5	9 »	3 50
Jardins de Versailles, Versailles (I) 12/5	9 »	5 »
Chanteurs célèbres, Paris (I) (6PJ) 19/5	14 »	25 »
Bloc, Paris (II) 19/5		22 »
Vieux Lyon, Lyon (I) 19/5	10 »	3 20
74e Congrès F.F.A.P. Tours, Tours (I) 1/6	7 »	3 »
Jean Vilar, Sète (I) 7/6	8 »	3 »
Jean Vilar, Avignon (I) 7/6	6 »	3 »
Vacances (TP gommé), Paris (I) 10/6		3 30
Vacances (TP autocol.), Aix en Provence (I) 10/6		3 30
Calais, Calais (I) 16/6	9 »	3 »
Demain l'Euro, Paris (I) 23/6	9 »	4 »
Strasbourg (II) 23/6		3 50
Albert Caquot, Vouziers (I) 30/6	8 »	3 50
Liberté d'Association, Paris (I) 1/7	10 »	3 »
Les Légendes du Rail, Paris (I) 6/7 (5PJ)	15 »	20 »
Dijon, Mulhouse (II) 6/7 - Chalindrey (II) 7/7 sur 5 PJ	9 »	22 »
Bloc, Paris (II) 6/7		17 »
Château de Grignan, Grignan (I) 7/7	9 »	4 »
Convention Genève Réfugiés, Paris (I) 28/7	9 »	3 50
Marianne du 14 Juillet TVP "RF", Paris (I) 1/8	13 »	4 »
Pierre de Fermat, Beaumont de Lomagne (I) 19/8	10 »	3 50
H. de Toulouse Lautrec, Albi 8/9	12 »	5 »
Le Siècle au fil du Timbre N° 4 Sciences,		
Paris (I) 22/9 (5 PJ)	12 »	17 »
Bande entière, Paris (I) 22/9		13 »
Val de Reuil, Val de Reuil (I) 29/9	9 »	3 »
Halloween, Paris ou Boulogne s/mer (I) 22/10	12 »	3 »
Bloc, Paris ou Boulogne s/mer (II) 22/10		13 »
J. Barthold Jongkind, La Côte St André (I) 27/10	12 »	5 50
Honfleur (II), 27/10		5 50
Croix Rouge, Paris (I) 8/11	7 »	4 »
Jean Pierre-Bloch, Paris (I) 8/11	7 »	4 »
Meilleurs Voeux, Bonne Année, Paris (I) 9/11	8 »	4 »
Albert Decaris, Paris (I) 9/11	12 »	5 »
Sotteville les Rouen (I) 9/11		5 »
Jacques Chaban-Delmas, Paris (I) 10/11	6 »	3 50
Bordeaux (I) 10/11		3 50
Ascain (II) 10/11		3 50
Blocs de Marianne en Francs, Paris (I) 10/11 (2 PJ)	32 »	32 »
Conseil de l'Europe, Strasbourg (I) 1/12	9 »	4 50
UNESCO, Paris (I) 1/12	14 »	8 »
France/Maroc, les Fontaines, Paris (I) 14/12 (2 PJ)	15 »	8 »
Maroc (II) 14/12 (2 PJ)		8 »

2002

	(Doc)	(1er j)
Marianne du 14 Juillet - 15 valeurs		
en Euro, Paris 1/1 (4 PJ)	32 »	30 »
Coeur 2002 - Yann Arthus Bertrand, Paris (I) 18/1	5 »	4 »
Bloc, Paris (I) 18/1		14 »
Salt Lake City, Albertville (I) 26/1	9 »	3 50
Gustav Klimt, Paris (I) 8/2	10 »	6 »
Blocs de Marianne en Euros, Paris (I) 8/2	32 »	28 »
Alain Bosquet, Paris (I) 16/2	9 »	3 50
Garçon - Fille - Oui, Paris (I) 23/2 (2 PJ)	9 »	8 »
Europa 2002 - Le Cirque, Strasbourg (I) 2/3	12 »	4 »
Fête du Timbre - Boule et Bill, Paris (II) 16/3	13 »	5 »
Paire carnet, Paris (II) 16/3		6 »
Bande carnet, Paris (II) 16/3		17 »
Bloc seul, Paris (II) 16/3		10 »
Les Arènes de Nîmes, Nîmes (I) 22/3	12 »	4 »
Le Siècle au fil du Timbre N° 5 Transports,		
Paris (I) 23/3 (5 PJ)	39 »	18 »
Bande entière, Paris (I) 23/3		15 »
France/Australie, Paris et St Martin de Ré		
(I) 4/4 (2 PJ)	20 »	8 »
Australie (II) 4/4 (2 PJ)		8 »
La Charité-sur-Loire, La Charité-sur-Loire (I) 6/4	7 »	3 50
Anniversaire - Invitation, Sevrier (I) 6/4 (2 PJ)	7 »	7 »
100e Course Paris-Roubaix, Compiègne (I) 13/4	11 »	4 »
Roubaix (I) 13/4		4 »
Fernando Botero, Paris (I) 27/4	15 »	6 »
Champions du Monde de Football, Paris (I) 27/4	15 »	4 50
Les Animaux Marins, Boulogne s/mer (I) 4/5	15 »	
ou Paris (I) 5/5 (4 PJ)		15 »
Bloc, Boulogne s/mer (II) 4/5 ou Paris (II) 5/5		14 »
75e Congrès F.F.A.P. Marseille, Marseille (I) 17/5	13 »	3 50
La Légion d'Honneur, Paris (I) 18/5	15 »	3 50
Longué - Jumelles (II) 18/5		4 50
Champions du Monde de Football	10 »	
(TP du bloc), St Denis (I) 18/5		4 50
Rocamadour, Rocamadour (I) 25/5	9 »	3 50
Louis Delgrès, Basse Terre (Guadeloupe) (I) 25/5	9 »	3 50
St Pierre (Martinique) (I) 25/5		3 50
Vacances (TP gommé), Paris (I) 8/6	5 »	3 50
Vacances (TP autocol.), La Rochelle (II) 8/6		3 50
Athlétisme Handisport, Villeneuve d'Ascq (I) 15/6	9 »	3 50
Chapelle Saint Ser, Puyloubier (I) 22/6	9 »	3 50
Collioure (Tableau Derain), Collioure (I) 22/6	8 »	4 »
Cathédrale de Metz (Vitrail Chagall), Metz (I) 6/7	9 »	4 50
Etoile du Jazz, Paris ou Juan les Pins (I) 6 PJ 13/7	12 »	24 »
Bloc, Paris ou Juan les Pins (I) 13/7		20 »
Locronan, Locronan (I) 13/7	9 »	3 50
Notre-Dame de la Salette, La Salette Fallavaux		
(I) 15/8	9 »	3 50
L'Art Chorégraphique, Lyon (I) 13/9	9 »	3 50
L'Art Chorégraphique, Grenoble (II) 13/9	10 »	3 50
Cylindrées et Carénages, Paris (I) 5 PJ 14/9		18 »
Cylindrées et Carénages, Magny Cours (I) 5 PJ 14/9		20 »
Bloc, Paris ou Magny Cours (I) 14/9		14 »
Georges Perec, Paris (I) 21/9	8 »	4 »
Georges Perec, Villard de Lans (II) 21/9		3 50
Le Siècle au Fil du Timbre n° 6 : Vie Quotidienne,		
Paris (I) 5 PJ 28/9	10 »	18 »
Bande entière, Paris (I) 28/9		13 »
Emile Zola, Paris (I) 5/10	8 »	3 50
Médan (II) 5/10		3 50
Neufchâteau (Vosges), Neufchâteau (I) 12/10	9 »	3 50
E. Vigée Lebrun (Tableau), Paris (I) 12/10	9 »	5 »

Avion Airbus A 300, Toulouse (I) 26/10	15 »	15 »
Croix Rouge, Paris (I) 7/11	5 »	4 »
Capitales européennes : ROME (4 TP du BF),		
Paris (I) 7/11	13 »	15 »
Bloc entier, Paris (I) 7/11		13 »
Meilleurs Voeux, Paris (I) 8/11	5 »	3 50
Timbre Entreprise, Paris (I) 8/11	5 »	3 50
Marianne du 14 Juillet TVP VERT, Paris (I) 9/11	10 »	3 20
Jesus Rafael Soto (Tableau), Paris (I) 11/11	9 »	4 50
Alexandre Dumas, Paris (I) 30/11	9 »	3 80
Alexandre Dumas, Villers Cotterêts (I) 30/11		3 50
Léopold Sédar Senghor, Paris (I) 20/12	8 »	3 50
Léopold Sédar Senghor, Verson (I) 20/12		3 50

2003	(Doc)	(1er j)
Coeur 2003 Torrente, Paris (I) 11/1	10 »	7 »
Bloc, Paris (I) 11/1	9 »	12 »
Naissance, Paris 11/1	9 »	3 50
Merci, Paris (I)	9 »	3 50
40e ann. Traité Franco/Allemand, Paris 16/1	9 »	3 50
Timbre allemand, Berlin 16/1	9 »	5 »
40 ans d'aménagement du territoire, Paris (I) 8/2		3 50
Geneviève de Gaulle-Anthonioz, Paris (I) 11/2	9 »	3 80
Chambre de Commerce et d'Industrie de Paris,		
Paris (I) 22/2	8 »	3 50
Fête du Timbre - Lucky Luke, Paris (II) 15/3	11 »	5 »
Paire carnet, Paris (II) 15/3	10 »	6 »
Bande carnet, Paris (II) 15/3	10 »	18 »
Bloc seul, Paris (II) 15/3	10 »	11 »
Les oiseaux d'outre-mer, Fort de France (I)		
St Denis (I) -		
Matoury (I) - Pointe à Pitre (I) - 4 PJ 22/3	8 »	15 »
Bloc entier, Paris (I) 22/3		12 »
Nantes - Loire Atlantique, Nantes (I) 4/4	9 »	3 50
Pierre Bérégovoy, Nevers (I) 30/4	9 »	3 80
Pierre Bérégovoy, Déville les Rouen (I) 30/4		3 80
France - Slovaquie (M. R. Stéfanik), Paris (I) 3/5	7 »	3 50
Slovaquie, Modra (II) 3/5		4 50
Europa 2003 - Art de l'Affiche, Strasbourg (I) 8/5	9 »	3 50
Charte des Droits Fondamentaux de l'Union		
Européenne Strasbourg (I) 8/5	9 »	3 50
Porte-avions Charles de Gaulle, Toulon (I) 8/5	10 »	4 50
Michel-Ange (Tableau les esclaves), Paris (I) 24/5	10 »	6 50
Portraits de Régions : n° 1 La France à Vivre		
(10 PJ) 24/5	35 »	35 »
Bloc découpé en deux sur 2 PJ, Paris (I) 24/5		22 »
Anniversaire - Le Marsupilami, Paris (I) 31/5	9 »	5 »
Bloc anniversaire, Paris (I) 31/5		13 »
Marianne du 14 Juillet (6 val.), Paris (2 PJ) 1/6	21 »	20 »
76e Congrès F.F.A.P. Mulhouse, Mulhouse (I) 6/6	7 »	3 50
Vacances (TP gommé), Paris (I) 14/6	9 »	3 50
Vacances (TP autocol.), Antibes, ou Canet en R.		
ou St Jean de Luz (II) 14/6		3 50
Poste aérienne - Jacqueline Auriol,		
Challans (I) 21/6	10 »	16 »
Paris (II) 21/6	10 »	17 »
Basilique Notre-Dame de l'Epine, l'Epine (I) 21/6	9 »	3 50
Tulle en Corrèze, Tulle (I) 21/6	9 »	3 50
Franc Maçonnerie Française, Lyon (I) 28/6	10 »	4 50
St Denis (II) 28/6	10 »	4 50
Tour de France (2 PJ), Paris et Montgeron (I), 28/6	21 »	8 »
5 PJ, Bordeaux, Nantes, Lyon, Toulouse,		
Marseille (I), 28/6		30 »
Kandinsky - tableau, Paris (I) 5/7	15 »	6 »
Signac - tableau, St Tropez (I) 5/7	15 »	6 »
Eglise de St Père (Yonne), St Père (I) 12/7	8 »	3 50
Athlétisme 2003, Paris (I) 19/7	7 »	3 50
St Denis (I) 19/7	8 »	3 80
Destinées romanesques (6 PJ), Paris (I) 30/8	10 »	22 »
Bloc, Paris (I) 30/8		18 »
Ahmad Shah Massoud, Paris (I) 9/9	5 »	3 50
Portaits de Régions n° 2 - La France à voir 10 PJ (I) 20/9		35 »
Bloc découpé en 2 sur 2 PJ, Paris (I) 20/9		22 »
Arras (Pas de Calais), Arras (I) 20/9	5 »	3 50
Les Jardins de France I - 2 PJ, Paris (I) 27/9	13 »	13 »
Bloc, Paris (I) 27/9		16 »
Pontarlier (Doubs), Pontarlier (I) 11/10	5 »	3 50
Conseil de l'Europe 2003, Strasbourg (I) 18/10	5 »	4 50
Utilitaires et Grandes Echelles - 5 PJ, Paris (I) 24/10	9 »	18 »
5 PJ autres villes (I et II), 24/10		20 »
Croix Rouge 2004, Paris (I) 6/11	12 »	4 50
Semeuse de Roty, Paris (I) 6/11	12 »	6 50
Vœux oiseau, Paris (I) 6/11	10 »	4 50
Vœux entreprise, Paris (I) 6/11		3 50
Capitales européennes II - Luxembourg - 4 PJ,		
Paris (I) 7/11	12 »	15 »
Bloc, Paris (I) 7/11		12 »
Andy Warhol - tableau, Paris (I) 8/11	10 »	7 »
Emission France/Inde - 2 PJ Paris (I) 29/11	10 »	7 50
2 PJ Inde (II) 29/11		10 »
UNESCO - Laponie/St Petersbourg 2 PJ Paris (I) 6/12	10 »	7 50
Queen Mary 2, St Nazaire (I) 12/12		5 »

2004	(Doc)	(1er j)
Cœur Chanel, Paris (I) 9/1	11 »	5 »
Bloc, Paris (I) 9/1		12 »
Naissance (2 TP), Paris (I) 9/1	11 »	4 »
Ceci est une invitation, Paris (I) 9/1		3 50
Un grand merci, Paris (I) 9/1		3 50
Lille, capitale européenne de la culture, Lille (I) 10/1	10 »	3 50
Lille (TGV - II) 10/1		5 »
Auguste Bartholdi - tableau, Paris (I) 21/2	10 »	5 »
Colmar (I) 21/2		5 »
Bloc couleurs de marianne, Paris (I) 28/2	20 »	20 »
Aliénor d'Aquitaine, Fontevraud (I) 28/2	10 »	4 »
Paris (II), 28/2		4 »
Fête du Timbre 2004 - Mickey, Paris (II) 6/3	11 »	5 »
Donald et Minnie - 2 PJ, Chessy (II) 6/3		11 »
Bande carnet, Paris (II) 6/3		22 »
Code Civil, Paris (I) 12/3	10 »	4 »
George Sand, Paris (I) 20/3		4 »
Nohant Vic (I) 20/3		4 »
Clermont Ferrand (Puy de Dôme),		
Clermont Ferrand (I) 26/3	10 »	3 50
Portraits de Région n° 3 - La France à vivre		
10 PJ (I) 26-27/3	12 »	35 »
Bloc découpé en 2 sur 2 PJ - Paris (I) 26/3		22 »
Entente Cordiale - Emission France/Angleterre 2 PJ,		
Paris (I) 6/4	16 »	8 »
2 PJ London (II) 6/4		8 »
La sécurité routière, Paris (I) 7/4	10 »	3 50
Jean Léon Gérôme - tableau, Vesoul (I) 17/4	10 »	6 »
Les animaux de la Ferme - 4 PJ (I) 24/4		15 »
Bloc Paris (I) 24/4	15 »	12 »
Bordeaux (Gironde), Bordeaux (I) 24/4	5 »	4 »
Elargissement Union Européenne, Paris ou		
Strasbourg (I) 1/5	10 »	3 50
Diên Biên Phu, Paris ou Pau (I) 7/5	10 »	3 50
Vacances - tableau de Dufy - Strasbourg (I) 9/5	10 »	4 50
TP autocol de carnet, Paris (I) 4/6		4 50
Blake et Mortimer - Emission France/Belgique 2 PJ		
Paris (I) 15/5	13 »	12 »
2 PJ Liège (Léodiphilex) (II) 15/5		12 »
Centenaire de la F.I.F.A., Paris (I) 21/5	5 »	4 »
Les Jardins de France II (2 Pj), Paris (I) 4/6	13 »	13 »
Bloc Paris (I) 4/6		16 »
Débarquement et Libération, Paris, Caen ou		
d'autres villes (I) 5/6	10 »	4 »
Ste Mère Eglise ou d'autres villes (II), 5/6		4 »
Salvador Dali - tableau, Perpignan (I) 19/6	6 »	5 50
Don d'organes, Paris (I) 22/6		3 50
Pierre Dugua de Mons - Emission France/Canada		
PJ Paris (I) 26/6	4 »	4 20
PJ Bayside (II) 26/6		4 »
Napoléon et la Garde impériale (6 PJ) Paris (I) 26/6	22 »	22 »
Napoléon (TP seul), Ajaccio (I) 26/6	4 »	4 »
Bloc Paris (I) 26/6		20 »
77e Congrès FFAP, Paris (I) 27/6	4 »	3 80
J.O. Athènes 2004 (2 TP du bloc), Paris (I) 28/6	8 »	7 50
Bloc entier, Paris (I) 28/6		18 »
Poste Aérienne - Marie Marvingt, Paris (I) 29/6	15 »	18 »
Aurillac (I) 29/6	14 »	18 »
Anniversaire, Paris (I) 30/6	8 »	3 50
Bloc Paris (I) 30/6		12 »
Une Marianne pour une grande cause, Paris (I) 1/7	4 »	3 50
Vincent Van Gogh - Tableau, Paris (I) 2/7	5 »	5 »
Auvers s/Oise (II) 2/7	5 »	5 »
Sports de Glisse (5 PJ), Paris (I) 3/7	17 »	17 50
Bloc Paris (I) 3/7		12 »
Vaux sur mer (Charente maritime), Vaux (I) 17/7	4 »	3 50
Portraits de Régions n° 4 - La France à voir -		
10 PJ - (I) 18/9	35 »	35 »
Bloc découpé en deux sur 2 PJ, Paris (I) 18/9		24 »

Cathédrale de Luçon, Luçon (I) 2/10	7 »	3 50
Halloween, Paris ou Angers (I) 9/10	7 »	3 50
Félix Eboué, Paris (I) 16/10	7 »	3 80
Paris Salon du Livre (II) 16-17/10		4 »
Phare d'Ouistreham, Ouistreham (I) 30/10	4 »	4 20
Croix-Rouge 2004, Paris (I) 10/11	4 »	5 »
Marianne d'Alger, Paris (II) 10/11	5 »	5 »
Capitales européennes - Athènes - 4 PJ Paris (I) 11/11	16 »	15 »
Bloc, Paris (I) 11/11		12 »
Vœux (autocollant de carnet), Paris (II) 12/11	4 »	3 80
Vœux entreprise, Paris (I) 12/11	4 »	3 50
Henri Wallon, Paris (I) 13/11	4 »	3 50
Viaduc de Millau (Aveyron), Millau (I) 14/12	15 »	5 50

2005	(Doc)	(1er j)
Marianne de Lamouche (12 val) - 4 PJ, Paris (I) 8/1	34 »	35 »
Marianne Solidarité Asie, Paris (I) 13/1		5 »
Rachi, Paris ou Troyes (I) 16/1	4 »	3 80
Année du Coq - Nouvel an chinois, Paris (I) 29/1	5 »	3 80
Cœur Cacharel - 2 PJ, Paris 29/1	8 »	8 »
Bloc, Paris (I) 29/1		12 »
Rotary club, Paris (I) 19/2	5 »	4 »
Fête du Timbre 2005 - Titeuf - Paris (II) 26/2	5 »	4 50
Bande carnet, Paris (II) 26/2		22 »
Marianne de Lamouche (6 val) - 2 PJ Paris (I) 1/3	17 »	18 »
Merci - Invitation, Paris (I) 1/3	7 »	4 »
Nicolas de Staël - Tableau, Grenoble (I) 5/3	7 »	5 50
Les Orchidées - 4 PJ, Paris (I) 11/3	14 »	15 »
Bloc, Paris (I) 11/3	13 »	12 »
Portraits de Régions n° 5 - La France à vivre - 10 PJ (I) 19/3	34 »	35 »
Bloc découpé en deux sur 2 PJ, Paris (I) 19/3		24 »
Aix-en-Provence (Fontaine 4 dauphins), Aix (I) 1/4	6 »	3 50
Anniversaire "Bécassine", Paris ou Aix (I) 2/4	4 »	5 »
Bloc, Paris ou Aix (I) 2/4		13 50
Albert Einstein, Paris (I) 16/4	5 »	3 80
Alexis de Tocqueville, Paris (I) 23/4		4 20
60e ann. Libération des Camps, Paris (I) 24/4	5 »	3 80
Lyon (II) 24/4		4 »
Emission commune France / République Tchèque : Napoléon et la bataille d'Austerlitz, Paris (I) 4/5	10 »	4 50
PJ Slavkov (II) 4/5		6 »
78e Congrès FFAP Nancy, Nancy (I) 5/5	7 »	3 50
Expo. Nat, Nancy (II) 5/5		4 »
Golfe du Morbihan, Vannes (I) 5/5	7 »	4 20
Europa 2005, Gastronomie, Strasbourg (I) 8/5	7 »	3 80
Jardin de Nîmes - 2 PJ, Nîmes (I) 15/5	7 »	14 »
Bloc Nîmes (I) 15/5		15 »
Vacances 2005, Paris (II) 21/5	4 »	3 50
Jules Verne - 6 PJ - Nantes (I) 28/5	24 »	25 »
6 PJ - Amiens (I) 28/5		25 »
6 PJ - Paris (I) 28/5		25 »
Bloc, Nantes - Amiens ou Paris (I) 28/5		20 »
Coupe Gordon Bennett - 3 PJ - Clermont Ferrand (I) 2/6	15 »	15 »
3 PJ, Paris (I) 2/6		15 »
Villefranche s/Mer (Alpes maritimes), Villefranche (I) 4/6	3 »	3 50
Charte de l'environnement, Paris (I) 5/6	3 »	3 50
Naissance (Garçon/Fille), Paris (II) 18/6	3 »	4 20
Loi pour les personnes handicapées, Paris (I) 18/6	3 »	3 50
François POMPON - tableau - Saulieu (I) 2/7	10 »	5 »
Le Haras du Pin, Le Pin au Haras (I) 16/7	8 »	3 80
La Roque Gageac (Dordogne), La Roque Gageac (I) 23/7	7 »	3 50
Capitales européennes - Berlin - 4 PJ Paris (I) 27/8	30 »	15 »
Bloc Paris (I) 27/8		12 »
Victor Baltard - tableau - Nogent sur marne (I) 17/9	10 »	5 50
Portraits de Régions n° 6 - La France à Voir - 10 PJ (I) 17/9	34 »	35 »
Bloc découpé sur 2 PJ Paris (I) 17/9		24 »
Conseil de l'Europe, Paris (I) 18/9	10 »	5 50
J.B. Greuze - tableau - Tournus (I) 24/9	10 »	5 »
Carnet sourrires - le chat - 3 PJ Courbevoie (II) 1/10	21 »	22 »
Dépistage du cancer du sein, Paris (I) 1/10		3 50
Raymond Aron, Paris (I) 7/10	7 »	3 50
Poste Aérienne - Adrienne Bolland, St Denis de l'Hôtel (I) 22/10	15 »	8 »
Croix Rouge 2005, Paris (I) 10/11	10 »	4 50
Emission France/Vatican - tableaux de Raphaël - 2 PJ Paris (I) 10/11	10 »	8 »
2 PJ Vatican (II) 10/11		12 »
Bloc Paris (I) 10/11		8 »
Marianne de Dulac, Paris (II) 11/11	10 »	5 50
Jeux vidéo - 5 PJ Paris (I) 11/11	17 »	17 50
Bloc Paris (I) 11/11		12 »
Meilleurs voeux autocollant - 2 PJ Paris (II) 12/11	10 »	10 »
Avicene, Paris (I) 12/11	7 »	3 50
Jacob Kaplan, Paris (I) 14/11	7 »	3 50
UNESCO - 2 PJ Paris (I) 26/11	7 »	7 50
Loi sur la sépartion des églises et de l'état, Paris (I) 3/12	7 »	3 50

2006	(Doc)	(1er j)
Coeur Scherrer - 2 PJ Paris (I) 7/1	10 »	8 »
Bloc, Paris (I) 7/1		12 »
Année du Chien - nouvel an chinois - Paris (I) 21/1	10 »	3 80
Les Impressionnistes - 10 PJ Paris (II) 21/1	40 »	40 »
J.O. Turin 2006, Paris (I) 4/2	7 »	3 50
Albertville (I) 4/2	7 »	3 80
Fête du Timbre 2006 - SPIROU - Paris (II) 25/2		4 50
Bande carnet - Paris (II) 25/2		22 »
Hommage aux mineurs, Courrières (I) 25/2	7 »	3 80
Ossuaire de Douaumont, Douaumont (I) 4/3	7 »	3 80
Portrais de Régions n° 7- La France à Vivre 10PJ (I) 25/3	35 »	35 »
Bloc découpé sur 2 PJ Paris (I) 25/3		24 »
Dijon (Côte d'or), Dijon (I) 7/4	7 »	3 50
Paul Cézanne - tableau, Aix en Provence (I) 8/4	10 »	6 »
Jeunes animaux domestiques - 4 PJ Paris (I) 22/4	10 »	15 »
Bloc, Paris (I) 22/4		12 »
Jardins des Hauts-de-Seine - 2 PJ Boulogne Billancourt et Chatenay Malabry (I) 22/4	10 »	14 »
Bloc Paris (I) 22/4		15 »
Pierre Bayle, Carla Bayle (I) 29/4	7 »	3 50
EUROPA 2006, l'intégration, Strasbourg (I) 30/4	7 »	3 50
Mémoires de l'esclavage et de son abolition, Paris 10/5	10 »	3 50
Coupe du Monde de Football, 3 PJ TP découpés Paris (I) 27/5	19 »	25 »
Bloc découpé en deux sur 2 PJ, Paris (I) 27/5		25 »
Vacances, Paris (II) 27/5	10 »	3 50
Grotte de Rouffignac - tableau - Rouffignac St Cernin de Reilhac (I) 27/5	10 »	5 »
Claude Viallat - tableau - Nîmes (I) 3/6	7 »	6 »
Marianne des Français en Argent, Paris (II) 17/6		15 »
Opéras de Mozart - 6 PJ Paris (I) 17/6		24 »
Bloc Paris(I) 17/6		20 »
Emission France / ONU - 2 PJ Mont Saint Michel (I) et Provins (I) 17/6	7 »	8 »
2 PJ ONU - Genève (II) 17/6	7 »	9 »
79° Congrès FFAP - Opéra Garnier Paris (I) 18/6		3 50
Congrès Paris (II) 18/6	7 »	4 »
Anniversaire "BABAR", Paris (I) 19/6	7 »	4 50
Bloc Paris (I) 19/6		13 »
Capitales européennes - Nicosie - 4 PJ Paris 20/6	12 »	15 »
Bloc Paris (I) 20/6		12 »
Emission France / Argentine Le Tango - Paris (I) 21/6	10 »	5 50
Agentine - Buenos Aires (II) 24/6		8 »
Fondation d'entreprise La Poste, Paris (I) 22/6	10 »	3 50
Poste Aérienne - Airbus A 380, Paris (I) 23/6	20 »	15 »
Toulouse ou St Nazaire (I) 23/6		15 »
Open de France de Golf - Paris (I)	10 »	3 80
Merci les Bleus - Paris (I) 5/7	9 »	4 »
Musée du Quai Branly Paris (I) 8/7	10 »	4 »
Réhabilitation du Capitaine Dreyfus Mulhouse ou autre ville (I) 12/7	8 »	3 80

Rouget de Lisle - Paris ou autre ville (I) 13/7	8 »	3 80
Lons le Saunier (II) 14/7	8 »	4 »
Antibes Juan-les-Pins (I)		
Antibes Juan-les-Pins 15/7	8 »	3 80
Pablo Casals - Prades (I) 29/7	8 »	4 »
Portraits de Régions n° 8 - La France à Voir		
10 PJ (I) 2/9	35 »	35 »
Bloc découpé sur 2 PJ Paris (I) 2/9	24 »	24 »
Pont Ecluse Thionville - Thionville (I) 16/9	8 »	3 80
Carnet sourires - Cubitus - 3 PJ Paris (II) 20/9	20 »	25 »
Emission France/Roumanie - Brancusi -		
2 PJ Paris (I) 25/9	11 »	10 »
Roumanie - 2 PJ Bucarest (II) 25/9	10 »	10 »
Marianne des Français - nouveaux tarifs -		
2 PJ Paris 1/10	25 »	25 »
Aviation sans Frontières - Paris (I) 7/10	8 »	3 80
Henri Moissan - Paris ou Melun (I) 14/10	8 »	3 80
Mémoire partagée - Paris (I) 26/10	8 »	3 80
Marianne de Gandon - Paris (II) 8/11	12 »	6 »
Machines volantes - 6 PJ Paris 9/11	15 »	25 »
Bloc Paris 9/11		15 »
Rembrandt - tableau 10/11	8 »	7 »
Tram Train - Les Pavillons sous Bois (I) 18/11	7 »	4 »
Croix Rouge 2006 - Paris (I) 25/11	7 »	5 50
Meilleurs voeux autocollant - 2 PJ Paris (II) 25/11	7 »	10 »
Grande Loge Nationale Française - Paris (I) 1/12	7 »	4 »
Alain Poher - Paris (I) 2/12	7 »	3 80
UNESCO - 2 PJ Paris (I) 7/12		8 »
Le Tramway à Paris - Paris (I) 16/12	7 »	4 »

2007	(Doc)	(1er j)
Coeur GIVENCHY - Paris (I) 6/1	8 »	5 50
Les Justes de France - Paris (I) 18/1	9 »	4 »
Année du Cochon - nouvel an Chinois -		
Paris (I) 27/1	9 »	3 80
Les antiquités - 10 PJ Paris (II) 27/1	30 »	40 »
Valenciennes - Valenciennes (I) 3/2	7 »	3 80
Bibliothèque Humaniste de Sélestat -		
Sélestat (I) 10/2	7 »	5 »
Poste aérienne - Hélicoptère EC 130 - Paris (I) 17/2	20 »	13 50
Marignane ou Châlons en Champagne (I) 17/2	8 »	13 50
Portraits de Régions n° 9 - La France à Voir		
10 PJ (I) 24/2	15 »	35 »
Fête du Timbre 2007 - Harry Potter - Paris (II) 10/3	15 »	4 50
Albert Londres - Périgueux (I) 16/3	7 »	3 80
Cour des Comptes - Paris 17/3	7 »	3 80
Traité de Rome - Paris 23/3	7 »	3 80
Limoges - Limoges (I) 23/3	7 »	3 80
Vauban - St Léger Vauban ou autre ville (I) 30/3	7 »	3 80
Allez les Petits - Rugby - Paris ou Souillac (I) 14/4	7 »	3 80
Parc de la Tête d'Or - 2 PJ Lyon (I) 28/4	7 »	14 »
Bloc - Lyon 28/4		14 »
Vacances (10 TP autocollants sur grande env.)		
Paris (II) 28/4	10 »	20 »
Espèces protégées d'outremer - 4 PJ paris ou		
villes des DOM 28/4	10 »	15 »
Bloc - Paris (I) 28/4		12 »
Europa 2007 - le scoutisme - Strasbourg (1) 1/5	7 »	4 »
Fédération internationale de voile - Paris (I) 4/5	7 »	4 20
Personnages de TINTIN - 3 PJ Paris (I) 12/5	16 »	16 »
Bloc Personnages de TINTIN - Paris (I) 12/5		22 »
Arcachon - Arcachon (I) 19/5	7 »	3 80
Emission France/Arménie - 2 PJ Paris 22/5	7 »	8 50
Arménie - 2 PJ 22/5		11 »
Sanglier-Enseigne Gaulois - tableau - Soulac		
s/mer 2/6	7 »	7 »
TGV EST Européen - Paris (I) 9/6	10 »	4 »
TGV EST Européen - Strasbourg (I) 9/6		4 »
TGV EST Européen - Reims, Metz ou Nancy (I) 9/6		4 50
80e Congrés FFAP - Poitiers (I) 15/6	6 »	3 80
Congrès de Poitiers (II) 16/6	4 »	4 »
Coupe du Monde de Rugby - 4 PJ Paris (I) 23/6	30 »	22 »
sur 10 PJ avec 10 oblit. différentes (I) 23/6		40 »
Conseil de l'Europe - Strasbourg (I) 23/6		6 »
Capitales européennes - Bruxelles -		
4 PJ Paris (I) 30/6	16 »	16 »
Bloc - Paris (I) 30/6		12 »
Associations maires de France - Paris (I) 5/7	7 »	3 80
Pierre Pflimlin - Strasbourg (I) 7/7	7 »	4 20
Castres - Castres (I) 19/7	7 »	3 80
Rugby (timbre lenticulaire) - St Denis ou autre ville (I) 5/9	20 »	12 »
Merci/Invitation - 2 PJ Paris (II) 8/9	7 »	9 »
Anniversaire Sylvain et Sylvette - Paris (I) 8/9	7 »	4 20
Bloc - Paris (I) 8/9		12 »
Sully Prudhomme - Paris (I) 15/9	7 »	6 »
Firminy Eglise St Pierre - Firminy (I) 15/9	7 »	4 »
Sourires 2007 - 2 PJ Paris (II) 20/9	8 »	10 »
Portraits de régionsn° 10 - la France à Vivre 10 PJ (I) 29/9	10 »	38 »
Conquète de l'espace - Paris ou autre ville (I) 4/10	7 »	4 50
Paul Sérusier - tableau - Paris (I) 14/10	7 »	5 50
Fondation recherche médicale - Paris ou autre ville (I) 20/10	7 »	3 80
Guy Môquet - Paris ou Châteaubriand (I) 22/10	7 »	4 »
Dole (Jura) - Dole (I) 2/11	7 »	3 80
Marianne de Cheffer - Paris (II) 8/11	9 »	6 »
Emission France/Groenland - Paris ou autres villes (I) 8/11	9 »	6 »
Groenland - (II) 8/11		6 »
Les phares - 6 PJ Paris ou autres villes (I) 9/11	25 »	25 »
Bloc - Paris (I) 9/11		15 »
Handball féminin - Paris (I) 10/11	10 »	3 80
Galerie des glaces - tableau - Paris ou Versailles (I) 10/11	10 »	5 50
Croix Rouge - Paris ou autres villes 24/11	7 »	5 50
Meilleurs vœux 2007 - 2 PJ Paris (II) 24/11	7 »	10 »
UNESCO - 2 PJ Paris (I) 13/12		8 50

2008	(Doc)	(1er j)
Cœur SORBIER - Paris (I) 5/1	8 »	6 »
Année du rat - nouvel an chinois - Paris (I) 26/1	8 »	4 »
Chefs-d'œuvre de la peinture - 10 PJ Paris (II) 26/1	10 »	42 50
Stade de France - St Denis (I) 28/1	9 »	4 »
Vendôme - Vendôme (I) 2/2	7 »	3 80
Les globes de Coronelli - tableau - Paris (I) 8/2	7 »	5 50
Abd el Kader - Paris (I) 20/2	7 »	3 80
Fête du Timbre 2008 - Droopy 3 PJ (II) 1/3	8 »	17 »
Bloc Droopy - (II) 1/3		12 50
Marianne des Français (6 valeurs) - Paris (I) 1/3	25 »	22 50
Bibliothèques sonores - Paris (I) 15/3	8 »	3 80
Portraits de régions n° 11 - la France à Voir -		
10 PJ (I) 29/3	10 »	38 »
Lyon Passerelle St Georges - Lyon (I) 4/4	8 »	4 »
La Rochelle, le vieux port - La Rochelle (I) 5/4	8 »	4 »
Jardins de Marseille - 2 PJ Marseille (I) 12/4	8 »	15 »
Bloc - Marseille (I) 12/4		15 »
Animaux de la Préhistoire - 4 PJ Paris (I) 19/4	8 »	16 »
Bloc - Montbéliard (II) 19/4		12 »
1° Greffe du cœur en Europe - Paris (I) 24/4	8 »	3 80
Cahors Pont Valentré - Cahors (I) 26/4	8 »	4 »
EUROPA 2008 - Strasbourg (I) 4/5	8 »	3 80
Emission France/Canada Fondation de		
Québec- Paris (I) 16/5	10 »	4 50
Canada - Québec (II) 16/5	»	4 »
Anniversaire OUI-OUI - Paris (I) 28/5	7 »	4 20
Bloc - Paris (I) 28/5		12 »
C'est un garçon/C'est une fille - Paris (II) 28/5	7 »	4 50
Vacances (10 TP autocol sur grande env) -		
Paris (II) 28/5		20 »
Evreux, le beffroi - Evreux (I) 31/5	7 »	3 80
Marianne et l'Europe 5€ argent - Paris Salon		
TP (II) 13/6	15 »	15 »
Carnet P.N.U.E. (10 TP autocol sur grande env.		
Paris (II) 14/6		20 »
81° Congrès FFAP Paris - Grand Palais - Paris (I) 14/6	7 »	4 »
Paix/Démocratie/Environnement en Europe +		
Marianne- 2 PJ		
(TP autocollants rouge et bleu de carnets) -		
Paris (II) 14/6		20 »
Personnages du cirque 3 PJ - Paris (I) 15/6	12 »	15 »
Bloc Paris (I) 15/6		20 »
J.O. été Beijing 2008 (4 TP du bloc) 2 PJ -		
Paris (I) 16/6	7 »	10 »
Marianne et l'Europe (13 valeurs) 4 PJ - Paris (I) 17/6	10 »	40 »
Mémorial de Gaulle - Paris (I) 18/6	7 »	4 20
Gérard Garouste - Tableau - Paris (I) 19/6	8 »	6 »
Grands Projets européens (4 TP du bloc)		
2 PJ Paris (I) 19/6	8 »	9 »
Bloc Paris (I) 19/6		10 »
Bateaux célèbres - 6 PJ Paris ou autres villes (I) 20/6	10 »	24 »
Bloc bateaux célèbres - Paris (I) 20/6		15 »
Emission France / Brésil - 2 PJ Paris (I) 21/6	10 »	8 »
Brésil (2 PJ) Rio de Janeiro (II) 21/6		9 »
Richelieu - Richelieu (I) 5/7	7 »	3 80
Toulon - Toulon (I) 5/7	7 »	3,80
Sommet de Paris pour le Méditerranée - Paris (I) 13/7	7 »	3 80

Portraits de régions n° 12 - la France à		
Vivre - 10 PJ (I) 6/9	12 »	38 »
Patrouille de France - Salon de Provence (I) 13/9	7 »	12 »
Sourires 2008 - TP autocol - 3 PJ Paris (II) 18/9		25 »
Josselin - Josselin (I) 20/9	7 »	3 80
Constitution de la V° République - Paris (I) 4/10	7 »	3 80
Je suis sport - La Courneuve ou autre ville (I) 4/10	7 »	3 80
Emission France / Vietnam - 2 PJ Paris et		
Bonifacio (I) 15/10	7 »	8 50
Vietnam (2 PJ) Ha Noi (II)15/10		8 50
Jean-Jacques Henner - tableau - Altkirch (I) 18/10	7 »	5 »
Les visages de la V° République - 3 PJ Paris (II) 6/11		25 »
Emission France / Israël - 2 PJ Paris (I) 6/11	10 »	8 50
Israël (2 PJ) Haïfa (II) 6/11		8 50
Capitales européennes - Prague - 4 PJ Paris (I) 7/11		16 »
Bloc, Paris (I) 7/11	10 »	12 »
Honoré Daumier - tableau - Paris (I) 7/11	7 »	6 50
Croix Rouge - Paris ou autre ville (I) 8/11		6 »
Bonnes fêtes - TP autocol - 4 PJ Paris (II) 8/11		32 »
90° ann. Armistice - PJ Paris (I) 11/11	7 »	4 »
PJ Verdun ou Compiègne (I) 11/11		4 »
Emission France / Liban - Paris (I) 20/11	7 »	4 50
Liban, Beyrouth (II) 25/11		5 50
UNESCO (2PJ) - Paris (II) 3/12	7 »	8 50

2009	(Doc)	(1er j)
Louis Braille - Coupvray (I) 4/1	7 »	3 80
Année du buffle - nouvel an chinois - Paris (I) 10/1	7 »	4 »
Métiers d'art - 12 TP Autocol - 6 PJ Paris (II) 10/1		35 »
René 1er d'Anjou - PJ Angers ou		
Aix en Provence (I) 16/1	7 »	3 80
Cœur UNGARO - PJ Paris (I) 17/1	7 »	6 50
bloc, Paris (I) 17/1		14 »
Championnats du Monde de ski alpin - 3 PJ Val d'Isère (I) 31/1		15 »
Bloc, Albertville (I) 31/1	10 »	15 »
Les Sables d'Olonne - Les Sables d'Olonnes (I) 31/1	7 »	3 80
Fondation de France - Paris ou autre ville (I) 5/2	7 »	3 80
Cathédrale Ste Cécile - tableau - Albi (I) 7/2	7 »	5 »
Menton - Menton 21/2	7 »	3 80
Fete du Timbre 2009 - Looney Tunes 3 PJ (II) 28/2	10 »	18 »
Bloc Looney Tunes (II) 28/2		11 50
Marianne et l'Europe (5 valeurs) 2 PJ - Paris (I) 28/2	15 »	22 50
Conseil Constitutionnel - Paris (I) 5/3	7 »	3 80
Avignon, le Palais des Papes - Avignon (I) 7/3	7 »	4 20
Journée de la Femme- 12 TP autocol - 3 PJ Paris (II) 9/3		30 »
Macon - Macon (I) 27/3	7 »	3 80
Protection des Poles - Paris ou Macon (I) 28/3		6 »
Bloc, Paris ou Macon (I) 28/3	10 »	12 »
Aimé Césaire - Paris ou Fort de France (I) 17/4	7 »	4 20
Flore des Régions - 24 TP autocol - 6 PJ (II) 25/4		50 »
Europa , l'Astronomie - Strasbourg (I) 3/5		6 »
bloc, PJ Strasbourg (I) 3/5	10 »	12 »
Vacances- 14 TP autocol - Paris (II) 13/5		30 »
La France en timbres - 8 TP autocol - Paris (II) 13/5		32 »
Chaumont - Chaumont (I) 16/5	7 »	3 80
Conseil de l'Europe - Strasbourg (I) 16/5	7 »	5 50
Jean Calvin - Noyon (I) 22/5	7 »	3 80
Le chocolat - 4 PJ Paris ou Bayonne (I) 23/5		22 50
bloc - Paris ou Bayonne (I) 23/5	12 »	20 »
Château de la Batie d'Urfé - St Etienne le Molard 6/6	7 »	3 80
82° congrès de la FFAP - Tarbes (I) 12/6	7 »	3 80
Christo et Jeanne-Claude - tableau - Paris (I) 13/6	7 »	6 50
Mémorial Jean Moulin - Caluire et Cuire (I) 20/6	7 »	4 00
Animaux disparus - 4 PJ Paris (I) 20/6		16 50
bloc, Paris (I) 20/6	10 »	14 »
Bordeaux - place de la Bourse - Bordeaux (I) 20/6	7 »	3 80
Coupe Gordon Bennett d'aviation - Bétheny (I) 27/6	7 »	3 80
Etienne Dolet - Orléans ou Lyon (I) 4/7	7 »	3 80

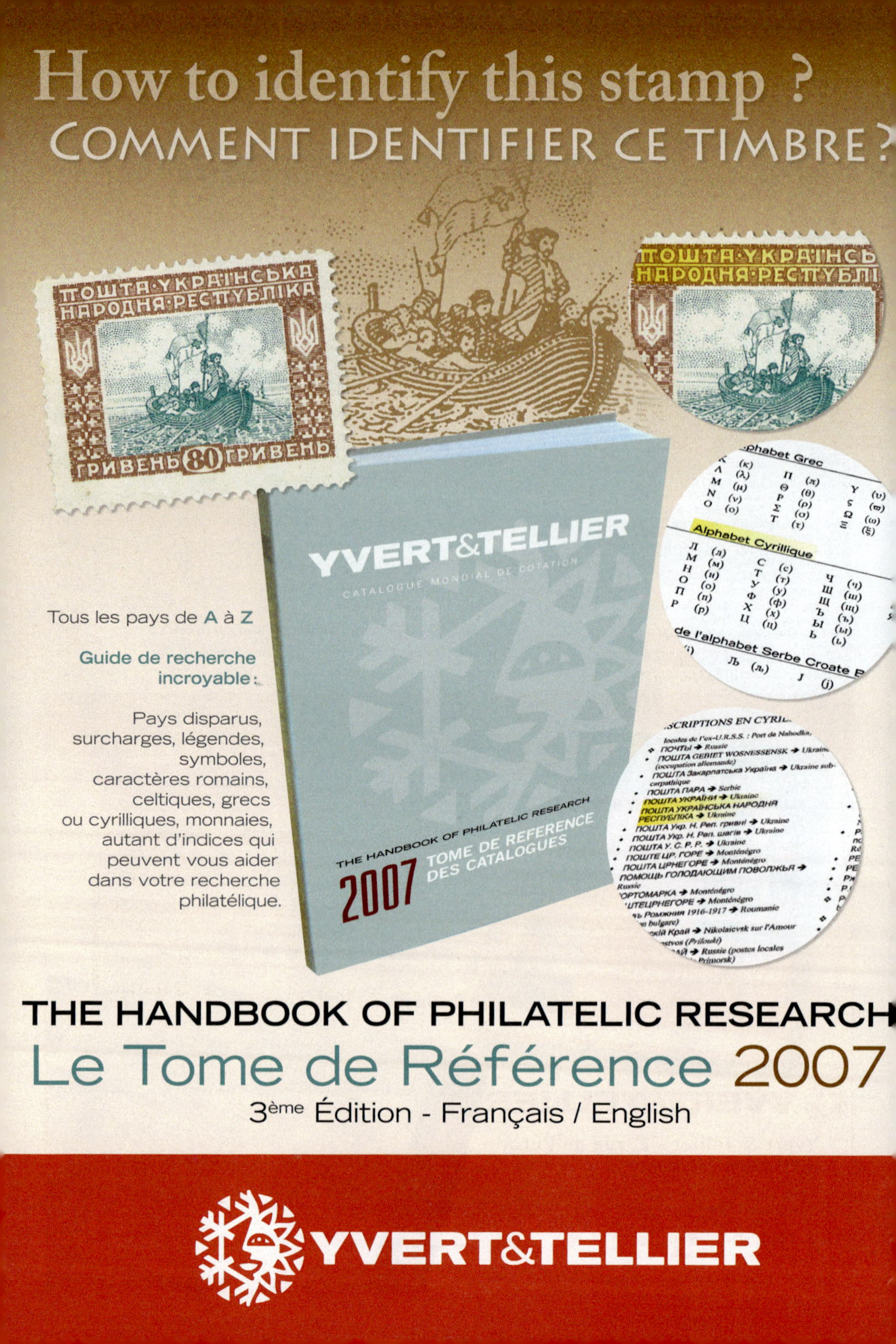
How to identify this stamp ?
COMMENT IDENTIFIER CE TIMBRE?
Tous les pays de A à Z
Guide de recherche incroyable :
Pays disparus, surcharges, légendes, symboles, caractères romains, celtiques, grecs ou cyrilliques, monnaies, autant d'indices qui peuvent vous aider dans votre recherche philatélique.
YVERT&TELLIER
CATALOGUE MONDIAL DE COTATION
THE HANDBOOK OF PHILATELIC RESEARCH
2007 TOME DE REFERENCE DES CATALOGUES
THE HANDBOOK OF PHILATELIC RESEARCH
Le Tome de Référence 2007
3ème Édition - Français / English
YVERT&TELLIER

TIMBRES POUR IMPRIMES DITS "PREOBLITERES"

Les numéros entre parenthèses renvoient aux numéros des timbres-poste.

1893. – *Timbres-poste au type Sage surchargés. Dentelés.*

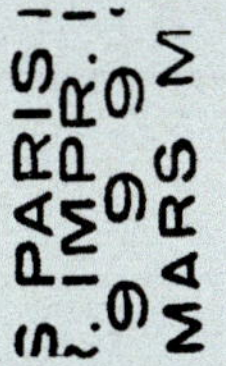

1re période.

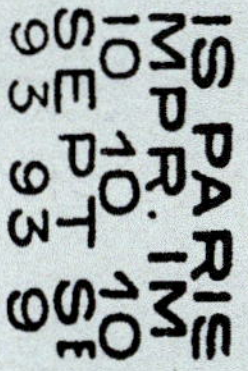

2e période.

Les Préoblitérés de 1893 sont rarement en bel état. Les prix donnés s'appliquent aux exemplaires sans gomme de qualité courante, c'est-à-dire présentant même de légers défauts.

I. - Première période (Janvier à Mars) Surcharge sur 4 lignes.

1	**2 c. brun-rouge (85)**	4 000 »
2	**4 c. lilas-brun (88)**	1 800 »
3	**5 c. vert (75)**	1 800 »
4	**10 c. noir sur lilas (89)**	2 500 »

5	**15 c. bleu (101)**	2 650 »
6	**20 c. brique sur vert (96)**	1 600 »
7	**25 c. noir sur rose (97)**	3 200 »
8	**30 c. brun (80)**	2 200 »

9	**40 c. rouge-orange sur paille (94)**	7 000 »
10	**50 c. rose (98)**	13 500 »
10A	**75 c. violet sur orange (99)**	27 500 »

II. - Seconde période (Septembre à Décembre) Surcharge sur 5 lignes.

2e période.

Dans cette période il existe des surcharges sur 4 lignes, sans le quantième, ligne de surcharge du milieu.

11	**1 c. noir sur azuré (83)**	2 500 »
12	**2 c. brun-rouge (85)**	2 750 »
13	**3 c. gris (87)**	750 »
14	**4 c. lilas-brun (88)**	800 »

15	**5 c. vert (75)**	650 »
16	**10 c. noir sur lilas (89)**	1 250 »
17	**15 c. bleu (101)**	1 850 »
18	**20 c. brique sur vert (96)**	1 500 »

19	**25 c. noir sur rose (97)**	2 850 »
20	**30 c. brun (80)**	2 000 »
21	**40 c. rouge-orange sur paille (94)**	5 750 »

22	**50 c. rose (98)**	8 500 »
23	**75 c. violet sur orange (99)**	18 500 »
23A	**1 f. olive (82)**	» »

On ne connait qu'un exemplaire, défectueux, de ce timbre.

Jusqu'en 1959 les cotes de la colonne de gauche concernent les timbres avec gomme d'origine intacte et sans charnière, celles de la colonne centrale les timbres avec gomme et charnière légère, celles de la colonne de droite les timbres sans gomme ou avec gomme altérée.

1920-22. – *Timbres-poste au type Semeuse, surchargés. Dentelés.*

POSTES PARIS 1920

24	**5 c. vert (137)**	750 »	400 »	170 »
25	**15 c. vert-olive (130)**	575 »	320 »	125 »

POSTES PARIS 1921

26	**5 c. vert (137)**	575 »	350 »	80 »
27	**5 c. orange (158)**	1 400 »	800 »	280 »
28	**15 c. vert-olive (130)**	1 200 »	750 »	180 »
29	**30 c. orange (141)**	950 »	525 »	80 »

POSTES PARIS 1922

30	**5 c. orange (158)**	350 »	185 »	20 »
31	**15 c. vert-olive (130)**	1 550 »	900 »	400 »
32	**30 c. rouge (160)**	1 300 »	750 »	200 »

POSTES FRANCE 1921

33	**5 c. orange (158)**	425 »	250 »	80 »
34	**15 c. vert-olive (130)**	3 500 »	2 250 »	950 »
35	**30 c. orange (141)**			6 500 »

POSTES FRANCE 1922

36	**5 c. orange (158)**	300 »	180 »	60 »
37	**15 c. olive (130)**	1 450 »	800 »	500 »
38	**30 c. rouge (160)**	2 100 »	1 100 »	750 »

Nos 24 à 38, très bon centrage (+30 %).

1922-47. – *Timbres-poste de 1900-46, surchargés. Dentelés.*

(p.) Surcharge à plat, fine, encre brillante.

(r.) Surcharge rotative lourde encre terne.

Reproduction agrandie du no 56 pour illustrer les deux types de surcharges.

Type Blanc.

39	**3 c. orange (p) (109)**	25 »	12 »	3 50
40	**4 c. brun (p) (110)**	4 50	2 »	1 »
	a. (r)	500 »	350 »	20 »
41	**5 c. vert (r) (111)**	12 »	5 »	0 50
	a. (p)	125 »	80 »	4 »
	b. (r)	125 »	80 »	15 »
	c. (Surcharge verte)		2 800 »	1 800 »
42	**7½ c. [lilas] (r)**	1 40	0 50	0 80
43	**10 c. violet (r) (233)**	2 60	1 55	0 30

Type Merson.

44	**45 c. vert et bleu (p) (143)**	100 »	50 »	45 »

Type Semeuse lignée.

45	**15 c. olive (p) (130c)**	4 »	2 30	2 30
46	**45 c. violet (r) (197)**	13 50	6 »	1 25
47	**55 c. sur 60 c. [violet] (p)**	350 »	175 »	70 »
48	**65 c. rose (p) (201)**	15 »	7 »	5 »
49	**65 c. olive (r) (234)**	35 »	15 »	5 »

Type Semeuse fond plein.

50	**5 c. orange (p) (158)**	120 »	45 »	1 25
51	**10 c. vert (r) (159)**	1 »	0 50	0 30
	a. (p)	75 »	50 »	3 50
	b. (r)	60 »	40 »	25 »
	c. (Premier s de Postes retouché)	320 »	250 »	215 »
52	**10 c. outremer (r) (279)**	1 25	0 80	0 30
	a. (IV) (r)	88 »	66 »	30 »
53	**15 c. brun-lilas (r) (189)**	1 »	0 50	0 50
	a. (p)	100 »	50 »	4 »
	b. (II) (r)	1 »	0 65	0 50
54	**20 c. lilas-brun (p) (139)**	160 »	85 »	15 »
	a. (p)	160 »	90 »	24 »
55	**20 c. lilas-rose (r) (190)**	18 »	7 »	0 50
	a. (V) (r)	10 »	5 »	0 50
56	**25 c. bleu (r) (140j)**	30 »	10 »	2 »
	a. (p)	70 »	40 »	4 »
57	**25 c. jaune-brun (r) (235)**	4 »	2 50	0 30
	a. (IIIB) (r)	100 »	65 »	3 50
58	**30 c. rouge (p) (160)**	320 »	160 »	8 »
59	**30 c. rose (p) (191)**	80 »	40 »	4 15
60	**30 c. bleu (r) (192)**	420 »	250 »	70 »
61	**30 c. rouge sombre (r) (360)**	2 30	1 70	1 70
62	**35 c. violet (p) (142)**	235 »	110 »	15 »
63	**35 c. vert (r) (361)**	15 »	8 »	3 »
64	**40 c. vermillon (r) (194)**	45 »	22 »	12 50

Type Pasteur.

65	**15 c. vert (p) (171)**	65 »	35 »	8 »
66	**30 c. vert (r) (174)**	60 »	32 »	7 »
67	**45 c. rouge (p) (175)**	45 »	22 »	3 50
68	**50 c. bleu (r) (176)**	285 »	150 »	30 »

Type Paix.

69	**30 c. vert (r) (280)**	8 500 »	5 750 »	
70	**40 c. lilas (p) (281)**	13 »	7 35	2 »
71	**45 c. bistre (r) (282)**	40 »	20 »	2 50
72	**60 c. bistre (r) (364)**	13 »	8 25	1 70
73	**65 c. violet-brun (r) (284)**	115 »	55 »	5 »
74	**80 c. sur 1 f. orange (r) (359)**	2 »	1 40	1 40
	a. (Surch. 80 c. renv)	600 »	450 »	
	b. (double surcharge)		1 400 »	900 »
75	**80 c. orange (r) (366)**	150 »	80 »	50 »
76	**1 f. rose (r) (369)**	20 »	10 »	3 »
77	**1 f. 40 lilas (r) (371)**	22 »	10 »	7 »

N°s 39 à 77, très bon centrage (+30 %).

Les surcharges des N°s 71 et 73 sont imprimées soit en haut, soit en bas des timbres (mêmes cotes).

Type Mercure.

78	**20 c. lilas (r) (410)**	1 »	0 50	0 50
79	**30 c. rouge (r) (412)**	5 »	2 30	2 30
80	**40 c. violet (r) (413)**	2 »	1 »	0 65
81	**40 c. violet (r) (548)**	1 »	0 50	0 50
82	**50 c. turquoise (r) (538)**	1 »	0 50	0 50
83	**60 c. rouge-orange (r) (415)**	48 »	27 »	26 »

Type Pétain.

84	**70 c. rouge-orange (r) (511)**	2 »	1 50	1 50
85	**1 f. 20 brun-rouge (r) (515)**	3 »	1 50	1 50
86	**2 f. vert (r) (518)**	6 »	3 »	3 »

Type Cérès de Mazelin.

87	**60 c. outremer (r) (674)**	0 50	0 50	0 50
88	**80 c. vert-jaune (r) (675)**	0 50	0 50	0 50
89	**90 c. [vert] (r)**	0 80	0 65	0 65
	a. (Non dentelé)		9 15	
90	**1 f. rose-rouge (r) (676)**	0 50	0 50	0 50
91	**1 f. 20 brun-noir (r) (677)**	0 80	0 80	0 80
91A	**1 f. 50 lilas (r) (679)**	0 65	0 30	0 30
92	**2 f. vert-jaune (r) (680)**	1 »	0 80	0 80
93	**2 f. 50 brun (r) (681)**	1 25	1 »	1 »

Type Marianne de Gandon.

94	**2 f. vert (r) (713)**	0 50	0 50	0 50
95	**2 f. 50 [brun] (r)**	2 60	1 50	1 35
96	**3 f. rose (r) (716)**	0 50	0 50	0 50
97	**4 f. violet (r) (718)**	0 50	0 50	0 50
98	**4 f. émeraude (r) (807)**	0 50	0 50	0 50
99	**4 f. orange (r) (808)**	1 40	0 80	0 80
100	**6 f. rose carminé (r) (721A)**	1 50	1 »	1 »
	a. (Mèches reliées)	80 »	40 »	40 »
	b. (Mèche croisée)	80 »	40 »	40 »
101	**8 f. bleu clair (r) (810)**	1 »	0 50	0 50
102	**10 f. lilas (r) (811)**	1 »	0 50	0 50
103	**12 f. outremer (r) (812)**	1 50	1 »	0 65
103A	**12 f. rouge-orange (r) (885)**	8 »	4 »	2 15
104	**15 f. rouge (r) (813)**	1 »	0 70	0 70

Armoiries.

105	**4 f. outremer, rouge et jaune (r) (838)**	0 30	0 30	0 30
	a. (p)	55 »	30 »	17 »
	N°s 39 à 105 (69 val.)	**11 440 85**	**7 255 50**	**441 70**

1953-59. – *Typographie. Dentelés 14 x 13½.*

Moissonneuse.

Coq Gaulois.

Le type "Coq Gaulois" n'existe qu'avec préoblitération.

(1) timbres émis en 1953

(2) timbres émis en 1957

(3) timbres émis en 1959

	Type Moissonneuse.			
106	**4 f. bleu-vert (1)**	0 30	0 20	0 20
	Type Coq Gaulois.			
107	**5 f. brun-olive (2)**	0 50	0 30	0 25
	Type Moissonneuse.			
108	**8 f. rouge-brun (1)**	6 90	3 »	1 50
	Type Coq Gaulois.			
109	**8 f. violet (3)**	0 80	0 50	0 30
110	**10 f. bleu (2)**	2 45	1 40	0 50
111	**12 f. rouge carminé (1)**	4 60	3 »	1 »
112	**15 f. lilas (2)**	3 05	1 60	1 »
113	**20 f. vert (3)**	2 30	1 50	1 25
114	**24 f. vert-bleu (1)**	24 50	13 »	6 »
115	**30 f. orange (2)**	14 25	6 »	4 »
116	**40 f. rouge-brun (3)**	5 35	3 »	3 »
117	**45 f. vert foncé (2)**	27 »	17 »	17 »
118	**55 f. vert-jaune (3)**	23 »	14 50	14 »
	N°s 106 à 118 (13 val.)	**115 »**	**65 »**	**50 »**
	La série, non dentelée		305 »	

A partir de 1960 les cotes de la colonne de gauche concernent les timbres avec gomme sans charnière, celles de la colonne de droite les timbres sans gomme.

1960. – ***Type Coq gaulois. Valeur en nouveau franc. Typographie. Dentelés 14 x 13½.***

119	**8 c. violet**	1 »	0 20
120	**20 c. vert**	3 »	0 70
121	**40 c. rouge-brun**	11 »	2 70
122	**55 c. vert-jaune**	35 »	20 »
	N°s 119 à 122 (4 val.)	**50 »**	**23 60**
	La série, non dentelée	110 »	

1964-69. – ***Monnaie gauloise. Typographie. Dentelés 13½ x 14.***

Monnaie gauloise

123	**10 c. vert et sépia**	0 50	0 30
124	**15 c. orange et brun**	0 30	0 30
125	**22 c. turquoise et outremer foncé**	0 70	0 50
126	**25 c. lilas et sépia**	0 50	0 65
127	**35 c. carmin et bleu**	1 50	0 80
128	**50 c. bleu et brun**	1 »	1 10
129	**70 c. bleu et brun-rouge**	6 50	3 85
	N°s 123 à 129 (7 val.)	**11 »**	**7 50**
	La série, non dentelée	92 »	

Le 15 c. existe avec surcharge brune.

1971. – ***Monnaie gauloise. Typographie. Dentelés 13½ x 14.***

130	**26 c. bistre et violet**	0 80	0 30
131	**30 c. bistre foncé et bistre clair**	0 80	0 80
132	**45 c. bistre et vert**	2 »	1 »
133	**90 c. bistre et rouge**	2 40	1 55
	N°s 130 à 133 (4 val.)	**6 »**	**3 65**
	La série, non dentelée	61 »	

A partir du n° 134 et jusqu'au n° 173, les timbres portent l'inscription FRANCE à la place de RÉPUBLIQUE FRANÇAISE.

1975. – ***Monnaie gauloise. Typographie. Dentelés 13½ x 14.***

134	**42 c. orange et carmin**	1 85	0 65
135	**48 c. bleu et brun**	1 50	1 50
136	**70 c. lilas-rose et rouge**	3 »	1 85
137	**1 f. 35 vert et brun**	3 25	2 »
	N°s 134 à 137 (4 val.)	**9 60**	**6 »**
	La série, non dentelée	34 50	

1976. – ***Monnaie gauloise. Typographie. Dentelés 13½ x 14.***

138	**50 c. émeraude et brun**	1 50	1 »
139	**52 c. rose et brun**	0 50	0 80
140	**60 c. brun-lilas et brun**	2 »	1 70
141	**62 c. lilas et brun**	1 50	1 50
142	**90 c. orange et brun**	3 »	2 20
143	**95 c. bistre et brun**	1 50	1 50
144	**1 f. 60 lilas et brun**	5 »	3 50
145	**1 f. 70 bleu et brun**	4 »	2 30
	N°s 138 à 145 (8 val.)	**19 »**	**14 50**
	La série, non dentelée	61 »	

1977. – ***Signes du Zodiaque. Taille-douce. Dentelés 13.***

Poissons.

Taureau.

146	**54 c. violet**	0 80	0 50
147	**68 c. brun foncé**	0 80	0 65

Scorpion.

Verseau.

148	**1 f. 05 lilas-rouge**	1 70	1 55
149	**1 f. 85 vert foncé**	3 70	2 »
	N°s 146 à 149 (4 val.)	**7 »**	**4 70**
	La série, non dentelée	54 »	

1978. – ***Signes du Zodiaque. Taille-douce. Dentelés 13.***

Cancer.

Bélier.

150	**58 c. vert-jaune**	1 »	0 50
151	**73 c. carmin**	1 50	1 »

Capricorne.

Vierge.

152	**1 f. 15 orange**	2 50	2 »
153	**2 f. vert-émeraude**	3 »	3 »
	N°s 150 à 153 (4 val.)	**8 »**	**6 50**
	La série, non dentelée	54 »	

1978. – *Signes du Zodiaque. Taille-douce. Dentelés 13.*

Sagittaire.

Balance.

154	**61 c. bleu**	0 65	0 50
155	**78 c. rouge**	1 »	0 65

Lion.

Gémeaux.

156	**1 f. 25 olive**	1 25	1 25
157	**2 f. 10 carmin**	1 85	1 55
	Nos 154 à 157 (4 val.)	**4 75**	**3 95**
	La série, non dentelée	54 »	

1979. – *Champignons. Taille-douce. Dentelés 13½ x 13.*

Oronge.

Trompette de la mort.

158	**64 c. orange**	0 65	0 30
159	**83 c. brun-olive**	0 65	0 50

Pleurote de l'olivier.

Clavaire chou-fleur.

160	**1 f. 30 ocre**	1 10	0 80
161	**2 f. 25 violet**	1 60	1 40
	Nos 158 à 161 (4 val.)	**4 »**	**3 »**
	La série, non dentelée	125 »	

1979. – *Monuments historiques. Taille-douce. Dentelés 13.*

Tour de la lanterne, La Rochelle.

Tours de la cathédrale de Chartres.

162	**68 c. lilas-brun**	0 50	0 50
163	**88 c. bleu-outremer**	0 50	0 65

Tours de la cathédrale de Bourges.

Tours de la cathédrale d'Amiens.

164	**1 f. 40 vert-olive**	1 »	0 80
165	**2 f. 35 brun-olive**	1 50	1 25
	Nos 162 à 165 (4 val.)	**3 50**	**3 20**
	La série, non dentelée	42 »	

1980. – *Monuments historiques. Taille-douce. Dentelés 13.*

Château d'Angers.

Château de Kerjean.

166	**76 c. bleu**	0 50	0 30
167	**99 c. vert-gris**	0 50	0 50

Château de Pierrefonds.

Château de Tarascon.

168	**1 f. 60 rose**	1 »	1 »
169	**2 f. 65 brun-orange**	1 50	1 25
	Nos 166 à 169 (4 val.)	**3 50**	**3 05**
	La série, non dentelée	34 50	

1981. – *Monuments historiques. Taille-douce. Dentelés 13.*

La chapelle impériale d'Ajaccio.

L'horloge astronomique de Besançon.

170	**88 c. lilas-rose**	0 50	0 30
171	**1 f. 14 bleu**	0 50	0 50

Les ruines du château de Coucy-le-Château.

La Grotte de Font-de-Gaune, à Les Eyzies-de-Tayac.

172	**1 f. 84 vert foncé**	1 »	1 »
173	**3 f. 05 rouge-brun**	1 50	1 25
	Nos 170 à 173 (4 val.)	**3 50**	**3 05**
	La série, non dentelée	34 50	

1982. – *Monuments historiques. Taille-douce. Dentelés 13.*

Château de Tanlay, Yonne.

Fort de Salses, Pyrénées-Orientales.

174	**97 c. olive**	0 50	0 30
175	**1 f. 25 rouge**	0 50	0 50

Tour de Montlhéry, Essonne.

Château d'If, Bouches-du-Rhône.

176	**2 f. 03 brun foncé**	1 »	1 »
177	**3 f. 36 bleu**	1 50	1 25
	Nos 174 à 177 (4 val.)	**3 50**	**3 05**
	La série, non dentelée	34 50	

1983. – *Les quatre saisons. Taille-douce. Dentelés 13.*

Printemps.

Eté.

178	**1 f. 05 vert-olive**	0 50	0 50
179	**1 f. 35 rouge**	0 50	0 50

Automne.

Hiver.

180	**2 f. 19 brun**	1 »	1 »
181	**3 f. 63 violet**	1 50	1 25
	Nos 178 à 181 (4 val.)	**3 50**	**3 25**
	La série, non dentelée	30 »	

1984. – *Cartes à jouer. Taille-douce. Dentelés 13.*

Coeur.

Pique.

182	**1 f. 14 noir, violet et rouge**	0 50	0 50
183	**1 f. 47 noir et bleu**	0 80	0 60

Carreau.

Trèfle.

184	**2 f. 38 noir, brun et rouge**	1 20	1 »
185	**3 f. 95 noir et vert**	1 50	1 40
	Nos 182 à 185 (4 val.)	**4 »**	**3 50**
	La série, non dentelée	30 50	

1985. – *Les mois de l'année (I). Taille-douce. Dentelés 13.*

Janvier.

Février.

186	**1 f. 22 lilas**	1 »	0 50
187	**1 f. 57 bleu et gris**	1 25	1 »

Mars.

Avril.

188	**2 f. 55 olive et brun**	1 50	1 50
189	**4 f. 23 brun-jaune et olive**	2 75	2 »
	Nos 186 à 189 (4 val.)	**6 50**	**5 »**
	La série, non dentelée	30 50	

1986. – *Les mois de l'année (II). Taille-douce. Dentelés 13.*

Mai.

Juin.

190	**1 f. 28 rose et vert foncé**	1 »	0 50
191	**1 f. 65 vert-bleu et vert**	1 »	1 »

Juillet.

Août.

192	**2 f. 67 rouge et bleu**	1 50	1 50
193	**4 f. 44 brun et orange**	3 »	2 »
	Nos 190 à 193 (4 val.)	**6 50**	**5 »**
	La série, non dentelée	30 50	

1987. – *Les mois de l'année (III). Taille-douce. Dentelés 13.*

Septembre.

Octobre.

194	**1 f. 31 brun-roux et lilas-brun**	1 »	0 50
195	**1 f. 69 lilas et brun-jaune**	1 25	1 »

Novembre.

Décembre.

196	**2 f. 74 bleu et gris**	1 75	1 50
197	**4 f. 56 lilas et vert foncé**	3 »	2 50
	Nos 194 à 197 (4 val.)	**7 »**	**5 50**
	La série, non dentelée	30 »	

1988. – *Les quatre éléments. Taille-douce. Dentelés 13.*

L'air.

L'eau.

198	**1 f. 36 noir et turquoise**	1 »	0 50
199	**1 f. 75 noir et bleu**	1 25	0 80

Le feu.

La terre.

200	**2 f. 83 noir et rouge-brun**	1 75	1 70
201	**4 f. 75 noir et olive**	3 »	3 »
	Nos 198 à 201 (4 val.)	**7 »**	**6 »**
	La série, non dentelée	35 »	

Le n° 201 a été vendu 4 f. 72.

1989. – *Les instruments de musique (I). Offset. Dentelés 12 x 12½.*

Harpe.

Piano.

202	**1 f. 39 bleu et noir**	1 »	0 50
203	**1 f. 79 brun-jaune et noir**	1 »	1 »

Trompette.

Violon.

204	**2 f. 90 orange et noir**	2 »	1 50
	a. (Dentelé 13)	350 »	150 »
205	**4 f. 84 brun-orange et noir**	3 »	3 »
	N°s 202 à 205 (4 val.)	**7 »**	**6 »**
	La série, non dentelée	42 »	

Au type du 2 f. 90 est paru un 1 f. 82 en 1993 (N° 228).

1990. – *Les instruments de musique (II). Offset. Dentelés 13.*

Accordéon.

Musette ou biniou.

206	**1 f. 46 émeraude, vert et noir**	1 25	1 »
207	**1 f. 89 orange, brun et noir**	1 50	1 »

Tambourin.

Vielle.

208	**3 f. 06 bleu clair, bleu et noir**	2 »	2 »
209	**5 f. 10 rose, lilas et noir**	3 25	3 »
	N°s 206 à 209 (4 val.)	**8 »**	**7 »**
	La série, non dentelée	45 75	

De nouvelles valeurs à ces types sont parues en 1992 (N°s 214, 216, 218 et 219) et en 1993 (N°s 229 et 230).

1990. – *Les instruments de musique (III). Offset. Dentelés 13.*

Harpe.

Piano.

Violon.

210	**1 f. 93 vert clair et noir**	1 25	1 »
211	**2 f. 39 rose et noir**	1 50	1 40
212	**2 f. 74 mauve et noir**	2 25	1 85
	La série, non dentelée	38 25	

De nouvelles valeurs à ces types sont parues en 1992 (N°s 220, 222 et 223).

1992. – *Les instruments de musique (IV). Types précédents et nouveaux instruments. Offset. Dentelés 13.*

Guitare électrique.

Accordéon.

Saxophone.

213	**1 f. 60 orange, brun et noir**	58 »	30 »
214	**1 f. 98 ocre, olive et noir (206)**	4 60	3 30
215	**2 f. 08 jaune, brun-jaune et noir**	2 30	1 85

Musette ou biniou.

Banjo.

Tambourin.

216	**2 f. 46 lilas, violet et noir (207)**	2 30	1 85
217	**2 f. 98 rose, violet et noir**	2 30	1 85
218	**3 f. 08 rouge, lie-de-vin et noir (208)**	6 80	4 30

Vielle.

Harpe.

Xylophone.

219	**3 f. 14 turquoise, vert et noir (209)**	3 »	2 30
220	**3 f. 19 gris et noir (210)**	8 »	4 85
221	**5 f. 28 vert-jaune, vert-bleu et noir**	5 »	3 70

Piano.

Violon.

222	**5 f. 30 bleu clair, bleu et noir (211)**	3 85	3 »
223	**5 f. 32 brun et noir (212)**	3 85	3 »
	N°s 213 à 223 (11 val.)	**100 »**	**60 »**
	La série, non dentelée	125 »	

Dentelés 12.

213a	1 f. 60	7 65	4 60
214a	1 f. 98	155 »	145 »
215a	2 f. 08	35 25	28 50
216a	2 f. 46	10 75	7 65
218a	3 f. 08	10 75	7 65
219a	3 f. 14	54 »	46 »
220a	3 f. 19	7 60	4 60
221a	5 f. 28	28 »	20 »
222a	5 f. 30	68 »	61 »
223a	5 f. 32	23 »	20 »
N°s 213a à 223a (10 val.)		400 »	345 »

Ces timbres portent le millésime 1991.

L'encre utilisée pour l'impression des textes et du fond pointillé des 1 f. 60, 2 f. 08, 2 f. 98 et 5 f. 28 est phosphorescente.

De nouvelles valeurs aux types des 1 f. 60, 2 f. 08, 2 f. 98 et 5 f. 28 sont parues en 1992 (N°s 224 à 227) et en 1993 (N° 231).

1992. – *Les instruments de musique (V). Types précédents. Offset. Dentelés 13.*

Guitare électrique.

Saxophone.

224	1 f. 73 vert-jaune, vert-bleu et noir (213)	1 »	0 65
225	2 f. 25 orange, brun-rouge et noir (215)	1 25	1 »

Banjo.

Xylophone.

226	3 f. 51 bleu clair, bleu et noir (217)	2 50	1 55
227	5 f. 40 rose, brun-rouge et noir (221)	3 »	2 30
	N°s 224 à 227 (4 val.)	**7 75**	**5 50**
	La série, non dentelée	42 »	

1993. – *Les instruments de musique (VI). Types précédents. Offset. Dentelés 13.*

Trompette.

Tambourin.

228	1 f. 82 gris, beige et noir (204)	1 »	0 65
229	2 f. 34 orange, brun-jaune et noir (208)	1 25	1 »

Vielle.

Xylophone.

230	3 f. 86 rose, rouge-brun et noir (209)	2 50	1 55
231	5 f. 93 rose, lilas et noir (221)	3 »	2 30
	N°s 228 à 231 (4 val.)	**7 75**	**5 50**
	La série, non dentelée	45 75	

1994. – *Feuilles d'arbres (I). Offset. Dentelés 13.*

Chêne.

Platane.

232	1 f. 91 olive, vert et noir	1 »	0 65
233	2 f. 46 vert sombre, vert et noir	1 25	0 80

Marronnier.

Houx.

234	4 f. 24 rouge, brun et noir	2 15	1 40
235	6 f. 51 vert-bleu foncé, bleu-vert et noir	3 35	2 60
	N°s 232 à 235 (4 val.)	**7 75**	**5 45**
	La série, non dentelée	45 75	

1996. – *Feuilles d'arbres (II). Offset. Dentelés 13.*

Frêne.

Hêtre.

236	1 f. 87 brun, vert et noir	1 10	0 50
237	2 f. 18 carmin, orange et noir	1 40	0 80

Noyer.

Orme.

238	4 f. 66 vert, jaune et noir	2 50	1 60
239	7 f. 11 bleu, bleu-vert et noir	3 50	2 60
	N°s 236 à 239 (4 val.)	**8 50**	**5 50**

1998. – *Fleurs sauvages. Offset. Dentelés 13.*

Liseron.

Coquelicot.

240	1 f. 87 multicolore	1 10	0 50
241	2 f. 18 multicolore	1 40	0 80

Violette.

Bouton d'or.

242	4 f. 66 multicolore	2 50	1 60
243	7 f. 11 multicolore	3 50	2 60
	N°s 240 à 243 (4 val.)	**8 50**	**5 50**

2002. – *Fleurs. Orchidées (I). Offset. Une bande de phosphore. Dentelés 13.*

Orchidée insulaire.

Orchidée Bourbon.

244	**0,29 € multicolore**	1 20	0 60
245	**0,33 € multicolore**	1 20	0 65

2003. – *Fleurs. Orchidées (II). Offset. Une bande de phosphore à gauche. Dentelés 13.*

Orchidée à fleurs vertes.

Orchidée de Savoie.

246	**0,30 € multicolore**	1 20	0 60
247	**0,35 € multicolore**	1 20	0 65

2004. – *Flore. Fleurs. Orchidées (IV). Offset. Une bande de phosphore à gauche. Dentelés 13.*

248	**0,39 € *Orchidée insulaire***	1 20	0 80

2004. – *Flore. Fleurs. Orchidées (IV). Offset. Une bande de phosphore à gauche. Dentelés 13.*

249	**0,42 € *Orchidée insulaire***	1 50	0 80

2007. – *Flore. Fleurs. Orchidées (V). Offset. Une bande de phosphore à gauche. Multicolore. Dentelés 13.*

250	**0,31 € *Orchidée à fleurs vertes (Platanthera chlorantha)* (246)**	1 »	0 50
251	**0,36 € *Orchidée de Savoie (Dactylorhiza savogiensis)* (247)**	1 20	0 80

252	**0,43 € *Orchidée insulaire (Orchis insularis)* (248)**	1 50	0 80

2008. – *Flore. Fleurs. Offset. Une bande de phosphore à gauche. Multicolore. Dentelés 13 x 13¼.*

253	**0,37 € *Ancolie (Aquilegia)***	0 75	0 35
254	**0,38 € *Tulipe (Tulipa sp.)***	0 75	0 35
255	**0,44 € *Pâquerette (Bellis perennis)***	1 »	0 45
256	**0,45 € *Primevère (Primula veris)***	1 »	0 45
	N°s 253 à 256 (4 val.)	**3 50**	**1 60**

2008. – *Flore. Fleurs. Offset. Une bande de phosphore à gauche. Multicolore. Dentelés 13 x 13¼.*

257	**0,31 € *Tournesol (Helianthus annuus)***	0 80	0 30
258	**0,33 € *Magnolia***	0 90	0 35

Tirage : 500 000 paires.

RADIODIFFUSION

Le ministère des P.T.T. a émis pendant trois années successives des timbres matérialisant la taxe mise à la charge des possesseurs d'appareil de radiodiffusion.

1935-37. – *Taille-douce. Dentelés 13.*

1	**(sans val.) bleu**	150 »	77 »	30 »
2	**(sans val.) rouge**	80 »	40 »	25 »
3	**(sans val.) vert**	50 »	25 »	» »

La radiodiffusion fut érigée en administration autonome en 1939.

ROULETTES

Certains timbres de grande consommation destinés aux machines distributrices ont été confectionnés en « bandes sans fin ». Ils se présentent alors sous forme de bobines d'abord de 600 (tirage à plat) ou 1200 (tirage par rotative) et, depuis 1929 en bobines de 500 ou 1000 exemplaires et exceptionnellement de 2000.

Les timbres provenant de ces bobines, dites « Roulettes », se collectionnent généralement par bande verticale de 6 ou 11, afin de pouvoir les différencier avec certitude (*).

Ces timbres se présentent généralement avec les dents coupées sur un ou deux côtés.

Des feuilles de Roulettes ont parfois servi à l'approvisionnement des Bureaux, qui, les ont détaillées au public. Il existe donc des bandes horizontales de 6 timbres des Roulettes n°s 11, 13, 15, 16, 17, 18, 19, 31, 37, 39, 42, 43, et 47.

N°	Timbre	Type	N° au catalogue	Bande de	verticale Cote	Bande horizont. de 6
	A. - IMPRESSION à PLAT					
1	5 c. Semeuse vert	I	137	6	245 »	
2	10 c. Semeuse rouge	IA	138	6	110 »	
3	15 c. Semeuse lignée vert-gris	IV	130c	6	1 650 »	
4	25 c. Semeuse bleu	I	140	6		
5	5 c. Semeuse orange	I	158	6	305 »	
6	10 c. Semeuse vert	IA	159a	6		
7	50 c. Semeuse lignée bleu	I	161	6	525 »	
	B. - IMPRESSION par ROTATIVE					
8	5 c. Semeuse orange	IIB	158c	6	185 »	
9	10 c. Pasteur vert		170	11	425 »	
10	15 c. Semeuse lignée vert	VI	130f	6		
11	50 c. Pasteur bleu		176a	6		3 250 »
12	15 c. Pasteur vert		171	11	210 »	
13	20 c. Semeuse lilas-brun	IV	139c	11	460 »	245 »
14	25 c. Semeuse bleu	IIIC	140k	11	680 »	
15	75 c. Pasteur bleu		177	6	2 450 »	2 450 »
16	5 c. Blanc vert	IIB	111	11	1 300 »	650 »
17	10 c. Semeuse vert	IV	159e	11	100 »	270 »
18	30 c. Semeuse bleu	IIC	192c	11	4 800 »	2 600 »
19	1 f. Pasteur bleu		179	11	950 »	650 »
20	15 c. Semeuse brun-lilas	I	189	11	750 »	
21	40 c. Semeuse vermillon	II	194	11	7 000 »	
22	30 c. Pasteur vert		174	11	500 »	
23	50 c. Semeuse lignée rouge	III	199f	11	400 »	
24	1 f. 50, Pasteur bleu		181	11	850 »	
25	25 c. Semeuse jaune-brun	IIIC	235a	11	900 »	
26	40 c. Semeuse violet	II	236	11	500 »	
27	40 c. Semeuse outremer	II	237	11	1 250 »	
28	30 c. Paix vert		280	11	500 »	
29	40 c. Paix lilas	II	281a	11	1 400 »	
30	20 c. Semeuse lilas-rose	IV	190a	11	360 »	
31	10 c. Semeuse outremer	IV	279a	11		115 »
32	50 c. Paix rose-rouge	IIB	283d	3	480 »	
33	65 c. Paix outremer	III	365c	11	675 »	
34	30 c. Mercure rouge	II	412a	11	725 »	
35	70 c. Mercure lilas-rose	II	416a	11	1 400 »	
36	90 c. Paix outremer	II	368b	11	1 000 »	
37	15 f. Marianne (Gandon) outremer	III	886d	11	530 »	3 200 »
38	6 f. Marianne (Muller) brun-rouge (N'existe qu'en roulettes).		1009A	11	45 »	
39	15 f. Marianne (Muller) rose carminé		1011	11	45 »	5 250 »
40	20 f. Marianne (Muller) bleu	I	1011B	11	250 »	
41	25 f. Marianne (Muller) rouge		1011C	11	250 »	
	Timbres préoblitérés					
42	4 c. Blanc, surch. « Affranchissement Postes »	II	40a	6	3 250 »	3 000 »
43	5 c. Blanc, id., surch. « Affranchissement Postes »	IIB	41b	11	1 400 »	775 »
44	10 c. Semeuse vert, surch. « Affranch. Postes »	IV	51b	11	600 »	
45	15 c. Semeuse brun-lilas, surch. « Affr. Postes »	I	53	11	5 250 »	
46	10 c. Blanc, surch. « Affranchissement Postes »	II	43	11	1 025 »	
47	25 c. Semeuse jne-br., surch. « Affranch. Postes »	IIIC	57a	11		460 »
48	10 c. Semeuse outremer, surch. « Affranch. Postes »	IV	52a	11	995 »	
49	20 c. Mercure lilas, surch. « Affranch. Postes »	I	78	11	1 500 »	

Remarque : la numérotation des roulettes 8 à 49 a été modifiée en séparant les roulettes de timbres préoblitérés.

N°	Timbre	Type	N° au catalogue	Bande de	verticale Cote	Bande horizont. de 6
	Timbres en nouveaux francs					
50	20 c. Semeuse (Piel) turquoise et rose	II	1233a	11	270 »	
51	25 c. Marianne à la Nef bleu et rouge		1234	11	210 »	
52	25 c. Marianne (Decaris) gris clair et carm. fcé		1263	11	65 »	
52a	25 c. Marianne (Decaris) rose clair et carm. fcé		1263a	11	340 »	

(Depuis 1962, un timbre sur dix des roulettes porte un numéro rouge inscrit au verso, sur la gomme, pour faciliter la comptabilité). (Après 1986, 1 timbre sur cinq).

N°	Timbre	Type	N° au catalogue	Bande de	verticale Cote	Bande horizont. de 6
53	25 c. Coq, outremer, carmin et brun dont 1 timbre avec n° vert au verso		1331	11	340 »	
53a	dont 1 timbre avec n° rouge au verso		1331	11	77 »	
54	30 c. Coq, vert, rouge et bistre		1331A	11	30 50	
55	25 c. Armoiries (Mont-de-Marsan), brun-rouge et bleu		1469	11	140 »	
56	25 c. Marianne (Cheffer), bleu		1535	11	92 »	
57	30 c. Marianne (Cheffer), lilas		1536	11	25 25	
58	30 c. Marianne (Cheffer), vert		1536A	11	9 15	
59	40 c. Marianne (Cheffer), rouge carminé		1536B	11	26 75	
60	5 c. Armoiries (Auch), bleu et rouge		1468	11	3 85	
61	50 c. Marianne (Béquet), carmin-rose		1664	11	38 25	
62	50 c. Marianne (Béquet), idem avec bandes phosphore		1664c	11	26 75	
63	40 c. La chapelle de Ronchamp (en raison du format le n° inscrit est porté 2 fois). vert, ocre et violet-brun		1435	11	» »	
64	20 c. Armoiries (Saint-Lô), multicolore		1510	11	19 25	
65	60 c. Marianne (Béquet), vert (gravé) avec bandes phosphore		1815a	11	95 »	
66	80 c. Marianne (Béquet), rouge avec bandes phosphore		1816b	11	45 75	
	Non dentelés verticalement					
67	80 c. Marianne (Béquet), vert avec 1 bande phosphore		1894	11	10 75	
68	1 f. Marianne (Béquet), rouge avec 3 bandes phosphore		1895	11	10 75	
69	80 c. Sabine, vert avec 1 bande phosphore		1980	11	24 50	
70	1 f. Sabine, rouge avec 2 bandes phosphore		1981	11	26 »	
71	1 f. Sabine, vert avec 1 bande phosphore		1981A	11	18 50	
72	1 f. 20, Sabine, rouge avec 2 bandes phosphore		1981B	11	20 »	
73	1 f. 10, Sabine, vert avec 1 bande phosphore		2062	11	27 50	
74	1 f. 30, Sabine, rouge avec 2 bandes phosphore		2063	11	27 50	
75	1 f. 20, Sabine, vert avec 1 bande phosphore		2103	11	10 »	
76	1 f. 40, Sabine, rouge avec 2 bandes phosphore		2104	11	11 50	
77	1 f. 40, Sabine, vert avec 1 bande phosphore		2157	11	10 »	
78	1 f. 60, Sabine, rouge avec 2 bandes phosphore		2158	11	10 75	
79	1 f. 40, Liberté, vert avec 1 bande phosphore		2191	11	24 50	
80	1 f. 60, Liberté, rouge avec 2 bandes phosphore		2192	11	24 50	
81	1 f. 60, Liberté, vert avec 1 bande phosphore		2222	11	11 50	
82	1 f. 80, Liberté, rouge avec 2 bandes phosphore		2223	11	13 »	
83	2 f. Liberté, rouge avec 2 bandes phosphore		2277	11	13 »	
84	1 f. 70, Liberté, vert avec 1 bande phosphore		2321	11	11 50	
84a	Idem. Gomme brillante		2321b	11	54 »	
85	2 f. 10, Liberté, rouge avec 2 bandes de phosphore		2322	11	13 75	
85a	Idem. Gomme brillante		2322b	11	84 »	
86	1 f. 80, Liberté, vert avec 1 bande de phsophore		2378	11	13 »	
86a	Idem. Numérotation tous les 5 timbres		2378	11	15 25	
86b	Idem. Gomme brillante		2378c	11	160 »	
87	2 f. 20, Liberté, rouge avec 2 bandes de phsophore		2379	11	15 25	
87a	Idem. Numérotation tous les 5 timbres		2379	11	13 75	
87b	Idem. Gomme brillante, jaunâtre		2379c	11	27 50	
88	1 f. 90, Liberté, vert avec 1 bande de phosphore		2426	11	23 »	
89	2 f. Liberté, vert avec 1 bande de phosphore		2487	11	11 50	
89a	Idem. Gomme brillante jaunâtre		2487b	11	20 »	
90	2 f. 10, Marianne du Bicentenaire, vert avec 1 bande de phosphore		2627	11	11 50	
91	2 f. 30, Marianne du Bicentenaire, rouge avec 2 bandes de phosphore		2628	11	13 75	

N°	Timbre	N° au catalogue	Bande de	verticale Cote	Bande horizont. de 6
92	2 f. 20, Marianne du Bicentenaire, vert avec 1 bande de phosphore	2718	11	18 »	
93	2 f. 50, Marianne du Bicentenaire, rouge avec 2 bandes de phosphore	2719	11	18 »	
94	2 f. 40, Marianne du Bicentenaire, vert avec 1 bande de phosphore	2823	11	22 »	
95	(sans valeur) Marianne du Bicentenaire, rouge avec 2 bandes de phosphore	2819	11	22 »	
96	2 f. 70, Marianne du Bicentenaire, vert avec 1 bande de phosphore	3008	11	30 »	
97	(sans valeur) Marianne du 14 Juillet, rouge avec 2 bandes de phosphore	3084	11	22 »	
98	2 f. 70, Marianne du 14 Juillet, vert avec 1 bande de phosphore	3100	11	22 »	
99	(sans valeur) Marianne du 14 Juillet « Mention RF », rouge avec 2 bandes de phosphore	3418	11	22 »	
100	0,41 €, Marianne du 14 Juillet « Mention RF », vert avec 1 bande de phosphore à droite	3458	11	23 »	
100a	0,41 €, avec n^{os} noirs au verso	3458b	11	22 »	
101	(sans valeur) Marianne du 14 Juillet « Mention RF », vert avec 1 bande de phosphore à droite	3535B	11	22 »	
101A	0,50 €, Flacon de parfum Chanel N°5 dans un coeur	3632C	7	1500 »	
101B	0,75 €, le tailleur Chanel sur fond avec la Tour Eiffel dans un coeur	3633C	7	1500 »	
102	(sans valeur) Marianne de Lamouche, vert avec 1 bande de phosphore à droite	3742	11	16 »	
102a	idem, légende philaposte	3742a	11	11 »	
103	(sans valeur) Marianne de Lamouche, rouge avec 2 bandes de phosphore	3743	11	19 »	
103a	idem, légende philaposte	3743a	11	12 »	
104	0,55 €, Marianne de Lamouche, bleu avec 2 bandes de phosphore	3807	11	22 »	
105	0,60 €, Marianne de Lamouche, bleu avec 2 bandes de phosphore	3973	11	13 »	
106	(sans valeur) Marianne de Lamouche, bleu avec 2 bandes de phosphore	4159	11	17 »	
107	(sans valeur) Marianne de Beaujard, vert avec 1 bande de phosphore à droite	4239	11	13 »	
108	(sans valeur) Marianne de Beaujard, rouge avec 2 bandes de phosphore à droite	4240	11	13 »	
109	(sans valeur) Marianne de Beaujard, bleu avec 1 bande de phosphore à droite	4241	11	17 »	

(*) A partir de la roulette n° 53, la bande de 11 n'est plus indispensable pour différencier avec certitude les timbres de roulette, avec les novations de 1962 (N^{os} au verso d'un timbre sur 10) et de 1976 (non dentelé verticalement) ; certains collectionneurs se contentent désormais d'une bande de 10 ; les cotes sont à diminuer de 15%. Avec la numérotation tous les cinq timbres, à partir de 1986, il est également loisible de collectionner une bande de 6 ou 5 timbres : les cotes sont à diminuer de 50% ou de 60%. Depuis 2002, roulette n° 101, tous ont un numéro noir au verso.

TIMBRES DE SERVICE

Pour les n°s 1 à 15 les cotes de la colonne de gauche concernent les timbres neufs avec gomme d'origine intacte et sans charnière, celles de la colonne de droite les timbres avec charnière ou sans gomme.

1943. – *Francisque. Typographie. Dentelure 14 x 13½, sauf n° 13, 14, 15 : 13½ x 14.*

Format 17 x 22. Dentelés 14 x 13½.

1	**10 c. *brun-orange***	80 »	35 »
2	**30 c. *outremer***	80 »	40 »
3	**40 c. *lilas***	125 »	32 »
4	**50 c. *bleu-vert***	125 »	45 »

5	**70 c. *gris-noir***	1 000 »	700 »
6	**1 f. *rose***	500 »	250 »
7	**1 f. 20 *bleu***	250 »	60 »
8	**1 f. 50 *brun-rouge***	100 »	45 »

9	**2 f. *vert***	50 »	26 »
10	**3 f. *orange***	110 »	35 »
11	**4 f. 50 *olive***	300 »	225 »
12	**5 f. *violet***	25 »	7 »

Format 22 x 36. Dentelés 13½ x 14.

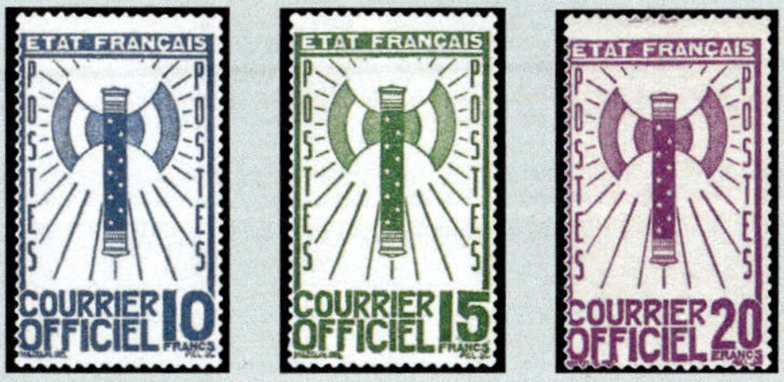

13	**10 f. *bleu***	80 »	60 »
14	**15 f. *vert***	35 »	20 »
15	**20 f. *lilas-rose***	40 »	20 »
	N°s 1 à 15 (15 val.)	**2 900 »**	**1 600 »**

Très bon centrage +100 %.

Ces timbres auraient dû être émis pour l'affranchissement du courrier des administrations, qui devaient perdre le droit à la franchise postale, à partir du 1er janvier 1942. Les réticences des ministères et administrations concernés entraînèrent le report de l'émission, et le tirage fut finalement détruit à la Libération.

Un petit stock de timbres avec gomme fut découvert au début des années soixante et les timbres sans gomme, souvent froissés, furent récupérés dans des bacs d'eau à la Libération, juste avant leur destruction.

En 1946, une étiquette gommée, bleue et rouge (dent. 12½) portant la mention "Affranchissement en compte avec l'Administration des Postes" fut mise en service pour affranchir les questionnaires du Service du Ravitaillement Général. Elle était oblitérée par le bureau de poste de départ.

15A	**bleu et rouge**	10 »	3 »

A partir du n° 16, les cotes de la colonne de gauche concernent les timbres neufs, sans charnière, celles de la colonne de droite, les timbres oblitérés.

1958. – *T.-P. de 1957 (Cathédrale de Rouen) surchargé.*

16	**35 f. rose et lie-de-vin (1129)**	1 50	3 »

1958-59. – *Conseil de l'Europe. Taille-douce. Dentelés 13.*
Drapeau du Conseil.

Drapeau du Conseil.

17	**8 f. violet, bleu foncé et orange**	0 30	0 30
18	**20 f. ocre, bleu foncé et jaune pâle**	0 30	0 30
19	**25 f. vert foncé, outremer et lilas-rose**	0 65	0 65
20	**35 f. rouge-brique et bleu foncé**	0 50	0 50
21	**50 f. lilas-rose et outremer**	1 25	1 25
	N°s 17 à 21 (5 val.)	**3 »**	**3 »**
	La série, non dentelée	535 »	

Les n°s 16 à 21 étaient réservés à l'affranchissement du courrier des membres du Conseil de l'Europe. Ils peuvent être utilisés sur du courrier privé déposé dans les bureaux du Conseil, à Strasbourg.

Huit nouvelles valeurs à ce type ont paru en 1963-71 (n°s 27 à 35), trois autres en 1975 (n°s 46 à 48) et une en 1976 (n° 49).

1960-65. – *Service de l'U.N.E.S.C.O., à Paris. Taille-douce. Dentelés 13.*
Tête de Bouddha et Hermés de Praxitèle.

Tête de Bouddha et Hermés de Praxitèle.

22	**20 c. noir, bleu et ocre**	0 50	0 50
23	**25 c. noir, vert et violet**	0 50	0 50
24	**30 c. bistre clair et bistre foncé**	1 25	1 »
25	**50 c. noir, violet et rouge**	1 25	1 25
26	**60 c. rouge-brun, carmin et bleu**	1 50	1 50
	N°s 22 à 26 (5 val.)	**5 »**	**4 75**
	La série, non dentelée	385 »	

1963-71. – *Type de 1958-59 (Conseil de l'Europe). Taille-douce. Dentelés 13.*

27	**20 c. brun, bleu et jaune**	1 25	1 25
28	**25 c. vert foncé, bleu et rose**	2 50	1 85
29	**25 c. bleu, jaune, vert et rouge**	1 25	1 »
30	**30 c. bleu, jaune et rouge**	1 »	1 »
	a. (Couleur jaune omise)	535 »	
	b. (jaune omis sur les étoiles)	155 »	
31	**40 c. gris, bleu, jaune et rouge**	1 50	1 40
32	**50 c. lilas-rose et bleu**	3 »	2 45
33	**50 c. vert, bleu, rouge et jaune**	3 »	2 »
34	**60 c. bleu, jaune, violet et rouge**	1 50	1 50
35	**70 c. brun-violet, bleu, jaune et rouge**	5 »	3 65
	N°s 27 à 35 (9 val.)	**20 »**	**16 10**
	La série, non dentelée	500 »	

Les étoiles du drapeau sont en blanc sur les n°s 27, 28 et 32, en jaune sur les autres valeurs.

1966. – *U.N.E.S.C.O. Campagne de l'alphabétisation. Taille-douce. Dentelés 13.*

36	**25 c. gris et noir**	0 50	0 50
37	**30 c. rouge-brique et brun-rouge**	0 75	0 75
38	**60 c. vert et vert foncé**	1 25	1 25
	La série, non dentelée	215 »	

1969-71. – *U.N.E.S.C.O. Déclaration universelle des Droits de l'Homme. Taille-douce. Dentelés 13.*

39	**30 c. vert foncé, rouge et brun**	0 80	0 80
40	**40 c. carmin, rouge et brun**	1 »	0 80
41	**50 c. outremer, carmin et brun**	1 60	1 40
42	**70 c. violet, rouge et ardoise**	2 60	2 60
	N°s 39 à 42 (4 val.)	**6 »**	**5 60**
	La série, non dentelée	230 »	

Du n° 43 au n° 65, les timbres portent l'inscription FRANCE à la place de République Française.

1975. – *U.N.E.S.C.O. Déclaration universelle des Droits de l'Homme. Taille-douce. Dentelés 13.*

43	**60 c. vert, brun-lilas et rouge**	1 50	1 25
44	**80 c. brun-orange, brun-rouge et rouge**	2 »	1 50
45	**1 f. 20 bleu-nuit, lilas-brun et rouge**	4 »	4 »
	La série, non dentelée	140 »	

1975. – *Conseil de l'Europe. Drapeau. Type de 1958-59. Dentelés 13.*

46	**60 c. vert-jaune, bleu, jaune et orange**	1 50	1 40
47	**80 c. grenat, jaune et bleu**	2 »	1 70
48	**1 f. 20 turquoise, bleu, jaune et rouge**	6 »	4 60
	La série, non dentelée	140 »	

1976. – *Conseil de l'Europe. Drapeau. Type de 1958-59. Dentelé 13.*

49	**1 f. olive, rouge, jaune et bleu**	4 »	4 »
	a. (Non dentelé)	61 »	

1976. – *U.N.E.S.C.O. Taille-douce. Dentelés 13.*

50	**80 c. vert-bleu, gris et bistre-olive**	1 »	1 »
51	**1 f. vert-jaune, bleu et orange**	0 50	0 50
52	**1 f. 40 brun, brun-orange et lilas-rose**	2 30	2 30
	La série, non dentelée	110 »	

1977. – *Conseil de l'Europe. Bâtiment du Conseil, à Strasbourg. Taille-douce. Dentelés 13.*

53	**80 c. ocre, brun-orange et rouge**	1 »	1 »
54	**1 f. bleu, vert foncé et brun**	0 50	0 50
55	**1 f. 40 vert foncé, olive et gris**	2 30	2 30
	La série, non dentelée	110 »	

1978. – ***U.N.E.S.C.O. Type de 1976. Dentelés 13.***

56	**1 f. 20 vert, outremer et brun-rouge**	0 65	0 65
57	**1 f. 70 rouge, vert-bleu et brun-rouge**	1 »	0 80

La paire, non dentelée 92 »

1978. – ***25e anniversaire de l'entrée en vigueur de la Convention Européenne des Droits de l'Homme. Conseil de l'Europe. Type de 1977 modifié. Taille-douce. Dentelés 13.***

58	**1 f. 20 lilas-rouge, vert foncé et gris-bleu**	0 65	0 65
59	**1 f. 70 bleu, émeraude et vert-bleu**	1 »	1 »

La paire, non dentelée 92 »

1980. – ***U.N.E.S.C.O. Patrimoine universel. Sites classés à protéger. Taille-douce. Dentelés 13.***

"La maison des esclaves", île de Gorée - Sénégal.

Site de Moenjodaro - Pakistan.

60	**1 f. 20 rose-bleu, bleu et vert**	0 75	0 75
61	**1 f. 40 vert-jaune, bleu et rose**	1 »	1 »

Palais de Sans-Souci - Haïti.

62	**2 f. rose-brun, violet et vert-gris**	1 25	1 25

La série, non dentelée 92 »

1980. – ***Conseil de l'Europe. Bâtiment du Conseil, à Strasbourg. Type de 1977. Dentelés 13.***

63	**1 f. 40 brun-olive**	1 »	1 »
64	**2 f. bleu-gris**	1 25	1 25

La paire, non dentelée 69 »

1981. – ***Conseil de l'Europe. Taille-douce. Dentelés 13.***

Palais de l'Europe : "Entrée et Hémicycle".

65	**1 f. 40 brun-rouge, bleu-gris foncé et violet**	0 80	0 80
66	**1 f. 60 brun-orange et olive**	0 80	0 80
67	**2 f. 30 bleu-vert, gris-bleu et olive foncé**	1 »	1 »

La série, non dentelée 92 »

1981. – ***U.N.E.S.C.O. Patrimoine universel. Sites classés à protéger. Taille-douce. Dentelés 13.***

Fès - Maroc.

Sukhotaï - Thaïlande.

68	**1 f. 40 bleu, roux et rose foncé**	0 80	0 80
69	**1 f. 60 rose foncé, bleu et olive**	0 80	0 80

Fort Saint-Elme - Malte.

70	**2 f. 30 olive, bleu et roux**	1 »	1 »

La série, non dentelée 92 »

1982. – ***U.N.E.S.C.O. Patrimoine universel. Sites classés à protéger. Taille-douce. Dentelés 13.***

Huê - Viet Nam.

São Miguel - Brésil.

71	**1 f. 80 lilas-rose, lilas et vert-bleu**	1 10	1 10
72	**2 f. 60 gris-bleu, sépia et rouge**	1 25	1 25

La paire, non dentelée 61 »

1982. – *Conseil de l'Europe. Type de 1981. Taille-douce. Dentelés 13.*

73	**1 f. 80 brun-violet, vert foncé et carmin**	1 10	1 10
74	**2 f. 60 bleu-vert, gris-bleu et violet**	1 25	1 25
	La paire, non dentelée	61 »	

1983. – *U.N.E.S.C.O. Patrimoine universel. Sites classés à protéger. Taille-douce. Dentelés 13.*

Mosquée de Chinguetti - Mauritanie.

Mur d'enceinte intérieur d'Istanbul - Turquie.

75	**2 f. bleu, brun et noir**	1 »	1 »
76	**2 f. 80 bleu, noir et brun**	1 25	1 25
	La paire, non dentelée	61 »	

1983. – *Conseil de l'Europe. Type de 1981. Taille-douce. Dentelés 13.*

77	**2 f. vert, carmin et bleu-vert**	1 »	1 »
78	**2 f. 80 violet, brun-rouge et bleu-vert**	1 25	1 25
	La paire, non dentelée	61 »	

1984. – *U.N.E.S.C.O. Patrimoine universel. Sites classés à protéger. Taille-douce. Dentelés 13.*

Eglise monolithique de Lalibela - Ethiopie.

Sanaa - République arabe du Yémen.

79	**1 f. 70 vert et brun-jaune**	1 »	1 »
80	**2 f. 10 bleu et brun**	1 10	1 10

Eglise Sainte-Marie Kotor - Yougoslavie.

81	**3 f. vert, brun-jaune et brun**	1 50	1 50
	La série, non dentelée	92 »	

1984. – *Conseil de l'Europe. Type de 1981. Taille-douce. Dentelés 13.*

82	**1 f. 70 vert**	1 »	1 »
83	**2 f. 10 rouge**	1 10	1 10
84	**3 f. bleu**	1 50	1 50
	La série, non dentelée	77 »	

1985. – *Conseil de l'Europe. Taille-douce. Dentelés 13.*

Pied chaussé sortant d'un oeuf.

85	**1 f. 80 vert**	1 »	1 »
86	**2 f. 20 rouge**	1 25	1 25
87	**3 f. 20 bleu**	1 50	1 50
	La série, non dentelée	77 »	

1985. – *U.N.E.S.C.O. Patrimoine universel. Sites classés à protéger. Taille-douce. Dentelés 13.*

Théâtre romain de Carthage - Tunisie.

Vieille place de La Havane - Cuba.

Temple d'Anuradhapura - Sri Lanka.

88	**1 f. 80 bleu, vert et brun**	1 10	1 10
89	**2 f. 20 bleu, vert et brun**	1 25	1 25
90	**3 f. 20 bleu, vert et brun**	2 »	2 »
	La série, non dentelée	92 »	

1986. – *U.N.E.S.C.O. Patrimoine universel. Sites classés à protéger. Taille-douce. Dentelés 13.*

Temple de Tikal - Guatemala.

Mosquée de Bagerhat - Bangladesh.

91	**1 f. 90 gris, brun clair et vert**	1 25	1 25
92	**3 f. 40 brun clair, gris et vert**	2 »	2 »
	La paire, non dentelée	61 »	

1986. – *Conseil de l'Europe. Offset. Dentelés 13.*

Bâtiment du Conseil.

93	**1 f. 90 vert**	1 25	1 25
94	**2 f. 20 rouge**	1 40	1 40
95	**3 f. 40 bleu**	2 »	2 »

La série, non dentelée 77 »

1987. – *Conseil de l'Europe. Offset. Dentelés 13.*

96	**2 f. vert**	1 25	1 25
97	**3 f. 60 bleu**	2 »	2 »

La paire, non dentelée 61 »

1987. – *U.N.E.S.C.O. Patrimoine universel. Sites classés à protéger. Taille-douce. Dentelés 13.*

Acropole d'Athènes - Grèce. Temple de Philae - Égypte.

98	**2 f. bleu, beige et brun**	1 25	1 25
99	**3 f. 60 bleu, beige et brun**	2 »	2 »

La paire, non dentelée 61 »

1989. – *40e anniversaire du Conseil de l'Europe. Valeur en Francs et ÉCU. Taille-douce sur fond offset. Dentelés 13.*

Allégorie.

100	**2 f. 20 rouge, lilas et jaune sur rose**	1 50	1 50
101	**3 f. 60 bleu, vert et jaune sur azuré**	2 »	2 »

La paire, non dentelée 77 »

1990. – *U.N.E.S.C.O. Patrimoine universel. Sites classés à protéger. Taille-douce. Dentelés 13.*

San Francisco de Lima - Pérou. Shibam - Yémen du Sud.

102	**2 f. 30 vert, brun-jaune et noir**	1 50	1 50
103	**3 f. 20 bleu, bleu clair et brun-roux**	2 »	2 »

La paire, non dentelée 61 »

1990. – *Conseil de l'Europe. Offset. Dentelés 13.*

Carte d'Europe et étoiles.

104	**2 f. 30 noir, vert, rouge bleu et jaune**	1 50	1 50
105	**3 f. 20 noir, rouge, bleu et jaune**	2 »	2 »

La paire, non dentelée 61 »

1991. – *Conseil de l'Europe. Type précédent. Offset. Dentelés 13.*

106	**2 f. 50 multicolore**	1 50	1 50
107	**3 f. 40 multicolore**	2 »	2 »

La paire, non dentelée 61 »

1991. – *U.N.E.S.C.O. Patrimoine universel. Sites classés à protéger. Taille-douce. Dentelés 13.*

Temple de Bagdaon - Népal. Citadelle d'Herat - Afghanistan.

108	**2 f. 50 brun et rouge**	1 50	1 50
109	**3 f. 40 vert, brun-olive et brun**	2 »	2 »

La paire, non dentelée 61 »

1993. – *U.N.E.S.C.O. Patrimoine universel. Sites classés à protéger. Offset. Dentelés 13.*

Parc archéologique d'Angkor - Cambodge.

Parc national du Tassili n'Ajjer - Algérie.

110	**2 f. 80 multicolore**	1 70	1 50
111	**3 f. 70 multicolore**	2 30	2 »
	La paire, non dentelée	61 »	

1994. – *Conseil de l'Europe. Offset. Dentelés 13.*

Détail de "36 têtes", oeuvre originale de Hundertwasser.

Détail de "36 têtes", oeuvre originale de Hundertwasser.

112	**2 f. 80 multicolore**	2 20	1 80
113	**3 f. 70 multicolore**	2 80	2 20
	La paire, non dentelée	61 »	

1996. – *U.N.E.S.C.O. Patrimoine universel. Sites classés à protéger. Offset. Dentelés 13.*

Parc national "Uluru"- Australie.

Parc national "Los Glaciares"- Argentine.

114	**3 f. multicolore**	2 50	2 50
115	**3 f. 80 multicolore**	3 »	3 »

1996. – *Conseil de l'Europe. Offset. Dentelés 13.*

Palais des Droits de l'Homme - Strasbourg.

Palais des Droits de l'Homme - Strasbourg.

116	**3 f. bleu clair, argent et rouge**	2 50	2 50
117	**3 f. 80 bleu clair, argent et bleu foncé**	3 »	3 »

1998. – *U.N.E.S.C.O. Patrimoine universel. Sites classés à protéger. Offset. Dentelés 13.*

Pompéi (femme cueillant des fleurs - peinture murale).

Ile de Pâques (statues).

118	**3 f. multicolore**	2 75	2 75
119	**3 f. 80 multicolore**	3 25	3 25

1999. – *Conseil de l'Europe. Héliogravure. Dentelés 13.*

Statue en bronze de l'aurige de Delphes.

Statue de la divinité grecque Niké, oeuvre de Petras Mazuras.

120	**3 f. (0,46 €) multicolore**	2 75	2 75
121	**3 f. 80 (0,58 €) multicolore**	3 25	3 25

2001. – *Conseil de l'Europe. Offset. Dentelés 13.*

"Je suis noir, je suis blanc, je suis noir et blanc", oeuvre de Tomi Ungerer.

"Je suis noir, je suis blanc, je suis noir et blanc", oeuvre de Tomi Ungerer.

122	**3 f. (0,46 €) multicolore**	3 »	3 »
123	**3 f. 80 (0,58 €) multicolore**	3 50	3 50

2001. – *UNESCO. Offset. Dentelés 13.*

Pyramides de Guizèh.

Parc national de Komodo.

124 **3 f. (0,46 €) multicolore** 3 » 3 »

125 **3 f. 80 (0,58 €) multicolore** 3 50 3 50

2003. – *Conseil de l'Europe. D'après l'oeuvre du dessinateur Tomi Ungerer "Le marcheur sur les étoiles". Offset. Dentelés 13.*

126 **0,50 € multicolore** 2 50 2 50

127 **0,75 € multicolore** 3 » 3 »

2003. – *UNESCO. Offset. Deux bandes de phosphore. Dentelés 13.*

Renne.

Eglise de la Résurrection, à Saint-Pétersbourg.

128 **0,50 € multicolore** 2 50 2 50

129 **0,75 € multicolore** 3 » 3 »

2005. – *Conseil de l'Europe. Offset. Deux bandes de phosphore. Dentelés 13x13¼.*

130 **0,55 €** ***"Jardinier semant des étoiles" - "Conseil de l'Europe semeur d'espoir", de Jean-Thomas Ungerer, dit Tomi Ungerer*** 2 50 2 50

131 **0,75 €** ***Drapeau avec nuages formant une carte de l'Europe, création de Rafal Olbinski*** 3 » 3 »

2005. – *U.N.E.S.C.O. Offset. Deux bandes de phosphore. Dentelés 13.*

132 **0,55 €** ***Bison de la forêt de Bialowieza (Pologne)*** 2 50 2 50

133 **0,90 €** ***Monument du Deir à Pétra (Jordanie)*** 3 » 3 »

2006. – *U.N.E.S.C.O. Offset. Deux bandes de phosphore. Dentelés 13.*

134 **0,60 €** ***Tigre de Sibérie*** 2 » 2 »

135 **0,85 €** ***Vat Xieng Tong (temple de la Cité d'Or) à Luang Prabang (Laos)*** 2 50 2 50

2007. – *Conseil de l'Europe. Offset. Deux bandes de phosphore. Multicolore. Dentelés 13.*

136 **0,60 €** ***Emblème et globe avec carte d'Europe*** 2 » 2 »

137 **0,85 €** ***Détail du monument aux Droits de l'Homme offert par le gouvernement espagnol au Conseil de l'Europe (sculpture de Mariano Gonzalez Beltrán)*** 2 50 2 50

2007. – *U.N.E.S.C.O. Offset. Deux bandes de phosphore. Multicolore. Dentelés 13.*

138 **0,60 €** ***Ksar d'Aït-Ben-Haddou, Maroc*** 2 » 2 »

139 **0,85 €** ***Koala (Australie)*** 2 50 2 50

2008. – *U.N.E.S.C.O.. Offset. Deux bandes de phosphore. Multicolore. Dentelés 13¼ x 13.*

140	**0,65 €** ***Gorille des montagnes d'Afrique avec jeune***	1 30	0 65
141	**0,85 €** ***Cité inca de Machu Picchu (Pérou)***	1 70	0 85

Tirage : 750 000 paires.

2009. – ***Conseil de l'Europe. Offset. Deux bandes de phosphore. Multicolore. Dentelés 13.***

142	**0,56 €** ***60e anniversaire du Conseil de l'Europe (nombre 60 et emblème)***	1 10	0 55
143	**0,70 €** ***Cinquantenaire de la Cour européenne des Droits de l'Homme (bâtiments stylisés)***	1 40	0 70

Tirage : 750 000 paires.

TIMBRES-SPÉCIMEN

Certains timbres-poste ou taxe existent avec la surcharge noire SPECIMEN, frappée horizontalement au moyen d'un cachet à main. Elle mesure généralement 16x3 mm.

On connaît les suivants :

Empire non lauré, dentelés.

1	**1 c. vert-olive (19)**	400 »
2	**5 c. vert (20)**	325 »
3	**10 c. bistre (21)**	280 »
4	**20 c. bleu (22)**	280 »
5	**20 c. et 20 c. (tête-bêche) (22b)**	14 500 »
6	**40 c. orange (23)**	350 »
7	**80 c. rose (24)**	350 »
8	**80 c. et 80 c. (tête-bêche) (24b)**	17 500 »

Empire lauré.

9	**1 c. vert-olive (25)**	850 »
10	**2 c. rouge-brun (26)**	265 »
11	**4 c. gris (27)**	265 »
12	**20 c. bleu (29)**	1 850 »
13	**30 c. brun (30)**	1 850 »
14	**40 c. orange (31)**	1 950 »
15	**80 c. rose (32)**	1 950 »
16	**5 f. violet-gris (33)**	3 400 »

Pour le 5 f. il existe deux types de surcharges.

Cérès gros chiffres.

17	**15 c. bistre (55)**	780 »

Idem, petits chiffres.

18	**15 c. bistre (59)**	780 »

Pour les timbres au Type Cérès ainsi que pour ceux au Type Sage il existe plusieurs types de surcharges.

Type Sage.

19	**1 c. noir s. azuré (83)**	500 »
20	**2 c. brun-rouge (85)**	500 »
21	**4 c. lilas-brun (88)**	800 »
22	**5 c. vert (75)**	1 100 »
23	**10 c. noir s. lilas (80)**	650 »
24	**15 c. bleu (90)**	550 »
25	**20 c. brun-lilas s. paille (67)**	1 100 »
26	**25 c. jaune clair (92)**	380 »
27	**30 c. brun-jaune (80)**	750 »
28	**40 c. rouge-orange (94)**	650 »
29	**75 c. carmin (71)**	1 250 »
30	**1 f. vert-bronze (72)**	1 000 »
31	**5 f. violet s. lilas (95)**	1 400 »

Chômeurs intellectuels.

32	**20 c.+10 c. brun carminé (330)**	85 »
33	**40 c.+10 c. vert (331)**	85 »
34	**50 c.+10 c. rouge-brique (332)**	85 »
35	**1 f. 50+50 c. outremer (333)**	85 »

Ces timbres sont normalement sans gomme.

Timbres-taxe.

36	**60 c. jaune-bistre (8)**	1 200 »
37	**60 c. bleu (9)**	700 »
38	**1 c. noir (10)**	100 »
39	**25 c. rose (32)**	120 »
40	**45 c. vert (36)**	120 »

TIMBRES-TAXE

Avant l'institution du timbre-poste en France, des "vignettes-taxe" avaient été employées officiellement, soit pour frapper d'une double-taxe les plis de service qui contenaient, à tort, une correspondance personnelle, soit pour servir de bordereau de décompte de taxe dans le cas des lettres réexpédiées de l'étranger.

Il existe deux séries de vignettes de double-taxe. L'une imprimée sur papier vieux rose en vertu de l'Ordonnance royale du 14 décembre 1825, était employée, soit entière, soit coupée par moitié, soit avec la seule mention TAXE A PERCEVOIR. La seconde série est du 12 février 1845 ; elle comporte trois types présentant tous le même aspect général, mais de couleurs différentes, rouge, bleu et jaune. (Valeur : à partir de 9150 »).

Quant aux vignettes-bordereaux de taxe, elles étaient imprimées sur papier jaune et réglementairement employées pour la taxe à percevoir des lettres réexpédiées de l'étranger en vertu des Instructions des Postes de juin 1832.

Le chapitre concerne les émissions aux chiffres taxe, aux timbres taxe et aux timbres de recouvrement.

1859. – *Chiffres taxe. Lithographie, sauf n° 2 : typographie. Non dentelés.*

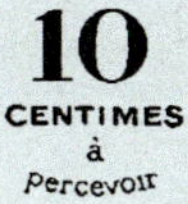

I

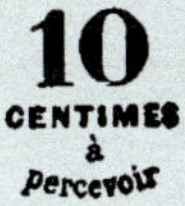

II

I. - Barre supérieure du 1 très légère ; mot "centimes" en lettres petites et espacées ; l'accent grave de l'à très léger et presque horizontal ; trait inférieur de la barre verticale du p de percevoir à peine visible.

II. - Barre supérieure du 1 très marquée ; mot "centimes" en lettres fortes et rapprochées ; accent grave de l'à presque vertical ; p de percevoir nettement imprimé.

I. - Lithographie.

1	**10 c. noir**	35 000 »	325 »
	(Sur lettre)		850 »
	(Neuf sans gomme)	7 500 »	

II. - Typographie.

2	**10 c. noir**	45 »	20 »
	(Sur lettre)		35 »
	⊞	200 »	475 »

Piquages.

2a	10 c. (B. - Percés en lignes)		270 »
2b	10 c. (D. - Piquage de Clamecy)	1 100 »	5 500 »

1863-70. – *Même type. Typographie, sauf n° 4 : lithographie. Non dentelés.*

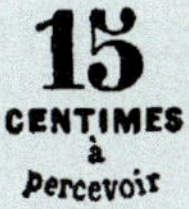

I

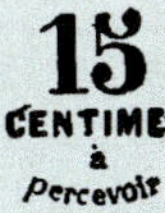

II

I. - Accent grave de l'à presque vertical ; mot "percevoir" légèrement cintré ; p nettement imprimé ; l'oeil de cette lettre est petit.

II. - Accent grave de l'à presque horizontal ; mot "percevoir" plus cintré ; trait inférieur de la barre verticale du p à peine visible ; l'oeil de cette lettre est assez fort.

I. - Typographie.

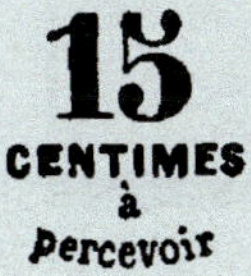

3	**15 c. noir**	50 »	15 »
	(Sur lettre)		35 »
	⊞	200 »	300 »
	a. (B. - Percés en lignes)		420 »
	b. (D. - Piquage de Clamecy)	1 000 »	5 000 »

Avec surcharge manuscrite.

3A	**25 sur 15 c. noir *(sur lettre)***		**3 200** »

II. - Lithographie.

4	**15 c. noir**	185 »	300 »
	(Sur lettre)		1 500 »
	⊞	800 »	

Avec surcharge manuscrite.

4A	**25 sur 15 c. noir**	600 »	4 600 »
	(Sur lettre)		4 600 »

1871-78. – *Idem. Typographie. Non dentelés.*

5	**25 c. noir**	200 »	65 »
	(Sur lettre)		120 »
	⊞	1 000 »	1 400 »
	a. (B. - Percés en lignes)		450 »
6	**30 c. noir**	300 »	160 »
	(Sur lettre)		300 »
	⊞	1 500 »	1 500 »
	a. (B. - Percés en lignes)		700 »
7	**40 c. bleu**	500 »	600 »
	(Sur lettre)		2 500 »
	⊞	2 200 »	
	a. outremer	8 500 »	8 000 »
	(Sur lettre)		23 000 »
	b. bleu de Prusse	3 250 »	
	c. (B. - Percés en lignes)		4 000 »

8	**60 c. jaune-bistre**	625 »	1 500 »
	(Sur lettre)		11 000 »
	⊞	3 000 »	
9	**60 c. bleu**	100 »	150 »
	(Sur lettre)		1 600 »
	⊞	450 »	900 »
	a. bleu très foncé	700 »	900 »
	⊞		
	b. bleu (B. - Percés en lignes)		3 500 »

NON ÉMIS

9A	20 c. *noir*	6 500 »
9B	60 c. *noir*	3 500 »

Piquages.

Les cotes ci-dessus s'entendent pour des timbres oblitérés sur lettre entière. (Les timbres sur très grand fragment valent le tiers).

Les timbres-taxe précédents ont eu un emploi restrictif (correspondances locales) jusqu'au 30 septembre 1882.

1881-92. – *Type Duval. Typographie. Dentelés 14 x 13½.*

Les timbres à ce type, non dentelés, appartiennent aux Colonies françaises. Le nº 10 a été imprimé jusqu'en 1907.

10	**1 c. noir**	3 »	2 50
	⊞	12 »	15 »
11	**2 c. noir**	50 »	30 »
	⊞	225 »	170 »
12	**3 c. noir**	70 »	28 »
	⊞	325 »	170 »
13	**4 c. noir**	90 »	45 »
	⊞	400 »	285 »

14	**5 c. noir**	180 »	35 »
	⊞	800 »	340 »
15	**10 c. noir**	225 »	2 50
	⊞	1 000 »	40 »
16	**15 c. noir**	125 »	12 »
	⊞	560 »	90 »
17	**20 c. noir**	500 »	150 »
	⊞	2 350 »	1 100 »

18	**30 c. noir**	315 »	2 50
	⊞	1 450 »	55 »
19	**40 c. noir**	215 »	70 »
	⊞	900 »	400 »
20	**50 c. noir**	900 »	240 »
	⊞	4 000 »	1 500 »
	a. (Non dentelé)	1 500 »	
21	**60 c. noir**	900 »	65 »
	⊞	4 000 »	1 150 »

22	**1 f. noir**	1 150 »	450 »
	⊞	5 000 »	3 250 »
23	**2 f. noir**	2 000 »	900 »
	⊞	9 000 »	5 500 »
24	**5 f. noir**	4 000 »	2 000 »
	⊞	22 000 »	12 500 »

Très bon centrage (+50 %).

Ces timbres et ceux des deux émissions suivantes sont souvent oblitérés par un cachet triangulaire.

Les 5 et 10 c. ont été surchargés au Maroc pour servir de T. -P. (voir Tome II 1re partie).

1884. – *Idem. Dentelés.*

25	**1 f. marron**	650 »	110 »
	⊞	3 000 »	1 100 »
26	**2 f. marron**	275 »	170 »
	⊞	975 »	900 »
27	**5 f. marron**	650 »	400 »
	⊞	2 700 »	2 100 »

A partir du nº 28 et jusqu'en 1959 les cotes de la colonne de gauche concernent les timbres neufs avec gomme d'origine intacte et sans charnière, celles de la colonne centrale les timbres neufs avec charnière légère, celles de la colonne de droite les timbres oblitérés.

1893-1935. – *Idem. Dentelés.*

28	**5 c. bleu**	0 60	0 30	0 45
29	**10 c. brun**	0 60	0 30	0 45
30	**15 c. vert-jaune**	65 »	35 »	1 60
31	**20 c. olive**	15 »	7 60	0 75

32	**25 c. rose**	13 »	7 50	4 50
33	**30 c. rouge carminé**	0 60	0 30	0 30
34	**30 c. rouge-orange**	1 300 »	750 »	100 »
35	**40 c. rose**	30 »	15 »	5 »

36	**45 c. vert**	25 »	10 »	5 50
37	**50 c. lilas**	1 »	0 50	0 50
38	**60 c. vert**	1 80	0 75	0 75
39	**1 f. rose s. paille**	1 300 »	750 »	475 »

40	**1 f. lilas-brun s. paille**	28 »	11 »	0 30
40A	**1 f. lilas-brun s. blanc**	2 50	1 35	0 45
41	**2 f. rouge-orange**	650 »	350 »	75 »

42	**2 f. violet**	1 40	0 75	1 05
42A	**3 f. lilas-rose**	1 40	0 75	1 20

N°s 34, 39 et 41. Très bon centrage (+30 %).

Un 5 f. rouge-orange a paru en 1941 (N° 66).

Papier G.C.

28a	5 c. bleu	2 50	0 90	1 50
29a	10 c. brun	2 50	0 90	0 90
30a	15 c. vert-jaune	45 »	22 50	1 50
31a	20 c. olive	10 50	5 25	0 90
33a	30 c. rouge carminé	2 70	1 20	0 90
37a	50 c. lilas	6 75	3 75	3 »

A la fin de 1916 et jusqu'en 1920 les timbres ont été imprimés sur un papier grisâtre ou jaunâtre de très mauvaise qualité, dit de "grande consommation" (G. C).

Les n°s 28, 29, 33, 37, 38 et 42 ont fait l'objet de tirage à plat et par rotatives ; seules les dimensions permettent de les distinguer. (Voir Catalogue Spécialisé Tome I Edit. 1975).

1908-25. – *Typographie. Dentelés 14 x 13½.*

43	**1 c. olive**	3 »	1 10	1 50
	a. olive (Papier G.C.)	3 75	2 50	1 50
44	**10 c. violet**	3 »	1 40	0 50
	a. (Non dentelé)		135 »	
	b. violet (Papier G.C.)	5 25	3 »	1 50
45	**20 c. bistre**	100 »	50 »	1 50
	a. bistre (Papier G.C.)	80 »	40 »	1 50

46	**30 c. bistre**	35 »	14 50	0 50
47	**50 c. rouge**	825 »	425 »	70 »
48	**60 c. rouge**	9 »	3 »	5 »
	N°s 43 à 48 (6 val.)	**975 »**	**495 »**	**79 »**

N° 47. Très bon centrage (+30 %).

Papier G.C. : Ces timbres servaient à taxer les valeurs dont le recouvrement, confié à la Poste, restait impayé.

1917. – *Timbres de 1908 surchargés. Dentelés.*

49	**20 c. s. 30 c. bistre (46)**	75 »	40 »	4 50
50	**40 c. s. 50 c. rouge (47)**	30 »	12 »	4 50
	a. (Sans point après c)	90 »	65 »	65 »
	b. (Chiffre 0 éloigné de 4)	120 »	90 »	90 »
	c. (Double surcharge)	750 »	600 »	

1926. – *Idem, surchargés. Dentelés.*

II *I*

51	**50 c. s. 10 c. violet (44)**	11 »	4 »	4 60
52	**60 c. s. 1 c. olive (I) (43)**	17 »	7 »	5 40
	a. (6 large) (II)	175 »	110 »	
53	**1 F. s. 60 c. rouge (48)**	45 »	23 »	15 »
54	**2 F. s. 60 c. rouge (48)**	45 »	23 »	15 »
	N°s 51 à 54 (4 val.)	**118 »**	**57 »**	**40 »**

1927-31. – *Typographie. Dentelés 14 x 13½.*

55	**1 c. olive**	2 50	1 50	1 60
56	**10 c. rose**	4 »	2 50	2 30
57	**30 c. bistre**	11 50	6 »	0 50
58	**60 c. rouge**	15 »	6 »	0 50

59	**1 f. lilas**	32 »	17 »	3 70
60	**1 f. bleu-vert**	40 »	20 »	0 90
61	**2 f. bleu**	260 »	100 »	50 »
62	**2 f. sépia**	335 »	180 »	30 50
	N°s 55 à 62 (8 val.)	**700 »**	**333 »**	**90 »**

1929-31. – *Timbres de 1927 avec nouvelle valeur en surcharge. Dentelés.*

63	**UN f. s. 60 c. rouge (58)**	85 »	35 »	2 »

Surcharge en chiffres

64	**1 f. 20 s. 2 f. bleu (C) (61)**	130 »	50 »	16 »
65	**5 f. s. 1 f. lilas (59)**	180 »	70 »	17 »

1941. – *Type Duval de 1881-92. Dentelé 14 x 13½.*

66	5 f. rouge-orange	3 50	2 50	2 75

1943-46. – *Type Gerbes. Légende FRANCE CHIFFRE-TAXE. Typographie. Dentelés 14 x 13½.*

67	10 c. sépia	0 15	0 15	0 15
68	30 c. lilas-rose	0 15	0 15	0 15
69	50 c. vert	0 15	0 15	0 15
70	1 f. bleu-violet	0 15	0 15	0 15

71	1 f. 50 rouge	0 30	0 15	0 30
72	2 f. bleu-vert	0 30	0 15	0 30
73	3 f. rouge-brun	0 50	0 15	0 30
74	4 f. violet	7 »	3 85	3 35

75	5 f. rose-lilas	0 65	0 30	0 35
76	10 f. rouge-orange	3 85	2 45	2 30
77	20 f. brun-olive	11 50	7 65	3 50
	Nos 67 à 77 (11 val.)	**24 70**	**15 30**	**11 »**

1946-55. – *Type Gerbes. Légende FRANCE TIMBRE TAXE. Typographie. Dentelés 14 x 13½.*

78	10 c. sépia	1 35	0 70	1 35
79	30 c. lilas-rose	1 35	0 70	1 35
80	50 c. vert	28 »	11 50	10 75
81	1 f. bleu-violet	0 30	0 30	0 30

82	2 f. bleu-vert	0 30	0 30	0 30
83	3 f. rouge-brun	0 30	0 30	0 30
84	4 f. violet	0 30	0 30	0 30
85	5 f. rose-lilas	0 30	0 30	0 30

86	10 f. rouge-orange	0 30	0 30	0 30
87	20 f. brun-olive	2 »	0 80	0 50
88	50 f. vert foncé	28 50	15 50	1 60
89	100 f. vert	87 »	54 »	7 65
	Nos 78 à 89 (12 val.)	**150 »**	**85 »**	**25 »**

A partir de 1960 les cotes de la colonne de gauche concernent les timbres neufs, sans charnières, celles de la colonne de droite les timbres oblitérés.

1960. – *Type Gerbes. Légende REPUBLIQUE FRANCAISE TIMBRE TAXE. Typographie. Dentelés 14 x 13½.*

90	5 c. rose-lilas	4 »	0 80
91	10 c. orange	6 »	0 70
92	20 c. brun-olive	5 »	0 30

93	50 c. vert foncé	15 »	1 40
94	1 f. vert	60 »	2 30
	Nos 90 à 94 (5 val.)	**90 »**	**5 50**

1964-71. – *Fleurs des Champs. Typographie. Dentelés 14 x 13½.*

Centaure jacée. Gentiane. Coquelicot.

95	5 c. lilas, rose, rouge et vert	0 15	0 15
96	10 c. carmin, vert et outremer	0 15	0 15
97	15 c. brun, vert et rouge	0 30	0 30

Pervenche.

Myosotis.

Ancolie.

98	**20 c. mauve, vert clair et vert foncé**	0 15	0 15
99	**30 c. brun, vert foncé et outremer**	0 15	0 15
100	**40 c. jaune, rouge et vert foncé**	0 30	0 30

Trèfle.

Soldanelle des Alpes.

101	**50 c. outremer, vert et rouge**	0 30	0 30
102	**1 f. outremer, vert et lilas**	0 80	0 30
	Nos 95 à 102 (8 val.)	**2 30**	**1 80**
	La série, non dentelée	92 »	

1982. – *Insectes. Coléoptères (I). Taille-douce. Dentelés 13.*

"Ampedus cinnabarinus".

"Dorcadion fuliginator".

"Pyrochroa coccinea".

103	**10 c. noir et brun-rouge foncé**	0 15	0 15
	a. (Double frappe)	25 »	
104	**20 c. noir**	0 15	0 15
	a. (Double frappe)	40 »	
105	**50 c. noir et rouge-brique**	0 30	0 30
	a. (Double frappe)	25 »	

"Scarites laevigatus".

"Trichius gallicus".

"Apoderus corily".

106	**1 f. noir**	0 50	0 50
	a. (Double frappe)	25 »	
107	**2 f. noir et brun-jaune**	1 »	0 80
108	**4 f. noir et rouge-brun**	2 20	0 80
	a. (Double frappe)	25 »	
	Nos 103 à 108 (6 val.)	**4 30**	**2 70**
	La série, non dentelée	61 »	

1983. – *Insectes. Coléoptères (II). Taille-douce. Dentelés 13.*

"Leplura cordigera".

"Paedurus littoralis".

109	**30 c. noir, brun et rouge**	0 30	0 30
110	**40 c. noir, bleu et brun-rouge**	0 50	0 30

"Adelia alpina".

"Tricodes alvearius".

111	**3 f. noir et brun-rouge**	1 55	0 50
112	**5 f. noir, bleu-lilas et rouge-brun**	2 30	0 50
	Nos 109 à 112 (4 val.)	**4 65**	**1 60**
	La série, non dentelée	54 »	

Les timbres-taxe ont été définitivement retirés le 18-11-1988.

TIMBRES-TELEGRAPHE

1868. - *Typographie.*

1	**25 c. rouge-carmin**	700 »	155 »
2	**50 c. vert**	700 »	245 »
3	**1 f. orange**	1 250 »	275 »
4	**2 f. violet**	1 250 »	200 »

Avec surcharge ÉPREUVE.

1a	25 c.	260 »	
3a	1 f.	340 »	
4a	2 f.	300 »	

BLOCS DE QUATRE

25 c.	3 500 »	2 100 »
50 c.	3 500 »	2 100 »
1 f.	6 500 »	2 600 »
2 f.	6 500 »	1 950 »

1868 (14 janvier). - *Idem. Dentelés 11½ x 12½.*

5	**25 c. rouge carminé**	1 000 »	110 »
6	**50 c. vert**	300 »	18 »
	a. vert clair	300 »	20 »
7	**1 f. orange**	300 »	15 50
	a. orange clair	350 »	20 »
8	**2 f. violet**	475 »	27 50
	a. violet clair	500 »	30 »

Avec surcharge ÉPREUVE.

6b	50 c.	110 »	
7b	1 f.	150 »	
8b	2 f.	175 »	

BLOCS DE QUATRE

	25 c.	5 000 »	765 »
	50 c.	1 550 »	460 »
	1 f.	1 550 »	460 »
	2 f.	2 300 »	500 »

TIMBRES-TELEPHONE

Les Timbres-Téléphone sont sans gomme.

1880. - ***Formules typographiques avec talon et nº d'ordre. Papier mince.***

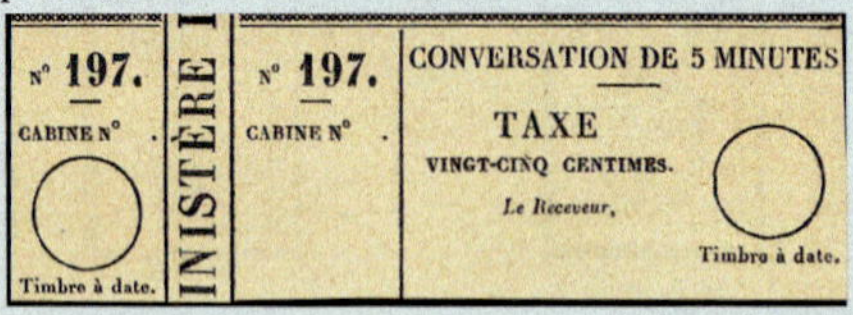

1	**25 c. noir sur bulle**	2 100 »	4 500 »
2	**50 c. noir sur bulle**	2 100 »	3 400 »

A. - Sur les nºs 3 à 15, le timbre porte dans le cartouche inférieur : TÉLÉGRAPHE.

1885-87. - ***Légende MINISTÈRE des POSTES et des TÉLÉGRAPHES-TÉLÉPHONES - Bulletin de conversation. Fond de sûreté formé des mots MINISTÈREDESPOSTESETDESTÉLÉGRAPHESTÉLÉPHONES. Typographie. Papier carte. Dentelés 13½.***

A partir des cabines téléphoniques ouvertes au public.

3	**25 c. bleu sur chamois**	260 »	13 »
4	**50 c. rouge sur rose**	325 »	30 »

Service téléphonique à longue distance.

5	**1 f. rouge sur azuré**	825 »	33 »

Service téléphonique international.

6	**3 f. noir sur vert**	700 »	80 »

1888-96. - ***Id. Légende POSTES ET TÉLÉGRAPHESTÉLÉPHONES - Bulletin de Conversation. Fond de sûreté formé des mots POSTESETTÉLÉGRAPHESTÉLÉPHONES. Typographie. Dentelés 13½.***

7	**25 c. bleu sur chamois**	285 »	20 »
8	**30 c. noir sur lilas**	170 »	18 »
8A	**30 c. vert sur gris**	200 »	88 »
9	**50 c. rouge sur rose**	180 »	17 »
	a. (Fond omis)	200 »	
	b. (Non dentelé)	300 »	
	c. (Non dentelé, noir sur rose)	325 »	
10	**1 f. rouge sur azuré**	190 »	17 »
11	**3 f. noir sur vert**	485 »	25 »

1896. - ***Timbres précédents avec "5 Minutes dans le service local 3 Minutes dans le service interurbain" en surcharge.***

12	**25 c. bleu s. chamois (3) (R)**	2 850 »	1 200 »
13	**25 c. bleu s. chamois (7) (R)**	525 »	180 »
14	**25 s. 50 c. rouge s. rose (9) (B)**	360 »	190 »

Id. BULLETIN de CONVERSATION.

15	**25 c. bleu et rouge s. chamois**	195 »	85 »

B. - Sur les nºs 16 à 30, le timbre porte dans le cartouche inférieur : TÉLÉPHONES.

1897. - ***Légende POSTES & TÉLÉGRAPHES -Bulletin de Communication. Fond de sûreté formé des mots POSTESETTÉLÉGRAPHESTÉLÉPHONES. Papier carte. Typographie. Dentelés 13½.***

16	**25 c. bleu sur chamois**	95 »	9 »
17	**30 c. brun-noir sur lilas**	155 »	50 »
18	**50 c. rouge sur rose**	130 »	9 »
19	**1 f. rouge sur azuré**	150 »	33 »
20	**3 f. noir sur vert**	800 »	170 »
	a. (Non dentelé)		240 »

Surcharge rouge : TAXE RÉDUITE à 0,15 centimes.

21	**0,15 sur 25 c. bleu sur chamois (16)**	95 »	17 »
	a. (Surcharge noire)	245 »	

1900-06. - ***Id. Sans fond de sûreté. Papier blanc ou crème. Typographie. Dentelés 13½.***

22	**10 c. violet**	85 »	6 »
23	**15 c. noir**	120 »	11 »
24	**25 c. bleu**	50 »	5 »
25	**30 c. brun**	120 »	13 »
26	**40 c. brun-rouge**	85 »	7 »
27	**50 c. orange**	70 »	7 »
28	**75 c. rose**	180 »	25 »
29	**1 f. rouge**	150 »	26 »
30	**3 f. vert**	8 200 »	920 »

Non dentelés.

22a	10 c.	185 »
23a	15 c.	300 »
24a	25 c.	185 »
25a	30 c.	300 »
26a	40 c.	155 »
27c	50 c.	460 »

Impression double.

23b	15 c.	460 »
26b	40 c.	460 »

DÉPARTEMENTS D'OUTRE-MER

A) Guadeloupe, Guyane, Martinique.

Ces départements utilisent depuis 1949 les timbres de la Métropole.

B) Réunion.

A utilisé les timbres de la Métropole, surchargés en francs C.F.A., (Voir Tome II 1re partie).

Depuis le 1er janvier 1975, il n'est plus émis de timbres exprimés en francs C.F.A. et les timbres métropolitains les remplacent.

C) Mayotte.

Collectivité territoriale depuis 1976. Les timbres métropolitains y ont été utilisés jusqu'en 1996.

Depuis cette date Mayotte émet ses propres timbres, voir au Tome 1 Bis.

D) Saint-Pierre-et-Miquelon.

Les timbres de la Métropole ont été utilisés entre 1976 et 1985. Collectivité territoriale depuis lors, Saint-Pierre-et-Miquelon utilise ses propres timbres (voir au tome 1 Bis).

COLONIES FRANÇAISES

1 f(ranc) = 100 c(entimes).

Les timbres métropolitains de 10 c., 25 c. et 1 f. carmin de l'émission 1849-1850 (France, nos 1, 4 et 6) ont été provisoirement utilisés de novembre 1851 à août 1853 en Guadeloupe et Martinique, et de mars 1852 à août 1855 à la Réunion. Les mêmes valeurs, et en outre le 25 c. type de 1852 (France no 10) ont servi à la Guyane en 1852 et jusqu'à la fin de 1853.

L'oblitération s'effectuant en France, l'origine ne peut être identifiée que sur les lettres, connues en petit nombre, dont la rareté croît dans l'ordre suivant : Guadeloupe, Martinique, Guyane, Réunion.

Oblitérations

Les premiers cachets oblitérants des colonies étaient constitués par des points (ronds ou carrés) assemblés en losanges ou en carrés. Certains de ces cachets sont muets, d'autres portent au centre l'abréviation en trois lettres du nom de la colonie (sauf pour INDE), selon le tableau ci-après :

ASI Assinié (Côte-d'Ivoire).
CCH Cochinchine.
GAB Gabon.
GOR Gorée (Sénégal).
GPE Guadeloupe.
INDE Inde.
MQE Martinique.
NSB Nossi-Bé.
OCN Océanie.
SNG Sénégal.
SPM Saint-Pierre-et-Miquelon.

Pour la cote des timbres sur lettre, voir l'introduction de notre Tome II 1re partie qui détaille chaque Colonie française.

Emissions générales

1859-65. – *Aigle impérial. Papier teinté.*

1	**1 c. olive**	25 »	30 »
	⊞	125 »	270 »
	a. (Paire intergalvano)	900 »	» »
2	**5 c. vert**	27 »	17 »
	⊞	135 »	230 »
	b. (Paire intergalvano)	600 »	» »
3	**10 c. bistre-jaune**	35 »	9 »
	⊞	170 »	80 »
	b. (double impression sans gomme)	80 »	
4	**20 c. bleu**	40 »	15 »
	⊞	185 »	200 »
	a. (double impression sans gomme)	100 »	
5	**40 c. vermillon**	30 »	15 »
	⊞	140 »	180 »
6	**80 c. rose**	125 »	70 »
	⊞	600 »	700 »

Paire dont un timbre couché.

3a	10 c. et 10 c.	1 100 »	600 »

Timbre sans parenthèses.

2a	5 c.	170 »	125 »

Dans le timbre normal, l'inscription se présente ainsi :

5 c. POSTES (5) c.

Ces timbres ont été réimprimés (valeur : 90 » pièce). Les réimpressions sont de nuances plus vives que les originaux et donnent, sous la lumière de Wood, la teinte jaune caractéristique des réimpressions Granet. La planche du 10 c. ne comporte pas de timbre couché.

De 1871 à 1880, les timbres des Colonies françaises sont les mêmes que les timbres de France, mais non dentelés.

1871-72. – *Napoléon III. Papier teinté.*

a

b

7	**1 c. vert-olive (a)**	90 »	90 »
	⊞	400 »	700 »
	a. (A la cigarette)	2 200 »	1 300 »
8	**5 c. vert-jaune**	1 100 »	500 »
	⊞	9 000 »	10 000 »
9	**30 c. brun (b)**	200 »	70 »
	⊞	850 »	450 »
10	**80 c. rose (b)**	1 200 »	130 »
	⊞	6 000 »	3 400 »

Le n° 8 (effigie non laurée) fut émis spécialement et fourni aux colonies en novembre 1871 ; il ressemble beaucoup au 5 c. vert de France de 1853. Il est aisé cependant de l'en distinguer par la nuance qui est semblable à celle du n° 35 (de France) et par l'état de la gravure usée.

Il existe différents types de surcharges "SPECIMEN" apposées sur les exemplaires d'exposition dans les bureaux de poste (rares), ces surcharges sont connues sur les types Cérès, Sage et Alphée Dubois, ainsi que sur les timbres Taxe au type Duval.

1871. – *Cérès. Idem.*

11	**10 c. bistre**	450 »	150 »
	⊞	2 000 »	2 000 »
	a. (tête-bêche)	50 000 »	23 000 »
12	**20 c. bleu**	600 »	140 »
	⊞	3 000 »	1 700 »
	a. (tête-bêche)	17 000 »	
13	**40 c. orange**	300 »	15 »
	⊞	2 000 »	600 »
	a. saumon	575 »	50 »

Chiffres 4 larges.

Pour la distinction de ce type, voir les clichés de France (1849-50).

13b	40 c. orange (Chiffres 4 larges)	3 850 »	700 »
13c	(Paire avec un normal)	8 000 »	2 000 »
13d	(Paire des deux timbres retouchés)	23 000 »	8 400 »

1872-77. – *Cérès. Papier teinté.*

A. - Grands chiffres dans les angles inférieurs.

14	**1 c. vert-olive**	15 »	17 »
	⊞	75 »	150 »
	a. (Cadre inférieur brisé)	90 »	» »
15	**2 c. rouge-brun**	550 »	900 »
	⊞	2 800 »	» »
	a. (à la barbiche)	2 300 »	3 000 »

16	**4 c. gris**	12 500 »	650 »
	⊞	» »	» »
17	**5 c. vert s. azuré**	20 »	11 »
	⊞	85 »	110 »
	a. (Papier filigrané LACROIX)	300 »	230 »

Les 2 c. et 4 c. ne furent fournis qu'à la Cochinchine. Ne pas confondre avec le 4 c. de France, non dentelé. Le 4 c. Colonies est gris jaunâtre, tandis que le 4 c. de France, non dentelé, est gris pâle. Quant au 4 c., essai, il est très facilement reconnaissable à une petite tâche sur la joue, due à un trait de burin.

B. - Type de 1871. Gros chiffres.

18	**10 c. brun s. rose**	280 »	15 »
	⊞	1 350 »	275 »
19	**15 c. bistre**	600 »	120 »
	⊞	3 000 »	1 400 »
20	**30 c. brun**	150 »	25 »
	⊞	650 »	230 »
21	**80 c. rose**	700 »	170 »
	⊞	3 400 »	1 100 »

C. - Même type. Petits chiffres.

22	**15 c. bistre**	380 »	15 »
	⊞	1 800 »	170 »
23	**25 c. bleu (I)**	200 »	15 »
	⊞	900 »	140 »
	a. (III)	450 »	30 »
	⊞	2 300 »	300 »

1877-79. – *Type Sage. Papier teinté.*

Type I.

24	**1 c. vert**	30 »	50 »
	⊞	200 »	300 »
25	**4 c. vert**	25 »	30 »
	⊞	120 »	150 »
26	**30 c. brun**	60 »	60 »
	⊞	280 »	300 »
27	**40 c. rouge-orange**	40 »	25 »
	⊞	200 »	230 »
28	**75 c. rose**	90 »	120 »
	⊞	430 »	600 »
	a. carmin	250 »	150 »
	⊞	1 200 »	850 »
29	**1 f. olive**	70 »	80 »
	⊞	300 »	400 »

Type II.

30	**2 c. vert**	20 »	15 »
	⊞	100 »	100 »
31	**5 c. vert**	25 »	6 »
	⊞	100 »	100 »
	a. vert sur vert	30 »	12 »
	⊞	125 »	125 »
32	**10 c. vert**	130 »	25 »
	⊞	600 »	150 »
33	**15 c. gris**	300 »	85 »
	⊞	1 500 »	1 400 »
34	**20 c. brun-lilas s. paille**	60 »	10 »
	⊞	280 »	125 »
35	**25 c. bleu**	5 000 »	200 »
	⊞	» »	3 000 »
36	**25 c. outremer**	60 »	10 »
	⊞	300 »	120 »
36A	**1 f. vert-bronze**	2 200 »	
	⊞	» »	» »

36A : quelques exemplaires furent envoyés au Tonkin entre 1884 et 1888 où ils reçurent une oblitération de complaisance.

Pour la distinction des types, se reporter aux clichés qui accompagnent l'émission de France de la même époque.

1878-80. – *Idem (Type II).*

37	**1 c. noir s. azuré**	25 »	25 »
	⊞	120 »	185 »
38	**2 c. lilas-brun s. paille**	25 »	35 »
	⊞	100 »	125 »
39	**4 c. lilas-brun s. gris**	35 »	50 »
	⊞	180 »	250 »
40	**10 c. noir s. lilas**	140 »	30 »
	⊞	650 »	250 »
41	**15 c. bleu**	40 »	20 »
	⊞	200 »	200 »
42	**20 c. brique s. vert**	100 »	20 »
	⊞	450 »	200 »
43	**25 c. noir s. rouge**	700 »	300 »
	⊞	3 500 »	» »

44	**25 c. jaune-bistre**	800 »	35 »
	⊞	4 200 »	460 »
45	**35 c. violet-noir s. jaune**	80 »	35 »
	⊞	400 »	275 »

Ne pas confondre le n° 43 avec la réimpression Granet ni avec le timbre de France non dentelé (qui est sur papier mince).

Le n° 44 est jaune-bistre sur jaune foncé, contrairement au n° 92b de France qui est jaune-bistre sur jaune clair.

Tirage spécial de 1900 sur bristol avec dentelure figurée.

L'Atelier du Timbre a procédé à un tirage de luxe des timbres de France, des Colonies françaises et des Bureaux français à l'étranger émis entre 1876 et 1892, en vue de la présentation à l'Exposition Universelle de 1900.

Lorsque les timbres originaux sont dentelés, le dentelure est figurée par une impression supplémentaire à l'encre sépia.

Pour les timbres des Colonies françaises et des Bureaux français à l'étranger, on ne connaîtrait que 2 panneaux de 25 timbres découpés.

Pour les sage ce tirage n'est pas avec dentelure figurée mais seulement sur bristol.

1881. – *Type Alphée Dubois. Papier teinté. Dentelés 14 x 13½.*

46	**1 c. noir s. azuré**	6 »	5 »
	⊞	30 »	100 »
47	**2 c. lilas-brun s. paille**	6 »	5 »
	⊞	30 »	100 »
48	**4 c. lilas-brun s. gris**	6 »	6 »
	⊞	30 »	100 »
49	**5 c. vert**	7 »	3 »
	⊞	35 »	60 »
50	**10 c. noir s. lilas**	12 »	5 »
	⊞	60 »	100 »
51	**15 c. bleu**	17 »	3 »
	⊞	85 »	100 »
52	**20 c. brique s. vert**	60 »	20 »
	⊞	280 »	280 »
53	**25 c. jaune-bistre**	20 »	6 »
	⊞	100 »	95 »
54	**25 c. noir s. rose**	30 »	3 »
	⊞	150 »	95 »
55	**30 c. brun**	50 »	25 »
	⊞	220 »	230 »
56	**35 c. violet-noir s. orange**	45 »	35 »
	⊞	225 »	275 »
	a. (sur jaune)	100 »	60 »
	⊞	500 »	400 »
57	**40 c. rouge-orange**	50 »	30 »
	⊞	250 »	285 »

58	**75 c. rose**	140 »	70 »
	⊞	700 »	1 000 »
59	**1 f. olive**	90 »	50 »
	⊞	420 »	460 »
	Type Alphée Dubois, la série de 14 valeurs avec dentelure figurée	1 500 »	

L'émission au type Alphée Dubois fut la dernière qui eut cours dans toutes les colonies françaises. Les variations du change dans quelques-unes de nos possessions obligèrent les pouvoirs publics à doter chaque colonie d'une série particulière ne servant que dans ses bureaux de poste ; on obtint d'abord ces timbres particuliers par des surcharges indiquant le nom de la colonie.

Dans certains cas la surcharge ne comportait que l'indication de la monnaie ainsi :

Sur timbres-poste ou timbres-taxe de France :

Surcharge en ANNAS, voir Zanzibar.

Surcharge en CENTIMOS, voir Maroc.

Surcharge en CENTS, voir Chine.

Surcharge en MILLIEMES, voir Alexandrie et Port-Saïd.

Surcharge en PIASTRES, voir Levant.

Surcharge chiffre et texte arabe, voir Maroc.

Surcharge 0.15 ou 15, voir Majunga.

Sur timbres-poste ou timbres-taxe des Colonies :

Sur émission Aigle, Napoléon, Cérès et Sage :

Surcharge chiffre et R, voir Réunion.

Sur émission Sage :

Surcharge 25, voir Nossi-Bé.

Surcharge 25 et deux barres, voir Tahiti.

Surcharge 20, 25 et GPE, voir Guadeloupe.

Sur émission Alphée Dubois :

Surcharge chiffre et A et T, voir Annam et Tonkin.

Surcharge 5, 15, avec ou sans C. CH., voir Cochinchine.

Surcharge violette 15, généralement oblique, voir Diégo-Suarez.

Surcharge 15, 25, voir Gabon.

Surcharge 05, 5, 15, 25, voir Madagascar.

Surcharge chiffre et MQE, voir Martinique.

Surcharge chiffre et NSB, voir Nossi-Bé.

Surcharge chiffre et R, voir Réunion.

Surcharge 2, voir Réunion.

Surcharge chiffre et SPM, voir Saint-Pierre-et-Miquelon.

Surcharge 5, 10, 15, voir Sénégal.

Sur timbre-taxe de 1893 :

Surcharge 10, voir Sénégal.

A partir de 1892, parut une émission d'un type général pour toutes les colonies, mais portant, dans un cartouche, le nom de chacune d'elles. Ce principe a été adopté depuis lors mais quelques timbres ont été imprimés par erreur sans nom de colonie. On connaît ainsi :

Type groupe, 25 c., voir Indochine (n° 10a).

Type groupe, 30 c., voir Diégo-Suarez (n° 46a).

Type Faidherbe, 1 c., voir Sénégal (n° 30a).

Type Faidherbe, 5 c., voir Côte-d'Ivoire (n° 24a).

Type Faidherbe, 10 c., voir Sénégal (n° 4a).

Exp. colon., tous, voir Cameroun (n°s 149a à 152a). 3 f. BF, voir Guadeloupe et Martinique.

Exposition de Paris, 20 c., 30 c., 90 c., 1 f. 50, voir Afrique Equatoriale (n°s 27 à 32).

Effigie de Caillé, 90 c., voir Côte-d'Ivoire (n°s 141a à 143a).

150e anniversaire de la Révolution, 2 f. 25 + 2 f., voir Afrique Equatoriale (n° 76a).

Effigie d'Eboué, 2 f., voir Afrique Equatoriale (n° 206a).

Poste aérienne 1940, 1 f. 90, 2 f. 90, 4 f. 50, 4 f. 90, et 6 f. 90, voir Côte-d'Ivoire (n°s 1a et suivants).

Protection de l'enfance indigène, voir Côte-d'Ivoire (n°s 6 à 8).

Voir aussi, à Afrique Occidentale (n° 75), un 20 f. sans nom de colonie portant la légende : OFFICE DES POSTES ET TELECOMMUNICATIONS.

Les timbres suivants, qui ne portent pas de nom de colonie, ont été émis par le Comité français de la libération nationale et mis en vente dans la plupart des colonies et en Corse.

Pour les n°s 60 à 66 et le P.A. n° 1, les cotes de la colonne de gauche concernent les timbres neufs avec gomme d'origine intacte et sans charnière, celles de la colonne centrale les timbres neufs avec charnière légère, celle de la colonne de droite les timbres oblitérés.

1943. – *Pour l'aide aux combattants. Dentelés 12.*

60	**0 f. 50+4 f. 50 émeraude**	1 50	1 »	2 »
61	**1 f. 50+8 f. 50 rose**	1 50	1 »	2 »
62	**3 f. +12 f. bleu clair**	1 50	1 »	2 »
63	**5 f. +15 f. gris-brun**	1 50	1 »	2 »

64	**9 f. +41 f. lilas**	4 »	2 50	3 50
	N°s 60 à 64 (5 val.)	**10 »**	**6 50**	**11 50**
	La série, non dentelée		40 »	

1943. – *Pour l'aide aux résistants. Percé en scie.*

Ce timbre a été imprimé par feuillets de 10 exemplaires, en deux rangées horizontales de cinq. Au dessus ou en dessous de chaque timbre se trouve un cadre en pointillés gris renfermant une croix de Lorraine bleu foncé.

65	**1 f. 50+98 f. 50 bleu foncé et gris**	55 »	40 »	55 »
	a. (sans vignette attenante)	25 »	15 »	15 »

1943. – ***Au profit des oeuvres de Solidarité française. Dentelé 12.***

66	**10 f. +40 f. bleu**	6 »	5 »	7 »
	a. (Non dentelé)	15 »		

TIMBRE POUR LA POSTE AERIENNE

1944. – ***Entraide de l'Aviation. Dentelé 12.***

1	**10 f. +40 f. gris-vert**	8 »	6 »	7 »
	a. (Non dentelé)	20 »		

TIMBRES-TAXE

1884. – ***Non dentelés.***

1	**1 c. noir**	4 »	4 »
2	**2 c. noir**	4 »	4 »
3	**3 c. noir**	4 »	4 »
4	**4 c. noir**	5 »	4 »
5	**5 c. noir**	7 »	3 »
6	**10 c. noir**	10 »	7 »
7	**15 c. noir**	15 »	12 »
8	**20 c. noir**	18 »	12 »
9	**30 c. noir**	20 »	10 »
10	**40 c. noir**	25 »	10 »
11	**60 c. noir**	35 »	20 »
12	**1 f. *noir***	350 »	
13	**2 f. *noir***	350 »	
14	**5 f. *noir***	500 »	

Les n°s 1 à 11 existent sur papier jaunâtre et sur papier blanc.
Tirage sur bristol (sans dentelure figurée)

N°s 1 à 14 (14 val.) 1 100 »

1884. – ***Idem. Dentelés.***

15	**1 f. marron**	50 »	40 »
16	**2 f. marron**	50 »	40 »
17	**5 f. marron**	130 »	90 »

On connaît des paires interpanneaux des 1 f., 2 f. et 5 f. en Aile de Moulin (Tête-Bêche).

Valeur d'une paire 750 »

Tirage sur bristol (sans dentelure figurée), les 3 valeurs 400 »

1893-1908. – ***Idem. Dentelés.***

18	**5 c. bleu**	1 50	1 50
19	**10 c. brun**	1 50	1 50
20	**15 c. vert-jaune**	2 »	2 »
21	**20 c. olive (1906)**	2 »	2 »
22	**30 c. rouge carminé**	3 »	2 »
23	**50 c. violet**	3 »	2 »
24	**60 c. brun jaunâtre**	5 »	3 »
	a. brun violacé	6 »	4 »
25	**1 f. rose s. paille**	36 »	25 »
26	**1 f. lilas-brun s. paille (1905)**	10 »	6 »
	N°s 18 à 26 (9 val.)	**64 »**	**45 »**

Tirage sur bristol (sans dentelure figurée) sauf les n°s 21 et 26, les 7 valeurs 300 »

Les 50 c. et 1 f. avec COLIS POSTAUX en surcharge sont catalogués à Côte-d'Ivoire

1945-46. – ***Dentelés 11½.***

27	**10 c. bleu**	0 30	0 30
28	**15 c. vert-jaune**	0 30	0 30
29	**25 c. jaune-orange**	0 30	0 30
30	**50 c. vert foncé**	0 80	0 65
31	**60 c. brun-rouge**	0 80	0 65
32	**1 f. lie-de-vin**	0 80	0 50
33	**2 f. rouge**	0 80	0 65
34	**4 f. gris**	3 35	2 75
35	**5 f. outremer**	3 35	2 75
36	**10 f. violet**	18 50	15 »
37	**20 f. brun**	3 80	3 »
38	**50 f. vert**	6 90	6 15
	N°s 27 à 38 (12 val.)	**40 »**	**33 »**

Les émissions générales des Colonies Françaises ont été de 1871 à 1881 aux mêmes types que les émissions de France, aussi sont-elles reprises dans le présent volume I. Toutefois le chapitre figure également en tête du volume II 1re partie.

FEUILLETS-SOUVENIR DE LA C.N.E.P.

Ces feuillets sont mis en vente par les professionnels membres de la Chambre Syndicale Française des Négociants et Experts en Philatélie (C.N.E.P.) à l'occasion des Salons Philatéliques organisés par celle-ci.

Ils n'ont pas pouvoir d'affranchissement.

1980. – ***Salon Philatélique de Strasbourg.***

1	**"ALSATEC"**	15 »

1981. – ***Salon Philatélique de Lyon.***

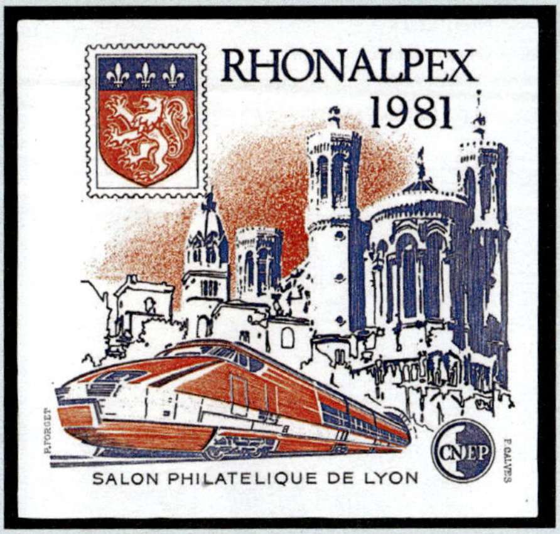

2	**"RHONALPEX"**	10 »

1982. – ***Salon Philatélique d'automne, à Paris. Dentelés.***

3	**"PARIPEX" (I)**	15 »

Idem. Dessin différent au-dessus de Notre-Dame. Pas de traits sur les toits des immeubles près du Pont Neuf.

3A	**"PARIPEX" (II)**	16 »

Idem. Dessin différent au-dessus de Notre-Dame. Pas de traits sur les toits des immeubles près du Pont Neuf.

1983. – ***Salon Philatélique de Lille.***

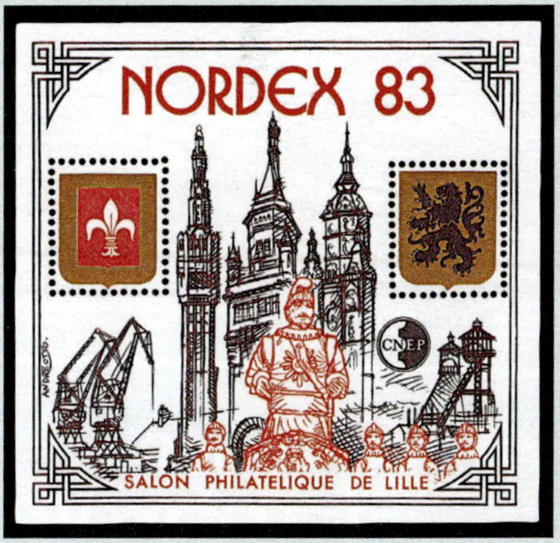

4	**"NORDEX" (Type I,**	
	3e clocher court extrémité sans croix)	8 »
	a. roue du derrik brisée (Type I)	10 »
4A	**"NORDEX" (Type II,**	
	3e clocher long extrémité avec croix)	9 »

1984. – ***Salon Philatélique de Toulouse. Dentelés.***

5 "AVIAPHIL" 22 »

Idem. Toit de l'église coupé.

5A "AVIAPHIL" (type 2) 25 »

1985. – ***Salon Philatélique de Marseille.***

6 "MASSILIA" 9 »

1986. – ***Salon Philatélique de Rennes.***

7 "BRETAGNE" 9 »

1987. – ***Salon Philatélique de Dijon.***

8 "BOURGOGNE" 14 »

1988. – ***Salon Philatélique de Metz.***

9 "LORRAINE" 20 »

1989. – ***Salon Philatélique de Lyon. Dentelés.***

10 **"LYONNAIS"** 20 »

Idem, avec surcharge rouge "ANNÉE DU BICENTENAIRE DE LA REVOLUTION FRANÇAISE".

11 **(sans val.)** 35 »

Le papier du n° 11 est plus blanc que celui du n° 10.

Idem, avec surcharge rouge "ANNÉE DU BICENTENAIRE DE LA REVOLUTION FRANÇAISE".

Le papier du n° 11 est plus blanc que celui du n° 10.

1990. – ***Salon Philatélique de Bordeaux.***

12 **"AQUITAINE"** 18 »

1991. – ***Salon Philatélique de Mulhouse.***

13 **"ALSACE"** 12 »

1992. – ***Salon Philatélique de Tours. Dentelés.***

14 **"TOURAINE"** 85 »

Idem, spécial Jeux olympiques.

15 **"ANNÉE OLYMPIQUE"** 85 »

1992. – *46ᵉ Salon Philatélique d'automne, à Paris.*

16 "DISNEY 92" 16 »

1993. – *Salon Philatélique de Strasbourg.*

17 "EUROPHILEX" 50 »

1994. – *Salon Philatélique de Lyon.*

18 "LUGDUNUM" 22 »

1994. – *48ᵉ Salon Philatélique d'automne, à Paris.*

19 "CHAMPS-ÉLYSÉES 94" 20 »

1995. – *Salon Philatélique de Toulouse.*

20 "TOLOSA 95" 48 »

1995. – *Hommage au Général de Gaulle.*

21 "PARIS 95" 13 »

1996. – *Salon Philatélique de Lille.*

22 "PHILAFLANDRE 96" 13 »

1996. – *50e Salon Philatélique d'automne, à Paris.*

23 "PARIS 1946-1996" 18 »

1997. – *Salon Philatélique de Mulhouse.*

24 "MULHOUSE-97" 20 »

1997. – *51e Salon Philatélique d'automne, à Paris.*

25 "PARIS 97" 25 »

1998. – *Salon Philatélique de Lyon. Dentelés.*

26 "Coupe du monde" 10 »

27 Idem surchargé 26 »

1998. – *52ᵉ Salon Philatélique d'automne, à Paris.*

28 "150ᵉ anniversaire du 1ᵉʳ Timbre-Poste français" 10 »

1999. – *Salon Philatélique de Strasbourg.*

29 "50ᵉ anniversaire du Conseil de l'Europe" 10 »

1999. – *"Philexfrance'99".*

30 "150ᵉ anniversaire du premier timbre-poste de France (Hologramme du 20 c. Cérès)" 11 »

2000. – *Salons Philatéliques Paris - Lyon.*

31 "An 2000" 10 »

2000. – *54ᵉ Salon Philatélique d'Automne, à Paris.*

32 "1900 à 2000" 10 »

2001. – *Salon Philatélique de Printemps, à Nancy.*

33 "Nancy 2001" 11 »

2001. – *55e Salon Philatélique d'Automne, à Paris.*

34 "2001 Hommage à Decaris" 9 »

2002. – *3e Biénnale Philatélique de Paris.*

35 "Adieu le Franc bonjour l'€uro" 9 »

2002. – *Salon Philatélique de Printemps, à Nîmes.*

36 "Nîmes 2002" 9 »

2002. – *Salon Philatélique d'Automne, à Paris.*

37 "Paris-Rome" 9 »

2003. – *Salon Philatélique de Printemps, à Nantes.*

38 "Nantes 2003" 9 »

2003. – *Salon Philatélique d'Automne, à Luxembourg.*

39 "Luxembourg 2003" 9 »

2004. – *Salon Philatélique de Printemps, à Clermont-Ferrand.*

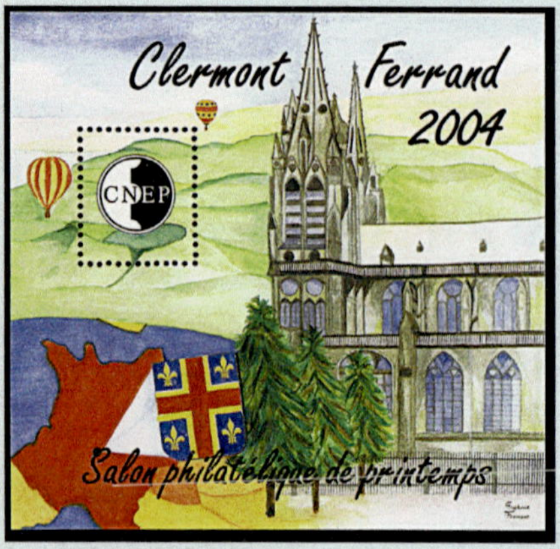

40 "Clermont-Ferrand" 9 »

2004. – *Salon du Timbre, à Paris.*

41 "Salon du Timbre 2004 (Parc Floral de Paris)" 9 »

2004. - *Salon Philatélique d'Automne, à Paris.*

42 "Paris" 9 »

2005. - *Salon Philatélique de Printemps, à Aix-en-Provence.*

43 "Aix-en-Provence 2005" 9 »

2005. - *Salon Philatélique d'Automne, à Paris.*

44 "Paris - Art du timbre gravé" 9 »

2006. - *Salon Philatélique de Printemps, à Dijon.*

45 "Dijon 2006" 9 »

2006. - *Salon du Timbre & de l'Ecrit, à Paris.*

46 "Salon du Timbre & de l'Ecrit 2006 (Parc Floral de Paris)" 9 »

2006. - *Salon Philatélique d'Automne à Paris.*

47 "60e anniversaire du Salon d'Automne à Paris" 9 »

2007. - *Salon Philatélique de Printemps à Limoges.*

48 "Limoges 2007" 8 »

2007. - *Salon Philatélique d'Automne.*

49 "Salon philatélique d'Automne 2007" 9 »

2008. - *Salon Philatélique de Printemps à Lyon.*

50 "Lyon" 9 »

2008. - *Salon du Timbre & de l'Ecrit, à Paris.*

51 "Salon du Timbre & de l'Ecrit 2008 (Parc Floral de Paris)" 9 »

2008. - *Salon Philatélique d'Automne.*

52 "Salon philatélique d'Automne 2008" 9 »

2009. - *Salon Philatélique de Printemps à Mâcon.*

53 "Macon 2009" 9 »

FEUILLETS-SOUVENIR DE LA FÉDÉRATION FRANÇAISE DES ASSOCIATIONS PHILATÉLIQUES (F.F.A.P.)

Ces feuillets sont mis en vente auprès des associations philatéliques fédérées et offerts aux abonnés de la revue "La Philatélie Française".

2007. - *80e Congrès Poitiers 2007.*

1 La Passion du Timbre.

Notre-Dame-La-Grande 9 »

2008. - *81e Congrès Paris 2008.*

2 La Passion du Timbre 8 »

2009. - *82 Congrès Tarbes 2009.*

3 **La Passion du Timbre** 8 »

FEUILLETS-SOUVENIR YVERT & TELLIER

Les Editions YVERT & TELLIER encouragent à travers un partenariat la Fédération Française des Associations Philatéliques. Elles encouragent également les artistes créateurs de beaux timbres par l'émission de Blocs-feuillets insérés dans son tome 1.

Ces feuillets sont l'oeuvre d'artistes ayant déjà créé des timbres-poste.

2008. – *Marc Taraskoff. percé en ligne.*

Logo soleil et neige.

1 **multicolore**

Peintre et dessinateur, **Marc Taraskoff** a réalisé plus de mille couvertures de livres et de nombreuses illustrations dans la presse (Le Monde, Libération, Jazzman, Le Point). Pour Phil@poste il est l'auteur de trente-cinq timbres dont les blocs "Rome", "Bruxelles", les portraits de Georges Perec, Massoud, André Malraux, Jean Vilar... Il est, depuis 2005, le Conseiller artistique pour la philatélie de Saint-Pierre et Miquelon.

2009. – *Christian Broutin. Dentelé.*

Logo (arbre en hiver / arbre en été).

2 **multicolore**

Christian Broutin commence sa carrière dans la publicité et la réalisation d'affiches de cinéma. Celle pour le film Jules et Jim de François Truffaut reçoit le Prix Toulouse-Lautrec en 1962. Son activité principale est la peinture mais il illustre aussi des magazines, des livres pour la jeunesse et réalise des reportages photographiques. Christian Broutin est l'auteur de nombreux timbres tels que : les roses anciennes, les jardins de France, Rouge-gorge, Charte de l'environnement, les animaux de la préhistoire.

2010. – *Marie-Laure Drillet. Dentelé.*

Logo (hiver/été).

3 **multicolore**

Marie-Laure Drillet vit et travaille à Bordeaux depuis 1997. L'artiste construit son univers à l'aide d'images présentes et passées, revisitant les mythes, entre rêves de petite fille et réalité de grande. Avec elle, l'élément quotidien se singularise.

Elle met en scène les femmes et les hommes dans des peintures/collages.

Entre pertinence et impertinence, son travail est narratif et suggestif, mêlant des couleurs chatoyantes à des histoires inattendues pour un résultat des plus facétieux. Elle met sa créativité au service de la poste de Saint-Pierre et Miquelon pour laquelle elle a créé notamment le timbre des 20 ans de la collectivité territoriale, les déferlantes et le bloc du port bloqué par les glaces.

Les points «club»

01 • AIN

01000 LIB MONTBARBON
Place de la Grenouillère
Bourg-en-Bresse
Tél 04 74 24 61 00

03 • ALLIER

03200 VICHY PHILATÉLIE
22 avenue P. Doumer
Vichy
Tél 04 70 31 65 41

06 • ALPES-MARITIMES

06000 ROLAND VESPA PHILATÉLIE
37 rue Gioffredo
Nice
Tél 04 93 62 26 10

06110 ED. LA ROSE DES VENTS
383 bd J. Monod
Rocheville
Tél 04 93 45 22 95

08 • ARDENNES

08000 VILLERS COLLECTIONS
8 rue Jules Lobet BP 45
Villers-Semeuse
Tél 03 24 37 31 97

09 • ARIEGE

09500 LOISIRS & COLLECTIONS
42-43 Place du Maréchal Leclerc
Sous les Couverts
Mirepoix
10ème anniversaire !
Magasin ouvert tous les jours
Tél 05 61 60 13 13
Fax 05 61 60 63 45
www.ariege-philatelie.com

11 • AUDE

11000 AUDE COLLECTIONS
24 rue Armagnac
Carcassonne
Tél 04 68 25 03 83

13 • BOUCHES-DU-RHÔNE

13001 MAISON DU TIMBRE
1 rue Pythéas
Marseille
Tél 04 91 33 76 16

13006 ESPACE YVERT & TELLIER
263 rue Paradis
Marseille
Tél : 04 91 58 22 22
Fax : 04 91 47 94 08

13100 ATOUT PHILATÉLIE
19 bis rue Emeric David
Aix-en-provence
Tél 04 42 91 40 39

13400 AUBAGNE PHILATÉLIE
Avenue Joseph Lafond
Le Verdi
Aubagne
Tél 04 42 03 02 88

14 • CALVADOS

14000 LE PHILATÉLISTE
24 rue Caponière
Caen
Tél 02 31 86 44 78

16 • CHARENTE

16000 PHILATÉLIE CHARENTAISE
12 place Delivertoux
Angoulême
Tél 05 45 92 59 35

17 • CHARENTE-MARITIME

17000 MONNAIES / MÉDAILLES 17
20 rue Gargoulleau
La Rochelle
Tél 05 46 41 40 01

17300 PHILARÊVE
51 rue Jean Jaurès
Rochefort
Tél 05 46 99 04 41

18 • CHER

18000 BERNADET PHILATÉLIE
20 rue Porte Jaune
Bourges
Tél. 02 48 24 10 00

21 • CÔTE-D'OR

21000 DIJON PHILATÉLIQUE
17 place Darcy
Dijon *(Sauf lundi)*
69ème anniversaire !
Achat - Vente - Timbres Poste - Lettres - Cartes postales - Monnaies
Tél/Fax 03 80 30 58 06

25 • DOUBS

25000 BESANCON PHIL.
3 rue Proudhon
Besançon
Tél 03 81 81 44 09

25000 ART ET PHILATÉLIE
32 rue Proudhon
Besançon
Tél 03 81.81.31.44

25200 PHILA CARTO NUMI
8 rue de la Sous préfecture
Montbéliard
Tél 03 81 97 10 09

26 • DROME

26000 L'AMATEUR TIMBROPHILE
1 Cité Chabert
Valence
Vente-Achat : Timbres Monnaies, Fournitures pour collectionneurs
Tél 04 75 43 36 63
Fax 04 75 43 38 38

26000 VALENCE COLLECTION
45 rue Faventines
Valence
Achat, Vente, Timbres Lettres, Cartes, Monnaies, Toutes fournitures
Tél 04 75 55 51 73
email: yannoffline@yahoo.fr

27 • EURE

27000 ESPACE COLLECTIONS
5 rue des Lombards
Evreux
Timbres et Monnaies de France, Euros et Monnaies de Paris
Tél/Fax 02 32 62 31 82

29 • FINISTÈRE

29000 ESPACE COLLECTIONS
Place au Beurre
QUIMPER
Timbres, Monnaies, Billets, Fournitures toutes collections
Tél 02 98 95 89 64
www.espace-collection.fr

29200 BREST PHILATÉLIE
18 rue de Lyon
Brest
Tél 02 98 44 31 71

30 • GARD

30100 LE COLLECTIONNEUR CÉVENOL
14, rue Taisson
Alès
Tél 04 66 52 90 99

30900 AS DE NÎMES COLLECTIONS
13, rue de la Curaterie
Nîmes
Tél 04 66 21 74 58

31 • HAUTE-GARONNE

31000 PHILATÉLIE DES CARMES
40 rue Pharaon
(métro Carmes)
Toulouse
Timbres: France, Monaco, Andorre, Espagne. Thématique, Matériel toutes collections
Tél 05 61 55 39 08
email : carmes.phila@wanadoo.fr
site web : www.philatélie-31.com

31000 CIRY PHILATÉLIE
9 ter, rue des Lois
Toulouse
Timbres, Matériel toutes marques
Tél/Fax 05 61 22 45 27

33 • GIRONDE

33000 PHILATÉLIE BORDELAISE
3, rue Louis Combes
Bordeaux
Nouveautés du Monde, Abonnements,Thématiques, Mancolistes - Matériel
Tél 05 56 81 20 47
Fax : 05 56 44 60 58

33000 ART ET PHILATÉLIE
31, rue Porte Dijeaux
Bordeaux
Tél 05 56 52 10 68

33000 BARRET PHILATÉLIE
30 rue des Remparts
Bordeaux
Tél 05 56 51 22 13

33000 LA MAISON DU COLL.
24 rue des Ayres
Bordeaux
Tél 05 56 51 11 64

33000 PHILATEXTE SARL
65 rue Georges Bonnac
Bordeaux
Achat-Vente Matériel, Timbres, Lettres, Cartes
Tél 05 56 51 42 36
email : philatexte@wanadoo.fr

34 • HÉRAULT

34500 BÉZIERS-PHILATÉLIE
12 rue Trencavel
Béziers
Tél 04 67 28 24 73

35 • ILLE-ET-VILAINE

35000 REN' COLLECTIONS
6 rue d'Argentré
Rennes
Timbres - Thématique - Matériel philatélique...
Tél 02 99 78 22 04
Fax 02 99 79 66 85
email : ren.collection@cegetel.net

36 • INDRE

36100 ISSOUDUN PHIL.
4 Bld. Roosevelt
Issoudun
Tél 02 54 21 02 19

37 • INDRE-ET-LOIRE

37000 PHILARAMA SARL
5, rue de Jérusalem
Tours
Achat-Vente de timbres de collection. Matériel philatélique et numismatique.
30 années d'expérience!
Tél 02 47 66 32 01
Fax 02 47 66 03 04
email : philarama@wanadoo.fr

38 • ISÈRE

38000 PHILATÉLIE RAPHAEL
33 Avenue Alsace Lorraine
Grenoble
Estimation, achat, vente, Timbres, monnaies, dépositaire toutes marques
Tél/Fax 04 76 87 10 74
email : alain.houplain@free.fr

41 • LOIR ET CHER

41000 ARTS ET PASSIONS
4, rue St-Lubin
Blois
Tél 02 54 78 61 61

42 • LOIRE

42000 M. J. RIOCREUX
29 rue de la République
St-Etienne
Tél 04 77 32 50 81

44 • LOIRE-ATLANTIQUE

44000 LA BOURSE AUX TIMBRES
19 passage Pommeraye
Nantes
Tél 02 40 48 52 04

44000 ARMEL HENRY PHILATÉLIE PLUS
2 rue des Deux Ponts
Nantes
Tél 02 40 20 45 71

49 • MAINE-ET-LOIRE

49000 ANJOU-PHILATÉLIE
53, rue Bressigny
Angers
Tél 02 41 88 55 45

50 • MANCHE

50100 PHILATÉLIE 50
9 rue Albert Mahieu
Cherbourg
Tél 02 33 93 55 91
Fax 02 33 93 56 74
www.philatelie50.com

51 • MARNE

51100 REIMS PHILATÉLIE
27 rue de Vesle
Reims
Tél 03 26 47 72 21

52 • HAUTE-MARNE

52000 SAINT DIZIER PHIL.
7 place Aristide Briand
Saint-Dizier
Tél 03 25 05 10 67

53 • MAYENNE

53000 PHILATÉLIE LAVALLOISE
47 Grande Rue
Laval
Tél. 02 43 67 15 41

54 • MEURTHE-ET-MOSELLE

54000 JEAN HECKLER
48 rue Stanislas
Nancy
Tél 03 83 32 20 86

54000 PHILATELOR
25, rue de mon Desert
Nancy
Tél 03 83 40 42 01

56 • MORBIHAN

56000 ATOUT'COLLECTIONS
1, ruelle du Recteur
Vannes
Tél 02 97 42 66 78
email : atoutcollec@orange.fr

57 • MOSELLE

57970 PHILA PASSION PLUS
111 av. des Nations
Yutz
Tél 03 82 56 52 12

59 • NORD

59000 MOLINEL PHILATÉLIE
127 rue du Molinel
Lille
Nouveautés d'Europe
Tél/Fax 03 20 57 40 89

59000 ESPACE YVERT & TELLIER
54 rue du Molinel
Lille
Tél 03 20 44 22 22
Fax 03 20 74 01 48

59140 DUNKERQUE PHILATÉLIE
33 rue Nationale
Dunkerque
Tél 03 28 69 56 20

59200 PHILATÉLIE M. BLOT
55, rue de Mouvaux
Tourcoing
Tél 03 20 26 95 12

60 • OISE

60000 PHILATÉLIE MALHERBE
18 rue de Malherbe
Beauvais
Achat-Vente-Estimation
Timbres-lettres
Tél 03 44 45 26 90

60200 PHILATEMARQ
20 rue des Cordeliers
Compiègne
Tél 03 44 23 18 76

61 • ORNE

61000 ART ET COLLECTION
4 place du 103ème R.I.
Alençon
Tél 02 33 32 17 25

62 • PAS-DE-CALAIS

62114 SAINS LOISIRS
50 Résidence
les Claires Fontaines
Sains en Gohelle
Tél/Fax 03 21 29 93 36

62600 JP LEPRETRE PHIL.
431 rue de l'Impératrice
Berck-sur-Mer
Tél 03 21 09 07 70

63 • PUY-DE-DOME

63000 CLERMONT COLLECTIONS
1 rue Saint Barthélemy
Clermont-Ferrand
Tél 04 73 37 88 31

64 • PYRÉNÉES-ATLANTIQUES

64000 LE TIMBRE EUROPÉEN
5 rue Lamothe
Pau
Tél 05 59 83 76 06

64000 BÉARN PHILATÉLIE
5 rue Samonzet
Pau
Tél 05 59 27 09 91

65 • PYRÉNÉES-ATLANTIQUES

65000 PYRÉNÉES PHILATÉLIE
40 rue Larrey
Tarbes
Tél 05 62 44 80 10

66 • PYRÉNÉES ORIENTALES

66000 COMPTOIR DU COLLECTIONNEUR
2 rue Brousse
Perpignan
Tél 04 68 34 52 09

67 • BAS-RHIN

67000 PHILATÉLIE SCHOTT
10 rue du Fbg de Pierre
Strasbourg
Tél 03 88 32 44 52

67000 STRAPHIL
24 rue de la 1ère armée
Strasbourg
Tél 03 88 24 18 99

68 • HAUT-RHIN

68100 EST-PHILATÉLIE
20 rue Henriette
Mulhouse
Tél 03 89 45 53 23
Fax 03 89 45 38 75

69 • RHÔNE

69002 ESPACE YVERT & TELLIER
48-50 rue de la Charité
Lyon
Tél 04 78 42 22 22
Fax 04 78 42 28 28

69002 PHILATÉLIE LAHITTE
39 rue Ste Hélène
Lyon
Tél 04 78 37 17 25

69160 DEMI LUNE PHILATÉLIE
138 rue Joliot Curie
Tassin la Demi lune
Tél 04 78 36 53 12

69219 BOURSE AUX TIMBRES
62 rue Auguste Comte
Lyon BP 2405
Tél 04 78 37 47 47

72 • SARTHE

72000 L'UNIVERS PHILATÉLIQUE
3 av. du Gal de Gaulle
Le Mans
Timbres et Monnaies
Achat - Vente
Tél 02 43 24 41 70

72190 PHILATÉLIE 72 SARL
8 rue du Champ Fleuri
Coulaines
Matériel, Timbres,
Monnaies Euro
Tél 02 43 23 27 55
Fax 02 43 87 05 32
www.philatelie72.com

73 • SAVOIE

73490 PHILATÉLIE SAVOISIENNE
226, RN6
La Ravoire
Achat-Vente-Timbres, Monnaies, Matériel toutes marques
Tél 04 79 71 35 44

73000 MARIANNE PHILATÉLIE
154 rue Croix d'or
Chambéry
Timbres - Monnaies - Achat Vente - Estimation -Dépositaire toutes marques
Tél 04 79 33 09 65
email : alain.houplain@free.fr

74 • HAUTE-SAVOIE

74100 AMORSI COLLECTIONS
8 Passage Jean Moulin
Annemasse
Tél 04 50 38 83 15

75 • PARIS

75002 AU MATÉRIEL DE COLLECTIONS
54 Passage des Panoramas
Paris
Tél 01 42 36 03 18

75005 ARPHI-DIF
15 bd St-Germain
Paris

75008 RENON
Gal. Elysées La Boétie,
52 av. Ch.Elysées
Paris
Tél 01 42 25 58 20

75009 BERNARD AUMONT
22 rue Drouot
Paris
Toutes marques, toutes collections, Magasin et par correspondance
Tél 01 47 70 63 34
Fax 01 42 46 25 32
www.bernard-aumont.com

75009 ESPACE YVERT & TELLIER
10 rue de Châteaudun
Paris
Tél 01 40 82 74 70
Fax 01 40 82 74 75

75009 STE PHILA. LANGUEDOCIENNE
22 rue la Fayette
Paris
Tél 01 42 46 99 30

75009 LA BOURSE DU TIMBRE
7, rue Drouot
Paris
Tél 01 47 70 87 60

75010 MAISON CHAMPION
62 bld de Strasbourg
Paris
Tél 01 42 46 70 38

76 • SEINE-MARITIME

76200 MINÉRAPHIL
6 et 8 rue Vauquelin
Dieppe
Tél. 02 35 84 10 04
Fax 02 32 90 11 89

76600 ESPACE YVERT & TELLIER
72 avenue Foch
Le Havre
Tél 02 35 41 22 22
Fax 02 35 42 07 58

76000 RÉP. PHILATÉLIE
60 rue de la République
Rouen
Tél 02 35 88 54 73

77 • SEINE-ET-MARNE

77000 LA BOURSE AUX COLLECTIONS
21 rue Carnot
Melun
Timbres - Monnaies - Matériel - Achat - Vente
Tél 01 64 39 94 49
www.labourseauxcollections.fr
contact@labourseauxcollections.fr

77170 MARC BESNARD PHILATÉLIE
9 rue des Halles
Brie Comte Robert
Tél/fax 01 64 05 80 81

78 • YVELINES

78000 VERSAILLES PHILATÉLIE
5 rue de la Paroisse
Versailles
Tél 01 39 25 03 59

78220 ARPHI
58 rue de Jouy
Viroflay
Tél 01 30 24 21 62

79 • DEUX-SÈVRES

79000 BUREAUTIQUE DU CENTRE-OUEST
3, rue du Temple
NIORT
Tél 05 49 25 68 14
Fax 05 49 75 97 48

80 • SOMME

80000 ESPACE YVERT ET TELLIER
26 rue au Lin
Amiens
Tél 03 22 92 33 32
Fax 03 22 72 02 08

81 - TARN

81100 TARN COLLECTIONS
31 rue Fuzies
Castres
Tél 05 63 59 98 78

83 • VAR

83000 TOULON PHILATÉLIE
1 rue Saunier
Toulon
Tél 04 94 91 92 04

84 • VAUCLUSE

84300 PHILATÉLIE CHABANNES
2 bis rue Diderot
Cavaillon
Tél 04 90 78 07 76

85 • VENDÉE

85003 AGORA SA
11 rue Clémenceau
La Roche-Sur-Yon
Tél 02 51 44 58 90

86 • VIENNE

86000 PHILADIRECT
8 rue Gaston Hulin
Poitiers
Tél 05 49 88 94 27

87 • HAUTE-VIENNE

87000 PHILATÉLIE 87
8 rue Jean Jaurès
Limoges
Tél 05 55 34 47 82

88 • VOSGES

88000 VOSGES-PHILATÉLIE
11 rue Mal Delattre
Épinal
Tél 03 29 64 11 30

91 • ESSONNE

91600 PHILATÉLIE 91
22 bis rue Charles Rossignol
Savigny sur Orge
Tél 01 69 24 32 05
www.philatelie91.fr

92 • HAUTS-DE-SEINE

92160 PHILATÉLIE SUD
5 rue Raymond Aron
Antony
Tél 01 43 50 52 22

92400 ÉD. FARCIGNY
36 av. de la République
Courbevoie
Tél 01 43 33 31 63

92600 AV ÉDITIONS DE MORANT
6 rue du Chalet
Asnières
Timbres, Matériel toute marque, Album encyclo--pédique France AV
Tél 01 47 93 61 16
Fax 01 47 33 24 65
email : avoacp@wanadoo.fr

95 • VAL-D'OISE

95170 VAL D'OISE DOCUMENTS ET COLLECTIONS
3, bis rue Charles de Gaulle
Deuil la Barre
Tél 01 39 84 14 95

95610 LE GRAND CERCLE
Centre Cial Art de Vivre
1 rue du Bois-Noyer
Eragny
Tél 01 34 30 48 00

Sélection de Timbres

Un ensemble de timbres pour enrichir en diversité votre collection. Plusieurs thèmes émis en France ou dans d'autres pays ont été sélectionnés avec passion, pour votre plus grand bonheur.

ANIMAUX

ANIMAUX

0174	POCH 100	**4,50€**
0175	POCH 200	**8,90€**
0176	POCH 300	**12,90€**
0177	POCH 500	**21,90€**
0178	POCH 1000	**46,90€**

ANIMAUX DE LA FERME

0723	POCH 100	**19,50€**

ANIMAUX POLAIRE

0724	POCH 100	**16,50€**

ANIMAUX PREHISTORIQUES

0725	POCH 100	**5,50€**

ANIMAUX SAUVAGES

0726	POCH 300	**19,50€**

ANIMAUX WWF

7011	POCH 100	**13,50€**

CAMELIDES ET CHAMEAUX

7033	POCH 50	**19,15**

CHASSE

0757	POCH 25	**8,30€**
7041	POCH 50	**15,25€**

CHATS

0355	POCH 200	**16,90€**

CHEVAUX

7042	POCH 100	**3,60€**
7043	POCH 200	**7,50€**
7044	POCH 300	**13,50€**
7045	POCH 500	**41,20€**
7046	POCH 800	**95,25€**
7047	POCH 1000	**152,95€**

CHIENS

0727	POCH 50	**2,90€**
0728	POCH 200	**16,90€**
0729	POCH 500	**189,00€**

ELEPHANTS

0731	POCH 50	**4,50€**

FELINS
0732 POCH 100 10,90€

GRENOUILLES
7084 POCH 25 3,60€

INSECTES
7100 POCH 100 4,50€
7101 POCH 200 13,50€
0733 POCH 300 41,90€

OISEAUX
0734 POCH 100 4,50€
7141 POCH 200 7,50€
0735 POCH 300 19,90€
7142 POCH 500 23,15€
7143 POCH 1000 57,55€
0736 POCH 1500 189,00€

OURS
0737 POCH 50 8,30€

PAPILLONS
7148 POCH 100 3,60€
0738 POCH 200 9,90€
7149 POCH 300 12,50€
0739 POCH 500 54,90€
7150 POCH 700 80,95€

PERROQUETS
0740 POCH 50 13,90€

RAPACES
0743 POCH 50 32,90€

REPTILES
0744 POCH 100 9,90€

RHINOCEROS
7185 POCH 25 6,90€

SINGES
0745 POCH 50 5,50€

TORTUES
0746 POCH 50 18,90€

ARTS ET LETTRES

ART EGYPTIEN
7014 POCH 25 4,50€

ARTISTES DE CINEMA
7015 POCH 25 4,50€

CELEBRITES
7037 POCH 500 21,75€

GAUGUIN
7077 POCH 25 4,50€

LITTERATURE
7119 POCH 100 9,10€

MANET
7123 POCH 15 5,70€

MUSIQUE ET MUSICIENS
0747 POCH 100 4,30€
0748 POCH 500 89,50€

INSTRUMENTS DE MUSIQUE
7102 POCH 50 9,10€

PICASSO
0750 POCH 50 8,30€

RENOIR
7166 POCH 25 4,50€

RUBENS
0751 POCH 50 8,30€

SCULPTURES
0749 POCH 100 11,20€

TABLEAUX
0193 POCH 100 4,50€
0194 POCH 200 8,90€
0195 POCH 300 12,90€
0196 POCH 500 25,90€
0197 POCH 1000 69,90€

TABLEAUX DE NUS
7206 POCH 100 9,10€
7207 POCH 200 19,05€

THEATRE
7214 POCH 50 9,10€

TOULOUSE LAUTREC
7217 POCH 20 5,70€

VAN GOGH
7224 POCH 25 10,50€

ENFANCE

CIRQUE
7250 POCH 25 3,20€

CONTES ET LEGENDES
0719 POCH 50 13,90€
0720 POCH 100 18,90€

DISNEY
0721 POCH 50 11,90€
0722 POCH 100 27,50€
7234 POCH 200 38,15€
7235 POCH 300 61,85€

NOEL
0356 POCH 50 13,90€
7140 POCH 100 16,25€

FLEURS ET FRUITS

CACTUS
0768 POCH 50 16,40€

CHAMPIGNONS
0769 POCH 50 2,90€
0770 POCH 200 38,50€

FLORE
0179 POCH 100 4,50€
0180 POCH 200 8,90€
0181 POCH 300 12,90€
0182 POCH 500 22,90€
0183 POCH 1000 62,90€

FRUITS

0771	POCH 200	24,90€

ORCHIDEES

0772	POCH 50	5,20€
7144	POCH 100	12,10€

ROSES

0773	POCH 50	3,90€
7186	POCH 100	6,90€

HISTOIRE ET CIVILISATION

ASTROLOGIE

0756	POCH 25	5,50€

AVIATEURS

7019	POCH 50	10,50€

CHATEAUX

0758	POCH 100	8,30€

COSTUMES

0761	POCH 200	12,10€

CROIX ROUGE

7061	POCH 100	10,50€

DE GAULLE

0752	POCH 100	16,90€
7064	POCH 200	36,40€

LADY DIANA

7111	POCH 50	10,50€
0753	POCH 100	32,90€

MASQUES

0762	POCH 100	21,90€

MEDECINE ET MEDECINS

7127	POCH 100	19,05€

MINERAUX ET FOSSILES

0763	POCH 50	11,20€
7131	POCH 100	15,50€

NAPOLEON

0754	POCH 100	11,20€
7136	POCH 200	23,15€

POMPIERS

0766	POCH 50	8,30€

PONTS

0767	POCH 50	13,90€

SCOUTISME

7191	POCH 200	21,25€

SECONDE GUERRE MONDIALE

7192	POCH 50	10,50€

SEPT MERVEILLES DU MONDE

7193	POCH 25	6,90€

TRIANGLES

7219	POCH 100	9,10€

ZEPPELIN

7239	POCH 50	5,40€

MER

BASES EN ANTARCTIQUE

0794	POCH 25	6,90€

BATEAUX ET NAVIRES

0779	POCH 100	4,50€
0780	POCH 500	38,50€

BATEAUX DE GUERRE

7024	POCH 25	3,05€

CETACES

7038	POCH 25	5,70€

COQUILLAGES

0730	POCH 50	3,90€

PECHE

7155	POCH 50	9,10€

PHARES

0765	POCH 25	8,30€

POISSONS

0741	POCH 100	4,50€
0742	POCH 300	19,30€
7158	POCH 500	41,95€
7159	POCH 700	80,95€

POISSONS ET FAUNE MARINE

7157	POCH 1000	135,55€

VOILIERS

7227	POCH 100	6,90€
0787	POCH 200	21,90€
7228	POCH 300	26,75€
7229	POCH 500	75,95€

RELIGIONS

NATIVITE VIERGE

0714	POCH 100	10,90€
0715	POCH 200	27,50€

PAPES

0712	POCH 25	5,50€
0713	POCH 50	13,90€

PAQUES

0764	POCH 50	13,90€

RELIGIONS DU MONDE

0716	POCH 100	4,50€
0717	POCH 200	12,90€
0718	POCH 300	32,90€

TEMPLES, MOSQUEES, PAGODES

7211	POCH 50	9,10€

SPORTS

ARTS MARTIAUX

0476	POCH 25	5,50€

BASKET-BALL

7022	POCH 25	4,50€
7023	POCH 50	11,50€

BOXE

0478	POCH 50	10,90€
7031	POCH 100	19,25€

CYCLISME

0479	POCH 50	3,90€
0480	POCH 100	13,90€

ECHECS

7065	POCH 50	3,60€
7066	POCH 100	15,25€

ESCRIME

7067	POCH 25	4,50€
7068	POCH 50	13,50€

FOOTBALL

0481	POCH 100	4,50€
0482	POCH 200	8,90€
0483	POCH 300	16,90€
7073	POCH 500	38,75€
7074	POCH 600	63,75€
7075	POCH 800	106,75€
7076	POCH 1000	190,55€

GYMNASTIQUE

0511	POCH 50	10,90€

HALTEROPHILIE

7090	POCH 25	4,50€

HAND BALL

7091	POCH 25	6,90€

HIPPISME

0489	POCH 50	7,90€
7092	POCH 100	19,05€

HOCKEY SUR GLACE

7093	POCH 50	11,50€

JUDO

0475	POCH 25	4,50€

LUTTE

0492	POCH 50	21,90€

NATATION

7137	POCH 100	19,05€

PATINAGE

7154	POCH 50	6,75€

SKI

7195	POCH 100	11,50€

SPORTS

0184	POCH 100	4,50€
0185	POCH 200	8,90€
0186	POCH 500	19,90€
0187	POCH 1000	59,90€

TENNIS

0493	POCH 25	2,90€
0473	POCH 50	10,90€

TIR A L'ARC

7215	POCH 25	6,90€

TIR ARME A FEU

7216	POCH 25	6,90€

VOLLEY-BALL

7233	POCH 25	6,90€

TRANSPORTS ET COMMUNICATION

ASTRONAUTIQUE

0188	POCH 100	4,50€
0190	POCH 300	12,90€
0191	POCH 500	27,50€
0192	POCH 1000	62,90€

ATTELAGES

7016	POCH 50	10,50€

AVIONS

0774	POCH 100	4,50€
0775	POCH 300	16,90€
0776	POCH 1000	137,20€

CONCORDE

0777	POCH 25	6,90€

HELICOPTERES

0778	POCH 50	16,90€

MOTOS

0782	POCH 100	11,20€

TRAINS

0783	POCH 100	4,50€
7218	POCH 200	8,15€
0784	POCH 300	13,10€
0785	POCH 500	59,90€
0786	POCH 800	192,10€

VOITURES

7230	POCH 100	3,60€
7231	POCH 200	9,10€
0357	POCH 300	21,50€
7232	POCH 500	55,95€

VOITURES DE COURSE

0788	POCH 50	19,90€

VOITURES FERRARI

0789	POCH 10	4,50€

VOITURES MERCEDES

0790	POCH 25	8,30€

FRANCE, MONACO ET DOM-TOM

FRANCE

0156	POCH 200	6,90€
0157	POCH 300	12,90€
0158	POCH 400	21,90€
0159	POCH 500	33,50€
0160	POCH 600	45,00€
0161	POCH 800	69,90€
0162	POCH 1000	89,90€
0164	POCH 1500	185,00€
0165	POCH 2000	335,00€

FRANCE EUROPA

0132	POCH 25	5,40€

FRANCE PRE-OBLITERES

0134	POCH 25	13,70€

FRANCE BLASONS

7174	POCH 50	9,60€

FRANCE CHATEAUX

7179	POCH 25	9,50€

FRANCE CROIX-ROUGE

7181	POCH 50	45,75€

FRANCE FICTIFS

7182	POCH 100	14,90€

FRANCE POSTE AERIENNE

7183	POCH 25	19,90€

FRANCE TABLEAUX

0131	POCH 100	76,90€

FRANCE TAXE

0137	POCH 50	24,90€

FRANCE TIMBRES DE ROULETTES

7184	POCH 25	11,25€

MONACO

0410	POCH 50	4,90€
0411	POCH 100	17,50€
0412	POCH 200	46,90€
7134	POCH 500	152,50€

GUADELOUPE

7085	POCH 50	24,80€

GUYANE FRANCAISE

0798	POCH 25	9,90€

MARTINIQUE

7126	POCH 50	25,30€

NOUVELLE-CALEDONIE

0416	POCH 50	16,90€

OCEANIE/POLYNESIE

0417	POCH 50	16,90€

REUNION/CFA

0418	POCH 25	10,90€
0419	POCH 50	35,90€
0420	POCH 100	79,90€

ST PIERRE & MIQUELON

7198	POCH 25	6,20€
7199	POCH 50	18,90€

TERRES AUSTRALES

0427	POCH 25	34,90€

WALLIS ET FUTUNA

0439	POCH 50	21,90€
0440	POCH 100	62,90€

AFRIQUE FRANCOPHONE

AFRIQUE EQUATORIALE FR.

7000	POCH 50	11,20€

AFRIQUE OCCIDENTALE FR.

7001	POCH 50	16,60€

ALGERIE
0261 POCH 100 9,90€
7003 POCH 200 19,50€
0262 POCH 300 54,90€

BENIN
0293 POCH 100 4,50€
7026 POCH 200 9,60€

BURKINA FASO
0295 POCH 50 4,90€

CAMEROUN
0268 POCH 50 4,50€
0269 POCH 100 16,90€
7034 POCH 200 44,80€

CENTRAFRIQUE
0270 POCH 50 4,50€
0271 POCH 100 9,50€
0272 POCH 200 29,90€

COLONIES FRANÇAISE AVANT INDEPENDANCE
7050 POCH 100 9,60€
7051 POCH 200 24,80€
7052 POCH 300 40,50€
7053 POCH 500 62,50€
7056 POCH 1000 212,50€

COMORES
0273 POCH 50 4,90€
0274 POCH 100 13,90€
0275 POCH 200 38,50€

CONGO
0276 POCH 50 5,50€
0277 POCH 100 18,90€
0278 POCH 200 54,90€

COTE D'IVOIRE
0279 POCH 50 6,90€
0280 POCH 100 18,90€
0281 POCH 200 52,00€

COTE FRANCAISES DES SOMALIS
7060 POCH 50 11,20€

DAHOMEY
0283 POCH 50 4,90€
0284 POCH 100 12,90€
0285 POCH 200 49,90€

DJIBOUTI
0286 POCH 50 3,90€
0287 POCH 100 7,90€
0288 POCH 200 18,90€

FEZZAN
7072 POCH 10 6,35€

GABON
0290 POCH 50 5,50€
0291 POCH 100 24,90€

GUINEE
0375 POCH 100 4,50€
0376 POCH 200 8,90€
0377 POCH 400 24,90€
0378 POCH 500 35,90€

HAUTE VOLTA
0381 POCH 100 7,90€
0382 POCH 200 23,90€

INDOCHINE
7097 POCH 100 22,95€

ININI
7099 POCH 10 2,60€

MADAGASCAR
0388 POCH 100 3,90€
0389 POCH 200 15,50€
0390 POCH 300 35,90€

MALI
0392 POCH 100 7,90€
0393 POCH 200 21,90€
0394 POCH 300 59,90€

MAROC
0396 POCH 100 7,90€
0397 POCH 200 19,90€
0398 POCH 300 43,90€

MAROC ESPAGNOL
7125 POCH 50 11,20€

TANGER
7208 POCH 25 16,90€

MAURITANIE
0407 POCH 50 3,90€
0408 POCH 100 11,50€
0409 POCH 200 32,90€

OUBANGUI
7145 POCH 25 12,50€

PAYS D'AFRIQUE FRANCOPHONE
0252 POCH 200 5,90€
0253 POCH 300 9,90€
0254 POCH 500 17,90€
0255 POCH 1000 45,00€
0256 POCH 2000 99,90€
0257 POCH 3000 169,90€
0258 POCH 5000 329,00€

NIGER
0413 POCH 50 3,90€
0414 POCH 100 10,90€
0415 POCH 200 31,90€

SENEGAL
0422 POCH 100 15,50€

SOUDAN FRANÇAIS
0801 POCH 25 9,30€

TCHAD
0424 POCH 100 6,90€
0425 POCH 200 12,90€
0426 POCH 300 27,50€

TOGO
0429 POCH 100 5,50€
0430 POCH 200 12,90€
0431 POCH 500 44,50€

TUNISIE
0433 POCH 100 7,90€
0434 POCH 200 21,90€
0435 POCH 300 45,00€

ZANZIBAR
7238 POCH 25 22,40€

EUROPE DU NORD ET SCANDINAVIE

ALAND

0346	POCH 10	8,90€

ALDERNEY

7002	POCH 25	14,15€

ALLEMAGNE AVANT 1945

7004	POCH 300	29,90€

ALLEMAGNE

0449	POCH 200	7,90€
0450	POCH 500	24,90€
0451	POCH 1000	62,90€

ALLEMAGNE EST

7006	POCH 1000	55,15€

ALLEMAGNE OUEST

7007	POCH 1000	75,95€

ANCIENNES POSSESSIONS ALLEMANDES

7005	POCH 10	24,40€

SARRE

7189	POCH 50	11,25€
7190	POCH 100	30,75€

BELGIQUE

0455	POCH 100	6,90€
0456	POCH 200	17,50€
0457	POCH 500	65,00€
0458	POCH 1000	99,90€

ANCIENNES POSSESSIONS BELGES

0593	POCH 100	5,50€
0594	POCH 200	10,90€
0595	POCH 300	18,90€

DANEMARK

0516	POCH 200	7,90€
0517	POCH 300	13,90€
0518	POCH 400	24,90€

FEROE

0347	POCH 25	27,50€

FINLANDE

0524	POCH 100	4,50€
0525	POCH 200	10,90€
0526	POCH 300	21,90€

GRANDE-BRETAGNE

0528	POCH 200	6,90€
0529	POCH 300	13,90€
0530	POCH 500	32,90€
7081	POCH 1000	75,95€

ANCIENNES POSSESSIONS BRITANNIQUES

0590	POCH 500	12,90€
0591	POCH 1000	36,90€
0592	POCH 2000	99,90€

GUERNESEY

0534	POCH 25	6,90€
0535	POCH 50	12,90€
0536	POCH 100	23,90€

GROENLAND

0348	POCH 25	19,90€

IRLANDE

0138	POCH 200	48,30€

ISLANDE

0349	POCH 25	4,90€

JERSEY

0531	POCH 25	6,90€
0532	POCH 50	12,90€
0533	POCH 100	23,90€

LUXEMBOURG

0548	POCH 100	10,90€
0549	POCH 200	27,50€
0550	POCH 300	43,90€
0551	POCH 500	99,90€

MAN (ILE DE)

7094	POCH 50	9,90€

NORVEGE

0554	POCH 100	4,50€
0555	POCH 200	10,90€
0556	POCH 300	23,90€

PAYS BAS

0557	POCH 100	3,90€
0558	POCH 200	6,90€
0559	POCH 500	39,90€

SUEDE

0573	POCH 200	7,90€
0350	POCH 300	11,50€
0351	POCH 400	16,90€

EUROPE CENTRALE

ALBANIE

0447	POCH 100	13,90€
0448	POCH 300	79,90€

AUTRICHE

0452	POCH 100	4,50€
0453	POCH 200	11,90€
0454	POCH 500	38,50€

BULGARIE

0512	POCH 100	3,90€
0513	POCH 500	27,50€
0514	POCH 1000	79,90€

HONGRIE

0541	POCH 200	4,50€
0542	POCH 500	14,90€
0543	POCH 1000	38,50€

LIECHTENSTEIN

0140	POCH 100	34,10€

MEMEL

7128	POCH 25	22,50€

POLOGNE

0561	POCH 500	16,90€
0562	POCH 1000	43,90€
7163	POCH 1500	99,95€

DANTZIG

7063	POCH 25	9,90€

ROUMANIE

0567	POCH 500	16,90€
0568	POCH 1000	41,90€
7247	POCH 2000	135,00€

SUISSE

0574	POCH 100	6,90€
0575	POCH 300	31,90€
7202	POCH 500	45,50€

TCHECOSLOVAQUIE

0577	POCH 200	5,50€
0578	POCH 300	8,90€
0579	POCH 1000	49,90€
7210	POCH 2000	137,50€

REPUBLIQUE TCHEQUE

7169	POCH 100	9,75€

SLOVAQUIE

7196	POCH 100	17,50€

BOHEME ET MORAVIE

7029	POCH 150	22,50€

TURQUIE

0581	POCH 200	4,50€
0582	POCH 500	17,50€
0583	POCH 1000	59,90€

PAYS DU BASSIN MEDITERRANEEN

ANDORRE

0263	POCH 25	5,50€
0264	POCH 50	21,90€
0265	POCH 100	69,90€

ANDORRE ESPAGNOL

7008	POCH 25	9,70€

BOSNIE

0127	POCH 25	9,50€

CHYPRE

7048	POCH 50	8,75€

EGYPTE

0646	POCH 100	5,90€
0647	POCH 200	13,90€
0648	POCH 500	69,90€

ESPAGNE

0519	POCH 100	4,50€
0520	POCH 200	10,90€
0521	POCH 300	19,90€
0522	POCH 500	41,90€
0523	POCH 1000	89,90€

ANCIENNES POSSESSIONS ESPAGNOLES

0596	POCH 100	17,90€
0597	POCH 200	42,90€

GIBRALTAR

7079	POCH 25	10,80€

GRECE

0537	POCH 100	7,90€
0538	POCH 200	18,90€
0539	POCH 300	32,90€

ISRAEL

0669	POCH 100	6,90€
0670	POCH 200	18,90€
7104	POCH 300	29,95€
0671	POCH 500	89,90€
7105	POCH 1000	170,15€

ITALIE

0545	POCH 200	6,90€
0546	POCH 500	41,90€
0547	POCH 1000	99,90€
7106	POCH 2000	275,35€

ANCIENNES POSSESSIONS ITALIENNES

0598	POCH 50	16,90€
0599	POCH 100	41,90€

LIBAN

7115	POCH 100	11,50€

LIBYE

0359	POCH 50	9,90€
7116	POCH 200	35,50€

MALTE

0552	POCH 100	6,90€
0553	POCH 200	18,90€

PORTUGAL

0563	POCH 100	6,90€
0564	POCH 200	13,90€
0565	POCH 500	54,90€

SLOVENIE

7197	POCH 25	5,55€

ST MARIN

0569	POCH 50	4,90€
0570	POCH 100	9,90€
0571	POCH 200	21,90€

SYRIE

7205	POCH 100	11,50€

VATICAN

0152	POCH 50	14,05€

YOUGOSLAVIE

0587	POCH 100	3,90€
0588	POCH 200	7,90€
0589	POCH 500	27,50€

SERBIE

0142	POCH 50	22,00€

RUSSIE ET EX-URSS

ARMENIE

0373	POCH 25	6,90€

AZERBAIDJAN

0327	POCH 50	3,90€
0363	POCH 75	7,90€
0328	POCH 100	18,90€

BIELORUSSIE

0330	POCH 50	10,90€

ESTONIE

0364	POCH 25	13,90€
0365	POCH 50	38,50€

KAZAKHSTAN

0366	POCH 15	5,50€

KIRGHIZISTAN

0331	POCH 25	2,90€
0332	POCH 50	5,50€

LETTONIE

0367	POCH 25	10,90€
0368	POCH 50	27,50€

LITUANIE

0369	POCH 25	10,90€
0370	POCH 50	24,90€

OUZBEKISTAN

0334	POCH 50	5,50€

RUSSIE

0371	POCH 25	5,50€

TADJIKISTAN

0335	POCH 25	2,90€

TURKMENISTAN

7222	POCH 10	9,75€

UKRAINE

0372	POCH 50	22,50€

URSS

0584	POCH 300	8,90€
0585	POCH 500	18,90€
0586	POCH 1000	46,90€

AFRIQUE

AFRIQUE DU SUD

0619	POCH 100	5,50€
0620	POCH 200	9,90€

ANGOLA

7009	POCH 50	8,15€

BURUNDI

0628	POCH 100	5,50€
0630	POCH 500	54,90€

CAP VERT

7036	POCH 50	4,80€

GHANA

7078	POCH 50	12,80€

GUINEE BISSAU

7087	POCH 200	9,10€

GUINEE EQUATORIALE

0657	POCH 100	3,90€

GUINEE ESPAGNOLE

7088	POCH 50	9,60€

KENYA

7109	POCH 50	13,50€

LESOTHO

7112	POCH 50	17,50€

LIBERIA
0676 POCH 100 10,90€
0677 POCH 300 54,90€

MAURICE (ILE)
7095 POCH 50 9,90€

MOZAMBIQUE
0682 POCH 100 10,90€

OUGANDA
7118 POCH 50 16,90€

RWANDA
7187 POCH 200 9,10€

SAHARA ESPAGNOL
0362 POCH 50 16,90€

SEYCHELLES
7194 POCH 25 14,90€

ST THOMAS ET PRINCE
0692 POCH 200 16,90€

STE HELENE
7200 POCH 25 16,25€

SWAZILAND
7204 POCH 50 18,60€

TANZANIE
7209 POCH 200 11,20€

ZAIRE
7236 POCH 100 13,50€

ZAMBIE
7237 POCH 50 11,30€

ZIMBABWE
7243 POCH 50 8,50€

AMERIQUE ET CARAÎBES

ANGUILLA
7010 POCH 50 14,90€

ANTIGUA ET BARBUDA
0336 POCH 25 4,50€
0337 POCH 50 10,90€

ARGENTINE
0625 POCH 500 23,90€
7013 POCH 1500 187,50€

BAHAMAS
7020 POCH 25 10,50€
7021 POCH 50 18,90€

BARBADE
0338 POCH 25 7,90€

BELIZE
7025 POCH 100 11,50€

BERMUDES
7027 POCH 100 37,50€

BOLIVIE
7030 POCH 100 15,50€

BRESIL
7032 POCH 500 45,80€

CANADA
0632 POCH 200 6,90€
0633 POCH 300 12,90€
7035 POCH 1000 95,35€

CAIMANES (ILES)
7096 POCH 50 17,65€

CHILI
0634 POCH 100 5,90€
0635 POCH 300 32,90€

COLOMBIE
0639 POCH 200 17,50€
7049 POCH 500 35,25€

COSTA RICA
7059 POCH 25 8,50€

CUBA
0643 POCH 200 6,90€
0659 POCH 300 11,90€
0644 POCH 500 24,90€
0645 POCH 1000 79,90€
7062 POCH 1500 187,50€

DOMINIQUE
0340 POCH 50 5,50€
0341 POCH 100 16,90€

EQUATEUR
0649 POCH 100 7,90€

ETATS-UNIS
0651 POCH 200 7,90€
0652 POCH 300 13,90€
0653 POCH 500 27,50€
0654 POCH 1000 69,90€
7069 POCH 2000 425,45€

FALKLAND
7070 POCH 25 12,50€

GRENADE
0656 POCH 100 10,90€

GRENADINES
0342 POCH 100 16,90€

GUATEMALA
7086 POCH 100 19,70€

GUYANE
7089 POCH 50 29,70€

HAITI
0658 POCH 100 13,90€

HONDURAS
7249 POCH 25 5,40€

JAMAIQUE
0344 POCH 25 4,50€
7107 POCH 50 7,50€

MEXIQUE

7130	POCH 300	36,25€

NICARAGUA

0683	POCH 100	3,90€
0684	POCH 300	13,90€

PANAMA

7147	POCH 100	9,90€

PARAGUAY

0687	POCH 100	7,90€
0689	POCH 300	27,50€
7153	POCH 500	49,50€

PEROU

7156	POCH 300	22,50€

REPUBLIQUE DOMINICAINE

7167	POCH 50	4,80€
7168	POCH 300	35,10€

SALVADOR

7188	POCH 50	9,50€

ST VINCENT DE GRENADINES

0352	POCH 100	17,50€

STE LUCIE

0353	POCH 25	4,50€
7201	POCH 100	20,45€

SURINAM

7203	POCH 50	24,40€

TERRE NEUVE

7212	POCH 25	20,20€

TRINITE ET TOBAGO

7220	POCH 50	10,40€
7221	POCH 100	32,50€

URUGUAY

0693	POCH 100	3,90€
0694	POCH 200	9,90€
7223	POCH 500	67,50€

VENEZUELA

0695	POCH 50	5,50€
7226	POCH 300	35,25€

ASIE ET OCEANIE

AFGHANISTAN

0617	POCH 100	5,50€
0618	POCH 200	16,90€

ARABIE SAOUDITE

7012	POCH 50	16,25€

AUSTRALIE

0626	POCH 100	3,90€
0627	POCH 200	6,90€
7018	POCH 500	24,90€

ANTARCTIQUE AUSTRALIEN

7017	POCH 25	15,90€

BHOUTAN

0703	POCH 100	15,50€

BIRMANIE

7028	POCH 50	19,90€

CAMBODGE

0704	POCH 300	15,50€

CEYLAN

7039	POCH 100	17,50€

CHINE

0636	POCH 100	13,90€
0705	POCH 200	29,90€
0637	POCH 300	56,90€

COREE DU NORD

0706	POCH 200	8,90€
0641	POCH 300	13,90€
7057	POCH 1000	62,55€

COREE DU SUD

7058	POCH 100	17,80€

INDE

0661	POCH 200	3,90€
0662	POCH 300	10,90€

INDONESIE

0663	POCH 100	3,90€
7098	POCH 300	21,50€

IRAK

0665	POCH 100	6,90€

IRAN

0666	POCH 100	5,90€
0667	POCH 200	13,90€
7103	POCH 300	21,80€

JAPON

0672	POCH 100	5,90€
0709	POCH 300	31,90€
7108	POCH 500	45,50€

KOWEIT

7110	POCH 50	21,25€

LAOS

0385	POCH 100	4,50€
0386	POCH 200	8,90€
0387	POCH 300	17,50€

MACAO

7121	POCH 25	12,80€

MALAISIE

7122	POCH 100	6,60€

MONGOLIE

0678	POCH 100	3,90€
0710	POCH 300	14,90€
0680	POCH 500	29,90€
7135	POCH 1000	112,50€

NEPAL

7139	POCH 200	17,50€

NOUVELLE-ZELANDE

0685	POCH 100	4,90€
7138	POCH 500	32,55€

PAKISTAN

7146	POCH 200	14,40€

PHILIPPINES

0690	POCH 100	8,90€

QUATAR

7164	POCH 25	112,50€

SINGAPOUR

0708	POCH 50	10,90€

THAILANDE

7213	POCH 50	7,20€

VIETNAM

0436	POCH 100	4,50€
0437	POCH 200	8,90€
0711	POCH 300	13,90€
0438	POCH 500	27,50€

RESTE DU MONDE ET EUROPE

EUROPA

0153	POCH 50	15,50€
0154	POCH 200	55,00€

EUROPE

0441	POCH 200	2,90€
0442	POCH 500	6,90€
0443	POCH 1000	16,90€
0444	POCH 2000	38,50€
0445	POCH 3000	62,90€
0446	POCH 5000	135,00€

TOUT PAYS

0166	POCH 300	3,90€
0167	POCH 500	5,50€
0168	POCH 1000	13,90€
0169	POCH 2000	29,90€
0170	POCH 3000	59,90€
0171	POCH 5000	99,90€
0172	POCH 10000	299,00€
0173	POCH 20000	890,00€

YVERT&TELLIER
2 RUE DE L'ÉTOILE
80094 AMIENS CEDEX 3
Tél (33) 03 22 71 71 78
Fax (33) 03 22 71 71 89
contact@yvert.com
S.A.S. au capital de 504 000 €
SIRET 551 721 343 B
RC AMIENS - CCP Paris 5 303 64 N

N° client : ⌊_⌊_⌊_⌊_⌊_⌊_⌋ *(1 lettre et 5 chiffres)* Nom :...Prénom :...................................

Adresse :..Code postal:..................................Ville :..

Pays :..Tél :..Email:..

BON DE COMMANDE SÉLECTION DE TIMBRES

Description	Référence	Prix unitaire	Qté	TOTAL

BON DE COMMANDE SÉLECTION DE TIMBRES

Description	Référence	Prix unitaire	Qté	TOTAL

RÈGLEMENT *(à joindre à votre commande)*

❑ Chèque bancaire ❑ C.C.P *(à l'ordre de Yvert & Tellier)* N°

❑ Carte bancaire (16 numéros + signature obligatoire)

N°

Expire fin Clé (les 3 derniers chiffres au dos de votre carte bancaire)

Signature :

AUTRE ADRESSE *cette adresse est :*

❑ Pour la livraison ❑ Ma nouvelle adresse

NOM PRÉNOM

ADRESSE

CODE POSTAL VILLE

T1bis10

▶ **MONTANT DE VOTRE COMMANDE** , €

▶ **FRAIS DE PORT ET D'EMBALLAGE** **+ 6 €**

Étranger et DOM-TOM sur devis minimum 6€

▶ **MONTANT TOTAL À PAYER**

Les informations qui vous sont demandées sont nécessaires au traitement de votre commande et pourront être communiquées à des tiers. Conformément à la Loi Informatique & Libertés du 06/01/78 (art.27), vous disposez d'un droit d'accès et de rectification des données vous concernant.

La collection des **Catalogues de cotation** du Monde entier

Depuis plus d'un siècle, nous avons le même désir de perfection pour offrir au monde de la philatélie les ouvrages de référence indispensables.

Aujourd'hui comme hier, tous les collaborateurs d'Yvert et Tellier travaillent dans ce même esprit, fidèles à notre réputation de sérieux et de compétence. Chaque rubrique est rédigée avec soin par un expert, soucieux de partager avec vous ses connaissances et sa passion. Nos experts vous guident au fil des pages, en mettant à votre service leur priorité : des informations précises, claires et fournies.

Chaque année, Yvert et Tellier réactualise une partie de ses ouvrages, pour coller au plus près de l'offre et de la demande. Les cotations sont mises à jour sans effet de mode, dans une perspective d'évolution à moyen terme, afin d'en assurer le sérieux et la fiabilité.
De plus, toujours à la recherche du meilleur, Yvert et Tellier a mis en place une base iconographique haute définition, en utilisant les technologies avancées de l'édition. Yvert et Tellier vous offre ainsi une représentation visuelle de haute qualité à partir de ses 400 000 images numérisées et destinées à la réalisation de nos ouvrages.